The Sporting News

BASEBALL GUIDE

1998 EDITION

Editors/Baseball Guide

CRAIG CARTER

DAVE SLOAN

The Sporting News

Efrem Zimbalist III, President and Chief Executive Officer, Times Mirror Magazines; **James H. Nuckols,** President, The Sporting News; **Francis X. Farrell,** Senior Vice President, Publisher; **John D. Rawlings,** Senior Vice President, Editorial Director; **John Kastberg,** Vice President, General Manager; **Kathy Kinkeade,** Vice President, Operations; **Steve Meyerhoff,** Executive Editor; **Mike Huguenin,** Assistant Managing Editor; **Joe Hoppel,** Senior Editor; **Sean Stewart,** Associate Editor; **Mark Bonavita and Brendan Roberts,** Assistant Editors; **Marilyn Kasal,** Production Director; **Terry Shea,** Database Analyst; **Michael Bruner,** Prepress Director; **Michael Behrens and Christen Webster,** Macintosh Production Artists.

A Times Mirror
Company

EXPLANATION OF STATISTICAL ABBREVIATIONS

A: assists. **AB:** at-bats. **Avg.:** batting average (hits divided by at-bats). **BB:** bases on balls. **Bk.:** balks. **CG:** complete games. **CS:** caught stealing. **E:** errors. **ER:** earned runs. **ERA:** earned-run average (earned runs times nine divided by innings pitched). **G:** games. **GB:** games behind. **GF:** games finished. **GDP:** grounding into double plays. **GS:** games started. **H:** hits. **HB:** hit batsmen. **HP:** hit by pitches. **HR:** home runs. **IBB:** intentional bases on balls. **IP:** innings pitched. **L:** losses. **OBP:** on-base percentage (hits plus bases on balls plus hit by pitches divided by at-bats plus bases on balls plus hit by pitches plus sacrifice flies). **Pct.:** winning percentage. **PO:** putouts. **Pos.:** position. **R:** runs. **RBI:** runs batted in. **SB:** stolen bases. **SF:** sacrifice flies (run-scoring flyouts). **SH:** sacrifice hits (bunts that advance one or more runners but result in the batter being retired at first base or reaching first on an error). **ShO:** shutouts. **Slg.:** slugging percentage (total bases divided by at-bats). **SO:** strikeouts. **Sv.:** saves. **TB:** total bases (hits plus doubles plus two times the number of triples plus three times the number of home runs). **TBF:** total batters faced. **TC:** total chances (putouts plus assists plus errors). **TPA:** total plate appearances (at-bats plus bases on balls plus sacrifice hits plus sacrifice flies plus hit by pitches plus times reaching base on catcher's interference). **W:** wins. **WP:** wild pitches. **2B:** doubles. **3B:** triples.

World Series, A.L. Championship Series, N.L. Championship Series, A.L. Division Series, N.L. Division Series and All-Star Game highlights written by Joe Hoppel and Ron Smith of THE SPORTING NEWS.

Major league statistics compiled by STATS, Inc., Lincolnwood, Ill.

Minor league statistics compiled by Howe Sportsdata International Inc., Boston.

ISBN: 0-89204-591-4

10 9 8 7 6 5 4 3 2 1

CONTENTS

ON THE COVER: Toronto's Roger Clemens led the major leagues with 21 victories in 1997. His 292 strike-outs and league-leading 2.05 earned-run average aided him in becoming the first American League pitcher to win four Cy Young awards. (Cover designed by Michael Behrens/THE SPORTING NEWS. Portrait by Robert Seale/THE SPORTING NEWS; action photo by Damian Strohmeyer/Allsport.)

Spine photo of Mark McGwire by Ed Nessen/THE SPORTING NEWS.

1998 SEASON

Major League Baseball directories

Team by team

MAJOR LEAGUE BASEBALL

Address
350 Park Avenue
New York, NY 10022
Telephone
212-339-7800
FAX
212-355-0007
COO, Major League Baseball
Paul Beeston
Executive director, market development
Kathleen Francis

Director, special events
Carolyn Taylor
Exec. dir., security/facility management
Kevin Hallinan
Executive director, public relations
Richard Levin
Executive director, baseball operations
William Murray
General counsel
Thomas J. Ostertag

Exec. director, minor league relations
Jimmie Lee Solomon
Chief financial officer
Jeffrey White
V.p., broadcasting and new media dev.
Leslie Sullivan
COO, MLB International
Timothy Brosnan

AMERICAN LEAGUE

Address
350 Park Avenue
New York, NY 10022
Telephone
212-339-7600
President
Gene A. Budig
Vice president
Gene Autry
Executive director of umpiring
Martin J. Springstead
Senior vice president
Phyllis Merhige
Vice president of finance
Derek Irwin
Director, waivers and player records
Kimberly J. Ng
Media relations assistant
Bill Melchior

Administrator of umpires/travel
Tess Basta-Marino
Administrative assistant
Carolyn Coen
Umpires
Larry Barnett
Joseph Brinkman
Gary Cederstrom
Alan Clark
Drew Coble
Derryl Cousins
Terry Craft
Donald Denkinger
James Evans
Dale Ford
Richard Garcia
Ted Hendry
John Hirschbeck
Mark Johnson
Jim Joyce

Kenneth Kaiser
Greg Kosc
Tim McClelland
Larry McCoy
James McKean
Chuck Meriwether
Durwood Merrill
Dan Morrison
David Phillips
Rick Reed
Michael Reilly
John (Rocky) Roe
Dale Scott
John Shulock
Tim Tschida
Tim Welke
Larry Young

NATIONAL LEAGUE

Address
350 Park Avenue
New York, NY 10022
Telephone
212-339-7700
President and treasurer
Leonard S. Coleman Jr.
Senior vice president and secretary
Katy Feeney
Executive director, public relations
Ricky Clemons
Director of umpire supervision
Paul Runge
Executive director, player records
Nancy Crofts
Executive secretary
Rita Aughavin

Administrative assistant, umpires
Cathy Davis
Public relations assistant
Glenn Wilburn
Umpires
Wally Bell
Greg Bonin
Jerry Crawford
Gary Darling
Bob Davidson
Gerry Davis
Dana DeMuth
Bruce Froemming
Brian Gorman
Eric Gregg
Tom Hallion
Angel Hernandez
Mark Hirschbeck

Bill Hohn
Jeff Kellogg
Jerry Layne
Randy Marsh
Ed Montague
Larry Poncino
Frank Pulli
Jim Quick
Ed Rapuano Jr.
Charlie Reliford
Rich Rieker
Steve Rippley
Terry Tata
Larry Vanover
Harry Wendelstedt
Joe West
Charlie Williams
Mike Winters

OTHER ORGANIZATIONS

PLAYER RELATIONS COMMITTEE

Address
350 Park Avenue
New York, NY 10022
Telephone
212-339-7400
212-371-2242 (FAX)

Chief labor negotiator and general counsel
Randy L. Levine
Associate counsels
Louis Melendez
John Westhoff

Contract administrator
John Ricco

NATIONAL ASSOCIATION OF PROFESSIONAL BASEBALL LEAGUES

Address
P.O. Box A
St. Petersburg, FL 33731
Telephone
813-822-6937
813-821-5819 (FAX)
President
Mike Moore
Vice president/administration
Pat O'Conner
Chief operating officer
Rob Dlugozima
General counsel
Ben Hayes
Director/licensing
Misann Ellmaker
Director/media relations
Jim Ferguson
Director of operations
Tim Brunswick
Director of marketing
Rod Meadows
Director of business/finance
Eric Krupa
General supervisor or Professional Baseball Umpire Corporation
Mike Fitzpatrick
Director of Professional Baseball Employment Opportunities
Ann Perkins

ASSOCIATION OF PROFESSIONAL BASEBALL PLAYERS OF AMERICA

Address
12062 Valley View, Suite 211
Garden Grove, CA 92645
Telephone
714-892-9900
714-897-0233 (FAX)
President
John J. McHale
Vice presidents
Joe DiMaggio
Arthur Richman
Robert Kennedy
Secretary/treasurer
Chuck Stevens

BASEBALL ASSISTANCE TEAM INC.

Address
350 Park Avenue
New York, NY 10022
Telephone
212-339-7884
Chairman
Ralph Branca
President
Joe Garagiola
Vice presidents
Joe Black
Earl Wilson
Executive director
James J. Martin
Secretary/treasurer
Tom Ostertag

NATIONAL BASEBALL HALL OF FAME AND MUSEUM

Address
P.O. Box 590
Cooperstown, NY 13326
Telephone
607-547-7200
607-547-2044 (FAX)
Chairman of Hall of Fame
Edward W. Stack
President
Donald C. Marr Jr.
Vice president
Frank Simio
Curator
William T. Spencer Jr.
Registrar
Peter P. Clark
Executive director of retail marketing
Barbara Shinn
Controller
Frances L. Althiser
Librarian
James L. Gates
Executive director of communications and education
Jeff Idelson

MAJOR LEAGUE BASEBALL MAJOR LEAGUE SCOUTING BUREAU

Address
23712 Birtcher Dr., Suite A
Lake Forest, CA 92630
Telephone
714-458-7600
714-458-9454 (FAX)
Director
Frank Marcos

MAJOR LEAGUE BASEBALL PLAYERS ASSOCIATION

Address
12 E. 49th St., 24th Floor
New York, NY 10017
Telephone
212-826-0808
212-752-3649 (FAX)
Executive director and general counsel
Donald M. Fehr
Special assistants
Mark Belanger
Tony Bernazard
Associate general counsel
Eugene D. Orza
Assistant general counsel
Doyle R. Pryor
Lauren Rich
Michael Weiner
Counsel
Arthur Schack
Robert Leneghan
Director of licensing
Judy Heeter
Director of communications
Richard A. Weiss

MAJOR LEAGUE BASEBALL PLAYERS ALUMNI ASSOC.

Address
1631 Mesa Ave., Suite C
Colorado Springs, CO 80906
Telephone
719-477-1870
719-477-1875 (FAX)
President
Brooks Robinson
Vice presidents
Bobby Bonds
Bob Boone
George Brett
Mike Hegan
Chuck Hinton
Al Kaline
Carl Erskine
Rusty Staub
Robin Yount
Secretary/treasurer
Fred Valentine

ELIAS SPORTS BUREAU

Address
500 Fifth Ave.
New York, NY 10110
Telephone
212-869-1530
212-354-0980 (FAX)
General manager
Seymour Siwoff

MAJOR LEAGUE UMPIRES ASSOCIATION

Address
1735 Market St., Suite 3420
Philadelphia, PA 19103
Telephone
215-979-3220
215-979-3201 (FAX)
General counsel
Richard G. Phillips

BASEBALL WRITERS' ASSOCIATION OF AMERICA

President
Jim Street, Seattle Post-Intelligencer
Vice president
Bob Elliott, Toronto Sun
Secretary/treasurer
Jack O'Connell, Hartford Courant

HOWE SPORTSDATA INTERNATIONAL INC.

Address
Boston Fish Pier
West Building No. 1, Suite 302
Boston, MA 02210
Telephone
617-951-0070
617-951-1379 (stats request)
617-737-9960 (FAX)
President
Jay Virshbo
Historical consultant
William Weiss

ANAHEIM ANGELS
AMERICAN LEAGUE WEST DIVISION

Angels Schedule

Home games shaded. *—All-Star Game at Coors Field (Colorado).
D—Day game (any game starting before 5 p.m.).

March
SUN	MON	TUE	WED	THU	FRI	SAT
		31				

April
SUN	MON	TUE	WED	THU	FRI	SAT
			1 NYY	2 NYY	3 CLE	4 CLE
5 D CLE	6 BOS	7	8 BOS	9	10 D CLE	11 D CLE
12 D CLE	13 NYY	14 NYY	15 D NYY	16 TB	17 TB	18 TB
19 D TB	20 BAL	21 BAL	22 BAL	23	24 TB	25 TB
26 D TB	27 BAL	28 BAL	29 BOS	30 BOS		

May
SUN	MON	TUE	WED	THU	FRI	SAT
					1 CWS	2 CWS
3 CWS	4 CWS	5 TOR	6 TOR	7	8 DET	9 DET
10 D DET	11	12 CWS	13 CWS	14 TOR	15 TOR	16 D DET
17 D DET	18 DET	19 OAK	20 OAK	21 OAK	22 MIN	23 MIN
24 MIN	25 D KC	26	27 KC	28	29 MIN	30 MIN
31 D MIN						

June
SUN	MON	TUE	WED	THU	FRI	SAT
	1 KC	2 KC	3 SEA	4 SEA	5 COL	6 COL
7 COL	8 D	9 ARZ	10 ARZ	11 ARZ	12 TEX	13 TEX
14 TEX	15 TEX	16 SEA	17 SEA	18 SEA	19 TEX	20 TEX
21 TEX	22 LA	23 LA	24 LA	25 LA	26 SD	27 SD
28 SD	29 D	30 SF				

July
SUN	MON	TUE	WED	THU	FRI	SAT
			1 SF	2 SF	3 OAK	4 OAK
5 D OAK	6	7 *	8	9 OAK	10 SEA	11 SEA
12 D SEA	13 OAK	14 D OAK	15 TB	16 TB	17 BAL	18 BAL
19 D BAL	20	21 MIN	22 MIN	23 D MIN	24 KC	25 KC
26 KC	27 D KC	28 NYY	29 NYY	30 NYY	31 BOS	

August
SUN	MON	TUE	WED	THU	FRI	SAT
						1 BOS
2 BOS	3 D CLE	4 CLE	5 D CLE	6 D	7 CWS	8 CWS
9 CWS	10 D DET	11 DET	12 DET	13 TOR	14 TOR	15 D TOR
16 TOR	17 D CWS	18 CWS	19 DET	20 DET	21 TOR	22 TOR
23 TOR	24 D	25 NYY	26 NYY	27 NYY	28 BOS	29 D BOS
30 BOS	31 D					

September
SUN	MON	TUE	WED	THU	FRI	SAT
		1 CLE	2 CLE	3	4 KC	5 KC
6 KC	7 D	8 MIN	9 MIN	10	11 BAL	12 BAL
13 BAL	14 D TB	15 TB	16 TEX	17 TEX	18 SEA	19 SEA
20 SEA	21 D TEX	22 TEX	23 TEX	24 OAK	25 OAK	26 D OAK
27 D OAK						

1998 SEASON
CLUB DIRECTORY

Owner
Gene Autry
Chairman and CEO, The Walt Disney Co.
Michael Eisner
President
Tony Tavares
Vice president and general manager
W.J. Bavasi
Assistant general manager
Tim Mead
Vice president of finance and admin.
Andy Roundtree
Vice president of business affairs
Kevin Gilmore
Vice president of sales and marketing
Ken Wachter
Special assistants to general manager
Preston Gomez
Bob Harrison
Legal counsel/contract negotiations
Mark Rosenthal
Director of player development
Ken Forsch
Director, scouting
Bob Fontaine Jr.
Manager, baseball operations
Jeff Parker
Equipment manager
Ken Higdon
Visiting clubhouse manager
Brian Harkins
Senior video coordinator
Diego Lopez
Director of communications
Bill Robertson
Manager, media services
Larry Babcock
Manager, publications
Doug Ward
Media relations coordinator
Luis Garcia
Director, broadcasting
Mark Vittorio

Director, entertainment
Marty Berg
Director of finance
Martin Greenspan
Medical director
Dr. Lewis Yocum
Team physician
Dr. Craig Milhouse
Head athletic trainer
Ned Bergert
Athletic trainer
Rick Smith
Strength and conditioning coach
Tom Wilson
Sports psychologist
Ken Ravizza
Dir. of advertising and broadcast sales
Bob Wagner
Director of stadium operations
Kevin Uhlich
Manager, ticket operations
Don Boudreau
Scouts
Don Archer, John Burden, Tom Burns, Pete Coachman, Marco Davalillo, Pompeyo Davalillo, Tom Davis, Red Gaskill, Jose Gomez, Steve Gruwell, Felipe Gutierrez, Ta Honda, Rick Ingalls, Hal Keller, Tim Kelly, Kris Kline, Tom Kotchman, Tony LaCava, George Lauzerique, Jose Leiva, Ron Marigny, Jim McLaughlin, Mario Mendoza, Darrell Miller, Jon Neiderer, Tom Osowski, Eusebio Perez, Paul Robinson, Rick Schlenker, Rick Schroeder, Jerry Streeter, Rip Tutor, Jack Uhey, Dick Wilson
Major league scouts
Dave Garcia, Jay Hankins, Bob Harrison, Nick Kamzic, Matt Keough, Joe McDonald, Tom Romenesko, Moose Stubing, Dale Sutherland

MINOR LEAGUE AFFILIATES

Class	Team	League	Manager
AAA	Vancouver	Pacific Coast	Mitch Seoane
AA	Midland	Texas	Don Long
A	Lake Elsinore	California	Mario Mendoza
A	Cedar Rapids	Midwest	Garry Templeton
A	Boise	Northwest	Tom Kotchman
Rookie	Butte	Pioneer	Bill Lachemann

BROADCAST INFORMATION

Radio: KRLA-AM (1110).
TV: KCAL-TV (Channel 9).
Cable TV: Fox Sports West.

SPRING TRAINING

Ballpark (city): Diablo Stadium (Tempe, Ariz.).
Ticket information: 888-HALOS.

Manager—Terry Collins (1).
Coaches—Larry Bowa (2), Rod Carew (29), Joe Coleman (47), Marcel Lachemann (53), Joe Maddon (70).

No.	PITCHERS	B/T	Ht./Wt.	Born	1997 clubs
	Bovee, Mike	R/R	5-10/200	8-21-73	Midland, Vancouver, Anaheim
43	Chavez, Tony	R/R	5-10/180	10-22-70	Midland, Vancouver, Anaheim
	Cooper, Brian	R/R	6-1/175	8-19-74	DID NOT PLAY
	DeLucia, Rich	R/R	6-0/190	10-7-64	San Francisco, Anaheim
19	Dickson, Jason	L/R	6-0/190	3-30-73	Anaheim
	Edsell, Geoff	R/R	6-2/190	12-12-71	Vancouver
31	Finley, Chuck	L/L	6-6/214	11-26-62	Anaheim, Lake Elsinore
	Freehill, Mike	R/R	6-3/185	6-1-71	Midland, Lake Elsinore
48	Harris, Pep	R/R	6-2/185	9-23-72	Anaheim
21	Hasegawa, Shigetoshi	R/R	5-11/160	8-1-68	Anaheim
44	Hill, Ken	R/R	6-2/205	12-14-65	Texas, Tulsa, Anaheim
65	Holtz, Mike	L/L	5-9/175	10-10-72	Anaheim
46	James, Mike	R/R	6-4/216	8-15-67	Anaheim
22	May, Darrell	L/L	6-2/170	6-13-72	Vancouver, Anaheim
	Olivares, Omar	R/R	6-1/193	7-6-67	Detroit, Seattle
40	Percival, Troy	R/R	6-3/200	8-9-69	Anaheim, Lake Elsinore
	Washburn, Jarrod	L/L	6-1/190	8-13-74	Midland
34	Watson, Allen	L/L	6-3/190	11-18-70	Anaheim

No.	CATCHERS	B/T	Ht./Wt.	Born	1997 clubs
2	Encarnacion, Angelo	R/R	5-8/180	4-18-73	Las Vegas, Anaheim
8	Greene, Todd	R/R	5-9/195	5-8-71	Anaheim, Vancouver
	Walbeck, Matt	B/R	5-11/191	10-2-69	Detroit, Lakeland, Toledo

No.	INFIELDERS	B/T	Ht./Wt.	Born	1997 clubs
	Baughman, Justin	R/R	5-11/175	8-1-74	Lake Elsinore
	Castro, Nelson	R/B	5-10/160	6-4-76	DID NOT PLAY
9	DiSarcina, Gary	R/R	6-1/178	11-19-67	Anaheim
	Eenhoorn, Robert	R/R	6-3/185	2-9-68	Vancouver, Anaheim
27	Erstad, Darin	L/L	6-2/210	6-4-74	Anaheim
	Fielder, Cecil	R/R	6-3/250	9-21-63	New York A.L.
10	Hollins, Dave	B/R	6-1/210	5-25-66	Anaheim
	Nevin, Phil	R/R	6-2/180	1-19-71	Lakeland, Toledo, Detroit
	Pritchett, Chris	L/R	6-4/185	1-31-70	Vancouver
18	Velarde, Randy	R/R	6-0/192	11-24-62	Anaheim

No.	OUTFIELDERS	B/T	Ht./Wt.	Born	1997 clubs
16	Anderson, Garret	L/L	6-3/190	6-30-72	Anaheim
25	Edmonds, Jim	L/L	6-1/190	6-27-70	Anaheim
	Hutchins, Norm	R/L	6-1/185	11-20-75	Lake Elsinore
3	Palmeiro, Orlando	L/R	5-11/155	1-19-69	Anaheim
15	Salmon, Tim	R/R	6-3/220	8-24-68	Anaheim

Ballpark (capacity, surface)
Edison International Field of Anaheim (45,000, grass)
Address
2000 Gene Autry Way
Anaheim, CA 92806
Business phone
714-940-2000
Ticket information
714-634-2000
Ticket prices
$18.50 (field MVP)
$15 (terrace MVP)
$14.50 (field box)
$12 (terrace box, terrace disabled MVP)
$9 (lower view MVP)
$8 (lower view box)
$7.50 (upper view, terrace disabled box)
$5 (terrace/club pavilion-adult)
$4 (LF pavilion-adult)
$2 (LF pavilion, terrace/club pavilion-children)
Field dimensions (from home plate)
To left field at foul line, 330 feet
To center field, 406 feet
To right field at foul line, 330 feet
First game played
April 19, 1966 (White Sox 3, Angels 1)

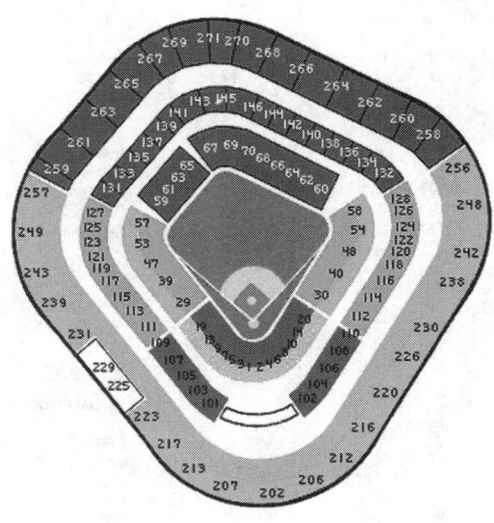

1998 SEASON Anaheim Angels

– 9 –

1998 SEASON *Anaheim Angels*

Date	Opp.	Res.	Score	(inn.*)	Hits	Opp. hits	Winning pitcher	Losing pitcher	Save	Record	Pos.	GB
4-2	Bos.	L	5-6		12	9	Mahomes	Percival	Slocumb	0-1	T3rd	1.0
4-3	Bos.	W	2-0		7	5	Dickson	Wakefield		1-1	T2nd	0.5
4-4	Cle.	W	8-6	(11)	14	9	Holtz	Shuey		2-1	T1st	....
4-5	Cle.	L	5-7		8	10	Ogea	Hasegawa	Shuey	2-2	T1st	....
4-6	Cle.	L	8-10		12	15	Kline	Percival	M. Jackson	2-3	T3rd	1.0
4-7	N.Y.	L	3-5		10	12	Pettitte	Langston	Rivera	2-4	T3rd	2.0
4-8	N.Y.	W	10-9	(12)	15	19	James	Nelson		3-4	T2nd	1.0
4-9	N.Y.	L	5-12		9	18	Wells	Watson		3-5	4th	2.0
4-11	At Cle.	L	3-15		7	20	Ogea	Gubicza		3-6	4th	3.0
4-13	At Cle.	W	8-3		13	10	Langston	McDowell		4-6	3rd	2.5
4-14	At N.Y.	W	5-1		7	5	Dickson	Rogers		5-6	3rd	1.5
4-15	At N.Y.	W	6-5		14	9	Hasegawa	Rivera	James	6-6	T3rd	1.5
4-16	At Min.	L	2-4		7	8	Robertson	Watson	Aguilera	6-7	4th	2.5
4-17	At Min.	L	3-4	(10)	11	11	Swindell	James		6-8	4th	3.5
4-19	At K.C.	L	3-7		5	12	Appier	Langston		6-9	4th	3.0
4-20	At K.C.	W	11-1		18	3	Dickson	Rusch		7-9	4th	3.0
4-21	Tor.	W	5-4	(13)	14	8	DeLucia	Spoljaric		8-9	4th	3.0
4-22	Tor.	L	6-7		7	10	Quantrill	James	Plesac	8-10	4th	4.0
4-23	Tor.	W	5-4	(10)	12	10	DeLucia	Spoljaric		9-10	4th	3.0
4-25	Det.	W	8-3		11	5	Dickson	Lira		10-10	T3rd	3.0
4-26	Det.	L	0-2		2	6	Moehler	Finley		10-11	4th	3.0
4-27	Det.	W	6-5		11	10	James	Myers		11-11	T3rd	3.0
4-29	At Bos.	W	5-4		12	11	Holtz	Henry	James	12-11	3rd	2.5
4-30	At Bos.	L	2-11		7	13	Hammond	Dickson		12-12	T3rd	2.5
5-3†	At Chi.	W	3-2		8	11	Watson	Baldwin	DeLucia	13-12		
5-3‡	At Chi.	L	2-4		3	9	Drabek	Springer	Hernandez	13-13	3rd	2.5
5-4	At Chi.	L	2-4		10	11	Navarro	Harris	Hernandez	13-14	3rd	3.5
5-5	At Bal.	W	7-2		8	9	Dickson	Kamieniecki	James	14-14	3rd	3.0
5-6	At Bal.	L	4-8		8	9	Erickson	Finley	Myers	14-15	3rd	4.0
5-7	At Bal.	L	0-3		8	7	Key	Watson	Myers	14-16	3rd	4.5
5-9	At Mil.	L	4-5		12	8	Eldred	Hasegawa	Jones	14-17	3rd	5.0
5-10	At Mil.	L	3-4	(10)	13	10	Jones	DeLucia		14-18	3rd	6.0
5-11	At Mil.	L	2-5		8	12	McDonald	Finley	Jones	14-19	3rd	6.0
5-12	Chi.	W	16-8		18	11	DeLucia	Levine		15-19	3rd	5.0
5-13	Chi.	W	8-7		13	11	Langston	Baldwin	James	16-19	3rd	5.0
5-14	Bal.	W	6-5		7	11	Springer	Boskie	Holtz	17-19	3rd	5.0
5-15	Bal.	W	3-2		9	3	Dickson	Kamieniecki	James	18-19	3rd	4.0
5-16	Mil.	W	5-1		8	5	Finley	McDonald		19-19	3rd	3.0
5-17	Mil.	W	6-5		8	11	Percival	Fetters		20-19	3rd	2.0
5-18	Mil.	W	5-4		6	7	Springer	Mercedes	James	21-19	3rd	2.0
5-19	Sea.	L	4-13		7	17	Moyer	Langston		21-20	3rd	2.5
5-20	Sea.	W	11-9		13	9	DeLucia	Manzanillo	Percival	22-20	3rd	2.5
5-21	Sea.	W	18-3		21	10	Finley	D. Martinez		23-20	2nd	1.5
5-23	At Tor.	W	12-2		17	7	Springer	Guzman		24-20	2nd	1.0
5-24	At Tor.	W	3-1		9	6	Watson	Williams	Percival	25-20	2nd	1.0
5-25	At Tor.	L	3-4	(11)	6	9	Timlin	DeLucia		25-21	2nd	1.0
5-26	At Det.	L	0-6		4	7	Olivares	Finley		25-22	2nd	1.0
5-27	At Det.	L	2-6		5	7	Thompson	Perisho	Myers	25-23	2nd	2.0
5-28	At Oak.	W	14-10		14	15	Percival	Mohler		26-23	2nd	1.0
5-29	At Oak.	W	7-1		12	6	Watson	Wengert		27-23	2nd	1.0
5-30	Min.	L	3-4		12	7	Tewksbury	Dickson	Aguilera	27-24	2nd	1.0
5-31	Min.	W	5-3		12	7	Finley	Aldred	Percival	28-24	2nd	1.0
6-1	Min.	L	4-5		9	12	Swindell	Hasegawa	Aguilera	28-25	2nd	1.0
6-3	K.C.	L	2-5		7	10	Belcher	Springer	Pichardo	28-26	3rd	1.5
6-4	K.C.	W	7-3		11	7	Watson	Rusch		29-26	2nd	1.0
6-5	At Min.	W	3-0		10	6	Dickson	Tewksbury	Percival	30-26	2nd	1.0
6-6	At Min.	L	7-9		10	15	Swindell	Harris	Aguilera	30-27	3rd	1.0
6-7	At Min.	L	1-6		6	13	Radke	Perisho		30-28	3rd	1.0
6-8	At Min.	W	8-6		11	6	Springer	Trombley	Percival	31-28	T2nd	1.0
6-9	At K.C.	W	12-5		18	8	Watson	Rusch		32-28	2nd	0.5
6-10	At K.C.	W	6-2		10	7	Dickson	Appier		33-28	1st	+0.5
6-11	At K.C.	L	1-6		8	8	Rosado	Finley		33-29	2nd	0.5
6-12	S.D.	W	8-4		17	9	James	Murray		34-29	2nd	0.5
6-13	S.D.	L	7-8	(14)	11	16	Bochtler	Hasegawa	Worrell	34-30	2nd	1.5
6-14	S.F.	L	3-10		14	10	Roa	Watson		34-31	3rd	2.5
6-15	S.F.	L	1-4		7	11	VanLandingham	Dickson	Beck	34-32	3rd	3.5
6-17	At L.A.	L	3-4		6	10	Hall	Percival		34-33	3rd	3.5
6-18	At L.A.	L	5-7		7	7	Dreifort	Holtz	Worrell	34-34	3rd	3.5
6-19	Oak.	W	4-3		9	9	James	Taylor		35-34	3rd	3.5
6-20	Oak.	W	5-2		6	4	Gross	Wengert	Percival	36-34	3rd	3.5
6-21	Oak.	W	5-3		6	12	DeLucia	Prieto	Percival	37-34	2nd	3.5
6-22	Oak.	W	7-6		13	6	Harris	Small	Percival	38-34	2nd	3.5

Date	Opp.	Res.	Score	(inn.*)	Hits	Opp. hits	Winning pitcher	Losing pitcher	Save	Record	Pos.	GB
6-23	At Tex.	W	1-0		7	7	Watson	Oliver	DeLucia	39-34	2nd	3.5
6-24	At Tex.	W	7-6		11	14	DeLucia	Hernandez	Percival	40-34	2nd	2.5
6-25	At Tex.	L	4-5		10	13	Gunderson	Holtz		40-35	2nd	3.5
6-26	At Sea.	L	3-6		7	14	Moyer	Dickson	Charlton	40-36	2nd	4.5
6-27	At Sea.	L	1-8		7	8	Fassero	Finley		40-37	2nd	5.5
6-28	At Sea.	W	6-1		9	3	Watson	Lowe		41-37	2nd	4.5
6-29	At Sea.	L	2-3		6	6	Ayala	DeLucia		41-38	2nd	5.5
6-30	At Col.	L	7-11		15	16	DiPoto	Gross		41-39	2nd	5.5
7-1	At Col.	W	4-1		10	6	Finley	Burke	Percival	42-39	2nd	5.5
7-2	L.A.	L	4-5		10	14	Radinsky	Percival	Worrell	42-40	2nd	5.5
7-3	L.A.	L	2-8		6	11	Nomo	Watson		42-41	2nd	5.5
7-4	Sea.	L	3-7		8	9	Johnson	Springer		42-42	3rd	6.5
7-5	Sea.	W	5-4		9	9	Percival	Charlton		43-42	3rd	5.5
7-6	Sea.	W	8-0		9	4	Finley	Fassero		44-42	2nd	4.5
7-10	At Oak.	W	8-4		12	4	Watson	Rigby	DeLucia	45-42	2nd	4.5
7-11	At Oak.	W	14-4		17	8	Dickson	Karsay		46-42	2nd	4.5
7-12	At Oak.	W	6-3		8	10	Finley	Prieto	Percival	47-42	2nd	3.5
7-13	At Oak.	W	5-3		9	4	Hasegawa	Oquist	Percival	48-42	2nd	2.5
7-14	Tex.	W	6-5		11	9	Gross	Wetteland		49-42	2nd	2.5
7-15	Tex.	W	6-2		12	9	Dickson	Hill		50-42	2nd	1.5
7-16	Det.	W	5-3		6	8	Finley	Moehler	Percival	51-42	2nd	1.5
7-17	Det.	W	9-4		12	8	Springer	Lira		52-42	2nd	0.5
7-18	Tor.	L	1-2		7	4	Williams	Watson	Escobar	52-43	2nd	1.5
7-19	Tor.	W	5-4		6	8	Percival	Timlin		53-43	2nd	0.5
7-20	Tor.	W	9-5		13	10	Finley	Andujar		54-43	2nd	0.5
7-22	At N.Y.	L	2-9		5	12	Cone	Springer		54-44	2nd	0.5
7-23	At N.Y.	L	4-5		9	10	Nelson	Hasegawa		54-45	2nd	1.5
7-25†	At Bos.	W	5-4		10	11	Finley	Gordon		55-45		
7-25‡	At Bos.	W	8-5		9	11	Holtz	Wakefield	Percival	56-45	2nd	1.5
7-26	At Bos.	L	6-7		14	13	Henry	Percival		56-46	2nd	2.5
7-27	At Bos.	L	5-6		7	9	Mahay	James		56-47	2nd	3.5
7-28†	At Cle.	W	2-0		9	8	Springer	Colon		57-47		
7-28‡	At Cle.	W	10-7		13	8	Harris	Weathers	Holtz	58-47	2nd	2.5
7-29	At Cle.	W	7-2		10	3	Finley	Clark		59-47	2nd	1.5
7-30	At Cle.	W	5-2		9	5	Hill	Nagy	James	60-47	2nd	0.5
7-31	Chi.	L	12-14		15	16	C. Castillo	Holtz	Karchner	60-48	2nd	0.5
8-1	Chi.	W	9-1		8	8	Watson	Eyre		61-48	1st	+0.5
8-2	Chi.	W	5-2		5	5	Springer	Clemons	Percival	62-48	1st	+0.5
8-3	Chi.	W	4-1		7	5	Finley	Baldwin	Percival	63-48	1st	+0.5
8-4	Mil.	L	2-5		6	14	Karl	Hill	Fetters	63-49	2nd	....
8-5	Mil.	W	6-5		8	11	Dickson	Florie	Percival	64-49	2nd	....
8-6	Mil.	W	8-6		9	11	Watson	Eldred	Percival	65-49	1st	+1.0
8-8	Bal.	L	2-6		5	12	Mussina	Springer	Myers	65-50	2nd	0.5
8-9	Bal.	W	4-3		6	7	Finley	Rhodes	Percival	66-50	1st	+0.5
8-10	Bal.	L	3-4		8	7	Benitez	James	Myers	66-51	1st	+0.5
8-12	At Chi.	L	5-8		9	13	Navarro	Dickson	T. Castillo	66-52	T1st	....
8-13	At Chi.	L	2-5		8	7	Eyre	Watson	Karchner	66-53	2nd	0.5
8-14	At Mil.	W	5-1		9	6	Springer	Mercedes		67-53	2nd	
8-15	At Mil.	W	5-3		10	9	Finley	Florie	Percival	68-53	1st	+0.5
8-16	At Bal.	L	9-10		12	13	Rhodes	May	Myers	68-54	2nd	0.5
8-17	At Bal.	L	4-5	(10)	10	12	Benitez	Hasegawa		68-55	2nd	1.0
8-18	At Bal.	L	1-2		7	8	Mills	Springer		68-56	2nd	1.0
8-19	N.Y.	W	12-4		12	7	Dickson	Wells		69-56	T1st	....
8-20†	N.Y.	L	3-7		6	12	Gooden	Hill	Mendoza	69-57		
8-20‡	N.Y.	L	5-8		9	12	Irabu	Langston	Rivera	69-58	2nd	1.5
8-21	N.Y.	L	3-4	(12)	12	10	Stanton	Harris	Nelson	69-59	2nd	2.5
8-22	Bos.	W	8-5		10	10	Watson	Saberhagen	Percival	70-59	2nd	2.5
8-23	Bos.	W	6-1		11	7	Dickson	Sele		71-59	2nd	1.5
8-24	Bos.	L	2-3		4	8	Wakefield	Hill	Gordon	71-60	2nd	2.5
8-26	Cle.	W	8-7		11	7	May	Plunk		72-60	2nd	2.0
8-27	Cle.	L	4-10		5	15	Wright	Watson		72-61	2nd	2.0
8-28	At S.D.	L	2-9		5	12	Menhart	Dickson		72-62	2nd	2.0
8-29	At S.D.	W	3-1		7	5	Hill	Smith	Percival	73-62	2nd	1.0
8-30	At S.F.	L	3-7		6	10	Estes	Springer		73-63	2nd	1.0
8-31	At S.F.	W	7-4		9	6	May	Alvarez	Percival	74-63	2nd	1.0
9-1	Col.	L	1-4		9	11	Thomson	Watson	DiPoto	74-64	2nd	2.0
9-2	Col.	L	2-7		9	12	Astacio	Dickson	Munoz	74-65	2nd	2.5
9-4	At Det.	L	4-5	(11)	5	9	Jones	Harris		74-66	2nd	3.0
9-5	At Det.	L	1-6		5	6	Thompson	Springer		74-67	2nd	4.0
9-6	At Det.	L	5-7		9	10	Moehler	Watson	Jones	74-68	2nd	5.0
9-7	At Det.	W	5-4	(15)	8	12	Hasegawa	Dishman		75-68	2nd	4.0
9-8	At Tor.	L	10-12		12	14	Plesac	James	Escobar	75-69	2nd	4.0
9-9	At Tor.	L	0-2		3	4	Carpenter	Hill		75-70	2nd	5.0
9-11	K.C.	L	2-4		11	7	Appier	Springer	Montgomery	75-71	2nd	5.5
9-12	K.C.	W	8-5		6	9	Harris	Bones	Percival	76-71	2nd	5.5

Date	Opp.	Res.	Score	(inn.*)	Hits	Opp. hits	Winning pitcher	Losing pitcher	Save	Record	Pos.	GB
9-13	K.C.	L	1-3	(13)	11	9	Olson	DeLucia	Bevil	76-72	2nd	5.5
9-14	K.C.	W	3-2		5	7	James	Service	Percival	77-72	2nd	5.5
9-15	Min.	W	8-5		9	8	Harris	Trombley		78-72	2nd	5.5
9-16	Min.	L	3-9		9	13	Radke	Hasegawa		78-73	2nd	6.0
9-17	Oak.	W	8-4		14	10	Watson	Ludwick		79-73	2nd	5.0
9-18	Oak.	L	3-7		9	9	Telgheder	Dickson		79-74	2nd	6.0
9-19	At Tex.	W	7-1		16	2	Hill	Witt		80-74	2nd	6.0
9-20	At Tex.	W	7-6		10	12	Springer	Helling	Percival	81-74	2nd	5.0
9-21	At Tex.	W	4-1		15	9	Harris	Pavlik	Percival	82-74	2nd	5.0
9-23	At Sea.	L	3-4		9	7	Johnson	Watson	Slocumb	82-75	2nd	6.5
9-24	At Sea.	W	9-3		13	5	Hill	Lira		83-75	2nd	5.5
9-25	Tex.	L	5-8		11	11	Witt	Dickson	Wetteland	83-76	2nd	6.0
9-26	Tex.	L	4-8		7	12	Helling	Holtz		83-77	2nd	6.0
9-27	Tex.	W	8-7		12	12	Percival	Santana		84-77	2nd	6.0
9-28	Tex.	L	0-4		3	9	Burkett	Watson		84-78	2nd	6.0

Monthly records: April (12-12), May (16-12), June (13-15), July (19-9), August (14-15), September (10-15).
*Innings, if other than nine. †First game of doubleheader. ‡Second game of doubleheader.

HIGHLIGHTS

High point: The team won 10 consecutive games, including three by surging lefthander Chuck Finley, from July 5-20 to move from 6½ games behind the first-place Seattle Mariners to one-half of a game back.

Low point: Reeling from Tony Phillips' drug arrest and season-ending injuries to Finley and catcher Todd Greene, the team lost eight of its first nine games in September to fall out of the division race.

Turning point: Phillips' August 10 arrest on felony possession of cocaine charges. The team was 66-50 the day Phillips was arrested but was never the same, going 18-28 after the arrest.

Most valuable player: Right fielder Tim Salmon. . . . again. Salmon was Mr. Clutch, hitting .348 with runners in scoring position and finishing with a .296 average, 33 homers and a career-high 129 RBIs.

Most valuable pitcher: Finley. He was 3-6 with a 5.71 ERA on June 27 but set a club record by winning his next 10 starts, improving to 13-6 with a 4.23 ERA before suffering a broken bone in his wrist on August 19.

Most improved player: Left fielder Garret Anderson. His power (eight homers) wasn't spectacular, but he may have been the team's most consistent hitter with a .303 average and 92 RBIs, and he batted .303 with runners in scoring position, compared to .242 in 1996.

Most pleasant surprise: Pitcher Jason Dickson. The rookie entered spring training as one of three candidates for the fifth spot in the rotation but opened as the team's No. 2 starter, going 10-4 with a 3.26 ERA in his first 20 games.

Biggest disappointment: Phillips and outfielder Rickey Henderson. Phillips let down his teammates, coaches and the organization in the middle of a pennant race, and Henderson hit .183 after the team acquired him from San Diego on August 13.

Key injuries: Finley and Greene suffered season-ending wrist injuries on consecutive nights, August 19-20; pitcher Mark

Langston was limited to nine starts because of elbow problems; pitcher Mark Gubicza's season ended after two starts because of a shoulder injury; and closer Troy Percival missed five weeks in April and May because of a nerve problem in his shoulder.

Notable: The team's 84 wins were a 14-game improvement over 1996 and the most for the franchise since 1989. . . . The team hit .278 with runners in scoring position, up from .258 in 1996; the team more than doubled its stolen base output, from 53 in 1996 to 126 in 1997; and it lowered its team ERA from 5.30 in 1996 to 4.52 in 1997. . . . Salmon became the first player in franchise history with four 30-homer seasons, and Anderson's 189 hits were the most by a lefthanded batter in club history. . . . The team led the major leagues with 27 blown saves.

—MIKE DiGIOVANNA

RECORDS

1997 regular-season record: 84-78 (2nd in A.L. West); 46-36 at home; 38-42 on road; 25-30 vs. East; 30-25 vs. Central; 29-23 vs. West; 18-23 vs. lefthanded starters; 66-55 vs. righthanded starters; 78-67 on grass; 6-11 on turf; 23-23 in daytime; 61-55 at night; 27-25 in one-run games; 5-8 in extra-inning games; 2-1-1 in doubleheaders.

Team record past five years: 350-395 (.470, ranks 10th in league in that span).

TEAM LEADERS

Batting average: Garret Anderson (.303).
At-bats: Garret Anderson (624).
Runs: Dave Hollins (101).
Hits: Garret Anderson (189).
Total bases: Tim Salmon (301).
Doubles: Garret Anderson (36).
Triples: Luis Alicea (7).
Home runs: Tim Salmon (33).
Runs batted in: Tim Salmon (129).
Stolen bases: Darin Erstad (23).
Slugging percentage: Tim Salmon (.517).
On-base percentage: Tim Salmon (.394).

Wins: Jason Dickson, Chuck Finley (13).
Earned-run average: Chuck Finley (4.23).
Complete games: Chuck Finley, Dennis Springer (3).
Shutouts: Jason Dickson, Chuck Finley, Dennis Springer (1).
Saves: Troy Percival (27).
Innings pitched: Jason Dickson (203.2).
Strikeouts: Chuck Finley (155).

GAMES BY POSITION

Catcher: Chad Kreuter 67, Jim Leyritz 58, Todd Greene 26, Jorge Fabregas 21, Angelo Encarnacion 11, Chris Turner 8.
First base: Darin Erstad 126, Jim Leyritz 15, Dave Hollins 14, Jack Howell 12, Jim Edmonds 11, Chris Turner 2.
Second base: Luis Alicea 105, Tony Phillips 43, Craig Grebeck 26, Robert Eenhoorn 3.
Third base: Dave Hollins 135, Jack Howell 24, Craig Grebeck 15, Luis Alicea 12, Robert Eenhoorn 5, George Arias 1, Tony Phillips 1.
Shortstop: Gary DiSarcina 153, Craig Grebeck 20, Robert Eenhoorn 2.
Outfield: Tim Salmon 153, Garret Anderson 148, Jim Edmonds 115, Orlando Palmeiro 52, Tony Phillips 35, Rickey Henderson 13, Craig Grebeck 3, Darin Erstad 1, Chris Turner 1.
Designated hitter: Eddie Murray 45, Tony Phillips 26, Jack Howell 22, Rickey Henderson 19, Jim Leyritz 13, Orlando Palmeiro 11, Darin Erstad 9, Jim Edmonds 8, Todd Greene 8, Luis Alicea 6, Garret Anderson 4, Tim Salmon 4, Chad Kreuter 2, George Arias 1, Chris Turner 1.

TOP DRAFT CHOICES

1. **Troy Glaus,** 3B, UCLA.
2. None.
3. **Heath Timmerman,** RHP, Northeastern Oklahoma A&M J.C.
4. **Joe Gangemi,** LHP, Seton Hall University.
5. **Michael Brunet,** RHP, Pasco-Hernando (Fla.) C.C.
6. **Matt Wise,** RHP, Cal State Fullerton.
7. **Matt Garrick,** C, Texas A&M University.
8. **Ryan Cummings,** RHP, Georgia Southern.
9. **Dwayne Dobson,** RHP, U. of South Florida.

BALTIMORE ORIOLES
AMERICAN LEAGUE EAST DIVISION

Orioles Schedule

Home games shaded. `—All-Star Game at Coors Field (Colorado).
D—Day game (any game starting before 5 p.m.).

March

SUN	MON	TUE	WED	THU	FRI	SAT
		31 D KC				

April

SUN	MON	TUE	WED	THU	FRI	SAT
			1 KC	2 KC	3 DET	4 D DET
5 D DET	6	7 KC	D 8	9 KC	10 DET	11 D DET
12 D DET	13	14 CWS	15 CWS	16 D CWS	17 TEX	18 TEX
19 D TEX	20 ANA	21 ANA	22 ANA	23	24 OAK	25 D OAK
26 OAK	27 ANA	28 ANA	29 CWS	30 D CWS		

May

SUN	MON	TUE	WED	THU	FRI	SAT
					1 MIN	2 D MIN
3 D MIN	4	5 CLE	6 CLE	7	8 TB	9 TB
10 D TB	11 MIN	12 CLE	13 CLE	14 CLE	15 TB	16 D TB
17 D TB	18 NYY	19 NYY	20 NYY	21 NYY	22 OAK	23 OAK
24 D OAK	25 SEA	26 D SEA	27	28 TEX	29 TEX	30 D TEX
31 D TEX						

June

SUN	MON	TUE	WED	THU	FRI	SAT
	1 SEA	2 SEA	3 BOS	4 BOS	5 ATL	6 ATL
7 D ATL	8 PHI	9 PHI	10 PHI	11	12 TOR	13 D TOR
14 D TOR	15 NYY	16 NYY	17 NYY	18 TOR	19 TOR	20 TOR
21 D TOR	22 NYM	23 NYM	24 NYM	25 NYM	26 MON	27 MON
28 D MON	29	30 FLA				

July

SUN	MON	TUE	WED	THU	FRI	SAT
			1 FLA	2 D FLA	3 NYY	4 D NYY
5 D NYY	6	7 *	8	9 BOS	10 BOS	11 BOS
12 D BOS	13 TOR	14 TOR	15 TEX	16 TEX	17 ANA	18 ANA
19 D ANA	20	21 OAK	22 OAK	23 OAK	24 SEA	25 SEA
26 D SEA	27	28 DET	29 DET	30 D DET	31 KC	

August

SUN	MON	TUE	WED	THU	FRI	SAT
						1 KC
2 D KC	3	4 DET	5 DET	D 6	7 MIN	8 MIN
9 D MIN	10 TB	11 TB	12 D TB	13 CLE	14 CLE	15 D CLE
16 D CLE	17 MIN	18 MIN	19 TB	20 TB	21 CLE	22 CLE
23 D CLE	24	25 CWS	26 CWS	27 CWS	28 KC	29 KC
30 D KC	31 CWS					

September

SUN	MON	TUE	WED	THU	FRI	SAT
		1 CWS	2 CWS	3	4 SEA	5 SEA
6 SEA	7 OAK	8 OAK	9 OAK	D 10	11 ANA	12 ANA
13 D ANA	14 TEX	15 TEX	16 BOS	17 BOS	18 NYY	19 NYY
20 D NYY	21 TOR	22 TOR	23 TOR	24 BOS	25 BOS	26 D BOS
27 D BOS						

1998 SEASON
CLUB DIRECTORY

Managing general partner
Peter Angelos
Vice chairman, business & finance
Joe Foss
General manager
Pat Gillick
Assistant general manager
Kevin Malone
Exec. dir., marketing & broadcasting
Mike Lehr
Director of player development
Syd Thrift
Asst. director of player development
Don Buford
Scouting director
Gary Nickels
Special assistant to the g.m.
Fred Uhlman Sr.
Scouting administrator
Matt Slater
Assistant, player development
Mike Wong
Director of finance
Robert Ames
Traveling secretary
Philip Itzoe
Director of public relations
John Maroon
Asst. director of public relations
Bill Stetka
Director of marketing and advertising
Scott Nickle
Director of stadium operations
Walter Gutowski
Director of community relations
Julie Wagner
Dir. of ballpark ent. & on-line services
Spiro Alafassos

Publishing director
Stephanie Parrillo
Director of computer services
James Kline
Director of ticket operations
Audrey Brown
Trainers
Richard Bancells
Brian Ebel
Strength and conditioning
Tim Bishop
Scouts
Dean Decillis
Lane Decker
Manny Estrada
John Gillette
John Green
Patrick Guerrero
Jesus Halabi
Ubaldo Heredia
Jim Howard
Deacon Jones
Ray Krawczik
Gil Kubski
Mike Ledna
Jeff Morris
Curt Motton
Lamar North
Fred Petersen
Salvador Ramirez
Arturo Sanchez
Harry Shelton
Ed Sprague
Marc Tramuta
Mike Tullier
Brett Ward
Don Welke
Logan White
Earl Winn
Marc Ziegler

MINOR LEAGUE AFFILIATES

Class	Team	League	Manager
AAA	Rochester	International	Marv Foley
AA	Bowie	Eastern	Joe Ferguson
A	Frederick	Carolina	Tommy Shields
A	Delmarva	South Atlantic	David Machemer
Rookie	Bluefield	Appalachian	To be announced
Rookie	Gulf Coast Orioles	Gulf Coast	To be announced

BROADCAST INFORMATION

Radio: WBAL-AM (1090).
TV: WJZ (Channel 13), WNUV
(Channel 54), WFTY (Channel 50,
Washington, D.C.).
Cable TV: Home Team Sports.

SPRING TRAINING

Ballpark (city): Ft. Lauderdale Stadium
(Ft. Lauderdale, Fla.).
Ticket information: 954-776-1921,
1-800-236-8908.

SPRING TRAINING ROSTER

Manager—Ray Miller (31).
Coaches—Carlos Bernhardt, Rick Down (48), Mike Flanagan, Elrod Hendricks (44), Eddie Murray, Sam Perlozzo (2).

No.	PITCHERS	B/T	Ht./Wt.	Born	1997 clubs
49	Benitez, Armando	R/R	6-4/225	11-3-72	Baltimore
	Charlton, Norm	B/L	6-3/205	1-6-63	Seattle
27	Coppinger, Rocky	R/R	6-5/225	3-19-74	Baltimore, Gulf Coast Orioles, Bowie
	Drabek, Doug	R/R	6-1/185	7-25-62	Chicago A.L.
19	Erickson, Scott	R/R	6-4/230	2-2-68	Baltimore
	Fussell, Chris	R/R	6-2/185	5-19-76	Bowie, Frederick
	Kamieniecki, Scott	R/R	6-0/195	4-19-64	Baltimore
21	Key, Jimmy	R/L	6-1/185	4-22-61	Baltimore
38	Krivda, Rick	R/L	6-1/180	1-19-70	Rochester, Baltimore
51	Mathews, Terry	L/R	6-2/225	10-5-64	Baltimore
75	Mills, Alan	B/R	6-1/195	10-18-66	Baltimore
	Montgomery, Steve	R/R	6-4/212	12-25-70	Edmonton, Oakland, Buffalo
	Moreno, Julio	R/R	6-1/145	10-23-75	Bowie
35	Mussina, Mike	R/R	6-1/180	12-8-68	Baltimore
47	Orosco, Jesse	R/L	6-2/205	4-21-57	Baltimore
	Percibal, Billy	R/R	6-1/156	2-2-74	Frederick, Bowie, Gulf Coast Orioles
	Ponson, Sydney	R/R	6-1/220	11-2-76	Bowie, Gulf Coast Orioles
	Ramirez, Hector	R/R	6-3/218	12-15-71	Rochester
53	Rhodes, Arthur	L/L	6-2/205	10-24-69	Baltimore
39	Rodriguez, Nerio	R/R	6-1/195	3-22-73	Rochester, Baltimore
	Stull, Everett	R/R	6-3/200	8-24-71	Ottawa, Montreal

No.	CATCHERS	B/T	Ht./Wt.	Born	1997 clubs
34	Greene, Charlie	R/R	6-2/190	1-23-71	Norfolk, Baltimore
23	Hoiles, Chris	R/R	6-0/215	3-20-65	Baltimore, Bowie
50	Rosario, Melvin	B/R	6-0/200	5-25-73	Bowie, Baltimore
	Webster, Lenny	R/R	5-9/202	2-10-65	Baltimore

No.	INFIELDERS	B/T	Ht./Wt.	Born	1997 clubs
12	Alomar, Roberto	B/R	6-0/185	2-5-68	Baltimore
14	Bordick, Mike	R/R	5-11/175	7-21-65	Baltimore
	Casimiro, Carlos	R/R	6-0/155	11-8-76	Delmarva
25	Palmeiro, Rafael	L/L	6-0/190	9-24-64	Baltimore
36	Reboulet, Jeff	R/R	6-0/174	4-30-64	Baltimore
8	Ripken, Cal	R/R	6-4/220	8-24-60	Baltimore

No.	OUTFIELDERS	B/T	Ht./Wt.	Born	1997 clubs
	Almonte, Wady	R/R	6-0/180	4-20-75	Bowie, Frederick
9	Anderson, Brady	L/L	6-1/190	1-18-64	Baltimore
3	Baines, Harold	L/L	6-2/195	3-15-59	Chicago A.L., Baltimore
	Carter, Joe	R/R	6-3/215	3-7-60	Toronto
37	Clyburn, Danny	R/R	6-3/220	4-6-74	Rochester, Baltimore
24	Davis, Eric	R/R	6-3/185	5-29-62	Baltimore
11	Hammonds, Jeffrey	R/R	6-0/195	3-5-71	Baltimore
	Kingsale, Gene	B/R	6-3/170	8-20-76	Bowie, Gulf Coast Orioles
17	Surhoff, B.J.	L/R	6-1/200	8-4-64	Baltimore
43	Tarasco, Tony	L/R	6-1/205	12-9-70	Baltimore, Rochester

BALLPARK INFORMATION

Ballpark (capacity, surface)
Oriole Park at Camden Yards (48,188, grass)
Address
333 W. Camden St.
Baltimore, MD 21201
Business phone
410-685-9800
Ticket information
410-481-SEAT
Ticket prices
$35 (club box)
$30 & $27 (field box)
$23 & $20 (terrace box)
$22 (left field club, lower box)
$18 (left field lower box, upper box)
$16 (left field upper box, lower reserve)
$13 (upper reserve, lower reserve)
$11 (left field upper reserve)
$9 (bleacher)
$7 (standing room)
Field dimensions (from home plate)
To left field at foul line, 333 feet
To center field, 400 feet
To right field at foul line, 318 feet
First game played
April 6, 1992 (Orioles 2, Indians 0)

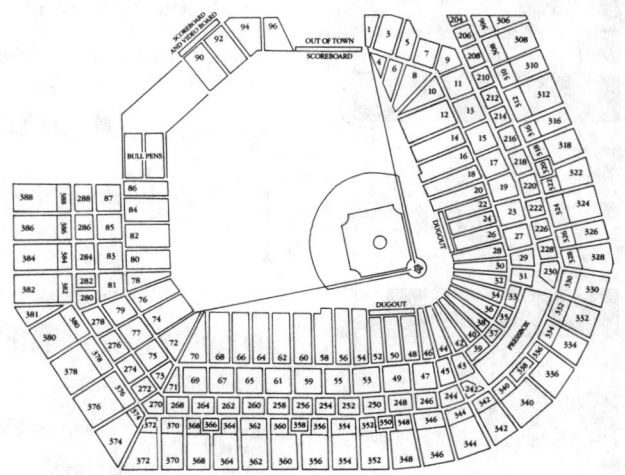

1998 SEASON *Baltimore Orioles*

Date	Opp.	Res.	Score	(inn.*)	Hits	Opp. hits	Winning pitcher	Losing pitcher	Save	Record	Pos.	GB
4-2	K.C.	W	4-2		10	7	Key	Walker	Myers	1-0	T1st	....
4-3	K.C.	W	6-4		9	8	Rhodes	Montgomery	Myers	2-0	1st	+1.0
4-4	At Tex.	W	5-4		9	5	Erickson	Patterson	Benitez	3-0	1st	+1.0
4-5	At Tex.	W	9-7		14	7	Rhodes	Oliver	Myers	4-0	1st	+1.0
4-6	At Tex.	L	3-9		6	13	Pavlik	Mussina		4-1	1st	+1.0
4-7	At K.C.	L	5-6		10	12	Walker	Benitez		4-2	1st	+1.0
4-9	At K.C.	W	4-2	(11)	8	8	Mills	Bevil	Myers	5-2	1st	+1.5
4-11	Tex.	W	9-3		16	4	Mussina	Burkett		6-2	1st	+1.5
4-13	Tex.	W	9-0		12	6	Key	Pavlik		7-2	1st	+2.5
4-14	Min.	W	4-2		9	6	Erickson	Tewksbury	Myers	8-2	1st	+3.0
4-15	Min.	W	3-1		5	2	Kamieniecki	Aldred	Myers	9-2	1st	+3.0
4-16	At Chi.	L	3-9		7	9	Drabek	Boskie		9-3	1st	+2.0
4-17	At Chi.	W	1-0		9	4	Mussina	D. Darwin	Myers	10-3	1st	+3.0
4-20	At Bos.	W	11-1		15	7	Key	Gordon		11-3	1st	+3.5
4-21	At Bos.	L	2-4		7	9	Sele	Erickson	Slocumb	11-4	1st	+3.0
4-22	Chi.	W	3-2		9	8	Mussina	D. Darwin	Myers	12-4	1st	+3.0
4-23	Chi.	L	9-11	(10)	9	15	T. Castillo	Benitez	Hernandez	12-5	1st	+3.0
4-24	Bos.	L	1-2	(12)	5	9	Trlicek	Mathews	Henry	12-6	1st	+2.0
4-25	Bos.	W	2-0		6	4	Erickson	Gordon	Myers	13-6	1st	+3.0
4-26	Bos.	W	14-5		18	10	Key	Sele	Johnson	14-6	1st	+4.0
4-27	Bos.	L	7-13		14	19	Henry	Rhodes		14-7	1st	+3.0
4-29	At Min.	W	6-4		12	7	Boskie	Swindell	Myers	15-7	1st	+4.0
4-30	At Min.	W	12-3		19	5	Kamieniecki	Tewksbury	Benitez	16-7	1st	+4.0
5-1	At Min.	W	3-2		5	5	Erickson	Aldred	Myers	17-7	1st	+4.5
5-2	Oak.	W	7-1		13	5	Key	Karsay		18-7	1st	+4.5
5-3	Oak.	L	3-4		9	7	Small	Myers	Taylor	18-8	1st	+4.5
5-4	Oak.	W	11-0		15	4	Coppinger	Prieto	Johnson	19-8	1st	+4.5
5-5	Ana.	L	2-7		9	8	Dickson	Kamieniecki	James	19-9	1st	+4.5
5-6	Ana.	W	8-4		9	8	Erickson	Finley	Myers	20-9	1st	+4.5
5-7	Ana.	W	3-0		7	8	Key	Watson	Myers	21-9	1st	+4.5
5-8	Sea.	W	13-3		13	5	Mussina	Johnson		22-9	1st	+4.5
5-9	Sea.	L	2-8		7	14	Moyer	Coppinger		22-10	1st	+4.5
5-10	Sea.	L	2-3	(11)	5	11	Charlton	Myers		22-11	1st	+3.5
5-11	Sea.	W	9-5		11	9	Erickson	D. Martinez		23-11	1st	+3.5
5-12	At Oak.	W	5-1		6	6	Key	Karsay	Benitez	24-11	1st	+4.0
5-13	At Oak.	W	7-3		13	7	Mussina	Mohler		25-11	1st	+4.0
5-14	At Ana.	L	5-6		11	7	Springer	Boskie	Holtz	25-12	1st	+3.0
5-15	At Ana.	L	2-3		3	9	Dickson	Kamieniecki	James	25-13	1st	+2.0
5-16	At Sea.	W	6-3		11	6	Erickson	D. Martinez		26-13	1st	+3.0
5-17	At Sea.	W	4-3		8	9	Key	Sanders	Benitez	27-13	1st	+3.0
5-18	At Sea.	W	8-7		8	12	Orosco	Charlton	Benitez	28-13	1st	+4.0
5-20	Det.	W	4-3		7	4	Kamieniecki	Olivares	Myers	29-13	1st	+5.0
5-21	Det.	W	2-0		5	5	Erickson	Thompson	Myers	30-13	1st	+6.0
5-23	At Cle.	L	1-6		2	12	Ogea	Key		30-14	1st	+6.5
5-24	At Cle.	W	8-3		15	9	Mussina	Kline		31-14	1st	+6.5
5-25	At Cle.	L	6-7		9	12	Nagy	Rhodes	Morman	31-15	1st	+6.0
5-26	At N.Y.	W	8-6		11	10	Boskie	Pettitte	Myers	32-15	1st	+6.5
5-27	At N.Y.	W	10-6		10	9	Kamieniecki	Rogers	Benitez	33-15	1st	+7.5
5-28	At Det.	W	8-1		10	7	Key	Moehler	Boskie	34-15	1st	+8.0
5-30	Cle.	W	3-0		9	1	Mussina	Nagy		35-15	1st	+8.5
5-31	Cle.	W	8-5		13	10	Boskie	Mesa	Myers	36-15	1st	+8.5
6-3	N.Y.	W	7-5	(10)	14	10	Myers	Mecir		37-15	1st	+8.5
6-4	N.Y.	W	9-7		10	13	Orosco	Nelson	Myers	38-15	1st	+9.5
6-6	At Chi.	L	3-7		12	11	Drabek	Erickson	Hernandez	38-16	1st	+8.5
6-7	At Chi.	L	0-1	(11)	9	8	Hernandez	Myers		38-17	1st	+7.5
6-8	At Chi.	W	2-1		9	7	Key	D. Darwin	Myers	39-17	1st	+7.5
6-9	At Chi.	W	10-2		13	5	Mussina	Baldwin		40-17	1st	+8.0
6-10†	At Bos.	W	7-2		12	7	Erickson	Eshelman		41-17		
6-10‡	At Bos.	W	4-2		9	12	Rhodes	Wakefield	Myers	42-17	1st	+8.5
6-11	At Bos.	L	1-10		4	14	Gordon	Johnson		42-18	1st	+7.5
6-12	At Bos.	L	5-9		8	11	Sele	Kamieniecki		42-19	1st	+7.0
6-13	At Atl.	W	4-3		8	7	Key	Maddux	Myers	43-19	1st	+8.0
6-14	At Atl.	W	6-4	(12)	10	8	Rhodes	Borowski	Myers	44-19	1st	+8.5
6-15	At Atl.	W	5-3	(10)	7	9	Mathews	Wohlers	Myers	45-19	1st	+9.0
6-16	Mon.	L	4-6		9	12	Hermanson	Boskie	Urbina	45-20	1st	+9.0
6-17	Mon.	W	5-4		10	10	Kamieniecki	Bullinger	Myers	46-20	1st	+9.0
6-18	Mon.	L	0-1		8	4	Perez	Key		46-21	1st	+8.0
6-20	At Tor.	L	0-3		6	10	Hentgen	Mussina		46-22	1st	+7.0
6-21	At Tor.	W	5-1		11	6	Erickson	Plesac		47-22	1st	+8.0
6-22	At Tor.	W	5-2		10	8	Kamieniecki	Person	Myers	48-22	1st	+9.0
6-23	At Mil.	L	0-5		4	11	D'Amico	Key		48-23	1st	+8.0

Date	Opp.	Res.	Score	(inn.*)	Hits	Opp. hits	Winning pitcher	Losing pitcher	Save	Record	Pos.	GB
6-24	At Mil.	W	6-2		8	4	Boskie	Karl	Rhodes	49-23	1st	+8.0
6-25	At Mil.	W	9-1		12	3	Mussina	Eldred		50-23	1st	+8.0
6-26	Tor.	L	0-3		6	6	Clemens	Erickson	Timlin	50-24	1st	+7.5
6-27	Tor.	L	1-2		5	6	Person	Kamieniecki	Spoljaric	50-25	1st	+6.5
6-28	Tor.	L	2-5		8	9	Williams	Key	Timlin	50-26	1st	+6.5
6-29	Tor.	L	2-3		5	7	Escobar	Benitez	Timlin	50-27	1st	+5.5
6-30	Phi.	W	8-1		8	6	Mussina	Maduro		51-27	1st	+5.5
7-1	Phi.	W	4-1		13	7	Erickson	Beech	Myers	52-27	1st	+6.5
7-2	Phi.	W	10-6		10	12	Rhodes	Spradlin		53-27	1st	+7.5
7-3	At Det.	W	10-1		15	5	Key	Lira		54-27	1st	+7.5
7-4†	At Det.	W	4-3		7	11	Rhodes	Keagle	Myers	55-27		
7-4‡	At Det.	L	8-11		8	9	Bautista	Mills	Jones	55-28	1st	+8.0
7-5	At Det.	L	5-6		8	8	Miceli	Orosco	Jones	55-29	1st	+7.0
7-6	At Det.	L	9-14		12	14	Blair	Erickson		55-30	1st	+7.0
7-11	Mil.	L	1-3		3	9	McDonald	Key	Jones	55-31	1st	+5.5
7-12	Mil.	L	2-3		6	12	Eldred	Erickson	Jones	55-32	1st	+4.5
7-13	Mil.	L	4-6		8	10	D'Amico	Mussina	Jones	55-33	1st	+4.5
7-14	Tor.	W	9-5		11	10	Mathews	Person		56-33	1st	+5.5
7-15	Tor.	W	8-4		13	6	Boskie	Guzman		57-33	1st	+5.5
7-16	Bos.	L	1-4		10	11	Avery	Key	Slocumb	57-34	1st	+4.5
7-17	Bos.	L	9-12		13	21	Mahay	Orosco	Slocumb	57-35	1st	+3.5
7-18	Chi.	L	0-3		3	10	Baldwin	Mussina	Hernandez	57-36	1st	+3.5
7-19	Chi.	W	8-3		9	9	Rhodes	Simas	Benitez	58-36	1st	+3.5
7-20	Chi.	L	2-10		9	19	Navarro	Boskie		58-37	1st	+3.5
7-21	At Tex.	W	5-1		8	8	Key	Oliver		59-37	1st	+3.5
7-22	At Tex.	W	9-3		16	12	Erickson	Burkett		60-37	1st	+3.5
7-23	At Tex.	W	3-2	(12)	11	9	Myers	Patterson		61-37	1st	+3.5
7-25	At Min.	L	2-5		7	8	Radke	Kamieniecki		61-38	1st	+3.5
7-26	At Min.	W	2-1	(12)	5	13	Orosco	Aguilera	Myers	62-38	1st	+4.5
7-27	At Min.	W	9-0		16	5	Erickson	Robertson		63-38	1st	+5.5
7-28	Tex.	W	7-2		13	8	Mussina	Witt	Benitez	64-38	1st	+5.5
7-29	Tex.	W	5-4		8	10	Krivda	Alberro	Myers	65-38	1st	+5.5
7-30	Tex.	W	3-1		6	3	Kamieniecki	Burkett	Myers	66-38	1st	+5.5
7-31	At Oak.	W	4-0	(11)	6	6	Benitez	Johnson		67-38	1st	+6.0
8-1	At Oak.	L	1-2		6	5	Mathews	Orosco		67-39	1st	+5.0
8-2	At Oak.	W	13-3		14	8	Mussina	Reyes		68-39	1st	+6.0
8-3	At Oak.	W	7-5		11	8	Boskie	Mathews	Myers	69-39	1st	+6.0
8-5	At Sea.	L	3-4		9	5	Charlton	Mathews		69-40	1st	+4.5
8-6	At Sea.	W	4-3	(11)	13	10	Orosco	Slocumb	Myers	70-40	1st	+5.5
8-8	At Ana.	W	6-2		12	5	Mussina	Springer	Myers	71-40	1st	+6.0
8-9	At Ana.	L	3-4		7	6	Finley	Rhodes	Percival	71-41	1st	+5.0
8-10	At Ana.	W	4-3		7	8	Benitez	James	Myers	72-41	1st	+5.0
8-12	Oak.	W	8-0		11	3	Erickson	Reyes		73-41	1st	+5.5
8-13	Oak.	L	2-4		8	8	Lorraine	Mussina	Mohler	73-42	1st	+4.5
8-15†	Sea.	W	4-3		4	8	Kamieniecki	Johnson	Myers	74-42		
8-15‡	Sea.	L	3-8		4	13	Cloude	Key		74-43	1st	+3.5
8-16	Ana.	W	10-9		13	12	Rhodes	May	Myers	75-43	1st	+4.5
8-17	Ana.	W	5-4	(10)	12	10	Benitez	Hasegawa		76-43	1st	+4.5
8-18	Ana.	W	2-1		8	7	Mills	Springer		77-43	1st	+5.0
8-19†	At K.C.	W	12-9		15	12	Mathews	Belcher		78-43		
8-19‡	At K.C.	L	2-9		7	13	Bones	Yan		78-44	1st	+5.5
8-20	At K.C.	W	4-2		8	5	Key	Rusch	Myers	79-44	1st	+5.0
8-21	At K.C.	W	4-3		9	7	Krivda	Appier	Myers	80-44	1st	+5.0
8-22	Min.	W	3-1		5	5	Erickson	Tewksbury	Myers	81-44	1st	+6.0
8-23	Min.	W	5-4		7	8	Orosco	Swindell	Myers	82-44	1st	+6.0
8-24	Min.	W	5-1		9	6	Kamieniecki	Hawkins	Benitez	83-44	1st	+7.0
8-26	K.C.	L	4-5		6	9	Whisenant	Benitez	Montgomery	83-45	1st	+6.0
8-27	K.C.	W	7-3		7	6	Rhodes	Carrasco		84-45	1st	+7.0
8-28	K.C.	L	1-5		6	7	Rosado	Mussina		84-46	1st	+6.5
8-29	N.Y. (NL)	W	4-3	(12)	10	9	Rhodes	J. Franco		85-46	1st	+7.5
8-30	N.Y. (NL)	L	6-13		9	19	Bohanon	Mathews	Lidle	85-47	1st	+7.5
8-31	N.Y. (NL)	L	1-4		6	8	Reed	Key	J. Franco	85-48	1st	+6.5
9-1	At Fla.	L	4-10		10	9	Heredia	Boskie		85-49	1st	+6.5
9-2	At Fla.	L	2-3	(10)	9	8	Vosberg	Mathews		85-50	1st	+6.5
9-3	At Fla.	L	6-7		9	13	Powell	Boskie		85-51	1st	+6.5
9-4	At N.Y.	W	5-2		14	8	Krivda	Wells	Myers	86-51	1st	+7.5
9-5	At N.Y.	W	13-9		15	16	Key	Irabu		87-51	1st	+8.5
9-6	At N.Y.	W	4-1		8	4	Erickson	Mendoza		88-51	1st	+9.5
9-7	At N.Y.	L	3-10		11	12	Rogers	Mussina		88-52	1st	+8.5
9-8	At Cle.	L	1-2		6	10	Assenmacher	Mills	Mesa	88-53	1st	+8.0
9-9	At Cle.	W	9-3		13	8	Krivda	Ogea		89-53	1st	+8.0
9-11	N.Y.	L	2-14		7	11	Pettitte	Key		89-54	1st	+7.5
9-12	N.Y.	L	5-13		12	17	Mendoza	Erickson		89-55	1st	+6.5
9-13	N.Y.	W	6-1		7	3	Mussina	Rogers		90-55	1st	+7.5
9-14	N.Y.	L	2-8		7	10	Gooden	Kamieniecki		90-56	1st	+6.5

Date	Opp.	Res.	Score	(inn.*)	Hits	Opp. hits	Winning pitcher	Losing pitcher	Save	Record	Pos.	GB
9-15†	Cle.	W	6-5		6	8	Benitez	Plunk	Myers	91-56		
9-15‡	Cle.	L	1-4		10	10	Ogea	Krivda	Mesa	91-57	1st	+6.0
9-16†	Cle.	L	2-4		7	9	Nagy	Rodriguez	Mesa	91-58		
9-16‡	Cle.	W	7-2		8	5	Key	Weathers		92-58	1st	+5.0
9-17	Mil.	L	3-8		9	14	D'Amico	Erickson		92-59	1st	+4.0
9-18	Mil.	W	4-3		7	9	Mussina	Karl	Myers	93-59	1st	+5.0
9-19	Det.	L	3-5	(10)	7	10	Jones	Mills		93-60	1st	+5.0
9-20	Det.	W	12-8		14	15	Rodriguez	Sanders		94-60	1st	+5.0
9-21	Det.	L	3-11		5	12	Thompson	Key		94-61	1st	+4.0
9-22	Det.	L	4-5		9	9	Gaillard	Benitez	Jones	94-62	1st	+3.0
9-23	At Tor.	W	3-2		9	3	Rodriguez	Clemens	Myers	95-62	1st	+4.0
9-24	At Tor.	W	9-3		12	7	Kamieniecki	Daal		96-62	1st	+4.0
9-25	At Tor.	L	3-4		13	11	Carpenter	Mussina	Escobar	96-63	1st	+3.0
9-26	At Mil.	L	2-4		6	10	Harnisch	Krivda	Jones	96-64	1st	+2.0
9-27	At Mil.	W	5-4		14	8	Mathews	Jones	Myers	97-64	1st	+2.0
9-28	At Mil.	W	7-6		10	13	Orosco	Reyes	Mathews	98-64	1st	+2.0

Monthly records: April (16-7), May (20-8), June (15-12), July (16-11), August (18-10), September (13-16).
*Innings, if other than nine. †First game of doubleheader. ‡Second game of doubleheader.

HIGHLIGHTS

High point: The Orioles defeated the Mariners in four games to win the Division Series and move on to the American League Championship Series for the second year in a row.

Low point: The June 17 announcement that outfielder Eric Davis had been diagnosed with colon cancer left the organization in shock, but Davis would come back to play in September and in the postseason.

Turning point: Opening day. The club got off to an outstanding start and never looked back. The roll didn't end until the underdog Cleveland Indians won the ALCS in six games.

Most valuable player: First baseman Rafael Palmeiro, who led the club in RBIs for the fourth consecutive season. Palmeiro hit 38 or more home runs for the third straight year and has a total of 432 RBIs in his four seasons in Baltimore.

Most valuable pitcher: Lefthanded reliever Randy Myers, who turned in one of the best performances of his career. He saved 45 games in 46 opportunities and led the league in both saves and save percentage (.978).

Most improved player: Outfielder Jeffrey Hammonds wasn't expected to play regularly, but he appeared in 118 games and hit a career-high 21 home runs.

Most pleasant surprise: Righthander Scott Kamieniecki wasn't even expected to make the club out of spring training, but he found himself in the starting rotation when injuries sidelined two starters in April. Kamieniecki went 10-6 working largely as the club's No. 4 starter, and he might have won 15 games with any kind of offensive support.

Biggest disappointment: Sophomore pitcher Rocky Coppinger was expected to make the club after winning 10 games in little more than half a season in 1996, but shoulder and elbow problems sidelined him for much of the season.

Key injuries: Outfielder Eric Davis was out for nearly three months recovering from abdominal surgery and colon cancer. Second baseman Roberto Alomar started the season on the sidelines with a sprained ankle and struggled throughout the year with a sore left shoulder. Brady Anderson opened the season with a broken rib and played through knee soreness to appear in 151 regular-season games. Catcher Chris Hoiles missed more than a month at midseason with a ligament strain in his right knee.

Notable: The Orioles became only the third team in the American League and the sixth team overall to spend every day of the regular season in first place.

—PETER SCHMUCK

RECORDS

1997 regular-season record: 98-64 (1st in A.L. East); 46-35 at home; 52-29 on road; 33-30 vs. East; 33-22 vs. Central; 32-12 vs. West; 33-19 vs. lefthanded starters; 65-45 vs. righthanded starters; 85-60 on grass; 13-4 on turf; 33-20 in daytime; 65-44 at night; 28-22 in one-run games; 10-6 in extra-inning games; 1-0-5 in doubleheaders.

Team record past five years: 405-337 (.546, ranks 3rd in league in that span).

TEAM LEADERS

Batting average: Brady Anderson (.288).
At-bats: Cal Ripken (615).
Runs: Brady Anderson (97).
Hits: Brady Anderson (170).
Total bases: Rafael Palmeiro (298).
Doubles: Brady Anderson (39).
Triples: Brady Anderson (7).
Home runs: Rafael Palmeiro (38).
Runs batted in: Rafael Palmeiro (110).
Stolen bases: Brady Anderson (18).
Slugging percentage: Rafael Palmeiro (.485).
On-base percentage: Brady Anderson (.393).
Wins: Scott Erickson, Jimmy Key (16).
Earned-run average: Mike Mussina (3.20).
Complete games: Mike Mussina (4).
Shutouts: Scott Erickson (2).
Saves: Randy Myers (45).
Innings pitched: Mike Mussina (224.2).
Strikeouts: Mike Mussina (218).

GAMES BY POSITION

Catcher: Lenny Webster 97, Chris Hoiles 87, Tim Laker 7, Charlie Greene 4, Mel Rosario 4.

First base: Rafael Palmeiro 155, Aaron Ledesma 5, Jerome Walton 5, Chris Hoiles 4, B.J. Surhoff 3.

Second base: Roberto Alomar 109, Jeff Reboulet 63, Aaron Ledesma 22.

Third base: Cal Ripken 162, Jeff Reboulet 12, Aaron Ledesma 11, B.J. Surhoff 3, Chris Hoiles 1.

Shortstop: Mike Bordick 153, Jeff Reboulet 22, Aaron Ledesma 4, Cal Ripken 3.

Outfield: B.J. Surhoff 133, Brady Anderson 124, Jeffrey Hammonds 114, Tony Tarasco 81, Geronimo Berroa 40, Eric Davis 30, Jerome Walton 19, Pete Incaviglia 18, David Dellucci 9, Danny Clyburn 1, Jeff Reboulet 1.

Designated hitter: Geronimo Berroa 42, Harold Baines 35, Pete Incaviglia 26, Brady Anderson 25, Eric Davis 12, B.J. Surhoff 9, Chris Hoiles 8, David Dellucci 5, Jeffrey Hammonds 4, Rafael Palmeiro 3, Roberto Alomar 2, Tony Tarasco 2, Jerome Walton 2, Lenny Webster 1.

TOP DRAFT CHOICES

1a. **Jayson Werth,** C, Glenwood H.S., Chatham, Ill.
1b. **Darnell McDonald,** OF, Cherry Creek H.S., Englewood, Colo.
1c. **Ntema Ndungidi,** OF, Edouard Montpetit H.S., Montreal.
2. **Sean Douglas,** RHP, Antelope Valley H.S., Lancaster, Calif.
3. **Matt Riley,** LHP, Liberty Union H.S., Oakley, Calif.
4. **Shannon Carter,** OF, El Reno (Okla.) H.S.
5. **Richard Bauer,** RHP, Treasure Valley (Ore.) C.C.
6. **Caleb Balbuena,** RHP, Cuesta (Calif.) J.C.
7. **Ray Casteel,** RHP, Northeast Texas C.C.
8. **Jay Spurgeon,** RHP, Univ. of Hawaii.
9. **Logan Cuellar,** RHP, Wharton County (Tex.) J.C.
10. **David Zwirchitz,** RHP, East H.S., Appleton, Wis.

BOSTON RED SOX
AMERICAN LEAGUE EAST DIVISION

1998 SEASON

Red Sox Schedule

Home games shaded. *—All-Star Game at Coors Field (Colorado).
D—Day game (any game starting before 5 p.m.)

March

SUN	MON	TUE	WED	THU	FRI	SAT
		31				

April

SUN	MON	TUE	WED	THU	FRI	SAT
			1 OAK	2 OAK	3 D SEA	4 SEA
5 D SEA	6 ANA	7 ANA	8 ANA	9	10 D SEA	11 SEA
12 SEA	13 OAK	14 OAK	15 OAK	16	17 CLE	18 D CLE
19 CLE	20 D CLE	21 DET	22 DET	23	24 CLE	25 D CLE
26 CLE	27 DET	28 DET	29 ANA	30 ANA		

May

SUN	MON	TUE	WED	THU	FRI	SAT
					1 TEX	2 D TEX
3 D TEX	4	5 MIN	6 MIN	7 KC	8 KC	9 KC
10 D KC	11 TEX	12 D MIN	13 MIN	14 D KC	15 KC	16 D KC
17 KC	18	19 CWS	20 CWS	21	22 NYY	23 D NYY
24 D NYY	25 D TOR	26 TOR	27	28 NYY	29 NYY	30 D NYY
31 D NYY						

June

SUN	MON	TUE	WED	THU	FRI	SAT
	1 TOR	2 TOR	3 BAL	4 BAL	5 NYM	6 D NYM
7 NYM	8 ATL	9 ATL	10 ATL	11	12 TB	13 D TB
14 TB	15 CWS	16 CWS	17 D CWS	18 TB	19 TB	20 TB
21 TB	22 D PHI	23 PHI	24 PHI	25 PHI	26 FLA	27 FLA
28 D FLA	29	30 MON				

July

SUN	MON	TUE	WED	THU	FRI	SAT
			1 MON	2 MON	3 CWS	4 CWS
5 D CWS	6	7 *	8 BAL	9 BAL	10 BAL	11 BAL
12 D BAL	13 TB	14 D TB	15 CLE	16 CLE	17 DET	18 DET
19 DET	20	21 CLE	22 CLE	23 TOR	24 TOR	25 D TOR
26 TOR	27	28 OAK	29 OAK	30 OAK	31 ANA	

August

SUN	MON	TUE	WED	THU	FRI	SAT
						1 ANA
2 ANA	3 D SEA	4 SEA	5	6 TEX	7 TEX	8 TEX
9 TEX	10	11 KC	12 KC	13 MIN	14 MIN	15 D MIN
16 D MIN	17 TEX	18 TEX	19 KC	20 KC	21 MIN	22 MIN
23 MIN	24	25 OAK	26 OAK	27 ANA	28 ANA	29 D ANA
30 ANA	31 SEA					

September

SUN	MON	TUE	WED	THU	FRI	SAT
		1 SEA	2 SEA	3 TOR	4 TOR	5 D TOR
6 TOR	7 NYY	8 NYY	9 NYY	10	11 DET	12 D DET
13 DET	14 NYY	15 NYY	16 BAL	17 BAL	18 CWS	19 CWS
20 D CWS	21 TB	22 TB	23 TB	24 BAL	25 BAL	26 D BAL
27 D BAL						

CLUB DIRECTORY

Chief executive officer
John L. Harrington
Exec. v.p. and general manager
Daniel F. Duquette
Exec. vice president administration
John S. Buckley
V.p. and chief financial officer
Robert C. Furbush
Vice president baseball operations
Michael D. Port
V.p. broadcasting and technology
James P. Healey
Vice president public affairs
Richard L. Bresciani
Vice president sales and marketing
Lawrence C. Cancro
Vice president stadium operations
Joseph F. McDermott
Assistant g.m. and legal counsel
Elaine W. Steward
Director of affiliate operations
Edward P. Kenney
Dir. of com. and baseball information
Kevin J. Shea
Dir. of human resources and office mgmt.
Michele Julian
Director of major league administration
Steven W. August
Director of player development
Robert W. Schaefer
Director of scouting
W. Wayne Britton
Exec. dir. of int'l baseball operations
R. Ray Poitevint
Coord. of baseball dev. and admin.
Kent A. Qualls
Director of Florida operations
Marci S. Blacker
Traveling secretary
John F. McCormick
Special asst. for player development
John M. Pesky
Major league scout
Frank J. Malzone
Major league special assignment scout
G. Edwin Haas
Medical director
Arthur M. Pappas, M.D.
Trainer
James W. Rowe Jr.
Physical therapist
Richard M. Zawacki
Strength and conditioning coordinator
Merle V. "B.J." Baker III
Baseball information manager
Fred Seymour Jr.
Baseball operations assistant
Thomas L. Moore
Communications credentials administrator
Kathleen J. Gordon
Instructors
Theodore S. Williams, Carl M. Yastrzemski

Executive administrative assistant
Lorraine Leong
Equip. manager and clubhouse operations
J. Joseph Cochran
Controller
Stanley H. Tran
Director of advertising and sponsorships
Jeffrey E. Goldenberg
Director of facilities management
Thomas L. Queenan Jr.
Director of food services
Patricia T. Flanagan
Director of sales
Robert G. Capilli
Director of ticket operations
Joseph P. Helyar
Executive consultant, public affairs
James "Lou" Gorman
Superintendent of grounds and maint.
Joseph P. Mooney
Box office manager
Richard J. Beaton Jr.
Broadcasting manager
James E. Shannahan
Community relations manager
Ronald E. Burton Jr.
Customer relations manager
Ann Marie C. Starzyk
Ground crew manager
Casey Erven
Group sales manager
Timothy J. Dalton
Promotions and special events manager
Susan P. Salerno
Property maintenance manager
John M. Caron
Publications manager
Debra A. Matson
Season ticket manager
Joseph L. Matthews
600 Club and suites manager
Daniel E. Lyons
Telephone sales manager
Jeffrey H. Connors
Central purchasing administrator
Eileen M. Murphy-Tagrin
Marketing administrator
Deborah A. McIntyre
Payroll administrator
Catherine A. Fahy
Public affairs administrator
Mary Jane Ryan
Executive administrative assistant
Jeanne A. Bill
Receptionist and switchboard
Helen B. Robinson
Staff accountant
Robin R. Yeingst
Scouts
Not available at press time

MINOR LEAGUE AFFILIATES

Class	Team	League	Manager
AAA	Pawtucket	International	Ken Macha
AA	Trenton	Eastern	DeMarlo Hale
A	Sarasota	Florida State	Bob Geren
A	Battle Creek	Midwest	Billy Gardner Jr.
A	Lowell	New York-Pennsylvania	Dick Berardino
Rookie	Gulf Coast Red Sox	Gulf Coast	Luis Aguayo

BROADCAST INFORMATION

Radio: WEEI-AM (680).
TV: WABU-TV (Channel 68).
Cable TV: New England Sports Network.

SPRING TRAINING

Ballpark (city): City of Palms Park (Ft. Myers, Fla.).
Ticket information: 941-334-4700.

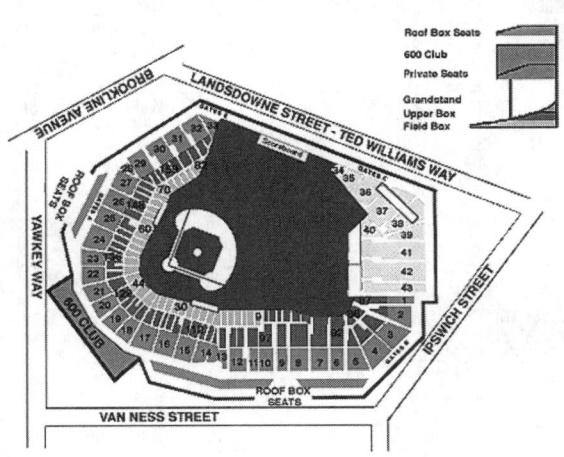

1998 SEASON *Boston Red Sox*

Manager—Jimy Williams (22).
Coaches—Dave Jauss (48), Joe Kerrigan (16), Wendell Kim (31), Grady Little (35), Jim Rice (14), Herm Starrette (23).

No.	PITCHERS	B/T	Ht./Wt.	Born	1997 clubs
33	Avery, Steve	L/L	6-4/205	4-14-70	Boston, Sarasota, Gulf Coast Red Sox, Pawtucket
	Barkley, Brian	L/L	6-2/180	12-8-75	Trenton
	Betancourt, Rafael	R/R	6-2/175	4-29-75	Michigan
	Bosio, Chris	R/R	6-3/225	4-3-63	Gulf Coast Red Sox, Sarasota
40	Checo, Robinson	R/R	6-1/185	9-9-71	Sarasota, Pawtucket, Trenton, Boston
	Corsi, Jim	R/R	6-1/220	9-9-61	Pawtucket, Boston, Gulf Coast Red Sox
43	Eckersley, Dennis	R/R	6-2/195	10-3-54	St. Louis
	Garces, Richard	R/R	6-0/215	5-18-71	Boston, Pawtucket
36	Gordon, Tom	R/R	5-9/180	11-18-67	Boston
27	Henry, Butch	L/L	6-1/205	10-7-68	Boston, Sarasota
54	Hudson, Joe	R/R	6-1/180	9-29-70	Pawtucket, Boston
	Lacy, Kerry	R/R	6-2/215	8-7-72	Pawtucket, Boston
43	Lowe, Derek	R/R	6-6/170	6-1-73	Tacoma, Seattle, Pawtucket, Boston
57	Mahay, Ron	L/L	6-2/190	6-28-71	Trenton, Pawtucket, Boston
	Martinez, Pedro J.	R/R	5-11/175	7-25-71	Montreal
	Munro, Peter	R/R	6-2/195	6-14-75	Trenton
	Rose, Brian	R/R	6-3/210	2-13-76	Pawtucket, Boston
	Saberhagen, Bret	R/R	6-1/200	4-11-64	Lowell, Trenton, Pawtucket, Boston
	Shouse, Brian	L/L	5-11/180	9-26-68	Rochester
49	Wakefield, Tim	R/R	6-2/206	8-2-66	Boston
46	Wasdin, John	R/R	6-2/193	8-5-72	Boston

No.	CATCHERS	B/T	Ht./Wt.	Born	1997 clubs
10	Hatteberg, Scott	L/R	6-1/195	12-14-69	Boston
	Leyritz, Jim	R/R	6-0/195	12-27-63	Anaheim, Texas
47	Varitek, Jason	B/R	6-2/210	4-11-72	Tacoma, Pawtucket, Boston

No.	INFIELDERS	B/T	Ht./Wt.	Born	1997 clubs
	Benjamin, Mike	R/R	6-0/169	11-22-65	Pawtucket, Boston
	Chamblee, Jim	R/R	6-4/175	5-6-75	Michigan
3	Frye, Jeff	R/R	5-9/165	8-31-66	Boston
5	Garciaparra, Nomar	R/R	6-0/167	7-23-73	Boston
18	Jefferson, Reggie	L/L	6-4/215	9-25-68	Boston
11	Naehring, Tim	R/R	6-2/203	2-1-67	Boston
29	Pozo, Arquimedez	R/R	5-10/160	8-24-73	Pawtucket, Boston
	Sadler, Donnie	R/R	5-6/165	6-17-75	Pawtucket
13	Valentin, John	R/R	6-0/180	2-18-67	Boston
42	Vaughn, Mo	L/R	6-1/240	12-15-67	Boston

No.	OUTFIELDERS	B/T	Ht./Wt.	Born	1997 clubs
56	Bragg, Darren	L/R	5-9/180	9-7-69	Boston
	Buford, Damon	R/R	5-10/170	6-12-70	Texas
44	Coleman, Michael	R/R	5-11/180	8-16-75	Trenton, Pawtucket, Boston
	Hurst, Jimmy	R/R	6-6/225	3-1-72	Jacksonville, Toledo, Detroit
	Lewis, Darren	R/R	6-0/189	8-28-67	Chicago A.L., Los Angeles
7	Nixon, Trot	L/L	6-2/196	4-11-74	Pawtucket
25	O'Leary, Troy	L/L	6-0/198	8-4-69	Boston

BALLPARK INFORMATION

Ballpark (capacity, surface)
Fenway Park (33,871, grass)
Address
4 Yawkey Way
Boston, MA 02215-3496
Business phone
617-267-9440
Ticket information
617-267-1700
Ticket prices
$30 (field box)
$27 (loge box and infield roof)
$25 (right-field boxes and right-field roof)
$20 (reserved grandstand)
$16 (outfield grandstand)
$12 (lower bleachers)
$10 (upper bleachers)
Field dimensions (from home plate)
To left field at foul line, 310 feet
To center field, 420 feet
To right field at foul line, 302 feet
First game played
April 20, 1912
(Red Sox 7, New York Highlanders 6)

1998 SEASON · *Boston Red Sox*

Date	Opp.	Res.	Score	(inn.*)	Hits	Opp. hits	Winning pitcher	Losing pitcher	Save	Record	Pos.	GB
4-2	At Ana.	W	6-5		9	12	Mahomes	Percival	Slocumb	1-0	T1st	....
4-3	At Ana.	L	0-2		5	7	Dickson	Wakefield		1-1	T2nd	1.0
4-4	At Sea.	W	10-5		15	7	Sele	Wolcott	Henry	2-1	T2nd	1.0
4-5	At Sea.	W	8-6		12	11	Trlicek	Charlton	Slocumb	3-1	2nd	1.0
4-6	At Sea.	L	7-8	(10)	11	9	Charlton	Trlicek		3-2	2nd	1.0
4-7	At Oak.	L	2-6		6	8	Lewis	Gordon	Taylor	3-3	T2nd	1.0
4-8	At Oak.	W	13-7		17	12	Trlicek	Wengert	Henry	4-3	2nd	0.5
4-9	At Oak.	L	3-4	(10)	10	10	Small	Trlicek		4-4	T2nd	1.5
4-11	Sea.	L	3-5		6	12	Johnson	Avery	Charlton	4-5	T4th	2.5
4-12	Sea.	L	1-5	(10)	2	7	Fassero	Corsi		4-6	5th	3.0
4-13	Sea.	W	7-1		11	5	Gordon	Sanders		5-6	T4th	3.0
4-14	Oak.	W	10-1		14	3	Wakefield	Adams		6-6	2nd	3.0
4-15	Oak.	W	7-2		11	7	Sele	Karsay		7-6	2nd	3.0
4-16	Cle.	W	11-6		16	10	Avery	Ogea		8-6	2nd	2.0
4-17	Cle.	L	3-4		10	10	Kline	Trlicek	Mesa	8-7	2nd	3.0
4-20	Bal.	L	1-11		7	15	Key	Gordon		8-8	3rd	4.0
4-21	Bal.	W	4-2		9	7	Sele	Erickson	Slocumb	9-8	2nd	3.0
4-22	At Cle.	W	8-2		15	4	Avery	Ogea	Henry	10-8	2nd	3.0
4-23	At Cle.	L	7-11		14	15	McDowell	Trlicek		10-9	2nd	3.0
4-24	At Bal.	W	2-1	(12)	9	5	Trlicek	Mathews	Henry	11-9	2nd	2.0
4-25	At Bal.	L	0-2		4	6	Erickson	Gordon	Myers	11-10	2nd	3.0
4-26	At Bal.	L	5-14		10	18	Key	Sele	Johnson	11-11	T2nd	4.0
4-27	At Bal.	W	13-7		19	14	Henry	Rhodes		12-11	2nd	3.0
4-29	Ana.	L	4-5		11	12	Holtz	Henry	James	12-12	T2nd	4.0
4-30	Ana.	W	11-2		13	7	Hammond	Dickson		13-12	T2nd	4.0
5-2	At Tex.	W	5-4		12	8	Henry	Patterson	Slocumb	14-12	T2nd	4.5
5-3	At Tex.	L	6-7		12	14	Vosberg	Slocumb		14-13	T2nd	4.5
5-4	At Tex.	L	6-7		9	13	Patterson	Henry	Wetteland	14-14	3rd	5.5
5-5	K.C.	L	0-2		5	7	Appier	Hammond		14-15	4th	5.5
5-6	K.C.	L	2-7		5	11	Rosado	Gordon	Pichardo	14-16	4th	6.5
5-7	Min.	W	11-3		14	8	Sele	Radke		15-16	4th	6.5
5-8	Min.	L	7-10		14	11	Robertson	Garces	Aguilera	15-17	4th	7.5
5-9	Tex.	L	1-5		5	10	Witt	Wasdin		15-18	4th	7.5
5-10	Tex.	L	5-11		11	15	Patterson	Slocumb		15-19	4th	7.5
5-11	Tex.	L	6-8		14	11	Santana	Gordon	Wetteland	15-20	4th	8.5
5-13	At K.C.	L	0-9		2	15	Belcher	Sele		15-21	5th	10.0
5-14	At K.C.	L	2-6		10	9	Veres	Wakefield	Pichardo	15-22	5th	10.0
5-16	At Min.	L	5-11		9	17	Aldred	Hammond		15-23	5th	10.5
5-17	At Min.	W	4-0		8	4	Gordon	Radke		16-23	5th	10.5
5-18	At Min.	L	5-7		8	11	Robertson	Sele	Aguilera	16-24	5th	11.5
5-20	At Chi.	L	1-10		7	10	Navarro	Wakefield		16-25	5th	13.5
5-21	At Chi.	L	5-10		11	11	Drabek	Hammond		16-26	5th	13.5
5-22	At N.Y.	W	8-2		19	9	Gordon	Wells		17-26	5th	13.0
5-23	At N.Y.	W	9-3		12	6	Sele	Nelson		18-26	5th	12.0
5-24	At N.Y.	L	2-4		6	8	Rivera	Wasdin		18-27	5th	13.0
5-26	Mil.	W	3-2		7	8	Hammond	Jones		19-27	5th	12.5
5-27	Mil.	W	7-6		10	8	Corsi	Adamson	Slocumb	20-27	5th	12.5
5-28	Chi.	W	5-3		5	6	Sele	Alvarez	Slocumb	21-27	5th	12.5
5-29	Chi.	L	2-5	(11)	7	13	Hernandez	Wasdin	Simas	21-28	5th	13.0
5-30	N.Y.	W	10-4		18	9	Hammond	Mendoza		22-28	5th	13.0
5-31	N.Y.	L	2-7		7	9	Pettitte	Wakefield		22-29	5th	14.0
6-1	N.Y.	L	6-11	(15)	17	16	Nelson	Lacy		22-30	5th	14.5
6-2	N.Y.	L	2-5		8	14	Wells	Sele	Rivera	22-31	5th	15.0
6-3	At Mil.	L	4-6		11	12	Wickman	Slocumb		22-32	5th	16.0
6-4	At Mil.	L	11-13		12	16	Eldred	Brandenburg	Jones	22-33	5th	17.0
6-5	At Mil.	W	2-1		6	7	Wakefield	McDonald	Lacy	23-33	5th	16.5
6-6	Cle.	L	3-7		11	10	Hershiser	Gordon		23-34	5th	16.5
6-7	Cle.	L	5-9		11	13	Colon	Sele		23-35	T5th	16.5
6-8	Cle.	W	12-6		16	8	Hudson	Ogea		24-35	5th	16.5
6-10†	Bal.	L	2-7		7	12	Erickson	Eshelman		24-36		
6-10‡	Bal.	L	2-4		12	9	Rhodes	Wakefield	Myers	24-37	5th	19.0
6-11	Bal.	W	10-1		14	4	Gordon	Johnson		25-37	5th	18.0
6-12	Bal.	W	9-5		11	8	Sele	Kamieniecki		26-37	5th	17.0
6-13	At N.Y. (NL)	W	8-4		11	12	Suppan	Reed	Lacy	27-37	5th	17.0
6-14	At N.Y. (NL)	L	2-5		3	11	Clark	Wakefield	J. Franco	27-38	5th	18.0
6-15	At N.Y. (NL)	W	10-1		13	5	Eshelman	Jones		28-38	5th	18.0
6-16	Phi.	W	5-4	(10)	15	11	Wasdin	Bottalico		29-38	5th	17.0
6-17	Phi.	W	12-6		16	10	Sele	Ruffcorn	Lacy	30-38	T4th	17.0
6-18	Phi.	W	4-2		8	5	Suppan	Schilling	Hammond	31-38	T4th	16.0
6-20	At Det.	L	6-12		10	16	Thompson	Wakefield	Sager	31-39	5th	16.0
6-21	At Det.	L	4-15		12	16	Bautista	Eshelman		31-40	5th	17.0
6-22	At Det.	W	2-1		6	7	Gordon	Blair	Slocumb	32-40	5th	17.0

Date	Opp.	Res.	Score	(inn.*)	Hits	Opp. hits	Winning pitcher	Losing pitcher	Save	Record	Pos.	GB
6-23	At Tor.	W	7-6		13	13	Sele	Williams	Slocumb	33-40	T4th	16.0
6-24	At Tor.	W	9-6		15	13	Wasdin	Andujar	Slocumb	34-40	4th	16.0
6-25	At Tor.	W	13-12		16	12	Wakefield	Hentgen	Slocumb	35-40	3rd	16.0
6-26	Det.	L	6-10		14	17	Moehler	Eshelman		35-41	4th	16.0
6-27	Det.	L	1-2	(11)	6	8	Miceli	Hammond	Jones	35-42	T4th	16.0
6-28	Det.	L	2-9		7	11	Lira	Sele		35-43	5th	16.0
6-29	Det.	W	8-6		9	13	Wasdin	Bautista	Slocumb	36-43	T4th	15.0
6-30	Fla.	L	5-8		7	9	Fernandez	Wakefield		36-44	5th	16.0
7-1	Fla.	W	9-2		14	9	Eshelman	Rapp	Corsi	37-44	5th	16.0
7-2	Fla.	L	2-3		8	5	Brown	Gordon	Nen	37-45	5th	17.0
7-3	At Chi.	W	4-1		7	7	Sele	Drabek		38-45	5th	17.0
7-4	At Chi.	L	5-6		8	9	Hernandez	Slocumb		38-46	5th	17.5
7-5	At Chi.	L	8-11		13	14	D. Darwin	Avery		38-47	5th	17.5
7-6	At Chi.	L	5-6		13	9	Baldwin	Wakefield	Hernandez	38-48	5th	17.5
7-10	Tor.	W	8-7	(11)	16	11	Eshelman	Timlin		39-48	5th	17.0
7-11	Tor.	L	4-8		11	12	Hentgen	Wasdin		39-49	5th	17.0
7-12	Tor.	L	1-3		4	6	Clemens	Sele	Spoljaric	39-50	5th	17.0
7-13	Tor.	L	2-3		7	6	Williams	Wakefield	Escobar	39-51	5th	17.0
7-14	Det.	W	18-4		21	8	Suppan	Jarvis		40-51	5th	17.0
7-15	Det.	L	5-7	(12)	14	14	Jones	Wasdin		40-52	5th	18.0
7-16	At Bal.	W	4-1		11	10	Avery	Key	Slocumb	41-52	5th	17.0
7-17	At Bal.	W	12-9		21	13	Mahay	Orosco	Slocumb	42-52	5th	16.0
7-18	At Cle.	W	7-0		14	6	Wakefield	Colon		43-52	5th	15.0
7-19	At Cle.	W	6-3		8	9	Suppan	Clark	Slocumb	44-52	5th	15.0
7-20	At Cle.	L	2-7		8	11	Nagy	Gordon		44-53	5th	15.0
7-21	At Cle.	W	3-1		8	4	Avery	Wright	Slocumb	45-53	5th	15.0
7-22	Oak.	W	4-3		12	9	Henry	Groom	Slocumb	46-53	5th	15.0
7-23	Oak.	L	2-5		11	11	Wengert	Wakefield	Taylor	46-54	5th	16.0
7-24	Oak.	W	3-0		10	6	Suppan	Rigby	Slocumb	47-54	5th	15.5
7-25†	Ana.	L	4-5		11	10	Finley	Gordon		47-55		
7-25‡	Ana.	L	5-8		11	9	Holtz	Wakefield	Percival	47-56	5th	16.0
7-26	Ana.	W	7-6		13	14	Henry	Percival		48-56	5th	16.0
7-27	Ana.	W	6-5		9	7	Mahay	James		49-56	4th	16.0
7-29	Sea.	W	4-0		8	5	Wakefield	Johnson		50-56	4th	16.5
7-30	Sea.	W	8-7	(10)	18	12	Corsi	Hurtado		51-56	4th	16.5
7-31	At K.C.	L	2-3	(10)	10	7	Carrasco	Slocumb		51-57	4th	17.5
8-1	At K.C.	W	10-3		15	7	Avery	Rosado		52-57	4th	16.5
8-2	At K.C.	L	3-10		9	13	Belcher	Sele		52-58	4th	17.5
8-3	At K.C.	L	2-5		7	6	Bones	Wakefield	Montgomery	52-59	5th	18.5
8-4	At Tex.	W	11-5		13	10	Henry	Patterson		53-59	3rd	18.0
8-5	At Tex.	W	17-1		24	5	Gordon	Alberro		54-59	3rd	17.0
8-6	At Min.	W	5-2		7	7	Wakefield	Robertson	Henry	55-59	3rd	17.0
8-7	At Min.	W	7-6		9	5	Sele	Bowers	Corsi	56-59	3rd	16.5
8-8	K.C.	W	8-2		15	7	Avery	Bones		57-59	3rd	16.5
8-9	K.C.	L	2-9		6	12	Rusch	Suppan		57-60	3rd	16.5
8-10	K.C.	W	6-4		10	9	Corsi	Carrasco		58-60	3rd	16.5
8-11	Tex.	L	3-8		9	15	Oliver	Wakefield		58-61	3rd	17.0
8-12	Tex.	L	2-12		10	17	Witt	Sele		58-62	4th	18.0
8-13	Tex.	L	6-7		15	7	Sturtze	Avery	Wetteland	58-63	4th	18.0
8-14	Min.	W	6-1		8	6	Suppan	Radke		59-63	4th	17.5
8-15	Min.	W	5-4	(10)	11	8	Lacy	Guardado		60-63	T3rd	17.0
8-16	Min.	W	12-4		12	10	Wakefield	Bowers		61-63	3rd	17.0
8-17	Min.	W	10-5		14	9	Sele	Tewksbury		62-63	3rd	17.0
8-20†	At Oak.	W	7-5		11	11	Wakefield	Haynes	Henry	63-63		
8-20‡	At Oak.	W	5-4	(13)	16	8	Hudson	Wengert	Gordon	64-63	3rd	17.0
8-21	At Oak.	L	6-13		10	17	Lorraine	Avery		64-64	3rd	18.0
8-22	At Ana.	L	5-8		10	10	Watson	Saberhagen	Percival	64-65	3rd	19.0
8-23	At Ana.	L	1-6		7	11	Dickson	Sele		64-66	3rd	20.0
8-24	At Ana.	W	3-2		8	4	Wakefield	Hill	Gordon	65-66	3rd	20.0
8-25	At Sea.	W	9-8		17	11	Hudson	Slocumb	Gordon	66-66	3rd	19.5
8-26	At Sea.	L	2-8		7	14	Moyer	Avery		66-67	3rd	19.5
8-27	At Sea.	W	9-5		14	7	Wasdin	Fassero	Gordon	67-67	3rd	19.5
8-29	Atl.	L	1-9		8	16	Smoltz	Sele		67-68	3rd	20.0
8-30	Atl.	L	2-15		7	19	Millwood	Wakefield		67-69	3rd	20.0
8-31	Atl.	L	3-7		6	13	Glavine	Avery		67-70	3rd	20.0
9-1	At Mon.	L	2-4	(10)	3	6	Urbina	Hudson		67-71	3rd	20.0
9-2	At Mon.	L	5-6		7	9	DeHart	Brandenburg	Urbina	67-72	3rd	20.0
9-3	At Mon.	L	0-1		2	1	Perez	Sele		67-73	3rd	20.0
9-5	Mil.	L	1-7		7	14	Eldred	Suppan		67-74	4th	21.5
9-6	Mil.	W	10-2		11	8	Wakefield	Harnisch		68-74	3rd	21.5
9-7	Mil.	W	11-2		14	11	Henry	D'Amico		69-74	3rd	20.5
9-9	N.Y.	L	6-8		9	13	Banks	Lowe	Rivera	69-75	5th	21.0
9-10	N.Y.	W	5-2		12	6	Sele	Wells	Gordon	70-75	T3rd	20.5
9-12	At Mil.	W	4-2		9	6	Suppan	D'Amico	Gordon	71-75	4th	19.0
9-13	At Mil.	W	2-1		9	4	Wakefield	Karl	Gordon	72-75	3rd	19.0

Date	Opp.	Res.	Score	(inn.*)	Hits	Opp. hits	Winning pitcher	Losing pitcher	Save	Record	Pos.	GB
9-14	At Mil.	W	2-1		4	7	Henry	Mercedes	Gordon	73-75	3rd	18.0
9-15	At N.Y.	L	6-7		12	11	Rivera	Corsi		73-76	4th	18.5
9-16†	At N.Y.	L	0-2		5	9	Pettitte	Wasdin	Rivera	73-77		
9-16‡	At N.Y.	L	3-4		7	9	Banks	Checo	Rivera	73-78	4th	19.5
9-17	Tor.	W	4-3		7	7	Mahay	Quantrill	Gordon	74-78	4th	18.5
9-18	Tor.	W	3-2		9	9	Corsi	Escobar		75-78	4th	18.5
9-19	Chi.	L	4-5	(10)	12	12	Foulke	Lowe	T. Castillo	75-79	4th	18.5
9-20	Chi.	L	4-6		13	12	McElroy	Avery	T. Castillo	75-80	4th	19.5
9-21	Chi.	W	5-2		10	10	Corsi	Fordham	Gordon	76-80	4th	18.5
9-23	At Det.	L	0-6		7	11	Keagle	Suppan		76-81	4th	19.0
9-24	At Det.	W	9-2		15	5	Wakefield	Blair		77-81	4th	19.0
9-25	At Det.	W	3-1		8	4	Checo	Sanders	Gordon	78-81	4th	18.0
9-26	At Tor.	L	0-3		10	6	Williams	Henry		78-82	4th	18.0
9-27	At Tor.	L	5-12		10	15	Janzen	Corsi		78-83	4th	19.0
9-28	At Tor.	L	2-3		8	8	Plesac	Gordon		78-84	4th	20.0

Monthly records: April (13-12), May (9-17), June (14-15), July (15-13), August (16-13), September (11-14).
*Innings, if other than nine. †First game of doubleheader. ‡Second game of doubleheader.

HIGHLIGHTS

High point: In a season of mediocrity, Fenway Park fans had little to cheer for. But on July 12, Roger Clemens had a stunning return to the place where he starred for 13 years. Clemens turned boos to cheers when he struck out 16 in a 3-1 Blue Jays victory. It was a brilliant way for the greatest pitcher in Red Sox history to return.

Low point: On June 11, outfielder Wilfredo Cordero was arrested for domestic violence when he hit and threatened to kill his wife Ana in their Cambridge, Mass. apartment. Cordero was unofficially placed on the restricted list, but the players association forced the team to reinstate him. He was released following the season.

Turning point: The team was 14-12 after 26 games, but consecutive 7-6 losses in Texas started a run in which the Red Sox lost 11 of 12 and were buried in the standings.

Most valuable player: Nomar Garciaparra produced the best season ever by a rookie shortstop and proved to be unlike any player the franchise has ever had. Besides playing outstanding defense, Garciaparra hit .306 with 30 homers, 98 RBIs, 22 stolen bases, 11 triples and 44 doubles.

Most valuable pitcher: Tom Gordon began the season as the opening day starter and ended it as the closer. In between, he was the team's most consistent pitcher. Gordon was 6-10, with a 3.74 ERA in 42 games, including 25 starts.

Most improved player: Second baseman Jeff Frye hit .286 in 105 games in '96, when he was a nice surprise as a utility player. But in '97, Frye established himself as an everyday player. He hit .312 with 19 stolen bases.

Most pleasant surprise: Even though the team believed Garciaparra could be a special player, he far exceeded expectations. At the very least, he was considered a strong defensive shortstop who might hit .280. Instead, he was one of the best all-around players in the game.

Biggest disappointment: After losing Roger Clemens, the Red Sox responded

by signing lefthander Steve Avery. The former 18-game winner for the Braves was a bust, though. Avery was 6-7, with a 6.42 ERA in 22 games, including 18 starts. He was sent to the bullpen, but manager Jimy Williams gave him a start late in the season that triggered an option in his contract. So Avery will be back in '98.

Key injuries: Third baseman Tim Naehring, one of the team's leaders, injured his elbow in late June. He had surgery in early July and missed the rest of the season. John Valentin moved to third and Frye became the everyday second baseman, but Naehring's professionalism was missed.

Notable: Garciaparra set several team and league records, the most notable a 30-game hitting streak that was the longest by an American League rookie.

—PAUL DOYLE

RECORDS

1997 regular-season record: 78-84 (4th in A.L. East); 39-42 at home; 39-42 on road; 28-35 vs. East; 28-27 vs. Central; 22-22 vs. West; 14-28 vs. lefthanded starters; 64-56 vs. righthanded starters; 68-74 on grass; 10-10 on turf; 22-28 in daytime; 56-56 at night; 24-20 in one-run games; 6-10 in extra-inning games; 1-3-0 in doubleheaders.

Team record past five years: 383-362 (.514, ranks 6th in league in that span).

TEAM LEADERS

Batting average: Reggie Jefferson (.319).
At-bats: Nomar Garciaparra (684).
Runs: Nomar Garciaparra (122).
Hits: Nomar Garciaparra (209).
Total bases: Nomar Garciaparra (365).
Doubles: John Valentin (47).
Triples: Nomar Garciaparra (11).
Home runs: Mo Vaughn (35).
Runs batted in: Nomar Garciaparra (98).
Stolen bases: Nomar Garciaparra (22).
Slugging percentage: Mo Vaughn (.560).
On-base percentage: Mo Vaughn (.420).
Wins: Aaron Sele (13).
Earned-run average: Tom Gordon (3.74).

Complete games: Tim Wakefield (4).
Shutouts: Tim Wakefield (2).
Saves: Heathcliff Slocumb (17).
Innings pitched: Tim Wakefield (201.1).
Strikeouts: Tom Gordon (159).

GAMES BY POSITION

Catcher: Scott Hatteberg 106, Bill Haselman 66, Mike Stanley 15, Walt McKeel 4, Jason Varitek 1.
First base: Mo Vaughn 131, Mike Stanley 31, Reggie Jefferson 12, Mike Benjamin 4, Jeff Frye 1, Walt McKeel 1.
Second base: Jeff Frye 80, John Valentin 79, Mike Benjamin 5, Wil Cordero 1.
Third base: Tim Naehring 68, John Valentin 64, Mike Benjamin 19, Jeff Frye 18, Arquimedez Pozo 4, Darren Bragg 1.
Shortstop: Nomar Garciaparra 153, Mike Benjamin 16, Jeff Frye 3.
Outfield: Darren Bragg 150, Troy O'Leary 142, Wil Cordero 137, Shane Mack 45, Jesus Tavarez 35, Rudy Pemberton 23, Jeff Frye 13, Michael Coleman 7, Jose Malave 4.
Designated hitter: Reggie Jefferson 119, Mike Stanley 53, Jeff Frye 11, Mo Vaughn 9, Shane Mack 5, Wil Cordero 2, Jesus Tavarez 2, Mike Benjamin 1, Scott Hatteberg 1, Tim Naehring 1, Troy O'Leary 1.

TOP DRAFT CHOICES

1a. **John Curtice,** LHP, Great Bridge, H.S., Chesapeake, Va.
1b. **Mark Fischer,** OF, Georgia Tech.
2a. **Aaron Capista,** SS, Joliet (Ill.) Catholic H.S.
2b. **Eric Glaser,** RHP, Highlands H.S., Fort Thomas, Ky.
3. **Travis Harper,** RHP, James Madison Univ.
4. **Ramon Santos,** SS, Miguel Melendez H.S., Cayey, P.R.
5. **Greg Miller,** LHP, Aurora H.S., West Aurora, Ill.
6. **Kris Wilken,** C, El Dorado H.S., Albuquerque, N.M.
7. **Jeff Taglienti,** RHP, Tufts (Mass.) Univ.
8. **Andrew Hazlett,** LHP, Univ. of Portland.
9. **Justin Wayne,** RHP, Punahou H.S., Honolulu.
10. **Marty McCleary,** RHP, Mount Vernon Nazarene (Ohio) College.

CHICAGO WHITE SOX
AMERICAN LEAGUE CENTRAL DIVISION

White Sox Schedule
Home games shaded. *—All-Star Game at Coors Field (Colorado). D—Day game (any game starting before 5 p.m.).

March
SUN	MON	TUE	WED	THU	FRI	SAT
		31 D TEX				

April
SUN	MON	TUE	WED	THU	FRI	SAT
			1 TEX	2 D TB	3 TB	4 TB
5 D TB	6 D TEX	7	8 TEX	9 D TEX	10 TB	11 D TB
12 D TB	13	14 BAL	15 BAL	16 BAL	17 D TOR	18 D TOR
19 D TOR	20	21 CLE	22 CLE	23 CLE	24 TOR	25 TOR
26 D TOR	27 CLE	28 CLE	29 BAL	30 D BAL		

May
SUN	MON	TUE	WED	THU	FRI	SAT
					1 ANA	2 ANA
3 D ANA	4 ANA	5 SEA	6 SEA	7	8 OAK	9 D OAK
10 OAK	11	12 ANA	13 ANA	14 SEA	15 SEA	16 SEA
17 OAK	18 D OAK	19 BOS	20 BOS	21	22 DET	23 DET
24 DET	25 NYY	26 NYY	27 NYY	28 DET	29 DET	30 DET
31 D DET						

June
SUN	MON	TUE	WED	THU	FRI	SAT
	1 NYY	2 NYY	3 KC	4 KC	5 D CUB	6 D CUB
7 D CUB	8 STL	9 STL	10 STL	11	12 MIN	13 MIN
14 MIN	15 BOS	16 BOS	17 BOS	18 D BOS	19 MIN	20 MIN
21 D MIN	22 PIT	23 PIT	24 CIN	25 CIN	26 MIL	27 MIL
28 D MIL	29	30 HOU				

July
SUN	MON	TUE	WED	THU	FRI	SAT
		1 HOU	2 HOU	3 BOS	4 D BOS	
5 D BOS	6	7	* 8	9 KC	10 KC	11 KC
12 KC	13 MIN	14 MIN	15 TOR	16 TOR	17 CLE	18 CLE
19 CLE	20 CLE	21 TOR	22 TOR	23	24 NYY	25 D NYY
26 D NYY	27	28 TB	29 TB	30	31 TEX	

August
SUN	MON	TUE	WED	THU	FRI	SAT
						1 TEX
2 TEX	3 TB	4 TB	5 TB	6	7 ANA	8 ANA
9 D ANA	10 OAK	11 OAK	12 D OAK	13	14 SEA	15 SEA
16 SEA	17 ANA	18 ANA	19 OAK	20 OAK	21 SEA	22 SEA
23 D SEA	24 SEA	25 BAL	26 BAL	27 BAL	28 TEX	29 TEX
30 D TEX	31 BAL					

September
SUN	MON	TUE	WED	THU	FRI	SAT
		1 BAL	2 BAL	3	4 NYY	5 NYY
6 D NYY	7 DET	8 DET	9 DET	10	11 CLE	12 D CLE
13 CLE	14 DET	15 DET	16 KC	17 KC	18 BOS	19 BOS
20 BOS	21 MIN	22 MIN	23 MIN	24 KC	25 KC	26 KC
27 D KC						

1998 SEASON
CLUB DIRECTORY

Chairman
Jerry Reinsdorf
Vice chairman
Eddie Einhorn
Executive vice president
Howard Pizer
Senior v.p., major league operations
Ron Schueler
Sr. v.p., marketing and broadcasting
Rob Gallas
Senior vice president, baseball
Jack Gould
Vice president, finance
Tim Buzard
Vice president, stadium operations
Terry Savarise
V.p., free agent and major league scouting
Larry Monroe
Vice president, player development
Ken Williams
Dir. of baseball operations/asst. g.m.
Dan Evans
Special assistants to Ron Schueler
Ed Brinkman
Mark Weidemaier
Dave Yoakum
Director of scouting
Duane Shaffer
Director of minor league administration
Steve Noworyta
Director of minor league instruction
Jim Snyder
Traveling secretary
Glen Rosenbaum
Asst. dir. of min. league & scouting admin.
Grace Guerrero Zwit
Asst. dir. of scouting & min. league op.
Daniel Fabian
Director of marketing and broadcasting
Bob Grim
Director of community relations
Christine Makowski

Director of sales
Jim Muno
Director of ticket operations
Bob Devoy
Dir. of management information services
Don Brown
Director of human resources
Moira Foy
Controller
Bill Waters
Director of public relations
Scott Reifert
Trainers
Herm Schneider
Mark Anderson
Director of conditioning
Steve Odgers
Team physicians
Dr. James Boscardin
Dr. Hugo Cuadros
Dr. Bernard Feldman
Dr. David Orth
Dr. Scott Price
Dr. Lowell Scott Weil
Scouting national cross-checker
George Bradley
Scouting supervisors
Doug Laumann
Ed Pebley
Full-time scouts
Juan Ramon Bernhardt, Joseph Butler, Scott Cerny, Hernan Cortes, Alex Cosmidis, Ed Crosby, Roberto Espinoza, Larry Grefer, Warren Hughes, Miguel Ibarra, Joe Karp, John Kazanas, Reginald Lewis, Jose Ortega, Gary Pellant, Paul Provas, Hector Rincones, Michael Sgobba, Ken Stauffer, John Tumminia
Part-time scouts
Tom Butler, Javier Ceteno, Mike Davenport, John Doldeorian, Joe Ingalls, Jack Jolly, George Kachigian, Dario Lodigiani, Donald Metzger, Al Otto, Michael Paris, Emanuel Upton

MINOR LEAGUE AFFILIATES

Class	Team	League	Manager
AAA	Calgary	Pacific Coast	Tom Spencer
AA	Birmingham	Southern	Dave Huppert
A	Hickory	South Atlantic	Mark Haley
A	Winston-Salem	Carolina	Chris Cron
Rookie	Bristol	Appalachian	Nick Capra
Rookie	Tucson White Sox	Arizona	To be announced

BROADCAST INFORMATION

Radio: WMVP-AM (1000).
TV: WGN-TV (Channel 9).
Cable TV: Fox Sports Chicago.

SPRING TRAINING

Ballpark (city): Tucson Electric Park (Tucson, Ariz.).
Ticket information: 888-683-3900.

SPRING TRAINING ROSTER

Manager—Jerry Manuel (6).
Coaches—Ron Jackson (52), Wallace Johnson, Art Kusyner (53), Bryan Little, Joe Nossek (21), Mike Pazik (25).

No.	PITCHERS	B/T	Ht./Wt.	Born	1997 clubs
	Ambrose, John	R/R	6-5/180	11-1-74	Winston-Salem
37	Baldwin, James	R/R	6-3/210	7-15-71	Chicago A.L.
	Barcelo, Lorenzo	R/R	6-4/180	8-10-77	San Jose, Shreveport, Birmingham
46	Bere, Jason	R/R	6-3/215	5-26-71	Gulf Coast White Sox, Hickory, Birmingham, Nashville, Chicago A.L.
	Bertotti, Mike	L/L	6-1/185	1-18-70	Chicago A.L., Nashville
	Castillo, Carlos	R/R	6-2/240	4-21-75	Chicago A.L., Nashville
49	Castillo, Tony	L/L	5-10/190	3-1-63	Chicago A.L.
60	Cruz, Nelson	R/R	6-1/175	9-13-72	Nashville, Chicago A.L.
36	Eyre, Scott	L/L	6-1/160	5-30-72	Birmingham, Chicago A.L.
32	Fordham, Tom	L/L	6-2/210	2-20-74	Nashville, Chicago A.L.
44	Foulke, Keith	R/R	6-0/195	10-19-72	Phoenix, San Francisco, Nashville, Chicago A.L.
	Hasselhoff, Derek	R/R	6-2/185	10-10-73	Nashville, Birmingham, Winston-Salem
	Howry, Bobby	L/R	6-5/210	8-4-73	Shreveport
47	Karchner, Matt	R/R	6-4/210	6-28-67	Nashville, Chicago A.L.
38	Navarro, Jaime	R/R	6-5/235	3-27-68	Chicago A.L.
	Olsen, Jason	R/R	6-4/210	3-16-75	Birmingham
	Rizzo, Todd	R/L	6-2/220	5-24-71	DID NOT PLAY
41	Simas, Bill	L/R	6-3/220	11-28-71	Chicago A.L.
33	Sirotka, Mike	L/L	6-1/200	5-13-71	Nashville, Chicago A.L.
	Snyder, John	R/R	6-3/185	8-16-74	DID NOT PLAY
	Ward, Bryan	L/L	6-2/210	1-28-72	Portland, Charlotte

No.	CATCHERS	B/T	Ht./Wt.	Born	1997 clubs
	Johnson, Mark	L/R	6-0/185	9-12-75	Winston-Salem, Gulf Coast White Sox
	Kreuter, Chad	B/R	6-2/200	8-26-64	Chicago A.L., Anaheim
55	Machado, Robert	R/R	6-1/205	6-3-73	Nashville, Chicago A.L.
	O'Brien, Charlie	R/R	6-2/205	5-1-61	Toronto

No.	INFIELDERS	B/T	Ht./Wt.	Born	1997 clubs
	Bautista, Juan	R/R	6-0/165	6-24-75	Birmingham, Gulf Coast Orioles, Bowie
	Caruso, Mike	B/R	6-0/172	5-27-77	San Jose, Winston-Salem
5	Durham, Ray	B/R	5-8/170	11-30-71	Chicago A.L.
	Gil, Benji	R/R	6-2/182	10-6-72	Texas
	Lee, Carlos	R/R	6-2/202	6-20-76	Winston-Salem
31	Norton, Greg	B/R	6-1/190	7-6-72	Nashville, Chicago A.L.
	Nunez, Sergio	R/R	5-11/155	1-3-75	Wichita, Gulf Coast Royals
27	Snopek, Chris	R/R	6-1/185	9-20-70	Chicago A.L., Nashville
35	Thomas, Frank	R/R	6-5/257	5-27-68	Chicago A.L.
34	Valdez, Mario	L/L	6-2/190	11-19-74	Nashville, Chicago A.L.
23	Ventura, Robin	L/R	6-1/198	7-14-67	Nashville, Birmingham, Chicago A.L.

No.	OUTFIELDERS	B/T	Ht./Wt.	Born	1997 clubs
45	Abbott, Jeff	R/L	6-2/190	8-17-72	Nashville, Chicago A.L.
8	Belle, Albert	R/R	6-2/225	8-25-66	Chicago A.L.
24	Cameron, Mike	R/R	6-2/190	1-8-73	Nashville, Chicago A.L.
30	Ordonez, Magglio	R/R	5-11/170	1-28-74	Nashville, Chicago A.L.
	Simmons, Brian	B/R	6-2/185	9-4-73	Birmingham

BALLPARK INFORMATION

Ballpark (capacity, surface)
Comiskey Park (44,321, grass)
Address
333 W. 35th St.
Chicago, IL 60616
Business phone
312-674-1000
Ticket information
312-674-1000
Ticket prices
$22 (lower deck box)
$20 (club level)
$17 (lower deck reserved)
$15 (upper deck box)
$14 (bleacher reserved)
$10 (upper deck reserved)
Field dimensions (from home plate)
To left field at foul line, 347 feet
To center field, 400 feet
To right field at foul line, 347 feet
First game played
April 18, 1991 (Tigers 16, White Sox 0)

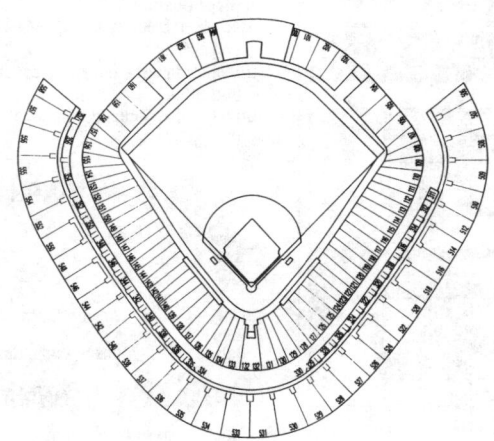

DAY BY DAY

Date	Opp.	Res.	Score	(inn.*)	Hits	Opp. hits	Winning pitcher	Losing pitcher	Save	Record	Pos.	GB
4-1	At Tor.	W	6-5	(10)	12	7	T. Castillo	Plesac	Hernandez	1-0	T1st	....
4-2	At Tor.	L	1-6		6	8	Clemens	Alvarez		1-1	3rd	1.0
4-4	Det.	L	7-8	(10)	10	10	Jones	Levine	Sager	1-2	T2nd	1.5
4-5	Det.	L	12-15		12	19	Blair	T. Castillo	Jones	1-3	T4th	2.5
4-6	Det.	W	5-3		10	8	Navarro	Brocail	Hernandez	2-3	T4th	1.5
4-9	Tor.	L	0-5		3	10	Clemens	Alvarez		2-4	5th	1.5
4-10	Tor.	L	0-4		4	5	Guzman	Baldwin		2-5	5th	2.0
4-11	At Det.	L	4-5		7	7	Olivares	Drabek	Jones	2-6	5th	2.5
4-13†	At Det.	W	11-8	(12)	12	10	Hernandez	Lira		3-6		
4-13‡	At Det.	L	2-4		8	8	Sager	Hernandez		3-7	5th	2.5
4-14	At Tex.	L	1-3		4	7	Patterson	Alvarez	Wetteland	3-8	5th	3.5
4-15	At Tex.	L	2-5		11	7	Witt	Baldwin	Wetteland	3-9	5th	3.5
4-16	Bal.	W	9-3		9	7	Drabek	Boskie		4-9	5th	3.5
4-17	Bal.	L	0-1		4	9	Mussina	D. Darwin	Myers	4-10	5th	4.5
4-18	N.Y.	L	4-10		10	14	Mendoza	Navarro		4-11	5th	5.5
4-19	N.Y.	L	2-3		4	4	Rogers	T. Castillo	Rivera	4-12	5th	5.5
4-20	N.Y.	W	8-7	(11)	16	12	Levine	Boehringer		5-12	5th	5.0
4-21	N.Y.	L	3-4		8	9	Cone	Drabek	Rivera	5-13	5th	5.0
4-22	At Bal.	L	2-3		8	9	Mussina	D. Darwin	Myers	5-14	5th	6.0
4-23	At Bal.	W	11-9	(10)	15	9	T. Castillo	Benitez	Hernandez	6-14	5th	5.0
4-25	At N.Y.	W	9-3		16	5	Alvarez	Wells		7-14	5th	4.0
4-26	At N.Y.	L	2-10		9	16	Cone	Baldwin	Rivera	7-15	5th	4.0
4-27	At N.Y.	L	1-7		4	9	Pettitte	Drabek		7-16	5th	4.5
4-29	Tex.	W	2-1		9	6	Navarro	Patterson		8-16	5th	5.0
4-30	Tex.	L	2-6	(7)	6	9	Witt	Alvarez		8-17	5th	5.0
5-3†	Ana.	L	2-3		11	8	Watson	Baldwin	DeLucia	8-18		
5-3‡	Ana.	W	4-2		9	3	Drabek	Springer	Hernandez	9-18	5th	5.0
5-4	Ana.	W	4-2		11	10	Navarro	Harris	Hernandez	10-18	5th	4.0
5-6	Sea.	L	6-7		8	14	Ayala	T. Castillo	Charlton	10-19	5th	5.0
5-8	Oak.	W	10-6		16	5	Baldwin	Mohler		11-19	5th	4.5
5-9	Oak.	W	3-2	(10)	11	7	Hernandez	Small		12-19	T4th	4.5
5-10	Oak.	W	9-8		17	7	Levine	Taylor		13-19	4th	4.5
5-11	Oak.	W	8-5		11	7	Alvarez	Adams	Hernandez	14-19	4th	4.5
5-12	At Ana.	L	8-16		11	18	DeLucia	Levine		14-20	4th	5.5
5-13	At Ana.	L	7-8		11	13	Langston	Baldwin	James	14-21	4th	5.5
5-14	At Sea.	L	7-9		12	15	Moyer	Navarro	Charlton	14-22	4th	5.5
5-15	At Sea.	W	4-3		10	7	Simas	Charlton	Hernandez	15-22	4th	5.0
5-16	At Oak.	W	6-2		10	10	Alvarez	Adams	Hernandez	16-22	4th	4.0
5-17	At Oak.	W	7-6		13	8	D. Darwin	Karsay	Hernandez	17-22	4th	3.0
5-18	At Oak.	W	10-4		12	6	Baldwin	Mohler		18-22	4th	2.0
5-20	Bos.	W	10-1		10	7	Navarro	Wakefield		19-22	4th	2.0
5-21	Bos.	W	10-5		11	11	Drabek	Hammond		20-22	T3rd	2.0
5-23	Mil.	L	1-4		3	8	Karl	Alvarez	Jones	20-23	3rd	3.5
5-24	Mil.	W	8-6		10	11	Simas	Fetters	Hernandez	21-23	3rd	2.5
5-25	Mil.	L	7-11		14	16	Adamson	Baldwin	Wickman	21-24	3rd	3.5
5-26	Cle.	L	4-10		6	13	Hershiser	Navarro		21-25	4th	4.5
5-27	Cle.	W	8-2		10	6	Drabek	Lopez		22-25	3rd	3.5
5-28	At Bos.	L	3-5		6	5	Sele	Alvarez	Slocumb	22-26	3rd	4.5
5-29	At Bos.	W	5-2	(11)	13	7	Hernandez	Wasdin	Simas	23-26	3rd	4.0
5-30	At Mil.	L	0-5		3	6	Eldred	Baldwin		23-27	T3rd	4.0
5-31	At Mil.	L	3-4		10	6	McDonald	Navarro	Jones	23-28	T3rd	4.0
6-1	At Mil.	L	4-7		9	12	Mercedes	Drabek	Jones	23-29	4th	4.5
6-2	At Mil.	W	8-5		14	8	Simas	Jones	Hernandez	24-29	4th	4.0
6-3	At Cle.	W	9-5		15	9	D. Darwin	Ogea		25-29	4th	3.0
6-4	At Cle.	W	9-4		13	6	Baldwin	Lopez		26-29	3rd	2.5
6-5	At Cle.	L	4-5	(11)	13	11	Shuey	C. Castillo		26-30	3rd	3.0
6-6	Bal.	W	7-3		11	12	Drabek	Erickson	Hernandez	27-30	3rd	3.0
6-7	Bal.	W	1-0	(11)	8	9	Hernandez	Myers		28-30	3rd	3.0
6-8	Bal.	L	1-2		7	9	Key	D. Darwin	Myers	28-31	4th	3.0
6-9	Bal.	L	2-10		5	13	Mussina	Baldwin		28-32	4th	3.5
6-10	At N.Y.	L	1-12		7	15	Pettitte	Navarro		28-33	4th	4.5
6-11	At N.Y.	L	5-7		8	9	Stanton	McElroy	Rivera	28-34	4th	5.5
6-13	At Cin.	W	3-1		3	7	Alvarez	Schourek	Hernandez	29-34	4th	4.5
6-14	At Cin.	L	1-5		7	9	Mercker	D. Darwin		29-35	5th	5.0
6-15	At Cin.	W	14-6		18	14	T. Castillo	Burba	C. Castillo	30-35	4th	5.0
6-16	Chi. (NL)	L	3-8		9	14	Foster	Navarro		30-36	5th	5.0
6-17	Chi. (NL)	W	5-3		7	7	Drabek	Gonzalez	Hernandez	31-36	4th	5.0
6-18	Chi. (NL)	W	3-0		6	4	Alvarez	Mulholland		32-36	4th	4.0
6-20	Min.	L	0-3		5	7	Tewksbury	D. Darwin	Aguilera	32-37	5th	4.0
6-21	Min.	W	5-3		8	5	Baldwin	Robertson	Hernandez	33-37	4th	4.0
6-22	Min.	W	2-1		8	9	Navarro	Hawkins	Hernandez	34-37	4th	4.0

Date	Opp.	Res.	Score	(inn.*)	Hits	Opp. hits	Winning pitcher	Losing pitcher	Save	Record	Pos.	GB
6-23	K.C.	W	7-6		10	14	Karchner	Pichardo	Hernandez	35-37	T3rd	3.0
6-24	K.C.	W	4-0		8	5	Alvarez	Pittsley	Hernandez	36-37	T2nd	3.0
6-25	K.C.	W	8-7	(10)	13	14	Karchner	Montgomery		37-37	2nd	2.5
6-26	At Min.	W	11-1		14	5	Baldwin	Hawkins		38-37	2nd	2.0
6-27	At Min.	W	10-6		15	8	Navarro	Tewksbury		39-37	2nd	1.0
6-28	At Min.	L	5-11		10	19	Radke	Drabek		39-38	2nd	2.0
6-29	At Min.	W	6-4		11	9	Alvarez	Stevens	Hernandez	40-38	2nd	1.0
6-30	At Pit.	L	1-3		5	9	Lieber	D. Darwin		40-39	2nd	2.0
7-1	At Pit.	L	0-3		5	8	Cooke	Baldwin	Loiselle	40-40	2nd	3.0
7-2	At Pit.	L	1-3		5	7	Schmidt	Navarro		40-41	2nd	3.0
7-3	Bos.	L	1-4		7	7	Sele	Drabek		40-42	2nd	3.5
7-4	Bos.	W	6-5		9	8	Hernandez	Slocumb		41-42	2nd	3.5
7-5	Bos.	W	11-8		14	13	D. Darwin	Avery		42-42	2nd	3.5
7-6	Bos.	W	6-5		9	13	Baldwin	Wakefield	Hernandez	43-42	2nd	3.5
7-10	At K.C.	W	6-3		12	8	Navarro	Appier	Hernandez	44-42	2nd	2.5
7-11	At K.C.	W	6-2		11	8	Alvarez	Rosado		45-42	2nd	2.5
7-12	At K.C.	W	11-7		14	14	D. Darwin	Belcher	Hernandez	46-42	2nd	2.5
7-13	At K.C.	W	7-6		9	10	C. Castillo	Pittsley	Hernandez	47-42	2nd	2.5
7-14	At Min.	L	3-5		8	8	Rodriguez	Drabek	Aguilera	47-43	2nd	3.5
7-15	At Min.	L	4-8		6	15	Radke	Navarro		47-44	2nd	3.5
7-16	N.Y.	L	5-11		9	12	Pettitte	Alvarez		47-45	2nd	4.5
7-17	N.Y.	L	2-4		8	9	Cone	D. Darwin	Rivera	47-46	2nd	5.5
7-18	At Bal.	W	3-0		10	3	Baldwin	Mussina	Hernandez	48-46	2nd	4.5
7-19	At Bal.	L	3-8		9	9	Rhodes	Simas	Benitez	48-47	2nd	4.5
7-20	At Bal.	W	10-2		19	9	Navarro	Boskie		49-47	2nd	4.5
7-21	At Det.	W	3-0		10	4	Alvarez	Thompson	Hernandez	50-47	2nd	3.5
7-22	At Det.	L	3-6		8	11	Moehler	D. Darwin	Jones	50-48	2nd	4.5
7-23	At Det.	L	6-8		11	10	Blair	Baldwin	Jones	50-49	2nd	4.5
7-24	Tex.	W	2-1		4	3	Karchner	Hill	Hernandez	51-49	2nd	3.5
7-25	Tex.	L	5-8		12	12	Patterson	Navarro	Wetteland	51-50	2nd	3.5
7-26	Tex.	L	1-4		5	10	Oliver	Alvarez	Wetteland	51-51	2nd	4.5
7-27	Tex.	L	4-5		9	11	Gunderson	T. Castillo	Wetteland	51-52	2nd	5.5
7-29	Det.	L	1-3		3	5	Blair	Baldwin		51-53	3rd	4.5
7-30	Det.	W	3-2		7	6	Drabek	Sanders	Hernandez	52-53	3rd	3.5
7-31	At Ana.	W	14-12		16	15	C. Castillo	Holtz	Karchner	53-53	3rd	3.0
8-1	At Ana.	L	1-9		8	8	Watson	Eyre		53-54	3rd	4.0
8-2	At Ana.	L	2-5		5	5	Springer	Clemons	Percival	53-55	3rd	5.0
8-3	At Ana.	L	1-4		5	7	Finley	Baldwin	Percival	53-56	3rd	5.0
8-5	At Oak.	W	3-0		8	7	Drabek	Karsay	Karchner	54-56	3rd	4.5
8-6	At Oak.	L	2-3		7	12	Mathews	Navarro	Taylor	54-57	3rd	4.5
8-7	At Sea.	L	2-3		6	3	Fassero	Eyre	Slocumb	54-58	3rd	4.5
8-8	At Sea.	L	0-5		5	10	Johnson	Clemons		54-59	3rd	4.5
8-9	At Sea.	W	5-2		4	7	Baldwin	Cloude	Karchner	55-59	3rd	4.0
8-10	At Sea.	W	2-1		8	3	Drabek	Olivares	Karchner	56-59	T2nd	3.0
8-12	Ana.	W	8-5		13	9	Navarro	Dickson	T. Castillo	57-59	2nd	3.0
8-13	Ana.	W	5-2		7	8	Eyre	Watson	Karchner	58-59	2nd	2.5
8-14	Oak.	L	5-12		9	15	Groom	McElroy		58-60	2nd	3.5
8-15	Oak.	L	6-11		8	14	Haynes	Baldwin		58-61	2nd	4.5
8-16†	Sea.	L	6-11		13	11	Ayala	Drabek		58-62	T2nd	5.5
8-17†	Sea.	L	3-5		9	10	Fassero	Navarro		58-63		
8-17‡	Sea.	W	4-2		7	8	Sirotka	Olivares	Karchner	59-63	3rd	5.0
8-18	Sea.	W	5-0		9	4	Eyre	Lira	Foulke	60-63	T2nd	5.0
8-19†	Tor.	L	5-6		13	9	Carpenter	Cruz	Escobar	60-64		
8-19‡	Tor.	W	5-3		9	7	Bere	Andujar	Karchner	61-64	3rd	5.5
8-20	Tor.	W	12-6		14	12	Baldwin	Person		62-64	3rd	4.5
8-21	Tor.	W	6-3		8	9	Drabek	Hentgen	Karchner	63-64	2nd	3.5
8-22	At Tex.	L	8-17		9	20	Oliver	Navarro		63-65	2nd	4.5
8-23	At Tex.	L	8-13		11	13	Patterson	Cruz		63-66	3rd	5.5
8-24	At Tex.	W	3-1		7	6	Bere	Helling	Karchner	64-66	3rd	4.5
8-26	At Tor.	W	8-5		17	9	Baldwin	Williams	Karchner	65-66	3rd	3.5
8-27	At Tor.	L	2-13		6	14	Hentgen	Drabek		65-67	3rd	4.5
8-28	At Tor.	L	2-3	(11)	9	11	Quantrill	McElroy		65-68	3rd	5.0
8-29	Hou.	W	5-4		8	9	Foulke	Hudek	Karchner	66-68	3rd	5.0
8-30	Hou.	W	9-2		14	3	Bere	Hampton		67-68	3rd	4.0
8-31	Hou.	W	3-1		9	7	Baldwin	Reynolds	Karchner	68-68	3rd	4.0
9-1	At St.L.	W	5-4		7	10	T. Castillo	Fossas	Karchner	69-68	3rd	4.0
9-2	At St.L.	L	1-6		7	11	An. Benes	Navarro		69-69	3rd	4.0
9-3	At St.L.	L	2-4		11	12	Aybar	Eyre	Eckersley	69-70	3rd	5.0
9-5	At Cle.	L	1-11		6	18	Nagy	Bere		69-71	3rd	6.0
9-6	At Cle.	L	7-9		11	12	Colon	Baldwin	Mesa	69-72	3rd	7.0
9-7	At Cle.	L	2-5		7	7	Wright	Drabek	Mesa	69-73	3rd	8.0
9-8	Mil.	L	5-8	(10)	7	14	Wickman	Karchner	Jones	69-74	3rd	9.0
9-9	Mil.	W	4-1		7	5	Eyre	Mercedes	T. Castillo	70-74	3rd	8.0
9-10	Mil.	W	3-1		7	5	Bere	Eldred	McElroy	71-74	3rd	7.5
9-11	Cle.	W	7-5		10	9	Foulke	Nagy	Karchner	72-74	3rd	6.5

Date	Opp.	Res.	Score	(inn.*)	Hits	Opp. hits	Winning pitcher	Losing pitcher	Save	Record	Pos.	GB
9-12	Cle.	L	0-9		3	14	Wright	Drabek		72-75	3rd	7.5
9-13	Cle.	W	7-6		10	16	Sirotka	Hershiser	Karchner	73-75	T2nd	6.5
9-14	Cle.	L	3-8		11	11	Shuey	J. Darwin		73-76	T2nd	7.5
9-15	At Mil.	L	10-11		14	13	Eldred	Eyre	Jones	73-77	3rd	8.0
9-17	At K.C.	W	8-4		14	9	Baldwin	Service	Foulke	74-77	3rd	8.0
9-18	At K.C.	W	9-2		14	6	Drabek	Pittsley		75-77	T2nd	8.0
9-19	At Bos.	W	5-4	(10)	9	12	Foulke	Lowe	T. Castillo	76-77	T2nd	7.5
9-20	At Bos.	W	6-4		12	13	McElroy	Avery	T. Castillo	77-77	2nd	6.5
9-21	At Bos.	L	2-5		10	10	Corsi	Fordham	Gordon	77-78	2nd	6.5
9-23	Min.	L	3-5		5	5	Tewksbury	Bere	Aguilera	77-79	2nd	7.5
9-24	Min.	L	2-7		7	11	Rodriguez	Baldwin	Aguilera	77-80	T2nd	7.5
9-25	Min.	W	10-5		16	7	Drabek	Hawkins		78-80	2nd	6.5
9-26	K.C.	W	7-2		9	7	Sirotka	Appier		79-80	2nd	6.5
9-27	K.C.	L	4-10		11	13	Bones	Navarro	Olson	79-81	2nd	7.0
9-28	K.C.	W	4-3		6	7	Eyre	Service	Foulke	80-81	2nd	6.0

Monthly records: April (8-17), May (15-11), June (17-11), July (13-14), August (15-15), September (12-13).
*Innings, if other than nine. †First game of doubleheader. ‡Second game of doubleheader.

HIGHLIGHTS

High point: After missing the first 99 games of the season with a dislocated right ankle and broken lower leg, third baseman Robin Ventura returned to the lineup on July 24. In his 1997 debut, Ventura's run-scoring double off Ken Hill with two outs in the eighth inning lifted the White Sox to a 2-1 win over the Rangers. **Low point:** On July 31, the White Sox rocked major league baseball by trading three of their top pitchers, Wilson Alvarez, Roberto Hernandez and Danny Darwin, to the Giants for six minor leaguers. The team was just 3 1/2 games out of first place at the time of the trade, but chairman Jerry Reinsdorf publicly said that it would be "crazy" to think the Sox could catch the Indians in the A.L. Central. **Turning point:** Two days after the 1997 season ended, manager Terry Bevington was fired. Many fans openly wondered why it took so long for G.M. Ron Schueler to pull the trigger. In his 2 1/2-year stay as manager, Bevington failed to gain the respect of his players or coaching staff, and he was pummeled by the media. New manager Jerry Manuel hardly has big shoes to fill. **Most valuable player:** Frank Thomas continued to put up monstrous offensive numbers (.347, 35 home runs, 125 RBIs) and also became the first White Sox player to win the batting crown since Luke Appling in 1943. **Most valuable pitcher:** The heart of the staff—Wilson Alvarez, Roberto Hernandez and Danny Darwin—was traded to the Giants on July 31. After that, new closer Matt Karchner stepped up and recorded 15 saves in as many tries. **Most improved player:** After failing to make much of an impression in brief stints with the team in 1995 and '96, lefthander Mike Sirotka finally broke through in '97. Sirotka made four starts for the White Sox and was 3-0 with a 2.45 ERA. **Most pleasant surprise:** Magglio Ordonez wasn't even on the team's 40-man roster at the start of the season. But after winning the American Association batting title with a .329 average at Class AAA Nashville, the 23-year-old right fielder joined the Sox in September and batted .319 over the final month.

Biggest disappointment: After signing a four-year, $20-million free-agent contract, Jaime Navarro was supposed to replace Alex Fernandez as the team's No. 1 starting pitcher. Navarro, though, was a huge flop. The righthander went 9-14 (5.79 ERA) and led the A.L. in hits allowed, runs allowed, opposing batting average and wild pitches. **Key injuries:** When Robin Ventura suffered a dislocated right ankle and broken lower leg during a routine slide into home during a March 21 spring training game, the team knew it was in trouble. Ventura is the White Sox' best all-around player, and the freak injury sidelined him for the first 99 games of the season. **Notable:** Frank Thomas (35 home runs, 125 RBIs) and Albert Belle (30 home runs, 116 RBIs) became the second duo in team history to hit 30 home runs and drive in 100 in the same season.

—SCOT GREGOR

RECORDS

1997 regular-season record: 80-81 (2nd in A.L. Central); 45-36 at home; 35-45 on road; 25-30 vs. East; 34-28 vs. Central; 21-23 vs. West; 19-23 vs. lefthanded starters; 61-58 vs. righthanded starters; 70-68 on grass; 10-13 on turf; 27-23 in daytime; 53-58 at night; 22-18 in one-run games; 9-4 in extra-inning games; 0-0-4 in doubleheaders.
Team record past five years: 394-348 (.531, ranks 4th in league in that span).

TEAM LEADERS

Batting average: Frank Thomas (.347).
At-bats: Albert Belle, Ray Durham (634).
Runs: Frank Thomas (110).
Hits: Frank Thomas (184).
Total bases: Frank Thomas (324).
Doubles: Albert Belle (45).
Triples: Ozzie Guillen, Dave Martinez (6).
Home runs: Frank Thomas (35).
Runs batted in: Frank Thomas (125).
Stolen bases: Ray Durham (33).
Slugging percentage: Frank Thomas (.611).
On-base percentage: Frank Thomas (.456).
Wins: James Baldwin, Doug Drabek (12).
Earned-run average: James Baldwin (5.27).

Complete games: Wilson Alvarez, Jaime Navarro (2).
Shutouts: Wilson Alvarez (1).
Saves: Roberto Hernandez (27).
Innings pitched: Jaime Navarro (209.2).
Strikeouts: Jaime Navarro (142).

GAMES BY POSITION

Catcher: Jorge Fabregas 92, Ron Karkovice 51, Tony Pena 30, Chad Kreuter 13, Robert Machado 10.
First base: Frank Thomas 97, Dave Martinez 52, Mario Valdez 47, Chad Kreuter 2, Jorge Fabregas 1.
Second base: Ray Durham 153, Norberto Martin 9, Chad Fonville 2.
Third base: Chris Snopek 82, Robin Ventura 54, Norberto Martin 17, Greg Norton 11, Tony Phillips 9, Tony Pena 1, Mario Valdez 1.
Shortstop: Ozzie Guillen 139, Norberto Martin 28, Chris Snopek 4, Chad Fonville 2.
Outfield: Albert Belle 154, Mike Cameron 112, Dave Martinez 105, Lyle Mouton 67, Darren Lewis 64, Tony Phillips 28, Magglio Ordonez 19, Jeff Abbott 10, Chad Fonville 3, Harold Baines 1.
Designated hitter: Harold Baines 86, Frank Thomas 49, Lyle Mouton 11, Albert Belle 7, Darren Lewis 6, Norberto Martin 6, Jeff Abbott 3, Mike Cameron 3, Greg Norton 2, Mario Valdez 2, Ray Durham 1, Chad Fonville 1.

TOP DRAFT CHOICES

1a. **Jason Dellaero,** SS, U. of South Florida.
1b. **Kyle Kane,** RHP, Saddleback (Calif.) C.C.
1c. **Brett Caradonna,** OF, El Capitan H.S., San Diego.
1d. **Aaron Myette,** RHP, Central Arizona J.C.
1e. **Jim Parque,** LHP, UCLA.
1f. **Rocky Biddle,** RHP, Long Beach State U.
2. **Jeff Weaver,** RHP, Fresno State Univ.
3. **J.R. Mounts,** OF, Key West (Fla.) H.S.
4. **Curtis Whitley,** LHP, Mount Olive (N.C.) College.
5. **Pat Daneker,** RHP, University of Virginia.
6. **Brian Scott,** RHP, San Diego State Univ.
7. **Jake Meyer,** RHP, UCLA.
8. **Tim Currens,** RHP, Lindsey Wilson (Ky.) College.
9. **Rolando Garza,** SS, Valley H.S., Coachella, Calif.
10. **Jamie Smith,** RHP-C, Texas A&M Univ.

CLEVELAND INDIANS
AMERICAN LEAGUE CENTRAL DIVISION

Indians Schedule
Home games shaded. *—All-Star Game at Coors Field (Colorado). D—Day game (any game starting before 5 p.m.).

March
SUN	MON	TUE	WED	THU	FRI	SAT
		31 D SEA				

April
SUN	MON	TUE	WED	THU	FRI	SAT
			1 SEA	2	3 ANA	4 ANA
5 D ANA	6 ANA	7	8 D OAK	9	10 D ANA	11 D ANA
12 D ANA	13 SEA	14 SEA	15 SEA	16	17 BOS	18 D BOS
19 D BOS	20 D BOS	21 CWS	22 CWS	23 CWS	24 BOS	25 D BOS
26 D BOS	27 CWS	28 CWS	29 D OAK	30 OAK		

May
SUN	MON	TUE	WED	THU	FRI	SAT
					1 TB	2 D TB
3 D TB	4	5 BAL	6 BAL	7 TEX	8 TEX	9 TEX
10 D TEX	11 TB	12 TB	13 BAL	14 BAL	15 D TEX	16 TEX
17 TEX	18	19 KC	20 KC	21 KC	22 TOR	23 D TOR
24 TOR	25 D DET	26 DET	27	28 TOR	29 TOR	30 D TOR
31 D TOR						

June
SUN	MON	TUE	WED	THU	FRI	SAT
	1 DET	2 DET	3 MIN	4 MIN	5 CIN	6 CIN
7 D CIN	8 PIT	9 PIT	10 PIT	11	12 NYY	13 D NYY
14 D NYY	15 KC	16 KC	17 KC	18 NYY	19 NYY	20 D NYY
21 NYY	22 CUB	23 D CUB	24 STL	25 STL	26 HOU	27 D HOU
28 D HOU	29	30 MIL				

July
SUN	MON	TUE	WED	THU	FRI	SAT
		1 MIL	2 MIL	3 KC	4 KC	
5 D KC	6	7 *	8	9 MIN	10 MIN	11 D MIN
12 D MIN	13 NYY	14 NYY	15 BOS	16 BOS	17 CWS	18 CWS
19 D CWS	20 D CWS	21 BOS	22 BOS	23 DET	24 DET	25 D DET
26 D DET	27	28 SEA	29 SEA	30 SEA	31 OAK	

August
SUN	MON	TUE	WED	THU	FRI	SAT
						1 D OAK
2 D OAK	3 ANA	4 ANA	5 D OAK	6	7 TB	8 TB
9 D TB	10	11 TEX	12 TEX	13 BAL	14 BAL	15 D BAL
16 D BAL	17 TB	18 TB	19 TEX	20 TEX	21 BAL	22 BAL
23 D BAL	24	25 SEA	26 SEA	27 SEA	28 OAK	29 D OAK
30 D OAK	31 OAK					

September
SUN	MON	TUE	WED	THU	FRI	SAT
		1 ANA	2 ANA	3 DET	4 DET	5 DET
6 D DET	7 D TOR	8	9 TOR	10	11 CWS	12 CWS
13 D CWS	14 TOR	15 TOR	16 MIN	17 MIN	18 KC	19 D KC
20 D KC	21	22 NYY	23 NYY	24 MIN	25 MIN	26 MIN
27 D MIN						

1998 SEASON
CLUB DIRECTORY

Board of directors
Richard E. Jacobs
Martin J. Cleary
Gary L. Bryenton
Chairman of the board and CEO
Richard E. Jacobs
Executive vice president, general manager
John Hart
Executive vice president, business
Dennis Lehman
V.p., marketing and communications
Jeff Overton
Vice president
Martin J. Cleary
Vice president, public relations
Bob DiBiasio
Vice president, finance
Ken Stefanov
Dir. of baseball operations/asst. g.m.
Dan O'Dowd
Director, scouting
Lee MacPhail
Director, team travel
Mike Seghi
Director, minor league operations
Mark Shapiro
Administrator, player personnel
Wendy Hoppel
Administrator, scouting
Brad Grant
Director, media relations
Bart Swain
Assistant director, media relations
Susie Giuliano
Director, community relations
Allen Davis
Manager, community relations
Melissa Zapanta
Manager, promotions
Chris Previte
Director, broadcasting
John Starrett
Manager, advertising/publications
Bernadette Repko
Controller
Ron McQuate

Director, ticket services
John Schulze
Director, ticket sales
Scott Sterneckert
Coordinator, season/group sales
Diane Stack
Director, ballpark operations
Jim Folk
Director, merchandising/licensing
Jayne Churchmack
Home clubhouse mgr./equipment mgr.
Ted Walsh
Equipment manager
Jeff Sipos
Visiting clubhouse manager
Cy Buynak
Medical director
William T. Wilder, M.D.
Head trainer
Paul Spicuzza
Assistant trainer
Jim Warfield
Strength and conditioning coach
Fernando Montes
Team physicians
Ronald Golovan M.D., Godofredo Domingo, M.D., K.V. Gopal, M.D., Zenos Vangelos, M.D.
Major league/spec. assignment scouts
Dan Carnevale, Dom Chiti, Tom Giordano, Ted Simmons, Bill Werle
National crosschecker
Bill Schmidt
West Coast supervisor
Jesse Flores
East Coast supervisor
Jerry Jordan
Midwest supervisor
Bob Mayer
Full-time scouts
Steve Abney, Steve Avila, Doug Baker, Keith Boeck, Ted Brzenk, Paul Cogan, Henry Cruz, Jim Gabella, Rene Gayo, Mark German, Chris Jefts, Guy Mader, Kasey McKeon, Chuck Ricci, Bill Schudlich, Max Semler, Rob Walton

MINOR LEAGUE AFFILIATES

Class	Team	League	Manager
AAA	Buffalo	International	Jeff Datz
AA	Akron	Eastern	Joel Skinner
A	Kinston	Carolina	To be announced
A	Columbus	South Atlantic	To be announced
A	Watertown	New York-Pennsylvania	To be announced
Rookie	Burlington	Appalachian	To be announced

BROADCAST INFORMATION
Radio: To be announced.
TV: WUAB-TV (Channel 43).
Cable TV: Fox Sports Ohio.

SPRING TRAINING
Ballpark (city): Chain O'Lakes (Winter Haven, Fla.).
Ticket information: 813-293-3900.

SPRING TRAINING ROSTER

Manager—Mike Hargrove (21).
Coaches—Al Bumbry, Johnny Goryl (54), Luis Isaac (4), Charlie Manuel (32), Jeff Newman (16), Mark Wiley (28).

No.	PITCHERS	B/T	Ht./Wt.	Born	1997 clubs
	Assenmacher, Paul	L/L	6-3/210	12-10-60	Cleveland
	Batchelor, Richard	R/R	6-1/195	4-8-67	St. Louis, Louisville, San Diego, Las Vegas
40	Colon, Bartolo	R/R	6-0/185	5-24-75	, Cleveland
	De La Rosa, Maximo	R/R	5-11/170	7-12-71	Buffalo, Akron
	Driskill, Travis	R/R	6-0/185	8-1-71	Buffalo
	Gooden, Dwight	R/R	6-3/210	11-16-64	New York A.L., Norwich, Columbus
42	Jackson, Mike	R/R	6-2/225	12-22-64	Cleveland
46	Jacome, Jason	L/L	6-1/185	11-24-70	Kansas City, Cleveland, Buffalo
	Karsay, Steve	R/R	6-3/205	3-24-72	Oakland
	Martin, Tom	L/L	6-1/185	5-21-70	Houston
	Matthews, Mike	L/L	6-2/175	10-24-73	Buffalo, Akron
	McDonald, Ben	R/R	6-7/214	11-24-67	Milwaukee
49	Mesa, Jose	R/R	6-3/230	5-22-66	Cleveland
51	Morman, Alvin	L/L	6-3/210	1-6-69	New Orleans, Cleveland, Buffalo
41	Nagy, Charles	L/R	6-3/200	5-5-67	Cleveland
37	Ogea, Chad	L/R	6-2/220	11-9-70	Cleveland, Buffalo
38	Plunk, Eric	R/R	6-6/220	9-3-63	Cleveland
	Rakers, Jason	R/R	6-2/200	6-29-73	Akron, Buffalo, Kinston
53	Shuey, Paul	R/R	6-3/215	9-16-70	Cleveland, Buffalo, Akron
	Smiley, John	L/L	6-4/210	3-17-65	Cincinnati, Cleveland
	Villone, Ron	L/L	6-3/235	1-16-70	Milwaukee
27	Wright, Jaret	R/R	6-2/220	12-29-75	Akron, Buffalo, Cleveland

No.	CATCHERS	B/T	Ht./Wt.	Born	1997 clubs
15	Alomar, Sandy	R/R	6-5/220	6-18-66	Cleveland
	Borders, Pat	R/R	6-2/200	5-14-63	Cleveland
2	Diaz, Einar	R/R	5-10/165	12-28-72	Buffalo, Cleveland

No.	INFIELDERS	B/T	Ht./Wt.	Born	1997 clubs
11	Branson, Jeff	L/R	6-0/180	1-26-67	Indianapolis, Cincinnati, Cleveland
	Branyan, Russell	L/R	6-3/195	12-19-75	Kinston, Akron
52	Casey, Sean	L/R	6-4/215	7-2-74	Akron, Buffalo, Cleveland
	Fonville, Chad	B/R	5-6/155	3-5-71	Los Angeles, Albuquerque, Chicago A.L.
	Fryman, Travis	R/R	6-1/194	3-25-69	Detroit
	Garcia, Carlos	R/R	6-1/197	10-15-67	Toronto
44	Sexson, Richie	R/R	6-6/205	12-29-74	Buffalo, Cleveland
25	Thome, Jim	L/R	6-4/225	8-27-70	Cleveland
13	Vizquel, Omar	B/R	5-9/170	4-24-67	Cleveland
35	Wilson, Enrique	B/R	5-11/160	7-27-75	Buffalo, Cleveland

No.	OUTFIELDERS	B/T	Ht./Wt.	Born	1997 clubs
56	Aven, Bruce	R/R	5-9/180	3-4-72	Buffalo, Cleveland
22	Giles, Brian	L/L	5-11/200	1-21-71	Cleveland
23	Justice, David	L/L	6-3/200	4-14-66	Cleveland
	Lofton, Kenny	L/L	6-0/190	5-31-67	Atlanta
	Morgan, Scott	R/R	6-7/230	7-19-73	Akron, Kinston
	Ramirez, Alex	R/R	5-11/180	10-3-74	Buffalo
24	Ramirez, Manny	R/R	6-0/200	5-30-72	Cleveland

BALLPARK INFORMATION

Ballpark (capacity, surface)
Jacobs Field (42,865, grass)
Address
2401 Ontario St.
Cleveland, OH 44115
Business phone
216-420-4200
Ticket information
216-241-8888
Ticket prices
$26 (field box)
$20 (lower box & view box)
$17 (lower reserved, upper box
& mezzanine seating)
$12 (bleachers)
$10 (upper reserved)
$6 (reserved g.a., standing room only)
Field dimensions (from home plate)
To left field at foul line, 325 feet
To center field, 405 feet
To right field at foul line, 325 feet
First game played
April 4, 1994
(Indians 4, Mariners 3, 11 innings)

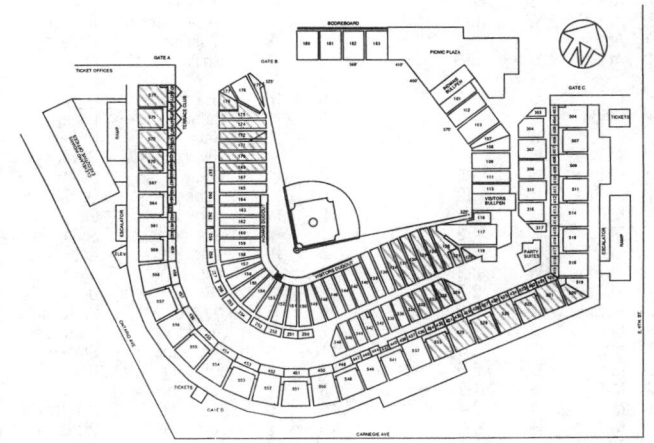

1998 SEASON · *Cleveland Indians*

Date	Opp.	Res.	Score	(inn.*)	Hits	Opp. hits	Winning pitcher	Losing pitcher	Save	Record	Pos.	GB
4-2	At Oak.	W	9-7		13	11	Kline	Wengert	Shuey	1-0	2nd	0.5
4-3	At Oak.	L	4-5		6	8	Lewis	Plunk	Taylor	1-1	T2nd	1.5
4-4	At Ana.	L	6-8	(11)	9	14	Holtz	Shuey		1-2	T2nd	1.5
4-5	At Ana.	W	7-5		10	8	Ogea	Hasegawa	Shuey	2-2	2nd	1.5
4-6	At Ana.	W	10-8		15	12	Kline	Percival	M. Jackson	3-2	2nd	0.5
4-7	At Sea.	W	8-3		9	11	Nagy	Sanders		4-2	1st	+0.5
4-8	At Sea.	L	8-14		18	17	Hurtado	Lopez		4-3	T1st	....
4-9	At Sea.	L	1-11		9	13	Wolcott	Colon		4-4	T2nd	0.5
4-11	Ana.	W	15-3		20	7	Ogea	Gubicza		5-4	T1st	....
4-13	Ana.	L	3-8		10	13	Langston	McDowell		5-5	3rd	0.5
4-14	Sea.	L	1-6		2	10	D. Martinez	Nagy		5-6	4th	1.5
4-15	Sea.	L	4-8		9	14	Wells	M. Jackson	Charlton	5-7	4th	1.5
4-16	At Bos.	L	6-11		10	16	Avery	Ogea		5-8	4th	2.5
4-17	At Bos.	W	4-3		10	10	Kline	Trlicek	Mesa	6-8	4th	2.5
4-18	Mil.	L	2-10		6	13	McDonald	McDowell		6-9	4th	3.5
4-19	Mil.	W	11-6		17	10	Nagy	Eldred		7-9	4th	2.5
4-20	Mil.	W	6-4		7	7	Hershiser	Wickman	Mesa	8-9	T3rd	1.5
4-22	Bos.	L	2-8		4	15	Avery	Ogea	Henry	8-10	3rd	2.5
4-23	Bos.	W	11-7		15	14	McDowell	Trlicek		9-10	3rd	1.5
4-24	At Mil.	W	6-3		14	11	Nagy	Eldred	Mesa	10-10	2nd	0.5
4-25	At Mil.	W	11-4		14	6	Hershiser	Karl		11-10	1st	+0.5
4-26	At Mil.	L	8-9		12	11	Jones	Mesa		11-11	1st	+0.5
4-27	At Mil.	L	5-6		8	13	Jones	Plunk		11-12	T2nd	0.5
4-29	Oak.	W	10-4		12	8	Nagy	Prieto	M. Jackson	12-12	T2nd	1.0
4-30	Oak.	L	9-11	(10)	15	15	Taylor	Mesa	Wengert	12-13	T2nd	1.0
5-1	Oak.	W	7-1		8	4	McDowell	Adams		13-13	T2nd	0.5
5-3	Det.	W	7-6		10	5	Plunk	Brocail		14-13	T1st	....
5-4	Det.	L	0-2		5	6	Blair	Nagy	Brocail	14-14	T1st	....
5-6	Tex.	W	5-4		6	9	Hershiser	Pavlik	M. Jackson	15-14	1st	....
5-7	Tor.	W	7-1		15	7	McDowell	Person		16-14	1st	+0.5
5-8	Tor.	L	3-4		8	10	Guzman	Ogea	Quantrill	16-15	T1st	....
5-9	At Det.	W	5-0		8	7	Nagy	Sager		17-15	T1st	....
5-10	At Det.	L	0-6		3	8	Olivares	Colon		17-16	T2nd	1.0
5-11	At Det.	L	3-11		4	15	Thompson	Hershiser		17-17	T2nd	2.0
5-12	At Tex.	L	2-4		9	5	Burkett	McDowell	Wetteland	17-18	3rd	3.0
5-13	At Tex.	W	7-3		12	8	Ogea	Oliver	Morman	18-18	3rd	2.0
5-14	At Tex.	L	3-4	(10)	8	13	Wetteland	Lopez		18-19	3rd	2.0
5-16	At Tor.	L	2-5		7	10	Clemens	Hershiser	Timlin	18-20	3rd	2.0
5-17	At Tor.	W	8-1		9	9	Lopez	Williams		19-20	3rd	1.0
5-18	At Tor.	W	8-6		11	8	Ogea	Carpenter	M. Jackson	20-20	T1st	....
5-20	K.C.	W	4-3		12	10	Shuey	Walker	M. Jackson	21-20	1st	+1.0
5-21	K.C.	W	1-0		2	6	Hershiser	Appier	M. Jackson	22-20	1st	+1.5
5-22	K.C.	W	9-1		12	6	Lopez	Rosado		23-20	1st	+2.0
5-23	Bal.	W	6-1		12	2	Ogea	Key		24-20	1st	+2.0
5-24	Bal.	L	3-8		9	15	Mussina	Kline		24-21	1st	+2.0
5-25	Bal.	W	7-6		12	9	Nagy	Rhodes	Morman	25-21	1st	+2.0
5-26	At Chi.	W	10-4		13	6	Hershiser	Navarro		26-21	1st	+3.0
5-27	At Chi.	L	2-8		6	10	Drabek	Lopez		26-22	1st	+3.0
5-28	At K.C.	W	10-3		16	6	Assenmacher	Belcher		27-22	1st	+4.0
5-30	At Bal.	L	0-3		1	9	Mussina	Nagy		27-23	1st	+2.5
5-31	At Bal.	L	5-8		10	13	Boskie	Mesa	Myers	27-24	1st	+1.5
6-3	Chi.	L	5-9		9	15	D. Darwin	Ogea		27-25	1st	+0.5
6-4	Chi.	L	4-9		6	13	Baldwin	Lopez		27-26	2nd	0.5
6-5	Chi.	W	5-4	(11)	11	13	Shuey	C. Castillo		28-26	1st	+0.5
6-6	At Bos.	W	7-3		10	11	Hershiser	Gordon		29-26	1st	+1.5
6-7	At Bos.	W	9-5		13	11	Colon	Sele		30-26	1st	+2.5
6-8	At Bos.	L	6-12		8	16	Hudson	Ogea		30-27	1st	+2.5
6-10	Mil.	W	5-4		9	11	Nagy	Eldred	M. Jackson	31-27	1st	+3.5
6-11	Mil.	W	4-3	(11)	11	5	Assenmacher	Jones		32-27	1st	+4.0
6-12	Mil.	L	2-6		6	10	Mercedes	Anderson		32-28	1st	+3.5
6-14†	At St.L.	W	8-3		14	7	Lopez	Mathews		33-28		
6-14‡	At St.L.	L	2-5		5	11	Morris	Ogea	Eckersley	33-29	1st	+3.5
6-15	At St.L.	W	9-2		9	5	Nagy	Stottlemyre		34-29	1st	+3.5
6-16	Cin.	L	1-4		7	7	Tomko	Hershiser		34-30	1st	+2.5
6-17	Cin.	W	5-1		11	5	Anderson	Smiley		35-30	1st	+3.5
6-18	Cin.	L	2-5		7	11	Remlinger	Ogea		35-31	1st	+2.5
6-20	N.Y.	L	1-7		5	12	Gooden	Nagy		35-32	1st	+1.5
6-21	N.Y.	W	13-4		15	10	Hershiser	Pettitte		36-32	1st	+2.0
6-22	N.Y.	W	5-2		10	8	Anderson	Wells	M. Jackson	37-32	1st	+3.0
6-23	Min.	L	2-7		7	16	Radke	Ogea		37-33	1st	+2.0
6-24	Min.	W	10-5		13	9	Wright	Stevens		38-33	1st	+3.0

Date	Opp.	Res.	Score	(inn.*)	Hits	Opp. hits	Winning pitcher	Losing pitcher	Save	Record	Pos.	GB
6-27	At N.Y.	L	2-3		7	7	Gooden	Hershiser	Rivera	38-34	1st	+1.0
6-28	At N.Y.	W	12-8		19	12	Plunk	Rogers		39-34	1st	+2.0
6-29	At N.Y.	L	10-11		13	15	Rivera	Mesa		39-35	1st	+1.0
6-30	At Hou.	W	6-4		9	8	Mesa	Martin	M. Jackson	40-35	1st	+2.0
7-1	At Hou.	W	8-6		15	10	Plunk	Lima	M. Jackson	41-35	1st	+3.0
7-2	At Hou.	L	2-6		10	10	Hampton	Hershiser		41-36	1st	+3.0
7-4	K.C.	W	7-6		13	12	Anderson	Pichardo	M. Jackson	42-36	1st	+3.5
7-5	K.C.	W	8-4		15	6	Nagy	Pittsley		43-36	1st	+3.5
7-6	K.C.	W	8-7		10	9	M. Jackson	Casian		44-36	1st	+3.5
7-10	At Min.	L	2-8		8	14	Radke	Nagy		44-37	1st	+2.5
7-11	At Min.	W	5-1		4	9	Jacome	Robertson		45-37	1st	+2.5
7-12	At Min.	W	7-2		13	8	Hershiser	Tewksbury		46-37	1st	+2.5
7-13	At Min.	W	12-5		15	7	Colon	Hawkins		47-37	1st	+2.5
7-14	At N.Y.	W	3-2	(10)	10	8	M. Jackson	Rivera		48-37	1st	+3.5
7-15	At N.Y.	L	6-12		13	17	Irabu	Nagy	Mendoza	48-38	1st	+3.5
7-16	At Mil.	W	4-3		8	6	Wright	McDonald	M. Jackson	49-38	1st	+4.5
7-17	At Mil.	W	3-2		5	6	Hershiser	Eldred	M. Jackson	50-38	1st	+5.5
7-18	Bos.	L	0-7		6	14	Wakefield	Colon		50-39	1st	+4.5
7-19	Bos.	L	3-6		9	8	Suppan	Clark	Slocumb	50-40	1st	+4.5
7-20	Bos.	W	7-2		11	8	Nagy	Gordon		51-40	1st	+4.5
7-21	Bos.	L	1-3		4	8	Avery	Wright	Slocumb	51-41	1st	+3.5
7-22	Sea.	W	6-2		10	4	Weathers	Fassero	M. Jackson	52-41	1st	+4.5
7-23	Sea.	L	3-6		11	11	Olivares	Colon	Holzemer	52-42	1st	+4.5
7-24	Sea.	L	1-11		8	12	Johnson	Clark		52-43	1st	+3.5
7-25	Oak.	L	1-2		5	6	Small	M. Jackson	Taylor	52-44	1st	+3.5
7-26	Oak.	W	6-3		12	6	Wright	Karsay		53-44	1st	+4.5
7-27	Oak.	W	4-2		7	6	Jacome	Haynes	Assenmacher	54-44	1st	+5.5
7-28†	Ana.	L	0-2		8	9	Springer	Colon		54-45		
7-28‡	Ana.	L	7-10		8	13	Harris	Weathers	Holtz	54-46	1st	+4.5
7-29	Ana.	L	2-7		3	10	Finley	Clark		54-47	1st	+3.5
7-30	Ana.	L	2-5		5	9	Hill	Nagy	James	54-48	1st	+3.0
8-1	At Tex.	W	8-5		15	10	Mesa	Gunderson	Assenmacher	55-48	1st	+2.5
8-2	At Tex.	W	7-3		11	6	Smiley	Witt		56-48	1st	+3.5
8-3	At Tex.	L	7-8		15	13	Wetteland	M. Jackson		56-49	1st	+3.5
8-4	At Det.	W	7-2		13	8	Nagy	Sanders		57-49	1st	+3.5
8-5	At Det.	L	4-6		9	8	Thompson	Plunk	Jones	57-50	1st	+3.5
8-6	At Tor.	L	3-6		13	10	Hentgen	Lopez	Escobar	57-51	1st	+3.5
8-7	At Tor.	L	0-4		5	9	Clemens	Smiley		57-52	1st	+3.5
8-8	Tex.	L	5-6		6	7	Bailes	M. Jackson	Wetteland	57-53	1st	+3.0
8-9†	Tex.	L	3-4		6	8	T. Clark	Nagy	Wetteland	57-54		
8-9‡	Tex.	W	4-2		9	7	Assenmacher	Moody	Mesa	58-54	1st	+3.5
8-10	Tex.	L	6-7		13	9	Whiteside	Juden	Wetteland	58-55	1st	+3.0
8-12	Det.	W	7-4		13	8	Plunk	Keagle	Mesa	59-55	1st	+3.0
8-13†	Det.	L	3-13		9	17	Blair	Smiley		59-56		
8-13‡	Det.	W	9-1		14	7	Hershiser	Dishman		60-56	1st	+2.5
8-14	Det.	W	12-1		15	4	Nagy	Sanders		61-56	1st	+3.5
8-15	Tor.	W	5-4	(10)	10	10	Assenmacher	Crabtree		62-56	1st	+4.5
8-16	Tor.	W	8-4		10	7	Shuey	Quantrill		63-56	1st	+5.5
8-17	Tor.	L	5-10		8	14	Clemens	Wright		63-57	1st	+4.5
8-18	Tor.	W	5-3		9	3	Hershiser	Williams	Mesa	64-57	1st	+5.0
8-19	At Sea.	W	7-5		8	10	Smiley	Cloude	Mesa	65-57	1st	+5.0
8-20	At Sea.	L	0-1		2	9	Johnson	Nagy	Slocumb	65-58	1st	+4.0
8-21	At Sea.	L	6-7		12	8	Moyer	Colon	Slocumb	65-59	1st	+3.5
8-22	At Oak.	W	5-3		12	6	Wright	Prieto	Mesa	66-59	1st	+4.5
8-23	At Oak.	W	7-4		17	8	Hershiser	Rigby	Mesa	67-59	1st	+5.0
8-24	At Oak.	L	1-4		5	6	Haynes	Smiley	Mathews	67-60	1st	+4.0
8-26	At Ana.	L	7-8		7	11	May	Plunk		67-61	1st	+2.5
8-27	At Ana.	W	10-4		15	5	Wright	Watson		68-61	1st	+3.5
8-29	Chi. (NL)	W	7-6		11	13	Mesa	Stevens		69-61	1st	+3.5
8-30	Chi. (NL)	L	4-9		8	15	Tapani	Smiley		69-62	1st	+3.5
8-31	Chi. (NL)	W	9-5		11	13	Nagy	Batista	Assenmacher	70-62	1st	+3.5
9-1	At Pit.	W	7-5		12	9	Ogea	Cooke	Mesa	71-62	1st	+3.5
9-2	At Pit.	L	4-6		11	9	Silva	Wright	Loiselle	71-63	1st	+2.5
9-3	At Pit.	W	7-3		7	8	Hershiser	Loaiza		72-63	1st	+3.5
9-5	Chi.	W	11-1		18	6	Nagy	Bere		73-63	1st	+3.5
9-6	Chi.	W	9-7		12	11	Colon	Baldwin	Mesa	74-63	1st	+4.5
9-7	Chi.	W	5-2		7	7	Wright	Drabek	Mesa	75-63	1st	+5.5
9-8	Bal.	W	2-1		10	6	Assenmacher	Mills	Mesa	76-63	1st	+5.5
9-9	Bal.	L	3-9		8	13	Krivda	Ogea		76-64	1st	+5.5
9-11	At Chi.	W	5-7		9	10	Foulke	Nagy	Karchner	76-65	1st	+5.5
9-12	At Chi.	W	9-0		14	3	Wright	Drabek		77-65	1st	+6.5
9-13	At Chi.	L	6-7		16	10	Sirotka	Hershiser	Karchner	77-66	1st	+6.5
9-14	At Chi.	W	8-3		11	11	Shuey	J. Darwin		78-66	1st	+7.5
9-15†	At Bal.	L	5-6		8	6	Benitez	Plunk	Myers	78-67		
9-15‡	At Bal.	W	4-1		10	10	Ogea	Krivda	Mesa	79-67	1st	+7.0

Date	Opp.	Res.	Score	(inn.*)	Hits	Opp. hits	Winning pitcher	Losing pitcher	Save	Record	Pos.	GB
9-16†	At Bal.	W	4-2		9	7	Nagy	Rodriguez	Mesa	80-67		
9-16‡	At Bal.	L	2-7		5	8	Key	Weathers		80-68	1st	+7.0
9-17	At Min.	W	7-6		9	11	Wright	T. Miller	Mesa	81-68	1st	+7.0
9-18	At Min.	W	4-1		11	4	Hershiser	Tewksbury	M. Jackson	82-68	1st	+8.0
9-19†	At K.C.	L	3-10		9	12	Belcher	Colon		82-69		
9-19‡	At K.C.	W	6-2		16	8	Anderson	Bones	Assenmacher	83-69	1st	+7.5
9-20	At K.C.	L	2-5		10	6	Olson	Lopez	Montgomery	83-70	1st	+6.5
9-21	At K.C.	L	0-1		5	5	Bevil	M. Jackson		83-71	1st	+6.5
9-23	N.Y.	W	10-9		12	13	Mesa	Nelson		84-71	1st	+7.5
9-24	N.Y.	L	4-8		9	13	Gooden	Anderson		84-72	1st	+7.5
9-25	N.Y.	L	4-5	(10)	6	9	Mendoza	Shuey	Stanton	84-73	1st	+6.5
9-26	Min.	W	7-2		8	12	Ogea	Radke		85-73	1st	+6.5
9-27†	Min.	W	10-6		16	14	Colon	T. Miller		86-73		
9-27‡	Min.	L	4-6	(10)	12	12	Aguilera	Lopez		86-74	1st	+7.0
9-28	Min.	L	1-5		6	9	Tewksbury	Nagy		86-75	1st	+6.0

Monthly records: April (12-13), May (15-11), June (13-11), July (14-13), August (16-14), September (16-13).
*Innings, if other than nine. †First game of doubleheader. ‡Second game of doubleheader.

HIGHLIGHTS

High point: Tony Fernandez's home run in the top of the 10th gave the Indians a 1-0 win over the Orioles in Game 6 of the ALCS and put them in the World Series for the second time in three years. All four of the Indians' wins in the series were by one run and three came in their last at-bat.

Low point: The Indians took a 2-1 lead over the Marlins into the ninth inning of Game 7 of the World Series and were two outs away from their first championship since 1948. But the Marlins tied the game in the ninth against Jose Mesa and won it in the 11th off Charles Nagy.

Turning point: August 13. The Indians were 59-56, their lead had shrunk to 2½ games and rumors were swirling that manager Mike Hargrove's job was in jeopardy. The Indians then won four straight and began to pull away from the division.

Most valuable player: Sandy Alomar had a dream season with career highs in batting average (.324), home runs (21) and RBIs (83). He also had a 30-game hitting streak, and he hit the game-winning home run and was MVP of the All-Star Game, played at Jacobs Field. Alomar's heroics continued in the postseason. His home run off Mariano Rivera tied Game 4 of the Division Series. He also had the winning hit in Game 4 of the ALCS.

Most valuable pitcher: Mike Jackson held the bullpen together. When Mesa pitched himself out of the closer's job early in the season, Jackson took over and recorded a career-high 15 saves. When Mesa reclaimed the closer's job in August, Jackson continued to pitch well in the setup role.

Most improved player: David Justice missed most of 1996 with a shoulder injury but bounced back to have a big season. He drove in 101 runs and batted a career high .329.

Most pleasant surprise: No one expected 21-year-old righthander Jaret Wright to make an impact in 1997. Because of several injuries to the pitching staff, the Indians called him up in late June. Wright responded by going 8-3 with a 4.38 ERA. He was even better in the postseason, going 3-0 in four starts.

Biggest disappointment: While the Indians are primarily noted for their hitting, their pitching led the league in ERA in 1995 and 1996. That changed dramatically last season. Their 4.73 ERA was ninth in the league and the big reason the team's win total dipped from 99 to 86.

Key injuries: Jack McDowell didn't pitch again after having elbow surgery in late May, Chad Ogea missed three months with elbow and knee problems, Orel Hershiser was on the disabled list with a stiff back and John Smiley broke his left arm while warming up for a start in September.

Notable: The Indians became the first American League team in history to hit 200 or more home runs in three straight seasons. They hit a club-record 220 homers last season.

—STEVE HERRICK

RECORDS

1997 regular-season record: 86-75 (1st in A.L. Central); 44-37 at home; 42-38 on road; 27-28 vs. East; 40-22 vs. Central; 19-25 vs. West; 22-19 vs. lefthanded starters; 64-56 vs. righthanded starters; 73-65 on grass; 13-10 on turf; 29-24 in daytime; 57-51 at night; 19-19 in one-run games; 4-5 in extra-inning games; 0-1-7 in doubleheaders.

Team record past five years: 427-314 (.576, ranks 1st in league in that span).

TEAM LEADERS

Batting average: David Justice (.329).
At-bats: Matt Williams (596).
Runs: Jim Thome (104).
Hits: Manny Ramirez (184).
Total bases: Manny Ramirez (302).
Doubles: Manny Ramirez (40).
Triples: Marquis Grissom, Omar Vizquel (6).
Home runs: Jim Thome (40).
Runs batted in: Matt Williams (105).
Stolen bases: Omar Vizquel (43).
Slugging percentage: David Justice (.596).
On-base percentage: Jim Thome (.423).
Wins: Charles Nagy (15).
Earned-run average: Charles Nagy (4.28).
Complete games: Bartolo Colon, Orel Hershiser, Charles Nagy, Chad Ogea (1).

Shutouts: Charles Nagy (1).
Saves: Jose Mesa (16).
Innings pitched: Charles Nagy (227.0).
Strikeouts: Charles Nagy (149).

GAMES BY POSITION

Catcher: Sandy Alomar 119, Pat Borders 53, Einar Diaz 5.
First base: Jim Thome 145, Kevin Seitzer 19, Jeff Manto 6, Richie Sexson 2, Sean Casey 1, Julio Franco 1.
Second base: Tony Fernandez 109, Julio Franco 35, Jeff Branson 19, Bip Roberts 13, Casey Candaele 9, Damian Jackson 1, Enrique Wilson 1.
Third base: Matt Williams 151, Kevin Seitzer 13, Jeff Manto 7, Jeff Branson 6, Casey Candaele 1.
Shortstop: Omar Vizquel 152, Tony Fernandez 10, Damian Jackson 5, Enrique Wilson 4, Jeff Branson 2.
Outfield: Manny Ramirez 146, Marquis Grissom 144, Brian S. Giles 115, David Justice 78, Chad Curtis 19, Bruce Aven 13, Bip Roberts 10, Trent Hubbard 6, Jeff Manto 1, Kevin Mitchell 1.
Designated hitter: David Justice 61, Julio Franco 42, Kevin Seitzer 24, Kevin Mitchell 16, Brian S. Giles 9, Manny Ramirez 4, Sean Casey 3, Sandy Alomar 1, Jeff Branson 1, Casey Candaele 1, Tony Fernandez 1, Richie Sexson 1.

TOP DRAFT CHOICES

1a. **Tim Drew,** RHP, Lowndes County H.S., Hahira, Ga.
1b. **Jason Fitzgerald,** OF, Tulane University.
2a. **Edgar Cruz,** C, Vocational Tech, Juncos P.R.
2b. **Rob Vael,** RHP, J.C. of Eastern Utah.
3. **Rob Pugmire,** RHP, Cascade H.S., Snohomish, Wash.
4. **Erick Thompson,** OF, Westover H.S., Fayetteville, N.C.
5. **Jonathan Hamilton,** OF-LHP, Ohlone (Calif.) J.C.
6. **Brian Benefield,** 2B, Texas A&M Univ.
7. **Mark Turnbow,** RHP, Hardin County H.S., Saltillo, Tenn.
8. **Johnnie Wheeler,** LHP, Connors State (Okla.) J.C.
9. **Dustan Mohr,** OF, University of Alabama.
10. **Joe Gilburg,** 2B-OF, Stanford University.

The Royals' Shane Halter looks to get his way out of a rundown.
(Photo by Ed Nessen/THE SPORTING NEWS)

As usual, Cal Ripken returns for another season in Baltimore.
(Photo by Ezra O. Shaw for THE SPORTING NEWS)

Houston's Craig Biggio led the National League in runs scored for the second time in his career. (Photo by Robert Seale/The Sporting News)

Pedro Martinez won the N.L. Cy Young but left the Expos and the National League for the Red Sox this season. (Photo by THE SPORTING NEWS)

Giants first baseman J.T. Snow won his third consecutive Gold Glove last season. (Photo by Ed Nessen/THE SPORTING NEWS)

L.A.'s Hideo Nomo had 14 wins in '97, tying him with Chan Ho Park for the team lead.
(Photo by THE SPORTING NEWS)

Shortstop Neifi Perez is a budding star who will step in to start for the Rockies this season. (Photo by Albert Dickson/The Sporting News)

Royce Clayton and the Cardinals couldn't catch Jeff Bagwell and the Astros, as Houston came away as NL Central champs in '97. (Photo by Ed Nessen/THE SPORTING NEWS)

DETROIT TIGERS
AMERICAN LEAGUE CENTRAL DIVISION

Tigers Schedule
Home games shaded. *—All-Star Game at Coors Field (Colorado).
D—Day game (any game starting before 5 p.m.).

March

SUN	MON	TUE	WED	THU	FRI	SAT
		31 D TB				

April

SUN	MON	TUE	WED	THU	FRI	SAT
			1 TB	2 TB	3 BAL	4 D BAL
5 D BAL	6	7 D TB	8	9 D TB	10 BAL	11 D BAL
12 D BAL	13 TEX	14 TEX	15 TEX	16	17 NYY	18 D NYY
19 D NYY	20	21 BOS	22 BOS	23	24 NYY	25 D NYY
26 NYY	27 BOS	28 BOS	29 TEX	30 D TEX		

May

SUN	MON	TUE	WED	THU	FRI	SAT
					1 SEA	2 SEA
3 D SEA	4	5 OAK	6 D OAK	7 D OAK	8 ANA	9 ANA
10 D ANA	11	12 SEA	13 SEA	14 OAK	15 OAK	16 D ANA
17 D ANA	18 ANA	19 MIN	20 MIN	21 D MIN	22 CWS	23 CWS
24 D CWS	25 D CLE	26 CLE	27	28 CWS	29 CWS	30 CWS
31 D CWS						

June

SUN	MON	TUE	WED	THU	FRI	SAT
	1 CLE	2 CLE	3 TOR	4 TOR	5 D MIL	6 MIL
7 D MIL	8 HOU	9 HOU	10 HOU	11	12 KC	13 KC
14 D KC	15 MIN	16 MIN	17 MIN	18 KC	19 KC	20 KC
21 D KC	22 STL	23 STL	24 CUB	25 CUB	26 CIN	27 CIN
28 D CIN	29	30 PIT				

July

SUN	MON	TUE	WED	THU	FRI	SAT
		1 PIT	2 PIT	3 MIN	4 D MIN
5 D MIN	6	7	8 D TOR	9 TOR	10 TOR	11 TOR
12 D TOR	13 KC	14 D KC	15 NYY	16 NYY	17 BOS	18 BOS
19 D BOS	20 NYY	21 NYY	22 D NYY	23 CLE	24 CLE	25 D CLE
26 D CLE	27	28 BAL	29 BAL	30 D BAL	31 TB	

August

SUN	MON	TUE	WED	THU	FRI	SAT
						1 TB
2 D TB	3	4 BAL	5 D BAL	6 SEA	7 SEA	8 SEA
9 D SEA	10 ANA	11 ANA	12 ANA	13	14 OAK	15 OAK
16 D OAK	17 SEA	18 SEA	19 ANA	20 ANA	21 OAK	22 D OAK
23 D OAK	24 TEX	25 TEX	26 TEX	27	28 TB	29 TB
30 D TB	31 TEX					

September

SUN	MON	TUE	WED	THU	FRI	SAT
		1 TEX	2 TEX	3 CLE	4 CLE	5 D CLE
6 D CLE	7 CWS	8 CWS	9 CWS	10	11 BOS	12 D BOS
13 D BOS	14 CLE	15 TOR	16 TOR	17 TOR	18 MIN	19 D MIN
20 D MIN	21 KC	22 KC	23 KC	24	25 TOR	26 D TOR
27 D TOR						

1998 SEASON
CLUB DIRECTORY

Owners
Michael Ilitch
President, chief executive officer
John McHale Jr.
Vice president, baseball operations/g.m.
Randy Smith
Vice president, business operations
David H. Glazier
Assistant general manager
Steve Lubratich
Assistant to baseball operations
Ricky Bennett
Special assistants to the g.m.
Al Hargesheimer
Randy Johnson
Director of scouting
Greg Smith
Director minor league operations
Dave Miller
Advance scout
Tom Runnells
Special assignment scout
Larry Bearnarth
Traveling secretary
Bill Brown
Director of public relations
Tyler Barnes
Assistant director of public relations
David Matheson
Manager, community relations
Celia Bobrowsky
Coordinator, community relations
Herman Jenkins
Coordinator, public relations
Giovanni Loria
Asst., public relations-publications
Merrill Cain
Asst., public relations-administrative
Erikka Cullum
Coordinator, community relations
Christina Branham
Sr. director, marketing and operations
Michael Dietz
Director of stadium operations
Tom Folk

Head groundskeeper
Frank Feneck
Senior director, corporate sales
Gary Vitto
Director of corporate sales
Martin Pawlusiak
Controller
Jennifer Marosso
Director of ticket services
Ken Marchetti
Group/season ticket sales manager
Kevin Marcy
Season ticket manager
Kevin Marcy
Director of merchandise
Kayla French
Head trainer
Russ Miller
Assistant trainer
Steve Carter
Strength and conditioning coach
Brad Andress
Manager, home clubhouse
Jim Schmakel
Assistant manager, visiting clubhouse
John Nelson
Team physicians
Clarence Livingood, M.D.
David Collon, M.D.
Terry Lock, M.D.
Louis Saco, M.D. (Florida)
Scouts
Larry Bearnarth, Ricky Bennett, Bill Buck, Tom Chandler, Nathan Durst, Louis Eljaua, Rob Guzik, Jack Hays, Ray Hayward, Mike Humphreys, Lou Laslo, Steve Lemke, Dennis Lieberthal, Jeff Malinoff, James Merriweather, John Mirabelli, Mark Monahan, Glenn Murdock, Jim Olander, David Owen, Ramon Pena, Rusty Pendergrass, Dave Roberts, Tom Runnells, Mike Stafford, Chuck Stone, Dan Warthen, Clyde Weir, Jeff Wetherby, Rob Wilfong, Gary York

MINOR LEAGUE AFFILIATES

Class	Team	League	Manager
AAA	Toledo	International	Gene Roof
AA	Jacksonville	Southern	Dave Anderson
A	Lakeland	Florida State	Mark Meleski
A	West Michigan	Midwest	Bruce Fields
A	Jamestown	New York-Pennsylvania	Tim Torricelli
Rookie	Gulf Coast Tigers	Gulf Coast	Kevin Bradshaw

BROADCAST INFORMATION

Radio: WJR-AM (760).
TV: WKBD (Channel 50).
Cable TV: Pro Am Sports Systems.

SPRING TRAINING

Ballpark (city): Marchant Stadium (Lakeland, Fla.).
Ticket information: 941-603-6278.

SPRING TRAINING ROSTER

Manager—Buddy Bell (25).
Coaches—Rick Adair (35), Larry Herndon (31), Perry Hill (13), Fred Kendall (18), Larry Parrish (15), Jerry White (48).

No.	PITCHERS	B/T	Ht./Wt.	Born	1997 clubs
26	Brocail, Doug	L/R	6-5/235	5-16-67	Detroit
	Castillo, Frank	R/R	6-1/200	4-1-69	Chicago N.L., Colorado
	Cordero, Francisco	R/R	6-2/160	8-11-77	West Michigan
	Crow, Dean	L/R	6-4/215	8-21-72	Tacoma, Toledo
	Drews, Matt	R/R	6-8/230	8-29-74	Jacksonville, Toledo
	Drumright, Mike	L/R	6-4/210	4-19-74	Jacksonville, Toledo
55	Duran, Roberto	L/L	6-0/167	3-6-73	Jacksonville, Detroit
	Florie, Bryce	R/R	5-11/190	5-21-70	Milwaukee
54	Gaillard, Eddie	R/R	6-1/180	8-13-70	Toledo, Detroit
	Garcia, Apostol	B/R	6-0/155	8-3-76	West Michigan
59	Jones, Todd	L/R	6-3/200	4-24-68	Detroit
57	Keagle, Greg	R/R	6-1/185	6-20-71	Toledo, Detroit
38	Moehler, Brian	R/R	6-3/195	12-31-71	Detroit
	Powell, Brian	R/R	6-2/205	10-10-73	Lakeland
	Roberts, Willis	R/R	6-3/175	6-19-75	Jacksonville
	Rosengren, John	L/L	6-4/190	8-10-72	Toledo
	Runyan, Sean	L/L	6-3/200	6-21-74	Mobile
49	Sager, A.J.	R/R	6-4/220	3-3-65	Detroit
28	Sanders, Scott	R/R	6-4/220	3-25-69	Seattle, Detroit
22	Thompson, Justin	L/L	6-3/175	3-8-73	Detroit
	Worrell, Tim	R/R	6-4/220	7-5-67	San Diego

No.	CATCHERS	B/T	Ht./Wt.	Born	1997 clubs
	Bako, Paul	R/L	6-2/195	6-20-72	Indianapolis
33	Casanova, Raul	B/R	5-11/200	8-23-72	Toledo, Detroit
10	Jensen, Marcus	B/R	6-4/204	12-14-72	San Francisco, Toledo, Detroit
	Oliver, Joe	R/R	6-3/220	7-24-65	Indianapolis, Cincinnati

No.	INFIELDERS	B/T	Ht./Wt.	Born	1997 clubs
	Almanzar, Richard	R/R	5-10/155	4-3-76	Jacksonville
	Alvarez, Gabe	R/R	6-1/185	3-6-74	Mobile
29	Catalanotto, Frank	L/R	6-0/170	4-27-74	Toledo, Detroit
17	Clark, Tony	B/R	6-8/250	6-15-72	Detroit
37	Cruz, Deivi	R/R	5-11/160	6-11-75	Detroit
9	Easley, Damion	R/R	5-11/185	11-11-69	Detroit
	Garcia, Luis	R/R	6-0/175	5-20-75	Jacksonville
	Randa, Joe	R/R	5-11/185	12-18-69	Pittsburgh, Calgary
	Ripken, Billy	R/R	6-1/190	12-16-64	Texas
1	Roberts, Bip	B/R	5-7/165	10-27-63	Kansas City, Cleveland

No.	OUTFIELDERS	B/T	Ht./Wt.	Born	1997 clubs
39	Bartee, Kimera	B/R	6-0/175	7-21-72	Toledo, Detroit
	Beamon, Trey	L/R	6-0/192	2-11-74	Las Vegas, San Diego
34	Encarnacion, Juan	R/R	6-2/160	3-22-76	Jacksonville, Detroit
	Gonzalez, Luis	L/R	6-2/185	9-3-67	Houston
4	Higginson, Bobby	L/R	5-11/180	8-18-70	Detroit
21	Hunter, Brian	R/R	6-4/180	3-5-71	Detroit
	Kapler, Gabriel	R/R	6-2/190	8-31-75	Lakeland

BALLPARK INFORMATION

Ballpark (capacity, surface)
Tiger Stadium (46,945, grass)

Address
Tiger Stadium
Detroit, MI 48216

Business phone
313-962-4000

Ticket information
313-963-2050

Ticket prices
$15 and $10 (box seats)
$12 and $8 (reserved seats)
$8 (grandstand reserved seats)
$4 (bleacher seats)

Field dimensions (from home plate)
To left field at foul line, 340 feet
To center field, 440 feet
To right field at foul line, 325 feet

First game played
April 20, 1912
   (Tigers 6, Cleveland Naps 5, 11 innings)

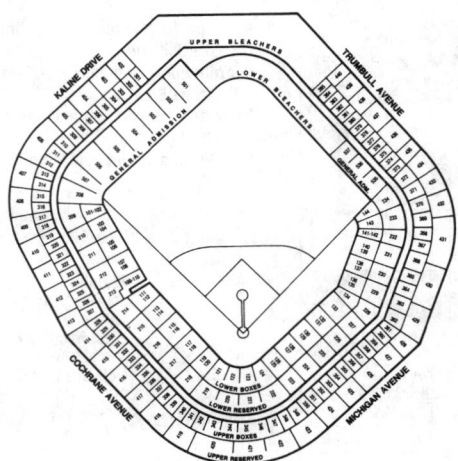

1998 SEASON · *Detroit Tigers*

Date	Opp.	Res.	Score	(inn.*)	Hits	Opp. hits	Winning pitcher	Losing pitcher	Save	Record	Pos.	GB
4-1	At Min.	L	5-7		12	13	Naulty	Miceli	Aguilera	0-1	T3rd	0.5
4-2	At Min.	L	6-7		10	8	Aguilera	Jones		0-2	5th	1.5
4-3	At Min.	L	6-10		14	10	Ritchie	Blair	Naulty	0-3	5th	2.5
4-4	At Chi.	W	8-7	(10)	10	10	Jones	Levine	Sager	1-3	5th	2.5
4-5	At Chi.	W	15-12		19	12	Blair	T. Castillo	Jones	2-3	5th	2.5
4-6	At Chi.	L	3-5		8	10	Navarro	Brocail	Hernandez	2-4	5th	2.5
4-7	Min.	W	10-4		9	9	Thompson	Rodriguez		3-4	T4th	1.5
4-9	Min.	W	10-5		10	9	Cummings	Ritchie		4-4	T2nd	1.5
4-10	Min.	L	3-7		6	14	Aldred	Blair		4-5	5th	2.0
4-11	Chi.	W	5-4		7	7	Olivares	Drabek	Jones	5-5	3rd	2.0
4-13†	Chi.	L	8-11	(12)	10	12	Hernandez	Lira		5-6	T4th	3.0
4-13‡	Chi.	W	4-2		8	8	Sager	Hernandez		6-6	T2nd	2.5
4-14	At Mil.	L	0-7		4	12	Eldred	Moehler		6-7	T3rd	3.5
4-15	At Mil.	W	3-1		8	6	Blair	Karl	Jones	7-7	3rd	3.5
4-16	Sea.	L	3-7		6	5	Johnson	Sager		7-8	T3rd	3.5
4-17	Sea.	L	6-8		11	16	Fassero	Bautista	Charlton	7-9	4th	4.5
4-18	Oak.	L	5-9		12	10	Groom	Myers		7-10	4th	5.0
4-19	Oak.	L	1-7		3	13	Adams	Thompson		7-11	5th	5.5
4-20	Oak.	W	9-2		12	8	Moehler	Karsay		8-11	4th	5.5
4-21	At Tex.	W	7-6		13	13	Sager	Vosberg	Miceli	9-11	4th	4.5
4-23	At Tex.	L	1-2		4	6	Wetteland	Brocail		9-12	5th	5.0
4-24	At Tex.	L	2-4		6	11	Pavlik	Thompson	Wetteland	9-13	5th	5.0
4-25	At Ana.	L	3-8		5	11	Dickson	Lira		9-14	5th	6.0
4-26	At Ana.	W	2-0		6	2	Moehler	Finley		10-14	5th	6.0
4-27	At Ana.	L	5-6		10	11	James	Myers		10-15	5th	6.0
4-29	Mil.	L	1-2		7	7	Eldred	Olivares	Jones	10-16	5th	7.0
4-30	Mil.	W	8-4		9	10	Thompson	Karl		11-16	5th	7.0
5-3	At Cle.	L	6-7		5	10	Plunk	Brocail		11-17	5th	8.0
5-4	At Cle.	W	2-0		6	5	Blair	Nagy	Brocail	12-17	5th	8.0
5-5	At Tor.	L	1-3		5	7	Clemens	Olivares		12-18	5th	8.0
5-6	At Tor.	L	1-2	(10)	4	11	Crabtree	Jones		12-19	5th	9.0
5-7	K.C.	W	12-3		11	9	Lira	Pittsley		13-19	5th	9.0
5-8	K.C.	L	0-4		5	7	Belcher	Moehler		13-20	5th	10.0
5-9	Cle.	L	0-5		7	8	Nagy	Sager		13-21	5th	10.0
5-10	Cle.	W	6-0		8	3	Olivares	Colon		14-21	5th	9.0
5-11	Cle.	W	11-3		15	4	Thompson	Hershiser		15-21	5th	9.0
5-13	Tor.	W	4-0		7	4	Lira	Guzman		16-21	4th	9.5
5-14	Tor.	L	2-7		5	12	Hentgen	Moehler		16-22	4th	9.5
5-15	At K.C.	L	9-10		7	15	Walker	Brocail		16-23	T4th	9.5
5-16	At K.C.	W	10-2		14	4	Thompson	Rosado		17-23	4th	9.5
5-17	At K.C.	W	9-2		11	5	Pugh	Pittsley		18-23	4th	9.5
5-18	At K.C.	W	6-5		15	6	Cummings	Belcher	Myers	19-23	4th	9.5
5-20	At Bal.	L	3-4		4	7	Kamieniecki	Olivares	Myers	19-24	4th	10.5
5-21	At Bal.	L	0-2		5	5	Erickson	Thompson	Myers	19-25	4th	11.5
5-23	Tex.	W	7-1		11	7	Moehler	Oliver		20-25	4th	10.5
5-24	Tex.	L	4-8		8	6	Hill	Pugh		20-26	4th	11.5
5-25	Tex.	W	13-5		13	9	Lira	Witt	Sager	21-26	4th	10.5
5-26	Ana.	W	6-0		7	4	Olivares	Finley		22-26	4th	10.5
5-27	Ana.	W	6-2		7	5	Thompson	Perisho	Myers	23-26	4th	10.5
5-28	Bal.	L	1-8		7	10	Key	Moehler	Boskie	23-27	4th	11.5
5-30	At Sea.	W	5-2		10	6	Lira	Fassero	Jones	24-27	4th	11.5
5-31	At Sea.	W	4-2		10	7	Olivares	Wolcott	Jones	25-27	4th	11.5
6-1	At Sea.	L	1-4		4	9	Sanders	Thompson	Ayala	25-28	4th	12.0
6-2	At Oak.	W	8-7		10	11	Moehler	Karsay	Brocail	26-28	4th	11.5
6-3	At Oak.	L	8-9		11	13	Small	Myers	Johnson	26-29	4th	12.5
6-5	Sea.	L	6-14		7	17	Fassero	Lira		26-30	4th	13.5
6-6	Sea.	L	3-6		8	9	Lowe	Olivares	Ayala	26-31	4th	13.5
6-7	Sea.	W	3-1		5	5	Thompson	Wolcott	Jones	27-31	4th	12.5
6-8	Sea.	L	0-2		2	8	Johnson	Moehler	Ayala	27-32	4th	13.5
6-10	Oak.	W	6-4		12	10	Blair	Prieto	Jones	28-32	4th	14.5
6-11	Oak.	W	4-2		8	7	Brocail	Small	Jones	29-32	4th	13.5
6-13	At Mon.	L	3-4		8	10	Perez	Olivares	Urbina	29-33	4th	14.0
6-14	At Mon.	L	0-1		3	6	Martinez	Thompson		29-34	4th	15.0
6-15	At Mon.	L	2-10		6	12	Juden	Moehler		29-35	4th	16.0
6-16	Fla.	L	3-7		6	13	Brown	Blair		29-36	4th	16.0
6-17	Fla.	L	2-3		4	6	Alfonseca	Jones	Nen	29-37	T4th	17.0
6-18	Fla.	W	6-2		8	4	Olivares	Leiter		30-37	T4th	16.0
6-20	Bos.	W	12-6		16	10	Thompson	Wakefield	Sager	31-37	4th	15.0
6-21	Bos.	W	15-4		16	12	Bautista	Eshelman		32-37	4th	15.0
6-22	Bos.	L	1-2		7	6	Gordon	Blair	Slocumb	32-38	4th	16.0
6-23	N.Y.	L	2-5		4	7	Cone	Lira	Rivera	32-39	T4th	16.0

Date	Opp.	Res.	Score	(inn.*)	Hits	Opp. hits	Winning pitcher	Losing pitcher	Save	Record	Pos.	GB
6-24	N.Y.	L	9-12		14	13	Lloyd	Myers	Rivera	32-40	5th	17.0
6-25	N.Y.	L	1-3		9	5	Stanton	Thompson	Rivera	32-41	5th	18.0
6-26	At Bos.	W	10-6		17	14	Moehler	Eshelman		33-41	5th	17.0
6-27	At Bos.	W	2-1	(11)	8	6	Miceli	Hammond	Jones	34-41	T4th	16.0
6-28	At Bos.	W	9-2		11	7	Lira	Sele		35-41	4th	15.0
6-29	At Bos.	L	6-8		13	9	Wasdin	Bautista	Slocumb	35-42	T4th	15.0
6-30	N.Y. (NL)	W	14-0		15	5	Thompson	Clark		36-42	4th	15.0
7-1	N.Y. (NL)	W	8-6		11	13	Moehler	B. Jones	T. Jones	37-42	4th	15.0
7-2	N.Y. (NL)	W	9-7		10	14	Blair	Mlicki	T. Jones	38-42	4th	15.0
7-3	Bal.	L	1-10		5	15	Key	Lira		38-43	4th	16.0
7-4†	Bal.	L	3-4		11	7	Rhodes	Keagle	Myers	38-44		
7-4‡	Bal.	W	11-8		9	8	Bautista	Mills	Jones	39-44	4th	16.0
7-5	Bal.	W	6-5		8	8	Miceli	Orosco	Jones	40-44	T3rd	15.0
7-6	Bal.	W	14-9		14	12	Blair	Erickson		41-44	T3rd	14.0
7-10	At N.Y.	L	3-10		8	10	Irabu	Olivares		41-45	T3rd	14.5
7-11	At N.Y.	L	0-3		6	6	Pettitte	Moehler	Rivera	41-46	4th	14.5
7-12	At N.Y.	L	2-6		4	15	Cone	Lira	Rivera	41-47	4th	14.5
7-13	At N.Y.	W	3-1		11	7	Blair	Gooden	Jones	42-47	4th	13.5
7-14	At Bos.	L	4-18		8	21	Suppan	Jarvis		42-48	4th	14.5
7-15	At Bos.	W	7-5	(12)	14	14	Jones	Wasdin		43-48	4th	14.5
7-16	At Ana.	L	3-5		8	6	Finley	Moehler	Percival	43-49	4th	14.5
7-17	At Ana.	L	4-9		8	12	Springer	Lira		43-50	4th	14.5
7-18	At Tex.	W	5-4		8	11	Blair	Witt	Jones	44-50	4th	13.5
7-19	At Tex.	W	6-5		10	9	Brocail	Hernandez	Jones	45-50	4th	13.5
7-20	At Tex.	L	6-7	(10)	11	16	Wetteland	Sager		45-51	4th	13.5
7-21	Chi.	L	0-3		4	10	Alvarez	Thompson	Hernandez	45-52	4th	14.5
7-22	Chi.	W	6-3		11	8	Moehler	D. Darwin	Jones	46-52	4th	14.5
7-23	Chi.	W	8-6		10	11	Blair	Baldwin	Jones	47-52	4th	14.5
7-25	Mil.	L	1-6		8	11	Karl	Sanders		47-53	4th	14.5
7-26	Mil.	L	1-3		6	5	Florie	Thompson	Fetters	47-54	4th	15.5
7-27	Mil.	L	7-11		9	18	Eldred	Moehler	Reyes	47-55	5th	16.5
7-29	At Chi.	W	3-1		5	3	Blair	Baldwin		48-55	5th	17.0
7-30	At Chi.	L	2-3		6	7	Drabek	Sanders	Hernandez	48-56	5th	18.0
7-31	Tor.	W	4-2		6	5	Thompson	Person	Jones	49-56	5th	18.0
8-1	Tor.	L	5-7		10	11	Hentgen	Miceli	Escobar	49-57	5th	18.0
8-2	Tor.	W	8-7		13	15	Brocail	Quantrill	Jones	50-57	5th	18.0
8-3	Tor.	W	5-2		9	9	Blair	Williams	Jones	51-57	T3rd	18.0
8-4	Cle.	L	2-7		8	13	Nagy	Sanders		51-58	T4th	18.5
8-5	Cle.	W	6-4		8	9	Thompson	Plunk	Jones	52-58	T4th	17.5
8-6	At K.C.	L	4-5		11	10	Rosado	Sager	Montgomery	52-59	5th	18.5
8-7	At K.C.	W	8-4		11	9	Dishman	Belcher		53-59	5th	18.0
8-8	At Tor.	L	3-6		11	12	Williams	Blair	Escobar	53-60	5th	19.0
8-9	At Tor.	W	3-2		9	4	Sanders	Carpenter	Jones	54-60	5th	18.0
8-10	At Tor.	W	4-2		4	8	Thompson	Person		55-60	T4th	18.0
8-11	At Tor.	L	2-8		10	11	Hentgen	Jarvis		55-61	5th	18.5
8-12	At Cle.	L	4-7		8	13	Plunk	Keagle	Mesa	55-62	5th	19.5
8-13†	At Cle.	W	13-3		17	9	Blair	Smiley		56-62		
8-13‡	At Cle.	L	1-9		7	14	Hershiser	Dishman		56-63	5th	19.0
8-14	At Cle.	L	1-12		4	15	Nagy	Sanders		56-64	5th	19.5
8-15	K.C.	L	3-5		6	10	Rusch	Thompson	Montgomery	56-65	5th	20.0
8-16	K.C.	L	1-2		9	7	Appier	Jarvis	Montgomery	56-66	5th	21.0
8-17	K.C.	W	8-4		8	7	Keagle	Rosado		57-66	5th	21.0
8-19	Min.	W	8-2		9	9	Blair	Hawkins		58-66	5th	21.0
8-20	Min.	L	1-11		3	14	Radke	Sanders		58-67	5th	22.0
8-21	At Mil.	W	2-1	(12)	9	5	Miceli	Wickman	Jones	59-67	5th	22.0
8-22	At Mil.	W	16-1		23	5	Moehler	Woodard	Gaillard	60-67	5th	22.0
8-23	At Mil.	L	2-5		10	11	Karl	Keagle	Jones	60-68	5th	23.0
8-24	At Mil.	L	0-6		4	9	Mercedes	Blair		60-69	5th	24.0
8-25	At Min.	W	7-6	(12)	11	12	Sager	Aguilera		61-69	5th	23.5
8-26	At Min.	L	2-8		7	11	Robertson	Thompson	Trombley	61-70	5th	23.5
8-27	At Min.	L	0-2		5	7	Tewksbury	Moehler		61-71	5th	24.5
8-29	Phi.	W	7-2		10	4	Blair	Green		62-71	5th	24.0
8-30	Phi.	L	0-2		8	8	Beech	Sanders	Bottalico	62-72	5th	24.0
8-31	Phi.	W	2-1		7	7	Thompson	Leiter	Jones	63-72	5th	23.0
9-1	At Atl.	W	4-2		10	6	Moehler	Maddux	Jones	64-72	5th	22.0
9-2	At Atl.	L	0-5		4	10	Neagle	Keagle		64-73	5th	22.0
9-3	At Atl.	W	12-4		15	10	Blair	Smoltz		65-73	T4th	21.0
9-4	Ana.	W	5-4	(11)	9	5	Jones	Harris		66-73	4th	21.0
9-5	Ana.	W	6-1		6	5	Thompson	Springer		67-73	3rd	21.0
9-6	Ana.	W	7-5		10	9	Moehler	Watson	Jones	68-73	3rd	21.0
9-7	Ana.	L	4-5	(15)	12	8	Hasegawa	Dishman		68-74	T4th	21.0
9-8	Tex.	W	6-2		7	5	Blair	Witt		69-74	3rd	20.0
9-9	Tex.	W	4-0		6	1	Sanders	Helling		70-74	T3rd	20.0
9-10	At Sea.	L	0-10		6	10	Moyer	Thompson		70-75	T3rd	20.5
9-11	At Sea.	W	3-1		5	5	Moehler	Fassero	Jones	71-75	3rd	19.5

Date	Opp.	Res.	Score	(inn.*)	Hits	Opp. hits	Winning pitcher	Losing pitcher	Save	Record	Pos.	GB
9-12	At Oak.	W	7-2		16	8	Keagle	Ludwick	Miceli	72-75	3rd	18.5
9-13	At Oak.	L	2-4		8	7	Telgheder	Blair	Mathews	72-76	4th	19.5
9-14	At Oak.	W	6-5		15	10	Sanders	Haynes	Jones	73-76	4th	18.5
9-15	At Oak.	W	6-3		11	10	Thompson	Oquist	Jones	74-76	3rd	18.0
9-17	At N.Y.	L	2-6		6	15	Mendoza	Moehler		74-77	3rd	18.0
9-18	At N.Y.	W	9-7	(11)	15	12	Jones	Borowski	Miceli	75-77	3rd	18.0
9-19	At Bal.	W	5-3	(10)	10	7	Jones	Mills		76-77	3rd	17.0
9-20	At Bal.	L	8-12		15	14	Rodriguez	Sanders		76-78	3rd	18.0
9-21	At Bal.	W	11-3		12	5	Thompson	Key		77-78	3rd	17.0
9-22	At Bal.	W	5-4		9	9	Gaillard	Benitez	Jones	78-78	3rd	16.0
9-23	Bos.	W	6-0		11	7	Keagle	Suppan		79-78	3rd	16.0
9-24	Bos.	L	2-9		5	15	Wakefield	Blair		79-79	3rd	17.0
9-25	Bos.	L	1-3		4	8	Checo	Sanders	Gordon	79-80	3rd	17.0
9-26	N.Y.	L	2-8		1	10	Rivera	Jones		79-81	3rd	17.0
9-27	N.Y.	L	1-6		6	11	Wells	Moehler		79-82	3rd	18.0
9-28	N.Y.	L	2-7		5	11	Irabu	Keagle		79-83	3rd	19.0

Monthly records: April (11-16), May (14-11), June (11-15), July (13-14), August (14-16), September (16-11).
*Innings, if other than nine. †First game of doubleheader. ‡Second game of doubleheader.

HIGHLIGHTS

High point: With three wins in a row, five of six and 18 of their last 26, the Tigers peaked above .500 on September 23 at 79-78. After losing 109 games in 1996, their goal—if not their dream—of finishing above .500 was within reach with five games remaining. But they lost all five.

Low point: On May 4 came the sickening sight and sound of a line drive off Julio Franco's bat in Cleveland that hit pitcher Willie Blair in the jaw. As Blair lay on the ground, and as Franco prayed at first base that he wasn't seriously hurt, no one knew if Blair's career was over. He hit .299, as it turned out, missed a month with a broken jaw and went on to win 16 games.

Turning point: The one game that proved to the Tigers that they could compete with good teams and beat good pitchers was a 4-2 victory against the Braves and Greg Maddux on September 1. Two days later, they beat John Smoltz, 12-4.

Most valuable player: It could be any one of a half-dozen players, but the one who combined offense and defense the best was Bob Higginson. He hit .299, drove in more than 100 runs (101) for the first time and led the majors with 20 outfield assists.

Most valuable pitcher: Todd Jones became the first righthander in the history of the Tigers to save more than 30 games. His 31 saves were fourth in the A.L. and he converted 23 of his last 24 save situations. In his final 38 games, he had a 1.99 ERA.

Most improved player: Second baseman Damion Easley went into the 1997 season just hoping to stay healthy enough to find out what he could do over a full season. He had hit only 17 home runs in five seasons with a career-high of 35 RBIs in 1994. Easley stayed healthy all right and hit .264 with 22 home runs and 72 RBIs, securing for himself a long-term future in Detroit.

Most pleasant surprise: The Tigers acquired shortstop Deivi Cruz in a December 1996 trade with the Dodgers after getting good reports about his defense. They didn't know he'd become their starting shortstop, but with a back injury to veteran Orlando Miller in spring training, that's exactly what happened. And Cruz turned out to be a bonanza. He started 133 games, made only 13 errors and hit .267 in the second half of the season en route to an overall .241 average.

Biggest disappointment: The Tigers finally ran out of patience with Melvin Nieves. They liked his power and his potential—but not his strikeouts. Nieves struck out 157 times in 359 at-bats while hitting .228. He was traded to Cincinnati following the season.

Key injuries: There were two. Miller's back injury in spring training opened the way for Cruz to become the starting shortstop. And Blair turned the adversity of his injury into a plus, rebounding with a 13-6 record after coming back on June 3.

Notable: Nineteen teams have lost 109 games in a season as the Tigers did in 1996, but none of the previous teams improved as much in the following season as the Tigers did in 1997. They finished four games under .500 after losing 109.
—TOM GAGE

RECORDS

1997 regular-season record: 79-83 (3rd in A.L. East); 42-39 at home; 37-44 on road; 29-34 vs. East; 26-29 vs. Central; 24-20 vs. West; 17-27 vs. lefthanded starters; 62-56 vs. righthanded starters; 73-69 on grass; 6-14 on turf; 32-31 in daytime; 47-52 at night; 17-19 in one-run games; 8-4 in extra-inning games; 0-0-3 in doubleheaders.

Team record past five years: 330-415 (.443, ranks 12th in league in that span).

TEAM LEADERS

Batting average: Bob Higginson (.299).
At-bats: Brian L. Hunter (658).
Runs: Brian L. Hunter (112).
Hits: Brian L. Hunter (177).
Total bases: Tony Clark (290).
Doubles: Damion Easley (37).
Triples: Brian L. Hunter (7).
Home runs: Tony Clark (32).
Runs batted in: Tony Clark (117).
Stolen bases: Brian L. Hunter (74).
Slugging percentage: Bob Higginson (.520).

On-base percentage: Bob Higginson (.379).
Wins: Willie Blair (16).
Earned-run average: Justin Thompson (3.02).
Complete games: Justin Thompson (4).
Shutouts: Omar Olivares (2).
Saves: Todd Jones (31).
Innings pitched: Justin Thompson (223.1).
Strikeouts: Justin Thompson (151).

GAMES BY POSITION

Catcher: Raul Casanova 92, Matt Walbeck 44, Brian Johnson 43, Marcus Jensen 8, Phil Nevin 1.
First base: Tony Clark 158, Bob Hamelin 7, Phil Nevin 7, Orlando Miller 3.
Second base: Damion Easley 137, Jody Reed 41, Frank Catalanotto 6.
Third base: Travis Fryman 153, Phil Nevin 17, Orlando Miller 4.
Shortstop: Deivi Cruz 147, Orlando Miller 31, Damion Easley 21.
Outfield: Brian L. Hunter 162, Bob Higginson 143, Melvin Nieves 99, Phil Nevin 40, Curtis Pride 35, Bubba Trammell 28, Jimmy Hurst 12, Juan Encarnacion 10, Kimera Bartee 6, Vince Coleman 3, Joe Hall 1.
Designated hitter: Bob Hamelin 95, Phil Nevin 30, Curtis Pride 23, Bubba Trammell 14, Melvin Nieves 12, Orlando Miller 11, Jody Reed 5, Damion Easley 4, Kimera Bartee 3, Frank Catalanotto 3, Brian Johnson 2, Raul Casanova 1, Tony Clark 1, Vince Coleman 1, Bob Higginson 1, Jimmy Hurst 1.

TOP DRAFT CHOICES

1. **Matt Anderson,** RHP, Rice University.
2. **Shane Loux,** RHP, Highland H.S., Gilbert, Ariz.
3. **Matt Boone,** 3B, Villa Park (Calif.) H.S.
4. **Alan Webb,** LHP, Durango H.S., Las Vegas.
5. **Heath Schesser,** SS, Kansas State Univ.
6. **Chris Parker,** C, Westlake H.S., Westlake Village, Calif.
7. **Mike Diebolt,** LHP, Univ. of Minnesota.
8. **Dan Lauterhahn,** 2B, William Paterson (N.J.) College.
9. **Bud Smith,** OF-LHP, St. John Bosco H.S., Lakewood, Calif.
10. **Rick Roberts,** LHP, Forest Hills, H.S., Summerhill, Pa.

KANSAS CITY ROYALS
AMERICAN LEAGUE CENTRAL DIVISION

Royals Schedule
Home games shaded. *—All-Star Game at Coors Field (Colorado).
D—Day game (any game starting before 5 p.m.).

March
SUN	MON	TUE	WED	THU	FRI	SAT
		31 D BAL				

April
SUN	MON	TUE	WED	THU	FRI	SAT
			1 BAL	2 BAL	3 MIN	4 MIN
5 D MIN	6	7 D BAL	8	9 BAL	10 MIN	11 D MIN
12 D MIN	13 TOR	14 TOR	15 TOR	16 OAK	17 OAK	18 D OAK
19 D OAK	20 SEA	21 SEA	22 SEA	23	24 TEX	25 TEX
26 TEX	27 SEA	28 SEA	29 TOR	30 D TOR		

May
SUN	MON	TUE	WED	THU	FRI	SAT
					1 NYY	2 D NYY
3 D NYY	4	5 TB	6 TB	7 BOS	8 BOS	9 BOS
10 D BOS	11 NYY	12 NYY	13 TB	14 TB	15 BOS	16 D BOS
17 BOS	18 CLE	19 CLE	20 CLE	21 CLE	22 TEX	23 TEX
24 D TEX	25 D ANA	26	27 ANA	28	29 OAK	30 OAK
31 D OAK						

June
SUN	MON	TUE	WED	THU	FRI	SAT
	1 ANA	2 ANA	3 CWS	4 D CWS	5 HOU	6 HOU
7 D HOU	8 MIL	9 MIL	10 MIL	11	12 DET	13 DET
14 D DET	15 CLE	16 CLE	17 CLE	18 DET	19 DET	20 DET
21 D DET	22 CIN	23 D CIN	24 PIT	25 PIT	26 CUB	27 CUB
28 CUB	29 STL	30 STL				

July
SUN	MON	TUE	WED	THU	FRI	SAT
		1 STL	2 STL	3 CLE	4 CLE	
5 D CLE	6	7	* 8	9 CWS	10 CWS	11 CWS
12 D CWS	13 DET	14 DET	15 D OAK	16 OAK	17 D SEA	18 SEA
19 D SEA	20	21 TEX	22 TEX	23 TEX	24 ANA	25 ANA
26 D ANA	27 ANA	28 MIN	29 MIN	30 MIN	31 BAL	

August
SUN	MON	TUE	WED	THU	FRI	SAT
						1 BAL
2 D BAL	3	4 MIN	5 MIN	6 MIN	7 D NYY	8 D NYY
9 D NYY	10	11 BOS	12 BOS	13 TB	14 TB	15 TB
16 D TB	17 NYY	18 NYY	19 BOS	20 D BOS	21 TB	22 TB
23 D TB	24 TOR	25 TOR	26 TOR	27 TOR	28 BAL	29 BAL
30 D BAL	31					

September
SUN	MON	TUE	WED	THU	FRI	SAT
		1 TOR	2 TOR	3	4 ANA	5 ANA
6 D ANA	7	8 TEX	9 TEX	10	11 SEA	12 SEA
13 SEA	14 OAK	15 OAK	16 CWS	17 CWS	18 CLE	19 D CLE
20 CLE	21 DET	22 DET	23 DET	24 CWS	25 CWS	26 CWS
27 D CWS						

1998 SEASON
CLUB DIRECTORY

Board of directors
David Glass
Richard Green
Mike Herman
Larry Kauffman
Janice Kreamer
Louis Smith
Joseph McGuff
Chairman of the board & CEO
David Glass
President
Mike Herman
Exec. v.p. and general manager
Spencer (Herk) Robinson
Sr. v.p., business operations & admin.
Art Chaudry
Vice president, finance
Dale Rohr
Vice president, baseball operations
George Brett
Vice president, player personnel
Larry Doughty
V.p., marketing and communications
Mike Levy
Sr. special assistant to g.m.
Art Stewart
Special assistant to general manager
Allard Baird
Assistant general manager
Jay Hinrichs
Director, media relations
Steve Fink
Director, community relations
Jim Lachimia
Director, scouting
Terry Wetzel
Director, minor league operations
Bob Hegman
Director, team travel
David Witty
Director, administration
John Johnson
Director, human resources
Lauris P. Hawthorne
Director, marketing and sales
Mike Behymer

Director, special markets
Vernice Givens
Director, stadium operations
Rodney Lewallen
Director, ticket operations
John Walker
Director, season ticket services
Joe Grigoli
Director, compensation
Tom Pfannenstiel
Director, season ticket sales
Chris Muehlbach
Director, information systems
Jim Edwards
Assistant director, player personnel
Dan Glass
Equipment manager
Mike Burkhalter
Team physician
Dr. Steve Joyce
Trainer
Nick Swartz
Assistant trainer
Steve Morrow
Major league scouts
Gail Henley
Dick Wiencek
Advance scout
Ron Clark
National crosschecker
Steve Flores
Regional crosscheckers
Carl Blando, Pat Jones, Jeff McKay
Territorial scouts
Frank Baez, Paul Baretta, Bob Bishop, Monte Bothwell, Jason Bryans, Balos Davis, Albert Gonzalez, Dave Herrera, Keith Hughes, Gary Johnson, Mike Lee, Cliff Pastornicky, Bill Price, Johnny Ramos, Wil Rutenschroer, Chet Sergo, Greg Smith, Gerald Turner, Dennis Woody
Latin American scouting supervisor
Luis Silverio
Canadian scouting supervisor
Jason Bryans

MINOR LEAGUE AFFILIATES

Class	Team	League	Manager
AAA	Omaha	Pacific Coast	Ron Johnson
AA	Wichita	Texas	John Mizerock
A	Wilmington	Carolina	Darrell Evans
A	Lansing	Midwest	Bob Herold
A	Spokane	Northwest	Jeff Garber
Rookie	Gulf Coast Royals	Gulf Coast	Andre David

BROADCAST INFORMATION
Radio: KMBZ-AM (980).
TV: KMBC (Channel 9), KCWB (Channel 29).
Cable TV: Fox Sports Rocky Mountain.

SPRING TRAINING
Ballpark (city): Baseball City Stadium (Davenport, Fla.).
Ticket information: 941-424-2500.

1998 SEASON *Kansas City Royals*

Manager—Tony Muser (40).
Coaches—Tom Burgmeier, Rich Dauer (37), Bruce Kison (54), Tom Poquette (38, Jamie Quirk (9), Frank White (20).

No.	PITCHERS	B/T	Ht./Wt.	Born	1997 clubs
17	Appier, Kevin	R/R	6-2/195	12-6-67	Kansas City
41	Belcher, Tim	R/R	6-3/225	10-19-61	Kansas City
47	Bevil, Brian	R/R	6-4/225	9-5-71	Wichita, Omaha, Kansas City
25	Bluma, Jamie	R/R	5-11/195	5-18-72	DID NOT PLAY
	Byrdak, Timothy	L/L	5-11/160	10-31-73	Wilmington
	De La Maza, Roland	R/R	6-2/195	11-11-71	DID NOT PLAY
	Evans, Bart	R/R	6-1/190	12-30-70	Wilmington, Wichita
	Flury, Patrick	R/R	6-1/220	3-14-74	Wichita, Omaha
33	Haney, Chris	L/L	6-3/205	11-16-68	Kansas City, Omaha, Wichita
21	Montgomery, Jeff	R/R	5-11/180	1-7-62	Kansas City, Omaha
35	Pichardo, Hipolito	R/R	6-1/185	8-22-69	Kansas City, Omaha
34	Pittsley, Jim	R/R	6-7/215	4-3-74	Omaha, Kansas City
	Ray, Ken	R/R	6-2/180	1-27-74	Omaha
50	Rosado, Jose	L/L	6-0/175	11-9-74	Kansas City
53	Rusch, Glendon	L/L	6-2/170	11-7-74	Kansas City, Omaha
	Santiago, Jose	R/R	6-3/215	11-5-74	Wilmington, Lansing, Kansas City, Wichita
46	Service, Scott	R/R	6-6/226	2-26-67	Cincinnati, Indianapolis, Omaha, Kansas City
57	Walker, Jamie	L/L	6-2/190	7-1-71	Kansas City, Wichita
56	Whisenant, Matt	R/L	6-3/215	6-8-71	Brevard County, Charlotte, Florida, Kansas City

No.	CATCHERS	B/T	Ht./Wt.	Born	1997 clubs
	Fasano, Sal	R/R	6-2/220	8-10-71	Omaha, Kansas City, Wichita
15	Macfarlane, Mike	R/R	6-1/210	4-12-64	Kansas City
29	Sweeney, Mike	R/R	6-2/215	7-22-73	Kansas City, Omaha

No.	INFIELDERS	B/T	Ht./Wt.	Born	1997 clubs
	Febles, Carlos	R/R	5-11/170	5-24-76	Wilmington
43	Halter, Shane	R/R	5-10/160	11-8-69	Omaha, Kansas City
2	Hansen, Jed	R/R	6-1/180	8-19-72	Omaha, Kansas City
7	King, Jeff	R/R	6-1/188	12-26-64	Kansas City
	Lopez, Mendy	R/R	6-2/165	10-15-74	Omaha, Wichita
36	Martinez, Felix	B/R	6-0/170	5-18-74	Omaha, Kansas City
	Morris, Hal	L/L	6-4/210	4-9-65	Cincinnati
30	Offerman, Jose	B/R	6-0/190	11-8-68	Kansas City
16	Palmer, Dean	R/R	6-1/210	12-27-68	Texas, Kansas City
22	Sutton, Larry	L/L	5-11/175	5-14-70	Omaha, Kansas City

No.	OUTFIELDERS	B/T	Ht./Wt.	Born	1997 clubs
	Conine, Jeff	R/R	6-1/220	6-27-66	Florida
18	Damon, Johnny	L/L	6-2/190	11-5-73	Kansas City
24	Dye, Jermaine	R/R	6-4/210	1-28-74	Kansas City, Omaha
	Long, Ryan	R/R	6-2/215	2-3-73	Omaha, Kansas City
31	Myers, Rod	L/L	6-1/190	1-14-73	Wichita, Kansas City, Omaha
	Quinn, Mark	R/R	6-1/175	5-21-74	Wilmington, Wichita
32	Vitiello, Joe	R/R	6-3/230	4-11-70	Kansas City, Omaha

BALLPARK INFORMATION

Ballpark (capacity, surface)
Kauffman Stadium (40,625, grass)

Address
P.O. Box 419969
Kansas City, MO 64141-6969

Business phone
816-921-8000

Ticket information
816-921-8000

Ticket prices
$15 (club box)
$14 (field box)
$12 (plaza reserved)
$11 (view upper box)
$10 (view upper reserved)
$5.50 (Royal nights)
$6 (general admission)

Field dimensions (from home plate)
To left field at foul line, 330 feet
To center field, 400 feet
To right field at foul line, 330 feet

First game played
April 10, 1973 (Royals 12, Rangers 1)

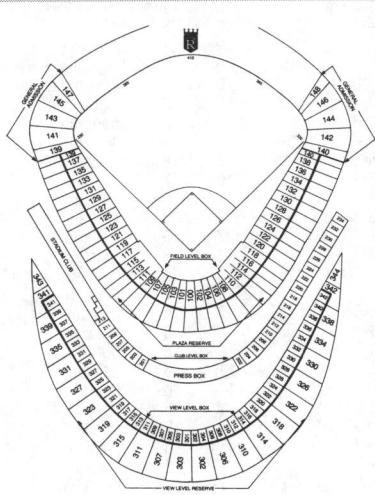

DAY BY DAY

Date	Opp.	Res.	Score	(inn.*)	Hits	Opp. hits	Winning pitcher	Losing pitcher	Save	Record	Pos.	GB
4-2	At Bal.	L	2-4		7	10	Key	Walker	Myers	0-1	T4th	1.5
4-3	At Bal.	L	4-6		8	9	Rhodes	Montgomery	Myers	0-2	5th	2.5
4-4	At Min.	W	2-1		7	8	Belcher	Tewksbury	Pichardo	1-2	T2nd	1.5
4-5	At Min.	L	5-7		9	12	Robertson	Haney	Aguilera	1-3	T4th	2.5
4-6	At Min.	W	12-2		15	5	Rusch	Radke		2-3	T4th	1.5
4-7	Bal.	W	6-5		12	10	Walker	Benitez		3-3	4th	1.0
4-9	Bal.	L	2-4	(11)	8	8	Mills	Bevil	Myers	3-4	4th	1.0
4-12	Min.	L	6-11		12	12	Ritchie	Belcher		3-5	4th	2.0
4-13	Min.	W	6-1		10	6	Appier	Rodriguez		4-5	4th	1.0
4-14	At Tor.	W	3-2		6	7	Rusch	Quantrill	Pichardo	5-5	T2nd	1.0
4-15	At Tor.	W	7-5		10	9	Rosado	Guzman	Pichardo	6-5	T1st	....
4-16	Tex.	L	0-2		10	4	Burkett	Pittsley	Wetteland	6-6	T2nd	1.0
4-17	Tex.	L	1-5		5	9	Oliver	Belcher		6-7	3rd	2.0
4-19	Ana.	W	7-3		12	5	Appier	Langston		7-7	3rd	1.5
4-20	Ana.	L	1-11		3	18	Dickson	Rusch		7-8	T3rd	1.5
4-21	At Sea.	L	5-6		7	9	Ayala	Bevil	Charlton	7-9	4th	2.0
4-22	At Sea.	L	2-7		5	10	Fassero	Belcher		7-10	4th	3.0
4-23	At Sea.	W	12-10		11	18	Veres	Hurtado	Pichardo	8-10	4th	2.0
4-25	At Oak.	W	10-3		13	8	Appier	Adams		9-10	3rd	1.0
4-26	At Oak.	L	6-7	(11)	14	15	Small	Mitch Williams		9-11	4th	1.0
4-27	At Oak.	W	7-1		13	6	Belcher	Mohler		10-11	T2nd	0.5
4-29	Tor.	W	6-5	(10)	10	8	Pichardo	Quantrill		11-11	T2nd	1.0
4-30	Tor.	L	0-1		4	5	Clemens	Appier	Spoljaric	11-12	T2nd	1.0
5-1	Tor.	W	8-0		12	4	Rosado	Williams		12-12	T2nd	0.5
5-2	N.Y.	L	1-9		7	7	Cone	Pittsley	Rivera	12-13	3rd	0.5
5-3	N.Y.	W	2-1		6	8	Belcher	Pettitte		13-13	3rd	0.5
5-4	N.Y.	L	5-13		8	19	Boehringer	Rusch		13-14	3rd	0.5
5-5	At Bos.	W	2-0		7	5	Appier	Hammond		14-14	T2nd	0.5
5-6	At Bos.	W	7-2		11	5	Rosado	Gordon	Pichardo	15-14	T1st	....
5-7	At Det.	L	3-12		9	11	Lira	Pittsley		15-15	3rd	1.0
5-8	At Det.	W	4-0		7	5	Belcher	Moehler		16-15	T1st	....
5-9	At N.Y.	W	7-5	(12)	9	12	Veres	Boehringer		17-15	T1st	....
5-10	At N.Y.	L	2-5		11	8	Mendoza	Appier	Rivera	17-16	T2nd	1.0
5-11	At N.Y.	L	2-3		5	7	Wells	Rosado	Rivera	17-17	T2nd	2.0
5-13	Bos.	W	9-0		15	2	Belcher	Sele		18-17	2nd	1.5
5-14	Bos.	W	6-2		9	10	Veres	Wakefield	Pichardo	19-17	2nd	0.5
5-15	Det.	W	10-9		15	7	Walker	Brocail		20-17	1st	+0.5
5-16	Det.	L	2-10		4	14	Thompson	Rosado		20-18	1st	+0.5
5-17	Det.	L	2-9		5	11	Pugh	Pittsley		20-19	1st	+0.5
5-18	Det.	L	5-6		6	15	Cummings	Belcher	Myers	20-20	T1st	....
5-20	At Cle.	L	3-4		10	12	Shuey	Walker	M. Jackson	20-21	2nd	1.0
5-21	At Cle.	L	0-1		6	2	Hershiser	Appier	M. Jackson	20-22	T3rd	2.0
5-22	At Cle.	L	1-9		6	12	Lopez	Rosado		20-23	4th	3.0
5-23	Sea.	L	4-8		10	13	Johnson	Belcher		20-24	4th	4.0
5-24	Sea.	W	11-5		13	12	Veres	Moyer	Pichardo	21-24	4th	3.0
5-25	Sea.	W	4-3	(11)	13	8	Walker	Ayala		22-24	3rd	3.0
5-26	Oak.	L	1-2	(11)	9	7	Adams	Mike Williams	Small	22-25	3rd	4.0
5-27	Oak.	L	6-8	(10)	10	7	Taylor	Pichardo	Johnson	22-26	4th	4.0
5-28	Cle.	L	3-10		6	16	Assenmacher	Belcher		22-27	4th	5.0
5-30	At Tex.	W	3-2		9	9	Rusch	Witt	Pichardo	23-27	T3rd	4.0
5-31	At Tex.	L	1-3		7	8	Santana	Appier	Wetteland	23-28	T3rd	4.0
6-1	At Tex.	W	6-2		13	8	Rosado	Burkett	Veres	24-28	3rd	3.5
6-3	At Ana.	W	5-2		10	7	Belcher	Springer	Pichardo	25-28	3rd	2.5
6-4	At Ana.	L	3-7		7	11	Watson	Rusch		25-29	4th	3.0
6-5	Tex.	L	3-6	(11)	8	8	Wetteland	Pichardo		25-30	4th	3.5
6-6	Tex.	W	2-1		7	5	Rosado	Burkett		26-30	4th	3.5
6-7	Tex.	W	10-4		12	5	Pittsley	Oliver		27-30	4th	3.5
6-8	Tex.	W	4-2		10	7	Belcher	Hill	Mike Williams	28-30	T2nd	2.5
6-9	Ana.	L	5-12		8	18	Watson	Rusch		28-31	3rd	3.0
6-10	Ana.	L	2-6		7	10	Dickson	Appier		28-32	3rd	4.0
6-11	Ana.	W	6-1		8	8	Rosado	Finley		29-32	2nd	4.0
6-13	At Pit.	L	3-5		9	8	Cordova	Mike Williams	Loiselle	29-33	3rd	4.0
6-14	At Pit.	W	8-3		11	8	Belcher	Lieber	Montgomery	30-33	T2nd	3.5
6-15	At Pit.	W	8-1		14	6	Appier	Cooke		31-33	2nd	3.5
6-16	Hou.	W	5-2		11	6	Rosado	Hampton		32-33	2nd	2.5
6-17	Hou.	L	2-10		4	15	Garcia	Haney		32-34	T2nd	3.5
6-18	Hou.	W	6-2		11	8	Pittsley	Wall		33-34	T2nd	2.5
6-20	At Mil.	L	5-7		7	12	Eldred	Belcher	Jones	33-35	3rd	2.5
6-22	At Mil.	W	6-5		7	13	Pichardo	Wickman	Montgomery	34-35	T2nd	3.0
6-23	At Chi.	L	6-7		14	10	Karchner	Pichardo	Hernandez	34-36	T3rd	3.0
6-24	At Chi.	L	0-4		5	8	Alvarez	Pittsley	Hernandez	34-37	4th	4.0

Date	Opp.	Res.	Score	(inn.*)	Hits	Opp. hits	Winning pitcher	Losing pitcher	Save	Record	Pos.	GB
6-25	At Chi.	L	7-8	(10)	14	13	Karchner	Montgomery		34-38	4th	4.5
6-26	Mil.	W	4-3		5	8	Haney	Mercedes	Montgomery	35-38	T3rd	4.0
6-27	Mil.	W	16-3		15	8	Appier	McDonald		36-38	3rd	3.0
6-28	Mil.	L	3-5		12	10	D'Amico	Rosado	Jones	36-39	T3rd	4.0
6-29	Mil.	L	2-3		10	12	Wickman	Montgomery	Jones	36-40	4th	4.0
6-30	At Chi. (NL)	L	7-8		11	17	Pisciotta	Bones	Rojas	36-41	4th	5.0
7-1	At Chi. (NL)	L	1-6		5	11	Castillo	Rusch		36-42	4th	6.0
7-2	At Chi. (NL)	L	2-3		9	9	Foster	Appier	Rojas	36-43	4th	6.0
7-4	At Cle.	L	6-7		12	13	Anderson	Pichardo	M. Jackson	36-44	4th	7.0
7-5	At Cle.	L	4-8		6	15	Nagy	Pittsley		36-45	4th	8.0
7-6	At Cle.	L	7-8		9	10	M. Jackson	Casian		36-46	4th	9.0
7-10	Chi.	L	3-6		8	12	Navarro	Appier	Hernandez	36-47	5th	9.0
7-11	Chi.	L	2-6		8	11	Alvarez	Rosado		36-48	5th	10.0
7-12	Chi.	L	7-11		14	14	D. Darwin	Belcher	Hernandez	36-49	5th	11.0
7-13	Chi.	L	6-7		10	9	C. Castillo	Pittsley	Hernandez	36-50	5th	12.0
7-14	Mil.	W	2-1	(14)	11	7	Perez	Jones		37-50	5th	12.0
7-15	Mil.	L	2-5		9	8	Karl	Appier		37-51	5th	12.0
7-16	At Oak.	L	3-11		7	8	Wengert	Rosado		37-52	5th	13.0
7-17	At Oak.	L	3-11		5	16	Karsay	Belcher		37-53	5th	14.0
7-18	At Sea.	L	4-5		9	7	Johnson	Bones		37-54	5th	14.0
7-19	At Sea.	W	9-6		10	11	Montgomery	Ayala		38-54	5th	13.0
7-20	At Sea.	L	4-5		9	6	Moyer	Appier	Wells	38-55	5th	14.0
7-22	At Min.	L	2-3		9	9	Swindell	Rosado	Aguilera	38-56	5th	14.5
7-23	At Min.	W	5-1		10	7	Belcher	Hawkins		39-56	5th	13.5
7-24	At Min.	W	5-3		9	6	Bones	Stevens	Montgomery	40-56	5th	12.5
7-25	At Tor.	L	1-2		10	5	Person	Rusch	Escobar	40-57	5th	12.5
7-26	At Tor.	L	5-6		8	8	Timlin	Carrasco		40-58	5th	13.5
7-27	At Tor.	W	3-2		6	2	Olson	Quantrill		41-58	5th	13.5
7-28†	Min.	W	10-3		17	6	Belcher	Rodriguez		42-58		
7-28‡	Min.	W	5-2		7	3	Pittsley	T. Miller	Montgomery	43-58	5th	11.5
7-29	Min.	L	8-11		13	14	Hawkins	Bones		43-59	5th	11.5
7-30	Min.	L	1-11		3	14	Radke	Rusch		43-60	5th	11.5
7-31	Bos.	W	3-2	(10)	7	10	Carrasco	Slocumb		44-60	5th	11.0
8-1	Bos.	L	3-10		7	15	Avery	Rosado		44-61	5th	12.0
8-2	Bos.	W	10-3		13	9	Belcher	Sele		45-61	5th	12.0
8-3	Bos.	W	5-2		6	7	Bones	Wakefield	Montgomery	46-61	5th	11.0
8-4	N.Y.	L	4-5		7	8	Wells	Rusch	Rivera	46-62	5th	12.0
8-5	N.Y.	L	1-4		11	9	Rogers	Appier		46-63	5th	12.0
8-6	Det.	W	5-4		10	11	Rosado	Sager	Montgomery	47-63	5th	11.0
8-7	Det.	L	4-8		9	11	Dishman	Belcher		47-64	5th	11.0
8-8	At Bos.	L	2-8		7	15	Avery	Bones		47-65	5th	11.0
8-9	At Bos.	W	9-2		12	6	Rusch	Suppan		48-65	5th	10.5
8-10	At Bos.	L	4-6		9	10	Corsi	Carrasco		48-66	5th	10.5
8-12	At N.Y.	W	6-4		12	11	Perez	Cone	Montgomery	49-66	5th	10.5
8-13	At N.Y.	L	3-9		11	12	Irabu	Belcher		49-67	5th	11.0
8-14	At N.Y.	L	5-10		10	13	Wells	Olson	Rivera	49-68	5th	12.0
8-15	At Det.	W	5-3		10	6	Rusch	Thompson	Montgomery	50-68	4th	12.0
8-16	At Det.	W	2-1		7	9	Appier	Jarvis	Montgomery	51-68	4th	12.0
8-17	At Det.	L	4-8		7	8	Keagle	Rosado		51-69	4th	12.0
8-19†	Bal.	L	9-12		12	15	Mathews	Belcher		51-70		
8-19‡	Bal.	W	9-2		13	7	Bones	Yan		52-70	4th	13.0
8-20	Bal.	L	2-4		5	8	Key	Rusch	Myers	52-71	4th	13.0
8-21	Bal.	L	3-4		7	9	Krivda	Appier	Myers	52-72	4th	13.0
8-22	Tor.	L	3-5		8	10	Clemens	Rosado	Escobar	52-73	4th	14.0
8-23	Tor.	L	5-6		10	8	Janzen	Walker	Quantrill	52-74	4th	15.0
8-24	Tor.	L	8-11	(13)	15	21	Crabtree	Casian		52-75	4th	15.0
8-26	At Bal.	W	5-4		9	6	Whisenant	Benitez	Montgomery	53-75	4th	14.0
8-27	At Bal.	L	3-7		6	7	Rhodes	Carrasco		53-76	T4th	15.0
8-28	At Bal.	W	5-1		7	6	Rosado	Mussina		54-76	4th	14.5
8-29	St.L.	L	7-9		8	11	Beltran	Carrasco	Eckersley	54-77	4th	15.5
8-30	St.L.	W	16-5		15	7	Belcher	Aybar		55-77	4th	14.5
8-31	St.L.	L	4-5		8	9	Osborne	Olson	Eckersley	55-78	5th	15.5
9-1	At Cin.	W	7-4		10	8	Appier	Remlinger	Pichardo	56-78	5th	15.5
9-2	At Cin.	L	0-4		7	9	Burba	Rosado	Shaw	56-79	5th	15.5
9-3	At Cin.	L	3-6		5	8	Tomko	Bones	Shaw	56-80	5th	16.5
9-4	Oak.	W	7-6	(12)	11	10	Olson	Wengert		57-80	4th	16.0
9-5	Oak.	L	6-9		15	16	Oquist	Carrasco	Taylor	57-81	4th	17.0
9-6	Oak.	L	3-9		12	15	Lorraine	Appier	Wengert	57-82	4th	18.0
9-7	Oak.	L	4-9		11	14	Ludwick	Rosado		57-83	5th	19.0
9-8	Sea.	W	9-2		15	6	Pittsley	Olivares		58-83	5th	19.0
9-9	Sea.	L	3-4		8	9	Timlin	Pichardo	Slocumb	58-84	5th	19.0
9-11	At Ana.	W	4-2		7	11	Appier	Springer	Montgomery	59-84	4th	18.0
9-12	At Ana.	L	5-8		9	6	Harris	Bones	Percival	59-85	4th	19.0
9-13	At Ana.	W	3-1	(13)	9	11	Olson	DeLucia	Bevil	60-85	4th	18.0
9-14	At Ana.	L	2-3		7	5	James	Service	Percival	60-86	4th	19.0

Date	Opp.	Res.	Score	(inn.*)	Hits	Opp. hits	Winning pitcher	Losing pitcher	Save	Record	Pos.	GB
9-15	At Tex.	W	11-9		19	16	Pichardo	Patterson	Montgomery	61-86	4th	18.5
9-16	At Tex.	L	2-4		9	8	Whiteside	Olson	Wetteland	61-87	4th	19.0
9-17	Chi.	L	4-8		9	14	Baldwin	Service	Foulke	61-88	4th	20.0
9-18	Chi.	L	2-9		6	14	Drabek	Pittsley		61-89	4th	21.0
9-19†	Cle.	W	10-3		12	9	Belcher	Colon		62-89		
9-19‡	Cle.	L	2-6		8	16	Anderson	Bones	Assenmacher	62-90	4th	21.0
9-20	Cle.	W	5-2		6	10	Olson	Lopez	Montgomery	63-90	4th	20.0
9-21	Cle.	W	1-0		5	5	Bevil	M. Jackson		64-90	4th	19.0
9-23†	At Mil.	L	4-7		8	10	Reyes	Carrasco	Jones	64-91		
9-23‡	At Mil.	W	6-2		9	7	Pittsley	Adamson		65-91	T4th	19.5
9-24	At Mil.	L	3-4	(15)	10	12	Wagner	Montgomery		65-92	5th	19.5
9-25	At Mil.	W	2-1		7	4	Rusch	Eldred	Pichardo	66-92	T4th	18.5
9-26	At Chi.	L	2-7		7	9	Sirotka	Appier		66-93	T4th	19.5
9-27	At Chi.	W	10-4		13	11	Bones	Navarro	Olson	67-93	4th	19.0
9-28	At Chi.	L	3-4		7	6	Eyre	Service	Foulke	67-94	5th	19.0

Monthly records: April (11-12), May (12-16), June (13-13), July (8-19), August (11-18), September (12-16).
*Innings, if other than nine. †First game of doubleheader. ‡Second game of doubleheader.

HIGHLIGHTS

High point: Rookie lefthander Jose Rosado. He compiled a 7-4 record with a 3.39 ERA in the first half and earned a trip to the All-Star Game as Kansas City's only representative. Rosado led the starting rotation to a 27-30 record and a 4.04 ERA before the break.

Low point: Bob Boone, the popular former Kansas City player, was fired as manager during the All-Star break with the Royals wallowing in an eight-game losing streak.

Turning point: The team lost its first four games under new manager Tony Muser to finish out a season-worst, 12-game losing streak that began with Boone still in charge. There was essentially no burst of enthusiasm with the change in leadership. The slow start under Muser reminded everyone there would be no quick fixes.

Most valuable player: Shortstop Jay Bell. Rock solid at shortstop, he added a career year at the plate in his first and only season in Kansas City. He hit .291 with 21 homers and 92 RBIs, and committed only 10 errors in 153 games.

Most valuable pitcher: Righthander Kevin Appier. He wound up in the top 10 of several A.L. pitching categories, including earned-run average (3.40), games started (34), innings pitched (235⅔) and strikeouts (196). The only thing missing was a big number of victories (he was 9-13), largely because Appier had poor run support throughout the season.

Most improved player: Closer Jeff Montgomery. He shook off a terrible first half to lead the team in saves with 14 for the season.

Most pleasant surprise: Righthanded reliever Hipolito Pichardo. Because Montgomery struggled to come back from a season-ending shoulder injury the year before and Jaime Bluma, his heir apparent, began having shoulder problems during spring training and did not play at all, Pichardo was forced to set aside his own ambition to be a starter. He became the interim closer and recorded 11 saves in 47 games.

Biggest disappointment: Outfielder Jermaine Dye. He didn't show anything near the promise that traveled with him to Kansas City from the Braves organization. Touted as a power-hitting right fielder with a strong arm, Dye hit only .236 with seven homers and 22 RBIs in 75 games.

Key injuries: Montgomery almost immediately went on the disabled list to start the season because he wasn't completely recovered from a shoulder injury in 1996. He came back at the beginning of May and pitched well down the stretch, but it didn't matter by that time. The loss of Bluma for the season just compounded the bullpen's troubles, forcing the Royals to use Pichardo, a middle relief guy, as the closer. Lefty Chris Haney missed close to four months with a fractured ankle and a sore pitching shoulder that forced a reshuffling of pitchers in the starting rotation.

Notable: The starting rotation went 27-30 with a 4.04 ERA and the bullpen had a 6.16 ERA in the first half. In the second half, they switched. Starters were only 20-31 with a 5.76 ERA, while the bullpen settled down and finished with a 3.24 ERA.

— LUCIANA CHAVEZ

RECORDS

1997 regular-season record: 67-94 (5th in A.L. Central); 33-47 at home; 34-47 on road; 25-30 vs. East; 23-39 vs. Central; 19-25 vs. West; 17-34 vs. lefthanded starters; 50-60 vs. righthanded starters; 55-83 on grass; 12-11 on turf; 21-31 in daytime; 46-63 at night; 20-29 in one-run games; 7-8 in extra-inning games; 1-0-3 in doubleheaders.

Team record past five years: 360-383 (.485, ranks 8th in league in that span).

TEAM LEADERS

Batting average: Jay Bell (.291).
At-bats: Jay Bell (573).
Runs: Jay Bell (89).
Hits: Jay Bell (167).
Total bases: Jay Bell (264).
Doubles: Jeff King (30).
Triples: Johnny Damon (8).
Home runs: Chili Davis (30).
Runs batted in: Jeff King (112).

Stolen bases: Tom Goodwin (34).
Slugging percentage: Chili Davis (.509).
On-base percentage: Chili Davis (.386).
Wins: Tim Belcher (13).
Earned-run average: Kevin Appier (3.40).
Complete games: Kevin Appier (4).
Shutouts: Kevin Appier, Tim Belcher (1).
Saves: Jeff Montgomery (14).
Innings pitched: Kevin Appier (235.2).
Strikeouts: Kevin Appier (196).

GAMES BY POSITION

Catcher: Mike Macfarlane 81, Mike Sweeney 76, Tim Spehr 17, Sal Fasano 12, Andy Stewart 4.
First base: Jeff King 150, Larry Sutton 12, Scott Cooper 8, Joe Vitiello 1.
Second base: Jose Offerman 101, David Howard 34, Jed Hansen 31, Shane Halter 18.
Third base: Craig Paquette 72, Dean Palmer 48, Scott Cooper 39, Shane Halter 12, Bip Roberts 10, David Howard 7, Jay Bell 4.
Shortstop: Jay Bell 149, Felix Martinez 12, David Howard 5, Shane Halter 5.
Outfield: Johnny Damon 136, Tom Goodwin 96, Bip Roberts 84, Jermaine Dye 75, Yamil Benitez 52, Shane Halter 32, Joe Vitiello 28, Rod Myers 26, David Howard 23, Jon Nunnally 9, Ryan Long 5, Craig Paquette 4, Larry Sutton 1.
Designated hitter: Chili Davis 133, Joe Vitiello 12, Scott Cooper 5, Johnny Damon 5, David Howard 5, Shane Halter 4, Larry Sutton 3, Mike Sweeney 3, Jeff King 2, Sal Fasano 1, Ryan Long 1, Jose Offerman 1, Dean Palmer 1, Andy Stewart 1.

TOP DRAFT CHOICES

1. **Dan Reichert,** RHP, University of Pacific.
2. **Dane Sardinha,** C, Kamehameha H.S., Kahuku, Hawaii.
3. **Jeremy Affeldt,** SS, Northwest Christian H.S., Spokane, Wash.
4. **Goefrey Tomlinson,** OF, U. of Houston.
5. **Jason Gooding,** LHP, Texas Tech.
6. **Jason Anderson,** RHP, Danville (Ill.) H.S.
7. **Joe Dillon,** 1B, Texas Tech.
8. **Eric Yanz,** RHP, Kansas State University.
9. **Kris Wilson,** RHP, Georgia Tech.
10. **David Willis,** 1B, UC Santa Barbara.

MINNESOTA TWINS
AMERICAN LEAGUE CENTRAL DIVISION

1998 SEASON
CLUB DIRECTORY

Owner
Carl R. Pohlad
President
Jerry Bell
Chairman of executive committee
Howard Fox
Directors
Carl R. Pohlad
Eloise Pohlad
James O. Pohlad
Robert C. Pohlad
William M. Pohlad
T. Geron (Jerry) Bell
Kirby Puckett
Chris Clouser
Vice president, general manager
Terry Ryan
Vice president, asst. general manager
Bill Smith
Executive vice president, baseball
Kirby Puckett
Vice president, operations
Matt Hoy
Director of minor leagues
Jim Rantz
Director of scouting
Mike Radcliff
Director of baseball operations
Rob Antony
Traveling secretary
Remzi Kiratli

Manager, media relations
Sean Harlin
Club physicians
Dr. Leonard J. Michienzi
Dr. John Steubs
Scouts
Ellsworth Brown
Ray Coley
Gene DeBoer
Cal Ermer
Marty Esposito
Vern Followell (west supervisor)
Earl Frishman (east supervisor)
Scott Groot
Bill Harford
Deron Johnson
Wayne Krivsky
John Leavitt
Joel Lepel
Bill Lohr
Bill Milos
Kevin Murphy
Tim O'Neil
Mark Quimuyog
Clair Rierson
Eddie Robinson
Mike Ruth (midwest supervisor)
Ricky Taylor
Brad Weitzel
John Wilson
International scouts
Enrique Brito
Howard Norsetter
Johnny Sierra

MINOR LEAGUE AFFILIATES

Class	Team	League	Manager
AAA	Salt Lake	Pacific Coast	Phil Roof
AA	New Britain	Eastern	John Russell
A	Fort Myers	Florida State	Mike Boulanger
A	Fort Wayne	Midwest	Jose Marzan
Rookie	Elizabethton	Appalachian	Jon Mathews
Rookie	Gulf Coast Twins	Gulf Coast	Steve Liddle

BROADCAST INFORMATION

Radio: WCCO-AM (830).
TV: WCCO-TV (Channel 4).
Cable TV: Midwest SportsChannel.

SPRING TRAINING

Ballpark (city): Lee County Sports
Complex (Fort Myers, Fla.).
Ticket information: 800-33-TWINS.

SPRING TRAINING ROSTER

Manager—Tom Kelly (10).
Coaches—Terry Crowley (46), Ron Gardenhire (35), Rick Stelmaszek (43), Dick Such (44), Scott Ullger (45).

No.	PITCHERS	B/T	Ht./Wt.	Born	1997 clubs
38	Aguilera, Rick	R/R	6-5/210	12-31-61	Minnesota
	Cumberland, Chris	R/L	6-1/190	1-15-73	Norwich, New Britain
18	Guardado, Eddie	R/L	6-0/195	10-2-70	Minnesota
	Harris, Jeff	R/R	6-0/180	7-4-74	Fort Myers, New Britain
32	Hawkins, LaTroy	R/R	6-5/201	12-21-72	Salt Lake, Minnesota
20	Miller, Travis	R/L	6-3/207	11-2-72	Salt Lake, Minnesota
	Morgan, Mike	R/R	6-2/220	10-8-59	Cincinnati
31	Naulty, Dan	R/R	6-6/223	1-6-70	Minnesota, Gulf Coast Twins, Salt Lake
	Perkins, Dan	R/R	6-2/193	3-15-75	New Britain
22	Radke, Brad	R/R	6-2/185	10-27-72	Minnesota
	Rath, Fred	R/R	6-3/205	1-5-73	Fort Myers, New Britain, Salt Lake
	Redman, Mark	L/L	6-5/220	1-5-74	Salt Lake
23	Ritchie, Todd	R/R	6-3/205	11-7-71	Minnesota
33	Rodriguez, Frank	R/R	6-0/197	12-11-72	Minnesota
	Sampson, Benj	L/L	6-1/205	4-27-75	New Britain
16	Serafini, Dan	B/L	6-1/191	1-25-74	Salt Lake, Minnesota
17	Swindell, Greg	R/L	6-3/225	1-2-65	Minnesota
19	Tewksbury, Bob	R/R	6-4/205	11-30-60	Minnesota
21	Trombley, Mike	R/R	6-2/203	4-14-67	Minnesota

No.	CATCHERS	B/T	Ht./Wt.	Born	1997 clubs
	Pierzynski, A.J.	L/R	6-3/202	12-30-76	Fort Myers
36	Steinbach, Terry	R/R	6-1/195	3-2-62	Minnesota
	Turner, Chris	R/R	6-1/190	3-23-69	Lake Elsinore, Vancouver, Anaheim
26	Valentin, Javier	B/R	5-10/191	9-19-75	New Britain, Minnesota

No.	INFIELDERS	B/T	Ht./Wt.	Born	1997 clubs
8	Coomer, Ron	R/R	5-11/225	11-18-66	Minnesota
	Davidson, Cleatus	B/R	5-10/160	11-1-76	Fort Wayne
	Gates, Brent	B/R	6-1/191	3-14-70	Seattle, Tacoma
7	Hocking, Denny	B/R	5-10/180	4-2-70	Minnesota
11	Knoblauch, Chuck	R/R	5-9/169	7-7-68	Minnesota
	Koskie, Corey	L/R	6-3/215	6-28-73	New Britain
2	Meares, Pat	R/R	6-0/187	9-6-68	Minnesota
	Mientkiewicz, Douglas	L/R	6-2/195	6-19-74	New Britain
4	Molitor, Paul	R/R	6-0/193	8-22-56	Minnesota
27	Ortiz, David	L/L	6-4/230	11-18-75	Fort Myers, New Britain, Salt Lake, Minnesota
12	Walker, Todd	L/R	6-0/177	5-25-73	Minnesota, Salt Lake

No.	OUTFIELDERS	B/T	Ht./Wt.	Born	1997 clubs
40	Cordova, Marty	R/R	6-0/201	7-10-69	Minnesota, Salt Lake
	Hunter, Torii	R/R	6-2/205	7-18-75	New Britain, Minnesota
59	Latham, Chris	B/R	6-0/185	5-26-73	Salt Lake, Minnesota
50	Lawton, Matt	L/R	5-10/200	11-3-71	Minnesota
	Lewis, Marc	R/R	6-2/175	5-20-75	Greenville
	Merced, Orlando	L/R	5-11/190	11-2-66	Toronto
	Nixon, Otis	B/R	6-2/180	1-9-59	Toronto, Los Angeles
	Ochoa, Alex	R/R	6-0/185	3-29-72	New York N.L.
	Radmanovich, Ryan	L/R	6-2/192	8-9-71	Salt Lake

BALLPARK INFORMATION

Ballpark (capacity, surface)
Hubert H. Humphrey Metrodome (48,678, artific

Address
34 Kirby Puckett Place
Minneapolis, MN 55415

Business phone
612-375-1366

Ticket information
1-800-33-TWINS

Ticket prices
$19 (VIP level, lower deck club level)
$16 (lower deck club)
$13 (lower deck reserved)
$11 (upper deck club level)
$7 (g.a., lower left field)
$4 (g.a., upper deck)

Field dimensions (from home plate)
To left field at foul line, 343 feet
To center field, 408 feet
To right field at foul line, 327 feet

First game played
April 6, 1982 (Mariners 11, Twins 7)

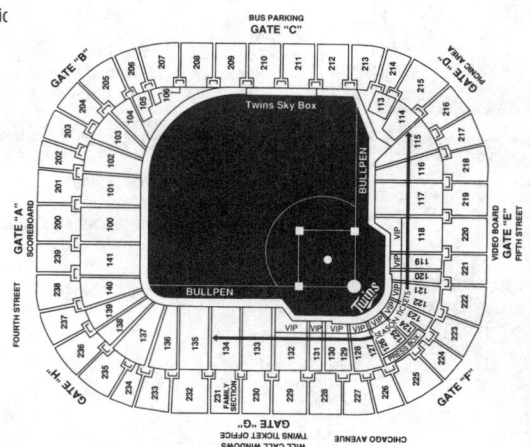

Minnesota Twins

1998 SEASON

Date	Opp.	Res.	Score	(inn.*)	Hits	Opp. hits	Winning pitcher	Losing pitcher	Save	Record	Pos.	GB
4-1	Det.	W	7-5		13	12	Naulty	Miceli	Aguilera	1-0	T1st	....
4-2	Det.	W	7-6		8	10	Aguilera	Jones		2-0	1st	+0.5
4-3	Det.	W	10-6		10	14	Ritchie	Blair	Naulty	3-0	1st	+1.5
4-4	K.C.	L	1-2		8	7	Belcher	Tewksbury	Pichardo	3-1	1st	+1.5
4-5	K.C.	W	7-5		12	9	Robertson	Haney	Aguilera	4-1	1st	+1.5
4-6	K.C.	L	2-12		5	15	Rusch	Radke		4-2	1st	+0.5
4-7	At Det.	L	4-10		9	9	Thompson	Rodriguez		4-3	T2nd	0.5
4-9	At Det.	L	5-10		9	10	Cummings	Ritchie		4-4	T2nd	0.5
4-10	At Det.	W	7-3		14	6	Aldred	Blair		5-4	1st	+0.5
4-12	At K.C.	W	11-6		12	12	Ritchie	Belcher		6-4	1st	+0.5
4-13	At K.C.	L	1-6		6	10	Appier	Rodriguez		6-5	T1st	...
4-14	At Bal.	L	2-4		6	9	Erickson	Tewksbury	Myers	6-6	T2nd	1.0
4-15	At Bal.	L	1-3		2	5	Kamieniecki	Aldred	Myers	6-7	3rd	1.0
4-16	Ana.	W	4-2		8	7	Robertson	Watson	Aguilera	7-7	T2nd	1.0
4-17	Ana.	W	4-3	(10)	11	11	Swindell	James		8-7	2nd	1.0
4-18	At Sea.	W	10-3		10	8	Rodriguez	Sanders		9-7	2nd	1.0
4-19	At Sea.	W	4-0		10	6	Tewksbury	D. Martinez		10-7	T1st	....
4-20	At Sea.	L	6-10		12	11	Wolcott	Ritchie	Charlton	10-8	T1st	....
4-22	At Oak.	W	5-3		7	5	Radke	Mohler	Aguilera	11-8	1st	+1.0
4-23	At Oak.	L	1-6		11	6	Prieto	Robertson	Small	11-9	1st	+1.0
4-24	At Oak.	L	11-12	(11)	21	19	Wengert	Aguilera		11-10	1st	+0.5
4-25	Tex.	L	3-6		6	11	Hill	Tewksbury	Wetteland	11-11	2nd	0.5
4-26	Tex.	L	1-6		7	11	Witt	Aldred	Gunderson	11-12	T2nd	0.5
4-27	Tex.	L	3-7		7	11	Patterson	Naulty		11-13	4th	1.0
4-29	Bal.	L	4-6		7	12	Boskie	Swindell	Myers	11-14	4th	2.5
4-30	Bal.	L	3-12		5	19	Kamieniecki	Tewksbury	Benitez	11-15	4th	2.5
5-1	Bal.	L	2-3		5	5	Erickson	Aldred	Myers	11-16	4th	3.0
5-2	At Tor.	W	3-2	(10)	7	6	Radke	Crabtree	Aguilera	12-16	4th	2.0
5-3	At Tor.	L	5-6		10	10	Quantrill	Ritchie		12-17	4th	3.0
5-4	At Tor.	L	0-1		4	4	Hentgen	Tewksbury		12-18	4th	3.0
5-5	At N.Y.	W	9-8		12	9	Swindell	Mecir		13-18	4th	3.0
5-6	At N.Y.	L	2-7		8	10	Wells	Aldred		13-19	4th	3.5
5-7	At Bos.	L	3-11		8	14	Sele	Radke		13-20	4th	4.5
5-8	At Bos.	W	10-7		11	14	Robertson	Garces	Aguilera	14-20	4th	3.5
5-9	Tor.	L	1-4		6	8	Hentgen	Rodriguez	Timlin	14-21	T4th	4.5
5-10	Tor.	L	4-6		10	8	Clemens	Swindell	Crabtree	14-22	5th	5.5
5-11	Tor.	L	2-3		8	7	Williams	Aldred	Timlin	14-23	5th	6.5
5-12	Tor.	L	12-2		20	10	Radke	Carpenter		15-23	5th	6.5
5-13	N.Y.	L	2-11		11	15	Cone	Robertson		15-24	5th	6.5
5-14	N.Y.	L	5-6	(12)	13	12	Boehringer	Guardado	Rivera	15-25	5th	6.5
5-16	Bos.	W	11-5		17	9	Aldred	Hammond		16-25	5th	5.5
5-17	Bos.	L	0-4		4	8	Gordon	Radke		16-26	5th	5.5
5-18	Bos.	W	7-5		11	8	Robertson	Sele	Aguilera	17-26	5th	4.5
5-20	At Mil.	W	4-3		8	7	Trombley	Eldred	Aguilera	18-26	5th	4.5
5-21	At Mil.	L	4-5		8	7	McDonald	Aldred	Jones	18-27	5th	5.5
5-23	Oak.	L	4-8		9	11	Karsay	Radke	Taylor	18-28	5th	7.0
5-24	Oak.	W	7-4		13	8	Robertson	Mohler	Aguilera	19-28	5th	6.0
5-25	Oak.	W	7-6	(10)	9	11	Aguilera	Taylor		20-28	5th	6.0
5-26	Sea.	L	8-13		13	14	Sanders	Aldred		20-29	5th	7.0
5-27	Sea.	W	11-10		14	12	Aguilera	Charlton		21-29	5th	6.0
5-28	Mil.	W	3-1		7	6	Radke	Karl	Aguilera	22-29	5th	6.0
5-29	Mil.	L	4-7		9	12	D'Amico	Robertson		22-30	5th	6.5
5-30	At Ana.	W	4-3		7	12	Tewksbury	Dickson	Aguilera	23-30	5th	5.5
5-31	At Ana.	L	3-5		7	12	Finley	Aldred	Percival	23-31	5th	5.5
6-1	At Ana.	W	5-4		12	9	Swindell	Hasegawa	Aguilera	24-31	5th	5.0
6-2	At Tex.	L	0-8		5	18	Oliver	Radke		24-32	5th	5.5
6-3	At Tex.	W	5-4		12	13	Robertson	Hill	Aguilera	25-32	5th	4.5
6-5	Ana.	L	0-3		6	10	Dickson	Tewksbury	Percival	25-33	5th	5.0
6-6	Ana.	W	9-7		15	10	Swindell	Harris	Aguilera	26-33	5th	5.0
6-7	Ana.	W	6-1		13	6	Radke	Perisho		27-33	5th	5.0
6-8	Ana.	L	6-8		6	11	Springer	Trombley	Percival	27-34	5th	5.0
6-10	Tex.	W	10-1		13	8	Tewksbury	Witt		28-34	5th	5.0
6-11	Tex.	L	6-9		12	18	Burkett	Aldred	Wetteland	28-35	5th	6.0
6-13	At Hou.	W	8-1		10	6	Radke	Wall		29-35	5th	5.0
6-14	At Hou.	W	6-1		12	9	Robertson	Kile		30-35	4th	4.5
6-15	At Hou.	L	2-3		8	6	Wagner	Guardado		30-36	5th	5.5
6-16	Pit.	L	6-8		9	15	Schmidt	Aldred	Loiselle	30-37	5th	5.5
6-17	Pit.	W	13-1		17	4	Hawkins	Loaiza		31-37	5th	5.5
6-18	Pit.	W	8-2		9	8	Radke	Cordova		32-37	5th	4.5
6-20	At Chi.	W	3-0		7	5	Tewksbury	D. Darwin	Aguilera	33-37	4th	3.5
6-21	At Chi.	L	3-5		5	8	Baldwin	Robertson	Hernandez	33-38	5th	4.5

Date	Opp.	Res.	Score	(inn.*)	Hits	Opp. hits	Winning pitcher	Losing pitcher	Save	Record	Pos.	GB
6-22	At Chi.	L	1-2		9	8	Navarro	Hawkins	Hernandez	33-39	5th	5.5
6-23	At Cle.	W	7-2		16	7	Radke	Ogea		34-39	5th	4.5
6-24	At Cle.	L	5-10		9	13	Wright	Stevens		34-40	5th	5.5
6-26	Chi.	L	1-11		5	14	Baldwin	Hawkins		34-41	5th	6.0
6-27	Chi.	L	6-10		8	15	Navarro	Tewksbury		34-42	5th	6.0
6-28	Chi.	W	11-5		19	10	Radke	Drabek		35-42	5th	6.0
6-29	Chi.	L	4-6		9	11	Alvarez	Stevens	Hernandez	35-43	5th	6.0
6-30	At St.L.	L	1-2		12	6	Morris	Robertson	Eckersley	35-44	5th	7.0
7-1	At St.L.	L	0-2		5	7	Stottlemyre	Hawkins	Eckersley	35-45	5th	8.0
7-2	At St.L.	L	1-2	(10)	5	10	Petkovsek	Guardado		35-46	5th	8.0
7-3	At Mil.	W	8-5		12	6	Radke	D'Amico	Aguilera	36-46	5th	7.5
7-4	At Mil.	W	13-1		23	10	Stevens	Karl		37-46	5th	7.5
7-5	At Mil.	L	1-2		4	5	Eldred	Robertson	Jones	37-47	5th	8.5
7-6	At Mil.	L	2-6		5	11	McDonald	Hawkins		37-48	5th	9.5
7-10	Cle.	W	8-2		14	8	Radke	Nagy		38-48	4th	8.5
7-11	Cle.	L	1-5		9	4	Jacome	Robertson		38-49	4th	9.5
7-12	Cle.	L	2-7		8	13	Hershiser	Tewksbury		38-50	4th	10.5
7-13	Cle.	L	5-12		7	15	Colon	Hawkins		38-51	4th	11.5
7-14	Chi.	W	5-3		8	8	Rodriguez	Drabek	Aguilera	39-51	4th	11.5
7-15	Chi.	W	8-4		15	6	Radke	Navarro		40-51	4th	10.5
7-16	At Sea.	L	7-8		10	14	Sanders	Aguilera		40-52	4th	11.5
7-17	At Sea.	W	9-7	(12)	11	17	Aguilera	Charlton	Guardado	41-52	4th	11.5
7-18	At Oak.	W	7-3		14	8	Hawkins	Wojciechowski		42-52	4th	10.5
7-19	At Oak.	W	7-6		11	12	Swindell	Wengert	Aguilera	43-52	4th	9.5
7-20	At Oak.	W	1-0		5	5	Radke	Reyes		44-52	4th	9.5
7-22	K.C.	W	3-2		9	9	Swindell	Rosado	Aguilera	45-52	4th	9.0
7-23	K.C.	L	1-5		7	10	Belcher	Hawkins		45-53	4th	9.0
7-24	K.C.	L	3-5		6	9	Bones	Stevens	Montgomery	45-54	4th	9.0
7-25	Bal.	W	5-2		8	7	Radke	Kamieniecki		46-54	4th	8.0
7-26	Bal.	L	1-2	(12)	13	5	Orosco	Aguilera	Myers	46-55	4th	9.0
7-27	Bal.	L	0-9		5	16	Erickson	Robertson		46-56	4th	10.0
7-28†	At K.C.	L	3-10		6	17	Belcher	Rodriguez		46-57		
7-28‡	At K.C.	L	2-5		3	7	Pittsley	T. Miller	Montgomery	46-58	4th	10.0
7-29	At K.C.	W	11-8		14	13	Hawkins	Bones		47-58	4th	9.0
7-30	At K.C.	W	11-1		14	3	Radke	Rusch		48-58	4th	8.0
8-1	At N.Y.	L	3-8		13	14	Pettitte	Robertson		48-59	4th	9.0
8-2	At N.Y.	W	5-4		6	9	Swindell	Cone	Aguilera	49-59	4th	9.0
8-3	At N.Y.	L	5-6		7	9	Gooden	Hawkins	Rivera	49-60	4th	9.0
8-4	Tor.	W	9-3		14	7	Radke	Carpenter		50-60	4th	9.0
8-5	Tor.	L	3-8		8	11	Person	T. Miller		50-61	4th	9.0
8-6	Bos.	L	2-5		7	7	Wakefield	Robertson	Henry	50-62	4th	9.0
8-7	Bos.	L	6-7		5	9	Sele	Bowers	Corsi	50-63	4th	9.0
8-8	N.Y.	W	9-1		13	11	Hawkins	Gooden		51-63	4th	8.0
8-9	N.Y.	L	1-4		8	8	Wells	Radke	Rivera	51-64	4th	8.5
8-10	N.Y.	L	6-9		13	16	Mendoza	T. Miller	Rivera	51-65	4th	8.5
8-11	N.Y.	L	0-11		5	21	Pettitte	Robertson		51-66	4th	9.0
8-12	At Tor.	L	1-9		8	11	Clemens	Bowers		51-67	4th	10.0
8-13	At Tor.	L	2-3		12	10	Quantrill	Trombley		51-68	4th	10.5
8-14	At Bos.	L	1-6		6	8	Suppan	Radke		51-69	4th	11.5
8-15	At Bos.	L	4-5	(10)	8	11	Lacy	Guardado		51-70	5th	12.5
8-16	At Bos.	L	4-12		10	12	Wakefield	Bowers		51-71	5th	13.5
8-17	At Bos.	L	5-10		9	14	Sele	Tewksbury		51-72	5th	13.5
8-19	At Det.	L	2-8		9	9	Blair	Hawkins		51-73	5th	15.0
8-20	At Det.	W	11-1		14	3	Radke	Sanders		52-73	5th	14.0
8-22	At Bal.	L	1-3		5	5	Erickson	Tewksbury	Myers	52-74	5th	14.5
8-23	At Bal.	L	4-5		8	7	Orosco	Swindell	Myers	52-75	5th	15.5
8-24	At Bal.	L	1-5		6	9	Kamieniecki	Hawkins	Benitez	52-76	5th	15.5
8-25	Det.	L	6-7	(12)	12	11	Sager	Aguilera		52-77	5th	16.0
8-26	Det.	W	8-2		11	7	Robertson	Thompson	Trombley	53-77	5th	15.0
8-27	Det.	W	2-0		7	5	Tewksbury	Moehler		54-77	T4th	15.0
8-29	Cin.	L	3-5		7	9	Tomko	Rodriguez	Shaw	54-78	5th	16.0
8-30	Cin.	W	4-1		7	7	Hawkins	Morgan	Aguilera	55-78	5th	15.0
8-31	Cin.	W	8-6		11	12	Radke	White	Aguilera	56-78	4th	15.0
9-1	At Chi. (NL)	W	7-6		13	12	Trombley	Stevens	Aguilera	57-78	4th	15.0
9-2	At Chi. (NL)	L	3-9		8	14	M. Clark	Tewksbury		57-79	4th	15.0
9-3	At Chi. (NL)	L	6-10		10	15	Gonzalez	Rodriguez		57-80	4th	16.0
9-4	Sea.	L	6-9		8	17	Cloude	Hawkins	Slocumb	57-81	5th	16.5
9-5	Sea.	L	6-10		10	15	Moyer	Radke		57-82	5th	17.5
9-6	Sea.	L	0-9		4	10	Fassero	Robertson		57-83	5th	18.5
9-7	Sea.	W	9-6		8	12	Tewksbury	Lira		58-83	4th	18.5
9-8	Oak.	W	7-2		15	5	Serafini	Telgheder		59-83	4th	18.5
9-9	Oak.	L	1-5		4	12	Haynes	Hawkins		59-84	4th	18.5
9-11	At Tex.	L	0-7		2	12	Pavlik	Radke		59-85	5th	18.5
9-12	At Tex.	L	5-6		9	8	Santana	Swindell	Wetteland	59-86	5th	19.5
9-13	At Tex.	L	3-9		8	12	Oliver	Tewksbury		59-87	5th	19.5

Date	Opp.	Res.	Score	(inn.*)	Hits	Opp. hits	Winning pitcher	Losing pitcher	Save	Record	Pos.	GB
9-14	At Tex.	W	11-1		21	10	Serafini	Witt		60-87	5th	19.5
9-15	At Ana.	L	5-8		8	9	Harris	Trombley		60-88	5th	20.0
9-16	At Ana.	W	9-3		13	9	Radke	Hasegawa		61-88	5th	19.5
9-17	Cle.	L	6-7		11	9	Wright	T. Miller	Mesa	61-89	5th	20.5
9-18	Cle.	L	1-4		4	11	Hershiser	Tewksbury	M. Jackson	61-90	5th	21.5
9-19	Mil.	L	4-7		7	11	Mercedes	Serafini	Jones	61-91	5th	22.0
9-20	Mil.	W	6-1		12	2	Hawkins	Eldred	Swindell	62-91	5th	21.0
9-21	Mil.	W	2-1	(10)	8	6	Radke	Fetters		63-91	5th	20.0
9-22	Mil.	W	5-2		6	6	T. Miller	D'Amico	Aguilera	64-91	5th	19.5
9-23	At Chi.	W	5-3		5	5	Tewksbury	Bere	Aguilera	65-91	T4th	19.5
9-24	At Chi.	W	7-2		11	7	Rodriguez	Baldwin	Aguilera	66-91	4th	18.5
9-25	At Chi.	L	5-10		7	16	Drabek	Hawkins		66-92	T4th	18.5
9-26	At Chi.	L	2-7		12	8	Ogea	Radke		66-93	T4th	19.5
9-27†	At Cle.	L	6-10		14	16	Colon	T. Miller		66-94		
9-27‡	At Cle.	W	6-4	(10)	12	12	Aguilera	Lopez		67-94	5th	19.5
9-28	At Cle.	W	5-1		9	6	Tewksbury	Nagy		68-94	4th	18.5

Monthly records: April (11-15), May (12-16), June (12-13), July (13-14), August (8-20), September (12-16).
*Innings, if other than nine. †First game of doubleheader. ‡Second game of doubleheader.

HIGHLIGHTS

High point: Brad Radke recorded his 20th victory of the season by lasting 10 innings in a 2-1 victory over Milwaukee at the Metrodome. A crowd of only 13,262 watched the Twins, who were 20 games out of first place, but the exuberance of Radke's teammates as the champagne flowed in the clubhouse was easily the best moment of the season.

Low point: A four-game sweep by Boston were losses No. 6 through 9 in a 10-game, August skid, the longest of the season. The last two games at Fenway Park, 12-4 and 10-5 defeats, were particularly painful, with the pitchers being roasted and Marty Cordova's hitting problems affecting his play in left field to the point that he was benched during the series.

Turning point: The Twins were eight games out of first after beating the Yankees, 9-1, at the Metrodome on August 8. A 4-1 loss to the Yankees the next day began their 10-game tailspin. By the time it ended, they were 14 games out.

Most valuable player: You'd never know Paul Molitor was in his 40s by watching him last season. Despite missing two weeks with an abdominal strain that bothered him most of the season, the DH led the team in hitting, doubles, RBIs, sacrifice flies and intentional walks.

Most valuable pitcher: Radke came into his own in 1997, his 20-10 record putting him alongside the game's top pitchers. He also had a major league-best, 12-start, winning streak.

Most improved player: Reliever Greg Swindell, who made only 11 total appearances in 1996 with Houston and Cleveland, was signed as a free agent in December of that year. He came through in a big way, making a career-high 65 appearances and leading the league in relief innings. He even recorded the first save of his career.

Most pleasant surprise: Todd Walker was penciled in at third base going into spring training, but Ron Coomer took over when Walker was sent down in late May. The nine-year minor leaguer played steady defense and was an effective hitter in his second full major league season, setting career highs in nearly every offensive category. He was second in hitting, doubles and RBIs and led the league in batting average vs. lefthanders (.415).

Biggest disappointment: Cordova was the Rookie of the Year in 1995, then hit .309 with 111 RBIs in 1996. That made his miserable 1997 all the more difficult to take. He suffered a foot injury in the spring that troubled him all season, limiting him to 103 games. He was on the disabled list for five weeks in April and May.

Key injuries: Cordova's foot problem was one of many. First baseman Scott Stahoviak suffered a broken finger on opening day and missed six weeks, reliever Dan Naulty was out for three months with a back injury and starter Bob Tewksbury went on the D.L. twice.

Notable: In a sign of the team's power shortage, Cordova was the home run leader with only 15. The Twins hit the fewest homers in the league for the second straight year.

— JOHN MILLEA

RECORDS

1997 regular-season record: 68-94 (4th in A.L. Central); 35-46 at home; 33-48 on road; 17-38 vs. East; 29-34 vs. Central; 22-22 vs. West; 16-17 vs. lefthanded starters; 52-77 vs. righthanded starters; 27-41 on grass; 41-53 on turf; 19-29 in daytime; 49-65 at night; 16-23 in one-run games; 6-6 in extra-inning games; 0-1 in doubleheaders.

Team record past five years: 326-417 (.439, ranks 14th in league in that span).

TEAM LEADERS

Batting average: Paul Molitor (.305).
At-bats: Chuck Knoblauch (611).
Runs: Chuck Knoblauch (117).
Hits: Chuck Knoblauch (178).
Total bases: Chuck Knoblauch (251).
Doubles: Paul Molitor (32).
Triples: Chuck Knoblauch (10).
Home runs: Marty Cordova (15).
Runs batted in: Paul Molitor (89).
Stolen bases: Chuck Knoblauch (62).
Slugging percentage: Ron Coomer (.438).

On-base percentage: Chuck Knoblauch (.390).
Wins: Brad Radke (20).
Earned-run average: Brad Radke (3.87).
Complete games: Bob Tewksbury (5).
Shutouts: Bob Tewksbury (2).
Saves: Rick Aguilera (26).
Innings pitched: Brad Radke (239.2).
Strikeouts: Brad Radke (174).

GAMES BY POSITION

Catcher: Terry Steinbach 116, Greg Myers 38, Damian Miller 20, Javier Valentin 4.
First base: Scott Stahoviak 81, Greg Colbrunn 64, Brent Brede 15, Paul Molitor 12, David Ortiz 11, Ron Coomer 9, Terry Steinbach 2, Denny Hocking 1.
Second base: Chuck Knoblauch 154, Denny Hocking 15, Todd Walker 8.
Third base: Ron Coomer 119, Todd Walker 40, Denny Hocking 39.
Shortstop: Pat Meares 134, Denny Hocking 44, Chuck Knoblauch 1.
Outfield: Matt Lawton 138, Rich Becker 128, Marty Cordova 101, Roberto Kelly 59, Darrin Jackson 44, Brent Brede 42, Denny Hocking 20, Chris Latham 10, Ron Coomer 7.
Designated hitter: Paul Molitor 122, Roberto Kelly 12, Greg Myers 10, Ron Coomer 7, Scott Stahoviak 5, Damian Miller 3, Greg Colbrunn 2, Marty Cordova 2, Todd Walker 2, Brent Brede 1, Denny Hocking 1, Chuck Knoblauch 1, Terry Steinbach 1.

TOP DRAFT CHOICES

1a. **Michael Cuddyer,** SS, Great Bridge H.S., Chesapeake, Va.
1b. **Matthew LeCroy,** C, Clemson University.
2. **Mike Restovich,** OF, Mayo H.S., Rochester, Minn.
3. **Greg Withelder,** LHP, Strath Haven H.S., Wallingford, Pa.
4. **Bob Davies,** LHP, Marietta (Ohio) College.
5. **Peter Blake,** LHP, Indianola (Iowa) H.S.
6. **Nate Melson,** RHP, Rogers (Ark.) H.S.
7. **Matt Carnes,** RHP, Univ. of Arkansas.
8. **Ben Thomas,** LHP, Wichita State Univ.
9. **Jon Schaeffer,** C, Stanford University.
10. **Josh Gandy,** LHP, Univ. of Georgia.

NEW YORK YANKEES
AMERICAN LEAGUE EAST DIVISION

Yankees Schedule

Home games shaded. *—All-Star Game at Coors Field (Colorado).
D—Day game (any game starting before 5 p.m.).

March

SUN	MON	TUE	WED	THU	FRI	SAT
			31			

April

SUN	MON	TUE	WED	THU	FRI	SAT
			1 ANA	2 ANA	3 OAK	4 D OAK
5 D OAK	6 SEA	7 SEA	8 D SEA	9	10 D OAK	11 OAK
12 D OAK	13 ANA	14 ANA	15 ANA	16 D	17 DET	18 D DET
19 D DET	20 TOR	21 TOR	22 TOR	23	24 DET	25 D DET
26 D DET	27 TOR	28 TOR	29 SEA	30 SEA		

May

SUN	MON	TUE	WED	THU	FRI	SAT
					1 KC	2 KC
3 D KC	4	5 TEX	6 TEX	7	8 MIN	9 MIN
10 D MIN	11 KC	12 TEX	13 TEX	14 TEX	15 MIN	16 D MIN
17 D MIN	18	19 BAL	20 BAL	21 BAL	22 BOS	23 D BOS
24 D BOS	25 CWS	26 CWS	27 CWS	28 BOS	29 BOS	30 D BOS
31 D BOS						

June

SUN	MON	TUE	WED	THU	FRI	SAT
	1 CWS	2 CWS	3 TB	4 TB	5 FLA	6 D FLA
7 D FLA	8	9 MON	10 MON	11 MON	12 CLE	13 D CLE
14 CLE	15 BAL	16 BAL	17 BAL	18 CLE	19 CLE	20 D CLE
21 D CLE	22 ATL	23 ATL	24 ATL	25 ATL	26 NYM	27 D NYM
28 D NYM	29	30 PHI				

July

SUN	MON	TUE	WED	THU	FRI	SAT
			1 PHI	2 PHI	3 BAL	4 D BAL
5 D BAL	6	7 *	8	9 TB	10 TB	11 TB
12 D TB	13 CLE	14 CLE	15 DET	16 DET	17 TOR	18 D TOR
19 D TOR	20 DET	21 DET	22 DET	23 D	24 CWS	25 D CWS
26 D CWS	27	28 ANA	29 ANA	30 ANA	31 SEA	

August

SUN	MON	TUE	WED	THU	FRI	SAT
						1 D SEA
2 D SEA	3 OAK	4 OAK	5 D OAK	6	7 KC	8 D KC
9 KC	10 MIN	11 MIN	12 D MIN	13 TEX	14 TEX	15 TEX
16 TEX	17 KC	18 KC	19 MIN	20 MIN	21 TEX	22 TEX
23 TEX	24	25 ANA	26 ANA	27 ANA	28 SEA	29 D SEA
30 D SEA	31					

September

SUN	MON	TUE	WED	THU	FRI	SAT
		1 OAK	2 OAK	3	4 CWS	5 CWS
6 CWS	7	8 BOS	9 BOS	10 TOR	11 TOR	12 D TOR
13 TOR	14 BOS	15 BOS	16 TB	17 TB	18 BAL	19 BAL
20 BAL	21	22 CLE	23 CLE	24 TB	25 TB	26 D TB
27 D TB						

1998 SEASON
CLUB DIRECTORY

Principal owner
George M. Steinbrenner III
General partners
Joseph A. Molloy, Harold Z. Steinbrenner,
Steven W. Swindal
Executive v.p., general counsel
Lonn Trost
Vice president, ticket operations
Frank Swaine
Vice president, business development
Derek Schiller
Vice president, chief financial officer
Mike Macaluso
Controller
Robert Brown
Special advisory group
Reggie Jackson, Clyde King,
Dick Williams
Vice president, general manager
Robert Watson
Vice president, player development
Mark Newman
Director of major league scouting
Gene Michael
Assistant general manager
Brian Cashman
Major league administrator
Tom May
Traveling secretary
David Szen
Director of stadium operations
Sonny Hight
Director of customer service
Joel White
Dir. of office administration nd services
Harvey C. Winston
Manager, stadium operations
Kirk Randazzo
Assistant, stadium operations
Bob Pelegrino
Stadium superintendent
Bob Wilkinson
Head groundskeeper
Dan Cunningham
Director, video and broadcast operations
Doyal Martin
Asst. dir., video and broadcast operations
Joe Pullia
Public address announcer
Bob Sheppard
Stadium organist
Eddie Layton
Executive director of ticket operations
Jeff Kline
Ticket director
Ken Skrypek

Director of media relations and publicity
Rick Cerrone
Asst. dir. of media relations and publicity
John Thursby
Senior advisor
Arthur Richman
Director of marketing
Deborah A. Tymon
Director of community relations
Brian Smith
Director of Yankee Alumni Association
Jim Ogle
Director of entertainment
Stanley Kay
Special assistant
Joe Pepitone
Dir. of television and video production
Joe Violone
Director of publications and multimedia
Kara McGovern
Team photographer
Steve Crandall
Assistant director of scouting
Joe Caro
Coord. of Latin American player dev.
Ken Dominguez
Team physician
Dr. Stuart Hershon
Head trainer
Gene Monahan
Assistant trainer
Steve Donohue
Strength & conditioning coach
Paul Mastropasqua
Cross-checkers
John Cox, Damon Oppenheimer,
Donnie Rowland
Special assignment scouts
Ket Barber, Bill Emslie
Scouts
Rich Arena, Joe Arnold, Mike Baker, Mark
Batchko, Bobby Dejardin, Lee Elder, Tim
Kelly, Greg Orr, Scott Pleis, Cesar Presbott,
Joe Robison, Phil Rossi, Steve Webber, J.
Leon Wurth, Bill Young
Coordinator of international scouting
Gordon Blakeley
Coordinator of Canadian scouting
Dick Groch
Foreign scouts
Karl Heron, Ricardo Heron, Ruddy Jabalera,
Francisco Lugo, Victor Mata, Manuel
Medina, Roberto Morillo, Jorge Oquendo,
Raul Ortega, Jim Patterson, Marc Picard,
Jose Quintero, Luis Ramos, Arquimedes
Rojas, Dale Tilleman, Modesto Ulloa

MINOR LEAGUE AFFILIATES

Class	Team	League	Manager
AAA	Columbus	International	To be announced
AA	Norwich	Eastern	Trey Hillman
A	Tampa	Florida State	Lee Mazzilli
A	Greensboro	South Atlantic	Tom Nieto
A	Oneonta	New York-Pennsylvania	To be announced
Rookie	Gulf Coast Yankees	Gulf Coast	To be announced

BROADCAST INFORMATION

Radio: WABC-AM (770).
TV: WPIX-TV.
Cable TV: Madison Square Garden Network.

SPRING TRAINING

Ballpark (city): Legends Field (Tampa, Fla.).
Ticket information: 813-875-7753.

Manager—Joe Torre (6).
Coaches—Jose Cardenal (53), Chris Chambliss (50), Tony Cloninger (40), Willie Randolph (30), Mel Stottlemyre (34), Don Zimmer (48).

No.	PITCHERS	B/T	Ht./Wt.	Born	1997 clubs
	Alberro, Jose	R/R	6-2/190	6-29-69	Oklahoma City, Texas, Columbus
62	Banks, Willie	R/R	6-1/195	2-27-69	Columbus, New York A.L.
52	Borowski, Joe	R/R	6-2/225	5-4-71	Atlanta, Richmond, New York A.L.
	Buddie, Mike	R/R	6-3/210	12-12-70	Norwich, Columbus
36	Cone, David	L/R	6-1/190	1-2-63	New York A.L.
	Einertson, Darrell	R/R	6-2/190	9-4-72	Tampa
	Holmes, Darren	R/R	6-0/202	4-25-66	Colorado
35	Irabu, Hideki	R/R	6-4/240	5-5-69	Tampa, Norwich, Columbus, New York A.L.
	Jerzembeck, Mike	R/R	6-1/185	5-18-72	Norwich, Columbus
27	Lloyd, Graeme	L/L	6-7/234	4-9-67	New York A.L.
55	Mendoza, Ramiro	R/R	6-2/154	6-15-72	Columbus, New York A.L.
	Milton, Eric	L/L	6-3/200	8-4-75	Tampa, Norwich
43	Nelson, Jeff	R/R	6-8/235	11-17-66	New York A.L.
46	Pettitte, Andy	L/L	6-5/235	6-15-72	New York A.L.
	Rios, Dan	R/R	6-2/190	11-11-72	Columbus, New York A.L.
42	Rivera, Mariano	R/R	6-2/168	11-29-69	New York A.L.
29	Stanton, Mike	L/L	6-1/215	6-2-67	New York A.L.
33	Wells, David	L/L	6-4/225	5-20-63	New York A.L.

No.	CATCHERS	B/T	Ht./Wt.	Born	1997 clubs
63	Figga, Mike	R/R	6-0/200	7-31-70	Columbus, New York A.L.
25	Girardi, Joe	R/R	5-11/195	10-14-64	New York A.L.
22	Posada, Jorge	B/R	6-2/205	8-17-71	New York A.L.

No.	INFIELDERS	B/T	Ht./Wt.	Born	1997 clubs
	Brosius, Scott	R/R	6-1/202	8-15-66	Oakland, Modesto
	Bush, Homer	R/R	5-10/175	11-12-72	Las Vegas, Columbus, New York A.L.
47	Cruz, Ivan	L/L	6-3/210	5-3-68	Columbus, New York A.L.
18	Fox, Andy	L/R	6-4/205	1-12-71	Columbus, New York A.L.
2	Jeter, Derek	R/R	6-3/185	6-26-74	New York A.L.
	Lowell, Mike	R/R	6-4/195	2-24-74	Norwich, Columbus
	Martinez, Gabby	B/R	6-2/170	1-7-74	Norwich, Gulf Coast Yankees
24	Martinez, Tino	L/R	6-2/210	12-7-67	New York A.L.
	Sojo, Luis	R/R	5-11/175	1-3-66	New York A.L.
	Sveum, Dale	B/R	6-3/185	11-23-63	Pittsburgh

No.	OUTFIELDERS	B/T	Ht./Wt.	Born	1997 clubs
	Buchanan, Brian	R/R	6-4/220	7-21-73	Norwich, Colorado Springs
28	Curtis, Chad	R/R	5-10/185	11-6-68	Cleveland, Akron, New York A.L.
	Davis, Chili	B/R	6-3/217	1-17-60	Kansas City
	Ledee, Ricky	L/L	6-1/160	11-22-73	Columbus, Gulf Coast Yankees
	McDonald, Donzell	B/R	5-11/165	2-20-75	Tampa
21	O'Neill, Paul	L/L	6-4/215	2-25-63	New York A.L.
31	Raines, Tim	B/R	5-8/186	9-16-59	Tampa, New York A.L., Columbus, Norwich, Gulf Coast Yankees
	Singleton, Chris	L/L	6-2/195	8-15-72	Shreveport
	Spencer, Shane	R/R	5-11/210	2-20-72	Columbus
	Strawberry, Darryl	L/L	6-6/215	3-12-62	New York A.L., Norwich, Columbus, Tampa
51	Williams, Bernie	B/R	6-2/205	9-13-68	New York A.L.

1998 SEASON *New York Yankees*

Ballpark (capacity, surface)
Yankee Stadium (57,545, grass)

Address
Yankee Stadium
E. 161 St. and River Ave.
Bronx, NY 10451

Business phone
718-293-4300

Ticket information
718-293-6000

Ticket prices
$25 (field, main and loge boxes)
$23 (main and loge boxes)
$23 (main reserved-infield)
$20 (tier boxes, main reserved-outfield)
$12 (tier reserved)
$7 (bleachers)
$2 (senior citizens)

Field dimensions (from home plate)
To left field at foul line, 318 feet
To center field, 408 feet
To right field at foul line, 314 feet

First game played
April 18, 1923 (Yankees 4, Red Sox 1)

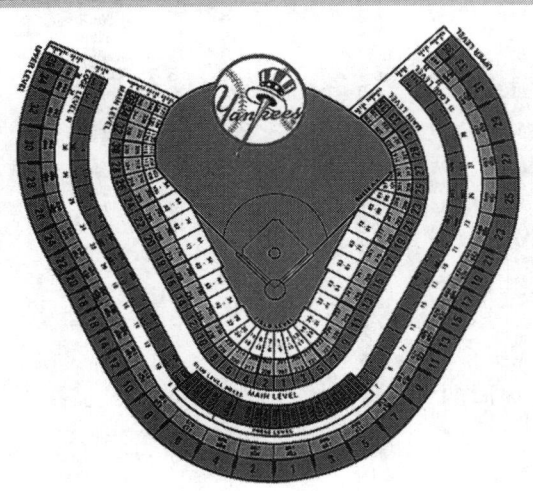

1997 REVIEW
DAY BY DAY

Date	Opp.	Res.	Score	(inn.*)	Hits	Opp. hits	Winning pitcher	Losing pitcher	Save	Record	Pos.	GB
4-1	At Sea.	L	2-4		8	7	Fassero	Cone	Charlton	0-1	T3rd	0.5
4-2	At Sea.	W	16-2		14	8	Pettitte	Sanders		1-1	T3rd	0.5
4-4	At Oak.	L	2-4		11	9	Acre	Weathers	Taylor	1-2	4th	2.0
4-5	At Oak.	W	10-5		13	10	Gooden	Mohler	Rivera	2-2	T3rd	2.0
4-6	At Oak.	L	0-3		7	4	Acre	Nelson	Taylor	2-3	T3rd	2.0
4-7	At Ana.	W	5-3		12	10	Pettitte	Langston	Rivera	3-3	T2nd	1.0
4-8	At Ana.	L	9-10	(12)	19	15	James	Nelson		3-4	T3rd	1.5
4-9	At Ana.	W	12-5		18	9	Wells	Watson		4-4	T2nd	1.5
4-11	Oak.	L	1-3	(12)	7	7	Small	Nelson		4-5	T4th	2.5
4-13†	Oak.	W	3-2		11	6	Pettitte	Telgheder	Rivera	5-5	T2nd	2.5
4-13‡	Oak.	L	4-7		8	14	Prieto	Mendoza	Taylor	5-6	T4th	3.0
4-14	Ana.	L	1-5		5	7	Dickson	Rogers		5-7	5th	4.0
4-15	Ana.	L	5-6		9	14	Hasegawa	Rivera	James	5-8	5th	5.0
4-16	At Mil.	L	4-7		7	12	Mercedes	Cone	Jones	5-9	5th	5.0
4-17	At Mil.	L	4-5		8	12	Wickman	Lloyd		5-10	5th	6.0
4-18	At Chi.	W	10-4		14	10	Mendoza	Navarro		6-10	5th	5.5
4-19	At Chi.	W	3-2		4	4	Rogers	T. Castillo	Rivera	7-10	4th	5.0
4-20	At Chi.	L	7-8	(11)	12	16	Levine	Boehringer		7-11	5th	6.0
4-21	At Chi.	W	4-3		9	8	Cone	Drabek	Rivera	8-11	5th	5.0
4-22	Mil.	W	10-2		14	6	Pettitte	D'Amico		9-11	T4th	5.0
4-23	Mil.	W	10-5		13	7	Rogers	McDonald	Lloyd	10-11	4th	4.0
4-25	Chi.	L	3-9		5	16	Alvarez	Wells		10-12	4th	4.5
4-26	Chi.	W	10-2		16	9	Cone	Baldwin	Rivera	11-12	4th	4.5
4-27	Chi.	W	7-1		9	4	Pettitte	Drabek		12-12	3rd	3.5
4-28	Sea.	W	6-5		13	9	Nelson	Ayala	Rivera	13-12	T2nd	3.0
4-29	Sea.	L	5-7		9	12	McCarthy	Mecir		13-13	T2nd	4.0
4-30	Sea.	W	3-2		8	8	Wells	D. Martinez	Rivera	14-13	T2nd	4.0
5-2	At K.C.	W	9-1		7	7	Cone	Pittsley	Rivera	15-13	T2nd	4.5
5-3	At K.C.	L	1-2		8	6	Belcher	Pettitte		15-14	T2nd	4.5
5-4	At K.C.	W	13-5		19	8	Boehringer	Rusch		16-14	2nd	4.5
5-5	Min.	L	8-9		9	12	Swindell	Mecir		16-15	2nd	4.5
5-6	Min.	W	7-2		10	8	Wells	Aldred		17-15	2nd	4.5
5-7	Tex.	W	5-2		8	9	Cone	Burkett	Rivera	18-15	2nd	4.5
5-8	Tex.	W	5-4		10	11	Pettitte	Oliver	Rivera	19-15	2nd	4.5
5-9	K.C.	L	5-7	(12)	12	9	Veres	Boehringer		19-16	2nd	4.5
5-10	K.C.	W	5-2		8	11	Mendoza	Appier	Rivera	20-16	2nd	3.5
5-11	K.C.	W	3-2		7	5	Wells	Rosado	Rivera	21-16	2nd	3.5
5-13	At Min.	W	11-2		15	11	Cone	Robertson		22-16	2nd	4.0
5-14	At Min.	W	6-5	(12)	12	13	Boehringer	Guardado	Rivera	23-16	2nd	3.0
5-15	At Tex.	W	8-2		11	9	Rogers	Alberro		24-16	2nd	2.0
5-16	At Tex.	L	0-6		4	6	Santana	Wells	Patterson	24-17	2nd	3.0
5-17	At Tex.	W	11-5		20	12	Mendoza	Burkett		25-17	2nd	3.0
5-18	At Tex.	L	2-4		9	8	Oliver	Cone	Wetteland	25-18	2nd	4.0
5-20	Tor.	L	0-2		5	8	Hentgen	Pettitte		25-19	2nd	5.0
5-21	Tor.	L	1-4		4	9	Clemens	Rogers		25-20	2nd	6.0
5-22	Bos.	L	2-8		9	19	Gordon	Wells		25-21	T2nd	6.5
5-23	Bos.	L	3-9		6	12	Sele	Nelson		25-22	T2nd	6.5
5-24	Bos.	W	4-2		8	6	Rivera	Wasdin		26-22	2nd	6.5
5-26	Bal.	L	6-8		10	11	Boskie	Pettitte	Myers	26-23	3rd	7.0
5-27	Bal.	L	6-10		9	10	Kamieniecki	Rogers	Benitez	26-24	3rd	8.0
5-28	At Tor.	W	6-4		6	5	Wells	Guzman	Rivera	27-24	2nd	8.0
5-29	At Tor.	W	4-0		10	5	Cone	Williams	Nelson	28-24	2nd	7.5
5-30	At Bos.	L	4-10		9	18	Hammond	Mendoza		28-25	2nd	8.5
5-31	At Bos.	W	7-2		9	7	Pettitte	Wakefield		29-25	2nd	8.5
6-1	At Bos.	W	11-6	(15)	16	17	Nelson	Lacy		30-25	2nd	8.0
6-2	At Bos.	W	5-2		14	8	Wells	Sele	Rivera	31-25	2nd	7.5
6-3	At Bal.	L	5-7	(10)	10	14	Myers	Mecir		31-26	2nd	8.5
6-4	At Bal.	L	7-9		13	10	Orosco	Nelson	Myers	31-27	2nd	9.5
6-6	Mil.	W	6-3		11	6	Rogers	Mercedes	Rivera	32-27	2nd	8.5
6-7	Mil.	W	2-0		5	4	Wells	Karl	Rivera	33-27	2nd	7.5
6-8	Mil.	W	3-1		7	8	Cone	D'Amico	Rivera	34-27	2nd	7.5
6-10	Chi.	W	12-1		15	7	Pettitte	Navarro		35-27	2nd	8.5
6-11	Chi.	W	7-5		9	8	Stanton	McElroy	Rivera	36-27	2nd	7.5
6-13	At Fla.	L	1-2	(12)	5	6	Cook	Mecir		36-28	2nd	8.0
6-15†	At Fla.	W	8-5		9	7	Stanton	Cook	Rivera	37-28		
6-15‡	At Fla.	L	5-6		9	10	Nen	Rivera		37-29		9.0
6-16	N.Y. (NL)	L	0-6		9	9	Mlicki	Pettitte		37-30	2nd	9.0
6-17	N.Y. (NL)	W	6-3		11	7	Wells	Reynoso	Rivera	38-30	2nd	9.0
6-18	N.Y. (NL)	W	3-2	(10)	8	3	Stanton	McMichael		39-30	2nd	8.0
6-20	At Cle.	W	7-1		12	5	Gooden	Nagy		40-30	2nd	7.0
6-21	At Cle.	L	4-13		10	15	Hershiser	Pettitte		40-31	2nd	8.0

Date	Opp.	Res.	Score	(inn.*)	Hits	Opp. hits	Winning pitcher	Losing pitcher	Save	Record	Pos.	GB
6-22	At Cle.	L	2-5		8	10	Anderson	Wells	M. Jackson	40-32	2nd	9.0
6-23	At Det.	W	5-2		7	4	Cone	Lira	Rivera	41-32	2nd	8.0
6-24	At Det.	W	12-9		13	14	Lloyd	Myers	Rivera	42-32	2nd	8.0
6-25	At Det.	W	3-1		5	9	Stanton	Thompson	Rivera	43-32	2nd	8.0
6-27	Cle.	W	3-2		7	7	Gooden	Hershiser	Rivera	44-32	2nd	6.5
6-28	Cle.	L	8-12		12	19	Plunk	Rogers		44-33	2nd	6.5
6-29	Cle.	W	11-10		15	13	Rivera	Mesa		45-33	2nd	5.5
6-30	Atl.	W	1-0	(10)	12	6	Stanton	Bielecki		46-33	2nd	5.5
7-1	Atl.	L	1-3		6	10	Neagle	Mendoza	Wohlers	46-34	2nd	6.5
7-2	Atl.	L	0-2		3	7	Maddux	Gooden		46-35	2nd	7.5
7-3	At Tor.	W	3-1		10	6	Wells	Williams	Rivera	47-35	2nd	7.5
7-4	At Tor.	L	0-1		2	6	Escobar	Cone		47-36	2nd	8.0
7-5	At Tor.	W	8-0		14	6	Pettitte	Hentgen		48-36	2nd	7.0
7-6	At Tor.	L	0-2		4	6	Clemens	Mendoza		48-37	2nd	7.0
7-10	Det.	W	10-3		10	8	Irabu	Olivares		49-37	2nd	6.5
7-11	Det.	W	3-0		6	6	Pettitte	Moehler	Rivera	50-37	2nd	5.5
7-12	Det.	W	6-2		15	4	Cone	Lira	Rivera	51-37	2nd	4.5
7-13	Det.	L	1-3		7	11	Blair	Gooden	Jones	51-38	2nd	4.5
7-14	Cle.	L	2-3	(10)	8	10	M. Jackson	Rivera		51-39	2nd	5.5
7-15	Cle.	W	12-6		17	13	Irabu	Nagy	Mendoza	52-39	2nd	5.5
7-16	At Chi.	W	11-5		12	9	Pettitte	Alvarez		53-39	2nd	4.5
7-17	At Chi.	W	4-2		9	8	Cone	D. Darwin	Rivera	54-39	2nd	3.5
7-18	At Mil.	L	4-6		10	11	D'Amico	Gooden	Fetters	54-40	2nd	3.5
7-19	At Mil.	W	8-0		14	3	Wells	Mercedes		55-40	2nd	3.5
7-20	At Mil.	L	2-6		8	7	Karl	Irabu		55-41	2nd	3.5
7-21	At Mil.	W	7-3		12	9	Pettitte	Florie	Stanton	56-41	2nd	3.5
7-22	Ana.	W	9-2		12	5	Cone	Springer		57-41	2nd	3.5
7-23	Ana.	W	5-4		10	9	Nelson	Hasegawa		58-41	2nd	3.5
7-25	Sea.	L	1-8		9	10	Moyer	Wells		58-42	2nd	3.5
7-26	Sea.	L	7-9		10	11	Ayala	Irabu	Charlton	58-43	2nd	4.5
7-27	Sea.	L	2-3		9	9	Fassero	Pettitte	Wells	58-44	2nd	5.5
7-28	Oak.	W	4-3		7	6	Rivera	Small		59-44	2nd	5.5
7-29	Oak.	W	7-4		9	8	Gooden	Reyes	Rivera	60-44	2nd	5.5
7-30	Oak.	W	7-0		13	3	Wells	Karsay		61-44	2nd	5.5
8-1	Min.	W	8-3		14	13	Pettitte	Robertson		62-44	2nd	5.0
8-2	Min.	L	4-5		9	6	Swindell	Cone	Aguilera	62-45	2nd	6.0
8-3	Min.	W	6-5		9	7	Gooden	Hawkins	Rivera	63-45	2nd	6.0
8-4	At K.C.	W	5-4		8	7	Wells	Rusch	Rivera	64-45	2nd	5.5
8-5	At K.C.	W	4-1		9	11	Rogers	Appier		65-45	2nd	4.5
8-6	At Tex.	L	2-6		11	10	Oliver	Pettitte		65-46	2nd	5.5
8-7	At Tex.	W	4-2		11	4	Cone	Witt	Rivera	66-46	2nd	5.0
8-8	At Min.	L	1-9		11	13	Hawkins	Gooden		66-47	2nd	6.0
8-9	At Min.	W	4-1		8	8	Wells	Radke	Rivera	67-47	2nd	5.0
8-10	At Min.	W	9-6		16	13	Mendoza	T. Miller	Rivera	68-47	2nd	5.0
8-11	At Min.	W	11-0		21	5	Pettitte	Robertson		69-47	2nd	4.5
8-12	K.C.	L	4-6		11	12	Perez	Cone	Montgomery	69-48	2nd	5.5
8-13	K.C.	W	9-3		12	11	Irabu	Belcher		70-48	2nd	4.5
8-14	K.C.	W	10-5		13	10	Wells	Olson	Rivera	71-48	2nd	4.0
8-15	Tex.	W	5-2		12	5	Gooden	T. Clark	Rivera	72-48	2nd	3.5
8-16	Tex.	L	5-8	(10)	6	14	Wetteland	Mendoza		72-49	2nd	4.5
8-17	Tex.	W	8-0		13	3	Mendoza	Witt		73-49	2nd	4.5
8-19	At Ana.	L	4-12		7	12	Dickson	Wells		73-50	2nd	5.5
8-20†	At Ana.	W	7-3		12	6	Gooden	Hill	Mendoza	74-50		
8-20‡	At Ana.	W	8-5		12	9	Irabu	Langston	Rivera	75-50	2nd	5.0
8-21	At Ana.	W	4-3	(12)	10	12	Stanton	Harris	Nelson	76-50	2nd	5.0
8-22	At Sea.	L	5-9		7	14	Fassero	Rogers		76-51	2nd	6.0
8-23	At Sea.	W	10-8	(11)	16	14	Rivera	Slocumb	Stanton	77-51	2nd	6.0
8-24	At Sea.	L	3-5		6	7	Ayala	Wells	Timlin	77-52	2nd	7.0
8-26	At Oak.	W	18-2		22	7	Pettitte	Oquist		78-52	2nd	6.0
8-27	At Oak.	L	7-8		14	15	Mathews	Nelson		78-53	2nd	7.0
8-29	Mon.	L	3-4		8	9	Telford	Rivera	Urbina	78-54	2nd	7.5
8-30	Mon.	W	2-7		5	11	Martinez	Wells		78-55	2nd	7.5
8-31	Mon.	W	3-2		8	9	Pettitte	Johnson	Rivera	79-55	2nd	6.5
9-1	At Phi.	L	1-5		7	11	Schilling	Irabu		79-56	2nd	6.5
9-2	At Phi.	L	0-5		3	10	Grace	Rogers		79-57	2nd	6.5
9-3	At Phi.	L	4-5		7	11	Spradlin	Stanton		79-58	2nd	6.5
9-4	Bal.	L	2-5		8	14	Krivda	Wells	Myers	79-59	2nd	7.5
9-5	Bal.	L	9-13		16	15	Key	Irabu		79-60	2nd	8.5
9-6	Bal.	L	1-4		4	8	Erickson	Mendoza		79-61	2nd	9.5
9-7	Bal.	W	10-3		12	11	Rogers	Mussina		80-61	2nd	8.5
9-9	At Bos.	W	8-6		13	9	Banks	Lowe	Rivera	81-61	2nd	8.0
9-10	At Bos.	L	2-5		6	12	Sele	Wells	Gordon	81-62	2nd	8.5
9-11	At Bal.	W	14-2		11	7	Pettitte	Key		82-62	2nd	7.5
9-12	At Bal.	W	13-5		17	12	Mendoza	Erickson		83-62	2nd	6.5
9-13	At Bal.	L	1-6		3	7	Mussina	Rogers		83-63	2nd	7.5
9-14	At Bal.	W	8-2		10	7	Gooden	Kamieniecki		84-63	2nd	6.5

Date	Opp.	Res.	Score	(inn.*)	Hits	Opp. hits	Winning pitcher	Losing pitcher	Save	Record	Pos.	GB
9-15	Bos.	W	7-6		11	12	Rivera	Corsi		85-63	2nd	6.0
9-16†	Bos.	W	2-0		9	5	Pettitte	Wasdin	Rivera	86-63		
9-16‡	Bos.	W	4-3		9	7	Banks	Checo	Rivera	87-63	2nd	5.0
9-17	Det.	W	6-2		15	6	Mendoza	Moehler		88-63	2nd	4.0
9-18	Det.	L	7-9	(11)	12	15	Jones	Borowski	Miceli	88-64	2nd	5.0
9-19	Tor.	L	0-3		8	6	Daal	Gooden	Escobar	88-65	2nd	5.0
9-20	Tor.	W	4-3	(11)	10	10	Banks	Janzen		89-65	2nd	5.0
9-21	Tor.	W	5-4	(10)	11	10	Boehringer	Almanzar		90-65	2nd	4.0
9-22	Tor.	W	8-1		11	7	Wells	Hentgen		91-65	2nd	3.0
9-23	At Cle.	L	9-10		13	12	Mesa	Nelson		91-66	2nd	4.0
9-24	At Cle.	W	8-4		13	9	Gooden	Anderson		92-66	2nd	4.0
9-25	At Cle.	W	5-4	(10)	9	6	Mendoza	Shuey	Stanton	93-66	2nd	3.0
9-26	At Det.	W	8-2		10	1	Rivera	Jones		94-66	2nd	2.0
9-27	At Det.	W	6-1		11	6	Wells	Moehler		95-66	2nd	2.0
9-28	At Det.	W	7-2		11	5	Irabu	Keagle		96-66	2nd	2.0

Monthly records: April (14-13), May (15-12), June (17-8), July (15-11), August (18-11), September (17-11).
*Innings, if other than nine. †First game of doubleheader. ‡Second game of doubleheader.

HIGHLIGHTS

High point: The Yankees clinched their third straight postseason berth with a 4-3 victory over Toronto at Yankee Stadium on September 20. The Yankees won nine of their final 10 games and appeared strong heading into the playoffs as the A.L. wild-card team.

Low point: The Yankees lost their chance to repeat as World Champions with a 4-3 defeat to the Indians in Game 5 of the Division Series, one day after a heartbreaking, 3-2 defeat in which they lost a 2-1 lead when closer Mariano Rivera allowed an opposite-field home run to Sandy Alomar.

Turning point: David Cone left an 8-0 victory August 17 over Texas in the second inning, complaining of pain in his right shoulder. The Yankees did not know at that time that the problem would hamper Cone the remainder of the season.

Most valuable player: Tino Martinez. He emerged as one of the top power hitters in the game, challenging ex-teammate Ken Griffey Jr. for the home run title until the beginning of August and winding up with 44 homers.

Most valuable pitcher: Andy Pettitte. He followed his brilliant sophomore campaign with another superb season, going 18-7 with a 2.88 ERA. Pettitte pitched 240 ⅓ innings, allowing 233 hits, walking 65 and striking out 166.

Most improved player: David Martinez. Few had any idea he could become this kind of power threat in his second year in the Bronx. He provided a preview of things to come April 2, in the second game of the season, with three homers in Seattle.

Most pleasant surprises: Martinez, Luis Sojo, Rey Sanchez, Chad Curtis and Jorge Posada. Sojo and Sanchez played admirably at second base, which had been considered a position of concern. Curtis played wonderfully in center field and left field after his acquisition from the Indians, a move that was suggested by club owner George Steinbrenner. Posada showed good pop and looks like he has a chance to be the club's catcher of the future.

Biggest disappointments: Hideki Irabu, Cecil Fielder. Both fit this category in more ways than one. The rotund Irabu

bombed in his first season after a big bidding war and a huge buildup, showing a questionable repertoire of pitches and a hellacious temper. The beefy Fielder showed little at all after making a ruckus during spring training over his contract situation.

Key injuries: Cone's shoulder problem that surfaced August 17 and rendered him out or ineffective thereafter cost the Yankees dearly. Darryl Strawberry's knee injury ruined his season and he wound up with only three hits in 29 at-bats. Fielder missed two months after tearing a ligament in his right thumb. Bernie Williams had two stays on the disabled list with hamstring problems. Tim Raines missed almost half the year with various hamstring troubles. Pat Kelly missed the final two months with a nerve problem in his lower left leg. Mariano Rivera had some shoulder pain at year's end but never went on the D.L.

Notables: Wade Boggs became the 37th player in major league history to reach 2,800 hits with his final hit of the season, a single off the Tigers' Brian Moehler.

—JON HEYMAN

RECORDS

1997 regular-season record: 96-66 (2nd in A.L. East); 47-33 at home; 49-33 on road; 34-29 vs. East; 38-17 vs. Central; 24-20 vs. West; 24-26 vs. lefthanded starters; 72-40 vs. righthanded starters; 85-57 on grass; 11-9 on turf; 37-23 in daytime; 59-43 at night; 23-16 in one-run games; 9-9 in extra-inning games; 2-0 in doubleheaders.

Team record past five years: 425-318 (.572, ranks 2nd in league in that span).

TEAM LEADERS

Batting average: Bernie Williams (.328).
At-bats: Derek Jeter (654).
Runs: Derek Jeter (116).
Hits: Derek Jeter (190).
Total bases: Tino Martinez (343).
Doubles: Paul O'Neill (42).
Triples: Derek Jeter (7).
Home runs: Tino Martinez (44).
Runs batted in: Tino Martinez (141).

Stolen bases: Derek Jeter (23).
Slugging percentage: Tino Martinez (.577).
On-base percentage: Bernie Williams (.408).
Wins: Andy Pettitte (18).
Earned-run average: David Cone (2.82).
Complete games: David Wells (5).
Shutouts: David Wells (2).
Saves: Mariano Rivera (43).
Innings pitched: Andy Pettitte (240.1).
Strikeouts: David Cone (222).

GAMES BY POSITION

Catcher: Joe Girardi 111, Jorge Posada 60, Mike Figga 1.
First base: Tino Martinez 150, Mike Stanley 12, Cecil Fielder 8, Ivan Cruz 3, Paul O'Neill 2, Luis Sojo 2.
Second base: Luis Sojo 72, Pat Kelly 48, Mariano Duncan 41, Rey Sanchez 37, Homer Bush 8, Andy Fox 5, Charlie Hayes 5.
Third base: Charlie Hayes 98, Wade Boggs 76, Andy Fox 11, Luis Sojo 3.
Shortstop: Derek Jeter 159, Rey Sanchez 6, Luis Sojo 4, Andy Fox 2.
Outfield: Paul O'Neill 146, Bernie Williams 128, Chad Curtis 92, Tim Raines 57, Mark Whiten 57, Scott Pose 45, Mariano Duncan 6, Darryl Strawberry 4, Andy Fox 2, Ivan Cruz 1.
Designated hitter: Cecil Fielder 89, Wade Boggs 19, Pat Kelly 16, Mike Stanley 16, Tim Raines 13, Tino Martinez 7, Mark Whiten 7, Pete Incaviglia 5, Scott Pose 5, Ivan Cruz 4, Darryl Strawberry 4, Mariano Duncan 2, Andy Fox 2, Paul O'Neill 2, Mike Figga 1.

TOP DRAFT CHOICES

1a. **Tyrell Godwin,** OF, East Bladen H.S., N.C.
1b. **Ryan Bradley,** RHP, Arizona State Univ.
2. **Jason Henry,** RHP, U. of Illinois-Chicago.
3. **Mike Knowles,** RHP, Palatka (Fla.) H.S.
4. **Dion Washington,** OF, J.C. of Southern Idaho.
5. **Randy Choate,** LHP, Florida State Univ.
6. **John Darjean,** OF, Dallas Baptist Univ.
7. **Scott Wiggins,** LHP, Northern Kentucky U.
8. **Jeremy Morris,** OF, Florida State Univ.
9. **Randy Flores,** LHP, Univ. of Southern California.
10. **David Parrish,** C, Esperanza H.S., Yorba Linda, Calif.

OAKLAND ATHLETICS
AMERICAN LEAGUE WEST DIVISION

Athletics Schedule

Home games shaded. *—All-Star Game at Coors Field (Colorado). D—Day game (any game starting before 5 p.m.).

March

SUN	MON	TUE	WED	THU	FRI	SAT
	31					

April

SUN	MON	TUE	WED	THU	FRI	SAT
			1 BOS	2 D BOS	3 NYY	4 D NYY
5 D NYY	6 CLE	7	8 D CLE	9	10 D NYY	11 D NYY
12 D NYY	13 BOS	14 BOS	15 BOS	16 KC	17 KC	18 D KC
19 D KC	20 MIN	21 MIN	22 D MIN	23	24 BAL	25 D BAL
26 D BAL	27 TB	28 TB	29 D CLE	30 CLE		

May

SUN	MON	TUE	WED	THU	FRI	SAT
					1 TOR	2 D TOR
3 D TOR	4 TOR	5 DET	6 D DET	7 DET	8 CWS	9 D CWS
10 D CWS	11	12 TOR	13 TOR	14 DET	15 DET	16 CWS
17 D CWS	18 D CWS	19 ANA	20 ANA	21 ANA	22 BAL	23 BAL
24 D BAL	25 D TB	26 D TB	27	28	29 KC	30 KC
31 D KC						

June

SUN	MON	TUE	WED	THU	FRI	SAT
	1 MIN	2 D MIN	3 TEX	4 D TEX	5 ARZ	6 D ARZ
7 D ARZ	8 LA	9 LA	10 LA	11 SEA	12 D SEA	13 D SEA
14 D SEA	15	16 TEX	17 TEX	18 D TEX	19 SEA	20 SEA
21 SEA	22 SF	23 D SF	24 D SF	25 SF	26 COL	27 COL
28 D COL	29	30 D SD				

July

SUN	MON	TUE	WED	THU	FRI	SAT
			1 D SD	2 D SD	3 ANA	4 ANA
5 D ANA	6	7	* 8	9 TEX	10 D TEX	11 D TEX
12 D TEX	13 ANA	14 D ANA	15 KC	16 KC	17 MIN	18 D MIN
19 D MIN	20	21 BAL	22 BAL	23 BAL	24 TB	25 TB
26 D TB	27 TB	28 BOS	29 D BOS	30 BOS	31 CLE	

August

SUN	MON	TUE	WED	THU	FRI	SAT
						1 CLE
2 D CLE	3 NYY	4 NYY	5 NYY	6 D	7 TOR	8 D TOR
9 D TOR	10 CWS	11 CWS	12 D CWS	13	14 DET	15 DET
16 D DET	17 TOR	18 TOR	19 CWS	20 CWS	21 DET	22 D DET
23 DET	24 BOS	25 BOS	26 BOS	27 CLE	28 CLE	29 D CLE
30 CLE	31 CLE					

September

SUN	MON	TUE	WED	THU	FRI	SAT
		1 NYY	2 NYY	3	4 TB	5 TB
6 D TB	7	8 BAL	9 D BAL	10	11 MIN	12 MIN
13 MIN	14 KC	15 KC	16 SEA	17 D SEA	18 TEX	19 TEX
20 D TEX	21 SEA	22 SEA	23 SEA	24 ANA	25 ANA	26 D ANA
27 D ANA						

1998 SEASON
CLUB DIRECTORY

Owners
Stephen C. Schott
Ken Hofmann
President
Sandy Alderson
Chief financial officer
Michael Crowley
Special assistants to the g.m.
Bill Rigney, J.P. Ricciardi
General manager
Billy Beane
Director of player development
Keith Lieppman
Director of scouting
Grady Fuson
Assistant director of scouting
Dave Seifert
Director of baseball administration
Pam Pitts
Traveling secretary
Mickey Morabito
Baseball information manager
Mike Selleck
Admin. asst., baseball operations
J. Raki Bogan
Sr. dir. of broadcasting communications
Ken Pries
Broadcasting manager
Robert Buan
Public relations manager
Eric Carrington
Sr. director of stadium operations
David Rinetti
Director of corporate sales
Franklin Lowe

Director of sales and marketing
David Alioto
Director of events and promotions
Susan Bress
Director of ticket sales
Paul Solby
Admin. assistant, executive office
Erin Buckert
Director of information resources
David Lozow
Team physician
Dr. Allan Pont
Team orthopedist
Dr. Jerrald Goldman
Trainers
Steven Sayles
Larry Davis
Equipment manager
Steve Vucinich
Visiting clubhouse manager
Mike Thalblum
Special assignment scout
Dick Bogard
National crosschecker
Ron Hopkins
Pacific Rim coordinator
Eric Kubota
Scouts
Tony Arias, Steve Bowden, Tom Clark, Ron Elam, Ruben Escalera, Tim Holt, John Kuehl, Rick Magnante, Gary McGraw, Billy Merkel, Chris Pittaro, John Poloni, Jim Pransky, Will Schock, Mike Soper, Rich Sparks, Ron Vaughn

MINOR LEAGUE AFFILIATES

Class	Team	League	Manager
AAA	Edmonton	Pacific Coast	Mike Quade
AA	Huntsville	Southern	Jeffrey Leonard
A	Modesto	California	To be announced
A	Visalia	California	To be announced
A	Southern Oregon	Northwest	Greg Sparks
Rookie	Scotttsdale A's	Arizona	John Kuehl

BROADCAST INFORMATION

Radio: KNEW-AM (910).
TV: KRON-TV (Channel 4).
Cable TV: Fox Sports Bay Area.

SPRING TRAINING

Ballpark (city): Phoenix Stadium (Phoenix, Ariz.).
Ticket information: 602-392-0074.

SPRING TRAINING ROSTER

Manager—Art Howe (18).
Coaches—Bob Cluck (3), Duffy Dyer (9), Brad Fischer (35), Gary Jones (47), Denny Walling, Ron Washington (38).

No.	PITCHERS	B/T	Ht./Wt.	Born	1997 clubs
40	Adams, Willie	R/R	6-7/211	10-8-72	Oakland, Edmonton
60	Bennett, Tom	R/R	6-4/180	5-13-76	Modesto
44	Bochtler, Doug	R/R	6-3/200	7-5-70	San Diego
49	Candiotti, Tom	R/R	6-2/221	8-31-57	Los Angeles
63	D'Amico, Jeff	R/R	6-3/195	11-9-74	Edmonton, Modesto
36	Fetters, Mike	R/R	6-4/224	12-19-64	Milwaukee, Tucson
24	Groom, Buddy	L/L	6-2/205	7-10-65	Oakland
51	Haynes, Jimmy	R/R	6-4/185	9-5-72	Rochester, Edmonton, Oakland
62	King, Bill	R/R	6-5/215	2-18-73	Huntsville
58	Kubinski, Tim	L/L	6-4/205	1-20-72	Edmonton, Oakland
29	Mathews, T.J.	R/R	6-2/200	1-19-70	St. Louis, Oakland
32	Mohler, Mike	R/L	6-2/209	7-26-68	Oakland
45	Oquist, Mike	R/R	6-2/170	5-30-68	Edmonton, Oakland, Modesto
48	Prieto, Ariel	R/R	6-3/230	10-22-69	Oakland, Edmonton
57	Rigby, Brad	R/R	6-6/195	5-14-73	Edmonton, Oakland
37	Rogers, Kenny	L/L	6-1/205	11-10-64	New York A.L.
30	Small, Aaron	R/R	6-5/214	11-23-71	Edmonton, Oakland
59	Stein, Blake	R/R	6-7/210	8-3-73	Arkansas, Huntsville
22	Taylor, Bill	R/R	6-8/232	10-16-61	Oakland
52	Witasick, Jay	R/R	6-4/234	8-28-72	Modesto, Edmonton, Oakland

No.	CATCHERS	B/T	Ht./Wt.	Born	1997 clubs
	Berryhill, Damon	B/R	6-0/205	12-3-63	San Francisco, Phoenix
61	Hernandez, Ramon	R/R	6-0/170	5-20-76	Visalia, Huntsville
	Hinch, A.J.	R/R	6-1/195	5-15-74	Modesto, Edmonton
19	Williams, George	B/R	5-10/190	4-22-69	Oakland, Modesto, Edmonton

No.	INFIELDERS	B/T	Ht./Wt.	Born	1997 clubs
7	Abbott, Kurt	R/R	6-0/190	6-2-69	Florida
10	Bellhorn, Mark	B/R	6-0/190	8-23-74	Edmonton, Oakland
6	Blowers, Mike	R/R	6-2/210	4-24-65	Seattle
26	Bournigal, Rafael	R/R	5-11/165	5-12-66	Oakland, Modesto
16	Giambi, Jason	L/R	6-2/218	1-8-71	Oakland
17	Magadan, Dave	L/R	6-4/210	9-30-62	Oakland
2	McDonald, Jason	B/R	5-8/185	3-20-72	Edmonton, Oakland
21	Spiezio, Scott	B/R	6-2/205	9-21-72	Oakland, Southern Oregon
4	Tejada, Miguel	R/R	5-10/170	5-25-76	Huntsville, Oakland
39	Velandia, Jorge	R/R	5-9/160	1-12-75	Las Vegas, San Diego

No.	OUTFIELDERS	B/T	Ht./Wt.	Born	1997 clubs
8	Christenson, Ryan	R/R	5-11/175	3-28-74	Visalia, Huntsville, Edmonton
14	Grieve, Ben	L/R	6-4/200	5-4-76	Huntsville, Edmonton, Oakland
20	Lesher, Brian	R/L	6-5/205	3-5-71	Edmonton, Oakland
5	Mack, Shane	R/R	6-0/190	12-7-63	Boston
12	Stairs, Matt	L/R	5-9/212	2-27-68	Oakland
11	Young, Ernie	R/R	6-1/214	7-8-69	Oakland, Edmonton

BALLPARK INFORMATION

Ballpark (capacity, surface)
Oakland-Alameda County Coliseum (43,662, grass)

Address
Oakland Athletics
7677 Oakport St., Suite 200
Oakland, CA 94621

Business phone
510-638-4900

Ticket information
510-638-4627

Ticket prices
$22 (plaza club)
$20 (MVP infield)
$17.50 (MVP)
$14 (field level-infield)
$13 (field level, plaza-infield)
$9 (plaza)
$5 (upper reserved)
$4 (bleachers)

Field dimensions (from home plate)
To left field at foul line, 330 feet
To center field, 400 feet
To right field at foul line, 330 feet

First game played
April 17, 1968 (Orioles 4, Athletics 1)

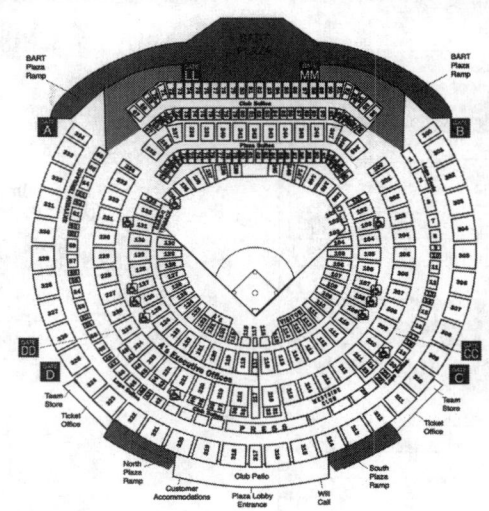

1998 SEASON *Oakland Athletics*

Date	Opp.	Res.	Score	(inn.*)	Hits	Opp. hits	Winning pitcher	Losing pitcher	Save	Record	Pos.	GB
4-2	Cle.	L	7-9		11	13	Kline	Wengert	Shuey	0-1	T3rd	1.0
4-3	Cle.	W	5-4		8	6	Lewis	Plunk	Taylor	1-1	T2nd	0.5
4-4	N.Y.	W	4-2		9	11	Acre	Weathers	Taylor	2-1	T1st	....
4-5	N.Y.	L	5-10		10	13	Gooden	Mohler	Rivera	2-2	T1st	....
4-6	N.Y.	W	3-0		4	7	Acre	Nelson	Taylor	3-2	1st	+0.5
4-7	Bos.	W	6-2		8	6	Lewis	Gordon	Taylor	4-2	1st	+1.5
4-8	Bos.	L	7-13		12	17	Trlicek	Wengert	Henry	4-3	1st	+1.0
4-9	Bos.	W	4-3	(10)	10	10	Small	Trlicek		5-3	1st	+1.0
4-11	At N.Y.	W	3-1	(12)	7	7	Small	Nelson		6-3	1st	+1.0
4-13†	At N.Y.	L	2-3		6	11	Pettitte	Telgheder	Rivera	6-4		
4-13‡	At N.Y.	W	7-4		14	8	Prieto	Mendoza	Taylor	7-4	1st	+1.0
4-14	At Bos.	L	1-10		3	14	Wakefield	Adams		7-5	T1st	....
4-15	At Bos.	L	2-7		7	11	Sele	Karsay		7-6	2nd	1.0
4-16	At Tor.	L	3-4		10	9	Crabtree	Taylor		7-7	3rd	2.0
4-17	At Tor.	L	4-5		7	13	Quantrill	Groom	Timlin	7-8	3rd	3.0
4-18	At Det.	W	9-5		10	12	Groom	Myers		8-8	3rd	2.0
4-19	At Det.	W	7-1		13	3	Adams	Thompson		9-8	2nd	1.0
4-20	At Det.	L	2-9		8	12	Moehler	Karsay		9-9	3rd	2.0
4-22	Min.	L	3-5		5	7	Radke	Mohler	Aguilera	9-10	3rd	3.5
4-23	Min.	W	6-1		6	11	Prieto	Robertson	Small	10-10	3rd	2.5
4-24	Min.	W	12-11	(11)	19	21	Wengert	Aguilera		11-10	3rd	2.0
4-25	K.C.	L	3-10		8	13	Appier	Adams		11-11	T3rd	3.0
4-26	K.C.	W	7-6	(11)	15	14	Small	M. Williams		12-11	3rd	2.0
4-27	K.C.	L	1-7		6	13	Belcher	Mohler		12-12	T3rd	3.0
4-29	At Cle.	L	4-10		8	12	Nagy	Prieto	M. Jackson	12-13	4th	3.5
4-30	At Cle.	W	11-9	(10)	15	15	Taylor	Mesa	Wengert	13-13	T3rd	2.5
5-1	At Cle.	L	1-7		4	8	McDowell	Adams		13-14	4th	3.0
5-2	At Bal.	L	1-7		5	13	Key	Karsay		13-15	4th	4.0
5-3	At Bal.	W	4-3		7	9	Small	Myers	Taylor	14-15	4th	3.0
5-4	At Bal.	L	0-11		4	15	Coppinger	Prieto	Johnson	14-16	4th	4.0
5-5	At Mil.	L	7-11		13	11	Karl	Telgheder		14-17	4th	4.5
5-6	At Mil.	W	6-5		12	9	Adams	Florie	Taylor	15-17	4th	4.5
5-7	At Mil.	L	0-1		4	7	Fetters	Montgomery	Jones	15-18	4th	5.0
5-8	At Chi.	L	6-10		5	16	Baldwin	Mohler		15-19	4th	5.0
5-9	At Chi.	L	2-3	(10)	7	11	Hernandez	Small		15-20	4th	6.0
5-10	At Chi.	L	8-9		7	17	Levine	Taylor		15-21	4th	7.0
5-11	At Chi.	L	5-8		7	11	Alvarez	Adams	Hernandez	15-22	4th	7.0
5-12	Bal.	L	1-5		6	6	Key	Karsay	Benitez	15-23	4th	7.0
5-13	Bal.	L	3-7		7	13	Mussina	Mohler		15-24	4th	8.0
5-14	Mil.	W	7-4		11	8	Prieto	Eldred		16-24	4th	8.0
5-15	Mil.	W	6-5		12	13	Wengert	Wickman	Taylor	17-24	4th	7.0
5-16	Chi.	L	2-6		10	10	Alvarez	Adams	Hernandez	17-25	4th	7.0
5-17	Chi.	L	6-7		8	13	D. Darwin	Karsay	Hernandez	17-26	4th	7.0
5-18	Chi.	L	4-10		6	12	Baldwin	Mohler		17-27	4th	8.0
5-20	At Tex.	L	3-8		7	14	Witt	Prieto		17-28	4th	9.0
5-21	At Tex.	W	7-3		9	9	Telgheder	Santana		18-28	4th	8.0
5-22	At Tex.	L	7-10		13	14	Burkett	Oquist	Wetteland	18-29	4th	9.0
5-23	At Min.	W	8-4		11	9	Karsay	Radke	Taylor	19-29	4th	8.0
5-24	At Min.	L	4-7		8	13	Robertson	Mohler	Aguilera	19-30	4th	9.0
5-25	At Min.	L	6-7	(10)	11	9	Aguilera	Taylor		19-31	4th	9.0
5-26	At K.C.	W	2-1	(11)	7	9	Adams	M. Williams	Small	20-31	4th	8.0
5-27	At K.C.	W	8-6	(10)	7	10	Taylor	Pichardo	Johnson	21-31	4th	8.0
5-28	Ana.	L	10-14		15	14	Percival	Mohler		21-32	4th	8.0
5-29	Ana.	L	1-7		6	12	Watson	Wengert		21-33	4th	9.0
5-30	Tor.	W	12-7		14	12	Prieto	Hentgen		22-33	4th	8.0
5-31	Tor.	L	3-13		11	19	Clemens	Telgheder		22-34	4th	9.0
6-1	Tor.	W	8-2		9	10	Oquist	Person		23-34	4th	8.0
6-2	Det.	L	7-8		11	10	Moehler	Karsay	Brocail	23-35	4th	9.0
6-3	Det.	W	9-8		13	11	Small	Myers	Johnson	24-35	4th	8.0
6-5	At Tor.	W	4-3		8	8	Reyes	Hentgen	Taylor	25-35	4th	8.0
6-6	At Tor.	L	1-4		8	6	Clemens	Oquist	Quantrill	25-36	4th	8.0
6-7	At Tor.	L	1-3		6	6	Person	Karsay	Quantrill	25-37	4th	8.0
6-8	At Tor.	W	7-5		10	10	Wengert	Andujar	Taylor	26-37	4th	8.0
6-10	At Det.	L	4-6		10	12	Blair	Prieto	Jones	26-38	4th	8.5
6-11	At Det.	L	2-4		7	8	Brocail	Small	Jones	26-39	4th	9.0
6-12	L.A.	W	5-4		6	10	Telgheder	Nomo	Taylor	27-39	4th	9.0
6-13	L.A.	L	4-6		8	11	Hall	Small	Worrell	27-40	4th	10.0
6-14	Col.	L	1-7		8	9	Bailey	Wengert		27-41	4th	11.0
6-15	Col.	W	5-2		10	8	Prieto	Ritz	Taylor	28-41	4th	11.0
6-17	At S.D.	W	10-3		12	8	Johnson	Smith	Small	29-41	4th	10.0
6-18	At S.D.	W	11-9		12	13	Reyes	Bochtler	Groom	30-41	4th	9.0

Date	Opp.	Res.	Score	(inn.*)	Hits	Opp. hits	Winning pitcher	Losing pitcher	Save	Record	Pos.	GB
6-19	At Ana.	L	3-4		9	9	James	Taylor		30-42	4th	10.0
6-20	At Ana.	L	2-5		4	6	Gross	Wengert	Percival	30-43	4th	11.0
6-21	At Ana.	L	3-5		12	6	DeLucia	Prieto	Percival	30-44	4th	12.0
6-22	At Ana.	L	6-7		6	13	Harris	Small	Percival	30-45	4th	13.0
6-23	At Sea.	L	5-6		8	11	Lowe	Telgheder	Charlton	30-46	4th	14.0
6-24	At Sea.	W	4-1		11	5	Karsay	Johnson		31-46	4th	13.0
6-25	At Sea.	L	4-9		12	12	Wolcott	Wengert		31-47	4th	14.0
6-26	Tex.	W	6-3		8	10	Prieto	Santana	Taylor	32-47	4th	14.0
6-27	Tex.	W	7-4		13	9	Oquist	Burkett	Taylor	33-47	4th	14.0
6-28	Tex.	L	0-2		5	7	Oliver	Rigby	Wetteland	33-48	4th	14.0
6-29	Tex.	W	7-5		11	10	Reyes	Hernandez	Groom	34-48	4th	14.0
6-30	S.D.	L	6-15		8	19	Ashby	Wengert		34-49	4th	14.0
7-1	S.D.	W	8-6		11	15	Small	Bochtler		35-49	4th	14.0
7-2	At S.F.	W	8-1		12	5	Johnson	Rueter	Groom	36-49	4th	13.0
7-3	At S.F.	L	4-6		6	12	Creek	Rigby	Beck	36-50	4th	13.0
7-4	At Tex.	L	6-7		11	11	Hill	Karsay	Wetteland	36-51	4th	14.0
7-5	At Tex.	L	1-8		3	12	Witt	Wengert		36-52	4th	14.0
7-6	At Tex.	W	9-8		9	11	Johnson	Whiteside	Taylor	37-52	4th	13.0
7-10	Ana.	L	4-8		4	12	Watson	Rigby	DeLucia	37-53	4th	14.0
7-11	Ana.	L	4-14		8	17	Dickson	Karsay		37-54	4th	15.0
7-12	Ana.	L	3-6		10	8	Finley	Prieto	Percival	37-55	4th	15.0
7-13	Ana.	L	3-5		4	9	Hasegawa	Oquist	Percival	37-56	4th	15.0
7-14	Sea.	L	2-6		11	14	Wolcott	Wojciechowski		37-57	4th	16.0
7-15	Sea.	W	8-5		11	10	Mohler	Moyer	Taylor	38-57	4th	15.0
7-16	K.C.	W	11-3		8	7	Wengert	Rosado		39-57	4th	15.0
7-17	K.C.	W	11-3		16	5	Karsay	Belcher		40-57	4th	14.0
7-18	Min.	L	3-7		8	14	Hawkins	Wojciechowski		40-58	4th	15.0
7-19	Min.	L	6-7		12	11	Swindell	Wengert	Aguilera	40-59	4th	15.0
7-20	Min.	L	0-1		5	5	Radke	Reyes		40-60	4th	16.0
7-22	At Bos.	L	3-4		9	12	Henry	Groom	Slocumb	40-61	4th	16.0
7-23	At Bos.	W	5-2		11	11	Wengert	Wakefield	Taylor	41-61	4th	16.0
7-24	At Bos.	L	0-3		6	10	Suppan	Rigby	Slocumb	41-62	4th	17.0
7-25	At Cle.	W	2-1		6	5	Small	M. Jackson	Taylor	42-62	4th	17.0
7-26	At Cle.	L	3-6		6	12	Wright	Karsay		42-63	4th	18.0
7-27	At Cle.	L	2-4		6	7	Jacome	Haynes	Assenmacher	42-64	4th	19.0
7-28	At N.Y.	L	3-4		6	7	Rivera	Small		42-65	4th	19.5
7-29	At N.Y.	L	4-7		8	9	Gooden	Reyes	Rivera	42-66	4th	19.5
7-30	At N.Y.	L	0-7		3	13	Wells	Karsay		42-67	4th	19.5
7-31	Bal.	L	0-4	(11)	6	6	Benitez	Johnson		42-68	4th	19.5
8-1	Bal.	W	2-1		5	6	Mathews	Orosco		43-68	4th	19.0
8-2	Bal.	L	3-13		8	14	Mussina	Reyes		43-69	4th	20.0
8-3	Bal.	L	5-7		8	11	Boskie	Mathews	Myers	43-70	4th	21.0
8-5	Chi.	L	0-3		7	8	Drabek	Karsay	Karchner	43-71	4th	21.5
8-6	Chi.	W	3-2		12	7	Mathews	Navarro	Taylor	44-71	4th	21.5
8-7	Mil.	W	5-4	(13)	10	10	Johnson	Jones		45-71	4th	21.0
8-9	Mil.	W	3-2		8	5	Mathews	Wickman	Taylor	46-71	4th	20.5
8-10†	Mil.	W	4-3		10	11	Taylor	Wickman		47-71		
8-10‡	Mil.	L	5-9		10	14	Florie	Haynes		47-72	4th	20.0
8-12	At Bal.	L	0-8		3	11	Erickson	Reyes		47-73	4th	20.0
8-13	At Bal.	W	4-2		8	8	Lorraine	Mussina	Mohler	48-73	4th	19.5
8-14	At Chi.	W	12-5		15	9	Groom	McElroy		49-73	4th	19.0
8-15	At Chi.	W	11-6		14	8	Haynes	Baldwin		50-73	4th	19.0
8-16	At Mil.	L	5-6		9	8	Jones	Mohler		50-74	4th	19.5
8-17	At Mil.	L	2-5		7	9	Woodard	Prieto	Jones	50-75	4th	20.0
8-20†	Bos.	L	5-7		11	11	Wakefield	Haynes	Henry	50-76		
8-20‡	Bos.	L	4-5	(13)	8	16	Hudson	Wengert	Gordon	50-77	4th	20.5
8-21	Bos.	W	13-6		17	10	Lorraine	Avery		51-77	4th	20.5
8-22	Cle.	L	3-5		6	12	Wright	Prieto	Mesa	51-78	4th	21.5
8-23	Cle.	L	4-7		8	17	Hershiser	Rigby	Mesa	51-79	4th	21.5
8-24	Cle.	W	4-1		6	5	Haynes	Smiley	Mathews	52-79	4th	21.5
8-26	N.Y.	L	2-18		7	22	Pettitte	Oquist		52-80	4th	22.0
8-27	N.Y.	W	8-7		15	14	Mathews	Nelson		53-80	4th	21.0
8-28	At L.A.	L	1-7		4	10	Nomo	Ludwick		53-81	4th	21.0
8-29	At L.A.	L	4-5	(10)	8	8	Osuna	Mathews		53-82	4th	21.0
8-30	At Col.	L	3-4		9	10	Dipoto	Mohler		53-83	4th	21.0
8-31	At Col.	L	4-10		10	13	Holmes	Oquist		53-84	4th	22.0
9-1	S.F.	L	2-8		10	10	Rueter	Lorraine		53-85	4th	23.0
9-3	S.F.	W	12-3		11	9	Rigby	Darwin	Small	54-85	4th	22.0
9-4	At K.C.	L	6-7	(12)	10	11	Olson	Wengert		54-86	4th	23.0
9-5	At K.C.	W	9-6		16	15	Oquist	Carrasco	Taylor	55-86	4th	23.0
9-6	At K.C.	W	9-3		15	12	Lorraine	Appier	Wengert	56-86	4th	23.0
9-7	At K.C.	W	9-4		14	11	Ludwick	Rosado		57-86	4th	22.0
9-8	At Min.	L	2-7		5	15	Serafini	Telgheder		57-87	4th	22.0
9-9	At Min.	W	5-1		12	4	Haynes	Hawkins		58-87	4th	22.0
9-10	Tor.	W	3-2		6	3	Mathews	Plesac		59-87	4th	22.0

Date	Opp.	Res.	Score	(inn.*)	Hits	Opp. hits	Winning pitcher	Losing pitcher	Save	Record	Pos.	GB
9-11	Tor.	W	8-7		11	13	Mathews	Escobar		60-87	4th	21.0
9-12	Det.	L	2-7		8	16	Keagle	Ludwick	Miceli	60-88	4th	22.0
9-13	Det.	W	4-2		7	8	Telgheder	Blair	Mathews	61-88	4th	21.0
9-14	Det.	L	5-6		10	15	Sanders	Haynes	Jones	61-89	4th	22.0
9-15	Det.	L	3-6		10	11	Thompson	Oquist	Jones	61-90	4th	23.0
9-17	At Ana.	L	4-8		10	14	Watson	Ludwick		61-91	4th	23.0
9-18	At Ana.	W	7-3		9	9	Telgheder	Dickson		62-91	4th	23.0
9-19	Sea.	L	4-9		9	12	Moyer	Haynes		62-92	4th	24.0
9-20	Sea.	W	4-3	(15)	11	10	Small	Lira		63-92	4th	23.0
9-21	Sea.	L	2-9		9	14	Cloude	Rigby		63-93	4th	24.0
9-22	Sea.	L	2-4		10	9	Fassero	Ludwick	Slocumb	63-94	4th	25.0
9-23	Tex.	L	6-14		11	20	Burkett	Telgheder		63-95	4th	26.0
9-24	Tex.	L	4-8		7	13	Oliver	Haynes		63-96	4th	26.0
9-26	At Sea.	W	8-5		12	7	Oquist	Moyer	Mathews	64-96	4th	25.0
9-27	At Sea.	L	3-9		10	13	Johnson	Rigby		64-97	4th	26.0
9-28	At Sea.	W	9-7		11	11	Small	Charlton	Taylor	65-97	4th	25.0

Monthly records: April (13-13), May (9-21), June (12-15), July (8-19), August (11-16), September (12-13).
*Innings, if other than nine. †First game of doubleheader. ‡Second game of doubleheader.

HIGHLIGHTS

High point: The closest the A's came to a high was June 24 when Mark McGwire hit a 538-foot home run to help beat Randy Johnson in Seattle. Johnson struck out 19 Athletics that night, one strikeout short of the major league record, but still lost the game, 4-1.
Low point: On July 31 the A's held the Orioles scoreless for 10 innings, then gave up four runs in the 11th to lose their sixth straight game and drop their record to 42-68. Earlier in the day they abandoned all hope for the season by trading McGwire to the Cardinals.
Turning point: The day after splitting a doubleheader with the Yankees, the A's lost to the Red Sox on April 14, 10-1. The A's, who entered the day alone in first place, ended it tied for the division lead. This began a four-game losing streak, and the A's were never heard from in the A.L. West again.
Most valuable player: Jason Giambi, in his second full season, broke the club record for doubles with 41 and hit .293 with 20 homers and 81 RBIs. He began the season out of position in left field, but moved to first base when McGwire was traded to St. Louis on July 31.
Most valuable pitcher: If one player must be picked, the choice would be Aaron Small, who led the staff with nine victories. That total was the fifth-best by an Oakland rookie. He had four saves and was the team's most effective set-up man.
Most improved player: Outfielder Matt Stairs, in his first full season, was the team's most consistent hitter for the first five months before slumping in September. Nevertheless, he finished the year with a .298 average, 27 homers and 73 RBIs.
Most pleasant surprise: Catcher Brent Mayne, who was cut by the Mariners in spring training. Mayne was signed by the A's and finished the season with career highs in batting average (.289), runs (29) and home runs (six).
Biggest disappointment: Scott Brosius, who posted career highs in virtually every offensive category in 1996, was a total loss at the plate. His average dropped from .304 to .203, making him the fourth player in history to see his

average drop more than 100 points in one season.
Key injuries: Jose Canseco played only seven games over the last two months because of back problems. Ariel Prieto, the opening night starter, made only five starts after June 26 because of shoulder problems. Steve Karsay, another member of the projected rotation, was put on the shelf for the season on August 6 with tendinitis in his right elbow. Opening night catcher George Williams missed 47 games over two trips to the D.L. And that doesn't count the 25 games he missed in September. He strained his left groin in April and his right bicep in July.
Notable: A's starters won only 29 games, making them just the fifth team in history to get fewer than 30 wins from its starters.

—DAVID BUSH

RECORDS

1997 regular-season record: 65-97 (4th in A.L. West); 35-46 at home; 30-51 on road; 22-33 vs. East; 25-30 vs. Central; 18-34 vs. West; 17-26 vs. lefthanded starters; 48-71 vs. righthanded starters; 58-87 on grass; 7-10 on turf; 30-38 in daytime; 35-59 at night; 22-23 in one-run games; 9-6 in extra-inning games; 0-1-2 in doubleheaders.
Team record past five years: 329-415 (.442, ranks 13th in league in that span).

TEAM LEADERS

Batting average: Jason Giambi (.293).
At-bats: Scott Spiezio (538).
Runs: Jason Giambi (66).
Hits: Jason Giambi (152).
Total bases: Jason Giambi (257).
Doubles: Jason Giambi (41).
Triples: Jason McDonald, Scott Spiezio (4).
Home runs: Mark McGwire (34).
Runs batted in: Jason Giambi, Mark McGwire (81).
Stolen bases: Jason McDonald (13).
Slugging percentage: Jason Giambi (.495).
On-base percentage: Jason Giambi (.362).
Wins: Aaron Small (9).

Earned-run average: None.
Complete games: Mike Oquist, Don Wengert (1).
Shutouts: None.
Saves: Billy Taylor (23).
Innings pitched: Don Wengert (134.0).
Strikeouts: Steve Karsay (92).

GAMES BY POSITION

Catcher: Brent Mayne 83, George Williams 67, Izzy Molina 48.
First base: Mark McGwire 101, Jason Giambi 51, Dave Magadan 30, Matt Stairs 7, Brian Lesher 3.
Second base: Scott Spiezio 146, Mark Bellhorn 17, Rafael Bournigal 7, Tilson Brito 2, Tony Batista 1, Scott Sheldon 1.
Third base: Scott Brosius 107, Dave Magadan 49, Mark Bellhorn 40, Tilson Brito 10, Tony Batista 4, Scott Sheldon 1, Scott Spiezio 1.
Shortstop: Rafael Bournigal 74, Tony Batista 61, Scott Brosius 30, Miguel Tejada 26, Scott Sheldon 12, Tilson Brito 6, Mark Bellhorn 1.
Outfield: Damon Mashore 89, Matt Stairs 89, Jason McDonald 74, Jason Giambi 68, Ernie Young 66, Jose Canseco 44, Geronimo Berroa 43, Patrick Lennon 36, Brian Lesher 32, Ben Grieve 24, Scott Brosius 22.
Designated hitter: Jose Canseco 60, Geronimo Berroa 27, Jason Giambi 25, Dave Magadan 25, Patrick Lennon 17, Matt Stairs 17, Mark Bellhorn 3, Brian Lesher 3, Tony Batista 1, George Williams 1.

TOP DRAFT CHOICES

1a. **Chris Enochs**, RHP, West Virginia Univ.
1b. **Eric DuBose**, LHP, Mississippi State U.
1c. **Nathan Haynes**, OF, Pinole Valley H.S., Hercules, Calif.
1d. **Denny Wagner**, RHP, Virginia Tech.
2. **Chad Harville**, RHP, Univ. of Memphis.
3. **Marcus Jones**, RHP, Long Beach State U.
4. **Jason Anderson**, LHP, Radford Univ.
5. **Andy Kimball**, RHP, University of Wisconsin-Oshkosh.
6. **Tim Hudson**, RHP, Auburn University.
7. **Roberto Vaz**, OF, University of Alabama.
8. **Adam Piatt**, 3B, Mississippi State Univ.
9. **Jared Jensen**, RHP, Brigham Young U.
10. **Javier Flores**, C, Oklahoma University.

SEATTLE MARINERS
AMERICAN LEAGUE WEST DIVISION

Mariners Schedule
Home games shaded. *—All-Star Game at Coors Field (Colorado).
D—Day game (any game starting before 5 p.m.).

March
SUN	MON	TUE	WED	THU	FRI	SAT
					31 D CLE	

April
SUN	MON	TUE	WED	THU	FRI	SAT
			1 CLE	2	3 BOS	4 BOS
5 D BOS	6 NYY	7 NYY	8 D NYY	9	10 D BOS	11 BOS
12 D BOS	13 CLE	14 CLE	15 CLE	16 MIN	17 MIN	18 MIN
19 D MIN	20 KC	21 KC	22 KC	23	24 MIN	25 MIN
26 D MIN	27 KC	28 KC	29 NYY	30 NYY		

May
SUN	MON	TUE	WED	THU	FRI	SAT
					1 DET	2 DET
3 D DET	4	5 CWS	6 CWS	7 TOR	8 TOR	9 TOR
10 D TOR	11	12 DET	13 DET	14 CWS	15 CWS	16 D TOR
17 D TOR	18 D TOR	19 TEX	20 TEX	21 TEX	22 TB	23 TB
24 TB	25 BAL	26 D BAL	27	28 TB	29 TB	30 TB
31 D TB						

June
SUN	MON	TUE	WED	THU	FRI	SAT
	1 BAL	2 BAL	3 ANA	4 ANA	5 LA	6 LA
7 D LA	8 SF	9 SF	10 D ANA	11 OAK	12 OAK	13 D OAK
14 OAK	15	16 ANA	17 ANA	18 ANA	19 OAK	20 OAK
21 D OAK	22 SD	23 D SD	24 SD	25 D SD	26 ARZ	27 ARZ
28 D ARZ	29 COL	30 COL				

July
SUN	MON	TUE	WED	THU	FRI	SAT
			1 COL	2 COL	3 D TEX	4 TEX
5 TEX	6	7	*8	9 ANA	10 ANA	11 ANA
12 D ANA	13 TEX	14 TEX	15 MIN	16 MIN	17 KC	18 KC
19 D KC	20	21 TB	22 TB	23	24 BAL	25 BAL
26 D BAL	27	28 CLE	29 CLE	30 CLE	31 NYY	

August
SUN	MON	TUE	WED	THU	FRI	SAT
						1 D NYY
2 D NYY	3 BOS	4 BOS	5	6 DET	7 DET	8 DET
9 D DET	10 D	11 TOR	12 D TOR	13	14 CWS	15 CWS
16 D CWS	17 DET	18 DET	19 TOR	20 TOR	21 CWS	22 CWS
23 CWS	24 D CWS	25 CLE	26 CLE	27 CLE	28 NYY	29 D NYY
30 NYY	31 BOS					

September
SUN	MON	TUE	WED	THU	FRI	SAT
		1 BOS	2 BOS	3	4 BAL	5 BAL
6 BAL	7	8 TB	9 D	10	11 KC	12 KC
13 KC	14 D MIN	15 MIN	16 D OAK	17 OAK	18 ANA	19 ANA
20 D ANA	21 D OAK	22 OAK	23 OAK	24 TEX	25 TEX	26 TEX
27 D TEX						

1998 SEASON
CLUB DIRECTORY

Board of directors
John Ellis, chairman; Minoru Arakawe; Chris Larson; Howard Lincoln; John McCaw; Frank Shrontz; Craig Watjen

Chairman and chief executive officer
John Ellis

President and chief operating officer
Chuck Armstrong

Vice president, baseball operations
Woody Woodward

Vice president, communications
Randy Adamack

V.p., finance and administration
Kevin Mather

Vice president, business development
Paul Isaki

V.p., scouting and player development
Roger Jongewaard

V.p., ballpark planning and development
John Palmer

Controller
Tim Kornegay

Vice president, baseball administration
Lee Pelekoudas

Assistants to v.p., baseball operations
George Zuraw
Larry Beinfest

Director of player development
Benny Looper

Coordinator of minor league instruction
Mike Goff

Director, team travel
Ron Spellacy

Director, community relations
To be announced

Vice president, sales
Bob Aylward

Director, sales
Joe Chard

Director, merchandising
Todd Vecchio

Director, public relations
Dave Aust

Director, stadium operations
Tony Pereira

Assistant director, public relations
Tim Hevly

Exec. asst., ownership/business dev.
Janet O'Brien

Manager, payroll and benefits admin.
Shirley Shreve

Trainers
Rick Griffin, Tom Newberg

Video coordinator
Carl Hamilton

Home clubhouse manager
Scott Gilbert

Visiting clubhouse manager
Henry Genzale

Strength and conditioning coach
Allen Wirtala

Club physicians
Dr. Larry Pedegana
Dr. Mitchel Storey

Club dentist
Dr. Richard Leshgold

Public address announcer
Tom Hutyler

Director of professional scouting
Ken Compton

Director of scouting
Frank Mattox

Major lg. and special assignment scouts
Bill Kearns
Ken Compton

Scouting supervisors
Ken Madeja, Steve Pope, Carroll Sembera

Area scouts
Dave Alexander, Maximo Alvarez, Fernando Arguelles, Brian Ballentine, Jeff Brissom, Mark Brown, Darrin Chamberlain, Rodney Davis, Ramon de los Santos, Curtis Dishman, Orlando Gomez, Ron Hafner, Larry Harper, Guadalupe Jabalara, Steve Jungewaard, Stan Lewis, Wilmer Mardera, John McMichen, Tom McNamara, Mauro Mazzotti, Billy Merkel, Julio Molina, Omer Munoz, Myron Pines, Don Poplin, Phil Pote, Alex Smith, Chris Smith, Jim Stewart, Roberto Valdez, Ray Vince, Curtis Wallace, Ken Wandzel, Craig Weissmann, Darren Wittcke, Selwyn Young

MINOR LEAGUE AFFILIATES

Class	Team	League	Manager
AAA	Tacoma	Pacific Coast	Dave Myers
AA	Orlando	Southern	Dan Rohn
A	Lancaster	California	Rick Burleson
A	Wisconsin	Midwest	Gary Varsho
A	Everett	Northwest	To be announced
Rookie	Peoria Mariners	Arizona	Darrin Garner

BROADCAST INFORMATION
Radio: KIRO-AM (710).
TV: KIRO-TV (Channel 7).
Cable TV: Fox Sports Northwest.

SPRING TRAINING
Ballpark: Peoria Stadium (Peoria, Ariz.).
Ticket information: 602-784-4444.

Manager—Lou Piniella (14).
Coaches—Jesse Barfield, Nardi Contreras (54), John McLaren (7), Sam Mejias (49), Matt Sinatro (15), Steve Smith (2).

No.	PITCHERS	B/T	Ht./Wt.	Born	1997 clubs
31	Ayala, Bobby	R/R	6-3/210	7-8-69	Seattle
22	Carmona, Rafael	L/R	6-2/185	10-2-72	Tacoma, Seattle
27	Cloude, Ken	R/R	6-1/180	1-9-75	Memphis, Seattle
47	Davis, Tim	L/L	5-11/165	7-14-70	Tacoma, Seattle
13	Fassero, Jeff	L/L	6-1/195	1-5-63	Seattle
	Fossas, Tony	L/L	6-0/198	9-23-57	St. Louis
	Hinchliffe, Brett	R/R	6-4/205	7-21-74	Memphis
	Hurtado, Edwin	R/R	6-3/215	2-1-70	Seattle, Tacoma
51	Johnson, Randy	R/L	6-10/225	9-10-63	Seattle
41	Lira, Felipe	R/R	6-0/170	4-26-72	Detroit, Seattle, Everett, Tacoma
	Marte, Damasco	L/L	6-0/170	2-14-75	Lancaster
39	McCarthy, Greg	L/L	6-2/215	10-30-68	Tacoma, Seattle
	Montane, Ivan	R/R	6-2/195	6-3-73	Memphis, Lancaster
50	Moyer, Jamie	L/L	6-0/170	11-18-62	Tacoma, Seattle
52	Slocumb, Heathcliff	R/R	6-3/220	6-7-66	Boston, Seattle
	Smith, Cam	R/R	6-3/190	9-20-73	Mobile
23	Spoljaric, Paul	R/L	6-3/210	9-24-70	Dunedin, Toronto, Seattle
	Suzuki, Makoto	R/R	6-3/195	5-31-75	Tacoma
40	Timlin, Mike	R/R	6-4/210	3-10-66	Toronto, Seattle
46	Wells, Bob	R/R	6-0/180	11-1-66	Seattle
	Zimmerman, Jordan	R/L	6-0/200	4-28-75	Everett, Wisconsin

No.	CATCHERS	B/T	Ht./Wt.	Born	1997 clubs
17	Marzano, John	R/R	5-11/195	2-14-63	Seattle
	Wilkins, Rick	L/R	6-2/215	6-4-67	San Francisco, Tacoma, Seattle
6	Wilson, Dan	R/R	6-3/190	3-25-69	Seattle

No.	INFIELDERS	B/T	Ht./Wt.	Born	1997 clubs
28	Cora, Joey	B/R	5-8/155	5-14-65	Seattle
18	Davis, Russ	R/R	6-0/195	9-13-69	Seattle
34	Guevara, Giomar	B/R	5-8/150	10-23-72	Tacoma, Memphis, Seattle
	Huson, Jeff	L/R	6-3/180	8-15-64	Colorado Springs, Milwaukee
	Listach, Pat	B/R	5-9/180	9-12-67	Houston, Buffalo
11	Martinez, Edgar	R/R	5-11/190	1-2-63	Seattle
3	Rodriguez, Alex	R/R	6-3/190	7-27-75	Seattle
35	Rohrmeier, Dan	R/R	6-0/195	1-27-65	Tacoma, Seattle
	Segui, David	B/L	6-1/202	7-19-66	Montreal

No.	OUTFIELDERS	B/T	Ht./Wt.	Born	1997 clubs
8	Amaral, Rich	R/R	6-0/175	4-1-62	Seattle
19	Buhner, Jay	R/R	6-3/210	8-13-64	Seattle
	Conner, Decomba	R/R	5-10/185	7-17-73	Jacksonville, Lakeland
29	Ducey, Rob	L/R	6-2/180	5-24-65	Tacoma, Seattle
	Gipson, Charles	R/R	6-1/188	12-16-72	Memphis, Tacoma
24	Griffey Jr., Ken	L/L	6-3/205	11-21-69	Seattle
38	Ibanez, Raul	L/R	6-2/200	6-2-72	Tacoma, Seattle
	Monahan, Shane	L/R	6-1/200	8-12-74	Memphis, Tacoma

BALLPARK INFORMATION

Ballpark (capacity, surface)
The Kingdome (59,856, artificial)

Address
P.O. Box 4100
83 King St.
Seattle, WA 98104

Business phone
206-346-4000

Ticket information
206-628-3555

Ticket prices
$25 (box)
$22 (field)
$20 (club)
$14 (view box)
$12 (view)
$10 (view, children 14 and under)
$9 (outfield reserved, family)
$7 (family, children 14 and under)
$7 (of reserved, children 14 and under)
$6 (Southwest Airlines Cloud Crowd)

Field dimensions (from home plate)
To left field at foul line, 331 feet
To center field, 405 feet
To right field at foul line, 312 feet

First game played
April 6, 1977 (Angels 7, Mariners 0)

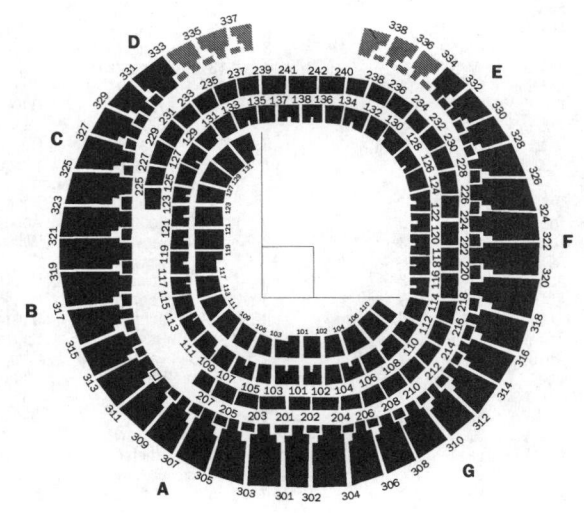

1998 SEASON Seattle Mariners

DAY BY DAY

Seattle Mariners

1998 SEASON

Date	Opp.	Res.	Score	(inn.*)	Hits	Opp. hits	Winning pitcher	Losing pitcher	Save	Record	Pos.	GB
4-1	N.Y.	W	4-2		7	8	Fassero	Cone	Charlton	1-0	T1st	....
4-2	N.Y.	L	2-16		8	14	Pettitte	Sanders		1-1	2nd	0.5
4-4	Bos.	L	5-10		7	15	Sele	Wolcott	Henry	1-2	4th	1.0
4-5	Bos.	L	6-8		11	12	Trlicek	Charlton	Slocumb	1-3	4th	1.0
4-6	Bos.	W	8-7	(10)	9	11	Charlton	Trlicek		2-3	T3rd	1.0
4-7	Cle.	L	3-8		11	9	Nagy	Sanders		2-4	T3rd	2.0
4-8	Cle.	W	14-8		17	18	Hurtado	Lopez		3-4	T2nd	1.0
4-9	Cle.	W	11-1		13	9	Wolcott	Colon		4-4	2nd	1.0
4-11	At Bos.	W	5-3		12	6	Johnson	Avery	Charlton	5-4	2nd	1.0
4-12	At Bos.	W	5-1	(10)	7	2	Fassero	Corsi		6-4	2nd	0.5
4-13	At Bos.	L	1-7		5	11	Gordon	Sanders		6-5	2nd	1.0
4-14	At Cle.	W	6-1		10	2	D. Martinez	Nagy		7-5	T1st	....
4-15	At Cle.	W	8-4		14	9	Wells	M. Jackson	Charlton	8-5	1st	+1.0
4-16	At Det.	W	7-3		5	6	Johnson	Sager	Charlton	9-5	1st	+1.5
4-17	At Det.	W	8-6		16	11	Fassero	Bautista	Charlton	10-5	1st	+1.5
4-18	Min.	L	3-10		8	10	Rodriguez	Sanders		10-6	1st	+1.5
4-19	Min.	L	0-4		6	10	Tewksbury	D. Martinez		10-7	1st	+1.0
4-20	Min.	W	10-6		11	12	Wolcott	Ritchie	Charlton	11-7	1st	+1.5
4-21	K.C.	W	6-5		9	7	Ayala	Bevil	Charlton	12-7	1st	+2.5
4-22	K.C.	W	7-2		10	5	Fassero	Belcher		13-7	1st	+3.0
4-23	K.C.	L	10-12		18	11	Veres	Hurtado	Pichardo	13-8	1st	+2.0
4-25	At Tor.	W	13-8		17	10	Ayala	Plesac		14-8	1st	+1.5
4-26	At Tor.	L	3-4		8	12	Quantrill	Lowe		14-9	1st	+0.5
4-27	At Tor.	W	2-1		6	7	Johnson	Person	Charlton	15-9	1st	+0.5
4-28	At N.Y.	L	5-6		9	13	Nelson	Ayala	Rivera	15-10	1st	+0.5
4-29	At N.Y.	W	7-5		12	9	McCarthy	Mecir		16-10	1st	+1.5
4-30	At N.Y.	L	2-3		8	8	Wells	D. Martinez	Rivera	16-11	1st	+0.5
5-2	Mil.	W	8-1		10	3	Johnson	D'Amico		17-11	1st	+1.5
5-3	Mil.	L	4-17		14	17	Florie	Fassero		17-12	1st	+0.5
5-4	Mil.	W	9-0		12	6	Moyer	Eldred		18-12	1st	+0.5
5-6	At Chi.	W	7-6		14	8	Ayala	T. Castillo	Charlton	19-12	1st	+1.5
5-8	At Bal.	L	3-13		5	13	Mussina	Johnson		19-13	1st	+2.0
5-9	At Bal.	W	8-2		14	7	Moyer	Coppinger		20-13	1st	+2.0
5-10	At Bal.	W	3-2	(11)	11	5	Charlton	Myers		21-13	1st	+2.0
5-11	At Bal.	L	5-9		9	11	Erickson	D. Martinez		21-14	1st	+1.0
5-12	At Mil.	L	8-9		12	11	D'Amico	Wolcott	Jones	21-15	2nd	....
5-13	At Mil.	W	2-1		3	6	Johnson	Fetters	Charlton	22-15	1st	+1.0
5-14	Chi.	W	9-7		15	12	Moyer	Navarro	Charlton	23-15	1st	+1.0
5-15	Chi.	L	3-4		7	10	Simas	Charlton	Hernandez	23-16	1st	+1.0
5-16	Bal.	L	3-6		6	11	Erickson	D. Martinez		23-17	2nd	....
5-17	Bal.	L	3-4		9	8	Key	Sanders	Benitez	23-18	2nd	....
5-18	Bal.	L	7-8		12	8	Orosco	Charlton	Benitez	23-19	2nd	1.0
5-19	At Ana.	W	13-4		17	7	Moyer	Langston		24-19	2nd	0.5
5-20	At Ana.	L	9-11		9	13	DeLucia	Manzanillo	Percival	24-20	2nd	1.5
5-21	At Ana.	L	3-18		10	21	Finley	D. Martinez		24-21	3rd	1.5
5-23	At K.C.	W	8-4		13	10	Johnson	Belcher		25-21	3rd	1.0
5-24	At K.C.	L	5-11		12	13	Veres	Moyer	Pichardo	25-22	3rd	2.0
5-25	At K.C.	L	3-4	(11)	8	13	Walker	Ayala		25-23	3rd	2.0
5-26	At Min.	W	13-8		14	13	Sanders	Aldred		26-23	3rd	1.0
5-27	At Min.	L	10-11		12	14	Aguilera	Charlton		26-24	3rd	2.0
5-28	Tex.	W	5-0		7	4	Johnson	Oliver		27-24	3rd	1.0
5-29	Tex.	L	2-8		8	13	Hill	Moyer		27-25	3rd	2.0
5-30	Det.	L	2-5		6	10	Lira	Fassero	Jones	27-26	3rd	2.0
5-31	Det.	L	2-4		7	10	Olivares	Wolcott	Jones	27-27	3rd	3.0
6-1	Det.	W	4-1		9	4	Sanders	Thompson	Ayala	28-27	3rd	2.0
6-2	Tor.	W	3-0		9	2	Johnson	Andujar		29-27	3rd	2.0
6-3	Tor.	W	6-3		12	7	Moyer	Williams		30-27	2nd	1.0
6-5	At Det.	W	14-6		17	7	Fassero	Lira		31-27	3rd	1.0
6-6	At Det.	W	6-3		9	8	Lowe	Olivares	Ayala	32-27	2nd	....
6-7	At Det.	L	1-3		5	5	Thompson	Wolcott	Jones	32-28	2nd	....
6-8	At Det.	W	2-0		8	2	Johnson	Moehler	Ayala	33-28	1st	+1.0
6-10	At Tor.	L	3-8		11	8	Hentgen	Sanders		33-29	2nd	0.5
6-11	At Tor.	W	5-1		9	5	Fassero	Clemens		34-29	1st	+0.5
6-12	Col.	W	12-11		12	18	Wells	Munoz	Ayala	35-29	1st	+0.5
6-13	Col.	W	6-1		7	4	Johnson	Wright		36-29	1st	+1.5
6-14	L.A.	W	9-8		11	11	Ayala	Osuna		37-29	1st	+2.0
6-15	L.A.	W	8-2		10	6	Moyer	Valdes	Sanders	38-29	1st	+2.0
6-17	At S.F.	L	3-4		9	10	Rueter	Fassero	Beck	38-30	1st	+1.0
6-18	At S.F.	L	2-4		4	10	Gardner	Lowe	Beck	38-31	1st	+1.0
6-19	At Tex.	W	2-1		9	5	Johnson	Hill	Ayala	39-31	1st	+2.0
6-20	At Tex.	W	5-4		7	8	Wolcott	Witt	Sanders	40-31	1st	+3.0

Date	Opp.	Res.	Score	(inn.*)	Hits	Opp. hits	Winning pitcher	Losing pitcher	Save	Record	Pos.	GB
6-21	At Tex.	W	15-8		13	16	Maddux	Vosberg		41-31	1st	+3.5
6-22	At Tex.	W	6-4		12	10	Fassero	Burkett	Ayala	42-31	1st	+3.5
6-23	Oak.	W	6-5		11	8	Lowe	Telgheder	Charlton	43-31	1st	+3.5
6-24	Oak.	L	1-4		5	11	Karsay	Johnson		43-32	1st	+2.5
6-25	Oak.	W	9-4		12	12	Wolcott	Wengert		44-32	1st	+3.5
6-26	Ana.	W	6-3		14	7	Moyer	Dickson	Charlton	45-32	1st	+4.5
6-27	Ana.	W	8-1		8	7	Fassero	Finley		46-32	1st	+5.5
6-28	Ana.	L	1-6		3	9	Watson	Lowe		46-33	1st	+4.5
6-29	Ana.	W	3-2		6	6	Ayala	DeLucia		47-33	1st	+5.5
6-30	S.F.	L	6-8	(10)	13	14	Beck	Charlton	Henry	47-34	1st	+5.5
7-1	S.F.	W	15-4		16	8	Moyer	VanLandingham		48-34	1st	+5.5
7-2	At S.D.	L	5-8		12	11	Hamilton	Fassero		48-35	1st	+5.5
7-3	At S.D.	L	8-10		10	9	Batchelor	McCarthy	Hoffman	48-36	1st	+5.5
7-4	At Ana.	W	7-3		9	8	Johnson	Springer		49-36	1st	+6.0
7-5	At Ana.	L	4-5		9	9	Percival	Charlton		49-37	1st	+5.0
7-6	At Ana.	L	0-8		4	9	Finley	Fassero		49-38	1st	+4.5
7-10	Tex.	W	12-9		18	11	Moyer	Hill	Charlton	50-38	1st	+4.5
7-11	Tex.	W	8-7		13	11	Ayala	Hernandez		51-38	1st	+4.5
7-12	Tex.	L	2-9		8	12	Burkett	Lowe		51-39	1st	+3.5
7-13	Tex.	L	2-4		8	7	Patterson	Ayala	Wetteland	51-40	1st	+2.5
7-14	At Oak.	W	6-2		14	11	Wolcott	Wojciechowski		52-40	1st	+2.5
7-15	At Oak.	L	5-8		10	11	Mohler	Moyer	Taylor	52-41	1st	+1.5
7-16	Min.	W	8-7		14	10	Sanders	Aguilera		53-41	1st	+1.5
7-17	Min.	L	7-9	(12)	17	11	Aguilera	Charlton	Guardado	53-42	1st	+0.5
7-18	K.C.	W	5-4		7	9	Johnson	Bones		54-42	1st	+1.5
7-19	K.C.	L	6-9		11	10	Montgomery	Ayala		54-43	1st	+0.5
7-20	K.C.	W	5-4		6	9	Moyer	Appier	Wells	55-43	1st	+0.5
7-22	At Cle.	L	2-6		4	10	Weathers	Fassero	M. Jackson	55-44	1st	+0.5
7-23	At Cle.	W	6-3		11	11	Olivares	Colon	Holzemer	56-44	1st	+1.5
7-24	At Cle.	W	11-1		12	8	Johnson	Clark		57-44	1st	+2.0
7-25	At N.Y.	W	8-1		10	9	Moyer	Wells		58-44	1st	+1.5
7-26	At N.Y.	W	9-7		11	10	Ayala	Irabu	Charlton	59-44	1st	+2.5
7-27	At N.Y.	W	3-2		9	9	Fassero	Pettitte	Wells	60-44	1st	+3.5
7-29	At Bos.	L	0-4		5	8	Wakefield	Johnson		60-45	1st	+1.5
7-30	At Bos.	L	7-8	(10)	12	18	Corsi	Hurtado		60-46	1st	+0.5
7-31	At Mil.	L	1-2		6	6	Wickman	Moyer		60-47	1st	+0.5
8-1	At Mil.	L	3-8		4	14	Eldred	Wolcott		60-48	2nd	0.5
8-2	At Mil.	W	14-4		15	12	Fassero	Woodard		61-48	2nd	0.5
8-3	At Mil.	W	6-5		11	7	Johnson	Reyes	Slocumb	62-48	2nd	0.5
8-5	Bal.	W	4-3		5	9	Charlton	Mathews		63-48	1st	0.0
8-6	Bal.	L	3-4	(11)	10	13	Orosco	Slocumb	Myers	63-49	2nd	1.0
8-7	Chi.	W	3-2		3	6	Fassero	Eyre	Slocumb	64-49	2nd	0.5
8-8	Chi.	W	5-0		10	5	Johnson	Clemons		65-49	1st	+0.5
8-9	Chi.	L	2-5		7	4	Baldwin	Cloude	Karchner	65-50	2nd	0.5
8-10	Chi.	L	1-2		3	8	Drabek	Olivares	Karchner	65-51	2nd	0.5
8-11	Mil.	W	11-1		14	4	Moyer	Eldred		66-51	T1st	....
8-12	Mil.	L	3-5		6	7	Woodard	Fassero	Jones	66-52	T1st	....
8-15†	At Bal.	L	3-4		8	4	Kamieniecki	Johnson	Myers	66-53		
8-15‡	At Bal.	W	8-3		13	4	Cloude	Key		67-53	2nd	0.5
8-16†	At Chi.	W	11-6		11	13	Ayala	Drabek		68-53	1st	+0.5
8-17†	At Chi.	W	5-3		10	9	Fassero	Navarro		69-53		
8-17‡	At Chi.	L	2-4		8	7	Sirotka	Olivares	Karchner	69-54	1st	+1.0
8-18	At Chi.	L	0-5		4	9	Eyre	Lira	Foulke	69-55	1st	+1.0
8-19	Cle.	L	5-7		10	8	Smiley	Cloude	Mesa	69-56	T1st	....
8-20	Cle.	W	1-0		9	2	Johnson	Nagy	Slocumb	70-56	1st	+1.5
8-21	Cle.	W	7-6		8	12	Moyer	Colon	Slocumb	71-56	1st	+2.5
8-22	N.Y.	W	9-5		14	7	Fassero	Rogers		72-56	1st	+2.5
8-23	N.Y.	L	8-10	(11)	14	16	Rivera	Slocumb	Stanton	72-57	1st	+1.5
8-24	N.Y.	W	5-3		7	6	Ayala	Wells	Timlin	73-57	1st	+2.5
8-25	Bos.	L	8-9		11	17	Hudson	Slocumb	Gordon	73-58	1st	+2.0
8-26	Bos.	W	8-2		14	7	Moyer	Avery		74-58	1st	+2.0
8-27	Bos.	L	5-9		7	14	Wasdin	Fassero	Gordon	74-59	1st	+2.0
8-28	At Col.	L	5-9		10	12	Astacio	Olivares		74-60	1st	+2.0
8-29	At Col.	L	5-6		7	11	Dipoto	Timlin		74-61	1st	+1.0
8-30	At L.A.	L	2-11		5	14	Martinez	Wolcott	Dreifort	74-62	1st	+1.0
8-31	At L.A.	W	3-1	(10)	6	3	Timlin	Worrell	Ayala	75-62	1st	+1.0
9-1	S.D.	W	9-6		11	7	Fassero	Hamilton		76-62	1st	+2.0
9-3	S.D.	L	5-6		5	12	D. Veras	Timlin	Hoffman	76-63	1st	+2.0
9-4	At Min.	W	9-6		17	8	Cloude	Hawkins	Slocumb	77-63	1st	+3.0
9-5	At Min.	W	10-6		15	10	Moyer	Radke		78-63	1st	+4.0
9-6	At Min.	W	9-0		10	4	Fassero	Robertson		79-63	1st	+5.0
9-7	At Min.	L	6-9		12	8	Tewksbury	Lira		79-64	1st	+4.0
9-8	At K.C.	L	2-9		6	15	Pittsley	Olivares		79-65	1st	+4.0
9-9	At K.C.	W	4-3		9	8	Timlin	Pichardo	Slocumb	80-65	1st	+5.0
9-10	Det.	W	10-0		10	6	Moyer	Thompson		81-65	1st	+5.5

Date	Opp.	Res.	Score	(inn.*)	Hits	Opp. hits	Winning pitcher	Losing pitcher	Save	Record	Pos.	GB
9-11	Det.	L	1-3		5	5	Moehler	Fassero	Jones	81-66	1st	+5.5
9-12	Tor.	W	7-3		10	8	Ayala	Clemens		82-66	1st	+5.5
9-13	Tor.	L	3-6		7	6	Escobar	Ayala		82-67	1st	+5.5
9-14	Tor.	W	3-2		7	6	Timlin	Risley	Slocumb	83-67	1st	+5.5
9-15	Tor.	W	7-3		10	9	Cloude	Williams	Slocumb	84-67	1st	+5.5
9-17	At Tex.	L	4-5		8	11	Patterson	Slocumb		84-68	1st	+5.0
9-18	At Tex.	W	6-3		9	10	Johnson	Oliver	Ayala	85-68	1st	+6.0
9-19	At Oak.	W	9-4		12	9	Moyer	Haynes		86-68	1st	+6.0
9-20	At Oak.	L	3-4	(15)	10	11	Small	Lira		86-69	1st	+5.0
9-21	At Oak.	W	9-2		14	9	Cloude	Rigby		87-69	1st	+5.0
9-22	At Oak.	W	4-2		9	10	Fassero	Ludwick	Slocumb	88-69	1st	+5.5
9-23	Ana.	W	4-3		7	9	Johnson	Watson	Slocumb	89-69	1st	+6.5
9-24	Ana.	L	3-9		5	13	Hill	Lira		89-70	1st	+5.5
9-26	Oak.	L	5-8		7	12	Oquist	Moyer	Mathews	89-71	1st	+6.0
9-27	Oak.	W	9-3		13	10	Johnson	Rigby		90-71	1st	+6.0
9-28	Oak.	L	7-9		11	11	Small	Charlton	Taylor	90-72	1st	+6.0

Monthly records: April (16-11), May (11-16), June (20-7), July (13-13), August (15-15), September (15-10).
*Innings, if other than nine. †First game of doubleheader. ‡Second game of doubleheader.

HIGHLIGHTS

High point: Prior to the 1997 season, the Mariners had been in first place only 106 days (total) during their 20-year franchise history. In '97, they spent 140 of the 180 days either tied for or in sole possession of top spot in the AL West. The Mariners moved into first place on August 15 and never were caught.
Low point: July 31, only a few hours before the trading deadline, rookie left fielder Jose Cruz Jr. was traded to the Blue Jays for pitchers Mike Timlin and Paul Spoljaric. After using more than 50 players in left field since 1989, the Mariners appeared finally to have solved the transient position with Cruz. But instead of a fixture, the former No. 1 draft pick became just another number.
Turning point: After being hammered by the Dodgers, 11-2, on August 30, manager Lou Piniella called a meeting with his veteran position players the following afternoon in Los Angeles. It worked: the Mariners won their next 14 games to open a six-game lead over the Angels.
Most valuable player: Center fielder Ken Griffey Jr. had his first injury-free season in three years and responded with eye-popping numbers. His 56 homers were the eighth-most in major league history; his 147 RBIs were the sixth-highest total over the past 48 years and his 393 total bases set a club record.
Most valuable pitcher: Lefthander Randy Johnson bounced back from career-threatening back surgery to become the franchise's first 20-game winner, posting a 20-4 record. He twice struck out 19 batters in a game during his comeback season and he held opposing hitters to a league-low .193 average.
Most improved player: Third baseman Russ Davis established career bests in batting average (.271), home runs (20) and RBIs (63), despite missing the last 32 games of the regular season because of a sprained ankle.
Most pleasant surprise: Righthander Ken Cloude began the season at Class AA Memphis and finished it with the Mariners, contributing four wins to the September pennant drive.
Biggest disappointment: The bullpen in general and lefthander Norm Charlton in particular. After going 9-for-9 in save opportunities April 11-May 14, he failed in five consecutive save situations and never fully recovered from the skid, finishing the season with 14 saves in 25 save chances and an ugly 7.27 ERA in 71 appearances.
Key injuries: Lefthander Jamie Moyer began the season on the DL with a strained left forearm and missed the first month. Shortstop Alex Rodriguez missed more than two weeks in June with a bruised chest, and it took him another two weeks to regain his batting stroke. Johnson missed four September starts because of tendinitis in the middle finger of his left hand.
Notable: Griffey hit two home runs on opening night, giving fans a sneak preview of what would become an awesome power display. Half his 56 homers traveled at least 400 feet, the longest being a 473-foot bomb against the White Sox.
—JIM STREET

RECORDS

1997 regular-season record: 90-72 (1st in A.L. West); 45-36 at home; 45-36 on road; 30-25 vs. East; 32-23 vs. Central; 28-24 vs. West; 24-18 vs. lefthanded starters; 66-54 vs. righthanded starters; 38-32 on grass; 52-40 on turf; 30-21 in daytime; 60-51 at night; 25-21 in one-run games; 4-7 in extra-inning games; 0-2 in doubleheaders.
Team record past five years: 385-357 (.519, ranks 5th in league in that span).

TEAM LEADERS

Batting average: Edgar Martinez (.330).
At-bats: Ken Griffey Jr. (.608).
Runs: Ken Griffey Jr. (125).
Hits: Ken Griffey Jr. (185).
Total bases: Ken Griffey Jr. (393).
Doubles: Joey Cora, Alex Rodriguez (40).
Triples: Joey Cora (4).
Home runs: Ken Griffey Jr. (56).
Runs batted in: Ken Griffey Jr. (147).
Stolen bases: Alex Rodriguez (29).
Slugging percentage: Ken Griffey Jr. (.646).
On-base percentage: Edgar Martinez (.456).
Wins: Randy Johnson (20).
Earned-run average: Randy Johnson (2.28).
Complete games: Randy Johnson (5).
Shutouts: Randy Johnson (2).

Saves: Norm Charlton (14).
Innings pitched: Jeff Fassero (234.1).
Strikeouts: Randy Johnson (291).

GAMES BY POSITION

Catcher: Dan Wilson 144, John Marzano 37, Rick Wilkins 3.
First base: Paul Sorrento 139, Mike Blowers 49, Rich Amaral 14, Edgar Martinez 7, Dan Rohrmeier 3, Brent Gates 1.
Second base: Joey Cora 142, Brent Gates 21, Alvaro Espinoza 11, Rich Amaral 11, Giomar Guevara 2, Andy Sheets 2, Brian Raabe 1.
Third base: Russ Davis 117, Brent Gates 32, Andy Sheets 21, Mike Blowers 10, Brian Raabe 2, Rich Amaral 1, Alvaro Espinoza 1, Edgar Martinez 1.
Shortstop: Alex Rodriguez 140, Alvaro Espinoza 17, Andy Sheets 9, Brent Gates 5, Rich Amaral 1, Giomar Guevara 1.
Outfield: Jay Buhner 154, Ken Griffey Jr 153, Rob Ducey 69, Rich Amaral 52, Jose Cruz Jr 49, Lee Tinsley 41, Roberto Kelly 29, Raul Ibanez 8, Mike Blowers 6, Brent Gates 1.
Designated hitter: Edgar Martinez 144, Ken Griffey Jr 4, Dan Rohrmeier 4, Lee Tinsley 4, Rich Amaral 3, Jay Buhner 2, Giomar Guevara 2, Rick Wilkins 2, Mike Blowers 1, Russ Davis 1, Brent Gates 1, Raul Ibanez 1, Roberto Kelly 1, John Marzano 1, Alex Rodriguez 1, Paul Sorrento 1.

TOP DRAFT CHOICES

1. **Ryan Anderson,** LHP, Divine Child H.S., Westland, Mich.
2a. **Brandon Parker,** RHP, University of Southern Mississippi.
2b. **Patrick Boyd,** OF, Central Catholic H.S., Clearwater, Fla.
3. **Patrick Dunham,** RHP, Auburn Univ.
4. **Scott Prouty,** RHP, Pekin H.S., Marquette Heights, Ill.
5. **Jermaine Clark,** 2B, U. of San Francisco.
6. **Harvey Hargrove,** 2B, Sacramento State University.
7. **Sam Walton,** LHP, W.W. Samuell H.S., Dallas.
8. **Larry Simpson,** RHP, Taft (Calif.) J.C.
9. **Frank Corr,** C, Father Lopez H.S., Deltona, Fla.
10. **Peter Duprey,** LHP, Forest H.S., Ocala, Fla.

TAMPA BAY DEVIL RAYS
AMERICAN LEAGUE EAST DIVISION

Devil Rays Schedule

Home games shaded. *—All-Star Game at Coors Field (Colorado).
D—Day game (any game starting before 5 p.m.).

March

SUN	MON	TUE	WED	THU	FRI	SAT
		31 D DET				

April

SUN	MON	TUE	WED	THU	FRI	SAT
			1 DET	2 D DET	3 CWS	4 CWS
5 D CWS	6	7 D DET	8	9 D DET	10 CWS	11 D CWS
12 D CWS	13 MIN	14 MIN	15	16 ANA	17 ANA	18 ANA
19 D ANA	20	21 TEX	22 TEX	23 D TEX	24 ANA	25 ANA
26 D ANA	27 OAK	28 OAK	29 MIN	30 D MIN		

May

SUN	MON	TUE	WED	THU	FRI	SAT
					1 CLE	2 D CLE
3 D CLE	4	5 KC	6 KC	7	8 BAL	9 BAL
10 D BAL	11 CLE	12 CLE	13 KC	14 KC	15 BAL	16 D BAL
17 D BAL	18 BAL	19 TOR	20 TOR	21 D TOR	22 SEA	23 SEA
24 SEA	25 D OAK	26 D OAK	27	28 SEA	29 SEA	30 SEA
31 D SEA						

June

SUN	MON	TUE	WED	THU	FRI	SAT
	1 TEX	2 TEX	3 NYY	4 NYY	5 D MON	6 MON
7 MON	8 NYM	9 NYM	10 NYM	11	12 BOS	13 D BOS
14 BOS	15 TOR	16 TOR	17 BOS	18 BOS	19 BOS	20 BOS
21 BOS	22 FLA	23 FLA	24 FLA	25 PHI	26 PHI	27 PHI
28 D PHI	29	30 ATL				

July

SUN	MON	TUE	WED	THU	FRI	SAT
			1 ATL	2 ATL	3 TOR	4 D TOR
5 D TOR	6	7 *	8	9 NYY	10 NYY	11 NYY
12 NYY	13 BOS	14 BOS	15 ANA	16 ANA	17 TEX	18 TEX
19 TEX	20	21 SEA	22 SEA	23	24 OAK	25 OAK
26 OAK	27 OAK	28 CWS	29 CWS	30	31 DET	

August

SUN	MON	TUE	WED	THU	FRI	SAT
						1 DET
2 D DET	3 CWS	4 CWS	5 CWS	6	7 CLE	8 D CLE
9 CLE	10 BAL	11 BAL	12 D BAL	13 KC	14 KC	15 KC
16 KC	17 CLE	18 CLE	19 BAL	20 BAL	21 KC	22 KC
23 KC	24	25 MIN	26 MIN	27 DET	28 DET	29
30 D DET	31 MIN					

September

SUN	MON	TUE	WED	THU	FRI	SAT
		1 MIN	2 MIN	3 MIN	4 D OAK	5 OAK
6 D OAK	7	8 SEA	9 D SEA	10	11 TEX	12 TEX
13 TEX	14 ANA	15 ANA	16 NYY	17 NYY	18 TOR	19 TOR
20 TOR	21 BOS	22 BOS	23 NYY	24 NYY	25 NYY	26 D NYY
27 D NYY						

1998 SEASON
CLUB DIRECTORY

Managing general partner/CEO
Vincent J. Naimoli
Sr. v.p. of baseball operations/g.m.
Chuck LaMar
Senior vice president/CFO
Raymond Naimoli
Senior vice president/general counsel
John P. Higgins
Vice president/public relations
Rick Vaughn
V.p./stadia operations & facilities
Rick Nafe
General manager/sales & marketing
David Auker
Admin. asst., managing gen. partner/CEO
Cass Halpin
Asst. g.m./baseball operations
Bart Braun
Asst. general manager/administration
Scott Proefrock
Director of player personnel
Bill Livesey
Special assistants to the g.m.
Bill Geivett, Bart Johnson, Mickey White
Director of scouting
Dan Jennings
Asst./scouting & player development
Michael Hill
Director of minor league operations
Tom Foley
Director of community development
Orestes Destrade
Director of ticket operations
Robert Bennett
Director of ticket sales
Dick Barry
Director of corporate sales
Larry McCabe
Director of corporate sales
John Brown
Director of merchandising
Rob Katz
Accountant
Sheryl Evans
Office administrator
Bill Wiener, Jr.
Media relations manager
Andrew Maraniss

Public relations assistant
Steve Matesich
Marketing coordinator
Noel Beaulieu
Ticket sales coordinator
Jim Cook
Director of community relations
Julie Williamson
Community relations assistant
Liz Lauck
Publications director
Mike Flanagan
Assistant publications director
Raul Alsina
Dir. of event productions & entertainment
John Franzone
Traveling secretary
Ken Lehner
Medical director
Dr. James Andrews
Trainers
Jamie Reed, Ken Crenshaw
Strength and conditioning coach
Kevin Harmon
Team physicians
Dr. William Carson, Dr. Michael Reilly, Dr. Koco Eaton
Head groundskeeper
Mike Williams
Equipment manager
Carlos Ledezma
Visiting clubhouse manager
Guy Gallagher
Major League scouts
Jerry Gardner, Al LaMacchia, Don Lindeberg, Don Williams
Crosscheckers
Jack Gillis, R.J. Harrison, Stan Meek, Shawn Pender
Area scouts
Fernando Arango, Skip Bundy, Tim Corcoran, Matt Dodd, Kevin Elfering, Paul Faulk, Doug Gassaway, Matt Kinzer, Paul Kirsch, Blaise Kozeniewski, Mark McKnight, Pat O'Neil, Edwin Rodriguez, Nelson Rood, Rudy Santin, Charles Scott, Craig F. Weissmann
Part-time scouts
Jorge Calvo Sr., Jorge Calvo Jr., Philip Elhage, Mark Lummus, Gustavo Rodriguez, Freddy Torres, Mel Zitter

MINOR LEAGUE AFFILIATES

Class	Team	League	Manager
AAA	Durham	International	To be announced
AA	Orlando	Southern	Dan Rohn
A	St. Petersburg	Florida State	Roy Silver
A	Charleston (W.Va.)	South Atlantic	Greg Mahlberg
Rookie	Hudson Valley	New York-Penn	Charlie Montoyo
Rookie	Princeton	Appalachian	David Howard
Rookie	Gulf Coast Devil Rays	Gulf Coast	Bobby Ramos

BROADCAST INFORMATION

Radio: WFLA-AM (970).
TV: WWWB (Channel 32).
Cable TV: SportsChannel Florida.

SPRING TRAINING

Ballpark (city): Al Lang Stadium (St. Petersburg, Fla.).
Ticket information: 813-825-3250.

TOP DRAFT CHOICES

1. **Jason Standridge,** RHP, Hewitt Trussville H.S., Trussville, Ala.
2. **Kenny Kelly,** OF, Tampa Catholic H.S.
3. **Barrett Wright,** RHP, Myers Park H.S., Charlotte.
4. **Todd Belitz,** LHP, Washington State Univ.
5. **Marquis Roberts,** LHP-OF, McLane H.S., Fresno, Calif.
6. **Doug Mansfield,** OF, Jacksonville H.S., Sherwood, Ark.
7. **Eddie Reyes,** RHP, University of Miami.
8. **Jack Joffrion,** SS, Lamar University.
9. **Toby Hall,** C, U. of Nevada-Las Vegas.
10. **Carl Hutchens,** RHP, Anderson H.S., Austin.

SPRING TRAINING ROSTER

Manager—Larry Rothschild.
Coaches—Billy Hatcher, Steve Henderson, Frank Howard, Greg Riddoch, Rick Williams.

No.	PITCHERS	B/T	Ht./Wt.	Born	1997 clubs
	Alvarez, Wilson	L/L	6-1/235	3-24-70	Chicago A.L., San Francisco
	Arrojo, Rolando	R/R	6-4/210	7-18-68	St. Petersburg
	Carlson, Dan	R/R	6-1/200	1-26-70	San Francisco, Bakersfield, Phoenix
	Eshelman, Vaughn	L/L	6-3/215	5-22-69	Pawtucket, Boston
	Gorecki, Rick	R/R	6-3/167	8-27-73	San Bernardino, San Antonio, Los Angeles
	Hernandez, Roberto	R/R	6-4/235	11-11-64	Chicago A.L., San Francisco
	Hernandez, Santos	R/R	6-2/180	11-3-72	San Jose, Shreveport
	Johnson, Jason	R/R	6-6/215	10-27-73	Lynchburg, Carolina, Pittsburgh
	LeRoy, John	R/R	6-3/175	4-19-75	Greenville, Atlanta
	Lopez, Albie	R/R	6-2/235	8-18-71	Cleveland, Buffalo, Akron
	Mecir, Jim	B/R	6-1/195	5-16-70	Columbus, New York A.L.
	Paniagua, Jose	R/R	6-2/185	8-20-73	West Palm Beach, Ottawa, Montreal
	Rekar, Bryan	R/R	6-3/210	6-3-72	Colorado Springs, Colorado
	Saunders, Tony	L/L	6-2/205	4-29-74	Florida, Portland, Charlotte
	Springer, Dennis	R/R	5-10/190	2-12-65	Anaheim, Vancouver
	Tatis, Ramon	L/L	6-2/185	1-5-73	Chicago N.L.
	Wade, Terrell	L/L	6-3/205	1-25-73	Atlanta, Greenville
	Yan, Esteban	R/R	6-4/230	6-22-74	Rochester, Baltimore

No.	CATCHERS	B/T	Ht./Wt.	Born	1997 clubs
	Difelice, Mike	R/R	6-2/205	5-28-69	Arkansas, St. Louis, Louisville
	Flaherty, John	R/R	6-1/205	10-21-67	San Diego

No.	INFIELDERS	B/T	Ht./Wt.	Born	1997 clubs
12	Boggs, Wade	L/R	6-2/197	6-15-58	New York A.L.
	Cairo, Miguel	R/R	6-0/192	5-4-74	Iowa, Chicago N.L.
	Cox, Steve	L/L	6-4/223	10-31-74	Edmonton
	Ledesma, Aaron	R/R	6-2/200	6-3-71	Rochester, Baltimore
	McGriff, Fred	L/L	6-3/215	10-31-63	Atlanta
	Perry, Herbert	R/R	6-2/215	9-15-69	DID NOT PLAY
	Smith, Bobby	R/R	6-3/190	5-10-74	Richmond
	Sorrento, Paul	L/R	6-2/220	11-17-65	Seattle
	Stocker, Kevin	B/R	6-1/175	2-13-70	Philadelphia

No.	OUTFIELDERS	B/T	Ht./Wt.	Born	1997 clubs
	Butler, Rich	L/R	6-1/180	5-1-73	Syracuse, Toronto
	Kelly, Mike	R/R	6-4/195	6-2-70	Indianapolis, Cincinnati, Chattanooga
	Kieschnick, Brooks	L/R	6-4/230	6-6-72	Iowa, Chicago N.L.
	Martinez, Dave	L/L	5-10/175	9-26-64	Chicago A.L.
	McCracken, Quinton	B/R	5-7/173	3-16-70	Colorado
	Mendoza, Carlos	L/L	5-11/160	11-4-74	Binghamton, Norfolk, New York N.L., Gulf Coast Devil Rays
	Robinson, Kerry	L/L	6-0/170	10-3-73	Arkansas, Louisville
	Trammell, Bubba	R/R	6-3/205	11-6-71	Detroit, Toledo
	Wilcox, Luke	L/R	6-4/195	11-15-73	Tampa, Norwich
	Winn, Randy	B/R	6-2/175	6-9-74	Brevard, Portland

BALLPARK INFORMATION

Ballpark (capacity, surface)
Tropicana Field (45,200, artificial)
Address
One Tropicana Drive
St. Petersburg, FL 33705
Business phone
813-825-3137
Ticket information
813-825-3250
Ticket prices
$27 (club field, club loge)
$19 (main box, loge box)
$16.50 (tier box)
$16 (main reserved)
$11.50 (tier reserved)
$6 (bleachers)
Field dimensions (from home plate)
To left field at foul line, 315 feet
To center field, 407 feet
To right field at foul line, 322 feet
First game played
Scheduled for March 31, 1998 vs. Detroit

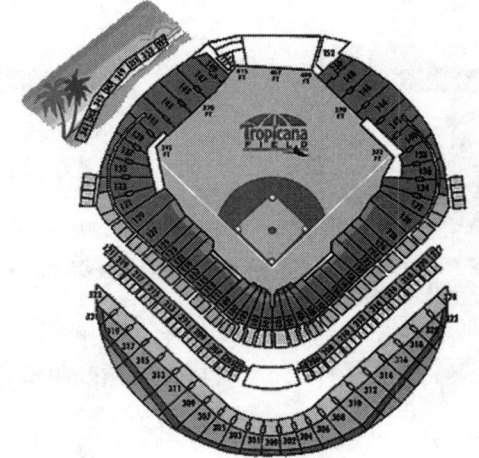

TEXAS RANGERS
AMERICAN LEAGUE WEST DIVISION

Rangers Schedule

Home games shaded. *—All-Star Game at Coors Field (Colorado). D—Day game (any game starting before 5 p.m.)

March
SUN	MON	TUE	WED	THU	FRI	SAT
		31 D CWS				

April
SUN	MON	TUE	WED	THU	FRI	SAT
			1 CWS	2 CWS	3 TOR	4 D TOR
5 D TOR	6 D CWS	7	8 CWS	9 D CWS	10 TOR	11 TOR
12 TOR	13 DET	14 DET	15 DET	16	17 BAL	18 BAL
19 BAL	20	21 TB	22 TB	23 D TB	24 KC	25 KC
26 D KC	27 MIN	28 MIN	29 DET	30 D DET		

May
SUN	MON	TUE	WED	THU	FRI	SAT
					1 BOS	2 D BOS
3 D BOS	4	5 NYY	6 NYY	7 CLE	8 CLE	9 CLE
10 D CLE	11 BOS	12 D NYY	13 NYY	14 NYY	15 CLE	16 D CLE
17 CLE	18	19 SEA	20 SEA	21 SEA	22 KC	23 KC
24 D KC	25 MIN	26	27 D MIN	28 BAL	29 BAL	30 D BAL
31 D BAL						

June
SUN	MON	TUE	WED	THU	FRI	SAT
	1 TB	2 TB	3 OAK	4 OAK	5 D SD	6 SD
7 SD	8 COL	9 COL	10 COL	11	12 ANA	13 ANA
14 ANA	15 ANA	16 OAK	17 OAK	18 OAK	19 D ANA	20 ANA
21 ANA	22 ARZ	23 ARZ	24 ARZ	25 SF	26 SF	27 D SF
28 D SF	29	30 LA				

July
SUN	MON	TUE	WED	THU	FRI	SAT
			1 LA	2 LA	3 SEA	4 SEA
5 SEA	6	7 *	8 D OAK	9 OAK	10 D OAK	11 D OAK
12 OAK	13 SEA	14 SEA	15 BAL	16 BAL	17 TB	18 TB
19 TB	20	21 KC	22 KC	23 KC	24 MIN	25 MIN
26 D MIN	27	28 TOR	29 TOR	30 TOR	31 CWS	

August
SUN	MON	TUE	WED	THU	FRI	SAT
						1 CWS
2 CWS	3	4 TOR	5 TOR	6 BOS	7 BOS	8 BOS
9 BOS	10	11 CLE	12 CLE	13 NYY	14 NYY	15 D NYY
16 D NYY	17 BOS	18 D BOS	19 CLE	20 CLE	21 NYY	22 NYY
23 NYY	24 DET	25 DET	26 DET	27	28 CWS	29 CWS
30 D CWS	31 DET					

September
SUN	MON	TUE	WED	THU	FRI	SAT
		1 DET	2 DET	3	4 MIN	5 MIN
6 MIN	7 MIN	8 D KC	9 KC	10	11 TB	12 TB
13 TB	14 BAL	15 BAL	16 ANA	17 ANA	18 OAK	19 OAK
20 OAK	21 ANA	22 ANA	23 ANA	24 SEA	25 SEA	26 SEA
27 D SEA						

1998 SEASON
CLUB DIRECTORY

General partners
Edward W. (Rusty) Rose
J. Thomas Schieffer

President
J. Thomas Schieffer

Exec. v.p., general manager
R. Douglas Melvin

Exec. v.p., bus. operations/treasurer
John F. McMichael

Vice president, marketing
Charles Searphin

Vice president, public relations
John C. Blake

Vice president, community development
Norman B. Lyons

Vice president, information technology
Steve McNeill

Vice president, human resources
Kimberly A. Smith

General counsel
Gerald W. Haddock

Dir., Legends of the Game baseball museum
Tom Smith

Assistant v.p., controller
Chip Sawicki

Assistant v.p., facilities
Billy Ray Johnson

Assistant v.p., customer service
Tim Murphy

Dir. of major league field operations
Tim Burns

Assistant general manager
Dan O'Brien III

Director of amateur scouting
Chuck McMichael

Director, player development
Reid Nichols

Director of travel
Chris Lyngos

Dir. of major league administration
Judy Johns

Asst. dir., professional and int'l scouting
Monty Clegg

Director of medical services
Dr. Mike Mycoskie

Visiting clubhouse manager
Joe Macko

Equipment and home clubhouse manager
Zack Minasian

Director, corporate sales
Mike Phillips

Director, camps and clinics
Jack Lazorko

Director, in-park entertainment
Chuck Morgan

Director, merchandising
Nancy Hill

Director, ticket operations
Marty Schueren

Director, sales
Ross Scott

Director, player relations
Taunee Taylor

Dir., Spanish broadcasting and Latin American liasion
Luis R. Mayoral

Director, publications
Eric Kolb

Assistant directors, public relations
Charley Green
Lydia Traina

Assistant, special projects
Bobby Bragan

Admin. asst., public relations
Amy Gunter

National crosscheckers
Tim Hallgren
David Klipstein
Jeff Taylor

Scouts
Manuel Batista (coordinator, Latin America), Dave Birecki, Mike Cadahia, Mike Daughtry, Jay Eddings, Kip Fagg, Jim Fairey, Mark Giegler, Joel Grampietro, Mike Grouse, Todd Guggiana, Doug Harris, Bob Heck, Larry Izzo, Jim Lentine, Randy Taylor, Greg Whitworth

MINOR LEAGUE AFFILIATES

Class	Team	League	Manager
AAA	Oklahoma	Pacific Coast	Greg Biagini
AA	Tulsa	Texas	Bobby Jones
A	Charlotte	Florida State	To be announced
A	Savannah	South Atlantic	James Byrd
Rookie	Pulaski	Appalachian	Paul Carey
Rookie	Gulf Coast Rangers	Gulf Coast	Daryl Kennedy

BROADCAST INFORMATION

Radio: KRLD-AM (1080); KMRT-AM (1480); KMRT-FM (106.7, Spanish language).
TV: KXAS-TV (Channel 5); KXTX-TV (Channel 39).
Cable TV: Fox Sports Southwest.

SPRING TRAINING

Ballpark (city): Charlotte County Stadium (Port Charlotte, Fla.).
Ticket information: 941-625-9500.

SPRING TRAINING ROSTER

Manager—Johnny Oates (26).
Coaches—Dick Bosman (17), Bucky Dent (20), Larry Hardy (25), Rudy Jaramillo (8), Ed Napoleon, Jerry Narron (5).

No.	PITCHERS	B/T	Ht./Wt.	Born	1997 clubs
	Bailes, Scott	L/L	6-2/171	12-18-62	Oklahoma City, Texas
	Brandenburg, Mark	R/R	6-0/180	7-14-70	Sarasota, Boston, Pawtucket
33	Burkett, John	R/R	6-3/215	11-28-64	Texas, Oklahoma City
	Glynn, Ryan	R/R	6-3/200	11-1-74	Charlotte, Tulsa
53	Gunderson, Eric	R/L	6-0/190	3-29-66	Texas
32	Helling, Rick	R/R	6-3/220	12-15-70	Florida, Texas
31	Hernandez, Xavier	L/R	6-2/195	8-16-65	Texas
	Johnson, Jonathon	R/R	6-0/180	7-16-74	Tulsa
	Knight, Brandon	L/L	6-0/170	10-1-75	Charlotte, Tulsa
	Kolb, Dan	R/R	6-4/185	3-29-75	Charlotte, Tulsa
54	Levine, Alan	L/R	6-3/180	5-22-68	Chicago A.L., Nashville
45	Moody, Eric	R/R	6-6/185	1-6-71	Oklahoma City, Texas
28	Oliver, Darren	R/L	6-2/200	10-6-70	Texas
56	Patterson, Danny	R/R	6-0/185	2-17-71	Texas, Tulsa
59	Pavlik, Roger	R/R	6-2/220	10-4-67	Texas, Gulf Coast Rangers, Tulsa, Oklahoma City
	Perisho, Matt	L/L	6-0/175	6-8-75	Midland, Anaheim, Vancouver
60	Santana, Julio	R/R	6-0/185	1-20-74	Texas, Oklahoma City
	Sele, Aaron	R/R	6-5/215	6-25-70	Boston
35	Smith, Danny	L/L	6-5/195	4-20-69	Tulsa, Oklahoma City
	Sturtze, Tanyon	R/R	6-5/205	10-12-70	Oklahoma City, Texas
	Thomas, Larry	R/L	6-1/195	10-25-69	Nashville, Chicago A.L.
35	Wetteland, John	R/R	6-2/215	8-21-66	Texas
27	Whiteside, Matt	R/R	6-0/205	8-8-67	Oklahoma City, Texas

No.	CATCHERS	B/T	Ht./Wt.	Born	1997 clubs
44	Brown, Kevin	R/R	6-2/200	4-21-73	Oklahoma City, Texas
37	Haselman, Bill	R/R	6-3/223	5-25-66	Boston, Gulf Coast Red Sox, Trenton
7	Rodriguez, Ivan	R/R	5-9/205	11-30-71	Texas

No.	INFIELDERS	B/T	Ht./Wt.	Born	1997 clubs
10	Alicea, Luis	B/R	5-9/176	7-29-65	Anaheim
1	Cedeno, Domingo	B/R	6-0/170	11-4-68	Texas, Tulsa, Oklahoma City
22	Clark, Will	L/L	6-1/200	3-13-64	Texas
19	Elster, Kevin	R/R	6-2/200	8-3-64	Pittsburgh
3	McLemore, Mark	B/R	5-11/207	10-4-64	Texas, Charlotte, Oklahoma City
	Sasser, Rob	R/R	6-4/190	3-9-75	Cedar Rapids
11	Stevens, Lee	L/L	6-4/219	7-10-67	Texas
4	Tatis, Fernando	L/R	6-1/175	1-1-75	Tulsa, Texas

No.	OUTFIELDERS	B/T	Ht./Wt.	Born	1997 clubs
19	Gonzalez, Juan	R/R	6-3/220	10-16-69	Texas
24	Goodwin, Tom	L/R	6-1/175	7-27-68	Kansas City, Texas
29	Greer, Rusty	L/L	6-0/190	1-21-69	Texas
5	Kelly, Roberto	R/R	6-2/198	10-1-64	Fort Myers, Minnesota, Seattle
	Little, Mark	R/R	6-0/195	7-11-72	Oklahoma City
	Simms, Mike	R/R	6-4/185	1-12-67	Oklahoma City, Texas

BALLPARK INFORMATION

Ballpark (capacity, surface)
The Ballpark in Arlington (49,166, grass)

Address
1000 Ballpark Way
Arlington, TX 76011

Business phone
817-273-5222

Ticket information
817-273-5100

Ticket prices
$25 (lower box, club box)
$20 (corner box, club box)
$15 (terrace club box)
$12 (upper box, left field reserved,
    lower home run porch)
$10 (upper box, upper reserved,
    upper home run porch)
$8 (bleachers, adults)
$6 (grandstand reserved, adults)
$4 (grandstand, adults and bleachers,
    children 13 and under)
$3 (grandstand reserved, children 13 and under)
$2 (grandstand, children 13 and under)

Field dimensions (from home plate)
To left field at foul line, 332 feet
To center field, 400 feet
To right field at foul line, 325 feet

First game played
April 11, 1994 (Brewers 4, Rangers 3)

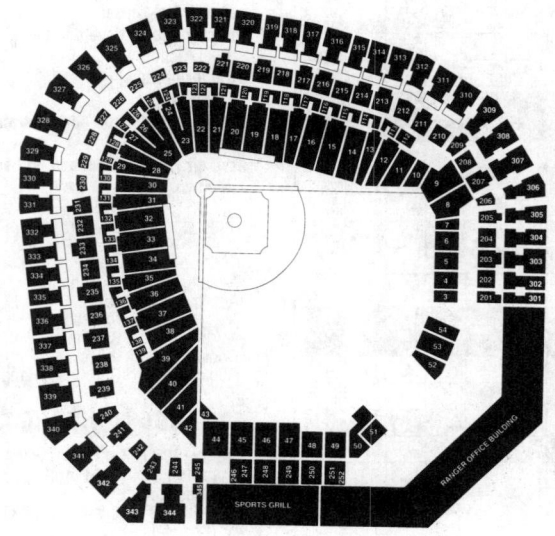

Date	Opp.	Res.	Score	(inn.*)	Hits	Opp. hits	Winning pitcher	Losing pitcher	Save	Record	Pos.	GB
4-1	Mil.	W	6-2		7	7	Hill	McDonald		1-0	T1st	....
4-4	Bal.	L	4-5		5	9	Erickson	Patterson	Benitez	1-1	3rd	0.5
4-5	Bal.	L	7-9		7	14	Rhodes	Oliver	Myers	1-2	3rd	0.5
4-6	Bal.	W	9-3		13	6	Pavlik	Mussina		2-2	2nd	0.5
4-7	At Mil.	L	3-5		7	7	Eldred	Hill	Jones	2-3	2nd	1.5
4-10	At Mil.	W	2-0		7	3	Witt	Karl	Wetteland	3-3	T2nd	1.0
4-11	At Bal.	L	3-9		4	16	Mussina	Burkett		3-4	3rd	2.0
4-13	At Bal.	L	0-9		6	12	Key	Pavlik		3-5	4th	2.5
4-14	Chi.	W	3-1		7	4	Patterson	Alvarez	Wetteland	4-5	4th	1.5
4-15	Chi.	W	5-2		7	11	Witt	Baldwin	Wetteland	5-5	T3rd	1.5
4-16	At K.C.	W	2-0		4	10	Burkett	Pittsley	Wetteland	6-5	2nd	1.5
4-17	At K.C.	W	5-1		9	5	Oliver	Belcher		7-5	2nd	1.5
4-18	Tor.	L	5-6		9	4	Hentgen	Pavlik	Timlin	7-6	2nd	1.5
4-19	Tor.	L	0-6		4	12	Clemens	Hill		7-7	3rd	1.5
4-20	Tor.	W	10-5		13	13	Witt	Guzman		8-7	2nd	1.5
4-21	Det.	L	6-7		13	13	Sager	Vosberg	Miceli	8-8	T2nd	2.5
4-23	Det.	W	2-1		6	4	Wetteland	Brocail		9-8	2nd	2.0
4-24	Det.	W	4-2		11	6	Pavlik	Thompson	Wetteland	10-8	2nd	1.5
4-25	At Min.	W	6-3		11	6	Hill	Tewksbury	Wetteland	11-8	2nd	1.5
4-26	At Min.	W	6-1		11	7	Witt	Aldred	Gunderson	12-8	2nd	0.5
4-27	At Min.	W	7-3		11	7	Patterson	Naulty		13-8	2nd	0.5
4-28	At Mil.	L	8-14		10	15	McDonald	Oliver		13-9	2nd	0.5
4-29	At Chi.	L	1-2		6	9	Navarro	Patterson		13-10	2nd	1.5
4-30	At Chi.	W	6-2	(7)	9	6	Witt	Alvarez		14-10	2nd	0.5
5-2	Bos.	L	4-5		8	12	Henry	Patterson	Slocumb	14-11	2nd	1.5
5-3	Bos.	W	7-6		14	12	Vosberg	Slocumb		15-11	2nd	0.5
5-4	Bos.	W	7-6		13	9	Patterson	Henry	Wetteland	16-11	2nd	0.5
5-6	At Cle.	L	4-5		9	6	Hershiser	Pavlik	M. Jackson	16-12	2nd	1.5
5-7	At N.Y.	L	2-5		9	8	Cone	Burkett	Rivera	16-13	2nd	2.0
5-8	At N.Y.	L	4-5		11	10	Pettitte	Oliver	Rivera	16-14	2nd	2.0
5-9	At Bos.	W	5-1		10	5	Witt	Wasdin		17-14	2nd	2.0
5-10	At Bos.	W	11-5		15	11	Patterson	Slocumb		18-14	2nd	2.0
5-11	At Bos.	W	8-6		11	14	Santana	Gordon	Wetteland	19-14	2nd	1.0
5-12	Cle.	W	4-2		5	9	Burkett	McDowell	Wetteland	20-14	1st	0.0
5-13	Cle.	L	3-7		8	12	Ogea	Oliver	Morman	20-15	2nd	1.0
5-14	Cle.	W	4-3	(10)	13	8	Wetteland	Lopez		21-15	2nd	1.0
5-15	N.Y.	L	2-8		9	11	Rogers	Alberro		21-16	2nd	1.0
5-16	N.Y.	W	6-0		6	4	Santana	Wells	Patterson	22-16	1st	0.0
5-17	N.Y.	L	5-11		12	20	Mendoza	Burkett		22-17	1st	0.0
5-18	N.Y.	W	4-2		8	9	Oliver	Cone	Wetteland	23-17	1st	+1.0
5-20	Oak.	W	8-3		14	7	Witt	Prieto		24-17	1st	+1.5
5-21	Oak.	L	3-7		9	9	Telgheder	Santana		24-18	1st	+1.5
5-22	Oak.	W	10-7		14	13	Burkett	Oquist	Wetteland	25-18	1st	+2.0
5-23	At Det.	L	1-7		7	11	Moehler	Oliver		25-19	1st	+1.0
5-24	At Det.	W	8-4		6	8	Hill	Pugh		26-19	1st	+1.0
5-25	At Det.	L	5-13		9	13	Lira	Witt	Sager	26-20	1st	+1.0
5-26	At Tor.	L	1-8		5	13	Clemens	Santana		26-21	1st	+1.0
5-27	At Tor.	W	15-5		16	10	Burkett	Person		27-21	1st	+2.0
5-28	At Sea.	L	0-5		4	7	Johnson	Oliver		27-22	1st	+1.0
5-29	At Sea.	W	8-2		13	8	Hill	Moyer		28-22	1st	+1.0
5-30	K.C.	L	2-3		9	9	Rusch	Witt	Pichardo	28-23	1st	+1.0
5-31	K.C.	W	3-1		8	7	Santana	Appier	Wetteland	29-23	1st	+1.0
6-1	K.C.	L	2-6		8	13	Rosado	Burkett	Veres	29-24	1st	+1.0
6-2	Min.	W	8-0		18	5	Oliver	Radke		30-24	1st	+1.5
6-3	Min.	L	4-5		13	12	Robertson	Hill	Aguilera	30-25	1st	+1.0
6-5	At K.C.	W	6-3	(11)	8	8	Wetteland	Pichardo		31-25	1st	+1.0
6-6	At K.C.	L	1-2		5	7	Rosado	Burkett		31-26	1st	0.0
6-7	At K.C.	L	4-10		5	12	Pittsley	Oliver		31-27	1st	0.0
6-8	At K.C.	L	2-4		7	10	Belcher	Hill	M. Williams	31-28	T2nd	1.0
6-10	At Min.	L	1-10		8	13	Tewksbury	Witt		31-29	3rd	1.5
6-11	At Min.	W	9-6		18	12	Burkett	Aldred	Wetteland	32-29	3rd	1.0
6-12	S.F.	L	3-4		8	9	Gardner	Oliver	Beck	32-30	3rd	2.0
6-13	S.F.	W	6-5		10	14	Wetteland	Rodriguez		33-30	3rd	2.0
6-14	S.D.	W	8-6		8	10	Whiteside	Jackson	Wetteland	34-30	2nd	2.0
6-15	S.D.	W	7-4		12	9	Witt	Ashby	Wetteland	35-30	2nd	2.0
6-17	At Col.	W	10-8	(11)	17	17	Patterson	S. Reed		36-30	2nd	1.0
6-18	At Col.	L	9-10		11	14	Leskanic	Wetteland		36-31	2nd	1.0
6-19	Sea.	L	1-2		5	9	Johnson	Hill	Ayala	36-32	2nd	2.0
6-20	Sea.	L	4-5		8	7	Wolcott	Witt	Sanders	36-33	2nd	3.0
6-21	Sea.	L	8-15		16	13	Maddux	Vosberg		36-34	3rd	4.0

Date	Opp.	Res.	Score	(inn.*)	Hits	Opp. hits	Winning pitcher	Losing pitcher	Save	Record	Pos.	GB
6-22	Sea.	L	4-6		10	12	Fassero	Burkett	Ayala	36-35	3rd	5.0
6-23	Ana.	L	0-1		7	7	Watson	Oliver	DeLucia	36-36	3rd	6.0
6-24	Ana.	L	6-7		14	11	DeLucia	Hernandez	Percival	36-37	3rd	6.0
6-25	Ana.	W	5-4		13	10	Gunderson	Holtz		37-37	3rd	6.0
6-26	At Oak.	L	3-6		10	8	Prieto	Santana	Taylor	37-38	3rd	7.0
6-27	At Oak.	L	4-7		9	13	Oquist	Burkett	Taylor	37-39	3rd	8.0
6-28	At Oak.	W	2-0		7	5	Oliver	Rigby	Wetteland	38-39	3rd	7.0
6-29	At Oak.	L	5-7		10	11	Reyes	Hernandez	Groom	38-40	3rd	8.0
6-30	At L.A.	W	3-2		9	6	Witt	Valdes	Wetteland	39-40	3rd	7.0
7-1	At L.A.	L	3-6		10	12	Dreifort	Santana	Worrell	39-41	3rd	8.0
7-2	Col.	W	9-1		12	4	Burkett	Thomson		40-41	3rd	7.0
7-3	Col.	W	8-3		11	4	Oliver	Ritz		41-41	3rd	6.0
7-4	Oak.	W	7-6		11	11	Hill	Karsay	Wetteland	42-41	2nd	6.0
7-5	Oak.	W	8-1		12	3	Witt	Wengert		43-41	2nd	5.0
7-6	Oak.	L	8-9		11	9	Johnson	Whiteside	Taylor	43-42	3rd	5.0
7-10	At Sea.	L	9-12		11	18	Moyer	Hill	Charlton	43-43	3rd	6.0
7-11	At Sea.	L	7-8		11	13	Ayala	Hernandez		43-44	3rd	7.0
7-12	At Sea.	W	9-2		12	8	Burkett	Lowe		44-44	3rd	6.0
7-13	At Sea.	W	4-2		7	8	Patterson	Ayala	Wetteland	45-44	3rd	5.0
7-14	At Ana.	L	5-6		9	11	Gross	Wetteland		45-45	3rd	6.0
7-15	At Ana.	L	2-6		9	12	Dickson	Hill		45-46	3rd	6.0
7-16	Tor.	W	6-0		10	8	Oliver	Hentgen		46-46	3rd	6.0
7-17	Tor.	L	1-9		5	15	Clemens	Burkett		46-47	3rd	6.0
7-18	Det.	L	4-5		11	8	Blair	Witt	Jones	46-48	3rd	7.0
7-19	Det.	L	5-6		9	10	Brocail	Hernandez	Jones	46-49	3rd	7.0
7-20	Det.	W	7-6	(10)	16	11	Wetteland	Sager		47-49	3rd	7.0
7-21	Bal.	L	1-5		8	8	Key	Oliver		47-50	3rd	7.5
7-22	Bal.	L	3-9		12	16	Erickson	Burkett		47-51	3rd	7.5
7-23	Bal.	L	2-3	(12)	9	11	Myers	Patterson		47-52	3rd	8.5
7-24	At Chi.	L	1-2		3	4	Karchner	Hill	Hernandez	47-53	3rd	9.5
7-25	At Chi.	W	8-5		12	12	Patterson	Navarro	Wetteland	48-53	3rd	9.5
7-26	At Chi.	W	4-1		10	5	Oliver	Alvarez	Wetteland	49-53	3rd	9.5
7-27	At Chi.	W	5-4		11	9	Gunderson	T. Castillo	Wetteland	50-53	3rd	9.5
7-28	At Bal.	L	2-7		8	13	Mussina	Witt	Benitez	50-54	3rd	10.0
7-29	At Bal.	L	4-5		10	8	Krivda	Alberro	Myers	50-55	3rd	10.0
7-30	At Bal.	L	1-3		3	6	Kamieniecki	Burkett	Myers	50-56	3rd	10.0
8-1	Cle.	L	5-8		10	15	Mesa	Gunderson	Assenmacher	50-57	3rd	10.0
8-2	Cle.	L	3-7		6	11	Smiley	Witt		50-58	3rd	11.0
8-3	Cle.	W	8-7		13	15	Wetteland	M. Jackson		51-58	3rd	11.0
8-4	Bos.	L	5-11		10	13	Henry	Patterson		51-59	3rd	11.0
8-5	Bos.	L	1-17		5	24	Gordon	Alberro		51-60	3rd	12.0
8-6	N.Y.	W	6-2		10	11	Oliver	Pettitte		52-60	3rd	12.0
8-7	N.Y.	L	2-4		4	11	Cone	Witt	Rivera	52-61	3rd	12.5
8-8	At Cle.	W	6-5		7	6	Bailes	M. Jackson	Wetteland	53-61	3rd	12.0
8-9†	At Cle.	W	4-3		8	6	T. Clark	Nagy	Wetteland	54-61		
8-9‡	At Cle.	L	2-4		7	9	Assenmacher	Moody	Mesa	54-62	3rd	12.0
8-10	At Cle.	W	7-6		9	13	Whiteside	Juden	Wetteland	55-62	3rd	11.0
8-11	At Bos.	W	8-3		15	9	Oliver	Wakefield		56-62	3rd	10.5
8-12	At Bos.	W	12-2		17	10	Witt	Sele		57-62	3rd	9.5
8-13	At Bos.	W	7-6		7	15	Sturtze	Avery	Wetteland	58-62	3rd	9.0
8-15	At N.Y.	L	2-5		5	12	Gooden	T. Clark	Rivera	58-63	3rd	10.0
8-16	At N.Y.	W	8-5	(10)	14	6	Wetteland	Mendoza		59-63	3rd	9.5
8-17	At N.Y.	L	0-8		3	13	Mendoza	Witt		59-64	3rd	10.0
8-18†	Mil.	L	5-8		9	12	Karl	Sturtze	Jones	59-65		
8-18‡	Mil.	W	2-0		7	1	Helling	Adamson	Wetteland	60-65	3rd	9.5
8-19	Mil.	L	2-8		7	11	Mercedes	Santana		60-66	3rd	9.5
8-20	Mil.	L	2-6		3	10	Florie	T. Clark	Jones	60-67	3rd	10.5
8-22	Chi.	W	17-8		20	9	Oliver	Navarro		61-67	3rd	11.0
8-23	Chi.	W	13-8		13	11	Patterson	Cruz		62-67	3rd	10.0
8-24	Chi.	L	1-3		6	7	Bere	Helling	Karchner	62-68	3rd	11.0
8-25	At Mil.	L	2-7		5	12	Adamson	T. Clark		62-69	3rd	11.0
8-26	At Mil.	L	10-11	(12)	19	20	Jones	Eversgerd		62-70	3rd	12.0
8-27	At Mil.	W	7-1		14	7	Oliver	Woodard		63-70	3rd	11.0
8-28	At S.F.	W	11-5		13	9	Whiteside	Beck		64-70	3rd	10.0
8-29	At S.F.	L	4-5	(12)	10	9	Rodriguez	Eversgerd		64-71	3rd	10.0
8-30	At S.D.	L	1-4		8	6	Ashby	T. Clark	Hoffman	64-72	3rd	10.0
8-31	At S.D.	L	3-5		9	12	Hitchcock	Burkett	Hoffman	64-73	3rd	11.0
9-2	L.A.	W	13-12		20	18	Heredia	Worrell		65-73	3rd	11.0
9-3	L.A.	W	5-2		11	8	Patterson	Dreifort	Wetteland	66-73	3rd	10.0
9-4	At Tor.	W	6-2		9	7	Helling	Carpenter		67-73	3rd	10.0
9-5	At Tor.	L	1-5		4	9	Williams	Pavlik		67-74	3rd	11.0
9-6	At Tor.	L	1-2		6	8	Hentgen	Burkett	Escobar	67-75	3rd	12.0
9-7	At Tor.	L	0-4		2	8	Clemens	Oliver		67-76	3rd	12.0
9-8	At Det.	L	2-6		5	7	Blair	Witt		67-77	3rd	12.0
9-9	At Det.	L	0-4		1	6	Sanders	Helling		67-78	3rd	13.0

– 68 –

Date	Opp.	Res.	Score	(inn.*)	Hits	Opp. hits	Winning pitcher	Losing pitcher	Save	Record	Pos.	GB
9-11	Min.	W	7-0		12	2	Pavlik	Radke		68-78	3rd	12.5
9-12	Min.	W	6-5		8	9	Santana	Swindell	Wetteland	69-78	3rd	12.5
9-13	Min.	W	9-3		12	8	Oliver	Tewksbury		70-78	3rd	11.5
9-14	Min.	L	1-11		10	21	Serafini	Witt		70-79	3rd	12.5
9-15	K.C.	L	9-11		16	19	Pichardo	Patterson	Montgomery	70-80	3rd	13.5
9-16	K.C.	W	4-2		8	9	Whiteside	Olson	Wetteland	71-80	3rd	13.0
9-17	Sea.	W	5-4		11	8	Patterson	Slocumb		72-80	3rd	12.0
9-18	Sea.	L	3-6		10	9	Johnson	Oliver	Ayala	72-81	3rd	13.0
9-19	Ana.	L	1-7		2	16	Hill	Witt		72-82	3rd	14.0
9-20	Ana.	L	6-7		12	10	Springer	Helling	Percival	72-83	3rd	14.0
9-21	Ana.	L	1-4		9	15	Harris	Pavlik	Percival	72-84	3rd	15.0
9-23	At Oak.	W	14-6		20	11	Burkett	Telgheder		73-84	3rd	15.5
9-24	At Oak.	W	8-4		13	7	Oliver	Haynes		74-84	3rd	14.5
9-25	At Ana.	W	8-5		11	11	Witt	Dickson	Wetteland	75-84	3rd	13.0
9-26	At Ana.	W	8-4		12	7	Helling	Holtz		76-84	3rd	13.0
9-27	At Ana.	L	7-8		12	12	Percival	Santana		76-85	3rd	14.0
9-28	At Ana.	W	4-0		9	3	Burkett	Watson		77-85	3rd	13.0

Monthly records: April (14-10), May (15-13), June (10-17), July (11-16), August (14-17), September (13-12).
*Innings, if other than nine. †First game of doubleheader. ‡Second game of doubleheader.

HIGHLIGHTS

High point: In April and May, the Rangers were executing their plan the way they wanted. Although the pitching started to struggle, the club hit .281 in May. They were 29-23 after May and led the A.L. West by one game over Anaheim and three games over Seattle.

Low point: A seven-game losing streak from June 18-24 sent the Rangers reeling and produced a 10-17 record for the month. During the seven-game skid, five losses came by only one run.

Turning point: On June 18, the losing streak began when the Rangers could not hold a 7-2 lead in Denver and closer John Wetteland was unable to close out a 9-6 ninth-inning lead. Wetteland did not record an out, and Colorado rallied for four runs in the bottom of the ninth to win, 10-9.

Most valuable player: Outfielder Juan Gonzalez. He had a torn ligament in his left thumb, which prevented him from playing until May. Despite the injury, he still managed to put up MVP-type numbers (.296, 42 home runs, 131 RBIs).

Most valuable pitcher: Darren Oliver. The promising lefthander reached an important threshold in his career last season—200 innings. Oliver crossed that barrier for the first time since being converted to a starter and might have ended worries about past arm injuries. He went 13-12 with a 4.20 ERA, but pitched better than the 14-6, 4.66 ERA he had in 1996.

Most improved player: Catcher Ivan Rodriguez. That may be hard to believe because of what he has accomplished in his career. But consider this: His offense is nearly as dangerous as his defense. He hit a career-high .313 and set a club record for home runs in a season by a catcher with 20. Most importantly, he signed a five-year deal with the Rangers hours before the trading deadline.

Most pleasant surprise: First baseman Lee Stevens. No one would have thought Stevens would put together a .300 season with 21 home runs and 74 RBIs. If not for his production off the bench, the Rangers would have faced an even tougher 1997 than the one they encountered.

Biggest disappointment: Take your pick, because this club had several. After lead-ing the majors with 75 wins in 1996, the starting rotation had the A.L.'s third-lowest win total at 49 and also allowed a league-high 1,132 hits. Injuries and lack of power limited first baseman Will Clark to 110 games, 12 home runs and 51 RBIs. The whispers of his brittleness have not silenced.

Key injuries: McLemore (torn ligament, right hand; torn cartilage, knee); Gonzalez (torn ligament, left thumb); Clark (bone bruise, left wrist; torn tissue, right heel); righthander Ken Hill (strained right shoulder); righthander Roger Pavlik (bone chips and spur in right elbow).

Notable: On Friday, May 2, Dean Palmer's two-run single in the bottom of the ninth capped a four-run rally to give the Rangers a 7-6 victory over the Boston Red Sox. That snapped a string of 106 consecutive losses when the Rangers trailed after eight innings.

—KEVIN LONNQUIST

RECORDS

1997 regular-season record: 77-85 (3rd in A.L. West); 39-42 at home; 38-43 on road; 21-34 vs. East; 31-24 vs. Central; 25-27 vs. West; 23-26 vs. lefthanded starters; 54-59 vs. righthanded starters; 68-77 on grass; 9-8 on turf; 21-16 in daytime; 56-69 at night; 18-29 in one-run games; 5-3 in extra-inning games; 0-0-2 in doubleheaders.

Team record past five years: 379-365 (.509, ranks 7th in league in that span).

TEAM LEADERS

Batting average: Rusty Greer (.321).
At-bats: Rusty Greer (601).
Runs: Rusty Greer (112).
Hits: Rusty Greer (193).
Total bases: Rusty Greer (319).
Doubles: Rusty Greer (42).
Triples: Domingo Cedeno (6).
Home runs: Juan Gonzalez (42).
Runs batted in: Juan Gonzalez (131).
Stolen bases: Damon Buford (18).
Slugging percentage: Juan Gonzalez (.589).
On-base percentage: Rusty Greer (.405).
Wins: Darren Oliver (13).
Earned-run average: Darren Oliver (4.20).

Complete games: Darren Oliver, Bobby Witt (3).
Shutouts: Darren Oliver (1).
Saves: John Wetteland (31).
Innings pitched: Bobby Witt (209.0).
Strikeouts: John Burkett (139).

GAMES BY POSITION

Catcher: Ivan Rodriguez 143, Henry Mercedes 23, Jim Leyritz 11, Kevin L. Brown 4.
First base: Will Clark 100, Lee Stevens 62, Jim Leyritz 9, Billy Ripken 9, Mike Simms 2, Alex Diaz 1, Marc Sagmoen 1.
Second base: Mark McLemore 89, Domingo Cedeno 65, Billy Ripken 25, Alex Diaz 1, Hanley Frias 1.
Third base: Dean Palmer 93, Fernando Tatis 60, Billy Ripken 13, Domingo Cedeno 3, Dave Silvestri 1.
Shortstop: Benji Gil 106, Domingo Cedeno 43, Billy Ripken 31, Hanley Frias 12, Dave Silvestri 1.
Outfield: Rusty Greer 153, Damon Buford 117, Juan Gonzalez 64, Warren Newson 58, Tom Goodwin 51, Mike Devereaux 28, Alex Diaz 23, Lee Stevens 22, Mike Simms 19, Marc Sagmoen 17, Mark McLemore 1.
Designated hitter: Juan Gonzalez 69, Lee Stevens 38, Mike Simms 28, Mickey Tettleton 13, Jim Leyritz 9, Warren Newson 9, Will Clark 7, Ivan Rodriguez 5, Damon Buford 3, Benji Gil 3, Domingo Cedeno 2, Rusty Greer 2.

TOP DRAFT CHOICES

1. **Jason Romano,** 3B, Hillsborough H.S., Tampa.
2a. **Jason Grabowski,** C, U. of Connecticut.
2b. **Chris Tynan,** RHP, Hudson's Bay H.S., Vancouver, Wash.
3. **Brandon Warriax,** SS, Purnell Swett H.S., Pembroke, N.C.
4. **David Elder,** RHP, Georgia Tech.
5. **Trey Poland,** LHP, University of Southwestern Louisiana.
6. **Dan DeYoung,** RHP, U. of Mississippi.
7. **Mike Lamb,** C, Cal State Fullerton.
8. **Billy Diaz,** RHP, Academia Adventista H.S., Caguas, P.R.
9. **Carlos Figueroa,** LHP, Jose Lazaro H.S., Carolina, P.R.
10. **Kevin Harris,** OF, Tampa Bay Tech H.S.

TORONTO BLUE JAYS
AMERICAN LEAGUE EAST DIVISION

Blue Jays Schedule
Home games shaded. *—All-Star Game at Coors Field (Colorado).
D—Day game (any game starting before 5 p.m.).

March

SUN	MON	TUE	WED	THU	FRI	SAT
		31				

April

SUN	MON	TUE	WED	THU	FRI	SAT
			1 MIN	2 MIN	3 D TEX	4 D TEX
5 D TEX	6	7 MIN	8 MIN	9 MIN	10 TEX	11 TEX
12 D TEX	13 KC	14 KC	15 KC	16	17 CWS	18 D CWS
19 CWS	20 D NYY	21 NYY	22 NYY	23	24 CWS	25 CWS
26 D CWS	27 NYY	28 NYY	29 KC	30 D KC		

May

SUN	MON	TUE	WED	THU	FRI	SAT
					1 OAK	2 D OAK
3 D OAK	4 OAK	5 ANA	6 ANA	7 SEA	8 SEA	9 SEA
10 SEA	11	12 OAK	13 OAK	14 ANA	15 ANA	16 D SEA
17 D SEA	18 SEA	19 TB	20 TB	21 D TB	22 CLE	23 D CLE
24 D CLE	25 BOS	26 BOS	27	28 CLE	29 CLE	30 D CLE
31 D CLE						

June

SUN	MON	TUE	WED	THU	FRI	SAT
	1 BOS	2 BOS	3 DET	4 DET	5 D PHI	6 D PHI
7 PHI	8 FLA	9 FLA	10 FLA	11	12 BAL	13 D BAL
14 D BAL	15 TB	16 TB	17 TB	18 BAL	19 BAL	20 BAL
21 D BAL	22 MON	23 MON	24 MON	25 MON	26 ATL	27 ATL
28 D ATL	29	30 NYM				

July

SUN	MON	TUE	WED	THU	FRI	SAT
			1 NYM	2 D NYM	3 TB	4 D TB
5 D TB	6	7	* 8	9 DET	10 DET	11 DET
12 DET	13 BAL	14 BAL	15 CWS	16 D CWS	17 D NYY	18 D NYY
19 D NYY	20	21 CWS	22 CWS	23 BOS	24 BOS	25 D BOS
26 D BOS	27	28 TEX	29 TEX	30 TEX	31 MIN	

August

SUN	MON	TUE	WED	THU	FRI	SAT
						1 MIN
2 D MIN	3	4 TEX	5 TEX	6	7 OAK	8 D OAK
9 D OAK	10	11 SEA	12 SEA	13 ANA	14 ANA	15 D ANA
16 D ANA	17 OAK	18 D OAK	19 SEA	20 SEA	21 ANA	22 ANA
23 ANA	24 D KC	25 KC	26 KC	27 KC	28 MIN	29 D MIN
30 D MIN	31					

September

SUN	MON	TUE	WED	THU	FRI	SAT
		1 KC	2 KC	3 BOS	4 BOS	5 D BOS
6 D BOS	7 D CLE	8 CLE	9 CLE	10 NYY	11 NYY	12 D NYY
13 NYY	14 CLE	15 CLE	16 DET	17 DET	18 TB	19 TB
20 D TB	21 BAL	22 BAL	23 BAL	24	25 DET	26 D DET
27 D DET						

1998 SEASON
CLUB DIRECTORY

Chairman and chief executive officer
Sam Pollock
Vice president, business
Bob Nicholson
Vice president, general manager
Gord Ash
Vice president, baseball
Bob Mattick
Senior advisor, baseball operations
Bob Engle
Special asst. to v.p., baseball, g.m.
Al Widmar
Gordon Lakey
Moose Johnson
Assistant general manager
Tim McCleary
Director, public relations
Howard Starkman
Director, stadium and ticket operations
George Holm
Director, finance
Susan Quigley
Director, scouting
Tim Wilken
Director, international scouting
Wayne Morgan
Director, player development
Jim Hoff
Director, Canadian scouting
Bill Byckowski
Director, minor league business
Ken Carson
Director, baseball administration
Bob Nelson
Asst. dir., tickets and box office mgr.
Randy Low
Director, Latin America operations
Herb Raybourn

Manager, group sales
Maureen Haffey
Manager, team travel
John Brioux
Manager, promotions and advertising
Rick Amos
Manager, accounting
Cathy McNamara
Manager, employee compensation
Perry Nicoletta
Manager, game operations
Mario Coutinho
Supervisor, office service
Mick Bazinet
Trainers
Tommy Craig
Scott Shannon
Strength and conditioning coordinator
To be announced
Team physicians
Dr. Ron Taylor
Dr. Anthony Miniaci
Dr. Allan Gross
Dr. Steve Mirabello
Advance scout
Darren Balsley
Scouts
Tony Arias, David Blume, Chris Bourjos, Chris Buckley, Bus Campbell, John Cole, Ellis Dungan, Joe Ford, Tom Hinkle, Jim Hughes, Ted Lekas, Ben McLure, Marty Miller, Bill Moore, Andy Pienovi, Alvin Rittman, Jorge Rivera, Joe Siers, Mark Snipp, Jerry Sobeck, Ron Tostenson, Steve Williams

MINOR LEAGUE AFFILIATES

Class	Team	League	Manager
AAA	Syracuse	International	Terry Bevington
AA	Knoxville	Southern	Omar Malave
A	Dunedin	Florida State	Rocket Wheeler
A	Hagerstown	South Atlantic	Marty Pevey
A	St. Catharines	New York-Penn.	Duane Larson
Rookie	Medicine Hat	Pioneer	Rolando Pino

BROADCAST INFORMATION
Radio: CHUM (1050).
TV: CBC-TV.
Cable TV: The Sports Network.

SPRING TRAINING
Ballpark (city): Dunedin Stadium at Grant Field (Dunedin, Fla.).
Ticket information: 800-707-8269; 813-733-0429

Manager—Tim Johnson.
Coaches—Sal Butera, Jack Hubbard (7), Jim Lett (10), Gary Matthews (36), Mel Queen (34), Eddie Rodriguez.

No.	PITCHERS	B/T	Ht./Wt.	Born	1997 clubs
40	Almanzar, Carlos	R/R	6-2/165	11-6-73	Knoxville, Syracuse, Toronto
50	Carpenter, Christopher	R/R	6-5/215	4-21-75	Syracuse, Toronto
21	Clemens, Roger	R/R	6-4/230	8-4-62	Toronto
37	Crabtree, Tim	R/R	6-4/200	10-13-69	St. Catharines, , Syracuse
	Davey, Tom	R/R	6-7/215	9-11-73	Dunedin, Knoxville
45	Escobar, Kelvim	R/R	6-1/205	4-11-76	Knoxville, Dunedin, Toronto
	Glover, Gary	R/R	6-5/180	12-3-76	Hagerstown
57	Guzman, Juan	R/R	5-11/195	10-28-66	Toronto, Dunedin
39	Hanson, Erik	R/R	6-6/215	5-18-65	Dunedin, Toronto
41	Hentgen, Pat	R/R	6-2/200	11-13-68	Toronto
	Myers, Randy	L/L	6-1/225	9-19-62	Baltimore
31	Person, Robert	R/R	6-0/185	10-6-69	Toronto, Syracuse
19	Plesac, Dan	L/L	6-5/220	2-4-62	Toronto
48	Quantrill, Paul	L/R	6-1/185	11-3-68	Toronto
55	Risley, Bill	R/R	6-2/220	5-29-67	Dunedin, Syracuse, Toronto
52	Robinson, Ken	R/R	5-9/170	11-3-69	Syracuse, Toronto
	Sinclair, Steve	L/L	6-2/175	8-2-71	Syracuse, Dunedin
30	Williams, Woody	R/R	6-0/190	8-19-66	Toronto
	Young, Joe	R/R	6-4/205	4-28-75	Knoxville

No.	CATCHERS	B/T	Ht./Wt.	Born	1997 clubs
	Fletcher, Darrin	L/R	6-1/200	10-3-66	Montreal
	Mosquera, Julio	R/R	6-0/190	1-29-72	Knoxville, Syracuse, Toronto
18	Santiago, Benito	R/R	6-1/185	3-9-65	Toronto
	Stanley, Mike	R/R	6-0/190	6-25-63	Boston, New York A.L.

No.	INFIELDERS	B/T	Ht./Wt.	Born	1997 clubs
3	Crespo, Felipe	B/R	5-11/200	3-5-73	Toronto, Syracuse
25	Delgado, Carlos	L/R	6-3/225	6-25-72	Toronto
28	Evans, Tom	R/R	6-1/208	7-9-74	Dunedin, Syracuse, Toronto
	Fernandez, Tony	B/R	6-2/175	6-30-62	Cleveland
	Freel, Ryan	R/R	5-10/175	3-8-76	Knoxville, Dunedin
8	Gonzalez, Alex	R/R	6-0/190	4-8-73	Toronto
	Grebeck, Craig	R/R	5-7/148	12-29-64	Anaheim
	Jones, Ryan	R/R	6-3/225	11-5-74	Knoxville, Syracuse
	Peeples, Mike	R/R	6-0/160	9-3-76	Dunedin
1	Perez, Tomas	B/R	5-11/172	12-29-73	Syracuse, Toronto
33	Sprague, Ed	R/R	6-2/205	7-25-67	Toronto
	Witt, Kevin	L/R	6-4/185	1-5-76	Knoxville

No.	OUTFIELDERS	B/T	Ht./Wt.	Born	1997 clubs
23	Cruz, Jose	B/R	6-0/190	4-19-74	Tacoma, Seattle, Toronto
15	Green, Shawn	L/L	6-4/195	11-10-72	Toronto
17	Perez, Robert	R/R	6-3/220	6-4-69	Toronto
	Samuel, Juan	R/R	5-11/185	12-9-60	Toronto
	Sanders, Anthony	R/R	6-2/190	3-2-74	Knoxville, Dunedin
	Saturria, Louis	R/R	6-2/165	7-21-76	Peoria
7	Stewart, Shannon	R/R	6-1/194	2-25-74	Toronto, Syracuse

BALLPARK INFORMATION

Ballpark (capacity, surface)
SkyDome (50,516, artificial)

Address
One Blue Jays Way
Suite 3200
Toronto, Ontario M5V 1J1

Business phone
416-341-1000

Ticket information
416-341-1111

Ticket prices
$27.50 (esplanade IF, club level OF)
$20 (skydeck IF, esplanade OF)
$13 (skydeck)
$4 (skydeck outfield)

Field dimensions (from home plate)
To left field at foul line, 330 feet
To center field, 400 feet
To right field at foul line, 330 feet

First game played
June 5, 1989 (Brewers 5, Blue Jays 3)

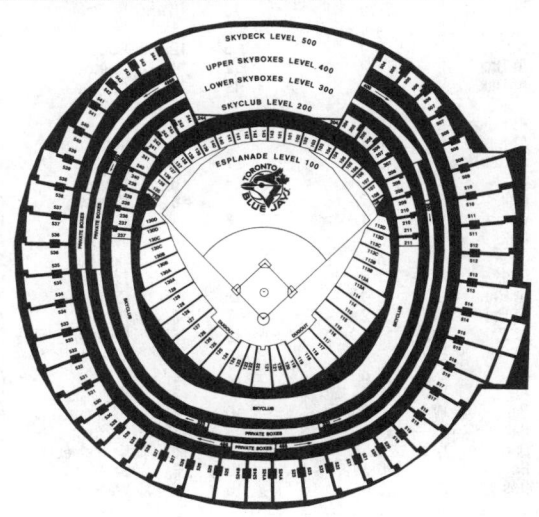

1998 SEASON *Toronto Blue Jays*

Date	Opp.	Res.	Score	(inn.*)	Hits	Opp. hits	Winning pitcher	Losing pitcher	Save	Record	Pos.	GB
4-1	Chi.	L	5-6	(10)	7	12	T. Castillo	Plesac	Hernandez	0-1	T3rd	0.5
4-2	Chi.	W	6-1		8	6	Clemens	Alvarez		1-1	T3rd	0.5
4-4	Mil.	W	6-2		9	5	Guzman	Karl	Crabtree	2-1	T2nd	1.0
4-5	Mil.	L	2-5		8	9	McAndrew	Williams	Jones	2-2	T3rd	2.0
4-6	Mil.	L	2-4		5	10	McDonald	Hentgen	Jones	2-3	T3rd	2.0
4-9	At Chi.	W	5-0		10	3	Clemens	Alvarez		3-3	T2nd	1.5
4-10	At Chi.	W	4-0		5	4	Guzman	Baldwin		4-3	2nd	1.0
4-13	At Mil.	L	2-3		6	10	Wickman	Crabtree		4-4	T2nd	2.5
4-14	K.C.	L	2-3		7	6	Rusch	Quantrill	Pichardo	4-5	T3rd	3.5
4-15	K.C.	L	5-7		9	10	Rosado	Guzman	Pichardo	4-6	4th	4.5
4-16	Oak.	W	4-3		9	10	Crabtree	Taylor		5-6	3rd	3.5
4-17	Oak.	W	5-4		13	7	Quantrill	Groom	Timlin	6-6	3rd	3.5
4-18	At Tex.	W	6-5		4	9	Hentgen	Pavlik	Timlin	7-6	T2nd	3.0
4-19	At Tex.	W	6-0		12	4	Clemens	Hill		8-6	2nd	2.5
4-20	At Tex.	L	5-10		13	13	Witt	Guzman		8-7	2nd	3.5
4-21	At Ana.	L	4-5	(13)	8	14	DeLucia	Spoljaric		8-8	3rd	3.5
4-22	At Ana.	W	7-6		10	7	Quantrill	James	Plesac	9-8	3rd	3.5
4-23	At Ana.	L	4-5	(10)	10	12	DeLucia	Spoljaric		9-9	3rd	3.5
4-25	Sea.	L	8-13		10	17	Ayala	Plesac		9-10	3rd	4.0
4-26	Sea.	W	4-3		12	8	Quantrill	Lowe		10-10	T2nd	4.0
4-27	Sea.	L	1-2		7	6	Johnson	Person	Charlton	10-11	4th	4.0
4-29	At K.C.	L	5-6	(10)	8	10	Pichardo	Quantrill		10-12	4th	5.0
4-30	At K.C.	W	1-0		5	4	Clemens	Appier	Spoljaric	11-12	4th	5.0
5-1	At K.C.	L	0-8		4	12	Rosado	Williams		11-13	4th	6.0
5-2	Min.	L	2-3	(10)	6	7	Radke	Crabtree	Aguilera	11-14	4th	7.0
5-3	Min.	W	6-5		10	10	Quantrill	Ritchie		12-14	4th	6.0
5-4	Min.	W	1-0		4	4	Hentgen	Tewksbury		13-14	4th	6.0
5-5	Det.	W	3-1		7	5	Clemens	Olivares		14-14	3rd	5.0
5-6	Det.	W	2-1	(10)	11	4	Crabtree	Jones		15-14	3rd	5.0
5-7	At Cle.	L	1-7		7	15	McDowell	Person		15-15	3rd	6.0
5-8	At Cle.	W	4-3		10	8	Guzman	Ogea	Quantrill	16-15	3rd	6.0
5-9	At Min.	W	4-1		8	6	Hentgen	Rodriguez	Timlin	17-15	3rd	5.0
5-10	At Min.	W	6-4		8	10	Clemens	Swindell	Crabtree	18-15	3rd	4.0
5-11	At Min.	W	3-2		7	8	Williams	Aldred	Timlin	19-15	3rd	4.0
5-12	At Min.	L	2-12		10	20	Radke	Carpenter		19-16	3rd	5.0
5-13	At Det.	L	0-4		4	7	Lira	Guzman		19-17	3rd	6.0
5-14	At Det.	W	7-2		12	5	Hentgen	Moehler		20-17	3rd	5.0
5-16	Cle.	W	5-2		10	7	Clemens	Hershiser	Timlin	21-17	3rd	4.5
5-17	Cle.	L	1-8		9	9	Lopez	Williams		21-18	3rd	5.5
5-18	Cle.	L	6-8		8	11	Ogea	Carpenter	M. Jackson	21-19	3rd	6.5
5-20	At N.Y.	W	2-0		8	5	Hentgen	Pettitte		22-19	3rd	6.5
5-21	At N.Y.	W	4-1		9	4	Clemens	Rogers		23-19	3rd	6.5
5-23	Ana.	L	2-12		7	17	Springer	Guzman		23-20	T2nd	6.5
5-24	Ana.	L	1-3		6	9	Watson	Williams	Percival	23-21	3rd	7.5
5-25	Ana.	W	4-3	(11)	9	6	Timlin	DeLucia		24-21	3rd	6.5
5-26	Tex.	W	8-1		13	5	Clemens	Santana		25-21	2nd	6.5
5-27	Tex.	L	5-15		10	16	Burkett	Person		25-22	2nd	7.5
5-28	N.Y.	L	4-6		5	6	Wells	Guzman	Rivera	25-23	3rd	8.5
5-29	N.Y.	L	0-4		5	10	Cone	Williams	Nelson	25-24	3rd	9.0
5-30	At Oak.	L	7-12		12	14	Prieto	Hentgen		25-25	3rd	10.0
5-31	At Oak.	W	13-3		19	11	Clemens	Telgheder		26-25	3rd	10.0
6-1	At Oak.	L	2-8		10	9	Oquist	Person		26-26	3rd	10.5
6-2	At Sea.	L	0-3		2	9	Johnson	Andujar		26-27	3rd	11.0
6-3	At Sea.	L	3-6		7	12	Moyer	Williams		26-28	3rd	12.0
6-5	Oak.	L	3-4		8	8	Reyes	Hentgen	Taylor	26-29	3rd	13.0
6-6	Oak.	W	4-1		6	8	Clemens	Oquist	Quantrill	27-29	3rd	12.0
6-7	Oak.	W	3-1		6	6	Person	Karsay	Quantrill	28-29	3rd	11.0
6-8	Oak.	L	5-7		10	10	Wengert	Andujar	Taylor	28-30	3rd	12.0
6-10	Sea.	W	8-3		8	11	Hentgen	Sanders		29-30	3rd	13.0
6-11	Sea.	L	1-5		5	9	Fassero	Clemens		29-31	3rd	13.0
6-13	At Phi.	L	3-4		10	7	Gomes	Spoljaric	Bottalico	29-32	3rd	13.5
6-14	At Phi.	W	3-2		7	8	Person	Nye	Quantrill	30-32	3rd	13.5
6-15	At Phi.	W	11-1		12	6	Hentgen	Leiter		31-32	3rd	13.5
6-16	Atl.	L	0-3		5	8	Neagle	Clemens		31-33	3rd	13.5
6-17	Atl.	L	7-8		12	12	Maddux	Andujar	Wohlers	31-34	3rd	14.5
6-18	Atl.	L	5-3		7	3	Williams	Smoltz	Timlin	32-34	3rd	13.5
6-20	Bal.	W	3-0		10	6	Hentgen	Mussina		33-34	3rd	12.5
6-21	Bal.	L	1-5		6	11	Erickson	Plesac		33-35	3rd	13.5
6-22	Bal.	L	2-5		8	10	Kamieniecki	Person	Myers	33-36	3rd	14.5
6-23	Bos.	L	6-7		13	13	Sele	Williams	Slocumb	33-37	3rd	14.5
6-24	Bos.	L	6-9		13	15	Wasdin	Andujar	Slocumb	33-38	3rd	15.5

Date	Opp.	Res.	Score	(inn.*)	Hits	Opp. hits	Winning pitcher	Losing pitcher	Save	Record	Pos.	GB
6-25	Bos.	L	12-13		12	16	Wakefield	Hentgen	Slocumb	33-39	4th	16.5
6-26	At Bal.	W	3-0		6	6	Clemens	Erickson	Timlin	34-39	3rd	15.5
6-27	At Bal.	W	2-1		6	5	Person	Kamieniecki	Spoljaric	35-39	3rd	14.5
6-28	At Bal.	W	5-2		9	8	Williams	Key	Timlin	36-39	3rd	13.5
6-29	At Bal.	W	3-2		7	5	Escobar	Benitez	Timlin	37-39	3rd	12.5
6-30	Mon.	L	1-2		3	6	Martinez	Hentgen		37-40	3rd	13.5
7-1	Mon.	L	1-2		2	10	Juden	Clemens	Urbina	37-41	3rd	14.5
7-2	Mon.	W	7-6	(13)	15	10	Timlin	Telford		38-41	3rd	14.5
7-3	N.Y.	L	1-3		6	10	Wells	Williams	Rivera	38-42	3rd	15.5
7-4	N.Y.	W	1-0		6	2	Escobar	Cone		39-42	3rd	15.0
7-5	N.Y.	L	0-8		6	14	Pettitte	Hentgen		39-43	3rd	15.0
7-6	N.Y.	W	2-0		6	4	Clemens	Mendoza		40-43	T3rd	14.0
7-10	At Bos.	L	7-8	(11)	11	16	Eshelman	Timlin		40-44	T3rd	14.5
7-11	At Bos.	W	8-4		12	11	Hentgen	Wasdin		41-44	3rd	13.5
7-12	At Bos.	W	3-1		6	4	Clemens	Sele	Spoljaric	42-44	3rd	12.5
7-13	At Bos.	W	3-2		6	7	Williams	Wakefield	Escobar	43-44	3rd	11.5
7-14	At Bal.	L	5-9		10	11	Mathews	Person		43-45	3rd	12.5
7-15	At Bal.	L	4-8		6	13	Boskie	Guzman		43-46	3rd	13.5
7-16	At Tex.	L	0-6		8	10	Oliver	Hentgen		43-47	3rd	13.5
7-17	At Tex.	W	9-1		15	5	Clemens	Burkett		44-47	3rd	12.5
7-18	At Ana.	W	2-1		4	7	Williams	Watson	Escobar	45-47	3rd	11.5
7-19	At Ana.	L	4-5		8	6	Percival	Timlin		45-48	3rd	12.5
7-20	At Ana.	L	5-9		10	13	Finley	Andujar		45-49	3rd	12.5
7-22	Mil.	W	5-2		4	5	Hentgen	Eldred	Escobar	46-49	3rd	13.0
7-23	Mil.	W	8-0		4	8	Clemens	McAndrew		47-49	3rd	13.0
7-24	Mil.	W	5-4		8	9	Williams	Mercedes	Escobar	48-49	3rd	12.5
7-25	K.C.	W	2-1		5	10	Person	Rusch	Escobar	49-49	3rd	11.5
7-26	K.C.	W	6-5		8	8	Timlin	Carrasco		50-49	3rd	11.5
7-27	K.C.	L	2-3		2	6	Olson	Quantrill		50-50	3rd	12.5
7-28†	At Mil.	L	0-1		1	4	Woodard	Clemens	Fetters	50-51		
7-28‡	At Mil.	L	3-9		11	19	Adamson	Flener		50-52	3rd	14.0
7-29†	At Mil.	L	0-2		4	5	Mercedes	Williams	Fetters	50-53		
7-29‡	At Mil.	L	2-4		6	11	Karl	Carpenter	Fetters	50-54	3rd	15.5
7-31	At Det.	L	2-4		5	6	Thompson	Person	Jones	50-55	3rd	17.0
8-1	At Det.	W	7-5		11	10	Hentgen	Miceli	Escobar	51-55	3rd	16.0
8-2	At Det.	L	7-8		15	13	Brocail	Quantrill	Jones	51-56	3rd	17.0
8-3	At Det.	L	2-5		9	9	Blair	Williams	Jones	51-57	T3rd	18.0
8-4	At Min.	L	3-9		7	14	Radke	Carpenter		51-58	T4th	18.5
8-5	At Min.	W	8-3		11	8	Person	T. Miller		52-58	T4th	17.5
8-6	Cle.	W	6-3		10	13	Hentgen	Lopez	Escobar	53-58	4th	17.5
8-7	Cle.	W	4-0		9	5	Clemens	Smiley		54-58	4th	17.0
8-8	Det.	W	6-3		12	11	Williams	Blair	Escobar	55-58	4th	17.0
8-9	Det.	L	2-3		4	9	Sanders	Carpenter	Jones	55-59	4th	17.0
8-10	Det.	L	2-4		8	4	Thompson	Person		55-60	T4th	18.0
8-11	Det.	W	8-2		11	10	Hentgen	Jarvis		56-60	4th	17.5
8-12	Min.	W	9-1		11	8	Clemens	Bowers		57-60	3rd	17.5
8-13	Min.	W	3-2		10	12	Quantrill	Trombley		58-60	3rd	16.5
8-15	At Cle.	L	4-5	(10)	10	10	Assenmacher	Crabtree		58-61	T3rd	18.0
8-16	At Cle.	L	4-8		7	10	Shuey	Quantrill		58-62	4th	18.0
8-17	At Cle.	W	10-5		14	8	Clemens	Wright		59-62	4th	18.0
8-18	At Cle.	L	3-5		3	9	Hershiser	Williams	Mesa	59-63	4th	19.0
8-19†	At Chi.	W	6-5		9	13	Carpenter	Cruz	Escobar	60-63		
8-19‡	At Chi.	L	3-5		7	9	Bere	Andujar	Karchner	60-64	4th	19.0
8-20	At Chi.	L	6-12		12	14	Baldwin	Person		60-65	4th	20.0
8-21	At Chi.	L	3-6		9	8	Drabek	Hentgen	Karchner	60-66	4th	21.0
8-22	At K.C.	W	5-3		10	8	Clemens	Rosado	Escobar	61-66	4th	21.0
8-23	At K.C.	W	6-5		8	10	Janzen	Walker	Quantrill	62-66	4th	21.0
8-24	At K.C.	W	11-8	(13)	21	15	Crabtree	Casian		63-66	4th	21.0
8-26	Chi.	L	5-8		9	17	Baldwin	Williams	Karchner	63-67	4th	21.0
8-27	Chi.	W	13-2		14	6	Hentgen	Drabek		64-67	4th	21.0
8-28	Chi.	W	3-2	(11)	11	9	Quantrill	McElroy		65-67	4th	20.0
8-29	Fla.	L	0-8		5	10	Leiter	Person		65-68	4th	21.0
8-30	Fla.	L	1-4		3	10	Fernandez	Carpenter	Nen	65-69	4th	21.0
8-31	Fla.	L	3-8		9	10	Hernandez	Williams		65-70	4th	21.0
9-1	At N.Y. (NL)	L	0-3		2	6	Isringhausen	Hentgen	J. Franco	65-71	4th	21.0
9-2	At N.Y. (NL)	L	5-8		7	12	Acevedo	Clemens	Wendell	65-72	4th	21.0
9-3	At N.Y. (NL)	L	2-4		5	10	Mlicki	Quantrill	J. Franco	65-73	T4th	21.0
9-4	Tex.	L	2-6		7	9	Helling	Carpenter		65-74	5th	22.0
9-5	Tex.	W	5-1		9	4	Williams	Pavlik		66-74	5th	22.0
9-6	Tex.	W	2-1		8	6	Hentgen	Burkett	Escobar	67-74	5th	22.0
9-7	Tex.	W	4-0		8	2	Clemens	Oliver		68-74	T4th	21.0
9-8	Ana.	W	12-10		14	12	Plesac	James	Escobar	69-74	T3rd	20.0
9-9	Ana.	W	2-0		4	3	Carpenter	Hill		70-74	3rd	20.0
9-10	At Oak.	L	2-3		3	6	Mathews	Plesac		70-75	T3rd	20.5
9-11	At Oak.	L	7-8		13	11	Mathews	Escobar		70-76	5th	20.5

1998 SEASON Toronto Blue Jays

Date	Opp.	Res.	Score	(inn.*)	Hits	Opp. hits	Winning pitcher	Losing pitcher	Save	Record	Pos.	GB
9-12	At Sea.	L	3-7		8	10	Ayala	Clemens		70-77	5th	20.5
9-13	At Sea.	W	6-3		6	7	Escobar	Ayala		71-77	5th	20.5
9-14	At Sea.	L	2-3		6	7	Timlin	Risley	Slocumb	71-78	5th	20.5
9-15	At Sea.	L	3-7		9	10	Cloude	Williams	Slocumb	71-79	5th	21.0
9-17	At Bos.	L	3-4		7	7	Mahay	Quantrill	Gordon	71-80	5th	21.0
9-18	At Bos.	L	2-3		9	9	Corsi	Escobar		71-81	5th	22.0
9-19	At N.Y.	W	3-0		6	8	Daal	Gooden	Escobar	72-81	5th	21.0
9-20	At N.Y.	L	3-4	(11)	10	10	Banks	Janzen		72-82	5th	22.0
9-21	At N.Y.	L	4-5	(10)	10	11	Boehringer	Almanzar		72-83	5th	22.0
9-22	At N.Y.	L	1-8		7	11	Wells	Hentgen		72-84	5th	22.0
9-23	Bal.	L	2-3		3	9	Rodriguez	Clemens	Myers	72-85	5th	23.0
9-24	Bal.	L	3-9		7	12	Kamieniecki	Daal		72-86	5th	24.0
9-25	Bal.	W	4-3		11	13	Carpenter	Mussina	Escobar	73-86	5th	23.0
9-26	Bos.	W	3-0		6	10	Williams	Henry		74-86	5th	22.0
9-27	Bos.	W	12-5		15	10	Janzen	Corsi		75-86	5th	22.0
9-28	Bos.	W	3-2		8	8	Plesac	Gordon		76-86	5th	22.0

Monthly records: April (11-12), May (15-13), June (11-15), July (13-15), August (15-15), September (11-16).
*Innings, if other than nine. †First game of doubleheader. ‡Second game of doubleheader.

HIGHLIGHTS

High point: On a July 12 afternoon filled with drama, Roger Clemens struck out 16 over eight innings at Fenway Park, defeating the Red Sox, 3-1, in his first appearance in Boston against his former team.
Low point: Opening day—April Fool's Day. Chicago pinch hitter Norberto Martin hit Mike Timlin's first pitch of the season for a game-tying solo homer in the ninth inning and the White Sox went on to a 6-5 victory in 10 innings.
Turning point: After hurdling the .500 mark (50-49) July 26 with a 6-5 win over Kansas City to cap a five-game win streak, Toronto lost six straight, then three of the next four to fall 18 ½ games behind. The team scored nine runs in the six consecutive losses, getting shut out twice.
Most valuable player: Carlos Delgado topped the Blue Jays with 42 doubles, 30 home runs and 274 total bases, all career highs. He also led the team with a .528 slugging percentage.
Most valuable pitcher: Roger Clemens became the first American Leaguer in 52 years to capture the pitcher's version of the Triple Crown. He led in wins (21), ERA (2.05) and a career-high 292 strikeouts to earn a fourth Cy Young Award.
Most improved player: Armed with a new forkball, reliever Paul Quantrill found his niche by pitching well in a variety of situations, from long relief to closing games. He rebounded from a 5-14, 5.43 ERA performance in '96 with a 6-7 record, five saves and a 1.94 ERA.
Most disappointing player: Half the roster qualified as candidates, but third baseman Ed Sprague, second baseman Carlos Garcia and catcher Benito Santiago were the runaway leaders. Sprague played hurt and sunk from 36 homers to 14 and from 101 RBIs to 48. Garcia, who had hit .278 over three seasons in Pittsburgh before his trade to Toronto, hit .163 in April, lost his starting second-base job in July, got 28 at-bats in August and finished with a .220 average. Santiago signed a three-year, $10 million deal after hitting 30 homers and collecting 85 RBIs for Philadelphia in 1996. He slid to 13 homers and 42 RBIs.
Key injuries: Righthander Erik Hanson opened the season on the D.L. with a tired arm, then made two starts before returning to the D.L. After undergoing rotator cuff surgery, he returned in September to make one relief appearance. . . . Righthander Juan Guzman fractured his right thumb on May 28. He returned June 27 but went back on the D.L. on July 26 with a shoulder strain and missed the remainder of the season. He had a large bone spur removed and a slight labrum tear repaired September 11. . . . Right fielder Orlando Merced went on the D.L. on July 30 and underwent surgery to repair a torn labrum in his throwing shoulder. . . . Sprague had a detached labrum in his throwing shoulder repaired September 10. . . . Shortstop Alex Gonzalez missed 30 games after his right index finger was fractured August 13 by a pitched ball.
Notable: The .244 team batting average, second-lowest in the club's 21-year history, trailed Boston's A.L.-leading mark by 47 points.

—TOM MALONEY

RECORDS

1997 regular-season record: 76-86 (5th in A.L. East); 42-39 at home; 34-47 on road; 27-36 vs. East; 29-26 vs. Central; 20-24 vs. West; 24-28 vs. lefthanded starters; 52-58 vs. righthanded starters; 27-39 on grass; 49-47 on turf; 24-35 in daytime; 52-51 at night; 29-30 in one-run games; 5-9 in extra-inning games; 0-2-1 in doubleheaders.
Team record past five years: 356-389 (.478, ranks 9th in league in that span).

TEAM LEADERS

Batting average: Carlos Delgado (.262).
At-bats: Joe Carter (612).
Runs: Carlos Delgado (79).
Hits: Joe Carter (143).
Total bases: Carlos Delgado (274).
Doubles: Carlos Delgado (42).
Triples: Shannon Stewart (7).
Home runs: Carlos Delgado (30).
Runs batted in: Joe Carter (102).
Stolen bases: Otis Nixon (47).
Slugging percentage: Carlos Delgado (.528).
On-base percentage: Carlos Delgado (.350).

Wins: Roger Clemens (21).
Earned-run average: Roger Clemens (2.05).
Complete games: Roger Clemens, Pat Hentgen (9).
Shutouts: Roger Clemens, Pat Hentgen (3).
Saves: Kelvim Escobar (14).
Innings pitched: Roger Clemens, Pat Hentgen (264.0).
Strikeouts: Roger Clemens (292).

GAMES BY POSITION

Catcher: Benito Santiago 95, Charlie O'Brien 69, Sandy Martinez 3, Julio Mosquera 3.
First base: Carlos Delgado 119, Joe Carter 42, Juan Samuel 7, Orlando Merced 1.
Second base: Carlos Garcia 96, Mariano Duncan 39, Tilson Brito 25, Tomas Perez 8, Juan Samuel 4, Felipe Crespo 1.
Third base: Ed Sprague 129, Tilson Brito 17, Tom Evans 12, Juan Samuel 9, Felipe Crespo 7, Carlos Garcia 4.
Shortstop: Alex Gonzalez 125, Tomas Perez 32, Tilson Brito 8, Carlos Garcia 5.
Outfield: Otis Nixon 102, Orlando Merced 96, Shawn Green 91, Jose Cruz Jr 55, Joe Carter 51, Jacob Brumfield 47, Shannon Stewart 41, Robert Perez 25, Ruben Sierra 7, Rich Butler 3, Juan Samuel 2.
Designated hitter: Joe Carter 64, Shawn Green 35, Carlos Delgado 33, Juan Samuel 16, Ed Sprague 8, Robert Perez 7, Ruben Sierra 6, Jacob Brumfield 4, Felipe Crespo 2, Rich Butler 1, Orlando Merced 1, Otis Nixon 1, Benito Santiago 1, Shannon Stewart 1.

TOP DRAFT CHOICES

1. **Vernon Wells**, OF, Bowie H.S., Arlington, Texas.
2. None.
3. **Billy Brown**, OF, Florida Atlantic Univ.
4. **Woody Heath**, RHP, Green River (Wash.) C.C.
5. **Michael Young**, SS, UC Santa Barbara.
6. **Paul Chiaffredo**, C, Santa Clara Univ.
7. **Matt McClellan**, RHP, Oakland (Mich.) U.
8. **Joe Casey**, RHP, Twin Valley H.S., Elverson, Pa.
9. **Carlos Ortiz**, C, Loara H.S., Anaheim, Calif.
10. **Matt Bowser**, 1B, Tarpon Springs H.S., Palm Harbor, Fla.

ARIZONA DIAMONDBACKS
NATIONAL LEAGUE WEST DIVISION

Diamondbacks Schedule
Home games shaded. *—All-Star Game at Coors Field (Colorado).
D—Day game (any game starting before 5 p.m.).

March

SUN	MON	TUE	WED	THU	FRI	SAT
					31 D COL	

April

SUN	MON	TUE	WED	THU	FRI	SAT
			1 COL	2 COL	3 SF	4 D SF
5 SF	D 6	7 LA	D 8 LA	9 LA	10 SD	11 SD
12 D SD	13 SD	14 STL	15 STL	16 D STL	17 FLA	18 D FLA
19 D FLA	20 FLA	21	22 ATL	23 ATL	24 ATL	25 FLA
26 D FLA	27	28 ATL	29 ATL	30		

May

SUN	MON	TUE	WED	THU	FRI	SAT
					1 MON	2 MON
3 MON	D 4 NYM	5 NYM	6 NYM	7 PHI	8 PHI	9 PHI
10 D PHI	11 CUB	12 CUB	13 MIL	14 MIL	15 PIT	16 PIT
17 PIT	18 D PIT	19	20 FLA	21 FLA	22 D LA	23 LA
24 D LA	25 SD	26 SD	27 SD	28 SF	29 SF	30 D SF
31 D SF						

June

SUN	MON	TUE	WED	THU	FRI	SAT
	1 COL	2 COL	3 COL	4 OAK	5 OAK	6 D OAK
7 OAK	D 8	9 ANA	10 ANA	11 ANA	12 STL	13 STL
14 D STL	15	16 CIN	17 CIN	18 D CIN	19 STL	20 D STL
21 D STL	22 TEX	23 TEX	24 TEX	25 TEX	26 SEA	27 SEA
28 D SEA	29	30 CUB				

July

SUN	MON	TUE	WED	THU	FRI	SAT
			1 D CUB	2 D CUB	3 HOU	4 HOU
5 D HOU	6	7 *	8	9	10 CIN	11 CIN
12 CIN	13 HOU	14 HOU	15 HOU	16	17 COL	18 COL
19 COL	20 SF	21 SF	22 SD	23 D SD	24 D LA	25 D LA
26 LA	27 CUB	28 CUB	29 CUB	30 D MIL	31 MIL	

August

SUN	MON	TUE	WED	THU	FRI	SAT
						1 MIL
2 D MIL	3 CUB	4 CUB	5 D CUB	6	7 MON	8 MON
9 D MON	10 PHI	11 PHI	12 PHI	13	14 NYM	15 NYM
16 NYM	17 D MON	18 MON	19 D MON	20 PHI	21 PHI	22 NYM
23 D NYM	24 D NYM	25 PIT	26 PIT	27 MIL	28 MIL	29 MIL
30 MIL	31					

September

SUN	MON	TUE	WED	THU	FRI	SAT
		1 PIT	2 PIT	3 D PIT	4 HOU	5 D HOU
6 D HOU	7 LA	8 LA	9 LA	10	11 CIN	12 D CIN
13 CIN	14 SF	15 SF	16 SF	17 ATL	18 ATL	19 ATL
20 D ATL	21	22 COL	23 COL	24	25 SD	26 D SD
27 D SD						

1998 SEASON
CLUB DIRECTORY

Managing general partner
Jerry Colangelo
President
Richard Dozer
Vice president and general manager
Joe Garagiola Jr.
Senior executive vice president
Roland Hemond
Vice president, sales and marketing
Scott Brubaker
Vice president, finance
Thomas Harris
V.p., tickets and special events
Dianne Aquilar
Director of player development
Mel Didier
Director of baseball administration
Ralph Nelson
Director of sales and marketing
Blake Edwards
Director of Hispanic marketing
Richard Saenz
Director of Tucson operations
Mark Fernandez
Stadium project coordinator
John Wasson
Director of public relations
Mike Swanson
Director of public affairs
Craig Pletenik
Director of ballpark services
Russ Amaral
Director of suite services
Diney Mahoney
Director of team travel
Roger Riley

Director of field operations
Tommy Jones
Director of scouting
Don Mitchell
Director of Pacific Rim operations
Jim Marshall
Trainer
Paul Lessard
Assistant trainer
Dave Edwards
Club physician
Dr. David Zeman
National scouting supervisors
Kendall Carter, Clay Daniel, Howard McCullough, Steve Springer
Area, int'l scouting supervisors
Oswaldo Alvarez, Tony Arango, David Cassidy, Arnold Cochran, Ray Corbett, Bill Earnhart, Jesse Flores, Brian Guinn, Scott Jaster, James Keller, Chris Knabenshue, Greg Lonigro, Jim Marshall, David May, Louie Medina, Junior Naboa, Mike Piatnik, Carlos Porte, Mac Siebert, Steve Swail, Brad Vaughn, John Wadsworth, Harold Zonder
Part-time scouts
Rogel Andrade, Robert Burguillos, Baldemar Carmona, Tom Couston, Gary Davenport, Doc Edwards, Jack Grant, David Andrew Hall, Scott Jamieson, Hal Kurtzman, Cesar Lopez, Rafael Mena, Ulloa Modesto, Francisco Moet, Arturo Pena, Jose Diaz Perez, Juan Carlos Salabarria, Tomas Santana, Williams Jose Sarmiento, Jorge Urribari, Roberto Perez Vilchis, Doyle Wilson, John Wright

MINOR LEAGUE AFFILIATES

Class	Team	League	Manager
AAA	Tucson	Pacific Coast	Chris Speier
AAA	Monterrey	Mexican	Derek Bryant
A	High Desert	California	Dick Scott
A	South Bend	Midwest	Don Wakamatsu
Rookie	Lethbridge	Pioneer	Joe Almaraz
Rookie	Peoria	Arizona	Mike Brumley

BROADCAST INFORMATION

Radio: KTAR-AM (620).
TV: KTVK (Channel 3)
Cable TV: Fox Sports Arizona.

SPRING TRAINING

Ballpark (city): Tuscon Electric Park (Tucson, Ariz.).
Ticket information: 800-638-4253, 520-325-8601, 520-325-8635, 888-683-3900.

TOP DRAFT CHOICES

1. **Jack Cust**, 1B, Immaculata H.S., Flemington, N.J.
2. **Jason Royer**, RHP, Del City (Okla.) H.S.
3. **Jeffrey Brooks**, 1B, Solanco H.S., Quarryville, Pa.
4. **Chase Voshell**, SS, Milford (Ohio) H.S.
5. **Matt Riethmaier**, RHP, Arkadelphia (Ark.) H.S.
6. **Mike Rooney**, RHP, St. John's University.
7. **Brian Gordon**, OF, Round Rock (Texas) H.S.
8. **Ron Calloway**, OF, Canada (Calif.) J.C.
9. **Justin Singleton**, SS, St. Paul's H.S., Lutherville, Md.
10. **Casey Cuntz**, SS, Louisiana State Univ.

SPRING TRAINING ROSTER

Manager—Buck Showalter (11).
Coaches—Brian Butterfield (55), Mark Connor (52), Dwayne Murphy (21), Jim Presley (17), Glenn Sherlock (53).

No.	PITCHERS	B/T	Ht./Wt.	Born	1997 clubs
	Adamson, Joel	L/L	6-4/185	7-2-71	Tucson, Milwaukee
	Anderson, Brian	B/L	6-1/190	4-26-72	Buffalo, Cleveland
	Blair, Willie	R/R	6-1/185	12-18-65	Detroit, West Michigan, Toledo
	Boyd, Jason	R/R	6-2/165	2-23-73	Reading
	Carrasco, Hector	R/R	6-2/180	10-22-69	Indianapolis, Cincinnati, Kansas City
	Clemons, Chris	R/R	6-4/215	10-31-72	Nashville, Chicago A.L.
	Corey, Bryan	R/R	6-0/160	10-21-73	Jacksonville
	Daal, Omar	L/L	6-3/185	3-1-72	Montreal, Ottawa, Toronto, Syracuse
	De La Cruz, Ynocencio	R/R	6-2/158	2-28-77	Gulf Coast Mets, Kingsport
	Erdos, Todd	R/R	6-1/190	11-21-73	Mobile, San Diego
	Ford, Ben	R/R	6-7/200	8-15-75	Tampa, Norwich
	Hansell, Greg	R/R	6-5/224	3-12-71	Tucson, Milwaukee
	Janzen, Marty	R/R	6-3/200	5-31-73	Syracuse, Toronto
	Lidle, Cory	R/R	5-11/180	3-22-72	Norfolk, New York N.L.
	Manuel, Barry	R/R	5-11/185	8-12-65	New York N.L., Norfolk
	Nunez, Vladimir	R/R	6-5/240	3-15-75	High Desert
	Ojala, Kirt	L/L	6-2/210	12-24-68	Charlotte, Florida
	Rodriguez, Felix	R/R	6-1/180	12-5-72	Indianapolis, Cincinnati
	Sanchez, Martin	R/R	6-2/175	1-19-77	Kane County
	Sodowsky, Clint	L/R	6-4/200	7-13-72	Calgary, Pittsburgh
	Springer, Russ	R/R	6-4/205	11-7-68	Houston, Jackson
	Suppan, Jeff	R/R	6-2/210	1-2-75	Pawtucket, Boston
	Weber, Neil	L/L	6-5/215	12-6-72	Ottawa, Harrisburg
	Wolcott, Bob	R/R	6-0/195	9-8-73	Seattle, Tacoma

No.	CATCHERS	B/T	Ht./Wt.	Born	1997 clubs
	Fabregas, Jorge	L/R	6-3/205	3-13-70	Anaheim, Chicago A.L.
	Miller, Damian	R/R	6-3/202	10-13-69	Salt Lake, Minnesota
	Stinnett, Kelly	R/R	5-11/195	2-14-70	Tucson, Milwaukee

No.	INFIELDERS	B/T	Ht./Wt.	Born	1997 clubs
	Batista, Tony	R/R	6-0/195	12-9-73	Oakland, Edmonton
	Bell, Jay	R/R	6-0/185	12-11-65	Kansas City
	Bell, Mike	R/R	6-2/185	12-7-74	Oklahoma City, Tulsa
	Diaz, Edwin	R/R	5-11/172	1-15-75	Oklahoma City, Tulsa
	Frias, Hanley	B/R	6-0/160	12-5-73	Oklahoma City, Texas
	Klassen, Dan	R/R	6-0/175	9-22-75	El Paso
	Lee, Travis	L/L	6-3/210	5-26-75	Tucson, High Desert
	Williams, Matt	R/R	6-2/216	11-28-65	Cleveland

No.	OUTFIELDERS	B/T	Ht./Wt.	Born	1997 clubs
	Benitez, Yamil	R/R	6-2/195	5-10-72	Omaha, Kansas City
	Brede, Brent	L/L	6-4/208	9-13-71	Salt Lake, Minnesota
	Dellucci, David	L/L	5-10/180	10-31-73	Bowie, Baltimore
	Garcia, Karim	L/L	6-0/172	10-29-75	Albuquerque, Los Angeles
	Jones, Chris	R/R	6-2/205	12-16-65	San Diego
	White, Devon	B/R	6-2/195	12-29-62	Florida

BALLPARK INFORMATION

Ballpark (capacity, surface)
Bank One Ballpark (48,500)
Address
401 East Jefferson
Phoenix, AZ 85003
Business phone
602-514-8500
Ticket information
602-514-8400
Ticket prices
$9 to $50 (lower deck)
$$1 to 13.50 (upper deck)
Field dimensions (from home plate)
To left field at foul line, 330 feet
To center field, 407 feet
To right field at foul line, 334 feet
First game played
Scheduled for March 31, 1998 vs. Colorado

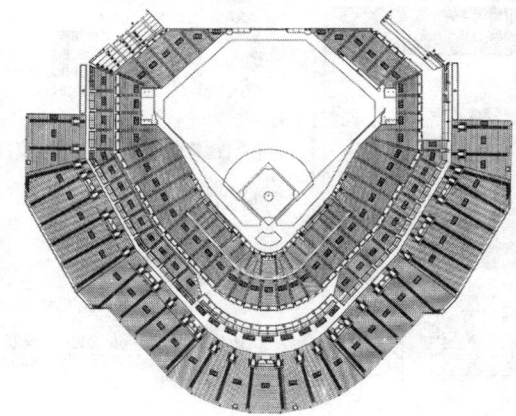

ATLANTA BRAVES
NATIONAL LEAGUE EAST DIVISION

Braves Schedule

Home games shaded. *—All-Star Game at Coors Field (Colorado).
D—Day game (any game starting before 5 p.m.).

March

SUN	MON	TUE	WED	THU	FRI	SAT
					31 D MIL	

April

SUN	MON	TUE	WED	THU	FRI	SAT
			1	2 MIL	3 D PHI	4 PHI
5 D PHI	6	7 PIT	8 D PIT	9 PIT	10 D PHI	11 PHI
12 D PHI	13 PHI	14 PIT	15 D PIT	16 D PIT	17 COL	18 D COL
19 D COL	20 COL	21	22 ARZ	23 ARZ	24 ARZ	25 COL
26 COL	27	28 ARZ	29 ARZ	30 SF		

May

SUN	MON	TUE	WED	THU	FRI	SAT
					1 SF	2 SF
3 D SF	4 LA	5 LA	6 D LA	7 SD	8 SD	9 SD
10 D SD	11 CIN	12 CIN	13 STL	14 STL	15 HOU	16 HOU
17 D HOU	18 D HOU	19	20 COL	21 COL	22 CUB	23 CUB
24 D CUB	25 D CUB	26 MON	27 MON	28 MON	29 D CUB	30 D CUB
31 D CUB						

June

SUN	MON	TUE	WED	THU	FRI	SAT
	1 MIL	2 MIL	3 MIL	4	5 BAL	6 BAL
7 D BAL	8 BOS	9 BOS	10 BOS	11	12 MON	13 MON
14 D MON	15	16 FLA	17 FLA	18 D FLA	19 MON	20 MON
21 D MON	22 NYY	23 NYY	24 NYY	25 NYY	26 TOR	27 TOR
28 D TOR	29	30 TB				

July

SUN	MON	TUE	WED	THU	FRI	SAT
			1 TB	2 D TB	3 NYM	4 NYM
5 D NYM	6	7	* 8	9 FLA	10 FLA	11 FLA
12 D FLA	13	14 NYM	15 D NYM	16 MIL	17 MIL	18 MIL
19 D MIL	20 CUB	21 CUB	22 PHI	23 PHI	24 PIT	25 PIT
26 D PIT	27 CIN	28 CIN	29 CIN	30 D CIN	31 STL	

August

SUN	MON	TUE	WED	THU	FRI	SAT
						1 STL
2 STL	3	4 CIN	5 CIN	6 CIN	7 SF	8 D SF
9 SF	10	11 SD	12 D SD	13 D SD	14 LA	15 LA
16 LA	17	18 SF	19 SF	20 SD	21 SD	22 LA
23 D LA	24 LA	25 HOU	26 HOU	27 STL	28 STL	29 STL
30 D STL	31 HOU					

September

SUN	MON	TUE	WED	THU	FRI	SAT
		1 HOU	2 D HOU	3	4 NYM	5 D NYM
6 NYM	7 D MON	8 D MON	9 MON	10 MON	11 FLA	12 FLA
13 FLA	14 PHI	15 PHI	16 D PHI	17 ARZ	18 ARZ	19 ARZ
20 ARZ	21 FLA	22 FLA	23	24	25 NYM	26 NYM
27 D NYM						

1998 SEASON
CLUB DIRECTORY

Owner
R.E. Turner III

Chairman of the board of directors
William C. Bartholomay

President
Stanley H. Kasten

Exec. v.p. and general manager
John Schuerholz

Sr. v.p. and asst. to the president
Henry L. Aaron

Senior v.p., administration
Bob Wolfe

V.p., dir. of marketing and broadcasting
Wayne Long

Vice president
Lee Douglas

Vice president of development
Janet Marie Smith

Assistant general manager
Dean Taylor

Dir. of scouting and player development
Paul Snyder

Director of minor league operations
Deric Ladnier

Assistant director of scouting
Dayton Moore

Baseball operations assistant
Tyrone Brooks

Special assistants to general manager
Bill Lajoie, Brian Murphy

Special assistant to g.m./player dev.
Jose Martinez

Dir. of team travel and equipment manager
Bill Acree

Executive assistant
June Cornillaud

Sr. dir. of promotions and civic affairs
Miles McRea

Controller
Chip Moore

Director of ticket sales
Paul Adams

Dir. of minor league business operations
Bruce Baldwin

Dir. of stadium operations and security
Larry Bowman

Director of Braves Foundation
Danny Goodwin

Field director
Ed Mangan

Director of ticket operations
Ed Newman

Team counsel
David Payne

Dir. of advertising
Amy Richter

Dir. of community rel. and fan dev.
Dexter Santos

Director of sports human resources
Lisa Stricklin

Director of public relations
Jim Schultz

Media relations manager
Glen Serra

Trainer
Dave Pursley

Assistant trainer
Jeff Porter

Club physician
Dr. David T. Watson

Associate physicians
Dr. John Cantwell, Dr. Robert Crow, Dr. Norman Elliott

Club orthopedist
Dr. Joe Chandler

Major league scouts
Dick Balderson, Scott Nethery, Fred Shaffer, Bill Wight, Bobby Wine

National supervisors
Roy Clark, Bob Wadsworth

Regional supervisors
Butch Baccala, Harold Cronin, John Flannery

International supervisor
Bill Clark

Area scouting supervisors
Stu Cann, Sherard Clinkscales, Phil Dale, Bob Dunning, Rene Francisco, Rod Gilbreath, John Hagemann, Dexter Harris, J. Harrison, Ray Jackson, Kurt Kemp, Brian Kohlscheen, Jim Martz, Marco Paddy, Julian Perez, Rolando Petit, John Ramey, John Stewart, Reyes Vizcaino

Scouts
Mike Baker, Jim Buchert, Joe Caputo, Rob English, Edgar Fernandez, Pedro Flores, Felix Francisco, Bill Froberg, Ruben Garcia, Ralph Garr, Gil Garrido, Luis Herrera, Bob Isabelle, Al Kubski, Duk Jung Lee, Jose Leon, Robert Lucas, William Marcot, Giorgio Moretti, Dario Paulino, Ernie Pedersen, Ubaldo Salinas, Charlie Smith, Doug Smith, Marvin Throneberry, Carlos Torres, Bob Turzilli, Giovanni Viceisza, Fernando Villaescusa

MINOR LEAGUE AFFILIATES

Class	Team	League	Manager
AAA	Richmond	International	Jeff Cox
AA	Greenville	Southern	Randy Ingle
A	Danville	Carolina	Paul Runge
A	Macon	South Atlantic	Brian Snitker
A	Eugene	Northwest	Jim Saul
Rookie	Danville	Appalachian	Franklin Stubbs
Rookie	Gulf Coast Braves	Gulf Coast	Rick Albert

BROADCAST INFORMATION

Radio: WSB-AM (750).
TV: TBS-TV (Channel 17).
Cable TV: SportSouth.

SPRING TRAINING

Ballpark (city): Disney's Wide World of Sports Baseball Stadium (Kissimmee, Fla.).
Ticket information: 407-839-3900, 407-828-3267, 407-939-1500.

SPRING TRAINING ROSTER

Manager—Bobby Cox (6).
Coaches—Jim Beauchamp (37), Pat Corrales (39), Bobby Dews (22), Clarence Jones (28), Leo Mazzone (54), Ned Yost.

No.	PITCHERS	B/T	Ht./Wt.	Born	1997 clubs
51	Borbon, Pedro	L/L	6-1/205	11-15-67	DID NOT PLAY
	Bowie, Micah	L/L	6-4/185	11-10-74	Durham
45	Byrd, Paul	R/R	6-1/185	12-3-70	Atlanta, Richmond
38	Cather, Mike	R/R	6-2/195	12-17-70	Greenville, Richmond, Atlanta
	Chen, Bruce	B/L	6-1/150	6-19-77	Macon
30	Clontz, Brad	R/R	6-1/180	4-25-71	Atlanta, Richmond
	Ebert, Derrin	R/L	6-3/175	8-21-76	Greenville
	Edmondson, Brian	R/R	6-2/175	1-29-73	Binghamton, Norfolk
32	Embree, Alan	L/L	6-2/190	1-23-70	Atlanta
47	Glavine, Tom	L/L	6-1/185	3-25-66	Atlanta
	Jacobs, Dwayne	R/R	6-6/185	7-17-76	Durham
46	Ligtenberg, Kerry	R/R	6-2/205	5-11-71	Greenville, Richmond, Atlanta
31	Maddux, Greg	R/R	6-0/175	4-14-66	Atlanta
34	Millwood, Kevin	R/R	6-4/205	12-24-74	Greenville, Richmond, Atlanta
	Moss, Damian	L/R	6-0/187	11-24-76	Greenville
15	Neagle, Denny	L/L	6-2/225	9-13-68	Atlanta
	Rocker, John	R/L	6-4/210	10-17-74	Durham, Greenville
29	Smoltz, John	R/R	6-3/185	5-15-67	Atlanta
43	Wohlers, Mark	R/R	6-4/207	1-23-70	Atlanta

No.	CATCHERS	B/T	Ht./Wt.	Born	1997 clubs
8	Lopez, Javy	R/R	6-3/200	11-5-70	Atlanta
	Lunar, Fernando	R/R	6-1/190	5-25-77	Macon
	Matos, Pascual	R/R	6-2/160	12-23-74	Durham
12	Perez, Eddie	R/R	6-1/175	5-4-68	Atlanta

No.	INFIELDERS	B/T	Ht./Wt.	Born	1997 clubs
2	Belliard, Rafael	R/R	5-6/160	10-24-61	Atlanta
	Galarraga, Andres	R/R	6-3/235	6-18-61	Colorado
14	Graffanino, Tony	R/R	6-1/175	6-6-72	Atlanta
	Helms, Wes	R/R	6-4/210	5-12-76	Richmond, Greenville
10	Jones, Chipper	B/R	6-3/195	4-24-72	Atlanta
1	Lockhart, Keith	L/R	5-10/170	11-10-64	Atlanta
33	Simon, Randall	L/L	6-0/180	5-26-75	Richmond, Atlanta
	Weiss, Walt	B/R	6-0/175	11-28-63	Colorado
	Williams, Glenn	B/R	6-2/170	7-18-77	Macon

No.	OUTFIELDERS	B/T	Ht./Wt.	Born	1997 clubs
17	Bautista, Danny	R/R	5-11/170	5-24-72	Richmond, Atlanta
19	Gregg, Tommy	L/L	6-1/190	7-29-63	Richmond, Atlanta
	Hollins, Damon	R/L	5-11/180	6-12-74	Richmond
25	Jones, Andruw	R/R	6-1/185	4-23-77	Atlanta
18	Klesko, Ryan	L/L	6-3/220	6-12-71	Atlanta
	Lombard, George	L/R	6-0/210	9-14-75	Durham
24	Tucker, Michael	L/R	6-2/185	6-25-71	Atlanta
	Williams, Gerald	R/R	6-2/190	8-10-66	Milwaukee

BALLPARK INFORMATION

Ballpark (capacity, surface)
Turner Field (50,528, grass)

Address
P.O. Box 4064
Atlanta, GA 30302

Business phone
404-522-7630

Ticket information
404-522-7630

Ticket prices
$30 (dugout level)
$25 (club level)
$20 (field level, terrace level)
$15 (field pavilion, terrace pavilion)
$10 (upper level)
$5 (upper pavilion)
$1 (skyline)

Field dimensions (from home plate)
To left field at foul line, 335 feet
To center field, 401 feet
To right field at foul line, 330 feet

First game played
April 4, 1997 (Braves 5, Cubs 4)

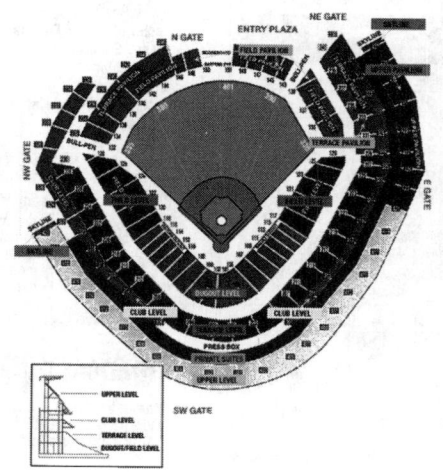

1998 SEASON *Atlanta Braves*

Date	Opp.	Res.	Score	(inn.*)	Hits	Opp. hits	Winning pitcher	Losing pitcher	Save	Record	Pos.	GB
4-1	At Hou.	L	1-2		8	8	Reynolds	Smoltz	Wagner	0-1	T4th	1.0
4-2	At Hou.	L	3-4		8	10	Hampton	Maddux	Wagner	0-2	T4th	2.0
4-3	At Hou.	W	3-2		2	8	Glavine	Kile	Wohlers	1-2	T3rd	2.0
4-4	Chi.	W	5-4		15	7	Clontz	Adams	Wohlers	2-2	3rd	1.0
4-5	Chi.	W	11-5		17	9	Smoltz	Casian		3-2	T2nd	1.0
4-6	Chi.	W	4-0		8	3	Maddux	Mulholland		4-2	2nd	1.0
4-8	Hou.	W	4-2		10	6	Glavine	Hampton	Wohlers	5-2	2nd	1.0
4-9	Hou.	W	4-3	(12)	8	8	Embree	Lima		6-2	2nd	0.5
4-10	Hou.	L	3-5		14	8	Holt	Smoltz	Hudek	6-3	2nd	1.5
4-12	At Chi.	W	2-1		8	5	Bielecki	Patterson	Wohlers	7-3	2nd	1.0
4-13	At Chi.	W	6-4		10	7	Clontz	Wendell	Wohlers	8-3	T1st	....
4-14	Cin.	W	15-5		19	9	Neagle	Schourek		9-3	1st	+0.5
4-15	Cin.	W	3-0		9	6	Smoltz	Mercker		10-3	1st	+1.5
4-16	Cin.	W	7-1		12	3	Byrd	Smiley		11-3	1st	+1.5
4-18	At Col.	W	14-0		23	8	Glavine	Wright		12-3	1st	+2.0
4-19	At Col.	W	8-7		15	10	Neagle	Ritz	Bielecki	13-3	1st	+3.0
4-20	At Col.	L	2-9		8	20	Holmes	Smoltz		13-4	1st	+3.0
4-22	At S.F.	W	4-0		7	5	Maddux	VanLandingham		14-4	1st	+4.0
4-23	At S.F.	L	3-4		8	10	Henry	Embree		14-5	1st	+4.0
4-25	S.D.	W	5-4		8	4	Neagle	Cunnane	Wohlers	15-5	1st	+4.0
4-26	S.D.	W	3-2	(10)	8	9	Wohlers	Hoffman		16-5	1st	+4.0
4-27	S.D.	W	2-0	(5)	7	1	Maddux	Valenzuela		17-5	1st	+4.0
4-28	L.A.	W	14-0		18	5	Glavine	Martinez		18-5	1st	+4.0
4-29	L.A.	L	2-6		7	13	Park	Wade		18-6	1st	+3.0
4-30	At Cin.	W	12-3		17	10	Neagle	Mercker		19-6	1st	+4.0
5-1	At Cin.	W	4-2		8	6	Smoltz	Burba	Wohlers	20-6	1st	+5.0
5-2	Pit.	L	2-3		7	6	Peters	Bielecki	Loiselle	20-7	1st	+5.0
5-3	Pit.	L	0-3		4	7	Loaiza	Glavine	Rincon	20-8	1st	+4.0
5-4	Pit.	W	3-1		6	8	Wade	Cordova	Wohlers	21-8	1st	+5.0
5-5	At St.L.	W	2-1		7	6	Neagle	Al. Benes	Wohlers	22-8	1st	+5.0
5-6	At St.L.	L	3-4		4	10	Mathews	Bielecki	Eckersley	22-9	1st	+5.0
5-7	At Fla.	W	3-2	(10)	8	9	Byrd	Powell	Bielecki	23-9	1st	+5.5
5-8	At Fla.	L	1-5		6	7	Saunders	Glavine		23-10	1st	+4.5
5-9	At Pit.	L	0-9		7	12	Cordova	Wade		23-11	1st	+4.0
5-10	At Pit.	W	9-3		12	7	Neagle	Lieber		24-11	1st	+5.0
5-11	At Pit.	W	8-2		13	6	Smoltz	Cooke		25-11	1st	+5.0
5-12	At Pit.	W	10-2		14	12	Maddux	Schmidt		26-11	1st	+5.0
5-13	Fla.	L	5-11		8	13	Saunders	Wade		26-12	1st	+4.0
5-14	Fla.	L	3-4		10	10	Brown	Bielecki	Nen	26-13	1st	+3.0
5-16	St.L.	W	1-0	(13)	7	11	Borowski	Frascatore		27-13	1st	+3.0
5-17	St.L.	W	11-6		19	7	Smoltz	Morris		28-13	1st	+3.0
5-18	St.L.	W	5-1		8	7	Glavine	An. Benes		29-13	1st	+3.0
5-19	St.L.	W	7-3		9	10	Neagle	Stottlemyre		30-13	1st	+3.5
5-20	Mon.	W	4-2		9	9	Wade	Hermanson	Wohlers	31-13	1st	+3.5
5-21	Mon.	W	3-2		5	8	Maddux	Urbina		32-13	1st	+4.5
5-23	At L.A.	W	4-2		8	7	Smoltz	Astacio	Wohlers	33-13	1st	+5.5
5-24	At L.A.	L	3-10		3	14	Martinez	Glavine		33-14	1st	+4.5
5-25	At L.A.	L	0-2		3	6	Valdes	Neagle	Worrell	33-15	1st	+3.5
5-26	At S.D.	W	12-5		16	11	Borowski	Worrell		34-15	1st	+4.5
5-27	At S.D.	W	9-2		10	12	Maddux	Hamilton		35-15	1st	+4.5
5-29	S.F.	L	2-4		5	10	Estes	Smoltz	Beck	35-16	1st	+4.5
5-30	S.F.	W	3-2		9	6	Wohlers	Henry		36-16	1st	+4.5
5-31	S.F.	L	4-6		8	9	Poole	Borowski	Beck	36-17	1st	+4.5
6-1	S.F.	W	4-3		9	9	Bielecki	Poole	Wohlers	37-17	1st	+5.5
6-2	S.D.	L	4-5		10	10	Murray	Maddux	Hoffman	37-18	1st	+4.5
6-3	S.D.	L	2-5		8	8	Smith	Wohlers	Hoffman	37-19	1st	+4.5
6-4	At Mon.	W	6-3		10	8	Glavine	Juden		38-19	1st	+4.5
6-5	At Mon.	W	9-0		13	6	Neagle	Hermanson		39-19	1st	+5.5
6-6	At S.F.	W	9-5		15	9	Byrd	Roa		40-19	1st	+6.0
6-7	At S.F.	W	5-2		6	2	Maddux	Henry	Wohlers	41-19	1st	+6.0
6-8	At S.F.	L	3-5		9	8	Poole	Smoltz	Beck	41-20	1st	+5.5
6-9	At Col.	L	3-8		13	12	Bailey	Glavine		41-21	1st	+5.5
6-10	At Col.	W	8-3		12	5	Neagle	Ritz		42-21	1st	+5.5
6-11	At Col.	L	6-9		11	16	Thomson	Clontz		42-22	1st	+4.5
6-13	Bal.	L	3-4		7	8	Key	Maddux	Myers	42-23	1st	+3.5
6-14	Bal.	L	4-6	(12)	8	10	Rhodes	Borowski	Myers	42-24	1st	+3.0
6-15	Bal.	L	3-5	(10)	9	7	Mathews	Wohlers	Myers	42-25	1st	+2.5
6-16	At Tor.	W	3-0		8	5	Neagle	Clemens		43-25	1st	+2.5
6-17	At Tor.	W	8-7		12	12	Maddux	Andujar	Wohlers	44-25	1st	+2.5
6-18	At Tor.	L	3-5		3	7	Williams	Smoltz	Timlin	44-26	1st	+2.5
6-20	At Phi.	W	4-1		8	7	Glavine	Leiter		45-26	1st	+2.5

Date	Opp.	Res.	Score	(inn.*)	Hits	Opp. hits	Winning pitcher	Losing pitcher	Save	Record	Pos.	GB
6-21	At Phi.	W	9-8		10	14	Clontz	Blazier	Wohlers	46-26	1st	+3.5
6-22	At Phi.	W	12-5		17	10	Maddux	Stephenson		47-26	1st	+3.5
6-23	At N.Y.	L	2-3		6	10	Reed	Smoltz		47-27	1st	+3.5
6-24	At N.Y.	L	5-6		12	11	McMichael	Wohlers		47-28	1st	+2.5
6-25	At N.Y.	W	14-7		17	9	Glavine	Jones		48-28	1st	+2.5
6-26	Phi.	W	5-4		7	9	Neagle	Beech	Wohlers	49-28	1st	+3.5
6-27	Phi.	W	7-1		10	6	Maddux	Stephenson		50-28	1st	+4.5
6-28	Phi.	W	9-1		11	8	Smoltz	Schilling		51-28	1st	+4.5
6-29	Phi.	W	6-5		7	10	Bielecki	Brewer	Wohlers	52-28	1st	+4.5
6-30	At N.Y. (AL)	L	0-1	(10)	6	12	Stanton	Bielecki		52-29	1st	+3.5
7-1	At N.Y. (AL)	W	3-1		10	6	Neagle	Mendoza	Wohlers	53-29	1st	+4.5
7-2	At N.Y. (AL)	W	2-0		7	3	Maddux	Gooden		54-29	1st	+4.5
7-3	At Mon.	W	15-2		19	7	Smoltz	Bullinger		55-29	1st	+4.5
7-4	At Mon.	W	6-3		11	6	Clontz	Urbina	Wohlers	56-29	1st	+5.5
7-5	At Mon.	W	5-3		8	8	Glavine	Martinez	Wohlers	57-29	1st	+6.5
7-6	At Mon.	L	2-6		6	11	Juden	Neagle		57-30	1st	+6.5
7-10	N.Y.	L	7-10		11	15	McMichael	Bielecki	J. Franco	57-31	1st	+5.5
7-11	N.Y.	L	7-9		11	12	Lidle	Glavine	J. Franco	57-32	1st	+5.5
7-12	N.Y.	W	7-4		10	7	Maddux	Clark	Wohlers	58-32	1st	+6.0
7-13	N.Y.	L	6-7	(10)	12	9	McMichael	Bielecki	J. Franco	58-33	1st	+5.0
7-14	Phi.	W	10-6		9	6	Millwood	Brewer	Wohlers	59-33	1st	+5.0
7-15	Phi.	L	1-8		4	10	Stephenson	Smoltz		59-34	1st	+5.0
7-16	Col.	W	2-1		9	5	Glavine	DiPoto	Wohlers	60-34	1st	+5.0
7-17	Col.	W	8-2		13	9	Maddux	Swift		61-34	1st	+5.0
7-18	L.A.	W	4-1		9	7	Neagle	Reyes	Wohlers	62-34	1st	+6.0
7-19	L.A.	L	1-4		4	8	Astacio	Millwood	Radinsky	62-35	1st	+5.0
7-20	L.A.	L	3-8		7	11	Park	Smoltz		62-36	1st	+5.0
7-21	L.A.	W	5-4	(10)	14	6	Embree	Dreifort		63-36	1st	+6.0
7-22†	At Chi.	W	4-1		8	5	Maddux	Gonzalez		64-36			
7-22‡	At Chi.	L	4-5		9	10	Bottenfield	Cather	Rojas	64-37	1st	+6.5
7-23	At Chi.	L	1-3		5	7	Tapani	Millwood	Rojas	64-38	1st	+5.5
7-25	At Cin.	W	7-3		9	2	Smoltz	Schourek		65-38	1st	+5.5
7-26	At Cin.	L	6-7	(11)	10	12	Shaw	Wohlers		65-39	1st	+5.5
7-27	At Cin.	W	3-2		5	6	Maddux	Burba	Wohlers	66-39	1st	+6.5
7-28	Chi.	W	6-0		9	3	Neagle	Tapani		67-39	1st	+7.0
7-29	Chi.	W	7-2		10	12	Millwood	Trachsel		68-39	1st	+7.5
7-30	Chi.	W	6-5		10	11	Embree	Rojas		69-39	1st	+7.5
7-31	At Fla.	L	0-1		4	6	Saunders	Byrd	Nen	69-40	1st	+6.5
8-1	At Fla.	L	2-3	(12)	5	10	Powell	Cather		69-41	1st	+5.5
8-2	At Fla.	W	4-2		6	7	Neagle	Leiter	Wohlers	70-41	1st	+6.5
8-3	At Fla.	L	4-8		7	10	Fernandez	Millwood		70-42	1st	+5.5
8-4	At Pit.	W	6-0		8	4	Smoltz	Cooke		71-42	1st	+5.5
8-5	At Pit.	L	4-5		6	8	Schmidt	Glavine	Loiselle	71-43	1st	+4.5
8-6	St.L.	W	4-3		7	11	Wohlers	Petkovsek		72-43	1st	+4.5
8-7	St.L.	W	3-0		8	7	Neagle	Stottlemyre	Wohlers	73-43	1st	+5.5
8-8	Fla.	L	4-6		9	11	Fernandez	Byrd	Nen	73-44	1st	+4.5
8-9	Fla.	W	4-3		9	7	Smoltz	Stanifer	Wohlers	74-44	1st	+5.5
8-10	Fla.	L	2-4	(10)	6	9	Powell	Bielecki	Nen	74-45	1st	+4.5
8-11	Fla.	W	2-1		4	5	Wohlers	Heredia		75-45	1st	+5.5
8-12	Pit.	L	2-5		8	9	Sodowsky	Wohlers	Loiselle	75-46	1st	+5.5
8-13	Pit.	L	1-2		6	7	Lieber	Smoltz	Loiselle	75-47	1st	+4.5
8-15	At St.L.	L	2-3	(12)	6	7	King	Cather		75-48	1st	+3.5
8-16	At St.L.	W	5-3		10	7	Maddux	Morris	Wohlers	76-48	1st	+4.5
8-17	At St.L.	L	1-3		6	7	King	Neagle	Eckersley	76-49	1st	+3.5
8-19	At Hou.	W	4-3		11	8	Smoltz	Hampton	Wohlers	77-49	1st	+4.0
8-20	At Hou.	W	3-1		6	4	Giavine	Reynolds	Wohlers	78-49	1st	+4.0
8-22	Cin.	W	6-2		8	11	Maddux	Remlinger		79-49	1st	+5.0
8-23	Cin.	W	10-3		10	8	Neagle	Tomko		80-49	1st	+5.0
8-24	Cin.	L	4-6	(10)	7	10	Shaw	Fox	Belinda	80-50	1st	+4.0
8-26	Hou.	W	7-6	(11)	9	13	Clontz	Wagner		81-50	1st	+4.5
8-27	Hou.	L	4-6	(13)	9	13	Hudek	Byrd	Lima	81-51	1st	+3.5
8-28	Hou.	W	4-2		7	5	Neagle	Kile	Wohlers	82-51	1st	+4.5
8-29	At Bos.	W	9-1		16	8	Smoltz	Sele		83-51	1st	+4.5
8-30	At Bos.	W	15-2		19	7	Millwood	Wakefield		84-51	1st	+4.5
8-31	At Bos.	W	7-3		13	6	Glavine	Avery		85-51	1st	+4.5
9-1	Det.	L	2-4		6	10	Moehler	Maddux	Jones	85-52	1st	+3.5
9-2	Det.	W	5-0		10	4	Neagle	Keagle		86-52	1st	+3.5
9-3	Det.	L	4-12		10	15	Blair	Smoltz		86-53	1st	+2.5
9-4	At S.D.	W	8-7	(11)	17	11	Wohlers	Worrell		87-53	1st	+3.0
9-5	At S.D.	L	2-6		2	12	Ashby	Glavine		87-54	1st	+3.0
9-6	At S.D.	W	9-1		11	5	Maddux	Hitchcock		88-54	1st	+4.0
9-7	At S.D.	W	4-0		7	4	Neagle	Hamilton		89-54	1st	+5.0
9-9	At L.A.	W	4-3		9	6	Smoltz	Valdes	Wohlers	90-54	1st	+5.5
9-10	At L.A.	W	7-0		8	4	Glavine	Martinez		91-54	1st	+6.5
9-12	Col.	L	1-3		8	7	Munoz	Wohlers	DiPoto	91-55	1st	+6.5

Date	Opp.	Res.	Score	(inn.*)	Hits	Opp. hits	Winning pitcher	Losing pitcher	Save	Record	Pos.	GB
9-13	Col.	L	6-10		12	12	Holmes	Cather	DeJean	91-56	1st	+5.5
9-14	Col.	L	0-4		4	10	Astacio	Smoltz		91-57	1st	+4.5
9-15	S.F.	W	5-4		8	5	Ligtenberg	Beck		92-57	1st	+5.5
9-16	S.F.	W	6-4		8	6	Millwood	Alvarez		93-57	1st	+5.5
9-17	N.Y.	W	10-2		14	6	Maddux	Jones		94-57	1st	+6.0
9-18	N.Y.	W	11-4		17	4	Byrd	Isringhausen		95-57	1st	+6.0
9-19	Mon.	W	2-1		3	5	Smoltz	Perez		96-57	1st	+6.0
9-20	Mon.	W	3-1		6	2	Glavine	Martinez		97-57	1st	+7.0
9-21	Mon.	L	1-7		10	11	DeHart	Neagle		97-58	1st	+7.0
9-22	Mon.	W	3-2	(11)	12	13	Cather	Bennett		98-58	1st	+8.0
9-23	At Phi.	W	6-0		11	3	Millwood	Leiter		99-58	1st	+8.0
9-24	At Phi.	L	1-5		4	10	Stephenson	Byrd		99-59	1st	+7.0
9-25	At Phi.	W	3-2	(10)	9	7	Cather	Spradlin	Clontz	100-59	1st	+8.0
9-26	At N.Y.	W	7-6	(11)	12	7	LeRoy	Rojas	Ligtenberg	101-59	1st	+9.0
9-27	At N.Y.	L	1-2		5	4	Crawford	Wohlers		101-60	1st	+9.0
9-28	At N.Y.	L	2-8		7	11	Acevedo	Neagle		101-61	1st	+9.0

Monthly records: April (19-6), May (17-11), June (16-12), July (17-11), August (16-11), September (16-10).
*Innings, if other than nine. †First game of doubleheader. ‡Second game of doubleheader.

HIGHLIGHTS

High point: The team clinched an unprecedented sixth consecutive division championship with a 3-2 victory in 11 innings over the Expos on September 22.

Low point: Hosting the Orioles in the first interleague series at Turner Field June 13-15, the team lost all three games, two in extra innings, and committed three errors.

Turning point: The Braves won 10 of 12 games heading into the All-Star break, extending a 2 ½-game division lead to 6 ½ games.

Most valuable player: Third baseman Chipper Jones. He hit 21 homers, scored 100 runs and drove in a career-high 111 runs. His 41 doubles were the most ever by a Braves player.

Most valuable pitcher: Denny Neagle. He was the league's only 20-game winner and posted a career-best 2.97 ERA. He started the season 7-0, equaling a team record.

Most improved player: Tony Graffanino. The young second baseman hit .174 in 22 games in 1996. A year later he took over for Mark Lemke in August and finished with a .258 average, eight homers and 20 RBIs.

Most pleasant surprise: Jeff Blauser. After two disappointing seasons, he rebounded to hit .308 with 17 homers and 70 RBIs. He had 41 multi-hit games and hit everywhere in the batting order except cleanup.

Biggest disappointment: Ryan Klesko. His average dropped 21 points, his home runs fell by 10 and he had nine fewer RBIs than in '96. He had a stretch of 32 games without a homer.

Key injuries: Kenny Lofton missed six weeks with a groin injury, Lemke suffered torn ligaments in his right ankle that ended his season in August, Terrell Wade had rotator cuff surgery and didn't pitch after June and Javier Lopez suffered a fractured thumb in the All-Star Game and was out for two weeks.

Notable: The Braves did not win fewer than 16 games in any month or lose more than 12. Their 19 wins in April set a major league record. . . . Atlanta had the best record (101-61) of any major league team. . . . Greg Maddux (19-4) won at least 15 games for the 10th straight season and ended the year with the highest winning percentage (.730) and lowest ERA (2.13) of any pitcher in club history. . . . Lofton became only the third Brave (after Felipe Alou and Denis Menke) to hit leadoff homers in back-to-back games. . . . Rafael Belliard ended a 10-year drought (1,869 at-bats) by homering against the Mets on September 26. . . . Klesko's grand slam against the Mets on September 17 was the team's 12th of the season, setting a major league record. . . . The team won its 100th game with a 3-2 victory over the Phillies on September 25, marking just the fourth time in franchise history that the Braves had reached the century mark in wins. . . . Bobby Cox moved into 24th place on the all-time managerial wins list with 1,312 victories. His 957 wins are the most by a Braves manager in the modern era (since 1900).

—BILL ZACK

RECORDS

1997 regular-season record: 101-61 (1st in N.L. East); 50-31 at home; 51-30 on road; 37-26 vs. East; 38-17 vs. Central; 26-18 vs. West; 27-14 vs. lefthanded starters; 74-47 vs. righthanded starters; 78-53 on grass; 23-8 on turf; 27-21 in daytime; 74-40 at night; 33-20 in one-run games; 10-10 in extra-inning games; 0-0-1 in doubleheaders.

Team record past five years: 459-285 (.617, ranks 1st in league in that span).

TEAM LEADERS

Batting average: Kenny Lofton (.333).
At-bats: Chipper Jones (597).
Runs: Chipper Jones (100).
Hits: Chipper Jones (176).
Total bases: Chipper Jones (286).
Doubles: Chipper Jones (41).
Triples: Michael Tucker (7).
Home runs: Ryan Klesko (24).
Runs batted in: Chipper Jones (111).
Stolen bases: Kenny Lofton (27).
Slugging percentage: Ryan Klesko (.490).
On-base percentage: Kenny Lofton (.409).
Wins: Denny Neagle (20).

Earned-run average: Greg Maddux (2.20).
Complete games: John Smoltz (7).
Shutouts: Denny Neagle (4).
Saves: Mark Wohlers (33).
Innings pitched: John Smoltz (256.0).
Strikeouts: John Smoltz (241).

GAMES BY POSITION

Catcher: Javy Lopez 117, Eddie Perez 64, Tim Spehr 7, Greg Myers 2.
First base: Fred McGriff 149, Ryan Klesko 22, Greg Colbrunn 14, Eddie Perez 6, Randall Simon 6, Mike Mordecai 3, Tony Graffanino 1, Tommy Gregg 1.
Second base: Mark Lemke 104, Tony Graffanino 75, Keith Lockhart 20, Rafael Belliard 7, Mike Mordecai 4, Ed Giovanola 1.
Third base: Chipper Jones 152, Mike Mordecai 19, Keith Lockhart 11, Ed Giovanola 8, Tony Graffanino 2.
Shortstop: Jeff Blauser 149, Rafael Belliard 53, Mike Mordecai 4, Tony Graffanino 2, Ed Giovanola 1.
Outfield: Andruw Jones 147, Ryan Klesko 130, Michael Tucker 129, Kenny Lofton 122, Danny Bautista 57, Tommy Gregg 6, Chipper Jones 5, Mike Mordecai 1.
Designated hitter: Keith Lockhart 4, Greg Colbrunn 3, Jeff Blauser 1, Mike Mordecai 1.

TOP DRAFT CHOICES

1. **Troy Cameron,** SS, St. Thomas Aquinas H.S., Fort Lauderdale.
2. **Joey Nation,** LHP, Putnam City H.S., Oklahoma City.
3. **Juan Velazquez,** SS, Jose Campeche H.S., San Lorenzo, P.R.
4. **Cory Aldridge,** OF, Cooper H.S., Abilene, Texas.
5. **Horatio Ramirez,** LHP, Inglewood (Calif.) H.S.
6. **Brett Groves,** SS, Tampa Bay Tech H.S.
7. **Bry Ewen,** C, Belton (Texas) H.S.
8. **Ryan Lehr,** C-3B, Grossmont H.S., La Mesa, Calif.
9. **Ryan Snare,** LHP, East Lake H.S., Palm Harbor, Fla.
10. **Gary Loudon,** RHP, Shippensburg (Pa.) University.

CHICAGO CUBS
NATIONAL LEAGUE CENTRAL DIVISION

Cubs Schedule

Home games shaded. *—All-Star Game at Coors Field (Colorado). D—Day game (any game starting before 5 p.m.).

March

SUN	MON	TUE	WED	THU	FRI	SAT
		31 D FLA				

April

SUN	MON	TUE	WED	THU	FRI	SAT
			1 FLA	2 D FLA	3 D MON	4 D MON
5 MON	6 MON	7	8 D NYM	9 D NYM	10 MON	11 D MON
12 MON	13	14 NYM	15 NYM	16 D NYM	17 D LA	18 D LA
19 D LA	20	21 SD	22 D SD	23 D SD	24 LA	25 LA
26 D LA	27 SD	28 SD	29	30 STL		

May

SUN	MON	TUE	WED	THU	FRI	SAT
					1 STL	2 D STL
3 D STL	4	5 HOU	6 D HOU	7 SF	8 D SF	9 D SF
10 SF	11 ARZ	12 ARZ	13 COL	14 COL	15 CIN	16 CIN
17 CIN	18 D	19 LA	20 D LA	21 LA	22 ATL	23 ATL
24 ATL	25 ATL	26	27 PHI	28 D PHI	29 D PHI	30 D PHI
31 ATL						

June

SUN	MON	TUE	WED	THU	FRI	SAT
	1 FLA	2 D FLA	3 D FLA	4	5 CWS	6 D CWS
7 CWS	8 MIN	9 MIN	10 MIN	11	12 PHI	13 PHI
14 PHI	15 MIL	16 D MIL	17 D MIL	18 D PHI	19 D PHI	20 D PHI
21 PHI	22 D CLE	23 D CLE	24 DET	25 DET	26 KC	27 KC
28 D KC	29	30 ARZ				

July

SUN	MON	TUE	WED	THU	FRI	SAT
			1 D ARZ	2 D ARZ	3 D PIT	4 D PIT
5 D PIT	6	7	* 8	9 D MIL	10 MIL	11 MIL
12 D MIL	13 PIT	14 PIT	15 PIT	16	17 FLA	18 FLA
19 D FLA	20 ATL	21 ATL	22 MON	23 D MON	24 D NYM	25 D NYM
26 D NYM	27 ARZ	28 ARZ	29 ARZ	30 D ARZ	31 COL	

August

SUN	MON	TUE	WED	THU	FRI	SAT
						1 D COL
2 COL	3 D ARZ	4 ARZ	5 D SF	6	7 STL	8 STL
9 STL	10 SF	11 D SF	12 D SF	13	14 HOU	15 HOU
16 D HOU	17	18 STL	19 D STL	20 D SF	21 D SF	22 D HOU
23 HOU	24 D HOU	25 CIN	26 D CIN	27 COL	28 COL	29 COL
30 COL	31 CIN					

September

SUN	MON	TUE	WED	THU	FRI	SAT
		1 CIN	2 D CIN	3 D	4 PIT	5 PIT
6 PIT	7 STL	8 D STL	9 PIT	10 PIT	11 MIL	12 MIL
13 MIL	14 SD	15 SD	16 SD	17 D CIN	18 CIN	19 D CIN
20 CIN	21	22 MIL	23 D MIL	24	25 HOU	26 HOU
27 D HOU						

1998 SEASON
CLUB DIRECTORY

Board of directors
James Dowdle
Andrew B. MacPhail
Andrew McKenna
President and chief executive officer
Andrew B. MacPhail
General manager
Ed Lynch
Director, baseball administration
Scott Nelson
Special assistants to the g.m.
Larry Himes
Ken Kravec
Special player consultant
Hugh Alexander
Major league advance scout
Keith Champion
Traveling secretary
Jimmy Bank
Director, minor leagues
David Wilder
Field coordinator
Alan Regier
Hitting coordinator
To be determined
Pitching coordinator
Lester Strode
Roving infield instructor
Sandy Alomar
Roving outfield instructor
Jimmy Piersall
Equipment manager
Michael Burkhart
Director, scouting
Jim Hendry
Regional scouting supervisors
John Stockstill
Tony DeMacio
Larry Maxie
Latin American coordinator
Oneri Fleita
Director, media relations
Sharon Pannozzo
Media information coordinator
Chuck Wasserstrom
Media relations assistant
Wanda Taylor
Team physicians
John Marquardt, M.D.
Michael Schafer, M.D.

Head trainer
David Tumbas
Assistant trainer
Steve Melendez
Strength coordinator
Bruce Hammel
Equipment manager
Yosh Kawano
Assistant equipment manager
Dana Noeltner
Visiting clubhouse manager
Tom Hellmann
Exec. v.p., business operations
Mark McGuire
V.p., marketing and broadcasting
John McDonough
Director, promotions and advertising
Jay Blunk
Dir., special events and community rel.
Connie Kowal
Mgr., Cubs Care/community relations
Rebecca Polihronis
Director, publications/special projects
Ernie Roth
Manager, publications
Lena McDonagh
Photographer
Stephen Green
Director, stadium operations
Tom Cooper
Assistant director, stadium operations
Paul Rathje
Director, ticket operations
Frank Maloney
Scouts
Mark Adair, Billy Blitzer, Tom Bourque, Moi Camacho, Bill Capps, Jim Crawford, Oneri Fleita, Steve Fuller, Al Geddes, John Gracio, Gene Handley, Bill Harford, Steve Hinton, Joe Housey, Sam Hughes, Spider Jorgensen, Buzzy Keller, Brad Kelley, Scott May, Brian Milner, Tad Powers, Alberto Rondon, Marc Russo, Jose Sera, Mark Servais, Billy Swoope, Jose Trujillo

MINOR LEAGUE AFFILIATES

Class	Team	League	Manager
AAA	Iowa	Pacific Coast	Terry Kennedy
AA	West Tenn	Southern	Dave Trembley
A	Daytona	Florida State	Steve Roadcap
A	Rockford	Midwest	Ruben Amaro
A	Williamsport	New York-Pennsylvania	Bob Ralston
Rookie	Mesa Cubs	Arizona	To be announced

BROADCAST INFORMATION

Radio: WGN-AM (720).
TV: WGN-TV (Channel 9).
Cable TV: CLTV.

SPRING TRAINING

Ballpark (city): HoHoKam Park (Mesa, Ariz.).
Ticket information: 800-638-4253.

SPRING TRAINING ROSTER

Manager—Jim Riggleman (5).
Coaches—Dave Bialas, Tom Gamboa (39), Jeff Pentland (2), Dan Radison (3) Phil Regan (27), Billy Williams (26).

No.	PITCHERS	B/T	Ht./Wt.	Born	1997 clubs
51	Adams, Terry	R/R	6-3/205	3-6-73	Chicago N.L.
48	Clark, Mark	R/R	6-5/225	5-12-68	New York N.L., Chicago N.L.
	Espinal, Jose	R/R	6-1/165	8-31-76	Rockford
31	Foster, Kevin	R/R	6-1/165	1-13-69	Chicago N.L.
54	Gonzalez, Jeremi	R/R	6-1/180	1-8-75	Iowa, Chicago N.L.
	Mahaffey, Alan	L/R	6-1/198	2-2-74	Fort Myers, New Britain
	Miller, Kurt	R/R	6-5/220	8-24-72	Brevard County, Charlotte, Florida
59	Myers, Rod	R/R	6-1/210	6-26-69	Iowa, Chicago N.L.
35	Patterson, Bob	R/L	6-1/195	5-16-59	Chicago N.L.
41	Pisciotta, Marc	R/R	6-5/227	8-7-70	Iowa, Chicago N.L.
	Rain, Steve	R/R	6-6/245	6-2-75	Iowa, Orlando
	Ryan, Jason	B/R	6-3/185	1-23-76	Daytona
	Speier, Justin	R/R	6-4/200	11-6-73	Orlando, Iowa
	Swartzbaugh, Dave	R/R	6-2/205	2-11-68	Chicago N.L., Iowa
36	Tapani, Kevin	R/R	6-0/189	2-18-64	Rockford, Orlando, Daytona, Iowa, Chicago N.L.
	Telemaco, Amaury	R/R	6-3/215	1-19-74	Iowa, Chicago N.L., Orlando
46	Trachsel, Steve	R/R	6-4/200	10-31-70	Chicago N.L.
	Wood, Kerry	R/R	6-5/195	6-16-77	Orlando, Iowa

No.	CATCHERS	B/T	Ht./Wt.	Born	1997 clubs
	Cline, Pat	R/R	6-3/225	10-9-74	Orlando, Iowa
7	Houston, Tyler	L/R	6-1/205	1-17-71	Iowa, Rockford, Chicago N.L.
6	Hubbard, Mike	R/R	6-1/200	2-16-71	Iowa, Chicago N.L.
	Martinez, Sandy	L/R	6-2/205	10-3-72	Syracuse, Toronto
9	Servais, Scott	R/R	6-2/205	6-4-67	Chicago N.L.

No.	INFIELDERS	B/T	Ht./Wt.	Born	1997 clubs
24	Alexander, Manny	R/R	5-10/160	3-20-71	New York N.L., St. Lucie, Chicago N.L.
	Blauser, Jeff	R/R	6-1/180	11-8-65	Atlanta
37	Brown, Brant	L/L	6-3/205	6-22-71	Chicago N.L., Iowa
17	Grace, Mark	L/L	6-2/195	6-28-64	Chicago N.L.
12	Hardtke, Jason	B/R	5-10/175	9-15-71	Norfolk, New York N.L., Binghamton
18	Hernandez, Jose	R/R	6-1/180	7-14-69	Chicago N.L.
	Maxwell, Jason	R/R	6-1/175	3-21-72	Orlando
19	McCall, Rod	L/R	6-7/235	11-4-71	Buffalo, Orlando, Iowa
	Morandini, Mickey	L/R	5-11/176	4-22-66	Philadelphia
	Nieves, Jose	R/R	6-1/170	6-16-75	Daytona
15	Orie, Kevin	R/R	6-4/210	9-1-72	Chicago N.L., Orlando, Iowa

No.	OUTFIELDERS	B/T	Ht./Wt.	Born	1997 clubs
29	Jennings, Robin	L/L	6-2/210	4-11-72	Iowa, Chicago N.L.
1	Johnson, Lance	L/L	5-11/160	7-6-63	New York N.L., Chicago N.L.
10	Lowery, Terrell	R/R	6-3/180	10-25-70	Iowa, Chicago N.L.
	Mieske, Matt	R/R	6-0/192	2-13-68	Milwaukee
21	Sosa, Sammy	R/R	6-0/200	11-12-68	Chicago N.L.
	Valdes, Pedro	L/L	6-1/180	6-29-73	Iowa

BALLPARK INFORMATION

Ballpark (capacity, surface)
Wrigley Field (38,902, grass)

Address
1060 W. Addison St.
Chicago, IL 60613-4397

Business phone
773-404-2827

Ticket information
773-404-2827

Ticket prices
$21 (club box, field box)
$17 (terrace box, upper deck box, family section)
$14 (terrace reserved)
$12 (bleachers)
$9 (adult upper deck reserved)
$6 (under 14 upper deck reserved)
All weekday afternoon games in April, May and
September are less.

Field dimensions (from home plate)
To left field at foul line, 355 feet
To center field, 400 feet
To right field at foul line, 353 feet

First game played
April 20, 1916 (Cubs 7, Reds 6)

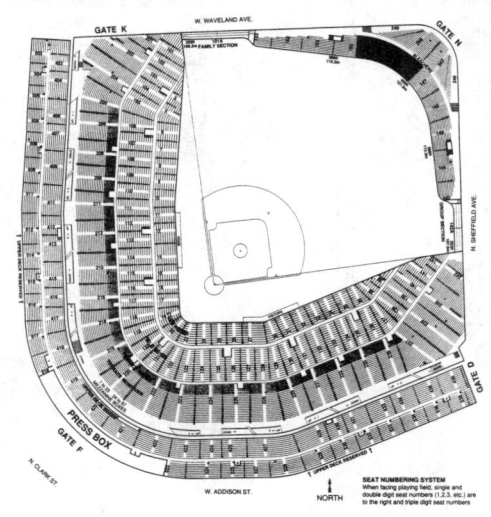

1997 REVIEW

DAY BY DAY

Date	Opp.	Res.	Score	(inn.*)	Hits	Opp. hits	Winning pitcher	Losing pitcher	Save	Record	Pos.	GB
4-1	At Fla.	L	2-4		3	10	Brown	Mulholland		0-1	T4th	1.0
4-2	At Fla.	L	3-4		5	11	Leiter	Trachsel	Nen	0-2	T4th	2.0
4-3	At Fla.	L	2-8		7	10	Fernandez	Castillo		0-3	T4th	2.0
4-4	At Atl.	L	4-5		7	15	Clontz	Adams	Wohlers	0-4	T4th	3.0
4-5	At Atl.	L	5-11		9	17	Smoltz	Casian		0-5	T4th	4.0
4-6	At Atl.	L	0-4		3	8	Maddux	Mulholland		0-6	T4th	5.0
4-8	Fla.	L	3-5		7	8	Leiter	Trachsel	Nen	0-7	5th	5.0
4-10	Fla.	L	0-1		1	7	Fernandez	Castillo		0-8	5th	5.5
4-12	Atl.	L	1-2		5	8	Bielecki	Patterson	Wohlers	0-9	5th	6.0
4-13	Atl.	L	4-6		7	10	Clontz	Wendell	Wohlers	0-10	5th	6.0
4-15	Col.	L	7-10		9	10	Thompson	Foster		0-11	5th	6.5
4-16	Col.	L	0-4		5	6	Bailey	Castillo		0-12	5th	7.5
4-19	At N.Y.	L	3-6		7	8	Clark	Wendell	J. Franco	0-13	5th	8.0
4-20†	At N.Y.	L	2-8		5	13	Jones	Trachsel		0-14		
4-20‡	At N.Y.	W	4-3		12	8	Foster	Mlicki	Wendell	1-14	5th	8.5
4-21	At N.Y.	W	6-4		8	5	Castillo	McMichael	Adams	2-14	5th	8.0
4-22	At Mon.	L	1-5		7	8	Hermanson	Swartzbaugh		2-15	5th	9.0
4-23	At Mon.	L	3-4		8	12	Bullinger	Mulholland	Smith	2-16	5th	10.0
4-24	Pit.	L	3-4		7	6	Loiselle	Rojas		2-17	5th	10.5
4-25	Pit.	W	11-1		14	5	Foster	Lieber		3-17	5th	10.5
4-26	Pit.	W	7-6		14	12	Patterson	Rincon	Rojas	4-17	5th	9.5
4-27	Pit.	L	0-7		5	10	Schmidt	Telemaco		4-18	5th	9.5
4-28	Mon.	W	5-2		8	8	Mulholland	Hermanson	Rojas	5-18	5th	8.5
4-29	Mon.	W	14-8		14	11	Trachsel	Bullinger		6-18	5th	8.5
4-30	At Col.	L	5-11		12	8	Ritz	Foster		6-19	5th	8.5
5-1	At Col.	L	4-5		8	9	Swift	Castillo	S. Reed	6-20	5th	8.5
5-2	At L.A.	L	7-8	(10)	12	11	Candiotti	Patterson		6-21	5th	9.5
5-3	At L.A.	W	2-1		5	8	Mulholland	Valdes	Adams	7-21	5th	8.5
5-4	At L.A.	L	2-5		5	12	Park	Trachsel	Worrell	7-22	5th	9.5
5-6	At S.D.	W	2-1		5	8	Foster	Ashby	Rojas	8-22	5th	9.0
5-7	At S.D.	L	3-6		11	12	Cunnane	Castillo	Hoffman	8-23	5th	9.0
5-8	At S.D.	W	6-2		16	8	Mulholland	Valenzuela		9-23	5th	9.0
5-9	At S.F.	W	5-3	(14)	12	7	Bottenfield	Roa		10-23	5th	8.5
5-10	At S.F.	L	2-4		8	10	Rueter	Telemaco		10-24	5th	9.0
5-11	At S.F.	L	5-11		11	10	Gardner	Foster	Henry	10-25	5th	9.0
5-13	L.A.	W	2-1		6	7	Wendell	Astacio	Rojas	11-25	T4th	7.5
5-14	L.A.	L	4-6		7	12	Osuna	Rojas	Worrell	11-26	T4th	8.5
5-15	S.D.	W	8-2		11	3	Castillo	Hitchcock		12-26	4th	8.5
5-16	S.D.	W	16-7		21	9	Foster	Worrell		13-26	4th	8.0
5-17	S.F.	L	1-4		7	5	Gardner	Telemaco	Beck	13-27	4th	8.0
5-18	S.F.	W	5-3		13	7	Wendell	Tavarez	Adams	14-27	4th	7.0
5-19	S.F.	W	15-4		18	12	Trachsel	Fernandez		15-27	4th	7.0
5-20	Phi.	L	2-3		6	10	Leiter	Castillo	Bottalico	15-28	4th	7.0
5-21	Phi.	W	7-0		10	4	Foster	Ramos		16-28	4th	7.0
5-23	At Cin.	W	3-1		4	5	Mulholland	Mercker	Adams	17-28	4th	6.0
5-24	At Cin.	L	1-4	(12)	6	12	Shaw	Wendell		17-29	4th	7.0
5-25	At Cin.	L	5-7		8	12	Schourek	Bottenfield	Shaw	17-30	4th	7.0
5-26	At Pit.	W	2-1		6	3	Foster	Cordova	Adams	18-30	4th	6.0
5-27	At Pit.	W	8-7		12	12	Gonzalez	Lieber	Adams	19-30	4th	5.0
5-28	At Pit.	L	1-4		6	8	Cooke	Mulholland		19-31	4th	5.5
5-29	Cin.	W	2-1		6	4	Trachsel	Belinda	Adams	20-31	4th	5.5
5-30	Cin.	L	1-5		5	15	Schourek	Castillo		20-32	4th	6.0
5-31	Cin.	W	7-4		11	7	Foster	Morgan	Rojas	21-32	4th	5.0
6-1	Cin.	W	7-1		13	6	Gonzalez	Smiley		22-32	4th	5.0
6-2	Pit.	W	3-2		7	6	Mulholland	Lieber	Adams	23-32	4th	4.0
6-3	Pit.	L	1-3		5	10	Cooke	Trachsel	Loiselle	23-33	4th	5.0
6-4	At Phi.	W	5-1		10	6	Castillo	Stephenson		24-33	4th	4.5
6-5	At Phi.	L	8-9	(10)	14	10	Ryan	Adams		24-34	4th	5.0
6-6	At Mon.	L	0-3		6	10	Bullinger	Gonzalez		24-35	4th	6.0
6-7	At Mon.	L	0-5		7	6	Perez	Mulholland		24-36	T4th	7.0
6-8	At Mon.	L	4-5		6	11	Telford	Adams		24-37	5th	7.0
6-9	At Mon.	L	5-6		10	8	Juden	Castillo	Urbina	24-38	5th	7.5
6-10	N.Y.	L	6-10		12	13	Mlicki	Foster		24-39	5th	7.5
6-11	N.Y.	W	5-4		13	7	Adams	McMichael		25-39	5th	6.5
6-13	Mil.	L	2-4		5	9	D'Amico	Mulholland	Jones	25-40	5th	7.5
6-14	Mil.	W	9-5		14	10	Trachsel	Karl	Wendell	26-40	5th	6.5
6-15	Mil.	W	4-3		5	10	Castillo	Eldred	Wendell	27-40	5th	5.5
6-16	At Chi. (AL)	W	8-3		14	9	Foster	Navarro		28-40	5th	5.5
6-17	At Chi. (AL)	L	3-5		7	7	Drabek	Gonzalez	Hernandez	28-41	5th	5.5
6-18	At Chi. (AL)	L	0-3		4	6	Alvarez	Mulholland		28-42	5th	5.5
6-20	At Hou.	L	3-7		9	13	Kile	Trachsel		28-43	5th	6.5

Date	Opp.	Res.	Score	(inn.*)	Hits	Opp. hits	Winning pitcher	Losing pitcher	Save	Record	Pos.	GB
6-21	At Hou.	L	3-7		6	12	Holt	Castillo		28-44	5th	7.5
6-22	At Hou.	L	1-3		6	5	Hampton	Foster	Wagner	28-45	5th	8.5
6-23	At St.L.	W	3-0		8	4	Gonzalez	Valenzuela		29-45	5th	7.5
6-24	At St.L.	L	2-7		5	15	An. Benes	Mulholland		29-46	5th	7.5
6-25	At St.L.	L	1-3		6	7	Mathews	Patterson		29-47	5th	8.5
6-26	Hou.	L	6-7	(10)	13	14	Wagner	Adams	Minor	29-48	5th	9.5
6-27	Hou.	W	2-1		6	7	Foster	Hampton	Wendell	30-48	5th	8.5
6-28	Hou.	W	5-2		6	2	Gonzalez	Garcia	Bottenfield	31-48	5th	7.5
6-29	Hou.	L	8-10		16	11	Minor	Mulholland	Wagner	31-49	5th	8.5
6-30	K.C.	W	8-7		17	11	Pisciotta	Bones	Rojas	32-49	5th	7.5
7-1	K.C.	W	6-1		11	5	Castillo	Rusch		33-49	5th	7.5
7-2	K.C.	W	3-2		9	9	Foster	Appier	Rojas	34-49	5th	7.5
7-3	At Phi.	W	5-4		10	8	Gonzalez	Schilling	Rojas	35-49	5th	6.5
7-4	At Phi.	W	9-3		12	10	Mulholland	Ruffcorn	Bottenfield	36-49	5th	5.5
7-5	At Phi.	L	7-9		9	14	Harris	Patterson	Bottalico	36-50	5th	6.5
7-6	At Phi.	W	8-4		14	9	Castillo	Leiter	Rojas	37-50	5th	6.5
7-10	St.L.	L	2-3		5	5	Al. Benes	Wendell	Eckersley	37-51	5th	6.5
7-11	St.L.	W	7-1		8	5	Gonzalez	Morris		38-51	5th	6.5
7-12	St.L.	L	1-2	(12)	7	10	Mathews	Wendell	Eckersley	38-52	5th	6.5
7-13	St.L.	L	5-11		6	20	Stottlemyre	Trachsel		38-53	5th	7.5
7-14	Hou.	L	7-9	(15)	18	14	Wagner	Tatis	Springer	38-54	5th	8.5
7-15	Hou.	L	3-5		8	9	Kile	Rojas	Magnante	38-55	5th	9.5
7-16	At N.Y.	W	6-5		10	7	Gonzalez	Reynoso	Rojas	39-55	5th	8.5
7-17	At N.Y.	L	3-4	(10)	9	12	J. Franco	Bottenfield		39-56	5th	8.5
7-19†	Col.	W	7-0		11	4	Trachsel	Wright		40-56		
7-19‡	Col.	W	6-5		8	13	Wendell	McCurry	Rojas	41-56	5th	8.5
7-20	Col.	L	5-9		12	12	Leskanic	Adams	Holmes	41-57	5th	9.5
7-22†	Atl.	L	1-4		5	8	Maddux	Gonzalez		41-58		
7-22‡	Atl.	W	5-4		10	9	Bottenfield	Cather	Rojas	42-58	5th	10.0
7-23	Atl.	W	3-1		7	5	Tapani	Millwood	Rojas	43-58	5th	10.0
7-24	At Col.	L	1-7		6	8	Wright	Trachsel		43-59	5th	11.0
7-25	At Col.	L	3-9		12	13	Castillo	Foster		43-60	5th	12.0
7-26	At Col.	L	3-6		9	9	Bailey	Mulholland	Holmes	43-61	5th	13.0
7-27	At Col.	L	0-4		7	7	Thomson	Gonzalez		43-62	5th	14.0
7-28	At Atl.	L	0-6		3	9	Neagle	Tapani		43-63	5th	14.0
7-29	At Atl.	L	2-7		12	10	Millwood	Trachsel		43-64	5th	15.0
7-30	At Atl.	L	5-6		11	10	Embree	Rojas		43-65	5th	16.0
7-31	L.A.	L	1-4		4	7	Park	Mulholland	Worrell	43-66	5th	16.5
8-1	L.A.	L	9-13		14	20	Nomo	Gonzalez		43-67	5th	16.5
8-2	L.A.	W	5-1		11	10	Tapani	Candiotti		44-67	5th	16.5
8-3	L.A.	W	4-3	(12)	11	9	Tatis	Worrell		45-67	5th	16.5
8-5	S.F.	L	2-8		5	11	Tavarez	Patterson		45-68	5th	16.0
8-6	S.F.	L	4-7		8	10	Rapp	Mulholland		45-69	5th	16.0
8-7	S.F.	W	6-3		11	5	Gonzalez	Alvarez		46-69	5th	15.0
8-8	S.D.	W	3-1		11	9	Pisciotta	Bochtler		47-69	5th	14.0
8-9	S.D.	L	5-7		10	12	Cunnane	Adams	Hoffman	47-70	5th	15.0
8-10	S.D.	L	3-4		11	6	Bochtler	Bottenfield	Hoffman	47-71	5th	16.0
8-11	At L.A.	L	1-2		4	7	Park	Batista		47-72	5th	17.0
8-12	At L.A.	W	4-2		9	10	M. Clark	Nomo	Adams	48-72	5th	17.0
8-13	At S.F.	W	6-5		10	10	Gonzalez	Gardner	Adams	49-72	5th	16.0
8-14	At S.F.	L	3-7		7	11	Estes	Tapani		49-73	5th	16.5
8-15	At S.D.	L	1-5		4	10	Hitchcock	Trachsel		49-74	5th	16.5
8-16	At S.D.	L	3-4	(10)	9	10	Hoffman	Adams		49-75	5th	16.5
8-17	At S.D.	W	6-5		12	8	M. Clark	Menhart	Adams	50-75	5th	16.5
8-19	At Fla.	L	1-8		4	5	Fernandez	Gonzalez		50-76	5th	16.5
8-20	At Fla.	L	5-6		11	9	Hernandez	Tapani	Nen	50-77	5th	16.5
8-22	Mon.	W	3-1		5	5	Trachsel	Kline	Adams	51-77	5th	17.0
8-23	Mon.	L	5-9		7	13	Telford	Patterson		51-78	5th	17.0
8-24	Mon.	W	12-3		15	8	Gonzalez	Perez		52-78	5th	17.0
8-25	Fla.	W	3-1		11	8	Tapani	Fernandez	Adams	53-78	5th	16.5
8-26	Fla.	L	0-11		4	17	Hernandez	Batista		53-79	5th	16.5
8-27	Fla.	L	3-4		9	6	Nen	Adams		53-80	5th	17.5
8-28	Fla.	W	4-3	(10)	10	7	Adams	Alfonseca		54-80	5th	16.5
8-29	At Cle.	L	6-7		13	11	Mesa	Stevens		54-81	5th	16.5
8-30	At Cle.	W	9-4		15	8	Tapani	Smiley		55-81	5th	15.5
8-31	At Cle.	L	5-9		13	11	Nagy	Batista	Assenmacher	55-82	5th	15.5
9-1	Min.	L	6-7		12	13	Trombley	Stevens	Aguilera	55-83	5th	15.5
9-2	Min.	W	9-3		14	8	M. Clark	Tewksbury		56-83	5th	14.5
9-3	Min.	W	10-6		15	10	Gonzalez	Rodriguez		57-83	5th	14.5
9-5	N.Y.	W	8-3		8	9	Tapani	Bohanon		58-83	5th	14.0
9-6	N.Y.	W	7-5		10	9	Pisciotta	J. Franco	Adams	59-83	5th	13.0
9-7	N.Y.	L	2-9		8	13	Jones	Trachsel		59-84	5th	13.0
9-8	At Cin.	W	8-1		13	3	M. Clark	Tomko		60-84	5th	12.5
9-9	At Cin.	L	2-5		8	8	Morgan	Gonzalez	Shaw	60-85	5th	13.5
9-10	At Cin.	W	3-1		11	6	Tapani	Mercker	Adams	61-85	5th	12.5

Date	Opp.	Res.	Score	(inn.*)	Hits	Opp. hits	Winning pitcher	Losing pitcher	Save	Record	Pos.	GB
9-12	At Pit.	L	1-3		6	5	Schmidt	Batista	Loiselle	61-86	5th	13.5
9-13	At Pit.	W	4-1		9	7	Trachsel	Cordova	Adams	62-86	5th	13.5
9-14	At Pit.	W	3-2		7	6	M. Clark	Rincon	Adams	63-86	5th	12.5
9-15	Cin.	L	1-4		6	9	Morgan	Gonzalez	Shaw	63-87	5th	12.5
9-16	Cin.	W	5-0		8	1	Tapani	Mercker		64-87	5th	12.5
9-17	St.L.	L	9-12		11	13	Morris	Batista		64-88	5th	13.5
9-18	St.L.	W	4-3		10	9	Trachsel	Lowe		65-88	5th	12.5
9-19	Phi.	L	5-10	(6)	9	13	Winston	M. Clark		65-89	5th	12.5
9-20	Phi.	L	2-3		6	6	Gomes	Adams	Bottalico	65-90	5th	13.5
9-21	Phi.	W	11-3		15	8	Tapani	Schilling		66-90	5th	13.5
9-23	At Hou.	L	3-5		6	11	Kile	Trachsel	Wagner	66-91	5th	15.0
9-24	At Hou.	W	3-1		11	8	M. Clark	Holt	Adams	67-91	5th	14.0
9-25	At Hou.	L	1-9		4	8	Hampton	Gonzalez		67-92	5th	15.0
9-26	At St.L.	W	5-2		14	6	Tapani	Busby		68-92	5th	15.0
9-27	At St.L.	L	4-12		7	12	Morris	Foster		68-93	5th	16.0
9-28	At St.L.	L	1-2		4	7	Painter	Pisciotta		68-94	5th	16.0

Monthly records: April (6-19), May (15-13), June (11-17), July (11-17), August (12-16), September (13-12).
*Innings, if other than nine. †First game of doubleheader. ‡Second game of doubleheader.

HIGHLIGHTS

High point: September 28. It marked the end of the season, one of the worst in franchise history.

Low point: In a season with many, it had to be the N.L.-record 14-game losing streak to start the season. In 121 previous campaigns, the Cubs' worst start was 0-7, in 1962.

Turning point: No. 1 starter Kevin Tapani's lingering finger injury finally led to surgery during spring training, leaving the team without a staff leader before the season had even begun.

Most valuable player: Mark Grace, who was the Cubs' lone representative at the All-Star Game. He hit .319 to finish in the top 10 in the league for the eighth time in 10 big-league seasons and was spectacular again at first base.

Most valuable pitcher: Tapani, who returned to the field after missing the first three-plus months, went 9-3 in 13 starts with a 3.39 ERA. He finished the season on a seven-game winning streak.

Most improved player: Doug Glanville, who hit .300 in his first full major league season after batting .241 in 1996.

Most pleasant surprise: Reliever Marc Pisciotta, who made his major league debut at age 27 and was superb in the set-up role.

Biggest disappointment: Closer Mel Rojas, who was shipped off to the Mets after a horrible four months in a Cubs uniform. He went 0-4 for the team with six blown saves in 19 chances.

Key injuries: Tapani, who was lost for nearly four months after finger surgery; Grace, who went down in Game 3 with a ripped hamstring; and Ryne Sandberg, who missed a couple of weeks in April after getting beaned in the dugout by a foul ball off the bat of Brant Brown.

Notable: The Cubs used a total of 42 players, including 16 who were on the roster for the first time. Nine players who were on the opening-day roster did not finish the season with the team. . . . Right fielder Sammy Sosa (week ending May 18) and pitcher Mark Clark (September 14) were named N.L. Players of the Week. . . . Sandberg retired after a Hall of Fame career that saw him set the record for home runs by a second baseman (277). He also is the all-time leader in fielding percentage at the position (.989) and finished 91st on the all-time hits list (2,386), 86th in homers (282) and 95th in steals (344). He is one of three players ever, along with Willie Mays and Andre Dawson, to compile 1,000 RBIs, 280 home runs, 300 stolen bases and 2,300 hits. He won nine Gold Gloves and played in 10 All-Star Games, starting nine. . . . Jeremi Gonzalez (11 wins) became the first rookie (excluding strike-shortened seasons) to lead the club in victories since Ken Holtzman in 1966. . . . Dave Clark set a club record with 22 pinch-hit RBIs. . . . Sammy Sosa set a club record and led the N.L. with 174 strikeouts. . . . On May 15 against San Diego, the Cubs hit four triples in a game for the first time since April 28, 1996. . . . Cub pitchers struck out a team-record 1,072 batters and allowed a team-record 185 homers.

—BARRY ROZNER

RECORDS

1997 regular-season record: 68-94 (5th in N.L. Central); 42-39 at home; 26-55 on road; 20-35 vs. East; 30-33 vs. Central; 18-26 vs. West; 50-74 vs. lefthanded starters; 56-76 on grass; 12-18 on turf; 44-47 in daytime; 24-47 at night; 24-26 in one-run games; 3-8 in extra-inning games; 1-0-2 in doubleheaders.

Team record past five years: 350-393 (.471, ranks 11th in league in that span).

TEAM LEADERS

Batting average: Mark Grace (.319).
At-bats: Sammy Sosa (642).
Runs: Sammy Sosa (90).
Hits: Mark Grace (177).
Total bases: Sammy Sosa (308).
Doubles: Mark Grace (32).
Triples: Doug Glanville, Mark Grace, Jose Hernandez, Brian McRae, Kevin Orie (5).
Home runs: Sammy Sosa (36).
Runs batted in: Sammy Sosa (119).
Stolen bases: Shawon Dunston (29).
Slugging percentage: Sammy Sosa (.480).
On-base percentage: Mark Grace (.409).
Wins: Jeremi Gonzalez (11).
Earned-run average: Steve Trachsel (4.51).
Complete games: Mark Clark (2).
Shutouts: Jeremi Gonzalez, Kevin Tapani (1).
Saves: Terry Adams (18).
Innings pitched: Steve Trachsel (201.1).
Strikeouts: Steve Trachsel (160).

GAMES BY POSITION

Catcher: Scott Servais 118, Tyler Houston 41, Mike Hubbard 20.
First base: Mark Grace 148, Brant Brown 12, Dave Hansen 4, Tyler Houston 2, Jose Hernandez 1, Scott Servais 1.
Second base: Ryne Sandberg 126, Rey Sanchez 32, Jose Hernandez 20, Miguel Cairo 9, Manny Alexander 4, Dave Hansen 1, Tyler Houston 1.
Third base: Kevin Orie 112, Dave Hansen 51, Jose Hernandez 47, Tyler Houston 12, Mike Hubbard 1, Rey Sanchez 1.
Shortstop: Shawon Dunston 108, Rey Sanchez 63, Manny Alexander 28, Jose Hernandez 21, Kevin Orie 3, Miguel Cairo 2, Tyler Houston 1.
Outfield: Sammy Sosa 161, Doug Glanville 138, Brian McRae 107, Lance Johnson 39, Brant Brown 27, Brooks Kieschnick 27, Dave Clark 25, Shawon Dunston 7, Jose Hernandez 6, Terrell Lowery 6, Robin Jennings 5.
Designated hitter: Dave Clark 4, Scott Servais 2, Jose Hernandez 1, Lance Johnson 1, Ryne Sandberg 1.

TOP DRAFT CHOICES

1. **Jon Garland,** RHP, Kennedy H.S., Granada Hills, Calif.
2. None.
3. **Scott Downs,** LHP, Univ. of Kentucky.
4. **Nathan Teut,** LHP, Iowa State University.
5. **Jaisen Randolph,** OF, Hillsborough H.S., Tampa.
6. **Matt Mauck,** 3B, Jasper (Ind.) H.S.
7. **Paul Vracar,** RHP, Orchard Park H.S., Stoney Creek, Ontario.
8. **Ron Walker,** 3B, Old Dominion Univ.
9. **Gary Johnson,** OF, University of Nevada.
10. **Mike Amrhein,** C, Univ. of Notre Dame.

CINCINNATI REDS
NATIONAL LEAGUE CENTRAL DIVISION

Reds Schedule
Home games shaded. *—All-Star Game at Coors Field (Colorado).
D—Day game (any game starting before 5 p.m.).

March
SUN	MON	TUE	WED	THU	FRI	SAT
		31 D SD	D			

April
SUN	MON	TUE	WED	THU	FRI	SAT
			1 SD	2 SD	3 LA	4 D LA
5 D LA	6	7 D SD	8 SD	9 D SD	10 COL	11 D COL
12 D COL	13 COL	14	15 HOU	16 HOU	17 NYM	18 D NYM
19 D NYM	20	21 PHI	22 PHI	23 PHI	24 NYM	25 D NYM
26 D NYM	27 PHI	28 PHI	29 D PHI	30		

May
SUN	MON	TUE	WED	THU	FRI	SAT
					1 MIL	2 D MIL
3 D MIL	4 MON	5 MON	6 MON	7 PIT	8 PIT	9 PIT
10 PIT	11 ATL	12 ATL	13 FLA	14 FLA	15 CUB	16 CUB
17 D CUB	18	19 NYM	20 NYM	21 NYM	22 COL	23 D COL
24 COL	25 D SF	26 SF	27 SF	28 D LA	29 LA	30 LA
31 D LA						

June
SUN	MON	TUE	WED	THU	FRI	SAT
	1 SF	2 SF	3 D SF	4 D	5 CLE	6 CLE
7 D CLE	8 D SD	9 SD	10 SD	11	12 HOU	13 HOU
14 D HOU	15 HOU	16 ARZ	17 ARZ	18 D ARZ	19 HOU	20 HOU
21 D HOU	22 KC	23 D KC	24 CWS	25 CWS	26 DET	27 DET
28 D DET	29	30 MIN				

July
SUN	MON	TUE	WED	THU	FRI	SAT
			1 MIN	2 MIN	3 STL	4 STL
5 D STL	6	7	* 8	9	10 ARZ	11 ARZ
12 ARZ	13 STL	14 STL	15 STL	16	17 SD	18 SD
19 SD	20 LA	21 LA	22 COL	23 COL	24 SF	25 D SF
26 D SF	27 ATL	28 ATL	29 ATL	30 D ATL	31 FLA	

August
SUN	MON	TUE	WED	THU	FRI	SAT
						1 FLA
2 D FLA	3	4 ATL	5 ATL	6 ATL	7 MIL	8 MIL
9 D MIL	10	11 PIT	12 PIT	13 PIT	14 MON	15 MON
16 D MON	17	18 MIL	19 D MIL	20 PIT	21 PIT	22 MON
23 MON	24 D MON	25 CUB	26 D CUB	27 FLA	28 FLA	29 FLA
30 D FLA	31 CUB					

September
SUN	MON	TUE	WED	THU	FRI	SAT
		1 CUB	2 D CUB	3 D	4 STL	5 STL
6 D STL	7 HOU	8 D HOU	9 STL	10 STL	11 ARZ	12 D ARZ
13 ARZ	14 MIL	15 MIL	16 MIL	17	18 D CUB	19 D CUB
20 D CUB	21 PHI	22 PHI	23 PHI	24	25 PIT	26 D PIT
27 D PIT						

1998 SEASON
CLUB DIRECTORY

General partner
Marge Schott

President and chief executive officer
Marge Schott

Managing executive
John Allen

General manager
Jim Bowden

Assistant/baseball operations
Brad Kullman

Special assistant to the general manager
Gene Bennett

Senior advisor/baseball operations
Larry Barton Jr.

Controller
Anthony Ward

Director, stadium operations
Jody Pettyjohn

Director, ticket department
John O'Brien

Director, season ticket sales
Pat McCaffrey

Director, group sales
Barb McManus

Marketing consultant
Cal Levy

Dir., public relations and publications
Mike Ringering

Director, media relations
Rob Butcher

Publicity assistant
Charles Henderson

Administrative assistant/publicity
Kelly Lippincott

Director, player development
Sheldon "Chief" Bender

Senior advisor/player personnel
Bob Boone

Sr. dir./scouting and player development
Al Goldis

Sr. advisor/baseball operations
Bob Zuk

Traveling secretary
Gary Wahoff

Assistant ticket director
Ken Ayer

Chief administrative assistant
Joyce Pfarr

Administrative assistant, business
Ginny Kamp

Chief administrator, scouting dept.
Wilma Mann

Admin. assistant, player development
Lois Schneider

Scouting secretary
Lois Hudson

Head trainer
Greg Lynn

Assistant trainer
Mark Mann

Field superintendent
To be announced

Sr. clubhouse & equipment manager
Bernie Stowe

Reds clubhouse & equipment manager
Rick Stowe

Visiting clubhouse & equip. manager
Mark Stowe

Cross-checkers
Jeff Barton, Hank Sargent, Thomas Wilson

Scouting supervisors
Johnny Almaraz, Ray Bellino, John Brickley, George Brill, Bobby Filotei, Jerry Flowers, Chris Gill, Jimmy Gonzales, Dick Hager, David Jennings, Robert Koontz, Steve Kring, Mike Mangan, Tom Severtson, Bob Szymkowski, Marion "Bo" Trumbo, Mike Wallace, Brian Wilson

Scouts
Fred Blair, Felix Delgado, Jim Grief, Don Hill, Don Gust, Fred Hayes, Thomas Herrera, Les Houser, Fred Leone, Anthony Dion Lowe, Armando Morales, Jose Moreno, Denny Nagel, Jerry Raddatz, Glenn Serviente, R. Douglas Stuart, Marlon Styles, Lee Toole, John Walsh, Murray Zuk

MINOR LEAGUE AFFILIATES

Class	Team	League	Manager
AAA	Indianapolis	International	Dave Miley
AA	Chattanooga	Southern	Mark Berry
A	Burlington	Midwest	Phillip Wellman
A	Charleston (WV)	South Atlantic	Barry Lyons
Rookie	Billings	Pioneer	Russ Nixon

BROADCAST INFORMATION

Radio: WLW-AM (700).
TV: WSTR-TV (Channel 64); WKRC-TV (Channel 12).
Cable TV: Fox Sports Ohio.

SPRING TRAINING

Ballpark (city): Ed Smith Stadium (Sarasota, Fla.).
Ticket information: 941-954-4101.

SPRING TRAINING ROSTER

Manager—Jack McKeon (31).
Coaches—Harry Dunlop, Ken Griffey Sr. (30), Don Gullett (35), Tom Hume, Denis Menke (19), Ron Oester (0).

No.	PITCHERS	B/T	Ht./Wt.	Born	1997 clubs
	Atchley, Justin	L/L	6-3/200	9-5-73	Chattanooga
37	Belinda, Stan	R/R	6-3/215	8-6-66	Cincinnati
34	Burba, Dave	R/R	6-4/240	7-7-66	Cincinnati
	Cooke, Steve	R/L	6-6/230	1-14-70	Pittsburgh
50	Crowell, Jim	L/L	6-4/225	5-14-74	Kinston, Akron, Chattanooga, Indianapolis, Cincinnati
	Glauber, Keith	R/R	6-2/190	1-18-72	Arkansas, Louisville
32	Graves, Danny	R/R	5-11/200	8-7-73	Buffalo, Cleveland, Indianapolis, Cincinnati
	Hutton, Mark	R/R	6-6/240	2-6-70	Florida, Colorado
	Lyons, Curt	R/R	6-5/240	10-17-74	Iowa, Orlando
	Priest, Eddie	R/L	6-1/195	4-8-74	Chattanooga, Charleston, W.Va.
43	Remlinger, Mike	L/L	6-0/195	3-26-66	Cincinnati
41	Shaw, Jeff	R/R	6-2/200	7-7-66	Cincinnati
56	Sullivan, Scott	R/R	6-4/210	3-13-71	Cincinnati, Indianapolis
40	Tomko, Brett	R/R	6-4/205	4-7-73	Indianapolis, Cincinnati
	Weathers, Dave	R/R	6-3/220	9-25-69	New York A.L., Columbus, Buffalo, Cleveland
48	White, Gabe	L/L	6-2/200	11-20-71	Indianapolis, Cincinnati
	Williams, Todd	R/R	6-3/185	2-13-71	Chattanooga, Indianapolis
	Winchester, Scott	R/R	6-2/210	4-20-73	Kinston, Chattanooga, Indianapolis, Cincinnati

No.	CATCHERS	B/T	Ht./Wt.	Born	1997 clubs
6	Fordyce, Brook	R/R	6-1/185	5-7-70	Cincinnati, Indianapolis
	LaRue, Jason	R/R	5-11/190	3-19-74	Charleston (W.Va.)
10	Taubensee, Eddie	L/R	6-4/205	10-31-68	Cincinnati
	Towle, Justin	R/R	6-2/210	2-21-74	Chattanooga

No.	INFIELDERS	B/T	Ht./Wt.	Born	1997 clubs
17	Boone, Aaron	R/R	6-2/190	3-9-73	Indianapolis, Cincinnati
29	Boone, Bret	R/R	5-10/180	4-6-69	Cincinnati, Indianapolis
12	Greene, Willie	L/R	5-11/185	9-23-71	Cincinnati
28	Harris, Lenny	L/R	5-10/210	10-28-64	Cincinnati
4	Jackson, Damian	R/R	5-10/160	8-16-73	Buffalo, Cleveland, Indianapolis, Cincinnati
11	Larkin, Barry	R/R	6-0/195	4-28-64	Cincinnati
	Owens, Eric	R/R	6-1/185	2-3-71	Cincinnati, Indianapolis
39	Perez, Eduardo	R/R	6-4/215	9-11-69	Cincinnati
3	Reese, Pokey	R/R	5-11/180	6-10-73	Cincinnati, Indianapolis
20	Stynes, Chris	R/R	5-9/175	1-19-73	Omaha, Indianapolis, Cincinnati
	Young, Dmitri	B/R	6-2/210	10-11-73	St. Louis, Louisville

No.	OUTFIELDERS	B/T	Ht./Wt.	Born	1997 clubs
	Ingram, Darron	R/R	6-3/210	6-7-76	Burlington
	Nieves, Melvin	B/R	6-2/210	12-28-71	Detroit
22	Nunnally, Jon	L/R	5-10/190	11-9-71	Omaha, Kansas City, Cincinnati
16	Sanders, Reggie	R/R	6-1/185	12-1-67	Cincinnati, , Chattanooga
	Timmons, Ozzie	R/R	6-2/225	9-18-70	Cincinnati, Indianapolis
44	Watkins, Pat	R/R	6-2/185	9-2-72	Chattanooga, Indianapolis, Cincinnati

BALLPARK INFORMATION

Ballpark (capacity, surface)
Cinergy Field (52,953, artificial)

Address
100 Cinergy Field
Cincinnati, OH 45202

Business phone
513-421-4510

Ticket information
513-421-7337, 1-800-829-5353

Ticket prices
$14 (blue level box seats)
$11 (green level box seats)
$11 (yellow level box seats)
$9 (red level box seats)
$8 (green level reserved seats)
$6 (red level reserved seats)
$3 ("top six" reserved seats)

Field dimensions (from home plate)
To left field at foul line, 330 feet
To center field, 404 feet
To right field at foul line, 330 feet

First game played
June 30, 1970 (Braves 8, Reds 2)

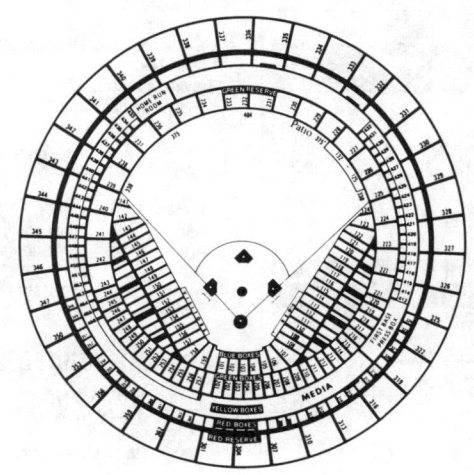

DAY BY DAY

Date	Opp.	Res.	Score	(inn.*)	Hits	Opp. hits	Winning pitcher	Losing pitcher	Save	Record	Pos.	GB
4-1	Col.	W	11-4		15	8	Smiley	Ritz	Jarvis	1-0	T1st	....
4-2	Col.	W	5-3		12	6	Burba	Swift	Shaw	2-0	T1st	....
4-3	Col.	L	1-7		6	8	Thompson	Schourek		2-1	T1st	....
4-4	At Fla.	W	9-7		9	14	Mercker	Hutton	Shaw	3-1	T1st	....
4-5	At Fla.	L	3-4	(11)	7	10	Nen	Jarvis		3-2	2nd	1.0
4-6	At Fla.	L	2-3		7	8	Brown	Smiley	Nen	3-3	2nd	2.0
4-7	At Col.	L	2-13		3	19	Swift	Burba	Holmes	3-4	2nd	2.5
4-9	At Col.	L	4-13		11	19	Thompson	Bones		3-5	3rd	2.0
4-11	Fla.	L	0-10		5	9	Rapp	Smiley		3-6	3rd	2.5
4-12	Fla.	W	2-1	(10)	8	4	Carrasco	Helling		4-6	3rd	2.5
4-13	Fla.	W	6-4		6	3	Burba	Leiter	Shaw	5-6	3rd	1.5
4-14	At Atl.	L	5-15		9	19	Neagle	Schourek		5-7	T2nd	2.5
4-15	At Atl.	L	0-3		6	9	Smoltz	Mercker		5-8	3rd	2.5
4-16	At Atl.	L	1-7		3	12	Byrd	Smiley		5-9	3rd	3.5
4-17	At Pit.	L	2-3		8	5	Loaiza	Morgan	Ericks	5-10	3rd	4.0
4-18	At Pit.	W	6-1		8	5	Burba	Cordova		6-10	3rd	3.0
4-19	At Pit.	L	5-6		12	8	Rincon	Remlinger		6-11	4th	4.0
4-20	At Pit.	L	3-5		9	7	Lieber	Mercker	Ericks	6-12	4th	5.0
4-22	At N.Y.	L	2-7		7	10	Reed	Smiley		6-13	4th	6.0
4-23	At N.Y.	L	2-10		7	14	Clark	Morgan		6-14	4th	7.0
4-25	Phi.	L	7-10		13	15	Leiter	Burba	Bottalico	6-15	4th	8.0
4-26	Phi.	W	10-2		12	3	Schourek	Schilling		7-15	4th	7.0
4-28	N.Y.	L	2-15		6	17	Reed	Smiley		7-16	4th	6.5
4-29	N.Y.	L	1-3		7	9	Clark	Morgan	J. Franco	7-17	4th	7.5
4-30	Atl.	L	3-12		10	17	Neagle	Mercker		7-18	4th	7.5
5-1	Atl.	L	2-4		6	8	Smoltz	Burba	Wohlers	7-19	4th	7.5
5-2	At S.F.	W	6-2		13	3	Schourek	Fernandez		8-19	4th	7.5
5-3	At S.F.	W	3-1		6	9	Smiley	Rodriguez	Brantley	9-19	4th	6.5
5-4	At S.F.	L	1-2	(10)	6	8	Beck	Brantley		9-20	4th	7.5
5-5	At L.A.	L	1-3		5	9	Nomo	Carrasco	Worrell	9-21	4th	8.5
5-6	At L.A.	W	3-2	(11)	8	9	Brantley	Guthrie	Remlinger	10-21	4th	7.5
5-7	At L.A.	L	2-4		7	5	Martinez	Schourek	Worrell	10-22	4th	7.5
5-9	At S.D.	W	7-2		11	6	Smiley	Worrell		11-22	4th	7.5
5-10	At S.D.	L	6-9		8	10	Hitchcock	Morgan	Hoffman	11-23	4th	8.0
5-11	At S.D.	L	4-5	(11)	8	8	Hoffman	Remlinger		11-24	4th	8.0
5-13	S.F.	L	1-4		6	8	Estes	Burba	Beck	11-25	T4th	7.5
5-14	S.F.	L	2-4	(10)	9	10	Beck	Remlinger	Rodriguez	11-26	T4th	8.5
5-15	L.A.	L	1-2		5	6	Valdes	Smiley	Worrell	11-27	5th	9.5
5-16	L.A.	W	4-2		9	6	Morgan	Park	Shaw	12-27	5th	9.0
5-17	S.D.	L	2-6		6	12	Hamilton	Mercker	Hoffman	12-28	5th	9.0
5-18	S.D.	W	5-0		9	9	Burba	Valenzuela		13-28	5th	8.0
5-19	S.D.	L	6-13		12	16	Cunnane	Schourek		13-29	5th	9.0
5-20	At Hou.	W	7-4		14	9	Smiley	Springer	Shaw	14-29	5th	8.0
5-21	At Hou.	L	3-4	(14)	14	11	Martin	Sullivan		14-30	5th	9.0
5-23	Chi.	L	1-3		5	4	Mulholland	Mercker	Adams	14-31	5th	9.0
5-24	Chi.	W	4-1	(12)	12	6	Shaw	Wendell		15-31	5th	9.0
5-25	Chi.	W	7-5		12	8	Schourek	Bottenfield	Shaw	16-31	5th	8.0
5-26†	Phi.	W	8-5		14	8	Smiley	Leiter	Remlinger	17-31		
5-26‡	Phi.	W	8-4		10	8	Morgan	Beech		18-31	5th	6.5
5-27	Phi.	L	1-2		7	6	Schilling	Tomko		18-32	5th	6.5
5-28	Phi.	W	2-0		7	8	Mercker	Stephenson	Shaw	19-32	5th	6.0
5-29	At Chi.	L	1-2		4	6	Trachsel	Belinda	Adams	19-33	5th	7.0
5-30	At Chi.	W	5-1		15	5	Schourek	Castillo		20-33	5th	6.5
5-31	At Chi.	L	4-7		7	11	Foster	Morgan	Rojas	20-34	5th	6.5
6-1	At Chi.	L	1-7		6	13	Gonzalez	Smiley		20-35	5th	7.5
6-3	At Phi.	W	3-2		6	5	Mercker	Schilling	Shaw	21-35	5th	7.0
6-4	Hou.	L	2-5		10	9	Holt	Burba	Wagner	21-36	5th	7.5
6-5	Hou.	W	6-5		11	7	Schourek	Reynolds	Shaw	22-36	5th	7.0
6-6	N.Y.	W	5-2		10	7	Tomko	Reed	Shaw	23-36	5th	7.0
6-7	N.Y.	W	10-5		16	9	Sullivan	Lidle		24-36	T4th	7.0
6-9	N.Y.	L	2-4		7	9	Jones	Belinda	J. Franco	24-37	4th	7.0
6-10	Pit.	W	8-5		15	9	Remlinger	Rincon	Shaw	25-37	4th	6.0
6-11	Pit.	W	2-1		6	6	Tomko	Loaiza	Shaw	26-37	4th	5.0
6-13	Chi. (AL)	L	1-3		7	3	Alvarez	Schourek	Hernandez	26-38	4th	6.0
6-14	Chi. (AL)	W	5-1		9	7	Mercker	D. Darwin		27-38	4th	5.0
6-15	Chi. (AL)	L	6-14		14	18	T. Castillo	Burba	C. Castillo	27-39	4th	5.0
6-16	At Cle.	W	4-1		7	7	Tomko	Hershiser		28-39	4th	5.0
6-17	At Cle.	L	1-5		5	11	Anderson	Smiley		28-40	4th	5.0
6-18	At Cle.	W	5-2		11	7	Remlinger	Ogea		29-40	4th	4.0
6-20	At St.L.	W	4-2		9	7	Mercker	Morris	Shaw	30-40	4th	4.0
6-21	At St.L.	L	2-6		9	13	Stottlemyre	Burba		30-41	4th	5.0

Date	Opp.	Res.	Score	(inn.*)	Hits	Opp. hits	Winning pitcher	Losing pitcher	Save	Record	Pos.	GB
6-22	At St.L.	L	2-5		4	9	Al. Benes	Sullivan	Eckersley	30-42	4th	6.0
6-23	At Mon.	L	0-5		4	8	Bullinger	Smiley		30-43	4th	6.0
6-24	At Mon.	W	7-6	(10)	12	13	Shaw	Veres		31-43	4th	5.0
6-25	At Mon.	W	2-1	(11)	6	9	Remlinger	Telford	Shaw	32-43	4th	5.0
6-26	St.L.	L	3-5		6	10	Stottlemyre	Burba	Eckersley	32-44	4th	6.0
6-27	St.L.	W	5-3		5	5	Tomko	Al. Benes	Shaw	33-44	4th	5.0
6-28	St.L.	L	6-12		9	18	Petkovsek	Smiley		33-45	4th	5.0
6-29	St.L.	L	5-6	(12)	13	11	Frascatore	Carrasco	Eckersley	33-46	4th	6.0
6-30	Mil.	W	4-3		9	9	Mercker	Fetters	Shaw	34-46	4th	5.0
7-1	Mil.	W	9-1		8	3	Burba	Mercedes		35-46	4th	5.0
7-2	Mil.	W	7-4		12	6	Tomko	McDonald	Sullivan	36-46	4th	5.0
7-3	At Hou.	W	4-3		8	7	Smiley	Garcia	Shaw	37-46	4th	4.0
7-4	At Hou.	W	4-2		7	5	Morgan	Greene	Shaw	38-46	4th	3.0
7-5	At Hou.	L	1-2		3	4	Kile	Mercker	Wagner	38-47	4th	4.0
7-6	At Hou.	L	5-6		11	9	Wagner	Remlinger		38-48	4th	5.0
7-11	Mon.	L	2-5		12	8	Bullinger	Burba	Urbina	38-49	4th	5.5
7-12	Mon.	W	4-3		8	6	Smiley	Perez	Shaw	39-49	4th	4.5
7-13	Mon.	L	0-2		1	4	Martinez	Morgan		39-50	4th	5.5
7-14	St.L.	W	4-2		5	7	Mercker	Valenzuela	Shaw	40-50	4th	5.5
7-15	St.L.	L	4-7		12	9	Al. Benes	Tomko	Eckersley	40-51	4th	6.5
7-16	At Pit.	W	7-3		11	8	Burba	Loaiza		41-51	4th	5.5
7-17	At Pit.	W	9-5		17	11	Smiley	Cordova		42-51	4th	4.5
7-18	At N.Y.	L	3-4		5	7	Crawford	Morgan	J. Franco	42-52	4th	5.5
7-19	At N.Y.	L	3-5		7	5	Reed	Tomko	McMichael	42-53	4th	6.5
7-20	At N.Y.	L	1-10		7	15	Mlicki	Mercker		42-54	4th	7.5
7-21	At N.Y.	L	3-5		7	4	McMichael	Sullivan	J. Franco	42-55	4th	8.0
7-22	Fla.	W	7-6		9	8	Smiley	Heredia	Shaw	43-55	4th	8.0
7-23	Fla.	L	1-8		7	12	Fernandez	Morgan		43-56	4th	9.0
7-25	Atl.	L	3-7		2	9	Smoltz	Schourek		43-57	4th	10.5
7-26	Atl.	W	7-6	(11)	12	10	Shaw	Wohlers		44-57	4th	10.5
7-27	Atl.	L	2-3		6	5	Maddux	Burba	Wohlers	44-58	4th	11.5
7-28	At Fla.	W	4-0		7	8	Belinda	Powell		45-58	4th	10.5
7-29	At Fla.	L	1-7		9	10	Fernandez	Morgan		45-59	4th	11.5
7-30	At Fla.	L	0-6		4	14	Hernandez	Schourek		45-60	4th	12.5
8-1	S.F.	L	7-8		7	11	Alvarez	Mercker	Beck	45-61	4th	12.5
8-2	S.F.	W	5-1		10	2	Tomko	Gardner		46-61	4th	12.5
8-3	S.F.	L	3-8	(10)	8	11	Hernandez	Shaw		46-62	4th	13.5
8-4	S.F.	L	1-9		7	10	Rueter	Carrara		46-63	4th	13.5
8-5	S.D.	W	7-3		12	8	Remlinger	Hitchcock		47-63	4th	12.5
8-6	S.D.	L	3-6		8	7	Hamilton	Belinda	Hoffman	47-64	4th	12.5
8-7	S.D.	W	7-0		11	4	Tomko	Jackson		48-64	4th	11.5
8-8	L.A.	L	5-10		11	15	Candiotti	Morgan	Dreifort	48-65	4th	11.5
8-9	L.A.	W	3-2		7	6	White	Valdes	Shaw	49-65	4th	11.5
8-10	L.A.	W	8-1		10	4	Remlinger	Astacio		50-65	4th	11.5
8-11	At S.F.	W	7-4		13	5	Mercker	Rapp		51-65	4th	11.5
8-12	At S.F.	L	3-7		8	10	Alvarez	Tomko	Hernandez	51-66	4th	12.5
8-13	At S.D.	W	2-0		6	1	Morgan	Smith	Shaw	52-66	4th	11.5
8-14	At S.D.	L	4-5	(10)	9	10	Hoffman	Shaw		52-67	4th	12.0
8-15	At L.A.	W	5-3		7	7	Remlinger	Astacio	Shaw	53-67	4th	11.0
8-16	At L.A.	L	3-5		7	4	Park	Mercker	Worrell	53-68	4th	11.0
8-17	At L.A.	W	5-0		10	7	Tomko	Nomo		54-68	4th	11.0
8-19	Col.	W	6-5		8	10	Morgan	Wright	Shaw	55-68	4th	10.0
8-20	Col.	L	3-5		5	9	Castillo	White	DiPoto	55-69	4th	10.0
8-22	At Atl.	L	2-6		11	8	Maddux	Remlinger		55-70	4th	11.5
8-23	At Atl.	L	3-10		8	10	Neagle	Tomko		55-71	4th	11.5
8-24	At Atl.	W	6-4	(10)	10	7	Shaw	Fox	Belinda	56-71	4th	11.5
8-25†	At Col.	W	7-6		13	12	Martinez	Castillo	Shaw	57-71		
8-25‡	At Col.	W	6-4		17	12	White	Hutton	Shaw	58-71	4th	10.5
8-26	At Col.	L	5-9		10	10	DeJean	Martinez		58-72	4th	10.5
8-27	At Col.	L	5-7		6	11	Thomson	Remlinger	DiPoto	58-73	4th	11.5
8-29	At Min.	W	5-3		9	7	Tomko	Rodriguez	Shaw	59-73	4th	10.0
8-30	At Min.	L	1-4		7	7	Hawkins	Morgan	Aguilera	59-74	4th	10.0
8-31	At Min.	L	6-8		12	11	Radke	White	Aguilera	59-75	4th	10.0
9-1	K.C.	L	4-7		8	10	Appier	Remlinger	Pichardo	59-76	4th	10.0
9-2	K.C.	W	4-0		9	7	Burba	Rosado	Shaw	60-76	4th	9.0
9-3	K.C.	W	6-3		8	5	Tomko	Bones	Shaw	61-76	4th	9.0
9-4	Pit.	W	5-2		7	7	Morgan	Lieber	Shaw	62-76	4th	9.0
9-5	Pit.	W	8-6		10	13	Sullivan	Wilkins	Shaw	63-76	4th	8.0
9-6	Pit.	L	4-13		11	15	Cordova	Remlinger		63-77	4th	8.0
9-7	Pit.	W	6-3		11	8	Burba	Silva	Shaw	64-77	4th	7.0
9-8	Chi.	L	1-8		3	13	M. Clark	Tomko		64-78	4th	7.5
9-9	Chi.	W	5-2		8	8	Morgan	Gonzalez	Shaw	65-78	4th	7.5
9-10	Chi.	L	1-3		6	11	Tapani	Mercker	Adams	65-79	4th	7.5
9-12†	At Phi.	W	4-2		9	8	Remlinger	Stephenson	Shaw	66-79		
9-12‡	At Phi.	L	1-9		5	14	Leiter	Schourek		66-80	4th	8.0

Date	Opp.	Res.	Score	(inn.*)	Hits	Opp. hits	Winning pitcher	Losing pitcher	Save	Record	Pos.	GB
9-13	At Phi.	W	3-0		7	4	Burba	Grace	Shaw	67-80	4th	8.0
9-14	At Phi.	W	6-4		9	8	Tomko	Green	Shaw	68-80	4th	7.0
9-15	At Chi.	W	4-1		9	6	Morgan	Gonzalez	Shaw	69-80	T3rd	6.0
9-16	At Chi.	L	0-5		1	8	Tapani	Mercker		69-81	T3rd	7.0
9-17	Mon.	L	1-4		7	8	Bullinger	Belinda	Urbina	69-82	4th	8.0
9-18	Mon.	W	6-3		12	8	Sullivan	Hermanson	Shaw	70-82	T3rd	7.0
9-19	Hou.	W	5-4		12	8	Burba	Holt	Shaw	71-82	T3rd	6.0
9-20	Hou.	L	1-4		5	10	Hampton	Tomko	Wagner	71-83	T3rd	7.0
9-21	Hou.	L	3-8		7	14	Garcia	Morgan		71-84	T3rd	8.0
9-22	Hou.	L	3-6		8	11	Springer	Belinda	Wagner	71-85	T3rd	9.0
9-23	At St.L.	W	8-6		13	8	Sullivan	King	Shaw	72-85	3rd	9.0
9-24	At St.L.	W	5-4		8	9	Burba	Fossas	Shaw	73-85	3rd	8.0
9-25	At St.L.	W	4-3	(14)	9	9	Sullivan	Petkovsek	White	74-85	3rd	8.0
9-26	At Mon.	W	7-1		11	3	Morgan	Johnson		75-85	3rd	8.0
9-27	At Mon.	L	5-8		10	14	Thurman	Crowell	Telford	75-86	3rd	9.0
9-28	At Mon.	W	11-3		12	4	Remlinger	Hermanson		76-86	3rd	8.0

Monthly records: April (7-18), May (13-16), June (14-12), July (11-14), August (14-15), September (17-11).
*Innings, if other than nine. †First game of doubleheader. ‡Second game of doubleheader.

HIGHLIGHTS

High point: On Labor Day, Pete Rose Jr. returned to his hometown for his major league debut, as Cincinnati saluted the son of the Hit King with one ovation after another. Rose Jr., who had toiled in the minor leagues for nine years, went 1-for-3 plus a walk, hustling to first base in tribute to the Old Man, who was sitting in the front row alongside another suspended figure, team owner Marge Schott.

Low point: On July 6 pitcher Mike Morgan ripped then-manager Ray Knight, saying, "I've lost respect for that guy, (and) I think the whole club has. That should be the writing on the wall right there." Morgan had been furious over Knight removing him from a game two days earlier, and the two then had words in the locker room. Morgan just took public what many of the players were saying privately.

Turning point: On July 25, the Reds decided they needed to make a change in manager, as Knight's intrusive, controlling manner had left the club growing ever more disenchanted. Cincinnati turned to Jack McKeon, who eased the tension in the clubhouse and took the team to an over-.500 record the rest of the way.

Most valuable player: This wasn't even close. Jeff Shaw, promoted from setup man to closer when Jeff Brantley missed most of the season because of rotator cuff problems, succeeded Brantley as the National League Rolaids Relief Award winner. Thanks to Shaw, the Reds lost only two of 72 games they led after eight innings.

Most valuable pitcher: Shaw again. Not only did he lead the league in saves, but his total (42) was only two shy of the club record set by Brantley in 1996.

Most improved player: Third baseman Willie Greene had a breakthrough season, leading the team in half a dozen offensive categories, including homers (26), RBIs (91) and runs scored (62).

Most pleasant surprise: Righthander Brett Tomko. After spending only two years in the minor leagues, he burst on the major league scene by winning 11 games, the most by a Reds rookie since Tom Browning won 20 in 1985.

Biggest disappointment: Second baseman

Bret Boone. After hitting .320 in 1994, Boone looked like a future star. Instead, he has regressed. His batting average has declined the past three seasons, bottoming out at .223 in 1997.

Key injuries: Brantley spent two stints on the disabled list with shoulder and rotator cuff ailments and did not pitch after May 19. . . . Right fielder Reggie Sanders also spent two stints on the D.L.—with disk, ankle and knee problems. . . . Shortstop Barry Larkin missed the final month with an injured left heel. . . . First baseman Hal Morris did not play after July 30 because of an injured right shoulder.

Notable: The Reds led the league with 190 stolen bases and 106 errors. . . . Despite not playing after September 4 to attend to his football duties, center fielder Deion Sanders led the team with 35 multi-hit games. . . . Boone set major league records for fielding percentage by a second baseman playing at least 100 games (.9967) and most games by a second baseman with two or fewer errors (136).

—MIKE BASS

RECORDS

1997 regular-season record: 76-86 (3rd in N.L. Central); 40-41 at home; 36-45 on road; 23-32 vs. East; 33-30 vs. Central; 20-24 vs. West; 14-18 vs. lefthanded starters; 62-68 vs. righthanded starters; 21-34 on grass; 55-52 on turf; 21-39 in daytime; 55-47 at night; 18-17 in one-run games; 8-8 in extra-inning games; 2-0-1 in doubleheaders.

Team record past five years: 381-363 (.512, ranks 6th in league in that span).

TEAM LEADERS

Batting average: Deion Sanders (.273).
At-bats: Willie Greene (495).
Runs: Willie Greene (62).
Hits: Deion Sanders (127).
Total bases: Willie Greene (227).
Doubles: Bret Boone (25).
Triples: Deion Sanders (7).
Home runs: Willie Greene (26).
Runs batted in: Willie Greene (91).
Stolen bases: Deion Sanders (56).

Slugging percentage: Willie Greene (.459).
On-base percentage: Willie Greene (.354).
Wins: Dave Burba, Brett Tomko (11).
Earned-run average: Mike Morgan (4.78).
Complete games: Dave Burba, Mike Remlinger (2).
Shutouts: None.
Saves: Jeff Shaw (42).
Innings pitched: Mike Morgan (162.0).
Strikeouts: Mike Remlinger (145).

GAMES BY POSITION

Catcher: Joe Oliver 106, Eddie Taubensee 64, Brook Fordyce 30.
First base: Hal Morris 89, Eduardo Perez 67, Lenny Harris 11, Willie Greene 7, Eddie Taubensee 7, Joe Oliver 4, Pete Rose Jr 1.
Second base: Bret Boone 136, Lenny Harris 20, Jeff Branson 14, Pokey Reese 8, Chris Stynes 8, Damian Jackson 3, Eric Owens 2, Aaron Boone 1.
Third base: Willie Greene 103, Terry Pendleton 32, Jeff Branson 27, Aaron Boone 13, Lenny Harris 13, Eduardo Perez 8, Pokey Reese 8, Chris Stynes 3, Pete Rose Jr 2.
Shortstop: Pokey Reese 110, Barry Larkin 63, Jeff Branson 11, Damian Jackson 6, Willie Greene 3.
Outfield: Deion Sanders 113, Reggie Sanders 85, Curtis Goodwin 71, Jon Nunnally 60, Mike Kelly 59, Lenny Harris 42, Willie Greene 39, Chris Stynes 38, Ruben Sierra 24, Eric Owens 18, Pat Watkins 15, Eduardo Perez 12, Eddie Taubensee 11, Ozzie Timmons 1.
Designated hitter: Eddie Taubensee 3, Barry Larkin 2, Brook Fordyce 1, Eduardo Perez 1.

TOP DRAFT CHOICES

1. **Brandon Larson,** SS, Louisiana State U.
2. **Travis Dawkins,** SS, Newberry (S.C.) H.S.
3. **Thad Markray,** 3B, Springhill (La.) H.S.
4. **Monte Roundtree,** LHP, Rose H.S., Greenville, N.C.
5. **DeWayne Wise,** OF, Chapin (S.C.) H.S.
6. **Toby Sanchez,** 1B, Long Beach State U.
7. **Mike Frank,** LHP-OF, Santa Clara Univ.
8. **John Borne,** RHP, Univ. of Kentucky.
9. **Scott Williamson,** RHP, Oklahoma State U.
10. **David Runk,** RHP, Tussey Mountain H.S., Saxton, Pa.

COLORADO ROCKIES
NATIONAL LEAGUE WEST DIVISION

Rockies Schedule
Home games shaded. *—All-Star Game at Coors Field (Colorado). D—Day game (any game starting before 5 p.m.).

March

SUN	MON	TUE	WED	THU	FRI	SAT
		31 D ARZ				

April

SUN	MON	TUE	WED	THU	FRI	SAT
		1 ARZ	2 ARZ	3 HOU	4 HOU	
5 HOU	6 D HOU	7 D STL	8 STL	9 STL	10 CIN	11 CIN
12 CIN	13 CIN	14 LA	15 LA	16	17 ATL	18 D ATL
19 ATL	20 ATL	21	22 FLA	23 FLA	24 FLA	25 ATL
26 ATL	27 D FLA	28 FLA	29	30 NYM		

May

SUN	MON	TUE	WED	THU	FRI	SAT
					1 NYM	2 D NYM
3 NYM	4 D PHI	5 PHI	6 PHI	7 MON	8 MON	9 MON
10 MON	11 D PIT	12 PIT	13 CUB	14 CUB	15 MIL	16 D MIL
17 MIL	18 MIL	19	20 ATL	21 ATL	22 CIN	23 D CIN
24 CIN	25 D STL	26	27 STL	28 STL	29 D HOU	30 D HOU
31 D HOU						

June

SUN	MON	TUE	WED	THU	FRI	SAT
	1 ARZ	2 ARZ	3 ARZ	4 ARZ	5 ANA	6 ANA
7 ANA	8 D TEX	9 TEX	10 TEX	11	12 LA	13 LA
14 LA	15 SF	16 SF	17 D SF	18 LA	19 LA	20 LA
21 LA	22 MIL	23 D MIL	24 D HOU	25 HOU	26 D OAK	27 OAK
28 OAK	29	30 SEA				

July

SUN	MON	TUE	WED	THU	FRI	SAT
		1 SEA	2 SEA	3 D SD	4 SD	
5 SD	6 D	7	*8	9	10 SF	11 SF
12 SF	13 D SD	14 SD	15 SD	16	17 ARZ	18 ARZ
19 ARZ	20 HOU	21 HOU	22 CIN	23 CIN	24 STL	25 STL
26 STL	27 D PIT	28 PIT	29 PIT	30	31 D CUB	

August

SUN	MON	TUE	WED	THU	FRI	SAT
						1 D CUB
2 D CUB	3 PIT	4 PIT	5 PIT	6 D PIT	7 NYM	8 NYM
9 NYM	10 D MON	11 MON	12 MON	13	14 PHI	15 PHI
16 PHI	17 D NYM	18 NYM	19 MON	20 MON	21 PHI	22 PHI
23 PHI	24 PHI	25 MIL	26 MIL	27 CUB	28 CUB	29 CUB
30 CUB	31					

September

SUN	MON	TUE	WED	THU	FRI	SAT
		1 MIL	2 MIL	3 MIL	4 SD	5 SD
6 SD	7 D FLA	8 D FLA	9 FLA	10 FLA	11 D SF	12 SF
13 SF	14 LA	15 LA	16	17 SD	18 SD	19 SD
20 SD	21	22 ARZ	23 ARZ	24	25 SF	26 D SF
27 D SF						

1998 SEASON
CLUB DIRECTORY

Chairman, president and CEO
Jerry McMorris
Exec. vice president/general manager
Bob Gebhard
Sr. v.p./secretary and corporate counsel
Clark Weaver
Sr. vice president/chief financial officer
Hal Roth
Sr. vice president/business operations
Keli McGregor
Assistant general manager
Tony Siegle
Vice president/finance
Michael Kent
Director/player personnel
Paul Egins
Vice president/sales and marketing
Greg Feasel
Vice president/scouting
Pat Daugherty
Vice president/ticket operations
Sue Ann McClaren
Director, broadcasting
Eric Brummond
Dir., management information systems
Mary Burns
Dir., promotions and special events
Alan Bossart
Director, public relations
Jay Alves
Director, publications
Jimmy Oldham
Director, stadium services
Kevin Kahn
Director, team travel
John Howell
Director, ticket operations
Chuck Javernick

Dir., charitable and community affairs
Roger Kinney
Director, int'l & professional scouting
Jeff Schugel
Assistant director, player personnel
Marc Gustafson
Assistant director, scouting
Coley Brannan
Head groundskeeper
Mark Razum
Coordinator of instruction
Rick Mathews
National cross-checkers
Dave Holliday
Bill Gayton
Regional cross-checkers
Bruce Andrew
Jay Darnell
Robyn Lynch
Major league scouts
Jack Bloomfield, Jim Fanning, Bill Harford, Larry High, Bill Wood
Scouts
John Cedarburg, Ty Coslow, Dar Cox, Mike Ericson, Abe Flores, Mike Garlatti, Bert Holt, Greg Hopkins, Bill Hughes, Damon Iannelli, Bill Mackenzie, Danny Montgomery, Lance Nichols, Steve Payne, Art Pontarelli, Ed Santa, Nick Venuto, Tom Wheeler
International scouts
Phil Allen, Dario Arias, Roland de Lima Gamez, Cristobal A. Giron, Jim Hovorka, Oscar Martinez, Brian McRobie, Atanacio Mendez, Jimmy Moreno, Jorge Posada, Jesus Rizales, Reed Spencer, Ron Steele, Herminio Toribio

---

MINOR LEAGUE AFFILIATES

Class	Team	League	Manager
AAA	Colorado Springs	Pacific Coast	Paul Zuvella
AA	New Haven	Eastern	Tim Blackwell
A	Salem	Carolina	Jay Loviglio
A	Asheville	South Atlantic	Ron Gideon
A	Portland	Northwest	Jim Eppard
Rookie	Rockies	Arizona	P.J. Carey

BROADCAST INFORMATION

Radio: KOA-AM (850).
TV: KWGN-TV (Channel 2).
Cable TV: Fox Sports Rocky Mountain.

SPRING TRAINING

Ballpark (city): Hi Corbett Field (Tucson, Ariz.).
Ticket information: 1-800-388-ROCK.

SPRING TRAINING ROSTER

Manager—Don Baylor (25).
Coaches—Paul Carey, Frank Funk (49), Gene Glynn (2), Bill Hayes, Clint Hurdle (13), Jackie Moore (4).

No.	PITCHERS	B/T	Ht./Wt.	Born	1997 clubs
34	Astacio, Pedro	R/R	6-2/195	11-28-69	Los Angeles, Colorado
31	Bailey, Roger	R/R	6-1/180	10-3-70	Colorado
41	Beckett, Robbie	R/L	6-5/225	7-16-72	Colorado Springs, Colorado
	Brownson, Mark	L/R	6-2/180	6-17-75	Nashville
	Burke, John	B/R	6-4/215	2-9-70	Colorado, Colorado Springs
44	DeJean, Mike	R/R	6-2/205	9-28-70	Colorado Springs, Colorado, New Haven
45	DiPoto, Jerry	R/R	6-2/200	5-24-68	Colorado
	Gonzalez, Lariel	R/R	6-1/180	5-25-76	Salem
	Hackman, Luther	R/R	6-4/195	10-6-74	New Haven, Salem
	Jones, Bobby	R/L	6-0/175	4-11-72	Colorado Springs, Colorado
	Kile, Darryl	R/R	6-5/185	12-2-68	Houston
16	Leskanic, Curtis	R/R	6-0/180	4-2-68	Salem, Colorado, Colorado Springs
	McElroy, Chuck	L/L	6-0/195	10-1-67	Anaheim, Chicago A.L.
43	Munoz, Mike	L/L	6-2/192	7-12-65	Colorado
	Randall, Scott	R/R	6-3/180	10-29-75	Salem
30	Ritz, Kevin	R/R	6-4/222	6-8-65	Colorado
18	Ruffin, Bruce	B/L	6-2/215	10-4-63	Colorado, Colorado Springs
	Saipe, Mike	R/R	6-1/190	9-10-73	Nashville, Colorado Springs
	Shoemaker, Steve	L/R	6-1/195	2-3-73	Salem, Nashville, Colorado Springs
32	Thompson, Mark	R/R	6-2/205	4-7-71	Colorado, Asheville, Colorado Springs
52	Thomson, John	R/R	6-3/175	10-1-73	Colorado Springs, Colorado
	Vavrek, Mike	L/L	6-2/185	4-23-74	Nashville
	Veres, Dave	R/R	6-2/195	10-19-66	Montreal
19	Wright, Jamey	R/R	6-5/203	12-24-74	Colorado, Salem, Colorado Springs

No.	CATCHERS	B/T	Ht./Wt.	Born	1997 clubs
8	Manwaring, Kirt	R/R	5-11/203	7-15-65	Colorado
	Reed, Jeff	L/R	6-2/190	11-12-62	Colorado

No.	INFIELDERS	B/T	Ht./Wt.	Born	1997 clubs
6	Bates, Jason	B/R	5-10/185	1-5-71	Colorado, Colorado Springs
9	Castilla, Vinny	R/R	6-1/200	7-4-67	Colorado
	Colbrunn, Greg	R/R	6-0/200	7-26-69	Minnesota, Atlanta
	Coolbaugh, Mike	R/R	6-1/185	6-5-72	Huntsville
17	Helton, Todd	L/L	6-2/190	8-20-73	Colorado Springs, Colorado
	Lansing, Mike	R/R	6-0/185	4-3-68	Montreal
	Liriano, Nelson	B/R	5-10/185	6-3-64	Los Angeles
5	Perez, Neifi	L/R	6-0/173	2-2-75	Colorado Springs, Colorado
	Sexton, Christopher	R/R	5-11/175	8-3-71	Nashville, Colorado Springs

No.	OUTFIELDERS	B/T	Ht./Wt.	Born	1997 clubs
10	Bichette, Dante	R/R	6-3/230	11-18-63	Colorado
26	Burks, Ellis	R/R	6-2/198	9-11-64	Colorado
	Echevarria, Angel	R/R	6-3/219	5-25-71	Colorado Springs, Colorado
	Gibson, Derrick	R/R	6-2/230	2-5-75	New Haven, Colorado Springs
	Goodwin, Curtis	L/L	5-11/180	9-30-72	Indianapolis, Cincinnati
35	Vander Wal, John	L/L	6-2/198	4-29-66	Colorado, Colorado Springs
	Velazquez, Edgard	R/R	5-11/170	12-15-75	Colorado Springs
33	Walker, Larry	L/R	6-3/225	12-1-66	Colorado

BALLPARK INFORMATION

Ballpark (capacity, surface)
Coors Field (50,200, grass)
Address
2001 Blake St.
Denver, CO 80205-2000
Business phone
303-292-0200
Ticket information
303-762-5437
Ticket prices
$30 (club level)
$25 (infield box)
$20 (outfield box)
$13/14 (lower reserved)
$12 (upper reserved, RF box)
$10 (RF mezzanine)
$8 (lower pavilion)
$6 (lower RF reserved)
$5 (upper RF reserved)
$4 (rockpile)
$1 (rockpile)
Field dimensions (from home plate)
To left field at foul line, 347 feet
To center field, 415 feet
To right field at foul line, 350
First game played
April 26, 1995 (Rockies 11, Mets 9, 14 innings)

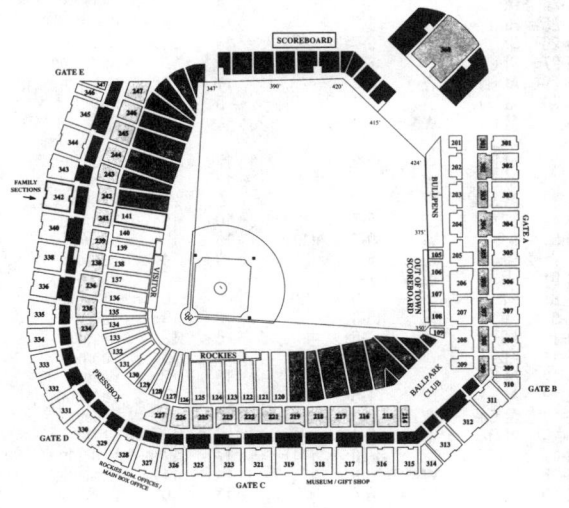

1998 SEASON *Colorado Rockies*

Date	Opp.	Res.	Score	(inn.*)	Hits	Opp. hits	Winning pitcher	Losing pitcher	Save	Record	Pos.	GB
4-1	At Cin.	L	4-11		8	15	Smiley	Ritz	Jarvis	0-1	T2nd	1.0
4-2	At Cin.	L	3-5		6	12	Burba	Swift	Shaw	0-2	T3rd	2.0
4-3	At Cin.	W	7-1		8	6	Thompson	Schourek		1-2	4th	1.0
4-4	At Mon.	W	5-4		8	9	Wright	Valdes	Ruffin	2-2	4th	1.0
4-5	At Mon.	W	15-3		15	10	Bailey	Cormier		3-2	T3rd	1.0
4-6	At Mon.	W	6-2		12	8	Ritz	Bullinger		4-2	T1st	....
4-7	Cin.	W	13-2		19	3	Swift	Burba	Holmes	5-2	T1st	....
4-9	Cin.	W	13-4		19	11	Thompson	Bones		6-2	1st	+0.5
4-12	Mon.	W	12-8		13	14	Wright	Bullinger	DiPoto	7-2	1st	+0.5
4-13	Mon.	L	3-8		8	17	Perez	Ritz	Daal	7-3	T2nd	0.5
4-14	Mon.	W	10-8		13	13	DiPoto	Stull	Ruffin	8-3	T1st	....
4-15	At Chi.	W	10-7		10	9	Thompson	Foster		9-3	T1st	....
4-16	At Chi.	W	4-0		6	5	Bailey	Castillo		10-3	T1st	....
4-18	Atl.	L	0-14		8	23	Glavine	Wright		10-4	T2nd	1.0
4-19	Atl.	L	7-8		10	15	Neagle	Ritz	Bielecki	10-5	T2nd	2.0
4-20	Atl.	W	9-2		20	8	Holmes	Smoltz		11-5	2nd	2.0
4-22	Fla.	W	13-4		19	6	Bailey	Rapp		12-5	2nd	1.0
4-23	Fla.	W	7-3		15	11	Wright	Brown	Ruffin	13-5	2nd	1.0
4-25	At St.L.	W	5-4		7	9	Ritz	Al. Benes	Ruffin	14-5	T1st	....
4-26	At St.L.	W	4-2		7	8	Swift	Morris	Ruffin	15-5	T1st	....
4-27	At St.L.	L	2-6		9	9	Osborne	Thompson		15-6	2nd	1.0
4-28	At Hou.	W	7-6	(10)	11	9	McCurry	Wagner	Ruffin	16-6	T1st	....
4-29	At Hou.	L	1-3		7	6	Wall	Bailey	Hudek	16-7	T1st	....
4-30	Chi.	W	11-5		8	12	Ritz	Foster		17-7	T1st	....
5-1	Chi.	W	5-4		9	8	Swift	Castillo	S. Reed	18-7	1st	+1.0
5-2	Phi.	L	4-7		5	9	Munoz	Thompson	Bottalico	18-8	1st	+1.0
5-3	Phi.	W	7-3		7	6	Wright	Portugal		19-8	1st	+2.0
5-4	Phi.	W	9-0		13	9	Bailey	Maduro		20-8	1st	+2.0
5-5	N.Y.	L	1-6		7	8	Jones	Ritz		20-9	1st	+1.0
5-6	N.Y.	W	12-11		14	20	Swift	Borland	S. Reed	21-9	1st	+2.0
5-7	Pit.	L	3-14		11	17	Wilkins	Thompson		21-10	1st	+2.0
5-8	Pit.	L	8-10		15	14	Loaiza	Wright	Loiselle	21-11	1st	+1.5
5-9	At Phi.	L	1-3		5	7	Maduro	Bailey	Bottalico	21-12	1st	+1.5
5-10	At Phi.	L	4-5	(10)	7	9	Bottalico	S. Reed		21-13	1st	+0.5
5-11	At Phi.	L	1-3		4	5	Schilling	Thomson		21-14	2nd	0.5
5-12	At Phi.	W	9-2		14	7	DeJean	Munoz		22-14	2nd	....
5-14	At Pit.	L	10-15		11	13	Wilkins	S. Reed		22-15	2nd	1.5
5-15	At Pit.	L	3-4		9	6	Cordova	Bailey	Rincon	22-16	3rd	1.5
5-16	At N.Y.	W	2-1		7	8	Munoz	McMichael	Ruffin	23-16	2nd	0.5
5-17	At N.Y.	L	1-3		8	10	Jones	Thomson	J. Franco	23-17	3rd	1.5
5-18	At N.Y.	L	4-10		8	9	Kashiwada	Ruffin		23-18	2nd	1.5
5-19	At N.Y.	L	3-4		3	11	Lidle	McCurry		23-19	3rd	1.5
5-20	At S.F.	L	3-6		6	10	VanLandingham	Bailey	Beck	23-20	3rd	2.5
5-21	At S.F.	W	10-7		10	11	Ritz	Rueter	S. Reed	24-20	2nd	1.5
5-22	At S.F.	L	2-7		7	11	Gardner	Thomson		24-21	2nd	2.5
5-23	Hou.	W	8-7		11	13	Jones	Wall	S. Reed	25-21	2nd	2.5
5-24	Hou.	L	0-7		4	8	Kile	Burke		25-22	2nd	2.5
5-25	Hou.	W	8-5		14	9	Bailey	Garcia	Munoz	26-22	2nd	1.5
5-26	St.L.	W	9-7		13	14	DeJean	Petkovsek	S. Reed	27-22	2nd	1.5
5-27	St.L.	L	6-8		14	13	Al. Benes	Thomson	Eckersley	27-23	2nd	2.5
5-29	At Fla.	W	6-5		11	9	Holmes	Nen	S. Reed	28-23	2nd	2.5
5-30	At Fla.	L	3-4	(12)	5	10	Hutton	DiPoto		28-24	2nd	2.5
5-31	At Fla.	W	8-4		11	13	Ritz	Brown	DeJean	29-24	2nd	2.5
6-1	At Fla.	W	9-2		17	7	Thomson	Helling		30-24	2nd	1.5
6-2	At St.L.	W	11-7		12	11	Burke	Jackson		31-24	2nd	0.5
6-3	At St.L.	L	4-15		5	21	Morris	Jones		31-25	2nd	1.5
6-4	S.D.	L	5-7		10	10	Cunnane	Bailey	Bochtler	31-26	2nd	1.5
6-5	S.D.	W	9-7	(11)	16	18	S. Reed	Burrows		32-26	2nd	1.5
6-7†	Fla.	L	5-7		9	14	Heredia	Holmes	Nen	32-27	2nd	1.0
6-8†	Fla.	W	7-2		11	5	Burke	Leiter	DiPoto	33-27		
6-8‡	Fla.	L	1-9	(8)	5	10	Fernandez	Wright		33-28	2nd	1.5
6-9	Atl.	W	8-3		12	13	Bailey	Glavine		34-28	2nd	1.5
6-10	Atl.	L	3-8		5	12	Neagle	Ritz		34-29	2nd	1.5
6-11	Atl.	W	9-6		16	11	Thomson	Clontz		35-29	2nd	0.5
6-12	At Sea.	L	11-12		18	12	Wells	Munoz	Ayala	35-30	2nd	1.5
6-13	At Sea.	L	1-6		4	7	Johnson	Wright		35-31	2nd	1.5
6-14	At Oak.	W	7-1		9	8	Bailey	Wengert		36-31	2nd	1.5
6-15	At Oak.	L	2-5		8	10	Prieto	Ritz	Taylor	36-32	2nd	2.5
6-17	Tex.	L	8-10	(11)	17	17	Patterson	S. Reed		36-33	2nd	3.5
6-18	Tex.	W	10-9		14	11	Leskanic	Wetteland		37-33	2nd	3.5
6-19	At S.D.	W	8-4		13	10	Bailey	Jackson		38-33	2nd	3.5

Date	Opp.	Res.	Score	(inn.*)	Hits	Opp. hits	Winning pitcher	Losing pitcher	Save	Record	Pos.	GB
6-20	At S.D.	L	2-5		9	11	Ashby	Munoz	Hoffman	38-34	2nd	3.5
6-21	At S.D.	W	9-4		16	8	Rekar	Bergman		39-34	2nd	2.5
6-22	At S.D.	L	2-4		4	5	Worrell	Ruffin	Hoffman	39-35	2nd	3.5
6-23	At L.A.	L	3-5		7	8	Nomo	Ritz	Hall	39-36	2nd	3.5
6-24	At L.A.	W	6-2		7	6	Holmes	Astacio		40-36	2nd	3.5
6-25	At L.A.	L	0-2		4	7	Valdes	Burke	Hall	40-37	2nd	4.5
6-26	S.F.	W	7-6		11	11	DeJean	Foulke	Leskanic	41-37	2nd	3.5
6-27	S.F.	L	3-6		8	10	Rueter	Thomson	Beck	41-38	2nd	4.5
6-28	S.F.	W	9-2		9	6	Ritz	Gardner		42-38	2nd	3.5
6-29	S.F.	L	4-7		10	16	Estes	Bailey		42-39	2nd	4.5
6-30	Ana.	W	11-7		16	15	DiPoto	Gross		43-39	2nd	4.5
7-1	Ana.	L	1-4		6	10	Finley	Burke	Percival	43-40	2nd	4.5
7-2	At Tex.	L	1-9		4	12	Burkett	Thomson		43-41	2nd	4.5
7-3	At Tex.	L	3-8		4	11	Oliver	Ritz		43-42	2nd	5.5
7-4	At S.F.	L	0-4		1	11	Estes	Wright	Beck	43-43	3rd	6.5
7-5	At S.F.	L	1-2		6	8	Tavarez	Munoz	Beck	43-44	3rd	7.5
7-6	At S.F.	L	0-7		5	9	Gardner	Burke		43-45	3rd	8.5
7-10	S.D.	L	5-11		9	16	Ashby	Burke		43-46	3rd	8.5
7-11	S.D.	W	6-5	(11)	11	11	DiPoto	Hoffman		44-46	3rd	7.5
7-12	S.D.	L	7-11		16	15	Hamilton	Swift	Hoffman	44-47	3rd	8.5
7-13	S.D.	L	11-13		14	18	Batchelor	McCurry	Hoffman	44-48	3rd	8.5
7-14	L.A.	L	12-14	(10)	18	22	Radinsky	S. Reed	Worrell	44-49	3rd	8.5
7-15	L.A.	L	5-6		11	12	Park	Bailey	Worrell	44-50	3rd	9.5
7-16	At Atl.	L	1-2		5	9	Glavine	DiPoto	Wohlers	44-51	3rd	9.5
7-17	At Atl.	L	2-8		9	13	Maddux	Swift		44-52	4th	10.5
7-19†	At Chi.	L	0-7		4	11	Trachsel	Wright		44-53		
7-19‡	At Chi.	L	5-6		13	8	Wendell	McCurry	Rojas	44-54	4th	10.5
7-20	At Chi.	W	9-5		12	12	Leskanic	Adams	Holmes	45-54	4th	10.5
7-21	At Mon.	L	4-8		10	10	Urbina	Holmes		45-55	4th	10.5
7-22	At Mon.	W	11-9	(12)	19	15	S. Reed	Veres		46-55	4th	10.5
7-24	Chi.	W	7-1		8	6	Wright	Trachsel		47-55	4th	10.0
7-25	Chi.	W	9-3		13	12	Castillo	Foster		48-55	4th	9.0
7-26	Chi.	W	6-3		9	9	Bailey	Mulholland	Holmes	49-55	4th	8.0
7-27	Chi.	W	4-0		7	7	Thomson	Gonzalez		50-55	4th	7.5
7-28	Mon.	L	2-3		6	6	Perez	Swift	Urbina	50-56	4th	8.0
7-29	Mon.	L	0-3		5	7	Martinez	Wright		50-57	4th	9.0
7-30	Mon.	W	12-6		17	17	Castillo	Juden		51-57	4th	8.0
7-31	At Pit.	L	1-4		7	5	Schmidt	Bailey	Loiselle	51-58	4th	8.5
8-1	At Pit.	W	7-6		10	13	S. Reed	Rincon	DiPoto	52-58	4th	8.5
8-2	At Pit.	L	5-6		13	5	Cordova	Swift	Loiselle	52-59	4th	8.5
8-3	At Pit.	L	4-8		9	14	Ruebel	S. Reed		52-60	4th	9.5
8-4	At Phi.	L	3-7		3	11	Green	Castillo		52-61	4th	10.5
8-5	At Phi.	W	4-2		13	7	Holmes	Bottalico	DiPoto	53-61	4th	10.5
8-6	At N.Y.	W	4-0		12	4	Thomson	Mlicki		54-61	4th	10.5
8-7	At N.Y.	L	4-12		8	16	Clark	Swift		54-62	4th	10.5
8-8	Pit.	W	5-3		10	11	Wright	Lieber	DiPoto	55-62	3rd	10.5
8-9	Pit.	W	8-7		11	12	Munoz	Rincon		56-62	3rd	9.5
8-10	Pit.	W	8-7		13	12	Leskanic	Wilkins	DiPoto	57-62	3rd	9.5
8-12	Phi.	L	0-5		5	10	Beech	Thomson		57-63	4th	10.0
8-13	Phi.	L	8-12		13	17	Leiter	Wright		57-64	4th	10.0
8-15	N.Y.	W	6-2		12	8	Castillo	Reed		58-64	4th	10.5
8-16	N.Y.	W	7-5		13	12	Holmes	McMichael	DiPoto	59-64	4th	9.5
8-17	N.Y.	W	6-4		9	9	Thomson	Mlicki	DiPoto	60-64	T3rd	9.5
8-19	At Cin.	L	5-6		10	8	Morgan	Wright	Shaw	60-65	3rd	10.0
8-20	At Cin.	W	5-3		9	5	Castillo	White	DiPoto	61-65	3rd	9.5
8-21	At Hou.	L	4-10		8	15	Holt	Bailey		61-66	3rd	10.0
8-22	At Hou.	L	1-9		7	12	Kile	Thomson		61-67	T3rd	10.0
8-23	At Hou.	W	6-3		14	10	S. Reed	Hudek	DiPoto	62-67	3rd	9.0
8-24	At Hou.	L	1-3		4	4	Hampton	Wright		62-68	T3rd	10.0
8-25†	Cin.	L	6-7		12	13	Martinez	Castillo	Shaw	62-69		
8-25‡	Cin.	L	4-6		12	17	White	Hutton	Shaw	62-70	T3rd	11.0
8-26	Cin.	W	9-5		10	10	DeJean	Martinez		63-70	3rd	11.0
8-27	Cin.	W	7-5		11	6	Thomson	Remlinger	DiPoto	64-70	3rd	11.0
8-28	Sea.	W	9-5		12	10	Astacio	Olivares		65-70	3rd	11.0
8-29	Sea.	W	6-5		11	7	DiPoto	Timlin		66-70	3rd	11.0
8-30	Oak.	W	4-3		10	9	DiPoto	Mohler		67-70	3rd	11.0
8-31	Oak.	W	10-4		13	10	Holmes	Oquist		68-70	3rd	10.0
9-1	At Ana.	W	4-1		11	9	Thomson	Watson	DiPoto	69-70	3rd	9.5
9-2	At Ana.	W	7-2		12	9	Astacio	Dickson	Munoz	70-70	3rd	8.5
9-5	St.L.	W	11-4		16	7	Castillo	Osborne		71-70	3rd	8.0
9-6†	St.L.	L	7-10	(13)	9	16	Eckersley	McCurry	Petkovsek	71-71		
9-6‡	St.L.	W	7-6		13	12	Holmes	King		72-71	3rd	8.5
9-7	St.L.	W	7-4		12	6	Astacio	Petkovsek		73-71	3rd	8.5
9-9	Hou.	L	4-7		8	11	Hampton	Wright	Springer	73-72	3rd	8.0
9-10	Hou.	W	9-7		11	11	Leskanic	Magnante	DiPoto	74-72	3rd	7.0

Date	Opp.	Res.	Score	(inn.*)	Hits	Opp. hits	Winning pitcher	Losing pitcher	Save	Record	Pos.	GB
9-12	At Atl.	W	3-1		7	8	Munoz	Wohlers	DiPoto	75-72	3rd	7.0
9-13	At Atl.	W	10-6		12	12	Holmes	Cather	DeJean	76-72	3rd	6.0
9-14	At Atl.	W	4-0		10	4	Astacio	Smoltz		77-72	3rd	5.0
9-15	At Fla.	W	7-1		7	11	Wright	Fernandez		78-72	3rd	5.0
9-16	At Fla.	L	6-9		8	13	Powell	DiPoto		78-73	3rd	6.0
9-17	At S.D.	L	4-5		5	10	Ashby	Thomson	Hoffman	78-74	3rd	6.0
9-18	At S.D.	L	6-7		11	8	Menhart	Bailey	Hoffman	78-75	3rd	6.0
9-19	At L.A.	W	6-4		7	11	Astacio	Nomo	DiPoto	79-75	3rd	6.0
9-20	At L.A.	W	2-1		6	9	Wright	Osuna	DiPoto	80-75	3rd	5.0
9-21	At L.A.	W	10-5		11	8	Castillo	Martinez		81-75	3rd	5.0
9-23	S.F.	W	7-6		14	13	Holmes	Darwin	Leskanic	82-75	3rd	4.5
9-24	S.F.	L	3-4		5	8	Hernandez	S. Reed		82-76	3rd	5.5
9-25	L.A.	L	5-9		7	13	Nomo	Astacio		82-77	3rd	6.0
9-26	L.A.	L	4-10		7	15	Valdes	Wright		82-78	3rd	7.0
9-27	L.A.	W	1-6		7	8	Martinez	Castillo		82-79	3rd	8.0
9-28	L.A.	W	13-9		18	11	DeJean	Reyes		83-79	3rd	7.0

Monthly records: April (17-7), May (12-17), June (14-15), July (8-19), August (17-12), September (15-9).
*Innings, if other than nine. †First game of doubleheader. ‡Second game of doubleheader.

HIGHLIGHTS

High point: After struggling at the plate in most of their 1996 road games, the Rockies sent an early message that 1997 would be different, pounding out a club-record seven homers in a 15-3 rout at Montreal April 5.

Low point: The club ended the first half with a 7-0 loss in San Francisco July 6. It came in the midst of a 1-15 stretch that knocked Colorado from the race and ended a five-game trip in which the team scored only five runs.

Turning point: The 15 losses in 16 games in early July. The Rockies fell from 43-39 and 4 ½ games behind to 44-54 and 10 ½ games behind. They never got closer than 4 ½ games the rest of the way.

Most valuable player: Right fielder Larry Walker. It's not too hard to figure, since he was the league's MVP. All he did was lead the majors in total bases, slugging percentage and extra-base hits and the league in home runs, on-base percentage and at-bats per home run ratio.

Most valuable pitcher: Jerry DiPoto, who grabbed the closer role in the second half and finished with 16 saves. He worked a club-record 18 consecutive scoreless innings from June 15 through July 10.

Most improved player: After starting the season as the club's fifth starter, Roger Bailey emerged as the staff ace in the first half of the season. He led the club in starts, innings, complete games and shutouts.

Most pleasant surprise: Rookie John Thomson won seven games and was one of the team's best starters after being called up from Class AAA Colorado Springs in May. He picked up his first big-league victory by allowing two runs and seven hits in a complete-game triumph over the Marlins in Miami in which he also went 4-for-4 at the plate.

Biggest disappointment: Maybe he shouldn't have been counted on, but Bill Swift suffered through another injury-filled season before being released in August.

Key injuries: Injuries to Swift (shoulder), Kevin Ritz (shoulder surgery), Bruce Ruffin (elbow surgery) and Ellis Burks (groin, hamstring) were pivotal to the team's fortunes.

Notable: Colorado led the league in both offense (.288 batting average) and defense (.983 fielding percentage). In addition to average, Rockie batsmen led the N.L. in runs, hits, total bases, home runs, RBIs, slugging percentage and on-base percentage. . . . Walker became the first National League player since Hank Aaron in 1959 and the first major leaguer since Jim Rice in 1978 to have 400 total bases. Walker's 409 total bases were the highest of any player since Stan Musial's 429 in 1948. . . . No starting pitcher who was with the team all season won as many as 10 games. Pedro Astacio and Frank Castillo both finished with 12 wins, but at least half came with their former teams—the Dodgers and Cubs, respectively. . . . The Rockies won a club-record 36 road games. . . . The Rockies led the majors in attendance for the fifth consecutive year (3,888,453). . . . The Rockies ended their fifth season with the best five-year aggregate winning percentage (363-384, .486) in history. The Kansas City Royals were 386-418, .480 through their first five seasons. . . . Colorado exceeded the 200-mark in both home runs (239) and double plays (202), a major league first.

—TONY DeMARCO

RECORDS

1997 regular-season record: 83-79 (3rd in N.L. West); 47-34 at home; 36-45 on road; 30-25 vs. East; 31-24 vs. Central; 22-30 vs. West; 20-19 vs. lefthanded starters; 63-60 vs. righthanded starters; 72-60 on grass; 11-19 on turf; 42-35 in daytime; 41-44 at night; 19-17 in one-run games; 4-5 in extra-inning games; 0-2-2 in doubleheaders.

Team record past five years: 363-384 (.486, ranks 8th in league in that span).

TEAM LEADERS

Batting average: Larry Walker (.366).
At-bats: Vinny Castilla (612).
Runs: Larry Walker (143).
Hits: Larry Walker (208).
Total bases: Larry Walker (409).
Doubles: Larry Walker (46).
Triples: Neifi Perez (10).
Home runs: Larry Walker (49).
Runs batted in: Andres Galarraga (140).
Stolen bases: Larry Walker (33).
Slugging percentage: Larry Walker (.720).
On-base percentage: Larry Walker (.452).
Wins: Roger Bailey, Darren Holmes (9).
Earned-run average: Roger Bailey (4.29).
Complete games: Roger Bailey (5).
Shutouts: Roger Bailey (2).
Saves: Jerry DiPoto (16).
Innings pitched: Roger Bailey (191.0).
Strikeouts: John Thomson (106).

GAMES BY POSITION

Catcher: Kirt Manwaring 100, Jeff Reed 78.
First base: Andres Galarraga 154, Todd Helton 8, John Vander Wal 5, Larry Walker 3.
Second base: Eric Young 117, Neifi Perez 41, Jason Bates 22, Brian Raabe 1.
Third base: Vinny Castilla 157, Jason Bates 6, Darnell Coles 3, Neifi Perez 2, Rene Gonzales 1.
Shortstop: Walt Weiss 119, Neifi Perez 45, Jason Bates 16.
Outfield: Larry Walker 151, Dante Bichette 139, Quinton McCracken 132, Ellis Burks 112, Harvey Pulliam 33, Todd Helton 15, John Vander Wal 9, Angel Echevarria 7, Darnell Coles 2.
Designated hitter: Dante Bichette 5, John Vander Wal 2, Larry Walker 1.

TOP DRAFT CHOICES

1. **Mark Mangum,** RHP, Kingwood (Tex.) H.S.
2. **Aaron Cook,** RHP, Hamilton (Ohio) H.S.
3. **Todd Sears,** 1B, University of Nebraska.
4. **Chone Figgins,** SS, Brandon (Fla.) H.S.
5. **Justin Miller,** RHP, Los Angeles Harbor J.C.
6. **Sam Smith,** SS, Jasper (Texas) H.S.
7. **Jake Kringen,** LHP, Univ. of Washington.
8. **Jeremy Jackson,** OF, Univ. of Arkansas.
9. **Dave Johnson,** RHP, Kansas State Univ.
10. **Derrick Vargas,** LHP, Chabot (Calif.) J.C.

FLORIDA MARLINS
NATIONAL LEAGUE EAST DIVISION

Marlins Schedule

Home games shaded. *—All-Star Game at Coors Field (Colorado).
D—Day game (any game starting before 5 p.m.).

March

SUN	MON	TUE	WED	THU	FRI	SAT
		31 D CUB				

April

SUN	MON	TUE	WED	THU	FRI	SAT
			1 CUB	2 D CUB	3 MIL	4 MIL
5 MIL	6 D MIL	7 D PHI	8 PHI	9 PHI	10 PIT	11 D PIT
12 D PIT	13 PIT	14	15 PHI	16 D PHI	17 ARZ	18 D ARZ
19 ARZ	20 D ARZ	21	22 COL	23 COL	24 COL	25 ARZ
26 D ARZ	27 COL	28 COL	29	30 SD		

May

SUN	MON	TUE	WED	THU	FRI	SAT
					1 SD	2 SD
3 SD	4 D SF	5 SF	6 D SF	7 LA	8 LA	9 LA
10 LA	11 D HOU	12 HOU	13 D CIN	14 CIN	15 STL	16 STL
17 D STL	18 D STL	19	20 ARZ	21 D ARZ	22 D PIT	23 PIT
24 PIT	25	26 NYM	27 NYM	28	29 MIL	30 MIL
31 D MIL						

June

SUN	MON	TUE	WED	THU	FRI	SAT
	1 CUB	2 D CUB	3 CUB	4 D		5 NYY	6 D NYY
7 NYY	8 D TOR	9 TOR	10 TOR	11 NYM	12 NYM	13 NYM
14 D NYM	15	16 ATL	17 ATL	18 D ATL	19 NYM	20 D NYM
21 NYM	22 TB	23 D TB	24 TB	25 D BOS	26 BOS	27 BOS
28 D BOS	29 BAL	30 D BAL				

July

SUN	MON	TUE	WED	THU	FRI	SAT
			1 BAL	2 D BAL	3 MON	4 MON
5 D MON	6	7 *	8	9 ATL	10 ATL	11 ATL
12 D ATL	13 MON	14 D MON	15 MON	16	17 CUB	18 CUB
19 D CUB	20 MIL	21 D MIL	22 PIT	23 PIT	24 PHI	25 PHI
26 D PHI	27 HOU	28 HOU	29 HOU	30 D HOU	31 CIN	

August

SUN	MON	TUE	WED	THU	FRI	SAT
						1 CIN
2 D CIN	3 HOU	4 HOU	5 D HOU	6	7 SD	8
9 D SD	10 SD	11 LA	12 LA	13 LA	14 SF	15 D SF
16 SF	17	18 SD	19 SD	20 LA	21 LA	22 SF
23 D SF	24 D STL	25 STL	26 STL	27 CIN	28 CIN	29 CIN
30 D CIN	31 STL					

September

SUN	MON	TUE	WED	THU	FRI	SAT
		1 STL	2 STL	3	4 MON	5 MON
6 MON	7 D COL	8 D COL	9 COL	10 D ATL	11 ATL	12 ATL
13 ATL	14 D MON	15 MON	16 MON	17	18 NYM	19 D NYM
20 NYM	21	22 ATL	23 ATL	24 PHI	25 PHI	26 PHI
27 D PHI						

1998 SEASON
CLUB DIRECTORY

Chairman
H. Wayne Huizenga

President
Donald A. Smiley

Exec. vice president and general manager
David Dombrowski

Vice president of finance & administration
Jonathan Mariner

Vice president of sales and marketing
Jim Ross

V.p. and assistant general manager
Frank Wren

Vice president of player personnel
Gary Hughes

Vice president of player development
John Boles

Senior adviser, player personnel
Whitey Lockman

Dir. of Latin American operations
Al Avila

Director of minor league administration
Dan Lunetta

Director of scouting
Orrin Freeman

Director of team travel
Bill Beck

Special asst. to the general manager
Tony Perez

Director of season & group sales
Lou De Paoli

Director of communications
Mark Geddis

Director of marketing partnerships
Ben Creed

Dir. of baseball information and publicity
Ron Colangelo

Asst. dir. of baseball info. and publicity
Julio C. Sarmiento

Director of Brevard County operations
Andy Dunn

Equipment manager
Mike Wallace

Team physician
Dr. Dan Kanell

Head trainer
Larry Starr

Assistant in baseball operations
Mike Carr

Major league scout
Scott Reid

International crosschecker
Tim Schmidt

National crosschecker
Jax Robertson

Regional crosscheckers
Dick Egan, Murray Cook, Greg Zunino

Scouts
Ed Bockman, Richard Bordi, Kelvin Bowles, Ty Brown, Joe Campise, John Castleberry, David Chadd, Jon Deeble, Whitey Dehart, Brad Del Barba, David Finley, Lou Fitzgerald, William George, Matthew King, Robert Laurie, Steve McFarland, Steve Minor, Deni Pacini, Cucho Rodriguez, Mike Russell, Stan Saleski, Bill Scherrer, Charlie Silvera, Keith Snider, Wally Walker, Stan Zielinski

Director Dominican Republic operations
Jesus Alou

Dominican Republic scouts
Carlos de la Cruz, Pablo Lantigua

Puerto Rico scouts
Cucho Rodriguez, Pedro Cintron

Venezuela scout
Miguel-Angel Garcia

Colombia scout
Holbert Cabrera

Panama scout
Ramon Webster

MINOR LEAGUE AFFILIATES

Class	Team	League	Manager
AAA	Charlotte	International	Fredi Gonzalez
AA	Portland	Eastern	Lynn Jones
A	Brevard County	Florida State	Rick Renteria
A	Kane County	Midwest	Juan Bustabad
A	Utica	New York-Pennsylvania	Ken Joyce
Rookie	Gulf Coast Marlins	Gulf Coast	Jon Deeble

BROADCAST INFORMATION

Radio: WQAM-AM (560); WCMQ-AM (1210, Spanish language).
TV: WBFS-TV (Channel 33).
Cable TV: SportsChannel.

SPRING TRAINING

Ballpark (city): Space Coast Stadium (Viera, Fla.).
Ticket information: 407-633-9200.

1998 SEASON *Florida Marlins*

Manager—Jim Leyland (11).
Coaches—Lorenzo Bundy, Rich Donnelly (45), Rich Dubee (31), Bruce Kimm (12), Milt May, Tommy Sandt (37).

No.	PITCHERS	B/T	Ht./Wt.	Born	1997 clubs
57	Alfonseca, Antonio	R/R	6-0/235	4-16-72	Charlotte, Florida
48	Barrios, Manuel	R/R	6-0/170	9-21-74	New Orleans, Houston
40	Darensbourg, Vic	L/L	5-10/165	11-13-70	Charlotte
32	Fernandez, Alex	R/R	6-1/215	8-13-69	Florida
41	Henriquez, Oscar	R/R	6-6/220	1-28-74	New Orleans, Houston
49	Heredia, Felix	L/L	6-0/175	6-18-76	Florida
61	Hernandez, Livan	R/R	6-2/220	2-20-75	Portland, Charlotte, Florida
36	Larkin, Andy	R/R	6-4/190	6-27-74	Charlotte
25	Leiter, Al	L/L	6-3/220	10-23-65	Florida
	Ludwick, Eric	R/R	6-5/220	12-14-71	St. Louis, Louisville, Edmonton, Oakland
35	Martinez, Jesus	L/L	6-2/145	3-13-74	Albuquerque
34	Meadows, Brian	R/R	6-4/200	11-21-75	Portland
47	Medina, Rafael	R/R	6-3/195	2-15-75	Rancho Cucamonga, Las Vegas
51	Mull, Blaine	R/R	6-4/210	8-14-76	Wilmington
39	Powell, Jay	R/R	6-4/225	1-19-72	Florida
38	Stanifer, Rob	R/R	6-3/205	3-10-72	Charlotte, Florida
50	Villano, Mike	R/R	6-0/200	8-10-71	Shreveport, Phoenix

No.	CATCHERS	B/T	Ht./Wt.	Born	1997 clubs
23	Johnson, Charles	R/R	6-2/220	7-20-71	Florida
9	Zaun, Gregg	B/R	5-10/180	4-14-71	Florida

No.	INFIELDERS	B/T	Ht./Wt.	Born	1997 clubs
24	Bonilla, Bobby	B/R	6-4/240	2-23-63	Florida
2	Booty, Josh	R/R	6-3/220	4-29-75	Portland, Florida
1	Castillo, Luis	B/R	5-11/175	9-12-75	Florida, Charlotte
30	Counsell, Craig	L/R	6-0/170	8-21-70	Colorado Springs, Colorado, Florida
26	Cromer, Brandon	L/R	6-2/175	1-25-74	Calgary, Carolina
20	Garcia, Amaury	R/R	5-10/160	5-20-75	Brevard County
22	Gonzalez, Alex	R/R	6-0/170	2-15-77	Portland
27	Lee, Derrek	R/R	6-5/205	9-6-75	Las Vegas, San Diego
21	Milliard, Ralph	R/R	5-11/170	12-30-73	Charlotte, Florida, Portland
16	Renteria, Edgar	R/R	6-1/180	8-7-75	Florida

No.	OUTFIELDERS	B/T	Ht./Wt.	Born	1997 clubs
7	Bates, Fletcher	B/R	6-1/195	3-24-74	St. Lucie
28	Cangelosi, John	B/L	5-8/160	3-10-63	Florida
17	Dunwoody, Todd	L/L	6-1/195	4-11-75	Charlotte, Florida
8	Eisenreich, Jim	L/L	5-11/195	4-18-59	Florida
15	Floyd, Cliff	L/R	6-4/235	12-5-72	Florida, Charlotte
3	Jackson, Ryan	L/L	6-3/185	11-11-71	Portland
4	Kotsay, Mark	L/L	6-0/180	12-2-75	Portland, Florida
44	Ramirez, Julio	R/R	5-11/170	8-10-77	Kane County
10	Sheffield, Gary	R/R	5-11/205	11-18-68	Florida

BALLPARK INFORMATION

Ballpark (capacity, surface)
Pro Player Stadium (42,531, grass)
Address
2267 N.W. 199th St.
Miami, Fla. 33056
Business phone
305-626-7400
Ticket information
305-930-HITS
Ticket prices
$28 (club level section A)
$21 (infield box)
$20 (club level section B)
$15 (club level section C)
$12.50 (terrace box, mezzanine box)
$9 (outfield reserved, adult)
$7 (mezzanine reserved)
$2 (outfield res., 12 and under, fish tank-adults)
$1.50 (fish tank, 12 and under)
Field dimensions (from home plate)
To left field at foul line, 330 feet
To center field, 434 feet
To right field at foul line, 345 feet
First game played
April 5, 1993 (Marlins 6, Dodgers 3)

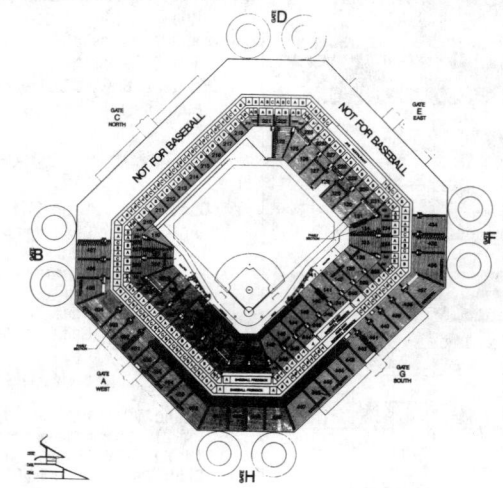

Date	Opp.	Res.	Score	(inn.*)	Hits	Opp. hits	Winning pitcher	Losing pitcher	Save	Record	Pos.	GB
4-1	Chi.	W	4-2		10	3	Brown	Mulholland		1-0	T1st	....
4-2	Chi.	W	4-3		11	5	Leiter	Trachsel	Nen	2-0	T1st	....
4-3	Chi.	W	8-2		10	7	Fernandez	Castillo		3-0	T1st	....
4-4	Cin.	L	7-9		14	9	Mercker	Hutton	Shaw	3-1	T1st	....
4-5	Cin.	W	4-3	(11)	10	7	Nen	Jarvis		4-1	1st	+1.0
4-6	Cin.	W	3-2		8	7	Brown	Smiley	Nen	5-1	1st	+1.0
4-8	At Chi.	W	5-3		8	7	Leiter	Trachsel	Nen	6-1	1st	+1.0
4-10	At Chi.	W	1-0		7	1	Fernandez	Castillo		7-1	1st	+1.5
4-11	At Cin.	W	10-0		9	5	Rapp	Smiley		8-1	1st	+2.0
4-12	At Cin.	L	1-2	(10)	4	8	Carrasco	Helling		8-2	1st	+1.0
4-13	At Cin.	L	4-6		3	6	Burba	Leiter	Shaw	8-3	T1st	....
4-15	St.L.	L	3-9		9	12	Raggio	Fernandez		8-4	2nd	1.5
4-16	St.L.	W	2-1		8	5	Rapp	Osborne	Nen	9-4	2nd	1.5
4-17	St.L.	W	2-1		7	4	Hutton	Petkovsek		10-4	2nd	1.0
4-18	At S.F.	L	4-5		9	10	Henry	Nen		10-5	2nd	2.0
4-19	At S.F.	L	2-3		4	6	Estes	Saunders	Beck	10-6	2nd	3.0
4-20	At S.F.	L	0-2		7	5	Fernandez	Fernandez	Beck	10-7	2nd	3.0
4-22	At Col.	L	4-13		6	19	Bailey	Rapp		10-8	2nd	4.0
4-23	At Col.	L	3-7		11	15	Wright	Brown	Ruffin	10-9	2nd	4.0
4-25	L.A.	W	4-2		5	4	Leiter	Nomo	Nen	11-9	2nd	4.0
4-26	L.A.	W	8-3		12	9	Fernandez	Valdes		12-9	2nd	4.0
4-27	L.A.	W	4-3		7	9	Hutton	Hall		13-9	2nd	4.0
4-28	S.D.	W	12-9		12	10	Heredia	Scott	Nen	14-9	2nd	4.0
4-29	S.D.	W	2-1		3	8	Brown	Hoffman	Nen	15-9	2nd	3.0
4-30	At St.L.	L	2-6		9	8	Al. Benes	Leiter		15-10	2nd	4.0
5-1	At St.L.	L	2-3		6	9	Morris	Fernandez	Eckersley	15-11	2nd	5.0
5-2	At Hou.	L	1-2		8	8	Reynolds	Rapp	Wagner	15-12	2nd	5.0
5-3	At Hou.	W	9-8	(13)	11	17	Heredia	Garcia	Powell	16-12	2nd	4.0
5-4	At Hou.	L	0-1		4	5	Kile	Brown		16-13	2nd	5.0
5-5	Pit.	W	3-0		7	4	Helling	Lieber	Nen	17-13	2nd	5.0
5-6	Pit.	L	0-4		4	10	Cooke	Fernandez		17-14	2nd	5.0
5-7	Atl.	L	2-3	(10)	9	8	Byrd	Powell	Bielecki	17-15	3rd	6.0
5-8	Atl.	W	5-1		7	6	Saunders	Glavine		18-15	T2nd	5.0
5-9	Hou.	W	3-2		7	7	Nen	Lima		19-15	2nd	4.0
5-10	Hou.	L	2-4		9	8	Holt	Helling	Wagner	19-16	2nd	5.0
5-11	Hou.	W	6-3		7	8	Fernandez	Wall	Nen	20-16	2nd	5.0
5-12	Hou.	W	11-4		14	10	Stanifer	Reynolds		21-16	2nd	5.0
5-13	At Atl.	W	11-5		13	8	Saunders	Wade		22-16	2nd	4.0
5-14	At Atl.	W	4-3		10	10	Brown	Bielecki	Nen	23-16	2nd	3.0
5-16	At Pit.	W	3-1		6	5	Fernandez	Lieber	Nen	24-16	2nd	3.0
5-17	At Pit.	W	11-1		19	8	Rapp	Cooke		25-16	2nd	3.0
5-18	At Pit.	W	5-3	(10)	12	8	Nen	Loiselle	Stanifer	26-16	2nd	3.0
5-20	N.Y.	W	6-5		12	11	Nen	J. Franco		27-16	2nd	3.5
5-21	N.Y.	L	1-2		8	6	Clark	Leiter	McMichael	27-17	2nd	4.5
5-23	At S.D.	L	3-6		11	9	Valenzuela	Fernandez		27-18	2nd	5.5
5-24	At S.D.	W	9-7		17	8	Powell	Bochtler	Nen	28-18	2nd	4.5
5-25	At S.D.	W	6-2		6	12	Brown	Hitchcock		29-18	2nd	3.5
5-26	At L.A.	L	3-5		8	8	Park	Helling	Worrell	29-19	2nd	4.5
5-27	At L.A.	W	8-5		17	7	Leiter	Nomo	Nen	30-19	2nd	4.5
5-29	Col.	L	5-6		9	11	Holmes	Nen	S. Reed	30-20	2nd	4.5
5-30	Col.	W	4-3	(12)	10	5	Hutton	DiPoto		31-20	2nd	4.5
5-31	Col.	L	4-8		13	11	Ritz	Brown	DeJean	31-21	2nd	4.5
6-1	Col.	L	2-9		7	17	Thomson	Helling		31-22	2nd	5.5
6-2	S.F.	W	4-2		7	9	Leiter	Gardner	Nen	32-22	2nd	4.5
6-3	S.F.	L	1-9	(7)	2	14	Estes	Fernandez		32-23	2nd	4.5
6-4	At N.Y.	W	5-2		11	5	Rapp	Mlicki	Nen	33-23	2nd	4.5
6-5	At N.Y.	L	0-6		5	12	Reynoso	Brown		33-24	2nd	5.5
6-7†	At Col.	W	7-5		14	9	Heredia	Holmes	Nen	34-24	2nd	6.0
6-8†	At Col.	L	2-7		5	11	Burke	Leiter	DiPoto	34-25		
6-8‡	At Col.	W	9-1	(8)	10	5	Fernandez	Wright		35-25	2nd	5.5
6-9	At S.F.	L	4-7		7	11	Foulke	Rapp		35-26	2nd	5.5
6-10	At S.F.	W	9-0		8	0	Brown	VanLandingham		36-26	2nd	5.5
6-11	At S.F.	W	6-3		13	9	Helling	Rueter	Nen	37-26	2nd	4.5
6-13	N.Y. (AL)	W	2-1	(12)	6	5	Cook	Mecir		38-26	2nd	3.5
6-15†	N.Y. (AL)	L	5-8		7	9	Stanton	Cook	Rivera	38-27		
6-15‡	N.Y. (AL)	W	6-5		10	9	Nen	Rivera		39-27	2nd	2.5
6-16	At Det.	W	7-3		13	6	Brown	Blair		40-27	2nd	2.5
6-17	At Det.	W	3-2		6	4	Alfonseca	Jones	Nen	41-27	2nd	2.5
6-18	At Det.	L	2-6		4	8	Olivares	Leiter		41-28	2nd	2.5
6-20	At Mon.	W	2-1		5	3	Fernandez	Martinez		42-28	2nd	2.5
6-21	At Mon.	L	3-4		10	13	Juden	Rapp	Urbina	42-29	2nd	3.5

Date	Opp.	Res.	Score	(inn.*)	Hits	Opp. hits	Winning pitcher	Losing pitcher	Save	Record	Pos.	GB
6-22	At Mon.	W	2-0		6	6	Heredia	Urbina	Nen	43-29	2nd	3.5
6-23	At Phi.	L	3-9		8	9	Schilling	Helling		43-30	2nd	3.5
6-24	At Phi.	W	4-1		10	6	Leiter	Ruffcorn	Nen	44-30	2nd	2.5
6-25	At Phi.	W	7-5		14	9	Fernandez	Harris	Nen	45-30	2nd	2.5
6-26	Mon.	L	2-5		4	10	Juden	Rapp		45-31	2nd	3.5
6-27	Mon.	L	0-2		6	10	Valdes	Brown	Urbina	45-32	2nd	4.5
6-28	Mon.	W	4-2		6	3	Hernandez	Bullinger	Nen	46-32	2nd	4.5
6-29	Mon.	W	5-3		7	6	Leiter	Perez	Nen	47-32	2nd	4.5
6-30	At Bos.	W	8-5		9	7	Fernandez	Wakefield		48-32	2nd	3.5
7-1	At Bos.	L	2-9		9	14	Eshelman	Rapp	Corsi	48-33	2nd	4.5
7-2	At Bos.	W	3-2		5	8	Brown	Gordon	Nen	49-33	2nd	4.5
7-3	At N.Y.	W	10-4		14	11	Hernandez	Reynoso		50-33	2nd	4.5
7-4	At N.Y.	L	2-6		8	8	Reed	Leiter	McMichael	50-34	2nd	5.5
7-5	At N.Y.	L	3-5		12	11	Clark	Fernandez	J. Franco	50-35	2nd	6.5
7-6	At N.Y.	L	2-3	(12)	8	10	Acevedo	Cook		50-36	2nd	6.5
7-10	Phi.	W	8-7		10	10	Nen	Spradlin		51-36	2nd	5.5
7-11	Phi.	L	3-13		8	15	Schilling	Brown		51-37	2nd	5.5
7-13	Phi.	W	9-3		8	6	Fernandez	Leiter		52-37	2nd	5.0
7-14	Mon.	W	5-4	(12)	10	9	Nen	Daal		53-37	2nd	5.0
7-15	Mon.	L	0-5		5	10	Hermanson	Saunders		53-38	2nd	5.0
7-16	L.A.	W	5-1		9	1	Brown	Nomo		54-38	2nd	5.0
7-17	L.A.	W	8-7		14	14	Leiter	Candiotti	Nen	55-38	2nd	5.0
7-18	S.D.	L	3-5		11	9	Smith	Fernandez	Worrell	55-39	2nd	6.0
7-19	S.D.	W	8-5		12	5	Hernandez	Jackson		56-39	2nd	5.0
7-20	S.D.	L	0-3		6	4	Ashby	Saunders	Hoffman	56-40	2nd	5.0
7-21	S.D.	L	2-10		5	15	Hitchcock	Brown		56-41	2nd	6.0
7-22	At Cin.	L	6-7		8	9	Smiley	Heredia	Shaw	56-42	2nd	6.5
7-23	At Cin.	W	8-1		12	7	Fernandez	Morgan		57-42	2nd	5.5
7-25	At St.L.	W	5-4		9	6	Hernandez	Al. Benes	Nen	58-42	T2nd	5.5
7-26	At St.L.	L	1-3		6	5	Morris	Helling	Eckersley	58-43	T2nd	5.5
7-27	At St.L.	L	4-6		7	9	An. Benes	Brown	Eckersley	58-44	T2nd	6.5
7-28	Cin.	L	0-4		8	7	Belinda	Powell		58-45	3rd	7.5
7-29	Cin.	W	7-1		10	9	Fernandez	Morgan		59-45	2nd	7.5
7-30	Cin.	W	6-0		14	4	Hernandez	Schourek		60-45	2nd	7.5
7-31	Atl.	W	1-0		6	4	Saunders	Byrd	Nen	61-45	2nd	6.5
8-1	Atl.	W	3-2	(12)	10	5	Powell	Cather		62-45	2nd	5.5
8-2	Atl.	L	2-4		7	6	Neagle	Leiter	Wohlers	62-46	2nd	6.5
8-3	Atl.	W	8-4		10	7	Fernandez	Millwood		63-46	2nd	5.5
8-4	Hou.	W	4-1		5	4	Hernandez	Holt	Powell	64-46	2nd	5.5
8-5	Hou.	W	6-5		11	8	Nen	Wagner		65-46	2nd	4.5
8-6	At Pit.	W	12-3		18	10	Brown	Loaiza		66-46	2nd	4.5
8-7	At Pit.	L	1-5		7	9	Wilkins	Leiter		66-47	2nd	5.5
8-8	At Atl.	W	6-4		11	9	Fernandez	Byrd	Nen	67-47	2nd	4.5
8-9	At Atl.	L	3-4		7	9	Smoltz	Stanifer	Wohlers	67-48	2nd	5.5
8-10	At Atl.	W	4-2	(10)	9	6	Powell	Bielecki	Nen	68-48	2nd	4.5
8-11	At Atl.	L	1-2		5	4	Wohlers	Heredia		68-49	2nd	5.5
8-12	At Hou.	L	2-13		6	16	Hampton	Leiter		68-50	2nd	5.5
8-13	At Hou.	W	8-6		14	11	Fernandez	Lima	Nen	69-50	2nd	4.5
8-15	Pit.	W	6-5		12	13	Powell	Loiselle		70-50	2nd	3.5
8-16	Pit.	L	5-10		9	12	Cordova	Saunders		70-51	2nd	4.5
8-17	Pit.	W	10-2		12	9	Brown	Cooke		71-51	2nd	3.5
8-18	Pit.	L	2-7		7	11	Loaiza	Alfonseca		71-52	2nd	4.0
8-19	Chi.	W	8-1		5	4	Fernandez	Gonzalez		72-52	2nd	4.0
8-20	Chi.	W	6-5		9	11	Hernandez	Tapani	Nen	73-52	2nd	4.0
8-22	St.L.	L	3-7		8	9	Morris	Saunders	.	73-53	2nd	5.0
8-23	St.L.	W	3-0		4	5	Brown	An. Benes		74-53	2nd	5.0
8-24	St.L.	W	7-1		9	8	Ojala	Stottlemyre		75-53	2nd	4.0
8-25	At Chi.	L	1-3		8	11	Tapani	Fernandez	Adams	75-54	2nd	4.5
8-26	At Chi.	W	11-0		17	4	Hernandez	Batista		76-54	2nd	4.5
8-27	At Chi.	W	4-3		6	9	Nen	Adams		77-54	2nd	3.5
8-28	At Chi.	L	3-4	(10)	7	10	Adams	Alfonseca		77-55	2nd	4.5
8-29	At Tor.	W	8-0		10	5	Leiter	Person		78-55	2nd	4.5
8-30	At Tor.	W	4-1		10	3	Fernandez	Carpenter	Nen	79-55	2nd	4.5
8-31	At Tor.	W	8-3		10	9	Hernandez	Williams		80-55	2nd	4.5
9-1	Bal.	W	10-4		9	10	Heredia	Boskie		81-55	2nd	3.5
9-2	Bal.	W	3-2	(10)	8	9	Vosberg	Mathews		82-55	2nd	3.5
9-3	Bal.	W	7-6		13	9	Powell	Boskie		83-55	2nd	2.5
9-5	At L.A.	L	4-7		6	10	Martinez	Fernandez	Worrell	83-56	2nd	3.0
9-6	At L.A.	L	5-9		10	12	Hall	Miller		83-57	2nd	4.0
9-7	At L.A.	L	5-9		6	12	Candiotti	Saunders		83-58	2nd	5.0
9-8	At L.A.	W	8-4		9	15	Brown	Nomo		84-58	2nd	4.5
9-9	At S.D.	L	6-7	(13)	9	15	Worrell	Ojala		84-59	2nd	5.5
9-10	At S.D.	L	3-4		8	10	Bruske	Vosberg		84-60	2nd	6.5
9-12	S.F.	L	0-1		8	6	Rueter	Hernandez	Beck	84-61	2nd	6.5
9-13	S.F.	W	8-1		10	3	Brown	Gardner		85-61	2nd	5.5

Date	Opp.	Res.	Score	(inn.*)	Hits	Opp. hits	Winning pitcher	Losing pitcher	Save	Record	Pos.	GB
9-14	S.F.	W	5-4		6	8	Powell	Hernandez	Nen	86-61	2nd	4.5
9-15	Col.	L	1-7		11	7	Wright	Fernandez		86-62	2nd	5.5
9-16	Col.	W	9-6		13	8	Powell	DiPoto		87-62	2nd	5.5
9-17†	Phi.	L	2-5		6	10	Stephenson	Hernandez	Bottalico	87-63		
9-17‡	Phi.	W	5-2		8	9	Saunders	Leiter	Nen	88-63	2nd	6.0
9-18	Phi.	W	8-2		15	10	Brown	Grace		89-63	2nd	6.0
9-19	N.Y.	W	5-2		6	5	Leiter	Mlicki		90-63	2nd	6.0
9-20	N.Y.	L	3-7		6	10	Bohanon	Fernandez		90-64	2nd	7.0
9-21	N.Y.	L	1-2		5	8	Reed	Ojala	Rojas	90-65	2nd	7.0
9-22	N.Y.	L	3-10		7	11	Jones	Hernandez		90-66	2nd	8.0
9-23	At Mon.	W	6-3		11	9	Brown	Hermanson	Nen	91-66	2nd	8.0
9-24	At Mon.	W	10-9		8	11	Leiter	Perez	Vosberg	92-66	2nd	7.0
9-25	At Mon.	L	2-3		6	4	Kline	Nen		92-67	2nd	8.0
9-26	At Phi.	L	3-5		5	10	Schilling	Alfonseca	Bottalico	92-68	2nd	9.0
9-27	At Phi.	L	7-8		8	14	Spradlin	Stanifer		92-69	2nd	9.0
9-28	At Phi.	L	7-8		9	10	Gomes	Heredia	Bottalico	92-70	2nd	9.0

Monthly records: April (15-10), May (16-11), June (17-11), July (13-13), August (19-10), September (12-15).
*Innings, if other than nine. †First game of doubleheader. ‡Second game of doubleheader.

HIGHLIGHTS

High point: South Florida could go a long time without reaching as high a point as it did just after midnight on October 26, when Edgar Renteria lined a single through the Pro Player Stadium infield to win the World Series for the Marlins in the 11th inning of a dramatic seventh game against Cleveland.

Low point: Eleven days after winning the World Series, team owner Wayne Huizenga announced he was selling the team to a syndicate headed by team president Don Smiley, and that the payroll would have to be slashed dramatically. That led to an offseason that saw the team trade away Moises Alou, Robb Nen, Devon White, Jeff Conine, Kevin Brown and Dennis Cook, among other key components to their championship season.

Turning point: In June, the team traded Pat Rapp to the Giants for two low minor-league prospects. The most important thing that did was clear a spot in the rotation for Livan Hernandez, the Cuban rookie who won his first nine decisions before becoming a playoff and World Series hero.

Most valuable player: Alou was the only everyday player who was steady and reliable all season. He overcame his injury-plagued past by playing in a career-high 150 games, scoring 88 runs, collecting 157 hits, hitting 23 home runs and driving in 115 runs.

Most valuable pitcher: Hernandez, whose ability to step in for the injured Alex Fernandez in the playoffs and World Series keyed the Marlins' defeat of both the Braves and Indians.

Most improved player: Catcher Charles Johnson won his third Gold Glove in as many seasons and finished the season with a major-league record 171 consecutive errorless games.

Most pleasant surprise: Nobody knew anything about second baseman Craig Counsell on July 27 when the Marlins acquired him from the Rockies in a trade for relief pitcher Mark Hutton, but they sure knew who he was three months later. After sparking the offense from the No. 8 spot by hitting .299 in the final two months of the regular season, Counsell took on the hero's role in Game 7 of the World Series, driving in the tying run with a ninth-inning sacrifice fly and scoring the winning run on Renteria's single in the 11th.

Biggest disappointment: Right fielder Gary Sheffield, who received a staggering six-year, $61 million contract extension on the second day of the season in reward for his big 1996 season. But he struggled all season at the plate, hitting .250 with 21 homers and 71 RBIs.

Key injuries: Center fielder Devon White missed a large chunk of the season with calf and knee injuries, but returned in time for the stretch drive. First baseman/outfielder Cliff Floyd was bothered all season by hamstring problems. Righthander Alex Fernandez had surgery to repair a partially torn rotator cuff after the season ended. The injury was discovered after Game 2 of the NLCS against the Braves, and Fernandez is expected to miss the 1998 season.

Notable: The Marlins became the first wild-card team to play in or win the World Series.

—DAN GRAZIANO

RECORDS

1997 regular-season record: 92-70 (2nd in N.L. East); 52-29 at home; 40-41 on road; 37-26 vs. East; 34-21 vs. Central; 21-23 vs. West; 18-15 vs. lefthanded starters; 74-55 vs. righthanded starters; 75-57 on grass; 17-13 on turf; 24-28 in daytime; 68-42 at night; 32-22 in one-run games; 9-5 in extra-inning games; 0-3 in doubleheaders.
Team record past five years: 354-390 (.476, ranks 10th in league in that span).

TEAM LEADERS

Batting average: Bobby Bonilla (.297).
At-bats: Edgar Renteria (617).
Runs: Edgar Renteria (90).
Hits: Edgar Renteria (171).
Total bases: Moises Alou (265).
Doubles: Bobby Bonilla (39).
Triples: Moises Alou (5).
Home runs: Moises Alou (23).
Runs batted in: Moises Alou (115).
Stolen bases: Edgar Renteria (32).
Slugging percentage: Moises Alou (.493).
On-base percentage: Gary Sheffield (.424).
Wins: Alex Fernandez (17).
Earned-run average: Kevin Brown (2.69).
Complete games: Kevin Brown (6).
Shutouts: Kevin Brown (2).
Saves: Robb Nen (35).
Innings pitched: Kevin Brown (237.1).
Strikeouts: Kevin Brown (205).

GAMES BY POSITION

Catcher: Charles Johnson 123, Gregg Zaun 50, Bob Natal 4.
First base: Jeff Conine 145, Darren Daulton 39, Jim Eisenreich 29, Cliff Floyd 9, Bobby Bonilla 2, Russ Morman 1, Gregg Zaun 1.
Second base: Luis Castillo 70, Kurt Abbott 54, Craig Counsell 51, Ralph Milliard 8.
Third base: Bobby Bonilla 149, Alex Arias 37, John Wehner 6, Kurt Abbott 4, Josh Booty 4.
Shortstop: Edgar Renteria 153, Alex Arias 11, Kurt Abbott 7.
Outfield: Moises Alou 150, Gary Sheffield 132, Devon White 71, John Cangelosi 58, Jim Eisenreich 55, Cliff Floyd 38, John Wehner 27, Todd Dunwoody 14, Mark Kotsay 14, Kurt Abbott 10, Darren Daulton 3, Billy McMillon 2, Russ Morman 2, Jeff Conine 1.
Designated hitter: Jim Eisenreich 4, Bobby Bonilla 3, Kurt Abbott 2, Darren Daulton 1, Gary Sheffield 1.

TOP DRAFT CHOICES

1. **Aaron Akin**, RHP, Cowley County (Kan.) C.C.
2. **Jeff Bailey**, C, Kelso (Wash.) H.S.
3. **Chris Aguila**, 3B, McQueen H.S., Reno, Nev.
4. **Brandon Harper**, C, Dallas Baptist Univ.
5. **Paul Avery**, LHP, Fresno C.C.
6. **Brian Reed**, OF, Green Valley H.S., Henderson, Nev.
7. **Matt Erickson**, 3B, Univ. of Arkansas.
8. **Clifton Lee**, LHP, Benton (Ark.) H.S.
9. **Jon Heinrichs**, OF, UCLA.
10. **Kelly Washington**, SS, Shenandoah H.S., Stephens City, Va.

HOUSTON ASTROS
NATIONAL LEAGUE CENTRAL DIVISION

Astros Schedule

Home games shaded. *—All-Star Game at Coors Field (Colorado).
D—Day game (any game starting before 5 p.m.).

March

SUN	MON	TUE	WED	THU	FRI	SAT
				31 D SF		

April

SUN	MON	TUE	WED	THU	FRI	SAT
			1 SF	2 SF	3 COL	4 COL
5 D COL	6 D COL	7 D SF	8 SF	9 SF	10 LA	11 LA
12 LA	13 LA	14	15 CIN	16 CIN	17 MON	18 MON
19 D MON	20		22 NYM	23 NYM	24 MON	25 MON
26 D MON	27	28 NYM	29 NYM	30		

May

SUN	MON	TUE	WED	THU	FRI	SAT
					1 PHI	2 PHI
3 D PHI	4	5 CUB	6 D CUB	7	8 MIL	9 MIL
10 D MIL	11 FLA	12 FLA	13 PIT	14 PIT	15 ATL	16 ATL
17 ATL	18 D ATL	19 MON	20 MON	21 D MON	22 SD	23 SD
24 SD	25 D LA	26 LA	27 LA	28	29 COL	30 D COL
31 D COL						

June

SUN	MON	TUE	WED	THU	FRI	SAT
	1	2 SD	3 SD	4	5 D KC	6 KC
7 D KC	8 DET	9 D DET	10 DET	11	12 CIN	13 CIN
14 CIN	15 CIN	16 STL	17 STL	18 STL	19 CIN	20 CIN
21 CIN	22 D MIN	23 MIN	24 COL	25 D COL	26 CLE	27 D CLE
28 D CLE	29	30 CWS				

July

SUN	MON	TUE	WED	THU	FRI	SAT
		1 CWS	2 CWS	3 ARZ	4 ARZ	
5 D ARZ	6	7	* 8	9 STL	10 STL	11 STL
12 D STL	13 ARZ	14 ARZ	15 ARZ	16	17 SF	18 SF
19 D SF	20 COL	21 COL	22 LA	23 LA	24 SD	25 SD
26 D SD	27 FLA	28 FLA	29 FLA	30 D FLA	31 PIT	

August

SUN	MON	TUE	WED	THU	FRI	SAT
						1 PIT
2 D PIT	3 FLA	4 FLA	5 FLA	6	7 PHI	8 PHI
9 D PHI	10 D MIL	11 MIL	12 MIL	13 MIL	14 CUB	15 CUB
16 D CUB	17 PHI	18 PHI	19 PHI	20 MIL	21 MIL	22 D CUB
23 D CUB	24 D CUB	25 ATL	26 ATL	27	28 PIT	29 PIT
30 D PIT	31 ATL					

September

SUN	MON	TUE	WED	THU	FRI	SAT
		1 ATL	2 ATL	3	4 ARZ	5 D ARZ
6 ARZ	7 D CIN	8 CIN	9 MIL	10 MIL	11 STL	12 STL
13 STL	14 NYM	15 NYM	16 NYM	17 D PIT	18 PIT	19 PIT
20 D PIT	21	22 STL	23 STL	24	25 CUB	26 CUB
27 D CUB						

1998 SEASON
CLUB DIRECTORY

Chairman and CEO
Drayton McLane
President
Tal Smith
Sr. vice president, business operations
Bob McClaren
General manager
Gerry Hunsicker
Assistant general manager
Tim Purpura
Spec. asst. to g.m. for int'l scouting & dev.
Andres Reiner
Director of scouting
David Lakey
Director of baseball administration
Barry Waters
Vice president of marketing
Pam Gardner
Director of media relations
Rob Matwick
Assistant director of media relations
Darrell Simon
Coordinator of publications
Alyson Footer
Director of broadcasting & promotions
Jamie Hildreth
Director of community development
Gene Pemberton
Director of ticket sales & services
John Sorrentino
Controller
Robert McBurnett
Scouts
Ricardo Aponte
Jesus Aristimno
Stan Benjamin
Bob Blair
Stan Boroski

Ralph Bratton
Rueben Cabrera
Rafael Cariel
Alexis Corro
Gerry Craft
Traci Dearing
Doug Deutsch
James Farrar
Brian Granger
David Henderson
Dan Huston
Mark Johnson
Brian Keenan
Bill Kelso
Bob King
David Lakey
Julio Linares
Mike Maggert
Domingo Mercedes
Tom Mooney
Pat Murphy
Fred Nelson
Mel Nelson
Joe Pittman
Bob Poole
Jim Pransky
Andres Reiner
Anibal Reluz
Joe Robinson
Adriano Rodriguez
Deron Rombach
Bob Skinner
Tad Slowik
Steve Smith
Scipio Spinks
Lynwood Stallings
Frankie Thon
Tim Tolman
Pablo Torrealba
Paul Weaver
Grant Weir
Gene Wellman
Tom Wiedenbauer

MINOR LEAGUE AFFILIATES

Class	Team	League	Manager
AAA	New Orleans	Pacific Coast	John Tamargo
AA	Jackson	Texas	Gary Allenson
A	Kissimmee	Florida State	To be announced
A	Quad City	Midwest	Mike Rojas
A	Auburn	New York-Pennsylvania	To be announced
Rookie	Gulf Coast Astros	Gulf Coast	To be announced

BROADCAST INFORMATION

Radio: KILT-AM (610); KXYZ-AM (1320, Spanish language).
TV: KTXH-TV (Channel 20).
Cable TV: Fox Sports Southwest.

SPRING TRAINING

Ballpark (city): Osceola County Stadium (Kissimmee, Fla.).
Ticket information: 407-933-2520.

1998 SEASON *Houston Astros*

Manager—Larry Dierker (49).
Coaches—Alan Ashby, Jose Cruz (25), Mike Cubbage (24), Matt Galante (1), Tom McCraw (16), Vern Ruhle (48).

No.	PITCHERS	B/T	Ht./Wt.	Born	1997 clubs
51	Cabrera, Jose	R/R	6-0/160	3-24-72	Buffalo, New Orleans, Houston
	Elarton, Scott	R/R	6-7/240	2-23-76	Jackson, New Orleans
	Garcia, Freddy	R/R	6-4/235	10-6-76	Kissimmee
59	Garcia, Ramon	R/R	6-2/200	12-9-69	Houston
23	Grzanich, Mike	R/R	6-1/180	8-24-72	Jackson
	Halama, John	L/L	6-5/195	2-22-72	New Orleans
10	Hampton, Mike	R/L	5-10/180	9-9-72	Houston
	Henry, Doug	R/R	6-4/205	12-10-63	San Francisco
45	Holt, Chris	R/R	6-4/205	9-18-71	Houston
42	Lima, Jose	R/R	6-2/170	9-30-72	Houston
52	Magnante, Mike	L/L	6-1/195	6-17-65	New Orleans, Houston
46	Miller, Trever	R/L	6-3/175	5-29-73	New Orleans
47	Nitkowski, C.J.	L/L	6-3/190	3-3-73	New Orleans
37	Reynolds, Shane	R/R	6-3/210	3-26-68	Houston, New Orleans
	Sikorski, Brian	R/R	6-1/190	7-27-73	Kissimmee, Jackson
13	Wagner, Billy	L/L	5-11/180	6-25-71	Houston
58	Walter, Mike	R/R	6-1/190	10-23-74	Jackson

No.	CATCHERS	B/T	Ht./Wt.	Born	1997 clubs
11	Ausmus, Brad	R/R	5-11/190	4-14-69	Houston
	Castro, Ramon	R/R	6-2/225	3-1-76	Kissimmee
20	Eusebio, Tony	R/R	6-2/210	4-27-67	Houston
	Meluskey, Mitch	B/R	6-0/185	9-18-73	Jackson, New Orleans

No.	INFIELDERS	B/T	Ht./Wt.	Born	1997 clubs
5	Bagwell, Jeff	R/R	6-0/195	5-27-68	Houston
7	Biggio, Craig	R/R	5-11/180	12-14-65	Houston
27	Bogar, Tim	R/R	6-2/198	10-28-66	Houston
64	Guillen, Carlos	R/R	6-1/180	9-30-75	Jackson, New Orleans
12	Gutierrez, Ricky	R/R	6-1/175	5-23-70	New Orleans, Houston
	Hernandez, Carlos	R/R	5-9/175	12-12-75	Jackson
	Howell, Jack	L/R	6-0/190	8-18-61	Anaheim
19	Johnson, Russ	R/R	5-10/180	2-22-73	New Orleans, Houston
	Spiers, Bill	L/R	6-2/190	6-5-66	Houston
	Ward, Daryle	L/L	6-2/240	6-27-75	Jackson, New Orleans

No.	OUTFIELDERS	B/T	Ht./Wt.	Born	1997 clubs
18	Alou, Moises	R/R	6-3/195	7-3-66	Florida
14	Bell, Derek	R/R	6-2/215	12-11-68	Houston, New Orleans
	Clark, Dave	L/R	6-2/213	9-3-62	Chicago N.L.
	Everett, Carl	B/R	6-0/190	6-3-71	New York N.L.
15	Hidalgo, Richard	R/R	6-3/190	7-2-75	New Orleans, Houston
39	Montgomery, Ray	R/R	6-3/195	8-8-69	Houston, New Orleans
6	Mouton, James	R/R	5-9/175	12-29-68	Houston

BALLPARK INFORMATION

Ballpark (capacity, surface)
The Astrodome (54,370, artificial)

Address
P.O. Box 288
Houston, TX 77001-0288

Business phone
713-799-9500

Ticket information
713-799-9555

Ticket prices
$21 (star deck)
$17 (field level)
$15 (mezzanine)
$12 (outfield mezzanine, sky box)
$11 (loge)
$7 (upper box)
$5 (upper reserved)
$4 (adult pavilion)
$1 (youth pavilion)

Field dimensions (from home plate)
To left field at foul line, 325 feet
To center field, 400 feet
To right field at foul line, 325 feet

First game played
April 12, 1965 (Phillies 2, Astros 0)

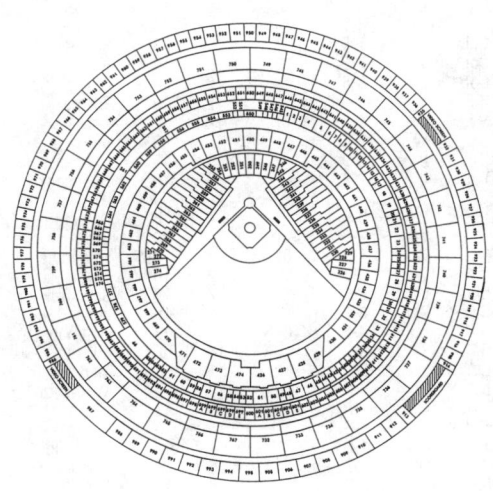

1998 SEASON *Houston Astros*

Date	Opp.	Res.	Score	(inn.*)	Hits	Opp. hits	Winning pitcher	Losing pitcher	Save	Record	Pos.	GB
4-1	Atl.	W	2-1		8	8	Reynolds	Smoltz	Wagner	1-0	T1st	....
4-2	Atl.	W	4-3		10	8	Hampton	Maddux	Wagner	2-0	T1st	....
4-3	Atl.	L	2-3		8	2	Glavine	Kile	Wohlers	2-1	T1st	....
4-4	St.L.	W	3-2	(11)	14	9	Springer	Ludwick		3-1	T1st	....
4-5	St.L.	W	6-2		7	7	Fernandez	Osborne	Garcia	4-1	1st	+1.0
4-6	St.L.	W	3-2		7	7	Martin	Frascatore	Wagner	5-1	1st	+2.0
4-8	At Atl.	L	2-4		6	10	Glavine	Hampton	Wohlers	5-2	1st	+2.0
4-9	At Atl.	L	3-4	(12)	8	8	Embree	Lima		5-3	1st	+1.0
4-10	At Atl.	W	5-3		8	14	Holt	Smoltz	Hudek	6-3	1st	+1.5
4-11	At St.L.	L	2-4		8	6	Batchelor	Reynolds	Eckersley	6-4	1st	+1.5
4-12	At St.L.	W	7-5		6	8	Garcia	Stottlemyre	Wagner	7-4	1st	+2.0
4-13	At St.L.	L	2-6		7	7	Al. Benes	Hampton	Eckersley	7-5	1st	+1.5
4-14	At St.L.	W	4-2	(10)	11	6	Wagner	Eckersley	Hudek	8-5	1st	+2.5
4-15	Mon.	L	5-7		7	9	Martinez	Holt		8-6	1st	+1.5
4-16	Mon.	W	10-2		10	3	Reynolds	Valdes		9-6	1st	+2.5
4-18	At L.A.	L	3-5		9	12	Martinez	Hampton	Worrell	9-7	1st	+2.0
4-19	At L.A.	W	2-1		5	8	Kile	Nomo	Wagner	10-7	1st	+2.0
4-20	At L.A.	W	3-1		6	6	Holt	Candiotti	Hudek	11-7	1st	+2.0
4-22	At S.D.	W	12-3		15	7	Reynolds	Valenzuela		12-7	1st	+3.0
4-23	At S.D.	W	11-7		18	10	Garcia	Worrell		13-7	1st	+3.0
4-25	S.F.	W	5-4		8	6	Wagner	Roa		14-7	1st	+3.5
4-26	S.F.	L	0-2		2	4	Estes	Holt		14-8	1st	+3.5
4-27	S.F.	L	2-3		7	7	Fernandez	Reynolds	Beck	14-9	1st	+2.5
4-28	Col.	L	6-7	(10)	9	11	McCurry	Wagner	Ruffin	14-10	1st	+1.5
4-29	Col.	W	3-1		6	7	Wall	Bailey	Hudek	15-10	1st	+2.5
4-30	At Mon.	L	6-8		11	13	Perez	Kile	Urbina	15-11	1st	+2.5
5-1	At Mon.	L	0-4		3	8	Martinez	Holt		15-12	1st	+1.5
5-2	Fla.	W	2-1		8	8	Reynolds	Rapp	Wagner	16-12	1st	+1.5
5-3	Fla.	L	8-9	(13)	17	11	Heredia	Garcia	Powell	16-13	1st	+0.5
5-4	Fla.	W	1-0		5	4	Kile	Brown		17-13	1st	+1.5
5-5	Phi.	W	9-2		8	7	Holt	Leiter		18-13	1st	+2.5
5-6	Phi.	L	1-5		9	9	Schilling	Garcia		18-14	1st	+1.5
5-7	N.Y.	L	1-4		4	10	Reynoso	Martin	J. Franco	18-15	1st	+0.5
5-8	N.Y.	W	4-2		11	8	Hampton	Reed	Wagner	19-15	1st	+0.5
5-9	At Fla.	L	2-3		7	7	Nen	Lima		19-16	2nd	0.5
5-10	At Fla.	W	4-2		8	9	Holt	Helling	Wagner	20-16	1st	+0.5
5-11	At Fla.	L	3-6		8	7	Fernandez	Wall	Nen	20-17	1st	+0.5
5-12	At Fla.	L	4-11		10	14	Stanifer	Reynolds		20-18	1st	+0.5
5-13	At N.Y.	L	3-4		7	8	McMichael	Springer	J. Franco	20-19	T1st	....
5-14	At N.Y.	W	1-0		7	4	Kile	McMichael	Wagner	21-19	T1st	....
5-16	At Phi.	W	12-7		11	13	Holt	Leiter		22-19	1st	+0.5
5-17	At Phi.	L	2-4		4	8	Schilling	Reynolds	Bottalico	22-20	1st	+0.5
5-18	At Phi.	L	3-5		9	8	Stephenson	Hampton	Bottalico	22-21	1st	+0.5
5-19	At Phi.	W	9-5		11	10	Kile	Maduro		23-21	1st	+1.0
5-20	Cin.	L	4-7		9	14	Smiley	Springer	Shaw	23-22	1st	+1.0
5-21	Cin.	W	4-3	(14)	11	14	Martin	Sullivan		24-22	1st	+1.0
5-23	At Col.	L	7-8		13	11	Jones	Wall	S. Reed	24-23	1st	+0.5
5-24	At Col.	W	7-0		8	4	Kile	Burke		25-23	1st	+1.5
5-25	At Col.	L	5-8		9	14	Bailey	Garcia	Munoz	25-24	1st	+0.5
5-26	At S.F.	L	3-4		7	9	Tavarez	Lima		25-25	1st	+0.5
5-27	At S.F.	L	4-5	(10)	12	7	Beck	Wagner		25-26	1st	+0.5
5-29	S.D.	W	10-6		12	10	Kile	Valenzuela		26-26	1st	+0.5
5-30	S.D.	L	2-9		6	13	Cunnane	Holt	Worrell	26-27	2nd	0.5
5-31	S.D.	L	5-12		10	16	Hitchcock	Reynolds	Smith	26-28	2nd	0.5
6-1	S.D.	L	3-6		7	8	Hamilton	Wagner	Hoffman	26-29	2nd	1.5
6-2	L.A.	W	2-0		6	6	Wall	Nomo	Lima	27-29	2nd	0.5
6-3	L.A.	W	4-3	(10)	7	10	Magnante	Radinsky		28-29	2nd	0.5
6-4	At Cin.	W	5-2		9	10	Holt	Burba	Wagner	29-29	1st	+0.5
6-5	At Cin.	L	5-6		7	11	Schourek	Reynolds	Shaw	29-30	2nd	0.5
6-6	At S.D.	W	8-7		12	15	Lima	Hamilton	Wagner	30-30	2nd	0.5
6-7	At S.D.	L	4-5	(10)	7	13	Hoffman	Garcia		30-31	2nd	1.5
6-8	At S.D.	W	9-0		14	5	Kile	Valenzuela		31-31	2nd	0.5
6-9	At L.A.	L	3-8		11	8	Martinez	Holt		31-32	2nd	1.0
6-10	At L.A.	W	6-3		13	9	Magnante	Osuna	Wagner	32-32	T1st	....
6-11	At L.A.	L	5-10		10	12	Park	Hampton		32-33	T1st	....
6-13	Min.	L	1-8		6	10	Radke	Wall		32-34	2nd	1.0
6-14	Min.	L	1-6		9	12	Robertson	Kile		32-35	T2nd	1.0
6-15	Min.	W	3-2		6	8	Wagner	Guardado		33-35	T1st	....
6-16	At K.C.	L	2-5		6	11	Rosado	Hampton		33-36	2nd	1.0
6-17	At K.C.	W	10-2		15	4	Garcia	Haney		34-36	T1st	....
6-18	At K.C.	L	2-6		8	11	Pittsley	Wall		34-37	T1st	....

Date	Opp.	Res.	Score	(inn.*)	Hits	Opp. hits	Winning pitcher	Losing pitcher	Save	Record	Pos.	GB
6-20	Chi.	W	7-3		13	9	Kile	Trachsel		35-37	1st	+1.5
6-21	Chi.	W	7-3		12	6	Holt	Castillo		36-37	1st	+2.5
6-22	Chi.	W	3-1		5	6	Hampton	Foster	Wagner	37-37	1st	+3.0
6-23	Pit.	L	0-6		2	8	Cordova	Garcia		37-38	1st	+2.5
6-24	Pit.	L	3-8		5	13	Lieber	Wall		37-39	1st	+1.5
6-25	Pit.	W	5-1		9	6	Kile	Sodowsky		38-39	1st	+2.0
6-26	At Chi.	W	7-6	(10)	14	13	Wagner	Adams	Minor	39-39	1st	+2.0
6-27	At Chi.	L	1-2		7	6	Foster	Hampton	Wendell	39-40	1st	+1.0
6-28	At Chi.	L	2-5		2	6	Gonzalez	Garcia	Bottenfield	39-41	1st	+1.0
6-29	At Chi.	W	10-8		11	16	Minor	Mulholland	Wagner	40-41	1st	+1.0
6-30	Cle.	L	4-6		8	9	Mesa	Martin	M. Jackson	40-42	T1st	....
7-1	Cle.	L	6-8		10	15	Plunk	Lima	M. Jackson	40-43	2nd	1.0
7-2	Cle.	W	6-2		10	10	Hampton	Hershiser		41-43	2nd	1.0
7-3	Cin.	L	3-4		7	8	Smiley	Garcia	Shaw	41-44	T2nd	1.0
7-4	Cin.	L	2-4		5	7	Morgan	Greene	Shaw	41-45	3rd	1.0
7-5	Cin.	W	2-1		4	3	Kile	Mercker	Wagner	42-45	T2nd	1.0
7-6	Cin.	W	6-5		9	11	Wagner	Remlinger		43-45	2nd	1.0
7-10	At Pit.	W	7-0		12	6	Kile	Schmidt		44-45	T1st	....
7-11	At Pit.	W	10-0		14	5	Hampton	Loaiza		45-45	1st	+1.0
7-12	At Pit.	L	0-3	(10)	0	6	Rincon	Hudek		45-46	T1st	....
7-13	At Pit.	L	3-5		6	10	Sodowsky	Springer	Loiselle	45-47	T2nd	1.0
7-14	At Chi.	W	9-7	(15)	14	18	Wagner	Tatis	Springer	46-47	2nd	1.0
7-15	At Chi.	W	5-3		9	8	Kile	Rojas	Magnante	47-47	2nd	1.0
7-16	S.F.	W	8-1		11	4	Hampton	Foulke		48-47	T1st	....
7-17	S.F.	L	1-3		5	9	Gardner	Holt	Beck	48-48	T1st	....
7-18	At Mon.	W	2-0		8	6	Garcia	Martinez	Wagner	49-48	1st	+1.0
7-19	At Mon.	W	8-6		16	8	Reynolds	Juden	Wagner	50-48	1st	+1.0
7-20	At Mon.	W	9-0		8	4	Kile	Hermanson		51-48	1st	+2.0
7-22	At St.L.	W	4-2		6	5	Hampton	An. Benes	Wagner	52-48	1st	+2.5
7-23	At St.L.	W	7-2		11	5	Magnante	Stottlemyre		53-48	1st	+3.5
7-24	Mon.	W	10-5		11	7	Martin	Telford		54-48	1st	+4.5
7-25	Mon.	W	5-2		6	7	Kile	Juden		55-48	1st	+4.5
7-26	Mon.	W	9-8	(10)	13	10	Wagner	Urbina		56-48	1st	+4.5
7-27	Mon.	W	7-2		8	8	Hampton	Bullinger		57-48	1st	+5.0
7-28	St.L.	L	1-2		6	6	Stottlemyre	Holt	Eckersley	57-49	1st	+5.0
7-29	St.L.	W	5-4		10	8	Reynolds	Osborne	Wagner	58-49	1st	+6.0
7-30	St.L.	W	7-4		11	11	Kile	Fossas	Martin	59-49	1st	+6.5
8-1	N.Y.	L	5-8	(10)	10	11	J. Franco	Lima		59-50	1st	+6.0
8-2	N.Y.	W	6-0		10	3	Hampton	Jones		60-50	1st	+6.0
8-3	N.Y.	W	3-2		7	6	Martin	McMichael		61-50	1st	+6.0
8-4	At Fla.	L	1-4		4	5	Hernandez	Holt	Powell	61-51	1st	+6.0
8-5	At Fla.	L	5-6		8	11	Nen	Wagner		61-52	1st	+5.0
8-6	At Phi.	L	4-6		9	8	Stephenson	Garcia	Bottalico	61-53	1st	+5.0
8-7	At Phi.	L	5-6	(11)	9	9	Brewer	Martin		61-54	1st	+4.0
8-8	At N.Y.	L	1-6		3	13	Bohanon	Reynolds		61-55	1st	+4.0
8-9	At N.Y.	W	8-3		11	4	Springer	Rojas		62-55	1st	+5.0
8-10	At N.Y.	W	11-8		14	11	Kile	Reed	Martin	63-55	1st	+6.0
8-11	At N.Y.	W	8-3		11	11	Garcia	Harnisch		64-55	1st	+6.5
8-12	Fla.	W	13-2		16	6	Hampton	Leiter		65-55	1st	+6.5
8-13	Fla.	L	6-8		11	14	Fernandez	Lima	Nen	65-56	1st	+5.5
8-15	Phi.	L	1-5		5	8	Schilling	Holt		65-57	1st	+5.5
8-16	Phi.	L	3-5		5	12	Spradlin	Wagner	Bottalico	65-58	1st	+4.5
8-17	Phi.	W	11-6		12	11	Martin	Gomes	Springer	66-58	1st	+5.5
8-19	Atl.	L	3-4		8	11	Smoltz	Hampton	Wohlers	66-59	1st	+4.0
8-20	Atl.	L	1-3		4	6	Glavine	Reynolds	Wohlers	66-60	1st	+3.0
8-21	Col.	W	10-4		15	8	Holt	Bailey		67-60	1st	+4.0
8-22	Col.	W	9-1		12	7	Kile	Thomson		68-60	1st	+4.0
8-23	Col.	L	3-6		10	14	S. Reed	Hudek	DiPoto	68-61	1st	+3.0
8-24	Col.	W	3-1		4	4	Hampton	Wright		69-61	1st	+3.0
8-26	At Atl.	L	6-7	(11)	13	9	Clontz	Wagner		69-62	1st	+3.0
8-27	At Atl.	W	6-4	(13)	13	9	Hudek	Byrd	Lima	70-62	1st	+4.0
8-28	At Atl.	L	2-4		5	7	Neagle	Kile	Wohlers	70-63	1st	+3.5
8-29	At Chi. (AL)	L	4-5		9	8	Foulke	Hudek	Karchner	70-64	1st	+3.5
8-30	At Chi. (AL)	L	2-9		3	14	Bere	Hampton		70-65	1st	+2.5
8-31	At Chi. (AL)	L	1-3		7	9	Baldwin	Reynolds	Karchner	70-66	1st	+2.5
9-1	Mil.	L	2-3		8	7	Adamson	Holt	Jones	70-67	1st	+2.5
9-2	Mil.	L	2-4		5	5	Villone	Kile	Jones	70-68	1st	+1.5
9-3	Mil.	W	4-0		7	5	Garcia	Karl		71-68	1st	+2.5
9-4	At S.F.	W	14-2		17	7	Hampton	Gardner		72-68	1st	+3.5
9-5	At S.F.	L	1-4		5	9	Hernandez	Reynolds	Beck	72-69	1st	+3.5
9-6	At S.F.	L	3-5		8	5	Tavarez	Wagner	Hernandez	72-70	1st	+2.5
9-7	At S.F.	L	1-5		9	5	Rueter	Kile		72-71	1st	+2.5
9-9	At Col.	W	7-4		11	8	Hampton	Wright	Springer	73-71	1st	+3.5
9-10	At Col.	L	7-9		11	11	Leskanic	Magnante	DiPoto	73-72	1st	+3.5
9-12	L.A.	W	10-3		10	9	Reynolds	Park		74-72	1st	+3.5

Date	Opp.	Res.	Score	(inn.*)	Hits	Opp. hits	Winning pitcher	Losing pitcher	Save	Record	Pos.	GB
9-13	L.A.	W	5-1		7	5	Kile	Candiotti		75-72	1st	+4.5
9-14	L.A.	L	3-4	(10)	6	7	Radinsky	Wagner	Worrell	75-73	1st	+4.5
9-15	S.D.	L	3-4		7	11	Smith	Hampton	Hoffman	75-74	1st	+3.5
9-16	S.D.	W	15-3		16	8	Garcia	Hitchcock		76-74	1st	+3.5
9-17	At Pit.	W	8-4		15	8	Reynolds	Schmidt		77-74	1st	+4.5
9-18	At Pit.	L	3-12		5	12	Cordova	Kile		77-75	1st	+3.5
9-19	At Cin.	L	4-5		8	12	Burba	Holt	Shaw	77-76	1st	+3.5
9-20	At Cin.	W	4-1		10	5	Hampton	Tomko	Wagner	78-76	1st	+3.5
9-21	At Cin.	W	8-3		14	7	Garcia	Morgan		79-76	1st	+3.5
9-22	At Cin.	W	6-3		11	8	Springer	Belinda	Wagner	80-76	1st	+3.5
9-23	Chi.	W	5-3		11	6	Kile	Trachsel	Wagner	81-76	1st	+3.5
9-24	Chi.	L	1-3		8	11	M. Clark	Holt	Adams	81-77	1st	+3.5
9-25	Chi.	W	9-1		8	4	Hampton	Gonzalez		82-77	1st	+4.0
9-26	Pit.	W	2-0		3	6	Garcia	Loaiza	Wagner	83-77	1st	+5.0
9-27	Pit.	W	8-1		12	8	Reynolds	Schmidt		84-77	1st	+6.0
9-28	Pit.	L	4-5	(11)	11	7	Christiansen	Henriquez	Loiselle	84-78	1st	+5.0

Monthly records: April (15-11), May (11-17), June (14-14), July (19-7), August (11-17), September (14-12).
*Innings, if other than nine.

HIGHLIGHTS

High point: The Astros had one of their best months ever when they went 19-7 in July. They began the month tied with Pittsburgh for first place in the division but finished with a 6 ½-game lead and were never caught.

Low point: For just about every Astro but Darryl Kile, May was a horrible month. While Kile went 5-0, the rest of the pitchers were 6-17, and the team fell two games behind Pittsburgh.

Turning point: After a season-worst six-game losing streak, the team's lead in the division dropped from 6 ½ games to 1 ½ on September 2. But No. 5 starter Ramon Garcia stopped the slide with a 4-0, five-hit shutout of Milwaukee. After that, the lead was never threatened.

Most valuable player: Second baseman Craig Biggio. He played brilliantly throughout the season, stole 47 bases, scored a league-high 146 runs and drove in 81 as a leadoff batter. He also became the first major leaguer not to ground into a double play in a 162-game season, and he won his fourth consecutive Gold Glove.

Most valuable pitcher: Kile. He won 19 games (10 in a row at one point), pitched 255⅔ innings and struck out 205. He lasted at least seven innings in 31 of his 34 starts.

Most improved player: Third baseman Bill Spiers. After batting .252 in 1996, he hit a career-best .320 in '97 with 27 doubles and a .438 on-base percentage. He hit .449 with runners in scoring position.

Most pleasant surprise: Mike Magnante. He was released by Kansas City at the end of the 1996 season and failed to make the Astros' roster in spring training, but the lefthander, 31, soon became the club's best middle reliever, going 3-1 with a 2.27 ERA in 40 appearances.

Biggest disappointment: Right fielder Derek Bell. After driving in 86 runs in 1995 and 113 in 1996, he slipped to 71 RBIs in 1997.

Key injuries: Opening-day starter Shane Reynolds sustained a knee injury in May and never fully recovered. Bell missed four weeks after surgery in May to remove a hematoma from his left calf. Shortstop Tim Bogar was having a career year before suf-

fering a broken left forearm on September 4. Third baseman Sean Berry made a slow recovery from rotator cuff surgery in October 1996, and he also was limited by elbow, finger, groin and calf injuries.

Notable: Jeff Bagwell established club records for homers (43), RBIs (135), total bases (335) and extra-base hits (85) in a season. He also became the first 30-30 player who played exclusively at first base. . . . Reliever Billy Wagner averaged 14.4 strikeouts per nine innings, the most ever for a pitcher with a minimum 50 innings pitched. . . . Biggio's 146 runs were the most by an N.L. player in 65 years. . . . Spiers reached base safely in 13 consecutive plate appearances (June 3-11)—one short of the N.L. record set by Pedro Guerrero in 1985. . . . Luis Gonzalez hit in 23 consecutive games (May 26-June 20), tying the club record set by Art Howe in 1981. It was the league's longest hitting streak in 1997. . . . The Astros clinched the N.L. Central on September 25, 11 years to the day after Mike Scott clinched the N.L. West for the team with a no-hit victory over the Giants in 1986.

—ALAN TRUEX

RECORDS

1997 regular-season record: 84-78 (1st in N.L. Central); 46-35 at home; 38-43 on road; 27-28 vs. East; 35-28 vs. Central; 22-22 vs. West; 14-27 vs. lefthanded starters; 70-51 vs. righthanded starters; 26-32 on grass; 58-46 on turf; 27-23 in daytime; 57-55 at night; 19-25 in one-run games; 8-11 in extra-inning games; 0-0-0 in doubleheaders.

Team record past five years: 393-352 (.528, ranks 4th in league in that span).

TEAM LEADERS

Batting average: Craig Biggio (.309).
At-bats: Craig Biggio (619).
Runs: Craig Biggio (146).
Hits: Craig Biggio (191).
Total bases: Jeff Bagwell (335).
Doubles: Jeff Bagwell (40).

Triples: Craig Biggio (8).
Home runs: Jeff Bagwell (43).
Runs batted in: Jeff Bagwell (135).
Stolen bases: Craig Biggio (47).
Slugging percentage: Jeff Bagwell (.592).
On-base percentage: Jeff Bagwell (.425).
Wins: Darryl Kile (19).
Earned-run average: Darryl Kile (2.57).
Complete games: Mike Hampton (7).
Shutouts: Darryl Kile (4).
Saves: Billy Wagner (23).
Innings pitched: Darryl Kile (255.2).
Strikeouts: Darryl Kile (205).

GAMES BY POSITION

Catcher: Brad Ausmus 129, Tony Eusebio 43, Tony Pena 8, Randy Knorr 3.
First base: Jeff Bagwell 159, Bill Spiers 8, J.R. Phillips 3, Randy Knorr 2, Tim Bogar 1, Luis Gonzalez 1.
Second base: Craig Biggio 160, Ricky Gutierrez 9, Bill Spiers 4, Russ Johnson 3, Luis Rivera 1.
Third base: Sean Berry 85, Bill Spiers 84, Ricky Gutierrez 22, Tim Bogar 14, Russ Johnson 14.
Shortstop: Tim Bogar 80, Ricky Gutierrez 64, Pat Listach 31, Bill Spiers 28, Luis Rivera 6.
Outfield: Luis Gonzalez 146, Derek Bell 125, Thomas Howard 62, James Mouton 61, Chuck Carr 59, Bob Abreu 53, Richard Hidalgo 19, Ray Montgomery 18, Pat Listach 6, J.R. Phillips 3, Ken Ramos 2.
Designated hitter: Sean Berry 3, Jeff Bagwell 1, Derek Bell 1, Craig Biggio 1.

TOP DRAFT CHOICES

1. **Lance Berkman,** 1B-OF, Rice University.
2. **Camron Hahn,** C, Male H.S., Louisville.
3. **Scott Barrett,** LHP, Mayde Creek H.S., Houston.
4. **Eric Byrnes,** OF, UCLA.
5. **Derek Stanford,** RHP, Temple (Tex.) H.S.
6. **Joe Messman,** RHP, Oregon State Univ.
7. **Rob Bystrowski,** OF, Sacramento C.C.
8. **Ryan Dunn,** OF, Texas Christian Univ.
9. **Don Thomas,** LHP, Kennesaw State (Ga.) College.
10. **Peter Fredericks,** RHP, Saguaro H.S., Scottsdale, Ariz.

LOS ANGELES DODGERS
NATIONAL LEAGUE WEST DIVISION

Dodgers Schedule

Home games shaded. *—All-Star Game at Coors Field (Colorado). D—Day game (any game starting before 5 p.m.).

March

SUN	MON	TUE	WED	THU	FRI	SAT
		31 D STL				

April

SUN	MON	TUE	WED	THU	FRI	SAT
			1	2 D STL	3 CIN	4 D CIN
5 D CIN	6	7 ARZ	8 D ARZ	9 ARZ	10 HOU	11 HOU
12 HOU	13 HOU	14 COL	15 COL	16	17 D CUB	18 D CUB
19 CUB	20 D	21 MIL	22 MIL	23 D MIL	24 CUB	25 CUB
26 CUB	27 MIL	28 MIL	29	30 PIT		

May

SUN	MON	TUE	WED	THU	FRI	SAT
					1 PIT	2 PIT
3 D PIT	4 ATL	5 ATL	6 D ATL	7 FLA	8 FLA	9 FLA
10 FLA	11 PHI	12 PHI	13 PHI	14 PHI	15 MON	16 MON
17 MON	18	19 CUB	20 D CUB	21 D ARZ	22 ARZ	23 ARZ
24 D ARZ	25 D HOU	26 HOU	27 HOU	28 CIN	29 CIN	30 CIN
31 D CIN						

June

SUN	MON	TUE	WED	THU	FRI	SAT
	1	2 STL	3 STL	4 STL	5 D SEA	6 SEA
7 SEA	8 D OAK	9 OAK	10 OAK	11	12 COL	13 COL
14 D COL	15	16 SD	17 SD	18 SD	19 COL	20 COL
21 COL	22 ANA	23 ANA	24 D ANA	25 ANA	26 PIT	27 PIT
28 PIT	29	30 TEX				

July

SUN	MON	TUE	WED	THU	FRI	SAT
			1 TEX	2 TEX	3 SF	4 D SF
5 D SF	6	7	* 8	9 D SD	10 SD	11 SD
12 D SD	13 SF	14 SF	15 D SF	16 STL	17 STL	18 STL
19 D STL	20 CIN	21 CIN	22 HOU	23 HOU	24 ARZ	25 D ARZ
26 ARZ	27	28 PHI	29 PHI	30 PHI	31 NYM	

August

SUN	MON	TUE	WED	THU	FRI	SAT
						1 NYM
2 D NYM	3 D NYM	4 MON	5 MON	6 MON	7 D PIT	8 PIT
9 PIT	10	11 D FLA	12 FLA	13 FLA	14 ATL	15 ATL
16 ATL	17	18 PIT	19 PIT	20 FLA	21 FLA	22 ATL
23 ATL	24 D MON	25 MON	26 MON	27 MON	28 NYM	29 NYM
30 NYM	31					

September

SUN	MON	TUE	WED	THU	FRI	SAT
		1 PHI	2 PHI	3	4 SF	5 SF
6 SF	7 D ARZ	8 ARZ	9 ARZ	10 D SD	11 SD	12 SD
13 SD	14 D COL	15 COL	16 COL	17	18 SF	19 D SF
20 SF	21	22 SD	23 SD	24 MIL	25 MIL	26 MIL
27 D MIL						

1998 SEASON
CLUB DIRECTORY

Board of directors
Peter O'Malley
Roland Seidler
Mrs. Roland (Terry) Seidler

President
Peter O'Malley

Executive vice president
Fred Claire

Vice president, communications
Tom Hawkins

Executive vice president
Bob Graziano

Vice president, marketing
Barry Stockhamer

Director, stadium operations
Doug Duennes

Vice president, treasurer
Roland Seidler

Vice president, Campo Las Palmas
Ralph Avila

Assistant secretary and general counsel
Santiago Fernandez

Director, accounting and finance
Bill Foltz

Director, advertising and special events
Paul Kalil

Director, broadcasting and publications
Brent Shyer

Director, community relations
Don Newcombe

Director, community affairs
Monique Brandon

Dir., management information services
Mike Mularky

Vice president, minor league operations
Charlie Blaney

Director, scouting
Terry Reynolds

Director, publicity
Derrick Hall

Assistant director, publicity
Shaun Rachau

Traveling secretary
Bill DeLury

Director, ticket operations
Debra Duncan

Club physicians
Dr. Frank W. Jobe
Dr. Michael F. Mellman

Scouts
Eleodoro Arias, Eddie Bane, Bill Barkley, John Barr, Rick Birmingham, Gib Bodet, Flores Bolivar, Mike Brito, Jim Chapman, Bob Darwin, Eddie Fajardo Rodriguez, Joe Ferrone, Rafael Gonzalez, Carl Greene, Michael Hankins, Dennis Haren, Hank Jones, Lon Joyce, John Keenan, Don LeJohn, Carl Lowenstine, Marty Maier, Teodoro Mata, Ed Mathes, Dale McReynolds, Tommy Mixon, Alberto Osorio, Deni Pacini, Camilo Pasqual, Pablo Peguero, Claude Pelletier, Bill Pleis, Silvano Quesada, Ross Sapp, Mark Sheehy, Bill Singer, Jim Stoeckel, Tom Thomas, Glen Van Proyen

Coordinator of professional scouting
Gary Sutherland

MINOR LEAGUE AFFILIATES

Class	Team	League	Manager
AAA	Albuquerque	Pacific Coast	Glenn Hoffman
AA	San Antonio	Texas	Ron Roenicke
A	San Bernardino	California	Mickey Hatcher
A	Vero Beach	Florida State	John Shoemaker
A	Yakima	Northwest	Tony Harris
Rookie	Great Falls	Pioneer	Dino Ebel

BROADCAST INFORMATION

Radio: KXTA-AM (1150); KWKW-AM (1330, Spanish language).
TV: KTLA-TV (Channel 5); Fox Sports West 2.

SPRING TRAINING

Ballpark (city): Holman Stadium (Vero Beach, Fla.).
Ticket information: 561-569-6858.

SPRING TRAINING ROSTER

Manager—Bill Russell (18).
Coaches—Joe Amalfitano (8), Mark Cresse (58), Glenn Gregson, Mike Scioscia (14), Reggie Smith (9).

No.	PITCHERS	B/T	Ht./Wt.	Born	1997 clubs
	Brunson, Will	L/L	6-6/185	3-20-70	Albuquerque, San Antonio
55	Bruske, Jim	R/R	6-1/185	10-7-64	Las Vegas, San Diego
	Deschenes, Marc	R/R	6-0/175	1-6-73	Columbus, Kinston
37	Dreifort, Darren	R/R	6-2/205	5-3-72	Los Angeles, Albuquerque
	Flores, Ignacio	R/R	6-2/180	5-8-75	San Antonio
	Gubicza, Mark	R/R	6-5/230	8-14-62	Anaheim, Lake Elsinore
44	Guthrie, Mark	R/L	6-4/207	9-22-65	Los Angeles
52	Hall, Darren	R/R	6-3/205	7-14-64	Los Angeles
	Judd, Michael	R/R	6-1/200	6-30-75	Vero Beach, San Antonio, Los Angeles
	Lankford, Frank	R/R	6-2/190	2-26-71	Norwich, Columbus
48	Martinez, Ramon J.	B/R	6-4/186	3-22-68	Los Angeles
16	Nomo, Hideo	R/R	6-2/210	8-31-68	Los Angeles
13	Osuna, Antonio	R/R	5-11/160	4-12-73	Albuquerque, Los Angeles
61	Park, Chan Ho	R/R	6-2/195	6-30-73	Los Angeles
36	Radinsky, Scott	L/L	6-3/204	3-3-68	Los Angeles
57	Reyes, Dennis	L/L	6-3/245	4-19-77	San Antonio, Albuquerque, Los Angeles
59	Valdes, Ismael	R/R	6-3/207	8-21-73	Los Angeles

No.	CATCHERS	B/T	Ht./Wt.	Born	1997 clubs
54	Blanco, Henry	R/R	5-11/168	8-29-71	Albuquerque, Los Angeles
	LoDuca, Paul	R/R	5-10/185	4-12-72	San Antonio
	Pena, Angel	R/R	5-10/225	2-16-75	San Bernardino
31	Piazza, Mike	R/R	6-3/215	9-4-68	Los Angeles
15	Prince, Tom	R/R	5-11/202	8-13-64	Los Angeles

No.	INFIELDERS	B/T	Ht./Wt.	Born	1997 clubs
60	Castro, Juan	R/R	5-10/163	6-20-72	Albuquerque, Los Angeles
41	Cromer, Tripp	R/R	6-2/165	11-21-67	Albuquerque, Los Angeles
30	Guerrero, Wilton	R/R	5-11/145	10-24-74	Los Angeles, Albuquerque
56	Ingram, Garey	R/R	5-11/185	7-25-70	San Antonio, Los Angeles
23	Karros, Eric	R/R	6-4/222	11-4-67	Los Angeles
66	Konerko, Paul	R/R	6-3/205	3-5-76	Albuquerque, Los Angeles
	Metcalfe, Mike	R/R	5-10/175	1-2-73	San Bernardino
	Richardson, Brian	R/R	6-2/198	8-31-75	San Antonio
51	Riggs, Adam	R/R	6-0/194	10-4-72	Albuquerque, Los Angeles
10	Vizcaino, Jose	B/R	6-1/180	3-26-68	San Francisco
26	Young, Eric	R/R	5-9/170	5-18-67	Colorado, Los Angeles
27	Zeile, Todd	R/R	6-1/200	9-9-65	Los Angeles

No.	OUTFIELDERS	B/T	Ht./Wt.	Born	1997 clubs
21	Ashley, Billy	R/R	6-7/235	7-11-70	Los Angeles
	Cedeno, Roger	B/R	6-1/165	8-16-74	Los Angeles, Albuquerque
	Gibbs, Kevin	B/R	6-2/185	4-3-74	San Antonio
28	Hollandsworth, Todd	L/L	6-2/193	4-20-73	Los Angeles, Albuquerque, San Bernardino
	Hubbard, Trenidad	R/R	5-8/183	5-11-66	Buffalo, Cleveland
	Luke, Matt	L/L	6-5/220	2-26-71	Columbus
43	Mondesi, Raul	R/R	5-11/212	3-12-71	Los Angeles

BALLPARK INFORMATION

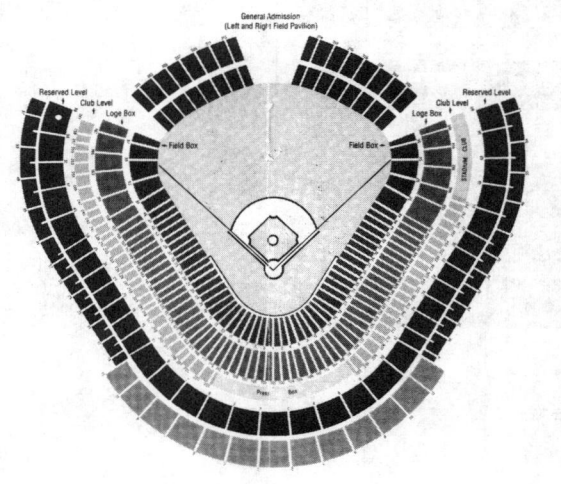

Ballpark (capacity, surface)
Dodger Stadium (56,000, grass)
Address
1000 Elysian Park Ave.
Los Angeles, CA 90012
Business phone
213-224-1500
Ticket information
213-224-1448
Ticket prices
$21 (preferred box-field)
$20 (preferred box-loge)
$18 (middle box-field)
$15 (middle box-loge)
$14 (box seats-field)
$12 (box seats-loge)
$12 (preferred reserved)
$8 (reserved)
$6 (top deck and pavilion)
$3 (g.a., youth 12 and under)
Field dimensions (from home plate)
To left field at foul line, 330 feet
To center field, 395 feet
To right field at foul line, 330 feet
First game played
April 10, 1962 (Reds 6, Dodgers 3)

1998 SEASON Los Angeles Dodgers

Date	Opp.	Res.	Score	(inn.*)	Hits	Opp. hits	Winning pitcher	Losing pitcher	Save	Record	Pos.	GB
4-1	Phi.	L	0-3		2	7	Schilling	Martinez	Bottalico	0-1	T2nd	1.0
4-2	Phi.	W	5-1		8	6	Nomo	Maduro	Dreifort	1-1	2nd	1.0
4-3	Phi.	W	2-1		7	5	Valdes	Leiter	Worrell	2-1	T1st	....
4-4	Pit.	W	5-3		8	5	Candiotti	Wainhouse	Worrell	3-1	T1st	....
4-5	Pit.	L	1-3		6	9	Cordova	Park	Ericks	3-2	T3rd	1.0
4-6	Pit.	W	6-3		11	8	Dreifort	Rincon	Worrell	4-2	T1st	....
4-7	N.Y.	W	3-2	(15)	12	7	Astacio	Crawford		5-2	T1st	....
4-8	N.Y.	L	3-5		5	9	Jones	Valdes	McMichael	5-3	T2nd	0.5
4-9	N.Y.	W	3-2	(14)	6	4	Candiotti	Bohanon		6-3	2nd	0.5
4-11	At Pit.	W	7-1		8	8	Martinez	Cordova		7-3	2nd	....
4-13	At Pit.	W	14-5		18	9	Nomo	Schmidt		8-3	1st	+0.5
4-15	At N.Y.	L	0-5		8	10	Reynoso	Valdes	Borland	8-4	3rd	1.0
4-16	At N.Y.	W	5-2		11	1	Astacio	Reed	Worrell	9-4	3rd	1.0
4-18	Hou.	W	5-3		12	9	Martinez	Hampton	Worrell	10-4	T2nd	1.0
4-19	Hou.	L	1-2		8	5	Kile	Nomo	Wagner	10-5	T2nd	2.0
4-20	Hou.	L	1-3		6	6	Holt	Candiotti	Hudek	10-6	3rd	3.0
4-22	St.L.	L	4-6		10	11	Frascatore	Worrell	Eckersley	10-7	3rd	3.0
4-23	St.L.	W	2-1		8	3	Guthrie	Petkovsek	Worrell	11-7	3rd	3.0
4-25	At Fla.	L	2-4		4	5	Leiter	Nomo	Nen	11-8	3rd	3.0
4-26	At Fla.	L	3-8		9	12	Fernandez	Valdes		11-9	3rd	4.0
4-27	At Fla.	L	3-4		9	7	Hutton	Hall		11-10	3rd	5.0
4-28	At Atl.	L	0-14		5	18	Glavine	Martinez		11-11	3rd	5.0
4-29	At Atl.	W	6-2		13	7	Park	Wade		12-11	3rd	4.0
4-30	At Phi.	W	7-5		13	11	Nomo	Leiter	Worrell	13-11	3rd	4.0
5-1	At Phi.	W	5-0		4	9	Astacio	Schilling		14-11	3rd	4.0
5-2	Chi.	W	8-7	(10)	11	12	Candiotti	Patterson		15-11	3rd	3.0
5-3	Chi.	L	1-2		8	5	Mulholland	Valdes	Adams	15-12	3rd	4.0
5-4	Chi.	W	5-2		12	5	Park	Trachsel	Worrell	16-12	3rd	4.0
5-5	Cin.	W	3-1		9	5	Nomo	Carrasco	Worrell	17-12	3rd	3.0
5-6	Cin.	L	2-3	(11)	9	8	Brantley	Guthrie	Remlinger	17-13	3rd	4.0
5-7	Cin.	W	4-2		5	7	Martinez	Schourek	Worrell	18-13	3rd	3.0
5-9	Mon.	W	5-1		8	7	Radinsky	Urbina		19-13	T2nd	1.5
5-10	Mon.	W	2-1		6	5	Radinsky	Veres		20-13	T2nd	0.5
5-11	Mon.	L	3-6	(10)	9	10	Daal	Candiotti	Valdes	20-14	3rd	1.0
5-13	At Chi.	L	1-2		7	6	Wendell	Astacio	Rojas	20-15	3rd	2.0
5-14	At Chi.	W	6-4		12	7	Osuna	Rojas	Worrell	21-15	3rd	1.0
5-15	At Cin.	W	2-1		6	5	Valdes	Smiley	Worrell	22-15	2nd	1.0
5-16	At Cin.	L	2-4		6	9	Morgan	Park	Shaw	22-16	3rd	1.0
5-17	At Mon.	W	8-3		11	6	Nomo	Perez		23-16	2nd	1.0
5-18	At Mon.	L	4-7		8	14	Martinez	Astacio	Urbina	23-17	2nd	1.0
5-19	At Mon.	L	1-2		7	7	Juden	Martinez	Urbina	23-18	2nd	1.0
5-20	At S.D.	L	3-7		8	11	Hitchcock	Valdes		23-19	2nd	2.0
5-21	At S.D.	L	4-5	(11)	9	6	Hoffman	Osuna		23-20	3rd	2.0
5-22	At S.D.	L	1-4		7	10	Hamilton	Nomo	Bochtler	23-21	3rd	3.0
5-23	Atl.	L	2-4		7	8	Smoltz	Astacio	Wohlers	23-22	3rd	4.0
5-24	Atl.	W	10-3		14	3	Martinez	Glavine		24-22	3rd	3.0
5-25	Atl.	W	2-0		6	3	Valdes	Neagle	Worrell	25-22	3rd	2.0
5-26	Fla.	W	5-3		8	8	Park	Helling	Worrell	26-22	3rd	2.0
5-27	Fla.	L	5-8		7	17	Leiter	Nomo	Nen	26-23	3rd	3.0
5-29	At St.L.	L	2-4		10	7	Morris	Astacio	Eckersley	26-24	3rd	4.0
5-30	At St.L.	L	1-2		7	6	Mathews	Hall		26-25	3rd	4.0
5-31	At St.L.	L	3-6		6	11	Stottlemyre	Valdes	Eckersley	26-26	3rd	5.0
6-1	At St.L.	W	6-1		9	11	Park	Al. Benes		27-26	3rd	4.0
6-2	At Hou.	L	0-2		6	6	Wall	Nomo	Lima	27-27	3rd	4.0
6-3	At Hou.	L	3-4	(10)	10	7	Magnante	Radinsky		27-28	3rd	5.0
6-4	S.F.	W	5-1		8	6	Martinez	Foulke		28-28	3rd	4.0
6-5	S.F.	L	4-5		6	7	VanLandingham	Valdes	Beck	28-29	3rd	5.0
6-6	St.L.	L	1-3		7	8	Al. Benes	Park	Eckersley	28-30	3rd	5.0
6-7	St.L.	W	5-2		14	6	Nomo	Jackson		29-30	3rd	4.0
6-8	St.L.	L	3-9		13	13	Morris	Astacio		29-31	3rd	5.0
6-9	Hou.	W	8-3		8	11	Martinez	Holt		30-31	3rd	5.0
6-10	Hou.	L	3-6		9	13	Magnante	Osuna	Wagner	30-32	3rd	5.0
6-11	Hou.	W	10-5		12	10	Park	Hampton		31-32	3rd	4.0
6-12	At Oak.	L	4-5		10	6	Telgheder	Nomo	Taylor	31-33	3rd	5.0
6-13	At Oak.	W	6-4		11	8	Hall	Small	Worrell	32-33	3rd	4.0
6-14	At Sea.	L	8-9		11	11	Ayala	Osuna		32-34	3rd	5.0
6-15	At Sea.	L	2-8		6	10	Moyer	Valdes	Sanders	32-35	3rd	6.0
6-17	Ana.	W	4-3		10	6	Hall	Percival		33-35	3rd	6.0
6-18	Ana.	W	7-5		7	7	Dreifort	Holtz	Worrell	34-35	3rd	6.0
6-19	At S.F.	L	2-5		4	5	Estes	Astacio		34-36	3rd	7.0
6-20	At S.F.	W	11-7	(10)	13	11	Worrell	Henry		35-36	3rd	6.0

Date	Opp.	Res.	Score	(inn.*)	Hits	Opp. hits	Winning pitcher	Losing pitcher	Save	Record	Pos.	GB
6-21	At S.F.	W	11-0		15	5	Candiotti	VanLandingham		36-36	3rd	5.0
6-22	At S.F.	L	2-4		7	5	Rueter	Park	Beck	36-37	3rd	6.0
6-23	Col.	W	5-3		8	7	Nomo	Ritz	Hall	37-37	3rd	5.0
6-24	Col.	L	2-6		6	7	Holmes	Astacio		37-38	3rd	6.0
6-25	Col.	W	2-0		7	4	Valdes	Burke	Hall	38-38	3rd	6.0
6-26	S.D.	L	7-9		11	9	Bergman	Guthrie	Hoffman	38-39	3rd	6.0
6-27	S.D.	L	5-7		12	12	Hamilton	Park	Hoffman	38-40	3rd	7.0
6-28	S.D.	L	3-9		8	13	Smith	Nomo		38-41	3rd	7.0
6-29	S.D.	W	10-4		12	8	Astacio	Jackson		39-41	3rd	7.0
6-30	Tex.	L	2-3		6	9	Witt	Valdes	Wetteland	39-42	3rd	8.0
7-1	Tex.	W	6-3		12	10	Dreifort	Santana	Worrell	40-42	3rd	7.0
7-2	At Ana.	W	5-4		14	10	Radinsky	Percival	Worrell	41-42	3rd	6.0
7-3	At Ana.	W	8-2		11	6	Nomo	Watson		42-42	3rd	6.0
7-4	At S.D.	W	5-2		12	8	Astacio	Jackson	Worrell	43-42	2nd	6.0
7-5	At S.D.	W	7-3		12	8	Valdes	Ashby		44-42	2nd	6.0
7-6	At S.D.	W	5-2		8	6	Candiotti	Bergman	Worrell	45-42	2nd	6.0
7-10	S.F.	W	11-0		16	3	Park	Rueter		46-42	2nd	5.0
7-11	S.F.	W	6-2		10	11	Nomo	Foulke	Worrell	47-42	2nd	4.0
7-12	S.F.	L	5-8		9	15	Tavarez	Worrell		47-43	2nd	5.0
7-13	S.F.	W	9-3		13	6	Reyes	Estes		48-43	2nd	4.0
7-14	At Col.	W	14-12	(10)	22	18	Radinsky	S. Reed	Worrell	49-43	2nd	3.0
7-15	At Col.	W	6-5		12	11	Park	Bailey	Worrell	50-43	2nd	3.0
7-16	At Fla.	L	1-5		1	9	Brown	Nomo		50-44	2nd	3.0
7-17	At Fla.	L	7-8		14	14	Leiter	Candiotti	Nen	50-45	2nd	4.0
7-18	At Atl.	L	1-4		7	9	Neagle	Reyes	Wohlers	50-46	2nd	4.0
7-19	At Atl.	W	4-1		8	4	Astacio	Millwood	Radinsky	51-46	2nd	3.0
7-20	At Atl.	W	8-3		11	7	Park	Smoltz		52-46	2nd	3.0
7-21	At Atl.	L	4-5	(10)	6	14	Embree	Dreifort		52-47	2nd	3.0
7-22	N.Y.	W	8-3		11	5	Candiotti	Clark		53-47	2nd	3.0
7-23	N.Y.	L	1-2		4	9	Bohanon	Reyes	J. Franco	53-48	2nd	4.0
7-24	N.Y.	L	1-3		4	10	Reed	Guthrie	J. Franco	53-49	2nd	4.0
7-25	Phi.	W	8-1		14	6	Park	Stephenson		54-49	2nd	3.0
7-26	Phi.	W	4-1		8	4	Dreifort	Schilling	Worrell	55-49	2nd	2.0
7-27	Phi.	W	7-1		10	8	Candiotti	Beech		56-49	2nd	1.5
7-28	Pit.	W	4-2		9	10	Valdes	Lieber	Worrell	57-49	2nd	1.0
7-29	Pit.	W	3-1		8	7	Astacio	Cooke	Worrell	58-49	2nd	1.0
7-31	At Chi.	W	4-1		7	4	Park	Mulholland	Worrell	59-49	T1st	....
8-1	At Chi.	W	13-9		20	14	Nomo	Gonzalez		60-49	T1st	....
8-2	At Chi.	L	1-5		10	11	Tapani	Candiotti		60-50	T1st	....
8-3	At Chi.	L	3-4	(12)	9	11	Tatis	Worrell		60-51	2nd	1.0
8-5	At Mon.	W	5-4	(10)	9	11	Worrell	Urbina		61-51	2nd	1.5
8-6	At Mon.	L	3-7		8	10	Hermanson	Park		61-52	2nd	2.5
8-7	At Mon.	W	9-4		14	13	Nomo	Bullinger		62-52	2nd	1.5
8-8	At Cin.	W	10-5		15	11	Candiotti	Morgan	Dreifort	63-52	2nd	1.5
8-9	At Cin.	L	2-3		6	7	White	Valdes	Shaw	63-53	2nd	1.5
8-10	At Cin.	L	1-8		4	10	Remlinger	Astacio		63-54	2nd	2.5
8-11	Chi.	W	2-1		7	4	Park	Batista		64-54	2nd	1.5
8-12	Chi.	L	2-4		10	9	M. Clark	Nomo	Adams	64-55	2nd	2.5
8-13	Mon.	W	3-1		9	4	Candiotti	Perez	Worrell	65-55	2nd	1.5
8-14	Mon.	W	1-0		5	4	Valdes	Martinez	Radinsky	66-55	2nd	1.5
8-15	Cin.	L	3-5		7	7	Remlinger	Astacio	Shaw	66-56	2nd	2.5
8-16	Cin.	W	5-3		4	7	Park	Mercker	Worrell	67-56	2nd	1.5
8-17	Cin.	L	0-5		7	10	Tomko	Nomo		67-57	2nd	2.5
8-19	At N.Y.	W	4-2		9	9	Valdes	Bohanon	Worrell	68-57	2nd	2.0
8-21†	At N.Y.	L	1-3		5	6	Crawford	Candiotti	J. Franco	68-58		
8-21‡	At N.Y.	W	4-3		7	7	Park	Reed	Worrell	69-58	2nd	2.0
8-22	At Phi.	W	5-3		7	7	Osuna	Bottalico	Worrell	70-58	2nd	1.0
8-23	At Phi.	W	4-3		9	9	Nomo	Green	Worrell	71-58	T1st	....
8-24	At Phi.	W	5-1		8	6	Valdes	Beech		72-58	1st	+1.0
8-25†	At Pit.	W	8-2		13	5	Martinez	Schmidt	Guthrie	73-58		
8-25‡	At Pit.	L	3-4		8	6	Wilkins	Worrell		73-59	1st	+0.5
8-26	At Pit.	W	6-4		13	6	Dreifort	Rincon		74-59	1st	+0.5
8-27	At Pit.	W	9-5		18	10	Reyes	Cooke		75-59	1st	+1.5
8-28	Oak.	W	7-1		10	4	Nomo	Ludwick		76-59	1st	+2.5
8-29	Oak.	W	5-4	(10)	8	8	Osuna	Mathews		77-59	1st	+2.5
8-30	Sea.	W	11-2		14	5	Martinez	Wolcott	Dreifort	78-59	1st	+2.5
8-31	Sea.	L	1-3	(10)	3	6	Timlin	Worrell	Ayala	78-60	1st	+2.5
9-2	At Tex.	L	12-13		18	20	Heredia	Worrell		78-61	1st	+1.5
9-3	At Tex.	L	2-5		8	11	Patterson	Dreifort	Wetteland	78-62	1st	+1.5
9-5	Fla.	W	7-4		10	6	Martinez	Fernandez	Worrell	79-62	1st	+2.0
9-6	Fla.	W	9-5		12	10	Hall	Miller		80-62	1st	+2.0
9-7	Fla.	W	9-5		12	6	Candiotti	Saunders		81-62	1st	+2.0
9-8	Fla.	L	4-8		15	9	Brown	Nomo		81-63	1st	+1.5
9-9	Atl.	L	3-4		6	9	Smoltz	Valdes	Wohlers	81-64	1st	+1.5
9-10	Atl.	L	0-7		4	8	Glavine	Martinez		81-65	1st	+0.5

Date	Opp.	Res.	Score	(inn.*)	Hits	Opp. hits	Winning pitcher	Losing pitcher	Save	Record	Pos.	GB
9-12	At Hou.	L	3-10		9	10	Reynolds	Park		81-66	2nd	1.0
9-13	At Hou.	L	1-5		5	7	Kile	Candiotti		81-67	2nd	1.0
9-14	At Hou.	W	4-3	(10)	7	6	Radinsky	Wagner	Worrell	82-67	T1st	....
9-15	At St.L.	W	7-6	(15)	11	12	Harkey	Raggio	Dreifort	83-67	1st	+1.0
9-16	At St.L.	W	7-6		11	8	Gorecki	Eckersley	Radinsky	84-67	1st	+2.0
9-17	At S.F.	L	1-2		4	3	Rueter	Park	Hernandez	84-68	1st	+1.0
9-18	At S.F.	L	5-6	(12)	15	12	Beck	Guthrie		84-69	T1st	....
9-19	Col.	L	4-6		11	7	Astacio	Nomo	DiPoto	84-70	2nd	1.0
9-20	Col.	L	1-2		9	6	Wright	Osuna	DiPoto	84-71	2nd	1.0
9-21	Col.	L	5-10		8	11	Castillo	Martinez		84-72	2nd	2.0
9-23	S.D.	W	6-2		12	7	Park	Menhart		85-72	2nd	1.5
9-24	S.D.	L	1-4		5	9	Hamilton	Candiotti	Hoffman	85-73	2nd	2.5
9-25	At Col.	W	9-5		13	7	Nomo	Astacio		86-73	2nd	2.0
9-26	At Col.	W	10-4		15	7	Valdes	Wright		87-73	2nd	2.0
9-27	At Col.	W	6-1		8	7	Martinez	Castillo		88-73	2nd	2.0
9-28	At Col.	L	9-13		11	18	DeJean	Reyes		88-74	2nd	2.0

Monthly records: April (13-11), May (13-15), June (13-16), July (20-7), August (19-11), September (10-14).
*Innings, if other than nine. †First game of doubleheader. ‡Second game of doubleheader.

HIGHLIGHTS

High point: When the Dodgers concluded a 20-7 month of July—one win shy of the best month in club history—to finally catch the Giants in the standings after chasing them for 108 days. The Dodgers began the month eight games back.

Low point: September 18 in San Francisco. With a chance to go two games up on the Giants with nine to play, the Dodgers failed to score—despite having the bases loaded and nobody out in the 10th inning. The Giants won on Brian Johnson's 12th-inning homer, handing the Dodgers their second loss of a five-game losing streak from which they never recovered.

Turning point: The collapse of the bullpen in late August and early September. That collapse was epitomized September 2 when the bullpen gave up six runs in the ninth inning in Texas, allowing the Rangers to rally for a 13-12 victory.

Most valuable player: No contest. Catcher Mike Piazza had career bests in average (.362), home runs (40) and RBIs (124), and a solid year behind the plate.

Most valuable pitcher: A surprise. Struggling to win the fifth spot in the rotation in the spring, righthander Chan Ho Park went on to win 14 games (tying Hideo Nomo for team-high honors) while losing eight with a 3.38 ERA. Down the stretch, Park was the stopper.

Most improved player: After a shaky start, both at bat and in the field, Todd Zeile came on strong to give the Dodgers their best power-hitting third baseman since Pedro Guerrero played the position in 1983. Zeile had a career high in homers with 31 and drove in 90.

Most pleasant surprise: Tripp Cromer, considered a journeyman backup, surprised the Dodgers by temporarily winning the second base job with a .291 average, surprising power and smooth fielding. But an elbow injury ended his season in July.

Biggest disappointment: Touted as yet another Rookie-of-the-Year candidate in the spring, second baseman Wilton Guerrero wound up the season on the bench because of bonehead baserunning and an inability to effectively turn the double play. Todd Worrell and Todd Hollandsworth also deserve strong consideration in this category.

Key injuries: The most crucial was suffered by ace righthander Ramon Martinez, who missed two months because of a torn rotator cuff in his throwing shoulder. Cromer's season ended in July because of a strained right elbow. Center fielder Roger Cedeno's season ended in August because of a fractured toe. Center fielder Brett Butler was in and out of the lineup because of shoulder problems. Left fielder Todd Hollandsworth missed large chunks of playing time because of both knee and elbow injuries.

Notable: For the second time in Dodger history, the club had four players hit 30 or more home runs: Piazza (40), Zeile (31), Eric Karros (31), and Raul Mondesi (30). Mondesi also became the first 30-30 Dodger, reaching that mark in both home runs and stolen bases (32).

—STEVE SPRINGER

RECORDS

1997 regular-season record: 88-74 (2nd in N.L. West); 47-34 at home; 41-40 on road; 32-23 vs. East; 29-26 vs. Central; 27-25 vs. West; 26-25 vs. lefthanded starters; 62-49 vs. righthanded starters; 72-61 on grass; 16-13 on turf; 27-20 in daytime; 61-54 at night; 19-24 in one-run games; 9-8 in extra-inning games; 0-0-2 in doubleheaders.

Team record past five years: 395-349 (.531, ranks 3rd in league in that span).

TEAM LEADERS

Batting average: Mike Piazza (.362).
At-bats: Eric Karros (628).
Runs: Mike Piazza (104).
Hits: Mike Piazza (201).
Total bases: Mike Piazza (355).
Doubles: Raul Mondesi (42).
Triples: Wilton Guerrero (9).
Home runs: Mike Piazza (40).
Runs batted in: Mike Piazza (124).
Stolen bases: Raul Mondesi (32).
Slugging percentage: Mike Piazza (.638).

On-base percentage: Mike Piazza (.431).
Wins: Hideo Nomo, Chan Ho Park (14).
Earned-run average: Ismael Valdes (2.65).
Complete games: Pedro Astacio, Chan Ho Park (2).
Shutouts: Pedro Astacio (1).
Saves: Todd Worrell (35).
Innings pitched: Hideo Nomo (207.1).
Strikeouts: Hideo Nomo (233).

GAMES BY POSITION

Catcher: Mike Piazza 139, Tom Prince 45.
First base: Eric Karros 162, Nelson Liriano 2, Henry Blanco 1, Paul Konerko 1.
Second base: Wilton Guerrero 90, Eric Young 37, Tripp Cromer 17, Nelson Liriano 17, Juan Castro 14, Adam Riggs 8, Chad Fonville 3.
Third base: Todd Zeile 160, Juan Castro 3, Chip Hale 2, Henry Blanco 1, Tripp Cromer 1, Paul Konerko 1, Nelson Liriano 1.
Shortstop: Greg Gagne 143, Juan Castro 22, Tripp Cromer 10, Wilton Guerrero 5, Nelson Liriano 1.
Outfield: Raul Mondesi 159, Todd Hollandsworth 99, Brett Butler 91, Roger Cedeno 71, Otis Nixon 42, Billy Ashley 35, Wayne Kirby 26, Darren Lewis 25, Eric Anthony 21, Karim Garcia 12, Garey Ingram 7.
Designated hitter: Mike Piazza 7, Brett Butler 1.

TOP DRAFT CHOICES

1. **Glenn Davis**, 1B, Vanderbilt University.
2a. **Chase Utley**, SS, Poly H.S., Long Beach, Calif.
2b. **Steve Colyer**, LHP, Fort Zumwalt South H.S., St. Peters, Mo.
3. **Ricky Bell**, SS, Moeller H.S., Cincinnati.
4. **John Hernandez**, C, Nogales H.S., La Puente, Calif.
5. **Kip Harkrider**, SS, University of Texas.
6. **Will McCrotty**, C, Russellville (Ark.) H.S.
7. **Miles Durham**, OF, Cooper H.S., Abilene, Texas.
8. **Beau Parker**, RHP, Prairie H.S., Brush Prairie, Wash.
9. **Jamie Goudie**, SS, Hardaway H.S., Columbus, Ga.
10. **Joe Patterson**, OF, Ontario (Calif.) H.S.

MILWAUKEE BREWERS
NATIONAL LEAGUE CENTRAL DIVISION

Brewers Schedule

Home games shaded. *—All-Star Game at Coors Field (Colorado).
D—Day game (any game starting before 5 p.m.).

March

SUN	MON	TUE	WED	THU	FRI	SAT
		31 D ATL				

April

SUN	MON	TUE	WED	THU	FRI	SAT
			1	2 ATL	3 FLA	4 FLA
5 D FLA	6 D FLA	7 D MON	8 MON	9 D MON	10 NYM	11 D NYM
12 NYM	13 NYM	14 MON	15 MON	16 MON	17 D SF	18 D SF
19 SF	20 D	21 LA	22 LA	23 D LA	24 SF	25 D SF
26 SF	27 D LA	28 LA	29	30		

May

SUN	MON	TUE	WED	THU	FRI	SAT
					1 CIN	2 D CIN
3 D CIN	4 SD	5 SD	6 D SD	7	8 HOU	9 HOU
10 HOU	11 D STL	12 STL	13 ARZ	14 ARZ	15 COL	16 D COL
17 COL	18 D COL	19 SF	20 SF	21 SF	22 NYM	23 D NYM
24 NYM	25	26 PIT	27 PIT	28	29 FLA	30 FLA
31 D FLA						

June

SUN	MON	TUE	WED	THU	FRI	SAT
	1 ATL	2 ATL	3 ATL	4	5 DET	6 DET
7 D DET	8 KC	9 KC	10 KC	11	12 PIT	13 PIT
14 D PIT	15 CUB	16 D CUB	17 CUB	18 D PIT	19 PIT	20 PIT
21 D PIT	22 COL	23 D COL	24 MIN	25 MIN	26 D CWS	27 CWS
28 D CWS	29	30 CLE				

July

SUN	MON	TUE	WED	THU	FRI	SAT
		1 CLE	2 CLE	3 PHI	4 PHI	
5 D PHI	6	7	* 8	9 CUB	10 CUB	11 CUB
12 D CUB	13 PHI	14 PHI	15 D PHI	16 ATL	17 ATL	18 ATL
19 D ATL	20 FLA	21 D FLA	22 NYM	23 D NYM	24 MON	25 D MON
26 D MON	27	28 STL	29 STL	30 STL	31 ARZ	

August

SUN	MON	TUE	WED	THU	FRI	SAT
						1 ARZ
2 D ARZ	3 STL	4 STL	5 STL	6	7 CIN	8 CIN
9 CIN	10 D HOU	11 HOU	12 HOU	13 HOU	14 SD	15 SD
16 D SD	17 D	18 CIN	19 D CIN	20 HOU	21 HOU	22 SD
23 SD	24 D SD	25 COL	26 COL	27 ARZ	28 ARZ	29 ARZ
30 ARZ	31					

September

SUN	MON	TUE	WED	THU	FRI	SAT
		1 COL	2 COL	3 D COL	4 PHI	5 PHI
6 D PHI	7 D PIT	8 D PIT	9 HOU	10 HOU	11 CUB	12 D CUB
13 CUB	14 CIN	15 CIN	16 D CIN	17	18 STL	19 STL
20 D STL	21 D	22 CUB	23 D CUB	24 LA	25 LA	26 LA
27 D LA						

CLUB DIRECTORY

President, chief executive officer
Allan H. (Bud) Selig
Sr. vice president, baseball operations
Sal Bando
Vice president & general counsel
Wendy Selig-Prieb
Assistant general counsel
Eugene (Pepi) Randolph
V.p., new ballpark development
Michael Bucek
Vice president, stadium operations
Scott Jenkins
Vice president, corporate affairs
Laurel Prieb
Vice president, finance
Paul Baniel
V.p., administration & human resources
Tom Gausden
Vice president, ticket sales
Bob Voight
Director, community relations
Michael Downs
Director, stadium operations
Terry Ann Peterson
Director, grounds
Gary Vandenberg
Director, media relations
Jon Greenberg
Director, player development
Cecil Cooper
Director of Brewers Gold Club
Mike Harlan
Director of publications
Mario Ziino
Director of ticket operations
John Barnes
Traveling secretary
Dan Larrea
Trainers
John Adam
Al Price

Strength and conditioning coach
John Rewolinski
Team physicians
Dr. Dennis Sullivan
Dr. Drew Palin
Scouting director
Ken Califano
Pro. scouting and special assignments
Dee Fondy
Larry Haney
Chuck Tanner
Special assignments
Felix Delgado
Paul Tretiak
Walter Youse
Midwest supervisor/crosschecker
Fred Beene
Southeast supervisor/crosschecker
Russ Bove
West coast supervisor/crosschecker
Kevin Christman
Northeast supervisor/crosschecker
Ron Rizzi
Southwest supervisor/crosschecker
Ric Wilson
International supervisor
Epy Guerrero
Scouts
Walter Boggen, Jeff Brookens,
Domingo Carrasquel, Rich Chiles,
Ramon Conde, Steve Connelly, Dick
Fanning, Mike Farrell, Dick Foster,
Danny Garcia, Mike Gibbons,
Manolo Hernandez, Elvio Jimenez,
Brian Johnson, Harvey Kuenn Jr.,
John Logan, Demie Mainieri, Alex
Morales, Douglas Reynolds, Corey
Rodriguez, Bruce Seid, Bob Sloan,
Jonathan Story, Tom Tanous, John
Viney, Red Whitsett, David Young

MINOR LEAGUE AFFILIATES

Class	Team	League	Manager
AAA	Louisville	International	Gary Allenson
AA	El Paso	Texas	Ed Romero
A	Stockton	California	Bernie Mancallo
A	Beloit	Midwest	Don Money
Rookie	Helena	Pioneer	Tom Houk
Rookie	Ogden	Pioneer	Ed Sedar

BROADCAST INFORMATION

Radio: WTMJ-AM (620).
TV: WVTV-TV (Channel 24).
Cable TV: Midwest Sports Channel.

SPRING TRAINING

Ballpark (city): Maryvale Baseball
Park (Maryvale, Ariz.).
Ticket information: 602-784-4444.

Manager—Phil Garner (3).
Coaches—Chris Bando (12), Bill Castro (35), Lamar Johnson (28), Doug Mansolino, Don Rowe (45), Joel Youngblood.

No.	PITCHERS	B/T	Ht./Wt.	Born	1997 clubs
13	D'Amico, Jeff	R/R	6-7/245	12-27-75	Milwaukee, Beloit
	De Los Santos, Valerio	L/L	6-2/180	9-6-75	El Paso
21	Eldred, Cal	R/R	6-4/235	11-24-67	Milwaukee
	Estrada, Horacio	R/R	6-0/160	10-19-75	El Paso
	Fox, Chad	R/R	6-3/183	9-3-70	Richmond, Atlanta
	Jones, Doug	R/R	6-2/225	6-24-57	Milwaukee
	Juden, Jeff	R/R	6-8/265	1-19-71	Montreal, Cleveland
42	Karl, Scott	L/L	6-2/195	8-9-71	Milwaukee
	Maloney, Sean	R/R	6-7/210	5-25-71	Tucson, Milwaukee
41	Mercedes, Jose	R/R	6-1/199	3-5-71	Milwaukee
	Myers, Mike	L/L	6-3/197	6-26-69	Detroit
	Pasqualicchio, Michael	R/L	6-1/205	8-17-74	Stockton
47	Reyes, Al	R/R	6-1/193	4-10-71	Tucson, Milwaukee
46	Wagner, Paul	R/R	6-1/210	11-14-67	Carolina, Pittsburgh, Milwaukee
27	Wickman, Bob	R/R	6-1/212	2-6-69	Milwaukee
37	Woodard, Steve	L/R	6-4/225	5-15-75	El Paso, Tucson, Milwaukee

No.	CATCHERS	B/T	Ht./Wt.	Born	1997 clubs
	Hughes, Bobby	R/R	6-4/237	3-10-71	Tucson
16	Levis, Jesse	L/R	5-9/180	4-14-68	Milwaukee
22	Matheny, Mike	R/R	6-3/205	9-22-70	Milwaukee

No.	INFIELDERS	B/T	Ht./Wt.	Born	1997 clubs
	Belliard, Ronnie	R/R	5-8/180	7-4-76	Tucson
26	Cirillo, Jeff	R/R	6-2/188	9-23-69	Milwaukee
32	Jaha, John	R/R	6-1/222	5-27-66	Milwaukee
	Kinkade, Mike	R/R	6-1/210	5-6-73	El Paso
8	Loretta, Mark	R/R	6-0/175	8-14-71	Milwaukee
14	Nilsson, Dave	L/R	6-3/231	12-14-69	Milwaukee
	Perez, Santiago	B/R	6-2/150	12-30-75	Lakeland
2	Valentin, Jose	B/R	5-10/166	10-12-69	Milwaukee, Beloit
1	Vina, Fernando	L/R	5-9/170	4-16-69	Milwaukee, Stockton, Tucson
	Williamson, Antone	L/R	6-1/195	7-18-73	Tucson, Milwaukee

No.	OUTFIELDERS	B/T	Ht./Wt.	Born	1997 clubs
7	Banks, Brian	B/R	6-3/200	9-28-70	Tucson, Milwaukee
20	Burnitz, Jeromy	L/R	6-0/180	4-15-69	Milwaukee
18	Dunn, Todd	R/R	6-5/220	7-29-70	Tucson, Milwaukee
	Grissom, Marquis	R/R	5-11/190	4-17-67	Cleveland
	Jackson, Darrin	R/R	6-0/185	8-22-63	Salt Lake, Minnesota, Milwaukee
	Jenkins, Geoffrey	L/R	6-1/200	7-21-74	Tucson
	Krause, Scott	R/R	6-1/180	8-16-73	El Paso
10	Newfield, Marc	R/R	6-4/205	10-19-72	Milwaukee, Tucson

Ballpark (capacity, surface)
County Stadium (53,192, grass)

Address
County Stadium
P.O. Box 3099 Milwaukee, WI
53201-3099

Business phone
414-933-4114

Ticket information
414-933-9000

Ticket prices
$22 (diamond box, diamond mezzanine)
$18 (lower box)
$14 (upper box, lower grandstand)
$14 (upper grandstand)
$7 (general admission)
$5 (bleachers)

Field dimensions (from home plate)
To left field at foul line, 315 feet
To center field, 402 feet
To right field at foul line, 315 feet

First game played
April 7, 1970 (Angels 12, Brewers 0)

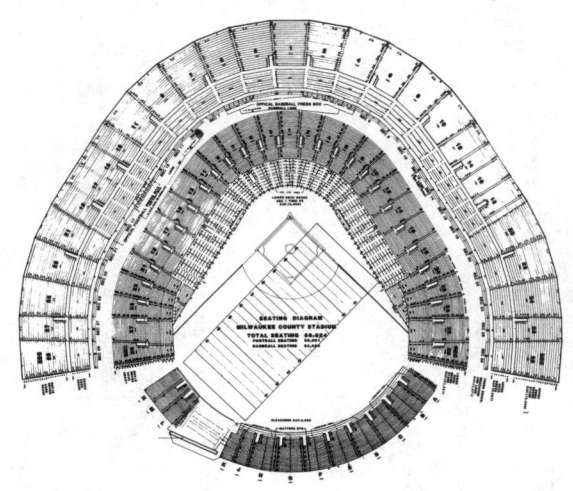

1998 SEASON Milwaukee Brewers

1997 REVIEW

DAY BY DAY

Date	Opp.	Res.	Score	(inn.*)	Hits	Opp. hits	Winning pitcher	Losing pitcher	Save	Record	Pos.	GB
4-1	At Tex.	L	2-6		7	7	Hill	McDonald		0-1	5th	1.0
4-4	At Tor.	L	2-6		5	9	Guzman	Karl	Crabtree	0-2	5th	2.0
4-5	At Tor.	W	5-2		9	8	McAndrew	Williams	Jones	1-2	3rd	2.0
4-6	At Tor.	W	4-2		10	5	McDonald	Hentgen	Jones	2-2	3rd	1.0
4-7	Tex.	W	5-3		7	7	Eldred	Hill	Jones	3-2	T2nd	0.5
4-10	Tex.	L	0-2		3	7	Witt	Karl	Wetteland	3-3	T2nd	0.5
4-13	Tor.	W	3-2		10	6	Wickman	Crabtree		4-3	T1st	....
4-14	Det.	W	7-0		12	4	Eldred	Moehler		5-3	1st	+1.0
4-15	Det.	L	1-3		6	8	Blair	Karl	Jones	5-4	T1st	....
4-16	N.Y.	W	7-4		12	7	Mercedes	Cone	Jones	6-4	1st	+1.0
4-17	N.Y.	W	5-4		12	8	Wickman	Lloyd		7-4	1st	+1.0
4-18	At Cle.	W	10-2		13	6	McDonald	McDowell		8-4	1st	+1.0
4-19	At Cle.	L	6-11		10	17	Nagy	Eldred		8-5	T1st	....
4-20	At Cle.	L	4-6		7	7	Hershiser	Wickman	Mesa	8-6	T1st	....
4-22	At N.Y.	L	2-10		6	14	Pettitte	D'Amico		8-7	2nd	1.0
4-23	At N.Y.	L	5-10		7	13	Rogers	McDonald	Lloyd	8-8	2nd	1.0
4-24	Cle.	L	3-6		11	14	Nagy	Eldred	Mesa	8-9	3rd	1.0
4-25	Cle.	L	4-11		6	14	Hershiser	Karl		8-10	4th	1.5
4-26	Cle.	W	9-8		11	12	Jones	Mesa		9-10	T2nd	0.5
4-27	Cle.	W	6-5		13	8	Jones	Plunk		10-10	1st	+0.5
4-28	Tex.	W	14-8		15	10	McDonald	Oliver		11-10	1st	+1.0
4-29	At Det.	W	2-1		7	7	Eldred	Olivares	Jones	12-10	1st	+1.0
4-30	At Det.	L	4-8		10	9	Thompson	Karl		12-11	1st	+1.0
5-2	At Sea.	L	1-8		3	10	Johnson	D'Amico		12-12	T1st	....
5-3	At Sea.	W	17-4		17	14	Florie	Fassero		13-12	T1st	....
5-4	At Sea.	L	0-9		6	12	Moyer	Eldred		13-13	T1st	....
5-5	Oak.	W	11-7		11	13	Karl	Telgheder		14-13	1st	+0.5
5-6	Oak.	L	5-6		9	12	Adams	Florie	Taylor	14-14	3rd	0.5
5-7	Oak.	W	1-0		7	4	Fetters	Montgomery	Jones	15-14	2nd	0.5
5-9	Ana.	W	5-4		8	12	Eldred	Hasegawa	Jones	16-14	T1st	....
5-10	Ana.	W	4-3	(10)	10	13	Jones	DeLucia		17-14	1st	+1.0
5-11	Ana.	W	5-2		12	8	McDonald	Finley	Jones	18-14	1st	+2.0
5-12	Sea.	W	9-8		11	12	D'Amico	Wolcott	Jones	19-14	1st	+2.5
5-13	Sea.	L	1-2		6	3	Johnson	Fetters	Charlton	19-15	1st	+1.5
5-14	At Oak.	L	4-7		8	11	Prieto	Eldred		19-16	1st	+0.5
5-15	At Oak.	L	5-6		13	12	Wengert	Wickman	Taylor	19-17	2nd	0.5
5-16	At Ana.	L	1-5		5	8	Finley	McDonald		19-18	2nd	0.5
5-17	At Ana.	L	5-6		11	8	Percival	Fetters		19-19	2nd	0.5
5-18	At Ana.	L	4-5		7	6	Springer	Mercedes	James	19-20	3rd	0.5
5-20	Min.	L	3-4		7	8	Trombley	Eldred	Aguilera	19-21	3rd	1.5
5-21	Min.	W	5-4		7	8	McDonald	Aldred	Jones	20-21	2nd	1.5
5-23	At Chi.	W	4-1		8	3	Karl	Alvarez	Jones	21-21	2nd	2.0
5-24	At Chi.	L	6-8		11	10	Simas	Fetters	Hernandez	21-22	2nd	2.0
5-25	At Chi.	W	11-7		16	14	Adamson	Baldwin	Wickman	22-22	2nd	2.0
5-26	At Bos.	L	2-3		8	7	Hammond	Jones		22-23	2nd	3.0
5-27	At Bos.	L	6-7		8	10	Corsi	Adamson	Slocumb	22-24	2nd	3.0
5-28	At Min.	L	1-3		6	7	Radke	Karl	Aguilera	22-25	2nd	4.0
5-29	At Min.	W	7-4		12	9	D'Amico	Robertson		23-25	2nd	3.5
5-30	Chi.	W	5-0		6	3	Eldred	Baldwin		24-25	2nd	2.5
5-31	Chi.	W	4-3		6	10	McDonald	Navarro	Jones	25-25	2nd	1.5
6-1	Chi.	W	7-4		12	9	Mercedes	Drabek	Jones	26-25	2nd	1.0
6-2	Chi.	L	5-8		8	14	Simas	Jones	Hernandez	26-26	2nd	1.5
6-3	Bos.	W	6-4		12	11	Wickman	Slocumb		27-26	2nd	0.5
6-4	Bos.	W	13-11		16	12	Eldred	Brandenburg	Jones	28-26	1st	+0.5
6-5	Bos.	L	1-2		7	6	Wakefield	McDonald	Lacy	28-27	2nd	0.5
6-6	At N.Y.	L	3-6		6	11	Rogers	Mercedes	Rivera	28-28	2nd	1.5
6-7	At N.Y.	L	0-2		4	5	Wells	Karl	Rivera	28-29	2nd	2.5
6-8	At N.Y.	L	1-3		8	7	Cone	D'Amico	Rivera	28-30	T2nd	2.5
6-10	At Cle.	L	4-5		11	9	Nagy	Eldred	M. Jackson	28-31	2nd	3.5
6-11	At Cle.	L	3-4	(11)	5	11	Assenmacher	Jones		28-32	3rd	4.5
6-12	At Cle.	W	6-2		10	6	Mercedes	Anderson		29-32	T2nd	3.5
6-13	At Chi. (NL)	W	4-2		9	5	D'Amico	Mulholland	Jones	30-32	2nd	3.0
6-14	At Chi. (NL)	L	5-9		10	14	Trachsel	Karl	Wendell	30-33	T2nd	3.5
6-15	At Chi. (NL)	L	3-4		10	5	Castillo	Eldred	Wendell	30-34	3rd	4.5
6-16	St.L.	W	1-0		4	5	Wickman	Al. Benes		31-34	3rd	3.5
6-17	St.L.	W	4-3		7	11	Adamson	Valenzuela	Jones	32-34	T2nd	3.5
6-18	St.L.	W	8-4		14	7	D'Amico	An. Benes		33-34	T2nd	2.5
6-20	K.C.	W	7-5		12	7	Eldred	Belcher	Jones	34-34	2nd	1.5
6-22	K.C.	L	5-6		13	7	Pichardo	Wickman	Montgomery	34-35	T2nd	3.0
6-23	Bal.	W	5-0		11	4	D'Amico	Key		35-35	2nd	2.0
6-24	Bal.	L	2-6		4	8	Boskie	Karl	Rhodes	35-36	T2nd	3.0
6-25	Bal.	L	1-9		3	12	Mussina	Eldred		35-37	3rd	3.5

Date	Opp.	Res.	Score	(inn.*)	Hits	Opp. hits	Winning pitcher	Losing pitcher	Save	Record	Pos.	GB
6-26	At K.C.	L	3-4		8	5	Haney	Mercedes	Montgomery	35-38	T3rd	4.0
6-27	At K.C.	L	3-16		8	15	Appier	McDonald		35-39	4th	4.0
6-28	At K.C.	W	5-3		10	12	D'Amico	Rosado	Jones	36-39	T3rd	4.0
6-29	At K.C.	W	3-2		12	10	Wickman	Montgomery	Jones	37-39	3rd	3.0
6-30	At Cin.	L	3-4		9	9	Mercker	Fetters	Shaw	37-40	3rd	4.0
7-1	At Cin.	L	1-9		3	8	Burba	Mercedes		37-41	3rd	5.0
7-2	At Cin.	L	4-7		6	12	Tomko	McDonald	Sullivan	37-42	3rd	5.0
7-3	Min.	L	5-8		6	12	Radke	D'Amico	Aguilera	37-43	3rd	5.5
7-4	Min.	L	1-13		10	23	Stevens	Karl		37-44	3rd	6.5
7-5	Min.	W	2-1		5	4	Eldred	Robertson	Jones	38-44	3rd	6.5
7-6	Min.	W	6-2		11	5	McDonald	Hawkins		39-44	3rd	6.5
7-11	At Bal.	W	3-1		9	3	McDonald	Key	Jones	40-44	3rd	6.0
7-12	At Bal.	W	3-2		12	6	Eldred	Erickson	Jones	41-44	3rd	6.0
7-13	At Bal.	W	6-4		10	8	D'Amico	Mussina	Jones	42-44	3rd	6.0
7-14	At K.C.	L	1-2	(14)	7	11	Perez	Jones		42-45	3rd	7.0
7-15	At K.C.	W	5-2		8	9	Karl	Appier		43-45	3rd	6.0
7-16	Cle.	L	3-4		6	8	Wright	McDonald	M. Jackson	43-46	3rd	7.0
7-17	Cle.	L	2-3		6	5	Hershiser	Eldred	M. Jackson	43-47	3rd	8.0
7-18	N.Y.	W	6-4		11	10	D'Amico	Gooden	Fetters	44-47	3rd	7.0
7-19	N.Y.	L	0-8		3	14	Wells	Mercedes		44-48	3rd	7.0
7-20	N.Y.	W	6-2		7	8	Karl	Irabu		45-48	3rd	7.0
7-21	N.Y.	L	3-7		9	12	Pettitte	Florie	Stanton	45-49	3rd	7.0
7-22	At Tor.	L	2-5		5	4	Hentgen	Eldred	Escobar	45-50	3rd	8.0
7-23	At Tor.	L	0-8		8	4	Clemens	McAndrew		45-51	3rd	8.0
7-24	At Tor.	L	4-5		9	8	Williams	Mercedes	Escobar	45-52	3rd	8.0
7-25	At Det.	W	6-1		11	8	Karl	Sanders		46-52	3rd	7.0
7-26	At Det.	W	3-1		5	6	Florie	Thompson	Fetters	47-52	3rd	7.0
7-27	At Det.	W	11-7		18	9	Eldred	Moehler	Reyes	48-52	3rd	7.0
7-28†	Tor.	W	1-0		4	1	Woodard	Clemens	Fetters	49-52		
7-28‡	Tor.	W	9-3		19	11	Adamson	Flener		50-52	3rd	5.0
7-29†	Tor.	W	2-0		5	4	Mercedes	Williams	Fetters	51-52		
7-29‡	Tor.	W	4-2		11	6	Karl	Carpenter	Fetters	52-52	2nd	3.5
7-31	Sea.	W	2-1		6	6	Wickman	Moyer		53-52	2nd	2.5
8-1	Sea.	W	8-3		14	4	Eldred	Wolcott		54-52	2nd	2.5
8-2	Sea.	L	4-14		12	15	Fassero	Woodard		54-53	2nd	3.5
8-3	Sea.	L	5-6		7	11	Johnson	Reyes	Slocumb	54-54	2nd	3.5
8-4	At Ana.	W	5-2		14	6	Karl	Hill	Fetters	55-54	2nd	3.5
8-5	At Ana.	L	5-6		11	8	Dickson	Florie	Percival	55-55	2nd	3.5
8-6	At Ana.	L	6-8		11	9	Watson	Eldred	Percival	55-56	2nd	3.5
8-7	At Oak.	L	4-5	(13)	10	10	Johnson	Jones		55-57	2nd	3.5
8-9	At Oak.	L	2-3		5	8	Mathews	Wickman	Taylor	55-58	2nd	3.5
8-10†	At Oak.	L	3-4		11	10	Taylor	Wickman		55-59		
8-10‡	At Oak.	W	9-5		14	10	Florie	Haynes		56-59	T2nd	3.0
8-11	At Sea.	L	1-11		4	14	Moyer	Eldred		56-60	3rd	3.5
8-12	At Sea.	W	5-3		7	6	Woodard	Fassero	Jones	57-60	3rd	3.5
8-14	Ana.	L	1-5		6	9	Springer	Mercedes		57-61	3rd	4.5
8-15	Ana.	L	3-5		9	10	Finley	Florie	Percival	57-62	3rd	5.5
8-16	Oak.	W	6-5		8	9	Jones	Mohler		58-62	T2nd	5.5
8-17	Oak.	W	5-2		9	7	Woodard	Prieto	Jones	59-62	2nd	4.5
8-18†	At Tex.	W	8-5		12	7	Karl	Sturtze	Jones	60-62		
8-18‡	At Tex.	L	0-2		1	7	Helling	Adamson	Wetteland	60-63	T2nd	5.0
8-19	At Tex.	W	8-2		11	7	Mercedes	Santana		61-63	2nd	5.0
8-20	At Tex.	W	6-2		10	3	Florie	T. Clark	Jones	62-63	2nd	4.0
8-21	Det.	L	1-2	(12)	5	9	Miceli	Wickman	Jones	62-64	3rd	4.0
8-22	Det.	L	1-16		5	23	Moehler	Woodard	Gaillard	62-65	3rd	5.0
8-23	Det.	W	5-2		11	10	Karl	Keagle	Jones	63-65	2nd	5.0
8-24	Det.	W	6-0		9	4	Mercedes	Blair		64-65	2nd	4.0
8-25	Tex.	W	7-2		12	5	Adamson	T. Clark		65-65	2nd	3.5
8-26	Tex.	W	11-10	(12)	20	19	Jones	Eversgerd		66-65	2nd	2.5
8-27	Tex.	L	1-7		7	14	Oliver	Woodard		66-66	2nd	3.5
8-29	Pit.	W	4-1		6	8	Karl	Loaiza	Jones	67-66	2nd	3.5
8-30	Pit.	L	1-3		6	10	Lieber	Mercedes	Loiselle	67-67	2nd	3.5
8-31	Pit.	W	3-2		11	7	Jones	Wilkins		68-67	2nd	3.5
9-1	At Hou.	W	3-2		7	8	Adamson	Holt	Jones	69-67	2nd	3.5
9-2	At Hou.	W	4-2		5	5	Villone	Kile	Jones	70-67	2nd	2.5
9-3	At Hou.	L	0-4		5	7	Garcia	Karl		70-68	2nd	3.5
9-5	At Bos.	W	7-1		14	7	Eldred	Suppan		71-68	2nd	3.5
9-6	At Bos.	L	2-10		8	11	Wakefield	Harnisch		71-69	2nd	4.5
9-7	At Bos.	L	2-11		11	14	Henry	D'Amico		71-70	2nd	5.5
9-8	At Chi.	W	8-5	(10)	14	7	Wickman	Karchner	Jones	72-70	2nd	5.5
9-9	At Chi.	L	1-4		5	7	Eyre	Mercedes	T. Castillo	72-71	2nd	5.5
9-10	At Chi.	L	1-3		5	7	Bere	Eldred	McElroy	72-72	2nd	6.0
9-12	Bos.	L	2-4		6	9	Suppan	D'Amico	Gordon	72-73	2nd	6.5
9-13	Bos.	L	1-2		4	9	Wakefield	Karl	Gordon	72-74	T2nd	6.5
9-14	Bos.	L	1-2		7	4	Henry	Mercedes	Gordon	72-75	T2nd	7.5

Date	Opp.	Res.	Score	(inn.*)	Hits	Opp. hits	Winning pitcher	Losing pitcher	Save	Record	Pos.	GB
9-15	Chi.	W	11-10		13	14	Eldred	Eyre	Jones	73-75	2nd	7.0
9-17	At Bal.	W	8-3		14	9	D'Amico	Erickson		74-75	2nd	7.0
9-18	At Bal.	L	3-4		9	7	Mussina	Karl	Myers	74-76	T2nd	8.0
9-19	At Min.	W	7-4		11	7	Mercedes	Serafini	Jones	75-76	T2nd	7.5
9-20	At Min.	L	1-6		2	12	Hawkins	Eldred	Swindell	75-77	3rd	7.5
9-21	At Min.	L	1-2	(10)	6	8	Radke	Fetters		75-78	3rd	7.5
9-22	At Min.	L	2-5		6	6	T. Miller	D'Amico	Aguilera	75-79	3rd	8.0
9-23†	K.C.	W	7-4		10	8	Reyes	Carrasco	Jones	76-79		
9-23‡	K.C.	L	2-6		7	9	Pittsley	Adamson		76-80	3rd	8.5
9-24	K.C.	W	4-3	(15)	12	10	Wagner	Montgomery		77-80	T2nd	7.5
9-25	K.C.	L	1-2		4	7	Rusch	Eldred	Pichardo	77-81	3rd	7.5
9-26	Bal.	W	4-2		10	6	Harnisch	Krivda	Jones	78-81	3rd	7.5
9-27	Bal.	L	4-5		8	14	Mathews	Jones	Myers	78-82	3rd	8.0
9-28	Bal.	L	6-7		13	10	Orosco	Reyes	Mathews	78-83	3rd	8.0

Monthly records: April (12-11), May (13-14), June (12-15), July (16-12), August (15-15), September (10-16).
*Innings, if other than nine. †First game of doubleheader. ‡Second game of doubleheader.

HIGHLIGHTS

High point: After being swept in a three-game series July 22-24 in Toronto, the club reeled off a nine-game winning streak that featured back-to-back double-header sweeps over the Blue Jays.

Low point: First baseman John Jaha and left fielder Marc Newfield, the club's best power threats from the right side of the plate, were sidelined with shoulder injuries during the final weekend in May. Jaha didn't return, Newfield's late comeback bid was aborted and the rest of the offense never picked up the slack.

Turning point: During an eight-day span in September, the club saw its playoff hopes fizzle during five deflating losses to Boston.

Most valuable player: Right fielder Jeromy Burnitz started the season in a platoon setup with Matt Mieske, but quickly won the everyday job and enjoyed a breakthrough season. His 27 homers and 85 RBIs were team highs.

Most valuable pitcher: With six victories and a club-record 36 saves, veteran reliever Doug Jones figured in 42 of the team's 78 victories. The 40-year-old righthander drove opposing hitters crazy with his fluttering changeup and sneaky fastball. He blew two save chances and walked only nine batters in 80 1/3 innings.

Most improved player: When spring training ended, righthander Jose Mercedes barely made the big-league roster as a middle reliever. By the end of the season, he'd established himself in the starting rotation. His 7-10 record was misleading because the club averaged just 1.8 runs in his 10 losses.

Most pleasant surprise: After a stellar first half with Class AA El Paso and seven scoreless innings with Class AAA Tucson, rookie righthander Steve Woodard was promoted to the big leagues on July 28 and turned in one of the more spectacular debut performances in history. After giving up a double to leadoff batter Otis Nixon, he struck out 12 and shut the Blue Jays out for eight innings without allowing another hit. His stunning 1-0 victory, which came against childhood hero Roger Clemens, was a highlight of a nine-game winning streak.

Biggest disappointment: David Nilsson avoided the disabled list for the first time, played in a team-high 156 games and hit 20 homers with 81 RBIs. Still, the campaign was a disappointment. When the club needed him most down the stretch, he did not hit a homer after August 5.

Key injuries: In addition to Jaha and Newfield, the club lost second baseman Fernando Vina for half the season due to a broken ankle, and righthander Ben McDonald, the ace of the starting staff, appeared in just 21 games before undergoing season-ending surgery on his rotator cuff on July 29. Shortstop Jose Valentin missed three weeks with a broken finger. Mercedes missed the final two weeks with tendinitis in his middle finger. Lefty Scott Karl was bothered by tendinitis in his thumb and a strained ligament in his left big toe.

Notable: After six seasons, Phil Garner has managed more games (906) and recorded more victories (437) and losses (469) than any skipper in franchise history.

—DREW OLSON

RECORDS

1997 regular-season record: 78-83 (3rd in A.L. Central); 47-33 at home; 31-50 on road; 27-28 vs. East; 30-32 vs. Central; 21-23 vs. West; 23-29 vs. lefthanded starters; 55-54 vs. righthanded starters; 70-68 on grass; 8-15 on turf; 27-33 in daytime; 51-50 at night; 24-32 in one-run games; 4-5 in extra-inning games; 2-0-3 in doubleheaders.

Team record past five years: 345-399 (.464, ranks 11th in league in that span).

TEAM LEADERS

Batting average: Jeff Cirillo (.288).
At-bats: Jeff Cirillo (580).
Runs: Jeromy Burnitz (85).
Hits: Jeff Cirillo (167).
Total bases: Jeromy Burnitz (273).
Doubles: Jeff Cirillo (46).
Triples: Jeromy Burnitz (8).
Home runs: Jeromy Burnitz (27).
Runs batted in: Jeromy Burnitz (85).
Stolen bases: Gerald Williams (23).
Slugging percentage: Jeromy Burnitz (.553).
On-base percentage: Jeromy Burnitz (.382).

Wins: Cal Eldred (13).
Earned-run average: Scott Karl (4.47).
Complete games: Jose Mercedes (2).
Shutouts: Jeff D'Amico, Cal Eldred, Jose Mercedes (1).
Saves: Doug Jones (36).
Innings pitched: Cal Eldred (202.0).
Strikeouts: Cal Eldred (122).

GAMES BY POSITION

Catcher: Mike Matheny 121, Jesse Levis 78, Kelly Stinnett 25.
First base: Dave Nilsson 74, John Jaha 27, Tim Unroe 23, Jeff Huson 21, Mark Loretta 19, Jack Voigt 19, Antone Williamson 14, Julio Franco 13, Brian Banks 5, Mike Matheny 2.
Second base: Fernando Vina 77, Mark Loretta 63, Jeff Huson 32, Eddy Diaz 14, Tim Unroe 1.
Third base: Jeff Cirillo 150, Mark Loretta 15, Jack Voigt 6, Jeff Huson 2, Tim Unroe 2, Brian Banks 1, Eddy Diaz 1.
Shortstop: Jose Valentin 134, Mark Loretta 44, Eddy Diaz 1.
Outfield: Gerald Williams 154, Jeromy Burnitz 149, Matt Mieske 74, Jack Voigt 40, Marc Newfield 28, Todd Dunn 27, Darrin Jackson 26, Chuck Carr 23, Dave Nilsson 22, Brian Banks 15, Jeff Huson 9, Tim Unroe 2.
Designated hitter: Dave Nilsson 59, Julio Franco 28, John Jaha 20, Marc Newfield 18, Todd Dunn 14, Jesse Levis 8, Matt Mieske 5, Jeff Huson 4, Antone Williamson 4, Jeff Cirillo 2, Brian Banks 1, Kelly Stinnett 1, Jose Valentin 1, Fernando Vina 1, Jack Voigt 1, Gerald Williams 1.

TOP DRAFT CHOICES

1. **Kyle Peterson,** RHP, Stanford University.
2. **Alvin Morrow,** OF, Kirkwood (Mo.) H.S.
3. **Jeff Deardorff,** 3B, South Lake H.S., Clermont, Fla.
4. **Tommy Warren,** OF, Westchester H.S., Inglewood, Calif.
5. **Frank Candela,** OF, Peabody (Mass.) H.S.
6. **Jake Eye,** RHP, Ohio University.
7. **Bucky Jacobsen,** OF, Lewis-Clark State (Ida.) College.
8. **Todd Incantalupo,** LHP, Providence College.
9. **Matt Childers,** RHP, Westside H.S., Augusta, Ga.
10. **Chris Patton,** SS, McClintock H.S., Tempe, Ariz.

MONTREAL EXPOS
NATIONAL LEAGUE EAST DIVISION

Expos Schedule

Home games shaded. *—All-Star Game at Coors Field (Colorado).
D—Day game (any game starting before 5 p.m.).

March

SUN	MON	TUE	WED	THU	FRI	SAT
		31				

April

SUN	MON	TUE	WED	THU	FRI	SAT
			1 PIT	2 D PIT	3 D CUB	4 D CUB
5 D CUB	6 D CUB	7 D MIL	8 D MIL	9 D MIL	10 CUB	11 D CUB
12 D CUB	13	14 MIL	15 MIL	16 D MIL	17 D HOU	18 HOU
19 D HOU	20	21 STL	22 STL	23 STL	24 HOU	25 HOU
26 D HOU	27 STL	28 STL	29 D STL	30		

May

SUN	MON	TUE	WED	THU	FRI	SAT
					1 ARZ	2 ARZ
3 D ARZ	4 CIN	5 CIN	6 CIN	7 COL	8 COL	9 COL
10 D COL	11 SF	12 SF	13 D SF	14 D LA	15 LA	16 LA
17 D LA	18	19 HOU	20 HOU	21 D HOU	22 PHI	23 PHI
24 D PHI	25 PHI	26 ATL	27 ATL	28 ATL	29 PIT	30 PIT
31 D PIT						

June

SUN	MON	TUE	WED	THU	FRI	SAT
	1 PHI	2 PHI	3 PHI	4	5 TB	6 TB
7 D TB	8	9 NYY	10 NYY	11 NYY	12 ATL	13 ATL
14 D ATL	15	16 NYM	17 NYM	18 NYM	19 ATL	20 ATL
21 D ATL	22 TOR	23 TOR	24 TOR	25 TOR	26 BAL	27 BAL
28 D BAL	29	30 BOS				

July

SUN	MON	TUE	WED	THU	FRI	SAT
			1 BOS	2 BOS	3 FLA	4 FLA
5 FLA	6	7	* 8	9 NYM	10 NYM	11 NYM
12 NYM	13 FLA	14 FLA	15 FLA	16 PIT	17 PIT	18 PIT
19 D PIT	20 PHI	21 PHI	22 CUB	23 D CUB	24 MIL	25 MIL
26 D MIL	27	28 SF	29 SF	30 SF	31 SD	

August

SUN	MON	TUE	WED	THU	FRI	SAT
						1 SD
2 D SD	3 D SD	4 D LA	5 LA	6 LA	7 ARZ	8 ARZ
9 D ARZ	10 COL	11 COL	12 COL	13	14 CIN	15 CIN
16 CIN	17 ARZ	18 ARZ	19 D ARZ	20 COL	21 COL	22 CIN
23 CIN	24 D CIN	25 LA	26 LA	27 LA	28 SD	29 SD
30 SD	31 SD					

September

SUN	MON	TUE	WED	THU	FRI	SAT
		1 SF	2 SF	3 D	4 FLA	5 FLA
6 D FLA	7	8 ATL	9 ATL	10 ATL	11 NYM	12 NYM
13 D NYM	14 FLA	15 FLA	16 FLA	17	18 PHI	19 PHI
20 D PHI	21	22 NYM	23 NYM	24	25 STL	26 D STL
27 D STL						

1998 SEASON
CLUB DIRECTORY

President and general partner
Claude R. Brochu

Chairman of the partnership committee
L. Jacques Menard

Vice chairmen of the partnership comm.
Raymond Bachand
Jocelyn Proteau
Louis A. Tanguay

Vice president, baseball operations
Bill Stoneman

Vice president and general manager
Jim Beattie

Executive vice president, development
Laurier M. Carpentier

Exec. director, finance and treasurer
Michel Bussiere

Dir., int'l op. & special asst. to the g.m.
Fred Ferreira

Director, scouting
Jim Fleming

Assistant director, scouting
Gregg Leonard

Director, player development
Dave Littlefield

Assistant director, player development
Chris Antonetti

V.p., marketing and communications
Richard Morency

Vice president, stadium operations
Claude Delorme

Vice president, sales
Lucien Baril

Director, media services
Monique Giroux

Director, media relations
P.J. Loyello

Directors, advertising sales
Luigi Carola
John Di Terlizzi
Danielle La Roche

Director, Olympic Stadium ticket office
Hubert Richard

Director, advertising
Johanne Heroux

Director, season ticket sales
Gilles Beauregard

Director, business development
Real Sureau

Club physician
Dr. Mike Thomassin

Club orthopedist
Dr. Larry Coughlin

Scouts
Alex Agostino, Matt Anderson, Mark Baca, Mike Berger, Dennis Cardoza, Robby Corsaro, Marc Del Piano, Phil Favia, Fred Ferreira, Jim Fleming, Dan Freed, Scott Goldby, John Hughes, Joe Jordan, Mark Leavitt, Jimmy Lester, Dave Malpass, Bob Oldis, Scott Stanley, Len Strelitz, William Wilson

MINOR LEAGUE AFFILIATES

Class	Team	League	Manager
AAA	Ottawa	International	Pat Kelly
AA	Harrisburg	Eastern	Rick Sweet
A	West Palm Beach	Florida State	Doug Sisson
A	Cape Fear	South Atlantic	To be announced
A	Vermont	New York-Pennsylvania	To be announced
Rookie	Gulf Coast Expos	Gulf Coast	Luis Dorante

BROADCAST INFORMATION

Radio: CIQC-AM (600); CKAC-AM (73, French language).
TV: CBFT (2, French language), TQS (5, French language).
Cable TV: The Sports Network; RDS (French language).

SPRING TRAINING

Ballpark (city): Roger Dean Stadium (Jupiter, Fla.).
Ticket information: 561-775-1818.

SPRING TRAINING ROSTER

Manager—Felipe Alou (17).

Coaches—Pierre Arsenault (67), Bobby Cuellar (26), Tommy Harper (1), Pete Mackanin (25), Luis Pujols (55), Jim Tracy (23).

No.	PITCHERS	B/T	Ht./Wt.	Born	1997 clubs
53	Baker, Jason	R/R	6-3/195	11-21-74	West Palm Beach, Gulf Coast Expos
48	Batista, Miguel	R/R	6-0/180	2-19-71	Iowa, Chicago N.L.
21	Bennett, Shayne	R/R	6-5/200	4-10-72	Harrisburg, Ottawa, Montreal
34	DeHart, Rick	L/L	6-1/180	3-21-70	Ottawa, Montreal
19	Falteisek, Steve	R/R	6-2/200	1-28-72	Ottawa, Montreal
30	Hermanson, Dustin	R/R	6-2/195	12-21-72	Montreal
47	Johnson, Mike	L/R	6-2/175	10-3-75	Baltimore, Montreal
44	Kline, Steve	B/L	6-2/200	8-22-72	Cleveland, Buffalo, Montreal
60	Moore, Trey	L/L	6-1/200	10-2-72	Harrisburg
45	Pavano, Carl	R/R	6-5/228	1-8-76	Pawtucket
33	Perez, Carlos	L/L	6-3/195	1-14-71	Montreal
61	Powell, Jeremy	R/R	6-6/225	6-18-76	West Palm Beach
32	Telford, Anthony	R/R	6-0/189	3-6-66	Montreal
35	Thurman, Mike	R/R	6-4/210	7-22-73	Harrisburg, Ottawa, Montreal
41	Urbina, Ugueth	R/R	6-2/185	2-15-74	Montreal
18	Valdes, Marc	R/R	6-0/187	12-20-71	Montreal
62	Vazquez, Javier	R/R	6-2/180	6-25-76	West Palm Beach, Harrisburg
46	Wagner, Matt	R/R	6-5/215	4-4-72	West Palm Beach

No.	CATCHERS	B/T	Ht./Wt.	Born	1997 clubs
12	Chavez, Raul	R/R	5-11/175	3-18-73	Ottawa, Montreal
54	Henley, Bob	R/R	6-2/190	1-30-73	Harrisburg
16	Widger, Chris	R/R	6-3/195	5-21-71	Montreal

No.	INFIELDERS	B/T	Ht./Wt.	Born	1997 clubs
11	Andrews, Shane	R/R	6-1/215	8-28-71	Montreal, West Palm Beach, Ottawa
56	Bocachica, Hiram	R/R	5-11/165	3-4-76	Harrisburg
2	Cabrera, Orlando	R/R	5-9/150	11-2-74	Montreal, Harrisburg, West Palm Beach, Ottawa
59	Coquillette, Trace	R/R	5-11/175	6-4-74	West Palm Beach, Harrisburg
27	Fernandez, Jose	R/R	6-2/190	11-2-74	West Palm Beach, Harrisburg
20	Fullmer, Brad	L/R	6-1/190	1-17-75	Harrisburg, Ottawa, Montreal
4	Grudzielanek, Mark	R/R	6-1/185	6-30-70	Montreal
51	McGuire, Ryan	L/L	6-2/210	11-23-71	Ottawa, Montreal
58	Seguignol, Fernando	B/R	6-5/190	1-17-75	West Palm Beach
37	Vidro, Jose	B/R	6-0/185	8-27-74	Ottawa, Montreal

No.	OUTFIELDERS	B/T	Ht./Wt.	Born	1997 clubs
27	Guerrero, Vladimir	R/R	6-2/195	2-9-76	West Palm Beach, Montreal
9	Jones, Terry	B/R	5-10/165	2-15-71	Colorado Springs
7	Santangelo, F.P.	B/R	5-10/170	10-24-67	Montreal
50	Stovall, DaRond	B/L	6-1/185	1-3-73	Harrisburg, Ottawa
22	White, Rondell	R/R	6-1/205	2-23-72	Montreal

BALLPARK INFORMATION

Ballpark (capacity, surface)
Olympic Stadium (46,500, artificial)

Address
4549 Pierre-de-Coubertin Ave.
Montreal, QC H1V 3N7

Business phone
514-253-3434

Ticket information
800-GO-EXPOS

Ticket prices
$30 (VIP box seats)
$20 (box seats)
$10 (terrace)
$5 (general admission)

Field dimensions (from home plate)
To left field at foul line, 325 feet
To center field, 404 feet
To right field at foul line, 325 feet

First game played
April 15, 1977 (Phillies 7, Expos 2)

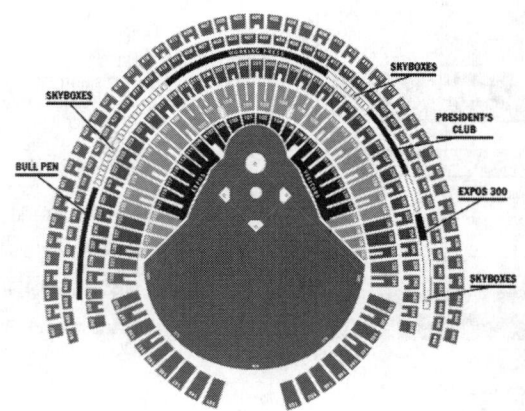

1998 SEASON *Montreal Expos*

Date	Opp.	Res.	Score	(inn.*)	Hits	Opp. hits	Winning pitcher	Losing pitcher	Save	Record	Pos.	GB
4-1	St.L.	W	2-1		7	7	Urbina	Batchelor		1-0	T1st	....
4-2	St.L.	W	4-1		9	2	Juden	Petkovsek	Smith	2-0	T1st	....
4-3	St.L.	W	9-4		14	7	Perez	Al. Benes		3-0	T1st	....
4-4	Col.	L	4-5		9	8	Wright	Valdes	Ruffin	3-1	T1st	....
4-5	Col.	L	3-15		10	15	Bailey	Cormier		3-2	T2nd	1.0
4-6	Col.	L	2-6		8	12	Ritz	Bullinger		3-3	3rd	2.0
4-8	At St.L.	L	1-2		6	7	Petkovsek	Urbina		3-4	3rd	3.0
4-12	At Col.	L	8-12		14	13	Wright	Bullinger	DiPoto	3-5	3rd	4.0
4-13	At Col.	W	8-3		17	8	Perez	Ritz	Daal	4-5	3rd	3.0
4-14	At Col.	L	8-10		13	13	DiPoto	Stull	Ruffin	4-6	3rd	4.0
4-15	At Hou.	W	7-5		9	7	Martinez	Holt		5-6	3rd	4.0
4-16	At Hou.	L	2-10		3	10	Reynolds	Valdes		5-7	3rd	5.0
4-18	At Phi.	L	3-8		6	10	Maduro	Bullinger		5-8	3rd	6.0
4-19	At Phi.	L	8-10		6	9	Leiter	Perez	Bottalico	5-9	3rd	7.0
4-20†	At Phi.	W	5-1		11	3	Juden	Munoz	Veres	6-9		
4-20‡	At Phi.	W	3-0		6	5	Martinez	Portugal	Urbina	7-9	3rd	5.5
4-22	Chi.	W	5-1		8	7	Hermanson	Swartzbaugh		8-9	3rd	5.5
4-23	Chi.	W	4-3		12	8	Bullinger	Mulholland	Smith	9-9	3rd	4.5
4-25	N.Y.	W	4-1		9	6	Perez	Jones		10-9	3rd	4.5
4-26	N.Y.	W	8-1		11	4	Martinez	Mlicki		11-9	3rd	4.5
4-27	N.Y.	L	3-5	(10)	9	12	McMichael	Smith	J. Franco	11-10	3rd	5.5
4-28	At Chi.	L	2-5		8	8	Mulholland	Hermanson	Rojas	11-11	3rd	6.5
4-29	At Chi.	L	8-14		11	14	Trachsel	Bullinger		11-12	3rd	6.5
4-30	Hou.	W	8-6		13	11	Perez	Kile	Urbina	12-12	3rd	6.5
5-1	Hou.	W	4-0		8	3	Martinez	Holt		13-12	3rd	6.5
5-2	At S.D.	W	5-4		9	11	Veres	Bochtler	Urbina	14-12	3rd	5.5
5-3	At S.D.	L	0-1		3	5	Worrell	Hermanson	Hoffman	14-13	3rd	5.5
5-4	At S.D.	W	9-3		17	4	Bullinger	Hitchcock		15-13	3rd	5.5
5-5	At S.F.	L	2-4		8	5	Gardner	Perez	Beck	15-14	3rd	6.5
5-6	At S.F.	W	10-3		12	5	Martinez	Estes		16-14	3rd	5.5
5-7	At S.F.	W	19-3		26	8	Juden	Fernandez		17-14	2nd	5.5
5-9	At L.A.	L	1-5		7	8	Radinsky	Urbina		17-15	3rd	5.0
5-10	At L.A.	L	1-2		5	6	Radinsky	Veres		17-16	3rd	6.0
5-11	At L.A.	W	6-3	(10)	10	9	Daal	Candiotti	Valdes	18-16	3rd	6.0
5-13	S.D.	W	7-3		11	11	Martinez	Valenzuela		19-16	3rd	5.5
5-14	S.D.	W	9-7		12	10	Valdes	Hoffman	Smith	20-16	3rd	4.5
5-15	S.F.	W	8-7		13	12	Telford	Tavarez	Urbina	21-16	3rd	4.0
5-16	S.F.	W	14-13		18	14	Urbina	Beck		22-16	3rd	4.0
5-17	L.A.	L	3-8		6	11	Nomo	Perez		22-17	3rd	5.0
5-18	L.A.	W	7-4		14	8	Martinez	Astacio	Urbina	23-17	3rd	5.0
5-19	L.A.	W	2-1		7	7	Juden	Martinez	Urbina	24-17	3rd	5.0
5-20	At Atl.	L	2-4		9	9	Wade	Hermanson	Wohlers	24-18	3rd	6.0
5-21	At Atl.	L	2-3		8	5	Maddux	Urbina		24-19	3rd	7.0
5-22	Pit.	L	3-9		8	10	Lieber	Perez	Rincon	24-20	T3rd	7.5
5-23	Pit.	W	4-1		7	5	Martinez	Cooke		25-20	3rd	7.5
5-24	Pit.	W	7-3		12	7	Juden	Schmidt	Urbina	26-20	3rd	6.5
5-25	Pit.	L	6-8		11	9	Wilkins	Daal	Loiselle	26-21	3rd	6.5
5-26	N.Y.	L	3-4		8	7	Lidle	Urbina	J. Franco	26-22	4th	7.5
5-27	N.Y.	W	5-4		12	7	Valdes	Clark	Smith	27-22	3rd	7.5
5-28	N.Y.	L	0-7		4	10	Jones	Martinez		27-23	4th	8.0
5-30	At Pit.	L	2-10		4	13	Peters	Juden		27-24	4th	8.5
5-31	At Pit.	W	4-2		7	6	Hermanson	Loaiza	Urbina	28-24	4th	7.5
6-1	At Pit.	L	2-11		10	12	Cordova	Bullinger		28-25	4th	8.5
6-2	At N.Y.	W	10-0		13	6	Perez	Clark		29-25	4th	7.5
6-3	At N.Y.	L	1-2		5	7	Jones	Martinez	J. Franco	29-26	4th	7.5
6-4	Atl.	L	3-6		8	10	Glavine	Juden		29-27	4th	8.5
6-5	Atl.	L	0-9		6	13	Neagle	Hermanson		29-28	4th	9.5
6-6	Chi.	W	3-0		10	6	Bullinger	Gonzalez		30-28	4th	9.5
6-7	Chi.	W	5-0		6	7	Perez	Mulholland		31-28	4th	9.5
6-8	Chi.	W	5-4		11	6	Telford	Adams		32-28	4th	8.5
6-9	Chi.	W	6-5		8	10	Juden	Castillo	Urbina	33-28	4th	7.5
6-10	Phi.	W	8-5		13	8	Veres	Bottalico	Smith	34-28	4th	7.5
6-11	Phi.	W	4-3		6	7	Bullinger	Spradlin	Urbina	35-28	T3rd	6.5
6-13	Det.	W	4-3		10	8	Perez	Olivares	Urbina	36-28	3rd	5.5
6-14	Det.	W	1-0		6	3	Martinez	Thompson		37-28	3rd	4.5
6-15	Det.	W	10-2		12	6	Juden	Moehler		38-28	3rd	3.5
6-16	At Bal.	W	6-4		12	9	Hermanson	Boskie	Urbina	39-28	3rd	3.5
6-17	At Bal.	L	4-5		10	10	Kamieniecki	Bullinger	Myers	39-29	3rd	4.5
6-18	At Bal.	W	1-0		4	8	Perez	Key		40-29	3rd	3.5
6-20	Fla.	L	1-2		3	5	Fernandez	Martinez		40-30	3rd	4.5
6-21	Fla.	W	4-3		13	10	Juden	Rapp	Urbina	41-30	3rd	4.5

Date	Opp.	Res.	Score	(inn.*)	Hits	Opp. hits	Winning pitcher	Losing pitcher	Save	Record	Pos.	GB
6-22	Fla.	L	0-2		6	6	Heredia	Urbina	Nen	41-31	3rd	5.5
6-23	Cin.	W	5-0		8	4	Bullinger	Smiley		42-31	3rd	4.5
6-24	Cin.	L	6-7	(10)	13	12	Shaw	Veres		42-32	4th	4.5
6-25	Cin.	L	1-2	(11)	9	6	Remlinger	Telford	Shaw	42-33	4th	5.5
6-26	At Fla.	W	5-2		10	4	Juden	Rapp		43-33	T3rd	5.5
6-27	At Fla.	W	2-0		10	6	Valdes	Brown	Urbina	44-33	3rd	5.5
6-28	At Fla.	L	2-4		3	6	Hernandez	Bullinger	Nen	44-34	T3rd	6.5
6-29	At Fla.	L	3-5		6	7	Leiter	Perez	Nen	44-35	4th	7.5
6-30	At Tor.	W	2-1		6	3	Martinez	Hentgen		45-35	T3rd	6.5
7-1	At Tor.	W	2-1		10	2	Juden	Clemens	Urbina	46-35	3rd	6.5
7-2	At Tor.	L	6-7	(13)	10	15	Timlin	Telford		46-36	3rd	7.5
7-3	Atl.	L	2-15		7	19	Smoltz	Bullinger		46-37	3rd	8.5
7-4	Atl.	L	3-6		6	11	Clontz	Urbina	Wohlers	46-38	T3rd	9.5
7-5	Atl.	L	3-5		8	8	Glavine	Martinez	Wohlers	46-39	4th	10.5
7-6	Atl.	W	6-2		11	6	Juden	Neagle		47-39	4th	9.5
7-11	At Cin.	W	5-2		8	12	Bullinger	Burba	Urbina	48-39	4th	8.0
7-12	At Cin.	L	3-4		6	8	Smiley	Perez	Shaw	48-40	4th	9.0
7-13	At Cin.	W	2-0		4	1	Martinez	Morgan		49-40	4th	8.0
7-14	At Fla.	L	4-5	(12)	9	10	Nen	Daal		49-41	4th	9.0
7-15	At Fla.	W	5-0		10	5	Hermanson	Saunders		50-41	4th	8.0
7-16	At Phi.	L	0-6		4	7	Schilling	Bullinger		50-42	4th	9.0
7-17	At Phi.	W	5-4		8	7	Perez	Beech	Urbina	51-42	4th	9.0
7-18	Hou.	L	0-2		6	8	Garcia	Martinez	Wagner	51-43	4th	10.0
7-19	Hou.	L	6-8		8	16	Reynolds	Juden	Wagner	51-44	4th	10.0
7-20	Hou.	L	0-9		4	8	Kile	Hermanson		51-45	4th	10.0
7-21	Col.	W	8-4		10	10	Urbina	Holmes		52-45	4th	10.0
7-22	Col.	L	9-11	(12)	15	19	S. Reed	Veres		52-46	4th	10.5
7-24	At Hou.	L	5-10		7	11	Martin	Telford		52-47	4th	10.5
7-25	At Hou.	L	2-5		7	6	Kile	Juden		52-48	4th	11.5
7-26	At Hou.	L	8-9	(10)	10	13	Wagner	Urbina		52-49	4th	11.5
7-27	At Hou.	L	2-7		8	8	Hampton	Bullinger		52-50	4th	12.5
7-28	At Col.	W	3-2		6	6	Perez	Swift	Urbina	53-50	4th	12.5
7-29	At Col.	W	3-0		7	5	Martinez	Wright		54-50	4th	12.5
7-30	At Col.	L	6-12		17	17	Castillo	Juden		54-51	4th	13.5
7-31	S.D.	W	9-2		8	9	Hermanson	Hitchcock	Valdes	55-51	4th	12.5
8-1	S.D.	L	2-8		4	16	Hamilton	Bullinger		55-52	4th	12.5
8-2	S.D.	W	6-0		8	5	Perez	Smith		56-52	4th	12.5
8-3	S.D.	W	6-3		12	3	Martinez	Ashby		57-52	4th	11.5
8-5	L.A.	L	4-5	(10)	11	9	Worrell	Urbina		57-53	4th	12.0
8-6	L.A.	W	7-3		10	8	Hermanson	Park		58-53	4th	12.0
8-7	L.A.	L	4-9		13	14	Nomo	Bullinger		58-54	4th	13.0
8-8	S.F.	L	0-4		2	9	Gardner	Perez		58-55	4th	13.0
8-9	S.F.	W	2-1		8	4	Martinez	Hernandez		59-55	4th	13.0
8-10	S.F.	L	3-6	(12)	11	12	Tavarez	Valdes	Henry	59-56	4th	13.0
8-11	At S.D.	W	6-3		12	7	Hermanson	Hamilton		60-56	4th	13.0
8-12	At S.D.	L	4-6		8	9	Bochtler	DeHart	Hoffman	60-57	4th	13.0
8-13	At L.A.	L	1-3		4	9	Candiotti	Perez	Worrell	60-58	4th	13.0
8-14	At L.A.	L	0-1		4	5	Valdes	Martinez	Radinsky	60-59	4th	13.5
8-15	At S.F.	L	2-6		9	10	Rueter	Johnson		60-60	4th	13.5
8-16	At S.F.	W	8-5		12	8	Hermanson	Rapp	Urbina	61-60	4th	13.5
8-17	At S.F.	L	6-8		7	11	Henry	Paniagua	Beck	61-61	4th	13.5
8-19	St.L.	L	5-12		9	16	Stottlemyre	Perez		61-62	4th	14.5
8-20	St.L.	L	3-6		10	8	King	Kline	Eckersley	61-63	4th	15.5
8-21	St.L.	W	3-2		9	2	Johnson	Osborne	Urbina	62-63	4th	15.0
8-22	At Chi.	L	1-3		5	5	Trachsel	Kline	Adams	62-64	4th	16.0
8-23	At Chi.	W	9-5		13	7	Telford	Patterson		63-64	4th	16.0
8-24	At Chi.	L	3-12		8	15	Gonzalez	Perez		63-65	4th	16.0
8-25	At St.L.	W	2-1		6	4	Martinez	Aybar	Urbina	64-65	4th	15.5
8-26	At St.L.	W	7-5		9	12	Valdes	Eckersley	Urbina	65-65	4th	15.5
8-27	At St.L.	L	3-4		10	7	Frascatore	Telford	Beltran	65-66	4th	15.5
8-28	At St.L.	L	5-11		7	15	An. Benes	Paniagua		65-67	4th	16.5
8-29	At N.Y. (AL)	W	4-3		9	8	Telford	Rivera	Urbina	66-67	4th	16.5
8-30	At N.Y. (AL)	W	7-2		11	5	Martinez	Wells		67-67	4th	16.5
8-31	At N.Y. (AL)	L	2-3		9	8	Pettitte	Johnson	Rivera	67-68	4th	17.5
9-1	Bos.	W	4-2	(10)	6	3	Urbina	Hudson		68-68	4th	16.5
9-2	Bos.	W	6-5		9	7	DeHart	Brandenburg	Urbina	69-68	4th	16.5
9-3	Bos.	W	1-0		1	2	Perez	Sele		70-68	4th	15.5
9-4	Phi.	L	4-6		10	8	Beech	Martinez	Bottalico	70-69	4th	16.5
9-5	Phi.	W	7-1		11	4	Johnson	Leiter		71-69	4th	15.5
9-6	Phi.	L	3-5		8	8	Schilling	Valdes		71-70	4th	16.5
9-7	Phi.	L	1-2		6	7	Karp	Telford	Bottalico	71-71	4th	17.5
9-9	Pit.	W	5-4	(10)	11	12	Urbina	Loiselle		72-71	4th	17.5
9-10	Pit.	W	5-4		8	10	Martinez	Lieber	Urbina	73-71	4th	17.5
9-11	At N.Y.	L	5-9		11	13	Reed	Johnson	J. Franco	73-72	4th	18.0
9-12	At N.Y.	W	3-2	(15)	7	12	Paniagua	Crawford	Urbina	74-72	4th	17.0
9-13	At N.Y.	L	6-9	(11)	14	9	J. Franco	Kline		74-73	4th	17.0

Date	Opp.	Res.	Score	(inn.*)	Hits	Opp. hits	Winning pitcher	Losing pitcher	Save	Record	Pos.	GB
9-14	At N.Y.	L	0-1		7	3	Mlicki	Perez	McMichael	74-74	4th	17.0
9-15	At Pit.	L	4-5	(10)	10	14	Wilkins	Telford		74-75	4th	18.0
9-16	At Pit.	L	2-8		6	11	Lieber	Johnson		74-76	4th	19.0
9-17	At Cin.	W	4-1		8	7	Bullinger	Belinda	Urbina	75-76	4th	19.0
9-18	At Cin.	L	3-6		8	12	Sullivan	Hermanson	Shaw	75-77	4th	20.0
9-19	At Atl.	L	1-2		5	3	Smoltz	Perez		75-78	4th	21.0
9-20	At Atl.	L	1-3		2	6	Glavine	Martinez		75-79	4th	22.0
9-21	At Atl.	W	7-1		11	10	DeHart	Neagle		76-79	4th	21.0
9-22	At Atl.	L	2-3	(11)	13	12	Cather	Bennett		76-80	4th	22.0
9-23	Fla.	L	3-6		9	11	Brown	Hermanson	Nen	76-81	4th	23.0
9-24	Fla.	L	9-10		11	8	Leiter	Perez	Vosberg	76-82	4th	23.0
9-25	Fla.	W	3-2		4	6	Kline	Nen		77-82	4th	23.0
9-26	Cin.	L	1-7		3	11	Morgan	Johnson		77-83	4th	24.0
9-27	Cin.	W	8-5		14	10	Thurman	Crowell	Telford	78-83	4th	23.0
9-28	Cin.	L	3-11		4	12	Remlinger	Hermanson		78-84	4th	23.0

Monthly records: April (12-12), May (16-12), June (17-11), July (10-16), August (12-17), September (11-16).
*Innings, if other than nine. †First game of doubleheader. ‡Second game of doubleheader.

HIGHLIGHTS

High point: The high point of the 1997 season came on July 1, Canada Day, when the Expos beat the Toronto Blue Jays and Roger Clemens 2-1 in front of 50,436 at SkyDome. It was the last time they would be 11 games over .500.

Low point: The Expos were forced to watch two National League East Division teams clinch post-season berths on back to back days: September 22, when the Atlanta Braves clinched the division title with an 11-inning win and September 23, when the Florida Marlins beat the Expos 6-3 to win the wild-card.

Turning point: One pitch turned around the Expos season. It was thrown by Cincinnati's Stan Belinda on July 11 and struck rookie right fielder Vladimir Guerrero on the left hand, breaking his fifth metacarpal and causing him to miss 16 games. Expos management, once again hamstrung by budgetary restraints, made no move to help the team.

Most valuable player: Mike Lansing was the anchor of the infield defense and the clubhouse leader while hitting .281 with 20 home runs and 70 runs batted in.

Most valuable pitcher: Pedro Martinez won the National League Cy Young Award with a 17-8 record, 305 strikeouts and a league-leading 1.90 ERA.

Most improved player: Who is Anthony Telford? A long-shot to make the roster out of spring training, Telford ended up logging 89 relief innings, fifth highest in the National League.

Most pleasant surprise: Righthander Dustin Hermanson never had started in his three-year professional career and had been a reliever in his final season at Kent University. Expos manager Felipe Alou turned him into a starter, and Hermanson developed a change-up. Hermanson finished 8-8 (3.69) and put together a 29-inning scoreless streak that was the longest in the National League.

Biggest disappointment: Henry Rodriguez continued to strike out at an alarming rate. He was a non-factor in the second half, hitting .197 with 10 home runs and 32 runs batted in while playing the same inconsistent defense.

Key injuries: Third baseman Shane Andrews, counted on to provide righthanded power and strong defense at third base, was lost to the team in early May after he pulled the long thoracic nerve in the back of his left shoulder. Vladimir Guerrero had three separate stints on the 15-day disabled list, beginning on the second-last day of spring training. He missed 52 games due to stints on the DL. Lefthander Rheal Cormier, meanwhile, was lost for the season after undergoing Tommy John tendon transplant surgery.

Notable: Shortstop Mark Grudzielanek tied Alex Rodriguez's major league record for doubles at the position (54), surpassing the National League record of 48 set by Dick Bartell in 1932.

—JEFF BLAIR

RECORDS

1997 regular-season record: 78-84 (4th in N.L. East); 45-36 at home; 33-48 on road; 30-33 vs. East; 26-29 vs. Central; 22-22 vs. West; 24-18 vs. lefthanded starters; 54-66 vs. righthanded starters; 23-33 on grass; 55-51 on turf; 26-26 in daytime; 52-58 at night; 28-25 in one-run games; 4-12 in extra-inning games; 1-0-0 in doubleheaders.

Team record past five years: 400-344 (.538, ranks 2nd in league in that span).

TEAM LEADERS

Batting average: David Segui (.307).
At-bats: Mark Grudzielanek (649).
Runs: Mike Lansing (86).
Hits: Mark Grudzielanek (177).
Total bases: Rondell White (283).
Doubles: Mark Grudzielanek (54).
Triples: F.P. Santangelo, Rondell White (5).
Home runs: Rondell White (28).
Runs batted in: Henry Rodriguez (83).
Stolen bases: Mark Grudzielanek (25).
Slugging percentage: David Segui (.505).
On-base percentage: David Segui (.380).
Wins: Pedro Martinez (17).
Earned-run average: Pedro Martinez (1.90).
Complete games: Pedro Martinez (13).
Shutouts: Carlos Perez (5).
Saves: Ugueth Urbina (27).
Innings pitched: Pedro Martinez (241.1).
Strikeouts: Pedro Martinez (305).

GAMES BY POSITION

Catcher: Chris Widger 85, Darrin Fletcher 83, Raul Chavez 13.
First base: David Segui 125, Ryan McGuire 30, Joe Orsulak 15, Brad Fullmer 8, Hensley Meulens 3, Henry Rodriguez 3, Doug Strange 1.
Second base: Mike Lansing 144, Andy Stankiewicz 25, F.P. Santangelo 7, Jose Vidro 5, Orlando Cabrera 4, Doug Strange 3.
Third base: Doug Strange 105, Jose Vidro 36, F.P. Santangelo 32, Shane Andrews 18, Andy Stankiewicz 3.
Shortstop: Mark Grudzielanek 156, Andy Stankiewicz 14, Orlando Cabrera 6, F.P. Santangelo 1.
Outfield: Rondell White 151, Henry Rodriguez 126, F.P. Santangelo 99, Vladimir Guerrero 85, Joe Orsulak 63, Ryan McGuire 44, Sherman Obando 15, Hensley Meulens 8, Brad Fullmer 2, Doug Strange 2.
Designated hitter: Jose Vidro 5, Ryan McGuire 3, Sherman Obando 2, Andy Stankiewicz 2, Joe Orsulak 1.

TOP DRAFT CHOICES

1a. **Donnie Bridges,** RHP, Oak Grove H.S., Hattiesburg, Miss.
1b. **Chris Stowe,** RHP, Chancellor H.S., Fredericksburg, Va.
1c. **Scott Hodges,** SS, Henry Clay H.S., Lexington, Ky.
1d. **Bryan Hebson,** RHP, Auburn University.
1e. **Thomas Pittman,** 1B, East St. John H.S., Garyville, Las.
1f. **T.J. Tucker,** RHP, River Ridge H.S., New Port Richey, Fla.
1g. **Shane Arthurs,** RHP, Westmoore H.S., Oklahoma City.
1h. **Tootie Myers,** OF, Petal (Miss.) H.S.
2. **Kris Tetz,** RHP, Lodi (Calif.) H.S.
3. **Josh Redding,** SS, Rancho Santiago (Calif.) J.C.
4. **Ronte Langs,** OF, Whitehaven H.S., Memphis, Tenn.
5. **Julio Perez,** RHP, Brito H.S., Miami.
6. **Scott Ackerman,** C, Oregon City (Ore.) H.S.
7. **Anthony Caracciolo,** SS, Basic H.S., Henderson, Nev.
8. **Ryan Becks,** LHP, West Valley (Calif.) J.C.
9. **Talmadge Nunnari,** 1B, Jacksonville U.
10. **Scott Strickland,** RHP, U. of New Mexico.

NEW YORK METS
NATIONAL LEAGUE EAST DIVISION

Mets Schedule
Home games shaded. *—All-Star Game at Coors Field (Colorado).
D—Day game (any game starting before 5 p.m.).

March

SUN	MON	TUE	WED	THU	FRI	SAT
		31 D PHI	D			

April

SUN	MON	TUE	WED	THU	FRI	SAT
			1	2 PHI	3 D PIT	4 D PIT
5 D PIT	6 D PIT	7 D CUB	8 D CUB	9 CUB	10 D MIL	11 D MIL
12 MIL	13 MIL	14 CUB	15 CUB	16 D CUB	17 CIN	18 D CIN
19 CIN	20	21 HOU	22 HOU	23 HOU	24 CIN	25 D CIN
26 CIN	27	28 HOU	29 HOU	30 COL		

May

SUN	MON	TUE	WED	THU	FRI	SAT
					1 COL	2 D COL
3 D COL	4 ARZ	5 ARZ	6 ARZ	7 STL	8 STL	9 D STL
10 D STL	11 SD	12 SD	13 SD	14 D SF	15 SF	16 D SF
17 D SF	18	19 CIN	20 CIN	21 CIN	22 MIL	23 D MIL
24 D MIL	25	26 FLA	27 FLA	28	29 PHI	30 PHI
31 D PHI						

June

SUN	MON	TUE	WED	THU	FRI	SAT
	1 PIT	2 PIT	3 PIT	4	5 BOS	6 BOS
7 D BOS	8 TB	9 TB	10 D TB	11 FLA	12 FLA	13 FLA
14 D FLA	15	16 MON	17 MON	18 MON	19 D FLA	20 D FLA
21 FLA	22 BAL	23 BAL	24 BAL	25 NYY	26 NYY	27 D NYY
28 NYY	29	30 TOR				

July

SUN	MON	TUE	WED	THU	FRI	SAT
			1 D TOR	2 TOR	3 ATL	4 ATL
5 ATL	6 D	7	*8	9 MON	10 MON	11 MON
12 MON	13	14 ATL	15 D ATL	16 PHI	17 PHI	18 PHI
19 PHI	20 PIT	21 PIT	22 MIL	23 D MIL	24 D CUB	25 D CUB
26 CUB	27	28 SD	29 SD	30 SD	31 LA	

August

SUN	MON	TUE	WED	THU	FRI	SAT
						1 LA
2 D LA	3 LA	4 SF	5 SF	6 SF	7 D COL	8 COL
9 D COL	10 STL	11 STL	12 STL	13	14 ARZ	15 ARZ
16 ARZ	17	18 COL	19 COL	20 STL	21 STL	22 ARZ
23 D ARZ	24 ARZ	25 SF	26 SF	27 D SF	28 LA	29 LA
30 LA	31 LA					

September

SUN	MON	TUE	WED	THU	FRI	SAT
		1 SD	2 SD	3	4 ATL	5 D ATL
6 D ATL	7 D PHI	8 PHI	9 PHI	10 PHI	11 MON	12 MON
13 MON	14 HOU	15 HOU	16 HOU	17 D HOU	18 FLA	19 D FLA
20 D FLA	21	22 MON	23 MON	24	25 ATL	26 ATL
27 D ATL						

1998 SEASON
CLUB DIRECTORY

Chairman of the board
Nelson Doubleday

President and chief executive officer
Fred Wilpon

Directors
Nelson Doubleday, Fred Wilpon, Saul B. Katz, Joe McIlvaine, Marvin B. Tepper

Special advisor to the board of directors
Richard Cummins

Senior v.p., general manager
Steve Phillips

Assistant general manager
Omar Minaya

Director of player personnel
Jim Duquette

Director of amateur scouting
Gary Larocque

Director of professional scouting
Carmen Fusco

Special assistants to general manager
Jack Zduriencik, Dave Wallace, Harry Minor

Assistant director of amateur scouting
Fred Wright

Assistant director of player personnel
Tom Hutchinson

Senior v.p. and treasurer
Harold W. O'Shaughnessy

V.p. bus. aff., gen. counsel & secretary
David Howard

Vice president, marketing
Mark Bingham

Vice president, stadium operations
Bob Mandt

Vice president, ticket sales and services
Bill Ianniciello

Senior v.p. and consultant
J. Frank Cashen

Director of marketing
Kit Geis

Director of marketing production
Tim Gunkel

Director of human resources
Ray Scott

General counsel
David Cohen

Dir., admin. and data processing
Russ Richardson

Director, community outreach
Jill Knee

Director of promotions
James Plummer

Director of media relations
Jay Horwitz

Director, ticket operations
Dan DeMato

Manager, customer relations
Joann Galardy

Club physicians
Dr. David Altchek

Club psychologist/E.A.P.
Dr. Allan Lans

Team trainers
Fred Hina, Scott Lawrenson

Special assignment scouts
Buddy Kerr, Darrell Johnson

Major league scouts
Dick Gernert, Howard Johnson, Roland Johnson, Bill Latham

National cross-checker
Jack Bowen

Regional scouting supervisors
Paul Ricciarini, Terry Tripp, Paul Fryer, Bob Minor

Scouting supervisors
Tom Allison, Kevin Blankenship, Quincy Boyd, Larry Chase, Joe DelliCarri, Chuck Hensley Jr., Bob Lavalee, Dave Lottsfeldt, Fred Mazuca, Marlin McPhail, Randy Milligan, Joe Nigro, Joe Norlen, Carlos Pascual, Jim Reeves, Junior Roman, Bob Rossi, Joe Salermo, Eddy Toledo, Terry Tripp, Greg Tubbs

Part-time scouts
Chet Atkins, Wilfredo Blanco, Joe Bogar, Marcos Briceno, David De La Cruz, Steve Free, Rich Hinell, Andy Lawrence, Gregorio Machado, Cookie Mitchell, Charlie Ready, Tim Rock, Felix Rodriguez, Doug Sisk, James Waddell, George Walden, Joe Willingham

MINOR LEAGUE AFFILIATES

Class	Team	League	Manager
AAA	Norfolk	International	Rick Dempsey
AA	Binghamton	Eastern	John Gibbons
A	St. Lucie	Florida State	Howie Freiling
A	Capital City	South Atlantic	Doug Davis
A	Pittsfield	New York-Pennsylvania	To be announced
Rookie	Kingsport	Appalachian	To be announced
Rookie	Gulf Coast Mets	Gulf Coast	John Stephenson

BROADCAST INFORMATION

Radio: WFAN-AM (660).
TV: WWOR-TV (Channel 9).
Cable TV: SportsChannel.

SPRING TRAINING

Ballpark (city): St. Lucie County Stadium (Port St. Lucie, Fla.).
Ticket information: 561-871-2115.

SPRING TRAINING ROSTER

Manager—Bobby Valentine (2).
Coaches—Bob Apodaca (34), Bruce Benedict (20), Randy Niemann, Tom Robson (53), Cookie Rojas (4), Mookie Wilson (51).

No.	PITCHERS	B/T	Ht./Wt.	Born	1997 clubs
39	Acevedo, Juan	R/R	6-2/218	5-5-70	Norfolk, New York N.L.
46	Bohanon, Brian	L/L	6-3/220	8-1-68	Norfolk, New York N.L.
	Cook, Dennis	L/L	6-3/190	10-4-62	Florida
	Dotel, Octavio	R/R	6-0/175	11-25-75	St. Lucie, Binghamton, Gulf Coast Mets
31	Franco, John	L/L	5-10/185	9-17-60	New York N.L.
	Gooch, Arnold	R/R	6-2/195	11-11-76	Binghamton
	Hudek, John	B/R	6-2/200	8-8-66	Houston, New Orleans
44	Isringhausen, Jason	R/R	6-3/196	9-7-72	Norfolk, St. Lucie, Gulf Coast Mets, New York N.L.
28	Jones, Bobby	R/R	6-4/225	2-10-70	New York N.L.
36	McMichael, Greg	R/R	6-3/215	12-1-66	New York N.L.
	Mercado, Hector	L/L	6-3/205	4-29-74	Portland, Charlotte
38	Mlicki, Dave	R/R	6-4/205	6-8-68	New York N.L.
	Pulsipher, Bill	L/L	6-3/200	10-9-73	Norfolk, St. Lucie, Binghamton, Gulf Coast Mets
35	Reed, Rick	R/R	6-0/200	8-16-64	New York N.L.
40	Reynoso, Armando	R/R	6-0/204	5-1-66	St. Lucie, New York N.L.
51	Rojas, Mel	R/R	5-11/195	12-10-66	Chicago N.L., New York N.L.
	Sanchez, Jesus	L/L	5-10/153	10-11-74	Binghamton
47	Wallace, Derek	R/R	6-3/215	9-1-71	Norfolk, St. Lucie, Gulf Coast Mets
99	Wendell, Turk	L/R	6-2/205	5-19-67	Chicago N.L., New York N.L.
	Wilson, Paul	R/R	6-5/235	3-28-73	Gulf Coast Mets, St. Lucie
	Yoshii, Masato	R/R	6-1/194	4-20-65	Yakult (Japan)

No.	CATCHERS	B/T	Ht./Wt.	Born	1997 clubs
30	Castillo, Alberto	R/R	6-0/184	2-10-70	New York N.L., Norfolk
9	Hundley, Todd	B/R	5-11/185	5-27-69	New York N.L.
43	Pratt, Todd	R/R	6-3/224	2-9-67	Norfolk, New York N.L.
	Wilson, Vance	R/R	5-11/190	3-17-73	Binghamton

No.	INFIELDERS	B/T	Ht./Wt.	Born	1997 clubs
13	Alfonzo, Ed	R/R	5-11/187	11-8-73	New York N.L.
8	Baerga, Carlos	B/R	5-11/200	11-4-68	New York N.L.
15	Franco, Matt	L/R	6-2/210	8-19-69	Norfolk, New York N.L.
17	Lopez, Luis	B/R	5-11/175	9-4-70	Norfolk, New York N.L.
	Olerud, John	L/L	6-5/220	8-5-68	New York N.L.
0	Ordonez, Rey	R/R	5-9/159	11-11-72	New York N.L.
10	Petagine, Roberto	L/L	6-1/170	6-2-71	Norfolk, New York N.L.

No.	OUTFIELDERS	B/T	Ht./Wt.	Born	1997 clubs
	Becker, Rich	L/L	5-10/192	2-1-72	Minnesota
23	Gilkey, Bernard	R/R	6-0/200	9-24-66	New York N.L.
	Hunter, Scott	R/R	6-2/195	12-17-75	Binghamton
42	Huskey, Butch	R/R	6-3/244	11-10-71	New York N.L.
	Long, Terrence	L/L	6-1/180	2-29-76	St. Lucie
56	McRae, Brian	B/R	6-0/195	8-27-67	Chicago N.L., New York N.L.
	Payton, Jay	R/R	5-10/185	11-22-72	DID NOT PLAY
	Wilson, Preston	R/R	6-2/193	7-19-74	St. Lucie, Binghamton

BALLPARK INFORMATION

Ballpark (capacity, surface)
Shea Stadium (55,777, grass)

Address
123-10 Roosevelt Ave.
Flushing, NY 11368-1699

Business phone
718-507-6387

Ticket information
718-507-8499

Ticket prices
$35 (Metropolitan Club seating)
$24 (inner field box, inner loge box)
$21 (outer field box, outer loge box,
      mezzanine box)
$18 (loge reserved)
$15 (mezzanine box, upper box)
$9 (upper reserved, back rows loge and mezzanine)

Field dimensions (from home plate)
To left field at foul line, 338 feet
To center field, 410 feet
To right field at foul line, 338 feet

First game played
April 17, 1964 (Pirates 4, Mets 3)

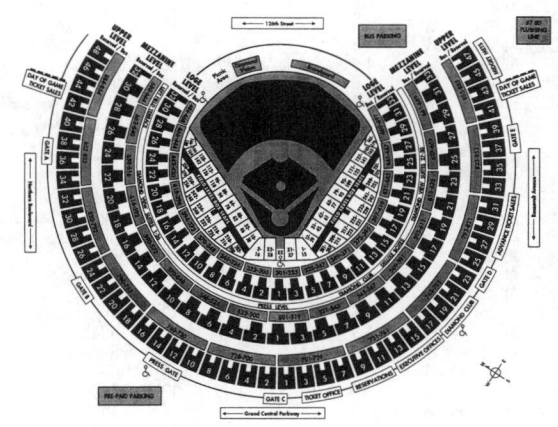

Date	Opp.	Res.	Score	(inn.*)	Hits	Opp. hits	Winning pitcher	Losing pitcher	Save	Record	Pos.	GB
4-1	At S.D.	L	5-12		9	11	Hamilton	Perez		0-1	T4th	1.0
4-2	At S.D.	L	5-6	(12)	5	12	Bergman	Jordan		0-2	T4th	2.0
4-3	At S.D.	W	4-1		8	7	Jones	Valenzuela	J. Franco	1-2	T3rd	2.0
4-4	At S.F.	L	4-6		9	10	Rodriguez	Jordan	Beck	1-3	T4th	2.0
4-5	At S.F.	L	0-2		3	6	Roa	Manuel	Beck	1-4	T4th	3.0
4-6	At S.F.	W	4-2		11	6	Bohanon	Gardner	J. Franco	2-4	T4th	3.0
4-7	At L.A.	L	2-3	(15)	7	12	Astacio	Crawford		2-5	T4th	3.5
4-8	At L.A.	W	5-3		9	5	Jones	Valdes	McMichael	3-5	T4th	3.5
4-9	At L.A.	L	2-3	(14)	4	6	Candiotti	Bohanon		3-6	T4th	4.0
4-13†	S.F.	L	1-5		9	10	Gardner	Clark		3-7		
4-13‡	S.F.	L	6-7		12	10	Estes	Jones	Beck	3-8	T4th	5.0
4-14	S.F.	L	2-3		7	7	Rodriguez	McMichael	Beck	3-9	5th	6.0
4-15	L.A.	W	5-0		10	8	Reynoso	Valdes	Borland	4-9	4th	6.0
4-16	L.A.	L	2-5		1	11	Astacio	Reed	Worrell	4-10	4th	7.0
4-19	Chi.	W	6-3		8	7	Clark	Wendell	J. Franco	5-10	T4th	7.5
4-20†	Chi.	W	8-2		13	5	Jones	Trachsel		6-10		
4-20‡	Chi.	L	3-4		8	12	Foster	Mlicki	Wendell	6-11	4th	7.0
4-21	Chi.	L	4-6		5	8	Castillo	McMichael	Adams	6-12	T4th	7.5
4-22	Cin.	W	7-2		10	7	Reed	Smiley		7-12	4th	7.5
4-23	Cin.	W	10-2		14	7	Clark	Morgan		8-12	4th	6.5
4-25	At Mon.	L	1-4		6	9	Perez	Jones		8-13	4th	7.5
4-26	At Mon.	L	1-8		4	11	Martinez	Mlicki		8-14	4th	8.5
4-27	At Mon.	W	5-3	(10)	12	9	McMichael	Smith	J. Franco	9-14	4th	8.5
4-28	At Cin.	W	15-2		17	6	Reed	Smiley		10-14	4th	8.5
4-29	At Cin.	W	3-1		9	7	Clark	Morgan	J. Franco	11-14	4th	7.5
4-30	S.D.	W	6-2		10	7	Jones	Hitchcock	J. Franco	12-14	4th	7.5
5-1	S.D.	L	3-7		8	12	Ashby	Mlicki		12-15	4th	8.5
5-2	St.L.	W	7-4		11	6	McMichael	Mathews	J. Franco	13-15	4th	7.5
5-3	St.L.	W	5-1		9	8	Reed	An. Benes		14-15	4th	6.5
5-4	St.L.	L	2-8		5	13	Stottlemyre	Clark		14-16	4th	7.5
5-5	At Col.	W	6-1		8	7	Jones	Ritz		15-16	4th	7.5
5-6	At Col.	L	11-12		20	14	Swift	Borland	S. Reed	15-17	4th	7.5
5-7	At Hou.	W	4-1		10	4	Reynoso	Martin	J. Franco	16-17	4th	7.5
5-8	At Hou.	L	2-4		8	11	Hampton	Reed	Wagner	16-18	4th	7.5
5-9	At St.L.	W	10-3		12	9	Clark	Stottlemyre		17-18	4th	6.5
5-10	At St.L.	W	2-0		9	3	Jones	Al. Benes	J. Franco	18-18	4th	6.5
5-11	At St.L.	W	6-4		9	9	Lidle	Eckersley	J. Franco	19-18	4th	6.5
5-13	Hou.	W	4-3		8	7	McMichael	Springer	J. Franco	20-18	4th	6.0
5-14	Hou.	L	0-1		4	7	Kile	McMichael	Wagner	20-19	4th	6.0
5-16	Col.	L	1-2		8	7	Munoz	McMichael	Ruffin	20-20	4th	7.0
5-17	Col.	W	3-1		10	8	Jones	Thomson	J. Franco	21-20	4th	7.0
5-18	Col.	W	10-4		9	8	Kashiwada	Ruffin		22-20	4th	7.0
5-19	Col.	W	4-3		11	3	Lidle	McCurry		23-20	4th	7.0
5-20	At Fla.	L	5-6		11	12	Nen	J. Franco		23-21	4th	8.0
5-21	At Fla.	W	2-1		6	8	Clark	Leiter	McMichael	24-21	4th	8.0
5-22	At Phi.	W	10-3		14	9	Jones	Schilling		25-21	T3rd	7.5
5-23	At Phi.	L	1-2		4	7	Stephenson	Mlicki	Bottalico	25-22	4th	8.5
5-24	At Phi.	W	8-4		11	13	Reynoso	Maduro	J. Franco	26-22	4th	7.5
5-26	At Mon.	W	4-3		7	8	Lidle	Urbina	J. Franco	27-22	3rd	7.0
5-27	At Mon.	L	4-5		7	12	Valdes	Clark	Smith	27-23	4th	8.0
5-28	At Mon.	W	7-0		10	4	Jones	Martinez		28-23	3rd	7.5
5-30	Phi.	W	7-3		9	8	Mlicki	Ramos		29-23	3rd	7.0
5-31	Phi.	W	10-3		16	10	Reynoso	Leiter		30-23	3rd	6.0
6-1	Phi.	W	8-5		10	12	Reed	Beech	Lidle	31-23	3rd	6.0
6-2	Mon.	L	0-10		6	13	Perez	Clark		31-24	3rd	6.0
6-3	Mon.	W	2-1		7	5	Jones	Martinez	J. Franco	32-24	3rd	5.0
6-4	Fla.	L	2-5		5	11	Rapp	Mlicki	Nen	32-25	3rd	6.0
6-5	Fla.	W	6-0		12	5	Reynoso	Brown		33-25	3rd	6.0
6-6	At Cin.	L	2-5		7	10	Tomko	Reed	Shaw	33-26	3rd	7.0
6-7	At Cin.	L	5-10		9	16	Sullivan	Lidle		33-27	3rd	8.0
6-9	At Cin.	W	4-2		9	7	Jones	Belinda	J. Franco	34-27	3rd	6.5
6-10	At Chi.	W	10-6		13	12	Mlicki	Foster		35-27	3rd	6.5
6-11	At Chi.	L	4-5		7	13	Adams	McMichael		35-28	T3rd	6.5
6-13	Bos.	L	4-8		12	11	Suppan	Reed	Lacy	35-29	4th	6.5
6-14	Bos.	W	5-2		11	3	Clark	Wakefield	J. Franco	36-29	4th	5.5
6-15	Bos.	L	1-10		5	13	Eshelman	Jones		36-30	4th	5.5
6-16	At N.Y. (AL)	W	6-0		9	9	Mlicki	Pettitte		37-30	4th	5.5
6-17	At N.Y. (AL)	L	3-6		7	11	Wells	Reynoso	Rivera	37-31	4th	6.5
6-18	At N.Y. (AL)	L	2-3	(10)	3	8	Stanton	McMichael		37-32	4th	6.5
6-19	Pit.	W	7-6		15	8	J. Franco	Rincon		38-32	4th	6.0
6-20	Pit.	W	1-0		9	6	Jones	Cooke	J. Franco	39-32	4th	6.0

– 124 –

Date	Opp.	Res.	Score	(inn.*)	Hits	Opp. hits	Winning pitcher	Losing pitcher	Save	Record	Pos.	GB
6-21	Pit.	W	3-2		6	8	Mlicki	Wilkins	McMichael	40-32	4th	6.0
6-22	Pit.	W	12-9	(10)	18	13	Kashiwada	Peters		41-32	4th	6.0
6-23	Atl.	W	3-2		10	6	Reed	Smoltz		42-32	4th	5.0
6-24	Atl.	W	6-5		11	12	McMichael	Wohlers		43-32	3rd	4.0
6-25	Atl.	L	7-14		9	17	Glavine	Jones		43-33	3rd	5.0
6-27	At Pit.	L	1-6		5	14	Schmidt	Mlicki		43-34	4th	6.5
6-28	At Pit.	W	8-3		11	9	Reynoso	Loaiza		44-34	T3rd	6.5
6-29	At Pit.	W	10-8		12	15	Jordan	Peters	J. Franco	45-34	3rd	6.5
6-30	At Det.	L	0-14		5	15	Thompson	Clark		45-35	T3rd	6.5
7-1	At Det.	L	6-8		13	11	Moehler	Jones	Jones	45-36	4th	7.5
7-2	At Det.	L	7-9		14	10	Blair	Mlicki	Jones	45-37	4th	8.5
7-3	Fla.	L	4-10		11	14	Hernandez	Reynoso		45-38	4th	9.5
7-4	Fla.	W	6-2		8	8	Reed	Leiter	McMichael	46-38	T3rd	9.5
7-5	Fla.	W	5-3		11	12	Clark	Fernandez	J. Franco	47-38	3rd	9.5
7-6	Fla.	W	3-2	(12)	10	8	Acevedo	Cook		48-38	3rd	8.5
7-10	At Atl.	W	10-7		15	11	McMichael	Bielecki	J. Franco	49-38	3rd	7.5
7-11	At Atl.	W	9-7		12	11	Lidle	Glavine	J. Franco	50-38	3rd	6.5
7-12	At Atl.	L	4-7		7	10	Maddux	Clark	Wohlers	50-39	3rd	7.5
7-13	At Atl.	W	7-6	(10)	9	12	McMichael	Bielecki	J. Franco	51-39	3rd	6.5
7-14	At Pit.	L	4-5		10	15	Rincon	McMichael	Loiselle	51-40	3rd	7.5
7-15	At Pit.	L	3-4		7	9	Christiansen	Acevedo	Loiselle	51-41	3rd	7.5
7-16	Chi.	L	5-6		7	10	Gonzalez	Reynoso	Rojas	51-42	3rd	8.5
7-17	Chi.	W	4-3	(10)	12	9	J. Franco	Bottenfield		52-42	3rd	8.5
7-18	Cin.	W	4-3		5	5	Crawford	Morgan	J. Franco	53-42	3rd	8.5
7-19	Cin.	W	5-3		5	7	Reed	Tomko	McMichael	54-42	3rd	7.5
7-20	Cin.	W	10-1		15	7	Mlicki	Mercker		55-42	3rd	6.5
7-21	Cin.	W	5-3		4	7	McMichael	Sullivan	J. Franco	56-42	3rd	6.5
7-22	At L.A.	L	3-8		5	11	Candiotti	Clark		56-43	3rd	7.0
7-23	At L.A.	W	2-1		9	4	Bohanon	Reyes	J. Franco	57-43	3rd	6.0
7-24	At L.A.	W	3-1		10	4	Reed	Guthrie	J. Franco	58-43	T2nd	5.5
7-25	At S.D.	W	4-2		8	4	Kashiwada	Worrell	McMichael	59-43	T2nd	5.5
7-26	At S.D.	L	3-5		7	8	Hitchcock	Jones	Hoffman	59-44	T2nd	5.5
7-27	At S.D.	L	3-5		6	13	Cunnane	Kashiwada	Hoffman	59-45	T2nd	6.5
7-29	At S.F.	L	2-5		5	9	Estes	McMichael	Beck	59-46	3rd	8.0
7-30	At S.F.	W	5-2		13	5	Reed	Tavarez	J. Franco	60-46	3rd	8.0
8-1	At Hou.	W	8-5	(10)	11	10	J. Franco	Lima		61-46	3rd	6.5
8-2	At Hou.	L	0-6		3	10	Hampton	Jones		61-47	3rd	7.5
8-3	At Hou.	L	2-3		6	7	Martin	McMichael		61-48	3rd	7.5
8-4	St.L.	W	4-2		8	6	Reed	Aybar	J. Franco	62-48	3rd	7.5
8-5	St.L.	W	5-4	(10)	7	10	Lidle	Fossas		63-48	3rd	6.5
8-6	Col.	L	0-4		4	12	Thomson	Mlicki		63-49	3rd	7.5
8-7	Col.	W	12-4		16	8	Clark	Swift		64-49	3rd	7.5
8-8	Hou.	W	6-1		13	3	Bohanon	Reynolds		65-49	3rd	6.5
8-9	Hou.	L	3-8		4	11	Springer	Rojas		65-50	3rd	7.5
8-10	Hou.	L	8-11		11	14	Kile	Reed	Martin	65-51	3rd	7.5
8-11	Hou.	L	3-8		11	11	Garcia	Harnisch		65-52	3rd	8.5
8-12	At St.L.	L	2-5		9	8	An. Benes	Mlicki	Eckersley	65-53	3rd	8.5
8-13	At St.L.	W	5-4	(10)	11	13	Lidle	Fossas	J. Franco	66-53	3rd	7.5
8-14	At St.L.	W	6-2		10	7	Jones	Osborne		67-53	3rd	7.0
8-15	At Col.	L	2-6		8	12	Castillo	Reed		67-54	3rd	7.0
8-16	At Col.	L	5-7		12	13	Holmes	McMichael	DiPoto	67-55	3rd	8.0
8-17	At Col.	L	4-6		9	9	Thomson	Mlicki	DiPoto	67-56	3rd	8.0
8-19	L.A.	L	2-4		9	9	Valdes	Bohanon	Worrell	67-57	3rd	9.0
8-21†	L.A.	W	3-1		6	5	Crawford	Candiotti	J. Franco	68-57		
8-21‡	L.A.	L	3-4		7	7	Park	Reed	Worrell	68-58	3rd	9.5
8-22	S.D.	W	9-8	(11)	13	12	J. Franco	Bochtler		69-58	3rd	9.5
8-23	S.D.	W	9-5		12	14	Mlicki	Menhart	J. Franco	70-58	3rd	9.5
8-24	S.D.	L	2-3		5	9	Smith	Bohanon	Hoffman	70-59	3rd	9.5
8-25	S.F.	L	1-7		6	11	Estes	Jones		70-60	3rd	10.0
8-26	S.F.	L	2-6		10	5	Alvarez	Reed		70-61	3rd	11.0
8-27	S.F.	W	15-6		17	14	Isringhausen	Tavarez		71-61	3rd	10.0
8-29	At Bal.	L	3-4	(12)	9	10	Rhodes	J. Franco		71-62	3rd	11.5
8-30	At Bal.	W	13-6		19	9	Bohanon	Mathews	Lidle	72-62	3rd	11.5
8-31	At Bal.	W	4-1		8	6	Reed	Key	J. Franco	73-62	3rd	11.5
9-1	Tor.	W	3-0		6	2	Isringhausen	Hentgen	J. Franco	74-62	3rd	10.5
9-2	Tor.	W	8-5		12	7	Acevedo	Clemens	Wendell	75-62	3rd	10.5
9-3	Tor.	W	4-2		10	5	Mlicki	Quantrill	J. Franco	76-62	3rd	9.5
9-5	At Chi.	L	3-8		4	8	Tapani	Bohanon		76-63	3rd	10.0
9-6	At Chi.	L	5-7		9	10	Pisciotta	J. Franco	Adams	76-64	3rd	11.0
9-7	At Chi.	W	9-2		13	8	Jones	Trachsel		77-64	3rd	11.0
9-8	Phi.	L	4-13		8	13	Grace	Isringhausen		77-65	3rd	11.5
9-9	Phi.	L	0-1		6	4	Green	Mlicki	Bottalico	77-66	3rd	12.5
9-10	Phi.	W	10-2		16	7	Bohanon	Beech		78-66	3rd	12.5
9-11	Mon.	W	9-5		13	11	Reed	Johnson	J. Franco	79-66	3rd	12.0
9-12	Mon.	L	2-3	(15)	12	7	Paniagua	Crawford	Urbina	79-67	3rd	12.0

Date	Opp.	Res.	Score	(inn.*)	Hits	Opp. hits	Winning pitcher	Losing pitcher	Save	Record	Pos.	GB
9-13	Mon.	W	9-6	(11)	9	14	J. Franco	Kline		80-67	3rd	11.0
9-14	Mon.	W	1-0		3	7	Mlicki	Perez	McMichael	81-67	3rd	10.0
9-15†	At Phi.	W	10-5	(10)	14	10	Lidle	Karp		82-67		
9-15‡	At Phi.	L	1-2		3	6	Winston	Crawford	Bottalico	82-68	3rd	10.5
9-16	At Phi.	L	2-3		3	5	Schilling	Reed		82-69	3rd	11.5
9-17	At Atl.	L	2-10		6	14	Maddux	Jones		82-70	3rd	12.5
9-18	At Atl.	L	4-11		4	17	Byrd	Isringhausen		82-71	3rd	13.5
9-19	At Fla.	L	2-5		5	6	Leiter	Mlicki		82-72	3rd	14.5
9-20	At Fla.	W	7-3		10	6	Bohanon	Fernandez		83-72	3rd	14.5
9-21	At Fla.	W	2-1		8	5	Reed	Ojala	Rojas	84-72	3rd	13.5
9-22	At Fla.	W	10-3		11	7	Jones	Hernandez		85-72	3rd	13.5
9-23	Pit.	L	4-5		4	7	Silva	Lidle	Loiselle	85-73	3rd	14.5
9-24	Pit.	W	7-5		8	8	Crawford	Cooke	Rojas	86-73	3rd	13.5
9-26	Atl.	L	6-7	(11)	7	12	LeRoy	Rojas	Ligtenberg	86-74	3rd	15.0
9-27	Atl.	W	2-1		4	5	Crawford	Wohlers		87-74	3rd	14.0
9-28	Atl.	W	8-2		11	7	Acevedo	Neagle		88-74	3rd	13.0

Monthly records: April (12-14), May (18-9), June (15-12), July (15-11), August (13-16), September (15-12).
*Innings, if other than nine. †First game of doubleheader. ‡Second game of doubleheader.

HIGHLIGHTS

High point: Just after the All-Star break, the team took three of four from the first-place Braves in Atlanta. The highlight came in the final game on July 13, which the Mets won 7-6 in 11 innings. Bobby Jones allowed six runs in the first inning, but then held the Braves scoreless for six innings. Butch Huskey hit two home runs off Denny Neagle, and Alex Ochoa smoked a pinch-hit home run to win it for New York in the 10th.

Low point: Late in the season, an internal disagreement became public. On August 21, Todd Hundley, widely respected in the clubhouse, chided manager Bobby Valentine one day after Valentine publicly asserted the catcher, 28, needed to take better care of his body. "We're the players," Hundley said. "We win and lose games. He doesn't. He just comes along for the ride. What he has to say doesn't matter that much."

Turning point: A 7-0 victory over the Expos and Pedro Martinez on May 28. Prior to the game, Martinez had been 10-0 against the Mets in his career.

Most valuable player: Hundley's inconsistent availability after the All-Star break created a void, and third baseman Edgardo Alfonzo (team-leading .315 average) filled it.

Most valuable pitcher: Rick Reed exceeded all expectations, especially for someone who wasn't even in the rotation at the start of the season. He finished sixth in the league in ERA, was second in fewest walks allowed per nine innings and worked a team-high 208 1/3 innings.

Most improved player: Huskey improved as the season went on. He batted .302 in his final 242 at-bats, making more consistent contact and showing a greater grasp of the strike zone.

Most pleasant surprise: Reed, a former replacement pitcher, emerged from his clubhouse exile to become the team's most consistent starting pitcher.

Biggest disappointment: Bernard Gilkey's .249 average, 18 home runs and 78 RBIs were all significantly down from 1996 (.317, 30, 117).

Key injuries: Hundley appeared in only 55 of the final 81 games because of the damage to and pain in his right elbow. Five starters—Bill Pulsipher (anxiety attacks), Paul Wilson (labrum surgery), Jason Isringhausen (broken hand and tuberculosis), Pete Harnisch (depression), Armando Reynoso (surgery on shoulder and elbow)—combined for 27 starts and 146 2/3 innings. Derek Wallace never pitched because of March surgery for an aneurysm. Jones' performance was compromised from June through September by a muscle problem in his back, shortstop Rey Ordonez missed six weeks because of broken finger and Lance Johnson (shin splints) played in only 72 games before being traded August 8.

Notable: John Olerud revitalized his career with 102 RBIs in his first National League season and became the seventh Mets player to hit for the cycle.

—MARTY NOBLE

RECORDS

1997 regular-season record: 88-74 (3rd in N.L. East); 50-31 at home; 38-43 on road; 36-27 vs. East; 34-21 vs. Central; 18-26 vs. West; 31-18 vs. lefthanded starters; 57-56 vs. righthanded starters; 75-60 on grass; 13-14 on turf; 38-26 in daytime; 50-48 at night; 21-27 in one-run games; 11-7 in extra-inning games; 0-1-3 in doubleheaders.

Team record past five years: 342-401 (.460, ranks 13th in league in that span).

TEAM LEADERS

Batting average: Edgardo Alfonzo (.315).
At-bats: John Olerud (524).
Runs: John Olerud (90).
Hits: Edgardo Alfonzo (163).
Total bases: John Olerud (256).
Doubles: John Olerud (34).
Triples: Lance Johnson (6).
Home runs: Todd Hundley (30).
Runs batted in: John Olerud (102).
Stolen bases: Carl Everett (17).
Slugging percentage: Todd Hundley (.549).
On-base percentage: John Olerud (.400).
Wins: Bobby Jones (15).

Earned-run average: Rick Reed (2.89).
Complete games: Bobby Jones, Rick Reed (2).
Shutouts: Bobby Jones, Dave Mlicki, Armando Reynoso (1).
Saves: John Franco (36).
Innings pitched: Rick Reed (208.1).
Strikeouts: Dave Mlicki (157).

GAMES BY POSITION

Catcher: Todd Hundley 122, Todd Pratt 36, Alberto Castillo 34, Steve Bieser 2.
First base: John Olerud 146, Butch Huskey 22, Matt Franco 13, Roberto Petagine 6.
Second base: Carlos Baerga 131, Manny Alexander 31, Jason Hardtke 21, Luis Lopez 20, Shawn Gilbert 8, Edgardo Alfonzo 3.
Third base: Edgardo Alfonzo 143, Matt Franco 39, Butch Huskey 15, Luis Lopez 4, Shawn Gilbert 3, Manny Alexander 1, Jason Hardtke 1, Kevin Morgan 1.
Shortstop: Rey Ordonez 118, Luis Lopez 45, Manny Alexander 26, Edgardo Alfonzo 12, Shawn Gilbert 6.
Outfield: Bernard Gilkey 136, Carl Everett 128, Butch Huskey 92, Alex Ochoa 88, Lance Johnson 66, Brian McRae 41, Steve Bieser 21, Gary Thurman 7, Carlos Mendoza 3, Andy Tomberlin 2, Matt Franco 1, Shawn Gilbert 1, Roberto Petagine 1.
Designated hitter: Butch Huskey 4, Bernard Gilkey 2, Todd Hundley 2, Matt Franco 1, Alex Ochoa 1.

TOP DRAFT CHOICES

1. **Geoff Goetz,** LHP, Jesuit H.S., Tampa.
2. **Tyler Walker,** RHP, Univ. of California.
3. **Cesar Crespo,** SS, Notre Dame H.S., Caguas, P.R.
4. **Michael Yancy,** OF, Morse H.S., San Diego.
5. **Brian Jenkins,** C, Port St. Joe (Fla.) H.S.
6. **Matt Lowe,** RHP, Walhalla (S.C.) H.S.
7. **Robert Weslowski,** RHP, Central H.S., Marcellus, N.Y.
8. **Vicente Rosario,** OF, George Washington H.S., New York.
9. **Kenny Miller,** SS, Univ. of Kentucky.
10. **Garrett Atkins,** 3B, University H.S., Irvine, Calif.

PHILADELPHIA PHILLIES
NATIONAL LEAGUE EAST DIVISION

Phillies Schedule

Home games shaded. *—All-Star Game at Coors Field (Colorado).
D—Day game (any game starting before 5 p.m.).

March

SUN	MON	TUE	WED	THU	FRI	SAT
		31 D NYM				

April

SUN	MON	TUE	WED	THU	FRI	SAT
			1	2 NYM	3 ATL	4 ATL
5 D ATL	6	7 FLA	8 FLA	9 FLA	10 ATL	11 ATL
12 D ATL	13 ATL	14	15 FLA	16 D FLA	17 STL	18 D STL
19 D STL	20	21 CIN	22 CIN	23 CIN	24 STL	25 STL
26 D STL	27 CIN	28 CIN	29 CIN	30		

May

SUN	MON	TUE	WED	THU	FRI	SAT
					1 HOU	2 HOU
3 D HOU	4 COL	5 COL	6 COL	7 ARZ	8 ARZ	9 ARZ
10 D ARZ	11 LA	12 LA	13 LA	14 LA	15 SD	16 SD
17 D SD	18	19 STL	20 STL	21 STL	22 MON	23 MON
24 D MON	25 MON	26	27 D CUB	28 D CUB	29 NYM	30 NYM
31 D NYM						

June

SUN	MON	TUE	WED	THU	FRI	SAT
	1 MON	2 MON	3 MON	4	5 TOR	6 D TOR
7 TOR	8 BAL	9 BAL	10 BAL	11	12 CUB	13 CUB
14 CUB	15 PIT	16 PIT	17 PIT	18 D CUB	19 D CUB	20 CUB
21 CUB	22 BOS	23 BOS	24 BOS	25 TB	26 TB	27 TB
28 D TB	29	30 NYY				

July

SUN	MON	TUE	WED	THU	FRI	SAT
			1 NYY	2 NYY	3 MIL	4 MIL
5 D MIL	6	7 *	8	9 MIL	10 PIT	11 PIT
12 D PIT	13 MIL	14 MIL	15 MIL	16 D NYM	17 NYM	18 NYM
19 NYM	20 MON	21 MON	22 ATL	23 ATL	24 FLA	25 FLA
26 D FLA	27	28 LA	29 LA	30 LA	31 SF	

August

SUN	MON	TUE	WED	THU	FRI	SAT
						1 SF
2 D SF	3 D SF	4 SD	5 SD	6 D SD	7 HOU	8 HOU
9 HOU	10 ARZ	11 ARZ	12 ARZ	13	14 COL	15 COL
16 COL	17 HOU	18 HOU	19 HOU	20 HOU	21 ARZ	22 ARZ
23 COL	24 SD	25 SD	26 SD	27 D SF	28 SF	29 D SF
30 SF	31 SF					

September

SUN	MON	TUE	WED	THU	FRI	SAT
		1 LA	2 LA	3	4 MIL	5 MIL
6 MIL	7	8 NYM	9 NYM	10 NYM	11 PIT	12 PIT
13 PIT	14 ATL	15 ATL	16 ATL	17	18 MON	19 MON
20 MON	21 CIN	22 CIN	23 CIN	24 FLA	25 FLA	26 FLA
27 D FLA						

1998 SEASON
CLUB DIRECTORY

Partners
Claire S. Betz
Tri-Play Associates (Alexander K. Buck, J. Mahlon Buck Jr., William C. Buck)
Double Play, Inc. (Herbert H. Middleton Jr.)
Fitz Eugene Dixon Jr.

Managing partner, president, CEO
David Montgomery

Chairman, general partner
Bill Giles

Sr. v.p.0, finance and planning
Jerry Clothier

Executive secretary
Nancy Nolan

Secretary and general counsel
William Y. Webb

Director, business development
Joseph W. Giles

Acting general manager
Ed Wade

Director, player development
Del Unser

Director, scouting
Mike Arbuckle

Senior advisor to general manager
Paul Owens

Traveling secretary
Eddie Ferenz

Vice president, public relations
Larry Shenk

Broadcaster/director speakers' bureau
Chris Wheeler

Director, community relations
Regina Castellani

Manager, publicity
Leigh Tobin

Manager, media relations
Gene Dias

Vice president, marketing
Dennis Mannion

Dir., broadcasting and video services
Rory McNeil

Advertising/Internet services manager
Jo-Ann Levy-Lamoreaux

V.p., ticket sales and operations
Richard Deats

Director, ticket department
Dan Goroff

Director, group sales
Kathy Killian

Director, stadium operations
Mike DiMuzio

Club physician
Dr. Phillip Marone

Club trainers
Jeff Cooper
Mark Andersen

National supervisor
Marti Wolever

Spec. assignment, major league scouts
Jimmy Stewart
Lee Elia

Advance scout, major leagues
Hank King

Special assignment scouts
Bing Devine, Dick Lawlor, Larry Rojas, Steve Schryver

Regular supervisor, scouts
Sonny Bowers, Dean Jongewood, Scott Trcka

Minor league and scouting
Karen Nocella

Regular scouts
Sal Agostinelli, Emil Belich, Jim Fregosi Jr., Steve Gillispie, Bill Harper, Tomas Herrera, Ken Hultzapple, Jerry Lafferty, Allan Lewis, Terry Logan, Miguel Machedo, Fred Manrique, Jesus Mendez, Lloyd Merritt, Willie Montanez, Arthur Parrack, Mark Ralston, Mitch Sokel, Doug Takaragawa, Roy Tanner, Wilfredo Tejada

MINOR LEAGUE AFFILIATES

Class	Team	League	Manager
AAA	Scranton/Wilkes-Barre	International	Marc Bombard
AA	Reading	Eastern	Al LeBoeuf
A	Clearwater	Florida State	Bill Dancy
A	Piedmont	South Atlantic	Ken Oberkfell
A	Batavia	New York-Pennsylvania	To be announced
Rookie	Martinsville	Appalachian	Greg Legg

BROADCAST INFORMATION

Radio: Talk Radio 1210.
TV: WPHL-TV (Channel 17).
Cable TV: Comcast Sportsnet.

SPRING TRAINING

Ballpark (city): Jack Russell Stadium (Clearwater, Fla.).
Ticket information: 215-463-1000, 813-442-8496.

SPRING TRAINING ROSTER

Manager—Terry Francona (7).
Coaches—Galen Cisco (43), Chuck Cottier (3), Ramon Henderson, Hal McRae (56), Brad Mills (9), John Vukovich (18).

No.	PITCHERS	B/T	Ht./Wt.	Born	1997 clubs
55	Beech, Matt	L/L	6-2/205	1-20-72	Clearwater, Scranton/Wilkes-Barre, Philadelphia
22	Blazier, Ron	R/R	6-5/205	7-30-71	Philadelphia, Scranton/Wilkes-Barre, Clearwater
52	Bottalico, Ricky	L/R	6-1/208	8-26-69	Philadelphia
	Burger, Rob	R/R	6-1/175	3-25-76	Clearwater
	Fiore, Tony	R/R	6-4/210	10-12-71	Reading, Scranton/Wilkes-Barre
61	Gomes, Wayne	R/R	6-4/220	1-15-73	Scranton/Wilkes-Barre, Philadelphia
44	Grace, Mike	R/R	6-4/220	6-20-70	Reading, Scranton/Wilkes-Barre, Philadelphia
28	Green, Tyler	R/R	6-5/211	2-18-70	Philadelphia, Scranton/Wilkes-Barre
31	Leiter, Mark	R/R	6-3/210	4-13-63	Philadelphia
	Loewer, Carlton	B/R	6-6/200	9-24-73	Scranton/Wilkes-Barre
	Maduro, Calvin	R/R	6-0/175	9-5-74	Philadelphia, Scranton/Wilkes-Barre
21	Portugal, Mark	R/R	6-0/190	10-30-62	Philadelphia
38	Schilling, Curt	R/R	6-4/226	11-14-66	Philadelphia
48	Spradlin, Jerry	B/R	6-7/240	6-14-67	Philadelphia
54	Stephenson, Garrett	R/R	6-4/195	1-2-72	Scranton/Wilkes-Barre, Philadelphia
	Welch, Mike	L/R	6-2/210	8-25-72	Norfolk
	Whiteman, Greg	L/L	6-2/180	6-12-73	Clearwater, Reading

No.	CATCHERS	B/T	Ht./Wt.	Born	1997 clubs
27	Estalella, Robert	R/R	6-1/195	8-23-74	Scranton/Wilkes-Barre, Philadelphia
24	Lieberthal, Mike	R/R	6-0/178	1-18-72	Philadelphia
8	Parent, Mark	R/R	6-5/245	9-16-61	Philadelphia

No.	INFIELDERS	B/T	Ht./Wt.	Born	1997 clubs
	Anderson, Marlon	L/R	5-11/190	1-6-74	Reading
2	Brogna, Rico	L/L	6-2/205	4-18-70	Philadelphia
	Doster, Dave	R/R	5-10/185	10-8-70	Scranton/Wilkes-Barre
	Held, Dan	R/R	6-1/200	8-29-71	Reading
14	Hudler, Rex	R/R	6-0/195	9-2-60	Reading, Philadelphia, Clearwater, Scranton/Wilkes-Barre
23	Jordan, Kevin	R/R	6-1/193	10-9-69	Scranton/Wilkes-Barre, Philadelphia
	Lewis, Mark	R/R	6-1/185	11-30-69	San Francisco
30	Relaford, Desi	B/R	5-8/155	9-16-73	Scranton/Wilkes-Barre, Philadelphia
17	Rolen, Scott	R/R	6-4/195	4-4-75	Philadelphia
11	Sefcik, Kevin	R/R	5-10/175	2-10-71	Philadelphia, Scranton/Wilkes-Barre

No.	OUTFIELDERS	B/T	Ht./Wt.	Born	1997 clubs
	Abreu, Bob	L/R	6-0/160	3-11-74	Houston, Jackson, New Orleans
53	Barron, Tony	R/R	6-0/185	8-17-66	Scranton/Wilkes-Barre, Philadelphia
	Carver, Steve	L/R	6-3/215	9-27-72	Reading
16	Cummings, Midre	L/R	6-0/195	10-14-71	Pittsburgh, Philadelphia
4	Dykstra, Lenny	L/L	5-10/188	2-10-63	DID NOT PLAY
	Glanville, Doug	R/R	6-2/175	8-25-70	Chicago N.L.
25	Jefferies, Gregg	B/R	5-10/184	8-1-67	Philadelphia
	Magee, Wendell	R/R	6-0/220	8-3-72	Philadelphia, Scranton/Wilkes-Barre
41	McMillon, Billy	L/L	5-11/180	11-17-71	Charlotte, Florida, Scranton/Wilkes-Barre, Philadelphia

BALLPARK INFORMATION

Ballpark (capacity, surface)
Veterans Stadium (62,409, artificial)

Address
P.O. Box 7575
Philadelphia, PA 19101

Business phone
215-463-6000

Ticket information
215-463-1000

Ticket prices
$16 (field box)
$14 (sections 258-274)
$14 (terrace box)
$14 (loge box)
$10 (reserved, 600 level)
$5 (reserved, 700 level)

Field dimensions (from home plate)
To left field at foul line, 330 feet
To center field, 408 feet
To right field at foul line, 330 feet

First game played
April 10, 1971 (Phillies 4, Expos 1)

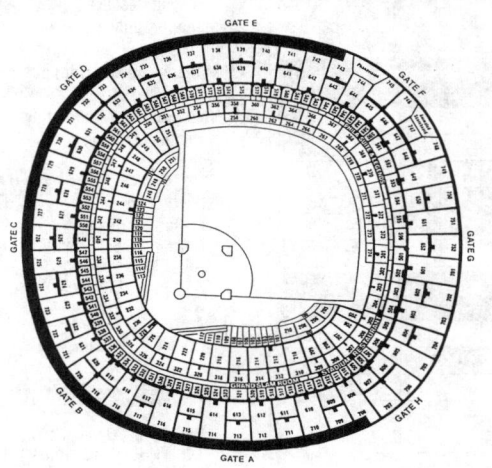

1998 SEASON *Philadelphia Phillies*

Date	Opp.	Res.	Score	(inn.*)	Hits	Opp. hits	Winning pitcher	Losing pitcher	Save	Record	Pos.	GB
4-1	At L.A.	W	3-0		7	2	Schilling	Martinez	Bottalico	1-0	T1st	....
4-2	At L.A.	L	1-5		6	8	Nomo	Maduro	Dreifort	1-1	3rd	1.0
4-3	At L.A.	L	1-2		5	7	Valdes	Leiter	Worrell	1-2	T3rd	2.0
4-4	At S.D.	L	3-13		7	13	Worrell	Munoz		1-3	T4th	2.0
4-5	At S.D.	L	1-4		1	7	Hitchcock	Mimbs	Hoffman	1-4	T4th	3.0
4-6	At S.D.	W	3-2		9	7	Schilling	Hamilton	Bottalico	2-4	T4th	3.0
4-7	At S.F.	L	3-4		7	5	Estes	Maduro	Beck	2-5	T4th	3.5
4-8	At S.F.	W	2-1		5	3	Leiter	Fernandez	Bottalico	3-5	T4th	3.5
4-9	At S.F.	L	0-3		5	9	Rueter	Munoz	Beck	3-6	T4th	4.0
4-11	S.D.	L	3-8		10	13	Hitchcock	Schilling		3-7	5th	5.5
4-13	S.D.	L	1-3		6	6	Scott	Bottalico	Hoffman	3-8	T4th	5.0
4-15	S.F.	L	4-8		8	12	VanLandingham	Munoz		3-9	5th	6.5
4-16	S.F.	L	5-6	(10)	10	9	Poole	Harris	Beck	3-10	5th	7.5
4-18	Mon.	W	8-3		10	6	Maduro	Bullinger		4-10	T4th	7.5
4-19	Mon.	W	10-8		9	6	Leiter	Perez	Bottalico	5-10	T4th	7.5
4-20†	Mon.	L	1-5		3	11	Juden	Munoz	Veres	5-11		
4-20‡	Mon.	L	0-3		5	6	Martinez	Portugal	Urbina	5-12	5th	8.0
4-21	At Pit.	W	10-2		14	9	Schilling	Cooke		6-12	T4th	7.5
4-23	At Pit.	L	2-3		7	6	Rincon	Spradlin		6-13	5th	8.0
4-25	At Cin.	W	10-7		15	13	Leiter	Burba	Bottalico	7-13	5th	8.0
4-26	At Cin.	L	2-10		3	12	Schourek	Schilling		7-14	5th	9.0
4-28	Pit.	L	4-9	(12)	14	13	Wilkins	Mimbs		7-15	5th	10.5
4-29	Pit.	W	8-2		11	9	Maduro	Ruebel		8-15	5th	9.5
4-30	L.A.	L	5-7		11	13	Nomo	Leiter	Worrell	8-16	5th	10.5
5-1	L.A.	L	0-5		9	4	Astacio	Schilling		8-17	5th	11.5
5-2	At Col.	W	7-4		9	5	Munoz	Thompson	Bottalico	9-17	5th	10.5
5-3	At Col.	L	3-7		6	7	Wright	Portugal		9-18	5th	10.5
5-4	At Col.	L	0-9		9	13	Bailey	Maduro		9-19	5th	11.5
5-5	At Hou.	L	2-9		7	8	Holt	Leiter		9-20	5th	12.5
5-6	At Hou.	W	5-1		9	9	Schilling	Garcia		10-20	5th	11.5
5-7	At St.L.	L	7-14		11	13	Frascatore	Harris		10-21	5th	12.5
5-8	At St.L.	L	2-6		6	6	An. Benes	Mimbs		10-22	5th	12.5
5-9	Col.	W	3-1		7	5	Maduro	Bailey	Bottalico	11-22	5th	11.5
5-10	Col.	W	5-4	(10)	9	7	Bottalico	S. Reed		12-22	5th	11.5
5-11	Col.	W	3-1		5	4	Schilling	Thomson		13-22	5th	11.5
5-12	Col.	L	2-9		7	14	DeJean	Munoz		13-23	5th	12.5
5-13	St.L.	W	3-2		6	3	Spradlin	Mathews	Bottalico	14-23	5th	11.5
5-14	St.L.	L	3-12		9	17	Stottlemyre	Maduro		14-24	5th	11.5
5-16	Hou.	L	7-12		13	11	Holt	Leiter		14-25	5th	12.5
5-17	Hou.	W	4-2		8	4	Schilling	Reynolds	Bottalico	15-25	5th	12.5
5-18	Hou.	W	5-3		8	9	Stephenson	Hampton	Bottalico	16-25	5th	12.5
5-19	Hou.	L	5-9		10	11	Kile	Maduro		16-26	5th	13.5
5-20	At Chi.	W	3-2		10	6	Leiter	Castillo	Bottalico	17-26	5th	13.5
5-21	At Chi.	L	0-7		4	10	Foster	Ramos		17-27	5th	14.5
5-22	N.Y.	L	3-10		9	14	Jones	Schilling		17-28	5th	15.0
5-23	N.Y.	W	2-1		7	4	Stephenson	Mlicki	Bottalico	18-28	5th	15.0
5-24	N.Y.	L	4-8		13	11	Reynoso	Maduro	J. Franco	18-29	5th	15.0
5-26†	At Cin.	L	5-8		8	14	Smiley	Leiter	Remlinger	18-30		
5-26‡	At Cin.	L	4-8		8	10	Morgan	Beech		18-31	5th	16.0
5-27	At Cin.	W	2-1		6	7	Schilling	Tomko		19-31	5th	16.0
5-28	At Cin.	L	0-2		8	7	Mercker	Stephenson	Shaw	19-32	5th	16.5
5-30	At N.Y.	L	3-7		8	9	Mlicki	Ramos		19-33	5th	17.0
5-31	At N.Y.	L	3-10		10	16	Reynoso	Leiter		19-34	5th	17.0
6-1	At N.Y.	L	5-8		12	10	Reed	Beech	Lidle	19-35	5th	18.0
6-3	Cin.	L	2-3		5	6	Mercker	Schilling	Shaw	19-36	5th	17.5
6-4	Chi.	L	1-5		6	10	Castillo	Stephenson		19-37	5th	18.5
6-5	Chi.	W	9-8	(10)	10	14	Ryan	Adams		20-37	5th	18.5
6-6	At Pit.	L	4-5	(10)	10	9	Wilkins	Spradlin		20-38	5th	19.5
6-7	At Pit.	L	2-9		5	10	Lieber	Nye		20-39	5th	20.5
6-8	At Pit.	W	3-2		9	6	Schilling	Cooke	Bottalico	21-39	5th	19.5
6-10	At Mon.	L	5-8		8	13	Veres	Bottalico	Smith	21-40	5th	20.0
6-11	At Mon.	L	3-4		7	6	Bullinger	Spradlin	Urbina	21-41	5th	20.0
6-13	Tor.	W	4-3		7	10	Gomes	Spoljaric	Bottalico	22-41	5th	19.0
6-14	Tor.	L	2-3		8	7	Person	Nye	Quantrill	22-42	5th	19.0
6-15	Tor.	L	1-11		6	12	Hentgen	Leiter		22-43	5th	19.0
6-16	At Bos.	L	4-5	(10)	11	15	Wasdin	Bottalico		22-44	5th	20.0
6-17	At Bos.	L	6-12		10	16	Sele	Ruffcorn	Lacy	22-45	5th	21.0
6-18	At Bos.	L	2-4		5	8	Suppan	Schilling	Hammond	22-46	5th	21.0
6-20	Atl.	L	1-4		7	8	Glavine	Leiter		22-47	5th	22.0
6-21	Atl.	L	8-9		14	10	Clontz	Blazier	Wohlers	22-48	5th	23.0
6-22	Atl.	L	5-12		10	17	Maddux	Stephenson		22-49	5th	24.0

Date	Opp.	Res.	Score	(inn.*)	Hits	Opp. hits	Winning pitcher	Losing pitcher	Save	Record	Pos.	GB
6-23	Fla.	W	9-3		9	8	Schilling	Helling		23-49	5th	23.0
6-24	Fla.	L	1-4		6	10	Leiter	Ruffcorn	Nen	23-50	5th	23.0
6-25	Fla.	L	5-7		9	14	Fernandez	Harris	Nen	23-51	5th	24.0
6-26	At Atl.	L	4-5		9	7	Neagle	Beech	Wohlers	23-52	5th	25.0
6-27	At Atl.	L	1-7		6	10	Maddux	Stephenson		23-53	5th	26.0
6-28	At Atl.	L	1-9		8	11	Smoltz	Schilling		23-54	5th	27.0
6-29	At Atl.	L	5-6		10	7	Bielecki	Brewer	Wohlers	23-55	5th	28.0
6-30	At Bal.	L	1-8		6	8	Mussina	Maduro		23-56	5th	28.0
7-1	At Bal.	L	1-4		7	13	Erickson	Beech	Myers	23-57	5th	29.0
7-2	At Bal.	L	6-10		12	10	Rhodes	Spradlin		23-58	5th	30.0
7-3	Chi.	L	4-5		8	10	Gonzalez	Schilling	Rojas	23-59	5th	31.0
7-4	Chi.	L	3-9		10	12	Mulholland	Ruffcorn	Bottenfield	23-60	5th	32.0
7-5	Chi.	W	9-7		14	9	Harris	Patterson	Bottalico	24-60	5th	32.0
7-6	Chi.	L	4-8		9	14	Castillo	Leiter	Rojas	24-61	5th	32.0
7-10	At Fla.	L	7-8		10	10	Nen	Spradlin		24-62	5th	32.0
7-11	At Fla.	W	13-3		15	8	Schilling	Brown		25-62	5th	31.0
7-13	At Fla.	L	3-9		6	8	Fernandez	Leiter		25-63	5th	31.5
7-14	At Atl.	L	6-10		6	9	Millwood	Brewer	Wohlers	25-64	5th	32.5
7-15	At Atl.	W	8-1		10	4	Stephenson	Smoltz		26-64	5th	31.5
7-16	Mon.	W	6-0		7	4	Schilling	Bullinger		27-64	5th	31.5
7-17	Mon.	L	4-5		7	8	Perez	Beech	Urbina	27-65	5th	32.5
7-18	Pit.	W	8-6		9	11	Leiter	Lieber	Bottalico	28-65	5th	32.5
7-19	Pit.	L	3-13		12	17	Cooke	Green		28-66	5th	32.5
7-20	Pit.	W	4-1		5	9	Stephenson	Schmidt	Bottalico	29-66	5th	31.5
7-21	Pit.	L	2-3		8	7	Loaiza	Schilling	Loiselle	29-67	5th	32.5
7-22	At S.F.	L	5-8		8	11	Gardner	Spradlin	Beck	29-68	5th	33.0
7-23	At S.F.	L	4-16		9	15	Estes	Leiter		29-69	5th	33.0
7-24	At S.F.	W	7-4		14	8	Gomes	Roa	Bottalico	30-69	5th	32.5
7-25	At L.A.	L	1-8		6	14	Park	Stephenson		30-70	5th	33.5
7-26	At L.A.	L	1-4		4	8	Dreifort	Schilling	Worrell	30-71	5th	33.5
7-27	At L.A.	L	1-7		8	10	Candiotti	Beech		30-72	5th	34.5
7-28	At S.D.	W	8-4		15	6	Leiter	Bergman		31-72	5th	34.5
7-29	At S.D.	W	6-5		10	9	Green	Ashby	Bottalico	32-72	5th	34.5
7-31	St.L.	W	2-1	(10)	9	4	Bottalico	Fossas		33-72	5th	34.0
8-1	St.L.	W	4-1		7	9	Stephenson	An. Benes	Bottalico	34-72	5th	33.0
8-2	St.L.	L	1-2		7	8	Stottlemyre	Beech	Eckersley	34-73	5th	34.0
8-3	St.L.	W	10-1		12	7	Leiter	Osborne		35-73	5th	33.0
8-4	Col.	W	7-3		11	3	Green	Castillo		36-73	5th	33.0
8-5	Col.	L	2-4		7	13	Holmes	Bottalico	DiPoto	36-74	5th	33.0
8-6	Hou.	W	6-4		8	9	Stephenson	Garcia	Bottalico	37-74	5th	33.0
8-7	Hou.	W	6-5	(11)	9	9	Brewer	Martin		38-74	5th	33.0
8-8	At St.L.	L	1-6		3	12	Osborne	Leiter		38-75	5th	33.0
8-9	At St.L.	W	3-2		9	3	Green	Aybar	Bottalico	39-75	5th	33.0
8-10	At St.L.	W	8-0		15	3	Schilling	Morris		40-75	5th	32.0
8-12	At Col.	W	5-0		10	5	Beech	Thomson		41-75	5th	31.5
8-13	At Col.	W	12-8		17	13	Leiter	Wright		42-75	5th	30.5
8-15	At Hou.	W	5-1		8	5	Schilling	Holt		43-75	5th	29.5
8-16	At Hou.	W	5-3		12	5	Spradlin	Wagner	Bottalico	44-75	5th	29.5
8-17	At Hou.	L	6-11		11	12	Martin	Gomes	Springer	44-76	5th	29.5
8-18	S.F.	W	12-3		16	6	Beech	Gardner		45-76	5th	29.0
8-19	S.F.	L	5-9		9	12	Estes	Leiter		45-77	5th	30.0
8-22	L.A.	L	3-5		7	7	Osuna	Bottalico	Worrell	45-78	5th	31.5
8-23	L.A.	L	3-4		9	9	Nomo	Green	Worrell	45-79	5th	32.5
8-24	L.A.	L	1-5		6	8	Valdes	Beech		45-80	5th	32.5
8-25†	S.D.	W	10-1		13	10	Leiter	Cunnane		46-80		
8-25‡	S.D.	W	6-4		10	5	Blazier	Ashby	Bottalico	47-80	5th	31.5
8-26	S.D.	W	4-2		9	7	Grace	Hitchcock	Bottalico	48-80	5th	31.5
8-27	S.D.	W	7-6	(12)	14	14	Gomes	Bruske		49-80	5th	30.5
8-29	At Det.	L	2-7		4	10	Blair	Green		49-81	5th	32.0
8-30	At Det.	W	2-0		8	8	Beech	Sanders	Bottalico	50-81	5th	32.0
8-31	At Det.	L	1-2		7	7	Thompson	Leiter	Jones	50-82	5th	33.0
9-1	N.Y. (AL)	W	5-1		11	7	Schilling	Irabu		51-82	5th	32.0
9-2	N.Y. (AL)	W	5-0		10	3	Grace	Rogers		52-82	5th	32.0
9-3	N.Y. (AL)	W	5-4		11	7	Spradlin	Stanton		53-82	5th	31.0
9-4	At Mon.	W	6-4		8	10	Beech	Martinez	Bottalico	54-82	5th	31.0
9-5	At Mon.	L	1-7		4	11	Johnson	Leiter		54-83	5th	31.0
9-6	At Mon.	W	5-3		8	8	Schilling	Valdes		55-83	5th	31.0
9-7	At Mon.	W	2-1		7	6	Karp	Telford	Bottalico	56-83	5th	31.0
9-8	At N.Y.	W	13-4		13	8	Grace	Isringhausen		57-83	5th	30.5
9-9	At N.Y.	W	1-0		4	6	Green	Mlicki	Bottalico	58-83	5th	30.5
9-10	At N.Y.	L	2-10		7	16	Bohanon	Beech		58-84	5th	31.5
9-11	S.F.	L	3-5		6	12	Hernandez	Spradlin	Beck	58-85	5th	32.0
9-12†	Cin.	L	2-4		8	9	Remlinger	Stephenson	Shaw	58-86		
9-12‡	Cin.	W	9-1		14	5	Leiter	Schourek		59-86	5th	31.5
9-13	Cin.	L	0-3		4	7	Burba	Grace	Shaw	59-87	5th	31.5

Date	Opp.	Res.	Score	(inn.*)	Hits	Opp. hits	Winning pitcher	Losing pitcher	Save	Record	Pos.	GB
9-14	Cin.	L	4-6		8	9	Tomko	Green	Shaw	59-88	5th	31.5
9-15†	N.Y.	L	5-10	(10)	10	14	Lidle	Karp		59-89		
9-15‡	N.Y.	W	2-1		6	3	Winston	Crawford	Bottalico	60-89	5th	32.0
9-16	N.Y.	W	3-2		5	3	Schilling	Reed		61-89	5th	32.0
9-17†	At Fla.	W	5-2		10	6	Stephenson	Hernandez	Bottalico	62-89		
9-17‡	At Fla.	L	2-5		9	8	Saunders	Leiter	Nen	62-90	5th	32.5
9-18	At Fla.	L	2-8		10	15	Brown	Grace		62-91	5th	33.5
9-19	At Chi.	W	10-5	(6)	13	9	Winston	M. Clark	Spradlin	63-91	5th	33.5
9-20	At Chi.	W	3-2		6	6	Gomes	Adams	Bottalico	64-91	5th	33.5
9-21	At Chi.	L	3-11		8	15	Tapani	Schilling		64-92	5th	33.5
9-23	Atl.	L	0-6		3	11	Millwood	Leiter		64-93	5th	35.0
9-24	Atl.	W	5-1		10	4	Stephenson	Byrd		65-93	5th	34.0
9-25	Atl.	L	2-3	(10)	7	9	Cather	Spradlin	Clontz	65-94	5th	35.0
9-26	Fla.	W	5-3		10	5	Schilling	Alfonseca	Bottalico	66-94	5th	35.0
9-27	Fla.	W	8-7		14	8	Spradlin	Stanifer		67-94	5th	34.0
9-28	Fla.	W	8-7		10	9	Gomes	Heredia	Bottalico	68-94	5th	33.0

Monthly records: April (8-16), May (11-18), June (4-22), July (10-16), August (17-10), September (18-12).
*Innings, if other than nine. †First game of doubleheader. ‡Second game of doubleheader.

HIGHLIGHTS

High point: The Phillies' three-game interleague sweep of the Yankees September 1-3 at Veterans Stadium. Before a Labor Day crowd of 50,869, Curt Schilling struck out a career-high 16. Righthander Mike Grace followed with a shutout. Clearly, the Phillies considered the Yankees series their equivalent of a divisional playoff, and they used it as a springboard to complete the second half with a 44-33 record.

Low point: For much of the season, the Phillies were the laughingstocks of baseball. The team was 4-22 in June and was 24-61 at the All-Star break.

Turning point: After being swept in a three-game series July 25-27 at Los Angeles, the Phillies agreed not to trade Schilling before the July 31 deadline. A two-game trip to San Diego produced two victories, and the Phillies went on to win 36 of their final 58 games.

Most valuable player: Third baseman Scott Rolen was the unanimous N.L. Rookie of the Year after hitting .283 with 35 doubles and team highs in home runs (21) and RBIs (92). He was the club's first rookie award recipient since Richie Allen in 1964, and he snapped the Dodgers' streak of five consecutive winners.

Most valuable pitcher: Schilling established an N.L. record for strikeouts by a righthander (319), also shattering Hall of Famer Steve Carlton's franchise season record of 310. Schilling finished fourth in the N.L. Cy Young voting, and his 17-11 record could have been better if teammates had nailed down a few more saves.

Most improved player: Catcher Mike Liebenthal hit 20 homers, drove in 77 runs and emerged as one of the best young receivers in the game. He also was durable, working 134 games.

Most pleasant surprise: Righthander Garrett Stephenson was an afterthought when he joined the Phillies in September 1996, also the player to be named in a trade with Baltimore. Joining the rotation in early May after injuries hit the staff, he struck out 12 Cardinals in his Phillies debut. As the fifth starter, he compiled an 8-6 record and a 3.15 ERA.

Biggest disappointment: Left fielder Gregg Jefferies wallowed through a sub-par season, hitting .256 with 11 homers and 48 RBIs. Jefferies' campaign was cut short by a left hamstring injury. In addition, free-agent righthander Mark Leiter lost an N.L.-high 17 games and compiled a 5.67 ERA.

Key injuries: Righthander Mark Portugal, signed as a free agent to be a key member of the rotation, missed 134 games and required elbow and knee surgery. On opening day, right fielder Danny Tartabull fouled a Ramon Martinez pitch off his left foot. He subsequently missed almost the entire season with a fracture (and is still looking for his first N.L. hit). In addition, outfielder Lenny Dykstra missed the season while rehabbing his back, and setup man Ken Ryan was sidelined for 73 games with elbow problems.

Notable: Rolen (21), Liebenthal (20) and first baseman Rico Brogna (20) gave the Phillies their first trio of players with 20 or more homers since 1987. . . . Catcher Bobby Estalella became the first Phillies rookie to hit three homers in a game, September 4 at Montreal.

—CHRIS EDWARDS

RECORDS

1997 regular-season record: 68-94 (5th in N.L. East); 38-43 at home; 30-51 on road; 24-39 vs. East; 26-29 vs. Central; 18-26 vs. West; 12-28 vs. lefthanded starters; 56-66 vs. righthanded starters; 20-39 on grass; 48-55 on turf; 20-31 in daytime; 48-63 at night; 23-20 in one-run games; 5-6 in extra-inning games; 1-2-3 in doubleheaders.

Team record past five years: 355-390 (.477, ranks 9th in league in that span).

TEAM LEADERS

Batting average: Mickey Morandini (.295).
At-bats: Scott Rolen (561).
Runs: Scott Rolen (93).
Hits: Mickey Morandini (163).
Total bases: Scott Rolen (263).
Doubles: Mickey Morandini (40).
Triples: Darren Daulton (6).
Home runs: Scott Rolen (21).
Runs batted in: Scott Rolen (92).

Stolen bases: Mickey Morandini, Scott Rolen (16).
Slugging percentage: Scott Rolen (.469).
On-base percentage: Scott Rolen (.377).
Wins: Curt Schilling (17).
Earned-run average: Curt Schilling (2.97).
Complete games: Curt Schilling (7).
Shutouts: Curt Schilling (2).
Saves: Ricky Bottalico (34).
Innings pitched: Curt Schilling (254.1).
Strikeouts: Curt Schilling (319).

GAMES BY POSITION

Catcher: Mike Liebenthal 129, Mark Parent 38, Bobby Estalella 11.
First base: Rico Brogna 145, Kevin Jordan 25, Mike Robertson 5, Darren Daulton 3, Ruben Amaro 1.
Second base: Mickey Morandini 146, Kevin Sefcik 22, Rex Hudler 6, Kevin Jordan 6.
Third base: Scott Rolen 155, Kevin Jordan 12, Kevin Sefcik 4.
Shortstop: Kevin Stocker 147, Desi Relaford 12, Kevin Sefcik 10, Mickey Morandini 1.
Outfield: Gregg Jefferies 124, Ruben Amaro 72, Darren Daulton 70, Derrick May 56, Midre Cummings 54, Tony Barron 53, Ricky Otero 42, Wendell Magee 38, Rex Hudler 35, Rob Butler 25, Billy McMillon 21, Mike Robertson 5, Danny Tartabull 3.
Designated hitter: Darren Daulton 6, Kevin Jordan 1, Mike Liebenthal 1, Mike Robertson 1.

TOP DRAFT CHOICES

1. **J.D. Drew,** OF, Florida State University.
2. **Randy Wolf,** LHP, Pepperdine University.
3. **Shomari Beverly,** OF, Encinal H.S., Alameda, Calif.
4. **Nick Marchant,** OF, Capital H.S., Boise, Idaho.
5. **Derrick Turnbow,** RHP, Franklin (Tenn.) H.S.
6. **Tom Jacquez,** LHP, UCLA.
7. **Derek Adair,** RHP, St. John's University.
8. **Brian Harris,** SS, Indiana University.
9. **Michael Schulte,** RHP, Cleveland H.S., Reseda, Calif.
10. **Bennie Bishop,** OF, Westchester H.S., Inglewood, Calif.

PITTSBURGH PIRATES
NATIONAL LEAGUE CENTRAL DIVISION

Pirates Schedule

Home games shaded. *—All-Star Game at Coors Field (Colorado). D—Day game (any game starting before 5 p.m.).

March

SUN	MON	TUE	WED	THU	FRI	SAT
		31				

April

SUN	MON	TUE	WED	THU	FRI	SAT
			1 MON	2 MON	3 D NYM	4 D NYM
5 D NYM	6 D NYM	7 ATL	8 ATL	9 ATL	10 FLA	11 D FLA
12 D FLA	13 FLA	14 ATL	15 ATL	16 ATL	17 D SD	18 D SD
19 D SD	20	21 SF	22 SF	23 SF	24 D SD	25 SD
26 D SD	27 SF	28 SF	29	30 LA		

May

SUN	MON	TUE	WED	THU	FRI	SAT
					1 LA	2 LA
3 D LA	4	5 STL	6 STL	7 CIN	8 CIN	9 CIN
10 D CIN	11 COL	12 COL	13 D HOU	14 HOU	15 ARZ	16 ARZ
17 ARZ	18 ARZ	19 D SD	20 SD	21 SD	22 FLA	23 FLA
24 D FLA	25	26 MIL	27 MIL	28	29 MON	30 MON
31 D MON						

June

SUN	MON	TUE	WED	THU	FRI	SAT
	1 NYM	2 NYM	3 NYM	4	5 MIN	6 MIN
7 D MIN	8 CLE	9 CLE	10 CLE	11	12 MIL	13 MIL
14 D MIL	15 PHI	16 PHI	17 D PHI	18 MIL	19 MIL	20 MIL
21 D MIL	22 CWS	23 CWS	24 KC	25 KC	26 LA	27 LA
28 LA	29	30 DET				

July

SUN	MON	TUE	WED	THU	FRI	SAT
			1 DET	2 DET	3 D CUB	4 D CUB
5 D CUB	6	7 *	8	9	10 PHI	11 PHI
12 D PHI	13 CUB	14 CUB	15 CUB	16 MON	17 MON	18 MON
19 MON	20 NYM	21 NYM	22 FLA	23 FLA	24 D ATL	25 ATL
26 D ATL	27 COL	28 COL	29 HOU	30	31 HOU	

August

SUN	MON	TUE	WED	THU	FRI	SAT
						1 HOU
2 D HOU	3 COL	4 COL	5 COL	6 COL	7 D LA	8 LA
9 LA	10	11 CIN	12 CIN	13 CIN	14 STL	15 STL
16 D STL	17	18 LA	19 LA	20 CIN	21 CIN	22 STL
23 D STL	24 D STL	25 ARZ	26 ARZ	27	28 HOU	29 HOU
30 D HOU	31					

September

SUN	MON	TUE	WED	THU	FRI	SAT
		1 ARZ	2 ARZ	3 D ARZ	4 D CUB	5 CUB
6 D CUB	7 D MIL	8 MIL	9 D CUB	10 CUB	11 PHI	12 PHI
13 PHI	14 STL	15 STL	16 STL	17 HOU	18 HOU	19 HOU
20 HOU	21 D SF	22 SF	23 D SF	24 D SF	25 CIN	26 D CIN
27 D CIN						

1998 SEASON
CLUB DIRECTORY

General partner
Kevin S. McClatchy
Board of directors
Donald Beaver
Frank Brenner
Chip Ganassi
Kevin S. McClatchy
Mayor Tom Murphy
G. Ogden Nutting
William E. Springer
Chief operating officer
Dick Freeman
Sr. v.p. and general manager
Cam Bonifay
Asst. general manager
John Sirignano
Sr. advisor/player personnel
Lenny Yochim
Special assistants to the g.m.
Chet Montgomery
Ken Parker
Roy Smith
Willie Stargell
V.p., finance and administration
Jim Plake
V.p., broadcasting and marketing
Vic Gregovits
V.p., communications
Steven N. Greenberg
Vice president, operations
Dennis DaPra
Director of finance
Patti Mistick
Traveling secretary
Greg Johnson
Dir. of corporate sales & broadcasting
Mark Ferraco
Director of Bradenton baseball operations
Jeff Podobnik
Director of community services & sales
Al Gordon
Director of corporate relations
Nellie Briles
Director of human resources
Linda Yenerall
Director of information systems
Terry Zeigler

Director of in-game entertainment
Eric Wolff
Director of marketing communications
Mike Gordon
Director of media relations
Jim Trdinich
Director of merchandising
Joe Billetdeaux
Director of player development
Paul Tinnell
Dir. of community & player relations
Kathy Guy
Dir. of promotions and advertising
Rick Orienza
Asst. director of player development
Bill Bryk
Director of sales
Gary Remlinger
Director of scouting
Leland Maddox
Club physician
Dr. Joseph Coroso
Team orthopedist
Dr. Jack Failla
Head trainer
Kent Biggerstaff
Equipment manager
Roger Wilson
Scouting coordinators
Tom Barnard, Ron King
Special assignment scouts
Jim Guinn, Boyd Odom, Roy Smith
Latin America coordinators
Pablo Cruz, Jose Luna
Scouting supervisors
Russell Bowen, Grant Brittain, Dana Brown, Dan Durst, Steve Fleming, Duane Gustavson, James House, Craig Kornfeld, Scott Littlefield, Jose Luna, Greg McClain, Jack Powell, Steve Riha, Ed Roebuck, Delvy Santiago, Robert Sidwell, George Swain, Michael Williams

MINOR LEAGUE AFFILIATES

Class	Team	League	Manager
AAA	Nashville	Pacific Coast	Trent Jewett
AA	Carolina	Southern	Jeff Banister
A	Lynchburg	Carolina	Jeff Richardson
A	Augusta	South Atlantic	Marty Brown
A	Erie	New York-Pennsylvania	Tracy Woodson
Rookie	Gulf Coast Pirates	Gulf Coast	Woody Huyke

BROADCAST INFORMATION

Radio: KDKA-AM (1020).
Cable TV: Fox Sports Pittsburgh.

SPRING TRAINING

Ballpark (city): McKechnie Field (Bradenton, Fla.).
Ticket information: 941-748-4610.

SPRING TRAINING ROSTER

Manager—Gene Lamont (32).
Coaches—Joe Jones (37), Jack Lind (45), Lloyd McClendon (23), Rick Renick, Pete Vuckovich (50), Spin Williams (54).

No.	PITCHERS	B/T	Ht./Wt.	Born	1997 clubs
	Anderson, Jimmy	L/L	6-1/180	1-22-76	Carolina, Calgary
	Benson, Kris	R/R	6-4/190	11-7-74	Rancho Cucamonga, Mobile
	Brazoban, Melvin	R/R	6-3/165	1-20-77	Gulf Coast Rangers
41	Christiansen, Jason	R/L	6-5/230	9-21-69	Pittsburgh, Carolina
67	Cordova, Francisco	R/R	6-1/171	4-26-72	Pittsburgh
	Davis, Kane	R/R	6-3/190	6-25-75	Carolina
71	Dessens, Elmer	R/R	6-0/185	1-13-72	Pittsburgh
	Hernandez, Elvin	R/R	6-1/165	8-20-77	Carolina, Lynchburg
	Lawrence, Sean	L/L	6-4/200	9-2-70	Calgary
47	Lieber, Jon	L/R	6-2/220	4-2-70	Pittsburgh
34	Loaiza, Esteban	R/R	6-2/195	12-31-71	Pittsburgh
51	Loiselle, Rich	R/R	6-5/240	1-12-72	Pittsburgh
	Martinez, Javier	R/R	6-2/210	2-5-77	Daytona, Rockford
38	Peters, Chris	L/L	6-1/169	1-28-72	Calgary, Pittsburgh
	Pett, Jose	R/R	6-6/200	1-8-76	Carolina, Calgary
	Phillips, Jason	R/R	6-5/220	3-22-74	Lynchburg
73	Rincon, Ricardo	L/L	6-0/190	4-13-70	Pittsburgh
42	Schmidt, Jason	R/R	6-5/207	1-29-73	Pittsburgh
56	Silva, Jose	R/R	6-5/210	12-19-73	Calgary, Pittsburgh
39	Wallace, Jeff	L/L	6-2/235	4-12-76	Lynchburg, Carolina, Pittsburgh
35	Wilkins, Marc	R/R	5-10/210	10-21-70	Pittsburgh

No.	CATCHERS	B/T	Ht./Wt.	Born	1997 clubs
18	Kendall, Jason	R/R	6-0/190	6-26-74	Pittsburgh
15	Osik, Keith	R/R	6-0/190	10-22-68	Pittsburgh

No.	INFIELDERS	B/T	Ht./Wt.	Born	1997 clubs
6	Collier, Lou	R/R	5-10/180	8-21-73	Calgary, Pittsburgh
22	Garcia, Freddy	R/R	6-2/205	8-1-72	Calgary, Pittsburgh, Carolina
48	Nunez, Abraham	B/R	5-11/170	3-16-76	Lynchburg, Carolina, Pittsburgh
2	Polcovich, Kevin	R/R	5-9/168	6-28-70	Carolina, Calgary, Pittsburgh
	Strange, Doug	B/R	6-1/185	4-13-64	Montreal, Ottawa
5	Womack, Tony	L/R	5-9/155	6-25-69	Pittsburgh
	Wright, Ron	R/R	6-0/210	1-21-76	Calgary
29	Young, Kevin	R/R	6-3/221	6-16-69	Pittsburgh

No.	OUTFIELDERS	B/T	Ht./Wt.	Born	1997 clubs
46	Allensworth, Jermaine	R/R	6-0/190	1-11-72	Pittsburgh, Calgary
13	Brown, Adrian	R/R	6-0/175	2-7-74	Carolina, Pittsburgh, Calgary
19	Brown, Emil	R/R	6-2/195	12-29-74	Pittsburgh
11	Guillen, Jose	R/R	5-11/185	5-17-76	Pittsburgh
28	Martin, Al	L/L	6-2/210	11-24-67	Pittsburgh, Carolina
	Martinez, Manny	R/R	6-2/170	10-3-70	Calgary
25	Smith, Mark	R/R	6-4/195	5-7-70	Calgary, Pittsburgh, Carolina
	Staton, T.J.	L/L	6-3/210	2-17-75	Calgary, Carolina
12	Ward, Turner	B/R	6-2/198	4-11-65	Calgary, Pittsburgh

BALLPARK INFORMATION

Ballpark (capacity, surface)
Three Rivers Stadium (47,972, artificial)

Address
600 Stadium Circle
Pittsburgh, PA 15212

Business phone
412-323-5000

Ticket information
800-BUY-BUCS

Ticket prices
$15 (club boxes)
$10 (terrace boxes)
$10 (family boxes)
$8 (reserved seats)
$5 (general admission)
$1 (g.a., children 14 and under)

Field dimensions (from home plate)
To left field at foul line, 335 feet
To center field, 400 feet
To right field at foul line, 335 feet

First game played
July 16, 1970 (Reds 3, Pirates 2)

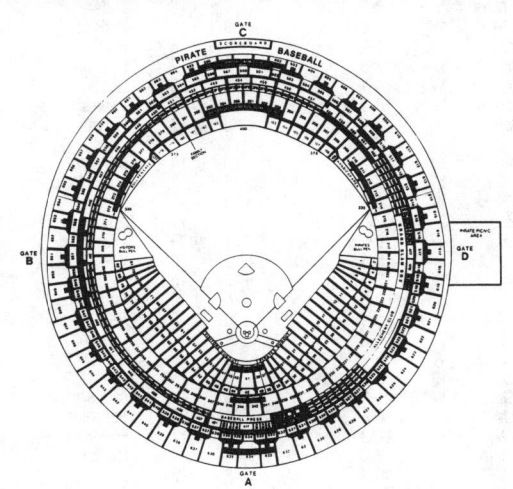

1998 SEASON *Pittsburgh Pirates*

Date	Opp.	Res.	Score	(inn.*)	Hits	Opp. hits	Winning pitcher	Losing pitcher	Save	Record	Pos.	GB
4-1	At S.F.	W	5-2		10	6	Ruebel	Rodriguez	Ericks	1-0	T1st	....
4-3	At S.F.	L	5-7		10	9	Fernandez	Cooke	Beck	1-1	3rd	0.5
4-4	At L.A.	L	3-5		5	8	Candiotti	Wainhouse	Worrell	1-2	3rd	1.5
4-5	At L.A.	W	3-1		9	6	Cordova	Park	Ericks	2-2	3rd	1.5
4-6	At L.A.	L	3-6		8	11	Dreifort	Rincon	Worrell	2-3	3rd	2.5
4-7	At S.D.	L	2-3	(10)	7	10	D. Veras	Ruebel		2-4	3rd	3.0
4-8	At S.D.	W	2-0		11	1	Cooke	Bergman	Ericks	3-4	T2nd	2.0
4-9	At S.D.	W	4-2		7	7	Loaiza	Worrell	Ericks	4-4	2nd	1.0
4-11	L.A.	L	1-7		8	8	Martinez	Cordova		4-5	2nd	1.5
4-13	L.A.	L	5-14		9	18	Nomo	Schmidt		4-6	3rd	2.0
4-15	S.D.	W	3-2		8	7	Ericks	Ashby		5-6	2nd	1.5
4-16	S.D.	L	5-7		11	7	Valenzuela	Cooke	Hoffman	5-7	2nd	2.5
4-17	Cin.	W	3-2		5	8	Loaiza	Morgan	Ericks	6-7	2nd	2.0
4-18	Cin.	L	1-6		5	8	Burba	Cordova		6-8	2nd	2.0
4-19	Cin.	W	6-5		8	12	Rincon	Remlinger		7-8	2nd	2.0
4-20	Cin.	W	5-3		7	9	Lieber	Mercker	Ericks	8-8	2nd	2.0
4-21	Phi.	L	2-10		9	14	Schilling	Cooke		8-9	2nd	2.5
4-23	Phi.	W	3-2		6	7	Rincon	Spradlin		9-9	2nd	3.0
4-24	At Chi.	W	4-3		6	7	Loiselle	Rojas		10-9	2nd	2.5
4-25	At Chi.	L	1-11		5	14	Foster	Lieber		10-10	2nd	3.5
4-26	At Chi.	L	6-7		12	14	Patterson	Rincon	Rojas	10-11	2nd	3.5
4-27	At Chi.	W	7-0		10	5	Schmidt	Telemaco		11-11	2nd	2.5
4-28	At Phi.	W	9-4	(12)	13	14	Wilkins	Mimbs		12-11	2nd	1.5
4-29	At Phi.	L	2-8		9	11	Maduro	Ruebel		12-12	2nd	2.5
4-30	S.F.	L	1-6		3	9	Gardner	Lieber		12-13	2nd	2.5
5-1	S.F.	W	3-2		6	8	Cooke	Estes	Rincon	13-13	2nd	1.5
5-2	At Atl.	W	3-2		6	7	Peters	Bielecki	Loiselle	14-13	2nd	1.5
5-3	At Atl.	W	3-0		7	4	Loaiza	Glavine	Rincon	15-13	2nd	0.5
5-4	At Atl.	L	1-3		8	6	Wade	Cordova	Wohlers	15-14	2nd	1.5
5-5	At Fla.	L	0-3		4	7	Helling	Lieber	Nen	15-15	2nd	2.5
5-6	At Fla.	W	4-0		10	4	Cooke	Fernandez		16-15	2nd	1.5
5-7	At Col.	W	14-3		17	11	Wilkins	Thompson		17-15	2nd	0.5
5-8	At Col.	W	10-8		14	15	Loaiza	Wright	Loiselle	18-15	2nd	0.5
5-9	Atl.	W	9-0		12	7	Cordova	Wade		19-15	1st	+0.5
5-10	Atl.	L	3-9		7	12	Neagle	Lieber		19-16	2nd	0.5
5-11	Atl.	L	2-8		6	13	Smoltz	Cooke		19-17	2nd	0.5
5-12	Atl.	L	2-10		12	14	Maddux	Schmidt		19-18	2nd	0.5
5-14	Col.	W	15-10		13	11	Wilkins	S. Reed		20-18	T1st	....
5-15	Col.	W	4-3		6	9	Cordova	Bailey	Rincon	21-18	1st	+0.5
5-16	Fla.	L	1-3		5	6	Fernandez	Lieber	Nen	21-19	2nd	0.5
5-17	Fla.	L	1-11		8	19	Rapp	Cooke		21-20	2nd	0.5
5-18	Fla.	L	3-5	(10)	8	12	Nen	Loiselle	Stanifer	21-21	2nd	0.5
5-20	At St.L.	L	1-3		4	7	Jackson	Loaiza	Eckersley	21-22	2nd	1.0
5-21	At St.L.	W	3-2		6	10	Ruebel	Fossas	Loiselle	22-22	2nd	1.0
5-22	At Mon.	W	9-3		10	8	Lieber	Perez	Rincon	23-22	2nd	0.5
5-23	At Mon.	L	1-4		5	7	Martinez	Cooke		23-23	2nd	0.5
5-24	At Mon.	L	3-7		7	12	Juden	Schmidt	Urbina	23-24	2nd	1.5
5-25	At Mon.	W	8-6		9	11	Wilkins	Daal	Loiselle	24-24	2nd	0.5
5-26	Chi.	L	1-2		3	6	Foster	Cordova	Adams	24-25	2nd	0.5
5-27	Chi.	L	7-8		12	12	Gonzalez	Lieber	Adams	24-26	2nd	0.5
5-28	Chi.	W	4-1		8	6	Cooke	Mulholland		25-26	T1st	....
5-30	Mon.	W	10-2		13	4	Peters	Juden		26-26	1st	+0.5
5-31	Mon.	L	2-4		6	7	Hermanson	Loaiza	Urbina	26-27	1st	+0.5
6-1	Mon.	W	11-2		12	10	Cordova	Bullinger		27-27	1st	+1.5
6-2	At Chi.	L	2-3		6	7	Mulholland	Lieber	Adams	27-28	1st	+0.5
6-3	At Chi.	W	3-1		10	5	Cooke	Trachsel	Loiselle	28-28	1st	+0.5
6-4	St.L.	L	0-10		7	11	An. Benes	Schmidt		28-29	2nd	0.5
6-5	St.L.	W	9-3		11	9	Loaiza	Stottlemyre		29-29	1st	+0.5
6-6	Phi.	W	5-4	(10)	9	10	Wilkins	Spradlin		30-29	1st	+0.5
6-7	Phi.	W	9-2		10	5	Lieber	Nye		31-29	1st	+1.5
6-8	Phi.	L	2-3		6	9	Schilling	Cooke	Bottalico	31-30	1st	+0.5
6-10	At Cin.	L	5-8		9	15	Remlinger	Rincon	Shaw	31-31	T1st	....
6-11	At Cin.	L	1-2		6	6	Tomko	Loaiza	Shaw	31-32	T1st	....
6-13	K.C.	W	5-3		8	9	Cordova	Mike Williams	Loiselle	32-32	1st	+1.0
6-14	K.C.	L	3-8		8	11	Belcher	Lieber	Montgomery	32-33	1st	+1.0
6-15	K.C.	L	1-8		6	14	Appier	Cooke		32-34	T1st	....
6-16	At Min.	W	8-6		15	9	Schmidt	Aldred	Loiselle	33-34	1st	+1.0
6-17	At Min.	L	1-13		4	17	Hawkins	Loaiza		33-35	T1st	....
6-18	At Min.	L	2-8		8	9	Radke	Cordova		33-36	T1st	....
6-19	At N.Y.	L	6-7		8	15	J. Franco	Rincon		33-37	2nd	0.5
6-20	At N.Y.	L	0-1		6	9	Jones	Cooke	J. Franco	33-38	2nd	1.5

Date	Opp.	Res.	Score	(inn.*)	Hits	Opp. hits	Winning pitcher	Losing pitcher	Save	Record	Pos.	GB
6-21	At N.Y.	L	2-3		8	6	Mlicki	Wilkins	McMichael	33-39	2nd	2.5
6-22	At N.Y.	L	9-12	(10)	13	18	Kashiwada	Peters		33-40	3rd	3.5
6-23	At Hou.	W	6-0		8	2	Cordova	Garcia		34-40	2nd	2.5
6-24	At Hou.	W	8-3		13	5	Lieber	Wall		35-40	2nd	1.5
6-25	At Hou.	L	1-5		6	9	Kile	Sodowsky		35-41	3rd	2.5
6-27	N.Y.	W	6-1		14	5	Schmidt	Mlicki		36-41	T2nd	2.0
6-28	N.Y.	L	3-8		9	11	Reynoso	Loaiza		36-42	3rd	2.0
6-29	N.Y.	L	8-10		15	12	Jordan	Peters	J. Franco	36-43	3rd	3.0
6-30	Chi. (AL)	W	3-1		9	5	Lieber	D. Darwin		37-43	3rd	2.0
7-1	Chi. (AL)	W	3-0		8	5	Cooke	Baldwin	Loiselle	38-43	3rd	2.0
7-2	Chi. (AL)	W	3-1		7	5	Schmidt	Navarro		39-43	3rd	2.0
7-3	At St.L.	W	6-4		12	11	Loaiza	Valenzuela	Loiselle	40-43	T2nd	1.0
7-4	At St.L.	W	7-5	(10)	10	11	Wilkins	Eckersley	Loiselle	41-43	T1st	....
7-5	At St.L.	W	4-3		9	9	Lieber	Morris	Wilkins	42-43	1st	+1.0
7-6	At St.L.	W	6-3		8	11	Cooke	Stottlemyre		43-43	1st	+1.0
7-10	Hou.	L	0-7		6	12	Kile	Schmidt		43-44	T1st	....
7-11	Hou.	L	0-10		5	14	Hampton	Loaiza		43-45	2nd	1.0
7-12	Hou.	W	3-0	(10)	6	0	Rincon	Hudek		44-45	T1st	....
7-13	Hou.	W	5-3		10	6	Sodowsky	Springer	Loiselle	45-45	1st	+1.0
7-14	N.Y.	W	5-4		15	10	Rincon	McMichael	Loiselle	46-45	1st	+1.0
7-15	N.Y.	W	4-3		9	7	Christiansen	Acevedo	Loiselle	47-45	1st	+1.0
7-16	Cin.	L	3-7		8	11	Burba	Loaiza		47-46	T1st	....
7-17	Cin.	L	5-9		11	17	Smiley	Cordova		47-47	T1st	....
7-18	At Phi.	L	6-8		11	9	Leiter	Lieber	Bottalico	47-48	2nd	1.0
7-19	At Phi.	W	13-3		17	12	Cooke	Green		48-48	2nd	1.0
7-20	At Phi.	L	1-4		9	5	Stephenson	Schmidt	Bottalico	48-49	2nd	2.0
7-21	At Phi.	W	3-2		7	8	Loaiza	Schilling	Loiselle	49-49	2nd	1.5
7-22	At S.D.	L	2-3		6	11	Hoffman	Loiselle		49-50	2nd	2.5
7-23	At S.D.	L	1-9		6	14	Smith	Lieber		49-51	2nd	3.5
7-24	At S.D.	L	6-8		10	12	Bruske	Sodowsky	Hoffman	49-52	2nd	4.5
7-25	At S.F.	W	5-2		9	6	Schmidt	Rueter	Loiselle	50-52	2nd	4.5
7-26	At S.F.	W	10-3		11	8	Loaiza	Creek		51-52	2nd	4.5
7-27†	At S.F.	L	5-6	(13)	15	13	Henry	Wilkins		51-53		
7-27‡	At S.F.	W	10-7		14	12	Cordova	VanLandingham		52-53	2nd	5.0
7-28	At L.A.	L	2-4		10	9	Valdes	Lieber	Worrell	52-54	T2nd	5.0
7-29	At L.A.	L	1-3		7	8	Astacio	Cooke	Worrell	52-55	T2nd	6.0
7-31	Col.	W	4-1		5	7	Schmidt	Bailey	Loiselle	53-55	2nd	6.0
8-1	Col.	L	6-7		13	10	S. Reed	Rincon	DiPoto	53-56	2nd	6.0
8-2	Col.	W	6-5		5	13	Cordova	Swift	Loiselle	54-56	2nd	6.0
8-3	Col.	W	8-4		14	9	Ruebel	S. Reed		55-56	2nd	6.0
8-4	Atl.	L	0-6		4	8	Smoltz	Cooke		55-57	2nd	6.0
8-5	Atl.	W	5-4		8	6	Schmidt	Glavine	Loiselle	56-57	2nd	5.0
8-6	Fla.	L	3-12		10	18	Brown	Loaiza		56-58	2nd	5.0
8-7	Fla.	W	5-1		9	7	Wilkins	Leiter		57-58	2nd	4.0
8-8	At Col.	L	3-5		11	10	Wright	Lieber	DiPoto	57-59	2nd	4.0
8-9	At Col.	L	7-8		12	11	Munoz	Rincon		57-60	2nd	5.0
8-10	At Col.	L	7-8		12	13	Leskanic	Wilkins	DiPoto	57-61	2nd	6.0
8-12	At Atl.	W	5-2		9	8	Sodowsky	Wohlers	Loiselle	58-61	2nd	6.5
8-13	At Atl.	W	2-1		7	6	Lieber	Smoltz	Loiselle	59-61	2nd	5.5
8-15	At Fla.	L	5-6		13	12	Powell	Loiselle		59-62	2nd	5.5
8-16	At Fla.	W	10-5		12	9	Cordova	Saunders		60-62	2nd	4.5
8-17	At Fla.	L	2-10		9	12	Brown	Cooke		60-63	2nd	5.5
8-18	At Fla.	W	7-2		11	7	Loaiza	Alfonseca		61-63	2nd	5.0
8-19	S.D.	L	5-3		7	7	Lieber	Smith	Loiselle	62-63	2nd	4.0
8-20	S.D.	W	7-3		14	7	Schmidt	Ashby		63-63	2nd	3.0
8-21	S.D.	L	4-9		6	13	Hitchcock	Cordova		63-64	2nd	4.0
8-22	S.F.	W	3-2		6	8	Cooke	Rueter	Loiselle	64-64	2nd	4.0
8-23	S.F.	W	6-4		10	8	Loaiza	Darwin	Loiselle	65-64	2nd	3.0
8-24	S.F.	W	9-6		13	12	Christiansen	Henry	Wilkins	66-64	2nd	3.0
8-25†	L.A.	L	2-8		5	13	Martinez	Schmidt	Guthrie	66-65		
8-25‡	L.A.	W	4-3		6	8	Wilkins	Worrell		67-65	2nd	3.0
8-26	L.A.	L	4-6		6	13	Dreifort	Rincon		67-66	2nd	3.0
8-27	L.A.	L	5-9		10	18	Reyes	Cooke		67-67	2nd	4.0
8-29	At Mil.	L	1-4		8	6	Karl	Loaiza	Jones	67-68	2nd	3.5
8-30	At Mil.	W	3-1		10	6	Lieber	Mercedes	Loiselle	68-68	2nd	2.5
8-31	At Mil.	L	2-3		7	11	Jones	Wilkins		68-69	2nd	2.5
9-1	Cle.	L	5-7		9	12	Ogea	Cooke	Mesa	68-70	2nd	2.5
9-2	Cle.	W	6-4		9	11	Silva	Wright	Loiselle	69-70	2nd	1.5
9-3	Cle.	L	3-7		8	7	Hershiser	Loaiza		69-71	2nd	2.5
9-4	At Cin.	L	2-5		7	7	Morgan	Lieber	Shaw	69-72	2nd	3.5
9-5	At Cin.	L	6-8		13	10	Sullivan	Wilkins	Shaw	69-73	2nd	3.5
9-6	At Cin.	W	13-4		15	11	Cordova	Remlinger		70-73	2nd	2.5
9-7	At Cin.	L	3-6		8	11	Burba	Silva	Shaw	70-74	2nd	2.5
9-9	At Mon.	L	4-5	(10)	12	11	Urbina	Loiselle		70-75	2nd	3.5
9-10	At Mon.	L	4-5		10	8	Martinez	Lieber	Urbina	70-76	2nd	3.5

Date	Opp.	Res.	Score	(inn.*)	Hits	Opp. hits	Winning pitcher	Losing pitcher	Save	Record	Pos.	GB
9-12	Chi.	W	3-1		5	6	Schmidt	Batista	Loiselle	71-76	2nd	3.5
9-13	Chi.	L	1-4		7	9	Trachsel	Cordova	Adams	71-77	2nd	4.5
9-14	Chi.	L	2-3		6	7	M. Clark	Rincon	Adams	71-78	2nd	4.5
9-15	Mon.	W	5-4	(10)	14	10	Wilkins	Telford		72-78	2nd	3.5
9-16	Mon.	W	8-2		11	6	Lieber	Johnson		73-78	2nd	3.5
9-17	Hou.	L	4-8		8	15	Reynolds	Schmidt		73-79	2nd	4.5
9-18	Hou.	W	12-3		12	5	Cordova	Kile		74-79	2nd	3.5
9-19	St.L.	L	5-6	(11)	12	13	King	Loiselle	Eckersley	74-80	2nd	3.5
9-20	St.L.	W	10-1		12	6	Loaiza	Beltran		75-80	2nd	3.5
9-21	St.L.	W	14-2		14	4	Lieber	Busby		76-80	2nd	3.5
9-22	St.L.	W	3-1		7	6	Schmidt	Morris	Loiselle	77-80	2nd	3.5
9-23	At N.Y.	W	5-4		7	4	Silva	Lidle	Loiselle	78-80	2nd	3.5
9-24	At N.Y.	L	5-7		8	8	Crawford	Cooke	Rojas	78-81	2nd	3.5
9-26	At Hou.	L	0-2		6	3	Garcia	Loaiza	Wagner	78-82	2nd	5.0
9-27	At Hou.	L	1-8		8	12	Reynolds	Schmidt		78-83	2nd	6.0
9-28	At Hou.	W	5-4	(11)	7	11	Christiansen	Henriquez	Loiselle	79-83	2nd	5.0

Monthly records: April (12-13), May (14-14), June (11-16), July (16-12), August (15-14), September (11-14).
*Innings, if other than nine. †First game of doubleheader. ‡Second game of doubleheader.

HIGHLIGHTS

High point: Francisco Cordova and Ricardo Rincon combined to throw a 10-inning no-hitter against the Astros on July 12. Pinch hitter Mark Smith won the game with a three-run homer in the 10th off John Hudek. It was the first combined extra inning no-hitter in major league history and came before the first non-opener sellout crowd in 20 years. It also allowed the Pirates to tie the Astros for first place.

Low point: The club's faint hopes of winning the National League Central were effectively ended when the Astros beat Jason Schmidt, 8-4, on September 17 at Three Rivers. The club fell 4½ games behind the Astros with 10 games remaining.

Turning point: The Pirates blew a 3-0 lead on September 9 in Montreal and lost, 5-4, in 10 innings. The loss was the club's fifth in six games. The Pirates had taken a lead in the top of the 10th, but Rich Loiselle, who had converted 25-of-28 save opportunities to that point, couldn't hold the lead and the team fell another game behind Houston.

Most valuable player: Second baseman Tony Womack. He wasn't even a lock to make the club in the spring and he wound up being the team's most consistent offensive player. Womack played in 155 games, solidified the leadoff spot and led the National League with 60 stolen bases.

Most valuable pitcher: Righthander Rich Loiselle. John Ericks' neck injury early in the season left the closer's spot up for grabs and Loiselle took it. His 29 saves (in 34 opportunities) were the second-highest total posted by a major league rookie since saves became an official stat in 1969. Like the rest of the staff, he had some rough spots, but Loiselle was a plus in a key role.

Most improved player: First baseman Kevin Young. He hit .300 with 18 home runs and 74 RBIs—not bad for a player who had been released by the organization the previous spring. Young went from a reserve to the club's cleanup hitter.

Most pleasant surprise: Right fielder Jose Guillen. The organization took a chance by promoting Guillen from Class A and was rewarded with a good season as Guillen hit .267 with 14 home runs and 70 RBIs.

Biggest disappointment: Center fielder Jermaine Allensworth. He took the job in 1996 and looked like he would be one of the main components in the club's rebuilding program. Allensworth regressed last year as a wrist injury took a big toll on his season. By September, he had effectively lost the job to journeyman Turner Ward.

Key injuries: Shortstop Kevin Elster's season ended on May 16, when he broke his right wrist. Ericks, who was counted on to be the closer, didn't pitch after April 28. A sprained right hand cost Al Martin 30 games, and Allensworth was out for 34. Young was lost for 35 games down the stretch when he tore a ligament in his right thumb.

Notable: Womack stole a club-record 32 consecutive bases between April 6 and July 4. The old record of 31 by Max Carey had stood since 1922.

—JOHN MEHNO

RECORDS

1997 regular-season record: 79-83 (2nd in N.L. Central); 43-38 at home; 36-45 on road; 26-29 vs. East; 31-32 vs. Central; 22-22 vs. West; 21-14 vs. lefthanded starters; 58-69 vs. righthanded starters; 26-28 on grass; 53-55 on turf; 26-28 in daytime; 53-55 at night; 22-21 in one-run games; 6-6 in extra-inning games; 0-0-2 in doubleheaders.

Team record past five years: 338-406 (.454, ranks 14th in league in that span).

TEAM LEADERS

Batting average: Jason Kendall (.294).
At-bats: Tony Womack (641).
Runs: Tony Womack (85).
Hits: Tony Womack (178).
Total bases: Tony Womack (240).
Doubles: Jason Kendall (36).
Triples: Joe Randa, Tony Womack (9).
Home runs: Kevin Young (18).
Runs batted in: Kevin Young (74).
Stolen bases: Tony Womack (60).
Slugging percentage: Jason Kendall (.434).
On-base percentage: Jason Kendall (.391).
Wins: Francisco Cordova, Jon Lieber, Esteban Loaiza (11).
Earned-run average: Francisco Cordova (3.63).
Complete games: Francisco Cordova, Jason Schmidt (2).
Shutouts: Francisco Cordova (2).
Saves: Rich Loiselle (29).
Innings pitched: Esteban Loaiza (196.1).
Strikeouts: Jon Lieber (160).

GAMES BY POSITION

Catcher: Jason Kendall 142, Keith Osik 32.
First base: Kevin Young 77, Mark Johnson 63, Eddie Williams 26, Dale Sveum 21, Mark Smith 9, Freddy Garcia 2, Keith Osik 1.
Second base: Tony Womack 152, Joe Randa 13, Abraham Nunez 9, Keith Osik 4, Kevin Polcovich 2, Dale Sveum 2.
Third base: Joe Randa 120, Dale Sveum 47, Kevin Young 12, Freddy Garcia 10, Keith Osik 1, Kevin Polcovich 1.
Shortstop: Kevin Polcovich 80, Kevin Elster 39, Dale Sveum 28, Lou Collier 18, Shawon Dunston 18, Abraham Nunez 12, Tony Womack 4.
Outfield: Jose Guillen 136, Al Martin 110, Jermaine Allensworth 104, Turner Ward 54, Emil Brown 42, Mark Smith 42, Adrian Brown 38, Midre Cummings 25, Kevin Young 11.
Designated hitter: Mark Smith 5, Mark Johnson 1.

TOP DRAFT CHOICES

1. **J.J. Davis,** 1B-RHP, Baldwin Park H.S., Pomona, Calif.
2. **Jose Nicolas,** OF, Westminster Christian H.S., Miami.
3. **John Grabow,** LHP, San Gabriel (Calif.) H.S.
4. **Maurice Washington,** OF, Chapparral H.S., Las Vegas, Nev.
5. **Chris Combs,** RHP-OF, North Carolina State University.
6. **Andy Bausher,** LHP, Kutztown (Pa.) Univ.
7. **Korwin Dehaan,** OF, Morningside (Iowa) College.
8. **Paul Stabile,** LHP, Brookdale (N.J.) C.C.
9. **Michael Parkerson,** LHP, Columbus (Ga.) H.S.
10. **Rico Washington,** SS, Jones County H.S., Gray, Ga.

ST. LOUIS CARDINALS
NATIONAL LEAGUE CENTRAL DIVISION

Cardinals Schedule
Home games shaded. *—All-Star Game at Coors Field (Colorado).
D—Day game (any game starting before 5 p.m.).

March
SUN	MON	TUE	WED	THU	FRI	SAT
		31 D LA				

April
SUN	MON	TUE	WED	THU	FRI	SAT
			1	2 D LA	3 D SD	4 SD
5 D SD	6	7 COL	8 D COL	9 COL	10 SF	11 D SF
12 SF	13 D SF	14 ARZ	15 ARZ	16 D ARZ	17 PHI	18 D PHI
19 PHI	20	21 MON	22 MON	23 MON	24 PHI	25 PHI
26 PHI	27 MON	28 MON	29 D MON	30 CUB		

May
SUN	MON	TUE	WED	THU	FRI	SAT
					1 D CUB	2 D CUB
3 D CUB	4	5 PIT	6 PIT	7 NYM	8 NYM	9 D NYM
10 NYM	11 MIL	12 MIL	13 ATL	14 ATL	15 FLA	16 FLA
17 FLA	18 D FLA	19 PHI	20 PHI	21 PHI	22 SF	23 SF
24 SF	25 D COL	26	27 COL	28 COL	29 D SD	30 SD
31 D SD						

June
SUN	MON	TUE	WED	THU	FRI	SAT
	1 SD	2 LA	3 LA	4 D LA	5 SF	6 SF
7 SF	8 D CWS	9 CWS	10 CWS	11	12 ARZ	13 ARZ
14 D ARZ	15	16 HOU	17 HOU	18 HOU	19 ARZ	20 D ARZ
21 ARZ	22 D DET	23 DET	24 CLE	25 CLE	26 MIN	27 MIN
28 D MIN	29	30 KC				

July
SUN	MON	TUE	WED	THU	FRI	SAT
			1 KC	2 KC	3 CIN	4 CIN
5 D CIN	6	7	* 8	9 HOU	10 HOU	11 HOU
12 D HOU	13 D CIN	14 CIN	15 CIN	16 LA	17 LA	18 LA
19 D LA	20 SD	21 SD	22 SF	23 D SF	24 COL	25 COL
26 D COL	27	28 MIL	29 MIL	30 MIL	31 ATL	

August
SUN	MON	TUE	WED	THU	FRI	SAT
						1 ATL
2 ATL	3 MIL	4 MIL	5 MIL	6	7 CUB	8 CUB
9 D CUB	10 NYM	11 NYM	12 NYM	13	14 PIT	15 PIT
16 D PIT	17	18 CUB	19 D CUB	20 NYM	21 NYM	22 PIT
23 D PIT	24 D FLA	25 FLA	26 FLA	27 ATL	28 ATL	29 ATL
30 D ATL	31 FLA					

September
SUN	MON	TUE	WED	THU	FRI	SAT
		1 FLA	2 FLA	3	4 CIN	5 CIN
6 D CIN	7 D CUB	8 CUB	9 CIN	10 CIN	11 HOU	12 HOU
13 D HOU	14 PIT	15 PIT	16 PIT	17	18 MIL	19 MIL
20 D MIL	21	22 HOU	23 HOU	24	25 MON	26 MON
27 D MON						

1998 SEASON
CLUB DIRECTORY

Chairman of the board/general partner
William O. DeWitt Jr.
Chairman
Frederick O. Hanser
President
Mark C. Lamping
Vice president, general manager
Walt Jocketty
Admin. asst. to the president
Julie Laningham
Sr. exec. asst. to v.p., general manager
Judy Carpenter-Barada
Secretary-treasurer
Andrew N. Baur
Director, merchandising
Bill DeWitt III
Director, ticket operations
Josie Arnold
Group director, sales
Kevin Wade
Manager, season sales
Mark Murray
Director, group sales
Joe Strohm
Vice president, corporate sales
Dan Farrell
Admin. asst. to v.p./corporate sales
Gail Ruhling
Vice president, community relations
Marty Hendin
Admin. asst. to the v.p., com. relations
Mary Ellen Edmiston
Director, promotions
Thane van Breusegen
Controller
Brad Wood
Director, media relations
Brian Bartow
Media relations assistants
Shawn Bertani
Mary Donovan
Steve Zesch

Vice president/player personnel
Jerry Walker
Coord. of int'l scouting & player dev.
Tim Hanser
Director, scouting
Ed Creech
Major league trainer
Barry Weinberg
Assistant major league trainer
Brad Henderson
Equipment manager
Buddy Bates
Assistant equipment manager
Rip Rowan
Traveling secretary
C.J. Cherre
Special assignment scouts
Fred McAlister, Jeff Scott, Joe Sparks,
Mike Squires
National cross checker
Marty Keough
East region cross checker
Michael Roberts
Assistant director of scouting
John Mozeliak
Director, player development
Mike Jorgensen
Player development assistant
John Vuch
Mgr., bus. operations for baseball
Scott Smulczenski
Scouts
Randy Benson, Doug Carpenter, Tim
Conroy, Roberto Diaz, Chuck Fick,
Ben Galante, Steve Grilli, Manny
Guerra, Dave Karaff, Tom
McCormack, Scott Melvin, Scott
Nichols, Jay North, Joe Rigoli,
Roger Smith, Duane Walker

MINOR LEAGUE AFFILIATES

Class	Team	League	Manager
AAA	Memphis	Pacific Coast	Gaylen Pitts
AA	Arkansas	Texas	Chris Maloney
A	Prince William	Carolina	Joe Cunningham
A	Peoria	Midwest	Jeff Shireman
A	New Jersey	New York-Pennsylvania	Jose Oquendo
Rookie	Johnson City	Appalachian	Steve Turco

BROADCAST INFORMATION

Radio: KMOX-AM (1120).
TV: KPLR-TV (Channel 11).
Cable TV: Fox Sports Midwest.

SPRING TRAINING

Ballpark (city): Roger Dean Stadium
(Jupiter, Fla.).
Ticket information: 1-888-447-4824.

SPRING TRAINING ROSTER

Manager—Tony La Russa (10).
Coaches—Mark DeJohn (44), Dave Duncan (18), Rene Lachemann (15), Dave McKay (39), Dave Parker.

No.	PITCHERS	B/T	Ht./Wt.	Born	1997 clubs
	Almanza, Armando	L/L	6-3/205	10-26-72	Prince William
38	Aybar, Manuel	R/R	6-1/165	10-5-74	Louisville, St. Louis
53	Beltran, Rigo	L/L	5-11/185	11-13-69	Louisville, St. Louis
41	Benes, Alan	R/R	6-5/215	1-21-72	St. Louis
	Bottenfield, Kent	B/R	6-3/245	11-14-68	Chicago N.L.
	Brantley, Jeff	R/R	5-10/180	9-5-63	Cincinnati
	Busby, Mike	R/R	6-4/210	12-27-72	Louisville, St. Louis
	Croushore, Rich	R/R	6-4/210	8-7-70	Arkansas, Louisville
50	Frascatore, John	R/R	6-1/210	2-4-70	St. Louis
	Heiserman, Rick	R/R	6-7/225	2-22-73	Arkansas, Louisville
57	King, Curtis	R/R	6-5/200	10-25-70	Arkansas, Louisville, St. Louis
	Looper, Braden	R/R	6-4/220	10-28-74	Prince William, Arkansas
34	Lowe, Sean	R/R	6-2/205	3-29-71	Louisville, St. Louis
	Mercker, Kent	L/L	6-2/195	2-1-68	Cincinnati
35	Morris, Matt	R/R	6-5/210	8-9-74	St. Louis
31	Osborne, Donovan	L/L	6-2/195	6-21-69	St. Louis, Louisville
28	Painter, Lance	L/L	6-1/197	7-21-67	St. Louis, Louisville
46	Petkovsek, Mark	R/R	6-0/185	11-18-65	St. Louis
64	Raggio, Brady	R/R	6-4/210	9-17-72	Louisville, St. Louis
30	Stottlemyre, Todd	L/R	6-3/200	5-20-65	St. Louis

No.	CATCHERS	B/T	Ht./Wt.	Born	1997 clubs
49	Lampkin, Tom	L/R	5-11/185	3-4-64	St. Louis
26	Marrero, Eli	R/R	6-1/180	11-17-73	Louisville, St. Louis
19	Pagnozzi, Tom	R/R	6-1/195	7-30-62	Arkansas, St. Louis, Louisville
12	Sheaffer, Danny	R/R	6-0/195	8-2-61	St. Louis

No.	INFIELDERS	B/T	Ht./Wt.	Born	1997 clubs
27	Bell, David	R/R	5-10/175	9-14-72	Arkansas, Louisville, St. Louis
11	Clayton, Royce	R/R	6-0/183	1-2-70	St. Louis
7	DeShields, Delino	L/R	6-1/175	1-15-69	St. Louis
8	Gaetti, Gary	R/R	6-0/205	8-19-58	St. Louis
	Howard, David	B/R	6-0/175	2-26-67	Kansas City
25	McGwire, Mark	R/R	6-5/250	10-1-63	Oakland, St. Louis
52	Ordaz, Luis	R/R	5-11/170	8-12-75	Arkansas, St. Louis
	Polanco, Placido	R/R	5-10/170	10-10-75	Arkansas
	Richard, Chris	L/L	6-2/190	6-7-74	Arkansas

No.	OUTFIELDERS	B/T	Ht./Wt.	Born	1997 clubs
5	Gant, Ron	R/R	6-0/200	3-2-65	St. Louis
	Green, Scarborough	R/R	5-10/170	6-9-74	Arkansas, Louisville, St. Louis
3	Jordan, Brian	R/R	6-1/205	3-29-67	St. Louis, Louisville
16	Lankford, Ray	L/L	5-11/198	6-5-67	Prince William, St. Louis
47	Mabry, John	L/R	6-4/195	10-17-70	St. Louis
51	McGee, Willie	B/R	6-1/185	11-2-58	St. Louis
	Munoz, Juan	L/L	5-10/170	3-27-74	Prince William, Arkansas

BALLPARK INFORMATION

Ballpark (capacity, surface)
Busch Stadium (49,676, grass)
Address
250 Stadium Plaza
St. Louis, MO 63102
Business phone
314-421-3060
Ticket information
314-421-2400
Ticket prices
$24 (field boxes-infield)
$22 (loge boxes-infield)
$20 (field boxes-outfield, loge boxes-outfield)
$16 (terrace boxes; loge reserved-infield)
$14 (loge reserved-outfield, terrace boxes-outfield)
$11 (terrace reserved-infield)
$11 (terrace reserved-outfield)
$6 (upper terrace reserved-outfield, bleachers)
$2 (upper terrace reserved-children)
Field dimensions (from home plate)
To left field at foul line, 330 feet
To center field, 402 feet
To right field at foul line, 330 feet
First game played
May 12, 1966 (Cardinals 4, Braves 3)

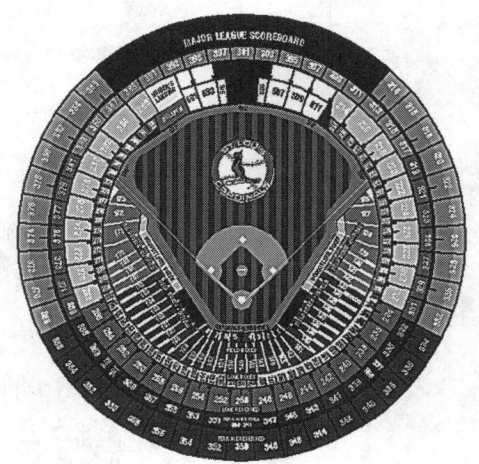

1998 SEASON *St. Louis Cardinals*

Date	Opp.	Res.	Score	(inn.*)	Hits	Opp. hits	Winning pitcher	Losing pitcher	Save	Record	Pos.	GB
4-1	At Mon.	L	1-2		7	7	Urbina	Batchelor		0-1	T4th	1.0
4-2	At Mon.	L	1-4		2	9	Juden	Petkovsek	Smith	0-2	T4th	2.0
4-3	At Mon.	L	4-9		7	14	Perez	Al. Benes		0-3	T4th	2.0
4-4	At Hou.	L	2-3	(11)	9	14	Springer	Ludwick		0-4	T4th	3.0
4-5	At Hou.	L	2-6		7	7	Fernandez	Osborne	Garcia	0-5	T4th	4.0
4-6	At Hou.	L	2-3		7	7	Martin	Frascatore	Wagner	0-6	T4th	5.0
4-8	Mon.	W	2-1		7	6	Petkovsek	Urbina		1-6	4th	4.0
4-11	Hou.	W	4-2		6	8	Batchelor	Reynolds	Eckersley	2-6	4th	3.0
4-12	Hou.	L	5-7		8	6	Garcia	Stottlemyre	Wagner	2-7	4th	4.0
4-13	Hou.	W	6-2		7	7	Al. Benes	Hampton	Eckersley	3-7	4th	3.0
4-14	Hou.	L	2-4	(10)	6	11	Wagner	Eckersley	Hudek	3-8	4th	4.0
4-15	At Fla.	W	9-3		12	9	Raggio	Fernandez		4-8	4th	3.0
4-16	At Fla.	L	1-2		5	8	Rapp	Osborne	Nen	4-9	4th	4.0
4-17	At Fla.	L	1-2		4	7	Hutton	Petkovsek		4-10	4th	4.5
4-19†	At S.D.§	W	1-0		7	6	Petkovsek	Hitchcock	Eckersley	5-10	4th	4.0
4-19‡	At S.D.§	W	2-1		7	3	Al. Benes	Worrell		6-10	3rd	3.5
4-20	At S.D.§	L	2-8		9	12	Ashby	Raggio		6-11	3rd	4.5
4-22	At L.A.	W	6-4		11	10	Frascatore	Worrell	Eckersley	7-11	3rd	4.5
4-23	At L.A.	L	1-2		3	8	Guthrie	Petkovsek	Worrell	7-12	3rd	5.5
4-25	Col.	L	4-5		9	7	Ritz	Al. Benes	Ruffin	7-13	3rd	6.5
4-26	Col.	L	2-4		8	7	Swift	Morris	Ruffin	7-14	3rd	6.5
4-27	Col.	W	6-2		9	9	Osborne	Thompson		8-14	3rd	5.5
4-28	S.F.	W	5-2		13	8	An. Benes	VanLandingham	Eckersley	9-14	3rd	4.5
4-29	S.F.	W	9-7		12	11	Fossas	Beck		10-14	3rd	4.5
4-30	Fla.	W	6-2		8	9	Al. Benes	Leiter		11-14	3rd	3.5
5-1	Fla.	W	3-2		9	6	Morris	Fernandez	Eckersley	12-14	3rd	2.5
5-2	At N.Y.	L	4-7		6	11	McMichael	Mathews	J. Franco	12-15	3rd	3.5
5-3	At N.Y.	L	1-5		8	9	Reed	An. Benes		12-16	3rd	3.5
5-4	At N.Y.	W	8-2		13	5	Stottlemyre	Clark		13-16	3rd	3.5
5-5	Atl.	L	1-2		6	7	Neagle	Al. Benes	Wohlers	13-17	3rd	4.5
5-6	Atl.	W	4-3		10	4	Mathews	Bielecki	Eckersley	14-17	3rd	3.5
5-7	Phi.	W	14-7		13	11	Frascatore	Harris		15-17	3rd	2.5
5-8	Phi.	W	6-2		6	6	An. Benes	Mimbs		16-17	3rd	2.5
5-9	N.Y.	L	3-10		9	12	Clark	Stottlemyre		16-18	3rd	3.0
5-10	N.Y.	L	0-2		3	9	Jones	Al. Benes	J. Franco	16-19	3rd	3.5
5-11	N.Y.	L	4-6		9	9	Lidle	Eckersley	J. Franco	16-20	3rd	3.5
5-13	At Phi.	L	2-3		3	6	Spradlin	Mathews	Bottalico	16-21	3rd	3.0
5-14	At Phi.	W	12-3		17	9	Stottlemyre	Maduro		17-21	3rd	3.0
5-16	At Atl.	L	0-1	(13)	11	7	Borowski	Frascatore		17-22	3rd	4.0
5-17	At Atl.	L	6-11		7	19	Smoltz	Morris		17-23	3rd	4.0
5-18	At Atl.	L	1-5		7	8	Glavine	An. Benes		17-24	3rd	4.0
5-19	At Atl.	L	3-7		10	9	Neagle	Stottlemyre		17-25	3rd	5.0
5-20	Pit.	W	3-1		7	4	Jackson	Loaiza	Eckersley	18-25	3rd	4.0
5-21	Pit.	L	2-3		10	6	Ruebel	Fossas	Loiselle	18-26	3rd	5.0
5-23	At S.F.	L	0-2		2	5	Estes	Morris		18-27	3rd	5.0
5-24	At S.F.	W	9-3		15	9	An. Benes	Roa		19-27	3rd	5.0
5-25	At S.F.	W	9-3		11	7	Stottlemyre	VanLandingham		20-27	3rd	4.0
5-26	At Col.	L	7-9		14	13	DeJean	Petkovsek	S. Reed	20-28	3rd	4.0
5-27	At Col.	W	8-6		13	14	Al. Benes	Thomson	Eckersley	21-28	3rd	3.0
5-29	L.A.	W	4-2		7	10	Morris	Astacio	Eckersley	22-28	3rd	3.0
5-30	L.A.	W	2-1		6	7	Mathews	Hall		23-28	3rd	2.5
5-31	L.A.	W	6-3		11	6	Stottlemyre	Valdes	Eckersley	24-28	3rd	1.5
6-1	L.A.	L	1-6		11	9	Park	Al. Benes		24-29	3rd	2.5
6-2	Col.	L	7-11		11	12	Burke	Jackson		24-30	3rd	2.5
6-3	Col.	W	15-4		21	5	Morris	Jones		25-30	3rd	2.5
6-4	At Pit.	W	10-0		11	7	An. Benes	Schmidt		26-30	3rd	2.0
6-5	At Pit.	L	3-9		9	11	Loaiza	Stottlemyre		26-31	3rd	2.5
6-6	At L.A.	W	3-1		8	7	Al. Benes	Park	Eckersley	27-31	3rd	2.5
6-7	At L.A.	L	2-5		6	14	Nomo	Jackson		27-32	4th	3.5
6-8	At L.A.	W	9-3		13	13	Morris	Astacio		28-32	3rd	2.5
6-9	At S.D.	W	9-1		14	5	An. Benes	Cunnane		29-32	3rd	2.0
6-10	At S.D.	L	5-6	(12)	8	15	Erdos	Beltran		29-33	3rd	2.0
6-11	At S.D.	W	8-3		11	6	Al. Benes	Burrows	Petkovsek	30-33	3rd	1.0
6-14†	Cle.	L	3-8		7	14	Lopez	Mathews		30-34		
6-14‡	Cle.	W	5-2		11	5	Morris	Ogea	Eckersley	31-34	T2nd	1.0
6-15	Cle.	L	2-9		5	9	Nagy	Stottlemyre		31-35	3rd	1.0
6-16	At Mil.	L	0-1		5	4	Wickman	Al. Benes		31-36	3rd	2.0
6-17	At Mil.	L	3-4		11	7	Adamson	Valenzuela	Jones	31-37	3rd	2.0
6-18	At Mil.	L	4-8		7	14	D'Amico	An. Benes		31-38	3rd	2.0
6-20	Cin.	L	2-4		7	9	Mercker	Morris	Shaw	31-39	3rd	3.0
6-21	Cin.	W	6-2		13	9	Stottlemyre	Burba		32-39	3rd	3.0

Date	Opp.	Res.	Score	(inn.*)	Hits	Opp. hits	Winning pitcher	Losing pitcher	Save	Record	Pos.	GB
6-22	Cin.	W	5-2		9	4	Al. Benes	Sullivan	Eckersley	33-39	2nd	3.0
6-23	Chi.	L	0-3		4	8	Gonzalez	Valenzuela		33-40	3rd	3.0
6-24	Chi.	W	7-2		15	5	An. Benes	Mulholland		34-40	3rd	2.0
6-25	Chi.	W	3-1		7	6	Mathews	Patterson		35-40	2nd	2.0
6-26	At Cin.	W	5-3		10	6	Stottlemyre	Burba	Eckersley	36-40	2nd	2.0
6-27	At Cin.	L	3-5		5	5	Tomko	Al. Benes	Shaw	36-41	T2nd	2.0
6-28	At Cin.	W	12-6		18	9	Petkovsek	Smiley		37-41	2nd	1.0
6-29	At Cin.	W	6-5	(12)	11	13	Frascatore	Carrasco	Eckersley	38-41	2nd	1.0
6-30	Min.	W	2-1		6	12	Morris	Robertson	Eckersley	39-41	T1st	....
7-1	Min.	W	2-0		7	5	Stottlemyre	Hawkins	Eckersley	40-41	1st	+1.0
7-2	Min.	W	2-1	(10)	10	5	Petkovsek	Guardado		41-41	1st	+1.0
7-3	Pit.	L	4-6		11	12	Loaiza	Valenzuela	Loiselle	41-42	1st	+1.0
7-4	Pit.	L	5-7	(10)	11	10	Wilkins	Eckersley	Loiselle	41-43	T1st	....
7-5	Pit.	L	3-4		9	9	Lieber	Morris	Wilkins	41-44	T2nd	1.0
7-6	Pit.	L	3-6		11	8	Cooke	Stottlemyre		41-45	3rd	2.0
7-10	At Chi.	W	3-2		5	5	Al. Benes	Wendell	Eckersley	42-45	3rd	1.0
7-11	At Chi.	L	1-7		5	8	Gonzalez	Morris		42-46	3rd	2.0
7-12	At Chi.	W	2-1	(12)	10	7	Mathews	Wendell	Eckersley	43-46	3rd	1.0
7-13	At Cin.	W	11-5		20	6	Stottlemyre	Trachsel		44-46	T2nd	1.0
7-14	At Cin.	L	2-4		7	5	Mercker	Valenzuela	Shaw	44-47	3rd	2.0
7-15	At Cin.	W	7-4		9	12	Al. Benes	Tomko	Eckersley	45-47	3rd	2.0
7-16	S.D.	L	3-4		7	8	Bruske	Mathews	Hoffman	45-48	3rd	2.0
7-17	S.D.	L	1-3		7	6	Hamilton	An. Benes	Hoffman	45-49	3rd	2.0
7-18	S.F.	W	6-5		7	10	Stottlemyre	Estes	Eckersley	46-49	3rd	2.0
7-19	S.F.	W	8-7		11	13	Frascatore	Henry	Eckersley	47-49	3rd	2.0
7-20	S.F.	L	2-9		8	13	Rueter	Al. Benes		47-50	3rd	3.0
7-21	S.F.	W	7-2		13	7	Morris	Foulke		48-50	3rd	2.5
7-22	Hou.	L	2-4		5	6	Hampton	An. Benes	Wagner	48-51	3rd	3.5
7-23	Hou.	L	2-7		5	11	Magnante	Stottlemyre		48-52	3rd	4.5
7-25	Fla.	L	4-5		6	9	Hernandez	Al. Benes	Nen	48-53	3rd	6.0
7-26	Fla.	W	3-1		5	6	Morris	Helling	Eckersley	49-53	3rd	6.0
7-27	Fla.	W	6-4		9	7	An. Benes	Brown	Eckersley	50-53	3rd	6.0
7-28	At Hou.	W	2-1		6	6	Stottlemyre	Holt	Eckersley	51-53	T2nd	5.0
7-29	At Hou.	L	4-5		8	10	Reynolds	Osborne	Wagner	51-54	T2nd	6.0
7-30	At Hou.	L	4-7		11	11	Kile	Fossas	Martin	51-55	3rd	7.0
7-31	At Phi.	L	1-2	(10)	4	9	Bottalico	Fossas		51-56	3rd	7.5
8-1	At Phi.	L	1-4		9	7	Stephenson	An. Benes	Bottalico	51-57	3rd	7.5
8-2	At Phi.	W	2-1		8	7	Stottlemyre	Beech	Eckersley	52-57	3rd	7.5
8-3	At Phi.	L	1-10		7	12	Leiter	Osborne		52-58	3rd	8.5
8-4	At N.Y.	L	2-4		6	8	Reed	Aybar	J. Franco	52-59	3rd	8.5
8-5	At N.Y.	L	4-5	(10)	10	7	Lidle	Fossas		52-60	3rd	8.5
8-6	At Atl.	L	3-4		11	7	Wohlers	Petkovsek		52-61	3rd	8.5
8-7	At Atl.	L	0-3		7	8	Neagle	Stottlemyre	Wohlers	52-62	3rd	8.5
8-8	Phi.	W	6-1		12	3	Osborne	Leiter		53-62	3rd	7.5
8-9	Phi.	L	2-3		3	9	Green	Aybar	Bottalico	53-63	3rd	8.5
8-10	Phi.	L	0-8		3	15	Schilling	Morris		53-64	3rd	9.5
8-12	N.Y.	W	5-2		8	9	An. Benes	Mlicki	Eckersley	54-64	3rd	10.0
8-13	N.Y.	L	4-5	(10)	13	11	Lidle	Fossas	J. Franco	54-65	3rd	10.0
8-14	N.Y.	L	2-6		7	10	Jones	Osborne		54-66	3rd	10.5
8-15	Atl.	W	3-2	(12)	7	6	King	Cather		55-66	3rd	9.5
8-16	Atl.	L	3-5		7	10	Maddux	Morris	Wohlers	55-67	3rd	9.5
8-17	Atl.	W	3-1		7	6	King	Neagle	Eckersley	56-67	3rd	9.5
8-19	At Mon.	W	12-5		16	9	Stottlemyre	Perez		57-67	3rd	8.5
8-20	At Mon.	W	6-3		8	10	King	Kline	Eckersley	58-67	3rd	7.5
8-21	At Mon.	L	2-3		2	9	Johnson	Osborne	Urbina	58-68	3rd	8.5
8-22	At Fla.	W	7-3		9	8	Morris	Saunders		59-68	3rd	8.5
8-23	At Fla.	L	0-3		5	4	Brown	An. Benes		59-69	3rd	8.5
8-24	At Fla.	L	1-7		8	9	Ojala	Stottlemyre		59-70	3rd	9.5
8-25	Mon.	L	1-2		4	6	Martinez	Aybar	Urbina	59-71	3rd	10.0
8-26	Mon.	L	5-7		12	9	Valdes	Eckersley	Urbina	59-72	3rd	10.0
8-27	Mon.	W	4-3		7	10	Frascatore	Telford	Beltran	60-72	3rd	10.0
8-28	Mon.	W	11-5		15	7	An. Benes	Paniagua		61-72	3rd	9.0
8-29	At K.C.	W	9-7		11	8	Beltran	Carrasco	Eckersley	62-72	3rd	8.0
8-30	At K.C.	L	5-16		7	15	Belcher	Aybar		62-73	3rd	8.0
8-31	At K.C.	W	5-4		9	8	Osborne	Olson	Eckersley	63-73	3rd	7.0
9-1	Chi. (AL)	L	4-5		10	7	T. Castillo	Fossas	Karchner	63-74	3rd	7.0
9-2	Chi. (AL)	W	6-1		11	7	An. Benes	Navarro		64-74	3rd	6.0
9-3	Chi. (AL)	W	4-2		12	11	Aybar	Eyre	Eckersley	65-74	3rd	6.0
9-5	At Col.	L	4-11		7	16	Castillo	Osborne		65-75	3rd	6.5
9-6†	At Col.	W	10-7	(13)	16	9	Eckersley	McCurry	Petkovsek	66-75		
9-6‡	At Col.	L	6-7		12	13	Holmes	King		66-76	3rd	6.0
9-7	At Col.	L	4-7		6	12	Astacio	Petkovsek		66-77	3rd	6.0
9-9	At S.F.	W	5-3		8	4	Aybar	Mulholland	Eckersley	67-77	3rd	6.0
9-10	At S.F.	L	6-7	(10)	9	12	Beck	Painter		67-78	3rd	6.0
9-12	S.D.	W	4-2		7	13	Morris	Ashby	Eckersley	68-78	3rd	6.0

Date	Opp.	Res.	Score	(inn.*)	Hits	Opp. hits	Winning pitcher	Losing pitcher	Save	Record	Pos.	GB
9-13	S.D.	L	3-8		6	11	Erdos	Lowe		68-79	3rd	7.0
9-14	S.D.	W	10-4		11	12	Fossas	Kroon		69-79	3rd	6.0
9-15	L.A.	L	6-7	(15)	12	11	Harkey	Raggio	Dreifort	69-80	T3rd	6.0
9-16	L.A.	L	6-7		8	11	Gorecki	Eckersley	Radinsky	69-81	T3rd	7.0
9-17	At Chi.	W	12-9		13	11	Morris	Batista		70-81	3rd	7.0
9-18	At Chi.	L	3-4		9	10	Trachsel	Lowe		70-82	T3rd	7.0
9-19	At Pit.	W	6-5	(11)	13	12	King	Loiselle	Eckersley	71-82	T3rd	6.0
9-20	At Pit.	L	1-10		6	12	Loaiza	Beltran		71-83	T3rd	7.0
9-21	At Pit.	L	2-14		4	14	Lieber	Busby		71-84	T3rd	8.0
9-22	At Pit.	L	1-3		6	7	Schmidt	Morris	Loiselle	71-85	T3rd	9.0
9-23	Cin.	L	6-8		8	13	Sullivan	King	Shaw	71-86	4th	10.0
9-24	Cin.	L	4-5		9	8	Burba	Fossas	Shaw	71-87	4th	10.0
9-25	Cin.	L	3-4	(14)	9	9	Sullivan	Petkovsek	White	71-88	4th	11.0
9-26	Chi.	L	2-5		6	14	Tapani	Busby		71-89	4th	12.0
9-27	Chi.	W	12-4		12	7	Morris	Foster		72-89	4th	12.0
9-28	Chi.	W	2-1		7	4	Painter	Pisciotta		73-89	4th	11.0

Monthly records: April (11-14), May (13-14), June (15-13), July (12-15), August (12-17), September (10-16).
*Innings, if other than nine. †First game of doubleheader. ‡Second game of doubleheader. §At Honolulu, Hawaii.

HIGHLIGHTS

High point: A three-game sweep of the Twins on June 30-July 2 brought the team to the .500 mark for the first time. But it was the team's only appearance at .500 all year. **Low point:** Starting the season with high hopes, the team lost six consecutive games in Montreal and Houston. The 0-6 start was the worst in franchise history. **Turning point:** After hitting the elusive .500 mark, the Cardinals lost four games in a row at home to Pittsburgh—they led in every game—before the All-Star break. Particularly galling was a 7-5 loss on July 4, a game the Cardinals would have won had left fielder Ron Gant not lost a fly ball in the sun with two outs in the top of the ninth inning, enabling the Pirates to tie the score. **Most valuable player:** Strangely, for a team that underachieved all season, it had two: Ray Lankford, who was the team's most consistent player all season, and Mark McGwire, who injected excitement into the final two months of a season that had gone south before his arrival from Oakland on July 31. **Most valuable pitcher:** Rookie righthander Matt Morris. When the club's other starters were dropping like flies, Morris persevered, finishing the season with 12 wins and a 3.19 ERA. He led all major league rookies in ERA, games started, innings, complete games and strikeouts. **Most improved player:** Catcher Mike Difelice, a career minor leaguer, took over the No. 1 job when Tom Pagnozzi was hurt and played beyond expectations. **Most pleasant surprise:** Second baseman Delino DeShields. After three off-years with Los Angeles because of injury and indifference, he rebounded to play 150 games and have the best offensive season of his career, regaining the form of his early years with the Expos. **Biggest disappointment:** Gant. He fanned 162 times—one for every game, had he played every game—and never got untracked. **Key injuries:** Brian Jordan dropped from 103 RBIs in 1996 to 10 because of back problems that finally shortened his season in August. Pagnozzi, the projected No. 1 catcher, played in only 25 games because of a torn hip flexor. Lefthander Donovan Osborne, bothered by a groin injury and a hernia, won just three games. Righthander Todd Stottlemyre missed the final six weeks with a "dead arm." **Notable:** McGwire ended the season with 58 homers, tying a major league record for most home runs in a season by a righthanded batter. Jimmie Foxx set the mark in 1932 and Hank Greenberg tied it in 1938. Only Roger Maris and Babe Ruth hit more homers in one season. . . . The Cardinals hit 144 homers, the most in club history. They also struck out a league-leading 1,191 times, their highest total ever and just 12 shy of the National League record set by the 1968 Mets. Three players—Gant, Lankford and Royce Clayton—struck out more times individually than the pitching staff did collectively. . . . DeShields hit a major-league-leading 14 triples.

—RICK HUMMEL

RECORDS

1997 regular-season record: 73-89 (4th in N.L. Central); 41-40 at home; 32-49 on road; 21-34 vs. East; 28-35 vs. Central; 24-20 vs. West; 21-17 vs. lefthanded starters; 52-72 vs. righthanded starters; 62-70 on grass; 11-19 on turf; 26-30 in daytime; 47-59 at night; 20-33 in one-run games; 6-11 in extra-inning games; 1-0-2 in doubleheaders.
Team record past five years: 363-380 (.489, ranks 7th in league in that span).

TEAM LEADERS

Batting average: Delino DeShields (.295).
At-bats: Royce Clayton (576).
Runs: Ray Lankford (94).
Hits: Delino DeShields (169).
Total bases: Ray Lankford (272).
Doubles: Royce Clayton (39).
Triples: Delino DeShields (14).
Home runs: Ray Lankford (31).
Runs batted in: Ray Lankford (98).
Stolen bases: Delino DeShields (55).
Slugging percentage: Ray Lankford (.585).
On-base percentage: Ray Lankford (.411).

Wins: Matt Morris, Todd Stottlemyre (12).
Earned-run average: Andy Benes (3.10).
Complete games: Matt Morris (3).
Shutouts: None.
Saves: Dennis Eckersley (36).
Innings pitched: Matt Morris (217.0).
Strikeouts: Andy Benes (175).

GAMES BY POSITION

Catcher: Mike Difelice 91, Tom Lampkin 86, Eli Marrero 17, Tom Pagnozzi 13, Danny Sheaffer 9.
First base: Dmitri Young 74, Mark McGwire 50, John Mabry 49, Gary Gaetti 20, Mark Sweeney 4, Tom Pagnozzi 2, Mike Difelice 1.
Second base: Delino DeShields 147, David Bell 23, Mike Gallego 11, Jeff Berblinger 4, Roberto Mejia 3, Danny Sheaffer 3, Steve Scarsone 2.
Third base: Gary Gaetti 132, David Bell 35, Danny Sheaffer 30, Mike Gallego 7, Mike Gulan 3, Scott Livingstone 2, John Mabry 1, Tom Pagnozzi 1, Steve Scarsone 1.
Shortstop: Royce Clayton 153, David Bell 13, Luis Ordaz 11, Mike Gallego 10.
Outfield: Ray Lankford 131, Ron Gant 128, Willie McGee 81, John Mabry 78, Brian Jordan 44, Phil Plantier 32, Mark Sweeney 25, Danny Sheaffer 22, Scarborough Green 19, Dmitri Young 17, Micah Franklin 13, Steve Scarsone 2, Scott Livingstone 1, Roberto Mejia 1.
Designated hitter: Willie McGee 3, Ron Gant 1, Scott Livingstone 1, Dmitri Young 1.

TOP DRAFT CHOICES

1. **Adam Kennedy,** SS, Cal State Northridge.
2. **Rick Ankiel,** LHP, Port St. Lucie (Fla.) H.S.
3. **Patrick Coogan,** RHP, Louisiana State U.
4. **Xavier Nady,** SS, Salinas (Calif.) H.S.
5. **Jason Navarro,** LHP, Tulane University.
6. **Bryan Rupert,** C, Limestone (S.C.) College.
7. **Joseph Secoda,** 2B, Rancho Santiago (Calif.) J.C.
8. **Jason Karnuth,** RHP, Illinois State Univ.
9. **Seth Etherton,** RHP, University of Southern California.
10. **Finley Woodward,** RHP, Auburn Univ.

SAN DIEGO PADRES
NATIONAL LEAGUE WEST DIVISION

Padres Schedule
Home games shaded. *—All-Star Game at Coors Field (Colorado).
D—Day game (any game starting before 5 p.m.).

March
SUN	MON	TUE	WED	THU	FRI	SAT
		31 D CIN				

April
SUN	MON	TUE	WED	THU	FRI	SAT
			1 CIN	2 CIN	3 STL	4 D STL
5 D STL	6	7 D CIN	8 CIN	9 D CIN	10 ARZ	11 ARZ
12 ARZ	13 ARZ	14 SF	15 SF	16	17 PIT	18 D PIT
19 PIT	20 D	21 CUB	22 D CUB	23 D CUB	24 PIT	25 PIT
26 PIT	27 D CUB	28 CUB	29	30 FLA		

May
SUN	MON	TUE	WED	THU	FRI	SAT
					1 FLA	2 FLA
3 FLA	4 D MIL	5 MIL	6 D MIL	7 ATL	8 ATL	9 ATL
10 ATL	11 NYM	12 NYM	13 NYM	14 NYM	15 PHI	16 PHI
17 PHI	18	19 PIT	20 PIT	21 PIT	22 HOU	23 HOU
24 HOU	25 D ARZ	26 ARZ	27 ARZ	28	29 STL	30 STL
31 D STL						

June
SUN	MON	TUE	WED	THU	FRI	SAT
	1 STL	2 HOU	3 HOU	4 D HOU	5 TEX	6 TEX
7 TEX	8 D CIN	9 CIN	10 CIN	11	12 SF	13 SF
14 D SF	15	16 LA	17 LA	18 D LA	19 SF	20 D SF
21 SF	22 D SEA	23 D SEA	24 SEA	25 ANA	26 D ANA	27 ANA
28 D ANA	29	30 D OAK				

July
SUN	MON	TUE	WED	THU	FRI	SAT
			1 D OAK	2 OAK	3 COL	4 COL
5 D COL	6	7	*8	9 D LA	10 LA	11 LA
12 LA	13 COL	14 COL	15 COL	16	17 CIN	18 CIN
19 CIN	20 D STL	21 STL	22 ARZ	23 ARZ	30 HOU	31 HOU
26 D HOU	27	28 NYM	29 NYM	30 NYM	31 MON	

August
SUN	MON	TUE	WED	THU	FRI	SAT
						1 MON
2 D MON	3 D MON	4 D PHI	5 PHI	6 D PHI	7 PHI	8
9 D FLA	10 FLA	11 ATL	12 ATL	13 D ATL	14 MIL	15 MIL
16 MIL	17	18 FLA	19 FLA	20 ATL	21 ATL	22 MIL
23 MIL	24 D MIL	25 PHI	26 D PHI	27 PHI	28 MON	29 MON
30 MON	31 MON					

September
SUN	MON	TUE	WED	THU	FRI	SAT
		1 NYM	2 NYM	3	4 COL	5 COL
6 D COL	7 D SF	8 SF	9 D LA	10 D LA	11 LA	12 LA
13 LA	14 D CUB	15 CUB	16 D CUB	17 CUB	18 D COL	19 COL
20 D COL	21	22 LA	23 LA	24	25 ARZ	26 D ARZ
27 ARZ						

1998 SEASON
CLUB DIRECTORY

Chairman
John Moores

President & chief executive officer
Larry Lucchino

Executive vice president
Bill Adams

Sr. v.p./baseball operations and g.m.
Kevin Towers

Sr. vice president/public affairs
Charles Steinberg

Vice president/corporate development
Michael Dee

Vice president/marketing
Don Johnson

Vice president/finance
Bob Wells

Assistant general manager
Fred Uhlman Jr.

Director/community relations
Michele Anderson

Director/merchandising
Michael Babida

Controller
Steve Fitch

Director/administrative services
Lucy Freeman

Director/ticket operations & services
Dave Gilmore

Director/stadium operations
Mark Guglielmo

Dir./Hispanic & multicultural marketing
Enrique Morones

Director/player development
Jim Skaalen

Director/minor league operations
Priscilla Oppenheimer

General counsel
Alan Ostfield

Director/team travel
Brian Prilaman

Director/public relations
Glenn Geffner

Director/fan services
Tim Katzman

Director/sales
Louie Ruvane

Director/scouting
Brad Sloan

Trainer
Todd Hutcheson

Assistant trainer
Jim Daniel

Strength and conditioning coach
Sam Gannelli

Club physicians
Cliff Colwell
Jan Fronek
Paul Hirshman
Blaine Phillips

Major league scouts
Ken Bracey
Ray Crone Sr.

Advance scout
Jeff Gardner

Supervisors
Bob Cummings, Andy Hancock, Jim Woodward

Full-time scouts
Joe Bochy, Chas Bolton, Howard Bowens, Ken Bracey, Ray Crone, Bob Cummings, Jimmy Dreyer, Denny Galehouse, Ronquito Garcia, Jeff Gardner, Rich Hacker, Andy Hancock, Gary Kendall, Don Lyle, Tim McWilliam, Bill Mele, Juan Melo, Rene Mons, Pat Murtaugh, Steve Nichols, Jack Pierce, Gary Roenicke, Brad Sloan, Van Smith, Mark Wasinger, Gene Watson, Jim Woodward

Part-time scouts
Freddy Barbosa, Cesar Berroteran, Bob Buob, Julio Coronado, Leroy Dreyer, Celestino Espinal, Robert Gutierrez, Timothy Harkness, William Killian, Steve Leavitt, Ramon Lopez, Darryl Milne, Chuck Pierce, Gene Thompson

MINOR LEAGUE AFFILIATES

Class	Team	League	Manager
AAA	Las Vegas	Pacific Coast	Jerry Royster
AA	Mobile	Southern	Mike Ramsey
A	Rancho Cucamonga	California	Mike Basso
A	Clinton	Midwest	Tom Le Vasseur
Rookie	Idaho Falls	Pioneer	Don Werner
Rookie	Peoria Padres	Arizona	Randy Whisler

BROADCAST INFORMATION
Radio: KFMB-AM (760).
TV: KUSI (Channel 9).
Cable TV: Channel 4 Padres.

SPRING TRAINING
Ballpark (city): Peoria Stadium (Peoria, Ariz.).
Ticket information: 602-878-4337.

SPRING TRAINING ROSTER

Manager—Bruce Bochy (15).
Coaches—Greg Booker, Tim Flannery (11), Davey Lopes (30), Rob Picciolo (5), Merv Rettenmund (16), Dave Stewart.

No.	PITCHERS	B/T	Ht./Wt.	Born	1997 clubs
43	Ashby, Andy	R/R	6-5/190	7-11-67	San Diego
40	Bergman, Sean	R/R	6-4/225	4-11-70	San Diego
	Boehringer, Brian	B/R	6-2/190	1-8-70	New York A.L., Gulf Coast Yankees, Tampa
	Brown, Kevin	R/R	6-4/200	3-14-65	Florida
	Clement, Matt	R/R	6-3/180	8-12-74	Rancho Cucamonga, Mobile
39	Cunnane, Will	R/R	6-2/175	4-24-74	San Diego
	Guzman, Domingo	R/R	6-0/180	4-5-75	Clinton, Rancho Cucamonga
50	Hamilton, Joey	R/R	6-4/230	9-9-70	San Diego
41	Hitchcock, Sterling	L/L	6-1/192	4-29-71	San Diego
51	Hoffman, Trevor	R/R	6-0/205	10-13-67	San Diego
	Kroon, Marc	R/R	6-2/195	4-2-73	Las Vegas, San Diego
54	Menhart, Paul	R/R	6-2/190	3-25-69	Tacoma, Las Vegas, San Diego
	Miceli, Dan	R/R	6-0/216	9-9-70	Detroit
	Murray, Heath	L/L	6-4/205	4-19-73	Las Vegas, San Diego
	Sak, Jim	R/R	6-1/195	8-18-73	Rancho Cucamonga
34	Smith, Pete	R/R	6-2/200	2-27-66	Las Vegas, San Diego
	Veras, Dario	R/R	6-1/155	3-13-73	San Diego, Las Vegas, Mobile, Rancho Cucamonga
	Vosberg, Ed	L/L	6-1/190	9-28-61	Texas, Florida
	Wall, Donne	R/R	6-1/180	7-11-67	New Orleans, Houston
	Wengert, Don	R/R	6-2/212	11-6-69	Oakland

No.	CATCHERS	B/T	Ht./Wt.	Born	1997 clubs
	Hernandez, Carlos	R/R	5-11/215	5-24-67	San Diego, Rancho Cucamonga
	Myers, Greg	L/R	6-2/208	4-14-66	Minnesota, Atlanta
	Romero, Mandy	B/R	5-11/196	10-19-67	Mobile, Las Vegas, San Diego

No.	INFIELDERS	B/T	Ht./Wt.	Born	1997 clubs
	Arias, George	R/R	5-11/190	3-12-72	Vancouver, Anaheim, Las Vegas, San Diego
21	Caminiti, Ken	B/R	6-0/200	4-21-63	San Diego
	Carmona, Cesarin	B/R	5-10/155	12-20-76	Clinton
	Cianfrocco, Archi	R/R	6-5/215	10-6-66	San Diego
11	Giovanola, Ed	L/R	5-10/170	3-4-69	Richmond, Atlanta
10	Gomez, Chris	R/R	6-1/195	6-16-71	San Diego
22	Joyner, Wally	L/L	6-2/200	6-16-62	San Diego, Las Vegas
	Melo, Juan	B/R	6-1/160	5-11-76	Mobile, Las Vegas
	Sheets, Andy	R/R	6-2/180	11-19-71	Tacoma, Seattle
4	Veras, Quilvio	B/R	5-9/166	4-3-71	San Diego

No.	OUTFIELDERS	B/T	Ht./Wt.	Born	1997 clubs
	Darr, Mike	L/R	6-3/205	3-21-76	Rancho Cucamonga
12	Finley, Steve	L/L	6-2/180	3-12-65	San Diego, Rancho Cucamonga, Mobile
19	Gwynn, Tony	L/L	5-11/220	5-9-60	San Diego
	Matthews, Gary	B/R	6-2/185	8-25-74	Rancho Cucamonga, Mobile
	Rivera, Ruben	R/R	6-3/200	11-14-73	Rancho Cucamonga, Las Vegas, San Diego
8	Sweeney, Mark	L/L	6-1/195	10-26-69	St. Louis, San Diego
25	Vaughn, Greg	R/R	6-0/202	7-3-65	San Diego

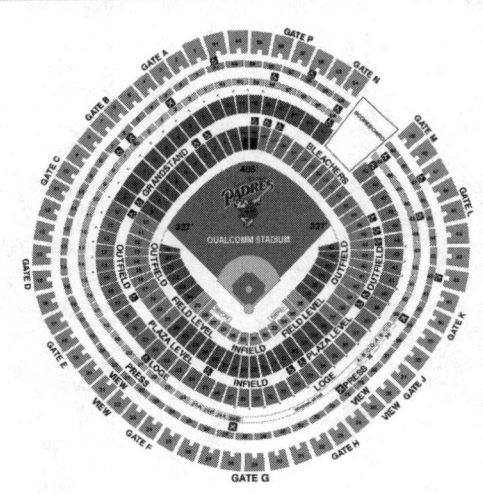

BALLPARK INFORMATION

Ballpark (capacity, surface)
Qualcomm Stadium (56,133, grass)

Address
P.O. Box 2000
San Diego, CA 92112-2000

Business phone
619-881-6500

Ticket information
619-881-6500, 888-723-7379

Ticket prices
$18 (sky boxes)
$16 (club level, field level, plaza level/IF)
$14 (plaza level, loge level)
$11 (press level)
$8 (LF & RF grandstand)
$7 (view level/IF)
$6 (view level)
$5 (RF & LF bleachers, view level/sand pit)

Field dimensions (from home plate)
To left field at foul line, 327 feet
To center field, 405 feet
To right field at foul line, 327 feet

First game played
April 8, 1969 (Padres 2, Astros 1)

1998 SEASON *San Diego Padres*

Date	Opp.	Res.	Score	(inn.*)	Hits	Opp. hits	Winning pitcher	Losing pitcher	Save	Record	Pos.	GB
4-1	N.Y.	W	12-5		11	9	Hamilton	Perez		1-0	1st	+1.0
4-2	N.Y.	W	6-5	(12)	12	5	Bergman	Jordan		2-0	1st	+1.0
4-3	N.Y.	L	1-4		7	8	Jones	Valenzuela	J. Franco	2-1	T1st	....
4-4	Phi.	W	13-3		13	7	Worrell	Munoz		3-1	T1st	....
4-5	Phi.	W	4-1		7	1	Hitchcock	Mimbs	Hoffman	4-1	1st	+0.5
4-6	Phi.	L	2-3		7	9	Schilling	Hamilton	Bottalico	4-2	T1st	....
4-7	Pit.	W	3-2	(10)	10	7	D. Veras	Ruebel		5-2	T1st	....
4-8	Pit.	L	0-2		1	11	Cooke	Bergman	Ericks	5-3	T2nd	0.5
4-9	Pit.	L	2-4		7	7	Loaiza	Worrell	Ericks	5-4	4th	1.5
4-11	At Phi.	W	8-3		13	10	Hitchcock	Schilling		6-4	4th	1.0
4-13	At Phi.	W	3-1		6	6	Scott	Bottalico	Hoffman	7-4	4th	1.0
4-15	At Pit.	L	2-3		7	8	Ericks	Ashby		7-5	4th	2.0
4-16	At Pit.	W	7-5		7	11	Valenzuela	Cooke	Hoffman	8-5	4th	2.0
4-19†	St.L.§	L	0-1		6	7	Petkovsek	Hitchcock	Eckersley	8-6		4.0
4-19‡	St.L.§	L	1-2		3	7	Al. Benes	Worrell		8-7	4th	4.0
4-20	St.L.§	W	8-2		12	9	Ashby	Raggio		9-7	4th	4.0
4-22	Hou.	L	3-12		7	15	Reynolds	Valenzuela		9-8	4th	4.0
4-23	Hou.	L	7-11		10	18	Garcia	Worrell		9-9	4th	5.0
4-25	At Atl.	L	4-5		4	8	Neagle	Cunnane	Wohlers	9-10	4th	5.0
4-26	At Atl.	L	2-3	(10)	9	8	Wohlers	Hoffman		9-11	4th	6.0
4-27	At Atl.	L	0-2	(5)	1	7	Maddux	Valenzuela		9-12	4th	7.0
4-28	At Fla.	L	9-12		10	12	Heredia	Scott	Nen	9-13	4th	7.0
4-29	At Fla.	L	1-2		8	3	Brown	Hoffman	Nen	9-14	4th	7.0
4-30	At N.Y.	L	2-6		7	10	Jones	Hitchcock	J. Franco	9-15	4th	8.0
5-1	At N.Y.	W	7-3		12	8	Ashby	Mlicki		10-15	4th	8.0
5-2	Mon.	L	4-5		11	9	Veres	Bochtler	Urbina	10-16	4th	8.0
5-3	Mon.	W	1-0		5	3	Worrell	Hermanson	Hoffman	11-16	4th	8.0
5-4	Mon.	L	3-9		4	17	Bullinger	Hitchcock		11-17	4th	9.0
5-6	Chi.	L	1-2		8	5	Foster	Ashby	Rojas	11-18	4th	9.5
5-7	Chi.	W	6-3		12	11	Cunnane	Castillo	Hoffman	12-18	4th	8.5
5-8	Chi.	L	2-6		8	16	Mulholland	Valenzuela		12-19	4th	8.5
5-9	Cin.	L	2-7		6	11	Smiley	Worrell		12-20	4th	8.5
5-10	Cin.	W	9-6		10	8	Hitchcock	Morgan	Hoffman	13-20	4th	7.5
5-11	Cin.	W	5-4	(11)	8	8	Hoffman	Remlinger		14-20	4th	7.0
5-13	At Mon.	L	3-7		11	11	Martinez	Valenzuela		14-21	4th	8.0
5-14	At Mon.	L	7-9		10	12	Valdes	Hoffman	Smith	14-22	4th	9.0
5-15	At Chi.	L	2-8		3	11	Castillo	Hitchcock		14-23	4th	9.0
5-16	At Chi.	L	7-16		9	21	Foster	Worrell		14-24	4th	9.0
5-17	At Cin.	W	6-2		12	6	Hamilton	Mercker	Hoffman	15-24	4th	9.0
5-18	At Cin.	L	0-5		9	9	Burba	Valenzuela		15-25	4th	9.0
5-19	At Cin.	W	13-6		16	12	Cunnane	Schourek		16-25	4th	8.0
5-20	L.A.	W	7-3		11	8	Hitchcock	Valdes		17-25	4th	8.0
5-21	L.A.	W	5-4	(11)	6	9	Hoffman	Osuna		18-25	4th	7.0
5-22	L.A.	W	4-1		10	7	Hamilton	Nomo	Bochtler	19-25	4th	7.0
5-23	Fla.	W	6-3		9	11	Valenzuela	Fernandez		20-25	4th	7.0
5-24	Fla.	L	7-9		8	17	Powell	Bochtler	Nen	20-26	4th	7.0
5-25	Fla.	L	2-6		12	6	Brown	Hitchcock		20-27	4th	7.0
5-26	Atl.	L	5-12		11	16	Borowski	Worrell		20-28	4th	8.0
5-27	Atl.	L	2-9		12	10	Maddux	Hamilton		20-29	4th	9.0
5-29	At Hou.	L	6-10		10	12	Kile	Valenzuela		20-30	4th	10.0
5-30	At Hou.	W	9-2		13	6	Cunnane	Holt	Worrell	21-30	4th	9.0
5-31	At Hou.	W	12-5		16	10	Hitchcock	Reynolds	Smith	22-30	4th	9.0
6-1	At Hou.	W	6-3		8	7	Hamilton	Wagner	Hoffman	23-30	4th	8.0
6-2	At Atl.	W	5-4		10	10	Murray	Maddux	Hoffman	24-30	4th	7.0
6-3	At Atl.	W	5-2		8	8	Smith	Wohlers	Hoffman	25-30	4th	7.0
6-4	At Col.	W	7-5		10	10	Cunnane	Bailey	Bochtler	26-30	4th	6.0
6-5	At Col.	L	7-9	(11)	18	16	S. Reed	Burrows		26-31	4th	7.0
6-6	Hou.	L	7-8		15	12	Lima	Hamilton	Wagner	26-32	4th	7.0
6-7	Hou.	W	5-4	(10)	13	7	Hoffman	Garcia		27-32	4th	6.0
6-8	Hou.	L	0-9		5	14	Kile	Valenzuela		27-33	4th	7.0
6-9	St.L.	L	1-9		5	14	An. Benes	Cunnane		27-34	4th	8.0
6-10	St.L.	W	6-5	(12)	15	8	Erdos	Beltran		28-34	4th	7.0
6-11	St.L.	L	3-8		6	11	Al. Benes	Burrows	Petkovsek	28-35	4th	7.0
6-12	At Ana.	L	4-8		9	17	James	Murray		28-36	4th	8.0
6-13	At Ana.	W	8-7	(14)	16	11	Bochtler	Hasegawa	Worrell	29-36	4th	7.0
6-14	At Tex.	L	6-8		10	8	Whiteside	Jackson	Wetteland	29-37	4th	8.0
6-15	At Tex.	L	4-7		9	12	Witt	Ashby	Wetteland	29-38	4th	9.0
6-17	Oak.	L	3-10		8	12	Johnson	Smith	Small	29-39	4th	10.0
6-18	Oak.	L	9-11		13	12	Reyes	Bochtler	Groom	29-40	4th	11.0
6-19	Col.	L	4-8		10	13	Bailey	Jackson		29-41	4th	12.0
6-20	Col.	W	5-2		11	9	Ashby	Munoz	Hoffman	30-41	4th	11.0

Date	Opp.	Res.	Score	(inn.*)	Hits	Opp. hits	Winning pitcher	Losing pitcher	Save	Record	Pos.	GB
6-21	Col.	L	4-9		8	16	Rekar	Bergman		30-42	4th	11.0
6-22	Col.	W	4-2		5	4	Worrell	Ruffin	Hoffman	31-42	4th	11.0
6-23	At S.F.	W	11-6		20	12	Bruske	Gardner	Hoffman	32-42	4th	10.0
6-24	At S.F.	L	1-4		7	8	Estes	Jackson	Beck	32-43	4th	11.0
6-25	At S.F.	L	7-14		11	17	Rodriguez	Ashby		32-44	4th	12.0
6-26	At L.A.	W	9-7		9	11	Bergman	Guthrie	Hoffman	33-44	4th	11.0
6-27	At L.A.	W	7-5		12	12	Hamilton	Park	Hoffman	34-44	4th	11.0
6-28	At L.A.	W	9-3		13	8	Smith	Nomo		35-44	4th	10.0
6-29	At L.A.	L	4-10		8	12	Astacio	Jackson		35-45	4th	11.0
6-30	At Oak.	W	15-6		19	8	Ashby	Wengert		36-45	4th	11.0
7-1	At Oak.	L	6-8		15	11	Small	Bochtler		36-46	4th	11.0
7-2	Sea.	W	8-5		11	12	Hamilton	Fassero		37-46	4th	10.0
7-3	Sea.	W	10-8		9	10	Batchelor	McCarthy	Hoffman	38-46	4th	10.0
7-4	L.A.	L	2-5		8	12	Astacio	Jackson	Worrell	38-47	4th	11.0
7-5	L.A.	L	3-7		8	12	Valdes	Ashby		38-48	4th	12.0
7-6	L.A.	L	2-5		6	8	Candiotti	Bergman	Worrell	38-49	4th	13.0
7-10	At Col.	W	11-5		16	9	Ashby	Burke		39-49	4th	12.0
7-11	At Col.	L	5-6	(11)	11	11	DiPoto	Hoffman		39-50	4th	12.0
7-12	At Col.	W	11-7		15	16	Hamilton	Swift	Hoffman	40-50	4th	11.0
7-13	At Col.	W	13-11		18	14	Batchelor	McCurry	Hoffman	41-50	4th	11.0
7-14	S.F.	W	5-3		8	8	Jackson	Creek	Hoffman	42-50	4th	10.0
7-15	S.F.	L	2-16		5	16	Rueter	Ashby		42-51	4th	11.0
7-16	At St.L.	W	4-3		8	7	Bruske	Mathews	Hoffman	43-51	4th	10.0
7-17	At St.L.	W	3-1		6	7	Hamilton	An. Benes	Hoffman	44-51	3rd	10.0
7-18	At Fla.	W	5-3		9	11	Smith	Fernandez	Worrell	45-51	3rd	9.0
7-19	At Fla.	L	5-8		5	12	Hernandez	Jackson		45-52	3rd	9.0
7-20	At Fla.	W	3-0		4	6	Ashby	Saunders	Hoffman	46-52	3rd	9.0
7-21	At Fla.	W	10-2		15	5	Hitchcock	Brown		47-52	3rd	8.0
7-22	Pit.	W	3-2		11	6	Hoffman	Loiselle		48-52	3rd	8.0
7-23	Pit.	W	9-1		14	6	Smith	Lieber		49-52	3rd	8.0
7-24	Pit.	W	8-6		12	10	Bruske	Sodowsky	Hoffman	50-52	3rd	7.0
7-25	N.Y.	L	2-4		4	8	Kashiwada	Worrell	McMichael	50-53	3rd	7.0
7-26	N.Y.	W	5-3		8	7	Hitchcock	Jones	Hoffman	51-53	3rd	6.0
7-27	N.Y.	W	5-3		13	6	Cunnane	Kashiwada	Hoffman	52-53	3rd	5.5
7-28	Phi.	L	4-8		6	15	Leiter	Bergman		52-54	3rd	7.0
7-29	Phi.	L	5-6		9	10	Green	Ashby	Bottalico	52-55	3rd	7.0
7-31	At Mon.	L	2-9		9	8	Hermanson	Hitchcock	Valdes	52-56	3rd	7.0
8-1	At Mon.	W	8-2		16	4	Hamilton	Bullinger		53-56	3rd	7.0
8-2	At Mon.	L	0-6		5	8	Perez	Smith		53-57	3rd	7.0
8-3	At Mon.	L	3-6		3	12	Martinez	Ashby		53-58	3rd	8.0
8-5	At Cin.	L	3-7		8	12	Remlinger	Hitchcock		53-59	3rd	9.5
8-6	At Cin.	W	6-3		7	8	Hamilton	Belinda	Hoffman	54-59	3rd	9.5
8-7	At Cin.	L	0-7		4	11	Tomko	Jackson		54-60	3rd	9.5
8-8	At Chi.	L	1-3		9	11	Pisciotta	Bochtler		54-61	4th	10.5
8-9	At Chi.	W	7-5		12	10	Cunnane	Adams	Hoffman	55-61	4th	9.5
8-10	At Chi.	W	4-3		6	11	Bochtler	Bottenfield	Hoffman	56-61	4th	9.5
8-11	Mon.	L	3-6		7	12	Hermanson	Hamilton		56-62	4th	9.5
8-12	Mon.	W	6-4		9	8	Bochtler	DeHart	Hoffman	57-62	3rd	9.5
8-13	Cin.	L	0-2		1	6	Morgan	Smith	Shaw	57-63	3rd	9.5
8-14	Cin.	W	5-4	(10)	10	9	Hoffman	Shaw		58-63	3rd	9.5
8-15	Chi.	W	5-1		10	4	Hitchcock	Trachsel		59-63	3rd	9.5
8-16	Chi.	W	4-3	(10)	10	9	Hoffman	Adams		60-63	3rd	8.5
8-17	Chi.	L	5-6		8	12	M. Clark	Menhart	Adams	60-64	T3rd	9.5
8-19	At Pit.	L	3-5		7	7	Lieber	Smith	Loiselle	60-65	4th	10.0
8-20	At Pit.	L	3-7		7	14	Schmidt	Ashby		60-66	4th	10.5
8-21	At Pit.	W	9-4		13	6	Hitchcock	Cordova		61-66	T3rd	10.0
8-22	At N.Y.	L	8-9	(11)	12	13	J. Franco	Bochtler		61-67	T3rd	10.0
8-23	At N.Y.	L	5-9		14	12	Mlicki	Menhart	J. Franco	61-68	4th	10.0
8-24	At N.Y.	W	3-2		9	5	Smith	Bohanon	Hoffman	62-68	T3rd	10.0
8-25†	At Phi.	L	1-10		10	13	Leiter	Cunnane		62-69		
8-25‡	At Phi.	L	4-6		5	10	Blazier	Ashby	Bottalico	62-70	T3rd	11.0
8-26	At Phi.	L	2-4		7	9	Grace	Hitchcock	Bottalico	62-71	4th	12.0
8-27	At Phi.	L	6-7	(12)	14	14	Gomes	Bruske		62-72	4th	13.0
8-28	Ana.	W	9-2		12	5	Menhart	Dickson		63-72	4th	13.0
8-29	Ana.	L	1-3		5	7	Hill	Smith	Percival	63-73	4th	14.0
8-30	Tex.	W	4-1		6	8	Ashby	T. Clark	Hoffman	64-73	4th	14.0
8-31	Tex.	W	5-3		12	9	Hitchcock	Burkett	Hoffman	65-73	4th	13.0
9-1	At Sea.	L	6-9		7	11	Fassero	Hamilton		65-74	4th	13.5
9-3	At Sea.	W	6-5		12	5	D. Veras	Timlin	Hoffman	66-74	4th	12.0
9-4	Atl.	L	7-8	(11)	11	17	Wohlers	Worrell		66-75	4th	12.5
9-5	Atl.	W	6-2		12	2	Ashby	Glavine		67-75	4th	12.5
9-6	Atl.	L	1-9		5	11	Maddux	Hitchcock		67-76	4th	13.5
9-7	Atl.	L	0-4		4	7	Neagle	Hamilton		67-77	4th	14.5
9-9	Fla.	W	7-6	(13)	15	9	Worrell	Ojala		68-77	4th	13.0
9-10	Fla.	W	4-3		10	8	Bruske	Vosberg		69-77	4th	12.0

Date	Opp.	Res.	Score	(inn.*)	Hits	Opp. hits	Winning pitcher	Losing pitcher	Save	Record	Pos.	GB
9-12	At St.L.	L	2-4		13	7	Morris	Ashby	Eckersley	69-78	4th	13.0
9-13	At St.L.	W	8-3		11	6	Erdos	Lowe		70-78	4th	12.0
9-14	At St.L.	L	4-10		12	11	Fossas	Kroon		70-79	4th	12.0
9-15	At Hou.	W	4-3		11	7	Smith	Hampton	Hoffman	71-79	4th	12.0
9-16	At Hou.	L	3-15		8	16	Garcia	Hitchcock		71-80	4th	13.0
9-17	Col.	W	5-4		10	5	Ashby	Thomson	Hoffman	72-80	4th	12.0
9-18	Col.	W	7-6		8	11	Menhart	Bailey	Hoffman	73-80	4th	11.0
9-19	S.F.	L	4-7		13	12	Darwin	Hamilton	Hernandez	73-81	4th	12.0
9-20	S.F.	W	12-2		12	8	Smith	Estes		74-81	4th	11.0
9-21	S.F.	L	5-8		7	13	Beck	D. Veras		74-82	4th	12.0
9-22	S.F.	L	5-11		11	12	Hernandez	Murray		74-83	4th	13.0
9-23	At L.A.	L	2-6		7	12	Park	Menhart		74-84	4th	13.0
9-24	At L.A.	W	4-1		9	5	Hamilton	Candiotti	Hoffman	75-84	4th	13.0
9-26	At S.F.	L	4-17		6	18	Estes	Smith		75-85	4th	14.0
9-27	At S.F.	L	1-6		4	7	Alvarez	Hitchcock		75-86	4th	15.0
9-28	At S.F.	W	5-3	(11)	12	7	Hamilton	Bailey		76-86	4th	14.0

Monthly records: April (9-15), May (13-15), June (14-15), July (16-11), August (13-17), September (11-13).
*Innings, if other than nine. †First game of doubleheader. ‡Second game of doubleheader. §At Honolulu, Hawaii.

HIGHLIGHTS

High point: The club began its title defense of the N.L. West in rousing fashion, getting consecutive home runs from Chris Gomez, Rickey Henderson and Quilvio Veras and beating the Mets 12-5 before an opening day sellout crowd at Jack Murphy Stadium (which was renamed Qualcomm Stadium later in the season).

Low point: In late August, the last-place Phillies swept a four-game series at Veterans Stadium. First baseman Wally Joyner, one of the team's least-combative players, was ejected by umpire Bob Davidson from the series finale after arguing a strike call. The club went on to lose the game 7-6 in 12 innings to fall 13 games out of first place.

Turning point: On July 28th, the club blew a chance to reach .500 for the first time since April when it let the Phillies rally from a 3-0 deficit to win 8-4. Philadelphia's rally began when Rico Brogna hit a game-tying three-run home run off reliever Sean Bergman in the sixth inning. The defeat was followed by a 2-7 skid that left the team 10½ games out of first place.

Most valuable player: Tony Gwynn. He finished sixth in the National League's MVP voting, set career marks for home runs (17) and RBIs (119) and won his eighth batting title with a .372 average.

Most valuable pitcher: Trevor Hoffman. He has more saves (110) over the last three seasons than John Wetteland or Rod Beck. He'd have even more on a team with decent middle relief.

Most improved player: Quilvio Veras. Demoted to the minors by the Marlins in 1996, he rescued his career with a solid season. The second baseman played in 145 games, stole 33 bases and hit .265 to go with a good defensive season.

Most pleasant surprise: Carlos Hernandez. After losing about 20 pounds in the offseason, the Dodgers' castoff hit a career-best .313 in 134 at-bats and impressed scouts with his footwork and quick throws.

Biggest disappointment: The bullpen. One year after it led the major leagues in ERA, the relievers had an ERA of 5.00. Beyond closer Trevor Hoffman, who had 37 saves, there were no reliable relievers. Left fielder Greg Vaughn also underachieved after signing a franchise-record $15-million contract before the season. Vaughn hit .216 with 110 strikeouts in 120 games.

Key injuries: Starting pitchers Andy Ashby, Joey Hamilton and Sterling Hitchcock were all placed on the 15-day disabled list in the first half of the season, as were third baseman Ken Caminiti and center fielder Steve Finley. Eighteen players went on the disabled list and missed a total of 549 games.

Notable: With his eighth batting title, Gwynn tied Honus Wagner's record for National League honors. Only Ty Cobb, with 12, has more. Gwynn has won four straight batting titles and has hit more than .300 in 15 consecutive seasons.
—TOM KRASOVIC

RECORDS

1997 regular-season record: 76-86 (4th in N.L. West); 39-42 at home; 37-44 on road; 22-33 vs. East; 27-28 vs. Central; 27-25 vs. West; 17-20 vs. lefthanded starters; 59-66 vs. righthanded starters; 63-68 on grass; 13-18 on turf; 27-29 in daytime; 49-57 at night; 21-16 in one-run games; 11-6 in extra-inning games; 0-2-0 in doubleheaders.

Team record past five years: 345-402 (.462, ranks 12th in league in that span).

TEAM LEADERS

Batting average: Tony Gwynn (.372).
At-bats: Tony Gwynn (592).
Runs: Steve Finley (101).
Hits: Tony Gwynn (220).
Total bases: Tony Gwynn (324).
Doubles: Tony Gwynn (49).
Triples: Steve Finley (5).
Home runs: Steve Finley (28).
Runs batted in: Tony Gwynn (119).
Stolen bases: Quilvio Veras (33).
Slugging percentage: Tony Gwynn (.547).
On-base percentage: Tony Gwynn (.409).
Wins: Joey Hamilton (12).

Earned-run average: Andy Ashby (4.13).
Complete games: Andy Ashby (2).
Shutouts: None.
Saves: Trevor Hoffman (37).
Innings pitched: Andy Ashby (200.2).
Strikeouts: Andy Ashby (144).

GAMES BY POSITION

Catcher: John Flaherty 124, Carlos Hernandez 44, Mandy Romero 19, Don Slaught 6.
First base: Wally Joyner 131, Archi Cianfrocco 39, Derrek Lee 21, Mark Sweeney 7, Carlos Hernandez 4, Craig Shipley 4, Scott Livingstone 2.
Second base: Quilvio Veras 142, Craig Shipley 16, Archi Cianfrocco 12, Terry Shumpert 7, Jorge Velandia 5, Scott Livingstone 1.
Third base: Ken Caminiti 133, Archi Cianfrocco 38, George Arias 8, Scott Livingstone 3, Jorge Velandia 3, Craig Shipley 2, Terry Shumpert 2.
Shortstop: Chris Gomez 150, Craig Shipley 21, Jorge Velandia 6, Archi Cianfrocco 5.
Outfield: Tony Gwynn 143, Steve Finley 140, Greg Vaughn 94, Rickey Henderson 78, Chris Jones 61, Trey Beamon 20, Mark Sweeney 20, Ruben Rivera 7, Phil Plantier 3, Terry Shumpert 3, Archi Cianfrocco 2.
Designated hitter: Tony Gwynn 3, Greg Vaughn 3, Rickey Henderson 2.

TOP DRAFT CHOICES

1. **Kevin Nicholson,** SS, Stetson University.
2. **Ben Howard,** RHP, Central Merry H.S., Jackson, Tenn.
3. **Jerry Darr,** RHP, Glen Rose H.S., Malvern, Ark.
4. **Tony Lawrence,** C, Louisiana Tech.
5. **Tim Hummel,** SS, Burke H.S., Montgomery, N.Y.
6. **Brittan Motley,** OF, Hickman Mills H.S., Kansas City, Mo.
7. **Douglas Young,** RHP, Sierra (Calif.) J.C.
8. **Jason Dunaway,** SS, Seward County (Kan.) C.C.
9. **Junior Herndon,** RHP, Moffat County H.S., Craig, Colo.
10. **Tony Cosentino,** C, West Torrance (Calif.) H.S.

SAN FRANCISCO GIANTS
NATIONAL LEAGUE WEST DIVISION

Giants Schedule

Home games studed. *—All-Star Game at Coors Field (Colorado).
D—Day game (any game starting before 5 p.m.).

March

SUN	MON	TUE	WED	THU	FRI	SAT
		31 D HOU				

April

SUN	MON	TUE	WED	THU	FRI	SAT
			1 HOU	2 HOU	3 ARZ	4 D ARZ
5 D ARZ	6	7 D HOU	8 D HOU	9 HOU	10 STL	11 D STL
12 D STL	13 D STL	14 SD	15 SD	16	17 MIL	18 D MIL
19 D MIL	20	21 PIT	22 PIT	23 D PIT	24 MIL	25 D MIL
26 MIL	27 PIT	28 PIT	29	30 ATL		

May

SUN	MON	TUE	WED	THU	FRI	SAT
					1 ATL	2 D ATL
3 D ATL	4 FLA	5 FLA	6 FLA	7	8 D CUB	9 D CUB
10 D CUB	11 D MON	12 MON	13 D MON	14 MON	15 D NYM	16 D NYM
17 NYM	18 MIL	19 MIL	20 MIL	21 D STL	22 STL	23 STL
24 D STL	25 D CIN	26 CIN	27 D CIN	28 D ARZ	29 ARZ	30 ARZ
31 D ARZ						

June

SUN	MON	TUE	WED	THU	FRI	SAT
	1 CIN	2 CIN	3 CIN	4 D	5 STL	6 STL
7 D STL	8 SEA	9 SEA	10 D SEA	11	12 SD	13 SD
14 D SD	15 COL	16 COL	17 D COL	18 D SD	19 SD	20 D SD
21 D SD	22 OAK	23 OAK	24 D OAK	25 OAK	26 TEX	27 D TEX
28 D TEX	29 ANA	30 ANA				

July

SUN	MON	TUE	WED	THU	FRI	SAT
			1 ANA	2 ANA	3 LA	4 D LA
5 D LA	6	7	* 8	9	10 COL	11 COL
12 D COL	13 LA	14 LA	15 D LA	16	17 HOU	18 HOU
19 D HOU	20 ARZ	21 ARZ	22 STL	23 D STL	24 D CIN	25 D CIN
26 D CIN	27	28 MON	29 MON	30 MON	31 PHI	

August

SUN	MON	TUE	WED	THU	FRI	SAT
						1 PHI
2 PHI	3 PHI	4 D NYM	5 NYM	6 D NYM	7 ATL	8 D ATL
9 ATL	10 CUB	11 D CUB	12 CUB	13	14 FLA	15 D FLA
16 FLA	17	18 ATL	19 ATL	20 CUB	21 D CUB	22 FLA
23 D FLA	24 D FLA	25 NYM	26 NYM	27 D NYM	28 PHI	29 D PHI
30 PHI	31 PHI					

September

SUN	MON	TUE	WED	THU	FRI	SAT
		1 MON	2 D MON	3	4 LA	5 LA
6 D LA	7 SD	8 SD	9 SD	10	11 COL	12 D COL
13 COL	14 ARZ	15 ARZ	16 ARZ	17	18 LA	19 D LA
20 D LA	21 PIT	22 PIT	23 D PIT	24 D PIT	25 COL	26 D COL
27 D COL						

1998 SEASON
CLUB DIRECTORY

President and managing general partner
Peter A. Magowan
Executive vice president/COO
Larry Baer
Senior v.p. and general manager
Brian Sabean
Sr. vice president, business operations
Pat Gallagher
Special assistant to the general manager
Jim Fregosi
Assistant general manager
Ned Colletti
Director of player personnel
Dick Tidrow
Director of player development
Jack Hiatt
Coordinator of international operations
Rick Ragazzo
Coordinator of Pacific Rim scouting
Masanon Murakami
Sr. v.p. and chief financial officer
John Yee
V.p., stadium operations/security
Jorge Costa
Vice president, communications
Bob Rose
Vice president, marketing/sales
Mario Alioto
General manager, retail/Internet
Connie Kullberg
Director of stadium operations
Gene Telucci

Vice president, ticket sales
Mark Norrelli
Vice president, ticket services
Russ Stanley
Director of travel
Reggie Younger Jr.
Vice president and general counsel
Jack Bair
Media relations manager
Jim Moorehead
National cross-checker
Randy Waddill
Eastern cross-checker
Paul Turco
Western cross-checker
Doug Mapson
Major league advance scouts
Cal Emery
Pat Dobson
Scouts
Jose Cassino, Richard Cole, Joe
DiCarlo, John Dipuglia, Mike
Keenan, Tom Korenek, Eric
Magnum, Alan Marr, Dan
McConnon, Doug McMillan, Tony
Michalak, Bob Myrick, Cesar
Navarro, Matt Nerland, Bo Osborne,
Hector Otero, John Shafer, Joe
Strain, Todd Thomas, Glenn Tufts,
Ciro Villalobos, Darren Wittake, Tom
Zimmer

MINOR LEAGUE AFFILIATES

Class	Team	League	Manager
AAA	Fresno	Pacific Coast	Jim Davenport
AA	Shreveport	Texas	Mike Hart
A	San Jose	California	Shane Turner
A	Bakersfield	California	Frank Reberger
Rookie	Salem-Keizer	Northwest	Carlos Lezcano

BROADCAST INFORMATION

Radio: KNBR-AM (680); KIQI-AM
(1010, Spanish language).
TV: KTVU-TV (Channel 2).
Cable TV: SportsChannel Pacific.

SPRING TRAINING

Ballpark (city): Scottsdale Stadium
(Scottsdale, Ariz.).
Ticket information: 602-990-7912.

SPRING TRAINING ROSTER

Manager— Dusty Baker (12).
Coaches—Carlos Alfonso (17), Gene Clines (20), Sonny Jackson (15), Ron Perranoski (16), Ron Wotus.

No.	PITCHERS	B/T	Ht./Wt.	Born	1997 clubs
41	Bailey, Cory	R/R	6-1/202	1-24-71	Oklahoma City, Phoenix, San Francisco
	Blood, Darin	R/R	6-2/200	8-13-74	Shreveport
	Brohawn, Troy	L/L	6-1/190	1-14-73	Shreveport
44	Darwin, Danny	R/R	6-3/200	10-25-55	Chicago A.L., San Francisco
55	Estes, Shawn	L/L	6-2/195	2-18-73	San Francisco
22	Fernandez, Osvaldo	R/R	6-2/193	11-4-68	San Francisco, Phoenix
26	Gardner, Mark	R/R	6-1/215	3-1-62	San Francisco
55	Hershiser, Orel	R/R	6-3/195	9-16-58	Cleveland
37	Johnstone, John	R/R	6-3/195	11-25-68	Phoenix, San Francisco, Oakland
	Nathan, Joe	R/R	6-4/195	11-22-74	Salem-Kaizer
	Nen, Robb	R/R	6-5/210	11-28-69	Florida
	Ortiz, Russ	R/R	6-1/190	6-5-74	Shreveport, Phoenix
	Pickett, Ricky	L/L	6-1/220	1-19-70	Phoenix
19	Poole, Jim	L/L	6-2/195	4-28-66	San Francisco
	Reed, Steve	R/R	6-2/212	3-11-66	Colorado
	Roa, Joe	R/R	6-1/195	10-11-71	San Francisco, Phoenix
	Rodriguez, Rich	L/L	6-0/200	3-1-63	San Francisco
46	Rueter, Kirk	L/L	6-3/207	12-1-70	San Francisco
52	Tavarez, Julian	R/R	6-2/190	5-22-73	San Francisco

No.	CATCHERS	B/T	Ht./Wt.	Born	1997 clubs
18	Johnson, Brian	R/R	6-2/210	1-8-68	Detroit, Toledo, San Francisco
	Mayne, Brent	L/R	6-1/190	4-19-68	Edmonton, Oakland
2	Mirabelli, Doug	R/R	6-0/215	10-18-70	Phoenix, San Francisco

No.	INFIELDERS	B/T	Ht./Wt.	Born	1997 clubs
35	Aurilia, Rich	R/R	6-1/182	9-2-71	San Francisco, Phoenix
36	Delgado, Wilson	B/R	5-11/155	7-15-75	San Francisco, Phoenix
	Felix, Pedro	R/R	6-1/180	4-27-77	Bakersfield
	Hayes, Charlie	R/R	6-0/215	5-29-65	New York A.L.
21	Kent, Jeff	R/R	6-1/190	3-7-68	San Francisco
	Martinez, Ramon	R/R	6-1/170	10-10-72	Shreveport, Phoenix
32	Mueller, Bill	B/R	5-10/170	3-17-71	San Francisco
6	Snow, J.T.	B/L	6-2/202	2-26-68	San Francisco

No.	OUTFIELDERS	B/T	Ht./Wt.	Born	1997 clubs
7	Benard, Marvin	L/L	5-9/183	1-20-70	San Francisco, Phoenix
25	Bonds, Barry	L/L	6-2/206	7-24-64	San Francisco
38	Cruz, Jacob	L/L	6-0/179	1-28-73	Phoenix, San Francisco
5	Hamilton, Darryl	L/R	6-1/185	12-3-64	San Francisco, Phoenix
	Javier, Stan	B/R	6-0/195	1-9-64	San Francisco
	Murray, Calvin	R/R	5-11/175	7-30-71	Shreveport
23	Powell, Dante	R/R	6-2/185	8-25-73	Phoenix, San Francisco
	Rios, Armando	L/L	5-9/185	9-13-71	Shreveport

BALLPARK INFORMATION

Ballpark (capacity, surface)
3Com Park at Candlestick Point (63,000, grass)

Address
3Com Park
San Francisco, CA 94124

Business phone
415-468-3700

Ticket information
415-467-8000

Ticket prices
$18 (lower box)
$13 (upper box)
$15 (lower reserved)
$7.50 (upper reserved)
$5 (pavilion)
$6 (reserved bleachers)

Field dimensions (from home plate)
To left field at foul line, 335 feet
To center field, 400 feet
To right field at foul line, 328 feet

First game played
April 12, 1960 (Giants 3, Cardinals 1)

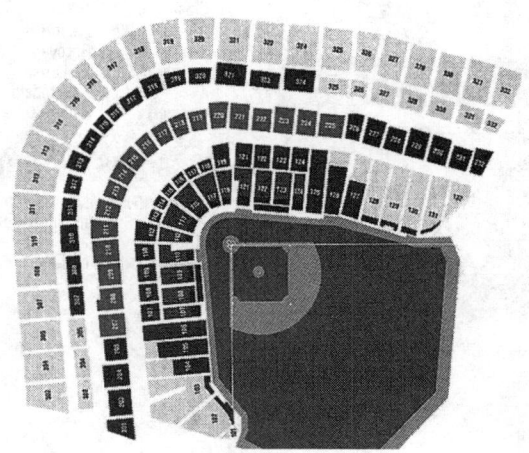

Date	Opp.	Res.	Score	(inn.*)	Hits	Opp. hits	Winning pitcher	Losing pitcher	Save	Record	Pos.	GB
4-1	Pit.	L	2-5		6	10	Ruebel	Rodriguez	Ericks	0-1	T2nd	1.0
4-3	Pit.	W	7-5		9	10	Fernandez	Cooke	Beck	1-1	3rd	0.5
4-4	N.Y.	W	6-4		10	9	Rodriguez	Jordan	Beck	2-1	3rd	0.5
4-5	N.Y.	W	2-0		6	3	Roa	Manuel	Beck	3-1	2nd	0.5
4-6	N.Y.	L	2-4		6	11	Bohanon	Gardner	J. Franco	3-2	4th	0.5
4-7	Phi.	W	4-3		5	7	Estes	Maduro	Beck	4-2	4th	0.5
4-8	Phi.	L	1-2		3	5	Leiter	Fernandez	Bottalico	4-3	4th	1.0
4-9	Phi.	W	3-0		9	5	Rueter	Munoz	Beck	5-3	3rd	1.0
4-13†	At N.Y.	W	5-1		10	9	Gardner	Clark		6-3		
4-13‡	At N.Y.	W	7-6		10	12	Estes	Jones	Beck	7-3	T2nd	0.5
4-14	At N.Y.	W	3-2		7	7	Rodriguez	McMichael	Beck	8-3	T1st	....
4-15	At Phi.	W	8-4		12	8	VanLandingham	Munoz		9-3	T1st	....
4-16	At Phi.	W	6-5	(10)	9	10	Poole	Harris	Beck	10-3	T1st	....
4-18	Fla.	W	5-4		10	9	Henry	Nen		11-3	1st	+1.0
4-19	Fla.	W	3-2		6	4	Estes	Saunders	Beck	12-3	1st	+2.0
4-20	Fla.	W	2-0		5	7	Fernandez	Fernandez	Beck	13-3	1st	+2.0
4-22	Atl.	L	0-4		5	7	Maddux	VanLandingham		13-4	1st	+1.0
4-23	Atl.	W	4-3		10	8	Henry	Embree		14-4	1st	+1.0
4-25	At Hou.	L	4-5		6	8	Wagner	Roa		14-5	T1st	....
4-26	At Hou.	W	2-0		4	2	Estes	Holt		15-5	T1st	....
4-27	At Hou.	W	3-2		7	7	Fernandez	Reynolds	Beck	16-5	1st	+1.0
4-28	At St.L.	L	2-5		8	13	An. Benes	VanLandingham	Eckersley	16-6	1st	....
4-29	At St.L.	L	7-9		11	12	Fossas	Beck		16-7	1st	....
4-30	At Pit.	W	6-1		9	3	Gardner	Lieber		17-7	T1st	....
5-1	At Pit.	L	2-3		8	6	Cooke	Estes	Rincon	17-8	2nd	1.0
5-2	Cin.	L	2-6		3	13	Schourek	Fernandez		17-9	2nd	1.0
5-3	Cin.	L	1-3		9	6	Smiley	Rodriguez	Brantley	17-10	2nd	2.0
5-4	Cin.	W	2-1	(10)	8	6	Beck	Brantley		18-10	2nd	2.0
5-5	Mon.	W	4-2		5	8	Gardner	Perez	Beck	19-10	2nd	1.0
5-6	Mon.	L	3-10		5	12	Martinez	Estes		19-11	2nd	2.0
5-7	Mon.	L	3-19		8	26	Juden	Fernandez		19-12	2nd	2.0
5-9	Chi.	L	3-5	(14)	7	12	Bottenfield	Roa		19-13	T2nd	1.5
5-10	Chi.	W	4-2		10	8	Rueter	Telemaco		20-13	T2nd	0.5
5-11	Chi.	W	11-5		10	11	Gardner	Foster	Henry	21-13	1st	+0.5
5-13	At Cin.	W	4-1		8	6	Estes	Burba	Beck	22-13	1st	+0.5
5-14	At Cin.	W	4-2	(10)	10	9	Beck	Remlinger	Rodriguez	23-13	1st	+1.5
5-15	At Mon.	L	7-8		12	13	Telford	Tavarez	Urbina	23-14	1st	+1.0
5-16	At Mon.	L	13-14		14	18	Urbina	Beck		23-15	1st	+0.5
5-17	At Chi.	W	4-1		5	7	Gardner	Telemaco	Beck	24-15	1st	+1.0
5-18	At Chi.	L	3-5		7	13	Wendell	Tavarez	Adams	24-16	1st	+1.0
5-19	At Chi.	L	4-15		12	18	Trachsel	Fernandez		24-17	1st	+1.0
5-20	Col.	W	6-3		10	6	VanLandingham	Bailey	Beck	25-17	1st	+2.0
5-21	Col.	L	7-10		11	10	Ritz	Rueter	S. Reed	25-18	1st	+1.5
5-22	Col.	W	7-2		11	7	Gardner	Thomson		26-18	1st	+2.5
5-23	St.L.	W	2-0		5	2	Estes	Morris		27-18	1st	+2.5
5-24	St.L.	L	3-9		9	15	An. Benes	Roa		27-19	1st	+2.5
5-25	St.L.	L	3-9		7	11	Stottlemyre	VanLandingham		27-20	1st	+1.5
5-26	Hou.	W	4-3		9	7	Tavarez	Lima		28-20	1st	+1.5
5-27	Hou.	W	5-4	(10)	7	12	Beck	Wagner		29-20	1st	+2.5
5-29	At Atl.	W	4-2		10	5	Estes	Smoltz	Beck	30-20	1st	+2.5
5-30	At Atl.	L	2-3		6	9	Wohlers	Henry		30-21	1st	+2.5
5-31	At Atl.	W	6-4		9	8	Poole	Borowski	Beck	31-21	1st	+2.5
6-1	At Atl.	L	3-4		9	9	Bielecki	Poole	Wohlers	31-22	1st	+1.5
6-2	At Fla.	L	2-4		9	7	Leiter	Gardner	Nen	31-23	1st	+0.5
6-3	At Fla.	W	9-1	(7)	14	2	Estes	Fernandez		32-23	1st	+1.5
6-4	At L.A.	L	1-5		6	8	Martinez	Foulke		32-24	1st	+1.5
6-5	At L.A.	W	5-4		7	6	VanLandingham	Valdes	Beck	33-24	1st	+1.5
6-6	Atl.	L	5-9		9	15	Byrd	Roa		33-25	1st	+1.0
6-7	Atl.	L	2-5		2	6	Maddux	Henry	Wohlers	33-26	1st	+1.0
6-8	Atl.	W	5-3		8	9	Poole	Smoltz	Beck	34-26	1st	+1.5
6-9	Fla.	W	7-4		11	7	Foulke	Rapp		35-26	1st	+1.5
6-10	Fla.	L	0-9		0	8	Brown	VanLandingham		35-27	1st	+1.5
6-11	Fla.	L	3-6		9	13	Helling	Rueter	Nen	35-28	1st	+0.5
6-12	At Tex.	W	4-3		9	8	Gardner	Oliver	Beck	36-28	1st	+1.5
6-13	At Tex.	L	5-6		14	10	Wetteland	Rodriguez	Beck	36-29	1st	+1.5
6-14	At Ana.	W	10-3		10	14	Roa	Watson		37-29	1st	+1.5
6-15	At Ana.	W	4-1		11	7	VanLandingham	Dickson	Beck	38-29	1st	+2.5
6-17	Sea.	W	4-3		10	9	Rueter	Fassero	Beck	39-29	1st	+3.5
6-18	Sea.	W	4-2		10	4	Gardner	Lowe	Beck	40-29	1st	+3.5
6-19	L.A.	W	5-2		5	4	Estes	Astacio		41-29	1st	+3.5
6-20	L.A.	L	7-11	(10)	11	13	Worrell	Henry		41-30	1st	+3.5

Date	Opp.	Res.	Score	(inn.*)	Hits	Opp. hits	Winning pitcher	Losing pitcher	Save	Record	Pos.	GB
6-21	L.A.	L	0-11		5	15	Candiotti	VanLandingham		41-31	1st	+2.5
6-22	L.A.	W	4-2		5	7	Rueter	Park	Beck	42-31	1st	+3.5
6-23	S.D.	L	6-11		12	20	Bruske	Gardner	Hoffman	42-32	1st	+3.5
6-24	S.D.	W	4-1		8	7	Estes	Jackson	Beck	43-32	1st	+3.5
6-25	S.D.	W	14-7		17	11	Rodriguez	Ashby		44-32	1st	+4.5
6-26	At Col.	L	6-7		11	11	DeJean	Foulke	Leskanic	44-33	1st	+3.5
6-27	At Col.	W	6-3		10	8	Rueter	Thomson	Beck	45-33	1st	+4.5
6-28	At Col.	L	2-9		6	9	Ritz	Gardner		45-34	1st	+3.5
6-29	At Col.	W	7-4		16	10	Estes	Bailey		46-34	1st	+4.5
6-30	At Sea.	W	8-6	(10)	14	13	Beck	Charlton	Henry	47-34	1st	+4.5
7-1	At Sea.	L	4-15		8	16	Moyer	VanLandingham		47-35	1st	+4.5
7-2	Oak.	L	1-8		5	12	Johnson	Rueter	Groom	47-36	1st	+4.5
7-3	Oak.	W	6-4		12	6	Creek	Rigby	Beck	48-36	1st	+5.5
7-4	Col.	W	4-0		11	1	Estes	Wright	Beck	49-36	1st	+6.0
7-5	Col.	W	2-1		8	6	Tavarez	Munoz	Beck	50-36	1st	+6.0
7-6	Col.	W	7-0		9	5	Gardner	Burke		51-36	1st	+6.0
7-10	At L.A.	L	0-11		3	16	Park	Rueter		51-37	1st	+5.0
7-11	At L.A.	L	2-6		11	10	Nomo	Foulke	Worrell	51-38	1st	+4.0
7-12	At L.A.	W	8-5		15	9	Tavarez	Worrell		52-38	1st	+5.0
7-13	At L.A.	L	3-9		6	13	Reyes	Estes		52-39	1st	+4.0
7-14	At S.D.	L	3-5		8	8	Jackson	Creek	Hoffman	52-40	1st	+3.0
7-15	At S.D.	W	16-2		16	5	Rueter	Ashby		53-40	1st	+3.0
7-16	At Hou.	L	1-8		4	11	Hampton	Foulke		53-41	1st	+3.0
7-17	At Hou.	W	3-1		9	5	Gardner	Holt	Beck	54-41	1st	+4.0
7-18	At St.L.	L	5-6		10	7	Stottlemyre	Estes	Eckersley	54-42	1st	+4.0
7-19	At St.L.	L	7-8		13	11	Frascatore	Henry	Eckersley	54-43	1st	+3.0
7-20	At St.L.	W	9-2		13	8	Rueter	Al. Benes		55-43	1st	+3.0
7-21	At St.L.	L	2-7		7	13	Morris	Foulke		55-44	1st	+3.0
7-22	Phi.	W	8-5		11	8	Gardner	Spradlin	Beck	56-44	1st	+3.0
7-23	Phi.	W	16-4		15	9	Estes	Leiter		57-44	1st	+4.0
7-24	Phi.	L	4-7		8	14	Gomes	Roa	Bottalico	57-45	1st	+4.0
7-25	Pit.	L	2-5		6	9	Schmidt	Rueter	Loiselle	57-46	1st	+3.0
7-26	Pit.	L	3-10		8	11	Loaiza	Creek		57-47	1st	+2.0
7-27†	Pit.	W	6-5	(13)	13	15	Henry	Wilkins		58-47		
7-27‡	Pit.	L	7-10		12	14	Cordova	VanLandingham		58-48	1st	+1.5
7-29	N.Y.	W	5-2		9	5	Estes	McMichael	Beck	59-48	1st	+1.5
7-30	N.Y.	L	2-5		5	13	Reed	Tavarez	J. Franco	59-49	1st	+0.5
8-1	At Cin.	W	8-7		11	7	Alvarez	Mercker	Beck	60-49	T1st	....
8-2	At Cin.	L	1-5		2	10	Tomko	Gardner		60-50	T1st	....
8-3	At Cin.	W	8-3	(10)	11	8	Hernandez	Shaw		61-50	1st	+1.0
8-4	At Cin.	W	9-1		10	7	Rueter	Carrara		62-50	1st	+1.5
8-5	At Chi.	W	8-2		11	5	Tavarez	Patterson		63-50	1st	+1.5
8-6	At Chi.	W	7-4		10	8	Rapp	Mulholland		64-50	1st	+2.5
8-7	At Chi.	L	3-6		5	11	Gonzalez	Alvarez		64-51	1st	+1.5
8-8	At Mon.	W	4-0		9	2	Gardner	Perez		65-51	1st	+1.5
8-9	At Mon.	L	1-2		4	8	Martinez	Hernandez		65-52	1st	+1.5
8-10	At Mon.	W	6-3	(12)	12	11	Tavarez	Valdes	Henry	66-52	1st	+2.5
8-11	Cin.	L	4-7		5	13	Mercker	Rapp		66-53	1st	+1.5
8-12	Cin.	W	7-3		10	8	Alvarez	Tomko	Hernandez	67-53	1st	+2.5
8-13	Chi.	L	5-6		10	10	Gonzalez	Gardner	Adams	67-54	1st	+1.5
8-14	Chi.	W	7-3		11	7	Estes	Tapani		68-54	1st	+1.5
8-15	Mon.	W	6-2		10	9	Rueter	Johnson		69-54	1st	+2.5
8-16	Mon.	L	5-8		8	12	Hermanson	Rapp	Urbina	69-55	1st	+1.5
8-17	Mon.	W	8-6		11	7	Henry	Paniagua	Beck	70-55	1st	+2.5
8-18	At Phi.	L	3-12		6	16	Beech	Gardner		70-56	1st	+2.0
8-19	At Phi.	W	9-5		12	9	Estes	Leiter		71-56	1st	+2.0
8-22	At Pit.	L	2-3		8	6	Cooke	Rueter	Loiselle	71-57	1st	+1.0
8-23	At Pit.	L	4-6		8	10	Loaiza	Darwin	Loiselle	71-58	T1st	....
8-24	At Pit.	L	6-9		12	13	Christiansen	Henry	Wilkins	71-59	2nd	1.0
8-25	At N.Y.	W	7-1		11	6	Estes	Jones		72-59	2nd	0.5
8-26	At N.Y.	W	6-2		5	10	Alvarez	Reed		73-59	2nd	0.5
8-27	At N.Y.	L	6-15		14	17	Isringhausen	Tavarez		73-60	2nd	1.5
8-28	Tex.	L	5-11		9	13	Whiteside	Beck		73-61	2nd	2.5
8-29	Tex.	W	5-4	(12)	9	10	Rodriguez	Eversgerd		74-61	2nd	2.5
8-30	Ana.	W	7-3		10	6	Estes	Springer		75-61	2nd	2.5
8-31	Ana.	L	4-7		6	9	May	Alvarez	Percival	75-62	2nd	2.5
9-1	At Oak.	W	8-2		10	10	Rueter	Lorraine		76-62	2nd	2.0
9-3	At Oak.	L	3-12		9	11	Rigby	Darwin	Small	76-63	2nd	1.5
9-4	Hou.	L	2-14		7	17	Hampton	Gardner		76-64	2nd	2.0
9-5	Hou.	W	4-1		9	5	Hernandez	Reynolds	Beck	77-64	2nd	2.0
9-6	Hou.	W	5-3		5	8	Tavarez	Wagner	Hernandez	78-64	2nd	2.0
9-7	Hou.	W	5-1		5	9	Rueter	Kile		79-64	2nd	2.0
9-9	St.L.	L	3-5		4	8	Aybar	Mulholland	Eckersley	79-65	2nd	1.5
9-10	St.L.	W	7-6	(10)	12	9	Beck	Painter		80-65	2nd	0.5
9-11	At Phi.	W	5-3		12	6	Hernandez	Spradlin	Beck	81-65	T1st	....

Date	Opp.	Res.	Score	(inn.*)	Hits	Opp. hits	Winning pitcher	Losing pitcher	Save	Record	Pos.	GB
9-12	At Fla.	W	1-0		6	8	Rueter	Hernandez	Beck	82-65	1st	+1.0
9-13	At Fla.	L	1-8		3	10	Brown	Gardner		82-66	1st	+1.0
9-14	At Fla.	L	4-5		8	6	Powell	Hernandez	Nen	82-67	T1st	....
9-15	At Atl.	L	4-5		5	8	Ligtenberg	Beck		82-68	2nd	1.0
9-16	At Atl.	L	4-6		6	8	Millwood	Alvarez		82-69	2nd	2.0
9-17	L.A.	W	2-1		3	4	Rueter	Park	Hernandez	83-69	2nd	1.0
9-18	L.A.	W	6-5	(12)	12	15	Beck	Guthrie		84-69	T1st	....
9-19	At S.D.	W	7-4		12	13	Darwin	Hamilton	Hernandez	85-69	1st	+1.0
9-20	At S.D.	L	2-12		8	12	Smith	Estes		85-70	1st	+1.0
9-21	At S.D.	W	8-5		13	7	Beck	D. Veras		86-70	1st	+2.0
9-22	At S.D.	W	11-5		12	11	Hernandez	Murray		87-70	1st	+2.5
9-23	At Col.	L	6-7		13	14	Holmes	Darwin	Leskanic	87-71	1st	+1.5
9-24	At Col.	W	4-3		8	5	Hernandez	S. Reed		88-71	1st	+2.5
9-26	S.D.	W	17-4		18	6	Estes	Smith		89-71	1st	+2.0
9-27	S.D.	W	6-1		7	4	Alvarez	Hitchcock		90-71	1st	+2.0
9-28	S.D.	L	3-5	(11)	7	12	Hamilton	Bailey		90-72	1st	+2.0

Monthly records: April (17-7), May (14-14), June (16-13), July (12-15), August (16-13), September (15-10).
*Innings, if other than nine. †First game of doubleheader. ‡Second game of doubleheader.

HIGHLIGHTS

High point: The Giants swept an emotional two-game series against their biggest rival, the Los Angeles Dodgers, at home September 17-18 to regain first place in the National League West. The second game ended in dramatic fashion—a leadoff homer by catcher Brian Johnson in the 12th inning to cap a 6-5 win. Rod Beck escaped a bases-loaded, no-outs jam in the 10th to keep San Francisco in the game.

Low point: The Giants' dream season seemed to be unraveling as the club, bereft of consistent starting pitching, lost eight of 12 games on a road trip to begin the second half. Despite the 4-8 trip, the team lost just two games off its division lead.

Turning point: On July 31 the team acquired pitchers Wilson Alvarez, Roberto Hernandez and Danny Darwin from the Chicago White Sox for six minor leaguers, infusing San Francisco with the pitching it needed to win five of its next six games and prosper down the stretch. It also showed the players that management would do whatever was necessary to help the team win.

Most valuable player: Second baseman Jeff Kent, whose career-high 29 homers and 121 RBIs gave the club consistent punch at the cleanup spot. His homer total was the highest ever by a Giants second baseman, eclipsing a record set 70 years earlier by Hall of Famer Rogers Hornsby.

Most valuable pitcher: Shawn Estes. The lefthander won 19 games, but more importantly went 9-0 with a 2.57 ERA in starts following a Giants loss. He also was named to the All-Star team in his first full season in the major leagues.

Most improved player: First baseman J.T. Snow. After a subpar 1996 with Anaheim (.257, 17 homers, 67 RBIs), Snow answered questions about his abilities with a great debut season in San Francisco (.281, 28, 104). He also won his third consecutive Gold Glove.

Most pleasant surprise: Starting pitcher Kirk Rueter pitched 190 innings and went 13-6, one season after the Montreal Expos gave

him to the Giants for practically nothing.

Biggest disappointment: Reliever Jim Poole. He was given a two-year contract before the season but he was the team's left-handed setup man, but he had the worst year of his career (7.11 ERA) and was rarely used late in the season. Of his 63 appearances, 41 came in the first half of the season.

Key injuries: Righthanded starter Osvaldo Fernandez made just 11 starts before he was lost for the season with bone chips in his pitching elbow, requiring surgery in June.

Notable: The Giants won 22 more games in 1997 than they did in 1996, the largest turnaround in the National League. They did not lose more than three games in a row until September, when they suffered a four-game losing streak at Florida and Atlanta. . . . The Giants became only the fourth team this century to win its division after finishing last the year before. . . . The Giants came from behind to win 46 times and lost just three times in the 76 games they led after eight innings.

—HENRY SCHULMAN

RECORDS

1997 regular-season record: 90-72 (1st in N.L. West); 48-33 at home; 42-39 on road; 31-24 vs. East; 27-28 vs. Central; 32-20 vs. West; 21-20 vs. lefthanded starters; 69-52 vs. righthanded starters; 74-60 on grass; 16-12 on turf; 41-33 in daytime; 49-39 at night; 23-17 in one-run games; 11-3 in extra-inning games; 1-0-1 in doubleheaders.

Team record past five years: 383-362 (.514, ranks 5th in league in that span).

TEAM LEADERS

Batting average: Barry Bonds (.291).
At-bats: Jeff Kent (580).
Runs: Barry Bonds (123).
Hits: Barry Bonds (155).
Total bases: Barry Bonds (311).
Doubles: Jeff Kent (38).

Triples: Jose Vizcaino (7).
Home runs: Barry Bonds (40).
Runs batted in: Jeff Kent (121).
Stolen bases: Barry Bonds (37).
Slugging percentage: Barry Bonds (.585).
On-base percentage: Barry Bonds (.446).
Wins: Shawn Estes (19).
Earned-run average: Shawn Estes (3.18).
Complete games: Shawn Estes (3).
Shutouts: Shawn Estes (2).
Saves: Rod Beck (37).
Innings pitched: Shawn Estes (201.0).
Strikeouts: Shawn Estes (181).

GAMES BY POSITION

Catcher: Rick Wilkins 57, Brian Johnson 55, Damon Berryhill 51, Marcus Jensen 28, Doug Mirabelli 6.
First base: J.T. Snow 156, Jeff Kent 13, Stan Javier 3, Brian Johnson 2, Damon Berryhill 1.
Second base: Jeff Kent 148, Mark Lewis 29, Jose Vizcaino 5, Wilson Delgado 3.
Third base: Bill Mueller 122, Mark Lewis 69.
Shortstop: Jose Vizcaino 147, Rich Aurilia 36, Wilson Delgado 1.
Outfield: Barry Bonds 159, Stan Javier 130, Darryl Hamilton 118, Glenallen Hill 97, Marvin Benard 36, Dante Powell 22, Jacob Cruz 11.
Designated hitter: Glenallen Hill 7, Marvin Benard 1, Mark Lewis 1.

TOP DRAFT CHOICES

1a. **Jason Grilli,** RHP, Seton Hall Univ.
1b. **Dan McKinley,** OF, Arizona State Univ.
2. **Scott Linebrink,** RHP, Southwest Texas State University.
3. **Jeff Andra,** LHP, Oklahoma University.
4. **Kevin McGerry,** RHP, Father Judge H.S., Philadelphia.
5. **Giuseppe Chiaramonte,** C, Fresno State U.
6. **Kevin Joseph,** RHP, Rice University.
7. **Joe Farley,** LHP, Capital H.S., Olympia, Wash.
8. **Brett Casper,** OF, Oral Roberts Univ.
9. **Todd Bellhorn,** LHP, U. of Central Florida.
10. **Joe Holland,** LHP, Bowling Green State University.

1997 REVIEW

Year in review

American League Division Series

National League Division Series

American League Championship Series

National League Championship Series

World Series

All-Star Game

Notable Performances

Transactions

Award Winners

Miscellaneous

Necrology

YEAR IN REVIEW

By STEVE GIETSCHIER
TSN Archivist

Baseball observed several important anniversaries in 1997, but the feeling pervading the sport as these occasions were marked was decidedly mixed. The game's past may still be golden to some, but its present remains shaky and its future uncertain. Fifty years ago, Jackie Robinson joined the Brooklyn Dodgers to become the first black to play major league baseball in the 20th century. Allan H. (Bud) Selig, Chairman of the Executive Council, helped celebrate the golden anniversary on April 15 by announcing that every major league team would retire Robinson's uniform number, 42, immediately, allowing only those currently wearing it to continue to do so. Yet, a fair assessment five decades after Robinson revolutionized the game must conclude that the sport continues to be burdened by substantial problems.

Some of baseball's ills, in fact, could be tied to the anniversaries noted in 1997. Robinson smashed the color line, but the sport still has not achieved racial equality anywhere but on the playing field. Forty years earlier, the Dodgers and the Giants brought major league baseball to the West Coast, ushering in a new era of prosperity for owners and players alike. Yet at year's end the Dodgers themselves were on the verge of being sold and, despite the initiation of revenue sharing, several other franchises were unstable, their owners threatening to move in search of new ballparks constructed at public expense.

Twenty-five years earlier, in 1972, the Major League Baseball Players Association staged the first strike in its history, and the U.S. Supreme Court decided the case of *Flood v. Kuhn et al.* in favor of the defendants, thereby denying outfielder Curt Flood's petition to overturn the reserve clause. Yet, in the year of Flood's death (January 20), baseball's labor relations had not been rationalized, and the prospect for renewed strife at the expiration of the current Basic Agreement seems almost inevitable.

Five years earlier, major league owners accepted the resignation of Commissioner Francis T. (Fay) Vincent under pressure and installed Selig, President and Chief Executive Officer of the Milwaukee Brewers, as the sport's de facto executive. Temporarily, it was said. But Selig is still Chairman of the Executive Council, and, despite occasional rumors to the contrary, baseball is apparently nowhere close to naming a new commissioner.

Normally, events transpiring on the field of play can divert the attention of fans away from the game's difficulties off the field. The 1997 season made a worthy effort in this regard but came up short. The introduction of interleague play jacked up attendance and fan interest, as did the quest of two of the game's most popular sluggers to break one of its most hallowed records. But the World Series, tra-ditionally the crown jewel of every season, seemed to lack its usual luster.

The odyssey of the Florida Marlins perhaps defines baseball's plight best. Florida advanced to the World Series as a wild-card team, thus reopening the debate over whether second-place teams should be playing in the postseason. The Marlins' success, though, was a result of the team's aggressive decision to commit a whopping $89 million in salaries to free agents during the previous offseason. Though the plan worked as intended, it appeared less than sporting to some. And then, Marlins Chairman H. Wayne Huizenga affirmed that, World Series triumph or not, his team had lost so much money during the year that he would be forced to sell it. The first thing he did after the Series was cut the payroll by trading the very players responsible for the Marlins' victory.

INTERLEAGUE PLAY BEGINS

The 1997 season marked the beginning of interleague play, the first time American League clubs met National League clubs in regular season play. The Basic Agreement approved in December 1996 called for interleague play on an experimental basis in 1997 only, with future years to be decided by negotiation.

The '97 schedule provided for three periods of interleague games: June 12-18, June 30-July 3 and August 28-September 3. Each team played 15 or 16 interleague games, three or four against each team in the corresponding division of the other league. A.L. umpires called games in A.L. parks, and N.L. umpires called games in N.L. parks. The designated-hitter rule was in force only in A.L. home games.

Overall, N.L. teams won 117 interleague games and lost 97. The Florida Marlins and Montreal Expos compiled the best interleague record among N.L. teams, winning 12 of their 15 games, while the Houston Astros compiled the worst mark (4-11). In the A.L., the Texas Rangers finished best at 10-6; the Toronto Blue Jays (4-11) and the Anaheim Angels (4-12) finished worst.

Interleague games proved to be a success at the gate with an average attendance of 33,407, more than 20 percent above the average for intraleague games.

1998 SCHEDULE

Following a season-long discussion of realignment prompted by the debut of the Arizona Diamondbacks and the Tampa Bay Devil Rays in 1998 (see EXPANSION TO 30 TEAMS below), the '98 schedule called for a continuation of interleague play. The American League retained a nearly balanced schedule with each team set to play 12 games against the other teams in its division, 11 games against teams in the other divisions and 15 interleague games, three each against teams in the corresponding N.L. division. The National League adopted an unbalanced schedule, complicated by having six teams in the N.L. Central. Each N.L. team will play 11 or 12 games against other teams in its division and nine games against teams in the other divisions, plus either 12 or 15 interleague games. Interleague play will occur during two periods in 1998: June 5-10 and June 22-July 1.

DUAL ASSAULT ON HOME RUN RECORD

One of the rites of every baseball spring is the hope that one or more of the game's sluggers will take aim at Roger Maris' single-season record of 61 homers. The 1997 season was no exception, with early attention focused on Ken Griffey of the Seattle Mariners. He hit two home runs on opening day against the Yankees and set major-league records for most homers through the end of April (13) and through the end of May (24).

Griffey wasn't the only long-ball force, however. The Yankees' Tino Martinez hit 20 home runs through the end of May, and Mark McGwire of the Oakland Athletics had 19. Jeff Bagwell of the Houston Astros, Tony Clark of the Detroit Tigers and Larry Walker of the Colorado Rockies lurked not far behind.

In June and July, though, all of these players fell considerably off record pace. Griffey hit only eight homers during these two months to give him 32. McGwire hit 10 in June but only five in July for a total of 34. Martinez hit eight each month for 36, giving him the major league lead. The collective slow-down took pressure off the hitters as the media circus generally expected to surround any attempt to break Maris' mark failed to materialize.

On July 31, McGwire was traded to the St. Louis Cardinals. Under baseball's record-keeping rules, he thus finished his A.L. season with 34 homers and began a new count in the N.L. He hit nine in August to give him 43, and while Griffey hit 12 for a total of 44, Maris' record appeared safe on September 1. But Griffey hit another 12 homers in September to finish with 56 and McGwire hit a remarkable 15 to end with 58.

McGwire, though he led neither league, tied the major league mark for most home runs by a righthanded hitter in a season, held by Jimmie Foxx (1932) and Hank Greenberg (1938). He became the sixth player to hit 50 or more home runs in more than one season and only the second (after Babe Ruth in 1920 and 1921, '27 and '28) to reach the 50 mark in consecutive seasons. For these achievements as well as his work off the field on behalf of abused children, The Sporting News named McGwire its Sportsman of the Year.

UMPIRES TAKE HARD LINE

Following the confrontation between Orioles second baseman Roberto Alomar and umpire John Hirschbeck in September 1996—an incident that resulted in a five-game suspension Alomar did not serve until the start of the 1997 season—players, owners and umpires agreed to meet in the hopes of formulating a code of conduct.

A meeting in early February resulted in the appointment of a committee to draft a code of conduct. Bud Selig declared that, even without such a code, baseball would not tolerate any abuse of

umpires by either players or managers. Yet, as the season began, the Major League Umpires Association unilaterally implemented a "get-tough" stance.

The draft committee met several times, but no code of conduct emerged from its deliberations. On September 30, the umpires association announced that the regular season's "low-tolerance" program would be replaced by a "no-tolerance" program for the postseason.

A chilly atmosphere prevailed throughout the playoffs and kept arguments to the barest minimum. At the same time, though, the hard line taken by the umpires exposed their decisions to heightened scrutiny. In particular, the dimensions and location of the strike zone became a subject for discussion, especially by television commentators. In Game 5 of the N.L. Championship Series, for example, the Atlanta Braves felt victimized by home plate umpire Eric Gregg, who seemed to call strikes for Florida Marlins pitcher Livan Hernandez on pitches that appeared to be well off the plate. Said Gregg in response to post-game criticism: "My strike zone has been like this for 25 years."

MARLINS WIN WORLD SERIES

The Florida Marlins defeated the Cleveland Indians, four games to three, to win the World Series in dramatic fashion. On Sunday night, October 26, Marlins shortstop Edgar Renteria, only the fourth native of Colombia to play in the majors, singled home second baseman Craig Counsell with the winning win to thwart the Indians, 3-2, in 11 innings.

The Florida franchise thus won a world title in just its fifth year of existence, reaching and winning the Series faster than any other expansion team. The Marlins also became the first wild-card team to advance to the Series.

Perhaps because some observers thought the Braves were still the best team in the National League, the 1997 World Series struck some as lacking appeal, especially as measured by television viewership. Only a large audience for Game 7 prevented the 1997 Series from finishing behind 1989's earthquake-interrupted Series with the lowest television ratings ever.

Dedicated fans, though, are primed to appreciate any World Series, and they took pleasure in this one because of the significant contributions made by Latino players on both teams, and because of the managerial success of Florida's Jim Leyland after 33 years of paying his baseball dues. The Marlins market themselves aggressively to south Florida's multiethnic community and also scout heavily in Latin America. Besides Renteria, players of Latino ethnicity in the Series for the Marlins included infielders Alex Arias and Bobby Bonilla, outfielders Moises Alou and Devon White and pitchers Antonio Alfonseca, Livan Hernandez and Felix Heredia. The Indians were represented in this regard by catcher Sandy Alomar Jr., infielders Tony Fernandez and Omar Vizquel, outfielder Manny Ramirez and pitcher Jose Mesa.

As for Leyland, knowing fans enjoyed his success after his 18 years of riding buses in the minors, his three consecutive division titles with the Pittsburgh Pirates (1990-92) that came up short of the

World Series each time, and his wrenching decision to leave the small-revenue Pirates after the 1996 season.

ATLANTA EXTENDS DIVISION STREAK

The Atlanta Braves celebrated their move from Atlanta-Fulton County Stadium to Turner Field by winning the N.L. East for the third year in a row. Discounting the abbreviated 1994 season that was not played to a conclusion, Atlanta has now won six consecutive division titles. The Braves won a major-league record 19 games in April, took over sole possession of first place on April 14 and clinched the division on September 22 by beating the Montreal Expos, 3-2, in 11 innings.

Atlanta batted .270 as a team (third in the N.L.), tied for second in home runs with 174 and third in runs scored. Kenny Lofton led the team in batting (.333, fourth in the league) and four Braves hit 20 or more home runs: Ryan Klesko (24), Javy Lopez (23), Fred McGriff (22) and Chipper Jones (21). Jones led the team in RBIs with 111 while McGriff drove in 97 and Klesko 84.

The Braves' pitching, once again, was outstanding. The staff finished first in the league in ERA, walks, shutouts, fewest hits allowed and fewest home runs allowed. Denny Neagle won 20 games (four by shutout) to lead the league, Greg Maddux won 19 (including 10 in a row), John Smoltz 15 and Tom Glavine 14. Smoltz finished third in the league in strikeouts with 241. Mark Wohlers saved 33 games.

MARLINS CAPTURE WILD CARD

Florida, having improved its record in each of its first five seasons of play, finished second in the N.L. East and captured the N.L.'s wild-card berth. The Marlins won 92 games and beat Atlanta eight of 12 times. They withstood a midseason challenge from the New York Mets to clinch a playoff spot with a 6-3 win over Montreal on September 23.

Florida's offense finished ninth in the N.L. in batting average (.259), 10th in home runs (136) and eighth in runs scored (740). Moises Alou hit .292 with 23 homers and 115 RBIs. Gary Sheffield hit 21 homers and Charles Johnson added 19. Bobby Bonilla drove in 96 runs.

Alex Fernandez won 17 games, and Kevin Brown won 16. Brown finished tied for fifth in the league in strikeouts and fifth in ERA. Fernandez finished seventh in strikeouts. Robb Nen earned 35 saves.

ASTROS TAKE N.L. CENTRAL CROWN

The Houston Astros won the N.L. Central title by five games over the resurgent Pittsburgh Pirates. With former pitcher and broadcaster Larry Dierker in his rookie season as manager, the Astros were never more than 1 1/2 games out of first place, which they took over for good on July 18. Houston clinched the division on September 25 by defeating the Chicago Cubs, 9-1. The Astros were led offensively by second baseman Craig Biggio, who hit .309 and led the league in runs scored with 146, and first baseman Jeff Bagwell, who finished second in the league in home runs (43) and RBIs (135).

Darryl Kile was Houston's best pitcher. He finished 19-7 with a 2.57 ERA, 205 strikeouts and a 10-game winning streak from June 20 through August

22. Mike Hampton added 15 wins, and Billy Wagner chalked up 23 saves. The surprising Pirates played .500 ball through August 30 only to fade just a bit in the final month.

The Chicago Cubs set a modern N.L record for most losses at the start of the season (14) before ending the streak on April 20 by winning the second game of a doubleheader against the Mets.

GIANTS GO WORST-TO-FIRST IN N.L. WEST

The San Francisco Giants became the fourth team this century to win a division title after finishing last the year before. For this achievement, The Sporting News named Dusty Baker N.L. Manager of the Year. The Giants held first place for 105 consecutive days (May 11 through August 23) but had trouble shaking the Los Angeles Dodgers in the final month. San Francisco did not clinch the N.L. West until September 27, the next-to-last day of the season.

The Giants hit .258 as a team while finishing fourth in runs scored and tied for fourth in home runs. Barry Bonds hit .291 with 40 homers and 101 RBIs. He walked a league-leading 145 times and stole 37 bases. Jeff Kent hit 29 homers (including three grand slams) and drove in 121 runs. J.T. Snow, despite being hit in the face with a pitched ball during spring training, added 28 homers and 104 RBIs.

Shawn Estes won 19 games, Kirk Rueter 13 and Mark Gardner 12. Estes struck out 181 (eighth in the N.L.) and held opponents to a .223 batting average (third). Rod Beck saved 37 games, tied for second in the league.

ORIOLES VICTORIOUS IN A.L. EAST

The Baltimore Orioles qualified for postseason play for the second straight season with a wire-to-wire triumph in the A.L. East, only the third team in A.L. history and the sixth in the majors to win in such fashion. Baltimore clinched the division on September 24 with a 9-3 win over the Toronto Blue Jays to finish two games ahead of the defending division and World Series champion New York Yankees.

The Orioles were led offensively by Rafael Palmeiro, who hit 38 home runs and drove in 110 runs despite batting only .254. Geronimo Berroa hit 26 homers and Jeffrey Hammond added 21. Berroa had 90 RBIs, B.J. Surhoff had 88 and Cal Ripken 84. Roberto Alomar hit .333 and Eric Davis hit .304 in 42 games, his season being interrupted by surgery on June 13 to combat colon cancer. Baltimore finished ninth in the A.L. in batting (.268), fourth in home runs (196) and sixth in runs scored (812). Brady Anderson, who hit 50 home runs in 1996, fell off to 18.

The strength of the Orioles was their pitching. The staff finished first in the A.L. in fewest hits and runs allowed, second in ERA, third in fewest home runs allowed and fourth in strikeouts. Jimmy Key and Scott Erickson led the team with 16 wins each. Mike Mussina added 15, and Scott Kamieniecki and Arthur Rhodes 10 each. Mussina was fourth in the league in strikeouts, and Randy Myers led the A.L. with 45 saves.

Cal Ripken played in all 162 Baltimore games, running his consecutive-games-played streak to 2,478.

YANKEES SETTLE FOR WILD CARD

The Yankees did not achieve in 1997 what they had in 1996 even though they won four more regular season games. They moved into second place in the A.L. East on April 28 and never got closer than two games to Baltimore until after the Orioles clinched the division title. The Yankees captured the wild-card playoff spot easily, clinching it on September 20.

INDIANS WIN THIRD A.L. CENTRAL TITLE

The Indians captured their third straight A.L. Central division title by six games over the Chicago White Sox. Cleveland grabbed first place for good on June 5 and was 3 1/2 games ahead of Chicago at the All-Star break. Curiously, the White Sox all but threw in the towel on July 31 by trading three key pitchers to the San Francisco Giants for six prospects. Chicago owner Jerry Reinsdorf said at the time, "Anyone who thinks this White Sox team will catch Cleveland is crazy," but he later pulled back from that statement a bit. The Indians built their lead over the White Sox steadily through the second half of the season and clinched the pennant on September 23 with a 10-9 win over New York.

The Indians hit a club-record 220 home runs and became the first A.L. team to hit 200 or more homers in three consecutive seasons. Jim Thome led the club with 40, David Justice added 33 and Matt Williams 32. Cleveland finished second in the league in home runs and third in batting average (.286) and runs scored. Sandy Alomar Jr. put together a 30-game hitting streak, the longest Indians streak since Napoleon Lajoie in 1906. Alomar hit .324 with 21 homers and 83 RBIs. Justice hit .329 with 101 RBIs and was named A.L. Comeback Player of the Year by The Sporting News. Williams drove in 105 runs and Thome 102. Omar Vizquel stole 43 bases, fifth in the league.

Cleveland's pitching was not nearly as effective as it had been in 1996. The staff finished ninth in the league in ERA (4.73), fewest hits allowed and fewest home runs allowed. Charles Nagy led the team with 15 wins and Orel Hershiser added 14, but no other pitcher won more than eight. Jose Mesa had 16 saves, far down from his 39 the year before.

SEATTLE WINS A.L. WEST

The Seattle Mariners set a franchise record by winning 90 games and captured their second A.L. West title in three years. They battled the Texas Rangers and the Anaheim Angels until taking over first place for good on August 16. Seattle clinched the pennant on September 23 by defeating the second-place Angels, 4-3.

The Mariners, who hit a major league record 264 homers, were led offensively by Ken Griffey. Besides his 56 home runs, Griffey batted .304 and drove in a league-leading 147 runs. He also finished first in the A.L. in runs scored, total bases, extrabase hits and slugging percentage en route to winning The Sporting News' Major League Player of the Year Award. Edgar Martinez hit .330 (second in the league) with 28 homers and 108 RBIs. Jay Buhner hit 40 homers with 109 RBIs, while Alex Rodriguez hit .300 with 23 homers and 84 RBIs.

Randy Johnson rebounded from back surgery in 1996 to win 20 games while losing only four. He had a 16-game winning streak ended on May 8 by the Orioles. He finished first in the A.L. in winning percentage and lowest opponents' batting average (.194) and second in wins (tied), strikeouts and ERA. Jamie Moyer won 17 games, and Jeff Fassero added 16. Heathcliff Slocumb earned 27 saves.

DIVISION SERIES MAY CHANGE FORMAT

Both N.L. Division Series ended in three-game sweeps. The Braves won the first two games at home before eliminating the Astros in Houston. The Marlins also opened at home in their sweep of the Giants. In the American League, the Orioles eliminated the Mariners in four games, beating Randy Johnson twice. The Indians defeated the Yankees, three games to two after trailing in the series two games to one. Jaret Wright, a 21-year-old rookie, won Games 2 and 5.

In November, baseball's general managers proposed that matchups for this first round of postseason play be determined not by rotation but by record, with the team having the best record opposing the team with the worst record regardless of whether or not these teams are in the same division. They also recommended that the current 2-3 format (with the team with the so-called "home-field advantage" having to play two games on the road before coming home) be switched to a 2-2-1 arrangement with the team having the better record playing Games 1, 2 and 5 (if necessary) at home. Alternatively, the general managers suggested expanding the Division Series from five games to seven. At year's end the Executive Committee had approved the matchups change and the new five-game format, but the owners had not yet acted upon this proposal.

MARLINS UPSET BRAVES IN SIX

The N.L. Championship Series began on an ominous note for the Braves as the Marlins beat Atlanta ace Greg Maddux, 5-3, in Game 1. Despite home runs from Chipper Jones and Ryan Klesko, the Braves were victimized by two errors that contributed to multi-run innings. The Braves won Game 2, 7-1, behind Tom Glavine, but when the Series moved to Miami, the Marlins won two games out of three. Rookie lefthander Tony Saunders outdueled John Smoltz, 5-2, in Game 3. Atlanta's Denny Neagle evened the Series by shuting out Florida, 4-0, in Game 4, but rookie righthander Livan Hernandez beat Maddux, 2-1, in Game 5.

Florida eliminated the Braves by winning Game 6, 7-4, behind Kevin Brown, who pitched a complete game despite battling a viral infection. Atlanta, touted by many as baseball's team of the '90s, thus failed in its attempt to reach a third consecutive World Series.

INDIANS WIN FOUR ONE-RUN GAMES

The Indians and the Orioles split the first two games of the A.L. Championship Series in Baltimore. The Orioles won Game 1, 3-0, as Brady Anderson saved a home run with a fine catch to end the top of the first inning and then led off the bottom of the first with a home run of his own. The Indians recovered to win Game 2, 5-4, on a three-run homer by Marquis Grissom.

Cleveland took a 3-1 lead in games when the Series shifted to Jacobs Field. The Indians won Game 3, 2-1, in a 12-inning affair that took 4 hours, 51 minutes to complete, the longest game in ALCS history. Grissom scored the winning run on Omar Vizquel's controversial squeeze-play attempt. Vizquel missed the bunt, but the ball nipped the top of catcher Lenny Webster's glove and fell into the dirt. Webster, thinking the ball was foul, stood by as Grissom crossed the plate.

The Indians also won Game 4, 8-7, on a ninth-inning single by Sandy Alomar Jr, but the Orioles stayed alive by taking Game 5, 4-2.

The decisive sixth game proved to be a postseason classic. Mike Mussina pitched magnificently for Baltimore, giving up only one hit and striking out 10 in eight innings, but his teammates failed to score a run in his behalf. In the 11th inning, Cleveland second baseman Tony Fernandez, starting in place of injured Bip Roberts, lined a forkball from Armando Benitez over the right-field fence for a homer to send the Indians to the World Series for the second time in three years.

MARLINS NIP INDIANS IN SEVEN

The World Series opened in Miami with the Marlins winning Game 1, 7-4. Livan Hernandez earned the victory, and Moises Alou hit a three-run homer in the fourth inning off Orel Hershiser. The Indians rebounded the next night, winning, 6-1. Sandy Alomar Jr. hit a two-run homer as Cleveland starter Chad Ogea outdueled Kevin Brown.

When the Series shifted to Cleveland, the teams were greeted by inordinately cold, blustery weather that made playing conditions precarious. The Marlins won an ugly Game 3, 14-11. Each team committed three errors, the Indians surrendered a 7-3 lead, the Marlins scored seven runs in the top of the ninth, and the Indians answered with four in their last at-bat. Cleveland bounced back from the debacle by winning Game 4, 10-3, behind the pitching of Jaret Wright. Florida then won Game 5, 8-7, with Hernandez again besting Hershiser and Alou again hitting a three-run homer.

Back in warm Florida, Cleveland staved off elimination by winning Game 6, 4-1, as Ogea again beat Brown. The Indians took a 2-0 lead in the third inning of Game 7 against Florida starter Al Leiter, but it wasn't enough despite a gutsy performance by Wright. Florida got one run in the seventh on a Bobby Bonilla home run and another in the eighth on a sacrifice fly. With one on and one out in the bottom of the 11th, Craig Counsell reached base when second baseman Fernandez muffed a grounder. He went to second on an intentional walk, advanced to third on a fielder's choice and scored on Renteria's bouncer up the middle to win the Series.

Each member of the Marlins voted a full World Series share received $188,467.55, down 13 percent from 1996. Cleveland's full shares came to $113,225.98, down 21 percent from 1996.

The smaller shares resulted from two factors. First, although the four Series games played at Pro Player Stadium in Miami drew the largest World Series crowds since 1963, many of the seats were sold for $25, a price much lower than at previous Series games. Second, under terms of the new collective bargaining agreement, the players' share of ticket receipts from postseason play dropped from 80 percent to 60 percent. The extra 20 percent will be held in escrow, to be paid to the players if the Major League Baseball Players Association exercises its option for a fifth year of the current agreement.

TWO NO-HITTERS

Kevin Brown pitched the second no-hitter in Marlins history by beating the Giants, 9-0, on June 10. He lost a perfect game with two out in the eighth inning when he hit pinch-hitter Marvin Benard with a pitch.

Francisco Cordova and Ricardo Rincon of the Pirates combined on a 10-inning no-hitter against Houston on July 12. Cordova pitched nine innings and struck out 10, but with the score tied 0-0 after nine innings, Rincon came on in relief and pitched a hitless 10th. Pinch-hitter Mark Smith, batting for Rincon, hit a three-run homer off John Hudek to win the game for Pittsburgh.

OTHER FEATS AND EVENTS

Tony Gwynn of the San Diego Padres led the N.L. in batting for the eighth time with a .372 average, tying Honus Wagner's N.L. record. Larry Walker led the league in homers (49), and teammate Andres Galarraga won the RBI crown (140). Frank Thomas of the White Sox won the A.L. batting title with a .347 mark.

Only four pitchers won 20 or more games: Roger Clemens of Toronto (21) and Randy Johnson, Brad Radke of Minnesota and Denny Neagle of Atlanta (20 each). Clemens led the A.L. in strikeouts with 292, and Curt Schilling of the Philadelphia Phillies led the N.L. with 319, a league record for a righthander. Johnson struck out 19 Oakland batters on June 24, an A.L. record for a lefthander, and then struck out 19 again on August 8, this time against the White Sox.

The Cardinals and the Padres took major league baseball to Hawaii for the first time by playing a three-game series in Honolulu on April 19-20. St. Louis swept a twi-night doubleheader, 1-0 and 2-1, and lost a single game, 8-2.

EXPANSION TO 30 TEAMS

The year's most vexing problem concerned the Arizona Diamondbacks and the Tampa Bay Devil Rays, baseball's newest expansion teams. Ever since the two franchises were awarded in 1995, prescient observers foresaw that two 15-team leagues would create scheduling difficulties. Either one team in each league would have to be idle each day of the season or, with interleague play in place, an interleague game would have to be scheduled every day.

Moreover, using the expansion teams to even out each league's 5-5-4 divisional alignment would require placing Tampa Bay in either the A.L. West or the N.L. West, certainly an affront to geography and not the best arrangement should the league to which the Devil Rays be assigned decide to adopt an unbalanced schedule.

On January 16, owners decided to put Arizona in the National League and Tampa Bay in the American. Six of the eight teams originally opposed to this decision relented upon the creation of a committee to examine the 1998 schedule and what soon came to be called "radical realignment." The Kansas City Royals and the Texas Rangers remained opposed to the plan, which included the understanding that the Diamondbacks would play in the N.L. West and the Devil Rays in the A.L. West.

The committee began meeting in February and started considering various plans to have substantial numbers of teams switch divisions and/or leagues. By the All-Star break, a far-reaching plan involving the move of perhaps as many as 14 teams from one league to the other was being discussed.

Though not a member of the committee, Selig publicly advocated radical realignment and cited surveys showing fan support for the concept. Still, no plan emanated from the committee with enough support to ensure passage. In particular, some owners took issue with the view that geographically contiguous teams, including those in the same city, should be placed in the same division.

A modified plan that apparently would have moved only seven teams failed to come to a vote at an owners meeting in mid-September. On October 15, owners finally agreed on a more modest proposal: Arizona to the N.L. West, Tampa Bay to the A.L. East, the Detroit Tigers from the A.L. East to the A.L. Central and one A.L. Central team to the N.L. Central, thus creating a 16-team National League and a 14-team American League.

The opportunity to move to the National League was offered first to the Royals. When they refused to switch, the Brewers agreed to do so, on November 5. "This is just the first phase. There will be more to come," Selig promised as he announced the Brewers' decision.

EXPANSION DRAFT

Rosters for the two new teams were filled by an expansion draft, held on November 18 in Phoenix. Arizona and Tampa Bay each got to draft 35 players in a three-round format. Each of the existing 28 clubs got to protect 15 players, including so-called "10-and-5" players and any players with no-trade clauses in their contracts—unless the players agreed to waive those rights.

Arizona won a coin toss and elected to reserve the second and third picks in the first round for itself and have Tampa Bay select first and fourth. Thereafter, the teams alternated picks until a total of 28 players, one from each existing team, had been selected. In the second round, existing teams got to protect three more players, and the new teams alternated picks, again taking one player from each exisiting team. For the third round, existing teams protected three more players, and the expansion teams alternated picks, selecting seven players each.

Tampa Bay selected Marlins pitcher Tony Saunders with its first pick. Arizona took Cleveland pitcher Brian Anderson with the second pick.

ATTENDANCE SECOND-HIGHEST EVER

Major league attendance for 1997 totalled 63,168,689, 5.1 percent higher than 1996 and the second-highest total ever, but still 10.1 percent behind 1993's record high. N.L. clubs outdrew A.L. clubs slightly, 31,885,368 to 31,283,321. Average attendance was 28,276, the third-highest ever.

Three teams in each league drew more than 3 million fans: Colorado (which led both leagues with 3,888,453, exceeding the 3 million mark for a record-tying fifth consecutive year), Atlanta and Los Angeles in the N.L. and Baltimore, Cleveland and Seattle in the A.L. Nine others clubs exceeded the 2-million mark, and all other clubs drew at least one million.

Baltimore, Cleveland, Seattle and Texas set single-season home attendance records. The Marlins showed the greatest increase, up 617,620 to 2,364,387, while the Phillies, last in attendance, also declined the most, down 294,452 to 1,490,638.

FIVE MANAGERIAL CHANGES

Three teams changed managers during the season, and two others made changes after the season. The Royals fired Bob Boone on July 9 and replaced him with Cubs coach Tony Muser. The Royals were in fourth place in the A.L. Central with a record of 36-46 when Boone was dismissed. They finished 31-48 under Muser and wound up in fifth place.

Cincinnati, mired in fourth place in the N.L. Central at 43-56, fired Ray Knight on July 25. Knight was replaced by Jack McKeon, the club's senior advisor for player personnel. Under McKeon, the Reds won 33 games and lost 30, climbing to third place.

Toronto fired Clarence (Cito) Gaston on September 24 with just five games left in the season. The Blue Jays, with a record of 72-85 and in last place in the A.L. East, replaced Gaston on an interim basis with pitching coach Mel Queen. On November 24, Toronto named Tim Johnson, a minor league manager and former Blue Jays player, as its next manager.

On September 30, two days after the close of a disappointing regular season, the White Sox fired Terry Bevington. Chicago had finished six games behind the Indians with a record of 80-81. On December 4, the White Sox named Florida bench coach Jerry Manuel as their new manager.

Davey Johnson resigned as manager of the Baltimore Orioles on November 5 after guiding the club to the A.L. East title and being named A.L. Manager of the Year by The Sporting News. He stepped down after feuding for some time with Managing General Partner Peter Angelos. The Orioles named pitching coach Ray Miller as Johnson's replacement on November 11.

The Devil Rays hired Marlins pitching coach Larry Rothschild as their first manager on November 7.

OWNERSHIP CHANGES AND BALLPARKS

On January 6, Peter O'Malley announced his intention to sell the Los Angeles Dodgers, the team his family had owned for 47 years. Estimates on the price of the sale, including the franchise, Dodger Stadium and its 300 surrounding acres, a spring training facility in Vero Beach, Fla., and other facilities in the Dominican Republic, ranged as high as

$300 million. In May, O'Malley said he was negotiating with the Fox Group, an affiliate of Rupert Murdoch's News Corporation. The two parties reached an agreement in principle on September 4 with a purchase price of $350 million, but at year's end final approval was still forthcoming.

H. Wayne Huizenga announced that the Marlins were for sale on June 26, but only to an individual or group that would keep the team in south Florida. Huizenga's decision to spend freely on free agents bumped the team's payroll from $30.1 million in 1996 to $53.5 million. Despite a 35 percent increase in attendance, the Marlins announced that they would lose more than $30 million. On November 6, Huizenga reached a tentative agreement to sell the club to a group represented by Marlins President Don Smiley.

Voters in King County, Washington, authorized $336 million in bonds to pay for a retractable-roof ballpark and parking garage, construction on which began in the spring. Mariners Chief Executive Officer John Ellis said the team needed the revenue from a new facility to remain competitive, but near the end of the year the Mariners announced their intention to trade star pitcher Randy Johnson rather than sign him to a contract extension.

Minnesota Twins owner Carl Pohlad tried in vain to secure public financing for a new ballpark. He offered a complicated arrangement involving transferring ownership of the team to a not-for-profit organization and eventually to the public, a lottery to fund construction and Pohlad's guarantee to cover the Twins' operating losses. After the Minnesota legislature refused to approve this package, Pohlad announced his intention to sell the club to parties in the Tri-Cities area (Greensboro, High Point and Winston-Salem) of North Carolina.

FIVE SALARY ARBITRATION CASES

Eighty players filed for salary arbitration, but only five cases proceeded all the way through the hearing and decision stage, the lowest total ever. A total of 48 players exchanged figures with their teams. Tim Wakefield of the Boston Red Sox was the only player to win his case, increasing his salary from $450,000 to $2,500,000. The other four (Tom Goodwin, Darryl Kile, Bill Risley and Aaron Sele) lost their cases but still got raises averaging 125 percent.

Ivan Rodriguez and the Rangers avoided arbitration by signing a one-year contract that will pay him $6.65 million in 1998, the largest one-year contract ever, surpassing the $6.5 million paid to Joe Carter by the Blue Jays in 1997.

Another star catcher, Mike Piazza, and the Dodgers avoided arbitration by agreeing to a two-year contract that will pay him $7 million in 1997 and $8 million in 1998. Piazza had filed an arbitration figure of $7.65 million, the highest salary ever asked for in arbitration. The Dodgers countered with an offer of $6.1 million, the highest ever offered until this year, when Baltimore's Mike Mussina asked for $7.1 million and the Orioles countered with $6.55 million.

Raises for the 80 players who filed for arbitration averaged 152.8 percent, more than double the average increase of the previous year. The average 1997 salary for these 80 players was $2,014,460.

SALARIES RISE

Figures released near the end of the year showed a marked increase in the average player salary from 1996 to 1997. According to the Player Relations Committee, the average salary in 1997 was $1,312,392, an increase of 19.2 percent over 1996. The Players' Association, which calculates salaries slightly differently, reported an increase of 19.3 percent from $1,119,981 to $1,336,609.

Two teams, the Yankees and Orioles, topped the $2 million mark in average salary. Twenty others paid an average salary of more than $1 million. The Pirates paid the lowest average salary, $380,443, according to the association.

Criticism of high salaries, rampant for years from fans and owners, took on a new dimension as studies showed that teams paying the highest salaries tended to make the playoffs. In fact, six of the year's eight playoff teams were in the top eight for salaries paid. These eight included the top five teams plus Seattle (eighth), San Francisco (11th) and Houston.

BONDS SIGNS RECORD CONTRACT

Barry Bonds led the march to yet higher salaries even before the 1997 season began when he signed a two-year contract extension with the Giants for 1999 and 2000 with an average salary of $11.45 million. It exceeded the salary agreed to by Albert Belle and the White Sox in 1996.

On April 2, the Marlins and Gary Sheffield agreed to a six-year contract extension worth $61 million with an option for a seventh year that would bring the contract's total worth to $72 million, the largest total package ever. Sheffield (average salary: $10,166,667) thus became the third-highest paid player behind Bonds and Belle.

Sammy Sosa passed Sheffield to become the third-highest paid player on June 25 when he signed a four-year contract extension with the Cubs worth $42.5 million. Following the settlement of his arbitration case, the Rangers' Ivan Rodriguez signed a five-year contract extension that made him the fifth-highest paid player with a package worth $42 million.

Greg Maddux of the Braves signed a five-year contract extension worth $57.5 million on August 10, thus vaulting him to the first rung on the salary ladder, ahead of Bonds and Belle, with an average salary of $11.5 million.

POST-SEASON CONTRACTS

On the eve of the expansion draft, the Diamondbacks jumpstarted a period of intense player transactions by signing free-agent shortstop Jay Bell to a five-year contract worth $34.5 million.

Following the draft, the Braves signed Andres Galarraga (three years, $24.75 million); Randy Myers left Baltimore for Toronto (three years, $18 million); Wilson Alvarez, obtained by the Giants from the White Sox at the trading deadline, signed with Arizona (five years, $35 million) and Darryl Kile left Houston for Colorado (three years, nearly $22 million). Kenny Lofton, traded from Cleveland to Atlanta on March 25, returned to the Indians as a free agent on December 8 (three years, $24 million).

Finally, pitcher Pedro Martinez, traded from the Montreal Expos to the Red Sox on November 18, signed a six-year contract worth a record $75 million with Boston on December 12, making him baseball's newest, highest-paid player.

RETIREMENTS

Last season marked the final one in the careers of four outstanding players. First baseman/DH Eddie Murray retired with a career batting average of .287, 504 home runs and 1,917 RBIs. Ryne Sandberg, who on April 27 hit his 267th home run as a second baseman to break Joe Morgan's major league record, also retired after the 1997 season. Sandberg finished his 16-year career with a batting average of .285, 282 homers (277 as a second baseman) and 1,061 RBIs.

Dennis Martinez, only the seventh pitcher to win 100 games in each league, retired on June 18 with a career record of 241-187. Lee Smith retired abruptly on July 15 after saving a major league record 478 games.

CONCLUSION

When the Marlins and Indians qualified for the World Series, Don Ohlmeyer, President of the West Coast Division of NBC, the network scheduled to televise the Series, said he would be happy if one team would sweep so NBC could resume its regular programming. "We're looking for four and out," he said. To which Dick Ebersol, President of NBC Sports, replied, "I guess a major NBC executive is supposed to say something stupid about baseball every two years, and this happens to be Don's turn."

Stupid or not, the relationship between television and baseball will continue. Here's how the game on the field ended up in 1997:

FINAL STANDINGS

AMERICAN LEAGUE

EAST DIVISION

Team	Bal.	N.Y.	Det.	Bos.	Tor.	Cle.	Chi.	Mil.	Min.	K.C.	Sea.	Ana.	Tex.	Oak.	Atl.	Fla.	N.Y.	Mon.	Phi.	W	L	Pct.	GB
Baltimore	....	8	6	5	6	6	5	5	10	7	7	7	10	8	3-0	0-3	1-2	1-2	3-0	98	64	.605	....
New York	4	....	10	8	7	6	9	7	8	8	4	7	7	6	1-2	1-2	2-1	1-2	1-0	96	66	.593	2.0
Detroit	6	2	....	7	6	5	7	4	4	6	4	6	7	7	2-1	1-2	3-0	0-3	2-1	79	83	.488	19.0
Boston	7	4	5	....	6	6	3	8	8	3	7	5	3	7	0-3	1-2	2-1	0-3	3-0	78	84	.481	20.0
Toronto	6	5	6	6	....	5	6	4	8	6	3	5	7	5	1-2	0-3	0-3	1-2	2-1	76	86	.469	22.0

CENTRAL DIVISION

Team	Cle.	Chi.	Mil.	Min.	K.C.	Bal.	N.Y.	Det.	Bos.	Tor.	Sea.	Ana.	Tex.	Oak.	Hou.	Pit.	Cin.	St.L.	Chi.	W	L	Pct.	GB
Cleveland	....	7	8	8	8	5	5	6	5	6	3	4	5	7	2-1	2-1	1-2	1-2	2-1	86	75	.534	....
Chicago	5	....	4	6	11	6	2	4	8	5	5	5	3	7	3-0	0-3	1-2	1-2	2-1	80	81	.497	6.0
Milwaukee	4	7	....	5	6	6	4	7	3	7	5	4	7	5	2-1	2-1	0-3	3-0	1-2	78	83	.484	8.0
Minnesota	4	6	7	....	5	1	3	7	3	3	5	7	3	7	2-1	2-1	2-1	0-3	1-2	68	94	.42	18.5
Kansas City	3	1	6	7	....	4	3	5	8	5	5	5	6	3	2-1	2-1	1-2	1-2	0-3	67	94	.416	19.0

WEST DIVISION

Team	Sea.	Ana.	Tex.	Oak.	Bal.	N.Y.	Det.	Bos.	Tor.	Cle.	Chi.	Mil.	Min.	K.C.	S.F.	L.A.	Col.	S.D.	W	L	Pct.	GB
Seattle	....	6	8	7	4	7	7	4	8	6	6	6	6	6	1-3	3-1	2-2	1-3	90	72	.556	....
Anaheim	6	....	8	11	4	4	5	6	6	7	6	7	4	6	1-3	0-4	1-3	2-2	84	78	.519	6.0
Texas	4	4	....	7	1	4	4	8	4	6	8	4	8	5	2-2	3-1	3-1	2-2	77	85	.475	13.0
Oakland	5	1	5	....	3	5	4	4	6	4	3	6	4	8	2-2	1-3	1-3	3-1	65	97	.401	25.0

NOTE: Read across for wins, down for losses.

Clinching dates: Baltimore (East)—September 24; Cleveland (Central)—September 23; Seattle (West)—September 23; New York (wild card)—September 23.

NATIONAL LEAGUE

EAST DIVISION

Team	Atl.	Fla.	N.Y.	Mon.	Phi.	Hou.	Pit.	Cin.	St.L.	Chi.	S.F.	L.A.	Col.	S.D.	Bal.	N.Y.	Det.	Bos.	Tor.	W	L	Pct.	GB
Atlanta	....	4	5	10	10	7	5	9	8	9	7	6	5	8	0-3	2-1	1-2	3-0	2-1	101	61	.623	....
Florida	8	....	4	7	6	7	7	6	5	9	5	7	4	5	3-0	2-1	2-1	2-1	3-0	92	70	.568	9.0
New York	7	8	....	7	7	4	7	9	9	5	3	5	5	5	2-1	1-2	0-3	1-2	3-0	88	74	.543	13.0
Montreal	2	5	5	....	6	3	5	5	6	7	6	4	4	8	2-1	2-1	3-0	0-3	1-2	78	84	.481	23.0
Philadelphia	2	6	5	6	....	7	5	3	6	5	3	1	7	7	0-3	3-0	1-2	0-3	1-2	68	94	.42	33.0

CENTRAL DIVISION

Team	Hou.	Pit.	Cin.	St.L.	Chi.	Atl.	Fla.	N.Y.	Mon.	Phi.	S.F.	L.A.	Col.	S.D.	Cle.	Chi.	Mil.	Min.	K.C.	W	L	Pct.	GB
Houston	....	6	7	9	9	4	4	7	8	4	3	7	6	6	1-2	0-3	1-2	1-2	1-2	84	78	.519	....
Pittsburgh	6	....	4	9	5	6	4	4	6	8	2	7	5	5	1-2	3-0	1-2	1-2	1-2	79	83	.488	5.0
Cincinnati	5	8	....	6	5	2	5	2	6	8	4	6	5	5	2-1	1-2	3-0	1-2	2-1	76	86	.469	8.0
St. Louis	3	3	6	....	8	3	6	2	5	8	6	4	6	4	1-2	2-1	0-3	3-0	2-1	73	89	.451	11.0
Chicago	3	7	7	4	....	2	2	6	4	6	5	5	2	6	1-2	1-2	2-1	2-1	3-0	68	94	.42	16.0

WEST DIVISION

Team	S.F.	L.A.	Col.	S.D.	Atl.	Fla.	N.Y.	Mon.	Phi.	Hou.	Pit.	Cin.	St.L.	Chi.	Sea.	Ana.	Tex.	Oak.	W	L	Pct.	GB
San Francisco	....	6	8	8	4	6	8	5	8	8	3	7	3	6	3-1	3-1	2-2	2-2	90	72	.556	....
Los Angeles	6	....	7	5	5	4	6	7	10	4	9	5	5	6	1-3	4-0	1-3	3-1	88	74	.543	2.0
Colorado	4	5	....	4	6	7	6	7	4	5	4	6	7	9	2-2	3-1	1-3	3-1	83	79	.512	7.0
San Diego	4	7	8	....	3	6	3	4	5	6	6	5	5	5	3-1	2-2	2-2	1-3	76	86	.469	14.0

NOTE: Read across for wins, down for losses.

Clinching dates: Atlanta (East)—September 22; Houston (Central)—September 25; San Francisco (West)—September 27; Florida (wild card)—September 23.

1997 REVIEW Year in review

BALTIMORE VS. SEATTLE

HIGHLIGHTS

The bottom line: The Baltimore Orioles, looking for their first American League pennant and World Series victory since 1983, stormed past the Seattle Mariners in a four-game Division Series test and claimed a spot in the A.L. Championship Series for the second straight year. Baltimore pitchers shut down the high-powered Mariners, who had set a regular-season record with 264 home runs and led the major leagues with 925 runs scored. The East Division-champion Orioles outscored the Mariners, 23-11, and closed the door on their principal power source. Seattle center fielder Ken Griffey, who hit 56 regular-season home runs, was 2-for-15 in the series without a homer.

Why the Orioles won: Because they were able to nullify Griffey, continue their mastery over intimidating lefthander Randy Johnson and take advantage of the Mariners' suspect bullpen. It took the Orioles only five innings to drive Johnson from the mound in a 9-3 opening-game victory and they handled him again in Game 4, posting a 3-1 series-clinching win. Johnson, who was 20-2 against the rest of the league while leading the Mariners to the A.L. West Division title, started five 1997 games against the Orioles and was 0-4. In the Division Series, Johnson was victimized in both starts by Baltimore ace Mike Mussina, who allowed only three runs and seven hits in 14 stellar innings. Two key Seattle relievers, Mike Timlin and Bobby Ayala, allowed 10 earned runs in two combined innings.

The turning points:

Game 1: The entire series turned when the Orioles jumped on Johnson for four fifth-inning runs, breaking a 1-1 tie and putting a major chink in the Mariners' pitching armor. Two of the runs scored on an Eric Davis single and another on Geronimo Berroa's home run as the Orioles took quick control of their post-season destiny. Baltimore also got a home run from Chris Hoiles in a four-run sixth against relievers Timlin and Paul Spoljaric. Mussina allowed only solo home runs to Edgar Martinez and Jay Buhner in a strong seven-inning stint.

Game 2: Like the opener, the turning point came in the fifth inning and concluded with another 9-3 Baltimore victory. The Orioles got a break when Seattle starter Jamie Moyer, leading 2-1, developed a sore elbow and had to leave the game with two out and runners on first and second base. Spoljaric replaced Moyer and Roberto Alomar greeted him with a drive to center that Griffey gloved but could not hold at the fence, allowing both runners to score. Brady Anderson added a two-run seventh-inning home run as the Orioles pulled away.

Game 3: This game belonged to Seattle lefthander Jeff Fassero, who did his best Houdini impressions in the first and third innings before settling down. Fassero's first moment of truth came when the Orioles loaded the bases with two out in the first and B.J. Surhoff hit a sharp grounder up the middle that the pitcher knocked down with his foot. Fassero spun around frantically, located the ball at the base of the mound and threw Surhoff out on a close play. The Baltimore third opened with an Anderson single and Alomar double, but Fassero struck out Berroa, got Rafael Palmeiro on a grounder to the mound and struck out Cal Ripken. The next 18 Orioles went down in order. The 4-2 victory, which featured back-to-back ninth-inning home runs by Buhner and Paul Sorrento, was not secured until after reliever Heathcliff Slocumb had surrendered a two-run bottom-of-the-ninth double to Baltimore's Jeffrey Hammonds.

Game 4: The Orioles gave Mussina two first-inning runs and he made them stand up for a clinching 3-1 victory. The first came from the unlikely bat of second baseman Jeff Reboulet, who was starting in place of Alomar because Johnson was on the mound. Reboulet hit a one-out home run and a Berroa double and Ripken single delivered the other. The only other scoring was provided by home runs—a second-inning blast by Martinez off Mussina and a fifth-inning shot by Berroa off Johnson. Despite allowing seven hits and striking out 13, Johnson came out on the short end to Mussina, who allowed only two hits over seven innings. Armando Benitez and Randy Myers each pitched a hitless inning to close out the two-hitter.

Notable:

Mariners: A Game 1 crowd of 59,579 set a Kingdome record. . . . Fassero, who pitched the Mariners to a series-extending 4-2 victory in Game 3, did not do it efficiently. When Fassero left after walking the first batter in the ninth inning, he had thrown a season-high 136 pitches. He threw 30 in the first inning. . . . To say catcher Dan Wilson had a tough series is an understatement. He finished 0-for-13 with nine strikeouts. Wilson is 2-for-46 lifetime in playoff action. . . . Seattle's version of murderer's row—Griffey, Martinez, Buhner and Alex Rodriguez—was a combined 13-for-60 in the series.

Orioles: The Game 3 crowd of 49,137 at Oriole Park at Camden Yards was a stadium record. . . . Mussina's two Division Series victories lifted his career record against the Mariners to 10-1. Mussina also became the first pitcher in Baltimore history to get two wins as a starter in a post-season series. His clinching victory marked the first time this season he had worked on three days rest. . . . Reboulet batted .237 in 99 regular-season games for the Orioles. But he hit .364 (4-for-11) with two home runs off Johnson.

Quotable:

Mariners: Fassero, after his Game 3 victory: "This is the biggest game I've ever pitched in my life . . . the biggest day of my life so far.". . . Johnson, after losing the Game 4 clincher: "I pitched my butt off. I got beat. I pitched as good a game as I have all year. Mike pitched better. Tip your hat to the Baltimore Orioles. Their pitching was much better."

Orioles: Manager Davey Johnson after Mussina's Game 1 win over Johnson: "I was happy the Big Unit was getting all the press. Everyone was talking about Randy Johnson and it was as if Mike Mussina was chopped liver. The greatest thing we had going for us was everyone thinking Mussina had no chance to beat Randy."

GAME 1 BOX SCORE

BALTIMORE 9, SEATTLE 3

WEDNESDAY, OCTOBER 1, AT SEATTLE

Baltimore	AB	R	H	RBI	PO	A
Anderson, cf	5	1	2	1	2	0
Reboulet, 2b	2	0	0	0	0	1
Alomar, ph-2b	1	1	0	0	1	0
Davis, rf	3	0	1	2	1	0
Surhoff, ph-lf	2	0	1	2	0	0
Berroa, dh	5	1	1	1	0	0
Ripken, 3b	5	0	3	0	1	0
Hoiles, c	2	1	1	1	6	0
Webster, c	2	0	1	0	5	0
Walton, 1b	2	0	0	0	3	1
Palmeiro, 1b	2	1	1	0	5	0
Hammonds, rf	2	2	0	0	1	0
Bordick, ss	3	2	2	2	1	4
Mussina, p	0	0	0	0	1	2
Orosco, p	0	0	0	0	0	0
Benitez, p	0	0	0	0	0	0
Totals	36	9	13	9	27	8

Seattle	AB	R	H	RBI	PO	A
Cora, 2b	4	0	1	0	3	4
Kelly, lf	4	0	1	0	0	0
Griffey, cf	4	0	0	0	5	0
Martinez, dh	4	1	1	1	0	0
Rodriguez, ss	4	1	2	1	1	1
Buhner, rf	3	1	1	1	2	0
Sorrento, 1b	4	0	1	0	8	1
Wilson, c	3	0	0	0	6	1
Blowers, 3b	2	0	0	0	1	1
Gates, ph-3b	1	0	0	0	0	0
Johnson, p	0	0	0	0	0	1
Timlin, p	0	0	0	0	0	0
Spoljaric, p	0	0	0	0	0	0
Wells, p	0	0	0	0	0	0
Charlton, p	0	0	0	0	1	0
Totals	33	3	7	3	27	9

Baltimore	0	0	1		0	4	4		0	0	0—9
Seattle	0	0	0		1	0	0		1	0	1—3

Baltimore	IP	H	R	ER	BB	SO
Mussina (W)	7.0	5	2	2	0	9
Orosco	1.0	1	0	0	0	0
Benitez	1.0	1	1	1	1	2

Seattle	IP	H	R	ER	BB	SO
Johnson (L)	5.0	7	5	5	4	3
Timlin	0.2	3	4	4	1	1
Spoljaric	0.1	1	0	0	0	0
Wells	1.1	1	0	0	0	1
Charlton	1.2	1	0	0	0	0

E—Sorrento. DP—Baltimore 1, Seattle 2. LOB—Baltimore 6, Seattle 4. 2B—Kelly, Bordick, Palmeiro, Surhoff, Sorrento. HR—Martinez, Berroa, Hoiles, Buhner, Rodriguez. SB—Anderson, Hammonds. T—3:14. A—59,579. U—McClelland, plate; Ford, first; Kaiser, second; Kosc, third; Phillips, left field; Roe, right field.

GAME 2 BOX SCORE

BALTIMORE 9, SEATTLE 3

THURSDAY, OCTOBER 2, AT SEATTLE

Baltimore	AB	R	H	RBI	PO	A
Anderson, cf	4	2	2	3	2	0
Alomar, 2b	5	0	1	2	2	4
Surhoff, lf	5	0	2	0	0	1
Davis, rf	2	0	0	0	0	0
Berroa, rf	2	0	2	0	0	0
Hammonds, pr-rf	1	1	0	0	0	0
Palmeiro, 1b	5	0	1	0	7	1
Ripken, 3b	4	1	2	0	1	2
Baines, dh	4	2	2	1	0	0
Webster, c	3	1	0	1	12	0
Bordick, ss	3	2	2	2	2	3
Erickson, p	0	0	0	0	1	0
Benitez, p	0	0	0	0	0	0
Orosco, p	0	0	0	0	0	0
Myers, p	0	0	0	0	0	0
Totals	38	9	14	9	27	11

Seattle	AB	R	H	RBI	PO	A
Cora, 2b	5	1	2	0	2	5
Kelly, lf	4	1	1	0	0	0
Griffey, cf	3	0	1	1	2	1
Martinez, dh	4	0	1	0	0	0
Rodriguez, ss	4	0	1	0	0	5
Buhner, rf	4	0	1	0	0	1
Sorrento, 1b	2	1	1	0	9	2
Amaral, ph-1b	1	0	0	0	1	1
Wilson, c	4	0	0	0	8	0
Sheets, 3b	2	0	1	0	0	0
Ducey, ph	1	0	1	1	0	0
Blowers, 3b	1	0	0	0	0	0
Moyer, p	0	0	0	0	2	1
Spoljaric, p	0	0	0	0	0	0
Ayala, p	0	0	0	0	0	0
Charlton, p	0	0	0	0	0	0
Slocumb, p	0	0	0	1	1	0
Totals	35	3	9	3	27	16

Baltimore	0	1	0		0	2	0		2	4	0—9
Seattle	2	0	0		0	0	0		1	0	0—3

Baltimore	IP	H	R	ER	BB	SO
Erickson (W)	6.2	7	3	3	2	6
Benitez	1.0	2	0	0	0	1
Orosco	0.1	0	0	0	0	1
Myers	1.0	0	0	0	0	3

Seattle	IP	H	R	ER	BB	SO
Moyer (L)	4.2	5	3	3	1	2
Spoljaric	1.1	3	0	0	0	1
Ayala	1.1	4	6	6	3	2
Charlton	0.2	1	0	0	0	1
Slocumb	1.0	1	0	0	1	0

DP—Seattle 1. LOB—Baltimore 7, Seattle 7. 2B—Kelly, Alomar, Ripken 2, Anderson, Palmeiro. HR—Baines, Anderson. SB—Griffey 2. PB—Webster. T—3:25. A—59,309. U—Ford, plate; Kaiser, first; Kosc, second; Phillips, third; Roe, left field; McClelland, right field.

GAME 3 BOX SCORE

SEATTLE 4, BALTIMORE 2

SATURDAY, OCTOBER 4, AT BALTIMORE

Seattle	AB	R	H	RBI	PO	A
Amaral, 1b	3	2	2	0	6	1
Sheets, 3b	1	0	0	0	0	0
Kelly, lf	4	0	2	1	2	0
Griffey, cf	4	0	1	1	4	0
Martinez, dh	4	0	1	0	0	0
Rodriguez, ss	4	0	2	0	4	3
Buhner, rf	4	1	1	1	1	0
Blowers, 3b	2	0	1	0	0	1
Sorrento, ph-1b	2	1	1	1	5	1
Wilson, c	4	0	0	0	4	0
Cora, 2b	4	0	0	0	0	1
Fassero, p	0	0	0	0	1	4
Slocumb, p	0	0	0	0	0	0
Totals	36	4	11	4	27	11

A.L. Division Series

1997 REVIEW

Baltimore	AB	R	H	RBI	PO	A
Anderson, cf	4	0	2	0	1	0
Alomar, 2b	3	0	1	0	0	2
Berroa, dh	2	1	0	0	0	0
Palmeiro, 1b	4	1	1	0	9	0
Ripken, 3b	3	0	0	0	1	1
Surhoff, lf	4	0	0	0	1	0
Hammonds, rf	4	0	1	2	4	1
Hoiles, c	3	0	0	0	10	0
Baines, ph	1	0	0	0	0	0
Bordick, ss	2	0	0	0	1	4
Key, p	0	0	0	0	0	1
Mills, p	0	0	0	0	0	1
Rhodes, p	0	0	0	0	0	0
Mathews, p	0	0	0	0	0	0
Totals	30	2	5	2	27	10

Seattle			0	0	1		0	1	0		0	0	2—4
Baltimore			0	0	0		0	0	0		0	0	2—2

Seattle	IP	H	R	ER	BB	SO
Fassero (W)	*8.0	3	1	1	4	3
Slocumb	1.0	2	1	1	0	0

Baltimore	IP	H	R	ER	BB	SO
Key (L)	4.2	8	2	2	0	4
Mills	1.0	1	0	0	0	1
Rhodes	2.1	0	0	0	0	4
Mathews	1.0	2	2	2	0	1

*Pitched to one batter in ninth.

LOB—Seattle 5, Baltimore 6. 2B—Kelly, Alomar, Rodriguez, Hammonds. HR—Buhner, Sorrento. SH—Alomar. WP—Key. T—3:26. A—49,137. U—Reed, plate; Scott, first; Garcia, second; Cousins, third; Tschida, left field; Morrison, right field.

GAME 4 BOX SCORE

BALTIMORE 3, SEATTLE 1
SUNDAY, OCTOBER 5, AT BALTIMORE

Seattle	AB	R	H	RBI	PO	A
Cora, 2b	4	0	0	0	2	1
Rodriguez, ss	4	0	0	0	0	1

Seattle	AB	R	H	RBI	PO	A
Griffey, cf	4	0	0	0	1	0
Martinez, dh	4	1	1	1	0	0
Sorrento, 1b	2	0	0	0	5	0
Kelly, ph	1	0	0	0	0	0
Buhner, rf	2	0	0	0	2	0
Ducey, lf	3	0	1	0	0	0
Gates, 3b	3	0	0	0	1	2
Wilson, c	2	0	0	0	11	0
Wilkins, ph-c	0	0	0	0	2	0
Johnson, p	0	0	0	0	0	2
Totals	29	1	2	1	24	6

Baltimore	AB	R	H	RBI	PO	A
Anderson, cf	4	0	0	0	1	0
Reboulet, 2b	3	1	1	1	2	2
Alomar, 2b	1	0	1	0	0	0
Berroa, dh	4	2	2	1	0	0
Davis, rf	4	0	1	0	0	0
Ripken, 3b	4	0	2	1	1	1
Hoiles, c	2	0	0	0	7	0
Webster, c	1	0	0	0	3	0
Walton, 1b	2	0	0	0	2	0
Palmeiro, 1b	1	0	0	0	7	0
Hammonds, lf	3	0	0	0	3	0
Bordick, ss	2	0	0	0	0	4
Mussina, p	0	0	0	0	1	2
Benitez, p	0	0	0	0	0	0
Myers, p	0	0	0	0	0	0
Totals	31	3	7	3	27	9

Seattle			0	1	0		0	0	0		0	0	0—1
Baltimore			2	0	0		0	1	0		0	0	x—3

Seattle	IP	H	R	ER	BB	SO
Johnson (L)	8.0	7	3	3	2	13

Baltimore	IP	H	R	ER	BB	SO
Mussina (W)	7.0	2	1	1	3	7
Benitez	1.0	0	0	0	1	1
Myers (S)	1.0	0	0	0	0	2

LOB—Seattle 5, Baltimore 6. 2B—Berroa. HR—Reboulet, Martinez, Berroa. T—2:42. A—48,766. U—Scott, plate; Garcia, first; Cousins, second; Tschida, third; Morrison, left field; Reed, right field.

STATISTICS

BALTIMORE ORIOLES' BATTING AND FIELDING AVERAGES

Player, position	G	AB	R	H	TB	2B	3B	HR	RBI	BB	IBB	SO	Avg.	PO	A	E	Avg.
Ripken, 3b	4	16	1	7	9	2	0	0	1	2	0	2	.438	4	4	0	1.000
Bordick, ss	4	10	4	4	5	1	0	0	4	4	0	2	.400	4	15	0	1.000
Baines, dh-ph	2	5	2	2	5	0	0	1	1	1	1	0	.400	0	0	0	.000
Berroa, dh-rf	4	13	4	5	12	1	0	2	2	2	0	0	.385	0	0	0	.000
Anderson, cf	4	17	3	6	10	1	0	1	4	1	0	4	.353	6	0	0	1.000
Alomar, 2b-ph	4	10	1	3	5	2	0	0	2	1	1	1	.300	3	6	0	1.000
Surhoff, lf-ph	3	11	0	3	4	1	0	0	2	0	0	2	.273	1	1	0	1.000
Palmeiro, 1b	4	12	2	3	5	2	0	0	0	0	0	2	.250	27	2	0	1.000
Davis, rf	3	9	0	2	2	0	0	0	2	0	0	5	.222	1	0	0	1.000
Reboulet, 2b	2	5	1	1	4	0	0	1	1	0	0	2	.200	2	3	0	1.000
Webster, c	3	6	1	1	1	0	0	0	1	1	0	0	.167	20	0	0	1.000
Hoiles, c	3	7	1	1	4	0	0	1	1	2	0	1	.143	23	0	0	1.000
Hammonds, lf-rf-pr	4	10	3	1	2	1	0	0	2	2	0	2	.100	8	1	0	1.000
Benitez, p	3	0	0	0	0	0	0	0	0	0	0	0	.000	0	0	0	.000
Erickson, p	1	0	0	0	0	0	0	0	0	0	0	0	.000	1	0	0	1.000
Key, p	1	0	0	0	0	0	0	0	0	0	0	0	.000	0	1	0	1.000
Mathews, p	1	0	0	0	0	0	0	0	0	0	0	0	.000	0	0	0	.000
Mills, p	1	0	0	0	0	0	0	0	0	0	0	0	.000	0	1	0	1.000
Mussina, p	2	0	0	0	0	0	0	0	0	0	0	0	.000	3	3	0	1.000
Myers, p	2	0	0	0	0	0	0	0	0	0	0	0	.000	0	0	0	.000
Orosco, p	2	0	0	0	0	0	0	0	0	0	0	0	.000	0	0	0	.000
Rhodes, p	1	0	0	0	0	0	0	0	0	0	0	0	.000	0	0	0	.000
Walton, 1b	2	4	0	0	0	0	0	0	0	0	0	2	.000	5	1	0	1.000
Totals	4	135	23	39	68	11	0	6	23	16	2	27	.289	108	38	0	1.000

SEATTLE MARINERS' BATTING AND FIELDING AVERAGES

Player, position	G	AB	R	H	TB	2B	3B	HR	RBI	BB	IBB	SO	Avg.	PO	A	E	Avg.
Amaral, 1b-ph	2	4	2	2	2	0	0	0	0	0	0	1	.500	7	2	0	1.000
Ducey, ph-lf	2	4	0	2	2	0	0	0	1	0	0	0	.500	0	0	0	.000
Sheets, 3b	2	3	0	1	1	0	0	0	0	0	0	2	.333	0	0	0	.000
Rodriguez, ss	4	16	1	5	9	1	0	1	1	0	0	5	.313	5	10	0	1.000
Kelly, lf-ph	4	13	1	4	7	3	0	0	1	0	0	3	.308	4	0	0	1.000
Sorrento, 1b-ph	4	10	2	3	7	1	0	1	1	2	0	3	.300	27	4	1	.969
Buhner, rf	4	13	2	3	9	0	0	2	2	3	0	6	.231	5	1	0	1.000
Blowers, 3b	3	5	0	1	1	0	0	0	0	0	0	3	.200	1	2	0	1.000
Martinez, dh	4	16	2	3	9	0	0	2	3	0	0	3	.188	0	0	0	.000
Cora, 2b	4	17	1	3	3	0	0	0	0	0	0	4	.176	7	11	0	1.000
Griffey, cf	4	15	0	2	2	0	0	0	2	1	0	3	.133	12	1	0	1.000
Ayala, p	1	0	0	0	0	0	0	0	0	0	0	0	.000	0	0	0	.000
Charlton, p	2	0	0	0	0	0	0	0	0	0	0	0	.000	1	0	0	1.000
Fassero, p	1	0	0	0	0	0	0	0	0	0	0	0	.000	1	4	0	1.000
Johnson, p	2	0	0	0	0	0	0	0	0	0	0	0	.000	0	3	0	1.000
Moyer, p	1	0	0	0	0	0	0	0	0	0	0	0	.000	2	1	0	1.000
Slocumb, p	2	0	0	0	0	0	0	0	0	0	0	0	.000	1	0	0	1.000
Spoljaric, p	2	0	0	0	0	0	0	0	0	0	0	0	.000	0	0	0	.000
Timlin, p	1	0	0	0	0	0	0	0	0	0	0	0	.000	0	0	0	.000
Wells, p	1	0	0	0	0	0	0	0	0	0	0	0	.000	0	0	0	.000
Wilkins, c-ph	1	0	0	0	0	0	0	0	0	0	1	0	.000	2	0	0	1.000
Gates, 3b-ph	2	4	0	0	0	0	0	0	0	0	0	0	.000	1	2	0	1.000
Wilson, c	4	13	0	0	0	0	0	0	0	0	0	9	.000	29	1	0	1.000
Totals	4	133	11	29	52	5	0	6	11	7	0	42	.218	105	42	1	.993

BALTIMORE ORIOLES' PITCHING RECORDS

Pitcher	G	GS	CG	IP	H	R	ER	HR	BB	IBB	SO	HB	WP	W	L	Pct.	ERA
Rhodes	1	0	0	2.1	0	0	0	0	0	0	4	0	0	0	0	.000	0.00
Myers	2	0	0	2.0	0	0	0	0	0	0	5	0	0	0	0	.000	0.00
Orosco	2	0	0	1.1	1	0	0	0	0	0	1	0	0	0	0	.000	0.00
Mills	1	0	0	1.0	1	0	0	0	0	0	1	0	0	0	0	.000	0.00
Mussina	2	2	0	14.0	7	3	3	3	3	0	16	0	0	2	0	1.000	1.93
Benitez	3	0	0	3.0	3	1	1	1	2	0	4	0	0	0	0	.000	3.00
Key	1	1	0	4.2	8	2	2	0	0	0	4	0	1	0	1	.000	3.86
Erickson	1	1	0	6.2	7	3	3	0	2	0	6	0	0	1	0	1.000	4.05
Mathews	1	0	0	1.0	2	2	2	2	0	0	1	0	0	0	0	.000	18.00
Totals	4	4	0	36.0	29	11	11	6	7	0	42	0	1	3	1	.750	2.75

No shutouts. Save—Myers.

SEATTLE MARINERS' PITCHING RECORDS

Pitcher	G	GS	CG	IP	H	R	ER	HR	BB	IBB	SO	HB	WP	W	L	Pct.	ERA
Charlton	2	0	0	2.1	2	0	0	0	0	0	1	0	0	0	0	.000	0.00
Spoljaric	2	0	0	1.2	4	0	0	0	0	0	1	0	0	0	0	.000	0.00
Wells	1	0	0	1.1	1	0	0	0	0	0	1	0	0	0	0	.000	0.00
Fassero	1	1	0	8.0	3	1	1	0	4	0	3	0	0	1	0	1.000	1.13
Slocumb	2	0	0	2.0	3	1	1	0	1	0	0	0	0	0	0	.000	4.50
Johnson	2	2	1	13.0	14	8	8	3	6	0	16	0	0	0	2	.000	5.54
Moyer	1	1	0	4.2	5	3	3	1	1	0	2	0	0	0	1	.000	5.79
Ayala	1	0	0	1.1	4	6	6	1	3	1	2	0	0	0	0	.000	40.50
Timlin	1	0	0	0.2	3	4	4	1	1	1	1	0	0	0	0	.000	54.00
Totals	4	4	1	35.0	39	23	23	6	16	2	27	0	0	1	3	.250	5.91

No shutouts or saves.

SCORE BY INNINGS

Baltimore	2	1	1	0	7	4	2	4	2—23
Seattle	2	1	1	1	1	0	2	0	3—11

MISCELLANEOUS STATISTICS

Sacrifice hits—Alomar, Reboulet.
Sacrifice flies—None.
Stolen bases—Griffey 2, Anderson, Hammonds.
Caught stealing—Bordick, Davis.
Double plays—Blowers, Cora and Sorrento; Bordick and Palmeiro; Rodriguez and Sorrento; Rodriguez, Cora and Sorrento.
Left on bases—Baltimore 6, 7, 6, 6—25; Seattle 4, 7, 5, 5—21.
Hit by pitcher—None.
Passed balls—Webster.
Balks—None.
Time of games—First game, 3:14; second game, 3:25; third game, 3:26; fourth game, 2:42.
Attendance—First game, 59,579; second game, 59,309; third game, 49,137; fourth game, 48,766.
Umpires—McClelland, Ford, Kaiser, Kosc, Phillips, Reed, Scott, Garcia, Cousins and Tschida.
Official scorers—Harland Beery, Jim Henneman.

CLEVELAND VS. NEW YORK

The bottom line: The Cleveland Indians claimed their second A.L. Championship Series berth in three years and dethroned the defending World Series-champion New York Yankees in a wild five-game Division Series filled with surprising comebacks and unexpected twists. The Central Division-champion Indians, who entered post-season play with the worst record (86-75) among A.L. playoff qualifiers, sloughed off a demoralizing Game 1 loss, broke through against the Yankees' vaunted bullpen in Game 4 and held off a frantic New York comeback bid in Game 5. The Yankees, who entered the series as the A.L. wild-card despite posting a 96-66 regular-season record, had been gunning for their record-extending 35th pennant and 24th World Series victory.

Why the Indians won: Because of the clutch work of a rookie pitcher and their Game 4 ability to break the stranglehold of a New York bullpen that had worked 11⅔ scoreless innings. Jaret Wright, the 21-year-old son of former big-league pitcher Clyde Wright, showed maturity beyond anybody's wildest expectations and posted victories in Games 2 and 5. The Game 4 breakthrough against Yankee right-handers Mariano Rivera and Ramiro Mendoza rallied the Indians from a 2-1 deficit to a 3-2 victory and put Wright at center stage in the first post-season game in Cleveland's long history where both teams faced elimination.

The turning points:

Game 1: A sixth-inning Yankee thunderclap wiped out the remnants of Cleveland's big early lead and gave New York first blood with an 8-6 victory at Yankee Stadium. Trailing 6-3 entering the inning, the Yankees cut their deficit to 6-4 on a Rey Sanchez single and vaulted into the lead on consecutive home runs by Tim Raines, Derek Jeter and Paul O'Neill—a post-season record. Raines' 415-foot blast off Eric Plunk tied a game the Indians had led 5-0 and 6-1. When Jeter connected off Plunk and O'Neill off Paul Assenmacher, the Yankees turned matters over to their reliable bullpen. The Indians had built their early lead with a five-run first inning keyed by Sandy Alomar's three-run homer off David Cone.

Game 2: Cleveland rebounded from its Game 1 stunner by raking Yankees lefthander Andy Pettitte for five runs in the fourth inning en route to a 7-5 victory. Wright, making his post-season debut, got off to an ominous beginning when he walked the bases loaded in the first inning and the Indians fell behind 3-0. But he settled down to hold the Yankees to three hits over six innings and the Indians vaulted ahead to stay in a fourth inning that was keyed by Matt Williams' two-run homer.

Game 3: The Yankees regained the momentum with a 6-1 victory at Cleveland's Jacobs Field, thanks to O'Neill's fourth-inning grand slam and David Wells' five-hit pitching. O'Neill, who had singled

home a run in the first inning, broke open a 2-1 game with his blast over the center-field wall off Chad Ogea after Indians starter Charles Nagy had walked the bases loaded. Wells took care of the rest, retiring the final 10 batters he faced after surrendering Dave Justice's double with two out in the sixth. He raised his post-season record to 4-0.

Game 4: The Yankees appeared to have matters well in hand when manager Joe Torre turned over a 2-1 lead to closer Rivera with one out in the eighth inning. New York relievers had not allowed a run in the series and the Yankees needed only five more outs to ensure a second straight Championship Series appearance. But lightning struck in the form of a Sandy Alomar game-tying homer in the eighth and the Indians completed their stunning comeback with a ninth-inning run off Mendoza. Marquis Grissom led off the ninth with a bloop single to right and Bip Roberts sacrificed him to second. Omar Vizquel's grounder hit Mendoza's glove and deflected past shortstop Jeter into left field, scoring Grissom and triggering a wild celebration at Jacobs Field. Starter Orel Hershiser, who allowed two first-inning runs, worked seven solid innings before Assenmacher and Mike Jackson finished up.

Game 5: Slugging first baseman Jim Thome made his presence felt with a sacrifice bunt and a seventh-inning defensive play that cut off a potential Yankee rally. Thome's fourth-inning bunt moved Alomar to third base, where he scored on a Tony Fernandez sacrifice fly to give the Indians a 4-0 lead. The Yankees had cut their deficit to 4-3 by the seventh, when Jeter led off with a single. Thome made a diving stab of O'Neill's hard hit grounder, got to his knees and threw Jeter out at second. With relievers Jackson, Assenmacher and Jose Mesa providing stellar work in relief of Wright, the Indians held on for the clinching victory.

Notable:

Yankees: The first-game crowd of 57,398 was the largest in the 22-year history of remodeled Yankee Stadium. . . . O'Neill's five RBIs in Game 3 were the most by a Yankee player in a playoff game since Thurman Munson drove in five during Game 5 of the 1978 World Series. His grand slam was the eighth in playoff history. . . . The Yankees entered the Division Series 15-5 at Jacobs Field. . . . Right-hander Doc Gooden made his first post-season start since 1988 in Game 4.

Indians: Wright was the first Indians rookie since 1948 to start a post-season game. Gene Bearden was a Cleveland starter in the fall classic against the Boston Braves. . . . Game 3 loser Nagy saw his 1997 record against the Yankees fall to 0-3 and his ERA rise to 15.63. . . . Cleveland's Game 4 victory snapped the Yankees' nine-game post-season road winning streak.

Quotable:

Yankees: Game 3 winner David Wells after the

Yankees had pulled within one victory of advancing to the ALCS: "It's party time. It's time to get down and dirty. It's three games and you're gone. This team doesn't want to go down early. They want to repeat.". . . Manager Torre, after the Yankees had lost in Game 5: "You're running and running, and all of a sudden there's a cliff. It's just a sudden stop. It's like you've crashed into a wall."

Indians: Game 5 winner Wright on the high-powered Cleveland crowd: "These fans were unbelievable. You can't tell me that they didn't make a difference last night and tonight. I guess they've been waiting a long time to beat the Yankees." . . . Infielder/outfielder Bip Roberts after Game 5: "They kept coming at us. I guess, since they were the world champions, they weren't going to go down easy. That was a heck of a game and a heck of a series."

GAME 1 BOX SCORE

NEW YORK 8, CLEVELAND 6

TUESDAY, SEPTEMBER 30, AT NEW YORK

Cleveland	AB	R	H	RBI	PO	A
Roberts, 2b	3	1	2	1	1	7
Vizquel, ss	3	0	1	0	4	2
Ramirez, rf	5	1	2	1	1	0
Thome, 1b	5	0	2	0	9	0
Justice, dh	4	1	1	0	0	0
M. Williams, 3b	4	1	0	0	1	2
Alomar, c	4	1	2	3	3	0
Giles, lf	4	0	0	0	3	0
Grissom, cf	4	1	1	0	2	0
Hershiser, p	0	0	0	0	0	1
Morman, p	0	0	0	0	0	0
Plunk, p	0	0	0	0	0	0
Assenmacher, p	0	0	0	0	0	0
Jackson, p	0	0	0	0	0	1
Totals	36	6	11	5	24	13

New York	AB	R	H	RBI	PO	A
Raines, dh	4	1	1	3	0	0
Jeter, ss	5	1	2	1	4	3
O'Neill, rf	3	1	1	1	2	0
B. Williams, cf	2	1	0	0	1	0
Martinez, 1b	4	1	2	1	9	3
Curtis, lf	2	0	1	0	1	0
Boggs, 3b	4	1	1	1	0	1
Hayes, 3b	0	0	0	0	0	0
Girardi, c	4	1	1	0	6	0
Sanchez, 2b	3	1	2	1	2	3
Cone, p	0	0	0	0	1	1
Mendoza, p	0	0	0	0	0	1
Stanton, p	0	0	0	0	0	0
Nelson, p	0	0	0	0	0	0
Rivera, p	0	0	0	0	1	0
Totals	31	8	11	8	27	12

Cleveland	5	0	0	1	0	0	0	0	0—6
New York	0	1	0	1	1	5	0	0	0—8

Cleveland	IP	H	R	ER	BB	SO
Hershiser (L)	4.1	6	3	3	2	1
Morman	0.0	0	0	0	1	0
Plunk (L)	1.1	4	4	4	0	1
Assenmacher	0.2	1	1	1	1	0
Jackson	1.2	0	0	0	1	1

New York	IP	H	R	ER	BB	SO
Cone	3.1	7	6	6	2	2
Mendoza (W)	3.1	1	0	0	0	2
Stanton	0.0	1	0	0	1	0
Nelson	1.0	1	0	0	1	0
Rivera (S)	1.1	1	0	0	0	1

DP—Cleveland 3, New York 1. LOB—Cleveland 9, New York 6. 2B—Justice, Sanchez. 3B—Grissom. HR—Alomar, Martinez, Raines, Jeter, O'Neill. SB—Roberts 2. SH—Vizquel. SF—Raines. HBP—By Cone (M.

Williams), by Assenmacher (B. Williams). WP—Cone. T—3:28. A—57,398. U—Tschida, plate; Morrison, first; Reed, second; Scott, third; Garcia, left field; Cousins, right field.

GAME 2 BOX SCORE

CLEVELAND 7, NEW YORK 5

THURSDAY, OCTOBER 2, AT NEW YORK

Cleveland	AB	R	H	RBI	PO	A
Roberts, lf	5	0	2	0	0	0
Vizquel, ss	5	2	3	0	2	1
Ramirez, rf	4	0	0	0	1	0
M. Williams, 3b	2	2	1	2	0	4
Justice, dh	4	1	1	1	0	0
Alomar, c	4	1	1	1	7	0
Thome, 1b	4	1	1	1	13	0
Fernandez, 2b	4	0	2	2	2	2
Grissom, cf	4	0	0	0	2	0
Wright, p	0	0	0	0	0	2
Jackson, p	0	0	0	0	0	0
Assenmacher, p	0	0	0	0	0	0
Mesa, p	0	0	0	0	0	0
Totals	36	7	11	7	27	9

New York	AB	R	H	RBI	PO	A
Raines, dh	5	0	1	0	0	0
Jeter, ss	4	2	2	1	4	3
O'Neill, rf	4	1	1	0	2	0
B. Williams, cf	3	2	1	0	1	0
Martinez, 1b	4	0	1	2	9	1
Hayes, 3b	3	0	1	1	0	2
Curtis, lf	3	0	0	0	2	0
Girardi, c	3	0	0	0	6	0
Stanley, ph	0	0	0	1	0	0
Fox, pr-2b	0	0	0	0	0	0
Sanchez, 2b	3	0	0	0	3	4
Boggs, ph	1	0	0	0	0	0
Posada, c	0	0	0	0	0	1
Pettitte, p	0	0	0	0	0	0
Boehringer, p	0	0	0	0	0	0
Lloyd, p	0	0	0	0	0	0
Nelson, p	0	0	0	0	0	0
Totals	33	5	7	5	27	12

Cleveland	0	0	0	5	2	0	0	0	0—7
New York	3	0	0	0	0	0	0	1	1—5

Cleveland	IP	H	R	ER	BB	SO
Wright (W)	6.0	3	3	3	4	5
Jackson	0.2	2	0	0	0	1
Assenmacher	0.2	0	1	1	1	0
Mesa	1.2	2	1	1	1	1

New York	IP	H	R	ER	BB	SO
Pettitte (L)	5.0	9	7	7	1	3
Boehringer	1.2	1	0	0	1	2
Lloyd	1.1	0	0	0	0	1
Nelson	1.0	1	0	0	0	0

E—Hayes, Wright, Boehringer. DP—Cleveland 1, New York 1. LOB—Cleveland 4, New York 9. 2B—Martinez, B. Williams, Fernandez. HR—M. Williams, Jeter. SB—Vizquel. SF—Hayes. HBP—By Mesa (Stanley). T—3:32. A—57,360. U—Morrison, plate; Reed, first; Scott, second; Garcia, third; Cousins, left field; Tschida, right field.

GAME 3 BOX SCORE

NEW YORK 6, CLEVELAND 1

SATURDAY, OCTOBER 4, AT CLEVELAND

New York	AB	R	H	RBI	PO	A
Raines, lf	2	2	0	0	3	0
Curtis, lf	1	0	0	0	1	0
Jeter, ss	3	2	0	0	3	3
O'Neill, rf	4	1	2	5	2	0
B. Williams, cf	4	0	0	0	1	0
Martinez, 1b	3	0	1	1	7	0
Fielder, dh	4	0	0	0	0	0
Hayes, 3b	4	0	0	0	1	4
Girardi, c	3	1	1	0	1	0
Sanchez, 2b	3	0	0	0	8	0
Wells, p	0	0	0	0	0	0
Totals	31	6	4	6	27	7

Cleveland	AB	R	H	RBI	PO	A
Roberts, lf	4	0	0	0	3	0
Seitzer, 1b	4	0	0	0	9	0
Ramirez, rf	4	0	0	0	1	0
M. Williams, 3b	4	1	1	0	1	2
Justice, dh	4	0	2	0	0	0
Alomar, c	4	0	0	0	2	1
Fernandez, 2b	3	0	0	1	4	2
Grissom, cf	3	0	1	0	6	0
Vizquel, ss	3	0	1	0	1	4
Nagy, p	0	0	0	0	0	1
Ogea, p	0	0	0	0	0	1
Totals	33	1	5	1	27	11

New York						
New York	1	0	1	4 0 0	0 0	0—6
Cleveland	0	1	0	0 0 0	0 0	0—1

New York	IP	H	R	ER	BB	SO
Wells (W)	9.0	5	1	1	0	1

Cleveland	IP	H	R	ER	BB	SO
Nagy (L)	3.2	2	5	4	6	1
Ogea	5.1	2	1	1	0	1

E—Nagy, Hayes. LOB—New York 5, Cleveland 5. 2B—Justice. HR—O'Neill. SB—Jeter. SH—Sanchez. T—2:59. A—45,274. U—Kaiser, plate; Kosc, first; Phillips, second; Roe, third; McClelland, left field; Ford, right field.

GAME 4 BOX SCORE

CLEVELAND 3, NEW YORK 2

SUNDAY, OCTOBER 5, AT CLEVELAND

New York	AB	R	H	RBI	PO	A
Raines, lf	4	0	1	0	1	0
Curtis, pr-lf	0	0	0	0	0	0
Jeter, ss	4	1	2	0	0	3
O'Neill, rf	4	1	2	1	2	0
B. Williams, cf	4	0	0	0	3	0
Martinez, 1b	3	0	0	0	9	0
Fielder, dh	4	0	1	1	0	0
Hayes, 3b	4	0	2	0	1	0
Girardi, c	3	0	0	0	8	0
Sanchez, 2b	4	0	1	0	1	4
Gooden, p	0	0	0	0	0	0
Lloyd, p	0	0	0	0	0	0
Nelson, p	0	0	0	0	0	0
Stanton, p	0	0	0	0	0	0
Rivera, p	0	0	0	0	0	0
Mendoza, p	0	0	0	0	0	0
Totals	34	2	9	2	25	7

Cleveland	AB	R	H	RBI	PO	A
Roberts, 2lf	4	0	0	0	1	1
Vizquel, ss	4	0	3	1	2	2
Ramirez, rf	4	0	0	0	0	0
Thome, 1b	4	0	0	0	12	1
Justice, dh	3	1	1	1	0	0
M. Williams, 3b	4	0	1	0	0	0
Alomar, c	4	1	2	1	8	0
Giles, lf	2	0	1	0	0	1
Fernandez, ph-2b	2	0	0	0	0	1
Grissom, cf	3	1	1	0	3	0
Hershiser, p	0	0	0	0	1	3
Assenmacher, p	0	0	0	0	0	0
Jackson, p	0	0	0	0	0	1
Totals	34	3	9	3	27	10

New York						
New York	2	0	0	0 0 0	0 0	0—2
Cleveland	0	1	0	0 0 0	0 1	1—3

New York	IP	H	R	ER	BB	SO
Gooden	5.2	5	1	1	3	5
Lloyd	0.0	0	0	0	0	0
Nelson	1.0	1	0	0	0	0

New York	IP	H	R	ER	BB	SO
Stanton	0.2	0	0	0	0	2
Rivera	0.2	1	1	1	0	0
Mendoza (L)	0.1	2	1	1	0	0

Cleveland	IP	H	R	ER	BB	SO
Hershiser	7.0	8	2	2	0	3
Assenmacher	0.2	1	0	0	0	2
Jackson (W)	1.1	0	0	0	0	2

E—Hayes. LOB—New York 7, Cleveland 10. 2B—Jeter, O'Neill, M. Williams. HR—Justice, Alomar. SB—Vizquel. SH—Girardi, Roberts. HBP—By Hershiser (Martinez). T—3:22. A—45,231. U—Kosc, plate; Phillips, first; Roe, second; McClelland, third; Ford, left field; Kaiser, right field.

GAME 5 BOX SCORE

CLEVELAND 4, NEW YORK 3

MONDAY, OCTOBER 6, AT CLEVELAND

New York	AB	R	H	RBI	PO	A
Raines, lf	4	1	1	0	3	0
Jeter, ss	5	0	1	0	1	3
O'Neill, rf	4	1	2	0	1	0
Pose, pr	0	0	0	0	0	0
B. Williams, cf	4	0	1	1	1	0
Martinez, 1b	4	0	0	0	14	2
Stanley, dh	4	1	3	0	0	0
Hayes, 32b	4	0	2	0	1	3
Fox, pr-2b	0	0	0	0	0	0
Girardi, c	2	0	0	0	0	0
Boggs, ph-3b	2	0	2	1	0	0
Sanchez, 2b	2	0	0	0	1	3
Posada, ph-c	2	0	0	0	1	0
Pettitte, p	0	0	0	0	1	4
Nelson, p	0	0	0	0	0	0
Stanton, p	0	0	0	0	0	0
Totals	37	3	12	2	24	17

Cleveland	AB	R	H	RBI	PO	A
Roberts, lf	3	0	2	0	0	0
Giles, lf	1	0	0	0	1	0
Vizquel, ss	3	1	1	0	3	5
Ramirez, rf	4	1	1	2	0	0
M. Williams, 3b	3	0	1	1	0	2
Justice, dh	4	0	0	0	0	0
Alomar, c	3	1	1	0	7	0
Thome, 1b	2	0	0	0	11	2
Fernandez, 2b	2	0	0	1	2	4
Grissom, cf	3	1	1	0	1	0
Wright, p	0	0	0	0	2	1
Jackson, p	0	0	0	0	0	0
Assenmacher, p	0	0	0	0	0	0
Mesa, p	0	0	0	0	0	0
Totals	28	4	7	4	27	15

New York						
New York	0	0	0	0 2 1	0 0	0—3
Cleveland	0	0	3	1 0 0	0 0	x—4

New York	IP	H	R	ER	BB	SO
Pettitte (L)	6.2	6	4	4	0	2
Nelson	1.0	0	0	0	1	0
Stanton	0.1	1	0	0	0	1

Cleveland	IP	H	R	ER	BB	SO
Wright W, 2-0	5.1	8	3	2	3	5
Jackson	*0.2	1	0	0	0	1
Assenmacher	1.1	0	0	0	0	0
Mesa (S)	1.2	3	0	0	0	1

*Pitched to one batter in seventh.

E—Alomar, Ramirez. DP—Cleveland 2. LOB—New York 10, Cleveland 4. 2B—Ramirez, Alomar, Stanley, O'Neill. SB—Raines 2, Vizquel 2. SH—Vizquel, Thome. SF—Fernandez. T—3:29. A—45,203. U—Phillips, plate; Roe, first; McClelland, second; Ford, third; Kaiser, left field; Kosc, right field.

STATISTICS

CLEVELAND INDIANS' BATTING AND FIELDING AVERAGES

Player, position	G	AB	R	H	TB	2B	3B	HR	RBI	BB	IBB	SO	Avg.	PO	A	E	Avg.
				BATTING											FIELDING		
Vizquel, ss	5	18	3	9	9	0	0	0	1	2	0	1	.500	12	14	0	1.000
Alomar, c	5	19	4	6	13	1	0	2	5	0	0	2	.316	28	1	1	.967
Roberts, 2b-lf	5	19	1	6	6	0	0	0	1	2	0	2	.316	5	8	0	1.000

1997 REVIEW A.L. Division Series

Player, position	G	AB	R	H	TB	2B	3B	HR	RBI	BB	IBB	SO	Avg.	PO	A	E	Avg.
Justice, dh	5	19	3	5	10	2	0	1	2	2	0	3	.263	0	0	0	.000
Grissom, cf	5	17	3	4	6	0	1	0	0	1	0	2	.235	14	0	0	1.000
M. Williams, 3b..............	5	17	4	4	8	1	0	1	3	3	0	3	.235	2	10	0	1.000
Thome, 1b	4	15	1	3	3	0	0	0	1	0	0	5	.200	44	3	0	1.000
Fernandez, 2b-ph	4	11	0	2	3	1	0	0	4	0	0	0	.182	8	9	0	1.000
Ramirez, rf	5	21	2	3	4	1	0	0	3	0	0	3	.143	3	0	1	.750
Giles, lf	3	7	0	1	1	0	0	0	0	0	0	1	.143	4	1	0	1.000
Assenmacher, p	4	0	0	0	0	0	0	0	0	0	0	0	.000	0	0	0	.000
Hershiser, p..................	2	0	0	0	0	0	0	0	0	0	0	0	.000	1	4	0	1.000
Jackson, p.....................	4	0	0	0	0	0	0	0	0	0	0	0	.000	0	1	0	1.000
Mesa, p	2	0	0	0	0	0	0	0	0	0	0	0	.000	0	1	0	1.000
Morman, p	1	0	0	0	0	0	0	0	0	0	0	0	.000	0	0	0	.000
Nagy, p	1	0	0	0	0	0	0	0	0	0	0	0	.000	0	1	1	.500
Ogea, p	1	0	0	0	0	0	0	0	0	0	0	0	.000	0	1	0	1.000
Plunk, p	1	0	0	0	0	0	0	0	0	0	0	0	.000	0	0	0	.000
Wright, p.......................	2	0	0	0	0	0	0	0	0	0	0	0	.000	2	3	1	.833
Seitzer, 1b	1	4	0	0	0	0	0	0	0	0	0	0	.000	9	0	0	1.000
Totals	5	167	21	43	63	6	1	4	20	10	0	22	.257	132	57	4	.979

NEW YORK YANKEES' BATTING AND FIELDING AVERAGES

Player, position	G	AB	R	H	TB	2B	3B	HR	RBI	BB	IBB	SO	Avg.	PO	A	E	Avg.
Stanley, ph-dh	2	4	1	3	4	1	0	0	1	0	0	1	.750	0	0	0	.000
Boggs, 3b-ph	3	7	1	3	3	0	0	0	2	0	0	0	.429	0	1	0	1.000
O'Neill, rf	5	19	5	8	16	2	0	2	7	3	0	0	.421	9	0	0	1.000
Jeter, ss	5	21	6	7	14	1	0	2	2	3	0	5	.333	12	15	0	1.000
Hayes, 3b-2b.................	5	15	0	5	5	0	0	0	1	0	0	2	.333	3	9	3	.800
Martinez, 1b	5	18	1	4	8	1	0	1	4	2	1	4	.222	48	6	0	1.000
Raines, dh-lf	5	19	4	4	7	0	0	1	3	3	1	1	.211	7	0	0	1.000
Sanchez, 2b	5	15	1	3	4	1	0	0	1	1	0	2	.200	15	14	0	1.000
Curtis, lf-pr	4	6	0	1	1	0	0	0	0	3	0	1	.167	4	0	0	1.000
Girardi, c	5	15	2	2	2	0	0	0	0	1	0	3	.133	21	2	0	1.000
Fielder, dh	2	8	0	1	1	0	0	0	1	0	0	3	.125	0	0	0	.000
B. Williams, cf...............	5	17	3	2	3	1	0	0	1	4	0	3	.118	7	0	0	1.000
Boehringer, p	1	0	0	0	0	0	0	0	0	0	0	0	.000	0	0	1	.000
Cone, p	1	0	0	0	0	0	0	0	0	0	0	0	.000	1	1	0	1.000
Fox, 2b-pr	2	0	0	0	0	0	0	0	0	0	0	0	.000	0	0	0	.000
Gooden, p	1	0	0	0	0	0	0	0	0	0	0	0	.000	0	0	0	.000
Lloyd, p........................	2	0	0	0	0	0	0	0	0	0	0	0	.000	0	0	0	.000
Mendoza, p	2	0	0	0	0	0	0	0	0	0	0	0	.000	0	1	0	1.000
Nelson, p.......................	4	0	0	0	0	0	0	0	0	0	0	0	.000	0	0	0	.000
Pettitte, p	2	0	0	0	0	0	0	0	0	0	0	0	.000	1	5	0	1.000
Pose, pr	1	0	0	0	0	0	0	0	0	0	0	0	.000	0	0	0	.000
Rivera, p	2	0	0	0	0	0	0	0	0	0	0	0	.000	1	0	0	1.000
Stanton, p	3	0	0	0	0	0	0	0	0	0	0	0	.000	0	0	0	.000
Wells, p........................	1	0	0	0	0	0	0	0	0	0	0	0	.000	0	0	0	.000
Posada, c-ph	2	2	0	0	0	0	0	0	0	0	0	1	.000	1	1	0	1.000
Totals	5	166	24	43	68	7	0	6	23	20	2	26	.259	130	55	4	.979

CLEVELAND INDIANS' PITCHING RECORDS

Pitcher	G	GS	CG	IP	H	R	ER	HR	BB	IBB	SO	HB	WP	W	L	Pct.	ERA
Jackson..........................	4	0	0	4.1	3	0	0	0	1	0	5	0	0	1	0	1.000	0.00
Ogea.............................	1	0	0	5.1	2	1	1	1	0	0	1	0	0	0	0	.000	1.69
Mesa..............................	2	0	0	3.1	5	1	1	1	1	0	2	1	0	0	0	.000	2.70
Hershiser	2	2	0	11.1	14	5	5	1	2	0	4	1	0	0	0	.000	3.97
Wright...........................	2	2	0	11.1	11	6	5	0	7	1	10	0	0	2	0	1.000	3.97
Assenmacher	4	0	0	3.1	2	2	2	1	2	0	2	1	0	0	0	.000	5.40
Nagy..............................	1	1	0	3.2	5	4	4	0	6	1	1	0	0	0	1	.000	9.82
Plunk.............................	1	0	0	1.1	4	4	4	2	0	0	1	0	0	0	1	.000	27.00
Morman	1	0	0	0.0	0	0	0	0	1	0	0	0	0	0	0	.000	0.00
Totals	5	5	0	44.0	43	24	22	6	20	2	26	3	0	3	2	.600	4.50

No shutouts. Save—Mesa.

NEW YORK YANKEES' PITCHING RECORDS

Pitcher	G	GS	CG	IP	H	R	ER	HR	BB	IBB	SO	HB	WP	W	L	Pct.	ERA
Nelson...........................	4	0	0	4.0	4	0	0	0	2	0	0	0	0	0	0	.000	0.00
Boehringer	1	0	0	1.2	1	0	0	0	1	0	2	0	0	0	0	.000	0.00
Lloyd.............................	2	0	0	1.1	0	0	0	0	0	0	1	0	0	0	0	.000	0.00
Stanton	3	0	0	1.0	1	0	0	0	1	0	3	0	0	0	0	.000	0.00
Wells.............................	1	1	1	9.0	5	1	1	0	0	0	1	0	0	1	0	1.000	1.00

Pitcher	G	GS	CG	IP	H	R	ER	HR	BB	IBB	SO	HB	WP	W	L	Pct.	ERA
Gooden	1	1	0	5.2	5	1	1	1	3	0	5	0	0	0	0	.000	1.59
Mendoza	2	0	0	3.2	3	1	1	0	0	0	2	0	0	1	1	.500	2.45
Rivera.............................	2	0	0	2.0	2	1	1	1	0	0	1	0	0	0	0	.000	4.50
Pettitte	2	2	0	11.2	15	11	11	1	1	0	5	0	0	0	2	.000	8.49
Cone..............................	1	1	0	3.1	7	6	6	1	2	0	2	1	1	0	0	.000	16.20
Totals	5	5	1	43.1	43	21	21	4	10	0	22	1	1	2	3	.400	4.36

No shutouts. Save—Rivera.

SCORE BY INNINGS

Cleveland...	5	2	3		7	2	0		0	1	1—21
New York..	6	1	1		5	3	6		0	1	1—24

MISCELLANEOUS STATISTICS

Sacrifice hits—Vizquel 2, Girardi, Roberts, Sanchez, Thome.
Sacrifice flies—Fernandez, Hayes, Raines.
Stolen bases—Vizquel 4, Raines 2, Roberts 2, Jeter.
Caught stealing—Grissom, Roberts.
Double plays—Roberts, Vizquel and Thome 2; Boggs, Sanchez and Martinez; Fernandez and Thome; Jeter and Martinez; Vizquel and
    Thome; M. Williams, Roberts and Thome; Wright, Fernandez, Vizquel and Thome.
Left on bases—Cleveland 9, 4, 5, 10, 4—32; New York 6, 9, 5, 7, 10—37.
Hit by pitcher—by Hershiser (Martinez), by Cone (M. Williams), by Assenmacher (B. Williams), by Mesa (Stanley).
Passed balls—None.
Balks—None.
Time of games—First game, 3:28; second game, 3:32; third game, 2:59; fourth game, 3:22; fifth game, 3:29.
Attendance—First game, 57,398; second game, 57,360; third game, 45,274; fourth game, 45,231; fifth game, 45,203.
Umpires—Tschida, Morrison, Reed, Scott, Garcia, Kaiser, Kosc, Phillips, Roe, McClelland and Ford.
Official scorers—Red Foley, Jim Ingraham, Hank Kozloski.

N.L. DIVISION SERIES
ATLANTA VS. HOUSTON

The bottom line: The Atlanta Braves earned a record sixth consecutive League Championship Series appearance with a quick-and-efficient three-game Division Series sweep of the Houston Astros in a battle between the East and Central division champions. The Braves, bidding for their fifth World Series berth of the decade, posted a 2-1 series-opening victory and methodically shut down Astros hitters behind the strong-armed tactics of their Greg Maddux, Tom Glavine and John Smoltz Cy Young threesome. Simply stated, the Astros were overmatched in their first post-season appearance since 1986. The Braves lifted their Division Series record to 9-1.

Why the Braves won: Because of the 1-2-3 pitching punch of Maddux, Glavine and Smoltz. That trio worked 24 innings, limited the Astros to five earned runs and shut down Houston's "Killer Bs" trio of Craig Biggio, Derek Bell and Jeff Bagwell, who combined for two hits and an .054 series average. The Astros managed only a .167 team average, which was inflated by a 3-for-5 plate performance by their pitchers. After the tense opening game, the Braves outscored the Astros 17-4 in the final two.

The turning points:

Game 1: The Braves' ability to manufacture two early runs against Houston 19-game winner Darryl Kile provided just enough fuel for Maddux's 2-1 victory at Atlanta's Turner Field. Center fielder Kenny Lofton created a first-inning run with his speed. He stretched a leadoff bloop hit into a double, moved to third on a fly ball to medium right field and scored on Chipper Jones' sacrifice fly to left. After Ryan Klesko hit the first pitch of the second inning into the right field bleachers to make the score 2-0, Kile shut down the Braves without a hit through the rest of his seven-inning stint. But that was enough support for Maddux, the four-time Cy Young Award winner who surrendered seven hits and only a fifth-inning run on Kile's single. Maddux, who held the Biggio-Bell-Bagwell threesome hitless in 12 at-bats, raised his 1997 daytime record to 10-0.

Game 2: With two out and nobody on base in the Braves' fifth inning, the Astros appeared to have the momentum that had evaded them in Game 1. After falling behind 3-0 on Jeff Blauser's third-inning three-run homer, Houston had fought back for a 3-3 tie and starting pitcher Mike Hampton appeared to be settling down. But Hampton inexplicably unraveled, as did Houston's hopes for a Division Series upset of the powerful Braves. Sixteen of Hampton's next 18 pitches missed the plate as walks to Chipper Jones, Fred McGriff, Javy Lopez and Andruw Jones forced in the lead run. Mike Magnante replaced Hampton and was greeted by Greg Colbrunn's

pinch single, increasing Atlanta's lead to 6-3. Five more sixth-inning runs, four of them unearned, gave Glavine more than enough cushion for a crushing 13-3 victory.

Game 3: The Braves took a 1-0 first-inning lead on Chipper Jones' long home run and then turned matters over to Smoltz, who struck out 11 and limited the Astros to three hits in an impressive 4-1 series-ending victory. Smoltz was masterful as he silenced the largest crowd (53,688) in the history of Houston's Astrodome and won his 10th post-season game, tying the record held by Whitey Ford and Dave Stewart. Smoltz needed only 104 pitches—77 were strikes—and never was in serious trouble. His only mistake came in the seventh when Chuckie Carr hit a home run into the right-field seats, cutting Atlanta's lead to 3-1 and giving the Astros brief hope. But all Houston could muster the rest of the way was a two-out Luis Gonzalez single in the ninth as Smoltz lifted his post-season record to 10-2.

Notable:

Astros: Houston has not won a playoff game since 1986, when it posted a 3-1 victory over the New York Mets in Game 4 of the N.L. Championship Series. . . . Hard-luck Game 1 loser Kile is used to coming out second best in head-to-head matchups with Maddux. In six career starts against the Braves ace, Kile is 1-4 with a 1.70 ERA. Maddux is 4-1 with a 1.08 ERA in games against Kile. . . . Houston's only run against Maddux was set up by slow-footed catcher Tony Eusebio, who singled and stole his first major league base before scoring on Kile's single. . . . Larry Dierker was the first rookie manager to take his team to the playoffs since Hal Lanier led the Astros to a post-season berth in 1986.

Braves: Atlanta failed to sell out either of its Division Series games against the Astros. The first-game crowd of 46,467 was about 3,000 short of Turner Field's capacity. The Game 2 crowd of 49,200 was several hundred short of capacity. . . . While Braves pitchers were holding the Astros to a .167 team batting average, Braves hitters weren't faring much better. They finished with a .217 mark. . . . As good as the Braves' pitchers were against the Astros, they were even better in their 1996 Division Series victory over the Los Angeles Dodgers. They compiled a 1.66 ERA against Houston; their ERA against the Dodgers was 0.96.

Quotable:

Astros: Manager Dierker, on his feelings after watching his team get swept in the Division Series: "Right now, I feel mostly disappointed. I don't feel happy about having a good season. I don't feel satisfied with losing three straight in the playoffs. It certainly leaves a sour taste in your mouth.". . . Hampton, on the wild streak that cost his team dearly in Game 2: "I was just trying to be a little too perfect and it wound up costing me. I probably just tried to nibble too much.". . . Kile, on his tough Game 1 loss to Maddux: "The only way you pitch better is if you win."

Braves: Smoltz, on his outstanding October success: "I've talked to Reggie (Jackson). This is the time of year. There's nobody I trust more than myself. When I'm in a car, I want to drive it. When I play golf, play basketball, I want the last shot.". . . Chipper Jones, on the Braves' subdued clubhouse after its sweep: "You didn't see a lot of jubilation. There are four steps. We've achieved two (winning the N.L. East and the Division Series). We've got two more to go."

GAME 1 BOX SCORE

ATLANTA 2, HOUSTON 1
TUESDAY, SEPTEMBER 30, AT ATLANTA

Houston	AB	R	H	RBI	PO	A
Biggio, 2b	4	0	0	0	1	1
Bell, rf	4	0	0	0	2	0
Bagwell, 1b	4	0	0	0	4	1
Gonzalez, lf	4	0	2	0	6	0
Spiers, 3b	4	0	0	0	0	0
Hidalgo, cf	3	0	0	0	2	0
Berry, ph	1	0	0	0	0	0
Eusebio, c	3	1	2	0	6	1
Gutierrez, ss	2	0	0	0	3	0
Kile, p	2	0	2	1	0	0
Abreu, ph	1	0	1	0	0	0
Springer, p	0	0	0	0	0	0
Martin, p	0	0	0	0	0	1
Totals	32	1	7	1	24	4

Atlanta	AB	R	H	RBI	PO	A
Lofton, cf	4	1	1	0	2	1
Lockhart, 2b	3	0	0	0	5	5
Graffanino, 2b	0	0	0	0	0	1
C. Jones, 3b	2	0	0	1	0	1
McGriff, 1b	3	0	0	0	11	2
Klesko, lf	3	1	1	1	2	0
A. Jones, rf	0	0	0	0	3	0
Tucker, rf	3	0	0	0	1	0
Bautista, lf	0	0	0	0	0	0
Perez, c	3	0	0	0	6	0
Blauser, ss	2	0	0	0	1	4
Maddux, p	2	0	0	0	1	1
Totals	25	2	2	2	27	15

Houston	0	0	0		0	1	0		0	0	0— 1
Atlanta	1	1	0		0	0	0		0	0	x— 2

Houston	IP	H	R	ER	BB	SO
Kile (L)	7.0	2	2	2	2	4
Springer	0.2	0	0	0	0	2
Martin	0.1	0	0	0	0	0

Atlanta	IP	H	R	ER	BB	SO
Maddux (W)	9.0	7	1	1	1	6

E—Biggio. DP—Atlanta 1. LOB—Houston 5, Atlanta 2. 2B—Lofton. HR—Klesko. SB—Eusebio, Abreu. SF—C. Jones. T—2:15. A—46,467. U—Bonin, plate; Rapuano, first; Reliford, second; Rippley, third; Wendelstedt, left field; Hernandez, right field.

GAME 2 BOX SCORE

ATLANTA 13, HOUSTON 3
WEDNESDAY, OCTOBER 1, AT ATLANTA

Houston	AB	R	H	RBI	PO	A
Biggio, 2b	4	0	1	0	1	3
Bell, rf	5	0	0	0	1	0
Bagwell, 1b	4	0	0	0	5	3
Gonzalez, lf	4	0	1	0	3	1
Hidalgo, cf	2	1	0	0	3	0
Magnante, p	0	0	0	0	0	0
Garcia, p	0	0	0	0	0	0
Lima, p	0	0	0	0	0	0
Howard, ph	0	0	0	0	0	0
Pena, c	0	0	0	0	2	0
Spiers, 3b	3	1	0	0	0	2
Gutierrez, ss	4	0	1	0	1	2
Ausmus, c	3	1	2	2	5	0
Abreu, ph	1	0	0	0	0	0
Wagner, p	0	0	0	0	0	0
Hampton, p	2	0	1	1	3	0
Carr, cf	1	0	0	0	0	0
Totals	33	3	6	3	24	11

Atlanta	AB	R	H	RBI	PO	A
Lofton, cf	4	1	0	0	2	0
Blauser, ss	5	2	2	3	1	3
C. Jones, 3b	2	2	1	0	1	1
McGriff, 1b	4	3	2	1	9	0
Lopez, c	3	2	1	1	7	0
A. Jones, rf	4	1	0	1	6	0
Klesko, lf	2	0	0	0	0	0
Colbrunn, ph	1	0	1	2	0	0
Bautista, lf	2	0	1	2	0	0
Graffanino, 2b	2	0	0	0	0	5
Glavine, p	3	2	2	0	1	1
Cather, p	1	0	0	0	0	0
Wohlers, p	0	0	0	0	0	0
Totals	33	13	10	10	27	11

Houston	0	0	0		3	0	0		0	0	0— 3
Atlanta	0	3	3		0	3	5		0	2	x—13

Houston	IP	H	R	ER	BB	SO
Hampton (L)	4.2	2	6	6	8	2
Magnante	1.0	4	3	1	0	2
Garcia	0.1	1	2	0	1	0
Lima	1.0	0	0	0	1	1
Wagner	1.0	3	2	2	0	2

Atlanta	IP	H	R	ER	BB	SO
Glavine (W)	6.0	5	3	3	5	4
Cather	2.0	0	0	0	1	2
Wohlers	1.0	1	0	0	0	1

E—Klesko, Bagwell, Gonzalez. DP—Houston 1. LOB—Houston 9, Atlanta 6. 2B—Ausmus, Lopez. HR—Blauser. SB—C. Jones. T—3:06. A—49,200. U—Rapuano, plate; Reliford, first; Rippley, second; Wendelstedt, third; Hernandez, left field; Bonin, right field.

GAME 3 BOX SCORE

ATLANTA 4, HOUSTON 1
FRIDAY, OCTOBER 3, AT HOUSTON

Atlanta	AB	R	H	RBI	PO	A
Lofton, cf	5	0	1	0	2	0
Lockhart, 2b	3	0	0	0	1	3
Graffanino, 2b	1	0	0	0	1	0
C. Jones, 3b	4	1	3	1	1	1
McGriff, 1b	2	1	0	0	7	0
Klesko, lf	3	1	1	0	1	0
Bautista, lf	1	0	0	0	0	0
Lopez, c	4	1	1	0	11	0
Tucker, rf	3	0	1	1	2	0
A. Jones, rf	1	0	0	0	1	0
Blauser, ss	3	0	1	1	0	3
Smoltz, p	4	0	0	0	0	0
Totals	34	4	8	3	27	7

Houston	AB	R	H	RBI	PO	A
Biggio, 2b	4	0	0	0	2	4
Bell, rf	4	0	0	0	0	0
Bagwell, 1b	4	0	1	0	8	2
Gonzalez, lf	4	0	1	0	4	0
Spiers, 3b	4	0	0	0	1	1
Carr, cf	3	1	1	1	2	0
Gutierrez, ss	2	0	0	0	1	3
Ausmus, c	2	0	0	0	8	0
Abreu, ph	0	0	0	0	0	0
Pena, c	0	0	0	0	0	0
Reynolds, p	1	0	0	0	1	1
Johnson, ph	1	0	0	0	0	0

Houston	AB	R	H	RBI	PO	A
Springer, p	0	0	0	0	0	0
Martin, p	0	0	0	0	0	0
Garcia, p	0	0	0	0	0	0
Howard, ph	1	0	0	0	0	0
Magnante, p	0	0	0	0	0	1
Totals	31	1	3	1	27	12

Atlanta									
Atlanta	1	1	0	0	0	0	1	1	0—4
Houston	0	0	0	0	0	0	1	0	0—1

Atlanta	IP	H	R	ER	BB	SO
Smoltz (W)	9.0	3	1	1	1	11

Houston	IP	H	R	ER	BB	SO
Reynolds (L)	6.0	5	2	2	1	5
Springer	1.0	2	1	1	1	1
Martin	0.1	1	1	0	1	0
Garcia	0.2	0	0	0	0	1
Magnante	1.0	0	0	0	0	0

E—Bagwell, Lockhart, C. Jones. DP—Atlanta 1, Houston 1. LOB—Atlanta 6, Houston 4. 2B—Klesko, Lopez. HR—C. Jones, Carr. PB—Ausmus. T—2:36. A—53:688. U—Hallion, plate; DeMuth, first; Tata, second; Gorman, third; Hirschbeck, left field; Darling, right field.

STATISTICS

ATLANTA BRAVES' BATTING AND FIELDING AVERAGES

Player, position	G	AB	R	H	TB	2B	3B	HR	RBI	BB	IBB	SO	Avg.	PO	A	E	Avg.
Colbrunn, ph	1	1	0	1	1	0	0	0	2	0	0	0	1.000	0	0	0	.000
Glavine, p	1	3	2	2	2	0	0	0	0	0	0	0	.667	1	1	0	1.000
C. Jones, 3b	3	8	3	4	7	0	0	1	2	3	0	2	.500	2	3	1	.833
Bautista, lf	3	3	0	1	1	0	0	0	2	0	0	1	.333	0	0	0	.000
Blauser, ss	3	10	2	3	6	0	0	1	4	2	0	2	.300	2	10	0	1.000
Lopez, c	2	7	3	2	4	2	0	0	1	2	0	1	.286	18	0	0	1.000
Klesko, lf	3	8	2	2	6	1	0	1	1	0	0	2	.250	3	0	1	.750
McGriff, 1b	3	9	4	2	2	0	0	0	1	3	0	2	.222	27	2	0	1.000
Tucker, rf	2	6	0	1	1	0	0	0	1	0	0	1	.167	3	0	0	1.000
Lofton, cf	3	13	2	2	3	1	0	0	0	1	0	1	.154	6	1	0	1.000
Wohlers, p	1	0	0	0	0	0	0	0	0	0	0	0	.000	0	0	0	.000
Cather, p	1	1	0	0	0	0	0	0	0	0	0	1	.000	0	0	0	.000
Maddux, p	1	2	0	0	0	0	0	0	0	1	0	1	.000	1	1	0	1.000
Graffanino, 2b	3	3	0	0	0	0	0	0	0	2	0	1	.000	1	6	0	1.000
Perez, c	1	3	0	0	0	0	0	0	0	0	0	1	.000	6	0	0	1.000
Smoltz, p	1	4	0	0	0	0	0	0	0	0	0	1	.000	0	0	0	.000
A. Jones, rf	3	5	1	0	0	0	0	0	1	1	0	1	.000	10	0	0	1.000
Lockhart, 2b	2	6	0	0	0	0	0	0	0	0	0	1	.000	1	8	1	.900
Totals	3	92	19	20	33	4	0	3	15	15	0	20	.217	81	32	3	.974

HOUSTON ASTROS' BATTING AND FIELDING AVERAGES

Player, position	G	AB	R	H	TB	2B	3B	HR	RBI	BB	IBB	SO	Avg.	PO	A	E	Avg.
Kile, p	1	2	0	2	2	0	0	0	1	0	0	0	1.000	0	0	0	.000
Eusebio, c	1	3	1	2	2	0	0	0	0	0	0	1	.667	6	1	0	1.000
Hampton, p	1	2	0	1	1	0	0	0	1	0	0	0	.500	3	0	0	1.000
Ausmus, c	2	5	1	2	3	1	0	0	2	0	0	1	.400	13	0	0	1.000
Gonzalez, lf	3	12	0	4	4	0	0	0	0	0	0	1	.333	13	1	1	.933
Abreu, ph	3	3	0	1	1	0	0	0	0	0	0	2	.333	0	0	0	.000
Carr, cf	2	4	1	1	4	0	0	1	1	1	0	3	.250	2	0	0	1.000
Gutierrez, ss	3	8	0	1	1	0	0	0	0	2	0	1	.125	5	5	0	1.000
Bagwell, 1b	3	12	0	1	1	0	0	0	0	0	0	5	.083	17	6	2	.920
Biggio, 2b	3	12	0	1	1	0	0	0	0	1	0	0	.083	4	8	1	.923
Garcia, p	2	0	0	0	0	0	0	0	0	0	0	0	.000	0	0	0	.000
Lima, p	1	0	0	0	0	0	0	0	0	0	0	0	.000	0	0	0	.000
Magnante, p	2	0	0	0	0	0	0	0	0	0	0	0	.000	0	1	0	1.000
Martin, p	2	0	0	0	0	0	0	0	0	0	0	0	.000	0	1	0	1.000
Pena, c	2	0	0	0	0	0	0	0	0	0	0	0	.000	2	0	0	1.000
Springer, p	2	0	0	0	0	0	0	0	0	0	0	0	.000	0	0	0	.000
Wagner, p	1	0	0	0	0	0	0	0	0	0	0	0	.000	0	0	0	.000
Berry, ph	1	1	0	0	0	0	0	0	0	0	0	0	.000	0	0	0	.000
Howard, ph	2	1	0	0	0	0	0	0	0	0	0	1	.000	0	0	0	.000
Johnson, ph	1	1	0	0	0	0	0	0	0	0	0	1	.000	0	0	0	.000
Reynolds, p	1	1	0	0	0	0	0	0	0	0	0	1	.000	1	1	0	1.000
Hidalgo, cf	2	5	1	0	0	0	0	0	0	1	0	2	.000	5	0	0	1.000
Spiers, 3b	3	11	1	0	0	0	0	0	0	1	0	2	.000	1	3	0	1.000
Bell, rf	3	13	0	0	0	0	0	0	0	0	0	3	.000	3	0	0	1.000
Totals	3	96	5	16	20	1	0	1	5	8	0	24	.167	75	27	4	.962

ATLANTA BRAVES' PITCHING RECORDS

Pitcher	G	GS	CG	IP	H	R	ER	HR	BB	IBB	SO	HB	WP	W	L	Pct.	ERA
Cather	1	0	0	2.0	0	0	0	0	1	0	2	0	0	0	0	.000	0.00
Wohlers	1	0	0	1.0	1	0	0	0	0	0	1	0	0	0	0	.000	0.00
Maddux	1	1	1	9.0	7	1	1	0	1	0	6	0	0	1	0	1.000	1.00

Pitcher	G	GS	CG	IP	H	R	ER	HR	BB	IBB	SO	HB	WP	W	L	Pct.	ERA
Smoltz....................	1	1	1	9.0	3	1	1	1	1	0	11	0	0	1	0	1.000	1.00
Glavine..................	1	1	0	6.0	5	3	3	0	5	0	4	0	0	1	0	1.000	4.50
Totals	3	3	2	27.0	16	5	5	1	8	0	24	0	0	3	0	1.000	1.67

No shutouts or saves.

HOUSTON ASTROS' PITCHING RECORDS

Pitcher	G	GS	CG	IP	H	R	ER	HR	BB	IBB	SO	HB	WP	W	L	Pct.	ERA
Garcia....................	2	0	0	1.0	1	2	0	0	1	0	1	0	0	0	0	.000	0.00
Lima......................	1	0	0	1.0	0	0	0	0	1	0	1	0	0	0	0	.000	0.00
Martin	2	0	0	0.2	1	1	0	0	1	0	0	0	0	0	0	.000	0.00
Kile	1	1	0	7.0	2	2	2	1	2	0	4	0	0	0	1	.000	2.57
Reynolds................	1	1	0	6.0	5	2	2	1	1	0	5	0	0	0	1	.000	3.00
Magnante................	2	0	0	2.0	4	3	1	0	0	0	2	0	0	0	0	.000	4.50
Springer.................	2	0	0	1.2	2	1	1	0	1	0	3	0	0	0	0	.000	5.40
Hampton	1	1	0	4.2	2	6	6	1	8	0	2	0	0	0	1	.000	11.57
Wagner..................	1	0	0	1.0	3	2	2	0	0	0	2	0	0	0	0	.000	18.00
Totals	3	3	0	25.0	20	19	14	3	15	0	20	0	0	0	3	.000	5.04

No shutouts or saves.

SCORE BY INNINGS

Atlanta...2	2	3		0	3	5		1	3	0—19
Houston 0	0	0		3	1	0		1	0	0 — 5

MISCELLANEOUS STATISTICS

Sacrifice hits—None.
Sacrifice flies—C. Jones.
Stolen bases—Abreu, Eusebio, C. Jones.
Caught stealing—Lofton.
Double plays—Biggio, Gutierrez and Bagwell; Blauser, Lockhart and McGriff; Gutierrez, Biggio and Bagwell; Lockhart, Blauser and McGriff.
Left on bases—Atlanta 2, 6, 6—14; Houston 5, 9, 4—18.
Hit by pitcher—None.
Passed balls—Ausmus.
Balks—None.
Time of games—First game, 2:15; second game, 3:06; third game, 2:36.
Attendance—First game, 46,467; second game, 49,200; third game, 53,688.
Umpires—Bonin, Rapuano, Reliford, Rippley, Wendelstedt, Hallion, DeMuth, Tata and Gorman.
Official scorers—Mark Frederickson, Ivy McLemore.

FLORIDA VS. SAN FRANCISCO

HIGHLIGHTS

The bottom line: The Florida Marlins, making the most of their first post-season opportunity, swept past the San Francisco Giants in the Division Series and claimed a Championship Series berth against the East Division-rival Atlanta Braves. The wild-card Marlins won the first two games with dramatic ninth-inning hits and put the West Division-champion Giants away in Game 3 with one sixth-inning swing of the bat. En route to becoming the youngest expansion team to win a playoff series, the 5-year-old Marlins extended the Giants' post-season losing streak to seven games. The Giants won the 1989 N.L. Championship Series before suffering a four-game World Series sweep by the Oakland A's.

Why the Marlins won: Because of a near-perfect combination of clutch hitting and pitching. "That was the story of the series," said Giants manager Dusty Baker. "They got clutch two-out hits. Whatever they needed, they got." Game 1 was decided by shortstop Edgar Renteria's two-out, ninth-inning single. Game 2 ended when Moises Alou lined a no-out, ninth-inning single to center. Game 3 took a dramatic twist when Devon White drove a two-out, sixth-inning grand slam into the left-field

seats at San Francisco's 3Com Park. Starters Kevin Brown and Alex Fernandez were solid in the first and third games. Livan Hernandez, the 21-year-old Cuban defector, contributed four innings of clutch relief work in Game 2.

The turning points:

Game 1: First baseman Jeff Conine's sixth-inning save might have been just as important as his contribution to the ninth-inning rally that produced a 2-1 victory. Conine made a diving stab of a Darryl Hamilton ground ball down the line, saving a run and preserving a scoreless tie. Then, after San Francisco's Bill Mueller and Florida's Charles Johnson traded seventh-inning solo home runs, Conine set up the winning rally with a leadoff single in the ninth. The verdict was not delivered until Renteria, batting with two out and the bases loaded, touched off a wild celebration at Pro Player Stadium when he drove a single through the right side of the infield, scoring Johnson. It marked the seventh time in 1997 that Renteria had delivered a winning hit in Florida's last at-bat. The hit, off Giants reliever Roberto Hernandez, made a winner of Dennis Cook, who pitched two scoreless innings in support of Brown's four-hit, seven-inning effort.

Game 2: The Marlins staged their second straight

ninth-inning rally, only this time Gary Sheffield and Alou took center stage. After the Giants had scored a solo run in the top of the ninth to forge a 6-6 tie, Sheffield led off the bottom of the inning with a single and surprised Giants reliever Hernandez by stealing second base. After Bobby Bonilla walked, Alou ended his 0-for-8 series slump by lining a 2-1 pitch to center field and Sheffield raced home, beating a strong throw from Dante Powell that caromed sideways off the mound. Sheffield had three hits, including a solo home run in the sixth inning. Bonilla also homered for the Marlins while catcher Brian Johnson went deep for the Giants.

Game 3: Lefthander Wilson Alvarez was sailing along with a 1-0 lead in the sixth inning when the roof caved in on the Giants' magical season. With two out, Alou singled, Conine singled off third baseman Mueller's glove and Johnson walked, loading the bases. White lined Alvarez's 113th pitch into the left-field bleachers, putting Fernandez in position to win his first game since August 30. Fernandez, who surrendered only a pair of solo home runs to Giants second baseman Jeff Kent, left after seven innings with a 4-2 lead and the Marlins added two runs in the eighth. Relievers Cook and Robb Nen completed the 6-2 victory.

Notable:
Giants: Mueller's Game 1 homer came in his first post-season game. He became the first Giants player to perform that feat since Tito Fuentes in 1971. . . . Hernandez and Alvarez, two of the three pitchers obtained from the Chicago White Sox in a late-season trade, surrendered the deciding hits in all three games. Hernandez finished the series with an unsightly 20.25 ERA. . . . The Giants scored first in each of the three games. . . . The crowd of 57,188 at the series finale at 3Com Park was the largest in San Francisco since opening day of 1994.
Marlins: The crowd of 42,167 at Pro Player Stadium for Florida's first playoff game was 2,519 below capacity. . . . When the Marlins erased 1-0, 3-2 and 4-3 Game 2 deficits, it marked the 45th time this season they had come from behind to win. . . . White's Game 3 grand slam was his third playoff home run. He hit two in 1993 when Toronto captured the World Series. . . . The Game 3 pitching matchup featured two long-time White Sox teammates: Alvarez vs. Fernandez. . . . Manager Jim Leyland finally won his first post-season series after three NLCS losses as manager of the Pittsburgh Pirates.

Quotable:
Giants: Reliever Rod Beck after his team had been swept out of the playoffs: "This was just a magical year, not just for me but for everyone in the clubhouse. No one expected us to do anything. And 20 other teams were watching us play baseball tonight. So I think we have a lot to be proud of.". . . Second baseman Kent: "I still don't feel like it's over. The Florida Marlins played better than we did for three given days. We have nothing to be ashamed of. We've just got to turn the page. It's over."

Marlins: Second-game starter Al Leiter, after watching his team win in the ninth inning for the second straight day: "If you could script these games, I don't think you could write a better story." . . . Game 3 winner Fernandez: "This is very special for everyone in south Florida. Everyone on our team has worked so hard to get to this point. It's just an unbelievable feeling."

GAME 1 BOX SCORE

FLORIDA 2, SAN FRANCISCO 1
TUESDAY, SEPTEMBER 30, AT FLORIDA

San Francisco	AB	R	H	RBI	PO	A
Hamilton, cf	4	0	0	0	3	0
Mueller, 3b	4	1	1	1	1	2
Bonds, lf	4	0	1	0	3	0
Snow, 1b	3	0	0	0	3	0
Kent, 2b	3	0	0	0	4	3
Javier, rf	3	0	1	0	6	0
Vizcaino, ss	3	0	0	0	0	0
B. Johnson, c	3	0	0	0	6	0
Rueter, p	2	0	1	0	0	1
Hill, ph	1	0	0	0	0	0
Tavarez, p	0	0	0	0	0	0
R. Hernandez, p	0	0	0	0	0	0
Totals	30	1	4	1	26	6

Florida	AB	R	H	RBI	PO	A
White, cf	5	0	0	0	1	0
Renteria, ss	5	0	2	1	1	3
Sheffield, rf	2	1	0	0	2	0
Bonilla, 3b	3	0	1	0	0	2
Alou, lf	4	0	0	0	2	0
Conine, 1b	4	0	1	0	9	2
C. Johnson, c	3	2	1	1	8	1
Counsell, 2b	2	0	1	0	2	1
Brown, p	2	0	0	0	2	1
Abbott, ph	1	0	0	0	0	0
Cook, p	0	0	0	0	0	0
Eisenreich, ph	0	0	0	0	0	0
Totals	31	2	7	2	27	10

San Francisco	0	0 0	0 0 0	1 0	0—1
Florida	0	0 0	0 0 0	1 0	1—2

San Francisco	IP	H	R	ER	BB	SO
Rueter	7.0	4	1	1	3	5
Tavarez (L)	*1.0	2	1	1	1	0
R. Hernandez	0.2	1	0	0	1	0

Florida	IP	H	R	ER	BB	SO
Brown	7.0	4	1	1	0	5
Cook (W)	2.0	0	0	0	0	3

*Pitched to two batters in ninth.
DP—San Francisco 1. LOB—San Francisco 2, Florida 9. 2B—Bonds, Sheffield. HR—Mueller, C. Johnson, SH—Counsell. HBP—By Tavarez (C. Johnson). T—2:48. A—42,167. U—Hirschbeck, plate; Darling, first; Hallion, second; DeMuth, third; Tata, left field; Gorman, right field.

GAME 2 BOX SCORE

FLORIDA 7, SAN FRANCISCO 6
WEDNESDAY, OCTOBER 1, AT FLORIDA

San Francisco	AB	R	H	RBI	PO	A
Javier, crf	5	2	4	1	1	0
Vizcaino, ss	4	1	1	0	1	5
Bonds, lf	4	0	2	2	1	0
Kent, 12b	3	0	0	0	14	1
Lewis, 2b	5	0	3	1	1	3
R. Hernandez, p	0	0	0	0	0	0
Hill, rf	3	0	0	0	1	0
Rodriguez, p	0	0	0	0	0	0
Powell, cf	0	0	0	0	0	0
Mueller, 3b	4	0	0	0	0	5
B. Johnson, c	3	2	1	1	5	0
Estes, p	1	0	0	0	0	1
Henry, p	0	0	0	0	0	0
Benard, ph	1	0	0	0	0	0

San Francisco	AB	R	H	RBI	PO	A
Tavarez, p	0	0	0	0	0	0
Hamilton, cf	1	0	0	0	0	0
Snow, 1b	0	0	0	0	0	0
Totals	34	6	11	5	24	15

Florida	AB	R	H	RBI	PO	A
Abbott, 2b	4	0	1	0	2	3
Counsell, 2b	1	0	0	0	1	0
Renteria, ss	3	1	0	0	3	5
Sheffield, rf	4	3	3	1	1	0
Bonilla, 3b	4	1	3	3	2	1
Alou, lf	5	0	1	1	2	0
Conine, 1b	3	1	1	0	8	0
C. Johnson, c	3	1	0	0	7	1
White, cf	2	0	0	0	1	0
Leiter, p	1	0	0	0	0	1
Arias, ph	1	0	1	1	0	0
L. Hernandez, p	1	0	0	0	0	0
Cangelosi, ph	1	0	0	0	0	0
Nen, p	0	0	0	0	0	0
Totals	33	7	10	6	27	11

San Francisco	1	1	1	1	0	0	1	0	1—6
Florida	2	0	1	2	0	1	0	0	1—7

San Francisco	IP	H	R	ER	BB	SO
Estes	*3.0	5	5	5	4	3
Henry	2.0	1	0	0	3	2
Tavarez	2.0	2	1	1	0	0
Rodriguez	1.0	0	0	0	0	0
R. Hernandez (L)	0.0	2	1	1	1	0

Florida	IP	H	R	ER	BB	SO
Leiter	4.0	7	4	4	3	3
L. Hernandez	4.0	3	1	1	0	3
Nen (W)	1.0	1	1	0	1	1

Pitched to four batters in fourth.
E—Conine, Counsell. DP—San Francisco 1, Florida 1. LOB—San Francisco 8, Florida 10. 2B—Javier, Conine, Vizcaino, Bonds. HR—Bonilla, B. Johnson, Sheffield. SB—Javier, Bonds, Sheffield. SH—Vizcaino, Estes. SF—Bonds. WP—Leiter. T—3:12. A—41,283. U—Darling, plate; Hallion, first; DeMuth, second; Tata, third; Gorman, left field; Hirschbeck, right field.

GAME 3 BOX SCORE

FLORIDA 6, SAN FRANCISCO 2
FRIDAY, OCTOBER 3, AT SAN FRANCISCO

Florida	AB	R	H	RBI	PO	A
Abbott, 2b	3	0	1	0	1	3
Counsell, 2b	2	0	1	1	2	1

Florida	AB	R	H	RBI	PO	A
Renteria, ss	5	0	0	0	5	3
Sheffield, rf	3	0	1	0	3	0
Wehner, pr-rf	0	0	0	0	0	0
Bonilla, 3b	5	0	0	0	1	2
Alou, lf	5	1	2	0	1	0
Conine, 1b	4	2	2	0	7	1
C. Johnson, c	2	2	1	1	6	1
White, cf	4	1	2	4	1	0
Fernandez, p	2	0	0	0	0	1
Eisenreich, ph	0	0	0	0	0	0
Cook, p	0	0	0	0	0	0
Nen, p	0	0	0	0	0	0
Totals	35	6	10	6	27	12

San Francisco	AB	R	H	RBI	PO	A
Javier, cf	4	0	0	0	4	0
Mueller, 3b	4	0	2	0	1	2
Bonds, lf	4	0	0	0	2	0
Kent, 2b	4	2	3	2	1	3
Snow, 1b	3	0	1	0	9	0
Hill, rf	3	0	0	0	1	0
Vizcaino, ss	4	0	1	0	2	5
B. Johnson, c	4	0	0	0	7	0
Alvarez, p	2	0	0	0	0	0
Tavarez, p	0	0	0	0	0	0
Benard, ph	1	0	0	0	0	0
R. Hernandez, p	0	0	0	0	0	0
Rodriguez, p	0	0	0	0	0	0
Beck, p	0	0	0	0	0	0
Berryhill, ph	1	0	0	0	0	0
Totals	34	2	7	2	27	10

Florida	0	0	0	0	0	4	0	2	0—6
San Francisco	0	0	0	1	0	1	0	0	0—2

Florida	IP	H	R	ER	BB	SO
Fernandez (W)	7.0	7	2	2	0	5
Cook	*1.0	0	0	0	1	0
Nen	1.0	0	0	0	1	1

San Francisco	IP	H	R	ER	BB	SO
Alvarez (L)	6.0	6	4	4	4	4
Tavarez	1.0	0	0	0	0	0
R. Hernandez	0.2	2	2	2	1	1
Rodriguez	0.0	1	0	0	0	0
Beck	1.1	1	0	0	0	1

*Pitched to one batter in ninth.
E—Renteria 2. DP—Florida 2, San Francisco 2. LOB—Florida 8, San Francisco 7. 2B—Alou, C. Johnson, Counsell. HR—Kent 2, White. WP—Nen. T—3:22. A—57,188. U—Reliford, plate; Rippley, first; Wendelstedt, second; Hernandez, third; Bonin, left field; Rapuano, right field.

STATISTICS

FLORIDA MARLINS' BATTING AND FIELDING AVERAGES

Player, position	G	AB	R	H	TB	2B	3B	HR	RBI	BB	IBB	SO	Avg.	PO	A	E	Avg.
Arias, ph	1	1	0	1	1	0	0	0	0	0	0	0	1.000	0	0	0	.000
Sheffield, rf	3	9	3	5	9	1	0	1	1	5	0	0	.556	6	0	0	1.000
Counsell, 2b	3	5	0	2	3	1	0	0	1	1	0	0	.400	5	2	1	.875
Conine, 1b	3	11	3	4	5	1	0	0	0	1	0	0	.364	24	3	1	.964
Bonilla, 3b	3	12	1	4	7	0	0	1	3	2	1	1	.333	3	5	0	1.000
Abbott, ph-2b	3	8	0	2	2	0	0	0	0	0	0	0	.250	8	6	0	1.000
C. Johnson, c	3	8	5	2	6	1	0	1	2	3	0	2	.250	21	3	0	1.000
Alou, lf	3	14	1	3	4	1	0	0	1	0	0	3	.214	5	0	0	1.000
White, cf	3	11	1	2	5	0	0	1	4	2	1	3	.182	3	0	0	1.000
Renteria, ss	3	13	1	2	2	0	0	0	1	2	0	4	.154	9	11	2	.909
Cook, p	2	0	0	0	0	0	0	0	0	0	0	0	.000	0	0	0	.000
Eisenreich, ph	2	0	0	0	0	0	0	0	0	0	2	1	.000	0	0	0	.000
Nen, p	2	0	0	0	0	0	0	0	0	0	0	0	.000	0	0	0	.000
Wehner, rf-pr	1	0	0	0	0	0	0	0	0	0	0	0	.000	0	0	0	.000
Cangelosi, ph	1	0	0	0	0	0	0	0	0	0	0	0	.000	0	0	0	.000
L. Hernandez, p	1	1	0	0	0	0	0	0	0	0	0	0	.000	0	0	0	.000
Leiter, p	1	1	0	0	0	0	0	0	0	0	0	0	.000	0	1	0	1.000
Brown, p	1	0	0	0	0	0	0	0	0	0	0	2	.000	2	1	0	1.000
Fernandez, p	1	2	0	0	0	0	0	0	0	0	1	1	.000	0	1	0	1.000
Totals	3	99	15	27	44	5	0	4	14	19	3	16	.273	81	33	4	.966

SAN FRANCISCO GIANTS' BATTING AND FIELDING AVERAGES

Player, position	G	AB	R	H	TB	2B	3B	HR	RBI	BB	IBB	SO	Avg.	PO	A	E	Avg.
Lewis, 2b	1	5	0	3	3	0	0	0	1	0	0	0	.600	1	3	0	1.000
Rueter, p	1	2	0	1	1	0	0	0	0	0	0	0	.500	0	1	0	1.000
Javier, rf-cf	3	12	2	5	6	1	0	0	1	0	0	2	.417	11	0	0	1.000
Kent, 2b-1b	3	10	2	3	9	0	0	2	2	2	0	1	.300	19	7	0	1.000
Bonds, lf	3	12	0	3	5	2	0	0	2	0	0	3	.250	6	0	0	1.000
Mueller, 3b	3	12	1	3	6	0	0	1	1	0	0	0	.250	2	9	0	1.000
Vizcaino, ss	3	11	1	2	3	1	0	0	0	0	0	5	.182	3	10	0	1.000
Snow, 1b	3	6	0	1	1	0	0	0	0	1	0	1	.167	12	0	0	1.000
B. Johnson, c	3	10	2	1	4	0	0	1	1	1	0	4	.100	18	0	0	1.000
Beck, p	1	0	0	0	0	0	0	0	0	0	0	0	.000	0	0	0	.000
Henry, p	1	0	0	0	0	0	0	0	0	0	0	0	.000	0	0	0	.000
R. Hernandez, p	3	0	0	0	0	0	0	0	0	0	0	0	.000	0	0	0	.000
Powell, cf	1	0	0	0	0	0	0	0	0	0	0	0	.000	0	0	0	.000
Rodriguez, p	2	0	0	0	0	0	0	0	0	0	0	0	.000	0	0	0	.000
Tavarez, p	3	0	0	0	0	0	0	0	0	0	0	0	.000	0	0	0	.000
Berryhill, ph	1	1	0	0	0	0	0	0	0	0	0	0	.000	0	0	0	.000
Estes, p	1	1	0	0	0	0	0	0	0	0	0	1	.000	0	1	0	1.000
Alvarez, p	1	2	0	0	0	0	0	0	0	0	0	0	.000	0	0	0	.000
Benard, ph	2	2	0	0	0	0	0	0	0	0	0	1	.000	0	0	0	.000
Hamilton, cf	2	5	1	0	0	0	0	0	0	0	0	1	.000	3	0	0	1.000
Hill, ph-rf	3	7	0	0	0	0	0	0	0	2	0	2	.000	2	0	0	1.000
Totals	3	98	9	22	38	4	0	4	8	6	0	21	.224	77	31	0	1.000

FLORIDA MARLINS' PITCHING RECORDS

Pitcher	G	GS	CG	IP	H	R	ER	HR	BB	IBB	SO	HB	WP	W	L	Pct.	ERA
Cook	2	0	0	3.0	0	0	0	0	1	0	3	0	0	1	0	1.000	0.00
Nen	2	0	0	2.0	1	1	0	0	2	0	2	0	1	1	0	1.000	0.00
Brown	1	1	0	7.0	4	1	1	1	0	0	5	0	0	0	0	.000	1.29
L. Hernandez	1	0	0	4.0	3	1	1	0	0	0	3	0	0	0	0	.000	2.25
Fernandez	1	1	0	7.0	7	2	2	2	0	0	5	0	0	1	0	1.000	2.57
Leiter	1	1	0	4.0	7	4	4	1	3	0	3	1	0	0	0	.000	9.00
Totals	3	3	0	27.0	22	9	8	4	6	0	21	0	2	3	0	1.000	2.67

No shutouts or saves.

SAN FRANCISCO GIANTS' PITCHING RECORDS

Pitcher	G	GS	CG	IP	H	R	ER	HR	BB	IBB	SO	HB	WP	W	L	Pct.	ERA
Henry	1	0	0	2.0	1	0	0	0	3	1	2	0	0	0	0	.000	0.00
Beck	1	0	0	1.1	1	0	0	0	0	1	0	0	0	0	0	.000	0.00
Rodriguez	2	0	0	1.0	1	0	0	0	0	0	0	0	0	0	0	.000	0.00
Rueter	1	1	0	7.0	4	1	1	1	3	0	5	0	0	0	0	.000	1.29
Tavarez	3	0	0	4.0	4	2	2	1	2	1	0	1	0	0	1	.000	4.50
Alvarez	1	1	0	6.0	6	4	4	1	4	0	4	0	0	0	1	.000	6.00
Estes	1	1	0	3.0	5	5	5	1	4	0	3	0	0	0	1	.000	15.00
R. Hernandez	3	0	0	1.1	5	3	3	0	3	1	1	0	0	0	1	.000	20.25
Totals	3	3	0	25.2	27	15	15	4	19	3	16	1	0	0	3	.000	5.26

No shutouts or saves.

SCORE BY INNINGS

Florida	2	0	1	2	0	5	1	2	2—15	
San Francisco	1	1	1	2	0	1	2	0	1— 9	

MISCELLANEOUS STATISTICS

Sacrifice hits—Counsell, Estes, Vizcaino.
Sacrifice flies—Bonds.
Stolen bases—Bonds, Javier, Sheffield.
Caught stealing—Javier, Lewis, Mueller.
Double plays—Abbott, Renteria and Conine; Kent, Vizcaino and Snow; Mueller, Kent and Snow; Renteria, Abbott and Conine; Vizcaino and Snow; Vizcaino, Lewis and Kent.
Left on bases—Florida 10, 10, 8—28; San Francisco 2, 8, 7—17.
Hit by pitcher—by Tavarez (Johnson).
Passed balls—None.
Balks—None.
Time of games—First game, 2:48; second game, 3:12; third game, 3:22.
Attendance—First game, 42,167; second game, 41,283; third game, 57,188.
Umpires—Hirschbeck, Darling, Hallion, DeMuth, Tata, Reliford, Rippley, Wendelstedt and Hernandez.
Official scorers—Dick O'Connor, Doug Pett.

1997 REVIEW N.L. Division Series

A.L. CHAMPIONSHIP SERIES

The bottom line: The Cleveland Indians, looking for their first championship since 1948, earned their second World Series appearance in three years with a pulsating six-game A.L. Championship Series victory over Baltimore, avenging their loss to the Orioles in the 1996 Division Series. The Indians, held to a .193 team average, claimed the franchise's fifth pennant with clutch pitching and timely hitting that produced four one-run victories over the A.L.'s winningest regular-season team. The Game 6 finale typified Cleveland's magical mystery tour through post-season victories over the defending-champion New York Yankees and Orioles: Outhit 10-3 by the Orioles and shut down on one hit through eight innings by Mike Mussina, the Indians persevered and won, 1-0, on an 11th-inning home run by Tony Fernandez.

Why the Indians won: Because they hit in the clutch and received a stellar performance from a bullpen that was considered inferior to Baltimore's. The Indians posted three victories in their final at-bat and a fourth on a three-run, eighth-inning home run by Marquis Grissom. The Fernandez and Grissom home runs and Sandy Alomar's Game 4-deciding ninth-inning single all were surrendered by Baltimore reliever Armando Benitez, who was outstanding during the regular season. Indians relievers worked 21 innings in the ALCS, compiling a 4-0 record, two saves and a 2.14 ERA.

The turning points:

Game 1: Baltimore's bid for its first pennant since 1983 got off to a rousing start, thanks to consecutive first-inning pitches that put Orioles starter Scott Erickson on course for the first shutout in the 1997 playoffs. With two out and nobody on base in the opening inning, Baltimore center fielder Brady Anderson grabbed the spotlight when he raced to the right-center field wall at Oriole Park at Camden Yards, leaped and robbed Manny Ramirez of a home run. Leading off the bottom of the first, Anderson ripped Chad Ogea's first pitch over the 25-foot scoreboard in right field for a home run. That was plenty of support for Erickson, who allowed four hits and used his sinker to produce 14 ground-ball outs in eight innings. Roberto Alomar's two-run homer provided the offensive icing for a 3-0 victory and closer Randy Myers completed the shutout with a scoreless ninth.

Game 2: Orioles fans might claim this game was decided on Benitez's 3-2 pitch to Jim Thome with two out and one man on base in the top of the eighth inning. Thome attempted to check his swing, third base umpire Larry McCoy signaled no swing on appeal and 49,131 fans and a dugout full of Orioles players and coaches let out a collective groan as Thome trotted to first base. Grissom, the next batter,

drove a 1-1 pitch over the center-field fence, wiping out a 4-2 Baltimore lead and providing the margin for a 5-4 Cleveland victory. The Indians' comeback had seemed unlikely against a team that was 79-4 in games it had led after seven innings during the regular season and a pitcher who successfully had protected 46 of the last 47 leads he had been entrusted with. Conversely, Cleveland relievers Alvin Morman, Jeff Juden, Paul Assenmacher, Mike Jackson and Jose Mesa worked 3 1/3 scoreless innings in relief of starter Charles Nagy after Mike Bordick had given the Orioles a 4-2 lead with a two-run, sixth-inning single. The teams had traded two-run homers by Ramirez and Cal Ripken in the first and second innings.

Game 3: The Indians claimed a pivotal victory on a controversial 12th-inning play on which ball never touched bat—at least by official accounts. With Grissom stationed at third and Fernandez on first with one out, Omar Vizquel tried to lay down a suicide squeeze bunt. Vizquel missed the bunt, Baltimore catcher Lenny Webster missed the ball and Grissom, running with the pitch, scored the winning run in a 2-1 victory at Jacobs Field. The Orioles argued vehemently that Vizquel had fouled the ball, but home plate umpire John Hirschbeck ruled otherwise and television replays seemed to confirm his call. The bizarre ending capped what had started as a pitching duel between Mussina and Orel Hershiser. Mussina worked seven innings, allowing three hits and one run, and struck out an LCS-record 15 batters. Hershiser allowed four hits in seven shutout innings. The Orioles tied the game in the ninth when center fielder Grissom lost Anderson's routine fly ball and let it fall for an RBI double.

Game 4: Cleveland catcher Sandy Alomar, 0-for-11 in the ALCS entering the game, took center stage with a home run, four RBIs and a game-deciding ninth-inning single that gave the Indians an 8-7 victory. But his most important contribution might have been as a baserunner on a bizarre fifth-inning play. After Alomar had singled home the tying run in a 5-5 game, he was stationed on second base with two out and the bases loaded. Orioles lefthander Arthur Rhodes bounced a pitch that deflected off catcher Webster and bounced about eight feet away as Dave Justice raced to score the go-ahead run. Webster chased the ball and flipped to Rhodes, who was upended by a sliding Justice. When the ball bounced away again, Alomar raced home, beating Rhodes' frantic toss to Ripken covering the plate. After the Orioles had fought back to tie with a ninth-inning run, Alomar, who had hit a two-run homer in the second, won the game with his two-out, ninth-inning single off Benitez.

Game 5: The Orioles sent the series back to Camden Yards with a 4-2 victory that was saved by second baseman Roberto Alomar's outstanding backhand play on Vizquel's sharp grounder up the middle with two out in the ninth and runners on second and third. Alomar's off-balance throw barely nipped Vizquel and ended a Cleveland threat that had already generated two runs off closer Randy Myers after surprise starter Scott Kamieniecki and Jimmy Key had shut out the Indians through eight innings. One Orioles' run came on a ninth-inning homer by Eric Davis, who is continuing his career while fighting a valiant battle against cancer.

Game 6: A seventh-inning defensive play set the stage for Fernandez's homer. Bordick and Anderson led off the inning with singles off Nagy and Alomar laid down a sacrifice bunt. But third baseman Matt Williams fielded the ball, wheeled around and fired to shortstop Vizquel covering third for a force. Geronimo Berroa followed by grounding into a double play and the Indians had survived another close call. The Orioles stranded 14 runners and were 0-for-12 with men in scoring position against Nagy and four relievers while the Indians managed only one hit and struck out 10 times in Mussina's brilliant eight-inning stint. Mussina pitched 15 ALCS innings and allowed one earned run on four hits. He struck out an LCS-record 25 batters but did not get a decision.

Notable:

Orioles: Erickson had been winless in six post-season starts before beating Seattle in the Division Series and the Indians in Game 1 of the ALCS. . . . Game 2 starter Key set an LCS record when he hit three Cleveland batters in the first inning. He had hit only five in 212 1/3 regular-season innings. . . . Harold Baines, Rafael Palmeiro and Anderson connected for third-inning Game 4 home runs, tying an LCS record. . . . Palmeiro batted in post-season play with 14 runners in scoring position. He stranded 13 of them.

Indians: The Game 1 loss was the fifth straight for the Indians in the opener of a post-season series. They are 3-2 in those series. . . . Game 6 hero Fernandez was a last-minute replacement at second base for Bip Roberts, who was injured in batting practice when Fernandez lined a shot off his thumb. . . . The switch-hitting Fernandez had not hit a left-handed home run this season before Game 6.

Quotable:

Orioles: Webster, on the Game 3 attempted squeeze that produced the winning run: "In defense of (umpire) John Hirschbeck, it was loud and probably impossible to hear. But he (Vizquel) definitely tipped the ball and deflected it off my glove.". . . Manager Davey Johnson on the surprising work of the Indians' bullpen: "I've been more surprised with the way we've swung at the Indians' pitches. I saw some hanging curveballs that we normally waffle. When I see hanging pitches in the strike zone, I figure that's not a good bullpen."

Indians: Manager Mike Hargrove to reporters after his team's exciting Game 6 victory: "You guys don't have to write this one. This one writes itself.". . . First baseman Thome: "Playing a series like this,

against a very good team like the Orioles, it gets you ready for the World Series. You're out there standing all by yourself in the ninth and 10th, with the game on the line. You're alone and everything's riding on it. That's pressure."

GAME 1 BOX SCORE

BALTIMORE 3, CLEVELAND 0

WEDNESDAY, OCTOBER 8, AT BALTIMORE

Cleveland	AB	R	H	RBI	PO	A
Roberts, 2b	4	0	1	0	2	3
Vizquel, ss	4	0	0	0	2	3
Ramirez, rf	3	0	0	0	0	0
Thome, 1b	3	0	0	0	10	1
Justice, dh	3	0	1	0	0	0
Williams, 3b	3	0	1	0	0	3
S. Alomar, c	3	0	0	0	5	0
Giles, lf	3	0	0	0	2	0
Grissom, cf	3	0	1	0	2	0
Ogea, p	0	0	0	0	0	0
Bri. Anderson, p	0	0	0	0	1	1
Totals	29	0	4	0	24	11

Baltimore	AB	R	H	RBI	PO	A
Bra. Anderson, cf	4	2	2	1	2	0
R. Alomar, 2b	3	1	1	2	0	1
Berroa, rf	3	0	0	0	0	0
Davis, rf	0	0	0	0	0	0
Palmeiro, 1b	4	0	0	0	13	0
Surhoff, lf	3	0	1	0	4	0
Ripken, 3b	3	0	1	0	1	6
Baines, dh	4	0	1	0	0	0
Webster, c	3	0	0	0	5	0
Bordick, ss	3	0	0	0	2	4
Erickson, p	0	0	0	0	0	2
Myers, p	0	0	0	0	0	0
Totals	30	3	6	3	27	13

Cleveland	0	0 0		0	0 0		0	0	0—0
Baltimore	1	0 2		0	0 0		0	0	x—3

Cleveland	IP	H	R	ER	BB	SO
Ogea (L)	6.0	6	3	3	3	3
Bri. Anderson	2.0	0	0	0	1	1

Baltimore	IP	H	R	ER	BB	SO
Erickson (W)	8.0	4	0	0	0	3
Myers (S)	1.0	0	0	0	0	2

E—Webster, Williams. DP—Cleveland 1, Baltimore 2. LOB—Cleveland 2, Baltimore 7. 2B—Anderson, Ripken. HR—Anderson, R. Alomar. SB—Roberts. T—2:33. A—49,029. U—Brinkman, plate; Joyce, first; Hirschbeck, second; Merrill, third; McCoy, left field; Reilly, right field.

GAME 2 BOX SCORE

CLEVELAND 5, BALTIMORE 4

THURSDAY, OCTOBER 9, AT BALTIMORE

Cleveland	AB	R	H	RBI	PO	A
Roberts, lf	5	0	0	0	3	0
Giles, lf	0	0	0	0	0	0
Vizquel, ss	3	1	0	0	3	2
Ramirez, rf	4	1	1	2	2	0
Williams, 3b	5	0	1	0	1	2
Justice, dh	2	0	1	0	0	0
Branson, ph-dh	2	0	0	0	0	0
S. Alomar, c	3	1	0	0	5	0
Fernandez, 2b	2	0	0	0	2	3
Seitzer, 1b	2	0	0	0	8	1
Thome, ph-1b	0	1	0	0	0	0
Grissom, cf	4	1	3	3	3	0
Nagy, p	0	0	0	0	0	1
Morman, p	0	0	0	0	0	0
Juden, p	0	0	0	0	0	0
Assenmacher, p	0	0	0	0	0	0
Jackson, p	0	0	0	0	0	0
Mesa, p	0	0	0	0	0	0
Totals	32	5	6	5	27	9

Baltimore	AB	R	H	RBI	PO	A
Bra. Anderson, cf	4	0	0	0	2	0
R. Alomar, 2b	5	0	0	0	2	4
Davis, rf	5	0	1	0	2	0
Palmeiro, 1b	4	1	2	0	10	0
Surhoff, lf	3	1	1	0	1	0
Ripken, 3b	4	2	2	2	0	2
Baines, dh	3	0	1	0	0	0
Berroa, ph-dh	1	0	0	0	0	0
Hoiles, c	3	0	0	0	10	1
Bordick, ss	3	0	1	2	0	2
Hammonds, ph	0	0	0	0	0	0
Key, p	0	0	0	0	0	0
Kamieniecki, p	0	0	0	0	0	1
Benitez, p	0	0	0	0	0	0
Mills, p	0	0	0	0	0	0
Totals	35	4	8	4	27	10

Cleveland	2	0	0		0	0	0	0	3	0—5
Baltimore	0	2	0		0	0	2	0	0	0—4

Cleveland	IP	H	R	ER	BB	SO
Nagy	5.2	8	4	4	2	1
Morman	0.2	0	0	0	0	0
Juden	0.1	0	0	0	0	0
Assenmacher (W)	0.2	0	0	0	1	2
Jackson	0.2	0	0	0	0	1
Mesa (S)	1.0	0	0	0	1	1

Baltimore	IP	H	R	ER	BB	SO
Key	4.0	5	2	2	2	4
Kamieniecki	3.0	0	0	0	1	1
Benitez (L)	1.0	1	3	3	2	3
Mills	1.0	1	0	0	1	2

E—Roberts, Fernandez, R. Alomar, Ramirez. DP—Cleveland 1, Baltimore 1. LOB—Cleveland 9, Baltimore 8. 2B—Palmeiro. HR—Ramirez, Ripken, Grissom. SB—Williams, Grissom. HBP—By Key 3 (Vizquel, Justice, Fernandez). T—3:53. A—49,131. U—Joyce, plate; Hirschbeck, first; Merrill, second; McCoy, third; Reilly, left field; Brinkman, right field.

GAME 3 BOX SCORE

CLEVELAND 2, BALTIMORE 1 (12 INNINGS)

SATURDAY, OCTOBER 11, AT CLEVELAND

Baltimore	AB	R	H	RBI	PO	A
Bra. Anderson, cf	4	0	2	1	1	0
R. Alomar, 2b	3	0	1	0	1	3
Davis, rf	4	0	0	0	1	0
Webster, c	1	0	1	0	5	0
Palmeiro, 1b	5	0	1	0	10	0
Surhoff, lf	5	0	0	0	1	0
Ripken, 3b	5	0	0	0	0	2
Baines, dh	1	0	1	0	0	0
Berroa, ph-dh	3	0	1	0	0	0
Hoiles, c	3	0	1	0	15	1
Reboulet, pr-ss	2	1	0	0	0	0
Bordick, ss	2	0	0	0	0	3
Hammonds, ph-rf	2	0	0	0	0	0
Mussina, p	0	0	0	0	0	0
Benitez, p	0	0	0	0	0	1
Orosco, p	0	0	0	0	0	0
Mills, p	0	0	0	0	0	0
Rhodes, p	0	0	0	0	0	0
Myers, p	0	0	0	0	0	0
Totals	40	1	8	1	34	10

Cleveland	AB	R	H	RBI	PO	A
Roberts, 2b	3	0	0	0	3	3
Fernandez, 2b	3	0	1	0	0	2
Vizquel, ss	4	0	0	0	4	2
Ramirez, rf	4	0	2	0	4	0
Thome, 1b	1	1	0	0	7	0
Seitzer, ph-1b	1	0	0	0	2	0
Justice, dh	5	0	1	0	0	0
Williams, 3b	4	0	2	1	1	5
S. Alomar, c	5	0	0	0	13	1
Giles, lf	5	0	0	0	0	0
Grissom, cf	4	1	0	0	2	0
Hershiser, p	0	0	0	0	0	0
Assenmacher, p	0	0	0	0	0	0
Jackson, p	0	0	0	0	0	0
Mesa, p	0	0	0	0	0	0

Cleveland	AB	R	H	RBI	PO	A
Juden, p	0	0	0	0	0	0
Morman, p	0	0	0	0	0	0
Plunk, p	0	0	0	0	0	0
Totals	39	2	6	1	36	13

Baltimore	0	0	0		0	0	0		0	0	1		0	0	0—1
Cleveland	0	0	0		0	0	0		1	0	0		0	0	1—2

Baltimore	IP	H	R	ER	BB	SO
Mussina	7.0	3	1	1	2	15
Benitez	*1.0	0	0	0	1	1
Orosco	0.2	0	0	0	1	1
Mills	0.1	1	0	0	0	0
Rhodes	†1.0	1	0	0	1	2
Myers (L)	1.1	1	1	0	2	2

Cleveland	IP	H	R	ER	BB	SO
Hershiser	7.0	4	0	0	1	7
Assenmacher	0.2	0	0	0	0	1
Jackson	0.1	0	0	0	0	0
Mesa	2.0	2	1	1	1	1
Juden	0.2	1	0	0	2	2
Morman	0.2	0	0	0	0	1
Plunk (W)	0.2	1	0	0	0	0

*Pitched to one batter in ninth.
†Pitched to two batters in 11th.

E—R. Alomar. DP—Cleveland 4. LOB—Baltimore 7, Cleveland 10. 2B—Bra. Anderson, Berroa. SB—Bra. Anderson, Grissom. WP—Rhodes. PB—Webster. T—4:51. A—45,047. U—Hirschbeck, plate; Merrill, first; McCoy, second; Reilly, third; Brinkman, left field; Joyce, right field.

GAME 4 BOX SCORE

CLEVELAND 8, BALTIMORE 7

SUNDAY, OCTOBER 12, AT CLEVELAND

Baltimore	AB	R	H	RBI	PO	A
Bra. Anderson, cf	4	2	2	1	3	0
R. Alomar, 2b	3	1	0	0	4	4
Berroa, rf	5	1	2	1	4	0
Hammonds, pr-rf	0	0	0	0	0	0
Baines, dh	3	1	1	2	0	0
Davis, ph-dh	2	0	0	0	0	0
Palmeiro, 1b	5	1	3	2	9	1
Ripken, 3b	4	1	1	0	0	1
Surhoff, lf	5	0	2	1	1	0
Webster, c	4	0	1	0	4	0
Bordick, ss	4	0	0	0	1	2
Erickson, p	0	0	0	0	0	3
Rhodes, p	0	0	0	0	0	0
Mills, p	0	0	0	0	0	0
Orosco, p	0	0	0	0	0	1
Benitez, p	0	0	0	0	0	0
Totals	39	7	12	7	26	12

Cleveland	AB	R	H	RBI	PO	A
Roberts, 2b	3	0	0	0	1	0
Fernandez, 2b	2	0	1	0	1	2
Vizquel, ss	4	0	0	0	1	2
Ramirez, rf	3	2	3	1	4	0
Thome, 1b	3	1	1	0	5	0
Seitzer, ph	0	0	0	0	0	0
Justice, dh	5	2	2	0	0	0
Williams, 3b	4	0	0	0	1	3
S. Alomar, c	5	2	3	4	10	0
Giles, lf	3	1	2	0	2	0
Grissom, cf	4	0	1	1	2	0
Wright, p	0	0	0	0	0	0
Bri. Anderson, p	0	0	0	0	0	1
Juden, p	0	0	0	0	0	0
Assenmacher, p	0	0	0	0	0	0
Jackson, p	0	0	0	0	0	0
Mesa, p	0	0	0	0	0	0
Totals	36	8	13	6	27	8

Baltimore	0	1	4		0	0	0		1	0	1—7
Cleveland	0	2	0		1	4	0		0	0	1—8

Baltimore	IP	H	R	ER	BB	SO
Erickson	4.2	11	7	6	1	3
Rhodes	1.1	1	0	0	2	0
Mills (L)	*2.0	0	1	1	1	1
Orosco	0.2	0	0	0	0	0
Benitez	0.0	1	0	0	1	0

Cleveland	IP	H	R	ER	BB	SO
Wright	3.0	6	5	5	2	3
Bri. Anderson	3.1	1	1	1	1	4
Juden	0.0	1	0	0	0	0
Assenmacher	0.1	1	0	0	0	0
Jackson	1.0	1	0	0	0	2
Mesa (W)	1.1	2	1	1	1	1

*Pitched to one batter in ninth.
E—Bra. Anderson, Webster. DP—Baltimore 1. LOB—Baltimore 9, Cleveland 9. 2B—Surhoff 2, Giles 2, Ramirez. HR—S. Alomar, Anderson, Baines, Palmeiro, Ramirez. SB—Bra. Anderson. SH—Vizquel, Seitzer. WP—Rhodes. T—3:32. A—45,081. U—Merrill, plate; McCoy, first; Reilly, second; Brinkman, third; Joyce, left field; Hirschbeck, right field.

GAME 5 BOX SCORE

BALTIMORE 4, CLEVELAND 2

MONDAY, OCTOBER 13, AT CLEVELAND

Baltimore	AB	R	H	RBI	PO	A
Bra. Anderson, cf	4	1	1	0	2	0
R. Alomar, 2b	3	0	1	0	1	3
Berroa, rf	4	0	1	2	2	0
Hammonds, rf	0	0	0	0	1	0
Baines, dh	3	0	1	0	0	0
Davis, ph-dh	1	1	1	1	0	0
Palmeiro, 1b	4	1	1	0	10	0
Ripken, 3b	4	0	2	1	0	2
Surhoff, lf	4	0	1	0	1	0
Hoiles, c	3	1	1	0	8	0
Bordick, ss	3	0	0	0	2	2
Kamieniecki, p	0	0	0	0	0	1
Key, p	0	0	0	0	0	0
Myers, p	0	0	0	0	0	0
Totals	33	4	10	4	27	8

Cleveland	AB	R	H	RBI	PO	A
Roberts, 2lf	5	0	2	0	2	1
Vizquel, ss	5	0	1	0	3	3
Ramirez, rf	3	0	0	0	4	0
Thome, 1b	3	0	0	0	5	1
Seitzer, ph-1b	1	0	0	0	1	0
Justice, dh	3	1	1	0	0	0
Williams, 3b	3	1	1	1	2	1
S. Alomar, c	4	0	0	0	5	0
Giles, lf	2	0	1	0	3	0
Fernandez, ph-2b	2	0	1	1	2	1
Grissom, cf	4	0	1	0	0	1
Ogea, p	0	0	0	0	0	1
Assenmacher, p	0	0	0	0	0	0
Jackson, p	0	0	0	0	0	0
Totals	35	2	8	2	27	9

Baltimore	0	0 2	0 0 0	0 0	2—4
Cleveland	0	0 0	0 0 0	0 0	2—2

Baltimore	IP	H	R	ER	BB	SO
Kamieniecki (W)	5.0	4	0	0	1	4
Key	3.0	0	0	0	1	3
Myers	1.0	4	2	2	0	1

Cleveland	IP	H	R	ER	BB	SO
Ogea (L)	8.0	6	2	2	2	4
Assenmacher	*0.0	4	2	2	0	0
Jackson	1.0	0	0	0	0	1

*Pitched to four batters in ninth.

E—Williams. DP—Cleveland 3. LOB—Baltimore 5, Cleveland 9. 2B—Roberts, Giles, Palmeiro, Williams, Fernandez. HR—Davis. SB—Grissom. SH—Bordick. HBP—By Kamieniecki (Ramirez). T—3:08. A—45,068. U—McCoy, plate; Reilly, first; Brinkman, second; Joyce, third; Hirschbeck, left field; Merrill, right field.

GAME 6 BOX SCORE

CLEVELAND 1, BALTIMORE 0 (11 INNINGS)

WEDNESDAY, OCTOBER 15, AT BALTIMORE

Cleveland	AB	R	H	RBI	PO	A
Vizquel, ss	5	0	0	0	3	3
Fernandez, 2b	5	1	2	1	4	2
Ramirez, rf	4	0	0	0	0	0
Justice, dh	3	0	1	0	0	0
Williams, 3b	4	0	0	0	1	4
Thome, 1b	4	0	0	0	8	0
S. Alomar, c	4	0	0	0	11	0
Giles, lf	3	0	0	0	2	0
Grissom, cf	4	0	0	0	4	0
Nagy, p	0	0	0	0	0	1
Assenmacher, p	0	0	0	0	0	0
Jackson, p	0	0	0	0	0	0
Bri. Anderson, p	0	0	0	0	0	0
Mesa, p	0	0	0	0	0	1
Totals	36	1	3	1	33	11

Baltimore	AB	R	H	RBI	PO	A
Bra. Anderson, cf	5	0	2	0	3	0
R. Alomar, 2b	5	0	1	0	2	2
Berroa, rf	5	0	2	0	3	0
Walton, rf	0	0	0	0	0	0
Baines, dh	3	0	1	0	0	0
Davis, ph-dh	1	0	0	0	0	0
Palmeiro, 1b	3	0	0	0	3	1
Hammonds, pr-lf	1	0	0	0	1	0
Ripken, 3b	3	0	2	0	0	1
Surhoff, l1b	5	0	0	0	5	0
Hoiles, c	5	0	0	0	14	0
Bordick, ss	4	0	2	0	0	1
Webster, ph	1	0	0	0	0	0
Mussina, p	0	0	0	0	2	1
Myers, p	0	0	0	0	0	0
Benitez, p	0	0	0	0	0	1
Totals	41	0	10	0	33	7

Cleveland	0 0 0	0 0 0	0 0 0	0 1—1
Baltimore	0 0 0	0 0 0	0 0 0	0 0—0

Cleveland	IP	H	R	ER	BB	SO
Nagy	7.1	9	0	0	3	4
Assenmacher	0.1	0	0	0	0	0
Jackson	1.1	0	0	0	1	3
Bri. Anderson (W)	1.0	0	0	0	1	2
Mesa (S)	1.0	1	0	0	0	2

Baltimore	IP	H	R	ER	BB	SO
Mussina	8.0	1	0	0	2	10
Myers	2.0	1	0	0	1	2
Benitez (L)	1.0	1	1	1	0	2

DP—Cleveland 2. LOB—Cleveland 5, Baltimore 14. 2B—Berroa, Bordick, Ripken, Justice. HR—Fernandez. SB—Hammonds. HBP—By Nagy (Palmeiro). T—3:52. A—49,075. U—Reilly, plate; Brinkman, first; Joyce, second; Hirschbeck, third; Merrill, left field; McCoy, right field.

STATISTICS

CLEVELAND INDIANS' BATTING AND FIELDING AVERAGES

Player, position	G	AB	R	H	TB	2B	3B	HR	RBI	BB	IBB	SO	Avg.	PO	A	E	Avg.
Fernandez, 2b-ph	5	14	1	5	9	1	0	1	2	1	0	2	.357	9	10	1	.950
Justice, dh	6	21	3	7	8	1	0	0	0	2	0	4	.333	0	0	0	.000
Ramirez, rf	6	21	3	6	13	1	0	2	3	5	1	5	.286	14	0	1	.933
Grissom, cf	6	23	2	6	9	0	0	1	4	1	0	9	.261	13	1	0	1.000
Williams, 3b	6	23	1	5	6	1	0	0	2	3	0	7	.217	6	18	2	.923
Giles, lf	6	16	1	3	6	0	0	0	0	2	0	6	.188	9	0	0	1.000
Roberts, 2b-lf	5	20	0	3	4	1	0	0	0	0	0	8	.150	11	7	1	.947
S. Alomar, c	6	24	3	3	6	0	0	1	4	1	0	3	.125	49	1	0	1.000

Player, position	G	AB	R	H	TB	2B	3B	HR	RBI	BB	IBB	SO	Avg.	PO	A	E	Avg.
							BATTING								**FIELDING**		
Thome, 1b-ph	6	14	3	1	1	0	0	0	0	5	0	4	.071	35	2	0	1.000
Vizquel, ss	6	25	1	1	1	0	0	0	0	2	0	10	.040	16	15	0	1.000
Bri. Anderson, p	3	0	0	0	0	0	0	0	0	0	0	0	.000	1	2	0	1.000
Assenmacher, p	5	0	0	0	0	0	0	0	0	0	0	0	.000	0	0	0	.000
Hershiser, p	1	0	0	0	0	0	0	0	0	0	0	0	.000	0	0	0	.000
Jackson, p	5	0	0	0	0	0	0	0	0	0	0	0	.000	0	0	0	.000
Juden, p	3	0	0	0	0	0	0	0	0	0	0	0	.000	0	0	0	.000
Mesa, p	4	0	0	0	0	0	0	0	0	0	0	0	.000	0	1	0	1.000
Morman, p	2	0	0	0	0	0	0	0	0	0	0	0	.000	0	0	0	.000
Nagy, p	2	0	0	0	0	0	0	0	0	0	0	0	.000	0	2	0	1.000
Ogea, p	2	0	0	0	0	0	0	0	0	0	0	0	.000	0	1	0	1.000
Plunk, p	1	0	0	0	0	0	0	0	0	0	0	0	.000	0	0	0	.000
Wright, p	1	0	0	0	0	0	0	0	0	0	0	0	.000	0	0	0	.000
Branson, dh	1	2	0	0	0	0	0	0	0	0	0	2	.000	0	0	0	.000
Seitzer, 1b-ph	4	4	0	0	0	0	0	0	0	1	0	2	.000	11	1	0	1.000
Totals	6	207	18	40	63	8	0	5	15	23	1	62	.193	174	61	5	.979

BALTIMORE ORIOLES' BATTING AND FIELDING AVERAGES

Player, position	G	AB	R	H	TB	2B	3B	HR	RBI	BB	IBB	SO	Avg.	PO	A	E	Avg.
							BATTING								**FIELDING**		
Bra. Anderson, cf	6	25	5	9	17	2	0	2	3	4	0	4	.360	13	0	1	.929
Baines, dh	6	17	1	6	9	0	0	1	2	2	0	1	.353	0	0	0	.000
Ripken, 3b	6	23	3	8	13	2	0	1	3	4	0	6	.348	1	14	0	1.000
Berroa, rf-dh	6	21	1	6	8	2	0	0	3	0	0	3	.286	9	0	0	1.000
Palmeiro, 1b	6	25	3	7	12	2	0	1	2	0	0	10	.280	55	2	0	1.000
Webster, c-ph	4	9	0	2	2	0	0	0	0	0	0	1	.222	14	0	2	.875
Surhoff, lf-1b	6	25	1	5	7	2	0	0	1	2	0	2	.200	13	0	0	1.000
R. Alomar, 2b	6	22	2	4	7	0	0	1	2	7	2	3	.182	10	17	2	.931
Bordick, ss	6	19	0	3	4	1	0	0	2	0	0	6	.158	5	14	0	1.000
Davis, rf-dh	6	13	1	2	5	0	0	1	1	1	1	3	.154	3	0	0	1.000
Hoiles, c	4	14	1	2	2	0	0	0	0	2	0	5	.143	47	2	0	1.000
Benitez, p	4	0	0	0	0	0	0	0	0	0	0	0	.000	0	1	0	1.000
Erickson, p	2	0	0	0	0	0	0	0	0	0	0	0	.000	0	5	0	1.000
Kamieniecki, p	2	0	0	0	0	0	0	0	0	0	0	0	.000	0	2	0	1.000
Key, p	2	0	0	0	0	0	0	0	0	0	0	0	.000	0	0	0	.000
Mills, p	3	0	0	0	0	0	0	0	0	0	0	0	.000	0	0	0	.000
Mussina, p	2	0	0	0	0	0	0	0	0	0	0	0	.000	2	1	0	1.000
Myers, p	4	0	0	0	0	0	0	0	0	0	0	0	.000	0	0	0	.000
Orosco, p	2	0	0	0	0	0	0	0	0	0	0	0	.000	0	2	0	1.000
Rhodes, p	2	0	0	0	0	0	0	0	0	0	0	0	.000	0	0	0	.000
Walton, rf	1	0	0	0	0	0	0	0	0	0	0	0	.000	0	0	0	.000
Reboulet, ss-pr	1	2	1	0	0	0	0	0	0	0	0	0	.000	0	0	0	.000
Hammonds, ph-rf-pr-lf	5	3	0	0	0	0	0	0	0	1	0	2	.000	2	0	0	1.000
Totals	6	218	19	54	86	11	0	7	19	23	3	47	.248	174	60	5	.979

CLEVELAND INDIANS' PITCHING RECORDS

Pitcher	G	GS	CG	IP	H	R	ER	HR	BB	IBB	SO	HB	WP	W	L	Pct.	ERA
Hershiser	1	1	0	7.0	4	0	0	0	1	0	7	0	0	0	0	.000	0.00
Jackson	5	0	0	4.1	1	0	0	0	1	0	7	0	0	0	0	.000	0.00
Morman	2	0	0	1.1	0	0	0	0	0	0	1	0	0	0	0	.000	0.00
Juden	3	0	0	1.0	2	0	0	0	2	1	2	0	0	0	0	.000	0.00
Plunk	1	0	0	0.2	1	0	0	0	0	0	0	0	0	1	0	1.000	0.00
Bri. Anderson	3	0	0	6.1	1	1	1	0	3	1	7	0	0	1	0	1.000	1.42
Nagy	2	2	0	13.0	17	4	4	1	5	0	5	1	0	0	0	.000	2.77
Ogea	2	2	0	14.0	12	5	5	2	5	0	7	0	0	0	2	.000	3.21
Mesa	4	0	0	5.1	5	2	2	0	3	1	5	0	0	1	0	1.000	3.38
Assenmacher	5	0	0	2.0	5	2	2	1	1	0	3	0	0	1	0	1.000	9.00
Wright	1	1	0	3.0	6	5	5	3	2	0	3	0	0	0	0	.000	15.00
Totals	6	6	0	58.0	54	19	19	7	23	3	47	1	0	4	2	.667	2.95

No shutouts. Saves—Mesa 2.

BALTIMORE ORIOLES' PITCHING RECORDS

Pitcher	G	GS	CG	IP	H	R	ER	HR	BB	IBB	SO	HB	WP	W	L	Pct.	ERA
Kamieniecki	2	1	0	8.0	4	0	0	0	2	0	5	1	0	1	0	1.000	0.00
Rhodes	2	0	0	2.1	2	0	0	0	3	1	2	0	2	0	0	.000	0.00
Orosco	2	0	0	1.1	0	0	0	0	1	0	1	0	0	0	0	.000	0.00
Mussina	2	2	0	15.0	4	1	1	0	4	0	25	0	0	0	0	.000	0.60
Key	2	1	0	7.0	5	2	2	1	3	0	7	3	0	0	0	.000	2.57
Mills	3	0	0	3.1	1	1	1	0	2	0	3	0	0	0	1	.000	2.70

Pitcher	G	GS	CG	IP	H	R	ER	HR	BB	IBB	SO	HB	WP	W	L	Pct.	ERA
Erickson	2	2	0	12.2	15	7	6	2	1	0	6	0	0	1	0	1.000	4.26
Myers	4	0	0	5.1	6	3	3	0	3	0	7	0	0	0	1	.000	5.06
Benitez	4	0	0	3.0	3	4	4	2	4	0	6	0	0	0	2	.000	12.00
Totals	6	6	0	58.0	40	18	17	5	23	1	62	4	2	2	4	.333	2.64

No shutouts. Save—Myers.

SCORE BY INNINGS

Cleveland	2 2 0	1 4 0	1 3 3	0 1 1—18
Baltimore	1 3 8	0 0 2	1 0 4	0 0 0—19

MISCELLANEOUS STATISTICS

Sacrifice hits—Bordick, Seitzer, Vizquel.
Sacrifice flies—None.
Stolen bases—Grissom 3, Bra. Anderson 2, Hammonds, Roberts, Williams.
Caught stealing—Baines.
Double plays—Ripken, R. Alomar and Palmeiro 2; Roberts, Vizquel and Thome 2; Vizquel and Thome 2; Vizquel, Roberts and Thome 2; Erickson, Bordick and Palmeiro; Ripken and Palmeiro; Vizquel, Fernandez and Seitzer; Williams and Seitzer; Williams, Fernandez and Thome; Williams, Roberts and Thome.
Left on bases—Cleveland 2, 9, 10, 9, 9, 5—44; Baltimore 7, 8, 7, 9, 5, 14—50.
Hit by pitcher—by Key 3 (Fernandez, Justice, Vizquel), by Nagy (Palmeiro), by Kamieniecki (Ramirez).
Passed balls—None.
Balks—None.
Time of games—First game, 3:53; second game, 4:51; third game, 3:32; fourth game, 2:33; fifth game, 3:08; sixth game, 3:52.
Attendance—First game, 49,131; second game, 45,047; third game, 45,081; fourth game, 49,029; fifth game, 45,068; sixth game, 49,075.
Umpires—Joyce, Hirschbeck, Merrill, McCoy, Reilly and Brinkman.
Official scorers—Jim Ingraham, Mark Jacobson, Hank Kosloski.

1997 REVIEW A.L. Championship Series

N.L. CHAMPIONSHIP SERIES

The bottom line: The Florida Marlins, who joined baseball's fast lane with an $89 million offseason facelift, became the first wild-card team to reach the World Series when they upended the defending N.L.-champion Atlanta Braves in a six-game N.L. Championship Series. The 5-year-old Marlins, the youngest expansion team to reach a World Series, gave the spring-training haven of South Florida its first Fall Classic and manager Jim Leyland his first Series appearance in a baseball career that spans 33 seasons. And they gave the Braves, who had played in four of the last five World Series, an early exit from their record sixth consecutive post-season appearance. The Marlins, who won 92 regular-season games and still finished nine games behind Atlanta in the A.L. East, didn't even exist when the Braves began their playoff run in 1991.

Why the Marlins won: Because they pitched well in the clutch and the Braves' usually reliable defense broke down in Games 1 and 3. The Marlins got two important victories from ace Kevin Brown and a stunning 15-strikeout, three-hit effort from 22-year-old rookie Livan Hernandez. Atlanta ace Greg Maddux started two games and allowed only two earned runs, but he did not win because of shoddy defensive play. John Smoltz also was victimized by defensive lapses that contributed to a 5-2 Game 3 loss. The Marlins ran their season record against the Braves to 12-6 despite batting .199.

The turning points:

Game 1: The opener at Atlanta's Turner Field was decided in the first inning when the Marlins touched Maddux for three unearned runs. The outburst was set up by first baseman Fred McGriff's error on a Jeff Conine grounder that loaded the bases with two out. Moises Alou followed with a sharp ground ball down the third base line that Atlanta's Chipper Jones should have fielded or at least knocked down. But it rolled untouched into the left-field corner and cleared the bases—an early hole the Braves never could climb out of. When the Marlins added a pair of unearned third-inning runs, which were set up by center fielder Kenny Lofton's three-base error on a Gary Sheffield drive, Brown and three relievers made it stand up for a 5-3 victory—the first playoff win in Florida's short history.

Game 2: The Braves, taking a cue from the Marlins, served notice with a three-run first inning that their shoddy play from the previous game was merely an illusion. Lofton led off the game with a bunt single and advanced to second on catcher Charles Johnson's throwing error. Keith Lockhart's triple and Ryan Klesko's home run made the score 3-0 and a two-run Chipper Jones homer in the third forced the earliest exit by Marlins starter Alex Fernandez since 1995. The five-run cushion was more than

enough for Braves lefthander Tom Glavine, who allowed only three hits in 7 2/3 innings and received sparkling defensive support en route to a 7-1 victory. The Marlins were jolted the next day by news that Fernandez had suffered a career-threatening rotator-cuff tear.

Game 3: Just when the Braves' express appeared to be back on track, another defensive lapse set up Florida's four-run sixth-inning explosion and a 5-2 victory over Smoltz. Playing before a record Pro Player Stadium baseball crowd of 53,857, the Braves held a 2-1 lead with two out and runners on first and second. Florida's Darren Daulton hit an apparent inning-ending line drive toward right fielder Andruw Jones, who misjudged the ball and watched it sail over his head for a game-tying double. Smoltz walked Devon White intentionally to face Johnson, who was 0-for-12 lifetime against Smoltz and 0-for-13 during the season with the bases loaded. But Johnson belted a 2-2 pitch into the left field gap for a bases-clearing double. Hernandez, who worked 1 2/3 scoreless innings in relief of Tony Saunders, earned the victory and set the stage for his Game 5 heroics.

Game 4: This game was decided in the first inning, when Fred McGriff singled home an Atlanta run and lefthander Denny Neagle began mowing down Marlins hitters en route to a 4-0 victory—the first NLCS complete-game shutout since 1991. Neagle, the No. 4 man in the Braves' rotation, retired the first nine batters and allowed only four hits and one walk in his impressive performance. McGriff drove in two runs and Chipper Jones contributed three hits off Al Leiter and two relievers. Leiter started in place of Brown, who was sidelined by a viral infection.

Game 5: Hernandez, who started because Brown still was ill, surrendered a triple to Lofton on his second pitch and walked Lockhart. But he set the tone for the game with consecutive strikeouts of Chipper Jones, McGriff and Klesko. Bolstered by that great escape, Hernandez allowed only two hits—one a Michael Tucker home run—the rest of the game and worked umpire Eric Gregg's expanded strike zone like a seasoned veteran. When he caught McGriff looking to end the game, he matched the LCS single-game strikeout record of 15 that Baltimore's Mike Mussina had set 24 hours earlier. Hernandez, working before a frenzied Pro Player Stadium crowd, outdueled Braves ace Maddux, who allowed only four hits and struck out nine in seven solid innings. One of those hits was a game-deciding seventh-inning single by Conine, the only player remaining from Florida's opening day lineup in its 1993 expansion season.

Game 6: The clincher was decided in a four-run Marlins first inning against Glavine, who failed to live up to his big-game reputation. The Marlins, taking advantage of Glavine's uncharacteristic wildness, scored two runs on Bobby Bonilla's bases-loaded single, one when Johnson was hit by a pitch with the bases full and another on Craig Counsell's grounder. That was enough for Brown, who would deliver a gutsy complete-game 11-hit performance while still recovering from a stomach flu. A three-run sixth sealed the verdict and raised Florida's post-season record to 7-2.

Notable:

Braves: Maddux has allowed 37 NLCS runs—only 25 earned. His NLCS record is 3-5. . . . Smoltz missed his chance to pass Whitey Ford and Dave Stewart as the all-time winningest pitcher in post-season history. The Game 3 loss dropped his playoff record to 10-3. . . . Neagle, who worked three score-less relief innings in Game 1, finished the NLCS with 12 shutout innings. . . . The Braves have won 20 NLCS games, one less than Los Angeles. The Oakland Athletics lead all teams with 23 wins.

Marlins: Catcher Charles Johnson's Game 2 error was his first of the season. . . . Hernandez's 15 Game 5 strikeouts fell two short of Bob Gibson's post-sea-son record of 17. Gibson performed his feat in Game 1 of the 1968 World Series against the Detroit Tigers. . . . Florida reached its first World Series three years faster than the expansion New York Mets, who held the previous record. . . . Hernandez became the first rookie to win an LCS MVP.

Quotable:

Braves: Smoltz after his Game 3 loss: "It was a tough game to lose. They hit two balls hard off me, and unfortunately it totaled five runs. But no one person is to blame.". . . Manager Bobby Cox on umpire Gregg's Game 5 strike zone: "Some of those pitches, I didn't think we had a chance to hit. But it wasn't decided by the umpires.". . . Cox after his team's elimination: "We've had a great year. These things are crapshoots. You hope you get hot."

Marlins: Conine, the only remaining original Marlin, on his feelings after delivering the deciding Game 5 hit: "Just standing there on second base and looking at the crowd going crazy, that's one of my most special moments in baseball.". . . Brown, after pitching his team into the World Series: "They talk about the money we spent, that we bought a cham-pionship. The money is not what won this series. The heart, the determination, the pursuit of the right goal got us there."

GAME 1 BOX SCORE

FLORIDA 5, ATLANTA 3

TUESDAY, OCTOBER 7, AT ATLANTA

Florida	AB	R	H	RBI	PO	A
White, cf	5	0	0	0	2	0
Renteria, ss	4	1	1	0	3	3
Sheffield, rf	3	2	1	0	0	0
Bonilla, 3b	3	1	0	0	1	1
Conine, 1b	4	1	0	0	12	2
Alou, lf	4	0	1	4	2	0
Johnson, c	4	0	1	1	4	1
Counsell, 2b	3	0	2	0	2	5
Brown, p	2	0	0	0	1	0
Cook, p	0	0	0	0	0	0
Powell, p	0	0	0	0	0	0

Florida	AB	R	H	RBI	PO	A
Daulton, ph	1	0	0	0	0	0
Nen, p	0	0	0	0	0	1
Totals	33	5	6	5	27	13

Atlanta	AB	R	H	RBI	PO	A
Lofton, cf	5	0	0	0	2	0
Lockhart, 2b	3	1	1	0	3	0
C. Jones, 3b	4	1	1	1	0	2
McGriff, 1b	4	0	1	1	7	0
Klesko, lf	3	1	1	1	1	0
Tucker, rf	0	0	0	0	3	1
A. Jones, ph-rf	1	0	0	0	0	0
Perez, c	0	0	0	0	3	0
Lopez, ph-c	4	0	0	0	7	1
Blauser, ss	3	0	1	0	1	2
Maddux, p	1	0	0	0	0	4
Gregg, ph	1	0	0	0	0	0
Neagle, p	0	0	0	0	0	0
Colbrunn, ph	1	0	0	0	0	0
Totals	30	3	5	3	27	10

Florida	3	0	2	0	0	0	0	0	0—5
Atlanta	1	0	1	0	0	1	0	0	0—3

Florida	IP	H	R	ER	BB	SO
Brown (W)	6.0	5	3	3	4	3
Cook	1.1	0	0	0	0	0
Powell	0.2	0	0	0	0	1
Nen (S)	1.0	0	0	0	0	0

Atlanta	IP	H	R	ER	BB	SO
Maddux (L)	6.0	5	5	0	3	7
Neagle	3.0	1	0	0	0	2

E—McGriff, Lofton. DP—Florida 1, Atlanta 1. LOB—Florida 6, Atlanta 7. 2B—Alou, Lockhart, Johnson. HR—C. Jones, Klesko. SB—Renteria. SH—Brown, Maddux. HBP—By Brown (Blauser), by Neagle (Renteria), by Cook (Lockhart). T—3:04. A—49,244. U—Froemming, plate; Williams, first; Winters, second; Layne, third; Gregg, left field; Pulli, right field.

GAME 2 BOX SCORE

ATLANTA 7, FLORIDA 1

WEDNESDAY, OCTOBER 8, AT ATLANTA

Florida	AB	R	H	RBI	PO	A
Abbott, 2b	4	0	2	0	2	1
Renteria, ss	3	0	0	0	0	0
Sheffield, rf	3	0	0	0	1	0
Bonilla, 3b	4	0	0	0	2	3
Conine, 1b	2	0	0	0	3	0
Vosberg, p	0	0	0	0	0	0
Counsell, ph	1	0	0	0	0	0
Eisenreich, lf	3	0	0	0	2	0
Johnson, c	2	1	0	0	10	1
Zaun, c	0	0	0	0	2	0
White, cf	3	0	1	1	1	0
Fernandez, p	1	0	0	0	0	0
Leiter, p	0	0	0	0	0	1
Cangelosi, ph	1	0	0	0	0	0
Heredia, p	0	0	0	0	0	0
Daulton, 1b	0	0	0	0	1	0
Totals	27	1	3	1	24	6

Atlanta	AB	R	H	RBI	PO	A
Lofton, cf	5	1	1	0	2	1
Lockhart, 2b	3	2	2	1	3	2
Graffanino, 2b	2	1	1	0	0	0
C. Jones, 3b	5	2	3	3	1	4
McGriff, 1b	3	0	1	0	11	0
Klesko, lf	3	1	1	2	1	0
Bautista, lf	0	0	0	0	0	0
Lopez, c	2	0	1	1	7	0
Tucker, rf	2	0	0	0	0	0
A. Jones, ph-rf	2	0	1	0	1	0
Blauser, ss	4	0	1	0	1	5
Glavine, p	2	0	0	0	0	1
Cather, p	0	0	0	0	0	0
Colbrunn, ph	1	0	1	0	0	0
Wohlers, p	0	0	0	0	0	0
Totals	34	7	13	7	27	13

Florida	0	0	0	0	0	0	0	1	0—1
Atlanta	3	0	2	0	0	0	2	0	x—7

Florida	IP	H	R	ER	BB	SO
Fernandez (L)	2.2	6	5	5	1	3
Leiter	2.1	3	0	0	0	1
Heredia	1.1	3	2	2	2	2
Vosberg	1.2	1	0	0	0	2

Atlanta	IP	H	R	ER	BB	SO
Glavine (W)	7.2	3	1	1	4	5
Cather	0.1	0	0	0	0	0
Wohlers	1.0	0	0	0	1	1

E—Johnson. DP—Florida 1, Atlanta 2. LOB—Florida 4, Atlanta 8. 2B—Lopez, Abbott, Graffanino, White. 3B—Lockhart. HR—Klesko, C. Jones. SH—Glavine. SF—Lopez. T—2:51. A—48,933. U—Williams, plate; Winters, first; Layne, second; Gregg, third; Pulli, left field; Froemming, right field.

GAME 3 BOX SCORE

FLORIDA 5, ATLANTA 2
FRIDAY, OCTOBER 10, AT FLORIDA

Atlanta	AB	R	H	RBI	PO	A
Lofton, cf	4	1	1	0	1	0
Blauser, ss	3	1	1	0	0	3
C. Jones, 3b	2	0	0	0	0	0
McGriff, 1b	3	0	1	1	6	0
Lopez, c	3	0	0	1	10	0
A. Jones, rf	2	0	1	0	4	1
Tucker, ph	1	0	0	0	0	0
Klesko, lf	4	0	1	0	2	0
Graffanino, 2b	2	0	0	0	0	0
Lockhart, ph-2b	2	0	1	0	1	0
Smoltz, p	2	0	0	0	0	1
Gregg, ph	1	0	0	0	0	0
Cather, p	0	0	0	0	0	0
Ligtenberg, p	0	0	0	0	0	1
Totals	29	2	6	2	24	6

Florida	AB	R	H	RBI	PO	A
Cangelosi, lf	3	0	0	0	2	0
Renteria, ss	4	1	1	0	3	2
Sheffield, rf	3	2	2	1	3	1
Bonilla, 3b	4	0	1	0	0	2
Arias, 3b	0	0	0	0	0	0
Daulton, 1b	3	1	1	1	7	0
Conine, 1b	1	0	0	0	1	1
White, cf	2	1	1	0	4	0
Johnson, c	3	0	1	3	6	0
Counsell, 2b	3	0	1	0	1	1
Saunders, p	2	0	0	0	0	1
Hernandez, p	1	0	0	0	0	1
Cook, p	0	0	0	0	0	1
Alou, ph	1	0	0	0	0	0
Nen, p	0	0	0	0	0	0
Totals	30	5	8	5	27	10

Atlanta	0	0	0	1	0	1	0	0	0—2
Florida	0	0	0	1	0	4	0	0	x—5

Atlanta	IP	H	R	ER	BB	SO
Smoltz (L)	6.0	5	5	5	5	9
Cather	1.0	2	0	0	0	0
Ligtenberg	1.0	1	0	0	0	1

Florida	IP	H	R	ER	BB	SO
Saunders	5.1	4	2	2	3	3
Hernandez (W)	1.2	2	0	0	0	1
Cook	1.0	0	0	0	0	2
Nen (S)	1.0	0	0	0	0	0

E—Counsell, Lofton. DP—Atlanta 1, Florida 1. LOB—Atlanta 6, Florida 7. 2B—Renteria, Daulton, Johnson. HR—Sheffield. SH—C. Jones, Johnson. SF—McGriff, Lopez. T—2:59. A—53,857. U—Winters, plate; Layne, first; Gregg, second; Pulli, third; Froemming, left field; Williams, right field.

GAME 4 BOX SCORE

ATLANTA 4, FLORIDA 0
SATURDAY, OCTOBER 11, AT FLORIDA

Atlanta	AB	R	H	RBI	PO	A
Lofton, cf	5	0	1	0	1	0
Blauser, ss	3	2	1	1	0	1
C. Jones, 3b	5	2	3	0	0	0
McGriff, 1b	3	0	2	2	3	1
Lopez, c	4	0	0	0	7	0
A. Jones, rf	4	0	2	1	7	0
Bautista, lf	4	0	1	0	4	0
Graffanino, 2b	4	0	1	0	4	2
Neagle, p	3	0	0	0	1	0
Totals	35	4	11	4	27	4

Florida	AB	R	H	RBI	PO	A
Abbott, 2b	4	0	1	0	2	0
Renteria, ss	4	0	1	0	3	5
Sheffield, rf	3	0	0	0	1	1
Bonilla, 3b	4	0	0	0	1	3
Conine, 1b	4	0	0	0	8	0
Alou, lf	3	0	0	0	0	0
Johnson, c	3	0	0	0	8	0
White, cf	3	0	0	0	3	0
Leiter, p	1	0	0	0	1	2
Arias, ph	1	0	1	0	0	0
Heredia, p	0	0	0	0	0	0
Cangelosi, ph	1	0	1	0	0	0
Vosberg, p	0	0	0	0	0	0
Totals	31	0	4	0	27	11

Atlanta	1	0	1	0	2	0	0	0	0—4
Florida	0	0	0	0	0	0	0	0	0—0

Atlanta	IP	H	R	ER	BB	SO
Neagle (W)	9.0	4	0	0	1	7

Florida	IP	H	R	ER	BB	SO
Leiter (L)	6.0	10	4	4	2	5
Heredia	2.0	0	0	0	0	2
Vosberg	1.0	1	0	0	1	1

DP—Florida 1. LOB—Atlanta 8, Florida 5. 2B—C. Jones, McGriff. HR—Blauser. SH—Neagle. T—2:40. A—54,890. U—Layne, plate; Gregg, first; Pulli, second; Froemming, third; Williams, left field; Winters, right field.

GAME 5 BOX SCORE

FLORIDA 2, ATLANTA 1
SUNDAY, OCTOBER 12, AT FLORIDA

Atlanta	AB	R	H	RBI	PO	A
Lofton, cf	3	0	1	0	1	0
Lockhart, 2b	3	0	0	0	2	1
C. Jones, 3b	4	0	0	0	0	2
McGriff, 1b	4	0	1	0	8	1
Klesko, lf	3	0	0	0	1	0
Tucker, rf	3	1	1	1	0	0
A. Jones, rf	0	0	0	0	0	0
Perez, c	3	0	0	0	11	0
Blauser, ss	3	0	0	0	1	4
Maddux, p	2	0	0	0	0	3
Gregg, ph	1	0	0	0	0	0
Cather, p	0	0	0	0	0	0
Totals	29	1	3	1	24	11

Florida	AB	R	H	RBI	PO	A
White, cf	3	1	0	0	2	0
Renteria, ss	4	0	0	0	3	2
Sheffield, rf	2	0	0	0	0	0
Bonilla, 3b	3	1	3	1	1	2
Conine, 1b	3	0	1	1	3	0
Alou, lf	3	0	0	0	0	0
Johnson, c	3	0	0	0	15	1
Counsell, 2b	3	0	1	0	2	0
Hernandez, p	2	0	0	0	1	0
Totals	26	2	5	2	27	5

Atlanta	0	1	0	0	0	0	0	0	0—1
Florida	1	0	0	0	0	0	1	0	x—2

Atlanta	IP	H	R	ER	BB	SO
Maddux (L)	7.0	4	2	2	1	9
Cather	1.0	1	0	0	0	1

Florida	IP	H	R	ER	BB	SO
Hernandez (W)	9.0	3	1	1	2	15

DP—Atlanta 1. LOB—Atlanta 3, Florida 3. 2B—Bonilla. 3B—Lofton. HR—Tucker. SB—White. SH—Hernandez. HBP—By Maddux (White). T—2:27. A—51,982. U—Gregg, plate; Pulli, first; Froemming, second; Williams, third; Winters, left field; Layne, right field.

GAME 6 BOX SCORE

FLORIDA 7, ATLANTA 4

TUESDAY, OCTOBER 14, AT ATLANTA

Florida	AB	R	H	RBI	PO	A
White, cf	5	2	2	0	4	0
Renteria, ss	3	2	2	0	1	4
Sheffield, rf	3	2	1	0	0	0
Bonilla, 3b	5	1	2	3	0	2
Arias, 3b	0	0	0	0	0	0
Conine, 1b	4	0	1	0	7	2
Alou, lf	4	0	0	1	1	0
Johnson, c	2	0	0	1	9	0
Counsell, 2b	4	0	2	2	3	2
Brown, p	4	0	0	0	2	2
Totals	34	7	10	7	27	12

Atlanta	AB	R	H	RBI	PO	A
Lofton, cf	5	1	1	1	2	0
Lockhart, 2b	5	1	4	2	5	2
C. Jones, 3b	4	0	0	0	0	0
McGriff, 1b	4	0	1	0	6	0
Klesko, lf	4	0	1	1	0	0
Lopez, c	4	0	0	0	9	2

Atlanta	AB	R	H	RBI	PO	A
Tucker, rf	4	0	0	0	2	0
Blauser, ss	4	2	2	0	3	4
Glavine, p	1	0	1	0	0	4
Cather, p	0	0	0	0	0	0
Gregg, ph	1	0	0	0	0	0
Ligtenberg, p	0	0	0	0	0	1
Embree, p	0	0	0	0	0	0
Colbrunn, ph	1	0	1	0	0	0
Totals	37	4	11	4	27	13

Florida	4 0 0	0 0 3	0 0 0	—7
Atlanta	1 2 0	0 0 0	0 0 1	—4

Florida	IP	H	R	ER	BB	SO
Brown (W)	9.0	11	4	4	1	8

Atlanta	IP	H	R	ER	BB	SO
Glavine (L)	5.2	10	7	7	7	4
Cather	0.1	0	0	0	0	1
Ligtenberg	2.0	0	0	0	0	3
Embree	1.0	0	0	0	1	1

E—Johnson, Blauser. DP—Atlanta 2. LOB—Florida 11, Atlanta 8. SB—Lofton. SH—Conine, Glavine, Brown. HBP—By Glavine (Johnson). T—3:10. A—50,446. U—Pulli, plate; Froemming, first; Williams, second; Winters, third; Layne, left field; Gregg, right field.

STATISTICS

FLORIDA MARLINS' BATTING AND FIELDING AVERAGES

Player, position	G	AB	R	H	TB	2B	3B	HR	RBI	BB	IBB	SO	Avg.	PO	A	E	Avg.
Arias, 3b-ph	3	1	0	1	1	0	0	0	0	0	0	0	1.000	0	0	0	.000
Counsell, 2b-ph	5	14	0	6	6	0	0	0	2	3	3	3	.429	7	9	1	.941
Abbott, 2b	2	8	0	3	4	1	0	0	0	0	0	2	.375	4	1	0	1.000
Bonilla, 3b	6	23	3	6	7	1	0	0	4	1	0	6	.261	5	13	0	1.000
Daulton, ph-1b	3	4	1	1	2	1	0	0	1	1	0	2	.250	8	1	0	1.000
Sheffield, rf	6	17	6	4	7	0	0	1	1	7	0	3	.235	5	2	0	1.000
Renteria, ss	6	22	4	5	6	1	0	0	0	3	0	6	.227	14	15	0	1.000
Cangelosi, ph-lf	3	5	0	1	1	0	0	0	0	1	0	0	.200	2	0	0	1.000
White, cf	6	21	4	4	5	1	0	0	1	2	1	7	.190	16	0	0	1.000
Johnson, c	6	17	1	2	4	2	0	0	5	3	1	8	.118	52	3	2	.965
Conine, 1b	6	18	1	2	2	0	0	0	1	1	0	4	.111	34	5	0	1.000
Alou, lf-ph	5	15	0	1	2	1	0	0	5	1	1	3	.067	3	0	0	1.000
Cook, p	2	0	0	0	0	0	0	0	0	0	0	0	.000	0	1	0	.000
Heredia, p	2	0	0	0	0	0	0	0	0	0	0	0	.000	0	0	0	.000
Nen, p	2	0	0	0	0	0	0	0	0	0	0	0	.000	0	1	0	1.000
Powell, p	1	0	0	0	0	0	0	0	0	0	0	0	.000	0	0	0	.000
Vosberg, p	2	0	0	0	0	0	0	•0	0	0	0	0	.000	0	0	0	.000
Zaun, c	1	0	0	0	0	0	0	0	0	0	0	0	.000	2	0	0	1.000
Fernandez, p	1	1	0	0	0	0	0	0	0	0	0	1	.000	0	0	0	.000
Leiter, p	2	1	0	0	0	0	0	0	0	0	0	1	.000	1	3	0	1.000
Saunders, p	1	2	0	0	0	0	0	0	0	0	0	2	.000	0	1	0	1.000
Eisenreich, lf	1	3	0	0	0	0	0	0	0	0	0	0	.000	2	0	0	1.000
Hernandez, p	2	3	0	0	0	0	0	0	0	0	0	0	.000	1	0	0	1.000
Brown, p	2	6	0	0	0	0	0	0	0	0	0	3	.000	3	2	0	1.000
Totals	6	181	20	36	47	8	0	1	20	23	6	52	.199	159	57	3	.986

ATLANTA BRAVES' BATTING AND FIELDING AVERAGES

Player, position	G	AB	R	H	TB	2B	3B	HR	RBI	BB	IBB	SO	Avg.	PO	A	E	Avg.
Colbrunn, ph	3	3	0	2	2	0	0	0	0	0	0	0	.667	0	0	0	.000
Lockhart, 2b-ph	5	16	4	8	11	1	1	0	3	1	0	1	.500	14	5	0	1.000
A. Jones, rf-ph	5	9	0	4	4	0	0	0	1	1	0	1	.444	12	1	0	1.000
McGriff, 1b	6	21	0	7	8	1	0	0	4	2	0	7	.333	41	2	1	.977
Glavine, p	2	3	0	1	1	0	0	0	0	0	0	2	.333	0	5	0	1.000
Blauser, ss	6	20	5	6	9	0	0	1	1	3	0	6	.300	6	19	1	.962
C. Jones, 3b	6	24	5	7	14	1	0	2	4	2	0	3	.292	1	8	0	1.000
Graffanino, 2b	3	8	1	2	3	1	0	0	0	0	0	3	.250	4	2	0	1.000
Bautista, lf	2	4	0	1	1	0	0	0	0	0	0	0	.250	4	0	0	1.000
Klesko, lf	5	17	2	4	10	0	0	2	4	2	0	3	.235	5	0	0	1.000
Lofton, cf	6	27	3	5	7	0	1	0	1	1	0	7	.185	9	1	2	.833
Tucker, rf-ph	5	10	1	1	4	0	0	0	1	3	0	4	.100	5	1	0	1.000
Lopez, c-ph	5	17	0	1	2	1	0	0	2	1	0	7	.059	40	3	0	1.000
Cather, p	4	0	0	0	0	0	0	0	0	0	0	0	.000	0	0	0	.000

Player, position	G	AB	R	H	TB	2B	3B	HR	RBI	BB	IBB	SO	Avg.	PO	A	E	Avg.
Embree, p	1	0	0	0	0	0	0	0	0	0	0	0	.000	0	0	0	.000
Ligtenberg, p	2	0	0	0	0	0	0	0	0	0	0	0	.000	0	2	0	1.000
Wohlers, p	1	0	0	0	0	0	0	0	0	0	0	0	.000	0	0	0	.000
Smoltz, p	1	2	0	0	0	0	0	0	0	0	0	1	.000	0	1	0	1.000
Maddux, p	2	3	0	0	0	0	0	0	0	0	0	2	.000	0	7	0	1.000
Neagle, p	2	3	0	0	0	0	0	0	0	0	0	1	.000	1	0	0	1.000
Perez, c	2	3	0	0	0	0	0	0	0	0	0	0	.000	14	0	0	1.000
Gregg, ph	4	4	0	0	0	0	0	0	0	0	0	1	.000	0	0	0	.000
Totals	6	194	21	49	76	5	2	6	21	16	0	49	.253	156	57	4	.982

FLORIDA MARLINS' PITCHING RECORDS

Pitcher	G	GS	CG	IP	H	R	ER	HR	BB	IBB	SO	HB	WP	W	L	Pct.	ERA
Vosberg	2	0	0	2.2	2	0	0	0	1	0	3	0	0	0	0	.000	0.00
Cook	2	0	0	2.1	0	0	0	0	0	0	2	1	0	0	0	.000	0.00
Nen	2	0	0	2.0	0	0	0	0	0	0	0	0	0	0	0	.000	0.00
Powell	1	0	0	0.2	0	0	0	0	0	0	1	0	0	0	0	.000	0.00
Hernandez	2	1	1	10.2	5	1	1	1	2	0	16	0	0	2	0	1.000	0.84
Saunders	1	1	0	5.1	4	2	2	0	3	0	3	0	0	0	0	.000	3.38
Brown	2	2	1	15.0	16	7	7	2	5	0	11	1	0	2	0	1.000	4.20
Leiter	2	1	0	8.1	13	4	4	1	2	0	6	0	0	0	1	.000	4.32
Heredia	2	0	0	3.1	3	2	2	0	2	0	4	0	0	0	0	.000	5.40
Fernandez	1	1	0	2.2	6	5	5	2	1	0	3	0	0	0	1	.000	16.88
Totals	6	6	2	53.0	49	21	21	6	16	0	49	2	0	4	2	.667	3.57

No shutouts. Saves—Nen 2.

ATLANTA BRAVES' PITCHING RECORDS

Pitcher	G	GS	CG	IP	H	R	ER	HR	BB	IBB	SO	HB	WP	W	L	Pct.	ERA
Neagle	2	1	1	12.0	5	0	0	0	1	0	9	1	0	1	0	1.000	0.00
Ligtenberg	2	0	0	3.0	1	0	0	0	0	0	4	0	0	0	0	.000	0.00
Cather	4	0	0	2.2	3	0	0	0	0	0	3	0	0	0	0	.000	0.00
Embree	1	0	0	1.0	0	0	0	0	1	0	1	0	0	0	0	.000	0.00
Wohlers	1	0	0	1.0	0	0	0	0	1	0	1	0	0	0	0	.000	0.00
Maddux	2	2	0	13.0	9	7	2	0	4	1	16	1	0	0	2	.000	1.38
Glavine	2	2	0	13.1	13	8	8	0	11	3	9	1	0	1	1	.500	5.40
Smoltz	1	1	0	6.0	5	5	5	1	5	2	9	0	0	0	1	.000	7.50
Totals	6	6	1	52.0	36	20	15	1	23	6	52	3	0	2	4	.333	2.60

Shutout—Neagle. No saves.

SCORE BY INNINGS

Florida	8	0	2	1	0	7	1	1	0	—20
Atlanta	6	3	4	1	2	2	2	0	1	—21

MISCELLANEOUS STATISTICS

Sacrifice hits—Brown 2, Glavine 2, Conine, Hernandez, Johnson, C. Jones, Maddux, Neagle.
Sacrifice flies—Lopez 2, McGriff.
Stolen bases—Lofton, Renteria, White.
Caught stealing—Johnson, Lofton.
Double plays—Blauser, Lockhart and McGriff 2; A. Jones and McGriff; Bonilla, Johnson and Daulton; Conine and Renteria; Leiter, Renteria and Conine; Ligtenberg, Blauser and McGriff; Maddux, Blauser and McGriff; Renteria, Counsell and Daulton.
Left on bases—Florida 6, 4, 7, 5, 3, 11—36; Atlanta 7, 8, 6, 8, 3, 8—40.
Hit by pitcher—by Maddux (White), by Brown (Blauser), by Glavine (Johnson), by Cook (Lockhart), by Neagle (Renteria).
Passed balls—None.
Balks—None.
Time of games—First game, 3:04; second game, 2:51; third game, 2:59; fourth game, 2:48; fifth game, 2:27; sixth game, 3:10.
Attendance—First game, 49,244; second game, 48,933; third game, 53,857; fourth game, 54,890; fifth game, 51,982; sixth game, 50,446.
Umpires—Froemming, Williams, C., Winters, Layne, Gregg and Pulli.
Official scorers—Scott McGregor, Doug Pett.

1997 REVIEW N.L. Championship Series

WORLD SERIES

GAME 1
HIGHLIGHTS

FLORIDA 7, CLEVELAND 4

Why the Marlins won: They went right after veteran Cleveland pitcher Orel Hershiser and got just enough solid mound work out of their temperamental rookie, Livan Hernandez, to make the difference. Moises Alou and Charles Johnson hit back-to-back home runs off Hershiser in the fourth inning, Alou's a three-run blast that ricocheted off the left-field foul pole at Pro Player Stadium. Hernandez, who had stood out in the League Championship Series, allowed three runs (two on homers) in 5 $^2/_3$ innings before being lifted. Visibly upset, Hernandez stormed off the mound and threw his glove in the dugout.

Why the Indians lost: Hershiser, known for his clutch postseason pitching (an 8-1 record and an ERA under 2.00), couldn't get the job done this time. Not only was he shelled for seven runs in 4 $^1/_3$ innings, he made a fielding blunder that a 39-year-old player should never commit. With the scored tied at 1 in the bottom of the fourth, Hershiser walked Bobby Bonilla on four pitchers, then was late covering first base when Darren Daulton hit a ground ball to the right side. Second baseman Bip Roberts fielded the ball but had no place to make a play. Hershiser then made another mistake, giving Alou a good pitch to hit on a 0-2 count. Hit it he did.

The turning points:

1. When Hershiser tried to beat out a bunt in the top half of the fourth—or so Cleveland manager Mike Hargrove insisted. Although the pitcher said the play was of no consequence, Hargrove believed that Hershiser's sprint to first base took something out of the righthander.

2. Johnson's towering home run, which seemed to prove conclusively that the night did not belong to Hershiser but that it did belong to the Marlins and their fans. The crowd reacted with a deafening roar to the back-to-back homers, thereby turning up the home-field advantage a notch or two.

Notable: Before homering off Hershiser, Alou had gone 1-for-12 against him in his career. . . . Moises' home run was the first by an Alou in World Series play. His father, Felipe, failed to connect in 26 at-bats for the Giants in the 1962 Series and uncles Matty (the Giants in '62, the A's in 1972) and Jesus (the A's in '73 and '74) went homerless in an combined 56 at-bats. . . . Alou was ecstatic over the scenario surrounding his home run. "It was awesome," he said. "My first World Series against a great pitcher like Orel. There's no better feeling than this.". . . Manny Ramirez's fifth-inning homer for Cleveland was his eighth in postseason play over three seasons. . . . Indians first baseman Jim Thome, experiencing a horrendous postseason to this point (.200 batting average in the Division Series and and a mark of .071

in the championship series), hit his first homer since September 14 when he connected off Hernandez in the sixth. He hit 40 homers in the regular season.

Quotable: Hernandez, who emphasized that he was not unhappy with manager Jim Leyland for removing him: "I did get a little angry. I got behind a few of the batters and showed emotion. I was angry at myself." . . . Leyland said he had no trouble with Hernandez's outburst "as long as it's for the right reason—and I'm sure it was. It's a time of tension for everybody." . . . Hershiser, responding to Hargrove's statement that his bunt attempt affected his strength: "I didn't feel tired at all. Running 90 feet is not going to make me tired."

BOX SCORE

SATURDAY, OCTOBER 18, AT FLORIDA

Cleveland	AB	R	H	RBI	PO	A
Roberts, 2b	4	1	2	0	3	1
Vizquel, ss	4	0	0	0	1	4
Ramirez, rf	3	1	1	1	2	0
Justice, lf	4	0	2	1	1	0
Williams, 3b	5	0	1	0	1	3
Thome, 1b	5	1	1	1	10	0
Alomar, c	5	0	1	0	4	1
Grissom, cf	3	1	2	0	1	0
Hershiser, p	2	0	0	0	1	1
Juden, p	0	0	0	0	0	0
*Branson, ph	1	0	0	0	0	0
Plunk, p	0	0	0	0	0	0
†Giles, ph	1	0	1	1	0	0
Assenmacher, p	0	0	0	0	0	0
Totals	**37**	**4**	**11**	**4**	**24**	**11**

Florida	AB	R	H	RBI	PO	A
White, cf	4	0	0	0	0	0
Renteria, ss	4	0	0	1	1	2
Sheffield, rf	2	1	0	0	4	0
Bonilla, 3b	3	2	2	0	0	2
Daulton, 1b	2	1	1	0	5	0
Conine, 1b	2	0	1	1	5	0
Alou, lf	3	1	1	3	1	0
Johnson, c	3	1	1	1	10	1
Counsell, 2b	3	1	1	0	1	1
Hernandez, p	2	0	0	0	0	2
Cook, p	0	0	0	0	0	0
Powell, p	0	0	0	0	0	0
‡Cangelosi, ph	1	0	0	0	0	0
Nen, p	0	0	0	0	0	0
Totals	**29**	**7**	**7**	**6**	**27**	**8**

Cleveland	1	0	0	0	1	1	0	1	0—4
Florida	0	0	1	4	2	0	0	0	x—7

Cleveland	IP	H	R	ER	BB	SO
Hershiser (L)	4.1	6	7	7	4	2
Juden	0.2	0	0	0	2	0
Plunk	2.0	1	0	0	1	1
Assenmacher	1.0	0	0	0	0	2

Florida	IP	H	R	ER	BB	SO
Hernandez (W)	5.2	8	3	3	2	5
Cook	1.2	0	0	0	1	2
Powell	0.2	1	1	1	2	1
Nen (S)	1.0	2	0	0	0	2

Bases on balls—Off Hershiser 4 (Sheffield 2, White, Bonilla), off Juden 2 (Johnson, Counsell), off Plunk 1 (Alou), off Hernandez 2 (Ramirez 2), off Cook 1 (Justice), off Powell 2 (Grissom, Roberts).

Strikeouts—By Hershiser 2 (Bonilla, Alou), by Plunk 1 (Sheffield), by Assenmacher 2 (Cangelosi, White), by Hernandez 5 (Alomar, Grissom, Hershiser, Williams, Branson), by Cook 2 (Vizquel, Thome), by Powell 1 (Vizquel), by Nen 2 (Thome, Alomar).

PLAY BY PLAY

FIRST INNING

Cleveland—Roberts doubled to right. Vizquel sacrificed Roberts to third, catcher to first baseman. Ramirez walked. Justice singled to center, scoring Roberts as Ramirez went to second. Williams popped to short. Thome grounded to second.

Florida—White grounded to the first baseman, who tossed to the pitcher. Renteria flied to right. Sheffield walked. Bonilla struck out.

SECOND INNING

Cleveland—Alomar, Grissom and Hershiser struck out.

Florida—Daulton flied to center. Alou struck out. Johnson grounded to third.

THIRD INNING

Cleveland—Roberts doubled to right-center. Vizquel flied to right, Roberts advancing to third. Ramirez walked. Justice flied to left. Williams struck out.

Florida—Counsell doubled to right. Hernandez sacrificed Counsell to second, pitcher to second baseman covering first. White walked. Renteria grounded to first as Counsell scored and White advanced to second. Sheffield grounded to third.

FOURTH INNING

Cleveland—Thome lined to first. Alomar grounded to third. Grissom doubled to right. Hershiser grounded to the pitcher.

Florida—Bonilla walked. Daulton singled to second, Bonilla advanced to second. Alou homered to left, scoring Bonilla and Daulton. Johnson homered to left. Counsell grounded to first. Hernandez popped to third. White flied to left.

FIFTH INNING

Cleveland—Conine now at first. Roberts grounded to the pitcher. Vizquel grounded to short. Ramirez homered to left. Justice popped to second.

Florida—Renteria grounded to third. Sheffield walked. Bonilla singled to right, Sheffield advancing to third. Conine singled to center, scoring Sheffield as Bonilla went to second. Juden now pitching. Alou forced Conine at second, shortstop to second baseman, as Bonilla went to third. Bonilla scored on a wild pitch and Alou went to second. Johnson and Counsell walked. Hernandez grounded to short.

SIXTH INNING

Cleveland—Williams grounded to third. Thome homered to left. Alomar singled to right. Grissom singled to left, Alomar advancing to second. Branson, pinch-hitting for Juden, struck out. Cook now pitching. Roberts flied to right.

Florida—Plunk now pitching. White popped to short. Renteria grounded to short. Sheffield struck out.

SEVENTH INNING

Cleveland—Vizquel struck out. Ramirez flied to right. Justice walked. Williams flied to right.

Florida—Bonilla singled to right. Conine grounded into a double play, shortstop to second baseman to first baseman. Alou walked. Johnson flied to left.

EIGHTH INNING

Cleveland—Thome struck out. Powell now pitching. Alomar popped foul to the first baseman. Grissom walked. Giles, pinch-hitting for Plunk, doubled to right-center and reached third on an error by the right fielder as Grissom scored. Roberts walked. Vizquel struck out.

Florida—Assenmacher now pitching. Counsell grounded to first. Cangelosi, pinch-hitting for Powell, struck out. White struck out and was retired on the dropped third strike, catcher to first baseman.

NINTH INNING

Cleveland—Nen now pitching. Ramirez grounded to short. Justice singled to right. Williams singled to third, Justice went to second. Thome and Alomar struck out.

CLEVELAND 6, FLORIDA 1

Why the Indians won: They got a stirring—and unexpected—lift from righthander Chad Ogea. Ogea spent two months on the disabled list during the regular season while struggling to an 8-9 record and a 4.99 ERA. Ogea yielded a first-inning run, then pitched shutout ball before being relieved with two outs in the seventh. He also executed a sacrifice bunt in the fifth that set up a two-run single by Bip Roberts.

Why the Marlins lost: Florida ace Kevin Brown, who won two games in the League Championship Series, was victimized by an Indians offense that was quietly effective in the fifth inning and explosively effective in the sixth. In the fifth, Cleveland parlayed four singles and Ogea's bunt into three runs and a 4-1 lead; in the sixth, the Indians' Sandy Alomar walloped a two-run homer.

The turning points:

1. With the score tied at 1 in the fourth and Florida's Moises Alou on second base after leading off with a double, catcher Alomar pounced on Charles Johnson's roller in front of the plate and threw out Alou trying to reach third. The play prevented the Marlins from possibly taking the lead and seizing momentum, and Cleveland struck for five runs in the next two innings.

2. With the game still within reach at 4-1 in the sixth, Florida third baseman Bobby Bonilla made an off-target throw on a potential double-play ball, getting only a forceout at second base and giving the Indians an extra out in the inning. The result: Alomar, who otherwise would not have batted (since Jim Thome flied out after Bonilla's play), drilled a two-run homer.

Notable: Marquis Grissom, whose fifth-inning single gave Cleveland a 2-1 lead, went 3-for-4 and extended his World Series hitting streak to 14 games, three off the record held by former Yankees star Hank Bauer. Grissom had played in the previous two World Series with the Braves. . . . Eleven of the Indians' 14 hits were singles. . . . Cleveland shortstop Omar Vizquel, 1-for-25 in the League Championship Series and 0-for-4 in Game 1 against the Marlins, doubled with one out in the first and scored the game's initial run on single by Dave Justice. It was the second consecutive night that the Indians had drawn first blood on a first-inning RBI single by Justice. . . . Jeff Conine, who played for the Marlins in the first game in franchise history in 1993, singled home Florida's run, in the first inning. . . . The game was a rare breather for Cleveland, whose four ALCS victories against Baltimore and its last two Division Series triumphs against the Yankees were by one run. The Indians' other postseason victory, against New York, was by two runs.

Quotable: Brown on his performance: "I threw decent. They killed me with grounders. I needed some luck and I didn't have any.". . . Alomar on nailing Alou at third base: "I saw Moises got a bad jump. I was lucky I made a low throw and Matt (Williams) was able to make the tag. I took a chance." . . . Ogea, unaccustomed to hitting except for limited interleague play, was impressed with Brown's repertoire but nonetheless able to lay down the key sacrifice. "The guy's got filthy stuff. I didn't have much of a chance to hit, but I got a bunt down. When you don't hit very often, it looks like they're throwing about 105 (mph)."

BOX SCORE

SUNDAY, OCTOBER 19, AT FLORIDA

Cleveland	AB	R	H	RBI	PO	A
Roberts, 2b	3	0	1	2	3	1
*Fernandez, ph-2b	2	0	2	0	1	1
Vizquel, ss	4	1	2	0	0	0
Ramirez, rf	5	0	0	0	4	0
Justice, lf	3	0	1	1	3	0
Williams, 3b	4	2	2	0	1	3
Thome, 1b	4	0	1	0	6	1
Alomar, c	4	2	2	2	7	1
Grissom, cf	4	1	3	1	1	0
Ogea, p	2	0	0	0	0	2
Jackson, p	1	0	0	0	0	0
Mesa, p	0	0	0	0	1	0
Totals	36	6	14	6	27	9

Florida	AB	R	H	RBI	PO	A
White, cf	5	0	2	0	2	0
Renteria, ss	4	1	2	0	1	3
Sheffield, rf	2	0	1	0	2	0
Bonilla, 3b	4	0	0	0	1	5
Conine, 1b	3	0	1	1	8	1
‡Daulton, ph-1b	1	0	0	0	1	0
Alou, lf	4	0	2	0	1	0
Johnson, c	3	0	0	0	5	1
§Zaun, c	1	0	0	0	0	0
Counsell, 2b	3	0	0	0	5	4
Brown, p	2	0	0	0	0	2
Heredia, p	0	0	0	0	1	0
†Eisenreich, ph	1	0	0	0	0	0
Alfonseca, p	0	0	0	0	0	0
∞Floyd, ph	1	0	0	0	0	0
Totals	34	1	8	1	27	16

Cleveland	1	0	0	0	3	2	0	0	0—6
Florida	1	0	0	0	0	0	0	0	0—1

Cleveland	IP	H	R	ER	BB	SO
Ogea (W)	6.2	7	1	1	1	4
Jackson	1.1	1	0	0	0	1
Mesa	1.0	0	0	0	1	1

Florida	IP	H	R	ER	BB	SO
Brown (L)	6.0	10	6	6	2	4
Heredia	1.0	1	0	0	0	1
Alfonseca	2.0	3	0	0	0	0

Bases on balls—Off Ogea 1 (Sheffield), off Mesa 1 (Counsell), off Brown 2 (Vizquel, Justice).

Strikeouts—By Ogea 4 (White, Johnson, Brown, Renteria), by Jackson 1 (Bonilla), by Mesa 1 (Floyd), by Brown 4 (Roberts, Justice, Thome, Ogea), by Heredia 1 (Ramirez).

*Doubled for Roberts in seventh. †Grounded out for Heredia in seventh. ‡Flied out for Conine in eighth. §Grounded out for Johnson in ninth. ∞Struck out for Alfonseca in ninth. DP—Cleveland 1, Florida 3. LOB—Cleveland 6, Florida 9. HR—Alomar. CS—Justice. SH—Ogea. HBP—By Ogea (Sheffield). U—Ford (A.L.), plate; West (N.L.), first; Kosc (A.L.), second; Marsh (N.L.), third; Kaiser (A.L.), left field; Montague (N.L.), right field. T—2:40. A—67,025.

PLAY BY PLAY

FIRST INNING

Cleveland—Roberts struck out. Vizquel doubled to right. Ramirez grounded to short, Vizquel advancing to third. Justice singled to right-center, scoring Vizquel. With Williams batting, Justice was caught trying to steal, catcher to second baseman.

Florida—White struck out. Renteria singled to center. Sheffield hit by pitch. Bonilla flied to center. Conine singled to center, scoring Renteria as Sheffield went to second. Alou flied to left.

SECOND INNING

Cleveland—Williams grounded to third. Thome singled to left. Alomar grounded into a double play, third baseman to second baseman to first baseman.

Florida—Johnson struck out. Counsell popped to second. Brown struck out.

THIRD INNING

Cleveland—Grissom grounded to the pitcher. Ogea grounded to third. Roberts grounded to short.

Florida—White grounded to first. Renteria doubled to left. Sheffield walked. Bonilla flied to left. Conine flied to right.

FOURTH INNING

Cleveland—Vizquel singled to center. Ramirez grounded into a double play, second baseman to shortstop to first baseman. Justice struck out.

Florida—Alou doubled to left-center. Johnson reached first on a fielder's choice as Alou was out trying to advance to third, catcher to third baseman. Counsell popped to second. Brown grounded to the pitcher.

FIFTH INNING

Cleveland—Williams singled to right-center. Thome struck out. Alomar singled to left, Williams advancing to second. Grissom singled to left, scoring Williams as Alomar went to second. Ogea sacrificed to the pitcher as Alomar went to third and Grissom to second. Roberts singled to center, scoring Alomar and Grissom. Vizquel walked. Ramirez flied to center.

Florida—White singled to center. Renteria struck out. Sheffield grounded into a double play, third baseman to second baseman to first baseman.

SIXTH INNING

Cleveland—Justice walked. Williams forced Justice at second, third baseman to second baseman. Thome flied to right. Alomar homered to left, scoring Williams. Grissom singled to third. Ogea struck out.

Florida—Bonilla flied to right. Conine fouled to the catcher. Alou doubled to left. Johnson grounded to third.

SEVENTH INNING

Cleveland—Heredia now pitching. Fernandez, pinch-hitting for Roberts, doubled to left-center. Vizquel flied to right. Ramirez struck out. Justice grounded to the first baseman, who tossed to the pitcher covering first.

Florida—Fernandez now at second. Counsell flied to right. Eisenreich, pinch-hitting for Heredia, grounded to the pitcher. White doubled to right. Jackson now pitching. Renteria flied to the right.

EIGHTH INNING

Cleveland—Alfonseca now pitching. Williams singled to left. Thome flied to left. Alomar flied to center. Grissom singled to right, Williams went to second. Jackson grounded to second.

Florida—Sheffield singled to left-center. Bonilla struck out. Daulton, pinch-hitting for Conine, flied to left. Alou forced Sheffield at second, third baseman to second baseman.

NINTH INNING

Cleveland—Daulton now at first. Fernandez singled to left. Vizquel popped foul to the third baseman. Ramirez grounded into a double play, third baseman to second baseman to first baseman.

Florida—Mesa now pitching. Zaun, pinch-hitting for Johnson, grounded to second. Counsell walked. Floyd, pinch-hitting for Alfonseca, struck out. White grounded to the first baseman, who tossed to the pitcher covering first.

GAME 3

HIGHLIGHTS

FLORIDA 14, CLEVELAND 11

Why the Marlins won: The warm-weather team survived the elements—temperatures in the 40s and wind-chill readings in the 20s—better than the cold-weather club did. Although both teams made three errors and got some terrible pitching, the Marlins banged out 16 hits and received a superlative performance from Gary Sheffield, who drove in five runs and made a sensational catch.

Why the Indians lost: Their miscues were particularly untimely, all coming in the ninth inning of what had been a 7-7 game, and their pitching—eight walks allowed, in addition to the hefty hits total—was somehow worse overall than Florida's.

The turning points:

1. When Cleveland's defense unraveled in the ninth. After leading 7-3 midway through the game, the Indians found themselves in a deadlocked game in the final inning—and soon wound up down by seven runs when errors by center fielder Marquis Grissom, first baseman Jim Thome and second baseman Tony Fernandez combined with four hits, three walks and a wild pitch to open the floodgates for Florida. Sheffield and Bobby Bonilla contributed two-run singles in the outburst.

2. With the Marlins having tied the score in the top of the seventh on RBI hits by Edgar Renteria and Sheffield, right fielder Sheffield climbed the wall in the bottom half of the inning and made a remarkable catch of Thome's smash. The play robbed Thome of at least an extra-base hit and foiled Cleveland's hopes of quickly recapturing the lead.

Notable: The 25-run game at Jacobs Field took 4 hours and 12 minutes to complete, making it the second highest-scoring and the second-longest game (in time) in World Series history. Only Game 4 of the 1993 Series, a 15-14 Blue Jays victory over the Phillies that consumed 4 hours and 14 minutes, surpassed this one in those categories. . . . Florida closer Robb Nen made things interesting in the bottom of the ninth, giving up three hits, two walks and four runs. . . . Sheffield began his big night with a first-inning home run. . . . Marlins pitchers walked nine batters, and starter Al Leiter threw 114 pitches in only 4 2/3 innings. . . . Indians starter Charles Nagy, trying to be too fine with his pitches, tied a World Series record in the third inning by walking three consecutive batters. . . . The Indians' Grissom extended his World Series batting streak to 15 games with a 2-for-3 performance.

Quotable: Indians manager Mike Hargrove: "It was as ugly a game as you'll ever see. It wasn't the weather. It was just poor play." . . . Sheffield on his dream of playing and excelling in the World Series: "I've been waiting nine years for this. I was finally able to come through."

BOX SCORE

TUESDAY, OCTOBER 21, AT CLEVELAND

Florida	AB	R	H	RBI	PO	A
White, cf	5	0	1	0	2	0
Renteria, ss	4	2	2	1	1	3
Sheffield, rf	5	2	3	5	5	0
Bonilla, 3b	5	1	1	2	0	4
Daulton, 1b	4	3	2	1	8	1
Conine, 1b	0	0	0	0	1	0
Alou, lf	5	0	0	0	1	0
Eisenreich, dh	3	1	2	2	0	0
*Abbott, ph-dh	1	0	0	0	0	0
†Floyd, ph-dh	0	1	0	0	0	0
Johnson, c	5	2	3	0	5	0
Counsell, 2b	5	2	2	1	3	3
Leiter, p	0	0	0	0	1	0
Heredia, p	0	0	0	0	0	0
Cook, p	0	0	0	0	0	0
Nen, p	0	0	0	0	0	0
Totals	42	14	16	12	27	11

Cleveland	AB	R	H	RBI	PO	A
Roberts, lf	5	1	1	2	0	0
Vizquel, ss	4	0	0	1	1	2
Ramirez, rf	5	0	1	1	2	0
Justice, dh	3	2	0	0	0	0
Williams, 3b	5	0	1	1	1	1
Alomar, c	3	2	2	1	8	0
‡Giles, ph	0	1	0	0	0	0
Thome, 1b	4	3	2	2	6	2
Fernandez, 2b	4	0	1	1	3	3
Grissom, cf	3	2	2	1	4	0
Nagy, p	0	0	0	0	1	1
Anderson, p	0	0	0	0	0	0
Jackson, p	0	0	0	0	1	0
Assenmacher, p	0	0	0	0	0	0
Plunk, p	0	0	0	0	0	0
Morman, p	0	0	0	0	0	0
Mesa, p	0	0	0	0	0	0
Totals	36	11	10	10	27	9

Florida	1	0	1	1	0	2	2	0 7—14
Cleveland	2	0	0	3	2	0	0	4—11

Florida	IP	H	R	ER	BB	SO
Leiter	4.2	6	7	4	6	3
Heredia	2.1	0	0	0	1	0
Cook (W)	1.0	1	0	0	0	1
Nen	1.0	3	4	4	2	1

Cleveland	IP	H	R	ER	BB	SO
Nagy	6.0	6	5	5	4	5
Anderson	0.1	1	1	1	0	0
Jackson	0.2	2	1	1	1	0
Assenmacher	0.2	3	0	0	0	1
Plunk (L)	0.2	2	4	3	2	1
Morman	0.1	0	2	0	1	1
Mesa	0.1	2	1	1	0	0

Bases on balls—Off Leiter 6 (Justice, Alomar, Thome, Grissom 2, Vizquel), off Heredia 1 (Vizquel), off Nen 2 (Justice, Giles), off Nagy 4 (White, Renteria, Sheffield, Daulton), off Jackson 1 (Daulton), off Plunk 2 (Bonilla, Floyd), off Morman 1 (Renteria). Strikeouts—By Leiter 3 (Thome, Roberts, Williams), by Cook 1 (Vizquel), by Nen 1 (Williams), by Nagy 5 (Alou 2, Counsell 2, Bonilla), by Assenmacher 1 (Abbott), by Plunk 1 (Alou), by Morman 1 (White). *Struck out for Eisenreich in eighth. †Intentionally walked for Abbott in ninth. ‡Walked for Alomar in ninth. E—Leiter, Bonilla 2, Grissom, Thome, Fernandez. DP—Florida 1, Cleveland 2. LOB—Florida 9, Cleveland 9. HR—Sheffield, Daulton, Thome, Eisenreich. SH—Roberts. SF—Fernandez. WP—Mesa. U—West (N.L.), plate; Kosc (A.L.), first; Marsh (N.L.), second; Kaiser (A.L.), third; Montague (N.L.), left field; Ford (A.L.), right field. T—4:12. A—44,880.

PLAY BY PLAY

FIRST INNING

Florida—White grounded to first. Renteria grounded to pitcher. Sheffield homered to left. Bonilla grounded to first.

Cleveland—Roberts reached first on an error by the pitcher. Vizquel grounded to second, Roberts advancing to second. Ramirez grounded to third. Justice walked. Williams singled to right-center, scoring Roberts as Justice went to third. Alomar singled to left, scoring Justice as Williams went to second. Thome struck out.

SECOND INNING

Florida—Daulton lined to right. Alou struck out. Eisenreich lined to center.

Cleveland—Fernandez singled to left. Grissom grounded into a double play, second baseman to shortstop to first baseman. Roberts lined to the pitcher.

THIRD INNING

Florida—Johnson singled to right. Counsell struck out. White, Renteria and Sheffield walked, Johnson scoring on the latter walk. Bonilla grounded into a double play, first baseman to shortstop to the pitcher covering first.

Cleveland—Vizquel flied to center. Ramirez reached first on an error by the third baseman. Justice flied to right. Williams forced Ramirez at second, shortstop to second baseman.

FOURTH INNING

Florida—Daulton homered to right-center. Alou flied to right. Eisenreich singled to right. Johnson forced Eisenreich at second, third baseman to second baseman. Counsell struck out.

Cleveland—Alomar and Thome walked. Fernandez flied to center, Alomar advancing to third and Thome to second. Grissom walked. Roberts struck out. Vizquel walked, scoring Alomar. Ramirez singled to third, scoring Thome as Grissom went to third. On the play, Grissom scored and Vizquel went to third on a throwing error by the third baseman. Justice forced Ramirez at second, third baseman to second baseman.

FIFTH INNING

Florida—White flied to center. Renteria singled to center. Sheffield grounded into a double play, shortstop to second baseman to first baseman.

Cleveland—Williams struck out. Alomar singled to the pitcher. Thome homered to right, scoring Alomar. Fernandez grounded to third. Grissom walked. Heredia now pitching. Roberts lined to right.

SIXTH INNING

Florida—Bonilla struck out. Daulton walked. Alou struck out. Eisenreich homered to right, scoring Daulton. Johnson grounded to second.

Cleveland—Vizquel walked. Ramirez flied to right. Justice grounded to first, Vizquel went to second. Williams grounded to third.

SEVENTH INNING

Florida—Anderson now pitching. Counsell singled to right. White grounded to second, Counsell advancing to second. Jackson now pitching. Renteria singled to center, scoring Counsell. Sheffield doubled to center, scoring Renteria. Bonilla grounded to the first baseman, who tossed to the pitcher covering first, Sheffield went to third. Daulton was walked intentionally. Alou flied to center.

Cleveland—Alomar and Thome flied to right. Fernandez grounded to short.

EIGHTH INNING

Florida—Assenmacher now pitching. Abbott, pinch-hitting for Eisenreich, struck out. Johnson singled to center. Counsell singled to right, Johnson went to second. White singled to third, Johnson advancing to third and Counsell to second. Renteria popped to second. Plunk now pitching. Sheffield forced Counsell at third, third baseman, unassisted.

Cleveland—Cook now pitching. Grissom singled to short. Roberts sacrificed Grissom to second, first baseman to second baseman covering first. Vizquel struck out. Ramirez popped foul to the first baseman.

NINTH INNING

Florida—Bonilla walked. Daulton singled to center and went to third on a throwing error by the center fielder. Bonilla scored on the play. Alou struck out. Floyd, pinch-hitting for Abbott, was walked intentionally. Daulton scored when the first baseman made an error on a pickoff attempt. Johnson singled to center, Floyd advancing to third. Morman now pitching. Counsell reached first on an error by the second baseman, Floyd scored, Johnson advancing to second. White struck out. Renteria walked. Mesa now pitching. Sheffield singled to right, scoring Johnson and Counsell as Renteria went to second. Renteria went to third and Sheffield to second on a wild pitch. Bonilla singled to right, scoring Renteria and Sheffield. Daulton lined to center.

Cleveland—Nen now pitching and Conine at first. Justice walked. Williams struck out. Giles, pinch-hitting for Alomar, walked. Thome singled to right, Justice advancing to third and Giles to second. Fernandez hit a sacrifice fly to left, scoring Justice. Grissom singled to short, scoring Giles as Thome went to second. Roberts doubled to right-center, scoring Thome and Grissom. Vizquel grounded to second.

CLEVELAND 10, FLORIDA 3

Why the Indians won: Their precocious rookie pitcher, Jaret Wright, warmed to the task—and then some—on a snowy night. A high school player just $3^{1}/_{2}$ years earlier and a Class AA pitcher in May, he went out in a pressure situation and, throwing in the mid-90s, held Florida in check over six innings as Cleveland tied the Series at two games apiece.

Why the Marlins lost: Marlins rookie starter Tony Saunders was as bad as Wright was good. While Wright allowed only three runs and five hits, Saunders was rocked for six runs and seven hits in two-plus innings.

The turning points:

1. When the Indians, after such an awful effort the night before, showed there would be no hangover effect by jumping on Saunders for three first-inning runs, two coming on Manny Ramirez's home run.

2. When Cleveland's bullpen, a kerosene-by-committee brigade in Game 3, came through. And it took only one man, Brian Anderson, to get the job done. After Wright was nicked for one run in the fourth inning and two in the sixth, lefthander Anderson was summoned and proceeded to pitch one-hit, shutout ball over the last three innings.

Notable: Cleveland center fielder Marquis Grissom saw his World Series hitting streak end at 15 games after going 0-for-4. He was the only Indians player to go hitless. . . . Indians third baseman Matt Williams, who hit a two-run homer in the eighth and was 3-for-3, made a nice hook slide around catcher Charles Johnson's tag in the first inning. He had singled and come around on Sandy Alomar's double. . . . Florida center fielder Devon White struck out four times in four at-bats. . . . Florida's defense came undone in the third inning, much as Cleveland's had in the ninth inning the night before. Saunders and shortstop Edgar Renteria committed throwing errors in a three-run Indians inning that put the Marlins in a 6-0 hole. . . . Williams and Alomar, Cleveland's No. 5 and 6 hitters, were a combined 6-for-8 with five RBIs. . . . The snowfall was the first at a World Series since the 1979 Orioles-Pirates matchup. Befitting the situation, "Jingle Bells" and "Let It Snow" were played over the stadium's speaker system. The game-time temperature was 38 (a World Series record low) and the wind chill read 18 degrees.

Quotable: Wright on the conditions: "This was the coldest weather I've pitched in. But it was the same for Tony Saunders. I was just fortunate that we got ahead early. I wasn't going to put any more pressure on myself because we lost last night." . . . Alomar, on Wright's outing: "Jaret was behind in the count a lot, but he got out of trouble with good sinking fastballs and good defense." . . . Williams, who had said it was crucial for Cleveland to seize an early lead, explained that he was merely being aggressive on the play that increased the Indians' lead to 3-0 in their first at-bat. With two outs, Williams was off and running when Alomar drove a Saunders pitch into left-center and never let up. "I saw Charles (Johnson) move up the line to catch the throw," he said, "so I tried to slide around him. Usually, I hurt myself trying to do that, but it worked OK tonight."

BOX SCORE

WEDNESDAY, OCTOBER 22, AT CLEVELAND

Florida	AB	R	H	RBI	PO	A
White, cf	4	0	0	0	2	0
Renteria, ss	4	0	1	0	0	3
Sheffield, rf	3	0	0	0	0	0
Bonilla, 3b	4	0	0	0	2	1
Daulton, 1b	3	2	2	0	8	0
Alou, lf	3	1	1	2	3	0
Eisenreich, dh	2	0	2	1	0	0
†Arias, ph-dh	1	0	0	0	0	0
Johnson, c	4	0	0	0	7	0
Counsell, 2b	2	0	0	0	2	1
‡Abbott, ph	1	0	0	0	0	0
Saunders, p	0	0	0	0	0	1
Alfonseca, p	0	0	0	0	0	0
Vosberg, p	0	0	0	0	0	1
Powell, p	0	0	0	0	0	1
Totals	31	3	6	3	24	8
Cleveland	AB	R	H	RBI	PO	A
Roberts, lf	4	0	1	0	1	0
Giles, lf	1	0	1	1	0	0
Vizquel, ss	5	2	2	0	2	3
Ramirez, rf	4	2	1	2	1	0
Justice, dh	3	2	1	0	0	0
Williams, 3b	3	3	3	2	0	2
Alomar, c	5	0	3	3	7	0
Thome, 1b	4	0	1	0	10	0
Fernandez, 2b	5	1	2	1	3	2
Grissom, cf	4	0	0	0	3	0
Wright, p	0	0	0	0	0	0
Anderson, p	0	0	0	0	0	1
Totals	38	10	15	9	27	8

Florida	0	0	0	1	0	2	0	0 0—	3
Cleveland	3	0	3	0	0	1	1	2 x—	10

Florida	IP	H	R	ER	BB	SO
Saunders (L)	*2.0	7	6	6	3	2
Alfonseca	3.0	3	0	0	0	4
Vosberg	2.0	3	2	2	2	1
Powell	1.0	2	2	2	1	0
Cleveland	IP	H	R	ER	BB	SO
Wright (W)	6.0	5	3	3	5	5
Anderson (S)	3.0	1	0	0	0	2

*Pitched to five batters in third.
Bases on balls—Off Saunders 3 (Ramirez, Williams, Thome), off Vosberg 2 (Justice, Williams), off Powell 1 (Justice), off Wright 5 (Sheffield, Eisenreich, Counsell, Alou, Daulton).
Strikeouts—By Saunders 2 (Roberts, Justice), by Alfonseca 4 (Grissom, Roberts, Justice, Thome), by Vosberg 1 (Ramirez), by Wright 5 (White 3, Johnson, Sheffield), by Anderson 2 (White, Sheffield).
†Popped out for Eisenreich in ninth. ‡Grounded out for Counsell in ninth. E—Renteria, Renteria. DP—Cleveland 2. LOB—Florida 6, Cleveland 10. HR—Ramirez, Alou, Williams. SB—Counsell, Vizquel. CS—Giles. WP—Wright. U—Kosc (A.L.), plate; Marsh (N.L.), first; Kaiser (A.L.), second; Montague (N.L.), third; Ford (A.L.), left field; West (N.L.), right field. T—3:15. A—44,877.

PLAY BY PLAY

FIRST INNING

Florida—White struck out. Renteria singled to right. Sheffield walked. Bonilla grounded into a double play, second baseman to shortstop to first baseman.

Cleveland—Roberts struck out. Vizquel singled to left-center. Ramirez homered to right, scoring Vizquel. Justice struck out. Williams singled to right. Alomar doubled to left-center, scoring Williams. Thome grounded to the pitcher.

SECOND INNING

Florida—Daulton grounded to second. Alou grounded to third. Eisenreich walked. Eisenreich went to second on a wild pitch. Johnson struck out.

Cleveland—Fernandez popped to third. Grissom flied to center. Roberts doubled to left. Vizquel grounded to second.

THIRD INNING

Florida—Counsell walked. White struck out as Counsell stole second. Renteria grounded to short, Counsell advancing to third. Sheffield struck out.

Cleveland—Ramirez walked and went to second on the pitcher's wild pickoff throw. Justice singled to short and reached second on the shortstop's wild throw, Ramirez scoring on the play. Williams walked. Alomar singled to right, scoring Justice as Williams went to second. Thome walked. Alfonseca now pitching. Fernandez singled to center, scoring Williams as Alomar went to third and Thome to second. Grissom and Roberts struck out. Vizquel popped to second.

FOURTH INNING

Florida—Bonilla lined to second. Daulton doubled to right-center. Alou walked. Eisenreich singled to left, scoring Daulton as Alou went to second. Johnson forced Eisenreich at second, shortstop to second baseman, Alou advancing to third. Counsell lined to center.

Cleveland—Ramirez grounded to short. Justice struck out. Williams singled to left. Alomar singled to right-center, Williams advancing to third. Thome struck out.

FIFTH INNING

Florida—White struck out. Renteria flied to right. Sheffield popped to second.

Cleveland—Fernandez flied to left. Grissom flied to center. Roberts grounded to first.

SIXTH INNING

Florida—Bonilla flied to center. Daulton walked. Alou homered to left, scoring Daulton. Eisenreich singled to left-center. Johnson lined into a double play, first baseman, unassisted.

Cleveland—Vosberg now pitching. Vizquel singled to right-center. Ramirez struck out. With Justice batting, Vizquel stole second. Justice and Williams walked. Alomar forced Justice at third, third baseman, unassisted, Vizquel scored as Williams went to second. Thome flied to left.

SEVENTH INNING

Florida—Anderson now pitching and Giles in left. Counsell popped to short. White struck out. Renteria lined to center.

Cleveland—Fernandez singled to right. Grissom grounded to third, Fernandez advancing to second. Giles singled to center, scoring Fernandez. With Vizquel batting, Giles caught stealing second, pitcher to first baseman. Vizquel lined to left.

EIGHTH INNING

Florida—Sheffield struck out. Bonilla popped to first. Daulton singled to center. Alou popped foul to the first baseman.

Cleveland—Powell now pitching. Ramirez grounded to short. Justice walked. Williams homered to left, scoring Justice. Alomar grounded to the pitcher. Thome singled to center. Fernandez forced Thome at second, shortstop to second baseman.

NINTH INNING

Florida—Arias, pinch-hitting for Eisenreich, popped to second. Johnson grounded to third. Abbott, pinch-hitting for Counsell, grounded to the pitcher.

GAME 5

HIGHLIGHTS

FLORIDA 8, CLEVELAND 7

Why the Marlins won: Moises Alou got the best of Indians veteran Orel Hershiser for the second time in this World Series—and it again proved crucial. Trying to protect a 4-2 lead in the sixth inning, Hershiser yielded a single to Gary Sheffield and a walk to Bobby Bonilla before being tagged for a go-ahead home run by Alou.

Why the Indians lost: They seemingly had Florida's Livan Hernandez on the ropes—they coaxed six walks from the righthander in the first three innings—but let him escape. The hyper rookie kept his composure—or at least regained it—and pitched into the ninth before giving way to Robb Nen.

The turning points:

1. With Cleveland behind 6-4 but still in the game, the Marlins got a big insurance run in the eighth when Alou reached on an infield single, stole second, moved to third on a groundout and scored on Charles Johnson's single.

2. With their lead now at three runs, Florida addedanother insurance run in the ninth when that man Alou singled home pinch runner Alex Arias.

Notable: The Marlins needed all the insurance runs they could muster when Nen allowed a two-run single to David Justice and a run-scoring single to Jim Thome in the ninth before closing out the Indians. . . . TV replays showed that first base umpire Ken Kaiser erred on a play that helped ignite Cleveland's last-ditch rally. Kaiser made a safe call on the Indians' Bip Roberts in the ninth, claiming that Hernandez had missed the bag when taking a throw from first baseman Jeff Conine on Roberts' grounder. The replay indicated Hernandez had touched the side of the bag with his foot, ahead of Roberts. . . . In the game's early going, Johnson, Florida pitching coach Larry Rothschild and ailing pitcher Alex Fernandez spent time between innings trying to keep the animated Hernandez, 22, from losing his cool. It seemed to work. After surrendering a three-run homer to Sandy Alomar in the third inning, Hernandez hurled five consecutive scoreless innings. His pitching line wasn't eye-popping—seven hits, eight walks, five earned runs and two strikeouts in eight-plus innings—but it was good enough to move the Marlins within one victory of a World Series title and boost his 1997 postseason record to 4-0.

Quotable: Alou said the game was "probably the biggest of my life." Acknowledging he had struggled in his first two at-bats (a popup and a strikeout), Alou said he made an adjustment before cracking the home run. "I stayed back (on the ball), trusted my hands and got a good pitch to hit," he said. "Actually, I got two good pitches to hit. He (Hershiser) threw me a hanging slider first, and I fouled it back. When he threw me another hanging slider, I was ready for it and got it good."

BOX SCORE

THURSDAY, OCTOBER 23, AT CLEVELAND

Florida	AB	R	H	RBI	PO	A
White, cf	4	0	2	2	2	0
Renteria, ss	5	0	1	0	2	8
Sheffield, rf	5	1	2	0	2	0
Bonilla, 3b	4	1	1	0	0	4
†Arias, pr-3b	0	1	0	0	0	0
Daulton, dh	5	1	2	0	0	0
Alou, lf	5	2	3	4	2	0
Conine, 1b	5	1	1	0	11	1
Johnson, c	5	1	3	2	3	0

Florida	AB	R	H	RBI	PO	A
Counsell, 2b	2	0	0	0	5	2
Hernandez, p	0	0	0	0	0	2
Nen, p	0	0	0	0	0	0
Totals	40	8	15	8	27	17

Cleveland	AB	R	H	RBI	PO	A
Roberts, 2b	3	1	0	0	2	5
Vizquel, ss	4	1	1	0	4	2
Ramirez, rf	5	0	1	0	1	1
Justice, dh	5	0	1	2	0	0
Williams, 3b	3	2	1	0	0	0
Thome, 1b	4	2	2	1	9	0
Alomar, c	5	1	2	4	7	0
Giles, lf	1	0	0	0	2	0
Grissom, cf	4	0	1	0	2	0
Hershiser, p	0	0	0	0	0	0
Morman, p	0	0	0	0	0	0
Plunk, p	0	0	0	0	0	0
Juden, p	0	0	0	0	0	0
Assenmacher, p	0	0	0	0	0	0
Mesa, p	0	0	0	0	0	0
Totals	34	7	9	7	27	8

Florida	0	2	0	0	0	4	0	1	1—8
Cleveland	0	1	3	0	0	0	0	0	3—7

Florida	IP	H	R	ER	BB	SO
Hernandez (W)	*8.0	7	6	5	8	2
Nen (S)	1.0	2	1	0	0	1

Cleveland	IP	H	R	ER	BB	SO
Hershiser (L)	5.2	9	6	6	2	3
Morman	0.0	0	0	0	1	0
Plunk	0.1	0	0	0	1	1
Juden	1.1	2	1	1	0	0
Assenmacher	0.2	1	0	0	0	1
Mesa	1.0	3	1	1	0	1

*Pitched to two batters in ninth.
Bases on balls—Off Hernandez 8 (Roberts 2, Giles 3, Williams 2, Thome), off Hershiser 2 (Counsell, Bonilla), off Morman 1 (Counsell), off Plunk 1 (White).
Strikeouts—By Hernandez 2 (Justice, Giles), by Nen 1 (Ramirez), by Hershiser 3 (Alou, Johnson, Renteria), by Plunk 1 (Renteria), by Assenmacher 1 (Counsell), by Mesa 1 (Johnson).
†Ran for Bonilla in ninth. E—Hernandez, Counsell. DP—Florida 2, Cleveland 1. LOB—Florida 9, Cleveland 9. HR—Alomar, Alou. SB—Alou, Daulton. SH—Vizquel. WP—Hernandez. U—Marsh (N.L.), plate; Kaiser (A.L.), first; Montague (N.L.), second; Ford (A.L.), third; West (N.L.), left field; Kosc (A.L.), right field. T—3:39. A—44,888.

PLAY BY PLAY

FIRST INNING

Florida—White grounded to second. Renteria singled to third. Sheffield singled to center, Renteria advancing to second. Bonilla grounded into a double play, second baseman to shortstop to first baseman.

Cleveland—Roberts walked. Vizquel sacrificed Roberts to second, third baseman to first baseman. Ramirez grounded to short. Justice grounded to the pitcher.

SECOND INNING

Florida—Daulton doubled to right. Alou popped to short. Conine grounded to first, Daulton advancing to third. Johnson singled to right-center, scoring Daulton. Counsell walked. White doubled to right-center, scoring Johnson as Counsell went to third. On the play, Counsell was out trying to score, right fielder to second baseman to catcher.

Cleveland—Williams grounded to short. Thome tripled to center. Alomar singled to right, scoring Thome. Giles walked. Grissom grounded to third, Alomar advancing to third and Giles to second. Roberts walked. Vizquel lined to center.

THIRD INNING

Florida—Renteria grounded to short. Sheffield lined to second. Bonilla lined to short.

Cleveland—Ramirez grounded to third. Justice struck out. Williams walked. Williams went to second on a wild pitch. Thome walked. Alomar homered to left, scoring Williams and Thome. Giles walked. Grissom singled to left, Giles advancing to second. Roberts lined to short.

FOURTH INNING

Florida—Daulton popped to first. Alou struck out. Conine lined to center.

Cleveland—Vizquel flied to right. Ramirez grounded to third. Justice lined to first.

FIFTH INNING

Florida—Johnson struck out. Counsell and White grounded to second.

Cleveland—Williams walked. Thome forced Williams at second, shortstop to second baseman. Alomar grounded into a double play, shortstop to second baseman to first baseman.

SIXTH INNING

Florida—Renteria struck out. Sheffield singled to left. Bonilla walked. Daulton lined to left. Alou homered to center, scoring Sheffield and Bonilla. Conine singled to left. Johnson singled to left, Conine advancing to second. Morman now pitching. Counsell walked. Plunk now pitching. White walked, scoring Conine. Renteria struck out.

Cleveland—Giles struck out. Grissom flied to center. Roberts lined to left.

SEVENTH INNING

Florida—Juden now pitching. Sheffield flied to center. Bonilla flied to right. Daulton popped foul to the first baseman.

Cleveland—Vizquel grounded to second. Ramirez singled to right. Justice grounded into a double play, pitcher to shortstop to first baseman.

EIGHTH INNING

Florida—Alou singled to the pitcher. With Conine batting, Alou stole second. Conine grounded to first, Alou advancing to third. Johnson singled to left-center, scoring Alou. Assenmacher now pitching. Counsell struck out. White doubled to left, Johnson advancing to third. Renteria flied to left.

Cleveland—Williams singled to center. Thome flied to left. Alomar forced Williams at second, shortstop to second baseman. Giles walked. Grissom forced Giles at second, shortstop to second baseman.

NINTH INNING

Florida—Mesa now pitching. Sheffield popped to short. Bonilla doubled to right. Arias now pinch-running for Bonilla. Daulton singled to right, Arias advancing to third. Alou singled to center, scoring Arias as Daulton went to second. With Conine batting, Daulton stole third. Conine popped to second. Johnson struck out.

Cleveland—Arias now at third. Roberts reached first on the pitcher's error (assist by the first baseman). Vizquel singled to right-center, Roberts went to third. Nen now pitching. Ramirez struck out. Vizquel went to second on defensive indifference. Justice singled to center, Roberts and Vizquel scoring. Williams forced Justice at second, shortstop to second baseman, and Williams went to second on a wild throw by the second baseman, scoring Williams. Thome singled to left-center, scoring Williams. Alomar flied to right.

GAME 6
HIGHLIGHTS

CLEVELAND 4, FLORIDA 1

Why the Indians won: Chad Ogea was too tough on the mound.

Why the Marlins lost: Chad Ogea was too tough with the bat.

The turning points:

1. When Ogea, who entered the game with exactly two at-bats in his major league career and said he had not collected a hit since his high school days nine years earlier, slapped a two-run single to right field off Florida's Kevin Brown in the second inning. As it turned out, it was all the offense Cleveland would need on the way to tying the Series at three victories apiece.

2. When, with Marlins players on second and third base and Cleveland trying to protect a 4-1 lead in the

sixth, Indians shortstop Omar Vizquel made a diving stop of Charles Johnson's grounder into the hole and threw out the Florida catcher to end the inning. If the ball had gotten through, it surely would have cut the deficit to one run.

Notable: Indians center fielder Marquis Grissom, on the dead run, made a sensational back-to-the-field, side-saddle basket catch of Jeff Conine's long drive in the second inning. The play was reminiscent of Willie Mays' catch against Cleveland in the 1954 Series. . . . Scintillating defensive play in this game seemed to make up for the sloppiness that was so prevalent in the first five games. Besides the great glove work by Vizquel and Grissom, Indians outfielders David Justice and Manny Ramirez and Florida third baseman Bobby Bonilla made outstanding plays. . . . Ogea, who pitched one-run, four-hit ball for five-plus innings, helped his cause again in the fifth when he doubled off Brown and eventually scored on Ramirez's second sacrifice fly of the game.

Quotable: Ogea, who beat Brown for the second time in this Series, was grateful for the opportunity to be given the ball in such a big game: "I was on the D.L. for two months this summer (with knee and elbow problems). In my wildest dreams, I didn't think I'd be in this situation. I worked hard on the D.L., came back healthy, rearranged my routine and got with it. And I started throwing the ball really well in September and it just carried into the postseason." . . . Florida manager Jim Leyland on Ogea's unexpected hitting prowess: "He's an athlete. He's very aggressive at the plate. I'm very impressed." . . . Vizquel on his big play: "That play (off Johnson in the sixth inning), I've done it before, probably about six, seven times." Still, he called the dive-and-throw acrobatics "the most important play of my career."

BOX SCORE

SATURDAY, OCTOBER 25, AT FLORIDA

Cleveland	AB	R	H	RBI	PO	A
Roberts, 2b	3	0	1	0	0	1
Fernandez, 2b	1	0	1	0	1	3
Vizquel, ss	4	1	1	0	2	2
Ramirez, rf	1	0	0	2	3	0
Justice, lf	4	0	0	0	4	0
Williams, 3b	4	1	2	0	1	1
Thome, 1b	3	1	0	0	7	1
Alomar, c	3	0	0	0	5	0
Grissom, cf	3	0	0	0	4	0
Ogea, p	2	1	2	2	0	0
Jackson, p	1	0	0	0	0	0
Assenmacher, p	0	0	0	0	0	0
▲Seitzer, ph	1	0	0	0	0	0
Mesa, p	0	0	0	0	0	0
Totals	30	4	7	4	27	8

Florida	AB	R	H	RBI	PO	A
White, cf	5	0	3	0	6	0
Renteria, ss	5	0	0	0	3	2
Sheffield, rf	3	0	0	0	1	0
Bonilla, 3b	4	0	0	0	0	3
Conine, 1b	2	0	0	0	5	0
§Eisenreich, ph-1b	1	0	0	0	2	1
Alou, lf	3	1	1	0	2	0
Johnson, c	4	0	2	0	8	0
Counsell, 2b	4	0	1	0	0	3
Brown, p	1	0	0	0	0	1
‡Daulton, ph	0	0	0	1	0	0

Florida	AB	R	H	RBI	PO	A
Heredia, p	0	0	0	0	0	0
∞Cangelosi, ph	1	0	1	0	0	0
Powell, p	0	0	0	0	0	0
Vosberg, p	0	0	0	0	0	0
◆Floyd, ph	1	0	0	0	0	0
Totals	**34**	**1**	**8**	**1**	**27**	**10**

Cleveland	0	2	1	0	1	0	0	0	0—4
Florida	0	0	0	0	1	0	0	0	0—1

Cleveland	IP	H	R	ER	BB	SO
Ogea (W)	*5.0	4	1	1	2	1
Jackson	2.0	2	0	0	2	2
Assenmacher	1.0	1	0	0	0	1
Mesa (S)	1.0	1	0	0	0	1

Florida	IP	H	R	ER	BB	SO
Brown (L)	5.0	5	4	4	3	2
Heredia	2.0	0	0	0	0	4
Powell	†1.0	2	0	0	0	1
Vosberg	1.0	0	0	0	1	1

*Pitched to one batter in sixth.
†Pitched to one batter in ninth.
Bases on balls—Off Ogea 2 (Alou, Sheffield), off Jackson 2 (Eisenreich, Sheffield), off Brown 3 (Ramirez, Thome, Grissom), off Vosberg 1 (Alomar). Strikeouts—By Ogea 1 (Counsell), by Jackson 2 (White, Renteria), by Assenmacher 1 (Eisenreich), by Mesa 1 (Renteria), by Brown 2 (Roberts, Grissom), by Heredia 4 (Williams, Thome, Alomar, Jackson), by Powell 1 (Justice), by Vosberg 1 (Thome).
‡Hit sacrifice fly for Brown in fifth. §Walked for Conine in sixth. ∞Singled for Heredia in seventh. ▲Grounded out for Assenmacher in ninth. ◆Grounded out for Vosberg in ninth. DP—Florida 1. LOB—Cleveland 5, Florida 11. SB—Vizquel 2, White. CS—Roberts. SF—Ramirez 2, Daulton. U—Kaiser (A.L.), plate; Montague (N.L.), first; Ford (A.L.), second; West (N.L.), third; Kosc (A.L.), left field; Marsh (N.L.), right field. T—3:15. A—67,498.

PLAY BY PLAY

FIRST INNING

Cleveland—Roberts struck out. Vizquel flied to center. Ramirez walked. Justice forced Ramirez at second, second baseman to shortstop.

Florida—White flied to center. Renteria fouled to right. Sheffield flied to left.

SECOND INNING

Cleveland—Williams singled to third. Thome walked. Alomar flied to center. Ogea singled to right, scoring Williams and Thome as Grissom advancing to second. Roberts grounded into a double play, second baseman to shortstop to first baseman.

Florida—Bonilla grounded to second. Conine flied to center. Alou walked. Johnson popped to third.

THIRD INNING

Cleveland—Vizquel doubled to right. Vizquel stole third. Ramirez hit a sacrifice fly to White, scoring Vizquel. Justice grounded to third. Williams flied to left.

Florida—Counsell struck out. Brown flied to left. White singled to left. White stole second. Renteria flied to center.

FOURTH INNING

Cleveland—Thome grounded to second. Alomar grounded to short. Grissom struck out.

Florida—Sheffield grounded to short. Bonilla flied to right. Conine lined to left.

FIFTH INNING

Cleveland—Ogea doubled to right. Roberts singled to left, Ogea went to third. Vizquel flied to center. Ramirez hit a sacrifice fly to center, scoring Ogea. Roberts caught stealing second, pitcher to first baseman.

Florida—Fernandez now at second. Alou singled to left. Johnson singled to left, Alou went to second. Counsell forced Johnson at second, first baseman to shortstop, as Alou went to third. Daulton, pinch-hitting for Brown, hit a sacrifice fly to right, scoring Alou. White singled to right, Counsell advancing to third. Renteria grounded to second.

SIXTH INNING

Cleveland—Heredia now pitching. Justice lined to left. Williams and Thome struck out.

Florida—Sheffield walked. Jackson now pitching. Bonilla popped to short. Eisenreich, now pinch-hitting for Conine, walked. Alou grounded to second, Sheffield went to third and Eisenreich to second. Johnson grounded to short.

SEVENTH INNING

Cleveland—Eisenreich now at first. Alomar struck out. Grissom grounded to third. Jackson struck out.

Florida—Counsell singled to center. Cangelosi, pinch-hitting for Heredia, singled to center, Counsell advancing to second. White and Renteria struck out. Sheffield walked. Bonilla flied to center.

EIGHTH INNING

Cleveland—Powell now pitching. Fernandez singled to center. Vizquel forced Fernandez at second, first baseman to shortstop. Ramirez flied to right. Vizquel stole second. Justice struck out.

Florida—Assenmacher now pitching. Eisenreich struck out. Alou flied to second. Johnson singled to left. Counsell flied to left.

NINTH INNING

Cleveland—Williams doubled to left-center. Vosberg now pitching. Thome struck out. Alomar was walked intentionally. Grissom flied to center, Williams advancing to third. Seitzer, pinch-hitting for Assenmacher, grounded to third.

Florida—Mesa now pitching. Floyd, pinch-hitting for Vosberg, grounded to second. White tripled to center. Renteria struck out. Sheffield grounded to third.

GAME 7
HIGHLIGHTS

FLORIDA 3, CLEVELAND 2 (11 INNINGS)

Why the Marlins won: With lefthander Al Leiter turning in a gutty performance and keeping things close, they never lost their cool despite being shut out and held to one hit over the first six innings by precocious righthander Jaret Wright. Leiter, who pitched terribly in Game 3, was almost certain to get a quick hook if he ran into trouble in this outing. But there was only one bump in the road—the third inning, when the Indians' Jim Thome walked, Marquis Grissom singled and, one out after Wright laid down a bunt, Tony Fernandez delivered a two-run single.

Why the Indians lost: Still ahead 2-1 after Wright was rocked for a leadoff homer by Bobby Bonilla in the seventh, they were victimized by shaky efforts from their final two relief pitchers (six hits allowed in 2⅔ innings) and a defensive lapse by second baseman Fernandez.

The turning points:

1. When Cleveland reliever Jose Mesa entered the game to lead off the ninth and couldn't nail down the victory. He allowed singles to Moises Alou and Charles Johnson and a one-out sacrifice fly to Craig Counsell that sent the game into extra innings.

2. When, with one out in the 11th and Bonilla aboard via a leadoff single, Fernandez let Counsell's grounder skip under his glove on a play in which Bonilla reached third base. An intentional walk to Jim Eisenreich loaded the bases, but Charles Nagy (who had come on in the 10th as the Indians' sixth pitcher of the night) got Devon White to hit into a ground-ball forceout at the plate. Edgar Renteria then whistled a single up the middle that scored Counsell, making the Marlins champions in their fifth season of play.

Notable: On a team vastly improved in the offsea-son because of the addition of $89 million worth of free-agent talent, it was a strange twist that Florida's Counsell, a minimum-wage man acquired in a late-July trade with the Rockies, and farm-system prod-uct Renteria played pivotal roles when the Marlins scored their tying and winning runs. . . . The Indians outscored (44-37), outhit (72-68) and outpitched (4.66 ERA to 5.48) the Marlins, but they failed to win their first Series crown since 1948. . . . Florida man-ager Jim Leyland, who had lost three League Championship Series as the Pirates' manager in the early 1990s, won the World Series in his first go-round. It was a momentous achievement for Leyland, whose playing talents were so limited that he never appeared in more than 82 games in one season in seven years as a minor league player. As a manager, he paid his dues with 11 seasons in the minors and 11 with Pittsburgh before hitting the jackpot in his first season with the Marlins. . . . Despite the Series title, Marlins owner H. Wayne Huizenga vowed to slash his payroll—and thereby move key members of his championship club—in the wake of what he termed heavy financial losses.
Quotable: Renteria said Nagy made a tactical mis-take in the fateful 11th: "He threw me a slider for the first pitch. I took it for a strike. I knew he was going to throw me another slider and I hit it. Too many breaking pitches." . . . Leyland on his feelings: "You're looking at a backup catcher (in the minor leagues). And I finally arrived at the pinnacle of this sport tonight, so there's hope for all those guys out there." . . . Marlins coach Rich Donnelly, on Leyland's impact on his club: "He absolutely willed this team to win."

BOX SCORE

SUNDAY, OCTOBER 26, AT FLORIDA

Cleveland	AB	R	H	RBI	PO	A
Vizquel, ss	5	0	1	0	1	3
Fernandez, 2b	5	0	2	2	1	5
Ramirez, rf	3	0	0	0	3	0
Justice, lf	5	0	0	0	1	0
Williams, 3b	2	0	0	0	1	0
Alomar, c	5	0	1	0	12	0
Thome, 1b	4	1	1	0	8	0
Grissom, cf	4	1	1	0	4	0
Wright, p	2	0	0	0	0	1
Assenmacher, p	0	0	0	0	0	0
Jackson, p	0	0	0	0	0	1
Anderson, p	0	0	0	0	0	0
§Giles, ph	1	0	0	0	0	0
Mesa, p	0	0	0	0	0	1
Nagy, p	0	0	0	0	1	0
Totals	36	2	6	2	32	11

Florida	AB	R	H	RBI	PO	A
White, cf	6	0	0	0	2	0
Renteria, ss	5	0	3	1	4	5
Sheffield, rf	4	0	1	0	2	0
Daulton, 1b	3	0	0	0	6	3
‡Conine, ph-1b	1	0	0	0	0	0
Nen, p	0	0	0	0	0	0
▲Cangelosi, ph	1	0	0	0	0	0
Powell, p	0	0	0	0	0	1
Alou, lf	5	1	1	0	1	0
Bonilla, 3b	5	1	2	1	0	1
Johnson, c	4	0	1	0	11	0

Florida	AB	R	H	RBI	PO	A
∞Zaun, pr-c	1	0	0	0	3	0
Counsell, 2b	3	1	0	1	2	1
Leiter, p	0	0	0	0	0	0
Cook, p	0	0	0	0	0	0
*Floyd, ph	0	0	0	0	0	0
†Abbott, ph	1	0	0	0	0	0
Alfonseca, p	0	0	0	0	1	1
Heredia, p	0	0	0	0	0	0
Eisenreich, 1b	1	0	0	0	1	0
Totals	40	3	8	3	33	12

Cleveland	0	0	2	0	0	0	0	0	0 0—2
Florida	0	0	0	0	0	1	0	1	0 1—3

Cleveland	IP	H	R	ER	BB	SO
Wright	6.1	2	1	1	5	7
Assenmacher	0.2	0	0	0	0	1
Jackson	0.2	0	0	0	0	1
Anderson	0.1	0	0	0	0	0
Mesa	1.2	4	1	1	0	2
Nagy (L)	1.0	2	1	0	1	0

Florida	IP	H	R	ER	BB	SO
Leiter	6.0	4	2	2	4	7
Cook	1.0	0	0	0	0	2
Alfonseca	1.1	0	0	0	1	1
Heredia	0.0	1	0	0	0	0
Nen	1.2	1	0	0	0	3
Powell (W)	1.0	0	0	0	0	0

Bases on balls—Off Wright 5 (Sheffield, Leiter 2, Renteria, Counsell), off Nagy 1 (Eisenreich), off Leiter 4 (Thome, Ramirez 2, Williams), off Alfonseca 1 (Williams), off Powell 1 (Williams).
Strikeouts—By Wright 7 (Johnson 2, White, Alou, Bonilla, Counsell, Sheffield), by Assenmacher 1 (White), by Jackson 1 (Sheffield), by Mesa 2 (Bonilla, Cangelosi), by Leiter 7 (Williams 2, Justice 2, Grissom, Wright, Fernandez), by Cook 2 (Wright, Vizquel), by Alfonseca 1 (Ramirez), by Nen 3 (Vizquel, Ramirez, Justice).
*Announced for Cook in seventh. †Flied out for Floyd in seventh. ‡Fouled out for Daulton in eighth. §Flied out for Anderson in ninth. ∞Ran for Johnson in ninth. ▲Struck out for Nen in 10th. E—Ramirez, Fernandez. DP—Cleveland 1, Florida 2. LOB—Cleveland 8, Florida 12. HR—Bonilla. SB—Vizquel 2. SH—Wright. SF—Counsell. U—Montague (N.L.), plate; Ford (A.L.), first; West (N.L.), second; Kosc (A.L.), third; Marsh (N.L.), left field; Kaiser (A.L.), right field. T—4:10. A—67,204.

PLAY BY PLAY

FIRST INNING
Cleveland—Vizquel grounded to third. Fernandez flied to cen-ter. Ramirez grounded to short.
Florida—White grounded to short. Renteria doubled to right. Sheffield walked. Daulton grounded into a double play, second baseman to shortstop to first baseman (Daulton was called out because Sheffield slid out of the baseline).

SECOND INNING
Cleveland—Justice grounded to first. Williams struck out. Alomar flied to center.
Florida—Alou popped to second. Bonilla grounded to second. Johnson struck out.

THIRD INNING
Cleveland—Thome walked. Grissom singled to left, Thome advancing to second. Wright sacrificed Thome to third and Grissom to second, first baseman to second baseman covering first. Vizquel popped to short. Fernandez singled to center, scor-ing Thome and Grissom. Ramirez walked. Justice struck out.
Florida—Counsell flied to center. Leiter walked. White struck out. Renteria walked. Sheffield popped to third.

FOURTH INNING
Cleveland—Williams struck out. Alomar singled to left. Thome flied to right. Grissom struck out.
Florida—Daulton grounded to second. Alou and Bonilla struck out.

FIFTH INNING
Cleveland—Wright struck out. Vizquel singled to left. Vizquel stole second. Fernandez struck out. Ramirez was walked inten-tionally. Vizquel stole third. Justice struck out.
Florida—Johnson grounded to the pitcher. Counsell struck out. Leiter walked. White flied to center.

SIXTH INNING

Cleveland—Williams walked. Alomar popped foul to the first baseman. Thome grounded into a double play, first baseman to shortstop to first baseman.

Florida—Renteria flied to center. Sheffield struck out. Daulton reached third on an error by the right fielder. Alou flied to center.

SEVENTH INNING

Cleveland—Cook now pitching. Grissom flied to right. Wright and Vizquel struck out.

Florida—Bonilla homered to right-center. Johnson struck out. Counsell walked. Floyd pinch hit for Cook. Assenmacher now pitching. Abbott, pinch-hitting for Floyd, flied to right. White struck out.

EIGHTH INNING

Cleveland—Alfonseca now pitching. Fernandez grounded to the pitcher. Ramirez struck out. Justice grounded to first.

Florida—Jackson now pitching. Renteria grounded to the pitcher. Sheffield struck out. Anderson now pitching. Conine, pinch-hitting for Daulton, fouled to Justice.

NINTH INNING

Cleveland—Conine now at first. Williams walked. Alomar forced Williams at second, shortstop to second baseman. Heredia now pitching. Thome singled to right, Alomar went to third. Nen now pitching, Eisenreich now at first. Grissom reached first on a fielder's choice, Alomar was out trying to score, shortstop to catcher. Thome went to second on the play. Giles, pinch-hitting for Anderson, flied to left.

Florida—Mesa now pitching. Alou singled to left-center. Bonilla struck out. Johnson singled to right, Alou advancing to third. Zaun now pinch-running for Johnson. Counsell hit a sacrifice fly to Ramirez, scoring Alou. Eisenreich grounded to second.

10TH INNING

Cleveland—Zaun now catching. Vizquel struck out. Fernandez singled to left. Ramirez and Justice struck out.

Florida—White grounded to the pitcher, who deflected the ball to shortstop, who threw to first. Renteria singled to left. Sheffield singled to short, Renteria went to second. Cangelosi, pinch-hitting for Nen, struck out. Nagy now pitching. Alou flied to right.

11TH INNING

Cleveland—Powell now pitching. Williams walked. Alomar forced at second, pitcher to shortstop. Thome grounded into a double play, second baseman to shortstop to first baseman.

Florida—Bonilla singled to center. Zaun popped to the pitcher. Counsell reached first on an error by the second baseman, Bonilla advancing to third. Eisenreich was walked intentionally. White reached first on a fielder's choice, Bonilla was out trying to score, second baseman to catcher. Counsell went to third and Eisenreich to second on the play. Renteria singled to center, scoring Counsell as Eisenreich went to third and White to second.

STATISTICS

FLORIDA MARLINS' BATTING AND FIELDING AVERAGES

Player, position	G	AB	R	H	TB	2B	3B	HR	RBI	BB	IBB	SO	Avg.	PO	A	E	Avg.
Eisenreich, ph-dh-1b.......	5	8	1	4	7	0	0	1	3	3	1	1	.500	3	1	0	1.000
Daulton, 1b-ph-dh..........	7	18	7	7	12	2	0	1	2	3	1	0	.389	28	4	0	1.000
Johnson, c	7	28	4	10	13	0	0	1	3	1	0	6	.357	49	2	0	1.000
Cangelosi, ph	3	3	0	1	1	0	0	0	0	0	0	2	.333	0	0	0	.000
Alou, lf	7	28	6	9	20	2	0	3	9	3	0	6	.321	11	0	0	1.000
Sheffield, rf	7	24	4	7	11	1	0	1	5	8	0	5	.292	16	0	1	.941
Renteria, ss	7	31	3	9	11	2	0	0	3	3	0	5	.290	12	26	1	.974
White, cf	7	33	0	8	13	3	1	0	2	3	0	10	.242	16	0	0	1.000
Conine, 1b-ph	6	13	1	3	3	0	0	0	2	0	0	5	.231	30	2	0	1.000
Bonilla, 3b.....................	7	29	5	6	10	1	0	1	3	3	0	5	.207	3	20	2	.920
Counsell, 2b....................	7	22	4	4	5	1	0	0	2	6	0	5	.182	18	15	1	.971
Alfonseca, p	3	0	0	0	0	0	0	0	0	0	0	0	.000	1	1	0	1.000
Cook, p	3	0	0	0	0	0	0	0	0	0	0	0	.000	0	0	0	.000
Heredia, p	4	0	0	0	0	0	0	0	0	0	0	0	.000	1	0	0	1.000
Leiter, p	2	0	0	0	0	0	0	0	0	2	0	0	.000	1	0	1	.500
Nen, p	4	0	0	0	0	0	0	0	0	0	0	0	.000	0	0	0	.000
Powell, p	4	0	0	0	0	0	0	0	0	0	0	0	.000	0	2	0	1.000
Saunders, p....................	1	0	0	0	0	0	0	0	0	0	0	0	.000	0	1	1	.500
Vosberg, p	2	0	0	0	0	0	0	0	0	0	0	0	.000	0	1	0	1.000
Arias, 3b-pr....................	2	1	0	0	0	0	0	0	0	0	0	0	.000	0	0	0	.000
Floyd, ph-dh...................	4	2	1	0	0	0	0	0	0	1	1	1	.000	0	0	0	.000
Hernandez, p...................	2	2	0	0	0	0	0	0	0	0	0	0	.000	0	4	1	.800
Zaun, ph-c-pr..................	2	2	0	0	0	0	0	0	0	0	0	0	.000	3	0	0	1.000
Abbott, dh-ph..................	3	3	0	0	0	0	0	0	0	0	0	1	.000	0	0	0	.000
Brown, p	2	3	0	0	0	0	0	0	0	0	0	1	.000	0	3	0	1.000
Totals	7	250	37	68	106	12	1	8	34	36	3	48	.272	192	82	8	.972

CLEVELAND INDIANS' BATTING AND FIELDING AVERAGES

Player, position	G	AB	R	H	TB	2B	3B	HR	RBI	BB	IBB	SO	Avg.	PO	A	E	Avg.
Giles, ph-lf	5	4	1	2	3	1	0	0	2	4	0	1	.500	2	0	0	1.000
Ogea, p	2	4	1	2	3	1	0	0	2	0	0	1	.500	0	2	0	1.000
Fernandez, 2b-ph	5	17	1	8	9	1	0	0	4	0	0	1	.471	9	14	2	.920
Williams, 3b...................	7	26	8	10	14	1	0	1	3	7	0	6	.385	5	9	0	1.000
Alomar, c.......................	7	30	5	11	18	1	0	2	10	2	1	3	.367	49	3	0	1.000
Grissom, cf	7	25	5	9	10	1	0	0	2	4	0	4	.360	19	0	1	.950
Thome, 1b......................	7	28	8	8	16	0	1	2	4	5	0	7	.286	57	5	1	.984
Roberts, 2b-lf..................	6	22	3	6	10	4	0	0	4	3	0	5	.273	8	8	0	1.000
Vizquel, ss.....................	7	30	5	7	9	2	0	0	1	3	0	5	.233	12	17	0	1.000
Justice, lf-dh...................	7	27	4	5	5	0	0	0	4	6	0	8	.185	9	0	0	1.000
Ramirez, rf	7	26	3	4	10	0	0	2	6	6	1	5	.154	16	1	1	.944

Player, position	G	AB	R	H	TB	2B	3B	HR	RBI	BB	IBB	SO	Avg.	PO	A	E	Avg.
Anderson, p	3	0	0	0	0	0	0	0	0	0	0	0	.000	0	1	0	1.000
Assenmacher, p	5	0	0	0	0	0	0	0	0	0	0	0	.000	0	0	0	.000
Juden, p	2	0	0	0	0	0	0	0	0	0	0	0	.000	0	0	0	.000
Mesa, p	5	0	0	0	0	0	0	0	0	0	0	0	.000	1	1	0	1.000
Morman, p	2	0	0	0	0	0	0	0	0	0	0	0	.000	0	0	0	.000
Nagy, p	2	0	0	0	0	0	0	0	0	0	0	0	.000	2	1	0	1.000
Plunk, p	3	0	0	0	0	0	0	0	0	0	0	0	.000	0	0	0	.000
Branson, ph	1	1	0	0	0	0	0	0	0	0	0	1	.000	0	0	0	.000
Seitzer, ph	1	1	0	0	0	0	0	0	0	0	0	0	.000	0	0	0	.000
Hershiser, p	2	2	0	0	0	0	0	0	0	0	0	1	.000	1	1	0	1.000
Jackson, p	4	2	0	0	0	0	0	0	0	0	0	1	.000	1	1	0	1.000
Wright, p	2	2	0	0	0	0	0	0	0	0	0	2	.000	0	1	0	1.000
Totals	7	247	44	72	107	12	1	7	42	40	2	51	.291	191	65	5	.981

FLORIDA MARLINS' PITCHING RECORDS

Pitcher	G	GS	CG	IP	H	R	ER	HR	BB	IBB	SO	HB	WP	W	L	Pct.	ERA
Alfonseca	3	0	0	6.1	6	0	0	0	1	0	5	0	0	0	0	.000	0.00
Heredia	4	0	0	5.1	2	0	0	0	1	0	5	0	0	0	0	.000	0.00
Cook	3	0	0	3.2	1	0	0	0	1	0	5	0	1	1	0	1.000	0.00
Leiter	2	2	0	10.2	10	9	6	1	10	1	10	0	0	0	0	.000	5.06
Hernandez	2	2	0	13.2	15	9	8	3	10	0	7	0	1	2	0	1.000	5.27
Vosberg	2	0	0	3.0	3	2	2	0	3	1	2	0	0	0	0	.000	6.00
Powell	4	0	0	3.2	5	3	3	1	4	0	2	0	0	1	0	1.000	7.36
Nen	4	0	0	4.2	8	5	4	0	2	0	7	0	0	0	0	.000	7.71
Brown	2	2	0	11.0	15	10	10	1	5	0	6	0	0	0	2	.000	8.18
Saunders	1	1	0	2.0	7	6	6	1	3	0	2	0	0	0	1	.000	27.00
Totals	7	7	0	64.0	72	44	39	7	40	2	51	0	1	4	3	.571	5.48

No shutouts. Saves—Nen 2.

CLEVELAND INDIANS' PITCHING RECORDS

Pitcher	G	GS	CG	IP	H	R	ER	HR	BB	IBB	SO	HB	WP	W	L	Pct.	ERA
Assenmacher	5	0	0	4.0	5	0	0	0	0	0	6	0	0	0	0	.000	0.00
Morman	2	0	0	0.1	0	2	0	0	2	0	1	0	0	0	0	.000	0.00
Ogea	2	2	0	11.2	11	2	2	0	3	0	5	1	0	2	0	1.000	1.54
Jackson	4	0	0	4.2	5	1	1	0	3	1	4	0	0	0	0	.000	1.93
Anderson	3	0	0	3.2	2	1	1	0	0	0	2	0	0	0	0	.000	2.45
Wright	2	2	0	12.1	7	4	4	2	10	0	12	0	1	1	0	1.000	2.92
Juden	2	0	0	2.0	2	1	1	0	2	0	1	0	0	0	0	.000	4.50
Mesa	5	0	0	5.0	10	3	3	0	1	0	5	0	1	0	0	.000	5.40
Nagy	2	1	0	7.0	8	6	5	3	5	1	5	0	0	0	1	.000	6.43
Plunk	3	0	0	3.0	3	4	3	0	4	1	3	0	0	0	1	.000	9.00
Hershiser	2	2	0	10.0	15	13	13	3	6	0	5	0	0	0	2	.000	11.70
Totals	7	7	0	63.2	68	37	32	8	36	3	48	1	3	3	4	.429	4.52

No shutouts. Saves—Anderson, Mesa.

SCORE BY INNINGS

Florida	2	2	2	6	3	8	3	1	9	0	1—37
Cleveland	7	3	9	3	7	4	1	3	7	0	0—44

MISCELLANEOUS STATISTICS

Sacrifice hits—Vizquel 2, Hernandez, Ogea, Roberts, Wright.
Sacrifice flies—Ramirez 2, Counsell, Daulton, Fernandez.
Stolen bases—Vizquel 5, Alou, Counsell, Daulton, White.
Caught stealing—Giles, Justice, Roberts.
Double plays—Counsell, Renteria and Conine 2; Fernandez, Vizquel and Thome 2; Roberts, Vizquel and Thome 2; Bonilla, Counsell and Conine; Bonilla, Counsell and Daulton; Counsell, Renteria and Daulton; Counsell, Renteria and Eisenreich; Daulton, Renteria and Daulton; Hernandez, Renteria and Conine; Renteria, Counsell and Conine; Thome (unassisted); Thome, Vizquel and Nagy; Vizquel, Fernandez and Thome; Williams, Roberts and Thome.
Left on bases—Florida 6, 9, 9, 6, 9, 11, 12—62; Cleveland 12, 6, 9, 10, 9, 5, 8—59.
Hit by pitcher—by Ogea (Sheffield).
Passed balls—None.
Balks—None.
Time of games—First game, 3:19; second game, 2:48; third game, 4:12; fourth game, 3:15; fifth game, 3:39; sixth game, 3:15; seventh game, 4:10.
Attendance—First game, 67,245; second game, 67,025; third game, 44,880; fourth game, 44,877; fifth game, 44,888; sixth game, 67,498; seventh game, 67,204.
Umpires—Montague, Ford, West, Kosc, Marsh and Kaiser.
Official scorers—Jim Ingraham, Hank Kozloski, Hal McCoy, Doug Pett.

ALL-STAR GAME

HIGHLIGHTS

AMERICAN LEAGUE 3, NATIONAL LEAGUE 1

Why the American League won: Because of the late-game heroics of catcher Sandy Alomar, who thrilled his hometown fans with a two-run, game-deciding home run in the seventh inning. Alomar, who entered the contest with a 30-game hitting streak, made his only at-bat a memorable one.

Why the National League lost: Because N.L. hitters, trying to add to their league's three-year winning streak, could manage only three hits off eight A.L. pitchers. Ironically, two of those hits and the N.L.'s only run came off Kansas City lefthander Jose Rosado—the winning pitcher.

The turning points:

1. After the A.L. had taken a second-inning lead on a solo home run by Seattle's Edgar Martinez, the N.L. ran itself out of a potential big inning. Yankees righthander David Cone opened the fourth by walking Barry Bonds and Mike Piazza. After Jeff Bagwell's line drive to right field advanced Bonds to third, the roof caved in on the N.L. rally. With Larry Walker at the plate, Piazza tried to go to second on a ball that bounced in front of catcher Ivan Rodriguez, who retrieved it and caught Piazza in a rundown. Piazza was tagged out and Cone got Walker on a grounder to end the inning.

2. After the N.L. had tied the game on a solo home run by Atlanta catcher Javier Lopez in the top of the seventh, the A.L. took control in the bottom of the inning. Bernie Williams drew a one-out walk and moved to second on a wild pitch by Giants lefthander Shawn Estes. Alomar became the first All-Star to earn MVP honors in his home ballpark when he blasted a two-out Estes pitch into the left field bleachers.

Notable: The most discussed All-Star sideshow was the second-inning comedy routine staged by A.L. starting pitcher Randy Johnson and N.L. slugger Larry Walker, former teammates in Montreal. Johnson's first pitch to Walker sailed about six feet over and behind his head. Walker, a lefthanded hitter, smiled broadly, turned his batting helmet backward and switched to the right side, taking Johnson's next pitch as the crowd roared. Walker reverted to his natural hitting side and eventually drew a walk. . . . The N.L. managed just one hit, a second-inning single by Jeff Blauser, before Lopez homered in the seventh. . . . Lopez became the 11th player to homer in his first All-Star at-bat. . . . The N.L.'s first three hitters—Craig Biggio, Tony Gwynn and Barry Bonds—were 0-for-8 against the A.L.'s first three pitchers—Johnson, Roger Clemens and Pat Hentgen. . . . Baltimore's Cal Ripken played in his 15th All-Star Game and made his 14th consecu-

tive start—but his first at third base. . . . The Alomar family All-Stars—Sandy and second baseman Roberto—wore black ribbons on their uniforms to honor their grandmother, who had died at age 96 two days before the All-Star Game. . . . Albert Belle, who left Cleveland to sign a $55 million contract with Chicago in the offseason, asked A.L. manager Joe Torre not to play him unless he really was needed. Belle had received rough treatment from Indians fans in an early season series at Cleveland and was booed lustily during introductions before the mid-summer classic.

Quotable: N.L. manager Bobby Cox on Sandy Alomar's MVP performance: "If you have to give up a game-winner, that's the way to do it. Give it up to the hometown boy.". . . Alomar on his game-winning blast: "To have the game-winning home run in your hometown is a once-in-a-lifetime dream. I was flying around the bases. I don't think I've ever run so fast around the bases." . . . Cox on the Johnson-Walker comedy show: "I think they had it planned." . . . Tigers lefthander Justin Thompson on his first All-Star performance: "I was pretty nervous. I was shaking. My legs were wobbling. Then when I started to warm up, I got that tunnel vision and I was all right."

BOX SCORE

National League	AB	R	H	RBI	PO	A
Biggio, 2b (Astros)	3	0	0	0	0	4
Womack, 2b (Pirates)	1	0	0	0	1	0
Gwynn, dh (Padres)	3	0	0	0	0	0
‡Galarraga, ph-dh (Rockies)	1	0	0	0	0	0
Bonds, lf (Giants)	2	0	0	0	2	0
Finley, lf (Padres)	1	0	0	0	1	0
Piazza, c (Dodgers)	1	0	0	0	2	0
Lopez, c (Braves)	1	1	1	1	4	1
C. Johnson, c (Marlins)	1	0	0	0	2	0
Bagwell, 1b (Astros)	3	0	0	0	8	1
Grace, 1b (Cubs)	1	0	0	0	1	0
Walker, rf (Rockies)	1	0	0	0	0	0
Alou, rf (Marlins)	2	0	1	0	1	0
Caminiti, 3b (Padres)	2	0	0	0	0	0
C. Jones, 3b (Braves)	1	0	0	0	0	1
Lankford, cf (Cardinals)	2	0	0	0	0	0
Blauser, ss (Braves)	2	0	1	0	1	1
Clayton, ss (Cardinals)	1	0	0	0	0	1
Maddux, p (Braves)	0	0	0	0	0	2
Schilling, p (Phillies)	0	0	0	0	1	0
Brown, p (Marlins)	0	0	0	0	0	1
P. Martinez, p (Expos)	0	0	0	0	0	0
Estes, p (Giants)	0	0	0	0	0	0
B. Jones, p (Mets)	0	0	0	0	0	0
Totals	29	1	3	1	24	12
American League	AB	R	H	RBI	PO	A
Anderson, lf-rf (Orioles)	4	2	2	0	1	0
A. Rodriguez, ss (Mariners)	3	0	1	0	0	1
Garciaparra, ss (Red Sox)	1	0	0	0	1	0
Griffey, cf (Mariners)	4	0	0	0	0	0
T. Martinez, 1b (Yankees)	2	0	0	0	10	0
McGwire, 1b (Athletics)	2	0	0	0	4	0
E. Martinez, dh (Mariners)	2	1	2	1	0	0
†Thome, ph-dh (Indians)	1	0	0	0	0	0
O'Neill, rf (Yankees)	2	0	0	0	1	0
Williams, lf (Yankees)	0	1	0	0	1	0
Ripken, 3b (Orioles)	2	0	1	0	0	4

American League	AB	R	H	RBI	PO	A
*Cora, pr-2b (Mariners).........	1	0	0	0	0	1
Knoblauch, 2b (Twins)...........	0	0	0	0	1	1
I. Rodriguez, c (Rangers).......	2	0	0	0	3	1
S. Alomar, c (Indians)..........	1	1	1	2	4	0
R. Alomar, 2b (Orioles).........	2	0	0	0	1	5
Cirillo, 3b (Brewers)...............	1	0	0	0	0	0
R. Johnson, p (Mariners).......	0	0	0	0	0	1
Clemens, p (Blue Jays).........	0	0	0	0	0	0
Cone, p (Yankees).................	0	0	0	0	0	0
Thompson, p (Tigers)	0	0	0	0	0	0
Hentgen, p (Blue Jays)	0	0	0	0	0	0
Rosado, p (Royals)...............	0	0	0	0	0	0
Myers, p (Orioles)...............	0	0	0	0	0	0
Rivera, p (Yankees).............	0	0	0	0	0	0
Totals................................	30	3	7	3	27	14

National League.............	0	0	0	0	0	0	1 0 0—1
American League	0	1	0	0	0	0	2 0 x—3

National League	IP	H	R	ER	BB	SO
Maddux (Braves)................	2	2	1	1	0	0
Schilling (Phillies)................	2	2	0	0	0	3
Brown (Marlins)...................	1	1	0	0	0	0
P. Martinez (Expos)............	1	0	0	0	0	2
Estes (Giants)	1	1	2	2	1	1
B. Jones (Mets)	1	1	0	0	0	2

American League	IP	H	R	ER	BB	SO
R. Johnson (Mariners)..........	2	0	0	0	1	2
Clemens (Blue Jays)	1	1	0	0	0	0
Cone (Yankees)....................	1	0	0	0	2	0
Thompson (Tigers)...............	1	0	0	0	0	1
Hentgen (Blue Jays).............	1	0	0	0	0	0
Rosado (Royals)	1	2	1	1	1	1
Myers (Orioles)...................	1	0	0	0	0	2
Rivera (Yankees)	1	0	0	0	0	1

Winning pitcher—Rosado. Losing pitcher—Estes. Save—Rivera.
*Ran for Ripken in fifth. †Grounded out for E. Martinez in seventh. ‡Struck out for Gwynn in eighth. LOB—N.L. 5, A.L. 4. 2B—Anderson. HR— E. Martinez, Lopez, S. Alomar. SB—Bonds. CS—E. Martinez. WP— Schilling, Estes. PB—Lopez. BB—Off Estes 1 (Williams), off R. Johnson 1 (Walker), off Cone 2 (Bonds, Piazza), off Rosado 1 (Lankford). SO—By Schilling 3 (A. Rodriguez, Griffey, O'Neill), by P. Martinez 2 (A. Rodriguez, McGwire), by Estes 1 (Cirillo), by B. Jones 2 (Griffey, McGwire), by R. Johnson 2 (Biggio, Bonds), by Thompson 1 (Lankford), Rosado 1 (Clayton), by Myers 2 (Galarraga, Finley), by Rivera 1 (C. Johnson). T—2:36. A— 44,916. U—Barnett (A.L.), plate; Davis (N.L.), first; Coble (A.L.), second; Kellogg (N.L.), third; Craft (A.L.), left field; Bell (N.L.), right field. Official scorers—Jim Ingraham, Hank Kozlosky, Hal McCoy.
Players listed on rosters but not used: N.L.—Beck (Giants), Glavine (Braves), Kile (Astros), Neagle (Braves); A.L.—Belle (White Sox), Dickson (Angels), Mussina (Orioles).

PLAY BY PLAY

FIRST INNING

N.L.—Biggio struck out. Gwynn grounded to the pitcher. Bonds struck out.

A.L.—Anderson grounded to second. A. Rodriguez singled to right. Griffey flied to left. T. Martinez grounded to second.

SECOND INNING

N.L.—Piazza and Bagwell grounded to second. Walker walked.

Caminiti forced Walker at second, shortstop to the second baseman.

A.L.—E. Martinez homered to left. O'Neill grounded to the pitcher. Ripken grounded to second. I. Rodriguez grounded to the pitcher.

THIRD INNING

N.L.—Clemens now pitching. Lankford grounded to second. Blauser singled to center. Biggio grounded to second, Blauser went to second. Gwynn grounded to third.

A.L.—Schilling now pitching. R. Alomar grounded to short. Anderson doubled to left. Anderson went to third on a wild pitch. A. Rodriguez and Griffey struck out.

FOURTH INNING

N.L.—Cone now pitching. Bonds walked and stole second. Piazza walked. Bagwell lined to right, Bonds went to third. Piazza out trying to advance to second, catcher to shortstop to first baseman. Walker grounded to second.

A.L.—Lopez now catching. T. Martinez grounded to first baseman, who tossed to the pitcher. E. Martinez singled to left. E. Martinez was caught trying to steal second, catcher to the shortstop. O''eill struck out.

FIFTH INNING

N.L.—Thompson now pitching. Caminiti grounded to third. Lankford struck out. Blauser grounded to third.

A.L.—Now pitching, C. Jones at third, Clayton at short, Alou in right field. Ripken singled to center. Cora now pinch-running for Ripken. I. Rodriguez grounded to second, Cora went to second. Cora went to third on a passed ball. R. Alomar grounded to the pitcher. Anderson flied to left.

SIXTH INNING

N.L.—Hentgen now pitching, McGwire at first, Cora at second, Cirillo at third, Williams in left field, Anderson moved to right field, S. Alomar catching. Biggio fouled to first. Gwynn grounded to second. Bonds flied to left.

A.L.—P. Martinez now pitching, Womack at second, Finley in left field. A. Rodriguez struck out. Griffey lined to right. McGwire struck out.

SEVENTH INNING

N.L.—Rosado now pitching, Garciaparra at shortstop. Lopez homered to left. Bagwell lined to short. Alou singled to right. C. Jones flied to right. Lankford walked. Clayton struck out.

A.L.—Estes now pitching, Grace at first. Thome, pinch-hitting for E. Martinez, grounded to short. Williams walked. Cora flied to left. Williams went to second on a wild pitch. S. Alomar homered to left, scoring Williams. Cirillo struck out.

EIGHTH INNING

N.L.—Myers now pitching, Knoblauch at second. Womack grounded to second. Galarraga, pinch-hitting for Gwynn, struck out. Finley struck out.

A.L.—B. Jones now pitching, C. Johnson catching. Anderson singled to left. Garciaparra forced Anderson at second, third baseman to second baseman. Griffey and McGwire struck out.

NINTH INNING

N.L.—Rivera now pitching. C. Johnson struck out. Grace grounded to first. Alou lined to second.

NOTABLE PERFORMANCES
BOX SCORES OF NO-HIT GAMES

KEVIN BROWN
JUNE 10
Florida 9, San Francisco 0 (D)

FLORIDA	AB	R	H	RBI	SAN FRANCISCO	AB	R	H	RBI
Castillo, 2b	5	1	1	0	Hamilton, cf	4	0	0	0
Renteria, ss	5	1	2	0	Vizcaino, ss	3	0	0	0
Eisenreich, lf	4	1	1	0	Snow, 1b	3	0	0	0
Wehner, 3b	1	0	0	0	Bonds, lf	3	0	0	0
Sheffield, rf	1	1	0	0	Kent, 2b	3	0	0	0
Alou, cf	4	1	1	2	Hill, rf	2	0	0	0
Bonilla, 3b	3	1	2	1	Benard, rf	0	0	0	0
Arias, 3b	0	0	0	0	Lewis, 3b	3	0	0	0
Conine, 1b	3	1	0	0	Berryhill, c	2	0	0	0
Johnson, c	4	1	1	2	Mueller, ph	1	0	0	0
Brown, p	3	1	0	0	VanLandingham, p	2	0	0	0
					Carlson, p	0	0	0	0
					Javier, ph	1	0	0	0
TOTALS	**33**	**9**	**8**	**7**	**TOTALS**	**27**	**0**	**0**	**0**

Florida	0	0	0	0	1	0	7	0	1—9
San Francisco	0	0	0	0	0	0	0	0	0—0

E—Lewis, Snow, Bonds. DP—San Francisco 1. LOB—Florida 7, San Francisco 1. 2B—Castillo, Eisenreich, Renteria. HR—Johnson. SB—Sheffield, Conine. CS—Renteria. SF—Alou.

FLORIDA	IP	H	R	ER	BB	SO
Brown (W, 6-4)	9	0	0	0	0	7

SAN FRANCISCO	IP	H	R	ER	BB	SO
VanLandingham (L, 3-4)	6 1/3	1	4	3	7	4
Carlson	2 2/3	7	5	4	2	2

HBP—By Brown (Benard). WP—VanLandingham 2. Balk—VanLandingham. T—2:21. A—10,257. Umpires—HP, Davidson; 1B, DeMuth; 2B, Pulli; 3B, Bonin.

FRANCISCO CORDOVA-RICARDO RINCON
JULY 12
Pittsburgh 3, Houston 0, 10 innings (N)

HOUSTON	AB	R	H	RBI	PITTSBURGH	AB	R	H	RBI
Biggio, 2b	4	0	0	0	Womack, 2b	4	0	2	0
Carr, cf	3	0	0	0	Allensworth, cf	4	0	0	0
Bagwell, 1b	3	0	0	0	Martin, lf	4	0	0	0
Gonzalez, lf	3	0	0	0	Young, 1b	4	0	0	0
Bell, rf	3	0	0	0	Sveum, 3b	4	0	0	0
Spiers, 3b	4	0	0	0	Kendall, c	2	1	1	0
Ausmus, c	4	0	0	0	Guillen, ss	4	0	0	0
Bogar, ss	3	0	0	0	Collier, ss	3	0	0	0
Wagner, p	0	0	0	0	Ward, ph	0	1	0	0
Hudek, p	0	0	0	0	Cordova, p	3	0	2	0
Holt, p	2	0	0	0	Rincon, p	0	0	0	0
Gutierrez, ss	1	0	0	0	Smith, ph	1	1	1	3
TOTALS	**30**	**0**	**0**	**0**	**TOTALS**	**33**	**3**	**6**	**3**

Houston	0 0 0	0 0 0	0 0 0	0—0
Pittsburgh	0 0 0	0 0 0	0 0 0	3—3

DP—Houston 1. LOB—Houston 4, Pittsburgh 4. HR—Smith. CS—Womack.

HOUSTON	IP	H	R	ER	BB	SO
Holt	7 2/3	5	0	0	1	1
Wagner	1 1/3	0	0	0	0	4
Hudek (L, 0-1)	2/3	1	3	3	2	1

PITTSBURGH	IP	H	R	ER	BB	SO
Cordova	9	0	0	0	2	10
Rincon (W, 3-4)	1	0	0	0	1	1

HBP—By Cordova (Carr). T—2:39. A—44,119. Umpires—HP, Hallion; 1B, Crawford; 2B, Montague; 3B, Bell.

LOW-HIT GAMES
AMERICAN LEAGUE

ONE-HIT GAMES
Date | **Pitcher(s), Team, Opponent, Result—Player with hit**
5-30 Mike Mussina, Baltimore vs. Cleveland, W 3-0—Sandy Alomar (single in ninth)
7-28 Steve Woodard (8 innings) and Mike Fetters (1 inning), Milwaukee vs. Toronto, W 1-0—Otis Nixon (double in first)
8-18 Rick Helling (8 innings) and John Wetteland (1 inning), Texas vs. Milwaukee, W 2-0—Fernando Vina (single in sixth)
9-3 Aaron Sele (7 innings) and Tom Gordon (1 inning), Boston at Montreal, L 0-1—Mike Lansing (home run in third)
9-9 Scott Sanders, Detroit vs. Texas, W 4-0—Domingo Cedeno (single in fifth)
9-26 Andy Pettitte (4 innings), Brian Boehringer (3 innings), Mariano Rivera (1 inning) and Jeff Nelson (1 inning), New York at Detroit, W 8-2—Travis Fryman (single in third)

TWO-HIT GAMES
Date | **Pitcher(s), Team, Opponent, Result—Player(s) with hit(s)**
4-12 Jeff Fassero (9 innings) and Norm Charlton (1 inning), Seattle at Boston, W 5-1—Mo Vaughn (single in first), Rudy Pemberton (double in eighth)
4-14 Dennis Martinez (6 innings), Edwin Hurtado (1 inning), Greg McCarthy (1 inning) and Bobby Ayala (1 inning), Seattle at Cleveland, W 6-1—Matt Williams (single in second and double in sixth)
4-15 Scott Kamieniecki (5 innings), Arthur Rhodes (3 innings) and Randy Myers (1 inning), Baltimore vs. Minnesota, W 3-1—Greg Colbrunn (single in second), Pat Meares (single in second)
4-26 Brian Moehler, Detroit at Anaheim, W 2-0—Luis Alicea (double in first), Jim Edmonds (double in fourth)
5-13 Tim Belcher, Kansas City vs. Boston, W 9-0—Mo Vaughn (single in seventh), John Valentin (single in sixth)
5-21 Kevin Appier, Kansas City at Cleveland, L 0-1—Jim Thome (single in fourth), Matt Williams (single in fourth)
5-23 Chad Ogea, Cleveland vs. Baltimore, W 6-1—Brady Anderson (double in first), B.J. Surhoff (single in second)
6-2 Randy Johnson, Seattle vs. Toronto, W 3-0—Alex Gonzalez (single in sixth), Tilson Brito (single in sixth)
6-8 Randy Johnson (8 innings) and Bobby Ayala (1 inning), Seattle at Detroit, W 2-0—Phil Nevin (single in eighth), Bob Hamelin (single in ninth)
7-1 Jeff Juden (8 1/3 innings) and Ugueth Urbina (2/3 inning), Montreal at Toronto, W 2-1—Orlando Merced (single in ninth), Shawn Green (home run in eighth)
7-4 Juan Guzman (5 innings) and Kelvim Escobar (4 innings), Toronto vs. New York, W 1-0—Derek Jeter (double in first), Tino Martinez (single in seventh)
7-27 Jose Rosado (7 innings), Mike Perez (1/3 inning), Larry Casian (1/3 inning) and Gregg Olson (1 1/3 innings), Kansas City at Toronto, W 3-2—Jacob Brumfield (single in sixth), Benito Santiago (single in fifth)
8-20 Randy Johnson (6 innings), Mike Timlin (1 1/3 innings), Norm Charlton (1/3 inning) and Heathcliff Slocumb (1 1/3 innings), Seattle vs. Cleveland, W 1-0—Tony Fernandez (single in seventh), Matt Williams (double in fifth)

Date	Pitcher(s), Team, Opponent, Result—Player(s) with hit(s)

Date   **Pitcher(s), Team, Opponent, Result—Player(s) with hit(s)**

9-1   Jason Isringhausen (6 innings), Greg McMichael (1 inning), Mel Rojas (1 inning) and John Franco (1 inning), New York vs. Toronto, W 3-0—Benito Santiago (single in seventh), Tomas Perez (single in second)

9-3   Carlos Perez, Montreal vs. Boston, W 1-0—John Valentin (double in fourth), Wil Cordero (single in second)

9-7   Roger Clemens, Toronto vs. Texas, W 4-0—Rusty Greer (single in sixth), Juan Gonzalez (single in fourth)

9-11   Roger Pavlik (6 innings), Scott Bailes (1 inning), Danny Patterson (1 inning) and John Wetteland (1 inning), Texas vs. Minnesota, W 7-0—Chuck Knoblauch (single in third), Ron Coomer (single in second)

9-19   Ken Hill, Anaheim at Texas, W 7-1—Tom Goodwin (single in first), Lee Stevens (single in second)

9-20   LaTroy Hawkins (6 innings), Mike Trombley (1 inning) and Greg Swindell (2 innings), Minnesota vs. Milwaukee, W 6-1—Jeff Cirillo (double in sixth), Julio Franco (single in sixth)

NATIONAL LEAGUE

ONE-HIT GAMES

Date   **Pitcher(s), Team, Opponent, Result—Player with hit**

4-5   Sterling Hitchcock (8 innings) and Trevor Hoffman (1 inning), San Diego vs. Philadelphia, W 4-1—Rico Brogna (double in fifth)

4-8   Steve Cooke (7 innings), Rich Loiselle (1 inning) and John Ericks (1 inning), Pittsburgh at San Diego, W 2-0—Steve Finley (single in first)

4-10   Alex Fernandez, Florida at Chicago, W 1-0—Dave Hansen (single in ninth)

4-16   Pedro Astacio (7 innings), Darren Dreifort (0 innings), Mark Guthrie (1 inning) and Todd Worrell (1 inning), Los Angeles at New York, W 5-2—Carlos Baerga (double in eighth)

4-27   Greg Maddux, Atlanta vs. San Diego, W 2-0—Ken Caminiti (single in second)

7-4   Shawn Estes (8 $2/3$ innings) and Rod Beck ($1/3$ inning), San Francisco vs. Colorado, W 4-0—Quinton McCracken (single in first)

7-13   Pedro Martinez, Montreal at Cincinnati, W 2-0—Bret Boone (single in fifth)

7-16   Kevin Brown, Florida vs. Los Angeles, W 5-1—Raul Mondesi (single in fifth)

8-13   Mike Morgan (7 innings), Stan Belinda (1 inning) and Jeff Shaw (1 inning), Cincinnati at San Diego, W 2-0—Mark Sweeney (single in seventh)

9-3   Aaron Sele (7 innings) and Tom Gordon (1 inning), Boston at Montreal, L 0-1—Mike Lansing (home run in third)

9-16   Kevin Tapani, Chicago vs. Cincinnati, W 5-0—Bret Boone (single in sixth)

TWO-HIT GAMES

Date   **Pitcher(s), Team, Opponent, Result—Player(s) with hit(s)**

4-1   Curt Schilling (8 innings) and Ricky Bottalico (1 inning), Philadelphia at Los Angeles, W 3-0—Brett Butler (single in third), Wilton Guerrero (single in first)

4-2   Jeff Juden (7 innings), Omar Daal (1 inning) and Lee Smith (1 inning), Montreal vs. St. Louis, W 4-1—Delino DeShields (single in first), Gary Gaetti (single in second)

4-3   Darryl Kile (8 innings) and Russ Springer (1 inning), Houston vs. Atlanta, L 2-3—Fred McGriff (home run in seventh), Mark Lemke (double in eighth)

4-26   Shawn Estes, San Francisco at Houston, W 2-0—Tony Eusebio (single in eighth), Pat Listach (single in sixth)

5-23   Shawn Estes, San Francisco vs. St. Louis, W 2-0—Delino DeShields (single in fourth), John Mabry (single in third)

6-3   Shawn Estes, San Francisco at Florida, W 9-1—Gary Sheffield (single in third), Bobby Bonilla (single in second)

6-7   Greg Maddux (8 innings) and Mark Wohlers (1 inning), Atlanta at San Francisco, W 5-2—Glenallen Hill (home run in eighth), Mark Gardner (single in sixth)

6-23   Francisco Cordova, Pittsburgh at Houston, W 6-0—Bill Spiers (single in seventh), Thomas Howard (single in second)

6-28   Jeremi Gonzalez (6 $1/3$ innings), Terry Adams ($1/3$ inning), Ramon Tatis (0 innings) and Kent Bottenfield (2 $1/3$ innings), Chicago vs. Houston, W 5-2—Luis Gonzalez (single in fourth), Brad Ausmus (single in seventh)

7-1   Jeff Juden (8 $1/3$ innings) and Ugueth Urbina ($2/3$ inning), Montreal at Toronto, W 2-1—Orlando Merced (single in ninth), Shawn Green (home run in eighth)

7-25   John Smoltz, Atlanta at Cincinnati, W 7-3—Hal Morris (single in fifth), Bret Boone (home run in fifth)

8-2   Brett Tomko (7 innings) and Jeff Shaw (2 innings), Cincinnati vs. San Francisco, W 5-1—Barry Bonds (home run in sixth), Jeff Kent (single in fourth)

8-8   Mark Gardner, San Francisco at Montreal, W 4-0—Vladimir Guerrero (double in seventh), Darrin Fletcher (single in eighth)

8-21   Mike Johnson (6 innings), Anthony Telford (2 innings) and Ugueth Urbina (1 inning), Montreal vs. St. Louis, W 3-2—Ron Gant (single in fourth), Mike Difelice (single in fifth)

9-1   Jason Isringhausen (6 innings), Greg McMichael (1 inning), Mel Rojas (1 inning) and John Franco (1 inning), New York vs. Toronto, W 3-0—Benito Santiago (single in seventh), Tomas Perez (single in second)

9-3   Carlos Perez, Montreal vs. Boston, W 1-0—John Valentin (double in fourth), Wil Cordero (single in second)

9-5   Andy Ashby, San Diego vs. Atlanta, W 6-2—Kenny Lofton (single in ninth), Fred McGriff (home run in ninth)

9-20   Tom Glavine, Atlanta vs. Montreal, W 3-1—Mark Grudzielanek (single in first), Ryan McGuire (double in sixth)

15-STRIKEOUT GAMES

Date	Pitcher, Team, Opponent	IP	H	R	ER	BB	SO	Result
5-28	Randy Johnson, Seattle A.L. vs. Texas	8	4	0	0	1	15	W 5-0
6-8	Randy Johnson, Seattle A.L. at Detroit	8	1	0	0	3	15	W 2-0
6-23	David Cone, New York A.L. at Detroit	8	4	2	2	2	16	W 5-2
6-24	Randy Johnson, Seattle A.L. vs. Oakland	9	11	4	4	0	19	L 1-4
7-12	Roger Clemens, Toronto A.L. at Boston	8	4	1	1	0	16	W 3-1
7-18	Randy Johnson, Seattle A.L. vs. Kansas City	9	9	4	4	3	16	W 5-4
7-21	Curt Schilling, Philadelphia N.L. vs. Pittsburgh	8	6	3	3	1	15	L 2-3
7-30	David Wells, New York A.L. vs. Oakland	9	3	0	0	3	16	W 7-0
8-8	Randy Johnson, Seattle A.L. vs. Chicago	9	5	0	0	3	19	W 5-0
9-1	Curt Schilling, Philadelphia N.L. vs. New York A.L.	8	7	1	1	0	16	W 5-1

10-STRIKEOUT GAMES

AMERICAN LEAGUE

Team	No.	Pitchers
Seattle	15	Randy Johnson 14, Jeff Fassero 1.
Toronto	15	Roger Clemens 14, Pat Hentgen 1.
New York	9	David Cone 6, Andy Pettitte 2, David Wells 1.
Baltimore	5	Mike Mussina 5.
Chicago	4	Wilson Alvarez 2, Jaime Navarro 1, James Baldwin 1.
Oakland	4	Mike Oquist 1, Steve Karsay 1, Ariel Prieto 1, Jimmy Haynes 1.
Boston	3	Tom Gordon 1, Tim Wakefield 1, Aaron Sele 1.
Anaheim	3	Chuck Finley 2, Ken Hill 1.
Kansas City	3	Kevin Appier 3.
Milwaukee	3	Ben McDonald 2, Steve Woodard 1.
Cleveland	1	Charles Nagy 1.
Detroit	1	Felipe Lira 1.
Minnesota	1	Brad Radke 1.
Texas	1	Rick Helling 1.

NATIONAL LEAGUE

Team	No.	Pitchers
Montreal	21	Pedro Martinez 18, Jeff Juden 2, Carlos Perez 1.
Philadelphia	20	Curt Schilling 17, Mark Leiter 1, Mike Grace 1, Garrett Stephenson 1.
St. Louis	12	Andy Benes 5, Alan Benes 4, Todd Stottlemyre 3.
San Francisco	8	Shawn Estes 4, Mark Gardner 2, Wilson Alvarez 2.
Florida	8	Alex Fernandez 4, Kevin Brown 2, Al Leiter 1, Tony Saunders 1.
Los Angeles	7	Hideo Nomo 6, Chan Ho Park 1.
Atlanta	5	John Smoltz 5.
Houston	5	Darryl Kile 2, Shane Reynolds 2, Ramon Garcia 1.
Cincinnati	4	Dave Burba 2, John Smiley 1, Brett Tomko 1.
Pittsburgh	4	Jon Lieber 2, Jason Schmidt 1, Francisco Cordova 1.
Chicago	2	Mark Clark 1, Kevin Foster 1.
San Diego	2	Andy Ashby 2.
Colorado	1	Pedro Astacio 1.
New York	0	None.

1-0 GAMES

AMERICAN LEAGUE

Date	Winner	Loser	Inn.*	Site
4-17	†Mike Mussina, Baltimore	Danny Darwin, Chicago	3	Chicago
4-30	†Roger Clemens, Toronto	Kevin Appier, Kansas City	2	Kansas City
5-4	Pat Hentgen, Toronto	Bob Tewksbury, Minnesota	4	Toronto
5-7	†Mike Fetters, Milwaukee	†Steve Montgomery, Oakland	7	Milwaukee
5-21	†Orel Hershiser, Cleveland	Kevin Appier, Kansas City	4	Cleveland
6-7	†Roberto Hernandez, Chicago	†Randy Myers, Baltimore	11	Chicago
6-14	Pedro Martinez, Montreal	†Justin Thompson, Detroit	4	Montreal
6-23	†Allen Watson, Anaheim	†Darren Oliver, Texas	5	Texas
7-4	†Kelvim Escobar, Toronto	†David Cone, New York	6	Toronto
7-20	Brad Radke, Minnesota	†Carlos Reyes, Oakland	2	Oakland
7-28‡	†Steve Woodard, Milwaukee	Roger Clemens, Toronto	4	Milwaukee
8-20	†Randy Johnson, Seattle	†Charles Nagy, Cleveland	4	Seattle
9-3	Carlos Perez, Montreal	†Aaron Sele, Boston	3	Montreal
9-21	†Brian Bevil, Kansas City	†Mike Jackson, Cleveland	9	Kansas City

PLAYERS HITTING HOME RUNS IN 1-0 GAMES: 4-30—Carlos Delgado, Toronto; 6-23—Jim Leyritz, Anaheim; 7-4—Orlando Merced, Toronto; 8-20—Edgar Martinez, Seattle; 9-3—Mike Lansing, Montreal.
*Inning in which run scored. †Did not pitch complete game. ‡First game of doubleheader.

NATIONAL LEAGUE

Date	Winner	Loser	Inn.*	Site
4-10	Alex Fernandez, Florida	†Frank Castillo, Chicago	1	Chicago
4-19‡	†Mark Petkovsek, St. Louis	†Sterling Hitchcock, San Diego	6	San Diego
5-3	†Tim Worrell, San Diego	†Dustin Hermanson, Montreal	1	San Diego
5-4	Darryl Kile, Houston	Kevin Brown, Florida	1	Houston
5-14	†Darryl Kile, Houston	†Greg McMichael, New York	9	New York
5-16	†Joe Borowski, Atlanta	†John Frascatore, St. Louis	13	Atlanta
6-16	†Bob Wickman, Milwaukee	Alan Benes, St. Louis	9	Milwaukee
6-18	Carlos Perez, Montreal	†Jimmy Key, Baltimore	6	Baltimore
6-20	†Bobby Jones, New York	†Steve Cooke, Pittsburgh	6	New York
6-30	†Mike Stanton, New York	†Mike Bielecki, Atlanta	10	New York
7-31	†Tony Saunders, Florida	†Paul Byrd, Atlanta	4	Florida
8-14	†Ismael Valdes, Los Angeles	†Pedro Martinez, Montreal	3	Los Angeles
9-9	†Tyler Green, Philadelphia	†Dave Mlicki, New York	8	New York
9-12	†Kirk Rueter, San Francisco	†Livan Hernandez, Florida	4	Florida
9-14	†Dave Mlicki, New York	†Carlos Perez, Montreal	5	New York

PLAYERS HITTING HOME RUNS IN 1-0 GAMES: 5-3—Tony Gwynn, San Diego; 6-16—Jeromy Burnitz, Milwaukee; 6-18—Sherman Obando, Montreal; 8-14—Mike Piazza, Los Angeles; 9-9—Rico Brogna, Philadelphia; 9-14—Luis Lopez, New York.
*Inning in which run scored. †Did not pitch complete game. ‡First game of doubleheader.

FOUR OR MORE HITS IN ONE GAME

AMERICAN LEAGUE

Team	No.	Hitters
New York	22	Tino Martinez 3, Bernie Williams 3, Tim Raines 2, Cecil Fielder 2, Paul O'Neill 2, Joe Girardi 2, Chad Curtis 2, Derek Jeter 2, Wade Boggs 1, Luis Sojo 1, Mark Whiten 1, Rey Sanchez 1.

Team	No.	Hitters
Minnesota	19	Paul Molitor 4, Chuck Knoblauch 3, Greg Colbrunn 2, Pat Meares 2, Ron Coomer 2, Brent Brede 2, Terry Steinbach 1, Greg Myers 1, Matt Lawton 1, Todd Walker 1.
Baltimore	17	Roberto Alomar 4, Eric Davis 3, B.J. Surhoff 3, Rafael Palmeiro 2, Jeffrey Hammonds 2, Cal Ripken 1, Brady Anderson 1, Jerome Walton 1.
Boston	17	Nomar Garciaparra 4, John Valentin 3, Reggie Jefferson 2, Mo Vaughn 2, Wil Cordero 2, Tim Naehring 1, Bill Haselman 1, Troy O'Leary 1, Scott Hatteberg 1.
Seattle	17	Joey Cora 5, Alex Rodriguez 3, Edgar Martinez 2, Ken Griffey Jr 2, Dan Wilson 2, Paul Sorrento 1, Rich Amaral 1, Russ Davis 1.
Kansas City	16	Bip Roberts 3, Jose Offerman 3, Jeff King 2, Chili Davis 1, Jay Bell 1, Tom Goodwin 1, Johnny Damon 1, Yamil Benitez 1, Jermaine Dye 1, Rod Myers 1, Shane Halter 1.
Anaheim	15	Tim Salmon 4, Gary DiSarcina 2, Jim Edmonds 2, Garret Anderson 2, Tony Phillips 1, Dave Hollins 1, Jim Leyritz 1, Todd Greene 1, Darin Erstad 1.
Texas	15	Ivan Rodriguez 5, Rusty Greer 2, Mark McLemore 1, Will Clark 1, Juan Gonzalez 1, Lee Stevens 1, Warren Newson 1, Tom Goodwin 1, Damon Buford 1, Fernando Tatis 1.
Cleveland	14	Manny Ramirez 4, Sandy Alomar 3, Marquis Grissom 3, Bip Roberts 1, Matt Williams 1, Omar Vizquel 1, David Justice 1.
Chicago	13	Frank Thomas 4, Dave Martinez 2, Albert Belle 2, Ray Durham 2, Ozzie Guillen 1, Jorge Fabregas 1, Chris Snopek 1.
Detroit	10	Bob Higginson 4, Tony Clark 3, Brian L. Hunter 2, Travis Fryman 1.
Oakland	7	Jose Canseco 1, Mark McGwire 1, Dave Magadan 1, Geronimo Berroa 1, Rafael Bournigal 1, Tony Batista 1, Mark Bellhorn 1.
Toronto	5	Carlos Garcia 1, Ed Sprague 1, Shannon Stewart 1, Tilson Brito 1, Jose Cruz Jr 1.
Milwaukee	4	Mark Loretta 2, Dave Nilsson 1, Jeff Cirillo 1.

NATIONAL LEAGUE

Team	No.	Hitters
Colorado	24	Larry Walker 5, Andres Galarraga 4, Dante Bichette 3, Vinny Castilla 3, Neifi Perez 2, Ellis Burks 1, Walt Weiss 1, Kirt Manwaring 1, Harvey Pulliam 1, Eric Young 1, Quinton McCracken 1, John Thomson 1.
New York	18	John Olerud 4, Carlos Baerga 3, Todd Hundley 2, Bernard Gilkey 2, Butch Huskey 2, Edgardo Alfonzo 2, Lance Johnson 1, Carl Everett 1, Alex Ochoa 1.
Atlanta	13	Kenny Lofton 5, Fred McGriff 3, Jeff Blauser 2, Ryan Klesko 1, Chipper Jones 1, Michael Tucker 1.
Montreal	13	Mike Lansing 3, Rondell White 3, David Segui 1, Henry Rodriguez 1, Mark Grudzielanek 1, Chris Widger 1, Vladimir Guerrero 1, Ryan McGuire 1, Jose Vidro 1.
St. Louis	13	Willie McGee 2, Ron Gant 2, Delino DeShields 2, Dmitri Young 2, Gary Gaetti 1, Mark McGwire 1, Ray Lankford 1, Royce Clayton 1, Mike Difelice 1.
Houston	10	Derek Bell 3, Craig Biggio 2, Bill Spiers 2, Luis Gonzalez 1, Ricky Gutierrez 1, Brad Ausmus 1.
Los Angeles	10	Mike Piazza 4, Brett Butler 2, Otis Nixon 1, Todd Zeile 1, Eric Karros 1, Eric Young 1.
Pittsburgh	10	Tony Womack 4, Turner Ward 1, Kevin Young 1, Al Martin 1, Mark Smith 1, Joe Randa 1, Jason Kendall 1.
San Diego	10	Tony Gwynn 4, Wally Joyner 2, Quilvio Veras 2, Steve Finley 1, Chris Gomez 1.
Cincinnati	9	Chris Stynes 2, Curtis Goodwin 2, Ruben Sierra 1, Deion Sanders 1, Bret Boone 1, Eduardo Perez 1, Aaron Boone 1.
Philadelphia	9	Mickey Morandini 2, Midre Cummings 2, Darren Daulton 1, Gregg Jefferies 1, Derrick May 1, Mike Lieberthal 1, Tony Barron 1.
Florida	7	Moises Alou 2, Devon White 1, John Cangelosi 1, Bobby Bonilla 1, Craig Counsell 1, Edgar Renteria 1.
Chicago	6	Sammy Sosa 2, Brian McRae 2, Lance Johnson 1, Kevin Orie 1.
San Francisco	5	Stan Javier 1, Darryl Hamilton 1, Jose Vizcaino 1, Marvin Benard 1, Bill Mueller 1.

FIVE- AND SIX-HIT GAMES

Date	Player, Team, Opponent	AB	R	H	2B	3B	HR	RBI	Result
4-14	Kenny Lofton, Atlanta N.L. vs. Cincinnati	6	5	5	0	0	0	2	W 15-5
4-15	Paul Sorrento, Seattle A.L. at Cleveland	5	1	5	2	0	0	4	W 8-4
4-16	Brett Butler, Los Angeles N.L. at New York	5	2	5	0	0	0	0	W 5-2
4-18	Kenny Lofton, Atlanta N.L. at Colorado	6	4	5	0	0	1	2	W 14-0
4-26	Cecil Fielder, New York A.L. vs. Chicago	5	1	5	2	0	1	5	W 10-2
4-30	Michael Tucker, Atlanta N.L. at Cincinnati	6	3	5	0	0	1	5	W 12-3
5-9	Joey Cora, Seattle A.L. at Baltimore	5	3	5	1	0	1	1	W 8-2
5-17	Kenny Lofton, Atlanta N.L. vs. St. Louis	5	2	5	0	1	0	2	W 11-6
5-18	Mike Lansing, Montreal N.L. vs. Los Angeles	5	3	5	2	0	1	3	W 7-4
5-22	Wil Cordero, Boston A.L. at New York	6	1	5	1	0	0	0	W 8-2
5-23	Paul Molitor, Minnesota A.L. at Oakland	5	1	5	1	0	0	1	L 4-8
6-3	Royce Clayton, St. Louis N.L. vs. Colorado	6	3	5	1	0	0	0	W 15-4
6-17	Ellis Burks, Colorado N.L. vs. Texas A.L.	6	2	5	1	0	1	3	L 8-10
6-24	Tino Martinez, New York A.L. at Detroit	5	4	5	1	0	2	4	W 12-9
6-27	Albert Belle, Chicago A.L. at Minnesota	5	4	5	1	0	1	2	W 10-6
6-28	Marquis Grissom, Cleveland A.L. at New York	6	1	5	2	0	0	3	W 12-8
6-30	Wally Joyner, San Diego N.L. at Oakland A.L.	6	2	5	1	0	0	2	W 15-6
7-22	Vinny Castilla, Colorado N.L. at Montreal	7	4	5	0	0	2	4	W 11-9
8-11	Chad Curtis, New York A.L. at Minnesota	5	1	5	2	0	0	1	W 11-0
8-22	Bob Higginson, Detroit A.L. at Milwaukee	6	2	5	1	0	0	1	W 16-1
8-27	Dave Magadan, Oakland A.L. vs. New York	5	2	5	0	0	1	2	W 8-7
8-27	Otis Nixon, Los Angeles N.L. at Pittsburgh	6	3	5	0	0	0	0	W 9-5
9-28	Neifi Perez, Colorado N.L. vs. Los Angeles	5	2	5	1	0	0	3	W 13-9

HITTING STREAKS OF 15 OR MORE GAMES

AMERICAN LEAGUE

G	Player, Team	Span of streak
30	Sandy Alomar, Cleveland	May 25-July 6
	Nomar Garciaparra, Boston	July 26-Aug. 29
27	Albert Belle, Chicago	May 3-June 1
25	Jason Giambi, Oakland	May 12-June 23
24	Joey Cora, Seattle	May 2-May 29
	Matt Williams, Cleveland	Aug. 13-Sep. 8
22	Reggie Jefferson, Boston	July 13-Aug. 8
19	Dave Martinez, Chicago	Aug. 5-Aug. 26
18	Julio Franco, Cleveland	Apr. 26-May 20
	Chuck Knoblauch, Minnesota	Aug. 7-Aug. 26
	Manny Ramirez, Cleveland	Aug. 30-Sep. 17
17	Edgar Martinez, Seattle	Apr. 22-May 12
	Garret Anderson, Anaheim	May 4-May 23
16	Alex Rodriguez, Seattle	June 1-July 3
	Paul O'Neill, New York	July 10-July 26
	Carlos Delgado, Toronto	Sep. 11-Sep. 28
15	Jeff Frye, Boston	July 27-Aug. 14
	John Valentin, Boston	Aug. 10-Aug. 25

NATIONAL LEAGUE

G	Player, Team	Span of streak
23	Luis Gonzalez, Houston	May 26-June 20
22	Vinny Castilla, Colorado	Aug. 9-Sep. 1
20	John Mabry, St. Louis	May 19-June 9
	Tony Gwynn, San Diego	May 20-June 10
	Edgardo Alfonzo, New York	June 10-July 10
	Butch Huskey, New York	Aug. 22-Sep. 13
19	Tony Gwynn, San Diego	June 21-July 14
18	F.P. Santangelo, Montreal	June 4-June 23
17	Mark Grudzielanek, Montreal	Apr. 13-May 2
16	Henry Rodriguez, Montreal	May 4-May 22
	Larry Walker, Colorado	May 11-May 29
	Michael Tucker, Atlanta	June 9-June 29
	Mark Grace, Chicago	Aug. 20-Sep. 6
15	Eric Young, Colorado	Apr. 4-Apr. 23
	Mark Grace, Chicago	May 6-May 21
	Kenny Lofton, Atlanta	May 26-June 10
	Kenny Lofton, Atlanta	June 15-Aug. 8
	Greg Gagne, Los Angeles	June 26-July 14
	Mike Lansing, Montreal	July 12-July 27

MULTI-HOMER GAMES

AMERICAN LEAGUE

Team	No.	Hitters
Texas	20	Juan Gonzalez 7, Rusty Greer 4, Lee Stevens 3, Warren Newson 2, Will Clark 1, Dean Palmer 1, Ivan Rodriguez 1, Fernando Tatis 1.
Seattle	18	Ken Griffey Jr 8, Jay Buhner 3, Edgar Martinez 2, Jose Cruz Jr 2, Roberto Kelly 1, Dan Wilson 1, Russ Davis 1.
Boston	15	Reggie Jefferson 3, Mo Vaughn 3, John Valentin 3, Nomar Garciaparra 3, Troy O'Leary 1, Darren Bragg 1, Scott Hatteberg 1.
Cleveland	14	Matt Williams 6, David Justice 3, Jim Thome 3, Sandy Alomar 1, Brian S. Giles 1.
Baltimore	10	Rafael Palmeiro 3, Jeffrey Hammonds 3, Eric Davis 1, Roberto Alomar 1, Jerome Walton 1, Chris Hoiles 1.
Kansas City	10	Chili Davis 3, Craig Paquette 2, Jay Bell 1, Mike Macfarlane 1, Jeff King 1, Dean Palmer 1, Mike Sweeney 1.
Oakland	10	Mark McGwire 3, Matt Stairs 3, Jose Canseco 2, Scott Brosius 1, Jason Giambi 1.
Toronto	10	Carlos Delgado 3, Benito Santiago 2, Shawn Green 2, Jose Cruz Jr 2, Ed Sprague 1.
Minnesota	9	Marty Cordova 3, Ron Coomer 2, Matt Lawton 2, Paul Molitor 1, Terry Steinbach 1.
New York	9	Tino Martinez 5, Paul O'Neill 1, Charlie Hayes 1, Bernie Williams 1, Derek Jeter 1.
Anaheim	8	Jack Howell 2, Jim Edmonds 2, Dave Hollins 1, Tim Salmon 1, Todd Greene 1, Darin Erstad 1.
Chicago	8	Frank Thomas 3, Albert Belle 2, Mike Cameron 2, Dave Martinez 1.
Detroit	8	Bob Higginson 3, Tony Clark 3, Damion Easley 1, Bob Hamelin 1.
Milwaukee	5	Dave Nilsson 3, John Jaha 1, Jeromy Burnitz 1.

NATIONAL LEAGUE

Team	No.	Hitters
Colorado	19	Larry Walker 8, Vinny Castilla 3, Jeff Reed 2, Andres Galarraga 2, Ellis Burks 2, Dante Bichette 2.
Los Angeles	15	Todd Zeile 5, Mike Piazza 4, Raul Mondesi 3, Eric Karros 2, Tripp Cromer 1.
New York	11	Todd Hundley 3, Carl Everett 3, John Olerud 2, Butch Huskey 2, Bernard Gilkey 1.
San Francisco	11	Barry Bonds 3, J.T. Snow 3, Jeff Kent 2, Glenallen Hill 1, Mark Lewis 1, Brian Johnson 1.
St. Louis	10	Mark McGwire 4, Ray Lankford 3, Gary Gaetti 1, Ron Gant 1, Delino DeShields 1.
Montreal	9	Rondell White 3, Henry Rodriguez 2, Mike Lansing 2, Darrin Fletcher 1, F.P. Santangelo 1.
San Diego	9	Steve Finley 4, Tony Gwynn 1, Wally Joyner 1, Ken Caminiti 1, Greg Vaughn 1, John Flaherty 1.
Florida	9	Moises Alou 3, Devon White 1, Gary Sheffield 1, Jeff Conine 1, Cliff Floyd 1, Charles Johnson 1, Edgar Renteria 1.
Atlanta	7	Fred McGriff 2, Ryan Klesko 1, Javy Lopez 1, Chipper Jones 1, Michael Tucker 1, Andruw Jones 1.
Houston	7	Jeff Bagwell 3, Craig Biggio 2, Luis Gonzalez 1, Bob Abreu 1.
Philadelphia	6	Rico Brogna 2, Scott Rolen 2, Mike Lieberthal 1, Bobby Estalella 1.
Chicago	4	Ryne Sandberg 2, Sammy Sosa 1, Brooks Kieschnick 1.
Pittsburgh	4	Shawon Dunston 1, Turner Ward 1, Kevin Young 1, Freddy Garcia 1.
Cincinnati	3	Reggie Sanders 1, Willie Greene 1, Eduardo Perez 1.

THREE-HOMER GAMES

Date	Player, Team, Opponent	AB	R	H	2B	3B	HR	RBI	Result
4-2	Tino Martinez, New York A.L. at Seattle	6	5	4	0	0	3	7	W16-2
4-5	Larry Walker, Colorado N.L. at Montreal	5	3	4	0	0	3	5	W15-3
4-25	Matt Williams, Cleveland A.L. at Milwaukee	5	3	3	0	0	3	4	W11-4
4-25	Ken Griffey Jr, Seattle A.L. at Toronto	5	3	3	0	0	3	3	W13-8

Date	Player, Team, Opponent	AB	R	H	2B	3B	HR	RBI	Result
4-26	Roberto Alomar, Baltimore A.L. vs. Boston	4	4	4	0	0	3	6	W 14-5
5-19	Steve Finley, San Diego N.L. at Cincinnati	5	3	3	0	0	3	3	W 13-6
5-30	Mo Vaughn, Boston A.L. vs. New York	4	3	4	0	0	3	3	W 10-4
6-23	Steve Finley, San Diego N.L. at San Francisco	5	4	4	0	0	3	4	W 11-6
6-30	Bob Higginson, Detroit A.L. vs. New York N.L.	3	4	3	0	0	3	7	W 14-0
9-4	Bobby Estalella, Philadelphia N.L. at Montreal	4	3	3	0	0	3	4	W 6-4
9-11	Ivan Rodriguez, Texas A.L. vs. Minnesota	4	3	3	0	0	3	5	W 7-0

GRAND SLAMS
AMERICAN LEAGUE

Date	Batter, Team	Pitcher, Team	Inn.*	Site
4-3	Paul Molitor, Minnesota	Willie Blair, Detroit	2	Minnesota
4-4	Tim Salmon, Anaheim	Paul Shuey, Cleveland	11	Anaheim
4-5	Paul O'Neill, New York	Mike Mohler, Oakland	3	Oakland
4-7	Mike Matheny, Milwaukee	Ken Hill, Texas	2	Milwaukee
4-8	Darren Bragg, Boston	Richie Lewis, Oakland	7	Oakland
4-9	Bob Higginson, Detroit	Eddie Guardado, Minnesota	8	Detroit
4-13	Tim Naehring, Boston	Scott Sanders, Seattle	3	Boston
4-18	Fernando Vina, Milwaukee	Jack McDowell, Cleveland	4	Cleveland
4-20	Dean Palmer, Texas	Juan Guzman, Toronto	3	Texas
4-23	Eric Davis, Baltimore	Jaime Navarro, Chicago	7	Baltimore
4-23	Scott Spiezio, Oakland	Rich Robertson, Minnesota	4	Oakland
4-25	Chili Davis, Kansas City	Richie Lewis, Oakland	6	Oakland
4-25	Carlos Delgado, Toronto	Dennis Martinez, Seattle	1	Toronto
4-30	Mike Simms, Texas	Wilson Alvarez, Chicago	1	Chicago
5-3	Tim Unroe, Milwaukee	Norm Charlton, Seattle	9	Seattle
5-4	Roberto Alomar, Baltimore	Don Wengert, Oakland	6	Baltimore
5-6	Cal Ripken, Baltimore	Pep Harris, Anaheim	7	Baltimore
5-8	Rudy Pemberton, Boston	Rich Robertson, Minnesota	2	Boston
5-10	Juan Gonzalez, Texas	Heathcliff Slocumb, Boston	9	Boston
5-11	Albert Belle, Chicago	Willie Adams, Oakland	3	Chicago
5-14	Charlie O'Brien, Toronto	Mike Myers, Detroit	8	Detroit
5-16	Darrin Jackson, Minnesota	Toby Borland, Boston	4	Minnesota
5-17	Jim Thome, Cleveland	Woody Williams, Toronto	3	Toronto
5-22	Jason Giambi, Oakland	John Burkett, Texas	4	Texas
5-24	Craig Paquette, Kansas City	Jamie Moyer, Seattle	6	Kansas City
5-25	Bob Higginson, Detroit	Eric Gunderson, Texas	8	Detroit
5-27	Albert Belle, Chicago	Albie Lopez, Cleveland	4	Chicago
5-30	Jeff Cirillo, Milwaukee	James Baldwin, Chicago	8	Milwaukee
6-4	Charlie Hayes, New York	Jesse Orosco, Baltimore	7	Baltimore
6-6	Carlos Delgado, Toronto	Mike Oquist, Oakland	1	Toronto
6-18	Jeff King, Kansas City	Donne Wall, Houston N.L.	1	Kansas City
6-20	Ken Griffey Jr, Seattle	Bobby Witt, Texas	5	Texas
6-21	Manny Ramirez, Cleveland	Graeme Lloyd, New York	8	Cleveland
6-26	Mark McGwire, Oakland	Julio Santana, Texas	1	Oakland
6-27	Jay Bell, Kansas City	Bryce Florie, Milwaukee	4	Kansas City
6-30	Cal Ripken, Baltimore	Calvin Maduro, Philadelphia N.L.	3	Baltimore
7-4†	Brian L. Hunter, Detroit	Mike Johnson, Baltimore	2	Detroit
7-6	Dave Hollins, Anaheim	Josias Manzanillo, Seattle	4	Anaheim
7-6	Manny Ramirez, Cleveland	Tim Belcher, Kansas City	3	Cleveland
7-10	Joe Carter, Toronto	Tom Gordon, Boston	5	Boston
7-16	Tino Martinez, New York	Wilson Alvarez, Chicago	7	Chicago
7-23	Joe Carter, Toronto	Joel Adamson, Milwaukee	4	Toronto
7-24	Carlos Delgado, Toronto	Jose Mercedes, Milwaukee	1	Toronto
7-28†	Garret Anderson, Anaheim	Orel Hershiser, Cleveland	4	Cleveland
8-2	Paul Sorrento, Seattle	Mike Misuraca, Milwaukee	6	Milwaukee
8-4	Greg Colbrunn, Minnesota	Omar Daal, Toronto	5	Minnesota
8-10	Chad Curtis, New York	Travis Miller, Minnesota	3	Minnesota
8-10†	Brian Banks, Milwaukee	Jimmy Haynes, Oakland	3	Oakland
8-11	Benito Santiago, Toronto	Mike Myers, Detroit	4	Toronto
8-19	David Justice, Cleveland	Ken Cloude, Seattle	5	Seattle
8-22	Albert Belle, Chicago	Darren Oliver, Texas	6	Texas
8-22	Rusty Greer, Texas	Jaime Navarro, Chicago	3	Texas
8-26	Brady Anderson, Baltimore	Glendon Rusch, Kansas City	4	Baltimore
8-27	Rafael Palmeiro, Baltimore	Hector Carrasco, Kansas City	8	Baltimore
8-27	Marquis Grissom, Cleveland	Allen Watson, Anaheim	4	Anaheim
8-30	Jermaine Dye, Kansas City	Mark Petkovsek, St. Louis N.L.	4	Kansas City
9-6	Bob Higginson, Detroit	Allen Watson, Anaheim	4	Detroit
9-7	Troy O'Leary, Boston	Jeff D'Amico, Milwaukee	3	Boston
9-19	Albert Belle, Chicago	Tom Gordon, Boston	9	Boston
9-22	Damian Miller, Minnesota	Jeff D'Amico, Milwaukee	2	Minnesota
9-26	Lee Stevens, Texas	Mike Holtz, Anaheim	7	Anaheim

Date	Batter, Team	Pitcher, Team	Inn.*	Site
9-27	Jeff King, Kansas City	Jeff Darwin, Chicago	6	Chicago
9-28	Jeromy Burnitz, Milwaukee	Jimmy Key, Baltimore	5	Milwaukee
9-28	Matt Stairs, Oakland	Norm Charlton, Seattle	7	Seattle

*Inning in which grand slam was hit. †Second game of doubleheader.

NATIONAL LEAGUE

Date	Batter, Team	Pitcher, Team	Inn.*	Site
4-3	Mark Johnson, Pittsburgh	Osvaldo Fernandez, San Francisco	5	San Francisco
4-3	Jeff Conine, Florida	Frank Castillo, Chicago	1	Florida
4-14	Javy Lopez, Atlanta	Stan Belinda, Cincinnati	7	Atlanta
4-20‡	Carl Everett, New York	Steve Trachsel, Chicago	3	New York
4-28	Gary Sheffield, Florida	Tim Scott, San Diego	6	Florida
4-28	Moises Alou, Florida	Tim Worrell, San Diego	1	Florida
4-30	Jeff Kent, San Francisco	Jon Lieber, Pittsburgh	1	Pittsburgh
4-30	Andres Galarraga, Colorado	Ramon Tatis, Chicago	6	Colorado
5-2	Rico Brogna, Philadelphia	Mark Thompson, Colorado	1	Colorado
5-7	Ray Lankford, St. Louis	Erik Plantenberg, Philadelphia	7	St. Louis
5-7	Henry Rodriguez, Montreal	Osvaldo Fernandez, San Francisco	5	San Francisco
5-10	Jeff Blauser, Atlanta	Jon Lieber, Pittsburgh	3	Pittsburgh
5-13	Bobby Bonilla, Florida	Paul Byrd, Atlanta	4	Atlanta
5-13	Jeff Kent, San Francisco	Dave Burba, Cincinnati	3	Cincinnati
5-14	Al Martin, Pittsburgh	Bruce Ruffin, Colorado	8	Pittsburgh
5-17	Ray Lankford, St. Louis	Brad Clontz, Atlanta	8	Atlanta
5-20	Jeff Kent, San Francisco	Roger Bailey, Colorado	1	San Francisco
5-25	Kevin Young, Pittsburgh	Lee Smith, Montreal	8	Montreal
5-31	Andres Galarraga, Colorado	Kevin Brown, Florida	4	Florida
6-14	Rich Aurilia, San Francisco	Allen Watson, Anaheim A.L.	2	Anaheim
6-25	Chipper Jones, Atlanta	Bobby Jones, New York	5	New York
6-26	Tony Gwynn, San Diego	Mark Guthrie, Los Angeles	7	Los Angeles
6-27	Willie Greene, Cincinnati	Alan Benes, St. Louis	6	Cincinnati
6-29	Keith Lockhart, Atlanta	Ron Blazier, Philadelphia	6	Atlanta
7-1	Terry Pendleton, Cincinnati	Bryce Florie, Milwaukee A.L.	7	Cincinnati
7-3	Steve Finley, San Diego	Derek Lowe, Seattle A.L.	1	San Diego
7-5	Chipper Jones, Atlanta	Pedro Martinez, Montreal	3	Montreal
7-10	Chipper Jones, Atlanta	Dave Mlicki, New York	5	Atlanta
7-14	Ryan Klesko, Atlanta	Billy Brewer, Philadelphia	6	Atlanta
7-14	Tim Spehr, Atlanta	Tyler Green, Philadelphia	5	Atlanta
7-14	Brad Ausmus, Houston	Kent Bottenfield, Chicago	7	Chicago
7-20	Luis Gonzalez, Houston	Omar Daal, Montreal	8	Montreal
7-21	Henry Rodriguez, Montreal	Darren Holmes, Colorado	9	Montreal
7-23	Barry Bonds, San Francisco	Mark Leiter, Philadelphia	3	San Francisco
7-25	Jeff Blauser, Atlanta	Pete Schourek, Cincinnati	2	Cincinnati
7-29	Mark Lewis, San Francisco	Greg McMichael, New York	7	San Francisco
8-14	Edgardo Alfonzo, New York	Donovan Osborne, St. Louis	5	St. Louis
8-18	Mike Lieberthal, Philadelphia	Terry Mulholland, San Francisco	6	Philadelphia
8-18	Billy McMillon, Philadelphia	Mark Gardner, San Francisco	3	Philadelphia
8-19	Bobby Bonilla, Florida	Ramon Tatis, Chicago	5	Florida
8-23	Todd Hundley, New York	Sean Bergman, San Diego	7	New York
8-24	Craig Counsell, Florida	Todd Stottlemyre, St. Louis	1	Florida
8-31	Andruw Jones, Atlanta	Steve Avery, Boston A.L.	2	Boston
9-1	Steve Finley, San Diego	Bobby Ayala, Seattle A.L.	9	Seattle
9-1	Devon White, Florida	Jesse Orosco, Baltimore A.L.	6	Florida
9-7	Todd Zeile, Los Angeles	Tony Saunders, Florida	1	Los Angeles
9-10	Dante Bichette, Colorado	John Hudek, Houston	7	Colorado
9-13	Carl Everett, New York	Ugueth Urbina, Montreal	9	New York
9-16	Eddie Perez, Atlanta	Wilson Alvarez, San Francisco	6	Atlanta
9-16	Bobby Bonilla, Florida	Jerry DiPoto, Colorado	9	Florida
9-17	Ryan Klesko, Atlanta	Bobby Jones, New York	1	Atlanta
9-20	Brian McRae, New York	Alex Fernandez, Florida	1	Florida
9-24	John Olerud, New York	Chris Peters, Pittsburgh	6	New York
9-26	Jon Nunnally, Cincinnati	Mike Johnson, Montreal	4	Montreal
9-28	Gary Sheffield, Florida	Matt Beech, Philadelphia	3	Philadelphia

*Inning in which grand slam was hit. ‡First game of doubleheader.

TRANSACTIONS

JANUARY 1, 1997-DECEMBER 31, 1997

JANUARY 2
Phillies released C Joe Kmak.

JANUARY 3
Indians organization signed IF Mike Busch.
Padres released 1B Jason Thompson.

JANUARY 4
Rangers signed OF Mike Devereaux.

JANUARY 6
A's organization signed C David Valle and P Richie Lewis.
Giants organization signed C Damon Berryhill.

JANUARY 7
Mariners signed P Rusty Meacham.
Padres re-signed P Fernando Valenzuela.

JANUARY 8
Giants signed P Doug Henry.

JANUARY 9
Angels signed P Shigetoshi Hasegawa.
Padres traded C Leroy McKinnis to Orioles for OF Mark Smith.
Yankees signed OF Mark Whiten.

JANUARY 10
White Sox re-signed OF Harold Baines.
White Sox organization signed P Roger McDowell and C Tony Pena.
White Sox traded P Scott Ruffcorn to Phillies for cash.
Mariners organization signed C Brent Mayne and P Paul Abbott.
Giants signed OF Darryl Hamilton.

JANUARY 13
Angels organization signed P Travis Buckley.

JANUARY 14
White Sox signed P Doug Drabek.
Royals organization signed P Mitch Williams.
Blue Jays organization signed OF Darrell Whitmore.
Reds organization signed OF/1B Brian R. Hunter.

JANUARY 15
Rangers organization signed IF Domingo Cedeno and IF Tom O'Malley.
Mets signed P Rudy Seanez.

JANUARY 16
Expos signed P Jim Bullinger.
Phillies organization signed P Jim Fortugno.

JANUARY 17
Indians organization signed IF Robby Thompson.
Tigers organization signed P Jason Grimsley.
Royals organization signed P Derek Lilliquist.
Padres organization signed OF Phil Plantier.

JANUARY 22
Red Sox signed P Steve Avery.
Orioles organization signed P Scott Kamieniecki.
Tigers organization signed P Jose Bautista.
Rangers organization signed C Scott Hemond and P Kevin Lomon.

Cubs organization signed IF Dave Hansen and IF Andujar Cedeno.
Padres traded C Sean Mulligan to Indians for cash.

JANUARY 23
A's organization signed IF Dave Magadan.
Rangers organization signed P Duane Ward.

JANUARY 24
Twins organization signed 1B Greg Colbrunn and IF Kevin Baez.
Mariners organization signed IF Mike Blowers.
Rangers signed P Eric Gunderson.
Rockies organization signed IF/OF Darnell Coles.
Expos signed P Pedro J. Martinez.

JANUARY 27
Red Sox traded OF Jose Canseco to A's for P John Wasdin and cash.
Reds organization signed 3B Terry Pendleton.
Mets signed P Dave Mlicki.

JANUARY 28
Royals traded P Melvin Bunch to Expos for OF Yamil Benitez.

JANUARY 29
Mariners organization signed 3B Chris Sabo.
Cubs organization signed OF Dave Clark.
Phillies organization signed OF Derrick May.

JANUARY 30
Orioles organization signed IF Jeff Reboulet.
Royals signed P Chris Haney.

JANUARY 31
Red Sox signed IF Mike Benjamin.
Blue Jays organization signed OF Mike Aldrete.
White Sox traded 1B Mike Robertson to Phillies for 1B Gene Schall.

FEBRUARY 3
Red Sox organization signed P Jim Corsi.
Red Sox released 2B Roberto Mejia.
Royals organization signed P Randy Tomlin.

FEBRUARY 4
Angels organization signed OF Kevin Bass.
Astros organization signed P Tommy Greene.
Expos organization signed IF Doug Strange.

FEBRUARY 7
White Sox organization signed P Danny Darwin.
Diamondbacks organization signed P Mark Davis.

FEBRUARY 8
Reds organization re-signed C Joe Oliver.

FEBRUARY 10
Blue Jays organization signed P Marvin Freeman.
Mets signed 3B Howard Johnson.

FEBRUARY 15
Red Sox organization signed P Mike Williams.
Pirates organization signed 1B Ricky Jordan.

FEBRUARY 17
Rockies signed P Robbie Beckett.
Reds re-signed OF Deion Sanders.

FEBRUARY 18
Dodgers organization re-signed P Mike Harkey.

FEBRUARY 20
Phillies signed OF Danny Tartabull.

FEBRUARY 22
Tigers organization signed OF Pedro Munoz.

FEBRUARY 28
Yankees signed P Julian Vasquez.

MARCH 1
Devil Rays signed OF Dwight Smith, P Jack Armstrong and P Kevin Morton.

MARCH 4
Royals released P Doug Linton.

MARCH 5
Mets organization signed P Roberto Ramirez.

MARCH 10
A's released OF Allen Battle.
Reds released P Billy Brewer and OF Scott Bullett.

MARCH 11
Angels organization signed IF Randy Ready.
Rangers released P Duane Ward.
A's released 2B Brent Gates.

MARCH 13
Expos released IF Geronimo Pena and OF Milt Cuyler.
Pirates released P Steve Parris.

MARCH 14
Royals claimed P Doug Johns on waivers from A's.

MARCH 15
Padres traded P Joey Eischen to Reds for a player to be named; Reds sent IF Ray Brown to Padres to complete deal (March 19).
Padres traded P Sean Runyan to Astros for IF Luis Lopez.
Mets released P John Habyan.

MARCH 16
Mariners signed IF Brent Gates.

MARCH 17
Rangers organization re-signed P Kevin Gross.
Dodgers released IF John Wehner.

MARCH 18
Royals released P Juan Agosto.
Giants released P Steven Bourgeois.

MARCH 19
Tigers released OF Pedro Munoz.
Mariners released IF Chris Sabo.
Astros released C Jeff Tackett.

MARCH 20
Orioles released P Jeff Williams.
Tigers released P Jason Grimsley.
Braves released IF/OF Hensley Meulens.
Astros released IF Tommy Gregg.

MARCH 21
Rangers organization signed C Jeff Tackett.
Phillies released OF Tony Longmire.

MARCH 22
Orioles traded IF Manny Alexander and IF Scott McLain to Mets for P Hector Ramirez.
Tigers traded OF Mike Darr and P Matt Skrmetta to Padres for 2B Jody Reed.

MARCH 23
Rangers released OF Tom O'Malley.

MARCH 24
Pirates released IF Esteban Beltre.

MARCH 25
Orioles claimed C Tim Laker on waivers from Expos.
Indians traded OF Kenny Lofton and P Alan Embree to Braves for OF Marquis Grissom and OF David Justice.

MARCH 26
Angels released P Todd Van Poppel.
Red Sox released IF Chris Donnels and P Mike Maddux.
Red Sox traded C Tim Spehr to Royals for cash.
Expos traded OF/1B Cliff Floyd to Marlins for OF Joe Orsulak and P Dustin Hermanson.
Mets announced the retirement of IF Howard Johnson.
Mets released IF Alvaro Espinoza.

MARCH 27
Tigers released P Jose Bautista.
Royals traded OF Michael Tucker and IF Keith Lockhart to Braves for OF Jermaine Dye and P Jamie Walker.
A's claimed P Scott Service on waivers from Reds.
Rangers claimed IF Dave Silvestri off waivers from Mariners.

MARCH 28
Dodgers returned 2B Jeff Berblinger to Cardinals.
Expos traded P Barry Manuel to Mets for cash.
Mariners released P Rusty Meacham and OF Lou Frazier.

MARCH 29
Rockies released P Mike Dyer.
Pirates traded OF Trey Beamon and C Angelo Encarnacion to Padres for OF Mark Smith and P Hal Garrett.

MARCH 31
Angels released P Jim Abbott.
Cubs traded OF Ozzie Timmons and P Jayson Peterson to Reds for P Curt Lyons.
Astros claimed IF Tim Bogar on waivers from Mets.
Mets claimed P Yorkis Perez on waivers from Braves.

APRIL 2
Mariners signed IF Alvaro Espinoza.

APRIL 4
Reds claimed P Scott Service on waivers from A's.

APRIL 14
Giants traded P Rich DeLucia to Angels for a player to be named; Angels sent P Travis Thurmond to Giants to complete deal (May 23).

APRIL 16
Tigers released OF Vince Coleman.

APRIL 18
Expos claimed P Salmon Torres on waivers from Mariners.

APRIL 21
Devil Rays signed P Rolando Arrojo.

APRIL 22

Padres traded rights to P Hideki Irabu, 2B Homer Bush, OF Gordon Amerson and a player to be named to Yankees for OF Ruben Rivera, P Rafael Medina, and $3 million; Padres sent OF Vernon Maxwell to Yankees to complete deal (June 9). Yankees completed deal by signing Irabu (May 29).

APRIL 23

Rockies traded IF Jeff Huson to Brewers for a player to be named.

APRIL 30

Mets traded P John Carter and P Erick Ojeda to Pirates for OF Wes Chamberlain and OF Ramon Espinoza.

MAY 2

Tigers claimed P Kevin Jarvis on waivers from Reds.

MAY 8

Indians claimed P Jason Jacome on waivers from Royals.

MAY 12

Red Sox traded P Rick Trlicek to Mets for P Toby Borland.

MAY 14

Orioles released P Giovanni Carrara.

MAY 16

Padres released P Tim Scott.

MAY 17

Reds organization signed P Giovanni Carrara.

MAY 27

Royals claimed P Larry Casian on waivers from Cubs.

JUNE 3

Indians released OF Kevin Mitchell.
Cubs traded IF Bobby Morris to Indians for 1B Rod McCall.

JUNE 5

Indians traded OF Ryan Thompson to Blue Jays for IF Jeff Manto.
Cubs organization signed P Lee D. Hancock.

JUNE 10

Mariners traded P Paul Menhart to Padres for P Andres Berumen.

JUNE 11

Rangers organization signed P Todd Van Poppel.

JUNE 13

Cardinals traded P Danny Jackson, P Rich Batchelor and OF Mark Sweeney to Padres for P Fernando Valenzuela, 3B Scott Livingstone and OF Phil Plantier.

JUNE 16

Blue Jays released OF Ruben Sierra.

JUNE 17

Tigers claimed P Kevin Jarvis on waivers from Twins.

JUNE 19

A's released P Richie Lewis

JUNE 23

Mariners released OF Craig Griffey.

JUNE 26

Brewers traded P Ricky Bones to Royals for cash.

JUNE 27

A's traded OF Geronimo Berroa to Orioles for P Jimmy Haynes and a player to be named; Orioles sent P Mark Seaver to A's to complete deal (September 2).

JULY 1

Astros released SS Pat Listach.

JULY 2

Indians claimed P Casey Whitten on waivers from Royals.

JULY 3

Indians organization signed P Angel Miranda.

JULY 6

Rangers announced retirement of DH Mickey Tettleton.

JULY 8

Phillies claimed OF Midre Cummings on waivers from Pirates.

JULY 12

Orioles released 3B Kelly Gruber.

JULY 15

Rangers organization signed IF Luis Ortiz.
Cubs traded P Frank Castillo to Rockies for P Matt Pool.
Reds traded P Hector Carrasco and P Scott Service to Royals for OF Jon Nunnally and IF/OF Chris Stynes.
Expos announced retirement of P Lee Smith.
Cardinals released P Fernando Valenzuela.

JULY 16

Tigers traded C Brian Johnson to Giants for C Marcus Jensen.
Tigers traded IF Dave Hajek to Padres for OF Earl Johnson.

JULY 18

Mariners traded P Scott Sanders, P Dean Crow and 3B Carlos Villalobos to Tigers for P Omar Olivares and P Felipe Lira.
Marlins traded P Pat Rapp to Giants for P Brandon Leese and P Bobby Rector.

JULY 19

Marlins organization signed P Bryan Harvey.

JULY 21

Tigers released P Jose Bautista.
Phillies traded OF/1B Darren Daulton to Marlins for OF Billy McMillon.

JULY 24

Blue Jays claimed P Omar Daal on waivers from Expos.

JULY 25

Yankees organization signed OF Pete Incaviglia.
Rangers traded 3B Dean Palmer to Royals for OF Tom Goodwin.

JULY 27

Marlins traded P Mark Hutton to Rockies for IF Craig Counsell.

JULY 29

White Sox traded DH Harold Baines to Orioles for a player to be named; Orioles sent SS Juan Bautista to White Sox to complete deal (August 18).
Rangers traded P Ken Hill to Angels for C Jim Leyritz and a player to be named; Angels sent IF Rob Sasser to Rangers to complete deal (October 31).
Rangers traded P Cory Bailey to Giants for P Chad Hartvigson.

Yankees traded IF/OF Mariano Duncan and cash to Blue Jays for OF Angel Ramirez.

Marlins traded P Matt Whisenant to Royals for C Matt Treanor.

JULY 31

Orioles traded P Mike Johnson to Expos for a player to be named; Expos sent P Everett Stull to Orioles to complete deal (October 31).

White Sox traded P Wilson Alvarez, P Danny Darwin and P Roberto Hernandez to Giants for SS Mike Caruso, OF Brian Manning, P Lorenzo Barcelo, P Keith Foulke, P Bob Howry and P Ken Vining.

Indians traded P Steve Kline and a player to be named to Expos for P Jeff Juden.

A's traded 1B Mark McGwire to Cardinals for P T.J. Mathews, P Eric Ludwick and P Blake Stein.

Mariners traded C Jason Varitek and P Derek Lowe to Red Sox for P Heathcliff Slocumb.

Blue Jays traded P Mike Timlin and P Paul Spoljaric to Mariners for OF Jose Cruz Jr.

Reds traded P John Smiley and IF Jeff Branson to Indians for P Danny Graves, P Jim Crowell, P Scott Winchester and IF Damian Jackson.

AUGUST 1

Giants released C Rick Wilkins.

AUGUST 2

Brewers released P Greg Hansell.

AUGUST 4

Rangers claimed P Terry Clark on waivers from Indians.

AUGUST 7

A's claimed P John Johnstone on waivers from Giants.

AUGUST 8

A's claimed SS/2B Tilson Brito on waivers from Blue Jays.

Giants claimed P Terry Mullholland on waivers from Cubs.

Mets traded OF Lance Johnson and two players to be named to Cubs for OF Brian McRae, P Mel Rojas and P Turk Wendell; Mets sent P Mark Clark (August 11) and IF Manny Alexander (August 14) to Cubs to complete deal.

AUGUST 9

Pirates traded P Hal Garrett to Dodgers for 1B Eddie Williams.

Padres announced retirement of P Danny Jackson.

AUGUST 12

Red Sox organization signed P Chris Bosio.

Rangers traded P Ed Vosberg to Marlins for P Rick Helling.

Blue Jays traded OF Otis Nixon to Dodgers for C Bobby Cripps.

AUGUST 13

Brewers signed DH Julio Franco.

Red Sox traded DH/C Mike Stanley and IF Randy Brown to Yankees for P Tony Armas and a player to be named.

Padres traded OF Rickey Henderson to Angels for P Ryan Hancock, P Stevenson Agosto and a player to be named; Angels sent 3B George Arias to Padres to complete deal (August 19).

AUGUST 14

Angels released DH Eddie Murray.

Twins traded 1B Greg Colbrunn to Braves for a player to be named; Braves sent OF Marc Lewis to Twins to complete deal (October 1).

AUGUST 15

Yankees released DH Pete Incaviglia.

Mariners signed C Rick Wilkins.

Astros traded P Julien Tucker to White Sox for C Tony Pena.

AUGUST 16

Cubs traded IF Rey Sanchez to Yankees for P Frisco Parotte.

AUGUST 19

Dodgers traded P Pedro Astacio to Rockies for 2B Eric Young.

AUGUST 20

Twins traded OF Roberto Kelly to Mariners for two players to named; Mariners sent P Joe Mays and P Jeromy Palki to Twins to complete deal (October 9).

Rockies released P Bill Swift.

Dodgers organization signed 1B Eddie Murray.

AUGUST 23

Angels traded IF/OF Aaron Guiel to Padres for C Angelo Encarnacion.

AUGUST 26

Orioles signed P Bill Swift.

AUGUST 27

White Sox traded OF Darren Lewis to Dodgers for a player to be named; Dodgers sent IF Chad Fonville to White Sox to complete deal (September 2).

AUGUST 29

Reds claimed 1B Mark Johnson on waivers from Pirates.

AUGUST 30

Cubs traded SS Shawon Dunston to Pirates for a player to be named.

Red Sox organization signed OF Curtis Pride.

Royals traded OF Bip Roberts to Indians for P Roland de la Maza.

Twins traded OF Darrin Jackson to Brewers for a player to be named; Brewers sent P Mick Fieldbinder to Twins to complete deal (September 4).

SEPTEMBER 2

Brewers signed P Paul Wagner.

Braves released OF Wonderful Monds.

SEPTEMBER 5

Twins traded C Greg Myers to Braves for a player to be named; Braves sent 1B Steve Hacker to Twins to complete deal (December 18).

SEPTEMBER 8

Mariners traded IF Brian Raabe to Rockies for P Donnie Schmidt.

SEPTEMBER 11

Orioles claimed C Charlie Greene on waivers from Mets.

SEPTEMBER 25

Red Sox claimed C B.J. Waszgis on waivers from Orioles.

SEPTEMBER 26

Cardinals announced retirement of P Rick Honeycutt.

SEPTEMBER 28

Red Sox released OF Wilfredo Cordero.

OCTOBER 3

Reds claimed P Curt Lyons on waivers from Cubs.

OCTOBER 6

Dodgers claimed P Jim Bruske on waivers from Padres.

OCTOBER 7

Reds claimed P Donne Wall on waivers from Astros.

OCTOBER 10

Mets released P Takashi Kashiwada.

OCTOBER 13

Padres claimed IF Ed Giovanola on waivers from Braves.

OCTOBER 14

Tigers claimed P Bill Hurst on waivers from Marlins.
White Sox claimed P Bryan Ward on waivers from Marlins.

OCTOBER 15

A's claimed P Vaughn Eshelman on waivers from Red Sox.
Cubs claimed 2B Jason Hardtke on waivers from Mets.
Pirates released IF Eddie Williams.

OCTOBER 16

Mariners released P Greg Hibbard.

OCTOBER 17

Mariners claimed OF Decomba Conner on waivers from Tigers.

OCTOBER 28

Red Sox signed P Brian Shouse.

OCTOBER 29

Blue Jays organization signed P Dane Johnson.

OCTOBER 31

Rangers traded IF Mike Bell to Angels for P Matt Perisho.

NOVEMBER 6

Red Sox traded P Aaron Sele, P Mark Brandenburg and C Bill Haselman to Rangers for C Jim Leyritz and OF Damon Buford.

NOVEMBER 7

Yankees traded P Kenny Rogers and cash to A's for a player to be named; A's sent 3B Scott Brosius to Yankees to complete deal (November 18).

NOVEMBER 10

Reds traded P Jeff Brantley to Cardinals for 1B Dmitri Young.

NOVEMBER 11

Blue Jays organization signed P Luis Andujar.
Marlins traded OF Moises Alou to Astros for P Oscar Henriquez, P Manuel Barrios and a player to be named; Astros sent P Mark Johnson to Marlins to complete deal (December 16).
Reds traded P Felix Rodriguez to Diamondbacks for a player to be named; Diamondbacks sent P Scott Winchester to Reds to complete deal (November 18).
Reds traded OF Mike Kelly to Devil Rays for a player to be named; Devil Rays sent 1B Dmitri Young to Reds to complete deal (November 18).
Tigers traded OF Mel Nieves to Reds for C Paul Bako and P Donne Wall.
Yankees traded 3B Charlie Hayes and cash to Giants for OF Chris Singleton and P Alberto Castillo.

NOVEMBER 15

Angels re-signed P Ken Hill.

NOVEMBER 17

Red Sox re-signed P Bret Saberhagen.
Diamondbacks signed SS Jay Bell.
Braves signed SS Walt Weiss.

NOVEMBER 18

Tigers traded 3B Travis Fryman to Diamondbacks for 3B Joe Randa, P Matt Drews and 3B Gabe Alvarez.
Brewers re-signed P Doug Jones.
Devil Rays signed P Roberto Hernandez to a four-year contract.
Braves traded 1B Fred McGriff to Devil Rays for a player to be named.
Marlins traded OF Devon White to Diamondbacks for P Jesus Martinez.
Rockies traded OF Harvey Pulliam to Diamondbacks for P Chuck McElroy.
Rockies re-signed C Jeff Reed.
Rockies organization signed IF Jeff Huson.
Marlins traded P Robb Nen to Giants for P Mike Villano, P Joe Fontenot and P Mick Pageler.
Marlins traded P Kurt Miller to Cubs for a player to be named.
Expos traded P Pedro J. Martinez to Red Sox for P Carl Pavano and a player to be named; Red Sox sent P Tony Armas Jr. to Expos to complete deal (December 18).
Rockies traded P Jake Westbrook, P John Nicholson and OF Mark Hamlin to Expos for 2B Mike Lansing.
Phillies traded SS Kevin Stocker to Devil Rays for OF Bob Abreu.
Padres traded C John Flaherty to Devil Rays for P Brian Boehringer and SS Andy Sheets.

NOVEMBER 19

Diamondbacks signed OF Chris Jones.
Padres traded OF Trey Beamon and P Tim Worrell to Tigers for P Dan Miceli, P Donne Wall and 3B Ryan Balfe.

NOVEMBER 20

Tigers traded 3B Phil Nevin and C Matt Walbeck to Angels for P Nick Skuse.
Braves signed 1B Andres Galarraga.
Marlins traded 1B/OF Jeff Conine to Royals for P Blaine Mull.
Brewers traded P Bryce Florie and a player to be named to Tigers for P Mike Myers, P Rick Greene and SS Santiago Perez.
Marlins traded P Ed Vosberg to Padres for P Chris Clark.

NOVEMBER 21

Red Sox re-signed SS Mike Benjamin.
White Sox sold contract of OF Lyle Mouton to Yakult of Japanese Central League.
Giants signed C Brent Mayne.

NOVEMBER 24

Astros signed OF Dave Clark.
Mets re-signed 1B John Olerud.

NOVEMBER 25

Indians claimed IF Chad Fonville on waivers from White Sox.
Royals re-signed C Mike Macfarlane.
Yankees signed IF Dale Sveum.
Padres signed C Greg Myers.
Padres released P Rich Batchelor.

NOVEMBER 26

White Sox released P Jeff Darwin.
A's traded P Don Wengert and IF David Newhan to Padres for P Doug Bochtler and IF Jorge Velandia.
Blue Jays signed P Randy Myers.
Blue Jays signed C Darrin Fletcher.
Astros signed P Doug Henry.

NOVEMBER 27

Blue Jays organization signed IF Craig Grebeck and IF Pat Kelly.

Reds organization signed P Toby Borland, P Ricardo Jordan, P Daron Kirkreit and P Ramon Fermin.

DECEMBER 1

Indians traded 3B Matt Williams to Diamondbacks for 3B Travis Fryman, P Tom Martin and cash.
Royals claimed SS Orlando Miller on waivers from Tigers.
Rangers organization signed C Rick Wrona.

DECEMBER 2

Mariners signed IF Aaron Holbert.
Pirates signed IF Doug Strange.

DECEMBER 3

Red Sox re-signed P Jim Corsi.
Devil Rays signed P Wilson Alvarez.

DECEMBER 4

White Sox sold contract of P Doug Creek to Hanshin of Japanese Pacific League.
Royals re-signed P Hipolito Pichardo.
Devil Rays signed OF Dave Martinez.
Rockies signed P Darryl Kile.
Dodgers announced retirement of P Todd Worrell.
Cardinals signed SS David Howard.

DECEMBER 5

Angels organization signed IF Steve Scarsone.
Orioles re-signed P Scott Kamieniecki.
Indians signed P Rich Batchelor.
Braves organization signed SS Rafael Belliard.
Marlins claimed IF Brandon Cromer on waivers from Pirates.
Cardinals re-signed OF Willie McGee.

DECEMBER 6

Angels re-signed P Rich DeLucia and P Mark Gubicza.
Orioles re-signed OF Brady Anderson.
Twins re-signed DH Paul Molitor.
Rangers signed P Scott Bailes.
Blue Jays organization re-signed IF/OF Juan Samuel.
Diamondbacks signed P Willie Blair.
Brewers organization re-signed OF Darrin Jackson.
Cardinals re-signed 3B Gary Gaetti.
Giants re-signed P Rich Rodriguez and P Danny Darwin.

DECEMBER 8

White Sox claimed 2B Sergio Nunez on waivers from Royals.
Indians signed OF Kenny Lofton and P Dwight Gooden.
Indians traded OF Marquis Grissom and P Jeff Juden to Brewers for P Ben McDonald, P Mike Fetters and Ron Villone.
A's traded P Steve Karsay to Indians for P Mike Fetters.
Blue Jays signed C Mike Stanley and 2B Tony Fernandez.
Devil Rays signed 1B Paul Sorrento.
Dodgers signed IF Jose Vizcaino.
Rangers signed SS Kevin Elster.

DECEMBER 9

Tigers signed OF Luis Gonzalez.
A's signed P Tom Candiotti.
Devil Rays signed 3B Wade Boggs.
Rangers signed IF Luis Alicea and OF Roberto Kelly.
Cubs signed SS Jeff Blauser.
Astros signed IF/OF Jack Howell.

DECEMBER 10

White Sox signed C Charlie O'Brien and C Chad Kreuter.
Yankees signed DH Chili Davis.
Reds traded OF Curtis Goodwin to Rockies for P Mark Hutton.

Expos traded P Dave Veres and a player to be named to Rockies for OF Terry Jones and a player to be named.
Pirates signed P Jeff Tabaka.

DECEMBER 11

Angels signed P Omar Olivares.
Orioles signed P Doug Drabek.
Orioles released P Brian Williams.
Tigers signed P Frank Castillo.
Twins signed OF Otis Nixon.
Blue Jays traded C Sandy Martinez to Cubs for a player to be named.
Braves traded P Chad Fox to Brewers for OF Gerald Williams.

DECEMBER 12

Orioles signed OF Joe Carter.
Tigers signed OF Bip Roberts.
Tigers released P Kevin Jarvis.
Mariners signed 1B David Segui.
Expos traded OF Henry Rodriguez to Cubs for P Miguel Batista.
Mets traded OF Alex Ochoa to Twins for OF Rich Becker.

DECEMBER 15

Orioles organization signed P Norm Charlton.
A's released OF Patrick Lennon.
Marlins traded P Kevin Brown to Padres for P Rafael Medina, P Steve Hoff and 1B Derrek Lee.
Mets traded P Mike Welch to Phillies for P Hector Mercado.
A's traded P Javier Martinez to Pirates for cash.
Pirates released P Steve Cooke.

DECEMBER 16

A's signed 1B/3B Mike Blowers.
Mariners signed P Tony Fossas and IF Pat Listach.
Cardinals signed P Kent Mercker.
Cardinals released IF Roberto Mejia.
Padres re-signed P Pete Smith.
Twins signed P Mike Morgan.

DECEMBER 17

Diamondbacks sold contract of OF Harvey Pulliam to Orix of Japanese Pacific League.
Rangers organization re-signed OF Mike Simms.

DECEMBER 18

Diamondbacks organization signed P Scott Brow, P Greg Hansell, P Barry Manuel and P Dave Pavlas.
Mets traded OF Fletcher Bates and P Scott Comer to Marlins for P Dennis Cook.
Rangers organization signed SS Domingo Cedeno.

DECEMBER 19

Angels signed DH Cecil Fielder.
Orioles re-signed DH Harold Baines.
Yankees re-signed OF Tim Raines.
Rangers traded SS Benji Gil to White Sox for P Al Levine and P Larry Thomas.
Rockies organization signed IF Nelson Liriano and OF Sherman Obando.
Marlins traded IF Kurt Abbott to A's for P Eric Ludwick.

DECEMBER 20

Reds signed P David Weathers.

DECEMBER 22

Royals signed 1B Hal Morris.
Yankees signed P Darren Holmes.
A's signed C Damon Berryhill and OF Shane Mack.

Reds signed P Steve Cooke.
Mets traded OF Carl Everett to Astros for P John Hudek.

DECEMBER 23

Red Sox signed OF Darren Lewis.
Rockies organization signed 1B Greg Colbrunn.
Phillies traded 2B Mickey Morandini to Cubs for OF Doug Glanville.
Mets organization signed 3B Craig Paquette.

DECEMBER 24

Giants signed P Steve Reed.

DECEMBER 26

Phillies signed IF Alex Arias.

DECEMBER 29

Cubs signed OF Matt Mieske.

DECEMBER 30

Astros organization signed P Bryan Harvey.

AWARD WINNERS

THE SPORTING NEWS

AMERICAN LEAGUE

Pitcher of the Year: Roger Clemens, Toronto
Rookie Player of the Year: Nomar Garciaparra, Boston, SS
Rookie Pitcher of the Year: Jason Dickson, Anaheim
Fireman of the Year: Mariano Rivera, New York
Comeback Player of the Year: David Justice, Cleveland
Manager of the Year: Dave Johnson, Baltimore

NATIONAL LEAGUE

Pitcher of the Year: Pedro Martinez, Montreal
Rookie Player of the Year: Scott Rolen, Philadelphia, 3B
Rookie Pitcher of the Year: Matt Morris, St. Louis
Fireman of the Year: Jeff Shaw, Cincinnati
Comeback Player of the Year: Darren Daulton, Phi.-Fla.
Manager of the Year: Dusty Baker, San Francisco

MAJOR LEAGUE

Player of the Year: Ken Griffey Jr., Seattle
Executive of the Year: Cam Bonifay, Pittsburgh

MINOR LEAGUE

Player of the Year: Ben Grieve, Huntsville, Southern; Edmonton, Pacific Coast
Manager of the Year: Marv Foley, Rochester, International
Executive of the Year: Andy Milovich, Erie, New York-Penn

BASEBALL WRITERS' ASSOCIATION OF AMERICA

AMERICAN LEAGUE

MOST VALUABLE PLAYER

Player, Team	1	2	3	4	5	6	7	8	9	10	Pts.
Ken Griffey Jr., Seattle	28	-	-	-	-	-	-	-	-	-	392
Tino Martinez, New York	-	24	2	4	3	-	-	-	-	-	248
Frank Thomas, Chicago	-	3	10	2	4	1	3	1	3	1	172
Randy Myers, Baltimore	-	-	8	3	3	3	1	1	1	1	128
David Justice, Cleveland	-	-	2	3	3	4	2	1	1	2	90
Jim Thome, Cleveland	-	-	1	5	2	3	4	-	1	1	89
Tim Salmon, Anaheim	-	1	1	2	3	2	3	2	2	3	84
Nomar Garciaparra, Boston	-	-	-	2	2	5	2	7	1	1	83
Juan Gonzalez, Texas	-	-	-	3	2	4	1	1	1	4	66
Roger Clemens, Toronto	-	-	1	1	2	2	1	3	3	-	56
Randy Johnson, Seattle	-	-	1	2	1	-	2	1	1	1	42
Paul O'Neill, New York	-	-	-	-	2	1	2	2	3	-	37
Rafael Palmeiro, Baltimore	-	-	-	2	1	1	1	1	-	4	36
Edgar Martinez, Seattle	-	-	-	-	2	-	-	1	3	1	22
Sandy Alomar Jr., Cleveland	-	-	-	2	-	-	-	2	1	-	22
Ivan Rodriguez, Texas	-	-	-	1	-	-	1	1	1	-	16
Bernie Williams, New York	-	-	-	-	1	-	1	1	-	1	14
Tony Clark, Detroit	-	-	-	-	-	-	1	-	4	1	13
Jay Buhner, Seattle	-	-	-	-	-	1	1	1	-	-	12
Doug Jones, Milwaukee	-	-	-	-	-	-	-	1	1	-	5
Arthur Rhodes, Baltimore	-	-	-	-	-	1	-	-	-	-	5
Roberto Alomar, Baltimore	-	-	-	-	-	-	-	1	-	-	4
Rusty Greer, Texas	-	-	-	-	-	-	1	-	-	-	4
Derek Jeter, New York	-	-	-	-	-	-	-	1	-	-	3
Mariano Rivera, New York	-	-	-	-	-	-	-	-	1	-	2
Brad Radke, Minnesota	-	-	-	-	-	-	-	-	-	2	2
Deivi Cruz, Detroit	-	-	-	-	-	-	-	-	-	2	2
Mo Vaughn, Boston	-	-	-	-	-	-	-	-	-	2	2
Jeromy Burnitz, Milwaukee	-	-	-	-	-	-	-	-	-	1	1

Fourteen points awarded for a first-place vote, nine for second and down to one for 10th.

CY YOUNG AWARD

Pitcher, Team	1	2	3	Pts.
Roger Clemens, Toronto	25	3	-	134
Randy Johnson, Seattle	2	21	4	77
Brad Radke, Minnesota	-	2	11	17
Randy Myers, Baltimore	1	1	6	14
Andy Pettitte, New York	-	1	6	9
Mike Mussina, Baltimore	-	-	1	1

Five points awarded for a first-place vote, three for second and one for third.

ROOKIE OF THE YEAR

Player, Team	1	2	3	Pts.
Nomar Garciaparra, Boston	28	-	-	140
Jose Cruz Jr., Sea.-Tor.	-	18	7	61
Jason Dickson, Anaheim	-	6	9	27
Deivi Cruz, Detroit	-	3	3	12
Jaret Wright, Cleveland	-	1	4	7
Mike Cameron, Chicago	-	-	5	5

Five points awarded for a first-place vote, three for second and one for third.

MANAGER OF THE YEAR

Manager, Team	1	2	3	Pts.
Dave Johnson, Baltimore	10	11	5	88
Buddy Bell, Detroit	4	7	9	50
Phil Garner, Milwaukee	5	5	2	42
Lou Piniella, Seattle	3	3	6	30
Terry Collins, Anaheim	4	1	1	24
Mike Hargrove, Cleveland	2	-	3	13
Joe Torre, New York	-	1	2	5

Five points awarded for a first-place vote, three for second and one for third.

MOST VALUABLE PLAYER

Player, Team	1	2	3	4	5	6	7	8	9	10	Pts.
Larry Walker, Colorado	22	3	3	-	-	-	-	-	-	-	359
Mike Piazza, Los Angeles	3	22	2	1	-	-	-	-	-	-	263
Jeff Bagwell, Houston	3	2	15	5	3	-	-	-	-	-	233
Craig Biggio, Houston	-	1	3	7	6	4	1	4	2	2	157
Barry Bonds, San Francisco	-	-	1	5	5	4	6	-	2	2	123
Tony Gwynn, San Diego	-	-	3	3	3	4	3	1	6	3	113
Andres Galarraga, Colorado	-	-	-	4	1	5	2	5	1	1	85
Jeff Kent, San Francisco	-	-	1	-	5	1	7	2	1	1	80
Chipper Jones, Atlanta	-	-	-	-	2	4	3	4	5	4	70
Moises Alou, Florida	-	-	-	2	2	4	-	4	-	2	60
Charles Johnson, Florida	-	-	-	1	-	-	1	2	1	3	22
Greg Maddux, Atlanta	-	-	-	-	1	1	-	1	1	-	16
Edgardo Alfonzo, New York	-	-	-	-	-	-	-	-	3	4	10
Curt Schilling, Philadelphia	-	-	-	-	-	1	-	1	-	1	9
Raul Mondesi, Los Angeles	-	-	-	-	-	1	-	2	-	8
Pedro Martinez, Montreal	-	-	-	-	-	-	-	1	1	1	6
Mark McGwire, St. Louis	-	-	-	-	-	-	-	1	-	2	6
Ray Lankford, St. Louis	-	-	-	-	-	-	1	-	1	-	6
Sammy Sosa, Chicago	-	-	-	-	-	-	1	-	-	1	5
Kevin Young, Pittsburgh	-	-	-	-	-	-	-	1	1	-	5
Jeff Blauser, Atlanta	-	-	-	-	-	-	1	-	-	-	4
Vinny Castilla, Colorado	-	-	-	-	-	-	-	1	-	-	3
Darryl Kile, Houston	-	-	-	-	-	-	-	1	-	-	3
Rod Beck, San Francisco	-	-	-	-	-	-	-	-	1	-	2
Tony Womack, Pittsburgh	-	-	-	-	-	-	-	-	1	-	2
Kenny Lofton, Atlanta	-	-	-	-	-	-	-	-	-	1	1
J.T. Snow, San Francisco	-	-	-	-	-	-	-	-	-	1	1

Fourteen points awarded for a first-place vote, nine for second and down to one for 10th.

MANAGER OF THE YEAR

Manager, Team	1	2	3	Pts.
Dusty Baker, San Francisco	17	7	4	110
Gene Lamont, Pittsburgh	10	13	3	92
Larry Dierker, Houston	1	5	14	34
Bobby Valentine, New York	-	2	1	7
Bobby Cox, Atlanta	-	1	3	6
Terry Francona, Philadelphia	-	-	2	2
Jim Leyland, Florida	-	-	1	1

Five points awarded for a first-place vote, three for second and one for third.

CY YOUNG AWARD

Pitcher, Team	1	2	3	Pts.
Pedro Martinez, Montreal	25	3	-	134
Greg Maddux, Atlanta	3	18	6	75
Denny Neagle, Atlanta	-	5	9	24
Curt Schilling, Philadelphia	-	1	9	12
Darryl Kile, Houston	-	1	4	7

Five points awarded for a first-place vote, three for second and one for third.

ROOKIE OF THE YEAR

Player, Team	1	2	3	Pts.
Scott Rolen, Philadelphia	28	-	-	140
Livan Hernandez, Florida	-	8	1	25
Matt Morris, St. Louis	-	7	4	25
Rich Loiselle, Pittsburgh	-	4	10	22
Andruw Jones, Atlanta	-	4	3	15
Vladimir Guerrero, Montreal	-	1	6	9
Jose Guillen, Pittsburgh	-	1	1	4
Brett Tomko, Cincinnati	-	1	1	4
Jeremi Gonzalez, Chicago	-	1	-	3
Tony Womack, Pittsburgh	-	1	-	3
Kevin Orie, Chicago	-	-	1	1
Neifi Perez, Colorado	-	-	1	1

Five points awarded for a first-place vote, three for second and one for third.

MISCELLANEOUS

ATTENDANCE

AMERICAN LEAGUE

	Home	Road
Baltimore	3,711,132	2,289,272
Cleveland	3,404,750	2,227,329
Seattle	3,192,237	2,409,664
Texas	2,945,228	2,142,471
Toronto	2,589,297	2,118,030
New York	2,580,325	2,643,175
Boston	2,226,136	2,139,097
Chicago	1,864,782	2,227,617
Anaheim	1,767,330	2,179,310
Kansas City	1,517,638	2,097,858
Milwaukee	1,444,027	2,161,263
Minnesota	1,411,064	2,095,535
Detroit	1,365,157	2,202,386
Oakland	1,264,218	2,362,054
Totals	**31,283,321**	**31,295,061**

NATIONAL LEAGUE

	Home	Road
Colorado	3,888,453	2,238,993
Atlanta	3,464,488	2,353,270
Los Angeles	3,319,504	2,579,741
St. Louis	2,634,014	2,184,564
Florida	2,364,387	2,169,072
Chicago	2,190,308	2,374,366
San Diego	2,089,333	2,201,113
Houston	2,046,781	2,115,796
Cincinnati	1,785,788	2,203,678
New York	1,766,174	2,382,838
San Francisco	1,690,869	2,425,975
Pittsburgh	1,657,022	2,132,337
Montreal	1,497,609	2,341,013
Philadelphia	1,490,638	2,170,872
Totals	**31,885,368**	**31,873,628**

DEBUTS

Player	Pos.	Team	Birth date	Birthplace	Debut
Abbott, Jeffrey William	LF	Chicago A.L.	8-17-72	Atlanta	6-10
Alfonseca, Antonio	P	Florida	4-16-72	La Romana, Dominican Republic	6-17
Almanzar, Carlos Manuel	P	Toronto	11-6-73	Santiago, Dominican Republic	9-4
Aven, David Bruce	LF	Cleveland	3-4-72	Orange, Texas	8-27
Aybar, Manuel Antonio	P	St. Louis	10-5-74	Bani, Dominican Republic	8-4
Barrios, Manuel	P	Houston	9-21-74	Cabecera, Panama	9-16
Bellhorn, Mark Christian	2B	Oakland	8-23-74	Boston	6-10
Beltran, Rigoberto	P	St. Louis	11-13-69	Tijuana, Mexico	6-2
Bennett, Shayne Anthony	P	Montreal	4-10-72	Adelaide, Australia	8-22
Berblinger, Jeffrey J.	2B	St. Louis	11-19-70	Wichita, Kansas	9-7
Bieser, Steven Ray	PH	New York N.L.	8-4-67	Perryville, Mo.	4-1
Blanco, Henry Ramon	PH	Los Angeles	8-29-71	Caracas, Venezuela	7-25
Boone, Aaron John	3B	Cincinnati	3-9-73	La Mesa, Calif.	6-20
Bovee, Michael Craig	P	Anaheim	8-21-73	San Diego	9-13
Bowers, Shane Patrick	P	Minnesota	7-27-71	Glendora, Calif.	7-26
Brock, Terrence Christopher	P	Atlanta	2-5-70	Orlando, Fla.	6-11
Brown, Adrian Demond	CF	Pittsburgh	2-7-74	McComb, Miss.	5-16
Brown, Emil Quincy	PH	Pittsburgh	12-29-74	Chicago, Ill.	4-3
Bush, Homer Giles	PR	New York A.L.	11-12-72	East St Louis, Ill.	8-16
Butler, Richard Dwight	LF	Toronto	5-1-73	Toronto	9-6
Cabrera, Jose Alberto	P	Houston	3-24-72	Santiago, Dominican Republic	7-15
Cabrera, Orlando	SS	Montreal	11-2-74	Cartagena, Columbia	9-3
Carpenter, Chistopher John	P	Toronto	4-27-75	Exeter, N.H.	5-12
Casey, Sean	PH	Cleveland	7-2-74	Willingsboro, N.J.	9-12
Castillo, Carlos	P	Chicago A.L.	4-21-75	Boston	4-2
Catalanotto, Frank John	PH	Detroit	4-27-74	Smithtown, N.Y.	9-3
Cather, Michael Peter	P	Atlanta	12-17-70	San Diego	7-13
Chavez, Anthony Francisco	P	Anaheim	10-22-70	Turlock, Calif.	9-2
Checo, Robinson Perez	P	Boston	9-9-71	Santo Domingo, Dominican Republic	9-16
Clemons, Chris Hale	P	Chicago A.L.	10-31-72	Baytown, Texas	7-23
Cloude, Kenneth Brian	P	Seattle	1-9-75	Baltimore, Md.	8-9
Clyburn, Danny	PH	Baltimore	4-6-74	Lancaster, S.C.	9-15
Coleman, Michael D.	CF	Boston	8-16-75	Nashville, Tenn.	9-1
Collier, Louis Keith	PH	Pittsburgh	8-21-73	Chicago	6-28
Colon, Bartolo	P	Cleveland	5-24-75	Altamira, Dominican Republic	4-4
Crawford, Joseph Randal	PH	New York N.L.	5-2-70	Gainesville, Fla.	4-7
Crowell, James	P	Cincinnati	5-14-74	Minneapolis	9-12
Cruz, Deivi	SS	Detroit	6-11-75	Nizao de Bani, Dominican Republic	4-1
Cruz Jr, Jose	LF	Seattle	4-19-74	Arroyo, Puerto Rico	5-31
Cruz, Luis Ivan	PH	New York A.L.	5-3-68	Fajardo, Puerto Rico	7-18
Cruz, Nelson	P	Chicago A.L.	9-13-72	Puerta Plaza, Dominican Republic	8-1
Cunnane, William Joseph	P	San Diego	4-24-74	Suffern, N.Y.	4-3
De La Maza, Roland Robert	P	Kansas City	11-11-71	Granada Hills, Calif.	9-26
DeHart, Richard A.	P	Montreal	3-21-70	Topeka, Kan.	7-16
DeJean, Michael Dwain	P	Colorado	9-28-70	Baton Rouge, La.	5-2
Dellucci, David Michael	DH	Baltimore	10-31-73	Baton Rouge, La.	6-3
Diaz, Eddy Javier	PH	Milwaukee	9-29-71	Barquisimeto, Venezuela	4-17

Player	Pos.	Team	Birth date	Birthplace	Debut
Dunwoody, Todd Franklin	PH	Florida	4-11-75	Lafayette, Ind.	5-10
Duran, Roberto	P	Detroit	3-6-73	Moca, Dominican Republic	7-6
Encarnacion, Juan DeDios	RF	Detroit	3-8-76	Las Matas de Faran, Dominican Rep.	9-2
Erdos, Todd Michael	P	San Diego	11-21-73	Washington, Pa.	6-8
Escobar, Kelvim Jose	P	Toronto	4-11-76	La Guaira, Venezuela	6-29
Evans, Thomas John	3B	Toronto	7-9-74	Kirkland, Wash.	9-2
Eyre, Scott Alan	P	Chicago A.L.	5-30-72	Inglewood, Calif.	8-1
Falteisek, Steven James	P	Montreal	1-28-72	Mineola, N.Y.	7-22
Figga, Michael Anthony	C	New York A.L.	7-31-70	Tampa, Fla.	9-16
Fordham, Thomas James	P	Chicago A.L.	2-20-74	San Diego	8-19
Foulke, Keith Charles	P	San Francisco	10-19-72	Ellsworth AFB, S.D.	5-21
Fox, Chad Douglas	P	Atlanta	9-3-70	Coronado, Calif.	7-13
Franklin, Micah Ishanti	RF	St. Louis	4-25-72	San Francisco	5-13
Frias, Hanley Acevedo	PH	Texas	12-5-73	Villa Ariagracia, Dominican Republic	6-21
Fullmer, Bradley Ryan	PH	Montreal	1-17-75	Chatsworth, Calif.	9-2
Gaillard, Julian Edward	P	Detroit	8-13-70	Camden, N.J.	8-11
Gilbert, Albert Shawn	PH	New York N.L.	3-12-68	Camden, N.J.	6-2
Gomes, Wayne M.	P	Philadelphia	1-15-73	Hampton, Va.	6-13
Gonzalez, Geremis Segundo	P	Chicago N.L.	1-8-75	Maracaibo, Venezuela	5-27
Gorecki, Richard John	P	Los Angeles	8-27-73	Evergreen, Ill.	9-10
Green, Bert Scarborough	CF	St. Louis	6-9-74	Creve Coeur, Mo.	8-2
Grieve, Benjamin	RF	Oakland	5-4-76	Arlington, Texas	9-3
Guevara, Giomar Antonio	PR	Seattle	10-23-72	Miranda, Venezuela	9-19
Guillen, Jose Manuel	RF	Pittsburgh	5-17-76	San Cristobal, Dominican Republic	4-1
Gulan, Michael Watts	3B	St. Louis	12-18-70	Stuebenville, Ohio	5-14
Halter, Shane David	PH	Kansas City	11-8-69	LaPlata, Md.	4-6
Hansen, Jed Ramon	PR	Kansas City	8-19-72	Tacoma, Wash.	7-29
Hasegawa, Shigetoshi	P	Anaheim	8-1-68	Kobe, Japan	4-5
Haught, Gary Allen	P	Oakland	9-29-70	Tacoma, Wash.	7-16
Helton, Todd Lynn	LF	Colorado	8-20-73	Knoxville, Tenn.	8-2
Henriquez, Oscar	P	Houston	1-28-74	LaGuaria, Venezuela	9-7
Hernandez, Fernando	P	Detroit	6-16-71	Santiago, Dominican Republic	4-3
Hidalgo, Richard	CF	Houston	7-2-75	Caracas, Venezuela	9-1
Hunter, Torii Kedar	PR	Minnesota	7-18-75	Pine Bluff, Ark.	8-22
Hurst, Jimmy O'Neal	RF	Detroit	3-1-72	Druid City, Ala.	9-10
Irabu, Hideki	P	New York A.L.	5-5-69	Hyogo, Japan	7-10
Johnson, Jason Michael	P	Pittsburgh	10-27-73	Santa Barbara, Calif.	8-27
Johnson, Michael Keith	P	Baltimore	10-3-75	Edmonton, Canada	4-6
Johnson, William Russell	3B	Houston	2-22-73	Baton Rouge, La.	4-8
Jones, Robert Mitchell	P	Colorado	4-11-72	Orange, N.J.	5-18
Judd, Michael	P	Los Angeles	6-30-75	San Diego, Calif.	9-28
Kashiwada, Takashi	P	New York N.L.	5-14-71	Tokyo, Japan	5-1
King, Curtis Albert	P	St. Louis	10-25-70	Norristown, Pa.	8-1
Kline, Steven James	P	Cleveland	8-22-72	Sunbury, Pa.	4-2
Konerko, Paul Henry	PH	Los Angeles	3-5-76	Providence, R.I.	9-8
Kotsay, Mark Steven	CF	Florida	12-2-75	Woodier, Calif.	7-11
Kubinski, Timothy Mark	P	Oakland	1-20-72	Pullman, Wash.	7-16
Latham, Christopher Joseph	PH	Minnesota	5-26-73	Coeur D'Alene, Idaho	4-12
Lee, Derrek Leon	1B	San Diego	9-6-75	Sacramento, Calif.	4-28
LeRoy, John Michael	P	Atlanta	4-19-75	Bellevue, Wash.	9-26
Lidle, Cory Fulton	P	New York N.L.	3-22-72	Hollywood, Calif.	5-8
Ligtenberg, Kerry Dale	P	Atlanta	5-11-71	Rapid City, S.D.	8-12
Long, Joey	P	San Diego	7-15-70	Sidney, Ohio	4-25
Long, Ryan Marcus	LF	Kansas City	2-3-73	Houston	7-16
Lowe, Derek Christopher	P	Seattle	6-1-73	Dearborn, Mich.	4-26
Lowe, Jonathan Sean	P	St. Louis	3-29-71	Dallas	8-29
Lowery, Quenton Terrell	PH	Chicago N.L.	10-25-70	Oakland	9-13
Maloney, Sean Patrick	P	Milwaukee	5-25-71	South Kingston, R.I.	4-28
Marrero, Elieser	C	St. Louis	11-17-73	Havana, Cuba	9-3
Martin, Thomas Edgar	P	Houston	5-21-70	Charleston, S.C.	4-2
Martinez, Felix Mata	PH	Kansas City	5-18-74	Nagua, Dominican Republic	9-3
McDill, Allen Gabriel	P	Kansas City	8-23-71	Greensville, Miss.	5-15
McDonald, Jason Adam	CF	Oakland	3-20-72	Modesto, Calif.	6-5
McGraw, Thomas Virgil	P	St. Louis	12-8-67	Portland, Ore.	5-7
McGuire, Ryan B.	1B	Montreal	11-23-71	Bellflower, Calif.	6-5
Mendoza, Carlos	PR	New York N.L.	11-14-74	Bolivar, Venezuela	9-3
Miller, Damian Donald	PH	Minnesota	10-13-69	La Crosse, Wis.	8-10
Millwood, Kevin Austin	P	Atlanta	12-24-74	Gastonia, N.C.	7-14
Misuraca, Michael William	P	Milwaukee	8-21-68	Long Beach, Calif.	7-27
Moody, Eric Lane	P	Texas	1-6-71	Greenville, S.C.	8-3
Morgan, Kevin Lee	PH	New York N.L.	3-3-70	Lafayette, La.	6-15
Morris, Matthew Christian	P	St. Louis	8-9-74	Middletown, N.Y.	4-4
Murray, Heath Robertson	P	San Diego	4-19-73	Troy, Ohio	5-24

Player	Pos.	Team	Birth date	Birthplace	Debut
Nunez, Abraham Orlando	SS	Pittsburgh	3-16-76	Santo Domingo, Dominican Republic	8-27
Nye, Ryan Craig	P	Philadelphia	6-24-73	Biloxi, Miss.	6-7
Ojala, Kirt Stanley	P	Florida	12-24-68	Kalamazoo, Mich.	8-18
Ordaz, Luis Javier	SS	St. Louis	8-12-75	Maracaibo, Venezuela	9-3
Ordonez, Magglio	RF	Chicago A.L.	1-28-74	Caracas, Venezuela	8-29
Orie, Kevin Leonard	3B	Chicago N.L.	9-1-72	West Chester, Pa.	4-1
Ortiz, David Americo	PH	Minnesota	11-18-75	Santo Domingo, Dominican Republic	9-2
Perisho, Matthew Alan	P	Anaheim	6-8-75	Burlington, Iowa	5-27
Pisciotta, Marc George	P	Chicago N.L.	8-7-70	Edison, N.J.	6-30
Polcovich, Kevin Michael	SS	Pittsburgh	6-28-70	Auburn, N.Y.	5-17
Powell, LeJon Dante	PH	San Francisco	8-25-73	Long Beach, Calif.	4-15
Raggio, Brady John	P	St. Louis	9-17-72	Los Angeles	4-15
Ramos, Edgar	P	Philadelphia	3-6-75	Cuinana, Edo Sucre, Venezuela	5-21
Ramos, Ken	PH	Houston	6-6-67	Sydney, Neb.	5-16
Reese, Calvin	SS	Cincinnati	6-10-73	Columbia, S.C.	4-1
Reyes, Dennis	P	Los Angeles	4-19-77	Higuera de Zaragoza, Mexico	7-13
Rigby, Bradley Kenneth	P	Oakland	5-14-73	Milwaukee, Wis.	6-28
Riggs, Adam	2B	Los Angeles	10-4-72	Steubenville, Ohio	8-7
Rincon, Ricardo	P	Pittsburgh	4-13-70	Veracruz, Mexico	4-3
Rios, Daniel	P	New York A.L.	11-11-72	Madrid, Spain	5-30
Ritchie, Todd Everett	P	Minnesota	11-7-71	Portsmouth, Va.	4-3
Rohrmeier, Daniel	PH	Seattle	1-27-65	Cincinnati	9-3
Romero, Armando	C	San Diego	10-29-67	Miami	7-15
Rosario, Melvin Gregario	C	Baltimore	5-25-73	Santo Domingo, Dominican Republic	9-11
Rose, Brian Leonard	P	Boston	2-13-76	New Bedford, Mass.	7-25
Rose Jr, Peter Edward	3B	Cincinnati	11-16-69	Cincinnati, Ohio	9-1
Rusch, Glendon James	P	Kansas City	11-7-74	Seattle	4-6
Sagmoen, Marc Richard	RF	Texas	4-16-71	Seattle	4-15
Santana, Julio Franklin	P	Texas	1-20-73	San Pedro de Macoris, D.R.	4-6
Santiago, Jose Rafael	P	Kansas City	11-5-74	Fajardo, Puerto Rico	6-7
Saunders, Anthony Scott	P	Florida	4-29-74	Baltimore	4-5
Sexson, Richmond Lockwood	PH	Cleveland	12-29-74	Portland, Ore.	9-14
Sheldon, Scott Patrick	SS	Oakland	11-28-68	Hammond, Ind.	5-18
Simon, Randall Carlito	PH	Atlanta	5-26-75	Willemstad, Curacao	9-1
Stanifer, Robert	P	Florida	3-10-72	Easley, S.C.	5-3
Stewart, Andrew David	PR	Kansas City	12-5-70	Oshawa, Canada	9-6
Stull, Everett James	P	Montreal	8-24-71	Fort Riley, Kan.	4-14
Sutton, Larry James	1B	Kansas City	5-14-70	West Covina, Calif.	8-17
Tatis, Fernando	3B	Texas	1-1-75	San Pedro de Macoris, D.R.	7-26
Tatis, Ramon Francisco	P	Chicago N.L.	5-2-73	Guayubin, Dominican Republic	4-5
Tejada, Miguel Odalis	SS	Oakland	5-25-76	Bani, Dominican Republic	8-27
Thomson, John Carl	P	Colorado	10-1-73	Vicksburg, Va.	5-11
Thurman, Michael Richard	P	Montreal	7-22-73	Corvallis, Ore.	9-2
Tomko, Brett Daniel	P	Cincinnati	4-7-73	Cleveland	5-27
Trammell, Thomas Bubba	DH	Detroit	11-6-71	Knoxville, Tenn.	4-1
Valdez, Mario A.	1B	Chicago A.L.	11-19-74	Obregon, Mexico	6-15
Valentin, Jose Javier	C	Minnesota	9-19-75	Manati, Puerto Rico	9-13
Varitek, Jason A.	PH	Boston	4-11-72	Rochester, Minn.	9-24
Velandia, Jorge Macias	2B	San Diego	1-12-75	Caracas, Venezuela	6-20
Vidro, Jose Angel	PH	Montreal	8-27-74	Mayaguez, Puerto Rico	6-8
Walker, Jamie Ross	P	Kansas City	7-1-71	McMinnville, Tenn.	4-2
Wallace, Jeffrey Allen	P	Pittsburgh	4-12-76	Wheeling, W.Va.	8-21
Watkins, William Patrick	CF	Cincinnati	9-2-72	Raleigh, N.C.	9-9
Whisenant, Matthew Michael	P	Florida	6-8-71	Los Angeles	7-4
Williamson, Antone	PH	Milwaukee	7-18-73	Harbor City, Calif.	5-31
Wilson, Enrique Martes	SS	Cleveland	7-27-75	Santo Domingo, Dominican Republic	9-24
Winchester, Scott	P	Cincinnati	4-20-73	Midland, Mich.	9-8
Winston, Darrin Alexander	P	Philadelphia	7-6-66	Passaic, N.J.	9-10
Woodard, Steve Larry	P	Milwaukee	5-15-75	Hartselle, Ala.	7-28
Wright, Jaret Samuel	P	Cleveland	12-29-75	Anaheim, Calif.	6-24

SALARY ARBITRATION RESULTS

WINNERS

Player, Team	Salary awarded	Team's offer
Tim Wakefield, Boston	$2,500,000	$1,550,000

LOSERS

Player, Team	Salary awarded	Player's request
Tom Goodwin, Kansas City	$1,050,000	$1,795,000
Darryl Kile, Houston	$1,700,000	$2,970,000
Bill Risley, Toronto	$380,000	$550,000
Aaron Sele, Boston	$1,126,000	$1,400,000

1997 FREE-AGENT FILINGS

AMERICAN LEAGUE

Anaheim: Luis Alicea, Rich DeLucia, Mark Gubicza, Rickey Henderson, Ken Hill, Jack Howell, Chad Kreuter, Mark Langston.
Baltimore: Brady Anderson, Harold Baines, Shawn Boskie, Scott Kamieniecki, Randy Myers, Jerome Walton, Lenny Webster.
Boston: Mike Benjamin, Jim Corsi, Chris Hammond, Shane Mack, Bret Saberhagen.
Chicago: Doug Drabek, Ozzie Guillen, Ron Karkovice, Dave Martinez.
Cleveland: Paul Assenmacher, Pat Borders, Tony Fernandez, Orel Hershiser, Jack McDowell, Bip Roberts, Kevin Seitzer.
Detroit: Willie Blair.
Kansas City: Jay Bell, Ricky Bones, Chili Davis, David Howard, Mike Macfarlane, Gregg Olson, Dean Palmer, Hipolito Pichardo.
Minnesota: Paul Molitor.
New York: Wade Boggs, Cecil Fielder, Dwight Gooden, Pat Kelly, Tim Raines, Rey Sanchez, Luis Sojo, Mike Stanley, Darryl Strawberry.
Oakland: Jose Canseco, Dave Magadan, Brent Mayne.
Seattle: Mike Blowers, Norm Charlton, Joey Cora, Roberto Kelly, John Marzano, Omar Olivares, Paul Sorrento, Rick Wilkins.
Texas: Scott Bailes, Bill Ripken, Bobby Witt.
Toronto: Joe Carter, Mariano Duncan, Orlando Merced, Charlie O'Brien, Juan Samuel.

NATIONAL LEAGUE

Atlanta: Rafael Belliard, Jeff Blauser, Mark Lemke, Kenny Lofton, Greg Myers.
Chicago: Dave Clark, Dave Hansen.
Cincinnati: Kent Mercker, Mike Morgan, Hal Morris, Joe Oliver, Jose Rijo, Deion Sanders.
Colorado: Frank Castillo, Andres Galarraga, Darren Holmes, Mike Munoz, Jeff Reed, Bruce Ruffin, Walt Weiss.
Florida: Darren Daulton.
Houston: Luis Gonzalez, Thomas Howard, Darryl Kile, Tony Pena, Luis Rivera, Bill Spiers.
Los Angeles: Brett Butler, Tom Candiotti, Darren Lewis, Eddie Murray, Otis Nixon, Todd Worrell.
Milwaukee: Mark Davis, Julio Franco, Pete Harnisch, Jeff Huson, Darrin Jackson, Doug Jones.
Montreal: Rheal Cormier, Darrin Fletcher, David Segui, Doug Strange.
New York: John Olerud.
Pittsburgh: Shawon Dunston, Kevin Elster, Dale Sveum.
St. Louis: Andy Benes, Dennis Eckersley, Tony Fossas, Gary Gaetti, Rick Honeycutt, Scott Livingstone, Willie McGee, Phil Plantier.
San Diego: Carlos Hernandez, Craig Shipley, Pete Smith.
San Francisco: Wilson Alvarez, Rod Beck, Damon Berryhill, Danny Darwin, Doug Henry, Roberto Hernandez, Glenallen Hill, Stan Javier, Terry Mulholland, Rich Rodriguez, Jose Vizcaino.

EXPANSION DRAFT OF NOVEMBER 18, 1997

TAMPA BAY DEVIL RAYS

FIRST ROUND

Pick Name, Position, Former team
1. Tony Saunders, LHP, Florida
2. Quinton McCracken, OF, Colorado
3. Bob Abreu, OF, Houston (traded to Philadelphia)
4. Miguel Cairo, 2B, Chicago Cubs
5. Rich Butler, OF, Toronto
6. Bobby Smith, SS, Atlanta
7. Jason Johnson, RHP, Pittsburgh
8. Dmitri Young, 1B/OF, Cincinnati (traded back to Cincinnati)
9. Esteban Yan, RHP, Baltimore
10. Mike Difelice, C, St. Louis
11. Bubba Trammell, OF, Detroit
12. Andy Sheets, SS, Seattle (traded to San Diego)
13. Dennis Springer, RHP, Anaheim
14. Dan Carlson, RHP, San Francisco

SECOND ROUND
15. Brian Boehringer, RHP, N.Y. Yankees (traded to San Diego)
16. Mike Duvall, LHP, Florida
17. John LeRoy, RHP, Atlanta
18. Jim Mecir, RHP, Boston
19. Bryan Rekar, RHP, Colorado
20. Rick Gorecki, RHP, Los Angeles
21. Ramon Tatis, LHP, Chicago Cubs
22. Kerry Robinson, OF, St. Louis
23. Steve Cox, 1B, Oakland

24. Albie Lopez, RHP, Cleveland
25. Jose Paniagua, RHP, Montreal
26. Carlos Mendoza, OF, New York Mets
27. Ryan Karp, LHP, Philadelphia
28. Santos Hernandez, RHP, San Francisco

THIRD ROUND
29. Randy Winn, OF, Florida
30. Terrell Wade, LHP, Atlanta
31. Aaron Ledesma, SS, Baltimore
32. Brooks Kieschnick, OF/1B, Chicago Cubs
33. Luke Wilcox, OF, New York Yankees;
34. Herbert Perry, 1B, Cleveland
35. Vaughn Eshelman, LHP, Boston

ARIZONA DIAMONDBACKS

FIRST ROUND

Pick Name, Position, Former team
1. Brian Anderson, LHP, Cleveland
2. Jeff Suppan, RHP, Boston
3. Gabe Alvarez, 3B, San Diego (traded to Detroit)
4. Jorge Fabregas, C, Chicago White Sox
5. Karim Garcia, OF, Los Angeles
6. Edwin Diaz, 2B, Texas
7. Cory Lidle, RHP, New York Mets
8. Joel Adamson, LHP, Milwaukee
9. Ben Ford, RHP, New York Yankees
10. Yamil Benitez, OF, Kansas City

11. Neil Weber, LHP, Montreal
12. Jason Boyd, RHP, Philadelphia
13. Brent Brede, OF/1B, Minnesota
14. Tony Batista, SS, Oakland

SECOND ROUND

15. Tom Martin, LHP, Houston
16. Omar Daal, LHP, Toronto
17. Scott Winchester, RHP, Cincinnati (traded back to Cin.)
18. Clint Sodowsky, RHP, Pittsburgh
19. Danny Klassen, SS, Milwaukee
20. Matt Drews, RHP, Detroit (traded back to Detroit)
21. Todd Erdos, RHP, San Diego
22. Chris Clemons, RHP, Chicago White Sox
23. David Dellucci, OF, Baltimore

24. Damian Miller, C, Minnesota
25. Hector Carrasco, RHP, Kansas City
26. Hanley Frias, SS, Texas
27. Bob Wolcott, RHP, Seattle
28. Mike Bell, 3B, Anaheim

THIRD ROUND

29. Joe Randa, 3B, Pittsburgh (traded to Detroit)
30. Jesus Martinez, LHP, Los Angeles (traded to Florida)
31. Russ Springer, RHP, Houston
32. Bryan Corey, RHP, Detroit
33. Kelly Stinnett, C, Milwaukee
34. Chuck McElroy, LHP, Chi. White Sox (traded to Colorado)
35. Marty Janzen, RHP, Toronto

MAJOR LEAGUE DRAFT

(Listed in order of selection)

Player	Pos.	Drafted by	Drafted from (major league organization)
Javier Martinez	P	Oakland	Iowa, American Association (Cubs)
Hector Mercado	P	Philadelphia	Charlotte, S.C., International League (Marlins)
Alan Mahaffey	P	Chicago N.L.	Salt Lake City, Pacific Coast League (Twins)
Luis Saturria	OF	Toronto	Louisville, American Association (Cardinals)
Keith Glauber	P	Cincinnati	Louisville, American Association (Cardinals)
Sean Runyan	P	Detroit	Las Vegas, Pacific Coast League (Padres)
Melvin Brazoban	P	Pittsburgh	Oklahoma City, American Association (Rangers)
Jeff Huson	2B-SS	Seattle	Colorado Springs, Pacific Coast League (Rockies)
Marc Deschenes	P	Los Angeles	Buffalo, American Association (Indians)
Brian Edmondson	P	Atlanta	Norfolk, International League (Mets)
Martin Sanchez	P	Arizona	Charlotte, S.C., International League (Marlins)
Frank Lankford	P	Los Angeles	Columbus, O., International League (Yankees)
Ynocencio De la Cruz	P	Arizona	Norfolk, International League (Mets)

NECROLOGY

Cal Abrams, 72, at Fort Lauderdale, Fla., on February 25. Outfielder Abrams, who batted .269 over eight big-league seasons, was a key figure in the climactic game of the 1950 National League pennant race. Playing for the Dodgers on the final day of the season when a victory over the league-leading Phillies would have tied Brooklyn for first place, Abrams was thrown out at the plate in the ninth inning of a 1-1 game while attempting to score from second base on Duke Snider's single. The Phils won the game—and the pennant—when Dick Sisler hit a three-run homer in the 10th inning.

Bobby Adams, 75, at Gig Harbor, Wash., on February 13. Adams, the Reds' regular third baseman in 1952 and 1953, spent 9½ of his 14 major league seasons with Cincinnati. He posted a career batting average of .269 and scored 99 runs for the '53 Reds.

Luis Aloma, 73, at Park Ridge, Ill., on April 7. From 1950-53, the White Sox's Aloma pitched in 116 big-league games—115 of them in relief—and compiled an 18-3 record before leaving the majors at age 30 because of shoulder problems. In his only start in the big leagues, Aloma tossed a shutout against the Athletics in 1951.

Richie Ashburn, 70, at New York on September 9. Hall of Famer Ashburn won two N.L. batting titles, hit .330 or higher five times and collected 2,574 hits in a 15-year major league career. The fleet outfielder spent 12 seasons with the Phillies and was a key member of the club's pennant-winning Whiz Kids of 1950. At the time of his death, Ashburn was in his 35th year as a Phils broadcaster.

Rex Barney, 72, at Baltimore, on August 12. Righthander Barney, who seldom could harness his blazing fastball, went 35-31 in six seasons with the Dodgers until control problems drove him out of the majors. Barney found a groove in 1948, winning 15 games and pitching a no-hitter against the Giants, but two years later he walked 48 batters in 33⅔ innings and disappeared from the big leagues. In the 1970s, he became public-address announcer for the Orioles and was serving in that capacity at the time of his death.

Ray Benge, 95, at Centerville, Texas, on June 27. Benge fashioned double-digit victory totals in six consecutive N.L. seasons and finished a 12-year major league career with a 101-130 record. He went 14-12 for the 1934 Dodgers.

Al Blanche, 87, at Melrose, Mass., on April 2. Blanche relieved in a total of 17 games for the Braves in 1935 and 1936.

Roger Bowman, 69, at Los Angeles, on July 21. Bowman made 50 pitching appearances in the majors—nine of them for the Giants' 1951 pennant-winning club.

Pidge Browne, 68, at Houston, on June 3. First baseman Browne, who had played for Houston teams in the Texas League and the American Association, saw his only big-league service for the Houston Colt .45s in 1962. He hit .210 in 65 games.

Bill Butland, 79, at Terre Haute, Ind., on September 19. A starter and reliever, Butland won seven of eight decisions for the 1942 Red Sox and was 9-3 overall in four major league seasons.

Bob Cain, 72, at Cleveland, on April 7. As a member of the Tigers, he pitched to (and walked) the Browns' 3-foot-7 Eddie Gaedel in 1951. Cain wound up winning 37 games over six major league seasons.

Dolph Camilli, 90, at San Mateo, Calif., on October 21. He was the National League's MVP in 1941, when he hit 34 home runs and drove in 120 runs for the pennant-winning Dodgers. Camilli, who spent eight full seasons in the minors before getting a look in the majors, hit 20 or more homers in eight consecutive big-league seasons and topped the 100-RBI mark five times.

Fred Chapman, 80, at Kannapolis, N.C., on March 27. Infielder Chapman appeared in 76 games for the Athletics from 1939 through 1941.

Lu Clinton, 60, at Wichita, Kan., on December 6. Outfielder Clinton played eight seasons in the majors and enjoyed his best year in 1962 when he batted .294 for the Red Sox with 18 home runs and 75 RBIs.

Joe Coleman, 74, at Fort Myers, Fla., on April 9. Coleman, a double-figure winner in three of his 10 big-league seasons, stood out for the Orioles in 1954 in the former St. Louis Browns franchise's first season in Baltimore. He was a 13-game winner for a team that lost 100 games and tossed four shutouts. His son, also Joe, pitched in the majors for 15 seasons.

Jeff Cross, 78, at Huntsville, Texas, on July 23. Infielder Cross played 49 of his 119 big-league games for the 1946 Cardinals, who were World Series champions.

Harry Davis, 88, Shreveport, La., on March 3. Davis was the No.1 first baseman for the Tigers in 1932 and the Browns in 1937. He batted .269 and .276 in those seasons.

Eddie Delker, 90, at Pottsville, Pa., on May 14. Infielder Delker played in a total of 98 games for the Cardinals and Phillies over four seasons (1929, 1931-33).

Johnny Dickshot, 87, at Waukegan, Ill., on November 4. Dickshot saw regular outfield duty for the 1945 White Sox, batting .302, and was in the majors for five other seasons.

George Dockins, 79, at Clyde, Kan., on January 22. Lefthander Dockins went 8-6 for the Cardinals in 1945 and had no decisions in a stint with the Dodgers in 1947.

Jerry Doggett, 80, at San Jose, Calif., on July 7. A Dodgers broadcaster from 1956 through 1987, Doggett and partner Vin Scully became celebrities when the club moved from Brooklyn to Los Angeles in 1958. It quickly became fashionable for Californians to take transistor radios to the ballpark to listen to Doggett and Scully describe what was unfolding before them.

Dick Donovan, 69, at Weymouth, Mass., on January 6. He won 122 games in a 15-year major league career. He went 16-6 for the White Sox in 1957, was a member of the pennant-winning Sox's rotation in 1959 and won 20 games for the Indians in 1962.

Gus Dugas, 90, at Norwich, Conn., on April 14. Outfielder Dugas had 218 at-bats (75 as a pinch hitter) over four big-league seasons in the early 1930s. He played for the Pirates, Phillies and Senators.

Woody English, 90, at Newark, Ohio, on September 26. English played 10 of his 12 big-league seasons for the Cubs. A shortstop/third baseman, he posted a career batting average of .286, played in the 1929 and 1932 World Series and appeared in the first All-Star game in 1933.

Hector Espino, 58, at Monterrey, Mexico, on September 7. First baseman Espino, who spent most of his 25 years of minor league ball in the Mexican League, ranks No. 1 in career homers in the minors with 484. He never played in the majors.

Curt Flood, 59, at Los Angeles on January 20. A gifted defensive outfielder who batted .293 over 15 major league seasons, he helped the Cardinals to three pennants and two World Series titles in a five-year span. As good a player as Flood was, his lasting impact came off the field when, after being traded to the Phillies in October 1969, he sued baseball over the legality of the reserve clause under which club owners controlled the movement of players. Although Flood lost his case, his challenge paved the way for the eventual stripping away of the renewal clause, the centerpiece of the reserve system, in 1975, which opened the door to free agency and megabucks contracts.

James "Rufe" Gentry, 79, at Winston-Salem. N.C., on July 3. Gentry threw four shutouts for the Tigers in 1944, a season in which he went 12-14. He was 1-3 while pitching in parts of three other seasons.

Connie Grob, 64, at Madison, Wis., on September 28. In his only major league season, the righthander compiled a 4-5 record for the Senators in 1956.

Sam Hairston, 77, at Birmingham, Ala., on October 31. Hairston was the first American-born black to play for the White Sox, appearing in four games in 1951. Sons Jerry and John also played in the majors.

Steve Hamilton, 62, at Morehead, Ky., on December 2. The 6-6 Hamilton, who spent two seasons with the NBA's Minneapolis Lakers, pitched in the majors for 12 seasons, principally in relief. In one four-year stretch (1963-66) with the Yankees, he went 23-7 and pitched in two World Series.

Bud Hardin, 75, at Rancho Santa Fe, Calif., on July 28. Infielder Hardin appeared in three games for the 1952 Cubs.

Buddy Hassett, 85, at Westwood, N.J., on August 23. First baseman Hassett, who played seven full years (1936 through 1942) in the majors and never struck out more than 19 times in one season, hit .292 in 929 big-league games. He was with the Dodgers, Braves and Yankees.

Joe Hauser, 98, at Sheboygan, Wis., on July 11. First baseman Hauser, a major leaguer for six seasons in the 1920s, is the only player in professional baseball history to record two 60-homer seasons. Hauser, who hit 27 home runs for the Athletics in 1924, smashed 63 homers for Baltimore of the International League in 1930 and 69 for Minneapolis of the American Association in 1933.

Jim Hickey, 76, at Manchester, Conn., on September 20. He pitched in a total of nine games for the Braves in 1942 and 1944.

Mark Holtz, 51, at Dallas on September 7. Holtz was the lead radio voice for Rangers broadcasts from 1982 through 1994 and was in his 17th season of radio or TV work for the club at the time of his death.

Duane Josephson, 54, at New Hampton, Iowa, on January 30. The White Sox's No. 1 catcher in 1968, Josephson hit .258 in eight big-league seasons.

Billy Jurges, 88, at Clearwater, Fla., on March 3. Jurges played 17 seasons in the majors—10 with the Cubs, for whom he stood out at shortstop and played in three World Series (1932, 1935 and 1938. He managed the Red Sox in the last half of 1959 and the first half of 1960.

Monte Kennedy, 74, at Midlothian, Va., on March 1. Kennedy pitched in 249 games for the Giants from 1946 through 1953. In 1949, he won 12 games and pitched four shutouts.

Austin Knickerbocker, 78, at Clinton Corners, N.Y., on February 18. An outfielder, Knickerbocker played in 21 games for the 1947 Athletics.

Alex Konikowski, 69, at Seymour, Conn., on September 28. Relief pitcher Konikowski appeared in a total of 35 games for the Giants in 1948, 1951 and 1954.

Bert Kuczynski, 77, at Allentown, Pa., on January 19. Kuczynski pitched in six games for the Athletics in 1943—the same year he played end for the NFL's Detroit Lions.

Bill Lawrence, 91, at Redwood City, Calif., on June 15. Lawrence saw brief outfield duty for the Tigers in 1932.

Thornton Lee, 90, at Tucson, Ariz., on June 9. Lefthander Lee won 117 games in 16 big-league seasons. His best year was 1941, when he won 22 games for the White Sox and posted an A.L.-leading 2.37 ERA. His son Don pitched in the majors for nine years.

Buck Leonard, 90, at Rocky Mount, N.C., on November 27. Hall of Famer Leonard was a slugging Negro leagues first baseman known as "the black Lou Gehrig." He spent 18 seasons with the Homestead Grays.

Dick Littlefield, 71, at Detroit, on November 20. The lefthander was one of the most-traveled players in big-league history. In a nine-year career in the majors, Littlefield pitched for the Red Sox, White Sox, Tigers, Browns/Orioles, Pirates, Cardinals, Giants, Cubs and Braves. In December 1956, the Giants traded Littlefield and cash to the Dodgers for Jackie Robinson—but the deal was voided when Robinson retired. Littlefield's career record: 33-54.

Vic Lombardi, 75, at Fresno, Calif., on December 3. A little left-hander, Lombardi won 12 games—and pitched three shutouts—for a 1947 Dodgers team that took the Yankees to seven games in the World Series before losing. Lombardi made two starts in that Series, going 0-1. He was a 50-51 pitcher in six big-league seasons.

Dwight Lowry, 39, at Jamestown, N.Y., on July 10. Lowry, a Tigers reserve catcher in the mid-1980s, was managing Detroit's New York-Penn League farm club in Jamestown at the time of his death.

Phil Marchildon, 83, at Toronto on January 10. The Canadian righthander compiled a 17-14 record in 1942 for the last-place Athletics. A prisoner during World War II, he encountered stress-related problems in his postwar career but experienced a notable season in 1947 when he won 19 games for the A's.

Stu Martin, 83, at Severn, N.C., on January 11. Martin was the Cardinals' No. 1 second baseman in 1938 and 1939, years in which he batted .278 and .268. He played six other seasons in the majors.

Roy McMillan, 67, at Bonham, Texas, on November 2. Shortstop McMillan was a three-time Gold Glove winner for the Reds and played 150 or more games in six consecutive seasons in the 1950s. He was interim manager of the Mets in 1975.

Bill McWilliams, 86, at Garland, Texas, on January 21. McWilliams had two at-bats for the 1931 Red Sox.

Art Merewether, 94, at Bayside, N.Y., on February 2. Infielder Merewether had one at-bat in the majors—for the 1922 Pirates.

Russ Meyer, 74, at Oglesby, Ill., on November 16. Meyer went 17-8 for the 1949 Phillies and won nine games for the pennant-winning Phils of 1950. In three seasons (1953-55) with Brooklyn, he compiled a 32-13 record. The righthander saw World Series duty in 1950, 1953 and 1955.

Eddie Miller, 80, at Lake Worth, Fla., on July 31. Shortstop Miller, who played a total of 14 years with the Reds, Braves, Phillies and Cardinals, played in four All-Star Games. He hit 19 homers and drove in 87 runs for the 1947 Reds.

Doug Million, 21, of an asthma attack at Mesa, Ariz., on September 24. Minor league pitcher Million was the Rockies' first-round draft choice in 1994.

Dee Moore, 83, at Williston, N.D., on July 2. In four seasons (1936-37, 1943, 1946) in the majors, Moore saw action at five positions—pitcher, catcher, third base, first base and the outfield.

Les Munns, 88, at Cedar Rapids, Iowa, on February 28. Munns pitched for the Dodgers in 1934 and 1935 and for the Cardinals in 1936. He lost 13 of his 17 career decisions.

Jerry Neudecker, 66, at Fort Walton Beach, Fla., on January 11. Neudecker was an American League umpire from 1965 through 1985.

Jose Oliva, 26, in a car accident near Santo Domingo, Dominican Republic, on December 22. Oliva played 89 games in the majors, 67 for the Braves in 1994 and 1995 and 22 for the Cardinals in '95. He batted only .178 overall but hit 13 home runs in 242 at-bats.

Don O'Riley, 52, in a shooting at Kansas City on May 2. O'Riley made 18 relief appearances for the Royals in the club's first season, 1969, and pitched nine times for Kansas City in 1970.

Loel Passe, 82, at Houston on July 15. Passe was an original member of the Colt 45s' broadcast team in 1962 and was a Colts/Astros radio voice through 1975.

Homer Peel, 94, at Shreveport, La., on April 8. Peel played in only 186 games over five major league seasons, but the outfielder did appear in two games for the Giants in the 1933 World Series.

George Pfister, 78, at Somerset, N.J., on August 14. Pfister, a catcher, appeared in one big-league game, for the Dodgers in 1941, and was a Brooklyn coach in 1952. He was working in the commissioner's office, where he had been employed for 23 years, at the time of his death.

Lou Possehl, 71, at Sarasota, Fla., on October 7. Although he pitched in only 15 games (all for the Phillies) in the majors, Possehl saw action in five big-league seasons (1946-47-48, 1951-52).

Stan Rojek, 78, at North Tonawanda, N.Y., on July 9. Rojek, a reserve infielder for the pennant-winning Dodgers of 1947, was the Pirates' regular shortstop in 1948 and 1949. He batted .266 over eight major league seasons.

Harry Rosenberg, 87, at San Mateo, Calif., on April 13. Outfielder Rosenberg had five hitless at-bats for the 1930 Giants.

Emile Roy, 89, at Crystal River, Fla., on January 5. Righthander Roy pitched in one game for the 1933 Athletics.

Manny Salvo, 83, at Vallejo, Calif., on February 7. Pitching for Boston in 1940, he shared the N.L. lead in shutouts with five. Salvo went 33-50 in five seasons with the Giants, Bees/Braves and Phillies.

Eddie Sawyer, 87, at Phoenixville, Pa., on September 22. Sawyer managed the Phillies' "Whiz Kids" to the 1950 N.L. pennant. He also directed the Phils in all or part of seven other seasons.

Lou Scoffic, 84, at Herrin, Ill., on August 28. An outfielder, Scoffic went 3-for-7 at the plate in four games with the 1936 Cardinals.

Vince Sherlock, 88, at Cheektowaga, N.Y., on May 11. This second baseman made the most of his only stint in the majors, batting .462 in nine games for the 1935 Dodgers.

Bill Smith, 62, at Clinton, Md., on March 30. Lefthander Smith appeared in a total of eight games for the Cardinals in 1958 and 1959 and in 24 games for the 1962 Phillies.

Milt Smith, 68, at San Diego on April 11. One of five players to play at least 25 games at third base for the Reds in 1955, Smith hit .196 in 36 games that season.

Glen "Gabby" Stewart, 84, at Memphis on February 11. Infielder Stewart broke into the majors with the Giants in 1940 and played extensively for the Phillies in 1943 and 1944.

Oadis Swigart, 82, at St. Joseph, Mo., on August 8. Swigart lost three of four decisions in brief duty with the Pirates in 1939 and 1940.

Moe Thacker, 63, at Louisville, Ky., on November 13. Thacker's most extensive duty in a five-year major league career came in 1962 when the catcher played 65 games for the Cubs.

Johnny Vander Meer, 82, at Tampa, on October 6. The Reds' Vander Meer is the only pitcher in big-league history to throw consecutive no-hitters, achieving the feat in 1938 against the Bees on June 11 in Cincinnati and the Dodgers on June 15 in the first night game in Brooklyn history. He led the National League in strikeouts three times and won 15 or more games five times en route to a career record of 119-121.

Jim Walkup, 87, at Danville, Ark., on February 7. Walkup, who was 16-38 in six big-league seasons, led the 1937 Browns in victories with nine despite an ERA of 7.36. He lost 12 games that season.

Hal Warnock, 85, at Tucson, Ariz., on February 8. Outfielder Warnock appeared in six games for the 1935 Browns.

Art "Butch" Weis, 94, at St. Louis on May 4. Weis saw pinch-hitting and reserve outfield duty with the Cubs from 1922-25.

Bob Whitcher, 80, at Akron, Ohio, on May 8. Whitcher pitched in six games for the 1945 Braves.

1997 A.L. STATISTICS

Batting

Designated hitting

Pinch-hitting

Pitching

Fielding

Miscellaneous

BATTING

TEAM

Team	Avg.	G	TPA	AB	R	H	TB	2B	3B	HR	RBI	SH	SF	HP	BB	IBB	SO	SB	CS	GDP	LOB	ShO	Slg.	OBP
Boston	.291	162	6430	5781	851	1684	2676	373	32	185	810	21	55	59	514	54	1044	68	48	155	1221	8	.463	.352
New York	.287	162	6527	5710	891	1636	2490	325	23	161	846	34	70	37	676	51	954	99	58	138	1276	9	.436	.362
Cleveland	.286	161	6304	5556	868	1589	2594	301	22	220	810	45	49	37	617	39	955	118	59	152	1181	8	.467	.358
Seattle	.280	162	6384	5614	925	1574	2720	312	21	264	890	46	49	49	626	53	1110	89	40	146	1149	4	.485	.355
Texas	.274	162	6265	5651	807	1547	2473	311	27	187	773	28	52	34	500	39	1116	72	37	118	1149	7	.438	.334
Chicago	.273	161	6200	5491	779	1498	2288	260	28	158	740	47	60	33	569	40	901	106	52	133	1148	8	.417	.341
Anaheim	.272	162	6387	5628	829	1531	2343	279	25	161	775	40	57	45	617	37	953	126	72	129	1203	5	.416	.346
Minnesota	.270	162	6265	5634	772	1522	2303	305	40	132	730	20	56	60	495	32	1121	151	52	117	1156	9	.409	.333
Baltimore	.268	162	6340	5584	812	1498	2394	264	22	196	780	46	59	65	586	44	952	63	26	121	1198	6	.429	.341
Kansas City	.264	161	6295	5599	747	1478	2278	256	35	158	711	51	42	42	561	34	1061	130	66	108	1176	5	.407	.333
Milwaukee	.260	161	6096	5444	681	1415	2168	294	27	135	643	48	52	58	494	31	967	103	55	123	1118	7	.398	.325
Oakland	.260	162	6369	5589	764	1451	2362	274	23	197	714	49	40	49	642	23	1181	71	36	133	1221	9	.423	.339
Detroit	.258	162	6189	5481	784	1415	2275	268	32	176	743	34	47	49	578	37	1164	61	72	120	1071	13	.431	.332
Toronto	.244	162	6109	5473	654	1333	2131	275	41	147	627	38	52	59	487	26	1138	134	50	102	1113	11	.389	.310
Totals	.271	1134	88160	78235	11164	21171	33495	4097	398	2477	10592	547	740	676	7962	540	14617	1491	723	1795	16380	109	.428	.340

INDIVIDUAL

TOP QUALIFIERS FOR BATTING CHAMPIONSHIP

Minimum 502 plate appearances. *Lefthanded batter. †Switch-hitter.

Player, Team	Avg.	G	TPA	AB	R	H	TB	2B	3B	HR	RBI	SH	SF	HP	BB	IBB	SO	SB	CS	GDP	Slg.	OBP
Thomas, Frank, Chicago	.347	146	649	530	110	184	324	35	0	35	125	0	7	3	109	9	69	1	1	15	.611	.456
Martinez, Edgar, Seattle	.330	155	678	542	104	179	300	35	1	28	108	0	6	11	119	11	86	2	4	21	.554	.456
Justice, David, Cleveland*	.329	139	582	495	84	163	295	31	1	33	101	0	7	0	80	11	79	3	5	12	.596	.418
Williams, Bernie, New York†	.328	129	591	509	107	167	277	35	6	21	100	0	8	1	73	7	80	15	8	10	.544	.408
Ramirez, Manny, Cleveland	.328	150	651	561	99	184	302	40	0	26	88	0	4	7	79	5	115	2	3	19	.538	.415
O'Neill, Paul, New York*	.324	149	637	553	89	179	284	42	0	21	117	0	9	0	75	8	92	10	7	16	.514	.399
Greer, Rusty, Texas*	.321	157	690	601	112	193	319	42	3	26	87	1	2	3	83	4	87	9	5	11	.531	.405
Jefferson, Reggie, Boston*†	.319	136	524	489	74	156	230	33	1	13	67	1	3	7	24	5	93	1	2	17	.470	.358
Vaughn, Mo, Boston*	.315	141	628	527	91	166	295	24	0	35	96	0	3	12	86	17	154	2	2	10	.560	.420
Rodriguez, Ivan, Texas	.313	150	648	597	98	187	289	34	4	20	77	1	4	8	38	7	89	7	3	18	.484	.360
O'Leary, Troy, Boston*	.309	146	545	499	65	154	239	32	4	15	80	1	4	2	39	7	70	0	5	13	.479	.358
Valentin, John, Boston	.306	143	644	575	95	176	287	47	5	18	77	1	5	5	58	5	66	7	4	21	.499	.372
Garciaparra, Nomar, Boston	.306	153	734	684	122	209	365	44	11	30	98	2	7	6	35	2	92	22	9	9	.534	.342
Molitor, Paul, Minnesota	.305	135	597	538	63	164	234	32	4	10	89	2	12	0	45	8	73	11	4	8	.435	.351
Griffey, Ken Jr., Seattle*	.304	157	704	608	125	185	393	34	3	56	147	0	12	8	76	23	121	15	4	12	.646	.382

DEPARTMENTAL LEADERS: G—Hunter, Det., Ripken, Bal., 162; AB—Garciaparra, Bos., 684; R—Griffey, Sea., 125; H—Garciaparra, Bos., 209; TB—Griffey, Sea., 393; 1B—Anderson, Ana., Jeter, N.Y., 142; 2B—Valentin, Bos., 47; 3B—Garciaparra, Bos., 11; HR—Griffey, Sea., 56; RBI—Griffey, Sea., 147; SH—Vizquel, Cle., 16; SF—Martinez, N.Y., 13; HP—Anderson, Bal., 19; BB—Thome, Cle., 120; IBB—Griffey, Sea., 23; SO—Buhner, Sea., 175; SB—Hunter, Det., 74; CS—Hunter, Det., 18; GIDP—Belle, Chi., 26; Slg. Pct.—Griffey, Sea., .646; OB. Pct.—Thomas, Chi., .456.

ALL PLAYERS

*Lefthanded batter. †Switch-hitter.

Player, Team	Avg.	G	TPA	AB	R	H	TB	2B	3B	HR	RBI	SH	SF	HP	BB	IBB	SO	SB	CS	GDP	Slg.	OBP
Abbott, Jeff, Chicago	.263	19	38	38	8	10	14	1	0	1	2	0	0	0	0	0	6	0	0	3	.368	.263
Adamson, Joel, Milwaukee*	.000	30	3	3	0	0	0	0	0	0	0	0	0	0	0	0	0	0	0	0	.000	.000
Alicea, Luis, Anaheim†	.253	128	471	388	59	98	143	16	7	5	37	4	2	8	69	3	65	22	8	4	.369	.375
Alomar, Roberto, Baltimore†.	.333	112	469	412	64	137	206	23	2	14	60	7	7	3	40	2	43	9	3	10	.500	.390
Alomar, Sandy Jr., Cleveland.	.324	125	480	451	63	146	246	37	0	21	83	6	1	3	19	2	48	0	2	16	.545	.354
Alvarez, Wilson, Chicago*	.000	22	3	3	0	0	0	0	0	0	0	0	0	0	0	0	2	0	0	0	.000	.000
Amaral, Rich, Seattle	.284	89	210	190	34	54	62	5	0	1	21	5	2	3	10	0	34	12	8	7	.326	.327
Anderson, Brady, Baltimore*	.288	151	696	590	97	170	277	39	7	18	73	2	1	19	84	6	105	18	12	1	.469	.393
Anderson, Garret, Anaheim*	.303	154	662	624	76	189	255	36	3	8	92	1	5	2	30	6	70	10	4	20	.409	.334
Appier, Kevin, Kansas City	.000	34	6	6	0	0	0	0	0	0	0	0	0	0	0	0	5	0	0	0	.000	.000
Arias, George, Anaheim	.333	3	6	6	1	2	2	0	0	0	1	0	0	0	0	0	0	0	0	0	.333	.333
Aven, Bruce, Cleveland	.211	13	20	19	4	4	5	1	0	0	2	0	0	0	1	0	5	0	1	0	.263	.250
Avery, Steve, Boston*	.000	24	1	1	1	0	0	0	0	0	0	0	0	0	0	0	0	0	0	0	.000	.000
Baines, Harold, Chi.-Bal.*	.301	137	510	452	55	136	207	23	0	16	67	0	3	0	55	11	62	0	1	12	.458	.375
Baldwin, James, Chicago	.000	32	4	3	0	0	0	0	0	0	0	0	0	0	0	0	2	0	0	0	.000	.000
Banks, Brian, Milwaukee†	.206	28	75	68	9	14	18	1	0	1	8	0	1	0	6	0	17	0	1	1	.265	.267
Bartee, Kimera, Detroit†	.200	12	8	5	4	1	1	0	0	0	0	0	0	1	2	0	2	3	1	0	.200	.500
Batista, Tony, Oakland	.202	68	207	188	22	38	62	10	1	4	18	3	0	2	14	0	31	2	2	8	.330	.265
Becker, Rich, Minnesota*	.264	132	510	443	61	117	175	22	3	10	45	2	2	1	62	1	130	17	5	4	.395	.354
Belcher, Tim, Kansas City	.000	32	6	6	0	0	0	0	0	0	0	0	0	0	0	0	1	0	0	1	.000	.000
Bell, Jay, Kansas City	.291	153	660	573	89	167	264	28	3	21	92	3	9	4	71	2	101	10	6	13	.461	.368
Belle, Albert, Chicago	.274	161	701	634	90	174	311	45	1	30	116	0	8	6	53	6	105	4	4	26	.491	.332
Bellhorn, Mark, Oakland†	.228	68	261	224	33	51	80	9	1	6	19	5	0	0	32	0	70	7	1	1	.357	.324
Benitez, Yamil, Kansas City	.267	53	204	191	22	51	84	7	1	8	21	2	0	1	10	0	49	2	2	2	.440	.307
Benjamin, Mike, Boston	.233	49	123	116	12	27	38	5	1	0	7	1	1	1	4	0	27	2	3	2	.328	.262
Berroa, Geronimo, Oak.-Bal.*	.283	156	648	561	88	159	262	25	0	26	90	0	7	4	76	4	120	4	4	18	.467	.369
Blair, Willie, Detroit	.000	29	4	4	0	0	0	0	0	0	0	0	0	0	0	0	3	0	0	0	.000	.000
Blowers, Mike, Seattle	.293	68	177	150	22	44	64	5	0	5	20	4	2	0	21	1	33	0	0	4	.427	.376
Boggs, Wade, New York*	.292	104	407	353	55	103	140	23	1	4	28	2	4	0	48	3	38	0	1	3	.397	.373

Player, Team	Avg.	G	TPA	AB	R	H	TB	2B	3B	HR	RBI	SH	SF	HP	BB	IBB	SO	SB	CS	GDP	Slg.	OBP
Borders, Pat, Cleveland..........	.296	55	170	159	17	47	68	7	1	4	15	0	0	2	9	0	27	0	2	5	.428	.341
Bordick, Mike, Baltimore........	.236	153	560	509	55	120	162	19	1	7	46	12	4	2	33	1	66	0	2	23	.318	.283
Bournigal, Rafael, Oakland......	.279	79	249	222	29	62	74	9	0	1	20	7	0	4	16	1	19	2	1	11	.333	.339
Bragg, Darren, Boston*..........	.257	153	586	513	65	132	198	35	2	9	57	5	4	3	61	5	102	10	6	16	.386	.337
Branson, Jeff, Cleveland*......	.264	29	82	72	5	19	29	4	0	2	7	0	2	1	7	0	17	0	2	1	.403	.329
Brede, Brent, Minnesota*......	.274	61	214	190	25	52	74	11	1	3	21	1	1	1	21	0	38	7	2	1	.389	.347
Brito, Tilson, Tor.-Oak...........	.238	66	188	172	17	41	54	5	1	2	14	2	2	2	10	0	38	1	0	2	.314	.285
Brosius, Scott, Oakland..........	.203	129	526	479	59	97	152	20	1	11	41	5	4	4	34	1	102	9	4	9	.317	.259
Brown, Kevin L., Texas...........	.400	4	5	5	1	2	5	0	0	1	1	0	0	0	0	0	0	0	0	0	1.000	.400
Brumfield, Jacob, Toronto......	.207	58	191	174	22	36	49	5	1	2	20	1	1	1	14	0	31	4	4	4	.282	.268
Buford, Damon, Texas...........	.224	122	404	366	49	82	124	18	0	8	39	3	2	3	30	0	83	18	7	8	.339	.287
Buhner, Jay, Seattle................	.243	157	665	540	104	131	273	18	2	40	109	0	1	5	119	3	175	0	0	23	.506	.383
Burkett, John, Texas..............	.200	30	5	5	1	1	1	0	0	0	0	0	0	0	0	0	1	0	0	0	.200	.200
Burnitz, Jeromy, Milwaukee*.	.281	153	577	494	85	139	273	37	8	27	85	3	0	5	75	8	111	20	13	8	.553	.382
Bush, Homer, New York..........	.364	10	11	11	2	4	4	0	0	0	3	0	0	0	0	0	0	0	0	0	.364	.364
Butler, Rich, Toronto*............	.286	7	16	14	3	4	5	1	0	0	2	0	0	0	2	0	3	0	1	0	.357	.375
Cameron, Mike, Chicago........	.259	116	446	379	63	98	164	18	3	14	55	2	5	5	55	1	105	23	2	8	.433	.356
Candaele, Casey, Cleveland†..	.308	14	27	26	5	8	9	1	0	0	4	0	0	0	1	0	1	1	0	0	.346	.333
Canseco, Jose, Oakland.........	.235	108	446	388	56	91	179	19	0	23	74	0	4	3	51	1	122	8	2	15	.461	.325
Carr, Chuck, Milwaukee†........	.130	26	50	46	3	6	9	3	0	0	0	1	0	1	2	0	11	1	0	0	.196	.184
Carter, Joe, Toronto..............	.234	157	668	612	76	143	244	30	4	21	102	0	9	7	40	5	105	8	2	12	.399	.284
Casanova, Raul, Detroit†........	.243	101	334	304	27	74	101	10	1	5	24	0	1	3	26	1	48	1	1	10	.332	.308
Casey, Sean, Cleveland*........	.200	6	12	10	1	2	2	0	0	0	1	0	0	1	1	0	2	0	0	0	.200	.333
Castillo, Carlos, Chicago........	1.000	37	1	1	0	1	1	0	0	0	0	0	0	0	0	0	0	0	0	0	1.000	1.000
Castillo, Tony J., Chicago*.....	.000	64	1	1	0	0	0	0	0	0	0	0	0	0	0	0	0	0	0	0	.000	.000
Catalanotto, Frank, Detroit*...	.308	13	29	26	2	8	10	2	0	0	3	0	0	0	3	0	7	0	0	0	.385	.379
Cedeno, Domingo, Texas†......	.282	113	397	365	49	103	146	19	6	4	36	2	1	2	27	0	77	3	3	5	.400	.334
Cirillo, Jeff, Milwaukee...........	.288	154	661	580	74	167	247	46	2	10	82	4	3	14	60	0	74	4	3	13	.426	.367
Clark, Terry, Cle.-Tex............	1.000	13	1	1	0	1	1	0	0	0	0	0	0	0	0	0	0	0	0	0	1.000	1.000
Clark, Tony, Detroit†..............	.276	159	681	580	105	160	290	28	3	32	117	0	5	3	93	13	144	1	3	11	.500	.376
Clark, Will, Texas*...................	.326	110	450	393	56	128	195	29	1	12	51	0	5	3	49	11	62	0	0	4	.496	.400
Clemens, Roger, Toronto.......	.500	34	3	2	1	1	2	1	0	0	0	0	0	0	1	0	0	0	0	0	1.000	.667
Cloude, Ken, Seattle..............	.000	10	2	2	0	0	0	0	0	0	0	0	0	0	0	0	0	0	0	0	.000	.000
Clyburn, Danny, Baltimore.....	.000	2	3	3	0	0	0	0	0	0	0	0	0	0	0	0	2	0	0	0	.000	.000
Colbrunn, Greg, Minnesota....	.281	70	228	217	24	61	90	14	0	5	26	0	2	1	8	1	38	1	2	7	.415	.307
Coleman, Michael, Boston.....	.167	8	25	24	2	4	5	1	0	0	2	1	0	0	0	0	11	1	0	0	.208	.167
Coleman, Vince, Detroit†.......	.071	6	15	14	0	1	1	0	0	0	0	0	0	0	1	0	3	0	0	1	.071	.133
Colon, Bartolo, Cleveland.......	.000	19	1	1	0	0	0	0	0	0	0	0	0	0	0	0	1	0	0	0	.000	.000
Cone, David, New York*.........	.000	29	3	3	0	0	0	0	0	0	0	0	0	0	0	0	2	0	0	0	.000	.000
Coomer, Ron, Minnesota.......	.298	140	550	523	63	156	229	30	2	13	85	0	5	0	22	5	91	4	3	11	.438	.324
Cooper, Scott, Kansas City*...	.201	75	182	159	12	32	49	6	1	3	15	2	2	2	17	0	32	1	1	4	.308	.283
Cora, Joey, Seattle†..............	.300	149	649	574	105	172	253	40	4	11	54	8	9	5	53	2	49	6	7	6	.441	.359
Cordero, Wilfredo, Boston.....	.281	140	609	570	82	160	246	26	3	18	72	0	4	4	31	7	122	1	3	11	.432	.320
Cordova, Marty, Minnesota....	.246	103	413	378	44	93	164	18	4	15	51	0	2	3	30	2	92	5	3	13	.434	.305
Crespo, Felipe, Toronto†........	.286	12	31	28	3	8	13	0	1	1	5	1	0	0	2	0	4	0	0	1	.464	.333
Cruz, Deivi, Detroit................	.241	147	467	436	35	105	137	26	0	2	40	14	3	0	14	0	55	3	6	9	.314	.263
Cruz, Ivan, New York*............	.250	11	22	20	0	5	6	1	0	0	3	0	0	0	2	0	4	0	0	0	.300	.318
Cruz, Jose Jr., Sea.-Tor.†.......	.248	104	442	395	59	98	197	19	1	26	68	1	5	0	41	2	117	7	2	5	.499	.315
Curtis, Chad, Cle.-N.Y............	.284	115	408	349	59	99	168	22	1	15	55	2	9	5	43	1	59	12	6	7	.481	.362
D'Amico, Jeff, Milwaukee.......	.000	23	5	4	0	0	0	0	0	0	0	1	0	0	0	0	3	0	0	0	.000	.000
Damon, Johnny, Kansas City*.	.275	146	524	472	70	130	182	12	8	8	48	6	1	3	42	2	70	16	10	3	.386	.338
Darwin, Danny, Chicago.........	.000	21	4	3	0	0	0	0	0	0	0	1	0	0	0	0	3	0	0	0	.000	.000
Davis, Chili, Kansas City†......	.279	140	567	477	71	133	243	20	0	30	90	0	4	1	85	16	96	6	3	15	.509	.386
Davis, Eric, Baltimore............	.304	42	176	158	29	48	83	11	0	8	25	0	3	1	14	0	47	6	0	2	.525	.358
Davis, Russ, Seattle...............	.271	119	454	420	57	114	205	29	1	20	63	3	2	2	27	2	100	6	2	11	.488	.317
Delgado, Carlos, Toronto*.....	.262	153	595	519	79	136	274	42	3	30	91	0	4	8	64	9	133	0	3	6	.528	.350
Dellucci, Dave, Baltimore*.....	.222	17	32	27	3	6	10	1	0	1	3	0	0	1	4	1	7	0	0	2	.370	.344
Devereaux, Mike, Texas..........	.208	29	80	72	8	15	18	3	0	0	7	0	1	0	7	0	10	1	0	0	.250	.275
Diaz, Alex, Texas†..................	.222	28	97	90	8	20	30	4	0	2	12	0	1	1	5	0	13	1	1	3	.333	.268
Diaz, Eddy, Milwaukee............	.220	16	51	50	4	11	15	2	1	0	7	0	0	0	1	0	5	0	0	3	.300	.235
Diaz, Einar, Cleveland............	.143	5	7	7	1	1	2	1	0	0	1	0	0	0	0	0	2	0	0	0	.286	.143
Dickson, Jason, Anaheim*......	.000	33	2	2	0	0	0	0	0	0	0	0	0	0	0	0	0	0	0	0	.000	.000
DiSarcina, Gary, Anaheim......	.246	154	583	549	52	135	179	28	2	4	47	8	5	4	17	0	29	7	8	18	.326	.271
Drabek, Doug, Chicago...........	.000	32	2	1	1	0	0	0	0	0	0	1	0	0	0	0	1	0	0	0	.000	.000
Ducey, Rob, Seattle*.............	.287	76	151	143	25	41	75	15	2	5	10	0	2	0	6	0	31	3	3	3	.524	.311
Duncan, Mariano, N.Y.-Tor.....	.236	89	355	339	36	80	97	14	0	1	25	1	0	3	12	0	78	6	3	6	.286	.268
Dunn, Todd, Milwaukee..........	.229	44	120	118	17	27	41	5	0	3	9	0	0	0	2	0	39	3	0	2	.347	.242
Durham, Ray, Chicago†..........	.271	155	711	634	106	172	242	27	5	11	53	2	8	6	61	0	96	33	16	14	.382	.337
Dye, Jermaine, Kansas City....	.236	75	283	263	26	62	97	14	0	7	22	1	1	1	17	0	51	2	1	6	.369	.284
Easley, Damion, Detroit...........	.264	151	620	527	97	139	248	37	3	22	72	4	5	16	68	3	102	28	13	18	.471	.362
Edmonds, Jim, Anaheim*.......	.291	133	571	502	82	146	251	27	0	26	80	0	5	4	60	5	80	5	7	8	.500	.368
Eenhoorn, Robert, Anaheim...	.350	11	21	20	2	7	11	1	0	1	6	0	1	0	0	0	2	0	0	0	.550	.333
Eldred, Cal, Milwaukee...........	.000	34	4	3	0	0	0	0	0	0	0	1	0	0	0	0	0	0	0	0	.000	.000
Encarnacion, Angelo, Anaheim	.412	11	17	17	2	7	11	1	0	1	4	0	0	0	0	0	1	2	0	1	.647	.412
Encarnacion, Juan, Detroit.....	.212	11	38	33	3	7	13	1	1	1	5	0	0	2	3	0	12	3	1	1	.394	.316
Erickson, Scott, Baltimore......	.000	34	5	2	0	0	0	0	0	0	0	2	0	0	1	0	2	0	0	0	.000	.333
Erstad, Darin, Anaheim*........	.299	139	605	539	99	161	251	34	4	16	77	5	6	4	51	4	86	23	8	5	.466	.360
Eshelman, Vaughn, Boston*..	.250	21	4	4	1	1	1	0	0	0	0	0	0	0	0	0	1	0	0	0	.250	.250
Espinoza, Alvaro, Seattle........	.181	33	78	72	3	13	14	1	0	0	7	3	0	1	2	0	12	1	1	2	.194	.213
Evans, Tom, Toronto..............	.289	12	41	38	7	11	16	2	0	1	2	0	0	1	2	0	10	0	1	0	.421	.341
Eyre, Scott, Chicago*.............	.500	11	2	2	0	1	1	0	0	0	0	0	0	0	0	0	0	0	0	0	.500	.500
Fabregas, Jorge, Ana.-Chi.*...	.258	121	385	360	33	93	127	11	1	7	51	6	4	1	14	0	46	1	1	16	.353	.285
Fasano, Sal, Kansas City........	.211	13	39	38	4	8	13	2	0	1	1	0	0	0	1	0	12	0	0	1	.342	.231

Player, Team	Avg.	G	TPA	AB	R	H	TB	2B	3B	HR	RBI	SH	SF	HP	BB	IBB	SO	SB	CS	GDP	Slg.	OBP
Fassero, Jeff, Seattle*	.200	35	5	5	0	1	1	0	0	0	0	0	0	0	0	0	2	0	0	0	.200	.200
Fernandez, Tony, Cleveland†	.286	120	442	409	55	117	173	21	1	11	44	6	3	2	22	0	47	6	6	11	.423	.323
Fielder, Cecil, New York	.260	98	425	361	40	94	148	15	0	13	61	0	6	7	51	3	87	0	0	14	.410	.358
Figga, Mike, New York	.000	2	4	4	0	0	0	0	0	0	0	0	0	0	0	0	3	0	0	0	.000	.000
Finley, Chuck, Anaheim*	.000	25	6	6	1	0	0	0	0	0	0	0	0	0	0	0	2	0	0	0	.000	.000
Fonville, Chad, Chicago†	.111	9	11	9	1	1	1	0	0	0	1	1	0	0	1	0	1	2	0	0	.111	.200
Fox, Andy, New York*	.226	22	40	31	13	7	8	1	0	0	1	2	0	0	7	0	9	2	1	1	.258	.368
Franco, Julio, Cle.-Mil.	.270	120	505	430	68	116	155	16	1	7	44	1	4	1	69	4	116	15	6	17	.360	.369
Frias, Hanley, Texas†	.192	14	27	26	4	5	6	1	0	0	1	0	0	0	1	0	4	0	0	1	.231	.222
Frye, Jeff, Boston	.312	127	442	404	56	126	175	36	2	3	51	2	7	2	27	1	44	19	8	12	.433	.352
Fryman, Travis, Detroit	.274	154	657	595	90	163	262	27	3	22	102	0	11	5	46	5	113	16	3	15	.440	.326
Garcia, Carlos, Toronto	.220	103	381	350	29	77	108	18	2	3	23	10	4	2	15	0	60	11	3	7	.309	.253
Garciaparra, Nomar, Boston	.306	153	734	684	122	209	365	44	11	30	98	2	7	6	35	2	92	22	9	9	.534	.342
Gates, Brent, Seattle†	.238	65	170	151	18	36	53	8	0	3	20	2	3	0	14	0	21	0	0	6	.351	.298
Giambi, Jason, Oakland*	.293	142	588	519	66	152	257	41	2	20	81	0	8	6	55	3	89	0	1	11	.495	.362
Gil, Benji, Texas	.224	110	345	317	35	71	103	13	2	5	31	6	4	1	17	0	96	1	2	3	.325	.263
Giles, Brian, Cleveland*	.268	130	451	377	62	101	173	15	3	17	61	3	7	1	63	2	50	13	3	10	.459	.368
Girardi, Joe, New York	.264	112	433	398	38	105	133	23	1	1	50	5	2	2	26	1	53	2	3	15	.334	.311
Gonzalez, Alex, Toronto	.239	126	478	426	46	102	165	23	2	12	35	11	2	5	34	1	94	15	6	9	.387	.302
Gonzalez, Juan, Texas	.296	133	579	533	87	158	314	24	3	42	131	0	10	3	33	7	107	0	0	12	.589	.335
Gooden, Dwight, New York	.000	20	4	4	0	0	0	0	0	0	0	0	0	0	0	0	1	0	0	0	.000	.000
Goodwin, Tom, K.C.-Tex.*	.260	150	635	574	90	149	193	26	6	3	39	11	3	3	44	1	88	50	16	7	.336	.314
Grebeck, Craig, Anaheim	.270	63	150	126	12	34	46	9	0	1	6	5	1	0	18	1	11	0	1	6	.365	.359
Green, Shawn, Toronto*	.287	135	471	429	57	123	201	22	4	16	53	1	4	1	36	4	99	14	3	4	.469	.340
Greene, Charlie, Baltimore	.000	5	2	2	0	0	0	0	0	0	0	1	0	0	0	0	1	0	0	0	.000	.000
Greene, Todd, Anaheim	.290	34	131	124	24	36	69	6	0	9	24	0	0	0	7	1	25	2	0	1	.556	.328
Greer, Rusty, Texas*	.321	157	690	601	112	193	319	42	3	26	87	1	2	3	83	4	87	9	5	11	.531	.405
Grieve, Ben, Oakland*	.312	24	108	93	12	29	44	6	0	3	24	1	0	1	13	1	25	0	0	1	.473	.402
Griffey, Ken Jr., Seattle*	.304	157	704	608	125	185	393	34	3	56	147	0	12	8	76	23	121	15	4	12	.646	.382
Grissom, Marquis, Cleveland	.262	144	622	558	74	146	221	27	6	12	66	6	9	6	43	1	89	22	13	12	.396	.317
Gross, Kevin, Anaheim	.000	12	1	1	0	0	0	0	0	0	0	0	0	0	0	0	0	0	0	0	.000	.000
Guevara, Giomar, Seattle	.000	5	4	4	0	0	0	0	0	0	0	0	0	0	0	0	2	1	0	0	.000	.000
Guillen, Ozzie, Chicago*	.245	142	527	490	59	120	165	21	6	4	52	11	4	0	22	1	24	5	3	7	.337	.275
Hall, Joe, Detroit	.500	2	4	4	1	2	3	1	0	0	3	0	0	0	0	0	0	0	0	0	.750	.500
Halter, Shane, Kansas City	.276	74	139	123	16	34	47	5	1	2	10	4	0	2	10	0	28	4	3	1	.382	.341
Hamelin, Bob, Detroit*	.270	110	369	318	47	86	155	15	0	18	52	0	2	1	48	3	72	2	1	8	.487	.366
Hammonds, Jeffrey, Baltimore	.264	118	434	397	71	105	193	19	3	21	55	0	2	3	32	1	73	15	1	6	.486	.323
Hansen, Jed, Kansas City	.309	34	111	94	11	29	40	6	1	1	14	2	1	1	13	0	29	3	2	2	.426	.394
Haselman, Bill, Boston	.236	67	232	212	22	50	83	15	0	6	26	1	2	2	15	2	44	0	2	8	.392	.290
Hatteberg, Scott, Boston*	.277	114	395	350	46	97	152	23	1	10	44	2	1	2	40	2	70	0	1	11	.434	.354
Hawkins, LaTroy, Minnesota	.000	20	1	1	0	0	0	0	0	0	0	0	0	0	0	0	1	0	0	0	.000	.000
Hayes, Charlie, New York	.258	100	398	353	39	91	140	16	0	11	53	0	4	1	40	2	66	3	2	13	.397	.332
Haynes, Jimmy, Oakland	.000	13	2	2	0	0	0	0	0	0	0	0	0	0	0	0	0	0	0	0	.000	.000
Helling, Rick, Texas	.000	10	3	3	0	0	0	0	0	0	0	0	0	0	0	0	0	0	0	0	.000	.000
Henderson, Rickey, Anaheim	.183	32	144	115	21	21	30	3	0	2	7	1	0	2	26	0	23	16	4	3	.261	.343
Henry, Butch, Boston*	.000	36	1	0	0	0	0	0	0	0	0	1	0	0	0	0	0	0	0	0	.000	.000
Hentgen, Pat, Toronto	.000	35	7	7	0	0	0	0	0	0	0	0	0	0	0	0	2	0	0	0	.000	.000
Hershiser, Orel, Cleveland	.000	32	5	3	0	0	0	0	0	0	0	1	0	1	0	0	1	0	0	0	.000	.000
Higginson, Bobby, Detroit*	.299	146	623	546	94	163	284	30	5	27	101	0	4	3	70	2	85	12	7	10	.520	.379
Hill, Ken, Tex.-Ana.	.500	31	3	2	0	1	2	1	0	0	2	1	0	0	0	0	1	0	0	0	1.000	.500
Hocking, Denny, Minnesota†	.257	115	278	253	28	65	91	12	4	2	25	5	1	1	18	0	51	3	5	6	.360	.308
Hoiles, Chris, Baltimore	.259	99	384	320	45	83	134	15	0	12	49	0	3	10	51	3	86	1	0	7	.419	.375
Hollins, Dave, Anaheim†	.288	149	648	572	101	165	246	29	2	16	85	1	5	8	62	2	124	16	6	12	.430	.363
Holtz, Mike, Anaheim*	.000	66	1	1	0	0	0	0	0	0	0	0	0	0	0	0	1	0	0	0	.000	.000
Howard, David, Kansas City†	.241	80	177	162	24	39	52	8	1	1	13	3	1	1	10	1	31	2	2	1	.321	.287
Howell, Jack, Anaheim*	.259	77	191	174	25	45	94	7	0	14	34	1	3	0	13	2	36	1	0	4	.540	.305
Hubbard, Trenidad, Cleveland	.250	7	13	12	3	3	4	1	0	0	0	0	0	0	1	0	3	2	0	0	.333	.308
Hunter, Brian, Detroit	.269	162	738	658	112	177	232	29	7	4	45	8	5	1	66	1	121	74	18	13	.353	.334
Hurst, Jimmy, Detroit	.176	13	19	17	1	3	7	1	0	1	1	0	0	0	2	0	6	0	0	0	.412	.263
Huson, Jeff, Milwaukee*	.203	84	153	143	12	29	32	3	0	0	11	2	1	2	5	0	15	3	0	7	.224	.238
Ibanez, Raul, Seattle*	.154	11	26	26	3	4	9	0	1	1	4	0	0	0	0	0	6	0	0	0	.346	.154
Incaviglia, Pete, Bal.-N.Y.	.247	53	169	154	19	38	57	4	0	5	12	0	1	3	11	2	46	0	0	1	.370	.308
Irabu, Hideki, New York	.000	13	1	1	0	0	0	0	0	0	0	0	0	0	0	0	0	0	0	0	.000	.000
Jackson, Damian, Cleveland	.111	8	10	9	2	1	1	0	0	0	0	0	0	0	1	0	1	1	0	0	.111	.200
Jackson, Darrin, Min.-Mil.	.261	75	224	211	26	55	81	9	1	5	36	5	2	0	6	0	31	4	1	5	.384	.279
Jaha, John, Milwaukee	.247	46	192	162	25	40	80	7	0	11	26	0	2	3	25	1	40	1	0	6	.494	.354
Jefferson, Reggie, Boston*	.319	136	524	489	74	156	230	33	1	13	67	1	3	7	24	5	93	1	2	17	.470	.358
Jensen, Marcus, Detroit†	.182	8	12	11	1	2	2	0	0	0	1	0	0	0	1	0	5	0	0	0	.182	.250
Jeter, Derek, New York	.291	159	748	654	116	190	265	31	7	10	70	8	2	10	74	0	125	23	12	14	.405	.370
Johnson, Brian, Detroit	.237	45	147	139	13	33	47	6	1	2	18	2	1	0	5	1	19	1	0	3	.338	.262
Jones, Doug, Milwaukee	.000	75	1	0	0	0	0	0	0	0	0	0	0	0	1	0	0	0	0	0	.000	1.000
Justice, David, Cleveland*	.329	139	582	495	84	163	295	31	1	33	101	0	7	0	80	11	79	3	5	12	.596	.418
Kamieniecki, Scott, Baltimore	.000	30	2	2	0	0	0	0	0	0	0	0	0	0	0	0	2	0	0	0	.000	.000
Karkovice, Ron, Chicago	.181	51	161	138	10	25	46	3	0	6	18	4	5	3	11	0	32	0	0	3	.333	.248
Karl, Scott, Milwaukee*	.000	32	4	4	0	0	0	0	0	0	0	0	0	0	0	0	3	0	0	0	.000	.000
Karsay, Steve, Oakland	.000	25	0	0	1	0	0	0	0	0	0	0	0	0	0	0	0	0	0	0	.000	.000
Keagle, Greg, Detroit	.000	11	1	1	0	0	0	0	0	0	0	0	0	0	0	0	1	0	0	0	.000	.000
Kelly, Pat, New York	.242	67	138	120	25	29	43	6	1	2	10	2	1	1	14	1	37	8	1	4	.358	.324
Kelly, Roberto, Min.-Sea.	.291	105	398	368	58	107	173	26	2	12	59	2	3	3	22	0	67	9	5	6	.470	.333
Key, Jimmy, Baltimore	.000	34	3	2	0	0	0	0	0	0	0	1	0	0	0	0	2	0	0	0	.000	.000
King, Jeff, Kansas City	.238	155	647	543	84	129	245	30	1	28	112	1	12	2	89	4	96	16	5	9	.451	.341
Knoblauch, Chuck, Minnesota	.291	156	716	611	117	178	251	26	10	9	58	0	4	17	84	6	84	62	10	11	.411	.390

Player, Team	Avg.	G	TPA	AB	R	H	TB	2B	3B	HR	RBI	SH	SF	HP	BB	IBB	SO	SB	CS	GDP	Slg.	OBP
Kreuter, Chad, Chi.-Ana.†	.231	89	285	255	25	59	87	9	2	5	21	1	0	0	29	0	66	0	3	7	.341	.310
Laker, Tim, Baltimore	.000	7	18	14	0	0	0	0	0	0	1	1	1	0	2	0	9	0	0	0	.000	.118
Latham, Chris, Minnesota†	.182	15	22	22	4	4	5	1	0	0	1	0	0	0	0	0	8	0	0	0	.227	.182
Lawton, Matt, Minnesota*	.248	142	548	460	74	114	191	29	3	14	60	1	1	10	76	3	81	7	4	7	.415	.366
Ledesma, Aaron, Baltimore	.352	43	104	88	24	31	44	5	1	2	11	1	1	1	13	0	9	1	0	1	.500	.437
Lennon, Patrick, Oakland	.293	56	131	116	14	34	45	6	1	1	14	0	0	0	15	0	35	0	1	3	.388	.374
Lesher, Brian, Oakland	.229	46	142	131	17	30	48	4	1	4	16	0	2	0	9	0	30	4	1	4	.366	.275
Levis, Jesse, Milwaukee*	.285	99	232	200	19	57	67	7	0	1	19	5	2	1	24	0	17	1	0	4	.335	.361
Lewis, Darren, Chicago	.234	81	93	77	15	18	19	1	0	0	5	5	0	0	11	0	14	11	4	2	.247	.330
Leyritz, Jim, Ana.-Tex.	.277	121	455	379	58	105	149	11	0	11	64	4	6	6	60	2	78	2	1	13	.393	.379
Long, Ryan, Kansas City	.222	6	10	9	2	2	2	0	0	0	2	0	0	1	0	0	3	0	0	0	.222	.300
Lopez, Albie, Cleveland	.000	37	1	1	0	0	0	0	0	0	0	0	0	0	0	0	1	0	0	0	.000	.000
Loretta, Mark, Milwaukee	.287	132	482	418	56	120	162	17	5	5	47	5	10	2	47	2	60	5	5	15	.388	.354
Lowe, Derek, Sea.-Bos.	.000	20	3	3	0	0	0	0	0	0	0	0	0	0	0	0	2	0	0	0	.000	.000
Ludwick, Eric, Oakland	.000	6	2	2	0	0	0	0	0	0	0	0	0	0	0	0	1	0	0	0	.000	.000
Macfarlane, Mike, Kansas City	.237	82	291	257	34	61	103	14	2	8	35	3	1	6	24	3	47	0	2	4	.401	.316
Machado, Robert, Chicago	.200	10	17	15	1	3	5	0	1	0	2	1	0	0	1	0	6	0	0	0	.333	.250
Mack, Shane, Boston	.315	60	146	130	13	41	57	7	0	3	17	2	2	3	9	1	24	2	1	3	.438	.368
Magadan, Dave, Oakland*	.303	128	328	271	38	82	106	10	1	4	30	4	1	2	50	1	40	1	0	7	.391	.414
Malave, Jose, Boston	.000	4	4	4	0	0	0	0	0	0	0	0	0	0	0	0	2	0	0	1	.000	.000
Manto, Jeff, Cleveland	.267	16	31	30	3	8	17	3	0	2	7	0	0	0	1	0	10	0	0	2	.567	.290
Manzanillo, Josias, Seattle	.000	16	1	1	0	0	0	0	0	0	0	0	0	0	0	0	0	0	0	0	.000	.000
Martin, Norberto, Chicago	.300	71	219	213	24	64	79	7	1	2	27	0	0	0	6	0	31	1	4	2	.371	.320
Martinez, Dave, Chicago*	.286	145	573	504	78	144	208	16	6	12	55	5	6	3	55	7	69	12	6	4	.413	.356
Martinez, Edgar, Seattle	.330	155	678	542	104	179	300	35	1	28	108	0	6	11	119	11	86	2	4	21	.554	.456
Martinez, Mata, Kansas City†	.226	16	38	31	3	7	10	1	1	0	3	1	0	0	6	0	8	0	0	1	.323	.351
Martinez, Sandy, Toronto*	.000	3	3	2	1	0	0	0	0	0	0	0	0	0	1	0	1	0	0	0	.000	.333
Martinez, Tino, New York*	.296	158	685	594	96	176	343	31	2	44	141	0	13	3	75	14	75	3	1	15	.577	.371
Marzano, John, Seattle	.287	39	96	87	7	25	31	3	0	1	10	2	0	0	7	0	15	0	0	2	.356	.340
Mashore, Damon, Oakland	.247	92	342	279	55	69	92	10	2	3	18	7	1	5	50	1	82	5	4	5	.330	.370
Matheny, Mike, Milwaukee	.244	123	356	320	29	78	108	16	1	4	32	9	3	7	17	0	68	0	1	9	.338	.294
May, Darrell, Anaheim*	.000	29	2	2	0	0	0	0	0	0	0	0	0	0	0	0	2	0	0	0	.000	.000
Mayne, Brent, Oakland*	.289	85	282	256	29	74	104	12	0	6	22	2	2	4	18	1	33	1	0	6	.406	.343
McDonald, Ben, Milwaukee	.000	21	1	1	0	0	0	0	0	0	0	0	0	0	0	0	1	0	0	0	.000	.000
McDonald, Jason, Oakland†	.263	78	276	236	47	62	93	11	4	4	14	2	1	1	36	0	49	13	8	0	.394	.361
McElroy, Chuck, Ana.-Chi.*	.000	62	0	0	1	0	0	0	0	0	0	0	0	0	0	0	0	0	0	0	.000	.000
McGwire, Mark, Oakland	.284	105	433	366	48	104	230	24	0	34	81	0	5	4	58	8	98	1	0	9	.628	.383
McKeel, Walt, Boston	.000	5	3	3	0	0	0	0	0	0	0	0	0	0	0	0	1	0	0	0	.000	.000
McLemore, Mark, Texas†	.261	89	399	349	47	91	115	17	2	1	25	6	2	2	40	1	54	7	5	5	.330	.338
Meares, Pat, Minnesota	.276	134	483	439	63	121	180	23	3	10	60	3	7	16	18	0	86	7	7	9	.410	.323
Merced, Orlando, Toronto*	.266	98	420	368	45	98	152	23	2	9	40	0	2	3	47	1	62	7	3	6	.413	.352
Mercedes, Henry, Texas	.213	23	56	47	4	10	14	4	0	0	4	3	0	0	6	0	25	0	0	0	.298	.302
Mercedes, Jose, Milwaukee	.000	29	2	2	0	0	0	0	0	0	0	0	0	0	0	0	2	0	0	0	.000	.000
Mieske, Matt, Milwaukee	.249	84	273	253	39	63	99	15	3	5	21	0	1	0	19	2	50	1	0	12	.391	.300
Miller, Damian, Minnesota	.273	25	71	66	5	18	25	1	0	2	13	0	3	0	2	0	12	0	0	2	.379	.282
Miller, Orlando, Detroit	.234	50	122	111	13	26	41	7	1	2	10	1	1	4	5	0	24	1	0	1	.369	.289
Mitchell, Kevin, Cleveland	.153	20	69	59	7	9	22	1	0	4	11	0	0	1	9	2	11	1	0	2	.373	.275
Moehler, Brian, Detroit	.000	31	3	3	0	0	0	0	0	0	0	0	0	0	0	0	2	0	0	0	.000	.000
Molina, Izzy, Oakland	.198	48	115	111	6	22	36	3	1	3	7	1	0	0	3	0	17	0	0	1	.324	.219
Molitor, Paul, Minnesota	.305	135	597	538	63	164	234	32	4	10	89	2	12	0	45	8	73	11	4	8	.435	.351
Morman, Alvin, Cleveland	.000	34	1	1	0	0	0	0	0	0	0	0	0	0	0	0	0	0	0	0	.000	.000
Mosquera, Julio, Toronto	.250	3	8	8	0	2	3	1	0	0	0	0	0	0	0	0	2	0	0	0	.375	.250
Mouton, Lyle, Chicago	.269	88	260	242	26	65	89	9	0	5	23	0	3	1	14	1	66	4	4	8	.368	.308
Moyer, Jamie, Seattle*	.333	30	3	3	0	1	1	0	0	0	0	0	0	0	0	0	0	0	0	0	.333	.333
Murray, Eddie, Anaheim†	.219	46	176	160	13	35	51	7	0	3	15	0	3	0	13	0	24	1	0	8	.319	.273
Mussina, Mike, Baltimore*	.250	33	4	4	0	1	1	0	0	0	0	0	0	0	0	0	1	0	0	0	.250	.250
Myers, Greg, Minnesota*	.267	62	183	165	24	44	72	11	1	5	28	0	2	0	16	2	29	0	0	4	.436	.328
Myers, Rod, Kansas City*	.257	31	121	101	14	26	39	7	0	2	9	2	0	1	17	0	22	4	0	2	.386	.370
Naehring, Tim, Boston	.286	70	301	259	38	74	121	18	1	9	40	0	3	1	38	0	40	1	1	10	.467	.375
Nagy, Charles, Cleveland*	.200	34	5	5	1	1	1	0	0	0	0	0	0	0	0	0	0	0	0	1	.200	.200
Navarro, Jaime, Chicago	.000	33	2	1	0	0	0	0	0	0	0	1	0	0	0	0	0	0	0	1	.000	.000
Nevin, Phil, Detroit	.235	93	278	251	32	59	104	16	1	9	35	0	1	1	25	1	68	0	1	5	.414	.306
Newfield, Marc, Milwaukee	.229	50	176	157	14	36	47	8	0	1	18	0	3	2	14	0	27	0	0	4	.299	.295
Newson, Warren, Texas*	.213	81	201	169	23	36	78	10	1	10	23	0	1	0	31	2	53	3	0	4	.462	.333
Nieves, Melvin, Detroit†	.228	116	405	359	46	82	162	18	1	20	64	0	2	5	39	6	157	1	7	3	.451	.311
Nilsson, Dave, Milwaukee*	.278	156	629	554	71	154	247	33	0	20	81	1	7	2	65	8	88	2	3	7	.446	.352
Nixon, Otis, Toronto†	.262	103	464	401	54	105	122	12	1	1	26	6	5	0	52	0	54	47	10	10	.304	.343
Norton, Greg, Chicago†	.265	18	37	34	5	9	15	2	2	0	1	1	0	0	2	0	8	0	0	0	.441	.306
Nunnally, Jon, Kansas City*	.241	13	34	29	8	7	12	0	1	1	4	0	0	0	5	0	7	0	0	0	.414	.353
O'Brien, Charlie, Toronto	.218	69	267	225	22	49	78	15	1	4	27	3	6	11	22	1	45	0	2	6	.347	.311
Offerman, Jose, Kansas City†	.297	106	471	424	59	126	167	23	6	2	39	6	0	41	3	64	9	10	5	.394	.359
Ogea, Chad, Cleveland	.000	21	4	2	0	0	0	0	0	0	0	2	0	0	0	0	1	0	0	0	.000	.000
O'Leary, Troy, Boston*	.309	146	545	499	65	154	239	32	4	15	80	1	4	2	39	7	70	0	5	13	.479	.358
Olivares, Omar, Det.-Sea.	.600	35	5	5	2	3	5	0	1	0	2	0	0	0	0	0	1	0	0	0	1.000	.600
Oliver, Darren, Texas	.500	32	3	2	1	1	1	0	0	0	2	1	0	0	0	0	1	0	0	0	.500	.667
O'Neill, Paul, New York*	.324	149	637	553	89	179	284	42	0	21	117	0	9	0	75	8	92	10	7	16	.514	.399
Oquist, Mike, Oakland	.250	21	5	4	0	1	1	0	0	0	0	0	0	0	0	0	0	0	0	0	.250	.250
Ordonez, Magglio, Chicago	.319	21	72	69	12	22	40	6	0	4	11	1	0	2	0	0	8	1	2	1	.580	.338
Orosco, Jesse, Baltimore	.000	71	1	0	0	0	0	0	0	0	0	0	0	0	1	0	0	0	0	0	.000	1.000
Ortiz, David, Minnesota*	.327	15	51	49	10	16	22	3	0	1	6	0	0	0	2	0	19	0	0	1	.449	.353
Palmeiro, Orlando, Anaheim*	.216	74	156	134	19	29	35	2	2	0	8	3	1	1	17	1	11	2	2	4	.261	.307
Palmeiro, Rafael, Baltimore*	.254	158	692	614	95	156	298	24	2	38	110	0	6	5	67	7	109	5	2	14	.485	.329

Player, Team	Avg.	G	TPA	AB	R	H	TB	2B	3B	HR	RBI	SH	SF	HP	BB	IBB	SO	SB	CS	GDP	Slg.	OBP
Palmer, Dean, Tex.-K.C.	.256	143	592	542	70	139	241	31	1	23	86	1	5	3	41	2	134	2	2	7	.445	.310
Paquette, Craig, Kansas City ..	.230	77	267	252	26	58	99	15	1	8	33	1	2	2	10	0	57	2	2	13	.393	.263
Pemberton, Rudy, Boston	.238	27	70	63	8	15	23	2	0	2	10	0	3	4	0	0	13	0	0	0	.365	.314
Pena, Tony, Chicago..............	.164	31	76	67	4	11	12	1	0	0	8	0	1	0	8	0	13	0	0	3	.179	.250
Perez, Robert, Toronto	.192	37	78	78	4	15	27	4	1	2	6	0	0	0	0	0	16	0	0	2	.346	.192
Perez, Tomas, Toronto†	.195	40	138	123	9	24	31	3	2	0	9	3	0	1	11	0	28	1	1	2	.252	.267
Perisho, Matt, Anaheim*........	.000	11	1	1	0	0	0	0	0	0	0	0	0	0	0	0	1	0	0	0	.000	.000
Person, Robert, Toronto	.000	23	5	4	0	0	0	0	0	0	0	1	0	0	0	0	1	0	0	0	.000	.000
Phillips, Tony, Chi.-Ana.†	.275	141	648	534	96	147	209	34	2	8	57	5	4	3	102	5	118	13	10	11	.391	.392
Pittsley, Jim, Kansas City	.500	21	2	2	0	1	2	1	0	0	0	0	0	0	0	0	1	0	0	0	1.000	.500
Plunk, Eric, Cleveland	.000	56	1	1	0	0	0	0	0	0	0	0	0	0	0	0	1	0	0	0	.000	.000
Posada, Jorge, New York†	.250	60	224	188	29	47	77	12	0	6	25	1	2	3	30	2	33	1	2	2	.410	.359
Pose, Scott, New York*	.218	54	96	87	19	19	23	2	1	0	5	0	0	0	9	0	11	3	1	1	.264	.292
Pozo, Arquimedez, Boston	.267	4	17	15	0	4	5	1	0	0	3	1	1	0	0	0	5	0	0	0	.333	.250
Pride, Curtis, Det.-Bos.*	.213	81	192	164	22	35	56	4	4	3	20	2	1	1	24	1	46	6	4	4	.341	.316
Quantrill, Paul, Toronto*	.000	77	1	1	0	0	0	0	0	0	0	0	0	0	0	0	1	0	0	0	.000	.000
Raabe, Brian, Seattle.............	.000	2	4	3	0	0	0	0	0	0	0	0	0	0	1	0	2	0	0	0	.000	.250
Radke, Brad, Minnesota	.000	35	4	3	0	0	0	0	0	0	0	1	0	0	0	0	1	0	0	0	.000	.000
Raines, Tim, New York†	.321	74	318	271	56	87	123	20	2	4	38	0	6	0	41	0	34	8	5	4	.454	.403
Ramirez, Manny, Cleveland	.328	150	651	561	99	184	302	40	0	26	88	0	4	7	79	5	115	2	3	19	.538	.415
Reboulet, Jeff, Baltimore	.237	99	265	228	26	54	75	9	0	4	27	11	2	1	23	0	44	3	0	3	.329	.307
Reed, Jody, Detroit	.196	52	129	112	6	22	24	2	0	0	8	3	1	3	10	0	15	3	2	2	.214	.278
Rhodes, Arthur, Baltimore*	.000	54	1	1	0	0	0	0	0	0	0	0	0	0	1	0	0	0	0	0	.000	.000
Rigby, Brad, Oakland	.000	14	3	3	0	0	0	0	0	0	0	0	0	0	0	0	2	0	0	0	.000	.000
Ripken, Billy, Texas	.276	71	218	203	18	56	76	9	1	3	24	1	5	0	9	0	32	0	1	7	.374	.300
Ripken, Cal, Baltimore............	.270	162	686	615	79	166	247	30	0	17	84	0	10	5	56	3	73	1	0	19	.402	.331
Ritchie, Todd, Minnesota	.000	42	2	2	0	0	0	0	0	0	0	0	0	0	0	0	1	0	0	0	.000	.000
Roberts, Bip, K.C.-Cle.†	.302	120	468	431	63	130	166	20	2	4	44	1	5	3	28	2	67	18	3	7	.385	.345
Robertson, Rich, Minnesota*	.200	31	5	5	0	1	1	0	0	0	0	0	0	0	0	0	2	0	0	1	.200	.200
Rodriguez, Alex, Seattle	.300	141	638	587	100	176	291	40	3	23	84	4	1	5	41	1	99	29	6	14	.496	.350
Rodriguez, Frankie, Minnesota ..	.000	43	1	1	0	0	0	0	0	0	0	0	0	0	0	0	0	0	0	0	.000	.000
Rodriguez, Ivan, Texas	.313	150	648	597	98	187	289	34	4	20	77	1	4	8	38	7	89	7	3	18	.484	.360
Rogers, Kenny, New York* ...	.000	31	3	3	0	0	0	0	0	0	0	0	0	0	0	0	0	0	0	0	.000	.000
Rohrmeier, Dan, Seattle	.333	7	11	9	4	3	3	0	0	0	2	0	0	0	2	0	4	0	0	0	.333	.455
Rosado, Jose, Kansas City* ...	.000	34	2	2	0	0	0	0	0	0	0	0	0	0	0	0	1	0	0	0	.000	.000
Rosario, Mel, Baltimore†	.000	4	3	3	0	0	0	0	0	0	0	0	0	0	0	0	0	0	0	0	.000	.000
Rusch, Glendon, Kansas City* ..	.000	30	3	3	0	0	0	0	0	0	0	0	0	0	0	0	2	0	0	0	.000	.000
Saberhagen, Bret, Boston	.000	6	1	1	0	0	0	0	0	0	0	0	0	0	0	0	0	0	0	0	.000	.000
Sagmoen, Marc, Texas*	.140	21	46	43	2	6	11	2	0	1	4	0	1	0	2	0	13	0	0	1	.256	.174
Salmon, Tim, Anaheim............	.296	157	695	582	95	172	301	28	1	33	129	0	11	7	95	5	142	9	12	7	.517	.394
Samuel, Juan, Toronto	.284	45	108	95	13	27	49	5	4	3	15	1	0	2	10	0	28	5	3	2	.516	.364
Sanchez, Rey, New York	.312	38	150	138	21	43	58	12	0	1	15	5	1	1	5	0	21	0	4	1	.420	.338
Santana, Julio, Texas	.500	30	2	2	0	1	1	0	0	0	0	0	0	0	0	0	0	0	0	0	.500	.500
Santiago, Benito, Toronto	.243	97	366	341	31	83	132	10	0	13	42	1	5	2	17	1	80	1	0	10	.387	.279
Seitzer, Kevin, Cleveland	.268	64	220	198	27	53	73	14	0	2	24	2	2	0	18	0	25	0	0	6	.369	.326
Sele, Aaron, Boston	.000	33	2	2	0	0	0	0	0	0	0	0	0	0	0	0	1	0	0	0	.000	.000
Sexson, Richie, Cleveland	.273	5	11	11	1	3	3	0	0	0	0	0	0	0	0	0	2	0	0	2	.273	.273
Sheets, Andy, Seattle	.247	32	102	89	18	22	37	3	0	4	9	5	1	0	7	0	34	2	0	1	.416	.299
Sheldon, Scott, Oakland	.250	13	27	24	2	6	9	0	0	1	2	1	0	1	1	0	6	0	0	0	.375	.308
Shuey, Paul, Cleveland	.000	40	1	1	0	0	0	0	0	0	0	0	0	0	0	0	1	0	0	0	.000	.000
Sierra, Ruben, Toronto†	.208	14	52	48	4	10	17	0	2	1	5	0	1	0	3	1	13	0	0	1	.354	.250
Silvestri, Dave, Texas	.000	2	4	4	0	0	0	0	0	0	0	0	0	0	0	0	1	0	0	0	.000	.000
Simms, Mike, Texas	.252	59	121	111	13	28	51	8	0	5	22	0	2	0	8	1	27	0	1	3	.459	.298
Sirotka, Mike, Chicago*	.000	7	1	1	0	0	0	0	0	0	0	0	0	0	0	0	1	0	0	0	.000	.000
Small, Aaron, Oakland............	.000	71	1	1	0	0	0	0	0	0	0	0	0	0	0	0	0	0	0	0	.000	.000
Snopek, Chris, Chicago	.218	86	323	298	27	65	95	15	0	5	35	4	2	1	18	0	51	3	2	4	.319	.263
Sojo, Luis, New York..............	.307	77	239	215	27	66	80	6	1	2	25	5	2	1	16	0	14	3	1	5	.372	.355
Sorrento, Paul, Seattle*	.269	146	513	457	68	123	235	19	0	31	80	0	2	3	51	9	112	0	2	13	.514	.345
Spehr, Tim, Kansas City	.171	17	38	35	3	6	9	0	0	1	2	0	0	1	2	0	12	0	0	0	.257	.237
Spiezio, Scott, Oakland†	.243	147	590	538	58	131	209	28	4	14	65	3	4	1	44	2	75	9	3	13	.388	.300
Spoljaric, Paul, Tor.-Sea.........	.000	57	1	1	0	0	0	0	0	0	0	0	0	0	0	0	0	0	0	0	.000	.000
Sprague, Ed Jr., Toronto	.228	138	562	504	63	115	194	29	4	14	48	0	1	6	51	0	102	0	1	10	.385	.306
Springer, Dennis, Anaheim.....	.000	32	3	3	0	0	0	0	0	0	0	0	0	0	0	0	3	0	0	0	.000	.000
Stahoviak, Scott, Minnesota	.229	91	309	275	33	63	110	17	0	10	33	0	4	6	24	1	73	5	2	7	.400	.301
Stairs, Matt, Oakland*............	.298	133	410	352	62	105	205	19	0	27	73	1	4	3	50	1	60	3	2	6	.582	.386
Stanley, Mike, Bos.-N.Y.	.297	125	415	347	61	103	176	25	0	16	65	0	8	6	54	1	72	0	1	13	.507	.393
Steinbach, Terry, Minnesota.....	.248	122	487	447	60	111	176	27	1	12	54	0	4	1	35	2	106	6	1	14	.394	.302
Stevens, Lee, Texas*	.300	137	454	426	58	128	219	24	2	21	74	1	3	1	23	2	83	1	3	18	.514	.336
Stewart, Andy, Kansas City	.250	5	8	8	1	2	3	1	0	0	0	0	0	0	0	0	0	0	0	1	.375	.250
Stewart, Shannon, Toronto	.286	44	193	168	25	48	75	13	7	0	22	0	2	4	19	1	24	10	3	3	.446	.368
Stinnett, Kelly, Milwaukee	.250	30	39	36	2	9	13	4	0	0	3	0	0	0	3	0	9	0	0	1	.361	.308
Strawberry, Darryl, New York* ..	.103	11	32	29	1	3	4	1	0	0	2	0	0	0	3	0	9	0	0	2	.138	.188
Suppan, Jeff, Boston..............	.000	23	2	2	0	0	0	0	0	0	0	0	0	0	0	0	0	0	0	0	.000	.000
Surhoff, B.J., Baltimore*..........	.284	147	595	528	80	150	242	30	4	18	88	3	10	5	49	14	60	1	1	7	.458	.345
Sutton, Larry, Kansas City*....	.290	27	75	69	9	20	28	2	0	2	8	1	0	0	5	0	12	0	0	0	.406	.338
Sweeney, Mike, Kansas City	.242	84	266	240	30	58	87	8	0	7	31	1	2	6	17	0	33	3	2	8	.363	.306
Tarasco, Tony, Baltimore*	.205	100	193	166	26	34	65	8	1	7	26	1	0	1	25	1	33	2	2	3	.392	.313
Tatis, Fernando, Texas...........	.256	60	241	223	29	57	90	9	0	8	29	2	2	0	14	0	42	3	0	6	.404	.297
Tavarez, Jesus, Boston†	.174	42	74	69	12	12	17	3	1	0	9	0	1	0	4	0	9	0	0	2	.246	.216
Tejada, Miguel, Oakland	.202	26	104	99	10	20	33	3	2	2	10	0	0	3	2	0	22	2	0	3	.333	.240
Telgheder, Dave, Oakland	.000	20	2	2	0	0	0	0	0	0	0	0	0	0	0	0	1	0	0	0	.000	.000
Tettleton, Mickey, Texas†	.091	17	48	44	5	4	14	1	0	3	4	0	0	1	3	1	12	0	0	1	.318	.167

Player, Team	Avg.	G	TPA	AB	R	H	TB	2B	3B	HR	RBI	SH	SF	HP	BB	IBB	SO	SB	CS	GDP	Slg.	OBP
Tewksbury, Bob, Minnesota ...	.200	26	5	5	0	1	1	0	0	0	1	0	0	0	0	0	1	0	0	0	.200	.200
Thomas, Frank, Chicago	.347	146	649	530	110	184	324	35	0	35	125	0	7	3	109	9	69	1	1	15	.611	.456
Thome, Jim, Cleveland*........	.286	147	627	496	104	142	287	25	0	40	102	0	8	3	120	9	146	1	1	9	.579	.423
Thompson, Justin, Detroit* ...	.000	32	2	2	0	0	0	0	0	0	0	0	0	0	0	0	1	0	0	0	.000	.000
Tinsley, Lee, Seattle†	.197	49	133	122	12	24	34	6	2	0	6	0	0	0	11	0	34	2	0	4	.279	.263
Trammell, Bubba, Detroit	.228	44	140	123	14	28	45	5	0	4	13	0	2	0	15	0	35	3	1	2	.366	.307
Trombley, Mike, Minnesota	.000	67	1	1	0	0	0	0	0	0	0	0	0	0	0	0	1	0	0	0	.000	.000
Turner, Chris, Anaheim	.261	13	29	23	4	6	12	1	1	1	2	1	0	0	5	0	8	0	0	0	.522	.393
Unroe, Tim, Milwaukee	.250	32	18	16	3	4	11	1	0	2	5	0	0	0	2	0	9	2	0	0	.688	.333
Valdez, Mario, Chicago*	.243	54	137	115	11	28	38	7	0	1	13	0	2	3	17	0	39	1	0	3	.330	.350
Valentin, Javier, Minnesota† ...	.286	4	7	7	1	2	2	0	0	0	0	0	0	0	0	0	3	0	0	0	.286	.286
Valentin, John, Boston	.306	143	644	575	95	176	287	47	5	18	77	1	5	5	58	5	66	7	4	21	.499	.372
Valentin, Jose, Milwaukee†	.253	136	546	494	58	125	201	23	1	17	58	4	5	4	39	4	109	19	8	5	.407	.310
Varitek, Jason, Boston†	1.000	1	1	1	0	1	1	0	0	0	0	0	0	0	0	0	0	0	0	0	1.000	1.000
Vaughn, Mo, Boston*	.315	141	628	527	91	166	295	24	0	35	96	0	3	12	86	17	154	2	2	10	.560	.420
Ventura, Robin, Chicago*	.262	54	220	183	27	48	78	10	1	6	26	0	3	0	34	5	21	0	0	3	.426	.373
Villone, Ron, Milwaukee*.......	.000	50	1	1	0	0	0	0	0	0	0	0	0	0	0	0	1	0	0	0	.000	.000
Vina, Fernando, Milwaukee*..	.275	79	348	324	37	89	117	12	2	4	28	2	3	7	12	1	23	8	7	4	.361	.312
Vitiello, Joe, Kansas City	.238	51	146	130	11	31	52	6	0	5	18	0	0	2	14	1	37	0	0	2	.400	.322
Vizquel, Omar, Cleveland†	.280	153	642	565	89	158	208	23	6	5	49	16	2	2	57	1	58	43	12	16	.368	.347
Voigt, Jack, Milwaukee..........	.245	72	174	151	20	37	74	9	2	8	22	2	1	1	19	2	36	1	2	5	.490	.331
Wakefield, Tim, Boston	.000	35	1	1	0	0	0	0	0	0	0	0	0	0	0	0	0	0	0	0	.000	.000
Walbeck, Matt, Detroit†	.277	47	151	137	18	38	50	3	0	3	10	0	2	0	12	0	19	3	3	4	.365	.331
Walker, Todd, Minnesota*......	.237	52	171	156	15	37	55	7	1	3	16	1	2	1	11	1	30	7	0	5	.353	.288
Walton, Jerome, Baltimore......	.294	26	74	68	8	20	30	1	0	3	9	2	0	0	4	0	10	0	0	3	.441	.333
Webster, Lenny, Baltimore	.255	98	287	259	29	66	97	8	1	7	37	3	1	2	22	0	46	0	1	10	.375	.317
Wells, Bob, Seattle	.000	46	1	0	1	0	0	0	0	0	0	0	0	0	1	0	0	0	0	0	.000	1.000
Wetteland, John, Texas	1.000	61	1	1	1	1	2	1	0	0	1	0	0	0	0	0	0	0	0	0	2.000	1.000
Whiten, Mark, New York†	.265	69	248	215	34	57	83	11	0	5	24	1	0	2	30	5	47	4	2	6	.386	.360
Wilkins, Rick, Seattle*	.250	5	14	12	2	3	7	1	0	1	4	0	1	0	1	0	2	0	0	0	.583	.286
Williams, Bernie, New York†..	.328	129	591	509	107	167	277	35	6	21	100	0	8	1	73	7	80	15	8	10	.544	.408
Williams, George, Oakland†....	.289	76	241	201	30	58	78	9	1	3	22	2	1	2	35	0	46	0	1	2	.388	.397
Williams, Gerald, Milwaukee...	.253	155	601	566	73	143	209	32	2	10	41	5	5	6	19	1	90	23	9	9	.369	.282
Williams, Matt, Cleveland......	.263	151	636	596	86	157	291	32	3	32	105	0	2	4	34	4	108	12	4	14	.488	.307
Williams, Woody, Toronto	.500	31	2	2	0	1	1	0	0	0	0	0	0	0	0	0	1	0	0	0	.500	.500
Williamson, Antone, Mil.*	.204	24	60	54	2	11	14	3	0	0	6	1	1	0	4	0	8	0	1	2	.259	.254
Wilson, Dan, Seattle.............	.270	146	563	508	66	137	215	31	1	15	74	8	3	5	39	1	72	7	2	12	.423	.326
Wilson, Enrique, Cleveland† ..	.333	5	15	15	2	5	5	0	0	0	1	0	0	0	0	0	2	0	0	0	.333	.333
Witt, Bobby, Texas	.333	35	6	6	1	2	6	1	0	1	2	0	0	0	0	0	1	0	0	0	1.000	.333
Wolcott, Bob, Seattle	.000	19	1	1	0	0	0	0	0	0	0	0	0	0	0	0	0	0	0	0	.000	.000
Wright, Jaret, Cleveland........	.000	16	5	3	0	0	0	0	0	0	0	0	0	0	0	0	0	0	0	0	.000	.000
Young, Ernie, Oakland...........	.223	71	200	175	22	39	61	7	0	5	15	2	2	2	19	0	57	1	3	6	.349	.303

AWARDED FIRST BASE ON OBSTRUCTION OR CATCHER'S INTERFERENCE—Steinbach, Minnesota 2 (Matheny, Marzano); R. Davis, Seattle (Johnson); Hamelin, Detroit (Sweeney); Huson, Milwaukee (Rosario); Leyritz, Texas (Johnson), Ordonez, Chicago (Alomar).

PLAYERS WITH TWO OR MORE TEAMS

Player, Team	Avg.	G	TPA	AB	R	H	TB	2B	3B	HR	RBI	SH	SF	HP	BB	IBB	SO	SB	CS	GDP	Slg.	OBP
Baines, Harold, Chicago*	.305	93	361	318	40	97	151	18	0	12	52	0	2	0	41	10	47	0	1	9	.475	.382
Baines, Harold, Baltimore......	.291	44	149	134	15	39	56	5	0	4	15	0	1	0	14	1	15	0	0	3	.418	.356
Berroa, Geronimo, Oakland...	.310	73	299	261	40	81	141	12	0	16	42	0	1	1	36	2	58	3	2	12	.540	.395
Berroa, Geronimo, Baltimore .	.260	83	349	300	48	78	121	13	0	10	48	0	6	3	40	2	62	1	2	6	.403	.347
Brito, Tilson, Toronto	.222	49	139	126	9	28	31	3	0	0	8	0	2	2	9	0	28	1	0	2	.246	.281
Brito, Tilson, Oakland...........	.283	17	49	46	8	13	23	2	1	2	6	2	0	0	1	0	10	0	0	0	.500	.298
Clark, Tony, Cleveland	.000	4	0	0	0	0	0	0	0	0	0	0	0	0	0	0	0	0	0	0	.000	.000
Clark, Tony, Texas	1.000	9	1	1	0	1	1	0	0	0	0	0	0	0	0	0	0	0	0	0	1.000	1.000
Cruz, Jose Jr., Seattle†	.268	49	198	183	28	49	99	12	1	12	34	1	1	0	13	0	45	1	0	3	.541	.315
Cruz, Jose Jr., Toronto†	.231	55	244	212	31	49	98	7	0	14	34	0	4	0	28	2	72	6	2	4	.462	.316
Curtis, Chad, Cleveland	.207	22	36	29	8	6	16	1	0	3	5	0	0	0	7	0	10	0	0	1	.552	.361
Curtis, Chad, New York	.291	93	372	320	51	93	152	21	1	12	50	2	9	5	36	1	49	12	6	6	.475	.362
Duncan, Mariano, New York ..	.244	50	179	172	16	42	53	8	0	1	13	1	0	0	6	0	39	2	1	2	.308	.270
Duncan, Mariano, Toronto	.228	39	176	167	20	38	44	6	0	0	12	0	0	3	6	0	39	4	2	4	.263	.267
Fabregas, Jorge, Anaheim*....	.079	21	43	38	2	3	4	1	0	0	3	2	0	0	3	0	3	0	0	2	.105	.146
Fabregas, Jorge, Chicago*.....	.280	100	342	322	31	90	123	10	1	7	48	4	4	1	11	0	43	1	1	14	.382	.302
Franco, Julio, Cleveland	.284	78	328	289	46	82	106	13	1	3	25	1	0	0	38	2	75	8	5	13	.367	.367
Franco, Julio, Milwaukee........	.241	42	177	141	22	34	49	3	0	4	19	0	4	1	31	2	41	7	1	4	.348	.373
Goodwin, Tom, Kansas City* .	.272	97	400	367	51	100	127	13	4	2	22	11	1	2	19	0	51	34	10	5	.346	.311
Goodwin, Tom, Texas*..........	.237	53	235	207	39	49	66	13	2	0	17	0	2	1	25	1	37	16	6	2	.319	.319
Hill, Ken, Texas....................	.000	19	0	0	0	0	0	0	0	0	0	0	0	0	0	0	0	0	0	0	.000	.000
Hill, Ken, Anaheim................	.500	12	3	2	0	1	2	1	0	0	2	1	0	0	0	0	1	0	0	0	1.000	.500
Incaviglia, Pete, Baltimore......	.246	48	153	138	18	34	53	4	0	5	12	0	1	3	11	2	43	0	0	1	.384	.314
Incaviglia, Pete, New York......	.250	5	16	16	1	4	4	0	0	0	0	0	0	0	0	0	3	0	0	0	.250	.250
Jackson, Darrin, Minnesota ...	.254	49	139	130	19	33	46	2	1	3	21	3	2	0	4	0	21	2	0	2	.354	.272
Jackson, Darrin, Milwaukee ...	.272	26	85	81	7	22	35	7	0	2	15	2	0	0	2	0	10	2	1	3	.432	.289
Kelly, Roberto, Minnesota	.287	75	269	247	39	71	109	19	2	5	37	1	2	2	17	0	50	7	4	4	.441	.336
Kelly, Roberto, Seattle...........	.298	30	129	121	19	36	64	7	0	7	22	1	1	1	5	0	17	2	1	2	.529	.328
Kreuter, Chad, Chicago†........	.216	19	45	37	6	8	15	2	1	1	3	0	0	0	8	0	9	0	1	0	.405	.356
Kreuter, Chad, Anaheim†	.234	70	240	218	19	51	72	7	1	4	18	1	0	0	21	0	57	0	2	7	.330	.301
Leyritz, Jim, Anaheim	.276	84	342	294	47	81	121	7	0	11	50	3	5	3	37	2	56	1	1	11	.412	.357
Leyritz, Jim, Texas	.282	37	113	85	11	24	28	4	0	0	14	1	1	3	23	0	22	1	0	2	.329	.446
Lowe, Derek, Seattle	.000	12	2	2	0	0	0	0	0	0	0	0	0	0	0	0	1	0	0	0	.000	.000

Player, Team	Avg.	G	TPA	AB	R	H	TB	2B	3B	HR	RBI	SH	SF	HP	BB	IBB	SO	SB	CS	GDP	Slg.	OBP
Lowe, Derek, Boston.............	.000	8	1	1	0	0	0	0	0	0	0		0	0	0	0	1	0	0	0	.000	.000
McElroy, Chuck, Anaheim*....	.000	13	0	0	0	0	0	0	0	0	0	0	0	0	0	0	0	0	0	0	.000	.000
McElroy, Chuck, Chicago*.....	.000	49	0	0	1	0	0	0	0	0	0	0	0	0	0	0	0	0	0	0	.000	.000
Olivares, Omar, Detroit..........	.667	22	3	3	2	2	4	0	1	0	0	0	0	0	0	0	0	0	0	0	1.333	.667
Olivares, Omar, Seattle...........	.500	13	2	2	0	1	1	0	0	0	2	0	0	0	0	0	1	0	0	0	.500	.500
Palmer, Dean, Texas...............	.245	94	386	355	47	87	150	21	0	14	55	1	3	1	26	2	84	1	0	4	.423	.296
Palmer, Dean, Kansas City	.278	49	206	187	23	52	91	10	1	9	31	0	2	2	15	0	50	1	2	3	.487	.335
Phillips, Tony, Chicago†........	.310	36	161	129	23	40	52	6	0	2	9	2	0	1	29	0	29	4	1	3	.403	.440
Phillips, Tony, Anaheim†........	.264	105	487	405	73	107	157	28	2	6	48	3	4	2	73	5	89	9	9	8	.388	.376
Pride, Curtis, Detroit*............	.210	79	190	162	21	34	52	4	4	2	19	2	1	1	24	1	45	6	4	4	.321	.314
Pride, Curtis, Boston*...........	.500	2	2	2	1	1	4	0	0	1	1	0	0	0	0	0	1	0	0	0	2.000	.500
Roberts, Bip, Kansas City†	.309	97	372	346	44	107	131	17	2	1	36	1	3	1	21	2	53	15	3	6	.379	.348
Roberts, Bip, Cleveland†........	.271	23	96	85	19	23	35	3	0	3	8	0	2	2	7	0	14	3	0	1	.412	.333
Spoljaric, Paul, Toronto..........	.000	37	1	1	0	0	0	0	0	0	0	0	0	0	0	0	0	0	0	0	.000	.000
Spoljaric, Paul, Seattle	.000	20	0	0	0	0	0	0	0	0	0	0	0	0	0	0	0	0	0	0	.000	.000
Stanley, Mike, Boston	.300	97	312	260	45	78	134	17	0	13	53	0	7	6	39	0	50	0	1	9	.515	.394
Stanley, Mike, New York	.287	28	103	87	16	25	42	8	0	3	12	0	1	0	15	4	22	0	0	4	.483	.388

DESIGNATED HITTING

TEAM

Team	Avg.	G	TPA	AB	R	H	TB	2B	3B	HR	RBI	SH	SF	HP	BB	IBB	SO	SB	CS	GDP	Slg.	OBP
Seattle	.315	154	699	562	107	177	291	34	1	26	113	1	6	11	119	11	98	4	4	20	.518	.440
Boston	.306	156	703	641	94	196	300	37	2	21	97	0	6	11	45	4	131	3	4	22	.468	.358
Chicago	.302	152	663	572	90	173	262	29	0	20	85	0	3	1	87	13	84	5	2	16	.458	.394
Cleveland	.297	152	668	595	88	177	276	31	1	22	84	1	3	2	67	5	107	7	4	16	.464	.369
Minnesota	.290	153	689	624	69	181	261	37	5	11	104	2	15	1	47	9	104	12	6	9	.418	.333
Oakland	.284	154	689	592	83	168	279	40	1	23	102	1	6	7	83	2	138	7	2	22	.471	.375
New York	.281	156	698	606	87	170	257	36	0	17	86	1	10	8	73	5	134	4	1	19	.424	.360
Kansas City	.277	152	660	560	88	155	281	24	0	34	106	0	6	2	92	16	116	8	3	16	.502	.377
Milwaukee	.263	152	641	562	68	148	213	23	0	14	71	1	11	4	63	3	126	9	3	10	.379	.336
Texas	.253	154	658	594	80	150	292	28	3	36	109	1	8	3	52	4	142	0	0	15	.492	.312
Baltimore	.250	156	684	595	86	149	227	24	3	16	70	0	6	9	74	8	131	5	5	10	.382	.339
Detroit	.248	156	654	568	82	141	252	30	3	25	92	1	6	1	78	5	146	4	5	14	.444	.337
Toronto	.237	156	656	598	70	142	248	25	3	25	95	0	3	8	47	3	129	7	5	8	.415	.300
Anaheim	.237	154	682	595	78	141	213	25	1	15	62	3	9	3	72	4	107	13	6	14	.358	.318
Totals	.274	2157	9444	8264	1170	2268	3652	423	23	305	1276	12	98	71	999	92	1693	88	50	211	.442	.354

INDIVIDUAL

TOP DESIGNATED HITTERS

Minimum 100 at-bats. *Lefthanded batter. †Switch-hitter.

Player, Team	Avg.	G	TPA	AB	R	H	TB	2B	3B	HR	RBI	SH	SF	HP	BB	IBB	SO	SB	CS	GDP	Slg.	OBP
Green, Shawn, Toronto*	.355	35	135	124	18	44	78	7	0	9	30	0	1	0	10	1	29	5	2	1	.629	.400
Justice, David, Cleveland*	.333	61	258	231	34	77	129	10	0	14	41	0	1	0	26	3	41	2	2	4	.558	.399
Martinez, Edgar, Seattle	.326	144	644	513	97	167	271	33	1	23	100	0	5	11	115	11	82	2	4	19	.528	.455
Jefferson, Reggie, Boston*	.325	119	481	452	66	147	217	29	1	13	62	0	2	6	21	3	86	1	2	15	.480	.362
Thomas, Frank, Chicago	.314	49	214	175	35	55	89	10	0	8	30	0	1	1	37	3	20	0	0	6	.509	.435
Molitor, Paul, Minnesota	.303	122	544	489	54	148	210	30	4	8	80	2	12	0	41	7	69	10	4	8	.429	.349
Franco, Julio, Cle.-Mil.	.295	70	302	261	47	77	109	12	1	6	30	0	4	0	37	2	63	9	3	6	.418	.377
Berroa, Geronimo, Oak.-Bal.	.295	69	297	258	41	76	118	15	0	9	41	0	3	2	34	0	51	2	2	9	.457	.377
Baines, Harold, Chi.-Bal.*	.293	121	495	437	53	128	195	22	0	15	62	0	3	0	55	11	62	0	1	10	.446	.370
Gonzalez, Juan, Texas	.282	69	303	277	43	78	164	13	2	23	67	0	5	0	21	2	65	0	0	7	.592	.327
Davis, Chili, Kansas City†	.280	133	560	472	71	132	242	20	0	30	90	0	4	1	83	16	93	6	3	15	.513	.386
Stevens, Lee, Texas*	.276	38	134	127	14	35	59	7	1	5	18	1	2	0	4	1	25	0	0	2	.465	.293
Hamelin, Bob, Detroit*	.275	95	347	298	47	82	151	15	0	18	51	0	2	1	46	2	66	2	1	7	.507	.372
Nilsson, Dave, Milwaukee*	.274	59	240	215	20	59	81	13	0	3	28	0	5	1	19	1	42	0	2	2	.377	.329
Stanley, Mike, Bos.-N.Y.	.264	69	218	182	26	48	80	11	0	7	28	0	4	5	27	2	46	0	0	7	.440	.367

ALL DESIGNATED HITTERS

*Lefthanded batter. †Switch-hitter.

Player, Team	Avg.	G	TPA	AB	R	H	TB	2B	3B	HR	RBI	SH	SF	HP	BB	IBB	SO	SB	CS	GDP	Slg.	OBP
Abbott, Jeff, Chicago	.444	3	9	9	3	4	4	0	0	0	0	0	0	0	0	0	1	0	0	0	.444	.444
Alicea, Luis, Anaheim†	.000	6	9	8	0	0	0	0	0	0	0	1	0	0	1	0	1	0	0	0	.000	.000
Alomar, Roberto, Baltimore†	.000	2	2	2	0	0	0	0	0	0	0	0	0	0	0	0	1	0	0	0	.000	.000
Alomar, Sandy Jr., Cleveland	.250	1	4	4	0	1	2	1	0	0	0	0	0	0	0	0	1	0	0	0	.500	.250
Amaral, Rich, Seattle	.000	3	1	0	2	0	0	0	0	0	0	1	0	0	0	0	0	1	0	0	.000	.000
Anderson, Brady, Baltimore*	.366	25	116	93	21	34	52	5	2	3	18	0	0	4	19	3	20	2	3	1	.559	.491
Anderson, Garret, Anaheim*	.385	4	15	13	3	5	8	3	0	0	1	0	0	0	2	0	3	0	0	0	.615	.467
Arias, George, Anaheim	.000	1	1	1	0	0	0	0	0	0	0	0	0	0	0	0	0	0	0	0	.000	.000
Baines, Harold, Chi.-Bal.*	.293	121	495	437	53	128	195	22	0	15	62	0	3	0	55	11	62	0	1	10	.446	.370
Banks, Brian, Milwaukee†	.000	1	3	3	0	0	0	0	0	0	0	0	0	0	0	0	0	0	0	0	.000	.000
Bartee, Kimera, Detroit†	.000	3	0	0	1	0	0	0	0	0	0	0	0	0	0	0	0	1	1	0	.000	.000
Batista, Tony, Oakland	.000	1	4	3	0	0	0	0	0	0	0	0	0	0	1	0	0	0	0	1	.000	.250
Belle, Albert, Chicago	.208	7	29	24	2	5	5	0	0	0	1	0	0	0	5	0	7	1	0	0	.208	.345
Bellhorn, Mark, Oakland†	.167	3	13	12	1	2	3	1	0	0	0	0	0	0	1	0	4	0	0	0	.250	.231
Benjamin, Mike, Boston	.000	1	1	1	0	0	0	0	0	0	0	0	0	0	0	0	1	0	0	0	.000	.000
Berroa, Geronimo, Oak.-Bal.	.295	69	297	258	41	76	118	15	0	9	41	0	3	2	34	0	51	2	2	9	.457	.377
Blowers, Mike, Seattle	.000	1	1	0	1	0	0	0	0	0	0	0	0	0	1	0	0	0	0	0	.000	1.000
Boggs, Wade, New York*	.394	19	73	66	9	26	35	6	0	1	3	1	0	0	6	1	12	0	1	1	.530	.444
Bones, Ricky, Kansas City	.000	1	0	0	0	0	0	0	0	0	0	0	0	0	0	0	0	0	0	0	.000	.000
Branson, Jeff, Cleveland*	.000	1	1	1	0	0	0	0	0	0	0	0	0	0	0	0	0	0	0	0	.000	.000
Brede, Brent, Minnesota*	1.000	1	1	1	0	1	2	1	0	0	0	0	0	0	0	0	0	0	0	0	2.000	1.000
Brumfield, Jacob, Toronto	.091	4	12	11	0	1	1	0	0	0	0	0	0	0	1	0	2	0	0	0	.091	.167
Buford, Damon, Texas	.000	3	1	1	1	0	0	0	0	0	0	0	0	0	0	0	0	0	0	0	.000	.000
Buhner, Jay, Seattle	.000	2	5	4	0	0	0	0	0	0	0	0	0	0	1	0	2	0	0	0	.000	.200
Bush, Homer, New York	.000	1	0	0	0	0	0	0	0	0	0	0	0	0	0	0	0	0	1	0	.000	.000
Butler, Rich, Toronto*	.000	1	2	1	0	0	0	0	0	0	0	0	0	0	1	0	1	0	1	0	.000	.500
Cameron, Mike, Chicago	.000	4	0	0	1	0	0	0	0	0	0	0	0	0	0	0	0	1	0	0	.000	.000
Candaele, Casey, Cleveland†	.000	1	1	1	0	0	0	0	0	0	0	0	0	0	0	0	0	0	0	0	.000	.000
Canseco, Jose, Oakland	.248	60	245	218	27	54	103	13	0	12	40	0	2	3	22	0	69	3	0	11	.472	.322
Carr, Chuck, Milwaukee†	.000	1	0	0	1	0	0	0	0	0	0	0	0	0	0	0	0	0	0	0	.000	.000
Carter, Joe, Toronto	.198	64	276	253	31	50	92	13	1	9	41	0	2	6	15	0	49	0	1	2	.364	.257
Casanova, Raul, Detroit†	.000	1	1	1	0	0	0	0	0	0	0	0	0	0	0	0	1	0	0	0	.000	.000
Casey, Sean, Cleveland*	.143	3	9	7	1	1	1	0	0	0	0	1	0	1	1	0	2	0	0	0	.143	.333
Catalanotto, Frank, Detroit*	.250	3	8	8	1	2	3	1	0	0	3	0	0	0	0	0	1	0	0	0	.375	.250
Cedeno, Domingo, Texas†	.500	2	2	2	1	1	4	0	0	1	1	0	0	0	0	0	0	0	0	0	2.000	.500
Cirillo, Jeff, Milwaukee	.250	2	9	8	0	2	2	0	0	0	2	0	0	0	1	0	0	0	0	1	.250	.333
Clark, Tony, Detroit†	.000	1	4	4	0	0	0	0	0	0	0	0	0	0	0	0	2	0	0	0	.000	.000
Clark, Will, Texas*	.217	7	26	23	2	5	8	0	0	1	1	0	0	0	3	0	3	0	0	1	.348	.308

Player, Team	Avg.	G	TPA	AB	R	H	TB	2B	3B	HR	RBI	SH	SF	HP	BB	IBB	SO	SB	CS	GDP	Slg.	OBP
Colbrunn, Greg, Minnesota....	.250	2	4	4	0	1	2	1	0	0	1	0	0	0	0	0	2	0	0	0	.500	.250
Coleman, Vince, Detroit†	.000	1	4	3	0	0	0	0	0	0	0	0	0	0	1	0	0	0	0	1	.000	.250
Coomer, Ron, Minnesota	.214	7	15	14	5	3	10	1	0	2	8	0	0	0	1	1	4	0	0	0	.714	.267
Cooper, Scott, Kansas City*...	.333	5	16	12	3	4	8	1	0	1	4	0	1	0	3	0	3	1	0	0	.667	.438
Cordero, Wilfredo, Boston	.000	2	7	7	0	0	0	0	0	0	0	0	0	0	0	0	1	0	0	0	.000	.000
Cordova, Marty, Minnesota....	.400	2	10	10	2	4	6	0	1	0	0	0	0	0	0	0	5	0	0	0	.600	.400
Crespo, Felipe, Toronto†	.000	2	1	1	0	0	0	0	0	0	0	0	0	0	0	0	1	0	0	0	.000	.000
Cruz, Ivan, New York*...........	.250	4	13	12	0	3	4	1	0	0	1	0	0	0	1	0	4	0	0	0	.333	.308
Damon, Johnny, Kansas City*.	.000	5	0	0	1	0	0	0	0	0	0	0	0	0	0	0	0	0	0	0	.000	.000
Davis, Chili, Kansas City†	.280	133	560	472	71	132	242	20	0	30	90	0	4	1	83	16	93	6	3	15	.513	.386
Davis, Eric, Baltimore............	.116	12	50	43	4	5	7	2	0	0	1	0	1	1	5	0	18	0	0	2	.163	.220
Davis, Russ, Seattle	.250	1	4	4	0	1	1	0	0	0	1	0	0	0	0	0	1	0	0	0	.250	.250
Delgado, Carlos, Toronto*	.250	33	102	88	14	22	41	4	0	5	15	0	0	1	13	2	20	0	0	1	.466	.353
Dellucci, Dave, Baltimore*	.000	5	9	7	0	0	0	0	0	0	0	0	0	0	2	1	4	0	0	0	.000	.222
Duncan, Mariano, New York ..	.286	2	7	7	0	2	2	0	0	0	0	0	0	0	0	0	1	0	0	0	.286	.286
Dunn, Todd, Milwaukee..........	.353	14	52	51	10	18	27	3	0	2	8	0	0	0	1	0	16	3	0	0	.529	.365
Durham, Ray, Chicago†	.000	1	5	3	1	0	0	0	0	0	0	0	0	0	2	0	0	0	0	0	.000	.400
Easley, Damion, Detroit..........	.250	4	17	16	2	4	11	2	1	1	2	0	0	0	1	0	2	0	0	1	.688	.294
Edmonds, Jim, Anaheim*	.250	8	36	28	1	7	8	1	0	0	2	0	0	1	7	0	7	0	0	1	.286	.417
Erstad, Darin, Anaheim*	.323	9	33	31	2	10	10	0	0	0	0	0	0	0	2	0	5	0	0	0	.323	.364
Fasano, Sal, Kansas City	.500	1	2	2	1	1	1	0	0	0	0	0	0	0	0	0	0	0	0	0	.500	.500
Fernandez, Tony, Cleveland† ..	1.000	1	1	1	0	1	1	0	0	0	0	0	0	0	0	0	0	0	0	0	1.000	1.000
Fielder, Cecil, New York..........	.263	89	392	334	39	88	141	14	0	13	58	0	6	7	45	2	78	0	0	13	.422	.357
Figga, Mike, New York	.000	1	1	1	0	0	0	0	0	0	0	0	0	0	0	0	1	0	0	0	.000	.000
Fonville, Chad, Chicago†	.000	1	0	0	0	0	0	0	0	0	0	0	0	0	0	0	0	1	0	0	.000	.000
Fox, Andy, New York*	.000	2	0	0	1	0	0	0	0	0	0	0	0	0	0	0	0	0	0	0	.000	.000
Franco, Julio, Cle.-Mil.	.295	70	302	261	47	77	109	12	1	6	30	0	4	0	37	2	63	9	3	6	.418	.377
Frye, Jeff, Boston....................	.300	11	12	10	2	3	6	0	0	1	2	0	1	0	1	0	1	2	2	1	.600	.333
Gates, Brent, Seattle†	.000	1	1	1	0	0	0	0	0	0	0	0	0	0	0	0	0	0	0	0	.000	.000
Giambi, Jason, Oakland*	.286	25	98	84	13	24	41	8	0	3	16	0	2	2	10	1	17	0	0	0	.488	.367
Gil, Benji, Texas......................	.000	4	0	0	2	0	0	0	0	0	0	0	0	0	0	0	0	0	0	0	.000	.000
Giles, Brian, Cleveland*	.200	9	27	20	4	4	5	1	0	0	0	0	0	0	7	0	4	1	0	1	.250	.407
Girardi, Joe, New York	.000	1	0	0	0	0	0	0	0	0	0	0	0	0	0	0	0	0	0	0	.000	.000
Gonzalez, Juan, Texas	.282	69	303	277	43	78	164	13	2	23	67	0	5	0	21	2	65	0	0	7	.592	.327
Grebeck, Craig, Anaheim.........	.000	2	0	0	0	0	0	0	0	0	0	0	0	0	0	0	0	0	0	0	.000	.000
Green, Shawn, Toronto*	.355	35	135	124	18	44	78	7	0	9	30	0	1	0	10	1	29	5	2	1	.629	.400
Greene, Todd, Anaheim..........	.308	8	29	26	5	8	10	2	0	0	4	0	0	0	3	1	5	1	0	0	.385	.379
Greer, Rusty, Texas*	.429	2	9	7	0	3	5	2	0	0	0	0	0	0	2	0	2	0	0	0	.714	.556
Griffey, Ken Jr., Seattle*.........	.125	4	17	16	2	2	8	0	0	2	3	0	0	0	1	0	6	0	0	0	.500	.176
Guevara, Giomar, Seattle........	.000	2	0	0	0	0	0	0	0	0	0	0	0	0	0	0	0	1	0	0	.000	.000
Halter, Shane, Kansas City	.000	4	0	0	1	0	0	0	0	0	0	0	0	0	0	0	0	1	0	0	.000	.000
Hamelin, Bob, Detroit*...........	.275	95	347	298	47	82	151	15	0	18	51	0	2	1	46	2	66	2	1	7	.507	.372
Hammonds, Jeffrey, Baltimore	.400	4	5	5	0	2	3	1	0	0	0	0	0	0	0	0	0	1	0	0	.600	.400
Hatteberg, Scott, Boston*......	.000	1	2	2	0	0	0	0	0	0	0	0	0	0	0	0	0	0	0	0	.000	.000
Henderson, Rickey, Anaheim .	.181	19	90	72	14	13	18	2	0	1	5	1	0	2	15	0	18	10	3	0	.250	.337
Higginson, Bobby, Detroit*	.000	1	1	1	0	0	0	0	0	0	0	0	0	0	0	0	1	0	0	0	.000	.000
Hocking, Denny, Minnesota† .	.000	1	1	1	0	0	0	0	0	0	0	0	0	0	0	0	1	0	0	0	.000	.000
Hoiles, Chris, Baltimore	.130	8	32	23	1	3	4	1	0	0	1	0	1	0	8	1	6	0	0	0	.174	.344
Howard, David, Kansas City†.	.000	5	0	0	2	0	0	0	0	0	0	0	0	0	0	0	0	0	0	0	.000	.000
Howell, Jack, Anaheim*	.264	22	80	72	12	19	45	2	0	8	15	1	1	0	6	1	11	0	0	1	.625	.316
Hurst, Jimmy, Detroit.............	.000	1	1	0	0	0	0	0	0	0	0	0	0	0	1	0	0	0	0	0	.000	1.000
Huson, Jeff, Milwaukee*	.000	4	5	4	0	0	0	0	0	0	0	0	0	1	0	0	1	0	0	0	.000	.200
Ibanez, Raul, Seattle*	.000	1	1	1	0	0	0	0	0	0	0	0	0	0	0	0	0	0	0	0	.000	.000
Incaviglia, Pete, Bal.-N.Y.	.239	31	115	109	12	26	37	2	0	3	8	0	0	3	3	1	32	0	0	0	.339	.278
Jaha, John, Milwaukee...........	.200	20	83	70	10	14	33	1	0	6	13	0	0	1	12	0	19	0	0	2	.471	.325
Jefferson, Reggie, Boston*....	.325	119	481	452	68	147	217	29	1	13	62	0	2	6	21	3	86	1	2	15	.480	.362
Johnson, Brian, Detroit..........	.000	2	2	2	0	0	0	0	0	0	0	0	0	0	0	0	1	0	0	0	.000	.000
Justice, David, Cleveland*	.333	61	258	231	34	77	129	10	0	14	41	0	1	0	26	3	41	2	2	4	.558	.399
Kelly, Pat, New York...............	.000	16	2	2	5	0	0	0	0	0	0	0	0	0	0	0	1	3	0	0	.000	.000
Kelly, Roberto, Min.-Sea.	.250	13	49	44	3	11	17	3	0	1	10	0	2	1	2	0	9	1	2	1	.386	.286
King, Jeff, Kansas City...........	.200	2	12	10	1	2	5	0	0	1	6	0	1	0	1	0	5	0	0	0	.500	.250
Knoblauch, Chuck, Minnesota	.250	1	5	4	1	1	1	0	0	0	1	0	0	0	1	1	0	1	0	0	.250	.400
Kreuter, Chad, Anaheim†	1.000	2	2	1	1	1	2	1	0	0	0	0	0	0	1	0	0	0	0	0	2.000	1.000
Lennon, Patrick, Oakland	.346	17	30	26	3	9	12	3	0	0	4	0	0	0	4	0	4	0	0	2	.462	.433
Lesher, Brian, Oakland...........	.000	3	5	4	1	0	0	0	0	0	0	0	0	0	1	0	0	1	0	0	.000	.200
Levis, Jesse, Milwaukee*........	.333	8	24	21	1	7	7	0	0	0	0	0	0	0	3	0	1	0	0	0	.333	.417
Lewis, Darren, Chicago...........	.000	6	3	3	2	0	0	0	0	0	0	0	0	0	0	0	0	1	0	0	.000	.000
Leyritz, Jim, Ana.-Tex.............	.159	22	88	69	8	11	14	0	0	1	9	0	2	2	15	0	20	0	0	2	.203	.318
Long, Ryan, Kansas City	.000	1	0	0	1	0	0	0	0	0	0	0	0	0	0	0	0	0	0	0	.000	.000
Loretta, Mark, Milwaukee.......	.000	1	0	0	0	0	0	0	0	0	0	0	0	0	0	0	0	0	0	0	.000	.000
Mack, Shane, Boston	.000	5	3	2	2	0	0	0	0	0	0	0	0	0	1	0	1	0	0	0	.000	.333
Magadan, Dave, Oakland*......	.310	25	108	87	18	27	37	5	1	1	12	1	0	1	19	1	10	0	0	2	.425	.439
Martin, Norberto, Chicago......	.429	6	15	14	2	6	6	0	0	0	2	0	0	0	1	0	1	1	0	0	.429	.467
Martinez, Dave, Chicago*	.000	1	0	0	0	0	0	0	0	0	0	0	0	0	0	0	0	0	0	0	.000	.000
Martinez, Edgar, Seattle	.326	144	644	513	97	167	271	33	1	23	100	0	5	11	115	11	82	2	4	19	.528	.455
Martinez, Mata, Kansas City†.	.000	2	0	0	0	0	0	0	0	0	0	0	0	0	0	0	0	0	0	0	.000	.000
Martinez, Tino, New York*	.261	7	25	23	1	6	10	1	0	1	5	0	1	0	1	0	2	0	0	0	.435	.280
Marzano, John, Seattle	.000	1	1	1	0	0	0	0	0	0	0	0	0	0	0	0	0	0	0	0	.000	.000
Merced, Orlando, Toronto*	.000	1	4	4	0	0	0	0	0	0	0	0	0	0	0	0	1	0	0	0	.000	.000
Mieske, Matt, Milwaukee........	.250	5	8	8	2	2	2	0	0	0	0	0	0	0	0	0	1	0	0	2	.250	.250
Miller, Damian, Minnesota	.200	3	10	10	0	2	2	0	0	0	0	0	0	0	0	0	3	0	0	0	.200	.200
Miller, Orlando, Detroit...........	.136	11	22	22	2	3	8	0	1	1	2	0	0	0	0	0	6	0	0	0	.364	.136
Mitchell, Kevin, Cleveland	.164	16	65	55	7	9	22	1	0	4	11	0	0	1	9	2	10	1	0	2	.400	.292
Molitor, Paul, Minnesota........	.303	122	544	489	54	148	210	30	4	8	80	2	12	0	41	7	69	10	4	8	.429	.349
Mouton, Lyle, Chicago	.267	11	31	30	5	8	12	1	0	1	3	0	0	0	1	0	7	0	1	2	.400	.290
Murray, Eddie, Anaheim†.......	.220	45	175	159	13	35	51	7	0	3	15	0	3	0	13	0	24	1	0	8	.321	.274
Myers, Greg, Minnesota*.......	.238	10	24	21	2	5	5	0	0	0	1	0	1	0	2	0	2	0	0	0	.238	.292
Naehring, Tim, Boston	.000	1	1	1	0	0	0	0	0	0	0	0	0	0	0	0	1	0	0	0	.000	.000
Nevin, Phil, Detroit................	.243	30	84	74	9	18	30	6	0	2	13	0	1	0	9	1	19	0	0	1	.405	.321
Newfield, Marc, Milwaukee	.183	18	66	60	3	11	13	2	0	0	4	0	2	1	3	0	14	0	0	1	.217	.227
Newson, Warren, Texas*........	.125	9	13	8	0	1	1	0	0	0	0	0	0	0	5	0	4	0	0	1	.125	.462

Player, Team	Avg.	G	TPA	AB	R	H	TB	2B	3B	HR	RBI	SH	SF	HP	BB	IBB	SO	SB	CS	GDP	Slg.	OBP
Nieves, Melvin, Detroit†	.303	12	38	33	6	10	17	1	0	2	9	0	0	0	5	2	19	0	1	0	.515	.395
Nilsson, Dave, Milwaukee*	.274	59	240	215	20	59	81	13	0	3	28	0	5	1	19	1	42	0	2	2	.377	.329
Nixon, Otis, Toronto†	.500	1	4	4	1	2	2	0	0	0	0	0	0	0	0	0	0	0	0	0	.500	.500
Norton, Greg, Chicago†	.000	2	1	1	0	0	0	0	0	0	0	0	0	0	0	0	0	0	0	0	.000	.000
Offerman, Jose, Kansas City†	.000	1	5	4	1	0	0	0	0	0	0	0	0	0	1	0	1	0	0	0	.000	.200
O'Leary, Troy, Boston*	.000	1	1	1	0	0	0	0	0	0	0	0	0	0	0	0	0	0	0	0	.000	.000
O'Neill, Paul, New York*	.250	2	4	4	0	1	1	0	0	0	0	0	0	0	0	0	1	0	0	0	.250	.250
Ortiz, David, Minnesota*	.400	1	5	5	0	2	2	0	0	0	1	0	0	0	0	0	2	0	0	0	.400	.400
Palmeiro, Orlando, Anaheim*	.313	11	18	16	4	5	7	0	1	0	1	0	1	0	1	1	1	0	0	1	.438	.333
Palmeiro, Rafael, Baltimore*	.333	3	14	12	2	4	5	1	0	0	1	0	0	0	2	0	2	1	1	0	.417	.429
Palmer, Dean, Kansas City	.000	1	1	0	0	0	0	0	0	0	0	0	0	0	1	0	0	0	0	0	.000	1.000
Perez, Robert, Toronto	.118	7	17	17	1	2	5	0	0	1	1	0	0	0	0	0	3	0	0	2	.294	.118
Phillips, Tony, Anaheim†	.245	26	126	110	17	27	36	6	0	1	14	1	2	0	13	1	19	1	3	2	.327	.320
Pose, Scott, New York*	.333	5	3	3	1	1	1	0	0	0	1	0	0	0	0	0	0	0	0	0	.333	.333
Pride, Curtis, Detroit*	.210	23	71	62	8	13	17	2	1	0	6	0	0	0	9	0	14	1	2	2	.274	.310
Raines, Tim, New York†	.364	13	65	55	15	20	34	8	0	2	14	0	2	0	8	0	4	1	0	1	.618	.431
Ramirez, Manny, Cleveland	.625	4	18	16	4	10	16	3	0	1	3	0	0	0	2	0	1	0	0	0	1.000	.667
Reboulet, Jeff, Baltimore	.000	1	0	0	0	0	0	0	0	0	0	0	0	0	0	0	0	0	0	0	.000	.000
Reed, Jody, Detroit	.167	5	8	6	0	1	1	0	0	0	2	1	1	0	0	0	0	0	0	0	.167	.143
Rodriguez, Alex, Seattle	.400	1	5	5	1	2	2	0	0	0	2	0	0	0	0	0	1	0	0	0	.400	.400
Rodriguez, Ivan, Texas	.350	5	21	20	1	7	7	0	0	0	2	0	0	0	1	0	5	0	0	1	.350	.381
Rohrmeier, Dan, Seattle	.333	4	7	6	2	2	2	0	0	0	1	0	0	0	1	0	2	0	0	0	.333	.429
Rosado, Jose, Kansas City*	.000	1	0	0	0	0	0	0	0	0	0	0	0	0	0	0	0	0	0	0	.000	.000
Sagmoen, Marc, Texas*	.000	1	0	0	0	0	0	0	0	0	0	0	0	0	0	0	0	0	0	0	.000	.000
Salmon, Tim, Anaheim	.214	4	18	14	3	3	7	1	0	1	1	0	0	0	4	0	2	0	0	0	.500	.389
Samuel, Juan, Toronto	.220	15	44	41	3	9	10	1	0	0	2	0	0	0	3	0	11	2	1	2	.244	.273
Sanders, Scott, Detroit	.000	1	0	0	0	0	0	0	0	0	0	0	0	0	0	0	0	0	0	0	.000	.000
Santiago, Benito, Toronto	.333	1	3	3	0	1	1	0	0	0	0	0	0	0	0	0	2	0	0	0	.333	.333
Seitzer, Kevin, Cleveland	.272	24	102	92	10	25	31	6	0	0	13	1	2	0	7	0	12	0	0	5	.337	.317
Sexson, Richie, Cleveland	.000	1	1	1	0	0	0	0	0	0	0	0	0	0	0	0	0	0	0	0	.000	.000
Sierra, Ruben, Toronto†	.200	6	21	20	1	4	8	0	2	0	3	0	0	0	1	0	5	0	0	0	.400	.238
Simms, Mike, Texas	.222	28	66	63	6	14	29	6	0	3	10	0	0	0	3	0	17	0	0	1	.460	.258
Sorrento, Paul, Seattle*	.333	1	3	3	0	1	1	0	0	0	2	0	0	0	0	0	1	0	0	0	.333	.333
Sprague, Ed Jr., Toronto	.241	8	33	29	1	7	10	0	0	1	3	0	0	1	3	0	6	0	0	0	.345	.333
Stahoviak, Scott, Minnesota*	.176	5	17	17	2	3	4	1	0	0	2	0	0	0	0	0	5	0	0	0	.235	.176
Stairs, Matt, Oakland*	.250	17	66	56	6	14	22	2	0	2	13	0	2	0	8	0	13	2	1	1	.393	.333
Stanley, Mike, Bos.-N.Y.	.264	69	218	182	26	48	80	11	0	7	28	0	4	5	27	2	46	0	0	7	.440	.367
Steinbach, Terry, Minnesota	.000	1	3	3	0	0	0	0	0	0	0	0	0	0	0	0	1	0	0	1	.000	.000
Stevens, Lee, Texas*	.276	38	134	127	14	35	59	7	1	5	18	1	2	0	4	1	25	0	0	2	.465	.293
Stewart, Andy, Kansas City	.000	1	2	2	0	0	0	0	0	0	0	0	0	0	0	0	0	0	0	0	.000	.000
Stewart, Shannon, Toronto	.000	1	2	2	0	0	0	0	0	0	0	0	0	0	0	0	0	0	0	0	.000	.000
Stinnett, Kelly, Milwaukee	.333	1	3	3	1	1	1	0	0	0	0	0	0	0	0	0	0	0	0	0	.333	.333
Strawberry, Darryl, New York*	.143	4	14	14	1	2	3	1	0	0	2	0	0	0	0	0	7	0	0	0	.214	.143
Surhoff, B.J., Baltimore*	.226	9	34	31	5	7	16	1	1	2	3	0	0	0	3	1	5	0	0	1	.516	.294
Sutton, Larry, Kansas City*	.364	3	11	11	3	4	5	1	0	0	0	0	0	0	0	0	2	0	0	0	.455	.364
Sweeney, Mike, Kansas City	.250	3	8	8	0	2	3	1	0	0	0	0	0	0	0	0	1	0	0	0	.375	.250
Tarasco, Tony, Baltimore*	.000	2	0	0	1	0	0	0	0	0	0	0	0	0	0	0	0	0	0	0	.000	.000
Tavarez, Jesus, Boston†	.333	2	3	3	2	1	3	0	1	0	2	0	0	0	0	0	1	0	0	0	1.000	.333
Tettleton, Mickey, Texas†	.075	13	44	40	5	3	12	0	0	3	4	0	0	1	3	1	11	0	0	1	.300	.159
Thomas, Frank, Chicago	.314	49	214	175	35	55	89	10	0	8	30	0	1	1	37	3	20	0	0	6	.509	.435
Tinsley, Lee, Seattle†	.000	5	0	0	1	0	0	0	0	0	0	0	0	0	0	0	0	0	0	0	.000	.000
Trammell, Bubba, Detroit	.211	14	46	38	6	8	14	3	0	1	4	0	2	0	6	0	11	0	0	2	.368	.304
Turner, Chris, Anaheim	.000	1	1	1	0	0	0	0	0	0	0	0	0	0	0	0	0	0	0	0	.000	.000
Valdez, Mario, Chicago*	.000	2	1	1	0	0	0	0	0	0	0	0	0	0	0	0	1	0	0	0	.000	.000
Valentin, Jose, Milwaukee†	.400	1	5	5	1	2	2	0	0	0	0	0	0	0	0	0	0	0	0	0	.400	.400
Vaughn, Mo, Boston*	.235	9	38	34	3	8	9	1	0	0	5	0	0	0	4	1	12	0	0	1	.265	.316
Vina, Fernando, Milwaukee*	.000	1	5	5	0	0	0	0	0	0	0	0	0	0	0	0	2	0	0	0	.000	.000
Vitiello, Joe, Kansas City	.256	12	43	39	3	10	17	1	0	2	6	0	0	1	3	0	11	0	0	1	.436	.326
Voigt, Jack, Milwaukee	.000	1	4	3	0	0	0	0	0	0	0	0	0	0	1	0	1	0	0	0	.000	.250
Walker, Todd, Minnesota*	.000	2	3	3	0	0	0	0	0	0	0	0	0	0	0	0	2	0	0	0	.000	.000
Walton, Jerome, Baltimore	.250	2	4	4	0	1	1	0	0	0	0	0	0	0	0	0	1	0	0	0	.250	.250
Webster, Lenny, Baltimore	.000	1	1	1	0	0	0	0	0	0	1	0	0	0	0	0	0	0	0	0	.000	.000
Whiten, Mark, New York†	.400	7	19	15	5	6	7	1	0	0	0	0	0	1	3	0	1	0	0	2	.467	.526
Wilkins, Rick, Seattle*	.333	2	7	6	1	2	6	1	0	1	4	0	1	0	0	0	2	0	0	0	1.000	.286
Williams, George, Oakland†	.000	1	1	0	0	0	0	0	0	0	0	0	0	0	1	0	0	0	0	0	.000	1.000
Williams, Gerald, Milwaukee	.000	1	0	0	0	0	0	0	0	0	0	0	0	0	0	0	0	0	0	0	.000	.000
Williamson, Antone, Mil.*	.364	4	13	11	0	4	5	1	0	0	0	1	0	0	1	0	2	0	0	0	.455	.417
Young, Ernie, Oakland	.000	1	1	1	0	0	0	0	0	0	0	0	0	0	0	0	0	0	0	0	.000	.000

DESIGNATED HITTERS WITH TWO OR MORE TEAMS

Player, Team	Avg.	G	TPA	AB	R	H	TB	2B	3B	HR	RBI	SH	SF	HP	BB	IBB	SO	SB	CS	GDP	Slg.	OBP
Baines, Harold, Chicago*	.304	86	355	312	39	95	146	18	0	11	49	0	2	0	41	10	47	0	1	8	.468	.383
Baines, Harold, Baltimore*	.264	35	140	125	14	33	49	4	0	4	13	0	1	0	14	1	15	0	0	2	.392	.336
Berroa, Geronimo, Oakland	.373	27	119	102	14	38	61	8	0	5	17	0	0	1	16	0	21	1	1	5	.598	.462
Berroa, Geronimo, Baltimore	.244	42	178	156	27	38	57	7	0	4	24	0	3	1	18	0	30	1	1	4	.365	.320
Franco, Julio, Cleveland	.295	42	181	166	28	49	69	9	1	3	14	0	0	0	15	0	36	3	2	4	.416	.354
Franco, Julio, Milwaukee	.295	28	121	95	19	28	40	3	0	3	16	0	4	0	22	2	27	6	1	2	.421	.413
Incaviglia, Pete, Baltimore	.237	26	99	93	11	22	33	2	0	3	8	0	0	3	3	1	29	0	0	0	.355	.283
Incaviglia, Pete, New York	.250	5	16	16	1	4	4	0	0	0	0	0	0	0	0	0	3	0	0	0	.250	.250
Kelly, Roberto, Minnesota	.262	12	47	42	3	11	17	3	0	1	10	0	2	1	2	0	8	1	2	0	.405	.298
Kelly, Roberto, Seattle	.000	1	2	2	0	0	0	0	0	0	0	0	0	0	0	0	1	0	0	1	.000	.000
Leyritz, Jim, Anaheim	.186	13	49	43	3	8	11	0	0	1	3	0	1	0	5	0	11	0	0	1	.256	.265
Leyritz, Jim, Texas	.115	9	39	26	5	3	3	0	0	0	6	0	1	2	10	0	9	0	0	1	.115	.385
Stanley, Mike, Boston	.289	53	154	128	17	37	65	7	0	7	26	0	3	5	18	0	27	0	0	5	.508	.390
Stanley, Mike, New York	.204	16	64	54	9	11	15	4	0	0	2	0	1	0	9	2	19	0	0	2	.278	.313

The following designated hitters, each of whom appeared in at least one game, had no plate appearances, runs scored or stolen base attempts: Damon, Johnny, Kansas City (5); Tinsley, Lee, Seattle (5); Cameron, Mike, Chicago (4); Howard, David, Kansas City (4); Bartee, Kimera, Detroit (3); Gil, Benji, Texas (3); Halter, Shane, Kansas City (3); Fox, Andy, New York (2); Grebeck, Craig, Anaheim (2); Martinez, Felix, Kansas City (2); Tarasco, Tony, Baltimore (2); Bones, Ricky, Kansas City; Bush, Homer, New York; Fonville, Chad, Chicago; Guevara, Giomar, Seattle; Long, Ryan, Kansas City; Loretta, Mark, Milwaukee; Martinez, Dave, Chicago; Rosado, Jose, Kansas City; Sagmoen, Marc, Texas; Sanders, Scott, Detroit; Williams, Gerald, Milwaukee; Garciaparra, Nomar, Boston.

PINCH-HITTING

TEAM

Team	Avg.	G	TPA	AB	R	H	TB	2B	3B	HR	RBI	SH	SF	HP	BB	IBB	SO	SB	CS	GDP	Slg.	OBP
Oakland	.345	113	195	165	21	57	70	4	0	3	31	0	1	3	26	1	37	1	0	4	.424	.441
Boston	.291	77	119	103	17	30	51	6	0	5	21	0	3	0	13	0	23	0	0	6	.495	.361
Minnesota	.250	89	157	140	15	35	49	8	0	2	17	2	1	1	13	1	39	4	2	8	.350	.316
Texas	.241	94	156	137	15	33	58	5	1	6	33	0	3	2	14	5	46	0	0	2	.423	.314
Milwaukee	.231	104	180	160	8	37	52	7	1	2	19	1	0	0	19	4	27	3	0	6	.325	.313
Detroit	.227	96	152	132	12	30	48	6	0	4	18	2	2	0	16	3	46	1	2	3	.364	.307
Baltimore	.222	76	99	90	10	20	28	5	0	1	11	0	1	0	8	2	23	1	0	3	.311	.283
Kansas City	.213	91	152	127	14	27	41	5	0	3	13	2	1	1	21	4	47	0	0	2	.323	.327
Anaheim	.211	63	82	71	9	15	20	5	0	0	8	1	1	0	9	2	19	0	0	1	.282	.296
Seattle	.208	87	146	125	17	26	46	4	2	4	20	2	3	0	16	1	35	0	0	3	.368	.292
New York	.194	57	74	62	8	12	17	2	0	1	8	0	0	0	12	1	17	0	0	4	.274	.324
Cleveland	.192	64	84	73	4	14	22	2	0	2	13	1	1	0	9	0	16	2	0	0	.301	.277
Chicago	.159	85	122	113	7	18	29	3	1	2	13	0	0	0	9	0	33	0	1	1	.257	.221
Toronto	.127	47	70	63	8	8	15	2	1	1	8	0	1	0	6	1	25	0	0	0	.238	.200
Totals	.232	1143	1788	1561	165	362	546	64	6	36	233	11	18	7	191	25	433	12	5	43	.350	.315

TOP PINCH-HITTERS

Minimum 20 at-bats. *Lefthanded batter. †Switch-hitter.

Player, Team	Avg.	G	TPA	AB	R	H	TB	2B	3B	HR	RBI	SH	SF	HP	BB	IBB	SO	SB	CS	GDP	Slg.	OBP
Stanley, Mike, Bos.-N.Y.	.357	34	34	28	5	10	19	3	0	2	9	0	2	0	4	0	5	0	0	2	.679	.412
Stairs, Matt, Oakland*	.353	42	41	34	6	12	15	0	0	1	5	0	0	2	5	1	6	0	0	0	.441	.463
Sorrento, Paul, Seattle*	.304	25	25	23	4	7	14	1	0	2	6	0	0	0	2	0	10	0	0	1	.609	.360
Stevens, Lee, Texas*	.304	27	26	23	3	7	12	2	0	1	6	0	0	0	3	1	5	0	0	1	.522	.385
Simms, Mike, Texas	.300	23	22	20	4	6	13	1	0	2	10	0	1	0	1	0	6	0	0	0	.650	.318
Magadan, Dave, Oakland*	.289	53	52	45	4	13	13	0	0	0	8	0	1	0	6	0	10	0	0	2	.289	.365
Pride, Curtis, Det.-Bos.*	.250	34	29	24	2	6	10	1	0	1	2	0	1	0	4	0	9	0	0	0	.417	.345
Levis, Jesse, Milwaukee*	.244	49	48	45	2	11	12	1	0	0	3	1	0	0	2	0	5	1	0	1	.267	.277
Huson, Jeff, Milwaukee*	.235	39	35	34	1	8	10	2	0	0	4	0	0	0	1	0	4	1	0	2	.294	.257
Amaral, Rich, Seattle	.200	23	23	20	3	4	5	1	0	0	2	1	1	0	1	0	4	0	0	1	.250	.227
Cooper, Scott, Kansas City*	.172	35	34	29	2	5	8	0	0	1	1	0	0	0	5	0	11	0	0	1	.276	.294
Howell, Jack, Anaheim*	.143	26	24	21	0	3	5	2	0	0	3	0	1	0	2	1	11	0	0	1	.238	.208
Newson, Warren, Texas*	.125	32	30	24	2	3	7	1	0	1	4	0	1	0	5	1	13	0	0	0	.292	.267

ALL PINCH-HITTERS

*Lefthanded batter. †Switch-hitter.

Player, Team	Avg.	G	TPA	AB	R	H	TB	2B	3B	HR	RBI	SH	SF	HP	BB	IBB	SO	SB	CS	GDP	Slg.	OBP
Abbott, Jeff, Chicago	.000	8	7	7	0	0	0	0	0	0	0	0	0	0	0	0	3	0	0	0	.000	.000
Alicea, Luis, Anaheim†	.000	8	8	8	0	0	0	0	0	0	0	0	0	0	0	0	2	0	0	0	.000	.000
Alomar, Roberto, Baltimore†.	.400	8	5	5	2	2	3	1	0	0	0	0	0	0	0	0	1	0	0	0	.600	.400
Alomar, Sandy Jr., Cleveland..	.143	7	7	7	0	1	1	0	0	0	0	0	0	0	0	0	1	0	0	0	.143	.143
Amaral, Rich, Seattle	.200	23	23	20	3	4	5	1	0	0	2	1	1	0	1	0	4	0	0	1	.250	.227
Anderson, Brady, Baltimore* .	.000	3	2	2	0	0	0	0	0	0	0	0	0	0	0	0	2	0	0	0	.000	.000
Anderson, Garret, Anaheim* ..	.500	2	2	2	1	1	2	1	0	0	0	0	0	0	0	0	0	0	0	0	1.000	.500
Arias, George, Anaheim	.000	2	2	2	0	0	0	0	0	0	0	0	0	0	0	0	0	0	0	0	.000	.000
Avery, Steve, Boston*	.000	1	1	1	0	0	0	0	0	0	0	0	0	0	0	0	0	0	0	0	.000	.000
Baines, Harold, Chi.-Bal.*	.533	16	15	15	2	8	12	1	0	1	5	0	0	0	0	0	1	0	0	1	.800	.533
Banks, Brian, Milwaukee†	.125	8	8	8	0	1	1	0	0	0	0	0	0	0	0	0	1	0	0	0	.125	.125
Bartee, Kimera, Detroit†	.000	2	2	1	0	0	0	0	0	0	0	0	0	1	0	0	1	0	0	0	.000	.500
Batista, Tony, Oakland	.000	3	3	3	0	0	0	0	0	0	0	0	0	0	0	0	2	0	0	0	.000	.000
Becker, Rich, Minnesota	.455	11	11	11	1	5	6	1	0	0	0	0	0	0	0	0	2	1	1	0	.545	.455
Bell, Jay, Kansas City	.000	5	5	4	0	0	0	0	0	0	0	0	0	0	1	0	1	0	0	0	.000	.000
Bellhorn, Mark, Oakland†	.556	9	9	9	2	5	9	1	0	1	3	0	0	0	0	0	3	0	0	0	1.000	.556
Benitez, Yamil, Kansas City	.000	1	1	1	0	0	0	0	0	0	0	0	0	0	0	0	1	0	0	0	.000	.000
Benjamin, Mike, Boston	.000	2	2	2	0	0	0	0	0	0	0	0	0	0	0	0	1	0	0	0	.000	.000
Berroa, Geronimo, Oak.-Bal. ..	.500	8	8	6	0	3	3	0	0	0	0	0	0	0	2	0	0	0	0	0	.500	.625
Blowers, Mike, Seattle	.214	18	18	14	2	3	3	0	0	0	2	0	1	0	3	0	4	0	0	0	.214	.333
Boggs, Wade, New York*	.000	14	14	13	0	0	0	0	0	0	0	0	0	0	1	1	4	0	0	0	.000	.071
Bournigal, Rafael, Oakland	.333	3	3	3	0	1	1	0	0	0	0	0	0	0	0	0	0	0	0	1	.333	.333
Bragg, Darren, Boston*	.222	11	11	9	2	2	3	1	0	0	0	0	0	0	2	0	1	0	0	1	.333	.364
Branson, Jeff, Cleveland*	.250	4	4	4	0	1	1	0	0	0	0	0	1	0	0	0	1	0	0	0	.250	.250
Brede, Brent, Minnesota*	.250	9	8	8	0	2	3	1	0	0	2	0	0	0	0	0	3	0	0	1	.375	.250
Brito, Tilson, Toronto	.000	1	1	0	0	0	0	0	0	0	0	0	1	0	0	0	0	0	0	0	.000	.000
Brosius, Scott, Oakland	.000	3	3	2	0	0	0	0	0	0	0	0	0	0	1	0	1	0	0	0	.000	.333
Brown, Kevin L., Texas	.000	1	1	1	0	0	0	0	0	0	0	0	0	0	0	0	1	0	0	0	.000	.000
Brumfield, Jacob, Toronto	.000	9	9	8	1	0	0	0	0	0	0	0	0	0	1	0	3	0	0	0	.000	.111
Buford, Damon, Texas	.000	4	4	4	0	0	0	0	0	0	0	0	0	0	0	0	2	0	0	0	.000	.000
Buhner, Jay, Seattle	.500	3	3	2	0	1	1	0	0	0	0	0	0	0	1	0	0	0	0	0	.500	.667
Burnitz, Jeromy, Milwaukee* .	.364	14	12	11	2	4	11	1	0	2	6	0	0	0	1	0	1	0	0	0	1.000	.417
Bush, Homer, New York	.500	2	2	2	1	1	1	0	0	0	0	0	0	0	0	0	1	0	0	0	.500	.500
Butler, Rich, Toronto*	.000	3	3	3	0	0	0	0	0	0	0	0	0	0	0	0	1	0	0	0	.000	.000
Cameron, Mike, Chicago	.000	1	1	1	0	0	0	0	0	0	0	0	0	0	0	0	1	0	0	0	.000	.000
Candaele, Casey, Cleveland† ..	.200	6	6	5	1	1	1	0	0	0	0	0	0	0	1	0	0	0	0	0	.200	.333
Canseco, Jose, Oakland	.000	4	4	4	0	0	0	0	0	0	0	0	0	0	0	0	4	0	0	0	.000	.000

Player, Team	Avg.	G	TPA	AB	R	H	TB	2B	3B	HR	RBI	SH	SF	HP	BB	IBB	SO	SB	CS	GDP	Slg.	OBP
Carr, Chuck, Milwaukee†	.000	2	2	1	0	0	0	0	0	0	0	0	0	0	1	0	0	0	0	0	.000	.500
Casanova, Raul, Detroit†	.182	13	13	11	3	2	3	1	0	0	0	0	0	0	2	0	7	0	0	1	.273	.308
Casey, Sean, Cleveland*	.667	3	3	3	1	2	2	0	0	0	0	0	0	0	0	0	0	0	0	0	.667	.667
Catalanotto, Frank, Detroit*	.000	6	6	5	0	0	0	0	0	0	0	0	0	0	1	0	2	0	0	0	.000	.167
Cedeno, Domingo, Texas†	.353	18	18	17	4	6	11	0	1	1	2	0	0	1	0	0	6	0	0	0	.647	.389
Cirillo, Jeff, Milwaukee	.000	4	4	4	0	0	0	0	0	0	0	0	0	0	0	0	1	0	0	0	.000	.000
Clark, Will, Texas*	.167	6	6	6	0	1	1	0	0	0	0	0	0	0	0	0	3	0	0	0	.167	.167
Clyburn, Danny, Baltimore	.000	1	1	1	0	0	0	0	0	0	0	0	0	0	0	0	0	0	0	0	.000	.000
Colbrunn, Greg, Minnesota	.250	16	16	16	2	4	7	0	0	1	4	0	0	0	0	0	4	0	0	1	.438	.250
Coleman, Vince, Detroit†	.000	4	4	4	0	0	0	0	0	0	0	0	0	0	0	0	0	0	0	0	.000	.000
Coomer, Ron, Minnesota	.000	9	9	7	0	0	0	0	0	0	0	0	0	0	2	1	4	0	0	0	.000	.222
Cooper, Scott, Kansas City*	.172	35	34	29	2	5	8	0	0	1	1	0	0	0	5	0	11	0	0	1	.276	.294
Cora, Joey, Seattle†	.143	11	11	7	0	1	2	1	0	0	0	0	0	0	4	1	0	0	0	0	.286	.455
Cordero, Wilfredo, Boston	.000	2	2	2	0	0	0	0	0	0	0	0	0	0	0	0	0	0	0	0	.000	.000
Cordova, Marty, Minnesota	.000	2	2	1	0	0	0	0	0	0	0	0	0	0	1	0	0	0	0	0	.000	.500
Crespo, Felipe, Toronto†	.333	3	3	3	1	1	1	0	0	0	2	0	0	0	0	0	0	0	0	0	.333	.333
Cruz, Ivan, New York*	.250	5	5	4	0	1	1	0	0	0	0	0	0	0	1	0	0	0	0	0	.250	.400
Cruz, Jose Jr., Seattle†	.000	1	1	1	0	0	0	0	0	0	0	0	0	0	0	0	0	0	0	0	.000	.000
Curtis, Chad, Cle.-N.Y.	.000	4	4	2	1	0	0	0	0	0	0	0	0	0	2	0	0	0	0	0	.000	.500
Damon, Johnny, Kansas City*	.143	8	8	7	1	1	4	0	0	1	1	1	0	0	0	0	0	0	0	0	.571	.143
Davis, Chili, Kansas City†	.167	9	9	6	0	1	1	0	0	0	1	0	1	0	2	0	4	0	0	0	.167	.333
Davis, Eric, Baltimore	.000	1	1	1	0	0	0	0	0	0	0	0	0	0	0	0	0	0	0	0	.000	.000
Davis, Russ, Seattle	.333	3	3	3	1	1	4	0	0	1	2	0	0	0	0	0	1	0	0	0	1.333	.333
Delgado, Carlos, Toronto*	.267	15	15	15	2	4	5	1	0	0	0	0	0	0	0	0	6	0	0	0	.333	.267
Dellucci, Dave, Baltimore*	.250	4	4	4	0	1	1	0	0	0	0	0	0	0	0	0	2	0	0	1	.250	.250
Devereaux, Mike, Texas	.000	4	4	4	0	0	0	0	0	0	0	0	0	0	0	0	0	0	0	0	.000	.000
Diaz, Alex, Texas†	.143	7	7	7	0	1	1	0	0	0	2	0	0	0	0	0	1	0	0	0	.143	.143
Diaz, Eddy, Milwaukee	.500	2	2	2	0	1	1	0	0	0	0	0	0	0	0	0	0	0	0	0	.500	.500
DiSarcina, Gary, Anaheim	.000	1	1	1	0	0	0	0	0	0	0	0	0	0	0	0	0	0	0	0	.000	.000
Ducey, Rob, Seattle*	.091	12	11	11	1	1	3	0	1	0	0	0	0	0	0	0	3	0	0	0	.273	.091
Duncan, Mariano, New York	.000	1	0	0	0	0	0	0	0	0	0	0	0	0	0	0	0	0	0	0	.000	.000
Dunn, Todd, Milwaukee	.333	3	3	3	0	1	1	0	0	0	0	0	0	0	0	0	1	0	0	0	.333	.333
Durham, Ray, Chicago†	.000	1	1	0	0	0	0	0	0	0	0	0	0	0	1	0	0	0	0	0	.000	1.000
Dye, Jermaine, Kansas City	.500	4	4	4	1	2	2	0	0	0	0	0	0	0	0	0	0	0	0	0	.500	.500
Easley, Damion, Detroit	.286	8	8	7	1	2	2	0	0	0	0	0	0	0	1	0	3	0	0	0	.286	.375
Edmonds, Jim, Anaheim*	.000	3	3	3	0	0	0	0	0	0	0	0	0	0	0	0	0	0	0	0	.000	.000
Eenhoorn, Robert, Anaheim	1.000	1	1	1	0	1	1	0	0	0	1	0	0	0	0	0	0	0	0	0	1.000	1.000
Erstad, Darin, Anaheim*	.667	5	4	3	0	2	3	1	0	0	4	0	0	0	1	0	0	0	0	0	1.000	.750
Espinoza, Alvaro, Seattle	.250	4	4	4	0	1	1	0	0	0	0	0	0	0	0	0	1	0	0	0	.250	.250
Fabregas, Jorge, Chicago*	.083	12	12	12	0	1	1	0	0	0	4	0	0	0	0	0	4	0	0	0	.083	.083
Fasano, Sal, Kansas City	.500	2	2	2	1	1	1	0	0	0	0	0	0	0	0	0	0	0	0	0	.500	.500
Fernandez, Tony, Cleveland†	.167	6	6	6	0	1	1	0	0	0	0	0	0	0	0	0	1	0	0	0	.167	.167
Fielder, Cecil, New York	.000	2	2	2	0	0	0	0	0	0	0	0	0	0	0	0	0	0	0	1	.000	.000
Figga, Mike, New York	.000	1	1	1	0	0	0	0	0	0	0	0	0	0	0	0	1	0	0	0	.000	.000
Franco, Julio, Cle.-Mil.	.000	2	2	0	0	0	0	0	0	0	1	0	0	0	2	0	0	0	0	0	.000	1.000
Frias, Hanley, Texas†	.000	1	1	1	0	0	0	0	0	0	0	0	0	0	0	0	1	0	0	0	.000	.000
Frye, Jeff, Boston	.444	9	9	9	3	4	7	0	0	1	1	0	0	0	0	0	2	0	0	0	.778	.444
Fryman, Travis, Detroit	.000	1	1	1	0	0	0	0	0	0	0	0	0	0	0	0	0	0	0	0	.000	.000
Garcia, Carlos, Toronto	.000	2	2	2	0	0	0	0	0	0	0	0	0	0	0	0	1	0	0	0	.000	.000
Gates, Brent, Seattle†	.214	17	17	14	3	3	6	0	0	1	1	1	0	0	2	0	3	0	0	0	.429	.313
Giambi, Jason, Oakland*	.250	5	5	4	0	1	1	0	0	0	0	0	0	1	0	0	3	0	0	0	.250	.400
Giles, Brian, Cleveland*	.250	17	16	12	0	3	4	1	0	0	4	0	1	0	3	0	3	2	0	0	.333	.375
Goodwin, Tom, Texas*	.000	4	4	3	0	0	0	0	0	0	0	0	0	0	1	0	1	0	0	0	.000	.250
Grebeck, Craig, Anaheim	.250	7	6	4	2	1	1	0	0	0	0	0	0	1	1	0	1	0	0	0	.250	.400
Green, Shawn, Toronto*	.000	17	14	12	0	0	0	0	0	0	0	0	0	0	2	0	7	0	0	0	.000	.143
Greene, Charlie, Baltimore	.000	1	1	1	0	0	0	0	0	0	0	0	0	0	0	0	1	0	0	0	.000	.000
Greene, Todd, Anaheim	.000	1	1	0	0	0	0	0	0	0	0	0	0	0	1	1	0	0	0	0	.000	1.000
Greer, Rusty, Texas*	.333	3	3	3	1	1	4	0	0	1	3	0	0	0	0	0	1	0	0	0	1.333	.333
Grieve, Ben, Oakland*	.500	2	2	2	1	1	1	0	0	0	0	0	0	0	0	0	1	0	0	0	.500	.500
Guillen, Ozzie, Chicago*	.200	5	5	5	1	1	1	0	0	0	0	0	0	0	0	0	0	0	0	0	.200	.200
Hall, Joe, Detroit	.000	1	1	1	0	0	0	0	0	0	0	0	0	0	0	0	0	0	0	0	.000	.000
Halter, Shane, Kansas City	.000	5	5	4	0	0	0	0	0	0	0	0	0	0	1	0	3	0	0	0	.000	.200
Hamelin, Bob, Detroit*	.214	16	15	14	0	3	3	0	0	0	1	0	0	0	1	0	4	0	0	1	.214	.267
Hammonds, Jeffrey, Bal.	.333	8	8	6	2	2	2	0	0	0	0	0	0	0	2	1	2	0	0	0	.333	.500
Haselman, Bill, Boston	.000	1	1	0	0	0	0	0	0	0	0	0	0	0	0	0	0	0	0	0	.000	.000
Hatteberg, Scott, Boston*	.222	14	11	9	2	2	5	0	0	1	2	0	0	0	2	0	2	0	0	1	.556	.364
Hayes, Charlie, New York	.200	8	8	5	1	1	4	0	0	1	4	0	0	0	3	0	0	0	0	1	.800	.500
Higginson, Bobby, Detroit*	.500	4	4	4	0	2	2	0	0	0	1	0	0	0	0	0	1	0	0	0	.500	.500
Hocking, Denny, Minnesota†	.176	22	22	17	1	3	3	0	0	0	1	1	0	1	3	0	5	1	0	0	.176	.333
Hoiles, Chris, Baltimore	.000	1	1	1	0	0	0	0	0	0	0	0	0	0	0	0	1	0	0	0	.000	.000
Hollins, Dave, Anaheim†	.000	2	2	2	0	0	0	0	0	0	0	0	0	0	0	0	1	0	0	0	.000	.000
Howard, David, Kansas City†	.000	9	9	6	2	0	0	0	0	0	0	0	0	0	3	1	3	0	0	0	.000	.333
Howell, Jack, Anaheim*	.143	26	24	21	0	3	5	2	0	0	3	0	0	0	2	1	11	0	0	1	.238	.208
Hubbard, Trinidad, Cleveland	.000	1	1	1	0	0	0	0	0	0	0	0	0	0	0	0	1	0	0	0	.000	.000
Hurst, Jimmy, Detroit	.000	1	1	0	0	0	0	0	0	0	0	0	0	0	1	0	0	0	0	0	.000	1.000
Huson, Jeff, Milwaukee*	.235	39	35	34	1	8	10	2	0	0	4	0	0	0	0	0	4	1	0	2	.294	.257
Ibanez, Raul, Seattle*	.000	3	3	3	0	0	0	0	0	0	0	0	0	0	0	0	1	0	0	0	.000	.000
Incaviglia, Pete, Bal.-N.Y.	.154	13	13	13	1	2	3	1	0	0	0	0	0	0	0	0	5	0	0	0	.231	.154
Jackson, Darrin, Minnesota	.167	8	7	6	1	1	1	0	0	0	0	0	0	0	1	0	0	0	0	0	.167	.167
Jaha, John, Milwaukee	.000	1	1	1	0	0	0	0	0	0	0	0	0	0	0	0	0	0	0	0	.000	.000
Jefferson, Reggie, Boston*	.300	12	12	10	2	3	4	1	0	0	2	0	1	0	1	0	4	0	0	1	.400	.333
Johnson, Brian, Detroit	.000	2	2	2	0	0	0	0	0	0	0	0	0	0	0	0	1	0	0	0	.000	.000

Player, Team	Avg.	G	TPA	AB	R	H	TB	2B	3B	HR	RBI	SH	SF	HP	BB	IBB	SO	SB	CS	GDP	Slg.	OBP
Justice, David, Cleveland*	.333	4	4	3	1	1	4	0	0	1	2	0	0	0	1	0	0	0	0	1	1.333	.500
Kelly, Pat, New York..............	.667	3	3	3	0	2	3	1	0	0	0	0	0	0	0	0	0	0	0	1	1.000	.667
Kelly, Roberto, Min.-Sea.	.286	17	16	14	2	4	5	1	0	0	4	0	1	0	1	0	4	0	1	1	.357	.313
King, Jeff, Kansas City	.000	5	5	4	0	0	0	0	0	0	0	0	0	0	1	1	2	0	0	0	.000	.200
Kreuter, Chad, Chi.-Ana.†	.222	12	12	9	3	2	4	2	0	0	0	0	0	0	3	0	2	0	0	0	.444	.417
Latham, Chris, Minnesota†	.000	5	4	4	1	0	0	0	0	0	0	0	0	0	0	0	2	0	0	0	.000	.000
Lawton, Matt, Minnesota*	.250	13	12	8	3	2	3	1	0	0	0	0	0	0	4	0	1	1	0	0	.375	.500
Ledesma, Aaron, Baltimore......	.250	4	4	4	0	1	1	0	0	0	0	0	0	0	0	0	0	0	0	0	.250	.250
Lennon, Patrick, Oakland	.417	17	17	12	2	5	6	1	0	0	6	0	0	0	5	0	3	0	0	1	.500	.588
Lesher, Brian, Oakland	.250	9	9	8	0	2	3	1	0	0	2	0	0	0	1	0	1	0	0	0	.375	.333
Levis, Jesse, Milwaukee*	.244	49	48	45	2	11	12	1	0	0	3	1	0	0	2	0	5	1	0	1	.267	.277
Lewis, Darren, Chicago	.200	12	11	10	0	2	2	0	0	0	0	0	0	0	1	0	1	0	0	0	.200	.273
Leyritz, Jim, Ana.-Tex...........	.444	13	13	9	1	4	4	0	0	0	2	0	1	1	2	0	3	0	0	1	.444	.538
Loretta, Mark, Milwaukee.......	.000	6	6	5	0	0	0	0	0	0	0	0	0	0	1	0	2	0	0	0	.000	.167
Macfarlane, Mike, Kansas City.	.333	3	3	3	0	1	1	0	0	0	0	0	0	0	0	0	1	0	0	0	.333	.333
Machado, Robert, Chicago........	.000	2	1	1	0	0	0	0	0	0	0	0	0	0	0	0	1	0	0	0	.000	.000
Mack, Shane, Boston	.200	12	12	10	0	2	2	0	0	0	1	0	0	0	2	0	2	0	0	1	.200	.333
Magadan, Dave, Oakland*.......	.289	53	52	45	4	13	13	0	0	0	8	0	1	0	6	0	10	0	0	2	.289	.365
Manto, Jeff, Cleveland...........	.200	5	5	5	0	1	2	1	0	0	1	0	0	0	0	0	2	0	0	0	.400	.200
Martin, Norberto, Chicago........	.125	18	18	16	1	2	5	0	0	1	2	0	0	0	2	0	2	0	0	0	.313	.222
Martinez, Dave, Chicago*	.200	13	12	10	1	2	4	0	1	0	1	0	0	0	2	0	3	0	0	0	.400	.333
Martinez, Edgar, Seattle	.000	3	3	2	0	0	0	0	0	0	0	0	0	0	1	0	0	0	0	0	.000	.333
Martinez, Mata, Kansas City†....	.000	1	1	1	0	0	0	0	0	0	0	0	0	0	0	0	1	0	0	0	.000	.000
Martinez, Tino, New York*	.000	2	2	2	0	0	0	0	0	0	0	0	0	0	0	0	2	0	0	0	.000	.000
Marzano, John, Seattle	.200	5	5	5	0	1	2	1	0	0	1	0	0	0	0	0	2	0	0	0	.400	.200
Matheny, Mike, Milwaukee	1.000	1	1	1	0	1	3	0	1	0	0	0	0	0	0	0	0	0	0	0	3.000	1.000
Mayne, Brent, Oakland*	.571	7	7	7	1	4	4	0	0	0	0	0	0	0	0	0	0	0	0	0	.571	.571
McDonald, Jason, Oakland† ..	.333	10	10	6	2	2	2	0	0	0	0	0	0	0	4	0	0	0	0	0	.333	.600
McGwire, Mark, Oakland	1.000	4	4	4	1	4	7	0	0	1	2	0	0	0	0	0	0	0	0	0	1.750	1.000
McKeel, Walt, Boston............	.000	1	1	1	0	0	0	0	0	0	0	0	0	0	0	0	1	0	0	0	.000	.000
McLemore, Mark, Texas†.........	.000	1	1	0	0	0	0	0	0	0	0	0	0	0	1	1	0	0	0	0	.000	1.000
Meares, Pat, Minnesota	.000	2	2	2	0	0	0	0	0	0	0	1	0	0	0	0	1	0	0	0	.000	.000
Merced, Orlando, Toronto*	.000	3	3	2	1	0	0	0	0	0	0	0	0	0	1	1	0	0	0	0	.000	.333
Mieske, Matt, Milwaukee.......	.167	15	15	12	1	2	2	0	0	0	0	0	0	0	3	1	1	1	1	2	.167	.333
Miller, Damian, Minnesota	.000	2	2	2	0	0	0	0	0	0	0	0	0	0	0	0	1	0	0	0	.000	.000
Miller, Orlando, Detroit	.250	10	8	8	1	2	6	1	0	1	4	0	0	0	0	0	2	0	0	0	.750	.250
Mitchell, Kevin, Cleveland	.000	4	4	4	0	0	0	0	0	0	0	0	0	0	0	0	2	0	0	0	.000	.000
Molina, Izzy, Oakland	.000	1	1	1	0	0	0	0	0	0	0	0	0	0	0	0	0	0	0	0	.000	.000
Molitor, Paul, Minnesota	.000	2	2	2	0	0	0	0	0	0	0	0	0	0	0	0	1	0	0	0	.000	.000
Mouton, Lyle, Chicago	.188	16	16	16	1	3	3	0	0	0	1	0	0	0	0	0	8	0	0	1	.188	.188
Murray, Eddie, Anaheim†	.000	3	3	3	0	0	0	0	0	0	0	0	0	0	0	0	0	0	0	0	.000	.000
Myers, Greg, Minnesota*........	.467	18	17	15	1	7	7	0	0	0	2	0	0	0	2	0	3	0	0	1	.467	.529
Myers, Rod, Kansas City*........	.333	7	7	6	0	2	2	0	0	0	0	0	1	0	0	0	3	0	0	0	.333	.333
Naehring, Tim, Boston	.000	2	2	2	0	0	0	0	0	0	0	0	0	0	0	0	1	0	0	0	.000	.000
Nevin, Phil, Detroit...............	.500	21	19	16	4	8	17	3	0	2	6	0	0	0	3	1	4	0	0	0	1.063	.579
Newfield, Marc, Milwaukee	.500	5	5	4	0	2	2	0	0	0	2	0	0	0	1	0	1	0	0	0	.500	.600
Newson, Warren, Texas*.........	.125	32	30	24	2	3	7	1	0	1	4	0	1	0	5	1	13	0	0	0	.292	.267
Nieves, Melvin, Detroit†	.063	19	18	16	1	1	4	0	0	1	3	0	0	0	2	1	11	0	0	1	.250	.167
Nilsson, Dave, Milwaukee*	.250	5	5	4	1	1	2	1	0	0	0	0	0	0	1	1	3	0	0	0	.500	.400
Norton, Greg, Chicago†	.000	7	7	6	0	0	0	0	0	0	0	0	0	0	1	0	2	0	0	0	.000	.143
Nunnally, Jon, Kansas City*.....	.000	4	4	3	0	0	0	0	0	0	0	0	0	0	1	0	1	0	0	0	.000	.250
Offerman, Jose, Kansas City†	.250	5	5	4	1	1	2	1	0	0	1	0	0	0	1	1	1	0	0	0	.500	.400
O'Leary, Troy, Boston*..........	.364	13	13	11	2	4	5	1	0	0	5	0	0	0	2	0	3	0	0	0	.455	.462
O'Neill, Paul, New York*	.250	4	4	4	0	1	1	0	0	0	0	0	0	0	0	0	1	0	0	1	.250	.250
Ordonez, Magglio, Chicago.......	.333	3	3	3	0	1	2	1	0	0	0	0	0	0	0	0	0	0	0	0	.667	.333
Ortiz, David, Minnesota*	.333	3	3	3	1	1	2	1	0	0	0	0	0	0	0	0	0	0	0	1	.667	.333
Palmeiro, Orlando, Anaheim*	.429	14	14	14	5	6	6	0	0	0	0	0	0	0	0	0	0	0	0	0	.429	.429
Palmeiro, Rafael, Baltimore*..	.000	3	3	2	0	0	0	0	0	0	0	1	0	0	1	0	0	0	0	0	.000	.000
Palmer, Dean, Tex.-K.C.	.500	3	3	2	0	1	1	0	0	0	1	0	0	0	1	0	1	0	0	0	.500	.667
Paquette, Craig, Kansas City ..	.333	6	6	6	1	2	3	1	0	0	2	0	0	0	0	0	1	0	0	1	.500	.333
Pemberton, Rudy, Boston........	.167	7	7	6	1	1	1	0	0	0	0	0	0	0	1	0	1	0	0	0	.167	.286
Pena, Tony, Chicago..............	.000	1	1	1	0	0	0	0	0	0	0	0	0	0	0	0	0	0	0	0	.000	.000
Perez, Robert, Toronto	.250	8	8	8	1	2	6	1	0	1	2	0	0	0	0	0	2	0	0	0	.750	.250
Phillips, Tony, Chi.-Ana.†	.000	4	4	3	0	0	0	0	0	0	0	0	0	0	1	0	1	0	0	0	.000	.250
Pose, Scott, New York*	.000	2	2	2	0	0	0	0	0	0	0	0	0	0	0	0	1	0	0	0	.000	.000
Pride, Curtis, Det.-Bos. *	.250	34	29	24	2	6	10	1	0	1	2	0	1	0	4	0	7	0	0	0	.417	.345
Raines, Tim, New York†	.000	7	7	5	1	0	0	0	0	0	0	0	0	0	2	0	2	0	0	0	.000	.286
Reboulet, Jeff, Baltimore........	.182	12	12	11	1	2	5	0	0	1	2	0	0	0	1	0	0	1	0	0	.455	.250
Reed, Jody, Detroit	.167	15	15	12	1	2	2	0	0	0	2	2	1	0	0	0	1	1	0	0	.167	.154
Ripken, Billy, Texas	.333	3	3	3	0	1	1	0	0	0	1	0	0	0	0	0	0	0	0	0	.333	.333
Roberts, Bip, K.C.-Cle.†	.250	12	12	8	1	2	2	0	0	0	2	0	0	1	3	0	1	0	0	0	.250	.500
Rodriguez, Ivan, Texas...........	.333	5	5	3	0	1	1	0	0	0	2	0	0	0	2	1	1	0	0	0	.333	.600
Rohrmeier, Dan, Seattle	.250	5	5	4	2	1	1	0	0	0	0	0	0	0	1	0	2	0	0	0	.250	.400
Sagmoen, Marc, Texas*	.000	3	2	2	0	0	0	0	0	0	0	0	0	0	0	0	1	0	0	1	.000	.000
Samuel, Juan, Toronto	.200	7	6	5	1	1	3	0	1	0	3	0	0	0	1	0	1	0	0	0	.600	.333
Santiago, Benito, Toronto........	.000	1	1	1	0	0	0	0	0	0	0	0	0	0	0	0	0	0	0	0	.000	.000
Seitzer, Kevin, Cleveland	.200	12	12	10	1	2	5	0	0	1	4	1	0	0	1	0	0	0	0	0	.500	.273
Sexson, Richie, Cleveland	.333	3	3	3	0	1	1	0	0	0	0	0	0	0	0	0	1	0	0	0	.333	.333
Sierra, Ruben, Toronto†..........	.000	1	1	1	0	0	0	0	0	0	0	0	0	0	0	0	0	0	0	0	.000	.000
Simms, Mike, Texas..............	.300	23	22	20	4	6	13	1	0	2	10	0	1	0	1	0	6	0	0	0	.650	.318
Snopek, Chris, Chicago..........	.667	3	3	3	0	2	3	1	0	0	1	0	0	0	0	0	0	0	0	1	1.000	.667
Sojo, Luis, New York..............	.000	3	3	3	0	0	0	0	0	0	0	0	0	0	0	0	0	0	0	0	.000	.000

Player, Team	Avg.	G	TPA	AB	R	H	TB	2B	3B	HR	RBI	SH	SF	HP	BB	IBB	SO	SB	CS	GDP	Slg.	OBP
Sorrento, Paul, Seattle*	.304	25	25	23	4	7	14	1	0	2	6	0	0	0	2	0	10	0	0	1	.609	.360
Spiezio, Scott, Oakland†	.000	3	3	2	0	0	0	0	0	0	0	0	0	0	1	0	0	0	0	0	.000	.333
Sprague, Ed Jr., Toronto	.000	1	1	1	0	0	0	0	0	0	0	0	0	0	0	0	0	0	0	0	.000	.000
Stahoviak, Scott, Minnesota*	.375	16	16	16	2	6	12	3	0	1	3	0	0	0	0	0	4	1	0	1	.750	.375
Stairs, Matt, Oakland*	.353	42	41	34	6	12	15	0	0	1	5	0	0	2	5	1	6	0	0	0	.441	.463
Stanley, Mike, Bos.-N.Y.	.357	34	34	28	5	10	19	3	0	2	9	0	2	0	4	0	5	0	0	2	.679	.412
Steinbach, Terry, Minnesota	.000	6	6	5	0	0	0	0	0	0	0	1	0	1	0	0	0	0	0	0	1.000	.000
Stevens, Lee, Texas*	.304	27	26	23	3	7	12	2	0	1	6	0	0	0	3	1	5	0	0	1	.522	.385
Stewart, Andy, Kansas City	1.000	1	1	1	1	1	2	1	0	0	0	0	0	0	0	0	0	0	0	0	2.000	1.000
Stewart, Shannon, Toronto	.000	3	3	2	1	0	0	0	0	0	0	0	0	0	1	0	0	0	0	0	.000	.333
Stinnett, Kelly, Milwaukee	.200	7	5	5	0	1	1	0	0	0	0	0	0	0	0	0	2	0	0	0	.200	.200
Strawberry, Darryl, New York*	1.000	3	3	1	0	1	1	0	0	0	0	0	0	0	2	0	0	0	0	0	1.000	1.000
Surhoff, B.J., Baltimore*	.000	4	4	2	1	0	0	0	0	0	0	0	0	0	2	1	1	0	0	0	.000	.500
Sutton, Larry, Kansas City*	.273	13	12	11	2	3	7	1	0	1	3	0	0	0	1	0	3	0	0	0	.636	.333
Sweeney, Mike, Kansas City	.333	8	7	6	0	2	3	1	0	0	0	0	0	0	1	0	1	0	0	0	.500	.429
Tarasco, Tony, Baltimore*	.176	20	19	17	2	3	5	2	0	0	5	0	0	0	2	0	5	0	0	0	.294	.263
Tavarez, Jesus, Boston†	.000	1	1	1	0	0	0	0	0	0	0	0	0	0	0	0	0	0	0	0	.000	.000
Tettleton, Mickey, Texas†	.167	6	6	6	0	1	2	1	0	0	0	0	0	0	0	0	2	0	0	0	.333	.167
Thome, Jim, Cleveland*	.000	7	6	6	0	0	0	0	0	0	0	0	0	0	0	0	2	0	0	0	.000	.000
Tinsley, Lee, Seattle†	.000	5	5	5	0	0	0	0	0	0	0	1	0	0	0	0	3	0	0	1	.000	.000
Trammell, Bubba, Detroit	.200	5	5	5	0	1	1	0	0	0	0	0	0	0	0	0	0	0	1	0	.200	.200
Turner, Chris, Anaheim	.000	3	3	2	0	0	0	0	0	0	0	0	0	0	1	0	0	0	0	0	.000	.333
Unroe, Tim, Milwaukee	.000	3	2	2	0	0	0	0	0	0	0	0	0	0	0	0	2	0	0	0	.000	.000
Valdez, Mario, Chicago*	.143	7	7	7	0	1	1	0	0	0	1	0	0	0	0	0	4	0	0	0	.143	.143
Valentin, John, Boston	.000	1	1	1	0	0	0	0	0	0	0	0	0	0	0	0	0	0	0	0	.000	.000
Valentin, Jose, Milwaukee†	.000	1	1	1	0	0	0	0	0	0	0	0	0	0	0	0	1	0	0	0	.000	.000
Varitek, Jason, Boston†	1.000	1	1	1	0	1	1	0	0	0	0	0	0	0	0	0	0	0	0	0	1.000	1.000
Vaughn, Mo, Boston*	.000	1	1	1	0	0	0	0	0	0	0	0	0	0	0	0	0	0	0	0	.000	.000
Vina, Fernando, Milwaukee*	.333	3	3	3	0	1	1	0	0	0	0	0	0	0	0	0	0	0	0	0	.333	.333
Vitiello, Joe, Kansas City	.273	12	12	11	1	3	3	0	0	0	2	0	0	0	1	1	2	0	0	0	.273	.333
Vizquel, Omar, Cleveland†	.000	2	2	2	0	0	0	0	0	0	0	0	0	0	0	0	0	0	0	0	.000	.000
Voigt, Jack, Milwaukee	.000	11	11	7	0	0	0	0	0	0	0	0	0	0	4	2	3	0	0	0	.000	.364
Walbeck, Matt, Detroit†	.667	3	3	3	0	2	2	0	0	0	0	0	0	0	0	0	0	0	0	1	.667	.667
Walker, Todd, Minnesota*	.000	5	5	5	0	0	0	0	0	0	0	0	0	0	0	0	3	0	0	0	.000	.000
Walton, Jerome, Baltimore	.000	7	7	7	0	0	0	0	0	0	0	0	0	0	0	0	3	0	0	1	.000	.000
Webster, Lenny, Baltimore	.000	1	1	1	0	0	0	0	0	0	0	1	0	0	0	0	0	0	0	0	.000	.000
Whiten, Mark, New York†	.556	10	10	9	3	5	6	1	0	0	3	0	0	0	1	0	3	0	0	0	.667	.600
Wilkins, Rick, Seattle*	.000	1	1	0	1	0	0	0	0	0	0	0	0	0	1	0	0	0	0	0	.000	1.000
Williams, Bernie, New York†	.000	1	1	1	0	0	0	0	0	0	0	0	0	0	0	0	0	0	0	0	.000	.000
Williams, George, Oakland†	.267	17	17	15	2	4	5	1	0	0	3	0	0	0	2	0	3	0	0	0	.333	.353
Williams, Gerald, Milwaukee	.000	1	1	1	0	0	0	0	0	0	0	0	0	0	0	0	0	0	0	0	.000	.000
Williams, Matt, Cleveland	.000	1	1	1	0	0	0	0	0	0	0	0	0	0	0	0	1	0	0	0	.000	.000
Williamson, Antone, Mil.*	.500	9	9	6	1	3	5	2	0	0	3	0	0	0	3	0	1	0	0	1	.833	.667
Wilson, Dan, Seattle	.400	5	5	5	0	2	4	0	1	0	2	0	0	0	0	0	0	0	0	0	.800	.400
Witt, Bobby, Texas	.000	1	1	0	0	0	0	0	0	0	0	0	0	0	0	0	1	0	0	0	.000	.000
Young, Ernie, Oakland	.500	3	2	2	0	1	1	0	0	0	1	0	0	0	0	0	0	0	0	0	.500	.500

PINCH-HITTERS WITH TWO OR MORE TEAMS

Player, Team	Avg.	G	TPA	AB	R	H	TB	2B	3B	HR	RBI	SH	SF	HP	BB	IBB	SO	SB	CS	GDP	Slg.	OBP
Baines, Harold, Chicago*	.333	7	6	6	1	2	5	0	0	1	3	0	0	0	0	0	0	0	0	0	.833	.333
Baines, Harold, Baltimore*	.667	9	9	9	1	6	7	1	0	0	2	0	0	0	0	0	0	0	0	1	.778	.667
Berroa, Geronimo, Oakland	1.000	3	3	2	2	2	2	0	0	0	1	0	0	0	1	0	0	0	0	0	1.000	1.000
Berroa, Geronimo, Baltimore	.250	5	5	4	0	1	1	0	0	0	0	0	0	0	1	0	0	0	0	0	.250	.400
Curtis, Chad, Cleveland	.000	2	2	1	0	0	0	0	0	0	0	0	0	0	1	0	0	0	0	0	.000	.500
Curtis, Chad, New York	.000	2	2	1	1	0	0	0	0	0	0	0	0	0	1	0	1	0	0	0	.000	.500
Franco, Julio, Cleveland	.000	1	1	0	0	0	0	0	0	0	1	0	0	0	1	0	0	0	0	0	.000	1.000
Franco, Julio, Milwaukee	.000	1	1	0	0	0	0	0	0	0	0	0	0	0	1	0	0	0	0	0	.000	1.000
Incaviglia, Pete, Baltimore	.167	12	12	12	1	2	3	1	0	0	0	0	0	0	0	0	4	0	0	0	.250	.167
Incaviglia, Pete, New York	.000	1	1	1	0	0	0	0	0	0	0	0	0	0	0	0	1	0	0	0	.000	.000
Kelly, Roberto, Minnesota	.333	14	13	12	2	4	5	1	0	0	3	0	0	0	1	0	3	0	1	1	.417	.385
Kelly, Roberto, Seattle	.000	3	3	2	0	0	0	0	0	0	0	1	0	1	0	0	1	0	0	0	.000	.000
Kreuter, Chad, Chicago†	.125	9	9	8	2	1	2	1	0	0	1	0	0	0	1	0	2	0	0	0	.250	.222
Kreuter, Chad, Anaheim†	1.000	3	3	1	1	1	2	1	0	0	0	0	0	0	2	0	0	0	0	0	2.000	1.000
Leyritz, Jim, Anaheim	.000	3	3	2	0	0	0	0	0	0	0	0	0	0	1	0	1	0	0	0	.000	.333
Leyritz, Jim, Texas	.571	10	10	7	1	4	4	0	0	0	2	0	1	1	2	0	2	0	0	0	.571	.600
Palmer, Dean, Texas	.500	2	2	2	0	1	1	0	0	0	1	0	0	0	0	0	1	0	0	0	.500	.500
Palmer, Dean, Kansas City	.000	1	1	1	0	0	0	0	0	0	0	0	0	0	1	0	0	0	0	0	.000	1.000
Phillips, Tony, Chicago†	.000	2	2	1	0	0	0	0	0	0	0	0	0	0	1	0	1	0	0	0	.000	.500
Phillips, Tony, Anaheim†	.000	2	2	2	0	0	0	0	0	0	0	0	0	0	0	0	1	0	0	0	.000	.000
Pride, Curtis, Detroit*	.227	32	27	22	1	5	6	1	0	0	1	0	1	0	4	0	8	0	0	0	.273	.333
Pride, Curtis, Boston*	.500	2	2	2	1	1	4	0	0	1	1	0	0	0	0	0	0	0	0	0	2.000	.500
Roberts, Bip, Kansas City†	.250	11	11	8	1	2	2	0	0	0	2	0	0	1	2	0	1	0	0	0	.250	.455
Roberts, Bip, Cleveland†	.000	1	1	0	0	0	0	0	0	0	0	0	0	0	1	0	0	0	0	0	.000	1.000
Stanley, Mike, Boston	.400	30	30	25	4	10	19	3	0	2	9	0	2	0	3	0	4	0	0	2	.760	.433
Stanley, Mike, New York	.000	4	4	3	1	0	0	0	0	0	0	0	0	0	1	0	1	0	0	0	.000	.250

PITCHING

TEAM

Team	W	L	Pct.	ERA	G	ShO	Rel.	Sv.	IP	H	TBF	R	ER	HR	SH	SF	HB	BB	IBB	SO	WP	Bk.
New York	96	66	.593	3.84	162	10	368	51	1467.2	1463	6279	688	626	144	42	34	45	532	41	1165	62	10
Baltimore	98	64	.605	3.91	162	10	400	59	1461.0	1404	6219	681	635	164	34	51	30	563	31	1139	43	4
Toronto	76	86	.469	3.92	162	16	336	34	1442.2	1453	6149	694	628	167	49	37	39	497	29	1150	54	5
Milwaukee	78	83	.484	4.22	161	8	367	44	1427.1	1419	6120	742	669	177	43	36	61	542	25	1016	46	5
Anaheim	84	78	.519	4.52	162	5	400	39	1454.2	1506	6365	794	730	202	46	56	54	605	34	1050	57	9
Detroit	79	83	.488	4.56	162	8	417	42	1445.2	1476	6246	790	732	178	37	61	43	552	33	982	51	3
Texas	77	85	.475	4.69	162	9	382	33	1429.2	1598	6309	823	745	169	30	58	38	541	40	925	55	6
Kansas City	67	94	.416	4.70	161	5	393	29	1443.0	1530	6277	820	753	186	51	57	54	531	42	961	62	6
Cleveland	86	75	.534	4.73	161	3	428	34	1425.2	1528	6260	815	749	181	45	52	51	575	53	1036	59	3
Chicago	80	81	.497	4.73	161	7	389	52	1422.1	1505	6262	833	748	175	43	52	32	575	45	961	71	9
Seattle	90	72	.556	4.78	162	8	392	38	1447.2	1500	6368	833	769	192	43	40	66	598	36	1207	57	5
Boston	78	84	.481	4.85	162	4	417	44	1451.2	1569	6440	857	782	149	32	57	70	611	52	987	51	1
Minnesota	68	94	.420	5.00	162	4	390	30	1434.0	1596	6250	861	796	187	34	47	33	495	31	908	66	6
Oakland	65	97	.401	5.48	162	1	480	38	1445.1	1734	6600	946	880	197	44	80	64	642	54	953	51	4
Totals	1122	1142	.496	4.56	2264	98	5559	568	20198.1	21281	88144	11177	10242	2468	573	718	680	7859	546	14440	785	76

NOTE—Totals for earned runs for several clubs do not agree with composite total for all pitchers of each respective club due to instances in which provisions of Section 10.18(i) of the Scoring Rules were applied. The following differences are to be noted: New York pitchers add to 627; Toronto pitchers add to 630; Milwaukee pitchers add to 671; Detroit pitchers add to 733; Texas pitchers add to 747; Kansas City pitchers add to 755; Chicago pitchers add to 749; Seattle pitchers add to 771; Boston pitchers add to 783; Minnesota pitchers add to 800; Oakland pitchers add to 881.

INDIVIDUAL

TOP QUALIFIERS FOR EARNED-RUN AVERAGE TITLE
Minimum 162 innings. *Throws lefthanded.

Pitcher, Team	W	L	Pct.	ERA	G	GS	CG	ShO	GF	Sv.	IP	H	TBF	R	ER	HR	SH	SF	HB	BB	IBB	SO	WP	Bk.
Clemens, Roger, Toronto	21	7	.750	2.05	34	34	9	3	0	0	264.0	204	1044	65	60	9	5	2	12	68	1	292	4	0
Johnson, Randy, Seattle*	20	4	.833	2.28	30	29	5	2	0	0	213.0	147	850	60	54	20	4	1	10	77	2	291	4	0
Cone, David, New York	12	6	.667	2.82	29	29	1	0	0	0	195.0	155	805	67	61	17	3	2	4	86	2	222	14	2
Pettitte, Andy, New York*	18	7	.720	2.88	35	35	4	1	0	0	240.1	233	986	86	77	7	6	2	3	65	0	166	7	0
Thompson, Justin, Detroit*	15	11	.577	3.02	32	32	4	0	0	0	223.1	188	891	82	75	20	5	10	2	66	1	151	4	0
Mussina, Mike, Baltimore	15	8	.652	3.20	33	33	4	1	0	0	224.2	197	905	87	80	27	3	2	3	54	3	218	5	0
Appier, Kevin, Kansas City	9	13	.409	3.40	34	34	4	1	0	0	235.2	215	972	96	89	24	4	4	4	74	2	196	14	1
Key, Jimmy, Baltimore*	16	10	.615	3.43	34	34	1	1	0	0	212.1	210	902	90	81	24	5	6	5	82	1	141	4	1
Fassero, Jeff, Seattle*	16	9	.640	3.61	35	35	2	1	0	0	234.1	226	1010	108	94	21	7	10	3	84	6	189	13	2
Hentgen, Pat, Toronto	15	10	.600	3.68	35	35	9	3	0	0	264.0	253	1085	116	108	31	9	3	7	71	2	160	6	2
Erickson, Scott, Baltimore	16	7	.696	3.69	34	33	3	2	0	0	221.2	218	922	100	91	16	3	4	5	31	5	131	11	0
Gordon, Tom, Boston	6	10	.375	3.74	42	25	2	1	16	11	182.2	155	774	85	76	18	3	4	3	78	1	159	11	0
Moyer, Jamie, Seattle*	17	5	.773	3.86	30	30	2	0	0	0	188.2	187	787	82	81	21	6	1	7	43	2	113	3	0
Radke, Brad, Minnesota	20	10	.667	3.87	35	35	4	1	0	0	239.2	238	989	114	103	28	2	9	3	48	1	174	1	1
Kamieniecki, Scott, Baltimore	10	6	.625	4.01	30	30	0	0	0	0	179.1	179	764	83	80	20	1	6	4	67	2	109	5	0

DEPARTMENTAL LEADERS: W—Clemens, Tor., 21; L—Baldwin, Chi., Eldred, Mil., Wakefield, Bos., 15; G—Myers, Det., 88; GS—Fassero, Sea., Hentgen, Tor., Pettitte, N.Y., Radke, Min., 35; CG—Clemens, Tor., Hentgen, Tor., 9; ShO—Clemens, Tor., Hentgen, Tor., 3; GF—Jones, Mil., 73; Sv.—Myers, Bal., 45; IP—Clemens, Tor., Hentgen, Tor., 264; H—Navarro, Chi., 267; TBF—Hentgen, Tor., 1085; R—Navarro, Chi., 135; ER—Navarro, Chi., 135; HR—Watson, Ana., 37; SH—T. Castillo, Chi., Hentgen, Tor., Mathews, Bal., Mohler, Oak., 9; SF—Navarro, Chi., 14; HB—Wakefield, Bos., 16; BB—Hill, Tex.-Ana., 95; IBB—Nelson, N.Y., 12; SO—Clemens, Tor., 292; WP—Appier, K.C., Baldwin, Chi., Cone, N.Y., Navarro, Chi., 14; Bk.—Baldwin, Chi., Hawkins, Min., Irabu, N.Y., Spoljaric, Tor.-Sea., 3.

ALL PITCHERS
*Throws lefthanded.

Pitcher, Team	W	L	Pct.	ERA	G	GS	CG	ShO	GF	Sv.	IP	H	TBF	R	ER	HR	SH	SF	HB	BB	IBB	SO	WP	Bk.
Acre, Mark, Oakland	2	0	1.000	5.74	15	0	0	0	5	0	15.2	21	75	10	10	1	0	3	0	8	0	12	0	0
Adams, Willie, Oakland	3	5	.375	8.18	13	12	0	0	0	0	58.1	73	282	53	53	9	3	5	4	32	1	37	2	0
Adamson, Joel, Milwaukee*	5	3	.625	3.54	30	6	0	0	3	0	76.1	78	324	36	30	13	4	2	5	19	0	56	0	1
Aguilera, Rick, Minnesota	5	4	.556	3.82	61	0	0	0	57	26	68.1	65	285	29	29	9	5	3	2	22	3	68	3	0
Alberro, Jose, Texas	0	3	.000	7.94	10	4	0	0	2	0	28.1	37	143	33	25	4	2	1	1	17	1	11	3	0
Aldred, Scott, Minnesota*	2	10	.167	7.68	17	15	0	0	0	0	77.1	102	350	66	66	20	2	1	3	28	2	33	7	0
Almanzar, Carlos, Toronto	0	1	.000	2.70	4	0	0	0	2	0	3.1	1	12	1	1	1	0	0	0	1	0	4	0	0
Alvarez, Wilson, Chicago*	9	8	.529	3.03	22	22	2	1	0	0	145.2	126	613	61	49	9	6	5	3	55	1	110	4	0
Anderson, Brian, Cleveland*	4	2	.667	4.69	8	8	0	0	0	0	48.0	55	199	28	25	7	0	5	0	11	0	22	1	0
Andujar, Luis, Toronto	0	6	.000	6.48	17	8	0	0	0	0	50.0	76	244	45	36	9	3	4	0	21	1	28	2	0
Appier, Kevin, Kansas City	9	13	.409	3.40	34	34	4	1	0	0	235.2	215	972	96	89	24	4	4	4	74	2	196	14	1
Assenmacher, Paul, Cleveland*	5	0	1.000	2.94	75	0	0	0	20	4	49.0	43	205	17	16	5	1	2	1	15	5	53	4	0
Avery, Steve, Boston*	6	7	.462	6.42	22	18	0	0	1	0	96.2	127	453	76	69	15	1	4	2	49	0	51	4	0
Ayala, Bobby, Seattle	10	5	.667	3.82	71	0	0	0	33	8	96.2	91	403	45	41	14	3	6	3	41	3	92	6	0
Bailes, Scott, Texas*	1	0	1.000	2.86	24	0	0	0	7	0	22.0	18	91	9	7	2	2	1	0	10	2	14	0	0
Bailey, Benjamin, Detroit	0	0	.000	0.00	0	0	0	0	0	0	0.0	0	0	0	0	0	0	0	0	0	0	0	0	0
Baldwin, James, Chicago	12	15	.444	5.27	32	32	1	0	0	0	200.0	205	879	128	117	19	3	6	5	83	3	140	14	3
Banks, Willie, New York	3	0	1.000	1.93	5	1	0	0	1	0	14.0	9	57	3	3	0	2	0	1	6	0	8	0	0
Bautista, Jose, Detroit	2	2	.500	6.69	21	0	0	0	4	0	40.1	55	185	32	30	6	1	0	2	12	3	19	1	1
Belcher, Tim, Kansas City	13	12	.520	5.02	32	32	3	1	0	0	213.1	242	927	128	119	31	7	4	5	70	2	113	7	1
Benitez, Armando, Baltimore	4	5	.444	2.45	71	0	0	0	26	9	73.1	49	307	22	20	7	2	4	1	43	5	106	1	0
Benjamin, Mike, Boston	0	0	.000	0.00	1	0	0	0	1	0	1.0	0	3	0	0	0	0	0	0	0	0	0	0	0

Pitcher, Team	W	L	Pct.	ERA	G	GS	CG	ShO	GF	Sv.	IP	H	TBF	R	ER	HR	SH	SF	HB	BB	IBB	SO	WP	Bk.
Bere, Jason, Chicago	4	2	.667	4.71	6	6	0	0	0	0	28.2	20	123	15	15	4	1	1	3	17	0	21	1	0
Bertotti, Mike, Chicago*	0	0	.000	7.36	9	0	0	0	2	0	3.2	9	23	3	3	0	0	1	0	2	0	4	0	1
Bevil, Brian, Kansas City	1	2	.333	6.61	18	0	0	0	11	1	16.1	16	72	13	12	1	0	2	1	9	2	13	2	0
Blair, Willie, Detroit	16	8	.667	4.17	29	27	2	0	0	0	175.0	186	739	85	81	18	3	6	3	46	2	90	6	1
Bluma, Jaime, Kansas City	0	0	.000	0.00	0	0	0	0	0	0	0.0	0	0	0	0	0	0	0	0	0	0	0	0	0
Boehringer, Brian, New York	3	2	.600	2.63	34	0	0	0	11	0	48.0	39	210	16	14	4	3	2	0	32	6	53	2	0
Boggs, Wade, New York	0	0	.000	0.00	1	0	0	0	1	0	1.0	0	4	0	0	0	0	0	0	1	0	1	0	0
Bones, Ricky, Kansas City	4	7	.364	5.97	21	11	1	0	2	0	78.1	102	352	59	52	10	2	6	5	25	2	36	1	0
Borland, Toby, Boston	0	0	.000	13.50	3	0	0	0	0	0	3.1	6	24	5	5	1	0	0	2	7	0	1	0	0
Borowski, Joe, New York	0	1	.000	9.00	1	0	0	0	1	0	2.0	2	12	2	2	0	0	0	0	4	1	2	0	0
Boskie, Shawn, Baltimore	6	6	.500	6.43	28	9	0	0	8	1	77.0	95	349	57	55	14	2	7	2	26	1	50	1	0
Bovee, Mike, Anaheim	0	0	.000	5.40	3	0	0	0	3	0	3.1	3	14	2	2	1	0	0	0	1	0	5	0	0
Bowers, Shane, Minnesota	0	3	.000	8.05	5	5	0	0	0	0	19.0	27	92	20	17	2	0	1	1	8	0	7	1	0
Brandenburg, Mark, Boston	0	2	.000	5.49	31	0	0	0	5	0	41.0	49	186	25	25	3	2	2	2	16	3	34	0	0
Brewer, Billy, Oakland*	0	0	.000	13.50	3	0	0	0	1	0	2.0	4	12	3	3	1	0	1	0	2	0	1	0	0
Brocail, Doug, Detroit	3	4	.429	3.23	61	4	0	0	20	2	78.0	74	332	31	28	10	1	3	3	36	4	60	6	0
Burkett, John, Texas	9	12	.429	4.56	30	30	2	0	0	0	189.1	240	828	106	96	20	4	7	4	30	1	139	1	0
Cadaret, Greg, Anaheim*	0	0	.000	3.29	15	0	0	0	6	0	13.2	11	61	5	5	1	1	0	2	8	2	11	3	0
Carmona, Rafael, Seattle	0	0	.000	3.18	4	0	0	0	1	0	5.2	3	22	3	2	1	0	0	0	2	0	6	1	0
Carpenter, Chris, Toronto	3	7	.300	5.09	14	13	1	1	1	0	81.1	108	374	55	46	7	1	2	2	37	0	55	7	1
Carrasco, Hector, Kansas City	1	6	.143	5.45	28	0	0	0	11	0	34.2	29	151	21	21	4	1	2	4	16	3	30	8	0
Casian, Larry, Kansas City*	0	2	.000	5.06	32	0	0	0	6	0	26.2	32	115	15	15	5	1	1	0	6	1	16	1	0
Castillo, Tony J., Chicago*	4	4	.500	4.91	64	0	0	0	20	4	62.1	74	283	48	34	6	9	0	1	23	7	42	0	0
Castillo, Carlos, Chicago	2	1	.667	4.48	37	2	0	0	14	1	66.1	68	295	35	33	9	0	4	1	33	3	43	3	0
Charlton, Norm, Seattle*	3	8	.273	7.27	71	0	0	0	38	14	69.1	89	343	59	56	7	7	0	4	47	2	55	7	1
Chavez, Anthony, Anaheim	0	0	.000	0.93	7	0	0	0	2	0	9.2	7	41	1	1	1	1	1	0	5	1	10	0	0
Checo, Robinson, Boston	1	1	.500	3.38	5	2	0	0	1	0	13.1	12	54	5	5	0	0	0	0	3	0	14	0	0
Clark, Terry, Cle.-Tex.	1	7	.125	6.00	13	9	0	0	2	0	57.0	70	256	41	38	6	1	2	2	23	1	24	1	0
Clemens, Roger, Toronto	21	7	.750	2.05	34	34	9	3	0	0	264.0	204	1044	65	60	9	5	2	12	68	1	292	4	0
Clemons, Chris, Chicago	0	2	.000	8.53	5	2	0	0	3	0	12.2	19	67	13	12	4	0	0	1	11	0	8	1	0
Cloude, Ken, Seattle	4	2	.667	5.12	10	9	0	0	0	0	51.0	41	219	32	29	8	1	1	3	26	0	46	2	0
Colon, Bartolo, Cleveland	4	7	.364	5.65	19	17	1	0	0	0	94.0	107	427	66	59	12	4	1	3	45	1	66	5	0
Cone, David, New York	12	6	.667	2.82	29	29	1	0	0	0	195.0	155	805	67	61	17	3	2	4	86	2	222	14	2
Converse, Jim, Kansas City	0	0	.000	3.60	3	0	0	0	1	0	5.0	4	23	2	2	2	0	0	0	5	0	3	0	0
Coppinger, Rocky, Baltimore	1	1	.500	6.30	5	4	0	0	1	0	20.0	21	95	14	14	2	0	1	1	16	1	22	1	0
Corsi, Jim, Boston	5	3	.625	3.43	52	0	0	0	14	2	57.2	56	251	26	22	1	3	3	4	21	7	40	2	0
Crabtree, Tim, Toronto	3	3	.500	7.08	37	0	0	0	16	2	40.2	65	199	32	32	7	4	2	2	17	3	26	4	0
Cruz, Nelson, Chicago	0	2	.000	6.49	19	0	0	0	5	0	26.1	29	116	19	19	6	1	0	0	9	1	23	3	0
Cummings, John, Detroit*	2	0	1.000	5.47	19	0	0	0	2	0	24.2	32	119	22	15	3	2	0	0	14	1	8	3	0
Daal, Omar, Toronto*	1	1	.500	4.00	9	3	0	0	0	0	27.0	34	120	13	12	3	2	0	0	6	0	28	1	0
D'Amico, Jeff, Milwaukee	9	7	.563	4.71	23	23	1	1	0	0	135.2	139	585	81	71	25	4	4	8	43	2	94	3	1
Darwin, Danny, Chicago	4	8	.333	4.13	21	17	1	0	0	0	113.1	130	496	60	52	21	4	5	1	31	1	62	1	2
Darwin, Jeff, Chicago	0	1	.000	5.27	14	0	0	0	6	0	13.2	17	65	8	8	1	0	1	0	7	0	9	3	0
Davis, Mark W., Milwaukee*	0	0	.000	5.51	19	0	0	0	3	0	16.1	21	72	10	10	4	1	0	1	5	0	14	0	0
Davis, Tim, Seattle*	0	0	.000	6.75	2	0	0	0	1	0	6.2	6	31	5	5	1	0	0	1	4	0	10	0	0
De La Maza, Roland, K.C.	0	0	.000	4.50	1	0	0	0	0	0	2.0	1	9	1	1	1	0	0	0	1	0	1	1	0
DeLucia, Rich, Anaheim	6	4	.600	3.61	33	0	0	0	13	3	42.1	29	174	18	17	5	2	2	1	27	2	42	1	0
Dickson, Jason, Anaheim	13	9	.591	4.29	33	32	2	1	1	0	203.2	236	888	111	97	32	4	5	7	56	3	115	4	1
Dishman, Glenn, Detroit*	1	2	.333	5.28	7	4	0	0	1	0	29.0	30	125	18	17	4	1	2	2	8	0	20	0	0
Drabek, Doug, Chicago	12	11	.522	5.74	31	31	0	0	0	0	169.1	170	731	109	108	30	4	2	4	69	5	85	12	2
Duran, Roberto, Detroit*	0	0	.000	7.59	13	0	0	0	1	0	10.2	7	56	9	9	0	0	1	3	15	0	11	1	1
Eldred, Cal, Milwaukee	13	15	.464	4.99	34	34	1	1	0	0	202.0	207	885	118	112	31	4	6	9	89	0	122	5	0
Erickson, Scott, Baltimore	16	7	.696	3.69	34	33	3	2	0	0	221.2	218	922	100	91	16	3	4	5	61	5	131	11	0
Escobar, Kelvim, Toronto	3	2	.600	2.90	27	0	0	0	23	14	31.0	28	139	12	10	1	2	0	0	19	2	36	0	0
Eshelman, Vaughn, Boston*	3	3	.500	6.33	21	6	0	0	6	0	42.2	58	198	32	30	3	1	2	2	17	5	18	2	0
Eversgerd, Bryan, Texas*	0	2	.000	20.25	3	0	0	0	1	0	1.1	5	12	3	3	0	0	0	0	3	0	2	0	0
Eyre, Scott, Chicago*	4	4	.500	5.04	11	11	0	0	0	0	60.2	62	267	36	34	11	1	2	1	31	1	36	2	0
Fassero, Jeff, Seattle*	16	9	.640	3.61	35	35	2	1	0	0	234.1	226	1010	108	94	21	7	10	3	84	6	189	13	2
Fetters, Mike, Milwaukee	1	5	.167	3.45	51	0	0	0	20	6	70.1	62	298	30	27	4	6	4	1	33	3	62	2	1
Finley, Chuck, Anaheim*	13	6	.684	4.23	25	25	3	1	0	0	164.0	152	690	79	77	20	3	4	5	65	0	155	10	2
Flener, Huck, Toronto*	0	1	.000	9.87	8	1	0	0	3	0	17.1	40	97	19	19	3	0	1	0	6	0	9	2	0
Florie, Bryce, Milwaukee	4	4	.500	4.32	32	8	0	0	6	0	75.0	74	332	43	36	4	1	4	3	42	2	53	4	1
Fordham, Tom, Chicago*	0	1	.000	6.23	7	1	0	0	1	0	17.1	17	78	13	12	2	1	2	1	10	2	10	0	0
Foulke, Keith, Chicago	3	0	1.000	3.45	16	0	0	0	5	3	28.2	28	117	11	11	4	1	1	0	5	1	21	0	0
Gaillard, Eddie, Detroit	1	0	1.000	5.31	16	0	0	0	5	1	20.1	16	88	12	12	2	0	2	0	10	2	12	0	0
Garces, Rich, Boston	0	1	.000	4.61	12	0	0	0	4	0	13.2	14	66	9	7	2	0	1	1	9	0	12	0	0
Gooden, Dwight, New York	9	5	.643	4.91	20	19	0	0	0	0	106.1	116	472	61	58	14	0	2	7	53	1	66	8	0
Gordon, Tom, Boston	6	10	.375	3.74	42	25	2	1	16	11	182.2	155	774	85	76	10	3	4	3	78	1	159	5	0
Graves, Danny, Cleveland	0	0	.000	4.76	5	0	0	0	2	0	11.1	15	56	8	6	2	0	1	0	9	0	4	0	0
Groom, Buddy, Oakland*	2	2	.500	5.15	78	0	0	0	7	3	64.2	75	285	38	37	9	0	4	0	24	1	45	3	0
Gross, Kevin, Anaheim	2	1	.667	6.75	12	3	0	0	2	0	25.1	30	121	20	19	4	2	2	1	20	1	20	2	1
Grundt, Ken, Boston*	0	0	.000	9.00	2	0	0	0	0	0	3.0	5	14	3	3	0	0	0	0	0	0	0	0	1
Guardado, Eddie, Minnesota*	0	4	.000	3.91	69	0	0	0	20	1	46.0	45	201	23	20	7	2	1	2	17	2	54	2	0
Gubicza, Mark, Anaheim	0	1	.000	25.07	2	2	0	0	0	0	4.2	13	30	13	13	2	0	0	0	3	0	5	0	0
Gunderson, Eric, Texas*	2	1	.667	3.26	60	0	0	0	11	1	49.2	45	209	19	18	5	2	3	2	15	3	31	2	1
Guzman, Juan, Toronto	3	6	.333	4.95	13	13	0	0	0	0	60.0	48	261	42	33	14	1	2	2	31	0	52	4	0
Hammond, Chris, Boston*	3	4	.429	5.92	29	8	0	0	6	1	65.1	81	293	45	43	5	0	3	2	27	4	48	2	0
Haney, Chris, Kansas City*	1	2	.333	4.38	8	3	0	0	1	0	24.2	29	110	16	12	1	2	1	2	5	2	16	1	0
Hansell, Greg, Milwaukee	0	0	.000	9.64	3	0	0	0	1	0	4.2	5	21	5	5	1	0	0	1	1	0	5	0	0
Hanson, Erik, Toronto	0	0	.000	7.80	3	2	0	0	1	0	15.0	15	65	13	13	3	0	0	0	6	0	18	1	0
Harnisch, Pete, Milwaukee	1	1	.500	5.14	4	3	0	0	0	0	14.0	13	65	9	8	1	0	0	0	12	0	10	1	0

Pitcher, Team	W	L	Pct.	ERA	G	GS	CG	ShO	GF	Sv.	IP	H	TBF	R	ER	HR	SH	SF	HB	BB	IBB	SO	WP	Bk.
Harris, Pep, Anaheim	5	4	.556	3.62	61	0	0	0	17	0	79.2	82	346	33	32	7	3	4	2	38	6	56	3	0
Hasegawa, Shigetoshi, Ana.	3	7	.300	3.93	50	7	0	0	17	0	116.2	118	497	60	51	14	5	5	4	46	6	83	2	1
Haught, Gary, Oakland	0	0	.000	7.15	6	0	0	0	2	0	11.1	12	52	9	9	3	0	1	2	6	0	11	1	0
Hawkins, LaTroy, Minnesota	6	12	.333	5.84	20	20	0	0	0	0	103.1	134	478	71	67	19	2	2	4	47	0	58	6	3
Haynes, Jimmy, Oakland	3	6	.333	4.42	13	13	0	0	0	0	73.1	74	329	38	36	7	1	4	2	40	1	65	4	1
Helling, Rick, Texas	3	3	.500	4.58	10	8	0	0	1	0	55.0	47	226	29	28	5	1	2	2	21	0	46	3	0
Henry, Butch, Boston*	7	3	.700	3.52	36	5	0	0	13	6	84.1	89	345	36	33	6	2	3	0	19	2	51	0	0
Hentgen, Pat, Toronto	15	10	.600	3.68	35	35	9	3	0	0	264.0	253	1085	116	108	31	9	3	7	71	2	160	6	2
Heredia, Wilson, Texas	1	0	1.000	3.20	10	0	0	0	3	0	19.2	14	89	9	7	2	0	2	0	16	0	8	0	0
Hernandez, Fernando, Detroit	0	0	.000	40.50	2	0	0	0	1	0	1.1	5	13	6	6	0	0	0	1	3	1	2	0	0
Hernandez, Xavier, Texas	0	4	.000	4.56	44	0	0	0	20	0	49.1	51	221	27	25	7	1	1	2	22	4	36	5	0
Hernandez, Roberto, Chicago	5	1	.833	2.44	46	0	0	0	43	27	48.0	38	203	15	13	5	1	1	1	24	4	47	2	0
Hershiser, Orel, Cleveland	14	6	.700	4.47	32	32	1	0	0	0	195.1	199	826	105	97	26	6	8	11	69	2	107	11	0
Hibbard, Greg, Seattle*	0	0	.000	0.00	0	0	0	0	0	0	0.0	0	0	0	0	0	0	0	0	0	0	0	0	0
Hill, Ken, Tex.-Ana.	9	12	.429	4.55	31	31	1	0	0	0	190.0	194	833	103	96	19	3	7	3	95	3	106	7	0
Holtz, Mike, Anaheim*	3	4	.429	3.32	66	0	0	0	11	0	43.1	38	187	21	16	7	1	2	2	15	4	40	1	0
Holzemer, Mark, Seattle*	0	0	.000	6.00	14	0	0	0	2	1	9.0	9	44	6	6	0	0	0	0	8	0	7	0	0
Hudson, Joe, Boston	3	1	.750	3.53	26	0	0	0	9	0	35.2	39	154	16	14	1	1	0	4	14	2	14	1	0
Huisman, Rick, Kansas City	0	0	.000	0.00	0	0	0	0	0	0	0.0	0	0	0	0	0	0	0	0	0	0	0	0	0
Hurtado, Edwin, Seattle	1	2	.333	9.00	13	1	0	0	2	0	19.0	25	94	19	19	5	0	1	2	15	0	10	2	0
Irabu, Hideki, New York	5	4	.556	7.09	13	9	0	0	0	0	53.1	69	246	47	42	15	1	2	1	20	0	56	4	3
Jackson, Mike R., Cleveland	2	5	.286	3.24	71	0	0	0	38	15	75.0	59	313	33	27	3	3	3	4	29	5	74	2	0
Jacome, Jason, K.C.-Cle.*	2	0	1.000	5.84	28	4	0	0	2	0	49.1	58	218	33	32	10	0	1	1	20	5	27	2	0
James, Mike, Anaheim	5	5	.500	4.31	58	0	0	0	22	7	62.2	69	284	32	30	3	6	1	5	28	4	57	1	0
Janzen, Marty, Toronto	2	1	.667	3.60	12	0	0	0	6	0	25.0	23	105	11	10	4	0	0	0	13	0	17	0	0
Jarvis, Kevin, Min.-Det.	0	3	.000	7.08	23	5	0	0	10	0	54.2	78	259	46	43	13	1	1	0	22	0	36	2	0
Johnson, Dane, Oakland	4	1	.800	4.53	38	0	0	0	12	2	45.2	49	217	28	23	4	0	4	2	31	4	43	4	1
Johnson, Mike, Baltimore	0	1	.000	7.94	14	5	0	0	5	2	39.2	52	183	36	35	12	0	2	1	16	2	29	1	0
Johnson, Randy, Seattle*	20	4	.833	2.28	30	29	5	2	0	0	213.0	147	850	60	54	20	4	1	10	77	2	291	4	0
Johnstone, John, Oakland	0	0	.000	2.84	5	0	0	0	1	0	6.1	7	32	2	2	0	1	0	0	4	0	7	0	0
Jones, Doug, Milwaukee	6	6	.500	2.02	75	0	0	0	73	36	80.1	62	307	20	18	4	1	5	3	9	1	82	2	0
Jones, Todd, Detroit	5	4	.556	3.09	68	0	0	0	51	31	70.0	60	301	29	24	3	1	4	1	35	2	70	7	0
Juden, Jeff, Cleveland	0	1	.000	5.46	8	5	0	0	0	0	31.1	32	141	21	19	6	2	2	1	15	0	29	1	0
Kamieniecki, Scott, Baltimore	10	6	.625	4.01	30	30	0	0	0	0	179.1	179	764	83	80	20	1	6	4	67	2	109	5	0
Karchner, Matt, Chicago	3	1	.750	2.91	52	0	0	0	25	15	52.2	50	224	18	17	4	3	1	0	26	4	30	6	0
Karl, Scott, Milwaukee*	10	13	.435	4.47	32	32	1	0	0	0	193.1	212	839	103	96	23	5	2	4	67	1	119	6	0
Karsay, Steve, Oakland	3	12	.200	5.77	24	24	0	0	0	0	132.2	166	609	92	85	20	2	5	8	47	3	92	7	0
Keagle, Greg, Detroit	3	5	.375	6.55	11	10	0	0	0	0	45.1	58	214	33	33	9	2	1	5	18	0	33	1	0
Key, Jimmy, Baltimore*	16	10	.615	3.43	34	34	1	1	0	0	212.1	210	902	90	81	24	5	6	5	82	1	141	4	1
Kline, Steve, Cleveland*	3	1	.750	5.81	20	1	0	0	0	0	26.1	42	130	19	17	6	1	0	1	13	1	17	3	1
Krivda, Rick, Baltimore*	4	2	.667	6.30	10	10	0	0	0	0	50.0	67	225	36	35	7	1	2	0	18	1	29	0	2
Kubinski, Tim, Oakland*	0	0	.000	5.68	11	0	0	0	3	0	12.2	12	56	9	8	2	0	2	1	6	1	10	0	0
Lacy, Kerry, Boston	1	1	.500	6.11	33	0	0	0	12	3	45.2	60	215	32	31	7	0	2	0	22	4	18	0	0
Langston, Mark, Anaheim*	2	4	.333	5.85	9	9	0	0	0	0	47.2	61	226	34	31	8	2	2	0	29	1	30	1	0
Levine, Al, Chicago	2	2	.500	6.91	25	0	0	0	6	0	27.1	35	133	22	21	4	1	2	2	16	1	22	2	0
Lewis, Richie, Oakland	2	0	1.000	9.64	14	0	0	0	5	0	18.2	24	94	21	20	7	1	1	1	15	0	12	2	0
Lira, Felipe, Det.-Sea.	5	11	.313	6.34	28	18	1	1	3	0	110.2	132	516	82	78	18	2	4	6	55	2	73	7	0
Lloyd, Graeme, New York*	1	1	.500	3.31	46	0	0	0	17	1	49.0	55	217	24	18	6	3	5	1	20	7	26	3	0
Lopez, Albie, Cleveland	3	7	.300	6.93	37	6	0	0	10	0	76.2	101	364	61	59	11	3	2	4	40	9	63	5	0
Lorraine, Andrew, Oakland*	3	1	.750	6.37	12	6	0	0	1	0	29.2	45	146	22	21	2	0	3	1	15	0	18	0	0
Lowe, Derek, Sea.-Bos.	2	6	.250	6.13	20	9	0	0	1	0	69.0	74	298	49	47	11	4	2	4	23	3	52	2	0
Ludwick, Eric, Oakland	1	4	.200	8.25	6	5	0	0	0	0	24.0	32	116	24	22	7	2	0	1	16	1	14	0	0
Maddux, Mike, Seattle	0	1	.000	10.13	6	0	0	0	1	0	10.2	20	59	12	12	1	0	1	8	2	7	1	0
Mahay, Ron, Boston*	3	0	1.000	2.52	28	0	0	0	7	0	25.0	19	105	7	7	3	1	0	0	11	0	22	3	0
Mahomes, Pat, Boston	1	0	1.000	8.10	10	0	0	0	2	0	10.0	15	54	10	9	2	0	1	2	10	1	5	1	0
Maloney, Sean, Milwaukee	0	0	.000	5.14	3	0	0	0	2	0	7.0	7	29	4	4	1	0	2	2	2	0	5	2	0
Manzanillo, Josias, Seattle	1	0	1.000	5.40	16	0	0	0	4	0	18.1	19	88	13	11	3	0	2	0	17	1	18	2	0
Martinez, Dennis, Seattle	1	5	.167	7.71	9	9	0	0	0	0	49.0	65	239	46	42	8	1	3	7	29	1	17	0	0
Mathews, Terry, Baltimore	4	4	.500	4.41	57	0	0	0	19	1	63.1	63	285	35	31	8	9	4	0	36	2	39	3	0
Mathews, T.J., Oakland	6	2	.750	4.40	24	0	0	0	14	3	28.2	34	132	18	14	5	2	1	1	12	1	24	0	0
May, Darrell, Anaheim*	2	1	.667	5.23	29	2	0	0	7	0	51.2	56	234	31	30	8	4	0	0	25	2	42	2	0
McAndrew, Jamie, Milwaukee	1	1	.500	8.38	5	4	0	0	0	0	19.1	24	104	19	18	1	0	2	0	23	0	8	2	0
McCarthy, Greg, Seattle*	1	1	.500	5.46	37	0	0	0	4	0	29.2	26	130	21	18	4	0	0	1	16	0	34	4	0
McDill, Allen, Kansas City*	0	0	.000	13.50	3	0	0	0	1	0	4.0	3	24	6	6	1	1	0	1	8	0	1	0	0
McDonald, Ben, Milwaukee	8	7	.533	4.06	21	21	1	0	0	0	133.0	120	551	68	60	13	3	1	5	36	2	110	3	0
McDowell, Jack, Cleveland	3	5	.500	5.09	8	6	0	0	0	0	40.2	44	181	25	23	6	4	2	1	18	1	38	1	0
McElroy, Chuck, Ana.-Chi.*	1	3	.250	3.84	61	0	0	0	16	1	75.0	73	320	36	32	5	3	3	2	22	1	62	1	0
Mecir, Jim, New York	0	4	.000	5.88	25	0	0	0	11	0	33.2	36	142	23	22	5	0	1	2	10	1	25	1	0
Mendoza, Ramiro, New York	8	6	.571	4.24	39	15	0	0	9	2	133.2	157	578	67	63	15	3	5	5	28	2	82	2	1
Mercedes, Jose, Milwaukee	7	10	.412	3.79	29	23	2	1	1	0	159.0	146	653	76	67	24	3	4	5	53	2	80	1	1
Mesa, Jose, Cleveland	4	4	.500	2.40	66	0	0	0	38	16	82.1	83	356	28	22	7	2	2	3	28	3	69	1	0
Miceli, Dan, Detroit	3	2	.600	5.01	71	0	0	0	24	3	82.2	77	357	49	46	13	5	3	1	38	4	79	3	0
Miller, Travis, Minnesota*	1	5	.167	7.63	13	7	0	0	1	0	48.1	64	227	49	41	8	1	2	1	23	2	26	5	0
Mills, Alan, Baltimore	2	3	.400	4.89	39	0	0	0	11	0	38.2	41	192	23	21	5	4	1	1	33	1	32	2	0
Miranda, Angel, Milwaukee*	0	1	.000	3.86	10	0	0	0	2	0	14.0	17	68	6	6	1	3	0	3	9	2	8	2	0
Misuraca, Mike, Milwaukee	0	0	.000	11.32	5	0	0	0	2	0	10.1	15	52	13	13	5	0	0	0	7	1	10	1	0
Moehler, Brian, Detroit	11	12	.478	4.67	31	31	2	1	0	0	175.1	198	770	97	91	22	1	8	5	61	1	97	3	0
Mohler, Mike, Oakland*	1	10	.091	5.13	62	10	0	0	16	1	101.2	116	462	65	58	11	9	7	7	54	8	66	4	0
Montgomery, Jeff, Kansas City	1	4	.200	3.49	55	0	0	0	37	14	59.1	53	245	24	23	9	4	2	0	18	5	48	5	0
Montgomery, Steve, Oakland	0	1	.000	9.95	4	0	0	0	2	0	6.1	10	35	7	7	2	0	1	0	8	2	1	0	0
Moody, Eric, Texas	0	1	.000	4.26	10	1	0	0	3	0	19.0	26	82	10	9	4	0	1	0	2	0	12	0	0

Pitcher, Team	W	L	Pct.	ERA	G	GS	CG	ShO	GF	Sv.	IP	H	TBF	R	ER	HR	SH	SF	HB	BB	IBB	SO	WP	Bk.
Morman, Alvin, Cleveland*	0	0	.000	5.89	34	0	0	0	7	2	18.1	19	86	13	12	2	0	0	1	14	3	13	1	0
Moyer, Jamie, Seattle*	17	5	.773	3.86	30	30	2	0	0	0	188.2	187	787	82	81	21	6	1	7	43	2	113	3	0
Mussina, Mike, Baltimore	15	8	.652	3.20	33	33	4	1	0	0	224.2	197	905	87	80	27	3	2	3	54	3	218	5	0
Myers, Mike, Detroit*	0	4	.000	5.70	88	0	0	0	23	2	53.2	58	246	36	34	12	4	3	2	25	2	50	0	0
Myers, Randy, Baltimore*	2	3	.400	1.51	61	0	0	0	57	45	59.2	47	241	12	10	2	2	0	0	22	2	56	3	0
Nagy, Charles, Cleveland	15	11	.577	4.28	34	34	1	1	0	0	227.0	253	991	115	108	27	5	6	7	77	4	149	5	0
Naulty, Dan, Minnesota	1	1	.500	5.87	29	0	0	0	8	1	30.2	29	128	20	20	8	0	4	0	10	0	23	3	0
Navarro, Jaime, Chicago	9	14	.391	5.79	33	33	2	0	0	0	209.2	267	957	155	135	22	2	14	3	73	6	142	14	1
Nelson, Jeff, New York	3	7	.300	2.86	77	0	0	0	22	2	78.2	53	327	32	25	7	7	2	4	37	12	81	4	0
Ogea, Chad, Cleveland	8	9	.471	4.99	21	21	1	0	0	0	126.1	139	552	79	70	13	3	5	5	47	4	80	4	2
Olivares, Omar, Det.-Sea.	6	10	.375	4.97	32	31	3	2	0	0	177.1	191	794	109	98	18	2	7	13	81	4	103	5	0
Oliver, Darren, Texas*	13	12	.520	4.20	32	32	3	1	0	0	201.1	213	887	111	94	29	2	5	11	82	3	104	7	0
Olson, Gregg, Min.-K.C.	4	3	.571	5.58	45	0	0	0	18	1	50.0	58	226	35	31	3	2	1	1	28	4	34	1	0
Oquist, Mike, Oakland	4	6	.400	5.02	19	17	1	0	0	0	107.2	111	473	62	60	15	3	3	6	43	3	72	2	0
Orosco, Jesse, Baltimore*	6	3	.667	2.32	71	0	0	0	12	0	50.1	29	205	13	13	6	1	2	0	30	0	46	1	1
Patterson, Danny, Texas	10	6	.625	3.42	54	0	0	0	17	1	71.0	70	296	29	27	3	4	3	0	23	4	69	7	1
Pavlik, Roger, Texas	3	5	.375	4.37	11	11	0	0	0	0	57.2	59	256	29	28	7	2	1	1	31	1	35	0	0
Percival, Troy, Anaheim	5	5	.500	3.46	55	0	0	0	46	27	52.0	40	224	20	20	6	1	0	4	22	2	72	5	0
Perez, Mike, Kansas City	2	0	1.000	3.54	16	0	0	0	4	0	20.1	15	80	8	8	2	1	0	1	8	0	17	1	0
Perisho, Matt, Anaheim*	0	2	.000	6.00	11	8	0	0	2	0	45.0	59	217	34	30	6	2	2	3	28	0	35	5	2
Person, Robert, Toronto	5	10	.333	5.61	23	22	0	0	0	0	128.1	125	566	86	80	19	4	6	5	60	2	99	7	0
Pettitte, Andy, New York*	18	7	.720	2.88	35	35	4	1	0	0	240.1	233	986	86	77	7	6	2	3	65	0	166	7	0
Pichardo, Hipolito, Kansas City.	3	5	.375	4.22	47	0	0	0	26	11	49.0	51	215	24	23	7	2	0	1	24	8	34	2	1
Pittsley, Jim, Kansas City	5	8	.385	5.46	21	21	0	0	0	0	112.0	120	501	72	68	15	2	6	6	54	1	52	3	0
Plesac, Dan, Toronto*	2	4	.333	3.58	73	0	0	0	18	1	50.1	47	215	22	20	8	2	1	0	19	4	61	2	0
Plunk, Eric, Cleveland	4	5	.444	4.66	55	0	0	0	22	0	65.2	62	293	37	34	12	1	2	1	36	7	66	6	0
Prieto, Ariel, Oakland	6	8	.429	5.04	22	22	0	0	0	0	125.0	155	588	84	70	16	3	4	5	70	3	90	7	1
Pugh, Tim, Detroit	1	1	.500	5.00	2	2	0	0	0	0	9.0	6	37	5	5	0	0	0	5	0	4	0	0
Quantrill, Paul, Toronto	6	7	.462	1.94	77	0	0	0	29	5	88.0	103	373	25	19	5	5	3	1	17	3	56	1	0
Radke, Brad, Minnesota	20	10	.667	3.87	35	35	4	1	0	0	239.2	238	989	114	103	28	2	9	3	48	1	174	1	1
Reyes, Carlos, Oakland	3	4	.429	5.82	37	6	0	0	9	0	77.1	101	352	52	50	13	3	2	2	25	2	43	2	1
Reyes, Al, Milwaukee	1	2	.333	5.46	19	0	0	0	7	1	29.2	32	131	19	18	4	2	0	3	9	0	28	1	0
Rhodes, Arthur, Baltimore*	10	3	.769	3.02	53	0	0	0	6	1	95.1	75	378	32	32	9	0	4	4	26	5	102	2	0
Rigby, Brad, Oakland	1	7	.125	4.87	14	14	0	0	0	0	77.2	92	339	44	42	14	2	8	2	22	2	34	3	0
Rios, Danny, New York	0	0	.000	19.29	2	0	0	0	1	0	2.1	9	19	5	5	3	0	0	1	2	0	1	0	0
Risley, Bill, Toronto	0	1	.000	8.31	3	0	0	0	1	0	4.1	3	18	4	4	2	0	0	0	2	0	2	0	0
Ritchie, Todd, Minnesota	2	3	.400	4.58	42	0	0	0	19	0	74.2	87	331	41	38	11	0	1	2	28	0	44	11	0
Rivera, Mariano, New York	6	4	.600	1.88	66	0	0	0	56	43	71.2	65	301	17	15	5	3	4	0	20	6	68	2	0
Robertson, Rich, Minnesota*	8	12	.400	5.69	31	26	0	0	2	0	147.0	169	666	105	93	19	3	8	6	70	3	69	10	0
Robinson, Ken, Toronto	0	0	.000	2.70	3	0	0	0	2	0	3.1	1	11	1	1	0	0	0	1	0	4	0	0
Rodriguez, Frankie, Minnesota	3	6	.333	4.62	43	15	0	0	5	0	142.1	147	613	82	73	12	4	2	4	60	9	65	6	0
Rodriguez, Nerio, Baltimore*	4	1	.667	4.91	6	2	0	0	1	0	22.0	21	98	15	12	2	1	1	1	8	0	11	1	0
Rogers, Kenny, New York*	6	7	.462	5.65	31	22	1	0	4	0	145.0	161	651	100	91	18	2	4	7	62	1	78	2	2
Rosado, Jose, Kansas City*	9	12	.429	4.69	33	33	2	0	0	0	203.1	208	881	117	106	26	6	11	4	73	3	129	4	2
Rose, Brian, Boston	0	0	.000	12.00	1	1	0	0	0	0	3.0	5	16	4	4	0	0	0	0	2	0	3	0	0
Rusch, Glendon, Kansas City*	6	9	.400	5.50	30	27	1	0	0	0	170.1	206	758	111	104	28	8	7	7	52	0	116	0	1
Saberhagen, Bret, Boston	0	1	.000	6.58	6	6	0	0	0	0	26.0	30	120	20	19	5	1	3	2	10	0	14	1	0
Sager, A.J., Detroit	3	4	.429	4.18	38	1	0	0	8	3	84.0	81	350	43	39	10	5	6	1	24	6	53	0	0
Sanders, Scott, Sea.-Det.	6	14	.300	5.86	47	20	1	1	15	2	139.2	152	626	92	91	30	3	10	4	62	6	120	8	0
Santana, Julio, Texas	4	6	.400	6.75	30	14	0	0	3	0	104.0	141	496	86	78	16	1	5	4	49	2	64	8	1
Santiago, Jose, Kansas City	0	0	.000	1.93	4	0	0	0	3	0	4.2	7	24	2	1	0	0	0	1	2	1	1	0	0
Sele, Aaron, Boston	13	12	.520	5.38	33	33	1	0	0	0	177.1	196	810	115	106	25	5	7	15	80	4	122	7	0
Serafini, Dan, Minnesota*	2	1	.667	3.42	6	4	1	0	1	0	26.1	27	111	11	10	1	1	0	0	11	0	15	1	0
Service, Scott, Kansas City	0	0	.000	4.76	12	0	0	0	1	0	17.0	17	69	9	9	1	1	1	0	5	0	19	0	0
Shuey, Paul, Cleveland	4	2	.667	6.20	40	0	0	0	16	2	45.0	52	212	31	31	5	4	2	1	28	3	46	2	0
Simas, Bill, Chicago	3	1	.750	4.14	40	0	0	0	11	1	41.1	46	193	23	19	6	1	1	2	24	3	38	2	0
Sirotka, Mike, Chicago*	3	0	1.000	2.25	7	4	0	0	1	0	32.0	36	130	9	8	4	0	0	1	5	1	24	0	0
Slocumb, Heathcliff, Bos.-Sea.	0	9	.000	5.16	76	0	0	0	61	27	75.0	84	353	45	43	6	4	2	4	49	5	64	10	0
Small, Aaron, Oakland	9	5	.643	4.28	71	0	0	0	22	4	96.2	109	425	50	46	6	5	3	6	40	6	57	4	0
Smiley, John, Cleveland*	2	4	.333	5.54	6	6	0	0	0	0	37.1	45	160	23	23	9	0	1	1	10	0	26	3	0
Sparks, Steve, Milwaukee	0	0	.000	0.00	0	0	0	0	0	0	0	0	0	0	0	0	0	0	0	0	0	0	0	0
Spoljaric, Paul, Tor.-Sea.*	0	3	.000	3.69	57	0	0	0	10	3	70.2	61	302	30	29	4	2	2	3	36	6	70	6	3
Springer, Dennis, Anaheim	9	9	.500	5.18	32	28	3	1	0	0	194.2	199	846	118	112	32	4	13	10	73	0	75	7	0
Stanton, Mike, New York*	6	1	.857	2.57	64	0	0	0	15	3	66.2	50	283	19	19	3	2	0	3	34	2	70	3	2
Stevens, Dave, Minnesota	1	3	.250	9.00	6	6	0	0	0	0	23.0	41	124	23	23	8	0	0	0	17	0	16	1	2
Sturtze, Tanyon, Texas	1	1	.500	8.27	9	5	0	0	1	0	32.2	45	155	30	30	6	4	3	0	18	0	18	1	1
Suppan, Jeff, Boston	7	3	.700	5.69	23	22	0	0	0	0	112.1	140	503	75	71	12	0	4	4	36	1	67	5	0
Swindell, Greg, Minnesota*	7	4	.636	3.58	65	1	0	0	12	1	115.2	102	460	46	46	12	3	2	25	3	75	0		
Taylor, Bill, Oakland	3	4	.429	3.82	72	0	0	0	45	23	73.0	70	320	32	31	3	1	2	5	36	9	66	0	0
Telgheder, Dave, Oakland	4	6	.400	6.06	20	19	0	0	0	0	101.0	134	458	71	68	15	0	7	2	35	1	55	4	0
Tewksbury, Bob, Minnesota	8	13	.381	4.22	26	26	5	2	0	0	168.2	200	721	83	79	12	8	7	1	31	1	92	2	0
Thomas, Larry, Chicago*	0	0	.000	8.10	5	0	0	0	3	0	3.1	3	15	3	3	1	1	0	0	2	0	0	0	0
Thompson, Justin, Detroit*	15	11	.577	3.02	32	32	4	0	0	0	223.1	188	891	82	75	20	5	10	2	66	1	151	4	0
Timlin, Mike, Tor.-Sea.	6	4	.600	3.22	64	0	0	0	31	10	72.2	69	297	30	26	8	1	1	20	5	45	1	1	
Torres, Salomon, Seattle	0	0	.000	27.00	2	0	0	0	1	0	3.1	7	21	10	10	0	0	1	3	0	0	0		
Trlicek, Rick, Boston	3	4	.429	4.63	18	0	0	0	8	0	23.1	26	111	14	12	1	1	1	18	4	10	2	0	
Trombley, Mike, Minnesota	2	3	.400	4.37	67	0	0	0	21	1	82.1	77	349	43	40	7	2	2	31	4	74	5	0	
Veres, Randy, Kansas City	4	0	1.000	3.31	24	0	0	0	7	1	35.1	36	152	17	13	4	5	5	3	7	1	28	4	0
Villone, Ron, Milwaukee*	1	0	1.000	3.42	50	0	0	0	15	0	52.2	54	238	23	20	4	0	1	36	2	40	3	0	
Vosberg, Ed, Texas*	1	2	.333	4.61	42	0	0	0	16	0	41.0	44	180	23	21	3	1	2	15	6	29	1	0	
Wagner, Paul, Milwaukee	1	0	1.000	9.00	2	0	0	0	1	0	2.0	3	8	2	2	1	0	0	0	0	0	4	0	0

Pitcher, Team	W	L	Pct.	ERA	G	GS	CG	ShO	GF	Sv.	IP	H	TBF	R	ER	HR	SH	SF	HB	BB	IBB	SO	WP	Bk.
Wakefield, Tim, Boston	12	15	.444	4.25	35	29	4	2	2	0	201.1	193	866	109	95	24	3	7	16	87	5	151	6	0
Walker, Jamie, Kansas City* ...	3	3	.500	5.44	50	0	0	0	15	0	43.0	46	197	28	26	6	2	2	3	20	3	24	2	0
Wasdin, John, Boston............	4	6	.400	4.40	53	7	0	0	10	0	124.2	121	534	68	61	18	4	7	3	38	4	84	4	0
Watson, Allen, Anaheim*	12	12	.500	4.93	35	34	0	0	0	0	199.0	220	880	121	109	37	5	6	8	73	0	141	8	2
Weathers, David, N.Y.-Cle........	1	3	.250	8.42	19	1	0	0	5	0	25.2	38	126	24	24	3	2	1	1	15	0	18	3	0
Wells, David, New York*	16	10	.615	4.21	32	32	5	2	0	0	218.0	239	922	109	102	24	7	3	6	45	0	156	8	0
Wells, Bob, Seattle	2	0	1.000	5.75	46	1	0	0	19	2	67.1	88	304	49	43	11	1	2	3	18	1	51	1	0
Wengert, Don, Oakland	5	11	.313	6.04	49	12	1	0	16	2	134.0	177	612	96	90	21	5	7	8	41	4	68	2	0
Wetteland, John, Texas	7	2	.778	1.94	61	0	0	0	58	31	65.0	43	259	18	14	5	1	1	0	21	3	63	1	0
Whisenant, Matt, Kansas City* .	1	0	1.000	2.84	24	0	0	0	3	0	19.0	15	86	7	6	0	0	0	3	12	0	16	3	0
Whiteside, Matt, Texas	4	1	.800	5.08	42	1	0	0	8	0	72.2	85	323	45	41	4	2	5	3	26	3	44	3	2
Wickman, Bob, Milwaukee	6	5	.538	2.73	74	0	0	0	20	1	95.2	89	405	32	29	8	6	2	3	41	7	78	8	0
Williams, Brian, Baltimore.......	0	0	.000	3.00	13	0	0	0	8	0	24.0	20	110	8	8	0	0	1	0	18	0	14	1	0
Williams, Woody, Toronto	9	14	.391	4.35	31	31	0	0	0	0	194.2	201	833	98	94	31	6	8	5	66	3	124	7	0
Williams, Mike, Kansas City	0	2	.000	6.43	10	0	0	0	4	1	14.0	20	70	11	10	1	0	1	1	8	1	10	0	0
Williams, Mitch, Kansas City*...	0	1	.000	10.80	7	0	0	0	4	0	6.2	11	38	8	8	2	0	1	0	7	1	10	2	0
Williams, Shad, Anaheim	0	0	.000	0.00	1	0	0	0	1	0	1.0	1	5	0	0	0	0	0	0	1	0	0	0	0
Witasick, Jay, Oakland	0	0	.000	5.73	8	0	0	0	1	0	11.0	14	53	7	7	2	1	0	0	6	0	8	0	0
Witt, Bobby, Texas..................	12	12	.500	4.82	34	32	3	0	1	0	209.0	245	919	118	112	33	3	7	2	74	4	121	7	0
Wojciechowski, Steve, Oak.*...	0	2	.000	7.84	2	2	0	0	0	0	10.1	17	46	9	9	2	1	0	1	5	0	5	0	0
Wolcott, Bob, Seattle..............	5	6	.455	6.03	19	18	0	0	0	0	100.0	129	451	71	67	22	4	2	5	29	2	58	0	0
Woodard, Steve, Milwaukee	3	3	.500	5.15	7	7	0	0	0	0	36.2	39	153	25	21	5	0	2	6	6	0	32	0	0
Wright, Jaret, Cleveland	8	3	.727	4.38	16	16	0	0	0	0	90.1	81	388	45	44	9	3	4	5	35	0	63	1	0
Yan, Esteban, Baltimore	0	1	.000	15.83	3	2	0	0	0	0	9.2	20	58	18	17	3	0	1	2	7	0	4	1	0

COMBINATION SHUTOUTS: **Anaheim (2)**—Dickson and Percival; Watson, Hasegawa, Holtz and DeLucia. **Baltimore (6)**—Erickson and Myers; Mussina and Myers; Coppinger and Johnson; Key, Orosco, Benitez and Myers; Erickson, Orosco and Myers; Key, Mathews, Rhodes, Benitez and Myers. **Boston (1)**—Suppan, Corsi and Slocumb. **Chicago (6)**—Alvarez, Karchner and Hernandez (2); Alvarez, Karchner, T. Castillo and Hernandez; Drabek, Cruz, T. Castillo and Karchner; Baldwin, T. Castillo and Hernandez; Eyre and Foulke. **Cleveland (2)**—Hershiser, Morman, Shuey and M. Jackson; Wright and Shuey. **Detroit (3)**—Blair, Cummings and Brocail; Thompson and Bautista; Keagle, Miceli and Gaillard. **Kansas City (3)**—Rosado, M. Williams and Converse; Belcher and Pichardo; Appier, Pichardo, Whisenant and Bevil. **Milwaukee (5)**—Eldred and Jones; D'Amico, Fetters and Jones; McDonald and Wickman; Woodard and Fetters; Mercedes, Wickman and Fetters. **Minnesota (1)**—Tewksbury, Swindell and Aguilera. **New York (7)**—Cone and Nelson; Pettitte, Rogers and Stanton; Wells and Rivera; Pettitte, Nelson and Rivera; Pettitte and Mecir; Cone, Mendoza and Rogers; Pettitte and Rivera. **Oakland (1)**—Telgheder, Groom, Acre and Taylor. **Seattle (5)**—Johnson and Ayala (2); Moyer and Sanders; Moyer, Timlin and Carmona; Johnson, Timlin, Charlton and Slocumb. **Texas (8)**—Burkett, Patterson and Wetteland; Santana and Patterson; Witt and Wetteland; Oliver and Whiteside; Oliver, Patterson, Gunderson and Wetteland; Helling and Wetteland; Pavlik, Bailes, Patterson and Wetteland; Burkett and Wetteland. **Toronto (9)**—Clemens, Andujar, Plesac and Crabtree; Guzman, Plesac, Crabtree and Timlin; Clemens, Spoljaric and Crabtree; Clemens, Plesac, Quantrill and Spoljaric; Clemens, Plesac and Quantrill; Clemens and Quantrill; Guzman and Escobar; Daal, Crabtree, Plesac, Quantrill and Escobar; Williams, Plesac and Escobar.

PITCHERS WITH TWO OR MORE TEAMS

Pitcher, Team	W	L	Pct.	ERA	G	GS	CG	ShO	GF	Sv.	IP	H	TBF	R	ER	HR	SH	SF	HB	BB	IBB	SO	WP	Bk.
Clark, Terry, Cleveland.............	0	3	.000	6.15	4	4	0	0	0	0	26.1	29	118	21	18	3	1	2	0	13	1	13	0	0
Clark, Terry, Texas	1	4	.200	5.87	9	5	0	0	2	0	30.2	41	138	20	20	3	0	0	2	10	0	11	1	0
Hill, Ken, Texas	5	8	.385	5.19	19	19	0	0	0	0	111.0	129	499	69	64	11	2	6	2	56	3	68	5	0
Hill, Ken, Anaheim..................	4	4	.500	3.65	12	12	1	0	0	0	79.0	65	334	34	32	8	1	1	1	39	0	38	2	0
Jacome, Jason, Kansas City*..	0	0	.000	9.45	7	0	0	0	0	0	6.2	13	35	7	7	2	0	0	1	5	1	3	0	0
Jacome, Jason, Cleveland*	2	0	1.000	5.27	21	4	0	0	2	0	42.2	45	183	26	25	8	0	1	0	15	4	24	2	0
Jarvis, Kevin, Minnesota	0	0	.000	12.46	6	2	0	0	1	0	13.0	23	70	18	18	4	0	0	0	8	0	9	2	0
Jarvis, Kevin, Detroit...............	0	3	.000	5.40	17	3	0	0	9	0	41.2	55	189	28	25	9	1	1	0	14	0	27	0	0
Lira, Felipe, Detroit.................	5	7	.417	5.77	20	15	1	1	1	0	92.0	101	415	61	59	15	2	2	2	45	2	64	7	0
Lira, Felipe, Seattle.................	4	4	.000	9.16	8	3	0	0	2	0	18.2	31	101	21	19	3	0	2	4	10	0	9	0	0
Lowe, Derek, Seattle...............	2	4	.333	6.96	12	9	0	0	1	0	53.0	59	234	43	41	11	2	1	2	20	2	39	2	0
Lowe, Derek, Boston...............	0	2	.000	3.38	8	0	0	0	0	0	16.0	15	64	6	6	0	2	1	2	3	1	13	0	0
McElroy, Chuck, Anaheim*	0	0	.000	3.45	13	0	0	0	3	0	15.2	17	66	7	6	2	0	0	0	3	0	18	0	0
McElroy, Chuck, Chicago*.......	1	3	.250	3.94	48	0	0	0	13	1	59.1	56	254	29	26	3	3	3	2	19	1	44	1	0
Olivares, Omar, Detroit...........	5	6	.455	4.70	19	19	3	2	0	0	115.0	110	502	68	60	8	2	4	9	53	1	74	5	0
Olivares, Omar, Seattle...........	1	4	.200	5.49	13	12	0	0	0	0	62.1	81	292	41	38	10	0	3	4	28	3	29	0	0
Olson, Gregg, Min...................	0	0	.000	18.36	11	0	0	0	5	0	8.1	19	55	17	17	0	0	0	0	11	1	6	0	0
Olson, Gregg, K.C.	4	3	.571	3.02	34	0	0	0	13	1	41.2	39	171	18	14	3	2	1	1	17	3	28	1	0
Sanders, Scott, Seattle............	3	6	.333	6.47	33	6	0	0	15	2	65.1	73	309	48	47	16	2	5	3	38	5	62	4	0
Sanders, Scott, Detroit............	3	8	.273	5.33	14	14	1	1	0	0	74.1	79	317	44	44	14	1	5	1	24	1	58	4	0
Slocumb, Heathcliff, Boston.....	0	5	.000	5.79	49	0	0	0	37	17	46.2	58	227	32	30	4	2	2	3	34	4	36	6	0
Slocumb, Heathcliff, Seattle.....	0	4	.000	4.13	27	0	0	0	24	10	28.1	26	126	13	13	2	2	0	1	15	1	28	4	0
Spoljaric, Paul, Toronto*	0	3	.000	3.19	37	0	0	0	10	3	48.0	37	198	17	17	3	1	2	2	21	4	43	5	1
Spoljaric, Paul, Seattle*	0	0	.000	4.76	20	0	0	0	6	0	22.2	24	104	13	12	1	1	0	1	15	2	27	1	2
Timlin, Mike, Toronto	3	2	.600	2.87	38	0	0	0	26	9	47.0	41	190	17	15	6	4	1	1	15	4	36	1	1
Timlin, Mike, Seattle...............	3	2	.600	3.86	26	0	0	0	5	1	25.2	28	107	13	11	2	0	0	5	1	9	0	0
Weathers, David, New York.....	0	1	.000	10.00	10	0	0	0	3	0	9.0	15	47	10	10	1	0	0	0	7	0	4	2	0
Weathers, David, Cleveland......	1	2	.333	7.56	9	1	0	0	2	0	16.2	23	79	14	14	2	2	1	1	8	0	14	1	0

FIELDING

TEAM

Team	Pct.	G	PO	A	E	TC	DP	PB	Team	Pct.	G	PO	A	E	TC	DP	PB
Detroit	.985	162	4337	1720	92	6149	146	11	Texas	.980	162	4289	1666	121	6076	155	6
Kansas City	.985	161	4329	1630	91	6050	168	14	Milwaukee	.980	161	4282	1655	121	6058	171	11
Toronto	.984	162	4328	1536	94	5958	150	11	Anaheim	.980	162	4364	1592	123	6079	140	19
Baltimore	.984	162	4383	1666	97	6146	148	7	Seattle	.979	162	4343	1572	126	6041	143	3
Minnesota	.983	162	4302	1694	101	6097	170	14	Chicago	.978	161	4267	1439	127	5833	131	16
New York	.983	162	4403	1704	104	6211	156	19	Boston	.978	162	4355	1696	135	6186	179	36
Cleveland	.983	161	4277	1728	106	6111	159	8	Totals	.982	1132	60595	23063	1560	85218	2186	180
Oakland	.980	162	4336	1765	122	6223	170	5									

TRIPLE PLAYS: Anaheim, Milwaukee.

INDIVIDUAL

FIRST BASEMEN

NOTE: All caps denotes fielding-percentage leader based on 81 games for catchers, 108 for all other non-pitchers and 162 innings for pitchers. *Throws lefthanded.

Player, Team	Pct.	G	PO	A	E	TC	DP
Amaral, Rich, Seattle	1.000	14	27	5	0	32	3
Banks, Brian, Milwaukee	.929	5	9	4	1	14	0
Benjamin, Mike, Boston	1.000	4	6	2	0	8	1
Blowers, Mike, Seattle	.990	49	263	25	3	291	27
Brede, Brent, Minnesota*	.992	15	121	9	1	131	9
Carter, Joe, Toronto	.997	42	325	22	1	348	24
Casey, Sean, Cleveland	1.000	1	2	0	0	2	0
Clark, Tony, Detroit	.993	158	1423	100	10	1533	131
Clark, Will, Texas*	.996	100	880	62	4	946	86
Colbrunn, Greg, Minnesota	.988	64	475	35	6	516	60
Coomer, Ron, Minnesota	1.000	9	40	5	0	45	5
Cooper, Scott, Kansas City	1.000	8	27	1	0	28	4
Cruz, Ivan, New York*	1.000	3	7	0	0	7	0
Delgado, Carlos, Toronto	.988	119	962	67	12	1041	98
Diaz, Alex, Texas	1.000	1	2	0	0	2	0
Edmonds, Jim, Anaheim*	1.000	11	84	7	0	91	5
Erstad, Darin, Anaheim*	.990	126	999	64	11	1074	92
Fabregas, Jorge, Chicago	1.000	1	1	0	0	1	0
Fielder, Cecil, New York	1.000	8	59	6	0	65	8
Franco, Julio, Cle.-Mil.	.992	14	109	11	1	121	20
Frye, Jeff, Boston	1.000	1	2	0	0	2	1
Gates, Brent, Seattle	.000	1	0	0	0	0	0
Giambi, Jason, Oakland	.989	51	399	39	5	443	49
Hamelin, Bob, Detroit*	1.000	7	29	1	0	30	1
Hocking, Denny, Minnesota	1.000	1	1	0	0	1	0
Hoiles, Chris, Baltimore	1.000	4	20	3	0	23	1
Hollins, Dave, Anaheim	1.000	14	107	8	0	115	10
Howell, Jack, Anaheim	.962	12	44	6	2	52	4
Huson, Jeff, Milwaukee	1.000	21	66	2	0	68	5
Jaha, John, Milwaukee	.992	27	220	14	2	236	26
Jefferson, Reggie, Boston*	.975	12	74	5	2	81	9
KING, Jeff, Kansas City	.996	150	1217	147	5	1369	135
Kreuter, Chad, Chicago	.750	2	2	1	1	4	1
Ledesma, Aaron, Baltimore	1.000	5	30	1	0	31	4
Lesher, Patrick, Oakland*	1.000	3	21	2	0	23	3
Leyritz, Jim, Ana.-Tex.	.986	24	139	7	2	148	21
Loretta, Mark, Milwaukee	.987	19	150	7	2	159	10
Magadan, Dave, Oakland	1.000	30	123	11	0	134	15
Manto, Jeff, Cleveland	1.000	6	35	1	0	36	4
Martinez, Tino, New York	.994	150	1302	105	8	1415	123
Martinez, Dave, Chicago*	.979	52	256	24	6	286	23
Martinez, Edgar, Seattle	.986	7	68	4	1	73	5
Matheny, Mike, Milwaukee	.000	2	0	0	0	0	0
McGwire, Mark, Oakland	.994	101	884	60	6	950	88
McKeel, Walt, Boston	1.000	1	2	0	0	2	0
Merced, Orlando, Toronto	1.000	1	3	0	0	3	0
Miller, Orlando, Detroit	1.000	3	6	0	0	6	0
Molitor, Paul, Minnesota	.991	12	99	7	1	107	6
Nevin, Phil, Detroit	.958	7	22	1	1	24	0
Nilsson, Dave, Milwaukee	.991	74	610	38	6	654	71
O'Neill, Paul, New York*	1.000	2	1	0	0	1	0
Ortiz, David, Minnesota*	.989	11	84	10	1	95	10
Palmeiro, Rafael, Baltimore*	.993	155	1304	112	10	1426	124
Ripken, Billy, Texas	1.000	9	34	4	0	38	4
Rohrmeier, Dan, Seattle	1.000	3	6	1	0	7	0
Sagmoen, Marc, Texas*	1.000	1	1	0	0	1	0
Samuel, Juan, Toronto	1.000	7	21	1	0	22	4
Seitzer, Kevin, Cleveland	1.000	19	146	13	0	159	17
Sexson, Richie, Cleveland	1.000	2	11	1	0	12	0
Simms, Mike, Texas	.933	2	13	1	1	15	2
Sojo, Luis, New York	1.000	2	4	0	0	4	1
Sorrento, Paul, Seattle	.996	139	929	86	4	1019	89
Stahoviak, Scott, Minnesota	.990	81	607	58	7	672	67
Stairs, Matt, Oakland	.958	7	20	3	1	24	2
Stanley, Mike, Bos.-N.Y.	.997	43	301	21	1	323	34
Steinbach, Terry, Minnesota	.750	2	3	0	1	4	0
Stevens, Lee, Texas*	.994	62	456	33	3	492	45
Surhoff, B.J., Baltimore	1.000	3	21	3	0	24	4
Sutton, Larry, Kansas City*	1.000	12	92	8	0	100	11
Thomas, Frank, Chicago	.986	97	739	49	11	799	70
Thome, Jim, Cleveland	.993	145	1233	95	10	1338	123
Turner, Chris, Anaheim	1.000	2	7	0	0	7	1
Unroe, Tim, Milwaukee	.969	23	57	6	2	65	5
Valdez, Mario, Chicago	1.000	47	256	12	0	268	19
Vaughn, Mo, Boston	.988	131	1088	75	14	1177	117
Vitiello, Joe, Kansas City	1.000	1	8	0	0	8	1
Voigt, Jack, Milwaukee	1.000	19	82	3	0	85	15
Walton, Jerome, Baltimore	1.000	5	23	1	0	24	1
Williamson, Antone, Milwaukee	.977	14	82	4	2	88	6

TRIPLE PLAYS: Erstad, Ana.; Nilsson, Mil.

FIRST BASEMEN WITH TWO OR MORE TEAMS

Player, Team	Pct.	G	PO	A	E	TC	DP
Franco, Julio, Cleveland	1.000	1	1	0	0	1	0
Franco, Julio, Milwaukee	.992	13	108	11	1	120	20
Leyritz, Jim, Anaheim	.977	15	79	5	2	86	17
Leyritz, Jim, Texas	1.000	9	60	2	0	62	4
Stanley, Mike, Boston	.996	31	231	18	1	250	26
Stanley, Mike, New York	1.000	12	70	3	0	73	8

SECOND BASEMEN

Player, Team	Pct.	G	PO	A	E	TC	DP
Alicea, Luis, Anaheim	.978	105	218	268	11	497	58
Alomar, Roberto, Baltimore	.988	109	203	300	6	509	66
Amaral, Rich, Seattle	.927	11	14	24	3	41	5
Batista, Tony, Oakland	1.000	1	2	4	0	6	0
Bellhorn, Mark, Oakland	.960	17	41	56	4	101	16
Benjamin, Mike, Boston	1.000	5	14	11	0	25	6
Bournigal, Rafael, Oakland	1.000	7	1	7	0	8	0
Branson, Jeff, Cleveland	.986	19	21	51	1	73	10
Brito, Tilson, Tor.-Oak.	.990	27	31	73	1	105	19
Bush, Homer, New York	.913	8	8	13	2	23	2
Candaele, Casey, Cleveland	1.000	9	10	25	0	35	4
Catalanotto, Frank, Detroit	1.000	6	7	9	0	16	0
Cedeno, Domingo, Texas	.960	65	100	162	11	273	28
Cora, Joey, Seattle	.973	142	307	310	17	634	81
Cordero, Wil, Boston	1.000	1	0	3	0	3	0
Crespo, Felipe, Toronto	1.000	1	1	3	0	4	0
Diaz, Alex, Texas	1.000	1	4	1	0	5	0
Diaz, Eddy, Milwaukee	1.000	14	27	35	0	62	10
Duncan, Mariano, N.Y.-Tor.	.980	80	139	210	7	356	44
Durham, Ray, Chicago	.974	153	270	395	18	683	77
Easley, Damion, Detroit	.981	137	234	389	12	635	82
Eenhoorn, Robert, Anaheim	.667	3	1	1	1	3	0
Espinoza, Alvaro, Seattle	.978	14	21	23	1	45	9
Fernandez, Tony, Cleveland	.980	109	207	295	10	512	59
Fonville, Chad, Chicago	1.000	2	0	1	0	1	0
Fox, Andy, New York	1.000	5	8	13	0	21	4
Franco, Julio, Cleveland	.983	35	69	107	3	179	23
Frias, Hanley, Texas	1.000	1	0	2	0	2	0
Frye, Jeff, Boston	.991	80	196	228	4	428	63
Garcia, Carlos, Toronto	.981	96	168	253	8	429	50

1997 A.L. STATISTICS Fielding

Player, Team	Pct.	G	PO	A	E	TC	DP
Gates, Brent, Seattle	.977	21	13	30	1	44	4
Grebeck, Craig, Anaheim	1.000	26	45	55	0	100	17
Guevara, Giomar, Seattle	.875	2	2	5	1	8	0
Halter, Shane, Kansas City	1.000	18	16	22	0	38	5
Hansen, Jed, Kansas City	.993	31	56	77	1	134	16
Hayes, Charlie, New York	1.000	5	2	1	0	3	1
Hocking, Denny, Minnesota	1.000	15	13	16	0	29	5
Howard, David, Kansas City	.973	34	65	81	4	150	25
Huson, Jeff, Milwaukee	.989	32	38	49	1	88	10
Jackson, Damian, Cleveland	.000	1	0	0	0	0	0
Kelly, Pat, New York	.981	48	63	92	3	158	26
Knoblauch, Chuck, Minnesota	.985	153	283	424	11	718	101
Ledesma, Aaron, Baltimore	.973	22	32	41	2	75	8
Loretta, Mark, Milwaukee	.980	63	125	170	6	301	52
Martin, Norberto, Chicago	.975	9	14	25	1	40	3
McLemore, Mark, Texas	.980	89	148	254	8	410	60
Offerman, Jose, Kansas City	.981	101	201	254	9	464	64
Perez, Tomas, Toronto	.959	8	15	32	2	49	3
Phillips, Tony, Anaheim	.968	43	78	101	6	185	21
Raabe, Brian, Seattle	.000	1	0	0	0	0	0
Reboulet, Jeff, Baltimore	.977	63	83	130	5	218	28
Reed, Jody, Detroit	.987	41	49	107	2	158	18
Ripken, Billy, Texas	.983	25	40	78	2	120	18
Roberts, Bip, Cleveland	.932	13	24	31	4	59	9
Samuel, Juan, Toronto	1.000	4	7	6	0	13	1
Sanchez, Rey, New York	.976	37	63	101	4	168	21
Sheets, Andy, Seattle	1.000	2	2	2	0	4	0
Sheldon, Scott, Oakland	1.000	1	1	2	0	3	1
Sojo, Luis, New York	.982	72	121	147	5	273	35
SPIEZIO, Scott, Oakland	.990	146	280	415	7	702	93
Unroe, Tim, Milwaukee	.000	1	0	0	0	0	0
Valentin, John, Boston	.976	79	180	259	11	450	67
Vina, Fernando, Milwaukee	.982	77	149	227	7	383	53
Walker, Todd, Minnesota	.964	8	11	16	1	28	5
Wilson, Enrique, Cleveland	1.000	1	1	3	0	4	0

TRIPLE PLAY: Loretta, Mil.

SECOND BASEMEN WITH TWO OR MORE TEAMS

Player, Team	Pct.	G	PO	A	E	TC	DP
Brito, Tilson, Toronto	.989	25	28	65	1	94	14
Brito, Tilson, Oakland	1.000	2	3	8	0	11	5
Duncan, Mariano, New York	.976	41	65	99	4	168	20
Duncan, Mariano, Toronto	.984	39	74	111	3	188	24

THIRD BASEMEN

Player, Team	Pct.	G	PO	A	E	TC	DP
Alicea, Luis, Anaheim	.960	12	5	19	1	25	1
Amaral, Rich, Seattle	.000	1	0	0	0	0	0
Arias, George, Anaheim	1.000	1	0	3	0	3	0
Banks, Brian, Milwaukee	1.000	1	2	3	0	5	0
Batista, Tony, Oakland	1.000	4	3	1	0	4	0
Bell, Jay, Kansas City	1.000	4	2	7	0	9	3
Bellhorn, Mark, Oakland	.951	40	31	66	5	102	8
Benjamin, Mike, Boston	.929	19	13	39	4	56	4
Blowers, Mike, Seattle	.929	10	3	10	1	14	1
Boggs, Wade, New York	.978	76	42	140	4	186	15
Bragg, Darren, Boston	.000	1	0	0	0	0	0
Branson, Jeff, Cleveland	1.000	6	2	8	0	10	2
Brito, Tilson, Tor.-Oak.	.961	27	20	29	2	51	5
Brosius, Scott, Oakland	.977	107	92	206	7	305	23
Candaele, Casey, Cleveland	.000	1	0	0	0	0	0
Cedeno, Domingo, Texas	1.000	3	2	6	0	8	2
Cirillo, Jeff, Milwaukee	.963	150	126	320	17	463	29
Coomer, Ron, Minnesota	.966	119	66	216	10	292	20
Cooper, Scott, Kansas City	1.000	39	21	54	0	75	4
Crespo, Felipe, Toronto	.933	7	8	6	1	15	1
Davis, Russ, Seattle	.939	117	56	219	18	293	24
Diaz, Eddy, Milwaukee	.000	1	0	0	0	0	0
Eenhoorn, Robert, Anaheim	.833	5	2	3	1	6	0
Espinoza, Alvaro, Seattle	.000	1	0	0	0	0	0
Evans, Tom, Toronto	.917	12	9	24	3	36	1
Fox, Andy, New York	1.000	11	5	13	0	18	1
Frye, Jeff, Boston	.878	18	11	32	6	49	2
FRYMAN, Travis, Detroit	.978	153	126	312	10	448	21
Garcia, Carlos, Toronto	.000	4	0	0	0	0	0
Gates, Brent, Seattle	.934	32	10	47	4	61	4
Grebeck, Craig, Anaheim	1.000	15	1	2	0	3	0
Halter, Shane, Kansas City	1.000	12	1	4	0	5	0
Hayes, Charlie, New York	.947	98	65	168	13	246	19
Hocking, Denny, Minnesota	1.000	39	14	32	0	46	2
Hoiles, Chris, Baltimore	.000	1	0	0	0	0	0
Hollins, Dave, Anaheim	.922	135	101	241	29	371	17

Player, Team	Pct.	G	PO	A	E	TC	DP
Howard, David, Kansas City	.867	7	3	10	2	15	1
Howell, Jack, Anaheim	.976	24	14	27	1	42	4
Huson, Jeff, Milwaukee	.000	2	0	0	0	0	0
Ledesma, Aaron, Baltimore	.923	11	5	7	1	13	1
Loretta, Mark, Milwaukee	.962	15	9	16	1	26	3
Magadan, Dave, Oakland	.940	49	25	54	5	84	7
Manto, Jeff, Cleveland	1.000	7	0	4	0	4	0
Martin, Norberto, Chicago	.973	17	9	27	1	37	2
Martinez, Edgar, Seattle	.000	1	0	0	0	0	0
Miller, Orlando, Detroit	.889	4	1	7	1	9	0
Naehring, Tim, Boston	.981	68	40	111	3	154	11
Nevin, Phil, Detroit	1.000	17	6	13	0	19	1
Norton, Greg, Chicago	.864	11	4	15	3	22	0
Palmer, Dean, Tex.-K.C.	.948	141	90	244	19	362	18
Paquette, Craig, Kansas City	.935	72	45	129	12	186	15
Pena, Tony, Cleveland	.000	1	0	0	0	0	0
Phillips, Tony, Chi.-Ana.	.952	10	7	13	1	21	1
Pozo, Arquimedez, Boston	.947	4	4	14	1	19	1
Raabe, Brian, Seattle	1.000	2	1	1	0	2	0
Reboulet, Jeff, Baltimore	.875	12	1	6	1	8	0
Ripken, Cal Jr., Baltimore	.949	162	98	314	22	434	25
Ripken, Billy, Texas	1.000	13	4	12	0	16	2
Roberts, Bip, Kansas City	1.000	10	3	12	0	15	1
Samuel, Juan, Toronto	1.000	9	3	7	0	10	2
Seitzer, Kevin, Cleveland	.885	13	3	20	3	26	0
Sheets, Andy, Seattle	.872	21	8	33	6	47	4
Sheldon, Scott, Oakland	.000	1	0	0	0	0	0
Silvestri, Dave, Texas	.000	1	0	0	0	0	0
Snopek, Chris, Chicago	.915	82	56	117	16	189	11
Sojo, Luis, New York	1.000	3	1	2	0	3	0
Spiezio, Scott, Oakland	.000	1	0	0	0	0	0
Sprague, Ed, Toronto	.945	129	106	202	18	326	19
Surhoff, B.J., Baltimore	1.000	3	0	2	0	2	1
Tatis, Fernando, Texas	.951	60	45	90	7	142	5
Unroe, Tim, Milwaukee	1.000	2	1	3	0	4	1
Valdez, Mario, Chicago	.000	1	0	0	0	0	0
Valentin, John, Boston	.942	64	59	121	11	191	15
Ventura, Robin, Chicago	.956	54	53	99	7	159	11
Voigt, Jack, Milwaukee	1.000	6	1	2	0	3	0
Walker, Todd, Minnesota	.969	40	24	70	3	97	4
Williams, Matt, Cleveland	.970	151	89	301	12	402	21

TRIPLE PLAY: Cirillo, Mil.

THIRD BASEMEN WITH TWO OR MORE TEAMS

Player, Team	Pct.	G	PO	A	E	TC	DP
Brito, Tilson, Toronto	1.000	17	12	14	0	26	3
Brito, Tilson, Oakland	.920	10	8	15	2	25	2
Palmer, Dean, Texas	.959	93	72	162	10	244	10
Palmer, Dean, Kansas City	.924	48	27	82	9	118	8
Phillips, Tony, Chicago	.950	9	7	12	1	20	1
Phillips, Tony, Anaheim	1.000	1	0	1	0	1	0

SHORTSTOPS

Player, Team	Pct.	G	PO	A	E	TC	DP
Amaral, Rich, Seattle	.000	1	0	0	0	0	0
Batista, Tony, Oakland	.970	61	91	169	8	268	38
Bell, Jay, Kansas City	.985	149	227	443	10	680	102
Bellhorn, Mark, Oakland	1.000	1	0	1	0	1	0
Benjamin, Mike, Boston	.958	16	17	29	2	48	4
Bordick, Mike, Baltimore	.980	153	223	425	13	661	95
Bournigal, Rafael, Oakland	.980	74	99	192	6	297	40
Branson, Jeff, Cleveland	1.000	2	0	1	0	1	0
Brito, Tilson, Tor.-Oak.	.951	14	18	21	2	41	7
Brosius, Scott, Oakland	.970	30	25	39	2	66	8
Cedeno, Domingo, Texas	.957	43	44	91	6	141	28
Cruz, Deivi, Detroit	.979	147	192	420	13	625	94
Diaz, Eddy, Milwaukee	.000	1	0	0	0	0	0
DiSarcina, Gary, Anaheim	.977	153	227	421	15	663	85
Easley, Damion, Detroit	1.000	21	9	16	0	25	0
Eenhoorn, Robert, Anaheim	.900	2	5	4	1	10	2
Espinoza, Alvaro, Seattle	.965	17	21	34	2	57	5
Fernandez, Tony, Cleveland	.974	10	12	26	1	39	7
Fonville, Chad, Boston	.800	2	2	2	1	5	0
Fox, Andy, New York	1.000	2	3	3	0	6	2
Frias, Hanley, Texas	1.000	12	12	11	0	23	2
Frye, Jeff, Boston	1.000	3	2	2	0	4	0
Garcia, Carlos, Toronto	.750	5	3	3	2	8	1
Garciaparra, Nomar, Boston	.971	153	249	450	21	720	113
Gates, Brent, Seattle	1.000	5	2	5	0	7	2
Gil, Benji, Texas	.963	106	163	328	19	510	71
GONZALEZ, Alex, Toronto	.986	125	209	341	8	558	77
Grebeck, Craig, Anaheim	.959	20	16	31	2	49	7

Player, Team	Pct.	G	PO	A	E	TC	DP
Guevara, Giomar, Seattle	1.000	1	0	1	0	1	0
Guillen, Ozzie, Chicago	.974	139	207	348	15	570	78
Halter, Shane, Kansas City	.957	5	9	13	1	23	3
Hocking, Denny, Minnesota	.975	44	61	96	4	161	28
Howard, David, Kansas City	.955	9	6	15	1	22	5
Jackson, Damian, Cleveland	1.000	5	7	7	0	14	2
Jeter, Derek, New York	.975	159	244	457	18	719	87
Knoblauch, Chuck, Minnesota	.833	1	2	3	1	6	1
Ledesma, Aaron, Baltimore	1.000	4	1	2	0	3	0
Loretta, Mark, Milwaukee	.957	44	50	84	6	140	23
Martin, Norberto, Chicago	.960	28	27	45	3	75	11
Martinez, Felix, Kansas City	.975	12	17	22	1	40	7
Meares, Pat, Minnesota	.969	134	211	415	20	646	93
Miller, Orlando, Detroit	.979	31	30	64	2	96	18
Perez, Tomas, Toronto	.993	32	43	91	1	135	22
Reboulet, Jeff, Baltimore	.979	22	20	27	1	48	4
Ripken, Cal Jr., Baltimore	1.000	3	2	0	0	2	0
Ripken, Billy, Texas	.971	31	38	64	3	105	15
Rodriguez, Alex, Seattle	.962	140	209	394	24	627	83
Sanchez, Rey, New York	1.000	6	3	9	0	12	1
Sheets, Andy, Seattle	.939	9	4	27	2	33	1
Sheldon, Scott, Oakland	.939	12	15	16	2	33	4
Silvestri, Dave, Texas	1.000	1	0	2	0	2	0
Snopek, Chris, Chicago	1.000	4	5	8	0	13	2
Sojo, Luis, New York	1.000	4	5	4	0	9	3
Tejada, Miguel, Oakland	.968	26	54	68	4	126	18
Valentin, Jose, Milwaukee	.967	134	208	383	20	611	86
Vizquel, Omar, Cleveland	.985	152	245	429	10	684	98
Wilson, Enrique, Cleveland	.941	4	6	10	1	17	4

TRIPLE PLAY: DiSarcina, Ana.

SHORTSTOPS WITH TWO OR MORE TEAMS

Player, Team	Pct.	G	PO	A	E	TC	DP
Brito, Tilson, Toronto	.929	8	13	13	2	28	6
Brito, Tilson, Oakland	1.000	6	5	8	0	13	1

OUTFIELDERS

Player, Team	Pct.	G	PO	A	E	TC	DP
Abbott, Jeff, Chicago*	1.000	10	15	0	0	15	0
Amaral, Rich, Seattle	1.000	52	62	0	0	62	0
Anderson, Brady, Baltimore*	.989	124	277	2	3	282	0
Anderson, Garret, Anaheim*	.992	148	343	14	3	360	2
Aven, Bruce, Cleveland	1.000	13	15	1	0	16	0
Baines, Harold, Chicago*	.000	1	0	0	0	0	0
Banks, Brian, Milwaukee	.950	15	19	0	1	20	0
Bartee, Kimera, Detroit	1.000	6	3	0	0	3	0
Becker, Rich, Minnesota*	.985	128	319	5	5	329	0
Belle, Albert, Chicago	.972	154	351	1	10	362	0
Benitez, Yamil, Kansas City	.965	52	111	0	4	115	0
Berroa, Geronimo, Oak.-Bal.	.973	83	141	2	4	147	0
Blowers, Mike, Seattle	1.000	6	5	0	0	5	0
Bragg, Darren, Boston	.987	150	365	11	5	381	3
Brede, Brent, Minnesota*	.957	42	67	0	3	70	0
Brosius, Scott, Oakland	.964	22	25	2	1	28	0
Brumfield, Jacob, Toronto	1.000	47	87	6	0	93	1
Buford, Damon, Texas	.990	117	282	7	3	292	4
BUHNER, Jay, Seattle	.997	154	295	5	1	301	3
Burnitz, Jeromy, Milwaukee	.975	149	256	13	7	276	3
Butler, Rich, Toronto	1.000	3	5	0	0	5	0
Cameron, Mike, Chicago	.985	112	334	5	5	344	2
Canseco, Jose, Oakland	.938	44	74	2	5	81	0
Carr, Chuck, Milwaukee	1.000	23	25	1	0	26	0
Carter, Joe, Toronto	.972	51	104	1	3	108	0
Clyburn, Danny, Baltimore	.000	1	0	0	0	0	0
Coleman, Michael, Boston	.941	7	16	0	1	17	0
Coleman, Vince, Detroit	1.000	3	3	0	0	3	0
Coomer, Ron, Minnesota	.950	7	17	2	1	20	2
Cordero, Wil, Boston	.992	137	248	8	2	258	4
Cordova, Marty, Minnesota	.991	101	217	12	2	231	2
Cruz, Jose Jr., Sea.-Tor.	.974	104	181	4	5	190	1
Cruz, Ivan, New York*	1.000	1	1	0	0	1	0
Curtis, Chad, Cle.-N.Y.	.980	111	188	6	4	198	1
Damon, Johnny, Kansas City*	.988	136	322	5	4	331	3
Davis, Eric, Baltimore	.975	30	39	0	1	40	0
Dellucci, David, Baltimore*	1.000	9	19	1	0	20	0
Devereaux, Mike, Texas	1.000	28	40	0	0	40	0
Diaz, Alex, Texas	.980	23	48	2	1	51	0
Ducey, Rob, Seattle	.986	69	66	3	1	70	1
Duncan, Mariano, New York	.889	6	7	1	1	9	0
Dunn, Todd, Milwaukee	.909	27	39	1	4	44	0
Dye, Jermaine, Kansas City	.966	75	164	7	6	177	3
Edmonds, Jim, Anaheim*	.985	115	312	9	5	326	2

Player, Team	Pct.	G	PO	A	E	TC	DP
Encarnacion, Angelo, Detroit	1.000	10	22	0	0	22	0
Erstad, Darin, Anaheim*	1.000	1	3	0	0	3	0
Fonville, Chad, Chicago	1.000	3	7	0	0	7	0
Fox, Andy, New York	.750	2	2	1	1	4	0
Frye, Jeff, Boston	.900	13	16	2	2	20	0
Gates, Brent, Seattle	1.000	1	1	0	0	1	0
Giambi, Jason, Oakland	.982	68	102	5	2	109	1
Giles, Brian, Cleveland*	.972	115	201	7	6	214	1
Gonzalez, Alex, Texas	.971	64	128	6	4	138	1
Goodwin, Tom, K.C.-Tex.	.992	147	370	6	3	379	0
Grebeck, Craig, Anaheim	1.000	3	6	0	0	6	0
Green, Shawn, Toronto*	.984	91	173	6	3	182	3
Greer, Rusty, Texas*	.965	153	318	9	12	339	0
Grieve, Ben, Oakland	1.000	24	39	1	0	40	1
Griffey, Ken Jr., Seattle*	.985	153	388	9	6	403	3
Grissom, Marquis, Cleveland	.992	144	356	7	3	366	3
Hall, Joe, Detroit	1.000	1	1	0	0	1	0
Halter, Shane, Kansas City	1.000	32	37	1	0	38	0
Hammonds, Jeffrey, Baltimore	.980	114	240	4	5	249	0
Henderson, Rickey, Anaheim*	1.000	13	26	0	0	26	0
Higginson, Bobby, Detroit	.972	143	287	20	9	316	5
Hocking, Denny, Minnesota	1.000	20	35	2	0	37	1
Howard, David, Kansas City	1.000	23	22	3	0	25	0
Hubbard, Trent, Cleveland	1.000	6	3	0	0	3	0
Hunter, Brian L., Detroit	.990	162	408	8	4	420	0
Hurst, Jimmy, Detroit	1.000	12	12	0	0	12	0
Huson, Jeff, Milwaukee	1.000	9	5	1	0	6	1
Ibanez, Raul, Seattle	1.000	8	9	0	0	9	0
Incaviglia, Pete, Baltimore	.952	18	20	0	1	21	0
Jackson, Darrin, Min.-Mil.	.994	70	148	6	1	155	2
Justice, David, Cleveland*	.984	78	120	3	2	125	0
Kelly, Roberto, Min.-Sea.	1.000	88	154	2	0	156	0
Latham, Chris, Minnesota	.917	10	11	0	1	12	0
Lawton, Matt, Minnesota	.976	138	278	9	7	294	3
Lennon, Patrick, Oakland	.948	36	55	0	3	58	0
Lesher, Patrick, Oakland*	.958	32	66	3	3	72	1
Lewis, Darren, Chicago	1.000	64	90	1	0	91	1
Long, Ryan, Kansas City	1.000	5	8	0	0	8	0
Mack, Shane, Boston	1.000	45	75	0	0	75	0
Malave, Jose, Boston	1.000	4	3	0	0	3	0
Manto, Jeff, Cleveland	.000	1	0	0	0	0	0
Martinez, Dave, Chicago*	.996	105	229	6	1	236	3
Mashore, Damon, Oakland	.991	89	203	10	2	215	3
McDonald, Jason, Oakland	.968	74	147	2	5	154	1
McLemore, Mark, Texas	.000	1	0	0	0	0	0
Merced, Orlando, Toronto	.985	96	190	10	3	203	4
Mieske, Matt, Milwaukee	.962	74	121	6	5	132	0
Mitchell, Kevin, Cleveland	.000	1	0	0	1	1	0
Mouton, Lyle, Chicago	.969	67	126	1	4	131	0
Myers, Rod, Kansas City*	.982	26	55	1	1	57	0
Nevin, Phil, Detroit	.986	40	65	4	1	70	2
Newfield, Milwaukee, Milwaukee	.977	28	43	0	1	44	0
Newson, Warren, Texas*	.949	58	93	1	5	99	0
Nieves, Melvin, Detroit	.979	99	187	4	4	195	1
Nilsson, Dave, Milwaukee	1.000	22	31	1	0	32	0
Nixon, Otis, Toronto	.996	102	254	1	1	256	0
Nunnally, Jon, Kansas City	1.000	9	12	0	0	12	0
O'Leary, Troy, Boston*	.979	142	266	8	6	280	0
O'Neill, Paul, New York*	.984	146	292	7	5	304	0
Ordonez, Magglio, Chicago	1.000	19	43	1	0	44	0
Palmeiro, Orlando, Anaheim*	.975	52	78	1	2	81	0
Paquette, Craig, Kansas City	1.000	4	6	1	0	7	1
Pemberton, Rudy, Boston	.949	23	35	2	2	39	1
Perez, Robert, Toronto	1.000	25	35	0	0	35	0
Phillips, Tony, Chi.-Ana.	.970	63	126	4	4	134	1
Pose, Scott, New York	1.000	45	44	2	0	46	1
Pride, Curtis, Detroit	.980	35	49	0	1	50	0
Raines, Tim, New York	.988	57	79	1	1	81	0
Ramirez, Manny, Cleveland	.975	146	259	10	7	276	2
Reboulet, Jeff, Baltimore	1.000	1	2	0	0	2	0
Roberts, Bip, K.C.-Cle.	.982	94	159	7	3	169	1
Sagmoen, Marc, Texas*	1.000	17	24	0	0	24	0
Salmon, Tim, Anaheim	.971	153	352	15	11	378	5
Samuel, Juan, Toronto	1.000	2	3	0	0	3	0
Sierra, Ruben, Toronto	.929	7	13	0	1	14	0
Simms, Mike, Texas	.958	19	23	0	1	24	0
Stairs, Matt, Oakland	.977	89	122	6	3	131	0
Stevens, Lee, Texas*	1.000	22	30	0	0	30	0
Stewart, Shannon, Toronto	.980	41	97	1	2	100	0
Strawberry, Darryl, New York*	1.000	4	5	0	0	5	0
Surhoff, B.J., Baltimore	.992	133	247	11	2	260	3
Sutton, Larry, Kansas City*	.000	1	0	0	0	0	0
Tarasco, Tony, Baltimore	.991	81	105	4	1	110	1

1997 A.L. STATISTICS Fielding

Player, Team	Pct.	G	PO	A	E	TC	DP
Tavarez, Jesus, Boston	.980	35	49	1	1	51	1
Tinsley, Lee, Seattle	1.000	41	68	2	0	70	2
Trammell, Bubba, Detroit	1.000	28	52	1	0	53	0
Turner, Chris, Anaheim	1.000	1	1	0	0	1	0
Unroe, Tim, Milwaukee	1.000	2	1	0	0	1	0
Vitiello, Joe, Kansas City	.980	28	48	0	1	49	0
Voigt, Jack, Milwaukee	.985	40	61	5	1	67	0
Walton, Jerome, Baltimore	1.000	19	29	0	0	29	0
Whiten, Mark, New York	.954	57	102	2	5	109	0
Williams, Bernie, New York	.993	128	270	2	2	274	1
Williams, Gerald, Milwaukee	.992	154	357	11	3	371	4
Young, Ernie, Oakland	.973	66	139	5	4	148	0

TRIPLE PLAY: Anderson, Ana.

OUTFIELDERS WITH TWO OR MORE TEAMS

Player, Team	Pct.	G	PO	A	E	TC	DP
Berroa, Geronimo, Oakland	.986	43	71	1	1	73	0
Berroa, Geronimo, Baltimore	.959	40	70	1	3	74	0
Cruz, Jose Jr., Seattle	.966	49	83	1	3	87	0
Cruz, Jose Jr., Toronto	.981	55	98	3	2	103	1
Curtis, Chad, Cleveland	1.000	19	20	0	0	20	0
Curtis, Chad, New York	.978	92	168	6	4	178	1
Goodwin, Tom, Kansas City	.996	96	232	3	1	236	0
Goodwin, Tom, Texas	.986	51	138	3	2	143	0
Jackson, Darrin, Minnesota	.990	44	93	4	1	98	1
Jackson, Darrin, Milwaukee	1.000	26	55	2	0	57	1
Kelly, Roberto, Minnesota	1.000	59	101	1	0	102	0
Kelly, Roberto, Seattle	1.000	29	53	1	0	54	0
Phillips, Tony, Chicago	.972	28	67	3	2	72	1
Phillips, Tony, Anaheim	.968	35	59	1	2	62	0
Roberts, Bip, Kansas City	.981	84	146	5	3	154	0
Roberts, Bip, Cleveland	1.000	10	13	2	0	15	1

CATCHERS

Player, Team	Pct.	G	PO	A	E	TC	DP	PB
Alomar, Sandy Jr., Cleveland	.985	119	743	40	12	795	8	3
Borders, Pat, Cleveland	1.000	53	312	19	0	331	2	5
Brown, Kevin L., Texas	.900	4	9	0	1	10	0	0
Casanova, Raul, Detroit	.985	92	543	38	9	590	6	8
Diaz, Einar, Cleveland	.955	5	18	3	1	22	0	0
Encarnacion, Angelo, Anaheim	.940	11	43	4	3	50	0	0
Fabregas, Jorge, Ana.-Chi.	.988	113	600	51	8	659	9	8
Fasano, Sal, Kansas City	.982	12	53	3	1	57	2	2
Figga, Mike, New York	1.000	1	6	0	0	6	0	0
Girardi, Joe, New York	.994	111	830	54	5	889	11	11
Greene, Charlie, Baltimore	1.000	4	4	0	0	4	0	0
Greene, Todd, Anaheim	1.000	26	153	7	0	160	2	5
Haselman, Bill, Boston	.983	66	373	40	7	420	4	17
Hatteberg, Scott, Boston	.983	106	574	46	11	631	13	17
HOILES, Chris, Baltimore	1.000	87	602	28	0	630	4	3
Jensen, Marcus, Detroit	.964	8	26	1	1	28	0	0
Johnson, Brian, Detroit	.987	43	217	9	3	229	2	0
Karkovice, Ron, Chicago	.996	51	261	13	1	275	1	2
Kreuter, Chad, Chi.-Ana.	.992	80	488	32	4	524	1	4
Laker, Tim, Baltimore	.966	7	28	0	1	29	0	0
Levis, Jesse, Milwaukee	.994	78	296	19	2	317	1	4
Leyritz, Jim, Ana.-Tex.	.998	69	417	45	1	463	4	10
Macfarlane, Mike, Kansas City	.991	81	439	20	4	463	3	9
Machado, Robert, Chicago	1.000	10	34	3	0	37	1	1
Martinez, Sandy, Toronto	.933	3	12	2	1	15	0	0
Marzano, John, Seattle	.976	37	191	13	5	209	4	2
Matheny, Mike, Milwaukee	.993	121	697	58	5	760	6	7
Mayne, Brent, Oakland	.996	83	419	36	2	457	5	1
McKeel, Walt, Boston	1.000	4	4	0	0	4	0	0
Mercedes, Henry, Texas	.988	23	78	4	1	83	2	2
Miller, Damian, Minnesota	1.000	20	85	3	0	88	1	3
Molina, Izzy, Oakland	.992	48	218	17	2	237	1	3
Mosquera, Julio, Toronto	.923	3	11	1	0	12	0	0
Myers, Greg, Minnesota	.986	38	196	11	3	210	2	2
Nevin, Phil, Detroit	1.000	1	1	0	0	1	0	0
O'Brien, Charlie, Toronto	.995	69	543	41	3	587	8	4
Pena, Tony, Chicago	1.000	30	143	8	0	151	2	5
Posada, Jorge, New York	.992	60	367	23	3	393	3	8
Rodriguez, Ivan, Texas	.992	143	821	75	7	903	11	3
Rosario, Mel, Baltimore	.875	4	7	0	1	8	0	0
Santiago, Benito, Toronto	.997	95	621	40	2	663	10	7
Spehr, Tim, Kansas City	1.000	17	78	7	0	85	1	0
Stanley, Mike, Boston	.982	15	53	3	1	57	0	2
Steinbach, Terry, Minnesota	.993	116	654	51	5	710	4	9
Stewart, Andy, Kansas City	1.000	4	10	1	0	11	0	0
Stinnett, Kelly, Milwaukee	.989	25	81	5	1	87	1	0
Sweeney, Mike, Kansas City	.993	76	425	31	3	459	13	3

Player, Team	Pct.	G	PO	A	E	TC	DP	PB
Turner, Chris, Anaheim	1.000	8	26	2	0	28	0	1
Valentin, Javier, Minnesota	1.000	4	11	2	0	13	0	0
Varitek, Jason, Boston	1.000	1	1	0	0	1	0	0
Walbeck, Matt, Detroit	.988	44	240	15	3	258	2	3
Webster, Lenny, Baltimore	.995	97	532	36	3	571	5	4
Wilkins, Rick, Seattle	1.000	3	9	1	0	10	0	0
Williams, George, Oakland	.984	67	337	27	6	370	3	1
Wilson, Dan, Seattle	.995	144	1051	72	6	1129	13	1

CATCHERS WITH TWO OR MORE TEAMS

Player, Team	Pct.	G	PO	A	E	TC	DP	PB
Fabregas, Jorge, Anaheim	.989	21	81	5	1	87	1	0
Fabregas, Jorge, Chicago	.988	92	519	46	7	572	8	8
Kreuter, Chad, Chicago	.984	13	57	3	1	61	0	0
Kreuter, Chad, Anaheim	.994	67	431	29	3	463	1	4
Leyritz, Jim, Anaheim	1.000	58	361	40	0	401	4	9
Leyritz, Jim, Texas	.984	11	56	5	1	62	0	1

PITCHERS

Player, Team	Pct.	G	PO	A	E	TC	DP
Acre, Mark, Oakland	1.000	15	1	1	0	2	0
Adams, Willie, Oakland	1.000	13	2	10	0	12	0
Adamson, Joel, Milwaukee*	.882	30	6	9	2	17	0
Aguilera, Rick, Minnesota	1.000	61	5	13	0	18	1
Alberro, Jose, Texas	.889	10	3	5	1	9	1
Aldred, Scott, Minnesota*	1.000	17	2	9	0	11	0
Almanzar, Carlos, Toronto	.000	4	0	0	0	0	0
Alvarez, Wilson, Chicago*	.958	22	6	17	1	24	0
Anderson, Brian, Cleveland*	1.000	8	0	11	0	11	0
Andujar, Luis, Toronto	1.000	17	1	7	0	8	0
Appier, Kevin, Kansas City	.976	34	24	17	1	42	3
Assenmacher, Paul, Cleveland*	1.000	75	5	6	0	11	0
Avery, Steve, Boston*	1.000	22	0	19	0	19	1
Ayala, Bobby, Seattle	1.000	71	11	7	0	18	1
Bailes, Scott, Texas*	1.000	24	2	6	0	8	1
Baldwin, James, Chicago	.949	32	15	22	2	39	0
Banks, Willie, New York	1.000	5	0	4	0	4	1
Bautista, Jose, Detroit	1.000	21	4	3	0	7	1
Belcher, Tim, Kansas City	1.000	32	23	22	0	45	1
Benitez, Armando, Baltimore	1.000	71	1	3	0	4	0
Benjamin, Mike, Boston*	.000	1	0	0	0	0	0
Bere, Jason, Chicago	.750	6	1	2	1	4	1
Bertotti, Mike, Chicago*	.000	9	0	0	0	0	0
Bevil, Brian, Kansas City	1.000	18	1	0	0	1	0
Blair, Willie, Detroit	.958	29	9	14	1	24	2
Boehringer, Brian, New York	1.000	34	2	5	0	7	1
Boggs, Wade, New York	.000	1	0	0	0	0	0
Bones, Ricky, Kansas City	.950	21	8	11	1	20	1
Borland, Toby, Boston	.000	3	0	0	0	0	0
Borowski, Joe, New York	1.000	1	0	0	0	0	0
Boskie, Shawn, Baltimore	1.000	28	6	11	0	17	1
Bovee, Mike, Anaheim	.000	3	0	0	0	0	0
Bowers, Shane, Minnesota	.800	5	2	2	1	5	0
Brandenburg, Mark, Boston	1.000	31	5	5	0	10	0
Brewer, Billy, Oakland*	.000	3	0	0	0	0	0
Brocail, Doug, Detroit	1.000	61	6	12	0	18	0
Burkett, John, Texas	.976	30	12	28	1	41	1
Cadaret, Greg, Anaheim*	1.000	15	1	0	0	1	0
Carmona, Rafael, Seattle	1.000	4	1	0	0	1	0
Carpenter, Chris, Toronto	.923	14	7	5	1	13	1
Carrasco, Hector, Kansas City	1.000	28	2	6	0	8	0
Casian, Larry, Kansas City*	1.000	32	1	5	0	6	0
Castillo, Tony, Chicago*	.880	64	3	19	3	25	0
Castillo, Carlos, Chicago	1.000	37	1	5	0	6	0
Charlton, Norm, Seattle*	.857	71	5	13	3	21	0
Chavez, Anthony, Anaheim	1.000	7	0	4	0	4	0
Checo, Robinson, Boston	.000	5	0	0	0	0	0
Clark, Terry, Cle.-Tex.	.952	13	9	11	1	21	2
Clemens, Roger, Toronto	.980	34	11	39	1	51	1
Clemons, Chris, Chicago	1.000	5	1	1	0	2	0
Cloude, Ken, Seattle	.900	10	5	4	1	10	0
Colon, Bartolo, Cleveland	.821	19	6	17	5	28	3
Cone, David, New York	.917	29	9	13	2	24	0
Converse, Jim, Kansas City	1.000	3	1	0	0	1	0
Coppinger, Rocky, Baltimore	1.000	5	1	1	0	2	0
Corsi, Jim, Boston	.938	52	6	9	1	16	0
Crabtree, Tim, Toronto	1.000	37	3	8	0	11	1
Cruz, Nelson, Chicago	1.000	19	3	1	0	4	0
Cummings, John, Detroit*	1.000	19	1	5	0	6	0
Daal, Omar, Toronto*	1.000	8	0	7	0	7	0
D'Amico, Jeff, Milwaukee	1.000	23	8	12	0	20	0
Darwin, Danny, Chicago	1.000	21	6	20	0	26	1

Player, Team	Pct.	G	PO	A	E	TC	DP
Darwin, Jeff, Chicago	1.000	14	0	1	0	1	0
Davis, Mark, Milwaukee*	1.000	19	2	5	0	7	1
Davis, Tim, Seattle*	1.000	2	0	1	0	1	0
De La Maza, Roland, Kansas City	.000	1	0	0	0	0	0
DeLucia, Rich, Anaheim	1.000	33	2	4	0	6	2
Dickson, Jason, Anaheim	.933	33	8	20	2	30	1
Dishman, Glenn, Detroit*	1.000	7	3	7	0	10	1
Drabek, Doug, Chicago	.971	31	14	20	1	35	0
Duran, Roberto, Detroit*	1.000	13	0	1	0	1	0
Eldred, Cal, Milwaukee	1.000	34	15	10	0	25	1
Erickson, Scott, Baltimore	.909	34	17	43	6	66	6
Escobar, Kelvim, Toronto	1.000	27	0	2	0	2	1
Eshelman, Vaughn, Boston*	.889	21	4	4	1	9	0
Eversgerd, Bryan, Texas*	.000	3	0	0	0	0	0
Eyre, Scott, Chicago*	1.000	11	0	6	0	6	0
Fassero, Jeff, Seattle*	.980	35	15	34	1	50	1
Fetters, Mike, Milwaukee	.933	51	2	12	1	15	0
Finley, Chuck, Anaheim*	1.000	25	2	17	0	19	0
Flener, Huck, Toronto*	.000	8	0	0	0	0	0
Florie, Bryce, Milwaukee	.800	32	5	3	2	10	1
Fordham, Tom, Chicago*	1.000	7	0	2	0	2	0
Foulke, Keith, Chicago	1.000	16	1	4	0	5	1
Gaillard, Eddie, Detroit	.000	16	0	0	0	0	0
Garces, Rich, Boston	1.000	12	1	2	0	3	0
Gooden, Dwight, New York	1.000	20	9	18	0	27	1
Gordon, Tom, Boston	.950	42	18	20	2	40	1
Graves, Danny, Cleveland	.000	5	0	0	0	0	0
Groom, Buddy, Oakland*	1.000	78	2	10	0	12	2
Gross, Kevin, Anaheim	1.000	12	0	4	0	4	0
Grundt, Ken, Boston*	1.000	2	2	0	0	2	0
Guardado, Eddie, Minnesota*	1.000	69	1	6	0	7	1
Gubicza, Mark, Anaheim	1.000	2	1	0	0	1	0
Gunderson, Eric, Texas*	1.000	60	1	3	0	4	0
Guzman, Juan, Toronto	.727	13	1	7	3	11	0
Hammond, Chris, Boston*	.929	29	3	10	1	14	1
Haney, Chris, Kansas City*	.875	8	1	6	1	8	0
Hansell, Greg, Milwaukee	.000	3	0	0	0	0	0
Hanson, Erik, Toronto	.000	3	0	0	0	0	0
Harnisch, Pete, Milwaukee	1.000	4	2	0	0	2	0
Harris, Pep, Anaheim	1.000	61	4	14	0	18	2
Hasegawa, Shigetoshi, Anaheim	.967	50	8	21	1	30	3
Haught, Gary, Oakland	1.000	6	1	1	0	2	0
Hawkins, LaTroy, Minnesota	.957	20	9	13	1	23	1
Haynes, Jimmy, Oakland	.889	13	6	10	2	18	2
Helling, Rick, Texas	1.000	10	1	1	0	2	0
Henry, Butch, Boston*	1.000	36	4	17	0	21	2
Hentgen, Pat, Toronto	.981	35	19	34	1	54	1
Heredia, Wilson, Texas	1.000	10	0	3	0	3	1
Hernandez, Fernando, Detroit	.000	2	0	0	0	0	0
Hernandez, Xavier, Texas	1.000	44	3	6	0	9	1
Hernandez, Roberto, Chicago	1.000	46	4	6	0	10	1
Hershiser, Orel, Cleveland	.925	32	20	29	4	53	2
Hill, Ken, Tex.-Ana.	1.000	31	17	37	0	54	2
Holtz, Mike, Anaheim*	.909	66	2	8	1	11	1
Holzemer, Mark, Seattle*	1.000	14	1	4	0	5	0
Hudson, Joe, Boston	1.000	26	2	7	0	9	2
Hurtado, Edwin, Seattle	1.000	13	0	6	0	6	1
Irabu, Hideki, New York	.750	13	1	5	2	8	1
Jackson, Mike, Cleveland	1.000	71	5	15	0	20	4
Jacome, Jason, K.C.-Cle.*	.941	28	4	12	1	17	1
James, Mike, Anaheim	1.000	58	2	9	0	11	0
Janzen, Marty, Toronto	1.000	12	3	1	0	4	0
Jarvis, Kevin, Min.-Det.	1.000	23	0	6	0	6	0
Johnson, Dane, Oakland	.714	38	1	4	2	7	0
Johnson, Mike, Baltimore	1.000	14	3	4	0	7	1
Johnson, Randy, Seattle*	.871	30	7	20	4	31	0
Johnstone, John, Oakland	1.000	5	1	0	0	1	0
Jones, Doug, Milwaukee	.857	75	4	8	2	14	1
Jones, Todd, Detroit	1.000	68	1	4	0	5	0
Juden, Jeff, Cleveland	1.000	8	1	2	0	3	0
Kamieniecki, Scott, Baltimore	.938	30	15	30	3	48	4
Karchner, Matt, Chicago	1.000	52	2	6	0	8	2
Karl, Scott, Milwaukee*	.892	32	5	28	4	37	5
Karsay, Steve, Oakland	.833	24	7	13	4	24	1
Keagle, Greg, Detroit	1.000	11	4	3	0	7	1
Key, Jimmy, Baltimore*	.961	34	12	37	2	51	2
Kline, Steve, Cleveland*	.750	20	2	1	1	4	0
Krivda, Rick, Baltimore*	1.000	10	6	5	0	11	1
Kubinski, Tim, Oakland*	1.000	11	2	1	0	3	1
Lacy, Kerry, Boston	.857	33	4	2	1	7	0
Langston, Mark, Anaheim*	.929	9	2	11	1	14	1
Levine, Al, Chicago	1.000	25	5	3	0	8	1
Lewis, Richie, Oakland	1.000	14	0	3	0	3	0
Lira, Felipe, Det.-Sea.	.935	28	8	21	2	31	4
Lloyd, Graeme, New York*	.800	46	3	9	3	15	0
Lopez, Albie, Cleveland	1.000	37	4	13	0	17	1
Lorraine, Andrew, Oakland*	1.000	12	4	2	0	6	1
Lowe, Derek, Sea.-Bos.	1.000	20	3	10	0	13	0
Ludwick, Eric, Oakland	1.000	6	2	3	0	5	1
Maddux, Mike, Seattle	1.000	6	1	1	0	2	0
Mahay, Ron, Boston*	1.000	28	1	2	0	3	0
Mahomes, Pat, Boston	.000	10	0	0	0	0	0
Maloney, Sean, Milwaukee	.000	3	0	0	0	0	0
Manzanillo, Josias, Seattle	1.000	16	1	1	0	2	0
Martinez, Dennis, Seattle	.857	9	6	6	2	14	0
Mathews, Terry, Baltimore	.938	57	5	10	1	16	0
Mathews, T.J., Oakland	.833	24	1	4	1	6	0
May, Darrell, Anaheim*	1.000	29	0	6	0	6	1
McAndrew, Jamie, Milwaukee	.800	5	3	1	1	5	0
McCarthy, Greg, Seattle*	1.000	37	2	4	0	6	0
McDill, Allen, Kansas City*	1.000	3	0	1	0	1	0
McDonald, Ben, Milwaukee	.957	21	6	16	1	23	3
McDowell, Jack, Cleveland	1.000	8	3	6	0	9	0
McElroy, Chuck, Ana.-Chi.*	1.000	61	1	12	0	13	1
Mecir, Jim, New York	1.000	25	5	2	0	7	0
Mendoza, Ramiro, New York	.947	39	11	25	2	38	2
Mercedes, Jose, Milwaukee	.880	29	6	16	3	25	2
Mesa, Jose, Cleveland	.923	66	5	7	1	13	2
Miceli, Dan, Detroit	1.000	71	4	6	0	10	0
Miller, Travis, Minnesota*	1.000	13	8	6	0	14	0
Mills, Alan, Baltimore	.778	39	3	4	2	9	0
Miranda, Angel, Milwaukee*	1.000	10	1	2	0	3	0
Misuraca, Mike, Milwaukee	.000	5	0	0	0	0	0
Moehler, Brian, Detroit	.975	31	16	23	1	40	2
Mohler, Mike, Oakland*	.962	62	7	18	1	26	0
Montgomery, Jeff, Kansas City	1.000	55	10	5	0	15	0
Montgomery, Steve, Oakland	1.000	4	1	0	0	1	0
Moody, Eric, Texas	1.000	10	1	2	0	3	0
Morman, Alvin, Cleveland*	1.000	34	0	2	0	2	0
Moyer, Jamie, Seattle*	1.000	30	14	34	0	48	1
Mussina, Mike, Baltimore	1.000	33	18	25	0	43	0
Myers, Mike, Detroit*	.857	88	4	8	2	14	0
Myers, Randy, Baltimore*	1.000	61	1	3	0	4	0
NAGY, Charles, Cleveland	1.000	34	16	45	0	61	0
Naulty, Dan, Minnesota	1.000	29	1	1	0	2	0
Navarro, Jaime, Chicago	.909	33	15	15	3	33	0
Nelson, Jeff, New York	1.000	77	4	17	0	21	0
Ogea, Chad, Cleveland	.833	21	8	17	5	30	1
Olivares, Omar, Det.-Sea.	.947	32	12	24	2	38	3
Oliver, Darren, Texas*	.938	32	7	23	2	32	0
Olson, Gregg, Min.-K.C.	.909	45	4	6	1	11	0
Oquist, Mike, Oakland	.947	19	8	10	1	19	2
Orosco, Jesse, Baltimore*	1.000	71	3	6	0	9	0
Patterson, Danny, Texas	1.000	54	4	7	0	11	1
Pavlik, Roger, Texas	.875	11	3	4	1	8	1
Percival, Troy, Anaheim	1.000	55	2	2	0	4	0
Perez, Mike, Kansas City	1.000	16	3	3	0	6	0
Perisho, Matt, Anaheim*	1.000	11	2	7	0	9	0
Person, Robert, Toronto	.923	23	4	8	1	13	1
Pettitte, Andy, New York*	.981	35	9	44	1	54	4
Pichardo, Hipolito, Kansas City	1.000	47	8	12	0	20	2
Pittsley, Jim, Kansas City	.941	21	6	10	1	17	0
Plesac, Dan, Toronto*	1.000	73	0	1	0	1	0
Plunk, Eric, Cleveland	.750	55	2	4	2	8	0
Prieto, Ariel, Oakland	.848	22	9	19	5	33	2
Pugh, Tim, Detroit	1.000	2	0	2	0	2	0
Quantrill, Paul, Toronto	.857	77	1	17	3	21	3
Radke, Brad, Minnesota	1.000	35	15	31	0	46	5
Reyes, Carlos, Oakland	1.000	37	6	11	0	17	1
Reyes, Al, Milwaukee	1.000	19	1	6	0	7	0
Rhodes, Arthur, Baltimore*	.952	53	4	16	1	21	1
Rigby, Brad, Oakland	.950	14	5	14	1	20	2
Rios, Danny, New York	1.000	2	1	0	0	1	0
Risley, Bill, Toronto	.000	3	0	0	0	0	0
Ritchie, Todd, Minnesota	1.000	42	3	10	0	13	1
Rivera, Mariano, New York	1.000	66	11	9	0	20	0
Robertson, Rich, Minnesota*	.905	31	6	13	2	21	2
Robinson, Ken, Toronto	1.000	3	1	2	0	3	1
Rodriguez, Frank, Minnesota	.944	43	10	24	2	36	2
Rodriguez, Nerio, Baltimore	1.000	6	0	5	0	5	0
Rogers, Kenny, New York*	.965	31	13	42	2	57	3
Rosado, Jose, Kansas City*	.972	33	11	24	1	36	2
Rose, Brian, Boston	.000	1	0	0	0	0	0
Rusch, Glendon, Kansas City*	1.000	30	8	13	0	21	1
Saberhagen, Bret, Boston	.750	6	1	2	1	4	1
Sager, A.J., Detroit	1.000	38	3	13	0	16	0

1997 A.L. STATISTICS Fielding

Player, Team	Pct.	G	PO	A	E	TC	DP
Sanders, Scott, Sea.-Det.	.941	47	6	10	1	17	0
Santana, Julio, Texas	1.000	30	6	15	0	21	3
Santiago, Jose, Kansas City	.000	4	0	0	0	0	0
Sele, Aaron, Boston	.972	33	10	25	1	36	2
Serafini, Dan, Minnesota*	1.000	6	0	1	0	1	0
Service, Scott, Kansas City	1.000	12	0	1	0	1	0
Shuey, Paul, Cleveland	1.000	40	3	7	0	10	0
Simas, Bill, Chicago	1.000	40	3	3	0	6	0
Sirotka, Mike, Chicago*	.800	7	1	3	1	5	0
Slocumb, Heathcliff, Bos.-Sea.	.929	76	7	6	1	14	1
Small, Aaron, Oakland	.952	71	5	15	1	21	2
Smiley, John, Cleveland*	1.000	6	0	4	0	4	0
Spoljaric, Paul, Tor.-Sea.*	1.000	57	6	11	0	17	1
Springer, Dennis, Anaheim	.949	32	12	25	2	39	3
Stanton, Mike, New York*	1.000	64	3	6	0	9	0
Stevens, Dave, Minnesota	1.000	6	2	1	0	3	0
Sturtze, Tanyon, Texas	1.000	9	0	1	0	1	0
Suppan, Jeff, Boston	.824	23	6	8	3	17	2
Swindell, Greg, Minnesota*	1.000	65	12	11	0	23	1
Taylor, Billy, Oakland	1.000	72	3	13	0	16	1
Telgheder, Dave, Oakland	1.000	20	9	24	0	33	4
Tewksbury, Bob, Minnesota	1.000	26	21	30	0	51	7
Thomas, Larry, Chicago*	1.000	5	1	0	0	1	0
Thompson, Justin, Detroit*	1.000	32	11	31	0	42	3
Timlin, Mike, Tor.-Sea.	.955	64	8	13	1	22	2
Torres, Salomon, Seattle	1.000	2	1	0	0	1	1
Trlicek, Ricky, Boston	1.000	18	3	3	0	6	1
Trombley, Mike, Minnesota	1.000	67	6	6	0	12	2
Veres, Randy, Kansas City	.857	24	0	6	1	7	0
Villone, Ron, Milwaukee	.900	50	3	6	1	10	2
Vosberg, Ed, Texas*	.833	42	1	4	1	6	0
Wagner, Paul, Milwaukee	1.000	2	0	1	0	1	0
Wakefield, Tim, Boston	.912	35	9	22	3	34	1
Walker, Jamie, Kansas City*	1.000	50	5	6	0	11	1
Wasdin, John, Boston	.889	53	5	11	2	18	0
Watson, Allen, Anaheim*	.927	35	4	34	3	41	1
Weathers, Dave, N.Y.-Cle.	1.000	19	2	2	0	4	0
Wells, David, New York*	.902	32	8	29	4	41	2
Wells, Bob, Seattle	1.000	46	7	6	0	13	0
Wengert, Don, Oakland	.967	49	13	16	1	30	2
Wetteland, John, Texas	1.000	61	1	6	0	7	0
Whisenant, Matt, Kansas City*	.750	24	0	3	1	4	1
Whiteside, Matt, Texas	.962	42	9	16	1	26	1
Wickman, Bob, Milwaukee	1.000	74	6	14	0	20	4
Williams, Brian, Baltimore	1.000	13	1	2	0	3	0
Williams, Woody, Toronto	.950	31	9	10	1	20	0
Williams, Mike, Kansas City	1.000	10	1	1	0	2	0
Williams, Mitch, Kansas City*	.000	7	0	0	0	0	0
Williams, Shad, Anaheim	.000	1	0	0	0	0	0
Witasick, Jay, Oakland	.000	8	0	0	0	0	0
Witt, Bobby, Texas	.974	34	10	27	1	38	2
Wojciechowski, Steve, Oakland*	1.000	2	0	4	0	4	0
Wolcott, Bob, Seattle	.944	19	4	13	1	18	2
Woodard, Steve, Milwaukee	1.000	7	0	2	0	2	0
Wright, Jaret, Cleveland	1.000	16	5	10	0	15	1
Yan, Esteban, Baltimore	.000	3	0	0	0	0	0

PITCHERS WITH TWO OR MORE TEAMS

Player, Team	Pct.	G	PO	A	E	TC	DP
Clark, Terry, Cleveland	1.000	4	3	4	0	7	0
Clark, Terry, Texas	.929	9	6	7	1	14	2
Hill, Ken, Texas	1.000	19	13	25	0	38	1
Hill, Ken, Anaheim	1.000	12	4	12	0	16	1
Jacome, Jason, Kansas City*	1.000	7	1	5	0	6	1
Jacome, Jason, Cleveland*	.909	21	3	7	1	11	0
Jarvis, Kevin, Minnesota	1.000	6	0	1	0	1	0
Jarvis, Kevin, Detroit	1.000	17	0	5	0	5	0
Lira, Felipe, Detroit	.929	20	7	19	2	28	3
Lira, Felipe, Seattle	1.000	8	1	2	0	3	1
Lowe, Derek, Seattle	1.000	12	2	6	0	8	0
Lowe, Derek, Boston	1.000	8	1	4	0	5	0
McElroy, Chuck, Anaheim*	.000	13	0	0	0	0	0
McElroy, Chuck, Chicago*	1.000	48	1	12	0	13	1
Olivares, Omar, Detroit	1.000	19	10	16	0	26	2
Olivares, Omar, Seattle	.833	13	2	8	2	12	1
Olson, Gregg, Minnesota	1.000	11	0	2	0	2	0
Olson, Gregg, Kansas City	.889	34	4	4	1	9	0
Sanders, Scott, Seattle	.750	33	2	1	1	4	0
Sanders, Scott, Detroit	1.000	14	4	9	0	13	0
Slocumb, Heathcliff, Boston	.889	49	4	4	1	9	1
Slocumb, Heathcliff, Seattle	1.000	27	3	2	0	5	0
Spoljaric, Paul, Toronto*	1.000	37	4	10	0	14	1
Spoljaric, Paul, Seattle*	1.000	20	2	1	0	3	0
Timlin, Mike, Toronto	1.000	38	5	8	0	13	2
Timlin, Mike, Seattle	.889	26	3	5	1	9	0
Weathers, Dave, New York	1.000	10	0	1	0	1	0
Weathers, Dave, Cleveland	1.000	9	2	1	0	3	0

MISCELLANEOUS

SHUTOUT GAMES

Read across for wins, down for losses.

Team	Sea.	Bal.	Tor.	Tex.	Mil.	N.Y.	Ana.	K.C.	Chi.	Det.	Bos.	Min.	Cle.	Oak.	N.L.	W	L	Pct.
Seattle	..	0	1	1	1	0	0	0	1	2	0	1	1	0	0	8	4	.667
Baltimore	0	..	0	1	0	0	1	0	1	1	1	1	1	3	0	10	6	.625
Toronto	0	2	..	2	1	4	1	1	2	0	1	1	1	0	0	16	11	.593
Texas	0	0	1	..	2	1	1	1	0	0	0	2	0	1	0	9	7	.563
Milwaukee	0	1	2	0	..	0	0	0	1	2	0	0	0	1	1	8	7	.533
New York	0	0	2	1	3	..	0	0	0	1	1	1	0	1	1	10	9	.526
Anaheim	1	0	0	1	0	0	..	0	0	0	1	1	1	0	0	5	5	.500
Kansas City	0	0	1	0	0	0	0	..	0	1	2	0	1	0	0	5	5	.500
Chicago	1	2	0	0	0	0	0	1	..	1	0	0	0	1	1	7	8	.467
Detroit	0	0	1	1	0	0	2	0	0	..	1	0	2	0	1	8	13	.381
Boston	1	0	0	0	0	0	0	0	0	0	..	1	1	1	0	4	8	.333
Minnesota	1	0	0	0	0	0	0	0	1	1	0	..	0	1	0	4	9	.308
Cleveland	0	0	0	0	0	0	0	1	1	1	0	0	..	0	0	3	8	.273
Oakland	0	0	0	0	0	1	0	0	0	0	0	0	0	..	0	1	9	.100
N.L. clubs	0	1	3	0	1	3	0	1	1	3	1	1	0	0	..	..	..	..
Lost	4	6	11	7	7	9	5	5	8	13	8	9	8	9	..	98	109	.473

A.L. shutouts vs. N.L. clubs (4): Chicago A.L. vs Chicago N.L., Detroit vs. New York N.L., Milwaukee vs. St. Louis, New York A.L. vs. Atlanta.

HOME RECORD

Read across for home wins, down for road losses.

Team	Mil.	N.Y.	Bal.	Ana.	Chi.	Sea.	Cle.	Det.	Tor.	Bos.	Tex.	Min.	Oak.	K.C.	N.L.	W	L	Pct.
Milwaukee	..	4	2	3	4	3	2	3	5	2	4	3	4	3	5	47	33	.588
New York	5	..	1	2	4	2	3	4	3	4	4	3	4	4	4	47	33	.588
Baltimore	1	3	..	5	2	3	4	3	2	2	5	5	3	3	5	46	35	.568
Anaheim	5	2	3	..	5	4	2	4	4	3	3	2	5	3	1	46	36	.561
Chicago	3	1	3	4	..	2	3	2	3	5	2	3	4	5	5	45	36	.556
Seattle	3	3	1	4	3	..	4	2	5	2	3	2	3	4	6	45	36	.556
Cleveland	4	3	3	1	4	1	..	4	4	2	2	3	4	6	3	44	37	.543
Detroit	1	0	3	5	4	1	3	..	4	3	4	3	3	2	6	42	39	.519
Toronto	4	2	2	3	3	2	3	4	..	3	4	4	2	2	2	42	39	.519
Boston	4	2	3	3	2	3	2	3	..	0	5	4	2	4		39	42	.481
Texas	2	3	1	1	4	1	3	3	2	2	..	4	4	2	7	39	42	.481
Minnesota	4	1	1	4	3	2	1	5	2	2	1	..	3	2	4	35	46	.432
Oakland	5	3	1	0	1	2	2	2	4	3	3	2	..	3	4	35	46	.432
Kansas City	3	1	2	2	0	3	3	2	2	5	3	3	1	..	3	33	47	.413
N.L. clubs	6	5	3	5	6	7	3	4	4	4	5	6	6	6	..	..	..	..
Lost on road	50	33	29	42	45	36	38	44	47	42	43	48	51	47	..	585	547	.517

HOME RECORDS IN INTERLEAGUE GAMES

Team	Atl.	Fla.	Mon.	N.Y.	Phi.	Team	Chi.	Cin.	Hou.	Pit.	St.L.	Team	Col.	L.A.	S.D.	S.F.
Baltimore	..	..	1-2	1-2	3-0	Chicago	2-1	..	3-0	..	..	Anaheim	0-2	0-2	1-1	0-2
Boston	0-3	1-2	..		3-0	Cleveland	2-1	1-2	..	..	..	Oakland	1-1	1-1	1-1	1-1
Detroit	..	1-2	..	3-0	2-1	Kansas City	..	..	2-1	..	1-2	Seattle	2-0	2-0	1-1	1-1
New York	1-2	..	1-2	2-1	..	Milwaukee	..	..	..	2-1	3-0	Texas	2-0	2-0	2-0	1-1
Toronto	1-2	0-3	1-2	..	..	Minnesota	..	2-1	..	2-1	..					

ROAD RECORD

Read across for road wins, down for home losses.

Team	Bal.	N.Y.	Sea.	Cle.	Bos.	Ana.	Tex.	Det.	Chi.	K.C.	Tor.	Min.	Mil.	Oak.	N.L.	W	L	Pct.
Baltimore	..	5	4	2	3	2	5	3	3	4	4	5	4	5	3	52	29	.642
New York	3	..	2	3	4	5	3	6	5	4	4	5	2	2	1	49	33	.598
Seattle	3	4	..	4	2	2	5	5	3	2	3	4	3	4	1	45	36	.556
Cleveland	2	2	2	..	3	3	3	2	3	2	2	5	4	3	6	42	38	.525
Boston	4	2	4	4	..	2	3	3	1	1	3	3	4	3	2	39	42	.481
Anaheim	1	2	2	5	3	..	5	1	1	3	2	2	2	6	3	38	42	.475
Texas	0	1	3	3	6	3	..	1	4	3	2	4	2	3	3	38	43	.469
Detroit	3	2	3	2	4	1	3	..	3	4	2	1	3	4	2	37	44	.457
Chicago	3	1	3	2	3	1	1	2	..	6	2	3	1	4	3	35	45	.438
Kansas City	2	2	2	0	3	3	3	3	1	..	3	4	3	2	3	34	47	.420
Toronto	4	3	1	2	3	2	3	2	3	4	..	4	0	1	2	34	47	.420
Minnesota	0	2	3	3	1	3	2	2	3	3	1	..	3	4	3	33	48	.407
Milwaukee	4	0	2	2	1	1	3	4	3	2	2	2	..	1	3	31	50	.383
Oakland	2	2	3	2	1	1	2	2	2	5	2	2	1	..	3	30	51	.370
N.L. clubs	4	5	2	3	5	7	1	3	1	3	7	2	1	4	..	..	..	..
Lost at home	35	33	36	37	42	36	42	39	36	47	39	46	33	46	..	537	595	.474

1997 A.L. STATISTICS *Miscellaneous*

ANAHEIM—84-78

Pitcher	Bal. W-L	Bos. W-L	Chi. W-L	Cle. W-L	Det. W-L	K.C. W-L	Mil. W-L	Min. W-L	N.Y. W-L	Oak. W-L	Sea. W-L	Tex. W-L	Tor. W-L	N.L. W-L	Totals W-L
Bovee, Mike	0-0	0-0	0-0	0-0	0-0	0-0	0-0	0-0	0-0	0-0	0-0	0-0	0-0	0-0	0-0
Cadaret, Greg	0-0	0-0	0-0	0-0	0-0	0-0	0-0	0-0	0-0	0-0	0-0	0-0	0-0	0-0	0-0
Chavez, Anthony	0-0	0-0	0-0	0-0	0-0	0-0	0-0	0-0	0-0	0-0	0-0	0-0	0-0	0-0	0-0
DeLucia, Rich	0-0	0-0	1-0	0-0	0-0	0-1	0-1	0-0	0-0	1-0	1-1	1-0	2-1	0-0	6-4
Dickson, Jason	2-0	2-1	0-1	0-0	1-0	2-0	1-0	1-1	2-0	1-1	0-1	1-1	0-0	0-3	13-9
Finley, Chuck	1-1	1-0	1-0	1-0	1-2	0-1	2-1	1-0	0-0	1-0	2-1	0-0	1-0	1-0	13-6
Gross, Kevin	0-0	0-0	0-0	0-0	0-0	0-0	0-0	0-0	0-0	1-0	0-0	1-0	0-0	0-1	2-1
Gubicza, Mark	0-0	0-0	0-0	0-1	0-0	0-0	0-0	0-0	0-0	0-0	0-0	0-0	0-0	0-0	0-1
Harris, Pep	0-0	0-0	0-1	1-0	0-1	1-0	0-0	1-1	0-1	1-0	0-0	0-0	0-0	0-0	5-4
Hasegawa, Shigetoshi	0-1	0-0	0-0	0-1	1-0	0-0	0-0	0-1	1-1	0-2	0-0	0-0	0-0	0-1	3-7
Hill, Ken	0-0	0-1	1-0	1-0	0-0	0-1	0-0	0-1	0-0	1-0	1-0	0-1	0-1	1-0	4-4
Holtz, Mike	0-0	2-0	0-1	1-0	0-0	0-1	0-0	0-0	0-1	0-0	0-0	0-2	0-0	0-1	3-4
James, Mike	0-1	0-1	0-0	0-0	1-0	1-0	0-0	0-1	1-0	1-0	0-0	0-2	0-0	1-0	5-5
Langston, Mark	0-0	0-0	1-0	0-0	0-0	0-1	0-0	0-0	0-2	0-0	0-1	0-0	0-0	0-0	2-4
May, Darrell	0-1	0-0	0-0	0-0	0-0	0-0	0-0	0-0	0-0	0-0	0-0	0-0	1-0	1-0	2-1
McElroy, Chuck	0-0	0-0	0-0	0-0	0-0	0-0	0-0	0-0	0-0	0-0	0-0	0-0	0-0	0-0	0-0
Percival, Troy	0-0	0-2	0-0	0-1	0-0	0-0	1-0	0-0	0-0	1-0	1-0	1-0	0-2	0-2	5-5
Perisho, Matt	0-0	0-0	0-0	0-0	0-1	0-0	0-0	0-1	0-0	0-0	0-0	0-0	0-0	0-0	0-2
Springer, Dennis	1-2	0-0	1-1	1-0	1-1	0-2	2-0	1-0	0-1	0-0	0-0	1-0	1-0	0-1	9-9
Watson, Allen	0-1	1-0	2-1	0-0	0-1	2-0	1-0	0-1	0-1	3-0	1-1	1-1	1-1	0-3	12-12
Williams, Shad	0-0	0-0	0-0	0-0	0-0	0-0	0-0	0-0	0-0	0-0	0-0	0-0	0-0	0-0	0-0
Totals	4-7	6-5	6-5	7-4	5-6	6-5	7-4	4-7	4-7	11-1	6-6	8-4	6-5	4-12	84-78

INTERLEAGUE BREAKDOWN: Holtz 0-1, Percival 0-2, Watson 0-1 vs. Dodgers; Dickson 0-1, Shigetoshi 0-1, Hill 1-0, James 1-0 vs. Padres; Dickson 0-1, May 1-0, Springer 0-1, Watson 0-1 vs. Giants; Dickson 0-1, Finley 1-0, Gross 0-1, Watson 0-1 vs. Rockies.

BALTIMORE—98-64

Pitcher	Ana. W-L	Bos. W-L	Chi. W-L	Cle. W-L	Det. W-L	K.C. W-L	Mil. W-L	Min. W-L	N.Y. W-L	Oak. W-L	Sea. W-L	Tex. W-L	Tor. W-L	N.L. W-L	Totals W-L
Benitez, Armando	2-0	0-0	0-1	1-0	0-1	0-2	0-0	0-0	0-0	1-0	0-0	0-0	0-1	0-0	4-5
Boskie, Shawn	0-1	0-0	0-2	1-0	0-0	0-0	1-0	1-0	1-0	1-0	0-0	0-0	1-0	0-3	6-6
Coppinger, Rocky	0-0	0-0	0-0	0-0	0-0	0-0	0-0	0-0	1-0	0-1	0-0	0-0	0-0	0-0	1-1
Erickson, Scott	1-0	2-1	0-1	0-0	1-1	0-0	0-2	4-0	1-1	1-0	2-0	2-0	1-1	1-0	16-7
Johnson, Mike	0-0	0-1	0-0	0-0	0-0	0-0	0-0	0-0	0-0	0-0	0-0	0-0	0-0	0-0	0-1
Kamieniecki, Scott	0-2	0-0	0-0	0-0	1-0	0-0	0-0	3-1	1-1	0-0	1-0	1-0	2-1	1-0	10-6
Key, Jimmy	1-0	2-1	1-0	1-1	2-1	2-0	0-2	0-0	1-1	2-0	1-1	0-0	0-0	1-2	16-10
Krivda, Rick	0-0	0-0	0-0	1-1	0-0	0-0	0-1	0-0	1-0	0-0	0-0	1-0	0-0	0-0	4-2
Mathews, Terry	0-0	0-1	0-0	0-0	0-0	1-0	1-0	0-0	0-0	0-0	0-1	0-0	1-0	1-2	4-4
Mills, Alan	1-0	0-0	0-0	0-1	0-2	1-0	0-0	0-0	0-0	0-0	0-0	0-0	0-0	0-0	2-3
Mussina, Mike	1-0	0-0	3-1	2-0	0-0	0-1	2-1	0-0	1-1	2-1	0-0	2-1	0-2	1-0	15-8
Myers, Randy	0-0	0-0	0-0	0-0	0-0	0-0	0-0	0-0	0-0	0-1	1-0	1-0	0-0	0-0	2-3
Orosco, Jesse	0-0	0-1	0-0	0-0	0-1	0-0	1-0	2-0	1-0	0-1	2-0	0-0	0-0	0-0	6-3
Rhodes, Arthur	1-1	1-1	1-0	0-1	1-0	2-0	0-0	0-0	0-0	0-0	1-0	0-0	0-0	3-0	10-3
Rodriguez, Nerio	0-0	0-0	0-0	0-1	1-0	0-0	0-0	0-0	0-0	0-0	0-0	0-0	1-0	0-0	2-1
Williams, Brian	0-0	0-0	0-0	0-0	0-0	0-0	0-0	0-0	0-0	0-0	0-0	0-0	0-0	0-0	0-0
Yan, Esteban	0-0	0-0	0-0	0-0	0-0	0-1	0-0	0-0	0-0	0-0	0-0	0-0	0-0	0-0	0-0
Totals	7-4	5-7	5-6	6-5	6-6	7-4	5-6	10-1	8-4	8-3	7-4	10-1	6-6	8-7	98-64

INTERLEAGUE BREAKDOWN: Key 1-0, Mathews 1-0, Rhodes 1-0 vs. Braves; Boskie 0-1, Kamieniecki 1-0, Key 0-1 vs. Expos; Key 0-1, Mathews 0-1, Rhodes 1-0 vs. Mets; Erickson 1-0, Mussina 1-0, Rhodes 1-0 vs. Phillies; Boskie 0-2, Mathews 0-1 vs. Marlins.

BOSTON—78-84

Pitcher	Ana. W-L	Bal. W-L	Chi. W-L	Cle. W-L	Det. W-L	K.C. W-L	Mil. W-L	Min. W-L	N.Y. W-L	Oak. W-L	Sea. W-L	Tex. W-L	Tor. W-L	N.L. W-L	Totals W-L
Avery, Steve	0-0	1-0	0-2	3-0	0-0	2-0	0-0	0-0	0-0	0-1	0-2	0-1	0-0	0-1	6-7
Benjamin, Mike	0-0	0-0	0-0	0-0	0-0	0-0	0-0	0-0	0-0	0-0	0-0	0-0	0-0	0-0	0-0
Borland, Toby	0-0	0-0	0-0	0-0	0-0	0-0	0-0	0-0	0-0	0-0	0-0	0-0	0-0	0-0	0-0
Brandenburg, Mark	0-0	0-0	0-0	0-0	0-0	0-0	0-1	0-0	0-0	0-0	0-0	0-0	0-0	0-1	0-2
Checo, Robinson	0-0	0-0	0-0	0-0	1-0	0-0	0-0	0-0	0-1	0-0	0-0	0-0	0-0	0-0	1-1
Corsi, Jim	0-0	0-0	1-0	0-0	0-0	1-0	1-0	0-0	0-1	0-0	1-1	0-0	1-1	0-0	5-3
Eshelman, Vaughn	0-0	0-1	0-0	0-0	0-2	0-0	0-0	0-0	0-0	0-0	0-0	1-0	2-0	0-0	3-3
Garces, Rich	0-0	0-0	0-0	0-0	0-0	0-0	0-1	0-0	0-0	0-0	0-0	0-0	0-0	0-0	0-1
Gordon, Tom	0-1	1-2	0-0	0-2	1-0	0-1	0-0	1-0	1-0	0-1	1-0	1-1	0-1	0-1	6-10
Grundt, Ken	0-0	0-0	0-0	0-0	0-0	0-0	0-0	0-0	0-0	0-0	0-0	0-0	0-0	0-0	0-0
Hammond, Chris	1-0	0-0	0-1	0-0	0-1	0-0	0-0	0-1	0-0	1-0	0-0	0-0	0-0	0-0	3-4
Henry, Butch	1-1	1-0	0-0	0-0	0-0	0-0	2-0	0-0	0-0	1-0	0-0	2-1	0-1	0-0	7-3
Hudson, Joe	0-0	0-0	0-0	1-0	0-0	0-0	0-0	1-0	0-0	1-0	0-0	0-0	0-1	0-1	3-1
Lacy, Kerry	0-0	0-0	0-0	0-0	0-0	0-0	1-0	0-1	0-0	0-0	0-0	0-0	0-0	0-0	1-1
Lowe, Derek	0-0	0-0	0-0	0-1	0-0	0-0	0-0	0-0	0-1	0-0	0-0	0-0	0-0	0-0	0-2
Mahay, Ron	1-0	1-0	0-0	0-0	0-0	0-0	0-0	0-0	0-0	0-0	0-0	0-0	1-0	0-0	3-0
Mahomes, Pat	1-0	0-0	0-0	0-0	0-0	0-0	0-0	0-0	0-0	0-0	0-0	0-0	0-0	0-0	1-0
Rose, Brian	0-0	0-0	0-0	0-0	0-0	0-0	0-0	0-0	0-0	0-0	0-0	0-0	0-0	0-0	0-0
Saberhagen, Bret	0-1	0-0	0-0	0-0	0-0	0-0	0-0	0-0	0-0	0-0	0-0	0-0	0-0	0-0	0-1
Sele, Aaron	0-1	2-1	2-0	0-1	0-1	0-2	0-0	3-1	2-1	1-0	1-0	0-1	1-1	1-2	13-12
Slocumb, Heathcliff	0-0	0-0	0-1	0-0	0-0	0-0	0-0	0-0	0-0	0-0	0-2	0-0	0-0	0-2	0-5
Suppan, Jeff	0-0	0-0	0-0	0-0	1-1	0-1	1-1	1-0	0-0	1-0	0-0	0-0	0-0	2-0	7-3
Trlicek, Ricky	0-0	1-0	0-0	0-2	0-0	0-0	0-0	0-0	1-1	1-1	0-0	0-0	0-0	0-0	3-4
Wakefield, Tim	1-2	0-1	0-2	1-0	1-1	0-1	3-0	2-0	1-1	1-0	0-1	1-1	0-1	0-3	12-15
Wasdin, John	0-0	0-0	0-1	0-0	1-1	0-0	0-0	0-0	0-2	0-0	1-0	0-1	1-1	1-0	4-6
Totals	5-6	7-5	3-8	6-5	5-7	3-8	8-3	8-3	4-8	7-4	7-4	3-8	6-6	6-9	78-84

INTERLEAGUE BREAKDOWN: Avery 0-1, Sele 0-1, Wakefield 0-1 vs. Braves; Brandenburg 0-1, Hudson 0-1, Sele 0-1 vs. Expos; Eshelman 1-0, Suppan 1-0, Wakefield 0-1 vs. Mets; Sele 1-0, Suppan 1-0, Wasdin 1-0 vs. Phillies; Eshelman 1-0, Gordon 0-1, Wakefield 0-1 vs. Marlins.

CHICAGO—80-81

Pitcher	Ana. W-L	Bal. W-L	Bos. W-L	Cle. W-L	Det. W-L	K.C. W-L	Mil. W-L	Min. W-L	N.Y. W-L	Oak. W-L	Sea. W-L	Tex. W-L	Tor. W-L	N.L. W-L	Totals W-L
Alvarez, Wilson	0-0	0-0	0-1	0-0	1-0	2-0	0-1	1-0	1-1	2-0	0-0	0-3	0-2	2-0	9-8
Baldwin, James	0-3	1-1	1-0	1-1	0-2	1-0	0-2	2-1	0-1	2-1	1-0	0-1	2-1	1-1	12-15
Bere, Jason	0-0	0-0	0-0	0-1	0-0	0-0	1-0	0-1	0-0	0-0	0-0	1-0	1-0	1-0	4-2
Bertotti, Mike	0-0	0-0	0-0	0-0	0-0	0-0	0-0	0-0	0-0	0-0	0-0	0-0	0-0	0-0	0-0
Castillo, Carlos	1-0	0-0	0-0	0-1	0-0	1-0	0-0	0-0	0-0	0-0	0-0	0-0	0-0	0-0	2-1
Castillo, Tony	0-0	1-0	0-0	0-0	0-1	0-0	0-0	0-0	0-1	0-0	0-1	0-1	1-0	2-0	4-4
Clemons, Chris	0-1	0-0	0-0	0-0	0-0	0-0	0-0	0-0	0-0	0-0	0-1	0-0	0-0	0-0	0-2
Cruz, Nelson	0-0	0-0	0-0	0-0	0-0	0-0	0-0	0-0	0-0	0-0	0-1	0-1	0-0	0-0	0-2
Darwin, Danny	0-0	0-3	1-0	1-0	0-1	1-0	0-0	0-1	0-1	1-0	0-0	0-0	0-0	0-2	4-8
Darwin, Jeff	0-0	0-0	0-0	0-1	0-0	0-0	0-0	0-0	0-0	0-0	0-0	0-0	0-0	0-0	0-1
Drabek, Doug	1-0	2-0	1-1	1-2	1-1	1-0	0-1	1-2	0-2	1-0	1-1	0-0	1-1	1-0	12-11
Eyre, Scott	1-1	0-0	0-0	0-0	0-0	1-1	1-1	0-0	0-0	0-0	1-1	0-0	0-0	0-1	4-4
Fordham, Tom	0-0	0-0	0-1	0-0	0-0	0-0	0-0	0-0	0-0	0-0	0-0	0-0	0-0	0-0	0-1
Foulke, Keith	0-0	0-0	1-0	1-0	0-0	0-0	0-0	0-0	0-0	0-0	0-0	0-0	0-0	1-0	3-0
Hernandez, Roberto	0-0	1-0	2-0	0-0	1-1	0-0	0-0	0-0	0-0	1-0	0-0	0-0	0-0	0-0	5-1
Karchner, Matt	0-0	0-0	0-0	0-0	0-0	2-0	0-1	0-0	0-0	0-0	1-0	0-0	0-0	0-0	3-1
Levine, Al	0-1	0-0	0-0	0-1	0-0	0-0	0-0	0-0	1-0	1-0	0-0	0-0	0-0	0-0	2-2
McElroy, Chuck	0-0	0-0	1-0	0-0	0-0	0-0	0-0	0-0	0-1	0-1	0-0	0-0	0-1	0-0	1-3
Navarro, Jaime	2-0	1-0	1-0	0-1	1-0	1-1	0-1	2-1	0-2	0-1	0-2	1-2	0-0	0-3	9-14
Simas, Bill	0-0	0-1	0-0	0-0	0-0	0-0	2-0	0-0	0-0	0-0	1-0	0-0	0-0	0-0	3-1
Sirotka, Mike	0-0	0-0	0-0	1-0	0-0	1-0	0-0	0-0	0-0	0-0	1-0	0-0	0-0	0-0	3-0
Thomas, Larry	0-0	0-0	0-0	0-0	0-0	0-0	0-0	0-0	0-0	0-0	0-0	0-0	0-0	0-0	0-0
Totals	5-6	6-5	8-3	5-7	4-7	11-1	4-7	6-6	2-9	8-3	5-6	3-8	5-6	8-7	80-81

INTERLEAGUE BREAKDOWN: Alvarez 1-0, Drabek 1-0, Navarro 0-1 vs. Cubs; Alvarez 1-0, T. Castillo 1-0, D. Darwin 0-1 vs. Reds; Baldwin 1-0, Bere 1-0, Foulke 1-0 vs. Astros; Baldwin 0-1, D. Darwin 0-1, Navarro 0-1 vs. Pirates; T. Castillo 1-0, Eyre 0-1, Navarro 0-1 vs. Cardinals.

CLEVELAND—86-75

Pitcher	Ana. W-L	Bal. W-L	Bos. W-L	Chi. W-L	Det. W-L	K.C. W-L	Mil. W-L	Min. W-L	N.Y. W-L	Oak. W-L	Sea. W-L	Tex. W-L	Tor. W-L	N.L. W-L	Totals W-L
Anderson, Brian	0-0	0-0	0-0	0-0	0-0	2-0	0-1	0-0	1-1	0-0	0-0	0-0	0-0	1-0	4-2
Assenmacher, Paul	0-0	1-0	0-0	0-0	0-0	1-0	1-0	0-0	0-0	0-0	1-0	1-0	0-0	0-0	5-0
Clark, Terry	0-1	0-0	0-0	0-0	0-0	0-0	0-0	0-0	0-0	0-1	0-0	0-0	0-0	0-0	0-3
Colon, Bartolo	0-1	0-0	1-1	1-0	0-1	0-1	0-0	2-0	0-0	0-0	0-3	0-0	0-0	0-0	4-7
Graves, Danny	0-0	0-0	0-0	0-0	0-0	0-0	0-0	0-0	0-0	0-0	0-0	0-0	0-0	0-0	0-0
Hershiser, Orel	0-0	0-0	1-0	1-1	1-1	0-0	3-0	2-0	1-1	1-0	0-0	1-0	1-1	1-2	14-6
Jackson, Mike	0-0	0-0	0-0	0-0	0-0	1-1	0-0	0-0	1-0	0-1	0-1	0-2	0-0	0-0	2-5
Jacome, Jason	0-0	0-0	0-0	0-0	0-0	0-0	0-0	1-0	0-0	1-0	0-0	0-0	0-0	0-0	2-0
Juden, Jeff	0-0	0-0	0-0	0-0	0-0	0-0	0-0	0-0	0-0	0-0	0-0	0-1	0-0	0-0	0-1
Kline, Steve	1-0	0-1	1-0	0-0	0-0	0-0	0-0	0-0	0-0	1-0	0-0	0-0	0-0	0-0	3-1
Lopez, Albie	0-0	0-0	0-0	0-2	0-0	1-1	0-0	0-1	0-0	0-0	0-1	1-1	1-0	0-0	3-7
McDowell, Jack	0-1	0-0	1-0	0-0	0-0	0-0	0-1	0-0	1-0	0-0	0-0	1-0	0-0	0-0	3-3
Mesa, Jose	0-0	0-1	0-0	0-0	0-0	0-0	0-1	0-0	1-1	0-1	0-0	1-0	0-0	2-0	4-4
Morman, Alvin	0-0	0-0	0-0	0-0	0-0	0-0	0-0	0-0	0-0	0-0	0-0	0-0	0-0	0-0	0-0
Nagy, Charles	0-1	2-1	1-0	1-1	3-1	1-0	3-0	0-2	0-2	1-0	1-2	0-1	0-0	2-0	15-11
Ogea, Chad	2-0	2-1	0-3	0-1	0-0	0-0	0-0	1-1	0-0	0-0	0-0	1-0	1-1	1-2	8-9
Plunk, Eric	0-1	0-1	0-0	0-0	2-1	0-0	0-1	0-0	1-0	0-1	0-0	0-0	0-0	1-0	4-5
Shuey, Paul	0-1	0-0	0-0	2-0	0-0	1-0	0-0	0-0	0-1	0-0	0-0	1-0	0-0	0-0	4-2
Smiley, John	0-0	0-0	0-0	0-0	0-1	0-0	0-0	0-0	0-1	0-0	1-0	1-0	0-1	0-1	2-4
Weathers, Dave	0-1	0-1	0-0	0-0	0-0	0-0	0-0	0-0	0-0	0-0	0-0	0-0	0-0	0-0	1-2
Wright, Jaret	1-0	0-0	0-1	2-0	0-0	0-0	1-0	2-0	0-0	2-0	0-0	0-0	0-1	0-1	8-3
Totals	4-7	5-6	5-6	7-5	6-5	8-3	8-4	8-4	5-6	7-4	3-8	5-6	6-5	9-6	86-75

INTERLEAGUE BREAKDOWN: Mesa 1-0, Nagy 1-0, Smiley 0-1 vs. Cubs; Anderson 1-0, Hershiser 0-1, Ogea 0-1 vs. Reds; Hershiser 0-1, Mesa 1-0, Plunk 1-0 vs. Astros; Hershiser 1-0, Ogea 1-0, Wright 0-1 vs. Pirates; Lopez 1-0, Nagy 1-0, Ogea 0-1 vs. Cardinals.

DETROIT—79-83

Pitcher	Ana. W-L	Bal. W-L	Bos. W-L	Chi. W-L	Cle. W-L	K.C. W-L	Mil. W-L	Min. W-L	N.Y. W-L	Oak. W-L	Sea. W-L	Tex. W-L	Tor. W-L	N.L. W-L	Totals W-L
Bautista, Jose	0-0	1-0	1-1	0-0	0-0	0-0	0-0	0-0	0-0	0-0	0-1	0-0	0-0	0-0	2-2
Blair, Willie	0-0	1-0	0-2	3-0	2-0	0-0	1-1	1-2	1-0	1-1	0-0	2-0	1-1	3-1	16-8
Brocail, Doug	0-0	0-0	0-0	0-1	0-1	0-1	0-0	0-0	0-0	1-0	0-0	1-1	1-0	0-0	3-4
Cummings, John	0-0	0-0	0-0	0-0	0-0	1-0	0-0	1-0	0-0	0-0	0-0	0-0	0-0	0-0	2-0
Dishman, Glenn	0-1	0-0	0-0	0-0	0-1	1-0	0-0	0-0	0-0	0-0	0-0	0-0	0-0	0-0	1-2
Duran, Roberto	0-0	0-0	0-0	0-0	0-0	0-0	0-0	0-0	0-0	0-0	0-0	0-0	0-0	0-0	0-0
Gaillard, Eddie	0-0	1-0	0-0	0-0	0-0	0-0	0-0	0-0	0-0	0-0	0-0	0-0	0-0	0-0	1-0
Hernandez, Fernando	0-0	0-0	0-0	0-0	0-0	0-0	0-0	0-0	0-0	0-0	0-0	0-0	0-0	0-0	0-0
Jarvis, Kevin	0-0	0-0	0-1	0-0	0-0	0-0	0-0	0-0	0-0	0-0	0-0	0-1	0-1	0-0	0-3
Jones, Todd	1-0	1-0	1-0	1-0	0-0	0-0	0-0	0-1	1-1	0-0	0-0	0-0	0-1	0-1	5-4
Keagle, Greg	0-0	0-1	1-0	0-0	0-1	0-0	0-1	0-0	0-1	1-0	0-0	0-0	0-0	0-1	3-5
Lira, Felipe	0-2	0-1	1-0	0-1	0-0	0-0	1-0	0-0	0-2	0-0	1-1	1-0	1-0	0-0	5-7
Miceli, Dan	0-0	1-0	1-0	0-0	0-0	0-0	1-0	0-1	0-1	0-0	0-0	0-0	0-0	0-0	3-1
Moehler, Brian	2-1	0-1	1-0	1-0	0-0	0-0	1-2	0-1	0-3	2-0	1-1	1-0	0-1	2-1	11-12
Myers, Mike	0-1	0-0	0-0	0-0	0-0	0-0	0-0	0-1	0-2	0-0	0-0	0-0	0-0	0-0	0-4
Olivares, Omar	1-0	0-1	0-0	1-0	1-0	0-0	0-1	0-0	0-1	0-0	0-0	0-1	1-1	0-1	5-6
Pugh, Tim	0-0	0-0	0-0	0-0	0-0	0-0	0-0	0-0	0-0	0-0	0-1	0-0	0-0	0-0	1-1
Sager, A.J.	0-0	0-0	0-0	1-0	0-1	0-1	0-0	1-0	0-0	0-0	0-1	1-1	0-0	0-0	3-4
Sanders, Scott	0-0	0-1	0-1	0-1	0-2	0-0	0-1	0-1	1-0	0-0	0-0	1-0	0-1	0-1	2-8
Thompson, Justin	2-0	1-1	1-0	0-0	2-0	1-1	1-1	1-1	0-1	1-1	1-2	0-1	2-0	2-1	15-11
Totals	6-5	6-6	7-5	7-4	5-6	6-5	4-7	4-7	2-10	7-4	4-7	7-4	6-6	8-7	79-83

INTERLEAGUE BREAKDOWN: Blair 1-0, Keagle 0-1, Moehler 1-0 vs. Braves; Moehler 0-1, Olivares 0-1, Thompson 0-1 vs. Expos; Blair 1-0, Moehler 1-0, Thompson 1-0 vs. Mets; Blair 1-0, Sanders 0-1, Thompson 1-0 vs. Phillies; Blair 0-1, Jones 0-1, Olivares 0-1 vs. Marlins.

KANSAS CITY—67-94

Pitcher	Ana. W-L	Bal. W-L	Bos. W-L	Chi. W-L	Cle. W-L	Det. W-L	Mil. W-L	Min. W-L	N.Y. W-L	Oak. W-L	Sea. W-L	Tex. W-L	Tor. W-L	N.L. W-L	Totals W-L
Appier, Kevin	2-1	0-1	1-0	0-2	0-1	1-0	1-1	1-0	0-2	1-1	0-1	0-1	0-1	2-1	9-13
Belcher, Tim	1-0	0-1	2-0	0-1	1-1	1-2	0-1	3-1	1-1	1-1	0-2	1-1	0-0	2-0	13-12
Bevil, Brian	0-0	0-1	0-0	0-0	1-0	0-0	0-0	0-0	0-0	0-0	0-1	0-0	0-0	0-0	1-2
Bones, Ricky	0-1	1-0	1-1	1-0	0-1	0-0	0-0	1-1	0-0	0-0	0-1	0-0	0-0	0-2	4-7
Carrasco, Hector	0-0	0-1	1-1	0-0	0-0	0-0	0-1	0-0	0-0	0-1	0-0	0-0	0-1	0-1	1-6
Casian, Larry	0-0	0-0	0-0	0-0	0-1	0-0	0-0	0-0	0-0	0-0	0-0	0-0	0-1	0-0	0-2
Converse, Jim	0-0	0-0	0-0	0-0	0-0	0-0	0-0	0-0	0-0	0-0	0-0	0-0	0-0	0-0	0-0
De La Maza, Roland	0-0	0-0	0-0	0-0	0-0	0-0	0-0	0-0	0-0	0-0	0-0	0-0	0-0	0-0	0-0
Haney, Chris	0-0	0-0	0-0	0-0	0-0	0-0	1-0	0-1	0-0	0-0	0-0	0-0	0-0	0-1	1-2
Jacome, Jason	0-0	0-0	0-0	0-0	0-0	0-0	0-0	0-0	0-0	0-0	0-0	0-0	0-0	0-0	0-0
McDill, Allen	0-0	0-0	0-0	0-0	0-0	0-0	0-0	0-0	0-0	0-0	0-0	0-0	0-0	0-0	0-0
Montgomery, Jeff	0-0	0-1	0-0	0-1	0-0	0-0	0-2	0-0	0-0	0-0	1-0	0-0	0-0	0-0	1-4
Olson, Gregg	1-0	0-0	0-0	0-0	1-0	0-0	0-0	0-0	0-1	1-0	0-0	0-1	1-0	0-1	4-3
Perez, Mike	0-0	0-0	0-0	0-0	0-0	0-0	1-0	0-0	1-0	0-0	0-0	0-0	0-0	0-0	2-0
Pichardo, Hipolito	0-0	0-0	0-0	0-1	0-1	0-0	1-0	0-0	0-0	0-1	0-1	1-1	1-0	0-0	3-5
Pittsley, Jim	0-0	0-0	0-0	0-3	0-1	0-2	1-0	1-0	0-1	0-0	1-0	1-1	0-0	1-0	5-8
Rosado, Jose	1-0	1-0	1-1	0-1	0-1	1-2	0-1	0-1	0-1	0-2	0-0	2-0	2-1	1-1	9-12
Rusch, Glendon	0-3	0-1	1-0	0-1	0-1	1-0	0-0	1-1	0-2	0-0	0-0	1-0	1-1	0-1	6-9
Santiago, Jose	0-0	0-0	0-0	0-0	0-0	0-0	0-0	0-0	0-0	0-0	0-0	0-0	0-0	0-0	0-0
Service, Scott	0-1	0-0	0-0	0-2	0-0	0-0	0-0	0-0	0-0	0-0	0-0	0-0	0-0	0-0	0-3
Veres, Randy	0-0	0-0	1-0	0-0	0-0	0-0	0-0	0-0	1-0	0-0	0-0	2-0	0-0	0-0	4-0
Walker, Jamie	0-0	1-1	0-0	0-0	0-1	0-0	0-0	0-0	0-0	0-0	1-0	0-0	0-1	0-0	3-3
Whisenant, Matt	0-0	1-0	0-0	0-0	0-0	0-0	0-0	0-0	0-0	0-0	0-0	0-0	0-0	0-0	1-0
Williams, Mike	0-0	0-0	0-0	0-0	0-0	0-0	0-0	0-0	0-0	0-1	0-0	0-0	0-0	0-1	0-2
Williams, Mitch	0-0	0-0	0-0	0-0	0-0	0-0	0-0	0-0	0-0	0-1	0-0	0-0	0-0	0-0	0-1
Totals	5-6	4-7	8-3	1-11	3-8	5-6	6-6	7-5	3-8	3-8	5-6	6-5	5-6	6-9	67-94

INTERLEAGUE BREAKDOWN: Appier 0-1, Bones 0-1, Rusch 0-1 vs. Cubs; Appier 1-0, Bones 0-1, Rosado 0-1 vs. Reds; Haney 0-1, Pittsley 1-0, Rosado 1-0 vs. Astros; Appier 1-0, Belcher 1-0, Mik. Williams 0-1 vs. Pirates; Belcher 1-0, Carrasco 0-1, Olson 0-1 vs. Cardinals.

MILWAUKEE—78-83

Pitcher	Ana. W-L	Bal. W-L	Bos. W-L	Chi. W-L	Cle. W-L	Det. W-L	K.C. W-L	Min. W-L	N.Y. W-L	Oak. W-L	Sea. W-L	Tex. W-L	Tor. W-L	N.L. W-L	Totals W-L
Adamson, Joel	0-0	0-0	0-1	1-0	0-0	0-0	0-1	0-0	0-0	0-0	0-0	1-1	1-0	2-0	5-3
D'Amico, Jeff	0-0	3-0	0-2	0-0	0-0	0-0	1-0	1-2	1-2	0-0	1-1	0-0	0-0	2-0	9-7
Davis, Mark	0-0	0-0	0-0	0-0	0-0	0-0	0-0	0-0	0-0	0-0	0-0	0-0	0-0	0-0	0-0
Eldred, Cal	1-1	1-1	2-0	2-1	0-4	3-0	1-1	1-2	0-0	0-1	1-2	1-0	0-1	0-1	13-15
Fetters, Mike	0-1	0-0	0-0	0-1	0-0	0-0	0-1	0-0	1-0	0-1	0-0	0-0	0-0	0-1	1-5
Florie, Bryce	0-2	0-0	0-0	0-0	0-0	1-0	0-0	0-0	0-1	1-1	1-0	1-0	0-0	0-0	4-4
Hansell, Greg	0-0	0-0	0-0	0-0	0-0	0-0	0-0	0-0	0-0	0-0	0-0	0-0	0-0	0-0	0-0
Harnisch, Pete	0-0	1-0	0-1	0-0	0-0	0-0	0-0	0-0	0-0	0-0	0-0	0-0	0-0	0-0	1-1
Jones, Doug	1-0	0-1	0-1	0-1	2-1	0-0	0-1	0-0	0-0	1-1	0-0	0-0	0-0	1-0	6-6
Karl, Scott	1-0	0-2	0-1	1-0	0-1	2-2	1-0	0-2	1-1	1-0	0-0	1-1	1-1	1-2	10-13
Maloney, Sean	0-0	0-0	0-0	0-0	0-0	0-0	0-0	0-0	0-0	0-0	0-0	0-0	1-0	0-0	1-0
McAndrew, Jamie	0-0	0-0	0-0	0-0	0-0	0-0	0-0	0-0	0-0	0-0	0-0	1-1	0-0	0-0	1-1
McDonald, Ben	1-1	1-0	0-1	1-0	1-1	0-0	0-1	2-0	0-1	0-0	0-0	1-1	1-0	0-1	8-7
Mercedes, Jose	0-2	0-0	0-1	1-1	1-0	1-0	0-1	1-0	1-2	0-0	0-0	1-0	1-1	0-2	7-10
Miranda, Angel	0-0	0-0	0-0	0-0	0-0	0-0	0-0	0-0	0-0	0-0	0-0	0-0	0-0	0-0	0-0
Misuraca, Mike	0-0	0-0	0-0	0-0	0-0	0-0	0-0	0-0	0-0	0-0	0-0	0-0	0-0	0-0	0-0
Reyes, Al	0-0	0-1	0-0	0-0	0-0	0-0	1-0	0-0	0-0	0-1	0-0	0-0	0-0	0-0	1-2
Villone, Ron	0-0	0-0	0-0	0-0	0-0	0-0	0-0	0-0	0-0	0-0	0-0	0-0	0-0	1-0	1-0
Wagner, Paul	0-0	0-0	0-0	0-0	0-0	0-0	1-0	0-0	0-0	0-0	0-0	0-0	0-0	0-0	1-0
Wickman, Bob	0-0	0-0	1-0	1-0	0-1	0-1	1-1	0-0	1-0	0-3	1-0	0-0	1-0	1-0	7-6
Woodard, Steve	0-0	0-0	0-0	0-0	0-0	0-1	0-0	0-0	0-0	0-0	1-1	0-1	1-0	0-0	3-3
Totals	4-7	6-5	3-8	7-4	4-8	7-4	6-6	5-7	4-7	5-6	5-6	7-4	7-4	8-7	78-83

INTERLEAGUE BREAKDOWN: D'Amico 1-0, Eldred 0-1, Karl 0-1 vs. Cubs; Fetters 0-1, McDonald 0-1, Mercedes 0-1 vs. Reds; Adamson 1-0, Karl 0-1, Villone 1-0 vs. Astros; Jones 1-0, Karl 1-0, Mercedes 0-1 vs. Pirates; Adamson 1-0, D'Amico 1-0, Wickman 1-0 vs. Cardinals.

MINNESOTA—68-94

Pitcher	Ana. W-L	Bal. W-L	Bos. W-L	Chi. W-L	Cle. W-L	Det. W-L	K.C. W-L	Mil. W-L	N.Y. W-L	Oak. W-L	Sea. W-L	Tex. W-L	Tor. W-L	N.L. W-L	Totals W-L
Aguilera, Rick	0-0	0-1	0-0	0-0	1-0	1-1	0-0	0-0	0-0	1-1	2-1	0-0	0-0	0-0	5-4
Aldred, Scott	0-1	0-2	1-0	0-0	0-0	1-0	0-0	0-1	0-1	0-0	0-1	0-2	0-1	0-1	2-10
Bowers, Shane	0-0	0-0	0-2	0-0	0-0	0-0	0-0	0-0	0-0	0-0	0-0	0-0	0-1	0-0	0-3
Guardado, Eddie	0-0	0-0	0-1	0-0	0-0	0-0	0-0	0-0	0-1	0-0	0-0	0-0	0-0	0-2	0-4
Hawkins, LaTroy	0-0	0-1	0-0	0-3	0-1	0-1	1-1	1-1	1-1	1-1	0-1	0-0	0-0	2-1	6-12
Jarvis, Kevin	0-0	0-0	0-0	0-0	0-0	0-0	0-0	1-0	0-1	0-0	0-0	0-0	0-1	0-0	1-5
Miller, Travis	0-0	0-0	0-0	0-0	0-2	0-0	0-1	1-0	0-1	0-0	0-0	0-0	0-1	0-0	1-5
Naulty, Dan	0-0	0-0	0-0	0-0	0-0	1-0	0-0	0-0	0-0	0-0	0-1	1-0	0-0	0-0	1-1
Olson, Gregg	0-0	0-0	0-0	0-0	0-0	0-0	0-0	0-0	0-0	0-0	0-0	0-0	0-0	0-0	0-0
Radke, Brad	2-0	1-0	0-3	2-0	2-1	1-0	1-1	3-0	0-1	2-1	0-1	0-2	3-0	3-0	20-10
Ritchie, Todd	0-0	0-0	0-0	0-0	0-0	1-0	1-0	0-0	0-0	0-0	0-1	0-0	0-1	0-0	2-3
Robertson, Rich	1-0	0-1	2-1	0-1	0-1	1-0	1-0	0-2	0-3	1-1	0-1	1-0	0-0	1-1	8-12
Rodriguez, Frank	0-0	0-0	0-0	2-0	0-0	0-1	0-2	0-0	0-0	0-0	1-0	0-0	0-1	0-2	3-6
Serafini, Dan	0-0	0-0	0-0	0-0	0-0	0-0	0-0	0-1	0-0	0-0	1-0	1-0	0-0	0-0	2-1
Stevens, Dave	0-0	0-0	0-0	0-1	0-0	0-1	0-1	1-0	0-0	0-0	0-0	0-0	0-0	0-0	1-3
Swindell, Greg	3-0	0-2	0-0	0-0	0-0	0-0	1-0	0-0	2-0	1-0	0-0	0-1	0-1	0-0	7-4
Tewksbury, Bob	1-1	0-3	0-1	2-1	1-2	0-1	0-1	0-0	0-0	0-0	2-0	1-2	0-1	1-0	8-13
Trombley, Mike	0-2	0-0	0-0	0-0	0-0	0-0	0-0	1-0	0-0	0-0	0-0	0-0	0-1	1-0	2-3
Totals	7-4	1-10	3-8	6-6	4-8	7-4	5-7	7-5	3-8	7-4	5-6	3-8	3-8	7-8	68-94

INTERLEAGUE BREAKDOWN: Rodriguez 0-1, Tewksbury 1-0, Trombley 1-0 vs. Cubs; Hawkins 1-0, Radke 1-0, Rodriguez 0-1 vs. Reds; Guardado 0-1, Radke 1-0, Robertson 1-0 vs. Astros; Aldred 0-1, Hawkins 1-0, Radke 1-0 vs. Pirates; Guardado 0-1, Hawkins 0-1, Robertson 0-1 vs. Cardinals.

NEW YORK—96-66

Pitcher	Ana. W-L	Bal. W-L	Bos. W-L	Chi. W-L	Cle. W-L	Det. W-L	K.C. W-L	Mil. W-L	Min. W-L	Oak. W-L	Sea. W-L	Tex. W-L	Tor. W-L	N.L. W-L	Totals W-L
Banks, Willie	0-0	0-0	2-0	0-0	0-0	0-0	0-0	0-0	0-0	0-0	0-0	0-0	1-0	0-0	3-0
Boehringer, Brian	0-0	0-0	0-0	0-1	0-0	0-0	1-1	0-0	1-0	0-0	0-0	0-0	1-0	0-0	3-2
Boggs, Wade	0-0	0-0	0-0	0-0	0-0	0-0	0-0	0-0	0-0	0-0	0-0	0-0	0-0	0-0	0-0
Borowski, Joe	0-0	0-0	0-0	0-0	0-0	0-1	0-0	0-0	0-0	0-0	0-0	0-0	0-0	0-0	0-1
Cone, David	1-0	0-0	0-0	3-0	0-0	2-0	1-1	1-1	1-1	0-0	0-1	2-1	1-1	0-0	12-6
Gooden, Dwight	1-0	1-0	0-0	0-0	3-0	0-1	0-0	0-1	1-1	2-0	0-0	1-0	0-1	0-1	9-5
Irabu, Hideki	1-0	0-1	0-0	0-0	1-0	2-0	1-0	0-1	1-0	0-0	0-1	0-0	0-0	0-1	5-4
Lloyd, Graeme	0-0	0-0	0-0	0-0	0-0	1-0	0-0	0-1	0-0	0-0	0-0	0-0	0-0	0-0	1-1
Mecir, Jim	0-0	0-1	0-0	0-0	0-0	0-0	0-0	0-0	0-1	0-0	0-1	0-0	0-0	0-1	0-4
Mendoza, Ramiro	0-0	1-1	0-1	1-0	1-0	1-0	1-0	0-0	1-0	0-1	0-0	2-1	0-1	0-1	8-6
Nelson, Jeff	1-1	0-1	1-1	0-0	0-1	0-0	0-0	0-0	0-0	0-3	1-0	0-0	0-0	0-0	3-7
Pettitte, Andy	1-0	1-1	2-0	3-0	1-0	1-0	0-1	2-0	2-0	2-0	1-1	1-1	1-1	1-1	18-7
Rios, Danny	0-0	0-0	0-0	0-0	0-0	0-0	0-0	0-0	0-0	0-0	0-0	0-0	0-0	0-0	0-0
Rivera, Mariano	0-1	0-0	2-0	0-0	1-1	1-0	0-0	0-0	0-0	1-0	0-0	0-0	0-0	0-2	6-4
Rogers, Kenny	0-1	1-2	0-0	1-0	0-0	0-0	1-0	2-0	0-0	0-0	0-1	1-0	0-0	0-1	6-7
Stanton, Mike	1-0	0-0	0-0	1-0	0-0	1-0	0-0	0-0	0-0	0-0	0-0	0-0	0-0	3-1	6-1
Weathers, Dave	0-0	0-0	0-0	0-0	0-0	0-0	0-0	0-0	0-0	0-1	0-0	0-0	0-0	0-0	0-1
Wells, David	1-1	0-1	1-2	0-1	0-1	1-0	3-0	2-0	2-0	1-0	1-2	0-1	3-0	1-1	16-10
Totals	7-4	4-8	8-4	9-2	6-5	10-2	8-3	7-4	8-3	6-5	4-7	7-4	7-5	5-10	96-66

INTERLEAGUE BREAKDOWN: Gooden 0-1, Mendoza 0-1, Stanton 1-0 vs. Braves; Pettitte 1-0, Rivera 0-1, Wells 0-1 vs. Expos; Pettitte 0-1, Stanton 1-0, Wells 1-0 vs. Mets; Irabu 0-1, Rogers 0-1, Stanton 0-1 vs. Phillies; Mecir 0-1, Rivera 0-1, Stanton 1-0 vs. Marlins..

OAKLAND—65-97

Pitcher	Ana. W-L	Bal. W-L	Bos. W-L	Chi. W-L	Cle. W-L	Det. W-L	K.C. W-L	Mil. W-L	Min. W-L	N.Y. W-L	Sea. W-L	Tex. W-L	Tor. W-L	N.L. W-L	Totals W-L
Acre, Mark	0-0	0-0	0-0	0-0	0-0	0-0	0-0	0-0	0-0	2-0	0-0	0-0	0-0	0-0	2-0
Adams, Willie	0-0	0-0	0-1	0-2	0-1	1-0	1-1	1-0	0-0	0-0	0-0	0-0	0-0	0-0	3-5
Brewer, Billy	0-0	0-0	0-0	0-0	0-0	0-0	0-0	0-0	0-0	0-0	0-0	0-0	0-0	0-0	0-0
Groom, Buddy	0-0	0-0	0-1	1-0	0-0	1-0	0-0	0-0	0-0	0-0	0-0	0-0	0-1	0-0	2-2
Haught, Gary	0-0	0-0	0-0	0-0	0-0	0-0	0-0	0-0	0-0	0-0	0-0	0-0	0-0	0-0	0-0
Haynes, Jimmy	0-0	0-0	0-1	1-0	1-1	0-1	0-0	0-1	1-0	0-0	0-1	0-1	0-0	0-0	3-6
Johnson, Dane	0-0	0-1	0-0	0-0	0-0	0-0	0-0	1-0	0-0	0-0	1-0	0-0	2-0	0-0	4-1
Johnstone, John	0-0	0-0	0-0	0-0	0-0	0-0	0-0	0-0	0-0	0-0	0-0	0-0	0-0	0-0	0-0
Karsay, Steve	0-1	0-2	0-1	0-2	0-1	0-2	1-0	0-0	1-0	0-1	1-0	0-1	0-1	0-0	3-12
Kubinski, Tim	0-0	0-0	0-0	0-0	0-0	0-0	0-0	0-0	0-0	0-0	0-0	0-0	0-0	0-0	0-0
Lewis, Richie	0-0	0-0	1-0	0-0	1-0	0-0	0-0	0-0	0-0	0-0	0-0	0-0	0-0	0-0	2-0
Lorraine, Andrew	0-0	1-0	0-0	0-0	0-0	0-0	1-0	0-0	0-0	0-0	0-0	0-0	0-0	0-1	3-1
Ludwick, Eric	0-1	0-0	0-0	0-0	0-0	0-1	1-0	0-0	0-0	0-1	0-0	0-0	0-0	0-1	1-4
Mathews, T.J.	0-0	1-1	0-0	1-0	0-0	0-0	0-0	1-0	0-0	0-0	0-0	2-0	0-0	0-1	6-2
Mohler, Mike	0-1	0-1	0-0	0-2	0-0	0-0	0-1	0-1	0-2	0-1	1-0	0-0	0-0	0-1	1-10
Montgomery, Steve	0-0	0-0	0-0	0-0	0-0	0-0	0-0	0-1	0-0	0-0	0-0	0-0	0-0	0-0	0-1
Oquist, Mike	0-1	0-0	0-0	0-0	0-0	0-0	1-0	0-0	0-0	0-1	1-1	1-1	0-0	0-1	4-6
Prieto, Ariel	0-2	0-1	0-0	0-0	0-2	0-1	0-0	1-1	1-0	1-0	0-0	1-1	1-0	1-0	6-8
Reyes, Carlos	0-0	0-2	0-0	0-0	0-0	0-0	0-0	0-0	0-1	1-0	0-0	1-0	1-0	1-0	3-4
Rigby, Brad	0-1	0-0	0-0	0-0	0-1	0-0	0-0	0-0	0-0	0-0	0-2	0-1	0-0	1-1	1-7
Small, Aaron	0-1	1-0	1-0	0-1	1-0	1-1	0-0	0-0	0-0	1-1	2-0	0-0	0-1	1-1	9-5
Taylor, Billy	0-1	0-0	0-0	0-1	1-0	0-0	0-0	1-0	0-1	0-0	0-0	0-0	0-1	0-0	3-4
Telgheder, Dave	1-0	0-0	0-0	0-0	0-0	1-0	0-0	0-1	0-1	0-0	0-1	1-1	0-1	1-0	4-6
Wengert, Don	0-2	0-0	0-1	0-2	0-0	0-1	0-0	1-1	1-1	0-0	0-1	0-1	1-0	0-2	5-11
Witasick, Jay	0-0	0-0	0-0	0-0	0-0	0-0	0-0	0-0	0-0	0-0	0-0	0-0	0-0	0-0	0-0
Wojciechowski, Steve	0-0	0-0	0-0	0-0	0-0	0-0	0-0	0-0	0-0	0-0	0-1	0-0	0-0	0-0	0-2
Totals	1-11	3-8	4-7	3-8	4-7	4-7	8-3	6-5	4-7	5-6	5-7	5-7	6-5	7-9	65-97

INTERLEAGUE BREAKDOWN: Ludwick 0-1, Mathews 0-1, Small 0-1, Telgheder 1-0 vs. Dodgers; Johnson 1-0, Reyes 1-0, Small 1-0, Wengert 0-1 vs. Padres; Johnson 1-0, Lorraine 0-1, Rigby 1-1 vs. Giants; Mohler 0-1, Oquist 0-1, Prieto 1-0, Wengert 0-1 vs. Rockies.

SEATTLE—90-72

Pitcher	Ana. W-L	Bal. W-L	Bos. W-L	Chi. W-L	Cle. W-L	Det. W-L	K.C. W-L	Mil. W-L	Min. W-L	N.Y. W-L	Oak. W-L	Tex. W-L	Tor. W-L	N.L. W-L	Totals W-L
Ayala, Bobby	1-0	0-0	0-0	2-0	0-0	0-0	1-2	0-0	0-0	2-1	0-0	1-1	2-1	1-0	10-5
Carmona, Rafael	0-0	0-0	0-0	0-0	0-0	0-0	0-0	0-0	0-0	0-0	0-0	0-0	0-0	0-0	0-0
Charlton, Norm	0-1	2-1	1-1	0-1	0-0	0-0	0-0	0-0	0-2	0-0	0-0	0-0	0-0	0-1	3-8
Cloude, Ken	0-0	1-0	0-0	0-0	0-1	0-0	0-0	0-0	1-0	0-0	0-0	1-0	1-0	0-0	4-2
Davis, Tim	0-0	0-0	0-0	0-0	0-0	0-0	0-0	0-0	0-0	0-0	0-0	0-0	0-0	0-0	0-0
Fassero, Jeff	1-1	0-0	1-1	2-0	0-1	2-2	1-0	1-2	1-0	3-0	1-0	1-0	1-0	1-2	16-9
Holzemer, Mark	0-0	0-0	0-1	0-0	0-0	0-0	0-0	0-0	0-0	0-0	0-0	0-0	0-0	0-0	0-1
Hurtado, Edwin	0-0	0-0	0-0	0-0	1-0	0-0	0-1	0-0	0-0	0-0	0-0	0-0	0-0	0-0	1-2
Johnson, Randy	2-0	0-2	1-1	1-0	2-0	2-0	2-0	3-0	0-0	0-0	1-1	3-0	2-0	1-0	20-4
Lira, Felipe	0-1	0-0	0-1	0-1	0-0	0-0	0-0	0-0	0-1	0-0	0-1	0-0	0-0	0-0	0-4
Lowe, Derek	0-1	0-0	0-0	0-0	0-0	1-0	0-0	0-0	0-0	1-0	0-1	0-1	0-0	0-1	2-4
Maddux, Mike	0-0	0-0	0-0	0-0	0-0	0-0	0-0	0-0	0-0	0-0	1-0	0-0	0-0	0-0	1-0
Manzanillo, Josias	0-1	0-0	0-0	0-0	0-0	0-0	0-0	0-0	0-0	0-0	0-0	0-0	0-0	0-0	0-1
Martinez, Dennis	0-1	0-2	0-0	0-0	1-0	0-0	0-0	0-0	0-1	0-1	0-0	0-0	0-0	0-0	1-5
McCarthy, Greg	0-0	0-0	0-0	0-0	0-0	0-0	0-0	0-0	0-0	1-0	0-0	0-0	0-1	0-0	1-1
Moyer, Jamie	2-0	1-0	1-0	1-0	1-0	1-0	1-1	2-1	1-0	1-0	1-2	1-1	1-0	2-0	17-5
Olivares, Omar	0-0	0-0	0-0	0-2	1-0	0-0	0-1	0-0	0-0	0-0	0-0	0-0	0-0	0-1	1-4
Sanders, Scott	0-0	0-1	0-1	0-0	0-1	1-0	0-0	0-0	2-1	0-1	0-0	0-0	0-1	0-0	3-6
Slocumb, Heathcliff	0-0	0-1	0-1	0-0	0-0	0-0	0-0	0-0	0-0	0-1	0-0	0-0	0-1	0-0	0-4
Spoljaric, Paul	0-0	0-0	0-0	0-0	0-0	0-0	0-0	0-0	0-0	0-0	0-0	0-0	0-0	0-0	0-0

Pitcher	Ana. W-L	Bal. W-L	Bos. W-L	Chi. W-L	Cle. W-L	Det. W-L	K.C. W-L	Mil. W-L	Min. W-L	N.Y. W-L	Oak. W-L	Tex. W-L	Tor. W-L	N.L. W-L	Totals W-L
Timlin, Mike	0-0	0-0	0-0	0-0	0-0	0-0	1-0	0-0	0-0	0-0	0-0	0-0	1-0	1-2	3-2
Torres, Salomon	0-0	0-0	0-0	0-0	0-0	0-0	0-0	0-0	0-0	0-0	0-0	0-0	0-0	0-0	0-0
Wells, Bob	0-0	0-0	0-0	0-0	1-0	0-0	0-0	0-0	0-0	0-0	0-0	0-0	0-0	1-0	2-0
Wolcott, Bob	0-0	0-0	0-1	0-0	1-0	0-2	0-0	0-2	1-0	0-0	2-0	1-0	0-0	0-1	5-6
Totals	6-6	4-7	4-7	6-5	8-3	7-4	6-5	6-5	6-5	7-4	7-5	8-4	8-3	7-9	90-72

INTERLEAGUE BREAKDOWN: Ayala 1-0, Moyer 1-0, Timlin 1-0, Wolcott 0-1 vs. Dodgers; Fassero 1-1, McCarthy 0-1, Timlin 0-1 vs. Padres; Charlton 0-1, Fassero 0-1, Lowe 0-1, Moyer 1-0 vs. Giants; Johnson 1-0, Olivares 0-1, Timlin 0-1, Wells 1-0 vs. Rockies.

TEXAS—77-85

Pitcher	Ana. W-L	Bal. W-L	Bos. W-L	Chi. W-L	Cle. W-L	Det. W-L	K.C. W-L	Mil. W-L	Min. W-L	N.Y. W-L	Oak. W-L	Sea. W-L	Tor. W-L	N.L. W-L	Totals W-L
Alberro, Jose	0-0	0-1	0-1	0-0	0-0	0-0	0-0	0-0	0-0	0-1	0-0	0-0	0-0	0-0	0-3
Bailes, Scott	0-0	0-0	0-0	0-0	1-0	0-0	0-0	0-0	0-0	0-0	0-0	0-0	0-0	0-0	1-0
Burkett, John	1-0	0-3	0-0	0-0	1-0	0-0	1-2	0-0	1-0	0-2	2-1	1-1	1-2	1-1	9-12
Clark, Terry	0-0	0-0	0-0	0-0	1-0	0-0	0-0	0-2	0-0	0-1	0-0	0-0	0-0	0-1	1-4
Eversgerd, Bryan	0-0	0-0	0-0	0-0	0-0	0-0	0-0	0-1	0-0	0-0	0-0	0-0	0-0	0-1	0-2
Gunderson, Eric	1-0	0-0	0-0	1-0	0-1	0-0	0-0	0-0	0-0	0-0	0-0	0-0	0-0	0-0	2-1
Helling, Rick	1-1	0-0	0-0	0-0	0-1	0-0	0-1	0-0	1-0	0-0	0-0	0-0	1-0	0-0	3-3
Heredia, Wilson	0-0	0-0	0-0	0-0	0-0	0-0	0-0	0-0	0-0	0-0	0-0	0-0	0-0	1-0	1-0
Hernandez, Xavier	0-1	0-0	0-0	0-0	0-1	0-0	0-0	0-0	0-0	0-1	0-1	0-0	0-0	0-0	0-4
Hill, Ken	0-1	0-0	0-0	0-1	0-0	0-1	0-1	1-1	1-1	0-0	1-0	1-2	0-1	0-0	5-8
Moody, Eric	0-0	0-0	0-0	0-0	0-0	0-0	0-0	0-0	0-0	0-0	0-0	0-0	0-0	0-1	0-1
Oliver, Darren	0-1	0-2	1-0	2-0	0-1	0-1	1-1	1-1	2-0	2-1	2-0	0-2	1-1	1-1	13-12
Patterson, Danny	0-0	0-2	2-2	3-1	0-0	0-0	0-1	0-0	1-0	0-0	2-0	0-0	2-0	2-0	10-6
Pavlik, Roger	0-1	1-1	0-0	0-0	0-1	0-0	0-0	0-0	0-0	0-0	0-0	0-2	0-0	0-0	3-5
Santana, Julio	0-1	0-0	1-0	0-0	0-0	0-0	1-0	0-1	1-0	1-0	0-2	0-0	0-1	0-1	4-6
Sturtze, Tanyon	0-0	0-0	1-0	0-0	0-0	0-0	0-0	0-1	0-0	0-0	0-0	0-0	0-0	0-0	1-1
Vosberg, Ed	0-0	0-0	1-0	0-0	0-0	0-1	0-0	0-0	0-0	0-0	0-0	0-0	0-0	0-0	1-2
Wetteland, John	0-1	0-0	0-0	0-0	2-0	2-0	0-0	0-0	0-0	1-0	0-0	0-0	0-0	1-1	7-2
Whiteside, Matt	0-0	0-0	0-0	0-0	1-0	0-0	1-0	0-0	0-0	0-0	0-1	0-0	0-0	2-0	4-1
Witt, Bobby	1-1	0-1	2-0	2-0	0-1	0-3	0-1	1-0	1-2	0-2	2-0	0-1	1-0	2-0	12-12
Totals	4-8	1-10	8-3	8-3	6-5	4-7	5-6	4-7	8-3	4-7	7-5	4-8	4-7	10-6	77-85

INTERLEAGUE BREAKDOWN: Heredia 1-0, Patterson 1-0, Santana 0-1, Witt 1-0 vs. Dodgers; Burkett 0-1, Clark 0-1, Whiteside 1-0, Witt 1-0 vs. Padres; Eversgerd 0-1, Oliver 0-1, Wetteland 1-0, Whiteside 1-0 vs. Giants; Burkett 1-0, Oliver 1-0, Patterson 1-0, Wetteland 0-1 vs. Rockies.

TORONTO—76-86

Pitcher	Ana. W-L	Bal. W-L	Bos. W-L	Chi. W-L	Cle. W-L	Det. W-L	K.C. W-L	Mil. W-L	Min. W-L	N.Y. W-L	Oak. W-L	Sea. W-L	Tex. W-L	N.L. W-L	Totals W-L
Almanzar, Carlos	0-0	0-0	0-0	0-0	0-0	0-0	0-0	0-0	0-0	0-1	0-0	0-0	0-0	0-0	0-1
Andujar, Luis	0-1	0-0	0-1	0-0	0-1	0-0	0-0	0-0	0-0	0-1	0-1	0-0	0-1	0-1	0-6
Carpenter, Chris	1-0	1-0	0-0	1-0	0-1	0-1	0-0	0-1	0-2	0-0	0-0	0-0	0-1	0-1	3-7
Clemens, Roger	0-0	1-1	1-0	2-0	3-0	1-0	2-0	1-1	2-0	2-0	2-0	0-2	4-0	0-3	21-7
Crabtree, Tim	0-0	0-0	0-0	0-0	0-0	0-1	1-0	1-0	0-1	0-1	0-0	1-0	0-0	0-0	3-3
Daal, Omar	0-0	0-1	0-0	0-0	0-0	0-0	0-0	0-0	0-0	1-0	0-0	0-0	0-0	0-0	1-1
Escobar, Kelvim	0-0	1-0	0-1	0-0	0-0	0-0	0-0	0-0	0-0	1-0	0-1	1-0	0-0	0-0	3-2
Flener, Huck	0-0	0-0	0-0	0-0	0-0	0-0	0-0	0-0	0-0	0-0	0-0	0-0	0-0	0-0	0-0
Guzman, Juan	0-1	0-1	0-0	1-0	1-0	0-0	0-1	1-0	0-0	0-0	0-0	0-0	0-0	0-2	3-6
Hanson, Erik	0-0	0-0	0-0	0-0	0-0	0-0	0-0	0-0	0-0	0-0	0-0	0-0	0-0	0-0	0-0
Hentgen, Pat	0-0	1-0	1-1	1-1	1-0	3-0	0-0	1-1	2-0	1-2	0-2	1-0	2-1	1-2	15-10
Janzen, Marty	0-0	0-0	1-0	0-0	0-0	0-0	1-0	0-0	0-0	0-0	0-0	0-0	0-0	0-1	2-1
Person, Robert	0-0	1-2	0-0	0-1	0-1	0-2	1-0	0-0	1-0	0-0	1-1	0-1	0-1	1-1	5-10
Plesac, Dan	1-0	0-1	1-0	0-1	0-0	0-0	0-0	0-0	0-0	0-1	0-1	0-0	0-0	0-2	2-7
Quantrill, Paul	1-0	0-0	0-1	1-0	0-1	0-1	0-3	0-0	2-0	0-0	1-0	1-0	0-0	0-1	6-7
Risley, Bill	0-0	0-0	0-0	0-0	0-0	0-0	0-0	0-0	0-0	0-1	0-0	0-0	0-0	0-0	0-1
Robinson, Ken	0-0	0-0	0-0	0-0	0-0	0-0	0-0	0-0	0-0	0-0	0-0	0-0	0-0	0-0	0-0
Spoljaric, Paul	0-2	0-0	0-0	0-0	0-0	0-0	0-0	0-0	0-0	0-0	0-0	0-0	0-0	0-1	0-3
Timlin, Mike	1-1	0-0	0-1	0-0	0-0	0-0	1-0	0-0	0-0	0-0	0-0	0-0	0-0	1-0	3-2
Williams, Woody	1-1	0-0	2-1	0-0	0-0	1-1	0-1	1-2	1-0	0-0	0-0	0-2	1-0	1-0	9-14
Totals	5-6	6-6	6-6	6-5	5-6	6-6	6-5	4-7	8-3	5-7	5-6	3-8	7-4	4-11	76-86

INTERLEAGUE BREAKDOWN: Andujar 0-1, Clemens 0-1, Williams 1-0 vs. Braves; Clemens 0-1, Hentgen 0-1, Timlin 1-0 vs. Expos; Clemens 0-1, Hentgen 0-1, Quantrill 0-1 vs. Mets; Hentgen 1-0, Person 1-0, Spoljaric 0-1 vs. Phillies; Carpenter 0-1, Person 0-1, Williams 0-1 vs. Marlins.

HOME RUNS BY PARKS

	At Ana.	At Bal.	At Bos.	At Chi.	At Cle.	At Det.	At K.C.	At Mil.	At Min.	At N.Y.	At Oak.	At Sea.	At Tex.	At Tor.	At N.L. Parks	Totals 1997	Totals 1996	HR Allow.
Anaheim	87	5	5	1	7	5	5	5	3	4	8	7	5	7	7	161	192	189
Baltimore	6	107	5	2	6	11	7	12	7	6	8	5	5	3	6	196	257	156
Boston	6	10	90	3	9	3	5	10	4	4	5	11	7	11	7	185	209	138
Chicago	4	5	4	73	11	4	10	7	8	5	4	5	8	3	7	158	195	167
Cleveland	11	5	8	9	96	6	4	16	6	10	10	9	12	6	12	220	218	176
Detroit	11	6	6	6	5	98	11	3	6	5	9	2	2	3	3	176	204	171
Kansas City	8	6	1	6	4	4	88	5	5	6	3	7	4	4	7	158	123	175
Milwaukee	10	6	1	7	9	9	5	56	3	3	3	6	5	6	6	135	178	172
Minnesota	6	2	7	5	5	4	9		59	9	4	9	4	1	8	132	118	180
New York	8	5	5	6	6	13	10	4	8	75	3	6	8	3	1	161	162	140
Oakland	3	5	4	9	7	7	6	4	5	2	107	10	9	6	13	197	243	188
Seattle	10	12	2	7	4	8	8	9	18	8	14	131	9	9	15	264	245	176
Texas	17	2	6	9	8	6	7	4	8	1	10	6	95	2	6	187	221	156

1997 A.L. STATISTICS — Miscellaneous

	At Ana.	At Bal.	At Bos.	At Chi.	At Cle.	At Det.	At K.C.	At Mil.	At Min.	At N.Y.	At Oak.	At Sea.	At Tex.	At Tor.	At N.L. Parks	Totals 1997	1996	HR Allow.
Toronto	9	8	6	2	3	8	9	2	6	2	6	4	8	68	6	147	177	163
N.L. clubs...............	14	12	9	4	5	2	3	2	5	6	9	15	5	8	....	99	....	125
1997 Totals	210	196	152	151	185	189	182	148	151	146	203	233	186	140	104	2576	....	2472
1996 Totals	227	229	214	166	177	230	140	186	182	152	*215	237	198	189	....	....	2742	....

*There were actually 192 home runs hit at Oakland in 1996. The totals include five home runs by the Blue Jays, eight by the Tigers and 10 by the Athletics at Cashman Field, Las Vegas.

AT ANAHEIM (210):

Anaheim (87)—Salmon 17, Hollins 15, Edmonds 14, Erstad 8, Anderson 5, Greene 5, Howell 5, Phillips 4, Leyritz 3, Alicea 2, DiSarcina 2, Kreuter 2, Murray 2, Eenhoorn 1, Grebeck 1, Henderson 1. **Baltimore (6)**—Anderson 2, Ripken 2, Bordick 1, Palmeiro 1. **Boston (6)**—Garciaparra 3, Naehring 1, Valentin 1, Vaughn 1. **Chicago (4)**—Cameron 1, Fabregas 1, Karkovice 1, Thomas 1. **Cleveland (11)**—Alomar 3, Justice 3, Grissom 2, Giles 1, Mitchell 1, Williams 1. **Detroit (11)**—Fryman 4, Nieves 2, Trammell 2, Clark 1, Easley 1, Hunter 1. **Kansas City (8)**—Palmer 2, Benitez 1, Dye 1, Goodwin 1, King 1, Macfarlane 1, Myers 1. **Milwaukee (10)**—Nilsson 4, Burnitz 2, Jaha 2, Valentin 1, Williams 1. **Minnesota (6)**—Cordova 2, Steinbach 2, Colbrunn 1, Coomer 1. **New York (8)**—Jeter 2, Boggs 1, Martinez 1, O'Neill 1, Posada 1, Sanchez 1, Williams 1. **Oakland (3)**—Berroa 1, Canseco 1, Mashore 1. **Seattle (10)**—Buhner 3, Griffey 2, Sorrento 2, Cora 1, Cruz 1, Martinez 1. **Texas (17)**—Gonzalez 3, Stevens 3, Newson 2, Brown 1, Buford 1, Clark 1, Diaz 1, Greer 1, Palmer 1, Ripken 1, Rodriguez 1, Tatis 1. **Toronto (9)**—Gonzalez 3, Sprague 2, Brumfield 1, Green 1, Merced 1, Santiago 1. **Colorado (4)**—Pulliam 1, Reed 1, Walker 1, Weiss 1. **Los Angeles (1)**—Karros 1. **San Diego (4)**—Flaherty 1, Henderson 1, Joyner 1, Vaughn 1. **San Francisco (5)**—Kent 2, Aurilia 1, Hamilton 1, Snow 1.

AT BALTIMORE (196):

Anaheim (5)—Salmon 2, Edmonds 1, Erstad 1, Greene 1. **Baltimore (107)**—Palmeiro 20, Alomar 10, Ripken 10, Surhoff 10, Hammonds 9, Hoiles 9, Anderson 8, Davis 7, Berroa 5, Bordick 5, Tarasco 4, Webster 3, Incaviglia 2, Reboulet 2, Baines 1, Ledesma 1, Walton 1. **Boston (10)**—Vaughn 3, Stanley 2, Cordero 1, Garciaparra 1, Haselman 1, Naehring 1, O'Leary 1. **Chicago (5)**—Baines 1, Belle 1, Martinez 1, Mouton 1, Thomas 1. **Cleveland (5)**—Borders 1, Grissom 1, Justice 1, Ramirez 1, Vizquel 1. **Detroit (6)**—Easley 3, Hamelin 1, Nevin 1, Nieves 1. **Kansas City (6)**—Bell 2, Davis 2, King 1, Sutton 1. **Milwaukee (6)**—Nilsson 2, Voigt 2, Jackson 1, Valentin 1. **Minnesota (2)**—Lawton 1, Molitor 1. **New York (5)**—Curtis 1, Fielder 1, Hayes 1, O'Neill 1, Williams 1. **Oakland (5)**—Hollborn 1, Giambi 1, Mayne 1, McDonald 1, Spiezio 1. **Seattle (12)**—Wilson 3, Cora 2, Griffey 2, Buhner 1, Davis 1, Martinez 1, Rodriguez 1, Sorrento 1. **Texas (2)**—Greer 2. **Toronto (8)**—Delgado 2, Garcia 2, Carter 1, Gonzalez 1, Green 1, Merced 1. **Montreal (4)**—Lansing 1, McGuire 1, Obando 1, Rodriguez 1. **New York (4)**—Gilkey 2, Franco 1, Huskey 1. **Philadelphia (4)**—Rolen 2, Amaro 1, Lieberthal 1.

AT BOSTON (152):

Anaheim (5)—Anderson 2, Howell 2, Salmon 1. **Baltimore (5)**—Surhoff 2, Hammonds 1, Hoiles 1, Palmeiro 1. **Boston (90)**—Vaughn 20, Cordero 11, Garciaparra 11, Valentin 11, Jefferson 6, Hatteberg 5, O'Leary 5, Stanley 5, Naehring 4, Bragg 3, Haselman 3, Frye 2, Mack 2, Pemberton 1, Pride 1. **Chicago (4)**—Belle 2, Fabregas 1, Thomas 1. **Cleveland (8)**—Thome 4, Williams 2, Borders 1, Justice 1. **Detroit (6)**—Nieves 3, Clark 1, Easley 1, Nevin 1. **Kansas City (1)**—Bell 1. **Milwaukee (1)**—Matheny 1. **New York (5)**—Boggs 2, O'Neill 2, Whiten 1. **Oakland (4)**—Batista 1, Brosius 1, Canseco 1, Mashore 1. **Seattle (2)**—Martinez 1, Rodriguez 1. **Texas (6)**—Gonzalez 3, Gil 1, Palmer 1, Rodriguez 1. **Toronto (6)**—Green 2, Carter 1, Cruz 1, Delgado 1, O'Brien 1. **Atlanta (7)**—McGriff 3, Colbrunn 1, Jones 1, Klesko 1, Lockhart 1. **Philadelphia (2)**—Daulton 1, Rolen 1.

AT CHICAGO (151):

Anaheim (1)—Howell 1. **Baltimore (2)**—Alomar 1, Hammonds 1. **Boston (3)**—Garciaparra 1, Jefferson 1, Mack 1. **Chicago (73)**—Thomas 16, Belle 14, Cameron 10, Baines 5, Karkovice 4, Mouton 4, Durham 3, Snopek 3, Ordonez 2, Ventura 2, Fabregas 1, Guillen 1, Kreuter 1, Martin 1, Phillips 1. **Cleveland (9)**—Thome 4, Alomar 1, Borders 1, Giles 1, Ramirez 1, Williams 1. **Detroit (6)**—Clark 2, Easley 2, Higginson 1, Nieves 1. **Kansas City (6)**—King 4, Bell 1, Sweeney 1. **Milwaukee (7)**—Jaha 2, Valentin 2, Cirillo 1, Loretta 1, Williams 1. **Minnesota (7)**—Cordova 3, Coomer 2, Brede 1, Lawton 1. **New York (6)**—Martinez 4, Boggs 1, O'Neill 1. **Oakland (9)**—Giambi 2, Stairs 2, Batista 1, Canseco 1, Magadan 1, Spiezio 1, Young 1. **Seattle (7)**—Buhner 2, Griffey 2, Martinez 2, Sorrento 1. **Texas (9)**—Palmer 2, Simms 2, Clark 1, Gil 1, McLemore 1, Newson 1, Tatis 1. **Toronto (2)**—Delgado 1, Perez 1. **Houston (4)**—Bagwell 2, Bell 1, Biggio 1.

AT CLEVELAND (185):

Anaheim (7)—Greene 2, Howell 2, Anderson 1, Edmonds 1, Murray 1. **Baltimore (6)**—Palmeiro 2, Anderson 1, Baines 1, Berroa 1, Surhoff 1. **Boston (9)**—Valentin 3, Frye 1, Garciaparra 1, Hatteberg 1, Jefferson 1, O'Leary 1, Vaughn 1. **Chicago (11)**—Thomas 3, Martinez 2, Belle 1, Cameron 1, Durham 1, Fabregas 1, Ordonez 1, Ventura 1. **Cleveland (96)**—Justice 17, Thome 17, Ramirez 14, Alomar 9, Fernandez 7, Giles 7, Williams 7, Grissom 5, Vizquel 3, Branson 2, Franco 2, Manto 2, Curtis 1, Mitchell 1, Roberts 1, Seitzer 1. **Detroit (5)**—Higginson 2, Clark 1, Easley 1, Nevin 1. **Kansas City (4)**—Damon 1, Davis 1, Macfarlane 1, Paquette 1. **Milwaukee (9)**—Jaha 2, Nilsson 2, Valentin 2, Burnitz 1, Cirillo 1, Vina 1. **Minnesota (5)**—Coomer 1, Cordova 1, Lawton 1, Meares 1, Stahoviak 1. **New York (6)**—Martinez 2, Fielder 1, Jeter 1, Posada 1, Raines 1. **Oakland (7)**—Canseco 3, McGwire 2, Berroa 1, Brosius 1. **Seattle (4)**—Davis 2, Cruz 1, Sorrento 1. **Texas (8)**—Gonzalez 3, Newson 2, Clark 1, Greer 1, Stevens 1. **Toronto (3)**—Cruz 1, Green 1, Sprague 1. **Chicago (3)**—Clark 1, Glanville 1, Grace 1. **Cincinnati (2)**—Greene 1, Perez 1.

AT DETROIT (189):

Anaheim (5)—Salmon 3, Edmonds 1, Leyritz 1. **Baltimore (11)**—Hammonds 3, Palmeiro 2, Tarasco 2, Alomar 1, Anderson 1, Berroa 1, Reboulet 1. **Boston (3)**—Vaughn 2, Hatteberg 1. **Chicago (4)**—Baines 1, Guillen 1, Snopek 1, Thomas 1. **Cleveland (6)**—Ramirez 2, Williams 2, Justice 1, Thome 1. **Detroit (98)**—Clark 18, Higginson 16, Fryman 13, Easley 12, Hamelin 10, Nieves 7, Casanova 5, Nevin 4, Hunter 2, Johnson 2, Miller 2, Pride 2, Trammell 2, Encarnacio 1, Hurst 1, Walbeck 1. **Kansas City (4)**—Damon 2, Bell 1, Dye 1. **Milwaukee (9)**—Nilsson 3, Burnitz 2, Williams 2, Jaha 1, Mieske 1. **Minnesota (5)**—Coomer 1, Hocking 1, Lawton 1, Miller 1, Steinbach 1. **New York (13)**—Martinez 4, Fielder 2, Stanley 2, Curtis 1, Hayes 1, O'Neill 1, Posada 1, Williams 1. **Oakland (7)**—Berroa 3, McGwire 2, Canseco 1, Magadan 1. **Seattle (8)**—Cruz 2, Griffey 2, Buhner 1, Davis 1, Rodriguez 1, Wilson 1. **Texas (6)**—Newson 2, Clark 1, Greer 1, Ripken 1, Rodriguez 1. **Toronto (8)**—Carter 2, Gonzalez 2, Cruz 1, Nixon 1, O'Brien 1, Sprague 1. **Florida (2)**—Bonilla 2.

AT KANSAS CITY (182):

Anaheim (5)—Salmon 2, Erstad 1, Kreuter 1, Leyritz 1. **Baltimore (7)**—Palmeiro 4, Anderson 1, Reboulet 1, Webster 1. **Boston (5)**—Jefferson 2, Garciaparra 1, Stanley 1, Vaughn 1. **Chicago (10)**—Durham 3, Thomas 3, Baines 1, Belle 1, Fabregas 1, Ventura 1. **Cleveland (4)**—Justice 2, Roberts 2. **Detroit (11)**—Clark 3, Higginson 2, Nieves 2, Easley 1, Fryman 1, Hamelin 1, Hunter 1. **Kansas City (88)**—Davis 21, King 11, Bell 10, Paquette 7, Benitez 5, Macfarlane 5, Sweeney 5, Palmer 4, Vitiello 4, Cooper 3, Damon 3, Dye 3, Offerman 2, Halter 1, Hansen 1, Myers 1, Nunnally 1, Sutton 1. **Milwaukee (5)**—Nilsson 2, Burnitz 1, Voigt 1, Williams 1. **Minnesota (4)**—Cordova 3, Meares 1. **New York (10)**—Martinez 3, Hayes 2, Williams 2, Fielder 1, O'Neill 1, Posada 1. **Oakland (6)**—Spiezio 2, Giambi 1, Lesher 1, McGwire 1, Molina 1. **Seattle (8)**—Buhner 2, Griffey 2, Sorrento 2, Ducey 1, Gates 1. **Texas (7)**—Buford 1, Cedeno 1, Gonzalez 1, Palmer 1, Rodriguez 1, Sagmoen 1, Stevens 1. **Toronto (9)**—Cruz 3, Sprague 3, Carter 1, Delgado 1, Merced 1. **Houston (1)**—Gonzalez 1. **St.. Louis (2)**—McGwire 1, Plantier 1.

AT MILWAUKEE (148):

Anaheim (5)—Erstad 1, Greene 1, Howell 1, Leyritz 1, Salmon 1. **Baltimore (12)**—Hammonds 3, Walton 2, Alomar 1, Baines 1, Davis 1, Dellucci 1, Incaviglia 1, Ledesma 1, Surhoff 1. **Boston (10)**—Garciaparra 3, Vaughn 2, Cordero 1, Haselman 1, Hatteberg 1, O'Leary 1, Valentin 1. **Chicago (7)**—Thomas 2, Abbott 1, Belle 1, Guillen 1, Martinez 1, Valdez 1. **Cleveland (16)**—Williams 5, Alomar 2, Giles 2, Justice 2, Borders 1, Curtis 1, Fernandez 1, Ramirez 1, Thome 1. **Detroit (3)**—Clark 1, Hamelin 1, Nieves 1. **Kansas City (5)**—King 2, Bell 1, Davis 1, Palmer 1. **Milwaukee (56)**—Burnitz 18, Cirillo 6, Nilsson 5, Voigt 5, Valentin 4, Franco 3, Williams 3, Dunn 2, Loretta 2, Matheny 2, Jackson 1, Jaha 1, Levis 1, Mieske 1, Unroe 1, Vina 1. **Minnesota (9)**—Stahoviak 2, Becker 1, Colbrunn 1, Coomer 1, Knoblauch 1, Meares 1, Molitor 1, Myers 1. **New York (4)**—Curtis 1, Kelly 1, Martinez 1, O'Neill 1. **Oakland (4)**—Brosius 1, Lesher 1, McGwire 1, Stairs 1. **Seattle (9)**—Ducey 2, Griffey 2, Buhner 1, Davis 1, Martinez 1, Rodriguez 1, Sorrento 1. **Texas (4)**—Gonzalez 2, Greer 1, Tettleton 1. **Toronto (2)**—Garcia 1, Samuel 1. **Pittsburgh (1)**—Smith 1. **St.. Louis (1)**—Lampkin 1.

– 259 –

AT MINNESOTA (151):

Anaheim (3)—Salmon 2, Edmonds 1. **Baltimore (7)**—Incaviglia 2, Surhoff 2, Anderson 1, Berroa 1, Palmeiro 1. **Boston (4)**—Bragg 1, Garciaparra 1, Haselman 1, O'Leary 1. **Chicago (8)**—Belle 2, Cameron 2, Martinez 2, Baines 1, Thomas 1. **Cleveland (6)**—Thome 2, Franco 1, Giles 1, Grissom 1, Justice 1. **Detroit (6)**—Nieves 2, Walbeck 2, Clark 1, Higginson 1. **Kansas City (5)**—Bell 1, Benitez 1, Roberts 1, Spehr 1, Sweeney 1. **Milwaukee (3)**—Cirillo 1, Loretta 1, Valentin 1. **Minnesota (59)**—Lawton 8, Steinbach 6, Kelly 5, Meares 5, Molitor 5, Becker 4, Coomer 4, Cordova 4, Stahoviak 4, Jackson 3, Myers 3, Brede 2, Colbrunn 2, Knoblauch 2, Miller 1, Walker 1. **New York (8)**—Martinez 3, Curtis 2, Hayes 1, O'Neill 1, Williams 1. **Oakland (5)**—McGwire 2, Berroa 1, Brosius 1, Spiezio 1. **Seattle (18)**—Griffey 5, Buhner 4, Martinez 3, Cora 1, Davis 1, Ducey 1, Gates 1, Sheets 1, Sorrento 1. **Texas (8)**—Gonzalez 2, Cedeno 1, Clark 1, Greer 1, Newson 1, Rodriguez 1, Stevens 1. **Toronto (6)**—Santiago 3, Carter 1, Cruz 1, Delgado 1. **Cincinnati (3)**—Greene 2, Stynes 1. **Pittsburgh (2)**—Polcovich 1, Smith 1.

AT NEW YORK (146):

Anaheim (4)—Leyritz 2, Erstad 1, Salmon 1. **Baltimore (6)**—Hammonds 2, Anderson 1, Berroa 1, Palmeiro 1, Ripken 1. **Boston (4)**—Stanley 2, Cordero 1, Vaughn 1. **Chicago (5)**—Belle 2, Thomas 2, Snopek 1. **Cleveland (10)**—Williams 5, Grissom 2, Fernandez 1, Giles 1, Thome 1. **Detroit (5)**—Higginson 2, Clark 1, Hamelin 1, Nevin 1. **Kansas City (6)**—Davis 3, Dye 1, King 1, Palmer 1. **Milwaukee (3)**—Cirillo 1, Dunn 1, Jaha 1. **Minnesota (9)**—Knoblauch 2, Steinbach 2, Becker 1, Meares 1, Molitor 1, Myers 1, Stahoviak 1. **New York (75)**—Martinez 18, Williams 13, O'Neill 10, Fielder 6, Hayes 5, Jeter 5, Whiten 4, Curtis 3, Raines 3, Posada 2, Sojo 2, Duncan 1, Girardi 1, Kelly 1, Stanley 1. **Oakland (2)**—McGwire 1, Young 1. **Seattle (8)**—Buhner 2, Griffey 2, Cruz 1, Martinez 1, Rodriguez 1, Wilson 1. **Texas (1)**—Stevens 1. **Toronto (2)**—Santiago 1, Sprague 1. **Atlanta (2)**—Klesko 2. **Montreal (3)**—Fletcher 1, Strange 1, White 1. **New York (1)**—Gilkey 1.

AT OAKLAND (203):

Anaheim (8)—Edmonds 2, Erstad 1, Hollins 1, Howell 1, Kreuter 1, Phillips 1, Salmon 1. **Baltimore (8)**—Anderson 1, Baines 1, Berroa 1, Bordick 1, Hoiles 1, Ripken 1, Surhoff 1, Tarasco 1. **Boston (5)**—Jefferson 2, Bragg 1, Naehring 1, Vaughn 1. **Chicago (4)**—Durham 1, Martinez 1, Thomas 1, Ventura 1. **Cleveland (10)**—Justice 4, Thome 3, Mitchell 2, Ramirez 1. **Detroit (9)**—Hamelin 3, Fryman 2, Clark 1, Cruz 1, Higginson 1, Nieves 1. **Kansas City (3)**—Bell 1, Davis 1, Macfarlane 1. **Milwaukee (3)**—Valentin 2, Banks 1. **Minnesota (4)**—Knoblauch 2, Hocking 1, Steinbach 1. **New York (3)**—Curtis 1, Martinez 1, O'Neill 1. **Oakland (107)**—Stairs 20, McGwire 17, Giambi 14, Canseco 10, Brosius 7, Berroa 6, Spiezio 6, Mayne 4, Bellhorn 3, Grieve 3, Young 3, Brito 2, Lesher 2, Magadan 2, Williams 2, Lennon 1, Mashore 1, McDonald 1, Molina 1, Sheldon 1, Tejada 1. **Seattle (14)**—Buhner 4, Griffey 3, Martinez 2, Amaral 1, Cora 1, Ducey 1, Kelly 1, Wilson 1. **Texas (10)**—Gonzalez 4, Stevens 2, Diaz 1, Greer 1, Palmer 1, Rodriguez 1. **Toronto (6)**—Carter 2, Gonzalez 1, Merced 1, Santiago 1, Sprague 1. **Colorado (4)**—Walker 2, Burks 1, Galarraga 1. **Los Angeles (1)**—Karros 1. **San Diego (3)**—Gwynn 1, Jones 1, Vaughn 1. **San Francisco (1)**—Bonds 1.

AT SEATTLE (233):

Anaheim (7)—Edmonds 2, Alicea 1, Disarcina 1, Howell 1, Leyritz 1, Turner 1. **Baltimore (5)**—Anderson 1, Hammonds 1, Hoiles 1, Surhoff 1, Webster 1. **Boston (11)**—Bragg 2, Cordero 2, Garciaparra 2, O'Leary 2, Hatteberg 1, Naehring 1, Stanley 1. **Chicago (5)**—Thomas 2, Baines 1, Phillips 1, Ventura 1. **Cleveland (9)**—Alomar 2, Ramirez 2, Curtis 1, Grissom 1, Justice 1, Thome 1, Williams 1. **Detroit (2)**—Higginson 1, Nevin 1. **Kansas City (7)**—King 2, Bell 1, Davis 1, Goodwin 1, Halter 1, Howard 1. **Milwaukee (6)**—Mieske 2, Jaha 1, Matheny 1, Newfield 1, Unroe 1. **Minnesota (9)**—Becker 2, Cordova 2, Colbrunn 1, Coomer 1, Knoblauch 1, Stahoviak 1, Walker 1. **New York (9)**—Martinez 3, Curtis 1, Jeter 1, Williams 1. **Oakland (10)**—Stairs 3, Bellhorn 1, Bournigal 1, Canseco 1, Giambi 1, McGwire 1, Molina 1, Spiezio 1, Williams 1. **Seattle (131)**—Griffey 27, Sorrento 18, Rodriguez 16, Buhner 13, Martinez 12, Davis 11, Wilson 9, Cruz 7, Blowers 5, Cora 4, Kelly 3, Sheets 2, Gates 1, Ibanez 1, Marzano 1, Wilkins 1. **Texas (6)**—Gonzalez 2, Buford 1, Clark 1, Palmer 1, Rodriguez 1. **Toronto (4)**—Delgado 2, Crespo 1, Cruz 1. **Colorado (1)**—Young 1. **Los Angeles (4)**—Karros 3, Piazza 1. **San Diego (5)**—Finley 2, Caminiti 1, Cianfrocco 1, Joyner 1. **San Francisco (5)**—Kent 2, Aurilia 1, Lewis 1, Snow 1.

AT TEXAS (186):

Anaheim (5)—Edmonds 1, Howell 1, Leyritz 1, Phillips 1, Salmon 1. **Baltimore (5)**—Palmeiro 3, Ripken 2. **Boston (7)**—Garciaparra 2, O'Leary 2, Cordero 1, Pemberton 1, Vaughn 1. **Chicago (8)**—Belle 3, Baines 1, Durham 1, Fabregas 1, Guillen 1, Karkovice 1. **Cleveland (12)**—Thome 3, Williams 3, Alomar 2, Giles 2, Fernandez 1, Ramirez 1. **Detroit (2)**—Fryman 2. **Kansas City (4)**—Damon 1, King 1, Palmer 1, Vitiello 1. **Milwaukee (5)**—Vina 2, Burnitz 1, Franco 1, Valentin 1. **Minnesota (4)**—Coomer 2, Arias 1, Walker 1. **New York (8)**—Martinez 2, Curtis 1, Fielder 1, Hayes 1, Jeter 1, O'Neill 1, Williams 1. **Oakland (9)**—Berroa 3, Canseco 2, Batista 1, Giambi 1, McDonald 1, McGwire 1. **Seattle (9)**—Buhner 3, Griffey 2, Kelly 2, Sorrento 2. **Texas (95)**—Gonzalez 18, Greer 18, Rodriguez 12, Stevens 12, Clark 6, Palmer 6, Tatis 6, Buford 4, Gil 3, Simms 3, Cedeno 2, Newson 2, Tettleton 2, Ripken 1. **Toronto (8)**—Delgado 4, Merced 2, Carter 1, Green 1. **Colorado (1)**—Castilla 1. **Los Angeles (1)**—Prince 1. **San Francisco (3)**—Bonds 1, Javier 1, Snow 1.

AT TORONTO (140):

Anaheim (7)—Erstad 3, Alicea 1, Disarcina 1, Leyritz 1, Salmon 1. **Baltimore (3)**—Alomar 1, Hammonds 1, Palmeiro 1. **Boston (11)**—Garciaparra 3, Bragg 2, Stanley 2, Cordero 1, Jefferson 1, Naehring 1, O'Leary 1. **Chicago (3)**—Belle 1, Martin 1, Thomas 1. **Cleveland (6)**—Williams 3, Thome 2, Alomar 1. **Detroit (3)**—Clark 1, Hamelin 1, Higginson 1. **Kansas City (4)**—Bell 2, Benitez 1, King 1. **Milwaukee (6)**—Nilsson 2, Jaha 1, Mieske 1, Valentin 1, Williams 1. **Minnesota (1)**—Knoblauch 1. **New York (3)**—Martinez 2, Fielder 1. **Oakland (6)**—McGwire 3, Berroa 1, Canseco 1, Spiezio 1. **Seattle (9)**—Griffey 4, Rodriguez 2, Buhner 1, Cora 1, Davis 1. **Texas (2)**—Gonzalez 2. **Toronto (68)**—Delgado 17, Carter 11, Green 10, Santiago 7, Sprague 5, Cruz 4, Gonzalez 4, Merced 3, O'Brien 2, Samuel 2, Brumfield 1, Evans 1, Sierra 1. **Atlanta (2)**—Jones 1, Klesko 1. **Florida (2)**—Johnson 1, Sheffield 1. **Montreal (4)**—Guerrero 2, Segui 1, White 1.

1997 N.L. STATISTICS

Batting

Designated hitting

Pinch-hitting

Pitching

Fielding

Miscellaneous

BATTING

TEAM

Team	Avg.	G	TPA	AB	R	H	TB	2B	3B	HR	RBI	SH	SF	HP	BB	IBB	SO	SB	CS	GDP	LOB	ShO	Slg.	OBP
Colorado	.288	162	6336	5603	923	1611	2677	269	40	239	869	73	35	63	562	35	1060	137	65	138	1124	8	.478	.357
San Diego	.271	162	6369	5609	795	1519	2282	275	16	152	761	63	58	35	604	40	1129	140	60	130	1207	9	.407	.342
Atlanta	.270	162	6312	5528	791	1490	2354	268	37	174	755	83	52	52	597	45	1160	108	58	143	1177	6	.426	.343
Los Angeles	.268	162	6216	5544	742	1488	2318	242	33	174	706	105	36	33	498	46	1079	131	64	109	1120	6	.418	.330
Chicago	.263	162	6095	5489	687	1444	2172	269	39	127	642	83	38	34	451	40	1003	116	60	119	1093	10	.396	.321
New York	.262	162	6248	5524	777	1448	2237	274	28	153	741	58	59	57	550	45	1029	97	74	122	1111	7	.405	.332
Pittsburgh	.262	162	6200	5503	725	1440	2222	291	52	129	686	77	47	92	481	27	1161	160	50	105	1168	7	.404	.329
Florida	.259	162	6299	5439	740	1410	2146	272	28	136	703	71	42	61	686	55	1074	115	58	132	1248	9	.395	.346
Houston	.259	162	6362	5502	777	1427	2220	314	40	133	720	74	53	100	633	63	1085	171	74	104	1221	4	.403	.344
Montreal	.258	162	6131	5426	691	1423	2346	339	34	172	659	72	40	73	420	40	1084	75	46	95	1091	10	.425	.316
San Francisco	.258	162	6296	5485	784	1415	2271	266	37	172	746	64	59	46	642	72	1120	121	49	111	1199	4	.414	.337
Philadelphia	.255	162	6126	5443	668	1390	2098	290	35	116	622	74	50	40	519	32	1032	92	56	105	1152	8	.385	.322
St. Louis	.255	162	6211	5524	689	1409	2188	269	39	144	654	58	44	42	543	54	1191	164	60	128	1140	8	.396	.324
Cincinnati	.253	162	6152	5484	651	1386	2135	269	27	142	612	75	30	45	518	35	1113	190	67	104	1144	10	.389	.321
Totals	.263	1134	87353	77203	10440	20300	31666	3907	485	2163	9876	1030	643	773	7704	629	15320	1817	841	1645	16195	102	.410	.333

INDIVIDUAL

TOP QUALIFIERS FOR BATTING CHAMPIONSHIP

Minimum 502 plate appearances. *Lefthanded batter. †Switch-hitter.

Player, Team	Avg.	G	TPA	AB	R	H	TB	2B	3B	HR	RBI	SH	SF	HP	BB	IBB	SO	SB	CS	GDP	Slg.	OBP
Gwynn, Tony, San Diego*	.372	149	651	592	97	220	324	49	2	17	119	1	12	3	43	12	28	12	5	12	.547	.409
Walker, Larry, Colorado*	.366	153	664	568	143	208	409	46	4	49	130	0	4	14	78	14	90	33	8	15	.720	.452
Piazza, Mike, Los Angeles	.362	152	633	556	104	201	355	32	1	40	124	0	5	3	69	11	77	5	1	19	.638	.431
Lofton, Kenny, Atlanta*	.333	122	564	493	90	164	211	20	6	5	48	2	3	2	64	5	83	27	20	10	.428	.409
Joyner, Wally, San Diego*	.327	135	518	455	59	149	221	29	2	13	83	0	10	2	51	5	51	3	5	14	.486	.390
Grace, Mark, Chicago*	.319	151	654	555	87	177	258	32	5	13	78	1	8	2	88	3	45	2	4	18	.465	.409
Galarraga, Andres, Colorado	.318	154	674	600	120	191	351	31	3	41	140	0	3	17	54	2	141	15	8	16	.585	.389
Alfonzo, Edgardo, New York	.315	151	599	518	84	163	224	27	2	10	72	8	5	5	63	0	56	11	6	4	.432	.391
Mondesi, Raul, Los Angeles	.310	159	670	616	95	191	333	42	5	30	87	1	3	6	44	7	105	32	15	11	.541	.360
Biggio, Craig, Houston	.309	162	744	619	146	191	310	37	8	22	81	0	7	34	84	6	107	47	10	0	.501	.415
Bichette, Dante, Colorado	.308	151	601	561	81	173	286	31	2	26	118	0	7	3	30	1	90	6	5	13	.510	.343
Blauser, Jeff, Atlanta	.308	151	623	519	90	160	250	31	4	17	70	5	9	20	70	6	101	5	1	13	.482	.405
Segui, David, Montreal†	.307	125	523	459	75	141	232	22	3	21	68	0	6	1	57	12	66	1	0	9	.505	.380
Castilla, Vinny, Colorado	.304	159	668	612	94	186	335	25	2	40	113	0	4	8	44	9	108	2	4	17	.547	.356
Dunston, Shawon, Chi.-Pit.	.300	132	511	490	71	147	221	22	5	14	57	5	5	3	8	0	75	32	8	9	.451	.312

DEPARTMENTAL LEADERS: G—Bagwell, Hou., Biggio, Hou., Karros, L.A., Sosa, Chi., 162; AB—Grudzielanek, Mon., 649; R—Biggio, Hou., 146; H—Gwynn, S.D., 220; TB—Walker, Col., 409; 1B—Gwynn, S.D., 152; 2B—Grudzielanek, Mon., 54; 3B—DeShields, St.L., 14; HR—Walker, Col., 49; RBI—Galarraga, Col., 140; SH—Renteria, Fla., 19; SF—Gilkey, N.Y., Gwynn, S.D., 12; HP—Biggio, Hou., 34; BB—Bonds, S.F., 145; IBB—Bonds, S.F., 34; SO—Sosa, Chi., 174; SB—Womack, Pit., 60; CS—Lofton, Atl., 20; GIDP—McGriff, Atl., 22; Slg. Pct.—Walker, Col., .720; OB. Pct.—Walker, Col., .452;

ALL PLAYERS

*Lefthanded batter. †Switch-hitter.

Player, Team	Avg.	G	TPA	AB	R	H	TB	2B	3B	HR	RBI	SH	SF	HP	BB	IBB	SO	SB	CS	GDP	Slg.	OBP
Abbott, Kurt, Florida	.274	94	273	252	35	69	109	18	2	6	30	6	0	1	14	3	68	3	1	5	.433	.315
Abreu, Bob, Houston*	.250	59	210	188	22	47	70	10	2	3	26	0	0	1	21	0	48	7	2	0	.372	.329
Acevedo, Juan, New York	.000	25	7	6	0	0	0	0	0	0	0	1	0	0	0	0	5	0	0	0	.000	.000
Adams, Terry, Chicago	.000	74	2	2	0	0	0	0	0	0	0	0	0	0	0	0	1	0	0	0	.000	.000
Alexander, Manny, N.Y.-Chi.	.266	87	272	248	37	66	95	12	4	3	22	3	1	3	17	3	54	13	1	6	.383	.320
Alfonseca, Antonio, Florida	.000	17	3	3	0	0	0	0	0	0	0	0	0	0	0	0	3	0	0	0	.000	.000
Alfonzo, Edgardo, New York	.315	151	599	518	84	163	224	27	2	10	72	8	5	5	63	0	56	11	6	4	.432	.391
Allensworth, Jermaine, Pit.	.255	108	435	369	55	94	125	18	2	3	43	9	6	7	44	1	79	14	7	5	.339	.340
Alou, Moises, Florida	.292	150	619	538	88	157	265	29	5	23	115	0	7	4	70	9	85	9	5	13	.493	.373
Alvarez, Wilson, San Fran.*	.130	11	26	23	1	3	3	0	0	0	1	1	0	0	2	0	5	0	0	0	.130	.200
Amaro, Ruben Jr., Phi.†	.234	117	200	175	18	41	55	6	1	2	21	0	2	2	21	0	24	1	1	4	.314	.320
Andrews, Shane, Montreal	.203	18	69	64	10	13	28	3	0	4	9	0	2	0	3	0	20	0	0	0	.438	.232
Anthony, Eric, Los Angeles*	.243	47	86	74	8	18	31	3	2	2	5	0	0	0	12	1	18	2	0	0	.419	.349
Arias, Alex, Florida	.247	74	112	93	13	23	28	2	0	1	11	4	0	3	12	0	12	0	0	1	.301	.352
Arias, George, San Diego	.227	11	22	22	2	5	6	1	0	0	2	0	0	0	0	0	4	0	0	2	.273	.227
Arocha, Rene, San Fran.	.000	6	1	1	0	0	0	0	0	0	0	0	0	0	0	0	1	0	0	0	.000	.000
Ashby, Andy, San Diego	.067	31	69	60	1	4	5	1	0	0	1	7	0	0	2	0	24	0	0	1	.083	.097
Ashley, Billy, Los Angeles	.244	71	140	131	12	32	57	7	0	6	19	0	0	1	8	0	46	0	0	2	.435	.293
Astacio, Pedro, L.A.-Col.	.130	33	65	54	2	7	8	1	0	0	1	11	0	0	0	0	24	0	0	0	.148	.130
Aurilia, Rich, San Fran.	.275	46	113	102	16	28	51	8	0	5	19	1	2	0	8	0	15	1	1	3	.500	.321
Ausmus, Brad, Houston	.266	130	478	425	45	113	152	25	1	4	44	6	6	3	38	4	78	14	6	8	.358	.326
Aybar, Manny, St. Louis	.143	12	21	21	0	3	3	0	0	0	1	0	0	0	0	0	9	0	0	0	.143	.143
Baerga, Carlos, New York†	.281	133	498	467	53	131	185	25	1	9	52	3	5	3	20	1	54	2	6	13	.396	.311
Bagwell, Jeff, Houston	.286	162	717	566	109	162	335	40	2	43	135	0	8	16	127	27	122	31	10	10	.592	.425
Bailey, Cory, San Fran.	1.000	7	1	1	0	1	1	0	0	0	0	0	0	0	0	0	0	0	0	0	1.000	1.000
Bailey, Roger, Colorado	.210	30	69	62	9	13	14	1	0	0	2	5	0	0	2	0	15	0	0	0	.226	.234
Barron, Tony, Philadelphia	.286	57	208	189	22	54	80	12	1	4	24	3	2	1	12	0	38	0	1	2	.423	.330

Player, Team	Avg.	G	TPA	AB	R	H	TB	2B	3B	HR	RBI	SH	SF	HP	BB	IBB	SO	SB	CS	GDP	Slg.	OBP
Bates, Jason, Colorado†	.240	62	139	121	17	29	48	10	0	3	11	0	0	3	15	1	27	0	1	3	.397	.338
Batista, Miguel, Chicago	.000	11	8	8	0	0	0	0	0	0	0	0	0	0	0	0	5	0	0	0	.000	.000
Bautista, Danny, Atlanta	.243	64	112	103	14	25	41	3	2	3	9	2	1	1	5	1	24	2	0	3	.398	.282
Beamon, Trey, San Diego*	.277	43	68	65	5	18	21	3	0	0	7	0	0	1	2	0	17	1	2	1	.323	.309
Beech, Matt, Philadelphia*	.167	24	41	30	1	5	6	1	0	0	1	11	0	0	0	0	14	0	0	0	.200	.167
Belinda, Stan, Cincinnati	.333	84	3	3	0	1	1	0	0	0	0	0	0	0	0	0	1	0	0	1	.333	.333
Bell, David, St. Louis	.211	66	155	142	9	30	44	7	2	1	12	2	1	0	10	2	28	1	0	2	.310	.261
Bell, Derek, Houston	.276	129	547	493	67	136	216	29	3	15	71	0	2	12	40	3	94	15	7	16	.438	.344
Belliard, Rafael, Atlanta	.211	72	77	71	9	15	21	3	0	1	3	4	1	0	1	0	17	0	1	1	.296	.219
Beltran, Rigo, St. Louis*	.143	35	7	7	1	1	2	1	0	0	0	0	0	0	0	0	1	0	0	0	.286	.143
Benard, Marvin, San Fran.*	.228	84	130	114	13	26	33	4	0	1	13	0	1	2	13	0	29	3	1	2	.289	.315
Benes, Alan, St. Louis	.173	23	54	52	1	9	11	2	0	0	3	2	0	0	0	0	16	0	0	0	.212	.173
Benes, Andy, St. Louis	.218	26	65	55	4	12	14	2	0	0	5	8	0	1	1	0	14	0	0	0	.255	.246
Bennett, Shayne, Montreal	.000	16	2	1	0	0	0	0	0	0	0	0	0	0	1	0	0	0	0	0	.000	.500
Berblinger, Jeff, St. Louis	.000	7	6	5	1	0	0	0	0	0	0	1	0	0	0	0	1	0	0	0	.000	.000
Bergman, Sean, San Diego	.231	44	16	13	2	3	4	1	0	0	3	0	0	0	0	0	7	0	0	0	.308	.231
Berry, Sean, Houston	.256	96	338	301	37	77	127	24	1	8	43	1	6	5	25	1	53	1	5	8	.422	.318
Berryhill, Damon, San Fran.†	.257	73	188	167	17	43	60	8	0	3	23	0	1	0	20	5	29	0	0	3	.359	.335
Bichette, Dante, Colorado	.308	151	601	561	81	173	286	31	2	26	118	0	7	3	30	1	90	6	5	13	.510	.343
Bielecki, Mike, Atlanta	.000	50	3	2	0	0	0	0	0	0	0	0	0	0	1	0	1	0	0	0	.000	.333
Bieser, Steve, New York*	.246	47	81	69	16	17	20	3	0	0	4	0	1	4	7	1	20	2	3	0	.290	.346
Biggio, Craig, Houston	.309	162	744	619	146	191	310	37	8	22	81	0	7	34	84	6	107	47	10	0	.501	.415
Blanco, Henry, Los Angeles	.400	3	5	5	1	2	5	0	0	1	1	0	0	0	0	0	1	0	0	0	1.000	.400
Blauser, Jeff, Atlanta	.308	151	623	519	90	160	250	31	4	17	70	5	9	20	70	6	101	5	1	13	.482	.405
Blazier, Ron, Philadelphia	.400	36	6	5	0	2	2	0	0	0	0	1	0	0	0	0	1	0	0	0	.400	.400
Bogar, Tim, Houston	.249	97	275	241	30	60	94	14	4	4	30	3	4	3	24	1	42	4	1	4	.390	.320
Bohanon, Brian, New York*	.182	21	35	33	0	6	6	0	0	0	4	1	1	0	0	0	15	0	0	0	.182	.176
Bonds, Barry, San Fran.*	.291	159	690	532	123	155	311	26	5	40	101	0	5	8	145	34	87	37	8	13	.585	.446
Bones, Ricky, Cincinnati	.000	9	2	2	0	0	0	0	0	0	0	0	0	0	0	0	0	0	0	0	.000	.000
Bonilla, Bobby, Florida†	.297	153	648	562	77	167	263	39	3	17	96	0	8	5	73	8	94	6	6	18	.468	.378
Boone, Aaron, Cincinnati	.245	16	52	49	5	12	13	1	0	0	5	1	0	0	2	0	5	1	0	1	.265	.275
Boone, Bret, Cincinnati	.223	139	501	443	40	99	147	25	1	7	46	4	5	4	45	4	101	5	5	11	.332	.298
Booty, Josh, Florida	.600	4	6	5	2	3	3	0	0	0	1	0	0	0	1	0	1	0	0	0	.600	.667
Borland, Toby, New York	.000	13	1	0	0	0	0	0	0	0	0	0	0	0	1	0	0	0	0	0	.000	.000
Bottalico, Ricky, Philadelphia*	.000	69	1	1	0	0	0	0	0	0	0	0	0	0	0	0	1	0	0	0	.000	.000
Bottenfield, Kent, Chicago	.000	64	8	4	0	0	0	0	0	0	0	4	0	0	0	0	3	0	0	0	.000	.000
Branson, Jeff, Cincinnati*	.153	65	106	98	9	15	23	3	1	1	5	1	0	0	7	1	23	1	0	3	.235	.210
Brewer, Billy, Philadelphia*	.000	25	1	1	0	0	0	0	0	0	0	0	0	0	0	0	0	0	0	0	.000	.000
Brock, Chris, Atlanta	.100	7	10	10	0	1	1	0	0	0	1	0	0	0	0	0	2	0	1	0	.100	.100
Brogna, Rico, Philadelphia*	.252	148	580	543	68	137	235	36	1	20	81	0	4	0	33	4	116	12	3	12	.433	.293
Brown, Adrian, Pittsburgh†	.190	48	167	147	17	28	37	6	0	1	10	2	1	4	13	0	18	8	4	3	.252	.273
Brown, Brant, Chicago*	.234	46	148	137	15	32	56	7	1	5	15	1	0	3	7	0	28	2	1	2	.409	.286
Brown, Emil, Pittsburgh	.179	66	112	95	16	17	27	2	1	2	6	0	0	7	10	1	32	5	1	1	.284	.304
Brown, Kevin, Florida	.125	33	83	72	4	9	10	1	0	0	4	6	0	0	5	0	25	0	0	0	.139	.182
Bruske, Jim, San Diego	.167	29	6	6	0	1	2	1	0	0	0	0	0	0	0	0	3	0	1	0	.333	.167
Bullinger, Jim, Montreal	.209	36	46	43	2	9	13	1	0	1	2	3	0	0	0	0	15	0	0	1	.302	.209
Burba, Dave, Cincinnati	.196	30	53	46	2	9	9	0	0	0	2	4	0	2	1	0	18	0	0	1	.196	.245
Burke, John, Colorado*	.158	18	21	19	1	3	3	0	0	0	2	2	0	0	0	0	6	0	0	0	.158	.158
Burks, Ellis, Colorado	.290	119	477	424	91	123	242	19	2	32	82	1	2	3	47	0	75	7	2	17	.571	.363
Busby, Mike, St. Louis	.500	3	4	4	0	2	2	0	0	0	0	0	0	0	0	0	2	0	0	0	.500	.500
Butler, Brett, Los Angeles*	.283	105	401	343	52	97	111	8	3	0	18	15	0	1	42	0	40	15	10	1	.324	.363
Butler, Rob, Philadelphia*	.292	43	95	89	10	26	37	9	1	0	13	0	1	0	5	0	8	1	0	2	.416	.326
Byrd, Paul, Atlanta	.143	31	9	7	0	1	1	0	0	0	1	2	0	0	0	0	2	0	0	0	.143	.143
Cabrera, Jose, Houston	.000	12	2	2	0	0	0	0	0	0	0	0	0	0	0	0	0	0	0	0	.000	.000
Cabrera, Orlando, Montreal	.222	16	20	18	4	4	4	0	0	0	2	1	0	0	1	0	3	1	2	1	.222	.263
Cairo, Miguel, Chicago	.241	16	32	29	7	7	8	1	0	0	1	0	0	1	2	0	3	1	0	1	.276	.313
Caminiti, Ken, San Diego†	.290	137	576	486	92	141	247	28	0	26	90	0	7	3	80	9	118	11	2	12	.508	.389
Candiotti, Tom, Los Angeles	.094	42	42	32	0	3	3	0	0	0	2	9	0	0	1	0	10	0	0	1	.094	.121
Cangelosi, John, Florida†	.245	103	216	192	28	47	58	8	0	1	12	1	1	3	19	1	33	5	1	3	.302	.321
Carlson, Dan, San Fran.	.000	6	3	3	0	0	0	0	0	0	0	0	0	0	0	0	0	0	0	0	.000	.000
Carr, Chuck, Houston†	.276	63	216	192	34	53	80	11	2	4	17	6	1	2	15	2	37	11	5	0	.417	.333
Carrara, Giovanni, Cincinnati	.000	2	4	2	0	0	0	0	0	0	0	2	0	0	0	0	2	0	0	0	.000	.000
Casian, Larry, Chicago	.000	12	1	1	0	0	0	0	0	0	0	0	0	0	0	0	0	0	0	0	.000	.000
Castilla, Vinny, Colorado	.304	159	668	612	94	186	335	25	2	40	113	0	4	8	44	9	108	2	4	17	.547	.356
Castillo, Alberto, New York	.203	35	71	59	3	12	13	1	0	0	7	2	1	0	9	0	16	0	1	3	.220	.304
Castillo, Frank, Chi.-Col.	.121	34	70	58	1	7	7	0	0	0	5	10	1	0	1	0	19	0	0	1	.121	.133
Castillo, Luis, Florida†	.240	75	291	263	27	63	71	8	0	0	8	1	0	0	27	0	53	16	10	6	.270	.310
Castro, Juan, Los Angeles	.147	40	84	75	3	11	16	3	1	0	4	2	0	0	7	1	20	0	0	2	.213	.220
Cather, Mike, Atlanta	.000	35	1	1	0	0	0	0	0	0	0	0	0	0	0	0	0	0	0	0	.000	.000
Cedeno, Roger, Los Angeles*†	.273	80	227	194	31	53	76	10	2	3	17	3	2	3	25	2	44	9	1	1	.392	.362
Chavez, Raul, Montreal	.269	13	27	26	0	7	7	0	0	0	1	0	0	0	5	1	0	0	0	0	.269	.259
Cianfrocco, Archi, San Diego	.245	89	251	220	25	54	78	12	0	4	26	1	2	3	25	1	80	7	1	11	.355	.328
Clark, Dave, Chicago*	.301	102	166	143	19	43	66	8	0	5	32	0	2	2	19	3	34	1	0	2	.462	.386
Clark, Mark, N.Y.-Chi.	.030	32	76	66	3	2	5	0	0	1	3	6	0	0	4	0	31	0	0	0	.076	.086
Clayton, Royce, St. Louis	.266	154	619	576	75	153	229	39	5	9	61	2	5	3	33	4	109	30	10	19	.398	.306
Clontz, Brad, Atlanta	.000	51	1	1	0	0	0	0	0	0	0	0	0	0	0	0	1	0	0	0	.000	.000
Colbrunn, Greg, Atlanta	.278	28	58	54	3	15	24	3	0	2	9	1	0	1	2	0	11	0	0	1	.444	.316
Coles, Darnell, Colorado	.318	21	23	22	1	7	11	1	0	1	2	0	0	1	0	0	6	0	0	0	.500	.348
Collier, Lou, Pittsburgh	.135	18	38	37	3	5	5	0	0	0	3	0	0	0	1	0	11	1	0	1	.135	.158
Conine, Jeff, Florida	.242	151	466	405	46	98	164	13	1	17	61	0	2	2	57	3	89	2	0	11	.405	.337
Cook, Dennis, Florida*	.556	61	9	9	2	5	8	0	0	1	2	0	0	0	0	0	0	0	0	0	.889	.556
Cooke, Steve, Pittsburgh	.058	32	59	52	2	3	4	1	0	0	1	7	0	0	0	0	18	0	0	1	.077	.058

Player, Team	Avg.	G	TPA	AB	R	H	TB	2B	3B	HR	RBI	SH	SF	HP	BB	IBB	SO	SB	CS	GDP	Slg.	OBP
Cordova, Francisco, Pittsburgh	.089	29	68	56	2	5	5	0	0	0	0	8	0	0	4	0	26	0	0	0	.089	.150
Counsell, Craig, Col.-Fla.*	.299	52	189	164	20	49	65	9	2	1	16	3	1	3	18	2	17	1	1	5	.396	.376
Crawford, Joe, New York*	.000	19	11	11	0	0	0	0	0	0	0	0	0	0	0	0	5	0	0	0	.000	.000
Creek, Doug, San Fran.*	.333	3	5	3	1	1	1	0	0	0	0	2	0	0	0	0	1	0	0	0	.333	.333
Cromer, Tripp, Los Angeles	.291	28	95	86	8	25	40	3	0	4	20	2	1	0	6	3	16	0	1	2	.465	.333
Crowell, James, Cincinnati	.000	2	2	2	0	0	0	0	0	0	0	0	0	0	0	0	0	0	0	0	.000	.000
Cruz, Jacob, San Fran.*	.160	16	29	25	3	4	5	1	0	0	3	0	1	0	3	0	4	0	0	3	.200	.241
Cummings, Midre, Pit.-Phi.*	.264	115	350	314	35	83	129	22	6	4	31	2	2	1	31	0	56	2	3	3	.411	.330
Cunnane, Will, San Diego	.357	55	17	14	4	5	7	0	1	0	4	1	0	0	2	0	4	0	0	0	.500	.438
Daal, Omar, Montreal*	.200	33	5	5	0	1	1	0	0	0	1	0	0	0	0	0	0	0	0	0	.200	.200
Darwin, Danny, San Fran.	.133	10	15	15	0	2	3	1	0	0	2	0	0	0	0	0	8	0	0	0	.200	.133
Daulton, Darren, Phi.-Fla.*	.263	136	482	395	68	104	183	21	8	14	63	0	9	2	76	5	74	6	1	4	.463	.378
DeHart, Rick, Montreal*	.000	23	2	2	0	0	0	0	0	0	0	0	0	0	2	0	0	0	0	0	.000	.000
DeJean, Mike, Colorado	.333	56	4	3	0	1	2	1	0	0	0	1	0	0	0	0	1	0	0	0	.667	.333
Delgado, Wilson, San Fran.†	.143	8	8	7	1	1	2	1	0	0	0	0	0	0	0	0	2	0	0	0	.286	.143
DeShields, Delino, St. Louis*	.295	150	643	572	92	169	256	26	14	11	58	7	6	3	55	1	72	55	14	5	.448	.357
Difelice, Mike, St. Louis	.238	93	289	260	16	62	86	10	1	4	30	6	1	3	19	0	61	1	1	11	.331	.297
DiPoto, Jerry, Colorado	.111	74	9	9	0	1	1	0	0	0	0	0	0	0	0	0	5	0	0	0	.111	.111
Dreifort, Darren, Los Angeles	.143	48	7	7	0	1	1	0	0	0	0	0	0	0	0	0	5	0	0	0	.143	.143
Dunston, Shawon, Chi.-Pit.	.300	132	511	490	71	147	221	22	5	14	57	5	5	3	8	0	75	32	8	9	.451	.312
Dunwoody, Todd, Florida*	.260	19	58	50	7	13	25	2	2	2	7	0	0	1	7	0	21	2	0	1	.500	.362
Echevarria, Angel, Colorado	.250	15	22	20	4	5	7	2	0	0	0	0	0	0	2	0	5	0	0	0	.350	.318
Eischen, Joey, Cincinnati*	.000	1	1	1	0	0	0	0	0	0	0	0	0	0	0	0	0	0	0	0	.000	.000
Eisenreich, Jim, Florida*	.280	120	331	293	36	82	109	19	1	2	34	3	4	1	30	4	28	0	0	7	.372	.345
Elster, Kevin, Pittsburgh	.225	39	164	138	14	31	62	6	2	7	25	2	2	1	21	0	39	0	2	1	.449	.327
Erdos, Todd, San Diego	.000	11	1	1	0	0	0	0	0	0	0	0	0	0	0	0	1	0	0	0	.000	.000
Estalella, Bobby, Philadelphia	.345	13	36	29	9	10	23	1	0	4	9	0	0	0	7	0	7	0	0	2	.793	.472
Estes, Shawn, San Fran.	.147	36	78	68	8	10	13	0	0	1	3	7	0	2	1	0	24	0	0	1	.191	.183
Eusebio, Tony, Houston	.274	60	187	164	12	45	50	2	0	1	18	0	0	4	19	1	27	0	1	4	.305	.364
Everett, Carl, New York†	.248	142	487	443	58	110	186	28	3	14	57	3	2	7	32	3	102	17	9	3	.420	.308
Falteisek, Steve, Montreal	.000	5	3	2	0	0	0	0	0	0	0	1	0	0	0	0	2	0	0	0	.000	.000
Fernandez, Alex, Florida	.152	33	80	66	3	10	16	6	0	0	4	7	1	0	6	0	20	0	0	1	.242	.219
Fernandez, Osvaldo, San Fran.	.000	12	21	17	0	0	0	0	0	0	0	2	0	1	1	0	13	0	0	0	.000	.105
Fernandez, Sid, Houston*	.000	1	1	1	0	0	0	0	0	0	0	0	0	0	0	0	1	0	0	0	.000	.000
Finley, Steve, San Diego*	.261	143	615	560	101	146	266	26	5	28	92	2	7	3	43	2	92	15	3	10	.475	.313
Flaherty, John, San Diego	.273	129	476	439	38	120	170	21	1	9	46	2	2	0	33	7	62	4	4	11	.387	.323
Fletcher, Darrin, Montreal*	.277	96	334	310	39	86	159	20	1	17	55	0	2	5	17	3	35	1	1	6	.513	.323
Floyd, Cliff, Florida*	.234	61	165	137	23	32	61	9	1	6	19	1	1	2	24	0	33	6	2	3	.445	.354
Fonville, Chad, Los Angeles†	.143	9	16	14	1	2	2	0	0	0	1	0	0	0	2	0	3	0	1	0	.143	.250
Fordyce, Brook, Cincinnati	.208	47	105	96	7	20	28	5	0	1	8	0	1	0	8	1	15	2	0	0	.292	.267
Foster, Kevin, Chicago	.128	30	59	47	3	6	7	1	0	0	4	11	0	0	1	0	20	0	0	0	.149	.146
Foulke, Keith, San Fran.	.154	11	15	13	0	2	2	0	0	0	0	2	0	0	0	0	4	0	0	0	.154	.154
Franco, Matt, New York*	.276	112	176	163	21	45	65	5	0	5	21	0	0	0	13	4	23	1	0	4	.399	.330
Franklin, Micah, St. Louis†	.324	17	37	34	6	11	17	0	0	2	2	0	0	0	3	0	10	0	0	0	.500	.378
Frascatore, John, St. Louis	.000	59	3	3	0	0	0	0	0	0	0	0	0	0	0	0	2	0	0	0	.000	.000
Fullmer, Brad, Montreal*	.300	19	43	40	4	12	23	2	0	3	8	0	0	1	2	1	7	0	0	0	.575	.349
Gaetti, Gary, St. Louis	.251	148	554	502	63	126	203	24	1	17	69	4	6	6	36	2	88	7	3	20	.404	.305
Gagne, Greg, Los Angeles	.251	144	553	514	49	129	182	20	3	9	57	3	1	4	31	4	120	2	5	13	.354	.298
Galarraga, Andres, Colorado	.318	154	674	600	120	191	351	31	3	41	140	0	3	17	54	2	141	15	8	16	.585	.389
Gallego, Mike, St. Louis	.163	27	46	43	6	7	9	2	0	0	1	1	1	0	1	0	6	0	0	2	.209	.178
Gant, Ron, St. Louis	.229	139	562	502	68	115	195	21	4	17	62	0	1	1	58	3	162	14	6	2	.388	.310
Garcia, Freddy, Pittsburgh	.150	20	42	40	4	6	16	1	0	3	5	0	0	0	2	0	17	0	0	0	.400	.190
Garcia, Karim, Los Angeles*	.128	15	46	39	5	5	8	0	0	1	8	0	1	0	6	1	14	0	0	0	.205	.239
Garcia, Ramon, Houston	.111	42	45	36	2	4	6	2	0	0	5	7	1	1	0	0	13	0	0	1	.167	.132
Gardner, Mark, San Fran.	.115	32	66	61	0	7	7	0	0	0	2	3	0	1	1	0	30	0	0	1	.115	.143
Gilbert, Shawn, New York	.136	29	23	22	3	3	6	0	0	1	1	0	0	0	1	0	8	1	0	0	.273	.174
Gilkey, Bernard, New York	.249	145	606	518	85	129	216	31	1	18	78	0	12	6	70	1	111	7	11	9	.417	.338
Giovanola, Ed, Atlanta*	.250	14	10	8	0	2	2	0	0	0	0	0	0	0	2	1	1	0	0	2	.250	.400
Glanville, Doug, Chicago	.300	146	510	474	79	142	186	22	5	4	35	9	2	1	24	0	46	19	11	9	.392	.333
Glavine, Tom, Atlanta*	.222	33	88	63	6	14	14	0	0	0	7	17	0	1	7	0	13	0	0	1	.222	.310
Gomes, Wayne, Philadelphia	.000	37	3	2	0	0	0	0	0	0	0	0	0	0	1	0	1	0	0	0	.000	.333
Gomez, Chris, San Diego	.253	150	586	522	62	132	170	19	2	5	54	9	1	0	53	1	114	5	8	16	.326	.326
Gonzales, Rene, Colorado	.500	2	2	2	0	1	1	0	0	0	0	0	0	0	0	0	0	0	0	0	.500	.500
Gonzalez, Jeremi, Chicago	.100	23	51	40	1	4	4	0	0	0	1	8	0	0	3	0	12	0	0	1	.100	.163
Gonzalez, Luis, Houston*	.258	152	631	550	78	142	207	31	2	10	68	0	5	3	71	7	67	10	7	12	.376	.345
Goodwin, Curtis, Cincinnati*	.253	85	297	265	27	67	81	11	0	1	12	6	1	1	24	0	53	22	13	6	.306	.316
Gorecki, Rick, Los Angeles	.000	4	1	0	1	0	0	0	0	0	0	1	0	0	0	0	0	0	0	0	.000	.000
Grace, Mark, Chicago*	.319	151	654	555	87	177	258	32	5	13	78	0	8	8	88	3	45	2	4	18	.465	.409
Grace, Mike, Philadelphia	.083	6	12	12	0	1	1	0	0	0	0	0	0	0	0	0	1	0	0	0	.083	.083
Graffanino, Tony, Atlanta	.258	104	221	186	33	48	83	9	1	8	20	3	5	1	26	1	46	6	4	3	.446	.344
Graves, Danny, Cincinnati	.000	10	1	1	0	0	0	0	0	0	0	0	0	0	0	0	1	0	0	0	.000	.000
Green, Scarborough, St. Louis	.097	20	33	31	5	3	3	0	0	0	0	0	0	0	2	0	5	0	0	0	.097	.152
Green, Tyler, Philadelphia	.308	14	27	26	2	8	11	3	0	0	2	1	0	0	0	0	5	0	0	0	.423	.308
Greene, Tommy, Houston	.333	2	4	3	1	1	2	1	0	0	1	0	0	0	0	0	0	0	0	0	.667	.333
Greene, Willie, Cincinnati*	.253	151	549	495	62	125	227	22	1	26	91	1	3	1	78	5	111	6	0	10	.459	.354
Gregg, Tommy, Atlanta*	.263	13	20	19	1	5	7	2	0	0	0	0	0	0	1	0	2	1	1	0	.368	.300
Grudzielanek, Mark, Montreal	.273	156	688	649	76	177	249	54	3	4	51	3	3	10	23	0	76	25	9	13	.384	.307
Guerrero, Vladimir, Montreal	.302	90	354	325	44	98	157	22	2	11	40	0	3	7	19	2	39	3	4	11	.483	.350
Guerrero, Wilton, Los Angeles†	.291	111	380	357	39	104	144	10	9	4	32	13	2	0	8	1	52	6	5	7	.403	.305
Guillen, Jose, Pittsburgh	.267	143	526	498	58	133	205	20	5	14	70	0	3	8	17	0	88	1	2	16	.412	.300
Gulan, Mike, St. Louis	.000	5	10	9	2	0	0	0	0	0	0	1	0	0	1	0	5	0	0	0	.000	.100
Guthrie, Mark, Los Angeles†	.250	62	5	4	0	1	1	0	0	0	0	0	0	0	0	0	0	0	0	0	.250	.250

Player, Team	Avg.	G	TPA	AB	R	H	TB	2B	3B	HR	RBI	SH	SF	HP	BB	IBB	SO	SB	CS	GDP	Slg.	OBP
Gutierrez, Ricky, Houston	.261	102	327	303	33	79	110	14	4	3	34	0	0	3	21	2	50	5	2	17	.363	.315
Gwynn, Tony, San Diego*	.372	149	651	592	97	220	324	49	2	17	119	1	12	3	43	12	28	12	5	12	.547	.409
Hale, Chip, Los Angeles*	.083	14	14	12	0	1	1	0	0	0	0	0	0	0	2	0	4	0	0	0	.083	.214
Hamilton, Darryl, San Fran.*	.270	125	529	460	78	124	168	23	3	5	43	6	2	0	61	1	61	15	10	6	.365	.354
Hamilton, Joey, San Diego	.130	31	66	54	4	7	13	0	0	2	6	9	2	0	1	0	26	0	0	0	.241	.140
Hampton, Mike, Houston	.137	34	89	73	6	10	13	1	1	0	8	10	1	0	5	0	21	0	1	0	.178	.190
Hansen, Dave, Chicago*	.311	90	186	151	19	47	68	8	2	3	21	2	1	1	31	1	32	1	2	0	.450	.429
Hardtke, Jason, New York†	.268	30	62	56	9	15	23	2	0	2	8	0	1	1	4	1	6	1	1	3	.411	.323
Harkey, Mike, Los Angeles	.000	10	3	1	0	0	0	0	0	0	0	2	0	0	0	0	1	0	0	0	.000	.000
Harnisch, Pete, New York	.000	6	9	8	0	0	0	0	0	0	0	1	0	0	0	0	3	0	0	0	.000	.000
Harris, Lenny, Cincinnati*	.273	120	263	238	32	65	89	13	1	3	28	3	2	2	18	1	18	4	3	10	.374	.327
Helling, Rick, Florida	.091	31	12	11	0	1	1	0	0	0	0	0	0	0	0	0	5	0	0	0	.091	.091
Helton, Todd, Colorado*	.280	35	101	93	13	26	45	2	1	5	11	0	0	0	8	0	11	0	1	1	.484	.337
Henderson, Rickey, San Diego	.274	88	365	288	63	79	108	11	0	6	27	0	2	4	71	2	62	29	4	7	.375	.422
Henry, Doug, San Fran.	.000	75	4	4	0	0	0	0	0	0	0	0	0	0	0	0	2	0	0	1	.000	.000
Heredia, Felix, Florida*	.500	56	3	2	0	1	1	0	0	0	0	1	0	0	0	0	1	0	0	0	.500	.500
Hermanson, Dustin, Montreal	.104	32	55	48	1	5	9	1	0	1	1	5	0	0	2	0	24	0	0	0	.188	.140
Hernandez, Carlos, San Diego	.313	50	138	134	15	42	60	7	1	3	14	1	0	0	3	0	27	0	2	5	.448	.328
Hernandez, Jose, Chicago	.273	121	199	183	33	50	89	8	5	7	26	1	1	0	14	2	42	2	5	5	.486	.323
Hernandez, Livan, Florida	.172	17	33	29	2	5	7	2	0	0	2	3	0	0	1	0	6	0	0	0	.241	.200
Hernandez, Roberto, San Fran.	.500	28	2	2	0	1	1	0	0	0	0	0	0	0	0	0	1	0	0	0	.500	.500
Hidalgo, Rich, Houston	.306	19	67	62	8	19	30	5	0	2	6	0	0	1	4	0	18	1	0	0	.484	.358
Hill, Glenallen, San Fran.	.261	128	428	398	47	104	173	28	4	11	64	0	7	4	19	0	87	7	4	8	.435	.297
Hitchcock, Sterling, S.D.*	.100	32	61	50	4	5	5	0	0	0	1	8	0	0	3	0	30	0	1	2	.100	.151
Hoffman, Trevor, San Diego	.333	70	3	3	0	1	1	0	0	0	1	0	0	0	0	0	1	0	0	0	.333	.333
Hollandsworth, Todd, L.A.*	.247	106	317	296	39	73	109	20	2	4	31	2	2	0	17	2	60	5	5	8	.368	.286
Holmes, Darren, Colorado	.158	42	23	19	2	3	6	0	0	1	2	3	1	0	0	0	9	0	0	0	.316	.150
Holt, Chris, Houston	.090	33	77	67	6	6	6	0	0	0	1	9	0	0	1	0	33	0	0	0	.090	.103
Houston, Tyler, Chicago*	.260	72	207	196	15	51	67	10	0	2	28	0	2	0	9	1	35	1	0	4	.342	.290
Howard, Thomas, Houston*	.247	107	286	255	24	63	90	16	1	3	22	1	1	3	26	1	48	1	2	3	.353	.323
Hubbard, Mike, Chicago	.203	29	66	64	4	13	16	0	0	1	2	0	0	0	2	1	21	0	0	1	.250	.227
Hudler, Rex, Philadelphia	.221	50	130	122	17	27	46	4	0	5	10	1	0	1	6	1	28	1	0	2	.377	.264
Hundley, Todd, New York†	.273	132	508	417	78	114	229	21	2	30	86	0	5	3	83	16	116	2	3	10	.549	.394
Huskey, Butch, New York	.287	142	505	471	61	135	237	26	2	24	81	0	8	1	25	5	84	8	5	21	.503	.319
Hutton, Mark, Fla.-Col.	.000	40	3	3	0	0	0	0	0	0	0	0	0	0	0	0	0	0	0	0	.000	.000
Ingram, Garey, Los Angeles	.444	12	10	9	2	4	4	0	0	0	0	0	0	0	1	0	3	1	0	0	.444	.500
Isringhausen, Jason, New York	.143	6	9	7	1	1	1	0	0	0	1	1	0	0	0	0	4	0	0	0	.143	.125
Jackson, Damian, Cincinnati	.222	12	32	27	6	6	13	2	1	1	2	1	0	0	4	1	7	1	1	0	.481	.323
Jackson, Danny, St.L.-S.D.	.100	17	22	20	1	2	2	0	0	0	0	1	0	0	1	0	8	0	1	0	.100	.143
Jarvis, Kevin, Cincinnati*	.000	9	1	1	0	0	0	0	0	0	0	0	0	0	0	0	0	0	0	0	.000	.000
Javier, Stan, San Fran.†	.286	142	510	440	69	126	174	16	4	8	50	2	7	5	56	1	70	25	3	5	.395	.368
Jefferies, Gregg, Philadelphia†	.256	130	531	476	68	122	186	25	3	11	48	0	2	0	53	7	27	12	6	8	.391	.333
Jennings, Robin, Chicago*	.167	9	19	18	1	3	4	1	0	0	2	0	1	0	0	0	2	0	0	0	.222	.158
Jensen, Marcus, San Fran.†	.149	30	81	74	5	11	16	2	0	1	3	0	0	0	7	1	23	0	0	2	.216	.222
Johnson, Brian, San Fran.	.279	56	201	179	19	50	94	7	2	11	27	3	3	2	14	7	26	0	1	8	.525	.333
Johnson, Charles, Florida	.250	124	484	416	43	104	189	26	1	19	63	3	2	3	60	6	109	0	2	13	.454	.347
Johnson, Jason, Pittsburgh	.000	3	1	1	0	0	0	0	0	0	0	0	0	0	0	0	1	0	0	0	.000	.000
Johnson, Lance, N.Y.-Chi.*	.307	111	454	410	60	126	173	16	8	5	39	0	2	0	42	3	31	20	12	8	.422	.370
Johnson, Mark, Pittsburgh*	.215	78	267	219	30	47	69	10	0	4	29	0	3	2	43	1	78	1	1	1	.315	.345
Johnson, Mike, Montreal*	.077	11	15	13	1	1	1	0	0	0	1	2	0	0	0	0	5	0	0	0	.077	.077
Johnson, Russ, Houston	.300	21	67	60	7	18	25	1	0	2	9	1	0	0	6	0	14	1	1	2	.417	.364
Johnstone, John, San Fran.	.000	13	2	2	0	0	0	0	0	0	0	0	0	0	0	0	1	0	0	0	.000	.000
Jones, Andruw, Atlanta	.231	153	467	399	60	92	166	18	1	18	70	5	3	4	56	2	107	20	11	11	.416	.329
Jones, Bobby M., Colorado	.200	4	7	5	1	1	1	0	0	0	1	0	0	0	1	0	0	0	0	0	.200	.333
Jones, Bobby, New York	.129	30	69	62	4	8	10	2	0	0	4	0	0	0	3	0	18	0	0	0	.161	.169
Jones, Chipper, Atlanta†	.295	157	679	597	100	176	286	41	3	21	111	0	6	0	76	8	88	20	5	19	.479	.371
Jones, Chris C., San Diego	.243	92	172	152	24	37	67	9	0	7	25	1	1	2	16	0	45	7	2	4	.441	.322
Jordan, Brian, St. Louis	.234	47	161	145	17	34	39	5	0	0	10	0	0	6	10	1	21	6	1	4	.269	.311
Jordan, Kevin, Philadelphia	.266	84	183	177	19	47	73	8	0	6	30	0	3	0	3	0	26	0	1	5	.412	.273
Jordan, Ricardo, New York*	.000	22	1	1	0	0	0	0	0	0	0	0	0	0	0	0	1	0	0	0	.000	.000
Joyner, Wally, San Diego*	.327	135	508	455	59	149	221	29	2	13	83	0	10	2	51	5	51	3	5	14	.486	.390
Judd, Michael, Los Angeles	.000	1	1	1	0	0	0	0	0	0	0	0	0	0	0	0	0	0	0	0	.000	.000
Juden, Jeff, Montreal	.140	22	47	43	1	6	8	2	0	0	4	2	0	1	1	0	24	0	0	0	.186	.178
Karros, Eric, Los Angeles	.266	162	700	628	86	167	288	28	0	31	104	0	9	2	61	2	116	15	7	10	.459	.329
Kashiwada, Takashi, New York*	.000	35	1	1	0	0	0	0	0	0	0	0	0	0	0	0	0	0	0	0	.000	.000
Kelly, Mike, Cincinnati	.293	73	151	140	27	41	76	13	2	6	19	0	1	0	10	0	30	6	1	3	.543	.338
Kendall, Jason, Pittsburgh	.294	144	572	486	71	143	211	36	4	8	49	1	5	31	49	2	53	18	6	11	.434	.391
Kent, Jeff, San Fran.	.250	155	651	580	90	145	274	38	2	29	121	0	10	13	48	6	133	11	3	14	.472	.316
Kieschnick, Brooks, Chicago*	.200	39	102	90	9	18	32	2	0	4	12	0	0	0	12	0	21	1	0	2	.356	.294
Kile, Darryl, Houston	.124	34	105	89	4	11	14	3	0	0	7	10	0	3	3	0	38	0	0	3	.157	.179
King, Curtis, St. Louis	.000	30	1	1	0	0	0	0	0	0	0	0	0	0	0	0	0	0	0	0	.000	.000
Kirby, Wayne, Los Angeles*	.169	46	75	65	6	11	13	2	0	0	4	0	0	0	10	0	12	0	0	1	.200	.280
Klesko, Ryan, Atlanta*	.261	143	522	467	67	122	229	23	6	24	84	1	2	4	48	5	130	4	4	12	.490	.334
Kline, Steve, Montreal†	.000	26	1	1	0	0	0	0	0	0	0	0	0	0	0	0	0	0	0	0	.000	.000
Knorr, Randy, Houston	.375	4	8	8	1	3	6	0	0	1	1	0	0	0	0	0	1	0	0	0	.750	.375
Konerko, Paul, Los Angeles	.143	6	8	7	0	1	1	0	0	0	1	0	0	0	1	0	3	0	0	0	.143	.250
Kotsay, Mark, Florida*	.192	14	57	52	5	10	13	1	1	0	4	1	0	0	4	0	7	3	0	1	.250	.250
Lampkin, Tom, St. Louis*	.245	108	267	229	28	56	87	8	1	7	22	4	2	4	28	5	30	2	1	8	.380	.335
Lankford, Ray, St. Louis*	.295	133	565	465	94	137	272	36	3	31	98	0	5	0	95	10	125	21	11	9	.585	.411
Lansing, Mike, Montreal	.281	144	631	572	86	161	270	45	2	20	70	6	3	5	45	2	92	11	5	9	.472	.338
Larkin, Barry, Cincinnati	.317	73	276	224	34	71	106	17	3	4	20	1	3	1	47	6	24	14	3	3	.473	.440
Lee, Derrek, San Diego	.259	22	63	54	9	14	20	3	0	1	4	0	0	0	9	0	24	0	0	1	.370	.365

Player, Team	Avg.	G	TPA	AB	R	H	TB	2B	3B	HR	RBI	SH	SF	HP	BB	IBB	SO	SB	CS	GDP	Slg.	OBP
Leiter, Al, Florida*	.104	27	53	48	2	5	5	0	0	0	1	2	0	0	3	0	25	0	0	3	.104	.157
Leiter, Mark, Philadelphia	.118	31	63	51	2	6	6	0	0	0	4	10	0	0	2	0	28	0	0	0	.118	.151
Lemke, Mark, Atlanta†	.245	109	397	351	33	86	111	17	1	2	26	8	5	0	33	2	51	2	0	10	.316	.306
Leskanic, Curtis, Colorado	.000	55	1	1	0	0	0	0	0	0	0	0	0	0	0	0	1	0	0	0	.000	.000
Lewis, Darren, Los Angeles	.299	26	85	77	7	23	31	3	1	1	10	2	0	0	6	0	17	3	2	1	.403	.349
Lewis, Mark, San Fran.	.267	118	372	341	50	91	147	14	6	10	42	1	3	4	23	2	62	3	2	8	.431	.318
Lewis, Richie, Cincinnati	1.000	4	1	1	0	1	1	0	0	0	0	0	0	0	0	0	0	0	0	0	1.000	1.000
Lidle, Cory, New York	.000	54	6	5	1	0	0	0	0	0	0	0	0	0	1	0	4	0	0	0	.000	.167
Lieber, Jon, Pittsburgh*	.121	33	64	58	1	7	9	2	0	0	8	2	0	0	4	0	23	0	0	4	.155	.177
Lieberthal, Mike, Philadelphia	.246	134	510	455	59	112	201	27	1	20	77	0	7	4	44	1	76	3	4	10	.442	.314
Lima, Jose, Houston	.000	52	5	3	0	0	0	0	0	0	0	2	0	0	0	0	3	0	0	0	.000	.000
Liriano, Nelson, Los Angeles†	.227	76	97	88	10	20	29	6	0	1	11	2	1	0	6	1	12	0	0	1	.330	.274
Listach, Pat, Houston†	.182	52	151	132	13	24	30	2	2	0	6	5	2	1	11	2	24	4	2	7	.227	.247
Livingstone, Scott, S.D.-St.L*	.164	65	72	67	4	11	13	2	0	0	6	0	2	0	3	0	11	1	0	1	.194	.194
Loaiza, Esteban, Pittsburgh	.167	33	69	60	4	10	11	1	0	0	5	8	0	0	1	0	17	0	0	1	.183	.180
Lockhart, Keith, Atlanta*	.279	96	169	147	25	41	70	5	3	6	32	3	4	1	14	0	17	0	0	4	.476	.337
Lofton, Kenny, Atlanta*	.333	122	564	493	90	164	211	20	6	5	48	2	3	2	64	5	83	27	20	10	.428	.409
Loiselle, Rich, Pittsburgh	.000	72	1	1	0	0	0	0	0	0	0	0	0	0	0	0	1	0	0	0	.000	.000
Lopez, Javier, Atlanta	.295	123	464	414	52	122	221	28	1	23	68	1	4	5	40	10	82	1	1	9	.534	.361
Lopez, Luis M., New York†	.270	78	196	178	19	48	65	12	1	1	19	2	0	4	12	2	42	2	4	2	.365	.330
Lowe, Sean, St. Louis	.333	6	3	3	0	1	1	0	0	0	0	0	0	0	0	0	1	0	0	0	.333	.333
Lowery, Terrell, Chicago	.286	9	17	14	2	4	4	0	0	0	0	0	0	0	3	0	3	1	0	0	.286	.412
Mabry, John, St. Louis*	.284	116	434	388	40	110	144	19	0	5	36	2	2	3	39	9	77	0	1	11	.371	.352
Maddux, Greg, Atlanta	.104	33	78	67	3	7	9	2	0	0	4	6	0	0	5	0	21	1	0	0	.134	.167
Maduro, Calvin, Philadelphia	.050	16	21	20	1	1	1	0	0	0	0	1	0	0	0	0	12	0	0	0	.050	.050
Magee, Wendell, Philadelphia	.200	38	126	115	7	23	30	4	0	1	9	0	2	0	9	1	20	1	4	8	.261	.254
Magnante, Mike, Houston*	.000	40	3	3	0	0	0	0	0	0	0	0	0	0	0	0	2	0	0	0	.000	.000
Manuel, Barry, New York	.000	19	2	2	0	0	0	0	0	0	0	0	0	0	0	0	1	0	0	0	.000	.000
Manwaring, Kirt, Colorado	.226	104	375	337	22	76	93	6	4	1	27	4	2	2	30	0	78	1	5	10	.276	.291
Marrero, Eli, St. Louis	.244	17	48	45	4	11	19	2	0	2	7	0	1	0	2	0	13	4	0	1	.422	.271
Martin, Al, Pittsburgh*	.291	113	477	423	64	123	200	24	7	13	59	1	5	3	45	7	83	23	7	7	.473	.359
Martin, Tom, Houston*	.000	55	3	3	0	0	0	0	0	0	0	0	0	0	0	0	1	0	0	0	.000	.000
Martinez, Pedro J., Montreal	.116	31	81	69	5	8	12	2	1	0	0	9	0	0	3	0	28	0	0	2	.174	.153
Martinez, Ramon, Los Angeles*	.190	22	47	42	5	8	9	1	0	0	1	5	0	0	0	0	11	0	0	0	.214	.190
Mathews, T.J., St. Louis	.000	40	1	1	0	0	0	0	0	0	0	0	0	0	0	0	0	0	0	0	.000	.000
May, Derrick, Philadelphia*	.228	83	158	149	8	34	44	5	1	1	13	0	1	0	8	3	26	4	1	4	.295	.266
McCracken, Quinton, Colorado†	.292	147	375	325	69	95	117	11	1	3	36	6	1	1	42	0	62	28	11	6	.360	.374
McCurry, Jeff, Colorado	.000	33	1	1	0	0	0	0	0	0	0	0	0	0	0	0	1	0	0	0	.000	.000
McGee, Willie, St. Louis†	.300	122	323	300	29	90	126	19	4	3	38	0	1	0	22	2	59	8	2	6	.420	.347
McGriff, Fred, Atlanta*	.277	152	641	564	77	156	249	25	1	22	97	0	5	4	68	4	112	5	0	22	.441	.356
McGuire, Ryan, Montreal*	.256	84	222	199	22	51	79	15	2	3	17	3	1	0	19	1	34	1	4	3	.397	.320
McGwire, Mark, St. Louis	.253	51	224	174	38	44	119	3	0	24	42	0	2	5	43	8	61	2	0	0	.684	.411
McMichael, Greg, New York	.667	73	3	3	0	2	2	0	0	0	0	0	0	0	0	0	1	0	0	0	.667	.667
McMillon, Billy, Fla.-Phi.*	.256	37	99	90	10	23	36	5	1	2	14	0	3	0	6	0	24	2	1	1	.400	.293
McRae, Brian, Chi.-N.Y.†	.242	153	639	562	86	136	215	32	7	11	43	4	2	6	65	2	84	17	10	13	.383	.326
Mejia, Roberto, St. Louis	.071	7	16	14	0	1	2	1	0	0	2	1	0	0	0	0	5	0	0	0	.143	.067
Mendoza, Carlos, New York*	.250	15	18	12	6	3	3	0	0	0	1	0	0	2	4	0	2	0	0	0	.250	.500
Menhart, Paul, San Diego	.000	9	14	12	0	0	0	0	0	0	0	2	0	0	0	0	4	0	0	0	.000	.000
Mercker, Kent, Cincinnati*	.156	31	53	45	3	7	10	1	1	0	1	4	0	0	4	0	23	0	0	2	.222	.224
Meulens, Hensley, Montreal	.292	16	29	24	6	7	14	1	0	2	6	0	1	0	4	0	10	0	1	0	.583	.379
Milliard, Ralph, Florida	.200	8	36	30	2	6	6	0	0	0	2	1	0	2	3	0	3	1	1	2	.200	.314
Millwood, Kevin, Atlanta	.000	12	14	12	0	0	0	0	0	0	0	1	0	0	1	0	8	0	0	0	.000	.077
Mimbs, Michael, Philadelphia*	.000	17	2	2	1	0	0	0	0	0	0	0	0	0	0	0	0	0	0	0	.000	.000
Mirabelli, Doug, San Fran.	.143	6	8	7	0	1	1	0	0	0	0	0	0	0	1	0	3	0	0	0	.143	.250
Mlicki, Dave, New York	.188	33	55	48	3	9	12	3	0	0	3	3	1	0	3	0	22	0	0	1	.250	.231
Mondesi, Raul, Los Angeles	.310	159	670	616	95	191	333	42	5	30	87	1	3	6	44	7	105	32	15	11	.541	.360
Montgomery, Ray, Houston	.235	29	76	68	8	16	22	4	1	0	4	0	3	0	5	0	18	0	0	2	.324	.276
Morandini, Mickey, Phi.*	.295	150	640	553	83	163	210	40	2	1	39	12	5	8	62	0	91	16	13	8	.380	.371
Mordecai, Mike, Atlanta	.173	61	89	81	8	14	18	2	1	0	3	1	1	0	6	0	16	0	1	4	.222	.227
Morgan, Kevin, New York	.000	1	1	1	0	0	0	0	0	0	0	0	0	0	0	0	0	0	0	0	.000	.000
Morgan, Mike, Cincinnati	.091	31	54	44	1	4	6	0	1	0	2	9	0	0	1	0	14	0	0	0	.136	.111
Morman, Russ, Florida	.286	4	7	7	3	2	6	1	0	1	2	0	0	0	0	0	2	1	0	0	.857	.286
Morris, Hal, Cincinnati*	.276	96	364	333	42	92	117	20	1	1	33	4	1	3	23	2	43	3	1	10	.351	.328
Morris, Matt, St. Louis	.205	34	80	73	4	15	17	2	0	0	6	2	0	0	5	0	36	0	1	0	.233	.256
Mouton, James, Houston	.211	86	204	180	24	38	58	9	1	3	23	2	2	2	18	0	30	9	7	3	.322	.287
Mueller, Bill, San Fran.†	.292	128	453	390	51	114	167	26	3	7	44	6	6	3	48	1	71	4	3	10	.428	.369
Mulholland, Terry, Chi.-S.F.	.164	40	59	55	1	9	12	3	0	0	2	4	0	0	0	0	27	0	0	1	.218	.164
Munoz, Bobby, Philadelphia	.300	8	11	10	2	3	4	1	0	0	1	1	0	0	0	0	1	0	0	0	.400	.364
Munoz, Mike, Colorado*	.000	64	2	1	0	0	0	0	0	0	0	0	0	0	1	0	0	0	0	0	.000	.500
Murray, Eddie, Los Angeles†	.286	9	9	7	0	2	2	0	0	0	3	0	0	0	2	0	2	0	0	2	.286	.444
Murray, Heath, San Diego*	.000	17	6	6	0	0	0	0	0	0	0	0	0	0	0	0	0	0	0	0	.000	.000
Myers, Greg, Atlanta*	.111	9	10	9	0	1	1	0	0	0	0	0	0	0	1	0	3	0	0	0	.111	.200
Natal, Bob, Florida	.500	4	7	4	2	2	6	1	0	1	3	0	1	0	2	0	0	0	0	0	1.500	.571
Neagle, Denny, Atlanta*	.153	34	85	72	6	11	15	1	0	1	7	9	0	0	4	0	35	0	0	1	.208	.197
Nixon, Otis, Los Angeles†	.274	42	191	175	30	48	61	6	2	1	18	2	1	0	13	0	24	12	2	2	.349	.323
Nomo, Hideo, Los Angeles	.159	33	75	69	3	11	16	5	0	0	2	5	0	0	1	0	32	0	0	0	.232	.171
Nunez, Abraham, Pittsburgh†‡	.225	19	45	40	3	9	15	2	2	0	6	0	1	0	3	0	10	1	0	1	.375	.289
Nunnally, Jon, Cincinnati*	.318	65	231	201	38	64	121	12	3	13	35	1	1	2	26	0	51	7	3	2	.602	.400
Nye, Ryan, Philadelphia	.000	4	3	2	0	0	0	0	0	0	0	1	0	0	0	0	1	0	0	0	.000	.000
Obando, Sherman, Montreal	.128	41	54	47	3	6	13	1	0	2	9	0	0	1	6	0	14	0	0	0	.277	.241
Ochoa, Alex, New York	.244	113	262	238	31	58	83	14	1	3	22	2	2	2	18	0	32	3	4	7	.349	.300
Ojala, Kirt, Florida*	.000	7	8	7	0	0	0	0	0	0	0	1	0	0	0	0	2	0	0	0	.000	.000

Player, Team	Avg.	G	TPA	AB	R	H	TB	2B	3B	HR	RBI	SH	SF	HP	BB	IBB	SO	SB	CS	GDP	Slg.	OBP
Olerud, John, New York*	.294	154	630	524	90	154	256	34	1	22	102	0	8	13	85	5	67	0	0	19	.489	.400
Oliver, Joe, Cincinnati	.258	111	386	349	28	90	145	13	0	14	43	2	5	5	25	1	58	1	3	7	.415	.313
Ordaz, Luis, St. Louis	.273	12	23	22	3	6	7	1	0	0	1	0	0	0	1	0	2	3	0	0	.318	.304
Ordonez, Rey, New York	.216	120	391	356	35	77	91	5	3	1	33	14	2	1	18	3	36	11	5	10	.256	.255
Orie, Kevin, Chicago	.275	114	415	364	40	100	157	23	5	8	44	3	4	5	39	3	57	2	2	13	.431	.350
Orsulak, Joe, Montreal*	.227	106	170	150	13	34	51	12	1	1	7	2	0	0	18	0	17	0	1	2	.340	.310
Osborne, Donovan, St. Louis*	.208	14	25	24	2	5	6	1	0	0	2	1	0	0	0	0	6	1	0	0	.250	.208
Osik, Keith, Pittsburgh	.257	49	117	105	10	27	38	9	1	0	7	2	0	1	9	1	21	0	1	1	.362	.322
Osuna, Antonio, Los Angeles	.500	48	2	2	0	1	1	0	0	0	0	0	0	0	0	0	0	0	0	0	.500	.500
Otero, Ricky, Philadelphia†	.252	50	174	151	20	38	48	6	2	0	3	3	0	1	19	0	15	0	3	2	.318	.339
Owens, Eric, Cincinnati	.263	27	61	57	8	15	15	0	0	0	3	0	0	0	4	0	11	3	2	2	.263	.311
Pagnozzi, Tom, St. Louis	.220	25	51	50	4	11	17	3	0	1	8	0	0	0	1	0	7	0	0	2	.340	.235
Painter, Lance, St. Louis*	.000	14	1	1	0	0	0	0	0	0	0	0	0	0	0	0	1	0	0	0	.000	.000
Pall, Donn, Florida	.000	2	1	1	0	0	0	0	0	0	0	0	0	0	0	0	1	0	0	0	.000	.000
Paniagua, Jose, Montreal	.000	9	5	5	0	0	0	0	0	0	0	0	0	0	0	0	3	0	0	0	.000	.000
Parent, Mark, Philadelphia	.150	39	121	113	4	17	20	3	0	0	8	0	1	0	7	0	39	0	1	3	.177	.198
Park, Chan Ho, Los Angeles	.176	32	66	51	5	9	13	4	0	0	2	11	0	0	4	0	21	0	0	0	.255	.236
Patterson, Bob, Chicago	.000	76	1	1	0	0	0	0	0	0	0	0	0	0	0	0	0	0	0	0	.000	.000
Pena, Tony, Houston	.211	9	22	19	2	4	7	3	0	0	2	0	1	0	2	0	3	0	0	0	.368	.273
Pendleton, Terry, Cincinnati†	.248	50	125	113	11	28	40	9	0	1	17	0	0	0	12	1	14	2	1	1	.354	.320
Perez, Carlos, Montreal*	.172	33	71	64	3	11	16	2	0	1	2	5	0	0	2	0	31	0	0	0	.250	.197
Perez, Eddie, Atlanta	.215	73	206	191	20	41	64	5	0	6	18	1	2	2	10	0	35	0	1	8	.335	.259
Perez, Eduardo, Cincinnati	.253	106	330	297	44	75	141	18	0	16	52	0	2	2	29	1	76	5	1	6	.475	.321
Perez, Neifi, Colorado†	.291	83	344	313	46	91	139	13	10	5	31	5	4	1	21	4	43	4	3	3	.444	.333
Perez, Yorkis, New York*	.000	9	1	1	0	0	0	0	0	0	0	0	0	0	0	0	0	0	0	0	.000	.000
Petagine, Roberto, New York*	.067	12	18	15	2	1	1	0	0	0	2	0	0	0	3	0	6	0	0	0	.067	.222
Peters, Chris, Pittsburgh*	.250	31	4	4	0	1	1	0	0	0	2	0	0	0	0	0	2	0	0	0	.250	.250
Petkovsek, Mark, St. Louis	.091	55	13	11	0	1	1	0	0	0	0	1	0	1	0	0	2	0	0	1	.091	.167
Phillips, J.R., Houston*	.133	13	16	15	2	2	5	0	0	1	4	0	1	0	0	0	7	0	0	0	.333	.125
Piazza, Mike, Los Angeles	.362	152	633	556	104	201	355	32	1	40	124	0	5	3	69	11	77	5	1	19	.638	.431
Pisciotta, Marc, Chicago	.000	24	1	1	0	0	0	0	0	0	0	0	0	0	0	0	1	0	0	0	.000	.000
Plantier, Phil, S.D.-St.L*	.248	52	139	121	13	30	53	8	0	5	18	0	2	3	13	1	30	0	3	5	.438	.331
Polcovich, Kevin, Pittsburgh	.273	84	279	245	37	67	97	16	1	4	21	2	2	9	21	4	45	2	2	11	.396	.350
Poole, Jim Ri., San Fran.*	.000	63	1	0	0	0	0	0	0	0	0	0	1	0	0	0	0	0	0	0	.000	.000
Portugal, Mark, Philadelphia	.000	3	4	4	0	0	0	0	0	0	0	0	0	0	0	0	2	0	0	0	.000	.000
Powell, Dante, San Fran.	.308	27	44	39	8	12	16	1	0	1	3	1	0	0	4	0	11	1	1	0	.410	.372
Powell, Jay, Florida	.500	74	4	4	0	2	2	0	0	0	1	0	0	0	0	0	1	0	0	1	.500	.500
Pratt, Todd, New York	.283	39	121	106	12	30	42	6	0	2	19	0	0	2	13	0	32	0	1	1	.396	.372
Prince, Tom, Los Angeles	.220	47	113	100	17	22	36	5	0	3	14	4	1	3	5	0	15	0	0	2	.360	.275
Pulliam, Harvey, Colorado	.284	59	72	67	15	19	31	3	0	3	9	0	0	0	5	0	15	0	1	2	.463	.333
Raabe, Brian, Colorado	.333	2	4	3	0	1	1	0	0	0	1	0	0	0	0	0	1	0	0	0	.333	.333
Radinsky, Scott, Los Angeles*	.000	75	4	4	0	0	0	0	0	0	0	0	0	0	0	0	4	0	0	0	.000	.000
Raggio, Brady, St. Louis	.000	15	4	3	0	0	0	0	0	0	0	1	0	0	0	0	1	0	0	0	.000	.000
Ramos, Edgar, Philadelphia	.000	4	4	3	0	0	0	0	0	0	0	0	0	0	0	0	2	0	0	0	.000	.000
Ramos, Ken, Houston*	.000	14	15	12	0	0	0	0	0	0	0	1	0	1	2	0	0	0	0	1	.000	.133
Randa, Joe, Pittsburgh	.302	126	499	443	58	134	200	27	9	7	60	4	5	6	41	1	64	4	2	10	.451	.366
Rapp, Pat, Fla.-S.F.	.106	27	51	47	3	5	8	0	0	1	2	4	0	0	0	0	16	0	0	0	.170	.106
Reed, Jeff, Colorado*	.297	90	298	256	43	76	137	10	0	17	47	5	0	2	35	1	55	2	1	8	.535	.386
Reed, Rick, New York	.175	33	66	57	6	10	18	5	0	1	5	6	0	0	3	0	18	0	0	0	.316	.217
Reed, Steve, Colorado	.000	63	1	1	0	0	0	0	0	0	0	0	0	0	0	0	0	0	0	0	.000	.000
Reese, Pokey, Cincinnati	.219	128	437	397	48	87	114	15	0	4	26	4	0	5	31	2	82	25	7	1	.287	.284
Rekar, Bryan, Colorado	.250	2	4	4	1	1	1	0	0	0	0	0	0	0	0	0	1	0	0	0	.250	.250
Relaford, Desi, Philadelphia†	.184	15	44	38	3	7	12	1	2	0	6	1	0	0	5	0	6	3	0	0	.316	.279
Remlinger, Mike, Cincinnati*	.095	71	26	21	1	2	4	2	0	0	6	3	0	0	2	0	11	0	0	1	.190	.174
Renteria, Edgar, Florida	.277	154	691	617	90	171	210	21	3	4	52	19	6	4	45	1	108	32	15	17	.340	.327
Reyes, Dennis, Los Angeles	.000	14	11	9	1	0	0	0	0	0	0	1	0	0	1	0	5	1	0	0	.000	.100
Reynolds, Shane, Houston	.113	30	62	53	3	6	9	3	0	0	2	7	0	0	2	0	31	0	0	0	.170	.145
Reynoso, Armando, New York	.241	16	32	29	3	7	10	0	0	1	3	0	1	0	2	0	15	0	0	0	.345	.281
Riggs, Adam, Los Angeles	.200	9	24	20	3	4	5	1	0	0	1	0	0	0	4	1	3	1	0	0	.250	.333
Rincon, Ricardo, Pittsburgh*	.000	62	2	1	0	0	0	0	0	0	0	0	0	0	0	0	1	0	0	0	.000	.000
Ritz, Kevin, Colorado	.057	18	41	35	4	2	2	0	0	0	0	2	0	0	4	0	15	1	0	0	.057	.154
Rivera, Luis, Houston	.231	7	15	13	2	3	5	0	1	0	3	1	0	0	1	0	6	0	0	0	.385	.286
Rivera, Ruben, San Diego	.250	17	22	20	2	5	6	1	0	0	1	0	0	0	9	2	1	0	0	0	.300	.318
Roa, Joe, San Fran.	.133	28	16	15	0	2	2	0	0	0	0	0	0	0	1	0	5	0	0	0	.133	.188
Robertson, Mike, Philadelphia*	.211	22	41	38	3	8	12	2	1	0	4	0	0	3	0	0	6	1	0	0	.316	.268
Rodriguez, Felix, Cincinnati	.000	26	4	3	0	0	0	0	0	0	0	1	0	0	0	0	0	0	0	0	.000	.000
Rodriguez, Henry, Montreal*	.244	132	523	476	55	116	228	28	3	26	83	0	3	2	42	5	149	3	3	6	.479	.306
Rodriguez, Rich, San Fran.*	.333	71	4	3	1	1	1	0	0	0	0	0	0	0	1	0	1	0	0	0	.333	.500
Rojas, Mel, Chi.-N.Y.	.000	77	1	1	0	0	0	0	0	0	0	0	0	0	0	0	1	0	0	0	.000	.000
Rolen, Scott, Philadelphia	.283	156	657	561	93	159	263	35	3	21	92	0	7	13	76	4	138	16	6	6	.469	.377
Romero, Mandy, San Diego†	.208	21	50	48	7	10	16	0	0	2	4	0	0	0	2	0	18	1	0	1	.333	.240
Rose, Pete Jr., Cincinnati*	.143	11	16	14	2	2	2	0	0	0	0	0	0	0	2	0	9	0	0	0	.143	.250
Ruebel, Matt, Pittsburgh*	.000	44	8	7	0	0	0	0	0	0	0	1	0	0	0	0	7	0	0	0	.000	.000
Rueter, Kirk, San Fran.*	.138	32	75	65	5	9	9	0	0	0	5	7	0	0	3	0	14	0	0	1	.138	.176
Ruffcorn, Scott, Philadelphia	.000	18	8	6	0	0	0	0	0	0	0	1	0	0	1	0	6	0	0	0	.000	.143
Sanchez, Rey, Chicago	.249	97	220	205	14	51	63	9	0	1	12	4	0	0	11	2	26	4	2	7	.307	.287
Sandberg, Ryne, Chicago	.264	135	480	447	54	118	180	26	0	12	64	0	3	2	28	3	94	7	4	5	.403	.308
Sanders, Deion, Cincinnati*	.273	115	509	465	53	127	169	13	7	5	23	2	2	6	34	2	67	56	13	4	.363	.329
Sanders, Reggie, Cincinnati	.253	86	358	312	52	79	159	19	2	19	56	1	0	3	42	3	93	13	7	9	.510	.347
Santangelo, F.P., Montreal†	.249	130	440	350	56	87	131	19	5	5	31	12	3	25	50	1	73	8	5	1	.374	.379
Saunders, Tony, Florida*	.081	22	40	37	2	3	6	0	0	1	1	0	0	0	2	0	19	0	0	0	.162	.128
Scarsone, Steve, St. Louis	.100	5	12	10	0	1	1	0	0	0	0	0	0	0	2	0	5	1	0	0	.100	.250

Player, Team	Avg.	G	TPA	AB	R	H	TB	2B	3B	HR	RBI	SH	SF	HP	BB	IBB	SO	SB	CS	GDP	Slg.	OBP
Schilling, Curt, Philadelphia......	.173	35	95	81	4	14	15	1	0	0	1	12	1	0	1	0	32	1	0	3	.185	.181
Schmidt, Jason, Pittsburgh.....	.107	32	67	56	2	6	8	2	0	0	2	9	0	0	2	0	26	0	0	1	.143	.138
Schourek, Pete, Cincinnati*......	.167	19	30	24	1	4	7	0	0	1	2	6	0	0	0	0	8	1	0	1	.292	.167
Sefcik, Kevin, Philadelphia......	.269	61	131	119	11	32	41	3	0	2	6	7	0	1	4	0	9	1	2	4	.345	.298
Segui, David, Montreal†	.307	125	523	459	75	141	232	22	3	21	68	0	6	1	57	12	66	1	0	9	.505	.380
Servais, Scott, Chicago	.260	122	425	385	36	100	139	21	0	6	45	7	3	6	24	7	56	0	1	7	.361	.311
Shaw, Jeff, Cincinnati	.000	78	4	3	0	0	0	0	0	0	0	1	0	0	0	0	3	0	0	0	.000	.000
Sheaffer, Danny, St. Louis........	.250	76	146	132	10	33	38	5	0	0	11	4	1	1	8	0	17	1	0	10	.288	.296
Sheffield, Gary, Florida........	.250	135	582	444	86	111	198	22	1	21	71	0	2	15	121	11	79	11	7	7	.446	.424
Shipley, Craig, San Diego	.273	63	148	139	22	38	62	9	0	5	19	1	1	0	7	0	20	1	1	1	.446	.306
Shumpert, Terry, San Diego......	.273	13	37	33	4	9	15	3	0	1	6	0	1	0	3	0	4	0	0	1	.455	.324
Sierra, Ruben, Cincinnati†	.244	25	96	90	6	22	35	5	1	2	7	0	0	0	6	1	21	0	0	1	.389	.292
Silva, Jose, Pittsburgh...........	.143	11	10	7	1	1	1	0	0	0	0	3	0	0	0	0	4	0	0	0	.143	.143
Simon, Randall, Atlanta*........	.429	13	15	14	2	6	7	1	0	0	1	0	0	0	1	0	2	0	0	1	.500	.467
Slaught, Don, San Diego..........	.000	20	26	20	2	0	0	0	0	0	0	1	0	0	5	0	4	0	0	1	.000	.200
Smiley, John, Cincinnati*........	.100	20	42	40	0	4	5	1	0	0	2	2	0	0	0	0	10	0	0	2	.125	.100
Smith, Mark, Pittsburgh........	.285	71	222	193	29	55	97	13	1	9	35	0	1	0	28	1	36	3	1	3	.503	.374
Smith, Pete J., San Diego	.167	38	37	30	2	5	8	1	1	0	3	6	0	0	1	0	16	0	0	0	.267	.194
Smoltz, John, Atlanta	.228	36	94	79	10	18	21	3	0	0	4	6	0	0	9	0	22	1	1	0	.266	.307
Snow, J.T., San Fran.†	.281	157	637	531	81	149	271	36	1	28	104	2	1	1	96	13	124	6	4	8	.510	.387
Sodowsky, Clint, Pittsburgh*...	.500	45	2	2	0	1	1	0	0	0	0	0	0	0	0	0	0	0	0	0	.500	.500
Sosa, Sammy, Chicago	.251	162	694	642	90	161	308	31	4	36	119	0	5	2	45	9	174	22	12	16	.480	.300
Spehr, Tim, Atlanta	.214	8	14	14	2	3	7	1	0	1	4	0	0	0	0	0	4	1	0	0	.500	.214
Spiers, Bill, Houston*	.320	132	355	291	51	93	140	27	4	4	48	1	1	1	61	6	42	10	5	4	.481	.438
Spradlin, Jerry, Philadelphia† ..	.000	76	1	1	0	0	0	0	0	0	0	0	0	0	0	0	1	0	0	0	.000	.000
Springer, Russ, Houston..........	.000	54	1	1	0	0	0	0	0	0	0	0	0	0	0	0	0	0	0	0	.000	.000
Stanifer, Rob, Florida	.667	36	4	3	1	2	3	1	0	0	1	0	0	0	1	0	0	0	0	0	1.000	.750
Stankiewicz, Andy, Montreal	.224	76	119	107	11	24	36	9	0	1	5	7	1	0	4	0	22	1	1	1	.336	.250
Stephenson, Garrett, Phi.........	.094	20	38	32	0	3	4	1	0	0	1	5	0	0	1	0	16	0	0	0	.125	.121
Stevens, Dave, Chicago	.000	10	1	1	0	0	0	0	0	0	0	0	0	0	0	0	0	0	0	0	.000	.000
Stocker, Kevin, Philadelphia†	.266	149	560	504	51	134	179	23	5	4	40	2	1	2	51	7	91	11	6	14	.355	.335
Stottlemyre, Todd, St. Louis* ...	.236	29	68	55	6	13	19	4	1	0	4	5	0	0	8	0	13	0	0	1	.345	.333
Strange, Doug, Montreal†	.257	118	372	327	40	84	140	16	2	12	47	5	2	2	36	9	76	0	2	4	.428	.332
Stull, Everett, Montreal	.000	3	1	0	0	0	0	0	0	0	0	1	0	0	0	0	0	0	0	0	.000	.000
Stynes, Chris, Cincinnati	.348	49	215	198	31	69	96	7	1	6	28	2	0	4	11	1	13	11	2	5	.485	.394
Sullivan, Scott, Cincinnati	.000	59	9	7	0	0	0	0	0	0	0	2	0	0	0	0	4	0	0	0	.000	.000
Sveum, Dale, Pittsburgh†	.261	126	339	306	30	80	138	20	1	12	47	4	2	0	27	2	81	0	3	8	.451	.319
Swartzbaugh, Dave, Chicago ...	.000	2	4	4	0	0	0	0	0	0	0	0	0	0	0	0	1	0	0	0	.000	.000
Sweeney, Mark, St.L.-S.D.*	.280	115	188	164	16	46	59	7	0	2	23	1	2	1	20	1	32	2	3	3	.360	.358
Swift, Bill C., Colorado	.211	16	28	19	2	4	5	1	0	0	2	4	0	1	4	0	4	0	0	1	.263	.375
Tapani, Kevin, Chicago............	.136	13	28	22	2	3	3	0	0	0	0	4	0	0	2	0	12	1	0	1	.136	.208
Tartabull, Danny, Philadelphia ..	.000	3	11	7	2	0	0	0	0	0	0	0	0	0	4	0	3	0	0	0	.000	.364
Tatis, Ramon, Chicago*	.000	56	4	3	0	0	0	0	0	0	0	0	0	0	1	0	3	0	0	0	.000	.250
Taubensee, Eddie, Cincinnati* ..	.268	108	283	254	26	68	116	18	0	10	34	1	5	1	22	2	66	0	1	2	.457	.323
Tavarez, Julian, San Fran.*	.000	89	1	1	0	0	0	0	0	0	0	0	0	0	0	0	0	0	0	0	.000	.000
Telemaco, Amaury, Chicago......	.222	10	10	9	0	2	2	0	0	0	0	1	0	0	0	0	6	0	0	0	.222	.300
Telford, Anthony, Montreal	.200	65	16	15	0	3	4	1	0	0	1	1	0	0	0	0	3	0	0	0	.267	.200
Thompson, Mark, Colorado	.182	6	13	11	1	2	6	1	0	1	1	2	0	0	0	0	5	0	0	0	.545	.182
Thomson, John, Colorado	.213	27	55	47	2	10	10	0	0	0	2	8	0	0	0	0	23	0	0	1	.213	.245
Thurman, Gary, New York........	.167	11	6	6	0	1	1	0	0	0	0	0	0	0	0	0	0	0	1	1	.167	.167
Thurman, Mike, Montreal	.500	5	3	2	1	1	1	0	0	0	0	1	0	0	0	0	0	0	0	0	.500	.500
Timmons, Ozzie, Cincinnati.......	.333	6	9	9	1	3	4	1	0	0	0	0	0	0	0	0	1	0	0	0	.444	.333
Tomberlin, Andy, New York*......	.286	6	8	7	0	2	2	0	0	0	0	0	0	0	1	0	3	0	0	0	.286	.375
Tomko, Brett, Cincinnati	.139	24	40	36	2	5	6	1	0	0	3	3	0	0	1	0	14	0	0	3	.167	.162
Torres, Salomon, Montreal	.000	12	6	6	0	0	0	0	0	0	0	0	0	0	0	0	4	0	0	0	.000	.000
Trachsel, Steve, Chicago	.117	34	76	60	5	7	10	3	0	0	4	11	0	0	5	0	19	0	0	3	.167	.185
Tucker, Michael, Atlanta*	.283	138	554	499	80	141	222	25	7	14	56	4	1	6	44	0	116	12	7	7	.445	.347
Urbina, Ugueth, Montreal	.000	63	5	5	0	0	0	0	0	0	0	0	0	0	0	0	4	0	0	0	.000	.000
Valdes, Ismael, Los Angeles	.088	30	67	57	0	5	6	1	0	0	1	7	0	0	3	0	17	1	0	2	.105	.133
Valdes, Marc, Montreal	.105	48	20	19	0	2	2	0	0	0	1	0	0	0	1	0	9	0	0	0	.105	.150
Valenzuela, Fernando, S.D.-St.L.*.	.182	19	28	22	1	4	4	0	0	0	0	6	0	0	0	0	3	0	0	0	.182	.182
Vander Wal, John, Colorado* ...	.174	76	102	92	7	16	21	2	0	1	11	0	0	0	10	0	33	1	1	2	.228	.255
VanLandingham, William, S.F. ..	.115	18	29	26	1	3	4	1	0	0	2	0	0	0	1	0	13	0	0	1	.154	.148
Vaughn, Greg, San Diego	.216	120	422	361	60	78	142	10	0	18	57	0	3	2	56	1	110	7	4	7	.393	.322
Velandia, Jorge, San Diego	.103	14	30	29	0	3	5	2	0	0	0	0	0	0	1	0	7	0	0	0	.172	.133
Veras, Quilvio, San Diego†	.265	145	631	539	74	143	177	23	1	3	45	9	4	7	72	0	84	33	12	9	.328	.357
Veres, Dave, Montreal	1.000	53	1	1	0	1	1	0	0	0	0	0	0	0	0	0	0	0	0	0	1.000	1.000
Vidro, Jose, Montreal†	.249	67	185	169	19	42	62	12	1	2	17	0	3	2	11	0	20	1	0	1	.367	.297
Vizcaino, Jose, San Fran.†	.266	151	630	568	77	151	199	19	7	5	50	13	1	0	48	1	87	8	8	13	.350	.323
Wade, Terrell, Atlanta*............	.250	12	15	12	0	3	3	0	0	0	1	1	0	0	2	0	5	0	0	0	.250	.357
Wagner, Billy, Houston*............	.000	62	1	1	0	0	0	0	0	0	0	0	0	0	0	0	0	0	0	0	.000	.000
Wagner, Paul, Pittsburgh	.000	14	1	1	0	0	0	0	0	0	0	0	0	0	0	0	0	0	0	0	.000	.000
Wainhouse, Dave, Pittsburgh* .	.000	25	2	2	0	0	0	0	0	0	0	0	0	0	0	0	0	0	0	0	.000	.000
Walker, Larry, Colorado*	.366	153	664	568	143	208	409	46	4	49	130	0	4	14	78	14	90	33	8	15	.720	.452
Wall, Donne, Houston..............	.100	8	12	10	0	1	1	0	0	0	0	1	0	0	1	0	4	0	0	0	.100	.182
Ward, Turner, Pittsburgh†	.353	71	191	167	33	59	98	16	1	7	33	1	1	2	18	2	17	4	1	1	.587	.420
Watkins, Pat, Cincinnati	.207	17	30	29	2	6	8	2	0	0	0	1	0	0	0	0	5	1	0	1	.276	.207
Wehner, John, Florida	.278	44	40	36	8	10	12	2	0	0	2	1	0	1	2	0	5	1	0	2	.333	.333
Weiss, Walt, Colorado†	.270	121	469	393	52	106	151	23	5	4	38	7	1	2	66	3	56	5	2	7	.384	.377
Wendell, Turk, Chi.-N.Y.*	.000	65	6	5	1	0	0	0	0	0	0	0	0	0	1	0	3	0	0	0	.000	.000
White, Devon, Florida†	.245	74	308	265	37	65	98	13	1	6	34	0	4	7	32	2	65	13	5	3	.370	.338
White, Gabe, Cincinnati*..........	.111	12	11	9	0	1	1	0	0	0	1	2	0	0	0	0	7	0	0	0	.111	.111

Player, Team	Avg.	G	TPA	AB	R	H	TB	2B	3B	HR	RBI	SH	SF	HP	BB	IBB	SO	SB	CS	GDP	Slg.	OBP
White, Rondell, Montreal	.270	151	638	592	84	160	283	29	5	28	82	1	4	10	31	3	111	16	8	18	.478	.316
Widger, Chris, Montreal	.234	91	305	278	30	65	112	20	3	7	37	2	2	1	22	1	59	2	0	7	.403	.290
Wilkins, Marc, Pittsburgh	.000	70	6	4	0	0	0	0	0	0	1	1	0	0	1	0	3	0	0	0	.000	.200
Wilkins, Rick, San Fran.*	.195	66	210	190	18	37	60	5	0	6	23	0	3	0	17	0	65	0	0	0	.316	.257
Williams, Eddie, L.A.-Pit.	.240	38	111	96	12	23	37	5	0	3	12	1	1	2	11	2	25	1	0	2	.385	.327
Winston, Darrin, Philadelphia	.500	7	3	2	0	1	1	0	0	0	1	0	0	0	1	0	0	0	0	0	.500	.667
Wohlers, Mark, Atlanta	.000	71	2	2	0	0	0	0	0	0	0	0	0	0	0	0	2	0	0	0	.000	.000
Womack, Tony, Pittsburgh*	.278	155	689	641	85	178	240	26	9	6	50	2	0	3	43	2	109	60	7	6	.374	.326
Worrell, Tim, San Diego	.200	60	17	15	3	3	3	0	0	0	1	0	0	0	2	0	8	0	0	0	.200	.294
Wright, Jamey, Colorado	.125	26	54	48	4	6	7	1	0	0	3	3	0	0	3	0	22	0	0	1	.146	.176
Young, Dmitri, St. Louis†	.258	110	377	333	38	86	121	14	3	5	34	1	3	2	38	3	63	6	5	8	.363	.335
Young, Eric, Col.-L.A.	.280	155	718	622	106	174	247	33	8	8	61	10	6	9	71	1	54	45	14	18	.397	.359
Young, Kevin, Pittsburgh	.300	97	362	333	59	100	178	18	3	18	74	1	8	4	16	1	89	11	2	6	.535	.332
Zaun, Gregg, Florida†	.301	58	172	143	21	43	63	10	2	2	20	1	0	2	26	4	18	1	0	3	.441	.415
Zeile, Todd, Los Angeles	.268	160	672	575	89	154	264	17	0	31	90	0	6	6	85	7	112	8	7	18	.459	.365

AWARDED FIRST BASE ON OBSTRUCTION OR CATCHER'S INTERFERENCE—Dauton, Phi.-Fla. 3 (Manwaring, Hundley, Fletcher); Gomez, San Diego 3 (Kendall, Taubensee, Marrero); Klesko, Atlanta 3 (J. Reed, Eusebio, Piazza); Orie, Chicago 3 (Widger 2, Osik); Barron, Philadelphia (Tomko); Berry, Houston (Zaun); Bichette, Colorado (Eusebio); Burks, Colorado (Zaun); Cianfrocco, San Diego (Zaun); Lankford, St. Louis (Alomar); May, Philadelphia (Spehr); Nunnally, Cincinnati (Kendall); Ward, Pittsburgh (Fletcher).

PLAYERS WITH TWO OR MORE TEAMS

Player, Team	Avg.	G	TPA	AB	R	H	TB	2B	3B	HR	RBI	SH	SF	HP	BB	IBB	SO	SB	CS	GDP	Slg.	OBP
Alexander, Manny, New York	.248	54	161	149	26	37	58	9	3	2	15	1	1	1	9	1	38	11	0	3	.389	.294
Alexander, Manny, Chicago	.293	33	111	99	11	29	37	3	1	1	7	2	0	2	8	2	16	2	1	3	.374	.358
Astacio, Pedro, Los Angeles	.146	26	51	41	2	6	7	1	0	0	1	10	0	0	0	0	16	0	0	0	.171	.146
Astacio, Pedro, Colorado	.077	7	14	13	0	1	1	0	0	0	0	1	0	0	0	0	8	0	0	0	.077	.077
Castillo, Frank, Chicago	.152	20	37	33	1	5	5	0	0	0	3	4	0	0	0	0	9	0	0	0	.152	.152
Castillo, Frank, Colorado	.080	14	33	25	0	2	2	0	0	0	2	6	1	0	1	0	10	0	0	0	.080	.111
Clark, Mark, New York	.047	23	49	43	1	2	5	0	0	1	2	4	0	0	2	0	19	0	0	0	.116	.089
Clark, Mark, Chicago	.000	9	27	23	2	0	0	0	0	0	1	2	0	0	2	0	12	0	0	0	.000	.080
Counsell, Craig, Colorado*	.000	1	0	0	0	0	0	0	0	0	0	0	0	0	0	0	0	0	0	0	.000	.000
Counsell, Craig, Florida*	.299	51	189	164	20	49	65	9	2	1	16	3	1	3	18	2	17	1	1	5	.396	.376
Cummings, Midre, Pittsburgh*	.189	52	116	106	11	20	39	6	2	3	8	1	0	1	8	0	26	0	0	1	.368	.252
Cummings, Midre, Phi.*	.303	63	234	208	24	63	90	16	4	1	23	1	2	0	23	0	30	2	3	2	.433	.369
Daulton, Darren, Philadelphia*	.264	84	331	269	46	71	129	13	6	11	42	0	7	1	54	4	57	4	0	3	.480	.381
Daulton, Darren, Florida*	.262	52	151	126	22	33	54	8	2	3	21	0	2	1	22	1	17	2	1	1	.429	.371
Dunston, Shawon, Chicago	.284	114	437	419	57	119	172	18	4	9	41	3	4	3	8	0	64	29	7	7	.411	.300
Dunston, Shawon, Pittsburgh	.394	18	74	71	14	28	49	4	1	5	16	2	1	0	0	0	11	3	1	2	.690	.389
Hutton, Mark, Florida	.000	32	0	0	0	0	0	0	0	0	0	0	0	0	0	0	0	0	0	0	.000	.000
Hutton, Mark, Colorado	.000	8	3	3	0	0	0	0	0	0	0	0	0	0	0	0	0	0	0	0	.000	.000
Jackson, Danny, St. Louis	.143	4	7	7	1	1	1	0	0	0	0	0	0	0	0	0	4	0	0	0	.143	.143
Jackson, Danny, San Diego	.077	13	15	13	0	1	1	0	0	0	0	1	0	0	1	0	4	0	1	0	.077	.143
Johnson, Lance, New York*	.309	72	299	265	43	82	107	10	6	1	24	0	1	0	33	2	21	15	10	6	.404	.385
Johnson, Lance, Chicago*	.303	39	155	145	17	44	66	6	2	4	15	0	1	0	9	1	10	5	2	2	.455	.342
Livingstone, Scott, San Diego*	.154	23	28	26	1	4	5	1	0	0	3	0	0	2	0	1	0	0	0	0	.192	.214
Livingstone, Scott, St. Louis*	.171	42	44	41	3	7	8	1	0	0	3	0	2	0	1	0	10	1	0	1	.195	.182
McMillon, Billy, Florida*	.111	13	18	18	0	2	3	1	0	0	1	0	0	0	0	0	7	0	0	0	.167	.111
McMillon, Billy, Philadelphia*	.292	24	81	72	10	21	33	4	1	2	13	0	3	0	6	0	17	2	1	1	.458	.333
McRae, Brian, Chicago†	.240	108	477	417	63	100	155	27	5	6	28	3	1	4	52	2	62	14	6	11	.372	.329
McRae, Brian, New York†	.248	45	162	145	23	36	60	5	2	5	15	1	1	2	13	0	22	3	4	2	.414	.317
Mulholland, Terry, Chicago	.163	25	52	49	0	8	10	2	0	0	2	3	0	0	0	0	24	0	0	0	.204	.163
Mulholland, Terry, San Fran.	.167	15	7	6	1	1	2	1	0	0	0	1	0	0	0	0	3	0	0	0	.333	.167
Plantier, Phil, San Diego*	.125	10	10	8	0	1	1	0	0	0	0	0	0	0	2	0	3	0	0	0	.125	.300
Plantier, Phil, St. Louis*	.257	42	129	113	13	29	52	8	0	5	18	0	2	3	11	1	27	0	3	5	.460	.333
Rapp, Pat, Florida	.143	19	39	35	3	5	8	0	0	0	1	2	4	0	0	0	12	0	0	0	.229	.143
Rapp, Pat, San Francisco	.000	8	12	12	0	0	0	0	0	0	0	0	0	0	0	0	4	0	0	0	.000	.000
Rojas, Mel, Chicago	.000	54	1	1	0	0	0	0	0	0	0	0	0	0	0	0	0	0	0	0	.000	.000
Rojas, Mel, New York	.000	23	0	0	0	0	0	0	0	0	0	0	0	0	0	0	0	0	0	0	.000	.000
Sweeney, Mark, St. Louis*	.213	44	73	61	5	13	16	3	0	0	4	1	1	1	9	1	14	0	1	2	.262	.319
Sweeney, Mark, San Diego*	.320	71	115	103	11	33	43	4	0	2	19	0	1	0	11	0	18	2	2	1	.417	.383
Valenzuela, Fernando, S.D.*	.176	14	21	17	0	3	3	0	0	0	1	4	0	0	0	0	3	0	0	0	.176	.176
Valenzuela, Fernando, St.L.*	.200	5	7	5	1	1	1	0	0	0	1	2	0	0	0	0	0	0	0	0	.200	.200
Wendell, Turk, Chicago*	.000	52	4	3	1	0	0	0	0	0	0	0	0	0	1	0	3	0	0	0	.000	.250
Wendell, Turk, New York*	.000	13	2	2	0	0	0	0	0	0	0	0	0	0	0	0	1	0	0	0	.000	.000
Williams, Eddie, Los Angeles	.143	8	8	7	0	1	1	0	0	0	0	1	0	0	1	1	1	0	0	0	.143	.250
Williams, Eddie, Pittsburgh	.247	30	103	89	12	22	36	5	0	3	11	1	1	2	10	1	24	1	0	2	.404	.333
Young, Eric, Colorado	.282	118	543	468	78	132	191	29	6	6	45	8	5	5	57	0	37	32	12	16	.408	.363
Young, Eric, Los Angeles	.273	37	175	154	28	42	56	4	2	2	16	2	1	4	14	1	17	13	2	2	.364	.347

DESIGNATED HITTING

TEAM

Team	Avg.	G	TPA	AB	R	H	TB	2B	3B	HR	RBI	SH	SF	HP	BB	IBB	SO	SB	CS	GDP	Slg.	OBP
Los Angeles	.441	8	37	34	4	15	20	3	1	0	7	1	1	0	1	0	3	0	0	0	.588	.444
Houston	.440	6	26	25	5	11	20	3	0	2	3	0	0	1	0	0	6	0	0	0	.800	.462
Chicago	.375	6	26	24	2	9	12	0	0	1	7	0	0	0	2	0	4	0	0	0	.500	.423
Pittsburgh	.304	6	24	23	4	7	14	1	0	2	5	0	0	0	1	0	1	0	1	0	.609	.333
New York	.258	9	39	31	5	8	14	0	0	2	7	0	0	1	7	1	6	2	0	1	.452	.410
Colorado	.258	8	35	31	6	8	11	0	0	1	1	0	0	1	3	1	5	2	1	1	.355	.343
San Francisco	.242	8	35	33	5	8	11	1	1	0	5	0	1	0	1	0	5	0	0	0	.333	.257
Atlanta	.231	9	40	39	3	9	16	2	1	1	9	0	0	0	1	0	4	0	0	4	.410	.250
Cincinnati	.227	6	23	22	2	5	7	2	0	0	0	0	0	0	1	0	2	0	0	0	.318	.261
San Diego	.216	8	42	37	6	8	18	1	0	3	8	0	0	0	5	1	10	0	0	0	.486	.310
Florida	.206	9	41	34	8	7	12	2	0	1	4	0	0	0	7	0	4	0	0	1	.353	.341
Philadelphia	.184	9	40	38	4	7	11	1	0	1	3	0	0	0	2	0	7	2	0	0	.289	.225
Montreal	.182	9	38	33	2	6	9	0	0	1	1	0	0	0	5	0	10	0	1	0	.273	.289
St. Louis	.160	6	25	25	0	4	6	0	1	0	3	0	0	0	0	0	4	0	0	0	.240	.160
Totals	.261	107	471	429	56	112	181	16	4	15	63	1	2	3	36	4	71	6	3	7	.422	.321

INDIVIDUAL

TOP DESIGNATED HITTERS

Minimum 15 at-bats. *Lefthanded batter. †Switch-hitter.

Player, Team	Avg.	G	TPA	AB	R	H	TB	2B	3B	HR	RBI	SH	SF	HP	BB	IBB	SO	SB	CS	GDP	Slg.	OBP
Piazza, Mike, Los Angeles	.484	7	32	31	4	15	20	3	1	0	6	0	1	0	0	0	2	0	0	0	.645	.469
Smith, Mark, Pittsburgh	.368	5	20	19	4	7	14	1	0	2	5	0	0	0	1	0	1	0	1	0	.737	.400
Lockhart, Keith, Atlanta*	.294	4	17	17	1	5	8	1	1	0	2	0	0	0	0	0	2	0	0	2	.471	.294
Bichette, Dante, Colorado	.286	5	22	21	4	6	6	0	0	0	0	0	0	0	1	0	3	0	0	0	.286	.318
Hill, Glenallen, San Francisco	.240	7	27	25	3	6	7	1	0	0	4	0	1	0	1	0	3	0	0	0	.280	.259
Vidro, Jose, Montreal†	.188	5	20	16	0	3	3	0	0	0	0	0	0	0	4	0	4	0	0	0	.188	.350
Daulton, Darren, Phi.-Fla.*	.167	7	31	30	3	5	9	1	0	1	2	0	0	0	1	0	3	0	0	0	.300	.194
Eisenreich, Jim, Florida*	.125	4	16	16	1	2	3	1	0	0	2	0	0	0	0	0	1	0	0	0	.188	.125
Huskey, Butch, New York	.125	4	16	16	0	2	2	0	0	0	1	0	0	0	0	0	3	1	0	1	.125	.125

ALL PINCH-HITTERS

*Lefthanded batter. †Switch-hitter.

Player, Team	Avg.	G	TPA	AB	R	H	TB	2B	3B	HR	RBI	SH	SF	HP	BB	IBB	SO	SB	CS	GDP	Slg.	OBP
Abbott, Kurt, Florida	.500	2	2	2	1	1	1	0	0	0	0	0	0	0	0	0	1	0	0	0	.500	.500
Bagwell, Jeff, Houston	.250	1	5	4	1	1	2	1	0	0	0	0	0	1	0	0	2	0	0	0	.500	.400
Bell, Derek, Houston	.250	1	4	4	1	1	4	0	0	1	1	0	0	0	0	0	1	0	0	0	1.000	.250
Benard, Marvin, San Fran.*	.000	1	3	3	0	0	0	0	0	0	0	0	0	0	0	0	1	0	0	0	.000	.000
Berry, Sean, Houston	.500	3	12	12	1	6	7	1	0	0	1	0	0	0	0	0	2	0	0	0	.583	.500
Bichette, Dante, Colorado	.286	5	22	21	4	6	6	0	0	0	0	0	0	0	1	0	3	0	0	0	.286	.318
Biggio, Craig, Houston	.600	1	5	5	2	3	7	1	0	1	1	0	0	0	0	0	1	0	0	0	1.400	.600
Blauser, Jeff, Atlanta	.250	1	4	4	0	1	1	0	0	0	2	0	0	0	0	0	1	0	0	0	.250	.250
Bonilla, Bobby, Florida†	.200	3	14	10	3	2	3	1	0	0	0	0	0	0	4	0	2	0	0	1	.300	.429
Butler, Brett, Los Angeles*	.000	1	5	3	0	0	0	0	0	0	0	1	1	0	1	0	1	0	0	0	.000	.250
Clark, Dave, Chicago*	.385	4	15	13	1	5	8	0	0	1	3	0	0	0	2	0	2	0	0	0	.615	.467
Colbrunn, Greg, Atlanta	.214	3	15	14	2	3	7	1	0	1	5	0	0	0	1	0	2	0	0	1	.500	.267
Daulton, Darren, Phi.-Fla.*	.167	7	31	30	3	5	9	1	0	1	2	0	0	0	1	0	3	0	0	0	.300	.194
Eisenreich, Jim, Florida*	.125	4	16	16	1	2	3	1	0	0	2	0	0	0	0	0	1	0	0	0	.188	.125
Fordyce, Brook, Cincinnati	.333	1	3	3	0	1	1	0	0	0	0	0	0	0	0	0	0	0	0	0	.333	.333
Franco, Matt, New York*	.500	1	4	2	1	1	4	0	0	1	2	0	0	0	2	1	0	0	0	0	2.000	.750
Gant, Ron, St. Louis	.000	1	4	4	0	0	0	0	0	0	0	0	0	0	0	0	3	0	0	0	.000	.000
Gilkey, Bernard, New York	.375	3	10	8	3	3	6	0	0	0	1	0	0	0	2	0	1	1	0	0	.750	.500
Gwynn, Tony, San Diego*	.143	3	14	14	0	2	3	1	0	0	2	0	0	0	0	0	0	0	0	0	.214	.143
Henderson, Rickey, San Diego.	.222	2	11	9	2	2	5	0	0	1	1	0	0	0	2	1	4	0	0	0	.556	.364
Hernandez, Jose, Chicago	.000	1	1	1	0	0	0	0	0	0	0	0	0	0	0	0	1	0	0	0	.000	.000
Hill, Glenallen, San Francisco	.240	7	27	25	3	6	7	1	0	0	4	0	1	0	1	0	3	0	0	0	.280	.259
Hundley, Todd, New York†	.500	2	8	4	1	2	2	0	0	0	0	0	0	1	3	0	1	0	0	0	.500	.750
Huskey, Butch, New York	.125	4	16	16	0	2	2	0	0	0	1	0	0	0	0	0	3	1	0	1	.125	.125
Johnson, Lance, Chicago*	.400	1	5	5	0	2	2	0	0	0	2	0	0	0	0	0	0	0	0	0	.400	.400
Johnson, Mark, Pittsburgh*	.000	1	4	4	0	0	0	0	0	0	0	0	0	0	0	0	0	0	0	0	.000	.000
Jordan, Kevin, Philadelphia	.250	2	5	4	1	1	1	0	0	0	0	0	0	0	1	0	2	0	0	0	.250	.400
Larkin, Barry, Cincinnati	.125	2	8	8	2	1	1	0	0	0	0	0	0	0	0	0	1	0	0	0	.125	.125
Lewis, Mark, San Francisco	.400	1	5	5	2	2	4	0	0	1	1	0	0	0	0	0	1	0	0	0	.800	.400
Lieberthal, Mike, Philadelphia	.250	1	4	4	0	1	1	0	0	0	0	0	0	0	0	0	2	1	0	0	.250	.250
Livingstone, Scott, St. Louis*	.250	1	4	4	0	1	1	0	0	0	0	0	0	0	0	0	0	0	0	0	.250	.250
Lockhart, Keith, Atlanta*	.294	4	17	17	1	5	8	1	1	0	2	0	0	0	0	0	2	0	0	2	.471	.294
McGee, Willie, St. Louis†	.154	3	13	13	0	2	4	0	1	0	0	0	0	0	0	0	2	0	0	2	.308	.154
McGuire, Ryan, Montreal*	.200	3	11	10	1	2	2	0	0	0	0	0	0	0	1	0	4	0	1	0	.200	.273
Mordecai, Mike, Atlanta	.000	1	4	4	0	0	0	0	0	0	0	0	0	0	0	0	1	0	0	0	.000	.000
Obando, Sherman, Montreal	.333	2	3	3	1	1	4	0	0	1	0	0	0	0	0	0	1	0	0	0	1.333	.333
Ochoa, Alex, New York	.000	1	1	1	0	0	0	0	0	0	0	0	0	0	0	0	0	0	0	0	.000	.000
Orsulak, Joe, Montreal*	.000	1	2	2	0	0	0	0	0	0	0	0	0	0	0	0	0	0	0	0	.000	.000
Perez, Eduardo, Cincinnati	.000	1	1	1	0	0	0	0	0	0	0	0	0	0	0	0	0	0	0	0	.000	.000

Player, Team	Avg.	G	TPA	AB	R	H	TB	2B	3B	HR	RBI	SH	SF	HP	BB	IBB	SO	SB	CS	GDP	Slg.	OBP
Piazza, Mike, Los Angeles......	.484	7	32	31	4	15	20	3	1	0	6	0	1	0	0	0	2	0	0	0	.645	.469
Robertson, Mike, Phi.*	.250	1	4	4	0	1	1	0	0	0	0	0	0	0	0	0	1	0	0	0	.250	.250
Sandberg, Ryne, Chicago......	.333	1	3	3	0	1	1	0	0	0	0	0	0	0	0	0	1	0	0	0	.333	.333
Servais, Scott, Chicago..........	.500	2	2	2	1	1	1	0	0	0	2	0	0	0	0	0	0	0	0	0	.500	.500
Sheffield, Gary, Florida...........	.500	1	5	2	3	1	4	0	0	1	2	0	0	0	3	0	0	0	0	0	2.000	.800
Smith, Mark, Pittsburgh.........	.368	5	20	19	4	7	14	1	0	2	5	0	0	0	1	0	1	0	1	0	.737	.400
Stankiewicz, Andy, Montreal ..	.000	2	2	2	0	0	0	0	0	0	0	0	0	0	0	0	1	0	0	0	.000	.000
Taubensee, Eddie, Cincinnati*	.300	3	11	10	0	3	5	2	0	0	0	0	0	0	1	0	2	0	0	0	.500	.364
Vander Wal, John, Colorado*	.143	2	8	7	0	1	1	0	0	0	0	0	0	0	1	0	2	1	1	1	.143	.250
Vaughn, Greg, San Diego.......	.286	3	17	14	4	4	10	0	0	2	5	0	0	0	3	0	5	0	0	0	.714	.412
Vidro, Jose, Montreal†	.188	5	20	16	0	3	3	0	0	0	0	0	0	0	4	0	4	0	0	0	.188	.350
Walker, Larry, Colorado*........	.333	1	5	3	2	1	4	0	0	1	1	0	0	1	1	1	0	1	0	0	1.333	.600
Young, Dmitri, St. Louis†.......	.250	1	4	4	0	1	1	0	0	0	0	0	0	0	0	0	1	0	0	0	.250	.250

DESIGNATED HITTERS WITH TWO OR MORE TEAMS

Player, Team	Avg.	G	TPA	AB	R	H	TB	2B	3B	HR	RBI	SH	SF	HP	BB	IBB	SO	SB	CS	GDP	Slg.	OBP
Daulton, Darren, Philadelphia* .	.154	6	27	26	3	4	8	1	0	1	2	0	0	0	1	0	3	0	0	0	.308	.185
Daulton, Darren, Florida*..........	.250	1	4	4	0	1	1	0	0	0	0	0	0	0	0	0	0	0	0	0	.250	.250

The following designated hitters, each of whom appeared in at least one game, had no plate appearances, runs scored or stolen base attempts: Kelly, Mike, Cincinnati; Lopez, Javy, Atlanta; McCracken, Quinton, Colorado; Park, Chan Ho, Los Angeles; Sanders, Deion, Cincinnati; Conine, Jeff, Florida.

PINCH-HITTING

TEAM

Team	Avg.	G	TPA	AB	R	H	TB	2B	3B	HR	RBI	SH	SF	HP	BB	IBB	SO	SB	CS	GDP	Slg.	OBP
Colorado	.271	120	216	188	25	51	77	12	1	4	25	3	1	1	23	0	57	0	1	2	.410	.352
San Francisco	.267	117	211	180	25	48	66	15	0	1	27	1	2	1	27	0	43	2	0	3	.367	.362
Florida	.253	128	252	217	23	55	80	11	1	4	25	6	1	4	24	1	49	2	0	10	.369	.337
Chicago	.249	135	269	241	29	60	92	12	1	6	47	3	3	1	21	1	69	1	0	4	.382	.308
New York	.248	138	304	274	40	68	108	7	0	11	45	0	3	7	20	2	69	2	2	5	.394	.313
San Diego	.248	141	286	250	33	62	93	10	0	7	43	2	2	1	31	0	79	6	2	5	.372	.331
Pittsburgh	.230	127	225	200	27	46	78	13	2	5	29	2	0	2	21	1	57	2	1	2	.390	.309
Houston	.223	130	262	224	19	50	71	13	1	2	38	2	4	4	28	1	51	1	3	7	.317	.315
Montreal	.211	114	197	171	13	36	60	10	1	4	22	8	2	2	14	0	42	0	2	1	.351	.275
Cincinnati	.201	142	307	278	23	56	77	13	1	2	25	2	3	1	23	3	63	5	2	6	.277	.262
Atlanta	.188	130	271	223	24	42	68	7	2	5	32	8	7	2	31	2	48	1	1	4	.305	.285
Los Angeles	.188	137	256	218	19	41	60	9	2	2	28	6	2	1	29	2	65	1	0	5	.275	.284
St. Louis	.188	141	297	261	22	49	75	13	2	3	29	2	6	2	26	4	67	2	0	9	.287	.261
Philadelphia	.184	134	284	245	21	45	70	16	0	3	26	7	3	4	25	2	57	2	1	7	.286	.267
Totals	.224	1834	3637	3170	343	709	1075	161	14	59	441	52	39	33	343	19	816	27	15	70	.339	.303

INDIVIDUAL

TOP PINCH-HITTERS

Minimum 20 at-bats. *Lefthanded batter. †Switch-hitter.

Player, Team	Avg.	G	TPA	AB	R	H	TB	2B	3B	HR	RBI	SH	SF	HP	BB	IBB	SO	SB	CS	GDP	Slg.	OBP
Spiers, Bill, Houston*	.455	40	40	33	6	15	24	6	0	1	11	0	0	0	7	1	4	1	1	0	.727	.550
Vidro, Jose, Montreal†	.450	21	21	20	5	9	13	4	0	0	4	0	0	0	1	0	2	0	0	0	.650	.476
Sweeney, Mark, St.L.-S.D.*	.367	73	72	60	10	22	29	1	0	2	14	0	2	1	9	1	13	2	1	1	.483	.444
Hill, Glenallen, San Francisco	.360	28	28	25	6	9	13	4	0	0	5	0	1	0	2	0	8	0	0	0	.520	.393
Abbott, Kurt, Florida	.350	24	24	20	4	7	8	1	0	0	1	1	0	0	3	0	7	0	0	0	.400	.435
Arias, Alex, Florida	.346	31	31	26	5	9	12	0	0	1	4	2	0	1	2	0	5	0	0	2	.462	.414
Benard, Marvin, San Fran.*	.341	49	48	44	7	15	18	3	0	0	6	0	0	0	4	0	7	2	0	1	.409	.396
Bates, Jason, Colorado†	.333	25	25	21	5	7	13	6	0	0	2	0	0	0	4	0	6	0	0	0	.619	.440
Ward, Turner, Pittsburgh†	.333	25	25	21	7	7	13	3	0	1	5	0	0	0	4	0	2	0	1	0	.619	.440
McGee, Willie, St. Louis†	.314	56	56	51	6	16	28	5	2	1	6	0	0	0	5	2	9	0	0	4	.549	.375
Clark, Dave, Chicago*	.308	76	72	65	8	20	31	2	0	3	22	0	1	0	6	0	19	0	0	2	.477	.361
Lopez, Luis M., New York†	.308	26	26	26	3	8	9	1	0	0	3	0	0	0	0	0	8	0	0	0	.346	.308
Franco, Matt, New York*	.306	71	66	62	7	19	31	3	0	3	13	0	0	0	4	1	9	0	0	2	.500	.348
Jordan, Kevin, Philadelphia	.289	47	47	45	6	13	23	4	0	2	12	0	0	0	2	0	10	0	0	1	.511	.319
Hansen, Dave, Chicago*	.286	45	40	35	3	10	17	2	1	1	2	0	0	0	5	0	6	0	0	0	.486	.375
Hernandez, Jose, Chicago	.286	33	33	28	6	8	12	1	0	1	4	0	1	0	4	0	9	1	0	0	.429	.364
Taubensee, Eddie, Cincinnati*	.286	38	37	35	2	10	14	4	0	0	6	0	0	0	2	0	10	0	0	0	.400	.324
Eisenreich, Jim, Florida*	.286	44	39	35	2	10	16	6	0	0	5	0	1	1	2	1	6	0	0	2	.457	.333
Jones, Chris C., San Diego	.286	34	34	28	4	8	12	4	0	0	6	0	0	1	4	0	14	0	0	0	.429	.394
Lewis, Mark, San Francisco	.286	24	24	21	3	6	8	2	0	0	2	0	0	0	3	0	2	0	0	0	.381	.375

ALL PINCH-HITTERS

*Lefthanded batter. †Switch-hitter.

Player, Team	Avg.	G	TPA	AB	R	H	TB	2B	3B	HR	RBI	SH	SF	HP	BB	IBB	SO	SB	CS	GDP	Slg.	OBP
Abbott, Kurt, Florida	.350	24	24	20	4	7	8	1	0	0	1	1	0	0	3	0	7	0	0	0	.400	.435
Abreu, Bob, Houston*	.444	11	10	9	4	4	6	0	1	0	4	0	0	0	1	0	2	0	0	0	.667	.500
Alexander, Manny, N.Y.-Chi.	.500	3	3	2	1	1	1	0	0	0	1	0	0	0	1	0	1	0	0	0	.500	.667
Alfonzo, Edgardo, New York	.200	6	6	5	1	1	2	1	0	0	2	0	1	0	0	0	3	0	0	0	.400	.167
Allensworth, Jermaine, Pit.	.000	4	4	3	0	0	0	0	0	0	0	1	0	0	0	0	2	0	0	0	.000	.000
Alou, Moises, Florida	.333	3	3	3	0	1	1	0	0	0	1	0	0	0	0	0	0	0	0	0	.333	.333
Amaro, Ruben Jr., Philadelphia†	.173	64	64	52	4	9	15	3	0	1	6	0	1	2	9	0	11	0	1	0	.288	.313
Anthony, Eric, Los Angeles*	.143	29	26	21	3	3	4	1	0	0	2	0	0	0	5	1	4	0	0	0	.190	.308
Arias, Alex, Florida	.346	31	31	26	5	9	12	0	0	1	4	2	0	1	2	0	5	0	0	2	.462	.414
Arias, George, San Diego	.000	3	3	3	0	0	0	0	0	0	0	0	0	0	0	0	1	0	0	0	.000	.000
Ashley, Billy, Los Angeles	.176	37	37	34	4	6	13	1	0	2	5	0	0	0	3	0	17	0	0	2	.382	.243
Aurilia, Rich, San Fran.	.444	11	11	9	1	4	5	1	0	0	3	0	0	0	2	0	1	0	0	0	.556	.545
Ausmus, Brad, Houston	.000	4	4	4	0	0	0	0	0	0	0	0	0	0	0	0	1	0	0	1	.000	.000
Baerga, Carlos, New York†	.250	8	8	8	0	2	2	0	0	0	1	0	0	0	0	0	1	0	0	0	.250	.250
Bagwell, Jeff, Houston	.333	3	3	3	0	1	2	1	0	0	2	0	0	0	0	0	0	0	0	0	.667	.333
Barron, Tony, Philadelphia	.250	4	4	4	0	1	2	1	0	0	0	0	0	0	0	0	1	0	0	0	.500	.250
Bates, Jason, Colorado†	.333	25	25	21	5	7	13	6	0	0	2	0	0	0	4	0	6	0	0	0	.619	.440
Bautista, Danny, Atlanta	.364	16	15	11	1	4	9	0	1	1	4	0	1	1	2	0	0	0	0	0	.818	.467
Beamon, Trey, San Diego*	.208	27	26	24	2	5	6	1	0	0	4	0	0	0	2	0	9	1	0	0	.250	.269
Bell, David, St. Louis	.000	6	5	5	0	0	0	0	0	0	0	0	0	0	0	0	1	0	0	0	.000	.000
Bell, Derek, Houston	.500	5	5	4	1	2	2	0	0	0	0	0	0	0	1	0	0	0	0	0	.500	.600
Belliard, Rafael, Atlanta	.000	5	5	4	0	0	0	0	0	0	0	1	0	0	0	0	1	0	0	0	.000	.000
Benard, Marvin, San Fran.*	.341	49	48	44	7	15	18	3	0	0	6	0	0	0	4	0	7	2	0	1	.409	.396
Berblinger, Jeff, St. Louis	.000	2	2	1	0	0	0	0	0	0	0	1	0	0	0	0	0	0	0	0	.000	.000
Berry, Sean, Houston	.000	12	12	9	0	0	0	0	0	0	0	1	0	1	0	0	1	0	0	1	.000	.167
Berryhill, Damon, San Fran.†	.263	23	23	19	1	5	7	2	0	0	5	0	0	0	3	0	0	0	0	0	.368	.391
Bichette, Dante, Colorado	.667	7	7	6	0	4	6	2	0	0	4	0	1	0	0	0	0	0	0	0	1.000	.571

Player, Team	Avg.	G	TPA	AB	R	H	TB	2B	3B	HR	RBI	SH	SF	HP	BB	IBB	SO	SB	CS	GDP	Slg.	OBP
Bieser, Steve, New York*	.136	26	25	22	5	3	3	0	0	0	0	0	0	1	2	0	8	0	0	0	.136	.240
Biggio, Craig, Houston	.000	3	3	2	0	0	0	0	0	0	1	0	1	0	0	0	1	0	0	0	.000	.000
Blanco, Henry, Los Angeles	.500	2	2	2	0	1	1	0	0	0	0	0	0	0	0	0	0	0	0	0	.500	.500
Blauser, Jeff, Atlanta	.500	3	3	2	0	1	1	0	0	0	1	0	1	0	0	0	1	0	0	0	.500	.333
Bogar, Tim, Houston	.000	4	4	4	0	0	0	0	0	0	0	0	0	0	0	0	2	0	0	0	.000	.000
Bohanon, Brian, New York*	.500	2	2	2	0	1	1	0	0	0	0	0	0	0	0	0	1	0	0	0	.500	.500
Bonilla, Bobby, Florida†	.000	1	1	0	0	0	0	0	0	0	0	0	0	1	0	0	0	0	0	0	.000	1.000
Boone, Aaron, Cincinnati	.250	4	4	4	1	1	1	0	0	0	0	0	0	0	0	0	1	0	0	0	.250	.250
Boone, Bret, Cincinnati	.200	5	5	5	0	1	1	0	0	0	0	0	0	0	0	0	0	0	0	0	.200	.200
Branson, Jeff, Cincinnati*	.150	24	22	20	3	3	3	0	0	0	0	0	0	2	0	0	4	0	0	0	.150	.227
Brogna, Rico, Philadelphia*	.000	7	7	7	0	0	0	0	0	0	0	0	0	0	0	0	2	0	0	0	.000	.000
Brown, Adrian, Pittsburgh†	.333	4	4	3	1	1	1	0	0	0	0	0	0	0	1	0	0	0	0	0	.333	.500
Brown, Brant, Chicago*	.143	7	7	7	0	1	1	0	0	0	0	0	0	0	0	0	4	0	0	0	.143	.143
Brown, Emil, Pittsburgh	.130	25	25	23	2	3	4	1	0	0	2	0	0	1	1	0	6	0	0	1	.174	.200
Bruske, Jim, San Diego	.000	1	1	1	0	0	0	0	0	0	0	0	0	0	0	0	1	0	0	0	.000	.000
Burke, John, Colorado*	.000	1	1	1	0	0	0	0	0	0	0	0	0	0	0	0	0	0	0	0	.000	.000
Burks, Ellis, Colorado	.000	9	9	7	0	0	0	0	0	0	1	0	0	0	2	0	2	0	0	1	.000	.222
Butler, Brett, Los Angeles*	.125	11	11	8	0	1	1	0	0	0	0	2	0	0	1	0	0	0	0	0	.125	.222
Butler, Rob, Philadelphia*	.176	20	20	17	2	3	5	2	0	0	3	0	1	0	2	0	3	0	0	0	.294	.250
Cabrera, Orlando, Montreal	1.000	1	1	1	1	1	1	0	0	0	1	0	0	0	0	0	0	0	0	0	1.000	1.000
Cairo, Miguel, Chicago	.000	5	5	4	1	0	0	0	0	0	0	0	0	0	1	0	0	0	0	0	.000	.200
Caminiti, Ken, San Diego†	.000	4	4	3	0	0	0	0	0	0	1	0	1	0	0	0	1	0	0	0	.000	.000
Candiotti, Tom, Los Angeles	.000	1	1	1	0	0	0	0	0	0	0	0	0	0	0	0	0	0	0	0	.000	.000
Cangelosi, John, Florida†	.178	48	48	45	4	8	13	2	0	1	2	0	0	0	3	0	8	1	0	1	.289	.229
Carr, Chuck, Houston†	.125	8	8	8	1	1	2	1	0	0	0	0	0	0	0	0	4	0	0	0	.250	.125
Castilla, Vinny, Colorado	.500	2	2	2	0	1	1	0	0	0	0	0	0	0	0	0	1	0	0	0	.500	.500
Castillo, Alberto, New York	.333	3	3	3	0	1	1	0	0	0	0	0	0	0	0	0	0	0	0	0	.333	.333
Castillo, Luis, Florida†	.250	5	5	4	1	1	1	0	0	0	0	0	0	0	1	0	0	0	0	0	.250	.400
Castro, Juan, Los Angeles	.000	2	2	1	0	0	0	0	0	0	0	1	0	0	0	0	1	0	0	0	.000	.000
Cedeno, Roger, Los Angeles†	.333	10	10	6	1	2	2	0	0	0	1	0	0	1	3	0	2	1	0	0	.333	.600
Chavez, Raul, Montreal	.000	2	2	2	0	0	0	0	0	0	0	0	0	0	0	0	0	0	0	0	.000	.000
Cianfrocco, Archi, San Diego	.143	8	7	7	1	1	1	0	0	0	0	0	0	0	0	0	4	0	0	0	.143	.143
Clark, Dave, Chicago*	.308	76	72	65	8	20	31	2	0	3	22	0	1	0	6	0	19	0	0	2	.477	.361
Clayton, Royce, St. Louis	.000	2	2	0	0	0	0	0	0	0	0	0	0	0	2	0	0	0	0	0	.000	1.000
Colbrunn, Greg, Atlanta	.500	17	17	16	1	8	12	1	0	1	2	1	0	0	0	0	3	0	0	0	.750	.500
Coles, Darnell, Colorado	.267	16	16	15	0	4	5	1	0	0	1	0	0	1	0	0	3	0	0	0	.333	.313
Collier, Lou, Pittsburgh	.500	2	2	2	1	1	1	0	0	0	0	0	0	0	0	0	0	0	0	0	.500	.500
Conine, Jeff, Florida	.188	19	19	16	1	3	6	0	0	1	1	0	0	0	3	0	5	0	0	2	.375	.316
Cook, Dennis, Florida*	1.000	2	2	2	1	2	2	0	0	0	1	0	0	0	0	0	0	0	0	1	1.000	1.000
Counsell, Craig, Florida*	.333	3	3	3	1	1	1	0	0	0	0	0	0	0	0	0	0	0	0	0	.333	.333
Crawford, Joe, New York*	.000	1	1	1	0	0	0	0	0	0	0	0	0	0	0	0	1	0	0	0	.000	.000
Cromer, Tripp, Los Angeles	.000	2	1	1	0	0	0	0	0	0	0	0	0	0	0	0	0	0	0	0	.000	.000
Cruz, Jacob, San Fran.*	.167	7	7	6	1	1	2	1	0	0	0	0	0	0	1	0	1	0	0	1	.333	.286
Cummings, Midre, Pit.-Phi.*	.189	39	39	37	2	7	14	2	1	1	6	0	0	2	0	0	11	0	0	0	.378	.231
Daulton, Darren, Phi.-Fla.*	.154	16	16	13	0	2	2	0	0	0	2	0	0	1	2	0	4	0	0	0	.154	.313
Delgado, Wilson, San Fran.†	.000	4	4	3	0	0	0	0	0	0	0	1	0	0	0	0	1	0	0	0	.000	.000
DeShields, Delino, St. Louis*	.375	8	8	8	3	3	9	0	0	2	3	0	0	0	0	0	2	1	0	1	1.125	.375
Difelice, Mike, St. Louis	.000	2	2	2	0	0	0	0	0	0	0	0	0	0	0	0	2	0	0	0	.000	.000
Dunston, Shawon, Chicago	.500	2	2	2	0	1	2	1	0	0	0	0	0	0	0	0	0	0	0	0	1.000	.500
Dunwoody, Todd, Florida*	.250	4	4	4	0	1	1	0	0	0	0	0	0	0	0	0	2	0	0	0	.250	.250
Echevarria, Angel, Colorado	.250	8	8	8	2	2	2	0	0	0	0	0	0	0	0	0	1	0	0	0	.250	.250
Eisenreich, Jim, Florida*	.286	44	39	35	2	10	16	6	0	0	5	0	1	1	2	1	6	0	0	2	.457	.333
Estalella, Bobby, Philadelphia	.000	3	3	3	0	0	0	0	0	0	0	0	0	0	0	0	2	0	0	1	.000	.000
Eusebio, Tony, Houston	.333	17	17	12	0	4	4	0	0	0	5	0	0	1	4	0	2	0	0	0	.333	.529
Everett, Carl, New York†	.200	28	28	25	3	5	8	0	0	1	3	0	0	0	3	1	8	1	0	0	.320	.286
Fernandez, Alex, Florida	.000	1	1	0	0	0	0	0	0	0	0	1	0	0	0	0	0	0	0	0	.000	.000
Finley, Steve, San Diego*	.500	10	10	8	3	4	4	0	0	0	2	0	0	0	2	0	1	2	0	0	.500	.600
Flaherty, John, San Diego	.333	5	5	3	0	1	1	0	0	0	0	0	0	0	2	0	0	0	0	1	.333	.600
Fletcher, Darrin, Montreal*	.214	15	15	14	1	3	7	1	0	1	1	0	0	1	0	0	4	0	0	0	.500	.267
Floyd, Cliff, Florida*	.056	24	24	18	2	1	3	0	1	0	1	0	0	0	6	0	4	1	0	0	.167	.292
Fonville, Chad, Los Angeles†	.333	4	4	3	0	1	1	0	0	0	1	0	0	0	1	0	1	0	0	0	.333	.500
Fordyce, Brook, Cincinnati	.167	14	13	12	0	2	2	0	0	0	0	0	0	1	0	0	2	0	0	0	.167	.231
Foster, Kevin, Chicago	.000	4	4	4	0	0	0	0	0	0	0	0	1	0	0	0	3	0	0	0	.000	.000
Franco, Matt, New York*	.306	71	66	62	7	19	31	3	0	3	13	0	0	4	1	0	9	0	0	2	.500	.348
Franklin, Micah, St. Louis†	.167	6	6	6	0	1	1	0	0	0	0	0	0	0	0	0	4	0	0	0	.167	.167
Fullmer, Brad, Montreal*	.273	11	11	11	2	3	10	1	0	2	3	0	0	0	0	0	2	0	0	1	.909	.273
Gaetti, Gary, St. Louis	.182	12	12	11	1	2	4	2	0	0	2	0	0	0	1	0	1	0	0	1	.364	.250
Gagne, Greg, Los Angeles	.000	1	1	1	0	0	0	0	0	0	0	0	0	0	0	0	0	0	0	0	.000	.000
Galarraga, Andres, Colorado	.000	1	1	1	0	0	0	0	0	0	0	0	0	0	0	0	1	0	0	0	.000	.000
Gallego, Mike, St. Louis	.200	5	5	5	1	1	1	0	0	0	0	0	0	0	0	0	1	0	0	0	.200	.200
Gant, Ron, St. Louis	.182	13	13	11	0	2	3	1	0	0	3	0	0	0	2	0	5	0	0	1	.273	.308
Garcia, Freddy, Pittsburgh	.000	8	8	8	0	0	0	0	0	0	0	0	0	0	0	0	7	0	0	0	.000	.000
Garcia, Karim, Los Angeles*	.000	5	5	4	0	0	0	0	0	0	1	0	1	0	0	0	4	0	0	0	.000	.000
Gardner, Mark, San Fran.	.000	2	2	1	0	0	0	0	0	0	0	0	0	0	1	0	0	0	0	0	.000	.500
Gilbert, Shawn, New York	.375	9	8	8	2	3	6	0	0	1	1	0	0	0	0	0	2	0	0	0	.750	.375
Gilkey, Bernard, New York	.200	8	8	5	2	1	4	0	0	1	5	0	1	1	1	0	1	0	0	0	.800	.375
Giovanola, Ed, Atlanta*	.000	4	4	4	0	0	0	0	0	0	0	0	0	0	0	0	1	0	0	2	.000	.000
Glanville, Doug, Chicago	.222	10	10	9	2	2	3	1	0	0	4	1	0	0	0	0	0	0	0	0	.333	.222
Gonzales, Rene, Colorado	.500	2	2	2	0	1	1	0	0	0	0	0	0	0	0	0	0	0	0	0	.500	.500
Gonzalez, Luis, Houston*	.167	7	7	6	0	1	1	0	0	0	1	0	0	0	1	0	1	0	0	0	.167	.286
Goodwin, Curtis, Cincinnati*	.133	17	16	15	0	2	3	1	0	0	0	0	0	0	1	0	5	0	1	0	.200	.188
Grace, Mark, Chicago*	.333	3	3	3	0	1	1	0	0	0	1	0	0	0	0	0	0	0	0	0	.333	.333

1997 N.L. STATISTICS — Pinch-hitting

Player, Team	Avg.	G	TPA	AB	R	H	TB	2B	3B	HR	RBI	SH	SF	HP	BB	IBB	SO	SB	CS	GDP	Slg.	OBP
Graffanino, Tony, Atlanta	.294	22	22	17	3	5	12	2	1	1	1	1	0	0	4	0	5	0	1	0	.706	.429
Green, Scarborough, St. Louis	.000	2	2	2	0	0	0	0	0	0	0	0	0	0	0	0	0	0	0	0	.000	.000
Greene, Willie, Cincinnati*	.091	12	12	11	0	1	1	0	0	0	0	2	0	0	1	0	1	1	0	0	.091	.167
Gregg, Tommy, Atlanta*	.000	8	8	8	0	0	0	0	0	0	0	0	0	0	0	0	0	0	0	0	.000	.000
Guerrero, Vladimir, Montreal	.000	5	5	5	0	0	0	0	0	0	0	0	0	0	0	0	0	0	0	0	.000	.000
Guerrero, Wilton, Los Angeles†	.250	13	13	12	2	3	5	0	1	0	0	0	0	0	1	0	4	0	0	0	.417	.308
Guillen, Jose, Pittsburgh	.375	8	8	8	2	3	3	0	0	0	0	0	0	0	0	0	1	0	0	0	.375	.375
Gulan, Mike, St. Louis	.000	4	4	3	0	0	0	0	0	0	0	0	0	0	1	0	3	0	0	0	.000	.250
Gutierrez, Ricky, Houston	.231	16	15	13	0	3	3	0	0	0	4	0	0	1	1	0	0	0	0	1	.231	.333
Gwynn, Tony, San Diego*	.667	3	3	3	0	2	2	0	0	0	3	0	0	0	0	0	0	0	0	0	.667	.667
Hale, Chip, Los Angeles*	.083	13	13	12	0	1	1	0	0	0	0	0	0	0	1	0	4	0	0	0	.083	.154
Hamilton, Darryl, San Fran.*	.143	8	8	7	0	1	1	0	0	0	0	0	0	0	1	0	2	0	0	0	.143	.250
Hansen, Dave, Chicago*	.286	45	40	35	3	10	17	2	1	1	2	0	0	0	5	0	6	0	0	0	.486	.375
Hardtke, Jason, New York†	.100	11	11	10	1	1	1	0	0	0	0	0	0	0	1	0	2	1	0	1	.100	.182
Harris, Lenny, Cincinnati*	.205	50	49	44	5	9	11	2	0	0	7	1	2	1	1	0	8	2	0	2	.250	.229
Helton, Todd, Colorado*	.250	13	13	12	1	3	6	0	0	1	2	0	0	0	1	0	3	0	0	0	.500	.308
Henderson, Rickey, San Diego	.143	10	10	7	2	1	4	0	0	1	1	0	0	0	3	0	3	0	0	0	.571	.400
Hernandez, Carlos, San Diego	.400	5	5	5	2	2	5	0	0	1	1	0	0	0	0	0	2	0	0	0	1.000	.400
Hernandez, Jose, Chicago	.286	33	33	28	6	8	12	1	0	1	4	0	1	0	4	0	9	1	0	0	.429	.364
Hidalgo, Rich, Houston	.000	2	2	1	0	0	0	0	0	0	0	0	0	0	1	0	1	0	0	0	.000	.500
Hill, Glenallen, San Fran.	.360	28	28	25	6	9	13	4	0	0	5	0	1	1	1	0	8	0	0	0	.520	.393
Hollandsworth, Todd, L.A.*	.429	15	15	14	2	6	8	2	0	0	3	0	0	0	1	0	3	0	0	0	.571	.467
Houston, Tyler, Chicago*	.158	21	20	19	0	3	5	2	0	0	4	0	0	0	1	0	6	0	0	1	.263	.200
Howard, Thomas, Houston*	.267	52	52	45	4	12	16	4	0	0	5	0	1	1	5	0	12	0	1	2	.356	.346
Hubbard, Mike, Chicago	.111	9	9	9	0	1	1	0	0	0	0	0	0	0	0	0	5	0	0	0	.111	.111
Hudler, Rex, Philadelphia	.067	17	17	15	1	1	1	0	0	0	0	0	0	0	2	0	6	0	0	0	.067	.176
Hundley, Todd, New York†	.273	12	12	11	1	3	3	0	0	0	0	0	0	0	1	0	3	0	0	0	.273	.333
Huskey, Butch, New York	.313	18	17	16	2	5	12	1	0	2	4	0	0	1	0	0	6	0	0	1	.750	.353
Ingram, Garey, Los Angeles	.000	2	1	1	0	0	0	0	0	0	0	0	0	0	0	0	1	0	0	0	.000	.000
Jackson, Damian, Cincinnati	.000	1	1	1	0	0	0	0	0	0	0	0	0	0	0	0	0	0	0	0	.000	.000
Javier, Stan, San Fran.†	.133	18	18	15	3	2	6	1	0	1	2	0	0	0	3	0	6	0	0	1	.400	.278
Jefferies, Gregg, Philadelphia†	.400	7	7	5	2	2	2	0	0	0	1	0	0	0	2	2	1	0	0	0	.400	.571
Jennings, Robin, Chicago*	.200	6	5	5	1	1	2	1	0	0	1	0	0	0	0	0	1	0	0	0	.400	.200
Jensen, Marcus, San Fran.†	.000	3	3	3	0	0	0	0	0	0	0	0	0	0	0	0	2	0	0	0	.000	.000
Johnson, Brian, San Fran.	.000	1	1	0	0	0	0	0	0	0	0	0	0	0	1	0	0	0	0	0	.000	1.000
Johnson, Charles, Florida	.000	1	1	1	0	0	0	0	0	0	0	0	0	0	0	0	0	0	0	0	.000	.000
Johnson, Lance, N.Y.-Chi.*	.300	11	11	10	1	3	3	0	0	0	2	0	1	0	0	0	2	0	1	0	.300	.273
Johnson, Mark, Pittsburgh*	.143	17	17	14	1	2	3	1	0	0	3	0	0	0	3	0	5	0	0	0	.214	.294
Johnson, Russ, Houston	.167	7	7	6	0	1	1	0	0	0	0	1	0	0	0	0	1	0	0	0	.167	.167
Jones, Andruw, Atlanta	.045	29	29	22	2	1	1	0	0	0	2	1	0	0	6	0	5	1	0	0	.045	.250
Jones, Chipper, Atlanta†	.500	3	3	2	0	1	1	0	0	0	0	0	0	0	1	1	0	0	0	0	.500	.667
Jones, Chris C., San Diego	.286	34	34	28	4	8	12	4	0	0	5	1	0	1	4	0	14	0	0	0	.429	.394
Jordan, Brian, St. Louis	.000	5	5	5	0	0	0	0	0	0	0	0	0	0	0	0	1	0	0	0	.000	.000
Jordan, Kevin, Philadelphia	.289	47	47	45	6	13	23	4	0	2	12	0	0	0	2	0	10	0	0	1	.511	.319
Joyner, Wally, San Diego*	.455	11	11	11	1	5	6	1	0	0	5	0	0	0	0	0	2	0	0	1	.545	.455
Kelly, Mike, Cincinnati	.167	26	26	24	3	4	10	1	1	1	4	0	1	0	1	0	5	0	0	0	.417	.192
Kendall, Jason, Pittsburgh	.500	2	2	2	0	1	1	0	0	0	0	0	0	0	0	0	1	0	0	0	.500	.500
Kent, Jeff, San Fran.	.000	2	2	2	0	0	0	0	0	0	0	0	0	0	0	0	0	0	0	0	.000	.000
Kieschnick, Brooks, Chicago*	.100	12	12	10	1	1	2	1	0	0	0	0	0	0	2	0	4	0	0	0	.200	.250
Kirby, Wayne, Los Angeles*	.059	22	21	17	2	1	1	0	0	0	2	0	0	0	4	0	6	0	0	0	.059	.238
Klesko, Ryan, Atlanta*	.000	8	8	7	1	0	0	0	0	0	0	0	0	0	1	1	3	0	0	0	.000	.125
Konerko, Paul, Los Angeles	.333	4	3	3	0	1	1	0	0	0	0	0	0	0	0	0	1	0	0	2	.333	.333
Lampkin, Tom, St. Louis*	.171	38	38	35	3	6	7	1	0	0	3	0	1	0	2	0	4	0	0	2	.200	.211
Lankford, Ray, St. Louis*	.000	2	2	2	1	0	0	0	0	0	0	0	0	0	0	0	0	0	0	0	.000	.000
Larkin, Barry, Cincinnati	.333	8	8	6	0	2	2	0	0	0	0	0	0	0	2	1	1	0	0	0	.333	.500
Lee, Derrek, San Diego	.167	6	6	6	1	1	2	1	0	0	0	0	0	0	0	0	3	0	0	0	.333	.167
Lemke, Mark, Atlanta†	.000	5	5	1	0	0	0	0	0	0	0	2	1	1	1	0	0	0	0	0	.000	.250
Lewis, Darren, Los Angeles	.750	4	4	4	2	3	5	0	1	0	2	0	0	0	0	0	0	0	0	1	1.250	.750
Lewis, Mark, San Fran.	.286	24	24	21	3	6	8	2	0	0	2	0	0	0	3	0	2	0	0	0	.381	.375
Lieberthal, Mike, Philadelphia	.111	9	9	9	1	1	1	0	0	0	0	0	0	0	0	0	1	0	0	1	.111	.111
Liriano, Nelson, Los Angeles†	.146	60	56	48	3	7	10	3	0	0	5	2	1	0	5	0	9	0	1	1	.208	.222
Listach, Pat, Houston†	.067	17	17	15	0	1	1	0	0	0	0	2	0	0	2	0	4	0	0	1	.067	.176
Livingstone, Scott, S.D.-St.L.*	.174	55	51	46	2	8	10	2	0	0	6	0	2	0	3	0	10	0	0	1	.217	.216
Lockhart, Keith, Atlanta*	.268	70	68	56	12	15	24	3	0	2	18	2	2	1	7	0	3	0	0	0	.429	.348
Lopez, Javier, Atlanta	.167	14	14	12	0	2	2	0	0	0	1	0	0	0	2	0	4	0	0	0	.167	.286
Lopez, Luis M., New York†	.308	26	26	26	3	8	9	1	0	0	3	0	0	0	0	0	8	0	0	0	.346	.308
Lowery, Terrell, Chicago	.400	6	6	5	1	2	2	0	0	0	0	0	0	0	1	0	2	0	0	0	.400	.500
Mabry, John, St. Louis*	.000	6	6	4	0	0	0	0	0	0	0	0	0	1	1	0	1	0	0	0	.000	.333
Manwaring, Kirt, Colorado	.000	3	3	2	0	0	0	0	0	0	0	0	0	0	1	0	0	0	0	0	.000	.333
Marrero, Eli, St. Louis	.000	1	1	0	0	0	0	0	0	0	0	0	1	0	0	0	0	0	0	0	.000	.000
Martin, Al, Pittsburgh*	.000	3	3	2	1	0	0	0	0	0	0	0	0	0	1	1	1	0	0	0	.000	.333
May, Derrick, Philadelphia*	.115	30	28	26	1	3	4	1	0	0	1	0	0	0	2	0	6	1	0	3	.154	.179
McCracken, Quinton, Colorado†	.333	15	14	12	4	4	4	0	0	0	0	0	0	0	2	0	3	0	0	0	.333	.429
McGee, Willie, St. Louis†	.314	56	56	51	6	16	28	5	2	1	6	0	0	0	5	2	9	0	0	4	.549	.375
McGriff, Fred, Atlanta*	.000	3	3	2	1	0	0	0	0	0	0	0	0	0	1	0	0	0	0	0	.000	.333
McGuire, Ryan, Montreal*	.250	10	9	8	0	2	2	0	0	0	1	0	0	0	1	0	4	0	1	0	.250	.333
McGwire, Mark, St. Louis	.000	2	2	1	0	0	0	0	0	0	0	0	0	0	1	0	0	0	0	0	.000	.500
McMillon, Billy, Fla.-Phi.*	.167	13	13	12	0	2	3	1	0	0	2	0	1	0	0	0	6	0	0	0	.250	.154
McRae, Brian, Chi.-N.Y.†	.500	9	9	6	4	3	6	0	0	1	4	0	1	1	1	0	2	0	0	0	1.000	.556
Mejia, Roberto, St. Louis	.000	3	3	3	0	0	0	0	0	0	0	0	0	0	0	0	1	0	0	0	.000	.000
Mendoza, Carlos, New York*	.250	5	5	4	1	1	1	0	0	0	0	0	0	0	1	0	0	0	0	0	.250	.400
Mercker, Kent, Cincinnati*	.000	2	2	0	0	0	0	0	0	0	0	1	0	0	1	0	0	0	0	0	.000	1.000

Player, Team	Avg.	G	TPA	AB	R	H	TB	2B	3B	HR	RBI	SH	SF	HP	BB	IBB	SO	SB	CS	GDP	Slg.	OBP
Meulens, Hensley, Montreal	.000	7	7	6	0	0	0	0	0	0	1	0	1	0	0	0	4	0	0	0	.000	.000
Mondesi, Raul, Los Angeles	1.000	1	1	1	0	1	2	1	0	0	0	0	0	0	0	0	0	0	0	0	2.000	1.000
Montgomery, Ray, Houston	.182	13	13	11	2	2	3	1	0	0	0	0	0	0	2	0	3	0	0	0	.273	.308
Morandini, Mickey, Phi.*	.333	4	4	3	0	1	2	1	0	0	0	0	0	1	0	0	1	1	0	0	.667	.500
Mordecai, Mike, Atlanta	.059	39	39	34	3	2	3	1	0	0	1	1	1	0	3	0	9	0	0	1	.088	.132
Morgan, Kevin, New York	.000	1	1	1	0	0	0	0	0	0	0	0	0	0	0	0	0	0	0	0	.000	.000
Morman, Russ, Florida	.000	2	2	2	0	0	0	0	0	0	0	0	0	0	0	0	2	0	0	0	.000	.000
Morris, Hal, Cincinnati*	.091	11	11	11	0	1	1	0	0	0	0	0	0	0	0	0	1	0	0	0	.091	.091
Morris, Matt, St. Louis	.000	1	1	1	0	0	0	0	0	0	0	0	0	0	0	0	1	0	0	0	.000	.000
Mouton, James, Houston	.111	19	19	18	0	2	2	0	0	0	0	1	0	0	0	0	8	0	1	0	.111	.111
Mueller, Bill, San Fran.†	.000	9	9	7	1	0	0	0	0	0	0	1	0	1	0	0	1	0	0	0	.000	.111
Murray, Eddie, Los Angeles†	.286	9	9	7	0	2	2	0	0	0	3	0	0	0	2	0	2	0	0	2	.286	.444
Myers, Greg, Atlanta*	.167	7	6	6	0	1	1	0	0	0	0	0	0	0	0	0	3	0	0	0	.167	.167
Nixon, Otis, Los Angeles†	.000	1	1	1	0	0	0	0	0	0	0	0	0	0	0	0	0	0	0	0	.000	.000
Nunnally, Jon, Cincinnati*	.000	11	10	10	0	0	0	0	0	0	0	0	0	0	0	0	5	1	0	0	.000	.000
Obando, Sherman, Montreal	.091	27	25	22	0	2	2	0	0	0	4	0	0	0	3	0	9	0	1	0	.091	.200
Ochoa, Alex, New York	.231	31	31	26	5	6	13	1	0	2	4	0	0	2	3	0	6	0	1	0	.500	.355
Olerud, John, New York*	.000	10	10	6	1	0	0	0	0	0	1	0	0	2	2	0	2	0	0	1	.000	.400
Oliver, Joe, Cincinnati	.125	8	8	8	0	1	1	0	0	0	0	0	0	0	0	0	1	0	0	0	.125	.125
Ordaz, Luis, St. Louis	.000	1	1	1	0	0	0	0	0	0	0	0	0	0	0	0	0	0	0	0	.000	.000
Ordonez, Rey, New York	.500	2	2	2	1	1	1	0	0	0	2	0	0	0	0	0	0	0	0	0	.500	.500
Orie, Kevin, Chicago	.500	4	4	4	2	2	5	0	1	1	0	0	0	0	0	0	1	0	0	0	1.250	.500
Orsulak, Joe, Montreal*	.167	32	30	24	0	4	7	3	0	0	0	0	0	0	6	0	3	0	1	0	.292	.333
Osik, Keith, Pittsburgh	.308	14	14	13	0	4	4	0	0	0	0	0	0	0	1	0	3	0	0	0	.308	.357
Otero, Ricky, Philadelphia†	.333	10	10	9	1	3	4	1	0	0	0	0	0	0	1	0	1	0	0	0	.444	.400
Owens, Eric, Cincinnati	.333	8	8	6	1	2	2	0	0	0	0	0	0	2	0	0	1	0	1	0	.333	.500
Pagnozzi, Tom, St. Louis	.300	11	10	10	1	3	5	2	0	0	2	0	0	0	0	0	2	0	0	0	.500	.300
Parent, Mark, Philadelphia	.000	1	1	1	0	0	0	0	0	0	0	0	0	0	0	0	1	0	0	0	.000	.000
Pena, Tony, Houston	.000	1	1	1	0	0	0	0	0	0	0	0	0	0	0	0	1	0	0	0	.000	.000
Pendleton, Terry, Cincinnati†	.200	24	24	20	0	4	6	2	0	0	4	0	0	0	4	1	4	0	0	1	.300	.333
Perez, Eddie, Atlanta	.000	3	3	3	0	0	0	0	0	0	0	0	0	0	0	0	1	0	0	0	.000	.000
Perez, Eduardo, Cincinnati	.238	27	24	21	3	5	9	1	0	1	2	0	0	3	0	0	3	0	0	2	.429	.333
Perez, Neifi, Colorado†	.000	2	2	2	0	0	0	0	0	0	0	0	0	0	0	0	1	0	0	0	.000	.000
Petagine, Roberto, New York*	.143	7	7	7	1	1	1	0	0	0	2	0	0	0	0	0	3	0	0	0	.143	.143
Phillips, J.R., Houston*	.125	8	8	8	1	1	4	0	0	1	3	0	0	0	0	0	3	0	0	0	.500	.125
Piazza, Mike, Los Angeles	.000	6	6	5	0	0	0	0	0	0	0	0	0	0	1	0	2	0	0	0	.000	.167
Plantier, Phil, S.D.-St.L.*	.100	17	13	10	0	1	1	0	0	0	0	0	0	0	3	0	5	0	0	0	.100	.308
Polcovich, Kevin, Pittsburgh	.000	1	1	1	0	0	0	0	0	0	0	0	0	0	0	0	0	0	0	0	.000	.000
Powell, Dante, San Fran.	.333	3	3	3	1	1	1	0	0	0	0	0	0	0	0	0	2	0	0	0	.333	.333
Pratt, Todd, New York	.000	3	3	3	0	0	0	0	0	0	0	0	0	0	0	0	1	0	0	0	.000	.000
Prince, Tom, Los Angeles	.500	3	3	2	0	1	2	1	0	0	2	1	0	0	0	0	1	0	0	0	1.000	.500
Pulliam, Harvey, Colorado	.269	29	28	26	6	7	13	0	0	2	4	0	0	0	2	0	8	0	1	1	.500	.321
Raabe, Brian, Colorado	.000	1	1	0	0	0	0	0	0	0	0	0	0	0	0	0	0	0	0	0	.000	.000
Ramos, Ken, Houston*	.000	14	14	11	0	0	0	0	0	0	1	0	1	0	2	0	0	0	0	1	.000	.143
Randa, Joe, Pittsburgh	1.000	1	1	1	0	1	1	0	0	0	0	0	0	0	0	0	0	0	0	0	1.000	1.000
Reed, Jeff, Colorado*	.333	18	18	12	2	4	4	0	0	0	2	1	0	0	5	0	4	0	1	0	.333	.529
Reese, Pokey, Cincinnati	.500	2	2	2	1	1	2	1	0	0	0	0	0	0	0	0	1	0	0	0	1.000	.500
Relaford, Desi, Philadelphia†	.000	3	3	2	0	0	0	0	0	0	0	0	0	0	1	0	0	0	0	0	.000	.333
Renteria, Edgar, Florida	.000	1	1	1	0	0	0	0	0	0	0	0	0	0	0	0	1	0	0	0	.000	.000
Riggs, Adam, Los Angeles	.000	1	1	1	0	0	0	0	0	0	0	0	0	0	0	0	0	0	0	0	.000	.000
Rivera, Luis, Houston	.000	1	1	1	0	0	0	0	0	0	0	0	0	0	0	0	1	0	0	0	.000	.000
Rivera, Ruben, San Diego	.143	7	7	7	0	1	2	1	0	0	0	0	0	0	0	0	3	0	0	0	.286	.143
Robertson, Mike, Philadelphia*	.000	12	11	10	0	0	0	0	0	0	0	0	0	1	0	0	2	0	0	0	.000	.091
Rodriguez, Henry, Montreal*	.000	5	5	5	0	0	0	0	0	0	0	0	0	0	0	0	4	0	0	0	.000	.000
Romero, Mandy, San Diego†	.000	6	6	5	0	0	0	0	0	0	0	0	0	1	0	0	4	0	0	0	.000	.167
Rose, Pete Jr., Cincinnati*	.125	9	9	8	1	1	1	0	0	0	0	0	0	0	1	0	5	0	0	0	.125	.222
Sanchez, Rey, Chicago	.000	12	12	11	0	0	0	0	0	0	0	1	0	0	0	0	2	0	0	0	.000	.000
Sandberg, Ryne, Chicago	.200	10	10	10	0	2	2	0	0	0	2	0	0	0	0	0	5	0	0	1	.200	.200
Sanders, Deion, Cincinnati*	.500	4	4	4	2	2	2	0	0	0	0	0	0	0	0	0	1	1	0	0	.500	.500
Sanders, Reggie, Cincinnati	1.000	1	1	1	0	1	1	0	0	0	0	0	0	0	0	0	0	0	0	0	1.000	1.000
Santangelo, F.P., Montreal†	.111	15	15	9	1	1	1	0	0	0	1	3	1	1	1	0	1	0	0	0	.111	.250
Sefcik, Kevin, Philadelphia	.316	30	29	19	3	6	8	2	0	0	0	7	0	0	3	0	3	0	0	0	.421	.409
Servais, Scott, Chicago	.333	7	7	6	2	2	3	1	0	0	3	0	0	0	1	1	1	0	0	0	.500	.429
Sheaffer, Danny, St. Louis	.120	28	26	25	1	3	3	0	0	0	2	1	0	0	0	0	4	1	0	1	.120	.120
Sheffield, Gary, Florida	1.000	2	2	2	0	2	2	0	0	0	3	0	0	0	0	0	0	0	0	0	1.000	1.000
Shipley, Craig, San Diego	.083	25	25	24	1	2	5	0	0	1	2	0	0	0	1	0	3	0	0	0	.208	.120
Shumpert, Terry, San Diego	.500	2	2	2	0	1	1	0	0	0	0	0	0	0	0	0	0	0	0	0	.500	.500
Sierra, Ruben, Cincinnati†	.000	3	3	2	0	0	0	0	0	0	0	0	0	0	1	1	0	0	0	0	.000	.333
Simon, Randall, Atlanta*	.333	7	7	6	0	2	2	0	0	0	0	0	0	0	1	0	0	0	0	1	.333	.429
Slaught, Don, San Diego	.000	16	16	12	1	0	0	0	0	0	0	0	0	0	3	0	3	0	0	1	.000	.200
Smith, Mark, Pittsburgh	.375	19	19	16	6	6	15	1	1	2	5	0	0	0	3	0	1	1	0	1	.938	.474
Snow, J.T., San Fran.†	.000	4	4	2	1	0	0	0	0	0	0	0	0	0	2	0	1	0	0	0	.000	.500
Sosa, Sammy, Chicago	.000	1	1	1	0	0	0	0	0	0	0	0	0	0	0	0	1	0	0	0	.000	.000
Spehr, Tim, Atlanta	.000	1	1	1	0	0	0	0	0	0	0	0	0	0	0	0	0	0	0	0	.000	.000
Spiers, Bill, Houston*	.455	40	40	33	6	15	24	6	0	1	11	0	0	0	7	1	4	1	0	0	.727	.550
Stankiewicz, Andy, Montreal	.167	39	36	30	2	5	9	1	0	1	3	4	0	0	2	0	6	0	0	0	.300	.219
Stocker, Kevin, Philadelphia†	.000	2	2	2	0	0	0	0	0	0	0	0	0	0	0	0	1	0	0	0	.000	.000
Stottlemyre, Todd, St. Louis*	.000	1	1	1	0	0	0	0	0	0	0	0	0	0	0	0	1	0	0	0	.000	.000
Strange, Doug, Montreal†	.750	9	9	8	1	6	8	0	1	0	7	1	0	0	0	0	0	0	0	0	1.000	.750
Sveum, Dale, Pittsburgh†	.220	48	48	41	2	9	17	5	0	1	7	1	0	0	6	0	17	0	0	0	.415	.319
Sweeney, Mark, St.L.-S.D.*	.367	73	72	60	10	22	29	1	0	2	14	0	2	1	9	1	13	2	1	1	.483	.444
Swift, Bill C., Colorado	.000	1	1	0	0	0	0	0	0	0	0	1	0	0	0	0	0	0	0	0	.000	.000

Player, Team	Avg.	G	TPA	AB	R	H	TB	2B	3B	HR	RBI	SH	SF	HP	BB	IBB	SO	SB	CS	GDP	Slg.	OBP
Taubensee, Eddie, Cincinnati*	.286	38	37	35	2	10	14	4	0	0	6	0	0	0	2	0	10	0	0	0	.400	.324
Thurman, Gary, New York	.250	5	4	4	0	1	1	0	0	0	0	0	0	0	0	0	0	0	0	0	.250	.250
Timmons, Ozzie, Cincinnati	.600	5	5	5	1	3	4	1	0	0	0	0	0	0	0	0	1	0	0	0	.800	.600
Tomberlin, Andy, New York*	.250	4	4	4	0	1	1	0	0	0	0	0	0	0	0	0	3	0	0	0	.250	.250
Tucker, Michael, Atlanta*	.000	12	11	9	0	0	0	0	0	0	0	0	0	0	2	0	3	0	0	0	.000	.182
Valenzuela, Fernando, S.D.*	1.000	1	1	1	0	1	1	0	0	0	0	0	0	0	0	0	0	0	0	0	1.000	1.000
Vander Wal, John, Colorado*	.185	60	58	54	3	10	15	2	0	1	7	0	0	0	4	0	24	0	0	0	.278	.241
Vaughn, Greg, San Diego	.217	28	28	23	6	5	11	0	0	2	3	0	0	0	5	0	9	1	1	0	.478	.357
Veras, Quilvio, San Diego†	.200	5	5	5	1	1	2	1	0	0	0	0	0	0	0	0	2	0	0	1	.400	.200
Vidro, Jose, Montreal†	.450	21	21	20	5	9	13	4	0	0	4	0	0	0	1	0	2	0	0	0	.650	.476
Vizcaino, Jose, San Fran.†	.333	6	6	6	0	2	2	0	0	0	0	0	0	0	0	0	0	0	0	0	.333	.333
Walker, Larry, Colorado*	.000	1	1	0	1	0	0	0	0	0	0	0	0	0	1	0	0	0	0	0	.000	1.000
Ward, Turner, Pittsburgh†	.333	25	25	21	7	7	13	3	0	1	5	0	0	0	4	0	2	0	1	0	.619	.440
Watkins, Pat, Cincinnati	.000	3	3	3	0	0	0	0	0	0	0	0	0	0	0	0	1	0	0	0	.000	.000
Wehner, John, Florida	.333	9	8	6	1	2	3	1	0	0	1	1	0	1	0	0	0	0	0	2	.500	.429
Weiss, Walt, Colorado†	.750	5	5	4	0	3	6	1	1	0	0	0	0	0	1	0	0	0	0	0	1.500	.800
White, Devon, Florida†	.000	4	4	4	0	0	0	0	0	0	0	0	0	0	0	0	2	0	0	0	.000	.000
Widger, Chris, Montreal	.000	6	6	6	0	0	0	0	0	0	0	0	0	0	0	0	2	0	0	1	.000	.000
Wilkins, Rick, San Fran.*	.286	10	10	7	0	2	3	1	0	0	3	0	0	0	3	0	3	0	0	0	.429	.500
Williams, Eddie, L.A.-Pit.	.091	13	13	11	0	1	1	0	0	0	2	0	0	0	2	1	3	0	0	0	.091	.231
Womack, Tony, Pittsburgh*	.333	3	3	3	1	1	1	0	0	0	0	0	0	0	0	0	0	1	0	0	.333	.333
Young, Dmitri, St. Louis†	.143	19	19	14	1	2	2	0	0	0	3	0	1	0	4	1	7	0	0	1	.143	.316
Young, Eric, Colorado	1.000	1	1	1	1	1	1	0	0	0	0	0	0	0	0	0	0	0	0	0	1.000	1.000
Young, Kevin, Pittsburgh	.250	8	8	8	1	2	3	1	0	0	2	0	0	0	0	0	2	0	0	0	.375	.250
Zaun, Gregg, Florida†	.500	8	8	6	1	3	6	0	0	1	2	1	0	0	1	0	0	0	0	0	1.000	.571
Zeile, Todd, Los Angeles	.000	1	1	1	0	0	0	0	0	0	0	0	0	0	0	0	1	0	0	0	.000	.000

PINCH-HITTERS WITH TWO OR MORE TEAMS

Player, Team	Avg.	G	TPA	AB	R	H	TB	2B	3B	HR	RBI	SH	SF	HP	BB	IBB	SO	SB	CS	GDP	Slg.	OBP
Alexander, Manny, New York	.000	2	2	1	1	0	0	0	0	0	1	0	0	0	1	0	1	0	0	0	.000	.500
Alexander, Manny, Chicago	1.000	1	1	1	0	1	1	0	0	0	0	0	0	0	0	0	0	0	0	0	1.000	1.000
Cummings, Midre, Pittsburgh*	.185	28	28	27	2	5	11	1	1	1	4	0	0	0	1	0	7	0	0	0	.407	.214
Cummings, Midre, Phi.*	.200	11	11	10	0	2	3	1	0	0	2	0	0	0	1	0	4	0	0	0	.300	.273
Daulton, Darren, Phi.*	.000	5	5	5	0	0	0	0	0	0	0	0	0	0	0	0	1	0	0	0	.000	.000
Daulton, Darren, Florida*	.250	11	11	8	0	2	2	0	0	0	2	0	0	1	2	0	3	0	0	0	.250	.455
Johnson, Lance, New York*	.250	8	8	8	1	2	2	0	0	0	1	0	0	0	0	0	2	0	1	0	.250	.250
Johnson, Lance, Chicago*	.500	3	3	2	0	1	1	0	0	0	1	0	1	0	0	0	0	0	0	0	.500	.333
Livingstone, Scott, San Diego*	.267	17	17	15	1	4	5	1	0	0	3	0	0	2	0	0	1	0	0	0	.333	.353
Livingstone, Scott, St. Louis*	.129	38	34	31	1	4	5	1	0	0	3	0	2	0	1	0	9	0	0	1	.161	.147
McMillon, Billy, Florida*	.182	11	11	11	0	2	3	1	0	0	1	0	0	0	0	0	4	0	0	0	.273	.182
McMillon, Billy, Philadelphia*	.000	2	2	1	0	0	0	0	0	0	0	0	1	0	0	0	0	0	0	0	.000	.000
McRae, Brian, Chicago†	.500	3	3	2	1	1	1	0	0	0	2	0	0	1	0	0	0	0	0	0	.500	.667
McRae, Brian, New York†	.500	6	6	4	2	2	5	0	0	1	2	0	1	0	1	0	1	0	0	0	1.250	.500
Plantier, Phil, San Diego*	.000	7	5	3	0	0	0	0	0	0	0	0	0	0	2	0	2	0	0	0	.000	.400
Plantier, Phil, St. Louis*	.143	10	8	7	0	1	1	0	0	0	0	0	0	0	1	0	3	0	0	0	.143	.250
Sweeney, Mark, St. Louis*	.313	23	23	16	3	5	6	1	0	0	1	0	1	1	5	1	3	0	0	0	.375	.478
Sweeney, Mark, San Diego*	.386	50	49	44	7	17	23	0	0	2	13	0	1	0	4	0	10	2	1	1	.523	.429
Williams, Eddie, Los Angeles	.143	8	8	7	0	1	1	0	0	0	1	0	0	0	1	1	1	0	0	0	.143	.250
Williams, Eddie, Pittsburgh	.000	5	5	4	0	0	0	0	0	0	1	0	0	0	1	0	2	0	0	0	.000	.200

PITCHING

TEAM

Team	W	L	Pct.	ERA	G	ShO	Rel.	Sv.	IP	H	TBF	R	ER	HR	SH	SF	HB	BB	IBB	SO	WP	Bk.
Atlanta	101	61	.623	3.18	162	17	374	37	1465.2	1319	6057	581	518	111	68	46	31	450	56	1196	38	4
Los Angeles	88	74	.543	3.62	162	6	412	45	1459.1	1325	6191	645	587	163	74	32	45	546	36	1232	36	14
Houston	84	78	.519	3.66	162	12	354	37	1459.0	1379	6166	660	594	134	76	42	52	511	25	1138	46	9
Florida	92	70	.568	3.83	162	10	404	39	1446.2	1353	6223	669	615	131	69	45	63	639	41	1188	41	4
St. Louis	73	89	.451	3.88	162	8	399	39	1455.2	1422	6222	708	627	124	81	52	59	536	34	1130	48	8
New York	88	74	.543	3.95	162	8	376	49	1459.1	1452	6210	709	640	160	63	44	47	504	43	982	47	7
Montreal	78	84	.481	4.14	162	14	390	37	1447.0	1365	6189	740	665	149	72	45	63	557	45	1138	52	4
Pittsburgh	79	83	.488	4.28	162	8	451	41	1436.0	1503	6291	760	683	143	78	47	64	560	71	1080	61	12
San Francisco	90	72	.556	4.39	162	9	481	45	1446.0	1494	6284	793	706	160	76	51	39	578	57	1044	48	10
Cincinnati	76	86	.469	4.41	162	8	423	49	1449.0	1408	6264	764	710	173	75	43	77	558	62	1159	64	7
Chicago	68	94	.420	4.44	162	4	441	37	1429.0	1451	6226	759	705	185	80	57	43	590	51	1072	35	8
Philadelphia	68	94	.420	4.85	162	7	409	35	1420.1	1441	6228	840	765	171	48	63	58	616	42	1209	73	12
San Diego	76	86	.469	4.98	162	2	426	43	1450.0	1581	6429	891	802	172	71	46	61	596	37	1059	58	7
Colorado	83	79	.512	5.25	162	5	426	38	1432.2	1697	6417	908	836	196	73	52	67	566	23	870	50	6
Totals	1144	1124	.504	4.20	2268	113	5766	571	20255.2	20190	87397	10427	9453	2172	1004	665	769	7807	623	15497	697	112

NOTE—Totals for earned runs for several clubs do not agree with composite total for all pitchers of each respective club due to instances in which provisions of Section 10.18(i) of the Scoring Rules were applied. The following differences are to be noted: Los Angeles pitchers add to 588; Houston pitchers add to 595; St. Louis pitchers add to 628; New York pitchers add to 641; San Francisco pitchers add to 712; Cincinnati pitchers add to 711; Philadelphia pitchers add to 768; San Diego pitchers add to 804.

INDIVIDUAL

TOP QUALIFIERS FOR EARNED-RUN AVERAGE TITLE

Minimum 162 innings. *Throws lefthanded.

Pitcher, Team	W	L	Pct.	ERA	G	GS	CG	ShO	GF	Sv.	IP	H	TBF	R	ER	HR	SH	SF	HB	BB	IBB	SO	WP	Bk.
Martinez, Pedro J., Montreal	17	8	.680	1.90	31	31	13	4	0	0	241.1	158	947	65	51	16	9	1	9	67	5	305	3	1
Maddux, Greg, Atlanta	19	4	.826	2.20	33	33	5	2	0	0	232.2	200	893	58	57	9	11	7	6	20	6	177	0	0
Kile, Darryl, Houston	19	7	.731	2.57	34	34	6	4	0	0	255.2	208	1056	87	73	19	17	10	10	94	2	205	7	1
Valdes, Ismael, Los Angeles	10	11	.476	2.65	30	30	0	0	0	0	196.2	171	795	68	58	16	11	3	3	47	1	140	3	2
Brown, Kevin, Florida	16	8	.667	2.69	33	33	6	2	0	0	237.1	214	976	77	71	10	5	1	14	66	7	205	7	1
Reed, Rick, New York	13	9	.591	2.89	33	31	2	0	0	0	208.1	186	824	76	67	19	7	3	5	31	4	113	0	0
Glavine, Tom, Atlanta*	14	7	.667	2.96	33	33	5	2	0	0	240.0	197	970	86	79	20	11	6	4	79	9	152	3	0
Neagle, Denny, Atlanta*	20	5	.800	2.97	34	34	4	4	0	0	233.1	204	947	87	77	18	12	6	6	49	5	172	3	0
Schilling, Curt, Philadelphia	17	11	.607	2.97	35	35	7	2	0	0	254.1	208	1009	96	84	25	8	8	5	58	3	319	5	1
Smoltz, John, Atlanta	15	12	.556	3.02	35	35	7	2	0	0	256.0	234	1043	97	86	21	10	3	1	63	9	241	10	1
Benes, Andy, St. Louis	10	7	.588	3.10	26	26	0	0	0	0	177.0	149	727	64	61	9	6	7	5	61	4	175	7	0
Estes, Shawn, San Francisco*	19	5	.792	3.18	32	32	3	2	0	0	201.0	162	849	80	71	12	13	2	8	100	2	181	10	2
Morris, Matt, St. Louis	12	9	.571	3.19	33	33	3	0	0	0	217.0	208	900	88	77	12	11	7	7	69	2	149	5	3
Park, Chan Ho, Los Angeles	14	8	.636	3.38	32	29	2	0	1	0	192.0	149	792	80	72	24	9	5	8	70	1	166	4	1
Rueter, Kirk, San Francisco*	13	6	.684	3.45	32	32	0	0	0	0	190.2	194	802	83	73	17	10	6	1	51	8	115	3	0

DEPARTMENTAL LEADERS: W—Neagle, Atl., 20; L—Leiter, Phi., 17; G—Tavarez, S.F., 89; GS—Schilling, Phi., Smoltz, Atl., 35; CG—Martinez, Mon., 13; ShO—Perez, Mon., 5; GF—Beck, S.F., 66; Sv.—Shaw, Cin., 42; IP—Smoltz, Atl., 256; H—Smoltz, Atl., 234; TBF—Kile, Hou., 1056; R—Leiter, Phi., 132; ER—Leiter, Phi., 115; HR—Trachsel, Chi., 32; SH—Cooke, Pit., 18; SF—Trachsel, Chi., 11; HB—Brown, Fla., 14; BB—Estes, S.F., 100; IBB—Cooke, Pit., 11; SO—Schilling, Phi., 319; WP—Remlinger, Cin., 12; Bk.—Nomo, L.A., 4.

ALL PITCHERS

*Throws lefthanded.

Pitcher, Team	W	L	Pct.	ERA	G	GS	CG	ShO	GF	Sv.	IP	H	TBF	R	ER	HR	SH	SF	HB	BB	IBB	SO	WP	Bk.
Acevedo, Juan, New York	3	1	.750	3.59	25	2	0	0	4	0	47.2	52	215	24	19	6	2	5	4	22	2	33	0	1
Adams, Terry, Chicago	2	9	.182	4.62	74	0	0	0	39	18	74.0	91	341	43	38	3	1	2	1	40	6	64	6	0
Alfonseca, Antonio, Florida	1	3	.250	4.91	17	0	0	0	2	0	25.2	36	123	16	14	3	1	0	1	10	3	19	1	0
Alston, Garvin, Colorado	0	0	.000	0.00	0	0	0	0	0	0	0.0	0	0	0	0	0	0	0	0	0	0	0	0	0
Alvarez, Wilson, San Fran.*	4	3	.571	4.48	11	11	0	0	0	0	66.1	54	283	36	33	9	4	1	1	36	3	69	1	1
Arocha, Rene, San Francisco	0	0	.000	11.32	6	0	0	0	2	0	10.1	17	54	14	13	2	1	1	1	5	2	7	0	0
Ashby, Andy, San Diego	9	11	.450	4.13	30	30	2	0	0	0	200.2	207	851	108	92	17	13	6	5	49	2	144	3	0
Astacio, Pedro, L.A.-Col.	12	10	.545	4.14	33	31	2	1	2	0	202.1	200	862	98	93	24	9	7	9	61	0	166	6	3
Aybar, Manny, St. Louis	2	4	.333	4.24	12	12	0	0	0	0	68.0	66	295	33	32	8	7	4	4	29	0	41	1	1
Bailey, Roger, Colorado	9	10	.474	4.29	29	29	5	2	0	0	191.0	210	835	103	91	27	7	4	13	70	2	84	4	0
Bailey, Cory, San Francisco	0	1	.000	8.38	7	0	0	0	4	0	9.2	15	45	9	9	1	0	1	0	4	0	6	0	0
Barber, Brian, St. Louis	0	0	.000	0.00	0	0	0	0	0	0	0.0	0	0	0	0	0	0	0	0	0	0	0	0	0
Barrios, Manuel, Houston	0	0	.000	12.00	2	0	0	0	1	0	3.0	6	18	4	4	0	0	0	2	3	0	2	0	0
Batchelor, Rich, St.L.-S.D.	3	1	.750	5.97	23	0	0	0	8	0	28.2	40	138	23	19	2	3	0	3	14	2	18	1	1
Batista, Miguel, Chicago	0	5	.000	5.70	11	6	0	0	2	0	36.1	36	168	24	23	4	4	4	1	24	2	27	2	0
Bautista, Jose, St. Louis	0	0	.000	6.57	11	0	0	0	3	0	12.1	15	56	10	9	2	3	0	1	2	1	4	1	0
Beck, Rod, San Francisco	7	4	.636	3.47	73	0	0	0	66	37	70.0	67	281	31	27	7	1	0	2	8	2	53	1	0
Beckett, Robbie, Colorado*	0	0	.000	5.40	2	0	0	0	1	0	1.2	1	7	1	1	0	0	0	0	1	1	2	0	0
Beech, Matt, Philadelphia*	4	9	.308	5.07	24	24	0	0	0	0	136.2	147	602	81	77	25	7	6	5	57	9	120	6	2
Belinda, Stan, Cincinnati	1	5	.167	3.71	84	0	0	0	18	1	99.1	84	420	42	41	11	6	5	9	33	6	114	5	0
Beltran, Rigo, St. Louis*	1	2	.333	3.48	35	4	0	0	16	1	54.1	47	224	25	21	3	6	3	0	17	0	50	1	0
Benes, Alan, St. Louis	9	9	.500	2.89	23	23	2	0	0	0	161.2	128	666	60	52	13	5	4	4	68	3	160	9	2
Benes, Andy, St. Louis	10	7	.588	3.10	26	26	0	0	0	0	177.0	149	727	64	61	9	6	7	5	61	4	175	7	0
Bennett, Shayne, Montreal	0	1	.000	3.18	16	0	0	0	3	0	22.2	21	98	9	8	2	1	3	0	9	3	8	0	0

Pitcher, Team	W	L	Pct.	ERA	G	GS	CG	ShO	GF	Sv.	IP	H	TBF	R	ER	HR	SH	SF	HB	BB	IBB	SO	WP	Bk.
Bergman, Sean, San Diego	2	4	.333	6.09	44	9	0	0	13	0	99.0	126	451	72	67	11	7	4	3	38	4	74	6	0
Bielecki, Mike, Atlanta	3	7	.300	4.08	50	0	0	0	7	2	57.1	56	250	33	26	9	3	1	1	21	3	60	1	0
Blazier, Ron, Philadelphia	1	1	.500	5.03	36	0	0	0	7	0	53.2	62	240	31	30	8	1	4	0	21	3	42	2	0
Bochtler, Doug, San Diego	3	6	.333	4.77	54	0	0	0	13	2	60.1	51	281	35	32	3	4	3	1	50	4	46	5	0
Bohanon, Brian, New York*	6	4	.600	3.82	19	14	0	0	0	0	94.1	95	412	49	40	9	6	0	4	34	2	66	3	1
Bones, Ricky, Cincinnati	0	1	.000	10.19	9	2	0	0	2	0	17.2	31	98	22	20	2	1	2	2	11	2	8	0	0
Borbon, Pedro Jr., Atlanta*	0	0	.000	0.00	0	0	0	0	0	0	0.0	0	0	0	0	0	0	0	0	0	0	0	0	0
Borland, Toby, New York	0	1	.000	6.08	13	0	0	0	5	1	13.1	11	65	9	9	1	0	0	1	14	0	7	3	0
Borowski, Joe, Atlanta	2	2	.500	3.75	20	0	0	0	8	0	24.0	27	111	11	10	2	1	0	0	16	4	6	0	0
Bottalico, Ricky, Philadelphia	2	5	.286	3.65	69	0	0	0	61	34	74.0	68	324	31	30	7	1	2	2	42	4	89	3	0
Bottenfield, Kent, Chicago	2	3	.400	3.86	64	0	0	0	20	2	84.0	82	361	39	36	13	4	4	2	35	7	74	2	0
Brantley, Jeff, Cincinnati	1	1	.500	3.86	13	0	0	0	9	1	11.2	9	53	5	5	2	0	0	2	7	1	16	2	0
Brewer, Billy, Philadelphia*	1	2	.333	3.27	25	0	0	0	4	0	22.0	15	93	8	8	2	0	2	0	11	0	16	1	0
Brock, Chris, Atlanta	0	0	.000	5.58	7	6	0	0	1	0	30.2	34	144	23	19	2	3	4	0	19	2	16	2	1
Brown, Kevin, Florida	16	8	.667	2.69	33	33	6	2	0	0	237.1	214	976	77	71	10	5	1	14	66	7	205	7	1
Bruske, Jim, San Diego	4	1	.800	3.63	28	0	0	0	6	0	44.2	37	193	22	18	4	2	3	1	25	1	32	4	0
Bullinger, Jim, Montreal	7	12	.368	5.56	36	25	2	2	4	0	155.1	165	697	106	96	17	8	6	12	74	5	87	7	0
Burba, Dave, Cincinnati	11	10	.524	4.73	30	27	2	0	1	0	160.0	157	706	88	84	22	6	3	9	73	10	131	6	0
Burke, John, Colorado	2	5	.286	6.56	17	9	0	0	1	0	59.0	83	288	46	43	13	1	3	6	26	0	39	4	0
Burrows, Terry, San Diego*	0	2	.000	10.45	13	0	0	0	4	0	10.1	12	52	13	12	1	1	0	1	8	1	8	0	0
Busby, Mike, St. Louis	0	2	.000	8.79	3	3	0	0	0	0	14.1	24	67	14	14	2	1	1	0	4	0	6	0	0
Byrd, Paul, Atlanta	4	4	.500	5.26	31	4	0	0	9	0	53.0	47	236	34	31	6	2	2	4	28	4	37	3	1
Cabrera, Jose, Houston	0	0	.000	1.17	12	0	0	0	6	0	15.1	6	57	2	2	1	0	3	0	6	0	18	0	0
Candiotti, Tom, Los Angeles	10	7	.588	3.60	41	18	0	0	6	0	135.0	128	573	60	54	21	3	2	11	40	4	89	4	0
Cangelosi, John, Florida*	0	0	.000	0.00	1	0	0	0	1	0	1.0	0	4	0	0	0	0	0	0	1	0	0	0	0
Carlson, Dan, San Francisco	0	0	.000	7.63	6	0	0	0	2	0	15.1	20	72	14	13	5	0	1	0	8	1	14	0	0
Carrara, Giovanni, Cincinnati	0	1	.000	7.84	2	2	0	0	0	0	10.1	14	49	9	9	4	1	0	0	6	1	5	0	0
Carrasco, Hector, Cincinnati	1	2	.333	3.68	38	0	0	0	11	0	51.1	51	237	25	21	3	3	1	4	25	2	46	3	2
Casian, Larry, Chicago*	0	1	.000	7.45	12	0	0	0	1	0	9.2	16	49	9	8	3	0	2	1	2	1	7	0	0
Castillo, Frank, Chi.-Col.	12	12	.500	5.42	34	33	0	0	0	0	184.1	220	830	121	111	25	17	2	8	69	4	126	3	0
Cather, Mike, Atlanta	2	4	.333	2.39	35	0	0	0	10	0	37.2	23	155	12	10	1	2	0	2	19	4	29	0	0
Christiansen, Jason, Pit.*	3	0	1.000	2.94	39	0	0	0	9	0	33.2	37	154	11	11	2	0	0	2	17	3	37	4	0
Clark, Mark, N.Y.-Chi.	14	8	.636	3.82	32	31	3	0	0	0	205.0	213	866	96	87	24	9	4	4	59	3	123	4	1
Clontz, Brad, Atlanta	5	1	.833	3.75	51	0	0	0	16	1	48.0	52	203	24	20	3	0	2	1	18	3	42	1	0
Cook, Dennis, Florida*	1	2	.333	3.90	59	0	0	0	12	0	62.1	64	272	28	27	4	1	1	2	28	4	63	0	0
Cooke, Steve, Pittsburgh*	9	15	.375	4.30	32	32	0	0	0	0	167.1	184	756	95	80	15	18	5	9	77	11	109	8	1
Cordova, Francisco, Pittsburgh	11	8	.579	3.63	29	29	2	2	0	0	178.2	175	744	80	72	14	3	7	9	49	4	121	4	0
Cormier, Rheal, Montreal*	0	1	.000	33.75	1	1	0	0	0	0	1.1	4	9	5	5	1	0	0	0	1	0	0	0	0
Crawford, Joe, New York*	4	3	.571	3.30	19	2	0	0	9	0	46.1	36	182	18	17	7	2	0	0	13	1	25	0	1
Creek, Doug, San Francisco*	1	2	.333	6.75	3	3	0	0	0	0	13.1	12	64	12	10	1	0	0	0	14	0	14	0	0
Crowell, James, Cincinnati*	0	1	.000	9.95	2	1	0	0	1	0	6.1	12	36	7	7	2	2	0	0	5	0	3	0	0
Cunnane, Will, San Diego	6	3	.667	5.81	54	8	0	0	16	0	91.1	114	430	69	59	11	1	1	5	49	3	79	3	0
Daal, Omar, Montreal*	1	2	.333	9.79	33	0	0	0	6	1	30.1	48	150	35	33	4	5	1	2	15	3	16	1	0
Darwin, Danny, San Francisco	1	3	.250	4.91	10	7	0	0	0	0	44.0	51	196	26	24	5	3	1	1	14	0	30	0	0
DeHart, Rick, Montreal*	2	1	.667	5.52	23	0	0	0	7	0	29.1	33	130	21	18	7	1	2	0	14	4	29	2	0
DeJean, Mike, Colorado	5	0	1.000	3.99	55	0	0	0	15	2	67.2	74	295	34	30	4	3	1	3	24	2	38	2	0
DeLucia, Rich, San Francisco	0	0	.000	10.80	3	0	0	0	0	0	1.2	6	12	3	2	0	0	0	0	0	0	2	1	0
Dessens, Elmer, Pittsburgh	0	0	.000	0.00	3	0	0	0	1	0	3.1	2	13	0	0	0	0	0	1	0	0	2	0	0
DiPoto, Jerry, Colorado	5	3	.625	4.70	74	0	0	0	33	16	95.2	108	422	56	50	6	3	7	4	33	5	74	4	1
Dreifort, Darren, Los Angeles	5	2	.714	2.86	48	0	0	0	15	4	63.0	45	265	21	20	3	5	2	1	34	2	63	3	1
Eckersley, Dennis, St. Louis	1	5	.167	3.91	57	0	0	0	47	36	53.0	49	218	24	23	9	2	0	2	8	0	45	2	0
Eischen, Joey, Cincinnati*	0	0	.000	6.75	1	0	0	0	0	0	1.1	2	7	2	1	0	0	0	0	1	0	2	1	0
Embree, Alan, Atlanta*	3	1	.750	2.54	66	0	0	0	15	0	46.0	36	190	13	13	1	4	1	2	20	2	45	3	1
Erdos, Todd, San Diego	2	0	1.000	5.27	11	0	0	0	2	0	13.2	17	64	9	8	1	0	0	2	4	0	13	3	0
Ericks, John, Pittsburgh	1	0	1.000	1.93	10	0	0	0	10	6	9.1	7	39	3	2	1	0	0	0	4	0	6	0	0
Estes, Shawn, San Francisco*	19	5	.792	3.18	32	32	3	2	0	0	201.0	162	849	80	71	12	13	2	8	100	2	181	10	2
Falteisek, Steve, Montreal	0	0	.000	3.38	5	0	0	0	2	0	8.0	8	34	4	3	0	0	2	1	3	0	2	0	0
Fernandez, Alex, Florida	17	12	.586	3.59	32	32	5	1	0	0	220.2	193	904	93	88	25	14	5	4	69	2	183	9	0
Fernandez, Sid, Houston*	1	0	1.000	3.60	1	1	0	0	0	0	5.0	4	21	2	2	1	0	0	0	2	0	3	0	0
Fernandez, Osvaldo, San Fran.	3	4	.429	4.95	11	11	0	0	0	0	56.1	74	256	39	31	9	4	1	0	15	2	31	2	1
Fossas, Tony, St. Louis*	2	7	.222	3.83	71	0	0	0	14	0	51.2	62	239	32	22	7	3	1	1	26	3	41	0	0
Foster, Kevin, Chicago	10	7	.588	4.61	26	25	1	0	0	0	146.1	141	637	79	75	27	9	7	2	66	4	118	3	0
Foulke, Keith, San Francisco	1	5	.167	8.26	11	8	0	0	0	0	44.2	60	209	41	41	9	2	0	4	18	1	33	1	0
Fox, Chad, Atlanta	0	1	.000	3.29	30	0	0	0	8	0	27.1	24	120	12	10	4	0	0	0	16	0	28	4	0
Franco, John, New York*	5	3	.625	2.55	59	0	0	0	53	36	60.0	49	244	18	17	3	5	1	1	20	2	53	6	0
Frascatore, John, St. Louis	5	2	.714	2.48	59	0	0	0	17	0	80.0	74	348	25	22	5	5	5	6	33	5	58	4	0
Gaetti, Gary, St. Louis	0	0	.000	0.00	1	0	0	0	1	0	0.1	1	3	0	0	0	0	0	1	0	0	0	0	0
Garcia, Ramon, Houston	9	8	.529	3.69	42	20	1	1	5	1	158.2	155	665	71	65	20	10	2	9	52	1	120	3	2
Gardner, Mark, San Francisco	12	9	.571	4.29	30	30	2	1	0	0	180.1	188	764	92	86	28	10	6	1	57	6	136	3	3
Glavine, Tom, Atlanta*	14	7	.667	2.96	33	33	5	2	0	0	240.0	197	970	86	79	20	11	6	4	79	9	152	3	0
Gomes, Wayne, Philadelphia	5	1	.833	5.27	37	0	0	0	13	0	42.2	45	191	26	25	4	2	0	1	24	0	24	2	0
Gonzalez, Jeremi, Chicago	11	9	.550	4.25	23	23	1	1	0	0	144.0	126	613	73	68	16	4	5	2	69	5	93	1	1
Gorecki, Rick, Los Angeles	1	0	1.000	15.00	4	1	0	0	2	0	6.0	9	32	10	10	3	0	0	0	6	1	6	0	0
Grace, Mike, Philadelphia	3	2	.600	3.46	6	6	1	1	0	0	39.0	32	151	16	15	3	0	1	1	10	1	26	2	0
Granger, Jeff, Pittsburgh*	0	0	.000	18.00	9	0	0	0	1	0	5.0	10	32	10	10	3	0	0	0	8	1	4	2	0
Graves, Danny, Cincinnati	0	0	.000	6.14	10	0	0	0	1	0	14.2	26	78	14	10	0	3	1	0	11	1	7	1	0
Green, Tyler, Philadelphia	4	4	.500	4.93	14	14	0	0	0	0	76.2	72	340	50	42	8	0	3	1	45	4	58	7	0
Greene, Tommy, Houston	0	1	.000	7.00	2	2	0	0	0	0	9.0	10	40	7	7	2	0	0	0	5	0	11	0	0
Guthrie, Mark, Los Angeles*	1	4	.200	5.32	62	0	0	0	18	1	69.1	71	305	44	41	12	10	3	0	30	6	42	2	1
Hall, Darren, Los Angeles	3	2	.600	2.30	63	0	0	0	20	2	54.2	58	233	15	14	3	1	1	0	26	7	39	0	0
Hamilton, Joey, San Diego	12	7	.632	4.25	31	29	1	0	1	0	192.2	199	831	100	91	22	8	8	12	69	2	124	7	0
Hampton, Mike, Houston*	15	10	.600	3.83	34	34	7	2	0	0	223.0	217	941	105	95	16	11	7	2	77	2	139	6	1

Pitcher, Team	W	L	Pct.	ERA	G	GS	CG	ShO	GF	Sv.	IP	H	TBF	R	ER	HR	SH	SF	HB	BB	IBB	SO	WP	Bk.
Harkey, Mike, Los Angeles	1	0	1.000	4.30	10	0	0	0	5	0	14.2	12	62	8	7	3	0	0	0	5	0	6	0	0
Harnisch, Pete, New York	0	1	.000	8.06	6	5	0	0	0	0	25.2	35	121	24	23	5	0	2	1	11	1	12	1	0
Harris, Reggie, Philadelphia	1	3	.250	5.30	50	0	0	0	13	0	54.1	55	264	33	32	1	3	4	5	43	1	45	5	1
Harvey, Bryan, Atlanta	0	0	.000	0.00	0	0	0	0	0	0	0.0	0	0	0	0	0	0	0	0	0	0	0	0	0
Helling, Rick, Florida	2	6	.250	4.38	31	8	0	0	8	0	76.0	61	324	38	37	12	2	7	4	48	2	53	0	0
Henriquez, Oscar, Houston	0	1	.000	4.50	4	0	0	0	1	0	4.0	2	17	2	2	0	1	0	1	3	0	3	0	0
Henry, Doug, San Francisco	4	5	.444	4.71	75	0	0	0	25	3	70.2	70	317	45	37	5	4	3	1	41	6	69	3	0
Heredia, Felix, Florida*	5	3	.625	4.29	56	0	0	0	10	0	56.2	53	259	30	27	3	2	2	5	30	1	54	2	0
Hermanson, Dustin, Montreal	8	8	.500	3.69	32	28	1	1	0	0	158.1	134	656	68	65	15	10	6	1	66	2	136	4	1
Hernandez, Livan, Florida	9	3	.750	3.18	17	17	0	0	0	0	96.1	81	405	39	34	5	4	7	3	38	1	72	0	0
Hernandez, Roberto, San Fran.	5	2	.714	2.48	28	0	0	0	7	4	32.2	29	137	9	9	2	1	0	0	14	1	35	1	0
Hitchcock, Sterling, S.D.*	10	11	.476	5.20	32	28	1	0	1	0	161.0	172	693	102	93	24	7	4	4	55	2	106	6	2
Hoffman, Trevor, San Diego	6	4	.600	2.66	70	0	0	0	59	37	81.1	59	322	25	24	9	2	1	0	24	4	111	7	0
Holmes, Darren, Colorado	9	2	.818	5.34	42	6	0	0	10	3	89.1	113	406	58	53	12	6	4	0	36	3	70	4	0
Holt, Chris, Houston	8	12	.400	3.52	33	32	0	0	0	0	209.2	211	883	98	82	17	7	5	8	61	4	95	1	0
Honeycutt, Rick, St. Louis*	0	0	.000	13.50	2	0	0	0	2	0	2.0	5	11	3	3	0	0	0	1	0	1	2	1	1
Hudek, John, Houston	1	3	.250	5.98	40	0	0	0	20	4	40.2	38	188	27	27	8	1	0	3	33	2	36	4	0
Hutton, Mark, Fla.-Col.	3	2	.600	4.48	40	1	0	0	9	0	60.1	72	272	34	30	10	7	4	6	26	3	39	3	1
Isringhausen, Jason, New York	2	2	.500	7.58	6	6	0	0	0	0	29.2	40	145	27	25	3	1	2	1	22	0	25	3	0
Jackson, Danny, St.L.-S.D.*	2	9	.182	7.58	17	13	0	0	0	0	67.2	98	321	64	57	11	4	5	5	28	3	32	2	0
Jarvis, Kevin, Cincinnati	0	1	.000	10.13	9	0	0	0	3	1	13.1	21	70	16	15	4	1	0	1	12	2	12	2	0
Johnson, Jason, Pittsburgh	0	0	.000	6.00	3	0	0	0	0	0	6.0	10	27	4	4	2	0	1	0	1	0	3	0	0
Johnson, Mike, Montreal	2	5	.286	5.94	11	11	0	0	0	0	50.0	54	220	34	33	8	2	2	0	21	2	28	4	0
Johnstone, John, San Fran.	0	0	.000	3.38	13	0	0	0	2	0	18.2	15	80	7	7	1	2	3	4	7	0	15	0	0
Jones, Bobby, New York	15	9	.625	3.63	30	30	2	1	0	0	193.1	177	806	88	78	24	6	4	2	63	3	125	3	1
Jones, Bobby M., Colorado*	1	1	.500	8.38	4	4	0	0	0	0	19.1	30	96	18	18	2	2	3	0	12	0	5	0	0
Jordan, Ricardo, New York*	1	2	.333	5.33	22	0	0	0	4	0	27.0	31	123	17	16	1	2	2	2	15	2	19	0	0
Judd, Michael, Los Angeles	0	0	.000	0.00	1	0	0	0	0	0	2.2	4	11	0	0	0	0	0	0	4	0	0	0	0
Juden, Jeff, Montreal	11	5	.688	4.22	22	22	3	0	0	0	130.0	125	565	64	61	17	5	4	9	57	2	107	7	1
Karp, Ryan, Philadelphia*	1	1	.500	5.40	15	1	0	0	1	0	15.0	12	67	12	9	2	1	0	2	9	0	18	1	0
Kashiwada, Takashi, N.Y.*	3	1	.750	4.31	35	0	0	0	11	0	31.1	35	145	15	15	4	1	3	2	18	0	19	4	0
Kile, Darryl, Houston	19	7	.731	2.57	34	34	6	4	0	0	255.2	208	1056	87	73	19	17	10	10	94	2	205	7	1
King, Curtis, St. Louis	4	2	.667	2.76	30	0	0	0	8	0	29.1	38	136	14	9	0	4	3	1	11	0	13	2	0
Kline, Steve, Montreal*	1	3	.250	6.15	26	0	0	0	7	0	26.1	31	118	18	18	4	3	2	1	10	3	20	1	0
Kroon, Marc, San Diego	0	1	.000	6.35	12	0	0	0	2	0	11.1	14	56	9	8	2	0	0	1	5	0	12	1	0
Leiter, Al, Florida*	11	9	.550	4.34	27	27	0	0	0	0	151.1	133	668	78	73	13	10	3	12	91	4	132	2	0
Leiter, Mark, Philadelphia	10	17	.370	5.67	31	31	3	0	0	0	182.2	216	832	132	115	25	11	8	9	64	4	148	11	2
Leroy, John, Atlanta	1	0	1.000	0.00	1	0	0	0	0	0	2.0	1	10	0	0	0	0	0	3	1	3	0	0	0
Leskanic, Curtis, Colorado	4	0	1.000	5.55	55	0	0	0	23	2	58.1	59	248	36	36	8	2	4	0	24	0	53	4	0
Lewis, Richie, Cincinnati	0	0	.000	6.35	4	0	0	0	0	0	5.2	4	25	5	4	3	2	0	0	3	0	4	0	0
Lidle, Cory, New York	7	2	.778	3.53	54	2	0	0	20	2	81.2	86	345	38	32	7	4	4	3	20	4	54	2	0
Lieber, Jon, Pittsburgh	11	14	.440	4.49	33	32	1	0	0	0	188.1	193	799	102	94	23	6	7	1	51	8	160	3	1
Ligtenberg, Kerry, Atlanta.	1	0	1.000	3.00	15	0	0	0	9	1	15.0	12	61	5	5	4	0	0	4	2	0	19	0	0
Lima, Jose, Houston	1	6	.143	5.28	52	1	0	0	15	2	75.0	79	321	45	44	9	6	3	5	16	2	63	2	0
Loaiza, Esteban, Pittsburgh	11	11	.500	4.13	33	32	1	0	0	0	196.1	214	851	99	90	17	10	7	12	56	9	122	2	3
Loiselle, Rich, Pittsburgh	1	5	.167	3.10	72	0	0	0	58	29	72.2	76	312	29	25	7	2	2	1	24	3	66	4	0
Long, Joey, San Diego*	0	0	.000	8.18	10	0	0	0	4	0	11.0	17	60	11	10	1	1	0	1	8	1	8	1	0
Lowe, Sean, St. Louis	0	2	.000	9.35	6	4	0	0	1	0	17.1	27	89	21	18	2	1	2	1	10	0	8	0	0
Ludwick, Eric, St. Louis	0	1	.000	9.45	5	0	0	0	3	0	6.2	12	36	7	7	1	0	0	0	6	0	7	0	0
Maddux, Greg, Atlanta	19	4	.826	2.20	33	33	5	2	0	0	232.2	200	893	58	57	9	11	7	6	20	6	177	0	0
Maduro, Calvin, Philadelphia	3	7	.300	7.23	15	13	0	0	0	0	71.0	83	331	59	57	12	1	4	3	41	5	31	6	2
Magnante, Mike, Houston*	3	1	.750	2.27	40	0	0	0	14	1	47.2	39	191	16	12	2	3	2	0	11	2	43	2	2
Mantei, Matt, Florida	0	0	.000	0.00	0	0	0	0	0	0	0.0	0	0	0	0	0	0	0	0	0	0	0	0	0
Manuel, Barry, New York	0	1	.000	5.26	19	0	0	0	6	0	25.2	35	123	18	15	6	1	0	1	13	1	21	0	1
Martin, Tom, Houston*	5	3	.625	2.09	55	0	0	0	18	2	56.0	52	236	13	13	2	6	1	1	23	2	36	3	0
Martinez, Pedro A., Cincinnati*	1	1	.500	9.45	8	0	0	0	1	0	6.2	8	37	9	7	1	0	1	1	7	0	4	0	0
Martinez, Pedro J., Montreal	17	8	.680	1.90	31	31	13	4	0	0	241.1	158	947	65	51	16	9	1	9	67	5	305	3	1
Martinez, Ramon, Los Angeles	10	5	.667	3.64	22	22	1	0	0	0	133.2	123	590	64	54	14	5	4	6	68	1	120	1	1
Mathews, T.J., St. Louis	4	4	.500	2.15	40	0	0	0	12	0	46.0	41	197	14	11	4	6	0	1	18	3	46	1	0
McCurry, Jeff, Colorado	1	4	.200	4.43	33	0	0	0	14	0	40.2	43	179	22	20	7	3	1	0	20	0	19	2	0
McGraw, Tom, St. Louis*	0	0	.000	0.00	2	0	0	0	2	0	1.2	2	8	0	0	0	0	1	0	1	0	0	0	0
McMichael, Greg, New York	7	10	.412	2.98	73	0	0	0	23	7	87.2	73	355	34	29	8	9	4	2	27	6	81	5	0
Menhart, Paul, San Diego	2	3	.400	4.70	9	8	0	0	0	0	44.0	42	180	23	23	6	2	1	0	13	0	22	4	0
Mercker, Kent, Cincinnati*	8	11	.421	3.92	28	25	0	0	0	0	144.2	135	616	65	63	16	8	4	2	62	6	75	2	1
Miller, Kurt, Florida	0	1	.000	9.82	7	0	0	0	1	0	7.1	12	41	8	8	2	0	0	1	7	0	7	0	0
Millwood, Kevin, Atlanta	5	3	.625	4.03	12	8	0	0	2	0	51.1	55	227	26	23	1	3	5	2	21	1	42	1	0
Mimbs, Michael, Philadelphia*	0	0	.000	7.53	17	1	0	0	4	0	28.2	31	146	27	24	6	2	0	3	27	1	29	4	0
Minchey, Nate, Colorado	0	0	.000	13.50	2	0	0	0	0	0	2.0	5	12	3	3	0	2	0	0	1	0	1	0	0
Minor, Blas, Houston	1	0	1.000	4.50	11	0	0	0	5	1	12.0	13	55	7	6	1	1	1	1	5	0	6	4	0
Mlicki, Dave, New York	8	12	.400	4.00	32	32	1	1	0	0	193.2	194	838	89	86	21	3	6	5	76	7	157	5	1
Morel, Ramon, Pit.-Chi.	2	0	1.000	4.76	8	0	0	0	5	0	11.1	14	53	6	6	3	0	0	0	7	1	7	0	0
Morgan, Mike, Cincinnati	9	12	.429	4.78	31	30	1	0	0	0	162.0	165	688	91	86	13	9	2	8	49	6	103	7	0
Morris, Matt, St. Louis	12	9	.571	3.19	33	33	3	0	0	0	217.0	208	900	88	77	17	11	7	7	69	2	149	5	3
Mulholland, Terry, Chi.-S.F.*	6	13	.316	4.24	40	27	1	0	5	0	186.2	190	794	100	88	24	17	4	11	51	3	99	3	0
Munoz, Mike, Colorado*	3	3	.500	4.53	64	0	0	0	16	2	45.2	52	192	25	23	4	0	0	13	0	26	3	0
Munoz, Bobby, Philadelphia	1	5	.167	8.91	8	7	0	0	1	0	33.1	47	161	35	33	4	3	2	15	1	20	3	1
Murray, Heath, San Diego*	1	2	.333	6.75	17	3	0	0	1	0	33.1	50	162	25	25	3	3	1	4	21	3	16	1	1
Myers, Rodney, Chicago	0	0	.000	6.00	5	1	0	0	2	0	9.0	12	44	6	6	1	1	1	1	6	0	6	0	0
Neagle, Denny, Atlanta*	20	5	.800	2.97	34	34	4	4	0	0	233.1	204	947	87	77	18	12	6	6	49	5	172	3	0
Nen, Robb, Florida	9	3	.750	3.89	73	0	0	0	65	35	74.0	72	332	35	32	7	1	3	0	40	7	81	5	0
Nomo, Hideo, Los Angeles	14	12	.538	4.25	33	33	1	0	0	0	207.1	193	904	104	98	23	7	1	9	92	2	233	10	4
Nye, Ryan, Philadelphia	0	2	.000	8.25	4	2	0	0	1	0	12.0	20	65	11	11	2	1	2	2	9	0	7	0	0

Pitcher, Team	W	L	Pct.	ERA	G	GS	CG	ShO	GF	Sv.	IP	H	TBF	R	ER	HR	SH	SF	HB	BB	IBB	SO	WP	Bk.
Ojala, Kirt, Florida*	1	2	.333	3.14	7	5	0	0	1	0	28.2	28	130	10	10	4	0	1	0	18	0	19	0	0
Osborne, Donovan, St. Louis*	3	7	.300	4.93	14	14	0	0	0	0	80.1	84	337	46	44	10	3	3	1	23	2	51	1	0
Osuna, Antonio, Los Angeles	3	4	.429	2.19	48	0	0	0	18	0	61.2	46	245	15	15	6	4	1	1	19	2	68	2	0
Painter, Lance, St. Louis*	1	1	.500	4.76	14	0	0	0	4	0	17.0	13	69	9	9	1	0	0	0	8	2	11	0	0
Pall, Donn, Florida	0	0	.000	3.86	2	0	0	0	1	0	2.1	3	11	1	1	1	0	0	0	1	0	0	0	0
Paniagua, Jose, Montreal	1	2	.333	12.00	9	3	0	0	0	0	18.0	29	100	24	24	2	1	1	4	16	1	8	1	0
Park, Chan Ho, Los Angeles	14	8	.636	3.38	32	29	2	0	1	0	192.0	149	792	80	72	24	9	5	8	70	1	166	4	1
Patterson, Bob, Chicago*	1	6	.143	3.34	76	0	0	0	12	0	59.1	47	231	23	22	9	5	4	0	10	1	58	1	0
Perez, Carlos, Montreal*	12	13	.480	3.88	33	32	8	5	0	0	206.2	206	857	109	89	21	5	7	4	48	1	110	2	1
Perez, Yorkis, New York*	0	1	.000	8.31	9	0	0	0	1	0	8.2	15	45	8	8	2	0	1	0	4	0	7	1	0
Peters, Chris, Pittsburgh*	2	2	.500	4.58	31	1	0	0	5	0	37.1	38	167	23	19	6	5	1	3	21	4	17	4	0
Petkovsek, Mark, St. Louis	4	7	.364	5.06	55	2	0	0	19	2	96.0	109	414	61	54	14	2	2	6	31	4	51	2	0
Pisciotta, Marc, Chicago	3	1	.750	3.18	24	0	0	0	7	0	28.1	20	119	10	10	1	1	1	1	16	0	21	2	0
Plantenberg, Erik, Phi.*	0	0	.000	4.91	35	0	0	0	9	0	25.2	25	113	14	14	1	1	1	2	10	1	12	2	0
Poole, Jim Ri., San Francisco*	3	1	.750	7.11	63	0	0	0	11	0	49.1	73	242	44	39	6	4	1	4	25	4	26	5	0
Portugal, Mark, Philadelphia	0	2	.000	4.61	3	3	0	0	0	0	13.2	17	60	8	7	0	1	1	0	5	0	2	0	0
Powell, Jay, Florida	7	2	.778	3.28	74	0	0	0	23	2	79.2	71	337	35	29	3	6	4	4	30	3	65	3	0
Pulsipher, Bill, New York*	0	0	.000	0.00	0	0	0	0	0	0	0.0	0	0	0	0	0	0	0	0	0	0	0	0	0
Radinsky, Scott, Los Angeles*	5	1	.833	2.89	75	0	0	0	14	3	62.1	54	258	22	20	4	3	4	1	21	5	44	0	0
Raggio, Brady, St. Louis	2	4	.333	6.89	15	4	0	0	5	0	31.1	44	151	24	24	1	1	2	1	16	0	21	3	0
Ramos, Edgar, Philadelphia	0	2	.000	5.14	4	2	0	0	1	0	14.0	15	60	9	8	3	1	0	1	6	0	4	1	0
Rapp, Pat, Fla.-S.F.	5	8	.385	4.83	27	25	1	1	0	0	141.2	158	638	83	76	16	6	6	5	72	4	92	8	0
Reed, Rick, New York	13	9	.591	2.89	33	31	2	0	0	0	208.1	186	824	76	67	19	7	3	5	31	4	113	0	0
Reed, Steve, Colorado	4	6	.400	4.04	63	0	0	0	23	6	62.1	49	260	28	28	10	3	1	5	27	1	43	0	0
Rekar, Bryan, Colorado	1	0	1.000	5.79	2	2	0	0	0	0	9.1	11	46	7	6	3	1	0	0	6	0	4	0	0
Remlinger, Mike, Cincinnati*	8	8	.500	4.14	69	12	2	0	10	2	124.0	100	525	61	57	11	6	4	7	60	6	145	12	2
Reyes, Dennis, Los Angeles*	2	3	.400	3.83	14	5	0	0	0	0	47.0	51	207	21	20	4	5	1	1	18	3	36	2	1
Reynolds, Shane, Houston	9	10	.474	4.23	30	30	2	0	0	0	181.0	189	773	92	85	19	9	5	3	47	5	152	5	2
Reynoso, Armando, New York	6	3	.667	4.53	16	16	1	1	0	0	91.1	95	388	47	46	7	3	5	6	29	4	47	4	1
Rijo, Jose, Cincinnati	0	0	.000	0.00	0	0	0	0	0	0	0	0	0	0	0	0	0	0	0	0	0	0	0	0
Rincon, Ricardo, Pittsburgh*	4	8	.333	3.45	62	0	0	0	23	4	60.0	51	254	26	23	5	5	1	2	24	6	71	2	3
Ritz, Kevin, Colorado	6	8	.429	5.87	18	18	1	0	0	0	107.1	142	486	72	70	16	4	5	1	46	3	56	7	0
Roa, Joe, San Francisco	2	5	.286	5.21	28	3	0	0	4	0	65.2	86	289	40	38	8	5	4	2	20	5	34	0	1
Rodriguez, Felix, Cincinnati	0	0	.000	4.30	26	1	0	0	13	0	46.0	48	212	23	22	2	0	1	6	28	2	34	4	1
Rodriguez, Rich, San Fran.*	4	3	.571	3.17	71	0	0	0	15	1	65.1	65	271	24	23	7	3	0	1	21	4	32	0	0
Rojas, Mel, Chi.-N.Y.	0	6	.000	4.64	77	0	0	0	50	15	85.1	78	370	47	44	15	2	2	7	36	2	93	3	0
Ruebel, Matt, Pittsburgh*	3	2	.600	6.32	44	0	0	0	9	0	62.2	77	296	50	44	8	5	5	2	27	3	50	4	0
Rueter, Kirk, San Francisco*	13	6	.684	3.45	32	32	0	0	0	0	190.2	194	802	83	73	17	10	6	1	51	8	115	3	0
Ruffcorn, Scott, Philadelphia	0	3	.000	7.71	18	4	0	0	7	0	39.2	42	202	40	34	4	1	5	7	36	1	33	6	1
Ruffin, Bruce, Colorado*	0	2	.000	5.32	23	0	0	0	15	7	22.0	18	102	15	13	3	2	0	0	18	0	31	2	0
Ryan, Ken, Philadelphia	1	0	1.000	9.58	22	0	0	0	10	0	20.2	31	108	23	22	5	1	2	2	13	1	10	0	0
Saunders, Tony, Florida*	4	6	.400	4.61	22	21	0	0	0	0	111.1	99	483	62	57	12	8	4	2	64	1	102	2	1
Schilling, Curt, Philadelphia	17	11	.607	2.97	35	35	7	2	0	0	254.1	208	1009	96	84	25	8	8	5	58	3	319	5	1
Schmidt, Jason, Pittsburgh	10	9	.526	4.60	32	32	2	0	0	0	187.2	193	825	106	96	16	10	3	9	76	2	136	8	0
Schourek, Pete, Cincinnati*	5	8	.385	5.42	18	17	0	0	0	0	84.2	78	371	59	51	18	4	1	4	38	0	59	2	0
Scott, Tim, S.D.-Col.	1	1	.500	8.14	17	0	0	0	2	0	21.0	30	101	20	19	2	1	1	3	7	0	16	0	0
Service, Scott, Cincinnati	0	0	.000	11.81	4	0	0	0	2	0	5.1	11	26	7	7	1	0	0	1	3	0	2	0	0
Shaw, Jeff, Cincinnati	4	2	.667	2.38	78	0	0	0	62	42	94.2	79	367	26	25	7	3	3	1	12	3	74	1	0
Silva, Jose, Pittsburgh	2	1	.667	5.94	11	4	0	0	1	0	36.1	52	174	26	24	4	4	3	1	16	3	30	0	1
Small, Mark, Houston	0	0	.000	0.00	0	0	0	0	0	0	0	0	0	0	0	0	0	0	0	0	0	0	0	0
Smiley, John, Cincinnati*	9	10	.474	5.23	20	20	0	0	0	0	117.0	139	514	76	68	17	6	1	6	31	3	94	2	0
Smith, Lee, Montreal	0	1	.000	5.82	25	0	0	0	14	5	21.2	28	100	16	14	2	0	1	8	0	15	0	0
Smith, Pete J., San Diego	7	6	.538	4.81	37	15	0	0	7	1	118.0	120	511	66	63	16	7	2	1	52	2	68	0	3
Smoltz, John, Atlanta	15	12	.556	3.02	35	35	7	2	0	0	256.0	234	1043	97	86	21	10	3	1	63	9	241	10	1
Sodowsky, Clint, Pittsburgh	2	2	.500	3.63	45	0	0	0	8	0	52.0	49	236	22	21	6	1	2	2	34	7	51	6	0
Spradlin, Jerry, Philadelphia	4	8	.333	4.74	76	0	0	0	23	1	81.2	86	345	45	43	9	1	2	1	27	3	67	5	2
Springer, Russ, Houston	3	3	.500	4.23	54	0	0	0	13	3	55.1	48	241	28	26	4	1	2	4	27	2	74	4	0
Stanifer, Rob, Florida	1	2	.333	4.60	36	0	0	0	10	1	45.0	43	188	23	23	9	4	0	3	16	0	28	1	0
Stephenson, Garrett, Phi.	8	6	.571	3.15	20	18	2	0	0	0	117.0	104	474	45	41	11	2	5	3	38	0	81	1	0
Stevens, Dave, Chicago	0	2	.000	9.64	10	0	0	0	1	0	9.1	13	50	11	10	0	0	1	1	9	0	13	0	1
Stottlemyre, Todd, St. Louis	12	9	.571	3.88	28	28	0	0	0	0	181.0	155	761	86	78	16	8	5	12	65	3	160	6	0
Stull, Everett, Montreal	0	1	.000	16.20	3	0	0	0	0	0	3.1	7	21	7	6	1	1	0	0	4	0	2	0	0
Sullivan, Scott, Cincinnati	5	3	.625	3.24	59	0	0	0	15	1	97.1	79	402	36	35	12	3	3	7	30	8	96	7	1
Swartzbaugh, Dave, Chicago	0	1	.000	9.00	2	2	0	0	0	0	8.0	12	42	8	8	1	0	1	1	7	0	4	0	0
Swift, Bill C., Colorado	4	6	.400	6.34	14	13	0	0	1	0	65.1	85	304	57	46	11	4	4	2	26	0	29	2	2
Tabaka, Jeff, Cincinnati*	0	0	.000	4.50	3	0	0	0	2	0	2.0	1	10	1	1	1	0	0	2	1	0	1	0	0
Tapani, Kevin, Chicago	9	3	.750	3.39	13	13	1	0	0	0	85.0	77	352	33	32	7	7	2	2	23	2	55	0	2
Tatis, Ramon, Chicago*	1	1	.500	5.34	56	0	0	0	12	0	55.2	66	255	36	33	13	6	3	3	29	6	33	4	2
Tavarez, Julian, San Francisco	6	4	.600	3.87	89	0	0	0	13	0	88.1	91	378	43	38	6	3	8	4	34	5	38	4	0
Telemaco, Amaury, Chicago	0	3	.000	6.16	10	5	0	0	2	0	38.0	47	169	26	26	4	2	1	0	11	0	29	1	0
Telford, Anthony, Montreal	4	6	.400	3.24	65	0	0	0	17	1	89.0	77	369	34	32	11	4	1	5	33	4	61	6	0
Thompson, Mark, Colorado	3	3	.500	7.89	6	0	0	0	0	0	29.2	40	146	27	26	8	3	2	4	19	0	9	0	1
Thomson, John, Colorado	7	9	.438	4.71	27	27	2	1	0	0	166.1	193	721	94	87	15	10	3	5	51	0	106	2	0
Thurman, Mike, Montreal	1	0	1.000	5.40	5	2	0	0	1	0	11.2	8	48	9	7	3	0	0	1	4	0	8	0	0
Tomko, Brett, Cincinnati	11	7	.611	3.43	22	19	0	0	1	0	126.0	106	519	50	48	14	5	4	9	47	4	95	5	0
Torres, Salomon, Montreal	0	0	.000	7.25	12	0	0	0	7	0	16.0	19	18	2	3	1	2	1	2	0	1	0	1	3	0
Trachsel, Steve, Chicago	8	12	.400	4.51	34	34	0	0	0	0	201.1	225	878	110	101	32	8	11	5	69	6	160	4	1
Trlicek, Rick, New York	0	0	.000	8.00	9	0	0	0	4	0	9.0	10	39	9	8	2	0	0	0	4	2	0	0	0
Urbina, Ugueth, Montreal	5	8	.385	3.78	63	0	0	0	50	27	64.1	52	276	29	27	9	3	0	1	29	2	84	2	0
Valdes, Ismael, Los Angeles	10	11	.476	2.65	30	30	0	0	0	0	196.2	171	795	68	58	16	11	3	4	47	1	140	3	2
Valdes, Marc, Montreal	4	4	.500	3.13	48	7	0	0	9	2	95.0	84	407	36	33	2	5	5	8	39	5	54	2	0
Valenzuela, F'do, S.D.-St.L.*	2	12	.143	4.96	18	18	1	0	0	0	89.0	106	419	61	49	12	7	2	5	46	0	61	4	0

Pitcher, Team	W	L	Pct.	ERA	G	GS	CG	ShO	GF	Sv.	IP	H	TBF	R	ER	HR	SH	SF	HB	BB	IBB	SO	WP	Bk.
VanLandingham, William, S.F...	4	7	.364	4.96	18	17	0	0	1	0	89.0	80	403	56	49	11	0	7	0	59	3	52	9	2
Veras, Dario, San Diego	2	1	.667	5.11	23	0	0	0	7	0	24.2	28	114	18	14	5	0	0	2	13	3	21	0	0
Veres, Dave, Montreal	2	3	.400	3.48	53	0	0	0	11	1	62.0	68	281	28	24	5	6	1	2	27	3	47	7	0
Vosberg, Ed, Florida*	1	1	.500	3.75	17	0	0	0	6	1	12.0	15	59	7	5	0	1	1	3	6	0	8	1	1
Wade, Terrell, Atlanta*	2	3	.400	5.36	12	9	0	0	1	0	42.0	60	197	31	25	6	2	5	2	16	1	35	1	0
Wagner, Matt, Montreal...........	0	0	.000	0.00	0	0	0	0	0	0	0.0	0	0	0	0	0	0	0	0	0	0	0	0	0
Wagner, Paul, Pittsburgh	0	0	.000	3.94	14	0	0	0	2	0	16.0	17	79	7	7	3	3	1	0	13	3	9	3	2
Wagner, Billy, Houston*	7	8	.467	2.85	62	0	0	0	49	23	66.1	49	277	23	21	5	3	1	3	30	1	106	3	0
Wainhouse, Dave, Pittsburgh...	0	1	.000	8.04	25	0	0	0	6	0	28.0	34	137	28	25	2	3	1	3	17	0	21	1	1
Wall, Donne, Houston	2	5	.286	6.26	8	8	0	0	0	0	41.2	53	186	31	29	8	0	0	2	16	0	25	2	1
Wallace, Derek, New York	0	0	.000	0.00	0	0	0	0	0	0	0.0	0	0	0	0	0	0	0	0	0	0	0	0	0
Wallace, Jeff, Pittsburgh*	0	0	.000	0.75	11	0	0	0	1	0	12.0	8	50	2	1	0	1	1	0	8	1	14	1	0
Wendell, Turk, Chi.-N.Y............	3	5	.375	4.36	65	0	0	0	21	5	76.1	68	345	42	37	7	4	3	2	53	6	64	4	0
Whisenant, Matt, Florida*	0	0	.000	16.88	4	0	0	0	2	0	2.2	4	19	6	5	0	1	0	0	6	0	4	0	0
White, Gabe, Cincinnati*	2	2	.500	4.39	12	6	0	0	2	1	41.0	39	168	20	20	6	3	2	1	8	1	25	0	0
Wilkins, Marc, Pittsburgh........	9	5	.643	3.69	70	0	0	0	21	2	75.2	65	310	33	31	7	4	0	4	33	2	47	5	0
Wilson, Paul, New York...........	0	0	.000	0.00	0	0	0	0	0	0	0.0	0	0	0	0	0	0	0	0	0	0	0	0	0
Winchester, Scott, Cincinnati ...	0	0	.000	6.00	5	0	0	0	4	0	6.0	9	30	5	4	1	2	0	1	2	0	3	0	0
Winston, Darrin, Philadelphia*.	2	0	1.000	5.25	7	1	0	0	1	0	12.0	8	50	8	7	4	0	0	2	3	1	8	0	0
Wohlers, Mark, Atlanta	5	7	.417	3.50	71	0	0	0	55	33	69.1	57	300	29	27	4	4	4	0	38	0	92	6	0
Worrell, Tim, San Diego	4	8	.333	5.16	60	10	0	0	14	3	106.1	116	483	67	61	14	6	6	7	50	2	81	2	1
Worrell, Todd, Los Angeles	2	6	.250	5.28	65	0	0	0	55	35	59.2	60	265	38	35	12	2	0	0	23	1	61	1	0
Wright, Jamey, Colorado	8	12	.400	6.25	26	26	1	0	0	0	149.2	198	698	113	104	19	8	3	11	71	3	59	6	2

COMBINATION SHUTOUTS: **Atlanta (7)**—Maddux, Wohlers, Bielecki, Byrd, Embree, Clontz and Borowski; Maddux and Wohlers; Maddux, Bielecki and Wohlers; Glavine, Byrd and Clontz; Neagle, Fox and Wohlers; Neagle, Embree and Wohlers; Millwood and Clontz; **Chicago (2)**—Foster, Patterson and Rojas; Trachsel and Wendell. **Cincinnati (8)**—Mercker, Carrasco, Remlinger and Shaw; Burba, Belinda, Shaw and Brantley; Tomko and Belinda; Smiley, Belinda and Shaw; Tomko and Sullivan; Morgan, Belinda and Shaw; Burba, Belinda and Shaw; Burba, Sullivan, Belinda and Shaw. **Colorado (2)**—Thomson and Holmes; Astacio and DiPoto. **Florida (6)**—Helling, Powell and Nen; Brown, Cook, Stanifer, Heredia and Nen; Hernandez and Cook; Saunders, Powell, Cook and Nen; Hernandez, Pall and Cook; Leiter, Heredia, Powell and Vosberg. **Houston (5)**—Kile and Wagner; Kile, Springer and Wagner; Wall and Lima; Garcia and Wagner; Garcia, Henriquez and Wagner. **Los Angeles (5)**—Valdes, Hall and Worrell; Candiotti and Dreifort; Valdes, Radinsky, Dreifort and Hall; Park, Dreifort and Osuna; Valdes and Radinsky. **Montreal (2)**—Martinez and Urbina; Hermanson, Valdes, Veres and Urbina. **New York (5)**—Jones and J. Franco (2); Reynoso and Borland; Isringhausen, McMichael, Rojas and J. Franco; Mlicki and McMichael. **Philadelphia (4)**—Beech, Brewer and Spradlin; Beech and Bottalico; Green and Bottalico; Schilling and Bottalico. **Pittsburgh (6)**—Cooke, Loiselle and Ericks; Schmidt, Rincon and Ericks; Loaiza and Rincon; Cooke, Morel and Loiselle; Cooke and Loiselle; Cordova and Rincon. **St. Louis (3)**—Morris, Petkovsek, Mathews and Eckersley; Stottlemyre, Mathews and Eckersley; A. Benes, Mathews and Fossas. **San Diego (2)**—Worrell and Hoffman; Ashby, Worrell and Hoffman. **San Francisco (6)**—VanLandingham, Roa, Poole and Beck; Rueter, Henry and Beck; Fernandez, Henry, Rodriguez and Beck; Gardner, Johnstone, Poole and Henry; Estes and Beck; Rueter, Tavarez, Hernandez and Beck.

PITCHERS WITH TWO OR MORE TEAMS

Pitcher, Team	W	L	Pct.	ERA	G	GS	CG	ShO	GF	Sv.	IP	H	TBF	R	ER	HR	SH	SF	HB	BB	IBB	SO	WP	Bk.
Astacio, Pedro, Los Angeles	7	9	.438	4.10	26	24	2	1	2	0	153.2	151	654	75	70	15	9	5	4	47	0	115	4	3
Astacio, Pedro, Colorado	5	1	.833	4.25	7	7	0	0	0	0	48.2	49	208	23	23	9	0	2	5	14	0	51	2	0
Batchelor, Rich, St. Louis	1	1	.500	4.50	10	0	0	0	3	0	16.0	21	76	12	8	0	2	0	2	7	1	8	0	1
Batchelor, Rich, San Diego......	2	0	1.000	7.82	13	0	0	0	5	0	12.2	19	62	11	11	2	1	0	1	7	1	10	1	0
Castillo, Frank, Chicago	6	9	.400	5.42	20	19	0	0	0	0	98.0	113	446	64	59	9	11	0	4	44	1	67	1	0
Castillo, Frank, Colorado	6	3	.667	5.42	14	14	0	0	0	0	86.1	107	384	57	52	16	6	2	4	25	3	59	2	0
Clark, Mark, New York..............	8	7	.533	4.25	23	22	1	0	0	0	142.0	158	608	74	67	18	9	2	3	47	2	72	4	0
Clark, Mark, Chicago	6	1	.857	2.86	9	9	2	0	0	0	63.0	55	258	22	20	6	0	2	1	12	1	51	0	1
Hutton, Mark, Florida	3	1	.750	3.78	32	0	0	0	9	0	47.2	50	204	24	20	7	5	3	2	19	3	29	3	1
Hutton, Mark, Colorado............	0	1	.000	7.11	8	1	0	0	0	0	12.2	22	68	10	10	3	2	1	4	7	0	10	0	0
Jackson, Danny, St. Louis *......	1	2	.333	7.71	4	4	0	0	0	0	18.2	26	88	17	16	3	1	2	2	8	1	13	0	0
Jackson, Danny, San Diego*.....	1	7	.125	7.53	13	9	0	0	0	0	49.0	72	233	47	41	8	3	3	20	2	19	2	0	
Morel, Ramon, Pittsburgh.........	0	0	.000	4.70	5	0	0	0	2	0	7.2	11	36	4	4	2	0	0	0	4	1	4	0	0
Morel, Ramon, Chicago	0	0	.000	4.91	3	0	0	0	3	0	3.2	3	17	2	2	1	0	0	0	3	0	3	0	0
Mulholland, Terry, Chicago*.....	6	12	.333	4.07	25	25	1	0	0	0	157.0	162	668	79	71	20	13	3	9	45	2	74	2	0
Mulholland, Terry, San Fran.* ...	0	1	.000	5.16	15	2	0	0	5	0	29.2	28	126	21	17	4	4	1	2	6	1	25	1	0
Rapp, Pat, Florida	4	6	.400	4.47	19	19	1	1	0	0	108.2	121	484	59	54	11	4	3	3	51	3	64	5	0
Rapp, Pat, San Francisco	1	2	.333	6.00	8	6	0	0	0	0	33.0	37	154	24	22	5	2	3	2	21	1	28	3	0
Rojas, Mel, Chicago	0	4	.000	4.42	54	0	0	0	38	13	59.0	54	259	30	29	11	2	1	5	30	1	61	2	0
Rojas, Mel, New York	0	2	.000	5.13	23	0	0	0	12	2	26.1	24	111	17	15	4	0	1	2	6	1	32	1	0
Scott, Tim, San Diego	1	1	.500	7.85	14	0	0	0	2	0	18.1	25	87	17	16	2	0	1	3	5	0	14	0	0
Scott, Tim, Colorado	0	0	.000	10.13	3	0	0	0	0	0	2.2	5	14	3	3	0	1	0	0	2	0	2	0	0
Valenzuela, Fernando, S.D.*.....	2	8	.200	4.75	13	13	1	0	0	0	66.1	84	313	42	35	10	3	2	4	32	0	51	2	0
Valenzuela, Fernando, St.L.*	0	4	.000	5.56	5	5	0	0	0	0	22.2	22	106	19	14	2	4	0	1	14	0	10	2	0
Wendell, Turk, Chicago.............	3	5	.375	4.20	52	0	0	0	18	4	60.0	53	269	32	28	4	3	3	1	39	5	54	4	0
Wendell, Turk, New York	0	0	.000	4.96	13	0	0	0	3	1	16.1	15	76	10	9	3	1	0	1	14	1	10	0	0

FIELDING

TEAM

Team	Pct.	G	PO	A	E	TC	DP	PB	Team	Pct.	G	PO	A	E	TC	DP	PB
Colorado	.983	162	4298	1946	111	6355	202	5	St. Louis	.980	162	4367	1739	123	6229	156	18
Cincinnati	.982	162	4347	1576	106	6029	129	13	San Francisco	.980	162	4338	1799	125	6262	157	9
Philadelphia	.982	162	4261	1547	108	5916	134	16	Houston	.979	162	4377	1874	131	6382	169	6
Atlanta	.982	162	4397	1669	114	6180	136	11	Pittsburgh	.979	162	4308	1833	131	6272	149	11
Chicago	.981	162	4287	1605	112	6004	117	16	San Diego	.979	162	4350	1819	132	6301	132	8
New York	.981	162	4378	1881	120	6379	165	10	Montreal	.979	162	4341	1697	132	6170	150	13
Florida	.981	162	4340	1650	116	6106	167	7	**Totals**	.981	1134	60767	24198	1677	86642	2067	154
Los Angeles	.981	162	4378	1563	116	6057	104	11									

TRIPLE PLAYS: Chicago, San Diego.

INDIVIDUAL

FIRST BASEMEN

NOTE: All caps denotes fielding-percentage leader based on 81 games for catchers, 108 for all other non-pitchers and 162 innings for pitchers. *Throws lefthanded.

Player, Team	Pct.	G	PO	A	E	TC	DP
Amaro, Ruben, Philadelphia	1.000	1	4	0	0	4	1
Bagwell, Jeff, Houston	.993	159	1404	137	11	1552	140
Berryhill, Damon, San Francisco	1.000	1	5	0	0	5	1
Blanco, Henry, Los Angeles	1.000	1	5	0	0	5	0
Bogar, Tim, Houston	.000	1	0	0	0	0	0
Bonilla, Bobby, Florida	1.000	2	2	0	0	2	0
Brogna, Rico, Philadelphia*	.994	145	1053	119	7	1179	100
Brown, Brant, Chicago*	.976	12	78	4	2	84	7
Cianfrocco, Archi, San Diego	.983	39	219	19	4	242	16
Colbrunn, Greg, Atlanta	.984	14	54	6	1	61	3
Conine, Jeff, Florida	.992	145	899	104	8	1011	101
Daulton, Darren, Phi.-Fla.	.986	42	259	17	4	280	22
Difelice, Mike, St. Louis	1.000	1	1	0	0	1	0
Eisenreich, Jim, Florida*	.993	29	136	11	1	148	15
Floyd, Cliff, Florida	.974	9	36	1	1	38	5
Franco, Matt, New York	1.000	13	50	4	0	54	5
Fullmer, Brad, Montreal	.982	8	49	7	1	57	6
Gaetti, Gary, St. Louis	1.000	20	61	6	0	67	8
Galarraga, Andres, Colorado	.991	154	1458	117	15	1590	176
Garcia, Freddy, Pittsburgh	1.000	2	14	0	0	14	2
Gonzalez, Luis, Houston	1.000	1	3	0	0	3	1
Grace, Mark, Chicago*	.995	148	1202	120	6	1328	93
Graffanino, Tony, Atlanta	1.000	1	1	0	0	1	0
Greene, Willie, Cincinnati	1.000	7	47	2	0	49	2
Gregg, Tommy, Atlanta*	1.000	1	3	0	0	3	0
Hansen, Dave, Chicago	.955	4	19	2	1	22	4
Harris, Lenny, Cincinnati	.982	11	51	5	1	57	1
Helton, Todd, Colorado*	1.000	8	68	10	0	78	7
Hernandez, Carlos, San Diego	1.000	4	5	3	0	8	0
Hernandez, Jose, Chicago	.857	1	6	0	1	7	0
Houston, Tyler, Chicago	1.000	2	8	2	0	10	1
Huskey, Butch, New York	.990	22	182	10	2	194	19
Javier, Stan, San Francisco	.955	3	21	0	1	22	2
Johnson, Brian, San Francisco	1.000	2	8	0	0	8	0
Johnson, Mark, Pittsburgh*	.992	63	542	44	5	591	48
Jordan, Kevin, Philadelphia	.987	25	148	9	2	159	12
JOYNER, Wally, San Diego*	.996	131	1027	89	4	1120	82
Karros, Eric, Los Angeles	.992	162	1318	121	11	1450	89
Kent, Jeff, San Francisco	1.000	13	80	4	0	84	6
Klesko, Ryan, Atlanta*	1.000	22	63	3	0	66	7
Knorr, Randy, Houston	1.000	2	7	2	0	9	1
Lee, Derrek, San Diego	1.000	21	131	13	0	144	12
Liriano, Nelson, Los Angeles	1.000	2	5	1	0	6	0
Livingstone, Scott, San Diego	1.000	2	16	1	0	17	1
Mabry, John, St. Louis	.997	49	346	22	1	369	33
McGriff, Fred, Atlanta*	.990	149	1191	96	13	1300	111
McGuire, Ryan, Montreal*	1.000	30	157	16	0	173	20
McGwire, Mark, St. Louis	.998	50	439	34	1	474	41
Meulens, Hensley, Montreal	1.000	3	9	0	0	9	1
Mordecai, Mike, Atlanta	1.000	3	11	2	0	13	0
Morman, Russ, Florida	1.000	1	3	0	0	3	0
Morris, Hal, Cincinnati*	.990	89	672	52	7	731	67
Olerud, John, New York*	.995	146	1292	120	7	1419	125
Oliver, Joe, Cincinnati	1.000	4	14	2	0	16	0
Orsulak, Joe, Montreal*	.992	15	112	10	1	123	4
Osik, Keith, Pittsburgh	1.000	1	2	0	0	2	0
Pagnozzi, Tom, St. Louis	1.000	2	6	0	0	6	1
Perez, Eddie, Atlanta	1.000	6	25	1	0	26	0
Perez, Eduardo, Cincinnati	.996	67	489	35	2	526	37
Petagine, Roberto, New York*	1.000	6	9	3	0	12	0
Phillips, J.R., Houston*	1.000	3	6	0	0	6	1
Robertson, Mike, Philadelphia*	1.000	5	20	1	0	21	1
Rodriguez, Henry, Montreal*	1.000	3	22	2	0	24	2
Rose, Pete Jr., Cincinnati	1.000	1	6	0	0	6	0
Segui, David, Montreal*	.995	125	1035	88	6	1129	104
Servais, Scott, Chicago	1.000	1	1	0	0	1	0
Shipley, Craig, San Diego	.933	4	28	0	2	30	0
Simon, Randall, Atlanta*	1.000	6	16	2	0	18	2
Smith, Mark, Pittsburgh	1.000	9	58	5	0	63	1
Snow, J.T., San Francisco*	.995	156	1308	108	7	1423	133
Spiers, Bill, Houston	1.000	8	32	1	0	33	5
Strange, Doug, Montreal	1.000	1	2	1	0	3	1
Sveum, Dale, Pittsburgh	1.000	21	105	5	0	110	10
Sweeney, Mark, St.L.-S.D.*	.973	11	32	4	1	37	6
Taubensee, Eddie, Cincinnati	1.000	7	42	1	0	43	4
Vander Wal, John, Colorado*	1.000	5	26	0	0	26	2
Walker, Larry, Colorado	1.000	3	22	2	0	24	3
Williams, Eddie, Pittsburgh	.991	26	201	9	2	212	18
Young, Dmitri, St. Louis	.985	74	601	45	10	656	50
Young, Kevin, Pittsburgh	.997	77	619	51	2	672	47
Zaun, Gregg, Florida	1.000	1	2	1	0	3	1

TRIPLE PLAY: Cianfrocco, S.D.

FIRST BASEMEN WITH TWO OR MORE TEAMS

Player, Team	Pct.	G	PO	A	E	TC	DP
Daulton, Darren, Philadelphia	1.000	3	29	0	0	29	0
Daulton, Darren, Florida	.984	39	230	17	4	251	22
Sweeney, Mark, St. Louis*	1.000	4	8	1	0	9	2
Sweeney, Mark, San Diego*	.964	7	24	3	1	28	4

SECOND BASEMEN

Player, Team	Pct.	G	PO	A	E	TC	DP
Abbott, Kurt, Florida	.969	54	101	116	7	224	21
Alexander, Manny, N.Y.-Chi.	.982	35	36	72	2	110	18
Alfonzo, Edgardo, New York	1.000	3	4	6	0	10	0
Baerga, Carlos, New York	.978	131	244	371	14	629	88
Bates, Jason, Colorado	1.000	22	27	25	0	52	12
Bell, David, St. Louis	.973	23	35	37	2	74	7
Belliard, Rafael, Atlanta	1.000	7	1	5	0	6	0
Berblinger, Jeff, St. Louis	1.000	4	4	4	0	8	2
Biggio, Craig, Houston	.979	160	341	504	18	863	108
Boone, Aaron, Cincinnati	.000	1	0	0	0	0	0
BOONE, Bret, Cincinnati	.997	136	271	334	2	607	74
Branson, Jeff, Cincinnati	.930	14	17	23	3	43	7
Cabrera, Orlando, Montreal	1.000	4	10	9	0	19	2
Cairo, Miguel, Chicago	1.000	9	15	15	0	30	5
Castillo, Luis, Florida	.971	70	129	177	9	315	44
Castro, Juan, Los Angeles	.977	14	15	28	1	44	4
Cianfrocco, Archi, San Diego	1.000	12	15	23	0	38	7
Counsell, Craig, Florida	.989	51	124	149	3	276	37
Cromer, Tripp, Los Angeles	.968	17	24	36	2	62	7
Delgado, Wilson, San Francisco	1.000	3	1	3	0	4	1
DeShields, Delino, St. Louis	.972	147	271	398	19	688	92
Fonville, Chad, Los Angeles	.833	3	0	5	1	6	0
Gallego, Mike, St. Louis	.962	11	9	16	1	26	3
Gilbert, Shawn, New York	.875	8	6	1	1	8	1
Giovanola, Ed, Atlanta	1.000	1	0	2	0	2	0
Graffanino, Tony, Atlanta	.982	75	88	178	5	271	29

Player, Team	Pct.	G	PO	A	E	TC	DP
Guerrero, Wilton, Los Angeles....	.989	90	140	221	4	365	24
Gutierrez, Ricky, Houston	1.000	9	9	3	0	12	2
Hansen, Dave, Chicago	.000	1	0	0	0	0	0
Hardtke, Jason, New York............	.981	21	25	26	1	52	7
Harris, Lenny, Cincinnati	.984	20	26	34	1	61	6
Hernandez, Jose, Chicago	.969	20	31	31	2	64	3
Houston, Tyler, Chicago	1.000	1	1	1	0	2	0
Hudler, Rex, Philadelphia	.952	6	11	9	1	21	2
Jackson, Damian, Cincinnati	.933	3	7	7	1	15	1
Johnson, Russ, Houston	1.000	3	9	2	0	11	1
Jordan, Kevin, Philadelphia	.882	6	4	11	2	17	1
Kent, Jeff, San Francisco	.979	148	325	425	16	766	104
Lansing, Mike, Montreal	.987	144	279	395	9	683	95
Lemke, Mark, Atlanta	.980	104	191	309	10	510	65
Lewis, Mark, San Francisco	.940	29	40	54	6	100	14
Liriano, Nelson, Los Angeles	.949	17	14	23	2	39	6
Livingstone, Scott, San Diego.....	1.000	1	0	3	0	3	0
Lockhart, Keith, Atlanta..............	.983	20	22	37	1	60	9
Lopez, Luis, New York	.961	20	34	40	3	77	8
Mejia, Roberto, St. Louis............	.900	3	3	6	1	10	3
Milliard, Ralph, Florida	1.000	8	14	32	0	46	9
Morandini, Mickey, Philadelphia .	.990	146	254	350	6	610	87
Mordecai, Mike, Atlanta	1.000	4	3	2	0	5	0
Nunez, Abraham, Pittsburgh.......	1.000	9	5	12	0	17	0
Osik, Keith, Pittsburgh	1.000	4	1	1	0	2	0
Owens, Eric, Cincinnati	.000	2	0	0	0	0	0
Perez, Neifi, Colorado	.992	41	106	130	2	238	39
Polcovich, Kevin, Pittsburgh.......	1.000	2	4	0	0	4	1
Raabe, Brian, Colorado	1.000	1	0	3	0	3	0
Randa, Joe, Pittsburgh	1.000	13	25	41	0	66	6
Reese, Pokey, Cincinnati	1.000	8	9	20	0	29	2
Riggs, Adam, Los Angeles..........	1.000	8	6	19	0	25	3
Rivera, Luis, Houston	1.000	1	3	1	0	4	0
Sanchez, Rey, Chicago................	.992	32	51	72	1	124	16
Sandberg, Ryne, Chicago............	.984	126	203	297	8	508	58
Santangelo, F.P., Montreal..........	1.000	7	5	6	0	11	2
Scarsone, Steve, St. Louis..........	1.000	2	4	2	0	6	0
Sefcik, Kevin, Philadelphia	.961	22	29	45	3	77	6
Sheaffer, Danny, St. Louis..........	1.000	3	3	3	0	6	2
Shipley, Craig, San Diego...........	.984	16	24	36	1	61	8
Shumpert, Terry, San Diego........	.973	7	21	15	1	37	4
Spiers, Bill, Houston	1.000	4	3	13	0	16	3
Stankiewicz, Andy, Montreal	.957	25	19	47	3	69	9
Strange, Doug, Montreal..............	1.000	3	6	5	0	11	1
Stynes, Chris, Cincinnati	1.000	8	9	19	0	28	2
Sveum, Dale, Pittsburgh	.889	2	3	5	1	9	1
Velandia, Jorge, San Diego	.929	5	7	6	1	14	1
Veras, Quilvio, San Diego	.984	142	276	407	11	694	65
Vidro, Jose, Montreal..................	.938	5	5	10	1	16	1
Vizcaino, Jose, San Francisco.....	1.000	5	4	4	0	8	0
Womack, Tony, Pittsburgh...........	.974	152	335	429	20	784	83
Young, Eric, Col.-L.A..................	.978	154	318	494	18	830	111

TRIPLE PLAY: Sandberg, Chi.

SECOND BASEMEN WITH TWO OR MORE TEAMS

Player, Team	Pct.	G	PO	A	E	TC	DP
Alexander, Manny, New York.......	.979	31	28	64	2	94	17
Alexander, Manny, Chicago.........	1.000	4	8	8	0	16	1
Young, Eric, Colorado	.978	117	258	414	15	687	93
Young, Eric, Los Angeles............	.979	37	60	80	3	143	18

THIRD BASEMEN

Player, Team	Pct.	G	PO	A	E	TC	DP
Abbott, Kurt, Florida	.750	4	2	1	1	4	0
Alexander, Manny, New York	1.000	1	0	1	0	1	0
Alfonzo, Edgardo, New York........	.967	143	82	269	12	363	29
Andrews, Shane, Montreal	.895	18	11	40	6	57	6
Arias, Alex, Florida	.971	37	13	20	1	34	3
Arias, George, San Diego	.941	8	4	12	1	17	0
Bates, Jason, Colorado	1.000	6	2	6	0	8	0
Bell, David, St. Louis..................	.913	35	10	32	4	46	1
Berry, Sean, Houston	.921	85	47	140	16	203	11
Blanco, Henry, Los Angeles........	.000	1	0	0	0	0	0
Bogar, Tim, Houston	.955	14	7	14	1	22	2
Bonilla, Bobby, Florida	.938	149	104	226	22	352	29
Boone, Aaron, Cincinnati	.917	13	11	22	3	36	0
Booty, Josh, Florida	.857	4	1	5	1	7	1
Branson, Jeff, Cincinnati	.971	27	12	22	1	35	4
Caminiti, Ken, San Diego	.941	133	90	291	24	405	20
Castilla, Vinny, Colorado	.954	157	112	323	21	456	41
Castro, Juan, Los Angeles	1.000	3	2	3	0	5	0

Player, Team	Pct.	G	PO	A	E	TC	DP
Cianfrocco, Archi, San Diego	.978	38	24	67	2	93	4
Coles, Darnell, Colorado	1.000	3	0	3	0	3	0
Cromer, Tripp, Los Angeles.........	.000	1	0	0	0	0	0
Franco, Matt, New York	.937	39	11	48	4	63	6
GAETTI, Gary, St. Louis..............	.978	132	72	243	7	322	24
Gallego, Mike, St. Louis..............	1.000	7	1	7	0	8	0
Garcia, Freddy, Pittsburgh	.842	10	7	9	3	19	1
Gilbert, Shawn, New York	1.000	3	1	3	0	4	0
Giovanola, Ed, Atlanta	1.000	8	0	3	0	3	0
Gonzales, Rene, Colorado...........	1.000	1	0	0	0	0	0
Graffanino, Tony, Atlanta.............	1.000	2	1	0	0	1	0
Greene, Willie, Cincinnati	.934	103	55	172	16	243	7
Gulan, Mike, St. Louis.................	1.000	3	1	1	0	2	1
Gutierrez, Ricky, Houston	1.000	22	10	35	0	45	3
Hale, Chip, Los Angeles..............	1.000	2	1	0	0	1	0
Hansen, Dave, Chicago	.922	51	26	45	6	77	5
Hardtke, Jason, New York............	.000	1	0	0	0	0	0
Harris, Lenny, Cincinnati	1.000	13	2	17	0	19	1
Hernandez, Jose, Chicago	.922	47	19	28	4	51	3
Houston, Tyler, Chicago	.963	12	8	18	1	27	2
Hubbard, Mike, Chicago..............	.000	1	0	0	0	0	0
Huskey, Butch, New York............	.848	15	17	22	7	46	3
Johnson, Russ, Houston	.963	14	4	22	1	27	2
Jones, Chipper, Atlanta...............	.955	152	77	241	15	333	17
Jordan, Kevin, Philadelphia.........	.889	12	5	11	2	18	0
Konerko, Paul, Los Angeles	.000	1	0	0	0	0	0
Lewis, Mark, San Francisco	.945	69	34	103	8	145	10
Liriano, Nelson, Los Angeles	.000	1	0	0	0	0	0
Livingstone, Scott, S.D.-St.L.	.778	5	1	6	2	9	0
Lockhart, Keith, Atlanta..............	.867	11	2	11	2	15	1
Lopez, Luis, New York	.944	4	4	13	1	18	1
Mabry, John, St. Louis................	.000	1	0	0	0	0	0
Mordecai, Mike, Atlanta	1.000	19	9	11	0	20	2
Morgan, Kevin, New York	1.000	1	0	1	0	1	0
Mueller, Bill, San Francisco	.956	122	85	218	14	317	18
Orie, Kevin, Chicago...................	.971	112	91	212	9	312	15
Osik, Keith, Pittsburgh	.000	1	0	0	0	0	0
Pagnozzi, Tom, St. Louis	.000	1	0	0	0	0	0
Pendleton, Terry, Cincinnati	.942	32	14	35	3	52	1
Perez, Eduardo, Cincinnati	1.000	8	6	14	0	20	1
Perez, Neifi, Colorado	.857	2	2	4	1	7	0
Polcovich, Kevin, Pittsburgh.......	.000	1	0	0	0	0	0
Randa, Joe, Pittsburgh	.937	120	66	247	21	334	24
Reese, Pokey, Cincinnati	1.000	8	2	3	0	5	0
Rolen, Scott, Philadelphia	.948	155	144	291	24	459	30
Rose, Pete Jr., Cincinnati	.600	2	0	3	2	5	0
Sanchez, Rey, Chicago................	.000	1	0	0	0	0	0
Santangelo, F.P., Montreal	.954	32	17	45	3	65	0
Scarsone, Steve, St. Louis..........	1.000	1	0	0	0	0	0
Sefcik, Kevin, Philadelphia	1.000	4	2	3	0	5	1
Sheaffer, Danny, St. Louis..........	.957	30	8	36	2	46	2
Shipley, Craig, San Diego...........	.000	2	0	0	0	0	0
Shumpert, Terry, San Diego........	.750	2	1	2	1	4	0
Spiers, Bill, Houston	.935	84	44	129	12	185	12
Stankiewicz, Andy, Montreal	1.000	3	1	2	0	3	1
Strange, Doug, Montreal..............	.947	105	62	170	13	245	13
Stynes, Chris, Cincinnati	1.000	3	1	9	0	10	1
Sveum, Dale, Pittsburgh	.941	47	17	78	6	101	4
Velandia, Jorge, San Diego	.833	3	0	5	1	6	0
Vidro, Jose, Montreal..................	.958	36	20	49	3	72	6
Wehner, John, Florida	1.000	6	1	3	0	4	0
Young, Kevin, Pittsburgh.............	.885	12	7	16	3	26	2
Zeile, Todd, Los Angeles............	.931	160	105	248	26	379	27

TRIPLE PLAY: Hernandez, Chi.

THIRD BASEMEN WITH TWO OR MORE TEAMS

Player, Team	Pct.	G	PO	A	E	TC	DP
Livingstone, Scott, San Diego......	.750	3	1	5	2	8	0
Livingstone, Scott, St. Louis.......	1.000	2	0	1	0	1	0

SHORTSTOPS

Player, Team	Pct.	G	PO	A	E	TC	DP
Abbott, Kurt, Florida	1.000	7	10	19	0	29	6
Alexander, Manny, N.Y.-Chi.	.959	54	61	148	9	218	21
Alfonzo, Edgardo, New York	1.000	12	12	15	0	27	3
Arias, Alex, Florida	.969	11	13	18	1	32	7
Aurilia, Rich, San Francisco	.979	36	47	91	3	141	19
Bates, Jason, Colorado	.945	16	15	37	3	55	12
Bell, David, St. Louis..................	.947	13	10	26	2	38	4
Belliard, Rafael, Atlanta	.990	53	36	64	1	101	14
Blauser, Jeff, Atlanta	.973	149	204	372	16	592	79

Player, Team	Pct.	G	PO	A	E	TC	DP
Bogar, Tim, Houston	.985	80	103	215	5	323	53
Branson, Jeff, Cincinnati	1.000	11	6	11	0	17	2
Cabrera, Orlando, Montreal	.875	6	1	6	1	8	1
Cairo, Miguel, Chicago	1.000	2	1	3	0	4	2
Castro, Juan, Los Angeles	1.000	22	19	34	0	53	6
Cianfrocco, Archi, San Diego	.909	5	3	7	1	11	0
Clayton, Royce, St. Louis	.973	153	228	452	19	699	93
Collier, Lou, Pittsburgh	1.000	18	9	36	0	45	7
Cromer, Tripp, Los Angeles	.980	10	23	25	1	49	4
Delgado, Wilson, San Francisco	1.000	1	1	0	0	1	0
Dunston, Shawon, Chi.-Pit.	.969	126	191	282	15	488	54
Elster, Kevin, Pittsburgh	.994	39	54	123	1	178	22
Gagne, Greg, Los Angeles	.971	143	174	358	16	548	54
Gallego, Mike, St. Louis	1.000	10	5	18	0	23	3
Gilbert, Shawn, New York	1.000	6	4	4	0	8	0
Giovanola, Ed, Atlanta	1.000	1	0	1	0	1	0
Gomez, Chris, San Diego	.978	149	226	433	15	674	79
Graffanino, Tony, Atlanta	1.000	2	0	2	0	2	0
Greene, Willie, Cincinnati	.000	3	0	0	0	0	0
Grudzielanek, Mark, Montreal	.955	156	237	446	32	715	99
Guerrero, Wilton, Los Angeles	1.000	5	8	10	0	18	2
Gutierrez, Ricky, Houston	.967	64	85	153	8	246	35
Hernandez, Jose, Chicago	.981	21	20	32	1	53	8
Houston, Tyler, Chicago	.000	1	0	0	0	0	0
Jackson, Damian, Cincinnati	1.000	6	6	14	0	20	2
Larkin, Barry, Cincinnati	.980	63	77	171	5	253	33
Liriano, Nelson, Los Angeles	.000	1	0	0	0	0	0
Listach, Pat, Houston	.951	31	26	71	5	102	12
Lopez, Luis, New York	.966	45	41	103	5	149	21
Morandini, Mickey, Philadelphia	.000	1	0	0	0	0	0
Mordecai, Mike, Atlanta	1.000	4	3	2	0	5	2
Nunez, Abraham, Pittsburgh	1.000	12	9	25	0	34	5
Ordaz, Luis, St. Louis	.964	11	9	18	1	28	4
ORDONEZ, Rey, New York	.983	118	171	355	9	535	71
Orie, Kevin, Chicago	1.000	3	0	1	0	1	0
Perez, Neifi, Colorado	.975	45	78	154	6	238	34
Polcovich, Kevin, Pittsburgh	.969	80	121	248	12	381	38
Reese, Pokey, Cincinnati	.966	110	171	261	15	447	56
Relaford, Desi, Philadelphia	.977	12	12	31	1	44	3
Renteria, Edgar, Florida	.975	153	242	415	17	674	95
Rivera, Luis, Houston	.875	6	6	8	2	16	4
Sanchez, Rey, Chicago	.964	63	49	85	5	139	12
Santangelo, F.P., Montreal	1.000	1	0	1	0	1	0
Sefcik, Kevin, Philadelphia	.957	10	8	14	1	23	2
Shipley, Craig, San Diego	.947	21	17	37	3	57	5
Spiers, Bill, Houston	.932	28	25	57	6	88	12
Stankiewicz, Andy, Montreal	1.000	14	13	19	0	32	4
Stocker, Kevin, Philadelphia	.981	147	190	376	11	577	74
Sveum, Dale, Pittsburgh	.988	28	29	54	1	84	14
Velandia, Jorge, San Diego	.941	6	4	12	1	17	4
Vizcaino, Jose, San Francisco	.976	147	202	446	16	664	94
Weiss, Walt, Colorado	.983	119	191	372	10	573	88
Womack, Tony, Pittsburgh	1.000	4	0	1	0	1	0

TRIPLE PLAY: Gomez, S.D.

SHORTSTOPS WITH TWO OR MORE TEAMS

Player, Team	Pct.	G	PO	A	E	TC	DP
Alexander, Manny, New York	.980	26	31	65	2	98	10
Alexander, Manny, Chicago	.942	28	30	83	7	120	11
Dunston, Shawon, Chicago	.970	108	163	227	12	402	46
Dunston, Shawon, Pittsburgh	.965	18	28	55	3	86	8

OUTFIELDERS

Player, Team	Pct.	G	PO	A	E	TC	DP
Abbott, Kurt, Florida	1.000	10	13	0	0	13	0
Abreu, Bob, Houston	.978	53	84	4	2	90	1
Allensworth, Jermaine, Pit.	.980	104	189	5	4	198	1
Alou, Moises, Florida	.988	150	248	4	3	255	1
Amaro, Ruben, Philadelphia	.987	72	75	2	1	78	0
Anthony, Eric, Los Angeles*	.966	21	26	2	1	29	1
Ashley, Billy, Los Angeles	.911	35	39	2	4	45	0
Barron, Tony, Philadelphia	.983	53	111	3	2	116	1
Bautista, Danny, Atlanta	.984	57	59	1	1	61	1
Beamon, Trey, San Diego	.909	20	17	3	2	22	0
Bell, Derek, Houston	.967	125	226	5	8	239	2
Benard, Marvin, San Francisco*	.967	36	27	2	1	30	0
Bichette, Dante, Colorado	.987	139	225	4	3	232	1
Bieser, Steve, New York	1.000	21	30	2	0	32	0
Bonds, Barry, San Francisco*	.984	159	290	10	5	305	0
Brown, Adrian, Pittsburgh	.987	38	74	3	1	78	1
Brown, Brant, Chicago*	1.000	27	43	3	0	46	0

Player, Team	Pct.	G	PO	A	E	TC	DP
Brown, Emil, Pittsburgh	.948	42	53	2	3	58	1
Burks, Ellis, Colorado	.982	112	207	6	4	217	1
Butler, Brett, Los Angeles*	1.000	91	163	4	0	167	2
Butler, Rob, Philadelphia*	1.000	25	33	3	0	36	2
Cangelosi, John, Florida*	1.000	58	84	1	0	85	0
Carr, Chuck, Houston	.966	59	111	3	4	118	1
Cedeno, Roger, Los Angeles	.987	71	148	1	2	151	0
Cianfrocco, Archi, San Diego	1.000	2	1	0	0	1	0
Clark, Dave, Chicago	.953	25	39	2	2	43	0
Coles, Darnell, Colorado	.000	2	0	0	0	0	0
Conine, Jeff, Florida	.000	1	0	0	0	0	0
Cruz, Jacob, San Francisco*	.933	11	12	2	1	15	1
Cummings, Midre, Pit.-Phi.	.993	79	150	2	1	153	0
Daulton, Darren, Phi.-Fla.	.979	73	133	6	3	142	1
Dunston, Shawon, Chicago	1.000	7	16	0	0	16	0
Dunwoody, Todd, Florida*	.929	14	26	0	2	28	0
Echevarria, Angel, Colorado	1.000	7	4	1	0	5	0
Eisenreich, Jim, Florida*	.987	55	75	2	1	78	1
Everett, Carl, New York	.971	128	226	8	7	241	3
Finley, Steve, San Diego*	.989	140	338	10	4	352	3
Floyd, Cliff, Florida	.970	38	60	4	2	66	2
Franco, Matt, New York	.000	1	0	0	0	0	0
Franklin, Micah, St. Louis	1.000	13	13	0	0	13	0
Fullmer, Brad, Montreal	.500	2	1	0	1	2	0
Gant, Ron, St. Louis	.977	128	247	4	6	257	1
Garcia, Karim, Los Angeles*	1.000	12	13	0	0	13	0
Gilbert, Shawn, New York	.000	1	0	0	0	0	0
Gilkey, Bernard, New York	.989	136	251	17	3	271	2
Glanville, Doug, Chicago	.989	138	247	12	3	262	3
Gonzalez, Luis, Houston	.982	146	263	10	5	278	2
Goodwin, Curtis, Cincinnati*	1.000	71	159	3	0	162	2
Green, Scarborough, St. Louis	.952	19	19	1	1	21	0
Greene, Willie, Cincinnati	.987	39	74	1	1	76	1
Gregg, Tommy, Atlanta*	1.000	6	2	0	0	2	0
Guerrero, Vladimir, Montreal	.929	85	148	10	12	170	3
Guillen, Jose, Pittsburgh	.963	136	226	9	9	244	3
Gwynn, Tony, San Diego*	.983	143	218	8	4	230	3
Hamilton, Darryl, San Francisco	.980	118	245	1	5	251	0
Harris, Lenny, Cincinnati	.977	42	41	1	1	43	0
Helton, Todd, Colorado*	1.000	15	16	2	0	18	0
Henderson, Rickey, San Diego*	.959	78	160	4	7	171	1
Hernandez, Jose, Chicago	1.000	6	4	0	0	4	0
Hidalgo, Richard, Houston	1.000	19	28	0	0	28	0
Hill, Glenallen, San Francisco	.947	97	158	2	9	169	0
Hollandsworth, Todd, Los Ang.*	.984	99	185	2	3	190	0
Howard, Thomas, Houston	1.000	62	107	5	0	112	1
Hudler, Rex, Philadelphia	.962	35	50	1	2	53	0
Huskey, Butch, New York	.968	92	178	6	6	190	1
Ingram, Garey, Los Angeles	1.000	7	4	0	0	4	0
Javier, Stan, San Francisco	.977	130	256	2	6	264	2
Jefferies, Gregg, Philadelphia	.986	124	211	5	3	219	2
Jennings, Robin, Chicago*	1.000	5	5	0	0	5	0
Johnson, Lance, N.Y.-Chi.*	.971	105	231	4	7	242	2
Jones, Andruw, Atlanta	.977	147	287	14	7	308	2
Jones, Chris, San Diego	.951	61	73	4	4	81	1
Jones, Chipper, Atlanta	1.000	5	6	0	0	6	0
Jordan, Brian, St. Louis	1.000	44	82	2	0	84	0
Kelly, Mike, Cincinnati	.978	59	88	2	2	92	0
Kieschnick, Brooks, Chicago	.952	27	39	1	2	42	0
Kirby, Wayne, Los Angeles	1.000	26	36	1	0	37	0
Klesko, Ryan, Atlanta*	.969	130	182	3	6	191	0
Kotsay, Mark, Florida*	1.000	14	31	2	0	33	1
Lankford, Ray, St. Louis*	.971	131	293	4	9	306	2
Lewis, Darren, Los Angeles	.980	25	49	1	1	51	0
Listach, Pat, Houston	.900	6	9	0	1	10	0
Livingstone, Scott, St. Louis	.000	1	0	0	0	0	0
Lofton, Kenny, Atlanta*	.983	122	290	5	5	300	1
Lowery, Terrell, Chicago	1.000	6	7	2	0	9	1
Mabry, John, St. Louis	1.000	78	109	8	0	117	1
Magee, Wendell, Philadelphia	.960	38	95	2	4	101	1
Martin, Al, Pittsburgh*	.957	110	125	8	6	139	1
May, Derrick, Philadelphia	.961	56	69	4	3	76	1
McCracken, Quinton, Colorado	.980	132	195	5	4	204	3
McGee, Willie, St. Louis	.981	81	100	6	2	108	3
McGuire, Ryan, Montreal	.960	44	69	3	3	75	1
McMillon, Billy, Fla.-Phi.*	.960	23	46	2	2	50	0
McRae, Brian, Chi.-N.Y.	.987	148	307	4	4	315	2
Mejia, Roberto, Chicago	.000	1	0	0	0	0	0
Mendoza, Carlos, New York*	1.000	3	5	0	0	5	0
Meulens, Hensley, Montreal	1.000	8	6	0	0	6	0
Mondesi, Raul, Los Angeles	.989	159	338	10	4	352	0
Montgomery, Ray, Houston	1.000	18	25	2	0	27	1

Player, Team	Pct.	G	PO	A	E	TC	DP
Mordecai, Mike, Atlanta	.000	1	0	0	0	0	0
Morman, Russ, Florida	1.000	2	0	1	0	1	0
Mouton, Lyle, Houston	1.000	61	86	1	0	87	1
Nixon, Otis, Los Angeles	.990	42	97	1	1	99	0
Nunnally, Jon, Cincinnati	.984	60	121	3	2	126	1
Obando, Sherman, Montreal	1.000	15	11	0	0	11	0
Ochoa, Alex, New York	.982	88	104	7	2	113	1
Orsulak, Joe, Montreal*	1.000	63	41	3	0	44	0
Otero, Ricky, Philadelphia*	1.000	42	95	4	0	99	1
Owens, Eric, Cincinnati	.938	18	15	0	1	16	0
Perez, Eduardo, Cincinnati	1.000	12	11	0	0	11	0
Petagine, Roberto, New York*	1.000	1	1	0	0	1	0
Phillips, J.R., Houston*	1.000	3	3	0	0	3	0
Plantier, Phil, S.D.-St.L.	.982	35	55	1	1	57	0
Powell, Dante, San Francisco	1.000	22	26	0	0	26	0
Pulliam, Harvey, Colorado	.962	33	23	2	1	26	0
Ramos, Ken, Houston*	.000	2	0	0	0	0	0
Rivera, Ruben, San Diego	1.000	7	13	0	0	13	0
Robertson, Mike, Philadelphia*	1.000	5	8	0	0	8	0
Rodriguez, Henry, Montreal*	.985	126	198	4	3	205	1
Sanders, Deion, Cincinnati*	.984	113	236	3	4	243	1
Sanders, Reggie, Cincinnati	.974	85	183	4	5	192	1
Santangelo, F.P., Montreal	1.000	99	153	4	0	157	2
Scarsone, Steve, St. Louis	.000	2	0	0	0	0	0
Sheaffer, Danny, St. Louis	1.000	22	13	0	0	13	0
Sheffield, Gary, Florida	.980	132	226	14	5	245	1
Shumpert, Terry, San Diego	1.000	3	1	0	0	1	0
Sierra, Ruben, Cincinnati	1.000	24	34	3	0	37	0
Smith, Mark, Pittsburgh	1.000	42	53	4	0	57	0
Sosa, Sammy, Chicago	.977	161	325	16	8	349	1
Strange, Doug, Montreal	.000	2	0	0	0	0	0
Stynes, Chris, Cincinnati	.976	38	76	5	2	83	0
Sweeney, Mark, St.L.-S.D.*	.976	45	40	0	1	41	0
Tartabull, Danny, Philadelphia	1.000	3	2	0	0	2	0
Taubensee, Eddie, Cincinnati	1.000	11	8	1	0	9	0
Thurman, Gary, New York	1.000	7	4	0	0	4	0
Timmons, Ozzie, Cincinnati	.000	1	0	0	1	1	0
Tomberlin, Andy, New York*	1.000	2	2	0	0	2	0
Tucker, Michael, Atlanta	.980	129	237	6	5	248	2
Vander Wal, John, Colorado*	.923	9	12	0	1	13	0
Vaughn, Greg, San Diego	.994	94	153	7	1	161	0
Walker, Larry, Colorado	.992	151	232	12	2	246	4
Ward, Turner, Pittsburgh	1.000	54	71	2	0	73	0
Watkins, Pat, Cincinnati	1.000	15	11	1	0	12	0
Wehner, John, Florida	1.000	27	13	0	0	13	0
White, Devon, Florida	.987	71	152	4	2	158	1
WHITE, Rondell, Montreal	.992	151	376	6	3	385	3
Young, Dmitri, St. Louis	.932	17	39	2	3	44	0
Young, Kevin, Pittsburgh	1.000	11	17	0	0	17	0

TRIPLE PLAY: McRae, Chi.

OUTFIELDERS WITH TWO OR MORE TEAMS

Player, Team	Pct.	G	PO	A	E	TC	DP
Cummings, Midre, Pittsburgh	1.000	25	37	1	0	38	0
Cummings, Midre, Philadelphia	.991	54	113	1	1	115	0
Daulton, Darren, Philadelphia	.979	70	133	6	3	142	1
Daulton, Darren, Florida	---	3	0	0	0	0	0
Johnson, Lance, New York*	.975	66	152	4	4	160	2
Johnson, Lance, Chicago*	.963	39	79	0	3	82	0
McMillon, Billy, Florida*	1.000	2	4	0	0	4	0
McMillon, Billy, Philadelphia*	.957	21	42	2	2	46	0
McRae, Brian, Chicago	.996	107	242	3	1	246	2
McRae, Brian, New York	.957	41	65	1	3	69	0
Plantier, Phil, San Diego	1.000	3	3	0	0	3	0
Plantier, Phil, St. Louis	.981	32	52	1	1	54	0
Sweeney, Mark, St. Louis*	1.000	25	23	0	0	23	0
Sweeney, Mark, San Diego*	.944	20	17	0	1	18	0

CATCHERS

Player, Team	Pct.	G	PO	A	E	TC	DP	PB
Ausmus, Brad, Houston	.992	129	807	73	7	887	16	6
Berryhill, Damon, San Fran.	.990	51	288	24	3	315	2	4
Bieser, Steve, New York	1.000	2	2	0	0	2	0	0
Castillo, Alberto, New York	.987	34	142	8	2	152	0	2
Chavez, Raul, Montreal	1.000	13	47	8	0	55	1	1
Difelice, Mike, St. Louis	.991	91	586	64	6	656	10	12
Estalella, Bobby, Philadelphia	1.000	11	49	3	0	52	0	1
Eusebio, Tony, Houston	.987	43	297	16	4	317	4	0
Flaherty, John, San Diego	.987	124	753	65	11	829	13	6
Fletcher, Darrin, Montreal	.994	83	606	26	4	636	4	4
Fordyce, Brook, Cincinnati	.983	30	162	12	3	177	1	2

Player, Team	Pct.	G	PO	A	E	TC	DP	PB
Hernandez, Carlos, San Diego..	.989	44	234	26	3	263	1	1
Houston, Tyler, Chicago	.986	41	263	16	4	283	1	6
Hubbard, Mike, Chicago	.992	20	120	8	1	129	0	2
Hundley, Todd, New York	.987	122	678	54	10	742	6	7
Jensen, Marcus, San Fran.	.983	28	106	10	2	118	1	2
Johnson, Brian, San Francisco	.995	55	344	24	2	370	5	2
JOHNSON, Charles, Florida	1.000	123	900	73	0	973	17	1
Kendall, Jason, Pittsburgh	.990	142	952	103	11	1066	20	7
Knorr, Randy, Houston	1.000	3	12	1	0	13	0	0
Lampkin, Tom, St. Louis	.989	86	413	37	5	455	6	6
Lieberthal, Mike, Philadelphia ..	.988	129	934	73	12	1019	8	12
Lopez, Javy, Atlanta	.993	117	792	56	6	854	7	9
Manwaring, Kirt, Colorado	.994	100	488	40	3	531	7	3
Marrero, Eli, St. Louis	.969	17	82	12	3	97	2	0
Mirabelli, Doug, San Francisco	1.000	6	16	0	0	16	0	0
Myers, Greg, Atlanta	1.000	2	11	2	0	13	0	0
Natal, Bob, Florida	1.000	4	15	1	0	16	0	0
Oliver, Joe, Cincinnati	.990	106	667	53	7	727	10	4
Osik, Keith, Pittsburgh	.989	32	160	13	2	175	3	4
Pagnozzi, Tom, St. Louis	1.000	13	57	2	0	59	0	0
Parent, Mark, Philadelphia	.996	38	225	21	1	247	2	3
Pena, Tony, Houston	1.000	8	48	6	0	54	1	0
Perez, Eddie, Atlanta	.988	64	392	23	5	420	1	2
Piazza, Mike, Los Angeles	.986	139	1045	74	16	1135	10	10
Pratt, Todd, New York	.990	36	186	22	2	210	3	1
Prince, Tom, Los Angeles	.996	45	221	25	1	247	5	1
Reed, Jeff, Colorado	.987	78	428	37	6	471	8	2
Romero, Mandy, San Diego	1.000	19	96	8	0	104	0	1
Servais, Scott, Chicago	.990	118	735	73	8	816	9	8
Sheaffer, Danny, St. Louis	1.000	9	19	1	0	20	0	0
Slaught, Don, San Diego	1.000	6	15	3	0	18	0	0
Spehr, Tim, Atlanta	.947	7	32	4	2	38	0	0
Taubensee, Eddie, Cincinnati..	.987	64	358	24	5	387	6	7
Widger, Chris, Montreal	.981	85	516	40	11	567	2	8
Wilkins, Rick, San Francisco	.986	57	326	37	5	368	5	1
Zaun, Gregg, Florida	.978	50	327	24	8	359	2	6

PITCHERS

Player, Team	Pct.	G	PO	A	E	TC	DP
Acevedo, Juan, New York	.923	25	3	9	1	13	0
Adams, Terry, Chicago	1.000	74	7	8	0	15	0
Alfonseca, Antonio, Florida	1.000	17	1	3	0	4	0
Alvarez, Wilson, San Francisco*	.889	11	2	6	1	9	0
Arocha, Rene, San Francisco	1.000	6	1	4	0	5	0
Ashby, Andy, San Diego	.980	30	16	34	1	51	0
Astacio, Pedro, L.A.-Col.	.983	33	20	38	1	59	3
Aybar, Manny, St. Louis	.867	12	3	10	2	15	0
BAILEY, Roger, Colorado	1.000	29	12	53	0	65	7
Bailey, Cory, San Francisco	.000	7	0	0	0	0	0
Barrios, Manuel, Houston	.000	2	0	0	0	0	0
Batchelor, Richard, St.L.-S.D.	.833	23	3	2	1	6	0
Batista, Miguel, Chicago	1.000	11	2	6	0	8	0
Bautista, Jose, St. Louis	1.000	11	1	0	0	1	0
Beck, Rod, San Francisco	.917	73	7	4	1	12	2
Beckett, Robbie, Colorado*	.000	2	0	0	0	0	0
Beech, Matt, Philadelphia*	1.000	24	6	18	0	24	2
Belinda, Stan, Cincinnati	1.000	84	3	4	0	7	0
Beltran, Rigo, St. Louis*	.933	35	4	10	1	15	0
Benes, Alan, St. Louis	1.000	23	13	12	0	25	3
Benes, Andy, St. Louis	.957	26	8	14	1	23	0
Bennett, Shayne, Montreal	1.000	16	1	1	0	2	0
Bergman, Sean, San Diego	.893	44	5	20	3	28	0
Bielecki, Mike, Atlanta	.917	50	4	7	1	12	1
Blazier, Ron, Philadelphia	1.000	36	4	1	0	5	1
Bochtler, Doug, San Diego	.818	54	4	5	2	11	0
Bohanon, Brian, New York*	1.000	19	2	13	0	15	0
Bones, Ricky, Cincinnati	.800	9	0	4	1	5	0
Borland, Toby, New York	.750	13	2	1	1	4	0
Borowski, Joe, Atlanta	1.000	20	4	3	0	7	2
Bottalico, Ricky, Philadelphia	1.000	69	4	5	0	9	1
Bottenfield, Kent, Chicago	1.000	64	5	5	0	10	0
Brantley, Jeff, Cincinnati	.000	13	0	0	0	0	0
Brewer, Billy, Philadelphia*	1.000	25	0	4	0	4	0
Brock, Chris, Atlanta	1.000	7	6	9	0	15	0
Brown, Kevin, Florida	.988	33	36	44	1	81	3
Bruske, Jim, San Diego	1.000	28	2	4	0	6	1
Bullinger, Jim, Montreal	1.000	36	12	30	0	42	2
Burba, Dave, Cincinnati	.974	30	13	24	1	38	0
Burke, John, Colorado	.909	17	4	6	1	11	1
Burrows, Terry, San Diego*	1.000	13	1	1	0	2	0
Busby, Mike, St. Louis	1.000	3	0	2	0	2	0

Player, Team	Pct.	G	PO	A	E	TC	DP
Byrd, Paul, Atlanta	.909	31	6	4	1	11	0
Cabrera, Jose, Houston	1.000	12	1	2	0	3	0
Candiotti, Tom, Los Angeles	.969	41	7	24	1	32	2
Cangelosi, John, Florida*	.000	1	0	0	0	0	0
Carlson, Dan, San Francisco	1.000	6	1	1	0	2	0
Carrara, Giovanni, Cincinnati	1.000	2	0	3	0	3	0
Carrasco, Hector, Cincinnati	.857	38	2	4	1	7	0
Casian, Larry, Chicago*	1.000	12	1	0	0	1	0
Castillo, Frank, Chi.-Col	.967	34	7	22	1	30	1
Cather, Mike, Atlanta	1.000	35	1	7	0	8	0
Christiansen, Jason, Pittsburgh*	.833	39	1	4	1	6	0
Clark, Mark, N.Y.-Chi	.956	32	11	32	2	45	1
Clontz, Brad, Atlanta	.714	51	0	5	2	7	0
Cook, Dennis, Florida*	1.000	59	3	9	0	12	2
Cooke, Steve, Pittsburgh*	.975	32	10	29	1	40	1
Cordova, Francisco, Pittsburgh	.941	29	16	32	3	51	3
Cormier, Rheal, Montreal*	.000	1	0	0	0	0	0
Crawford, Joe, New York*	1.000	19	1	9	0	10	0
Creek, Doug, San Francisco*	1.000	3	1	2	0	3	0
Crowell, Jim, Cincinnati*	1.000	2	2	2	0	4	0
Cunnane, Will, San Diego	.900	54	12	6	2	20	2
Daal, Omar, Montreal*	.875	33	7	7	2	16	0
Darwin, Danny, San Francisco	1.000	10	2	7	0	9	1
DeHart, Rick, Montreal*	1.000	23	1	5	0	6	0
DeJean, Mike, Colorado	.889	55	5	11	2	18	0
DeLucia, Rich, San Francisco	1.000	3	0	1	0	1	0
Dessens, Elmer, Pittsburgh	1.000	3	1	1	0	2	0
DiPoto, Jerry, Colorado	.947	74	7	11	1	19	0
Dreifort, Darren, Los Angeles	.957	48	4	18	1	23	0
Eckersley, Dennis, St. Louis	1.000	57	3	5	0	8	0
Eischen, Joey, Cincinnati*	.000	1	0	0	0	0	0
Embree, Alan, Atlanta*	1.000	66	1	7	0	8	0
Erdos, Todd, San Diego	1.000	11	2	2	0	4	0
Ericks, John, Pittsburgh	1.000	10	0	2	0	2	0
Estes, Shawn, San Francisco*	.978	32	10	34	1	45	2
Falteisek, Steve, Montreal	1.000	5	1	1	0	2	0
Fernandez, Alex, Florida	.984	32	20	40	1	61	3
Fernandez, Sid, Houston*	1.000	1	0	1	0	1	0
Fernandez, Osvaldo, San Fran.	.889	11	3	5	1	9	0
Fossas, Tony, St. Louis*	1.000	71	2	16	0	18	1
Foster, Kevin, Chicago	1.000	26	6	14	0	20	0
Foulke, Keith, San Francisco	.857	11	5	7	2	14	0
Fox, Chad, Atlanta	1.000	30	2	0	0	2	0
Franco, John, New York*	1.000	59	4	14	0	18	1
Frascatore, John, St. Louis	1.000	59	5	5	0	10	0
Gaetti, Gary, St. Louis	.000	1	0	0	0	0	0
Garcia, Ramon, Houston	.950	42	9	29	2	40	3
Gardner, Mark, San Francisco	1.000	30	12	28	0	40	1
Glavine, Tom, Atlanta*	.980	33	15	35	1	51	4
Gomes, Wayne, Philadelphia	1.000	37	2	2	0	4	0
Gonzalez, Jeremi, Chicago	.917	23	7	15	2	24	1
Gorecki, Rick, Los Angeles	.000	4	0	0	0	0	0
Grace, Mike, Philadelphia	1.000	6	3	3	0	6	0
Granger, Jeff, Pittsburgh*	.000	9	0	0	0	0	0
Graves, Danny, Cincinnati	.857	10	3	3	1	7	0
Green, Tyler, Philadelphia	.867	14	6	7	2	15	1
Greene, Tommy, Houston	.000	2	0	0	0	0	0
Guthrie, Mark, Los Angeles*	.938	62	2	13	1	16	0
Hall, Darren, Los Angeles	.944	63	3	14	1	18	2
Hamilton, Joey, San Diego	.967	31	10	19	1	30	0
Hampton, Mike, Houston*	.961	34	16	57	3	76	4
Harkey, Mike, Los Angeles	1.000	10	0	1	0	1	0
Harnisch, Pete, New York	1.000	6	3	4	0	7	2
Harris, Reggie, Philadelphia	1.000	50	3	3	0	6	0
Helling, Rick, Florida	.889	31	0	8	1	9	0
Henriquez, Oscar, Houston	1.000	4	2	0	0	2	0
Henry, Doug, San Francisco	.909	75	6	4	1	11	0
Heredia, Felix, Florida*	.500	56	1	0	1	2	0
Hermanson, Dustin, Montreal	.938	32	10	20	2	32	2
Hernandez, Livan, Florida	.960	17	8	16	1	25	4
Hernandez, Roberto, San Fran.	.800	28	0	4	1	5	0
Hitchcock, Sterling, San Diego*	.926	32	4	21	2	27	1
Hoffman, Trevor, San Diego	.875	70	2	5	1	8	0
Holmes, Darren, Colorado	.957	42	7	15	1	23	0
Holt, Chris, Houston	.980	33	13	36	1	50	1
Honeycutt, Rick, St. Louis*	.000	2	0	0	0	0	0
Hudek, John, Houston	1.000	40	1	6	0	7	1
Hutton, Mark, Fla.-Col	.000	40	6	11	0	17	1
Isringhausen, Jason, New York	1.000	6	3	1	0	4	0
Jackson, Danny, St.L.-S.D.*	.857	17	3	9	2	14	0
Jarvis, Kevin, Cincinnati	1.000	9	1	1	0	2	0
Johnson, Jason, Pittsburgh	.000	3	0	0	0	0	0
Johnson, Mike, Montreal	.917	11	2	9	1	12	0
Johnstone, John, San Francisco	1.000	13	1	3	0	4	0
Jones, Bobby, New York	.980	30	14	35	1	50	2
Jones, Bobby M., Colorado*	1.000	4	1	2	0	3	1
Jordan, Ricardo, New York*	1.000	22	0	5	0	5	1
Judd, Mike, Los Angeles	.000	1	0	0	0	0	0
Juden, Jeff, Montreal	.857	22	5	13	3	21	0
Karp, Ryan, Philadelphia*	.667	15	1	1	1	3	0
Kashiwada, Takashi, New York*	.900	35	4	5	1	10	0
Kile, Darryl, Houston	.985	34	28	39	1	68	3
King, Curtis, St. Louis	1.000	30	2	5	0	7	0
Kline, Steve, Montreal*	1.000	26	1	4	0	5	0
Kroon, Marc, San Diego	.000	12	0	0	0	0	0
Leiter, Al, Florida*	1.000	27	0	14	0	14	1
Leiter, Mark, Philadelphia	.930	31	10	30	3	43	4
Leroy, John, Atlanta	.000	1	0	0	0	0	0
Leskanic, Curtis, Colorado	1.000	55	5	5	0	10	1
Lewis, Richie, Cincinnati	.500	4	0	1	1	2	0
Lidle, Cory, New York	1.000	54	5	8	0	13	0
Lieber, Jon, Pittsburgh	.976	33	16	25	1	42	1
Ligtenberg, Kerry, Atlanta	1.000	15	1	0	0	1	0
Lima, Jose, Houston	1.000	52	5	4	0	9	0
Loaiza, Esteban, Pittsburgh	.949	33	11	26	2	39	1
Loiselle, Rich, Pittsburgh	.769	72	3	7	3	13	1
Long, Joey, San Diego*	1.000	10	2	1	0	3	0
Lowe, Sean, St. Louis	.667	6	1	3	2	6	0
Ludwick, Eric, St. Louis	.000	5	0	0	0	0	0
Maddux, Greg, Atlanta	.956	33	16	49	3	68	3
Maduro, Calvin, Philadelphia	.938	15	8	7	1	16	0
Magnante, Mike, Houston*	.889	40	1	7	1	9	0
Manuel, Barry, New York	.750	19	2	1	1	4	0
Martin, Tom, Houston*	.909	55	1	9	1	11	0
Martinez, Pedro A., Cincinnati*	1.000	8	1	0	0	1	0
Martinez, Pedro, Montreal	.974	31	7	31	1	39	1
Martinez, Ramon, Los Angeles	.968	22	10	20	1	31	1
Mathews, T.J., St. Louis	.900	40	5	4	1	10	0
McCurry, Jeff, Colorado	1.000	33	3	5	0	8	0
McGraw, Tom, St. Louis*	1.000	2	0	1	0	1	0
McMichael, Greg, New York	1.000	73	9	13	0	22	2
Menhart, Paul, San Diego	1.000	6	4	0	0	10	2
Mercker, Kent, Cincinnati*	1.000	28	11	22	0	33	0
Miller, Kurt, Florida	1.000	7	1	0	0	1	0
Millwood, Kevin, Atlanta	1.000	12	3	6	0	9	0
Mimbs, Michael, Philadelphia*	.500	17	0	2	2	4	0
Minchey, Nate, Colorado	1.000	2	0	2	0	2	0
Minor, Blas, Houston	1.000	11	1	2	0	3	0
Mlicki, Dave, New York	.933	32	11	17	2	30	1
Morel, Ramon, Pit.-Chi.	1.000	8	1	2	0	3	0
Morgan, Morgan, Cincinnati	1.000	31	10	23	0	33	1
Morris, Matt, St. Louis	.868	33	5	28	5	38	1
Mulholland, Terry, Chi.-S.F.*	.929	40	12	40	4	56	2
Munoz, Mike, Colorado*	.900	64	3	6	1	10	2
Munoz, Bobby, Philadelphia	.875	8	1	6	1	8	0
Murray, Heath, San Diego*	1.000	17	1	2	0	3	1
Myers, Rodney, Chicago	1.000	5	2	0	0	2	0
Neagle, Denny, Atlanta*	.978	34	9	35	1	45	1
Nen, Robb, Florida	.941	73	9	7	1	17	1
Nomo, Hideo, Los Angeles	.923	33	16	8	2	26	2
Nye, Ryan, Philadelphia	1.000	4	1	3	0	4	1
Ojala, Kirt, Florida*	1.000	7	4	4	0	8	1
Osborne, Donovan, St. Louis*	1.000	14	4	10	0	14	1
Osuna, Antonio, Los Angeles	.889	48	3	13	2	18	1
Painter, Lance, St. Louis*	1.000	14	4	3	0	7	1
Pall, Donn, Florida	.000	2	0	0	0	0	0
Paniagua, Jose, Montreal	1.000	9	3	1	0	4	0
Park, Cha Ho, Los Angeles	.946	32	7	28	2	37	1
Patterson, Bob, Chicago*	.923	76	4	8	1	13	1
Perez, Carlos, Montreal*	.949	33	19	37	3	59	4
Perez, Yorkis, Montreal*	.000	9	0	0	0	0	0
Peters, Chris, Pittsburgh*	1.000	31	2	8	0	10	0
Petkovsek, Mark, St. Louis	.968	55	11	19	1	31	3
Pisciotta, Marc, Chicago	1.000	24	2	4	0	6	0
Plantenberg, Erik, Philadelphia*	.800	35	2	2	1	5	0
Poole, Jim, San Francisco*	.800	63	2	6	2	10	0
Portugal, Mark, Philadelphia	.750	3	1	2	1	4	0
Powell, Jay, Florida	.840	74	5	16	4	25	2
Radinsky, Scott, Los Angeles*	1.000	75	3	8	0	11	2
Raggio, Brady, St. Louis	1.000	15	1	6	0	7	0
Ramos, Edgar, Philadelphia	1.000	4	0	2	0	2	0
Rapp, Pat, Fla.-S.F.	.903	27	8	20	3	31	2
Reed, Rick, New York	.961	33	22	27	2	51	2
Reed, Steve, Colorado	.929	63	1	12	1	14	0

Player, Team	Pct.	G	PO	A	E	TC	DP
Rekar, Bryan, Colorado	1.000	2	2	0	0	2	1
Remlinger, Mike, Cincinnati*	.964	69	6	21	1	28	0
Reyes, Dennis, Los Angeles*	.944	14	1	16	1	18	0
Reynolds, Shane, Houston	.911	30	10	31	4	45	4
Reynoso, Armando, New York	.960	16	7	17	1	25	1
Rincon, Ricardo, Pittsburgh*	1.000	62	3	6	0	9	0
Ritz, Kevin, Colorado	1.000	18	13	15	0	28	3
Roa, Joe, San Francisco	.957	28	6	16	1	23	4
Rodriguez, Felix, Cincinnati	1.000	26	0	2	0	2	0
Rodriguez, Rich, San Francisco*	.957	71	5	17	1	23	1
Rojas, Mel, Chi.-N.Y.	.900	77	2	7	1	10	0
Ruebel, Matt, Pittsburgh*	.800	44	3	9	3	15	0
Rueter, Kirk, San Francisco*	1.000	32	6	53	0	59	4
Ruffcorn, Scott, Philadelphia	.857	18	3	3	1	7	0
Ruffin, Bruce, Colorado*	1.000	23	1	2	0	3	0
Ryan, Ken, Philadelphia	1.000	22	3	2	0	5	0
Saunders, Tony, Florida*	.867	22	2	11	2	15	0
Schilling, Curt, Philadelphia	.980	35	20	28	1	49	2
Schmidt, Jason, Pittsburgh	1.000	32	13	19	0	32	0
Schourek, Pete, Cincinnati*	1.000	18	3	8	0	11	0
Scott, Tim, S.D.-Col.	1.000	17	4	5	0	9	0
Service, Service, Cincinnati	1.000	4	2	1	0	3	0
Shaw, Jeff, Cincinnati	1.000	78	12	13	0	25	1
Silva, Jose, Pittsburgh	1.000	11	3	1	0	4	0
Smiley, John, Cincinnati*	1.000	20	0	12	0	12	0
Smith, Lee, Montreal	1.000	25	1	4	0	5	0
Smith, Pete, San Diego	.968	37	6	24	1	31	1
Smoltz, John, Atlanta	.968	35	29	31	2	62	2
Sodowsky, Clint, Pittsburgh	1.000	45	3	5	0	8	0
Spradlin, Jerry, Philadelphia	1.000	76	9	2	0	11	0
Springer, Russ, Houston	.909	54	5	5	1	11	1
Stanifer, Robby, Florida*	.875	36	1	6	1	8	1
Stephenson, Garrett, Phi.	1.000	20	15	14	0	29	0
Stevens, Dave, Chicago	1.000	10	1	0	0	1	0
Stottlemyre, Todd, St. Louis	.971	28	12	21	1	34	0
Stull, Everett, Montreal	.000	3	0	0	0	0	0
Sullivan, Scott, Cincinnati	.882	59	4	11	2	17	0
Swartzbaugh, Dave, Chicago	1.000	2	0	1	0	1	0
Swift, Bill, Colorado	.963	14	4	22	1	27	2
Tabaka, Jeff, Cincinnati*	.000	3	0	0	0	0	0
Tapani, Kevin, Chicago	1.000	13	4	10	0	14	0
Tatis, Ramon, Chicago*	.941	56	6	10	1	17	2
Tavarez, Julian, San Francisco	.900	89	5	13	2	20	2
Telemaco, Amaury, Chicago	1.000	10	3	5	0	8	0
Telford, Anthony, Montreal	.968	65	7	23	1	31	1
Thompson, Mark, Colorado	1.000	6	2	5	0	7	0
Thomson, John, Colorado	.943	27	9	24	2	35	2
Thurman, Mike, Montreal	1.000	5	0	4	0	4	0
Tomko, Brett, Cincinnati	.882	22	6	9	2	17	1
Torres, Salomon, Montreal	1.000	12	3	5	0	8	0
Trachsel, Steve, Chicago	.956	34	17	26	2	45	0
Trlicek, Ricky, New York	1.000	9	1	2	0	3	0
Urbina, Ugueth, Montreal	.917	63	3	8	1	12	0
Valdes, Ismael, Los Angeles	.938	30	17	28	3	48	3
Valdes, Marc, Montreal	.950	48	9	10	1	20	1
Valenzuela, Fernando, S.D.-St.L.*	.935	18	5	24	2	31	0
VanLandingham, William, S.F.	1.000	18	6	3	0	9	2
Veras, Dario, San Diego	.000	23	0	0	0	0	0
Veres, Dave, Montreal	.917	53	5	6	1	12	0
Vosberg, Ed, Florida*	1.000	17	0	1	0	1	0
Wade, Terrell, Atlanta*	.875	12	2	5	1	8	0
Wagner, Paul, Pittsburgh	1.000	14	1	3	0	4	0
Wagner, Billy, Houston*	.900	62	2	7	1	10	0
Wainhouse, David, Pittsburgh	.857	25	2	4	1	7	0
Wall, Donne, Houston	1.000	8	2	6	0	8	1
Wallace, Jeff, Pittsburgh*	1.000	11	0	2	0	2	0
Wendell, Turk, Chi.-N.Y.	.905	65	6	13	2	21	2
Whisenant, Matt, Florida*	.000	4	0	0	1	1	0
White, Gabe, Cincinnati*	1.000	12	1	3	0	4	1
Wilkins, Marc, Pittsburgh	1.000	70	1	4	0	5	1
Winchester, Scott, Cincinnati	1.000	5	0	1	0	1	0
Winston, Darrin, Philadelphia*	1.000	7	1	0	0	1	0
Wohlers, Mark, Atlanta	.900	71	7	2	1	10	0
Worrell, Tim, San Diego	.867	60	8	18	4	30	2
Worrell, Todd, Los Angeles	.933	65	4	10	1	15	2
Wright, Jamey, Colorado	.927	26	19	19	3	41	1

TRIPLE PLAY: Ashby, S.D.

PITCHERS WITH TWO OR MORE TEAMS

Player, Team	Pct.	G	PO	A	E	TC	DP
Astacio, Pedro, Los Angeles	1.000	26	15	27	0	42	3
Astacio, Pedro, Colorado	.941	7	5	11	1	17	0
Batchelor, Richard, St. Louis	.500	10	0	1	1	2	0
Batchelor, Richard, San Diego	1.000	13	3	1	0	4	0
Castillo, Frank, Chicago	.952	20	7	13	1	21	0
Castillo, Frank, Colorado	1.000	14	0	9	0	9	1
Clark, Mark, New York	.966	23	6	22	1	29	1
Clark, Mark, Chicago	.938	9	5	10	1	16	0
Hutton, Mark, Florida	1.000	32	6	10	0	16	1
Hutton, Mark, Colorado	1.000	8	0	1	0	1	0
Jackson, Danny, St. Louis*	.800	4	0	4	1	5	0
Jackson, Danny, San Diego*	.889	13	3	5	1	9	0
Morel, Ramon, Pittsburgh	1.000	5	1	2	0	3	0
Morel, Ramon, Chicago	.000	3	0	0	0	0	0
Mulholland, Terry, Chicago*	.936	25	11	33	3	47	2
Mulholland, Terry, San Fran.*	.889	15	1	7	1	9	0
Rapp, Pat, Florida	.885	19	7	16	3	26	2
Rapp, Pat, San Francisco	1.000	8	1	4	0	5	0
Rojas, Mel, Chicago	.833	54	0	5	1	6	0
Rojas, Mel, New York	1.000	23	2	2	0	4	0
Scott, Tim, San Diego	1.000	14	4	4	0	8	0
Scott, Tim, Colorado	1.000	3	0	1	0	1	0
Valenzuela, Fernando, S.D.*	.952	13	4	16	1	21	0
Valenzuela, Fernando, St. Louis*	.900	5	1	8	1	10	0
Wendell, Turk, Chicago	.867	52	3	10	2	15	0
Wendell, Turk, New York	1.000	13	3	3	0	6	2

MISCELLANEOUS

SHUTOUT GAMES

Read across for wins, down for losses.

Team	Hou.	Atl.	S.F.	Mon.	Cin.	N.Y.	Pit.	Fla.	L.A.	Phi.	Col.	Chi.	St.L.	S.D.	A.L.	W	L	Pct.
Houston	..	0	0	2	0	2	3	1	1	0	1	0	0	1	1	12	4	.750
Atlanta	0	..	1	1	1	0	1	0	2	1	1	2	2	2	3	17	6	.739
San Francisco	1	0	..	1	0	1	0	2	0	1	2	0	1	0	0	9	4	.692
Montreal	1	0	0	..	2	1	0	2	0	1	1	2	0	1	3	14	10	.583
Cincinnati	0	0	0	0	..	0	0	1	1	2	0	0	0	3	1	8	6	.571
New York	0	0	0	2	0	..	1	1	1	0	0	0	1	0	2	8	7	.533
Pittsburgh	2	2	0	0	0	0	..	1	0	0	0	1	0	1	1	8	7	.533
Florida	0	1	1	1	2	0	1	..	0	0	0	2	1	0	1	10	9	.526
Los Angeles	0	1	2	1	0	0	0	0	..	1	1	0	0	0	0	6	6	.500
Philadelphia	0	0	0	1	0	1	0	0	0	..	1	0	1	0	2	7	8	.467
Colorado	0	1	0	0	0	0	0	0	1	0	..	2	0	0	0	5	8	.385
Chicago	0	0	0	0	1	0	0	0	0	0	1	..	1	0	0	4	10	.286
St Louis	0	0	0	0	0	0	1	0	0	0	0	0	..	1	1	3	8	.273
San Diego	0	0	0	1	0	0	0	1	0	0	0	0	0	..	0	2	9	.182
A.L. clubs	0	1	0	0	0	1	0	0	0	0	0	1	1	0	..	113	102	.526
Lost	4	6	4	10	6	7	7	9	6	8	8	10	8	9	..	113	102	.526

N.L. shutouts vs. A.L. clubs (15): Atlanta vs. Detroit, New York A.L. and Toronto; Cincinnati vs. Kansas City; Florida vs. Toronto; Houston vs. Milwaukee; Montreal vs. Baltimore, Boston and Detroit; New York N.L. vs. New York A.L. and Toronto; Philadelphia vs. Detroit and New York A.L.; Pittsburgh vs. Chicago A.L.; St. Louis vs. Minnesota.

HOME RECORD

Read across for home wins, down for road losses.

Team	Fla.	Atl.	N.Y.	S.F.	L.A.	Col.	Hou.	Mon.	Pit.	Chi.	St.L.	Cin.	S.D.	Phi.	A.L.	W	L	Pct.
Florida	..	4	2	5	3	5	5	3	3	5	4	4	3	4	5	52	29	.642
Atlanta	2	..	3	4	3	2	4	5	1	6	6	5	3	5	1	50	31	.617
New York	4	4	..	1	2	4	2	4	5	3	4	6	3	4	4	50	31	.617
San Francisco	4	2	3	..	4	5	5	3	2	3	2	2	4	4	5	48	33	.593
Los Angeles	4	2	3	4	..	2	3	4	4	3	2	3	2	5	6	47	34	.580
Colorado	3	3	4	3	1	..	3	3	3	6	4	4	2	2	6	47	34	.580
Houston	3	2	3	2	4	4	..	5	3	5	5	3	2	2	3	46	35	.568
Montreal	2	1	3	3	3	1	2	..	4	6	4	2	5	3	6	45	36	.556
Pittsburgh	1	2	3	4	1	5	3	4	..	2	4	3	3	5	5	43	38	.531
Chicago	2	2	3	3	3	2	4	3	3	..	2	4	3	2	7	42	39	.519
St Louis	4	3	1	5	3	2	2	3	1	4	..	2	2	3	6	41	40	.506
Cincinnati	3	1	2	1	3	3	2	2	5	3	2	..	3	4	6	40	41	.494
San Diego	3	1	4	2	3	4	1	2	4	3	2	3	..	2	5	39	42	.481
Philadelphia	4	1	3	1	4	4	3	3	2	4	1	4	..	4	4	38	43	.469
A.L. clubs	2	2	6	3	5	5	5	3	4	4	3	5	8	..	..	..	..	..
Lost on road	41	30	43	39	40	45	43	48	45	55	49	45	44	51	..	628	506	.554

HOME RECORDS IN INTERLEAGUE GAMES

Team	Bal.	Bos.	Det.	N.Y.	Tor.
Atlanta	0-3	..	1-2	..	..
Florida	3-0	..	..	2-1	..
Montreal	..	3-0	3-0	..	..
New York	..	1-2	..	..	3-0
Philadelphia	..	..	..	3-0	1-2

Team	Chi.	Cle.	K.C.	Mil.	Min.
Chicago	..	..	3-0	2-1	2-1
Cincinnati	1-2	..	2-1	3-0	..
Houston	..	1-2	..	1-2	1-2
Pittsburgh	3-0	1-2	1-2	..	..
St. Louis	2-1	1-2	..	..	3-0

Team	Ana.	Oak.	Sea.	Tex.
Colorado	1-1	2-0	2-0	1-1
Los Angeles	2-0	2-0	1-1	1-1
San Diego	1-1	0-2	2-0	2-0
San Francisco	1-1	1-1	2-0	1-1

ROAD RECORD

Read across for road wins, down for home losses.

Team	Atl.	S.F.	L.A.	Fla.	Hou.	N.Y.	S.D.	Cin.	Pit.	Col.	Mon.	St.L.	Phi.	Chi.	A.L.	W	L	Pct.
Atlanta	..	3	3	2	3	2	5	4	4	3	5	2	5	3	7	51	30	.630
San Francisco	2	..	2	2	3	5	4	5	1	3	2	1	4	3	6	42	39	.519
Los Angeles	3	2	..	0	1	3	3	2	5	5	3	3	5	3	3	41	40	.506
Florida	4	2	2	..	2	2	2	4	2	4	1	2	4	1	7	40	41	.494
Houston	2	1	3	1	..	4	4	4	3	2	3	2	4	1	3	38	43	.469
New York	3	2	3	4	2	..	2	3	2	1	3	5	3	2	3	38	43	.469
San Diego	2	2	4	3	4	2	..	3	2	4	1	3	2	2	3	37	44	.457
Cincinnati	1	3	3	2	3	0	2	..	3	2	4	4	4	2	3	36	45	.444
Pittsburgh	4	4	1	3	3	1	2	1	..	2	2	5	3	3	2	36	45	.444
Colorado	3	1	4	4	2	2	2	2	1	..	4	3	2	3	3	36	45	.444
Montreal	1	3	1	3	1	2	3	3	1	3	..	2	3	1	6	33	48	.407
St Louis	0	3	3	2	1	1	4	4	2	2	2	..	2	4	2	32	49	.395
Philadelphia	1	2	1	2	3	2	3	2	2	3	3	2	..	3	1	30	51	.370
Chicago	0	2	2	0	1	3	3	4	0	0	2	4	2	..	2	26	55	.321
A.L. clubs	5	3	2	1	6	2	3	3	4	2	0	3	2	2	..	..	..	..
Lost at home	31	33	34	29	35	31	42	41	38	34	36	40	43	39	..	516	618	.455

ATLANTA—101-61

Pitcher	Chi. W-L	Cin. W-L	Col. W-L	Fla. W-L	Hou. W-L	L.A. W-L	Mon. W-L	N.Y. W-L	Phi. W-L	Pit. W-L	St.L. W-L	S.D. W-L	S.F. W-L	A.L. W-L	Totals W-L
Bielecki, Mike	1-0	0-0	0-0	0-2	0-0	0-0	0-0	0-2	1-0	0-1	0-1	0-0	1-0	0-1	3-7
Borowski, Joe	0-0	0-0	0-0	0-0	0-0	0-0	0-0	0-0	0-0	0-0	1-0	1-0	0-1	0-1	2-2
Brock, Chris	0-0	0-0	0-0	0-0	0-0	0-0	0-0	0-0	0-0	0-0	0-0	0-0	0-0	0-0	0-0
Byrd, Paul	0-0	1-0	0-0	1-2	0-1	0-0	0-0	1-0	0-1	0-0	0-0	0-0	1-0	0-0	4-4
Cather, Mike	0-1	0-0	0-1	0-1	0-0	0-0	1-0	0-0	1-0	0-0	0-1	0-0	0-0	0-0	2-4
Clontz, Brad	2-0	0-0	0-1	0-0	1-0	0-0	1-0	0-0	1-0	0-0	0-0	0-0	0-0	0-0	5-1
Embree, Alan	1-0	0-0	0-0	0-0	1-0	1-0	0-0	0-0	0-0	0-0	0-0	0-0	0-1	0-0	3-1
Fox, Chad	0-0	0-1	0-0	0-0	0-0	0-0	0-0	0-0	0-0	0-0	0-0	0-0	0-0	0-0	0-1
Glavine, Tom	0-0	0-0	2-1	0-1	3-0	2-1	3-0	1-1	1-0	0-2	1-0	0-1	0-0	1-0	14-7
LeRoy, John	0-0	0-0	0-0	0-0	0-0	0-0	0-0	1-0	0-0	0-0	0-0	0-0	0-0	0-0	1-0
Ligtenberg, Kerry	0-0	0-0	0-0	0-0	0-0	0-0	0-0	0-0	0-0	0-0	0-0	1-0	0-0	0-0	1-0
Maddux, Greg	2-0	2-0	1-0	0-0	0-1	0-0	1-0	2-0	2-0	1-0	1-0	3-1	2-0	2-2	19-4
Millwood, Kevin	1-1	0-0	0-0	0-1	0-0	0-1	0-0	0-0	2-0	0-0	0-0	0-0	1-0	1-0	5-3
Neagle, Denny	1-0	3-0	2-0	1-0	1-0	1-1	1-2	0-1	1-0	1-0	3-1	2-0	0-0	3-0	20-5
Smoltz, John	1-0	3-0	0-2	1-0	1-2	2-1	2-0	0-1	1-1	2-1	1-0	0-0	0-2	1-2	15-12
Wade, Terrell	0-0	0-0	0-0	0-1	0-0	0-1	1-0	0-0	0-0	1-1	0-0	0-0	0-0	0-0	2-3
Wohlers, Mark	0-0	0-1	0-1	1-0	0-0	0-0	0-0	0-2	0-0	0-1	1-0	2-1	1-0	0-1	5-7
Totals	9-2	9-2	5-6	4-8	7-4	6-5	10-2	5-7	10-2	5-6	8-3	8-3	7-4	8-7	101-61

INTERLEAGUE BREAKDOWN: Borowski 0-1, Maddux 0-1, Wohlers 0-1 vs. Orioles; Glavine 1-0, Millwood 1-0, Smoltz 1-0 vs. Red Sox; Maddux 0-1, Neagle 1-0, Smoltz 0-1 vs. Tigers; Bielecki 0-1, Maddux 1-0, Neagle 1-0 vs. Yankees; Maddux 1-0, Neagle 1-0, Smoltz 0-1 vs. Blue Jays.

CHICAGO—68-94

Pitcher	Atl. W-L	Cin. W-L	Col. W-L	Fla. W-L	Hou. W-L	L.A. W-L	Mon. W-L	N.Y. W-L	Phi. W-L	Pit. W-L	St.L. W-L	S.D. W-L	S.F. W-L	A.L. W-L	Totals W-L
Adams, Terry	0-1	0-0	0-1	1-1	0-1	0-0	0-1	1-0	0-2	0-0	0-0	0-2	0-0	0-0	2-9
Batista, Miguel	0-0	0-0	0-0	0-1	0-0	0-1	0-0	0-0	0-0	0-1	0-1	0-0	0-0	0-1	0-5
Bottenfield, Kent	1-0	0-1	0-0	0-0	0-0	0-0	0-0	0-1	0-0	0-0	0-0	0-1	1-0	0-0	2-3
Casian, Larry	0-1	0-0	0-0	0-0	0-0	0-0	0-0	0-0	0-0	0-0	0-0	0-0	0-0	0-0	0-1
Castillo, Frank	0-0	0-1	0-2	0-2	0-1	0-0	0-1	1-0	2-1	0-0	0-0	1-1	0-0	2-0	6-9
Clark, Mark	0-0	1-0	0-0	0-0	1-0	1-0	0-0	0-0	0-1	1-0	0-0	1-0	0-0	1-0	6-1
Foster, Kevin	0-0	1-0	0-3	0-0	1-1	0-0	0-0	1-1	1-0	2-0	0-1	2-0	0-1	2-0	10-7
Gonzalez, Jeremi	0-1	1-2	0-1	0-1	1-1	0-1	1-1	1-0	1-0	0-0	2-0	0-0	2-0	1-1	11-9
Morel, Ramon	0-0	0-0	0-0	0-0	0-0	0-0	0-0	0-0	0-0	0-0	0-0	0-0	0-0	0-0	0-0
Mulholland, Terry	0-1	1-0	0-0	0-0	0-1	1-1	1-2	0-0	1-0	1-1	0-1	1-0	0-1	0-2	6-12
Myers, Rodney	0-0	0-0	0-0	0-0	0-0	0-0	0-0	0-0	0-0	0-0	0-0	0-0	0-0	0-0	0-0
Patterson, Bob	0-1	0-0	0-0	0-0	0-0	0-0	0-0	0-0	0-1	1-0	0-0	0-0	0-0	0-0	1-6
Pisciotta, Marc	0-0	0-0	0-0	0-0	0-0	0-0	0-0	0-0	0-0	0-0	0-1	1-0	0-0	1-0	3-1
Rojas, Mel	0-1	0-0	0-0	0-0	0-1	0-1	0-0	0-0	0-1	0-0	0-0	0-0	0-0	0-0	0-4
Stevens, Dave	0-0	0-0	0-0	0-0	0-0	0-0	0-0	0-0	0-0	0-0	0-0	0-0	0-2	0-0	0-2
Swartzbaugh, Dave	0-0	0-0	0-0	0-0	0-0	0-0	0-0	0-0	0-0	0-0	0-0	0-0	0-0	0-0	0-1
Tapani, Kevin	1-1	2-0	0-0	1-1	0-0	0-0	0-0	1-0	1-0	0-0	1-0	0-0	0-1	1-0	9-3
Tatis, Ramon	0-0	0-0	0-0	0-0	0-0	1-0	0-0	0-0	0-0	0-0	0-0	0-0	0-0	0-0	1-1
Telemaco, Amaury	0-0	0-0	0-0	0-0	0-0	0-0	0-0	0-0	0-1	0-0	0-0	0-2	0-0	0-0	0-3
Trachsel, Steve	0-1	1-0	1-1	0-2	0-1	0-1	2-0	0-2	0-0	1-1	1-1	0-1	1-0	1-0	8-12
Wendell, Turk	0-1	0-1	1-0	0-0	0-0	1-0	0-0	0-1	0-0	0-0	0-2	0-0	1-0	0-0	3-5
Totals	2-9	7-5	2-9	2-9	4-7	6-5	4-7	6-5	6-5	7-5	4-8	6-5	5-6	9-6	68-94

INTERLEAGUE BREAKDOWN: Foster 1-0, Gonzalez 0-1, Mulholland 0-1 vs. White Sox; Batista 0-1, Stevens 0-1, Tapani 1-0 vs. Indians; Castillo 1-0, Foster 1-0, Pisciotta 1-0 vs. Royals; Castillo 1-0, Mulholland 0-1, Trachsel 1-0 vs. Brewers; Clark 1-0, Gonzalez 1-0, Stevens 0-1 vs. Twins.

CINCINNATI—76-86

Pitcher	Atl. W-L	Chi. W-L	Col. W-L	Fla. W-L	Hou. W-L	L.A. W-L	Mon. W-L	N.Y. W-L	Phi. W-L	Pit. W-L	St.L. W-L	S.D. W-L	S.F. W-L	A.L. W-L	Totals W-L
Belinda, Stan	0-0	0-1	0-0	1-0	0-1	0-0	0-1	0-1	1-0	0-0	0-0	0-1	0-0	0-0	1-5
Bones, Ricky	0-0	0-0	0-1	0-0	0-0	0-0	0-0	0-0	0-0	0-0	0-0	0-0	0-0	0-0	0-1
Brantley, Jeff	0-0	0-0	0-0	0-0	0-0	1-0	0-0	0-0	0-0	0-0	0-0	0-1	0-0	0-1	1-2
Burba, Dave	0-2	0-0	1-1	1-0	1-1	0-0	0-1	1-1	3-0	1-2	1-0	0-1	0-1	2-1	11-10
Carrara, Giovanni	0-0	0-0	0-0	0-0	0-0	0-0	0-0	0-0	0-0	0-0	0-0	0-1	0-0	0-0	0-1
Carrasco, Hector	0-0	0-0	0-0	0-0	0-0	0-1	0-0	0-0	0-0	0-1	0-0	0-0	0-0	0-0	1-2
Crowell, Jim	0-0	0-0	0-0	0-0	0-0	0-0	0-0	0-0	0-0	0-0	0-0	0-0	0-0	0-0	0-1
Eischen, Joey	0-0	0-0	0-0	0-0	0-0	0-0	0-0	0-0	0-0	0-0	0-0	0-0	0-0	0-0	0-0
Graves, Danny	0-0	0-0	0-0	0-0	0-0	0-0	0-0	0-0	0-0	0-0	0-0	0-0	0-0	0-0	0-0
Jarvis, Kevin	0-0	0-0	0-0	0-1	0-0	0-0	0-0	0-0	0-0	0-0	0-0	0-0	0-0	0-0	0-1
Lewis, Richie	0-0	0-0	0-0	0-0	0-0	0-0	0-0	0-0	0-0	0-0	0-0	0-0	0-0	0-0	0-0
Martinez, Pedro A.	0-0	0-0	1-1	0-0	0-0	0-0	0-0	0-0	0-0	0-0	0-0	0-0	0-0	0-0	1-1
Mercker, Kent	0-2	0-3	0-0	1-0	0-1	0-1	0-0	0-1	2-0	0-1	2-0	0-1	1-1	2-0	8-11
Morgan, Mike	0-0	2-1	1-0	0-2	1-1	1-1	0-3	1-0	1-1	0-0	1-0	0-0	0-1	0-1	9-12
Remlinger, Mike	0-1	0-0	0-1	0-1	1-0	2-0	2-0	1-0	1-2	0-0	1-1	0-1	1-1	1-1	8-8
Rodriguez, Felix	0-0	0-0	0-0	0-0	0-0	0-0	0-0	0-0	0-0	0-0	0-0	0-0	0-0	0-0	0-0
Schourek, Pete	0-2	2-0	0-1	0-1	1-0	0-1	0-0	0-0	1-1	0-0	0-0	1-0	0-1	0-1	5-8
Service, Scott	0-0	0-0	0-0	0-0	0-0	0-0	0-0	0-0	0-0	0-0	0-0	0-0	0-0	0-0	0-0
Shaw, Jeff	2-0	1-0	0-0	0-0	0-0	0-0	0-0	0-0	0-0	0-0	0-1	0-0	0-1	0-0	4-2
Smiley, John	0-1	0-1	1-0	1-2	2-0	0-1	1-1	0-2	1-0	1-0	0-1	1-0	1-0	0-1	9-10
Sullivan, Scott	0-0	0-0	0-0	0-0	0-1	0-0	1-1	0-0	1-1	0-0	2-1	0-0	0-0	0-0	5-3
Tabaka, Jeff	0-0	0-0	0-0	0-0	0-0	0-0	0-0	0-0	0-0	0-0	0-0	0-0	0-0	0-0	0-0
Tomko, Brett	0-1	0-1	0-0	0-0	1-0	0-0	0-0	1-1	1-1	1-0	1-1	1-0	1-1	4-0	11-7
White, Gabe	0-0	0-0	1-1	0-0	0-0	0-0	0-0	0-0	0-0	0-0	0-0	0-0	0-0	0-0	2-2
Winchester, Scott	0-0	0-0	0-0	0-0	0-0	0-0	0-0	0-0	0-0	0-0	0-0	0-0	0-0	0-0	0-0
Totals	2-9	5-7	5-6	5-6	5-7	6-5	6-5	2-9	8-3	8-4	6-6	5-6	4-7	9-6	76-86

INTERLEAGUE BREAKDOWN: Burba 0-1, Mercker 1-0, Schourek 0-1 vs. White Sox; Remlinger 1-0, Smiley 0-1, Tomko 1-0 vs. Indians; Burba 1-0, Remlinger 0-1, Tomko 1-0 vs. Royals; Burba 0-1, Mercker 1-0, Tomko 1-0 vs. Brewers; Morgan 0-1, Tomko 1-0, White 0-1 vs. Twins.

COLORADO—83-79

Pitcher	Atl. W-L	Chi. W-L	Cin. W-L	Fla. W-L	Hou. W-L	L.A. W-L	Mon. W-L	N.Y. W-L	Phi. W-L	Pit. W-L	St.L. W-L	S.D. W-L	S.F. W-L	A.L. W-L	Totals W-L
Astacio, Pedro	1-0	0-0	0-0	0-0	0-0	1-1	0-0	0-0	0-0	0-0	1-0	0-0	0-0	2-0	5-1
Bailey, Roger	1-0	2-0	0-0	1-0	1-2	0-1	1-0	0-0	1-1	0-2	0-0	1-2	0-2	1-0	9-10
Beckett, Robbie	0-0	0-0	0-0	0-0	0-0	0-0	0-0	0-0	0-0	0-0	0-0	0-0	0-0	0-0	0-0
Burke, John	0-0	0-0	0-0	1-0	0-1	0-1	0-0	0-0	0-0	0-0	1-0	0-1	0-1	0-1	2-5
Castillo, Frank	0-0	1-0	1-1	0-0	0-0	1-0	1-0	1-0	0-1	0-0	0-0	0-0	0-0	0-0	6-3
DeJean, Mike	0-0	0-0	1-0	0-0	0-0	1-0	0-0	0-0	1-0	0-0	1-0	1-0	0-0	0-0	5-0
DiPoto, Jerry	0-1	0-0	0-0	0-2	0-0	0-0	1-0	0-0	0-0	0-0	1-0	0-0	0-0	3-0	5-3
Holmes, Darren	2-0	0-0	0-0	1-1	0-0	1-0	0-1	1-0	1-0	0-0	0-0	1-0	1-0	1-0	9-2
Hutton, Mark	0-0	0-0	0-1	0-0	0-0	0-0	0-0	0-0	0-0	0-0	0-0	0-0	0-0	0-0	0-1
Jones, Bobby M.	0-0	0-0	0-0	0-0	1-0	0-0	0-0	0-0	0-0	0-0	0-1	0-0	0-0	0-0	1-1
Leskanic, Curt	0-0	1-0	0-0	0-0	0-0	0-0	0-0	0-0	0-0	1-0	1-0	0-0	0-0	1-0	4-0
McCurry, Jeff	0-0	0-1	0-0	0-0	1-0	0-0	0-0	0-1	0-0	0-0	0-1	0-1	0-0	0-0	1-4
Minchey, Nate	0-0	0-0	0-0	0-0	0-0	0-0	0-0	0-0	0-0	0-0	0-0	0-0	0-0	0-0	0-0
Munoz, Mike	1-0	0-0	0-0	0-0	0-0	0-0	0-0	1-0	0-0	1-0	0-0	0-1	0-1	0-1	3-3
Reed, Steve	0-0	0-0	0-0	0-0	1-0	0-1	1-0	0-0	0-1	1-2	0-0	1-0	0-1	0-1	4-6
Rekar, Bryan	0-0	0-0	0-0	0-0	0-0	0-0	0-0	0-0	0-0	0-0	1-0	0-0	0-0	0-0	1-0
Ritz, Kevin	0-2	1-0	0-1	1-0	0-1	0-0	1-1	0-1	0-0	0-0	1-0	0-0	2-0	0-2	6-8
Ruffin, Bruce	0-0	0-0	0-0	0-0	0-0	0-0	0-0	0-0	0-0	0-0	0-1	0-1	0-0	0-0	0-2
Scott, Tim	0-0	0-0	0-0	0-0	0-0	0-0	0-0	0-0	0-0	0-0	0-0	0-0	0-0	0-0	0-0
Swift, Bill	0-1	1-0	1-1	0-0	0-0	0-1	0-1	1-1	0-0	0-1	1-0	0-0	0-0	0-0	4-6
Thompson, Mark	0-0	1-0	2-0	0-0	0-0	0-0	0-0	0-0	0-1	0-1	0-1	0-0	0-0	0-0	3-3
Thomson, John	1-0	1-0	1-0	1-0	0-1	0-0	0-0	2-1	0-2	0-0	0-1	0-1	0-2	1-1	7-9
Wright, Jamey	0-1	1-1	0-0	2-1	0-2	1-1	2-1	0-0	0-0	0-1	1-0	0-0	0-1	0-1	8-12
Totals	6-5	9-2	6-5	4-7	5-6	5-7	7-4	6-5	4-7	4-7	7-4	4-8	4-8	9-7	83-79

INTERLEAGUE BREAKDOWN: Astacio 1-0, Burke 0-1, DiPoto 1-0, Thomson 1-0 vs. Angels; Bailey 1-0, DiPoto 1-0, Holmes 1-0, Ritz 0-1 vs. A's; Astacio 1-0, DiPoto 1-0, Munoz 0-1, Wright 0-1 vs. Mariners; Leskanic 1-0, Reed 0-1, Ritz 0-1, Thomson 0-1 vs. Rangers.

FLORIDA—92-70

Pitcher	Atl. W-L	Chi. W-L	Cin. W-L	Col. W-L	Hou. W-L	L.A. W-L	Mon. W-L	N.Y. W-L	Phi. W-L	Pit. W-L	St.L. W-L	S.D. W-L	S.F. W-L	A.L. W-L	Totals W-L
Alfonseca, Antonio	0-0	0-1	0-0	0-0	0-0	0-0	0-0	0-0	0-1	0-1	0-0	0-0	0-0	1-0	1-3
Brown, Kevin	1-0	1-0	1-0	0-2	0-1	2-0	1-1	0-1	1-1	2-0	1-1	2-1	2-0	2-0	16-8
Cangelosi, John	0-0	0-0	0-0	0-0	0-0	0-0	0-0	0-0	0-0	0-0	0-0	0-0	0-0	0-0	0-0
Cook, Dennis	0-0	0-0	0-0	0-0	0-0	0-0	0-0	0-1	0-0	0-0	0-0	0-0	0-0	1-1	1-2
Fernandez, Alex	2-0	3-1	2-0	1-1	2-0	1-1	1-0	0-2	2-0	1-1	0-2	0-2	0-2	2-0	17-12
Helling, Rick	0-0	0-0	0-1	0-1	0-1	0-1	0-1	0-0	0-0	1-0	0-1	0-0	1-0	0-0	2-6
Heredia, Felix	0-1	0-0	0-1	1-0	1-0	0-0	1-0	0-0	0-1	0-0	1-0	0-0	0-0	1-0	5-3
Hernandez, Livan	0-0	2-0	1-0	1-0	1-0	0-0	1-0	1-1	0-1	0-0	1-0	0-0	0-1	1-0	9-3
Hutton, Mark	0-0	0-0	0-1	0-0	0-0	1-0	1-0	0-0	0-0	1-0	0-0	0-0	0-0	0-0	3-1
Leiter, Al	0-1	2-0	0-1	0-1	0-1	3-0	2-0	1-2	1-0	0-1	0-1	0-0	1-0	1-1	11-9
Miller, Kurt	0-0	0-0	0-0	0-0	0-0	0-1	0-0	0-0	0-0	0-0	0-0	0-0	0-0	0-0	0-1
Nen, Robb	0-0	1-0	1-0	0-1	2-0	0-0	1-1	1-0	1-0	0-0	0-0	0-1	1-0	1-0	9-3
Ojala, Kirt	0-0	0-0	0-0	0-0	0-0	0-0	0-0	0-1	0-0	0-0	0-1	1-0	0-0	0-0	1-2
Pall, Donn	0-0	0-0	0-0	0-0	0-0	0-0	0-0	0-0	0-0	0-0	0-0	0-0	0-0	0-0	0-0
Powell, Jay	2-1	0-0	0-1	1-0	0-0	0-0	0-0	0-0	0-0	0-0	1-0	1-0	1-0	1-0	7-2
Rapp, Pat	0-0	0-0	1-0	0-1	0-1	1-0	0-2	1-0	0-0	1-0	0-0	0-1	0-0	0-1	4-6
Saunders, Tony	3-0	0-0	0-0	0-1	0-0	0-0	0-1	0-0	1-0	0-1	0-1	0-1	0-1	0-0	4-6
Stanifer, Robby	0-1	0-0	0-0	0-0	1-0	0-0	0-0	0-0	0-1	0-0	0-0	0-0	0-0	0-0	1-2
Vosberg, Ed	0-0	0-0	0-0	0-0	0-0	0-0	0-0	0-0	0-0	0-0	0-0	0-0	0-1	1-0	1-1
Whisenant, Matt	0-0	0-0	0-0	0-0	0-0	0-0	0-0	0-0	0-0	0-0	0-0	0-0	0-0	0-0	0-0
Totals	8-4	9-2	6-5	4-7	7-4	7-4	7-5	8-3	6-6	6-6	5-6	5-6	5-6	12-3	92-70

INTERLEAGUE BREAKDOWN: Heredia 1-0, Powell 1-0, Vosberg 1-0 vs. Orioles; Brown 1-0, Fernandez 1-0, Rapp 0-1 vs. Red Sox; Alfonseca 1-0, Brown 1-0, Leiter 0-1 vs. Tigers; Cook 1-1, Nen 1-0 vs. Yankees; Fernandez 1-0, Hernandez 1-0, Leiter 1-0 vs. Blue Jays.

HOUSTON—84-78

Pitcher	Atl. W-L	Chi. W-L	Cin. W-L	Col. W-L	Fla. W-L	L.A. W-L	Mon. W-L	N.Y. W-L	Phi. W-L	Pit. W-L	St.L. W-L	S.D. W-L	S.F. W-L	A.L. W-L	Totals W-L
Barrios, Manuel	0-0	0-0	0-0	0-0	0-0	0-0	0-0	0-0	0-0	0-0	0-0	0-0	0-0	0-0	0-0
Cabrera, Jose	0-0	0-0	0-0	0-0	0-0	0-0	0-0	0-0	0-0	0-0	0-0	0-0	0-0	0-0	0-0
Fernandez, Sid	0-0	0-0	0-0	0-0	0-0	0-0	0-0	0-0	0-0	0-0	1-0	0-0	0-0	0-0	1-0
Garcia, Ramon	0-0	0-1	1-1	0-1	0-1	0-0	1-0	1-0	0-2	1-1	1-0	2-1	0-0	2-0	9-8
Greene, Tommy	0-0	0-0	0-1	0-0	0-0	0-0	0-0	0-0	0-0	0-0	0-0	0-0	0-0	0-0	0-1
Hampton, Mike	1-2	2-1	1-0	2-0	1-0	0-2	1-0	2-0	0-1	1-0	1-1	0-1	2-0	1-2	15-10
Henriquez, Oscar	0-0	0-0	0-0	0-0	0-0	0-1	0-0	0-0	0-0	0-0	0-0	0-0	0-0	0-0	0-1
Holt, Chris	1-0	1-1	1-1	1-0	1-1	1-1	0-2	0-0	0-0	2-1	0-1	0-1	0-2	0-1	8-12
Hudek, John	1-0	0-0	0-0	0-0	0-0	0-0	0-0	0-0	0-0	0-1	0-0	0-1	0-0	0-1	1-3
Kile, Darryl	0-2	3-0	1-0	2-0	1-0	2-0	2-1	2-0	1-0	2-1	1-0	2-0	0-1	0-2	19-7
Lima, Jose	0-1	0-0	0-0	0-1	0-0	0-2	0-0	0-0	0-1	0-0	1-0	0-0	0-0	0-1	1-6
Magnante, Mike	0-0	0-0	1-0	0-1	0-0	0-0	1-0	0-0	0-0	0-0	1-0	0-0	0-0	0-0	3-1
Martin, Tom	0-0	1-0	1-0	0-0	0-0	0-0	1-1	1-1	0-0	1-0	0-0	0-0	0-0	0-1	5-3
Minor, Blas	0-0	1-0	0-0	0-0	0-0	0-0	0-0	0-0	0-0	0-0	0-0	0-0	0-0	0-0	1-0
Reynolds, Shane	1-1	0-0	0-1	0-0	1-1	0-0	2-0	0-1	0-1	2-0	1-1	1-1	0-2	0-1	9-10
Springer, Russ	0-0	0-0	1-1	0-0	0-0	0-0	0-0	0-0	0-1	0-1	1-0	0-0	0-0	0-1	3-3
Wagner, Billy	0-1	2-0	1-0	0-1	0-1	0-1	1-0	0-0	0-1	1-0	0-0	0-1	1-2	1-0	7-8
Wall, Donne	0-0	0-0	0-0	1-1	0-1	1-0	0-0	0-0	0-0	0-1	0-0	0-0	0-0	0-2	2-5
Totals	4-7	9-3	7-5	6-5	4-7	7-4	8-3	7-4	4-7	6-6	9-3	6-5	3-8	4-11	84-78

INTERLEAGUE BREAKDOWN: Hampton 0-1, Hudek 0-1, Reynolds 0-1 vs. White Sox; Hampton 1-0, Lima 0-1, Martin 0-1 vs. Indians; Garcia 1-0, Hampton 0-1, Wall 0-1 vs. Royals; Garcia 1-0, Holt 0-1, Kile 0-1 vs. Brewers; Kile 0-1, Wagner 1-0, Wall 0-1 vs. Twins.

LOS ANGELES—88-74

Pitcher	Atl. W-L	Chi. W-L	Cin. W-L	Col. W-L	Fla. W-L	Hou. W-L	Mon. W-L	N.Y. W-L	Phi. W-L	Pit. W-L	St.L. W-L	S.D. W-L	S.F. W-L	A.L. W-L	Totals W-L
Astacio, Pedro	1-1	0-1	0-2	0-1	0-0	0-0	0-1	2-0	1-0	1-0	0-2	2-0	0-1	0-0	7-9
Candiotti, Tom	0-0	1-1	1-0	0-0	1-1	0-2	1-1	2-1	1-0	1-0	0-0	1-1	1-0	0-0	10-7
Dreifort, Darren	0-1	0-0	0-0	0-0	0-0	0-0	0-0	0-0	1-0	2-0	0-0	0-0	0-0	2-1	5-2
Gorecki, Rick	0-0	0-0	0-0	0-0	0-0	0-0	0-0	0-0	0-0	0-0	1-0	0-0	0-0	0-0	1-0
Guthrie, Mark	0-0	0-0	0-1	0-0	0-0	0-0	0-0	0-1	0-0	0-0	1-0	0-1	0-1	0-0	1-4
Hall, Darren	0-0	0-0	0-0	0-0	1-1	0-0	0-0	0-0	0-0	0-1	0-0	0-0	0-0	2-0	3-2
Harkey, Mike	0-0	0-0	0-0	0-0	0-0	0-0	0-0	0-0	0-0	0-0	1-0	0-0	0-0	0-0	1-0
Judd, Mike	0-0	0-0	0-0	0-0	0-0	0-0	0-0	0-0	0-0	0-0	0-0	0-0	0-0	0-0	0-0
Martinez, Ramon	1-2	0-0	1-0	1-1	1-0	2-0	0-1	0-0	0-1	2-0	0-0	0-0	1-0	1-0	10-5
Nomo, Hideo	0-0	1-1	1-1	2-1	0-4	0-2	2-0	0-0	3-0	1-0	1-0	0-2	1-0	2-1	14-12
Osuna, Antonio	0-0	1-0	0-0	0-1	0-0	0-1	0-0	0-0	1-0	0-0	0-0	0-1	0-0	1-1	3-4
Park, Chan Ho	2-0	3-0	1-1	1-0	1-0	1-1	0-1	1-0	1-0	0-1	1-1	1-1	1-2	0-0	14-8
Radinsky, Scott	0-0	0-0	0-0	1-0	0-0	1-1	2-0	0-0	0-0	0-0	0-0	0-0	0-0	1-0	5-1
Reyes, Dennis	0-1	0-0	0-0	0-1	0-0	0-0	0-0	0-1	0-0	1-0	0-0	0-0	1-0	0-0	2-3
Valdes, Ismael	1-1	0-1	1-1	2-0	0-1	0-0	1-0	1-2	2-0	1-0	0-1	1-1	0-1	0-2	10-11
Worrell, Todd	0-0	0-0	0-0	0-0	0-0	0-0	0-0	0-0	0-0	0-1	0-1	0-0	1-1	0-2	2-6
Totals	5-6	6-5	5-6	7-5	4-7	4-7	7-4	6-5	10-1	9-2	5-6	5-7	6-6	9-7	88-74

INTERLEAGUE BREAKDOWN: Dreifort 1-0, Hall 1-0, Nomo 1-0, Radinsky 1-0 vs. Angels; Hall 1-0, Nomo 1-1, Osuna 1-0 vs. A's; Martinez 1-0, Osuna 0-1, Valdes 0-1, Worrell 0-1 vs. Mariners; Dreifort 1-1, Valdes 0-1, Worrell 0-1 vs. Rangers.

MONTREAL—78-84

Pitcher	Atl. W-L	Chi. W-L	Cin. W-L	Col. W-L	Fla. W-L	Hou. W-L	L.A. W-L	N.Y. W-L	Phi. W-L	Pit. W-L	St.L. W-L	S.D. W-L	S.F. W-L	A.L. W-L	Totals W-L
Bennett, Shayne	0-1	0-0	0-0	0-0	0-0	0-0	0-0	0-0	0-0	0-0	0-0	0-0	0-0	0-0	0-1
Bullinger, Jim	0-1	2-1	3-0	0-2	0-1	0-1	0-1	0-0	1-2	0-1	0-0	1-1	0-0	0-1	7-12
Cormier, Rheal	0-0	0-0	0-0	0-1	0-0	0-0	0-0	0-0	0-0	0-0	0-0	0-0	0-0	0-0	0-1
Daal, Omar	0-0	0-0	0-0	0-0	0-0	1-0	0-0	0-0	0-1	0-0	0-0	0-0	0-0	1-0	1-2
DeHart, Rick	1-0	0-0	0-0	0-0	0-0	0-0	0-0	0-0	0-0	0-0	0-1	0-0	0-0	1-0	2-1
Falteisek, Steve	0-0	0-0	0-0	0-0	0-0	0-0	0-0	0-0	0-0	0-0	0-0	0-0	0-0	0-0	0-0
Hermanson, Dustin	0-2	1-1	0-2	0-0	1-1	0-1	1-0	0-0	0-0	1-0	0-0	2-1	1-0	1-0	8-8
Johnson, Mike	0-0	0-0	0-1	0-0	0-0	0-0	0-0	0-1	0-0	0-1	1-0	0-0	0-1	0-1	2-5
Juden, Jeff	1-1	1-0	0-0	0-1	2-0	0-2	1-0	0-0	1-0	1-1	1-0	0-0	1-0	2-0	11-5
Kline, Steve	0-0	0-1	0-0	0-0	1-0	0-0	0-0	0-1	0-0	0-0	0-1	0-0	0-0	0-0	1-3
Martinez, Pedro	0-2	0-0	1-0	1-0	0-1	2-1	1-1	1-2	1-1	2-0	1-0	2-0	2-0	3-0	17-8
Paniagua, Jose	0-0	0-0	0-0	0-0	0-0	0-0	0-0	1-0	0-0	0-0	0-1	0-0	0-1	0-0	1-2
Perez, Carlos	0-1	1-1	0-1	2-0	0-2	1-0	0-2	2-1	1-1	0-1	1-1	1-0	0-2	3-0	12-13
Smith, Lee	0-0	0-0	0-0	0-0	0-0	0-0	0-0	0-1	0-0	0-0	0-0	0-0	0-0	0-0	0-1
Stull, Everett	0-0	0-0	0-0	0-1	0-0	0-0	0-0	0-0	0-0	0-0	0-0	0-0	0-0	0-0	0-1
Telford, Anthony	0-0	2-0	0-1	0-0	0-0	0-1	0-0	0-0	0-1	0-1	0-1	0-0	1-0	1-1	4-6
Thurman, Mike	0-0	0-0	1-0	0-0	0-0	0-0	0-0	0-0	0-0	0-0	0-0	0-0	0-0	0-0	1-0
Torres, Salomon	0-0	0-0	0-0	0-0	0-0	0-0	0-0	0-0	0-0	0-0	0-0	0-0	0-0	0-0	0-0
Urbina, Ugueth	0-2	0-0	0-0	1-0	0-1	0-1	0-2	0-1	0-0	1-0	1-1	0-0	1-0	1-0	5-8
Valdes, Marc	0-0	0-0	0-0	0-1	1-0	0-0	1-0	0-0	1-0	0-0	1-0	0-1	0-1	0-0	4-4
Veres, Dave	0-0	0-0	0-1	0-1	0-0	0-0	0-0	0-1	0-0	1-0	0-0	0-0	1-0	0-0	2-3
Totals	2-10	7-4	5-6	4-7	5-7	3-8	4-7	5-7	6-6	5-6	6-5	8-3	6-5	12-3	78-84

INTERLEAGUE BREAKDOWN: Bullinger 0-1, Hermanson 1-0, Perez 1-0 vs. Orioles; DeHart 1-0, Perez 1-0, Urbina 1-0 vs. Red Sox; Juden 1-0, Martinez 1-0, Perez 1-0 vs. Tigers; Johnson 0-1, Martinez 1-0, Telford 1-0 vs. Yankees; Juden 1-0, Martinez 1-0, Telford 0-1 vs. Blue Jays.

NEW YORK—88-74

Pitcher	Atl. W-L	Chi. W-L	Cin. W-L	Col. W-L	Fla. W-L	Hou. W-L	L.A. W-L	Mon. W-L	Phi. W-L	Pit. W-L	St.L. W-L	S.D. W-L	S.F. W-L	A.L. W-L	Totals W-L
Acevedo, Juan	1-0	0-0	0-0	0-0	1-0	0-0	0-0	0-0	0-0	0-1	0-0	0-0	0-0	1-0	3-1
Bohanon, Brian	0-0	0-1	0-0	0-0	1-0	1-0	1-2	0-0	1-0	0-0	0-0	0-1	1-0	1-0	6-4
Borland, Toby	0-0	0-0	0-0	0-1	0-0	0-0	0-0	0-0	0-0	0-0	0-0	0-0	0-0	0-0	0-1
Clark, Mark	0-1	1-0	2-0	1-0	2-0	0-0	0-1	0-2	0-0	0-0	1-1	0-0	0-1	1-1	8-7
Crawford, Joe	1-0	0-0	1-0	0-0	0-0	0-0	1-1	0-1	0-1	1-0	0-0	0-0	0-0	0-0	4-3
Franco, John	0-0	1-1	0-0	0-0	0-1	1-0	0-0	1-0	0-0	0-0	1-0	0-0	0-0	0-1	5-3
Harnisch, Pete	0-0	0-0	0-0	0-0	0-0	0-1	0-0	0-0	0-0	0-0	0-0	0-0	0-0	0-0	0-1
Isringhausen, Jason	0-1	0-0	0-0	0-0	0-0	0-0	0-0	0-0	0-1	0-0	0-0	0-0	1-0	1-0	2-2
Jones, Bobby	0-2	2-0	1-0	2-0	1-0	0-1	1-0	2-1	1-0	1-0	2-0	2-1	0-2	0-2	15-9
Jordan, Ricardo	0-0	0-0	0-0	0-0	0-0	0-0	0-0	0-0	0-0	0-0	0-1	0-1	0-0	0-0	1-2
Kashiwada, Takashi	0-0	0-0	0-0	1-0	0-0	0-0	0-0	0-0	0-0	1-1	0-0	0-0	1-0	0-0	3-1
Lidle, Cory	1-0	0-0	0-1	1-0	0-0	0-0	1-0	1-0	0-1	3-0	0-0	0-0	0-0	0-0	7-2
Manuel, Barry	0-0	0-0	0-0	0-0	0-0	0-0	0-0	0-0	0-0	0-0	0-0	0-0	0-1	0-0	0-1
McMichael, Greg	3-0	0-2	1-0	0-2	0-0	1-2	0-0	1-0	0-0	0-1	1-0	0-0	0-2	0-1	7-10
Mlicki, Dave	0-0	1-1	1-0	0-2	0-2	0-0	0-0	1-1	1-2	1-1	0-1	1-1	0-0	2-1	8-12
Perez, Yorkis	0-0	0-0	0-0	0-0	0-0	0-0	0-0	0-0	0-0	0-1	0-0	0-0	0-0	0-0	0-1
Reed, Rick	1-0	0-0	3-1	0-1	2-0	0-2	1-2	1-0	1-1	0-0	2-0	0-0	1-1	1-1	13-9
Reynoso, Armando	0-0	0-1	0-0	0-0	1-1	1-0	1-0	0-0	0-0	2-0	1-0	0-0	0-0	0-1	6-3
Rojas, Mel	0-1	0-0	0-0	0-0	0-0	0-0	0-0	0-0	0-0	0-0	0-0	0-1	0-0	0-0	0-2
Trlicek, Ricky	0-0	0-0	0-0	0-0	0-0	0-0	0-0	0-0	0-0	0-0	0-0	0-0	0-0	0-0	0-0
Wendell, Turk	0-0	0-0	0-0	0-0	0-0	0-0	0-0	0-0	0-0	0-0	0-0	0-0	0-0	0-0	0-0
Totals	7-5	5-6	9-2	5-6	8-4	4-7	5-6	7-5	7-5	7-4	9-2	5-6	3-8	7-8	88-74

INTERLEAGUE BREAKDOWN: Bohanon 1-0, Franco 0-1, Reed 1-0 vs. Orioles; Clark 1-0, Jones 0-1, Reed 0-1 vs. Red Sox; Clark 0-1, Jones 0-1, Mlicki 0-1 vs. Tigers; McMichael 0-1, Mlicki 1-0, Reynoso 0-1 vs. Yankees; Acevedo 1-0, Isringhausen 1-0, Mlicki 1-0 vs. Blue Jays.

PHILADELPHIA—68-94

Pitcher	Atl. W-L	Chi. W-L	Cin. W-L	Col. W-L	Fla. W-L	Hou. W-L	L.A. W-L	Mon. W-L	N.Y. W-L	Pit. W-L	St.L. W-L	S.D. W-L	S.F. W-L	A.L. W-L	Totals W-L
Beech, Matt	0-1	0-0	0-1	1-0	0-0	0-0	0-2	1-1	0-2	0-0	0-1	0-0	1-0	1-1	4-9
Blazier, Ron	0-1	0-0	0-0	0-0	0-0	0-0	0-0	0-0	0-0	0-0	0-0	1-0	0-0	0-0	1-1
Bottalico, Ricky	0-0	0-0	0-0	1-1	0-0	0-0	0-1	0-1	0-0	0-0	1-0	0-1	0-0	0-1	2-5
Brewer, Billy	0-2	0-0	0-0	0-0	0-0	1-0	0-0	0-0	0-0	0-0	0-0	0-0	0-0	0-0	1-2
Gomes, Wayne	0-0	1-0	0-0	0-0	1-0	0-1	0-0	0-0	0-0	0-0	0-0	1-0	1-0	1-0	5-1
Grace, Mike	0-0	0-0	0-1	0-0	0-1	0-0	0-0	0-0	1-0	0-0	0-0	1-0	0-0	1-0	3-2
Green, Tyler	0-0	0-0	0-1	1-0	0-0	0-0	0-1	0-0	1-0	0-0	1-0	1-0	0-0	0-1	4-4
Harris, Reggie	0-0	1-0	0-0	0-0	0-1	0-0	0-0	0-0	0-0	0-0	0-1	0-0	0-1	0-0	1-3
Karp, Ryan	0-0	0-0	0-0	0-0	0-0	0-0	0-0	1-0	0-1	0-0	0-0	0-0	0-0	0-0	1-1
Leiter, Mark	0-2	1-1	2-1	1-0	0-2	0-2	0-2	1-1	0-1	1-0	1-1	2-0	1-2	0-2	10-17
Maduro, Calvin	0-0	0-0	0-0	1-1	0-0	0-1	0-1	1-0	0-1	1-0	0-1	0-0	0-1	0-1	3-7
Mimbs, Michael	0-0	0-0	0-0	0-0	0-0	0-0	0-0	0-0	0-0	0-1	0-1	0-1	0-0	0-0	0-3
Munoz, Bobby	0-0	0-0	0-0	1-1	0-0	0-0	0-0	0-1	0-0	0-0	0-0	0-1	0-2	0-0	1-5
Nye, Ryan	0-0	0-0	0-0	0-0	0-0	0-0	0-0	0-0	0-0	0-0	0-0	0-0	0-0	0-1	0-2
Plantenberg, Erik	0-0	0-0	0-0	0-0	0-0	0-0	0-0	0-0	0-0	0-0	0-0	0-0	0-0	0-0	0-0
Portugal, Mark	0-0	0-0	0-0	0-1	0-0	0-0	0-0	0-1	0-0	0-0	0-0	0-0	0-0	0-0	0-2
Ramos, Edgar	0-0	0-1	0-0	0-0	0-0	0-0	0-0	0-0	0-0	0-0	0-0	0-0	0-0	0-0	0-2
Ruffcorn, Scott	0-0	0-1	0-0	0-0	0-1	0-0	0-0	0-0	0-0	0-0	0-0	0-0	0-1	0-0	0-3
Ryan, Ken	0-0	1-0	0-0	0-0	0-0	0-0	0-0	0-0	0-0	0-0	0-0	0-0	0-0	0-0	1-0
Schilling, Curt	0-1	0-2	1-2	1-0	3-0	3-0	1-2	2-0	1-1	2-1	1-0	1-1	0-0	1-1	17-11
Spradlin, Jerry	0-1	0-0	0-0	0-0	1-1	1-0	0-0	0-1	0-0	0-2	1-0	0-0	0-2	1-1	4-8
Stephenson, Garrett	2-2	0-1	0-2	0-0	1-0	2-0	0-1	0-0	1-0	1-0	1-0	0-0	0-0	0-0	8-6
Winston, Darrin	0-0	1-0	0-0	0-0	0-0	0-0	0-0	0-0	0-0	0-0	0-0	0-0	0-0	0-0	1-0
Totals	2-10	5-6	3-8	7-4	6-6	7-4	1-10	6-6	5-7	5-6	6-5	7-4	3-8	5-10	68-94

INTERLEAGUE BREAKDOWN: Beech 0-1, Maduro 0-1, Spradlin 0-1 vs. Orioles; Bottalico 0-1, Ruffcorn 0-1, Schilling 0-1 vs. Red Sox; Beech 1-0, Green 0-1, Leiter 0-1 vs. Tigers; Grace 1-0, Schilling 1-0, Spradlin 1-0 vs. Yankees; Gomes 1-0, Leiter 0-1, Nye 0-1 vs. Blue Jays.

PITTSBURGH—79-83

Pitcher	Atl. W-L	Chi. W-L	Cin. W-L	Col. W-L	Fla. W-L	Hou. W-L	L.A. W-L	Mon. W-L	N.Y. W-L	Phi. W-L	St.L. W-L	S.D. W-L	S.F. W-L	A.L. W-L	Totals W-L
Christiansen, Jason	0-0	0-0	0-0	0-0	0-0	1-0	0-0	0-0	1-0	0-0	0-0	0-0	1-0	0-0	3-0
Cooke, Steve	0-2	2-0	0-0	0-0	1-2	0-0	0-2	0-1	0-2	1-2	1-0	1-1	2-1	1-2	9-15
Cordova, Francisco	1-1	0-2	1-2	2-0	1-0	2-0	1-1	1-0	0-0	0-0	0-1	1-0	1-1	1-1	11-8
Dessens, Elmer	0-0	0-0	0-0	0-0	0-0	0-0	0-0	0-0	0-0	0-0	0-0	0-0	0-0	0-0	0-0
Ericks, John	0-0	0-0	0-0	0-0	0-0	0-0	0-0	0-0	0-0	0-0	1-0	0-0	0-0	0-0	1-0
Granger, Jeff	0-0	0-0	0-0	0-0	0-0	0-0	0-0	0-0	0-0	0-0	0-0	0-0	0-0	0-0	0-0
Johnson, Jason	0-0	0-0	0-0	0-0	0-0	0-0	0-0	0-0	0-0	0-0	0-0	0-0	0-0	0-0	0-0
Lieber, Jon	1-1	0-3	1-1	0-1	0-2	1-0	0-1	2-1	0-0	1-1	2-0	1-1	0-1	2-1	11-14
Loaiza, Esteban	1-0	0-0	1-2	1-0	1-1	0-2	0-0	0-1	0-1	1-0	3-1	1-0	2-0	0-3	11-11
Loiselle, Rich	0-0	1-0	0-0	0-0	0-2	0-0	0-0	0-0	0-0	0-0	0-1	0-1	0-0	0-0	1-5
Morel, Ramon	0-0	0-0	0-0	0-0	0-0	0-0	0-0	0-0	0-0	0-0	0-0	0-0	0-0	0-0	0-0
Peters, Chris	1-0	0-0	0-0	0-0	0-0	0-0	0-0	1-0	0-0	0-0	0-0	0-0	0-0	0-0	2-2
Rincon, Ricardo	0-0	0-2	1-1	0-2	0-0	1-0	0-2	0-0	1-1	1-0	0-0	0-0	0-0	0-0	4-8
Ruebel, Matt	0-0	0-0	0-0	1-0	0-0	0-0	0-0	0-0	0-0	0-1	1-0	0-1	1-0	0-0	3-2
Schmidt, Jason	1-1	2-0	1-0	1-0	0-0	0-3	0-2	0-1	0-1	1-1	1-0	1-0	0-0	2-0	10-9
Silva, Jose	0-0	0-0	0-1	0-0	0-0	0-0	0-0	0-0	1-0	0-0	0-0	0-0	0-0	1-0	2-1
Sodowsky, Clint	1-0	0-0	0-0	0-0	0-0	1-1	0-0	0-0	0-0	0-0	0-0	0-0	0-0	0-0	2-2
Wagner, Paul	0-0	0-0	0-0	0-0	0-0	0-0	0-0	0-0	0-0	0-0	0-0	0-0	0-0	0-0	0-0
Wainhouse, David	0-0	0-0	0-0	0-0	0-0	0-0	0-1	0-0	0-0	0-0	0-0	0-0	0-0	0-0	0-1
Wallace, Jeff	0-0	0-0	0-0	0-0	0-0	0-0	0-0	0-0	0-0	0-0	0-0	0-0	0-0	0-0	0-0
Wilkins, Marc	0-0	0-0	0-2	2-1	0-0	0-0	1-0	2-0	0-0	1-0	0-0	0-0	0-1	0-1	9-5
Totals	6-5	5-7	4-8	7-4	4-7	6-6	2-9	6-5	4-7	6-5	9-3	5-6	8-3	7-8	79-83

INTERLEAGUE BREAKDOWN: Cooke 1-0, Lieber 1-0, Schmidt 1-0 vs. White Sox; Cooke 0-1, Loaiza 0-1, Silva 1-0 vs. Indians; Cooke 0-1, Cordova 1-0, Lieber 0-1 vs. Royals; Lieber 1-0, Loaiza 0-1, Wilkins 0-1 vs. Brewers; Cordova 0-1, Loaiza 0-1, Schmidt 1-0 vs. Twins.

ST. LOUIS—73-89

Pitcher	Atl. W-L	Chi. W-L	Cin. W-L	Col. W-L	Fla. W-L	Hou. W-L	L.A. W-L	Mon. W-L	N.Y. W-L	Phi. W-L	Pit. W-L	S.D. W-L	S.F. W-L	A.L. W-L	Totals W-L
Aybar, Manny	0-0	0-0	0-0	0-0	0-0	0-0	0-0	0-1	0-1	0-1	0-0	0-0	1-0	1-1	2-4
Batchelor, Richard	0-0	0-0	0-0	0-0	0-0	1-0	0-0	0-1	0-0	0-0	0-0	0-0	0-0	0-0	1-1
Bautista, Jose	0-0	0-0	0-0	0-0	0-0	0-0	0-0	0-0	0-0	0-0	0-0	0-0	0-0	0-0	0-0
Beltran, Rigo	0-0	0-0	0-0	0-0	0-0	0-0	0-0	0-0	0-0	0-1	0-1	0-0	1-0	1-0	1-2
Benes, Alan	0-1	1-0	2-1	1-1	1-1	1-0	1-1	0-1	0-1	0-0	0-0	2-0	0-1	0-1	9-9
Benes, Andy	0-1	1-0	0-0	0-0	1-1	0-1	0-0	1-0	1-1	1-1	1-0	1-1	2-0	1-1	10-7
Busby, Mike	0-0	0-1	0-0	0-0	0-0	0-0	0-0	0-0	0-0	0-1	0-0	0-0	0-0	0-0	0-2
Eckersley, Dennis	0-0	0-0	0-0	1-0	0-0	0-1	0-1	0-1	0-1	0-0	0-0	0-0	0-0	0-0	1-5
Fossas, Tony	0-0	0-0	0-1	0-0	0-0	0-1	0-0	0-2	0-1	1-0	0-0	1-0	1-0	0-1	2-7
Frascatore, John	0-1	0-0	1-0	0-0	0-0	0-1	1-0	1-0	0-0	1-0	0-0	0-0	1-0	0-0	5-2
Gaetti, Gary	0-0	0-0	0-0	0-0	0-0	0-0	0-0	0-0	0-0	0-0	0-0	0-0	0-0	0-0	0-0
Honeycutt, Rick	0-0	0-0	0-0	0-0	0-0	0-0	0-0	0-0	0-0	0-0	0-0	0-0	0-0	0-0	0-0
Jackson, Danny	0-0	0-0	0-0	0-1	0-0	0-0	0-1	0-0	0-0	0-0	1-0	0-0	0-0	0-0	1-2
King, Curtis	2-0	0-0	0-1	0-1	0-0	0-0	0-0	1-0	0-0	0-0	0-0	0-0	0-0	0-0	4-2
Lowe, Sean	0-0	0-1	0-0	0-0	0-0	0-0	0-0	0-0	0-0	0-0	0-1	0-0	0-0	0-0	0-2
Ludwick, Eric	0-0	0-0	0-0	0-0	0-0	0-1	0-0	0-0	0-0	0-0	0-0	0-0	0-0	0-0	0-1
Mathews, T.J.	1-0	2-0	0-0	0-0	0-0	0-0	1-0	0-0	0-1	0-1	0-0	0-1	0-0	0-1	4-4
McGraw, Tom	0-0	0-0	0-0	0-0	0-0	0-0	0-0	0-0	0-0	0-0	0-0	0-0	0-0	0-0	0-0
Morris, Matt	0-2	2-1	0-1	1-1	3-0	0-0	2-0	0-0	0-0	0-1	0-2	1-0	1-1	2-0	12-9
Osborne, Donovan	0-0	0-0	0-0	1-1	0-1	0-2	0-0	0-1	0-1	1-1	0-0	0-0	1-0	0-0	3-7
Painter, Lance	0-0	1-0	0-0	0-0	0-0	0-0	0-0	0-0	0-0	0-0	0-0	0-0	0-1	0-0	1-1

Pitcher	Atl. W-L	Chi. W-L	Cin. W-L	Col. W-L	Fla. W-L	Hou. W-L	L.A. W-L	Mon. W-L	N.Y. W-L	Phi. W-L	Pit. W-L	S.D. W-L	S.F. W-L	A.L. W-L	Totals W-L
Petkovsek, Mark	0-1	0-0	1-1	0-2	0-1	0-0	0-1	1-1	0-0	0-0	0-0	1-0	0-0	1-0	4-7
Raggio, Brady	0-0	0-0	0-0	0-0	1-0	0-0	0-1	0-0	0-0	0-0	0-0	0-1	0-0	0-0	1-2
Stottlemyre, Todd	0-2	1-0	2-0	0-0	0-1	1-2	1-0	1-0	1-1	2-0	0-2	0-0	2-0	1-1	12-9
Valenzuela, Fernando	0-0	0-1	0-1	0-0	0-0	0-0	0-0	0-0	0-0	0-0	0-1	0-0	0-0	0-1	0-4
Totals	3-8	8-4	6-6	4-7	6-5	3-9	6-5	5-6	2-9	5-6	3-9	6-5	8-3	8-7	73-89

INTERLEAGUE BREAKDOWN: Aybar 1-0, An. Benes 1-0, Fossas 0-1 vs. White Sox; Mathews 0-1, Morris 1-0, Stottlemyre 0-1 vs. Indians; Aybar 0-1, Beltran 1-0, Osborne 1-0 vs. Royals; Al. Benes 0-1, An. Benes 0-1, Valenzuela 0-1 vs. Brewers; Morris 1-0, Petkovsek 1-0, Stottlemyre 1-0 vs. Twins. Total: 8-7.

SAN DIEGO—76-86

Pitcher	Atl. W-L	Chi. W-L	Cin. W-L	Col. W-L	Fla. W-L	Hou. W-L	L.A. W-L	Mon. W-L	N.Y. W-L	Phi. W-L	Pit. W-L	St.L. W-L	S.F. W-L	A.L. W-L	Totals W-L
Ashby, Andy	1-0	0-1	0-0	3-0	1-0	0-0	0-1	0-1	1-0	0-2	0-2	1-1	0-2	2-1	9-11
Batchelor, Richard	0-0	0-0	0-0	1-0	0-0	0-0	0-0	0-0	0-0	0-0	0-0	0-0	0-0	1-0	2-0
Bergman, Sean	0-0	0-0	0-0	0-1	0-0	0-0	1-1	0-0	1-0	0-1	0-1	0-0	0-0	0-0	2-4
Bochtler, Doug	0-0	1-1	0-0	0-0	0-1	0-0	0-0	1-1	0-1	0-0	0-0	0-0	0-0	1-2	3-6
Bruske, Jim	0-0	0-0	0-0	0-0	1-0	0-0	0-0	0-0	0-1	1-0	1-0	1-0	0-0	0-0	4-1
Burrows, Terry	0-0	0-0	0-0	0-1	0-0	0-0	0-0	0-0	0-0	0-0	0-1	0-0	0-0	0-0	0-2
Cunnane, Will	0-1	2-0	1-0	0-0	0-0	1-0	0-0	0-0	1-0	0-1	0-0	0-1	0-0	0-0	6-3
Erdos, Todd	0-0	0-0	0-0	0-0	0-0	0-0	0-0	0-0	0-0	0-0	2-0	0-0	0-0	0-0	2-0
Hamilton, Joey	0-2	0-0	2-0	1-0	0-0	1-1	3-0	1-1	1-0	0-1	0-0	1-0	1-1	1-1	12-7
Hitchcock, Sterling	0-1	1-1	1-1	0-0	1-1	1-1	1-0	0-2	1-1	2-1	1-0	0-1	0-1	1-0	10-11
Hoffman, Trevor	0-1	1-0	2-0	0-1	0-1	1-0	1-0	0-1	0-0	0-0	1-0	0-0	0-0	0-0	6-4
Jackson, Danny	0-0	0-0	0-1	0-1	0-0	0-0	0-2	0-0	0-0	0-0	0-0	0-0	1-1	0-1	1-7
Kroon, Marc	0-0	0-0	0-0	0-0	0-0	0-0	0-0	0-0	0-0	0-0	0-0	0-1	0-0	0-0	0-1
Long, Joey	0-0	0-0	0-0	0-0	0-0	0-0	0-0	0-0	0-0	0-0	0-0	0-0	0-0	0-0	0-0
Menhart, Paul	0-0	0-1	0-0	1-0	0-0	0-0	0-1	0-0	0-1	0-0	0-0	0-0	0-0	1-0	2-3
Murray, Heath	1-0	0-0	0-0	0-0	0-0	0-0	0-0	0-0	0-0	0-0	0-0	0-0	0-1	0-1	1-2
Scott, Tim	0-0	0-0	0-0	0-0	0-0	0-0	0-0	0-0	0-0	1-0	0-0	0-0	0-0	0-0	1-1
Smith, Pete	1-0	0-0	0-1	0-0	1-0	1-0	0-0	0-1	1-0	0-0	1-1	0-0	1-1	0-2	7-6
Valenzuela, Fernando	0-1	0-1	0-1	0-0	1-0	0-3	0-0	0-1	0-1	0-0	1-0	0-0	0-0	0-0	2-8
Veras, Dario	0-0	0-0	0-0	0-0	0-0	0-0	0-0	0-0	0-0	0-0	1-0	0-0	1-0	1-0	2-1
Worrell, Tim	0-2	0-1	0-1	1-0	1-0	0-1	0-0	1-0	0-1	1-0	0-1	0-1	0-0	0-0	4-8
Totals	3-8	5-6	6-5	8-4	6-5	5-6	7-5	3-8	6-5	4-7	6-5	5-6	4-8	8-8	76-86

INTERLEAGUE BREAKDOWN: Bochtler 1-0, Menhart 1-0, Murray 0-1, Smith 0-1 vs. Angels; Ashby 1-0, Bochtler 0-2, Smith 0-1 vs. A's; Batchelor 1-0, Hamilton 1-1, Veras 1-0 vs. Mariners; Hitchcock 1-0, Jackson 0-1 vs. Rangers. Total: 8-8.

SAN FRANCISCO—90-72

Pitcher	Atl. W-L	Chi. W-L	Cin. W-L	Col. W-L	Fla. W-L	Hou. W-L	L.A. W-L	Mon. W-L	N.Y. W-L	Phi. W-L	Pit. W-L	St.L. W-L	S.D. W-L	A.L. W-L	Totals W-L
Alvarez, Wilson	0-1	0-1	2-0	0-0	0-0	0-0	0-0	0-0	1-0	0-0	0-0	0-0	1-0	0-1	4-3
Arocha, Rene	0-0	0-0	0-0	0-0	0-0	0-0	0-0	0-0	0-0	0-0	0-0	0-0	0-0	0-0	0-0
Bailey, Cory	0-0	0-0	0-0	0-0	0-0	0-0	0-0	0-0	0-0	0-0	0-0	0-0	0-1	0-0	0-1
Beck, Rod	0-1	0-0	2-0	0-0	0-0	1-0	1-0	0-1	0-0	0-0	0-0	1-1	1-0	1-1	7-4
Carlson, Dan	0-0	0-0	0-0	0-0	0-0	0-0	0-0	0-0	0-0	0-0	0-0	0-0	0-0	0-0	0-0
Creek, Doug	0-0	0-0	0-0	0-1	0-0	0-0	0-0	0-0	0-0	0-1	0-0	0-1	1-0	1-0	1-2
Darwin, Danny	0-0	0-0	0-0	0-1	0-0	0-0	0-0	0-0	0-0	0-0	0-0	0-0	1-0	0-1	1-3
DeLucia, Rich	0-0	0-0	0-0	0-0	0-0	0-0	0-0	0-0	0-0	0-0	0-0	0-0	0-0	0-0	0-0
Estes, Shawn	1-0	1-0	1-0	2-0	2-0	1-0	1-1	0-1	3-0	3-0	0-1	1-1	2-1	1-0	19-5
Fernandez, Osvaldo	0-0	0-1	0-1	0-0	1-0	1-0	0-0	0-0	0-1	1-0	0-0	0-0	0-0	0-0	3-4
Foulke, Keith	0-0	0-0	0-0	0-1	1-0	0-1	0-2	0-0	0-0	0-0	0-0	0-0	0-0	0-0	1-5
Gardner, Mark	0-0	2-1	0-1	2-1	0-2	1-1	0-0	2-0	1-1	1-1	1-0	0-0	0-1	2-0	12-9
Henry, Doug	1-2	0-0	0-0	0-0	1-0	0-0	0-1	1-0	0-0	0-0	1-1	0-1	0-0	0-0	4-5
Hernandez, Roberto	0-0	0-0	1-0	1-0	0-1	0-0	0-0	0-1	0-0	1-0	0-0	1-0	0-0	0-1	5-2
Johnstone, John	0-0	0-0	0-0	0-0	0-0	0-0	0-0	0-0	0-0	0-0	0-0	0-0	0-0	0-0	0-0
Mulholland, Terry	0-0	0-0	0-0	0-0	0-0	0-0	0-0	0-0	0-0	0-0	0-1	0-0	0-0	0-0	0-1
Poole, Jim	2-1	0-0	0-0	0-0	0-0	0-0	0-0	0-0	1-0	0-0	0-0	0-0	0-0	0-0	3-1
Rapp, Pat	0-0	1-0	0-1	0-0	0-0	0-0	0-0	0-0	0-0	0-0	0-0	0-0	0-0	0-0	1-2
Roa, Joe	0-1	0-1	0-0	0-0	0-0	0-1	0-0	1-0	0-1	0-0	0-0	0-1	1-0	0-0	2-5
Rodriguez, Rich	0-0	0-0	0-1	0-0	0-0	0-0	0-0	0-0	2-0	0-0	0-1	0-0	1-0	1-1	4-3
Rueter, Kirk	0-0	1-0	1-0	1-1	1-1	1-0	2-1	1-0	0-0	1-0	0-2	1-0	1-0	2-1	13-6
Tavarez, Julian	0-0	1-1	0-0	1-0	0-0	2-0	1-0	1-1	0-2	0-0	0-0	0-0	0-0	0-0	6-4
VanLandingham, William	0-1	0-0	0-0	1-0	0-1	0-0	1-1	0-0	0-0	1-0	0-1	0-2	0-0	1-1	4-7
Totals	4-7	6-5	7-4	8-4	6-5	8-3	6-6	5-6	8-3	8-3	3-8	3-8	8-4	10-6	90-72

INTERLEAGUE BREAKDOWN: Alvarez 0-1, Estes 1-0, Roa 1-0, VanLandingham 1-0 vs. Angels; Creek 1-0, Darwin 0-1, Rueter 1-1 vs. A's; Beck 1-0, Gardner 1-0, Rueter 1-0, VanLandingham 0-1 vs. Mariners; Beck 0-1, Gardner 1-0, Rodriguez 1-1 vs. Rangers. Total: 10-6.

HOME RUNS BY PARKS

	At Atl.	At Chi.	At Cin.	At Col.	At Fla.	At Hou.	At L.A.	At Mon.	At N.Y.	At Phi.	At Pit.	At St.L.	At S.D.	At S.F.	At A.L. Parks	Totals 1997	Totals 1996	HR Allow.
Atlanta	76	5	12	9	3	4	4	8	7	10	10	3	9	3	11	174	197	103
Chicago	0	79	5	7	3	4	3	1	2	7	2	1	3	7	3	127	175	179
Cincinnati	3	5	73	10	3	5	4	6	5	3	4	5	6	5	5	142	191	168
Colorado	3	11	8	124	13	8	7	13	7	5	8	4	11	7	10	239	221	191
Florida	7	7	7	6	63	3	11	4	2	5	4	6	2	5	4	136	150	126
Houston	5	7	6	4	4	59	4	4	6	10	5	4	7	3	5	133	129	128
Los Angeles	6	9	1	19	7	2	85	7	4	4	5	6	5	7	7	174	150	150
Montreal	7	13	4	8	1	5	2	81	8	5	3	3	12	9	11	172	148	141
New York	6	11	4	5	9	3	5	2	74	10	9	6	4	0	5	153	147	139

	At Atl.	At Chi.	At Cin.	At Col.	At Fla.	At Hou.	At L.A.	At Mon.	At N.Y.	At Phi.	At Pit.	At St.L.	At S.D.	At S.F.	At A.L. Parks	Totals 1997	1996	HR Allow.
Philadelphia	3	4	3	2	4	4	2	7	4	61	1	3	9	3	6	116	132	163
Pittsburgh	2	4	6	11	5	4	2	5	1	4	68	5	2	7	3	129	138	138
St. Louis	5	12	8	10	3	1	7	4	2	6	6	68	*5	4	3	144	142	113
San Diego	1	5	10	8	3	2	9	2	7	2	6	3	75	7	12	152	147	161
San Francisco	2	6	7	13	4	3	6	3	8	6	4	5	8	83	14	172	153	147
A.L. clubs	5	7	10	9	3	8	10	3	8	4	10	5	13	9		104		121
1997 Totals	131	185	164	245	128	115	161	150	145	142	145	127	*171	159	99	2267		2168
1996 Totals	172	188	175	271	117	123	111	157	136	137	155	151	†147	180			2220	

*There were actually 170 home runs hit at San Diego in 1997. The totals include one home run by the Cardinals at Aloha Stadium, Honolulu, Hawaii.
†There were actually 138 home runs hit at San Diego in 1996. The totals include one home run by the Mets and eight by the Padres at Monterrey Stadium, Mexico.

AT ATLANTA (131):

Atlanta (76)—Lopez 11, Klesko 10, Blauser 9, McGriff 8, C. Jones 7, Graffanino 5, A. Jones 5, Tucker 5, Perez 4, Lockhart 3, Lofton 3, Lemke 2, Bautista 1, Colbrunn 1, Neagle 1, Spehr 1. **Cincinnati (3)**—Kelly 1, Oliver 1, Sanders 1. **Colorado (3)**—Castilla 1, Vanderwal 1, Walker 1. **Florida (7)**—Bonilla 2, Johnson 2, Conine 1, Dunwoody 1, Sheffield 1. **Houston (5)**—Bagwell 2, Biggio 2, Carr 1, Spiers 1. **Los Angeles (6)**—Mondesi 3, Gagne 1, Karros 1, Piazza 1. **Montreal (7)**—Segui 2, White 2, Fullmer 1, Meulens 1, Vidro 1. **New York (6)**—Huskey 3, Alexander 1, Hundley 1, Ochoa 1. **Philadelphia (3)**—Brogna 1, Daulton 1, Lieberthal 1. **Pittsburgh (2)**—Martin 1, Williams 1. **St. Louis (5)**—Gant 2, Lankford 2, Franklin 1. **San Diego (1)**—Gwynn 1. **San Francisco (2)**—Hill 1, Kent 1. **Baltimore (3)**—Anderson 1, Palmeiro 1, Webster 1. **Detroit (2)**—Clark 1, Cruz 1.

AT CHICAGO (185):

Atlanta (5)—Bautista 2, A. Jones 2, Tucker 1. **Chicago (79)**—Sosa 25, Sandberg 9, Dunston 7, Grace 6, Orie 6, Hernandez 4, McRae 4, Servais 4, Brown 3, Johnson 3, Kieschnick 3, Glanville 2, Clark 1, Hansen 1, Sanchez 1. **Cincinnati (5)**—Larkin 3, Oliver 1, Perez 1. **Colorado (11)**—Walker 4, Castilla 2, Bichette 1, Galarraga 1, McCracken 1, Thompson 1, Young 1. **Florida (7)**—Conine 3, Sheffield 2, Alou 1, Johnson 1. **Houston (7)**—Ausmus 2, Bagwell 1, Bell 1, Berry 1, Biggio 1, Spiers 1. **Los Angeles (9)**—Mondesi 4, Zeile 2, Gagne 1, Guerrero 1, Liriano 1. **Montreal (13)**—Fletcher 3, Lansing 2, Rodriguez 2, Strange 2, Andrews 1, Grudzielanek 1, Stankiewicz 1, White 1. **New York (11)**—Huskey 3, Hundley 2, Olerud 2, Alexander 1, Alfonzo 1, Baerga 1, Gilkey 1. **Philadelphia (4)**—Rolen 2, Brogna 1, Jefferies 1. **Pittsburgh (4)**—Brown 1, Elster 1, Guillen 1, Johnson 1. **St. Louis (12)**—Gaetti 4, Lankford 2, Clayton 1, DeShields 1, Difelice 1, Marrero 1, McGwire 1, Plantier 1. **San Diego (5)**—Finley 1, Flaherty 1, Gomez 1, Joyner 1, Vaughn 1. **San Francisco (6)**—Aurilia 1, Hill 1, Kent 1, Lewis 1, Snow 1, Wilkins 1. **Kansas City (2)**—Dye 1, King 1. **Milwaukee (2)**—Burnitz 1, Valentin 1. **Minnesota (3)**—Becker 1, Meares 1, Molitor 1.

AT CINCINNATI (164):

Atlanta (12)—Lopez 3, McGriff 3, Tucker 2, Blauser 1, A. Jones 1, C. Jones 1, Klesko 1. **Chicago (5)**—Sosa 2, Glanville 1, Hernandez 1, Servais 1. **Cincinnati (73)**—Greene 13, Sanders 11, Oliver 7, Perez 7, Taubensee 7, Nunnally 6, B. Boone 4, Kelly 3, Reese 3, Harris 3, Sierra 2, Stynes 2, Branson 1, Fordyce 1, Goodwin 1, Morris 1, Pendleton 1, Schourek 1. **Colorado (8)**—Burks 3, Castilla 2, Walker 2, Galarraga 1. **Florida (7)**—Abbott 2, Bonilla 2, Alou 1, Conine 1, Johnson 1. **Houston (6)**—Bagwell 1, Bell 1, Biggio 1, Gonzalez 1, Hidalgo 1, Howard 1. **Los Angeles (1)**—Piazza 1. **Montreal (4)**—Segui 2, Rodriguez 1, White 1. **New York (4)**—Hundley 2, Everett 1, Huskey 1. **Philadelphia (3)**—Brogna 1, Jefferies 1, Jordan 1. **Pittsburgh (6)**—Garcia 3, Dunston 2, Kendall 1. **St. Louis (8)**—Lankford 4, Clayton 1, Difelice 1, Gaetti 1, Gant 1. **San Diego (10)**—Finley 4, Caminiti 1, Gwynn 1, Hernandez 1, Joyner 1, Shipley 1, Shumpert 1. **San Francisco (7)**—Bonds 2, Snow 2, Johnson 1, Kent 1, Vizcaino 1. **Chicago A.L. (6)**—Belle 2, Durham 2, Baines 1, Fabregas 1. **Kansas City (1)**—Damon 1. **Milwaukee (3)**—Burnitz 1, Loretta 1, Williams 1.

AT COLORADO (245):

Atlanta (9)—C. Jones 2, Klesko 2, A. Jones 1, Lofton 1, Lopez 1, McGriff 1, Perez 1. **Chicago (7)**—Sosa 2, Clark 1, Dunston 1, Grace 1, Houston 1, Servais 1. **Cincinnati (10)**—R. Sanders 4, Nunnally 2, B. Boone 1, Greene 1, Larkin 1, Perez 1. **Colorado (124)**—Castilla 21, Galarraga 21, Bichette 20, Walker 20, Burks 17, Reed 9, Helton 3, Perez 3, Pulliam 2, Weiss 2, Young 2, Bates 1, Holmes 1, Manwaring 1, McCracken 1. **Florida (6)**—Alou 2, Arias 1, Conine 1, Johnson 1, Sheffield 1. **Houston (4)**—Bagwell 1, Bell 1, Biggio 1, Spiers 1. **Los Angeles (19)**—Zeile 5, Piazza 4, Karros 3, Mondesi 3, Blanco 1, Gagne 1, Hollandsworth 1, Lewis 1, Young 1. **Montreal (8)**—Segui 2, White 2, Andrews 1, Perez 1, Rodriguez 1, Strange 1. **New York (5)**—Hundley 3, Gilkey 1, Olerud 1. **Philadelphia (2)**—Brogna 1, Lieberthal 1. **Pittsburgh (11)**—Elster 2, Guillen 2, Martin 2, Sveum 2, Kendall 1, Randa 1, Ward 1. **St. Louis (10)**—McGwire 4, Lankford 2, Gaetti 1, Gant 1, Lampkin 1, Plantier 1. **San Diego (8)**—Finley 4, Caminiti 2, Gwynn 2. **San Francisco (13)**—Snow 4, Bonds 3, Aurilia 1, Berryhill 1, Hamilton 1, Johnson 1, Kent 1, Vizcaino 1. **Anaheim (3)**—Edmonds 2, Alicea 1. **Oakland (2)**—Stairs 2. **Seattle (3)**—Kelly 1, Martinez 1, Sorrento 1. **Texas (1)**—Gonzalez 1.

AT FLORIDA (128):

Atlanta (3)—C. Jones 1, Lopez 1, McGriff 1. **Chicago (3)**—Grace 1, Johnson 1, Sosa 1. **Cincinnati (3)**—Kelly 1, Oliver 1, Sanders 1. **Colorado (13)**—Galarraga 5, Walker 3, Castilla 2, Bichette 1, McCracken 1, Weiss 1. **Florida (63)**—Sheffield 13, Alou 12, Bonilla 8, Conine 7, Johnson 7, White 4, Renteria 3, Eisenreich 2, Floyd 2, Abbott 1, Cangelosi 1, Counsell 1, Natal 1, Saunders 1. **Houston (4)**—Gutierrez 2, Bell 1, Biggio 1. **Los Angeles (2)**—Cromer 2, Karros 2, Gagne 1, Mondesi 1, Piazza 1. **Montreal (1)**—Rodriguez 1. **New York (9)**—Alfonzo 1, Baerga 1, Everett 1, Gilkey 1, Hardtke 1, Hundley 1, McRae 1, Ochoa 1, Olerud 1. **Philadelphia (4)**—Jefferies 2, Barron 1, Rolen 1. **Pittsburgh (5)**—Allenswortht 1, Guillen 1, Polcovich 1, Sveum 1, Williams 1. **St. Louis (3)**—McGwire 2, Gaetti 1. **San Diego (3)**—Gomez 1, Romero 1, Vaughn 1. **San Francisco (4)**—Benard 1, Estes 1, Mueller 1, Snow 1. **Baltimore (3)**—Palmeiro 1, Ripken 1, Webster 1.

AT HOUSTON (115):

Atlanta (4)—Blauser 1, C. Jones 1, Lopez 1, McGriff 1. **Chicago (4)**—Alexander 1, Houston 1, Kieschnick 1, Orie 1. **Cincinnati (5)**—Greene 2, Oliver 1, Sanders 1, Sanders 1. **Colorado (8)**—Burks 2, Castilla 2, Galarraga 2, Bates 1, Bichette 1. **Florida (3)**—Abbott 1, Conine 1, Zaun 1. **Houston (59)**—Bagwell 22, Bell 7, Biggio 7, Berry 4, Gonzalez 4, Abreu 3, Bogar 3, Carr 3, Johnson 2, Ausmus 1, Knorr 1, Mouton 1, Phillips 1. **Los Angeles (2)**—Piazza 1, Zeile 1. **Montreal (5)**—White 2, Hermanson 1, Lansing 1, Rodriguez 1. **New York (3)**—Hardtke 1, Hundley 1, Huskey 1. **Philadelphia (4)**—Brogna 2, Daulton 1, Jefferies 1. **Pittsburgh (4)**—Guillen 2, Martin 1, Young 1. **St. Louis (1)**—DeShields 1. **San Diego (2)**—Finley 1, Jones 1. **San Francisco (3)**—Bonds 1, Hill 1, Wilkins 1. **Cleveland (2)**—Giles 1, Ramirez 1, Seitzer 1, Williams 1. **Milwaukee (1)**—Valentin 1. **Minnesota (3)**—Lawton 2, Molitor 1.

AT LOS ANGELES (161):

Atlanta (4)—Klesko 3, Blauser 1. **Chicago (3)**—Hansen 1, Hernandez 1, Sosa 1. **Cincinnati (4)**—Perez 2, Sanders 1, Sanders 1. **Colorado (7)**—Burks 2, Reed 2, Castilla 1, Galarraga 1, Walker 1. **Florida (11)**—Floyd 3, Abbott 1, Alou 1, Bonilla 1, Conine 1, Daulton 1, Renteria 1, Sheffield 1, White 1. **Houston (4)**—Biggio 3, Howard 1. **Los Angeles (85)**—Piazza 22, Zeile 17, Mondesi 16, Karros 13, Ashley 4, Cedeno 3, Cromer 2, Gagne 2, Guerrero 2, Prince 2, Anthony 1, Hollandsworth 1. **Montreal (2)**—Lansing 1, Strange 1. **New York (5)**—Hundley 2, Alfonzo 1, Baerga 1, Huskey 1. **Philadelphia (2)**—Jefferies 1, Lieberthal 1. **Pittsburgh (2)**—Allensworth 1, Guillen 1. **St. Louis (7)**—Lankford 3, Clayton 1, DeShields 1, Gant 1, Lampkin 1. **San Diego (9)**—Finley 4, Gwynn 2, Caminiti 1, Flaherty 1, Hamilton 1. **San Francisco (6)**—Kent 2, Wilkins 2, Bonds 1, Lewis 1. **Anaheim (1)**—Salmon 1. **Oakland (2)**—Mayne 1, Tejada 1. **Seattle (3)**—Buhner 1, Griffey 1, Sheets 1. **Texas (4)**—Gonzalez 1, Palmer 1, Rodriguez 1, Witt 1.

AT MONTREAL (150):

Atlanta (8)—A. Jones 2, Lopez 2, Blauser 1, C. Jones 1, Lockhart 1, McGriff 1. **Chicago (1)**—Sosa 1. **Cincinnati (6)**—Nunnally 2, Greene 1, Jackson 1, Kelly 1, Perez 1. **Colorado (13)**—Castilla 4, Walker 4, Bichette 2, Burks 1, Galarraga 1, Reed 1. **Florida (4)**—Conine 1, Dunwoody 1, Johnson 1, Morman 1. **Houston (4)**—Gonzalez 2, Bagwell 1, Bogar 1. **Los Angeles (7)**—Piazza 3, Zeile 2, Gagne 1, Karros 1. **Montreal (81)**—Rodriguez 14, Lansing 11, Fletcher 10, Segui 10, White 9, Strange 6, Guerrero 5, Santangelo 5, Widger 4, Andrews 2, McGuire 2, Fullmer 1, Grudzielanek 1, Meulens 1. **New York (2)**—Alfonzo 1, Baerga 1. **Philadelphia (7)**—Estalella 1, Brogna 2, Jordan 1, Lieberthal 1. **Pittsburgh (5)**—Brown 1, Cummings 1, Randa 1, Sveum 1, Young 1. **St. Louis (4)**—Gaetti 1, Lampkin 1, Lankford 1, Young 1. **San Diego (2)**—Caminiti 1, Jones 1. **San Francisco (3)**—Bonds 1, Hill 1, Snow 1. **Boston (2)**—Valentin 1, Vaughn 1. **Detroit (1)**—Easley 1.

AT NEW YORK (145):

Atlanta (7)—C. Jones 2, Tucker 2, Belliard 1, Blauser 1, Graffanino 1. **Chicago (2)**—Clark 1, Grace 1. **Cincinnati (5)**—Greene 2, Nunnally 1, Oliver 1, Taubensee 1. **Colorado (7)**—Galarraga 3, Burks 1, Castilla 1, Reed 1, Walker 1. **Florida (2)**—Conine 1, Sheffield 1. **Houston (6)**—Bagwell 3, Bell 1, Berry 1, Mouton 1. **Los Angeles (4)**—Karros 2, Guerrero 1, Piazza 1. **Montreal (8)**—Fletcher 1, Guerrero 1, Lansing 1, Orsulak 1, Rodriguez 1, Segui 1, Vidro 1, White 1. **New York (74)**—Hundley 14, Olerud 13, Everett 11, Gilkey 7, Huskey 7, Alfonzo 4, Baerga 4, Franco 3, McRae 2, Clark 1, Gilbert 1, Johnson 1, Lopez 1, Ochoa 1, Ordonez 1, Pratt 1, Reed 1, Reynoso 1. **Philadelphia (4)**—Rolen 2, Brogna 1, Daulton 1. **Pittsburgh (1)**—Sveum 1. **St. Louis (2)**—Lankford 1, McGee 1. **San Diego (7)**—Caminiti 2, Flaherty 2, Finley 1, Shipley 1, Vaughn 1. **San Francisco (8)**—Kent 2, Lewis 2, Hill 1, Johnson 1, Snow 1, Vizcaino 1. **Boston (5)**—Garciaparr 1, Hatteberg 1, O'Leary 1, Valentin 1, Vaughn 1. **Toronto (3)**—Cruz 2, Delgado 1.

AT PHILADELPHIA (142):

Atlanta (10)—A. Jones 2, Tucker 2, Blauser 1, Graffanino 1, C. Jones 1, Lockhart 1, McGriff 1, Perez 1. **Chicago (7)**—Sandberg 2, Brown 1, Dunston 1, Grace 1, Hansen 1, Sosa 1. **Cincinnati (3)**—Greene 1, Perez 1, Stynes 1. **Colorado (5)**—Bates 1, Bichette 1, Castilla 1, Coles 1, Walker 1. **Florida (5)**—Abbott 1, Alou 1, Daulton 1, Johnson 1, Sheffield 1. **Houston (10)**—Bagwell 4, Biggio 4, Ausmus 1, Berry 1. **Los Angeles (4)**—Zeile 2, Piazza 1, Young 1. **Montreal (5)**—Lansing 1, Obando 1, Rodriguez 1, White 1, Widger 1. **New York (10)**—Gilkey 4, Huskey 3, McRae 2, Olerud 1. **Philadelphia (61)**—Lieberthal 11, Rolen 11, Brogna 9, Daulton 6, Hudler 5, Jordan 4, Barron 3, Jefferies 2, McMillon 2, Sefcik 2, Stocker 2, Amaro 1, Cummings 1, Estalella 1, Morandini 1. **Pittsburgh (4)**—Martin 1, Polcovich 1, Sveum 1, Young 1. **St. Louis (6)**—Clayton 1, DeShields 1, Franklin 1, Gaetti 1, Lampkin 1, Lankford 1. **San Diego (2)**—Caminiti 2. **San Francisco (6)**—Hill 2, Kent 2, Lewis 1, Wilkins 1. **New York A.L. (1)**—Curtis 1. **Toronto (3)**—Carter 1, Gonzalez 1, Perez 1.

AT PITTSBURGH (145):

Atlanta (10)—Lopez 3, Blauser 2, C. Jones 2, A. Jones 1, Klesko 1, Tucker 1. **Chicago (2)**—Brown 1, Sosa 1. **Cincinnati (4)**—Greene 1, Nunnally 1, Sanders 1, Taubensee 1. **Colorado (8)**—Walker 4, Helton 2, Perez (Dia 1, Young 1. **Florida (4)**—Alou 1, Daulton 1, Johnson 1, Rapp 1. **Houston (5)**—Bagwell 1, Bell 1, Gonzalez 1, Hidalgo 1, Spiers 1. **Los Angeles (5)**—Mondesi 2, Piazza 2, Hollandsworth 1. **Montreal (3)**—Fletcher 1, Fullmer 1, White 1. **New York (9)**—Hundley 2, Huskey 2, Olerud 2, Baerga 1, Franco 1, Pratt 1. **Philadelphia (1)**—Lieberthal 1. **Pittsburgh (68)**—Young 11, Martin 8, Smith 6, Guillen 5, Kendall 5, Randa 5, Sveum 5, Ward 5, Womack 5, Dunston 3, Elster 3, Cummings 2, Johnson 2, Allensworth 1, Brown 1, Williams 1. **St. Louis (6)**—Lankford 3, Marrero 1, McGwire 1, Young 1. **San Diego (6)**—Gwynn 2, Vaughn 2, Caminiti 1, Finley 1. **San Francisco (4)**—Kent 2, Johnson 1, Vizcaino 1. **Cleveland (6)**—Ramirez 2, Alomar 1, Fernandez 1, Vizquel 1, Williams 1. **Kansas City (4)**—King 3, Fasano 1.

AT ST. LOUIS (127):

Atlanta (3)—Klesko 1, McGriff 1, Tucker 1. **Chicago (1)**—Grace 1. **Cincinnati (5)**—B. Boone 1, Greene 1, Reese 1, D. Sanders 1, Stynes 1. **Colorado (4)**—Burks 1, Galarraga 1, Reed 1, Walker 1. **Florida (6)**—Alou 2, Johnson 2, Cook 1, Zaun 1. **Houston (4)**—Bagwell 1, Bell 1, Biggio 1, Howard 1. **Los Angeles (6)**—Piazza 2, Anthony 1, Hollandsworth 1, Karros 1, Zeile 1. **Montreal (3)**—Fletcher 1, Segui 1, White 1. **New York (6)**—Huskey 2, Alfonzo 1, Everett 1, Hundley 1, Olerud 1. **Philadelphia (3)**—Jefferies 2, Rolen 1. **Pittsburgh (5)**—Young 2, Guillen 1, Smith 1, Ward 1. **St. Louis (68)**—McGwire 13, Gant 11, Lankford 10, Gaetti 7, DeShields 6, Clayton 5, Mabry 5, Lampkin 2, McGee 2, Plantier 2, Young 2, Bell 1, Difelice 1, Pagnozzi 1. **San Diego (3)**—Finley 2, Joyner 1. **San Francisco (5)**—Bonds 1, Hamilton 1, Javier 1, Johnson 1, Mueller 1. **Cleveland (2)**—Giles 1, Thome 1. **Chicago A.L. (1)**—Ordonez 1. **Minnesota (2)**—Becker 1, Stahoviak 1.

AT SAN DIEGO (171):

Atlanta (9)—A. Jones 2, C. Jones 2, McGriff 2, Graffanino 1, Klesko 1, Lofton 1. **Chicago (3)**—Hernandez 1, Hubbard 1, McRae 1. **Cincinnati (6)**—Perez 2, B. Boone 1, Greene 1, Nunnally 1, Oliver 1. **Colorado (11)**—Walker 4, Galarraga 3, Burks 1, Perez 1, Reed 1, Young 1. **Florida (2)**—Bonilla 1, White 1. **Houston (7)**—Bagwell 3, Berry 1, Eusebio 1, Gonzalez 1, Mouton 1. **Los Angeles (5)**—Karros 2, Ashley 1, Mondesi 1, Zeile 1. **Montreal (12)**—White 3, Grudzielanek 2, Guerrero 2, Rodriguez 2, Bullinger 1, Segui 1, Widger 1. **New York (4)**—Alfonzo 1, Gilkey 1, Hundley 1, Olerud 1. **Philadelphia (9)**—Brogna 2, Lieberthal 2, Daulton 1, Magee 1, May 1, Rolen 1, Stocker 1. **Pittsburgh (2)**—Elster 1, Kendall 1. **St. Louis (5)**—DeShields 1, Difelice 1, *Gant 1, Lankford 1, Young 1. **San Diego (75)**—Caminiti 15, Vaughn 11, Gwynn 8, Joyner 6, Finley 5, Henderson 5, Flaherty 4, Jones 4, Cianfrocco 3, Shipley 3, Veras 3, Gomez 2, Hernandez 2, Sweeney 2, Hamilton 1, Romero 1. **San Francisco (8)**—Bonds 5, Hamilton 1, Hill 1, Snow 1. **Anaheim (1)**—Edmonds 1. **Oakland (5)**—Canseco 2, McGwire 2, McDonald 1. **Seattle (6)**—Martinez 2, Buhner 1, Cora 1, Davis 1, Sorrento 1. **Texas (1)**—Buford 1.

***Note:** The Cardinals actually hit four home runs at San Diego. Gant hit one homer at Honolulu, Hawaii.

AT SAN FRANCISCO (159):

Atlanta (3)—A. Jones 1, Klesko 1, Lopez 1. **Chicago (7)**—Sosa 2, Clark 1, Grace 1, McRae 1, Orie 1, Sandberg 1. **Cincinnati (5)**—Harris 1, Oliver 1, Sanders 1, Stynes 1, Taubensee 1. **Colorado (7)**—Burks 3, Castilla 2, Galarraga 1, Reed 1. **Florida (5)**—Alou 2, Bonilla 1, Floyd 1, Johnson 1. **Houston (3)**—Bagwell 1, Biggio 1, Gutierrez 1. **Los Angeles (7)**—Gagne 2, Ashley 1, Garcia 1, Karros 1, Mondesi 1, Nixon 1. **Montreal (9)**—Lansing 2, White 2, Guerrero 1, Rodriguez 1, Segui 1, Strange 1, Widger 1. **Philadelphia (3)**—Jefferies 1, Lieberthal 1, Stocker 1. **Pittsburgh (7)**—Young 2, Guillen 1, Johnson 1, Polcovich 1, Sveum 1, Womack 1. **St. Louis (4)**—McGwire 2, Gaetti 1, Lankford 1. **San Diego (2)**—Finley 3, Joyner 2, Gomez 1, Lee 1. **San Francisco (83)**—Bonds 24, Snow 14, Kent 13, Javier 6, Johnson 6, Mueller 5, Lewis 4, Hill 3, Berryhill 2, Aurilia 1, Hamilton 1, Jensen 1, Powell 1, Vizcaino 1, Wilkins 1. **Anaheim (2)**—Encarnacion 1, Henderson 1. **Oakland (4)**—Batista 1, Bellhorn 1, McGwire 1, Spiezio 1. **Seattle (3)**—Buhner 1, Davis 1, Martinez 1.

HISTORY

All-time results

Award winners

Hall of Fame

Team by team

ALL-TIME RESULTS

AMERICAN LEAGUE CHAMPIONS

Year	Team	Manager	Year	Team	Manager
1901	Chicago	Clark Griffith	1951	New York	Casey Stengel
1902	Philadelphia	Connie Mack	1952	New York	Casey Stengel
1903	Boston	Jimmy Collins	1953	New York	Casey Stengel
1904	Boston	Jimmy Collins	1954	Cleveland	Al Lopez
1905	Philadelphia	Connie Mack	1955	New York	Casey Stengel
1906	Chicago	Fielder Jones	1956	New York	Casey Stengel
1907	Detroit	Hugh Jennings	1957	New York	Casey Stengel
1908	Detroit	Hugh Jennings	1958	New York	Casey Stengel
1909	Detroit	Hugh Jennings	1959	Chicago	Al Lopez
1910	Philadelphia	Connie Mack	1960	New York	Casey Stengel
1911	Philadelphia	Connie Mack	1961	New York	Ralph Houk
1912	Boston	Jake Stahl	1962	New York	Ralph Houk
1913	Philadelphia	Connie Mack	1963	New York	Ralph Houk
1914	Philadelphia	Connie Mack	1964	New York	Yogi Berra
1915	Boston	Bill Carrigan	1965	Minnesota	Sam Mele
1916	Boston	Bill Carrigan	1966	Baltimore	Hank Bauer
1917	Chicago	Pants Rowland	1967	Boston	Dick Williams
1918	Boston	Ed Barrow	1968	Detroit	Mayo Smith
1919	Chicago	Kid Gleason	1969	Baltimore (East Division)	Earl Weaver
1920	Cleveland	Tris Speaker	1970	Baltimore (East Division)	Earl Weaver
1921	New York	Miller Huggins	1971	Baltimore (East Division)	Earl Weaver
1922	New York	Miller Huggins	1972	Oakland (West Division)	Dick Williams
1923	New York	Miller Huggins	1973	Oakland (West Division)	Dick Williams
1924	Washington	Bucky Harris	1974	Oakland (West Division)	Al Dark
1925	Washington	Bucky Harris	1975	Boston (East Division)	Darrell Johnson
1926	New York	Miller Huggins	1976	New York (East Division)	Billy Martin
1927	New York	Miller Huggins	1977	New York (East Division)	Billy Martin
1928	New York	Miller Huggins	1978	New York (East Division)	Billy Martin, Bob Lemon
1929	Philadelphia	Connie Mack	1979	Baltimore (East Division)	Earl Weaver
1930	Philadelphia	Connie Mack	1980	Kansas City (West Division)	Jim Frey
1931	Philadelphia	Connie Mack	1981	New York (East Division)	Gene Michael, Bob Lemon
1932	New York	Joe McCarthy	1982	Milwaukee (East Division)	Buck Rodgers, Harvey Kuenn
1933	Washington	Joe Cronin	1983	Baltimore (East Division)	Joe Altobelli
1934	Detroit	Mickey Cochrane	1984	Detroit (East Division)	Sparky Anderson
1935	Detroit	Mickey Cochrane	1985	Kansas City (West Division)	Dick Howser
1936	New York	Joe McCarthy	1986	Boston (East Division)	John McNamara
1937	New York	Joe McCarthy	1987	Minnesota (West Division)	Tom Kelly
1938	New York	Joe McCarthy	1988	Oakland (West Division)	Tony La Russa
1939	New York	Joe McCarthy	1989	Oakland (West Division)	Tony La Russa
1940	Detroit	Del Baker	1990	Oakland (West Division)	Tony La Russa
1941	New York	Joe McCarthy	1991	Minnesota (West Division)	Tom Kelly
1942	New York	Joe McCarthy	1992	Toronto (East Division)	Cito Gaston
1943	New York	Joe McCarthy	1993	Toronto (East Division)	Cito Gaston
1944	St. Louis	Luke Sewell	1994	None†	
1945	Detroit	Steve O'Neill	1995	Cleveland (Central Division)	Mike Hargrove
1946	Boston	Joe Cronin	1996	New York (East Division)	Joe Torre
1947	New York	Bucky Harris	1997	Cleveland (Central Division)	Mike Hargrove
1948	Cleveland*	Lou Boudreau			
1949	New York	Casey Stengel			
1950	New York	Casey Stengel			

*Defeated Boston in one-game playoff. †New York finished the strike-shortened season with the league's best record.

NATIONAL LEAGUE CHAMPIONS

Year	Team	Manager	Year	Team	Manager
1876	Chicago	Albert Spalding	1892	Boston	Frank Selee
1877	Boston	Harry Wright	1893	Boston	Frank Selee
1878	Boston	Harry Wright	1894	Baltimore	Edward Hanlon
1879	Providence	George Wright	1895	Baltimore	Edward Hanlon
1880	Chicago	Adrian Anson	1896	Baltimore	Edward Hanlon
1881	Chicago	Adrian Anson	1897	Boston	Frank Selee
1882	Chicago	Adrian Anson	1898	Boston	Frank Selee
1883	Boston	John Morrill	1899	Brooklyn	Edward Hanlon
1884	Providence	Frank Bancroft	1900	Brooklyn	Edward Hanlon
1885	Chicago	Adrian Anson	1901	Pittsburgh	Fred Clarke
1886	Chicago	Adrian Anson	1902	Pittsburgh	Fred Clarke
1887	Detroit	William Watkins	1903	Pittsburgh	Fred Clarke
1888	New York	James Mutrie	1904	New York	John McGraw
1889	New York	James Mutrie	1905	New York	John McGraw
1890	Brooklyn	William McGunnigle	1906	Chicago	Frank Chance
1891	Boston	Frank Selee	1907	Chicago	Frank Chance

Year	Team	Manager	Year	Team	Manager
1908	Chicago	Frank Chance	1956	Brooklyn	Walter Alston
1909	Pittsburgh	Fred Clarke	1957	Milwaukee	Fred Haney
1910	Chicago	Frank Chance	1958	Milwaukee	Fred Haney
1911	New York	John McGraw	1959	Los Angeles‡	Walter Alston
1912	New York	John McGraw	1960	Pittsburgh	Danny Murtaugh
1913	New York	John McGraw	1961	Cincinnati	Fred Hutchinson
1914	Boston	George Stallings	1962	San Francisco§	Al Dark
1915	Philadelphia	Pat Moran	1963	Los Angeles	Walter Alston
1916	Brooklyn	Wilbert Robinson	1964	St. Louis	Johnny Keane
1917	New York	John McGraw	1965	Los Angeles	Walter Alston
1918	Chicago	Fred Mitchell	1966	Los Angeles	Walter Alston
1919	Cincinnati	Pat Moran	1967	St. Louis	Red Schoendienst
1920	Brooklyn	Wilbert Robinson	1968	St. Louis	Red Schoendienst
1921	New York	John McGraw	1969	New York (East Division)	Gil Hodges
1922	New York	John McGraw	1970	Cincinnati (West Division)	Sparky Anderson
1923	New York	John McGraw	1971	Pittsburgh (East Division)	Danny Murtaugh
1924	New York	John McGraw	1972	Cincinnati (West Division)	Sparky Anderson
1925	Pittsburgh	Bill McKechnie	1973	New York (East Division)	Yogi Berra
1926	St. Louis	Rogers Hornsby	1974	Los Angeles (West Division)	Walter Alston
1927	Pittsburgh	Donie Bush	1975	Cincinnati (West Division)	Sparky Anderson
1928	St. Louis	Bill McKechnie	1976	Cincinnati (West Division)	Sparky Anderson
1929	Chicago	Joe McCarthy	1977	Los Angeles (West Division)	Tommy Lasorda
1930	St. Louis	Gabby Street	1978	Los Angeles (West Division)	Tommy Lasorda
1931	St. Louis	Gabby Street	1979	Pittsburgh (East Division)	Chuck Tanner
1932	Chicago	Charlie Grimm	1980	Philadelphia (East Division)	Dallas Green
1933	New York	Bill Terry	1981	Los Angeles (West Division)	Tommy Lasorda
1934	St. Louis	Frank Frisch	1982	St. Louis (East Division)	Whitey Herzog
1935	Chicago	Charlie Grimm	1983	Philadelphia (East Division)	Pat Corrales, Paul Owens
1936	New York	Bill Terry	1984	San Diego (West Division)	Dick Williams
1937	New York	Bill Terry	1985	St. Loius (East Division)	Whitey Herzog
1938	Chicago	Gabby Hartnett	1986	New York (East Division)	Dave Johnson
1939	Cincinnati	Bill McKechnie	1987	St. Louis (East Division)	Whitey Herzog
1940	Cincinnati	Bill McKechnie	1988	Los Angeles (West Division)	Tommy Lasorda
1941	Brooklyn	Leo Durocher	1989	San Francisco (West Division)	Roger Craig
1942	St. Louis	Billy Southworth	1990	Cincinnati (West Division)	Lou Piniella
1943	St. Louis	Billy Southworth	1991	Atlanta (West Division)	Bobby Cox
1944	St. Louis	Billy Southworth	1992	Atlanta (West Division)	Bobby Cox
1945	Chicago	Charlie Grimm	1993	Philadelphia (East Division)	Jim Fregosi
1946	St. Louis*	Eddie Dyer	1994	None∞	
1947	Brooklyn	Burt Shotton	1995	Atlanta (East Division)	Bobby Cox
1948	Boston	Billy Southworth	1996	Atlanta (East Division)	Bobby Cox
1949	Brooklyn	Burt Shotton	1997	Florida (East Division)	Jim Leyland
1950	Philadelphia	Eddie Sawyer			
1951	New York†	Leo Durocher			
1952	Brooklyn	Charlie Dressen			
1953	Brooklyn	Charlie Dressen			
1954	New York	Leo Durocher			
1955	Brooklyn	Walter Alston			

*Defeated Brooklyn, two games to none, in playoff for pennant.
†Defeated Brooklyn, two games to one, in playoff for pennant.
‡Defeated Milwaukee, two games to none, in playoff for pennant.
§Defeated Los Angeles, two games to one, in playoff for pennant.
∞Montreal finished the strike-shortened season with the league's best record.

WORLD SERIES

Year	Winner	Loser	Games	Year	Winner	Loser	Games
1903	Boston A.L.	Pittsburgh N.L.	5-3	1927	New York A.L.	Pittsburgh, N.L.	4-0
1904	No Series			1928	New York A.L.	St. Louis N.L.	4-0
1905	New York N.L.	Philadelphia A.L.	4-1	1929	Philadelphia A.L.	Chicago N.L.	4-1
1906	Chicago A.L.	Chicago N.L.	4-2	1930	Philadelphia A.L.	St. Louis N.L.	4-2
1907	Chicago N.L.	Detroit A.L.	*4-0	1931	St. Louis N.L.	Philadelphia A.L.	4-3
1908	Chicago N.L.	Detroit A.L.	4-1	1932	New York A.L.	Chicago N.L.	4-0
1909	Pittsburgh N.L.	Detroit A.L.	4-3	1933	New York N.L.	Washington A.L.	4-1
1910	Philadelphia A.L.	Chicago N.L.	4-1	1934	St. Louis N.L.	Detroit A.L.	4-3
1911	Philadelphia A.L.	New York N.L.	4-2	1935	Detroit A.L.	Chicago N.L.	4-2
1912	Boston A.L.	New York N.L.	*4-3	1936	New York A.L.	New York N.L.	4-2
1913	Philadelphia A.L.	New York N.L.	4-1	1937	New York A.L.	New York N.L.	4-1
1914	Boston N.L.	Philadelphia A.L.	4-0	1938	New York A.L.	Chicago N.L.	4-0
1915	Boston A.L.	Philadelphia N.L.	4-1	1939	New York A.L.	Cincinnati N.L.	4-0
1916	Boston A.L.	Brooklyn N.L.	4-1	1940	Cincinnati N.L.	Detroit A.L.	4-3
1917	Chicago A.L.	New York N.L.	4-2	1941	New York A.L.	Brooklyn N.L.	4-1
1918	Boston A.L.	Chicago N.L.	4-2	1942	St. Louis N.L.	New York A.L.	4-1
1919	Cincinnati N.L.	Chicago A.L.	5-3	1943	New York A.L.	St. Louis N.L.	4-1
1920	Cleveland A.L.	Brooklyn N.L.	5-2	1944	St. Louis N.L.	St. Louis A.L.	4-2
1921	New York N.L.	New York A.L.	5-3	1945	Detroit A.L.	Chicago N.L.	4-3
1922	New York N.L.	New York A.L.	*4-0	1946	St. Louis N.L.	Boston A.L.	4-3
1923	New York A.L.	New York N.L.	4-2	1947	New York A.L.	Brooklyn, N.L.	4-3
1924	Washington A.L.	New York N.L.	4-3	1948	Cleveland A.L.	Boston N.L.	4-2
1925	Pittsburgh N.L.	Washington A.L.	4-3	1949	New York A.L.	Brooklyn N.L.	4-1
1926	St. Louis N.L.	New York A.L.	4-3	1950	New York A.L.	Philadelphia N.L.	4-0

Year	Winner	Loser	Games
1951—New York A.L.	New York N.L.	4-2
1952—New York A.L.	Brooklyn N.L.	4-3
1953—New York A.L.	Brooklyn N.L.	4-2
1954—New York N.L.	Cleveland A.L.	4-0
1955—Brooklyn N.L.	New York A.L.	4-3
1956—New York A.L.	Brooklyn N.L.	4-3
1957—Milwaukee N.L.	New York A.L.	4-3
1958—New York A.L.	Milwaukee N.L.	4-3
1959—Los Angeles N.L.	Chicago A.L.	4-2
1960—Pittsburgh N.L.	New York A.L.	4-3
1961—New York A.L.	Cincinnati N.L.	4-1
1962—New York A.L.	San Francisco N.L.	4-3
1963—Los Angeles N.L.	New York A.L.	4-0
1964—St. Louis N.L.	New York A.L.	4-3
1965—Los Angeles N.L.	Minnesota A.L.	4-3
1966—Baltimore A.L.	Los Angeles N.L.	4-0
1967—St. Louis N.L.	Boston A.L.	4-3
1968—Detroit A.L.	St. Louis N.L.	4-3
1969—New York N.L.	Baltimore A.L.	4-1
1970—Baltimore A.L.	Cincinnati N.L.	4-1
1971—Pittsburgh N.L.	Baltimore A.L.	4-3
1972—Oakland A.L.	Cincinnati N.L.	4-3
1973—Oakland A.L.	New York N.L.	4-3
1974—Oakland A.L.	Los Angeles N.L.	4-1

Year	Winner	Loser	Games
1975—Cincinnati N.L.	Boston A.L.	4-3
1976—Cincinnati N.L.	New York A.L.	4-0
1977—New York A.L.	Los Angeles N.L.	4-2
1978—New York A.L.	Los Angeles N.L.	4-2
1979—Pittsburgh N.L.	Baltimore A.L.	4-3
1980—Philadelphia N.L.	Kansas City A.L.	4-2
1981—Los Angeles N.L.	New York A.L.	4-2
1982—St. Louis N.L.	Milwaukee A.L.	4-3
1983—Baltimore A.L.	Philadelphia N.L.	4-1
1984—Detroit A.L.	San Diego N.L.	4-1
1985—Kansas City A.L.	St. Louis N.L.	4-3
1986—New York N.L.	Boston A.L.	4-3
1987—Minnesota A.L.	St. Louis N.L.	4-3
1988—Los Angeles N.L.	Oakland A.L.	4-1
1989—Oakland A.L.	San Francisco N.L.	4-0
1990—Cincinnati N.L.	Oakland A.L.	4-0
1991—Minnesota A.L.	Atlanta N.L.	4-3
1992—Toronto A.L.	Atlanta N.L.	4-2
1993—Toronto A.L.	Philadelphia N.L.	4-2
1994—No Series		
1995—Atlanta N.L.	Cleveland A.L.	4-2
1996—New York A.L.	Atlanta N.L.	4-2
1997—Florida N.L.	Cleveland A.L.	4-3

*Includes tie game.

DIVISION SERIES

AMERICAN LEAGUE

Year	Winner (Division)	Loser (Division)	Games
1981—New York (East)	Milwaukee (East)	3-2
Oakland (West)	Kansas City (West)	3-0
1995—Cleveland (Central)	Boston (East)	3-0
Seattle (West)	New York* (East)	3-2
1996—New York (East)	Texas (West)	3-1
Baltimore (East)*	Cleveland (Central)	3-1
1997—Baltimore (East)	Seattle (West)	3-1
Cleveland (Central)	New York (East)*	3-2

NATIONAL LEAGUE

Year	Winner (Division)	Loser (Division)	Games
1981—Montreal (East)	Philadelphia (East)	3-2
Los Angeles (West)	Houston (West)	3-2
1995—Atlanta (East)	Colorado* (West)	3-1
Cincinnati (Central)	Los Angeles (West)	3-0
1996—Atlanta (East)	Los Angeles (West)*	3-0
St. Louis (Central)	San Diego (West)	3-0
1997—Atlanta (East)	Houston (Central)	3-0
Florida (East)*	San Francisco (West)	3-0

*Wild-card team.

CHAMPIONSHIP SERIES

AMERICAN LEAGUE

Year	Winner (Division)	Loser (Division)	Games
1969—Baltimore (East)	Minnesota (West)	3-0
1970—Baltimore (East)	Minnesota (West)	3-0
1971—Baltimore (East)	Oakland (West)	3-0
1972—Oakland (West)	Detroit (East)	3-2
1973—Oakland (West)	Baltimore (East)	3-2
1974—Oakland (West)	Baltimore (East)	3-1
1975—Boston (East)	Oakland (West)	3-0
1976—New York (East)	Kansas City (West)	3-2
1977—New York (East)	Kansas City (West)	3-2
1978—New York (East)	Kansas City (West)	3-1
1979—Baltimore (East)	California (West)	3-1
1980—Kansas City (West)	New York (East)	3-0
1981—New York (East)	Oakland (West)	3-0
1982—Milwaukee (East)	California (West)	3-2
1983—Baltimore (East)	Chicago (West)	3-1
1984—Detroit (East)	Kansas City (West)	3-0
1985—Kansas City (West)	Toronto (East)	4-3
1986—Boston (East)	California (West)	4-3
1987—Minnesota (West)	Detroit (East)	4-1
1988—Oakland (West)	Boston (East)	4-0
1989—Oakland (West)	Toronto (East)	4-1
1990—Oakland (West)	Boston (East)	4-0
1991—Minnesota (West)	Toronto (East)	4-1
1992—Toronto (East)	Oakland (West)	4-2
1993—Toronto (East)	Chicago (West)	4-2
1994—No series		
1995—Cleveland (Central)	Seattle (West)	4-2
1996—New York (East)	Baltimore (East)*	4-1
1997—Cleveland (Central)	Baltimore (East)	4-2

NATIONAL LEAGUE

Year	Winner (Division)	Loser (Division)	Games
1969—New York (East)	Atlanta (West)	3-0
1970—Cincinnati (West)	Pittsburgh (East)	3-0
1971—Pittsburgh (East)	San Francisco (West)	3-1
1972—Cincinnati (West)	Pittsburgh (East)	3-2
1973—New York (East)	Cincinnati (West)	3-2
1974—Los Angeles (West)	Pittsburgh (East)	3-1
1975—Cincinnati (West)	Pittsburgh (East)	3-0
1976—Cincinnati (West)	Philadelphia (East)	3-0
1977—Los Angeles (West)	Philadelphia (East)	3-1
1978—Los Angeles (West)	Philadelphia (East)	3-1
1979—Pittsburgh (East)	Cincinnati (West)	3-0
1980—Philadelphia (East)	Houston (West)	3-2
1981—Los Angeles (West)	Montreal (East)	3-2
1982—St. Louis (East)	Atlanta (West)	3-0
1983—Philadelphia (East)	Los Angeles (West)	3-1
1984—San Diego (West)	Chicago (East)	3-2
1985—St. Louis (East)	Los Angeles (West)	4-2
1986—New York (East)	Houston (West)	4-2
1987—St. Louis (East)	San Francisco (West)	4-3
1988—Los Angeles (West)	New York (East)	4-3
1989—San Francisco (West)	Chicago (East)	4-1
1990—Cincinnati (West)	Pittsburgh (East)	4-2
1991—Atlanta (West)	Pittsburgh (East)	4-3
1992—Atlanta (West)	Pittsburgh (East)	4-3
1993—Philadelphia (East)	Atlanta (West)	4-2
1994—No series		
1995—Atlanta (East)	Cincinnati (Central)	4-0
1996—Atlanta (East)	St. Louis (Central)	4-3
1997—Florida (East)*	Atlanta (East)	4-2

*Wild-card team.

Date	Site	Score (Winner)	Winning pitcher (Losing pitcher)	Winning manager (Losing manager)	Att.
7-6-33	Comiskey Park	4-2	Lefty Gomez, Yankees	Connie Mack, Athletics	47,595
	Chicago	(A.L.)	(Bill Hallahan, Cardinals)	(John McGraw, Giants)	
7-10-34	Polo Grounds	9-7	Mel Harder, Indians	Joe Cronin, Senators	48,363
	New York	(A.L.)	(Van Mungo, Dodgers)	(Bill Terry, Giants)	
7-8-35	Municipal Stadium	4-1	Lefty Gomez, Yankees	Mickey Cochrane, Tigers	69,831
	Cleveland	(A.L.)	(Bill Walker, Cardinals)	(Frankie Frisch, Cardinals)	
7-7-36	Braves Field	4-3	Dizzy Dean, Cardinals	Charlie Grimm, Cubs	25,556
	Boston	(N.L.)	(Lefty Grove, Red Sox)	(Joe McCarthy, Yankees)	
7-7-37	Griffith Stadium	8-3	Lefty Gomez, Yankees	Joe McCarthy, Yankees	31,391
	Washington	(A.L.)	(Dizzy Dean, Cardinals)	(Bill Terry, Giants)	
7-6-38	Crosley Field	4-1	Johnny Vander Meer, Reds	Bill Terry, Giants	27,067
	Cincinnati	(N.L.)	(Lefty Gomez, Yankees)	(Joe McCarthy, Yankees)	
7-11-39	Yankee Stadium	3-1	Tommy Bridges, Tigers	Joe McCarthy, Yankees	62,892
	New York	(A.L.)	(Bill Lee, Cubs)	(Gabby Hartnett, Cubs)	
7-9-40	Sportsman's Park	4-0	Paul Derringer, Reds	Bill McKechnie, Reds	32,373
	St. Louis	(N.L.)	(Red Ruffing, Yankees)	(Joe Cronin, Red Sox)	
7-8-41	Briggs Stadium	7-5	Ed Smith, White Sox	Del Baker, Tigers	54,674
	Detroit	(A.L.)	(Claude Passeau, Cubs)	(Bill McKechnie, Reds)	
7-6-42	Polo Grounds	3-1	Spud Chandler, Yankees	Joe McCarthy, Yankees	34,178
	New York	(A.L.)	(Mort Cooper, Cardinals)	(Leo Durocher, Dodgers)	
7-13-43	Shibe Park	5-3	Dutch Leonard, Senators	Joe McCarthy, Yankees	31,938
	Philadelphia	(A.L.)	(Mort Cooper, Cardinals)	(Billy Southworth, Cardinals)	
7-11-44	Forbes Field	7-1	Ken Raffensberger, Phillies	Billy Southworth, Cardinals	29,589
	Pittsburgh	(N.L.)	(Tex Hughson, Red Sox)	(Joe McCarthy, Yankees)	
1945	No game played.				
7-9-46	Fenway Park	12-0	Bob Feller, Indians	Steve O'Neill, Tigers	34,906
	Boston	(A.L.)	(Claude Passeau, Cubs)	(Charlie Grimm, Cubs)	
7-8-47	Wrigley Field	2-1	Frank Shea, Yankees	Joe Cronin, Red Sox	41,123
	Chicago	(A.L.)	(Johnny Sain, Braves)	(Eddie Dyer, Cardinals)	
7-13-48	Sportsman's Park	5-2	Vic Raschi, Yankees	Bucky Harris, Yankees	34,009
	St. Louis	(A.L.)	(Johnny Schmitz, Cubs)	(Leo Durocher, Dodgers)	
7-12-49	Ebbets Field	11-7	Virgil Trucks, Tigers	Lou Boudreau, Indians	32,577
	Brooklyn	(A.L.)	(Don Newcombe, Dodgers)	(Billy Southworth, Braves)	
7-11-50	Comiskey Park	4-3*	Ewell Blackwell, Reds	Burt Shotton, Dodgers	46,127
	Chicago	(N.L.)	(Ted Gray, Tigers)	(Casey Stengel, Yankees)	
7-10-51	Briggs Stadium	8-3	Sal Maglie, Giants	Eddie Sawyer, Phillies	52,075
	Detroit	(N.L.)	(Ed Lopat, Yankees)	(Casey Stengel, Yankees)	
7-8-52	Shibe Park	3-2†	Bob Rush, Cubs	Leo Durocher, Giants	32,785
	Philadelphia	(N.L.)	(Bob Lemon, Indians)	(Casey Stengel, Yankees)	
7-14-53	Crosley Field	5-1	Warren Spahn, Braves	Chuck Dressen, Dodgers	30,846
	Cincinnati	(N.L.)	(Allie Reynolds, Yankees)	(Casey Stengel, Yankees)	
7-13-54	Municipal Stadium	11-9	Dean Stone, Senators	Casey Stengel, Yankees	68,751
	Cleveland	(A.L.)	(Gene Conley, Braves)	(Walter Alston, Dodgers)	
7-12-55	Milwaukee Co. Stadium	6-5‡	Gene Conley, Braves	Leo Durocher, Giants	45,643
	Milwaukee	(N.L.)	(Frank Sullivan, Red Sox)	(Al Lopez, Indians)	
7-10-56	Griffith Stadium	7-3	Bob Friend, Pirates	Walter Alston, Dodgers	28,843
	Washington	(N.L.)	(Billy Pierce, White Sox)	(Casey Stengel, Yankees)	
7-9-57	Busch Stadium	6-5	Jim Bunning, Tigers	Casey Stengel, Yankees	30,693
	St. Louis	(A.L.)	(Curt Simmons, Phillies)	(Walter Alston, Dodgers)	
7-8-58	Memorial Stadium	4-3	Early Wynn, White Sox	Casey Stengel, Yankees	48,829
	Baltimore	(A.L.)	(Bob Friend, Pirates)	(Fred Haney, Braves)	
7-7-59	Forbes Field	5-4	Johnny Antonelli, Giants	Fred Haney, Braves	35,277
	Pittsburgh	(N.L.)	(Whitey Ford, Yankees)	(Casey Stengel, Yankees)	
8-3-59	Memorial Coliseum	5-3	Jerry Walker, Orioles	Casey Stengel, Yankees	55,105
	Los Angeles	(A.L.)	(Don Drysdale, Dodgers)	(Fred Haney, Braves)	
7-11-60	Municipal Stadium	5-3	Bob Friend, Pirates	Walter Alston, Dodgers	30,619
	Kansas City	(N.L.)	(Bill Monbouquette, Red Sox)	(Al Lopez, White Sox)	
7-13-60	Yankee Stadium	6-0	Vernon Law, Pirates	Walter Alston, Dodgers	38,362
	New York	(N.L.)	(Whitey Ford, Yankees)	(Al Lopez, White Sox)	
7-11-61	Candlestick Park	5-4§	Stu Miller, Giants	Danny Murtaugh, Pirates	44,115
	San Francisco	(N.L.)	(Hoyt Wilhelm, Orioles)	(Paul Richards, Orioles)	
7-31-61	Fenway Park	1-1		Paul Richards, Orioles (A.L.)	31,851
	Boston	(tie)		Danny Murtaugh, Pirates (N.L.)	
7-10-62	District of Col. Stad.	3-1	Juan Marichal, Giants	Fred Hutchinson, Reds	45,480
	Washington	(N.L.)	(Camilo Pascual, Twins)	(Ralph Houk, Yankees)	
7-30-62	Wrigley Field	9-4	Ray Herbert, White Sox	Ralph Houk, Yankees	38,359
	Chicago	(A.L.)	(Art Mahaffey, Phillies)	(Fred Hutchinson, Reds)	
7-9-63	Municipal Stadium	5-3	Larry Jackson, Cubs	Alvin Dark, Giants	44,160
	Cleveland	(N.L.)	(Jim Bunning, Tigers)	(Ralph Houk, Yankees)	
7-7-64	Shea Stadium	7-4	Juan Marichal, Giants	Walter Alston, Dodgers	50,850
	New York	(N.L.)	(Dick Radatz, Red Sox)	(Al Lopez, White Sox)	

HISTORY All-time results

Date	Site	Score (Winner)	Winning pitcher (Losing pitcher)	Winning manager (Losing manager)	Att.
7-13-65	Metropolitan Stadium Bloomington, Minn.	6-5 (N.L.)	Sandy Koufax, Dodgers (Sam McDowell, Indians)	Gene Mauch, Phillies (Al Lopez, White Sox)	46,706
7-12-66	Busch Stadium St. Louis	2-1§ (N.L.)	Gaylord Perry, Giants (Pete Richert, Senators)	Walter Alston, Dodgers (Sam Mele, Twins)	49,936
7-11-67	Anaheim Stadium Anaheim, Calif.	2-1∞ (N.L.)	Don Drysdale, Dodgers (Jim Hunter, Athletics)	Walter Alston, Dodgers (Hank Bauer, Orioles)	46,309
7-9-68	Astrodome Houston	1-0 (N.L.)	Don Drysdale, Dodgers (Luis Tiant, Indians)	Red Schoendienst, Cardinals (Dick Williams, Red Sox)	48,321
7-23-69	R.F.K. Stadium Washington	9-3 (N.L.)	Steve Carlton, Cardinals (Mel Stottlemyre, Yankees)	Red Schoendienst, Cardinals (Mayo Smith, Tigers)	45,259
7-14-70	Riverfront Stadium Cincinnati	5-4‡ (N.L.)	Claude Osteen, Dodgers (Clyde Wright, Angels)	Gil Hodges, Mets (Earl Weaver, Orioles)	51,838
7-13-71	Tiger Stadium Detroit	6-4 (A.L.)	Vida Blue, Athletics (Dock Ellis, Pirates)	Earl Weaver, Orioles (Sparky Anderson, Reds)	53,559
7-25-72	Atlanta Stadium Atlanta	4-3§ (N.L.)	Tug McGraw, Mets (Dave McNally, Orioles)	Danny Murtaugh, Pirates (Earl Weaver, Orioles)	53,107
7-24-73	Royals Stadium Kansas City	7-1 (N.L.)	Rick Wise, Cardinals (Bert Blyleven, Twins)	Sparky Anderson, Reds (Dick Williams, Athletics)	40,849
7-23-74	Three Rivers Stadium Pittsburgh	7-2 (N.L.)	Ken Brett, Pirates (Luis Tiant, Red Sox)	Yogi Berra, Mets (Dick Williams, Athletics)	50,706
7-15-75	Milwaukee Co. Stadium Milwaukee	6-3 (N.L.)	Jon Matlack, Mets (Jim Hunter, Yankees)	Walter Alston, Dodgers (Alvin Dark, Athletics)	51,480
7-13-76	Veterans Stadium Philadelphia	7-1 (N.L)	Randy Jones, Padres (Mark Fidrych, Tigers)	Sparky Anderson, Reds (Darrell Johnson, Red Sox)	63,974
7-19-77	Yankee Stadium New York	7-5 (N.L.)	Don Sutton, Dodgers (Jim Palmer, Orioles)	Sparky Anderson, Reds (Billy Martin, Yankees)	56,683
7-11-78	San Diego Stadium San Diego	7-3 (N.L.)	Bruce Sutter, Cubs (Rich Gossage, Yankees)	Tommy Lasorda, Dodgers (Billy Martin, Yankees)	51,549
7-17-79	Kingdome Seattle	7-6 (N.L.)	Bruce Sutter, Cubs (Jim Kern, Rangers)	Tommy Lasorda, Dodgers (Bob Lemon, Yankees)	58,905
7-8-80	Dodger Stadium Los Angeles	4-2 (N.L.)	Jerry Reuss, Dodgers (Tommy John, Yankees)	Chuck Tanner, Pirates (Earl Weaver, Orioles)	56,088
8-9-81	Municipal Stadium Cleveland	5-4 (N.L.)	Vida Blue, Giants (Rollie Fingers, Brewers)	Dallas Green, Phillies (Jim Frey, Royals)	72,086
7-13-82	Olympic Stadium Montreal	4-1 (N.L.)	Steve Rogers, Expos (Dennis Eckersley, Red Sox)	Tommy Lasorda, Dodgers (Billy Martin, Athletics)	59,057
7-6-83	Comiskey Park Chicago	13-3 (A.L.)	Dave Stieb, Blue Jays (Mario Soto, Reds)	Harvey Kuenn, Brewers (Whitey Herzog, Cardinals)	43,801
7-10-84	Candlestick Park San Francisco	3-1 (N.L.)	Charlie Lea, Expos (Dave Stieb, Blue Jays)	Paul Owens, Phillies (Joe Altobelli, Orioles)	57,756
7-16-85	Metrodome Minneapolis	6-1 (N.L.)	LaMarr Hoyt, Padres (Jack Morris, Tigers)	Dick Williams, Padres (Sparky Anderson, Tigers)	54,960
7-15-86	Astrodome Houston	3-2 (A.L.)	Roger Clemens, Red Sox (Dwight Gooden, Mets)	Dick Howser, Royals (Whitey Herzog, Cardinals)	45,774
7-14-87	Oak.-Alameda Co. Col. Oakland	2-0▲ (N.L.)	Lee Smith, Cubs (Jay Howell, Athletics)	Dave Johnson, Mets (John McNamara, Red Sox)	49,671
7-12-88	Riverfront Stadium Cincinnati	2-1 (A.L.)	Frank Viola, Twins (Dwight Gooden, Mets)	Tom Kelly, Twins (Whitey Herzog, Cardinals)	55,837
7-11-89	Anaheim Stadium Anaheim, Calif.	5-3 (A.L.)	Nolan Ryan, Rangers (John Smoltz, Braves)	Tony La Russa, Athletics (Tommy Lasorda, Dodgers)	64,036
7-10-90	Wrigley Field Chicago	2-0 (A.L.)	Bret Saberhagen, Royals (Jeff Brantley, Giants)	Tony La Russa, Athletics (Roger Craig, Giants)	39,071
7-9-91	SkyDome Toronto	4-2 (A.L.)	Jimmy Key, Blue Jays (Dennis Martinez, Expos)	Tony La Russa, Athletics (Lou Piniella, Reds)	52,383
7-14-92	Jack Murphy Stadium San Diego	13-6 (A.L.)	Kevin Brown, Rangers (Tom Glavine, Braves)	Tom Kelly, Twins (Bobby Cox, Braves)	59,372
7-13-93	Oriole Park at Camden Yards, Baltimore	9-3 (A.L.)	Jack McDowell, White Sox (John Burkett, Giants)	Cito Gaston, Blue Jays (Bobby Cox, Braves)	48,147
7-12-94	Three Rivers Stadium Pittsburgh	8-7§ (N.L.)	Doug Jones, Phillies (Jason Bere, White Sox)	Jim Fregosi, Phillies (Cito Gaston, Blue Jays)	59,568
7-11-95	Ballpark in Arlington Arlington, Texas	3-2 (N.L.)	Heathcliff Slocumb, Phillies (Steve Ontiveros, A's)	Felipe Alou, Expos (Buck Showalter, Yankees)	50,920
7-9-96	Veterans Stadium Philadelphia	6-0 (N.L.)	John Smoltz, Braves (Charles Nagy, Indians)	Bobby Cox, Braves (Mike Hargrove, Indians)	62,670
7-8-97	Jacobs Field Cleveland	3-1 (A.L.)	Jose Rosado, Royals (Shawn Estes, Giants)	Joe Torre, Yankees (Bobby Cox, Braves)	44,916

*14 innings. †5 innings (rain). ‡12 innings. §10 innings. ∞15 innings. ▲13 innings.

AWARD WINNERS

THE SPORTING NEWS
MOST VALUABLE PLAYER

AMERICAN LEAGUE

Year	Player	Team	Pos.	Points
1929—Al Simmons		Philadelphia	OF	40
1930—Joe Cronin		Washington	SS	52
1931—Lou Gehrig		New York	1B	40
1932—Jimmie Foxx		Philadelphia	1B	46
1933—Jimmie Foxx		Philadelphia	1B	49
1934—Lou Gehrig		New York	1B	51
1935—Hank Greenberg		Detroit	1B	64
1936—Lou Gehrig		New York	1B	55
1937—Charley Gehringer		Detroit	2B	78
1938—Jimmie Foxx		Boston	1B	304
1939—Joe DiMaggio		New York	OF	280
1940—Hank Greenberg		Detroit	OF	292
1941—Joe DiMaggio		New York	OF	291
1942—Joe Gordon		New York	2B	270
1943—Spud Chandler		New York	P	246
1944—Bobby Doerr		Boston	2B	
1945—Eddie Mayo		Detroit	2B	

NATIONAL LEAGUE

Year	Player	Team	Pos.	Points
1929—No selection				
1930—Bill Terry		New York	1B	47
1931—Chuck Klein		Philadelphia	OF	40
1932—Chuck Klein		Philadelphia	OF	46
1933—Carl Hubbell		New York	P	64
1934—Dizzy Dean		St. Louis	P	57
1935—Arky Vaughan		Pittsburgh	SS	42
1936—Carl Hubbell		New York	P	61
1937—Joe Medwick		St. Louis	OF	70
1938—Ernie Lombardi		Cincinnati	C	229
1939—Bucky Walters		Cincinnati	P	303
1940—Frank McCormick		Cincinnati	1B	274
1941—Dolf Camilli		Brooklyn	1B	300
1942—Mort Cooper		St. Louis	P	263
1943—Stan Musial		St. Louis	OF	267
1944—Marty Marion		St. Louis	SS	
1945—Tommy Holmes		Boston	OF	

PLAYER AND PITCHER OF THE YEAR

AMERICAN LEAGUE

Year	Player	Team	Pos.
1944—Bobby Doerr		Boston	2B
Hal Newhouser		Detroit	P
1945—Eddie Mayo		Detroit	2B
Hal Newhouser		Detroit	P
1946—No selections			
1947—No selections			
1948—Lou Boudreau		Cleveland	SS
Bob Lemon		Cleveland	P
1949—Ted Williams		Boston	OF
Ellis Kinder		Boston	P
1950—Phil Rizzuto		New York	SS
Bob Lemon		Cleveland	P
1951—Ferris Fain		Philadelphia	1B
Bob Feller		Cleveland	P
1952—Luke Easter		Cleveland	1B
Bobby Shantz		Philadelphia	P
1953—Al Rosen		Cleveland	3B
Bob Porterfield		Washington	P
1954—Bobby Avila		Cleveland	2B
Bob Lemon		Cleveland	P
1955—Al Kaline		Detroit	OF
Whitey Ford		New York	P
1956—Mickey Mantle		New York	OF
Billy Pierce		Chicago	P
1957—Ted Williams		Boston	OF
Billy Pierce		Chicago	P
1958—Jackie Jensen		Boston	OF
Bob Turley		New York	P
1959—Nellie Fox		Chicago	2B
Early Wynn		Chicago	P
1960—Roger Maris		New York	OF
Chuck Estrada		Baltimore	P
1961—Roger Maris		New York	OF
Whitey Ford		New York	P
1962—Mickey Mantle		New York	OF
Dick Donovan		Cleveland	P
1963—Al Kaline		Detroit	OF
Whitey Ford		New York	P
1964—Brooks Robinson		Baltimore	3B
Dean Chance		Los Angeles	P
1965—Tony Oliva		Minnesota	OF
Jim Grant		Minnesota	P
1966—Frank Robinson		Baltimore	OF
Jim Kaat		Minnesota	P

NATIONAL LEAGUE

Year	Player	Team	Pos.
1944—Marty Marion		St. Louis	SS
Bill Voiselle		New York	P
1945—Tommy Holmes		Boston	OF
Hank Borowy		Chicago	P
1946—No selections			
1947—No selections			
1948—Stan Musial		St. Louis	OF-1B
Johnny Sain		Boston	P
1949—Enos Slaughter		St. Louis	OF
Howard Pollet		St. Louis	P
1950—Ralph Kiner		Pittsburgh	OF
Jim Konstanty		Philadelphia	P
1951—Stan Musial		St. Louis	OF
Preacher Roe		Brooklyn	P
1952—Hank Sauer		Chicago	OF
Robin Roberts		Philadelphia	P
1953—Roy Campanella		Brooklyn	C
Warren Spahn		Milwaukee	P
1954—Willie Mays		New York	OF
Johnny Antonelli		New York	P
1955—Duke Snider		Brooklyn	OF
Robin Roberts		Philadelphia	P
1956—Hank Aaron		Milwaukee	OF
Don Newcombe		Brooklyn	P
1957—Stan Musial		St. Louis	1B
Warren Spahn		Milwaukee	P
1958—Ernie Banks		Chicago	SS
Warren Spahn		Milwaukee	P
1959—Ernie Banks		Chicago	SS
Sam Jones		San Francisco	P
1960—Dick Groat		Pittsburgh	SS
Vern Law		Pittsburgh	P
1961—Frank Robinson		Cincinnati	OF
Warren Spahn		Milwaukee	P
1962—Maury Wills		Los Angeles	SS
Don Drysdale		Los Angeles	P
1963—Hank Aaron		Milwaukee	OF
Sandy Koufax		Los Angeles	P
1964—Ken Boyer		St. Louis	3B
Sandy Koufax		Los Angeles	P
1965—Willie Mays		San Francisco	OF
Sandy Koufax		Los Angeles	P
1966—Roberto Clemente		Pittsburgh	OF
Sandy Koufax		Los Angeles	P

HISTORY *Award winners*

Year	Player	Team	Pos.
1967—	Carl Yastrzemski	Boston	OF
	Jim Lonborg	Boston	P
1968—	Ken Harrelson	Boston	OF
	Denny McLain	Detroit	P
1969—	Harmon Killebrew	Minnesota	1B-3B
	Denny McLain	Detroit	P
1970—	Harmon Killebrew	Minnesota	3B
	Sam McDowell	Cleveland	P
1971—	Tony Oliva	Minnesota	OF
	Vida Blue	Oakland	P
1972—	Dick Allen	Chicago	1B
	Wilbur Wood	Chicago	P
1973—	Reggie Jackson	Oakland	OF
	Jim Palmer	Baltimore	P
1974—	Jeff Burroughs	Texas	OF
	Jim Hunter	Oakland	P
1975—	Fred Lynn	Boston	OF
	Jim Palmer	Baltimore	P
1976—	Thurman Munson	New York	C
	Jim Palmer	Baltimore	P
1977—	Rod Carew	Minnesota	1B
	Nolan Ryan	California	P
1978—	Jim Rice	Boston	OF
	Ron Guidry	New York	P
1979—	Don Baylor	California	OF
	Mike Flanagan	Baltimore	P
1980—	George Brett	Kansas City	3B
	Steve Stone	Baltimore	P
1981—	Tony Armas	Oakland	OF
	Jack Morris	Detroit	P
1982—	Robin Yount	Milwaukee	SS
	Dave Stieb	Toronto	P
1983—	Cal Ripken Jr.	Baltimore	SS
	LaMarr Hoyt	Chicago	P
1984—	Don Mattingly	New York	1B
	Willie Hernandez	Detroit	P
1985—	Don Mattingly	New York	1B
	Bret Saberhagen	Kansas City	P
1986—	Don Mattingly	New York	1B
	Roger Clemens	Boston	P
1987—	George Bell	Toronto	OF
	Jimmy Key	Toronto	P
1988—	Jose Canseco	Oakland	OF
	Frank Viola	Minnesota	P
1989—	Ruben Sierra	Texas	OF
	Bret Saberhagen	Kansas City	P
1990—	Cecil Fielder	Detroit	1B
	Bob Welch	Oakland	P
1991—	Cal Ripken Jr.	Baltimore	SS
	Roger Clemens	Boston	P

Year	Player	Team	Pos.
1967—	Orlando Cepeda	St. Louis	1B
	Mike McCormick	San Francisco	P
1968—	Pete Rose	Cincinnati	OF
	Bob Gibson	St. Louis	P
1969—	Willie McCovey	San Francisco	1B
	Tom Seaver	New York	P
1970—	Johnny Bench	Cincinnati	C
	Bob Gibson	St. Louis	P
1971—	Joe Torre	St. Louis	3B
	Ferguson Jenkins	Chicago	P
1972—	Billy Williams	Chicago	OF
	Steve Carlton	Philadelphia	P
1973—	Bobby Bonds	San Francisco	OF
	Ron Bryant	San Francisco	P
1974—	Lou Brock	St. Louis	OF
	Mike Marshall	Los Angeles	P
1975—	Joe Morgan	Cincinnati	2B
	Tom Seaver	New York	P
1976—	George Foster	Cincinnati	OF
	Randy Jones	San Diego	P
1977—	George Foster	Cincinnati	OF
	Steve Carlton	Philadelphia	P
1978—	Dave Parker	Pittsburgh	OF
	Vida Blue	San Francisco	P
1979—	Keith Hernandez	St. Louis	1B
	Joe Niekro	Houston	P
1980—	Mike Schmidt	Philadelphia	3B
	Steve Carlton	Philadelphia	P
1981—	Andre Dawson	Montreal	OF
	Fernando Valenzuela	Los Angeles	P
1982—	Dale Murphy	Atlanta	OF
	Steve Carlton	Philadelphia	P
1983—	Dale Murphy	Atlanta	OF
	John Denny	Philadelphia	P
1984—	Ryne Sandberg	Chicago	2B
	Rick Sutcliffe	Chicago	P
1985—	Willie McGee	St. Louis	OF
	Dwight Gooden	New York	P
1986—	Mike Schmidt	Philadelphia	3B
	Mike Scott	Houston	P
1987—	Andre Dawson	Chicago	OF
	Rick Sutcliffe	Chicago	P
1988—	Andy Van Slyke	Pittsburgh	OF
	Orel Hershiser	Los Angeles	P
1989—	Kevin Mitchell	San Francisco	OF
	Mark Davis	San Diego	P
1990—	Barry Bonds	Pittsburgh	OF
	Doug Drabek	Pittsburgh	P
1991—	Barry Bonds	Pittsburgh	OF
	Tom Glavine	Atlanta	P

PITCHER OF THE YEAR

AMERICAN LEAGUE

Year	Pitcher	Team
1992—	Dennis Eckersley	Oakland
1993—	Jack McDowell	Chicago
1994—	Jimmy Key	New York
1995—	Randy Johnson	Seattle
1996—	Pat Hentgen	Toronto
1997—	Roger Clemens	Toronto

NATIONAL LEAGUE

Year	Pitcher	Team
1992—	Greg Maddux	Chicago
1993—	Greg Maddux	Atlanta
1994—	Greg Maddux	Atlanta
1995—	Greg Maddux	Atlanta
1996—	John Smoltz	Atlanta
1997—	Pedro Martinez	Montreal

ROOKIE OF THE YEAR

1946—Combined selection—Del Ennis, Philadelphia N.L., OF
1947—Combined selection—Jackie Robinson, Brooklyn N.L., 1B
1948—Combined selection—Richie Ashburn, Philadelphia N.L., OF

AMERICAN LEAGUE

Year	Player	Team	Pos.
1949—	Roy Sievers	St. Louis	OF
1950—	Whitey Ford	New York	P
1951—	Minnie Minoso	Chicago	OF
1952—	Clint Courtney	St. Louis	C
1953—	Harvey Kuenn	Detroit	SS

NATIONAL LEAGUE

Year	Player	Team	Pos.
1949—	Don Newcombe	Brooklyn	P
1950—	Combined A.L.-N.L. selection		
1951—	Willie Mays	New York	OF
1952—	Joe Black	Brooklyn	P
1953—	Jim Gilliam	Brooklyn	2B

Year	Player	Team	Pos.	Year	Player	Team	Pos.
1954—Bob Grim	New York	P		1954—Wally Moon	St. Louis	OF	
1955—Herb Score	Cleveland	P		1955—Bill Virdon	St. Louis	OF	
1956—Luis Aparicio	Chicago	SS		1956—Frank Robinson	Cincinnati	OF	
1957—Tony Kubek	New York	IF-OF		1957—Ed Bouchee	Philadelphia	1B	
(No pitcher named)				Jack Sanford	Philadelphia	P	
1958—Albie Pearson	Washington	OF		1958—Orlando Cepeda	San Francisco	1B	
Ryne Duren	New York	P		Carlton Willey	Milwaukee	P	
1959—Bob Allison	Washington	OF		1959—Willie McCovey	San Francisco	1B	
1960—Ron Hansen	Baltimore	SS		1960—Frank Howard	Los Angeles	OF	
1961—Dick Howser	Kansas City	SS		1961—Billy Williams	Chicago	OF	
Don Schwall	Boston	P		Ken Hunt	Cincinnati	P	
1962—Tom Tresh	New York	OF-SS		1962—Ken Hubbs	Chicago	2B	
1963—Pete Ward	Chicago	3B		1963—Pete Rose	Cincinnati	2B	
Gary Peters	Chicago	P		Ray Culp	Philadelphia	P	
1964—Tony Oliva	Minnesota	OF		1964—Dick Allen	Philadelphia	3B	
Wally Bunker	Baltimore	P		Billy McCool	Cincinnati	P	
1965—Curt Blefary	Baltimore	OF		1965—Joe Morgan	Houston	2B	
Marcelino Lopez	California	P		Frank Linzy	San Francisco	P	
1966—Tommie Agee	Chicago	OF		1966—Tommy Helms	Cincinnati	3B	
Jim Nash	Kansas City	P		Don Sutton	Los Angeles	P	
1967—Rod Carew	Minnesota	2B		1967—Lee May	Cincinnati	1B	
Tom Phoebus	Baltimore	P		Dick Hughes	St. Louis	P	
1968—Del Unser	Washington	OF		1968—Johnny Bench	Cincinnati	C	
Stan Bahnsen	New York	P		Jerry Koosman	New York	P	
1969—Carlos May	Chicago	OF		1969—Coco Laboy	Montreal	3B	
Mike Nagy	Boston	P		Tom Griffin	Houston	P	
1970—Roy Foster	Cleveland	OF		1970—Bernie Carbo	Cincinnati	OF	
Bert Blyleven	Minnesota	P		Carl Morton	Montreal	P	
1971—Chris Chambliss	Cleveland	1B		1971—Earl Williams	Atlanta	C	
Bill Parsons	Milwaukee	P		Reggie Cleveland	St. Louis	P	
1972—Carlton Fisk	Boston	C		1972—Dave Rader	San Francisco	C	
Dick Tidrow	Cleveland	P		Jon Matlack	New York	P	
1973—Al Bumbry	Baltimore	OF		1973—Gary Matthews	San Francisco	OF	
Steve Busby	Kansas City	P		Steve Rogers	Montreal	P	
1974—Mike Hargrove	Texas	1B		1974—Greg Gross	Houston	OF	
Frank Tanana	California	P		John D'Acquisto	San Francisco	P	
1975—Fred Lynn	Boston	OF		1975—Gary Carter	Montreal	OF-C	
Dennis Eckersley	Cleveland	P		John Montefusco	San Francisco	P	
1976—Butch Wynegar	Minnesota	C		1976—Larry Herndon	San Francisco	OF	
Mark Fidrych	Detroit	P		Butch Metzger	San Diego	P	
1977—Mitchell Page	Oakland	OF		1977—Andre Dawson	Montreal	OF	
Dave Rozema	Detroit	P		Bob Owchinko	San Diego	P	
1978—Paul Molitor	Milwaukee	2B		1978—Bob Horner	Atlanta	3B	
Rich Gale	Kansas City	P		Don Robinson	Pittsburgh	P	
1979—Pat Putnam	Texas 1B			1979—Jeff Leonard	Houston	OF	
Mark Clear	California	P		Rick Sutcliffe	Los Angeles	P	
1980—Joe Charboneau	Cleveland	OF		1980—Lonnie Smith	Philadelphia	OF	
Britt Burns	Chicago	P		Bill Gullickson	Montreal	P	
1981—Rich Gedman	Boston	C		1981—Tim Raines	Montreal	OF	
Dave Righetti	New York	P		Fernando Valenzuela	Los Angeles	P	
1982—Cal Ripken Jr.	Baltimore	SS-3B		1982—Johnny Ray	Pittsburgh	2B	
Ed Vande Berg	Seattle	P		Steve Bedrosian	Atlanta	P	
1983—Ron Kittle	Chicago	OF		1983—Darryl Strawberry	New York	OF	
Mike Boddicker	Baltimore	P		Craig McMurtry	Atlanta	P	
1984—Alvin Davis	Seattle	1B		1984—Juan Samuel	Philadelphia	2B	
Mark Langston	Seattle	P		Dwight Gooden	New York	P	
1985 Ozzie Gullen	Chicago	SS		1985—Vince Coleman	St. Louis	OF	
Teddy Higuera	Milwaukee	P		Tom Browning	Cincinnati	P	
1986—Jose Canseco	Oakland	OF		1986—Robby Thompson	San Francisco	2B	
Mark Eichhorn	Toronto	P		Todd Worrell	St. Louis	P	
1987—Mark McGwire	Oakland	1B		1987—Benito Santiago	San Diego	C	
Mike Henneman	Detroit	P		Mike Dunne	Pittsburgh	P	
1988—Walt Weiss	Oakland	SS		1988—Mark Grace	Chicago	1B	
Bryan Harvey	California	P		Tim Belcher	Los Angeles	P	
1989—Craig Worthington	Baltimore	3B		1989—Jerome Walton	Chicago	OF	
Tom Gordon	Kansas City	P		Andy Benes	San Diego	P	
1990—Sandy Alomar Jr.	Cleveland	C		1990—David Justice	Atlanta	OF	
Kevin Appier	Kansas City	P		Mike Harkey	Chicago	P	
1991—Chuck Knoblauch	Minnesota	2B		1991—Jeff Bagwell	Houston	1B	
Juan Guzman	Toronto	P		Al Osuna	Houston	P	
1992—Pat Listach	Milwaukee	SS		1992—Eric Karros	Los Angeles	1B	
Cal Eldred	Milwaukee	P		Tim Wakefield	Pittsburgh	P	
1993—Tim Salmon	California	OF		1993—Mike Piazza	Los Angeles	C	
Aaron Sele	Boston	P		Kirk Rueter	Montreal	P	
1994—Bob Hamelin	Kansas City	DH		1994—Raul Mondesi	Los Angeles	OF	
Brian Anderson	California	P		Steve Trachsel	Chicago	P	

Year	Player	Team	Pos.
1995—Garret Anderson	California	OF
	Julian Tavarez	Cleveland	P
1996—Derek Jeter	New York	SS
	James Baldwin	Chicago	P
1997—Nomar Garciaparra	Boston	SS
	Jason Dickson	Anaheim	P

Year	Player	Team	Pos.
1995—Chipper Jones	Atlanta	3B
	Hideo Nomo	Los Angeles	P
1996—Jason Kendall	Pittsburgh	C
	Alan Benes	St. Louis	P
1997—Scott Rolen	Philadelphia	3B
	Matt Morris	St. Louis	P

FIREMAN OF THE YEAR

AMERICAN LEAGUE

Year	Pitcher	Team
1960—Mike Fornieles	Boston
1961—Luis Arroyo	New York
1962—Dick Radatz	Boston
1963—Stu Miller	Baltimore
1964—Dick Radatz	Boston
1965—Eddie Fisher	Chicago
1966—Jack Aker	Kansas City
1967—Minnie Rojas	California
1968—Wilbur Wood	Chicago
1969—Ron Perranoski	Minnesota
1970—Ron Perranoski	Minnesota
1971—Ken Sanders	Milwaukee
1972—Sparky Lyle	New York
1973—John Hiller	Detroit
1974—Terry Forster	Chicago
1975—Rich Gossage	Chicago
1976—Bill Campbell	Minnesota
1977—Bill Campbell	Boston
1978—Rich Gossage	New York
1979—Mike Marshall	Minnesota
Jim Kern	Texas
1980—Dan Quisenberry	Kansas City
1981—Rollie Fingers	Milwaukee
1982—Dan Quisenberry	Kansas City
1983—Dan Quisenberry	Kansas City
1984—Dan Quisenberry	Kansas City
1985—Dan Quisenberry	Kansas City
1986—Dave Righetti	New York
1987—Dave Righetti	New York
Jeff Reardon	Minnesota
1988—Dennis Eckersley	Oakland
1989—Jeff Russell	Texas
1990—Bobby Thigpen	Chicago
1991—Dennis Eckersley	Oakland
Bryan Harvey	California
1992—Dennis Eckersley	Oakland
1993—Jeff Montgomery	Kansas City
1994—Lee Smith	Baltimore
1995—Jose Mesa	Cleveland
1996—John Wetteland	New York
1997—Mariano Rivera	New York

NATIONAL LEAGUE

Year	Pitcher	Team
1960— Lindy McDaniel	St. Louis
1961— Stu Miller	San Francisco
1962— Roy Face	Pittsburgh
1963— Lindy McDaniel	Chicago
1964— Al McBean	Pittsburgh
1965— Ted Abernathy	Chicago
1966— Phil Regan	Los Angeles
1967— Ted Abernathy	Cincinnati
1968— Phil Regan	L.A.-Chicago
1969— Wayne Granger	Cincinnati
1970— Wayne Granger	Cincinnati
1971— Dave Giusti	Pittsburgh
1972— Clay Carroll	Cincinnati
1973— Mike Marshall	Montreal
1974— Mike Marshall	Los Angeles
1975— Al Hrabosky	St. Louis
1976— Rawly Eastwick	Cincinnati
1977— Rollie Fingers	San Diego
1978— Rollie Fingers	San Diego
1979— Bruce Sutter	Chicago
1980— Rollie Fingers	San Diego
Tom Hume	Cincinnati
1981— Bruce Sutter	St. Louis
1982— Bruce Sutter	St. Louis
1983— Al Holland	Philadelphia
Lee Smith	Chicago
1984— Bruce Sutter	St. Louis
1985— Jeff Reardon	Montreal
1986— Todd Worrell	St. Louis
1987— Steve Bedrosian	Philadelphia
1988— John Franco	Cincinnati
1989— Mark Davis	San Diego
1990— John Franco	New York
1991— Lee Smith	St. Louis
1992— Doug Jones	Houston
Lee Smith	St. Louis
1993— Randy Myers	Chicago
1994— John Franco	New York
1995— Randy Myers	Chicago
1996— Trevor Hoffman	San Diego
1997— Jeff Shaw	Cincinnati

MAJOR LEAGUE PLAYER OF THE YEAR

Year	Player	Team	Year	Player	Team	Year	Player	Team
1936—Carl Hubbell	New York N.L.	1952—Robin Roberts	Philadelphia N.L.	1967—Carl Yastrzemski	Boston A.L.
1937—Johnny Allen	Cleveland A.L.	1953—Al Rosen	Cleveland A.L.	1968—Denny McLain	Detroit A.L.
1938—Johnny Vander Meer	Cincinnati N.L.	1954—Willie Mays	New York N.L.	1969—Willie McCovey	San Francisco N.L.
1939—Joe DiMaggio	New York A.L.	1955—Duke Snider	Brooklyn N.L.	1970—Johnny Bench	Cincinnati N.L.
1940—Bob Feller	Cleveland A.L.	1956—Mickey Mantle	New York A.L.	1971—Joe Torre	St. Louis N.L.
1941—Ted Williams	Boston A.L.	1957—Ted Williams	Boston A.L.	1972—Billy Williams	Chicago N.L.
1942—Ted Williams	Boston A.L.	1958—Bob Turley	New York A.L.	1973—Reggie Jackson	Oakland A.L.
1943—Spud Chandler	New York A.L.	1959—Early Wynn	Chicago A.L.	1974—Lou Brock	St. Louis N.L.
1944—Marty Marion	St. Louis N.L.	1960—Bill Mazeroski	Pittsburgh N.L.	1975—Joe Morgan	Cincinnati N.L.
1945—Hal Newhouser	Detroit A.L.	1961—Roger Maris	New York A.L.	1976—Joe Morgan	Cincinnati N.L.
1946—Stan Musial	St. Louis N.L.	1962—Maury Wills	Los Angeles N.L.	1977—Rod Carew	Minnesota A.L.
1947—Ted Williams	Boston A.L.	Don Drysdale	Los Angeles N.L.	1978—Ron Guidry	New York A.L.
1948—Lou Boudreau	Cleveland A.L.	1963—Sandy Koufax	Los Angeles N.L.	1979—Willie Stargell	Pittsburgh N.L.
1949—Ted Williams	Boston A.L.	1964—Ken Boyer	St. Louis N.L.	1980—George Brett	Kansas City A.L.
1950—Phil Rizzuto	New York A.L.	1965—Sandy Koufax	Los Angeles N.L.	1981—Fernando Valenzuela	Los Angeles N.L.
1951—Stan Musial	St. Louis N.L.	1966—Frank Robinson	Baltimore A.L.	1982—Robin Yount	Milwaukee A.L.

Year	Player	Team	Year	Player	Team	Year	Player	Team
1983—Cal Ripken Jr.	Baltimore A.L.		1988—Orel Hershiser	Los Angeles N.L.		1993—Frank Thomas	Chicago A.L.	
1984—Ryne Sandberg	Chicago N.L.		1989—Kevin Mitchell	San Francisco N.L.		1994—Jeff Bagwell	Houston N.L.	
1985—Don Mattingly	New York A.L.		1990—Barry Bonds	Pittsburgh N.L.		1995—Albert Belle	Cleveland A.L.	
1986—Roger Clemens	Boston A.L.		1991—Cal Ripken Jr.	Baltimore A.L.		1996—Alex Rodriguez	Seattle A.L.	
1987—George Bell	Toronto A.L.		1992—Gary Sheffield	San Diego N.L.		1997—Ken Griffey Jr.	Seattle A.L.	

MAJOR LEAGUE MANAGER OF THE YEAR

Year	Manager	Team	Year	Manager	Team	Year	Manager	Team
1936—Joe McCarthy	New York A.L.		1961—Ralph Houk	New York A.L.		1986—John McNamara	Boston A.L.	
1937—Bill McKechnie	Boston N.L.		1962—Bill Rigney	Los Angeles A.L.			Hal Lanier	Houston N.L.
1938—Joe McCarthy	New York A.L.		1963—Walter Alston	Los Angeles N.L.		1987—Sparky Anderson	Detroit A.L.	
1939—Leo Durocher	Brooklyn N.L.		1964—Johnny Keane	St. Louis N.L.			Buck Rodgers	Montreal N.L.
1940—Bill McKechnie	Cincinnati N.L.		1965—Sam Mele	Minnesota A.L.		1988—Tony La Russa	Oakland A.L.	
1941—Billy Southworth	St. Louis N.L.		1966—Hank Bauer	Baltimore A.L.			Tom Lasorda	L.A. N.L. (tie)
1942—Billy Southworth	St. Louis N.L.		1967—Dick Williams	Boston A.L.			Jim Leyland	Pit. N.L. (tie)
1943—Joe McCarthy	New York A.L.		1968—Mayo Smith	Detroit A.L.		1989—Frank Robinson	Baltimore A.L.	
1944—Luke Sewell	St. Louis A.L.		1969—Gil Hodges	New York N.L.			Don Zimmer	Chicago N.L.
1945—Ossie Bluege	Washington A.L.		1970—Danny Murtaugh	Pittsburgh N.L.		1990—Jeff Torborg	Chicago A.L.	
1946—Eddie Dyer	St. Louis N.L.		1971—Charlie Fox	San Francisco N.L.			Jim Leyland	Pittsburgh N.L.
1947—Bucky Harris	New York A.L.		1972—Chuck Tanner	Chicago A.L.		1991—Tom Kelly	Minnesota A.L.	
1948—Bill Meyer	Pittsburgh N.L.		1973—Gene Mauch	Montreal N.L.			Bobby Cox	Atlanta N.L.
1949—Casey Stengel	New York A.L.		1974—Bill Virdon	New York A.L.		1992—Tony La Russa	Oakland A.L.	
1950—Red Rolfe	Detroit A.L.		1975—Darrell Johnson	Boston A.L.			Jim Leyland	Pittsburgh N.L.
1951—Leo Durocher	New York N.L.		1976—Danny Ozark	Philadelphia N.L.		1993—Johnny Oates	Baltimore A.L.	
1952—Eddie Stanky	St. Louis N.L.		1977—Earl Weaver	Baltimore A.L.			Bobby Cox	Atlanta N.L.
1953—Casey Stengel	New York A.L.		1978—George Bamberger	Milwaukee A.L.		1994—Buck Showalter	New York A.L.	
1954—Leo Durocher	New York N.L.		1979—Earl Weaver	Baltimore A.L.			Felipe Alou	Montreal N.L.
1955—Walter Alston	Brooklyn N.L.		1980—Bill Virdon	Houston N.L.		1995—Mike Hargrove	Cleveland A.L.	
1956—Birdie Tebbetts	Cincinnati N.L.		1981—Billy Martin	Oakland A.L.			Don Baylor	Colorado N.L.
1957—Fred Hutchinson	St. Louis N.L.		1982—Whitey Herzog	St. Louis N.L.		1996—Johnny Oates	Texas A.L.	
1958—Casey Stengel	New York A.L.		1983—Tony La Russa	Chicago A.L.			Bruce Bochy	San Diego N.L.
1959—Walter A.L.ston	Los Angeles N.L.		1984—Jim Frey	Chicago N.L.		1997—Dave Johnson	Baltimore A.L.	
1960—Danny Murtaugh	Pittsburgh N.L.		1985—Bobby Cox	Toronto A.L.			Dusty Baker	San Fran. N.L.

MAJOR LEAGUE EXECUTIVE OF THE YEAR

Year	Executive	Team	Year	Executive	Team	Year	Executive	Team
1936—Branch Rickey	St. Louis N.L.		1957—Frank Lane	St. Louis N.L.		1978—Spec Richardson	San Francisco N.L.	
1937—Ed Barrow	New York A.L.		1958—Joe Brown	Pittsburgh N.L.		1979—Hank Peters	Baltimore A.L.	
1938—Warren Giles	Cincinnati N.L.		1959—Buzzie Bavasi	L.A. N.L.		1980—Tal Smith	Houston N.L.	
1939—Larry MacPhail	Brooklyn N.L.		1960—George Weiss	New York A.L.		1981—John McHale	Montreal N.L.	
1940—Walter Briggs Sr.	Detroit A.L.		1961—Dan Topping	New York A.L.		1982—Harry Dalton	Milwaukee A.L.	
1941—Ed Barrow	New York A.L.		1962—Fred Haney	Los Angeles A.L.		1983—Hank Peters	Baltimore A.L.	
1942—Branch Rickey	St. Louis N.L.		1963—Bing Devine	St. Louis N.L.		1984—Dallas Green	Chicago N.L.	
1943—Clark Griffith	Washington A.L.		1964—Bing Devine	St. Louis N.L.		1985—John Schuerholz	Kansas City A.L.	
1944—Billy DeWitt	St. Louis A.L.		1965—Cal Griffith	Minnesota A.L.		1986—Frank Cashen	New York N.L.	
1945—Phil Wrigley	Chicago N.L.		1966—Lee MacPhail	Commissioner's Office		1987—Al Rosen	San Francisco N.L.	
1946—Tom Yawkey	Boston A.L.		1967—Dick O'Connell	Boston A.L.		1988—Fred Claire	Los Angeles N.L.	
1947—Branch Rickey	Brooklyn N.L.		1968—Jim Campbell	Detroit A.L.		1989—Roland Hemond	Baltimore A.L.	
1948—Bill Veeck	Cleveland A.L.		1969—John Murphy	New York N.L.		1990—Bob Quinn	Cincinnati N.L.	
1949—Bob Carpenter	Philadelphia N.L.		1970—Harry Dalton	Baltimore A.L.		1991—Andy MacPhail	Minnesota A.L.	
1950—George Weiss	New York A.L.		1971—Cedric Tallis	Kansas City A.L.		1992—Dan Duquette	Montreal N.L.	
1951—George Weiss	New York A.L.		1972—Roland Hemond	Chicago A.L.		1993—Lee Thomas	Philadelphia N.L.	
1952—George Weiss	New York A.L.		1973—Bob Howsam	Cincinnati N.L.		1994—John Hart	Cleveland A.L.	
1953—Lou Perini	Milwaukee A.L.		1974—Gabe Paul	New York A.L.		1995—John Hart	Cleveland A.L.	
1954—Horace Stoneham	New York N.L.		1975—Dick O'Connell	Boston A.L.		1996—Doug Melvin	Texas A.L.	
1955—Walter O'Malley	Brooklyn N.L.		1976—Joe Burke	Kansas City A.L.		1997—Cam Bonifay	Pittsburgh N.L.	
1956—Gabe Paul	Cincinnati N.L.		1977—Bill Veeck	Chicago A.L.				

GOLD GLOVE TEAMS

1957	1958	NATIONAL LEAGUE
MAJORS	**AMERICAN LEAGUE**	P— Harvey Haddix, Cincinnati
P— Bobby Shantz, New York A.L.	P— Bobby Shantz, New York	C— Del Crandall, Milwaukee
C— Sherm Lollar, Chicago A.L.	C— Sherm Lollar, Chicago	1B— Gil Hodges, Los Angeles
1B— Gil Hodges, Brooklyn N.L.	1B— Vic Power, Cleveland	2B— Bill Mazeroski, Pittsburgh
2B— Nellie Fox, Chicago A.L.	2B— Frank Bolling, Detroit	3B— Ken Boyer, St. Louis
3B— Frank Malzone, Boston A.L.	3B— Frank Malzone, Boston	SS— Roy McMillan, Cincinnati
SS— Roy McMillan, Cincinnati N.L.	SS— Luis Aparicio, Chicago	OF— Frank Robinson, Cincinnati
OF— Minnie Minoso, Chicago A.L.	OF— Norm Siebern, New York	OF— Willie Mays, San Francisco
OF— Willie Mays, New York N.L.	OF— Jimmy Piersall, Boston	OF— Hank Aaron, Milwaukee
OF— Al Kaline, Detroit A.L.	OF— Al Kaline, Detroit	

HISTORY *Award winners*

1959
AMERICAN LEAGUE
P— Bobby Shantz, New York
C— Sherm Lollar, Chicago
1B— Vic Power, Cleveland
2B— Nellie Fox, Chicago
3B— Frank Malzone, Boston
SS— Luis Aparicio, Chicago
OF— Minnie Minoso, Cleveland
OF— Al Kaline, Detroit
OF— Jackie Jensen, Boston

NATIONAL LEAGUE
P— Harvey Haddix, Pittsburgh
C— Del Crandall, Milwaukee
1B— Gil Hodges, Los Angeles
2B— Charley Neal, Los Angeles
3B— Ken Boyer, St. Louis
SS— Roy McMillan, Cincinnati
OF— Jackie Brandt, San Francisco
OF— Willie Mays, San Francisco
OF— Hank Aaron, Milwaukee

1960
AMERICAN LEAGUE
P— Bobby Shantz, New York
C— Earl Battey, Washington
1B— Vic Power, Cleveland
2B— Nellie Fox, Chicago
3B— Brooks Robinson, Baltimore
SS— Luis Aparicio, Chicago
OF— Minnie Minoso, Chicago
OF— Jim Landis, Chicago
OF— Roger Maris, New York

NATIONAL LEAGUE
P— Harvey Haddix, Pittsburgh
C— Del Crandall, Milwaukee
1B— Bill White, St. Louis
2B— Bill Mazeroski, Pittsburgh
3B— Ken Boyer, St. Louis
SS— Ernie Banks, Chicago
OF— Wally Moon, Los Angeles
OF— Willie Mays, San Francisco
OF— Hank Aaron, Milwaukee

1961
AMERICAN LEAGUE
P— Frank Lary, Detroit
C— Earl Battey, Minnesota
1B— Vic Power, Cleveland
2B— Bobby Richardson, New York
3B— Brooks Robinson, Baltimore
SS— Luis Aparicio, Chicago
OF— Al Kaline, Detroit
OF— Jimmy Piersall, Cleveland
OF— Jim Landis, Chicago

NATIONAL LEAGUE
P— Bobby Shantz, Pittsburgh
C— John Roseboro, Los Angeles
1B— Bill White, St. Louis
2B— Bill Mazeroski, Pittsburgh
3B— Ken Boyer, St. Louis
SS— Maury Wills, Los Angeles
OF— Willie Mays, San Francisco
OF— Roberto Clemente, Pittsburgh
OF— Vada Pinson, Cincinnati

1962
AMERICAN LEAGUE
P— Jim Kaat, Minnesota
C— Earl Battey, Minnesota
1B— Vic Power, Minnesota
2B— Bobby Richardson, New York
3B— Brooks Robinson, Baltimore
SS— Luis Aparicio, Chicago
OF— Jim Landis, Chicago
OF— Mickey Mantle, New York
OF— Al Kaline, Detroit

NATIONAL LEAGUE
P— Bobby Shantz, St. Louis
C— Del Crandall, Milwaukee
1B— Bill White, St. Louis
2B— Ken Hubbs, Chicago
3B— Jim Davenport, San Francisco
SS— Maury Wills, Los Angeles
OF— Willie Mays, San Francisco
OF— Roberto Clemente, Pittsburgh
OF— Bill Virdon, Pittsburgh

1963
AMERICAN LEAGUE
P— Jim Kaat, Minnesota
C— Elston Howard, New York
1B— Vic Power, Minnesota
2B— Bobby Richardson, New York
3B— Brooks Robinson, Baltimore
SS— Zoilo Versalles, Minnesota
OF— Al Kaline, Detroit
OF— Carl Yastrzemski, Boston
OF— Jim Landis, Chicago

NATIONAL LEAGUE
P— Bobby Shantz, St. Louis
C— Johnny Edwards, Cincinnati
1B— Bill White, St. Louis
2B— Bill Mazeroski, Pittsburgh
3B— Ken Boyer, St. Louis
SS— Bobby Wine, Philadelphia
OF— Willie Mays, San Francisco
OF— Roberto Clemente, Pittsburgh
OF— Curt Flood, St. Louis

1964
AMERICAN LEAGUE
P— Jim Kaat, Minnesota
C— Elston Howard, New York
1B— Vic Power, Los Angeles
2B— Bobby Richardson, New York
3B— Brooks Robinson, Baltimore
SS— Luis Aparicio, Baltimore
OF— Al Kaline, Detroit
OF— Jim Landis, Chicago
OF— Vic Davalillo, Cleveland

NATIONAL LEAGUE
P— Bobby Shantz, Philadelphia
C— Johnny Edwards, Cincinnati
1B— Bill White, St. Louis
2B— Bill Mazeroski, Pittsburgh
3B— Ron Santo, Chicago
SS— Ruben Amaro, Philadelphia
OF— Willie Mays, San Francisco
OF— Roberto Clemente, Pittsburgh
OF— Curt Flood, St. Louis

1965
AMERICAN LEAGUE
P— Jim Kaat, Minnesota
C— Bill Freehan, Detroit
1B— Joe Pepitone, New York
2B— Bobby Richardson, New York
3B— Brooks Robinson, Baltimore
SS— Zoilo Versalles, Minnesota
OF— Al Kaline, Detroit
OF— Tom Tresh, New York
OF— Carl Yastrzemski, Boston

NATIONAL LEAGUE
P— Bob Gibson, St. Louis
C— Joe Torre, Atlanta
1B— Bill White, St. Louis
2B— Bill Mazeroski, Pittsburgh
3B— Ron Santo, Chicago
SS— Leo Cardenas, Cincinnati
OF— Willie Mays, San Francisco
OF— Roberto Clemente, Pittsburgh
OF— Curt Flood, St. Louis

1966
AMERICAN LEAGUE
P— Jim Kaat, Minnesota
C— Bill Freehan, Detroit
1B— Joe Pepitone, New York
2B— Bobby Knoop, California
3B— Brooks Robinson, Baltimore
SS— Luis Aparicio, Baltimore
OF— Al Kaline, Detroit
OF— Tommie Agee, Chicago
OF— Tony Oliva, Minnesota

NATIONAL LEAGUE
P— Bob Gibson, St. Louis
C— John Roseboro, Los Angeles
1B— Bill White, Philadelphia
2B— Bill Mazeroski, Pittsburgh
3B— Ron Santo, Chicago
SS— Gene Alley, Pittsburgh
OF— Willie Mays, San Francisco
OF— Curt Flood, St. Louis
OF— Roberto Clemente, Pittsburgh

1967
AMERICAN LEAGUE
P— Jim Kaat, Minnesota
C— Bill Freehan, Detroit
1B— George Scott, Boston
2B— Bobby Knoop, California
3B— Brooks Robinson, Baltimore
SS— Jim Fregosi, California
OF— Carl Yastrzemski, Boston
OF— Paul Blair, Baltimore
OF— Al Kaline, Detroit

NATIONAL LEAGUE
P— Bob Gibson, St. Louis
C— Randy Hundley, Chicago
1B— Wes Parker, Los Angeles
2B— Bill Mazeroski, Pittsburgh
3B— Ron Santo, Chicago
SS— Gene Alley, Pittsburgh
OF— Roberto Clemente, Pittsburgh
OF— Curt Flood, St. Louis
OF— Willie Mays, San Francisco

1968
AMERICAN LEAGUE
P— Jim Kaat, Minnesota
C— Bill Freehan, Detroit
1B— George Scott, Boston
2B— Bobby Knoop, California
3B— Brooks Robinson, Baltimore
SS— Luis Aparicio, Chicago
OF— Mickey Stanley, Detroit
OF— Carl Yastrzemski, Boston
OF— Reggie Smith, Boston

NATIONAL LEAGUE
P— Bob Gibson, St. Louis
C— Johnny Bench, Cincinnati
1B— Wes Parker, Los Angeles
2B— Glenn Beckert, Chicago
3B— Ron Santo, Chicago
SS— Dal Maxvill, St. Louis
OF— Willie Mays, San Francisco
OF— Roberto Clemente, Pittsburgh
OF— Curt Flood, St. Louis

1969
AMERICAN LEAGUE
P— Jim Kaat, Minnesota
C— Bill Freehan, Detroit
1B— Joe Pepitone, New York
2B— Dave Johnson, Baltimore
3B— Brooks Robinson, Baltimore
SS— Mark Belanger, Baltimore
OF— Paul Blair, Baltimore
OF— Mickey Stanley, Detroit
OF— Carl Yastrzemski, Boston

NATIONAL LEAGUE
P— Bob Gibson, St. Louis
C— Johnny Bench, Cincinnati
1B— Wes Parker, Los Angeles
2B— Felix Millan, Atlanta
3B— Clete Boyer, Atlanta
SS— Don Kessinger, Chicago
OF— Roberto Clemente, Pittsburgh
OF— Curt Flood, St. Louis
OF— Pete Rose, Cincinnati

1970
AMERICAN LEAGUE
P— Jim Kaat, Minnesota
C— Ray Fosse, Cleveland
1B— Jim Spencer, California
2B— Dave Johnson, Baltimore
3B— Brooks Robinson, Baltimore
SS— Luis Aparicio, Chicago
OF— Mickey Stanley, Detroit
OF— Paul Blair, Baltimore
OF— Ken Berry, Chicago

NATIONAL LEAGUE
P— Bob Gibson, St. Louis
C— Johnny Bench, Cincinnati
1B— Wes Parker, Los Angeles
2B— Tommy Helms, Cincinnati
3B— Doug Rader, Houston
SS— Don Kessinger, Chicago
OF— Roberto Clemente, Pittsburgh
OF— Tommie Agee, New York
OF— Pete Rose, Cincinnati

1971
AMERICAN LEAGUE
P— Jim Kaat, Minnesota
C— Ray Fosse, Cleveland
1B— George Scott, Boston
2B— Dave Johnson, Baltimore
3B— Brooks Robinson, Baltimore
SS— Mark Belanger, Baltimore
OF— Paul Blair, Baltimore
OF— Amos Otis, Kansas City
OF— Carl Yastrzemski, Boston

NATIONAL LEAGUE
P— Bob Gibson, St. Louis
C— Johnny Bench, Cincinnati
1B— Wes Parker, Los Angeles
2B— Tommy Helms, Cincinnati
3B— Doug Rader, Houston
SS— Bud Harrelson, New York
OF— Roberto Clemente, Pittsburgh
OF— Bobby Bonds, San Francisco
OF— Willie Davis, Los Angeles

1972
AMERICAN LEAGUE
P— Jim Kaat, Minnesota
C— Carlton Fisk, Boston
1B— George Scott, Milwaukee
2B— Doug Griffin, Boston
3B— Brooks Robinson, Baltimore
SS— Ed Brinkman, Detroit
OF— Paul Blair, Baltimore
OF— Bobby Murcer, New York
OF— Ken Berry, California

NATIONAL LEAGUE
P— Bob Gibson, St. Louis
C— Johnny Bench, Cincinnati
1B— Wes Parker, Los Angeles
2B— Felix Millan, Atlanta
3B— Doug Rader, Houston
SS— Larry Bowa, Philadelphia
OF— Roberto Clemente, Pittsburgh
OF— Cesar Cedeno, Houston
OF— Willie Davis, Los Angeles

1973
AMERICAN LEAGUE
P— Jim Kaat, Chicago
C— Thurman Munson, New York
1B— George Scott, Milwaukee
2B— Bobby Grich, Baltimore
3B— Brooks Robinson, Baltimore
SS— Mark Belanger, Baltimore
OF— Paul Blair, Baltimore
OF— Amos Otis, Kansas City
OF— Mickey Stanley, Detroit

NATIONAL LEAGUE
P— Bob Gibson, St. Louis
C— Johnny Bench, Cincinnati
1B— Mike Jorgensen, Montreal
2B— Joe Morgan, Cincinnati
3B— Doug Rader, Houston
SS— Roger Metzger, Houston
OF— Bobby Bonds, San Francisco
OF— Cesar Cedeno, Houston
OF— Willie Davis, Los Angeles

1974
AMERICAN LEAGUE
P— Jim Kaat, Chicago
C— Thurman Munson, New York
1B— George Scott, Milwaukee
2B— Bobby Grich, Baltimore
3B— Brooks Robinson, Baltimore
SS— Mark Belanger, Baltimore
OF— Paul Blair, Baltimore
OF— Amos Otis, Kansas City
OF— Joe Rudi, Oakland

NATIONAL LEAGUE
P— Andy Messersmith, Los Angeles
C— Johnny Bench, Cincinnati
1B— Steve Garvey, Los Angeles
2B— Joe Morgan, Cincinnati
3B— Doug Rader, Houston
SS— Dave Concepcion, Cincinnati
OF— Cesar Cedeno, Houston
OF— Cesar Geronimo, Cincinnati
OF— Bobby Bonds, San Francisco

1975
AMERICAN LEAGUE
P— Jim Kaat, Chicago
C— Thurman Munson, New York
1B— George Scott, Milwaukee
2B— Bobby Grich, Baltimore
3B— Brooks Robinson, Baltimore
SS— Mark Belanger, Baltimore
OF— Paul Blair, Baltimore
OF— Joe Rudi, Oakland
OF— Fred Lynn, Boston

NATIONAL LEAGUE
P— Andy Messersmith, Los Angeles
C— Johnny Bench, Cincinnati
1B— Steve Garvey, Los Angeles
2B— Joe Morgan, Cincinnati
3B— Ken Reitz, St. Louis
SS— Dave Concepcion, Cincinnati
OF— Cesar Cedeno, Houston
OF— Cesar Geronimo, Cincinnati
OF— Garry Maddox, Philadelphia

1976
AMERICAN LEAGUE
P— Jim Palmer, Baltimore
C— Jim Sundberg, Texas
1B— George Scott, Milwaukee
2B— Bobby Grich, Baltimore
3B— Aurelio Rodriguez, Detroit
SS— Mark Belanger, Baltimore
OF— Joe Rudi, Oakland
OF— Dwight Evans, Boston
OF— Rick Manning, Cleveland

NATIONAL LEAGUE
P— Jim Kaat, Philadelphia
C— Johnny Bench, Cincinnati
1B— Steve Garvey, Los Angeles
2B— Joe Morgan, Cincinnati
3B— Mike Schmidt, Philadelphia
SS— Dave Concepcion, Cincinnati
OF— Cesar Cedeno, Houston
OF— Cesar Geronimo, Cincinnati
OF— Garry Maddox, Philadelphia

1977
AMERICAN LEAGUE
P— Jim Palmer, Baltimore
C— Jim Sundberg, Texas
1B— Jim Spencer, Chicago
2B— Frank White, Kansas City
3B— Graig Nettles, New York
SS— Mark Belanger, Baltimore
OF— Juan Beniquez, Texas
OF— Carl Yastrzemski, Boston
OF— Al Cowens, Kansas City

NATIONAL LEAGUE
P— Jim Kaat, Philadelphia
C— Johnny Bench, Cincinnati
1B— Steve Garvey, Los Angeles
2B— Joe Morgan, Cincinnati
3B— Mike Schmidt, Philadelphia
SS— Dave Concepcion, Cincinnati
OF— Cesar Geronimo, Cincinnati
OF— Garry Maddox, Philadelphia
OF— Dave Parker, Pittsburgh

1978
AMERICAN LEAGUE
P— Jim Palmer, Baltimore
C— Jim Sundberg, Texas
1B— Chris Chambliss, New York
2B— Frank White, Kansas City
3B— Graig Nettles, New York
SS— Mark Belanger, Baltimore
OF— Fred Lynn, Boston
OF— Dwight Evans, Boston
OF— Rick Miller, California

NATIONAL LEAGUE
P— Phil Niekro, Atlanta
C— Bob Boone, Philadelphia
1B— Keith Hernandez, St. Louis
2B— Dave Lopes, Los Angeles
3B— Mike Schmidt, Philadelphia
SS— Larry Bowa, Philadelphia
OF— Garry Maddox, Philadelphia
OF— Dave Parker, Pittsburgh
OF— Ellis Valentine, Montreal

1979
AMERICAN LEAGUE
P— Jim Palmer, Baltimore
C— Jim Sundberg, Texas
1B— Cecil Cooper, Milwaukee
2B— Frank White, Kansas City
3B— Buddy Bell, Texas
SS— Rick Burleson, Boston
OF— Dwight Evans, Boston
OF— Sixto Lezcano, Milwaukee
OF— Fred Lynn, Boston

NATIONAL LEAGUE
P— Phil Niekro, Atlanta
C— Bob Boone, Philadelphia
1B— Keith Hernandez, St. Louis
2B— Manny Trillo, Philadelphia
3B— Mike Schmidt, Philadelphia
SS— Dave Concepcion, Cincinnati
OF— Garry Maddox, Philadelphia
OF— Dave Parker, Pittsburgh
OF— Dave Winfield, San Diego

1980
AMERICAN LEAGUE
P— Mike Norris, Oakland
C— Jim Sundberg, Texas
1B— Cecil Cooper, Milwaukee
2B— Frank White, Kansas City
3B— Buddy Bell, Texas
SS— Alan Trammell, Detroit
OF— Fred Lynn, Boston
OF— Dwayne Murphy, Oakland
OF— Willie Wilson, Kansas City

NATIONAL LEAGUE
P— Phil Niekro, Atlanta
C— Gary Carter, Montreal
1B— Keith Hernandez, St. Louis
2B— Doug Flynn, New York
3B— Mike Schmidt, Philadelphia
SS— Ozzie Smith, San Diego
OF— Andre Dawson, Montreal
OF— Garry Maddox, Philadelphia
OF— Dave Winfield, San Diego

1981
AMERICAN LEAGUE
P— Mike Norris, Oakland
C— Jim Sundberg, Texas
1B— Mike Squires, Chicago
2B— Frank White, Kansas City
3B— Buddy Bell, Texas
SS— Alan Trammell, Detroit
OF— Dwayne Murphy, Oakland
OF— Dwight Evans, Boston
OF— Rickey Henderson, Oakland

NATIONAL LEAGUE
P— Steve Carlton, Philadelphia
C— Gary Carter, Montreal
1B— Keith Hernandez, St. Louis
2B— Manny Trillo, Philadelphia
3B— Mike Schmidt, Philadelphia
SS— Ozzie Smith, San Diego
OF— Andre Dawson, Montreal
OF— Garry Maddox, Philadelphia
OF— Dusty Baker, Los Angeles

1982
AMERICAN LEAGUE
P— Ron Guidry, New York
C— Bob Boone, California
1B— Eddie Murray, Baltimore
2B— Frank White, Kansas City
3B— Buddy Bell, Texas
SS— Robin Yount, Milwaukee
OF— Dwight Evans, Boston
OF— Dave Winfield, New York
OF— Dwayne Murphy, Oakland

NATIONAL LEAGUE
P— Phil Niekro, Atlanta
C— Gary Carter, Montreal
1B— Keith Hernandez, St. Louis
2B— Manny Trillo, Philadelphia
3B— Mike Schmidt, Philadelphia
SS— Ozzie Smith, St. Louis
OF— Andre Dawson, Montreal
OF— Dale Murphy, Atlanta
OF— Garry Maddox, Philadelphia

1983
AMERICAN LEAGUE
P— Ron Guidry, New York
C— Lance Parrish, Detroit
1B— Eddie Murray, Baltimore
2B— Lou Whitaker, Detroit
3B— Buddy Bell, Texas
SS— Alan Trammell, Detroit
OF— Dwight Evans, Boston
OF— Dave Winfield, New York
OF— Dwayne Murphy, Oakland

NATIONAL LEAGUE
P— Phil Niekro, Atlanta
C— Tony Pena, Pittsburgh
1B— Keith Hernandez, St.L.-N.Y.
2B— Ryne Sandberg, Chicago
3B— Mike Schmidt, Philadelphia
SS— Ozzie Smith, St. Louis
OF— Andre Dawson, Montreal
OF— Dale Murphy, Atlanta
OF— Willie McGee, St. Louis

1984
AMERICAN LEAGUE
P— Ron Guidry, New York
C— Lance Parrish, Detroit
1B— Eddie Murray, Baltimore
2B— Lou Whitaker, Detroit
3B— Buddy Bell, Texas
SS— Alan Trammell, Detroit
OF— Dwight Evans, Boston
OF— Dave Winfield, New York
OF— Dwayne Murphy, Oakland

NATIONAL LEAGUE
P— Joaquin Andujar, St. Louis
C— Tony Pena, Pittsburgh
1B— Keith Hernandez, New York
2B— Ryne Sandberg, Chicago
3B— Mike Schmidt, Philadelphia
SS— Ozzie Smith, St. Louis
OF— Dale Murphy, Atlanta
OF— Bob Dernier, Chicago
OF— Andre Dawson, Montreal

1985
AMERICAN LEAGUE
P— Ron Guidry, New York
C— Lance Parrish, Detroit
1B— Don Mattingly, New York
2B— Lou Whitaker, Detroit
3B— George Brett, Kansas City
SS— Alfredo Griffin, Oakland
OF— Gary Pettis, California
OF— Dave Winfield, New York
OF— Dwight Evans, Boston (tie)
　　 Dwayne Murphy, Oakland (tie)

NATIONAL LEAGUE
P— Rick Reuschel, Pittsburgh
C— Tony Pena, Pittsburgh
1B— Keith Hernandez, New York
2B— Ryne Sandberg, Chicago
3B— Tim Wallach, Montreal
SS— Ozzie Smith, St. Louis
OF— Willie McGee, St. Louis
OF— Dale Murphy, Atlanta
OF— Andre Dawson, Montreal

1986
AMERICAN LEAGUE
P— Ron Guidry, New York
C— Bob Boone, California
1B— Don Mattingly, New York
2B— Frank White, Kansas City
3B— Gary Gaetti, Minnesota
SS— Tony Fernandez, Toronto
OF— Gary Pettis, California
OF— Jesse Barfield, Toronto
OF— Kirby Puckett, Minnesota

NATIONAL LEAGUE
P— Fernando Valenzuela, Los Angeles
C— Jody Davis, Chicago
1B— Keith Hernandez, New York
2B— Ryne Sandberg, Chicago
3B— Mike Schmidt, Philadelphia
SS— Ozzie Smith, St. Louis
OF— Tony Gwynn, San Diego
OF— Dale Murphy, Atlanta
OF— Willie McGee, St. Louis

1987
AMERICAN LEAGUE
P— Mark Langston, Seattle
C— Bob Boone, California
1B— Don Mattingly, New York
2B— Frank White, Kansas City
3B— Gary Gaetti, Minnesota
SS— Tony Fernandez, Toronto
OF— Jesse Barfield, Toronto
OF— Kirby Puckett, Minnesota
OF— Dave Winfield, New York

NATIONAL LEAGUE
P— Rick Reuschel, Pit.-S.F.
C— Mike LaValliere, Pittsburgh
1B— Keith Hernandez, New York
2B— Ryne Sandberg, Chicago
3B— Terry Pendleton, St. Louis
SS— Ozzie Smith, St. Louis
OF— Eric Davis, Cincinnati
OF— Tony Gwynn, San Diego
OF— Andre Dawson, Chicago

1988
AMERICAN LEAGUE
P— Mark Langston, Seattle
C— Bob Boone, California
1B— Don Mattingly, New York
2B— Harold Reynolds, Seattle
3B— Gary Gaetti, Minnesota
SS— Tony Fernandez, Toronto
OF— Kirby Puckett, Minnesota
OF— Devon White, California
OF— Gary Pettis, Detroit

NATIONAL LEAGUE
P— Orel Hershiser, Los Angeles
C— Benito Santiago, San Diego
1B— Keith Hernandez, New York
2B— Ryne Sandberg, Chicago
3B— Tim Wallach, Montreal
SS— Ozzie Smith, St. Louis
OF— Andy Van Slyke, Pittsburgh
OF— Eric Davis, Cincinnati
OF— Andre Dawson, Chicago

1989
AMERICAN LEAGUE
P— Bret Saberhagen, Kansas City
C— Bob Boone, Kansas City
1B— Don Mattingly, New York
2B— Harold Reynolds, Seattle
3B— Gary Gaetti, Minnesota
SS— Tony Fernandez, Toronto
OF— Kirby Puckett, Minnesota
OF— Devon White, California
OF— Gary Pettis, Detroit

NATIONAL LEAGUE
P— Ron Darling, New York
C— Benito Santiago, San Diego
1B— Andres Galarraga, Montreal
2B— Ryne Sandberg, Chicago
3B— Terry Pendleton, St. Louis
SS— Ozzie Smith, St. Louis
OF— Andy Van Slyke, Pittsburgh
OF— Tony Gwynn, San Diego
OF— Eric Davis, Cincinnati

1990
AMERICAN LEAGUE
P— Mike Boddicker, Boston
C— Sandy Alomar Jr., Cleveland
1B— Mark McGwire, Oakland
2B— Harold Reynolds, Seattle
3B— Kelly Gruber, Toronto
SS— Ozzie Guillen, Chicago
OF— Ken Griffey Jr., Seattle
OF— Ellis Burks, Boston
OF— Gary Pettis, Texas

NATIONAL LEAGUE
P— Greg Maddux, Chicago
C— Benito Santiago, San Diego
1B— Andres Galarraga, Montreal
2B— Ryne Sandberg, Chicago
3B— Tim Wallach, Montreal
SS— Ozzie Smith, St. Louis
OF— Barry Bonds, Pittsburgh
OF— Andy Van Slyke, Pittsburgh
OF— Tony Gwynn, San Diego

1991
AMERICAN LEAGUE
P— Mark Langston, California
C— Tony Pena, Boston
1B— Don Mattingly, New York
2B— Roberto Alomar, Toronto
3B— Robin Ventura, Chicago
SS— Cal Ripken, Baltimore
OF— Ken Griffey Jr., Seattle
OF— Kirby Puckett, Minnesota
OF— Devon White, Toronto

NATIONAL LEAGUE
P— Greg Maddux, Chicago
C— Tom Pagnozzi, St. Louis
1B— Will Clark, San Francisco
2B— Ryne Sandberg, Chicago
3B— Matt Williams, San Francisco
SS— Ozzie Smith, St. Louis
OF— Barry Bonds, Pittsburgh
OF— Andy Van Slyke, Pittsburgh
OF— Tony Gwynn, San Diego

1992
AMERICAN LEAGUE
P— Mark Langston, California
C— Ivan Rodriguez, Texas
1B— Don Mattingly, New York
2B— Roberto Alomar, Toronto
3B— Robin Ventura, Chicago
SS— Cal Ripken, Baltimore
OF— Ken Griffey Jr., Seattle
OF— Kirby Puckett, Minnesota
OF— Devon White, Toronto

NATIONAL LEAGUE
P— Greg Maddux, Chicago
C— Tom Pagnozzi, St. Louis
1B— Mark Grace, Chicago
2B— Jose Lind, Pittsburgh
3B— Terry Pendleton, Atlanta
SS— Ozzie Smith, St. Louis
OF— Barry Bonds, Pittsburgh
OF— Andy Van Slyke, Pittsburgh
OF— Larry Walker, Montreal

1993
AMERICAN LEAGUE
P— Mark Langston, California
C— Ivan Rodriguez, Texas
1B— Don Mattingly, New York
2B— Roberto Alomar, Toronto
3B— Robin Ventura, Chicago
SS— Omar Vizquel, Seattle
OF— Ken Griffey Jr., Seattle
OF— Kenny Lofton, Cleveland
OF— Devon White, Toronto

NATIONAL LEAGUE
P— Greg Maddux, Atlanta
C— Kirt Manwaring, San Francisco
1B— Mark Grace, Chicago
2B— Robby Thompson, San Fran.
3B— Matt Williams, San Francisco
SS— Jay Bell, Pittsburgh
OF— Barry Bonds, San Francisco
OF— Marquis Grissom, Montreal
OF— Larry Walker, Montreal

1994
AMERICAN LEAGUE
P— Mark Langston, California
C— Ivan Rodriguez, Texas
1B— Don Mattingly, New York
2B— Roberto Alomar, Toronto
3B— Wade Boggs, New York
SS— Omar Vizquel, Cleveland
OF— Ken Griffey Jr., Seattle
OF— Kenny Lofton, Cleveland
OF— Devon White, Toronto

NATIONAL LEAGUE
P— Greg Maddux, Atlanta
C— Tom Pagnozzi, St. Louis
1B— Jeff Bagwell, Houston
2B— Craig Biggio, Houston
3B— Matt Williams, San Francisco
SS— Barry Larkin, Cincinnati
OF— Barry Bonds, San Francisco
OF— Marquis Grissom, Montreal
OF— Darren Lewis, San Francisco

1995
AMERICAN LEAGUE
P— Mark Langston, California
C— Ivan Rodriguez, Texas
1B— J.T. Snow, California
2B— Roberto Alomar, Toronto
3B— Wade Boggs, New York
SS— Omar Vizquel, Cleveland
OF— Ken Griffey Jr., Seattle
OF— Kenny Lofton, Cleveland
OF— Devon White, Toronto

NATIONAL LEAGUE
P— Greg Maddux, Atlanta
C— Charles Johnson, Florida
1B— Mark Grace, Chicago
2B— Craig Biggio, Houston
3B— Ken Caminiti, San Diego
SS— Barry Larkin, Cincinnati
OF— Raul Mondesi, Los Angeles
OF— Marquis Grissom, Atlanta
OF— Steve Finley, San Diego

1996
AMERICAN LEAGUE
P— Mike Mussina, Baltimore
C— Ivan Rodriguez, Texas
1B— J.T. Snow, California
2B— Roberto Alomar, Baltimore
3B— Robin Ventura, Chicago
SS— Omar Vizquel, Cleveland
OF— Jay Buhner, Seattle
OF— Ken Griffey Jr., Seattle
OF— Kenny Lofton, Cleveland

NATIONAL LEAGUE
P— Greg Maddux, Atlanta
C— Charles Johnson, Florida
1B— Mark Grace, Chicago
2B— Craig Biggio, Houston
3B— Ken Caminiti, San Diego
SS— Barry Larkin, Cincinnati
OF— Barry Bonds, San Francisco
OF— Marquis Grissom, Atlanta
OF— Steve Finley, San Diego

1997
AMERICAN LEAGUE
P— Mike Mussina, Baltimore
C— Ivan Rodriguez, Texas
1B— Rafael Palmeiro, Baltimore
2B— Chuck Knoblauch, Minnesota
3B— Matt Williams, Cleveland
SS— Omar Vizquel, Cleveland
OF— Jim Edmonds, Anaheim
OF— Ken Griffey Jr., Seattle
OF— Bernie Williams, New York

NATIONAL LEAGUE
P— Greg Maddux, Atlanta
C— Charles Johnson, Florida
1B— J.T. Snow, San Francisco
2B— Craig Biggio, Houston
3B— Ken Caminiti, San Diego
SS— Rey Ordonez, New York
OF— Barry Bonds, San Francisco
OF— Raul Mondesi, Los Angeles
OF— Larry Walker, Colorado

SILVER SLUGGER TEAMS

1980
AMERICAN LEAGUE
1B— Cecil Cooper, Milwaukee
2B— Willie Randolph, New York
3B— George Brett, Kansas City
SS— Robin Yount, Milwaukee
OF— Ben Oglivie, Milwaukee
OF— Al Oliver, Texas
OF— Willie Wilson, Kansas City
C— Lance Parrish, Detroit
DH— Reggie Jackson, New York

NATIONAL LEAGUE
1B— Keith Hernandez, St. Louis
2B— Manny Trillo, Philadelphia
3B— Mike Schmidt, Philadelphia
SS— Garry Templeton, St. Louis
OF— Dusty Baker, Los Angeles
OF— Andre Dawson, Montreal
OF— George Hendrick, St. Louis

C— Ted Simmons, St. Louis
P— Bob Forsch, St. Louis

1981
AMERICAN LEAGUE
1B— Cecil Cooper, Milwaukee
2B— Bobby Grich, California
3B— Carney Lansford, Boston
SS— Rick Burleson, California
OF— Rickey Henderson, Oakland
OF— Dwight Evans, Boston
OF— Dave Winfield, New York
C— Carlton Fisk, Chicago
DH— Al Oliver, Texas

NATIONAL LEAGUE
1B— Pete Rose, Philadelphia
2B— Manny Trillo, Philadelphia
3B— Mike Schmidt, Philadelphia
SS— Dave Concepcion, Cincinnati

OF— Andre Dawson, Montreal
OF— George Foster, Cincinnati
OF— Dusty Baker, Los Angeles
C— Gary Carter, Montreal
P— Fernando Valenzuela, Los Angeles

1982
AMERICAN LEAGUE
1B— Cecil Cooper, Milwaukee
2B— Damaso Garcia, Toronto
3B— Doug DeCinces, California
SS— Robin Yount, Milwaukee
OF— Dave Winfield, New York
OF— Willie Wilson, Kansas City
OF— Reggie Jackson, California
C— Lance Parrish, Detroit
DH— Hal McRae, Kansas City

NATIONAL LEAGUE
1B— Al Oliver, Montreal
2B— Joe Morgan, San Francisco
3B— Mike Schmidt, Philadelphia
SS— Dave Concepcion, Cincinnati
OF— Dale Murphy, Atlanta
OF— Pedro Guerrero, Los Angeles
OF— Leon Durham, Chicago
C— Gary Carter, Montreal
P— Don Robinson, Pittsburgh

1983
AMERICAN LEAGUE
1B— Eddie Murray, Baltimore
2B— Lou Whitaker, Detroit
3B— Wade Boggs, Boston
SS— Cal Ripken Jr., Baltimore
OF— Jim Rice, Boston
OF— Dave Winfield, New York
OF— Lloyd Moseby, Toronto
C— Lance Parrish, Detroit
DH— Don Baylor, New York

NATIONAL LEAGUE
1B— George Hendrick, St. Louis
2B— Johnny Ray, Pittsburgh
3B— Mike Schmidt, Philadelphia
SS— Dickie Thon, Houston
OF— Andre Dawson, Montreal
OF— Dale Murphy, Atlanta
OF— Jose Cruz, Houston
C— Terry Kennedy, San Diego
P— Fernando Valenzuela, Los Angeles

1984
AMERICAN LEAGUE
1B— Eddie Murray, Baltimore
2B— Lou Whitaker, Detroit
3B— Buddy Bell, Texas
SS— Cal Ripken Jr., Baltimore
OF— Tony Armas, Boston
OF— Jim Rice, Boston
OF— Dave Winfield, New York
C— Lance Parrish, Detroit
DH— Andre Thornton, Cleveland

NATIONAL LEAGUE
1B— Keith Hernandez, New York
2B— Ryne Sandberg, Chicago
3B— Mike Schmidt, Philadelphia
SS— Garry Templeton, San Diego
OF— Dale Murphy, Atlanta
OF— Jose Cruz, Houston
OF— Tony Gwynn, San Diego
C— Gary Carter, Montreal
P— Rick Rhoden, Pittsburgh

1985
AMERICAN LEAGUE
1B— Don Mattingly, New York
2B— Lou Whitaker, Detroit
3B— George Brett, Kansas City
SS— Cal Ripken Jr., Baltimore
OF— Rickey Henderson, New York
OF— Dave Winfield, New York
OF— George Bell, Toronto
C— Carlton Fisk, Chicago
DH— Don Baylor, New York

NATIONAL LEAGUE
1B— Jack Clark, St. Louis
2B— Ryne Sandberg, Chicago
3B— Tim Wallach, Montreal
SS— Hubie Brooks, Montreal
OF— Willie McGee, St. Louis
OF— Dale Murphy, Atlanta
OF— Dave Parker, Cincinnati
C— Gary Carter, New York
P— Rick Rhoden, Pittsburgh

1986
AMERICAN LEAGUE
1B— Don Mattingly, New York
2B— Frank White, Kansas City
3B— Wade Boggs, Boston
SS— Cal Ripken Jr., Baltimore
OF— George Bell, Toronto
OF— Kirby Puckett, Minnesota
OF— Jesse Barfield, Toronto
C— Lance Parrish, Detroit
DH— Don Baylor, Boston

NATIONAL LEAGUE
1B— Glenn Davis, Houston
2B— Steve Sax, Los Angeles
3B— Mike Schmidt, Philadelphia
SS— Hubie Brooks, Montreal
OF— Tony Gwynn, San Diego
OF— Tim Raines, Montreal
OF— Dave Parker, Cincinnati
C— Gary Carter, New York
P— Rick Rhoden, Pittsburgh

1987
AMERICAN LEAGUE
1B— Don Mattingly, New York
2B— Lou Whitaker, Detroit
3B— Wade Boggs, Boston
SS— Alan Trammell, Detroit
OF— George Bell, Toronto
OF— Dwight Evans, Boston
OF— Kirby Puckett, Minnesota
C— Matt Nokes, Detroit
DH— Paul Molitor, Milwaukee

NATIONAL LEAGUE
1B— Jack Clark, St. Louis
2B— Juan Samuel, Philadelphia
3B— Tim Wallach, Montreal
SS— Ozzie Smith, St. Louis
OF— Andre Dawson, Chicago
OF— Eric Davis, Cincinnati
OF— Tony Gwynn, San Diego
C— Benito Santiago, San Diego
P— Bob Forsch, St. Louis

1988
AMERICAN LEAGUE
1B— George Brett, Kansas City
2B— Julio Franco, Cleveland
3B— Wade Boggs, Boston
SS— Alan Trammell, Detroit
OF— Kirby Puckett, Minnesota
OF— Jose Canseco, Oakland
OF— Mike Greenwell, Boston
C— Carlton Fisk, Chicago
DH— Paul Molitor, Milwaukee

NATIONAL LEAGUE
1B— Andres Galarraga, Montreal
2B— Ryne Sandberg, Chicago
3B— Bobby Bonilla, Pittsburgh
SS— Barry Larkin, Cincinnati
OF— Darryl Strawberry, New York
OF— Andy Van Slyke, Pittsburgh
OF— Kirk Gibson, Los Angeles
C— Benito Santiago, San Diego
P— Tim Leary, Los Angeles

1989
AMERICAN LEAGUE
1B— Fred McGriff, Toronto
2B— Julio Franco, Texas
3B— Wade Boggs, Boston
SS— Cal Ripken Jr., Baltimore
OF— Kirby Puckett, Minnesota
OF— Ruben Sierra, Texas
OF— Robin Yount, Milwaukee
C— Mickey Tettleton, Baltimore
DH— Harold Baines, Chi.-Tex.

NATIONAL LEAGUE
1B— Will Clark, San Francisco
2B— Ryne Sandberg, Chicago
3B— Howard Johnson, New York
SS— Barry Larkin, Cincinnati
OF— Kevin Mitchell, San Francisco
OF— Tony Gwynn, San Diego
OF— Eric Davis, Cincinnati
C— Craig Biggio, Houston
P— Don Robinson, San Francisco

1990
AMERICAN LEAGUE
1B— Cecil Fielder, Detroit
2B— Julio Franco, Texas
3B— Kelly Gruber, Toronto
SS— Alan Trammell, Detroit
OF— Rickey Henderson, Oakland
OF— Jose Canseco, Oakland
OF— Ellis Burks, Boston
C— Lance Parrish, California
DH— Dave Parker, Milwaukee

NATIONAL LEAGUE
1B— Eddie Murray, Los Angeles
2B— Ryne Sandberg, Chicago
3B— Matt Williams, San Francisco
SS— Barry Larkin, Cincinnati
OF— Barry Bonds, Pittsburgh
OF— Bobby Bonilla, Pittsburgh
OF— Darryl Strawberry, New York
C— Benito Santiago, San Diego
P— Don Robinson, San Francisco

1991
AMERICAN LEAGUE
1B— Cecil Fielder, Detroit
2B— Julio Franco, Texas
3B— Wade Boggs, Boston
SS— Cal Ripken Jr., Baltimore
OF— Jose Canseco, Oakland
OF— Joe Carter, Toronto
OF— Ken Griffey Jr., Seattle
C— Mickey Tettleton, Detroit
DH— Frank Thomas, Chicago

NATIONAL LEAGUE
1B— Will Clark, San Francisco
2B— Ryne Sandberg, Chicago
3B— Howard Johnson, New York
SS— Barry Larkin, Cincinnati
OF— Barry Bonds, Pittsburgh
OF— Bobby Bonilla, Pittsburgh
OF— Ron Gant, Atlanta
C— Benito Santiago, San Diego
P— Tom Glavine, Atlanta

1992
AMERICAN LEAGUE
1B— Mark McGwire, Oakland
2B— Roberto Alomar, Toronto
3B— Edgar Martinez, Seattle
SS— Travis Fryman, Detroit
OF— Joe Carter, Toronto
OF— Juan Gonzalez, Texas
OF— Kirby Puckett, Minnesota
C— Mickey Tettleton, Detroit
DH— Dave Winfield, Toronto

NATIONAL LEAGUE
1B— Fred McGriff, San Diego
2B— Ryne Sandberg, Chicago
3B— Gary Sheffield, San Diego
SS— Barry Larkin, Cincinnati
OF— Barry Bonds, Pittsburgh
OF— Andy Van Slyke, Pittsburgh
OF— Larry Walker, Montreal
C— Darren Daulton, Philadelphia
P— Dwight Gooden, New York

1993
AMERICAN LEAGUE
1B— Frank Thomas, Chicago
2B— Carlos Baerga, Cleveland
3B— Wade Boggs, New York
SS— Cal Ripken Jr., Baltimore
OF— Albert Belle, Cleveland
OF— Juan Gonzalez, Texas
OF— Ken Griffey Jr., Seattle
C— Mike Stanley, New York
DH— Paul Molitor, Toronto

NATIONAL LEAGUE
1B— Fred McGriff, S.D.-Atl.
2B— Robby Thompson, San Fran.
3B— Matt Williams, San Francisco
SS— Jay Bell, Pittsburgh
OF— Barry Bonds, San Francisco
OF— Lenny Dykstra, Philadelphia
OF— David Justice, Atlanta
C— Mike Piazza, Los Angeles
P— Orel Hershiser, Los Angeles

1994
AMERICAN LEAGUE
1B— Frank Thomas, Chicago
2B— Carlos Baerga, Cleveland
3B— Wade Boggs, New York
SS— Cal Ripken Jr., Baltimore
OF— Albert Belle, Cleveland
OF— Ken Griffey Jr., Seattle
OF— Kirby Puckett, Minnesota
C— Ivan Rodriguez, Texas
DH— Julio Franco, Chicago

NATIONAL LEAGUE
1B— Jeff Bagwell, Houston
2B— Craig Biggio, Houston

3B— Matt Williams, San Francisco
SS— Wil Cordero, Montreal
OF— Moises Alou, Montreal
OF— Barry Bonds, San Francisco
OF— Tony Gwynn, San Diego
C— Mike Piazza, Los Angeles
P— Mark Portugal, San Francisco

1995
AMERICAN LEAGUE
1B— Mo Vaughn, Boston
2B— Chuck Knoblauch, Minnesota
3B— Gary Gaetti, Kansas City
SS— John Valentin, Boston
OF— Albert Belle, Cleveland
OF— Tim Salmon, California
OF— Manny Ramirez, Cleveland
C— Ivan Rodriguez, Texas
DH— Edgar Martinez, Seattle

NATIONAL LEAGUE
1B— Eric Karros, Los Angeles
2B— Craig Biggio, Houston
3B— Vinny Castilla, Colorado
SS— Barry Larkin, Cincinnati
OF— Dante Bichette, Colorado
OF— Tony Gwynn, San Diego
OF— Sammy Sosa, Chicago
C— Mike Piazza, Los Angeles
P— Tom Glavine, Atlanta

1996
AMERICAN LEAGUE
1B— Mark McGwire, Oakland
2B— Roberto Alomar, Baltimore
3B— Jim Thome, Cleveland
SS— Alex Rodriguez, Seattle
OF— Albert Belle, Cleveland

OF— Juan Gonzalez, Texas
OF— Ken Griffey Jr., Seattle
C— Ivan Rodriguez, Texas
DH— Paul Molitor, Minnesota

NATIONAL LEAGUE
1B— Andres Galarraga, Colorado
2B— Eric Young, Colorado
3B— Ken Caminiti, San Diego
SS— Barry Larkin, Cincinnati
OF— Barry Bonds, San Francisco
OF— Ellis Burks, Colorado
OF— Gary Sheffield, Florida
C— Mike Piazza, Los Angeles
P— Tom Glavine, Atlanta

1997
AMERICAN LEAGUE
1B— Tino Martinez, New York
2B— Chuck Knoblauch, Minnesota
3B— Matt Williams, Cleveland
SS— Nomar Garciaparra, Boston
OF— Juan Gonzalez, Texas
OF— Ken Griffey Jr., Seattle
OF— David Justice, Cleveland
C— Ivan Rodriguez, Texas
DH— Edgar Martinez, Seattle

NATIONAL LEAGUE
1B— Jeff Bagwell, Houston
2B— Craig Biggio, Houston
3B— Vinny Castilla, Colorado
SS— Jeff Blauser, Atlanta
OF— Barry Bonds, San Francisco
OF— Tony Gwynn, San Diego
OF— Larry Walker, Colorado
C— Mike Piazza, Los Angeles
P— John Smoltz, Atlanta

MAJOR LEAGUE ALL-STAR TEAMS

1925
1B— Jim Bottomley, St. Louis N.L.
2B— Rogers Hornsby, St. Louis N.L.
SS— Glenn Wright, Pittsburgh N.L.
3B— Pie Traynor, Pittsburgh N.L.
OF— Kiki Cuyler, Pittsburgh N.L.
OF— Max Carey, Pittsburgh N.L.
OF— Goose Goslin, Washington A.L.
C— Mickey Cochrane, Phil. A.L.
P— Walter Johnson, Washington A.L.
P— Ed Rommel, Philadelphia A.L.
P— Dazzy Vance, Brooklyn N.L.

1926
1B— George Burns, Cleveland A.L.
2B— Rogers Hornsby, St. Louis N.L.
SS— Joe Sewell, Cleveland A.L.
3B— Pie Traynor, Pittsburgh N.L.
OF— Goose Goslin, Washington A.L.
OF— John Mostil, Chicago A.L.
OF— Babe Ruth, New York A.L.
C— Bob O'Farrell, St. Louis N.L.
P— Herb Pennock, New York A.L.
P— George Uhle, Cleveland A.L.
P— Grover Alexander, St. Louis N.L.

1927
1B— Lou Gehrig, New York A.L.
2B— Rogers Hornsby, New York N.L.
SS— Travis Jackson, New York N.L.
3B— Pie Traynor, Pittsburgh N.L.
OF— Babe Ruth, New York A.L.
OF— Al Simmons, Philadelphia A.L.
OF— Paul Waner, Pittsburgh N.L.
C— Gabby Hartnett, Chicago N.L.
P— Charley Root, Chicago N.L.
P— Ted Lyons, Chicago A.L.

1928
1B— Lou Gehrig, New York A.L.
2B— Rogers Hornsby, Boston N.L.
SS— Travis Jackson, New York N.L.
3B— Fred Lindstrom, New York N.L.
OF— Babe Ruth, New York A.L.
OF— Heinie Manush, St. Louis A.L.
OF— Paul Waner, Pittsburgh N.L.
C— Mickey Cochrane, Phil. A.L.
P— Lefty Grove, Philadelphia A.L.
P— Waite Hoyt, New York A.L.

1929
1B— Jimmie Foxx, Philadelphia A.L.
2B— Rogers Hornsby, Chicago N.L.
SS— Travis Jackson, New York N.L.
3B— Pie Traynor, Pittsburgh, N.L.
OF— Al Simmons, Philadelphia A.L.
OF— Hack Wilson, Chicago N.L.
OF— Babe Ruth, New York A.L.
C— Mickey Cochrane, Phil. A.L.
P— Lefty Grove, Philadelphia A.L.
P— Burleigh Grimes, Pittsburgh N.L.

1930
1B— Bill Terry, New York N.L.
2B— Frank Frisch, St. Louis N.L.
SS— Joe Cronin, Washington A.L.
3B— Fred Lindstrom, New York N.L.
OF— Al Simmons, Philadelphia A.L.
OF— Hack Wilson, Chicago N.L.
OF— Babe Ruth, New York A.L.
C— Mickey Cochrane, Phil. A.L.
P— Lefty Grove, Philadelphia A.L.
P— Wes Ferrell, Cleveland A.L.

1931
1B— Lou Gehrig, New York A.L.
2B— Frank Frisch, St. Louis N.L.

SS— Joe Cronin, Washington A.L.
3B— Pie Traynor, Pittsburgh N.L.
OF— Al Simmons, Philadelphia A.L.
OF— Earl Averill, Cleveland A.L.
OF— Babe Ruth, New York A.L.
C— Mickey Cochrane, Phil. A.L.
P— Lefty Grove, Philadelphia A.L.
P— George Earnshaw, Phil. A.L.

1932
1B— Jimmie Foxx, Philadelphia A.L.
2B— Tony Lazzeri, New York A.L.
SS— Joe Cronin, Washington A.L.
3B— Pie Traynor, Pittsburgh N.L.
OF— Lefty O'Doul, Brooklyn N.L.
OF— Earl Averill, Cleveland A.L.
OF— Chuck Klein, Philadelphia N.L.
C— Bill Dickey, New York A.L.
P— Lefty Grove, Philadelphia A.L.
P— Lon Warneke, Chicago N.L.

1933
1B— Jimmie Foxx, Philadelphia A.L.
2B— Charley Gehringer, Detroit A.L.
SS— Joe Cronin, Washington A.L.
3B— Pie Traynor, Pittsburgh N.L.
OF— Al Simmons, Chicago A.L.
OF— Wally Berger, Boston N.L.
OF— Chuck Klein, Philadelphia N.L.
C— Bill Dickey, New York A.L.
P— Alvin Crowder, Washington A.L.
P— Carl Hubbell, New York N.L.

1934
1B— Lou Gehrig, New York A.L.
2B— Charley Gehringer, Detroit A.L.
SS— Joe Cronin, Washington A.L.
3B— Mike Higgins, Philadelphia A.L.

OF— Al Simmons, Chicago A.L.
OF— Earl Averill, Cleveland A.L.
OF— Mel Ott, New York N.L.
C— Mickey Cochrane, Detroit A.L.
P— Lefty Gomez, New York A.L.
P— Schoolboy Rowe, Detroit A.L.
P— Dizzy Dean, St. Louis N.L.

1935
1B— Hank Greenberg, Detroit A.L.
2B— Charley Gehringer, Detroit A.L.
SS— Arky Vaughan, Pittsburgh N.L.
3B— Pepper Martin, St. Louis N.L.
OF— Joe Medwick, St. Louis N.L.
OF— Doc Cramer, Philadelphia A.L.
OF— Mel Ott, New York N.L.
C— Mickey Cochrane, Detroit A.L.
P— Carl Hubbell, New York N.L.
P— Dizzy Dean, St. Louis N.L.

1936
1B— Lou Gehrig, New York A.L.
2B— Charley Gehringer, Detroit A.L.
SS— Luke Appling, Chicago A.L.
3B— Mike Higgins, Philadelphia A.L.
OF— Joe Medwick, St. Louis N.L.
OF— Earl Averill, Cleveland A.L.
OF— Mel Ott, New York N.L.
C— Bill Dickey, New York A.L.
P— Carl Hubbell, New York N.L.
P— Dizzy Dean, St. Louis N.L.

1937
1B— Lou Gehrig, New York A.L.
2B— Charley Gehringer, Detroit A.L.
SS— Dick Bartell, New York N.L.
3B— Red Rolfe, New York A.L.
OF— Joe Medwick, St. Louis N.L.
OF— Joe DiMaggio, New York A.L.
OF— Paul Waner, Pittsburgh N.L.
C— Gabby Hartnett, Chicago N.L.
P— Carl Hubbell, New York N.L.
P— Red Ruffing, New York A.L.

1938
1B— Jimmie Foxx, Boston A.L.
2B— Charley Gehringer, Detroit A.L.
SS— Joe Cronin, Boston A.L.
3B— Red Rolfe, New York A.L.
OF— Joe Medwick, St. Louis N.L.
OF— Joe DiMaggio, New York A.L.
OF— Mel Ott, New York N.L.
C— Bill Dickey, New York A.L.
P— Red Ruffing, New York A.L.
P— Lefty Gomez, New York A.L.
P— Johnny Vander Meer, Cin. N.L.

1939
1B— Jimmie Foxx, Boston A.L.
2B— Joe Gordon, New York A.L.
SS— Joe Cronin, Boston A.L.
3B— Red Rolfe, New York A.L.
OF— Joe Medwick, St. Louis N.L.
OF— Joe DiMaggio, New York A.L.
OF— Ted Williams, Boston A.L.
C— Bill Dickey, New York A.L.
P— Red Ruffing, New York A.L.
P— Bob Feller, Cleveland A.L.
P— Bucky Walters, Cincinnati N.L.

1940
1B— Frank McCormick, Cincinnati N.L.
2B— Joe Gordon, New York A.L.
SS— Luke Appling, Chicago A.L.
3B— Stan Hack, Chicago N.L.
OF— Hank Greenberg, Detroit A.L.
OF— Joe DiMaggio, New York A.L.
OF— Ted Williams, Boston A.L.
C— Harry Danning, New York N.L.
P— Bob Feller, Cleveland A.L.
P— Bucky Walters, Cincinnati N.L.
P— Paul Derringer, Cincinnati N.L.

1941
1B— Dolf Camilli, Brooklyn N.L.
2B— Joe Gordon, New York A.L.
SS— Cecil Travis, Washington A.L.
3B— Stan Hack, Chicago N.L.
OF— Ted Williams, Boston A.L.
OF— Joe DiMaggio, New York A.L.
OF— Pete Reiser, Brooklyn N.L.
C— Bill Dickey, New York A.L.
P— Bob Feller, Cleveland A.L.
P— Whitlow Wyatt, Brooklyn N.L.
P— Thornton Lee, Chicago A.L.

1942
1B— Johnny Mize, New York N.L.
2B— Joe Gordon, New York A.L.
SS— Johnny Pesky, Boston A.L.
3B— Stan Hack, Chicago N.L.
OF— Ted Williams, Boston A.L.
OF— Joe DiMaggio, New York A.L.
OF— Enos Slaughter, St. Louis N.L.
C— Mickey Owen, Brooklyn N.L.
P— Mort Cooper, St. Louis N.L.
P— Tiny Bonham, New York A.L.
P— Tex Hughson, Boston A.L.

1943
1B— Rudy York, Detroit A.L.
2B— Billy Herman, Brooklyn N.L.
SS— Luke Appling, Chicago A.L.
3B— Billy Johnson, New York A.L.
OF— Dick Wakefield, Detroit A.L.
OF— Stan Musial, St. Louis N.L.
OF— Bill Nicholson, Chicago N.L.
C— Walker Cooper, St. Louis N.L.
P— Spud Chandler, New York A.L.
P— Mort Cooper, St. Louis N.L.
P— Rip Sewell, Pittsburgh N.L.

1944
1B— Ray Sanders, St. Louis N.L.
2B— Bobby Doerr, Boston A.L.
SS— Marty Marion, St. Louis N.L.
3B— Bob Elliott, Pittsburgh N.L.
OF— Stan Musial, St. Louis N.L.
OF— Dick Wakefield, Detroit A.L.
OF— Dixie Walker, Brooklyn, N.L.
C— Walker Cooper, St. Louis N.L.
P— Hal Newhouser, Detroit A.L.
P— Mort Cooper, St. Louis N.L.
P— Dizzy Trout, Detroit A.L.

1945
1B— Phil Cavarretta, Chicago N.L.
2B— George Stirnweiss, N.Y. A.L.
SS— Marty Marion, St. Louis N.L.
3B— Whitey Kurowski, St. Louis N.L.
OF— Tommy Holmes, Boston N.L.
OF— Andy Pafko, Chicago N.L.
OF— Goody Rosen, Brooklyn N.L.
C— Paul Richards, Detroit A.L.
P— Hal Newhouser, Detroit A.L.
P— Boo Ferriss, Boston A.L.
P— Hank Borowy, Chicago N.L.

1946
1B— Stan Musial, St. Louis N.L.
2B— Bobby Doerr, Boston A.L.
SS— Johnny Pesky, Boston A.L.
3B— George Kell, Detroit A.L.
OF— Ted Williams, Boston A.L.
OF— Dom DiMaggio, Boston A.L.
OF— Enos Slaughter, St. Louis N.L.
C— Aaron Robinson, New York A.L.
P— Hal Newhouser, Detroit A.L.
P— Bob Feller, Cleveland A.L.
P— Boo Ferriss, Boston A.L.

1947
1B— Johnny Mize, New York N.L.
2B— Joe Gordon, Cleveland A.L.

SS— Lou Boudreau, Cleveland A.L.
3B— George Kell, Detroit A.L.
OF— Ted Williams, Boston A.L.
OF— Joe DiMaggio, New York A.L.
OF— Ralph Kiner, Pittsburgh N.L.
C— Walker Cooper, New York N.L.
P— Ewell Blackwell, Cincinnati N.L.
P— Bob Feller, Cleveland A.L.
P— Ralph Branca, Brooklyn N.L.

1948
1B— Johnny Mize, New York N.L.
2B— Joe Gordon, Cleveland A.L.
SS— Lou Boudreau, Cleveland A.L.
3B— Bob Elliott, Boston N.L.
OF— Ted Williams, Boston A.L.
OF— Joe DiMaggio, New York A.L.
OF— Stan Musial, St. Louis N.L.
C— Birdie Tebbetts, Boston A.L.
P— Johnny Sain, Boston N.L.
P— Bob Lemon, Cleveland A.L.
P— Harry Brecheen, St. Louis N.L.

1949
1B— Tommy Henrich, New York A.L.
2B— Jackie Robinson, Brooklyn N.L.
SS— Phil Rizzuto, New York A.L.
3B— George Kell, Detroit A.L.
OF— Ted Williams, Boston A.L.
OF— Stan Musial, St. Louis N.L.
OF— Ralph Kiner, Pittsburgh N.L.
C— Roy Campanella, Brooklyn N.L.
P— Mel Parnell, Boston A.L.
P— Ellis Kinder, Boston A.L.
P— Joe Page, New York A.L.

1950
1B— Walt Dropo, Boston A.L.
2B— Jackie Robinson, Brooklyn N.L.
SS— Phil Rizzuto, New York A.L.
3B— George Kell, Detroit A.L.
OF— Stan Musial, St. Louis N.L.
OF— Ralph Kiner, Pittsburgh N.L.
OF— Larry Doby, Cleveland A.L.
C— Yogi Berra, New York A.L.
P— Vic Raschi, New York A.L.
P— Bob Lemon, Cleveland A.L.
P— Jim Konstanty, Phil. N.L.

1951
1B— Ferris Fain, Philadelphia A.L.
2B— Jackie Robinson, Brooklyn N.L.
SS— Phil Rizzuto, New York A.L.
3B— George Kell, Detroit A.L.
OF— Stan Musial, St. Louis N.L.
OF— Ted Williams, Boston A.L.
OF— Ralph Kiner, Pittsburgh N.L.
C— Roy Campanella, Brooklyn N.L.
P— Sal Maglie, New York N.L.
P— Preacher Roe, Brooklyn N.L.
P— Allie Reynolds, New York A.L.

1952
1B— Ferris Fain, Philadelphia A.L.
2B— Jackie Robinson, Brooklyn N.L.
SS— Phil Rizzuto, New York A.L.
3B— George Kell, Boston A.L.
OF— Stan Musial, St. Louis N.L.
OF— Hank Sauer, Chicago N.L.
OF— Mickey Mantle, New York A.L.
C— Yogi Berra, New York A.L.
P— Robin Roberts, Philadelphia N.L.
P— Bobby Shantz, Philadelphia A.L.
P— Allie Reynolds, New York A.L.

1953
1B— Mickey Vernon, Washington A.L.
2B— Red Schoendienst, St. Louis N.L.
SS— Pee Wee Reese, Brooklyn N.L.
3B— Al Rosen, Cleveland A.L.
OF— Stan Musial, St. Louis N.L.

OF— Duke Snider, Brooklyn N.L.
OF— Carl Furillo, Brooklyn N.L.
C— Roy Campanella, Brooklyn N.L.
P— Robin Roberts, Philadelphia N.L.
P— Warren Spahn, Milwaukee N.L.
P— Bob Porterfield, Washington A.L.

1954
1B— Ted Kluszewski, Cincinnati N.L.
2B— Bobby Avila, Cleveland A.L.
SS— Alvin Dark, New York N.L.
3B— Al Rosen, Cleveland A.L.
OF— Willie Mays, New York N.L.
OF— Stan Musial, St. Louis N.L.
OF— Duke Snider, Brooklyn N.L.
C— Yogi Berra, New York A.L.
P— Bob Lemon, Cleveland A.L.
P— Johnny Antonelli, New York N.L.
P— Robin Roberts, Philadelphia N.L.

1955
1B— Ted Kluszewski, Cincinnati N.L.
2B— Nellie Fox, Chicago A.L.
SS— Ernie Banks, Chicago N.L.
3B— Ed Mathews, Milwaukee N.L.
OF— Duke Snider, Brooklyn N.L.
OF— Ted Williams, Boston A.L.
OF— Al Kaline, Detroit A.L.
C— Roy Campanella, Brooklyn N.L.
P— Robin Roberts, Philadelphia N.L.
P— Don Newcombe, Brooklyn N.L.
P— Whitey Ford, New York A.L.

1956
1B— Ted Kluszewski, Cincinnati N.L.
2B— Nellie Fox, Chicago A.L.
SS— Harvey Kuenn, Detroit A.L.
3B— Ken Boyer, St. Louis N.L.
OF— Mickey Mantle, New York A.L.
OF— Hank Aaron, Milwaukee N.L.
OF— Ted Williams, Boston A.L.
C— Yogi Berra, New York A.L.
P— Don Newcombe, Brooklyn N.L.
P— Whitey Ford, New York A.L.
P— Billy Pierce, Chicago A.L.

1957
1B— Stan Musial, St. Louis N.L.
2B— Red Schoendienst, N.Y.-Mil. N.L.
SS— Gil McDougald, New York A.L.
3B— Ed Mathews, Milwaukee N.L.
OF— Mickey Mantle, New York A.L.
OF— Ted Williams, Boston A.L.
OF— Willie Mays, New York N.L.
C— Yogi Berra, New York A.L.
P— Warren Spahn, Milwaukee N.L.
P— Billy Pierce, Chicago N.L.
P— Jim Bunning, Detroit A.L.

1958
1B— Stan Musial, St. Louis N.L.
2B— Nellie Fox, Chicago A.L.
SS— Ernie Banks, Chicago N.L.
3B— Frank Thomas, Pittsburgh N.L.
OF— Ted Williams, Boston A.L.
OF— Willie Mays, San Francisco N.L.
OF— Hank Aaron, Milwaukee N.L.
C— Del Crandall, Milwaukee N.L.
P— Bob Turley, New York A.L.
P— Warren Spahn, Milwaukee N.L.
P— Bob Friend, Pittsburgh N.L.

1959
1B— Orlando Cepeda, S.F. N.L.
2B— Nellie Fox, Chicago A.L.
SS— Ernie Banks, Chicago N.L.
3B— Ed Mathews, Milwaukee N.L.
OF— Minnie Minoso, Cleveland A.L.
OF— Willie Mays, San Francisco N.L.
OF— Hank Aaron, Milwaukee N.L.

C— Sherm Lollar, Chicago A.L.
P— Early Wynn, Chicago A.L.
P— Sam Jones, San Francisco N.L.
P— Johnny Antonelli, S.F. N.L.

1960
1B— Bill Skowron, New York A.L.
2B— Bill Mazeroski, Pittsburgh N.L.
SS— Ernie Banks, Chicago N.L.
3B— Ed Mathews, Milwaukee N.L.
OF— Minnie Minoso, Chicago A.L.
OF— Willie Mays, San Francisco N.L.
OF— Roger Maris, New York A.L.
C— Del Crandall, Milwaukee N.L.
P— Vernon Law, Pittsburgh N.L.
P— Warren Spahn, Milwaukee N.L.
P— Ernie Broglio, St. Louis N.L.

1961
AMERICAN LEAGUE
1B— Norm Cash, Detroit
2B— Bobby Richardson, New York
SS— Tony Kubek, New York
3B— Brooks Robinson, Baltimore
OF— Mickey Mantle, New York
OF— Roger Maris, New York
OF— Rocky Colavito, Detroit
C— Elston Howard, New York
P— Whitey Ford, New York
P— Frank Lary, Detroit

NATIONAL LEAGUE
1B— Orlando Cepeda, San Francisco
2B— Frank Bolling, Milwaukee
SS— Maury Wills, Los Angeles
3B— Ken Boyer, St. Louis
OF— Willie Mays, San Francisco
OF— Frank Robinson, Cincinnati
OF— Roberto Clemente, Pittsburgh
C— Smoky Burgess, Pittsburgh
P— Joey Jay, Cincinnati
P— Warren Spahn, Milwaukee

1962
AMERICAN LEAGUE
1B— Norm Siebern, Kansas City
2B— Bobby Richardson, New York
SS— Tom Tresh, New York
3B— Brooks Robinson, Baltimore
OF— Leon Wagner, Los Angeles
OF— Mickey Mantle, New York
OF— Al Kaline, Detroit
C— Earl Battey, Minnesota
P— Ralph Terry, New York
P— Dick Donovan, Cleveland

NATIONAL LEAGUE
1B— Orlando Cepeda, San Francisco
2B— Bill Mazeroski, Pittsburgh
SS— Maury Wills, Los Angeles
3B— Ken Boyer, St. Louis
OF— Tommy Davis, Los Angeles
OF— Willie Mays, San Francisco
OF— Frank Robinson, Cincinnati
C— Del Crandall, Milwaukee
P— Don Drysdale, Los Angeles
P— Bob Purkey, Cincinnati

1963
AMERICAN LEAGUE
1B— Joe Pepitone, New York
2B— Bobby Richardson, New York
SS— Luis Aparicio, Baltimore
3B— Frank Malzone, Boston
OF— Carl Yastrzemski, Boston
OF— Albie Pearson, Los Angeles
OF— Al Kaline, Detroit
C— Elston Howard, New York
P— Whitey Ford, New York
P— Gary Peters, Chicago

NATIONAL LEAGUE
1B— Bill White, St. Louis
2B— Jim Gilliam, Los Angeles
SS— Dick Groat, St. Louis
3B— Ken Boyer, St. Louis
OF— Tommy Davis, Los Angeles
OF— Willie Mays, San Francisco
OF— Hank Aaron, Milwaukee
C— John Edwards, Cincinnati
P— Sandy Koufax, Los Angeles
P— Juan Marichal, San Francisco

1964
AMERICAN LEAGUE
1B— Dick Stuart, Boston
2B— Bobby Richardson, New York
SS— Jim Fregosi, Los Angeles
3B— Brooks Robinson, Baltimore
OF— Harmon Killebrew, Minnesota
OF— Mickey Mantle, New York
OF— Tony Oliva, Minnesota
C— Elston Howard, New York
P— Dean Chance, Los Angeles
P— Gary Peters, Chicago

NATIONAL LEAGUE
1B— Bill White, St. Louis
2B— Ron Hunt, New York
SS— Dick Groat, St. Louis
3B— Ken Boyer, St. Louis
OF— Billy Williams, Chicago
OF— Willie Mays, San Francisco
OF— Roberto Clemente, Pittsburgh
C— Joe Torre, Milwaukee
P— Sandy Koufax, Los Angeles
P— Jim Bunning, Philadelphia

1965
AMERICAN LEAGUE
1B— Fred Whitfield, Cleveland
2B— Bobby Richardson, New York
SS— Zoilo Versalles, Minnesota
3B— Brooks Robinson, Baltimore
OF— Carl Yastrzemski, Boston
OF— Jimmie Hall, Minnesota
OF— Tony Oliva, Minnesota
C— Earl Battey, Minnesota
P— Jim Grant, Minnesota
P— Mel Stottlemyre, New York

NATIONAL LEAGUE
1B— Willie McCovey, San Francisco
2B— Pete Rose, Cincinnati
SS— Maury Wills, Los Angeles
3B— Deron Johnson, Cincinnati
OF— Willie Stargell, Pittsburgh
OF— Willie Mays, San Francisco
OF— Hank Aaron, Milwaukee
C— Joe Torre, Milwaukee
P— Sandy Koufax, Los Angeles
P— Juan Marichal, San Francisco

1966
AMERICAN LEAGUE
1B— Boog Powell, Baltimore
2B— Bobby Richardson, New York
SS— Luis Aparicio, Baltimore
3B— Brooks Robinson, Baltimore
OF— Frank Robinson, Baltimore
OF— Al Kaline, Detroit
OF— Tony Oliva, Minnesota
C— Paul Casanova, Washington
P— Jim Kaat, Minnesota
P— Earl Wilson, Detroit

NATIONAL LEAGUE
1B— Felipe Alou, Atlanta
2B— Pete Rose, Cincinnati
SS— Gene Alley, Pittsburgh
3B— Ron Santo, Chicago
OF— Willie Stargell, Pittsburgh

OF— Willie Mays, San Francisco
OF— Roberto Clemente, Pittsburgh
C— Joe Torre, Atlanta
P— Sandy Koufax, Los Angeles
P— Juan Marichal, San Francisco

1967
AMERICAN LEAGUE
1B— Harmon Killebrew, Minnesota
2B— Rod Carew, Minnesota
SS— Jim Fregosi, California
3B— Brooks Robinson, Baltimore
OF— Carl Yastrzemski, Boston
OF— Al Kaline, Detroit
OF— Frank Robinson, Baltimore
C— Bill Freehan, Detroit
P— Jim Lonborg, Boston
P— Earl Wilson, Detroit

NATIONAL LEAGUE
1B— Orlando Cepeda, St. Louis
2B— Bill Mazeroski, Pittsburgh
SS— Gene Alley, Pittsburgh
3B— Ron Santo, Chicago
OF— Hank Aaron, Atlanta
OF— Jim Wynn, Houston
OF— Roberto Clemente, Pittsburgh
C— Tim McCarver, St. Louis
P— Mike McCormick, San Francisco
P— Ferguson Jenkins, Chicago

1968
AMERICAN LEAGUE
1B— Boog Powell, Baltimore
2B— Rod Carew, Minnesota
SS— Luis Aparicio, Chicago
3B— Brooks Robinson, Baltimore
OF— Ken Harrelson, Boston
OF— Willie Horton, Detroit
OF— Frank Howard, Washington
C— Bill Freehan, Detroit
P— Dave McNally, Baltimore
P— Denny McLain, Detroit

NATIONAL LEAGUE
1B— Willie McCovey, San Francisco
2B— Tommy Helms, Cincinnati
SS— Don Kessinger, Chicago
3B— Ron Santo, Chicago
OF— Billy Williams, Chicago
OF— Curt Flood, St. Louis
OF— Pete Rose, Cincinnati
C— Johnny Bench, Cincinnati
P— Bob Gibson, St. Louis
P— Juan Marichal, San Francisco

1969
AMERICAN LEAGUE
1B— Boog Powell, Baltimore
2B— Rod Carew, Minnesota
SS— Rico Petrocelli, Boston
3B— Harmon Killebrew, Minnesota
OF— Frank Howard, Washington
OF— Paul Blair, Baltimore
OF— Reggie Jackson, Oakland
C— Bill Freehan, Detroit
RHP— Denny McLain, Detroit
LHP— Mike Cuellar, Baltimore

NATIONAL LEAGUE
1B— Willie McCovey, San Francisco
2B— Glenn Beckert, Chicago
SS— Don Kessinger, Chicago
3B— Ron Santo, Chicago
OF— Cleon Jones, New York
OF— Matty Alou, Pittsburgh
OF— Hank Aaron, Atlanta
C— Johnny Bench, Cincinnati
RHP— Tom Seaver, New York
LHP— Steve Carlton, St. Louis

1970
AMERICAN LEAGUE
1B— Boog Powell, Baltimore
2B— Dave Johnson, Baltimore
SS— Luis Aparicio, Chicago
3B— Harmon Killebrew, Minnesota
OF— Frank Howard, Washington
OF— Reggie Smith, Boston
OF— Tony Oliva, Minnesota
C— Ray Fosse, Cleveland
RHP— Jim Perry, Minnesota
LHP— Sam McDowell, Cleveland

NATIONAL LEAGUE
1B— Willie McCovey, San Francisco
2B— Glenn Beckert, Chicago
SS— Don Kessinger, Chicago
3B— Tony Perez, Cincinnati
OF— Billy Williams, Chicago
OF— Bobby Tolan, Cincinnati
OF— Hank Aaron, Atlanta
C— Johnny Bench, Cincinnati
RHP— Bob Gibson, St. Louis
LHP— Jim Merritt, Cincinnati

1971
AMERICAN LEAGUE
1B— Norm Cash, Detroit
2B— Cookie Rojas, Kansas City
SS— Leo Cardenas, Minnesota
3B— Brooks Robinson, Baltimore
OF— Merv Rettenmund, Baltimore
OF— Bobby Murcer, New York
OF— Tony Oliva, Minnesota
C— Bill Freehan, Detroit
RHP— Jim Palmer, Baltimore
LHP— Vida Blue, Oakland

NATIONAL LEAGUE
1B— Lee May, Cincinnati
2B— Glenn Beckett, Chicago
SS— Bud Harrelson, New York
3B— Joe Torre, St. Louis
OF— Willie Stargell, Pittsburgh
OF— Willie Davis, Los Angeles
OF— Hank Aaron, Atlanta
C— Manny Sanguillen, Pittsburgh
RHP— Ferguson Jenkins, Chicago
LHP— Steve Carlton, St. Louis

1972
AMERICAN LEAGUE
1B— Dick Allen, Chicago
2B— Rod Carew, Minnesota
SS— Luis Aparicio, Boston
3B— Brooks Robinson, Baltimore
OF— Joe Rudi, Oakland
OF— Bobby Murcer, New York
OF— Richie Scheinblum, Kansas City
C— Carlton Fisk, Boston
RHP— Gaylord Perry, Cleveland
LHP— Wilbur Wood, Chicago

NATIONAL LEAGUE
1B— Willie Stargell, Pittsburgh
2B— Joe Morgan, Cincinnati
SS— Chris Speier, San Francisco
3B— Ron Santo, Chicago
OF— Billy Williams, Chicago
OF— Cesar Cedeno, Houston
OF— Roberto Clemente, Pittsburgh
C— Johnny Bench, Cincinnati
RHP— Ferguson Jenkins, Chicago
LHP— Steve Carlton, Philadelphia

1973
AMERICAN LEAGUE
1B— John Mayberry, Kansas City
2B— Rod Carew, Minnesota
SS— Bert Campaneris, Oakland

3B— Sal Bando, Oakland
OF— Reggie Jackson, Oakland
OF— Amos Otis, Kansas City
OF— Bobby Murcer, New York
C— Thurman Munson, New York
RHP— Jim Palmer, Baltimore
LHP— Ken Holtzman, Oakland

NATIONAL LEAGUE
1B— Tony Perez, Cincinnati
2B— Dave Johnson, Atlanta
SS— Bill Russell, Los Angeles
3B— Darrell Evans, Atlanta
OF— Bobby Bonds, San Francisco
OF— Cesar Cedeno, Houston
OF— Pete Rose, Cincinnati
C— Johnny Bench, Cincinnati
RHP— Tom Seaver, New York
LHP— Ron Bryant, San Francisco

1974
AMERICAN LEAGUE
1B— Dick Allen, Chicago
2B— Rod Carew, Minnesota
SS— Bert Campaneris, Oakland
3B— Sal Bando, Oakland
OF— Joe Rudi, Oakland
OF— Paul Blair, Baltimore
OF— Jeff Burroughs, Texas
C— Thurman Munson, New York
DH— Tommy Davis, Baltimore
RHP— Jim Hunter, Oakland
LHP— Mike Cuellar, Baltimore

NATIONAL LEAGUE
1B— Steve Garvey, Los Angeles
2B— Joe Morgan, Cincinnati
SS— Dave Concepcion, Cincinnati
3B— Mike Schmidt, Philadelphia
OF— Lou Brock, St. Louis
OF— Jim Wynn, Los Angeles
OF— Richie Zisk, Pittsburgh
C— Johnny Bench, Cincinnati
RHP— Andy Messersmith, Los Angeles
LHP— Don Gullett, Cincinnati

1975
AMERICAN LEAGUE
1B— John Mayberry, Kansas City
2B— Rod Carew, Minnesota
SS— Toby Harrah, Texas
3B— Graig Nettles, New York
OF— Jim Rice, Boston
OF— Fred Lynn, Boston
OF— Reggie Jackson, Oakland
C— Thurman Munson, New York
DH— Willie Horton, Detroit
RHP— Jim Palmer, Baltimore
LHP— Jim Kaat, Chicago

NATIONAL LEAGUE
1B— Steve Garvey, Los Angeles
2B— Joe Morgan, Cincinnati
SS— Larry Bowa, Philadelphia
3B— Bill Madlock, Chicago
OF— Greg Luzinski, Philadelphia
OF— Al Oliver, Pittsburgh
OF— Dave Parker, Pittsburgh
C— Johnny Bench, Cincinnati
RHP— Tom Seaver, New York
LHP— Randy Jones, San Diego

1976
AMERICAN LEAGUE
1B— Chris Chambliss, New York
2B— Bobby Grich, Baltimore
3B— George Brett, Kansas City
SS— Mark Belanger, Baltimore
OF— Joe Rudi, Oakland
OF— Mickey Rivers, New York
OF— Reggie Jackson, Baltimore

C— Thurman Munson, New York
DH— Hal McRae, Kansas City
RHP— Jim Palmer, Baltimore
LHP— Frank Tanana, California

NATIONAL LEAGUE
1B— Willie Montanez, S.F.-Atl.
2B— Joe Morgan, Cincinnati
3B— Mike Schmidt, Philadelphia
SS— Dave Concepcion, Cincinnati
OF— George Foster, Cincinnati
OF— Cesar Cedeno, Houston
OF— Ken Griffey, Cincinnati
C— Bob Boone, Philadelphia
RHP— Don Sutton, Los Angeles
LHP— Randy Jones, San Diego

1977
AMERICAN LEAGUE
1B— Rod Carew, Minnesota
2B— Willie Randolph, New York
3B— Graig Nettles, New York
SS— Rick Burleson, Boston
OF— Jim Rice, Boston
OF— Larry Hisle, Minnesota
OF— Bobby Bonds, California
C— Carlton Fisk, Boston
DH— Hal McRae, Kansas City
RHP— Nolan Ryan, California
LHP— Frank Tanana, California

NATIONAL LEAGUE
1B— Steve Garvey, Los Angeles
2B— Joe Morgan, Cincinnati
3B— Mike Schmidt, Philadelphia
SS— Garry Templeton, St. Louis
OF— George Foster, Cincinnati
OF— Dave Parker, Pittsburgh
OF— Greg Luzinski, Philadelphia
C— Ted Simmons, St. Louis
RHP— Rick Reuschel, Chicago
LHP— Steve Carlton, Philadelphia

1978
AMERICAN LEAGUE
1B— Rod Carew, Minnesota
2B— Frank White, Kansas City
3B— Graig Nettles, New York
SS— Robin Yount, Milwaukee
OF— Jim Rice, Boston
OF— Larry Hisle, Milwaukee
OF— Fred Lynn, Boston
C— Jim Sundberg, Texas
DH— Rusty Staub, Detroit
RHP— Jim Palmer, Baltimore
LHP— Ron Guidry, New York

NATIONAL LEAGUE
1B— Steve Garvey, Los Angeles
2B— Dave Lopes, Los Angeles
3B— Pete Rose, Cincinnati
SS— Larry Bowa, Philadelphia
OF— George Foster, Cincinnati
OF— Dave Parker, Pittsburgh
OF— Jack Clark, San Francisco
C— Ted Simmons, St. Louis
RHP— Gaylord Perry, San Diego
LHP— Vida Blue, San Francisco

1979
AMERICAN LEAGUE
1B— Cecil Cooper, Milwaukee
2B— Bobby Grich, California
3B— George Brett, Kansas City
SS— Roy Smalley, Minnesota
OF— Jim Rice, Boston
OF— Fred Lynn, Boston
OF— Ken Singleton, Baltimore
C— Darrell Porter, Kansas City
DH— Don Baylor, California

RHP— Jim Kern, Texas
LHP— Mike Flanagan, Baltimore

NATIONAL LEAGUE
1B— Keith Hernandez, St. Louis
2B— Dave Lopes, Los Angeles
3B— Mike Schmidt, Philadelphia
SS— Garry Templeton, St. Louis
OF— Dave Kingman, Chicago
OF— Omar Moreno, Pittsburgh
OF— Dave Winfield, San Diego
C— Ted Simmons, St. Louis
RHP— Joe Niekro, Houston
LHP— Steve Carlton, Philadelphia

1980
AMERICAN LEAGUE
1B— Cecil Cooper, Milwaukee
2B— Willie Randolph, New York
3B— George Brett, Kansas City
SS— Robin Yount, Milwaukee
OF— Ben Oglivie, Milwaukee
OF— Al Bumbry, Baltimore
OF— Reggie Jackson, New York
DH— Reggie Jackson, New York
C— Rick Cerone, New York
RHP— Steve Stone, Baltimore
LHP— Tommy John, New York

NATIONAL LEAGUE
1B— Keith Hernandez, St. Louis
2B— Manny Trillo, Philadelphia
3B— Mike Schmidt, Philadelphia
SS— Garry Templeton, St. Louis
OF— Dusty Baker, Los Angeles
OF— Cesar Cedeno, Houston
OF— George Hendrick, St. Louis
C— Gary Carter, Montreal
RHP— Jim Bibby, Pittsburgh
LHP— Steve Carlton, Philadelphia

1981
AMERICAN LEAGUE
1B— Cecil Cooper, Milwaukee
2B— Bobby Grich, California
3B— Buddy Bell, Texas
SS— Rick Burleson, California
OF— Rickey Henderson, Oakland
OF— Dwayne Murphy, Oakland
OF— Tony Armas, Oakland
C— Jim Sundberg, Texas
DH— Richie Zisk, Seattle
RHP— Jack Morris, Detroit
LHP— Ron Guidry, New York

NATIONAL LEAGUE
1B— Pete Rose, Philadelphia
2B— Manny Trillo, Philadelphia
3B— Mike Schmidt, Philadelphia
SS— Dave Concepcion, Cincinnati
OF— George Foster, Cincinnati
OF— Andre Dawson, Montreal
OF— Pedro Guerrero, Los Angeles
C— Gary Carter, Montreal
RHP— Tom Seaver, Cincinnati
LHP— Fernando Valenzuela, Los Angeles

1982
AMERICAN LEAGUE
1B— Cecil Cooper, Milwaukee
2B— Damaso Garcia, Toronto
3B— Doug DeCinces, California
SS— Robin Yount, Milwaukee
OF— Dave Winfield, New York
OF— Gorman Thomas, Milwaukee
OF— Dwight Evans, Boston
C— Lance Parrish, Detroit
DH— Hal McRae, Kansas City
RHP— Dave Stieb, Toronto
LHP— Geoff Zahn, California

NATIONAL LEAGUE
1B— Al Oliver, Montreal
2B— Manny Trillo, Philadelphia
3B— Mike Schmidt, Philadelphia
SS— Ozzie Smith, St. Louis
OF— Lonnie Smith, St. Louis
OF— Dale Murphy, Atlanta
OF— Pedro Guerrero, Los Angeles
C— Gary Carter, Montreal
RHP— Steve Rogers, Montreal
LHP— Steve Carlton, Philadelphia

1983
AMERICAN LEAGUE
1B— Eddie Murray, Baltimore
2B— Lou Whitaker, Detroit
3B— Wade Boggs, Boston
SS— Cal Ripken, Baltimore
OF— Jim Rice, Boston
OF— Dave Winfield, New York
OF— Lloyd Moseby, Toronto
C— Carlton Fisk, Chicago
DH— Greg Luzinski, Chicago
RHP— LaMarr Hoyt, Chicago
LHP— Ron Guidry, New York

NATIONAL LEAGUE
1B— George Hendrick, St. Louis
2B— Glenn Hubbard, Atlanta
3B— Mike Schmidt, Philadelphia
SS— Dickie Thon, Houston
OF— Dale Murphy, Atlanta
OF— Andre Dawson, Montreal
OF— Tim Raines, Montreal
C— Tony Pena, Pittsburgh
RHP— John Denny, Philadelphia
LHP— Larry McWilliams, Pittsburgh

1984
AMERICAN LEAGUE
1B— Don Mattingly, New York
2B— Lou Whitaker, Detroit
3B— Buddy Bell, Texas
SS— Cal Ripken, Baltimore
OF— Tony Armas, Boston
OF— Dwight Evans, Boston
OF— Dave Winfield, New York
C— Lance Parrish, Detroit
DH— Dave Kingman, Oakland
RHP— Mike Boddicker, Baltimore
LHP— Willie Hernandez, Detroit

NATIONAL LEAGUE
1B— Keith Hernandez, New York
2B— Ryne Sandberg, Chicago
3B— Mike Schmidt, Philadelphia
SS— Ozzie Smith, St. Louis
OF— Dale Murphy, Atlanta
OF— Jose Cruz, Houston
OF— Tony Gwynn, San Diego
C— Gary Carter, Montreal
RHP— Rick Sutcliffe, Chicago
LHP— Mark Thurmond, San Diego

1985
AMERICAN LEAGUE
1B— Don Mattingly, New York
2B— Damaso Garcia, Toronto
3B— Wade Boggs, Boston
SS— Cal Ripken, Baltimore
OF— Rickey Henderson, New York
OF— Harold Baines, Chicago
OF— Phil Bradley, Seattle
C— Carlton Fisk, Chicago
DH— Don Baylor, New York
RHP— Bret Saberhagen, Kansas City
LHP— Ron Guidry, New York

NATIONAL LEAGUE
1B— Keith Hernandez, New York
2B— Tom Herr, St. Louis

3B— Tim Wallach, Montreal
SS— Ozzie Smith, St. Louis
OF— Dave Parker, Cincinnati
OF— Willie McGee, St. Louis
OF— Dale Murphy, Atlanta
C— Gary Carter, New York
RHP— Dwight Gooden, New York
LHP— John Tudor, St. Louis

1986
AMERICAN LEAGUE
1B— Don Mattingly, New York
2B— Tony Bernazard, Cleveland
3B— Wade Boggs, Boston
SS— Tony Fernandez, Toronto
OF— Jim Rice, Boston
OF— George Bell, Toronto
OF— Kirby Puckett, Minnesota
C— Rich Gedman, Boston
DH— Don Baylor, Boston
RHP— Roger Clemens, Boston
LHP— Teddy Higuera, Milwaukee

NATIONAL LEAGUE
1B— Keith Hernandez, New York
2B— Steve Sax, Los Angeles
3B— Mike Schmidt, Philadelphia
SS— Ozzie Smith, St. Louis
OF— Tim Raines, Montreal
OF— Tony Gwynn, San Diego
OF— Dave Parker, Cincinnati
C— Gary Carter, New York
RHP— Mike Scott, Houston
LHP— Fernando Valenzuela, Los Angeles

1987
AMERICAN LEAGUE
1B— Don Mattingly, New York
2B— Willie Randolph, New York
3B— Wade Boggs, Boston
SS— Alan Trammell, Detroit
OF— George Bell, Toronto
OF— Kirby Puckett, Minnesota
OF— Dwight Evans, Boston
C— Matt Nokes, Detroit
DH— Paul Molitor, Milwaukee
RHP— Roger Clemens, Boston
LHP— Jimmy Key, Toronto

NATIONAL LEAGUE
1B— Jack Clark, St. Louis
2B— Juan Samuel, Philadelphia
3B— Tim Wallach, Montreal
SS— Ozzie Smith, St. Louis
OF— Andre Dawson, Chicago
OF— Tony Gwynn, San Diego
OF— Eric Davis, Cincinnati
C— Benito Santiago, San Diego
RHP— Rick Sutcliffe, Chicago
LHP— Zane Smith, Atlanta

1988
AMERICAN LEAGUE
1B— George Brett, Kansas City
2B— Johnny Ray, California
3B— Wade Boggs, Boston
SS— Alan Trammell, Detroit
OF— Kirby Puckett, Minnesota
OF— Mike Greenwell, Boston
OF— Jose Canseco, Oakland
C— Ernie Whitt, Toronto
DH— Harold Baines, Chicago
RHP— Dave Stewart, Oakland
LHP— Frank Viola, Minnesota

NATIONAL LEAGUE
1B— Will Clark, San Francisco
2B— Ryne Sandberg, Chicago
3B— Bobby Bonilla, Pittsburgh
SS— Barry Larkin, Cincinnati

OF— Darryl Strawberry, New York
OF— Andy Van Slyke, Pittsburgh
OF— Kevin McReynolds, New York
C— Mike LaValliere, Pittsburgh
RHP— Orel Hershiser, Los Angeles
LHP— Danny Jackson, Cincinnati

1989
AMERICAN LEAGUE
1B— Fred McGriff, Toronto
2B— Julio Franco, Texas
3B— Carney Lansford, Oakland
SS— Cal Ripken, Baltimore
OF— Ruben Sierra, Texas
OF— Kirby Puckett, Minnesota
OF— Robin Yount, Milwaukee
C— Mickey Tettleton, Baltimore
DH— Harold Baines, Chi.-Tex.
RHP— Bret Saberhagen, Kansas City
LHP— Chuck Finley, California

NATIONAL LEAGUE
1B— Will Clark, San Francisco
2B— Ryne Sandberg, Chicago
3B— Howard Johnson, New York
SS— Shawon Dunston, Chicago
OF— Tony Gwynn, San Diego
OF— Kevin Mitchell, San Francisco
OF— Eric Davis, Cincinnati
C— Benito Santiago, San Diego
RHP— Mike Scott, Houston
LHP— Mark Davis, San Diego

1990
AMERICAN LEAGUE
1B— Cecil Fielder, Detroit
2B— Julio Franco, Texas
3B— Kelly Gruber, Toronto
SS— Alan Trammell, Detroit
OF— Rickey Henderson, Oakland
OF— Jose Canseco, Oakland
OF— Ellis Burks, Boston
C— Carlton Fisk, Chicago
DH— Dave Parker, Milwaukee
RHP— Bob Welch, Oakland
LHP— Chuck Finley, California

NATIONAL LEAGUE
1B— Eddie Murray, Los Angeles
2B— Ryne Sandberg, Chicago
3B— Matt Williams, San Francisco
SS— Barry Larkin, Cincinnati
OF— Barry Bonds, Pittsburgh
OF— Bobby Bonilla, Pittsburgh
OF— Darryl Strawberry, New York
C— Mike Scioscia, Los Angeles
RHP— Doug Drabek, Pittsburgh
LHP— Frank Viola, New York

1991
AMERICAN LEAGUE
1B— Cecil Fielder, Detroit
2B— Julio Franco, Texas
3B— Wade Boggs, Boston
SS— Cal Ripken, Baltimore
OF— Jose Canseco, Oakland
OF— Joe Carter, Toronto
OF— Ken Griffey Jr., Seattle
C— Mickey Tettleton, Detroit
RHP— Roger Clemens, Boston
LHP— Jim Abbott, California

NATIONAL LEAGUE
1B— Will Clark, San Francisco
2B— Ryne Sandberg, Chicago
3B— Terry Pendleton, Atlanta
SS— Barry Larkin, Cincinnati
OF— Barry Bonds, Pittsburgh
OF— Bobby Bonilla, Pittsburgh
OF— Ron Gant, Atlanta

C— Benito Santiago, San Diego
RHP— Jose Rijo, Cincinnati
LHP— Tom Glavine, Atlanta

1992
AMERICAN LEAGUE
1B— Mark McGwire, Oakland
2B— Roberto Alomar, Toronto
3B— Edgar Martinez, Seattle
SS— Travis Fryman, Detroit
OF— Joe Carter, Toronto
OF— Mike Devereaux, Baltimore
OF— Kirby Puckett, Minnesota
C— Mickey Tettleton, Detroit
RHP— Jack McDowell, Chicago
LHP— Dave Fleming, Seattle

NATIONAL LEAGUE
1B— Fred McGriff, San Diego
2B— Ryne Sandberg, Chicago
3B— Gary Sheffield, San Diego
SS— Barry Larkin, Cincinnati
OF— Barry Bonds, Pittsburgh
OF— Andy Van Slyke, Pittsburgh
OF— Larry Walker, Montreal
C— Darren Daulton, Philadelphia
RHP— Greg Maddux, Chicago
LHP— Tom Glavine, Atlanta

1993
AMERICAN LEAGUE
1B— Frank Thomas, Chicago
2B— Carlos Baerga, Cleveland
3B— Travis Fryman, Detroit
SS— Cal Ripken Jr., Baltimore
OF— Albert Belle, Cleveland
OF— Juan Gonzalez, Texas
OF— Ken Griffey Jr., Seattle
C— Mike Stanley, New York
DH— Paul Molitor, Toronto
RHP— Jack McDowell, Chicago
LHP— Jimmy Key, New York

NATIONAL LEAGUE
1B— Fred McGriff, S.D.-Atl.
2B— Robby Thompson, San Francisco
3B— Matt Williams, San Francisco
SS— Jay Bell, Pittsburgh
OF— Barry Bonds, San Francisco
OF— Lenny Dykstra, Philadelphia
OF— David Justice, Atlanta
C— Mike Piazza, Los Angeles
RHP— Greg Maddux, Atlanta
LHP— Steve Avery, Atlanta

1994
AMERICAN LEAGUE
1B— Frank Thomas, Chicago
2B— Chuck Knoblauch, Minnesota
3B— Wade Boggs, New York
SS— Cal Ripken Jr., Baltimore
OF— Albert Belle, Cleveland
OF— Ken Griffey Jr., Seattle
OF— Kirby Puckett, Minnesota
C— Ivan Rodriguez, Texas
DH— Paul Molitor, Toronto
RHP— David Cone, Kansas City
LHP— Jimmy Key, New York

NATIONAL LEAGUE
1B— Jeff Bagwell, Houston
2B— Craig Biggio, Houston
3B— Matt Williams, San Francisco
SS— Barry Larkin, Cincinnati
OF— Moises Alou, Montreal
OF— Barry Bonds, San Francisco
OF— Tony Gwynn, San Diego
C— Mike Piazza, Los Angeles
RHP— Greg Maddux, Atlanta
LHP— Danny Jackson, Philadelphia

1995	**1996**	**1997**
AMERICAN LEAGUE	**AMERICAN LEAGUE**	**AMERICAN LEAGUE**
1B— Mo Vaughn, Boston	1B— Mark McGwire, Oakland	1B— Tino Martinez, New York
2B— Carlos Baerga, Cleveland	2B— Roberto Alomar, Baltimore	2B— Chuck Knoblauch, Minnesota
3B— Jim Thome, Cleveland	3B— Jim Thome, Cleveland	3B— Matt Williams, Cleveland
SS— Cal Ripken Jr., Baltimore	SS— Alex Rodriguez, Seattle	SS— Nomar Garciaparra, Boston
OF— Albert Belle, Cleveland	OF— Albert Belle, Cleveland	OF— Ken Griffey Jr., Seattle
OF— Tim Salmon, California	OF— Juan Gonzalez, Texas	OF— David Justice, Cleveland
OF— Jim Edmonds, California	OF— Ken Griffey Jr., Seattle	OF— Tim Salmon, Anaheim
C— Ivan Rodriguez, Texas	C— Ivan Rodriguez, Texas	C— Ivan Rodriguez, Texas
DH— Edgar Martinez, Seattle	DH— Paul Molitor, Minnesota	DH— Edgar Martinez, Seattle
RHP— Mike Mussina, Baltimore	RHP— Pat Hentgen, Toronto	RHP— Roger Clemens, Toronto
LHP— Randy Johnson, Seattle	LHP— Andy Pettitte, New York	LHP— Randy Johnson, Seattle
NATIONAL LEAGUE	**NATIONAL LEAGUE**	**NATIONAL LEAGUE**
1B— Eric Karros, Los Angeles	1B— Jeff Bagwell, Houston	1B— Jeff Bagwell, Houston
2B— Craig Biggio, Houston	2B— Eric Young, Colorado	2B— Craig Biggio, Houston
3B— Vinny Castilla, Colorado	3B— Ken Caminiti, San Diego	3B— Vinny Castillo, Colorado
SS— Barry Larkin, Cincinnati	SS— Barry Larkin, Cincinnati	SS— Jeff Blauser, Atlanta
OF— Reggie Sanders, Cincinnati	OF— Barry Bonds, San Francisco	OF— Barry Bonds, San Francisco
OF— Dante Bichette, Colorado	OF— Ellis Burks, Colorado	OF— Tony Gwynn, San Diego
OF— Sammy Sosa, Chicago	OF— Gary Sheffield, Florida	OF— Larry Walker, Colorado
C— Mike Piazza, Los Angeles	C— Mike Piazza, Los Angeles	C— Mike Piazza, Los Angeles
RHP— Greg Maddux, Atlanta	RHP— John Smoltz, Atlanta	RHP— Pedro Martinez, Montreal
LHP— Pete Schourek, Cincinnati	LHP— Al Leiter, Florida	LHP— Denny Neagle, Atlanta

MINOR LEAGUE PLAYER OF THE YEAR

Year	Player, Team, League
1936	John Vander Meer, Durham, Piedmont
1937	Charlie Keller, Newark, International
1938	Fred Hutchinson, Seattle, Pacific Coast
1939	Lou Novikoff, Tulsa, Texas; Los Angeles, Pacific Coast
1940	Phil Rizzuto, Kansas City, American Association
1941	John Lindell, Newark, International
1942	Dick Barrett, Seattle, Pacific Coast
1943	Chet Covington, Scranton, Eastern
1944	Rip Collins, Albany, Eastern
1945	Gil Coan, Chattanooga, Southern
1946	Sibby Sisti, Indianapolis, American Association
1947	Hank Sauer, Syracuse, International
1948	Gene Woodling, San Francisco, Pacific Coast
1949	Orie Arntzen, Albany, Eastern
1950	Frank Saucier, San Antonio, Texas
1951	Gene Conley, Hartford, Eastern
1952	Bill Skowron, Kansas City, American Association
1953	Gene Conley, Toledo, American Association
1954	Herb Score, Indianapolis, American Association
1955	John Murff, Dallas, Texas
1956	Steve Bilko, Los Angeles, Pacific Coast
1957	Norm Siebern, Denver, American Association
1958	Jim O'Toole, Nashville, Southern
1959	Frank Howard, Victoria-Spokane
1960	Willie Davis, Spokane, Pacific Coast
1961	Howie Koplitz, Birmingham, Southern
1962	Bob Bailey, Columbus, International
1963	Don Buford, Indianapolis, International
1964	Mel Stottlemyre, Richmond, International
1965	Joe Foy, Toronto, International
1966	Mike Epstein, Rochester, International
1967	Johnny Bench, Buffalo, International
1968	Merv Rettenmund, Rochester, International

Year	Player, Team, League
1969	Danny Walton, Oklahoma City, American Association
1970	Don Baylor, Rochester, International
1971	Bobby Grich, Rochester, International
1972	Tom Paciorek, Albuquerque, Pacific Coast
1973	Steve Ontiveros, Phoenix, Pacific Coast
1974	Jim Rice, Pawtucket, International
1975	Hector Cruz, Tulsa, American Association
1976	Pat Putnam, Asheville, Western Carolina
1977	Ken Landreaux, S.L.C., Pacific Coast; El Paso, Texas
1978	Champ Summers, Indianapolis, American Association
1979	Mark Bomback, Vancouver, Pacific Coast
1980	Tim Raines, Denver, American Association
1981	Mike Marshall, Albuquerque, Pacific Coast
1982	Ron Kittle, Edmonton, Pacific Coast
1983	Kevin McReynolds, Las Vegas, Pacific Coast
1984	Alan Knicely, Wichita, American Association
1985	Jose Canseco, Hunt., Southern-Tac., Pacific Coast
1986	Tim Pyznarski, Las Vegas, Pacific Coast
1987	Randy Milligan, Tidewater, International
1988	Sandy Alomar Jr., Las Vegas, Pacific Coast
	Gary Sheffield, Denver, American Association (tie)
1989	Sandy Alomar Jr., Las Vegas, Pacific Coast
1990	Jose Offerman, Albuquerque, Pacific Coast
1991	Pedro Martinez, Albuquerque, Pacific Coast
1992	Tim Salmon, Edmonton, Pacific Coast
1993	Cliff Floyd, Harrisburg, Eastern
1994	Derek Jeter, Tampa, Florida State; Albany, Eastern; Columbus, International
1995	Karim Garcia, Albuquerque, Pacific Coast
1996	Vladimir Guerrero, West Palm Beach, Florida State; Harrisburg, Eastern
1997	Ben Grieve, Huntsville, Southern; Edmonton, Pacific Coast

MINOR LEAGUE MANAGER OF THE YEAR

Year	Manager, Team, League
1936	Al Sothoron, Milwaukee, American Association
1937	Jake Flowers, Salisbury, Eastern Shore
1938	Paul Richards, Atlanta, Southern
1939	Bill Meyer, Kansas City, American Association
1940	Larry Gilbert, Nashville, Southern
1941	Burt Shotton, Columbus, American Association
1942	Eddie Dyer, Columbus, American Association
1943	Nick Cullop, Columbus, American Association
1944	Al Thomas, Baltimore, International
1945	Lefty O'Doul, San Francisco, Pacific Coast
1946	Clay Hopper, Montreal, International
1947	Nick Cullop, Milwaukee, American Association
1948	Casey Stengel, Oakland, Pacific Coast

Year	Manager, Team, League
1949	Fred Haney, Hollywood, Pacific Coast
1950	Rollie Hemsley, Columbus, American Association
1951	Charlie Grimm, Milwaukee, American Association
1952	Luke Appling, Memphis, Southern
1953	Bobby Bragan, Hollywood, Pacific Coast
1954	Kerby Farrell, Indianapolis, American Association
1955	Bill Rigney, Minneapolis, American Association
1956	Kerby Farrell, Indianapolis, American Association
1957	Ben Geraghty, Wichita, American Association
1958	Cal Ermer, Birmingham, Southern
1959	Pete Reiser, Victoria, Texas
1960	Mel McGaha, Toronto, International
1961	Kerby Farrell, Buffalo, International

Year	Manager, Team, League	Year	Manager, Team, League
1962	Ben Geraghty, Jacksonville, International	1980	Hal Lanier, Springfield, American Association
1963	Rollie Hemsley, Indianapolis, International	1981	Del Crandall, Albuquerque, Pacific Coast
1964	Harry Walker, Jacksonville, International	1982	George Scherger, Indianapolis, American Association
1965	Grady Hatton, Oklahoma City, Pacific Coast	1983	Bill Dancy, Reading, Eastern
1966	Bob Lemon, Seattle, Pacific Coast	1984	Bob Rodgers, Indianapolis, American Association
1967	Bob Skinner, San Diego, Pacific Coast	1985	Jim Fregosi, Louisville, American Association
1968	Jack Tighe, Toledo, International	1986	Joe Sparks, Indianapolis, American Association
1969	Clyde McCullough, Tidewater, International	1987	Terry Collins, Albuquerque, Pacific Coast
1970	Tom Lasorda, Spokane, Pacific Coast	1988	Joe Sparks, Indianapolis, American Association
1971	Del Rice, Salt Lake City, Pacific Coast	1989	Bob Bailor, Syracuse, International
1972	Hank Bauer, Tidewater, International	1990	Sal Rende, Omaha, American Association
1973	Joe Morgan, Charleston, International	1991	Chris Chambliss, Greenville, Southern
1974	Joe Altobelli, Rochester, International	1992	Grady Little, Greenville, Southern
1975	Joe Frazier, Tidewater, International	1993	Jim Tracy, Harrisburg, Eastern
1976	Vern Rapp, Denver, American Association	1994	Mike Jirschele, Wilmington, Carolina
1977	Tommy Thompson, Arkan., Texas	1995	Pete Mackanin, Ottawa, International
1978	Les Moss, Evansville, American Association	1996	John Mizerock, Wilmington, Carolina
1979	Vern Benson, Syracuse, International	1997	Marv Foley, Rochester, International

MINOR LEAGUE EXECUTIVE OF THE YEAR (HIGHER CLASSIFICATIONS, 1936-1992)

(Restricted to Class AAA starting in 1963)

Year	Executive, Team, League	Year	Executive, Team, League
1936	Earl Mann, Atlanta, Southern	1965	Harold Cooper, Columbus, International
1937	Robert LaMotte, Savannah, Sally	1966	John Quinn Jr., Hawaii, Pacific Coast
1938	Louis McKenna, St. Paul, American Association	1967	Hillman Lyons, Richmond, International
1939	Bruce Dudley, Louisville, American Association	1968	Gabe Paul Jr., Tulsa, Pacific Coast
1940	Roy Hamey, Kansas City, American Association	1969	Bill Gardner, Louisville, International
1941	Emil Sick, Seattle, Pacific Coast	1970	Dick King, Wichita, American Association
1942	Bill Veeck, Milwaukee, American Association	1971	Carl Steinfeldt Jr., Rochester, International
1943	Clarence Rowland, Los Angeles, Pacific Coast	1972	Don Labbruzzo, Evansville, American Association
1944	William Mulligan, Seattle, Pacific Coast	1973	Merle Miller, Tucson, Pacific Coast
1945	Bruce Dudley, Louisville, American Association	1974	John Carbray, Sacramento, Pacific Coast
1946	Earl Mann, Atlanta, Southern	1975	Stan Naccarato, Tacoma, Pacific Coast
1947	William Purnhage, Waterloo, I.I.I.	1976	Art Teece, Salt Lake City, Pacific Coast
1948	Edward Glennon, Birmingham, Southern	1977	George Sisler Jr., Columbus, International
1949	Ted Sullivan, Indianapolis, American Association	1978	Willie Sanchez, Albuquerque, Pacific Coast
1950	Clearnce (Brick) Laws, Oakland, Pacific Coast	1979	George Sisler Jr., Columbus, International
1951	Robert Howsam, Denver, West	1980	Jim Burris, Denver, American Association
1952	Jack Cooke, Toronto, International	1981	Pat McKernan, Albuquerque, Pacific Coast
1953	Richard Burnett, Dallas, Texas	1982	A. Ray Smith, Louisville, American Association
1954	Edward Stumpf, Indianapolis, American Association	1983	A. Ray Smith, Louisville, American Association
1955	Dewey Soriano, Seattle, Pacific Coast	1984	Mike Tamburro, Pawtucket, International
1956	Robert Howsam, Denver American Association	1985	Patty Cox Hampton, Oklahoma City, American Association
1957	John Stiglmeier, Buffalo, International	1986	Bob Goughan, Rochester, International
1958	Edward Glennon, Birmingham, Southern	1987	Stu Kehoe, Vancouver, Pacific Coast
1959	Edward Leishman, Salt Lake City, Pacific Coast	1988	Bob Rich, Buffalo, American Association
1960	Ray Winder, Little Rock, Southern	1989	Larry Schmittou, Nashville, American Association
1961	Elten Schiller, Omaha, American Association	1990	Greg Corns, Phoenix, Pacific Coast
1962	George Sisler Jr., Rochester, International	1991	Tom Maloney, Denver, American Association
1963	Lewis Matlin, Hawaii, Pacific Coast	1992	Lou Schwechheimer, Pawtucket, International
1964	Edward Leishman, San Diego, Pacific Coast		

MINOR LEAGUE EXECUTIVE OF THE YEAR (LOWER CLASSIFICATIONS, 1950-1990)

(Separate awards for Class AA and Class A started in 1963; for Short Class A in 1988)

Year	Executive, Team, League	Year	Executive, Team, League
1950	H. Cooper, Hutchinson, Western Association	1967	Robert Quinn, Reading, Eastern
1951	O. W. (Bill) Hayes, Triple, B.S.		Pat Williams, Spar'burg, W.C.
1952	Hillman Lyons, Danville, MOV	1968	Phil Howser, Charlotte, Southern
1953	Carl Roth, Peoria, I.I.I.		Merle Miller, Burlington, Midwest
1954	James Meagham, Cedar Rapids, I.I.I.	1969	Charlie Blaney, Albuquerque, Texas
1955	John Petrakis, Dubuque, MOV		Bill Gorman, Visalia, California
1956	Marvin Milkes, Fresno, California	1970	Carl Sawatski, Arkansas, Texas
1957	Richard Wagner, Lincoln, West.		Bob Williams, Bakersfield, California
1958	Gerald Waring, Macon, Sally	1971	Miles Wolff, Savannah, Dixie Association
1959	Clay Dennis, Des Moines, I.I.I.		Ed Holtz, Appleton, Midwest
1960	Hubert Kittle, Yakima, Northwest	1972	John Begzos, S. Antonio, Texas
1961	David Steele, Fresno, California		Bob Piccinini, Modesto, California
1962	John Quinn Jr., San Jose, California	1973	Dick Kravitz, Jacksonville, Southern
1963	Hugh Finnerty, Tulsa, Texas		Fritz Colschen, Clinton, Midwest
	Ben Jewell, M. Valley, Pioneer	1974	Jim Paul, El Paso, Texas
1964	Glynn West, Birmingham, Southern		Bing Russell, Portland, Northwest
	James Bayens, Rock Hill, W. Carolina	1975	Jim Paul, El Paso, Texas
1965	Dick Butler, Dallas-Ft. Worth, Texas		Cordy Jensen, Eugene, Northwest
	Ken. Blackman, Quad Cities, Midwest	1976	Woodrow Reid, Chattanooga, Southern
1966	Tom Fleming, Evansville, Southern		Don Buchheister, Cedar Rapids, Midwest
	Cappy Harada, Lodi, California	1977	Jim Paul, El Paso, Texas

HISTORY *Award winners*

Year	Executive, Team, League
	Harry Pells, Quad Cities, Midwest
1978	Larry Schmittou, Nashville, Southern
	Dave Hersh, Appleton, Midwest
1979	Bill Rigney Jr., Midland, Texas
	Tom Romenesko, Greensboro, W.C.
1980	Frances Crockett, Charlotte, Southern
	Tom Romenesko, Greensboro, W.C.
1981	Allie Prescott, Memphis, Southern
	Dan Overstreet, Hagerstown, Caro.
1982	Art Clarkson, Birmingham, Southern
	Bob Carruesco, Stockton, California
1983	Edward Kenney, New Britain, Eastern
	Terry Reynolds, Vero Beach, Florida State
1984	Bruce Baldwin, Greenville, Southern
	Dave Tarrolly, Beloit, Midwest

Year	Executive, Team, League
1985	Ben Bernard, Albany-Colonie, Eastern
	Pete Vonachen, Peoria, Midwest
1986	Bill Davidson, Midland, Texas
	Rob Dlugozima, Durham, Carolina
1987	Joe Preseren, Tulsa, Texas
	Skip Weisman, Greensboro, South Atlantic
1988	Bill Valentine, Arkansas, Texas
	Dennis Bastien, Charleston (W.Va.), South Atlantic
	Bob Beban, Eugene, Northwest
1989	Chuck Domino, Reading, Eastern
	John Baxter, South Bend, Midwest
	Bill Pereira, Boise, Northwest
1990	Joe Preseren, Tulsa, Texas
	Dan Chapman, Stockton, California
	Dave Baggott, Salt Lake City, Pioneer

MINOR LEAGUE EXECUTIVE OF THE YEAR

Year	Executive, Team, League
1993	Todd Vander Woude, Harrisburg, Eastern (AA)
1994	Scott Lane, West Michigan, Midwest (A)
1995	Jack and Mary Cain, Portland, Northwest (A)

Year	Executive, Team, League
1996	Wayne Hodes, Trenton, Eastern (AA)
1997	Andy Milovich, Erie, New York-Pennsylvania (A)

BASEBALL WRITERS' ASSOCIATION OF AMERICA
MOST VALUABLE PLAYER

AMERICAN LEAGUE

Year	Player	Team	Pos.	Points
1931	Lefty Grove	Philadelphia	P	78
1932	Jimmie Foxx	Philadelphia	1B	75
1933	Jimmie Foxx	Philadelphia	1B	74
1934	Mickey Cochrane	Detroit	C	67
1935	Hank Greenberg	Detroit	1B	*80
1936	Lou Gehrig	New York	1B	73
1937	Charley Gehringer	Detroit	2B	78
1938	Jimmie Foxx	Boston	1B	305
1939	Joe DiMaggio	New York	OF	280
1940	Hank Greenberg	Detroit	OF	292
1941	Joe DiMaggio	New York	OF	291
1942	Joe Gordon	New York	2B	270
1943	Spud Chandler	New York	P	246
1944	Hal Newhouser	Detroit	P	236
1945	Hal Newhouser	Detroit	P	236
1946	Ted Williams	Boston	OF	224
1947	Joe DiMaggio	New York	OF	202
1948	Lou Boudreau	Cleveland	SS	324
1949	Ted Williams	Boston	OF	272
1950	Phil Rizzuto	New York	SS	284
1951	Yogi Berra	New York	C	184
1952	Bobby Shantz	Philadelphia	P	280
1953	Al Rosen	Cleveland	3B	*336
1954	Yogi Berra	New York	C	230
1955	Yogi Berra	New York	C	218
1956	Mickey Mantle	New York	OF	*336
1957	Mickey Mantle	New York	OF	233
1958	Jackie Jensen	Boston	OF	233
1959	Nellie Fox	Chicago	2B	295
1960	Roger Maris	New York	OF	225
1961	Roger Maris	New York	OF	202
1962	Mickey Mantle	New York	OF	234
1963	Elston Howard	New York	C	248
1964	Brooks Robinson	Baltimore	3B	269
1965	Zoilo Versalles	Minnesota	SS	275
1966	Frank Robinson	Baltimore	OF	*280
1967	Carl Yastrzemski	Boston	OF	275
1968	Denny McLain	Detroit	P	*280
1969	Harmon Killebrew	Minnesota	1B-3B	294
1970	Boog Powell	Baltimore	1B	234
1971	Vida Blue	Oakland	P	268
1972	Dick Allen	Chicago	1B	321
1973	Reggie Jackson	Oakland	OF	*336
1974	Jeff Burroughs	Texas	OF	248
1975	Fred Lynn	Boston	OF	326
1976	Thurman Munson	New York	C	304
1977	Rod Carew	Minnesota	1B	273

NATIONAL LEAGUE

Year	Player	Team	Pos.	Points
1931	Frank Frisch	St. Louis	2B	65
1932	Chuck Klein	Philadelphia	OF	78
1933	Carl Hubbell	New York	P	77
1934	Dizzy Dean	St. Louis	P	78
1935	Gabby Hartnett	Chicago	C	75
1936	Carl Hubbell	New York	P	60
1937	Joe Medwick	St. Louis	OF	70
1938	Ernie Lombardi	Cincinnati	C	229
1939	Bucky Walters	Cincinnati	P	303
1940	Frank McCormick	Cincinnati	1B	274
1941	Dolf Camilli	Brooklyn	1B	300
1942	Mort Cooper	St. Louis	P	263
1943	Stan Musial	St. Louis	OF	267
1944	Marty Marion	St. Louis	SS	190
1945	Phil Cavarretta	Chicago	1B	279
1946	Stan Musial	St. Louis	1B	319
1947	Bob Elliott	Boston	3B	205
1948	Stan Musial	St. Louis	OF	303
1949	Jackie Robinson	Brooklyn	2B	264
1950	Jim Konstanty	Philadelphia	P	286
1951	Roy Campanella	Brooklyn	C	243
1952	Hank Sauer	Chicago	OF	226
1953	Roy Campanella	Brooklyn	C	297
1954	Willie Mays	New York	OF	283
1955	Roy Campanella	Brooklyn	C	226
1956	Don Newcombe	Brooklyn	P	223
1957	Hank Aaron	Milwaukee	OF	239
1958	Ernie Banks	Chicago	SS	283
1959	Ernie Banks	Chicago	SS	232 1/2
1960	Dick Groat	Pittsburgh	SS	276
1961	Frank Robinson	Cincinnati	OF	219
1962	Maury Wills	Los Angeles	SS	209
1963	Sandy Koufax	Los Angeles	P	237
1964	Ken Boyer	St. Louis	3B	243
1965	Willie Mays	San Francisco	OF	224
1966	Roberto Clemente	Pittsburgh	OF	218
1967	Orlando Cepeda	St. Louis	1B	*280
1968	Bob Gibson	St. Louis	P	242
1969	Willie McCovey	San Francisco	1B	265
1970	Johnny Bench	Cincinnati	C	326
1971	Joe Torre	St. Louis	3B	318
1972	Johnny Bench	Cincinnati	C	263
1973	Pete Rose	Cincinnati	OF	274
1974	Steve Garvey	Los Angeles	1B	270
1975	Joe Morgan	Cincinnati	2B	321 1/2
1976	Joe Morgan	Cincinnati	2B	311
1977	George Foster	Cincinnati	OF	291

Year	Player	Team	Pos.	Points	Year	Player	Team	Pos.	Points
1978—Jim Rice	Boston	OF	352		1978—Dave Parker	Pittsburgh	OF	320	
1979—Don Baylor	California	OF	347		1979—Willie Stargell	Pittsburgh	1B	216	
					Keith Hernandez	St. Louis	1B	216	
1980—George Brett	Kansas City	3B	335		1980—Mike Schmidt	Philadelphia	3B	*336	
1981—Rollie Fingers	Milwaukee	P	319		1981—Mike Schmidt	Philadelphia	3B	321	
1982—Robin Yount	Milwaukee	SS	385		1982—Dale Murphy	Atlanta	OF	283	
1983—Cal Ripken Jr.	Baltimore	SS	322		1983—Dale Murphy	Atlanta	OF	318	
1984—Willie Hernandez	Detroit	P	306		1984—Ryne Sandberg	Chicago	2B	326	
1985—Don Mattingly	New York	1B	367		1985—Willie McGee	St. Louis	OF	280	
1986—Roger Clemens	Boston	P	339		1986—Mike Schmidt	Philadelphia	3B	287	
1987—George Bell	Toronto	OF	332		1987—Andre Dawson	Chicago	OF	269	
1988—Jose Canseco	Oakland	OF	*392		1988—Kirk Gibson	Los Angeles	OF	272	
1989—Robin Yount	Milwaukee	OF	256		1989—Kevin Mitchell	San Francisco	OF	314	
1990—Rickey Henderson	Oakland	OF	317		1990—Barry Bonds	Pittsburgh	OF	331	
1991—Cal Ripken Jr.	Baltimore	SS	318		1991—Terry Pendleton	Atlanta	3B	274	
1992—Dennis Eckersley	Oakland	P	306		1992—Barry Bonds	Pittsburgh	OF	304	
1993—Frank Thomas	Chicago	1B	*392		1993—Barry Bonds	San Francisco	OF	372	
1994—Frank Thomas	Chicago	1B	372		1994—Jeff Bagwell	Houston	1B	*392	
1995—Mo Vaughn	Boston	1B	308		1995—Barry Larkin	Cincinnati	SS	281	
1996—Juan Gonzalez	Texas	OF	290		1996—Ken Caminiti	San Diego	3B	*392	
1997—Ken Griffey Jr.	Seattle	OF	*392		1997—Larry Walker	Colorado	OF	359	

*Unanimous selection.

CY YOUNG MEMORIAL AWARD

Year	Pitcher	Team	Votes	Year	Pitcher	Team	Votes
1956—Don Newcombe	Brooklyn	10		1980—A.L.—Steve Stone	Baltimore	100	
1957—Warren Spahn	Milwaukee	15		N.L.—Steve Carlton	Philadelphia	118	
1958—Bob Turley	New York A.L.	5		1981—A.L.—Rollie Fingers	Milwaukee	126	
1959—Early Wynn	Chicago A.L.	13		N.L.—Fernando Valenzuela	Los Angeles	70	
1960—Vernon Law	Pittsburgh	8		1982—A.L.—Pete Vuckovich	Milwaukee	87	
1961—Whitey Ford	New York A.L.	9		N.L.—Steve Carlton	Philadelphia	112	
1962—Don Drysdale	Los Angeles N.L.	14		1983—A.L.—LaMarr Hoyt	Chicago	116	
1963—Sandy Koufax	Los Angeles N.L.	*20		N.L.—John Denny	Philadelphia	103	
1964—Dean Chance	Los Angeles A.L.	17		1984—A.L.—Willie Hernandez	Detroit	88	
1965—Sandy Koufax	Los Angeles N.L.	*20		N.L.—Rick Sutcliffe	Chicago	*120	
1966—Sandy Koufax	Los Angeles N.L.	*20		1985—A.L.—Bret Saberhagen	Kansas City	127	
1967—A.L.—Jim Lonborg	Boston	18		N.L.—Dwight Gooden	New York	*120	
N.L.—Mike McCormick	San Francisco	18		1986—A.L.—Roger Clemens	Boston	*140	
1968—A.L.—Denny McLain	Detroit	*20		N.L.—Mike Scott	Houston	98	
N.L.—Bob Gibson	St. Louis	*20		1987—A.L.—Roger Clemens	Boston	124	
1969—A.L.—Denny McLain	Detroit	10		N.L.—Steve Bedrosian	Philadelphia	57	
Mike Cuellar	Baltimore	10		1988—A.L.—Frank Viola	Minnesota	138	
N.L.—Tom Seaver	New York	23		N.L.—Orel Hershiser	Los Angeles	*120	
1970—A.L.—Jim Perry	Minnesota	55		1989—A.L.—Bret Saberhagen	Kansas City	138	
N.L.—Bob Gibson	St. Louis	118		N.L.—Mark Davis	San Diego	107	
1971—A.L.—Vida Blue	Oakland	98		1990—A.L.—Bob Welch	Oakland	107	
N.L.—Fergie Jenkins	Chicago	97		N.L.—Doug Drabek	Pittsburgh	118	
1972—A.L.—Gaylord Perry	Cleveland	64		1991—A.L.—Roger Clemens	Boston	119	
N.L.—Steve Carlton	Philadelphia	*120		N.L.—Tom Glavine	Atlanta	110	
1973—A.L.—Jim Palmer	Baltimore	88		1992—A.L.—Dennis Eckersley	Oakland	107	
N.L.—Tom Seaver	New York	71		N.L.—Greg Maddux	Chicago	112	
1974—A.L.—Jim Hunter	Oakland	90		1993—A.L.—Jack McDowell	Chicago	124	
N.L.—Mike Marshall	Los Angeles	96		N.L.—Greg Maddux	Atlanta	119	
1975—A.L.—Jim Palmer	Baltimore	98		1994—A.L.—David Cone	Kansas City	108	
N.L.—Tom Seaver	New York	98		N.L.—Greg Maddux	Atlanta	*140	
1976—A.L.—Jim Palmer	Baltimore	108		1995—A.L.—Randy Johnson	Seattle	136	
N.L.—Randy Jones	San Diego	96		N.L.—Greg Maddux	Atlanta	*140	
1977—A.L.—Sparky Lyle	New York	56½		1996—A.L.—Pat Hentgen	Toronto	110	
N.L.—Steve Carlton	Philadelphia	*104		N.L.—John Smoltz	Atlanta	136	
1978—A.L.—Ron Guidry	New York	*140		1997—A.L.—Roger Clemens	Toronto	134	
N.L.—Gaylord Perry	San Diego	116		N.L.—Pedro Martinez	Montreal	134	
1979—A.L.—Mike Flanagan	Baltimore	136					
N.L.—Bruce Sutter	Chicago	72					

*Unanimous selection.

ROOKIE OF THE YEAR

1947—Combined selection—Jackie Robinson, Brooklyn N.L., 1B
1948—Combined selection—Alvin Dark, Boston N.L., SS

AMERICAN LEAGUE

Year	Player	Team	Pos.	Votes
1949—Roy Sievers	St. Louis	OF	10
1950—Walt Dropo	Boston	1B	15
1951—Gil McDougald	New York	3B	13
1952—Harry Byrd	Philadelphia	P	9
1953—Harvey Kuenn	Detroit	SS	23
1954—Bob Grim	New York	P	15

NATIONAL LEAGUE

Year	Player	Team	Pos.	Votes
1949—Don Newcombe	Brooklyn	P	21
1950—Sam Jethroe	Boston	OF	11
1951—Willie Mays	New York	OF	18
1952—Joe Black	Brooklyn	P	19
1953—Jim Gilliam	Brooklyn	2B	11
1954—Wally Moon	St. Louis	OF	17

Year	Player	Team	Pos.	Votes	Year	Player	Team	Pos.	Votes
1955—Herb Score	Cleveland	P	18		1955—Bill Virdon	St. Louis	OF	15	
1956—Luis Aparicio	Chicago	SS	22		1956—Frank Robinson	Cincinnati	OF	*24	
1957—Tony Kubek	New York	IF-OF	23		1957—Jack Sanford	Philadelphia	P	16	
1958—Albie Pearson	Washington	OF	14		1958—Orlando Cepeda	San Francisco	1B	*†21	
1959—Bob Allison	Washington	OF	18		1959—Willie McCovey	San Francisco	1B	*24	
1960—Ron Hansen	Baltimore	SS	22		1960—Frank Howard	Los Angeles	OF	12	
1961—Don Schwall	Boston	P	7		1961—Billy Williams	Chicago	OF	10	
1962—Tom Tresh	New York	OF-SS	13		1962—Ken Hubbs	Chicago	2B	19	
1963—Gary Peters	Chicago	P	10		1963—Pete Rose	Cincinnati	2B	17	
1964—Tony Oliva	Minnesota	OF	19		1964—Dick Allen	Philadelphia	3B	18	
1965—Curt Blefary	Baltimore	OF	12		1965—Jim Lefebvre	Los Angeles	2B	13	
1966—Tommie Agee	Chicago	OF	16		1966—Tommy Helms	Cincinnati	3B	12	
1967—Rod Carew	Minnesota	2B	19		1967—Tom Seaver	New York	P	11	
1968—Stan Bahnsen	New York	P	17		1968—Johnny Bench	Cincinnati	C	10½	
1969—Lou Piniella	Kansas City	OF	9		1969—Ted Sizemore	Los Angeles	2B	14	
1970—Thurman Munson	New York	C	23		1970—Carl Morton	Montreal	P	11	
1971—Chris Chambliss	Cleveland	1B	11		1971—Earl Williams	Atlanta	C	18	
1972—Carlton Fisk	Boston	C	*24		1972—Jon Matlack	New York	P	19	
1973—Al Bumbry	Baltimore	OF	13½		1973—Gary Matthews	San Francisco	OF	11	
1974—Mike Hargrove	Texas	1B	16½		1974—Bake McBride	St. Louis	OF	16	
1975—Fred Lynn	Boston	OF	23		1975—John Montefusco	San Francisco	P	12	
1976—Mark Fidrych	Detroit	P	22		1976—Butch Metzger	San Diego	P	11	
					Pat Zachry	Cincinnati	P	11	
1977—Eddie Murray	Baltimore	DH-1B	12½		1977—Andre Dawson	Montreal	OF	10	
1978—Lou Whitaker	Detroit	2B	21		1978—Bob Horner	Atlanta	3B	12½	
1979—John Castino	Minnesota	3B	7		1979—Rick Sutcliffe	Los Angeles	P	20	
Alfredo Griffin	Toronto	SS	7						
1980—Joe Charboneau	Cleveland	OF	103		1980—Steve Howe	Los Angeles	P	80	
1981—Dave Righetti	New York	P	127		1981—Fernando Valenzuela	Los Angeles	P	107	
1982—Cal Ripken	Baltimore	SS-3B	132		1982—Steve Sax	Los Angeles	2B	63	
1983—Ron Kittle	Chicago	OF	104		1983—Darryl Strawberry	New York	OF	109	
1984—Alvin Davis	Seattle	1B	134		1984—Dwight Gooden	New York	P	118	
1985—Ozzie Guillen	Chicago	SS	101		1985—Vince Coleman	St. Louis	OF	*120	
1986—Jose Canseco	Oakland	OF	110		1986—Todd Worrell	St. Louis	P	118	
1987—Mark McGwire	Oakland	1B	*140		1987—Benito Santiago	San Diego	C	*120	
1988—Walt Weiss	Oakland	SS	103		1988—Chris Sabo	Cincinnati	3B	79	
1989—Gregg Olson	Baltimore	P	136		1989—Jerome Walton	Chicago	OF	116	
1990—Sandy Alomar Jr.	Cleveland	C	*140		1990—Dave Justice	Atlanta	OF	118	
1991—Chuck Knoblauch	Minnesota	2B	136		1991—Jeff Bagwell	Houston	1B	118	
1992—Pat Listach	Milwaukee	SS	122		1992—Eric Karros	Los Angeles	1B	116	
1993—Tim Salmon	California	OF	*140		1993—Mike Piazza	Los Angeles	C	*140	
1994—Bob Hamelin	Kansas City	DH	134		1994—Raul Mondesi	Los Angeles	OF	*140	
1995—Marty Cordova	Minnesota	3B	105		1995—Hideo Nomo	Los Angeles	P	118	
1996—Derek Jeter	New York	SS	*140		1996—Todd Hollandsworth	Los Angeles	OF	105	
1997—Nomar Garciaparra	Boston	SS	*140		1997—Scott Rolen	Philadelphia	3B	*140	

*Unanimous selection. †Three writers did not vote.

MANAGER OF THE YEAR

AMERICAN LEAGUE

Year	Manager	Team	Points
1983—Tony La Russa	Chicago	17
1984—Sparky Anderson	Detroit	96
1985—Bobby Cox	Toronto	104
1986—John McNamara	Boston	95
1987—Sparky Anderson	Detroit	90
1988—Tony La Russa	Oakland	103
1989—Frank Robinson	Baltimore	125
1990—Jeff Torborg	Chicago	128
1991—Tom Kelly	Minnesota	138
1992—Tony La Russa	Oakland	132
1993—Gene Lamont	Chicago	72
1994—Buck Showalter	New York	132
1995—Lou Piniella	Seattle	86
1996—Johnny Oates	Texas	89
Joe Torre	New York	89
1997—Dave Johnson	Baltimore	88

NATIONAL LEAGUE

Year	Manager	Team	Points
1983— Tommy Lasorda	Los Angeles	10
1984— Jim Frey	Chicago	101
1985— Whitey Herzog	St. Louis	86
1986— Hal Lanier	Houston	108
1987— Buck Rodgers	Montreal	92
1988— Tommy Lasorda	Los Angeles	101
1989— Don Zimmer	Chicago	118
1990— Jim Leyland	Pittsburgh	99
1991— Bobby Cox	Atlanta	96
1992— Jim Leyland	Pittsburgh	109
1993— Dusty Baker	San Francisco	105
1994— Felipe Alou	Montreal	138
1995— Don Baylor	Colorado	122
1996— Bruce Bochy	San Diego	76
1997— Dusty Baker	San Francisco	110

EARLY MOST VALUABLE PLAYER AWARDS
CHALMERS AWARD

AMERICAN LEAGUE

Year	Player	Team	Pos.	Points
1911—Ty Cobb	Detroit	OF	64
1912—Tris Speaker	Boston	OF	59

NATIONAL LEAGUE

Year	Player	Team	Pos.	Points
1911—Frank Schulte	Chicago	OF	29
1912—Larry Doyle	New York	2B	48

Year	Player	Team	Pos.	Points		Year	Player	Team	Pos.	Points
1913—Walter Johnson	Washington	P	54		1913—Jake Daubert	Brooklyn	1B	50
1914—Eddie Collins	Philadelphia	2B	63		1914—Johnny Evers	Boston	2B	50

LEAGUE AWARDS

AMERICAN LEAGUE

Year	Player	Team	Pos.	Points
1922—George Sisler	St. Louis	1B	59
1923—Babe Ruth	New York	OF	64
1924—Walter Johnson	Washington	P	55
1925—Roger Peckinpaugh	Washington	SS	45
1926—George Burns	Cleveland	1B	63
1927—Lou Gehrig	New York	1B	56
1928—Mickey Cochrane	Philadelphia	C	53
1929—No selection			

NATIONAL LEAGUE

Year	Player	Team	Pos.	Points
1922—No selection			
1923—No selection			
1924—Dazzy Vance	Brooklyn	P	74
1925—Rogers Hornsby	St. Louis	2B	73
1926—Bob O'Farrell	St. Louis	C	79
1927—Paul Waner	Pittsburgh	OF	72
1928—Jim Bottomley	St. Louis	1B	76
1929—Rogers Hornsby	Chicago	2B	60

HALL OF FAME

ROSTER OF MEMBERS

Name	Des.*	Elec. year	Votes rec.†	Votes cast‡	% of vote	Teams as player
Aaron, Hank	P	1982	406	415	97.8	Milwaukee NL, Atlanta NL, Milwaukee AL
Alexander, Grover C.	P	1938	212	262	80.9	Philadelphia NL, Chicago NL, St. Louis NL
Alston, Walter	M	1983	CV	—	—	St. Louis NL
Anson, Cap	P	1939	C1	—	—	Chicago NL
Aparicio, Luis	P	1984	341	403	84.6	Chicago AL, Baltimore AL, Boston AL
Appling, Luke	P	1964	189	225	84	Chicago AL
Ashburn, Richie	P	1995	CV	—	—	Philadelphia NL, Chicago NL, New York NL
Averill, Earl	P	1975	CV	—	—	Cleveland AL, Detroit AL, Boston AL
Baker, Home Run	P	1955	CV	—	—	Philadelphia AL, New York AL
Bancroft, Dave	P	1971	CV	—	—	Philadelphia NL, New York NL, Boston NL, Brooklyn NL
Banks, Ernie	P	1977	321	383	83.8	Chicago NL
Barlick, Al	U	1989	CV	—	—	
Barrow, Ed	E	1953	CV	—	—	
Beckley, Jake	P	1971	CV	—	—	Pittsburgh NL, Pittsburgh PL, New York NL, Cincinnati NL, St. Louis NL
Bell, Cool Papa	P	1974	SCNL	—	—	Negro Leagues
Bench, Johnny	P	1989	431	447	96.4	Cincinnati NL
Bender, Chief	P	1953	CV	—	—	Philadelphia AL, Philadelphia NL, Chicago AL
Berra, Yogi	P	1972	339	396	85.6	New York AL, New York NL
Bottomley, Jim	P	1974	CV	—	—	St. Louis NL, Cincinnati NL, St. Louis AL
Boudreau, Lou	P	1970	232	300	77.3	Cleveland AL, Boston AL
Bresnahan, Roger	P	1945	C2	—	—	Washington NL, Chicago NL, Baltimore AL, New York NL, St. Louis NL
Brock, Lou	P	1985	315	395	79.7	Chicago NL, St. Louis NL
Brouthers, Dan	P	1945	C2	—	—	Troy NL, Buffalo NL, Detroit NL, Boston NL, Boston PL, Boston AA,Brooklyn NL, Baltimore NL,Louisville NL, Philadelphia NL, New York NL
Brown, Three Finger	P	1949	C2	—	—	St. Louis NL, Chicago NL, Cincinnati NL
Bulkeley, Morgan	E	1937	CC	—	—	
Bunning, Jim	P	1996	CV	—	—	Detroit AL, Philadelphia NL, Pittsburgh NL, Los Angeles NL
Burkett, Jesse	P	1946	C2	—	—	New York NL, Cleveland NL, St. Louis NL, St. Louis AL, Boston AL
Campanella, Roy	P	1969	270	340	79.4	Brooklyn NL
Carew, Rod	P	1991	401	447	89.7	Minnesota AL, California AL
Carey, Max	P	1961	CV	—	—	Pittsburgh NL, Brooklyn NL
Carlton, Steve	P	1994	436	455	95.8	St. Louis NL, Philadelphia NL, San Francisco NL, Chicago AL, Cleveland AL, Minnesota AL
Cartwright, Alexander	O	1938	CC	—	—	
Chadwick, Henry	O	1938	CC	—	—	
Chance, Frank	P	1946	C2	—	—	Chicago NL, New York AL
Chandler, Happy	E	1982	CV	—	—	
Charleston, Oscar	P	1976	SCNL	—	—	Negro Leagues
Chesbro, Jack	P	1946	C2	—	—	Pittsburgh NL, New York AL, Boston AL
Clarke, Fred	P	1945	C2	—	—	Louisville NL, Pittsburgh NL
Clarkson, John	P	1963	CV	—	—	Worcester NL, Chicago NL, Boston NL, Cleveland NL
Clemente, Roberto	P	1973	393	424	92.7	Pittsburgh NL
Cobb, Ty	P	1936	222	226	98.2	Detroit AL, Philadelphia AL
Cochrane, Mickey	P	1947	128	161	79.5	Philadelphia AL, Detroit AL
Collins, Eddie	P	1939	213	274	77.7	Philadelphia AL, Chicago AL
Collins, Jimmy	P	1945	C2	—	—	Boston NL, Louisville NL, Boston AL, Philadelphia AL
Combs, Earle	P	1970	CV	—	—	New York AL
Comiskey, Charley	F/P	1939	C1	—	—	St. Louis AA, Chicago PL, Cincinnati NL
Conlan, Jocko	U	1974	CV	—	—	Chicago AL
Connolly, Tommy	U	1953	CV	—	—	
Connor, Roger	P	1976	CV	—	—	Troy NL, New York NL, New York PL, Philadelphia NL, St. Louis NL
Coveleski, Stan	P	1969	CV	—	—	Philadelphia AL, Cleveland AL, Washington AL, New York AL
Crawford, Sam	P	1957	CV	—	—	Cincinnati NL, Detroit AL
Cronin, Joe	P	1956	152	193	78.8	Pittsburgh NL, Washington AL, Boston AL
Cummings, Candy	P	1939	C1	—	—	Hartford NL, Cincinnati NL
Cuyler, Kiki	P	1968	CV	—	—	Pittsburgh NL, Chicago NL, Cincinnati NL, Brooklyn NL
Dandridge, Ray	P	1987	CV	—	—	Negro Leagues
Day, Leon	P	1995	CV	—	—	Negro Leagues
Dean, Dizzy	P	1953	209	264	79.2	St. Louis NL, Chicago NL, St. Louis AL
Delahanty, Ed	P	1945	C2	—	—	Philadelphia NL, Cleveland PL, Washington AL
Dickey, Bill	P	1954	202	252	80.2	New York AL
Dihigo, Martin	P	1977	SCNL	—	—	Negro Leagues
DiMaggio, Joe	P	1955	223	251	88.8	New York AL

Name	Des.*	Elec. year	Votes rec.†	Votes cast‡	% of vote	Teams as player
Doerr, Bobby	P	1986	CV	—	—	Boston AL
Drysdale, Don	P	1984	316	403	78.4	Brooklyn NL, Los Angeles NL
Duffy, Hugh	P	1945	C2	—	—	Chicago NL, Chicago PL, Boston AA, Boston NL, Milwaukee AL, Philadelphia NL
Durocher, Leo	M	1994	CV	—	—	New York AL, Cincinnati NL, St. Louis NL, Brooklyn NL
Evans, Billy	U	1973	CV	—	—	
Evers, Johnny	P	1946	C2	—	—	Chicago NL, Boston NL, Philadelphia NL, Chicago AL
Ewing, Buck	P	1939	C1	—	—	Troy NL, New York NL, New York PL, Cleveland NL, Cincinnati NL
Faber, Red	P	1964	CV	—	—	Chicago AL
Feller, Bob	P	1962	150	160	93.8	Cleveland AL
Ferrell, Rick	P	1984	CV	—	—	St. Louis AL, Boston AL, Washington AL
Fingers, Rollie	P	1992	349	430	81.2	Oakland AL, San Diego NL, Milwaukee AL
Flick, Elmer	P	1963	CV	—	—	Philadelphia NL, Philadelphia AL, Cleveland AL
Ford, Whitey	P	1974	284	365	77.8	New York AL
Foster, Bill	P	1996	CV	—	—	Negro Leagues
Foster, Rube	P	1981	CV	—	—	Negro Leagues
Fox, Nellie	P	1997	CV	—	—	Philadelphia AL, Chicago AL, Houston NL
Foxx, Jimmie	P	1951	179	226	79.2	Philadelphia AL, Boston AL, Chicago NL, Philadelphia NL
Frick, Ford	E	1970	CV	—	—	
Frisch, Frank	P	1947	136	161	84.5	New York NL, St. Louis NL
Galvin, Pud	P	1965	CV	—	—	Buffalo NL, Pittsburgh AA, Pittsburgh NL, Pittsburgh PL, St. Louis NL
Gehrig, Lou	P	1939	SE	—	—	New York AL
Gehringer, Charley	P	1949	159	187	85.0	Detroit AL
Gibson, Bob	P	1981	337	401	84.0	St. Louis NL
Gibson, Josh	P	1972	SCNL	—	—	Negro Leagues
Giles, Warren	E	1979	CV	—	—	
Gomez, Lefty	P	1972	CV	—	—	New York AL, Washington AL
Goslin, Goose	P	1968	CV	—	—	Washington AL, St. Louis AL, Detroit AL
Greenberg, Hank	P	1956	164	193	85.0	Detroit AL, Pittsburgh NL
Griffith, Clark	M	1946	C2	—	—	St. Louis AA, Boston AA, Chicago NL, Chicago AL, New York AL, Cincinnati NL, Washington AL
Grimes, Burleigh	P	1964	CV	—	—	Pittsburgh NL, Brooklyn NL, New York NL, Boston NL, St. Louis NL, Chicago NL, New York AL
Grove, Lefty	P	1947	123	161	76.4	Philadelphia AL, Boston AL
Hafey, Chick	P	1971	CV	—	—	St. Louis NL, Cincinnati NL
Haines, Jesse	P	1970	CV	—	—	Cincinnati NL, St. Louis NL
Hamilton, Billy	P	1961	CV	—	—	Kansas City AA, Philadelphia NL, Boston NL
Hanlon, Ned	M	1996	CV	—	—	Cleveland NL, Detroit NL, Pittsburgh NL, Pittsburgh PL, Baltimore NL
Harridge, Will	E	1972	CV	—	—	
Harris, Bucky	M	1975	CV	—	—	Washington AL, Detroit AL
Hartnett, Gabby	P	1955	195	251	77.7	Chicago NL, New York NL
Heilmann, Harry	P	1952	203	234	86.8	Detroit AL, Cincinnati NL
Herman, Billy	P	1975	CV	—	—	Chicago NL, Brooklyn NL, Boston NL, Pittsburgh NL
Hooper, Harry	P	1971	CV	—	—	Boston AL, Chicago AL
Hornsby, Rogers	P	1942	182	233	78.1	St. Louis NL, New York NL, Boston NL, Chicago NL, St. Louis AL
Hoyt, Waite	P	1969	CV	—	—	New York NL, Boston AL, New York AL, Detroit AL, Philadelphia AL, Brooklyn NL, Pittsburgh NL
Hubbard, Cal	U	1976	CV	—	—	
Hubbell, Carl	P	1947	140	161	87.0	New York NL
Huggins, Miller	M	1964	CV	—	—	Cincinnati NL, St. Louis NL
Hulbert, William	F	1995	CV	—	—	
Hunter, Catfish	P	1987	315	413	76.3	Kansas City AL, Oakland AL, New York AL
Irvin, Monte	P	1973	SCNL	—	—	New York NL, Chicago NL, Negro Leagues
Jackson, Reggie	P	1993	396	423	93.6	Kansas City AL, Oakland AL, Baltimore AL, New York AL, California AL
Jackson, Travis	P	1982	CV	—	—	New York NL
Jenkins, Ferguson	P	1991	334	447	74.7	Philadelphia NL, Chicago NL, Texas AL, Boston AL
Jennings, Hugh	P	1945	C2	—	—	Louisville AA, Louisville NL, Baltimore NL, Brooklyn NL, Philadelphia NL, Detroit AL
Johnson, Ban	E	1937	CC	—	—	
Johnson, Judy	P	1975	SCNL	—	—	Negro Leagues
Johnson, Walter	P	1936	189	226	83.6	Washington AL
Joss, Addie	P	1978	CV	—	—	Cleveland AL
Kaline, Al	P	1980	340	385	88.3	Detroit AL
Keefe, Tim	P	1964	CV	—	—	Troy NL, New York AA, New York NL, New York PL, Philadelphia NL
Keeler, Willie	P	1939	207	274	75.5	New York NL, Brooklyn, NL, Baltimore NL, New York AL
Kell, George	P	1983	CV	—	—	Philadelphia AL, Detroit AL, Boston AL, Chicago AL, Baltimore AL

Name	Des.*	Elec. year	Votes rec.†	Votes cast‡	% of vote	Teams as player
Kelley, Joe	P	1971	CV	—	—	Boston NL, Pittsburgh NL, Baltimore NL, Brooklyn NL, Baltimore AL, Cincinnati NL
Kelly, George	P	1973	CV	—	—	New York NL, Pittsburgh NL, Cincinnati NL, Chicago NL, Brooklyn NL
Kelly, Mike	P	1945	C2	—	—	Cincinnati NL, Chicago NL, Boston NL, Boston PL, Cincinnati AA, Boston AA, New York NL
Killebrew, Harmon	P	1984	335	403	83.1	Washington AL, Minnesota AL, Kansas City AL
Kiner, Ralph	P	1975	273	362	75.4	Pittsburgh NL, Chicago NL, Cleveland AL
Klein, Chuck	P	1980	CV	—	—	Philadelphia NL, Chicago NL, Pittsburgh NL
Klem, Bill	U	1953	CV	—	—	
Koufax, Sandy	P	1972	344	396	86.9	Brooklyn NL, Los Angeles NL
Lajoie, Nap	P	1937	168	201	83.6	Philadelphia NL, Philadelphia AL, Cleveland AL
Landis, Kenesaw M.	E	1944	C2	—	—	
Lasorda, Tom	M	1997	CV	—	—	Brooklyn NL, Kansas City AL
Lazzeri, Tony	P	1991	CV	—	—	New York AL, Chicago NL, Brooklyn NL, New York NL
Lemon, Bob	P	1976	305	388	78.6	Cleveland AL
Leonard, Buck	P	1972	SCNL	—	—	Negro Leagues
Lindstrom, Fred	P	1976	CV	—	—	New York NL, Pittsburgh NL, Chicago NL, Brooklyn NL
Lloyd, John Henry	P	1977	SCNL	—	—	Negro Leagues
Lombardi, Ernie	P	1986	CV	—	—	Brooklyn NL, Cincinnati NL, Boston NL, New York NL
Lopez, Al	M	1977	CV	—	—	Brooklyn NL, Boston NL, Pittsburgh NL, Cleveland AL
Lyons, Ted	P	1955	217	251	86.5	Chicago AL
Mack, Connie	M	1937	CC	—	—	Washington NL, Buffalo PL, Pittsburgh NL
MacPhail, Larry	E	1978	CV	—	—	
Mantle, Mickey	P	1974	322	365	88.2	New York AL
Manush, Heinie	P	1964	CV	—	—	Detroit AL, St. Louis AL, Washington AL, Boston AL, Brooklyn NL, Pittsburgh NL
Maranville, Rabbit	P	1954	209	252	82.9	Boston NL, Pittsburgh NL, Chicago NL, Brooklyn NL, St. Louis NL
Marichal, Juan	P	1983	313	374	83.7	San Francisco NL, Boston AL, Los Angeles NL
Marquard, Rube	P	1971	CV	—	—	New York NL, Brooklyn NL, Cincinnati NL, Boston NL
Mathews, Eddie	P	1978	301	379	79.4	Boston NL, Milwaukee NL, Atlanta NL, Houston NL, Detroit AL
Mathewson, Christy	P	1936	205	226	90.7	New York NL, Cincinnati NL
Mays, Willie	P	1979	409	432	94.7	New York (Giants)NL, San Francisco NL, New York (Mets)NL
McCarthy, Joe	M	1957	CV	—	—	
McCarthy, Tommy	P	1946	C2	—	—	Boston UA, Boston NL, Philadelphia NL, St. Louis AA, Brooklyn NL
McCovey, Willie	P	1986	346	425	81.4	San Francisco NL, San Diego NL, Oakland AL
McGinnity, Joe	P	1946	C2	—	—	Baltimore NL, Brooklyn NL, Baltimore AL, New York NL
McGowan, Bill	U	1992	CV	—	—	
McGraw, John	M	1937	CC	—	—	Baltimore AA, Baltimore NL, St. Louis NL, Baltimore AL, New York NL
McKechnie, Bill	M	1962	CV	—	—	Pittsburgh NL, Boston NL, New York AL, New York NL, Cincinnati
Medwick, Joe	P	1968	240	283	84.8	St. Louis NL, Brooklyn NL, New York NL, Boston NL
Mize, Johnny	P	1981	CV	—	—	St. Louis NL, New York NL, New York AL
Morgan, Joe	P	1990	363	444	81.8	Houston NL, Cincinnati NL, San Francisco NL, Philadelphia NL, Oakland AL
Musial, Stan	P	1969	317	340	93.2	St. Louis NL
Newhouser, Hal	P	1992	CV	—	—	Detroit AL, Cleveland AL
Nichols, Kid	P	1949	C2	—	—	Boston NL, St. Louis NL, Philadelphia NL
Niekro, Phil	P	1997	380	473	80.3	Milwaukee NL, Atlanta NL, New York AL, Cleveland AL, Toronto AL
O'Rourke, Jim	P	1945	C2	—	—	Boston NL, Providence NL, Buffalo NL, New York NL, Washington NL, New York PL
Ott, Mel	P	1951	197	226	87.2	New York NL
Paige, Satchel	P	1971	SCNL	—	—	Cleveland AL, St. Louis AL, Kansas City AL, Negro Leagues
Palmer, Jim	P	1990	411	444	92.6	Baltimore AL
Pennock, Herb	P	1948	94	121	77.7	Philadelphia AL, Boston AL, New York AL
Perry, Gaylord	P	1991	342	447	76.5	San Francisco NL, Cleveland AL, Texas AL, San Diego NL, New York AL, Atlanta NL, Seattle AL, Kansas City AL
Plank, Eddie	P	1946	C2	—	—	Philadelphia AL, St. Louis AL
Radbourn, Hoss	P	1939	C1	—	—	Buffalo NL, Providence NL, Boston NL, Boston PL, Cincinnati NL
Reese, Pee Wee	P	1984	CV	—	—	Brooklyn NL, Los Angeles NL
Rice, Sam	P	1963	CV	—	—	Washington AL, Cleveland AL
Rickey, Branch	E	1967	CV	—	—	St. Louis AL, New York AL
Rixey, Eppa	P	1963	CV	—	—	Philadelphia NL, Cincinnati NL
Rizzuto, Phil	P	1994	CV	—	—	New York AL
Roberts, Robin	P	1976	337	388	86.9	Philadelphia NL, Baltimore AL, Houston NL, Chicago NL

HISTORY Hall of Fame

Name	Des.*	Elec. year	Votes rec.†	Votes cast‡	% of vote	Teams as player
Robinson, Brooks	P	1983	344	374	92.0	Baltimore AL
Robinson, Frank	P	1982	370	415	89.2	Cincinnati NL, Baltimore AL, Los Angeles NL, California AL, Cleveland AL
Robinson, Jackie	P	1962	124	160	77.5	Brooklyn NL
Robinson, Wilbert	M	1945	C2	—	—	Philadelphia AA, Baltimore AA, Baltimore NL, St. Louis NL, Baltimore AL
Roush, Edd	P	1962	CV	—	—	Chicago AL, New York NL, Cincinnati NL
Ruffing, Red	P	1967	266	306	86.9	Boston AL, New York AL, Chicago AL
Rusie, Amos	P	1977	CV	—	—	Indianapolis NL, New York NL, Cincinnati NL
Ruth, Babe	P	1936	215	226	95.1	Boston AL, New York AL, Boston NL
Schalk, Ray	P	1955	CV	—	—	Chicago AL, New York NL
Schmidt, Mike	P	1995	444	460	96.5	Philadelphia NL
Schoendienst, Red	P	1989	CV	—	—	St. Louis NL, New York (Giants) NL, Milwaukee NL
Seaver, Tom	P	1992	425	430	98.8	New York NL, Cincinnati NL, Chicago AL, Boston AL
Sewell, Joe	P	1977	CV	—	—	Cleveland AL, New York AL
Simmons, Al	P	1953	199	264	75.4	Philadelphia AL, Chicago AL, Detroit AL, Washington AL, Boston NL, Cincinnati NL, Boston AL
Sisler, George	P	1939	235	274	85.8	St. Louis AL, Washington AL, Boston NL
Slaughter, Enos	P	1985	CV	—	—	St. Louis NL, New York AL, Kansas City AL, Milwaukee NL
Snider, Duke	P	1980	333	385	86.5	Brooklyn NL, Los Angeles NL, New York NL, San Francisco NL
Spahn, Warren	P	1973	316	380	83.2	Boston NL, Milwaukee NL, New York NL, San Francisco NL
Spalding, Al	P	1939	C1	—	—	Chicago NL
Speaker, Tris	P	1937	165	201	82.1	Boston AL, Cleveland AL, Washington AL, Philadelphia AL
Stargell, Willie	P	1988	352	427	82.4	Pittsburgh NL
Stengel, Casey	M	1966	CV	—	—	Brooklyn NL, Pittsburgh NL, Philadelphia NL, New York NL, Boston NL
Sutton, Don	P	1998	386	473	81.6	Los Angeles NL, Houston NL, Milwaukee AL, Oakland AL, California AL
Terry, Bill	P	1954	195	252	77.4	New York NL
Thompson, Sam	P	1974	CV	—	—	Detroit NL, Philadelphia NL, Detroit AL
Tinker, Joe	P	1946	C2	—	—	Chicago NL, Cincinnati NL
Traynor, Pie	P	1948	93	121	76.9	Pittsburgh NL
Vance, Dazzy	P	1955	205	251	81.7	Pittsburgh NL, New York AL, Brooklyn NL, St. Louis NL, Cincinnati NL
Vaughan, Arky	P	1985	CV	—	—	Pittsburgh NL, Brooklyn NL
Veeck, Bill	E	1991	CV	—	—	
Waddell, Rube	P	1946	C2	—	—	Louisville NL, Pittsburgh NL, Chicago NL, Philadelphia AL, St. Louis AL
Wagner, Honus	P	1936	215	226	95.1	Louisville NL, Pittsburgh NL
Wallace, Bobby	P	1953	CV	—	—	Cleveland NL, St. Louis NL, St. Louis AL
Walsh, Ed	P	1946	C2	—	—	Chicago AL, Boston NL
Waner, Lloyd	P	1967	CV	—	—	Pittsburgh NL, Boston NL, Cincinnati NL, Philadelphia NL, Brooklyn NL
Waner, Paul	P	1952	195	234	83.3	Pittsburgh NL, Brooklyn NL, Boston NL, New York AL
Ward, John Montgomery	P	1964	CV	—	—	Providence NL, New York NL, Brooklyn PL, Brooklyn NL
Weaver, Earl	M	1996	CV	—	—	
Weiss, George	E	1971	CV	—	—	
Welch, Mickey	P	1973	CV	—	—	Troy NL, New York NL
Wells, Willie	P	1997	CV	—	—	
Wheat, Zack	P	1959	CV	—	—	Brooklyn NL, Philadelphia AL
Wilhelm, Hoyt	P	1985	331	395	83.8	New York NL, St. Louis NL, Cleveland AL, Baltimore AL, Chicago AL California AL, Atlanta NL, Chicago NL, Los Angeles NL
Williams, Billy	P	1987	354	413	85.7	Chicago NL, Oakland AL
Williams, Ted	P	1966	282	302	93.4	Boston AL
Willis, Vic	P	1995	CV	—	—	Boston NL, Pittsburgh NL, St. Louis NL
Wilson, Hack	P	1979	CV	—	—	New York NL, Chicago NL, Brooklyn NL, Philadelphia NL
Wright, George	M	1937	CC	—	—	Boston NL, Providence NL
Wright, Harry	M	1953	CV	—	—	Boston NL
Wynn, Early	P	1972	301	396	76.0	Washington AL, Cleveland AL, Chicago AL
Yastrzemski, Carl	P	1989	423	447	94.6	Boston AL
Yawkey, Tom	E	1980	CV	—	—	
Young, Cy	P	1937	153	201	76.1	Cleveland NL, St. Louis NL, Boston AL, Cleveland AL, Boston NL
Youngs, Ross	P	1972	CV	—	—	New York NL

*Designation for which he was honored. Abbreviations: E—executive; F—founder; M—manager; O—organizer; P—player; U—umpire.
†Where an abbreviation is listed rather than a vote total, the enshrinee was selected by one of the following groups: Centennial Commission (CC), committee of old-time players and writers (C1), committee on old-timers (C2), Committee on Veterans (CV), special election by Baseball Writers' Association of America (SE) or Special Committee on Negro Leagues (SCNL).
‡Votes cast by eligible members of the Baseball Writers' Association of America.
League abbreviations: AA—American Association; AL—American League; NL—National League; PL—Players League; UA—Union Association.

TEAM BY TEAM

AMERICAN LEAGUE

CALIFORNIA ANGELS

YEARLY FINISHES

Year	Position	W	L	Pct.	*GB	Manager	Attendance
1961†	8th	70	91	.435	38 1/2	Bill Rigney	603,510
1962†	3rd	86	76	.531	10	Bill Rigney	1,144,063
1963†	9th	70	91	.435	34	Bill Rigney	821,015
1964†	5th	82	80	.506	17	Bill Rigney	760,439
1965†	7th	75	87	.463	27	Bill Rigney	566,727
1966‡	6th	80	82	.494	18	Bill Rigney	1,400,321
1967‡	5th	84	77	.522	7 1/2	Bill Rigney	1,317,713
1968‡	8th	67	95	.414	36	Bill Rigney	1,025,956

WEST DIVISION

Year	Position	W	L	Pct.	*GB	Manager	Attendance
1969‡	3rd	71	91	.438	26	Bill Rigney, Lefty Phillips	758,388
1970‡	3rd	86	76	.531	12	Lefty Phillips	1,077,741
1971‡	4th	76	86	.469	25 1/2	Lefty Phillips	926,373
1972‡	5th	75	80	.484	18	Del Rice	744,190
1973‡	4th	79	83	.488	15	Bobby Winkles	1,058,206
1974‡	6th	68	94	.420	22	Bobby Winkles, Dick Williams	917,269
1975‡	6th	72	89	.447	25 1/2	Dick Williams	1,058,163
1976‡	4th (tied)	76	86	.469	14	Dick Williams, Norm Sherry	1,006,774
1977‡	5th	74	88	.457	28	Norm Sherry, Dave Garcia	1,432,633
1978‡	2nd (tied)	87	75	.537	5	Dave Garcia, Jim Fregosi	1,755,386
1979‡	1st§	88	74	.543	+3	Jim Fregosi	2,523,575
1980‡	6th	65	95	.406	31	Jim Fregosi	2,297,327
1981‡	4th/7th	51	59	.464	∞	Jim Fregosi, Gene Mauch	1,441,545
1982‡	1st§	93	69	.574	+3	Gene Mauch	2,807,360
1983‡	5th (tied)	70	92	.432	29	John McNamara	2,555,016
1984‡	2nd (tied)	81	81	.500	3	John McNamara	2,402,997
1985‡	2nd	90	72	.556	1	Gene Mauch	2,567,427
1986‡	1st§	92	70	.568	+5	Gene Mauch	2,655,872
1987‡	6th (tied)	75	87	.463	10	Gene Mauch	2,696,299
1988‡	4th	75	87	.463	29	Cookie Rojas	2,340,925
1989‡	3rd	91	71	.562	8	Doug Rader	2,647,291
1990‡	4th	80	82	.494	23	Doug Rader	2,555,688
1991‡	7th	81	81	.500	14	Doug Rader, Buck Rodgers	2,416,236
1992‡	5th (tied)	72	90	.444	24	Buck Rodgers	2,065,444
1993‡	5th (tied)	71	91	.438	23	Buck Rodgers	2,057,460
1994‡	4th	47	68	.409	5	Buck Rodgers, Marcel Lachemann	1,512,622
1995‡	2nd	78	67	.538	1	Marcel Lachemann	1,748,680
1996‡	4th	70	91	.435	19 1/2	Marcel Lachemann, John McNamara, Joe Maddon	1,820,521
1997	2nd	84	78	.519	6	Terry Collins	1,767,330

*Games behind winner. †Los Angeles Angels through September 1, 1965. ‡California Angels through 1996. §Lost championship series. ∞First half 31-29; second half 20-30.

MANAGERIAL RECORDS

Terry Collins 84-78, Jim Fregosi 237-249, Dave Garcia 60-66, Marcel Lachemann 161-170, Joe Maddon 8-14, Gene Mauch 379-332, John McNamara 161-191, Lefty Phillips 222-225, Doug Rader 232-216, Del Rice 75-80, Bill Rigney 625-707, Buck Rodgers 179-223, Cookie Rojas 75-87, Norm Sherry 76-71, Dick Williams 147-194, Bobby Winkles 109-127.

BALTIMORE ORIOLES

YEARLY FINISHES

Year	Position	W	L	Pct.	*GB	Manager	Attendance
1901†	8th	48	89	.350	35 1/2	Hugh Duffy	139,034
1902‡	2nd	78	58	.574	5	Jimmy McAleer	272,283
1903‡	6th	65	74	.468	26 1/2	Jimmy McAleer	380,405
1904‡	6th	65	87	.428	29	Jimmy McAleer	318,108
1905‡	8th	54	99	.354	40 1/2	Jimmy McAleer	339,112
1906‡	5th	76	73	.510	16	Jimmy McAleer	389,157
1907‡	6th	69	83	.454	24	Jimmy McAleer	419,025
1908‡	4th	83	69	.546	6 1/2	Jimmy McAleer	618,947
1909‡	7th	61	89	.407	36	Jimmy McAleer	366,274
1910‡	8th	47	107	.305	57	John O'Connor	249,889
1911‡	8th	45	107	.296	56 1/2	Bobby Wallace	207,984
1912‡	7th	53	101	.344	53	Bobby Wallace, George Stovall	214,070

Year	Position	W	L	Pct.	*GB	Manager	Attendance
1913‡	8th	57	96	.373	39	George Stovall, Branch Rickey	250,330
1914‡	5th	71	82	.464	28 1/2	Branch Rickey	244,714
1915‡	6th	63	91	.409	39 1/2	Branch Rickey	150,358
1916‡	5th	79	75	.513	12	Fielder Jones	335,740
1917‡	7th	57	97	.370	43	Fielder Jones	210,486
1918‡	5th	58	64	.475	15	Fielder Jones, Jimmy Austin, Jimmy Burke	122,076
1919‡	5th	67	72	.482	20 1/2	Jimmy Burke	349,350
1920‡	4th	76	77	.497	21 1/2	Jimmy Burke	419,311
1921‡	3rd	81	73	.526	17 1/2	Lee Fohl	355,978
1922‡	2nd	93	61	.604	1	Lee Fohl	712,918
1923‡	5th	74	78	.487	24	Lee Fohl, Jimmy Austin	430,296
1924‡	4th	74	78	.487	17	George Sisler	533,349
1925‡	3rd	82	71	.536	15	George Sisler	462,898
1926‡	7th	62	92	.403	29	George Sisler	283,986
1927‡	7th	59	94	.336	50 1/2	Dan Howley	247,879
1928‡	3rd	82	72	.532	19	Dan Howley	339,497
1929‡	4th	79	73	.520	26	Dan Howley	280,697
1930‡	6th	64	90	.416	38	Bill Killefer	152,088
1931‡	5th	63	91	.409	45	Bill Killefer	179,126
1932‡	6th	63	91	.409	44	Bill Killefer	112,558
1933‡	8th	55	96	.364	43 1/2	Bill Killefer, Allen Sothoron, Rogers Hornsby	88,113
1934‡	6th	67	85	.441	33	Rogers Hornsby	115,305
1935‡	7th	65	87	.428	28 1/2	Rogers Hornsby	80,922
1936‡	7th	57	95	.375	44 1/2	Rogers Hornsby	93,267
1937‡	8th	46	108	.299	56	Rogers Hornsby, Jim Bottomley	123,121
1938‡	7th	55	97	.362	44	Gabby Street	130,417
1939‡	8th	43	111	.279	64 1/2	Fred Haney	109,159
1940‡	6th	67	87	.435	23	Fred Haney	239,591
1941‡	6th (tied)	70	84	.455	31	Fred Haney, Luke Sewell	176,240
1942‡	3rd	82	69	.543	19 1/2	Luke Sewell	255,617
1943‡	6th	72	80	.474	25	Luke Sewell	214,392
1944‡	1st	89	65	.578	+1	Luke Sewell	508,644
1945‡	3rd	81	70	.536	6	Luke Sewell	482,986
1946‡	7th	66	88	.429	38	Luke Sewell, Zack Taylor	526,435
1947‡	8th	59	95	.383	38	Muddy Ruel	320,474
1948‡	6th	59	94	.386	37	Zack Taylor	335,546
1949‡	7th	53	101	.344	44	Zack Taylor	270,936
1950‡	7th	58	96	.377	40	Zack Taylor	247,131
1951‡	8th	52	102	.338	46	Zack Taylor	293,790
1952‡	7th	64	90	.416	31	Rogers Hornsby, Marty Marion	518,796
1953‡	8th	54	100	.351	46 1/2	Marty Marion	297,238
1954	7th	54	100	.351	57	Jimmie Dykes	1,060,910
1955	7th	57	97	.370	39	Paul Richards	852,039
1956	6th	69	85	.448	28	Paul Richards	901,201
1957	5th	76	76	.500	21	Paul Richards	1,029,581
1958	6th	74	79	.484	17 1/2	Paul Richards	829,991
1959	6th	74	80	.481	20	Paul Richards	891,926
1960	2nd	89	65	.578	8	Paul Richards	1,187,849
1961	3rd	95	67	.586	14	Paul Richards, Luman Harris	951,089
1962	7th	77	85	.475	19	Billy Hitchcock	790,254
1963	4th	86	76	.531	18 1/2	Billy Hitchcock	774,343
1964	3rd	97	65	.599	2	Hank Bauer	1,116,215
1965	3rd	94	68	.580	8	Hank Bauer	781,649
1966	1st	97	63	.606	+9	Hank Bauer	1,203,366
1967	6th (tied)	76	85	.472	15 1/2	Hank Bauer	955,053
1968	2nd	91	71	.562	12	Hank Bauer, Earl Weaver	943,977

EAST DIVISION

Year	Position	W	L	Pct.	*GB	Manager	Attendance
1969	1st§	109	53	.673	+19	Earl Weaver	1,058,168
1970	1st§	108	54	.667	+15	Earl Weaver	1,057,069
1971	1st§	101	57	.639	+12	Earl Weaver	1,023,037
1972	3rd	80	74	.519	5	Earl Weaver	899,950
1973	1st∞	97	65	.599	+8	Earl Weaver	958,667
1974	1st∞	91	71	.562	+2	Earl Weaver	962,572
1975	2nd	90	69	.566	4 1/2	Earl Weaver	1,002,157
1976	2nd	88	74	.543	10 1/2	Earl Weaver	1,058,609
1977	2nd (tied)	97	64	.602	2 1/2	Earl Weaver	1,195,769
1978	4th	90	71	.559	9	Earl Weaver	1,051,724
1979	1st§	102	57	.642	+8	Earl Weaver	1,681,009
1980	2nd	100	62	.617	3	Earl Weaver	1,797,438
1981	2nd/4th	59	46	.562	▲	Earl Weaver	1,024,652
1982	2nd	94	68	.580	1	Earl Weaver	1,613,031
1983	1st§	98	64	.605	+6	Joe Altobelli	2,042,071
1984	5th	85	77	.525	19	Joe Altobelli	2,045,784
1985	4th	83	78	.516	16	Joe Altobelli, Earl Weaver	2,132,387

Year	Position	W	L	Pct.	*GB	Manager	Attendance
1986	7th	73	89	.451	22½	Earl Weaver	1,973,176
1987	6th	67	95	.414	31	Cal Ripken Sr.	1,835,692
1988	7th	54	107	.335	34½	Cal Ripken Sr., Frank Robinson	1,660,738
1989	2nd	87	75	.537	2	Frank Robinson	2,535,208
1990	5th	76	85	.472	11½	Frank Robinson	2,415,189
1991	6th	67	95	.414	24	Frank Robinson, Johnny Oates	2,552,753
1992	3rd	89	73	.549	7	Johnny Oates	3,567,819
1993	3rd (tied)	85	77	.525	10	Johnny Oates	3,644,965
1994	2nd	63	49	.563	6½	Johnny Oates	2,535,359
1995	3rd	71	73	.493	15	Phil Regan	3,098,475
1996	2nd◆■∞	88	74	.543	4	Dave Johnson	3,646,950
1997	1st◆∞	98	64	.605	+2	Dave Johnson	3,711,132

*Games behind winner. †Milwaukee Brewers. ‡St. Louis Browns. §Won championship series. ∞Lost championship series. ▲First half 31-23; second half 28-23. ◆Wild-card playoff qualifier. ■Won division series.

MANAGERIAL RECORDS

Joe Altobelli 212-167, Jimmy Austin 29-38, Hank Bauer 407-318, Jim Bottomley 21-56, Jimmy Burke 172-180, Hugh Duffy 48-89, Jimmie Dykes 54-100, Lee Fohl 226-183, Fred Haney 125-227, Lum Harris 17-10, Billy Hitchcock 163-161, Rogers Hornsby 255-381, Dan Howley 220-239, Dave Johnson 186-138, Fielder Jones 158-196, Bill Killefer 224-329, Marty Marion 96-161, Jimmy McAleer 551-632, Johnny Oates 291-270, Jack O'Connor 47-107, Phil Regan 71-73, Paul Richards 517-539, Branch Rickey 139-179, Cal Ripken Sr. 67-101, Frank Robinson 230-285, Luke Sewell 432-410, George Sisler 218-241, Al Sothoron 2-6, George Stovall 91-158, Gabby Street 55-97, Zack Taylor 235-410, Bobby Wallace 57-134, Earl Weaver 1,481-1,060.

BOSTON RED SOX
YEARLY FINISHES

Year	Position	W	L	Pct.	*GB	Manager	Attendance
1901	2nd	79	57	.581	4	Jimmy Collins	289,448
1902	3rd	77	60	.562	6½	Jimmy Collins	348,567
1903	1st	91	47	.659	+14½	Jimmy Collins	379,338
1904	1st	95	59	.617	+1½	Jimmy Collins	623,295
1905	4th	78	74	.513	16	Jimmy Collins	468,828
1906	8th	49	105	.318	45½	Jimmy Collins, Chick Stahl	410,209
1907	7th	59	90	.396	32½	George Huff, Bob Unglaub, Deacon McGuire	436,777
1908	5th	75	79	.487	15½	Deacon McGuire, Fred Lake	473,048
1909	3rd	88	63	.583	9½	Fred Lake	668,965
1910	4th	81	72	.529	22½	Patsy Donovan	584,619
1911	5th	78	75	.510	24	Patsy Donovan	503,961
1912	1st	105	47	.691	+14	Jake Stahl	597,096
1913	4th	79	71	.527	15½	Jake Stahl, Bill Carrigan	437,194
1914	2nd	91	62	.595	8½	Bill Carrigan	481,359
1915	1st	101	50	.669	+2½	Bill Carrigan	539,885
1916	1st	91	63	.591	+2	Bill Carrigan	496,397
1917	2nd	90	62	.592	9	Jack Barry	387,856
1918	1st	75	51	.595	+2½	Ed Barrow	249,513
1919	6th	66	71	.482	20½	Ed Barrow	417,291
1920	5th	72	81	.471	25½	Ed Barrow	402,445
1921	5th	75	79	.487	23½	Hugh Duffy	279,273
1922	8th	61	93	.396	33	Hugh Duffy	259,184
1923	8th	61	91	.401	37	Frank Chance	229,668
1924	7th	67	87	.435	25	Lee Fohl	448,556
1925	8th	47	105	.309	49½	Lee Fohl	267,782
1926	8th	46	107	.301	44½	Lee Fohl	285,155
1927	8th	51	103	.331	59	Bill Carrigan	305,275
1928	8th	57	96	.373	43½	Bill Carrigan	396,920
1929	8th	58	96	.377	48	Bill Carrigan	394,620
1930	8th	52	102	.338	50	Heinie Wagner	444,045
1931	6th	62	90	.408	45	Shano Collins	350,975
1932	8th	43	111	.279	64	Shano Collins, Marty McManus	182,150
1933	7th	63	86	.423	34½	Marty McManus	268,715
1934	4th	76	76	.500	24	Bucky Harris	610,640
1935	4th	78	75	.510	16	Joseph Cronin	558,568
1936	6th	74	80	.481	28½	Joe Cronin	626,895
1937	5th	80	72	.526	21	Joe Cronin	559,659
1938	2nd	88	61	.591	9½	Joe Cronin	646,459
1939	2nd	89	62	.589	17	Joe Cronin	573,070
1940	4th (tied)	82	72	.532	8	Joe Cronin	716,234
1941	2nd	84	70	.545	17	Joe Cronin	718,497
1942	2nd	93	59	.612	9	Joe Cronin	730,340
1943	7th	68	84	.447	29	Joe Cronin	358,275
1944	4th	77	77	.500	12	Joe Cronin	506,975
1945	7th	71	83	.461	17½	Joe Cronin	603,794
1946	1st	104	50	.675	+12	Joe Cronin	1,416,944
1947	3rd	83	71	.539	14	Joe Cronin	1,427,315

Year	Position	W	L	Pct.	*GB	Manager	Attendance
1948	2nd†	96	59	.619	1	Joe McCarthy	1,558,798
1949	2nd	96	58	.623	1	Joe McCarthy	1,596,650
1950	3rd	94	60	.610	4	Joe McCarthy, Steve O'Neill	1,344,080
1951	3rd	87	67	.565	11	Steve O'Neill	1,312,282
1952	6th	76	78	.494	19	Lou Boudreau	1,115,750
1953	4th	84	69	.549	16	Lou Boudreau	1,026,133
1954	4th	69	85	.448	42	Lou Boudreau	931,127
1955	4th	84	70	.545	12	Pinky Higgins	1,203,200
1956	4th	84	70	.545	13	Pinky Higgins	1,137,158
1957	3rd	82	72	.532	16	Pinky Higgins	1,181,087
1958	3rd	79	75	.513	13	Pinky Higgins	1,077,047
1959	5th	75	79	.487	19	Pinky Higgins, Billy Jurges	984,102
1960	7th	65	89	.422	32	Billy Jurges, Pinky Higgins	1,129,866
1961	6th	76	86	.469	33	Pinky Higgins	850,589
1962	8th	76	84	.475	19	Pinky Higgins	733,080
1963	7th	76	85	.472	28	Johnny Pesky	942,642
1964	8th	72	90	.444	27	Johnny Pesky, Billy Herman	883,276
1965	9th	62	100	.383	40	Billy Herman	652,201
1966	9th	72	90	.444	26	Billy Herman, Pete Runnels	811,172
1967	1st‡	92	70	.568	+1	Dick Williams	1,727,832
1968	4th	86	76	.531	17	Dick Williams	1,940,788

EAST DIVISION

Year	Position	W	L	Pct.	*GB	Manager	Attendance
1969	3rd	87	75	.537	22	Dick Williams, Eddie Popowski	1,833,246
1970	3rd	87	75	.537	21	Eddie Kasko	1,595,278
1971	3rd	85	77	.525	18	Eddie Kasko	1,678,732
1972	2nd	85	70	.548	1/2	Eddie Kasko	1,441,718
1973	2nd	89	73	.549	8	Eddie Kasko	1,481,002
1974	3rd	84	78	.519	7	Darrell Johnson	1,556,411
1975	1st‡	95	65	.594	+4 1/2	Darrell Johnson	1,748,587
1976	3rd	83	79	.512	15 1/2	Darrell Johnson, Don Zimmer	1,895,846
1977	2nd (tied)	97	64	.602	2 1/2	Don Zimmer	2,074,549
1978	2nd§	99	64	.607	1	Don Zimmer	2,320,643
1979	3rd	91	69	.569	11 1/2	Don Zimmer	2,353,114
1980	4th	83	77	.519	19	Don Zimmer, Johnny Pesky	1,956,092
1981	5th/2nd (tied)	59	49	.546	∞	Ralph Houk	1,060,379
1982	3rd	89	73	.549	6	Ralph Houk	1,950,124
1983	6th	78	84	.481	20	Ralph Houk	1,782,285
1984	4th	86	76	.531	18	Ralph Houk	1,661,618
1985	5th	81	81	.500	18 1/2	John McNamara	1,786,633
1986	1st‡	95	66	.590	+5 1/2	John McNamara	2,147,641
1987	5th	78	84	.481	20	John McNamara	2,231,551
1988	1st▲	89	73	.549	+1	John McNamara, Joe Morgan	2,464,851
1989	3rd	83	79	.512	6	Joe Morgan	2,510,012
1990	1st▲	88	74	.543	+2	Joe Morgan	2,528,986
1991	2nd (tied)	84	78	.519	7	Joe Morgan	2,562,435
1992	7th	73	89	.451	23	Butch Hobson	2,468,574
1993	5th	80	82	.494	15	Butch Hobson	2,422,021
1994	4th	54	61	.470	17	Butch Hobson	1,775,818
1995	1st◆	86	58	.597	+7	Kevin Kennedy	2,164,410
1996	3rd	85	77	.525	7	Kevin Kennedy	2,315,231
1997	4th	78	84	.481	20	Jimy Williams	2,226,136

*Games behind winner. †Lost pennant playoff. ‡Won championship series. §Lost division playoff. ∞First half 30-26; second half 29-23. ▲Lost championship series. ◆Lost division series.

MANAGERIAL RECORDS

Ed Barrow 213-203, Jack Barry 90-62, Lou Boudreau 229-232, Bill Carrigan 489-500, Frank Chance 61-91, Jimmy Collins 455-376, Shano Collins 73-134, Joe Cronin 1,071-916, Patsy Donovan 159-147, Hugh Duffy 136-172, Lee Fohl 160-299, Bucky Harris 76-76, Billy Herman 128-182, Pinky Higgins 560-556, Butch Hobson 207-232, Ralph Houk 312-282, George Huff 2-6, Darrell Johnson 220-188, Billy Jurges 59-63, Eddie Kasko 346-295, Kevin Kennedy 171-135, Fred Lake 110-80, Joe McCarthy 223-145, Deacon McGuire 98-123, Marty McManus 95-153, John McNamara 297-273, Joe Morgan 301-262, Steve O'Neill 150-99, Johnny Pesky 147-179, Eddie Popowski 5-4, Pete Runnels 8-8, Chick Stahl 14-26, Jake Stahl 144-88, Bob Unglaub 9-20, Heinie Wagner 52-102, Dick Williams 260-217, Jimy Williams 78-84, Don Zimmer 411-304.

CHICAGO WHITE SOX
YEARLY FINISHES

Year	Position	W	L	Pct.	*GB	Manager	Attendance
1901	1st	83	53	.610	+4	Clark Griffith	354,350
1902	4th	74	60	.552	8	Clark Griffith	337,898
1903	7th	60	77	.438	30 1/2	Nixey Callahan	286,183
1904	3rd	89	65	.578	6	Nixey Callahan, Fielder Jones	557,123

Year	Position	W	L	Pct.	*GB	Manager	Attendance
1905	2nd	92	60	.605	2	Fielder Jones	687,419
1906	1st	93	58	.616	+3	Fielder Jones	585,202
1907	3rd	87	64	.576	5 1/2	Fielder Jones	666,307
1908	3rd	88	64	.579	1 1/2	Fielder Jones	636,096
1909	4th	78	74	.513	20	Billy Sullivan	478,400
1910	6th	68	85	.444	35 1/2	Hugh Duffy	552,084
1911	4th	77	74	.510	24	Hugh Duffy	583,208
1912	4th	78	76	.506	28	Nixey Callahan	602,241
1913	5th	78	74	.513	17 1/2	Nixey Callahan	644,501
1914	6th (tied)	70	84	.455	30	Nixey Callahan	469,290
1915	3rd	93	61	.604	9 1/2	Pants Rowland	539,461
1916	2nd	89	65	.578	2	Pants Rowland	679,923
1917	1st	100	54	.649	+9	Pants Rowland	684,521
1918	6th	57	67	.460	17	Pants Rowland	195,081
1919	1st	88	52	.629	+3 1/2	Kid Gleason	627,186
1920	2nd	96	58	.623	2	Kid Gleason	833,492
1921	7th	62	92	.403	36 1/2	Kid Gleason	543,650
1922	5th	77	77	.500	17	Kid Gleason	602,860
1923	7th	69	85	.448	30	Kid Gleason	573,778
1924	8th	66	87	.431	25 1/2	Johnny Evers	606,658
1925	5th	79	75	.513	18 1/2	Eddie Collins	832,231
1926	5th	81	72	.529	9 1/2	Eddie Collins	710,339
1927	5th	70	83	.458	29 1/2	Ray Schalk	614,423
1928	5th	72	82	.468	29	Ray Schalk, Lena Blackburne	494,152
1929	7th	59	93	.388	46	Lena Blackburne	426,795
1930	7th	62	92	.403	40	Donie Bush	406,123
1931	8th	56	97	.366	51	Donie Bush	403,550
1932	7th	49	102	.325	56 1/2	Lew Fonseca	233,198
1933	6th	67	83	.447	31	Lew Fonseca	397,789
1934	8th	53	99	.349	47	Lew Fonseca, Jimmie Dykes	236,559
1935	5th	74	78	.487	19 1/2	Jimmie Dykes	470,281
1936	3rd	81	70	.536	20	Jimmie Dykes	440,810
1937	3rd	86	68	.558	16	Jimmie Dykes	589,245
1938	6th	65	83	.439	32	Jimmie Dykes	338,278
1939	4th	85	69	.552	22 1/2	Jimmie Dykes	594,104
1940	4th (tied)	82	72	.532	8	Jimmie Dykes	660,336
1941	3rd	77	77	.500	24	Jimmie Dykes	677,077
1942	6th	66	82	.446	34	Jimmie Dykes	425,734
1943	4th	82	72	.532	16	Jimmie Dykes	508,962
1944	7th	71	83	.461	18	Jimmie Dykes	563,539
1945	6th	71	78	.477	15	Jimmie Dykes	657,981
1946	5th	74	80	.481	30	Jimmie Dykes, Ted Lyons	983,403
1947	6th	70	84	.455	27	Ted Lyons	876,948
1948	8th	51	101	.336	44 1/2	Ted Lyons	777,844
1949	6th	63	91	.409	34	Jack Onslow	937,151
1950	6th	60	94	.390	38	Jack Onslow, Red Corriden	781,330
1951	4th	81	73	.526	17	Paul Richards	1,328,234
1952	3rd	81	73	.526	14	Paul Richards	1,231,675
1953	3rd	89	65	.578	11 1/2	Paul Richards	1,191,353
1954	3rd	94	60	.610	17	Paul Richards, Marty Marion	1,231,629
1955	3rd	91	63	.591	5	Marty Marion	1,175,684
1956	3rd	85	69	.552	12	Marty Marion	1,000,090
1957	2nd	90	64	.584	8	Al Lopez	1,135,668
1958	2nd	82	72	.532	10	Al Lopez	797,451
1959	1st	94	60	.610	+5	Al Lopez	1,423,144
1960	3rd	87	67	.565	10	Al Lopez	1,644,460
1961	4th	86	76	.531	23	Al Lopez	1,146,019
1962	5th	85	77	.525	11	Al Lopez	1,131,562
1963	2nd	94	68	.580	10 1/2	Al Lopez	1,158,848
1964	2nd	98	64	.605	1	Al Lopez	1,250,053
1965	2nd	95	67	.586	7	Al Lopez	1,130,519
1966	4th	83	79	.512	15	Eddie Stanky	990,016
1967	4th	89	73	.549	3	Eddie Stanky	985,634
1968	8th (tied)	67	95	.414	36	Eddie Stanky, Al Lopez	803,775

WEST DIVISION

Year	Position	W	L	Pct.	*GB	Manager	Attendance
1969	5th	68	94	.420	29	Al Lopez, Don Gutteridge	589,546
1970	6th	56	106	.346	42	Don Gutteridge, Chuck Tanner	495,355
1971	3rd	79	83	.488	22 1/2	Chuck Tanner	833,891
1972	2nd	87	67	.565	5 1/2	Chuck Tanner	1,177,318
1973	5th	77	85	.475	17	Chuck Tanner	1,302,527
1974	4th	80	80	.500	9	Chuck Tanner	1,149,596
1975	5th	75	86	.466	22 1/2	Chuck Tanner	750,802
1976	6th	64	97	.398	25 1/2	Paul Richards	914,945
1977	3rd	90	72	.556	12	Bob Lemon	1,657,135

– 333 –

Year	Position	W	L	Pct.	*GB	Manager	Attendance
1978	5th	71	90	.441	20½	Bob Lemon, Larry Doby	1,491,100
1979	5th	73	87	.456	14	Don Kessinger, Tony La Russa	1,280,702
1980	5th	70	90	.438	26	Tony La Russa	1,200,365
1981	3rd/6th	54	52	.509	†	Tony La Russa	946,651
1982	3rd	87	75	.537	6	Tony La Russa	1,567,787
1983	1st‡	99	63	.611	+20	Tony La Russa	2,132,821
1984	5th (tied)	74	88	.457	10	Tony La Russa	2,136,988
1985	3rd	85	77	.525	6	Tony La Russa	1,669,888
1986	5th	72	90	.444	20	Tony La Russa, Jim Fregosi	1,424,313
1987	5th	77	85	.475	8	Jim Fregosi	1,208,060
1988	5th	71	90	.441	32½	Jim Fregosi	1,115,749
1989	7th	69	92	.429	29½	Jeff Torborg	1,045,651
1990	2nd	94	68	.580	9	Jeff Torborg	2,002,357
1991	2nd	87	75	.537	8	Jeff Torborg	2,934,154
1992	3rd	86	76	.531	10	Gene Lamont	2,681,156
1993	1st‡	94	68	.580	+8	Gene Lamont	2,581,091

CENTRAL DIVISION

Year	Position	W	L	Pct.	*GB	Manager	Attendance
1994	1st	67	46	.593	+1	Gene Lamont	1,697,398
1995	3rd	68	76	.472	32	Gene Lamont, Terry Bevington	1,609,773
1996	2nd	85	77	.525	14½	Terry Bevington	1,676,403
1997	2nd	80	81	.497	6	Terry Bevington	1,864,782

*Games behind winner. †First half 31-22; second half 23-30. ‡Lost championship series.

MANAGERIAL RECORDS

Terry Bevington 222-214, Lena Blackburne 99-133, Donie Bush 118-189, Nixey Callahan 309-329, Eddie Collins 160-147, Red Corriden 52-72, Larry Doby 37-50, Hugh Duffy 145-159, Jimmie Dykes 899-940, Johnny Evers 66-87, Lew Fonseca 120-196, Jim Fregosi 193-226, Kid Gleason 392-364, Clark Griffith 157-113, Don Gutteridge 109-172, Fielder Jones 426-293, Don Kessinger 46-60, Tony La Russa 522-510, Gene Lamont 258-210, Bob Lemon 124-112, Al Lopez 840-650, Ted Lyons 185-245, Marty Marion 179-138, Jack Onslow 71-133, Paul Richards 406-362, Pants Rowland 339-247, Ray Schalk 102-125, Eddie Stanky 206-197, Billy Sullivan 78-74, Chuck Tanner 401-414, Jeff Torborg 250-235.

CLEVELAND INDIANS
YEARLY FINISHES

Year	Position	W	L	Pct.	*GB	Manager	Attendance
1901	7th	54	82	.397	29	James McAleer	131,380
1902	5th	69	67	.507	14	Bill Armour	275,395
1903	3rd	77	63	.550	15	Bill Armour	311,280
1904	4th	86	65	.570	7½	Bill Armour	264,749
1905	5th	76	78	.494	19	Nap Lajoie	316,306
1906	3rd	89	64	.582	5	Nap Lajoie	325,733
1907	4th	85	67	.559	8	Nap Lajoie	382,046
1908	2nd	90	64	.584	½	Nap Lajoie	422,242
1909	6th	71	82	.464	27½	Nap Lajoie, Deacon McGuire	354,627
1910	5th	71	81	.467	32	Deacon McGuire	293,456
1911	3rd	80	73	.523	22	Deacon McGuire, George Stovall	406,296
1912	5th	75	78	.490	30½	Harry Davis, J.L. Birmingham	336,844
1913	3rd	86	66	.566	9½	J.L. Birmingham	541,000
1914	8th	51	102	.333	48½	J.L. Birmingham	185,997
1915	7th	57	95	.375	44½	J.L. Birmingham, Lee Fohl	159,285
1916	6th	77	77	.500	14	Lee Fohl	492,106
1917	3rd	88	66	.571	12	Lee Fohl	477,298
1918	2nd	73	54	.575	2½	Lee Fohl	295,515
1919	2nd	84	55	.604	3½	Lee Fohl, Tris Speaker	538,135
1920	1st	98	56	.636	+2	Tris Speaker	912,832
1921	2nd	94	60	.610	4½	Tris Speaker	748,705
1922	4th	78	76	.507	16	Tris Speaker	528,145
1923	3rd	82	71	.536	16½	Tris Speaker	558,856
1924	6th	67	86	.438	24½	Tris Speaker	481,905
1925	6th	70	84	.455	27½	Tris Speaker	419,005
1926	2nd	88	66	.571	3	Tris Speaker	627,426
1927	6th	66	87	.431	43½	Jack McAllister	373,138
1928	7th	62	92	.403	39	Roger Peckinpaugh	375,907
1929	3rd	81	71	.533	24	Roger Peckinpaugh	536,210
1930	4th	81	73	.536	21	Roger Peckinpaugh	528,657
1931	4th	78	76	.506	30	Roger Peckinpaugh	483,027
1932	4th	87	65	.572	19	Roger Peckinpaugh	468,953
1933	4th	75	76	.497	23½	Roger Peckinpaugh, Walter Johnson	387,936
1934	3rd	85	69	.552	16	Walter Johnson	391,338

Year	Position	W	L	Pct.	*GB	Manager	Attendance
1935	3rd	82	71	.536	12	Walter Johnson, Steve O'Neill	397,615
1936	5th	80	74	.519	22½	Steve O'Neill	500,391
1937	4th	83	71	.539	19	Steve O'Neill	564,849
1938	3rd	86	66	.566	13	Ossie Vitt	652,006
1939	3rd	87	67	.565	20½	Ossie Vitt	563,926
1940	2nd	89	65	.578	1	Ossie Vitt	902,576
1941	4th (tied)	75	79	.487	26	Roger Peckinpaugh	745,948
1942	4th	75	79	.487	28	Lou Boudreau	459,447
1943	3rd	82	71	.536	15½	Lou Boudreau	438,894
1944	5th (tied)	72	82	.468	17	Lou Boudreau	475,272
1945	5th	73	72	.503	11	Lou Boudreau	558,182
1946	6th	68	86	.442	36	Lou Boudreau	1,057,289
1947	4th	80	74	.519	17	Lou Boudreau	1,521,978
1948	1st†	97	58	.626	+1	Lou Boudreau	2,620,627
1949	3rd	89	65	.578	8	Lou Boudreau	2,233,771
1950	4th	92	62	.597	6	Lou Boudreau	1,727,464
1951	2nd	93	61	.604	5	Al Lopez	1,704,984
1952	2nd	93	61	.604	2	Al Lopez	1,444,607
1953	2nd	92	62	.597	8½	Al Lopez	1,069,176
1954	1st	111	43	.721	+8	Al Lopez	1,335,472
1955	2nd	93	61	.604	3	Al Lopez	1,221,780
1956	2nd	88	66	.571	9	Al Lopez	865,467
1957	6th	76	77	.497	21½	Kerby Farrell	722,256
1958	4th	77	76	.503	14½	Bobby Bragan, Joe Gordon	663,805
1959	2nd	89	65	.578	5	Joe Gordon	1,497,976
1960	4th	76	78	.494	21	Joe Gordon, Jimmie Dykes	950,985
1961	5th	78	83	.484	30½	Jimmie Dykes	725,547
1962	6th	80	82	.494	16	Mel McGaha	716,076
1963	5th (tied)	79	83	.488	25½	Birdie Tebbetts	562,507
1964	6th (tied)	79	83	.488	20	Birdie Tebbetts	653,293
1965	5th	87	75	.537	15	Birdie Tebbetts	934,786
1966	5th	81	81	.500	17	Birdie Tebbetts, George Strickland	903,359
1967	8th	75	87	.463	17	Joe Adcock	662,980
1968	3rd	86	75	.534	16½	Alvin Dark	857,994

EAST DIVISION

Year	Position	W	L	Pct.	*GB	Manager	Attendance
1969	6th	62	99	.385	46½	Alvin Dark	619,970
1970	5th	76	86	.469	32	Alvin Dark	729,752
1971	6th	60	102	.370	43	Alvin Dark, John Lipon	591,361
1972	5th	72	84	.462	14	Ken Aspromonte	626,354
1973	6th	71	91	.438	26	Ken Aspromonte	615,107
1974	4th	77	85	.475	14	Ken Aspromonte	1,114,262
1975	4th	79	80	.497	15½	Frank Robinson	977,039
1976	4th	81	78	.509	16	Frank Robinson	948,776
1977	5th	71	90	.441	28½	Frank Robinson, Jeff Torborg	900,365
1978	6th	69	90	.434	29	Jeff Torborg	800,584
1979	6th	81	80	.503	22	Jeff Torborg, Dave Garcia	1,011,644
1980	6th	79	81	.494	23	Dave Garcia	1,033,827
1981	6th/5th	52	51	.504	‡	Dave Garcia	661,395
1982	6th (tied)	78	84	.481	17	Dave Garcia	1,044,021
1983	7th	70	92	.432	28	Mike Ferraro, Pat Corrales	768,941
1984	6th	75	87	.463	29	Pat Corrales	734,079
1985	7th	60	102	.370	39½	Pat Corrales	655,181
1986	5th	84	78	.519	11½	Pat Corrales	1,471,805
1987	7th	61	101	.377	37	Pat Corrales, Doc Edwards	1,077,898
1988	6th	78	84	.481	11	Doc Edwards	1,411,610
1989	6th	73	89	.451	16	Doc Edwards, John Hart	1,285,542
1990	4th	77	85	.475	11	John McNamara	1,225,240
1991	7th	57	105	.352	34	John McNamara, Mike Hargrove	1,051,863
1992	4th (tied)	76	86	.469	20	Mike Hargrove	1,224,274
1993	6th	76	86	.469	19	Mike Hargrove	2,177,908

CENTRAL DIVISION

Year	Position	W	L	Pct.	*GB	Manager	Attendance
1994	2nd	66	47	.584	1	Mike Hargrove	1,995,174
1995	1st§∞	100	44	.694	+30	Mike Hargrove	2,842,745
1996	1st▲	99	62	.615	+14½	Mike Hargrove	3,318,174
1997	1st§∞	86	75	.534	+6	Mike Hargrove	3,404,750

*Games behind winner. †Won pennant playoff. ‡First half 26-24; second half 26-27. §Won division series. ∞Won championship series. ▲Lost division series.

MANAGERIAL RECORDS

Joe Adcock 75-87, Bill Armour 232-195, Ken Aspromonte 220-260, Joe Birmingham 170-191, Lou Boudreau 728-649, Bobby Bragan 31-36, Pat Corrales 280-355, Alvin Dark 266-321, Harry Davis 54-71, Jimmie Dykes 103-115, Doc Edwards 173-207, Kerby Farrell 76-77, Mike Ferraro 40-60, Lee Fohl 327-310, Dave Garcia 247-244, Joe Gordon 184-151, Mike Hargrove 535-453, John Hart 8-11, Walter Johnson 179-168, Nap Lajoie 377-309, Johnny Lipon 18-41, Al Lopez 570-354, Jimmy McAleer 54-82, Jack McCallister 66-87, Mel McGaha 80-82, Deacon McGuire 91-117, John McNamara 102-137, Steve O'Neill 199-168, Roger Peckinpaugh 490-481, Frank Robinson 186-189, Tris Speaker 617-520, George Stovall 74-62, George Strickland 15-24, Birdie Tebbetts 269-298, Jeff Torborg 157-201, Oscar Vitt 262-198.

DETROIT TIGERS
YEARLY FINISHES

Year	Position	W	L	Pct.	*GB	Manager	Attendance
1901	3rd	74	61	.548	8 1/2	George Stallings	259,430
1902	7th	52	83	.385	30 1/2	Frank Dwyer	189,469
1903	5th	65	71	.478	25	Ed Barrow	224,523
1904	7th	62	90	.408	32	Ed Barrow, Bobby Lowe	177,796
1905	3rd	79	74	.516	15 1/2	Bill Armour	193,384
1906	6th	71	78	.477	21	Bill Armour	174,043
1907	1st	92	58	.613	+1 1/2	Hughey Jennings	297,079
1908	1st	90	63	.588	+ 1/2	Hughey Jennings	436,199
1909	1st	98	54	.645	+3 1/2	Hughey Jennings	490,490
1910	3rd	86	68	.558	18	Hughey Jennings	391,288
1911	2nd	89	65	.578	13 1/2	Hughey Jennings	484,988
1912	6th	69	84	.451	36 1/2	Hughey Jennings	402,870
1913	6th	66	87	.431	30	Hughey Jennings	398,502
1914	4th	80	73	.523	19 1/2	Hughey Jennings	416,225
1915	2nd	100	54	.649	2 1/2	Hughey Jennings	476,105
1916	3rd	87	67	.565	4	Hughey Jennings	616,772
1917	4th	78	75	.510	21 1/2	Hughey Jennings	457,289
1918	7th	55	71	.437	20	Hughey Jennings	203,719
1919	4th	80	60	.571	8	Hughey Jennings	643,805
1920	7th	61	93	.396	37	Hughey Jennings	579,650
1921	6th	71	82	.464	27	Ty Cobb	661,527
1922	3rd	79	75	.513	15	Ty Cobb	861,206
1923	2nd	83	71	.539	16	Ty Cobb	911,377
1924	3rd	86	68	.558	6	Ty Cobb	1,015,136
1925	4th	81	73	.526	16 1/2	Ty Cobb	820,766
1926	6th	79	75	.513	12	Ty Cobb	711,914
1927	4th	82	71	.536	27 1/2	George Moriarty	773,716
1928	6th	68	86	.442	33	George Moriarty	474,323
1929	6th	70	84	.455	36	Bucky Harris	869,318
1930	5th	75	79	.487	27	Bucky Harris	649,450
1931	7th	61	93	.396	47	Bucky Harris	434,056
1932	5th	76	75	.503	29 1/2	Bucky Harris	397,157
1933	5th	75	79	.487	25	Del Baker	320,972
1934	1st	101	53	.656	+7	Mickey Cochrane	919,161
1935	1st	93	58	.616	+3	Mickey Cochrane	1,034,929
1936	2nd	83	71	.539	19 1/2	Mickey Cochrane	875,948
1937	2nd	89	65	.578	13	Mickey Cochrane	1,072,276
1938	4th	84	70	.545	16	Mickey Cochrane, Del Baker	799,557
1939	5th	81	73	.526	26 1/2	Del Baker	836,279
1940	1st	90	64	.584	+1	Del Baker	1,112,693
1941	4th (tied)	75	79	.487	26	Del Baker	684,915
1942	5th	73	81	.474	30	Del Baker	580,087
1943	5th	78	76	.506	20	Steve O'Neill	606,287
1944	2nd	88	66	.571	1	Steve O'Neill	923,176
1945	1st	88	65	.575	+1 1/2	Steve O'Neill	1,280,341
1946	2nd	92	62	.597	12	Steve O'Neill	1,722,590
1947	2nd	85	69	.552	12	Steve O'Neill	1,398,093
1948	5th	78	76	.506	18 1/2	Steve O'Neill	1,743,035
1949	4th	87	67	.565	10	Red Rolfe	1,821,204
1950	2nd	95	59	.617	3	Red Rolfe	1,951,474
1951	5th	73	81	.474	25	Red Rolfe	1,132,641
1952	8th	50	104	.325	45	Red Rolfe, Fred Hutchinson	1,026,846
1953	6th	60	94	.390	40 1/2	Fred Hutchinson	884,658
1954	5th	68	86	.442	43	Fred Hutchinson	1,079,847
1955	5th	79	75	.513	17	Bucky Harris	1,181,838
1956	5th	82	72	.532	15	Bucky Harris	1,051,182
1957	4th	78	76	.506	20	Jack Tighe	1,272,346
1958	5th	77	77	.500	15	Jack Tighe, Bill Norman	1,098,924

Year	Position	W	L	Pct.	*GB	Manager	Attendance
1959	4th	76	78	.494	18	Bill Norman, Jimmie Dykes	1,221,221
1960	6th	71	83	.461	26	Jimmie Dykes, Billy Hitchcock, Joe Gordon	1,167,669
1961	2nd	101	61	.623	8	Bob Scheffing	1,600,710
1962	4th	85	76	.528	10½	Bob Scheffing	1,207,881
1963	5th (tied)	79	83	.488	25½	Bob Scheffing, Charlie Dressen	821,952
1964	4th	85	77	.525	14	Charlie Dressen	816,139
1965	4th	89	73	.549	13	Charlie Dressen, Bob Swift	1,029,645
1966	3rd	88	74	.543	10	Charlie Dressen, Bob Swift, Frank Skaff	1,124,293
1967	2nd	91	71	.562	1	Mayo Smith	1,447,143
1968	1st	103	59	.636	+12	Mayo Smith	2,031,847

EAST DIVISION

Year	Position	W	L	Pct.	*GB	Manager	Attendance
1969	2nd	90	72	.556	19	Mayo Smith	1,577,481
1970	4th	79	83	.488	29	Mayo Smith	1,501,293
1971	2nd	91	71	.562	12	Billy Martin	1,591,073
1972	1st†	86	70	.551	+½	Billy Martin	1,892,386
1973	3rd	85	77	.525	12	Billy Martin, Joe Schultz	1,724,146
1974	6th	72	90	.444	19	Ralph Houk	1,243,080
1975	6th	57	102	.358	37½	Ralph Houk	1,058,836
1976	5th	74	87	.460	24	Ralph Houk	1,467,020
1977	4th	74	88	.457	26	Ralph Houk	1,359,856
1978	5th	86	76	.531	13½	Ralph Houk	1,714,893
1979	5th	85	76	.528	18	Les Moss, Dick Tracewski, Sparky Anderson	1,630,929
1980	5th	84	78	.519	19	Sparky Anderson	1,785,293
1981	4th/2nd (tied)	60	49	.550	‡	Sparky Anderson	1,149,144
1982	4th	83	79	.512	12	Sparky Anderson	1,636,058
1983	2nd	92	70	.568	6	Sparky Anderson	1,829,636
1984	1st§	104	58	.642	+15	Sparky Anderson	2,704,794
1985	3rd	84	77	.522	15	Sparky Anderson	2,286,609
1986	3rd	87	75	.537	8½	Sparky Anderson	1,899,437
1987	1st†	98	64	.605	+2	Sparky Anderson	2,061,830
1988	2nd	88	74	.543	1	Sparky Anderson	2,081,162
1989	7th	59	103	.364	30	Sparky Anderson	1,543,656
1990	3rd	79	83	.488	9	Sparky Anderson	1,495,785
1991	2nd	84	78	.519	7	Sparky Anderson	1,641,661
1992	6th	75	87	.463	21	Sparky Anderson	1,423,963
1993	3rd (tied)	85	77	.525	10	Sparky Anderson	1,971,421
1994	5th	53	62	.461	18	Sparky Anderson	1,184,783
1995	4th	60	84	.417	26	Sparky Anderson	1,180,979
1996	5th	53	109	.327	39	Buddy Bell	1,168,610
1997	3rd	79	83	.488	19	Buddy Bell	1,365,157

*Games behind winner. †Lost championship series. ‡First half 31-26; second half 29-23. §Won championship series.

MANAGERIAL RECORDS

Sparky Anderson 1,431-1,248, Bill Armour 150-152, Del Baker 392-336, Ed Barrow 97-117, Buddy Bell 132-192, Ty Cobb 479-444, Mickey Cochrane 379-278, Chuck Dressen 221-189, Frank Dwyer 52-83, Jimmie Dykes 118-115, Joe Gordon 26-31, Bucky Harris 516-557, Ralph Houk 366-443, Fred Hutchinson 155-235, Hugh Jennings 1,131-972, Bobby Lowe 30-44, Billy Martin 248-204, George Moriarty 150-157, Les Moss 27-26, Bill Norman 58-64, Steve O'Neill 509-414, Red Rolfe 278-256, Bob Scheffing 210-173, Joe Schultz 14-14, Frank Skaff 40-39, Mayo Smith 363-285, George Stallings 74-61, Bob Swift 56-43, Jack Tighe 99-104.

KANSAS CITY ROYALS
YEARLY FINISHES

WEST DIVISION

Year	Position	W	L	Pct.	*GB	Manager	Attendance
1969	4th	69	93	.429	28	Joe Gordon	902,414
1970	4th (tied)	65	97	.401	33	Charlie Metro, Bob Lemon	693,047
1971	2nd	85	76	.528	16	Bob Lemon	910,784
1972	4th	76	78	.494	16½	Bob Lemon	707,656
1973	2nd	88	74	.543	6	Jack McKeon	1,345,341
1974	5th	77	85	.475	13	Jack McKeon	1,173,292
1975	2nd	91	71	.562	7	Jack McKeon, Whitey Herzog	1,151,836
1976	1st†	90	72	.556	+2½	Whitey Herzog	1,680,265
1977	1st†	102	60	.630	+8	Whitey Herzog	1,852,603
1978	1st†	92	70	.568	+5	Whitey Herzog	2,255,493
1979	2nd	85	77	.525	3	Whitey Herzog	2,261,845
1980	1st‡	97	65	.599	+14	Jim Frey	2,288,714
1981	5th/1st∞	50	53	.485	§	Jim Frey, Dick Howser	1,279,403
1982	2nd	90	72	.556	3	Dick Howser	2,284,464
1983	2nd	79	83	.488	20	Dick Howser	1,963,875
1984	1st†	84	78	.519	+3	Dick Howser	1,810,018
1985	1st‡	91	71	.562	+1	Dick Howser	2,162,717

Year	Position	W	L	Pct.	*GB	Manager	Attendance
1986	3rd (tied)	76	86	.469	16	Dick Howser, Mike Ferraro	2,320,794
1987	2nd	83	79	.512	2	Billy Gardner, John Wathan	2,392,471
1988	3rd	84	77	.522	19 1/2	John Wathan	2,350,181
1989	2nd	92	70	.568	7	John Wathan	2,477,700
1990	6th	75	86	.466	27 1/2	John Wathan	2,244,956
1991	6th	82	80	.506	13	John Wathan, Hal McRae	2,161,537
1992	5th (tied)	72	90	.444	24	Hal McRae	1,867,689
1993	3rd	84	78	.519	10	Hal McRae	1,934,578

CENTRAL DIVISION

Year	Position	W	L	Pct.	*GB	Manager	Attendance
1994	3rd	64	51	.557	4	Hal McRae	1,400,494
1995	2nd	70	74	.486	30	Bob Boone	1,233,530
1996	5th	75	86	.466	24	Bob Boone	1,435,997
1997	5th	67	94	.416	19	Bob Boone, Tony Muser	1,517,638

*Games behind winner. †Lost championship series. ‡Won championship series. §First half 20-30; second half 30-23. ∞Lost division series.

MANAGERIAL RECORDS

Bob Boone 181-206, Mike Ferraro 36-38, Jim Frey 127-105, Billy Gardner 62-64, Joe Gordon 69-93, Whitey Herzog 410-304, Dick Howser 404-365, Bob Lemon 207-218, Jack McKeon 215-205, Hal McRae 286-277, Charlie Metro 19-33, Tony Muser 31-48, John Wathan 288-270.

MILWAUKEE BREWERS
YEARLY FINISHES

WEST DIVISION

Year	Position	W	L	Pct.	*GB	Manager	Attendance
1969†	6th	64	98	.395	33	Joe Schultz	677,944
1970	4th	65	97	.401	33	Dave Bristol	933,690
1971	6th	69	92	.429	32	Dave Bristol	731,531

EAST DIVISION

Year	Position	W	L	Pct.	*GB	Manager	Attendance
1972	6th	65	91	.417	21	Dave Bristol, Del Crandall	600,440
1973	5th	74	88	.457	23	Del Crandall	1,092,158
1974	5th	76	86	.469	15	Del Crandall	955,741
1975	5th	68	94	.420	28	Del Crandall	1,213,357
1976	6th	66	95	.410	32	Alex Grammas	1,012,164
1977	6th	67	95	.414	33	Alex Grammas	1,114,938
1978	3rd	93	69	.574	6 1/2	George Bamberger	1,601,406
1979	2nd	95	66	.590	8	George Bamberger	1,918,343
1980	3rd	86	76	.531	17	George Bamberger, Buck Rodgers	1,857,408
1981	3rd/1st§	62	47	.569	‡	Buck Rodgers	878,432
1982	1st∞	95	67	.586	+1	Buck Rodgers, Harvey Kuenn	1,978,896
1983	5th	87	75	.537	11	Harvey Kuenn	2,397,131
1984	7th	67	94	.416	36 1/2	Rene Lachemann	1,608,509
1985	6th	71	90	.441	28	George Bamberger	1,360,265
1986	6th	77	84	.478	18	George Bamberger, Tom Trebelhorn	1,265,041
1987	3rd	91	71	.562	7	Tom Trebelhorn	1,909,244
1988	3rd (tied)	87	75	.537	2	Tom Trebelhorn	1,923,238
1989	4th	81	81	.500	8	Tom Trebelhorn	1,970,735
1990	6th	74	88	.457	14	Tom Trebelhorn	1,752,900
1991	4th	83	79	.512	8	Tom Trebelhorn	1,478,729
1992	2nd	92	70	.568	4	Phil Garner	1,857,314
1993	7th	69	93	.426	26	Phil Garner	1,688,080

CENTRAL DIVISION

Year	Position	W	L	Pct.	*GB	Manager	Attendance
1994	5th	53	62	.461	15	Phil Garner	1,268,399
1995	4th	65	79	.451	35	Phil Garner	1,087,560
1996	3rd	80	82	.494	19 1/2	Phil Garner	1,327,155
1997	3rd	78	83	.484	8	Phil Garner	1,444,027

*Games behind winner. †Seattle Pilots. ‡First half 31-25; second half 31-22. §Lost division series. ∞Won championship series.

MANAGERIAL RECORDS

George Bamberger 377-351, Dave Bristol 144-209, Del Crandall 271-338, Phil Garner 437-469, Alex Grammas 133-190, Harvey Kuenn 160-118, Rene Lachemann 67-94, Buck Rodgers 124-102, Joe Schultz 64-98, Tom Trebelhorn 422-397.

Year	Position	W	L	Pct.	*GB	Manager	Attendance
1901†	6th	61	72	.459	20 1/2	Jimmy Manning	161,661
1902†	6th	61	75	.449	22	Tom Loftus	188,158
1903†	8th	43	94	.314	47 1/2	Tom Loftus	128,878
1904†	8th	38	113	.251	55 1/2	Patsy Donovan	131,744
1905†	7th	64	87	.421	29 1/2	Jake Stahl	252,027
1906†	7th	55	95	.367	37 1/2	Jake Stahl	129,903
1907†	8th	49	102	.325	43 1/2	Joe Cantillon	221,929
1908†	7th	67	85	.441	22 1/2	Joe Cantillon	264,252
1909†	8th	42	110	.276	56	Joe Cantillon	205,199
1910†	7th	66	85	.437	36 1/2	Jimmy McAleer	254,591
1911†	7th	64	90	.416	38 1/2	Jimmy McAleer	244,884
1912†	2nd	91	61	.599	14	Clark Griffith	350,663
1913†	2nd	90	64	.584	6 1/2	Clark Griffith	325,831
1914†	3rd	81	73	.526	19	Clark Griffith	243,888
1915†	4th	85	68	.556	17	Clark Griffith	167,332
1916†	7th	76	77	.497	14 1/2	Clark Griffith	177,265
1917†	5th	74	79	.484	25 1/2	Clark Griffith	89,682
1918†	3rd	72	56	.563	4	Clark Griffith	182,122
1919†	7th	56	84	.400	32	Clark Griffith	234,096
1920†	6th	68	84	.447	29	Clark Griffith	359,260
1921†	4th	80	73	.523	18	George McBride	456,069
1922†	6th	69	85	.448	25	Clyde Milan	458,552
1923†	4th	75	78	.490	23 1/2	Donie Bush	357,406
1924†	1st	92	62	.597	+2	Bucky Harris	534,310
1925†	1st	96	55	.636	+8 1/2	Bucky Harris	817,199
1926†	4th	81	69	.540	8	Bucky Harris	551,580
1927†	3rd	85	69	.552	25	Bucky Harris	528,976
1928†	4th	75	79	.487	26	Bucky Harris	378,501
1929†	5th	71	81	.467	34	Walter Johnson	355,506
1930†	2nd	94	60	.610	8	Walter Johnson	614,474
1931†	3rd	92	62	.597	16	Walter Johnson	492,657
1932†	3rd	93	61	.604	14	Walter Johnson	371,396
1933†	1st	99	53	.651	+7	Joe Cronin	437,533
1934†	7th	66	86	.434	34	Joe Cronin	330,074
1935†	6th	67	86	.438	27	Bucky Harris	255,011
1936†	4th	82	71	.536	20	Bucky Harris	379,525
1937†	6th	73	80	.477	28 1/2	Bucky Harris	397,799
1938†	5th	75	76	.497	23 1/2	Bucky Harris	522,694
1939†	6th	65	87	.428	41 1/2	Bucky Harris	339,257
1940†	7th	64	90	.416	26	Bucky Harris	381,241
1941†	6th (tied)	70	84	.455	31	Bucky Harris	415,663
1942†	7th	62	89	.411	39 1/2	Bucky Harris	403,493
1943†	2nd	84	69	.549	13 1/2	Ossie Bluege	574,694
1944†	8th	64	90	.416	25	Ossie Bluege	525,235
1945†	2nd	87	67	.565	1 1/2	Ossie Bluege	652,660
1946†	4th	76	78	.494	28	Ossie Bluege	1,027,216
1947†	7th	64	90	.416	33	Ossie Bluege	850,758
1948†	7th	56	97	.366	40	Joe Kuhel	795,254
1949†	8th	50	104	.325	47	Joe Kuhel	770,745
1950†	5th	67	87	.435	31	Bucky Harris	699,697
1951†	7th	62	92	.403	36	Bucky Harris	695,167
1952†	5th	78	76	.506	17	Bucky Harris	699,457
1953†	5th	76	76	.500	23 1/2	Bucky Harris	595,594
1954†	6th	66	88	.429	45	Bucky Harris	503,542
1955†	8th	53	101	.344	43	Chuck Dressen	425,238
1956†	7th	59	95	.383	38	Chuck Dressen	431,647
1957†	8th	55	99	.357	43	Chuck Dressen, Cookie Lavagetto	457,079
1958†	8th	61	93	.396	31	Cookie Lavagetto	475,288
1959†	8th	63	91	.409	31	Cookie Lavagetto	615,372
1960†	5th	73	81	.474	24	Cookie Lavagetto	743,404
1961	7th	70	90	.438	38	Cookie Lavagetto, Sam Mele	1,256,723
1962	2nd	91	71	.562	5	Sam Mele	1,433,116
1963	3rd	91	70	.565	13	Sam Mele	1,406,652
1964	6th (tied)	79	83	.488	20	Sam Mele	1,207,514
1965	1st	102	60	.630	+7	Sam Mele	1,463,258
1966	2nd	89	73	.549	9	Sam Mele	1,259,374
1967	2nd (tied)	91	71	.562	1	Sam Mele, Cal Ermer	1,483,547
1968	7th	79	83	.488	24	Cal Ermer	1,143,257

HISTORY Team by team

WEST DIVISION

Year	Position	W	L	Pct.	*GB	Manager	Attendance
1969	1st‡	97	65	.599	+9	Billy Martin	1,349,328
1970	1st‡	98	64	.605	+9	Bill Rigney	1,261,887
1971	5th	74	86	.463	26 1/2	Bill Rigney	940,858
1972	3rd	77	77	.500	15 1/2	Bill Rigney, Frank Quilici	797,901
1973	3rd	81	81	.500	13	Frank Quilici	907,499
1974	3rd	82	80	.506	8	Frank Quilici	662,401
1975	4th	76	83	.478	20 1/2	Frank Quilici	737,156
1976	3rd	85	77	.525	5	Gene Mauch	715,394
1977	4th	84	77	.522	17 1/2	Gene Mauch	1,162,727
1978	4th	73	89	.451	19	Gene Mauch	787,878
1979	4th	82	80	.506	6	Gene Mauch	1,070,521
1980	3rd	77	84	.478	19 1/2	Gene Mauch, Johnny Goryl	769,206
1981	7th/4th	41	68	.376	§	Johnny Goryl, Billy Gardner	469,090
1982	7th	60	102	.370	33	Billy Gardner	921,186
1983	5th (tied)	70	92	.432	29	Billy Gardner	858,939
1984	2nd (tied)	81	81	.500	3	Billy Gardner	1,598,422
1985	4th (tied)	77	85	.475	14	Billy Gardner, Ray Miller	1,651,814
1986	6th	71	91	.438	21	Ray Miller, Tom Kelly	1,255,453
1987	1st∞	85	77	.525	+2	Tom Kelly	2,081,976
1988	2nd	91	71	.562	13	Tom Kelly	3,030,672
1989	5th	80	82	.494	19	Tom Kelly	2,277,438
1990	7th	74	88	.457	29	Tom Kelly	1,751,584
1991	1st∞	95	67	.586	+8	Tom Kelly	2,293,842
1992	2nd	90	72	.556	6	Tom Kelly	2,482,428
1993	5th (tied)	71	91	.438	23	Tom Kelly	2,048,673

CENTRAL DIVISION

Year	Position	W	L	Pct.	*GB	Manager	Attendance
1994	4th	53	60	.469	14	Tom Kelly	1,398,565
1995	5th	56	88	.389	44	Tom Kelly	1,057,667
1996	4th	78	84	.481	21 1/2	Tom Kelly	1,437,352
1997	4th	68	94	.420	18 1/2	Tom Kelly	1,411,064

*Games behind winner. †Washington Senators (original club). ‡Lost championship series. §First half 17-39; second half 24-29. ∞Won championship series.

MANAGERIAL RECORDS

Ossie Bluege 375-394, Donie Bush 75-78, Joe Cantillon 158-297, Joe Cronin 165-139, Patsy Donovan 38-113, Chuck Dressen 116-212, Cal Ermer 145-129, Billy Gardner 268-353, Johnny Goryl 34-38, Clark Griffith 693-646, Bucky Harris 1,336-1,416, Walter Johnson 350-264, Tom Kelly 853-885, Joe Kuhel 106-201, Cookie Lavagetto 271-384, Tom Loftus 104-169, Jimmy Manning 61-72, Billy Martin 97-65, Gene Mauch 378-394, Jimmy McAleer 130-175, George McBride 80-73, Sam Mele 524-436, Clyde Milan 69-85, Ray Miller 109-130, Frank Quilici 280-287, Bill Rigney 208-184, Jake Stahl 119-182.

NEW YORK YANKEES
YEARLY FINISHES

Year	Position	W	L	Pct.	*GB	Manager	Attendance
1901†	5th	68	65	.511	13 1/2	John McGraw	141,952
1902	8th	50	88	.362	34	John McGraw, Wilbert Robinson	174,606
1903	4th	72	62	.537	17	Clark Griffith	211,808
1904	2nd	92	59	.609	1 1/2	Clark Griffith	438,919
1905	6th	71	78	.477	21 1/2	Clark Griffith	309,100
1906	2nd	90	61	.596	3	Clark Griffith	434,709
1907	5th	70	78	.473	21	Clark Griffith	350,020
1908	8th	51	103	.331	39 1/2	Clark Griffith, Kid Elberfeld	305,500
1909	5th	74	77	.490	23 1/2	George Stallings	501,000
1910	2nd‡	88	63	.583	14 1/2	George Stallings, Hal Chase	355,857
1911	6th	76	76	.500	25 1/2	Hal Chase	302,444
1912	8th	50	102	.329	55	Harry Wolverton	242,194
1913	7th	57	94	.377	38	Frank Chance	357,551
1914	6th (tied)	70	84	.455	30	Frank Chance, Roger Peckinpaugh	359,477
1915	5th	69	83	.454	32 1/2	Bill Donovan	256,035
1916	4th	80	74	.519	11	Bill Donovan	469,211
1917	6th	71	82	.464	28 1/2	Bill Donovan	330,294
1918	4th	60	63	.488	13 1/2	Miller Huggins	282,047
1919	3rd	80	59	.576	7 1/2	Miller Huggins	619,164
1920	3rd	95	59	.617	3	Miller Huggins	1,289,422
1921	1st	98	55	.641	+4 1/2	Miller Huggins	1,230,696
1922	1st	94	60	.610	+1	Miller Huggins	1,026,134
1923	1st	98	54	.645	+16	Miller Huggins	1,007,066
1924	2nd	89	63	.586	2	Miller Huggins	1,053,533
1925	7th	69	85	.448	30	Miller Huggins	697,267
1926	1st	91	63	.591	+3	Miller Huggins	1,027,095

Year	Position	W	L	Pct.	*GB	Manager	Attendance
1927	1st	110	44	.714	+19	Miller Huggins	1,164,015
1928	1st	101	53	.656	+2 1/2	Miller Huggins	1,072,132
1929	2nd	88	66	.571	18	Miller Huggins, Art Fletcher	960,148
1930	3rd	86	68	.558	16	Bob Shawkey	1,169,230
1931	2nd	94	59	.614	13 1/2	Joe McCarthy	912,437
1932	1st	107	47	.695	+13	Joe McCarthy	962,320
1933	2nd	91	59	.607	7	Joe McCarthy	728,014
1934	2nd	94	60	.610	7	Joe McCarthy	854,682
1935	2nd	89	60	.597	3	Joe McCarthy	657,508
1936	1st	102	51	.667	+19 1/2	Joe McCarthy	976,913
1937	1st	102	52	.662	+13	Joe McCarthy	998,148
1938	1st	99	53	.651	+9 1/2	Joe McCarthy	970,916
1939	1st	106	45	.702	+17	Joe McCarthy	859,785
1940	3rd	88	66	.571	2	Joe McCarthy	988,975
1941	1st	101	53	.656	+17	Joe McCarthy	964,722
1942	1st	103	51	.669	+9	Joe McCarthy	988,251
1943	1st	98	56	.636	+13 1/2	Joe McCarthy	645,006
1944	3rd	83	71	.539	6	Joe McCarthy	822,864
1945	4th	81	71	.533	6 1/2	Joe McCarthy	881,846
1946	3rd	87	67	.565	17	Joe McCarthy, Bill Dickey, Johnny Neun	2,265,512
1947	1st	97	57	.630	+12	Bucky Harris	2,178,937
1948	3rd	94	60	.610	2 1/2	Bucky Harris	2,373,901
1949	1st	97	57	.630	+1	Casey Stengel	2,281,676
1950	1st	98	56	.636	+3	Casey Stengel	2,081,380
1951	1st	98	56	.636	+5	Casey Stengel	1,950,107
1952	1st	95	59	.617	+2	Casey Stengel	1,629,665
1953	1st	99	52	.656	+8 1/2	Casey Stengel	1,537,811
1954	2nd	103	51	.669	8	Casey Stengel	1,475,171
1955	1st	96	58	.623	+3	Casey Stengel	1,490,138
1956	1st	97	57	.630	+9	Casey Stengel	1,491,784
1957	1st	98	56	.636	+8	Casey Stengel	1,497,134
1958	1st	92	62	.597	+10	Casey Stengel	1,428,438
1959	3rd	79	75	.513	15	Casey Stengel	1,552,030
1960	1st	97	57	.630	+8	Casey Stengel	1,627,349
1961	1st	109	53	.673	+8	Ralph Houk	1,747,725
1962	1st	96	66	.593	+5	Ralph Houk	1,493,574
1963	1st	104	57	.646	+10 1/2	Ralph Houk	1,308,920
1964	1st	99	63	.611	+1	Yogi Berra	1,305,638
1965	6th	77	85	.475	25	Johnny Keane	1,213,552
1966	10th	70	89	.440	26 1/2	Johnny Keane, Ralph Houk	1,124,648
1967	9th	72	90	.444	20	Ralph Houk	1,259,514
1968	5th	83	79	.512	20	Ralph Houk	1,185,666

EAST DIVISION

Year	Position	W	L	Pct.	*GB	Manager	Attendance
1969	5th	80	81	.497	28 1/2	Ralph Houk	1,067,996
1970	2nd	93	69	.574	15	Ralph Houk	1,136,879
1971	4th	82	80	.506	21	Ralph Houk	1,070,771
1972	4th	79	76	.510	6 1/2	Ralph Houk	966,328
1973	4th	80	82	.494	17	Ralph Houk	1,262,103
1974	2nd	89	73	.549	2	Bill Virdon	1,273,075
1975	3rd	83	77	.519	12	Bill Virdon, Billy Martin	1,288,048
1976	1st‡	97	62	.610	+10 1/2	Billy Martin	2,012,434
1977	1st‡	100	62	.617	+2 1/2	Billy Martin	2,103,092
1978	1st§‡	100	63	.613	+1	Billy Martin, Bob Lemon	2,335,871
1979	4th	89	71	.556	13 1/2	Bob Lemon, Billy Martin	2,537,765
1980	1st∞	103	59	.636	+3	Dick Howser	2,627,417
1981	1st/6th◆‡	59	48	.551	▲	Gene Michael, Bob Lemon	1,614,533
1982	5th	79	83	.488	16	Bob Lemon, Gene Michael, Clyde King	2,041,219
1983	3rd	91	71	.562	7	Billy Martin	2,257,976
1984	3rd	87	75	.537	17	Yogi Berra	1,821,815
1985	2nd	97	64	.602	2	Yogi Berra, Billy Martin	2,214,587
1986	2nd	90	72	.556	5 1/2	Lou Piniella	2,268,030
1987	4th	89	73	.549	9	Lou Piniella	2,427,672
1988	5th	85	76	.528	3 1/2	Billy Martin, Lou Piniella	2,633,701
1989	5th	74	87	.460	14 1/2	Dallas Green, Bucky Dent	2,170,485
1990	7th	67	95	.414	21	Bucky Dent, Stump Merrill	2,006,436
1991	5th	71	91	.438	20	Stump Merrill	1,863,733
1992	4th (tied)	76	86	.469	20	Buck Showalter	1,748,733
1993	2nd	88	74	.543	7	Buck Showalter	2,416,965
1994	1st	70	43	.619	+6 1/2	Buck Showalter	1,675,556
1995	2nd◆▼	79	65	.549	7	Buck Showalter	1,705,263
1996	1st■‡	92	70	.568	+4	Joe Torre	2,250,877
1997	2nd◆▼	96	66	.593	2	Joe Torre	2,580,325

*Games behind winner. †Baltimore Orioles. ‡Won championship series. §Won pennant playoff. ∞Lost championship series. ▲First half 34-22; second half 25-26. ◆Wild-card playoff qualifier. ■Won division series. ▼Lost division series.

HISTORY *Team by team*

MANAGERIAL RECORDS

Yogi Berra 192-148, Frank Chance 117-168, Hal Chase 86-80, Bucky Dent 36-53, Bill Dickey 57-48, Bill Donovan 220-239, Kid Elberfeld 27-71, Art Fletcher 6-5, Dallas Green 56-65, Clark Griffith 419-370, Bucky Harris 191-117, Ralph Houk 944-806, Dick Howser 103-59, Miller Huggins 1,067-719, Johnny Keane 81-101, Clyde King 29-33, Bob Lemon 99-73, Billy Martin 501-385, Joe McCarthy 1,460-867, John McGraw 94-96, Stump Merrill 120-155, Gene Michael 92-76, Johnny Neun 8-6, Roger Peckinpaugh 10-10, Lou Piniella 224-193, Wilbert Robinson 24-57, Bob Shawkey 86-68, Buck Showalter 311-268, George Stallings 152-136, Casey Stengel 1,149-696, Joe Torre 188-136, Bill Virdon 142-124, Harry Wolverton 50-102.

OAKLAND ATHLETICS
YEARLY FINISHES

Year	Position	W	L	Pct.	*GB	Manager	Attendance
1901†	4th	74	62	.544	9	Connie Mack	206,329
1902†	1st	83	53	.610	+5	Connie Mack	442,473
1903†	2nd	75	60	.556	14 1/2	Connie Mack	420,078
1904†	5th	81	70	.536	12 1/2	Connie Mack	512,294
1905†	1st	92	56	.622	+2	Connie Mack	554,576
1906†	4th	78	67	.538	12	Connie Mack	489,129
1907†	2nd	88	57	.607	1 1/2	Connie Mack	625,581
1908†	6th	68	85	.444	22	Connie Mack	455,062
1909†	2nd	95	58	.621	3 1/2	Connie Mack	674,915
1910†	1st	102	48	.680	+14 1/2	Connie Mack	588,905
1911†	1st	101	50	.669	+13 1/2	Connie Mack	605,749
1912†	3rd	90	62	.592	15	Connie Mack	517,653
1913†	1st	96	57	.627	+6 1/2	Connie Mack	571,896
1914†	1st	99	53	.651	+8 1/2	Connie Mack	346,641
1915†	8th	43	109	.283	58 1/2	Connie Mack	146,223
1916†	8th	36	117	.235	54 1/2	Connie Mack	184,471
1917†	8th	55	98	.359	44 1/2	Connie Mack	221,432
1918†	8th	52	76	.406	24	Connie Mack	177,926
1919†	8th	36	104	.257	52	Connie Mack	225,209
1920†	8th	48	106	.312	50	Connie Mack	287,888
1921†	8th	53	100	.346	45	Connie Mack	344,430
1922†	7th	65	89	.422	29	Connie Mack	425,356
1923†	6th	69	83	.454	29	Connie Mack	534,122
1924†	5th	71	81	.467	20	Connie Mack	531,992
1925†	2nd	88	64	.579	8 1/2	Connie Mack	869,703
1926†	3rd	83	67	.553	6	Connie Mack	714,308
1927†	2nd	91	63	.591	19	Connie Mack	605,529
1928†	2nd	98	55	.641	2 1/2	Connie Mack	689,756
1929†	1st	104	46	.693	+18	Connie Mack	839,176
1930†	1st	102	52	.662	+8	Connie Mack	721,663
1931†	1st	107	45	.704	+13 1/2	Connie Mack	627,464
1932†	2nd	94	60	.610	13	Connie Mack	405,500
1933†	3rd	79	72	.523	19 1/2	Connie Mack	297,138
1934†	5th	68	82	.453	31	Connie Mack	305,847
1935†	8th	58	91	.389	34	Connie Mack	233,173
1936†	8th	53	100	.346	49	Connie Mack	285,173
1937†	7th	54	97	.358	46 1/2	Connie Mack	430,733
1938†	8th	53	99	.349	46	Connie Mack	385,357
1939†	7th	55	97	.362	51 1/2	Connie Mack	395,022
1940†	8th	54	100	.351	36	Connie Mack	432,145
1941†	8th	64	90	.416	37	Connie Mack	528,894
1942†	8th	55	99	.357	48	Connie Mack	423,487
1943†	8th	49	105	.318	49	Connie Mack	376,735
1944†	5th (tied)	72	82	.468	17	Connie Mack	505,322
1945†	8th	52	98	.347	34 1/2	Connie Mack	462,631
1946†	8th	49	105	.318	55	Connie Mack	621,793
1947†	5th	78	76	.506	19	Connie Mack	911,566
1948†	4th	84	70	.545	12 1/2	Connie Mack	945,076
1949†	5th	81	73	.526	16	Connie Mack	816,514
1950†	8th	52	102	.338	46	Connie Mack	309,805
1951†	6th	70	84	.455	28	Jimmie Dykes	465,469
1952†	4th	79	75	.513	16	Jimmie Dykes	627,100
1953†	7th	59	95	.383	41 1/2	Jimmie Dykes	362,113
1954†	8th	51	103	.331	60	Ed Joost	304,666
1955‡	6th	63	91	.409	33	Lou Boudreau	1,393,054
1956‡	8th	52	102	.338	45	Lou Boudreau	1,015,154
1957‡	7th	59	94	.386	38 1/2	Lou Boudreau, Harry Craft	901,067
1958‡	7th	73	81	.474	19	Harry Craft	925,090
1959‡	7th	66	88	.429	28	Harry Craft	963,683
1960‡	8th	58	96	.377	39	Bob Elliot	774,944
1961‡	9th (tied)	61	100	.379	47 1/2	Joe Gordon, Hank Bauer	683,817
1962‡	9th	72	90	.444	24	Hank Bauer	635,675
1963‡	8th	73	89	.451	31 1/2	Ed Lopat	762,364

Year	Position	W	L	Pct.	*GB	Manager	Attendance
1964‡	10th	57	105	.352	42	Ed Lopat, Mel McGaha	642,478
1965‡	10th	59	103	.364	43	Mel McGaha, Haywood Sullivan	528,344
1966‡	7th	74	86	.463	23	Alvin Dark	773,929
1967‡	10th	62	99	.385	29 1/2	Alvin Dark, Luke Appling	726,639
1968	6th	82	80	.506	21	Bob Kennedy	837,466

WEST DIVISION

Year	Position	W	L	Pct.	*GB	Manager	Attendance
1969	2nd	88	74	.543	9	Hank Bauer, John McNamara	778,232
1970	2nd	89	73	.549	9	John McNamara	778,355
1971	1st§	101	60	.627	+16	Dick Williams	914,993
1972	1st∞	93	62	.600	+5 1/2	Dick Williams	921,323
1973	1st∞	94	68	.580	+6	Dick Williams	1,000,763
1974	1st∞	90	72	.556	+5	Alvin Dark	845,693
1975	1st§	98	64	.605	+7	Alvin Dark	1,075,518
1976	2nd	87	74	.540	2 1/2	Chuck Tanner	780,593
1977	7th	63	98	.391	38 1/2	Jack McKeon, Bobby Winkles	495,599
1978	6th	69	93	.426	23	Bobby Winkles, Jack McKeon	526,999
1979	7th	54	108	.333	34	Jim Marshall	306,763
1980	2nd	83	79	.512	14	Billy Martin	842,259
1981	1st/2nd◆§	64	45	.587	▲	Billy Martin	1,304,054
1982	5th	68	94	.420	25	Billy Martin	1,735,489
1983	4th	74	88	.457	25	Steve Boros	1,294,941
1984	4th	77	85	.475	7	Steve Boros, Jackie Moore	1,353,281
1985	4th (tied)	77	85	.475	14	Jackie Moore	1,334,599
1986	3rd (tied)	76	86	.469	16	Jackie Moore, Tony La Russa	1,314,646
1987	3rd	81	81	.500	4	Tony La Russa	1,678,921
1988	1st∞	104	58	.642	+13	Tony La Russa	2,287,335
1989	1st∞	99	63	.611	+7	Tony La Russa	2,667,225
1990	1st∞	103	59	.636	+9	Tony La Russa	2,900,217
1991	4th	84	78	.519	11	Tony La Russa	2,713,493
1992	1st§	96	66	.593	+6	Tony La Russa	2,494,160
1993	7th	68	94	.420	26	Tony La Russa	2,035,025
1994	2nd	51	63	.447	1	Tony La Russa	1,242,692
1995	4th	67	77	.465	11 1/2	Tony La Russa	1,174,310
1996	3rd	78	84	.481	12	Art Howe	1,148,380
1997	4th	65	97	.401	25	Art Howe	1,264,218

*Games behind winner. †Philadelphia Athletics. ‡Kansas City Athletics. §Lost championship series. ∞Won championship series. ▲First half 37-23; second half 27-22. ◆Won division series.

MANAGERIAL RECORDS

Luke Appling 10-30, Hank Bauer 187-226, Steve Boros 94-112, Lou Boudreau 151-260, Harry Craft 162-196, Alvin Dark 314-291, Jimmie Dykes 198-254, Bob Elliott 58-96, Joe Gordon 26-33, Art Howe 143-181, Eddie Joost 51-103, Bob Kennedy 82-80, Tony La Russa 695-614, Eddie Lopat 90-124, Connie Mack 3,582-3,814, Jim Marshall 54-108, Billy Martin 215-218, Mel McGaha 45-91, Jack McKeon 71-105, John McNamara 97-78, Jackie Moore 163-190, Haywood Sullivan 54-82, Chuck Tanner 87-74, Dick Williams 288-190, Bobby Winkles 61-86.

SEATTLE MARINERS
YEARLY FINISHES

WEST DIVISION

Year	Position	W	L	Pct.	*GB	Manager	Attendance
1977	6th	64	98	.395	38	Darrell Johnson	1,338,511
1978	7th	56	104	.350	35	Darrell Johnson	877,440
1979	6th	67	95	.414	21	Darrell Johnson	844,441
1980	7th	59	103	.364	38	Darrell Johnson, Maury Wills	836,204
1981	6th/5th	44	65	.404	†	Maury Wills, Rene Lachemann	636,276
1982	4th	76	86	.469	17	Rene Lachemann	1,070,404
1983	7th	60	102	.370	39	Rene Lachemann, Del Crandall	813,537
1984	5th (tied)	74	88	.457	10	Del Crandall, Chuck Cottier	870,372
1985	6th	74	88	.457	17	Chuck Cottier	1,128,696
1986	7th	67	95	.414	25	Chuck Cottier, Marty Martinez, Dick Williams	1,029,045
1987	4th	78	84	.481	7	Dick Williams	1,134,255
1988	7th	68	93	.422	35 1/2	Dick Williams, Jim Snyder	1,022,398
1989	6th	73	89	.451	26	Jim Lefebvre	1,298,443
1990	5th	77	85	.475	26	Jim Lefebvre	1,509,727
1991	5th	83	79	.512	12	Jim Lefebvre	2,147,905
1992	7th	64	98	.395	32	Bill Plummer	1,651,398
1993	4th	82	80	.506	12	Lou Piniella	2,051,853
1994	3rd	49	63	.438	2	Lou Piniella	1,104,206
1995	1st‡§	79	66	.545	+1	Lou Piniella	1,643,203
1996	2nd	85	76	.528	4 1/2	Lou Piniella	2,723,850
1997	1st∞	90	72	.556	+6	Lou Piniella	3,192,237

*Games behind winner. †First half 21-36; second half 23-29. ‡Won division series. §Lost championship series. ∞Lost division series.

MANAGERIAL RECORDS

Chuck Cottier 98-120, Del Crandall 93-141, Darrell Johnson 226-362, Rene Lachemann 140-180, Jim Lefebvre 233-253, Lou Piniella 385-357, Bill Plummer 64-98, Jimmy Snyder 45-60, Dick Williams 159-192, Maury Wills 26-56.

TEXAS RANGERS
YEARLY FINISHES

Year	Position	W	L	Pct.	*GB	Manager	Attendance
1961†	9th (tied)	61	100	.379	47 1/2	Mickey Vernon	597,287
1962†	10th	60	101	.373	35 1/2	Mickey Vernon	729,775
1963†	10th	56	106	.346	48 1/2	Mickey Vernon, Gil Hodges	535,604
1964†	9th	62	100	.383	37	Gil Hodges	600,106
1965†	8th	70	92	.432	32	Gil Hodges	560,083
1966†	8th	71	88	.447	25 1/2	Gil Hodges	576,260
1967†	6th (tied)	76	85	.472	15 1/2	Gil Hodges	770,863
1968†	10th	65	96	.404	37 1/2	Jim Lemon	546,661

EAST DIVISION

Year	Position	W	L	Pct.	*GB	Manager	Attendance
1969†	4th	86	76	.531	23	Ted Williams	918,106
1970†	6th	70	92	.432	38	Ted Williams	824,789
1971†	5th	63	96	.396	38 1/2	Ted Williams	655,156

WEST DIVISION

Year	Position	W	L	Pct.	*GB	Manager	Attendance
1972	6th	54	100	.351	38 1/2	Ted Williams	662,974
1973	6th	57	105	.352	37	Whitey Herzog, Del Wilber, Billy Martin	686,085
1974	2nd	84	76	.525	5	Billy Martin	1,193,902
1975	3rd	79	83	.488	19	Billy Martin, Frank Lucchesi	1,127,924
1976	4th (tied)	76	86	.469	14	Frank Lucchesi	1,164,982
1977	2nd	94	68	.580	8	Frank Lucchesi, Eddie Stanky, Connie Ryan, Billy Hunter	1,250,722
1978	2nd (tied)	87	75	.537	5	Billy Hunter, Pat Corrales	1,447,963
1979	3rd	83	79	.512	5	Pat Corrales	1,519,671
1980	4th	76	85	.472	20 1/2	Pat Corrales	1,198,175
1981	2nd/3rd	57	48	.543	‡	Don Zimmer	850,076
1982	6th	64	98	.395	29	Don Zimmer, Darrell Johnson	1,154,432
1983	3rd	77	85	.475	22	Doug Rader	1,363,469
1984	7th	69	92	.429	14 1/2	Doug Rader	1,102,471
1985	7th	62	99	.385	28 1/2	Doug Rader, Bobby Valentine	1,112,497
1986	2nd	87	75	.537	5	Bobby Valentine	1,692,002
1987	6th (tied)	75	87	.463	10	Bobby Valentine	1,763,053
1988	6th	70	91	.435	33 1/2	Bobby Valentine	1,581,901
1989	4th	83	79	.512	16	Bobby Valentine	2,043,993
1990	3rd	83	79	.512	20	Bobby Valentine	2,057,911
1991	3rd	85	77	.525	10	Bobby Valentine	2,297,720
1992	4th	77	85	.475	19	Bobby Valentine, Toby Harrah	2,198,231
1993	2nd	86	76	.531	8	Kevin Kennedy	2,244,616
1994	1st	52	62	.456	+1	Kevin Kennedy	2,503,198
1995	3rd	74	70	.514	4 1/2	Johnny Oates	1,985,910
1996	1st§	90	72	.556	+4 1/2	Johnny Oates	2,889,020
1997	3rd	77	85	.475	13	Johnny Oates	2,945,228

*Games behind winner. †Washington Senators (second club). ‡First half 33-22; second half 24-26. §Lost division series.

MANAGERIAL RECORDS

Pat Corrales 160-164, Toby Harrah 32-44, Whitey Herzog 47-91, Gil Hodges 321-444, Billy Hunter 146-108, Darrell Johnson 26-40, Kevin Kennedy 138-138, Jim Lemon 65-96, Frank Lucchesi 142-149, Billy Martin 137-141, Johnny Oates 241-227, Doug Rader 155-200, Connie Ryan 2-4, Eddie Stanky 1-0, Bobby Valentine 581-605, Mickey Vernon 135-227, Del Wilber 1-0, Ted Williams 273-364, Don Zimmer 95-106.

TORONTO BLUE JAYS
YEARLY FINISHES

EAST DIVISION

Year	Position	W	L	Pct.	*GB	Manager	Attendance
1977	7th	54	107	.335	45 1/2	Roy Hartsfield	1,701,052
1978	7th	59	102	.366	40	Roy Hartsfield	1,562,585
1979	7th	53	109	.327	50 1/2	Roy Hartsfield	1,431,651
1980	7th	67	95	.414	36	Bobby Mattick	1,400,327
1981	7th/7th	37	69	.349	†	Bobby Mattick	755,083

Year	Position	W	L	Pct.	*GB	Manager	Attendance
1982	6th (tied)	78	84	.481	17	Bobby Cox	1,275,978
1983	4th	89	73	.549	9	Bobby Cox	1,930,415
1984	2nd	89	73	.549	15	Bobby Cox	2,110,009
1985	1st‡	99	62	.615	+2	Bobby Cox	2,468,925
1986	4th	86	76	.531	9½	Jimy Williams	2,455,477
1987	2nd	96	66	.593	2	Jimy Williams	2,778,429
1988	3rd (tied)	87	75	.537	2	Jimy Williams	2,595,175
1989	1st‡	89	73	.549	+2	Jimy Williams, Cito Gaston	3,375,883
1990	2nd	86	76	.531	2	Cito Gaston	3,885,284
1991	1st‡	91	71	.562	+7	Cito Gaston	4,001,527
1992	1st§	96	66	.593	+4	Cito Gaston	4,028,318
1993	1st§	95	67	.586	+7	Cito Gaston	4,057,947
1994	3rd	55	60	.478	16	Cito Gaston	2,907,933
1995	5th	56	88	.389	30	Cito Gaston	2,826,483
1996	4th	74	88	.457	18	Cito Gaston	2,559,573
1997	5th	76	86	.469	22	Cito Gaston, Mel Queen	2,589,297

*Games behind winner. †First half 16-42; second half 21-27. ‡Lost championship series. §Won championship series.

MANAGERIAL RECORDS

Bobby Cox 355-292, Cito Gaston 702-650, Roy Hartsfield 166-318, Bobby Mattick 104-164, Mel Queen 4-1, Jimy Williams 281-241.

NATIONAL LEAGUE

ATLANTA BRAVES
YEARLY FINISHES

Year	Position	W	L	Pct.	*GB	Manager	Attendance
1901†	5th	69	69	.500	20½	Frank Selee	146,502
1902†	3rd	73	64	.533	29	Al Buckenberger	116,960
1903†	6th	58	80	.420	32	Al Buckenberger	143,155
1904†	7th	55	98	.359	51	Al Buckenberger	140,694
1905†	7th	51	103	.331	54½	Fred Tenney	150,003
1906†	8th	49	102	.325	66½	Fred Tenney	143,280
1907†	7th	58	90	.392	47	Fred Tenney	203,221
1908†	6th	63	91	.409	36	Joe Kelley	253,750
1909†	8th	45	108	.294	65½	Frank Bowerman, Harry Smith	195,188
1910†	8th	53	100	.346	50½	Fred Lake	149,027
1911†	8th	44	107	.291	54	Fred Tenney	116,000
1912†	8th	52	101	.340	52	Johnny Kling	121,000
1913†	5th	69	82	.457	31½	George Stallings	208,000
1914†	1st	94	59	.614	+10½	George Stallings	382,913
1915†	2nd	83	69	.546	7	George Stallings	376,283
1916†	3rd	89	63	.586	4	George Stallings	313,495
1917†	6th	72	81	.471	25½	George Stallings	174,253
1918†	7th	53	71	.427	28½	George Stallings	84,938
1919†	6th	57	82	.410	38½	George Stallings	167,401
1920†	7th	62	90	.408	30	George Stallings	162,483
1921†	4th	79	74	.516	15	Fred Mitchell	318,627
1922†	8th	53	100	.346	39½	Fred Mitchell	167,965
1923†	7th	54	100	.351	41½	Fred Mitchell	227,802
1924†	8th	53	100	.346	40	Dave Bancroft	117,478
1925†	5th	70	83	.458	25	Dave Bancroft	313,528
1926†	7th	66	86	.434	22	Dave Bancroft	303,598
1927†	7th	60	94	.390	34	Dave Bancroft	288,685
1928†	7th	50	103	.327	44½	Jack Slattery, Rogers Hornsby	227,001
1929†	8th	56	98	.364	43	Emil Fuchs	372,351
1930†	6th	70	84	.455	22	Bill McKechnie	464,835
1931†	7th	64	90	.416	37	Bill McKechnie	515,005
1932†	5th	77	77	.500	13	Bill McKechnie	507,606
1933†	4th	83	71	.539	9	Bill McKechnie	517,803
1934†	4th	78	73	.517	16	Bill McKechnie	303,205
1935†	8th	38	115	.248	61½	Bill McKechnie	232,754
1936†	6th	71	83	.461	21	Bill McKechnie	340,585
1937†	5th	79	73	.520	16	Bill McKechnie	385,339
1938†	5th	77	75	.507	12	Casey Stengel	341,149
1939†	7th	63	88	.417	32½	Casey Stengel	285,994
1940†	7th	65	87	.428	34½	Casey Stengel	241,616
1941†	7th	62	92	.403	38	Casey Stengel	263,680
1942†	7th	59	89	.399	44	Casey Stengel	285,332

Year	Position	W	L	Pct.	*GB	Manager	Attendance
1943†	6th	68	85	.444	36½	Casey Stengel	271,289
1944†	6th	65	89	.422	40	Bob Coleman	208,691
1945†	6th	67	85	.441	30	Bob Coleman, Del Bissonette	374,178
1946†	4th	81	72	.529	15½	Billy Southworth	969,673
1947†	3rd	86	68	.558	8	Billy Southworth	1,277,361
1948†	1st	91	62	.595	+6½	Billy Southworth	1,455,439
1949†	4th	75	79	.487	22	Billy Southworth	1,081,795
1950†	4th	83	71	.539	8	Billy Southworth	944,391
1951†	4th	76	78	.494	20½	Billy Southworth, Tommy Holmes	487,475
1952†	7th	64	89	.418	32	Tommy Holmes, Charlie Grimm	281,278
1953‡	2nd	92	62	.597	13	Charlie Grimm	1,826,397
1954‡	3rd	89	65	.578	8	Charlie Grimm	2,131,388
1955‡	2nd	85	69	.552	13½	Charlie Grimm	2,005,836
1956‡	2nd	92	62	.597	1	Charlie Grimm, Fred Haney	2,046,331
1957‡	1st	95	59	.617	+8	Fred Haney	2,215,404
1958‡	1st	92	62	.597	+8	Fred Haney	1,971,101
1959‡	2nd§	86	70	.551	2	Fred Haney	1,749,112
1960‡	2nd	88	66	.571	7	Chuck Dressen	1,497,799
1961‡	4th	83	71	.539	10	Chuck Dressen, Birdie Tebbetts	1,101,441
1962‡	5th	86	76	.531	15½	Birdie Tebbetts	766,921
1963‡	6th	84	78	.519	15	Bobby Bragan	773,018
1964‡	5th	88	74	.543	5	Bobby Bragan	910,911
1965‡	5th	86	76	.531	11	Bobby Bragan	555,584
1966	5th	85	77	.525	10	Bobby Bragan, Billy Hitchcock	1,539,801
1967	7th	77	85	.475	24½	Billy Hitchcock, Ken Silvestri	1,389,222
1968	5th	81	81	.500	16	Lum Harris	1,126,540

WEST DIVISION

Year	Position	W	L	Pct.	*GB	Manager	Attendance
1969	1st∞	93	69	.574	+3	Lum Harris	1,458,320
1970	5th	76	86	.469	26	Lum Harris	1,078,848
1971	3rd	82	80	.506	8	Lum Harris	1,006,320
1972	4th	70	84	.455	25	Lum Harris, Eddie Mathews	752,973
1973	5th	76	85	.472	22½	Eddie Mathews	800,655
1974	3rd	88	74	.543	14	Eddie Mathews, Clyde King	981,085
1975	5th	67	94	.416	40½	Clyde King, Connie Ryan	534,672
1976	6th	70	92	.432	32	Dave Bristol	818,179
1977	6th	61	101	.377	37	Dave Bristol, Ted Turner	872,464
1978	6th	69	93	.426	26	Bobby Cox	904,494
1979	6th	66	94	.413	23½	Bobby Cox	769,465
1980	4th	81	80	.503	11	Bobby Cox	1,048,411
1981	4th/5th	50	56	.472	▲	Bobby Cox	535,418
1982	1st∞	89	73	.549	+1	Joe Torre	1,801,985
1983	2nd	88	74	.543	3	Joe Torre	2,119,935
1984	2nd (tied)	80	82	.494	12	Joe Torre	1,724,892
1985	5th	66	96	.407	29	Eddie Haas, Bobby Wine	1,350,137
1986	6th	72	89	.447	23½	Chuck Tanner	1,387,181
1987	5th	69	92	.429	20½	Chuck Tanner	1,217,402
1988	6th	54	106	.338	39½	Chuck Tanner, Russ Nixon	848,089
1989	6th	63	97	.394	28	Russ Nixon	984,930
1990	6th	65	97	.401	26	Russ Nixon, Bobby Cox	980,129
1991	1st◆	94	68	.580	+1	Bobby Cox	2,140,217
1992	1st◆	98	64	.605	+8	Bobby Cox	3,077,400
1993	1st∞	104	58	.642	+1	Bobby Cox	3,884,725

EAST DIVISION

Year	Position	W	L	Pct.	*GB	Manager	Attendance
1994	2nd	68	46	.596	6	Bobby Cox	2,539,240
1995	1st■◆	90	54	.625	+21	Bobby Cox	2,561,831
1996	1st■◆	96	66	.593	+8	Bobby Cox	2,901,242
1997	1st■∞	101	61	.623	+9	Bobby Cox	3,464,488

*Games behind winner. †Boston Braves. ‡Milwaukee Braves. §Lost pennant playoff. ∞Lost championship series. ▲First half 25-29; second half 25-27. ◆Won championship series. ■Won division series.

MANAGERIAL RECORDS

Dave Bancroft 249-363, Del Bissonette 25-34, Frank Bowerman 23-55, Bobby Bragan 310-287, Dave Bristol 131-192, Al Buckenberger 186-242, Bob Coleman 107-140, Bobby Cox 957-797, Chuck Dressen 159-124, Emil Fuchs 56-98, Charlie Grimm 341-285, Eddie Haas 50-71, Fred Haney 341-231, Lum Harris 379-373, Billy Hitchcock 110-100, Tommy Holmes 61-69, Rogers Hornsby 39-83, Joe Kelley 63-91, Clyde King 52-101, Johnny Kling 52-101, Fred Lake 53-100, Eddie Mathews 149-161, Bill McKechnie 560-666, Fred Mitchell 186-274, Russ Nixon 130-216, Connie Ryan 9-18, Frank Selee 69-69, Ken Silvestri 0-3, Jack Slattery 11-20, Harry Smith 22-53, Billy Southworth 424-358, George Stallings 579-597, Casey Stengel 394-516, Chuck Tanner 153-208, Birdie Tebbetts 98-89, Fred Tenney 202-402, Joe Torre 257-229, Ted Turner 0-1, Bobby Wine 16-25.

YEARLY FINISHES

Year	Position	W	L	Pct.	*GB	Manager	Attendance
1901	6th	53	86	.381	37	Tom Loftus	205,071
1902	5th	68	69	.496	34	Frank Selee	263,700
1903	3rd	82	56	.594	8	Frank Selee	386,205
1904	2nd	93	60	.608	13	Frank Selee	439,100
1905	3rd	92	61	.601	13	Frank Selee, Frank Chance	509,900
1906	1st	116	36	.763	+20	Frank Chance	654,300
1907	1st	107	45	.704	+17	Frank Chance	422,550
1908	1st	99	55	.643	+1	Frank Chance	665,325
1909	2nd	104	49	.680	6 1/2	Frank Chance	633,480
1910	1st	104	50	.675	+13	Frank Chance	526,152
1911	2nd	92	62	.597	7 1/2	Frank Chance	576,000
1912	3rd	91	59	.607	11 1/2	Frank Chance	514,000
1913	3rd	88	65	.575	13 1/2	Johnny Evers	419,000
1914	4th	78	76	.506	16 1/2	Hank O'Day	202,516
1915	4th	73	80	.477	17 1/2	Roger Bresnahan	217,058
1916	5th	67	86	.438	26 1/2	Joe Tinker	453,685
1917	5th	74	80	.481	24	Fred Mitchell	360,218
1918	1st	84	45	.651	+10 1/2	Fred Mitchell	337,256
1919	3rd	75	65	.536	21	Fred Mitchell	424,430
1950	5th (tied)	75	79	.487	18	Fred Mitchell	480,783
1921	7th	64	89	.418	30	Johnny Evers, Bill Killefer	410,107
1922	5th	80	74	.519	13	Bill Killefer	542,283
1923	4th	83	71	.539	12 1/2	Bill Killefer	703,705
1924	5th	81	72	.529	12	Bill Killefer	716,922
1925	8th	68	86	.442	27 1/2	Bill Killefer, Rabbit Maranville, George Gibson	622,610
1926	4th	82	72	.532	7	Joe McCarthy	885,063
1927	4th	85	68	.556	8 1/2	Joe McCarthy	1,159,168
1928	3rd	91	63	.591	4	Joe McCarthy	1,143,740
1929	1st	98	54	.645	+10 1/2	Joe McCarthy	1,485,166
1930	2nd	90	64	.584	2	Joe McCarthy, Rogers Hornsby	1,463,624
1931	3rd	84	70	.545	17	Rogers Hornsby	1,086,422
1932	1st	90	64	.584	+4	Rogers Hornsby, Charlie Grimm	974,688
1933	3rd	86	68	.558	6	Charlie Grimm	594,112
1934	3rd	86	65	.570	8	Charlie Grimm	707,525
1935	1st	100	54	.649	+4	Charlie Grimm	692,604
1936	2nd (tied)	87	67	.565	5	Charlie Grimm	699,370
1937	2nd	93	61	.604	3	Charlie Grimm	895,020
1938	1st	89	63	.586	+2	Charlie Grimm, Gabby Hartnett	951,640
1939	4th	84	70	.545	13	Gabby Hartnett	726,663
1940	5th	75	79	.487	25 1/2	Gabby Hartnett	534,878
1941	6th	70	84	.455	30	Jimmy Wilson	545,159
1942	6th	68	86	.442	38	Jimmy Wilson	590,872
1943	5th	74	79	.484	30 1/2	Jimmy Wilson	508,247
1944	4th	75	79	.487	30	Jimmy Wilson, Charlie Grimm	640,110
1945	1st	98	56	.636	+3	Charlie Grimm	1,036,386
1946	3rd	82	71	.536	14 1/2	Charlie Grimm	1,342,970
1947	6th	69	85	.448	25	Charlie Grimm	1,364,039
1948	8th	64	90	.416	27 1/2	Charlie Grimm	1,237,792
1949	8th	61	93	.396	36	Charlie Grimm, Frankie Frisch	1,143,139
1950	7th	64	89	.418	26 1/2	Frankie Frisch	1,165,944
1951	8th	62	92	.403	34 1/2	Frankie Frisch, Phil Cavarretta	894,415
1952	5th	77	77	.500	19 1/2	Phil Cavarretta	1,024,826
1953	7th	65	89	.422	40	Phil Cavarretta	763,658
1954	7th	64	90	.416	33	Stan Hack	748,183
1955	6th	72	81	.471	26	Stan Hack	875,800
1956	8th	60	94	.390	33	Stan Hack	720,118
1957	7th (tied)	62	92	.403	33	Bob Scheffing	670,629
1958	5th (tied)	72	82	.468	20	Bob Scheffing	979,904
1959	5th (tied)	74	80	.481	13	Bob Scheffing	858,255
1960	7th	60	94	.390	35	Charlie Grimm, Lou Boudreau	809,770
1961	7th	64	90	.416	29	Vedie Himsl, Harry Craft, Elvin Tappe, Lou Klein	673,057
1962	9th	59	103	.364	42 1/2	Charlie Metro, Elvin Tappe, Lou Klein	609,802
1963	7th	82	80	.506	17	Bob Kennedy	979,551
1964	8th	76	86	.469	17	Bob Kennedy	751,647
1965	8th	72	90	.444	25	Bob Kennedy, Lou Klein	641,361
1966	10th	59	103	.364	36	Leo Durocher	635,891
1967	3rd	87	74	.540	14	Leo Durocher	977,226
1968	3rd	84	78	.519	13	Leo Durocher	1,043,409

EAST DIVISION

Year	Position	W	L	Pct.	*GB	Manager	Attendance
1969	2nd	92	70	.568	8	Leo Durocher	1,674,993
1970	2nd	84	78	.519	5	Leo Durocher	1,642,705

HISTORY *Team by team*

– 347 –

Year	Position	W	L	Pct.	*GB	Manager	Attendance
1971	3rd (tied)	83	79	.512	14	Leo Durocher	1,653,007
1972	2nd	85	70	.548	11	Leo Durocher, Whitey Lockman	1,299,163
1973	5th	77	84	.478	5	Whitey Lockman	1,351,705
1974	6th	66	96	.407	22	Whitey Lockman, Jim Marshall	1,015,378
1975	5th (tied)	75	87	.463	17 1/2	Jim Marshall	1,034,819
1976	4th	75	87	.463	26	Jim Marshall	1,026,217
1977	4th	81	81	.500	20	Herman Franks	1,439,834
1978	3rd	79	83	.488	11	Herman Franks	1,525,311
1979	5th	80	82	.494	18	Herman Franks, Joe Amalfitano	1,648,587
1980	6th	64	98	.395	27	Preston Gomez, Joe Amalfitano	1,206,776
1981	6th/5th	38	65	.369	†	Joe Amalfitano	565,637
1982	5th	73	89	.451	19	Lee Elia	1,249,278
1983	5th	71	91	.438	19	Lee Elia, Charlie Fox	1,479,717
1984	1st‡	96	65	.596	+6 1/2	Jim Frey	2,104,219
1985	4th	77	84	.478	23 1/2	Jim Frey	2,161,534
1986	5th	70	90	.438	37	Jim Frey, John Vukovich, Gene Michael	1,859,102
1987	6th	76	85	.472	18 1/2	Gene Michael, Frank Lucchesi	2,035,130
1988	4th	77	85	.475	24	Don Zimmer	2,089,034
1989	1st‡	93	69	.574	+6	Don Zimmer	2,491,942
1990	4th	77	85	.475	18	Don Zimmer	2,243,791
1991	4th	77	83	.481	20	Don Zimmer, Joe Altobelli, Jim Essian	2,314,250
1992	4th	78	84	.481	18	Jim Lefebvre	2,126,720
1993	4th	84	78	.519	13	Jim Lefebvre	2,653,763

CENTRAL DIVISION

Year	Position	W	L	Pct.	*GB	Manager	Attendance
1994	5th	49	64	.434	16 1/2	Tom Trebelhorn	1,845,208
1995	3rd	73	71	.507	12	Jim Riggleman	1,918,265
1996	4th	76	86	.469	12	Jim Riggleman	2,219,110
1997	5th	68	94	.420	16	Jim Riggleman	2,190,308

*Games behind winner. †First half 15-37; second half 23-28. ‡Lost championship series.

MANAGERIAL RECORDS

Joe Amalfitano 66-116, Lou Boudreau 54-83, Roger Bresnahan 73-80, Phil Cavarretta 169-213, Frank Chance 753-379, Harry Craft 7-9, Leo Durocher 535-526, Lee Elia 127-158, Jim Essian 59-63, Johnny Evers 130-121, Charlie Fox 17-22, Herman Franks 238-241, Jim Frey 196-182, Frank Frisch 141-196, George Gibson 12-14, Preston Gomez 38-52, Charlie Grimm 946-784, Stan Hack 196-265, Gabby Hartnett 203-176, Vedie Himsl 10-21, Rogers Hornsby 141-114, Roy Johnson 0-1, Bob Kennedy 182-198, Bill Killefer 299-292, Lou Klein 65-83, Jim Lefebvre 162-162, Whitey Lockman 157-162, Tom Loftus 53-86, Frank Lucchesi 8-17, Rabbit Maranville 23-30, Jim Marshall 175-218, Joe McCarthy 442-321, Charlie Metro 43-69, Gene Michael 114-124, Fred Mitchell 308-269, Hank O'Day 78-76, Jim Riggleman 217-251, Bob Scheffing 208-254, Frank Selee 295-223, Elvin Tappe 46-69, Joe Tinker 67-86, Tom Trebelhorn 49-64, John Vukovich 1-1, Jimmy Wilson 213-258, Don Zimmer 265-259.

CINCINNATI REDS
YEARLY FINISHES

Year	Position	W	L	Pct.	*GB	Manager	Attendance
1901	8th	52	87	.374	38	Bid McPhee	205,728
1902	4th	70	70	.500	33 1/2	Bid McPhee, Frank Bancroft, Joe Kelley	217,300
1903	4th	74	65	.532	16 1/2	Joe Kelley	351,680
1904	3rd	88	65	.575	18	Joe Kelley	391,915
1905	5th	79	74	.516	26	Joe Kelley	313,927
1906	6th	64	87	.424	51 1/2	Ned Hanlon	330,056
1907	6th	66	87	.431	41 1/2	Ned Hanlon	317,500
1908	5th	73	81	.474	26	John Ganzel	399,200
1909	4th	77	76	.503	33 1/2	Clark Griffith	424,643
1910	5th	75	79	.487	29	Clark Griffith	380,622
1911	6th	70	83	.458	29	Clark Griffith	300,000
1912	4th	75	78	.490	29	Hank O'Day	344,000
1913	7th	64	89	.418	37 1/2	Joe Tinker	258,000
1914	8th	60	94	.390	34 1/2	Buck Herzog	100,791
1915	7th	71	83	.461	20	Buck Herzog	218,878
1916	7th (tied)	60	93	.392	33 1/2	Buck Herzog, Christy Mathewson	255,846
1917	4th	78	76	.506	20	Christy Mathewson	269,056
1918	3rd	68	60	.531	15 1/2	Christy Mathewson, Heinie Groh	163,009
1919	1st	96	44	.686	+9	Pat Moran	532,501
1920	3rd	82	71	.536	10 1/2	Pat Moran	568,107
1921	6th	70	83	.458	24	Pat Moran	311,227
1922	2nd	86	68	.558	7	Pat Moran	493,754
1923	2nd	91	63	.591	4 1/2	Pat Moran	575,063
1924	4th	83	70	.542	10	Jack Hendricks	437,707
1925	3rd	80	73	.523	15	Jack Hendricks	464,920

HISTORY Team by team

Year	Position	W	L	Pct.	*GB	Manager	Attendance
1926	2nd	87	67	.565	2	Jack Hendricks	672,987
1927	5th	75	78	.490	18 1/2	Jack Hendricks	442,164
1928	5th	78	74	.513	16	Jack Hendricks	490,490
1929	7th	66	88	.429	33	Jack Hendricks	295,040
1930	7th	59	95	.383	33	Dan Howley	386,727
1931	8th	58	96	.377	43	Dan Howley	263,316
1932	8th	60	94	.390	30	Dan Howley	356,950
1933	8th	58	94	.382	33	Donie Bush	218,281
1934	8th	52	99	.344	42	Bob O'Farrell, Chuck Dressen	206,773
1935	6th	68	85	.444	31 1/2	Chuck Dressen	448,247
1936	5th	74	80	.481	18	Chuck Dressen	466,245
1937	8th	56	98	.364	40	Chuck Dressen, Bobby Wallace	411,221
1938	4th	82	68	.547	6	Bill McKechnie	706,756
1939	1st	97	57	.630	+4 1/2	Bill McKechnie	981,443
1940	1st	100	53	.654	+12	Bill McKechnie	850,180
1941	3rd	88	66	.571	12	Bill McKechnie	643,513
1942	4th	76	76	.500	29	Bill McKechnie	427,031
1943	2nd	87	67	.565	18	Bill McKechnie	379,122
1944	3rd	89	65	.578	16	Bill McKechnie	409,567
1945	7th	61	93	.396	37	Bill McKechnie	290,070
1946	6th	67	87	.435	30	Bill McKechnie	715,751
1947	5th	73	81	.474	21	Johnny Neun	899,975
1948	7th	64	89	.418	27	Johnny Neun, Bucky Walters	823,386
1949	7th	62	92	.403	35	Bucky Walters	707,782
1950	6th	66	87	.431	24 1/2	Luke Sewell	538,794
1951	6th	68	86	.442	28 1/2	Luke Sewell	588,268
1952	6th	69	85	.448	27 1/2	Luke Sewell, Rogers Hornsby	604,197
1953	6th	68	86	.442	37	Rogers Hornsby, Buster Mills	548,086
1954	5th	74	80	.481	23	Birdie Tebbetts	704,167
1955	5th	75	79	.487	23 1/2	Birdie Tebbetts	693,662
1956	3rd	91	63	.591	2	Birdie Tebbetts	1,125,928
1957	4th	80	74	.519	15	Birdie Tebbetts	1,070,850
1958	4th	76	78	.494	16	Birdie Tebbetts, Jimmie Dykes	788,582
1959	5th (tied)	74	80	.481	13	Mayo Smith, Fred Hutchinson	801,289
1960	6th	67	87	.435	28	Fred Hutchinson	663,486
1961	1st	93	61	.604	+4	Fred Hutchinson	1,117,603
1962	3rd	98	64	.605	3 1/2	Fred Hutchinson	982,085
1963	5th	86	76	.531	13	Fred Hutchinson	858,805
1964	2nd (tied)	92	70	.549	1	Fred Hutchinson, Dick Sisler	862,466
1965	4th	89	73	.549	8	Dick Sisler	1,047,824
1966	7th	76	84	.475	18	Don Heffner, Dave Bristol	742,958
1967	4th	87	75	.537	14 1/2	Dave Bristol	958,300
1968	4th	83	79	.512	14	Dave Bristol	733,354

WEST DIVISION

Year	Position	W	L	Pct.	*GB	Manager	Attendance
1969	3rd	89	73	.549	4	Dave Bristol	987,991
1970	1st†	102	60	.630	+14 1/2	Sparky Anderson	1,803,568
1971	4th (tied)	79	83	.488	11	Sparky Anderson	1,501,122
1972	1st†	95	59	.617	+10 1/2	Sparky Anderson	1,611,459
1973	1st‡	99	63	.611	+3 1/2	Sparky Anderson	2,017,601
1974	2nd	98	64	.605	4	Sparky Anderson	2,164,307
1975	1st†	108	54	.667	+20	Sparky Anderson	2,315,603
1976	1st†	102	60	.630	+10	Sparky Anderson	2,629,708
1977	2nd	88	74	.543	10	Sparky Anderson	2,519,670
1978	2nd	92	69	.571	2 1/2	Sparky Anderson	2,532,497
1979	1st‡	90	71	.559	+1 1/2	John McNamara	2,356,933
1980	3rd	89	73	.549	3 1/2	John McNamara	2,022,450
1981	2nd/2nd	66	42	.611	§	John McNamara	1,093,730
1982	6th	61	101	.377	28	John McNamara, Russ Nixon	1,326,528
1983	6th	74	88	.457	17	Russ Nixon	1,190,419
1984	5th	70	92	.432	22	Vern Rapp, Pete Rose	1,275,887
1985	2nd	89	72	.553	5 1/2	Pete Rose	1,834,619
1986	2nd	86	76	.531	10	Pete Rose	1,692,432
1987	2nd	84	78	.519	6	Pete Rose	2,185,205
1988	2nd	87	74	.540	7	Pete Rose	2,072,528
1989	5th	75	87	.463	17	Pete Rose, Tommy Helms	1,979,320
1990	1st†	91	71	.562	+5	Lou Piniella	2,400,892
1991	5th	74	88	.457	20	Lou Piniella	2,372,377
1992	2nd	90	72	.556	8	Lou Piniella	2,315,946
1993	5th	73	89	.451	31	Tony Perez, Dave Johnson	2,453,232

– 349 –

CENTRAL DIVISION

Year	Position	W	L	Pct.	*GB	Manager	Attendance
1994	1st................66		48	.579	+1/2	Dave Johnson..	1,897,681
1995	1st∞‡.............85		59	.590	+9	Dave Johnson..	1,837,649
1996	3rd................81		81	.500	7	Ray Knight..	1,861,428
1997	3rd................76		86	.469	8	Ray Knight, Jack McKeon	1,785,788

*Games behind winner. †Won championship series. ‡Lost championship series. §First half 35-21; second half 31-21. ∞Won division series.

MANAGERIAL RECORDS

Sparky Anderson 863-586, Frank Bancroft 9-7, Dave Bristol 298-265, Donie Bush 58-94, Chuck Dressen 214-282, Jimmie Dykes 24-17, John Ganzel 73-81, Clark Griffith 222-238, Heinie Groh 7-3, Ned Hanlon 130-174, Don Heffner 37-46, Tommy Helms 14-21, Jack Hendricks 469-450, Buck Herzog 165-226, Rogers Hornsby 91-106, Dan Howley 177-285, Fred Hutchinson 443-372, Dave Johnson 204-172, Joe Kelley 275-230, Ray Knight 124-137, Christy Mathewson 164-176, Bill McKechnie 747-632, Jack McKeon 33-30, John McNamara 279-244, Bid McPhee 79-124, Buster Mills 4-4, Pat Moran 425-329, Johnny Neun 117-137, Russ Nixon 101-131, Hank O'Day 75-78, Bob O'Farrell 30-60, Tony Perez 20-24, Lou Piniella 255-231, Vern Rapp 51-70, Pete Rose 426-388, Luke Sewell 176-234, Dick Sisler 121-94, Mayo Smith 35-45, Birdie Tebbetts 372-357, Joe Tinker 64-89, Bobby Wallace 5-20, Bucky Walters 81-123.

COLORADO ROCKIES
YEARLY FINISHES

WEST DIVISION

Year	Position	W	L	Pct.	*GB	Manager	Attendance
1993	6th 67		95	.414	37	Don Baylor...	4,483,350
1994	3rd................53		64	.453	6 1/2	Don Baylor...	3,281,511
1995	2nd†‡.............77		67	.535	1	Don Baylor...	3,390,037
1996	3rd................83		79	.512	8	Don Baylor...	3,891,014
1997	3rd................83		79	.512	7	Don Baylor...	3,888,453

*Games behind winner. †Wild-card playoff qualifier. ‡Lost division series.

MANAGERIAL RECORDS

Don Baylor 363-384.

FLORIDA MARLINS
YEARLY FINISHES

EAST DIVISION

Year	Position	W	L	Pct.	*GB	Manager	Attendance
1993	6th 64		98	.395	33	Rene Lachemann..	3,064,847
1994	5th 51		64	.443	23 1/2	Rene Lachemann..	1,937,467
1995	4th 67		76	.469	22 1/2	Rene Lachemann..	1,700,466
1996	3rd 80		82	.494	16	Rene Lachemann, John Boles	1,746,767
1997	2nd†‡§...........92		70	.568	9	Jim Leyland...	2,364,387

*Games behind winner. †Wild-card playoff qualifier. ‡Won division series. §Won championship series.

MANAGERIAL RECORDS

John Boles 40-35, Rene Lachemann 222-285, Jim Leyland 92-70.

HOUSTON ASTROS
YEARLY FINISHES

Year	Position	W	L	Pct.	*GB	Manager	Attendance
1962†	8th................64		96	.400	36 1/2	Harry Craft..	924,456
1963†	9th 66		96	.407	33	Harry Craft..	719,502
1964†	9th 66		96	.407	27	Harry Craft, Luman Harris................................	725,773
1965	9th 65		97	.401	32	Luman Harris...	2,151,470
1966	8th 72		90	.444	23	Grady Hatton..	1,872,108
1967	9th 69		93	.426	32 1/2	Grady Hatton..	1,348,303
1968	10th 72		90	.444	25	Grady Hatton, Harry Walker..............................	1,312,887

WEST DIVISION

Year	Position	W	L	Pct.	*GB	Manager	Attendance
1969	5th 81		81	.500	12	Harry Walker..	1,442,995
1970	4th 79		83	.488	23	Harry Walker..	1,253,444
1971	4th (tied) 79		83	.488	11	Harry Walker..	1,261,589
1972	2nd...............84		69	.549	10 1/2	Harry Walker, Leo Durocher, Salty Parker............	1,469,247
1973	4th 82		80	.506	17	Leo Durocher, Preston Gomez..........................	1,394,004
1974	4th 81		81	.500	21	Preston Gomez...	1,090,728
1975	6th 64		97	.398	43 1/2	Preston Gomez, Bill Virdon...............................	858,002

Year	Position	W	L	Pct.	*GB	Manager	Attendance
1976	3rd	80	82	.494	22	Bill Virdon	886,146
1977	3rd	81	81	.500	17	Bill Virdon	1,109,560
1978	5th	74	88	.457	21	Bill Virdon	1,126,145
1979	2nd	89	73	.549	1 1/2	Bill Virdon	1,900,312
1980	1st‡§	93	70	.571	+1	Bill Virdon	2,278,217
1981	3rd/1st▲	61	49	.555	∞	Bill Virdon	1,321,282
1982	5th	77	85	.475	12	Bill Virdon, Bob Lillis	1,558,555
1983	3rd	85	77	.525	6	Bob Lillis	1,351,962
1984	2nd (tied)	80	82	.494	12	Bob Lillis	1,229,862
1985	3rd (tied)	83	79	.512	12	Bob Lillis	1,184,314
1986	1st§	96	66	.593	+10	Hal Lanier	1,734,276
1987	3rd	76	86	.469	14	Hal Lanier	1,909,902
1988	5th	82	80	.506	12 1/2	Hal Lanier	1,933,505
1989	3rd	86	76	.531	6	Art Howe	1,834,908
1990	4th (tied)	75	87	.463	16	Art Howe	1,310,927
1991	6th	65	97	.401	29	Art Howe	1,196,152
1992	4th	81	81	.500	17	Art Howe	1,211,412
1993	3rd	85	77	.525	19	Art Howe	2,084,546

CENTRAL DIVISION

Year	Position	W	L	Pct.	*GB	Manager	Attendance
1994	2nd	66	49	.574	1/2	Terry Collins	1,561,136
1995	2nd	76	68	.528	9	Terry Collins	1,363,801
1996	2nd	82	80	.506	6	Terry Collins	1,975,888
1997	1st▲	84	78	.519	+5	Larry Dierker	2,046,781

*Games behind winner. †Houston Colt .45s. ‡Won division playoff. §Lost championship series. ∞First half 28-29; second half 33-20. ▲Lost division series.

MANAGERIAL RECORDS

Terry Collins 224-197, Harry Craft 191-280, Larry Dierker 84-78, Leo Durocher 98-95, Preston Gomez 128-161, Lum Harris 70-105, Grady Hatton 164-221, Art Howe 392-418, Hal Lanier 254-232, Bob Lillis 276-261, Bill Virdon 544-522, Harry Walker 355-353.

LOS ANGELES DODGERS
YEARLY FINISHES

Year	Position	W	L	Pct.	*GB	Manager	Attendance
1901†	3rd	79	57	.581	9 1/2	Ned Hanlon	189,200
1902†	2nd	75	63	.543	27 1/2	Ned Hanlon	199,868
1903†	5th	70	66	.515	19	Ned Hanlon	224,670
1904†	6th	56	97	.366	50	Ned Hanlon	214,600
1905†	8th	48	104	.316	56 1/2	Ned Hanlon	227,924
1906†	5th	66	86	.434	50	Patsy Donovan	227,400
1907†	5th	65	83	.439	40	Patsy Donovan	312,500
1908†	7th	53	101	.344	46	Patsy Donovan	275,600
1909†	6th	55	98	.359	55 1/2	Harry Lumley	321,300
1910†	6th	64	90	.416	40	Bill Dahlen	279,321
1911†	7th	64	86	.427	33 1/2	Bill Dahlen	269,000
1912†	7th	58	95	.379	46	Bill Dahlen	243,000
1913†	6th	65	84	.436	34 1/2	Bill Dahlen	347,000
1914†	5th	75	79	.487	19 1/2	Wilbert Robinson	122,671
1915†	3rd	80	72	.526	10	Wilbert Robinson	297,766
1916†	1st	94	60	.610	+2 1/2	Wilbert Robinson	447,747
1917†	7th	70	81	.464	26 1/2	Wilbert Robinson	221,619
1918†	5th	57	69	.452	25 1/2	Wilbert Robinson	83,831
1919†	5th	69	71	.493	27	Wilbert Robinson	360,721
1920†	1st	93	61	.604	+7	Wilbert Robinson	808,722
1921†	5th	77	75	.507	16 1/2	Wilbert Robinson	613,245
1922†	6th	76	78	.494	17	Wilbert Robinson	498,856
1923†	6th	76	78	.494	19 1/2	Wilbert Robinson	564,666
1924†	2nd	92	62	.597	1 1/2	Wilbert Robinson	818,883
1925†	6th (tied)	68	85	.444	27	Wilbert Robinson	659,435
1926†	6th	71	82	.464	17 1/2	Wilbert Robinson	650,819
1927†	6th	65	88	.425	28 1/2	Wilbert Robinson	637,230
1928†	6th	77	76	.503	17 1/2	Wilbert Robinson	664,863
1929†	6th	70	83	.458	28 1/2	Wilbert Robinson	731,886
1930†	4th	86	68	.558	6	Wilbert Robinson	1,097,339
1931†	4th	79	73	.520	21	Wilbert Robinson	753,133
1932†	3rd	81	73	.526	9	Max Carey	681,827
1933†	6th	65	88	.425	26 1/2	Max Carey	526,815
1934†	6th	71	81	.467	23 1/2	Casey Stengel	434,188
1935†	5th	70	83	.458	29 1/2	Casey Stengel	470,517
1936†	7th	67	87	.435	25	Casey Stengel	489,618
1937†	6th	62	91	.405	33 1/2	Burleigh Grimes	482,481

Year	Position	W	L	Pct.	*GB	Manager	Attendance
1938†	7th	69	80	.463	18 1/2	Burleigh Grimes	663,087
1939†	3rd	84	69	.549	12 1/2	Leo Durocher	955,668
1940†	2nd	88	65	.575	12	Leo Durocher	975,978
1941†	1st	100	54	.649	+2 1/2	Leo Durocher	1,214,910
1942†	2nd	104	50	.675	2	Leo Durocher	1,037,765
1943†	3rd	81	72	.529	23 1/2	Leo Durocher	661,739
1944†	7th	63	91	.409	42	Leo Durocher	605,905
1945†	3rd	87	67	.565	11	Leo Durocher	1,059,220
1946†	2nd‡	96	60	.615	2	Leo Durocher	1,796,824
1947†	1st	94	60	.610	+5	Clyde Sukeforth, Burt Shotton	1,807,526
1948†	3rd	84	70	.545	7 1/2	Leo Durocher, Burt Shotton	1,398,967
1949†	1st	97	57	.630	+1	Burt Shotton	1,633,747
1950†	2nd	89	65	.578	2	Burt Shotton	1,185,896
1951†	2nd‡	97	60	.618	1	Chuck Dressen	1,282,628
1952†	1st	96	57	.627	+4 1/2	Chuck Dressen	1,088,704
1953†	1st	105	49	.682	+13	Chuck Dressen	1,163,419
1954†	2nd	92	62	.597	5	Walter Alston	1,020,531
1955†	1st	98	55	.641	+13 1/2	Walter Alston	1,033,589
1956†	1st	93	61	.604	+1	Walter Alston	1,213,562
1957†	3rd	84	70	.545	11	Walter Alston	1,028,258
1958	7th	71	83	.461	21	Walter Alston	1,845,556
1959	1st§	88	68	.564	+2	Walter Alston	2,071,045
1960	4th	82	72	.532	13	Walter Alston	2,253,887
1961	2nd	89	65	.578	4	Walter Alston	1,804,250
1962	2nd‡	102	63	.618	1	Walter Alston	2,755,184
1963	1st	99	63	.611	+6	Walter Alston	2,538,602
1964	6th (tied)	80	82	.494	13	Walter Alston	2,228,751
1965	1st	97	65	.599	+2	Walter Alston	2,553,577
1966	1st	95	67	.586	+1 1/2	Walter Alston	2,617,029
1967	8th	73	89	.451	28 1/2	Walter Alston	1,664,362
1968	7th	76	86	.469	21	Walter Alston	1,581,093

WEST DIVISION

Year	Position	W	L	Pct.	*GB	Manager	Attendance
1969	4th	85	77	.525	8	Walter Alston	1,784,527
1970	2nd	87	74	.540	14 1/2	Walter Alston	1,697,142
1971	2nd	89	73	.549	1	Walter Alston	2,064,594
1972	3rd	85	70	.548	10 1/2	Walter Alston	1,860,858
1973	2nd	95	66	.590	3 1/2	Walter Alston	2,136,192
1974	1st∞	102	60	.630	+4	Walter Alston	2,632,474
1975	2nd	88	74	.543	20	Walter Alston	2,539,349
1976	2nd	92	70	.568	10	Walter Alston, Tommy Lasorda	2,386,301
1977	1st∞	98	64	.605	+10	Tommy Lasorda	2,955,087
1978	1st∞	95	67	.586	+2 1/2	Tommy Lasorda	3,347,845
1979	3rd	79	83	.488	11 1/2	Tommy Lasorda	2,860,954
1980	2nd▲	92	71	.564	1	Tommy Lasorda	3,249,287
1981	1st/4th§∞	63	47	.573	◆	Tommy Lasorda	2,381,292
1982	2nd	88	74	.543	1	Tommy Lasorda	3,608,881
1983	1st▼	91	71	.652	+3	Tommy Lasorda	3,510,313
1984	4th	79	83	.488	13	Tommy Lasorda	3,134,824
1985	1st▼	95	67	.586	+5 1/2	Tommy Lasorda	3,264,593
1986	5th	73	89	.451	23	Tommy Lasorda	3,023,208
1987	4th	73	89	.451	17	Tommy Lasorda	2,797,409
1988	1st∞	94	67	.584	+7	Tommy Lasorda	2,980,262
1989	4th	77	83	.481	14	Tommy Lasorda	2,944,653
1990	2nd	86	76	.531	5	Tommy Lasorda	3,002,396
1991	2nd	93	69	.574	1	Tommy Lasorda	3,348,170
1992	6th	63	99	.389	35	Tommy Lasorda	2,473,266
1993	4th	81	81	.500	23	Tommy Lasorda	3,170,392
1994	1st	58	56	.509	+3 1/2	Tommy Lasorda	2,279,355
1995	1st@	78	66	.542	+1	Tommy Lasorda	2,766,251
1996	2nd■@	90	72	.556	1	Tommy Lasorda, Bill Russell	3,188,454
1997	2nd	88	74	.543	2	Bill Russell	3,319,504

*Games behind winner. †Brooklyn Dodgers. ‡Lost pennant playoff. §Won division series. ∞Won championship series. ▲Lost division playoff. ◆First half 36-21; second half 27-26. ■Wild-card playoff qualifier. ▼Lost championship series. @Lost division series.

MANAGERIAL RECORDS

Walter Alston 2,040-1,613, Max Carey 146-161, Bill Dahlen 251-355, Patsy Donovan 184-270, Chuck Dressen 298-166, Leo Durocher 738-565, Burleigh Grimes 131-171, Ned Hanlon 328-387, Tommy Lasorda 1,599-1,439, Harry Lumley 55-98, Wilbert Robinson 1,375-1,341, Bill Russell 137-111, Burt Shotton 326-215, Casey Stengel 208-251, Clyde Sukeforth 2-0.

MONTREAL EXPOS
YEARLY FINISHES

EAST DIVISION

Year	Position	W	L	Pct.	*GB	Manager	Attendance
1969	6th	52	110	.321	48	Gene Mauch	1,212,608
1970	6th	73	89	.451	16	Gene Mauch	1,424,683
1971	5th	71	90	.441	25 1/2	Gene Mauch	1,290,963
1972	5th	70	86	.449	26 1/2	Gene Mauch	1,142,145
1973	4th	79	83	.488	3 1/2	Gene Mauch	1,246,863
1974	4th	79	82	.491	8 1/2	Gene Mauch	1,019,134
1975	5th (tied)	75	87	.463	17 1/2	Gene Mauch	908,292
1976	6th	55	107	.340	46	Karl Kuehl, Charlie Fox	646,704
1977	5th	75	87	.463	26	Dick Williams	1,433,757
1978	4th	76	86	.469	14	Dick Williams	1,427,007
1979	2nd	95	65	.594	2	Dick Williams	2,102,173
1980	2nd	90	72	.556	1	Dick Williams	2,208,175
1981	3rd/1st‡§	60	48	.556	†	Dick Williams, Jim Fanning	1,534,564
1982	3rd	86	76	.531	6	Jim Fanning	2,318,292
1983	3rd	82	80	.506	8	Bill Virdon	2,320,651
1984	5th	78	83	.484	18	Bill Virdon, Jim Fanning	1,606,531
1985	3rd	84	77	.522	16 1/2	Buck Rodgers	1,502,494
1986	4th	78	83	.484	29 1/2	Buck Rodgers	1,128,981
1987	3rd	91	71	.562	4	Buck Rodgers	1,850,324
1988	3rd	81	81	.500	20	Buck Rodgers	1,478,659
1989	4th	81	81	.500	12	Buck Rodgers	1,783,533
1990	3rd	85	77	.525	10	Buck Rodgers	1,373,087
1991	6th	71	90	.441	26 1/2	Buck Rodgers, Tom Runnells	934,742
1992	2nd	87	75	.537	9	Tom Runnells, Felipe Alou	1,669,077
1993	2nd	94	68	.580	3	Felipe Alou	1,641,437
1994	1st	74	40	.649	+6	Felipe Alou	1,276,250
1995	5th	66	78	.458	24	Felipe Alou	1,309,618
1996	2nd	88	74	.543	8	Felipe Alou	1,616,709
1997	4th	78	84	.481	23	Felipe Alou	1,497,609

*Games behind winner. †First half 30-25; second half 30-23. ‡Won division series. §Lost championship series.

MANAGERIAL RECORDS

Felipe Alou 470-399, Jim Fanning 116-103, Charlie Fox 12-22, Karl Kuehl 43-85, Gene Mauch 499-627, Buck Rodgers 520-499, Tom Runnells 68-81, Bill Virdon 146-147, Dick Williams 380-347.

NEW YORK METS
YEARLY FINISHES

Year	Position	W	L	Pct.	*GB	Manager	Attendance
1962	10th	40	120	.250	60 1/2	Casey Stengel	922,530
1963	10th	51	111	.315	48	Casey Stengel	1,080,108
1964	10th	53	109	.327	40	Casey Stengel	1,732,597
1965	10th	50	112	.309	47	Casey Stengel, Wes Westrum	1,768,389
1966	9th	66	95	.410	28 1/2	Wes Westrum	1,932,693
1967	10th	61	101	.377	40 1/2	Wes Westrum, Salty Parker	1,565,492
1968	9th	73	89	.451	24	Gil Hodges	1,781,657

EAST DIVISION

Year	Position	W	L	Pct.	*GB	Manager	Attendance
1969	1st†	100	62	.617	+8	Gil Hodges	2,175,373
1970	3rd	83	79	.512	6	Gil Hodges	2,697,479
1971	3rd (tied)	83	79	.512	14	Gil Hodges	2,266,680
1972	3rd	83	73	.532	13 1/2	Yogi Berra	2,134,185
1973	1st†	82	79	.509	+1 1/2	Yogi Berra	1,912,390
1974	5th	71	91	.438	17	Yogi Berra	1,722,209
1975	3rd (tied)	82	80	.506	10 1/2	Yogi Berra, Roy McMillan	1,730,566
1976	3rd	86	76	.531	15	Joe Frazier	1,468,754
1977	6th	64	98	.395	37	Joe Frazier, Joe Torre	1,066,825
1978	6th	66	96	.407	24	Joe Torre	1,007,328
1979	6th	63	99	.389	35	Joe Torre	788,905
1980	5th	67	95	.414	24	Joe Torre	1,192,073
1981	5th/4th	41	62	.398	‡	Joe Torre	704,244
1982	6th	65	97	.401	27	George Bamberger	1,323,036
1983	6th	68	94	.420	22	George Bamberger, Frank Howard	1,112,774
1984	2nd	90	72	.556	6 1/2	Dave Johnson	1,842,695
1985	2nd	98	64	.605	3	Dave Johnson	2,761,601

– 353 –

Year	Position	W	L	Pct.	*GB	Manager	Attendance
1986	1st†	108	54	.667	+21 1/2	Dave Johnson	2,767,601
1987	2nd	92	70	.568	3	Dave Johnson	3,034,129
1988	1st§	100	60	.625	+15	Dave Johnson	3,055,445
1989	2nd	87	75	.537	6	Dave Johnson	2,918,710
1990	2nd	91	71	.562	4	Dave Johnson, Bud Harrelson	2,732,745
1991	5th	77	84	.478	20 1/2	Bud Harrelson, Mike Cubbage	2,284,484
1992	5th	72	90	.444	24	Jeff Torborg	1,779,534
1993	7th	59	103	.364	38	Jeff Torborg, Dallas Green	1,873,183
1994	3rd	55	58	.487	18 1/2	Dallas Green	1,151,471
1995	2nd (tied)	69	75	.479	21	Dallas Green	1,273,183
1996	4th	71	91	.438	25	Dallas Green, Bobby Valentine	1,588,323
1997	3rd	88	74	.543	13	Bobby Valentine	1,766,174

*Games behind winner. †Won championship series. ‡First half 17-34; second half 24-28. §Lost championship series.

MANAGERIAL RECORDS

George Bamberger 81-127, Yogi Berra 292-296, Mike Cubbage 3-4, Joe Frazier 101-106, Dallas Green 229-283, Bud Harrelson 145-129, Gil Hodges 339-309, Frank Howard 52-64, Davey Johnson 595-417, Roy McMillan 26-27, Salty Parker 4-7, Casey Stengel 175-404, Jeff Torborg 85-115, Joe Torre 286-420, Bobby Valentine 100-93, Wes Westrum 142-237.

PHILADELPHIA PHILLIES
YEARLY FINISHES

Year	Position	W	L	Pct.	*GB	Manager	Attendance
1901	2nd	83	57	.593	7 1/2	Bill Shettsline	234,937
1902	7th	56	81	.409	46	Bill Shettsline	112,066
1903	7th	49	86	.363	39 1/2	Chief Zimmer	151,729
1904	8th	52	100	.342	53 1/2	Hugh Duffy	140,771
1905	4th	83	69	.546	21 1/2	Hugh Duffy	317,932
1906	4th	71	82	.464	45 1/2	Hugh Duffy	294,680
1907	3rd	83	64	.565	21 1/2	Bill Murray	341,216
1908	4th	83	71	.539	16	Bill Murray	420,660
1909	5th	74	79	.484	36 1/2	Bill Murray	303,177
1910	4th	78	75	.510	25 1/2	Red Dooin	296,597
1911	4th	79	73	.520	19 1/2	Red Dooin	416,000
1912	5th	73	79	.480	30 1/2	Red Dooin	250,000
1913	2nd	88	63	.583	12 1/2	Red Dooin	470,000
1914	6th	74	80	.481	20 1/2	Red Dooin	138,474
1915	1st	90	62	.592	+7	Pat Moran	449,898
1916	2nd	91	62	.595	2 1/2	Pat Moran	515,365
1917	2nd	87	65	.572	10	Pat Moran	354,428
1918	6th	55	68	.447	26	Pat Moran	122,266
1919	8th	47	90	.343	47 1/2	Jack Coombs, Gavvy Cravath	240,424
1920	8th	62	91	.405	30 1/2	Gavvy Cravath	330,998
1921	8th	51	103	.331	43 1/2	Bill Donovan, Kaiser Wilhelm	273,961
1922	7th	57	96	.373	35 1/2	Kaiser Wilhelm	232,471
1923	8th	50	104	.325	45 1/2	Art Fletcher	228,168
1924	7th	55	96	.364	37	Art Fletcher	299,818
1925	6th (tied)	68	85	.444	27	Art Fletcher	304,905
1926	8th	58	93	.384	29 1/2	Art Fletcher	240,600
1927	8th	51	103	.331	43	Stuffy McInnis	305,420
1928	8th	43	109	.283	51	Burt Shotton	182,168
1929	5th	71	82	.464	27 1/2	Burt Shotton	281,200
1930	8th	52	102	.338	40	Burt Shotton	299,007
1931	6th	66	88	.429	35	Burt Shotton	284,849
1932	4th	78	76	.506	12	Burt Shotton	268,914
1933	7th	60	92	.395	31	Burt Shotton	156,421
1934	7th	56	93	.376	37	Jimmy Wilson	169,885
1935	7th	64	89	.418	35 1/2	Jimmy Wilson	205,470
1936	8th	54	100	.351	38	Jimmy Wilson	249,219
1937	7th	61	92	.399	34 1/2	Jimmy Wilson	212,790
1938	8th	45	105	.300	43	Jimmy Wilson, Hans Lobert	166,111
1939	8th	45	106	.298	50 1/2	Doc Prothro	277,973
1940	8th	50	103	.327	50	Doc Prothro	207,177
1941	8th	43	111	.279	57	Doc Prothro	231,401
1942	8th	42	109	.278	62 1/2	Hans Lobert	230,183
1943	7th	64	90	.416	41	Bucky Harris, Fred Fitzsimmons	466,975
1944	8th	61	92	.399	43 1/2	Fred Fitzsimmons	369,586
1945	8th	46	108	.299	52	Fred Fitzsimmons, Ben Chapman	285,057
1946	5th	69	85	.448	28	Ben Chapman	1,045,247
1947	7th (tied)	62	92	.403	32	Ben Chapman	907,332
1948	6th	66	88	.429	25 1/2	Ben Chapman, Dusty Cooke, Eddie Sawyer	767,429
1949	3rd	81	73	.526	16	Eddie Sawyer	819,698

Year	Position	W	L	Pct.	*GB	Manager	Attendance
1950	1st.....................	91	63	.591	+2	Eddie Sawyer	1,217,035
1951	5th.....................	73	81	.474	23 1/2	Eddie Sawyer	937,658
1952	4th	87	67	.565	9 1/2	Eddie Sawyer, Steve O'Neill	775,417
1953	3rd (tied).................	83	71	.539	22	Steve O'Neill	853,644
1954	4th.....................	75	79	.487	22	Steve O'Neill, Terry Moore	738,991
1955	4th.....................	77	77	.500	21 1/2	Mayo Smith	922,886
1956	5th.....................	71	83	.461	22	Mayo Smith	934,798
1957	5th.....................	77	77	.500	19	Mayo Smith	1,146,230
1958	8th.....................	69	85	.448	23	Mayo Smith, Eddie Sawyer	931,110
1959	8th.....................	64	90	.416	23	Eddie Sawyer	802,815
1960	8th.....................	59	95	.383	36	Eddie Sawyer, Andy Cohen, Gene Mauch	862,205
1961	8th.....................	47	107	.305	46	Gene Mauch	590,039
1962	7th.....................	81	80	.503	20	Gene Mauch	762,034
1963	4th.....................	87	75	.537	12	Gene Mauch	907,141
1964	2nd (tied).................	92	70	.568	1	Gene Mauch	1,425,891
1965	6th.....................	85	76	.528	11 1/2	Gene Mauch	1,166,376
1966	4th.....................	87	75	.537	8	Gene Mauch	1,108,201
1967	5th.....................	82	80	.506	19 1/2	Gene Mauch	828,888
1968	7th (tied).................	76	86	.469	21	Gene Mauch, George Myatt, Bob Skinner	664,546

EAST DIVISION

Year	Position	W	L	Pct.	*GB	Manager	Attendance
1969	5th.....................	63	99	.389	37	Bob Skinner, George Myatt	519,414
1970	5th.....................	73	88	.453	15 1/2	Frank Lucchesi	708,247
1971	6th.....................	67	95	.414	30	Frank Lucchesi	1,511,223
1972	6th.....................	59	97	.378	37 1/2	Frank Lucchesi, Paul Owens	1,343,329
1973	6th.....................	71	91	.438	11 1/2	Danny Ozark	1,475,934
1974	3rd.....................	80	82	.494	8	Danny Ozark	1,808,648
1975	2nd.....................	86	76	.531	6 1/2	Danny Ozark	1,909,233
1976	1st†.....................	101	61	.623	+9	Danny Ozark	2,480,150
1977	1st†.....................	101	61	.623	+5	Danny Ozark	2,700,070
1978	1st†.....................	90	72	.556	+1 1/2	Danny Ozark	2,583,389
1979	4th.....................	84	78	.519	14	Danny Ozark, Dallas Green	2,775,011
1980	1st‡.....................	91	71	.562	+1	Dallas Green	2,651,650
1981	1st/3rd∞	59	48	.551	§	Dallas Green	1,638,752
1982	2nd.....................	89	73	.549	3	Pat Corrales	2,376,394
1983	1st‡.....................	90	72	.556	+6	Pat Corrales, Paul Owens	2,128,339
1984	4th.....................	81	81	.500	15 1/2	Paul Owens	2,062,693
1985	5th.....................	75	87	.463	26	John Felske	1,830,350
1986	2nd.....................	86	75	.534	21 1/2	John Felske	1,933,335
1987	4th (tied).................	80	82	.494	15	John Felske, Lee Elia	2,100,110
1988	6th.....................	65	96	.404	35 1/2	Lee Elia, John Vukovich	1,990,041
1989	6th.....................	67	95	.414	26	Nick Leyva	1,861,985
1990	4th (tied).................	77	85	.475	18	Nick Leyva	1,992,484
1991	3rd.....................	78	84	.481	20	Nick Leyva, Jim Fregosi	2,050,012
1992	6th.....................	70	92	.432	26	Jim Fregosi	1,927,448
1993	1st‡.....................	97	65	.599	+3	Jim Fregosi	3,137,674
1994	4th.....................	54	61	.470	20 1/2	Jim Fregosi	2,290,971
1995	2nd (tied).................	69	75	.479	21	Jim Fregosi	2,043,598
1996	5th.....................	67	95	.414	29	Jim Fregosi	1,801,677
1997	5th.....................	68	94	.420	33	Terry Francona	1,490,638

*Games behind winner. †Lost championship series. ‡Won championship series. §First half 34-21; second half 25-27. ∞Lost division series.

MANAGERIAL RECORDS

Ben Chapman 197-277, Andy Cohen 1-0, Dusty Cooke 6-6, Jack Coombs 18-44, Pat Corrales 132-115, Gavvy Cravath 91-137, Bill Donovan 31-71, Red Dooin 392-370, Hugh Duffy 206-251, Lee Elia 111-142, John Felske 190-194, Fred Fitzsimmons 102-179, Art Fletcher 231-378, Terry Francona 68-94, Jim Fregosi 431-463, Dallas Green 169-130, Bucky Harris 40-53, Nick Leyva 148-189, Hans Lobert 42-111, Frank Lucchesi 166-233, Gene Mauch 645-684, Stuffy McInnis 51-103, Terry Moore 35-42, Pat Moran 323-257, Bill Murray 240-214, George Myatt 21-35, Steve O'Neill 182-140, Paul Owens 161-158, Danny Ozark 594-510, Doc Prothro 138-320, Eddie Sawyer 390-424, Bill Shettsline 139-138, Burt Shotton 370-549, Bob Skinner 92-123, Mayo Smith 264-281, John Vukovich 5-4, Kaiser Wilhelm 77-128, Jimmy Wilson 280-477, Chief Zimmer 49-86.

PITTSBURGH PIRATES
YEARLY FINISHES

Year	Position	W	L	Pct.	*GB	Manager	Attendance
1901	1st.....................	90	49	.647	+7 1/2	Fred Clarke	251,955
1902	1st.....................	103	36	.741	+27 1/2	Fred Clarke	243,826
1903	1st.....................	91	49	.650	+6 1/2	Fred Clarke	326,855
1904	4th.....................	87	66	.569	19	Fred Clarke	340,615
1905	2nd.....................	96	57	.627	9	Fred Clarke	369,124
1906	3rd.....................	93	60	.608	23 1/2	Fred Clarke	394,877

Year	Position	W	L	Pct.	*GB	Manager	Attendance
1907	2nd	91	63	.591	17	Fred Clarke	319,506
1908	2nd	98	56	.636	1	Fred Clarke	382,444
1909	1st	110	42	.724	+6 1/2	Fred Clarke	534,950
1910	3rd	86	67	.562	17 1/2	Fred Clarke	436,586
1911	3rd	85	69	.552	14 1/2	Fred Clarke	432,000
1912	2nd	93	58	.616	10	Fred Clarke	384,000
1913	4th	78	71	.523	21 1/2	Fred Clarke	296,000
1914	7th	69	85	.448	25 1/2	Fred Clarke	139,620
1915	5th	73	81	.474	18	Fred Clarke	225,743
1916	6th	65	89	.422	29	Jimmy Callahan	289,132
1917	8th	51	103	.331	47	Jimmy Callahan, Honus Wagner, Hugo Bezdek	192,807
1918	4th	65	60	.520	17	Hugo Bezdek	213,610
1919	4th	71	68	.511	24 1/2	Hugo Bezdek	276,810
1920	4th	79	75	.513	14	George Gibson	429,037
1921	2nd	90	63	.588	4	George Gibson	701,567
1922	3rd (tied)	85	69	.552	8	George Gibson, Bill McKechnie	523,675
1923	3rd	87	67	.565	8 1/2	Bill McKechnie	611,082
1924	3rd	90	63	.588	3	Bill McKechnie	736,883
1925	1st	95	58	.621	+8 1/2	Bill McKechnie	804,354
1926	3rd	84	69	.549	4 1/2	Bill McKechnie	798,542
1927	1st	94	60	.610	+1 1/2	Donie Bush	869,720
1928	4th	85	67	.559	9	Donie Bush	495,070
1929	2nd	88	65	.575	10 1/2	Donie Bush, Jewel Ens	491,377
1930	5th	80	74	.519	12	Jewel Ens	357,795
1931	5th	75	79	.487	26	Jewel Ens	260,392
1932	2nd	86	68	.558	4	George Gibson	287,262
1933	2nd	87	67	.565	5	George Gibson	288,747
1934	5th	74	76	.493	19 1/2	George Gibson, Pie Traynor	322,622
1935	4th	86	67	.562	13 1/2	Pie Traynor	352,885
1936	4th	84	70	.545	8	Pie Traynor	372,524
1937	3rd	86	68	.558	10	Pie Traynor	459,679
1938	2nd	86	64	.573	2	Pie Traynor	641,033
1939	6th	68	85	.444	28 1/2	Pie Traynor	376,734
1940	4th	78	76	.506	22 1/2	Frankie Frisch	507,934
1941	4th	81	73	.526	19	Frankie Frisch	482,241
1942	5th	66	81	.449	36 1/2	Frankie Frisch	448,897
1943	4th	80	74	.519	25	Frankie Frisch	604,278
1944	2nd	90	63	.588	14 1/2	Frankie Frisch	498,740
1945	4th	82	72	.532	16	Frankie Frisch	604,694
1946	7th	63	91	.409	34	Frankie Frisch, Spud Davis	749,962
1947	7th (tied)	62	92	.403	32	Billy Herman, Bill Burwell	1,283,531
1948	4th	83	71	.539	8 1/2	Billy Meyer	1,517,021
1949	6th	71	83	.461	26	Billy Meyer	1,499,435
1950	8th	57	96	.373	33 1/2	Billy Meyer	1,166,267
1951	7th	64	90	.416	32 1/2	Billy Meyer	980,590
1952	8th	42	112	.273	54 1/2	Billy Meyer	686,673
1953	8th	50	104	.325	55	Fred Haney	572,757
1954	8th	53	101	.344	44	Fred Haney	475,494
1955	8th	60	94	.390	38 1/2	Fred Haney	469,397
1956	7th	66	88	.429	27	Bobby Bragan	949,878
1957	7th (tied)	62	92	.403	33	Bobby Bragan, Danny Murtaugh	850,732
1958	2nd	84	70	.545	8	Danny Murtaugh	1,311,988
1959	4th	78	76	.506	9	Danny Murtaugh	1,359,917
1960	1st	95	59	.617	+7	Danny Murtaugh	1,705,828
1961	6th	75	79	.487	18	Danny Murtaugh	1,199,128
1962	4th	93	68	.578	8	Danny Murtaugh	1,090,648
1963	8th	74	88	.457	25	Danny Murtaugh	783,648
1964	6th (tied)	80	82	.494	13	Danny Murtaugh	759,496
1965	3rd	90	72	.556	7	Harry Walker	909,279
1966	3rd	92	70	.568	3	Harry Walker	1,196,618
1967	6th	81	81	.500	20 1/2	Harry Walker, Danny Murtaugh	907,012
1968	6th	80	82	.494	17	Larry Shepard	693,485

EAST DIVISION

Year	Position	W	L	Pct.	*GB	Manager	Attendance
1969	3rd	88	74	.543	12	Larry Shepard, Alex Grammas	769,369
1970	1st†	89	73	.549	+5	Danny Murtaugh	1,341,947
1971	1st‡	97	65	.599	+7	Danny Murtaugh	1,501,132
1972	1st†	96	59	.619	+11	Bill Virdon	1,427,460
1973	3rd	80	82	.494	2 1/2	Bill Virdon, Danny Murtaugh	1,319,913
1974	1st†	88	74	.543	+1 1/2	Danny Murtaugh	1,110,552
1975	1st†	92	69	.571	+6 1/2	Danny Murtaugh	1,270,018
1976	2nd	92	70	.568	9	Danny Murtaugh	1,025,945
1977	2nd	96	66	.593	5	Chuck Tanner	1,237,349
1978	2nd	88	73	.547	1 1/2	Chuck Tanner	964,106

Year	Position	W	L	Pct.	*GB	Manager	Attendance
1979	1st‡	98	64	.605	+2	Chuck Tanner	1,435,454
1980	3rd	83	79	.512	8	Chuck Tanner	1,646,757
1981	4th/6th	46	56	.451	§	Chuck Tanner	541,789
1982	4th	84	78	.519	8	Chuck Tanner	1,024,106
1983	2nd	84	78	.519	6	Chuck Tanner	1,225,916
1984	6th	75	87	.463	21 1/2	Chuck Tanner	773,500
1985	6th	57	104	.354	43 1/2	Chuck Tanner	735,900
1986	6th	64	98	.395	44	Jim Leyland	1,000,917
1987	4th (tied)	80	82	.494	15	Jim Leyland	1,161,193
1988	2nd	85	75	.531	15	Jim Leyland	1,866,713
1989	5th	74	88	.457	19	Jim Leyland	1,374,141
1990	1st†	95	67	.586	+4	Jim Leyland	2,049,908
1991	1st†	98	64	.605	+14	Jim Leyland	2,065,302
1992	1st‡	96	66	.593	+9	Jim Leyland	1,829,395
1993	5th	75	87	.463	22	Jim Leyland	1,650,593

CENTRAL DIVISION

Year	Position	W	L	Pct.	*GB	Manager	Attendance
1994	3rd (tied)	53	61	.465	13	Jim Leyland	1,222,520
1995	5th	58	86	.403	27	Jim Leyland	905,517
1996	5th	73	89	.451	15	Jim Leyland	1,332,150
1997	2nd	79	83	.488	5	Gene Lamont	1,657,022

*Games behind winner. †Lost championship series. ‡Won championship series. §First half 25-23; second half 21-33.

MANAGERIAL RECORDS

Hugo Bezdek 166-187, Bobby Bragan 102-155, Bill Burwell 1-0, Donie Bush 246-178, Jimmy Callahan 85-129, Fred Clarke 1,343-909, Spud Davis 1-2, Jewel Ens 176-167, Frank Frisch 539-528, George Gibson 401-330, Alex Grammas 4-1, Fred Haney 163-299, Billy Herman 61-92, Gene Lamont 79-83, Jim Leyland 851-863, Bill McKechnie 409-293, Billy Meyer 317-452, Danny Murtaugh 1,115-950, Larry Shepard 164-155, Chuck Tanner 711-685, Pie Traynor 457-406, Bill Virdon 163-128, Honus Wagner 1-4, Harry Walker 224-184.

ST. LOUIS CARDINALS
YEARLY FINISHES

Year	Position	W	L	Pct.	*GB	Manager	Attendance
1901	4th	76	64	.543	14 1/2	Patsy Donovan	379,988
1902	6th	56	78	.418	44 1/2	Patsy Donovan	226,417
1903	8th	43	94	.314	46 1/2	Patsy Donovan	226,538
1904	5th	75	79	.487	31 1/2	Kid Nichols	386,750
1905	6th	58	96	.377	47 1/2	Kid Nichols, Jimmy Burke, Matt Robison	292,800
1906	7th	52	98	.347	63	John McCloskey	283,770
1907	8th	52	101	.340	55 1/2	John McCloskey	185,377
1908	8th	49	105	.318	50	John McCloskey	205,129
1909	7th	54	98	.355	56	Roger Bresnahan	299,982
1910	7th	63	90	.412	40 1/2	Roger Bresnahan	355,668
1911	5th	75	74	.503	22	Roger Bresnahan	447,768
1912	6th	63	90	.412	41	Roger Bresnahan	241,759
1913	8th	51	99	.340	49	Miller Huggins	203,531
1914	3rd	81	72	.529	13	Miller Huggins	256,099
1915	6th	72	81	.471	18 1/2	Miller Huggins	252,666
1916	7th (tied)	60	93	.392	33 1/2	Miller Huggins	224,308
1917	3rd	82	70	.539	15	Miller Huggins	288,491
1918	8th	51	78	.395	33	Jack Hendricks	110,599
1919	7th	54	83	.394	40 1/2	Branch Rickey	167,059
1920	5th (tied)	75	79	.487	18	Branch Rickey	326,836
1921	3rd	87	66	.569	7	Branch Rickey	384,773
1922	3rd (tied)	85	69	.552	8	Branch Rickey	536,998
1923	5th	79	74	.516	16	Branch Rickey	338,551
1924	6th	65	89	.422	28 1/2	Branch Rickey	272,885
1925	4th	77	76	.503	18	Branch Rickey, Rogers Hornsby	404,959
1926	1st	89	65	.578	+2	Rogers Hornsby	668,428
1927	2nd	92	61	.601	1 1/2	Bob O'Farrell	749,340
1928	1st	95	59	.617	+2	Bill McKechnie	761,574
1929	4th	78	74	.513	20	Bill McKechnie, Billy Southworth	399,887
1930	1st	92	62	.597	+2	Gabby Street	508,501
1931	1st	101	53	.656	+13	Gabby Street	608,535
1932	6th (tied)	72	82	.468	18	Gabby Street	279,219
1933	5th	82	71	.536	9 1/2	Gabby Street, Frankie Frisch	256,171
1934	1st	95	58	.621	+2	Frankie Frisch	325,056
1935	2nd	96	58	.623	4	Frankie Frisch	506,084
1936	2nd (tied)	87	67	.565	5	Frankie Frisch	448,078
1937	4th	81	73	.526	15	Frankie Frisch	430,811
1938	6th	71	80	.470	17 1/2	Frankie Frisch, Mike Gonzalez	291,418
1939	2nd	92	61	.601	4 1/2	Ray Blades	400,245

Year	Position	W	L	Pct.	*GB	Manager	Attendance
1940	3rd	84	69	.549	16	Ray Blades, Mike Gonzalez, Billy Southworth	324,078
1941	2nd	97	56	.634	2 1/2	Billy Southworth	633,645
1942	1st	106	48	.688	+2	Billy Southworth	553,552
1943	1st	105	49	.682	+18	Billy Southworth	517,135
1944	1st	105	49	.682	+14 1/2	Billy Southworth	461,968
1945	2nd	95	59	.617	3	Billy Southworth	594,630
1946	1st†	98	58	.628	+2	Eddie Dyer	1,061,807
1947	2nd	89	65	.578	5	Eddie Dyer	1,247,913
1948	2nd	85	69	.552	6 1/2	Eddie Dyer	1,111,440
1949	2nd	96	58	.623	1	Eddie Dyer	1,430,676
1950	5th	78	75	.510	12 1/2	Eddie Dyer	1,093,411
1951	3rd	81	73	.526	15 1/2	Marty Marion	1,013,429
1952	3rd	88	66	.571	8 1/2	Eddie Stanky	913,113
1953	3rd (tied)	83	71	.539	22	Eddie Stanky	880,242
1954	6th	72	82	.468	25	Eddie Stanky	1,039,698
1955	7th	68	86	.442	30 1/2	Eddie Stanky, Harry Walker	849,130
1956	4th	76	78	.494	17	Fred Hutchinson	1,029,773
1957	2nd	87	67	.565	8	Fred Hutchinson	1,183,575
1958	5th (tied)	72	82	.468	20	Fred Hutchinson, Stan Hack	1,063,730
1959	7th	71	83	.461	16	Solly Hemus	929,953
1960	3rd	86	68	.558	9	Solly Hemus	1,096,632
1961	5th	80	74	.519	13	Solly Hemus, Johnny Keane	855,305
1962	6th	84	78	.519	17 1/2	Johnny Keane	953,895
1963	2nd	93	69	.574	6	Johnny Keane	1,170,546
1964	1st	93	69	.574	+1	Johnny Keane	1,143,294
1965	7th	80	81	.497	16 1/2	Red Schoendienst	1,241,201
1966	6th	83	79	.512	12	Red Schoendienst	1,712,980
1967	1st	101	60	.627	+10 1/2	Red Schoendienst	2,090,145
1968	1st	97	65	.599	+9	Red Schoendienst	2,011,167

EAST DIVISION

Year	Position	W	L	Pct.	*GB	Manager	Attendance
1969	4th	87	75	.537	13	Red Schoendienst	1,682,783
1970	4th	76	86	.469	13	Red Schoendienst	1,629,736
1971	2nd	90	72	.556	7	Red Schoendienst	1,604,671
1972	4th	75	81	.481	21 1/2	Red Schoendienst	1,196,894
1973	2nd	81	81	.500	1 1/2	Red Schoendienst	1,574,046
1974	2nd	86	75	.534	1 1/2	Red Schoendienst	1,838,413
1975	3rd (tied)	82	80	.506	10 1/2	Red Schoendienst	1,695,270
1976	5th	72	90	.444	29	Red Schoendienst	1,207,079
1977	3rd	83	79	.512	18	Vern Rapp	1,659,287
1978	5th	69	93	.426	21	Vern Rapp, Jack Krol, Ken Boyer	1,278,215
1979	3rd	86	76	.531	12	Ken Boyer	1,627,256
1980	4th	74	88	.457	17	Ken Boyer, Jack Krol, Whitey Herzog, Red Schoendienst	1,385,147
1981	2nd/2nd	59	43	.578	‡	Whitey Herzog	1,010,247
1982	1st§	92	70	.568	+3	Whitey Herzog	2,111,906
1983	4th	79	83	.488	11	Whitey Herzog	2,317,914
1984	3rd	84	78	.519	12 1/2	Whitey Herzog	2,037,448
1985	1st§	101	61	.623	+3	Whitey Herzog	2,637,563
1986	3rd	79	82	.491	28 1/2	Whitey Herzog	2,471,974
1987	1st§	95	67	.586	+3	Whitey Herzog	3,072,122
1988	5th	76	86	.469	25	Whitey Herzog	2,892,799
1989	3rd	86	76	.531	7	Whitey Herzog	3,080,980
1990	6th	70	92	.432	25	Whitey Herzog, Red Schoendienst, Joe Torre	2,573,225
1991	2nd	84	78	.519	14	Joe Torre	2,448,699
1992	3rd	83	79	.512	13	Joe Torre	2,418,483
1993	3rd	87	75	.537	10	Joe Torre	2,844,328

CENTRAL DIVISION

Year	Position	W	L	Pct.	*GB	Manager	Attendance
1994	3rd (tied)	53	61	.465	13	Joe Torre	1,866,544
1995	4th	62	81	.434	22 1/2	Joe Torre, Mike Jorgensen	1,756,727
1996	1st∞▲	88	74	.543	+6	Tony La Russa	2,654,718
1997	4th	73	89	.451	11	Tony La Russa	2,634,014

*Games behind winner. †Won pennant playoff. ‡First half 30-20; second half 29-23. §Won championship series. ∞Won division series. ▲Lost championship series.

MANAGERIAL RECORDS

Ray Blades 106-85, Ken Boyer 166-190, Roger Bresnahan 255-352, Jimmy Burke 17-32, Patsy Donovan 175-236, Eddie Dyer 446-325, Frank Frisch 458-354, Mike Gonzalez 9-13, Stan Hack 3-7, Solly Hemus 190-192, Jack Hendricks 51-78, Whitey Herzog 835-739, Rogers Hornsby 153-116, Miller Huggins 346-415, Fred Hutchinson 232-220, Mike Jorgensen 42-54, Johnny Keane 317-249, Tony La Russa 161-163, Marty Marion 81-73, John McCloskey 153-304, Bill McKechnie 129-88, Kid Nichols 94-108, Bob O'Farrell 92-61, Vern Rapp 89-90, Branch Rickey 458-485, Stanley Robison 22-35, Red Schoendienst 1,028-944, Billy Southworth 620-346, Eddie Stanky 260-238, Gabby Street 312-242, Joe Torre 351-354, Harry Walker 51-67.

SAN DIEGO PADRES
YEARLY FINISHES

WEST DIVISION

Year	Position	W	L	Pct.	*GB	Manager	Attendance
1969	6th	52	110	.321	41	Preston Gomez	512,970
1970	6th	63	99	.389	39	Preston Gomez	643,679
1971	6th	61	100	.379	28½	Preston Gomez	557,513
1972	6th	58	95	.379	36½	Preston Gomez, Don Zimmer	644,273
1973	6th	60	102	.370	39	Don Zimmer	611,826
1974	6th	60	102	.370	42	John McNamara	1,075,399
1975	4th	71	91	.438	37	John McNamara	1,281,747
1976	5th	73	89	.451	29	John McNamara	1,458,478
1977	5th	69	93	.426	29	John McNamara, Bob Skinner, Alvin Dark	1,376,269
1978	4th	84	78	.519	11	Roger Craig	1,670,107
1979	5th	68	93	.422	22	Roger Craig	1,456,967
1980	6th	73	89	.451	19½	Jerry Coleman	1,139,026
1981	6th/6th	41	69	.373	†	Frank Howard	519,161
1982	4th	81	81	.500	8	Dick Williams	1,607,516
1983	4th	81	81	.500	10	Dick Williams	1,539,815
1984	1st†	92	70	.568	+12	Dick Williams	1,983,904
1985	3rd (tied)	83	79	.512	12	Dick Williams	2,210,352
1986	4th	74	88	.457	22	Steve Boros	1,805,716
1987	6th	65	97	.401	25	Larry Bowa	1,454,061
1988	3rd	83	78	.516	11	Larry Bowa, Jack McKeon	1,506,896
1989	2nd	89	73	.549	3	Jack McKeon	2,009,031
1990	4th (tied)	75	87	.463	16	Jack McKeon, Greg Riddoch	1,856,396
1991	3rd	84	78	.519	10	Greg Riddoch	1,804,289
1992	3rd	82	80	.506	16	Greg Riddoch, Jim Riggleman	1,722,102
1993	7th	61	101	.377	43	Jim Riggleman	1,375,432
1994	4th	47	70	.402	12½	Jim Riggleman	953,857
1995	3rd	70	74	.486	8	Bruce Bochy	1,041,805
1996	1st§	91	71	.562	+1	Bruce Bochy	2,187,886
1997	4th	76	86	.469	14	Bruce Bochy	2,089,333

*Games behind winner. †First half 23-33; second half 18-36. ‡Won championship series. §Lost division series.

MANAGERIAL RECORDS

Bruce Bochy 237-231, Steve Boros 74-88, Larry Bowa 81-127, Jerry Coleman 73-89, Roger Craig 152-171, Alvin Dark 49-65, Preston Gomez 180-316, Frank Howard 41-69, Jack McKeon 193-164, John McNamara 224-310, Greg Riddoch 200-194, Jim Riggleman 112-179, Dick Williams 337-311, Don Zimmer 114-190.

SAN FRANCISCO GIANTS
YEARLY FINISHES

Year	Position	W	L	Pct.	*GB	Manager	Attendance
1901†	7th	52	85	.380	37	George Davis	297,650
1902†	8th	48	88	.353	53½	Horace Fogel, Heinie Smith, John McGraw	302,875
1903†	2nd	84	55	.604	6½	John McGraw	579,530
1904†	1st	106	47	.693	+13	John McGraw	609,826
1905†	1st	105	48	.686	+9	John McGraw	552,700
1906†	2nd	96	56	.632	20	John McGraw	402,850
1907†	4th	82	71	.536	25½	John McGraw	538,350
1908†	2nd (tied)	98	56	.636	1	John McGraw	910,000
1909†	3rd	92	61	.601	18½	John McGraw	783,700
1910†	2nd	91	63	.591	13	John McGraw	511,785
1911†	1st	99	54	.647	+7½	John McGraw	675,000
1912†	1st	103	48	.682	+10	John McGraw	638,000
1913†	1st	101	51	.664	+12½	John McGraw	630,000
1914†	2nd	84	70	.545	10½	John McGraw	364,313
1915†	8th	69	83	.454	21	John McGraw	391,850
1916†	4th	86	66	.566	7	John McGraw	552,056
1917†	1st	98	56	.636	+10	John McGraw	500,264
1918†	2nd	71	53	.573	10½	John McGraw	256,618
1919†	2nd	87	53	.621	9	John McGraw	708,857
1920†	2nd	86	68	.558	7	John McGraw	929,609
1921†	1st	94	59	.614	+4	John McGraw	773,477
1922†	1st	93	61	.604	+7	John McGraw	945,809
1923†	1st	95	58	.621	+4½	John McGraw	820,780
1924†	1st	93	60	.608	+1½	John McGraw	844,068
1925†	2nd	86	66	.566	8½	John McGraw	778,993

Year	Position	W	L	Pct.	*GB	Manager	Attendance
1926†	5th	74	77	.490	13 1/2	John McGraw	700,362
1927†	3rd	92	62	.597	2	John McGraw	858,190
1928†	2nd	93	61	.604	2	John McGraw	916,191
1929†	3rd	84	67	.556	13 1/2	John McGraw	868,806
1930†	3rd	87	67	.565	5	John McGraw	868,714
1931†	2nd	87	65	.572	13	John McGraw	812,163
1932†	6th (tied)	72	82	.468	18	John McGraw, Bill Terry	484,868
1933†	1st	91	61	.599	+5	Bill Terry	604,471
1934†	2nd	93	60	.608	2	Bill Terry	730,851
1935†	3rd	91	62	.595	8 1/2	Bill Terry	748,748
1936†	1st	92	62	.597	+5	Bill Terry	837,952
1937†	1st	95	57	.625	+3	Bill Terry	926,887
1938†	3rd	83	67	.553	5	Bill Terry	799,633
1939†	5th	77	74	.510	18 1/2	Bill Terry	702,457
1940†	6th	72	80	.474	27 1/2	Bill Terry	747,852
1941†	5th	74	79	.484	25 1/2	Bill Terry	763,098
1942†	3rd	85	67	.559	20	Mel Ott	779,621
1943†	8th	55	98	.359	49 1/2	Mel Ott	466,095
1944†	5th	67	87	.435	38	Mel Ott	674,083
1945†	5th	78	74	.513	19	Mel Ott	1,016,468
1946†	8th	61	93	.396	36	Mel Ott	1,219,873
1947†	4th	81	73	.526	13	Mel Ott	1,600,793
1948†	5th	78	76	.506	13 1/2	Mel Ott, Leo Durocher	1,459,269
1949†	5th	73	81	.474	24	Leo Durocher	1,218,446
1950†	3rd	86	68	.558	5	Leo Durocher	1,008,876
1951†	1st‡	98	59	.624	+1	Leo Durocher	1,059,539
1952†	2nd	92	62	.597	4 1/2	Leo Durocher	984,940
1953†	5th	70	84	.455	35	Leo Durocher	811,518
1954†	1st	97	57	.630	+5	Leo Durocher	1,155,067
1955†	3rd	80	74	.519	18 1/2	Leo Durocher	824,112
1956†	6th	67	87	.435	26	Bill Rigney	629,179
1957†	6th	69	85	.448	26	Bill Rigney	653,923
1958	3rd	80	74	.519	12	Bill Rigney	1,272,625
1959	3rd	83	71	.539	4	Bill Rigney	1,422,130
1960	5th	79	75	.513	16	Bill Rigney, Tom Sheehan	1,795,356
1961	3rd	85	69	.552	8	Alvin Dark	1,390,679
1962	1st‡	103	62	.624	+1	Alvin Dark	1,592,594
1963	3rd	88	74	.543	11	Alvin Dark	1,571,306
1964	4th	90	72	.556	3	Alvin Dark	1,504,364
1965	2nd	95	67	.586	2	Herman Franks	1,546,075
1966	2nd	93	68	.578	1 1/2	Herman Franks	1,657,192
1967	2nd	91	71	.562	10 1/2	Herman Franks	1,242,480
1968	2nd	88	74	.543	9	Herman Franks	837,220

WEST DIVISION

Year	Position	W	L	Pct.	*GB	Manager	Attendance
1969	2nd	90	72	.556	3	Clyde King	873,603
1970	3rd	86	76	.531	16	Clyde King, Charlie Fox	740,720
1971	1st§	90	72	.556	+1	Charlie Fox	1,106,043
1972	5th	69	86	.445	26 1/2	Charlie Fox	647,744
1973	3rd	88	74	.543	11	Charlie Fox	834,193
1974	5th	72	90	.444	30	Charlie Fox, Wes Westrum	519,987
1975	3rd	80	81	.497	27 1/2	Wes Westrum	522,919
1976	4th	74	88	.457	28	Bill Rigney	626,868
1977	4th	75	87	.463	23	Joe Altobelli	700,056
1978	3rd	89	73	.549	6	Joe Altobelli	1,740,477
1979	4th	71	91	.438	19 1/2	Joe Altobelli, Dave Bristol	1,456,402
1980	5th	75	86	.466	17	Dave Bristol	1,096,115
1981	5th/3rd	56	55	.505	∞	Frank Robinson	632,274
1982	3rd	87	75	.537	2	Frank Robinson	1,200,948
1983	5th	79	83	.488	12	Frank Robinson	1,251,530
1984	6th	66	96	.407	26	Frank Robinson, Danny Ozark	1,001,545
1985	6th	62	100	.383	33	Jim Davenport, Roger Craig	818,697
1986	3rd	83	79	.512	13	Roger Craig	1,528,748
1987	1st§	90	72	.556	+6	Roger Craig	1,917,168
1988	4th	83	79	.512	11 1/2	Roger Craig	1,785,297
1989	1st▲	92	70	.568	+3	Roger Craig	2,059,701
1990	3rd	85	77	.525	6	Roger Craig	1,975,528
1991	4th	75	87	.463	19	Roger Craig	1,737,478
1992	5th	72	90	.444	26	Roger Craig	1,561,987
1993	2nd	103	59	.636	1	Dusty Baker	2,606,354
1994	2nd	55	60	.478	3 1/2	Dusty Baker	1,704,608
1995	4th	67	77	.465	11	Dusty Baker	1,241,500

Year	Position	W	L	Pct.	*GB	Manager	Attendance
1996	4th 68		94	.420	23	Dusty Baker 1,413,922
1997	1st◆ 90		72	.556	+2	Dusty Baker...1,690,869

*Games behind winner. †New York Giants. ‡Won pennant playoff. §Lost championship series. ∞First half 27-32; second half 29-23. ▲Won championship series.

MANAGERIAL RECORDS

Joe Altobelli 225-239, Dusty Baker 383-362, Dave Bristol 85-98, Roger Craig 586-566, Alvin Dark 366-277, Jim Davenport 56-88, George Davis 52-85, Leo Durocher 637-523, Horace Fogel 18-23, Charlie Fox 348-327, Herman Franks 367-280, Clyde King 109-95, John McGraw 2,604-1,801, Mel Ott 464-530, Danny Ozark 24-32, Bill Rigney 406-430, Frank Robinson 264-277, Tom Sheehan 46-50, Heinie Smith 5-27, Bill Terry 823-661, Wes Westrum 118-129.

MINOR LEAGUES

FARM SYSTEMS

AMERICAN LEAGUE

ANAHEIM (6): AAA—Vancouver. AA—Midland. A—Cedar Rapids, Lake Elsinore, Boise. Rookie—Butte.
BALTIMORE (6): AAA—Rochester. AA—Bowie. A—Delmarva, Frederick. Rookie—Bluefield, Gulf Coast Orioles.
BOSTON (6): AAA—Pawtucket. AA—Trenton. A—Sarasota, Michigan, Lowell. Rookie—Gulf Coast Red Sox.
CHICAGO (6): AAA—Calgary. AA—Birmingham. A—Hickory, Winston-Salem. Rookie—Bristol, White Sox (AZ).
CLEVELAND (6): AAA—Buffalo. AA—Akron. A—Kinston, Columbus, Watertown. Rookie—Burlington.
DETROIT (6): AAA—Toledo. AA—Jacksonville. A—Lakeland, Jamestown, West Michigan. Rookie—Gulf Coast Tigers.
KANSAS CITY (6): AAA—Omaha. AA—Wichita. A—Lansing, Wilmington, Spokane. Rookie—Gulf Coast Royals.
MINNESOTA (6): AAA—Salt Lake. AA—New Britain. A—Fort Myers, Fort Wayne. Rookie—Elizabethton, Gulf Coast Twins.
NEW YORK (6): AAA—Columbus. AA—Norwich. A—Tampa, Greensboro, Oneonta. Rookie—Gulf Coast Yankees.
OAKLAND (6): AAA—Edmonton. AA—Huntsville. A—Modesto, Visalia, Southern Oregon. Rookie—Phoenix A's.
SEATTLE (6): AAA—Tacoma. AA—Orlando. A—Lancaster, Wisconsin, Everett. Rookie—Peoria Mariners.
TAMPA BAY (6): AAA—Durham. A—St. Petersburg, Charleston (SC), Hudson Valley. Rookie—Princeton, Gulf Coast Devil Rays.
TEXAS (6): AAA—Oklahoma City. AA—Tulsa. A—Charlotte, Savannah. Rookie—Pulaski, Gulf Coast Rangers.
TORONTO (6): AAA—Syracuse. AA—Knoxville. A—Dunedin, Hagerstown, St. Catharines. Rookie—Medicine Hat.

NATIONAL LEAGUE

ARIZONA (5): AAA—Tucson. A—High Desert, South Bend. Rookie—Lethbridge, Peoria (AZ) Diamondbacks.
ATLANTA (7): AAA—Richmond. AA—Greenville. A—Durham, Macon, Eugene. Rookie—Danville, Gulf Coast Braves.
CHICAGO (6): AAA—Iowa. AA—West Tenn. A—Daytona Beach, Rockford, Williamsport. Rookie—Mesa Cubs.
CINCINNATI (5): AAA—Indianapolis. AA—Chattanooga. A—Burlington, Charleston (WV). Rookie—Billings.
COLORADO (6): AAA—Colorado Springs. AA—New Haven. A—Salem, Asheville, Portland (OR). Rookie—Mesa Rockies.
FLORIDA (6): AAA—Charlotte. AA—Portland (ME). A—Brevard County, Kane County, Utica. Rookie—Gulf Coast Marlins.
HOUSTON (6): AAA—New Orleans. AA—Jackson. A—Kissimmee, Quad City, Auburn. Rookie—Gulf Coast Astros.
LOS ANGELES (6): AAA—Albuquerque. AA—San Antonio. A—San Bernardino, Vero Beach, Yakima. Rookie—Great Falls.
MILWAUKEE (6): AAA—Louisville. AA—El Paso. A—Stockton, Beloit. Rookie—Helena, Ogden.
MONTREAL (6): AAA—Ottawa. AA—Harrisburg. A—Jupiter, Cape Fear, Vermont. Rookie—Gulf Coast Expos.
NEW YORK (7): AAA—Norfolk. AA—Binghamton. A—St. Lucie, Capital City, Pittsfield. Rookie—Kingsport, Gulf Coast Mets.
PHILADELPHIA (6): AAA—Scranton/Wilkes-Barre. AA—Reading. A—Clearwater, Piedmont, Batavia. Rookie—Martinsville.
PITTSBURGH (6): AAA—Nashville. AA—Carolina. A—Lynchburg, Augusta, Erie. Rookie—Gulf Coast Pirates.
ST. LOUIS (6): AAA—Memphis. AA—Arkansas. A—Prince William, Peoria (IL), New Jersey. Rookie—Johnson City.
SAN DIEGO (6): AAA—Las Vegas. AA—Mobile. A—Rancho Cucamonga, Clinton. Rookie—Idaho Falls, Peoria (AZ) Padres.
SAN FRANCISCO (5): AAA—Fresno. AA—Shreveport. A—Bakersfield, San Jose, Salem-Keizer.

AMERICAN ASSOCIATION

League disbanded after 1997 season. Teams will move to existing leagues in the following manner: Buffalo, Indianapolis and Louisville to the International League; Iowa, Nashville, New Orleans, Oklahoma and Omaha to the Pacific Coast League.

TEAMS

BUFFALO BISONS
General manager
Mike Buczowski
Manager
Jeff Datz
Ballpark (capacity, surface)
North AmeriCare Park (21,050, grass)
Affiliation
Indians
Address
P.O. Box 450
Buffalo, NY 14205
Phone
716-846-2003

INDIANAPOLIS INDIANS
President/CEO
Max Schumacher
General manager
Cal Burleson
Manager
Dave Miley
Ballpark (capacity, surface)
Victory Field (15,000, grass)
Affiliation
Reds
Address
501 W. Maryland St.
Indianapolis, IN 42225
Phone
317-269-3545

IOWA CUBS
General manager
Sam Bernabe
Manager
Terry Kennedy
Ballpark (capacity, surface)
Sec Taylor Stadium (10,500, grass)

Affiliation
Cubs
Address
350 SW 1 St.
Des Moines, IA 50309
Phone
515-243-6111

LOUISVILLE REDBIRDS
General manager
Dale Owens
Manager
Gary Allenson
Ballpark (capacity, surface)
Cardinal Stadium (33,000, artificial)
Affiliation
Brewers
Address
P.O. Box 36407
Louisville, KY 40233
Phone
502-367-9121

NASHVILLE SOUNDS
General manager
Dale Larsen
Manager
To be announced
Ballpark (capacity, surface)
Greer Stadium (11,500, grass)
Affiliation
Pirates
Address
P.O. Box 23290
Nashville, TN 37202
Phone
615-242-4371

NEW ORLEANS ZEPHYRS
General manager
Jay Miller

Manager
John Tamargo
Ballpark (capacity, surface)
Zephyr Field (10,000, grass)
Affiliation
Astros
Address
6000 Airline Highway
Metairie, LA 70003
Phone
504-734-5155

OKLAHOMA REDHAWKS
General Manager
David Vance
Manager
Greg Biagini
Ballpark (capacity, surface)
To be announced (13,300, grass)
Affiliation
Rangers
Address
To be announced
Phone
405-218-1000

OMAHA ROYALS
Vice president/general manager
Bill Gorman
Manager
Ron Johnson
Ballpark (capacity, surface)
Rosenblatt Stadium (23,000, grass)
Affiliation
Royals
Address
P.O. Box 3665
Omaha, NE 68103
Phone
402-734-2550

1997 FINAL STANDINGS

EASTERN DIVISION

Team	W	L	T	Pct.	GB
Buffalo (Indians)	87	57	0	.604	....
Indianapolis (Reds)	85	59	0	.590	2
Nashville (White Sox)	74	69	0	.517	12½
Louisville (Cardinals)	58	85	0	.406	28½

WESTERN DIVISION

Team	W	L	T	Pct.	GB
Iowa (Cubs)	74	69	0	.517	....
New Orleans (Astros)	74	70	0	.514	½
Oklahoma City (Rangers)	61	82	0	.427	13
Omaha (Royals)	61	83	0	.424	13½

COMPOSITE

Team	Buf.	Ind.	Nash.	Iowa	N.O.	O.C.	Oma.	Lou.	W	L	T	Pct.	GB
Buffalo (Indians)	....	15	13	7	12	11	13	16	87	57	0	.604	....
Indianapolis (Reds)	9	....	13	12	7	12	15	17	85	59	0	.590	2
Nashville (White Sox)	11	11	....	6	11	9	13	13	74	69	0	.517	12½
Iowa (Cubs)	11	6	11	....	13	12	10	11	74	69	0	.517	12½
New Orleans (Astros)	6	11	7	11	....	16	12	11	74	70	0	.514	13
Oklahoma City (Rangers)	7	6	9	12	8	....	11	8	61	82	0	.427	25½
Omaha (Royals)	5	3	5	14	12	13	....	9	61	83	0	.424	26
Louisville (Cardinals)	8	7	11	7	7	9	9	....	58	85	0	.406	28½

Major league affiliations in parentheses.
Iowa club represented Des Moines, Iowa.
PLAYOFFS: Buffalo defeated Indianapolis, three games to two; Iowa defeated New Orleans, three games to none; Buffalo defeated Iowa, three games to none, to win league championship.

CLASS AAA *American Association*

REGULAR-SEASON ATTENDANCE: Buffalo, 696,193; Indianapolis, 618,095; Iowa, 403,040; Louisville, 408,550; Nashville, 269,186; New Orleans, 507,164; Oklahoma City, 325,582; Omaha, 449,753. Total—3,677,563. Playoffs (11 games)—71,063. Class AAA All-Star Game at Des Moines—11,183.

MANAGERS: Buffalo, Brian Graham; Indianapolis, Dave Miley; Iowa, Tim Johnson; Louisville, Gaylen Pitts; Nashville, Tom Spencer; New Orleans, Steve Swisher; Oklahoma City, Greg Biagini; Omaha, Mike Jirschele.

ALL-STAR TEAM: 1B—Richie Sexson, Buffalo; 2B—Miguel Cairo, Iowa; 3B—Aaron Boone, Indianapolis; SS—Damian Jackson, Buffalo-Indianapolis; OF—Jeff Abbott, Nashville; Bruce Aven, Buffalo; Magglio Ordonez, Nashville; C—Eli Marrero, Louisville; DH—Bubba Smith, Oklahoma City; RHP—Giovanni Carrara, Indianapolis; LHP—John Halama, New Orleans; Relief Pitcher—Marc Pisciotta, Iowa; Most Valuable Player—Magglio Ordonez, Nashville; Rookie of the Year—Magglio Ordonez, Nashville; Manager of the Year—Dave Miley, Indianapolis.

1997 BATTING

TEAM

Team	Avg.	G	TPA	AB	R	H	TB	2B	3B	HR	RBI	SH	SF	HP	BB	IBB	SO	SB	CS	GDP	LOB	SHO	Slg.	OBP
Nashville	.269	143	5375	4797	706	1292	2043	246	23	153	659	45	36	43	454	19	859	81	49	120	982	14	.426	.336
Buffalo	.268	144	5459	4804	711	1286	2116	242	21	182	656	39	50	57	509	23	910	99	66	110	1027	6	.440	.342
Iowa	.265	143	5349	4779	666	1265	2011	254	21	150	627	34	36	47	453	29	893	91	52	116	959	9	.421	.332
Indianapolis	.264	144	5381	4758	669	1257	2010	233	35	150	621	35	47	26	515	26	928	122	70	101	994	6	.422	.336
Okla. City	.262	143	5470	4881	622	1278	2022	266	32	138	577	29	38	36	486	18	1055	134	62	119	1022	5	.414	.331
Omaha	.261	144	5288	4738	663	1235	2033	232	16	178	622	33	35	48	434	16	1014	75	41	115	941	6	.429	.327
New Orleans	.258	144	5528	4855	639	1253	1790	242	32	77	595	49	52	36	536	30	814	58	50	131	1041	7	.369	.333
Louisville	.253	143	5315	4724	611	1195	1883	220	39	130	560	37	34	41	479	15	953	93	65	117	949	13	.399	.325

INDIVIDUAL

TOP QUALIFIERS FOR BATTING CHAMPIONSHIP
Minimum 389 plate appearances. *Lefthanded batter. †Switch-hitter.

Player, Team	Avg.	G	TPA	AB	R	H	TB	2B	3B	HR	RBI	SH	SF	HP	BB	IBB	SO	SB	CS	GDP	Slg.	OBP
Ordonez, Magglio, Nashville	.329	135	570	523	65	172	249	29	3	14	90	2	9	2	32	5	61	14	10	18	.476	.364
Abbott, Jeff, Nashville	.327	118	518	465	88	152	226	35	3	11	63	2	3	5	41	0	52	12	7	12	.486	.385
Hubbard, Trenidad, Buffalo	.312	103	441	375	71	117	189	22	1	16	60	0	6	3	57	0	52	26	10	10	.504	.401
Wilson, Enrique, Buffalo†	.306	118	506	451	78	138	197	20	3	11	39	4	4	5	42	2	41	9	8	7	.437	.369
Costo, Tim, Louisville	.303	121	448	400	52	121	193	26	2	14	54	2	2	3	41	1	72	4	4	4	.483	.370
Lowery, Terrell, Iowa	.301	110	455	386	69	116	201	28	3	17	71	1	2	1	65	2	97	9	8	8	.521	.401
Sutton, Larry, Omaha*	.300	106	443	380	61	114	200	27	1	19	72	0	2	0	61	4	57	0	0	6	.526	.395
Boone, Aaron, Indianapolis	.290	131	523	476	79	138	242	30	4	22	75	3	1	4	40	3	81	12	4	11	.508	.344
Phillips, J.R., New Orleans*	.290	104	454	411	59	119	210	28	0	21	71	0	4	0	39	3	112	0	1	11	.511	.348
Jackson, Damian, Buf.-Ind.	.288	92	394	337	63	97	129	18	1	4	20	3	3	4	47	2	62	24	9	3	.383	.379
Aven, Bruce, Buffalo	.287	121	500	432	69	124	208	27	3	17	77	2	5	11	50	0	99	10	3	10	.481	.371
Owens, Eric, Indianapolis	.286	104	441	391	56	112	168	15	4	11	44	1	4	3	42	0	55	23	10	8	.430	.357
Diaz, Alex, Oklahoma City†	.286	105	465	426	65	122	187	25	2	12	49	0	3	3	33	3	53	26	7	19	.439	.340
Ramirez, Alex, Buffalo	.286	119	453	416	59	119	187	19	8	11	44	6	3	4	24	0	95	10	5	9	.450	.329
Stynes, Chris, Oma.-Ind.	.285	103	449	418	67	119	174	26	1	9	61	5	4	1	21	1	30	7	2	10	.416	.318

DEPARTMENTAL LEADERS: G—C. Smith, 140; AB—Cairo, 569; R—Abbott, 88; H—Ordonez, 172; TB—Hunter, Ordonez, 249 each; 2B—Hidalgo, 37; 3B—Ramirez, 8; HR—Sexson, 31; RBI—C. Smith, 94; SH—C. Wilson, 12; SF—Ordonez, 9; HP—Aven, Mora, 11 each; BB—Mitchell, 72; IBB—Colon, 6; SO—C. Smith, 139; SB—Cairo, 40; CS—Cairo, Frias, 15 each; GIDP—C. Wilson, 19; Slg.—Norton, .534; OBP—Lowery, T. Hubbard, .401 each.

ALL PLAYERS
*Lefthanded batter. †Switch-hitter.

Player, Team	Avg.	G	TPA	AB	R	H	TB	2B	3B	HR	RBI	SH	SF	HP	BB	IBB	SO	SB	CS	GDP	Slg.	OBP
Abbott, Jeff, Nashville	.327	118	518	465	88	152	226	35	3	11	63	2	3	5	41	0	52	12	7	12	.486	.385
Abreu, Bob, New Orleans*	.268	47	219	194	25	52	75	9	4	2	22	1	3	0	21	2	49	7	4	4	.387	.335
Anthony, Eric, O.C.*	.444	9	39	36	3	16	24	2	0	2	9	0	1	0	2	0	7	0	0	0	.667	.462
Arrandale, Matt, Louisville	.000	56	2	2	0	0	0	0	0	0	0	0	0	0	0	0	1	0	0	0	.000	.000
Aven, Bruce, Buffalo	.287	121	500	432	69	124	208	27	3	17	77	2	5	11	50	0	99	10	3	10	.481	.371
Aybar, Manny, Louisville	.040	22	28	25	1	1	2	1	0	0	1	3	0	0	0	0	8	0	0	0	.080	.040
Bako, Paul, Indianapolis*	.243	104	362	321	34	78	118	14	1	8	43	1	4	2	34	3	81	0	5	7	.368	.316
Barber, Brian, Louisville	.100	18	13	10	1	1	1	0	0	0	1	1	0	0	2	0	2	0	0	1	.100	.250
Barrios, Manuel, New Orleans	.000	57	1	1	0	0	0	0	0	0	0	0	0	0	0	0	0	0	0	0	.000	.000
Batista, Miguel, Iowa	.071	31	15	14	1	1	4	0	0	1	2	1	0	0	0	0	8	0	0	0	.286	.071
Battle, Allen, Nashville	.222	11	32	27	6	6	13	1	0	2	5	0	0	0	5	0	7	0	0	0	.481	.344
Belk, Tim, Indianapolis	.290	90	289	255	37	74	118	18	1	8	38	3	4	1	26	1	45	5	3	1	.463	.353
Bell, David, Louisville	.227	6	25	22	3	5	8	0	0	1	4	0	1	1	0	0	6	0	0	0	.364	.250
Bell, Derek, New Orleans	.154	5	14	13	0	2	2	0	0	0	1	0	0	0	1	0	1	0	0	3	.154	.214
Bell, Mike, Oklahoma City	.235	93	365	328	35	77	114	18	2	5	38	0	3	4	29	0	78	4	2	10	.348	.302
Beltran, Rigo, Louisville*	.000	9	2	2	0	0	0	0	0	0	0	0	0	0	0	0	1	0	0	0	.000	.000
Benitez, Yamil, Omaha	.295	92	358	329	61	97	176	14	1	21	71	0	4	1	24	1	82	12	3	8	.535	.341
Berblinger, Jeff, Louisville	.263	133	580	513	63	135	201	19	7	11	58	1	5	6	55	1	98	24	12	15	.392	.339
Berry, Sean, New Orleans	.333	3	12	9	1	3	3	0	0	0	0	0	0	3	0	0	3	0	0	0	.333	.500
Blosser, Greg, O.C.*	.303	54	207	178	33	54	103	11	1	12	37	0	2	0	27	0	46	6	2	2	.579	.391
Bolton, Rodney, Indianapolis	.100	28	31	30	1	3	3	0	0	0	1	0	0	0	0	0	12	0	0	2	.100	.100
Boone, Aaron, Indianapolis	.290	131	523	476	79	138	242	30	4	22	75	3	1	4	40	3	81	12	4	11	.508	.344
Boone, Bret, Indianapolis	.286	3	9	7	1	2	3	1	0	0	1	0	0	0	2	0	1	0	0	0	.429	.444
Bradshaw, Terry, Louisville*	.249	130	524	453	79	113	166	17	6	8	43	1	0	9	61	1	79	26	10	12	.366	.350
Brady, Doug, Nashville†	.238	106	399	370	43	88	127	12	3	7	36	8	1	2	18	0	47	13	4	4	.343	.276
Branson, Jeff, Indianapolis*	.211	15	64	57	7	12	18	3	0	1	4	1	0	0	6	0	10	0	0	1	.316	.286
Brewer, Rod, Buffalo*	.161	10	40	31	3	5	12	1	0	2	4	5	0	0	3	0	9	0	0	1	.387	.325
Bridges, Kary, New Orleans*..	.172	23	71	64	6	11	16	1	2	0	3	0	1	1	5	0	9	1	0	0	.250	.239
Brooks, Rayme, Omaha	.000	3	9	9	0	0	0	0	0	0	0	0	0	0	0	0	4	0	0	0	.000	.000
Brown, Brant, Iowa*	.301	71	291	256	51	77	150	19	3	16	51	1	2	1	31	2	44	6	6	5	.586	.379
Brown, Kevin, Oklahoma City	.241	116	449	403	56	97	176	18	2	19	50	1	2	5	38	1	111	2	2	11	.437	.313

Player, Team	Avg.	G	TPA	AB	R	H	TB	2B	3B	HR	RBI	SH	SF	HP	BB	IBB	SO	SB	CS	GDP	Slg.	OBP
Busby, Mike, Louisville	.214	15	15	14	1	3	6	0	0	1	2	0	0	0	1	0	6	0	0	1	.429	.267
Busch, Mike, Buffalo	.181	51	191	166	24	30	70	4	0	12	29	0	2	1	22	1	68	0	0	6	.422	.277
Cabrera, Jose, Buf.-N.O.	.200	36	6	5	1	1	1	0	0	0	0	1	0	0	0	0	3	0	0	0	.200	.200
Cairo, Miguel, Iowa	.279	135	608	569	82	159	217	35	4	5	46	6	3	6	24	0	54	40	15	9	.381	.314
Cameron, Mike, Nashville	.275	30	143	120	21	33	64	7	3	6	17	0	2	3	18	0	31	4	2	1	.533	.378
Candaele, Casey, Buffalo†	.228	79	351	311	39	71	113	21	0	7	38	4	4	1	31	2	43	1	6	12	.363	.297
Cappuccio, Carmine, Nashville*	.220	55	196	177	22	39	62	11	0	4	21	1	2	0	16	2	24	1	0	10	.350	.282
Caraballo, Ramon, Iowa†	.211	49	158	133	16	28	48	8	0	4	21	0	1	6	18	1	25	5	2	1	.361	.329
Carr, Chuck, New Orleans†	.246	19	73	65	8	16	17	1	0	0	3	0	0	0	8	0	14	5	3	1	.262	.329
Carr, Jeremy, Omaha	.267	35	139	120	17	32	45	3	2	2	9	1	0	3	15	0	17	12	3	3	.375	.362
Carrara, Giovanni, Ind.	.222	19	21	18	2	4	4	0	0	0	2	1	0	0	2	0	4	0	1	0	.222	.300
Carrasco, Hector, Ind.	.000	3	1	1	0	0	0	0	0	0	0	0	0	0	0	0	0	0	0	0	.000	.000
Casey, Sean, Buffalo*	.361	20	82	72	12	26	48	7	0	5	18	0	0	1	9	0	11	0	0	0	.667	.439
Castillo, Carlos, Nashville	.000	4	1	1	0	0	0	0	0	0	0	0	0	0	0	0	0	0	0	0	.000	.000
Castleberry, Kevin, O.C.*	.270	40	122	111	14	30	41	6	1	1	9	1	1	0	9	2	21	1	2	1	.369	.322
Cedeno, Domingo, O.C.†	.357	6	28	28	0	10	12	2	0	0	2	0	0	0	0	0	6	0	1	1	.429	.357
Cholowsky, Dan, Iowa	.185	36	74	65	12	12	17	2	0	1	4	0	0	0	9	0	17	2	1	2	.262	.284
Christopherson, Eric, N.Orlns..	.190	9	25	21	3	4	4	0	0	0	0	0	0	0	4	0	7	0	0	0	.190	.320
Cline, Pat, Iowa	.221	27	106	95	6	21	32	2	0	3	10	0	1	0	10	1	24	0	1	4	.337	.292
Colon, Dennis, New Orleans*	.270	129	458	400	49	108	151	23	1	6	64	2	8	6	42	6	48	2	2	10	.378	.342
Costo, Tim, Louisville	.303	121	448	400	52	121	193	26	2	14	54	2	2	3	41	1	72	4	4	4	.483	.370
Cotton, John, Nashville*	.269	94	350	323	45	87	140	14	3	11	50	1	2	0	24	1	94	8	2	7	.433	.318
Coughlin, Kevin, Louisville* ...	.257	12	36	35	2	9	10	1	0	0	2	0	0	0	1	0	7	0	1	0	.286	.278
Croushore, Rick, Louisville	.000	14	3	3	0	0	0	0	0	0	0	0	0	0	0	0	2	0	0	0	.000	.000
Crowell, Jim, Indianapolis*	.200	3	5	5	0	1	1	0	0	0	0	0	0	0	0	0	1	0	0	0	.200	.200
Curtis, Randy, Buffalo*	.270	41	128	111	14	30	52	7	0	5	15	0	0	3	14	1	22	1	1	2	.468	.367
Dalesandro, Mark, Iowa	.262	115	445	405	48	106	144	14	0	8	48	0	5	2	33	3	51	0	0	15	.356	.317
Detmers, Kris, Louisville†	.000	10	5	4	0	0	0	0	0	0	0	1	0	0	0	0	3	0	0	0	.000	.000
Diaz, Alex, Oklahoma City†	.286	105	465	426	65	122	187	25	2	12	49	0	3	3	33	3	53	26	7	19	.439	.340
Diaz, Edwin, Oklahoma City ...	.110	20	78	73	6	8	16	3	1	1	4	1	0	2	2	0	27	1	1	1	.219	.156
Diaz, Einar, Buffalo	.256	109	365	336	40	86	117	18	2	3	31	4	2	5	18	1	34	2	6	12	.348	.302
Difelice, Mike, Louisville	.250	1	4	4	1	1	4	0	0	1	1	0	0	0	0	0	1	0	0	0	1.000	.250
Dowler, Dee, Iowa	.230	42	114	100	14	23	31	2	0	2	12	1	1	2	10	0	16	6	1	2	.310	.310
Downs, Brian, Nashville	.222	7	18	18	1	4	4	0	0	0	1	0	0	0	0	0	5	0	1	0	.222	.222
Dye, Jermaine, Omaha	.306	39	155	144	21	44	80	6	0	10	25	0	1	1	9	1	25	0	2	3	.556	.348
Eischen, Joey, Indianapolis* ..	.000	26	2	2	0	0	0	0	0	0	0	0	0	0	0	0	0	0	0	0	.000	.000
Elarton, Scott, New Orleans ...	.333	9	6	6	2	2	3	1	0	0	0	0	0	0	0	0	2	0	0	0	.500	.333
Estrada, Osmani, Okla. City	.226	92	317	288	22	65	77	9	0	1	20	3	4	2	20	0	37	7	2	8	.267	.277
Evans, Jason, Nashville†	.284	65	249	194	38	55	70	10	1	1	27	2	0	4	49	1	45	6	3	1	.361	.437
Fasano, Sal, Omaha	.164	49	170	152	17	25	44	7	0	4	14	0	1	5	12	1	53	0	0	1	.289	.247
Fletcher, Paul, Iowa	.000	54	1	1	0	0	0	0	0	0	0	0	0	0	0	0	0	0	0	0	.000	.000
Flora, Kevin, New Orleans	.257	31	126	109	14	28	41	1	3	2	14	1	0	0	16	1	25	8	2	3	.376	.352
Fordyce, Brook, Indianapolis..	.234	12	53	47	7	11	19	2	0	2	6	0	0	1	5	0	6	1	1	3	.404	.321
Franklin, Micah, Louisville†	.221	99	383	326	49	72	124	14	1	12	48	0	3	3	51	4	74	2	0	9	.380	.329
Freeman, Ricky, Iowa	.169	31	88	77	7	13	16	0	0	1	4	0	0	3	8	0	20	1	0	4	.208	.273
Frias, Hanley, Oklahoma City†	.264	132	552	484	64	128	168	17	4	5	46	8	3	1	56	2	72	35	15	8	.347	.340
Gallego, Mike, Louisville	.278	6	23	18	0	5	6	1	0	0	1	0	1	1	3	1	5	1	1	1	.333	.391
Garcia, Guillermo, Indnpls.	.238	55	163	151	16	36	68	2	0	10	20	0	2	1	9	0	46	0	2	4	.450	.282
Gardiner, Mike, New Orleans..	.000	11	5	4	0	0	0	0	0	0	0	1	0	0	0	0	2	0	0	0	.000	.000
Giannelli, Ray, Louisville*	.221	39	112	95	12	21	34	4	0	3	12	0	0	0	17	0	18	0	0	3	.358	.339
Gonzalez, Jeremi, Iowa	.222	10	11	9	0	2	2	0	0	0	0	2	0	0	0	0	2	0	0	0	.222	.222
Goodwin, Curtis, Indianapolis*	.276	30	132	116	14	32	41	4	1	1	7	1	0	0	15	0	20	11	8	0	.353	.359
Grebeck, Brian, New Orleans .	.126	68	130	103	15	13	14	1	0	0	8	4	2	0	21	0	17	1	0	5	.136	.270
Green, Scarborough, Louisville†	.254	52	232	209	26	53	77	11	2	3	13	1	0	0	22	0	55	10	7	3	.368	.325
Greene, Tommy, New Orleans	.444	14	10	9	2	4	7	0	0	1	2	0	1	0	0	0	1	0	0	0	.778	.400
Guillen, Carlos, New Orleans†	.308	3	13	13	3	4	5	1	0	0	0	0	0	0	0	0	4	0	0	0	.385	.308
Gulan, Mike, Louisville	.267	116	447	412	50	110	184	20	6	14	61	1	3	3	28	0	121	5	2	12	.447	.316
Gutierrez, Ricky, New Orleans	.185	7	30	27	2	5	6	1	0	0	4	0	1	0	2	0	4	0	1	1	.222	.233
Halama, John, New Orleans*.	.231	26	27	26	2	6	10	2	1	0	0	1	0	0	0	0	5	0	0	1	.385	.231
Hall, Billy, Indianapolis†	.200	10	22	20	3	4	4	0	0	0	3	1	0	0	1	0	6	0	0	0	.200	.238
Halter, Shane, Omaha	.265	14	58	49	10	13	22	1	1	2	9	0	2	1	6	0	10	0	0	1	.449	.345
Haney, Todd, New Orleans	.282	115	517	454	63	128	159	25	0	2	63	10	7	3	43	0	50	5	2	10	.350	.343
Hansen, Jed, Omaha	.268	114	421	380	43	102	159	20	2	11	44	5	2	2	32	0	78	8	1	9	.418	.327
Hatcher, Chris, Omaha	.230	68	248	222	34	51	93	9	0	11	24	0	3	6	17	2	68	0	1	4	.419	.298
Henriquez, Oscar, N.Orleans ..	.000	60	3	3	1	0	0	0	0	0	1	0	0	0	0	0	1	0	0	0	.000	.000
Heredia, Gil, Iowa	.000	31	5	5	0	0	0	0	0	0	0	0	0	0	0	0	2	0	0	0	.000	.000
Hidalgo, Richard, N.Orleans ...	.279	134	576	526	74	147	227	37	5	11	78	0	7	8	35	3	57	6	10	16	.432	.330
Holbert, Aaron, Louisville	.255	93	338	314	32	80	112	14	3	4	32	3	4	2	15	1	56	9	5	9	.357	.290
Houston, Tyler, Iowa*	.217	6	23	23	0	5	7	2	0	0	4	0	0	0	0	0	2	0	0	0	.304	.217
Hubbard, Mike, Iowa	.280	50	200	186	24	52	87	15	1	6	26	1	2	0	11	0	23	2	0	2	.468	.317
Hubbard, Trenidad, Buffalo	.312	103	441	375	71	117	189	22	1	16	60	0	6	3	57	0	52	26	10	10	.504	.401
Hunter, Brian, Indianapolis	.281	139	562	506	74	142	249	36	4	21	85	2	8	4	42	2	76	9	6	9	.492	.336
Jackson, Damian, Buf.-Ind.	.288	92	394	337	63	97	129	18	1	4	20	3	3	4	47	2	62	24	9	3	.383	.379
Jackson, Danny, Louisville	.167	4	7	6	0	1	1	0	0	0	1	1	0	0	0	0	4	0	0	0	.167	.167
Jennings, Robin, Iowa*	.276	126	527	464	67	128	223	25	5	20	71	0	2	5	56	5	73	5	3	7	.481	.359
Johnson, Mark, Indianapolis*	.000	3	6	4	0	0	0	0	0	0	0	0	0	0	2	0	2	0	1	0	.000	.333
Johnson, Russ, New Orleans.	.276	122	516	445	72	123	163	16	6	4	49	2	2	1	66	1	78	7	4	10	.366	.370
Jordan, Brian, Louisville	.150	6	22	20	1	3	3	0	0	0	2	0	0	1	1	0	2	0	1	0	.150	.227
Kelly, Mike, Indianapolis	.348	27	115	92	28	32	61	8	0	7	18	0	0	0	23	2	23	7	1	0	.663	.478
Kieschnick, Brooks, Iowa*	.258	97	402	360	57	93	177	21	0	21	66	0	5	1	36	4	89	0	2	8	.492	.323
Klingenbeck, Scott, Ind.	.294	27	19	17	1	5	5	0	0	0	0	2	0	0	0	0	3	0	0	0	.294	.294
Kmak, Joe, Indianapolis	.158	16	44	38	6	6	9	0	0	1	2	0	1	0	5	0	6	0	0	2	.237	.250
Knorr, Randy, New Orleans	.238	72	268	244	22	58	83	10	0	5	27	1	1	0	22	3	38	0	0	13	.340	.300

Player, Team	Avg.	G	TPA	AB	R	H	TB	2B	3B	HR	RBI	SH	SF	HP	BB	IBB	SO	SB	CS	GDP	Slg.	OBP
Koslofski, Kevin, Louisville* ..	.211	106	337	285	37	60	107	14	3	9	27	5	2	2	43	2	78	1	9	6	.375	.316
Leius, Scott, Nashville............	.240	30	116	104	15	25	48	2	0	7	17	1	0	0	11	0	6	0	0	1	.462	.313
Lisanti, Bob, Iowa	.364	4	13	11	2	4	4	0	0	0	1	0	0	0	2	0	5	0	0	0	.364	.462
Listach, Pat, Buffalo†	.260	25	88	73	3	19	22	1	1	0	2	0	1	2	12	1	10	6	3	1	.301	.375
Little, Mark, Oklahoma City ...	.263	121	472	415	72	109	185	23	4	15	45	8	0	8	39	1	100	21	9	8	.446	.338
Livingstone, Scott, Louisville*	.360	9	29	25	4	9	10	1	0	0	2	1	1	0	2	0	3	0	0	0	.400	.393
Long, Ryan, Omaha	.265	113	442	411	48	109	192	26	0	19	56	3	3	7	18	2	98	2	4	14	.467	.305
Lopez, Mendy, Omaha............	.231	17	61	52	6	12	17	2	0	1	6	1	0	0	8	0	21	0	0	0	.327	.333
Lovullo, Torey, Buffalo†	.227	97	380	321	40	73	127	18	0	12	40	1	5	2	51	5	64	0	5	6	.396	.332
Lowe, Sean, Louisville	.263	26	20	19	1	5	6	1	0	0	1	1	0	0	0	0	7	0	0	0	.316	.263
Lowery, Terrell, Iowa	.301	110	455	386	69	116	201	28	3	17	71	1	2	1	65	2	97	9	8	8	.521	.401
Ludwick, Eric, Louisville	.250	24	9	8	1	2	3	1	0	0	1	1	0	0	0	0	2	0	0	0	.375	.250
Lyons, Curt, Iowa..................	.500	8	2	2	1	1	1	0	0	0	0	0	0	0	0	0	1	0	0	0	.500	.500
Maas, Kevin, Ind.-N.O.*	.219	86	313	260	38	57	103	23	1	7	34	0	2	3	48	4	56	0	0	3	.396	.345
Machado, Robert, Nashville ...	.269	84	328	308	43	83	125	18	0	8	30	5	2	1	12	0	61	5	0	6	.406	.297
Magdaleno, Ricky, Indnpls.....	.206	56	174	155	20	32	55	11	0	4	14	1	2	0	16	0	48	0	1	4	.355	.277
Manto, Jeff, Buffalo	.321	54	221	187	37	60	131	11	0	20	54	0	1	2	31	2	43	0	2	6	.701	.421
Marrero, Eli, Louisville	.273	112	429	395	60	108	203	21	7	20	68	1	5	3	25	2	53	4	4	8	.514	.318
Martinez, Felix, Omaha†	.254	112	452	410	55	104	137	19	4	2	36	5	1	7	29	0	86	21	11	11	.334	.313
Martinez, Pedro, Indianapolis*	.000	28	10	9	0	0	0	0	0	0	0	1	0	0	0	0	5	0	0	0	.000	.000
McCall, Rod, Buf.-Iowa*	.263	85	294	255	38	67	137	10	0	20	55	0	3	4	31	3	90	0	0	4	.537	.348
McIntosh, Tim, Iowa	.259	17	59	54	9	14	23	3	0	2	8	0	0	2	3	0	14	0	0	0	.426	.322
McLemore, Mark, O.C.†	.100	3	12	10	0	1	1	0	0	0	0	1	0	1	0	0	1	1	0	0	.100	.167
McNabb, Buck, New Orleans*	.158	11	20	19	2	3	5	0	1	0	0	0	0	0	1	0	6	0	0	0	.263	.200
Medrano, Tony, Omaha	.203	17	66	59	10	12	24	0	0	4	9	0	3	0	4	1	5	0	1	1	.407	.242
Mejia, Roberto, Louisville	.333	6	22	21	3	7	11	1	0	1	2	0	0	1	0	0	4	0	2	0	.524	.364
Meluskey, Mitch, N.Orleans† .	.250	51	199	172	22	43	59	7	0	3	21	0	1	1	25	1	38	0	0	6	.343	.347
Menechino, Frankie, Nashville	.230	37	146	113	20	26	42	4	0	4	11	0	1	6	26	1	31	3	2	2	.372	.397
Mercedes, Henry, O.C.	.246	16	66	57	6	14	20	3	0	1	4	0	0	0	9	0	12	0	0	3	.351	.348
Merchant, Mark, Omaha†.......	.000	2	5	5	0	0	0	0	0	0	0	0	0	0	0	0	4	0	0	0	.000	.000
Miller, Trever, New Orleans	.148	29	29	27	1	4	4	0	0	0	1	2	0	0	0	0	10	0	1	0	.148	.148
Mimbs, Mark, New Orleans*..	.000	22	1	1	0	0	0	0	0	0	0	0	0	0	0	0	0	0	0	0	.000	.000
Minor, Blas, New Orleans	.000	23	1	1	0	0	0	0	0	0	0	0	0	0	0	0	0	0	0	0	.000	.000
Mitchell, Keith, Indianapolis....	.265	124	487	407	72	108	179	24	1	15	60	1	6	1	72	1	65	10	4	11	.440	.372
Mlicki, Doug, New Orleans.....	.000	15	3	2	0	0	0	0	0	0	0	1	0	0	0	0	1	0	0	0	.000	.000
Molina, Jose, Iowa	.333	1	4	3	0	1	1	0	0	0	0	0	0	0	1	0	1	0	0	1	.333	.500
Montgomery, Ray, N.Orleans .	.288	20	84	73	17	21	44	5	0	6	13	0	0	0	11	0	15	1	1	2	.603	.381
Mora, Melvin, New Orleans	.257	119	439	370	55	95	122	15	3	2	38	9	2	11	47	0	52	7	7	7	.330	.356
Morris, Warren, O.C.*	.219	8	35	32	3	7	11	1	0	1	3	0	0	0	3	0	5	0	0	0	.344	.286
Mottola, Chad, Indianapolis ...	.289	83	306	284	33	82	125	10	6	7	45	0	2	4	16	2	43	12	4	6	.440	.333
Murphy, Mike, Oklahoma City	.329	73	291	243	37	80	118	13	5	5	25	4	2	4	38	1	66	14	5	1	.486	.425
Murray, Glenn, Indianapolis ...	.167	7	14	12	1	2	3	1	0	0	0	0	0	0	2	0	3	0	0	1	.250	.286
Myers, Rod, Omaha*	.254	38	162	142	21	36	52	10	0	2	10	4	1	0	15	0	37	6	4	0	.366	.323
Myers, Rodney, Iowa	.222	24	29	27	4	6	11	0	1	1	1	2	0	0	0	0	13	0	0	1	.407	.222
Nava, Lipso, Iowa	.266	109	350	319	37	85	131	17	1	9	36	0	2	7	22	0	53	2	3	16	.411	.326
Nevers, Tom, Louisville	.233	71	245	227	22	53	86	9	0	8	27	2	2	2	12	0	48	1	3	12	.379	.276
Nitkowski, C.J., New Orleans*	.042	28	26	24	1	1	1	0	0	0	0	2	0	0	0	0	15	0	1	2	.042	.042
Nix, James, Indianapolis	1.000	12	1	1	0	1	1	0	0	0	0	0	0	0	0	0	0	0	0	0	1.000	1.000
Norman, Les, Buffalo	.259	118	489	428	71	111	184	20	1	17	56	6	4	8	43	2	80	7	6	5	.430	.335
Norton, Greg, Nashville†	.275	114	479	414	82	114	221	27	1	26	76	1	3	4	57	2	101	3	5	9	.534	.366
Nunnally, Jon, Omaha*	.278	68	274	230	35	64	122	11	1	15	33	0	2	3	39	2	67	8	3	3	.530	.387
Oliver, Joe, Indianapolis	.333	2	9	9	1	3	6	0	0	1	1	0	0	0	0	0	1	0	0	0	.667	.333
O'Neill, Doug, Oklahoma City.	.194	11	34	31	2	6	9	3	0	0	1	0	0	0	3	0	10	1	1	1	.290	.265
Ordonez, Magglio, Nashville ..	.329	135	570	523	65	172	249	29	3	14	90	2	9	2	32	5	61	14	10	18	.476	.364
Orie, Kevin, Iowa..................	.375	9	38	32	7	12	19	4	0	1	8	0	0	0	5	0	5	0	0	0	.594	.459
Ortiz, Hector, Omaha.............	.190	21	76	63	7	12	15	3	0	0	3	0	0	0	13	0	15	0	0	1	.238	.329
Ortiz, Luis, Oklahoma City......	.305	22	90	82	9	25	33	5	0	1	11	0	3	0	5	0	7	1	1	2	.402	.333
Osborne, Donovan, Louisville*	.000	3	3	2	0	0	0	0	0	0	0	1	0	0	0	0	1	0	0	0	.000	.000
Owens, Eric, Indianapolis	.286	104	441	391	56	112	168	15	4	11	44	1	4	3	42	0	55	23	10	8	.430	.357
Pagnozzi, Tom, Louisville	.000	3	5	5	0	0	0	0	0	0	0	0	0	0	0	0	0	0	0	0	.000	.000
Painter, Lance, Louisville*	.000	18	1	1	0	0	0	0	0	0	0	0	0	0	0	0	0	0	0	0	.000	.000
Paquette, Craig, Omaha	.308	23	99	91	9	28	43	6	0	3	20	0	2	0	6	0	26	0	2	6	.473	.343
Parris, Steve, Indianapolis	.200	5	6	5	1	1	1	0	0	0	0	1	0	0	0	0	2	0	0	0	.200	.200
Patrick, Bronswell, N.Orleans.	.000	30	9	9	0	0	0	0	0	0	0	0	0	0	0	0	1	0	0	0	.000	.000
Pearson, Eddie, Nashville†.....	.223	41	156	148	17	33	49	4	0	4	16	1	1	0	6	1	23	1	1	3	.331	.252
Pegues, Steve, Iowa..............	.375	6	24	24	3	9	11	2	0	0	1	0	0	0	0	0	3	0	0	2	.458	.375
Pendleton, Terry, Ind.†..........	.167	4	17	12	2	2	2	0	0	0	2	0	1	0	4	1	1	0	0	1	.167	.353
Petersen, Chris, Iowa†	.240	119	436	391	49	94	123	16	2	3	33	4	3	6	32	4	89	1	6	15	.315	.306
Phillips, J.R., New Orleans*...	.290	104	454	411	59	119	210	28	0	21	70	0	4	0	39	3	112	0	1	11	.511	.348
Pisciotta, Marc, Iowa	.000	42	1	1	0	0	0	0	0	0	0	0	0	0	0	0	0	0	0	0	.000	.000
Plantier, Phil, Louisville*	.258	9	39	31	6	8	14	3	0	1	10	0	2	0	6	1	3	0	0	1	.452	.359
Polidor, Wil, Nashville†	.097	9	32	31	2	3	3	0	0	0	2	1	0	0	0	0	4	0	0	1	.097	.097
Pough, Pork Chop, Omaha	.252	124	489	433	63	109	197	20	1	22	59	2	0	1	53	0	113	0	1	15	.455	.335
Probst, Alan, New Orleans	.223	46	124	112	8	25	37	6	0	2	10	1	2	0	9	0	27	0	0	4	.330	.276
Raggio, Brady, Louisville........	.053	22	20	19	2	1	1	0	0	0	0	0	0	0	0	0	3	0	0	0	.053	.053
Ramirez, Alex, Buffalo	.286	119	453	416	59	119	187	19	8	11	44	6	3	4	24	0	95	10	5	9	.450	.329
Ramos, Ken, New Orleans* ...	.289	92	304	253	32	73	84	9	1	0	22	4	1	1	45	5	15	2	7	6	.332	.397
Ratliff, Jon, Iowa...................	.250	9	5	4	0	1	1	0	0	0	0	1	0	0	0	0	0	0	0	0	.250	.250
Reese, Pokey, Indianapolis	.236	17	81	72	12	17	31	2	0	4	11	0	0	0	9	0	12	4	0	2	.431	.321
Reynolds, Shane, N.Orleans...	.000	1	2	2	0	0	0	0	0	0	0	0	0	0	0	0	2	0	0	0	.000	.000
Rivera, Luis, New Orleans......	.238	124	432	382	46	91	131	23	4	3	45	5	8	3	34	2	51	5	4	12	.343	.300
Robinson, Kerry, Louisville* ..	.111	2	9	9	0	1	1	0	0	0	0	0	0	0	0	0	1	0	0	0	.111	.111
Robles, Oscar, New Orleans*.	.333	2	4	3	0	1	1	0	0	0	0	0	0	0	1	0	0	0	0	0	.333	.500

Player, Team	Avg.	G	TPA	AB	R	H	TB	2B	3B	HR	RBI	SH	SF	HP	BB	IBB	SO	SB	CS	GDP	Slg.	OBP
Rose, Pete, Indianapolis*	.225	12	42	40	2	9	11	2	0	0	1	0	0	0	2	0	11	0	0	1	.275	.262
Rupp, Brian, Louisville	.275	59	210	189	17	52	63	7	2	0	16	1	1	0	19	1	36	1	1	5	.333	.340
Russell, Lagrande, Iowa	.000	7	1	1	0	0	0	0	0	0	0	0	0	0	0	0	1	0	0	0	.000	.000
Sagmoen, Marc, O.C.*	.263	111	448	418	47	110	169	32	6	5	44	1	2	1	26	4	95	4	3	10	.404	.306
Salkeld, Roger, Indianapolis...	.000	36	10	10	0	0	0	0	0	0	0	0	0	0	0	0	3	0	0	0	.000	.000
Sanders, Reggie, Indianapolis	.211	5	20	19	1	4	4	0	0	0	1	0	0	0	1	0	6	0	0	0	.211	.250
Sauveur, Rich, Iowa*	1.000	39	1	1	0	1	1	0	0	0	0	0	0	0	0	0	0	0	0	0	1.000	1.000
Scarsone, Steve, Louisville	.154	10	35	26	5	4	7	0	0	1	3	0	0	2	7	0	10	0	0	0	.269	.371
Schall, Gene, Nashville	.196	33	125	112	11	22	39	0	1	5	17	1	0	1	11	0	32	1	1	1	.348	.274
Scutaro, Marcos, Buffalo	.263	21	65	57	8	15	21	3	0	1	6	1	1	0	6	0	8	0	1	4	.368	.328
Seitzer, Brad, Omaha	.190	21	69	63	4	12	15	3	0	0	4	0	1	0	5	0	10	0	0	4	.238	.246
Sexson, Richie, Buffalo	.260	115	472	434	57	113	230	20	2	31	88	3	4	4	27	1	87	5	1	11	.530	.307
Silvestri, Dave, O.C.	.240	124	530	467	54	112	194	25	3	17	68	2	6	0	55	1	104	4	6	9	.415	.316
Simms, Mike, Oklahoma City	.385	10	47	39	7	15	28	4	0	3	8	0	1	1	6	1	8	0	0	2	.718	.468
Sisco, Steve, Omaha	.261	54	200	188	23	49	66	8	0	3	12	3	1	0	8	0	34	2	1	4	.351	.289
Smith, Bubba, Oklahoma City	.255	140	575	514	60	131	244	30	1	27	94	0	4	4	53	2	139	2	2	16	.475	.327
Snopek, Chris, Nashville	.233	20	80	73	8	17	30	4	0	3	8	0	0	0	7	0	13	0	0	4	.411	.300
Soliz, Steve, Buffalo	.192	62	169	151	12	29	37	5	0	1	13	5	3	0	10	0	40	0	1	2	.245	.238
Steenstra, Kennie, Iowa	.056	25	26	18	2	1	1	0	0	0	0	0	0	0	2	0	10	0	0	0	.056	.150
Stefanski, Mike, Louisville	.305	57	213	197	26	60	88	10	0	6	22	2	1	1	12	0	20	0	1	6	.447	.346
Stewart, Andy, Omaha	.274	86	321	288	38	79	109	10	1	6	24	5	1	9	18	0	43	1	1	11	.378	.335
Stynes, Chris, Oma.-Ind.	.285	103	449	418	67	119	174	26	1	9	61	5	4	1	21	1	30	7	2	10	.416	.318
Sullivan, Scott, Indianapolis	.000	19	1	1	0	0	0	0	0	0	0	0	0	0	0	0	1	0	0	0	.000	.000
Sutton, Larry, Omaha*	.300	106	443	380	61	114	200	27	1	19	72	0	2	0	61	4	57	0	0	6	.526	.395
Swartzbaugh, Dave, Iowa	.087	24	26	23	0	2	2	0	0	0	0	0	2	1	0	0	8	0	0	0	.087	.083
Sweeney, Mike, Omaha	.236	40	167	144	22	34	74	8	1	10	29	0	3	2	18	1	20	0	2	3	.514	.323
Tabaka, Jeff, Indianapolis...	.000	58	1	1	0	0	0	0	0	0	0	0	0	0	0	0	0	0	0	0	.000	.000
Tackett, Jeff, Oklahoma City...	.273	64	236	209	23	57	87	15	0	5	19	0	0	1	26	0	49	4	1	6	.416	.356
Telemaco, Amaury, Iowa	.300	18	13	10	1	3	3	0	0	0	1	2	0	0	1	0	2	0	0	0	.300	.364
Tettleton, Mickey, O.C.†	.444	4	15	9	4	4	5	1	0	0	0	0	0	0	6	0	1	0	0	0	.556	.667
Thomas, Greg, Buffalo*	.077	11	16	13	1	1	2	1	0	0	2	0	0	0	3	0	6	0	0	0	.154	.250
Thomas, Larry, Nashville	.000	45	1	1	0	0	0	0	0	0	0	0	1	0	0	0	0	0	0	0	.000	.000
Thompson, Ryan, Buffalo	.242	24	71	66	10	16	19	0	0	1	6	0	0	0	5	1	16	2	0	1	.288	.296
Timmons, Ozzie, Indianapolis	.253	125	474	407	46	103	161	14	1	14	55	0	5	2	60	5	100	1	4	11	.396	.348
Tomko, Brett, Indianapolis	.000	10	5	4	1	0	0	0	0	0	0	0	1	0	0	0	1	0	0	1	.000	.000
Valdes, Pedro, Iowa*	.284	125	521	464	65	132	206	30	1	14	60	1	6	2	48	5	67	9	2	13	.444	.350
Valdez, Mario, Nashville*	.280	81	339	282	44	79	146	20	1	15	61	1	4	9	43	3	77	1	1	8	.518	.388
VanRyn, Ben, Iowa*	.000	51	3	3	0	0	0	0	0	0	0	0	0	0	0	0	3	0	0	0	.000	.000
Ventura, Robin, Nashville*	.400	5	17	15	3	6	13	1	0	2	5	0	0	2	2	0	1	0	1	0	.867	.471
Vinas, Julio, Nashville	.232	91	350	314	39	73	122	12	2	11	41	3	5	2	25	2	72	4	4	6	.389	.289
Vitiello, Joe, Omaha	.214	13	47	42	5	9	19	1	0	3	9	0	0	0	5	0	16	0	0	0	.452	.298
Walker, Mike, Indianapolis	.222	55	10	9	1	2	2	0	0	0	1	1	0	0	0	0	4	0	0	0	.222	.222
Wall, Donne, New Orleans	.167	17	18	12	3	2	2	0	0	0	0	0	1	0	5	0	2	0	0	1	.167	.412
Ward, Daryle, New Orleans*	.375	14	55	48	4	18	25	1	0	2	8	0	0	0	7	1	7	0	0	0	.521	.455
Warner, Ron, Louisville	.232	101	326	276	43	64	101	16	0	7	30	6	1	1	42	0	45	4	1	8	.366	.334
Watkins, Pat, Indianapolis	.280	84	354	325	46	91	146	14	2	9	35	3	1	1	24	2	55	13	9	10	.449	.330
White, Gabe, Indianapolis*	.111	20	20	18	0	2	3	1	0	0	0	0	2	0	0	0	12	0	0	0	.167	.111
Wiegandt, Scott, Louisville*	.333	40	6	6	1	2	3	1	0	0	0	0	0	0	0	0	1	0	0	0	.500	.333
Williams, Harold, Iowa*	.179	9	30	28	2	5	10	2	0	1	2	0	0	2	0	0	8	0	0	0	.357	.233
Wilson, Brandon, Ind.-Ia.	.236	87	270	242	28	57	73	5	4	1	17	7	0	1	20	2	48	8	6	4	.302	.297
Wilson, Craig, Nashville	.272	137	514	453	71	123	165	20	2	6	42	12	0	1	48	1	31	4	4	19	.364	.343
Wilson, Enrique, Buffalo†	.306	118	506	451	78	138	197	20	3	11	39	4	4	5	42	2	41	9	8	7	.437	.369
Wimmer, Chris, Louisville	.167	5	12	12	0	2	2	0	0	0	0	1	0	0	0	0	1	0	0	0	.167	.167
Wood, Kerry, Iowa	.000	10	7	5	0	0	0	0	0	0	0	0	0	0	0	0	0	0	0	0	.000	.000
Wrona, Rick, Nashville	.246	70	221	211	22	52	85	15	0	6	22	3	1	3	3	0	41	1	1	7	.403	.266
Young, Dmitri, Louisville†	.274	24	97	84	10	23	42	7	0	4	14	0	0	1	13	0	15	1	1	1	.500	.371

GRAND SLAMS: Aven, A. Boone, Costo, Lowery, 2 each; Benitez, Bradshaw, Brady, B. Brown, Fasano, Franklin, Frias, Garcia, Giannelli, Halter, Kieschnick, Long, Maa Mora, Nava, Phillips, Reese, Schall, Sexson, Silvestri, Stynes, Soliz, P. Watkins, 1 each.

AWARDED FIRST BASE ON CATCHER'S INTERFERENCE: Abbott 2 (Einar Diaz, Soliz); Little 2 (Soliz, Meluskey); Ordonez 2 (Tackett, Stefanski); D. Bell (Cline); M. Bel (H. Ortiz); McCall (Stefanski); Orie (H. Ortiz); Vinas (Soliz).

PLAYERS WITH TWO OR MORE TEAMS

Player, Team	Avg.	G	TPA	AB	R	H	TB	2B	3B	HR	RBI	SH	SF	HP	BB	IBB	SO	SB	CS	GDP	Slg.	OBP
Cabrera, Jose, Buffalo	.000	5	0	0	0	0	0	0	0	0	0	0	0	0	0	0	0	0	0	0	.000	.000
Cabrera, Jose, New Orleans...	.200	31	6	5	1	1	1	0	0	0	0	1	0	0	0	0	3	0	0	0	.200	.200
Jackson, Damian, Buffalo	.293	73	311	266	51	78	102	12	0	4	13	3	2	3	37	2	45	20	8	2	.383	.383
Jackson, Damian, Ind.	.268	19	83	71	12	19	27	6	1	0	7	0	1	1	10	0	17	4	1	1	.380	.361
Maas, Kevin, Indianapolis*	.224	31	95	67	14	15	25	4	0	2	7	0	1	2	25	2	15	0	0	0	.373	.442
Maas, Kevin, New Orleans*	.218	55	218	193	24	42	78	19	1	5	27	0	1	1	23	2	41	0	0	3	.404	.303
McCall, Rod, Buffalo*	.234	36	121	107	12	25	48	5	0	6	20	0	2	2	9	1	37	0	0	3	.449	.300
McCall, Rod, Iowa*	.284	49	173	148	26	42	89	5	0	14	35	0	1	2	22	2	53	0	0	1	.601	.382
Stynes, Chris, Omaha	.265	82	357	332	53	88	132	18	1	8	44	4	2	0	19	1	25	3	1	7	.398	.303
Stynes, Chris, Indianapolis	.360	21	92	86	14	31	42	8	0	1	17	1	2	1	2	0	5	4	1	3	.488	.374
Wilson, Brandon, Ind.	.228	68	205	180	24	41	55	3	4	1	14	6	0	1	18	2	38	5	4	3	.306	.302
Wilson, Brandon, Iowa	.258	19	65	62	4	16	18	2	0	0	3	1	0	0	2	0	10	3	2	1	.290	.281

1997 PITCHING
TEAM

Team	W	L	Pct.	ERA	G	CG	ShO	Sv.	IP	H	TBF	R	ER	HR	SH	SF	HB	BB	IBB	SO	WP	Bk.
New Orleans	74	70	.514	3.45	144	6	12	27	1287.0	1231	5349	560	494	103	59	49	29	387	30	1073	48	6
Indianapolis	85	59	.590	3.57	144	8	12	48	1249.0	1171	5298	567	495	126	43	32	44	438	20	959	64	9
Buffalo	87	57	.604	3.66	144	18	9	28	1255.2	1197	5327	593	510	156	30	38	27	469	8	900	63	7
Iowa	74	69	.517	4.11	143	13	11	33	1242.0	1201	5291	645	567	155	42	36	31	472	24	969	75	6
Louisville	58	85	.406	4.24	143	9	3	30	1243.0	1260	5371	651	586	139	40	37	56	465	28	944	54	8
Nashville	74	69	.517	4.64	143	11	4	41	1233.1	1287	5456	718	636	156	31	45	37	554	19	881	90	14
Oklahoma City	61	82	.427	4.67	143	10	8	34	1265.2	1398	5598	746	657	129	34	46	58	483	32	794	44	13
Omaha	61	83	.424	5.36	144	8	7	35	1215.2	1316	5486	807	724	194	22	45	52	598	15	906	62	9

INDIVIDUAL
TOP QUALIFIERS FOR EARNED-RUN AVERAGE TITLE
Minimum 115 innings. *Lefthanded pitcher.

Pitcher, Team	W	L	Pct.	ERA	G	GS	CG	ShO	GF	Sv.	IP	H	TBF	R	ER	HR	SH	SF	HB	BB	IBB	SO	WP	Bk.
Halama, John, New Orleans*	13	3	.813	2.58	26	24	1	0	2	0	171.0	150	673	57	49	9	4	7	1	32	1	126	2	2
Swartzbaugh, Dave, Iowa	8	7	.533	2.82	24	20	1	1	1	1	134.0	129	561	55	42	12	4	5	1	48	1	97	3	1
White, Gabe, Indianapolis*	7	4	.636	2.82	20	19	0	0	0	0	118.0	119	493	46	37	10	2	4	6	18	0	62	2	1
Keyser, Brian, Nashville	7	5	.583	2.87	44	9	3	0	7	1	119.0	114	500	44	38	10	6	1		45	1	68	7	0
DeLaMaza, Roland, Buffalo	9	4	.692	2.90	34	14	2	0	11	2	115.0	104	481	42	37	12	4	1	0	43	1	73	4	2
Miller, Trever, New Orleans*	6	7	.462	3.30	29	27	2	0	0	0	163.2	177	694	71	60	15	8	4	3	54	1	99	6	0
Aybar, Manny, Louisville	5	8	.385	3.48	22	22	3	2	0	0	137.0	131	579	60	53	10	2	2	4	45	2	114	7	3
Carrara, Giovanni, Ind.	12	5	.706	3.51	19	18	2	0	0	0	120.2	111	509	50	47	12	5	0	3	51	3	105	1	1
Steenstra, Kennie, Iowa	5	10	.333	3.92	25	25	4	0	0	0	160.2	161	663	85	70	15	4	9	0	41	4	111	7	0
Klingenbeck, Scott, Ind.	12	8	.600	3.96	27	27	2	0	0	0	170.2	180	727	85	75	23	5	6	5	41	0	119	2	2
Nitkowski, C.J., N.Orleans*	8	10	.444	3.98	28	28	1	0	0	0	174.1	183	738	82	77	10	6	8	6	56	2	141	6	3
Myers, Rodney, Iowa	7	8	.467	4.09	24	23	1	0	0	0	140.2	140	590	76	64	18	2	7	6	38	1	79	3	0
Raggio, Brady, Louisville	8	11	.421	4.17	22	22	2	0	0	0	138.0	145	576	68	64	18	5	3	6	32	0	91	3	1
Batista, Miguel, Iowa	9	4	.692	4.20	31	14	2	2	4	0	122.0	117	509	60	57	19	3	3	0	38	1	95	8	1
Bolton, Rodney, Indianapolis	9	8	.529	4.30	28	27	1	1	0	0	169.2	185	730	96	81	21	6	4	3	47	0	108	16	2

DEPARTMENTAL LEADERS: W—Halama, 13; L—D. Smith, 14; Pct.—Halama, .813; G—Henriquez, 60; GS—Harrison, 29; CG—Clark, Harrison, Steenstra, 4 each; ShO—Aybar, Batista, Telemaco, 2 each; GF—Service, 42; Sv.—Service, 24; IP—Harrison, 178.1; H—Harrison, 208; TBF—Harrison, 783; R—Harrison, 114; ER—Harrison, 100; HR—Klingenbeck, 23; SH—Barrios, 10; SF—Harrison, Steenstra, 9 each; HB—Harrison, Lowe, 10 each; BB—Bertotti, 105; IBB—Arrandale, Barrios, Davis, 9 each; SO—Nitkowski, 141; WP—Bolton, 16; BK—Pratt, 7.

ALL PITCHERS
*Lefthanded pitcher.

Pitcher, Team	W	L	Pct.	ERA	G	GS	CG	ShO	GF	Sv.	IP	H	TBF	R	ER	HR	SH	SF	HB	BB	IBB	SO	WP	Bk.
Alberro, Jose, Oklahoma City	5	6	.455	4.22	16	16	1	1	0	0	91.2	90	387	48	43	6	1	1	5	29	1	59	3	1
Anderson, Brian, Buffalo*	7	1	.875	3.05	15	15	1	1	0	0	85.2	78	348	33	29	13	2	1	1	15	0	60	1	1
Arrandale, Matt, Louisville	2	6	.250	3.67	56	1	0	0	15	1	83.1	84	360	38	34	9	5	2	3	38	9	32	5	0
Aybar, Manny, Louisville	5	8	.385	3.48	22	22	3	2	0	0	137.0	131	579	60	53	10	2	2	4	45	2	114	7	3
Badorek, Mike, Louisville	0	0	.000	18.00	1	0	0	0	0	0	2.0	4	12	4	4	2	0	0		2	0	3	0	0
Bailes, Scott, Oklahoma City*	2	3	.400	3.98	44	0	0	0	20	4	43.0	46	189	22	19	5	4	1	1	13	2	37	2	2
Bailey, Cory, Oklahoma City	3	4	.429	3.40	42	0	0	0	33	15	50.1	49	219	20	19	1	3	1	0	23	7	38	4	0
Barber, Brian, Louisville	4	8	.333	6.90	18	18	0	0	0	0	92.2	111	431	80	71	20	2	4	3	44	1	74	5	0
Barfield, John, Buffalo*	0	1	.000	27.00	1	0	0	0	0	0	1.0	3	6	3	3	1	0	0	0	0	0	1	0	0
Barrios, Manuel, New Orleans	4	8	.333	3.27	57	0	0	0	27	0	82.2	70	350	32	30	5	10	4	1	34	9	77	2	0
Batchelor, Rich, Louisville	0	2	.000	4.50	12	0	0	0	10	5	14.0	18	66	9	7	1	0	2	1	6	2	10	2	0
Batista, Miguel, Iowa	9	4	.692	4.20	31	14	2	2	4	0	122.0	117	509	60	57	19	3	3	0	38	1	95	8	1
Bautista, Jose, Louisville	2	0	1.000	0.00	11	0	0	0	2	0	17.1	3	56	0	0	0	3	0	2	1	11	0	0	
Beltran, Rigo, Louisville*	5	2	.714	2.32	9	8	1	0	1	0	54.1	45	227	17	14	7	0	1	1	21	0	46	0	0
Benes, Andy, Louisville	0	0	.000	1.80	1	1	0	0	0	0	5.0	3	18	1	1	0	0	0	0	0	5	0	0	
Bere, Jason, Nashville	1	1	.500	5.59	4	4	0	0	0	0	19.1	23	85	13	12	2	0	0	0	7	0	13	1	0
Bertotti, Mike, Nashville*	5	9	.357	5.35	21	20	1	0	0	0	107.2	91	505	70	64	17	1	7	2	105	0	87	15	0
Bevil, Brian, Omaha	2	1	.667	4.38	26	3	0	0	1	0	39.0	34	171	22	19	8	1	2	2	22	0	47	0	0
Blomdahl, Ben, Buffalo	7	8	.467	4.76	29	13	1	0	4	0	104.0	110	447	64	55	20	1	6	2	31	0	60	1	1
Blosser, Greg, O.C.*	0	0	.000	18.00	1	0	0	0	0	0	1.0	4	7	2	2	0	0	0	0	0	1	0	0	
Bolton, Rodney, Indianapolis	9	8	.529	4.30	28	27	1	1	0	0	169.2	185	730	96	81	21	6	4	3	47	0	108	16	2
Brewington, Jamie, Omaha	2	2	.500	8.31	7	4	0	0	0	0	21.2	21	98	21	20	10	0	1	1	13	0	20	1	1
Brower, Jim, Oklahoma City	2	1	.667	7.23	4	3	0	0	0	0	18.2	30	92	17	15	3	0	2	1	8	0	7	3	0
Buckles, Bucky, O.C.	0	0	.000	0.77	5	0	0	0	1	0	11.2	12	50	3	1	0	2	1	0	4	0	5	0	0
Burgos, John, O.C.*	2	0	1.000	2.57	7	3	0	0	0	0	28.0	27	116	8	8	3	0	1	2	8	0	15	0	0
Burkett, John, Oklahoma City	1	0	1.000	3.60	1	1	0	0	0	0	5.0	6	23	2	2	1	0	0	0	2	0	3	0	0
Busby, Mike, Louisville	4	8	.333	4.61	15	14	1	1	0	0	93.2	95	395	49	48	12	0	1	7	30	1	65	8	0
Busch, Mike, Buffalo	0	0	.000	0.00	1	0	0	0	1	0	1.0	0	3	0	0	0	0	0	0	0	0	0	0	0
Cabrera, Jose, Buf.-N.O.	5	2	.714	2.21	36	0	0	0	7	0	61.0	39	238	15	15	4	1	0	3	20	4	59	1	0
Cadaret, Greg, Buffalo*	2	2	.500	4.86	29	1	0	0	13	4	50.0	46	231	31	27	3	1	2	1	35	2	49	8	0
Carpenter, Brian, Louisville	0	0	.000	4.32	4	0	0	0	0	0	8.1	11	42	4	4	1	1	2	1	5	0	9	0	0
Carrara, Giovanni, Ind.	12	5	.706	3.51	19	18	2	0	0	0	120.2	111	509	50	47	12	5	0	3	51	3	105	1	1
Carrasco, Hector, Ind.	0	0	.000	6.23	3	0	0	0	0	0	4.1	5	20	3	3	1	0	0	0	4	0	4	0	0
Castillo, Carlos, Nashville	0	0	.000	1.50	4	0	0	0	1	0	6.0	4	24	1	1	0	0	0	0	4	0	4	0	0
Christopherson, Eric, N.O.	0	0	.000	0.00	1	0	0	0	0	0	1.0	2	6	0	0	0	0	0	1	0	1	0	0	
Clark, Terry, Buffalo	7	3	.700	2.85	25	10	4	1	7	3	94.2	86	390	34	30	8	3	2	2	30	0	63	4	0
Clemons, Chris, Nashville	5	5	.500	4.55	22	21	1	0	0	0	124.2	115	543	73	63	15	2	3	4	65	0	70	6	1
Colon, Bartolo, Buffalo	7	1	.875	2.22	10	10	1	1	0	0	56.2	45	230	15	14	4	2	1	0	23	0	54	1	1

CLASS AAA American Association

Pitcher, Team	W	L	Pct.	ERA	G	GS	CG	ShO	GF	Sv.	IP	H	TBF	R	ER	HR	SH	SF	HB	BB	IBB	SO	WP	Bk.
Converse, Jim, Omaha	2	1	.667	6.75	6	3	0	0	1	0	17.1	18	75	13	13	3	0	2	1	9	0	13	0	0
Croushore, Rick, Louisville	1	2	.333	2.47	14	6	0	0	3	1	43.2	37	173	14	12	3	0	0	0	13	0	41	4	0
Crowell, Jim, Indianapolis*	1	1	.500	2.75	3	3	1	1	0	0	19.2	19	85	7	6	1	0	2	0	8	0	6	1	0
Cruz, Nelson, Nashville	11	7	.611	5.11	21	20	1	0	0	0	123.1	139	533	75	70	20	1	4	9	31	0	93	1	2
Darwin, Jeff, Nashville	4	3	.571	4.53	47	0	0	0	36	22	53.2	60	244	32	27	8	3	1	2	24	4	44	6	0
Davis, Clint, Oklahoma City	6	1	.857	3.20	40	1	0	0	11	0	70.1	55	309	28	25	4	0	3	5	46	9	53	1	0
Dedrick, Jim, Oklahoma City	0	0	.000	5.91	8	0	0	0	4	3	10.2	16	57	7	7	0	0	0	0	10	0	2	1	0
DeLaMaza, Roland, Buffalo	9	4	.692	2.90	34	14	2	0	11	2	115.0	104	481	42	37	12	4	1	0	43	1	73	4	2
DeLaRosa, Maximo, Buffalo	2	2	.500	6.49	15	4	0	0	3	0	43.0	43	208	34	31	10	2	3	9	33	0	31	1	0
Detmers, Kris, Louisville*	3	3	.500	7.20	10	5	0	0	0	0	35.0	43	164	28	28	3	0	2	2	17	0	22	1	0
Diaz, Alex, Oklahoma City	0	0	.000	0.00	1	0	0	0	1	0	1.0	0	7	1	0	0	0	0	0	3	0	1	1	0
Dougherty, Anthony, Buffalo	2	0	1.000	3.77	18	0	0	0	7	2	28.2	31	128	17	12	2	1	0	0	18	0	21	5	0
Driskill, Travis, Buffalo	8	7	.533	4.65	29	24	1	0	1	0	147.0	159	645	86	76	22	2	6	3	60	0	102	15	1
Eischen, Joey, Indianapolis*	1	0	1.000	1.27	26	5	0	0	7	2	42.2	41	173	7	6	1	2	0	1	13	1	26	2	0
Elarton, Scott, New Orleans	4	4	.500	5.33	9	9	0	0	0	0	54.0	51	228	36	32	5	3	1	1	17	1	50	4	0
Estrada, Osmani, O.C.	0	0	.000	0.00	2	0	0	0	2	0	2.0	0	6	0	0	0	0	0	0	0	0	2	0	0
Eversgerd, Bryan, O.C.*	1	3	.250	4.24	26	7	0	0	5	0	76.1	91	339	48	36	12	4	2	2	24	2	43	5	1
Fernandez, Sid, New Orleans*	0	1	.000	4.32	2	2	0	0	0	0	8.1	7	34	4	4	0	0	0	0	3	0	7	2	0
Fletcher, Paul, Iowa	10	6	.625	3.56	54	0	0	0	14	0	78.1	63	330	32	31	11	4	1	1	39	1	67	15	0
Flury, Pat, Omaha	1	0	1.000	6.08	18	0	0	0	7	0	26.2	29	124	18	18	5	2	0	2	16	2	24	1	0
Fordham, Tom, Nashville*	6	7	.462	4.74	21	20	2	0	0	0	114.0	113	493	64	60	14	1	5	1	53	1	90	6	1
Foulke, Keith, Nashville	0	0	.000	5.79	1	1	0	0	0	0	4.2	8	20	3	3	1	0	0	0	0	0	4	1	0
Gardiner, Mike, New Orleans	2	1	.667	8.13	11	4	0	0	3	0	31.0	43	147	32	28	3	1	2	1	14	0	24	0	0
Glauber, Keith, Louisville	1	3	.250	5.17	15	0	0	0	12	5	15.2	18	71	14	9	2	1	0	1	4	0	14	0	0
Gonzalez, Jeremi, Iowa	2	2	.500	3.48	10	10	1	1	0	0	62.0	47	249	27	24	8	1	1	1	21	0	58	2	0
Graves, Danny, Buf.-Ind.	3	3	.500	3.95	30	3	0	0	14	7	54.2	52	225	25	24	4	1	3	4	16	0	26	1	0
Greene, Tommy, New Orleans	5	3	.625	3.38	13	13	0	0	0	0	74.2	59	305	30	28	12	2	3	2	25	0	75	1	0
Grimsley, Jason, Omaha	1	5	.167	6.68	7	6	0	0	0	0	31.0	36	156	26	23	3	0	1	3	29	0	22	3	0
Gross, Kevin, Oklahoma City	2	3	.400	4.83	6	6	0	0	0	0	31.2	35	134	18	17	4	0	1	1	6	0	26	0	2
Gutierrez, Jim, New Orleans	0	1	.000	3.27	7	0	0	0	5	0	11.0	11	46	4	4	1	0	1	0	2	0	8	2	0
Halama, John, New Orleans*	13	3	.813	2.58	26	24	1	0	2	0	171.0	150	673	57	49	9	4	7	1	32	1	126	2	2
Haney, Chris, Omaha*	1	0	1.000	3.79	4	3	0	0	0	0	19.0	16	82	12	8	3	0	0	2	6	0	7	1	0
Harrison, Brian, Omaha	10	12	.455	5.05	30	29	4	0	0	0	178.1	208	783	114	100	20	0	9	10	55	0	83	6	0
Hart, Jason, Iowa	0	1	.000	18.00	1	0	0	0	0	0	1.0	1	6	2	2	0	0	0	0	2	0	3	0	0
Hartvigson, Chad, O.C.*	2	2	.500	6.66	14	1	0	0	6	2	25.2	35	121	21	19	5	1	1	0	9	0	22	0	0
Hasselhoff, Derek, Nashville	1	1	.500	9.82	6	0	0	0	1	0	7.1	9	37	8	8	2	0	0	0	7	0	2	0	0
Heathcott, Mike, Nashville	2	3	.400	7.33	17	0	0	0	7	0	27.0	39	129	23	22	5	1	0	0	12	0	23	6	0
Heiserman, Rick, Louisville	0	0	.000	4.50	1	0	0	0	1	0	2.0	2	10	1	1	1	0	0	0	1	0	0	0	0
Henriquez, Oscar, N.Orleans	4	5	.444	2.80	60	0	0	0	37	12	74.0	65	313	28	23	4	6	3	5	27	3	80	7	1
Heredia, Gil, Iowa	4	2	.667	3.86	31	1	0	0	14	1	46.2	54	197	22	20	6	2	1	0	9	0	30	3	0
Heredia, Wilson, O.C.	7	12	.368	4.97	27	26	2	0	0	0	168.1	167	733	106	93	22	3	6	7	70	1	113	10	2
Hudek, John, New Orleans	0	0	.000	0.44	19	0	0	0	16	7	20.2	3	67	1	1	1	0	1	0	3	0	26	0	0
Huisman, Rick, Omaha	1	5	.167	3.62	37	1	0	0	8	2	59.2	59	268	29	24	7	1	3	3	35	1	57	7	0
Ilsley, Blaise, Buffalo*	0	0	.000	2.19	9	0	0	0	4	0	12.1	12	49	3	3	1	0	0	0	1	0	7	0	0
Jackson, Danny, Louisville*	1	0	1.000	1.80	4	4	0	0	0	0	25.0	20	100	6	5	3	2	0	0	8	0	14	0	0
Jacome, Jason, Buffalo*	3	1	.750	3.16	7	7	1	0	0	0	37.0	41	151	14	13	7	1	3	1	10	0	23	0	1
Johns, Doug, Omaha*	1	5	.167	7.56	9	6	1	0	1	0	41.2	58	189	36	35	7	1	2	1	11	0	24	1	2
Johnson, Barry, Nashville	4	1	.800	3.55	14	0	0	0	5	2	25.1	24	108	10	10	1	1	1	0	11	1	10	3	0
Johnson, Jonathan, O.C.	1	8	.111	7.29	13	12	1	0	1	1	58.0	83	276	54	47	6	1	3	1	29	3	33	2	1
Jones, Stacy, Nashville	0	0	.000	54.00	1	0	0	0	0	0	0.1	4	6	3	2	0	0	0	0	0	0	0	0	0
Karchner, Matt, Nashville	2	1	.667	1.93	13	0	0	0	8	3	18.2	12	78	5	4	1	2	1	1	6	0	11	1	0
Kell, Rob, Oklahoma City*	1	0	1.000	8.86	11	2	0	0	5	0	21.1	30	115	24	21	3	0	0	4	16	1	20	3	1
Keyser, Brian, Nashville	7	5	.583	2.87	44	9	3	0	7	1	119.0	114	500	44	38	10	4	6	1	45	1	68	7	0
King, Curt, Louisville	2	1	.667	2.05	16	0	0	0	9	3	22.0	19	89	5	5	1	5	0	0	6	1	9	0	0
Kirkreit, Daron, Buffalo	1	0	1.000	0.00	1	1	1	1	0	0	7.0	3	23	0	0	0	0	0	0	1	0	2	0	0
Kline, Steven, Buffalo*	3	3	.500	4.03	20	4	0	0	5	1	51.1	53	219	26	23	4	3	0	3	13	1	41	5	0
Klingenbeck, Scott, Ind.	12	8	.600	3.96	27	27	2	0	0	0	170.2	180	727	85	75	23	5	6	5	41	0	119	2	2
Levine, Alan, Nashville	1	1	.500	7.13	26	0	0	0	9	2	35.1	58	171	32	28	3	1	2	1	11	1	29	5	0
Lewis, Richie, Indianapolis	0	1	.000	1.52	27	0	0	0	17	9	29.2	22	120	7	5	0	1	2	2	7	2	33	3	0
Lopez, Albie, Buffalo	1	0	1.000	0.00	7	0	0	0	6	1	11.1	6	43	0	0	0	0	0	1	2	0	13	2	0
Lowe, Sean, Louisville	6	10	.375	4.37	26	23	1	0	2	1	131.2	142	581	74	64	13	3	3	10	53	4	117	5	2
Ludwick, Eric, Louisville	6	8	.429	2.93	24	11	1	0	12	4	80.0	67	325	31	26	7	1	1	4	26	0	85	4	0
Lyons, Curt, Iowa	0	2	.000	6.37	8	8	0	0	0	0	29.2	35	145	23	21	8	0	0	4	21	0	26	2	0
Magnante, Mike, N.Orleans*	2	3	.400	4.50	17	0	0	0	6	1	24.0	31	107	14	12	0	2	1	0	5	0	23	2	0
Manning, David, O.C.	1	3	.250	4.40	5	5	1	0	0	0	28.2	33	130	17	14	6	0	0	2	9	0	15	1	0
Manzanillo, Josias, N.Orleans	0	0	.000	4.40	11	0	0	0	5	0	14.1	17	63	7	7	3	0	0	1	6	0	11	0	0
Martinez, Pedro A., Ind.*	4	3	.571	3.47	28	11	1	1	2	0	80.1	70	341	37	31	9	3	1	0	35	0	36	1	0
Matranga, Jeff, Louisville	3	3	.500	5.57	37	0	0	0	8	0	53.1	75	252	34	33	5	2	3	5	13	1	30	1	0
Matthews, Mike, Buffalo*	0	2	.000	7.71	5	5	0	0	0	0	21.0	32	106	19	18	7	0	2	0	10	0	17	1	0
Maxcy, Brian, Louisville	2	2	.500	3.76	30	0	0	0	20	9	38.1	36	176	18	16	4	3	2	4	24	3	22	2	0
McDill, Allen, Omaha*	5	2	.714	5.88	23	6	0	0	5	2	64.1	80	295	42	42	10	2	1	5	26	2	51	2	0
McGraw, Tom, Louisville*	1	4	.200	5.33	45	0	0	0	18	0	49.0	55	226	34	29	3	4	2	0	26	2	39	3	0
Miller, Trever, New Orleans*	6	7	.462	3.30	29	27	2	0	0	0	163.2	177	694	71	60	15	8	4	3	54	1	99	6	0
Mimbs, Mark, New Orleans*	1	2	.333	4.36	22	3	0	0	5	1	33.0	36	144	19	16	2	3	2	3	9	1	26	0	0
Minor, Blas, New Orleans	3	3	.500	2.27	23	0	0	0	15	6	31.2	20	122	8	8	1	3	2	0	9	3	27	3	0
Miranda, Angel, Buf.-O.C.*	0	3	.000	11.30	11	0	0	0	3	0	14.1	24	71	19	18	3	0	1	1	6	0	11	2	0
Mlicki, Doug, New Orleans	4	3	.571	3.60	14	3	0	0	4	0	30.0	27	124	12	12	4	0	0	1	10	0	18	1	0
Montgomery, Jeff, Omaha	0	0	.000	0.00	2	0	0	0	1	0	2.0	1	8	0	0	0	0	0	0	1	0	2	0	0
Montgomery, Steve, Buffalo	1	2	.333	5.63	7	0	0	0	6	1	8.0	12	37	6	5	2	1	0	0	3	0	5	0	0
Moody, Eric, Oklahoma City	5	6	.455	3.46	35	10	1	1	10	1	112.0	114	469	49	43	13	5	1	4	21	1	72	1	0
Moore, Marcus, Buffalo	5	3	.625	2.54	10	10	3	1	0	0	71.0	54	291	26	20	6	1	0	0	31	1	72	0	0
Mora, Melvin, New Orleans	0	0	.000	9.00	1	0	0	0	1	0	1.0	2	6	1	1	0	0	1	0	1	0	0	0	0
Morman, Alvin, N.O.-Buf.*	0	1	.000	3.38	11	0	0	0	2	0	13.1	13	54	5	5	1	1	1	0	2	1	17	1	0
Mounce, Tony, New Orleans*	0	0	.000	1.93	1	1	0	0	0	0	4.2	2	21	1	1	1	0	0	0	6	0	6	0	0

Pitcher, Team	W	L	Pct.	ERA	G	GS	CG	ShO	GF	Sv.	IP	H	TBF	R	ER	HR	SH	SF	HB	BB	IBB	SO	WP	Bk.
Myers, Rodney, Iowa	7	8	.467	4.09	24	23	1	0	0	0	140.2	140	590	76	64	18	2	7	6	38	1	79	3	0
Nitkowski, C.J., N.Orleans*	8	10	.444	3.98	28	28	1	0	0	0	174.1	183	738	82	77	10	6	8	6	56	2	141	6	3
Nix, James, Indianapolis	3	0	1.000	8.82	12	0	0	0	1	0	16.1	18	80	16	16	0	0	2	0	16	0	13	1	0
Ogea, Chad, Buffalo	1	1	.500	4.29	4	4	0	0	0	0	21.0	24	88	10	10	2	0	0	0	6	0	11	0	0
Olsen, Steve, Omaha	4	5	.444	5.76	22	13	0	0	2	0	84.1	96	402	67	54	11	2	3	3	48	3	43	5	1
Olson, Gregg, Omaha	3	1	.750	3.31	9	5	0	0	2	0	35.1	30	140	13	13	4	0	0	0	10	0	20	1	0
Osborne, Donovan, Louisville*	0	1	.000	4.73	3	3	0	0	0	0	13.1	13	58	7	7	2	1	1	0	5	1	13	1	0
Painter, Lance, Louisville*	1	0	1.000	5.23	18	2	0	0	7	0	20.2	18	85	14	12	2	2	1	1	4	0	22	0	1
Parque, Jim, Nashville*	1	0	1.000	4.22	2	2	0	0	0	0	10.2	9	49	5	5	0	0	1	0	9	0	5	1	0
Parris, Steve, Indianapolis	2	3	.400	3.57	5	5	1	1	0	0	35.1	26	143	15	14	4	1	1	2	11	1	27	0	0
Patrick, Bronswell, N.Orleans	6	5	.545	3.22	30	12	1	1	10	0	100.2	108	426	45	36	10	6	2	0	30	4	88	5	0
Patterson, Ken, Omaha*	2	2	.500	4.11	22	0	0	0	13	4	30.2	34	132	17	14	5	0	0	0	10	0	28	2	0
Pavlik, Roger, Oklahoma City	0	0	.000	0.00	1	1	0	0	0	0	6.0	2	21	0	0	0	0	0	0	0	0	4	0	0
Pennington, Brad, Omaha*	2	1	.667	4.32	35	1	0	0	6	0	50.0	41	230	28	24	6	3	4	3	41	0	48	4	0
Perez, Mike, Omaha	4	1	.800	4.71	34	0	0	0	22	8	36.1	38	166	22	19	4	2	1	2	18	3	29	2	0
Pichardo, Hipolito, Omaha	0	0	.000	5.79	5	1	0	0	2	1	4.2	5	22	3	3	1	0	0	0	3	0	3	0	1
Pisciotta, Marc, Iowa	6	2	.750	2.36	42	0	0	0	38	22	45.2	29	194	12	12	2	4	0	2	23	3	48	6	0
Pittsley, Jim, Omaha	1	2	.333	4.42	7	7	0	0	0	0	38.2	36	173	21	19	3	0	1	2	20	0	30	2	0
Powell, John, Oklahoma City	0	0	.000	4.50	1	0	0	0	0	0	4.0	5	16	2	2	0	0	0	0	1	1	2	0	0
Pratt, Rich, Nashville*	9	8	.529	4.58	29	24	2	0	1	0	149.1	165	649	89	76	22	3	5	8	50	1	71	6	7
Probst, Alan, New Orleans	0	0	.000	0.00	1	0	0	0	1	0	1.0	2	4	0	0	0	0	0	0	0	0	1	0	0
Raggio, Brady, Louisville	8	11	.421	4.17	22	22	2	0	0	0	138.0	145	576	68	64	18	5	3	6	32	0	91	3	1
Rain, Steve, Iowa	7	1	.875	5.89	40	0	0	0	17	1	44.1	51	217	30	29	8	2	1	0	34	4	50	4	1
Rakers, Jason, Buffalo	1	0	1.000	0.00	1	1	0	0	0	0	7.0	5	26	0	0	0	0	0	0	1	0	3	0	0
Ratliff, Jon, Iowa	1	3	.250	5.57	9	4	0	0	1	1	32.1	30	134	20	20	6	1	0	2	7	0	25	2	0
Ray, Ken, Omaha	5	12	.294	6.37	25	21	2	0	1	0	113.0	131	516	86	80	21	2	5	4	63	2	96	8	1
Reed, Chris, Indianapolis	0	1	.000	5.79	3	3	0	0	0	0	14.0	19	68	11	9	3	0	1	1	9	0	4	1	0
Reynolds, Shane, N.Orleans	1	0	1.000	0.00	1	1	0	0	0	0	5.0	3	19	0	0	0	0	0	1	1	0	6	0	0
Rizzo, Todd, Nashville*	4	5	.444	3.57	54	0	0	0	23	6	70.2	63	318	39	28	6	3	1	3	33	3	60	9	0
Rodriguez, Felix, Ind.	3	3	.500	1.01	23	0	0	0	7	1	26.2	22	124	10	3	0	2	0	2	16	1	26	1	3
Rupp, Brian, Louisville	0	0	.000	36.00	1	0	0	0	1	0	1.0	3	7	4	4	2	0	0	0	1	0	0	0	0
Rusch, Glendon, Omaha*	0	1	.000	4.50	1	1	0	0	0	0	6.0	7	25	3	3	3	0	0	0	1	0	2	1	0
Russell, Lagrande, Iowa	0	3	.000	12.54	7	3	0	0	1	0	18.2	36	93	26	26	5	0	1	0	8	0	3	1	0
Salkeld, Roger, Indianapolis	4	8	.333	6.75	36	11	0	0	7	1	88.0	91	421	75	66	16	2	2	5	60	2	88	6	0
Santana, Julio, Oklahoma City	0	0	.000	15.00	1	1	0	0	0	0	3.0	9	20	6	5	0	0	0	0	2	0	1	0	0
Sauveur, Rich, Iowa*	1	3	.250	3.38	39	1	0	0	19	2	45.1	46	198	19	17	4	2	1	3	21	5	37	0	0
Schall, Gene, Nashville	0	0	.000	18.00	1	0	0	0	1	0	1.0	2	7	2	2	0	0	0	0	2	0	1	1	0
Scott, Darryl, Buffalo	5	6	.455	2.88	48	0	0	0	35	12	65.2	52	272	24	21	10	4	1	0	28	2	29	4	0
Seanez, Rudy, Omaha	2	5	.286	6.51	28	3	0	0	8	0	47.0	53	226	42	34	13	1	2	2	25	0	46	2	0
Service, Scott, Ind.-Oma.	3	2	.600	2.59	49	0	0	0	42	24	48.2	39	205	15	14	5	4	0	2	16	1	69	2	0
Sexton, Jeff, Buffalo	2	1	.667	5.32	15	0	0	0	11	0	23.2	17	100	14	14	3	1	0	0	12	0	15	2	0
Shuey, Paul, Buffalo	0	0	.000	3.60	2	0	0	0	0	0	5.0	4	23	2	2	0	0	1	0	4	0	6	0	0
Sirotka, Mike, Nashville*	7	5	.583	3.28	19	19	1	0	0	0	112.1	115	469	49	41	13	2	3	1	22	0	92	2	1
Small, Mark, New Orleans	1	1	.500	5.79	7	0	0	0	4	0	9.1	11	43	9	6	1	0	1	0	3	1	7	1	0
Smith, Chuck, Nashville	0	3	.000	8.81	20	1	0	0	12	0	31.2	39	156	33	31	8	2	3	2	23	2	29	8	2
Smith, Dan, Oklahoma City*	3	14	.176	5.64	23	23	3	1	0	0	129.1	154	574	88	81	11	2	5	5	42	0	67	3	1
Smith, Toby, Omaha	1	3	.250	7.84	17	0	0	0	12	3	20.2	24	96	19	18	6	1	1	0	15	2	11	3	1
Speier, Justin, Iowa	2	0	1.000	0.00	8	0	0	0	4	1	12.1	5	41	0	0	0	1	0	0	1	0	9	0	0
Steenstra, Kennie, Iowa	5	10	.333	3.92	25	25	4	0	0	0	160.2	161	663	85	70	15	4	9	0	41	4	111	7	0
Stefanski, Mike, Louisville	0	0	.000	9.00	1	0	0	0	1	0	1.0	3	6	1	1	1	0	0	0	0	0	1	0	1
Stevens, Dave, Iowa	1	1	.500	4.70	6	0	0	0	5	1	7.2	8	34	4	4	0	1	0	0	5	1	8	0	0
Sturtze, Tanyon, O.C.	8	6	.571	5.10	25	19	1	0	3	0	114.2	133	515	76	65	10	1	7	9	47	1	79	3	1
Sullivan, Scott, Indianapolis	3	1	.750	1.30	19	0	0	0	10	2	27.2	16	96	4	4	0	3	2	1	4	1	23	1	0
Swartzbaugh, Dave, Iowa	8	7	.533	2.82	24	20	1	1	1	1	134.0	129	561	55	42	12	4	5	1	48	1	97	3	1
Tabaka, Jeff, Indianapolis*	3	2	.600	2.65	58	0	0	0	23	3	57.2	44	228	19	17	5	1	2	1	19	3	68	8	0
Tapani, Kevin, Iowa	0	1	.000	4.00	1	1	1	0	0	0	9.0	5	32	4	4	1	0	0	0	1	0	4	0	0
Telemaco, Amaury, Iowa	5	9	.357	4.51	18	18	3	2	0	0	113.2	121	501	70	57	20	3	3	4	38	1	75	6	1
Thomas, Larry, Nashville*	3	2	.600	3.94	44	1	0	0	12	2	48.0	47	208	21	21	6	2	1	1	18	4	53	2	0
Tomko, Brett, Indianapolis	6	3	.667	2.95	10	10	0	0	0	0	61.0	53	239	21	20	7	0	1	1	9	0	60	0	0
Toth, Robert, Omaha	5	2	.714	2.75	15	7	0	0	1	0	52.1	50	225	18	16	6	0	1	1	19	0	30	0	0
Urbani, Thomas, O.C.*	3	2	.600	4.19	21	3	0	0	4	1	43.0	53	187	21	20	7	0	3	0	13	1	21	0	0
Van Poppel, Todd, Omaha	1	5	.167	8.03	11	6	0	0	1	0	37.0	50	188	36	33	10	2	3	3	24	0	27	2	0
VanRyn, Ben, Iowa*	2	2	.500	4.59	51	5	0	0	12	3	80.1	88	343	43	41	10	5	3	1	25	2	64	5	0
Veres, Randy, Omaha	1	1	.500	6.60	11	1	0	0	5	0	15.0	15	66	11	11	2	0	0	0	5	0	19	0	0
Walker, Mike, Indianapolis	9	6	.600	2.98	55	5	0	0	19	7	102.2	80	431	35	34	7	4	1	6	46	4	80	13	0
Wall, Donne, New Orleans	8	7	.533	3.85	17	17	1	0	0	0	110.0	109	446	49	47	13	3	5	1	24	0	84	3	0
Warner, Ron, Louisville	0	0	.000	18.00	1	0	0	0	0	0	1.0	2	6	2	2	1	0	0	0	2	0	0	0	0
Warren, Brian, Oklahoma City	5	5	.500	3.62	41	0	0	0	22	6	69.2	73	295	30	28	6	7	5	7	22	2	39	1	0
Watkins, Scott, Omaha*	0	0	.000	6.46	9	0	0	0	4	0	15.1	19	72	13	11	4	0	1	0	6	0	15	2	1
Weathers, David, Buffalo	4	3	.571	3.15	11	11	2	1	0	0	68.2	71	290	37	24	7	1	5	0	17	0	51	4	0
White, Gabe, Indianapolis*	7	4	.636	2.82	20	19	0	0	0	0	118.0	119	493	46	37	10	2	4	6	18	0	62	2	1
Whiteside, Matt, O.C.	1	1	.500	3.54	10	1	0	0	3	1	28.0	30	124	14	11	1	0	2	0	13	0	11	0	1
Whitten, Casey, Buffalo*	0	0	.000	0.00	2	0	0	0	0	0	1.0	1	4	0	0	0	0	0	0	0	0	0	0	0
Wiegandt, Scott, Louisville*	1	3	.250	4.45	40	3	0	0	10	0	64.2	57	280	34	32	5	1	2	3	36	0	55	3	0
Williams, Mike, Omaha	3	6	.333	4.22	20	11	1	0	6	5	79.0	71	335	41	37	10	2	2	1	38	0	68	5	0
Williams, Mitch, Omaha*	0	0	.000	2.08	3	0	0	0	1	0	8.2	6	33	2	2	1	0	0	0	5	0	8	0	0
Williams, Todd, Indianapolis	2	0	1.000	2.13	12	0	0	0	5	2	12.2	11	54	4	3	0	1	0	1	6	1	11	2	0
Winchester, Scott, Ind.	0	0	.000	0.00	4	0	0	0	0	0	5.2	2	21	0	0	0	0	0	0	2	0	2	0	0
Wood, Kerry, Iowa	4	2	.667	4.68	10	10	0	0	0	0	57.2	35	254	35	30	2	3	0	6	52	0	80	8	2
Woods, Brian, Nashville	1	2	.333	7.71	14	1	0	0	5	0	23.1	34	124	24	20	2	2	1	1	20	1	22	3	0
Wright, Jaret, Buffalo	4	1	.800	1.80	7	7	1	1	0	0	45.0	30	183	16	9	4	0	1	1	19	0	47	2	0
York, Mike, Oklahoma City	0	1	.000	8.10	4	2	0	0	0	0	10.0	12	54	9	9	0	0	0	1	12	0	1	0	0
Zimmerman, Mike, Omaha	1	3	.250	10.59	7	6	0	0	1	0	26.1	41	133	32	31	8	0	0	1	20	0	17	1	1

COMBINATION SHUTOUTS: **Buffalo (2)**—Rakers-Sexton, Ogea-Sexton. **Indianapolis (8)**—Tomko-Walker-Sullivan, White-Sullivan, Tomko-Sullivan-Service, Martinez-Rodriguez-Service, Klingenbeck-Service, Tomko-Rodriguez, Carrara-Lewis, Martinez-Tabaka-Walker. **Iowa (5)**—Telemaco-Fletcher, Lyons-Fletcher-Pisciotta, Myers-Heredia, Myers-Swartzbaugh, Wood-Heredia-Pisciotta. **Louisville (0)**—None. **Nashville (3)**—Cruz-Heathcott, Pratt-Darwin-Thomas, Sirotka-Darwin. **New Orleans (11)**—Wall-Patrick, Wall-Henriquez, Miller-Minor, Halama-Minor, Fernandez-Halama, Gardiner-Barrios-Henriquez, Halama-Gutierrez, Nitkowski-Barrios-Henriquez, Miller-Henriquez-Mimbs-Hudek, Miller-Mimbs-Henriquez-Hudek, Halama-Henriquez. **Oklahoma City (5)**—Gross-Urbani-Whiteside-Bailes, Sturtze-Bailes-Whiteside, Sturtze-Urbani, Sturtze-Bailey-Bailes, Alberro-Moody-Bailes. **Omaha (7)**—Converse-McDill, Olson-Patterson-Huisman, Harrison-Perez, Harrison-Service, Olsen-Huisman-Bevil, Toth-Bevil-Service, Harrison-Veres-Service.

NO-HIT GAMES: Converse (6²/₃ innings) and McDill (2¹/₃ innings), Omaha, defeated Oklahoma City, 2-0, April 17; Martinez (5²/₃ innings), Rodriguez (¹/₃ inning) and Service (one inning), Indianapolis, defeated Louisville, 1-0, second game, May 25; Colon, Buffalo, defeated New Orleans, 4-0, June 20.

PITCHERS WITH TWO OR MORE TEAMS

Pitcher, Team	W	L	Pct.	ERA	G	GS	CG	ShO	GF	Sv.	IP	H	TBF	R	ER	HR	SH	SF	HB	BB	IBB	SO	WP	Bk.
Cabrera, Jose, Buffalo	3	0	1.000	1.20	5	0	0	0	2	0	15.0	8	57	2	2	0	1	1	7	1	1	11	1	0
Cabrera, Jose, New Orleans .	2	2	.500	2.54	31	0	0	0	5	0	46.0	31	181	13	13	2	1	0	2	13	3	48	0	0
Graves, Danny, Buffalo.....	2	3	.400	4.19	19	3	0	0	6	2	43.0	45	178	21	20	3	0	2	2	11	0	21	0	0
Graves, Danny, Indianapolis .	1	0	1.000	3.09	11	0	0	0	8	5	11.2	7	47	4	4	1	1	1	2	5	0	5	1	0
Miranda, Angel, Buffalo* ...	0	2	.000	10.03	9	0	0	0	3	0	11.2	20	58	14	13	3	0	1	0	5	0	9	2	0
Miranda, Angel, O.C.*	0	1	.000	16.88	2	0	0	0	0	0	2.2	4	13	5	5	0	0	0	1	1	0	2	0	0
Morman, Alvin, N.Orleans*..	0	0	.000	4.50	8	0	0	0	1	0	10.0	11	42	5	5	1	1	0	2	1	14	1	0	0
Morman, Alvin, Buffalo*....	0	0	.000	0.00	3	0	0	0	1	0	3.1	2	12	0	0	0	0	0	0	0	3	0	0	0
Service, Scott, Indianapolis .	3	2	.600	3.71	33	0	0	0	28	15	34.0	30	148	15	14	5	4	0	2	12	1	53	2	0
Service, Scott, Omaha	0	0	.000	0.00	16	0	0	0	14	9	14.2	9	57	0	0	0	0	0	0	4	0	16	0	0

1997 FIELDING
TEAM

Team	Pct.	G	PO	A	E	TC	DP	PB	Team	Pct.	G	PO	A	E	TC	DP	PB
Iowa	.979	143	3726	1468	109	5303	146	11	Oklahoma City .	.973	143	3797	1613	149	5559	149	9
New Orleans....	.978	144	3861	1586	122	5569	134	11	Nashville..........	.972	143	3700	1525	149	5374	129	12
Louisville	.977	143	3729	1537	122	5388	137	5	Omaha.............	.967	144	3647	1421	172	5240	163	15
Indianapolis.....	.973	144	3747	1416	141	5304	120	19	TRIPLE PLAYS: Buffalo 2, Indianapolis.								
Buffalo.............	.973	144	3767	1520	145	5432	152	8									

INDIVIDUAL

FIRST BASEMEN

NOTE: All caps denotes fielding-percentage leader based on 72 games for catchers, 96 for all other non-pitchers and 144 innings for pitchers. *Throws lefthanded.

Player, Team	Pct.	G	PO	A	E	TC	DP
Anthony, Eric, Oklahoma City*....	1.000	2	14	1	0	15	1
Belk, Tim, Indianapolis..........	.992	69	462	24	4	490	43
Bell, Mike, Oklahoma City	.923	5	12	0	1	13	3
Brewer, Rod, Buffalo*	.947	2	18	0	1	19	1
Brown, Brant, Iowa*	.979	17	128	13	3	144	11
Brown, Kevin, Oklahoma City....	1.000	15	111	15	0	126	7
Busch, Mike, Buffalo	.991	13	104	6	1	111	13
Casey, Sean, Buffalo	1.000	2	17	1	0	18	1
Colon, Dennis, New Orleans	.990	97	806	71	9	886	58
Costo, Tim, Louisville	.995	88	752	54	4	810	68
Cotton, John, Nashville..............	1.000	2	5	2	0	7	2
Dalesandro, Mark, Iowa	.994	19	140	13	1	154	16
Freeman, Ricky, Iowa	1.000	23	192	13	0	205	18
Garcia, Guillermo, Indianapolis....	1.000	4	11	0	0	11	0
Giannelli, Ray, Iowa	.970	4	29	3	1	33	2
Gulan, Mike, Louisville	1.000	1	5	0	0	5	0
Hunter, Brian, Indianapolis*........	.988	81	635	52	8	695	61
Johnson, Mark, Indianapolis*.....	1.000	3	17	2	0	19	0
Kieschnick, Brooks, Iowa..........	.991	63	531	38	5	574	66
Leius, Scott, Nashville	.980	6	49	1	1	51	4
Little, Mark, Oklahoma City	1.000	1	2	0	0	2	0
Livingstone, Scott, Louisville......	.971	4	31	3	1	35	3
Lovullo, Torey, Buffalo	1.000	3	16	1	0	17	1
Maas, Kevin, Ind.-N.O.*	.981	21	144	9	3	156	11
Manto, Jeff, Buffalo	1.000	5	43	0	0	43	9
McCall, Rod, Buf.-Ia.*	.996	31	250	11	1	262	19
McIntosh, Tim, Iowa	.947	2	17	1	1	19	3
Mitchell, Keith, Indianapolis	1.000	2	8	0	0	8	0
Nava, Lipso, Iowa	1.000	6	25	3	0	28	1
Norman, Les, Buffalo	1.000	3	17	1	0	18	4
Ortiz, Luis, Oklahoma City	.989	9	85	2	1	88	6
Pearson, Eddie, Nashville..........	.993	37	281	16	2	299	33
Phillips, J.R., New Orleans*.......	.989	49	329	31	4	364	38
Pough, Pork Chop, Omaha	.992	16	114	13	1	128	13
Rupp, Brian, Louisville..............	.996	25	213	9	1	223	20
Sagmoen, Marc, Oklahoma City*	.963	13	92	12	4	108	11
Schall, Gene, Nashville..............	1.000	8	45	5	0	50	9
SEXSON, Richie, Buffalo............	.996	110	922	77	4	1003	105
Silvestri, Dave, Oklahoma City....	.985	13	124	11	2	137	20
Sisco, Steve, Omaha	.960	3	23	1	1	25	4
Smith, Bubba, Oklahoma City	.994	83	729	46	5	780	72
Stefanski, Mike, Louisville	.982	8	47	9	1	57	8

Player, Team	Pct.	G	PO	A	E	TC	DP
Stewart, Andy, Omaha	.991	27	189	32	2	223	19
Sutton, Larry, Omaha*	.994	102	839	54	5	898	103
Tackett, Jeff, Oklahoma City.......	1.000	16	130	6	0	136	10
Thomas, Greg, Buffalo*	1.000	2	6	0	0	6	1
Valdez, Mario, Nashville.............	.991	75	616	44	6	666	48
Vinas, Julio, Nashville................	.986	16	129	8	2	139	14
Ward, Daryle, New Orleans*.......	.976	9	75	6	2	83	9
Warner, Ron, Louisville..............	.989	23	166	14	2	182	23
Williams, Harold, Iowa...............	1.000	1	7	0	0	7	1
Wrona, Rick, Nashville...............	1.000	12	64	8	0	72	11
Young, Dmitri, Louisville.............	1.000	5	36	1	0	37	1
TRIPLE PLAYS: Sexson 2, Hunter.							

FIRST BASEMEN WITH TWO OR MORE TEAMS

Player, Team	Pct.	G	PO	A	E	TC	DP
Maas, Kevin, Indianapolis*	.975	10	72	5	2	79	2
Maas, Kevin, New Orleans*	.987	11	72	4	1	77	9
McCall, Rod, Buffalo*	1.000	10	74	3	0	77	5
McCall, Rod, Iowa*	.995	21	176	8	1	185	14

SECOND BASEMEN

Player, Team	Pct.	G	PO	A	E	TC	DP
Bell, David, Louisville..................	1.000	2	5	3	0	8	1
Bell, Mike, Oklahoma City	.957	47	88	112	9	209	25
Berblinger, Jeff, Louisville...........	.981	128	258	362	12	632	93
Boone, Aaron, Indianapolis.........	.900	6	19	8	3	30	0
Boone, Bret, Indianapolis...........	1.000	3	6	10	0	16	2
Brady, Doug, Nashville................	.983	90	211	200	7	418	66
Bridges, Kary, New Orleans	.936	16	35	38	5	78	13
Cairo, Miguel, Iowa	.979	105	201	305	11	517	80
Candaele, Casey, Buffalo............	.980	55	95	155	5	255	35
Caraballo, Ramon, Iowa..............	.972	33	60	79	4	143	18
Castleberry, Kevin, O.C..............	1.000	4	8	9	0	17	3
Cedeno, Domingo, O.C...............	1.000	6	13	20	0	33	6
Cotton, John, Nashville...............	.952	11	16	24	2	42	7
Diaz, Alex, Oklahoma City	.939	21	36	41	5	82	12
Diaz, Edwin, Oklahoma City	.934	17	37	48	6	91	12
Estrada, Osmani, Oklahoma City.	.990	43	94	111	2	207	27
Garcia, Guillermo, Indianapolis ...	1.000	10	13	18	0	31	5
Grebeck, Brian, New Orleans	1.000	10	13	8	0	21	5
Hall, Billy, Indianapolis...............	1.000	6	15	15	0	30	4
Halter, Shane, Omaha	.933	4	9	5	1	15	1
HANEY, Todd, New Orleans	.990	115	213	259	5	477	64
Hansen, Jed, Omaha	.960	85	164	243	17	424	69
Holbert, Aaron, Louisville............	.957	4	14	8	1	23	2

Player, Team	Pct.	G	PO	A	E	TC	DP
Jackson, Damian, Buf.-Ind.........	.967	18	38	50	3	91	12
Listach, Pat, Buffalo.................	1.000	2	1	4	0	5	1
Lovullo, Torey, Buffalo	.967	28	50	67	4	121	22
McLemore, Mark, Oklahoma City	1.000	2	2	3	0	5	1
Medrano, Tony, Omaha	.941	10	25	23	3	51	3
Mejia, Roberto, Louisville	1.000	3	8	3	0	11	0
Menechino, Frankie, Nashville	.949	32	74	74	8	156	19
Mora, Melvin, New Orleans........	1.000	9	17	19	0	36	5
Morris, Warren, Oklahoma City...	1.000	8	17	31	0	48	7
Murphy, Mike, Oklahoma City.....	1.000	1	0	1	0	1	0
Nevers, Tom, Louisville..............	1.000	3	9	10	0	19	3
Norton, Greg, Nashville..............	1.000	6	7	9	0	16	1
Owens, Eric, Indianapolis...........	.955	84	157	201	17	375	35
Petersen, Chris, Iowa................	1.000	4	8	8	0	16	2
Polidor, Wil, Nashville...............	.974	9	17	21	1	39	4
Reese, Pokey, Indianapolis	1.000	4	10	11	0	21	2
Rivera, Luis, New Orleans..........	.800	1	1	3	1	5	0
Robles, Oscar, New Orleans.......	1.000	1	0	2	0	2	0
Scarsone, Steve, Louisville	.957	4	11	11	1	23	2
Scutaro, Marcos, Buffalo	1.000	12	18	27	0	45	10
Silvestri, Dave, Oklahoma City ...	.986	12	36	34	1	71	13
Sisco, Steve, Omaha.................	.973	30	46	63	3	112	17
Stynes, Chris, Oma.-Ind.............	.980	44	88	104	4	196	36
Warner, Ron, Louisville..............	1.000	3	2	3	0	5	0
Wilson, Brandon, Ind.-Ia............	1.000	15	16	34	0	50	5
Wilson, Craig, Nashville	.982	10	32	24	1	57	8
Wilson, Enrique, Buffalo	.970	51	117	143	8	268	31
Wimmer, Chris, Louisville	1.000	3	2	4	0	6	0

TRIPLE PLAYS: Candaele, Lovullo, Owens.

SECOND BASEMEN WITH TWO OR MORE TEAMS

Player, Team	Pct.	G	PO	A	E	TC	DP
Jackson, Damian, Buffalo	.968	6	13	17	1	31	5
Jackson, Damian, Indianapolis ...	.967	12	25	33	2	60	7
Stynes, Chris, Omaha................	.977	23	41	43	2	86	19
Stynes, Chris, Indianapolis	.982	21	47	61	2	110	17
Wilson, Brandon, Indianapolis	1.000	12	14	28	0	42	4
Wilson, Brandon, Iowa..............	1.000	3	2	6	0	8	1

THIRD BASEMEN

Player, Team	Pct.	G	PO	A	E	TC	DP
Belk, Tim, Indianapolis...............	.885	9	10	13	3	26	1
Bell, David, Louisville.................	1.000	2	0	4	0	4	1
Bell, Mike, Oklahoma City	.914	35	28	78	10	116	13
Berry, Sean, New Orleans	1.000	3	0	6	0	6	0
Boone, Aaron, Indianapolis	.943	122	76	241	19	336	27
Brady, Doug, Nashville...............	.625	5	1	4	3	8	0
Branson, Jeff, Indianapolis	1.000	2	1	2	0	3	0
Busch, Mike, Buffalo.................	.857	5	5	7	2	14	2
Candaele, Casey, Buffalo	.899	26	24	47	8	79	3
Caraballo, Ramon, Iowa.............	.778	4	3	4	2	9	0
Cholowsky, Dan, Iowa...............	1.000	8	2	4	0	6	1
Cotton, John, Nashville..............	.000	3	0	0	1	1	0
Dalesandro, Mark, Iowa.............	1.000	40	19	58	0	77	3
Diaz, Einar, Buffalo...................	.909	3	3	7	1	11	1
Estrada, Osmani, Oklahoma City.	.957	22	12	32	2	46	7
Garcia, Guillermo, Indianapolis ...	.909	6	3	7	1	11	0
Grebeck, Brian, New Orleans	.941	13	3	29	2	34	1
GULAN, Mike, Louisville	.948	107	73	221	16	310	22
Halter, Shane, Omaha	.667	5	1	1	1	3	0
Haney, Todd, New Orleans	1.000	1	0	1	0	1	0
Hansen, Jed, Omaha..................	1.000	3	2	5	0	7	2
Houston, Tyler, Iowa..................	.833	4	2	8	2	12	2
Hubbard, Trenidad, Buffalo	.967	11	8	21	1	30	3
Johnson, Russ, New Orleans......	.932	106	60	230	21	311	17
Kieschnick, Brooks, Iowa...........	.875	7	5	16	3	24	1
Leius, Scott, Nashville	.895	13	8	26	4	38	1
Listach, Pat, Buffalo..................	1.000	5	1	6	0	7	1
Lopez, Mendy, Omaha	.898	17	15	38	6	59	5
Lovullo, Torey, Buffalo	.958	66	49	134	8	191	13
Magdaleno, Ricky, Indianapolis ..	1.000	1	1	1	0	2	0
Manto, Jeff, Buffalo...................	.918	28	13	54	6	73	9
Mejia, Roberto, Louisville	.857	3	1	5	1	7	0
Menechino, Frankie, Nashville	.941	4	4	12	1	17	0
Mora, Melvin, New Orleans........	.888	34	17	54	9	80	3
Nava, Lipso, Iowa	.940	85	52	135	12	199	18
Nevers, Tom, Louisville..............	1.000	8	9	10	0	19	2
Norton, Greg, Nashville..............	.896	94	62	189	29	280	25
Orie, Kevin, Iowa......................	.938	6	2	13	1	16	2
Ortiz, Luis, Oklahoma City	.750	5	0	6	2	8	0
Owens, Eric, Indianapolis...........	1.000	3	0	1	0	1	0
Paquette, Craig, Omaha	.953	19	12	29	2	43	3
Pendleton, Terry, Indianapolis.....	1.000	4	3	10	0	13	0

Player, Team	Pct.	G	PO	A	E	TC	DP
Petersen, Chris, Iowa................	1.000	4	4	4	0	8	0
Pough, Pork Chop, Omaha........	.909	69	41	138	18	197	20
Rivera, Luis, New Orleans..........	.875	5	3	11	2	16	1
Rose, Pete, Indianapolis	.957	10	3	19	1	23	2
Rupp, Brian, Louisville...............	.875	13	8	13	3	24	1
Scarsone, Steve, Louisville	1.000	4	2	9	0	11	0
Schall, Gene, Nashville	.636	3	2	5	4	11	0
Scutaro, Marcos, Buffalo	.889	7	6	10	2	18	1
Seitzer, Brad, Omaha.................	.885	20	16	30	6	52	3
Silvestri, Dave, Oklahoma City ...	.940	88	52	216	17	285	19
Sisco, Steve, Omaha.................	.913	6	9	12	2	23	3
Snopek, Chris, Nashville	1.000	1	2	1	0	3	0
Stynes, Chris, Omaha	.875	15	8	34	6	48	4
Tackett, Jeff, Oklahoma City.......	1.000	2	2	3	0	5	0
Ventura, Robin, Nashville...........	1.000	4	1	12	0	13	0
Vinas, Julio, Nashville................	.857	6	9	9	3	21	0
Warner, Ron, Louisville..............	.950	20	11	27	2	40	4
Wilson, Brandon, Ind.-Ia............	.929	16	9	17	2	28	2
Wilson, Craig, Nashville	1.000	17	12	37	0	49	2
Wilson, Enrique, Buffalo	1.000	2	2	4	0	6	1
Wimmer, Chris, Louisville	1.000	1	1	1	0	2	0
Wrona, Rick, Nashville...............	.875	12	4	24	4	32	3

TRIPLE PLAYS: Boone, Manto.

THIRD BASEMEN WITH TWO OR MORE TEAMS

Player, Team	Pct.	G	PO	A	E	TC	DP
Wilson, Brandon, Indianapolis	.500	4	1	0	1	2	0
Wilson, Brandon, Iowa..............	.962	12	8	17	1	26	2

SHORTSTOPS

Player, Team	Pct.	G	PO	A	E	TC	DP
Bell, David, Louisville.................	.800	1	1	3	1	5	1
Boone, Aaron, Indianapolis	.949	11	17	20	2	39	3
Brady, Doug, Nashville...............	.500	1	0	1	1	2	0
Branson, Jeff, Indianapolis	.979	14	17	30	1	48	7
Cairo, Miguel, Iowa...................	.934	30	47	81	9	137	15
Candaele, Casey, Buffalo	1.000	1	0	1	0	1	0
Diaz, Alex, Oklahoma City	1.000	1	0	2	0	2	0
Estrada, Osmani, Oklahoma City.	.971	16	22	46	2	70	10
Frias, Hanley, Oklahoma City	.947	129	176	414	33	623	81
Gallego, Mike, Louisville	.955	6	8	13	1	22	1
Grebeck, Brian, New Orleans	.947	22	22	49	4	75	9
Guillen, Carlos, New Orleans	1.000	3	5	6	0	11	1
Gutierrez, Ricky, New Orleans.....	.971	7	12	21	1	34	3
Halter, Shane, Omaha	1.000	4	2	8	0	10	3
Hansen, Jed, Omaha..................	.950	27	39	75	6	120	16
Holbert, Aaron, Louisville............	.934	81	115	253	26	394	52
Jackson, Damian, Buf.-Ind..........	.938	73	124	251	25	400	58
Johnson, Russ, New Orleans......	1.000	18	26	39	0	65	8
Listach, Pat, Buffalo..................	.929	12	20	32	4	56	6
Lovullo, Torey, Buffalo	1.000	1	0	1	0	1	1
Magdaleno, Ricky, Indianapolis ..	.941	54	62	147	13	222	24
Martinez, Felix, Omaha..............	.931	112	175	312	36	523	81
Medrano, Tony, Omaha	1.000	8	18	19	0	37	5
Mora, Melvin, New Orleans........	.667	2	2	2	2	6	0
Nava, Lipso, Iowa	1.000	4	4	7	0	11	0
Nevers, Tom, Louisville..............	.963	57	72	162	9	243	36
Norton, Greg, Nashville..............	.875	18	14	49	9	72	11
Owens, Eric, Indianapolis...........	.863	19	24	39	10	73	5
PETERSON, Chris, Iowa.............	.9730	111	164	341	14	519	84
Reese, Pokey, Indianapolis	.955	13	33	31	3	67	5
Rivera, Luis, New Orleans..........	.9725	106	144	352	14	510	70
Scutaro, Marcos, Buffalo	.900	2	3	6	1	10	2
Silvestri, Dave, Oklahoma City ...	.667	1	2	2	2	6	1
Snopek, Chris, Nashville	.963	18	27	51	3	81	11
Warner, Ron, Louisville..............	.941	9	10	22	2	34	3
Wilson, Brandon, Ind.-Ia............	.946	50	62	97	9	168	24
Wilson, Craig, Nashville	.962	113	145	336	19	500	67
Wilson, Enrique, Buffalo	.959	64	99	185	12	296	45

TRIPLE PLAY: E. Wilson.

SHORTSTOPS WITH TWO OR MORE TEAMS

Player, Team	Pct.	G	PO	A	E	TC	DP
Jackson, Damian, Buffalo	.940	66	113	229	22	364	53
Jackson, Damian, Indianapolis ...	.917	7	11	22	3	36	5
Wilson, Brandon, Indianapolis	.942	47	58	88	9	155	21
Wilson, Brandon, Iowa..............	1.000	3	4	9	0	13	3

OUTFIELDERS

Player, Team	Pct.	G	PO	A	E	TC	DP
ABBOTT, Jeff, Nashville*...........	1.000	113	237	6	0	243	0
Abreu, Bob, New Orleans...........	.990	47	99	4	1	104	0

Player, Team	Pct.	G	PO	A	E	TC	DP
Anthony, Eric, Oklahoma City*	1.000	5	4	1	0	5	0
Aven, Bruce, Buffalo	.991	108	219	3	2	224	1
Battle, Allen, Nashville	1.000	10	9	1	0	10	0
Bell, Derek, New Orleans	1.000	5	10	0	0	10	0
Benitez, Yamil, Omaha	.963	89	150	6	6	162	1
Blosser, Greg, Oklahoma City*	.979	29	44	2	1	47	0
Bradshaw, Terry, Louisville	.990	122	187	5	2	194	0
Brady, Doug, Nashville	.935	15	29	0	2	31	0
Brewer, Rod, Buffalo*	.500	1	1	0	1	2	0
Brown, Brant, Iowa*	.987	47	74	0	1	75	0
Cameron, Mike, Nashville	.985	29	63	3	1	67	0
Cappuccio, Carmine, Nashville	1.000	38	56	1	0	57	0
Carr, Chuck, New Orleans	1.000	18	35	1	0	36	0
Carr, Jeremy, Omaha	.983	33	57	2	1	60	2
Castleberry, Kevin, O.C.	1.000	30	56	5	0	61	0
Cholowsky, Dan, Iowa	1.000	2	1	1	0	2	0
Cotton, John, Nashville	.983	63	106	7	2	115	2
Coughlin, Kevin, Louisville*	1.000	12	17	0	0	17	0
Curtis, Randy, Buffalo*	1.000	27	48	1	0	49	0
Dalesandro, Mark, Iowa	1.000	5	3	0	0	3	0
Diaz, Alex, Oklahoma City	.968	81	144	9	5	158	2
Dowler, Dee, Iowa	1.000	31	60	3	0	63	0
Dye, Jermaine, Omaha	1.000	29	41	2	0	43	0
Estrada, Osmani, Oklahoma City.	.973	14	35	1	1	37	0
Evans, Jason, Nashville	.992	63	115	6	1	122	1
Flora, Kevin, New Orleans	1.000	28	45	2	0	47	0
Franklin, Micah, Louisville	.978	94	128	7	3	138	1
Giannelli, Ray, Louisville	1.000	14	28	0	0	28	0
Goodwin, Curtis, Indianapolis*	1.000	30	57	2	0	59	0
Green, Scarborough, Louisville	.993	52	138	7	1	146	4
Halter, Shane, Omaha	1.000	5	10	0	0	10	0
Hatcher, Chris, Omaha	.921	39	56	2	5	63	0
Hidalgo, Richard, New Orleans	.968	127	261	15	9	285	3
Hubbard, Trenidad, Buffalo	.996	89	228	5	1	234	2
Hunter, Brian, Indianapolis*	.990	58	99	4	1	104	0
Jackson, Damian, Buffalo	1.000	1	2	0	0	2	0
Jennings, Robin, Iowa*	.986	119	197	10	3	210	3
Jordan, Brian, Louisville	1.000	4	6	0	0	6	0
Kelly, Mike, Louisville	.963	25	51	1	2	54	0
Kieschnick, Brooks, Iowa	1.000	14	26	0	0	26	0
Koslofski, Kevin, Louisville	.985	99	195	8	3	206	3
Listach, Pat, Buffalo	1.000	6	12	0	0	12	0
Little, Mark, Oklahoma City	.973	116	280	9	8	297	1
Long, Ryan, Omaha	.956	104	186	9	9	204	1
Lowery, Terrell, Iowa	.988	104	244	8	3	255	1
Maas, Kevin, Ind.-N.O.*	1.000	17	18	0	0	18	0
Manto, Jeff, Buffalo	1.000	2	3	0	0	3	0
McIntosh, Tim, Iowa	1.000	2	1	0	0	1	0
McNabb, Buck, New Orleans	1.000	2	4	0	0	4	0
Menechino, Frankie, Nashville	1.000	1	1	0	0	1	0
Merchant, Mark, Omaha	1.000	1	1	0	0	1	0
Mitchell, Keith, Indianapolis	.978	83	169	6	4	179	4
Montgomery, Ray, New Orleans	.971	13	33	0	1	34	0
Mora, Melvin, New Orleans	1.000	80	125	5	0	130	1
Mottola, Chad, Indianapolis	.947	75	136	8	8	152	3
Murphy, Mike, Oklahoma City	1.000	70	139	5	0	144	2
Murray, Glenn, Indianapolis	1.000	2	4	0	0	4	0
Myers, Rod, Omaha*	.989	38	89	3	1	93	1
Nevers, Tom, Louisville	1.000	2	2	0	0	2	0
Norman, Les, Buffalo	.995	107	206	6	1	213	1
Nunnally, Jon, Omaha	.963	66	173	8	7	188	2
O'Neill, Doug, Oklahoma City	1.000	10	16	0	0	16	0
Ordonez, Magglio, Nashville	.983	121	278	8	5	291	0
Owens, Eric, Indianapolis	1.000	4	3	0	0	3	0
Pegues, Steve, Iowa	.833	4	4	1	1	6	1
Phillips, J.R., New Orleans*	.967	63	82	5	3	90	0
Plantier, Phil, Louisville	1.000	7	7	0	0	7	0
Ramirez, Alex, Buffalo	.946	99	167	8	10	185	3
Ramos, Ken, New Orleans*	.993	79	129	4	1	134	0
Robinson, Kerry, Louisville*	1.000	2	3	0	0	3	0
Rupp, Brian, Louisville	1.000	13	21	0	0	21	0
Sagmoen, Marc, Oklahoma City*	.986	99	205	9	3	217	2
Sanders, Reggie, Indianapolis	.750	5	6	0	2	8	0
Silvestri, Dave, Oklahoma City	1.000	1	1	0	0	1	0
Simms, Mike, Oklahoma City	1.000	7	17	1	0	18	0
Sisco, Steve, Omaha	.957	19	22	0	1	23	0
Stewart, Andy, Omaha	1.000	4	3	0	0	3	0
Stynes, Chris, Omaha	.965	23	52	3	2	57	0
Thompson, Ryan, Buffalo	.955	15	20	1	1	22	0
Timmons, Ozzie, Indianapolis	.983	97	172	3	3	178	1
Valdes, Pedro, Iowa*	.989	116	256	13	3	272	6
Vitiello, Joe, Omaha	1.000	1	1	0	0	1	0
Warner, Ron, Louisville	.976	32	40	1	1	42	0
Watkins, Pat, Indianapolis	.989	83	170	5	2	177	1
Young, Dmitri, Louisville	.967	19	28	1	1	30	0

OUTFIELDERS WITH TWO OR MORE TEAMS

Player, Team	Pct.	G	PO	A	E	TC	DP
Maas, Kevin, Indianapolis*	1.000	1	1	0	0	1	0
Maas, Kevin, New Orleans*	1.000	16	17	0	0	17	0

CATCHERS

Player, Team	Pct.	G	PO	A	E	TC	DP	PB
Bako, Paul, Indianapolis	.9913	99	622	64	6	692	10	9
Brooks, Rayme, Omaha	1.000	1	1	0	0	1	0	0
BROWN, Kevin, O.C.	.9914	95	529	47	5	581	10	5
Candaele, Casey, Buffalo	1.000	2	0	0	0	2	0	0
Cholowsky, Dan, Iowa	.980	14	92	7	2	101	1	0
Christopherson, Eric, N.O.	1.000	6	46	2	0	48	0	0
Cline, Pat, Iowa	.990	27	188	11	2	201	0	1
Dalesandro, Mark, Iowa	.991	51	305	19	3	327	2	3
Diaz, Einar, Buffalo	.975	105	650	60	18	728	8	3
Difelice, Mike, Louisville	1.000	1	3	1	0	4	0	0
Downs, Brian, Nashville	1.000	6	16	1	0	17	0	0
Fasano, Sal, Omaha	.988	47	296	34	4	334	4	7
Fordyce, Brook, Indianapolis	1.000	11	73	8	0	81	0	2
Garcia, Guillermo, Ind.	1.000	35	189	6	0	195	3	8
Houston, Tyler, Iowa	1.000	1	4	1	0	5	0	0
Hubbard, Mike, Iowa	.994	46	310	22	2	334	6	4
Kmak, Joe, Indianapolis	.976	13	71	11	2	84	0	0
Knorr, Randy, New Orleans	.984	72	502	54	9	565	7	5
Lisanti, Bob, Iowa	1.000	4	22	2	0	24	1	2
Machado, Robert, Nashville	.988	72	461	49	6	516	7	9
Marrero, Eli, Louisville	.9907	100	675	68	7	750	8	5
McIntosh, Tim, Iowa	.969	8	57	6	2	65	1	1
Meluskey, Mitch, N.O.	.989	49	323	26	4	353	6	4
Mercedes, Henry, O.C.	.989	14	78	13	1	92	3	1
Molina, Jose, Iowa	1.000	1	3	0	0	3	0	0
Oliver, Joe, Indianapolis	1.000	2	21	4	0	25	0	0
Ortiz, Hector, Omaha	.978	21	130	6	3	139	1	0
Pagnozzi, Tom, Louisville	1.000	3	8	3	0	11	1	0
Probst, Alan, New Orleans	.996	35	210	16	1	227	2	2
Soliz, Steve, Buffalo	.974	60	276	24	8	308	2	5
Stefanski, Mike, Louisville	.978	47	271	34	7	312	2	0
Stewart, Andy, Omaha	.994	49	285	26	2	313	6	4
Sweeney, Mike, Omaha	.996	33	229	15	1	245	2	4
Tackett, Jeff, Oklahoma City	.985	39	238	31	4	273	6	3
Vinas, Julio, Nashville	.986	31	193	15	3	211	0	1
Wrona, Rick, Nashville	.986	44	243	30	4	277	1	2

PITCHERS

Player, Team	Pct.	G	PO	A	E	TC	DP
Alberro, Jose, Oklahoma City	.964	16	9	18	1	28	0
Anderson, Brian, Buffalo*	1.000	15	6	11	0	17	1
Arrandale, Matt, Louisville	.929	56	1	12	1	14	0
Aybar, Manny, Louisville	1.000	22	3	16	0	19	1
Bailes, Scott, Oklahoma City*	.750	44	0	9	3	12	1
Bailey, Cory, Oklahoma City	1.000	42	3	10	0	13	0
Barber, Brian, Louisville	.941	18	7	9	1	17	1
Barfield, John, Buffalo*	1.000	1	0	1	0	1	0
Barrios, Manuel, New Orleans	1.000	57	6	16	0	22	0
Batchelor, Rich, Louisville	1.000	12	0	3	0	3	1
Batista, Miguel, Iowa	.923	31	8	16	2	26	1
Bautista, Jose, Louisville	1.000	11	2	3	0	5	0
Beltran, Rigo, Louisville*	1.000	9	3	7	0	10	0
Bere, Jason, Nashville	1.000	4	0	2	0	2	0
Bertotti, Mike, Nashville*	1.000	21	4	15	0	19	0
Bevil, Brian, Omaha	.800	26	1	3	1	5	0
Blomdahl, Ben, Buffalo	1.000	29	3	16	0	19	3
Bolton, Rodney, Indianapolis	1.000	28	15	25	0	40	3
Brewington, Jamie, Omaha	1.000	7	0	1	0	1	0
Brower, Jim, Oklahoma City	1.000	4	2	4	0	6	1
Buckles, Bucky, Oklahoma City	1.000	5	2	5	0	7	0
Burgos, John, Oklahoma City*	1.000	7	0	2	0	2	0
Burkett, John, New Orleans	1.000	1	1	0	0	1	0
Busby, Mike, Louisville	1.000	15	9	10	0	19	3
Cabrera, Jose, Buf.-N.O.	1.000	36	1	4	0	5	1
Cadaret, Greg, Buffalo*	.833	29	1	4	1	6	0
Carpenter, Brian, Louisville	1.000	4	1	1	0	2	0
Carrara, Giovanni, Indianapolis	.958	19	9	14	1	24	2
Clark, Terry, Buffalo	1.000	25	7	14	0	21	1
Clemons, Chris, Nashville	1.000	22	7	17	0	24	0
Colon, Bartolo, Buffalo	.933	10	5	9	1	15	2
Converse, Jim, Omaha	1.000	6	1	1	0	2	0
Croushore, Rick, Louisville	.667	14	2	0	1	3	0
Crowell, Jim, Indianapolis*	1.000	3	1	9	0	10	1
Cruz, Nelson, Nashville	1.000	21	6	19	0	25	0

Player, Team	Pct.	G	PO	A	E	TC	DP
Darwin, Jeff, Nashville	1.000	47	3	6	0	9	0
Davis, Clint, Oklahoma City	1.000	40	3	11	0	14	0
Dedrick, Jim, Oklahoma City	1.000	8	2	2	0	4	0
Detmers, Kris, Louisville*	1.000	10	0	4	0	4	0
DeLaMaza, Roland, Buffalo	1.000	34	8	18	0	26	1
DeLaRosa, Maximo, Buffalo	.727	15	3	5	3	11	0
Dougherty, Anthony, Buffalo	.667	18	0	2	1	3	0
Driskill, Travis, Buffalo	1.000	29	14	8	0	22	2
Eischen, Joey, Indianapolis*	1.000	26	1	4	0	5	0
Elarton, Scott, New Orleans	.909	9	5	5	1	11	0
Eversgerd, Bryan, O.C.*	.938	26	6	9	1	16	0
Fernandez, Sid, New Orleans*	1.000	2	0	1	0	1	0
Fletcher, Paul, Iowa	.938	54	3	12	1	16	1
Flury, Pat, Omaha	1.000	18	4	4	0	8	0
Fordham, Tom, Nashville*	.917	21	4	18	2	24	1
Foulke, Keith, Nashville	1.000	1	0	1	0	1	1
Gardiner, Mike, New Orleans	1.000	11	5	4	0	9	0
Glauber, Keith, Louisville	.833	15	1	4	1	6	0
Gonzalez, Jeremi, Iowa	.923	10	6	6	1	13	0
Graves, Danny, Buf.-Ind.	.952	30	4	16	1	21	2
Greene, Tommy, New Orleans	.947	13	4	14	1	19	0
Grimsley, Jason, Omaha	1.000	7	2	2	0	4	0
Gross, Kevin, Oklahoma City	1.000	6	2	1	0	3	0
Gutierrez, Jim, New Orleans	1.000	7	1	2	0	3	0
Halama, John, New Orleans*	.976	26	7	33	1	41	2
Haney, Chris, Omaha*	.900	4	1	8	1	10	0
Harrison, Brian, Omaha	1.000	30	14	24	0	38	3
Hartvigson, Chad, O.C.*	1.000	14	1	3	0	4	0
Hasselhoff, Derek, Nashville	1.000	6	0	2	0	2	0
Heathcott, Mike, Nashville	.500	17	0	1	1	2	0
Henriquez, Oscar, New Orleans	.818	60	5	4	2	11	0
Heredia, Gil, Iowa	1.000	31	1	17	0	18	2
Heredia, Wilson, Oklahoma City	.909	27	9	21	3	33	0
Hudek, John, New Orleans	1.000	19	1	1	0	2	0
Huisman, Rick, Omaha	.818	37	1	8	2	11	1
Ilsley, Blaise, Buffalo*	1.000	9	0	1	0	1	0
Jackson, Danny, Louisville*	1.000	4	3	4	0	7	0
Jacome, Jason, Buffalo*	.833	7	2	3	1	6	0
Johns, Doug, Omaha*	1.000	9	3	4	0	7	2
Johnson, Barry, Nashville	1.000	14	1	8	0	9	0
Johnson, Jonathan, O.C.	1.000	13	7	7	0	14	0
Karchner, Matt, Nashville	1.000	13	1	2	0	3	0
Kell, Rob, Oklahoma City*	1.000	11	0	1	0	1	0
Keyser, Brian, Nashville	.927	44	8	30	3	41	1
King, Curt, Louisville	1.000	16	3	4	0	7	0
Kline, Steven, Buffalo*	1.000	20	1	7	0	8	0
Klingenbeck, Scott, Indianapolis	.960	27	10	14	1	25	0
Levine, Alan, Nashville	.900	26	1	8	1	10	0
Lewis, Richie, Indianapolis	1.000	27	2	4	0	6	1
Lopez, Albie, Buffalo	1.000	7	2	1	0	3	0
Lowe, Sean, Louisville	.913	26	8	13	2	23	0
Ludwick, Eric, Louisville	1.000	24	4	5	0	9	1
Lyons, Curt, Iowa	1.000	8	2	3	0	5	0
Magnante, Mike, New Orleans*	1.000	17	4	8	0	12	0
Manning, David, Oklahoma City	1.000	5	0	3	0	3	0
Martinez, Pedro A., Ind.*	.952	28	5	15	1	21	2
Matranga, Jeff, Louisville	.944	37	4	13	1	18	0
Matthews, Mike, Buffalo*	.667	5	1	1	1	3	0
Maxcy, Brian, Louisville	1.000	30	4	7	0	11	0
McDill, Allen, Omaha*	1.000	23	5	5	0	10	0
McGraw, Tom, Louisville*	.813	45	5	8	3	16	0
Miller, Trever, New Orleans*	.951	29	9	30	2	41	1
Mimbs, Mark, New Orleans*	1.000	22	4	6	0	10	2
Minor, Blas, New Orleans	.917	23	1	10	1	12	2
Miranda, Angel, Buf.-O.C.*	1.000	11	2	2	0	4	0
Mlicki, Doug, New Orleans	1.000	14	4	1	0	5	0
Montgomery, Steve, Buffalo	1.000	7	1	4	0	5	0
Moody, Eric, Oklahoma City	.957	35	10	12	1	23	0
Moore, Marcus, Buffalo	1.000	10	4	9	0	13	1
Morman, Alvin, N.O.-Buf.*	1.000	11	0	3	0	3	0
Myers, Rodney, Iowa	.886	24	8	23	4	35	1
Nitkowski, C.J., New Orleans*	.939	28	10	36	3	49	2
Nix, James, Indianapolis	1.000	12	0	4	0	4	0
Ogea, Chad, Buffalo	1.000	4	0	3	0	3	0
Olsen, Steve, Omaha	1.000	22	9	7	0	16	1
Olson, Gregg, Omaha	1.000	9	1	6	0	7	0
Osborne, Donovan, Louisville*	.750	3	1	2	1	4	0
Painter, Lance, Louisville*	1.000	18	1	4	0	5	0
Parque, Jim, Nashville*	1.000	2	0	3	0	3	1
Parris, Steve, Indianapolis	1.000	5	2	3	0	5	1
Patrick, Bronswell, New Orleans	1.000	30	7	14	0	21	3
Patterson, Ken, Omaha*	1.000	22	0	2	0	2	0
Pavlik, Roger, Oklahoma City	1.000	1	0	2	0	2	0
Pennington, Brad, Omaha*	.714	35	1	4	2	7	1
Perez, Mike, Omaha	1.000	34	0	5	0	5	0
Pichardo, Hipolito, Omaha	1.000	5	1	1	0	2	0
Pisciotta, Marc, Iowa	.857	42	2	4	1	7	0
Pittsley, Jim, Omaha	1.000	7	2	1	0	3	0
PRATT, Rich, Nashville*	1.000	29	7	35	0	42	1
Raggio, Brady, Louisville	.976	22	9	31	1	41	4
Rain, Steve, Iowa	1.000	40	0	3	0	3	0
Rakers, Jason, Buffalo	1.000	1	0	2	0	2	0
Ratliff, Jon, Iowa	1.000	9	6	4	0	10	0
Ray, Ken, Omaha	.913	25	9	12	2	23	2
Reed, Chris, Indianapolis	1.000	3	1	2	0	3	0
Rizzo, Todd, Nashville*	.857	54	0	6	1	7	1
Rodriguez, Felix, Indianapolis	1.000	23	0	3	0	3	0
Russell, Lagrande, Iowa	1.000	7	1	5	0	6	1
Salkeld, Roger, Indianapolis	.950	36	9	10	1	20	1
Santana, Julio, Oklahoma City	1.000	1	0	1	0	1	0
Sauveur, Rich, Iowa*	.917	39	4	7	1	12	0
Scott, Darryl, Buffalo	.944	48	5	12	1	18	1
Seanez, Rudy, Omaha	1.000	28	3	3	0	6	0
Service, Scott, Ind.-Oma.	.857	49	0	6	1	7	0
Sexton, Jeff, Buffalo	.857	15	5	1	1	7	0
Sirotka, Mike, Nashville*	.960	19	9	15	1	25	0
Smith, Chuck, Nashville	.900	20	2	7	1	10	0
Smith, Dan, Oklahoma City*	.895	23	1	16	2	19	0
Smith, Toby, Omaha	1.000	17	1	0	0	1	1
Speier, Justin, Iowa	1.000	8	0	1	0	1	0
Steenstra, Kennie, Iowa	.967	25	5	24	1	30	4
Stevens, Dave, Iowa	1.000	6	1	2	0	3	1
Sturtze, Tanyon, Oklahoma City	.864	25	7	12	3	22	3
Sullivan, Scott, Indianapolis	1.000	19	2	6	0	8	3
Swartzbaugh, Dave, Iowa	1.000	24	10	20	0	30	1
Tabaka, Jeff, Indianapolis*	1.000	58	2	3	0	5	0
Tapani, Kevin, Iowa	.800	1	4	0	1	5	0
Telemaco, Amaury, Iowa	.906	18	12	17	3	32	0
Thomas, Larry, Nashville*	.875	44	0	7	1	8	0
Tomko, Brett, Indianapolis	1.000	10	1	8	0	9	0
Toth, Robert, Omaha	1.000	15	9	2	0	11	0
Urbani, Thomas, O.C.*	.917	21	3	8	1	12	0
Van Poppel, Todd, Omaha	.833	11	2	3	1	6	2
VanRyn, Ben, Iowa*	.917	51	1	10	1	12	0
Veres, Randy, Omaha	1.000	11	0	1	0	1	0
Walker, Mike, Indianapolis	.963	55	8	18	1	27	0
Wall, Donne, New Orleans	1.000	17	11	20	0	31	1
Warren, Brian, Oklahoma City	.938	41	14	16	2	32	2
Watkins, Scott, Omaha*	1.000	9	0	1	0	1	0
Weathers, David, Buffalo	.933	11	5	9	1	15	1
White, Gabe, Indianapolis*	1.000	20	3	7	0	10	0
Whiteside, Matt, Oklahoma City	1.000	10	3	4	0	7	0
Wiegandt, Scott, Louisville*	1.000	40	2	2	0	4	0
Williams, Mike, Omaha	.947	20	4	14	1	19	2
Williams, Mitch, Omaha*	1.000	3	0	3	0	3	0
Williams, Todd, Indianapolis	.667	12	0	2	1	3	0
Wood, Kerry, Iowa	.889	10	2	6	1	9	1
Woods, Brian, Nashville	.700	14	3	4	3	10	0
Wright, Jaret, Buffalo	.875	7	1	6	1	8	0
York, Mike, Oklahoma City	1.000	4	1	1	0	2	0
Zimmerman, Mike, Omaha	.750	7	3	0	1	4	0

PITCHERS WITH TWO OR MORE TEAMS

Player, Team	Pct.	G	PO	A	E	TC	DP
Cabrera, Jose, Buffalo	1.000	5	0	1	0	1	0
Cabrera, Jose, New Orleans	1.000	31	1	3	0	4	1
Graves, Danny, Buffalo	1.000	19	3	16	0	19	2
Graves, Danny, Indianapolis	.500	11	1	0	1	2	0
Miranda, Angel, Buffalo*	1.000	9	1	2	0	3	0
Miranda, Angel, Oklahoma City*	1.000	2	1	0	0	1	0
Morman, Alvin, New Orleans*	1.000	8	0	3	0	3	0
Morman, Alvin, Buffalo*	.000	3	0	0	0	0	0
Service, Scott, Indianapolis	1.000	33	0	4	0	4	0
Service, Scott, Omaha	.667	16	0	2	1	3	0

The following players did not have any fielding statistics at the positions indicated or appeared only as a designated hitter, pinch-hitter or pinch-runner: Badorek, p; Benes, p; Berblinger, of; Blosser, p; Busch, p; Candaele, c; Carrasco, p; Castillo, p; Christopherson, p; Castleberry, 3b; A. Diaz, p; Osmani Estrada, p; Gulan, of; Hart, p; Heiserman, p; M. Hubbard, of; Jones, p; Kirkreit, p; Manzanillo, p; J. Montgomery, p; Mora, p; Mounce, p; Powell, p; Probst, p; Reynolds, p; Rupp, p; Rusch, p; Saylor, 3b; Schall, p; Shuey, p; Small, p; Stefanski, p; Tettleton, dh; R. Warner, p; Whitten, p; Winchester, p; Wrona, of.

LEAGUE CHAMPIONS

Year	Team	Pct.	Year	Team	Pct.	Year	Team	Pct.
1902—	Indianapolis	.683	1943—	Milwaukee	.596	1974—	Indianapolis	.578
1903—	St. Paul	.657		Columbus (3rd)‡	.532		Tulsa*	.567
1904—	St. Paul	.646	1944—	Milwaukee	.667	1975—	Evansville*	.566
1905—	Columbus	.658		Louisville (3rd)‡	.574		Denver	.569
1906—	Columbus	.615	1945—	Milwaukee	.604	1976—	Denver*	.632
1907—	Columbus	.584		Louisville (3rd)‡	.545		Omaha	.574
1908—	Indianapolis	.601	1946—	Louisville†	.601	1977—	Omaha	.563
1909—	Louisville	.554	1947—	Kansas City	.608		Denver*	.522
1910—	Minneapolis	.637		Milwaukee (3rd)†	.513	1978—	Indianapolis	.578
1911—	Minneapolis	.600	1948—	Indianapolis	.649		Omaha*	.489
1912—	Minneapolis	.636		St. Paul (3rd)‡	.558	1979—	Evansville*	.574
1913—	Milwaukee	.599	1949—	St. Paul	.608		Oklahoma City	.533
1914—	Milwaukee	.590		Indianapolis (2nd)‡	.604	1980—	Denver	.676
1915—	Minneapolis	.597	1950—	Minneapolis	.584		Springfield*	.551
1916—	Louisville	.605		Columbus (3rd)‡	.549	1981—	Omaha	.581
1917—	Indianapolis	.588	1951—	Milwaukee†	.623		Denver*	.559
1918—	Kansas City	.589	1952—	Milwaukee	.656	1982—	Indianapolis*	.551
1919—	St. Paul	.610		Kansas City (2nd)‡	.578		Omaha	.518
1920—	St. Paul	.701	1953—	Toledo	.584	1983—	Louisville	.578
1921—	Louisville	.583		Kansas City (2nd)‡	.571		Denver‡	.545
1922—	St. Paul	.641	1954—	Indianapolis	.625	1984—	Denver	.513
1923—	Kansas City	.675		Louisville (2nd)‡	.556		Louisville‡	.510
1924—	St. Paul	.578	1955—	Minneapolis†	.597	1985—	Oklahoma City	.556
1925—	Louisville	.635	1956—	Indianapolis†	.597		Louisville*	.521
1926—	Louisville	.629	1957—	Wichita	.604	1986—	Indianapolis*	.563
1927—	Toledo	.601		Denver (2nd)†	.584		Denver	.535
1928—	Indianapolis	.593	1958—	Charleston	.589	1987—	Denver	.564
1929—	Kansas City	.665		Minneapolis (3rd)‡	.536		Indianapolis‡	.536
1930—	Louisville	.608	1959—	Louisville§	.599	1988—	Indianapolis	.627
1931—	St. Paul	.623		Omaha§	.516		Omaha	.570
1932—	Minneapolis	.595		Minneapolis (2nd)‡	.586	1989—	Indianapolis*	.596
1933—	Columbus*	.604	1960—	Denver	.571		Omaha	.507
	Minneapolis	.562		Louisville (2nd)‡	.556	1990—	Omaha*	.589
1934—	Minneapolis	.570	1961—	Indianapolis	.573		Nashville	.585
	Columbus*	.556		Louisville (2nd)‡	.553	1991—	Buffalo	.566
1935—	Minneapolis	.591	1962—	Indianapolis	.605		Denver*	.549
1936—	Milwaukee†	.584		Louisville (4th)‡	.486	1992—	Buffalo	.604
1937—	Columbus†	.584	1963-1968—Did not operate.				Oklahoma City*	.514
1938—	St. Paul	.596	1969—	Omaha	.607	1993—	Iowa*	.590
	Kansas City (2nd)‡	.556	1970—	Omaha*	.529		Nashville	.566
1939—	Kansas City	.695		Denver	.504	1994—	Indianapolis‡	.601
	Louisville (4th)‡	.490	1971—	Indianapolis	.604		Nashville	.576
1940—	Kansas City	.625		Denver*	.521	1995—	Indianapolis	.611
	Louisville (4th)‡	.500	1972—	Wichita	.621		Louisville‡	.514
1941—	Columbus†	.621		Evansville*	.593	1996—	Buffalo	.583
1942—	Kansas City	.549	1973—	Iowa	.610		Oklahoma City‡	.514
	Columbus (3rd)‡	.532		Tulsa*	.504	1997—	Buffalo‡	.604
							Iowa	.517

*Won playoff (East vs. West). †Won championship and four-team playoff. ‡Won four-team playoff. §Respective Eastern and Western division winners.

CLASS AAA *American Association*

INTERNATIONAL LEAGUE

The International League will expand to 14 teams in 1998. In addition to the 10 teams that played in the league in 1997, Class AAA newcomer Durham and three teams from the disbanded American Association will join. The 1998 directories for those three former American Association teams—Buffalo, Indianapolis and Louisville—can be found on page 365.

LEAGUE OFFICE

President
Randy Mobley

Address
55 S. High St., Suite 202
Dublin, OH 43017

Phone
614-791-9300

TEAMS

CHARLOTTE KNIGHTS
V.P./general manager
Marty Steele
Manager
Fredi Gonzalez
Ballpark (capacity, surface)
Knights Castle (10,005, grass)
Affiliation
Marlins
Address
P.O. Box 1207
Fort Mill, SC 29716-1207
Phone
803-548-8050

COLUMBUS CLIPPERS
General manager
Ken Schnacke
Manager
To be announced
Ballpark (capacity, surface)
Cooper Stadium (15,000, artificial)
Affiliation
Yankees
Address
1155 W. Mound St.
Columbus, OH 43223
Phone
614-462-5250

DURHAM BULLS
General manager
Peter Anlyan
Manager
To be announced
Ballpark (capacity, surface)
Durham Bulls Athletic Park
(10,000, grass)
Affiliation
Devil Rays
Address
409 Blackwell St.
Durham, NC 27702
Phone
919-687-6500

NORFOLK TIDES
General manager
Dave Rosenfield
Manager
To be announced
Ballpark (capacity, surface)
Harbor Park (12,059, grass)
Affiliation
Mets

Address
150 Park Ave.
Norfolk, VA 23510
Phone
757-622-2222

OTTAWA LYNX
Director of baseball operations
Joe Bohringer
Manager
Pat Kelly
Ballpark (capacity, surface)
Jetform Park (10,332, grass)
Affiliation
Expos
Address
300 Coventry Rd.
Ottawa, Ontario K1K 4P5
Phone
613-747-5969

PAWTUCKET RED SOX
General manager
Lou Schwechheimer
Manager
Ken Macha
Ballpark (capacity, surface)
McCoy Stadium (7,002, grass)
Affiliation
Red Sox
Address
P.O. Box 2365
Pawtucket, RI 02861
Phone
401-724-7300

RICHMOND BRAVES
General manager
Bruce Baldwin
Manager
Jeff Cox
Ballpark (capacity, surface)
The Diamond (12,156, grass)
Affiliation
Braves
Address
P.O. Box 6667
Richmond, VA 23230
Phone
804-359-4444

ROCHESTER RED WINGS
General manager
Dan Mason
Manager
Marv Foley

Ballpark (capacity, surface)
Frontier Field (10,600, grass)
Affiliation
Orioles
Address
1 Morrie Silver Way
Rochester, NY 14608
Phone
716-454-1001

SCRANTON/WILKES-BARRE RED BARONS
General manager
Rick Muntean
Manager
To be announced
Ballpark (capacity, surface)
Lackawanna County Stadium (10,832, artificial)
Affiliation
Phillies
Address
P.O. Box 3449
Scranton, PA 18505
Phone
717-969-2255

SYRACUSE SKY CHIEFS
General manager
John Simone
Manager
Terry Bevington
Ballpark (capacity, surface)
P&C Stadium (11,100, artificial)
Affiliation
Blue Jays
Address
P&C Stadium
Syracuse, NY 13208
Phone
315-474-7833

TOLEDO MUD HENS
General manager
Gene Cook
Manager
Gene Roof
Ballpark (capacity, surface)
Ned Skeldon Stadium (10,025, grass)
Affiliation
Tigers
Address
P.O. Box 6212
Toledo, OH 43614
Phone
419-893-9483

EAST DIVISION

Team	W	L	T	Pct.	GB
Rochester (Orioles)	83	58	0	.589	....
Pawtucket (Red Sox)	81	60	0	.574	2
Scranton/Wilkes-Barre (Phillies)	66	76	0	.465	17¹/₂
Syracuse (Blue Jays)	55	87	0	.387	28¹/₂
Ottawa (Expos)	54	86	0	.386	28¹/₂

WEST DIVISION

Team	W	L	T	Pct.	GB
Columbus (Yankees)	79	63	0	.556	....
Charlotte (Marlins)	76	65	0	.539	2¹/₂
Norfolk (Mets)	75	67	0	.528	4
Richmond (Braves)	70	72	0	.493	9
Toledo (Tigers)	68	73	0	.482	10¹/₂

COMPOSITE

Team	Roc.	Paw.	Col.	Char.	Nor.	Rich.	Tol.	SWB	Syr.	Ott.	W	L	T	Pct.	GB
Rochester (Orioles)	....	5	9	8	8	8	8	9	15	13	83	58	0	.589	....
Pawtucket (Red Sox)	12	....	4	7	8	6	11	10	12	11	81	60	0	.574	2
Columbus (Yankees)	5	10	....	7	11	10	9	9	8	10	79	63	0	.556	4¹/₂
Charlotte (Marlins)	6	7	11	....	7	12	8	9	7	9	76	65	0	.539	7
Norfolk (Mets)	6	6	7	11	....	7	10	8	10	10	75	67	0	.528	8¹/₂
Richmond (Braves)	6	8	8	6	11	....	9	7	5	10	70	72	0	.493	13¹/₂
Toledo (Tigers)	6	3	9	10	8	9	....	8	8	7	68	73	0	.482	15
Scranton/Wilkes-Barre (Phillies)	9	8	5	5	6	7	6	....	12	8	66	76	0	.465	17¹/₂
Syracuse (Blue Jays)	3	6	6	7	4	9	6	6	....	8	55	87	0	.387	28¹/₂
Ottawa (Expos)	5	7	4	4	4	4	6	10	10	....	54	86	0	.386	28¹/₂

Major league affiliations in parentheses.

PLAYOFFS: Rochester defeated Pawtucket, three games to one; Columbus defeated Charlotte, three games to one; Rochester defeated Columbus, three games to two, to win league championship.

REGULAR-SEASON ATTENDANCE: Charlotte, 318,102; Columbus, 507,810; Norfolk, 507,328; Ottawa, 266,568; Pawtucket, 474, 557; Richmond, 512,727; Rochester, 512,570; Scranton/Wilkes-Barre, 441,413; Syracuse, 400,804; Toledo, 325,532. Total—4,267,411. Playoffs (13 games)—47,074. Class AAA All-Star Game at Des Moines—11,183.

MANAGERS: Charlotte, Carlos Tosca; Columbus, Stump Merrill; Norfolk, Rick Dempsey; Ottawa, Pat Kelly; Pawtucket, Ken Macha; Richmond, Bill Dancy; Rochester, Marv Foley; Scranton/Wilkes-Barre, Marc Bombard; Syracuse, Garth Iorg; Toledo, Glenn Ezell (through June 5) and Gene Roof (June 6 through end of season). Managerial record of teams with more than one manager: Toledo, Ezell, 33-24, Roof, 35-49.

ALL-STAR TEAM: 1B—Roberto Petagine, Norfolk; 2B—Frank Catalanotto, Toledo; 3B—Arquimedez Pozo, Pawtucket; SS—Matt Howard, Columbus; OF—Danny Clyburn, Rochester; Tony Barron, Scranton/Wilkes-Barre; Todd Dunwoody, Charlotte; C—Bobby Estalella, Scranton/Wilkes-Barre; DH—Russ Morman, Charlotte; Utility—Randall Simon, Richmond; Starting pitcher—Brian Rose, Pawtucket; Relief pitcher—Eddie Gaillard, Toledo; Most Valuable Player—Roberto Petagine, Norfolk; Most Valuable Pitcher—Brian Rose, Pawtucket; Rookie of the Year—Brian Rose, Pawtucket; Manager of the Year—Marv Foley, Rochester.

1997 BATTING

TEAM

Team	Avg.	G	TPA	AB	R	H	TB	2B	3B	HR	RBI	SH	SF	HP	BB	IBB	SO	SB	CS	GDP	LOB	ShO	Slg.	OBP
Scr./Wil.-Bar.	.277	142	5346	4714	715	1304	2033	303	36	118	664	35	48	53	496	17	867	70	43	113	992	9	.431	.349
Rochester	.273	141	5367	4750	702	1295	1930	248	39	103	621	38	38	56	485	15	879	116	46	136	1022	6	.406	.345
Richmond	.271	142	5342	4735	680	1284	1952	266	36	110	625	60	37	38	472	22	963	70	50	114	952	6	.412	.340
Columbus	.268	142	5450	4751	768	1274	2109	266	46	159	728	25	33	54	587	24	920	124	70	109	1004	7	.444	.353
Charlotte	.268	141	5170	4529	720	1214	2045	268	28	169	676	54	38	41	508	35	1013	125	52	94	906	9	.452	.345
Norfolk	.267	142	5405	4727	659	1260	1940	245	21	131	610	48	38	48	544	27	993	91	58	104	1035	5	.410	.346
Ottawa	.260	140	5153	4530	636	1177	1813	240	30	112	592	51	47	42	483	31	915	131	65	126	889	11	.400	.334
Pawtucket	.256	141	5325	4692	692	1200	1933	212	19	161	632	33	33	38	529	15	974	105	60	119	944	9	.412	.334
Syracuse	.254	142	5371	4695	617	1191	1868	245	24	128	566	45	32	62	537	25	1008	81	58	85	1054	13	.398	.336
Toledo	.245	141	5193	4615	596	1132	1781	224	31	121	552	44	41	40	453	18	1030	107	56	91	928	10	.386	.316

INDIVIDUAL

TOP QUALIFIERS FOR BATTING CHAMPIONSHIP

Minimum 383 plate appearances. *Lefthanded batter. †Switch-hitter.

Player, Team	Avg.	G	TPA	AB	R	H	TB	2B	3B	HR	RBI	SH	SF	HP	BB	IBB	SO	SB	CS	GDP	Slg.	OBP
Gregg, Tommy, Richmond*	.332	115	435	385	52	128	193	36	1	9	54	0	3	1	46	6	64	3	3	7	.501	.402
Matos, Francisco, Rochester	.324	101	414	389	51	126	163	17	4	4	51	9	3	4	9	0	42	8	2	15	.419	.343
Morman, Russ, Charlotte	.319	117	462	395	82	126	246	17	2	33	99	0	5	4	58	11	89	3	2	6	.623	.407
Petagine, Roberto, Norfolk*	.317	129	543	441	90	140	267	32	1	31	100	1	8	8	85	3	92	0	1	6	.605	.430
Zuber, Jon, Scr./W.-B.*	.315	126	522	435	85	137	196	37	2	6	64	1	3	3	79	0	53	3	4	11	.451	.421
Doster, David, Scr./W.-B.	.315	108	453	410	70	129	213	32	2	16	79	2	3	8	30	1	60	5	5	9	.520	.370
Howard, Matt, Columbus	.312	122	548	478	90	149	209	28	7	6	67	3	10	54	1	33	22	7	12	.437	.391
Agbayani, Benny, Norfolk	.310	127	544	468	90	145	206	24	2	11	51	0	3	6	67	0	106	29	14	13	.440	.401
Simon, Randall, Richmond*	.308	133	542	519	62	160	249	45	1	14	102	1	1	4	17	2	76	1	6	18	.480	.335
Davis, Tommy, Rochester	.304	119	487	438	74	133	204	22	2	15	62	3	1	2	43	2	90	6	1	16	.466	.368
Clyburn, Danny, Rochester	.300	137	583	520	91	156	259	33	5	20	76	0	2	8	53	3	107	14	4	7	.498	.372
Catalanotto, Frank, Toledo*	.300	134	564	500	75	150	236	32	3	16	68	1	6	10	47	6	80	12	11	9	.472	.368
Butler, Rich, Syracuse*	.300	137	607	537	93	161	281	30	9	24	87	3	3	4	60	2	107	20	7	11	.523	.373
Cruz, Ivan, Columbus*	.300	116	497	417	69	125	234	35	1	24	95	0	4	11	65	10	78	4	5	6	.561	.404
Robertson, Mike, Scr./W.-B.*	.298	121	485	416	61	124	183	17	3	12	72	1	6	4	58	4	67	0	2	9	.440	.384

DEPARTMENTAL LEADERS: G—Rich Butler, Clyburn, 137 each; AB—Rich Butler, 537; R—Rich Butler, 93; H—Rich Butler, 161; TB—Rich Butler, 281; 2B—Simon, 45; 3B—Tyler, 10; HR—Morman, 33; RBI—Simon, 102; SH—T. Perez, 14; SF—Daubach, 10; HP—Barron, 12; BB—Petagine, 85; IBB—Morman, 11; SO—Bartee, 154; SB—Bartee, 33; CS—Agbayani, Sadler, 14 each; GIDP—Simon, 18; Slg.—Morman, .623; OBP—Petagine, .430.

CLASS AAA International League

ALL PLAYERS

*Lefthanded batter. †Switch-hitter.

Player, Team	Avg.	G	TPA	AB	R	H	TB	2B	3B	HR	RBI	SH	SF	HP	BB	IBB	SO	SB	CS	GDP	Slg.	OBP
Abad, Andy, Pawtucket*	.273	68	267	227	28	62	96	7	0	9	32	1	1	2	36	1	47	3	2	4	.423	.376
Acevedo, Juan, Norfolk	.211	18	23	19	4	4	5	1	0	0	1	3	0	0	1	0	3	0	0	0	.263	.250
Agbayani, Benny, Norfolk	.310	127	544	468	90	145	206	24	2	11	51	0	3	6	67	0	106	29	14	13	.440	.401
Aldrete, Mike, Syracuse*	.297	27	93	74	8	22	27	5	0	0	8	1	1	0	17	0	15	0	0	2	.365	.424
Alfonseca, Antonio, Charlotte	.333	46	3	3	0	1	1	0	0	0	0	0	0	0	0	0	0	0	0	0	.333	.333
Allison, Chris, Pawtucket	.280	8	26	25	2	7	9	2	0	0	1	0	0	0	1	0	0	0	1	1	.360	.308
Alvarez, Tavo, Ottawa	.000	37	10	8	0	0	0	0	0	0	0	0	1	0	1	0	3	0	0	0	.000	.111
Amador, Manuel, Scr./W.-B.†	.343	23	79	70	12	24	32	5	0	1	9	0	2	1	6	0	11	0	0	2	.457	.392
Andrews, Shane, Ottawa	.250	3	13	12	3	3	6	0	0	1	1	0	0	0	1	0	0	0	0	1	.500	.308
Angeli, Doug, Scr./W.-B.	.224	78	275	241	24	54	75	11	2	2	19	3	3	1	27	3	53	0	3	4	.311	.301
Aude, Rich, Syracuse	.283	100	390	350	48	99	171	23	2	15	59	0	3	11	26	2	88	3	0	9	.489	.349
Ayrault, Joe, Richmond	.286	18	61	56	11	16	27	2	0	3	5	1	0	0	4	0	17	0	0	0	.482	.333
Azuaje, Jesus, Norfolk	.306	22	58	49	11	15	21	3	0	1	6	0	0	2	7	1	8	1	0	2	.429	.414
Banks, Willie, Columbus	.000	35	2	2	1	0	0	0	0	0	0	0	0	0	0	0	1	0	0	0	.000	.000
Barker, Glen, Toledo	.191	21	55	47	9	9	13	1	0	1	3	2	0	1	5	0	15	6	2	0	.277	.283
Barker, Tim, Columbus	.279	65	240	208	36	58	87	10	2	5	30	0	0	0	32	0	41	14	6	5	.418	.375
Barron, Tony, Scr./W.-B.	.328	92	371	329	51	108	191	21	4	18	78	0	3	12	27	4	64	3	4	11	.581	.396
Bartee, Kimera, Toledo†	.218	136	574	501	67	109	145	13	7	3	33	12	4	4	52	1	154	33	9	3	.289	.294
Bautista, Danny, Richmond	.282	46	193	170	28	48	70	10	3	2	28	2	1	1	19	0	30	1	0	9	.412	.356
Beech, Matt, Scr./W.-B.*	.200	5	5	5	0	1	1	0	0	0	1	0	0	0	0	0	3	0	0	0	.200	.200
Bellinger, Clay, Columbus	.274	111	460	416	55	114	187	31	3	12	59	2	1	7	34	2	74	10	4	10	.450	.338
Benjamin, Mike, Pawtucket	.248	33	117	105	12	26	44	4	1	4	12	2	0	2	8	0	20	4	1	2	.419	.313
Bennett, Gary, Pawtucket	.214	71	246	224	16	48	69	7	1	4	22	1	1	2	18	0	39	1	1	10	.308	.278
Bennett, Shayne, Ottawa	.000	25	1	1	0	0	0	0	0	0	0	0	0	0	0	0	0	0	0	0	.000	.000
Berg, David, Charlotte	.295	117	495	424	76	125	190	26	6	9	47	10	3	3	55	1	71	16	7	13	.448	.377
Berry, Mike, Rochester	.299	54	192	177	23	53	73	11	3	1	19	0	1	1	13	0	31	1	1	4	.412	.349
Bieser, Steve, Norfolk*	.164	41	138	122	6	20	25	5	0	0	4	2	0	5	9	0	20	4	3	1	.205	.250
Blum, Geoffrey, Ottawa†	.248	118	480	407	59	101	135	21	2	3	35	12	6	3	52	1	73	14	6	6	.332	.333
Bohanon, Brian, Norfolk*	.000	16	14	11	0	0	0	0	0	0	0	3	0	0	0	0	3	0	0	0	.000	.000
Borowski, Joe, Richmond	.000	21	3	3	0	0	0	0	0	0	0	0	0	0	0	0	0	0	0	0	.000	.000
Borrero, Richie, Pawtucket	.255	15	54	51	4	13	20	1	0	2	6	1	1	0	1	0	17	0	1	0	.392	.264
Bowers, Brent, Scr./W.-B.*	.255	39	120	110	15	28	39	2	0	3	7	0	1	1	8	0	28	1	1	1	.355	.308
Bream, Scott, Toledo†	.231	30	104	91	11	21	22	1	0	0	0	0	0	0	13	0	31	0	1	2	.242	.327
Brito, Jorge, Syracuse	.233	8	37	30	3	7	16	3	0	2	4	2	0	2	3	0	10	1	0	1	.533	.343
Brock, Chris, Richmond	.148	21	28	27	1	4	5	1	0	0	0	1	0	0	0	0	4	0	0	1	.185	.148
Brow, Scott, Richmond	.000	61	4	1	0	0	0	0	0	0	0	2	0	0	1	0	1	0	0	0	.000	.500
Brown, Ron, Columbus	.182	10	36	33	4	6	8	0	1	0	1	1	0	0	2	0	3	1	0	0	.242	.229
Bryant, Pat, Pawtucket	.294	9	35	34	3	10	14	2	1	0	4	0	0	0	1	0	11	2	0	2	.412	.314
Buchanan, Brian, Columbus	.279	18	70	61	8	17	30	1	0	4	7	1	1	3	4	0	11	2	1	3	.492	.348
Bullett, Scott, Rochester*	.250	136	566	512	73	128	195	24	8	9	58	0	2	7	45	2	112	19	11	17	.381	.318
Bullinger, Kirk, Ottawa	.000	22	1	1	0	0	0	0	0	0	0	0	0	0	0	0	0	0	0	0	.000	.000
Bunch, Mel, Ottawa	.273	17	14	11	1	3	3	0	0	0	0	1	0	0	2	0	4	0	1	0	.273	.385
Burton, Darren, Scr./W.-B.†	.249	70	280	253	34	63	109	16	3	8	39	1	4	3	19	1	40	3	0	6	.431	.305
Bush, Homer, Columbus	.247	74	312	275	36	68	90	10	3	2	26	7	4	1	25	0	56	12	7	6	.327	.308
Butler, Rich, Syracuse*	.300	137	607	537	93	161	281	30	9	24	87	3	3	4	60	2	107	20	7	11	.523	.373
Butler, Rob, Scr./W.-B.*	.282	21	72	71	8	20	24	4	0	0	9	0	0	1	0	0	9	0	0	4	.338	.292
Byrd, Paul, Richmond	.000	3	2	1	0	0	0	0	0	0	0	1	0	0	0	0	0	0	0	1	.000	.000
Cabrera, Jolbert, Ottawa	.283	68	207	191	28	54	72	10	4	0	12	4	1	0	11	0	31	15	5	5	.377	.320
Cabrera, Orlando, Ottawa	.262	31	135	122	17	32	47	5	2	2	14	1	3	2	7	0	16	8	1	0	.385	.306
Carey, Todd, Pawtucket*	.216	113	424	380	35	82	134	16	0	12	58	4	4	2	34	1	114	1	2	11	.353	.281
Carlyle, Ken, Richmond	.167	16	8	6	0	1	1	0	0	0	1	1	0	1	0	0	1	0	0	0	.167	.286
Carney, Bartt, Rochester†	.000	4	9	6	1	0	0	0	0	0	0	0	0	0	3	0	2	0	0	0	.000	.333
Carpenter, Bubba, Columbus*	.280	85	323	271	47	76	114	12	4	6	39	3	1	0	48	0	46	4	8	3	.421	.388
Casanova, Raul, Toledo	.195	12	45	41	1	8	11	0	0	1	3	0	1	0	3	0	8	0	0	1	.268	.244
Castillo, Alberto, Norfolk	.217	34	104	83	4	18	22	1	0	1	8	3	1	0	17	1	16	1	0	5	.265	.347
Castillo, Luis, Toledo	.354	37	149	130	25	46	51	5	0	0	5	3	0	0	16	1	22	8	6	2	.392	.425
Catalanotto, Frank, Toledo*	.300	134	564	500	75	150	236	32	3	16	68	1	6	10	47	6	80	12	11	9	.472	.368
Cather, Mike, Richmond	.000	13	2	2	0	0	0	0	0	0	0	0	0	0	0	0	1	0	0	0	.000	.000
Chamberlain, Wes, Norfolk	.274	97	371	336	33	92	133	16	2	7	50	0	1	10	24	1	58	7	2	13	.396	.340
Chavez, Raul, Ottawa	.245	92	338	310	31	76	105	17	0	4	46	3	3	4	18	1	42	1	3	9	.339	.293
Chergey, Dan, Charlotte	.333	27	4	3	0	1	1	0	0	0	0	0	0	0	1	0	1	0	0	0	.333	.500
Clapinski, Chris, Charlotte†	.262	110	405	340	62	89	153	24	2	12	52	6	2	9	48	4	64	14	2	9	.450	.366
Clyburn, Danny, Rochester	.300	137	583	520	91	156	259	33	5	20	76	0	2	8	53	0	107	14	4	17	.498	.372
Cole, Alex, Charlotte*	.210	39	126	105	20	22	33	5	0	2	7	2	0	1	18	0	20	4	1	1	.314	.331
Coleman, Michael, Pawtucket	.319	28	128	113	27	36	70	9	2	7	19	0	1	2	12	0	27	4	2	2	.619	.391
Cornelius, Reid, Charlotte	.103	22	32	29	2	3	3	0	0	0	1	2	1	0	0	0	12	0	0	0	.103	.100
Correia, Rod, Pawtucket	.195	35	137	128	17	25	34	4	1	1	15	1	1	2	5	0	14	3	0	4	.266	.235
Cradle, Rickey, Syracuse	.120	11	29	25	4	3	6	0	0	1	3	0	0	2	2	0	9	0	1	0	.240	.241
Crawford, Joe, Norfolk*	.136	17	25	22	0	3	4	1	0	0	0	3	0	0	0	0	4	0	0	1	.182	.136
Crespo, Felipe, Syracuse†	.259	80	344	290	53	75	123	12	0	12	26	2	2	4	46	0	38	7	7	1	.424	.365
Crow, Dean, Toledo	.000	18	1	1	0	0	0	0	0	0	0	0	0	0	0	0	0	0	0	0	.000	.000
Cruz, Ivan, Columbus*	.300	116	497	417	69	125	234	35	1	24	95	0	4	11	65	10	78	4	5	5	.561	.404
Daal, Omar, Ott.-Syr.*	.333	7	3	3	0	1	1	0	0	0	0	0	0	0	0	0	0	0	0	0	.333	.333
Daubach, Brian, Charlotte*	.278	136	543	461	66	128	235	40	2	21	93	1	10	6	65	4	126	1	8	7	.510	.367
Davis, Tommy, Rochester	.304	119	487	438	74	133	204	22	2	15	62	3	1	2	43	2	90	6	1	16	.466	.368
Delgado, Alex, Charlotte	.211	14	45	38	1	8	9	1	0	0	2	1	0	0	3	0	7	0	0	1	.237	.262
DeLaCruz, Lorenzo, Syracuse	.219	39	134	128	11	28	47	4	0	5	13	0	0	0	6	1	35	1	2	0	.367	.254
Delvecchio, Nick, Columbus*	.179	31	113	95	16	17	32	5	1	3	4	1	0	0	17	0	39	1	0	3	.337	.310
Diaz, Alex, Norfolk†	.077	7	28	26	0	2	3	1	0	0	1	0	0	0	2	0	3	0	0	2	.115	.143

Player, Team	Avg.	G	TPA	AB	R	H	TB	2B	3B	HR	RBI	SH	SF	HP	BB	IBB	SO	SB	CS	GDP	Slg.	OBP
Dodson, Bo, Pawtucket*	.295	17	67	61	8	18	24	6	0	0	6	0	0	1	5	0	11	0	0	0	.393	.358
Doster, David, Scr./W.-B.	.315	108	453	410	70	129	213	32	2	16	79	2	3	8	30	1	60	5	5	9	.520	.370
Dougherty, Jim, Norfolk	.250	49	5	4	2	1	1	0	0	0	1	1	0	0	0	0	0	0	0	0	.250	.250
Dunwoody, Todd, Charlotte*	.262	107	444	401	74	105	204	16	7	23	62	0	1	3	39	2	129	25	3	8	.509	.331
Dyer, Mike, Richmond	.000	29	1	1	0	0	0	0	0	0	0	0	0	0	0	0	1	0	0	0	.000	.000
Edmondson, Brian, Norfolk	.200	31	6	5	1	1	1	0	0	0	0	0	1	0	0	0	3	0	0	0	.200	.200
Espinosa, Ramon, Norfolk	.338	27	80	77	7	26	31	3	1	0	8	0	0	1	2	1	10	2	1	1	.403	.363
Estalella, Bobby, Scr./W.-B.	.233	123	500	433	63	101	181	32	0	16	65	0	2	9	56	0	109	3	0	14	.418	.332
Evans, Tom, Syracuse	.263	107	442	376	60	99	163	17	1	15	65	1	3	9	53	1	104	1	2	4	.434	.365
Falteisek, Steve, Ottawa	.200	22	19	15	0	3	3	0	0	0	1	2	0	1	1	0	2	0	0	1	.200	.294
Figga, Mike, Columbus	.244	110	414	390	48	95	153	14	4	12	54	1	3	2	18	0	104	3	3	9	.392	.278
Fiore, Tony, Scr./W.-B.	.000	9	6	4	0	0	0	0	0	0	0	0	0	1	0	1	0	3	0	0	.000	.200
Flores, Jose, Scr./W.-B.	.250	71	241	204	32	51	70	14	1	1	18	5	2	2	28	1	51	3	1	2	.343	.343
Floyd, Cliff, Charlotte*	.366	39	142	131	27	48	85	10	0	9	33	0	0	1	10	1	29	7	2	3	.649	.415
Forbes, P.J., Rochester	.272	116	486	434	67	118	168	22	2	8	54	8	3	6	35	0	42	15	4	11	.387	.333
Fortugno, Tim, Scr./W.-B.*	.000	19	1	1	0	0	0	0	0	0	0	0	0	0	0	0	1	0	0	0	.000	.000
Foster, Jim, Rochester	.556	3	12	9	4	5	7	2	0	0	4	0	0	0	3	0	0	0	0	1	.778	.667
Fox, Andy, Columbus*	.274	95	377	318	66	87	124	11	4	6	33	2	1	1	54	5	64	28	11	5	.390	.380
Fox, Chad, Richmond	.000	13	2	1	0	0	0	0	0	0	0	0	1	0	0	0	0	0	0	0	.000	.000
Fox, Eric, Roch.-S./W.-B.†	.280	92	288	264	41	74	106	17	3	3	26	0	3	0	21	1	50	2	3	10	.402	.330
Franco, Matt, Norfolk*	.269	7	29	26	5	7	9	2	0	0	0	0	0	1	2	1	2	0	0	0	.346	.345
Frazier, Lou, Rochester†	.248	84	345	302	40	75	101	12	4	2	39	3	3	1	36	1	68	24	6	9	.334	.327
Fullmer, Brad, Ottawa*	.297	24	101	91	13	27	43	7	0	3	17	0	5	2	3	0	10	1	1	3	.473	.317
Geisler, Phil, Norfolk*	.256	109	367	336	28	86	137	24	0	9	57	0	6	1	24	4	90	2	5	8	.408	.302
Giannelli, Ray, Syracuse*	.175	38	103	80	9	14	18	4	0	0	8	2	2	1	18	1	20	1	1	3	.225	.327
Gilbert, Shawn, Norfolk	.264	78	337	288	53	76	115	13	1	8	33	3	1	2	43	1	64	16	4	2	.399	.362
Giovanola, Ed, Richmond*	.291	116	478	395	65	115	154	23	5	2	46	11	7	1	64	0	56	2	2	8	.390	.385
Gomes, Wayne, Scr./W.-B.	.000	26	2	2	0	0	0	0	0	0	0	0	0	0	0	0	1	0	0	0	.000	.000
Gonzalez, Gabe, Charlotte†	.000	37	2	2	0	0	0	0	0	0	0	0	0	0	0	0	1	0	0	0	.000	.000
Grace, Mike, Scr./W.-B.	.000	12	8	7	0	0	0	0	0	0	0	0	0	0	0	0	3	0	0	1	.000	.000
Green, Tyler, Scr./W.-B.	.154	12	14	13	1	2	2	0	0	0	1	1	0	0	0	0	6	0	0	1	.154	.154
Greene, Charlie, Norfolk	.206	76	251	238	27	49	80	7	0	8	28	0	2	2	9	0	54	1	0	4	.336	.239
Gregg, Tommy, Richmond*	.332	115	435	385	52	128	193	36	1	9	54	0	3	1	46	6	64	3	3	7	.501	.402
Gresham, Kris, Rochester	.107	13	30	28	1	3	4	1	0	0	0	0	0	0	2	0	8	0	0	1	.143	.167
Gruber, Kelly, Rochester	.250	38	163	144	26	36	55	9	2	2	23	1	1	2	15	0	14	1	1	5	.382	.327
Hajek, Dave, Toledo	.217	72	278	253	27	55	85	14	2	4	32	2	2	0	21	0	18	0	2	7	.336	.275
Hall, Joe, Toledo	.251	75	299	271	35	68	108	18	2	6	30	0	4	2	22	0	48	2	1	10	.399	.308
Hamelin, Bob, Toledo*	.242	27	118	91	14	22	47	7	0	6	24	0	0	0	27	2	24	0	0	1	.516	.415
Hardtke, Jason, Norfolk†	.276	97	433	388	46	107	169	23	3	11	45	4	1	0	40	1	54	3	6	9	.436	.343
Hare, Shawn, Tol.-Col.*	.188	34	107	85	12	16	24	5	0	1	8	0	0	0	22	2	34	0	0	1	.282	.355
Harnisch, Pete, Norfolk	.667	3	3	3	0	2	2	0	0	0	1	0	0	0	0	0	1	0	0	0	.667	.667
Harrison, Tommy, Richmond	.125	22	21	16	1	2	2	0	0	0	0	0	3	0	2	0	9	0	0	1	.125	.222
Hartgraves, Dean, Richmond	.000	50	3	2	0	0	0	0	0	0	0	0	0	0	0	0	1	0	0	0	.000	.000
Hawblitzel, Ryan, Scr./W.-B.	.286	34	16	14	2	4	5	1	0	0	1	0	0	1	0	0	4	0	0	0	.357	.333
Heflin, Bronson, Scr./W.-B.	.000	35	1	1	0	0	0	0	0	0	0	0	0	0	0	0	0	0	0	0	.000	.000
Helms, Wes, Richmond	.191	32	126	110	11	21	34	4	0	3	15	0	1	5	10	1	34	1	1	4	.309	.286
Henderson, Rod, Ottawa	.200	26	20	15	1	3	8	2	0	1	5	4	0	0	1	0	5	0	0	0	.533	.250
Henry, Santiago, Syracuse	.241	44	121	116	15	28	41	5	1	2	16	1	1	1	2	0	21	5	1	3	.353	.258
Hernandez, Fernando, Toledo.	1.000	55	2	1	1	1	1	0	0	0	1	1	0	0	0	0	0	0	0	0	1.000	1.000
Hernandez, Livan, Charlotte	.357	14	14	14	1	5	7	2	0	0	0	0	0	0	0	0	1	0	0	0	.500	.357
Holbert, Ray, Toledo	.242	109	417	372	43	90	143	18	7	7	37	7	2	4	32	0	109	16	7	7	.384	.307
Hollins, Damon, Richmond	.265	134	553	498	73	132	229	31	3	20	63	6	1	3	45	4	84	7	2	18	.460	.329
Holman, Craig, Scr./W.-B.†	.000	48	2	2	0	0	0	0	0	0	0	0	0	0	0	0	0	0	0	0	.000	.000
Hostetler, Mike, Richmond	.000	5	2	1	0	0	0	0	0	0	0	0	0	0	0	0	1	0	0	0	.000	.000
Howard, Matt, Columbus	.312	122	548	478	90	149	209	28	7	6	67	3	3	10	54	1	33	22	7	12	.437	.391
Hudler, Rex, Scr./W.-B.	.333	3	9	9	0	3	3	0	0	0	0	0	0	0	0	0	0	0	0	0	.333	.333
Hurst, Jimmy, Toledo	.271	110	431	377	51	102	173	11	3	18	58	1	4	0	47	1	115	14	5	11	.459	.348
Hyers, Tim, Toledo*	.274	121	473	424	61	116	180	22	3	12	55	4	3	1	41	3	65	1	2	8	.425	.337
Hyzdu, Adam, Pawtucket	.276	119	492	413	77	114	206	21	1	23	84	1	2	4	72	0	113	10	6	6	.499	.387
Incaviglia, Pete, Columbus	.308	3	13	13	1	4	5	1	0	0	2	0	0	0	0	0	4	0	0	0	.385	.308
Isringhausen, Jason, Norfolk	.000	3	2	1	0	0	0	0	0	0	0	0	0	0	0	0	0	0	0	0	.000	.000
Jaime, Angel, Norfolk	.192	16	29	26	3	5	6	1	0	0	5	3	0	0	0	0	7	0	1	0	.231	.192
Jensen, Marcus, Toledo†	.175	24	91	80	5	14	19	5	0	0	9	2	0	0	9	0	25	0	0	0	.238	.258
Jimenez, D'Angelo, Col.†	.143	2	8	7	1	1	1	0	0	0	0	0	0	1	0	0	1	0	0	1	.143	.125
Johns, Keith, Rochester	.000	1	2	1	0	0	0	0	0	0	0	0	0	0	1	0	0	0	0	0	.000	.500
Johnson, Brian, Toledo	.143	7	22	21	0	3	5	2	0	0	1	0	1	0	0	0	2	0	0	0	.238	.136
Jones, Ryan, Syracuse	.138	41	147	123	8	17	33	5	1	3	16	0	4	3	15	0	28	0	2	2	.268	.241
Jordan, Kevin, Scr./W.-B.	.300	7	32	30	5	9	15	2	2	0	2	0	0	0	2	0	6	2	0	1	.500	.344
Jordan, Ricardo, Norfolk*	.000	34	2	1	0	0	0	0	0	0	0	0	0	0	0	0	1	0	0	0	.000	.000
Juelsgaard, Jarod, Charlotte	.111	21	10	9	1	1	1	0	0	0	0	2	1	0	0	0	3	0	0	1	.111	.111
Karp, Ryan, Scr./W.-B.*	.167	34	14	12	2	2	3	1	0	0	1	0	0	0	0	0	4	0	0	0	.250	.231
Kelly, Pat, Columbus	.341	11	48	44	8	15	25	4	0	2	6	0	0	0	4	1	6	1	1	1	.568	.396
Kmak, Joe, Charlotte	.237	36	107	93	7	22	30	6	1	0	12	2	1	0	11	1	28	1	0	3	.323	.314
Komminsk, Brad, Toledo	.667	1	3	3	0	2	3	1	0	0	1	0	0	0	0	0	0	0	0	0	1.000	.667
Kuilan, Hector, Charlotte	.103	14	41	39	3	4	4	0	0	0	3	0	0	0	2	0	8	0	0	2	.103	.146
Laker, Tim, Rochester	.259	79	333	290	45	75	121	11	1	11	37	0	4	5	34	1	49	1	2	4	.417	.342
Larkin, Andy, Charlotte	.048	28	23	21	0	1	1	0	0	0	1	0	1	0	0	0	11	0	0	0	.048	.091
Lawrence, Brian, Charlotte	.233	17	48	43	9	10	12	0	1	0	7	2	0	0	3	0	8	1	1	1	.279	.283
Ledee, Ricky, Columbus*	.306	43	192	170	38	52	96	12	1	10	39	0	0	1	21	0	49	4	0	5	.565	.385
Ledesma, Aaron, Rochester	.325	85	373	326	40	106	143	26	1	3	43	2	7	3	35	3	48	12	2	10	.439	.388
Lewis, T.R., Richmond	.295	117	413	363	65	107	158	20	5	7	58	1	7	5	37	2	71	8	3	9	.435	.362
Lidle, Cory, Norfolk	.125	7	9	8	0	1	1	0	0	0	0	1	0	0	0	0	5	0	0	1	.125	.125

Player, Team	Avg.	G	TPA	AB	R	H	TB	2B	3B	HR	RBI	SH	SF	HP	BB	IBB	SO	SB	CS	GDP	Slg.	OBP
Loewer, Carlton, Scr./W.-B.† ..	.053	29	23	19	1	1	1	0	0	0	0	2	0	1	1	0	8	0	0	0	.053	.143
Long, R.D., Columbus†	.184	19	52	49	6	9	17	2	0	2	6	0	1	0	2	0	18	2	0	0	.347	.212
Lopez, Jose, Norfolk	.333	2	6	6	1	2	2	0	0	0	0	0	0	0	0	0	2	0	0	0	.333	.333
Lopez, Luis, Norfolk†	.330	48	217	203	32	67	93	12	1	4	19	2	2	1	9	2	29	2	6	1	.458	.358
Lott, Billy, Ottawa	.222	32	119	108	12	24	35	5	0	2	18	1	2	0	8	1	22	1	1	5	.324	.271
Lovullo, Torey, Ottawa†	.141	28	72	64	6	9	12	3	0	0	6	0	1	1	6	0	13	0	0	3	.188	.222
Lowell, Mike, Columbus	.276	57	243	210	36	58	118	13	1	15	45	1	6	3	23	0	34	2	4	6	.562	.347
Lucca, Lou, Charlotte	.284	96	319	292	40	83	161	22	1	18	51	0	3	2	22	4	56	5	4	7	.551	.335
Luebbers, Larry, Richmond	.227	27	22	22	2	5	6	1	0	0	3	0	0	0	0	0	4	0	0	2	.273	.227
Lukachyk, Rob, Ottawa*	.248	82	323	286	39	71	125	16	1	12	39	1	1	3	32	3	69	18	5	10	.437	.329
Luke, Matt, Columbus*	.228	87	371	337	42	77	126	19	3	8	45	0	1	4	29	1	64	0	3	9	.374	.296
Luzinski, Ryan, Rochester	.208	42	149	125	12	26	41	7	1	2	16	1	1	3	19	0	49	0	1	5	.328	.324
Maduro, Calvin, Scr./W.-B.	.077	13	17	13	0	1	1	0	0	0	0	4	0	0	0	0	3	0	0	0	.077	.077
Magee, Wendell, Scr./W.-B.	.245	83	329	294	39	72	124	20	1	10	39	0	5	0	30	1	56	4	7	10	.422	.310
Makarewicz, Scott, Toledo	.235	100	366	340	34	80	118	15	1	7	38	3	3	6	14	0	68	0	5	13	.347	.275
Malave, Jose, Pawtucket	.297	115	489	427	87	127	206	24	2	17	70	0	5	2	55	1	78	12	4	12	.482	.376
Malloy, Marty, Richmond*	.285	108	461	414	66	118	153	19	5	2	25	5	0	1	41	1	61	17	7	6	.370	.351
Manto, Jeff, Syracuse	.205	40	156	132	18	27	43	5	1	3	11	1	0	1	22	1	30	1	2	3	.326	.323
Manuel, Barry, Norfolk	.000	19	9	8	0	0	0	0	0	0	0	1	0	0	0	0	2	0	0	0	.000	.000
Martin, Jim, Norfolk*	.250	37	115	104	10	26	43	4	2	3	18	1	1	1	8	2	44	5	2	0	.413	.307
Martinez, Eddy, Rochester	.074	12	29	27	0	2	3	1	0	0	3	1	0	0	1	0	8	0	0	0	.111	.107
Martinez, Pablo, Richmond†..	.257	96	332	296	32	76	104	14	1	4	20	8	2	0	26	0	77	9	11	3	.351	.315
Martinez, Sandy, Syracuse* ..	.224	96	359	322	28	72	98	12	1	4	29	3	2	5	27	2	76	7	2	9	.304	.292
Matos, Francisco, Rochester..	.324	101	414	389	51	126	163	17	4	4	51	9	3	4	9	0	42	8	2	15	.419	.343
McClain, Scott, Norfolk	.280	127	504	429	71	120	216	29	2	21	64	1	8	2	64	5	93	1	3	8	.503	.370
McGuire, Ryan, Ottawa*	.299	50	222	184	37	55	77	11	1	3	15	0	2	0	36	2	29	5	2	4	.418	.410
McKeel, Walt, Pawtucket	.253	66	275	237	34	60	93	15	0	6	30	1	2	1	34	3	39	0	1	8	.392	.347
McMillon, Billy, Char.-S./W.-B.*	.284	83	342	296	52	84	148	26	1	12	47	0	1	1	44	1	75	10	0	4	.500	.377
Melhuse, Adam, Syracuse†	.237	38	132	118	7	28	41	5	1	2	9	0	1	1	12	0	18	1	1	2	.347	.311
Mendoza, Carlos, Norfolk*	.143	10	40	35	3	5	7	0	1	0	0	1	0	1	3	0	4	1	0	1	.200	.231
Mendoza, Reynol, Charlotte	.154	46	14	13	1	2	2	0	0	0	1	1	0	0	0	0	2	0	0	0	.154	.154
Mercado, Hector, Charlotte* ..	.000	1	1	0	1	0	0	0	0	0	0	0	0	0	1	0	0	0	0	0	.000	1.000
Merloni, Lou, Pawtucket	.297	49	186	165	24	49	74	10	0	5	24	1	1	4	15	2	20	0	2	4	.448	.368
Meulens, Hensley, Ottawa	.274	121	495	423	81	116	212	20	2	24	75	0	5	5	62	4	119	19	5	11	.501	.370
Millan, Adan, Scr./W.-B.	.500	1	3	2	0	1	1	0	0	0	1	0	0	0	1	0	0	0	0	0	.500	.667
Miller, Kurt, Charlotte	.000	21	1	0	0	0	0	0	0	0	0	0	0	0	1	0	0	0	0	0	.000	.000
Miller, Orlando, Toledo	.267	8	32	30	3	8	12	1	1	0	5	0	0	0	2	0	5	2	1	1	.400	.313
Milliard, Ralph, Charlotte	.265	33	148	132	19	35	54	5	1	4	18	4	0	3	9	0	21	5	3	1	.409	.326
Millwood, Kevin, Richmond ...	.385	9	14	13	4	5	10	2	0	1	0	0	0	0	1	0	3	0	0	0	.769	.429
Mimbs, Mike, Scr./W.-B.*	.200	11	5	5	0	1	1	0	0	0	0	0	0	0	0	0	1	0	0	1	.200	.200
Mitchell, Tony, Toledo†	.186	22	86	70	7	13	21	2	0	2	9	0	0	0	16	1	19	1	1	3	.300	.337
Moore, Mike, Norfolk	.241	34	92	83	10	20	30	4	0	2	6	0	0	0	9	0	33	1	0	3	.361	.315
Morales, Francisco, Ottawa	.111	7	19	18	2	2	7	0	1	1	4	0	0	0	1	0	6	0	0	0	.389	.158
Mordecai, Mike, Richmond	.311	31	135	122	23	38	57	10	0	3	15	2	1	1	9	0	17	0	1	0	.467	.361
Morgan, Kevin, Norfolk	.273	71	283	256	34	70	89	11	1	2	20	0	0	0	27	1	26	6	5	5	.348	.343
Morman, Russ, Charlotte	.319	117	462	395	82	126	246	17	2	33	99	0	5	4	58	11	89	3	2	6	.623	.407
Mosquera, Julio, Syracuse	.229	10	38	35	5	8	9	1	0	0	1	0	0	1	2	0	5	0	0	2	.257	.289
Mummau, Rob, Syracuse	.255	103	382	333	47	85	130	17	2	8	40	5	2	7	35	3	60	2	3	3	.390	.337
Myers, Jimmy, Norfolk	.000	45	3	2	0	0	0	0	0	0	0	1	0	0	0	0	0	0	0	0	.000	.000
Natal, Rob, Charlotte	.267	78	273	251	34	67	121	17	2	11	49	0	2	1	19	0	37	2	2	9	.482	.319
Nevin, Phil, Toledo	.158	5	21	19	1	3	6	0	0	1	3	0	0	0	2	1	9	0	0	1	.316	.238
Nixon, Trot, Pawtucket*	.244	130	552	475	80	116	200	18	3	20	61	9	4	1	63	2	86	11	4	11	.421	.331
Norris, Joe, Charlotte	.000	9	1	1	0	0	0	0	0	0	0	0	0	0	0	0	1	0	0	0	.000	.000
Northeimer, Jamie, Scr./W.-B.	.154	4	14	13	1	2	2	0	0	0	0	1	0	0	0	0	6	0	0	1	.154	.214
Nye, Ryan, Scr./W.-B.	.214	17	17	14	0	3	3	0	0	0	1	1	0	1	0	0	3	0	0	0	.214	.313
Obando, Sherman, Ottawa	.238	7	27	21	5	5	14	0	0	3	8	0	0	1	5	0	7	0	0	3	.667	.407
Ojala, Kirt, Charlotte*	.056	27	23	18	0	1	2	1	0	0	2	3	0	0	2	0	10	0	0	0	.111	.150
Ojeda, Augie, Rochester†	.234	15	58	47	5	11	16	3	1	0	6	3	0	0	8	0	4	1	2	2	.340	.345
Olmeda, Jose, Charlotte†	.207	83	272	242	24	50	66	11	1	1	29	2	5	2	21	1	41	3	2	7	.273	.270
Otanez, Willis, Rochester	.208	49	186	168	20	35	59	9	0	5	25	0	3	0	15	0	35	0	0	8	.351	.269
Otero, Ricky, Scr./W.-B.†	.331	38	176	160	24	53	76	10	5	1	15	0	3	0	13	0	13	5	4	1	.475	.375
Pall, Donn, Charlotte	.500	59	2	2	0	1	1	0	0	0	0	0	0	0	0	0	0	0	0	0	.500	.500
Paniagua, Jose, Ottawa	.100	22	23	20	1	2	5	0	0	1	1	2	0	0	1	0	11	0	0	0	.250	.143
Patzke, Jeff, Syracuse†	.285	96	373	316	38	90	125	25	2	2	29	3	2	1	51	3	66	0	3	4	.396	.384
Pegues, Steve, Ottawa	.300	66	203	190	19	57	80	12	1	3	28	0	3	1	9	1	29	4	4	12	.421	.330
Perez, Tomas, Syracuse†	.224	89	355	303	32	68	84	13	0	1	20	14	1	0	37	1	67	3	4	9	.277	.308
Petagine, Roberto, Norfolk* ...	.317	129	543	441	90	140	267	32	1	31	100	1	8	8	85	3	92	0	1	6	.605	.430
Pose, Scott, Columbus*	.308	57	266	227	50	70	100	10	7	2	32	2	0	5	32	0	29	13	5	2	.441	.405
Pozo, Arquimedez, Pawtucket	.284	101	422	377	61	107	193	18	1	22	70	0	1	7	37	4	55	4	4	9	.512	.358
Pratt, Todd, Norfolk	.301	59	237	206	42	62	103	8	3	9	34	2	1	2	26	1	48	1	2	8	.500	.383
Pride, Curtis, Pawtucket*	.000	1	3	3	0	0	0	0	0	0	0	0	0	0	0	0	2	0	0	0	.000	.000
Pulido, Carlos, Ottawa*	.000	44	1	1	0	0	0	0	0	0	0	0	0	0	0	0	0	0	0	0	.000	.000
Pulsipher, Bill, Norfolk*	.000	8	2	1	0	0	0	0	0	0	0	1	0	0	0	0	1	0	0	0	.000	.000
Pye, Eddie, Norfolk	.083	3	16	12	3	1	1	0	0	0	0	0	0	0	4	0	2	0	0	1	.083	.313
Raines, Tim, Columbus†	.154	4	16	13	1	2	2	0	0	0	0	0	0	0	3	0	0	0	0	0	.154	.313
Ramirez, Angel, Syracuse	.174	7	25	23	4	4	5	1	0	0	0	0	0	0	0	0	7	0	0	1	.217	.174
Redmond, Mike, Charlotte	.213	22	67	61	6	13	23	5	1	1	2	2	0	3	1	1	10	0	1	1	.377	.262
Relaford, Desi, Scr./W.-B.† ..	.267	131	576	517	82	138	207	34	4	9	53	4	5	7	43	0	77	29	8	12	.400	.329
Ricci, Chuck, Ottawa	.000	22	1	1	0	0	0	0	0	0	0	0	0	0	0	0	0	0	0	0	.000	.000
Roberts, Chris, Norfolk	.000	7	6	5	0	0	0	0	0	0	0	1	0	0	0	0	2	0	0	0	.000	.000
Roberts, Lonell, Syracuse†	.156	77	194	173	17	27	40	4	0	3	10	2	0	0	19	0	50	6	7	1	.231	.240
Robertson, Mike, Scr./W.-B.* .	.298	121	485	416	61	124	183	17	3	12	72	1	6	4	58	4	67	0	2	9	.440	.384

Player, Team	Avg.	G	TPA	AB	R	H	TB	2B	3B	HR	RBI	SH	SF	HP	BB	IBB	SO	SB	CS	GDP	Slg.	OBP
Rodarte, Raul, Richmond......	.242	41	106	95	13	23	27	4	0	0	10	0	0	1	10	0	22	2	2	5	.284	.321
Rodriguez, Adam, Toledo	.200	29	75	70	4	14	19	2	0	1	3	1	0	1	3	0	17	0	1	3	.271	.243
Rodriguez, Luis, Syracuse	.000	3	2	2	0	0	0	0	0	0	0	0	0	0	0	0	2	0	0	0	.000	.000
Rodriguez, Maximo, Charlotte	.048	7	22	21	2	1	1	0	0	0	0	0	0	0	1	0	7	0	0	1	.048	.091
Rodriguez, Steve, Toledo	.233	107	466	425	57	99	143	30	1	4	38	6	5	4	26	0	58	18	5	6	.336	.280
Rodriguez, Tony, Pawtucket ...	.249	82	298	285	27	71	89	12	0	2	19	2	0	2	9	0	47	5	2	12	.312	.277
Ronan, Marc, Columbus*	.276	55	184	156	16	43	58	12	0	1	19	0	0	1	27	3	24	1	3	9	.372	.386
Rossy, Rico, Ottawa.............	.251	117	428	375	56	94	147	23	0	10	52	8	4	4	37	2	64	5	0	14	.392	.321
Ruffcorn, Scott, Scr./W.-B.....	.000	5	7	6	0	0	0	0	0	0	0	1	0	0	0	0	2	0	0	0	.000	.000
Russo, Paul, Columbus......	.136	9	27	22	3	3	9	0	0	2	4	0	0	0	5	0	6	0	0	2	.409	.296
Sadler, Donnie, Pawtucket	.212	125	549	481	74	102	157	18	2	11	36	3	6	2	57	0	121	20	14	11	.326	.295
Saffer, Jon, Ottawa*	.267	134	570	483	81	129	212	20	9	15	60	0	3	8	76	1	74	13	6	12	.439	.374
Samuels, Scott, Ottawa*	.345	20	63	55	6	19	25	3	0	1	7	1	0	0	7	3	12	2	0	2	.455	.419
Sauerbeck, Scott, Norfolk.	.000	1	2	1	1	0	0	0	0	0	0	0	0	0	1	0	1	0	0	0	.000	.500
Saunders, Chris, Norfolk......	.249	68	215	173	24	43	52	9	0	0	24	2	1	2	37	2	37	2	2	6	.301	.385
Saunders, Tony, Charlotte*	.000	3	2	2	0	0	0	0	0	0	0	0	0	0	0	0	1	0	0	0	.000	.000
Schu, Rick, Ottawa................	.190	8	21	21	3	4	8	1	0	1	3	0	0	0	0	0	4	0	0	1	.381	.190
Schutz, Carl, Richmond*	.000	27	10	10	0	0	0	0	0	0	0	0	0	0	0	0	4	0	0	0	.000	.000
Seefried, Tate, Norfolk*	.229	33	109	96	11	22	39	6	1	3	13	0	0	0	13	0	31	2	0	3	.406	.321
Seelbach, Chris, Charlotte......	.182	16	11	11	2	2	2	0	0	0	0	0	0	0	0	0	3	0	0	0	.182	.182
Sefcik, Kevin, Scr./W.-B. ...	.333	29	134	123	19	41	59	11	2	1	7	2	0	0	9	0	11	5	1	1	.480	.379
Seitzer, Brad, Ottawa.........	.250	18	65	56	4	14	18	1	0	1	7	0	0	1	8	0	11	1	2	3	.321	.354
Sheff, Chris, Charlotte............	.255	120	372	322	54	82	140	23	1	11	43	2	3	1	43	1	76	16	4	5	.435	.341
Shepherd, Keith, Norfolk.........	.067	19	17	15	0	1	1	0	0	0	1	1	0	1	0	0	5	0	0	0	.067	.125
Siddall, Joe, Ottawa	.274	57	186	164	18	45	62	12	1	1	16	0	1	1	21	3	42	1	2	2	.378	.360
Sierra, Ruben, Syracuse†	.219	8	34	32	5	7	12	2	0	1	5	0	0	0	2	1	6	0	0	0	.375	.265
Simon, Randall, Richmond* ..	.308	133	542	519	62	160	249	45	1	14	102	1	1	4	17	2	76	1	6	18	.480	.335
Smith, Bobby, Richmond	.246	100	412	357	47	88	138	10	2	12	47	2	1	7	44	2	109	6	5	4	.387	.340
Smith, Ira, Toledo..................	.243	39	163	148	19	36	47	8	0	1	13	2	0	2	11	0	29	0	1	3	.318	.304
Soriano, Fred, Syracuse†........	.114	17	48	44	3	5	8	1	0	0	4	2	0	1	1	0	7	2	0	0	.182	.152
Spehr, Tim, Richmond	.192	36	135	120	13	23	37	5	0	3	14	0	2	1	12	0	37	0	0	1	.308	.267
Spencer, Shane, Columbus	.241	125	534	452	78	109	241	34	4	30	86	1	5	4	71	1	105	0	2	8	.533	.346
Stanifer, Robby, Charlotte	.000	23	1	0	1	0	0	0	0	0	0	0	0	0	0	0	0	0	0	0	.000	.000
Stephenson, Garrett, Scr./W.-B.	.500	7	5	2	1	1	2	1	0	0	1	3	0	0	0	0	0	0	0	1	1.000	.500
Stewart, Shannon, Syracuse ..	.346	58	249	208	41	72	102	13	1	5	24	1	0	4	36	3	26	9	6	1	.490	.452
Stovall, Darond, Ottawa†	.243	98	382	342	40	83	122	23	2	4	48	3	4	2	31	3	114	10	13	6	.357	.306
Strange, Doug, Ottawa†........	.429	2	8	7	3	3	4	1	0	0	0	0	0	1	0	0	1	0	0	2	.571	.500
Strawberry, Darryl, Col.*........	.289	11	47	38	8	11	32	3	0	6	19	0	1	0	8	0	10	0	0	1	.842	.404
Stull, Everett, Ottawa.............	.200	27	18	15	1	3	3	0	0	0	1	2	0	0	1	0	5	0	0	0	.200	.250
Tam, Jeff, Norfolk	.083	40	13	12	0	1	2	1	0	0	0	1	0	0	0	0	6	0	0	0	.167	.083
Tarasco, Tony, Rochester*	.200	10	43	35	4	7	13	0	0	2	6	0	1	0	7	0	7	0	0	1	.371	.326
Tavarez, Jesus, Pawtucket† ...	.266	59	263	229	43	61	82	6	3	3	20	6	0	1	27	1	31	22	9	3	.358	.346
Tejero, Fausto, Richmond	.231	76	256	225	31	52	81	11	0	6	28	2	2	4	23	2	41	0	1	6	.360	.311
Thobe, Tom, Richmond............	.000	19	10	9	0	0	0	0	0	0	0	1	0	0	0	0	7	0	0	0	.000	.000
Thompson, Ryan, Syracuse	.288	83	357	330	37	95	168	23	1	16	58	0	3	3	21	1	59	4	3	10	.509	.333
Thurman, Gary, Nor.-Ott.......	.228	66	221	184	23	42	52	8	1	0	17	4	2	2	29	1	44	12	5	5	.283	.336
Thurman, Mike, Ottawa..........	.000	4	5	5	0	0	0	0	0	0	0	0	0	0	0	0	3	0	0	0	.000	.000
Tolentino, Jose, Rochester*.....	.211	20	73	57	6	12	17	2	0	1	9	0	1	1	14	1	11	0	0	5	.298	.370
Torres, Tony, Charlotte	.279	29	76	68	9	19	25	3	0	1	8	1	0	0	7	0	26	3	2	0	.368	.347
Toth, Dave, Richmond............	.196	14	50	46	6	9	12	3	0	0	5	0	0	0	4	0	8	0	0	3	.261	.260
Trammell, Bubba, Toledo	.251	90	366	319	56	80	181	15	1	28	75	0	4	5	38	1	91	2	2	1	.567	.336
Troilo, Jason, Columbus	.136	8	27	22	1	3	5	2	0	0	1	1	0	0	4	0	9	0	0	1	.227	.269
Tyler, Brad, Richmond*	.264	129	451	383	69	101	190	15	10	18	77	3	7	3	55	2	110	13	6	4	.496	.355
Urbani, Thomas, Ottawa*	.000	30	1	0	0	0	0	0	0	0	0	1	0	0	0	0	0	0	0	0	.000	.000
Valle, Dave, Richmond	.211	12	40	38	2	8	8	0	0	0	2	0	1	0	1	0	7	0	0	3	.211	.225
Valrie, Kerry, Ottawa	.221	34	118	113	12	25	46	6	3	3	20	0	1	0	4	0	22	3	4	2	.407	.246
Varitek, Jason, Pawtucket†† ...	.197	20	74	66	6	13	21	5	0	1	5	0	0	0	8	0	12	0	0	4	.318	.284
Vidro, Jose, Ottawa†	.323	73	305	279	40	90	146	17	0	13	47	0	3	1	22	5	40	2	0	6	.523	.370
Walbeck, Matt, Toledo†..........	.305	17	65	59	6	18	25	2	1	1	8	0	2	0	4	0	15	0	0	1	.424	.338
Ward, Bryan, Charlotte*	.250	15	12	12	1	3	3	0	0	0	0	0	0	0	0	0	4	0	0	1	.250	.250
Waszgis, B.J., Rochester	.260	100	388	315	61	82	138	15	1	13	48	4	4	9	56	1	78	1	1	5	.438	.383
Wawruck, Jim, Rochester*	.271	94	378	339	47	92	133	20	3	5	35	1	1	3	34	1	64	12	6	10	.392	.342
Weber, Neil, Ottawa*	.250	9	9	8	1	2	2	0	0	0	1	1	0	0	0	0	5	0	0	0	.250	.250
Wedge, Eric, Scr./W.-B.	.256	47	154	129	25	33	64	8	1	7	36	0	3	0	22	0	40	0	0	1	.496	.357
Wehner, John, Charlotte..........	.280	31	100	93	16	26	40	5	0	3	11	1	0	0	6	1	18	3	1	1	.430	.323
Whitmore, Darrell, Syracuse* ...	.256	58	222	195	23	50	77	15	0	4	21	0	2	1	24	3	54	7	4	4	.395	.338
Williams, Juan, Pawtucket* ...	.198	27	103	81	11	16	29	4	0	3	10	0	1	1	20	0	35	2	3	1	.358	.359
Wilson, Pookie, Charlotte*	.253	60	169	146	27	37	51	6	1	2	13	5	0	1	17	1	26	1	2	2	.349	.335
Wilson, Tom, Columbus...........	.000	1	4	3	0	0	0	0	0	0	0	0	0	0	1	0	0	0	0	0	.000	.250
Winston, Darrin, Scr./W.-B.....	.000	39	7	7	1	0	0	0	0	0	0	0	0	0	0	0	1	0	0	0	.000	.000
Withem, Shannon, Norfolk.......	.000	29	23	21	0	0	0	0	0	0	0	2	0	0	0	0	10	0	0	0	.000	.000
Woodall, Brad, Richmond†	.143	28	32	28	3	4	7	0	0	1	6	4	0	0	0	0	4	0	0	2	.250	.143
Woods, Tyrone, Pawtucket	.352	29	118	105	16	37	69	3	1	9	28	0	2	0	11	0	35	1	1	4	.657	.407
Yarnall, Ed, Norfolk*	.000	1	1	0	0	0	0	0	0	0	0	1	0	0	0	0	0	0	0	0	.000	.000
Zuber, Jon, Scr./W.-B.*	.315	126	522	435	85	137	196	37	2	6	64	1	3	3	79	0	53	3	4	11	.451	.421

GRAND SLAMS: Trammell, 3; Cruz, Daubach, Malave, Robertson, Thompson, 2 each; Barron, Bautista, G. Bennett, Catalanotto, Davis, Estalella, Figga, Gilbert, Henderson, Hollins, Ledee, Magee, Matos, McMillon, Morman, Natal, Saffer, B. Smith, Spencer, Tavarez, 1 each.

AWARDED FIRST BASE ON CATCHER'S INTEFERENCE: J. Hurst 2 (Tejero, Waszgis), Jones 2 (Gresham, Waszgis); Bartee (Castillo); A. Fox (Estalella); Sheff (Adam Rodriguez); Bobby Smith (Borrero); Spencer (Makarewicz); Zuber (Kuilan).

PLAYERS WITH TWO OR MORE TEAMS

Player, Team	Avg.	G	TPA	AB	R	H	TB	2B	3B	HR	RBI	SH	SF	HP	BB	IBB	SO	SB	CS	GDP	Slg.	OBP
Daal, Omar, Ottawa*	.333	2	3	3	0	1	1	0	0	0	0	0	0	0	0	0	0	0	0	0	.333	.333
Daal, Omar, Syracuse*	.000	5	0	0	0	0	0	0	0	0	0	0	0	0	0	0	0	0	0	0	.000	.000
Fox, Eric, Rochester†	.222	5	20	18	2	4	5	1	0	0	0	0	0	0	2	0	2	0	0	0	.278	.300
Fox, Eric, Scr./W.-B.†	.285	87	268	246	39	70	101	16	3	3	26	0	3	0	19	1	48	2	3	10	.411	.332
Hare, Shawn, Toledo*	.180	23	79	61	9	11	18	4	0	1	6	0	0	0	18	2	25	0	0	0	.295	.367
Hare, Shawn, Columbus*	.208	11	28	24	3	5	6	1	0	0	2	0	0	0	4	0	9	0	0	1	.250	.321
McMillon, Billy, Charlotte*	.279	57	238	204	34	57	99	18	0	8	26	0	1	1	32	1	51	8	0	3	.485	.378
McMillon, Billy, Scr./W.-B.*	.293	26	104	92	18	27	49	8	1	4	21	0	0	0	12	0	24	2	0	1	.533	.375
Thurman, Gary, Norfolk	.250	23	94	80	7	20	24	4	0	0	12	1	2	0	11	0	16	4	1	2	.300	.333
Thurman, Gary, Ottawa	.212	43	127	104	16	22	28	4	1	0	5	3	0	2	18	1	28	8	4	3	.269	.339

1997 PITCHING
TEAM

Team	W	L	Pct.	ERA	G	CG	ShO	Sv.	IP	H	TBF	R	ER	HR	SH	SF	HB	BB	IBB	SO	WP	Bk.
Norfolk	75	67	.528	3.76	142	7	9	37	1232.1	1238	5329	616	515	105	49	37	49	509	25	952	48	14
Rochester	83	58	.589	3.93	141	13	13	43	1226.0	1112	5173	605	535	134	33	40	49	441	9	1108	51	14
Pawtucket	81	60	.574	4.07	141	11	7	38	1242.1	1198	5342	636	562	135	38	40	53	491	32	991	65	5
Columbus	79	63	.556	4.16	142	9	9	45	1234.2	1288	5304	654	571	108	40	37	38	426	10	975	60	11
Richmond	70	72	.493	4.33	142	6	10	34	1234.0	1252	5302	671	594	143	51	34	24	470	20	922	59	2
Toledo	68	73	.482	4.42	141	6	10	38	1223.0	1211	5398	689	600	129	52	41	59	581	22	979	58	10
Scranton/W.-B.	66	76	.465	4.59	142	20	7	32	1208.2	1248	5289	700	617	142	44	32	31	488	38	964	60	6
Syracuse	55	87	.387	4.71	142	9	11	23	1218.2	1218	5352	720	638	135	36	45	52	582	11	902	68	11
Charlotte	76	65	.539	4.95	141	6	4	43	1190.0	1278	5289	744	655	150	40	39	55	535	32	895	68	7
Ottawa	54	86	.386	5.03	140	5	5	28	1197.1	1288	5354	750	669	131	50	40	62	571	30	874	73	3

INDIVIDUAL
TOP QUALIFIERS FOR EARNED-RUN AVERAGE TITLE
Minimum 114 innings. *Lefthanded pitcher.

Pitcher, Team	W	L	Pct.	ERA	G	GS	CG	ShO	GF	Sv.	IP	H	TBF	R	ER	HR	SH	SF	HB	BB	IBB	SO	WP	Bk.
Rose, Brian, Pawtucket	17	5	.773	3.02	27	26	3	0	0	0	190.2	188	787	74	64	21	1	5	7	46	2	116	5	0
Yan, Esteban, Rochester	11	5	.688	3.10	34	12	0	0	8	2	119.0	107	490	54	41	13	1	6	5	37	0	131	5	0
Pavano, Carl, Pawtucket	11	6	.647	3.12	23	23	0	0	0	0	161.2	148	663	62	56	13	1	3	6	34	2	147	7	1
Brock, Chris, Richmond	10	6	.625	3.34	20	19	0	0	0	0	118.2	97	497	50	44	9	8	4	1	51	0	83	8	1
Krivda, Rick, Rochester*	14	2	.875	3.39	22	21	6	3	0	0	146.0	122	589	61	55	13	0	2	5	34	0	128	2	2
Ojala, Kirt, Charlotte*	8	7	.533	3.50	25	24	0	0	1	0	149.0	148	627	74	58	13	4	1	3	55	1	119	4	0
Jerzembeck, Mike, Columbus	7	5	.583	3.59	20	20	2	0	0	0	130.1	125	540	55	52	14	5	2	37	0	118	4	0	
Keagle, Greg, Toledo	11	7	.611	3.81	23	23	3	1	0	0	151.1	136	645	68	64	8	4	2	10	61	0	140	4	1
Acevedo, Juan, Norfolk	6	6	.500	3.86	18	18	1	0	0	0	116.2	111	487	55	50	7	4	3	4	34	1	99	2	4
Dishman, Glenn, Toledo*	7	6	.538	3.87	21	18	1	0	2	1	114.0	112	467	53	49	12	3	3	2	32	0	77	4	1
Rodriguez, Nerio, Rochester	11	10	.524	3.90	27	27	1	1	0	0	168.1	124	688	82	73	23	6	0	8	62	0	160	4	3
Falteisek, Steve, Ottawa	6	9	.400	3.96	22	22	1	0	0	0	125.0	135	555	67	55	10	7	7	5	54	1	56	12	1
Harriger, Denny, Toledo	11	8	.579	3.99	27	27	2	1	0	0	167.0	159	717	87	74	19	5	1	5	63	2	109	3	0
Flener, Huck, Syracuse*	6	6	.500	4.14	20	20	1	1	0	0	124.0	126	524	71	57	14	3	3	2	43	1	58	6	2
Harrison, Tommy, Richmond	9	7	.563	4.20	22	22	1	0	0	0	122.0	118	519	64	57	21	2	4	5	40	2	92	3	0

DEPARTMENTAL LEADERS: W—B. Rose, 17; L—Luebbers, 14; Pct.—Dougherty, .909; G—Polley, 62; GS—Loewer, 29; CG—Krivda, 6; ShO—Krivda, 3; GF—Brow, 50; Sv.—Gaillard, 28; IP—B. Rose, 190.2; H—Loewer, 198; TBF—Loewer, 797; R—Loewer, 120; ER—Stull, 103; HR—Stull, 25; SH—Hartgraves, Woodall, 9 each; SF—Brandow, 12; HB—Larkin, 15; BB—Drumright, Brandow, 91 each; IBB—Barnes, Karp, Loewer, 6 each; SO—N. Rodriguez, 160; WP—Ricken, 16; BK—Acevedo, Drumright, Urso, 4 each.

ALL PITCHERS
*Lefthanded pitcher.

Pitcher, Team	W	L	Pct.	ERA	G	GS	CG	ShO	GF	Sv.	IP	H	TBF	R	ER	HR	SH	SF	HB	BB	IBB	SO	WP	Bk.
Acevedo, Juan, Norfolk	6	6	.500	3.86	18	18	1	0	0	0	116.2	111	487	55	50	7	4	3	4	34	1	99	2	4
Alberro, Jose, Columbus	0	1	.000	3.38	1	1	0	0	0	0	8.0	5	32	4	3	1	0	1	1	1	0	6	0	0
Alfonseca, Antonio, Charlotte	7	2	.778	4.32	46	0	0	0	20	7	58.1	58	246	34	28	8	2	2	2	20	3	45	3	2
Almanzar, Carlos, Syracuse	5	1	.833	1.41	32	0	0	0	17	3	51.0	30	189	9	8	2	2	1		8	0	47	2	0
Alvarez, Tavo, Ottawa	4	8	.333	4.82	37	13	0	0	6	1	106.1	123	470	61	57	11	6	3	3	42	3	86	6	0
Andujar, Luis, Syracuse	1	6	.143	5.54	13	5	1	0	7	1	39.0	37	169	25	24	6	2	3	14	1	29	1	1	
Arocha, Rene, Columbus	1	0	1.000	1.86	4	1	0	0	1	0	9.2	7	37	2	2	0	0	1	0	2	0	10	0	0
Aucoin, Derek, Ottawa	0	1	.000	22.74	8	0	0	0	6	0	6.1	5	54	16	16	0	0	1	0	10	2	5	2	0
Avery, Steve, Pawtucket*	1	0	1.000	0.00	1	1	0	0	0	0	5.0	1	19	0	0	0	0	0	0	3	0	1	0	0
Banks, Willie, Columbus	14	5	.737	4.27	33	24	1	0	5	3	154.0	164	662	87	73	18	3	3	4	45	0	130	7	0
Barnes, Brian, Toledo*	7	10	.412	6.71	32	18	0	0	4	0	115.1	143	540	100	86	16	2	8	7	57	6	86	9	0
Baxter, Bob, Ottawa*	0	0	.000	12.79	4	0	0	0	1	0	6.1	11	35	10	9	1	1	1	1	3	1	4	0	0
Beech, Matt, Scr./W.-B.*	3	1	.750	5.70	5	5	1	0	0	0	30.0	24	127	20	19	5	0	1	0	10	0	38	2	0
Bennett, Chris, Rochester	4	2	.667	3.54	25	0	0	0	7	0	40.2	40	166	17	16	0	3	4	2	7	1	28	1	0
Bennett, Shayne, Ottawa	1	2	.333	1.57	25	0	0	0	21	14	34.1	23	142	8	6	0	2	1	2	21	1	29	2	0
Blair, Willie, Toledo	0	0	.000	0.00	1	1	0	0	0	0	7.0	1	25	1	0	0	0	0	0	2	0	4	0	0
Blais, Mike, Pawtucket	1	4	.200	8.31	10	0	0	0	2	0	13.0	10	64	15	12	3	2	0	3	10	1	10	3	0
Blazier, Ron, Scr./W.-B.	0	3	.000	3.68	11	0	0	0	8	1	14.2	17	68	9	6	4	1	0	3	10	0	10	0	0
Bogott, Kurtiss, Syracuse*	1	3	.250	7.89	16	0	0	0	0	0	21.2	23	106	20	19	2	2	2	3	15	1	16	1	0
Bohanon, Brian, Norfolk*	9	3	.750	2.63	15	14	4	2	0	0	96.0	88	404	37	28	9	2	1	3	32	0	84	2	0
Borland, Toby, Pawtucket	2	0	1.000	3.99	28	2	0	0	13	2	47.1	50	213	22	21	5	0	0	2	25	3	46	5	0
Borowski, Joe, Richmond	1	2	.333	3.58	21	0	0	0	4	2	37.2	32	159	16	15	3	2	0	1	19	2	34	4	0
Bowen, Ryan, Columbus	0	1	.000	9.00	2	1	0	0	0	0	10.0	15	49	10	10	1	1	3	1	5	0	7	0	0
Brandenburg, Mark, Paw.	2	1	.667	2.41	9	0	0	0	4	0	18.2	13	73	6	5	2	0	1	1	3	1	23	0	0
Brandow, Derek, Syracuse	7	11	.389	5.41	31	25	1	0	0	0	143.0	161	677	103	86	14	5	12	11	91	1	120	10	1

CLASS AAA International League

Pitcher, Team	W	L	Pct.	ERA	G	GS	CG	ShO	GF	Sv.	IP	H	TBF	R	ER	HR	SH	SF	HB	BB	IBB	SO	WP	Bk.
Brewer, Billy, Scr./W.-B.*	2	1	.667	3.00	11	0	0	0	6	1	9.0	10	41	7	3	2	2	0	0	5	1	9	0	0
Brock, Chris, Richmond	10	6	.625	3.34	20	19	0	0	0	0	118.2	97	497	50	44	9	8	4	1	51	0	83	8	1
Brow, Scott, Richmond	5	9	.357	4.45	61	1	0	0	50	18	83.0	89	369	48	41	12	1	1	2	35	2	62	6	1
Brown, Chad, Syracuse*	0	3	.000	6.34	22	0	0	0	14	0	38.1	41	178	32	27	5	1	1	2	26	0	26	1	0
Buddie, Mike, Columbus	6	6	.500	2.64	53	0	0	0	13	2	75.0	85	319	24	22	4	4	3	2	25	0	67	5	0
Bullinger, Kirk, Ottawa	3	4	.429	1.71	22	0	0	0	14	5	31.2	17	119	7	6	0	2	1	0	10	0	15	1	0
Bunch, Mel, Ottawa	4	4	.500	6.35	16	14	0	0	0	0	78.0	102	369	63	55	13	1	7	2	45	5	58	8	0
Byrd, Paul, Richmond	2	1	.667	3.18	3	3	0	0	0	0	17.0	14	64	6	6	2	1	0	1	1	0	14	1	0
Cain, Tim, Paw.-Syr.	3	5	.375	5.68	30	1	0	0	10	2	52.1	60	245	35	33	10	2	5	7	26	0	27	1	0
Carlyle, Ken, Richmond	4	1	.800	2.84	16	11	1	1	1	0	69.2	69	284	26	22	4	0	1	1	19	0	48	0	0
Carpenter, Chris, Syracuse	4	9	.308	4.50	19	19	3	2	0	0	120.0	113	499	64	60	16	2	1	3	53	0	97	8	0
Carrara, Giovanni, Rochester	4	2	.667	4.44	8	8	1	0	0	0	46.2	45	196	23	23	4	1	3	2	16	0	48	1	0
Castro, Tony, Charlotte	0	0	.000	4.91	2	0	0	0	1	0	3.2	2	14	2	2	1	0	0	0	2	0	1	0	0
Cather, Mike, Richmond	0	0	.000	1.73	13	0	0	0	10	3	26.0	17	102	6	5	1	2	0	1	9	1	22	0	0
Checo, Robinson, Pawtucket	4	2	.667	3.42	9	9	2	1	0	0	55.1	41	220	22	21	8	1	0	0	16	0	56	3	0
Chergey, Dan, Charlotte	3	1	.750	3.14	27	4	0	0	9	6	43.0	37	174	18	15	5	1	4	2	9	1	40	2	0
Clontz, Brad, Richmond	0	0	.000	0.00	16	0	0	0	11	6	22.0	10	77	1	0	0	2	0	1	2	1	24	0	0
Converse, Jim, Columbus	0	2	.000	3.32	10	1	0	0	5	1	19.0	22	86	8	7	1	0	0	0	11	1	13	1	0
Coppinger, Rocky, Rochester	1	2	.333	5.52	3	3	0	0	0	0	14.2	16	69	10	9	2	0	0	0	11	0	9	0	0
Corbin, Archie, Rochester	4	3	.571	4.00	43	1	0	0	22	5	69.2	47	314	32	31	5	2	3	1	62	0	66	10	0
Cornelius, Reid, Charlotte	12	5	.706	5.10	22	22	1	0	0	0	130.2	134	555	82	74	19	5	8	4	43	1	80	5	1
Corsi, Jim, Pawtucket	0	0	.000	0.00	2	0	0	0	1	1	2.1	2	10	0	0	0	0	0	0	1	0	3	0	0
Crabtree, Tim, Syracuse	0	0	.000	9.82	3	0	0	0	2	1	3.2	7	19	4	4	1	1	0	0	1	0	3	0	0
Crawford, Joe, Norfolk*	8	2	.800	3.52	16	16	0	0	0	0	99.2	109	431	45	39	6	5	5	1	31	0	72	4	2
Crow, Dean, Toledo	3	0	1.000	7.85	18	0	0	0	10	2	18.1	26	90	16	16	1	2	1	2	10	1	10	0	0
Cummings, John, Toledo*	2	1	.667	2.76	19	0	0	0	5	0	16.1	13	70	6	5	2	2	2	1	6	1	7	0	0
Czajkowski, Jim, Syracuse	0	2	.000	3.18	16	0	0	0	6	0	22.2	21	101	11	8	2	1	0	0	14	1	13	0	0
Daal, Omar, Ott.-Syr.*	3	1	.750	1.51	7	7	1	1	0	0	41.2	28	164	8	7	1	0	1	0	11	0	38	3	1
Dace, Derek, Toledo*	0	0	.000	3.60	5	0	0	0	3	0	10.0	13	48	8	4	0	1	0	1	6	0	6	1	0
Darensbourg, Vic, Charlotte*	4	2	.667	4.38	27	0	0	0	6	2	24.2	22	110	12	12	4	2	0	2	15	3	21	1	0
Dedrick, Jim, Ottawa	0	1	.000	7.07	8	0	0	0	2	0	14.0	15	68	12	11	2	1	0	0	13	0	14	0	0
DeHart, Rick, Ottawa*	0	4	.000	4.00	43	0	0	0	14	2	63.0	60	264	33	28	6	2	1	4	22	2	57	1	0
Dishman, Glenn, Toledo*	7	6	.538	3.87	21	18	1	0	2	1	114.0	112	467	53	49	12	3	3	2	32	0	77	4	1
Dixon, Timothy, Ottawa*	1	1	.500	9.64	5	0	0	0	1	0	9.1	12	45	10	10	2	1	1	0	5	1	8	2	0
Doman, Roger, Syracuse	1	2	.333	7.59	8	0	0	0	1	0	10.2	11	50	9	9	3	1	0	0	6	0	8	1	0
Dougherty, Jim, Norfolk	10	1	.909	1.45	49	0	0	0	24	4	62.0	45	259	11	10	3	4	2	2	43	3	59	4	0
Drews, Matt, Toledo	0	2	.000	6.60	3	3	0	0	0	0	15.0	14	72	11	11	2	2	0	0	14	1	7	2	0
Drumright, Mike, Toledo	5	10	.333	5.06	23	23	0	0	0	0	133.1	134	612	78	75	22	8	8	4	91	1	115	5	4
Dyer, Mike, Richmond	2	1	.667	4.87	29	0	0	0	8	1	40.2	42	183	25	22	5	3	1	0	24	1	23	2	0
Edenfield, Ken, Columbus	1	0	1.000	6.92	9	0	0	0	3	0	13.0	23	74	19	10	2	0	1	1	8	0	11	3	0
Edmondson, Brian, Norfolk	4	3	.571	2.90	31	4	0	0	8	1	68.1	62	296	27	22	5	3	3	4	37	2	65	4	1
Eiland, Dave, Columbus	4	2	.667	6.64	13	11	0	0	2	0	62.1	80	277	47	46	8	0	0	0	14	0	43	0	0
Eshelman, Vaughn, Paw.*	3	4	.429	4.86	14	13	0	0	1	1	66.2	63	281	38	36	4	7	4	5	22	0	57	3	0
Falteisek, Steve, Ottawa	6	9	.400	3.96	22	22	1	0	0	0	125.0	135	555	67	55	10	7	7	5	54	1	56	12	1
Farrell, Jim, Pawtucket	0	0	.000	0.00	1	1	0	0	0	0	5.0	4	21	0	0	0	1	0	0	2	0	6	1	0
Fermin, Ramon, Toledo	4	2	.667	4.93	41	8	0	0	12	0	80.1	103	376	53	44	10	5	5	4	33	3	46	4	0
Fernandez, Jared, Pawtucket	0	3	.000	5.79	11	11	0	0	0	0	60.2	76	281	45	39	7	2	2	5	28	1	33	4	0
Fiore, Tony, Scr./W.-B.	3	5	.375	3.86	9	9	1	0	0	0	60.2	60	268	34	26	3	3	1	0	26	1	56	6	1
Fleetham, Ben, Ottawa	1	2	.333	2.00	9	0	0	0	6	1	9.0	2	40	3	2	1	0	0	1	10	0	14	2	0
Flener, Huck, Syracuse*	6	6	.500	4.14	20	20	1	1	0	0	124.0	126	524	71	57	14	3	3	2	43	1	58	6	2
Fortugno, Tim, Scr./W.-B.*	0	1	.000	6.62	19	0	0	0	12	3	17.2	21	82	13	13	4	0	1	0	8	1	15	6	2
Fox, Chad, Richmond	1	0	1.000	3.70	13	0	0	0	7	0	24.1	24	105	10	10	1	2	1	0	14	0	25	4	0
Freeman, Marvin, Syracuse	0	0	.000	9.00	1	0	0	0	0	0	1.0	1	4	1	1	0	1	0	0	1	0	0	0	0
Gaillard, Eddie, Toledo	1	4	.200	4.25	55	0	0	0	46	28	53.0	52	235	27	25	7	3	1	2	24	2	54	4	1
Gallaher, Kevin, Toledo	1	1	.500	4.74	9	0	0	0	2	0	19.0	16	88	12	10	1	1	0	2	17	0	13	2	1
Garces, Rich, Pawtucket	2	1	.667	1.45	26	0	0	0	16	5	31.0	24	126	5	5	0	3	0	1	13	3	42	4	0
Gardiner, Mike, Columbus	5	4	.556	3.92	14	13	1	0	0	0	85.0	83	348	40	37	10	5	2	3	24	0	65	3	0
Geisler, Phil, Norfolk*	0	0	.000	6.75	1	0	0	0	1	0	2.2	6	18	6	2	2	0	0	0	3	0	2	0	0
Giannelli, Ray, Syracuse	0	0	.000	54.00	1	0	0	0	1	0	1.0	4	10	6	6	1	0	0	0	3	0	0	0	0
Goldsmith, Gary, Toledo	0	0	.000	4.50	1	0	0	0	1	0	2.0	2	8	1	1	1	0	0	0	0	0	1	0	0
Gomes, Wayne, Scr./W.-B.	3	1	.750	2.37	26	0	0	0	15	7	38.0	31	166	11	10	2	1	1	0	24	2	36	2	0
Gonzalez, Gabe, Charlotte*	2	2	.500	2.74	37	1	0	0	11	3	42.2	38	176	15	13	3	1	2	2	14	1	24	0	0
Gooden, Dwight, Columbus	1	1	.500	3.75	2	2	0	0	0	0	12.0	7	50	5	5	1	0	0	2	4	0	10	2	0
Grace, Mike, Scr./W.-B.	5	6	.455	4.56	12	12	4	0	0	0	75.0	84	331	43	38	0	3	5	3	27	1	55	1	0
Green, Tyler, Scr./W.-B.	4	8	.333	6.10	12	12	3	0	0	0	72.1	80	322	54	49	13	1	0	1	29	3	40	4	0
Greene, Rick, Toledo	6	8	.429	2.83	57	0	0	0	14	1	70.0	49	289	29	22	4	7	2	5	32	3	51	8	0
Greer, Ken, Rochester	0	2	.000	5.79	15	0	0	0	7	1	23.1	30	105	15	15	4	1	1	2	5	0	14	0	0
Grundt, Ken, Pawtucket*	4	2	.667	5.32	49	1	0	0	15	3	47.1	59	224	30	28	9	5	2	5	22	5	28	0	0
Hajek, Dave, Toledo	0	0	.000	0.00	1	0	0	0	1	0	1.0	1	4	0	0	0	0	0	0	1	0	0	0	0
Halladay, Roy, Syracuse	7	10	.412	4.58	22	22	2	2	0	0	125.2	132	537	74	64	13	4	1	1	53	1	64	8	3
Harnisch, Pete, Norfolk	1	1	.500	5.40	3	3	0	0	0	0	16.2	16	74	12	10	4	0	0	0	10	0	16	1	0
Harriger, Denny, Toledo	11	8	.579	3.99	27	27	2	1	0	0	167.0	159	717	87	74	19	5	1	5	63	2	109	3	0
Harrison, Tommy, Richmond	9	7	.563	4.20	22	22	1	0	0	0	122.0	118	519	64	57	21	2	4	5	40	2	92	3	0
Hartgraves, Dean, Rich.*	7	4	.636	4.48	50	0	0	0	16	3	72.1	76	324	38	36	6	9	4	1	39	3	56	0	0
Harvey, Bryan, Charlotte	0	0	.000	0.00	2	0	0	0	0	0	1.1	0	4	0	0	0	0	0	0	0	0	0	0	0
Hawblitzel, Ryan, Scr./W.-B.	6	9	.400	4.99	34	15	1	1	9	2	115.1	132	498	65	64	16	3	4	4	33	3	80	1	0
Haynes, Jimmy, Rochester	5	4	.556	3.44	16	16	2	1	0	0	102.0	89	435	49	39	9	4	3	1	55	0	113	8	1
Heflin, Bronson, Scr./W.-B.	1	1	.500	2.28	35	0	0	0	27	13	43.1	29	185	17	11	3	2	1	0	25	2	36	2	0
Henderson, Rod, Ottawa	5	9	.357	4.95	26	20	2	1	3	1	123.2	136	542	72	68	18	4	2	6	49	3	103	6	0
Heredia, Gil, Ottawa	0	4	.000	4.70	28	0	0	0	9	0	44.0	50	189	29	23	5	2	1	0	9	2	41	1	0
Hernandez, Fernando, Toledo	6	5	.545	4.11	55	1	0	0	18	4	76.2	71	350	44	35	5	4	2	1	51	1	98	1	1
Hernandez, Livan, Charlotte	5	3	.625	3.98	14	14	0	0	0	0	81.1	76	352	39	36	5	2	1	3	38	2	58	1	1

Pitcher, Team	W	L	Pct.	ERA	G	GS	CG	ShO	GF	Sv.	IP	H	TBF	R	ER	HR	SH	SF	HB	BB	IBB	SO	WP	Bk.
Holman, Craig, Scr./W.-B.	3	1	.750	4.64	48	0	0	0	18	3	75.2	100	346	44	39	7	3	1	4	27	4	75	6	0
Hostetler, Mike, Richmond	1	2	.333	9.43	5	5	0	0	0	0	21.0	33	101	23	22	7	1	0	1	9	0	14	1	0
Hudson, Joe, Pawtucket	2	1	.667	2.25	29	0	0	0	17	7	32.0	25	148	22	8	1	2	2	3	23	3	14	3	0
Hurst, Bill, Charlotte	1	2	.333	7.76	27	0	0	0	14	3	29.0	39	147	27	25	3	0	4	1	22	2	15	5	0
Irabu, Hideki, Columbus	2	0	1.000	1.67	4	4	1	1	0	0	27.0	19	101	7	5	1	1	1	0	5	0	28	2	3
Isringhausen, Jason, Norfolk	0	2	.000	4.05	3	3	0	0	0	0	20.0	20	87	10	9	4	1	1	2	8	0	17	1	0
Janzen, Marty, Syracuse	0	5	.000	7.20	22	9	0	0	6	1	65.0	76	304	58	52	12	3	3	3	36	0	56	8	0
Jarvis, Kevin, Toledo	0	1	.000	6.75	2	2	0	0	0	0	8.0	7	36	6	6	0	0	0	1	4	0	5	0	0
Jerzembeck, Mike, Columbus	7	5	.583	3.59	20	20	2	0	0	0	130.1	125	540	55	52	14	4	5	2	37	0	118	4	0
Johns, Doug, Rochester*	3	1	.750	3.74	9	8	2	1	0	0	55.1	57	233	25	23	5	1	2	1	13	1	42	1	1
Jordan, Ricardo, Norfolk*	0	1	.000	2.79	34	0	0	0	10	1	29.0	20	128	11	9	1	0	1	2	24	2	34	1	0
Juelsgaard, Jarod, Charlotte	1	3	.250	6.04	21	6	0	0	3	0	50.2	65	251	41	34	5	2	1	2	39	3	31	3	0
Karp, Ryan, Scr./W.-B.*	4	3	.571	4.19	32	5	0	0	6	1	73.0	72	326	35	34	9	4	1	2	42	6	55	5	0
Kashiwada, Takashi, Norfolk*	0	1	.000	4.73	14	0	0	0	7	0	13.1	11	58	9	7	0	4	1	2	5	0	12	1	1
Keagle, Greg, Toledo	11	7	.611	3.81	23	23	3	1	0	0	151.1	136	645	68	64	8	4	2	10	61	0	140	4	1
Krivda, Rick, Rochester*	14	2	.875	3.39	22	21	6	3	0	0	146.0	122	589	61	55	13	0	2	5	34	0	128	2	2
Lacy, Kerry, Pawtucket	5	3	.625	4.73	23	0	0	0	19	8	32.1	36	144	18	17	4	1	0	2	11	1	21	1	0
Lankford, Frank, Columbus	7	4	.636	2.69	15	13	1	1	2	0	93.2	84	374	33	28	2	3	1	2	22	1	40	1	0
Larkin, Andy, Charlotte	6	11	.353	6.05	28	27	3	0	0	0	144.1	166	669	109	97	23	3	3	15	76	2	103	4	1
Lidle, Cory, Norfolk	4	2	.667	3.64	7	7	1	0	0	0	42.0	46	181	20	17	1	4	1	1	10	0	34	0	0
Ligtenberg, Kerry, Richmond	0	3	.000	4.32	14	0	0	0	6	1	25.0	21	94	13	12	3	1	2	0	2	0	35	3	0
Loewer, Carlton, Scr./W.-B.	5	13	.278	4.60	29	29	4	0	0	0	184.0	198	797	120	94	20	8	4	7	50	6	152	3	0
Lomon, Kevin, Columbus	1	1	.500	6.28	3	3	0	0	0	0	14.1	21	71	12	10	2	1	1	2	7	0	14	1	0
Lowe, Derek, Pawtucket	4	0	1.000	2.37	6	5	0	0	1	0	30.1	23	121	8	8	3	1	0	1	11	0	21	0	0
Luebbers, Larry, Richmond	3	14	.176	5.38	27	26	2	0	1	0	144.0	180	634	101	86	20	2	6	3	44	2	91	6	0
Lukasiewicz, Mark, Syracuse*	2	3	.400	5.17	30	0	0	0	9	0	31.1	37	146	22	18	7	1	2	2	13	1	31	1	0
Maduro, Calvin, Scr./W.-B.	6	4	.600	4.99	13	13	2	0	0	0	79.1	71	354	48	44	10	5	2	1	57	1	53	6	0
Mahay, Ron, Pawtucket*	1	0	1.000	0.00	2	0	0	0	0	0	4.2	3	18	0	0	0	0	0	0	1	0	6	0	0
Mahomes, Pat, Pawtucket	5	1	.833	2.84	18	1	0	0	10	7	31.2	22	129	11	10	2	1	0	0	17	0	40	3	0
Manuel, Barry, Norfolk	2	5	.286	4.87	19	8	0	0	4	0	61.0	60	259	36	33	9	0	2	6	21	1	52	5	1
Meacham, Rusty, Pawtucket	3	3	.500	4.78	28	2	0	0	9	1	43.1	54	196	23	23	6	2	2	2	15	2	42	5	0
Mecir, Jim, Columbus	1	1	.500	1.00	24	0	0	0	17	11	27.0	14	98	4	3	0	1	0	2	6	0	34	0	0
Mendoza, Ramiro, Columbus	0	0	.000	5.68	1	1	0	0	0	0	6.1	7	31	6	4	1	0	0	0	1	0	4	0	0
Mendoza, Reynol, Charlotte	7	8	.467	5.49	46	17	0	0	15	9	114.2	134	526	79	70	14	4	3	2	57	4	93	15	1
Mercado, Hector, Charlotte*	0	1	.000	9.00	1	1	0	0	0	0	5.0	5	25	5	5	2	0	0	0	5	0	1	1	0
Miller, Kurt, Charlotte	2	1	.667	3.58	21	0	0	0	2	0	27.2	25	129	12	11	2	1	1	2	22	0	31	5	0
Millwood, Kevin, Richmond	7	0	1.000	1.93	9	9	1	0	0	0	60.2	38	232	13	13	2	2	0	1	16	0	46	2	0
Mimbs, Mark, Pawtucket*	3	8	.273	5.06	15	14	0	0	0	0	83.2	97	376	58	47	11	1	3	2	35	3	81	2	2
Mimbs, Mike, Scr./W.-B.*	4	2	.667	5.98	11	8	1	0	2	0	43.2	52	199	33	29	8	1	2	1	20	0	41	5	1
Montgomery, Steve, Roch.	0	2	.000	12.15	2	1	0	0	0	0	6.2	15	39	12	9	1	0	0	0	3	0	2	0	0
Myers, Jimmy, Norfolk	2	4	.333	1.83	45	0	0	0	14	2	69.0	57	288	23	14	1	2	1	4	33	5	31	4	2
Norris, Joe, Charlotte	0	0	.000	11.81	9	1	0	0	3	0	16.0	23	84	22	21	4	1	0	4	13	0	10	2	0
Nye, Ryan, Scr./W.-B.	4	10	.286	5.52	17	17	0	0	0	0	109.1	117	465	70	67	20	2	2	2	32	1	85	2	1
Ojala, Kirt, Charlotte*	8	7	.533	3.50	25	24	0	0	1	0	149.0	148	627	74	58	13	4	1	3	55	2	119	4	0
Orellano, Rafael, Pawtucket*	3	5	.375	7.14	16	12	1	0	0	0	69.1	65	323	58	55	12	2	7	2	55	0	46	4	0
Pall, Donn, Charlotte	4	7	.364	3.39	59	0	0	0	28	8	79.2	82	334	40	30	10	2	1	5	11	2	70	3	0
Paniagua, Jose, Ottawa	8	10	.444	4.64	22	22	1	0	0	0	137.2	164	618	79	71	13	5	6	7	44	1	87	5	0
Pavano, Carl, Pawtucket	11	6	.647	3.12	23	23	3	0	0	0	161.2	148	663	62	56	13	1	3	6	34	2	147	7	1
Pavlas, Dave, Columbus	1	3	.250	4.62	26	0	0	0	25	12	25.1	33	116	14	13	3	2	1	0	4	2	34	0	0
Perez, Yorkis, Norfolk*	1	0	1.000	3.48	17	0	0	0	8	3	20.2	22	89	9	8	2	2	2	0	7	0	24	0	0
Person, Robert, Syracuse	1	0	1.000	0.00	1	1	0	0	0	0	7.0	4	26	1	0	0	0	0	0	2	0	5	0	0
Peterson, Dean, Pawtucket	0	1	.000	3.00	2	0	0	0	2	0	3.0	2	13	1	1	1	0	0	0	1	0	2	0	1
Plantenberg, Erik, Scr./W.-B.*	0	2	.000	7.53	18	0	0	0	8	0	14.1	22	74	12	12	1	1	1	0	9	2	12	1	0
Polley, Dale, Columbus*	2	2	.500	3.75	62	0	0	0	13	2	48.0	47	202	20	20	2	1	3	3	20	1	49	2	0
Press, Gregg, Charlotte	0	0	.000	4.50	1	1	0	0	0	0	6.0	5	26	3	3	1	0	0	0	4	0	2	0	0
Pugh, Tim, Toledo	3	5	.375	4.29	19	17	0	0	1	0	109.0	115	460	60	52	18	2	3	5	28	0	97	4	0
Pulido, Carlos, Ottawa*	5	2	.714	5.42	44	5	0	0	17	0	76.1	84	333	47	46	10	0	2	2	25	2	44	2	0
Pulsipher, Bill, Norfolk*	0	5	.000	7.81	8	5	0	0	1	0	27.2	23	142	29	24	1	3	0	1	38	0	18	5	1
Ramirez, Hector, Rochester	8	7	.533	4.91	39	9	0	0	10	3	102.2	114	456	65	56	11	1	8	7	38	2	50	11	3
Reyes, Carlos, Columbus	0	0	.000	18.00	1	1	0	0	0	0	2.0	5	12	4	4	0	0	0	1	0	0	2	0	0
Rhine, Kendall, Syracuse	0	0	.000	9.00	1	0	0	0	1	0	2.0	2	12	2	2	0	0	1	1	3	0	0	0	0
Ricci, Chuck, Ottawa	2	2	.500	4.67	22	0	0	0	9	0	27.0	22	125	16	14	1	3	1	1	25	3	27	6	0
Ricken, Ray, Columbus	11	7	.611	5.54	26	26	0	0	0	0	152.2	172	701	104	94	12	3	3	6	81	2	99	16	1
Rios, Dan, Columbus	7	4	.636	3.08	58	0	0	0	14	3	84.2	73	351	37	29	8	3	4	1	31	1	53	5	0
Risley, Bill, Syracuse	1	2	.333	8.22	11	1	0	0	4	0	15.1	19	78	15	14	5	0	0	3	10	0	20	2	0
Roberts, Chris, Norfolk*	0	4	.000	2.89	7	6	0	0	1	0	37.1	38	164	17	12	2	2	1	2	17	0	21	0	1
Robinson, Ken, Syracuse	7	7	.500	2.56	56	0	0	0	41	17	81.0	44	319	24	23	6	4	2	0	36	1	96	5	0
Rodarte, Raul, Richmond	0	0	.000	9.00	1	0	0	0	1	0	1.0	2	5	1	1	1	0	0	0	0	0	0	1	0
Rodriguez, Nerio, Rochester	11	10	.524	3.90	27	27	1	1	0	0	168.1	124	688	82	73	23	6	0	8	62	0	160	4	3
Rodriguez, Tony, Pawtucket	0	0	.000	18.00	1	0	0	0	1	0	1.0	4	7	2	2	0	0	0	0	0	0	0	0	0
Rogers, Bryan, Richmond	1	1	.500	5.17	21	0	0	0	9	0	38.1	45	178	26	22	4	0	1	0	16	2	25	2	0
Rogers, Kevin, Richmond*	0	2	.000	7.36	10	0	0	0	4	0	11.0	15	53	11	9	2	0	1	0	5	0	9	1	0
Romano, Michael, Syracuse	2	4	.333	4.25	40	12	0	0	9	0	108.0	100	487	56	51	10	1	3	6	74	2	83	7	0
Rose, Brian, Pawtucket	17	5	.773	3.02	27	26	3	0	0	0	190.2	188	787	74	64	21	1	5	7	46	2	116	5	0
Rose, Scott, Columbus	2	2	.500	3.70	26	0	0	0	22	11	24.1	24	99	11	10	2	2	1	0	6	1	13	0	0
Rosengren, John, Toledo*	1	3	.250	3.99	54	0	0	0	16	2	56.1	44	266	29	25	1	1	3	7	49	1	53	7	1
Rossy, Rico, Ottawa	0	0	.000	0.00	1	0	0	0	1	0	1.0	0	4	0	0	0	0	0	0	1	0	0	1	0
Ruffcorn, Scott, Scr./W.-B.	2	0	1.000	1.16	5	5	2	2	0	0	31.0	22	126	6	4	0	2	0	1	10	0	20	0	0
Ruffin, Johnny, Pawtucket	0	1	.000	4.50	6	1	0	0	2	0	14.0	5	60	7	7	0	0	0	0	16	0	16	4	0
Rumer, Tim, Columbus*	4	7	.364	6.16	17	12	1	0	2	0	68.2	79	315	54	47	8	2	2	2	41	1	46	3	3
Ryan, Ken, Scr./W.-B.	1	0	1.000	4.50	3	0	0	0	1	1	4.0	5	18	2	2	0	0	0	0	3	0	3	0	0
Saberhagen, Bret, Pawtucket	0	1	.000	3.27	2	2	0	0	0	0	11.0	11	45	4	4	1	0	0	1	1	0	9	0	0

Pitcher, Team	W	L	Pct.	ERA	G	GS	CG	ShO	GF	Sv.	IP	H	TBF	R	ER	HR	SH	SF	HB	BB	IBB	SO	WP	Bk.
Sackinsky, Brian, Rochester .	1	0	1.000	5.11	2	2	0	0	0	0	12.1	12	49	7	7	3	0	0	0	3	0	6	0	0
Sauerbeck, Scott, Norfolk* ..	1	0	1.000	3.60	1	0	0	0	0	0	5.0	3	20	2	2	0	0	1	0	4	0	4	1	0
Saunders, Tony, Charlotte* ..	1	0	1.000	2.77	3	3	0	0	0	0	13.0	9	50	4	4	1	1	0	0	6	0	9	0	0
Schmidt, Curt, Ottawa	0	3	.000	6.61	31	0	0	0	23	5	31.1	44	157	24	23	2	5	0	2	22	5	18	1	0
Schrenk, Steve, Rochester .	4	7	.364	4.66	25	24	1	0	0	0	125.2	127	539	73	65	21	2	1	6	36	0	99	3	2
Schutz, Carl, Richmond* ...	4	6	.400	5.33	27	10	0	0	7	0	79.1	83	366	56	47	12	1	2	2	51	2	66	6	0
Seanez, Rudy, Norfolk	1	0	1.000	4.05	9	0	0	0	0	0	13.1	12	63	8	6	1	0	0	0	11	0	17	0	0
Seelbach, Chris, Charlotte .	5	0	1.000	6.26	16	6	0	0	1	0	50.1	58	241	36	35	7	3	3	1	34	2	50	3	0
Shepherd, Keith, Norfolk ...	8	8	.500	4.37	19	18	0	0	1	0	107.0	119	482	61	52	10	3	2	3	55	1	78	3	1
Shouse, Brian, Rochester* ..	6	2	.750	2.27	54	0	0	0	29	9	71.1	48	282	21	18	6	5	1	3	21	4	81	2	0
Sievert, Mark, Syracuse	0	0	.000	3.38	1	1	0	0	0	0	5.1	5	23	3	2	0	0	0	0	2	0	5	0	0
Sinclair, Steve, Syracuse* ..	0	0	.000	6.00	1	0	0	0	1	0	9.0	11	40	6	6	0	0	0	0	3	0	9	0	0
Smith, Brian, Syracuse....	7	11	.389	5.37	31	21	0	0	2	0	137.1	169	619	89	82	12	2	6	8	51	1	73	4	3
Stanifer, Robby, Charlotte...	4	0	1.000	4.88	22	0	0	0	16	5	27.2	34	123	16	15	3	1	1	1	7	0	25	2	0
Steph, Rod, Charlotte.....	3	3	.500	4.25	41	0	0	0	32	14	48.2	49	208	24	23	6	3	4	2	12	1	51	2	0
Stephenson, Garrett, Scr./W.-B.	3	1	.750	5.90	7	3	0	0	1	0	29.0	27	125	19	19	6	0	1	0	12	0	27	2	0
Stull, Everett, Ottawa	8	10	.444	5.82	27	27	1	0	0	0	159.1	166	710	110	103	25	4	4	13	86	0	130	9	0
Suppan, Jeff, Pawtucket....	5	1	.833	3.71	9	9	2	1	0	0	60.2	51	239	26	25	7	0	4	1	15	0	40	2	1
Swift, Billy, Rochester	1	0	1.000	4.91	2	0	0	0	0	0	3.2	2	16	2	2	0	0	0	0	3	0	2	0	0
Tam, Jeff, Norfolk.	7	5	.583	4.67	40	11	0	0	15	6	111.2	137	480	72	58	9	6	4	7	14	4	67	5	0
Thobe, Tom, Richmond*	5	2	.714	4.14	19	10	0	0	1	0	71.2	70	297	37	33	9	3	3	0	22	1	36	3	0
Thurman, Mike, Ottawa	1	3	.250	5.49	4	4	0	0	0	0	19.2	17	85	13	12	1	0	0	1	9	0	15	2	1
Torres, Salomon, Ottawa ...	0	0	.000	5.40	2	1	0	0	0	0	5.0	7	24	5	3	0	0	0	0	2	0	2	0	1
Urbani, Thomas, Ottawa* ..	3	1	.750	2.61	30	1	0	0	7	0	41.1	37	166	13	12	2	2	0	0	12	0	25	1	0
Urso, Sal, Columbus *	0	3	.000	4.73	24	2	0	0	9	0	45.2	59	211	29	24	4	3	1	3	19	0	44	5	4
Valdez, Carlos, Pawtucket...	0	4	.000	4.69	35	8	0	0	6	1	78.2	73	346	49	41	7	3	4	0	46	4	64	5	0
Walker, Pete, Pawtucket....	0	0	.000	5.40	7	0	0	0	2	0	11.2	14	57	8	7	2	0	0	0	7	1	8	1	0
Wallace, Derek, Norfolk	0	1	.000	9.00	1	0	0	0	1	0	1.0	2	6	2	1	0	0	0	0	1	0	0	0	0
Ward, Bryan, Charlotte* ...	2	9	.182	6.93	15	14	2	0	0	0	75.1	102	349	62	58	17	5	4	4	30	4	48	5	1
Weathers, David, Columbus .	2	2	.500	3.19	5	5	1	0	0	0	36.2	35	148	18	13	3	1	0	0	7	0	35	0	0
Weber, Neil, Ottawa*	2	5	.286	7.94	9	9	0	0	0	0	39.2	46	204	46	35	7	2	1	2	40	0	27	2	0
Welch, Mike, Norfolk	2	2	.500	3.66	46	0	0	0	38	20	51.2	53	216	21	21	6	2	2	1	16	2	35	0	0
Whisenant, Matt, Charlotte* .	2	1	.667	7.20	16	0	0	0	4	0	15.0	16	73	12	12	0	0	0	1	12	0	19	4	0
Williams, Brian, Rochester ..	4	3	.571	3.89	22	9	0	0	1	0	69.1	68	299	33	30	8	3	2	4	23	0	78	1	2
Wilson, Pookie, Charlotte* ..	0	0	.000	0.00	1	0	0	0	1	0	1.0	0	4	0	0	0	0	0	0	1	0	0	0	0
Winston, Darrin, Scr./W.-B.* .	7	4	.636	3.43	39	9	1	0	9	1	89.1	74	371	38	34	9	2	3	5	36	4	66	6	1
Withem, Shannon, Norfolk ..	9	10	.474	4.34	29	27	1	0	2	0	155.2	167	668	85	75	21	2	4	4	48	1	109	5	0
Woodall, Brad, Richmond* ..	8	11	.421	5.51	28	26	1	0	0	0	148.2	177	659	100	91	19	9	3	3	52	1	117	6	0
Yan, Esteban, Rochester....	11	5	.688	3.10	34	12	0	0	8	2	119.0	107	490	54	41	13	1	6	5	37	0	131	5	0
Yarnall, Ed, Norfolk*	0	1	.000	14.40	1	1	0	0	0	0	5.0	11	29	8	8	1	0	0	7	2	2	5	0	0

COMBINATION SHUTOUTS: **Charlotte (4)**—Ojala-Juelsgaard-Darensbourg-Stanifer-Hurst, Hernandez-Mendoza, Hernandez-Alfonseca-Darensbourg-Stanifer, Chergey-Pall. **Columbus (7)**—Banks-Rios-Pavlas, Banks-Rios-Polley-Rose, Converse-Rios-Buddie-Mecir, Gardiner-Rios, Irabu-Rios-Banks, Banks-Buddie, Arocha-Mecir-Polley-Rios. **Norfolk (7)**—Lidle-Welch, Lidle-Myers-Kashiwada, Shepherd-Tam, Crawford-Jordan-Welch, Bohanon-Myers-Perez, Shepherd-Edmondson-Dougherty, Withem-Perez. **Ottawa (4)**—Falteisek-Pulido, Paniagua-Bennett, Thurman-Bennett, Falteisek-Urbani-Bullinger. **Pawtucket (5)**—Pavano-Grundt-Mahomes, Avery-Meacham-Borland-Garces, Grundt-Brandenburg-Lacy, Lowe-Rose-Borland, Eshelman-Borland-Lacy. **Richmond (9)**—Woodall-Brow, Harrison-Hartgraves, Millwood-Fox, Harrison-Brow, Millwood-Fox, Byrd-Ligtenberg-Brow, Woodall-Clontz-Brow, Thobe-Clontz, Harrison-Brow. **Rochester (7)**—Schrenk-Steph-Yan-Williams, Rodriguez-Ramirez-Shouse, Haynes-Shouse-Williams, Yan-Bennett, Yan-Bennett-Shouse, Rodriguez-Ramirez, Johns-Corbin. **Scranton/Wilkes-Barre (4)**—Maduro-Heflin, Fiore-Holman, Winston-Hawblitzel-Heflin, Loewer-Mimbs-Holman-Heflin. **Syracuse (5)**—Smith-Robinson-Brown, Halladay-Smith-Robinson, Halladay-Lukasiewicz-Robinson, Flener-Robinson, Daal-Almanzar. **Toledo (8)**—Keagle-Fermin-Rosengren-Gaillard, Dishman-Hernandez-Greene-Gaillard, Harriger-Greene-Gaillard, Barnes-Dishman-Greene-Gaillard, Keagle-Hernandez-Rosengren, Dishman-Fermin, Dishman-Gaillard, Harriger-Hernandez.

NO-HIT GAMES: None.

PITCHERS WITH TWO OR MORE TEAMS

Pitcher, Team	W	L	Pct.	ERA	G	GS	CG	ShO	GF	Sv.	IP	H	TBF	R	ER	HR	SH	SF	HB	BB	IBB	SO	WP	Bk.
Cain, Tim, Pawtucket	3	3	.500	5.93	17	0	0	0	4	2	30.1	34	138	22	20	6	2	1	4	12	0	13	0	0
Cain, Tim, Syracuse	0	2	.000	5.32	13	1	0	0	6	0	22.0	26	107	13	13	4	0	4	3	14	0	14	1	0
Daal, Omar, Ottawa*	0	1	.000	5.63	2	2	0	0	0	0	8.0	10	36	6	5	1	0	0	1	9	0	9	1	0
Daal, Omar, Syracuse*	3	0	1.000	0.53	5	5	1	1	0	0	33.2	18	128	2	2	0	0	1	0	10	0	29	2	1

1997 FIELDING

TEAM

Team	Pct.	G	PO	A	E	TC	DP	PB	Team	Pct.	G	PO	A	E	TC	DP	PB
Columbus	.980	142	3704	1534	106	5344	131	19	Ottawa	.974	140	3592	1570	140	5302	139	14
Charlotte..........	.977	141	3570	1521	118	5209	145	17	Toledo..............	.973	141	3669	1468	145	5282	116	8
Pawtucket........	.976	141	3727	1471	126	5324	120	22	Norfolk..............	.971	142	3697	1574	156	5427	166	13
Rochester........	.975	141	3678	1268	127	5073	84	14	Scranton/W.-B....	.971	142	3626	1424	150	5200	118	8
Syracuse	.975	142	3656	1549	136	5341	176	6	TRIPLE PLAYS: Norfolk, Scranton/W.-B., Toledo.								
Richmond........	.974	142	3702	1509	138	5349	138	9									

INDIVIDUAL

FIRST BASEMEN

NOTE: All caps denotes fielding-percentage leader based on 71 games for catchers, 95 for all other non-pitchers and 142 innings for pitchers. *Throws lefthanded.

Player, Team	Pct.	G	PO	A	E	TC	DP
Abad, Andy, Pawtucket*	.984	33	275	25	5	305	24
Aldrete, Mike, Syracuse*......	.989	22	173	10	2	185	18

Player, Team	Pct.	G	PO	A	E	TC	DP
Aude, Rich, Syracuse	.984	68	587	34	10	631	78
Bellinger, Clay, Columbus	1.000	9	65	2	0	67	7
Bennett, Gary, Pawtucket	1.000	6	48	3	0	51	1
Bream, Scott, Toledo.........	1.000	3	26	1	0	27	2
Carey, Todd, Pawtucket.......	.993	52	369	31	3	403	40
Correia, Rod, Pawtucket	.949	4	34	3	2	39	5

Player, Team	Pct.	G	PO	A	E	TC	DP
Crespo, Felipe, Syracuse	.976	19	151	11	4	166	16
Cruz, Ivan, Columbus*	.992	114	974	83	8	1065	89
Daubach, Brian, Charlotte	.991	101	870	62	8	940	92
DAVIS, Tommy, Rochester	.994	116	875	72	6	953	56
Dodson, Bo, Pawtucket*	.987	16	141	13	2	156	12
Floyd, Cliff, Charlotte	.971	3	32	1	1	34	7
Franco, Matt, Norfolk	1.000	2	11	3	0	14	1
Fullmer, Brad, Ottawa	.995	19	172	12	1	185	17
Giannelli, Ray, Syracuse	1.000	6	25	1	0	26	2
Gregg, Tommy, Richmond*	.994	20	148	9	1	158	15
Gruber, Kelly, Rochester	.968	8	56	5	2	63	6
Hall, Joe, Toledo	.988	11	74	10	1	85	1
Hamelin, Bob, Toledo*	.984	14	121	5	2	128	12
Hare, Shawn, Columbus*	.944	5	30	4	2	36	4
Hyers, Tim, Toledo*	.990	113	879	94	10	983	80
Jones, Ryan, Syracuse	.991	40	333	16	3	352	43
Jordan, Kevin, Scr./W.-B.	1.000	1	17	0	0	17	2
Ledesma, Aaron, Rochester	1.000	1	3	1	0	4	1
Lukachyk, Rob, Ottawa	.995	24	192	13	1	206	22
Luke, Matt, Columbus*	.989	18	157	15	2	174	14
Malave, Jose, Pawtucket	.983	17	165	9	3	177	12
Manto, Jeff, Syracuse	1.000	2	13	4	0	17	2
Martin, Jim, Norfolk	1.000	1	1	0	0	1	0
McClain, Scott, Norfolk	.985	8	58	8	1	67	7
McGuire, Ryan, Ottawa*	.996	50	421	52	2	475	36
McKeel, Walt, Pawtucket	.968	20	144	7	5	156	12
Meulens, Hensley, Ottawa	.980	38	320	21	7	348	32
Morman, Russ, Charlotte	.986	50	339	26	5	370	35
Nevin, Phil, Toledo	1.000	3	19	3	0	22	4
Otanez, Willis, Rochester	.977	7	39	3	1	43	2
Petagine, Roberto, Norfolk*	.990	116	1002	68	11	1081	117
Robertson, Mike, Scr./W.-B.*	.987	120	951	97	14	1062	82
Rodriguez, Adam, Toledo	.946	5	33	2	2	37	3
Rodriguez, Tony, Pawtucket	1.000	2	17	1	0	18	3
Ronan, Marc, Columbus	1.000	3	18	2	0	20	4
Saunders, Chris, Norfolk	1.000	5	31	3	0	34	4
Schu, Rick, Ottawa	1.000	1	8	1	0	9	1
Seefried, Tate, Norfolk	1.000	21	158	11	0	169	21
Seitzer, Brad, Ottawa	.992	15	112	14	1	127	11
Simon, Randall, Richmond*	.988	127	1063	72	14	1149	115
Tolentino, Jose, Rochester*	.959	12	66	5	3	74	7
Waszgis, B.J., Rochester	1.000	3	23	2	0	25	2
Wedge, Eric, Scr./W.-B.	.895	4	16	1	2	19	1
Wehner, John, Charlotte	1.000	2	8	0	0	8	1
Woods, Tyrone, Pawtucket	1.000	2	22	0	0	22	0
Zuber, Jon, Scr./W.-B.*	.995	23	189	15	1	205	19

TRIPLE PLAYS: Hyers, McClain, Robertson.

SECOND BASEMEN

Player, Team	Pct.	G	PO	A	E	TC	DP
Allison, Chris, Pawtucket	.970	8	12	20	1	33	3
Angeli, Doug, Scr./W.-B.	.963	20	29	50	3	82	14
Azuaje, Jesus, Norfolk	.940	11	22	25	3	50	6
Barker, Tim, Columbus	.985	31	54	74	2	130	16
Bellinger, Clay, Columbus	1.000	3	8	8	0	16	1
Benjamin, Mike, Pawtucket	1.000	1	0	3	0	3	0
Berg, David, Charlotte	1.000	2	1	2	0	3	0
Berry, Mike, Rochester	1.000	6	1	6	0	7	0
Bieser, Steve, Norfolk	1.000	3	4	7	0	11	0
Blum, Geoffrey, Ottawa	.975	70	156	197	9	362	50
Bream, Scott, Toledo	.962	17	31	45	3	79	4
Bush, Homer, Columbus	.978	74	153	253	9	415	62
Cabrera, Jolbert, Ottawa	1.000	7	20	19	0	39	1
Cabrera, Orlando, Ottawa	1.000	10	18	27	0	45	6
Carey, Todd, Pawtucket	.952	13	15	45	3	63	11
Castillo, Luis, Charlotte	.970	36	66	97	5	168	24
CATALANOTTO, Frank, Toledo	.984	96	152	276	7	435	51
Clapinski, Chris, Charlotte	.969	40	89	96	6	191	27
Crespo, Felipe, Syracuse	.962	28	47	78	5	130	20
Doster, David, Scr./W.-B.	.979	74	123	200	7	330	37
Flores, Jose, Scr./W.-B.	.987	33	65	92	2	159	19
Forbes, P.J., Rochester	.979	58	102	131	5	238	28
Fox, Andy, Columbus	.982	22	46	66	2	114	13
Gilbert, Shawn, Norfolk	.921	8	13	22	3	38	7
Gruber, Kelly, Rochester	.963	21	31	48	3	82	8
Hajek, Dave, Toledo	1.000	9	17	19	0	36	3
Hardtke, Jason, Norfolk	.981	95	187	319	10	516	76
Henry, Santiago, Syracuse	.949	8	16	21	2	39	6
Howard, Matt, Columbus	1.000	5	6	13	0	19	2
Hudler, Rex, Scr./W.-B.	1.000	1	1	5	0	6	1
Jaime, Angel, Norfolk	1.000	1	2	2	0	4	1
Jordan, Kevin, Scr./W.-B.	1.000	3	5	11	0	16	2
Kelly, Pat, Columbus	1.000	10	15	39	0	54	6
Lawrence, Chip, Rochester	.889	2	2	6	1	9	0
Lopez, Luis, Norfolk	.974	8	14	24	1	39	7
Lovullo, Torey, Ottawa	1.000	14	31	35	0	66	6
Malloy, Marty, Richmond	.975	101	195	278	12	485	67
Martinez, Pablo, Richmond	.986	30	62	78	2	142	20
Matos, Francisco, Rochester	.975	66	100	135	6	241	17
Melhuse, Adam, Syracuse	1.000	1	1	3	0	4	1
Merloni, Lou, Pawtucket	.986	33	50	94	2	146	17
Milliard, Ralph, Charlotte	.994	32	71	91	1	163	33
Mordecai, Mike, Richmond	1.000	11	21	35	0	56	10
Morgan, Kevin, Norfolk	.968	22	27	63	3	93	11
Mummau, Rob, Syracuse	.977	35	68	103	4	175	23
Olmeda, Jose, Charlotte	.981	23	46	55	2	103	16
Patzke, Jeff, Syracuse	.975	78	153	238	10	401	74
Pozo, Arquimedez, Pawtucket	1.000	5	5	9	0	14	1
Pye, Eddie, Norfolk	1.000	1	2	2	0	4	0
Rodriguez, Steve, Toledo	.991	21	42	63	1	106	14
Rodriguez, Tony, Pawtucket	.944	9	16	18	2	36	2
Rossy, Rico, Ottawa	.947	24	38	52	5	95	16
Sadler, Donnie, Pawtucket	.971	78	173	234	12	419	51
Sefcik, Kevin, Scr./W.-B.	.973	16	33	40	2	75	8
Soriano, Fred, Syracuse	.875	2	2	5	1	8	1
Torres, Tony, Charlotte	1.000	19	24	44	0	68	13
Tyler, Brad, Richmond	.900	4	2	7	1	10	0
Vidro, Jose, Ottawa	.958	21	40	52	4	96	14
Wehner, John, Charlotte	1.000	1	0	2	0	2	0

TRIPLE PLAY: Catalanotto.

THIRD BASEMEN

Player, Team	Pct.	G	PO	A	E	TC	DP
Amador, Manuel, Scr./W.-B.	.895	20	14	37	6	57	3
Andrews, Shane, Ottawa	1.000	3	2	4	0	6	1
Angeli, Doug, Scr./W.-B.	.867	46	23	94	18	135	6
Azuaje, Jesus, Norfolk	1.000	8	1	15	0	16	1
Bellinger, Clay, Columbus	.918	48	28	84	10	122	9
Benjamin, Mike, Pawtucket	1.000	2	1	2	0	3	0
Berg, David, Charlotte	1.000	1	0	4	0	4	2
Berry, Mike, Rochester	.936	44	33	69	7	109	4
Bieser, Steve, Norfolk	.500	2	0	1	1	2	0
Blum, Geoffrey, Ottawa	1.000	6	7	8	0	15	1
Cabrera, Jolbert, Ottawa	.962	46	23	102	5	130	8
Carey, Todd, Pawtucket	.917	28	17	49	6	72	1
Catalanotto, Frank, Toledo	.890	36	14	75	11	100	3
Clapinski, Chris, Charlotte	.969	24	17	45	2	64	3
Correia, Rod, Pawtucket	1.000	7	7	21	0	28	3
Crespo, Felipe, Syracuse	1.000	3	2	10	0	12	1
Doster, David, Scr./W.-B.	.917	34	29	48	7	84	5
EVANS, Tom, Syracuse	.964	104	83	242	12	337	27
Flores, Jose, Scr./W.-B.	.897	30	25	45	8	78	4
Forbes, P.J., Rochester	.952	57	43	95	7	145	4
Fox, Andy, Columbus	.934	49	26	101	9	136	6
Gilbert, Shawn, Norfolk	1.000	7	1	14	0	15	3
Giovanola, Ed, Richmond	.957	79	51	148	9	208	21
Hajek, Dave, Toledo	.899	53	33	83	13	129	11
Helms, Wes, Richmond	.902	32	18	65	9	92	5
Holbert, Ray, Toledo	.947	6	4	14	1	19	0
Jordan, Kevin, Scr./W.-B.	.889	4	1	7	1	9	0
Kmak, Joe, Charlotte	1.000	1	0	1	0	1	0
Lawrence, Chip, Rochester	1.000	4	3	9	0	12	0
Long, R.D., Columbus	.700	8	2	5	3	10	1
Lopez, Jose, Norfolk	.900	2	2	7	1	10	1
Lovullo, Torey, Ottawa	1.000	1	0	7	0	7	0
Lowell, Mike, Columbus	.954	43	31	73	5	109	5
Lucca, Lou, Charlotte	.946	91	43	201	14	258	15
Manto, Jeff, Syracuse	.947	7	3	15	1	19	2
Martinez, Pablo, Richmond	.903	28	13	52	7	72	5
McClain, Scott, Norfolk	.949	92	64	194	14	272	19
Merloni, Lou, Pawtucket	.955	8	6	15	1	22	0
Meulens, Hensley, Ottawa	.916	45	29	91	11	131	11
Mordecai, Mike, Richmond	1.000	11	2	17	0	19	2
Mummau, Rob, Syracuse	1.000	30	18	55	0	73	3
Nevin, Phil, Toledo	1.000	1	0	1	0	1	0
Olmeda, Jose, Charlotte	.918	21	13	54	6	73	10
Otanez, Willis, Rochester	.894	44	28	65	11	104	2
Patzke, Jeff, Syracuse	1.000	1	2	2	0	4	1
Pozo, Arquimedez, Pawtucket	.957	86	61	161	10	232	8
Roberts, Lonell, Syracuse	1.000	1	2	2	0	4	0
Rodriguez, Adam, Toledo	1.000	1	0	2	0	2	0
Rodriguez, Steve, Toledo	.917	48	19	80	9	108	7
Rodriguez, Tony, Pawtucket	.955	21	15	48	3	66	7
Russo, Paul, Columbus	1.000	1	1	2	0	3	0
Saunders, Chris, Norfolk	.926	37	19	56	6	81	7

Player, Team	Pct.	G	PO	A	E	TC	DP
Schu, Rick, Ottawa	1.000	4	1	5	0	6	0
Seefried, Tate, Norfolk	.846	8	0	11	2	13	1
Sefcik, Kevin, Scr./W.-B.	.879	13	14	15	4	33	0
Seitzer, Brad, Ottawa	.800	2	0	8	2	10	1
Spencer, Shane, Columbus	1.000	2	1	2	0	3	0
Strange, Doug, Ottawa	1.000	1	2	3	0	5	0
Troilo, Jason, Columbus	.750	2	1	2	1	4	0
Vidro, Jose, Ottawa	.972	47	30	109	4	143	11
Wehner, John, Charlotte	.975	14	8	31	1	40	5

TRIPLE PLAY: S. Rodriguez.

SHORTSTOPS

Player, Team	Pct.	G	PO	A	E	TC	DP
Angeli, Doug, Scr./W.-B.	.976	11	10	31	1	42	3
Barker, Tim, Columbus	.778	3	2	5	2	9	2
Bellinger, Clay, Columbus	.945	11	13	39	3	55	2
Benjamin, Mike, Pawtucket	.962	27	45	81	5	131	15
Berg, David, Charlotte	.954	108	135	318	22	475	70
Blum, Geoffrey, Ottawa	.952	35	60	100	8	168	18
Bream, Scott, Toledo	.897	9	16	19	4	39	4
Cabrera, Jolbert, Ottawa	.867	4	8	5	2	15	1
Cabrera, Orlando, Ottawa	.969	22	27	67	3	97	14
Carey, Todd, Pawtucket	.867	5	6	7	2	15	2
Clapinski, Chris, Charlotte	.971	32	42	93	4	139	19
Correia, Rod, Pawtucket	.960	20	33	63	4	100	13
Flores, Jose, Scr./W.-B.	.938	7	3	12	1	16	0
Forbes, P.J., Rochester	1.000	6	5	11	0	16	3
Fox, Andy, Columbus	.964	17	30	51	3	84	9
Gilbert, Shawn, Norfolk	.939	38	60	95	10	165	29
Giovanola, Ed, Richmond	.939	25	28	79	7	114	13
Henry, Santiago, Syracuse	.928	32	57	84	11	152	24
Holbert, Ray, Toledo	.952	104	183	288	24	495	58
HOWARD, Matt, Columbus	.989	110	154	293	5	452	69
Jimenez, D'Angelo, Columbus	.833	2	2	8	2	12	0
Johns, Keith, Rochester	1.000	1	0	1	0	1	0
Lawrence, Chip, Rochester	.929	9	11	15	2	28	1
Ledesma, Aaron, Rochester	.959	81	118	184	13	315	39
Lopez, Luis, Norfolk	.927	40	65	99	13	177	31
Lowell, Mike, Columbus	.833	3	5	10	3	18	3
Martinez, Eddy, Rochester	.969	12	6	25	1	32	4
Martinez, Pablo, Richmond	.975	22	30	48	2	80	11
Matos, Francisco, Rochester	.975	28	31	48	2	81	7
McClain, Scott, Norfolk	.964	22	39	68	4	111	15
Merloni, Lou, Pawtucket	.947	7	5	13	1	19	3
Miller, Orlando, Toledo	.957	7	10	12	1	23	1
Mordecai, Mike, Richmond	.938	4	6	9	1	16	4
Morgan, Kevin, Norfolk	.945	50	73	150	13	236	32
Mummau, Rob, Syracuse	.887	17	25	38	8	71	10
Ojeda, Augie, Rochester	.922	15	24	35	5	64	6
Olmeda, Jose, Charlotte	.857	1	4	2	1	7	1
Perez, Tomas, Syracuse	.973	89	158	274	12	444	78
Pye, Eddie, Norfolk	1.000	1	1	4	0	5	0
Relaford, Desi, Scr./W.-B.	.942	130	180	373	34	587	81
Rodriguez, Steve, Toledo	.933	24	42	55	7	104	13
Rodriguez, Tony, Pawtucket	.973	42	73	105	5	183	25
Rossy, Rico, Ottawa	.959	85	116	236	15	367	53
Sadler, Donnie, Pawtucket	.985	46	79	120	3	202	24
Smith, Bobby, Richmond	.952	98	161	297	23	481	59
Soriano, Fred, Syracuse	.947	14	19	35	3	57	8

TRIPLE PLAYS: Lopez, Relaford.

OUTFIELDERS

Player, Team	Pct.	G	PO	A	E	TC	DP
Abad, Andy, Pawtucket*	.942	34	48	1	3	52	0
Agbayani, Benny, Norfolk	.978	120	207	12	5	224	1
Aldrete, Mike, Syracuse*	1.000	2	3	0	0	3	0
Angeli, Doug, Scr./W.-B.	1.000	2	3	0	0	3	0
Aude, Rich, Syracuse	1.000	2	3	0	0	3	0
Banks, Willie, Columbus	.000	1	0	0	1	1	0
Barker, Glen, Toledo	1.000	17	24	1	0	25	0
Barker, Tim, Columbus	1.000	19	40	3	0	43	1
Barron, Tony, Scr./W.-B.	.963	70	102	3	4	109	1
Bartee, Kimera, Toledo	.997	135	336	4	1	341	1
Bautista, Danny, Richmond	1.000	42	104	4	0	108	3
Bellinger, Clay, Columbus	.975	37	73	4	2	79	0
Bieser, Steve, Norfolk	.935	21	29	0	2	31	0
Bowers, Brent, Scr./W.-B.	.964	20	25	2	1	28	0
Brown, Ron, Columbus	1.000	10	16	0	0	16	0
Bryant, Pat, Pawtucket	.882	8	15	0	2	17	0
Buchanan, Brian, Columbus	.947	12	17	1	1	19	0
Bullett, Scott, Rochester*	.972	122	232	8	7	247	2
Burton, Darren, Scr./W.-B.	.980	63	138	9	3	150	0
Butler, Rich, Syracuse	.968	135	236	8	8	252	4
Butler, Rob, Scr./W.-B.*	1.000	15	23	1	0	24	0
Cabrera, Jolbert, Ottawa	1.000	1	0	1	0	1	0
Carney, Bartt, Rochester	1.000	3	7	0	0	7	0
Carpenter, Bubba, Columbus*	.994	79	164	6	1	171	3
Castillo, Alberto, Norfolk	.000	1	0	0	1	1	0
Catalanotto, Frank, Toledo	1.000	2	2	0	0	2	0
Chamberlain, Wes, Norfolk	.942	61	75	6	5	86	0
Clyburn, Danny, Rochester	.961	133	241	5	10	256	1
Cole, Alex, Charlotte*	.980	34	46	2	1	49	1
Coleman, Michael, Pawtucket	.932	28	53	2	4	59	0
Correia, Rod, Pawtucket	.500	1	1	0	1	2	0
Cradle, Rickey, Syracuse	1.000	7	9	1	0	10	0
Crespo, Felipe, Syracuse	.944	30	47	4	3	54	2
Delvecchio, Nick, Columbus	1.000	3	3	0	0	3	0
DeLaCruz, Lorenzo, Syracuse	1.000	9	16	2	0	18	0
Diaz, Alex, Norfolk	.923	6	10	2	1	13	0
Dunwoody, Todd, Charlotte*	.992	105	231	5	2	238	1
Espinosa, Ramon, Norfolk	1.000	23	31	1	0	32	0
Floyd, Cliff, Charlotte	1.000	36	47	4	0	51	0
Fox, Andy, Columbus	1.000	6	9	0	0	9	0
Fox, Eric, Roch.-S./W.-B.*	.991	54	106	2	1	109	1
Franco, Matt, Norfolk	1.000	3	2	1	0	3	0
Frazier, Lou, Rochester	.981	83	204	6	4	214	0
Fullmer, Brad, Ottawa	1.000	1	1	0	0	1	0
Geisler, Phil, Norfolk*	.994	93	171	6	1	178	3
Gilbert, Shawn, Norfolk	.946	31	50	3	3	56	1
Giovanola, Ed, Richmond	1.000	5	8	0	0	8	0
Gregg, Tommy, Richmond*	.988	52	82	3	1	86	2
Gruber, Kelly, Rochester	1.000	6	14	0	0	14	0
Hall, Joe, Toledo	1.000	38	61	5	0	66	1
Hare, Shawn, Tol.-Col.*	1.000	16	22	2	0	24	1
Hollins, Damon, Richmond*	.977	133	319	14	8	341	2
Hurst, Jimmy, Toledo	.962	106	210	18	9	237	3
Hyers, Tim, Toledo*	.933	11	13	1	1	15	0
Hyzdu, Adam, Pawtucket	.978	92	170	10	4	184	0
Incaviglia, Pete, Columbus	1.000	3	7	1	0	8	0
Jaime, Angel, Norfolk	1.000	9	10	2	0	12	1
Ledee, Ricky, Columbus*	.966	34	56	0	2	58	0
Lewis, T.R., Richmond	.984	100	179	6	3	188	1
Lott, Billy, Ottawa	1.000	29	52	2	0	54	0
Lukachyk, Rob, Ottawa	.971	54	93	7	3	103	1
Luke, Matt, Columbus*	.983	63	106	8	2	116	0
Magee, Wendell, Scr./W.-B.	.983	80	167	3	3	173	0
Malave, Jose, Pawtucket	.970	63	94	3	3	100	2
Manto, Jeff, Syracuse	1.000	5	7	0	0	7	0
Martin, Jim, Norfolk	1.000	23	39	3	0	42	0
McMillon, Billy, Char.-S./W.-B.*	.986	81	133	8	2	143	0
Mendoza, Carlos, Norfolk*	1.000	9	17	0	0	17	0
Meulens, Hensley, Ottawa	.949	18	35	2	2	39	1
Mitchell, Tony, Toledo	.967	18	27	2	1	30	1
Moore, Mike, Norfolk	.957	26	45	0	2	47	0
Morman, Russ, Charlotte	1.000	41	59	3	0	62	0
Mummau, Rob, Syracuse	.952	16	20	0	1	21	0
Natal, Rob, Charlotte	1.000	1	5	0	0	5	0
Nixon, Trot, Pawtucket*	.986	129	268	10	4	282	4
Obando, Sherman, Ottawa	1.000	1	3	0	0	3	0
Olmeda, Jose, Charlotte	.982	28	52	4	1	57	0
Otero, Ricky, Scr./W.-B.*	.979	38	90	5	2	97	0
Pegues, Steve, Ottawa	.938	31	40	5	3	48	0
Petagine, Roberto, Norfolk*	1.000	16	21	0	0	21	0
Pose, Scott, Columbus	.992	56	113	6	1	120	2
Pride, Curtis, Pawtucket	1.000	1	2	0	0	2	0
Raines, Tim, Columbus	1.000	4	4	0	0	4	0
Ramirez, Angel, Syracuse	.727	7	8	0	3	11	0
Roberts, Lonell, Syracuse	.966	67	83	3	3	89	0
Rodarte, Raul, Richmond	1.000	19	24	1	0	25	0
Rodriguez, Steve, Toledo	1.000	5	5	2	0	7	0
Saffer, Jon, Ottawa	.968	125	226	15	8	249	8
Samuels, Scott, Ottawa	1.000	17	24	2	0	26	0
Sefcik, Kevin, Scr./W.-B.	1.000	1	4	1	0	5	0
SHEFF, Chris, Charlotte	1.000	105	154	5	0	159	0
Sierra, Ruben, Syracuse	.923	8	10	2	1	13	1
Smith, Ira, Toledo	1.000	16	33	0	0	33	0
Spencer, Shane, Columbus	.980	109	188	5	4	197	0
Stewart, Shannon, Syracuse	.983	55	115	1	2	118	0
Stovall, Darond, Ottawa*	.965	96	181	10	7	198	4
Tarasco, Tony, Rochester	1.000	10	19	1	0	20	0
Tavarez, Jesus, Pawtucket	.978	57	127	7	3	137	1
Thompson, Ryan, Syracuse	.992	76	117	4	1	122	0
Thurman, Gary, Nor.-Ott.	.982	63	108	3	2	113	0
Trammell, Bubba, Toledo	.972	75	103	3	3	109	1
Tyler, Brad, Richmond	.967	109	170	7	6	183	0

Player, Team	Pct.	G	PO	A	E	TC	DP
Valrie, Kerry, Ottawa	.973	30	67	4	2	73	1
Wawruck, Jim, Rochester*	.984	64	118	6	2	126	0
Wehner, John, Charlotte	.941	13	16	0	1	17	0
Whitmore, Darrell, Syracuse ...	.986	39	69	1	1	71	0
Williams, Juan, Pawtucket	.971	18	33	0	1	34	0
Wilson, Pookie, Charlotte*	1.000	47	75	2	0	77	1
Zuber, Jon, Scr./W.-B.*	1.000	77	111	3	0	114	0

OUTFIELDERS WITH TWO OR MORE TEAMS

Player, Team	Pct.	G	PO	A	E	TC	DP
Fox, Eric, Rochester*	1.000	4	8	0	0	8	0
Fox, Eric, Scr./W.-B.*	.990	50	98	2	1	101	1
Hare, Shawn, Toledo*	1.000	12	15	1	0	16	1
Hare, Shawn, Columbus*	1.000	4	7	1	0	8	0
McMillon, Billy, Charlotte*	.978	57	84	5	2	91	0
McMillon, Billy, Scr./W.-B.*	1.000	24	49	3	0	52	0
Thurman, Gary, Norfolk......	.981	23	51	2	1	54	0
Thurman, Gary, Ottawa	.983	40	57	1	1	59	0

CATCHERS

Player, Team	Pct.	G	PO	A	E	TC	DP	PB
Ayrault, Joe, Richmond......	.978	18	83	7	2	92	1	2
Bennett, Gary, Pawtucket	.985	65	480	33	8	521	0	1
Bieser, Steve, Norfolk........	.909	2	8	2	1	11	0	0
Borrero, Richie, Pawtucket	.983	15	107	9	2	118	0	8
Brito, Jorge, Syracuse............	.969	8	58	5	2	65	1	0
Casanova, Raul, Toledo	.977	12	77	8	2	87	0	1
Castillo, Alberto, Norfolk......	.973	33	197	16	6	219	4	4
Chavez, Raul, Ottawa	.978	89	593	77	15	685	9	9
Delgado, Alex, Charlotte.......	.990	14	88	11	1	100	1	2
Estalella, Bobby, Scr./W.-B....	.986	117	844	71	13	928	9	7
Figga, Mike, Columbus...........	.986	102	706	62	11	779	6	12
Foster, Jim, Rochester	1.000	1	10	1	0	11	0	0
Greene, Charlie, Norfolk........	.985	75	475	49	8	532	8	5
Gresham, Kris, Rochester	.985	12	56	8	1	65	0	0
Jensen, Marcus, Toledo	.994	22	149	6	1	156	2	0
Johnson, Brian, Toledo	1.000	5	38	4	0	42	0	1
Kmak, Joe, Charlotte............	.985	33	187	13	3	203	1	4
Kuilan, Hector, Charlotte	.988	14	76	9	1	86	2	2
Laker, Tim, Rochester	.980	33	283	17	6	306	1	1
Luzinski, Ryan, Rochester......	.993	35	270	27	2	299	5	4
MAKAREWICZ, Scott, Toledo.	.9913	88	624	59	6	689	9	4
Martinez, Sandy, Syracuse	.986	92	588	50	9	647	8	4
McKeel, Walt, Pawtucket.......	.997	48	303	32	1	336	8	10
Melhuse, Adam, Syracuse......	.991	36	211	20	2	233	3	2
Millan, Adan, Scr./W.-B.	1.000	1	5	1	0	6	0	0
Morales, Francisco, Ottawa.....	1.000	5	31	4	0	35	1	0
Mosquera, Julio, Syracuse......	.984	10	55	5	1	61	0	0
Mummau, Rob, Syracuse......	1.000	1	0	1	0	1	0	0
Natal, Rob, Charlotte...........	.9908	72	396	34	4	434	4	8
Northeimer, Jamie, Scr./W.-B.	1.000	4	26	2	0	28	0	0
Pratt, Todd, Norfolk..............	.988	48	317	24	4	345	4	4
Redmond, Mike, Charlotte	.985	20	119	13	2	134	1	1
Rodriguez, Adam, Toledo......	.975	12	73	4	2	79	0	0
Rodriguez, Luis, Syracuse	1.000	3	6	0	0	6	0	0
Rodriguez, Maximo, Charlotte	.981	6	49	3	1	53	0	0
Ronan, Marc, Columbus........	.990	48	249	36	3	288	3	5
Russo, Paul, Columbus.........	.000	1	0	0	0	0	0	1
Siddall, Joe, Ottawa	.987	56	278	32	4	314	2	5
Spehr, Tim, Richmond	.983	35	262	36	5	303	1	2
Tejero, Fausto, Richmond	.981	75	471	49	10	530	9	2
Toth, Dave, Richmond.........	.974	13	72	2	2	76	0	1
Troilo, Jason, Columbus	1.000	4	26	6	0	32	1	1
Valle, Dave, Richmond	.986	12	66	6	1	73	0	2
Varitek, Jason, Pawtucket	.993	19	123	10	1	134	1	3
Walbeck, Matt, Toledo.........	.955	10	55	9	3	67	0	2
Waszgis, B.J., Rochester.......	.980	70	538	37	12	587	1	9
Wedge, Eric, Scr./W.-B.	.985	21	121	8	2	131	1	1
Wilson, Tom, Columbus........	1.000	1	8	0	0	8	0	0

PITCHERS

Player, Team	Pct.	G	PO	A	E	TC	DP
Acevedo, Juan, Norfolk........	1.000	18	4	10	0	14	0
Alberro, Jose, Columbus......	1.000	1	3	1	0	4	0
Alfonseca, Antonio, Charlotte ..	.917	46	4	7	1	12	2
Almanzar, Carlos, Syracuse ...	1.000	32	1	5	0	6	0
Alvarez, Tavo, Ottawa	1.000	37	6	14	0	20	2
Andujar, Luis, Syracuse.......	.875	13	1	6	1	8	0
Avery, Steve, Pawtucket*	1.000	1	0	1	0	1	0
Banks, Willie, Columbus	.946	33	14	21	2	37	0
Barnes, Brian, Toledo*	.875	32	9	19	4	32	1
Baxter, Bob, Ottawa*..........	1.000	4	1	4	0	5	0
Beech, Matt, Scr./W.-B.*	1.000	5	0	1	0	1	0
Bennett, Chris, Rochester	.933	25	5	9	1	15	2
Bennett, Shayne, Ottawa......	1.000	25	1	3	0	4	0
Blair, Willie, Toledo...........	1.000	1	2	2	0	4	0
Blais, Mike, Pawtucket	1.000	10	2	7	0	9	0
Blazier, Ron, Scr./W.-B.......	1.000	11	1	0	0	1	0
Bogott, Kurtiss, Syracuse*	.857	16	1	5	1	7	0
Bohanon, Brian, Norfolk*	.944	15	6	11	1	18	0
Borland, Toby, Pawtucket	1.000	28	1	3	0	4	0
Borowski, Joe, Richmond	1.000	21	0	4	0	4	0
Bowen, Ryan, Columbus.......	1.000	2	2	1	0	3	0
Brandenburg, Mark, Pawtucket.	1.000	9	0	3	0	3	0
Brandow, Derek, Syracuse	.846	31	2	9	2	13	1
Brewer, Billy, Scr./W.-B.*	1.000	11	0	1	0	1	0
Brock, Chris, Richmond	.892	20	7	26	4	37	1
Brow, Scott, Richmond	1.000	61	5	16	0	21	1
Brown, Chad, Syracuse*	1.000	22	2	5	0	7	0
Buddie, Mike, Columbus.......	1.000	53	7	15	0	22	1
Bullinger, Kirk, Ottawa........	1.000	22	2	8	0	10	1
Bunch, Mel, Ottawa...........	1.000	16	7	5	0	12	0
Byrd, Paul, Richmond.........	1.000	3	0	5	0	5	0
Cain, Tim, Paw.-Syr...........	.929	30	6	7	1	14	1
Carlyle, Ken, Richmond........	1.000	16	3	8	0	11	1
Carpenter, Chris, Syracuse	1.000	19	5	16	0	21	4
Carrara, Giovanni, Rochester...	1.000	8	6	5	0	11	1
Castro, Tony, Charlotte	1.000	2	1	0	0	1	0
Cather, Mike, Richmond	1.000	13	2	6	0	8	1
Checo, Robinson, Pawtucket...	1.000	9	2	3	0	5	0
Chergey, Dan, Charlotte.......	.875	27	0	7	1	8	0
Clontz, Brad, Richmond	1.000	16	1	2	0	3	0
Converse, Jim, Columbus	1.000	10	1	2	0	3	1
Coppinger, Rocky, Rochester...	.500	3	1	0	1	2	0
Corbin, Archie, Rochester	1.000	43	1	7	0	8	0
Cornelius, Reid, Charlotte	.976	22	11	30	1	42	2
Crabtree, Tim, Syracuse	1.000	3	0	1	0	1	0
Crawford, Joe, Norfolk*	.952	16	3	17	1	21	1
Crow, Dean, Toledo...........	1.000	18	0	1	0	1	0
Cummings, John, Toledo*.....	1.000	19	0	3	0	3	0
Czajkowski, Jim, Syracuse	1.000	16	0	3	0	3	0
Daal, Omar, Ott.-Syr.*	1.000	7	2	6	0	8	0
Dace, Derek, Toledo*	1.000	5	1	4	0	5	0
Darensbourg, Vic, Charlotte* ..	1.000	27	1	4	0	5	1
Dedrick, Jim, Ottawa..........	1.000	8	0	3	0	3	0
DeHart, Rick, Ottawa*.........	.889	43	3	5	1	9	0
Dishman, Glenn, Toledo*	.917	21	9	24	3	36	2
Dixon, Timothy, Ottawa*......	1.000	5	0	2	0	2	0
Doman, Roger, Syracuse......	1.000	8	3	3	0	6	0
Dougherty, Jim, Norfolk	1.000	49	5	14	0	19	3
Drews, Matt, Toledo	1.000	3	0	2	0	2	0
Drumright, Mike, Toledo	.914	23	11	21	3	35	4
Dyer, Mike, Richmond.........	1.000	29	2	5	0	7	0
Edenfield, Ken, Columbus	1.000	9	2	0	0	2	0
Edmondson, Brian, Norfolk....	.769	31	4	6	3	13	1
Eiland, Dave, Columbus	1.000	13	5	11	0	16	0
Eshelman, Vaughn, Pawtucket*.	1.000	14	4	10	0	14	0
Falteisek, Steve, Ottawa.......	.931	22	10	17	2	29	3
Farrell, Jim, Pawtucket	1.000	1	0	2	0	2	0
Fermin, Ramon, Toledo.......	1.000	41	5	7	0	12	0
Fernandez, Jared, Pawtucket...	.933	11	4	10	1	15	0
Fiore, Tony, Scr./W.-B.........	.867	9	3	10	2	15	0
Fleetham, Ben, Ottawa	.500	9	0	1	1	2	0
Flener, Huck, Syracuse*	.912	20	6	25	3	34	4
Fortugno, Tim, Scr./W.-B.*	1.000	19	0	1	0	1	0
Fox, Chad, Richmond	.833	13	2	3	1	6	0
Gaillard, Eddie, Toledo	1.000	55	3	11	0	14	2
Gallaher, Kevin, Toledo	1.000	9	3	3	0	6	0
Garces, Rich, Pawtucket	1.000	26	2	1	0	3	0
Gardiner, Mike, Columbus	1.000	14	3	11	0	14	1
Geisler, Phil, Norfolk*	1.000	1	0	1	0	1	0
Gomes, Wayne, Scr./W.-B.....	1.000	26	2	7	0	9	1
Gonzalez, Gabe, Charlotte*	.944	37	6	11	1	18	1
Gooden, Dwight, Columbus....	1.000	2	1	3	0	4	0
Grace, Mike, Scr./W.-B........	.867	12	3	10	2	15	2
Green, Tyler, Scr./W.-B........	.833	12	7	3	2	12	1
Greene, Rick, Toledo..........	.966	57	10	18	1	29	3
Greer, Ken, Rochester	1.000	15	0	4	0	4	0
Grundt, Ken, Pawtucket*......	1.000	49	1	8	0	9	1
Hajek, Dave, Toledo...........	1.000	1	0	1	0	1	0
Halladay, Roy, Syracuse	.962	22	9	16	1	26	1
Harnisch, Pete, Norfolk.......	1.000	3	0	2	0	2	0
Harriger, Denny, Toledo.......	.960	27	26	22	2	50	2
Harrison, Tommy, Richmond...	1.000	22	12	8	0	20	0

Player, Team	Pct.	G	PO	A	E	TC	DP
Hartgraves, Dean, Richmond*..	.867	50	3	10	2	15	0
Harvey, Bryan, Charlotte	1.000	2	1	0	0	1	0
Hawblitzel, Ryan, Scr./W.-B.	1.000	34	12	9	0	21	1
Haynes, Jimmy, Rochester	.963	16	8	18	1	27	2
Heflin, Bronson, Scr./W.-B.	.909	35	7	3	1	11	0
Henderson, Rod, Ottawa	1.000	26	7	14	0	21	3
Heredia, Gil, Ottawa	.875	28	10	11	3	24	2
Hernandez, Fernando, Toledo	1.000	55	3	7	0	10	0
Hernandez, Livan, Charlotte	.950	14	4	15	1	20	1
Holman, Craig, Scr./W.-B.	1.000	48	3	8	0	11	0
Hostetler, Mike, Richmond	1.000	5	1	2	0	3	0
Hudson, Joe, Pawtucket	1.000	29	2	9	0	11	2
Hurst, Bill, Charlotte	1.000	27	0	3	0	3	0
Irabu, Hideki, Columbus	1.000	4	0	3	0	3	0
Isringhausen, Jason, Norfolk	1.000	3	1	5	0	6	0
Janzen, Marty, Syracuse	.938	22	4	11	1	16	0
Jarvis, Kevin, Toledo	1.000	2	2	3	0	5	0
Jerzembeck, Mike, Columbus	1.000	20	5	9	0	14	1
Johns, Doug, Rochester*	1.000	9	4	11	0	15	1
Jordan, Ricardo, Norfolk*	1.000	34	0	4	0	4	0
Juelsgaard, Jarod, Charlotte	.867	21	5	8	2	15	0
Karp, Ryan, Scr./W.-B.*	1.000	32	3	11	0	14	0
Kashiwada, Takashi, Norfolk*	1.000	14	0	5	0	5	0
Keagle, Greg, Toledo	.943	23	7	26	2	35	6
Krivda, Rick, Rochester*	.968	22	9	21	1	31	1
Lacy, Kerry, Pawtucket	.909	23	5	5	1	11	0
Lankford, Frank, Columbus	.955	15	9	12	1	22	2
Larkin, Andy, Charlotte	.938	28	10	20	2	32	1
Lidle, Cory, Norfolk	1.000	7	4	10	0	14	0
Ligtenberg, Kerry, Richmond	1.000	14	0	2	0	2	0
Loewer, Carlton, Scr./W.-B.	.971	29	15	19	1	35	0
Lomon, Kevin, Columbus	1.000	3	1	4	0	5	0
Lowe, Derek, Pawtucket	1.000	6	4	2	0	6	0
Luebbers, Larry, Richmond	.966	27	7	21	1	29	1
Lukasiewicz, Mark, Syracuse*	1.000	30	1	2	0	3	1
Maduro, Calvin, Scr./W.-B.	1.000	13	2	12	0	14	1
Mahomes, Pat, Pawtucket	1.000	18	2	0	0	2	1
Manuel, Barry, Norfolk	.769	19	6	4	3	13	0
Meacham, Rusty, Pawtucket	1.000	28	2	6	0	8	1
Mecir, Jim, Columbus	1.000	24	1	6	0	7	0
Mendoza, Reynol, Charlotte	.939	46	12	19	2	33	3
Miller, Kurt, Charlotte	.500	21	0	1	1	2	0
Millwood, Kevin, Richmond	1.000	9	2	8	0	10	1
Mimbs, Mark, Pawtucket*	.889	15	2	14	2	18	0
Mimbs, Mike, Scr./W.-B.*	1.000	11	3	3	0	6	1
Montgomery, Steve, Rochester	.500	2	0	1	1	2	0
Myers, Jimmy, Norfolk	.778	45	4	10	4	18	2
Norris, Joe, Charlotte	1.000	9	0	2	0	2	0
Nye, Ryan, Scr./W.-B.	.966	17	13	15	1	29	3
Ojala, Kirt, Charlotte*	.893	25	6	19	3	28	3
Orellano, Rafael, Pawtucket*	.909	16	2	8	1	11	0
Pall, Donn, Charlotte	.857	59	4	14	3	21	0
Paniagua, Jose, Ottawa	.879	22	9	20	4	33	1
Pavano, Carl, Pawtucket	1.000	23	8	17	0	25	0
Pavlas, Dave, Columbus	.667	26	2	0	1	3	0
Perez, Yorkis, Norfolk*	.667	17	2	2	2	6	1
Person, Robert, Syracuse	1.000	1	1	1	0	2	0
Plantenberg, Erik, Scr./W.-B.*	1.000	18	3	2	0	5	0
Polley, Dale, Columbus*	1.000	62	2	8	0	10	0
Press, Gregg, Charlotte	1.000	1	1	0	0	1	0
Pugh, Tim, Toledo	.920	19	16	7	2	25	0
Pulido, Carlos, Ottawa*	1.000	44	1	10	0	11	0
Pulsipher, Bill, Norfolk*	.933	8	3	11	1	15	0
Ramirez, Hector, Rochester	1.000	39	6	12	0	18	0
Reyes, Carlos, Columbus	1.000	1	1	1	0	2	0
Ricci, Chuck, Ottawa	.875	22	2	5	1	8	0
Ricken, Ray, Columbus	.944	26	15	19	2	36	1
Rios, Dan, Columbus	1.000	58	9	12	0	21	0
Roberts, Chris, Norfolk*	1.000	7	2	6	0	8	0
Robinson, Ken, Syracuse	1.000	56	3	8	0	11	0
RODRIGUEZ, Nerio, Rochester	1.000	27	11	29	0	40	3
Rogers, Bryan, Rochester	1.000	21	3	3	0	6	0
Rogers, Kevin, Richmond*	.500	10	1	0	1	2	0
Romano, Michael, Syracuse	1.000	40	6	10	0	16	1
Rose, Brian, Pawtucket	.952	27	14	26	2	42	5
Rose, Scott, Columbus	1.000	26	2	5	0	7	0
Rosengren, John, Toledo*	.833	54	2	13	3	18	0
Ruffcorn, Scott, Scr./W.-B.	1.000	5	5	2	0	7	0
Ruffin, Johnny, Pawtucket	1.000	6	0	1	0	1	0
Rumer, Tim, Columbus*	1.000	17	1	7	0	8	0
Saberhagen, Bret, Pawtucket	1.000	2	1	1	0	2	0
Sackinsky, Brian, Rochester	1.000	2	3	2	0	5	0
Sauerbeck, Scott, Norfolk*	1.000	1	0	2	0	2	1
Saunders, Tony, Charlotte*	1.000	3	0	1	0	1	0
Schmidt, Curt, Ottawa	1.000	31	4	7	0	11	0
Schrenk, Steve, Rochester	.963	25	7	19	1	27	0
Schutz, Carl, Richmond*	1.000	27	0	7	0	7	1
Seanez, Rudy, Norfolk	1.000	9	0	1	0	1	0
Seelbach, Chris, Charlotte	1.000	16	6	3	0	9	0
Shepherd, Keith, Norfolk	.944	19	4	13	1	18	0
Shouse, Brian, Rochester*	1.000	54	3	13	0	16	1
Sievert, Mark, Syracuse	1.000	1	0	2	0	2	0
Sinclair, Steve, Syracuse*	.750	6	1	2	1	4	0
Smith, Brian, Syracuse	1.000	31	6	19	0	25	0
Stanifer, Robby, Charlotte	1.000	22	2	2	0	4	0
Steph, Rod, Rochester	1.000	41	1	6	0	7	0
Stephenson, Garrett, Scr./W.-B..	1.000	7	2	5	0	7	0
Stull, Everett, Ottawa	.969	27	8	23	1	32	2
Suppan, Jeff, Pawtucket	.900	9	2	7	1	10	1
Swift, Billy, Rochester	1.000	2	0	2	0	2	0
Tam, Jeff, Norfolk	.920	40	5	18	2	25	4
Thobe, Tom, Richmond*	1.000	19	2	17	0	19	0
Thurman, Mike, Ottawa	1.000	4	2	2	0	4	0
Urbani, Thomas, Ottawa*	.917	30	2	9	1	12	0
Urso, Sal, Columbus*	1.000	24	1	9	0	10	1
Valdez, Carlos, Pawtucket	.923	35	4	8	1	13	0
Walker, Pete, Pawtucket	1.000	7	2	2	0	4	0
Ward, Bryan, Charlotte*	.889	15	3	13	2	18	2
Weathers, David, Columbus	.800	5	3	1	1	5	0
Weber, Neil, Ottawa*	.875	9	3	4	1	8	0
Welch, Mike, Norfolk	.875	46	5	2	1	8	1
Whisenant, Matt, Charlotte*	.833	16	1	4	1	6	1
Williams, Brian, Rochester	1.000	22	1	10	0	11	0
Winston, Darrin, Scr./W.-B.*	.958	39	8	15	1	24	1
Withem, Shannon, Norfolk	.977	29	26	16	1	43	1
Woodall, Brad, Richmond*	.923	26	9	27	3	39	0
Yan, Esteban, Rochester	.923	34	12	12	2	26	2
Yarnall, Ed, Norfolk*	1.000	1	1	4	0	5	1

PITCHERS WITH TWO OR MORE TEAMS

Player, Team	Pct.	G	PO	A	E	TC	DP
Cain, Tim, Pawtucket	1.000	17	3	0	0	3	0
Cain, Tim, Syracuse	.909	13	3	7	1	11	1
Daal, Omar, Ottawa*	1.000	2	0	1	0	1	0
Daal, Omar, Syracuse*	1.000	5	2	5	0	7	0

The following players did not have any fielding statistics at the positions indicated or appeared only as a designated hitter, pinch-hitter, or pinch-runner: Arocha, p; Aucoin, p; Bream, of; Rich Butler, 3b; Clapinski, of; Corsi, p; Forbes, of; Franco, 3b; Freeman, p; Giannelli, p; Goldsmith, p; Hyers, 3b; Kmak, 1b; Komminsk, dh; Mahay, p; Melhuse, of; Ramiro Mendoza, p; Mercado, p; Peterson, p; Rhine, p; Risley, p; L. Roberts, 2b; Robertson, of; Rodarte, p; Ant. Rodriguez, p; Rossy, p; Ryan, p; Sadler, of; Strawberry, dh; Torres, p; Wallace, p; P. Wilson, p.

LEAGUE CHAMPIONS

Year	Team	Pct.	Year	Team	Pct.	Year	Team	Pct.
1884—	Trenton	.520	1893—	Erie	.606	1904—	Buffalo	.657
1885—	Syracuse	.584	1894—	Providence	.696	1905—	Providence	.638
1886—	Utica	.646	1895—	Springfield	.687	1906—	Buffalo	.607
1887—	Toronto	.644	1896—	Providence	.602	1907—	Toronto	.619
1888—	Syracuse	.723	1897—	Syracuse	.632	1908—	Baltimore	.593
1889—	Detroit	.649	1898—	Montreal	.586	1909—	Rochester	.596
1890—	Detroit	.617	1899—	Rochester	.624	1910—	Rochester	.601
1891—	Buffalo (reg. season)	.727	1900—	Providence	.616	1911—	Rochester	.645
	Buffalo (supplemental)	.680	1901—	Rochester	.642	1912—	Toronto	.595
1892—	Providence	.615	1902—	Toronto	.669	1913—	Newark	.625
	Binghamton*	.667	1903—	Jersey City	.742	1914—	Providence	.617

CLASS AAA International League

Year	Team	Pct.
1915—	Buffalo	.632
1916—	Buffalo	.586
1917—	Toronto	.604
1918—	Toronto	.693
1919—	Baltimore	.671
1920—	Baltimore	.719
1921—	Baltimore	.717
1922—	Baltimore	.689
1923—	Baltimore	.677
1924—	Baltimore	.709
1925—	Baltimore	.633
1926—	Toronto	.657
1927—	Buffalo	.667
1928—	Rochester	.549
1929—	Rochester	.613
1930—	Rochester	.629
1931—	Rochester	.601
1932—	Newark	.649
1933—	Newark	.622
	Buffalo (4th)†	.494
1934—	Newark	.608
	Toronto (3rd)†	.559
1935—	Montreal	.597
	Syracuse (2nd)†	.565
1936—	Buffalo‡	.610
1937—	Newark‡	.717
1938—	Newark‡	.684
1939—	Jersey City	.582
	Rochester (2nd)†	.556
1940—	Rochester	.611
	Newark (2nd)†	.594
1941—	Newark	.649
	Montreal (2nd)†	.584
1942—	Newark	.601
	Syracuse (3rd)†	.513
1943—	Toronto	.625
	Syracuse (3rd)†	.536
1944—	Baltimore‡	.553
1945—	Montreal	.621
	Newark (2nd)†	.582
1946—	Montreal‡	.649
1947—	Jersey City	.610
	Syracuse (3rd)†	.575
1948—	Montreal‡	.614

Year	Team	Pct.
1949—	Buffalo	.584
	Montreal (3rd)†	.545
1950—	Rochester	.609
	Baltimore (3rd)†	.556
1951—	Montreal‡	.617
1952—	Montreal	.629
	Rochester (3rd)†	.619
1953—	Rochester	.630
	Montreal (2nd)†	.586
1954—	Toronto	.630
	Syracuse (4th)§	.510
1955—	Montreal	.617
	Rochester (4th)†	.497
1956—	Toronto	.566
	Rochester (2nd)†	.553
1957—	Toronto	.575
	Buffalo (2nd)†	.571
1958—	Montreal‡	.588
1959—	Buffalo	.582
	Havana (3rd)†	.523
1960—	Toronto‡	.649
1961—	Columbus	.597
	Buffalo (3rd)†	.559
1962—	Jacksonville	.610
	Atlanta (3rd)†	.539
1963—	Syracuse∞	.533
	Indianapolis‡	.562
1964—	Jacksonville	.589
	Rochester (4th)†	.532
1965—	Columbus	.582
	Toronto (3rd)†	.556
1966—	Rochester	.565
	Toronto (2nd-tied)†	.558
1967—	Richmond	.574
	Toledo (3rd)†	.525
1968—	Toledo	.565
	Jacksonville (4th)†	.514
1969—	Tidewater	.563
	Syracuse (3rd)†	.536
1970—	Syracuse‡	.600
1971—	Rochester‡	.614
1972—	Louisville	.563
	Tidewater (3rd)†	.545
1973—	Charleston	.586
	Pawtucket▲†	.534

Year	Team	Pct.
1974—	Memphis	.613
	Rochester ∞‡	.611
1975—	Tidewater‡	.610
1976—	Rochester	.638
	Syracuse (2nd)†	.590
1977—	Pawtucket	.571
	Charleston (2nd)‡	.557
1978—	Charleston	.607
	Richmond (4th)†	.511
1979—	Columbus‡	.612
1980—	Columbus‡	.593
1981—	Columbus‡	.633
1982—	Richmond	.590
	Tidewater (3rd)†	.540
1983—	Columbus	.593
	Tidewater (4th)†	.511
1984—	Columbus	.590
	Pawtucket (4th)†	.536
1985—	Syracuse	.564
	Tidewater (4th)†	.540
1986—	Richmond‡	.571
1987—	Tidewater	.579
	Columbus†	.550
1988—	Columbus◆	.546
	Tidewater	.546
1989—	Syracuse	.572
	Richmond◆	.555
1990—	Rochester◆	.614
	Columbus	.596
1991—	Columbus◆	.590
	Pawtucket	.552
1992—	Columbus◆	.660
	Scr. W.B.	.592
1993—	Charlotte◆	.610
	Rochester	.525
1994—	Richmond◆	.567
	Pawtucket	.549
1995—	Norfolk	.606
	Ottawa◆	.507
1996—	Columbus◆	.599
	Rochester	.511
1997—	Rochester◆	.589
	Columbus	.556

*Won split-season playoff. †Won four-team playoff. ‡Won championship and four-team playoff. §Defeated Havana in game to decide fourth place, then won four-team playoff. ∞League was divided into Northern, Southern divisions. ▲League divided into American, National divisions. ◆League divided into Eastern, Western divisions; won playoffs. (NOTE—Known as Eastern League in 1884, New York State League in 1885, International League in 1886-87, International Association in 1888, International League in 1889-90, Eastern Association in 1891 and Eastern League from 1892 until 1912.)

CLASS AAA *International League*

MEXICAN LEAGUE

1997 FINAL STANDINGS

FIRST HALF

NORTHERN ZONE

Team	W	L	T	Pct.	GB
Reynosa	36	23	1	.610	....
Monterrey	36	26	0	.581	1¹/₂
Monclova	33	28	0	.541	4
Nuevo Laredo	29	31	2	.483	7¹/₂
Saltillo	25	35	0	.417	11¹/₂
Torreon	25	36	0	.410	12

CENTRAL ZONE

Team	W	L	T	Pct.	GB
Mexico City Tigers	42	20	0	.677	....
Mexico City Red Devils	39	22	0	.639	2¹/₂
Poza Rica	37	24	0	.607	4¹/₂
Oaxaca	24	38	0	.387	18
Aguascalientes	21	40	1	.344	20¹/₂

SOUTHERN ZONE

Team	W	L	T	Pct.	GB
Quintana Roo	33	29	0	.530	....
Yucatan	29	32	1	.475	3¹/₂
Tabasco	29	33	0	.468	4
Campeche	26	34	1	.433	6
Minatitlan	24	37	0	.393	8¹/₂

SECOND HALF

NORTHERN ZONE

Team	W	L	T	Pct.	GB
Monterrey	32	26	0	.552	....
Monclova	32	28	0	.533	1
Saltillo	30	29	1	.508	2¹/₂
Nuevo Laredo	26	33	1	.441	6¹/₂
Reynosa	24	34	1	.414	8
Torreon	23	34	1	.404	8¹/₂

CENTRAL ZONE

Team	W	L	T	Pct.	GB
Mexico City Red Devils	44	16	0	.733	....
Mexico City Tigers	35	20	2	.636	6¹/₂
Poza Rica	30	28	0	.517	13
Oaxaca	29	31	0	.483	15
Aguascalientes	25	33	1	.431	18

SOUTHERN ZONE

Team	W	L	T	Pct.	GB
Tabasco	38	19	0	.667	....
Quintana Roo	28	27	2	.509	9
Yucatan	25	32	1	.439	13
Campeche	20	30	0	.400	14¹/₂
Minatitlan	18	39	2	.316	20

COMPOSITE

NORTHERN ZONE

Team	W	L	T	Pct.	GB
Monterrey	68	52	0	.567	....
Monclova	65	56	0	.537	3¹/₂
Reynosa	60	57	2	.513	6¹/₂
Saltillo	55	64	1	.462	12¹/₂
Nuevo Laredo	55	64	3	.462	12¹/₂
Torreon	48	70	1	.407	19

CENTRAL ZONE

Team	W	L	T	Pct.	GB
Mexico City Red Devils	83	38	0	.686	....
Mexico City Tigers	77	40	2	.658	4
Poza Rica	67	52	0	.563	15
Oaxaca	53	69	0	.434	30¹/₂
Aguascalientes	46	73	2	.387	36

SOUTHERN ZONE

Team	W	L	T	Pct.	GB
Tabasco	67	52	0	.563	....
Quintana Roo	61	56	2	.521	5
Yucatan	54	64	2	.458	12¹/₂
Campeche	46	64	1	.418	16¹/₂
Minatitlan	42	76	2	.356	24¹/₂

PLAYOFFS—Mexico City Red Devils defeated Reynosa, four games to none; Tabasco defeated Monclova, four games to none; Mexico City Tigers defeated Poza Rica, four games to none; Quintana Roo defeated Monterrey, four games to two, in the first round; Mexico City Tigers defeated Tabasco, four games to one; Mexico City Red Devils defeated Quintana Roo, four games to two, in the second round; Mexico City Tigers defeated Mexico City Red Devils, four games to one, in final series to capture league championship.

(Compiled by Ana Luisa Perea Talarico, League Statistician, Mexico, D.F.)

1997 BATTING

TEAM

Team	Avg.	G	TPA	AB	R	H	TB	2B	3B	HR	RBI	SH	SF	HP	BB	IBB	SO	SB	CS	GDP	LOB	ShO	Slg.	OBP
M.C. Red Devils	.305	121	4787	4084	769	1245	1780	190	30	95	709	51	40	37	575	36	515	96	30	127	961	9	.436	.392
M.C. Tigers	.292	119	4606	3963	658	1158	1676	202	44	76	594	78	40	48	477	54	570	100	59	112	885	8	.423	.372
Oaxaca	.287	122	4679	4043	582	1160	1538	202	25	42	510	75	40	37	484	41	484	74	53	126	938	7	.380	.365
Monterrey	.280	120	4586	4041	509	1132	1537	173	32	56	464	63	26	20	436	47	452	92	67	131	906	9	.380	.351
Reynosa	.278	119	4393	3840	455	1069	1453	166	49	40	420	91	33	40	389	47	431	51	53	125	881	9	.378	.348
Torreon	.276	119	4463	3932	478	1084	1394	166	30	28	425	63	22	38	408	23	486	36	21	146	891	10	.355	.348
Poza Rica	.276	119	4348	3862	486	1064	1375	178	35	21	448	55	42	30	359	36	474	78	51	111	836	15	.356	.338
Yucatan	.270	120	4492	3870	474	1043	1338	139	27	34	414	94	30	42	456	47	485	70	47	94	935	10	.346	.350
Tabasco	.269	119	4395	3739	462	1004	1301	146	14	41	405	86	31	41	498	36	450	46	50	129	911	8	.348	.358
Aguascalientes	.267	122	4543	3967	467	1065	1433	142	20	62	415	76	36	51	413	35	468	59	69	125	893	10	.361	.342
Saltillo	.266	120	4437	3872	490	1031	1357	150	37	34	444	96	31	25	413	34	521	52	31	117	862	15	.350	.338
Monclova	.265	121	4536	3916	536	1037	1532	194	26	83	488	64	38	38	480	32	492	56	42	103	905	7	.391	.348
Nuevo Laredo	.265	122	4544	3952	443	1049	1343	143	23	35	398	83	36	41	432	32	492	73	49	113	934	14	.340	.341
Quintana Roo	.265	119	4412	3810	483	1011	1382	169	29	48	428	82	35	41	444	34	512	84	69	143	832	9	.363	.345
Campeche	.258	111	4108	3586	416	925	1245	136	17	50	368	85	21	26	390	31	428	38	41	128	794	11	.347	.333
Minatitlan	.244	120	4485	3826	440	935	1252	147	19	44	407	93	17	36	513	31	529	45	44	130	887	10	.327	.338

TOP QUALIFIERS FOR BATTING CHAMPIONSHIP

Minimum 313 plate appearances.

Player, Team	Avg.	G	TPA	AB	R	H	TB	2B	3B	HR	RBI	SH	SF	HP	BB	IBB	SO	SB	CS	GDP	Slg.	OBP
Garcia, Cornelio, Mont.	.382	115	531	448	86	171	214	24	8	1	34	10	1	2	70	6	47	22	17	7	.478	.466
Polonia, Luis, Tig.	.377	110	495	408	105	154	214	29	5	7	59	5	3	4	75	12	33	48	12	13	.525	.476
Magallanes, Ever, Mont.	.359	88	373	334	47	120	150	17	2	3	46	5	3	1	30	5	35	3	3	11	.449	.410
Gainey, Ty, Mex.	.353	107	479	399	97	141	238	18	2	25	108	0	3	4	73	11	65	8	0	11	.596	.455
Salas, Heriberto, Tor.	.349	87	383	338	59	118	148	16	4	2	32	5	0	1	39	2	22	3	4	5	.438	.418
Wood, Tyrone, Min.	.342	85	367	304	58	104	182	20	2	18	73	0	2	2	59	8	49	0	2	8	.599	.450
Alvarez, Hector, Oax.	.341	88	364	317	50	108	144	20	5	2	52	5	5	2	35	3	34	3	3	11	.454	.404
Carter, Michael, Lar.	.341	110	492	454	69	155	195	27	5	1	33	5	3	3	27	3	26	41	17	9	.430	.380
Arredondo, Luis, Yuc.	.337	119	540	481	79	162	212	16	11	4	49	5	2	1	51	6	41	31	17	3	.441	.400
Stark, Matt, Yuc.	.337	109	458	362	53	122	166	23	0	7	57	0	5	11	80	17	30	2	1	12	.459	.465
Garcia, Omar, P.R.	.336	117	482	434	57	146	185	25	7	0	65	1	9	1	37	4	30	4	0	11	.426	.383
Mendez, Roberto C., Oax.	.328	103	423	357	67	117	170	21	4	8	69	8	5	5	48	6	35	13	6	12	.476	.410
Michel, Domingo, Cam.	.327	107	446	343	64	112	153	13	2	8	54	4	2	3	94	7	54	8	1	6	.446	.473
Sherman, Darrell, Rey.	.327	97	445	355	72	116	147	17	7	0	16	9	0	5	76	3	33	19	13	7	.414	.452
Zazueta, Juan Carlos, Tor.	.327	91	367	333	47	109	128	15	2	0	24	7	0	2	25	1	17	3	4	17	.384	.378

DEPARTMENTAL LEADERS: G—G. Sanchez, 122; AB—L. Arredondo, 481; R—D. Fernandez, 107; H—Co. Garcia, 171; TB—Gainey, 238; 2B—Azocar, 35; 3B—Jorge Valle, 13; HR—Gainey, 25; RBI—Gainey, 108; SH—A. Castro, 25; SF—Aganza, 11; HP—Ef. Ramirez, 12; BB—Michel, 94; IBB—Stark, 17; SO—Chance, 93; SB—Polonia, 48; CS—Peguero, 18; GIDP—Cazarin, 24; Slg.—Wood, 599; OBP—D. Gonzalez, .477.

ALL PLAYERS

Player, Team	Avg.	G	TPA	AB	R	H	TB	2B	3B	HR	RBI	SH	SF	HP	BB	IBB	SO	SB	CS	GDP	Slg.	OBP
Abrego, Jesus, Rey.	.252	77	280	226	25	57	80	13	2	2	24	8	3	5	38	4	37	4	2	8	.354	.368
Acuna, Jose, Mont.	.207	37	68	58	11	12	15	3	0	0	3	2	0	0	8	0	15	1	2	0	.259	.303
Aganza, Ruben, Monc.	.302	121	482	430	53	130	193	28	1	11	75	3	11	1	37	2	47	4	4	12	.449	.351
Aguilar, Enrique, Yuc.	.290	76	250	214	25	62	86	9	0	5	30	3	6	5	22	1	12	2	1	3	.402	.360
Aguilera, Antonio, Tab.	.272	108	438	363	54	98	116	12	0	2	26	23	2	3	47	2	49	6	2	8	.322	.357
Aguilera, Armando, Sal.	.240	97	308	267	37	64	84	8	3	2	27	11	2	1	27	0	37	7	2	14	.315	.310
Alfonso, Edgar, Tab.	.282	108	442	394	48	111	147	25	1	3	53	5	6	7	30	2	47	2	2	23	.373	.339
Almeida, Shammar, Agua.	.215	94	328	256	28	55	88	12	0	7	34	3	5	4	60	5	52	0	3	8	.344	.366
Almendra, Gregorio, Tab.	.000	6	7	7	0	0	0	0	0	0	0	0	0	0	0	0	0	0	0	0	.000	.000
Alvarez, Hector, Oax.	.341	88	364	317	50	108	144	20	5	2	52	5	5	2	35	3	34	3	3	11	.454	.404
Amador, Alonso, Agua.	.000	5	4	3	1	0	0	0	0	0	1	0	0	0	1	0	0	0	1	0	.000	.250
Amezcua, Adan, Rey.	.316	86	321	275	32	87	127	14	4	6	50	6	8	2	30	2	37	2	1	16	.462	.378
Arano, Eloy, P.R.	.274	99	343	307	37	84	98	8	3	0	24	7	3	0	26	4	36	10	6	8	.319	.327
Arano, Wilfredo, Lar.	.221	94	245	204	19	45	48	9	3	0	21	4	3	1	33	2	16	2	1	10	.235	.328
Arauz, Leobardo, Yuc.	.209	15	51	43	4	9	11	0	1	0	3	1	0	1	6	0	11	1	3	1	.256	.320
Arevalo, Guadalupe, Cam.	.204	49	117	108	11	22	33	5	0	2	11	2	1	0	6	0	11	1	0	8	.306	.243
Arias, Everardo, Q.R.	.077	12	16	13	2	1	1	0	0	0	2	3	0	0	0	0	3	0	1	0	.077	.077
Armenta, Fernando, Min.	.074	22	31	27	4	2	2	0	0	0	1	0	0	0	4	0	10	1	2	0	.074	.194
Armenta, Guillermo, Mex.	.329	68	244	222	37	73	88	11	2	0	27	4	2	1	15	1	12	5	1	5	.396	.371
Arredondo, Jesus, Agua.	.250	114	434	372	46	93	112	9	2	2	25	10	1	4	47	1	28	6	4	9	.301	.340
Arredondo, Luis, Yuc.	.337	119	540	481	79	162	212	16	11	4	49	5	2	1	51	6	41	31	17	3	.441	.400
Arvizu, Javier, Oax.	.236	62	175	140	12	33	44	6	1	1	17	1	2	1	31	1	33	1	1	1	.314	.374
Arzate, Martin, Cam.	.000	3	8	7	1	0	0	0	0	0	0	1	0	0	0	0	1	0	0	0	.000	.000
Atwell, Sergio, Monc.	.279	26	48	43	10	12	15	1	1	0	2	0	1	0	4	0	5	0	0	1	.349	.354
Avila, Ruben, Tor.	.249	100	376	329	27	82	107	16	0	3	44	4	5	3	35	3	57	2	1	9	.325	.323
Aviles, Alejandro, Sal.	.182	61	147	132	12	24	29	3	1	0	8	3	0	1	11	2	39	2	0	3	.220	.250
Azocar, Oscar, P.R.	.312	116	488	452	62	141	206	35	3	8	85	1	9	5	21	11	18	8	4	17	.456	.343
Balderas, Abelardo, P.R.	.500	2	2	2	0	1	1	0	0	0	0	0	0	0	0	0	1	0	0	0	.500	.500
Barrera, Nelson, Oax.	.310	120	499	445	57	138	203	30	1	11	82	2	9	5	38	6	67	5	2	16	.456	.364
Battle, Allen, Sal.	.136	8	27	22	2	3	3	0	0	0	2	1	0	1	3	0	5	1	0	0	.136	.269
Beltran, Gerardo, Min.	.226	73	245	217	20	49	57	6	1	0	24	6	2	2	18	1	27	0	3	5	.263	.289
Bojorquez, Victor, Mex.	.213	56	62	61	15	13	14	1	0	0	2	0	0	1	0	0	6	0	0	2	.230	.226
Briley, Greg, P.R.	.245	61	246	216	20	53	63	8	1	0	16	2	3	1	24	4	30	7	5	8	.292	.320
Brinkley, Darrell, Mex.	.340	14	55	50	13	17	27	1	0	3	8	0	0	0	5	0	3	4	2	1	.540	.400
Brito, Bernardo, Mont.	.197	21	87	76	10	15	28	1	0	4	10	0	0	0	11	1	17	0	0	4	.368	.299
Buccheri, Jim, Tig.	.310	56	263	226	36	70	94	8	5	2	27	5	2	1	29	2	31	16	6	3	.416	.388
Burton, Essex, Monc.	.236	15	61	55	8	13	14	1	0	0	4	1	0	2	3	0	9	4	2	1	.255	.300
Bustillos, Luis, Oax.	.197	62	148	127	22	25	29	4	0	0	10	9	0	1	11	0	24	2	2	6	.228	.266
Cabrales, Gabriel, Oax.	.000	1	2	2	0	0	0	0	0	0	0	0	0	0	0	0	2	0	0	0	.000	.000
Cabrera, Alex, Tig.	.314	104	421	395	52	124	231	28	5	23	84	0	3	6	17	5	60	6	4	16	.585	.349
Cairo, Sergio, Tab.	.271	48	189	155	22	42	55	7	0	2	19	1	1	1	31	1	25	2	2	8	.355	.394
Camacho, Adulfo, Min.	.177	57	218	164	31	29	38	9	0	0	15	4	1	3	46	2	27	3	3	4	.232	.364
Canate, William, Min.	.231	31	140	130	17	30	39	4	1	1	13	1	0	1	8	0	12	3	3	4	.300	.281
Canizalez, Juan, Mont.	.291	60	251	227	23	66	89	13	2	2	30	1	2	1	20	6	26	1	3	9	.392	.348
Carranza, Pedro, Rey.	.219	40	121	105	10	23	32	4	1	1	9	5	1	0	10	1	17	0	1	3	.305	.284
Carrasco, Alejandro, Oax.	.000	1	1	1	0	0	0	0	0	0	0	0	0	0	0	0	1	0	0	0	.000	.000
Carrasco, Ernesto, Lar.	.270	111	399	344	41	93	115	20	1	0	25	7	5	2	41	2	35	5	6	9	.334	.347
Carrillo, Matias, Tig.	.326	119	504	417	83	136	224	22	3	20	102	2	5	1	79	15	33	6	7	13	.537	.430
Carter, Michael, Lar.	.341	110	492	454	69	155	195	27	5	1	33	5	3	3	27	3	26	41	17	9	.430	.380
Castaneda, Rafael, Sal.	.275	113	443	382	46	105	116	9	1	0	28	9	3	2	47	0	34	2	4	7	.304	.355
Castaneda, Hector, Oax.	.243	74	259	214	29	52	69	9	1	2	21	0	4	1	37	3	38	3	1	6	.322	.343
Castro, Arnoldo, Q.R.	.229	118	505	437	48	100	116	8	0	2	34	25	4	2	35	0	38	2	3	16	.261	.285
Castro, Eddie, Min.	.276	110	442	352	44	97	120	14	0	3	55	2	2	6	80	4	52	2	3	12	.341	.416
Cazarin, Manuel, Q.R.	.286	114	455	416	42	119	168	26	1	7	61	6	2	4	27	2	28	1	4	24	.404	.330
Cedeno, Ramon, Monc.	.278	6	19	18	1	5	6	1	0	0	0	0	0	0	1	0	7	0	0	0	.333	.316

Player, Team	Avg.	G	TPA	AB	R	H	TB	2B	3B	HR	RBI	SH	SF	HP	BB	IBB	SO	SB	CS	GDP	Slg.	OBP
Cervantes, Fernando, Agua.	.000	3	4	4	0	0	0	0	0	0	0	0	0	0	0	0	0	0	0	0	.000	.000
Cervantes, Refugio, Lar.	.000	5	8	8	0	0	0	0	0	0	0	0	0	0	0	0	1	0	0	0	.000	.000
Cervera, Francisco, Cam.	.269	89	352	297	32	80	117	8	1	9	45	13	2	9	31	3	40	5	4	16	.394	.354
Chan, Armando, Monc.	.112	48	104	89	5	10	12	2	0	0	2	2	1	0	12	1	16	0	1	3	.135	.216
Chance, Tony, Monc.	.288	118	500	399	76	115	212	20	4	23	78	2	5	5	89	7	93	5	4	11	.531	.420
Clark, Tim, Sal.	.326	112	450	386	59	126	206	30	4	14	78	1	6	3	54	9	65	2	1	15	.534	.408
Cobos, Rogelio, P.R.	.242	84	232	211	20	51	70	6	2	3	17	5	1	1	14	0	52	1	0	5	.332	.291
Contreras, Jose, Mont.	.194	47	108	98	5	19	22	3	0	0	5	2	0	1	7	0	4	0	1	4	.224	.255
Cookson, Brent, Lar.	.301	28	113	93	17	28	57	3	1	8	16	0	0	0	20	3	15	1	0	4	.613	.425
Cox, Darron, Tig.	.287	107	409	352	47	101	137	19	4	3	46	11	7	8	31	0	42	1	5	7	.389	.352
Cruz, Luis, Rey.	.238	83	300	265	13	63	85	12	2	2	26	8	3	5	19	4	23	0	0	12	.321	.298
Cruz, G. Marco A., Tor.	.265	109	410	347	31	92	125	24	0	3	31	7	0	10	46	2	56	1	0	16	.360	.367
Cuevas, Jorge, Tig.	.083	6	14	12	2	1	1	0	0	0	0	1	0	0	1	0	5	0	0	1	.083	.154
Deak, Darrel, Oax.	.319	89	374	304	45	97	133	27	0	3	48	1	5	1	63	5	47	9	7	7	.438	.432
De La Cruz, Hector, Q.R.	.261	110	452	402	51	105	157	15	5	9	59	3	5	2	40	3	51	23	11	17	.391	.327
De La Nuez, Rex, Tor.	.316	30	122	98	11	31	43	9	0	1	13	0	0	5	19	0	13	2	0	4	.439	.451
De La Rosa, Juan, Cam.	.212	39	167	151	13	32	44	9	0	1	13	5	3	0	8	1	17	2	3	0	.291	.247
Delgado, Juan, Tor.	.000	1	0	0	0	0	0	0	0	0	0	0	0	0	0	0	0	0	0	0	.000	.000
Delgado, Tomas, Yuc.	.059	12	17	17	2	1	1	0	0	0	2	0	0	0	0	0	3	0	0	1	.059	.059
De Lima, Rafael, P.R.	.269	88	393	324	51	87	113	13	5	1	29	3	5	0	61	2	53	16	10	7	.349	.379
Denson, Drew, Monc.	.291	54	218	182	39	53	88	8	0	9	35	0	3	4	29	4	17	0	0	7	.484	.394
Devarez, Cesar, Tig.	.188	6	21	16	3	3	3	0	0	0	4	0	0	0	5	0	3	0	0	1	.188	.381
Diaz, Luis, Lar.	.296	92	339	291	34	86	112	14	0	4	36	4	2	4	38	6	45	1	3	6	.385	.382
Diaz, Mario, Yuc.	.250	18	66	64	2	16	20	4	0	0	8	0	0	0	2	1	6	0	1	2	.313	.273
Diaz, Pedro Ivan, Tig.	.167	16	31	30	4	5	6	1	0	0	2	1	0	0	0	0	5	0	0	1	.200	.167
Diaz, Remigio, Mont.	.287	116	460	408	57	117	142	13	0	4	42	12	0	4	36	3	22	22	3	11	.348	.350
Dominguez, David, Q.R.	.242	64	226	186	29	45	70	10	0	5	20	1	2	1	36	1	25	1	1	8	.376	.364
Dominguez, Fausto, Agua.	.200	16	15	15	1	3	3	0	0	0	0	0	0	0	0	0	5	0	0	0	.200	.200
Duarte, Rene, Cam.	.243	60	187	169	9	41	48	7	0	0	15	7	2	2	7	1	21	0	0	3	.284	.278
Duran, Felipe, Oax.	.298	47	167	151	16	45	53	5	0	1	20	8	2	0	6	0	17	3	2	7	.351	.321
Durazo, Erubiel, Mont.	.282	110	415	358	47	101	166	21	10	8	61	0	4	1	52	11	43	3	7	13	.464	.371
Escalante, Marcelo, Agua.	.182	13	23	22	2	4	5	1	0	0	2	1	0	0	0	0	3	0	0	2	.227	.182
Espino, Daniel, Agua.	.290	70	208	183	19	53	59	4	1	0	19	5	3	5	12	0	23	6	5	4	.322	.345
Espinoza, Javier, Min.	.213	93	268	211	18	45	50	5	0	0	12	10	0	3	44	2	29	3	2	4	.237	.357
Espinoza, Jose, Lar.	.230	103	330	296	26	68	83	4	4	1	25	10	2	3	19	1	39	3	5	8	.280	.281
Espinoza, Ramon, Tor.	.143	20	28	28	3	4	4	0	0	0	2	0	0	0	0	0	10	0	0	1	.143	.143
Esquer, Ramon, Rey.	.296	116	482	416	66	123	154	13	6	2	39	13	1	2	50	6	42	5	8	7	.370	.373
Estrada, Hector, Monc.	.298	107	395	352	30	105	138	19	1	4	50	12	3	2	26	0	24	1	0	13	.392	.347
Estrada, Ricardo, Agua.	.000	3	3	3	0	0	0	0	0	0	0	0	0	0	0	0	1	0	0	0	.000	.000
Facundo, Armando, Tab.	.000	2	1	1	1	0	0	0	0	0	0	0	0	0	0	0	0	0	0	0	.000	.000
Felder, Mike, Monc.	.305	81	334	305	50	93	135	13	7	5	32	1	1	2	25	4	25	12	5	9	.443	.360
Felix, Arturo, Yuc.	.171	51	132	117	12	20	27	1	0	2	11	4	1	1	9	0	21	0	1	3	.231	.234
Felix, Junior, Yuc.	.323	99	422	356	53	115	169	16	4	10	77	2	4	7	53	4	57	3	2	13	.475	.417
Fentanes, Oscar, Tab.	.312	118	478	426	41	133	166	20	5	1	48	8	3	6	35	3	33	6	6	17	.390	.370
Fermin, Carlos, Tor.	.107	15	33	28	1	3	4	1	0	0	1	1	0	0	4	0	2	0	0	1	.143	.219
Fernandez, Daniel, Mex.	.319	115	544	442	107	141	172	18	5	1	39	7	3	1	91	6	49	24	6	9	.389	.434
Fernandez, Fabian, Rey.	.189	24	39	37	3	7	8	1	0	0	2	2	0	0	0	0	2	0	0	0	.216	.189
Figueroa, Marco Antonio, Min.	.316	28	67	57	5	18	18	0	0	0	6	2	0	0	8	1	14	0	2	3	.316	.400
Figueroa, Ricardo, Cam.	.077	15	16	13	1	1	2	1	0	0	1	1	0	0	2	0	2	0	1	0	.154	.200
Flores, Miguel, Mont.	.305	85	379	334	51	102	146	23	3	5	41	2	0	2	41	4	22	15	7	20	.437	.385
Franco, Manuel, Sal.	.173	27	55	52	1	9	11	0	1	0	2	0	0	0	3	0	11	0	1	0	.212	.218
Francois, Manuel, Oax.	.250	32	139	120	21	30	41	5	0	2	16	1	0	0	18	0	13	6	1	4	.342	.348
Gainey, Ty, Mex.	.353	107	479	399	97	141	238	18	2	25	108	0	3	4	73	11	65	8	0	11	.596	.455
Garcia, Carlos, Tab.	.170	67	157	135	20	23	33	6	2	0	8	3	1	0	18	0	29	5	1	1	.244	.266
Garcia, Cornelio, Mont.	.382	115	531	448	86	171	214	24	8	1	34	10	1	2	70	6	47	22	17	7	.478	.466
Garcia, Hector, Tor.	.272	98	390	346	55	94	110	9	2	1	25	5	0	1	38	1	25	6	1	10	.318	.345
Garcia, Heriberto, P.R.	.259	95	389	347	51	90	114	10	7	0	27	6	1	3	32	0	25	8	6	13	.329	.326
Garcia, Omar, P.R.	.336	117	482	434	57	146	185	25	7	0	65	1	9	1	37	4	30	4	0	11	.426	.383
Garza, Fidel, Mont.	.000	2	2	2	0	0	0	0	0	0	0	0	0	0	0	0	0	0	0	0	.000	.000
Garza, Gerardo, Lar.	.239	115	417	368	29	88	103	7	1	2	50	9	5	1	34	1	27	2	4	10	.280	.301
Garzon, Eliseo, Tab.	.265	109	381	325	40	86	97	6	1	1	36	5	6	1	44	2	46	0	2	16	.298	.348
Gastelum, Carlos, Monc.	.247	52	81	73	5	18	20	2	0	0	6	4	0	0	4	0	9	0	0	2	.274	.286
Gastelum, Sergio, Tig.	.305	91	369	331	48	101	128	15	0	4	45	4	2	8	24	2	30	7	1	15	.387	.364
Gavia, Jesus, Cam.	.241	76	253	232	15	56	77	10	1	3	24	4	1	1	15	0	20	1	1	10	.332	.289
Giles, Brian, P.R.	.297	76	292	246	27	73	87	12	1	0	26	2	0	5	39	2	44	3	5	9	.354	.403
Gomez, Ever, Tab.	.234	80	232	201	22	47	56	4	1	1	19	13	0	4	14	0	30	5	5	7	.279	.297
Gonzalez, Denio, Tab.	.295	88	354	258	48	76	133	9	0	16	52	2	2	5	87	2	29	1	3	6	.516	.477
Gonzalez, Gilberto, Tor.	.500	1	2	2	1	1	1	0	0	0	0	0	0	0	0	0	1	0	0	0	.500	.500
Gonzalez, Jesus, Cam.	.323	107	457	402	63	130	197	21	2	14	55	5	1	5	44	4	46	7	6	10	.490	.396
Gonzalez, Jose, Agua.	.265	87	351	313	44	83	121	11	3	7	38	0	4	1	33	1	41	12	11	6	.387	.333
Gonzalez, Roman, Min.	.036	18	29	28	1	1	1	0	0	0	0	1	0	0	0	0	11	0	0	0	.036	.036
Guerrero, Francisco, Q.R.	.288	90	327	267	35	77	98	15	0	2	30	11	2	2	45	0	59	7	6	6	.367	.392
Guerrero, Jaime, Agua.	.271	79	188	170	18	46	56	7	0	1	11	5	1	1	11	0	35	1	3	5	.329	.317
Guerrero, Javier, Agua.	.125	7	10	8	0	1	1	0	0	0	0	2	0	0	0	0	4	0	0	0	.125	.125
Guerrero, Jose, Q.R.	.097	22	32	31	1	3	3	0	0	0	1	0	0	0	1	0	7	2	0	1	.097	.125
Guizar, Hector, Cam.	.283	106	436	400	51	113	136	9	1	4	30	11	3	0	22	0	22	1	6	17	.340	.318
Gutierrez, Felipe, Oax.	.182	8	23	22	0	4	4	0	0	0	2	1	0	0	0	0	3	0	0	1	.182	.182
Gutierrez, Said, Yuc.	.000	1	0	0	0	0	0	0	0	0	0	0	0	0	0	0	0	0	0	0	.000	.000
Guzman, Marco, Yuc.	.271	65	203	181	16	49	64	9	0	2	19	4	3	0	15	1	15	0	1	3	.354	.322
Hansen, Terrell, Tor.	.249	59	237	217	27	54	86	11	0	7	41	1	2	10	7	2	54	0	0	7	.396	.301
Hernandez, Cesar, Tor.	.286	10	25	21	1	6	6	0	0	0	2	0	0	0	4	0	5	0	0	2	.286	.400
Hernandez, Gerardo, Tig.	.163	49	102	86	18	14	23	3	0	2	8	1	0	1	14	0	33	0	2	0	.267	.287

Player, Team	Avg.	G	TPA	AB	R	H	TB	2B	3B	HR	RBI	SH	SF	HP	BB	IBB	SO	SB	CS	GDP	Slg.	OBP
Hernandez, Julio, Oax.	.000	1	1	1	0	0	0	0	0	0	0	0	0	0	0	0	0	0	0	0	.000	.000
Hernandez, Miguel, P.R.	.152	58	135	112	18	17	17	0	0	0	11	7	0	1	15	0	8	0	0	5	.152	.258
Herrera, Isidro, Oax.	.280	54	238	193	36	54	64	6	2	0	20	1	2	2	40	3	11	7	8	4	.332	.405
Hosey, Steve, Agua.	.244	26	99	82	14	20	32	3	0	3	11	2	1	2	12	1	15	2	1	2	.390	.351
Howell, Patrick, Mex.	.318	52	221	198	31	63	75	4	4	0	18	13	0	1	9	1	20	11	3	2	.379	.351
Hurst, Jonathan, Agua.	.000	1	1	1	0	0	0	0	0	0	0	0	0	0	0	0	0	0	0	0	.000	.000
Hurtado, Hector, Min.	.182	58	176	165	8	30	40	4	0	2	12	1	0	1	9	2	33	1	2	10	.242	.229
Ingram, Ricardo, Mont.	.154	7	29	26	1	4	5	1	0	0	0	0	0	0	3	0	5	0	0	1	.192	.241
Iturbe, Pedro, Tig.	.287	37	139	115	21	33	47	2	3	2	11	1	2	1	20	2	25	4	3	3	.409	.391
Jerald, Clack, Tab.	.400	4	16	15	4	6	12	0	0	2	6	0	0	0	1	0	3	0	0	1	.800	.438
Jimenez, Alfonso, Mex.	.276	62	288	246	47	68	99	9	2	6	31	7	3	0	32	0	28	3	1	9	.402	.356
Jimenez, Eduardo, Mex.	.291	103	434	333	78	97	182	17	1	22	91	0	6	9	86	5	68	2	0	12	.547	.442
Johnson, Roy, Cam.	.219	13	38	32	3	7	12	2	0	1	6	0	0	0	6	2	4	0	0	0	.375	.342
Jones, Bobby, Tor.	.182	11	37	33	2	6	6	0	0	0	4	0	0	0	4	0	8	0	1	3	.182	.270
Jones, Ron, Tab.	.232	32	137	112	10	26	39	2	1	3	17	1	0	0	24	4	14	0	1	1	.348	.368
Jose, Felix, Cam.	.269	92	374	308	54	83	131	16	1	10	41	0	3	2	61	12	60	8	5	12	.425	.390
Leal, Jose, Cam.	.267	87	296	258	30	69	95	8	3	4	26	5	0	0	33	7	35	1	0	11	.368	.351
Lewis, Anthony, Sal.	.248	74	299	270	29	67	110	13	0	10	45	1	0	2	26	2	53	0	3	13	.407	.319
Leyva, German, Yuc.	.289	117	469	401	43	116	141	17	4	0	40	8	4	4	52	9	32	7	4	12	.352	.373
Linares, Rigoberto, Min.	.217	86	257	217	22	47	56	4	1	1	11	14	0	1	25	0	33	0	3	7	.258	.300
Lopez, Fabian, Oax.	.276	94	320	294	42	81	93	9	0	1	21	4	3	2	17	6	22	6	3	9	.316	.316
Lopez, Gonzalo, Monc.	.245	53	168	139	15	34	42	6	1	0	14	8	3	1	17	1	12	0	0	5	.302	.325
Lopez, Jose Jaime, P.R.	.000	5	5	5	1	0	0	0	0	0	0	0	0	0	0	0	1	0	0	0	.000	.000
Lopez, Miguel, Yuc.	.000	4	2	2	0	0	0	0	0	0	0	0	0	0	0	0	0	0	0	0	.000	.000
Lopez, Salvador, Agua.	.245	72	222	188	28	46	60	9	1	1	11	5	1	0	28	0	21	3	9	4	.319	.341
Lopez, Victor, Oax.	.228	52	144	136	13	31	37	4	1	0	11	1	0	1	6	1	12	3	3	1	.272	.266
Loredo, Jorge Luis, Oax.	.260	108	451	388	49	101	138	20	4	3	42	9	3	7	44	1	55	2	3	14	.356	.344
Luna, Jose, Mont.	.198	52	90	81	6	16	17	1	0	0	7	3	0	0	6	0	7	0	1	2	.210	.253
Lydy, Scott, Mex.	.306	121	524	458	93	140	234	30	5	18	107	1	5	5	55	4	70	20	5	11	.511	.382
Machiria, Pablo, Mont.	.284	97	384	341	45	97	128	10	3	5	36	6	2	6	29	3	18	3	6	13	.375	.349
Mack, Quinn, Sal.	.276	109	431	399	58	110	137	19	4	0	55	1	3	3	25	8	36	16	8	13	.343	.321
Magallanes, Ever, Mont.	.359	88	373	334	47	120	150	17	2	3	46	5	3	1	30	5	35	3	3	11	.449	.410
Magallanes, Roberto, Mex.	.286	23	61	49	10	14	17	3	0	0	7	0	0	0	12	1	10	1	1	2	.347	.426
Magana, Gabriel, Yuc.	.188	15	16	16	3	3	3	0	0	0	0	0	0	0	0	0	2	1	0	2	.188	.188
Malpica, Enrique, P.R.	.125	26	47	40	5	5	5	0	0	0	6	2	1	1	3	0	12	0	1	0	.125	.200
Martinez, Abel, Q.R.	.154	48	71	65	11	10	15	1	2	0	3	1	0	0	5	0	14	6	1	1	.231	.214
Martinez, Cesar, Mont.	.000	1	1	0	0	0	0	0	0	0	0	0	0	0	0	0	1	0	0	0	.000	.000
Martinez, Enrique, Agua.	.261	75	299	261	36	68	90	6	2	4	26	6	4	3	25	1	34	7	5	7	.345	.328
Martinez, Grimaldo, Monc.	.272	112	491	426	57	116	176	34	4	6	40	10	3	6	46	0	33	6	8	8	.413	.349
Martinez, Jose, Yuc.	.000	1	0	0	0	0	0	0	0	0	0	0	0	0	0	0	0	0	0	1	.000	.000
Martinez, Julian, Oax.	.281	17	68	57	9	16	19	1	1	0	4	1	1	0	9	0	10	2	1	2	.333	.373
Martinez, Raul, P.R.	.108	45	96	83	3	9	12	3	0	0	4	1	1	1	10	2	8	0	1	6	.145	.211
Martinez, Ray, Mex.	.307	83	360	296	63	91	114	20	0	1	49	4	3	3	54	0	35	3	3	15	.385	.416
Mata, Noe, P.R.	.200	5	6	5	0	1	1	0	0	0	1	0	0	0	1	0	2	0	0	0	.200	.333
McGriff, Terry, Lar.	.206	68	245	208	19	52	68	10	0	2	24	1	1	2	33	2	22	2	1	9	.279	.357
Medina, Jose R., Cam.	.275	90	327	298	39	82	112	16	4	2	28	6	0	0	23	1	49	0	5	9	.376	.327
Meggers, Mike, Q.R.	.205	11	53	44	11	9	14	2	0	1	4	0	1	0	8	0	17	0	0	1	.318	.321
Mendez, Ramon, Agua.	.311	17	46	45	3	14	19	3	1	0	5	0	0	0	1	0	5	0	0	4	.422	.326
Mendez, Roberto C., Oax.	.328	103	423	357	67	117	170	21	4	8	69	8	5	5	48	6	35	13	6	12	.476	.410
Mendiola, Juan Carlos, Min.	.000	2	4	4	0	0	0	0	0	0	0	0	0	0	0	0	0	0	0	0	.000	.000
Mendoza, Omar, Lar.	.196	55	161	143	12	28	34	6	0	0	15	3	2	2	11	0	31	0	0	5	.238	.259
Mere, Pedro, P.R.	.264	106	369	322	48	85	116	13	3	4	45	12	2	4	29	0	41	6	2	11	.360	.331
Meza, Alfredo, Mont.	.239	76	244	230	16	55	65	5	1	1	21	5	1	2	6	0	18	3	3	3	.283	.264
Michel, Domingo, Cam.	.327	107	446	343	64	112	153	13	2	8	54	4	2	3	94	7	54	8	1	6	.446	.473
Monell, Johnny, Q.R.	.291	60	246	206	31	60	74	9	1	1	22	0	1	1	38	6	18	3	0	6	.359	.402
Monroy, Victor, Min.	.000	1	1	1	0	0	0	0	0	0	0	0	0	0	0	0	0	0	0	0	.000	.000
Montalvo, Ivan, Tig.	.304	108	440	365	53	111	170	28	8	5	63	6	6	5	58	11	72	2	6	10	.466	.401
Montanez, Lardaniel, Q.R.	.083	19	15	12	1	1	1	0	0	0	1	0	0	1	2	0	3	0	0	0	.083	.154
Mora, Andres, Lar.	.429	17	39	28	3	12	12	0	0	0	5	1	1	0	9	3	3	0	0	0	.429	.553
Morales, Florentino, Lar.	.233	89	290	240	26	56	68	7	1	1	17	5	0	2	43	0	26	3	2	10	.283	.354
Morejon, Oswaldo, Yuc.	.244	74	226	205	15	50	53	1	1	0	18	1	0	2	18	0	36	2	1	3	.259	.285
Moreno, David, Rey.	.220	22	46	41	2	9	9	0	0	0	1	0	1	0	4	0	2	0	1	1	.220	.304
Moreno, Leonardo, Oax.	.279	81	249	226	27	63	76	8	1	1	22	7	0	2	14	1	22	0	1	6	.336	.326
Morones, Martin, P.R.	.300	86	289	250	36	75	97	12	2	2	30	3	4	1	31	4	24	6	4	5	.388	.374
Mota, Manny Jr., Sal.	.289	22	83	76	12	22	24	2	0	0	4	2	0	1	4	0	13	3	3	0	.316	.333
Munoz, Jose, Tab.	.301	115	506	438	59	132	160	20	1	2	40	7	2	3	56	6	24	14	15	8	.365	.383
Munoz, Jose De J., Sal.	.272	100	362	309	47	84	104	11	3	1	22	10	2	0	41	0	36	3	3	7	.337	.355
Munoz, Noe, Mex.	.298	97	376	309	42	92	116	16	1	2	52	4	6	4	53	2	36	2	1	14	.375	.401
Navarrete, Alejandro, Agua.	.222	6	10	9	2	2	4	0	1	0	0	0	0	0	1	0	1	0	0	0	.444	.300
Noris, Rogelio, Rey.	.000	1	1	1	0	0	0	0	0	0	0	0	0	0	0	0	0	0	0	0	.000	.000
Norton, Christopher, Tig.	.281	17	76	64	15	18	30	4	1	2	12	1	0	1	10	2	17	0	0	2	.469	.387
Nunez, Dimmerson, Tor.	.164	19	72	67	4	11	12	1	0	0	8	0	2	0	3	0	13	2	3	5	.179	.194
Nunez, A. Jose Juan, Oax.	.500	2	2	2	0	1	1	0	0	0	0	0	0	0	0	0	0	0	0	0	.500	.500
Nunez, G. Jose Juan, Oax.	.138	18	34	29	2	4	4	0	0	0	1	0	0	0	3	0	6	1	1	1	.138	.219
O'Brien, John, Q.R.	.207	9	38	29	2	6	7	1	0	0	4	1	0	0	8	0	9	0	0	1	.241	.378
Ochoa, Edgar, Tig.	.227	31	80	75	5	17	26	6	0	1	7	1	1	0	3	1	16	0	1	3	.347	.253
Ojeda, Miguel, Mex.	.266	92	323	289	41	77	110	14	2	5	45	1	1	1	31	3	44	4	2	11	.381	.339
Olvera, Sergio, Monc.	.231	89	304	286	29	66	80	6	4	0	16	5	1	4	8	0	24	5	6	9	.280	.261
Orantes, Ramon, Agua.	.261	95	360	341	20	89	125	11	2	7	41	4	2	3	10	5	40	1	5	18	.367	.287
Ortega, Antonio, Mex.	.476	16	21	21	2	10	17	2	1	1	8	0	0	0	0	0	2	0	0	1	.810	.476
Ortiz, Alejandro, Q.R.	.242	105	393	339	32	82	111	15	1	4	34	4	4	5	41	3	39	3	3	23	.327	.329
Osuna, Hector, Yuc.	.221	30	78	68	5	15	16	1	0	0	4	5	0	1	4	0	12	0	0	0	.235	.274

Player, Team	Avg.	G	TPA	AB	R	H	TB	2B	3B	HR	RBI	SH	SF	HP	BB	IBB	SO	SB	CS	GDP	Slg.	OBP
Pacho, Carlos, Yuc.	.169	34	95	89	6	15	20	1	2	0	7	4	0	0	2	0	19	0	0	6	.225	.187
Pacho, Juan Jose, Yuc.	.257	105	404	350	40	90	98	8	0	0	24	22	1	2	29	0	22	4	3	7	.280	.317
Paez, Raul, Rey.	.315	89	356	305	30	96	131	13	5	4	57	6	5	3	37	7	47	5	3	5	.430	.389
Pantoja, Rigel, Yuc.	.250	1	4	4	0	1	1	0	0	0	1	0	0	0	0	0	0	0	0	0	.250	.250
Pardo, Victor, Min.	.182	65	217	181	16	33	43	6	2	0	18	5	1	1	29	4	21	2	0	5	.238	.297
Payro, Edison, Agua.	.251	93	354	315	36	79	90	8	0	1	17	10	0	1	28	0	46	2	9	14	.286	.314
Peguero, Julio, Q.R.	.318	116	528	450	67	143	192	20	7	5	58	5	5	3	65	12	53	16	18	12	.427	.403
Pena, Carlos, Tab.	.065	24	37	31	4	2	5	0	0	1	4	0	1	0	5	0	5	0	0	1	.161	.189
Pena, Luis A., Sal.	.279	34	75	68	6	19	29	1	0	3	10	1	1	0	5	0	19	0	0	3	.426	.324
Perez, Alfredo, Cam.	.221	90	311	272	22	60	69	9	0	0	21	11	4	2	22	0	20	1	1	10	.254	.280
Perez, Francisco, Mex.	.267	54	121	116	7	31	46	5	2	2	16	2	0	0	3	1	19	4	2	3	.397	.286
Perez, Juan, Tor.	.171	36	75	70	4	12	15	3	0	0	4	2	0	0	3	0	22	0	1	3	.214	.205
Perez, Noel, Sal.	.000	2	1	1	0	0	0	0	0	0	0	0	0	0	0	0	0	0	0	0	.000	.000
Polonia, Luis, Tig.	.377	110	495	408	105	154	214	29	5	7	59	5	3	4	75	12	33	48	12	13	.525	.476
Precichi, Jorge, Sal.	.167	14	13	12	0	2	3	1	0	0	2	0	0	0	1	0	0	1	0	0	.250	.231
Quintana, Carlos, Sal.	.148	8	30	27	1	4	4	0	0	0	1	0	0	0	3	0	7	1	0	0	.148	.233
Quintero, Allan, Yuc.	.285	49	164	151	20	43	59	11	1	1	11	5	0	1	7	0	24	0	1	7	.391	.321
Quintero, Edgar, Mont.	.240	10	27	25	2	6	6	0	0	0	1	0	0	0	2	0	8	0	0	0	.240	.296
Quintero, Guillermo, Mont.	.168	76	187	155	14	26	28	2	0	0	7	11	3	1	17	1	23	5	3	4	.181	.250
Quiroz, Jose Julian, Sal.	.000	2	2	2	1	0	0	0	0	0	0	0	0	0	0	0	1	0	0	0	.000	.000
Ramirez, Efren, Agua.	.228	82	245	202	22	46	62	11	1	1	20	4	0	12	27	1	29	1	2	6	.307	.353
Ramirez, Enrique, Monc.	.214	56	175	159	16	34	37	3	0	0	8	5	0	1	10	0	10	4	2	3	.233	.265
Ramirez, Jesus, P.R.	.296	80	246	226	34	67	83	7	3	1	13	5	0	3	12	0	27	5	3	3	.367	.340
Ramirez, Omar, Min.	.233	43	176	146	20	34	38	4	0	0	5	6	1	1	22	1	10	3	0	6	.260	.335
Ramon, Reyes, Tab.	.248	51	135	117	11	29	33	4	0	0	13	4	1	2	11	2	16	1	1	5	.282	.321
Ramsey, Fernando, Rey.	.259	53	216	205	25	53	65	6	3	0	17	1	1	2	7	1	20	7	9	2	.317	.288
Rathiff, Darryl, Tor.	.382	29	120	110	19	42	49	3	2	0	17	0	0	0	10	0	13	2	0	4	.445	.433
Resendez, Carlos, Monc.	.167	6	6	6	1	1	1	0	0	0	0	0	0	0	0	0	1	0	0	0	.167	.167
Reyes, Gilberto, Min.	.291	36	143	127	10	37	44	4	0	1	12	2	1	1	12	1	24	0	1	5	.346	.355
Robles, Benito, P.R.	.000	1	0	0	0	0	0	0	0	0	0	0	0	0	0	0	0	0	0	0	.000	.000
Robles, Gerardo, Cam.	.130	18	25	23	2	3	4	1	0	0	1	0	0	0	2	0	4	0	1	1	.174	.200
Robles, Javier, Tig.	.280	113	478	414	57	116	179	25	7	8	75	3	6	6	49	4	66	7	6	16	.432	.360
Robles, Trinidad, Lar.	.246	118	406	342	40	84	115	7	6	4	28	11	2	5	46	1	85	7	6	6	.336	.342
Rodriguez, Fernando, Tor.	.295	110	444	400	42	118	168	22	2	8	75	4	5	4	31	5	52	0	3	17	.421	.348
Rodriguez, Jose Luis, Sal.	.233	16	30	30	1	7	12	0	1	1	1	0	0	0	0	0	4	0	0	0	.400	.233
Rodriguez, Noel, Tab.	.000	1	4	4	0	0	0	0	0	0	0	0	0	0	0	0	0	0	0	0	.000	.000
Rodriguez, Serafin, Q.R.	.283	102	373	321	35	91	125	14	7	2	32	11	2	8	31	1	43	14	7	4	.389	.359
Rojas, Francisco, Tab.	.222	36	47	45	6	10	12	2	0	0	1	0	0	1	1	0	9	0	1	1	.267	.255
Rojas, Homar, Yuc.	.252	41	165	151	18	38	52	8	0	2	21	1	4	1	8	1	17	0	0	3	.344	.287
Romero, Israel, Lar.	.163	41	58	49	4	8	9	1	0	0	3	2	0	0	7	0	14	0	0	1	.184	.268
Romero, Marco, Yuc.	.264	107	422	371	44	98	146	21	0	9	38	2	2	4	43	4	44	1	4	15	.394	.345
Romero, Oscar, Monc.	.246	103	406	342	45	84	131	23	3	6	45	3	2	4	55	6	56	9	5	6	.383	.355
Rosario, Victor, Q.R.	.295	77	306	285	34	84	109	16	3	1	27	4	1	3	13	3	44	7	8	10	.382	.331
Rubio, Sergio, Yuc.	.221	72	185	154	21	34	40	2	2	0	8	11	0	3	17	0	23	6	3	6	.260	.310
Ruiz, Juan De Dios, Min.	.217	51	156	138	9	30	36	6	0	0	6	5	0	1	12	0	13	0	2	2	.261	.285
Ruiz, Placido, Mont.	.200	5	6	5	1	1	1	0	0	0	0	0	0	0	1	0	0	0	0	0	.200	.333
Russel, Omar, Min.	.100	20	23	20	0	2	2	0	0	0	1	1	0	1	1	0	8	0	0	1	.100	.182
Saenz, Ricardo, Monc.	.267	102	426	359	60	96	163	22	3	13	52	5	2	3	57	3	66	2	0	6	.454	.371
Salas, Heriberto, Tor.	.349	87	383	338	59	118	148	16	4	2	32	5	0	1	39	2	22	3	4	5	.438	.418
Sanchez, Armando, Mont.	.216	73	226	185	17	40	50	7	0	1	18	14	0	0	27	0	12	0	1	13	.270	.316
Sanchez, Gerardo, Lar.	.303	122	528	462	59	140	191	20	2	9	74	6	8	10	42	5	46	6	3	16	.413	.368
Sanchez, Ismael, P.R.	.182	41	70	66	7	12	17	5	0	0	8	0	0	0	4	0	21	1	0	3	.258	.229
Sanchez, Raul, Q.R.	.254	80	210	185	34	47	63	10	3	0	17	8	1	2	14	0	28	4	4	7	.341	.312
Sanchez, Roque, Rey.	.259	100	355	332	33	86	114	9	8	1	22	13	1	2	7	1	22	2	4	14	.343	.278
Sandoval, Jose, Sal.	.272	111	414	360	34	98	133	20	3	3	34	4	3	2	45	5	52	1	2	15	.369	.354
Sandoval, Octavio, Tig.	.242	74	256	231	25	56	71	5	2	2	16	8	0	2	15	0	32	2	2	5	.307	.294
Santana, Mario, Agua.	.305	53	136	128	11	39	50	7	2	0	12	2	0	0	6	0	20	0	1	4	.391	.336
Saucedo, Roberto, Mont.	.229	71	183	170	13	39	68	6	1	7	26	2	0	0	11	3	20	0	0	4	.400	.276
Scott, Gary, Q.R.	.120	7	31	25	4	3	5	0	1	0	0	0	0	0	6	0	7	0	0	2	.200	.290
Sherman, Darrell, Rey.	.327	97	445	355	72	116	147	17	7	0	16	9	0	5	76	3	33	19	13	7	.414	.452
Sievers, Carlos, Yuc.	.212	27	35	33	7	7	7	0	0	0	3	0	0	0	2	1	3	0	0	0	.212	.257
Soriano, Ricardo, Tor.	.248	78	236	214	21	53	64	7	2	0	22	4	2	1	15	0	32	1	0	4	.299	.297
Stark, Matt, Yuc.	.337	109	458	362	53	122	166	23	0	7	57	0	5	11	80	17	30	2	1	12	.459	.465
Steverson, Todd, Lar.	.231	34	131	104	11	24	28	4	0	0	5	0	0	1	26	3	27	1	1	3	.269	.389
Tejeda, Arturo, Lar.	.222	71	127	117	16	26	32	4	1	0	6	4	0	0	6	0	11	0	0	2	.274	.260
Tellez, Alonso, Rey.	.317	119	501	445	55	141	219	27	6	13	67	1	4	2	49	11	45	2	4	16	.492	.384
Texidor, Jose, Rey.	.161	16	63	62	5	10	14	1	0	1	2	1	0	0	0	0	10	0	0	1	.226	.161
Tiquet, Lazaro, Tab.	.254	72	199	177	21	45	60	10	1	1	15	4	0	3	15	1	30	2	1	9	.339	.323
Torres, Eduardo, Monc.	.236	82	261	212	29	50	63	4	0	3	25	3	2	2	42	4	24	4	2	8	.297	.364
Torres, Raymundo, Yuc.	.194	45	154	124	12	24	40	4	0	4	20	0	0	1	29	2	51	0	0	0	.323	.351
Trapaga, Julio, Tig.	.259	117	516	448	74	116	155	15	3	6	48	18	3	5	42	1	86	7	3	9	.346	.327
Valdez, Edgar, Q.R.	.333	3	3	3	0	1	1	0	0	0	0	0	0	0	0	0	0	0	0	0	.333	.333
Valdez, Francisco, Rey.	.269	57	188	156	16	42	56	9	1	1	13	7	0	4	21	1	15	2	3	3	.359	.370
Valdez, Jesus, Cam.	.168	44	138	119	6	20	22	2	0	0	9	4	0	2	13	1	10	0	1	7	.185	.261
Valdez, Ramon, Min.	.263	93	311	247	44	65	66	1	0	0	13	7	1	7	49	0	26	13	6	6	.267	.398
Valencia, Carlos, Sal.	.285	97	340	302	29	86	101	9	0	2	35	10	4	4	20	2	22	2	2	9	.334	.333
Valenzuela, Armando, Rey.	.244	115	440	402	45	98	112	10	2	0	24	9	3	2	24	2	28	8	9	14	.279	.288
Valenzuela, Eduardo, Sal.	.272	80	198	169	16	46	55	6	0	1	24	7	2	0	20	2	14	0	0	6	.325	.346
Valenzuela, Jose Luis, Tab.	.000	3	4	3	0	0	0	0	0	0	0	0	0	0	1	0	1	0	0	0	.000	.250
Valenzuela, Mario, Sal.	.250	19	45	40	7	10	16	2	2	0	4	1	0	1	3	0	9	1	1	0	.400	.318
Valle, Jorge, Tor.	.247	118	423	381	45	94	137	11	13	2	35	14	2	2	24	0	45	4	2	11	.360	.293
Valle, Jose, Min.	.271	94	331	295	26	80	93	9	2	0	27	12	1	1	22	1	16	2	4	10	.315	.323

Player, Team	Avg.	G	TPA	AB	R	H	TB	2B	3B	HR	RBI	SH	SF	HP	BB	IBB	SO	SB	CS	GDP	Slg.	OBP
Valle, Roberto, Tor.	.154	10	17	13	1	2	2	0	0	0	0	1	0	1	2	0	2	1	1	0	.154	.313
Valrie, Kerry, Oax.	.335	62	287	254	56	85	112	18	3	1	23	2	2	1	28	3	23	7	4	3	.441	.400
Vargas, Hector, Rey.	.307	66	288	228	37	70	91	10	1	3	34	2	1	5	52	2	25	4	4	14	.399	.444
Vazquez, Felipe, Oax.	.180	42	133	111	7	20	22	0	1	0	6	10	0	1	11	0	14	0	0	4	.198	.260
Vega, Edgar, Min.	.209	69	214	182	12	38	49	6	1	1	11	4	0	2	26	1	22	0	1	8	.269	.314
Vela, Manuel, Rey.	.243	24	43	37	5	9	11	2	0	0	1	3	0	0	3	0	12	0	1	0	.297	.300
Velazquez, Guillermo, Mont. .	.301	82	334	286	40	86	139	15	1	12	57	0	5	1	42	5	46	1	3	12	.486	.386
Velez, Manuel, Tig.	.251	75	226	199	30	50	59	9	0	0	24	9	2	1	15	0	14	0	4	7	.296	.304
Verdugo, Vicente, Mex.	.288	113	426	385	47	111	132	13	1	2	54	8	7	3	23	0	16	3	3	13	.343	.328
Villa, Carlos, Lar.	.000	5	5	5	0	0	0	0	0	0	0	0	0	0	0	0	1	0	0	0	.000	.000
Villanueva, Hector, Q.R.	.300	54	226	180	26	54	84	12	0	6	29	0	3	2	41	5	25	1	1	2	.467	.429
Villarreal, Alejandro, Lar.	.265	95	302	264	24	70	93	9	1	4	25	11	2	7	18	1	29	0	1	6	.352	.326
Villegas, Fernando, Sal.	.294	109	455	401	61	118	140	4	9	0	49	14	2	4	34	3	46	2	1	11	.349	.354
Vizcarra, Marco, Sal.	.228	119	454	390	45	89	105	8	4	0	41	19	4	2	39	0	27	4	4	6	.269	.299
Vizcarra, Roberto, Agua.	.294	121	519	449	54	132	177	17	2	8	44	8	4	6	52	9	29	15	9	15	.394	.372
Walker, Steve, P.R.	.264	44	175	159	14	42	55	11	1	0	19	1	0	2	13	4	36	6	6	5	.346	.328
Williams, Harold, P.R.	.254	49	197	177	8	45	68	14	0	3	25	0	3	2	15	1	31	0	3	3	.384	.315
Williams, Reggie, Mont.	.257	59	252	218	23	56	76	13	2	1	20	2	3	0	29	3	37	10	4	8	.349	.340
Wong, Julian, Cam.	.230	79	296	248	32	57	75	15	0	1	23	6	4	2	36	1	25	2	0	9	.302	.328
Wood, Tyrone, Min.	.342	85	367	304	58	104	182	20	2	18	73	0	2	9	58	8	49	0	2	8	.599	.450
Worthington, Craig, Mont.	.259	23	101	85	10	22	29	4	0	1	12	2	2	0	12	0	15	0	1	2	.341	.343
Wright, George, Agua.	.260	96	411	334	56	87	119	12	1	6	52	0	4	2	71	6	35	9	6	13	.356	.389
Wright, Tom, Cam.	.000	3	10	10	0	0	0	0	0	0	0	0	0	0	0	0	2	0	0	1	.000	.000
Yan, Julian, Agua.	.302	68	274	258	31	78	128	15	1	11	36	1	3	1	11	4	48	0	1	5	.496	.330
Yuriar, Jesus, Yuc.	.235	57	180	153	12	36	42	6	0	0	19	4	3	1	19	0	23	1	1	8	.275	.318
Zambrano, Roberto, Q.R.	.311	27	116	103	19	32	56	6	0	6	14	0	1	4	8	1	13	0	1	2	.544	.379
Zamudio, Rafael, Min.	.241	101	384	344	43	83	121	12	7	4	35	11	0	3	26	3	52	5	3	9	.352	.300
Zazueta, Juan Carlos, Tor.	.327	91	367	333	47	109	128	15	2	0	24	7	0	2	25	1	17	3	4	17	.384	.378
Zazueta, Mauricio, Tor.	.252	116	481	408	53	103	130	14	2	3	36	9	4	2	58	3	36	6	0	21	.319	.345
Zupcic, Bob, Rey.	.000	2	6	6	0	0	0	0	0	0	0	0	0	0	0	0	0	0	0	0	.000	.000

GRAND SLAMS: E. Jimenez, 3; Aganza, Gainey, Norton, J. Robles, Scott, 2 each; Canizalez, Carrillo, Esquer, A. Jimenez, Orantes, G. Sanchez, Wood, Wright, 1 each.
AWARD FIRST BASE ON CATCHER'S INTEFERENCE: De Lima (H. Estrada); Esquer (H. Estrada); S. Lopez (N. Munoz); A. Martinez (Russell); Morones (Cazarin); En. Ramirez (Cobos); F. Valdez (Santana).

1997 PITCHING

TEAM

Team	W	L	Pct.	ERA	G	CG	ShO	Sv.	IP	H	TBF	R	ER	HR	SH	SF	HB	BB	IBB	SO	WP	Bk.
Tabasco	67	52	.563	3.04	119	28	11	29	1015.2	952	4207	408	343	32	96	22	51	349	53	470	21	13
Monterrey	68	52	.567	3.26	120	13	2	30	1067.0	1008	4512	435	386	36	87	31	37	467	46	593	38	6
Quintana Roo	61	56	.521	3.30	119	41	12	23	1036.1	1050	4374	454	380	63	73	18	41	362	19	434	40	5
Poza Rica	67	52	.563	3.33	119	15	7	34	1015.2	993	4296	448	376	46	71	32	31	414	34	376	28	12
M.C. Red Devils	83	38	.686	3.41	121	8	1	29	1043.0	1049	4549	491	395	30	73	25	27	503	24	538	47	11
M.C. Tigers	77	40	.658	3.44	119	13	6	34	1038.1	984	4431	474	397	50	60	35	27	514	27	523	53	3
Reynosa	60	57	.513	3.49	119	18	7	31	1019.2	966	4262	457	395	40	...	26	35	491	38	528	63	3
Campeche	46	64	.418	3.53	111	12	1	18	953.2	932	4089	437	374	51	78	42	31	452	27	382	64	9
Monclova	65	56	.537	3.59	121	16	7	32	1036.2	1020	4489	511	414	60	62	33	34	482	26	555	61	13
Nuevo Laredo....	55	64	.462	3.71	122	10	5	28	1051.2	1130	4526	500	434	70	85	28	45	391	67	513	54	13
Yucatan	54	64	.458	3.86	120	10	4	23	1022.0	1026	4442	511	438	46	95	39	36	478	39	493	54	11
Saltillo	55	64	.462	4.22	120	6	0	26	1021.2	1126	4453	557	479	56	67	29	36	438	41	510	36	12
Minatitlan	42	76	.356	4.28	120	11	0	15	1038.0	1174	4581	583	494	56	79	41	32	424	52	429	34	13
Torreon	48	70	.407	4.40	119	8	3	17	1019.2	1136	4506	581	498	55	53	30	33	451	26	498	56	8
Aguascalientes ..	46	73	.387	4.50	121	18	5	21	1050.0	1213	4629	607	525	42	77	45	54	448	32	447	43	3
Oaxaca	53	69	.434	4.83	122	14	3	23	1045.0	1253	4774	694	561	56	76	42	41	503	45	505	65	12

INDIVIDUAL

TOP QUALIFIERS FOR EARNED-RUN AVERAGE TITLE
Minimum 93 innings.

Pitcher, Team	W	L	Pct.	ERA	G	GS	CG	ShO	GF	Sv.	IP	H	TBF	R	ER	HR	SH	SF	HB	BB	IBB	SO	WP	Bk.
Lopez, Emigdio, Tab.	15	5	.750	1.91	24	24	10	4	0	0	183.1	155	664	46	39	4	15	2	8	47	9	74	2	0
Osuna, Roberto, Sal.	4	2	.667	1.92	75	0	0	0	75	24	98.1	88	359	24	21	4	7	1	0	27	6	60	1	3
Valdez, Efrain, Q.R.	14	7	.667	2.07	24	24	13	5	0	0	187.0	149	667	55	43	7	11	1	7	54	2	75	2	0
Purata, Julio, Rey.	16	8	.667	2.18	25	25	7	3	0	0	190.1	155	660	55	46	5	23	2	3	74	8	98	5	0
Aguirre, Gaudencio, Tab.	12	4	.750	2.30	28	18	6	3	10	1	133.1	118	479	46	34	1	8	3	9	37	5	59	0	1
Hernandez, Martin, Q.R.	14	4	.778	2.41	24	23	10	3	1	0	171.2	147	624	55	46	7	8	0	1	55	0	83	8	1
Tejeda, Felix, P.R.	13	6	.684	2.42	23	23	2	2	0	0	141.1	137	531	44	38	3	11	1	1	24	2	34	1	0
Hernandez, Jose, Lar.	13	8	.619	2.44	23	23	5	4	0	0	155.0	149	568	51	42	5	14	2	3	44	4	65	7	1
Perez, David, Mont.	8	5	.615	2.45	23	20	6	2	1	0	139.2	122	510	44	38	5	9	2	4	52	6	61	2	1
Osuna, Ricardo, Tab.	13	8	.619	2.51	25	24	6	3	1	0	168.2	147	612	53	47	4	16	3	5	51	4	89	7	3
Cano, Jose, Yuc.	13	5	.722	2.54	22	22	5	1	0	0	142.0	143	539	50	40	2	11	1	7	64	2	69	13	1
Mora, Eleazar, P.R.	16	3	.842	2.59	27	23	2	0	4	0	152.2	128	550	49	44	8	13	3	7	40	1	56	0	1
Lara, Jorge, Sal.	10	6	.625	2.64	38	15	1	0	23	0	133.0	125	491	42	39	4	7	3	4	39	2	79	2	1
Gonzalez, Arturo, Mont.	8	6	.571	2.68	21	20	2	0	1	0	127.2	132	470	43	38	6	14	3	3	28	6	39	2	0

DEPARTMENTAL LEADERS: W—Dessens, Purata, 16; L—Cuervo, Mattson, 14; Pct.—Mora, .842; G—Ro. Osuna, 75; GS—F. Garcia, 27; CG—E. Valdez, 13; ShO—H. Lara, 5; GF—Ro. Osuna, 75; Sv.—I. Marquez, 30; IP—Mattson, 191.1; H—F. Soto, 194; TBF—Mattson, F. Soto, 695; R—Cuervo, 100; ER—Pina, 79; HR—F. Soto, 20; SH—Purata, 23; SF—F. Garcia, Man. Hernandez, 8; HB—Mattson, 14; BB—F. Garcia, 85; IBB—M. Garcia, 10; SO—Rios, 121; WP—A. Acosta, G. Gonzalez, Pina, 15; BK—Quintanilla, 6.

ALL PITCHERS

Pitcher, Team	W	L	Pct.	ERA	G	GS	CG	ShO	GF	Sv.	IP	H	TBF	R	ER	HR	SH	SF	HB	BB	IBB	SO	WP	Bk.
Abreu, Alvaro, Yuc.	0	0	.000	3.60	3	1	0	0	2	0	5.0	3	18	2	2	0	0	0	0	4	0	3	1	0
Acosta, Aaron, Monc.	9	8	.529	3.09	22	22	3	3	0	0	137.0	143	529	61	47	1	9	2	4	60	3	82	15	2
Acosta, Gerardo, Oax.	3	2	.600	3.63	27	3	0	0	24	0	67.0	66	255	34	27	1	2	2	1	35	1	27	12	1
Adam, David, Tig.	13	5	.722	2.89	24	24	0	0	0	0	152.2	137	566	62	49	5	7	4	5	53	3	84	5	0
Aguilar, Miguel, Tab.	1	4	.200	4.94	35	3	0	0	32	1	27.1	30	111	18	15	0	4	1	3	15	3	10	1	2
Aguirre, Gaudencio, Tab.	12	4	.750	2.30	28	18	6	3	10	1	133.1	118	479	46	34	1	8	3	9	37	5	59	0	1
Alicea, Miguel, Min.	1	2	.333	2.42	23	0	0	0	23	9	22.1	22	84	9	6	1	4	2	0	13	3	13	0	1
Almeida, Rousel, Lar.	0	0	.000	15.75	5	0	0	0	5	0	4.0	4	15	7	7	1	0	1	0	5	0	2	0	0
Alvarez, Juan Carlos, Tab.	3	10	.231	4.48	25	12	0	0	12	3	92.1	120	346	58	46	8	6	7	8	29	5	23	1	1
Alvarez, Juan, Tab.	7	13	.350	3.27	28	22	4	0	6	1	150.0	151	555	69	57	6	19	2	11	57	9	67	3	1
Anderson, Mike, Mont.	2	0	1.000	0.90	7	0	0	0	7	0	10.0	5	32	1	1	0	1	0	0	7	1	8	1	0
Angulo, Luis, Sal.	0	0	.000	5.54	13	0	0	0	13	0	13.0	18	56	12	11	2	0	0	1	12	0	7	0	0
Antunez, Martin, P.R.	0	3	.000	5.91	24	2	0	0	22	0	32.0	40	129	24	21	0	1	3	1	23	2	21	3	0
Armenta, Alejandro, Tig.	3	1	.750	4.08	33	0	0	0	33	0	35.1	29	123	24	16	3	1	1	0	28	2	13	9	0
Arzate, Martin, Cam.	0	1	.000	10.38	1	1	0	0	0	0	4.1	6	17	5	5	0	0	2	3	0	1	0	0
Atilano, Juan, P.R.	0	0	.000	5.87	11	0	0	0	11	0	15.1	14	55	15	10	0	0	2	1	19	2	8	0	0
Austin, James, Agua.	1	2	.333	2.63	23	0	0	0	23	6	24.0	25	98	9	7	0	3	0	1	18	3	18	2	0
Avila, Jose, Sal.	2	2	.500	3.80	9	8	1	0	1	0	42.2	44	160	19	18	2	0	2	2	32	0	29	0	1
Ayala, Luis I., Sal.	7	5	.583	4.62	37	2	0	0	35	0	62.1	76	237	37	32	3	1	7	3	21	4	30	2	1
Baez, Sixto, P.R.	1	1	.500	2.01	24	0	0	0	24	0	22.1	14	75	6	5	1	0	0	1	14	0	7	0	3
Baker, Scott, Tor.	7	7	.500	4.35	29	19	1	0	10	0	109.2	131	441	63	53	7	8	2	1	43	1	55	1	1
Barfield, John, Lar.	5	2	.714	2.35	45	2	0	0	43	21	61.1	55	217	18	16	2	8	1	1	20	7	18	0	0
Barraza, Ernesto, Tig.	9	5	.643	2.96	19	18	5	1	1	0	112.2	107	411	48	37	2	9	4	2	64	2	55	2	0
Barrera, Sigfrido, Tig.	1	0	1.000	3.79	17	0	0	0	17	0	38.0	34	132	17	16	2	2	2	0	29	2	11	1	0
Barron, Avelino, Cam.	4	4	.500	3.00	32	0	0	0	32	2	60.0	50	222	25	20	1	2	3	2	26	3	31	6	0
Baxter, Robert, Tig.	0	0	.000	3.18	2	2	0	0	0	0	5.2	5	21	2	2	0	0	0	1	5	0	4	1	0
Beatty, Blaine, Mex.	2	3	.400	4.91	6	5	2	0	1	0	29.1	40	121	21	16	3	6	1	3	20	1	19	1	1
Burgos, John, Yuc.	4	5	.444	4.09	30	15	1	0	15	1	105.2	100	400	51	48	9	7	2	0	39	3	64	3	2
Cabrales, Gabriel, Oax.	1	0	1.000	5.40	14	0	0	0	14	0	20.0	31	83	16	12	1	2	0	0	7	1	16	0	0
Calderon, Manaces, Min.	0	0	.000	17.18	3	0	0	0	3	0	3.2	9	18	7	7	0	0	0	0	2	0	0	0	0
Camacho, Adrian, Sal.	0	0	.000	7.67	13	1	0	0	11	0	27.0	35	110	29	23	2	0	1	2	25	1	6	4	0
Camacho, Placido, Q.R.	0	0	.000	12.46	4	0	0	0	4	0	4.1	8	22	7	6	0	0	0	0	4	0	5	0	0
Camara, Pedro, Tab.	0	0	.000	3.00	7	0	0	0	7	0	3.0	1	9	1	1	0	0	0	1	4	1	3	0	0
Campillo, Jorge, Tig.	1	0	1.000	4.50	2	0	0	0	2	0	4.0	2	14	2	2	0	0	0	0	5	0	4	1	0
Campos, Francisco, Cam.	9	10	.474	2.92	25	25	5	0	0	0	179.0	144	623	62	58	11	14	7	2	67	1	70	12	2
Campos, Frank, Min.	0	2	.000	7.59	5	2	0	0	3	0	10.2	11	39	9	9	0	1	1	0	13	0	3	1	0
Cano, Jose, Yuc.	13	5	.722	2.54	22	22	5	1	0	0	142.0	143	539	50	40	2	11	1	7	64	2	69	13	1
Carranza, Javier, Q.R.	2	3	.400	4.14	22	6	0	0	16	1	54.1	59	211	29	25	4	6	2	1	31	2	37	6	0
Carrazco, Alejandro, Cam.	10	8	.556	4.80	30	23	1	0	7	0	140.2	174	574	93	75	13	5	4	7	43	3	49	7	1
Castaneda, Aurelio, Cam.	7	6	.538	3.64	34	5	0	0	29	7	64.1	58	232	29	26	2	4	5	3	40	5	38	6	0
Castillo, Felipe, Cam.	0	1	.000	2.45	8	0	0	0	8	1	11.0	5	38	4	3	0	2	0	1	8	2	4	1	0
Castillo, Juan Fco., Monc.	4	6	.400	5.10	13	12	1	0	1	0	77.2	80	298	49	44	5	4	3	3	48	1	32	6	1
Catedral, Raul, Sal.	1	2	.333	8.10	9	2	0	0	7	2	13.1	15	54	12	12	1	1	0	1	15	0	10	1	0
Cazares, Rosario, Tab.	3	2	.600	3.96	39	0	0	0	39	14	38.2	31	137	18	17	4	2	3	3	12	0	22	0	1
Cazares, Tomas, Monc.	1	3	.250	6.00	10	3	0	0	7	0	24.0	29	96	17	16	0	1	1	2	13	0	16	2	0
Cecena, Jose, Monc.	2	0	1.000	4.06	21	2	0	0	19	0	37.2	33	144	19	17	3	1	1	2	17	0	22	3	1
Cerros, Juan, Rey.	2	1	.667	3.49	38	2	0	0	36	2	67.0	57	238	31	26	2	8	0	7	42	2	27	3	0
Chavez, Rafael, Oax.	0	2	.000	5.95	9	2	0	0	7	0	19.2	24	74	14	13	1	3	1	3	8	2	8	1	0
Clayton, Royal, Tor.	4	7	.364	4.03	16	14	2	1	2	0	80.1	87	314	43	36	3	3	2	1	19	0	37	1	1
Conde, Ricardo, Yuc.	0	0	.000	9.00	1	0	0	0	1	0	1.0	1	4	1	1	0	0	0	0	2	0	1	0	0
Coronado, Jorge, Oax.	2	3	.400	3.79	28	4	0	0	24	0	38.0	48	147	22	16	0	3	4	5	23	2	24	0	1
Cota, Marino, Sal.	0	3	.000	11.42	13	3	0	0	10	0	26.0	55	120	34	33	1	2	4	2	8	4	17	0	0
Couoh, Enrique, Tig.	8	6	.571	3.39	41	15	1	0	26	1	127.1	128	475	64	48	12	8	5	2	49	2	58	6	0
Cruz, Javier, Mex.	5	2	.714	1.99	38	3	0	0	35	2	63.1	49	231	14	14	2	2	0	0	29	1	36	1	2
Cruz, Juan Diego, Yuc.	0	0	.000	3.18	4	0	0	0	8	0	5.2	3	18	2	2	0	0	1	1	3	0	2	0	0
Cuervo, Bernardo, Oax.	6	14	.300	4.80	26	23	2	1	3	0	133.0	181	562	100	71	5	14	4	7	49	4	52	6	0
Del Toro, Miguel, Mex.	0	0	.000	3.75	26	0	0	0	26	0	36.0	21	120	18	15	1	2	3	3	32	1	30	2	0
Delfin, Adolfo, Tor.	0	3	.000	5.06	26	1	0	0	25	1	32.0	49	135	23	18	5	3	1	0	14	2	12	3	0
Dessens, Elmer, Mex.	16	5	.762	3.56	26	25	3	1	1	0	159.1	156	602	73	63	1	12	4	5	51	1	61	4	0
Diaz, Alejandro, Oax.	2	1	.667	4.19	49	1	0	0	48	0	81.2	106	337	48	38	9	4	3	4	34	2	35	2	5
Diaz, Cesar, Lar.	1	1	.500	3.31	36	1	0	0	35	4	51.2	55	195	20	19	3	5	1	4	15	6	25	2	0
Diaz, Marco, Q.R.	4	2	.667	4.05	21	12	2	1	9	2	73.1	82	290	34	33	4	1	0	1	33	0	33	1	0
Diaz, Rafael, Mont.	7	7	.500	3.34	22	19	2	0	3	0	122.0	105	440	48	45	3	5	6	3	75	4	72	8	0
Dominguez, Herminio, Cam.	6	2	.750	3.28	30	3	0	0	27	1	46.2	52	172	18	17	1	8	1	2	18	4	18	2	1
Duarte, Miguel, Sal.	0	0	.000	1.69	5	0	0	0	5	0	10.2	9	36	2	2	0	0	1	0	8	0	6	0	0
Duncan, Chip, Oax.	6	8	.429	3.59	23	23	6	0	0	0	138.0	122	490	61	55	4	10	5	2	68	3	87	12	0
Elvira, Narciso, Mont.	0	0	.000	3.44	6	4	0	0	2	0	18.1	17	66	11	7	2	3	0	0	10	0	8	0	0
Enriquez, Martin, Mont.	5	3	.625	2.86	42	0	0	0	42	0	63.0	48	227	22	20	0	3	1	2	31	7	22	4	0
Escarrega, Guillermo, Min.	1	1	.500	3.10	17	1	0	0	16	0	20.1	19	76	11	7	0	0	2	1	8	1	3	2	1
Espana, Roberto, P.R.	0	1	.000	3.12	7	1	0	0	6	0	8.2	7	31	3	3	0	1	1	0	5	0	2	0	0
Espejo, Ramon, Agua.	0	0	.000	9.24	10	0	0	0	10	0	12.2	15	52	13	13	0	0	1	0	12	0	7	0	0
Espino, Jorge, Tor.	0	0	.000	4.26	4	0	0	0	4	0	6.1	7	26	5	3	0	1	0	0	4	1	0	0	0
Esquer, Mercedes, Mont.	13	3	.813	3.78	23	22	0	0	1	0	128.2	135	489	55	54	6	10	4	3	62	3	58	1	1
Fajardo, Hector, Monc.	2	3	.400	6.23	7	7	1	1	0	0	34.2	33	131	29	24	5	2	2	0	20	0	14	1	1
Federico, Gustavo, Min.	2	7	.222	4.01	16	15	0	0	1	0	83.0	101	326	48	37	6	6	3	2	29	1	33	5	2
Flores, Ignacio, Tor.	5	4	.556	4.55	46	1	0	0	45	0	95.0	98	359	55	48	6	4	3	3	53	8	45	5	1
Galvez, Rosario, Lar.	3	6	.333	4.18	48	0	0	0	48	0	64.2	60	237	36	30	5	5	4	2	35	6	45	2	1
Gamez, Francisco, Mont.	3	2	.600	2.24	46	2	0	0	44	2	72.1	58	256	19	18	0	4	2	3	34	1	34	3	0
Garcia, Adolfo, Cam.	0	0	.000	4.50	1	0	0	0	1	0	2.0	1	7	1	1	0	0	0	0	0	0	0	0	0
Garcia, Francisco, Mex.	14	6	.700	3.19	27	27	1	0	0	0	141.0	136	522	75	50	4	11	8	4	85	3	78	13	1
Garcia, Jose, Lar.	6	12	.333	3.72	28	24	3	0	4	0	155.0	166	604	75	64	10	12	1	7	43	5	81	4	1

Pitcher, Team	W	L	Pct.	ERA	G	GS	CG	ShO	GF	Sv.	IP	H	TBF	R	ER	HR	SH	SF	HB	BB	IBB	SO	WP	Bk.
Garcia, Zenon, Cam.	0	0	.000	8.53	1	1	0	0	0	0	6.1	9	26	6	6	1	1	1	0	2	0	3	0	0
Garcia, Miguel, Min.	2	6	.250	4.58	59	2	0	0	57	2	110.0	110	406	60	56	7	9	2	4	67	10	31	4	0
Garibaldi, Cecilio, Tig.	1	1	.500	6.60	18	1	0	0	17	1	30.0	32	113	22	22	4	3	2	2	22	0	11	4	0
Garibay, Daniel, Tig.	13	8	.619	3.51	26	26	5	3	0	0	159.0	140	575	70	62	7	9	2	5	67	0	95	6	0
Garibay, Roberto, Q.R.	2	7	.222	3.50	30	4	0	0	26	5	61.2	73	248	31	24	1	8	3	6	34	4	14	7	1
Garibay, Salvador, Cam.	0	2	.000	3.55	21	0	0	0	21	1	25.1	17	85	16	10	2	2	3	2	14	1	8	3	0
Garza, Alejandro, Rey.	1	2	.333	4.71	16	1	0	0	15	0	21.0	22	78	12	11	0	2	2	1	14	1	22	4	0
Garza, Roberto, Lar.	2	3	.400	3.95	49	1	0	0	48	1	70.2	79	273	36	31	8	6	4	7	31	9	27	0	4
Gomez, Martin, Tab.	0	1	.000	27.00	9	0	0	0	9	2	4.2	18	31	14	14	0	0	0	0	3	0	1	0	0
Gomez, Jesus, Lar.	0	0	.000	8.53	7	0	0	0	7	0	6.1	9	27	6	6	2	0	0	0	7	0	2	1	0
Gonzalez, Arturo, Mont.	8	6	.571	2.68	21	20	2	0	1	0	127.2	132	470	43	38	6	14	4	5	29	4	53	3	0
Gonzalez, Gilberto, Tor.	4	10	.286	3.51	33	21	2	1	12	1	130.2	119	481	61	51	4	4	5	3	81	2	83	15	4
Gonzalez, Victor, P.R.	3	2	.600	6.06	44	2	0	0	42	0	62.1	88	259	45	42	2	6	1	4	36	5	16	2	1
Gracia, Edmundo, Sal.	4	7	.364	6.26	25	9	1	0	16	0	69.0	88	278	58	48	6	5	1	2	33	2	18	3	0
Grajales, Norberto, Tor.	3	2	.600	3.20	41	3	0	0	39	0	81.2	93	325	35	29	1	4	0	2	22	4	32	2	0
Gray, Dennis, Tor.	0	1	.000	1.88	15	1	0	0	14	6	24.0	15	81	7	5	0	3	0	0	10	0	21	0	0
Green, Ottis, Mex.	3	2	.600	1.97	34	0	0	0	34	6	45.2	35	161	10	10	1	1	1	0	26	3	39	2	0
Guereca, Guillermo, Oax.	3	4	.429	6.26	51	0	0	0	51	1	64.2	75	258	51	45	7	3	3	2	40	4	36	6	0
Guerrero, Omar, Rey.	0	5	.000	3.38	28	1	0	0	27	0	50.2	47	184	25	19	3	9	5	4	24	3	17	4	0
Heredia, Hector, Agua.	7	7	.500	3.50	23	23	2	1	0	0	141.1	169	552	64	55	9	10	6	2	35	2	46	3	0
Hernandez, Dimas, Monc.	0	0	.000	4.15	3	0	0	0	3	0	8.2	6	28	7	4	1	0	1	2	11	0	5	4	0
Hernandez, Jesus, Min.	2	7	.222	4.88	12	9	1	0	3	0	59.0	67	234	35	32	3	3	2	0	28	4	36	0	0
Hernandez, Jose, Lar.	13	8	.619	2.44	23	23	5	4	0	0	155.0	149	568	51	42	5	14	2	3	44	4	65	7	1
Hernandez, Julio, Oax.	2	5	.286	6.02	35	6	0	0	29	0	83.2	106	337	69	56	3	2	4	3	56	6	42	6	3
Hernandez, Manuel, Oax.	8	8	.500	4.76	27	26	3	1	1	0	132.1	158	519	86	70	5	12	8	4	72	3	63	8	1
Hernandez, Martin, Q.R.	14	4	.778	2.41	24	23	10	3	1	0	171.2	147	624	55	46	7	8	0	1	55	0	83	8	1
Herrera, Alberto, Lar.	0	0	.000	40.50	1	0	0	0	1	0	0.2	1	3	3	3	0	0	0	0	3	0	0	0	0
Herrera, Calixto, Monc.	2	1	.667	2.88	50	0	0	0	50	2	56.1	49	205	23	18	3	1	1	4	34	3	35	6	2
Herrera, Enrique, Tab.	0	2	.000	3.26	37	0	0	0	37	6	38.2	32	139	14	14	1	6	1	2	21	8	31	2	4
Holman, Shawn, Mex.	0	1	.000	10.29	2	2	0	0	0	0	7.0	10	31	9	8	1	0	0	0	6	0	4	0	0
Huerta, Luis, Lar.	9	7	.563	3.13	25	25	1	0	0	0	149.2	165	596	63	52	12	7	2	3	46	5	63	12	0
Hurst, Jonathan, Agua.	1	4	.200	3.08	32	0	0	0	32	6	38.0	32	134	17	13	2	7	0	2	20	2	25	0	0
Ilsley, Blaise, Cam.	4	5	.444	3.10	16	16	1	0	0	0	98.2	107	374	38	34	7	14	2	0	22	0	32	2	0
Izabal, Luis, Q.R.	0	0	.000	9.82	9	0	0	0	9	0	11.0	19	50	12	12	1	1	0	3	11	0	6	1	0
Jasso, Oscar, Rey.	0	1	0.000	4.12	16	1	0	0	15	0	19.2	17	73	13	9	0	1	0	3	18	1	3	5	0
Jersild, Aaron, Yuc.	0	1	.000	9.82	2	2	0	0	0	0	3.2	10	22	5	4	0	0	0	2	0	2	2	0
Jimenez, German, Agua.	2	11	.154	7.10	18	17	0	0	1	0	64.2	94	269	58	51	5	6	4	3	33	0	28	3	0
Jimenez, Isaac, P.R.	7	13	.350	3.42	23	23	2	0	0	0	139.1	133	514	62	53	8	6	5	2	61	4	57	6	0
Jimenez, Jesus, Tor.	0	0	.000	2.56	24	0	0	0	24	0	31.2	22	110	10	9	1	2	1	1	18	0	18	2	1
Jimenez, Manuel, Tor.	0	0	.000	5.40	2	0	0	0	2	0	3.1	3	12	2	2	1	0	0	1	0	0	0	0	0
Juarez, Fernando, Tor.	0	1	.000	5.40	3	0	0	0	3	0	1.2	2	6	1	1	0	1	0	1	0	0	0	1	0
Kelly, Richard, Rey.	4	9	.308	4.26	19	18	0	0	1	0	95.0	101	367	62	45	5	6	2	1	50	3	51	2	0
Lara, Hugo, P.R.	13	4	.765	2.50	26	24	8	5	2	0	158.1	151	583	55	44	7	8	5	3	29	5	69	3	2
Lara, Jorge, Sal.	10	6	.625	2.64	38	15	1	0	23	0	133.0	125	491	42	39	4	7	3	4	39	2	79	2	1
Leal, Gerardo, Monc.	13	7	.650	3.91	23	23	1	0	0	0	131.1	135	486	72	57	9	7	6	6	73	2	49	7	5
Leftwich, Philip, Lar.	6	7	.462	3.64	19	18	1	1	1	0	111.1	121	421	54	45	5	17	3	6	39	9	80	9	0
Leon, Juan, Tor.	0	1	.000	7.84	17	0	0	0	17	0	20.2	32	85	18	18	3	0	0	0	14	0	7	1	0
Lewis, Scott, Tig.	6	3	.667	2.47	13	13	2	2	0	0	87.1	93	331	29	24	5	2	4	2	12	0	36	2	0
Lezama, Rafael, Tab.	0	0	.000	8.10	7	0	0	0	7	0	3.1	4	12	3	3	1	0	1	0	2	0	2	0	0
Lizarraga, Andres, Lar.	1	0	1.000	4.64	23	1	0	0	22	0	21.1	28	86	13	11	3	0	1	0	12	0	7	5	0
Llanes, Emeterio, Yuc.	0	0	.000	3.63	9	1	0	0	6	0	17.1	16	60	7	7	0	2	1	1	8	4	17	1	0
Loaiza, Sabino, Cam.	7	10	.412	3.72	22	21	4	0	1	0	128.1	135	483	58	53	6	6	4	4	59	2	39	4	1
Lopez, Dionisio, Agua.	0	0	.000	2.70	4	0	0	0	4	0	6.2	5	23	3	2	0	0	1	2	6	0	1	0	0
Lopez, Emigdio, Tab.	15	5	.750	1.91	24	24	10	4	0	0	183.1	155	664	46	39	4	15	2	8	47	9	74	2	0
Lopez, Gilberto, P.R.	0	1	.000	7.36	5	1	0	0	4	0	7.1	12	33	7	6	0	0	2	1	4	1	1	0	0
Lopez, Jesus Nain, Rey.	1	1	.500	5.32	28	0	0	0	28	1	23.2	26	89	16	14	2	2	1	1	13	1	10	1	0
Lopez, Jonas, Agua.	6	6	.500	4.46	18	17	1	1	1	0	82.2	92	314	49	41	5	9	4	4	25	2	24	0	2
Lopez, Jose Juan, Mex.	4	4	.500	2.01	49	0	0	0	49	20	62.2	70	241	19	14	2	6	0	0	22	7	33	2	2
Luevano, Juan, P.R.	4	2	.667	1.75	57	0	0	0	57	28	61.2	49	218	14	12	2	3	2	3	27	3	30	1	0
Lugo, Javier, Lar.	0	0	.000	0.00	3	0	0	0	3	0	2.1	2	9	0	0	0	0	0	0	1	0	1	0	0
Magre, Pete, Q.R.	0	0	.000	3.00	3	0	0	0	1	0	3.0	2	7	1	1	1	1	0	0	0	0	1	0	0
Manrique, Alberto, Agua.	0	1	.000	7.97	12	0	0	0	12	0	20.1	37	89	22	18	1	2	3	1	10	1	4	3	0
Manzano, Adrian, Tig.	6	3	.667	3.45	19	10	0	0	9	0	73.0	63	264	31	28	3	2	2	2	33	1	39	3	2
Marquez, Isidro, Tig.	8	2	.800	3.41	51	0	0	0	51	30	63.1	61	228	24	24	4	9	4	2	29	5	30	5	1
Marquez, Jose, Tor.	0	0	.000	135.00	1	0	0	0	1	0	0.1	3	4	5	5	0	0	0	2	0	0	0	0	0
Martinez, Cesar, Mont.	1	2	.333	5.08	34	0	0	0	34	0	28.1	39	117	16	16	0	2	3	21	4	15	1	0	
Martinez, Jose, Yuc.	0	0	.000	3.18	10	0	0	0	10	1	17.0	18	69	8	6	2	0	1	1	8	3	6	2	1
Martinez, Uriel, P.R.	1	2	.333	4.66	9	1	0	0	8	0	19.1	17	68	11	10	2	2	1	2	13	1	6	2	1
Mattson, Rob, Agua.	11	14	.440	2.87	27	26	12	3	1	1	191.1	181	695	71	61	3	8	6	14	49	3	73	6	0
Melendez, Jose, Yuc.	7	6	.538	3.26	28	0	0	0	28	6	60.2	48	213	23	22	3	11	4	4	27	8	60	0	0
Mendez, Luis, Yuc.	6	5	.545	3.17	16	16	1	0	0	0	82.1	84	316	39	29	2	5	0	1	29	1	44	3	1
Metoyer, Tony, Rey.	8	4	.667	3.23	52	0	0	0	52	29	81.2	60	282	27	23	3	11	2	2	44	3	62	11	2
Meza, Leobardo, P.R.	0	0	.000	9.45	4	2	0	0	2	0	6.2	10	29	7	7	2	0	0	4	0	1	0	0	
Miranda, Julio, Yuc.	6	9	.400	3.54	54	0	0	0	54	14	76.1	77	290	34	30	5	5	3	1	33	5	46	4	2
Mora, Eleazar, P.R.	16	3	.842	2.59	27	23	2	0	4	0	152.2	128	550	49	44	8	13	3	7	40	1	56	0	1
Morales, Luis, Q.R.	1	0	1.000	5.68	6	0	0	0	6	0	6.1	10	26	5	4	1	0	2	1	2	0	1	0	0
Moreno, Angel, Yuc.	5	10	.333	3.18	25	24	2	0	1	0	164.0	158	608	63	58	3	16	4	5	64	3	68	7	0
Moreno, Jesus, Yuc.	0	0	.000	0.00	1	0	0	0	1	0	1.0	0	3	0	0	0	0	0	0	1	0	1	0	0
Moreno, Leobardo, Mex.	7	1	.875	2.99	24	11	0	0	13	0	87.1	82	325	34	29	3	5	0	2	42	1	37	7	0
Moreno, Ricardo, Oax.	0	0	.000	4.15	6	0	0	0	6	0	8.2	10	37	7	4	0	0	0	4	7	1	4	0	0
Morton, Kevin, Tig.	2	1	.667	6.84	7	7	0	0	0	0	26.1	34	110	24	20	4	0	0	0	24	1	10	0	0
Murillo, Felipe, Monc.	4	7	.364	3.60	45	0	0	0	45	21	45.0	53	178	27	18	1	6	3	1	18	4	23	0	0

Pitcher, Team	W	L	Pct.	ERA	G	GS	CG	ShO	GF	Sv.	IP	H	TBF	R	ER	HR	SH	SF	HB	BB	IBB	SO	WP	Bk.
Munoz, Jaime, Tig.	5	1	.833	2.39	45	0	0	0	45	1	49.0	35	170	16	13	0	5	0	1	29	4	45	3	0
Munoz, Leonardo, Agua.	3	2	.600	3.38	54	1	0	0	53	2	48.0	48	181	25	18	2	5	5	2	28	1	20	3	1
Munoz, Miguel, Rey.	0	1	.000	5.73	4	2	0	0	2	0	11.0	14	43	7	7	0	1	0	0	6	0	2	0	0
Munoz, Pablo Roberto, Q.R.	0	0	.000	21.60	5	0	0	0	5	0	1.2	8	13	4	4	0	0	0	0	0	0	2	0	0
Navarro, Luis, Yuc.	6	8	.429	4.42	20	13	0	0	7	0	91.2	95	340	52	45	4	5	7	3	29	0	24	3	0
Neri, Braulio, Monc.	0	0	.000	4.73	17	0	0	0	17	0	13.1	11	44	7	7	0	0	2	1	10	0	4	4	0
Neri, Eduardo, P.R.	3	4	.429	3.01	65	0	0	0	65	5	74.2	72	278	33	25	2	8	4	2	43	3	36	3	3
Nieblas, Omar, Tab.	0	0	.000	10.80	5	0	0	0	5	0	3.1	8	17	4	4	0	0	0	0	4	0	1	0	0
Nunez, A. Jose Juan, Oax.	0	0	.000	6.35	23	0	0	0	23	0	11.1	12	40	8	8	0	0	2	0	16	2	10	0	0
Nunez, G. Jose Juan, Oax.	0	0	.000	5.06	7	0	0	0	7	0	10.2	13	43	8	6	1	0	0	0	8	1	10	1	0
Ochoa, Pablo Joel, Rey.	4	3	.571	13.50	20	1	1	0	10	0	87.0	82	318	31	27	3	8	4	0	48	6	40	4	0
Olague, Jesus, Mont.	2	2	.500	4.86	20	5	0	0	15	1	46.1	44	167	27	25	2	4	1	3	30	2	25	4	4
Orea, Flavio, Agua.	1	1	.500	11.12	9	1	0	0	8	1	11.1	21	56	14	14	1	0	1	0	10	0	10	1	0
Orozco, Gabriel, Yuc.	0	0	.000	10.13	1	0	0	0	1	0	2.2	6	13	3	3	2	0	0	0	1	0	0	0	0
Orozco, Jaime, Min.	12	9	.571	3.54	26	26	3	0	0	0	160.0	177	624	85	63	6	8	6	4	31	4	65	2	5
Ortega, Raul, Yuc.	0	1	.000	27.00	1	0	0	0	1	0	1.0	4	6	4	3	0	0	0	0	3	0	0	1	0
Ortega, Roberto, Min.	2	3	.400	4.85	19	4	0	0	15	0	29.2	27	108	19	16	0	3	1	1	31	1	18	2	1
Ortega, Wilbert, Yuc.	0	2	.000	5.09	17	0	0	0	17	0	17.2	20	68	16	10	1	3	0	0	10	0	11	3	1
Osuna, Ricardo, Tab.	13	8	.619	2.51	25	24	6	3	1	0	168.2	147	612	53	47	4	16	3	5	51	4	89	7	3
Osuna, Roberto, Sal.	4	2	.667	1.92	75	0	0	0	75	24	98.1	88	359	24	21	4	7	1	0	27	6	60	1	3
Palacios, Israel, Oax.	0	3	.000	16.68	12	3	0	0	9	0	11.1	26	60	24	21	2	1	0	3	12	0	10	4	0
Palacios, Vicente, Mont.	11	4	.733	3.59	23	22	3	0	1	0	148.0	143	548	66	59	5	11	5	5	51	3	120	4	0
Palafox, Juan, Tor.	4	8	.333	5.17	30	13	0	0	17	1	92.1	117	368	61	53	3	7	5	10	28	2	41	9	0
Parra, Julio, Tig.	0	2	.000	3.50	32	0	0	0	32	1	36.0	35	132	15	14	1	2	3	1	38	4	12	3	0
Perez, David, Mont.	8	5	.615	2.45	23	20	6	2	3	0	139.2	122	510	44	38	5	9	2	4	52	6	61	2	1
Perez, Edgar, Min.	1	4	.200	4.48	17	10	3	0	7	0	68.1	65	251	36	34	3	7	2	3	34	2	49	7	0
Perez, Leonardo, Tab.	2	5	.286	5.64	29	9	1	0	20	2	81.1	103	320	59	51	1	6	3	4	40	5	38	3	0
Perez, Vladimir, Sal.	3	3	.500	4.68	40	2	1	0	38	1	59.2	61	222	34	31	3	6	4	0	36	4	31	3	1
Pena, Joel, Mont.	0	0	.000	13.50	1	0	0	0	1	0	1.1	3	7	3	2	0	1	0	3	2	0	2	0	0
Pimentel, Roberto, Sal.	7	5	.583	3.08	36	17	2	0	19	0	117.0	125	442	53	40	7	6	3	2	44	2	46	9	0
Pineda, Gabriel, P.R.	5	10	.333	4.86	27	17	1	0	10	1	96.1	100	360	66	52	8	10	1	2	71	3	33	7	0
Pina, Rafael, Rey.	7	12	.368	5.22	28	22	5	0	6	0	136.1	156	534	87	79	11	9	3	4	67	4	80	15	0
Powell, Dennis, Mont.	4	7	.364	3.72	53	0	0	0	53	17	55.2	55	205	24	23	2	7	2	2	26	7	46	3	0
Pulido, Raymundo, Tig.	0	0	.000	40.50	1	1	0	0	0	0	0.2	4	5	3	3	0	0	0	1	0	0	0	0	0
Purata, Julio, Rey.	16	8	.667	2.18	25	25	7	3	0	0	190.1	155	679	55	46	5	23	2	3	74	8	98	5	0
Quijada, Mario, Tor.	0	0	.000	27.00	4	0	0	0	4	0	2.0	5	11	6	6	1	0	0	0	5	0	1	0	0
Quintanilla, Enrique, Lar.	6	13	.316	4.49	31	23	0	0	8	1	130.1	153	513	73	65	9	6	3	11	43	8	59	6	6
Quiroz, Aaron, Mex.	7	5	.583	3.70	21	19	3	1	2	0	107.0	114	415	54	44	4	10	2	1	56	4	49	5	0
Quiroz, Jose Julian, Sal.	0	0	.000	3.00	5	0	0	0	5	0	3.0	3	11	1	1	0	2	0	0	3	1	2	0	0
Quinones, Enrique, Yuc.	2	4	.333	4.15	9	9	0	0	0	0	39.0	35	143	22	18	1	5	2	3	28	2	11	1	1
Ramirez, Emilio, Agua.	0	0	.000	9.00	3	0	0	0	3	0	1.0	1	4	1	1	0	0	0	0	2	0	2	0	0
Ramirez, Roberto, Mex.	12	4	.750	3.76	24	24	1	0	0	0	150.2	157	571	71	63	8	10	3	4	64	2	82	3	2
Ramos, Jorge, Q.R.	3	0	1.000	4.97	11	0	0	0	11	0	12.2	11	46	7	7	0	1	0	0	9	1	1	0	0
Raygoza, Martin, Sal.	7	6	.538	3.87	20	20	0	0	0	0	114.0	123	441	56	49	9	11	2	4	27	3	49	2	5
Renteria, Hilario, Q.R.	1	5	.167	4.38	27	2	0	0	25	6	49.1	66	193	27	24	2	7	1	0	8	5	19	2	1
Retes, Lorenzo, Cam.	4	9	.308	4.28	24	22	1	1	2	0	113.2	130	444	61	54	6	9	4	3	57	1	35	7	2
Revening, Todd, Tor.	4	0	1.000	5.51	26	0	0	0	26	4	32.2	36	126	21	20	3	2	0	1	8	0	16	0	0
Reyes, Flavio, Min.	2	2	.500	3.92	37	3	0	0	34	0	57.1	55	218	27	25	4	4	1	5	19	1	25	2	0
Rios, Jesus, Monc.	12	5	.706	2.90	24	24	8	3	0	0	167.2	139	613	61	54	16	10	3	5	57	3	121	3	0
Rivera, Carlos, Oax.	0	1	.000	7.24	10	0	0	0	10	0	13.2	19	56	13	11	1	2	1	0	8	0	6	3	0
Rivera, Oscar, Rey.	3	3	.500	4.14	25	10	0	0	15	0	74.0	77	275	38	34	2	7	2	5	42	4	42	7	0
Rivera, Paul, Agua.	0	0	.000	11.57	6	1	0	0	5	0	4.2	9	23	7	6	1	0	0	0	4	1	0	0	0
Rodriguez, Manuel, Min.	0	1	.000	9.55	16	1	0	0	15	0	21.2	30	86	26	23	2	0	6	1	25	1	10	4	1
Rodriguez, Mario A., P.R.	0	0	.000	9.00	5	0	0	0	5	0	5.0	11	22	5	5	1	2	0	0	3	1	1	0	0
Rodriguez, Raul, Monc.	8	4	.667	3.45	16	16	0	0	0	0	99.0	99	376	44	38	7	6	1	1	32	0	45	2	0
Rodriguez, Rene, Tor.	1	1	.500	3.00	11	0	0	0	11	0	12.0	13	48	6	4	2	1	1	2	5	0	2	1	0
Rodriguez, Rosario, Min.	1	0	1.000	0.00	8	0	0	0	8	0	2.1	3	11	0	0	0	0	1	1	2	1	0	0	0
Rodriguez, Salvador, Yuc.	7	5	.583	2.91	17	16	4	3	1	0	105.0	101	385	41	34	3	16	2	1	44	4	42	3	0
Rojo, Oscar, Cam.	2	6	.250	3.22	30	11	0	0	19	1	103.1	111	381	44	37	10	9	7	3	42	3	43	5	0
Romero, Juan, Min.	2	3	.400	3.71	19	3	1	0	16	1	34.0	45	139	19	14	0	4	0	1	16	3	21	3	0
Romo, Guillermo, Tab.	0	0	.000	5.40	4	0	0	0	4	0	3.1	3	12	3	2	0	1	0	0	4	0	1	0	0
Ruiz, Cecilio, Tab.	9	6	.600	2.98	21	21	2	1	0	0	130.0	136	497	51	43	2	14	4	1	28	5	50	1	0
Saenz, Alfredo, Tor.	2	8	.200	4.68	28	10	1	0	18	0	77.0	92	310	44	40	6	4	3	1	31	2	30	1	0
Saldana, Edgardo, Tab.	3	1	.750	4.46	18	2	0	0	16	0	34.1	35	130	21	17	6	1	1	1	13	0	19	1	1
Salgado, Eduardo, Agua.	0	1	.000	5.73	7	1	0	0	6	0	11.0	11	40	7	7	2	0	0	2	7	0	7	1	0
Sanchez, Alejandro, Q.R.	1	1	.500	2.45	6	2	0	0	4	0	22.0	24	94	7	6	3	1	0	0	7	1	14	0	0
Sanchez, Efrain, Tab.	2	3	.400	3.86	19	5	0	0	14	0	46.2	46	171	29	20	1	7	1	5	26	4	13	2	1
Sanchez, Hector, Agua.	2	10	.167	4.91	42	6	0	0	37	9	73.1	91	280	43	40	4	13	5	0	24	9	26	2	0
Sanchez, Pablo, Sal.	0	1	.000	4.56	8	5	0	0	3	0	23.2	19	83	13	12	2	2	0	0	23	2	9	1	0
Sandoval, Carlos, Min.	0	2	.000	4.50	17	2	0	0	15	0	22.0	34	96	15	11	0	1	0	0	11	1	7	0	0
Sandoval, Guillermo, Yuc.	2	4	.333	4.66	20	12	0	0	8	0	73.1	87	288	48	38	4	7	3	3	44	3	29	5	0
Sangeado, Juan C., Min.	1	4	.200	7.15	12	5	0	0	7	0	22.2	27	92	22	18	0	1	0	0	25	0	22	3	0
Sangilbert, Mario, Cam.	1	3	.250	3.22	8	4	1	0	4	2	22.1	16	78	11	8	3	0	1	21	2	11	3	1	
Santana, Manuel, Cam.	0	0	.000	5.14	6	0	0	0	6	0	7.0	8	26	4	4	1	0	0	7	0	5	0	0	
Sauveur, Richard, Tab.	0	2	.000	3.86	9	0	0	0	3	0	9.1	7	32	5	4	1	1	0	0	8	2	7	1	0
Scanlan, Robert, Mex.	1	2	.333	5.93	12	1	0	0	11	1	13.2	25	63	19	9	2	1	0	0	11	0	4	1	0
Schullstrom, Erik, Mont.	3	1	.750	0.31	29	0	0	0	29	2	28.2	19	103	4	1	0	2	0	0	13	2	39	1	1
Serna, Ramon, Agua.	1	0	1.000	5.40	4	2	0	0	2	0	11.2	9	42	9	7	0	1	0	2	7	0	5	0	0
Sierra, Abel, Oax.	1	2	.333	3.96	7	4	1	0	3	0	25.0	29	101	14	11	0	0	0	4	10	0	10	1	0
Sinohui, David, Q.R.	0	0	.000	2.25	15	0	0	0	15	1	20.0	25	82	5	5	0	1	0	2	10	1	15	6	0
Solano, Julio, Oax.	8	7	.533	3.30	46	0	0	0	46	22	62.2	62	232	28	23	2	9	2	1	28	9	23	1	1
Solarte, Jose, Monc.	0	4	.000	11.02	18	0	0	0	18	5	16.1	25	71	23	20	1	2	0	0	13	0	11	1	0

Pitcher, Team	W	L	Pct.	ERA	G	GS	CG	ShO	GF	Sv.	IP	H	TBF	R	ER	HR	SH	SF	HB	BB	IBB	SO	WP	Bk.
Solis, Ricardo, Min.	2	11	.154	5.05	22	20	3	0	2	0	112.1	148	452	69	63	8	8	2	0	35	6	32	3	0
Sombra, Francisco, Tor.	1	6	.143	7.05	19	7	0	0	12	0	37.0	68	166	33	29	3	5	1	4	7	1	13	1	0
Soto, Cruz A., Q.R.	2	3	.400	2.27	30	0	0	0	30	7	47.2	39	177	19	12	4	2	2	2	20	0	34	2	1
Soto, Daniel, Mex.	8	2	.800	3.32	38	4	0	0	34	0	81.1	85	308	37	30	2	5	3	4	30	1	38	1	2
Soto, Fernando, Q.R.	10	10	.500	3.55	24	24	10	2	0	0	177.1	194	695	80	70	20	9	4	9	23	2	70	1	0
Sulu, Mario, Cam.	0	0	.000	4.83	12	0	0	0	12	0	31.2	39	122	19	17	1	1	2	1	19	0	9	3	0
Tejeda, Felix, P.R.	13	6	.684	2.42	23	23	2	2	0	0	141.1	137	531	44	38	3	11	1	1	24	2	34	1	0
Tejeda, Juan, Tab.	0	0	.000	3.86	9	0	0	0	9	1	4.2	10	22	2	2	1	0	0	0	3	0	0	0	0
Turgeon, David, Rey.	9	6	.600	3.19	18	18	4	3	0	0	118.1	122	447	45	42	3	9	0	0	31	2	68	5	0
Uribe, Juan C., Yuc.	1	4	.200	4.99	33	3	0	0	30	2	48.2	54	187	34	27	1	7	3	3	23	4	27	4	1
Valdez, Armando, Agua.	3	3	.500	6.11	34	4	0	0	30	0	53.0	78	223	50	36	0	3	2	3	27	1	30	3	0
Valdez, Efrain, Q.R.	14	7	.667	2.07	24	24	13	5	0	0	187.0	149	667	55	43	7	17	1	7	54	2	75	2	0
Valdez, Rodolfo, Monc.	4	3	.571	3.58	31	0	0	0	31	0	65.1	66	248	32	26	5	4	3	2	24	2	24	1	0
Valencia, Jorge, Monc.	0	0	.000	2.55	11	0	0	0	11	0	17.2	17	62	8	5	0	2	2	1	7	0	5	1	0
Valenzuela, Saul, Q.R.	6	13	.316	3.93	24	24	6	1	0	0	153.1	171	584	85	67	13	13	3	9	58	2	39	7	0
Valerio, Juan C., Monc.	0	3	.000	3.44	46	4	0	0	42	2	36.2	41	148	20	14	1	3	1	0	15	5	18	0	0
Vargas, Ignacio, Yuc.	6	7	.462	3.75	46	6	0	0	40	0	100.2	93	360	49	42	5	12	7	3	57	9	40	0	2
Vargas, Joel, Tab.	2	2	.500	4.17	18	3	0	0	15	0	41.0	37	148	20	19	0	2	1	4	20	1	18	1	0
Vazquez, Aguedo, Tor.	0	0	.000	3.60	3	3	0	0	0	0		9	38	8	4	2	1	0	0	10	0	4	3	0
Vega, Obed, Lar.	3	5	.375	5.75	44	4	0	0	40	1	67.1	83	258	45	43	5	5	5	1	48	3	38	6	0
Velazquez, Ernesto A., Yuc.	2	0	1.000	3.45	25	0	0	0	25	0	44.1	39	165	20	17	2	2	1	2	22	1	14	1	2
Velazquez, Israel, Agua.	5	7	.417	3.99	31	9	0	0	22	0	88.0	88	340	47	39	5	6	1	4	37	2	56	4	0
Verdugo, Hugo, Sal.	5	7	.417	5.22	33	10	0	0	23	0	91.1	101	353	61	53	7	8	2	9	47	6	57	6	0
Verdugo, Orlando, Yuc.	0	0	.000	5.79	14	0	0	0	14	0	28.0	32	110	19	18	4	1	2	2	13	0	16	2	1
Villarreal, Antonio, Tor.	9	13	.409	3.87	27	24	1	0	3	0	146.1	179	591	78	63	5	5	6	4	51	5	58	5	0
Villegas, Jose A., Agua.	4	4	.500	4.00	50	1	0	0	49	0	108.0	120	413	55	48	3	9	1	9	49	5	37	6	0
Williams, Jeff, Sal.	8	10	.444	4.15	22	22	1	1	0	0	130.0	128	479	69	60	3	13	4	6	66	4	47	1	1
York, Michael, Tor.	10	6	.625	4.59	19	18	2	1	1	1	100.0	101	372	57	51	2	5	2	1	74	1	68	7	0
Zamudio, Jovanni, Mex.	0	0	.000	9.00	4	0	0	0	4	0	4.0	4	14	4	4	0	0	1	1	0	0	2	0	0
Zappelli, Mark, Sal.	3	5	.375	3.24	10	10	1	0	0	0	58.1	62	223	24	21	2	4	0	2	18	1	28	2	1
Zavala, Marco, Tig.	0	2	.000	3.20	15	2	0	0	13	0	25.1	23	95	13	9	0	0	1	1	17	1	9	1	0
Zimmerman, Mike, Cam.	1	1	.500	1.69	12	0	0	0	12	2	16.0	11	54	6	3	0	1	2		15	1	11	6	0

COMBINATION SHUTOUTS: A total of 87 combination shutouts were pitched in the Mexican League in 1997. Poza Rica led the league with 9.
NO-HIT GAMES: Mattson, Aguascalientes, defeated Poza Rica, 2-0, March 24; Fajardo, Monclova, defeated Torreon, 3-0, April 20.

1997 FIELDING

TEAM

Team	Pct.	G	PO	A	E	TC	DP	PB
Monterrey	.984	120	3201	1459	77	4737	118	6
Aguascalientes	.979	121	3150	1549	101	4800	144	7
M.C. Tigers	.979	119	3115	1430	98	4643	144	9
Poza Rica	.978	119	3047	1444	100	4591	123	8
Reynosa	.977	119	3059	1435	104	4598	126	10
Nuevo Laredo	.975	122	3155	1397	117	4669	131	11
Yucatan	.975	120	3066	1355	112	4533	117	9
Torreon	.974	119	3058	1501	122	4681	146	12
Tabasco	.974	119	3047	1464	119	4630	104	3
Minatitlan	.974	120	3114	1349	118	4581	105	22
Quintana Roo	.974	119	3109	1329	118	4556	116	17
Campeche	.973	111	2861	1302	116	4279	127	3
Saltillo	.971	120	3066	1422	132	4620	130	11
Monclova	.970	121	3110	1293	137	4540	115	15
M.C. Red Devils	.970	121	3129	1433	143	4705	142	12
Oaxaca	.966	122	3135	1590	166	4891	138	3

TRIPLE PLAYS: Yucatan 2, Mex. City Red Devils, Tabasco.

INDIVIDUAL

FIRST BASEMEN

Player, Team	Pct.	G	PO	A	E	TC	DP
Aganza, Ruben, Monc.	.989	116	1050	83	13	1146	97
Aguilar, Enrique, Yuc.	1.000	2	17	1	0	18	3
Aguilera, Antonio, Tab.	1.000	1	2	0	0	2	0
Aguilera, Armando, Sal.	1.000	1	1	0	0	1	0
Alfonso, Edgar, Tab.	1.000	4	16	1	0	17	1
Almeida, Shammar, Agua.	.994	70	633	48	4	685	59
Arano, Wilfredo, Lar.	1.000	1	6	0	0	6	0
Arevalo, Guadalupe, Cam.	1.000	1	2	0	0	2	0
Arvizu, Javier, Oax.	.998	49	396	42	1	439	35
Avila, Ruben, Tor.	.993	78	760	61	6	827	71
Aviles, Alejandro, Sal.	1.000	2	2	0	0	2	0
Azocar, Oscar, P.R.	.995	41	401	30	2	433	29
Barrera, Nelson, Oax.	.985	52	477	51	8	536	53
Beltran, Gerardo, Min.	1.000	3	18	1	0	19	0
Bustillos, Luis, Oax.	.857	1	2	4	1	7	1
Cabrera, Alex, Tig.	1.000	60	518	33	0	551	46
Cairo, Sergio A., Tab.	.994	19	159	13	1	173	12
Carranza, Pedro, Rey.	1.000	3	4	1	0	5	0
Castaneda, Hector, Oax.	1.000	2	4	0	0	4	0
Castaneda, Rafael, Sal.	.990	11	95	7	1	103	8
Castro, Eddie, Min.	.994	39	319	23	2	344	33
Cervantes, Refugio, Lar.	1.000	2	12	1	0	13	0
Chan, Armando, Monc.	1.000	7	44	2	0	46	6
Clark, Tim, Sal.	.996	77	623	66	3	692	72
Cobos, Rogelio, P.R.	1.000	5	13	0	0	13	0
Cruz, G. Marco A., Tor.	1.000	2	11	0	0	11	2
Cruz, Luis A., Rey.	.996	27	245	22	1	268	22
Deak, Darrel, Oax.	.987	23	137	14	2	153	17
De La Cruz, Hector, Q.R.	.966	4	27	1	1	29	3
Diaz, Luis F., Lar.	1.000	3	19	0	0	19	2
Diaz, Pedro Ivan, Tig.	1.000	11	49	1	0	50	4
Duarte, Rene, Cam.	1.000	5	43	0	0	43	4
Durazo, Erubiel, Mont.	.994	52	453	47	3	503	49
Espino, Daniel, Agua.	1.000	10	64	2	0	66	12
Espinoza, Javier, Min.	1.000	6	43	4	0	47	2
Espinoza, Ramon A., Tor.	1.000	2	9	0	0	9	2
Federico, Gustavo A., Min.	1.000	1	1	2	0	3	0
Fermin, Carlos E., Tor.	1.000	4	26	2	0	28	1
Garcia, Heriberto, P.R.	1.000	1	6	0	0	7	0
Garcia, Omar, P.R.	.994	73	761	39	5	805	61
Gavia, Jesus, Cam.	1.000	5	28	2	0	30	3
Gonzalez, Denio, Tab.	.998	75	761	49	2	812	62
Gonzalez, Jesus, Cam.	.996	24	208	23	1	232	20
Iturbe, Pedro, Tig.	.987	9	67	10	1	78	9
Leal, Jose G., Lar.	1.000	1	3	0	0	3	0
Lewis, Anthony, Sal.	1.000	2	13	2	0	15	2
Lopez, Jose Jaime, P.R.	1.000	2	2	0	0	2	0
Lydy, Scott, Mex.	.990	118	1088	70	12	1170	121
Machiria, Pablo, Mont.	1.000	8	69	4	0	73	7
Magallanes, Ever, Mont.	1.000	1	1	1	0	2	0
Magallanes, Roberto, Mex.	1.000	5	18	1	0	19	2
Martinez, Enrique, Agua.	1.000	5	12	0	0	12	0
Martinez, Raul, P.R.	1.000	1	2	0	0	2	0

Player, Team	Pct.	G	PO	A	E	TC	DP
McGriff, Terry, Lar.	1.000	6	36	3	0	39	5
Meggers, Mike, Q.R.	.982	5	54	2	1	57	4
Mendez, Roberto C., Oax.	.952	5	18	2	1	21	4
Michel, Domingo, Cam.	.986	82	766	54	12	832	73
Monell, Johnny, Q.R.	1.000	1	1	0	0	1	0
Morton, Kevin, Tig.	1.000	1	10	0	0	10	1
Norton, Christopher, Tig.	.988	16	159	10	2	171	19
O'Brien, John, Q.R.	1.000	9	85	9	0	94	7
Ochoa, Edgar, Tig.	1.000	4	12	1	0	13	1
Ojeda, Miguel, Mex.	1.000	2	24	2	0	26	3
Ortiz, Alejandro, Q.R.	1.000	23	201	17	0	218	18
Paez, Raul, Rey.	.992	90	866	33	7	906	80
Pardo, Victor M., Min.	.983	7	56	1	1	58	4
Peguero, Julio, Q.R.	.987	44	364	23	5	392	25
Pena, Luis A., Sal.	1.000	11	73	2	0	75	11
Perez, Francisco, Mex.	.750	1	3	0	1	4	1
Perez, Juan L., Tor.	1.000	2	5	1	0	6	1
Quintana, Carlos, Sal.	.984	6	57	6	1	64	5
Quintero, Allan, Yuc.	1.000	3	13	0	0	13	2
Quiroz, Jose Julian, Sal.	1.000	1	5	0	0	5	0
Reyes, Gilberto, Min.	.982	6	54	2	1	57	5
Rodriguez, Fernando, Tor.	1.000	2	6	0	0	6	0
Rojas, Francisco, Tab.	1.000	32	140	14	0	154	11
Rojas, Homar, Yuc.	1.000	1	1	0	0	1	0
Romero, Marco A., Yuc.	.991	79	685	75	7	767	66
SANCHEZ, Gerardo, Lar.	.995	114	1063	58	6	1127	112
Sanchez, Raul, Q.R.	1.000	2	2	0	0	2	0
Sievers, Carlos, Yuc.	.988	16	75	10	1	86	7
Soriano, Ricardo, Tor.	.875	1	7	0	1	8	1
Stark, Matt, Yuc.	.992	50	471	24	4	499	49
Tejeda, Arturo, Lar.	1.000	3	11	3	0	14	0
Torres, Eduardo, Monc.	1.000	2	6	0	0	6	2
Trapaga, Julio, Tig.	.991	57	510	39	5	554	60
Valdez, Francisco J., Rey.	1.000	1	3	0	0	3	0
Valdez, Jesus, Cam.	1.000	6	29	3	0	32	10
Valencia, Carlos, Sal.	1.000	9	80	3	0	83	9
Valenzuela, Eduardo, Sal.	.968	15	82	8	3	93	9
Vargas, Hector, Rey.	1.000	6	45	10	0	55	7
Velazquez, Guillermo, Mont.	.993	67	628	55	5	688	44
Velazquez, Israel, Agua.	1.000	1	12	4	0	16	2
Villanueva, Hector, Q.R.	.993	28	257	21	2	280	29
Villegas, Fernando, Sal.	1.000	1	9	0	0	9	0
Williams, Harold, P.R.	.957	5	42	3	2	47	1
Wood, Tyrone, Min.	.997	40	336	18	1	355	23
Worthington, Craig, Mont.	.978	9	81	7	2	90	8
Yan, Julian, Agua.	.995	53	520	43	3	566	61
Zambrano, Roberto, Q.R.	.984	6	54	6	1	61	7
Zamudio, Rafael, Min.	.989	22	175	12	2	189	16
Zazueta, Mauricio, Tor.	.973	3	35	1	1	37	2
Zazueta, Juan, Carlos, Tor.	.992	36	362	20	3	385	49

TRIPLE PLAYS: Arvizu, Stark.

SECOND BASEMEN

Player, Team	Pct.	G	PO	A	E	TC	DP
Alfonso, Edgar, Tab.	1.000	1	0	2	0	2	0
Arano, Eloy, P.R.	.974	26	56	56	3	115	20
Arano, Wilfredo, Lar.	1.000	1	1	1	0	2	1
Arevalo, Guadalupe, Cam.	.984	26	26	34	1	61	8
Armenta, Fernando, Min.	1.000	1	2	4	0	6	3
Armenta, Guillermo, Mex.	1.000	8	8	8	0	16	3
Arredondo, Jesus, Agua.	1.000	8	14	9	0	23	2
Aviles, Alejandro, Sal.	1.000	3	2	1	0	3	0
Bustillos, Luis, Oax.	1.000	4	4	6	0	10	1
Camacho, Adulfo, Min.	.982	54	138	139	5	282	29
Carranza, Pedro, Rey.	1.000	6	16	17	0	33	3
Carrasco, Ernesto, Lar.	.970	44	115	114	7	236	28
Castro, Arnoldo, Q.R.	.986	117	323	325	9	657	71
Contreras, Jose, Mont.	1.000	1	1	0	0	1	0
Cruz, G. Marco A., Tor.	1.000	1	5	0	0	5	0
Cuevas, Jorge, Tig.	.941	2	8	8	1	17	2
Diaz, Luis F., Lar.	1.000	2	1	0	0	1	0
Diaz, Mario, Yuc.	.967	13	28	31	2	61	7
Esquer, Ramon, Rey.	.975	115	295	324	16	635	76
Estrada, Hector, Monc.	1.000	1	6	0	0	6	0
Facundo, Armando, Tab.	1.000	1	1	1	0	2	1
Felix, Arturo, Yuc.	.972	20	38	31	2	71	12
Fernandez, Fabian, Rey.	1.000	6	6	6	0	12	1
Figueroa, Ricardo, Cam.	.250	2	1	0	3	4	0
Flores, Miguel, Mont.	.987	71	190	193	5	388	42
Francois, Manuel, Oax.	.986	13	27	42	1	70	8
Garcia, Carlos, Tab.	.935	27	31	41	5	77	7
Garza, Fidel, Mont.	1.000	1	0	1	0	1	0

Player, Team	Pct.	G	PO	A	E	TC	DP
Garza, Gerardo, Lar.	1.000	1	1	0	0	1	0
Gastelum, Sergio O., Tig.	.978	42	142	120	6	268	43
Giles, Brian, P.R.	1.000	1	1	0	0	1	0
Gonzalez, Denio, Tab.	1.000	1	3	0	0	3	0
Gonzalez, Roman, Min.	1.000	2	7	3	0	10	3
Howell, Patrick, Mex.	1.000	6	16	14	0	30	2
Hurtado, Hector, Min.	1.000	1	5	1	0	6	0
Iturbe, Pedro, Tig.	1.000	1	2	0	0	2	0
Linares, Rigoberto, Min.	.994	39	73	86	1	160	12
Lopez, Fabian, Oax.	.955	12	27	36	3	66	8
Lopez, Gonzalo, Monc.	.981	13	25	28	1	54	4
Lopez, Miguel, Yuc.	1.000	3	2	1	0	3	0
Loredo, Jorge Luis, Oax.	.970	102	249	325	18	592	77
Magallanes, Ever, Mont.	.986	18	32	38	1	71	11
Magallanes, Roberto, Mex.	1.000	2	5	1	0	6	0
Malpica, Enrique, P.R.	1.000	2	0	1	0	1	0
Martinez, Abel, Q.R.	1.000	5	5	9	0	14	2
Martinez, Grimaldo, Monc.	.977	112	264	320	14	598	75
Martinez, Ray, Mex.	.974	8	19	19	1	39	2
Medina, Jose R., Cam.	1.000	2	0	1	0	1	0
Mendoza, Omar, Lar.	.969	48	121	98	7	226	30
MERE, Pedro, P.R.	.987	99	241	276	7	524	60
Montanez, Lardaniel, Q.R.	1.000	1	1	0	0	1	0
Morales, Florentino, Lar.	.971	57	112	119	7	238	34
Morejon, Oswaldo, Yuc.	.973	72	149	179	9	337	39
Munoz, Jose, Tab.	.976	99	231	287	13	531	52
Navarrete, Alejandro, Agua.	1.000	1	1	0	0	1	0
Pardo, Victor M., Min.	.978	26	57	58	0	115	15
Perez, Alfredo, Cam.	.978	83	219	229	10	458	63
Precichi, Jorge, Sal.	1.000	6	8	7	0	15	3
Quintero, Allan, Yuc.	1.000	1	3	0	0	3	0
Quintero, Edgar, Mont.	1.000	1	1	2	0	3	0
Quintero, Guillermo, Mont.	.995	43	91	103	1	195	20
Ramirez, Enrique, Monc.	1.000	5	0	1	0	1	0
Ramirez, Jesus, P.R.	1.000	3	2	7	0	9	1
Robles, Gerardo, Cam.	1.000	2	3	2	0	5	1
Rodriguez, Rosario, Min.	1.000	1	3	3	0	6	1
Rosario, Victor, Q.R.	.917	6	12	10	2	24	4
Ruiz, Juan De Dios, Mex.	.975	12	16	23	1	40	4
Sanchez, Armando, Mont.	.986	15	29	39	1	69	6
Sanchez, Gerardo, Lar.	.727	2	5	3	3	11	0
Santana, Mario, Agua.	1.000	1	5	1	0	6	0
Tiquet, Lazaro, Tab.	1.000	1	4	0	0	4	0
Trapaga, Julio, Tig.	.978	57	149	156	7	312	45
Valdez, Francisco J., Rey.	1.000	1	7	0	0	7	0
Valdez, Ramon, Min.	1.000	1	1	0	0	1	0
Valle, Jorge L., Tor.	1.000	1	0	1	0	1	0
Valle, Roberto, Tor.	1.000	1	1	0	0	1	0
Vargas, Hector, Rey.	1.000	2	1	2	0	3	0
Vela, Manuel, Rey.	1.000	2	4	5	0	9	2
Velez, Manuel, Tig.	.993	29	69	75	1	145	17
Verdugo, Hugo, Sal.	.900	2	6	3	1	10	0
Verdugo, Vicente, Mex.	.977	105	303	338	15	656	98
Vizcarra, Marco A., Sal.	.973	113	258	352	17	627	96
Vizcarra, Roberto, Agua.	.981	119	325	361	13	699	97
Wong, Julian, Cam.	.981	53	118	140	5	263	27
Zazueta, Juan Carlos, Tor.	1.000	13	25	24	0	49	11
Zazueta, Mauricio, Tor.	.986	112	282	369	9	660	94

TRIPLE PLAYS: Morejon, Munoz.

THIRD BASEMEN

Player, Team	Pct.	G	PO	A	E	TC	DP
Aganza, Ruben, Monc.	.900	5	4	14	2	20	2
Aguilar, Enrique, Yuc.	.935	13	9	20	2	31	3
Aguilera, Armando, Sal.	.667	3	1	1	1	3	0
Alfonso, Edgar, Tab.	.953	67	44	160	10	214	12
Amador, Alonso, Agua.	1.000	1	2	0	0	2	0
Arano, Eloy, P.R.	.955	58	55	135	9	199	11
Arevalo, Guadalupe, Cam.	.935	19	12	31	3	46	2
Arias, Everardo, Q.R.	.857	6	1	5	1	7	0
Armenta, Guillermo, Mex.	.923	12	9	15	2	26	6
Aviles, Alejandro, Sal.	.929	41	34	44	6	84	6
Balderas, Abelardo, P.R.	.750	1	0	3	1	4	0
Barrera, Nelson, Oax.	.800	2	0	4	1	5	1
Bustillos, Luis, Oax.	.905	19	6	32	4	42	6
Camacho, Adulfo, Min.	1.000	3	2	1	0	3	0
Carranza, Pedro, Rey.	.936	23	20	53	5	78	8
Carrasco, Ernesto, Lar.	.948	68	46	119	9	174	13
Castaneda, Rafael, Sal.	.944	102	108	231	20	359	29
Cervera, Francisco, Cam.	.952	86	92	168	13	273	12
Contreras, Jose, Mont.	.978	39	31	58	2	91	6
Cruz, Luis A., Rey.	1.000	1	2	1	0	3	1

CLASS AAA Mexican League

Player, Team	Pct.	G	PO	A	E	TC	DP
Deak, Darrel, Oax.	.920	61	22	105	11	138	13
Diaz, Luis F., Lar.	1.000	1	1	0	0	1	0
Diaz, Pedro Ivan, Tig.	1.000	2	0	3	0	3	0
Diaz, Remigio, Mont.	1.000	1	2	4	0	6	1
Duran, Felipe, Oax.	1.000	1	3	3	0	6	3
Espino, Daniel, Agua.	1.000	1	1	3	0	4	1
Felix, Arturo, Yuc.	1.000	5	7	7	0	14	0
Franco, Manuel, Sal.	.900	11	9	18	3	30	2
Francois, Manuel, Oax.	.810	13	11	23	8	42	4
Garcia, Carlos, Tab.	.915	31	10	44	5	59	2
Garcia, Heriberto, P.R.	1.000	3	5	9	0	14	2
Giles, Brian, P.R.	.940	54	48	139	12	199	9
Gonzalez, Roman, Min.	.833	8	1	4	1	6	1
Guerrero, Francisco, Q.R.	.962	42	43	84	5	132	7
Guerrero, Jaime, Agua.	.970	40	29	69	3	101	12
Guizar, Hector, Cam.	1.000	1	4	3	0	7	0
Gutierrez, Felipe, Oax.	.900	3	1	8	1	10	0
Hernandez, Cesar, Tor.	.895	5	3	14	2	19	2
Leyva, Darren, Yuc.	.931	116	105	270	28	403	25
Linares, Rigoberto, Min.	.917	5	1	10	1	12	1
Lopez, Fabian, Oax.	.892	44	31	76	13	120	6
Lopez, Gonzalo, Monc.	1.000	16	14	15	0	29	0
Lopez, Jose Jaime, P.R.	1.000	3	1	4	0	5	0
Magallanes, Ever, Mont.	.953	71	65	157	11	233	15
Magallanes, Roberto, Mex.	.885	10	6	17	3	26	2
Malpica, Enrique, P.R.	.957	19	12	33	2	47	3
Martinez, Abel, Q.R.	.960	29	17	31	2	50	0
Martinez, Julian, Oax.	.857	4	4	2	1	7	1
Martinez, Ray, Mex.	.899	66	37	124	18	179	16
Mendiola, Juan Carlos, Min.	.500	2	0	1	1	2	0
Mere, Pedro, P.R.	1.000	3	0	2	0	2	0
MONTALVO, Ivan, Tig.	.959	104	67	215	12	294	14
Montanez, Lardaniel, Q.R.	1.000	4	1	1	0	2	0
Munoz, Noe, Mex.	1.000	2	0	3	0	3	0
Navarrete, Alejandro, Agua.	.938	5	4	11	1	16	0
Nunez, G. Jose Juan, Oax.	1.000	3	2	3	0	5	0
Ojeda, Miguel, Mex.	.946	41	22	84	6	112	6
Orantes, Ramon, Agua.	.950	89	80	225	16	321	17
Ortiz, Alejandro, Q.R.	.931	63	51	98	11	160	6
Pardo, Victor, M., Min.	.917	21	13	31	4	48	2
Precichi, Jorge, Sal.	1.000	3	1	4	0	5	0
Ramirez, Enrique, Monc.	1.000	2	1	4	0	5	1
Reyes, Ramon, Tab.	1.000	1	1	2	0	3	0
Robles, Gerardo, Cam.	.833	5	6	4	2	12	0
Robles, Javier, Lar.	1.000	1	1	3	0	4	1
Robles, Trinidad, Lar.	1.000	2	2	5	0	7	1
Rodriguez, Rosario, Min.	1.000	2	0	3	0	3	0
Romero, Oscar, Monc.	.944	102	104	199	18	321	22
Rosario, Victor, Q.R.	.800	5	3	9	3	15	2
Ruiz, Cecilio, Tab.	.800	1	4	0	1	5	0
Ruiz, Juan De Dios, Min.	.922	34	34	60	8	102	5
Salas, Heriberto, Tor.	.974	8	12	26	1	39	3
Sanchez, Armando, Mont.	.957	42	31	59	4	94	6
Sanchez, Roque, Rey.	.945	98	103	243	20	366	17
Sandoval, Jose L., Sal.	.833	1	3	2	1	6	0
Scott, Gary, Q.R.	.800	3	1	3	1	5	0
Texidor, Jose, Rey.	1.000	1	2	0	0	2	0
Valenzuela, Armando, Rey.	1.000	2	2	4	0	6	1
Valenzuela, Eduardo, Sal.	1.000	3	1	6	0	7	0
Valle, Jorge L., Tor.	.956	91	62	242	14	318	33
Valle, Jose L., Min.	1.000	3	5	0	0	8	0
Valle, Roberto, Tor.	.895	6	5	12	2	19	1
Vela, Manuel, Rey.	1.000	1	2	3	0	5	0
Velez, Manuel, Tig.	.934	20	12	45	4	61	5
Verdugo, Vicente, Mex.	.947	8	3	15	1	19	0
Villarreal, Alejandro, Lar.	.949	84	54	150	11	215	14
Wong, Julian, Cam.	.964	25	12	41	2	55	7
Wood, Tyrone, Min.	.936	34	24	64	6	94	6
Worthington, Craig, Mont.	.882	8	6	9	2	17	3
Wright, George, Agua.	.667	2	1	1	1	3	0
Zazueta, Juan Carlos, Tor.	.921	15	7	28	3	38	4
Zazueta, Mauricio, Tor.	1.000	1	0	1	0	1	0
Balderas, Abelardo, P.R.	1.000	1	1	0	0	1	0
Bustillos, Luis, Oax.	.926	34	47	66	9	122	15
Carranza, Pedro, Rey.	1.000	1	1	2	0	3	1
Carrasco, Ernesto, Lar.	.839	10	8	18	5	31	3
Castaneda, Rafael, Sal.	.778	1	3	4	2	9	0
Cervera, Francisco, Cam.	1.000	2	1	7	0	8	1
Chan, Armando, Monc.	.667	2	0	2	1	3	0
Clayton, Royal, Tor.	.875	1	2	5	1	8	1
Contreras, Jose, Mont.	1.000	1	0	2	0	2	0
Cuevas, Jorge, Tig.	1.000	1	0	1	0	1	0
Deak, Darrel, Oax.	1.000	1	2	5	0	7	1
DIAZ, Remigio, Mont.	.985	115	186	394	9	589	65
Duran, Felipe, Oax.	.971	43	91	143	7	241	30
Espinoza, Jose M., Lar.	1.000	1	0	1	0	1	0
Felix, Arturo, Yuc.	.972	24	22	47	2	71	8
Fermin, Carlos E., Tor.	.960	5	11	13	1	25	2
Fernandez, Daniel, Mex.	1.000	1	4	0	0	4	0
Franco, Manuel, Sal.	1.000	1	0	1	0	1	0
Garcia, Carlos, Tab.	.947	11	12	24	2	38	3
Garcia, Heriberto, P.R.	.968	90	168	322	16	506	50
Garza, Fidel, Mont.	1.000	1	1	3	0	4	0
Giles, Brian, P.R.	.981	23	32	71	2	105	9
Gomez, Ever, Tab.	.955	76	118	221	16	355	38
Gonzalez, Roman, Min.	1.000	1	1	2	0	3	0
Guerrero, Francisco, Q.R.	.967	51	98	163	9	270	31
Guerrero, Jaime, Agua.	.977	36	51	75	3	129	19
Guizar, Hector, Cam.	.949	102	207	354	30	591	78
Gutierrez, Felipe, Oax.	1.000	5	4	11	0	15	1
Hernandez, Cesar, Tor.	1.000	3	2	3	0	5	0
Jimenez, Alfonso, Mex.	.956	62	102	223	15	340	50
Leyva, German, Yuc.	.500	2	0	1	1	2	0
Linares, Rigoberto, Min.	.962	39	51	128	7	186	17
Lopez, Fabian, Oax.	.964	28	42	92	5	139	15
Loredo, Jorge Luis, Oax.	.935	6	11	18	2	31	3
Magallanes, Roberto, Mex.	.500	2	1	0	1	2	0
Magana, Gabriel, Yuc.	.706	11	4	8	5	17	3
Malpica, Enrique, P.R.	.750	1	0	3	1	4	2
Martinez, Abel, Q.R.	1.000	3	3	4	0	7	1
Martinez, Julian, Oax.	.956	16	20	45	3	68	11
Martinez, Ray, Mex.	.951	15	35	42	4	81	11
Montalvo, Ivan, Tig.	1.000	1	1	2	0	3	0
Montanez, Lardaniel, Q.R.	1.000	9	7	14	0	21	3
Morejon, Oswaldo, Yuc.	1.000	2	1	1	0	2	0
Munoz, Jose, Tab.	.930	24	29	51	6	86	6
Nunez, G.Jose Juan, Oax.	.918	14	20	36	5	61	9
Olvera, Sergio, Monc.	.947	88	132	225	20	377	49
Ortega, Antonio, Mex.	1.000	1	1	2	0	3	0
Pacho, Juan Jose, Tab.	.970	104	172	318	15	505	57
Pardo, Victor M., Min.	1.000	1	1	5	0	6	0
Perez, Alfredo, Cam.	.974	8	14	24	1	39	4
Quintero, Guillermo, Mont.	1.000	9	11	21	0	32	7
Ramirez, Enrique, Monc.	.949	52	62	124	10	196	22
Robles, Javier, Tig.	.967	111	214	393	21	628	92
Robles, Trinidad, Lar.	.949	118	188	370	30	588	73
Rosario, Victor, Q.R.	.937	64	132	211	23	366	44
Salas, Heriberto, Tor.	.934	79	125	260	27	412	54
Sanchez, Armando, Mont.	1.000	1	1	4	0	5	0
Sanchez, Roque, Rey.	1.000	4	4	6	0	10	2
Sandoval, Jose L., Sal.	.966	112	211	332	19	562	70
Scott, Gary, Q.R.	.750	1	2	1	1	4	0
Trapaga, Julio, Tig.	.931	11	19	35	4	58	11
Valdez, Jesus, Cam.	1.000	1	1	2	0	3	2
Valdez, Ramon, Min.	1.000	2	1	2	0	3	1
Valenzuela, Armando, Rey.	.962	113	187	366	22	575	68
Valenzuela, Eduardo, Sal.	.000	1	0	0	1	1	0
Valle, Jorge L., Tor.	.976	10	6	34	1	41	0
Valle, Jose L., Min.	.961	87	145	271	17	433	37
Valle, Roberto, Tor.	.867	5	11	15	4	30	5
Vela, Manuel, Rey.	1.000	8	5	9	0	14	3
Villarreal, Alejandro, Lar.	.909	4	1	9	1	11	2
Wong, Julian, Cam.	1.000	2	1	2	0	3	0
Wood, Tyrone, Min.	1.000	1	1	2	0	3	0
Zazueta, Juan Carlos, Tor.	.937	28	49	84	9	142	15

TRIPLE PLAYS: Gomez, Magana, R. Martinez, Pacho.

SHORTSTOPS

Player, Team	Pct.	G	PO	A	E	TC	DP
Alfonso, Edgar, Tab.	.953	39	66	117	9	192	16
Amador, Alonso, Agua.	1.000	2	0	1	0	1	0
Arano, Eloy, P.R.	.957	12	17	27	2	46	7
Arias, Everardo, Q.R.	.769	6	2	8	3	13	3
Armenta, Guillermo, Mex.	.909	47	72	159	23	254	24
Arredondo, Jesus, Agua.	.970	108	181	366	17	564	74
Aviles, Alejandro, Sal.	.984	17	26	37	1	64	9

OUTFIELDERS

Player, Team	Pct.	G	PO	A	E	TC	DP
Abrego, Jesus, Rey.	1.000	11	11	2	0	13	0
Acuna, Jose L., Mont.	.944	27	48	3	3	54	0
Aguilar, Miguel, Tab.	1.000	2	4	0	0	4	0
Aguilera, Antonio, Tab.	.967	105	141	7	5	153	0
Aguilera, Armando, Sal.	1.000	4	4	1	0	5	0

Player, Team	Pct.	G	PO	A	E	TC	DP
Almeida, Shammar, Agua.	1.000	1	1	1	0	2	0
Alvarez, Hector, Oax.	.988	83	146	12	2	160	3
Arano, Wilfredo, Lar.	.983	73	105	8	2	115	2
Arauz, Leobardo, Yuc.	.923	14	22	2	2	26	3
Armenta, Fernando, Min.	.917	20	21	1	2	24	0
Arredondo, Luis, Yuc.	.993	119	266	10	2	278	1
Arzate, Martin, Cam.	1.000	3	3	0	0	3	0
Atwell, Sergio, Monc.	.950	21	19	0	1	20	0
Azocar, Oscar, P.R.	.975	45	75	3	2	80	0
Battle, Allen, Sal.	.950	7	19	0	1	20	0
Beltran, Gerardo, Min.	1.000	43	91	4	0	95	0
Bojorquez, Victor, Mex.	.979	57	45	2	1	48	0
Briley, Greg, P.R.	.987	61	145	2	2	149	0
Brinkley, Darrell, Mex.	1.000	15	24	0	0	24	0
Buccheri, Jim, Tig.	.963	13	25	1	1	27	0
Burton, Essex, Monc.	.970	18	31	1	1	33	0
Bustillos, Luis, Oax.	.500	3	1	0	1	2	0
Cabrera, Alex, Tig.	.958	46	86	5	4	95	2
Cairo, Sergio A., Tab.	1.000	27	63	1	0	64	0
Camacho, Adulfo, Min.	1.000	2	2	3	0	5	0
Canate, William, Min.	.965	31	79	4	3	86	1
Canizalez, Juan C., Mont.	.990	53	94	2	1	97	0
CARRILLO, Matias, Tig.	1.000	116	216	4	0	220	2
Carter, Michael, Lar.	.990	110	270	15	3	288	1
Castaneda, Hector, Oax.	1.000	3	3	1	0	4	0
Chan, Armando, Monc.	.900	6	9	0	1	10	0
Chance, Tony, Monc.	.939	118	227	4	15	246	0
Clark, Tim, Sal.	.962	21	22	3	1	26	1
Cookson, Brent, Lar.	.972	18	30	5	1	36	1
Cruz, Luis A., Rey.	.984	34	58	4	1	63	0
Cuervo, Bernardo, Oax.	1.000	1	1	0	0	1	0
Cuevas, Jorge, Tig.	1.000	1	1	0	0	1	0
Deak, Darrel, Oax.	.944	14	17	0	1	18	1
De La Cruz, Hector, Q.R.	.976	96	200	7	5	212	3
De La Nuez, Rex, Tor.	.913	27	41	1	4	46	0
De La Rosa, Juan, Cam.	.971	39	93	6	3	102	1
Delgado, Tomas, Yuc.	1.000	5	5	2	0	7	0
Delima, Rafael, P.R.	.969	97	175	14	6	195	0
Diaz, Luis F., Lar.	.972	78	98	8	3	109	2
Diaz, Mario, Yuc.	1.000	5	9	1	0	10	0
Diaz, Pedro Ivan, Tig.	1.000	2	6	0	0	6	1
Dominguez, David, Q.R.	.985	46	62	5	1	68	0
Durazo, Erubiel, Mont.	1.000	20	27	1	0	28	0
Escalante, Marcelo, Agua.	1.000	11	7	0	0	7	0
Espino, Daniel, Agua.	1.000	17	21	0	0	21	0
Espinoza, Javier, Min.	.981	87	157	2	3	162	0
Espinoza, Jose M., Lar.	.978	93	162	15	4	181	4
Felder, Mike, Monc.	.988	79	164	5	2	171	2
Felix, Arturo, Yuc.	1.000	2	2	1	0	3	0
Felix, Junior F., Yuc.	.974	95	139	9	4	152	1
Fentanes, Oscar, Tab.	.963	113	199	10	8	217	1
Fernandez, Daniel, Mex.	.988	114	237	9	3	249	0
Figueroa, Marco Antonio, Min.	1.000	24	28	2	0	30	0
Flores, Miguel, Mont.	1.000	16	29	1	0	30	0
Franco, Manuel, Sal.	1.000	1	1	0	0	1	0
Garcia, Carlos, Tab.	1.000	1	1	0	0	1	0
Garcia, Cornelio, Mont.	.951	114	187	6	10	203	0
Garcia, Hector, Tor.	.986	96	189	15	3	207	2
Garza, Gerardo, Lar.	1.000	1	0	2	0	2	0
Gastelum, Sergio O., Tig.	.962	20	25	0	1	26	0
Gonzalez, Jesus, Cam.	1.000	13	23	3	0	26	2
Gonzalez, Jose, Agua.	.973	83	176	4	5	185	2
Gonzalez, Roman, Min.	1.000	4	4	0	0	4	0
Green, Ottis, Mex.	.900	6	9	0	1	10	0
Guizar, Hector, Cam.	1.000	1	1	0	0	1	0
Hernandez, Gerardo, Tig.	.956	51	62	3	3	68	0
Herrera, Isidro, Oax.	.955	50	80	4	4	88	0
Hosey, Steve, Agua.	1.000	19	30	1	0	31	0
Howell, Patrick, Mex.	.975	48	75	3	2	80	0
Ingram, Ricardo, Mont.	1.000	5	9	0	0	9	0
Iturbe, Pedro, Tig.	.973	24	35	1	1	37	1
Jimenez, Eduardo, Mex.	.984	97	172	10	3	185	2
Jones, Bobby, Tor.	.750	10	9	0	3	12	0
Jose, Felix, Tab.	.977	47	82	4	2	88	1
Leal, Jose G., Cam.	1.000	82	163	10	0	173	3
Lewis, Anthony, Sal.	1.000	14	25	0	0	25	0
Lopez, Fabian, Oax.	1.000	8	4	2	0	6	0
Lopez, Gonzalo, Monc.	.750	8	1	2	1	4	0
Lopez, Salvador, Agua.	.980	56	92	5	2	99	1
Lopez, Victor M., Oax.	1.000	13	13	0	0	13	0
Luevano, Juan, P.R.	1.000	1	2	0	0	2	0
Lydy, Scott, Mex.	1.000	7	9	0	0	9	0
Machiria, Pablo, Mont.	.979	72	131	6	3	140	3

Player, Team	Pct.	G	PO	A	E	TC	DP
Mack, Quinn, Sal.	.990	117	196	9	2	207	2
Martinez, Abel, Q.R.	1.000	4	4	0	0	4	0
Martinez, Enrique, Agua.	.986	76	141	5	2	148	2
Mata, Noe, P.R.	1.000	4	2	0	0	2	0
Medina, Jose R., Cam.	.967	81	158	17	6	181	0
Mendez, Roberto C., Oax.	.939	103	148	5	10	163	0
Mendoza, Omar, Lar.	1.000	1	0	1	0	1	0
Monell, Johnny, Q.R.	.972	14	35	0	1	36	0
Montalvo, Ivan, Tig.	1.000	4	7	0	0	7	0
Moreno, David, Rey.	1.000	20	27	1	0	28	0
Moreno, Leonardo, Oax.	.974	79	144	7	4	155	1
Morones, Martin, P.R.	.972	73	99	6	3	108	1
Mota, Manny Jr., Sal.	1.000	22	42	1	0	43	0
Munoz, Jose, Tab.	.929	5	8	5	1	14	1
Munoz, Jose De J., Sal.	.981	97	185	17	4	206	1
Munoz, Noe, Mex.	1.000	1	1	0	0	1	0
Nunez, A. Jose Juan, Oax.	.000	1	0	0	1	1	0
Nunez, Dimmerson, Tor.	1.000	12	10	0	0	10	0
Ochoa, Edgar, Tig.	1.000	1	2	0	0	2	0
Ojeda, Miguel, Mex.	1.000	17	24	1	0	25	0
Pardo, Victor M., Min.	.944	11	17	0	1	18	0
Payro, Edison, Agua.	.944	90	124	10	8	142	0
Peguero, Julio, Q.R.	.975	76	182	11	5	198	0
Perez, Francisco, Mex.	.942	35	46	3	3	52	0
Perez, Juan L., Tor.	1.000	16	14	1	0	15	0
Polonia, Luis, Tig.	.972	103	166	8	5	179	1
Quintero, Allan, Yuc.	.963	44	72	5	3	80	0
Quintero, Edgar, Mont.	1.000	1	2	0	0	2	0
Quintero, Guillermo, Mont.	1.000	6	4	1	0	5	0
Ramirez, Jesus, P.R.	.984	72	119	3	2	124	0
Ramirez, Omar, Min.	.978	41	88	2	2	92	0
Ramsey, Fernando, Rey.	.974	52	108	4	3	115	1
Rathiff, Darryl, Tor.	.978	30	41	3	1	45	1
Reyes, Ramon, Tab.	.938	18	12	3	1	16	1
Robles, Gerardo, Cam.	1.000	4	3	0	0	3	0
Rodriguez, Fernando, Tor.	.982	93	153	8	3	164	3
Rodriguez, Jose Luis, Sal.	1.000	7	9	0	0	9	0
Rodriguez, Rene, Tor.	1.000	1	2	0	0	2	0
Rodriguez, Serafin, Q.R.	.981	91	196	6	4	206	0
Rubio, Sergio, Yuc.	.965	67	80	2	3	85	0
Ruiz, Placido, Mont.	1.000	3	6	0	0	6	0
Saenz, Ricardo, Monc.	.976	91	195	10	5	210	1
Salgado, Eduardo, Agua.	1.000	1	5	0	0	5	0
Sanchez, Gerardo, Lar.	1.000	7	5	2	0	7	0
Sanchez, Ismael, P.R.	1.000	21	25	1	0	26	0
Sanchez, Raul, Q.R.	.961	64	118	4	5	127	0
Sandoval, Octavio, Tig.	.984	70	117	7	2	126	0
Sherman, Darrell, Rey.	.987	96	214	11	3	228	0
Soriano, Ricardo, Tor.	.989	60	88	2	1	91	1
Tejeda, Arturo, Lar.	.979	44	44	2	1	47	0
Tellez, Alonso, Rey.	1.000	118	158	15	0	173	4
Texidor, Jose, Rey.	1.000	15	33	1	0	34	1
Tlquet, Lazaro, Tab.	.961	44	43	6	2	51	0
Torres, Eduardo, Monc.	.986	71	136	3	2	141	2
Valdez, Jesus, Cam.	.980	33	46	3	1	50	1
Valdez, Ramon, Min.	.976	82	159	6	4	169	0
Valencia, Carlos, Sal.	1.000	69	104	5	0	109	1
Valenzuela, Mario, Sal.	.958	14	21	2	1	24	1
Valle, Jorge L., Tor.	1.000	17	22	1	0	23	0
Valle, Jose L., Min.	.833	1	1	4	1	6	1
Valrie, Kerry, Oax.	.954	62	142	4	7	153	1
Vargas, Hector, Rey.	.963	63	102	2	4	108	0
Velez, Manuel, Tig.	1.000	1	0	1	0	1	0
Verdugo, Vicente, Mex.	.900	2	3	6	1	10	1
Villa, Carlos, Lar.	1.000	2	1	0	0	1	0
Villegas, Fernando, Sal.	.978	94	168	9	4	181	1
Walker, Steve, P.R.	.938	45	103	3	7	113	0
Williams, Harold, P.R.	.714	2	5	0	2	7	0
Williams, Reggie, Mont.	.961	59	117	7	5	129	2
Wong, Julian, Cam.	1.000	1	0	3	0	3	0
Wright, George, Agua.	.976	95	195	8	5	208	3
Wright, Tom, Cam.	1.000	3	5	1	0	6	0
Yuriar, Jesus, Yuc.	.990	55	97	5	1	103	1
Zambrano, Roberto, Q.R.	1.000	14	32	2	0	34	1
Zamudio, Rafael, Min.	.948	80	158	6	9	173	0
Zupcic, Bob, Rey.	1.000	2	3	0	0	3	0

CATCHERS

Player, Team	Pct.	G	PO	A	E	TC	DP	PB
Abrego, Jesus, Rey.	.969	10	53	9	2	64	1	1
Aguilera, Antonio, Tab.	1.000	1	1	0	0	1	0	0
Aguilera, Armando, Sal.	.953	90	370	59	21	450	4	10
Amezcua, Adan, Rey.	.978	69	312	52	8	372	3	7

Player, Team	Pct.	G	PO	A	E	TC	DP	PB
Camacho, Adulfo, Min.	1.000	1	2	1	0	3	0	0
Carrasco, Ernesto, Lar.	.889	1	7	1	1	9	0	0
Castaneda, Hector, Oax.	.984	62	246	54	5	305	1	6
Cazarin, Manuel, Q.R.	.982	106	416	87	9	512	5	10
Cervantes, Fernando, Agua.	1.000	3	1	1	0	2	0	0
Cobos, Rogelio, P.R.	.987	79	254	40	4	298	1	4
COX, Darron, Tig.	.994	103	473	69	3	545	5	7
Cruz, G. Marco A., Tor.	.980	104	453	49	10	512	10	8
Devarez, Cesar, Tig.	.929	6	25	1	2	28	0	1
Dominguez, Fausto, Agua.	.976	15	34	6	1	41	2	0
Duarte, Rene, Cam.	.984	49	149	30	3	182	2	1
Espinoza, Ramon A., Tor.	1.000	11	22	0	0	22	0	2
Estrada, Hector, Monc.	.981	104	464	59	10	533	5	12
Estrada, Ricardo, Agua.	1.000	1	1	0	0	1	0	0
Figueroa, Ricardo, Cam.	1.000	8	11	1	0	12	1	0
Franco, Manuel, Sal.	1.000	2	0	3	0	3	0	0
Garza, Gerardo, Lar.	.991	113	495	46	5	546	9	9
Garzon, Eliseo, Tab.	.989	108	460	77	6	543	4	2
Gastelum, Carlos, Monc.	.978	53	119	14	3	136	1	3
Gastelum, Sergio O., Tig.	1.000	2	10	6	0	16	3	0
Gavia, Jesus, Cam.	.990	66	246	49	3	298	2	1
Gonzalez, Jesus, Cam.	.800	2	4	0	1	5	0	0
Guerrero, Jose, Q.R.	1.000	18	29	0	0	29	0	3
Guzman, Marco A., Yuc.	.979	62	210	25	5	240	6	2
Hernandez, Miguel, P.R.	1.000	60	153	23	0	176	0	4
Hurtado, Hector, Min.	.977	51	174	34	5	213	2	4
Lopez, Fabian, Oax.	1.000	1	1	0	0	1	0	0
Lopez, Victor M., Oax.	.969	32	109	16	4	129	1	1
Loredo, Jorge Luis, Oax.	.833	1	3	2	1	6	0	0
Luna, Jose L., Mont.	1.000	49	130	12	0	142	0	0
Martinez, Raul, P.R.	.991	38	93	16	1	110	1	0
McGriff, Terry, Lar.	.975	23	100	18	3	121	2	0
Mendez, Ramon, Agua.	.980	14	40	8	1	49	0	1
Meza, Alfredo, Mont.	.991	67	306	39	3	348	4	1
Morejon, Oswaldo, Yuc.	1.000	1	1	1	0	2	0	0
Munoz, Noe, Mex.	.980	94	443	38	10	491	1	7
Nunez, Dimmerson, Tor.	1.000	5	45	1	0	46	0	0
Ochoa, Edgar, Tig.	1.000	16	46	3	0	49	1	1
Ojeda, Miguel, Mex.	.986	35	124	15	2	141	2	1
Ortega, Antonio, Mex.	.962	15	23	2	1	26	0	0
Osuna, Hector, Yuc.	.981	29	89	14	2	105	0	4
Pacho, Carlos, Yuc.	.986	33	129	16	2	147	1	2
Pantoja, Rigel, Yuc.	1.000	2	3	3	0	6	0	0
Pena, Carlos, Tab.	1.000	22	38	5	0	43	0	1
Perez, Alfredo, Cam.	1.000	1	4	3	0	7	0	0
Perez, Juan L., Tor.	1.000	14	35	2	0	37	1	1
Perez, Noel, Sal.	1.000	2	2	0	0	2	0	0
Powell, Dennis, Mont.	1.000	2	4	3	0	7	0	0
Quintero, Guillermo, Mont.	1.000	1	3	1	0	4	0	0
Ramirez, Efren, Agua.	.988	82	278	59	4	341	6	3
Resendez, Carlos, Monc.	1.000	5	10	2	0	12	0	0
Reyes, Gilberto, Min.	.938	11	39	6	3	48	1	4
Rojas, Homar, Yuc.	.981	40	183	19	4	206	3	2
Romero, Israel, Lar.	1.000	35	76	10	0	86	0	2
Ruiz, Juan De Dios, Min.	1.000	1	5	2	0	7	1	0
Russel, Omar, Min.	.958	15	22	1	1	24	0	4
Santana, Mario, Agua.	.955	46	146	25	8	179	2	3
Saucedo, Roberto, Mont.	.987	48	196	30	3	229	0	5
Soriano, Ricardo, Tor.	1.000	1	3	1	0	4	0	0
Valdez, Francisco J., Rey.	.988	49	196	46	3	245	2	2
Valenzuela, Eduardo, Sal.	.985	26	116	13	2	131	0	0
Vazquez, Felipe, Oax.	.991	41	190	30	2	222	5	0
Vega, Edgar, Min.	.965	59	211	39	9	259	5	8
Velez, Manuel, Tig.	1.000	2	0	3	0	3	1	0
Villanueva, Hector, Q.R.	1.000	3	9	0	0	9	0	0
Vizcarra, Marco A., Sal.	.800	1	2	2	1	5	1	0

PITCHERS

Player, Team	Pct.	G	PO	A	E	TC	DP
Acosta, Aaron, Monc.	.861	22	4	27	5	36	2
Acosta, Gerardo, Oax.	1.000	27	5	13	0	18	2
Adam, David, Tig.	.875	24	11	17	4	32	2
Aguilar, Miguel, Tab.	.900	35	3	6	1	10	0
Aguirre, Gaudencio, Tab.	.964	28	8	46	2	56	4
Alicea, Miguel, Min.	1.000	23	1	0	0	1	0
Alvarez, Juan Carlos, Tab.	.933	24	3	11	1	15	0
Alvarez, Juan J., Tab.	.891	29	4	37	5	46	1
Anderson, Mike, Mont.	1.000	7	1	4	0	5	0
Antunez, Martin, P.R.	1.000	24	0	4	0	4	0
Armenta, Alejandro, Tig.	1.000	33	2	8	0	10	1
Arzate, Martin, Cam.	.000	1	0	0	1	1	0
Austin, James, Agua.	1.000	23	3	5	0	8	0

Player, Team	Pct.	G	PO	A	E	TC	DP
Avila, Jose, Sal.	1.000	9	3	2	0	5	1
Ayala, Luis, Sal.	1.000	37	4	10	0	14	2
Baez, Sixto, P.R.	1.000	24	1	4	0	5	0
Baker, Scott, Tor.	.967	29	8	21	1	30	1
Barfield, John D., Lar.	1.000	44	2	17	0	19	0
Barraza, Ernesto, Tig.	.902	19	9	28	4	41	5
Barrera, Sigfrido, Tig.	1.000	17	1	7	0	8	0
Barron, Avelino, Cam.	1.000	32	3	9	0	12	0
Baxter, Robert, Tig.	1.000	2	1	1	0	2	0
Beatty, Blaine, Mex.	.889	6	0	8	1	9	0
Burgos, John, Yuc.	1.000	30	3	14	0	17	1
Cabrales, Gabriel, Oax.	1.000	14	1	2	0	3	0
Camacho, Adrian, Sal.	1.000	13	4	2	0	6	0
Camacho, Placido, Q.R.	.500	4	0	1	1	2	0
Campos, Francisco, Cam.	.943	26	15	35	3	53	4
Campos, Frank, Min.	1.000	5	0	1	0	1	0
Cano, Jose, Yuc.	.923	22	9	27	3	39	1
Carranza, Javier, Q.R.	.933	22	2	12	1	15	3
Carrazco, Alejandro, Oax.	.977	30	14	28	1	43	0
Castaneda, Aurelio, Cam.	.800	33	1	3	1	5	0
Castillo, Felipe, Cam.	1.000	8	1	3	0	4	0
Castillo, Juan Fco., Monc.	.905	13	6	13	2	21	0
Catedral, Raul, Sal.	1.000	9	1	2	0	3	0
Cazares, Rosario, Tab.	.833	38	1	4	1	6	1
Cazares, Tomas, Monc.	1.000	10	0	2	0	2	0
Cecena, Jose I., Monc.	1.000	21	1	4	0	5	0
Cerros, Juan, Rey.	1.000	38	7	11	0	18	2
Chance, Tony, Monc.	1.000	1	0	4	0	4	1
Chavez, Rafael, Oax.	1.000	9	1	7	0	8	0
Clayton, Royal, Tor.	.882	16	12	18	4	34	0
Coronado, Jorge, Oax.	1.000	27	3	12	0	15	2
Cota, Marino, Sal.	1.000	13	2	5	0	7	0
Couoh, Enrique, Tig.	.933	41	5	23	2	30	2
Cruz, Javier, Mex.	1.000	38	6	7	0	13	0
Cuervo, Bernardo, Oax.	.947	25	15	39	3	57	2
Delfin, Adolfo, Tor.	1.000	26	1	5	0	6	3
Del Toro, Miguel A., Mex.	.857	26	2	4	1	7	0
Dessens, Elmer, Mex.	1.000	26	12	31	0	43	4
Diaz, Alejandro, Oax.	1.000	49	6	14	0	20	1
Diaz, Cesar, Lar.	.923	36	1	11	1	13	0
Diaz, Marco A., Q.R.	1.000	21	6	15	0	21	1
Diaz, Rafael, Mont.	.933	21	11	17	2	30	2
Diaz, Remigio, Mont.	1.000	1	1	0	0	1	0
Dominguez, Herminio, Cam.	1.000	29	4	15	0	19	0
Duarte, Miguel, Sal.	1.000	5	1	0	0	1	0
Duncan, Chip, Oax.	.978	23	6	39	1	46	0
Elvira, Narciso, Mont.	1.000	6	1	5	0	6	1
Enriquez, Martin, Mont.	1.000	42	4	13	0	17	0
Escarrega, Guillermo, P.R.	1.000	18	3	3	0	6	1
Espana, Roberto, P.R.	1.000	7	0	1	0	1	0
Espejo, Ramon, Agua.	1.000	9	0	1	0	1	0
Espino, Jorge, Tor.	1.000	4	0	2	0	2	0
Esquer, Mercedes, Mont.	1.000	23	2	20	0	22	1
Fajardo, Hector, Monc.	1.000	7	2	6	0	8	0
Federico, Gustavo A., Min.	.938	15	7	23	2	32	2
Flores, Ignacio, Tor.	.955	45	6	15	1	22	0
Galvez, Rosario, Lar.	1.000	47	0	14	0	14	1
Gamez, Francisco, Mont.	1.000	44	4	20	0	24	1
Garcia, Francisco J., Mex.	.886	27	10	29	5	44	3
Garcia, Jose L., Lar.	.950	28	12	45	3	60	3
Garcia, Omar, P.R.	1.000	1	6	0	0	6	1
Garcia, Miguel, Min.	1.000	59	9	31	0	40	5
Garibaldi, Cecilio, Tig.	1.000	17	1	6	0	7	0
Garibay, Daniel, Tig.	1.000	27	8	28	0	36	2
Garibay, Roberto, Q.R.	1.000	30	3	11	0	14	0
Garibay, Salvador, Cam.	1.000	21	0	2	0	2	0
Garza, Alejandro, Rey.	1.000	16	5	1	0	6	0
Garza, Roberto, Lar.	.833	49	3	2	1	6	0
Gomez, Martin, Tab.	1.000	9	1	2	0	3	0
Gonzalez, Arturo, Mont.	.967	20	3	26	1	30	3
Gonzalez, Gilberto, Tor.	.953	32	8	33	2	43	0
Gonzalez, Jesus, Cam.	1.000	1	0	4	0	4	0
Gonzalez, Victor, P.R.	.895	44	4	13	2	19	0
Gracia, Edmundo, Sal.	.955	25	6	15	1	22	2
Grajales, Norberto, Tor.	1.000	42	2	14	0	16	0
Gray, Dennis, Min.	1.000	15	0	4	0	4	1
Green, Ottis, Mex.	1.000	34	6	7	0	13	1
Guerca, Guillermo, Oax.	1.000	51	0	13	0	13	1
Guerrero, Omar, Rey.	1.000	28	2	5	0	7	0
Heredia, Hector, Agua.	.917	23	4	18	2	24	1
Hernandez, Dimas C., Monc.	1.000	3	0	2	0	2	0
Hernandez, Gerardo, Tig.	1.000	1	0	1	0	1	0

Player, Team	Pct.	G	PO	A	E	TC	DP
Hernandez, Jesus, Min.	.833	12	2	3	1	6	0
Hernandez, Jose M., Lar.	1.000	23	14	42	0	56	7
Hernandez, Julio, Oax.	.789	35	5	10	4	19	1
Hernandez, Manuel, Oax.	.973	27	7	29	1	37	4
Hernandez, Martin, Q.R.	1.000	24	9	21	0	30	0
Herrera, Calixto, Monc.	1.000	49	5	9	0	14	1
Herrera, Enrique, Tab.	.882	36	5	10	2	17	0
Holman, Shawn, Mex.	1.000	2	0	2	0	2	0
Huerta, Luis E., Lar.	.973	25	10	26	1	37	1
Hurst, Jonathan, Agua.	1.000	32	5	6	0	11	0
Ilsley, Blaise, Cam.	.964	16	5	22	1	28	2
Izabal, Luis A., Q.R.	1.000	9	4	2	0	6	0
Jasso, Oscar, Rey.	.833	15	1	4	1	6	0
Jersild, Aaron, Yuc.	1.000	2	1	0	0	1	0
Jimenez, German, Agua.	.867	18	0	13	2	15	1
Jimenez, Isaac, P.R.	.953	24	6	35	2	43	3
Jimenez, Jesus, Tor.	1.000	24	0	4	0	4	0
Jimenez, Manuel, Tab.	1.000	2	0	1	0	1	0
Kelly, Richard, Rey.	.815	18	5	17	5	27	2
Lara, Hugo, P.R.	1.000	26	11	23	0	34	2
Lara, Jorge, Sal.	1.000	38	7	16	0	23	0
Leal, Gerardo, Monc.	.923	22	3	21	2	26	0
Leftwich, Philip, Lar.	1.000	19	5	22	0	27	1
Leon, Juan A., Tor.	1.000	17	0	1	0	1	0
Lewis, Scott, Tig.	1.000	13	3	17	0	20	1
Lezama, Rafael, Tab.	1.000	7	0	1	0	1	0
Lizarraga, Andres, Lar.	1.000	23	2	3	0	5	0
Llanes, Emeterio, Yuc.	1.000	9	1	0	0	1	0
Loaiza, Sabino, Cam.	.903	22	11	17	3	31	2
Lopez, Emigdio, Min.	.960	24	17	31	2	50	2
Lopez, Gilberto, P.R.	.667	5	0	2	1	3	0
Lopez, Jesus Nain, Rey.	.875	26	2	5	1	8	1
Lopez, Jonas, Agua.	1.000	18	7	21	0	28	0
Lopez, Jose Juan, Mex.	.923	49	5	7	1	13	0
Luevano, Juan, P.R.	1.000	56	0	8	0	8	1
Magre, Pete, Q.R.	1.000	3	0	1	0	1	0
Manrique, Alberto, Agua.	1.000	12	0	2	0	2	1
Manzano, Adrian, Tig.	.938	19	2	13	1	16	0
Marquez, Isidro, Tig.	1.000	50	3	15	0	18	1
Martinez, Cesar, Mont.	.667	32	0	2	1	3	0
Martinez, Grimaldo, Monc.	1.000	1	1	3	0	4	1
Martinez, Jose A., Yuc.	.500	9	1	0	1	2	0
Martinez, Uriel, P.R.	1.000	8	0	6	0	6	0
Mattson, Rob, Agua.	.984	27	11	51	1	63	3
Melendez, Jose, Yuc.	1.000	28	1	11	0	12	1
Mendez, Luis F., Yuc.	1.000	16	8	11	0	19	2
Metoyer, Tony, Rey.	.960	52	7	17	1	25	0
Meza, Alfredo, Mont.	1.000	1	8	2	0	10	0
Meza, Leobardo, P.R.	.000	4	0	0	1	1	0
Miranda, Julio C., Yuc.	1.000	54	1	14	0	15	1
Mora, Eleazar, P.R.	.973	27	5	31	1	37	2
Morales, Luis F., Q.R.	1.000	6	1	0	0	1	0
Moreno, Angel, Yuc.	.985	25	14	50	1	65	6
Moreno, Leobardo, Mex.	1.000	24	4	21	0	25	2
Morton, Kevin, Tig.	.857	7	1	5	1	7	1
Munoz, Jaime, Tig.	1.000	44	5	9	0	14	0
Munoz, Leonardo, Agua.	1.000	53	2	9	0	11	1
Munoz, Miguel, Rey.	1.000	4	0	5	0	5	0
Murillo, Felipe, Monc.	1.000	45	0	7	0	7	0
Navarro, Luis, Yuc.	.895	20	3	14	2	19	2
Neri, Braulio, Monc.	.000	17	0	0	1	1	0
Neri, Eduardo, P.R.	.808	64	4	17	5	26	0
Nunez, A. Jose Juan, Oax.	1.000	23	0	3	0	3	0
Nunez, G. Jose Juan, Oax.	.333	7	0	1	2	3	0
Ochoa, Pablo Joel, Rey.	.857	20	4	14	3	21	1
Olague, Jesus, Mont.	1.000	21	3	7	0	10	3
Orozco, Jaime, Min.	.907	26	12	27	4	43	2
Ortega, Raul, Min.	1.000	1	1	1	0	2	1
Ortega, Roberto, Min.	1.000	19	1	4	0	5	0
Ortega, Wilbert, Yuc.	1.000	17	0	4	0	4	0
Osuna, Ricardo, Tab.	.967	25	14	45	2	61	1
Osuna, Roberto, Sal.	1.000	75	9	19	0	28	1
Paez, Raul, Rey.	1.000	1	0	1	0	1	0
Palacios, Israel, Oax.	1.000	12	0	1	0	1	0
Palacios, Vicente, Mont.	1.000	23	7	22	0	29	0
Palafox, Juan M., Tor.	.967	30	5	24	1	30	4
Parra, Julio, Tig.	.833	32	3	2	1	6	0
Perez, David, Mont.	.972	23	5	30	1	36	0
Perez, Edgar, Min.	1.000	7	2	0	0	2	0

Player, Team	Pct.	G	PO	A	E	TC	DP
Perez, Leonardo, Tab.	.941	30	6	10	1	17	0
Perez, Vladimir, Sal.	1.000	40	6	10	0	16	2
Pimentel, Roberto, Sal.	1.000	34	10	24	0	34	2
Pina, Rafael, Rey.	1.000	28	1	27	0	28	2
Pineda, Gabriel, P.R.	1.000	27	3	24	0	27	1
Powell, Dennis, Mont.	1.000	53	11	24	0	35	3
Purata, Julio, Rey.	.983	25	11	46	1	58	1
Quijada, Mario, Tor.	1.000	4	0	1	0	1	0
Quinones, Enrique, Yuc.	.875	9	3	4	1	8	0
Quintanilla, Enrique, Lar.	.889	31	7	17	3	27	3
Quiroz, Aaron, Mex.	1.000	21	3	26	0	29	2
RAMIREZ, Roberto, Mex.	1.000	24	6	37	0	43	3
Ramos, Jorge L., Q.R.	1.000	11	1	1	0	2	0
Raygoza, Martin, Sal.	.913	20	6	15	2	23	1
Renteria, Hilario, Q.R.	1.000	27	2	7	0	9	0
Retes, Lorenzo, Cam.	.957	25	5	17	1	23	0
Revening, Todd, Tor.	1.000	25	1	3	0	4	0
Reyes, Flavio, Min.	1.000	37	2	4	0	6	0
Rios, Jesus, Monc.	.867	24	5	21	4	30	1
Rivera, Oscar, Rey.	1.000	24	3	23	0	26	2
Rivera, Paul, Agua.	1.000	6	1	0	0	1	0
Rodriguez, Manuel, Min.	1.000	16	1	4	0	5	0
Rodriguez, Raul, Monc.	.963	16	1	25	1	27	3
Rodriguez, Rene, Tor.	1.000	11	1	5	0	6	0
Rodriguez, Rosario, Min.	.000	8	0	0	1	1	0
Rodriguez, Salvador, Yuc.	.968	17	6	24	1	31	2
Rojo, Oscar, Cam.	.966	30	8	20	1	29	2
Romero, Juan, Min.	.875	19	0	7	1	8	0
Romo, Guillermo, Tab.	1.000	4	0	2	0	2	0
Ruiz, Cecilio, Tab.	.971	21	7	26	1	34	0
Saenz, Alfredo, Tor.	1.000	28	5	10	0	15	1
Saldana, Edgardo, Tab.	1.000	18	1	4	0	5	0
Salgado, Eduardo, Agua.	1.000	7	1	2	0	3	1
Sanchez, Alejandro, Q.R.	1.000	6	3	2	0	5	0
Sanchez, Efrain, Tab.	.913	17	6	15	2	23	2
Sanchez, Hector, Agua.	.967	42	9	20	1	30	3
Sanchez, Pablo, Sal.	1.000	8	1	6	0	7	0
Sandoval, Carlos, Min.	.667	17	0	2	1	3	1
Sandoval, Guillermo, Yuc.	.958	19	8	15	1	24	1
Sangeado, Juan C., Cam.	1.000	12	1	5	0	6	0
Sangilbert, Mario, Cam.	.889	8	1	7	1	9	0
Scanlan, Robert, Mex.	.500	12	0	2	2	4	0
Schullstrom, Erik, Mont.	1.000	29	0	1	0	1	0
Serna, Ramon, Agua.	.500	4	0	1	1	2	0
Sierra, Abel, Oax.	1.000	7	3	3	0	6	0
Sinohui, David, Q.R.	1.000	15	1	1	0	2	0
Solano, Julio, Oax.	1.000	46	5	9	0	14	1
Solarte, Jose, Monc.	1.000	18	1	2	0	3	0
Solis, Ricardo, Min.	.964	22	7	20	1	28	0
Sombra, Francisco, Tor.	1.000	21	2	9	0	11	1
Soto, Cruz A., Q.R.	1.000	30	2	15	0	17	1
Soto, Daniel, Mex.	.957	38	6	16	1	23	1
Soto, Fernando, Q.R.	1.000	24	2	23	0	25	2
Sulu, Mario, Cam.	1.000	12	1	3	0	4	0
Tejeda, Felix, P.R.	1.000	23	2	15	0	17	1
Tejeda, Juan, Tab.	1.000	9	0	2	0	2	0
Turgeon, David, Rey.	.929	18	9	17	2	28	2
Uribe, Juan C., Yuc.	1.000	33	2	11	0	13	1
Valdez, Armando, Agua.	1.000	35	4	3	0	7	0
Valdez, Efrain, Q.R.	.941	24	16	32	3	51	0
Valdez, Rodolfo, Monc.	1.000	29	2	3	0	5	0
Valencia, Jorge, Monc.	1.000	11	0	3	0	3	1
Valenzuela, Saul, Q.R.	.927	23	7	31	3	41	2
Valerio, Julio C., Monc.	.889	46	2	6	1	9	0
Vargas, Ignacio, Min.	1.000	46	3	19	0	22	2
Vargas, Joel, Tab.	1.000	18	4	3	0	7	0
Vazquez, Aguedo, Tor.	.500	3	0	1	1	2	0
Vega, Obed, Lar.	.875	43	3	11	2	16	0
Velazquez, Ernesto A., Yuc.	1.000	25	3	3	0	6	1
Velazquez, Israel, Agua.	.952	30	3	17	1	21	0
Verdugo, Hugo, Sal.	1.000	34	8	16	0	24	1
Verdugo, Orlando, Yuc.	1.000	14	2	3	0	5	0
Villarreal, Antonio, Tor.	.943	27	6	27	2	35	3
Villegas, Jose A., Agua.	.889	49	7	17	3	27	2
Williams, Jeff, Sal.	.861	22	13	18	5	36	3
York, Michael, Tor.	1.000	19	6	21	0	27	1
Zappelli, Mark, Sal.	.938	10	2	13	1	16	0
Zimmerman, Mike, Cam.	.500	11	1	0	1	2	0

TRIPLE PLAY: A. Moreno.

LEAGUE CHAMPIONS

Year	Team	Pct.
1955—	Mexico City Tigers*	.539
1956—	Mexico City Reds	.692
1957—	Yucatan	.567
	Mex. C. Reds (2nd)†	.550
1958—	Nuevo Laredo	.625
1959—	Poza Rica	.575
	Mex. C. Reds (3rd)†	.507
1960—	Mexico City Tigers	.538
1961—	Veracruz	.575
1962—	Monterrey	.592
1963—	Puebla	.606
1964—	Mexico City Reds	.586
1965—	Mexico City Tigers	.590
1966—	Mexico City Tigers‡	.614
	Mexico City Reds	.571
1967—	Jalisco	.607
1968—	Mexico City Reds	.586
1969—	Reynosa	.591
1970—	Aguila§	.580
	Mexico City Reds	.607
1971—	Jalisco§	.558
	Saltillo	.593
1972—	Saltillo	.636
	Cordoba§	.541
1973—	Saltillo	.656
	Mexico City Reds∞	.590
1974—	Jalisco	.627
	Mexico City Reds∞	.551
1975—	Tampico∞	.541
	Cordoba	.649
1976—	Mexico City Reds∞	.543
	Union Laguna	.547
1977—	Mexico City Reds	.623
	Nuevo Laredo∞	.507
1978—	Aguascalientes∞	.589
	Union Laguna	.523
1979—	Saltillo	.704
	Puebla∞	.628
1980—	No champion▲	
1981—	Mexico City Reds	.615
	Reynosa	.492
1982—	Ciudad Juarez∞	.570
	Mexico City Tigers	.508
1983—	Campeche◆	.614
	Ciudad Juarez	.535
1984—	Yucatan◆	.560
	Ciudad Juarez	.509
1985—	Mexico City Reds◆	.606
	Nuevo Laredo	.5275
1986—	Puebla◆	.682
	Monclova	.598
1987—	Mexico City Reds◆	.605
	Monterrey	.536
1988—	Mexico City Reds◆	.646
	Nuevo Laredo	.602
1989—	Nuevo Laredo◆	.621
	Yucatan	.539
1990—	Nuevo Laredo	.618
	Leon◆	.565
1991—	Monterrey◆	.683
	Mexico City Reds	.627
1992—	Mexico City Tigers◆	.594
	Nuevo Laredo	.538
1993—	Nuevo Laredo	.589
	Tabasco◆	.528
1994—	Mexico City Red Devils◆	.646
	Monterrey Sultans	.608
1995—	Mexico City Red Devils	.708
	Monterrey Sultans◆	.570
1996—	Monterrey Sultans	.713
	Mexico City Reds◆	.619
1997—	Mexico City Red Devils	.686
	Mexico City Tigers■	.658

*Defeated Nuevo Laredo, two games to none, in playoff for pennant. †Won four-team playoff. ‡Won split-season playoff. §League divided into Northern, Southern divisions; won two-team playoff. ∞League divided into Northern, Southern zones; sub-divided into Eastern, Western divisions, won eight-team play-off. ▲A players strike on July 1 forced the cancellation of the regular season and playoff schedule. ◆ League divided into Northern, Southern zones; four clubs from each zone qualified for postseason play. Won final series for league championship. ■ League divided into Northern, Central and Southern zones; played split season, with top eight teams qualifying for playoffs. Won final series for league championship.

PACIFIC COAST LEAGUE

The Pacific Coast League will expand to 16 teams in 1998. In addition to the 10 teams that played in the league in 1997, Class AAA newcomer Memphis and five teams from the disbanded American Association will join. The 1998 directories for those five former American Association teams—Iowa, Nashville, New Orleans, Oklahoma and Omaha—can be found on page 365.

LEAGUE OFFICE

President
Branch Rickey

Address
1631 Mesa Ave.
Colorado Springs, CO 80906

Phone
719-636-3399

TEAMS

ALBUQUERQUE DUKES

General manager
Pat McKernan
Manager
Glenn Hoffman
Ballpark (capacity, surface)
Albuquerque Sports Stadium (10,510, grass)
Affiliation
Dodgers
Address
1601 Stadium Blvd. SE
Albuquerque, NM 87106
Phone
505-243-1791

CALGARY CANNONS

Vice president, baseball operations
John Traub
Manager
Tom Spencer
Ballpark (capacity, surface)
Burn Stadium (8,000, grass)
Affiliation
White Sox
Address
2255 Crowchild Trail N.W.
Calgary, Alberta T2M 4S7
Phone
403-284-1111

COLORADO SPRINGS SKY SOX

General manager/president
Robert Goughan
Manager
Paul Zuvella
Ballpark (capacity, surface)
Sky Sox Stadium (8,500, grass)
Affiliation
Rockies
Address
4385 Tutt Blvd.
Colorado Springs, CO 80922
Phone
719-597-1449

EDMONTON TRAPPERS

President/general manager
Mel Kowalchuk
Manager
To be announced
Ballpark (capacity, surface)
Teluf Field (10,000; artificial infield, grass outfield)

Affiliation
Athletics
Address
10233 96th Ave.
Edmonton, Alberta T5K 0A5
Phone
403-429-2934

FRESNO GRIZZLIES

Vice president/general manager
Craig Pletenik
Manager
Jim Davenport
Ballpark (capacity, surface)
To be announced
Affiliation
Giants
Address
To be announced
Phone
520-615-9630

LAS VEGAS STARS

General manager
Don Logan
Manager
Jerry Royster
Ballpark (capacity, surface)
Cashman Field (9,370, grass)
Affiliation
Padres
Address
850 Las Vegas Blvd. N
Las Vegas, NV 89101
Phone
702-386-7200

MEMPHIS REDBIRDS

President/general manager
Allie Prescott
Manager
Gaylen Pitts
Ballpark (capacity, surface)
Tim McCarver Stadium (9,000; artificial infield, grass outfield)
Affiliation
Cardinals
Address
800 Home Run Lane
Memphis, TN 38104
Phone
901-721-6000

SALT LAKE BUZZ

Assistant general managers
Dorsena Picknell, Rob White

Manager
Phil Roof
Ballpark (capacity, surface)
Franklin-Quest Field (15,500, grass)
Affiliation
Twins
Address
P.O. Box 4108
Salt Lake City, UT 84110
Phone
801-485-3800

TACOMA RAINIERS

Executive vice president
Mel Taylor
Manager
Dave Myers
Ballpark (capacity, surface)
Cheney Stadium (10,106, grass)
Affiliation
Mariners
Address
P.O. Box 11087
Tacoma, WA 98411
Phone
206-752-7707

TUCSON SIDEWINDERS

General manager
Mike Feder
Manager
Chris Speier
Ballpark (capacity, surface)
Tucson Electric Park (11,000, grass)
Affiliation
Diamondbacks
Address
P.O. Box 27045
Tucson, AZ 85716
Phone
To be announced

VANCOUVER CANADIANS

Vice president/general manager
Gary Arthur
Manager
Mitch Seoane
Ballpark (capacity, surface)
Nat Bailey Stadium (6,500, grass)
Affiliation
Angels
Address
4601 Ontario St.
Vancouver, B.C. V5V 3H4
Phone
604-872-5232

1997 FINAL STANDINGS
FIRST HALF

NORTHERN DIVISION

Team	W	L	T	Pct.	GB
Vancouver (Angels)	39	32	0	.549	....
Edmonton (Athletics)	39	33	0	.542	1/2
Tacoma (Mariners)	35	35	0	.500	3 1/2
Salt Lake (Twins)	34	38	0	.472	5 1/2
Calgary (Pirates)	29	38	0	.433	8

SOUTHERN DIVISION

Team	W	L	T	Pct.	GB
Colorado Springs (Rockies)	45	23	0	.662	....
Phoenix (Giants)	39	33	0	.542	8
Albuquerque (Dodgers)	33	36	0	.478	12 1/2
Tucson (Brewers)	34	38	0	.472	13
Las Vegas (Padres)	25	46	0	.352	21 1/2

SECOND HALF

NORTHERN DIVISION

Team	W	L	T	Pct.	GB
Edmonton (Athletics)	41	31	0	.569	....
Tacoma (Mariners)	40	31	0	.563	1/2
Salt Lake (Twins)	38	33	0	.535	2 1/2
Vancouver (Angels)	36	36	0	.500	5
Calgary (Pirates)	31	40	0	.437	9 1/2

SOUTHERN DIVISION

Team	W	L	T	Pct.	GB
Phoenix (Giants)	49	22	0	.690	....
Las Vegas (Padres)	31	39	0	.443	17 1/2
Colorado Springs (Rockies)	31	41	0	.431	18 1/2
Tucson (Brewers)	30	40	0	.429	18 1/2
Albuquerque (Dodgers)	29	43	0	.403	20 1/2

COMPOSITE

Team	Phx.	Edm.	C.S.	Tac.	Van.	SLC	Tuc.	Alb.	Cal.	L.V.	W	L	T	Pct.	GB
Phoenix (Giants)	....	9	11	9	9	11	8	11	11	9	88	55	0	.615	....
Edmonton (Athletics)	7	....	10	6	11	9	8	10	9	10	80	64	0	.556	8 1/2
Colorado Springs (Rockies)	5	6	....	7	11	9	10	7	8	13	76	64	0	.543	10 1/2
Tacoma (Mariners)	7	10	8	....	4	9	7	9	12	9	75	66	0	.532	12
Vancouver (Angels)	7	5	5	12	....	10	11	11	8	6	75	68	0	.524	13
Salt Lake (Twins)	5	7	7	7	6	....	10	10	10	10	72	71	0	.503	16
Tucson (Brewers)	7	8	6	8	5	6	....	8	7	9	64	78	0	.451	23 1/2
Albuquerque (Dodgers)	5	6	9	7	4	6	8	....	6	11	62	79	0	.440	25
Calgary (Pirates)	5	7	5	4	8	6	9	8	....	8	60	78	0	.435	25 1/2
Las Vegas (Padres)	7	6	3	6	10	5	7	5	7	....	56	85	0	.397	31

Major league affiliations in parentheses.

PLAYOFFS: Edmonton defeated Vancouver, three games to none; Phoenix defeated Colorado Springs, three games to none; Edmonton defeated Phoenix, three games to one, to win league championship.

REGULAR-SEASON ATTENDANCE: Albuquerque, 307,760; Calgary, 291,918; Colorado Springs, 216,716; Edmonton, 432,504; Las Vegas, 313,128; Phoenix, 209,698; Salt Lake, 578,107; Tacoma, 305,281; Tucson, 285,817; Vancouver, 303,148. Total—3,244,077. Playoffs (10 games)—43,933. Class AAA All-Star Game at Des Moines—11,183.

MANAGERS: Albuquerque, Glenn Hoffman; Calgary, Trent Jewett; Colorado Springs, Paul Zuvella; Edmonton, Gary Jones; Las Vegas, Jerry Royster; Phoenix, Ron Wotus; Salt Lake, Phil Roof; Tacoma, Dave Myers; Tucson, Tim Ireland (through June 22) and Bob Mariano (June 23 through end of season); Vancouver, Bruce Hines. Managerial record of team with more than one manager: Tucson, Ireland, 36-41; Mariano, 28-37.

ALL-STAR TEAM: 1B—Todd Helton, Colorado Springs; 2B—Brian Raabe, Tacoma; 3B—Paul Konerko, Albuquerque; SS—Neifi Perez, Colorado Springs; OF—Jacob Cruz, Phoenix; Manny Martinez, Calgary; Ryan Radmanovich, Salt Lake; C—Todd Greene, Vancouver; DH—Dan Rohrmeier, Tacoma; RHP—Dan Carlson, Phoenix; LHP—Doug Creek, Phoenix; Relief Pitcher—John Johnstone, Phoenix; Most Valuable Player—Paul Konerko, Albuquerque; Manager of the Year—Ron Wotus, Phoenix.

1997 BATTING
TEAM

Team	Avg.	G	TPA	AB	R	H	TB	2B	3B	HR	RBI	SH	SF	HP	BB	IBB	SO	SB	CS	GDP	LOB	ShO	Slg.	OBP
Colo. Springs	.305	140	5615	4937	924	1506	2390	326	39	160	863	48	43	60	527	32	986	93	34	99	1093	3	.484	.376
Edmonton	.303	144	5558	4733	878	1433	2324	305	44	166	826	41	40	52	692	26	922	95	49	135	1130	3	.491	.395
Salt Lake	.297	144	5677	4998	889	1482	2371	295	54	162	835	27	49	56	547	18	1034	117	57	106	1047	4	.474	.369
Tacoma	.295	141	5422	4853	770	1430	2267	316	28	155	731	30	44	42	453	28	864	42	42	117	1030	7	.467	.357
Calgary	.294	138	5260	4677	787	1375	2208	340	38	139	731	36	30	44	465	34	888	111	55	118	934	3	.472	.361
Phoenix	.294	143	5459	4918	816	1445	2214	296	46	127	752	38	34	49	530	40	928	134	57	117	1067	9	.450	.366
Tucson	.292	142	5613	4911	829	1433	2271	359	43	131	780	25	51	69	557	14	936	58	39	134	1080	4	.462	.368
Vancouver	.288	143	5450	4839	766	1396	2181	293	42	136	703	68	36	62	445	34	855	124	72	125	969	4	.451	.354
Albuquerque	.286	141	5442	4815	820	1379	2273	246	51	182	770	44	35	43	505	22	853	121	65	103	945	2	.472	.357
Las Vegas	.282	141	5492	4888	686	1376	2064	290	34	110	618	48	37	46	473	29	971	113	54	117	1070	7	.422	.348

INDIVIDUAL

TOP QUALIFIERS FOR BATTING CHAMPIONSHIP

Minimum 389 plate appearances. *Lefthanded batter. †Switch-hitter.

Player, Team	Avg.	G	TPA	AB	R	H	TB	2B	3B	HR	RBI	SH	SF	HP	BB	IBB	SO	SB	CS	GDP	Slg.	OBP
Cruz, Jacob, Phoenix*	.361	127	565	493	97	178	265	45	3	12	95	0	5	3	64	9	64	18	3	11	.538	.434
McCarty, Dave, Phoenix	.353	121	488	434	85	153	256	27	5	22	92	1	2	2	49	5	75	9	4	18	.590	.419
Helton, Todd, Col. Springs*	.352	99	460	392	87	138	221	31	2	16	88	1	6	0	61	4	68	3	1	10	.564	.434
Raabe, Brian, Tacoma	.352	135	607	543	101	191	276	35	4	14	80	1	9	16	38	5	20	1	6	12	.508	.404
Wilson, Desi, Phoenix*	.344	121	502	451	76	155	215	27	6	7	53	0	3	4	44	5	73	16	3	11	.477	.404
Counsell, Craig, Col. Springs*	.335	96	440	376	77	126	184	31	6	5	63	7	6	6	45	3	38	12	2	6	.489	.409
Martinez, Manny, Calgary	.331	109	456	420	78	139	223	34	1	16	66	2	1	0	33	4	80	17	9	3	.531	.379
Collier, Lou, Calgary	.330	112	451	397	65	131	175	31	5	1	48	8	3	6	37	2	47	12	7	13	.441	.393
Shave, Jon, Salt Lake	.329	103	449	395	75	130	184	27	3	7	60	1	8	6	39	0	62	6	6	9	.466	.391

Player, Team	Avg.	G	TPA	AB	R	H	TB	2B	3B	HR	RBI	SH	SF	HP	BB	IBB	SO	SB	CS	GDP	Slg.	OBP
Diaz, Eddy, Tucson	.329	94	402	356	65	117	174	24	3	9	70	3	8	9	26	0	25	0	1	7	.489	.381
Beamon, Trey, Las Vegas*........	.328	90	390	329	64	108	150	19	4	5	49	2	2	9	48	1	58	14	6	11	.456	.425
Lee, Derrek, Las Vegas.............	.324	125	534	472	86	153	225	29	2	13	64	0	2	0	60	4	116	17	3	9	.477	.399
White, Derrick, Vancouver.........	.324	116	468	414	64	134	206	35	2	11	65	1	2	7	44	2	73	11	7	12	.498	.396
Konerko, Paul, Albuquerque	.323	130	560	483	97	156	300	31	1	37	127	0	5	8	64	3	61	2	3	16	.621	.407
Lesher, Brian, Edmonton	.323	110	484	415	85	134	234	27	5	21	78	0	2	3	64	3	86	14	3	14	.564	.415

DEPARTMENTAL LEADERS: G—Raabe, 135; AB—Raabe, 543; R—Raabe, 101; H—Raabe, 191; TB—Konerko, 300; 2B—Ja. Cruz, 45; 3B—Carvajal, 20; HR—Konerko, 37; RBI—Konerko, 127; SH—Caceres, Eenhoorn, 12 each; SF—Cox, Raabe, 9 each; HP—Raabe, 16; BB—Cox, 88; IBB—Ja. Cruz, Zinter, 9 each; SO—Radmanovich, 138; SB—T. Jones, 36; CS—Latham, 19; GIDP—Wood, 21; Slg.—Konerko, .621; OBP—Ja. Cruz, Helton, .434.

ALL PLAYERS
*Lefthanded batter. †Switch-hitter.

Player, Team	Avg.	G	TPA	AB	R	H	TB	2B	3B	HR	RBI	SH	SF	HP	BB	IBB	SO	SB	CS	GDP	Slg.	OBP
Ahearne, Pat, Albuquerque	.100	21	13	10	0	1	1	0	0	0	1	3	0	0	0	0	4	0	0	0	.100	.100
Allensworth, Jermaine, Cal.	.400	5	22	20	5	8	13	3	1	0	1	0	0	0	2	0	4	1	1	0	.650	.455
Alvarez, Rafael, Salt Lake*	.271	17	55	48	10	13	16	1	1	0	5	1	0	0	6	0	9	5	0	1	.333	.352
Anderson, Jimmy, Calgary* ...	.091	21	12	11	1	1	1	0	0	0	1	0	0	0	1	0	5	0	0	0	.091	.167
Andreopoulos, Alex, Tucson*.	.400	10	15	15	3	6	7	1	0	0	1	0	0	0	0	0	1	0	0	0	.467	.400
Anthony, Eric, Albuquerque*..	.343	27	117	105	18	36	65	6	1	7	27	0	1	0	11	1	28	2	3	0	.619	.402
Arias, George, Van.-L.V.	.283	115	483	431	75	122	198	32	4	12	65	1	5	4	42	4	59	3	4	18	.459	.349
Arocha, Rene, Phoenix...........	.000	18	14	11	1	0	0	0	0	0	0	3	0	0	0	0	5	0	0	0	.000	.000
Aurilia, Rich, Phoenix	.294	8	39	34	9	10	15	2	0	1	5	0	0	0	5	0	4	2	1	1	.441	.385
Baez, Kevin, Salt Lake	.274	112	425	383	38	105	151	25	3	5	54	3	6	4	29	0	74	3	4	7	.394	.327
Bailey, Cory, Phoenix	.000	13	1	1	0	0	0	0	0	0	0	0	0	0	0	0	1	0	0	0	.000	.000
Ball, Jeff, Phoenix	.321	126	542	470	90	151	249	38	3	18	103	1	7	5	58	5	84	10	4	12	.530	.396
Banks, Brian, Tucson†	.296	98	421	378	53	112	174	26	3	10	63	2	5	1	35	2	83	7	3	6	.460	.353
Barry, Jeff, Col. Springs†	.300	81	309	273	46	82	140	13	3	13	70	0	2	4	30	2	45	5	0	5	.513	.375
Bass, Kevin, Vancouver†	.333	4	15	12	4	4	7	0	0	1	1	0	0	0	3	1	2	0	1	0	.583	.467
Bates, Jason, Col. Springs†	.237	35	152	135	21	32	49	6	1	3	18	1	1	2	13	0	36	1	3	1	.363	.311
Batista, Tony, Edmonton	.315	33	145	124	25	39	60	10	1	3	21	1	2	1	17	0	18	2	2	4	.484	.396
Battle, Howard, Albuquerque .	.237	50	147	139	14	33	49	3	2	3	16	0	2	0	6	0	23	1	2	3	.353	.265
Beamon, Trey, Las Vegas*	.328	90	390	329	64	108	150	19	4	5	49	2	2	9	48	1	58	14	6	11	.456	.425
Beasley, Tony, Calgary............	.273	75	250	220	36	60	80	7	5	1	28	1	2	2	25	0	23	11	6	4	.364	.349
Beckett, Robbie, Col. Springs ..	.500	45	2	2	1	1	1	0	0	0	0	1	0	0	0	0	0	0	0	0	.500	.500
Bellhorn, Mark, Edmonton† ...	.328	70	310	241	54	79	136	18	3	11	46	3	0	2	64	2	59	6	6	4	.564	.472
Belliard, Ronnie, Tucson	.282	118	523	443	80	125	180	35	4	4	55	3	5	11	61	1	69	10	7	13	.406	.379
Benard, Marvin, Phoenix*	.333	17	72	60	14	20	25	5	0	0	5	0	0	1	11	0	9	4	3	3	.417	.444
Berryhill, Damon, Phoenix† ...	.385	4	15	13	0	5	5	0	0	0	1	0	0	0	2	2	1	0	0	1	.385	.467
Berumen, Andres, L.V.-Tac......	.000	34	2	1	0	0	0	0	0	0	0	1	0	0	0	0	0	0	0	0	.000	.000
Betten, Randy, Vancouver	.279	23	71	61	9	17	24	4	0	1	12	3	0	0	7	0	21	1	1	1	.393	.353
Blanco, Henry, Albuquerque..	.313	91	336	294	38	92	132	20	1	6	47	1	3	1	37	2	63	7	4	7	.449	.388
Boever, Joe, Cal.-Edm.............	.000	53	4	4	0	0	0	0	0	0	0	0	0	0	0	0	0	0	0	0	.000	.000
Bolick, Frank, Vancouver†	.304	102	412	362	61	110	193	27	4	16	66	1	2	1	46	4	70	4	1	12	.533	.382
Bolton, Tom, Cal.-Tuc. *	.286	23	8	7	0	2	3	1	0	0	0	0	0	0	1	0	3	0	0	0	.429	.375
Bonds, Bobby, Phoenix	.000	1	1	1	0	0	0	0	0	0	0	0	0	0	0	0	0	0	0	0	.000	.000
Bonnici, Jim, Tacoma..............	.250	1	5	4	0	1	1	0	0	0	1	0	0	0	1	0	1	0	0	0	.250	.400
Bost, Heath, Col. Springs.......	.000	2	1	1	0	0	0	0	0	0	0	0	0	0	0	0	1	0	0	0	.000	.000
Boston, D.J., Col. Springs*	.333	2	6	6	1	2	2	0	0	0	0	0	0	0	0	0	3	0	0	0	.333	.333
Bourgeois, Steve, Col. Springs	.269	36	29	26	4	7	9	2	0	0	5	2	0	0	1	0	7	0	0	0	.346	.296
Boze, Marshall, Las Vegas	.000	14	6	6	0	0	0	0	0	0	0	0	0	0	0	0	4	0	0	0	.000	.000
Brede, Brent, Salt Lake*	.354	84	382	328	82	116	178	27	4	9	76	0	5	2	47	0	62	4	2	8	.543	.432
Bridges, Kary, Calgary*...........	.263	33	103	95	9	25	29	4	0	0	6	1	0	0	7	1	6	1	0	3	.305	.314
Briggs, Stoney, Las Vegas	.269	119	473	435	58	117	181	21	5	11	57	0	4	6	28	1	122	18	12	10	.416	.319
Brown, Adrian, Calgary†	.319	62	279	248	53	79	94	10	1	1	19	2	2	0	27	1	38	20	4	9	.379	.393
Brown, Alvin, Albuquerque	.400	12	5	5	0	2	2	0	0	0	1	0	0	0	0	0	0	0	0	0	.400	.400
Brown, Jarvis, Tucson.............	.265	112	448	385	65	102	147	21	3	6	35	3	6	2	52	0	84	14	6	15	.382	.351
Brown, Ray, Las Vegas*	.257	41	153	140	12	36	55	13	0	2	15	1	0	1	11	1	28	1	0	11	.393	.316
Brunson, William, Alb.*	.000	27	1	1	0	0	0	0	0	0	0	0	0	0	0	0	1	0	0	0	.000	.000
Bruske, Jim, Las Vegas..........	.400	18	15	10	0	4	5	1	0	0	3	4	1	0	0	0	3	0	0	0	.500	.364
Burke, Jamie, Vancouver	.296	8	31	27	4	8	9	1	0	0	3	0	1	0	3	0	2	0	0	1	.333	.387
Burke, John, Col. Springs	.000	4	6	6	0	0	0	0	0	0	0	0	0	0	0	0	5	0	0	0	.000	.000
Burrows, Terry, L.V.-Edm.*	.333	45	3	3	0	1	1	0	0	0	0	0	0	0	0	0	0	0	0	0	.333	.333
Bush, Homer, Las Vegas	.277	38	169	155	25	43	64	10	1	3	14	1	4	2	7	0	40	5	1	1	.413	.310
Caceres, Edgar, Vancouver†....	.310	82	293	258	30	80	99	13	0	2	37	12	3	1	19	0	23	6	6	8	.384	.356
Canizaro, Jay, Phoenix	.198	23	91	81	12	16	29	7	0	2	12	1	0	0	9	0	24	2	2	2	.358	.278
Carlson, Dan, Phoenix.............	.083	30	15	12	1	1	1	0	0	0	0	0	0	0	1	0	7	0	0	0	.083	.154
Carter, John, Calgary..............	.000	15	2	1	0	0	0	0	0	0	0	0	0	0	1	0	1	0	0	0	.000	.500
Carvajal, Jovino, Vancouver†....	.285	131	510	480	80	137	203	20	20	2	51	4	1	4	21	3	85	28	9	10	.423	.320
Castellano, Pedro, Salt Lake ...	.358	43	189	165	29	59	91	9	1	7	36	0	2	2	20	1	31	0	1	4	.552	.429
Castillo, Marino, Las Vegas.....	.167	30	20	18	1	3	6	0	0	1	2	2	0	0	0	0	7	0	0	1	.333	.167
Castro, Jose A., Edmonton† ..	.167	2	7	6	0	1	1	0	0	0	0	1	0	0	0	0	1	0	0	0	.167	.286
Castro, Jose L., Tacoma*	.000	2	1	1	0	0	0	0	0	0	0	0	0	0	0	0	0	0	0	0	.000	.000
Castro, Juan, Albuquerque	.307	27	108	101	11	31	46	5	2	2	11	1	2	0	4	0	20	1	0	5	.455	.327
Cedeno, Roger, Alb.†	.354	29	136	113	21	40	58	4	4	2	9	0	0	1	22	0	16	5	5	1	.513	.463
Chamberlain, Wes, Calgary....	.317	18	60	60	7	19	29	4	0	2	9	0	0	0	0	0	14	1	0	1	.483	.317
Cholowsky, Dan, Col. Springs	.333	26	100	84	17	28	49	6	0	5	19	0	0	1	15	1	21	1	1	1	.583	.440
Christenson, Ryan, Edm.	.286	16	62	49	12	14	26	2	2	2	9	0	0	1	11	0	11	2	0	1	.531	.435
Christian, Eddie, Tacoma†.......	.319	35	152	135	16	43	53	5	1	1	9	3	0	0	14	0	24	3	2	3	.393	.383
Colbert, Craig, Las Vegas.......	1.000	2	2	2	0	2	3	1	0	0	0	0	0	0	0	0	0	0	0	0	1.500	1.000

CLASS AAA Pacific Coast League

Player, Team	Avg.	G	TPA	AB	R	H	TB	2B	3B	HR	RBI	SH	SF	HP	BB	IBB	SO	SB	CS	GDP	Slg.	OBP
Collier, Lou, Calgary..............	.330	112	451	397	65	131	175	31	5	1	48	8	3	6	37	2	47	12	7	13	.441	.393
Cordova, Marty, Salt Lake......	.375	6	26	24	5	9	16	4	0	1	4	0	0	0	2	0	3	1	0	0	.667	.423
Corps, Edwin, Phoenix..........	.000	7	5	4	0	0	0	0	0	0	0	0	0	0	0	0	3	0	0	0	.000	.200
Counsell, Craig, Col. Springs*	.335	96	440	376	77	126	184	31	6	5	63	7	6	6	45	3	38	12	2	6	.489	.409
Cox, Steve, Edmonton*..........	.274	131	568	467	84	128	209	34	1	15	93	2	9	2	88	4	90	1	3	16	.448	.385
Crawford, Carlos, Calgary	.231	10	14	13	1	3	3	0	0	0	0	0	0	0	0	0	3	0	0	0	.231	.286
Creek, Doug, Phoenix*..........	.250	25	24	24	5	6	8	2	0	0	0	0	0	0	0	0	7	0	0	0	.333	.250
Cromer, Brandon, Calgary*....	.232	68	251	228	30	53	96	15	2	8	36	1	3	0	19	2	46	3	1	5	.421	.288
Cromer, Tripp, Albuquerque ...	.321	43	159	140	25	45	80	8	6	5	24	1	3	1	14	1	34	4	1	0	.571	.380
Cruz, Fausto, Vancouver	.288	118	444	413	52	119	182	28	1	11	67	4	4	5	18	0	81	5	8	10	.441	.323
Cruz, Jacob, Phoenix*..........	.361	127	565	493	97	178	265	45	3	12	95	0	5	3	64	9	64	18	3	11	.538	.434
Cruz, Jose, Tacoma†.............	.268	50	226	190	33	51	89	16	2	6	30	1	0	1	34	1	44	3	0	4	.468	.382
Dascenzo, Doug, Las Vegas†.	.277	109	486	433	61	120	178	23	4	9	45	6	1	1	45	4	42	16	8	7	.411	.346
Daspit, Jamie, L.V.-Edm........	.000	13	1	1	0	0	0	0	0	0	0	0	0	0	0	0	0	0	0	0	.000	.000
Decker, Steve, Tacoma	.297	99	378	350	44	104	161	25	1	10	52	0	5	1	22	0	37	0	0	10	.460	.336
Delgado, Wilson, Phoenix†....	.288	119	451	416	47	120	177	22	4	9	59	6	4	1	24	4	70	9	3	9	.425	.326
Demetral, Chris, Alb.*..........	.250	12	30	24	1	6	11	2	0	1	1	0	0	0	6	0	3	0	1	1	.458	.400
Diaz, Eddy, Tucson	.329	94	402	356	65	117	174	24	3	9	70	3	8	9	26	0	25	0	1	7	.489	.381
Drahman, Brian, Las Vegas....	.000	33	1	1	0	0	0	0	0	0	0	0	0	0	0	0	1	0	0	0	.000	.000
Dreifort, Darren, Albuquerque	.000	2	1	1	0	0	0	0	0	0	0	0	0	0	0	0	1	0	0	0	.000	.000
Dressendorfer, Kirk, Alb.........	.000	7	2	1	0	0	0	0	0	0	0	1	0	0	0	0	1	0	0	0	.000	.000
Ducey, Rob, Tacoma*............	.324	23	85	74	8	24	32	8	0	0	11	0	0	3	8	2	15	0	0	0	.432	.412
Dunn, Todd, Tucson	.304	93	380	332	66	101	194	31	4	18	66	0	1	8	39	1	83	5	5	11	.584	.389
Durant, Mike, Salt Lake..........	.206	66	250	223	33	46	85	13	1	8	36	0	0	6	21	0	42	4	1	8	.381	.292
Echevarria, Angel, Col. Springs	.322	77	334	295	59	95	158	24	0	13	80	1	4	6	28	0	47	6	2	8	.536	.387
Edge, Tim, Calgary	.235	62	208	187	23	44	70	13	2	3	22	3	0	5	13	2	50	0	2	2	.374	.302
Eenhoorn, Robert, Vancouver	.308	120	504	455	77	140	215	29	5	12	58	12	5	7	25	2	59	1	4	10	.473	.350
Encarnacion, Angelo, L.V........	.245	79	270	253	27	62	85	12	1	3	23	1	0	1	15	1	32	1	5	9	.336	.290
Espinoza, Alvaro, Tacoma.......	.333	4	14	12	1	4	4	0	0	0	1	0	0	0	2	0	1	0	0	0	.333	.429
Farmer, Michael, Col. Springs†	.417	22	12	12	4	5	12	1	0	2	4	0	0	0	0	0	4	0	0	0	1.000	.417
Felix, Lauro, Tucson	.319	19	54	47	7	15	23	5	0	1	5	2	0	0	5	0	15	0	0	0	.489	.385
Ferguson, Jeff, Salt Lake........	.282	65	273	241	51	68	115	19	2	8	35	1	1	6	24	0	48	4	2	5	.477	.360
Fernandez, Osvaldo, Phoenix .	.400	2	5	5	0	2	2	0	0	0	0	0	0	0	0	0	1	0	0	0	.400	.400
Florez, Tim, Phoenix...............	.301	114	440	402	57	121	174	24	4	7	61	5	1	8	32	2	68	6	3	5	.433	.363
Fonville, Chad, Albuquerque†	.218	102	409	371	49	81	90	5	2	0	22	3	2	3	30	0	39	23	10	3	.243	.281
Foulke, Keith, Phoenix............	.100	12	11	10	1	1	3	0	1	0	0	0	0	0	1	0	2	0	0	0	.300	.182
Frontera, Chad, Phoenix.........	.200	5	6	5	0	1	1	0	0	0	0	1	0	0	0	0	1	0	0	0	.200	.200
Gajkowski, Steve, Tacoma......	.500	44	2	2	0	1	1	0	0	0	0	0	0	0	0	0	0	0	0	0	.500	.500
Garcia, Freddy, Calgary	.240	35	133	121	21	29	50	6	0	5	17	0	2	1	9	3	20	0	0	8	.413	.293
Garcia, Jose, Albuquerque	.000	33	1	1	0	0	0	0	0	0	0	0	0	0	0	0	1	0	0	0	.000	.000
Garcia, Karim, Albuquerque* .	.305	71	286	262	53	80	169	17	6	20	66	1	0	0	23	4	70	11	5	4	.645	.361
Garrison, Webster, Edmonton	.289	125	494	429	70	124	197	24	2	15	80	2	4	2	57	5	91	5	3	6	.459	.372
Gates, Brent, Tacoma†...........	.455	7	37	33	7	15	18	3	0	0	6	0	0	4	0	2	2	0	0	0	.545	.514
Gibson, Derrick, Col. Springs.	.423	21	83	78	14	33	49	7	0	3	12	0	0	0	5	1	9	0	2	1	.628	.458
Gipson, Charles, Tacoma........	.314	11	40	35	5	11	13	2	0	0	5	0	0	1	4	0	3	0	1	0	.371	.400
Gonzales, Frank, Calgary........	.000	25	1	1	0	0	0	0	0	0	0	0	0	0	0	0	1	0	0	0	.000	.000
Gonzales, Rene, L.V.-C.S........	.283	98	395	339	50	96	128	21	1	3	42	4	5	4	43	0	49	2	4	10	.378	.366
Granger, Jeff, Calgary	.300	30	10	10	0	3	4	1	0	0	2	0	0	0	0	0	4	0	0	0	.400	.300
Greene, Todd, Vancouver	.354	64	287	260	51	92	189	22	0	25	75	0	2	5	20	8	31	5	1	6	.727	.404
Grieve, Ben, Edmonton*	.426	27	123	108	27	46	80	11	1	7	28	1	1	1	12	0	16	0	1	4	.741	.484
Griffey, Craig, Tacoma............	.333	3	3	3	1	1	3	0	1	0	0	0	0	0	0	0	1	0	0	0	1.000	.333
Gubanich, Creighton, Edm.-Tuc.-C.S.	.310	81	301	277	40	86	150	19	0	15	57	1	1	3	19	0	79	1	2	10	.542	.360
Guerrero, Wilton, Alb.†	.400	10	48	45	9	18	20	0	1	0	5	0	1	0	2	1	3	3	0	1	.444	.417
Guevara, Giomar, Tacoma	.244	54	187	176	29	43	56	5	1	2	13	5	0	1	5	0	39	3	7	2	.318	.269
Hajek, Dave, Las Vegas	.340	41	171	156	25	53	69	14	1	0	25	0	1	0	14	1	6	7	2	7	.442	.392
Hale, Chip, Albuquerque*	.267	88	313	247	43	66	88	16	0	2	30	4	2	2	58	0	26	3	3	9	.356	.408
Hall, Billy, Col. Springs†.........	.255	13	54	51	6	13	17	0	2	0	6	0	0	0	3	0	11	3	1	2	.333	.296
Halperin, Mike, Calgary*.........	.000	15	3	2	0	0	0	0	0	0	0	0	0	0	1	0	0	0	0	0	.000	.333
Hamilton, Darryl, Phoenix*.....	.286	3	14	14	1	4	8	1	0	1	2	0	0	0	0	0	2	0	0	0	.571	.286
Hancock, Lee, Phoenix*.........	.500	7	2	2	1	1	1	0	0	0	0	0	0	0	0	0	1	0	0	0	.500	.500
Haney, Todd, Tacoma.............	.353	4	19	17	3	6	10	4	0	0	2	0	0	2	0	0	2	0	0	0	.588	.421
Harkey, Mike, Albuquerque	.000	49	2	2	1	0	0	0	0	0	0	0	0	0	0	0	0	0	0	0	.000	.000
Hartvigson, Chad, Phoenix*...	.000	17	11	9	0	0	0	0	0	0	0	0	0	0	0	0	5	0	0	1	.000	.182
Hazlett, Steve, Calgary	.298	37	110	94	18	28	53	12	2	3	15	1	1	2	12	2	19	1	0	1	.564	.385
Helfand, Eric, Las Vegas*	.315	80	274	238	31	75	116	21	1	6	33	2	0	6	28	1	47	1	1	9	.487	.401
Helton, Todd, Col. Springs*	.352	99	460	392	87	138	221	31	2	16	88	1	6	0	61	4	68	3	1	10	.564	.434
Henderson, Ryan, Alb.-C.S.	.667	19	3	3	1	2	2	0	0	0	0	0	0	0	0	0	1	0	0	0	.667	.667
Herges, Matt, Albuquerque* ..	.167	31	7	6	1	1	1	0	0	0	1	0	0	0	1	0	3	0	0	0	.167	.286
Hernandez, Carlos, Las Vegas	.400	3	12	10	1	4	7	0	0	1	5	0	1	0	1	0	3	0	0	0	.700	.417
Herrera, Jose, Edmonton*	.297	122	473	421	64	125	162	21	2	4	41	7	2	1	42	2	64	7	5	12	.385	.361
Hinch, A.J., Edmonton	.376	39	148	125	23	47	66	7	0	4	24	0	0	3	20	1	13	2	0	7	.528	.473
Hollandsworth, Todd, Alb.*.....	.429	13	60	56	13	24	37	4	3	1	14	0	0	0	4	0	4	2	3	0	.661	.467
Hook, Chris, Las Vegas	.000	19	6	5	0	0	0	0	0	0	0	1	0	0	0	0	4	0	0	0	.000	.167
Hope, John, Col. Springs........	.333	48	20	18	5	6	9	0	0	1	1	2	0	0	0	0	5	0	0	0	.500	.333
Horn, Jeff, Salt Lake	.333	23	90	78	16	26	35	6	0	1	13	0	0	0	11	0	22	0	0	4	.449	.422
Howitt, Dann, Col. Springs*	.332	102	349	316	57	105	176	29	0	14	62	0	1	0	32	4	71	2	2	7	.557	.393
Hubbs, Dan, Albuquerque	.000	62	3	3	0	0	0	0	0	0	0	0	0	0	0	0	2	0	0	0	.000	.000
Huckaby, Ken, Albuquerque	.199	69	215	201	14	40	47	5	1	0	18	3	2	0	9	1	36	1	0	5	.234	.231
Hughes, Bobby, Tucson	.310	89	327	290	43	90	144	29	2	7	51	0	4	9	24	1	46	0	0	9	.497	.376
Huson, Jeff, Col. Springs*	.350	9	22	20	3	7	13	3	0	1	5	0	0	0	2	0	2	0	0	1	.650	.409
Iapoce, Anthony, Tucson†.......	.333	7	22	21	5	7	11	4	0	0	3	0	0	0	1	0	4	0	0	1	.524	.364
Ibanez, Raul, Tacoma*	.304	111	478	438	84	133	218	30	5	15	84	3	4	1	32	1	75	7	5	12	.498	.349

Player, Team	Avg.	G	TPA	AB	R	H	TB	2B	3B	HR	RBI	SH	SF	HP	BB	IBB	SO	SB	CS	GDP	Slg.	OBP
Jackson, Darrin, Salt Lake	.300	19	86	80	14	24	36	3	3	1	12	0	0	1	5	0	17	3	0	0	.450	.349
Jenkins, Geoff, Tucson*	.236	93	383	347	44	82	142	24	3	10	56	0	0	3	33	1	87	0	2	7	.409	.308
Johns, Keith, Tucson	.264	112	386	333	45	88	130	21	3	5	36	6	2	2	43	0	61	4	2	7	.390	.350
Johnson, Barry, Calgary	.000	34	1	1	0	0	0	0	0	0	0	0	0	0	0	0	1	0	0	0	.000	.000
Johnson, J.J., Salt Lake	.146	26	88	82	6	12	15	1	1	0	5	1	0	1	4	0	24	2	2	2	.183	.195
Johnson, Mark, Calgary*	.339	34	139	115	28	39	70	11	1	6	16	0	1	1	22	4	28	4	2	2	.609	.446
Jones, Bobby, Col. Springs	.071	25	18	14	0	1	1	0	0	0	0	1	0	0	3	0	8	0	0	0	.071	.235
Jones, Dax, Phoenix	.255	93	318	271	48	69	95	7	5	3	28	3	4	1	39	0	39	9	10	6	.351	.346
Jones, Terry, Col. Springs	.270	92	396	363	70	98	123	14	4	1	25	6	2	0	25	0	49	36	6	3	.339	.315
Joyner, Wally, Las Vegas*	.250	3	8	8	1	2	2	0	0	0	1	0	0	0	0	0	1	0	0	1	.250	.250
Kaufman, Brad, Las Vegas	.000	6	4	4	0	0	0	0	0	0	0	0	0	0	0	0	2	0	0	0	.000	.000
Keefe, Jamie, Las Vegas	.190	42	72	58	10	11	20	2	2	1	6	1	0	3	10	0	24	0	1	0	.345	.338
Kellner, Frank, Tucson†	.287	67	254	230	31	66	88	14	4	0	25	5	2	1	16	0	38	2	1	6	.383	.333
Kennedy, Darryl, Phoenix	.173	32	108	98	10	17	21	4	0	0	8	1	2	1	6	1	13	1	1	2	.214	.224
Kirby, Wayne, Albuquerque*	.335	68	299	269	57	90	146	16	5	10	43	1	2	1	26	0	33	18	5	5	.543	.393
Konerko, Paul, Albuquerque	.323	130	560	483	97	156	300	31	1	37	127	0	5	8	64	3	61	2	3	16	.621	.407
Kramer, Tom, Col. Springs	.000	51	4	3	0	0	0	0	0	0	0	1	0	0	0	0	2	0	0	0	.000	.000
Kroon, Marc, Las Vegas†	.000	46	1	0	0	0	0	0	0	0	0	1	0	0	0	0	0	1	0	0	.000	.000
Kubenka, Jeff, Albuquerque	.000	8	1	0	0	0	0	0	0	0	0	1	0	0	0	0	0	0	0	0	.000	.000
Latham, Chris, Salt Lake†	.309	118	559	492	78	152	208	22	5	8	58	4	1	4	58	0	110	21	19	8	.423	.386
Lawrence, Sean, Calgary*	.182	26	28	22	1	4	4	0	0	0	2	5	0	0	1	0	8	0	0	0	.182	.217
Leach, Jalal, Tacoma*	.308	115	453	415	56	128	187	26	3	9	55	2	3	1	32	2	74	6	6	11	.451	.357
Lee, Derek, Las Vegas*	.294	75	265	231	22	68	101	16	1	5	35	0	2	0	32	4	35	4	1	6	.437	.377
Lee, Derrek, Las Vegas	.324	125	534	472	86	153	225	29	2	13	64	0	2	0	60	4	116	17	3	9	.477	.399
Lee, Mark, Col. Springs*	.000	48	5	3	0	0	0	0	0	0	1	1	0	0	1	0	2	0	0	0	.000	.250
Lee, Travis, Tucson*	.300	59	261	227	42	68	130	16	2	14	46	0	1	2	31	2	46	2	0	10	.573	.387
Lennon, Patrick, Edmonton	.343	39	160	134	28	46	80	7	0	9	35	0	2	2	22	4	34	0	0	5	.597	.438
Lesher, Brian, Edmonton	.323	110	484	415	85	134	234	27	5	21	78	0	2	3	64	3	86	14	3	14	.564	.415
Leskanic, Curt, Col. Springs	.000	10	1	1	0	0	0	0	0	0	0	0	0	0	0	0	0	0	0	0	.000	.000
Long, Joey, Las Vegas	.000	16	1	1	0	0	0	0	0	0	0	0	0	0	0	0	0	0	0	0	.000	.000
Lott, Billy, Calgary	.314	71	280	239	45	75	138	18	0	15	55	1	2	3	35	6	56	6	0	9	.577	.405
Maddux, Mike, Tac.-L.V.*	.500	4	3	2	0	1	1	0	0	0	0	0	0	0	1	0	0	0	0	0	.500	.667
Marrero, Oreste, Alb.*	.262	96	288	263	38	69	116	20	0	9	42	0	1	0	24	2	70	1	1	8	.441	.323
Martinez, Greg, Tucson†	.417	3	12	12	2	5	7	2	0	0	3	0	0	0	0	0	1	0	0	0	.583	.417
Martinez, Jesus, Alb.*	.125	26	16	16	0	2	3	1	0	0	3	0	0	0	0	0	6	0	0	0	.188	.125
Martinez, Manny, Calgary	.331	109	456	420	78	139	223	34	1	16	66	2	1	0	33	4	80	17	9	3	.531	.379
Martinez, Ramon, Phoenix	.281	18	64	57	6	16	21	2	0	1	7	1	1	0	5	0	9	1	0	1	.368	.333
Martins, Eric, Edmonton	.280	27	96	82	17	23	35	7	1	1	8	2	0	1	11	0	19	0	0	3	.427	.372
Marx, Tim, Calgary	.250	90	330	300	42	75	106	18	2	3	40	1	1	5	23	1	42	9	1	16	.353	.313
Maurer, Ron, Albuquerque	.275	114	402	349	61	96	149	21	4	8	50	2	5	7	39	0	59	3	3	10	.427	.355
Mayes, Craig, Phoenix*	.095	7	22	21	2	2	3	1	0	0	0	0	0	0	1	0	5	0	0	2	.143	.136
Mayne, Brent, Edmonton*	.000	2	3	3	0	0	0	0	0	0	0	0	0	0	0	0	1	0	0	0	.000	.000
McCarty, Dave, Phoenix	.353	121	488	434	85	153	256	27	5	22	92	1	2	2	49	5	75	9	4	18	.590	.419
McDonald, Jason, Edm.†	.264	79	366	276	74	73	111	14	6	4	30	8	1	7	74	0	58	31	9	4	.402	.430
Medina, Rafael, Las Vegas	.222	13	9	9	0	2	2	0	0	0	1	0	0	0	0	0	2	0	0	0	.222	.222
Melo, Juan, Las Vegas†	.271	12	51	48	6	13	20	4	0	1	6	0	1	1	1	0	10	0	0	0	.417	.294
Menhart, Paul, Tac.-L.V.	.333	27	10	6	2	2	2	0	0	0	0	3	0	0	1	0	2	0	0	0	.333	.429
Miller, Damian, Salt Lake	.338	85	350	314	48	106	164	19	3	11	82	1	3	3	29	0	62	6	1	7	.522	.395
Millette, Joe, Tacoma	.211	46	133	123	12	26	30	2	1	0	5	0	0	2	8	0	23	1	1	1	.244	.271
Minchey, Nate, Col. Springs	.136	27	29	22	1	3	3	0	0	0	2	4	0	0	3	0	14	0	0	1	.136	.240
Mintz, Steve, Las Vegas*	.000	27	1	0	0	0	0	0	0	0	0	0	0	0	1	0	0	0	0	0	.000	1.000
Mirabelli, Doug, Phoenix	.265	100	401	332	49	88	139	23	2	8	48	3	1	7	58	2	69	1	2	9	.419	.384
Molina, Izzy, Edmonton	.261	61	231	218	33	57	92	11	3	6	34	1	0	0	12	0	27	2	0	4	.422	.300
Monahan, Shane, Tacoma*	.294	21	93	85	15	25	35	4	0	2	12	2	0	1	5	0	21	5	1	1	.412	.341
Montgomery, Steve, Edm	.000	30	1	1	0	0	0	0	0	0	0	0	0	0	0	0	1	0	0	0	.000	.000
Montoya, Norm, Tucson*	.000	27	1	1	0	0	0	0	0	0	0	0	0	0	0	0	0	0	0	0	.000	.000
Monzon, Jose, Vancouver	.234	17	53	47	2	11	13	2	0	0	6	1	1	0	4	0	8	1	0	2	.277	.288
Moore, Joel, Col. Springs*	.200	5	7	5	0	1	1	0	0	0	2	1	0	0	1	0	2	0	0	0	.200	.333
Morales, Willie, Edmonton	.291	56	196	179	23	52	79	12	0	5	35	3	3	0	11	0	27	0	2	4	.441	.326
Morel, Ramon, Calgary	.300	27	11	10	1	3	3	0	0	0	0	1	0	0	0	0	3	0	0	0	.300	.300
Munoz, Bobby, L.V.-Alb.	.000	35	2	1	0	0	0	0	0	0	0	1	0	0	0	0	0	0	0	1	.000	.000
Murray, Eddie, Albuquerque†	.308	9	29	26	4	8	15	1	0	2	9	0	0	0	3	0	3	0	0	0	.577	.379
Murray, Heath, Las Vegas*	.111	19	19	18	1	2	2	0	0	0	1	0	0	0	1	0	6	0	0	1	.111	.158
Neill, Mike, Edmonton*	.190	7	30	21	3	4	4	0	0	0	3	2	0	0	7	0	7	1	1	1	.190	.393
Newfield, Marc, Tucson	.323	8	35	31	4	10	14	1	0	1	3	0	0	0	4	1	6	0	0	1	.452	.400
Norton, Chris, Vancouver	.200	1	5	5	1	1	4	0	0	1	1	0	0	0	0	0	2	0	0	0	.800	.200
Ogden, Jamie, Salt Lake*	.286	97	404	367	67	105	175	18	5	14	53	0	0	2	35	2	99	14	3	11	.477	.351
Ortiz, David, Salt Lake*	.214	10	44	42	5	9	22	1	0	4	10	0	0	0	2	0	11	0	1	4	.524	.250
Ortiz, Russ, Phoenix	.231	14	17	13	0	3	3	0	0	0	2	2	0	1	1	0	6	0	0	0	.231	.333
Owens, Jayhawk, Col. Springs	.260	95	358	289	57	75	122	17	0	10	34	1	2	11	55	4	98	4	1	3	.422	.395
Parker, Rick, Albuquerque	.272	49	166	151	33	41	72	7	3	6	21	0	0	5	10	0	26	6	0	4	.477	.337
Parra, Jose, Salt Lake	.000	50	1	1	0	0	0	0	0	0	0	0	0	0	0	0	0	0	0	0	.000	.000
Pennyfeather, William, Alb.	.254	115	433	402	59	102	182	21	4	17	54	2	2	1	26	1	73	11	11	9	.453	.299
Perez, Neifi, Col. Springs†	.363	68	323	303	68	110	164	24	3	8	46	0	3	0	17	0	27	8	2	3	.541	.393
Peters, Chris, Calgary*	.556	14	10	9	2	5	6	1	0	0	1	1	0	0	0	0	2	0	0	0	.667	.556
Pett, Jose, Calgary	.000	3	2	2	0	0	0	0	0	0	0	0	0	0	0	0	1	0	0	0	.000	.000
Phillips, Randy, Phoenix	.125	21	9	8	1	1	1	0	0	0	0	0	0	0	1	0	5	0	0	0	.125	.222
Phillips, Tony, Tuc.-Edm.	.000	41	4	4	0	0	0	0	0	0	0	0	0	0	0	0	0	0	0	0	.000	.000
Pickett, Ricky, Phoenix*	.000	61	3	2	0	0	0	0	0	0	0	0	0	0	1	0	2	0	0	0	.000	.333
Plantier, Phil, Las Vegas*	.429	15	60	56	13	24	45	6	0	5	9	0	0	0	4	0	8	1	1	0	.804	.467
Poe, Charles, Las Vegas	.261	54	209	180	28	47	86	9	3	8	34	1	4	2	22	4	32	1	2	7	.478	.341
Polcovich, Kevin, Calgary	.306	17	65	62	7	19	26	4	0	1	9	0	1	1	1	0	7	0	0	1	.419	.323
Powell, Dante, Phoenix	.241	108	510	452	91	109	174	24	4	11	42	3	0	3	52	1	105	34	10	9	.385	.323
Pritchett, Chris, Vancouver*	.279	109	437	383	60	107	164	30	3	7	47	5	2	5	42	6	72	5	3	9	.428	.356

Player, Team	Avg.	G	TPA	AB	R	H	TB	2B	3B	HR	RBI	SH	SF	HP	BB	IBB	SO	SB	CS	GDP	Slg.	OBP
Pulliam, Harvey, Col. Springs.	.401	40	162	137	44	55	105	10	2	12	43	0	0	4	21	3	19	1	0	1	.766	.494
Purdy, Shawn, Phoenix..........	.000	56	4	4	0	0	0	0	0	0	0	0	0	0	0	0	1	0	0	1	.000	.000
Pyc, Dave, Albuquerque*.......	.182	31	25	22	2	4	6	0	1	0	2	3	0	0	0	0	8	0	0	0	.273	.182
Quinlan, Tom, Col. Springs....	.285	134	580	509	85	145	254	36	2	23	113	1	8	12	50	4	117	1	1	15	.499	.358
Raabe, Brian, Tacoma...........	.352	135	607	543	101	191	276	35	4	14	80	1	9	16	38	5	20	1	6	12	.508	.404
Radmanovich, Ryan, S.L.*.....	.264	133	562	485	92	128	245	25	4	28	78	1	5	4	67	7	138	11	4	4	.505	.355
Randa, Joe, Calgary..............	.364	3	14	11	4	4	8	1	0	1	4	0	0	0	3	0	4	0	0	1	.727	.500
Rapp, Pat, Phoenix...............	.500	3	3	2	0	1	1	0	0	0	0	1	0	0	0	0	1	0	0	0	.500	.500
Rath, Gary, Albuquerque*......	.158	24	26	19	0	3	3	0	0	0	1	7	0	0	0	0	6	0	0	0	.158	.158
Reimer, Kevin, Tacoma*.........	.345	46	185	168	21	58	85	18	0	3	21	0	3	2	12	0	22	0	3	8	.506	.389
Rekar, Bryan, Col. Springs.....	.100	28	23	20	2	2	3	1	0	0	0	2	0	0	1	0	8	0	0	1	.150	.143
Reyes, Dennis, Albuquerque*	.400	10	7	5	1	2	3	1	0	0	2	2	0	0	0	0	1	0	0	0	.600	.400
Riggs, Adam, Albuquerque....	.304	57	259	227	59	69	122	8	3	13	28	0	0	3	29	1	39	12	2	2	.537	.390
Riley, Marquis, Vancouver† ...	.264	65	287	242	33	64	70	6	0	0	8	6	2	1	36	0	27	27	7	4	.289	.359
Rivera, Ruben, Las Vegas......	.250	12	50	48	6	12	22	5	1	1	6	0	0	1	1	0	20	1	0	0	.458	.280
Roa, Joe, Phoenix.................	.143	6	9	7	1	1	1	0	0	0	0	1	0	0	1	0	4	0	0	0	.143	.250
Roach, Petie, Albuquerque*...	.250	31	6	4	1	1	1	0	0	0	2	1	0	0	1	0	2	0	0	0	.250	.400
Roberson, Kevin, Phoenix†....	.287	109	399	349	60	100	171	19	5	14	67	0	2	11	37	2	98	9	5	6	.490	.371
Rohrmeier, Dan, Tacoma........	.297	125	522	471	86	140	290	43	4	33	120	0	6	0	45	2	81	1	0	14	.616	.354
Romero, Mandy, Las Vegas† .	.308	33	104	91	19	28	43	4	1	3	13	0	1	1	11	1	19	0	0	4	.473	.385
Rowland, Rich, Phoenix.........	.237	19	66	59	10	14	25	5	0	2	13	0	0	0	7	0	13	0	0	2	.424	.318
Rupp, Chad, Salt Lake..........	.272	117	491	426	77	116	245	19	7	32	94	3	6	7	49	1	112	2	1	10	.575	.352
Saipe, Mike, Col. Springs.......	.100	10	13	10	0	1	1	0	0	0	1	3	0	0	0	0	1	0	0	1	.100	.100
Sanford, Chance, Calgary*.....	.292	89	373	325	58	95	158	27	9	6	60	1	5	3	39	0	82	9	7	5	.486	.368
Scanlan, Bob, Las Vegas........	.500	36	2	2	0	1	1	0	0	0	0	0	0	0	0	0	0	0	0	0	.500	.500
Scarsone, Steve, Las Vegas...	.231	82	296	251	37	58	106	13	1	11	35	2	2	3	38	0	78	2	2	1	.422	.337
Schmidt, Curt, Calgary...........	1.000	25	1	1	0	1	1	0	0	0	0	0	0	0	0	0	0	0	1	0	1.000	1.000
Schmitt, Todd, Las Vegas......	.000	48	1	1	0	0	0	0	0	0	0	0	0	0	0	0	1	0	0	0	.000	.000
Sealy, Scot, Tacoma...............	.273	18	63	55	8	15	27	3	0	3	10	0	1	2	5	0	13	0	1	2	.491	.349
Secrist, Reed, Calgary*..........	.264	40	136	121	19	32	60	7	3	5	18	1	0	0	14	0	32	0	1	3	.496	.341
Seitzer, Brad, Tucson............	.316	62	263	234	50	74	120	13	3	9	42	0	4	3	22	0	33	0	1	9	.513	.376
Sexton, Chris, Col. Springs....	.268	33	129	112	18	30	38	3	1	1	8	1	0	0	16	0	21	1	1	4	.339	.359
Shave, Jon, Salt Lake............	.329	103	449	395	75	130	184	27	3	7	60	1	8	6	39	0	62	6	6	9	.466	.391
Shaw, Curtis, Calgary*..........	.000	21	1	1	0	0	0	0	0	0	0	0	0	0	0	0	1	0	0	0	.000	.000
Sheets, Andy, Tacoma...........	.259	113	456	401	57	104	169	23	0	14	53	5	2	2	46	1	97	7	2	9	.421	.337
Sheldon, Scott, Edmonton.....	.315	118	494	422	89	133	241	39	6	19	77	3	3	6	59	4	104	5	2	11	.571	.404
Shepherd, Keith, Calgary.......	.333	10	3	3	1	1	1	0	0	0	0	0	0	0	0	0	1	0	0	0	.333	.333
Shipley, Craig, Las Vegas.......	.316	6	19	19	0	6	9	3	0	0	1	0	0	0	0	0	5	0	0	0	.474	.316
Shoemaker, Stephen, C.S.*....	.000	5	3	2	1	0	0	0	0	0	0	1	0	0	0	0	2	0	0	0	.000	.000
Shumpert, Terry, L.V.-C.S.	.288	42	163	146	26	42	61	11	1	2	18	1	2	3	11	1	27	3	0	2	.418	.346
Silva, Jose, Calgary...............	.250	17	15	12	2	3	4	1	0	0	0	2	0	0	1	0	6	0	0	1	.333	.308
Silvestre, Juan, Tacoma.........	.250	8	30	28	5	7	10	3	0	0	0	0	0	0	2	0	9	0	0	0	.357	.300
Simons, Mitch, Salt Lake.......	.299	115	528	462	87	138	207	34	10	5	59	9	5	5	47	4	48	26	5	7	.448	.366
Singleton, Duane, Vancouver*	.206	108	432	383	56	79	117	17	3	5	36	6	2	4	37	1	79	15	12	15	.305	.282
Smith, Demond, Edmonton†..	.219	42	182	151	22	33	59	3	4	5	22	1	4	3	23	0	31	10	3	3	.391	.326
Smith, Jeff, Salt Lake*...........	.250	7	13	12	2	3	5	2	0	0	2	0	0	0	1	0	3	0	0	0	.417	.308
Smith, Mark, Calgary.............	.372	39	160	137	37	51	109	14	1	14	42	0	0	2	21	1	15	2	1	5	.796	.463
Smith, Pete, Las Vegas..........	.143	6	8	7	0	1	1	0	0	0	0	1	0	0	0	0	1	0	0	0	.143	.143
Soderstrom, Steve, Phoenix..	.214	31	15	14	0	3	3	0	0	0	0	1	0	0	0	0	4	0	0	0	.214	.214
Sodowsky, Clint, Calgary*.....	.000	8	2	2	0	0	0	0	0	0	0	0	0	0	0	0	1	0	0	0	.000	.000
Spearman, Vernon, Alb.*.......	.217	30	111	92	13	20	25	3	1	0	8	3	0	2	14	0	11	5	1	1	.272	.333
Spencer, Stan, Las Vegas.......	.333	8	10	6	1	2	3	1	0	0	1	2	0	0	2	0	1	0	0	0	.500	.500
Stahoviak, Scott, Salt Lake*..	.214	8	34	28	5	6	12	0	0	2	10	0	0	1	5	0	8	0	0	1	.429	.353
Staton, T.J., Calgary*............	.236	65	225	199	30	47	67	14	0	2	22	1	1	2	22	0	51	3	3	6	.337	.317
Steed, Dave, Albuquerque......	.213	25	51	47	8	10	17	4	0	1	4	0	0	0	4	1	19	0	0	0	.362	.275
Stidham, Phil, Col. Springs....	.000	26	5	4	0	0	0	0	0	0	0	1	0	0	0	0	2	0	0	1	.000	.000
Stinnett, Kelly, Tucson...........	.321	64	259	209	50	67	118	15	3	10	43	0	2	6	42	1	46	1	1	2	.565	.444
Strittmatter, Mark, C.S..........	.246	45	135	114	16	28	42	8	0	2	12	4	1	5	11	3	21	0	1	4	.368	.336
Swift, Billy, Col. Springs.........	1.000	1	1	1	0	1	3	0	1	0	2	0	0	0	0	0	0	0	0	0	3.000	1.000
Tatum, Jim, Las Vegas...........	.317	44	173	161	21	51	92	12	1	9	25	0	2	1	8	0	39	1	2	1	.571	.349
Taulbee, Andy, Phoenix..........	.000	19	5	5	0	0	0	0	0	0	0	0	0	0	0	0	3	0	0	0	.000	.000
Taylor, Kerry, Las Vegas.........	.059	23	21	17	0	1	1	0	0	0	0	3	0	0	1	0	13	0	0	0	.059	.111
Taylor, Scott, L.V.-Cal............	.200	42	5	5	0	1	1	0	0	0	2	0	0	0	0	0	2	0	0	0	.200	.200
Thobe, Steve, Calgary............	.255	34	119	102	16	26	49	8	0	5	14	0	0	2	15	0	25	2	1	1	.480	.361
Thompson, Mark, C.S..............	.000	1	1	1	0	0	0	0	0	0	0	0	0	0	0	0	1	0	0	0	.000	.000
Thomson, John, Col. Springs	.143	7	8	7	0	1	1	0	0	0	1	1	0	0	0	0	2	0	0	0	.143	.143
Thurston, Jerrey, Vancouver..	.236	65	217	195	17	46	63	3	1	4	19	8	2	4	8	0	59	3	2	2	.323	.278
Tinsley, Lee, Tacoma†............	.181	31	117	105	15	19	29	2	1	2	7	0	0	0	12	0	34	1	4	0	.276	.265
Tolentino, Jose, Calgary*.......	.308	88	344	305	52	94	166	24	0	16	69	0	6	2	31	3	49	2	5	10	.544	.369
Torres, Paul, Tacoma.............	.301	59	234	209	24	63	97	19	0	5	22	3	5	3	14	1	31	1	0	4	.464	.346
Treadwell, Jody, Albuquerque	.280	27	28	25	3	7	10	0	0	1	5	2	0	0	1	0	10	0	0	0	.400	.308
Tredaway, Chad, Las Vegas†..	.257	116	452	409	58	105	151	23	1	7	50	3	6	0	34	2	63	6	4	9	.369	.310
Turner, Chris, Vancouver........	.370	37	151	135	26	50	72	10	0	4	22	0	0	2	14	0	22	0	0	5	.533	.437
Unrat, Chris, Phoenix*...........	.500	1	3	2	0	1	1	0	0	0	0	0	0	0	1	0	0	0	0	0	.500	.667
Unroe, Tim, Tucson...............	.291	63	247	234	45	68	114	17	1	9	46	0	2	2	9	0	62	3	3	6	.487	.320
Vanderwal, John, C.S.*...........	.408	25	114	103	29	42	65	12	1	3	19	0	0	0	11	1	28	1	1	1	.631	.465
Vanderweele, Doug, Phoenix.	.000	36	6	6	0	0	0	0	0	0	0	0	0	0	0	0	3	0	0	0	.000	.000
VanLandingham, William, Pho.	.000	4	5	5	0	0	0	0	0	0	0	0	0	0	0	0	1	0	0	0	.000	.000
Varitek, Jason, Tacoma†........	.254	87	351	307	54	78	136	13	0	15	48	4	4	2	34	2	71	0	1	13	.443	.329
Velandia, Jorge, Las Vegas....	.272	114	447	405	46	110	138	15	2	3	35	8	1	4	29	3	62	13	3	5	.341	.326
Velazquez, Edgard, C.S..........	.281	120	481	438	70	123	218	24	10	17	73	1	2	6	34	2	119	6	3	8	.498	.340
Villano, Mike, Phoenix............	.500	13	14	12	3	6	7	1	0	0	3	1	0	0	1	0	2	0	0	0	.583	.538
Vina, Fernando, Tucson*........	.474	6	24	19	3	9	15	3	0	1	5	0	0	2	3	0	1	0	1	0	.789	.583
Voigt, Jack, Tucson................	.272	66	281	235	36	64	99	20	0	5	40	0	2	1	43	1	57	4	3	4	.421	.384
Wachter, Derek, Tucson.........	.289	46	170	142	24	41	59	12	0	2	28	1	6	3	18	0	28	2	2	6	.415	.367

Player, Team	Avg.	G	TPA	AB	R	H	TB	2B	3B	HR	RBI	SH	SF	HP	BB	IBB	SO	SB	CS	GDP	Slg.	OBP
Wainhouse, David, Calgary* ..	.500	25	2	2	0	1	1	0	0	0	0	0	0	0	0	0	1	0	0	0	.500	.500
Walker, Todd, Salt Lake*	.345	83	378	322	69	111	166	20	1	11	53	2	7	1	46	3	49	5	5	10	.516	.420
Ward, Turner, Calgary†	.340	59	241	209	44	71	122	18	3	9	44	0	1	5	24	0	26	7	1	5	.584	.418
Weaver, Eric, Albuquerque	.125	21	10	8	0	1	1	0	0	0	0	2	0	0	0	0	2	0	0	0	.125	.125
White, Derrick, Vancouver	.324	116	468	414	64	134	206	35	2	11	65	1	2	7	44	2	73	11	7	12	.498	.396
Wilkins, Rick, Tacoma*	.338	17	77	68	16	23	34	8	0	1	14	0	1	0	8	2	12	0	0	4	.500	.403
Williams, Eddie, Albuquerque	.366	76	326	279	73	102	206	17	0	29	76	0	2	8	37	4	45	0	2	9	.738	.451
Williams, George, Edm.†	.000	3	8	7	0	0	0	0	0	0	0	0	0	0	1	0	1	0	0	0	.000	.125
Williams, Keith, Phoenix	.200	3	5	5	0	1	1	0	0	0	0	0	0	0	0	0	2	0	0	0	.200	.200
Williams, Reggie, Van.†	.250	12	46	40	10	10	19	3	0	2	5	0	0	0	6	0	13	3	2	0	.475	.348
Williamson, Antone, Tucson*.	.286	83	357	304	53	87	132	20	5	5	41	0	1	3	49	3	41	3	1	12	.434	.389
Wilson, Desi, Phoenix*	.344	121	502	451	76	155	215	27	6	7	53	0	3	4	44	5	73	16	3	11	.477	.404
Wilson, Gary, Calgary	.222	21	12	9	1	2	4	2	0	0	0	3	0	0	0	0	3	0	0	0	.444	.222
Witasick, Jay, Edmonton	.000	13	1	1	0	0	0	0	0	0	0	0	0	0	0	0	0	0	0	0	.000	.000
Witte, Trey, Tacoma	.000	33	1	1	0	0	0	0	0	0	0	0	0	0	0	0	0	0	0	0	.000	.000
Wojciechowski, Steve, Edm.*	1.000	26	2	1	0	1	1	0	0	0	0	1	0	0	0	0	0	0	0	0	1.000	1.000
Wolff, Mike, Vancouver	.282	91	337	266	58	75	153	15	0	21	64	4	3	11	53	3	75	6	4	1	.575	.417
Wood, Jason, Edmonton	.321	130	564	505	83	162	268	35	7	19	87	2	4	8	45	0	74	2	4	21	.531	.383
Woods, Ken, Phoenix	1.000	1	1	1	0	1	1	0	0	0	1	0	0	0	0	0	0	0	0	0	1.000	1.000
Wright, Jamey, Col. Springs ..	.000	2	2	2	0	0	0	0	0	0	0	0	0	0	0	0	1	0	0	0	.000	.000
Wright, Ron, Calgary	.304	91	368	336	50	102	181	31	0	16	63	0	6	2	24	2	81	0	2	4	.539	.348
Young, Ernie, Edmonton	.323	54	241	195	39	63	100	10	0	9	45	1	2	6	37	1	46	5	2	7	.513	.442
Zancanaro, Dave, Las Vegas†	.000	3	2	1	0	0	0	0	0	0	0	0	1	0	0	0	0	0	0	0	.000	.000
Zinter, Alan, Tacoma†	.287	110	473	404	69	116	203	19	4	20	70	1	1	3	64	9	113	3	1	7	.502	.388
Zosky, Eddie, Phoenix	.278	86	261	241	38	67	112	10	4	9	45	1	2	1	16	2	38	3	3	5	.465	.323

GRAND SLAMS: Blanco, K. Garcia, Konerko, McCarty, Rohrmeier, 2 each; Arias, Barry, Bellhorn, Belliard, Cox, B. Cromer, Ja. Cruz, Daszenzo, Echevarria, Ferguson, Florez, Greene, Grieve, Hazlett, Herrera, Latham, M. Martinez, R. Martinez, D. Miller, Perez, Powell, Quinlan, Roberson, Scarsone, Sheldon, M. Smith, Stahoviak, Tredaway, E. Williams, Wood, Wright, Young, Zosky, 1 each.

AWARDED FIRST BASE ON CATCHER'S INTERFERENCE: Ward 2 (D. Miller, Varitek); Ball (Owens); Sheldon (Varitek); Tatum (Owens).

PLAYERS WITH TWO OR MORE TEAMS

Player, Team	Avg.	G	TPA	AB	R	H	TB	2B	3B	HR	RBI	SH	SF	HP	BB	IBB	SO	SB	CS	GDP	Slg.	OBP
Arias, George, Vancouver.......	.279	105	450	401	71	112	179	28	3	11	60	1	5	4	39	4	51	3	4	17	.446	.345
Arias, George, Las Vegas.......	.333	10	33	30	4	10	19	4	1	1	5	0	0	0	3	0	8	0	0	1	.633	.394
Berumen, Andres, Las Vegas .	.000	18	2	1	0	0	0	0	0	0	0	1	0	0	0	0	0	0	0	0	.000	.000
Berumen, Andres, Tacoma......	.000	16	0	0	0	0	0	0	0	0	0	0	0	0	0	0	0	0	0	0	.000	.000
Boever, Joe, Calgary	.000	36	2	2	0	0	0	0	0	0	0	0	0	0	0	0	0	0	0	0	.000	.000
Boever, Joe, Edmonton	.000	17	2	2	0	0	0	0	0	0	0	0	0	0	0	0	0	0	0	0	.000	.000
Bolton, Tom, Calgary*...........	.286	8	8	7	0	2	3	1	0	0	0	0	0	1	0	3	0	0	0	.429	.375
Bolton, Tom, Tucson*	.000	15	0	0	0	0	0	0	0	0	0	0	0	0	0	0	0	0	0	0	.000	.000
Burrows, Terry, Las Vegas* ..	.000	31	1	1	0	0	0	0	0	0	0	0	0	0	0	0	0	0	0	0	.000	.000
Burrows, Terry, Edmonton* ..	.500	14	2	2	0	1	1	0	0	0	0	0	0	0	0	0	0	0	0	0	.500	.500
Daspit, Jamie, Las Vegas	.000	10	1	1	0	0	0	0	0	0	0	0	0	0	0	0	0	0	0	0	.000	.000
Daspit, Jamie, Edmonton	.000	3	0	0	0	0	0	0	0	0	0	0	0	0	0	0	0	0	0	0	.000	.000
Gonzales, Rene, Las Vegas	.186	13	50	43	2	8	9	1	0	0	3	0	0	1	6	0	6	0	0	4	.209	.300
Gonzales, Rene, Col. Springs .	.297	85	345	296	48	88	119	20	1	3	39	4	5	3	37	0	43	2	4	6	.402	.375
Gubanich, Creighton, Edm.....	.331	43	163	145	23	48	82	13	0	7	34	1	1	2	14	0	42	0	2	4	.566	.395
Gubanich, Creighton, Tuc......	.341	24	87	85	13	29	49	5	0	5	17	0	1	1	0	0	19	1	0	2	.576	.356
Gubanich, Creighton, C.S......	.191	14	51	47	4	9	19	1	0	3	6	0	0	0	4	0	18	0	0	4	.404	.255
Henderson, Ryan, Alb.............	.000	13	0	0	0	0	0	0	0	0	0	0	0	0	0	0	0	0	0	0	.000	.000
Henderson, Ryan, C.S............	.667	6	3	3	1	2	2	0	0	0	0	0	0	0	0	0	1	0	0	0	.667	.667
Maddux, Mike, Tacoma*	.000	1	0	0	0	0	0	0	0	0	0	0	0	0	0	0	0	0	0	0	.000	.000
Maddux, Mike, Las Vegas*	.500	3	3	2	0	1	1	0	0	0	0	0	0	1	0	0	0	0	0	0	.500	.667
Menhart, Paul, Tacoma	.000	15	0	0	0	0	0	0	0	0	0	0	0	0	0	0	0	0	0	0	.000	.000
Menhart, Paul, Las Vegas	.333	12	10	6	2	2	2	0	0	0	0	3	0	1	0	0	2	0	0	0	.333	.429
Munoz, Bobby, Las Vegas	.000	17	2	1	0	0	0	0	0	0	0	1	0	0	0	0	0	0	0	1	.000	.000
Munoz, Bobby, Albuquerque ..	.000	18	0	0	0	0	0	0	0	0	0	0	0	0	0	0	0	0	0	0	.000	.000
Phillips, Tony, Tucson	.000	29	1	1	0	0	0	0	0	0	0	0	0	0	0	0	0	0	0	0	.000	.000
Phillips, Tony, Edmonton	.000	12	3	3	0	0	0	0	0	0	0	0	0	0	0	0	0	0	0	0	.000	.000
Shumpert, Terry, Las Vegas ...	.284	32	124	109	18	31	44	2	8	1	1	16	1	2	3	9	1	20	3	0	1	.404	.350
Shumpert, Terry, Col. Springs	.297	10	39	37	8	11	17	3	0	1	2	0	0	0	2	0	7	0	0	1	.459	.333
Taylor, Scott, Las Vegas	.000	2	0	0	0	0	0	0	0	0	0	0	0	0	0	0	0	0	0	0	.000	.000
Taylor, Scott, Calgary	.200	40	5	5	0	1	1	0	0	0	2	0	0	0	0	0	2	0	0	0	.200	.200

1997 PITCHING
TEAM

Team	W	L	Pct.	ERA	G	CG	ShO	Sv.	IP	H	TBF	R	ER	HR	SH	SF	HB	BB	IBB	SO	WP	Bk.
Tacoma	75	66	.532	4.65	141	9	8	33	1211.1	1294	5358	694	626	134	43	33	57	512	19	1017	54	12
Phoenix	88	55	.615	4.77	143	3	3	46	1241.2	1405	5494	721	658	128	43	32	47	493	17	926	59	11
Vancouver..........	75	68	.524	4.91	143	16	6	37	1237.0	1331	5534	767	675	134	37	44	59	591	17	836	84	7
Edmonton...........	80	64	.556	5.35	144	8	7	45	1193.0	1400	5302	783	709	158	33	48	32	402	33	866	64	7
Salt Lake	72	71	.503	5.45	143	7	5	34	1251.0	1511	5651	855	757	141	36	36	52	472	30	893	79	7
Tucson	64	78	.451	5.48	142	1	4	31	1229.1	1444	5582	869	748	148	45	44	51	541	33	843	81	12
Albuquerque	62	79	.440	5.54	141	7	6	30	1221.0	1518	5611	849	751	143	52	48	46	527	23	992	76	3
Calgary	60	78	.435	5.66	138	2	1	27	1173.2	1479	5461	844	738	135	50	43	55	507	43	909	56	12
Las Vegas	56	85	.397	5.90	141	6	3	30	1230.0	1467	5635	902	806	161	42	42	58	565	38	993	77	9
Colo. Springs.....	76	64	.543	5.92	140	6	3	27	1203.0	1406	5475	881	791	186	24	37	66	584	24	962	73	6

CLASS AAA Pacific Coast League

TOP QUALIFIERS FOR EARNED-RUN AVERAGE TITLE

Minimum 115 innings. *Lefthanded pitcher.

Pitcher, Team	W	L	Pct.	ERA	G	GS	CG	ShO	GF	Sv.	IP	H	TBF	R	ER	HR	SH	SF	HB	BB	IBB	SO	WP	Bk.
Hurtado, Edwin, Tacoma.........	10	6	.625	3.88	20	20	5	3	0	0	132.1	139	567	60	57	9	2	5	3	37	1	100	7	0
Lawrence, Sean, Calgary*.......	8	9	.471	4.21	26	26	2	0	0	0	143.1	154	641	83	67	17	9	6	3	57	3	116	6	0
Taylor, Kerry, Las Vegas	7	9	.438	4.31	22	22	3	0	0	0	144.0	150	628	84	69	15	8	8	11	55	3	103	4	0
Minchey, Nate, Col. Springs.....	15	6	.714	4.51	27	21	3	0	0	0	157.2	172	678	87	79	17	5	3	6	53	1	107	4	0
Miller, Travis, Salt Lake*........	10	6	.625	4.73	21	21	0	0	0	0	125.2	140	558	73	66	11	5	2	4	57	0	86	5	0
Lorraine, Andrew, Edmonton* .	8	6	.571	4.74	23	20	2	2	2	0	117.2	143	520	72	62	12	3	7	2	34	1	75	3	0
Creek, Doug, Phoenix*	8	6	.571	4.93	25	23	2	1	0	0	129.2	140	583	76	71	15	6	0	4	66	0	137	7	2
Serafini, Dan, Salt Lake*.......	9	7	.563	4.97	28	24	2	0	1	0	152.0	166	660	87	84	18	4	3	8	55	0	118	3	0
Buckley, Travis, Vancouver	7	11	.389	5.11	32	25	1	0	4	1	176.0	223	785	116	100	25	6	8	8	51	3	119	6	0
Treadwell, Jody, Albuquerque ..	10	5	.667	5.12	27	21	2	0	2	1	128.1	143	575	80	73	16	4	2	4	54	2	108	3	0
Jones, Bobby, Col. Springs*....	7	11	.389	5.14	25	21	0	0	2	0	133.0	135	593	89	76	16	1	5	12	71	2	104	2	0
Castillo, Marino, Las Vegas	6	5	.545	5.14	30	19	0	0	0	0	126.0	146	567	88	72	18	2	4	2	43	2	102	3	2
Edsell, Geoff, Vancouver.........	14	11	.560	5.15	30	29	6	1	0	0	183.1	196	826	121	105	11	5	6	12	96	1	95	8	0
Pyc, Dave, Albuquerque*........	12	12	.500	5.33	31	23	3	2	1	1	152.0	181	675	104	90	18	4	6	5	50	2	106	5	1
Rekar, Bryan, Col. Springs......	10	9	.526	5.46	28	25	0	0	0	0	145.0	169	636	96	88	21	1	3	10	39	2	116	7	0

DEPARTMENTAL LEADERS: W—Minchey, 15; L—Redman, 15; Pct.—Carlson, .813; G—Hubbs, 62; GS—Edsell, 29; CG—Edsell, 6; ShO—Hurtado, 3; GF—Boever, 36; Sv.—Johnstone, 24; IP—Edsell, 183.1; H—Buckley, 223; TBF—Edsell, 826; R—Redman, 123; ER—Nichting, 113; HR—Buckley, 25; SH—Lawrence, Menhart, 9 each; SF—Buckley, Misuraca, K. Taylor, 8 each; HB—Edsell, Jones, 12 each; BB—Edsell, 96; IBB—Parra, 7; SO—Creek, 137; WP—Grimsley, 20; BK—J. Anderson, J. McAndrew, 4 each.

ALL PITCHERS

*Lefthanded pitcher.

Pitcher, Team	W	L	Pct.	ERA	G	GS	CG	ShO	GF	Sv.	IP	H	TBF	R	ER	HR	SH	SF	HB	BB	IBB	SO	WP	Bk.
Abbott, Paul, Tacoma	8	4	.667	4.13	17	14	3	0	0	0	93.2	80	391	48	43	11	3	2	6	29	1	117	6	0
Acre, Mark, Edmonton	3	4	.429	4.15	43	0	0	0	26	11	47.2	48	209	27	22	5	3	1	1	20	5	46	2	0
Adams, Willie, Edmonton	5	4	.556	6.45	13	12	0	0	0	0	75.1	105	345	57	54	13	2	4	2	19	3	58	3	1
Adamson, Joel, Tucson* . . .	2	1	.667	4.36	6	6	0	0	0	0	33.0	38	138	16	16	4	1	1	2	8	0	24	3	1
Ahearne, Pat, Albuquerque . .	2	4	.333	4.90	20	8	0	0	3	0	60.2	82	280	43	33	9	4	2	1	20	1	44	2	0
Aldred, Scott, Salt Lake* . . .	3	3	.500	7.03	7	7	0	0	0	0	39.2	56	187	39	31	4	1	2	1	16	1	23	7	0
Anderson, Jimmy, Calgary* .	7	6	.538	5.68	21	21	0	0	0	0	103.0	124	486	78	65	9	6	5	5	64	3	71	9	4
Anderson, Mike, Albuquerque	0	0	.000	10.80	6	0	0	0	2	1	10.0	18	49	12	12	2	0	0	1	9	0	9	0	0
Arocha, Rene, Phoenix	7	3	.700	4.76	18	18	1	0	0	0	111.2	121	470	59	59	17	3	2	4	27	0	68	3	0
Ausanio, Joe, Col. Springs . .	0	0	.000	29.45	3	0	0	0	1	0	3.2	14	28	13	12	3	0	0	0	3	0	3	0	0
Baez, Kevin, Salt Lake	0	0	.000	0.00	2	0	0	0	2	0	2.0	1	9	0	0	0	0	0	0	2	0	1	1	0
Bailey, Cory, Phoenix	4	0	1.000	1.56	13	0	0	0	11	3	17.1	16	70	4	3	0	1	1	0	6	1	14	1	0
Baptist, Travis, Salt Lake*. . .	4	1	.800	2.08	7	6	1	1	0	0	47.2	47	194	16	11	3	0	1	1	9	0	28	2	1
Baron, Jim, Las Vegas* . . .	0	0	.000	11.25	4	0	0	0	2	0	4.0	8	21	5	5	2	0	0	0	3	0	3	0	0
Batchelor, Rich, Las Vegas . .	3	0	1.000	6.43	15	0	0	0	4	0	21.0	23	93	15	15	2	1	1	1	8	2	19	5	0
Battle, Howard, Albuquerque	0	0	.000	0.00	1	0	0	0	1	0	0.1	1	2	0	0	0	0	0	0	0	0	1	0	0
Beatty, Blaine, Calgary*	1	2	.333	23.63	3	2	0	0	0	0	5.1	18	37	14	14	3	0	0	1	3	0	2	0	0
Beckett, Robbie, Col. Springs*	1	3	.250	6.79	45	1	0	0	17	1	54.1	61	260	49	41	12	1	3	2	47	2	67	13	0
Bene, Bill, Vancouver	0	1	.000	7.24	19	0	0	0	8	0	27.1	28	141	25	22	6	1	1	3	26	0	29	10	0
Berumen, Andres, L.V.-Tac. .	9	4	.692	4.91	34	16	0	0	2	0	113.2	127	527	71	62	13	2	1	7	64	1	114	13	2
Boever, Joe, Cal.-Edm.	10	8	.556	4.99	53	3	0	0	36	9	92.0	112	408	54	51	13	1	7	0	23	3	81	2	0
Bolton, Tom, Cal.-Tuc.*	5	10	.333	6.92	23	15	0	0	1	0	95.0	142	443	80	73	11	5	1	3	32	2	71	4	0
Bones, Ricky, Tucson	5	0	1.000	2.79	8	7	0	0	1	0	42.0	40	173	18	13	2	0	0	3	8	0	22	0	1
Bost, Heath, Col. Springs . . .	0	1	.000	21.00	2	0	0	0	0	0	3.0	10	21	8	7	1	0	1	0	1	0	3	0	0
Bourgeois, Steve, Col. Springs	9	7	.563	5.99	33	18	2	2	5	0	121.2	154	571	96	81	18	2	3	5	66	3	86	7	0
Bovee, Mike, Vancouver	4	3	.571	3.44	12	12	1	0	0	0	89.0	92	377	38	34	7	4	2	7	25	0	71	4	0
Bowers, Shane, Salt Lake . . .	6	2	.750	4.79	9	9	1	0	0	0	56.1	64	247	35	30	12	1	4	3	14	0	46	2	0
Boze, Marshall, Las Vegas . .	0	7	.000	7.62	14	8	0	0	2	0	52.0	68	252	51	44	11	1	4	1	29	2	44	2	0
Brewer, Billy, Edmonton* . . .	0	0	.000	5.63	7	1	0	0	2	1	8.0	8	36	5	5	2	0	0	1	6	0	11	1	0
Brewington, Jamie, Tucson. . .	1	3	.250	10.18	6	5	0	0	0	0	20.1	33	112	26	23	2	0	1	2	17	0	13	0	0
Briscoe, John, Calgary	0	1	.000	12.27	4	0	0	0	2	0	7.1	18	41	11	10	1	0	1	0	2	1	7	2	0
Brown, Alvin, Albuquerque . .	4	6	.400	6.13	12	11	1	1	0	0	61.2	74	291	50	42	9	4	2	1	35	0	43	6	1
Browne, Byron, Tucson	0	1	.000	5.23	3	3	0	0	0	0	10.1	13	52	9	6	0	0	0	0	8	0	7	1	1
Brunson, William, Alb.*	1	1	.500	6.49	27	0	0	0	7	0	26.1	39	125	19	19	3	1	1	1	10	1	25	0	0
Bruske, Jim, Las Vegas	5	4	.556	4.90	16	9	0	0	0	0	68.0	73	294	41	37	8	2	1	3	22	1	67	2	0
Buckley, Travis, Vancouver . .	7	11	.389	5.11	32	25	1	0	4	1	176.0	223	785	116	100	25	6	8	8	51	3	119	6	0
Burke, John, Col. Springs. . .	1	2	.333	5.82	3	3	0	0	0	0	17.0	23	85	14	11	1	0	0	0	14	0	15	2	0
Burrows, Terry, L.V.-Edm.*. .	3	7	.300	6.08	44	1	0	0	13	2	60.2	79	287	42	41	5	2	2	1	34	5	50	3	1
Cadaret, Greg, Vancouver* . .	0	1	.000	3.14	9	0	0	0	3	0	14.1	11	56	5	5	1	0	0	0	4	0	16	1	0
Carlson, Dan, Phoenix	13	3	.813	3.88	29	14	0	0	7	3	109.0	102	451	53	47	12	3	3	2	36	1	108	6	1
Carmona, Rafael, Tacoma . . .	2	5	.286	3.79	32	5	0	0	19	4	59.1	52	263	31	25	7	2	1	2	35	2	56	3	2
Carter, John, Calgary	1	2	.333	14.57	15	2	0	0	3	0	25.1	45	150	41	41	6	3	4	3	27	2	18	4	0
Castillo, Marino, Las Vegas .	6	5	.545	5.14	30	19	0	0	0	0	126.0	146	567	88	72	18	2	4	2	43	2	102	3	2
Chavez, Anthony, Vancouver. .	4	3	.571	2.54	28	0	0	0	26	15	28.1	21	111	8	8	2	0	1	1	6	0	22	3	0
Chouinard, Bobby, Edmonton	6	6	.500	6.03	25	21	1	0	1	0	100.0	129	446	80	67	19	1	1	0	26	0	58	6	0
Corps, Edwin, Phoenix	2	1	.667	5.68	7	2	0	0	0	0	19.0	26	88	14	12	0	0	0	2	8	1	8	0	0
Crawford, Carlos, Calgary . . .	1	5	.167	5.94	9	9	0	0	0	0	50.0	60	228	43	33	8	1	1	3	19	3	26	3	0
Creek, Doug, Phoenix*.	8	6	.571	4.93	25	23	2	1	0	0	129.2	140	583	76	71	15	6	0	4	66	0	137	7	2
Crow, Dean, Tacoma.	4	2	.667	4.78	33	0	0	0	23	7	43.1	56	200	25	23	3	2	3	1	19	1	36	3	0
D'Amico, Jeffrey, Edmonton .	0	2	.333	8.22	10	7	0	0	1	0	30.2	42	141	29	28	7	1	2	2	6	2	19	3	0
Dascenzo, Doug, Las Vegas*	0	0	.000	6.75	1	0	0	0	0	0	1.1	3	8	2	1	0	0	0	0	1	0	0	0	0
Daspit, Jamie, L.V.-Edm. . . .	0	2	.000	6.83	13	2	0	0	0	0	27.2	31	119	22	21	6	1	0	0	9	3	14	4	0
Davis, Mark, Tucson*	0	2	.000	3.57	17	0	0	0	10	2	22.2	19	96	9	9	1	1	3	1	12	1	19	1	1
Davis, Tim, Tacoma*	1	0	1.000	3.60	1	1	0	0	0	0	5.0	4	22	2	2	0	1	0	1	3	0	5	0	0
DeJean, Mike, Col. Springs. .	0	1	.000	5.40	10	0	0	0	4	0	10.0	17	50	6	6	0	0	1	0	7	1	9	0	0

Pitcher, Team	W	L	Pct.	ERA	G	GS	CG	ShO	GF	Sv.	IP	H	TBF	R	ER	HR	SH	SF	HB	BB	IBB	SO	WP	Bk.
Drahman, Brian, Las Vegas .	2	1	.667	6.33	33	0	0	0	6	1	42.2	51	205	32	30	5	2	3	2	28	4	39	2	0
Dreifort, Darren, Albuquerque	0	0	.000	1.59	2	2	0	0	0	0	5.2	2	19	1	1	1	0	0	0	1	0	3	0	0
Dressendorfer, Kirk, Alb.. . . .	0	2	.000	4.50	7	7	0	0	0	0	30.0	43	141	18	15	5	1	3	1	10	0	14	1	0
Dreyer, Steve, Salt Lake	1	0	1.000	7.36	27	0	0	0	12	2	44.0	65	202	38	36	4	2	3	1	10	2	34	1	0
Dunbar, Matt, Edm.-Van.* . .	1	0	1.000	6.85	14	1	0	0	4	0	23.2	32	112	18	18	4	1	3	1	14	1	20	2	0
Duncan, Calvin, Salt Lake . . .	0	0	.000	7.94	5	1	0	0	1	0	11.1	17	55	13	10	1	0	1	0	3	0	16	6	1
Edsell, Geoff, Vancouver. . . .	14	11	.560	5.15	30	29	6	1	1	0	183.1	196	826	121	105	11	5	6	12	96	1	95	8	0
Ellis, Robert, Vancouver	9	10	.474	5.92	29	23	3	0	1	0	149.0	185	698	108	98	15	6	6	7	83	1	70	15	1
Elvira, Narciso, Albuquerque*	0	0	.000	16.88	4	0	0	0	0	0	2.2	5	17	6	5	2	0	0	0	3	0	4	1	0
Ericks, John, Calgary	0	0	.000	12.86	6	0	0	0	1	0	7.0	14	39	11	10	0	0	1	2	1	0	10	1	0
Farmer, Michael, Col. Springs*	5	5	.500	6.75	18	8	0	0	3	0	54.2	70	243	42	41	14	3	1	5	18	0	29	4	1
Felix, Lauro, Tucson	0	0	.000	27.00	1	0	0	0	1	0	1.0	4	8	3	3	1	0	0	0	1	0	1	0	0
Fernandez, Osvaldo, Phoenix	0	0	.000	3.00	2	2	0	0	0	0	12.0	10	47	5	4	1	1	2	0	3	1	4	1	0
Fetters, Mike, Tucson	0	0	.000	10.80	2	0	0	0	0	0	1.2	1	8	2	2	0	0	1	0	1	0	0	2	0
Fortugno, Tim, Vancouver*. .	4	2	.667	5.23	34	0	0	0	11	0	31.0	29	137	21	18	2	2	0	2	17	0	36	3	0
Foulke, Keith, Phoenix	5	4	.556	4.50	12	12	0	0	0	0	76.0	79	321	38	38	11	2	5	6	15	0	54	1	2
Franklin, Ryan, Tacoma	5	5	.500	4.18	14	14	0	0	0	0	90.1	97	386	48	42	11	7	2	8	24	1	59	1	1
Frey, Steve, Vancouver*	3	3	.500	5.01	31	1	0	0	10	4	41.1	45	183	23	23	6	3	0	1	21	1	28	0	0
Frontera, Chad, Phoenix	2	0	1.000	6.20	5	5	0	0	0	0	24.2	32	114	19	17	2	0	2	2	9	0	13	3	1
Gajkowski, Steve, Tacoma . .	5	3	.625	3.87	44	3	0	0	10	2	93.0	100	394	43	40	11	2	1	5	24	0	48	3	1
Gandarillas, Gus, Salt Lake . .	1	0	1.000	3.18	11	2	0	0	2	2	22.2	22	93	8	8	1	0	0	1	6	1	13	1	0
Garcia, Jose, Albuquerque . .	3	3	.500	5.12	33	0	0	0	13	0	45.2	57	203	27	26	5	3	1	3	14	2	44	6	0
Gardner, Scott, Tucson	1	0	1.000	3.00	1	1	0	0	0	0	6.0	6	26	2	2	0	0	1	0	3	0	6	0	0
Garrison, Webster, Edmonton	0	0	.000	0.00	2	0	0	0	2	0	1.1	1	6	0	0	0	0	0	0	1	0	1	0	0
Gohr, Greg, Vancouver	5	1	.833	3.80	8	7	0	0	0	0	47.1	51	202	23	20	3	0	3	1	14	0	27	3	0
Gonzales, Frank, Calgary* . .	1	0	1.000	7.26	25	0	0	0	11	1	31.0	43	143	25	25	5	1	4	1	9	2	24	0	1
Granger, Jeff, Calgary*	1	7	.125	5.55	30	12	0	0	7	1	82.2	111	387	63	51	7	3	1	3	33	5	68	6	0
Greer, Ken, Calgary	0	3	.000	8.46	15	0	0	0	4	0	22.1	33	107	22	21	7	2	2	1	7	1	16	1	0
Grimsley, Jason, Tucson. . . .	5	10	.333	5.70	36	10	0	0	18	4	85.1	96	397	70	54	6	2	3	4	43	2	65	20	0
Gross, Kevin, Vancouver . . .	1	0	1.000	1.64	2	2	0	0	0	0	11.0	7	38	2	2	1	0	0	0	0	0	5	0	0
Grott, Matt, Tucson*	3	1	.750	4.79	55	0	0	0	18	4	88.1	94	395	57	47	11	4	2	2	33	6	58	10	0
Gubanich, Creighton, Tucson	0	0	.000	13.50	2	0	0	0	2	0	2.0	5	11	3	3	0	0	0	0	0	0	0	0	0
Halperin, Mike, Calgary*. . . .	1	0	1.000	6.43	15	4	0	0	3	0	28.0	44	148	24	20	3	3	1	1	24	0	18	0	2
Hancock, Lee, Phoenix*	0	1	.000	6.10	7	0	0	0	1	0	10.1	23	53	7	7	0	0	0	0	4	0	9	0	0
Hancock, Ryan, Van.-L.V. . . .	3	3	.500	4.20	43	2	0	0	19	2	79.1	81	355	44	37	5	2	2	3	40	1	63	1	1
Hansell, Greg, Tucson	2	3	.400	4.64	40	9	0	0	13	2	87.1	99	378	52	45	15	1	2	6	27	2	76	4	0
Harikkala, Tim, Tacoma	6	8	.429	6.43	21	21	0	0	0	0	113.1	160	538	93	81	11	3	5	4	50	2	86	7	0
Harkey, Mike, Albuquerque . .	2	2	.500	2.10	47	0	0	0	33	15	55.2	50	222	14	13	4	2	3	2	11	1	57	0	0
Hartvigson, Chad, Phoenix* .	2	2	.500	5.37	17	4	0	0	4	0	53.2	63	238	34	32	4	1	1	2	17	0	52	2	1
Haught, Gary, Edmonton . . .	1	1	.500	3.59	30	2	0	0	21	11	42.2	37	174	20	17	7	0	1	5	13	1	35	1	1
Hawkins, LaTroy, Salt Lake . .	9	4	.692	5.45	14	13	2	1	1	0	76.0	100	346	53	46	4	2	2	4	16	1	53	8	1
Haynes, Jimmy, Edmonton . .	0	2	.000	4.85	5	5	0	0	0	0	29.2	36	135	22	16	4	2	0	1	11	0	24	4	0
Henderson, Ryan, Alb.-C.S. .	2	4	.333	8.90	19	1	0	0	6	0	30.1	40	154	32	30	3	3	0	2	23	4	29	1	0
Herges, Matt, Albuquerque . .	0	8	.000	8.89	31	12	0	0	5	0	85.0	120	417	92	84	13	5	4	9	46	1	61	5	0
Holdridge, David, Tacoma. . .	1	1	.500	2.96	15	0	0	0	8	1	24.1	21	105	9	8	0	1	1	1	13	0	24	0	0
Hollins, Stacy, Edmonton . . .	0	0	.000	10.13	1	1	0	0	0	0	2.2	5	17	4	3	0	0	0	0	3	0	2	0	0
Holzemer, Mark, Tacoma* . .	1	0	1.000	2.20	37	0	0	0	26	13	41.0	32	165	10	10	1	0	2	0	10	3	38	1	0
Hook, Chris, Las Vegas	0	7	.000	8.79	19	8	0	0	7	0	56.1	80	294	64	55	9	3	2	5	49	2	35	11	0
Hope, John, Col. Springs . . .	4	3	.571	7.22	43	9	0	0	5	0	99.2	115	473	85	80	15	2	1	11	65	1	67	12	0
Howitt, Dann, Col. Springs . .	0	0	.000	27.00	1	0	0	0	1	0	1.0	3	6	3	3	1	0	0	0	1	0	0	0	0
Hubbs, Dan, Albuquerque. . .	6	4	.600	3.90	62	3	0	0	19	3	94.2	103	411	45	41	11	4	5	4	38	2	87	2	0
Huber, Jeff, Tucson*	3	7	.300	4.74	40	2	0	0	15	5	62.2	67	274	36	33	11	6	2	1	22	1	37	3	0
Hurtado, Edwin, Tacoma. . . .	10	6	.625	3.88	20	20	5	3	0	0	132.1	139	567	60	57	9	2	5	3	37	1	100	7	0
Janicki, Pete, Vancouver. . . .	1	4	.200	7.80	42	0	0	0	19	1	47.1	48	232	43	41	9	2	3	1	44	4	43	6	0
Jimenez, Miguel, Edmonton .	0	2	.000	11.15	7	2	0	0	4	1	15.1	29	85	19	19	6	0	1	0	11	0	11	0	0
Johnson, Barry, Calgary	5	2	.714	4.13	34	1	0	0	12	1	56.2	55	247	30	26	7	1	3	1	23	2	51	3	0
Johnson, Dane, Edmonton . .	1	1	.500	5.63	14	0	0	0	11	6	16.0	17	72	11	10	1	1	0	0	8	1	13	0	0
Johnstone, John, Phoenix . .	0	3	.000	4.03	38	0	0	0	34	24	38.0	34	161	17	17	3	0	0	1	15	3	30	4	0
Jones, Bobby, Col. Springs*.	7	11	.389	5.14	25	21	0	0	2	0	133.0	135	593	89	76	16	1	5	12	71	2	104	2	0
Kaufman, Brad, Las Vegas . .	0	5	.000	8.07	6	6	0	0	0	0	32.1	40	151	37	29	9	0	1	1	15	0	19	1	0
Kellner, Frank, Tucson	0	0	.000	0.00	2	0	0	0	2	0	2.0	2	8	0	0	0	0	0	0	0	0	2	0	0
Kjos, Ryan, Edmonton	0	1	.000	36.00	1	0	0	0	1	0	2.0	6	15	8	8	2	0	0	0	3	0	2	1	0
Klingenbeck, Scott, Salt Lake	0	0	.000	1.29	1	1	0	0	0	0	7.0	6	26	1	1	1	0	0	0	0	0	6	0	0
Kramer, Tom, Col. Springs . .	3	2	.600	5.23	51	0	0	0	34	11	62.0	57	279	42	36	10	2	5	2	40	1	56	4	1
Kroon, Marc, Las Vegas	1	3	.250	4.54	46	0	0	0	33	15	41.2	34	175	22	21	5	2	2	3	22	0	53	6	0
Kubenka, Jeff, Albuquerque*	0	2	.000	8.59	8	0	0	0	6	2	7.1	11	37	9	7	2	0	0	0	2	0	10	3	0
Kubinski, Tim, Edmonton* . .	4	4	.500	4.50	47	0	0	0	17	7	76.0	64	315	39	38	8	6	1	1	34	4	53	7	2
Lawrence, Sean, Calgary* . .	8	9	.471	4.21	26	26	2	0	0	0	143.1	154	641	83	67	17	9	6	3	57	3	116	6	0
Lee, Mark, Col. Springs* . . .	1	2	.333	6.28	48	0	0	0	16	3	67.1	93	309	49	47	15	1	3	2	21	2	63	0	0
Legault, Kevin, Salt Lake . . .	1	3	.250	7.52	16	0	0	0	5	0	26.1	39	120	24	22	2	1	0	0	7	3	18	0	0
Leskanic, Curt, Col. Springs .	0	0	.000	3.79	10	3	0	0	6	2	19.0	11	81	9	8	1	0	0	0	18	0	20	1	0
Lewis, Richie, Edmonton . . .	1	1	.500	5.85	11	1	0	0	4	1	20.0	24	96	13	13	2	1	1	1	14	1	25	3	0
Linebarger, Keith, Salt Lake .	4	6	.400	6.63	41	7	0	0	17	5	97.2	135	468	79	72	10	4	2	4	42	4	59	5	0
Lira, Felipe, Tacoma	2	0	1.000	3.43	3	3	0	0	0	0	21.0	21	87	8	8	1	1	1	0	5	1	17	0	0
Long, Joey, Las Vegas*	0	0	.000	4.82	16	0	0	0	2	0	18.2	17	83	10	10	3	0	0	0	12	2	13	2	0
Looney, Brian, Salt Lake* . . .	0	2	.000	2.19	17	0	0	0	6	1	24.2	20	103	7	6	4	1	0	0	10	2	21	2	0
Lorraine, Andrew, Edmonton*	8	6	.571	4.74	23	20	2	2	2	0	117.2	143	520	72	62	12	3	7	2	34	1	75	3	0
Lott, Billy, Calgary	0	0	.000	13.50	2	0	0	0	2	0	1.1	4	8	2	2	0	0	1	0	0	0	1	0	0
Lowe, Derek, Tacoma	3	4	.429	3.45	10	9	1	0	0	0	57.1	53	242	26	22	3	0	1	2	20	0	49	1	0
Ludwick, Eric, Edmonton . . .	1	1	.500	3.32	6	3	0	0	0	0	19.0	22	84	7	7	1	1	1	1	4	0	20	2	0
Macey, Fausto, Vancouver . .	1	3	.250	8.10	9	8	0	0	0	0	40.0	47	197	39	36	9	1	2	3	32	1	23	4	1
Maddux, Mike, Tac.-L.V.	0	2	.000	4.29	4	4	0	0	0	0	21.0	24	95	11	10	0	1	2	1	11	1	18	0	0
Maloney, Sean, Tucson.	0	2	.000	4.82	15	0	0	0	10	5	18.2	24	82	10	10	3	5	0	0	3	3	21	1	0
Manzanillo, Josias, Tacoma .	0	0	.000	6.43	11	0	0	0	4	1	14.0	16	65	10	10	4	0	1	0	8	0	15	0	0
Manzanillo, Ravelo, Tacoma*	2	1	.667	6.52	18	0	0	0	11	1	29.0	34	138	22	21	2	1	0	2	22	2	25	2	2

Pitcher, Team	W	L	Pct.	ERA	G	GS	CG	ShO	GF	Sv.	IP	H	TBF	R	ER	HR	SH	SF	HB	BB	IBB	SO	WP	Bk.
Martinez, Jesus, Alb.*	7	1	.875	6.21	26	12	0	0	6	0	84.0	112	404	64	58	8	3	1	1	52	0	80	15	1
May, Darrell, Vancouver*	7	5	.583	3.26	13	12	2	2	0	0	80.0	65	330	31	29	10	2	4	1	31	0	62	0	1
McAndrew, Jamie, Tucson	7	8	.467	6.79	22	21	0	0	0	0	108.2	132	512	87	82	10	2	3	0	65	1	63	8	4
McCarthy, Greg, Tacoma*	2	1	.667	3.27	22	0	0	0	10	3	22.0	21	103	8	8	3	1	0	2	16	2	34	1	0
McCurry, Jeff, Col. Springs	1	1	.500	5.09	16	0	0	0	8	3	17.2	17	77	12	10	2	1	1	1	6	1	13	4	0
Medina, Rafael, Las Vegas	4	5	.444	7.56	13	13	0	0	0	0	66.2	90	321	60	56	12	1	1	2	39	1	50	8	2
Menhart, Paul, Tac.-L.V.	4	14	.222	6.06	26	21	1	0	2	1	127.2	154	579	92	86	18	9	4	6	55	2	95	6	2
Miller, Travis, Salt Lake*	10	6	.625	4.73	21	21	0	0	0	0	125.2	140	558	73	66	11	5	2	4	57	0	86	5	0
Minchey, Nate, Col. Springs	15	6	.714	4.51	27	21	3	0	0	0	157.2	172	678	87	79	17	5	3	6	53	1	107	4	0
Minor, Blas, Tucson	2	2	.500	4.03	12	3	0	0	4	1	29.0	36	137	21	13	3	1	0	2	15	1	21	2	0
Mintz, Steve, Las Vegas	5	2	.714	8.05	27	0	0	0	16	5	34.2	50	171	31	31	7	1	2	2	17	3	28	2	0
Misuraca, Mike, Tucson	8	7	.533	4.98	33	10	0	0	8	1	108.1	119	472	68	60	15	1	8	5	39	3	62	2	1
Molina, Izzy, Edmonton	0	0	.000	0.00	1	0	0	0	1	0	0.1	0	1	0	0	0	0	0	0	0	0	0	0	0
Montgomery, Steve, Edm.	2	1	.667	5.79	30	0	0	0	13	3	46.2	61	216	30	30	6	1	1	1	17	2	38	4	0
Montoya, Norm, Tucson*	6	10	.375	6.25	27	24	0	0	2	0	131.0	175	589	100	91	16	5	4	4	38	0	75	6	2
Moore, Joel, Col. Springs	3	1	.750	7.76	5	5	0	0	0	0	26.2	47	133	26	23	4	0	3	1	12	1	20	0	0
Morel, Ramon, Calgary	6	7	.462	5.75	27	18	0	0	3	0	101.2	131	466	71	65	13	3	2	4	42	1	72	4	2
Moyer, Jamie, Tacoma*	1	0	1.000	0.00	1	1	0	0	0	0	5.0	1	16	0	0	0	0	0	0	0	0	6	0	0
Munoz, Bobby, L.V.-Alb.	0	5	.000	6.71	35	1	0	0	12	0	53.2	73	253	43	40	4	0	3	0	26	3	33	2	0
Murray, Heath, Las Vegas*	6	8	.429	5.45	19	19	2	1	0	0	109.0	142	493	72	66	10	1	2	5	41	1	99	8	1
Naulty, Dan, Salt Lake	0	1	.000	11.37	6	0	0	0	2	0	6.1	11	34	10	8	4	1	0	0	2	0	5	2	0
Nichting, Chris, Edmonton	7	13	.350	7.76	33	24	3	0	3	1	131.0	170	602	120	113	21	0	7	3	46	2	90	8	1
Niedermaier, Brad, Salt Lake.	2	1	.667	5.88	16	0	0	0	5	0	26.0	29	118	22	17	7	2	0	0	13	2	20	1	0
Ohme, Kevin, Salt Lake*	2	5	.286	5.62	56	0	0	0	34	11	73.2	70	324	49	46	6	5	1	6	34	4	45	4	1
Oquist, Mike, Edmonton	6	1	.857	3.25	9	9	1	0	0	0	52.2	57	225	23	19	3	2	1	0	16	0	37	0	0
Ortiz, Russ, Phoenix	4	3	.571	5.51	14	14	0	0	0	0	85.0	96	376	57	52	11	2	3	2	34	0	70	3	1
Osuna, Antonio, Albuquerque	1	1	.500	1.93	13	0	0	0	12	6	14.0	9	55	3	3	0	0	0	0	4	0	26	1	0
Pace, Scotty, Tucson*	0	0	.000	1.59	2	0	0	0	1	0	5.2	6	25	2	1	0	0	0	0	4	0	2	1	0
Pacheco, Alexander, Tacoma.	0	2	.000	8.78	15	2	0	0	4	0	27.2	45	143	27	27	4	0	0	3	15	1	21	1	0
Parra, Jose, Salt Lake	2	8	.200	6.03	50	4	0	0	31	8	94.0	126	441	73	63	8	3	5	9	30	7	61	9	0
Perisho, Matt, Vancouver*	4	4	.500	5.33	9	9	1	0	0	0	52.1	68	254	42	31	3	3	2	3	29	1	47	5	3
Peters, Chris, Calgary*	2	4	.333	4.38	14	9	0	0	1	1	51.1	52	243	32	25	5	0	2	5	30	1	55	2	0
Peterson, Mark, Phoenix*	0	0	.000	7.36	3	0	0	0	1	0	3.2	6	21	4	3	0	0	0	1	1	0	2	0	0
Pett, Jose, Calgary	0	3	.000	9.64	3	3	0	0	0	0	14.0	25	74	15	15	4	0	0	0	8	0	8	0	0
Phillips, Randy, Phoenix	5	4	.556	3.04	21	3	0	0	4	0	47.1	44	198	20	16	5	2	0	2	18	2	27	2	0
Phillips, Tony, Tuc.-Edm.	4	2	.667	5.44	40	2	0	0	15	0	81.0	95	358	56	49	11	4	2	7	27	5	46	1	2
Pickett, Ricky, Phoenix*	3	3	.500	3.19	61	0	0	0	29	12	67.2	52	302	27	24	2	4	1	4	49	3	85	4	0
Price, Jamey, Edmonton	2	0	1.000	1.64	2	1	0	0	1	0	11.0	9	44	3	2	0	1	0	0	1	0	10	0	0
Prieto, Ariel, Edmonton	0	0	.000	1.50	2	2	0	0	0	0	6.0	4	22	1	1	0	0	0	0	1	0	7	1	0
Purdy, Shawn, Phoenix	10	3	.769	4.37	56	0	0	0	26	2	82.1	103	367	45	40	8	4	0	2	33	1	42	3	1
Pyc, Dave, Albuquerque*	12	12	.500	5.33	31	23	3	2	1	1	152.0	181	675	104	90	18	4	6	5	50	2	106	5	1
Quinlan, Tom, Col. Springs	0	0	.000	2.70	4	0	0	0	4	0	3.1	3	13	1	1	0	0	0	0	0	0	0	0	0
Rapp, Pat, Phoenix	2	0	1.000	3.60	3	3	0	0	0	0	15.0	16	69	6	6	2	0	0	1	9	0	6	0	0
Rath, Fred, Salt Lake	0	1	.000	1.64	10	0	0	0	9	3	11.0	11	46	2	2	1	0	0	0	2	0	11	0	0
Rath, Gary, Albuquerque*	7	11	.389	6.05	24	24	0	0	0	0	132.1	177	615	107	89	17	7	4	4	49	1	100	7	0
Redman, Mark, Salt Lake*	8	15	.348	6.31	29	28	0	0	1	1	158.1	204	739	123	111	19	3	6	4	80	3	125	12	2
Rekar, Bryan, Col. Springs	10	9	.526	5.46	28	25	0	0	0	0	145.0	169	636	96	88	21	1	3	10	39	2	116	7	0
Reyes, Alberto, Tucson	2	4	.333	5.02	38	0	0	0	17	7	57.1	52	262	39	32	12	4	3	7	34	2	70	1	0
Reyes, Carlos, Edmonton	2	0	1.000	3.48	5	4	1	0	0	0	31.0	30	123	14	12	2	0	2	0	3	1	23	0	0
Reyes, Dennis, Albuquerque*	6	3	.667	5.65	10	10	1	0	0	0	57.1	70	271	40	36	4	1	5	1	33	0	45	5	0
Ricci, Chuck, Edmonton	0	0	.000	16.88	4	0	0	0	3	0	5.1	10	33	10	10	3	1	1	1	6	0	5	4	0
Rigby, Brad, Edmonton	8	4	.667	4.37	15	15	0	0	0	0	82.1	95	370	49	40	10	3	3	3	26	4	49	5	0
Roa, Joe, Phoenix	3	1	.750	4.75	6	5	0	0	0	0	36.0	43	158	21	19	4	1	0	1	11	0	16	0	0
Roach, Petie, Albuquerque*	0	5	.000	5.29	31	0	0	0	6	1	49.1	56	232	31	29	6	3	4	6	27	3	33	8	0
Roberson, Sid, Tucson*	0	2	.000	11.45	10	4	0	0	4	0	22.0	47	129	29	28	5	0	2	4	14	3	8	1	0
Roberts, Brett, Salt Lake	1	3	.250	6.90	24	6	0	0	7	1	58.2	89	286	51	45	11	0	2	2	33	0	33	4	0
Rodriguez, Frankie, Tucson	3	1	.750	4.40	12	6	1	1	1	0	47.0	53	204	25	23	1	2	1	2	19	1	41	1	0
Rohrmeier, Dan, Tacoma	0	0	.000	0.00	1	0	0	0	1	0	1.0	2	5	1	0	0	0	0	0	0	0	0	0	0
Ruffin, Bruce, Col. Springs*	0	0	.000	3.38	2	0	.0	0	1	0	2.2	1	9	1	1	1	0	0	0	0	0	2	0	0
Sadler, Al, Tucson	1	0	1.000	1.50	1	1	0	0	0	0	6.0	7	28	1	1	0	0	0	0	4	0	1	2	0
Saipe, Mike, Col. Springs	4	3	.571	5.52	10	10	1	0	0	0	60.1	74	278	42	37	10	1	0	4	24	3	40	2	3
Scanlan, Bob, Las Vegas	3	1	.750	3.53	36	1	0	0	11	1	51.0	51	218	24	20	4	1	0	6	17	1	20	1	0
Schmidt, Curt, Calgary	2	3	.400	4.26	25	0	0	0	17	7	31.2	43	152	19	15	3	1	0	3	14	4	30	1	0
Schmidt, Jeff, Vancouver	1	2	.333	5.32	27	0	0	0	16	10	22.0	22	104	14	13	2	0	1	0	20	2	14	6	0
Schmitt, Todd, Las Vegas	5	2	.714	5.03	48	0	0	0	27	4	53.2	55	254	34	30	7	4	2	6	38	4	59	2	1
Scott, Tim, Col. Springs	0	0	.000	1.23	12	0	0	0	9	3	14.2	7	52	2	2	1	1	1	0	3	0	18	1	1
Seitzer, Brad, Tucson	0	0	.000	0.00	1	0	0	0	1	0	1.0	1	5	0	0	0	0	0	0	1	0	0	0	0
Serafini, Dan, Salt Lake*	9	7	.563	4.97	28	24	2	0	1	0	152.0	166	660	87	84	18	4	3	8	55	0	118	3	0
Shaw, Curtis, Calgary*	0	3	.000	5.23	21	0	0	0	8	2	31.0	31	147	26	18	0	2	1	2	18	1	23	2	1
Shepherd, Keith, Calgary	0	1	.000	7.64	10	1	0	0	4	0	17.2	23	88	16	15	1	1	0	1	14	3	16	1	0
Shoemaker, Stephen, C.S. . 1	1	.500	8.41	5	4	0	0	0	0	20.1	23	101	19	19		5	0	1	3	17	0	27	1	0
Silva, Jose, Calgary	5	1	.833	3.41	17	11	0	0	1	0	66.0	74	288	27	25	3	3	1	3	22	0	54	2	1
Skuse, Nick, Vancouver	0	0	.000	0.00	1	0	0	0	1	0	1.0	0	3	0	0	0	0	0	0	0	0	2	0	0
Small, Aaron, Edmonton	1	0	1.000	0.00	1	1	0	0	0	0	5.0	1	16	0	0	0	0	0	0	0	0	4	0	0
Smith, Pete, Las Vegas	3	2	.600	4.28	6	6	0	0	0	0	33.2	38	138	16	16	5	2	0	0	6	0	24	0	1
Smith, Ryan, Tacoma	1	0	1.000	0.00	1	1	0	0	0	0	5.0	4	17	0	0	0	0	0	0	1	0	2	0	0
Soderstrom, Steve, Phoenix	4	8	.333	6.47	31	15	0	0	8	1	105.2	141	498	81	76	12	2	2	6	52	1	78	10	1
Sodowsky, Clint, Calgary	0	1	.000	6.59	8	0	0	0	1	1	13.2	19	64	10	10	1	0	0	0	6	0	9	1	0
Spencer, Stan, Las Vegas	3	2	.600	3.75	8	8	0	0	0	0	48.0	48	208	23	20	5	1	0	1	18	2	47	1	0
Springer, Dennis, Vancouver.	1	1	.500	3.00	2	2	2	0	0	0	15.0	12	63	6	5	1	0	0	1	6	0	7	0	0
Steed, Dave, Albuquerque	0	0	.000	0.00	1	0	0	0	1	0	1.0	1	3	0	0	0	0	0	0	0	0	1	0	0
Stevens, Dave, Salt Lake	9	3	.750	4.30	16	14	1	0	0	0	90.0	93	395	52	43	10	1	2	4	31	0	71	4	1
Stidham, Phil, Col. Springs	5	2	.714	9.91	26	0	0	0	10	0	36.1	55	182	43	40	8	2	2	1	26	2	20	7	0
Suzuki, Mac, Tacoma	4	9	.308	5.94	32	10	0	0	7	0	83.1	79	384	60	55	13	2	1	0	64	1	63	6	1
Swift, Billy, Col. Springs	0	1	.000	12.00	1	1	0	0	0	0	3.0	4	16	4	4	1	0	0	0	3	0	4	0	0

Pitcher, Team	W	L	Pct.	ERA	G	GS	CG	ShO	GF	Sv.	IP	H	TBF	R	ER	HR	SH	SF	HB	BB	IBB	SO	WP	Bk.
Taulbee, Andy, Phoenix. . . .	2	2	.500	7.52	19	6	0	0	5	0	40.2	64	195	41	34	4	4	0	0	14	0	20	0	0
Taylor, Kerry, Las Vegas . .	7	9	.438	4.31	22	22	3	0	0	0	144.0	150	628	84	69	15	8	8	11	55	3	103	4	0
Taylor, Scott, L.V.-Cal.	5	4	.556	2.59	42	0	0	0	13	4	76.1	69	311	29	22	6	2	1	3	19	4	53	2	1
Thompson, Mark, Col. Springs	0	0	.000	12.00	1	1	0	0	0	0	3.0	6	14	4	4	1	0	0	0	1	0	1	0	0
Thomson, John, Col. Springs	4	2	.667	3.43	7	7	0	0	0	0	42.0	36	169	18	16	4	1	0	0	14	1	49	2	0
Thurston, Jerrey, Vancouver .	0	0	.000	45.00	1	0	0	0	1	0	1.0	4	8	5	5	2	0	0	0	1	0	0	0	0
Tolentino, Jose, Calgary* . . .	0	0	.000	36.00	1	0	0	0	1	0	1.0	6	9	4	4	0	0	0	0	0	0	0	0	0
Treadwell, Jody, Albuquerque	10	5	.667	5.12	27	21	2	0	2	1	128.1	143	575	80	73	16	4	2	4	54	2	108	3	0
Tyler, Josh, Tucson.	0	0	.000	0.00	1	0	0	0	1	0	1.0	0	3	0	0	0	0	0	0	0	0	0	0	0
Vanderweele, Doug, Phoenix	6	4	.600	4.59	36	2	0	0	8	1	68.2	99	313	38	35	6	2	3	5	18	2	35	3	0
VanEgmond, Tim, Tucson. . .	1	0	1.000	9.00	1	0	0	0	0	0	1.0	3	6	1	1	0	0	0	0	0	0	0	0	0
VanLandingham, William, Pho.	1	1	.500	9.00	4	4	0	0	0	0	17.0	20	92	19	17	2	2	3	0	21	0	7	4	1
Veras, Dario, Las Vegas	0	2	.000	5.02	12	0	0	0	5	2	14.1	14	59	8	8	1	0	0	0	6	0	13	3	0
Villano, Mike, Phoenix	5	3	.625	4.16	13	11	0	0	1	0	71.1	75	309	36	33	7	3	2	2	27	1	41	2	0
Wainhouse, David, Calgary. .	2	0	1.000	5.92	25	0	0	0	9	1	38.0	46	174	25	25	5	1	1	3	13	2	24	3	0
Ware, Jeff, Tucson	5	8	.385	6.71	25	21	0	0	1	0	106.0	127	513	98	79	16	4	5	2	80	1	69	6	0
Washburn, Jarrod, Vancouver*	0	0	.000	3.60	1	1	0	0	0	0	5.0	4	21	2	2	0	0	0	2	0	6	2	0
Weaver, Eric, Albuquerque . .	3	0	.000	6.42	21	8	0	0	5	0	68.2	101	335	53	49	6	3	4	2	38	1	54	4	0
Williams, Shad, Vancouver. .	6	2	.750	3.82	40	10	0	0	7	1	99.0	98	424	52	42	13	0	4	5	41	2	52	5	0
Wilson, Gary, Calgary.	6	3	.667	5.87	21	11	0	0	2	0	84.1	115	387	59	55	10	4	3	5	22	1	54	1	0
Witasick, Jay, Edmonton . . .	3	2	.600	4.28	13	1	0	0	4	0	27.1	25	121	13	13	3	1	2	0	15	3	17	2	0
Witte, Trey, Tacoma	5	1	.833	5.29	32	4	0	0	7	0	66.1	82	304	49	39	14	7	3	4	26	0	52	1	0
Wojciechowski, Steve, Edm.*	8	2	.800	3.84	26	7	0	0	3	1	65.2	68	286	33	28	6	1	1	2	23	1	49	2	1
Wolcott, Bob, Tacoma	1	3	.250	5.11	7	7	0	0	0	0	37.0	40	157	23	21	4	4	2	3	7	0	29	0	2
Woodard, Steve, Tucson. . . .	1	0	1.000	0.00	1	1	0	0	0	0	7.0	3	26	0	0	0	0	0	1	1	0	6	1	0
Wright, Jamey, Col. Springs .	1	0	1.000	1.64	2	2	0	0	0	0	11.0	9	44	3	2	1	0	0	5	0	11	0	0
Zancanaro, Dave, Las Vegas*	0	3	.000	15.53	3	3	0	0	0	0	13.1	27	77	24	23	3	0	0	2	8	0	9	0	0

COMBINATION SHUTOUTS: **Albuquerque (3)**—Rath-Ahearne-Osuna, Hubbs-Treadwell-Ahearne, Reyes-Brown-Harkey-Hubbs. **Calgary (1)**—Peters-Taylor. **Colorado Springs (1)**—Bourgeois-Lee-Kramer. **Edmonton (5)**—Haught-Nichting-Kubinski, Rigby-Acre-Haught, Lorraine-Acre, Boever-Acre, Nichting-Acre. **Las Vegas (2)**—Bruske-Drahman-Baron-Schmitt, Castillo-Schmitt. **Phoenix (2)**—Carlson-Vanderweele, Creek-Pickett. **Salt Lake (3)**—Miller-Linebarger, Stevens-Dreyer, Redman-Roberts-Ohme. **Tacoma (5)**—Moyer-Suzuki-Holzemer-Crow, Smith-Holzemer, Hurtado-Manzanillo, Suzuki-Gajkowski-Holzemer, Gajkowski-Suzuki-Holdridge. **Tucson (3)**—Ware-Huber-Roberson, Bones-Grott, Montoya-Huber-Hansell. **Vancouver (3)**—Gohr-Buckley, Ellis-Buckley, Bovee-Fortugno-Chavez.

NO-HIT GAMES: May, Vancouver, defeated Salt Lake, 4-0 (second game), June 27.

PITCHERS WITH TWO OR MORE TEAMS

Pitcher, Team	W	L	Pct.	ERA	G	GS	CG	ShO	GF	Sv.	IP	H	TBF	R	ER	HR	SH	SF	HB	BB	IBB	SO	WP	Bk.
Berumen, Andres, Las Vegas . .	2	0	1.000	5.45	18	1	0	0	2	0	33.0	49	164	26	20	2	0	1	16	1	35	6	0
Berumen, Andres, Tacoma	7	4	.636	4.69	16	15	0	0	0	0	80.2	78	363	45	42	11	2	1	6	48	0	79	7	2
Boever, Joe, Calgary	4	5	.444	5.01	36	0	0	0	31	8	46.2	59	217	28	26	5	1	2	0	19	3	55	2	0
Boever, Joe, Edmonton	6	3	.667	4.96	17	3	0	0	5	1	45.1	53	191	26	25	8	0	5	0	4	0	26	0	0
Bolton, Tom, Calgary*	6	2	.250	8.29	8	8	0	0	0	0	38.0	67	188	38	35	6	3	1	3	12	1	29	0	0
Bolton, Tom, Tucson*	3	4	.429	6.00	15	7	0	0	1	0	57.0	75	255	42	38	5	2	0	20	1	42	4	0
Burrows, Terry, Las Vegas* . . .	1	5	.167	6.42	31	1	0	0	10	2	33.2	44	160	24	24	3	1	0	1	19	3	26	1	1
Burrows, Terry, Edmonton*	2	2	.500	5.67	13	0	0	0	3	0	27.0	35	127	18	17	2	1	2	0	15	2	24	2	0
Daspit, Jamie, Las Vegas	0	1	.000	7.20	10	2	0	0	0	0	20.0	22	88	17	16	5	1	0	7	2	12	4	0
Daspit, Jamie, Edmonton	0	1	.000	5.87	3	0	0	0	0	0	7.2	9	31	5	5	1	0	0	2	1	2	0	0
Dunbar, Matt, Edmonton*	1	0	1.000	4.98	12	1	0	0	3	0	21.2	29	98	12	12	2	1	3	1	8	1	18	0	0
Dunbar, Matt, Vancouver*	0	0	.000	27.00	2	0	0	0	1	0	2.0	3	14	6	6	2	0	0	6	0	2	2	0
Hancock, Ryan, Vancouver	3	3	.500	3.63	39	2	0	0	18	2	74.1	72	330	37	30	4	2	1	3	36	1	60	1	1
Hancock, Ryan, Las Vegas	0	0	.000	12.60	4	0	0	0	1	0	5.0	9	25	7	7	1	0	1	0	4	0	3	0	0
Henderson, Ryan, Alb.	1	3	.250	6.23	13	0	0	0	4	0	17.1	20	87	14	12	0	3	0	1	14	3	17	1	0
Henderson, Ryan, Col. Springs	1	1	.500	12.46	6	1	0	0	2	0	13.0	20	67	18	18	3	0	0	1	9	1	12	0	0
Maddux, Mike, Tacoma	0	0	.000	0.00	1	1	0	0	0	0	5.0	1	18	0	0	0	0	1	2	0	5	0	0
Maddux, Mike, Las Vegas	0	2	.000	5.63	3	3	0	0	0	0	16.0	23	77	11	10	0	1	2	0	9	1	13	0	0
Menhart, Paul, Tacoma	4	7	.364	6.16	15	10	0	0	2	1	61.1	76	285	46	42	11	2	1	4	34	1	51	4	1
Menhart, Paul, Las Vegas	0	7	.000	5.97	11	11	1	0	0	0	66.1	78	294	46	44	7	7	3	2	21	1	44	2	1
Munoz, Bobby, Las Vegas	0	2	.000	9.93	17	1	0	0	6	0	22.2	30	108	26	25	2	0	2	0	11	0	13	1	0
Munoz, Bobby, Albuquerque	0	3	.000	4.35	18	0	0	0	6	0	31.0	43	145	17	15	2	0	1	0	15	3	20	1	0
Phillips, Tony, Tucson	3	2	.600	5.59	29	1	0	0	10	0	58.0	67	258	43	36	9	4	2	3	21	5	32	1	1
Phillips, Tony, Edmonton	1	0	1.000	5.09	11	1	0	0	6	0	23.0	28	100	13	13	2	0	0	4	6	0	14	0	1
Taylor, Scott, Las Vegas	0	0	.000	18.00	2	0	0	0	0	0	1.0	4	9	2	2	0	0	1	1	0	1	0	0
Taylor, Scott, Calgary	5	4	.556	2.39	40	0	0	0	13	4	75.1	65	302	27	20	6	2	0	2	18	4	52	2	1

1997 FIELDING

TEAM

Team	Pct.	G	PO	A	E	TC	DP	PB	Team	Pct.	G	PO	A	E	TC	DP	PB
Tacoma	.978	141	3634	1402	114	5150	145	19	Salt Lake	.972	143	3753	1632	156	5541	163	7
Phoenix	.977	143	3725	1490	121	5336	156	4	Albuquerque	.969	141	3663	1578	167	5408	144	17
Col. Springs . . .	.977	140	3609	1468	118	5195	158	12	Calgary	.968	138	3521	1495	165	5181	132	17
Edmonton	.977	144	3579	1401	119	5099	132	17	Tucson	.967	142	3688	1653	183	5524	157	18
Las Vegas	.973	141	3690	1552	145	5387	139	22	TRIPLE PLAY: Tucson.								
Vancouver	.973	143	3711	1407	144	5262	129	18									

FIRST BASEMEN

NOTE: All caps denotes fielding-percentage leader based on 72 games for catchers, 96 for all other non-pitchers and 144 innings for pitchers. *Throws lefthanded.

Player, Team	Pct.	G	PO	A	E	TC	DP
Anthony, Eric, Albuquerque*	1.000	1	1	0	0	1	0
Ball, Jeff, Phoenix	.963	3	20	6	1	27	2
Battle, Howard, Albuquerque	1.000	1	6	0	0	6	3
Blanco, Henry, Albuquerque	1.000	7	39	4	0	43	5
Bolick, Frank, Vancouver	.996	29	208	15	1	224	22
Bonnici, Jim, Tacoma	.889	1	8	0	1	9	0
Boston, D.J., Col. Springs*	1.000	1	3	1	0	4	0
Brede, Brent, Salt Lake*	.990	39	374	25	4	403	50
Brown, Ray, Las Vegas	1.000	12	92	3	0	95	9
Caceres, Edgar, Vancouver	1.000	1	5	2	0	7	1
Cholowsky, Dan, Col. Springs	1.000	2	10	0	0	10	0
Cox, Steve, Edmonton*	.991	128	1043	70	10	1123	104
Decker, Steve, Tacoma	1.000	9	76	7	0	83	9
Echevarria, Angel, Col. Springs	1.000	4	29	3	0	32	1
Ferguson, Jeff, Salt Lake	1.000	1	1	0	0	1	0
Garrison, Webster, Edmonton	1.000	12	85	3	0	88	6
Gonzales, Rene, Col. Springs	.973	22	167	13	5	185	23
Greene, Todd, Vancouver	1.000	3	15	1	0	16	1
Gubanich, Creighton, Tucson	1.000	2	14	1	0	15	2
Hale, Chip, Albuquerque	.995	49	379	32	2	413	40
Helton, Todd, Col. Springs*	.986	78	585	61	9	655	78
Howitt, Dann, Col. Springs	.990	25	179	17	2	198	23
Johnson, Mark, Calgary*	1.000	22	181	25	0	206	14
Joyner, Wally, Las Vegas*	1.000	3	16	1	0	17	0
Kellner, Frank, Tucson	.991	13	107	7	1	115	11
Konerko, Paul, Albuquerque	.982	29	206	15	4	225	17
LEE, Derrek, Las Vegas	.992	124	1069	111	9	1189	108
Lee, Travis, Tucson*	.995	39	379	32	2	413	33
Lesher, Brian, Edmonton*	1.000	7	35	0	0	35	4
Marrero, Oreste, Albuquerque*	.986	32	195	18	3	216	24
Maurer, Ron, Albuquerque	1.000	16	100	5	0	105	8
McCarty, Dave, Phoenix*	.995	75	561	53	3	617	71
Morales, Willie, Edmonton	1.000	3	25	1	0	26	4
Murray, Eddie, Albuquerque	.966	7	56	1	2	59	7
Norton, Chris, Vancouver	1.000	1	6	0	0	6	2
Ogden, Jamie, Salt Lake*	.995	23	195	10	1	206	27
Ortiz, David, Salt Lake*	1.000	8	71	2	0	73	7
Parker, Rick, Albuquerque	1.000	1	5	0	0	5	0
Pritchett, Chris, Vancouver	.991	79	607	51	6	664	62
Reimer, Kevin, Tacoma	.990	15	97	4	1	102	13
Rivera, Ruben, Las Vegas	1.000	1	1	0	0	1	0
Rohrmeier, Dan, Tacoma	.991	40	315	27	3	345	39
Romero, Mandy, Las Vegas	1.000	4	32	1	0	33	5
Rupp, Chad, Salt Lake	.995	63	563	33	3	599	58
Scarsone, Steve, Las Vegas	1.000	4	30	2	0	32	1
Sealy, Scot, Tacoma	1.000	8	57	4	0	61	8
Secrist, Reed, Calgary	.980	8	44	4	1	49	3
Seitzer, Brad, Tucson	1.000	23	208	24	0	232	28
Shave, Jon, Salt Lake	.988	10	77	7	1	85	5
Stahoviak, Scott, Salt Lake	1.000	7	72	7	0	79	5
Stinnett, Kelly, Tucson	1.000	1	1	0	0	1	0
Tatum, Jim, Las Vegas	.960	4	22	2	1	25	3
Thobe, Steve, Calgary	.960	2	22	2	1	25	3
Tolentino, Jose, Calgary*	.991	40	311	16	3	330	31
Torres, Paul, Tacoma	1.000	1	9	0	0	9	2
Turner, Chris, Vancouver	.991	23	203	11	2	216	15
Vanderwal, John, Col. Springs*	.976	18	153	10	4	167	16
Voigt, Jack, Tucson	.982	9	51	5	1	57	8
Wachter, Derek, Tucson	1.000	3	24	4	0	28	3
Ward, Turner, Calgary	1.000	2	5	1	0	6	0
White, Derrick, Vancouver	1.000	11	70	7	0	77	8
Wilkins, Rick, Tacoma	1.000	1	7	0	0	7	1
Williams, Eddie, Albuquerque	.996	31	232	15	1	248	25
Williamson, Antone, Tucson	.985	63	543	40	9	592	52
Wilson, Desi, Phoenix*	.991	75	592	43	6	641	74
Wolff, Mike, Vancouver	.980	8	44	6	1	51	6
Wright, Ron, Calgary	.995	78	610	44	3	657	67
Zinter, Alan, Tacoma	.990	72	565	48	6	619	61

TRIPLE PLAY: T. Lee.

SECOND BASEMEN

Player, Team	Pct.	G	PO	A	E	TC	DP
Ball, Jeff, Phoenix	.857	2	3	3	1	7	0
Bates, Jason, Col. Springs	.980	10	19	30	1	50	10
Beasley, Tony, Calgary	.960	57	105	158	11	274	37
Bellhorn, Mark, Edmonton	.970	42	74	118	6	198	24
Belliard, Ronnie, Tucson	.961	114	229	358	24	611	92
Betten, Randy, Vancouver	.940	11	24	23	3	50	5
Bolick, Frank, Vancouver	1.000	2	5	2	0	7	0
Bridges, Kary, Calgary	.985	16	32	33	1	66	8
Bush, Homer, Las Vegas	.978	36	73	103	4	180	25
Caceres, Edgar, Vancouver	.982	55	100	123	4	227	31
Canizaro, Jay, Phoenix	.969	15	25	37	2	64	7
Castellano, Pedro, Salt Lake	1.000	1	1	0	0	1	0
Castro, Jose, Edmonton	.923	2	3	9	1	13	1
Castro, Juan, Albuquerque	1.000	3	6	13	0	19	2
Collier, Lou, Calgary	.931	27	59	63	9	131	15
Counsell, Craig, Col. Springs	.980	90	204	239	9	452	69
Cromer, Brandon, Calgary	.978	28	51	85	3	139	13
Cruz, Fausto, Vancouver	.962	81	180	199	15	394	50
Delgado, Wilson, Phoenix	1.000	5	11	15	0	26	3
Demetral, Chris, Albuquerque	1.000	7	14	26	0	40	7
Diaz, Eddy, Tucson	.933	6	3	11	1	15	2
Eenhoorn, Robert, Vancouver	1.000	4	4	9	0	13	0
Espinoza, Alvaro, Tacoma	1.000	2	3	4	0	7	1
Felix, Lauro, Tucson	.929	12	21	31	4	56	8
Ferguson, Jeff, Salt Lake	.958	56	92	183	12	287	45
FLOREZ, Tim, Phoenix	.982	105	189	313	9	511	92
Fonville, Chad, Albuquerque	.963	30	53	77	5	135	17
Garrison, Webster, Edmonton	.988	58	105	132	3	240	35
Gates, Brent, Tacoma	.889	4	4	4	1	9	0
Gipson, Charles, Tacoma	.750	1	1	2	1	4	1
Gonzales, Rene, Col. Springs	.961	34	58	114	7	179	22
Guerrero, Wilton, Albuquerque	.952	4	8	12	1	21	2
Guevara, Giomar, Tacoma	.959	42	86	102	8	196	27
Hajek, Dave, Las Vegas	.989	39	64	121	2	187	24
Hale, Chip, Albuquerque	.990	27	40	56	1	97	21
Hall, Billy, Col. Springs	.920	6	10	13	2	25	3
Hazlett, Steve, Calgary	.938	6	11	19	2	32	2
Huson, Jeff, Col. Springs	1.000	3	2	4	0	6	2
Keefe, Jamie, Las Vegas	.882	6	3	12	2	17	2
Kellner, Frank, Tucson	.967	10	14	15	1	30	2
Konerko, Paul, Albuquerque	1.000	1	3	3	0	6	1
Martinez, Ramon, Phoenix	.957	14	25	41	3	69	11
Martins, Eric, Edmonton	.959	19	29	42	3	74	8
Maurer, Ron, Albuquerque	.991	26	47	59	1	107	13
Millette, Joe, Tacoma	1.000	7	8	17	0	25	4
Parker, Rick, Albuquerque	.862	8	8	17	4	29	2
Raabe, Brian, Tacoma	.988	92	163	248	5	416	62
Riggs, Adam, Albuquerque	.973	56	129	162	8	299	35
Sanford, Chance, Calgary	.985	15	28	38	1	67	10
Scarsone, Steve, Las Vegas	.990	42	70	131	2	203	22
Seitzer, Brad, Tucson	.833	2	3	2	1	6	1
Shave, Jon, Salt Lake	.986	16	26	42	1	69	9
Sheets, Andy, Tacoma	1.000	4	4	11	0	15	3
Sheldon, Scott, Edmonton	.992	31	43	85	1	129	21
Shipley, Craig, Las Vegas	1.000	1	2	1	0	3	0
Shumpert, Terry, L.V.-C.S.	.926	12	18	32	4	54	6
Simons, Mitch, Salt Lake	.986	75	168	242	6	416	69
Torres, Paul, Tacoma	.939	23	39	54	6	99	14
Tredaway, Chad, Las Vegas	1.000	8	12	11	0	23	5
Unroe, Tim, Tucson	.923	6	8	16	2	26	5
Vina, Fernando, Tucson	1.000	1	0	1	0	1	0
Voigt, Jack, Tucson	1.000	2	5	4	0	9	1
Williams, Reggie, Vancouver	.952	16	33	27	3	63	7
Zosky, Eddie, Phoenix							

TRIPLE PLAY: Belliard.

SECOND BASEMEN WITH TWO OR MORE TEAMS

Player, Team	Pct.	G	PO	A	E	TC	DP
Shumpert, Terry, Las Vegas	.925	9	15	22	3	40	4
Shumpert, Terry, Col. Springs	.929	3	3	10	1	14	2

THIRD BASEMEN

Player, Team	Pct.	G	PO	A	E	TC	DP
Arias, George, Van.-L.V.	.952	108	99	218	16	333	23
Ball, Jeff, Phoenix	.938	107	46	166	14	226	13
Battle, Howard, Albuquerque	.892	33	23	51	9	83	3
Bellhorn, Mark, Edmonton	1.000	5	1	9	0	10	1
Bolick, Frank, Vancouver	1.000	24	12	53	0	65	6
Bridges, Kary, Calgary	.857	2	1	5	1	7	2
Burke, Jamie, Vancouver	.875	3	1	6	1	8	1

Player, Team	Pct.	G	PO	A	E	TC	DP
Caceres, Edgar, Vancouver	.920	19	15	31	4	50	4
Canizaro, Jay, Phoenix	1.000	6	7	9	0	16	1
Castellano, Pedro, Salt Lake ...	.981	38	22	80	2	104	6
Cholowsky, Dan, Col. Springs ..	1.000	1	1	1	0	2	0
Cromer, Brandon, Calgary	.857	5	1	5	1	7	0
Decker, Steve, Tacoma	.921	24	18	40	5	63	2
Diaz, Eddy, Tucson	.948	69	31	153	10	194	17
Espinoza, Alvaro, Tacoma	1.000	1	1	0	0	1	0
Felix, Lauro, Tucson	1.000	4	1	6	0	7	0
Ferguson, Jeff, Salt Lake......	.750	5	1	8	3	12	3
Florez, Tim, Phoenix	.778	3	1	6	2	9	1
Garcia, Freddy, Calgary	.855	33	18	53	12	83	1
Garrison, Webster, Edmonton ..	.933	23	16	40	4	60	1
Gipson, Charles, Tacoma......	.917	7	8	14	2	24	2
Gonzales, Rene, L.V.-C.S.	.911	21	6	35	4	45	3
Hale, Chip, Albuquerque	1.000	7	4	11	0	15	3
Haney, Todd, Tacoma	1.000	2	4	5	0	9	1
Hughes, Bobby, Tucson.......	1.000	1	0	3	0	3	0
Huson, Jeff, Col. Springs	1.000	4	3	4	0	7	0
Kellner, Frank, Tucson........	.938	12	7	23	2	32	5
Kennedy, Darryl, Phoenix	1.000	2	2	2	0	4	0
Konerko, Paul, Albuquerque ...	.925	105	48	198	20	266	21
Maurer, Ron, Albuquerque	1.000	9	4	17	0	21	1
Millette, Joe, Tacoma	.949	19	5	32	2	39	4
Morales, Willie, Edmonton	1.000	5	3	5	0	8	1
Parker, Rick, Albuquerque.....	1.000	1	1	0	0	1	0
QUINLAN, Tom, Col. Springs...	.960	131	91	269	15	375	30
Raabe, Brian, Tacoma........	.976	46	28	92	3	123	14
Randa, Joe, Calgary	.900	3	2	7	1	10	1
Riggs, Adam, Albuquerque	1.000	1	1	0	0	1	0
Romero, Mandy, Las Vegas....	.667	5	1	1	1	3	0
Rupp, Chad, Salt Lake........	.826	7	5	14	4	23	2
Sanford, Chance, Calgary	.924	70	38	132	14	184	11
Scarsone, Steve, Las Vegas ...	.873	24	9	39	7	55	4
Secrist, Reed, Calgary........	.889	13	9	23	4	36	2
Seitzer, Brad, Tucson	.932	24	15	53	5	73	4
Shave, Jon, Salt Lake	.946	22	14	56	4	74	5
Sheets, Andy, Tacoma........	1.000	2	0	5	0	5	1
Shipley, Craig, Las Vegas	1.000	1	0	1	0	1	0
Shumpert, Terry, L.V.-C.S.	.969	15	9	22	1	32	2
Tatum, Jim, Las Vegas	1.000	8	7	9	0	16	0
Thobe, Steve, Calgary	.859	23	19	42	10	71	8
Torres, Paul, Tacoma	.926	47	21	66	7	94	3
Tredaway, Chad, Las Vegas....	.924	89	66	141	17	224	26
Unroe, Tim, Tucson..........	.931	35	20	75	7	102	9
Voigt, Jack, Tucson..........	.667	6	0	2	1	3	0
Walker, Todd, Salt Lake	.901	74	44	174	24	242	20
Williamson, Antone, Tucson ...	.848	13	7	21	5	33	1
Wood, Jason, Edmonton	.954	117	88	222	15	325	30
Zinter, Alan, Tacoma	.875	8	1	20	3	24	1
Zosky, Eddie, Phoenix	.953	42	16	65	4	85	13

TRIPLE PLAY: Diaz.

THIRD BASEMEN WITH TWO OR MORE TEAMS

Player, Team	Pct.	G	PO	A	E	TC	DP
Arias, George, Vancouver	.955	99	93	203	14	310	22
Arias, George, Las Vegas	.913	9	6	15	2	23	1
Gonzales, Rene, Las Vegas	.935	12	4	25	2	31	2
Gonzales, Rene, Col. Springs ..	.857	9	2	10	2	14	1
Shumpert, Terry, Las Vegas ...	1.000	14	9	21	0	30	2
Shumpert, Terry, Col. Springs ..	.500	1	0	1	1	2	0

SHORTSTOPS

Player, Team	Pct.	G	PO	A	E	TC	DP
Arias, George, Vancouver	1.000	3	3	10	0	13	2
Aurilia, Rich, Phoenix	1.000	8	14	22	0	36	8
Baez, Kevin, Salt Lake........	.957	109	164	345	23	532	74
Bates, Jason, Col. Springs	.955	25	41	65	5	111	20
Batista, Tony, Edmonton	.952	32	40	78	6	124	16
Battle, Howard, Albuquerque...	1.000	2	2	1	0	3	0
Beasley, Tony, Calgary.......	1.000	6	2	12	0	14	3
Bellhorn, Mark, Edmonton	.928	23	30	60	7	97	11
Belliard, Ronnie, Tucson......	.882	7	4	11	2	17	3
Caceres, Edgar, Vancouver	.857	3	3	9	2	14	1
Castro, Juan, Albuquerque	.915	24	27	70	9	106	15
Collier, Lou, Calgary	.938	83	128	252	25	405	46
Counsell, Craig, Col. Springs...	1.000	6	9	21	0	30	5
Cromer, Brandon, Calgary.....	.955	33	43	106	7	156	19
Cromer, Tripp, Albuquerque....	.966	42	65	106	6	177	23
Cruz, Fausto, Vancouver	.939	29	45	62	7	114	11
Delgado, Wilson, Phoenix	.967	114	197	332	18	547	86
Diaz, Eddy, Tucson	.926	14	15	35	4	54	12

Player, Team	Pct.	G	PO	A	E	TC	DP
Eenhoorn, Robert, Vancouver ..	.955	115	153	293	21	467	56
Espinoza, Alvaro, Tacoma	.333	1	1	0	2	3	0
Felix, Lauro, Tucson	1.000	3	2	5	0	7	0
Ferguson, Jeff, Salt Lake......	.778	4	3	11	4	18	3
Florez, Tim, Phoenix	1.000	4	4	10	0	14	1
Fonville, Chad, Albuquerque ...	.935	26	31	70	7	108	10
Gates, Brent, Tacoma........	.824	4	6	8	3	17	3
Gonzales, Rene, Col. Springs ..	.914	10	13	19	3	35	7
Guerrero, Wilton, Albuquerque .	.895	7	8	26	4	38	7
Guevara, Giomar, Tacoma	.935	12	16	27	3	46	5
Haney, Todd, Tacoma	1.000	1	0	4	0	4	0
Johns, Keith, Tucson.........	.941	108	154	308	29	491	66
Keefe, Jamie, Las Vegas	.875	1	6	1	1	8	1
Kellner, Frank, Tucson........	.942	33	40	91	8	139	22
Martinez, Ramon, Phoenix	1.000	2	1	3	0	4	0
Maurer, Ron, Albuquerque	.949	59	79	184	14	277	45
Melo, Juan, Las Vegas	.936	12	11	33	3	47	7
Millette, Joe, Tacoma	.956	19	35	52	4	91	14
Parker, Rick, Albuquerque.....	1.000	4	4	3	0	7	0
Perez, Neifi, Col. Springs......	.975	67	119	198	8	325	56
Polcovich, Kevin, Calgary	.930	16	27	53	6	86	11
Sanford, Chance, Calgary	.964	5	8	19	1	28	4
Scarsone, Steve, Las Vegas ...	.929	12	15	37	4	56	11
Sexton, Chris, Col. Springs	.966	32	57	87	5	149	20
Shave, Jon, Salt Lake	.933	26	42	84	9	135	17
SHEETS, Andy, Tacoma........	.973	107	170	298	13	481	69
Sheldon, Scott, Edmonton	.970	81	96	228	10	334	44
Shipley, Craig, Las Vegas	1.000	2	1	3	0	4	0
Shumpert, Terry, L.V.-C.S.	.913	14	18	24	4	46	8
Simons, Mitch, Salt Lake	.985	13	26	39	1	66	12
Unroe, Tim, Tucson..........	1.000	1	0	1	0	1	0
Velandia, Jorge, Las Vegas	.961	113	170	347	21	538	69
Wood, Jason, Edmonton.......	.966	11	15	42	2	59	7
Zosky, Eddie, Phoenix	.966	30	44	69	4	117	18

SHORTSTOPS WITH TWO OR MORE TEAMS

Player, Team	Pct.	G	PO	A	E	TC	DP
Shumpert, Terry, Las Vegas ...	.966	9	13	15	1	29	5
Shumpert, Terry, Col. Springs ..	.824	5	5	9	3	17	3

OUTFIELDERS

Player, Team	Pct.	G	PO	A	E	TC	DP
Allensworth, Jermaine, Calgary .	1.000	5	8	0	0	8	0
Alvarez, Rafael, Salt Lake*	.920	15	22	1	2	25	0
Anthony, Eric, Albuquerque*...	.968	23	29	1	1	31	0
Banks, Brian, Tucson	.986	78	138	8	2	148	0
Barry, Jeff, Col. Springs	1.000	70	130	11	0	141	1
Bass, Kevin, Vancouver.......	1.000	3	3	0	0	3	0
Beamon, Trey, Las Vegas	.967	77	111	7	4	122	1
Beasley, Tony, Calgary.......	.800	6	4	0	1	5	0
Benard, Marvin, Phoenix*.....	.966	17	26	2	1	29	0
Betten, Randy, Vancouver.....	1.000	7	10	0	0	10	0
Brede, Brent, Salt Lake*	.961	42	71	2	3	76	0
Bridges, Kary, Calgary........	1.000	1	4	0	0	4	0
Briggs, Stoney, Las Vegas.....	.932	110	181	10	14	205	2
Brown, Adrian, Calgary	.993	60	130	3	1	134	1
Brown, Jarvis, Tucson........	.966	107	218	12	8	238	3
Brown, Ray, Las Vegas	.938	27	30	0	2	32	0
Carvajal, Jovino, Vancouver ...	.958	126	262	9	12	283	3
Castro, Jose, Tacoma*	1.000	2	1	0	0	1	0
Cedeno, Roger, Albuquerque...	.964	29	53	1	2	56	0
Chamberlain, Wes, Calgary....	.789	9	13	2	4	19	1
Christenson, Ryan, Edmonton..	1.000	16	42	1	0	43	1
Christian, Eddie, Tacoma*.....	.985	31	65	2	1	68	2
Cordova, Marty, Salt Lake	.750	2	3	0	1	4	0
Cruz, Fausto, Vancouver	.923	8	12	0	1	13	0
Cruz, Jacob, Phoenix*	.970	117	239	16	8	263	4
Cruz, Jose, Tacoma..........	1.000	48	70	3	0	73	1
DASCENZO, Doug, Las Vegas* .	.992	105	238	6	2	246	0
Diaz, Eddy, Tucson	.900	5	9	0	1	10	0
Ducey, Rob, Tacoma.........	.940	23	44	3	3	50	1
Dunn, Todd, Tucson	.961	88	143	4	6	153	0
Echevarria, Angel, Col. Springs .	.991	63	106	6	1	113	0
Encarnacion, Angelo, Las Vegas	.667	5	2	0	1	3	0
Felix, Lauro, Tucson	1.000	1	1	0	0	1	0
Fonville, Chad, Albuquerque ...	.968	49	89	2	3	94	2
Garcia, Karim, Albuquerque*...	.952	64	97	3	5	105	0
Garrison, Webster, Edmonton ..	.967	20	29	0	1	30	0
Gibson, Derrick, Col. Springs ..	.968	18	30	0	1	31	0
Gipson, Charles, Tacoma......	1.000	3	6	0	0	6	0
Greene, Todd, Vancouver	1.000	2	3	0	0	3	0
Grieve, Ben, Edmonton	.964	27	51	2	2	55	1

Player, Team	Pct.	G	PO	A	E	TC	DP
Griffey, Craig, Tacoma	1.000	2	4	0	0	4	0
Hale, Chip, Albuquerque	1.000	2	4	0	0	4	0
Hall, Billy, Col. Springs	.938	7	15	0	1	16	0
Hamilton, Darryl, Phoenix	1.000	3	6	0	0	6	0
Haney, Todd, Tacoma	1.000	1	1	0	0	1	0
Hazlett, Steve, Calgary	1.000	21	15	0	0	15	0
Helton, Todd, Col. Springs*	1.000	22	37	3	0	40	0
Herrera, Jose, Edmonton*	.965	114	210	9	8	227	1
Hinch, A.J., Edmonton	1.000	3	4	0	0	4	0
Hollandsworth, Todd, Alb.*	1.000	13	32	1	0	33	0
Howitt, Dann, Col. Springs	1.000	20	29	2	0	31	1
Iapoce, Anthony, Tucson*	1.000	7	18	0	0	18	0
Ibanez, Raul, Tacoma	.976	110	192	12	5	209	1
Jackson, Darrin, Salt Lake	1.000	18	26	2	0	28	1
Jenkins, Geoff, Tucson	.961	72	115	7	5	127	1
Johnson, J.J., Salt Lake	.958	26	22	1	1	24	0
Johnson, Mark, Calgary*	1.000	3	2	0	0	2	0
Jones, Dax, Phoenix	.968	81	146	6	5	157	2
Jones, Terry, Col. Springs	.993	87	139	11	1	151	3
Keefe, Jamie, Las Vegas	.952	11	20	0	1	21	0
Kirby, Wayne, Albuquerque	.967	66	138	9	5	152	2
Latham, Chris, Salt Lake	.961	118	262	6	11	279	1
Leach, Jalal, Tacoma*	.977	101	205	8	5	218	1
Lee, Derek, Las Vegas	1.000	37	46	8	0	54	2
Lee, Travis, Tucson*	.750	2	3	0	1	4	0
Lennon, Patrick, Edmonton	1.000	10	13	1	0	14	0
Lesher, Brian, Edmonton*	.970	99	185	6	6	197	2
Lott, Billy, Calgary	.990	65	94	6	1	101	0
Marrero, Oreste, Albuquerque*	.884	41	36	2	5	43	0
Martinez, Greg, Tucson	1.000	3	4	0	0	4	0
Martinez, Manny, Calgary	.976	102	196	7	5	208	2
Maurer, Ron, Albuquerque*	1.000	5	3	1	0	4	0
McCarty, Dave, Phoenix*	1.000	1	2	0	0	2	0
McDonald, Jason, Edmonton	.975	78	187	10	5	202	3
Monahan, Shane, Tacoma	.961	21	46	3	2	51	1
Neill, Mike, Edmonton*	.857	5	6	0	1	7	0
Ogden, Jamie, Salt Lake*	1.000	71	129	9	0	138	0
Owens, Jayhawk, Col. Springs	1.000	11	16	0	0	16	0
Parker, Rick, Albuquerque	.946	33	34	1	2	37	0
Pennyfeather, William, Alb.	.960	111	207	8	9	224	1
Plantier, Phil, Las Vegas	1.000	9	17	2	0	19	0
Poe, Charles, Las Vegas	1.000	43	63	4	0	67	0
Powell, Dante, Phoenix	.986	108	266	7	4	277	1
Pritchett, Chris, Vancouver	.933	9	14	0	1	15	0
Pulliam, Harvey, Col. Springs	.957	32	44	0	2	46	0
Radmanovich, Ryan, Salt Lake	.963	130	226	7	9	242	3
Reimer, Kevin, Tacoma	1.000	2	1	0	0	1	0
Riggs, Adam, Albuquerque	1.000	1	1	0	0	1	0
Riley, Marquis, Vancouver	.995	65	177	4	1	182	2
Roberson, Kevin, Phoenix	.980	92	139	7	3	149	0
Rohrmeier, Dan, Tacoma	.979	64	89	4	2	95	0
Scarsone, Steve, Las Vegas	1.000	1	2	0	0	2	0
Secrist, Reed, Calgary	1.000	4	3	0	0	3	0
Shave, Jon, Salt Lake	1.000	16	32	3	0	35	0
Shipley, Craig, Las Vegas	1.000	1	1	0	0	1	0
Silvestre, Juan, Tacoma	.750	7	9	0	3	12	0
Simons, Mitch, Salt Lake	1.000	7	10	0	0	10	0
Singleton, Duane, Vancouver	.978	100	209	15	5	229	2
Smith, Demond, Edmonton	.958	29	67	2	3	72	0
Smith, Mark, Calgary	.982	33	55	1	1	57	1
Spearman, Vernon, Alb.*	.976	26	36	5	1	42	1
Staton, T.J., Calgary*	.988	61	78	3	1	82	0
Tatum, Jim, Las Vegas	1.000	30	27	2	0	29	0
Thobe, Steve, Calgary	.667	1	2	0	1	3	0
Tinsley, Lee, Tacoma	.917	23	32	1	3	36	1
Tolentino, Jose, Calgary*	1.000	20	32	0	0	32	0
Torres, Paul, Tacoma	1.000	5	8	1	0	9	0
Turner, Chris, Vancouver	1.000	1	1	0	0	1	0
Unroe, Tim, Tucson	1.000	21	33	5	0	38	1
Vanderwal, John, Col. Springs*	1.000	4	5	0	0	5	0
Velazquez, Edgard, Col. Springs	.974	114	208	13	6	227	5
Voigt, Jack, Tucson	1.000	40	61	2	0	63	1
Wachter, Derek, Tucson	.958	39	65	3	3	71	0
Ward, Turner, Calgary	.967	53	82	5	3	90	1
White, Derrick, Vancouver	.979	85	183	7	4	194	0
Williams, Reggie, Vancouver	1.000	9	22	1	0	23	1
Wilson, Desi, Phoenix*	.960	38	66	6	3	75	1
Wolff, Mike, Vancouver	.944	40	64	4	4	72	2
Young, Ernie, Edmonton	.991	43	100	5	1	106	2

TRIPLE PLAY: Banks.

CATCHERS

Player, Team	Pct.	G	PO	A	E	TC	DP	PB
Andreopoulos, Alex, Tucson	1.000	7	16	1	0	17	0	0
Banks, Brian, Tucson	.984	13	56	5	1	62	2	1
Berryhill, Damon, Phoenix	1.000	3	14	1	0	15	0	0
Blanco, Henry, Albuquerque	.995	28	568	64	3	635	11	10
Burke, Jamie, Vancouver	.935	4	27	2	2	31	0	0
Cholowsky, Dan, Col. Springs	.987	20	142	12	2	156	3	3
Decker, Steve, Tacoma	.997	44	306	21	1	328	2	5
Durant, Mike, Salt Lake	1.000	51	326	23	0	349	4	4
Edge, Tim, Calgary	.984	53	327	34	6	367	8	8
Encarnacion, Angelo, L.V.	.983	69	453	61	9	523	6	9
Greene, Todd, Vancouver	.992	56	313	42	3	358	4	4
Gubanich, Creighton, Edm.-Tuc.-C.S.	.976	57	364	39	10	413	6	13
Helfand, Eric, Las Vegas	.987	65	434	30	6	470	3	10
Hernandez, Carlos, Las Vegas	1.000	3	15	2	0	17	0	0
Hinch, A.J., Edmonton	.986	31	197	7	3	207	3	1
Horn, Jeff, Salt Lake	.993	23	129	5	1	135	0	1
Huckaby, Ken, Albuquerque	.975	63	359	25	10	394	2	7
Hughes, Bobby, Tucson	.977	80	455	45	12	512	5	11
Kennedy, Darryl, Phoenix	.980	30	182	12	4	198	0	0
Marx, Tim, Calgary	.989	82	564	40	7	611	6	8
Mayes, Craig, Phoenix	1.000	5	23	3	0	26	0	0
Mayne, Brent, Edmonton	1.000	1	5	0	0	5	0	0
Miller, Damian, Salt Lake	.988	70	445	35	6	486	8	2
Mirabelli, Doug, Phoenix	.994	99	629	47	4	680	6	2
Molina, Izzy, Edmonton	.995	55	330	32	2	364	6	6
Monzon, Jose, Vancouver	.980	17	87	11	2	100	1	2
Morales, Willie, Edmonton	.976	32	153	7	4	164	1	2
Owens, Jayhawk, Col. Springs	.988	82	529	52	7	588	6	5
Romero, Mandy, Las Vegas	.983	20	112	6	2	120	2	3
Rowland, Rich, Phoenix	1.000	16	115	6	0	121	0	2
Sealy, Scot, Tacoma	.971	6	34	0	1	35	0	1
Secrist, Reed, Calgary	.985	12	61	4	1	66	1	1
Smith, Jeff, Salt Lake	1.000	6	23	4	0	27	0	0
Steed, Dave, Albuquerque	.989	19	86	8	1	95	0	0
Stinnett, Kelly, Tucson	.993	45	255	34	2	291	3	3
Strittmatter, Mark, C.S.	.996	44	241	15	1	257	2	2
Thurston, Jerry, Vancouver	.977	64	353	30	9	392	0	10
Turner, Chris, Vancouver	.968	14	87	4	3	94	1	2
Unrat, Chris, Phoenix	.500	1	2	0	2	4	0	0
VARITEK, Jason, Tacoma	.995	49	613	49	3	665	6	12
Wilkins, Rick, Tacoma	.988	11	75	4	1	80	0	1
Williams, George, Edmonton	1.000	2	8	1	0	9	0	0
Zinter, Alan, Tacoma	1.000	2	11	0	0	11	0	0

CATCHERS WITH TWO OR MORE TEAMS

Player, Team	Pct.	G	PO	A	E	TC	DP	PB
Gubanich, Creighton, Edm.	.991	29	194	17	2	213	3	8
Gubanich, Creighton, Tucson	.950	15	81	14	5	100	1	3
Gubanich, Creighton, C.S.	.970	13	89	8	3	100	2	2

PITCHERS

Player, Team	Pct.	G	PO	A	E	TC	DP
Abbott, Paul, Tacoma	.947	17	8	10	1	19	1
Acre, Mark, Edmonton	.875	43	3	4	1	8	0
Adams, Willie, Edmonton	1.000	13	3	8	0	11	1
Adamson, Joel, Tucson*	1.000	6	2	6	0	8	1
Ahearne, Pat, Albuquerque	.813	20	3	10	3	16	1
Aldred, Scott, Salt Lake*	1.000	7	2	7	0	9	0
Anderson, Jimmy, Calgary*	.975	21	7	32	1	40	4
Arocha, Rene, Phoenix	.815	18	9	13	5	27	0
Baez, Kevin, Salt Lake	1.000	2	0	1	0	1	0
Bailey, Cory, Phoenix	1.000	13	1	4	0	5	0
Baptist, Travis, Salt Lake*	1.000	7	1	6	0	7	0
Batchelor, Rich, Las Vegas	1.000	15	5	4	0	9	0
Beckett, Robbie, Col. Springs*	.625	45	2	3	3	8	0
Bene, Bill, Vancouver	1.000	19	1	1	0	2	0
Berumen, Andres, L.V.-Tac.	.920	34	10	13	2	25	0
Boever, Joe, Cal.-Edm.	.933	53	7	7	1	15	2
Bolton, Tom, Cal.-Tuc.*	.920	23	11	12	2	25	2
Bones, Ricky, Tucson	1.000	8	3	1	0	4	1
Bourgeois, Steve, Col. Springs	.862	33	12	13	4	29	1
Bovee, Mike, Vancouver	1.000	12	6	13	0	19	1
Bowers, Shane, Salt Lake	.857	9	3	3	1	7	0
Boze, Marshall, Las Vegas	1.000	14	2	6	0	8	0
Brewer, Billy, Edmonton*	1.000	9	0	2	0	2	0
Brewington, Jamie, Tucson	1.000	6	0	2	0	2	0
Brown, Alvin, Albuquerque	.786	12	8	3	3	14	0
Browne, Byron, Tucson	.667	3	0	2	1	3	0
Brunson, William, Albuquerque*	1.000	27	1	5	0	6	0
Bruske, Jim, Las Vegas	1.000	16	5	10	0	15	1

$- 422 -$

Player, Team	Pct.	G	PO	A	E	TC	DP
Buckley, Travis, Vancouver	.971	32	9	25	1	35	2
Burke, John, Col. Springs	1.000	3	1	2	0	3	1
Burrows, Terry, L.V.-Edm.*	.800	44	2	6	2	10	0
Cadaret, Greg, Vancouver*	1.000	9	1	0	0	1	0
Carlson, Dan, Phoenix.	1.000	29	9	9	0	18	2
Carmona, Rafael, Tacoma	1.000	32	4	10	0	14	0
Carter, John, Calgary.	.889	15	4	4	1	9	0
Castillo, Marino, Las Vegas	.900	30	9	9	2	20	3
Chavez, Anthony, Vancouver ...	1.000	28	1	6	0	7	0
Chouinard, Bobby, Edmonton ...	1.000	25	1	12	0	13	1
Corps, Edwin, Phoenix	1.000	7	2	0	0	2	0
Crawford, Carlos, Calgary	.917	9	4	7	1	12	0
Creek, Doug, Phoenix*	.880	25	2	20	3	25	0
Crow, Dean, Tacoma	1.000	33	2	4	0	6	1
D'Amico, Jeffrey, Edmonton ...	1.000	10	2	2	0	4	0
Daspit, Jamie, L.V.-Edm.	1.000	13	1	5	0	6	0
Davis, Mark, Tucson*	1.000	17	1	3	0	4	0
Davis, Tim, Tacoma*	1.000	1	0	2	0	2	0
Drahman, Brian, Las Vegas	1.000	33	1	5	0	6	1
Dreifort, Darren, Albuquerque ..	1.000	2	0	2	0	2	0
Dressendorfer, Kirk, Alb.......	1.000	7	3	6	0	9	0
Dreyer, Steve, Salt Lake	.909	27	4	6	1	11	0
Dunbar, Matt, Edm.-Van.*	1.000	14	3	3	0	6	0
Duncan, Calvin, Salt Lake	1.000	5	1	0	0	1	0
Edsell, Geoff, Vancouver	.875	30	9	26	5	40	1
Ellis, Robert, Vancouver	.833	29	11	19	6	36	2
Ericks, John, Calgary	1.000	6	2	1	0	3	0
Farmer, Michael, Col. Springs* .	1.000	18	2	4	0	6	0
Fernandez, Osvaldo, Phoenix...	1.000	2	2	4	0	6	0
Fortugno, Tim, Vancouver*	.857	34	2	4	1	7	0
Foulke, Keith, Phoenix.	.917	12	2	9	1	12	0
Franklin, Ryan, Tacoma	.900	14	9	9	2	20	1
Frey, Steve, Vancouver*	1.000	31	1	6	0	7	0
Frontera, Chad, Phoenix	.750	5	1	2	1	4	0
Gajkowski, Steve, Tacoma.....	1.000	44	10	16	0	26	3
Gandarillas, Gus, Salt Lake	1.000	11	4	2	0	6	0
Garcia, Jose, Albuquerque.....	.909	33	2	8	1	11	2
Gardner, Scott, Tucson	1.000	1	1	0	0	1	0
Gohr, Greg, Vancouver	1.000	8	7	4	0	11	1
Gonzales, Frank, Calgary*	.800	25	3	1	1	5	0
Granger, Jeff, Calgary*	.842	30	5	11	3	19	0
Greer, Ken, Calgary	1.000	15	4	3	0	7	0
Grimsley, Jason, Tucson	.750	36	11	10	7	28	1
Gross, Kevin, Vancouver	1.000	2	2	2	0	4	0
Grott, Matt, Tucson*	.938	55	5	10	1	16	0
Halperin, Mike, Calgary*	1.000	15	2	11	0	13	0
Hancock, Lee, Phoenix*	1.000	7	1	1	0	2	1
Hancock, Ryan, Van.-L.V.	1.000	43	5	12	0	17	4
Hansell, Greg, Tucson.......	.952	40	9	11	1	21	2
Harikkala, Tim, Tacoma	1.000	21	7	11	0	18	1
Harkey, Mike, Albuquerque	1.000	48	2	4	0	6	0
Hartvigson, Chad, Phoenix* ...	1.000	17	1	4	0	5	0
Haught, Gary, Edmonton	1.000	30	3	7	0	10	1
Hawkins, LaTroy, Salt Lake	.917	14	6	16	2	24	1
Haynes, Jimmy, Edmonton	1.000	5	1	9	0	10	1
Henderson, Ryan, Alb.-C.S....	1.000	19	1	5	0	6	0
Herges, Matt, Albuquerque	.923	31	2	10	1	13	3
Holdridge, David, Tacoma	1.000	15	3	2	0	5	0
Holzemer, Mark, Tacoma*	.923	37	4	8	1	13	0
Hook, Chris, Las Vegas	.813	19	7	6	3	16	0
Hope, John, Col. Springs	1.000	43	13	13	0	26	1
Hubbs, Dan, Albuquerque	.962	62	6	19	1	26	0
Huber, Jeff, Tucson*	.882	40	7	8	2	17	0
Hurtado, Edwin, Tacoma......	.955	20	11	10	1	22	0
Janicki, Pete, Vancouver*	1.000	42	1	5	0	6	0
Johnson, Barry, Calgary	1.000	34	5	7	0	12	0
Johnson, Dane, Edmonton	1.000	14	1	3	0	4	0
Johnstone, John, Phoenix.....	1.000	38	1	3	0	4	1
Jones, Bobby, Col. Springs* ...	.968	25	11	19	1	31	2
Kaufman, Brad, Las Vegas	1.000	6	1	9	0	10	0
Klingenbeck, Scott, Salt Lake ..	1.000	1	0	1	0	1	0
Kramer, Tom, Col. Springs	1.000	51	1	4	0	5	0
Kroon, Marc, Las Vegas	1.000	46	2	4	0	6	0
Kubenka, Jeff, Albuquerque* ...	.500	8	1	0	1	2	0
Kubinski, Tim, Edmonton*	1.000	47	7	18	0	25	2
Lawrence, Sean, Calgary*	.947	26	1	17	1	19	0
Lee, Mark, Col. Springs*	1.000	48	0	3	0	3	1
Legault, Kevin, Salt Lake	1.000	16	3	5	0	8	0
Leskanic, Curt, Col. Springs ...	1.000	10	2	0	0	4	2
Lewis, Richie, Edmonton.....	1.000	11	0	2	0	2	0
Linebarger, Keith, Salt Lake ...	.900	41	7	11	2	20	2
Lira, Felipe, Tacoma	1.000	3	1	4	0	5	0
Long, Joey, Las Vegas*	1.000	16	5	2	0	7	1
Looney, Brian, Salt Lake*	1.000	17	1	3	0	4	0
Lorraine, Andrew, Edmonton*..	.938	23	2	13	1	16	4
Lowe, Derek, Tacoma	.929	10	4	9	1	14	1
Ludwick, Eric, Edmonton	1.000	6	0	4	0	4	0
Macey, Fausto, Vancouver.....	1.000	9	1	7	0	8	0
Maddux, Mike, Tac.-L.V.	1.000	4	2	5	0	7	1
Maloney, Sean, Tucson	.800	15	1	3	1	5	0
Manzanillo, Josias, Tacoma....	1.000	11	2	0	0	2	0
Manzanillo, Ravelo, Tacoma* ...	1.000	18	0	5	0	5	1
Martinez, Jesus, Albuquerque* .	.900	26	4	14	2	20	0
May, Darrell, Vancouver*	1.000	13	3	8	0	11	0
McAndrew, Jamie, Tucson	.957	22	11	11	1	23	1
McCarthy, Greg, Tacoma*	1.000	22	2	3	0	5	0
McCurry, Jeff, Col. Springs	.800	16	1	3	1	5	0
Medina, Rafael, Las Vegas	.929	13	5	8	1	14	1
Menhart, Paul, Tac.-L.V.	.842	26	11	21	6	38	1
Miller, Travis, Salt Lake*	.960	21	2	22	1	25	0
MINCHEY, Nate, Col. Springs .	1.000	27	11	23	0	34	1
Minor, Blas, Tucson	1.000	12	3	4	0	7	2
Mintz, Steve, Las Vegas	.889	27	3	5	1	9	0
Misuraca, Mike, Tucson	1.000	33	13	10	0	23	2
Montgomery, Steve, Edmonton .	1.000	30	4	6	0	10	2
Montoya, Norm, Tucson*	.978	27	6	38	1	45	2
Moore, Joel, Col. Springs	1.000	5	1	4	0	5	1
Morel, Ramon, Calgary	.960	27	8	16	1	25	2
Munoz, Bobby, L.V.-Alb.	.941	35	7	9	1	17	1
Murray, Heath, Las Vegas*	1.000	19	5	15	0	20	3
Naulty, Dan, Salt Lake	1.000	6	1	0	0	1	0
Nichting, Chris, Edmonton	.889	33	11	13	3	27	0
Niedermaier, Brad, Salt Lake ..	.667	16	1	1	1	3	0
Ohme, Kevin, Salt Lake*	1.000	56	3	16	0	19	0
Oquist, Mike, Edmonton	1.000	9	1	11	0	12	0
Ortiz, Russ, Phoenix	.889	14	9	7	2	18	1
Osuna, Antonio, Albuquerque ..	1.000	13	2	2	0	4	0
Pace, Scotty, Tucson*	1.000	2	0	1	0	1	0
Pacheco, Alexander, Tacoma ..	1.000	15	1	0	0	1	0
Parra, Jose, Salt Lake	.833	50	2	13	3	18	1
Perisho, Matt, Vancouver*	.909	9	4	6	1	11	0
Peters, Chris, Calgary*	1.000	14	2	8	0	10	0
Peterson, Mark, Phoenix*	.000	3	0	0	1	1	0
Pett, Jose, Calgary	1.000	3	0	1	0	1	0
Phillips, Randy, Phoenix	1.000	21	7	4	0	11	0
Phillips, Tony, Tuc.-Edm.	1.000	40	6	13	0	19	4
Pickett, Ricky, Phoenix*	1.000	61	3	3	0	6	0
Price, Jamey, Edmonton	1.000	2	0	1	0	1	0
Prieto, Ariel, Edmonton	1.000	2	0	1	0	1	0
Purdy, Shawn, Phoenix	.938	56	1	14	1	16	3
Pyc, Dave, Albuquerque*	.978	31	14	31	1	46	1
Rapp, Pat, Phoenix	1.000	3	2	2	0	4	0
Rath, Fred, Salt Lake.	1.000	10	0	1	0	1	0
Rath, Gary, Albuquerque*	.966	24	2	26	1	29	1
Redman, Mark, Salt Lake*	.926	29	5	20	2	27	0
Rekar, Bryan, Col. Springs	.964	28	17	10	1	28	1
Reyes, Alberto, Tucson	.923	38	2	10	1	13	0
Reyes, Carlos, Edmonton	.750	5	1	5	2	8	0
Reyes, Dennis, Albuquerque* ..	.900	10	2	7	1	10	0
Ricci, Chuck, Edmonton	1.000	4	1	1	0	2	0
Rigby, Brad, Edmonton	.826	15	8	11	4	23	0
Roa, Joe, Phoenix.	.833	6	0	5	1	6	0
Roach, Petie, Albuquerque* ...	1.000	31	1	11	0	12	0
Roberson, Sid, Tucson*	1.000	10	4	1	0	5	0
Roberts, Brett, Salt Lake	.818	24	3	6	2	11	1
Rodriguez, Frankie, Tucson ...	1.000	12	5	6	0	11	0
Rohrmeier, Dan, Tacoma......	1.000	1	0	1	0	1	0
Sadler, Al, Tucson	1.000	1	1	0	0	1	0
Saipe, Mike, Col. Springs	.929	10	2	11	1	14	1
Scanlan, Bob, Las Vegas	1.000	36	10	11	0	21	0
Schmidt, Curt, Calgary	.750	25	1	2	1	4	0
Schmidt, Jeff, Vancouver	1.000	27	1	1	0	2	0
Schmitt, Todd, Las Vegas	.889	48	3	5	1	9	0
Scott, Tim, Col. Springs	1.000	12	1	4	0	5	0
Serafini, Dan, Salt Lake	.931	28	3	24	2	29	0
Shaw, Curtis, Calgary*	.692	21	2	7	4	13	4
Shepherd, Keith, Calgary.	1.000	10	3	2	0	5	0
Shoemaker, Stephen, C.S.	1.000	5	0	1	0	1	0
Silva, Jose, Calgary.	1.000	17	11	7	0	18	0
Smith, Pete, Las Vegas	1.000	6	3	3	0	6	0
Smith, Ryan, Tacoma	1.000	1	0	2	0	2	0
Soderstrom, Steve, Phoenix ...	.963	31	8	18	1	27	2
Sodowsky, Clint, Calgary.....	1.000	8	2	3	0	5	0
Spencer, Stan, Las Vegas	1.000	8	0	7	0	7	0
Springer, Dennis, Vancouver ..	1.000	2	5	2	0	7	0
Stevens, Dave, Salt Lake......	.880	16	14	8	3	25	0

CLASS AAA Pacific Coast League

Player, Team	Pct.	G	PO	A	E	TC	DP
Stidham, Phil, Col. Springs	1.000	26	2	4	0	6	0
Suzuki, Mac, Tacoma	.905	32	12	7	2	21	0
Taulbee, Andy, Phoenix	1.000	19	5	6	0	11	0
Taylor, Kerry, Las Vegas	.926	22	9	16	2	27	1
Taylor, Scott, L.V.-Cal.	.964	42	9	18	1	28	2
Thompson, Mark, Col. Springs	1.000	1	1	2	0	3	1
Thomson, John, Col. Springs	1.000	7	4	6	0	10	0
Tolentino, Jose, Calgary*	1.000	1	0	1	0	1	0
Treadwell, Jody, Albuquerque	.926	27	8	17	2	27	2
Vanderweele, Doug, Phoenix	.941	36	2	14	1	17	1
VanLandingham, William, Pho.	1.000	4	2	1	0	3	0
Veras, Dario, Las Vegas	1.000	12	2	0	0	2	0
Villano, Mike, Phoenix	1.000	13	9	12	0	21	2
Wainhouse, David, Calgary	1.000	25	1	4	0	5	0
Ware, Jeff, Tucson	.950	25	10	9	1	20	2
Weaver, Eric, Albuquerque	.944	21	7	10	1	18	0
Williams, Shad, Vancouver	.960	40	13	11	1	25	1
Wilson, Gary, Calgary	1.000	21	14	17	0	31	1
Witasick, Jay, Edmonton	1.000	13	2	4	0	6	0
Witte, Trey, Tacoma	1.000	32	4	10	0	14	0
Wojciechowski, Steve, Edm.*	1.000	26	3	10	0	13	0
Wolcott, Bob, Tacoma	1.000	7	1	7	0	8	0
Woodard, Steve, Tucson	1.000	1	0	6	0	6	0
Wright, Jamey, Col. Springs	1.000	2	2	1	0	3	0
Zancanaro, Dave, Las Vegas*	1.000	3	1	4	0	5	0

PITCHERS WITH TWO OR MORE TEAMS

Player, Team	Pct.	G	PO	A	E	TC	DP
Berumen, Andres, Las Vegas	.875	18	2	5	1	8	0
Berumen, Andres, Tacoma	.941	16	8	8	1	17	0
Boever, Joe, Calgary	1.000	36	2	5	0	7	2
Boever, Joe, Edmonton	.875	17	5	2	1	8	0
Bolton, Tom, Calgary*	.923	8	4	8	1	13	2
Bolton, Tom, Tucson*	.917	15	7	4	1	12	0
Burrows, Terry, Las Vegas*	.800	31	1	3	1	5	0
Burrows, Terry, Edmonton*	.800	13	1	3	1	5	0
Daspit, Jamie, Las Vegas	1.000	10	0	5	0	5	0
Daspit, Jamie, Edmonton	1.000	3	1	0	0	1	0
Dunbar, Matt, Edmonton*	1.000	12	3	3	0	6	0
Hancock, Ryan, Vancouver	1.000	39	5	12	0	17	4
Henderson, Ryan, Albuquerque	1.000	13	1	1	0	2	0
Henderson, Ryan, Col. Springs	1.000	6	0	4	0	4	0
Maddux, Mike, Tacoma	1.000	1	0	3	0	3	0
Maddux, Mike, Las Vegas	1.000	3	2	2	0	4	1
Menhart, Paul, Tacoma	.875	15	6	8	2	16	1
Menhart, Paul, Las Vegas	.818	11	5	13	4	22	0
Munoz, Bobby, Las Vegas	1.000	17	4	5	0	9	1
Munoz, Bobby, Albuquerque	.875	18	3	4	1	8	0
Phillips, Tony, Tucson	1.000	29	3	11	0	14	3
Phillips, Tony, Edmonton	1.000	11	3	2	0	5	1
Taylor, Scott, Las Vegas	.000	2	0	0	0	0	0
Taylor, Scott, Calgary	.964	40	9	18	1	28	2

The following players did not have any fielding statistics at the positions indicated or appeared only as a designated hitter, pinch-hitter or pinch-runner: Ahearne, of; M. Anderson, p; Ausanio, p; Baron, p; Battle, of, p; Beatty, of; Blanco, of; Bonds, of; Bost, p; Briscoe, p; Castellano, ss; Colbert, dh; Dascenzo, p; DeJean, p; Demetral, of; Edge, 3b; Elvira, p; Felix, p; Fetters, p; Garrison, p; Gipson, ss; Gubanich, 3b, p; Harkey, of; Hollins, p; Howitt, 3b, p; Jenkins, ss; Jimenez, p; Kellner, p; Kjos, p; Lott, p; Molina, p; Moyer, p; Marx, of; Newfield, dh; Owens, 3b; Quinlan, p; Radmanovich, 3b; Ruffin, p; Seitzer, ss, p; Shumpert, of; Skuse, p; Small, p; Steed, 3b, p; Swift, p; Thurston, p; Tyler, p; VanEgmond, p; E. Williams, 3b; K. Williams, of; Wolff, 3b; Woods, 3b.

LEAGUE CHAMPIONS

Year	Team	Pct.
1903—	Los Angeles	.630
1904—	Tacoma	.589
	Tacoma§	.571
	Los Angeles§	.571
1905—	Tacoma	.583
	Los Angeles*	.604
1906—	Portland	.657
1907—	Los Angeles	.608
1908—	Los Angeles	.585
1909—	San Francisco	.623
1910—	Portland	.567
1911—	Portland	.589
1912—	Oakland	.591
1913—	Portland	.559
1914—	Portland	.574
1915—	San Francisco	.570
1916—	Los Angeles	.601
1917—	San Francisco	.561
1918—	Vernon	.569
	Los Angeles (2nd)◆	.548
1919—	Vernon	.613
1920—	Vernon	.556
1921—	Los Angeles	.574
1922—	San Francisco	.638
1923—	San Francisco	.617
1924—	Seattle	.545
1925—	Los Angeles	.643
1926—	Los Angeles	.599
1927—	Oakland	.615
1928—	San Francisco*	.630
	Sacramento∞	.626
	San Francisco∞	.626
1929—	Mission	.643
	Hollywood*	.592
1930—	Los Angeles	.576
	Hollywood*	.650
1931—	Hollywood	.626
	San Francisco*	.608
1932—	Portland	.587
1933—	Los Angeles	.610
1934—	Los Angeles▼	.786
	Los Angeles▼	.689
1935—	Los Angeles	.648
	San Francisco*	.608
1936—	Portland‡	.549
1937—	Sacramento	.573
	San Diego (3rd)†	.545

Year	Team	Pct.
1938—	Los Angeles	.590
	Sacramento (3rd)†	.537
1939—	Seattle	.589
	Sacramento (4th)†	.500
1940—	Seattle‡	.629
1941—	Seattle‡	.598
1942—	Sacramento	.590
	Seattle (3rd)†	.539
1943—	Los Angeles	.710
	S. Francisco (2nd)†	.574
1944—	Los Angeles	.586
	S. Francisco (3rd)†	.509
1945—	Portland	.622
	S. Francisco (4th)†	.525
1946—	San Francisco‡	.628
1947—	Los Angeles▲	.567
1948—	Oakland‡	.606
1949—	Hollywood‡	.583
1950—	Oakland	.590
1951—	Seattle‡	.593
1952—	Hollywood	.606
1953—	Hollywood	.589
1954—	San Diego■	.604
1955—	Seattle	.552
1956—	Los Angeles	.637
1957—	San Francisco	.601
1958—	Phoenix	.578
1959—	Salt Lake City	.552
1960—	Spokane	.601
1961—	Tacoma	.630
1962—	San Diego	.604
1963—	Spokane	.620
	Oklahoma City•	.632
1964—	Arkansas	.609
	San Diego•	.576
1965—	Oklahoma City	.628
	Portland	.547
1966—	Seattle•	.561
	Tulsa	.578
1967—	San Diego•	.574
	Spokane	.541
1968—	Tulsa•	.642
	Spokane	.586
1969—	Tacoma•	.589
	Eugene	.603

Year	Team	Pct.
1970—	Spokane•	.644
	Hawaii	.671
1971—	Salt Lake City	.534
	Tacoma	.545
1972—	Albuquerque	.622
	Eugene	.534
1973—	Tucson	.583
	Spokane•	.563
1974—	Spokane•	.549
	Albuquerque	.535
1975—	Salt Lake City	.556
	Hawaii•	.611
1976—	Salt Lake City	.625
	Hawaii•	.531
1977—	Phoenix•	.579
	Hawaii	.541
1978—	Tacoma††	.584
	Albuquerque††	.557
1979—	Albuquerque	.581
	Salt Lake City‡‡	.541
1980—	Albuquerque	.578
	Hawaii	.539
1981—	Albuquerque*	.712
	Tacoma	.561
1982—	Albuquerque*	.594
	Spokane	.545
1983—	Albuquerque	.594
	Portland*	.528
1984—	Hawaii	.621
	Edmonton*	.486
1985—	Vancouver*	.522
	Phoenix	.563
1986—	Vancouver	.616
	Las Vegas*	.563
1987—	Calgary	.596
	Albuquerque*	.542
1988—	Vancouver	.599
	Las Vegas*	.529
1989—	Albuquerque	.563
	Vancouver*	.514
1990—	Albuquerque*	.641
	Edmonton	.553
1991—	Tucson*	.580
	Tucson*	.564
1992—	Colorado Springs*	.596
	Portland	.576

CLASS AAA *Pacific Coast League*

Year	Team	Pct.	Year	Team	Pct.	Year	Team	Pct.
1993—	Portland	.608	1995—	Salt Lake	.549	1997—	Phoenix	.615
	Tucson*	.580		Colorado Springs*	.538		Edmonton*	.556
1994—	Albuquerque*	.597	1996—	Edmonton*	.592			
	Vancouver	.542		Phoenix	.479			

*Won split-season playoff. †Won four-team playoff. ‡Won pennant and four-team playoff. §Tied for second-half title with Tacoma winning playoff. ∞Tied for second-half title, with Sacramento winning playoff. ▲Ended regular season in tie with San Francisco and won one-game playoff for pennant, then won four-club playoff. ◆Won playoff from first-place Vernon and awarded championship. ■Defeated Hollywood in one-game playoff for pennant. ▼Won both halves, no playoff. •League was divided into Northern, Southern divisions in 1963, 1969-70-71, and Eastern, Western divisions in 1964 through 1968 and 1972 through 1977, won two-team playoff. ††League divided into Eastern and Western divisions, Tacoma and Albuquerque declared co-champions following cancellation of four-team playoff due to continuing rain and wet grounds. ‡‡Won second-half title and defeated Hawaii in four-team playoff.

CLASS AAA *Pacific Coast League*

EASTERN LEAGUE

LEAGUE OFFICE

President
Bill Troubh

Address
P.O. Box 9711
Portland, ME 04104

Phone
207-761-2700

TEAMS

AKRON AEROS
General manager/vice president
Jeff Auman
Manager
Joel Skinner
Ballpark (capacity, surface)
Canal Park (8,900, grass)
Affiliation
Indians
Address
300 S. Main St.
Akron, OH 44308
Phone
330-253-5151

BINGHAMTON METS
General manager
R.C. Reuteman
Manager
John Gibbons
Ballpark (capacity, surface)
Binghamton Municipal Stadium (6,064, grass)
Affiliation
Mets
Address
P.O. Box 598
Binghamton, NY 13902
Phone
607-723-6387

BOWIE BAYSOX
General manager
Jon Danos
Manager
To be announced
Ballpark (capacity, surface)
Prince George's Stadium (10,000, grass)
Affiliation
Orioles
Address
P.O. Box 1661
Bowie, MD 20717
Phone
301-805-6000

HARRISBURG SENATORS
General manager
Todd Vander Woude
Manager
Rick Sweet
Ballpark (capacity, surface)
RiverSide Stadium (6,300, grass)
Affiliation
Expos
Address
P.O. Box 15757
Harrisburg, PA 17105
Phone
717-231-4444

NEW BRITAIN ROCK CATS
General manager
Gerry Berthiaume
Manager
John Russell
Ballpark (capacity, surface)
New Britain Stadium (6,146, grass)
Affiliation
Twins
Address
P.O. Box 1718
New Britain, CT 06050
Phone
860-224-8383

NEW HAVEN RAVENS
General manager
Chris Canetti
Manager
Tim Blackwell
Ballpark (capacity, surface)
Yale Field (6,200, grass)
Affiliation
Rockies
Address
252 Darby Ave.
West Haven, CT 06516
Phone
1-800-728-3671

NORWICH NAVIGATORS
General manager
Brian Mahoney
Manager
Trey Hillman
Ballpark (capacity, surface)
Dodd Stadium (7,000, grass)
Affiliation
Yankees
Address
P.O. Box 6003
Yantic, CT 06389

Phone
860-887-7962

PORTLAND SEA DOGS
General manager
Charles Eshbach
Manager
Lynn Jones
Ballpark (capacity, surface)
Hadlock Field (6,000, grass)
Affiliation
Marlins
Address
P.O. Box 636
Portland, ME 04104
Phone
207-874-9300

READING PHILLIES
General manager
Chuck Domino
Manager
Al LeBoeuf
Ballpark (capacity, surface)
Municipal Memorial Stadium (8,500, grass)
Affiliation
Phillies
Address
P.O. Box 15050
Reading, PA 19612
Phone
610-375-8469

TRENTON THUNDER
General manager
Wayne Hodes
Manager
DeMarlo Hale
Ballpark (capacity, surface)
Mercer County Waterfront Park (6,300, grass)
Affiliation
Red Sox
Address
One Thunder Road
Trenton, NJ 08611
Phone
609-394-8326

CLASS AA *Eastern League*

NORTHERN DIVISION

Team	W	L	T	Pct.	GB
Portland (Marlins)	79	63	0	.556	....
Norwich (Yankees)	73	69	0	.514	6
New Britain (Twins)	70	72	0	.493	9
Binghamton (Mets)	66	76	0	.465	13
New Haven (Rockies)	64	78	0	.451	15

SOUTHERN DIVISION

Team	W	L	T	Pct.	GB
Harrisburg (Expos)	86	56	0	.606	....
Bowie (Orioles)	75	67	0	.528	11
Reading (Phillies)	74	68	0	.521	12
Trenton (Red Sox)	71	70	0	.504	14½
Akron (Indians)	51	90	0	.362	34½

COMPOSITE

Team	Har.	Por.	Bow.	Rea.	Nor.	Tre.	N.B.	Bin.	N.H.	Akr.	W	L	T	Pct.	GB
Harrisburg (Expos)	....	8	9	15	7	11	6	11	7	12	86	56	0	.606	....
Portland (Marlins)	6	....	7	5	8	10	12	11	11	9	79	63	0	.556	7
Bowie (Orioles)	9	7	....	9	8	8	5	9	6	14	75	67	0	.528	11
Reading (Phillies)	3	9	9	....	7	7	12	10	8	9	74	68	0	.521	12
Norwich (Yankees)	7	10	6	7	....	9	9	6	9	10	73	69	0	.514	13
Trenton (Red Sox)	7	4	10	11	5	....	7	10	7	10	71	70	0	.504	14½
New Britain (Twins)	8	6	9	2	9	7	....	7	10	12	70	72	0	.493	16
Binghamton (Mets)	3	7	5	4	12	4	11	....	13	7	66	76	0	.465	20
New Haven (Rockies)	7	7	8	6	9	7	8	5	....	7	64	78	0	.451	22
Akron (Indians)	6	5	4	9	4	7	2	7	7	....	51	90	0	.362	34½

Major league affiliations in parentheses.

PLAYOFFS: Portland defeated Norwich, three games to two; Harrisburg defeated Bowie, three games to two; Harrisburg defeated Portland, three games to one, to win league championship.

REGULAR-SEASON ATTENDANCE: Akron, 473,232; Binghamton, 200,513; Bowie, 409,285; Harrisburg, 242,431; New Britain, 151,718; New Haven, 232,101; Norwich, 244,246; Portland, 397,117; Reading, 398,182; Trenton, 446,527. Total—3,195,352. Playoffs (14 games)—42,157. Class AA All-Star Game at San Antonio—7,114.

MANAGERS: Akron, Jeff Datz; Binghamton, Rick Sweet; Bowie, Joe Ferguson; Harrisburg, Rick Sofield; New Britain, Al Newman; New Haven, Bill Hayes; Norwich, Trey Hillman; Portland, Fredi Gonzalez; Reading, Al LeBoeuf; Trenton, Demarlo Hale.

ALL-STAR TEAM: 1B—Kevin Millar, Portland; 2B—Rudy Gomez, Norwich; 3B—Corey Koskie, New Britain; SS—Alex Gonzalez, Portland; OF—Mark Kotsay, Portland; David Dellucci, Bowie; Derrick Gibson, New Haven; C—Bob Henley, Harrisburg; DH—Chan Perry, Akron; Utility—Lionel Hastings, Portland; RHP—Mike Saipe, New Haven; Steve Montgomery, Bowie; LHP—Mike Vavrek, New Haven; Jesus Sanchez, Binghamton; Relief pitcher—Ben Fleetham, Harrisburg; Player of the Year—Kevin Millar, Portland; Pitcher of the Year—Mike Vavrek, New Haven; Rookie of the Year—Mark Kotsay, Portland; Manager of the Year—Al LeBoeuf, Reading.

1997 BATTING

TEAM

Team	Avg.	G	TPA	AB	R	H	TB	2B	3B	HR	RBI	SH	SF	HP	BB	IBB	SO	SB	CS	GDP	LOB	ShO	Slg.	OBP
Portland	.288	142	5522	4890	824	1407	2304	262	31	191	765	47	34	41	510	28	971	103	79	110	994	4	.471	.358
Norwich	.283	142	5524	4806	784	1359	2040	234	30	129	718	32	39	71	576	9	917	109	64	112	1080	8	.424	.365
Harrisburg	.270	142	5308	4721	692	1274	2006	227	35	145	631	52	39	65	431	27	829	143	69	87	933	5	.425	.337
Trenton	.270	141	5473	4726	766	1274	2002	236	33	142	697	55	38	76	578	19	977	125	70	93	1021	4	.424	.356
Akron	.268	141	5409	4671	758	1254	1984	245	28	143	717	39	40	66	593	20	936	73	57	113	1010	5	.425	.356
Bowie	.267	142	5499	4809	701	1283	1977	260	16	134	644	53	38	59	580	14	1001	72	47	103	1063	6	.411	.346
New Haven	.262	142	5291	4637	663	1216	1828	211	22	119	612	78	47	47	482	24	957	77	69	95	960	10	.394	.335
Binghamton	.257	142	5277	4662	654	1197	2002	223	18	182	608	59	36	56	464	29	1097	139	71	89	927	12	.429	.329
Reading	.250	142	5392	4721	658	1182	1810	201	35	119	595	69	32	77	493	27	965	86	63	103	970	4	.383	.329
New Britain	.250	142	5270	4543	670	1137	1752	242	29	105	616	53	41	48	585	22	914	121	67	92	966	8	.386	.339

INDIVIDUAL

TOP QUALIFIERS FOR BATTING CHAMPIONSHIP

Minimum 383 plate appearances. *Lefthanded batter. †Switch-hitter.

Player, Team	Avg.	G	TPA	AB	R	H	TB	2B	3B	HR	RBI	SH	SF	HP	BB	IBB	SO	SB	CS	GDP	Slg.	OBP
Millar, Kevin, Portland	.342	135	594	511	94	175	309	34	2	32	131	0	7	10	66	9	53	2	3	11	.605	.423
Dellucci, David, Bowie*	.327	107	449	385	71	126	221	29	3	20	55	0	1	5	58	1	69	11	4	6	.574	.421
Gibson, Derrick, New Haven	.317	119	509	461	91	146	243	24	2	23	75	0	2	10	36	7	100	20	13	8	.527	.377
Perry, Chan, Akron	.315	119	516	476	74	150	248	34	2	20	96	1	6	5	28	0	61	3	3	14	.521	.355
Seefried, Tate, Binghamton*	.313	96	393	335	59	105	208	16	0	29	79	0	4	0	54	10	99	9	4	2	.621	.405
Jackson, Ryan, Portland*	.312	134	546	491	87	153	267	28	4	26	98	1	0	3	51	2	85	2	5	6	.544	.380
Fullmer, Brad, Harrisburg*	.311	94	398	357	60	111	196	24	2	19	62	0	4	7	30	5	25	6	4	11	.549	.372
Buchanan, Brian, Norwich	.309	116	519	470	75	145	204	25	2	10	69	0	6	11	32	0	85	11	9	11	.434	.362
Roskos, John, Portland	.308	123	509	451	66	139	244	31	1	24	84	2	6	0	50	2	81	4	6	17	.541	.373
Kotsay, Mark, Portland*	.306	114	516	438	103	134	225	27	2	20	77	0	3	0	75	3	65	17	5	16	.514	.405
Coleman, Michael, Trenton	.301	102	444	385	56	116	191	17	8	14	58	9	4	5	41	1	89	20	7	5	.496	.372
Miller, David, Akron*	.301	134	569	509	84	153	210	27	9	4	61	6	4	2	48	2	77	22	11	5	.413	.361
Gomez, Rudy, Norwich	.300	102	468	393	65	118	165	18	7	5	52	1	3	10	61	0	64	11	7	8	.420	.405
Sexton, Chris, New Haven	.297	98	439	360	65	107	140	22	4	1	38	11	4	2	62	0	37	8	16	8	.389	.400
Wilson, Tom, Norwich	.296	124	514	419	88	124	216	21	4	21	80	0	5	4	86	0	126	1	4	8	.516	.416

DEPARTMENTAL LEADERS: G—J. Garcia, 141; AB—Anderson, 553; R—Kotsay, 103; H—Millar, 175; TB—Millar, 309; 2B—Millar, Perry, 34 each; 3B—D. Miller 9; HR—Raleigh, 37; RBI—Millar, 131; SH—J. Garcia, 24; SF—R. Lane, Millar, K. Curtis, 7 each; HP—Held, 18; BB—Mientkiewicz, 98; IBB—Seefried, Koskie, 10 each; SO—Raleigh, 169; SB—Fuller, 40; CS—Winn, 20; GIDP—Moyle, 17; Slg.—Seefried, .621; OBP—Millar, .423.

CLASS AA *Eastern League*

*Lefthanded batter. †Switch-hitter.

Player, Team	Avg.	G	TPA	AB	R	H	TB	2B	3B	HR	RBI	SH	SF	HP	BB	IBB	SO	SB	CS	GDP	Slg.	OBP
Abad, Andy, Trenton*	.303	45	201	165	37	50	87	13	0	8	24	0	1	2	33	3	27	2	4	2	.527	.423
Alcantara, Israel, Harrisburg	.282	89	336	301	48	85	179	9	2	27	68	0	3	3	29	1	84	4	5	5	.595	.348
Allen, Chad, New Britain	.252	30	126	115	20	29	52	9	1	4	18	1	1	0	9	0	21	2	0	3	.452	.304
Almonte, Wady, Bowie	.207	69	255	222	25	46	75	7	2	6	25	0	1	5	27	0	64	2	4	6	.338	.306
Alvarez, Rafael, New Britain*	.255	16	54	47	5	12	18	0	0	2	7	1	0	1	5	0	9	1	4	0	.383	.340
Amador, Manuel, Reading†	.243	63	197	169	17	41	58	9	1	2	22	2	2	4	20	1	29	0	0	5	.343	.333
Anderson, Marlon, Reading*	.266	137	615	553	88	147	207	18	6	10	62	9	1	10	42	1	77	27	15	8	.374	.328
Angeli, Doug, Reading	.223	42	171	148	25	33	55	5	1	5	19	3	1	2	16	2	28	1	2	3	.372	.305
Arroyo, Luis, Binghamtom*	.000	7	1	1	0	0	0	0	0	0	0	0	0	0	0	0	0	0	0	0	.000	.000
Ashby, Chris, Norwich	.249	136	546	457	92	114	208	20	1	24	82	0	3	6	80	2	95	10	7	14	.455	.366
Azuaje, Jesus, Binghamtom	.278	100	396	331	50	92	127	15	1	6	37	8	4	8	45	1	42	11	9	13	.384	.374
Bady, Edward, Harrisburg†	.210	97	299	267	36	56	75	8	4	1	22	10	0	1	21	3	62	15	5	3	.281	.270
Barbao, Joe, Reading	.000	52	6	5	0	0	0	0	0	0	0	0	1	0	0	0	2	0	0	0	.000	.000
Barry, Jeff, New Haven†	.219	40	155	146	21	32	51	4	0	5	12	1	1	3	4	0	34	3	2	3	.349	.253
Barthol, Blake, New Haven	.243	109	379	325	42	79	113	12	2	6	39	11	2	10	31	0	76	5	3	6	.348	.326
Bates, Fletcher, Binghamtom†	.257	68	275	245	44	63	117	14	2	12	34	1	2	1	26	0	71	9	3	2	.478	.328
Bautista, Juan, Bowie	.250	21	75	68	9	17	18	1	0	0	3	1	1	0	5	0	17	1	2	2	.265	.297
Bennett, Shayne, Harrisburg	.333	23	6	6	0	2	2	0	0	0	0	0	0	0	0	0	1	0	0	0	.333	.333
Benz, Jacob, Harrisburg*	.500	23	4	2	3	1	2	1	0	0	0	0	0	0	2	0	0	0	0	0	1.000	.750
Bernhardt, Steve, New Haven	.213	101	358	315	35	67	99	14	0	6	38	8	5	3	27	0	46	2	2	5	.314	.277
Berry, Mike, Bowie	.230	53	234	204	34	47	81	10	0	8	30	1	2	3	24	0	53	1	1	6	.397	.318
Betts, Todd, Akron*	.246	128	522	439	65	108	195	25	1	20	69	1	5	4	73	8	97	1	3	6	.444	.355
Betzsold, James, Akron	.265	118	506	434	76	115	203	21	5	19	79	0	2	10	60	2	119	4	5	12	.468	.366
Bierek, Kurt, Norwich*	.271	133	541	473	77	128	218	32	2	18	78	0	2	7	56	2	89	4	4	8	.461	.355
Bocachica, Hiram, Harrisburg	.278	119	501	443	82	123	181	19	3	11	35	1	3	13	41	1	98	29	12	3	.409	.354
Bogle, Bryan, Bowie	.255	102	421	384	50	98	154	17	0	13	58	1	4	5	27	1	92	3	4	15	.401	.310
Booty, Josh, Portland	.210	122	480	448	42	94	177	19	2	20	69	0	4	1	27	1	166	2	2	12	.395	.254
Borrero, Richie, Trenton	.251	57	222	203	31	51	74	12	1	3	23	2	1	3	13	0	46	2	2	7	.365	.305
Bost, Heath, New Haven	.000	38	3	3	0	0	0	0	0	0	0	0	0	0	0	0	2	0	0	0	.000	.000
Boston, D.J., New Haven*	.287	83	346	293	53	84	123	14	2	7	49	0	4	0	49	2	63	1	5	5	.420	.384
Boyd, Jason, Reading	.077	48	14	13	1	1	1	0	0	0	0	0	0	0	1	0	5	0	0	0	.077	.143
Brannan, Ryan, Reading	.000	45	1	1	0	0	0	0	0	0	0	0	0	0	0	0	1	0	0	0	.000	.000
Branyan, Russell, Akron*	.234	41	168	137	26	32	72	4	0	12	30	0	1	2	28	1	56	0	0	1	.526	.369
Brinkley, Josh, Harrisburg	.315	22	56	54	8	17	25	2	0	2	6	0	1	0	1	0	12	0	1	1	.463	.321
Brown, Armann, New Britain	.152	14	55	46	4	7	10	3	0	0	1	0	0	9	0	13	1	2	0	.217	.291
Brown, Randy, Tren.-Nor.	.250	116	456	396	61	99	153	3	4	11	57	3	4	6	47	3	124	11	8	7	.386	.334
Brown, Ron, Norwich	.287	100	403	362	47	104	142	17	3	5	50	3	2	1	35	1	59	5	7	11	.392	.350
Brownson, Mark, New Haven*	.143	31	34	28	2	4	4	0	0	0	1	2	0	0	4	0	10	0	0	1	.143	.250
Bryant, Pat, Trenton	.288	104	452	379	73	109	192	20	3	19	77	2	2	9	60	1	76	18	7	3	.507	.396
Buchanan, Brian, Norwich	.309	116	519	470	75	145	204	25	2	10	69	0	6	11	32	0	85	11	9	11	.434	.362
Bullinger, Kirk, Harrisburg	.000	21	2	2	0	0	0	0	0	0	0	0	0	0	0	0	2	0	0	0	.000	.000
Bunch, Mel, Harrisburg	.143	9	8	7	0	1	1	0	0	0	0	1	0	0	0	0	3	0	0	1	.143	.143
Burgus, Travis, Portland*	.143	16	11	7	1	1	1	0	0	0	0	0	0	0	4	0	3	0	0	0	.143	.333
Burton, Darren, Reading†	.315	45	201	184	23	58	99	11	3	8	34	2	3	3	9	2	39	1	1	1	.538	.352
Byrd, Matt, New Haven†	.000	10	4	3	0	0	0	0	0	0	0	1	0	0	0	0	1	0	0	1	.000	.000
Cabrera, Jolbert, Harrisburg	.251	48	203	171	28	43	58	9	0	2	11	3	0	1	28	0	28	8	5	4	.339	.360
Cabrera, Orlando, Harrisburg	.308	35	149	133	34	41	73	13	2	5	20	1	0	0	15	0	18	7	2	0	.549	.378
Campos, Jesus, Harrisburg	.308	82	308	286	33	88	117	12	1	5	36	6	6	2	8	0	24	6	8	9	.409	.325
Carney, Bartt, Bowie†	.269	66	195	156	27	42	47	5	0	0	8	4	1	3	31	1	31	8	5	0	.301	.398
Carpenter, Brian, Binghamtom	.000	17	3	3	0	0	0	0	0	0	0	0	0	0	0	0	3	0	0	0	.000	.000
Carter, John, Bing.-Ak.	.000	19	1	1	0	0	0	0	0	0	0	0	0	0	0	0	1	0	0	0	.000	.000
Carvajal, Jhonny, Harrisburg	.259	116	416	378	36	98	115	12	1	1	31	4	3	4	27	3	66	10	7	8	.304	.313
Carver, Steve, Reading*	.262	79	322	282	41	74	136	11	3	15	43	0	1	3	36	9	69	2	2	8	.482	.351
Casey, Sean, Akron*	.386	62	270	241	38	93	144	19	1	10	66	0	1	5	23	2	34	0	1	5	.598	.448
Castro, Tony, Portland	.333	27	3	3	1	1	4	0	0	1	1	0	0	0	0	0	1	0	0	0	1.333	.333
Censale, Silvio, Reading*	.000	20	29	21	2	0	0	0	0	0	0	4	0	0	4	0	7	0	0	0	.000	.160
Chergey, Dan, Portland	.500	32	2	2	0	1	1	0	0	0	0	0	0	0	0	0	0	0	0	0	.500	.500
Clark, Howie, Bowie*	.287	105	351	314	39	90	133	16	0	9	37	1	3	1	32	2	38	2	2	5	.424	.351
Claudio, Patricio, Akron	.212	17	37	33	6	7	8	1	0	0	6	0	0	1	3	0	14	2	2	1	.242	.297
Cole, Jason, Harrisburg	.000	37	1	0	0	0	0	0	0	0	0	0	0	0	1	0	0	0	0	0	.000	.000
Coleman, Michael, Trenton	.301	102	444	385	56	116	191	17	5	14	58	9	4	5	41	1	89	20	7	5	.496	.372
Cook, Hayward, Portland	.295	69	183	166	37	49	77	13	0	5	21	2	1	1	13	0	44	2	5	3	.464	.348
Coquillette, Trace, Harrisburg	.259	81	334	293	46	76	129	17	3	10	51	1	1	14	25	0	40	9	4	5	.440	.345
Cornelius, Reid, Portland	.375	6	9	8	3	3	5	2	0	0	0	0	0	0	0	0	2	0	0	0	.625	.375
Correia, Rod, Trenton	.293	67	282	249	40	73	114	18	1	7	33	4	1	6	22	0	32	4	2	7	.458	.363
Costa, Tony, Reading	.353	28	25	17	5	6	7	1	0	0	2	4	0	0	4	0	5	0	0	1	.412	.476
Costello, Brian, Reading	.194	16	41	36	6	7	14	2	1	1	5	1	0	2	2	0	12	0	1	0	.389	.275
Curtis, Chad, Akron	.389	4	19	18	5	7	17	1	0	3	6	0	0	1	0	0	3	0	1	1	.944	.421
Curtis, Kevin, Bow.-N.H.	.273	127	484	429	65	117	201	30	0	18	82	1	7	6	41	0	104	1	3	9	.469	.340
Curtis, Randy, Akron*	.237	29	119	93	19	22	40	3	0	5	15	2	2	0	22	0	27	2	3	1	.430	.376
Daedelow, Craig, Bowie	.000	1	1	1	0	0	0	0	0	0	0	0	0	0	0	0	1	0	0	0	.000	.000
Dawkins, Walt, New Britain	.239	106	377	331	48	79	118	13	1	8	40	6	3	2	35	0	90	4	5	6	.356	.313
Dellucci, David, Bowie*	.327	107	449	385	71	126	221	29	3	20	55	0	1	5	58	1	69	11	4	6	.574	.421
Dennis, Les, Norwich	.333	10	37	30	4	10	11	1	0	0	2	2	0	0	5	0	11	1	1	0	.367	.429
Depastino, Joe, Trenton	.254	79	316	276	51	70	137	14	1	17	55	0	1	7	32	0	63	1	2	12	.496	.345
Derosso, Tony, Trenton	.216	102	390	357	50	77	139	14	1	14	40	3	2	2	26	0	94	13	1	5	.389	.271
Dixon, Timothy, Harrisburg*	.333	37	9	9	1	3	4	1	0	0	0	0	0	0	0	0	3	0	0	0	.444	.333
Dodd, Robert, Reading*	.000	63	5	5	0	0	0	0	0	0	0	0	0	0	0	0	2	0	0	0	.000	.000
Donato, Daniel, Norwich*	.275	96	385	349	44	96	129	16	1	5	43	0	1	9	26	2	44	7	4	13	.370	.340

Player, Team	Avg.	G	TPA	AB	R	H	TB	2B	3B	HR	RBI	SH	SF	HP	BB	IBB	SO	SB	CS	GDP	Slg.	OBP
Dotel, Octavio, Binghamtom ..	.000	12	6	5	0	0	0	0	0	0	0	0	0	0	1	0	0	0	0	0	.000	.167
Dukart, Derek, Norwich*	.344	9	38	32	4	11	13	2	0	0	5	0	0	3	3	0	4	0	0	1	.406	.447
Duvall, Mike, Portland	.000	45	2	2	0	0	0	0	0	0	0	0	0	0	0	0	1	0	0	0	.000	.000
Edmondson, Brian, Bing.	.000	14	1	0	1	0	0	0	0	0	0	1	0	0	0	0	0	0	0	0	.000	.000
Epperson, Chad, Trenton†	.333	3	9	9	2	3	4	1	0	0	1	0	0	0	0	0	2	1	0	0	.444	.333
Espinosa, Ramon, Bing.	.271	67	276	255	32	69	111	7	1	11	37	2	2	4	13	1	39	10	1	10	.435	.314
Faggett, Ethan, Trenton*	.286	17	68	56	10	16	24	2	0	2	8	2	1	1	8	0	17	2	0	0	.429	.379
Ferguson, Jeff, New Britain	.244	36	150	135	19	33	40	4	0	1	21	1	1	1	12	0	31	1	1	2	.296	.309
Fernandez, Jose, Harrisburg ..	.229	29	108	96	10	22	39	3	1	4	11	0	0	1	11	0	28	2	0	4	.406	.315
Fesh, Sean, Binghamtom *	.000	45	2	2	0	0	0	0	0	0	0	0	0	0	0	0	2	0	0	0	.000	.000
Feuerstein, Dave, New Haven..	.260	26	111	104	8	27	37	4	3	0	10	0	0	0	7	0	20	2	1	4	.356	.306
Figueroa, Nelson, Bing.†	.227	34	24	22	1	5	5	0	0	0	2	2	0	0	0	0	2	0	0	0	.227	.227
Fiore, Tony, Reading	.231	17	18	13	0	3	3	0	0	0	1	4	0	0	1	0	5	0	0	1	.231	.286
Fithian, Grant, Norwich	.281	79	295	253	38	71	113	16	1	8	51	0	1	0	41	0	52	1	1	3	.447	.380
Fleetham, Ben, Harrisburg	.000	49	2	2	0	0	0	0	0	0	0	0	0	0	0	0	1	0	0	0	.000	.000
Forster, Scott, Harrisburg.......	.091	17	12	11	1	1	2	1	0	0	0	1	0	0	0	0	5	0	0	0	.182	.091
Fortin, Troy, New Britain	.234	12	55	47	11	11	13	2	0	0	4	1	0	4	3	0	7	0	0	1	.277	.333
Foster, Jim, Bowie..................	.275	63	253	211	36	58	91	12	0	7	41	1	2	1	36	0	31	1	1	6	.431	.380
Foster, Mark, Reading*	.500	10	2	2	0	1	2	1	0	0	0	0	0	0	0	0	0	0	0	0	1.000	.500
Fraser, Joe, New Britain	.239	79	280	238	33	57	73	11	1	1	16	8	2	1	29	0	50	11	6	3	.307	.322
Frazier, Lou, Bowie†	.233	25	127	103	20	24	32	4	2	0	8	3	0	0	21	0	20	13	1	2	.311	.363
Fuller, Aaron, Trenton†	.260	128	590	481	87	125	172	17	6	6	46	5	4	4	95	4	84	40	15	8	.358	.384
Fullmer, Brad, Harrisburg*	.311	94	398	357	60	111	196	24	2	19	62	0	4	7	30	5	25	6	4	11	.549	.372
Garcia, Jesse, Bowie..............	.236	141	507	437	52	103	138	18	1	5	42	24	2	6	38	0	71	7	7	9	.316	.304
Garcia, Vicente, New Haven ...	.155	22	73	58	9	9	17	2	0	2	11	1	2	0	12	0	19	0	1	1	.293	.292
Gibralter, David, Trenton	.274	123	536	478	70	131	200	25	1	14	86	1	4	9	44	0	103	3	5	10	.418	.344
Gibson, Derrick, New Haven ..	.317	119	509	461	91	146	243	24	2	23	75	0	2	10	36	7	100	20	13	8	.527	.377
Giudice, John, New Haven	.250	63	236	216	26	54	81	8	2	5	30	0	1	3	16	1	49	5	1	4	.375	.309
Glass, Chip, Akron*	.259	113	462	394	74	102	142	17	4	5	37	3	1	7	56	1	61	16	10	11	.360	.360
Gomez, Rudy, Norwich	.300	102	468	393	65	118	165	18	7	5	52	1	3	10	61	0	64	11	7	8	.420	.405
Gonzalez, Alex, Portland	.254	133	489	449	69	114	195	16	4	19	65	3	3	7	27	5	83	4	7	7	.434	.305
Gonzalez, Gabe, Portland†	.000	29	2	2	0	0	0	0	0	0	0	0	0	0	0	0	1	0	0	1	.000	.000
Gonzalez, Juan, Portland........	.000	17	3	2	0	0	0	0	0	0	0	1	0	0	0	0	1	0	0	0	.000	.000
Gooch, Arnold, Binghamtom...	.000	27	26	17	2	0	0	0	0	0	0	4	0	1	4	0	7	0	0	0	.000	.227
Grace, Mike, Reading	.333	4	3	3	0	1	1	0	0	0	0	0	0	0	0	0	0	0	0	0	.333	.333
Grifol, Pedro, Binghamtom	.200	61	218	200	15	40	55	6	0	3	15	3	3	3	9	0	29	1	1	9	.275	.242
Gross, Rafael, Akron	.286	19	51	49	7	14	18	4	0	0	2	0	0	0	2	0	13	3	3	3	.367	.314
Grunewald, Keith, N.H.†	.242	103	347	310	41	75	88	11	1	0	24	6	5	1	25	1	78	7	3	8	.284	.296
Guerra, Mark, Binghamtom.....	.400	48	11	10	0	4	5	1	0	0	0	0	0	1	0	2	0	0	0	5	.500	.455
Guiliano, Matt, Reading..........	.226	119	416	367	38	83	125	15	3	7	37	8	2	5	34	4	99	7	6	8	.341	.299
Gunderson, Shane, New Brit...	.256	33	142	117	17	30	49	7	3	2	10	4	0	1	19	0	31	7	2	1	.419	.365
Haas, Matt, Harrisburg*	.211	8	24	19	2	4	8	1	0	1	4	0	1	0	4	0	2	1	0	1	.421	.333
Hackman, Luther, New Haven	.111	10	10	9	1	1	1	0	0	0	0	1	0	0	0	0	2	0	0	0	.111	.111
Hall, Billy, New Haven†	.220	17	66	59	8	13	20	2	1	1	7	0	0	0	7	0	10	7	1	1	.339	.303
Hardtke, Jason, Binghamtom†	.385	6	28	26	3	10	15	2	0	1	4	0	0	0	2	0	2	0	0	0	.577	.429
Harriss, Robin, Akron	.267	49	175	146	24	39	50	8	0	1	17	7	2	0	20	0	36	0	1	8	.342	.351
Haselman, Bill, Trenton	.231	7	28	26	3	6	13	1	0	2	3	0	0	0	2	0	2	0	0	1	.500	.286
Hastings, Lionel, Portland.......	.344	93	327	279	55	96	147	21	0	10	35	3	3	3	39	1	53	6	3	6	.527	.426
Hawkins, Kraig, Norwich.........	.261	51	220	188	36	49	57	6	1	0	16	3	2	1	26	0	37	12	2	1	.303	.350
Haynes, Heath, Tren.-N.H.-Por.	.000	47	2	2	0	0	0	0	0	0	0	0	0	0	0	0	2	0	0	0	.000	.000
Held, Dan, Reading	.272	138	589	525	80	143	260	31	4	26	86	0	4	18	42	1	116	1	3	14	.495	.345
Henderson, Ryan, New Haven	.000	24	3	3	0	0	0	0	0	0	0	0	0	0	0	0	0	0	0	0	.000	.000
Henley, Bob, Harrisburg.........	.304	79	321	280	41	85	140	19	0	12	49	0	4	5	32	2	40	5	1	7	.500	.380
Henthorne, Kevin, Norwich† ..	.000	34	2	2	0	0	0	0	0	0	0	0	0	0	0	0	1	0	0	0	.000	.000
Hernandez, Livan, Portland.....	.000	1	1	1	0	0	0	0	0	0	0	0	0	0	0	0	0	0	0	0	.000	.000
Hinds, Rob, Norwich..............	.244	51	138	119	15	29	35	4	1	0	12	3	2	2	12	0	31	1	1	5	.294	.319
Hoiles, Chris, Bowie	.143	3	10	7	1	1	2	1	0	0	2	0	0	0	3	0	2	0	0	0	.286	.400
Holdren, Nate, New Haven	.183	25	86	82	9	15	29	2	0	4	9	0	0	1	3	0	28	0	2	2	.354	.221
Horn, Jeff, New Britain...........	.255	56	214	184	17	47	69	10	0	4	26	2	2	7	19	0	24	2	4	7	.375	.344
Howard, Chris, Binghamtom...	.000	13	1	1	0	0	0	0	0	0	0	0	0	0	0	0	0	0	0	0	.000	.000
Hudler, Rex, Reading	.348	6	24	23	5	8	13	2	0	1	5	0	0	0	1	0	2	0	0	0	.565	.375
Huff, Larry, Reading	.264	124	473	425	58	112	154	21	3	5	41	6	0	6	36	3	57	24	7	10	.362	.330
Hunter, Rich, Reading	.053	29	23	19	2	1	1	0	0	0	0	2	0	0	2	0	6	0	0	0	.053	.143
Hunter, Scott, Binghamtom.....	.256	80	323	289	45	74	120	12	2	10	31	1	4	4	25	1	52	24	9	6	.415	.320
Hunter, Torii, New Britain	.231	127	528	471	57	109	159	22	2	8	56	6	1	3	47	1	94	8	8	6	.338	.305
Isom, Johnny, Bowie..............	.274	135	579	518	70	142	239	29	4	20	91	2	4	11	44	4	121	1	5	12	.461	.341
Jackson, Gavin, Trenton	.272	100	369	301	46	82	97	12	0	1	46	12	2	6	48	0	36	2	6	11	.322	.381
Jackson, Ryan, Portland*	.312	134	546	491	87	153	267	28	4	26	98	1	0	3	51	2	85	2	5	6	.544	.381
Jacobsen, Joe, Portland	.000	47	3	3	0	0	0	0	0	0	0	0	0	0	0	0	2	0	0	0	.000	.000
Jarrett, Link, New Haven†	.303	88	292	261	19	79	93	9	1	1	27	11	1	1	18	3	30	2	2	3	.356	.349
Johnson, J.J., New Britain	.236	103	407	356	60	84	110	11	3	3	42	3	6	4	38	1	94	13	1	6	.309	.312
Kingsale, Eugene, Bowie†	.413	13	53	46	8	19	25	6	0	0	4	1	0	1	5	0	4	5	1	2	.543	.481
Kirgan, Chris, Bowie	.230	139	569	504	72	116	198	25	0	19	71	0	3	2	60	1	141	0	0	13	.393	.313
Knowles, Eric, Binghamtom ...	.236	51	176	157	16	37	56	10	0	3	22	0	2	1	16	1	34	7	0	2	.357	.307
Koeyers, Ramsey, Portland.....	.259	83	305	286	37	74	126	14	1	12	50	1	1	2	15	2	67	0	3	5	.441	.299
Koskie, Corey, New Britain* ...	.286	131	536	437	88	125	232	26	6	23	79	0	2	7	90	10	106	9	5	13	.531	.414
Kotsay, Mark, Portland*	.306	114	516	438	103	134	225	27	2	20	77	0	3	0	75	0	65	17	5	16	.514	.405
Kusiewicz, Mike, New Haven...	.000	10	2	2	0	0	0	0	0	0	0	0	0	0	0	0	0	0	0	0	.000	.000
Lamb, David, Bowie†	.331	73	315	269	46	89	125	20	2	4	38	4	4	4	34	0	35	0	0	3	.465	.408
Lane, Ryan, New Britain	.259	128	503	444	63	115	160	26	2	5	56	8	7	1	43	0	79	18	7	5	.360	.321
Lasater, Chris, Bowie	.250	3	4	4	0	1	1	0	0	0	0	0	0	0	0	0	1	0	0	0	.250	.250
Lawrence, Chip, Bowie...........	.231	7	14	13	1	3	3	0	0	0	0	0	0	0	1	0	3	0	0	0	.231	.286

Player, Team	Avg.	G	TPA	AB	R	H	TB	2B	3B	HR	RBI	SH	SF	HP	BB	IBB	SO	SB	CS	GDP	Slg.	OBP
LeCronier, Jason, Bowie*......	.300	6	11	10	0	3	3	0	0	0	2	0	1	0	0	0	4	0	0	0	.300	.273
LeGree, Keith, New Britain* ...	.242	113	407	343	46	83	133	19	2	9	58	1	4	3	56	5	70	10	4	15	.388	.350
Lewis, Anthony, New Haven*.	.228	51	183	167	32	38	83	9	0	12	36	0	3	0	13	0	39	1	1	1	.497	.279
Light, Tal, New Haven	.241	25	89	83	10	20	41	6	0	5	11	1	0	0	5	0	36	0	1	1	.494	.284
Liniak, Cole, Trenton	.280	53	222	200	20	56	73	11	0	2	18	3	1	1	17	0	29	0	1	6	.365	.338
Lobaton, Jose, Norwich	.193	68	218	197	16	38	47	6	0	1	15	5	2	2	12	0	60	2	3	4	.239	.244
Long, R.D., Norwich†	.281	34	107	89	18	25	38	5	1	2	17	2	1	1	13	0	21	5	3	2	.427	.375
Lopez, Jose, Binghamtom......	.246	66	221	207	31	51	96	10	1	11	26	0	1	0	13	1	63	4	2	4	.464	.290
Lowell, Mike, Norwich	.344	78	343	285	60	98	160	17	0	15	47	1	5	4	48	1	30	2	1	11	.561	.439
Lukachyk, Rob, Harrisburg*..	.275	42	169	153	26	42	75	6	3	7	26	1	1	3	11	0	26	5	3	2	.490	.333
Luzinski, Ryan, Bowie	.284	30	91	81	12	23	42	4	0	5	15	0	0	0	10	1	17	3	0	1	.519	.363
Macca, Chris, New Haven	.000	46	1	1	0	0	0	0	0	0	0	0	0	0	0	0	1	0	0	0	.000	.000
Madonna, Chris, Trenton*......	.341	14	47	41	7	14	17	3	0	0	6	0	0	0	6	0	11	2	2	1	.415	.426
Mahalik, John, Binghamtom ..	.217	74	208	189	19	41	56	12	0	1	18	2	2	4	11	1	39	2	3	6	.296	.272
Maness, Dwight, Bing...........	.189	74	294	259	33	49	83	13	3	5	31	4	2	5	24	1	73	4	4	2	.320	.269
Manning, Len, Reading*.........	.000	28	5	4	0	0	0	0	0	0	0	0	1	0	0	0	2	0	0	0	.000	.000
Martin, Jim, Binghamtom*......	.233	36	108	90	17	21	47	2	0	8	14	0	0	2	16	0	37	6	4	0	.522	.361
Martin, Lincoln, Bowie†	.292	12	27	24	3	7	9	2	0	0	3	0	0	0	3	0	2	0	1	0	.375	.370
Martinez, Eddy, Bowie	.156	16	54	45	3	7	10	3	0	0	1	3	0	0	6	0	12	2	0	0	.222	.255
Martinez, Gabby, Norwich	.321	77	341	312	49	100	140	12	5	6	54	10	3	5	11	0	44	21	6	5	.449	.350
Martinez, Ramiro, Harrisburg*	.250	37	9	8	1	2	2	0	0	0	0	1	0	0	0	0	1	0	0	0	.250	.250
McCommon, Jason, Har........	.100	29	13	10	1	1	4	0	0	1	1	2	0	0	1	0	6	0	0	0	.400	.182
McKeel, Walt, Trenton	.160	7	27	25	0	4	6	2	0	0	4	1	0	0	1	0	2	0	0	0	.240	.192
Meadows, Brian, Portland.*	.038	29	32	26	0	1	1	0	0	0	0	0	2	0	4	0	14	0	0	0	.038	.167
Mendoza, Carlos, Bin.*	.382	59	253	228	36	87	106	12	2	1	13	7	0	4	14	1	25	14	12	4	.465	.427
Mercado, Hector, Portland*..	.182	31	13	11	2	2	2	0	0	0	0	0	0	0	0	0	7	0	0	0	.182	.182
Mercedes, Guillermo, Akron†.	.208	97	336	288	37	60	69	7	1	0	27	10	5	5	28	0	38	2	3	9	.240	.285
Merloni, Lou, Trenton............	.310	69	302	255	49	79	119	17	4	5	37	1	4	12	30	1	43	3	2	4	.467	.402
Mientkiewicz, Doug, N.B.*	.255	132	579	467	87	119	196	28	2	15	61	5	2	7	98	2	67	21	8	8	.420	.390
Millan, Adan, Reading	.244	95	318	266	43	65	102	10	0	9	43	2	4	2	44	0	52	0	0	5	.383	.351
Millar, Kevin, Portland	.342	135	594	511	94	175	309	34	2	32	131	0	7	10	66	9	53	2	3	11	.605	.423
Miller, David, Akron*	.301	134	569	509	84	153	210	27	9	4	61	6	4	2	48	2	77	22	11	5	.413	.361
Milliard, Ralph, Portland	.275	19	80	69	13	19	24	1	2	0	5	3	0	1	7	0	8	3	2	2	.348	.351
Million, Doug, New Haven*....	.250	10	10	8	0	2	3	1	0	0	0	1	0	0	1	0	1	0	0	0	.375	.333
Mitchell, Scott, Harrisburg	.200	4	5	5	0	1	1	0	0	0	1	0	0	0	0	0	1	0	0	0	.200	.200
Mix, Greg, Portland...............	.067	30	18	15	0	1	1	0	0	0	1	0	3	0	0	0	8	0	0	0	.067	.067
Montgomery, Steve, Bowie	.500	24	3	2	0	1	1	0	0	0	0	1	0	0	0	0	1	0	0	0	.500	.500
Moore, Joel, New Haven*	.250	19	8	8	0	2	2	0	0	0	1	0	0	0	0	0	2	0	0	0	.250	.250
Moore, Mike, Binghamtom	.300	50	150	130	19	39	58	11	1	2	13	0	1	1	18	1	47	7	3	2	.446	.387
Moore, Trey, Harrisburg*	.190	27	21	21	1	4	6	0	1	0	2	0	0	0	0	0	4	0	0	0	.286	.190
Morales, Elvin, Binghamtom ..	.250	1	4	4	0	1	1	0	0	0	0	0	0	0	0	0	1	0	0	0	.250	.250
Morales, Francisco, Harrisburg	.204	16	54	49	5	10	17	1	0	2	4	0	1	1	3	1	22	0	0	3	.347	.259
Morgan, Kevin, Binghamtom .	.194	51	216	191	16	37	47	7	0	1	10	3	0	3	19	1	25	11	2	3	.246	.277
Morgan, Scott, Akron............	.174	21	79	69	11	12	21	3	0	2	6	0	1	1	8	0	20	1	0	0	.304	.266
Moriarty, Mike, New Britain ...	.221	135	492	421	60	93	143	22	5	6	48	10	5	3	53	1	68	12	5	10	.340	.309
Morris, Bobby, Akron*	.252	42	146	119	17	30	44	9	1	1	15	2	1	2	22	0	21	1	2	3	.370	.375
Moyle, Mike, Akron...............	.231	104	404	342	56	79	142	15	0	16	53	1	2	6	53	1	71	3	0	17	.415	.342
Mulligan, Sean, Akron...........	.429	2	8	7	1	3	4	1	0	0	1	0	0	0	1	0	0	0	0	0	.571	.500
Neal, Mike, Akron	.282	126	532	457	77	129	208	24	2	17	69	5	3	12	55	0	103	8	7	7	.455	.372
Newstrom, Doug, New Haven*	.266	95	290	244	29	65	80	10	1	1	43	2	4	1	39	1	32	9	5	8	.328	.365
Norman, Scott, New Haven....	.000	29	1	1	0	0	0	0	0	0	0	0	0	0	0	0	1	0	0	0	.000	.000
Norris, Joe, Portland	.000	9	1	1	0	0	0	0	0	0	0	0	0	0	0	0	0	0	0	0	.000	.000
Northeimer, Jamie, Reading...	.200	44	132	100	14	20	29	6	0	1	16	2	0	5	25	1	22	0	0	2	.290	.385
Ojeda, Augie, Bowie†	.294	58	246	204	33	60	77	9	1	2	23	4	3	3	31	1	17	7	0	6	.377	.390
Ortiz, Bo, Harrisburg	.223	60	206	188	24	42	71	2	3	7	21	2	2	0	12	0	25	5	0	3	.378	.267
Ortiz, David, New Britain*	.322	69	285	258	40	83	151	22	2	14	56	0	2	4	21	1	78	2	6	5	.585	.379
Ortiz, Nick, Trenton	.281	87	331	288	47	81	126	17	2	8	53	6	5	7	27	1	55	3	2	8	.438	.348
Osborne, Mark, New Haven*..	.000	3	7	5	1	0	0	0	0	0	0	0	0	0	2	0	4	0	0	0	.000	.286
Otanez, Willis, Bowie	.333	19	88	78	13	26	44	9	0	3	13	0	1	0	9	0	19	0	1	3	.564	.398
Pachot, John, Harrisburg	.279	94	355	323	40	90	140	23	3	7	50	2	5	3	22	0	42	6	6	10	.433	.326
Pagano, Scott, Reading†	.274	117	530	468	77	128	159	16	3	3	44	2	4	8	48	3	62	17	13	11	.340	.348
Parisi, Mike, Portland............	.167	9	6	6	0	1	1	0	0	0	0	0	0	0	0	0	5	0	0	0	.167	.167
Parra, Franklin, Binghamtom†	.200	5	16	15	2	3	4	1	0	0	1	1	0	0	0	0	5	0	0	0	.267	.200
Paxton, Chris, Bowie*...........	.136	12	23	22	1	3	4	1	0	0	1	0	0	0	1	0	7	0	0	1	.182	.174
Peever, Lloyd, New Haven......	.231	20	17	13	0	3	3	0	0	0	1	3	1	0	0	0	5	0	0	0	.231	.214
Perez, Yorkis, Binghamtom*..	.000	12	1	1	0	0	0	0	0	0	0	0	0	0	0	0	0	0	0	0	.000	.000
Perry, Chan, Akron	.315	119	516	476	74	150	248	34	2	20	96	1	6	5	28	0	61	3	3	14	.521	.355
Peterson, Nate, Harrisburg*..	.243	52	159	140	17	34	54	4	2	4	18	1	0	1	17	5	27	1	0	5	.386	.329
Phelps, Tom, Harrisburg*	.158	18	22	19	1	3	3	0	0	0	1	3	0	0	0	0	5	0	0	0	.158	.158
Pledger, Kinnis, New Haven*.	.254	61	235	201	35	51	95	10	2	10	26	2	1	1	30	2	53	2	2	7	.473	.352
Polanco, Enohel, Binghamtom	.300	82	290	263	34	79	109	13	4	3	32	5	0	5	17	2	59	7	5	3	.414	.354
Pool, Matt, New Haven†	.000	29	3	2	0	0	0	0	0	0	0	1	0	0	0	0	1	0	0	0	.000	.000
Post, Dave, Harrisburg..........	.263	48	189	156	26	41	60	10	0	3	18	3	1	5	24	0	24	5	1	1	.385	.376
Press, Gregg, Portland..........	.111	28	21	18	2	2	2	0	0	0	0	0	0	0	2	0	4	0	0	0	.111	.200
Price, Tom, New Haven*........	.000	48	1	1	0	0	0	0	0	0	0	0	0	0	0	0	0	0	0	0	.000	.000
Raines, Tim, Norwich†	.286	2	7	7	0	2	3	1	0	0	2	0	0	0	0	0	2	0	0	0	.429	.286
Raleigh, Matt, Binghamtom ...	.196	122	479	398	71	78	204	15	0	37	74	0	1	1	79	6	169	0	2	7	.513	.330
Ramirez, Angel, Norwich	.000	2	1	1	0	0	0	0	0	0	0	0	0	0	0	0	1	0	0	0	.000	.000
Rector, Bobby, Portland	.333	6	3	3	0	1	1	0	0	0	0	0	0	0	0	0	0	0	0	0	.333	.333
Reeves, Glenn, Portland........	.351	66	267	222	53	78	114	14	2	6	35	0	2	4	39	0	43	9	4	3	.514	.453
Riggs, Kevin, Akron*	.225	53	218	178	34	40	52	9	0	1	20	1	2	3	34	2	35	3	1	5	.292	.355
Roberts, Chris, Binghamtom..	.077	23	30	26	2	2	6	1	0	1	5	3	0	0	1	0	10	0	0	0	.231	.111

Player, Team	Avg.	G	TPA	AB	R	H	TB	2B	3B	HR	RBI	SH	SF	HP	BB	IBB	SO	SB	CS	GDP	Slg.	OBP
Rodriguez, Victor, Portland	.277	113	444	401	63	111	146	18	4	3	38	10	3	0	30	0	43	13	7	15	.364	.325
Roque, Rafael, Binghamtom*	.000	16	1	1	0	0	0	0	0	0	0	0	0	0	0	0	0	0	0	0	.000	.000
Rosario, Mel, Bowie†	.263	123	471	430	68	113	177	26	1	12	60	1	4	9	27	2	106	4	7	5	.412	.317
Rose, Scott, Norwich	.000	22	1	1	0	0	0	0	0	0	0	0	0	0	0	0	0	0	0	0	.000	.000
Roskos, John, Portland.........	.308	123	509	451	66	139	244	31	1	24	84	2	6	0	50	2	81	4	6	17	.541	.373
Royster, Aaron, Reading	.257	112	468	412	59	106	179	18	5	15	62	0	2	1	53	0	104	2	3	12	.434	.342
Saipe, Mike, New Haven	.238	19	25	21	5	5	12	1	0	2	5	4	0	0	0	0	2	0	0	0	.571	.238
Samuels, Scott, Harrisburg* ..	.296	64	259	223	32	66	102	19	1	5	32	1	0	1	34	3	43	13	4	0	.457	.391
Sanchez, Jesus, Binghamtom*	.231	26	35	26	4	6	6	0	0	0	0	7	0	0	2	0	8	1	0	0	.231	.286
Sauerbeck, Scott, Bin...........	.100	27	13	10	0	1	1	0	0	0	1	2	0	0	1	0	4	0	0	0	.100	.182
Saunders, Chris, Binghamtom	.324	30	129	111	16	36	58	13	0	3	22	0	4	2	12	1	20	3	1	2	.523	.388
Schaeffer, Jon, New Britain....	.207	10	31	29	1	6	8	2	0	0	4	0	0	0	2	0	7	1	1	1	.276	.258
Seefried, Tate, Binghamtom* .	.313	96	393	335	59	105	208	16	0	29	79	0	4	0	54	10	99	9	4	2	.621	.405
Sexton, Chris, New Haven.....	.297	98	439	360	65	107	140	22	4	1	38	11	4	2	62	0	37	8	16	8	.389	.400
Shoemaker, Stephen, N.H.* ...	.250	14	20	16	0	4	4	0	0	0	1	4	0	0	0	0	5	0	1	0	.250	.250
Short, Barry, Binghamtom	1.000	6	1	1	1	1	1	0	0	0	0	0	0	0	0	0	0	0	0	0	1.000	1.000
Shumpert, Terry, New Haven .	.235	5	17	17	2	4	7	0	0	1	1	0	0	0	0	0	0	0	0	1	.412	.235
Smart, J.D., Harrisburg	.000	12	9	7	0	0	0	0	0	0	0	2	0	0	0	0	1	0	0	0	.000	.000
Smith, Jeff, New Britain*	.222	5	20	18	1	4	5	1	0	0	3	0	0	0	2	0	4	0	0	0	.278	.300
Smith, Sloan, Norwich†	.200	2	8	5	1	1	1	0	0	0	1	1	0	0	2	0	2	0	0	0	.200	.429
Stevenson, Rodney, Har.........	.000	4	1	1	0	0	0	0	0	0	0	0	0	0	0	0	0	0	0	0	.000	.000
Stovall, Darond, Harrisburg† ..	.284	45	195	169	29	48	81	4	1	9	39	0	3	0	23	1	30	4	0	3	.479	.364
Stowers, Chris, Harrisburg	.288	19	65	59	9	17	25	4	2	0	5	1	0	0	5	2	11	3	1	1	.424	.344
Strawberry, Darryl, Norwich* .	.000	1	2	2	0	0	0	0	0	0	0	0	0	0	0	0	1	0	0	0	.000	.000
Taylor, Jamie, New Haven*	.325	104	375	329	43	107	150	17	1	8	41	5	4	2	35	7	49	2	3	5	.456	.389
Tebbs, Nate, Trenton†	.313	5	18	16	2	5	5	0	0	0	0	0	0	0	2	0	1	0	1	0	.313	.389
Thomas, Evan, Reading	.111	15	10	9	1	1	1	0	0	0	0	1	0	0	0	0	2	0	0	0	.111	.111
Thomas, Greg, Akron*	.244	67	274	242	27	59	97	13	2	7	42	0	2	0	29	1	50	2	1	4	.401	.322
Thurman, Mike, Harrisburg.....	.154	20	14	13	2	2	3	1	0	0	2	0	0	0	0	0	6	0	0	0	.231	.154
Tolar, Kevin, Binghamtom	.000	22	1	1	0	0	0	0	0	0	0	0	0	0	0	0	1	0	0	0	.000	.000
Torres, Tony, Portland	.260	29	61	50	12	13	23	2	1	2	4	1	0	2	8	0	15	2	3	0	.460	.383
Townsend, Dave, Portland	.167	15	12	12	1	2	3	1	0	0	0	0	0	0	0	0	5	0	0	0	.250	.167
Tremie, Chris, Reading	.203	97	346	295	20	60	79	11	1	2	31	5	5	5	36	0	61	0	5	7	.268	.296
Troutman, Keith, Reading.......	.286	57	8	7	1	2	5	0	0	1	1	1	0	0	0	0	3	0	0	0	.714	.286
Turrentine, Rich, Binghamtom	.000	61	1	1	0	0	0	0	0	0	0	0	0	0	0	0	1	0	0	0	.000	.000
Valdez, Trovin, Harrisburg......	.310	13	47	42	8	13	15	2	0	0	4	1	0	0	4	0	9	2	1	1	.357	.370
Valentin, Javier, New Britain† .	.243	102	409	370	41	90	131	17	0	8	50	2	6	1	30	1	61	2	3	5	.354	.297
Vavrek, Mike, New Haven*	.063	17	17	16	2	1	1	0	0	0	0	0	0	0	0	0	4	0	0	0	.063	.063
Vazquez, Javier, Harrisburg....	.000	6	6	5	0	0	0	0	0	0	0	1	0	0	0	0	2	0	0	0	.000	.000
Ward, Bryan, Portland*	.143	13	10	7	2	1	1	0	0	0	0	1	0	0	2	0	2	0	1	0	.143	.333
Watkins, Scott, New Haven* ..	1.000	13	1	1	0	1	2	1	0	0	0	0	0	0	0	0	0	0	0	0	2.000	1.000
Weber, Neil, Harrisburg*	.077	18	16	13	1	1	1	0	0	0	1	2	0	0	1	0	4	0	0	0	.077	.143
Wells, Forry, New Haven*	.224	39	123	98	16	22	32	4	0	2	7	0	1	3	21	0	37	1	2	2	.327	.374
Wesemann, Jason, Reading....	.182	7	14	11	4	2	2	0	0	0	1	0	0	1	2	0	2	0	0	1	.182	.357
Westbrook, Destry, Reading ...	.000	26	2	1	0	0	0	0	0	0	0	1	0	0	0	0	1	0	0	0	.000	.000
Whiteman, Greg, Reading*	.000	9	8	6	0	0	0	0	0	0	0	2	0	0	0	0	3	0	0	0	.000	.000
Wilcox, Luke, Norwich*	.277	74	323	300	45	83	116	13	1	6	34	1	1	3	18	1	36	13	3	6	.387	.323
Williams, Juan, Trenton*	.200	63	235	200	34	40	83	5	1	12	30	1	1	0	33	2	63	0	4	2	.415	.312
Wilson, Pookie, Portland*	.252	45	128	115	15	29	44	6	0	3	14	2	0	0	11	1	15	2	3	1	.383	.317
Wilson, Preston, Binghamton..	.286	70	285	259	37	74	145	12	1	19	47	0	3	2	21	0	71	7	1	5	.560	.340
Wilson, Tom, Norwich............	.296	124	514	419	88	124	216	21	4	21	80	0	5	4	86	0	126	1	4	8	.516	.416
Wilson, Vance, Binghamtom ..	.276	92	352	322	46	89	151	17	0	15	40	3	1	5	20	0	46	2	5	6	.469	.328
Winn, Randy, Portland	.292	96	440	384	66	112	163	15	6	8	36	6	1	7	42	2	92	35	20	4	.424	.371
Yarnall, Ed, Binghamtom	.000	5	5	5	0	0	0	0	0	0	0	0	0	0	0	0	3	0	0	0	.000	.000
Zolecki, Mike, New Haven	.000	16	6	4	0	0	0	0	0	0	0	1	0	1	0	0	0	0	0	0	.000	.200
Zorrilla, Julio, Binghamtom†..	.125	7	24	24	2	3	4	1	0	0	0	0	0	0	0	0	5	0	0	0	.167	.125

GRAND SLAMS: Ashby, Seefried, 3 each; Casey, Rosario, Roskos, T. Wilson, 2 each; Alcantara, Anderson, Barthol, Bates, Bernhardt, Bogle, Bierek, Buchanan, Carver Cook, Coquillette, K. Curtis, Dawkins, Espinosa, Gibraltar, Gomez, Guiliano, Isom, R. Jackson, Kirgan, Mientkiewicz, Moriarty, Moyle, D. Ortiz, N. Ortiz, Perry, Raleigh, Saunders, Wilcox, 1 each.

AWARDED FIRST BASE ON CATCHER'S INTERFERENCE: Bierek 3 (Pachot 2, Barthol); Foster 2 (Borrero 2); Fraser 2 (Borrero, Grifol); Ortiz 2 (Roskos 2); Angeli (V. Wilson); Fuller (Grifol); Glass (Northeimer) Gunders

PLAYERS WITH TWO OR MORE TEAMS

Player, Team	Avg.	G	TPA	AB	R	H	TB	2B	3B	HR	RBI	SH	SF	HP	BB	IBB	SO	SB	CS	GDP	Slg.	OBP
Brown, Randy, Trenton	.256	97	385	336	51	86	129	11	4	8	49	3	4	4	38	3	102	9	7	6	.384	.335
Brown, Randy, Norwich............	.217	19	71	60	10	13	24	2	0	3	8	0	0	2	9	0	22	2	1	1	.400	.338
Carter, John, Binghamtom	.000	9	1	1	0	0	0	0	0	0	0	0	0	0	0	0	0	0	0	0	.000	.000
Carter, John, Akron..................	.000	10	0	0	0	0	0	0	0	0	0	0	0	0	0	0	0	0	0	0	.000	.000
Curtis, Kevin, Bowie	.269	22	76	67	7	18	27	6	0	1	13	1	1	0	7	0	22	1	1	0	.403	.333
Curtis, Kevin, New Haven	.273	105	408	362	58	99	174	24	0	17	69	0	6	6	34	0	82	0	2	9	.481	.341
Haynes, Heath, Trenton	.000	14	0	0	0	0	0	0	0	0	0	0	0	0	0	0	0	0	0	0	.000	.000
Haynes, Heath, New Haven........	.000	5	1	1	0	0	0	0	0	0	0	0	0	0	0	0	1	0	0	0	.000	.000
Haynes, Heath, Portland........	.000	28	1	1	0	0	0	0	0	0	0	0	0	0	0	0	1	0	0	0	.000	.000

1997 PITCHING

TEAM

Team	W	L	Pct.	ERA	G	CG	ShO	Sv.	IP	H	TBF	R	ER	HR	SH	SF	HB	BB	IBB	SO	WP	Bk.
Harrisburg	86	56	.606	3.78	142	5	8	42	1243.2	1135	5359	644	522	145	64	37	68	513	11	1087	49	3
Norwich	73	69	.514	4.14	142	9	11	29	1222.1	1235	5351	681	562	107	32	39	50	490	9	999	82	17
Bowie	75	67	.528	4.14	142	5	5	37	1250.2	1215	5391	681	576	156	41	41	71	553	42	1029	77	14
New Britain	70	72	.493	4.32	142	10	6	38	1209.2	1196	5220	666	581	125	49	41	50	521	13	888	102	6
New Haven	64	78	.451	4.43	142	11	9	31	1214.2	1200	5273	696	598	143	59	37	64	515	29	949	75	11
Portland	79	63	.556	4.49	142	7	5	41	1245.0	1365	5479	728	621	164	61	34	66	426	33	919	75	6
Binghamton	66	76	.465	4.51	142	11	8	28	1227.2	1258	5392	732	615	136	58	32	37	553	16	983	62	11
Reading	74	68	.521	4.60	142	3	4	42	1257.1	1309	5528	741	643	169	67	34	69	538	27	959	48	9
Trenton	71	70	.504	4.92	141	6	5	36	1229.1	1313	5487	760	672	132	42	43	52	555	15	900	66	9
Akron	51	90	.362	5.26	141	16	5	19	1197.0	1357	5503	841	700	132	64	46	79	588	24	851	69	17

INDIVIDUAL

TOP QUALIFIERS FOR EARNED-RUN AVERAGE TITLE

Minimum 114 innings. *Lefthanded pitcher.

Pitcher, Team	W	L	Pct.	ERA	G	GS	CG	ShO	GF	Sv.	IP	H	TBF	R	ER	HR	SH	SF	HB	BB	IBB	SO	WP	Bk.
Vavrek, Mike, New Haven*	12	3	.800	2.57	17	17	2	0	0	0	122.2	94	491	38	35	7	8	4	1	34	0	101	4	0
Saipe, Mike, New Haven	8	5	.615	3.10	19	19	4	2	0	0	136.2	127	550	57	47	18	3	1	5	29	2	123	4	1
Montgomery, Steve, Bowie	10	5	.667	3.10	24	23	2	0	0	0	136.1	116	569	56	47	15	2	3	5	52	3	127	5	1
Lomon, Kevin, Norwich	9	7	.563	3.21	18	18	2	1	0	0	115.0	104	487	51	41	5	1	5	6	50	0	117	5	1
Bell, Jason, New Britain	11	9	.550	3.39	28	28	3	1	0	0	164.2	163	700	71	62	19	3	2	5	64	0	142	13	2
Thurman, Mike, Harrisburg	9	6	.600	3.81	20	20	1	0	0	0	115.2	102	474	54	49	16	3	7	5	30	0	85	3	0
Moreno, Julio, Bowie	9	6	.600	3.83	27	25	1	0	0	0	138.2	141	596	76	59	20	2	3	6	64	4	106	6	3
Mercado, Hector, Portland*	11	3	.786	3.96	31	17	1	1	6	0	129.2	129	565	66	57	10	6	1	3	54	5	125	16	2
Cumberland, Chris, Nor.-N.B.*	12	10	.545	3.99	26	26	3	1	0	0	160.1	193	708	102	71	12	5	3	5	61	1	83	12	4
Moore, Trey, Harrisburg*	11	6	.647	4.15	27	27	2	2	0	0	162.2	152	701	91	75	15	6	3	10	66	1	137	4	0
Brownson, Mark, New Haven	10	9	.526	4.19	29	29	2	0	0	0	184.2	172	779	101	86	24	8	5	14	55	1	170	5	2
Sampson, Benj, New Britain*	10	6	.625	4.19	25	20	0	0	1	0	118.0	112	498	56	55	12	2	5	1	49	1	92	4	2
Sanchez, Jesus, Binghamton*	13	10	.565	4.30	26	26	3	0	0	0	165.1	146	693	87	79	25	4	6	5	61	2	176	4	3
Figueroa, Nelson, Binghamton	5	11	.313	4.34	33	22	0	0	3	0	143.0	137	617	76	69	14	7	2	6	68	1	116	7	0
Farrell, Jim, Trenton	12	7	.632	4.37	26	26	0	0	0	0	162.2	173	706	93	79	24	1	5	7	57	0	110	11	0

DEPARTMENTAL LEADERS: W—Sanchez, 13; L—Gooch, Costa, 12; Pct.—Vavrek, .800; G—Snyder, 67; GS—Meadows, Barkley, Brownson, 29 each; CG—Delarosa, 5; ShO—Saipe, W. Moore, 2 each; GF—Tessmer, 49; Sv.—Fleetham, 30; IP—Brownson, 184.2; H—Barkley, 208; TBF—Barkley, 797; R—Barkley, 113; ER—Barkley, 98; HR—Sanchez, 25; SH—Munro, 10; SF—Yennaco, 10; HB—Brownson, 14; BB—Barkley, 79; IBB—Bullard, 9; SO—Sanchez, 176; WP—Turrentine, Resz, 17 each; BK—Several pitchers tied with 4 each.

ALL PITCHERS

*Lefthanded pitcher.

Pitcher, Team	W	L	Pct.	ERA	G	GS	CG	ShO	GF	Sv.	IP	H	TBF	R	ER	HR	SH	SF	HB	BB	IBB	SO	WP	Bk.
Arroyo, Luis, Binghamton*	0	0	.000	3.07	7	0	0	0	1	0	14.2	14	60	6	5	2	2	1	0	6	0	9	0	1
Badorek, Mike, Akron	1	2	.333	6.12	4	4	1	0	0	0	25.0	40	122	22	17	0	2	3	0	6	1	15	3	0
Baker, Scott, Akron*	2	1	.667	3.42	4	4	1	0	0	0	26.1	25	108	11	10	2	2	3	0	4	0	12	0	0
Baptist, Travis, New Britain*	5	6	.455	3.41	36	3	0	0	7	0	60.2	49	247	27	23	6	8	1	2	26	2	50	4	0
Barbao, Joe, Reading	2	3	.400	5.23	52	0	0	0	16	2	75.2	101	359	53	44	12	6	1	8	28	3	33	3	0
Barcelo, Marc, New Britain	0	1	.000	8.61	7	4	0	0	1	1	23.0	27	118	22	22	2	1	3	1	28	0	9	4	0
Barkley, Brian, Trenton*	12	9	.571	4.94	29	29	4	0	0	0	178.2	208	797	113	98	18	3	6	3	79	0	121	3	2
Bell, Jason, New Britain	11	9	.550	3.39	28	28	3	1	0	0	164.2	163	700	71	62	19	3	2	5	64	0	142	13	2
Bennett, Chris, Bowie	2	1	.667	2.89	10	0	0	0	3	0	18.2	15	79	9	6	1	0	1	1	11	2	9	0	0
Bennett, Erik, Akron	2	3	.400	4.81	11	1	0	0	5	0	24.1	26	107	13	13	1	0	0	1	9	1	20	1	1
Bennett, Joel, Bowie.	6	8	.429	3.18	44	10	0	0	12	4	113.1	89	461	45	40	12	6	3	4	40	6	146	2	1
Bennett, Shayne, Harrisburg	4	2	.667	4.40	23	1	0	0	7	2	47.0	47	210	28	23	6	3	1	4	20	0	38	1	0
Benz, Jacob, Harrisburg*	4	1	.800	2.33	23	0	0	0	8	2	38.2	39	168	12	10	0	3	1	1	20	0	36	4	0
Betti, Rich, Trenton*	2	0	1.000	6.35	30	0	0	0	14	3	39.2	42	179	29	28	7	1	1	3	17	0	30	3	0
Beverlin, Jason, Norwich	1	0	1.000	7.78	25	0	0	0	8	0	41.2	50	203	38	36	10	0	0	6	24	0	42	3	0
Blais, Mike, Trenton	2	2	.500	3.32	18	0	0	0	14	5	21.2	26	104	11	8	1	0	0	1	12	0	14	4	0
Bost, Heath, New Haven	2	2	.500	4.40	38	0	0	0	32	20	43.0	44	180	18	17	3	0	0	0	10	1	45	5	0
Bowers, Shane, New Britain	7	2	.778	3.41	14	13	1	1	0	0	71.1	65	299	29	27	6	2	3	4	22	0	59	2	0
Boyd, Jason, Reading	10	6	.625	4.82	48	7	0	0	9	0	115.2	113	509	65	62	16	2	3	5	64	7	98	1	2
Brannan, Ryan, Reading	4	2	.667	3.10	45	0	0	0	41	20	52.1	52	223	18	18	2	7	1	5	20	2	39	3	2
Brinkley, Josh, Harrisburg	0	0	.000	0.00	1	0	0	0	1	0	1.0	1	5	0	0	0	0	0	0	1	0	0	0	0
Brownson, Mark, New Haven	10	9	.526	4.19	29	29	2	0	0	0	184.2	172	779	101	86	24	8	5	14	55	1	170	5	2
Buddie, Mike, Norwich	0	0	.000	0.00	1	0	0	0	0	0	1.0	0	3	0	0	0	0	0	0	3	0	0	0	0
Bullard, Jason, Bowie	7	2	.778	2.62	61	0	0	0	15	9	92.2	84	392	39	27	6	3	4	10	39	9	77	10	0
Bullinger, Kirk, Harrisburg	3	0	1.000	2.87	21	0	0	0	12	6	27.0	22	106	9	8	4	1	0	1	6	2	29	0	0
Bunch, Mel, Harrisburg	3	3	.500	4.20	9	9	0	0	0	0	49.1	45	210	27	23	7	5	0	4	22	0	50	2	0
Burgus, Travis, Portland*	4	3	.571	6.75	9	9	0	0	0	0	52.0	63	244	47	39	12	0	1	4	26	1	29	0	0
Byrd, Matt, New Haven	1	3	.250	5.40	10	3	0	0	0	0	23.1	22	105	15	13	3	1	0	0	12	1	17	1	0
Cafaro, Rocco, Bowie	3	3	.500	5.40	13	6	0	0	0	0	48.1	50	208	34	29	9	1	2	1	16	0	43	2	4
Calmus, Lance, Akron	1	1	.500	6.10	5	1	0	0	0	0	10.1	6	46	7	7	3	0	0	1	9	0	10	1	0
Camp, Jared, Akron	2	8	.200	6.19	12	12	1	0	0	0	64.0	79	293	49	44	13	4	1	1	26	1	39	4	0
Cannon, Kevan, Trenton*	1	1	.500	2.81	13	0	0	0	7	1	16.0	7	67	7	5	1	0	1	1	11	1	11	2	0
Carpenter, Brian, Binghamton	0	1	.000	9.00	17	0	0	0	9	0	23.0	37	112	23	23	4	0	2	0	12	2	22	2	0
Carrasco, Troy, New Britain*	4	4	.500	4.96	31	3	0	0	16	1	65.1	69	305	53	36	11	4	2	2	44	4	46	4	1
Carter, John, Bing.-Ak.	1	2	.333	9.00	19	0	0	0	6	0	39.0	51	195	45	39	7	1	3	7	26	1	24	5	0

CLASS AA Eastern League

Pitcher, Team	W	L	Pct.	ERA	G	GS	CG	ShO	GF	Sv.	IP	H	TBF	R	ER	HR	SH	SF	HB	BB	IBB	SO	WP	Bk.
Castro, Tony, Portland	1	2	.333	4.58	27	0	0	0	6	0	39.1	47	176	21	20	5	4	1	3	17	1	21	4	0
Cederblad, Brett, Trenton	0	0	.000	8.68	6	0	0	0	2	0	9.1	12	42	10	9	1	0	0	0	2	0	7	1	0
Censale, Silvio, Reading*	9	4	.692	4.36	20	20	0	0	0	0	107.1	88	456	58	52	21	4	1	4	56	0	102	5	1
Chavez, Carlos, Portland	2	1	.667	5.26	30	0	0	0	13	1	39.1	35	169	23	23	4	1	1	3	16	1	32	9	0
Checo, Robinson, Trenton	1	0	1.000	2.35	1	1	0	0	0	0	7.2	6	29	3	2	0	0	1	0	1	0	9	0	0
Chergey, Dan, Portland	2	0	1.000	3.23	32	0	0	0	18	7	39.0	30	154	14	14	5	1	0	0	7	0	44	1	1
Clark, Howie, Bowie	0	0	.000	16.88	2	0	0	0	0	0	2.2	5	17	5	5	1	0	0	1	3	0	3	1	0
Cobb, Trevor, New Britain*	6	4	.600	3.43	19	13	3	0	1	1	94.1	77	386	41	36	6	4	3	4	39	0	68	12	0
Cole, Jason, Harrisburg	2	3	.400	3.57	37	0	0	0	16	0	58.0	52	254	31	23	5	3	1	3	19	2	31	1	0
Coppinger, Rocky, Bowie	1	1	.500	4.80	3	3	0	0	0	0	15.0	15	65	9	8	4	1	0	1	3	0	15	0	0
Cornelius, Reid, Portland	5	0	1.000	2.73	6	6	0	0	0	0	33.0	32	146	11	10	1	0	0	1	17	0	24	1	0
Costa, Tony, Reading	7	12	.368	5.24	28	28	2	0	0	0	165.0	174	736	111	96	24	7	4	12	72	0	110	8	0
Croghan, Andy, Norwich	2	1	.667	5.72	42	1	0	0	13	4	67.2	72	308	48	43	9	1	3	1	36	2	85	3	0
Crowell, Jim, Akron*	1	0	1.000	4.50	3	3	0	0	0	0	18.0	13	80	12	9	2	1	1	1	11	0	7	1	0
Cumberland, Chris, Nor.-N.B.*	12	10	.545	3.99	26	26	3	1	0	0	160.1	193	708	102	71	12	5	3	5	61	1	83	12	4
Curtis, Chris, Bowie	6	1	.857	3.62	36	6	0	0	14	2	87.0	100	361	41	35	10	3	2	2	17	1	48	4	2
DaSilva, Fernando, Harrisburg	0	3	.000	13.83	12	0	0	0	6	0	13.2	21	75	23	21	6	1	1	1	10	0	11	0	0
Dedrick, Jim, Harrisburg	2	1	.667	2.79	15	0	0	0	7	1	19.1	18	78	8	6	1	1	0	0	8	0	17	0	1
DeJean, Mike, New Haven	0	1	.000	6.00	2	0	0	0	0	0	3.0	3	14	2	2	0	0	0	1	2	0	2	0	0
De Los Santos, Luis, Norwich	1	1	.500	2.52	4	4	0	0	0	0	25.0	23	104	9	7	4	1	1	0	7	0	15	0	1
DeLaCruz, Francisco, Norwich	0	1	.000	3.24	2	2	0	0	0	0	8.1	8	39	3	3	0	1	0	2	7	0	0	0	0
De La Rosa, Maximo, Akron	4	9	.308	4.44	17	13	5	0	2	0	97.1	112	435	63	48	11	8	4	5	32	3	70	2	4
Dixon, Timothy, Harrisburg*	5	2	.714	3.38	37	2	0	0	6	0	69.1	66	296	34	26	6	4	3	4	24	2	75	4	0
Dodd, Robert, Reading*	9	4	.692	3.25	63	0	0	0	23	8	80.1	61	314	29	29	8	6	0	0	21	1	94	1	0
Dotel, Octavio, Binghamton	3	4	.429	5.98	12	12	0	0	0	0	55.2	66	266	50	37	5	1	0	0	38	1	40	2	1
Dougherty, Anthony, Akron	0	2	.000	2.54	28	0	0	0	26	8	39.0	31	163	11	11	2	1	2	1	19	1	31	0	0
Duvall, Mike, Portland*	4	6	.400	1.84	45	0	0	0	25	18	68.1	63	291	20	14	4	9	1	2	20	2	49	2	0
Dykhoff, Radhames, Bowie*	0	0	.000	8.31	7	0	0	0	4	0	8.2	10	43	9	8	2	0	0	0	7	0	7	0	0
Edmondson, Brian, Bin.	2	0	1.000	1.23	14	0	0	0	7	3	22.0	17	85	4	3	0	2	0	0	7	0	18	1	0
Falkenborg, Brian, Bowie	0	1	.000	16.20	1	1	0	0	0	0	1.2	3	11	3	3	0	0	0	0	3	0	0	0	0
Farrell, Jim, Trenton	12	7	.632	4.37	26	26	0	0	0	0	162.2	173	706	93	79	24	1	5	7	57	0	110	11	0
Fernandez, Jared, Trenton	4	6	.400	5.41	21	16	1	0	4	0	121.1	138	560	90	73	12	2	2	0	66	0	73	14	0
Fesh, Sean, Binghamton*	3	1	.750	3.25	45	0	0	0	13	4	55.1	60	255	26	20	3	0	1	2	24	0	37	2	3
Figueroa, Nelson, Binghamton	5	11	.313	4.34	33	22	0	0	3	0	143.0	137	617	76	69	14	7	2	6	68	1	116	7	0
Fiore, Tony, Reading	8	3	.727	3.01	17	16	0	0	0	0	104.2	89	434	47	35	6	8	4	5	40	0	64	10	1
Fleetham, Ben, Harrisburg	2	1	.667	3.04	49	0	0	0	46	30	50.1	28	216	21	17	4	3	2	2	33	2	69	4	0
Ford, Ben, Norwich	4	3	.571	4.22	28	0	0	0	14	1	42.2	35	183	28	20	1	1	2	3	19	1	38	4	0
Forster, Scott, Harrisburg*	3	6	.333	2.27	17	15	0	0	2	0	79.1	77	365	45	20	7	7	6	6	48	0	71	4	0
Foster, Mark, Reading*	2	2	.500	6.35	9	0	0	0	6	1	17.0	20	80	16	12	4	0	1	0	8	2	9	0	0
Fussell, Chris, Bowie	1	8	.111	7.11	19	18	0	0	0	0	82.1	102	398	71	65	12	1	5	10	58	3	71	7	0
Gallaher, Kevin, Bowie	1	5	.167	4.46	26	1	0	0	20	8	42.1	50	187	27	21	2	1	2	5	15	1	36	6	0
Gandarillas, Gus, New Britain	2	4	.333	4.70	17	7	1	0	2	0	61.1	67	253	34	32	6	0	2	3	15	0	29	5	0
Gonzales, Frank, Trenton*	3	1	.750	5.88	14	0	0	0	8	2	26.0	29	122	18	17	3	2	0	2	16	2	14	1	0
Gonzalez, Gabe, Portland*	3	2	.600	2.11	29	0	0	0	10	3	42.2	43	171	12	10	1	3	3	0	5	1	28	1	0
Gonzalez, Juan, Portland	0	1	.000	6.75	17	0	0	0	7	0	29.1	32	131	25	22	10	1	2	2	10	0	21	2	0
Gooch, Arnold, Binghamton	10	12	.455	5.09	27	27	4	1	0	0	161.0	179	727	106	91	12	4	7	5	76	3	98	12	0
Gooden, Dwight, Norwich	3	0	1.000	3.00	3	3	0	0	0	0	18.0	13	74	6	6	3	0	0	2	5	0	14	0	0
Gordon, Mike, Akron	1	2	.333	4.15	6	6	0	0	0	0	30.1	37	147	28	14	3	1	0	2	14	0	16	2	0
Gourdin, Tom, New Britain	2	2	.500	5.31	49	0	0	0	40	15	61.0	62	271	36	36	8	1	3	3	29	0	32	16	0
Grace, Mike, Reading	1	3	.250	5.75	4	4	0	0	0	0	20.1	28	93	17	13	4	1	0	0	6	0	10	1	0
Granata, Chris, Akron	1	0	1.000	7.20	4	0	0	0	1	0	5.0	8	27	5	4	0	0	0	0	4	0	3	1	0
Gray, Dennis, Akron*	0	2	.000	12.27	10	0	0	0	3	0	7.1	13	42	10	10	2	1	0	0	9	0	5	1	0
Greer, Ken, Bowie	1	1	.500	4.08	11	0	0	0	4	0	17.2	17	71	9	8	1	0	1	1	3	1	12	0	0
Guerra, Mark, Binghamton	4	8	.333	3.23	48	7	1	0	17	7	94.2	96	403	46	34	10	3	2	1	30	1	74	2	0
Guiliano, Matt, Reading	0	0	.000	49.50	2	0	0	0	1	0	2.0	5	17	11	11	4	0	1	0	6	0	0	0	0
Haas, Matt, Harrisburg	0	0	.000	0.00	1	0	0	0	1	0	1.0	1	4	0	0	0	0	0	0	0	0	0	0	0
Hackman, Luther, New Haven	0	6	.000	7.82	10	10	0	0	0	0	50.2	58	241	49	44	11	5	2	5	34	1	34	4	3
Hale, Chad, Trenton*	0	0	.000	8.31	3	0	0	0	1	0	4.1	5	22	5	4	1	0	0	0	5	0	2	0	0
Harris, Jeff, New Britain	2	1	.667	2.34	28	0	0	0	14	3	42.1	30	175	15	11	2	3	2	3	16	0	44	3	0
Haynes, Heath, Tren.-N.H.-Por.	5	1	.833	2.97	47	0	0	0	15	3	72.2	69	306	25	24	6	4	2	5	16	7	73	0	2
Hecker, Doug, Trenton	1	0	1.000	2.57	4	0	0	0	1	0	7.0	5	34	2	2	0	0	0	0	9	1	7	0	0
Henderson, Ryan, New Haven	2	5	.286	4.80	24	4	0	0	7	0	50.2	54	228	29	27	2	2	2	3	27	2	46	6	0
Henthorne, Kevin, Norwich	2	1	.667	3.31	33	6	0	0	12	2	73.1	72	313	32	27	8	0	4	4	14	0	64	2	0
Hernandez, Francis, Bowie	0	0	.000	1.59	6	0	0	0	2	0	5.2	7	26	1	1	0	0	0	0	4	1	2	0	0
Hernandez, Livan, Portland	0	0	.000	2.25	1	1	0	0	0	0	4.0	2	21	1	1	0	0	0	1	7	0	2	0	0
Howard, Chris, Binghamton*	0	0	.000	1.15	13	0	0	0	2	1	15.2	6	55	2	2	1	1	0	0	7	0	16	0	0
Hubbard, Mark, Norwich*	0	0	.000	15.43	2	0	0	0	2	0	2.1	6	13	4	4	1	0	0	0	1	0	0	0	0
Huff, Larry, Reading	0	0	.000	9.00	1	0	0	0	1	0	1.0	1	6	1	1	0	0	0	1	1	0	0	0	0
Hunter, Rich, Reading	6	11	.353	4.69	29	28	1	1	0	0	163.0	191	730	100	85	20	4	6	13	60	4	104	2	0
Hurst, Bill, Portland	0	0	.000	0.00	2	0	0	0	1	0	2.0	1	7	0	0	0	0	0	1	0	0	2	0	0
Irabu, Hideki, Norwich	1	1	.500	4.50	2	2	0	0	0	0	10.0	13	41	5	5	1	0	0	0	0	0	9	0	2
Jacobsen, Joe, Portland	5	5	.500	5.09	47	1	0	0	29	11	58.1	76	270	44	33	7	1	2	2	23	4	48	5	0
Jerzembeck, Mike, Norwich	2	1	.667	1.71	8	8	0	0	0	0	42.0	21	164	10	8	1	2	0	0	16	0	42	2	1
Kammerer, James, N.H.*	0	0	.000	3.60	1	1	0	0	0	0	5.0	3	21	2	2	1	1	0	0	3	0	1	0	0
Kirgan, Chris, Bowie	1	0	1.000	6.75	5	0	0	0	5	0	4.0	4	17	3	3	1	0	0	0	1	0	2	0	0
Kirkreit, Daron, Akron	8	9	.471	5.20	26	20	1	0	3	0	117.2	131	562	96	68	15	9	4	13	69	3	83	10	1
Kohlmeier, Ryan, Bowie	0	0	.000	0.00	2	0	0	0	1	1	2.2	0	9	0	0	0	0	0	0	2	0	5	0	1
Kusiewicz, Mike, New Haven*	2	4	.333	6.35	10	4	0	0	0	0	28.1	41	138	28	20	2	2	2	6	10	1	11	1	0
Lane, Aaron, Bowie*	0	1	.000	7.94	7	0	0	0	2	0	5.2	6	30	5	5	2	0	0	2	6	0	4	0	0
Lankford, Frank, Norwich	4	2	.667	2.90	11	11	2	0	0	0	68.1	58	277	28	22	3	1	1	2	15	1	39	1	1
Legault, Kevin, New Britain	5	1	.833	4.50	40	1	0	0	13	3	70.0	74	305	37	35	6	4	3	3	26	3	40	4	0
LeCronier, Jason, Bowie	0	0	.000	0.00	1	0	0	0	0	0	1.2	0	6	0	0	0	0	0	0	1	0	2	0	0
Linebarger, Keith, New Britain	0	1	.000	7.20	1	1	0	0	0	0	5.0	5	24	4	4	0	1	0	0	3	0	1	0	0

Pitcher, Team	W	L	Pct.	ERA	G	GS	CG	ShO	GF	Sv.	IP	H	TBF	R	ER	HR	SH	SF	HB	BB	IBB	SO	WP	Bk.
Lomon, Kevin, Norwich	9	7	.563	3.21	18	18	2	1	0	0	115.0	104	487	51	41	5	1	5	6	50	0	117	5	1
Lopez, Albie, Akron	0	0	.000	0.00	1	0	0	0	0	0	1.0	2	5	0	0	0	0	0	0	0	0	2	0	0
Macca, Chris, New Haven	0	4	.000	7.77	46	0	0	0	32	9	44.0	47	237	40	38	3	1	3	7	55	1	29	8	0
Maeda, Katsuhiro, Norwich	8	10	.444	4.56	25	21	1	1	2	0	124.1	117	545	75	63	14	4	2	8	62	1	76	11	2
Mahaffey, Alan, New Britain*	1	2	.333	3.57	13	1	0	0	5	1	22.2	19	98	11	9	2	1	3	0	10	0	29	4	0
Mahalik, John, Binghamton	0	0	.000	0.00	3	0	0	0	3	0	3.0	0	10	0	0	0	0	0	0	1	0	4	0	0
Mahay, Ron, Trenton*	3	3	.500	3.10	17	4	0	0	9	5	40.2	29	165	16	14	0	0	0	1	13	0	47	2	0
Maine, Dalton, Bowie	0	0	.000	0.00	9	0	0	0	5	0	12.2	4	45	0	0	0	0	0	1	6	1	11	2	0
Manning, Len, Reading*	3	1	.750	5.34	28	7	0	0	8	0	62.1	66	295	40	37	4	2	2	7	46	0	41	3	1
Mantei, Matt, Portland	1	0	1.000	6.75	5	0	0	0	1	0	4.0	1	21	3	3	0	1	0	0	8	0	7	0	0
Martinez, Johnny, Akron	1	8	.111	4.96	32	0	0	0	18	2	49.0	63	244	32	27	9	3	2	4	26	4	31	5	0
Martinez, Ramiro, Harrisburg*	4	4	.500	3.69	37	3	0	0	15	1	75.2	64	330	36	31	11	3	2	5	33	1	69	2	0
Matthews, Mike, Akron*	6	8	.429	3.82	19	19	3	1	0	0	113.0	116	492	62	48	13	3	0	7	57	0	69	5	4
McCommon, Jason, Har.	6	3	.667	5.01	29	8	0	0	7	0	82.2	81	358	50	46	13	0	0	3	39	0	58	4	1
Meadows, Brian, Portland	9	7	.563	4.61	29	29	4	0	0	0	175.2	204	763	99	90	23	9	2	4	48	4	115	7	1
Mercado, Hector, Portland*	11	3	.786	3.96	31	17	1	1	6	0	129.2	129	565	66	57	10	6	1	3	54	5	125	16	2
Mesa, Rafael, Akron	0	1	.000	4.21	14	0	0	0	4	0	25.2	36	114	13	12	1	1	0	3	9	0	7	1	0
Million, Doug, New Haven*	0	5	.000	9.23	10	10	0	0	0	0	40.0	64	213	46	41	7	6	0	3	36	0	19	4	2
Milton, Eric, Norwich*	6	3	.667	3.13	14	14	1	0	0	0	77.2	59	322	29	27	2	1	4	0	36	0	67	3	4
Mitchell, Larry, Norwich	9	9	.500	3.49	57	0	0	0	12	0	95.1	98	430	45	37	10	5	2	3	37	1	99	10	0
Mitchell, Scott, Harrisburg	1	0	1.000	3.63	4	3	0	0	0	0	17.1	11	67	7	7	3	1	0	1	3	0	13	1	0
Mix, Greg, Portland	7	7	.500	4.73	30	13	0	0	4	0	102.2	121	461	70	54	16	7	5	8	32	0	74	5	0
Montgomery, Steve, Bowie	10	5	.667	3.10	24	23	2	0	0	0	136.1	116	569	56	47	15	2	3	5	52	3	127	5	1
Montoya, Wilmer, Akron	0	0	.000	11.57	2	0	0	0	1	0	2.1	4	14	3	3	0	0	0	0	2	0	2	1	0
Moore, Joel, New Haven	6	4	.600	3.84	19	12	1	0	3	0	77.1	77	331	38	33	12	0	3	3	35	3	47	7	0
Moore, Marcus, Akron	3	5	.375	4.94	13	10	1	0	0	0	71.0	84	323	50	39	9	5	3	1	32	1	63	4	1
Moore, Trey, Harrisburg*	11	6	.647	4.15	27	27	2	2	0	0	162.2	152	701	91	75	15	6	3	10	66	1	137	4	0
Moreno, Julio, Bowie	9	6	.600	3.83	27	25	1	0	0	0	138.2	141	596	76	59	20	2	3	6	64	4	106	6	3
Morse, Paul, New Britain	3	11	.214	5.98	37	17	0	0	9	1	111.1	124	508	91	74	16	4	2	6	70	2	75	11	0
Mott, Tom, New Britain	0	0	.000	0.00	1	0	0	0	0	0	1.1	2	5	0	0	0	0	0	0	0	0	0	0	0
Munro, Peter, Trenton	7	10	.412	4.95	22	22	1	0	0	0	116.1	113	506	76	64	12	10	6	8	47	0	109	6	3
Najera, Noe, Akron*	4	8	.333	6.06	25	14	1	0	4	0	84.2	96	383	63	57	3	3	1	3	40	1	50	2	1
Norman, Scott, New Haven	1	5	.167	6.75	29	0	0	0	9	1	41.1	58	192	38	31	3	2	2	2	15	2	21	3	0
Norris, Joe, Portland	2	0	1.000	6.75	9	0	0	0	1	0	12.0	11	53	9	9	2	0	1	1	5	0	14	0	0
Orellano, Rafael, Trenton*	0	1	.000	17.05	2	2	0	0	0	0	6.1	14	42	12	12	1	0	1	0	7	0	5	1	1
Osteen, Gavin, Bowie*	1	1	.500	2.05	18	2	0	0	2	0	30.2	20	119	7	7	1	0	0	0	11	0	22	2	0
Parisi, Mike, Portland	1	3	.250	7.08	9	9	0	0	0	0	40.2	56	193	36	32	8	4	1	5	14	3	27	1	0
Parrish, John, Bowie*	1	0	1.000	1.80	1	1	0	0	0	0	5.0	3	20	1	1	0	0	0	0	2	0	3	0	0
Paxton, Chris, Bowie	0	0	.000	0.00	1	0	0	0	1	0	2.0	1	7	0	0	0	0	0	0	0	0	1	0	0
Peever, Lloyd, New Haven	5	5	.500	5.50	20	10	0	0	2	0	73.2	70	310	49	45	14	4	1	5	24	2	46	2	0
Pena, Juan, Trenton	5	6	.455	4.73	16	14	0	0	2	0	97.0	98	418	56	51	13	6	3	2	31	0	79	5	1
Percibal, Billy, Bowie	0	1	.000	3.00	1	1	1	0	0	0	6.0	5	22	2	2	0	0	1	0	1	0	5	0	0
Perez, David, New Britain	0	1	.000	6.75	1	1	0	0	0	0	4.0	5	17	3	3	0	0	1	0	1	0	3	0	0
Perez, Julio, Akron	1	0	1.000	5.63	9	0	0	0	4	1	24.0	27	115	16	15	3	0	1	2	13	0	23	1	1
Perez, Yorkis, Binghamton*	2	1	.667	0.66	12	3	0	0	4	0	27.1	15	104	4	2	1	1	0	0	12	1	39	1	0
Perkins, Dan, New Britain	7	10	.412	4.91	24	24	2	0	0	0	144.2	158	644	94	79	17	8	2	11	53	1	114	10	0
Peterson, Dean, Trenton	1	3	.250	4.60	33	1	0	0	19	5	58.2	67	268	30	30	4	4	2	4	30	3	48	5	1
Phelps, Tom, Harrisburg*	10	6	.625	4.71	18	18	0	0	0	0	101.1	115	462	68	53	14	8	5	5	39	1	86	3	1
Pierson, Jason, Binghamton*	2	2	.500	7.88	13	0	0	0	4	0	16.0	33	88	22	14	3	3	2	1	7	0	7	0	0
Ponson, Sidney, Bowie	2	7	.222	5.42	13	13	1	1	0	0	74.2	77	328	51	45	11	4	3	3	32	2	56	1	1
Pool, Matt, New Haven	3	5	.375	4.28	29	1	0	0	9	0	48.1	57	217	36	23	9	2	1	1	16	3	23	2	0
Press, Gregg, Portland	7	11	.389	4.98	28	25	1	0	1	0	144.2	178	648	101	80	19	6	4	9	41	5	93	11	1
Price, Tom, New Haven*	1	3	.250	3.16	48	1	0	0	18	0	57.0	55	246	25	20	6	5	3	3	21	2	48	1	0
Pulsipher, Bill, Binghamton*	0	0	.000	1.42	10	0	0	0	4	0	12.2	11	55	3	2	0	2	0	0	7	1	12	0	0
Rakers, Jason, Akron	1	4	.200	4.39	7	7	1	1	0	0	41.0	36	168	21	20	3	1	2	4	11	0	31	1	0
Ramirez, Felix, Trenton*	4	2	.667	5.44	18	3	0	0	6	2	41.1	43	186	28	25	7	2	3	1	20	1	29	1	0
Rath, Fred, New Britain	3	3	.500	2.68	33	0	0	0	23	12	50.1	43	200	17	15	1	1	3	1	13	0	33	3	0
Rector, Bobby, Portland	2	2	.500	4.81	6	6	0	0	0	0	33.2	45	155	20	18	7	2	1	1	11	0	23	2	0
Resz, Greg, Norwich	5	4	.556	4.70	25	13	0	0	6	0	90.0	94	410	59	47	9	3	6	3	43	0	75	17	0
Ricken, Ray, Norwich	0	2	.000	6.75	2	2	0	0	0	0	10.2	12	48	8	8	0	2	0	0	5	0	13	0	0
Roberts, Chris, Binghamton*	5	8	.385	4.96	19	19	1	0	0	0	105.1	103	448	69	58	18	6	2	8	33	0	66	1	1
Roque, Rafael, Binghamton*	1	1	.500	6.84	16	0	0	0	5	0	26.1	35	126	26	20	7	2	0	1	17	1	23	1	0
Rose, Brian, Trenton	2	1	.667	2.84	15	0	0	0	6	0	25.1	23	107	8	8	4	0	0	0	10	0	18	0	0
Rose, Scott, Norwich	0	2	.000	2.67	21	0	0	0	12	4	30.1	34	129	17	9	1	1	1	0	8	0	20	5	0
Rushing, Will, New Britain*	1	2	.333	3.97	3	2	0	0	0	0	11.1	14	50	5	5	0	0	0	0	3	0	9	0	1
Ryan, Ken, Reading	0	0	.000	0.00	2	2	0	0	0	0	2.0	1	7	0	0	0	0	0	0	1	0	0	0	0
Saberhagen, Bret, Trenton	0	0	.000	0.00	2	2	0	0	0	0	8.0	2	27	0	0	0	0	0	1	1	0	9	0	0
Saipe, Mike, New Haven	8	5	.615	3.10	19	19	4	2	0	0	136.2	127	550	57	47	18	3	1	5	29	2	123	4	1
Sampson, Ben, New Britain*	10	6	.625	4.19	25	20	0	0	1	0	118.0	112	498	56	55	12	2	5	1	49	1	92	4	2
Sanchez, Jesus, Binghamton*	13	10	.565	4.30	26	26	3	0	0	0	165.1	146	693	87	79	25	4	6	5	61	2	176	4	3
Saneaux, Francisco, Bowie	0	0	.000	8.56	8	0	0	0	1	0	13.2	8	81	14	13	1	1	1	5	32	0	13	7	0
Sauerbeck, Scott, Bin.*	8	9	.471	4.93	27	20	2	0	1	0	131.1	144	575	89	72	15	7	1	3	50	0	88	4	2
Saunders, Tony, Portland*	0	0	.000	9.00	1	1	0	0	0	0	2.0	3	10	2	2	0	0	0	0	1	0	3	0	0
Schlomann, Brett, Norwich	1	4	.200	7.85	10	10	0	0	0	0	47.0	66	224	43	41	6	0	3	3	17	0	36	1	0
Sexton, Jeff, Akron	2	0	1.000	4.75	16	3	0	0	5	1	47.1	55	215	27	25	4	4	4	5	15	1	38	1	2
Shepherd, Alvie, Bowie	10	6	.625	5.33	22	19	0	0	0	0	106.1	98	460	68	63	19	3	5	2	57	1	80	10	1
Shoemaker, Stephen, N.H.	6	4	.600	3.02	14	14	1	0	0	0	95.1	64	389	36	32	6	5	2	3	53	3	111	5	1
Short, Barry, Binghamton	2	0	1.000	2.61	6	0	0	0	2	0	10.1	9	45	3	3	1	1	0	0	4	0	6	0	0
Shuey, Paul, Akron	0	0	.000	3.38	3	0	0	0	1	0	8.0	10	32	3	3	1	0	0	0	0	0	9	1	0
Smart, J.D., Harrisburg	6	3	.667	3.69	12	12	0	0	0	0	70.2	75	308	34	29	7	6	3	3	24	0	43	3	0
Smetana, Steve, Trenton*	1	2	.333	2.95	18	0	0	0	10	3	21.1	25	97	9	7	2	2	1	2	7	1	16	1	0
Smith, Hut, Bowie	5	4	.556	4.22	14	13	0	0	1	0	81.0	90	347	45	38	14	4	2	7	22	1	46	2	0

Pitcher, Team	W	L	Pct.	ERA	G	GS	CG	ShO	GF	Sv.	IP	H	TBF	R	ER	HR	SH	SF	HB	BB	IBB	SO	WP	Bk.
Snyder, Matt, Bowie	7	5	.583	4.16	67	0	0	0	45	19	80.0	89	366	48	37	11	8	4	4	42	5	68	10	0
Steph, Rod, Bowie	1	0	1.000	1.32	7	0	0	0	0	0	13.2	6	50	3	2	1	1	0	0	3	1	9	0	0
Stevenson, Rodney, Har.	0	0	.000	3.86	4	0	0	0	2	0	7.0	9	33	5	3	1	0	0	0	5	1	6	1	0
Stidham, Phil, New Haven	0	0	.000	3.72	8	0	0	0	4	1	9.2	10	47	4	4	1	1	1	0	8	1	7	0	0
Tessmer, Jay, Norwich	3	6	.333	5.31	55	0	0	0	49	17	62.2	78	289	41	37	7	3	2	2	24	2	51	4	0
Thomas, Evan, Reading	3	6	.333	4.12	15	15	0	0	0	0	83.0	98	377	51	38	10	5	2	7	32	1	83	3	2
Thurman, Mike, Harrisburg	9	6	.600	3.81	20	20	1	0	0	0	115.2	102	474	54	49	16	3	7	5	30	0	85	3	0
Tolar, Kevin, Binghamton*	1	1	.500	5.12	22	0	0	0	9	0	31.2	38	157	20	18	3	4	1	2	22	1	26	6	0
Townsend, Dave, Portland	3	7	.300	4.87	15	13	1	0	0	0	77.2	86	350	49	42	9	1	4	11	36	1	30	2	0
Trinidad, Hector, New Britain	0	2	.000	6.33	6	3	0	0	0	0	21.1	26	95	18	15	5	2	1	1	8	0	11	1	0
Troutman, Keith, Reading	6	5	.545	3.77	57	3	0	0	19	7	107.1	94	440	48	45	17	8	4	2	34	6	103	4	0
Turrentine, Rich, Binghamton	2	4	.333	5.23	61	0	0	0	45	13	62.0	66	292	38	36	3	4	1	2	54	2	58	17	0
Tweedlie, Brad, Trenton	4	6	.400	5.77	41	0	0	0	26	5	57.2	62	275	41	37	10	1	2	6	44	3	30	1	0
Urso, Sal, Norwich*	1	1	.500	1.26	7	2	0	0	3	1	14.1	14	59	2	2	0	0	0	0	5	0	13	1	1
Vasquez, Leoner, Bin.*	0	1	.000	10.13	1	1	0	0	0	0	5.1	7	26	6	6	3	1	2	0	2	0	2	0	0
Vaught, Jay, Akron	2	3	.400	5.22	29	4	0	0	9	1	70.2	65	312	43	41	8	6	6	5	40	1	56	4	0
Vavrek, Mike, New Haven*	12	3	.800	2.57	17	17	2	0	0	0	122.2	94	491	38	35	7	8	4	1	34	0	101	4	0
Vazquez, Javier, Harrisburg	4	0	1.000	1.07	6	6	1	0	0	0	42.0	15	155	5	5	2	0	1	2	12	0	47	2	0
Walker, Pete, Trenton	0	0	.000	4.05	8	0	0	0	3	0	13.1	14	61	6	6	1	3	0	0	7	0	13	0	0
Ward, Bryan, Portland*	6	3	.667	3.91	12	12	0	0	0	0	76.0	71	316	39	33	17	2	2	2	19	1	69	6	0
Warrecker, Teddy, Akron	1	5	.167	11.53	10	7	0	0	0	2	32.0	44	192	50	41	3	1	4	9	40	0	25	4	1
Watkins, Scott, New Haven*	0	2	.000	3.52	13	0	0	0	8	0	15.1	9	58	6	6	1	1	1	3	8	3	8	3	0
Weber, Lenny, Akron	1	0	1.000	15.43	6	0	0	0	0	0	9.1	22	59	17	16	3	0	3	0	9	0	8	0	0
Weber, Neil, Harrisburg*	7	6	.538	3.83	18	18	1	0	0	0	112.2	93	477	56	48	17	6	1	8	51	1	121	6	0
Wertz, Bill, Akron	1	0	1.000	9.61	11	1	0	0	2	0	19.2	32	105	24	21	2	1	0	2	12	0	7	0	0
Westbrook, Destry, Reading	0	2	.000	8.20	26	3	0	0	15	4	45.0	70	226	49	41	11	3	3	1	22	1	38	1	0
Whiteman, Greg, Reading*	4	4	.500	4.05	9	9	0	0	0	0	53.1	57	226	27	24	6	4	1	1	21	0	31	3	0
Whitten, Casey, Akron*	1	3	.250	5.87	4	4	0	0	0	0	15.1	20	71	12	10	1	1	0	0	11	0	14	1	0
Wilson, Pookie, Portland*	0	0	.000	0.00	1	0	0	0	1	0	1.0	0	5	0	0	0	0	0	2	0	0	0	0	0
Winchester, Scott, Akron	0	0	.000	3.86	6	0	0	0	6	1	7.0	8	32	3	3	1	0	0	1	2	1	8	1	0
Wright, Jaret, Akron	3	3	.500	3.67	8	8	1	0	0	0	54.0	43	221	26	22	4	5	0	0	23	2	59	2	1
Yarnall, Ed, Binghamton*	3	2	.600	3.06	5	5	0	0	0	0	32.1	20	127	11	11	2	2	1	0	11	0	32	0	0
Yennaco, Jay, Trenton	5	11	.313	6.33	21	21	0	0	0	0	122.1	146	557	89	86	8	3	10	8	54	0	73	5	0
Young, Tim, Harrisburg*	0	0	.000	0.00	1	0	0	0	1	0	2.0	1	7	0	0	0	0	0	0	0	0	3	0	0
Zolecki, Mike, New Haven	3	5	.375	5.08	16	7	1	0	2	0	56.2	64	255	38	32	10	2	4	1	32	3	32	10	2

COMBINATION SHUTOUTS: **Akron (3)**—Camp-Vaught-Briscoe, Crowell-Lopez-Martinez, Baker-Vaught-Briscoe. **Binghamton (7)**—Sanchez-Edmondson 2, Sauerbeck-Guerra-Fesh, Perez-Pierson-Fesh-Turrentine, Guerra-Howard-Perez, Sauerbeck-Pulsipher, Yarnall-Howard-Guerra. **Bowie (4)**—Shepherd-Bullard-Bennett-Snyder, Shepherd-Gallaher, Moreno-Greer-Osteen, Montgomery-Snyder-Gallaher. **Harrisburg (5)**—Thurman-Cole, Forster-Bennett-Bullinger, Moore-Dixon-Bullinger, Smart-Benz, Dixon-Benz-Fleetham. **New Britain (4)**—Sampson-Legault-Gourdin, Sampson-Rath, Carrasco-Morse-Gourdin, Bell-Harris. **New Haven (7)**—Saipe-Zolecki-Macca, Brownson-Bost, Saipe-Macca, Shoemaker-Norman, Vavrek-Pool-Bost, Shoemaker-Macca-Henderson, Vavrek-Stidham-Bost. **Norwich (8)**—Lankford-Buddie-Tessmer-Croghan, Resz-Tessmer, Lankford-Croghan-Beverlin, Irabu-Mitchell-Beverlin, Maeda-Ford-Tessmer, Milton-Mitchell-Resz, Lomon-Resz-Maeda, Urso-Ford. **Portland (4)**—Press-Chergey-Gonzalez, Press-Chergey-Jacobsen, Mercado-Duvall, Press-Haynes-Burgus-Mantei. **Reading (3)**—Fiore-Barbao, Hunter-Barbao-Dodd, Hunter-Dodd-Brannan. **Trenton (5)**—Mahay-Peterson, Munro-Haynes, Pena-Blais, Saberhagen-Pena, Munro-Peterson-Betti.

NO-HIT GAMES: None.

PITCHERS WITH TWO OR MORE TEAMS

Pitcher, Team	W	L	Pct.	ERA	G	GS	CG	ShO	GF	Sv.	IP	H	TBF	R	ER	HR	SH	SF	HB	BB	IBB	SO	WP	Bk.
Carter, John, Binghamton	0	0	.000	6.59	9	0	0	0	4	0	13.2	19	66	15	10	4	1	1	4	0	14	0	0
Carter, John, Akron	1	2	.333	10.30	10	0	0	0	1	0	25.1	32	129	30	29	3	0	2	6	22	1	10	5	0
Cumberland, Chris, Norwich*	11	10	.524	4.02	25	25	3	1	0	0	154.2	188	686	100	69	12	5	3	5	59	1	81	10	4
Cumberland, Chris, N.B.*	1	0	1.000	3.18	1	1	0	0	0	0	5.2	5	22	2	2	0	0	0	0	2	0	2	2	0
Haynes, Heath, Trenton	1	1	.500	2.36	14	0	0	0	3	2	26.2	26	116	8	7	1	0	2	8	3	26	0	1
Haynes, Heath, New Haven	0	0	.000	1.13	5	0	0	0	1	0	8.0	7	31	1	1	0	0	1	0	8	0	1
Haynes, Heath, Portland	4	0	1.000	3.79	28	0	0	0	11	1	38.0	36	159	16	16	4	3	2	3	7	4	39	0	1

1997 FIELDING

TEAM

Team	Pct.	G	PO	A	E	TC	DP	PB	Team	Pct.	G	PO	A	E	TC	DP	PB
New Britain	.977	142	3629	1575	123	5327	153	25	Norwich	.966	142	3667	1514	181	5362	115	20
Trenton	.974	141	3688	1433	139	5260	115	26	Binghamton	.966	142	3683	1627	189	5499	146	21
Reading	.972	142	3772	1547	155	5474	115	21	Akron	.963	141	3591	1488	194	5273	105	20
Bowie	.971	142	3752	1545	156	5453	131	20	Harrisburg	.963	142	3731	1365	195	5291	89	10
New Haven	.971	142	3644	1564	155	5363	144	16	TRIPLE PLAYS: Reading.								
Portland	.971	142	3735	1637	162	5534	155	25									

INDIVIDUAL

FIRST BASEMEN

NOTE: All caps denotes fielding-percentage leader based on 71 games for catchers, 95 for all other non-pitchers and 142 innings for pitchers. *Throws lefthanded.

Player, Team	Pct.	G	PO	A	E	TC	DP
Abad, Andy, Trenton*	.989	21	167	14	2	183	13
Alcantara, Israel, Harrisburg	.979	30	222	11	5	238	14
Ashby, Chris, Norwich	.983	117	994	75	19	1088	92
Barry, Jeff, New Haven	.971	6	57	10	2	69	5
Betts, Todd, Akron	.900	2	8	1	1	10	0
Bierek, Kurt, Norwich	.991	27	209	17	2	228	14

Player, Team	Pct.	G	PO	A	E	TC	DP
Boston, D.J., New Haven*	.990	81	665	59	7	731	77
Brinkley, Josh, Harrisburg	1.000	1	8	0	0	8	1
Casey, Sean, Akron	.988	52	405	22	5	432	35
Clark, Howie, Bowie	1.000	7	8	4	0	12	1
Curtis, Kevin, Bow.-N.H.	.986	17	127	16	2	145	23
Derosso, Tony, Trenton	.985	7	57	9	1	67	4
Donato, Daniel, Norwich	1.000	1	14	0	0	14	1
Epperson, Chad, Trenton	1.000	1	6	0	0	6	0
Fernandez, Jose, Harrisburg	1.000	3	23	2	0	25	1
Fithian, Grant, Norwich	1.000	2	2	0	0	2	0
Fortin, Troy, New Britain	1.000	2	17	0	0	17	2

Player, Team	Pct.	G	PO	A	E	TC	DP
Foster, Jim, Bowie	1.000	2	17	0	0	17	2
Fraser, Joe, New Britain	1.000	1	1	0	0	1	0
Fullmer, Brad, Harrisburg	.991	68	507	41	5	553	39
Gibralter, David, Trenton	.990	114	942	74	10	1026	86
Grifol, Pedro, Binghamtom	1.000	1	3	0	0	3	1
Grunewald, Keith, New Haven	.986	18	130	7	2	139	12
Guiliano, Matt, Reading	1.000	2	2	0	0	2	0
Haas, Matt, Harrisburg	1.000	1	12	1	0	13	0
Hastings, Lionel, Portland	.500	1	1	0	1	2	0
Held, Dan, Reading	.994	130	1123	76	7	1206	89
Holdren, Nate, New Haven	.960	20	161	9	7	177	16
Horn, Jeff, New Britain	.938	2	13	2	1	16	3
Jackson, Ryan, Portland*	.979	8	44	3	1	48	5
Kirgan, Chris, Bowie	.992	139	1228	89	11	1328	111
Madonna, Chris, Trenton	1.000	2	1	0	0	1	0
Mahalik, John, Binghamtom	1.000	8	30	2	0	32	3
Martin, Jim, Binghamtom	.962	3	24	1	1	26	1
McKeel, Walt, Trenton	1.000	1	5	1	0	6	1
MIENTKIEWICZ, Doug, N.B.	.995	106	963	59	5	1027	98
Millan, Adan, Reading	.984	20	116	7	2	125	16
Millar, Kevin, Portland	.990	122	1140	93	13	1246	116
Miller, David, Akron*	1.000	2	15	1	0	16	0
Newstrom, Doug, New Haven	1.000	11	83	14	0	97	8
Northeimer, Jamie, New Haven	1.000	1	1	0	0	1	0
Ortiz, David, New Britain*	.990	33	268	16	3	287	32
Pachot, John, Harrisburg	.991	26	195	25	2	222	15
Paxton, Chris, Bowie	1.000	3	4	0	0	4	1
Perry, Chan, Akron	.994	56	427	34	3	464	32
Peterson, Nate, Harrisburg	.983	11	53	6	1	60	6
Post, Dave, Harrisburg	.973	11	60	12	2	74	4
Raleigh, Matt, Binghamtom	.983	45	374	25	7	406	43
Roskos, John, Portland	1.000	18	161	10	0	171	19
Saunders, Chris, Binghamtom	.971	3	31	3	1	35	2
Seefried, Tate, Binghamtom	.984	91	830	55	14	899	83
Taylor, Jim, New Britain	1.000	1	1	0	0	1	0
Thomas, Greg, Akron*	.963	39	296	19	12	327	25
Wilson, Pookie, Portland*	1.000	1	1	0	0	1	1
Wilson, Tom, Norwich	1.000	2	13	1	0	14	1

TRIPLE PLAY: Held.

FIRST BASEMEN WITH TWO OR MORE TEAMS

Player, Team	Pct.	G	PO	A	E	TC	DP
Curtis, Kevin, Bowie	1.000	5	22	1	0	23	5
Curtis, Kevin, New Haven	.984	12	105	15	2	122	18

SECOND BASEMEN

Player, Team	Pct.	G	PO	A	E	TC	DP
Anderson, Marlon, Reading	.961	137	323	396	29	748	87
Azuaje, Jesus, Binghamtom	.981	92	178	239	8	425	64
Bernhardt, Steve, New Haven	.974	80	177	199	10	386	59
Bocachica, Hiram, Harrisburg	.963	28	64	67	5	136	9
Brown, Randy, Trenton	.944	17	35	50	5	90	9
Cabrera, Jolbert, Harrisburg	.968	26	71	50	4	125	12
Cabrera, Orlando, Harrisburg	1.000	1	4	2	0	6	1
Carvajal, Jhonny, Harrisburg	.938	19	40	36	5	81	8
Clark, Howie, Bowie	.962	20	24	27	2	53	4
Coquillette, Trace, Harrisburg	.957	56	105	137	11	253	21
Correia, Rod, Trenton	.949	28	43	69	6	118	15
Ferguson, Jeff, New Britain	.875	8	6	15	3	24	1
Fraser, Joe, New Britain	.952	14	33	26	3	62	13
Fuller, Aaron, Trenton	1.000	2	4	6	0	10	1
GARCIA, Jesse, Bowie	.985	134	277	362	10	649	84
Garcia, Vicente, New Haven	.988	21	44	35	1	80	15
Gomez, Rudy, Norwich	.979	92	177	244	9	430	48
Gross, Rafael, Akron	1.000	6	15	8	0	23	5
Grunewald, Keith, New Haven	.992	29	47	75	1	123	17
Hall, Billy, New Haven	.930	11	9	31	3	43	4
Hastings, Lionel, Portland	.975	43	79	120	5	204	29
Hinds, Rob, Norwich	.922	21	28	31	5	64	4
Huff, Larry, Reading	1.000	8	13	19	0	32	5
Jackson, Gavin, Trenton	.981	27	39	67	2	108	12
Jarrett, Link, New Haven	1.000	11	29	19	0	48	6
Knowles, Eric, Binghamtom	.944	10	19	32	3	54	6
Lamb, David, Bowie	.941	4	8	8	1	17	6
Lane, Ryan, New Britain	.975	126	245	372	16	633	94
Lawrence, Chip, Bowie	1.000	1	1	0	0	1	0
Lobaton, Jose, Norwich	.983	15	19	40	1	60	10
Long, R.D., Norwich	.893	14	22	28	6	56	8
Mahalik, John, Binghamtom	.976	27	43	80	3	126	18
Martin, Lincoln, Bowie	.950	8	7	12	1	20	0
Martinez, Gabby, Norwich	.929	19	34	57	7	98	17
Merloni, Lou, Trenton	.981	12	23	28	1	52	8
Milliard, Ralph, Portland	.989	19	37	53	1	91	10
Morgan, Kevin, Binghamtom	.986	13	37	35	1	73	14
Morris, Bobby, Akron	.927	32	69	84	12	165	11
Neal, Mike, Akron	.967	72	167	158	11	336	34
Ortiz, Nick, Trenton	.984	63	129	176	5	310	36
Parra, Franklin, Binghamtom	.600	2	1	2	2	5	0
Post, Dave, Harrisburg	.976	19	40	40	2	82	9
Riggs, Kevin, Akron	.916	40	79	73	14	166	18
Rodriguez, Victor, Portland	.978	87	178	220	9	407	62
Shumpert, Terry, New Haven	1.000	4	8	17	0	25	7
Tebbs, Nate, Trenton	1.000	2	7	3	0	10	1
Torres, Tony, Portland	1.000	9	12	13	0	25	2
Zorrilla, Julio, Binghamtom	.967	6	12	17	1	30	4

TRIPLE PLAY: Anderson.

THIRD BASEMEN

Player, Team	Pct.	G	PO	A	E	TC	DP
Alcantara, Israel, Harrisburg	.877	41	31	69	14	114	4
Amador, Manuel, Reading	.889	32	22	42	8	72	3
Azuaje, Jesus, Binghamtom	1.000	6	3	8	0	11	1
Bernhardt, Steve, New Haven	.750	3	0	3	1	4	0
Berry, Mike, Bowie	.927	52	32	108	11	151	11
Betts, Todd, Akron	.904	94	75	178	27	280	17
Bierek, Kurt, Norwich	.800	3	2	6	2	10	0
Booty, Josh, Portland	.934	113	75	262	24	361	38
Branyan, Russell, Akron	.921	39	31	98	11	140	7
Brinkley, Josh, Harrisburg	.815	14	4	18	5	27	2
Brown, Randy, Norwich	.800	1	0	4	1	5	0
Carvajal, Jhonny, Harrisburg	.933	58	37	88	9	134	4
Clark, Howie, Bowie	.882	66	29	106	18	153	10
Coquillette, Trace, Harrisburg	.896	16	11	32	5	48	0
Derosso, Tony, Trenton	.876	41	20	72	13	105	8
Donato, Daniel, Norwich	.937	63	37	127	11	175	6
Dukart, Derek, Norwich	.875	7	6	8	2	16	0
Ferguson, Jeff, New Britain	1.000	5	3	3	0	6	0
Fernandez, Jose, Harrisburg	.887	22	18	29	6	53	1
Fithian, Grant, New Haven	.500	2	0	1	1	2	0
Fraser, Joe, New Britain	.917	16	12	21	3	36	4
Garcia, Jesse, Bowie	1.000	1	1	0	0	1	0
Gomez, Rudy, Norwich	.950	9	3	16	1	20	1
Gross, Rafael, Akron	.889	3	0	8	1	9	0
Grunewald, Keith, New Haven	.855	25	7	40	8	55	6
Guiliano, Matt, Reading	.940	18	5	42	3	50	5
Haas, Matt, Harrisburg	1.000	2	1	3	0	4	0
Hastings, Lionel, Portland	.938	26	17	58	5	80	5
Held, Dan, Reading	.933	5	4	10	1	15	1
Huff, Larry, Reading	.930	98	62	202	20	284	17
Jarrett, Link, New Britain	1.000	4	0	3	0	3	0
Knowles, Eric, Binghamtom	.904	19	8	39	5	52	2
Koskie, Corey, New Britain	.933	125	72	234	22	328	14
Lamb, David, Bowie	.933	29	13	29	3	45	3
Lawrence, Chip, Bowie	.909	5	4	6	1	11	0
Light, Tal, New Haven	.816	24	14	57	16	87	4
Liniak, Cole, Trenton	.929	46	35	82	9	126	11
Lopez, Jose, Binghamtom	.903	32	15	69	9	93	6
Lowell, Mike, Norwich	.923	65	48	120	14	182	10
Mahalik, John, Binghamtom	.968	21	6	24	1	31	5
Merloni, Lou, Trenton	.948	53	45	102	8	155	8
Millar, Kevin, Portland	.895	13	6	28	4	38	1
Neal, Mike, Akron	.947	9	5	13	1	19	0
Ortiz, Nick, Trenton	.833	4	3	7	2	12	0
Otanez, Willis, Bowie	.955	7	1	20	1	22	2
Pachot, John, Harrisburg	.786	6	2	9	3	14	2
Parra, Franklin, Binghamtom	1.000	2	0	4	0	4	1
Perry, Chan, Akron	1.000	1	1	2	0	3	0
Post, Dave, Harrisburg	.667	2	1	3	2	6	0
Raleigh, Matt, Binghamtom	.939	56	28	110	9	147	10
Saunders, Chris, Binghamtom	.986	25	11	57	1	69	3
Seefried, Tate, Binghamtom	1.000	1	1	0	0	1	0
TAYLOR, Jamie, New Haven	.955	98	60	218	13	291	20
Tebbs, Nate, Trenton	1.000	1	0	1	0	1	0
Valentin, Javier, New Britain	.750	1	3	0	1	4	0
Wesemann, Jason, Reading	1.000	6	2	7	0	9	1
Wilson, Tom, Norwich	.750	1	0	3	1	4	0

TRIPLE PLAY: Amador.

SHORTSTOPS

Player, Team	Pct.	G	PO	A	E	TC	DP
Angeli, Doug, Reading	.966	41	55	116	6	177	19
Bautista, Juan, Bowie	.942	21	25	73	6	104	15
Bocachica, Hiram, Harrisburg	.876	57	71	119	27	217	18
Brinkley, Josh, Harrisburg	1.000	1	0	2	0	2	0
Brown, Randy, Tren.-Nor.	.955	77	122	194	15	331	41
Cabrera, Jolbert, Harrisburg	.904	17	21	26	5	52	8
Cabrera, Orlando, Harrisburg	.964	34	53	81	5	139	15

Player, Team	Pct.	G	PO	A	E	TC	DP
Carvajal, Jhonny, Harrisburg	.946	42	54	105	9	168	17
Dennis, Les, Norwich	.917	8	13	31	4	48	7
Dukart, Derek, Norwich	.833	2	2	3	1	6	0
Ferguson, Jeff, New Britain	.833	3	7	3	2	12	0
Fraser, Joe, New Britain	1.000	6	7	8	0	15	0
Garcia, Jesse, Bowie	.900	10	12	15	3	30	3
Gomez, Rudy, Norwich	.933	5	4	10	1	15	1
Gonzalez, Alex, Portland	.943	133	192	423	37	652	87
Gross, Rafael, Akron	.769	3	3	7	3	13	2
Grunewald, Keith, New Haven	.906	11	14	34	5	53	8
Guiliano, Matt, Reading	.960	95	120	266	16	402	49
Hall, Billy, New Haven	1.000	1	1	2	0	3	0
Hastings, Lionel, Portland	.917	14	9	35	4	48	3
Huff, Larry, Reading	1.000	11	15	23	0	38	4
Jackson, Gavin, Trenton	.947	73	113	175	16	304	27
Jarrett, Link, New Haven	.982	64	80	189	5	274	46
Knowles, Eric, Binghamtom	.880	21	31	42	10	83	12
Lamb, David, Bowie	.963	46	60	122	7	189	20
Lane, Ryan, New Britain	1.000	1	1	2	0	3	0
Lawrence, Chip, Bowie	1.000	1	2	1	0	3	1
Lobaton, Jose, Norwich	.955	51	68	100	8	176	26
Long, R.D., Norwich	.898	16	16	37	6	59	6
Lowell, Mike, Norwich	.957	7	9	13	1	23	2
Mahalik, John, Binghamtom	.911	11	12	29	4	45	6
Martinez, Eddy, Bowie	.943	16	17	49	4	70	9
Martinez, Gabby, Norwich	.956	53	65	152	10	227	33
Mercedes, Guillermo, Akron	.963	97	161	283	17	461	42
Morgan, Kevin, Binghamtom	.943	39	75	139	13	227	28
MORIARTY, Mike, New Britain	.973	135	210	475	19	704	114
Neal, Mike, Akron	.923	49	78	127	17	222	23
Ojeda, Augie, Bowie	.967	58	84	176	9	269	37
Ortiz, Nick, Trenton	.944	12	20	31	3	54	6
Parra, Franklin, Binghamtom	.667	1	0	2	1	3	1
Polanco, Enohel, Binghamtom	.939	81	119	250	24	393	56
Rodriguez, Victor, Portland	1.000	1	0	1	0	1	0
Sexton, Chris, New Haven	.961	72	120	199	13	332	45
Tebbs, Nate, Trenton	1.000	1	0	3	0	3	0
Torres, Tony, Portland	.781	6	10	15	7	32	6

SHORTSTOPS WITH TWO OR MORE TEAMS

Player, Team	Pct.	G	PO	A	E	TC	DP
Brown, Randy, Trenton	.945	59	92	149	14	255	33
Brown, Randy, Norwich	.987	18	30	45	1	76	8

OUTFIELDERS

Player, Team	Pct.	G	PO	A	E	TC	DP
Abad, Andy, Trenton*	.971	19	33	1	1	35	0
Alcantara, Israel, Harrisburg	1.000	1	1	0	0	1	0
Allen, Chad, New Britain	.973	29	35	1	1	37	0
Almonte, Wady, Bowie	.916	68	94	4	9	107	0
Alvarez, Rafael, New Britain*	1.000	16	29	2	0	31	0
Bady, Edward, Harrisburg	.951	89	149	5	8	162	1
Barry, Jeff, New Haven	.943	30	65	1	4	70	0
Bates, Fletcher, Binghamtom	.963	62	96	7	4	107	0
Betzsold, James, Akron	.960	117	197	17	9	223	1
Bierek, Kurt, Norwich	.952	93	157	3	8	168	0
Bogle, Bryan, Bowie	.958	95	152	9	7	168	0
Brinkley, Josh, Harrisburg	1.000	1	0	1	0	1	0
Brown, Armann, New Britain	.944	13	17	0	1	18	0
Brown, Randy, Trenton	1.000	4	3	0	0	3	0
Brown, Ron, Norwich	.960	96	160	7	7	174	0
Bryant, Pat, Trenton	.985	96	197	6	3	206	2
Buchanan, Brian, Norwich	.962	114	192	11	8	211	1
Burton, Darren, Reading	.972	45	98	7	3	108	0
Cabrera, Jolbert, Harrisburg	1.000	6	6	0	0	6	0
Campos, Jesus, Harrisburg	.974	81	176	11	5	192	1
Carney, Bartt, Bowie	.971	59	95	4	3	102	1
Carver, Steve, Reading	.943	74	116	0	7	123	0
Claudio, Patricio, Akron	1.000	12	25	0	0	25	0
Coleman, Michael, Trenton	.981	100	259	6	5	270	1
Cook, Hayward, Portland	.955	50	59	5	3	67	1
Correia, Rod, Trenton	1.000	16	27	3	0	30	0
Costello, Brian, Reading	.926	9	23	2	2	27	0
Curtis, Chad, Akron	1.000	4	5	2	0	7	0
Curtis, Kevin, Bow.-N.H.	.964	81	128	4	5	137	1
Curtis, Randy, Akron*	.923	21	47	1	4	52	0
Dawkins, Walt, Reading	.972	86	134	4	4	142	0
Dellucci, David, Bowie*	.994	91	162	2	1	165	1
Derosso, Tony, Trenton	1.000	18	25	1	0	26	0
Espinosa, Ramon, Binghamtom.	.939	62	86	6	6	98	0
Faggett, Ethan, Trenton*	.950	14	19	0	1	20	0
Fraser, Joe, New Britain	.955	23	21	0	1	22	0

Player, Team	Pct.	G	PO	A	E	TC	DP
Frazier, Lou, Bowie	.917	25	52	3	5	60	0
Fuller, Aaron, Trenton	.976	122	232	11	6	249	1
Fullmer, Brad, Harrisburg	.969	18	31	0	1	32	0
Gibson, Derrick, New Haven	.947	115	188	8	11	207	0
Giudice, John, New Haven	.969	58	123	4	4	131	0
Glass, Chip, Akron*	.962	101	191	11	8	210	1
Gross, Rafael, Akron	1.000	5	14	0	0	14	0
Gunderson, Shane, New Britain..	.985	33	63	2	1	66	1
Haas, Matt, Harrisburg	1.000	2	3	0	0	3	0
Harriss, Robin, Akron	1.000	2	1	0	0	1	0
Hastings, Lionel, Portland	1.000	9	4	0	0	4	0
Hawkins, Kraig, Norwich	.983	50	112	1	2	115	0
Henthorne, Kevin, Norwich	1.000	1	1	0	0	1	0
Hinds, Rob, Norwich	.923	9	12	0	1	13	0
Hudler, Rex, Reading	1.000	4	4	1	0	5	0
Huff, Larry, Reading	1.000	6	9	0	0	9	0
Hunter, Scott, Binghamtom	.991	77	109	7	1	117	0
Hunter, Torii, New Britain	.974	124	252	7	7	266	4
Isom, Johnny, Bowie	.975	99	148	5	4	157	3
Jackson, Ryan, Portland*	.979	103	183	6	4	193	3
Johnson, J.J., New Britain	.977	94	168	5	4	177	2
Kingsale, Eugene, Bowie	.958	12	23	0	1	24	0
KOTSAY, Mark, Portland*	.992	113	230	12	2	244	4
LeCronier, Jason, Bowie	1.000	4	6	0	0	6	0
LeGree, Keith, New Britain	.963	97	176	8	7	191	1
Lewis, Anthony, New Haven*	.978	28	45	0	1	46	0
Lukachyk, Rob, Harrisburg	.970	38	60	4	2	66	0
Mahalik, John, Binghamtom	1.000	1	2	1	0	3	0
Maness, Dwight, Binghamtom	.993	72	140	2	1	143	0
Martin, Jim, Binghamtom	.968	25	29	1	1	31	0
Martin, Lincoln, Bowie	1.000	3	8	0	0	8	0
Mendoza, Carlos, Binghamtom*.	.988	46	79	5	1	85	0
Mientkiewicz, Doug, New Britain	1.000	16	26	4	0	30	1
Miller, David, Akron*	.980	132	230	9	5	244	0
Moore, Mike, Binghamtom	.953	43	57	4	3	64	1
Morgan, Scott, Akron	.976	21	37	4	1	42	1
Ortiz, Bo, Harrisburg	.990	54	95	3	1	99	0
Pagano, Scott, Reading	.975	115	302	13	8	323	4
Perry, Chan, Akron	1.000	14	31	2	0	33	0
Peterson, Nate, Harrisburg	.980	36	47	1	1	49	0
Pledger, Kinnis, New Haven	.990	55	95	3	1	99	0
Post, Dave, Harrisburg	1.000	4	2	1	0	3	0
Raines, Tim, Norwich	1.000	2	2	0	0	2	0
Ramirez, Angel, Norwich	1.000	2	3	0	0	3	0
Reeves, Glenn, Portland	.989	61	84	3	1	88	1
Royster, Aaron, Reading	.975	105	153	4	4	161	0
Samuels, Scott, Harrisburg	.976	64	116	4	3	123	1
Sexton, Chris, New Haven	.983	26	58	1	1	60	0
Smith, Sloan, Norwich	.800	2	4	0	1	5	0
Stovall, Darond, Harrisburg*	.990	44	93	3	1	97	1
Stowers, Chris, Harrisburg*	.929	18	37	2	3	42	1
Thomas, Greg, Akron*	.958	13	23	0	1	24	0
Valdez, Trovin, Harrisburg	.846	11	9	2	2	13	0
Wells, Forry, New Haven	.912	24	26	5	3	34	0
Wilcox, Luke, Norwich	.980	72	141	6	3	150	1
Williams, Juan, Trenton	.990	48	100	4	1	105	1
Wilson, Pookie, Portland*	.933	34	40	2	3	45	0
Wilson, Preston, Binghamtom	.952	65	116	3	6	125	0
Winn, Randy, Portland	.979	93	182	6	4	192	0

OUTFIELDERS WITH TWO OR MORE TEAMS

Player, Team	Pct.	G	PO	A	E	TC	DP
Curtis, Kevin, Bowie	.667	1	2	0	1	3	0
Curtis, Kevin, New Haven	.970	80	126	4	4	134	1

CATCHERS

Player, Team	Pct.	G	PO	A	E	TC	DP	PB
Barthol, Blake, New Haven	.984	107	671	71	12	754	5	13
Borrero, Richie, Trenton	.983	56	373	39	7	419	1	17
Brinkley, Josh, Harrisburg	1.000	4	6	0	0	6	0	0
Chavez, Eric, Bowie	1.000	1	0	1	0	1	0	0
Depastino, Joe, Trenton	.988	71	447	45	6	498	4	7
Epperson, Chad, Trenton	1.000	1	4	0	0	4	0	0
Fithian, Grant, Norwich	.988	45	298	42	4	344	0	7
Fortin, Troy, New Britain	1.000	8	50	13	0	63	2	2
Foster, Jim, Bowie	.981	39	284	29	6	319	4	1
Grifol, Pedro, Binghamtom	.977	55	383	47	10	440	5	7
Harriss, Robin, Akron	.991	47	294	29	3	326	2	3
Haselman, Bill, Trenton	1.000	4	30	2	0	32	0	0
HENLEY, Bob, Harrisburg	.995	75	574	77	3	654	6	5
Hoiles, Chris, Bowie	1.000	2	12	0	0	12	0	0
Horn, Jeff, New Britain	.996	43	239	38	1	278	1	10
Koeyers, Ramsey, Portland	.988	75	450	42	6	498	4	17

Player, Team	Pct.	G	PO	A	E	TC	DP	PB
Lasater, Chris, Bowie	1.000	2	5	0	0	5	0	3
Luzinski, Ryan, Bowie	.985	18	114	16	2	132	1	4
Madonna, Chris, Trenton	1.000	11	69	5	0	74	0	1
Mahalik, John, Binghamtom	1.000	1	3	0	0	3	0	1
McKeel, Walt, Trenton	1.000	2	12	0	0	12	0	1
Millan, Adan, Reading	.981	42	236	26	5	267	1	11
Morales, Elvin, Binghamtom	1.000	1	7	0	0	7	0	0
Morales, Francisco, Har.	1.000	14	95	6	0	101	0	1
Moyle, Mike, Akron	.993	99	592	80	5	677	10	17
Mulligan, Sean, Akron	1.000	2	11	0	0	11	0	0
Newstrom, Doug, New Haven	.985	52	296	36	5	337	3	3
Northeimer, Jamie, Reading	.969	22	113	14	4	131	1	5
Pachot, John, Harrisburg	.972	64	437	44	14	495	3	4
Paxton, Chris, Bowie	.957	5	19	3	1	23	0	0
Rosario, Mel, Bowie	.986	92	621	87	10	718	7	12
Roskos, John, Portland	.984	73	469	27	8	504	2	8
Schaeffer, Jon, New Britain	.985	10	57	10	1	68	0	1
Smith, Jeff, New Britain	.956	5	42	1	2	45	0	0
Tremie, Chris, Reading	.995	97	650	84	4	738	6	5
Valentin, Javier, New Britain	.991	85	513	65	5	583	8	12
Wilson, Tom, Norwich	.991	103	694	80	7	781	5	13
Wilson, Vance, Binghamtom	.984	91	604	69	11	684	4	13

PITCHERS

Player, Team	Pct.	G	PO	A	E	TC	DP
Arroyo, Luis, Binghamtom*	1.000	7	0	2	0	2	0
Badorek, Mike, Akron	1.000	4	1	2	0	3	0
Baker, Scott, Akron*	1.000	4	1	2	0	3	0
Baptist, Travis, New Britain*	.962	36	6	19	1	26	3
Barbao, Joe, Reading	.857	52	4	8	2	14	0
Barcelo, Marc, New Britain	1.000	7	0	2	0	2	0
Barkley, Brian, Trenton*	.878	29	7	29	5	41	3
Bell, Jason, New Britain	1.000	28	6	19	0	25	2
Bennett, Chris, Bowie	.667	10	0	2	1	3	1
Bennett, Erik, Akron	1.000	11	1	4	0	5	0
Bennett, Joel, Bowie	.913	44	5	16	2	23	0
Bennett, Shayne, Harrisburg	.917	23	4	7	1	12	0
Benz, Jacob, Harrisburg*	1.000	23	0	10	0	10	1
Betti, Rich, Trenton*	.667	30	1	3	2	6	1
Beverlin, Jason, Norwich	1.000	25	4	5	0	9	0
Blais, Mike, Trenton	1.000	18	1	0	0	1	0
Bost, Heath, New Haven	.909	38	2	8	1	11	0
Bowers, Shane, New Britain	.933	14	6	8	1	15	0
Boyd, Jason, Reading	.917	48	10	12	2	24	0
Brannan, Ryan, Reading	.933	45	6	8	1	15	1
Briscoe, John, Akron	.833	33	2	3	1	6	0
Brownson, Mark, New Haven	.941	29	14	18	2	34	0
Bullard, Jason, Bowie	.833	61	4	11	3	18	1
Bullinger, Kirk, Harrisburg	1.000	21	1	10	0	11	1
Bunch, Mel, Harrisburg	.917	9	4	7	1	12	1
Burgus, Travis, Portland*	1.000	16	3	11	0	14	1
Byrd, Matt, New Haven	.857	10	3	3	1	7	1
Cafaro, Rocco, Bowie	.875	13	3	4	1	8	0
Calmus, Lance, Akron	1.000	5	0	2	0	2	0
Camp, Jared, Akron	1.000	12	4	6	0	10	0
Cannon, Kevan, Trenton*	1.000	13	0	1	0	1	0
Carpenter, Brian, Binghamtom	1.000	17	1	3	0	4	0
Carrasco, Troy, New Britain*	.786	31	1	10	3	14	2
Carter, John, Bing.-Ak.	.846	19	1	10	2	13	0
Castro, Tony, Portland	1.000	27	2	4	0	6	0
Censale, Silvio, Reading*	.895	20	7	10	2	19	1
Chavez, Carlos, Portland	1.000	30	2	5	0	7	0
Chergey, Dan, Portland	1.000	32	1	4	0	5	0
Clark, Howie, Bowie	1.000	2	1	0	0	1	0
Cobb, Trevor, New Britain*	.947	19	9	9	1	19	0
Cole, Jason, Harrisburg	.882	37	6	9	2	17	1
Coppinger, Rocky, Bowie	1.000	3	1	2	0	3	0
Cornelius, Reid, Portland	1.000	6	2	3	0	5	2
Costa, Troy, Reading	.947	28	9	27	2	38	2
Croghan, Andy, Norwich	1.000	42	2	8	0	10	0
Crowell, Jim, Akron*	1.000	3	0	4	0	4	0
Cumberland, Chris, Nor.-N.B.*	.855	26	12	35	8	55	4
Curtis, Chris, Bowie	.889	37	10	14	3	27	0
DaSilva, Fernando, Harrisburg	1.000	12	2	1	0	3	0
Dedrick, Jim, Harrisburg	.857	15	1	5	1	7	0
DeJean, Mike, New Haven	1.000	2	0	3	0	3	0
DeLosSantos, Luis, Norwich	.833	4	2	3	1	6	0
DeLaCruz, Francisco, Norwich	1.000	2	0	2	0	2	0
DeLaRosa, Maximo, Akron	.880	17	6	16	3	25	1
Dixon, Timothy, Harrisburg*	.833	37	5	5	2	12	0
Dodd, Robert, Reading*	.941	63	2	14	1	17	0
Dotel, Octavio, Binghamtom	.632	12	4	8	7	19	1
Dougherty, Anthony, Akron	1.000	28	4	7	0	11	0
Duvall, Mike, Portland*	.828	45	5	19	5	29	3
Dykhoff, Radhames, Bowie*	1.000	7	2	0	0	2	0
Edmondson, Brian, Binghamtom	1.000	14	1	2	0	3	0
Falkenborg, Brian, Bowie	1.000	1	0	1	0	1	0
FARRELL, Jim, Trenton	1.000	26	12	27	0	39	4
Fernandez, Jared, Trenton	.969	21	8	23	1	32	0
Fesh, Sean, Binghamtom*	.944	45	3	14	1	18	0
Figueroa, Nelson, Binghamtom	.919	33	12	22	3	37	1
Fiore, Tony, Reading	1.000	17	8	24	0	32	1
Fleetham, Ben, Harrisburg	.909	49	4	6	1	11	0
Ford, Ben, Norwich	.600	28	1	5	4	10	0
Forster, Scott, Harrisburg*	.829	17	7	22	6	35	1
Foster, Mark, Reading*	1.000	9	2	3	0	5	0
Fussell, Chris, Bowie	1.000	19	1	15	0	16	0
Gallaher, Kevin, Bowie	1.000	26	4	8	0	12	1
Gandarillas, Gus, New Britain	.957	17	7	15	1	23	1
Gonzales, Frank, Trenton*	1.000	14	1	6	0	7	0
Gonzalez, Gabe, Portland*	1.000	29	1	11	0	12	1
Gonzalez, Juan, Portland	1.000	17	0	4	0	4	0
Gooch, Arnold, Binghamtom	.891	27	10	31	5	46	1
Gooden, Dwight, Norwich	1.000	3	1	1	0	2	0
Gordon, Mike, Akron	.867	6	3	10	2	15	0
Gourdin, Tom, New Britain	.941	49	4	12	1	17	1
Grace, Mike, Reading	1.000	4	1	2	0	3	0
Granata, Chris, Akron	1.000	4	1	1	0	2	1
Gray, Dennis, Akron*	1.000	10	0	1	0	1	0
Greer, Ken, Bowie	1.000	11	1	2	0	3	1
Guerra, Mark, Binghamtom	.913	48	9	12	2	23	0
Hackman, Luther, New Haven	1.000	10	2	5	0	7	0
Hale, Chad, Trenton*	1.000	3	2	1	0	3	0
Harris, Jeff, New Britain	1.000	28	5	9	0	14	0
Haynes, Heath, Tren.-N.H.-Por.	.923	47	3	9	1	13	0
Hecker, Doug, Trenton	1.000	4	1	0	0	1	0
Henderson, Ryan, New Haven	1.000	24	6	7	0	13	1
Henthorne, Kevin, Norwich	1.000	33	4	13	0	17	0
Hernandez, Francis, Bowie	1.000	6	1	0	0	1	0
Hernandez, Livan, Portland	1.000	1	1	0	0	1	0
Howard, Chris, Binghamtom*	1.000	13	3	1	0	4	0
Huff, Larry, Binghamtom	1.000	1	0	2	0	2	0
Hunter, Rich, Reading	.886	29	9	22	4	35	2
Jacobsen, Joe, Portland	.913	47	5	16	2	23	3
Jerzembeck, Mike, Norwich	.818	8	3	6	2	11	0
Kirgan, Chris, Bowie	1.000	5	1	0	0	1	0
Kirkreit, Daron, Akron	.957	26	7	15	1	23	0
Kohlmeier, Ryan, Bowie	1.000	2	0	2	0	2	0
Kusiewicz, Mike, New Haven*	1.000	10	2	11	0	13	0
Lane, Aaron, Bowie*	1.000	7	0	4	0	4	0
Lankford, Frank, Norwich	1.000	11	9	17	0	26	0
Legault, Kevin, New Britain	1.000	40	5	14	0	19	0
Linebarger, Keith, New Britain	1.000	1	2	1	0	3	0
Lomon, Kevin, Norwich	1.000	18	9	13	0	22	1
Macca, Chris, New Haven	1.000	46	4	6	0	10	0
Maeda, Katsuhiro, Norwich	.970	25	12	20	1	33	2
Mahaffey, Alan, New Britain*	.500	13	0	1	1	2	0
Mahalik, John, Binghamtom	1.000	3	0	1	0	1	0
Mahay, Ron, Trenton*	1.000	17	1	4	0	5	0
Manning, Len, Reading*	.500	28	1	2	3	6	0
Martinez, Johnny, Akron	.933	32	4	10	1	15	0
Martinez, Ramiro, Harrisburg*	1.000	37	4	14	0	18	0
Matthews, Mike, Akron*	1.000	19	4	29	0	33	1
McCommon, Jason, Harrisburg..	1.000	29	2	8	0	10	1
Meadows, Brian, Portland	1.000	29	12	23	0	35	2
Mercado, Hector, Portland*	.821	31	4	19	5	28	0
Mesa, Rafael, Akron	1.000	14	4	9	0	13	1
Million, Doug, New Haven*	1.000	10	1	13	0	14	2
Milton, Eric, Norwich*	.938	14	2	13	1	16	0
Mitchell, Larry, Norwich	.905	57	4	15	2	21	0
Mitchell, Scott, Harrisburg	1.000	4	2	4	0	6	1
Mix, Greg, Portland	.955	30	3	18	1	22	0
Montgomery, Steve, Bowie	.966	24	11	17	1	29	0
Montoya, Wilmer, Akron	1.000	2	1	0	0	1	0
Moore, Joel, New Haven	.833	19	3	7	2	12	2
Moore, Marcus, Akron	.750	13	4	11	5	20	1
Moore, Trey, Harrisburg*	.919	27	12	22	3	37	0
Moreno, Julio, Bowie	.950	27	8	11	1	20	2
Morse, Paul, New Britain	1.000	37	8	13	0	21	3
Munro, Peter, Trenton	1.000	22	10	24	0	34	0
Najera, Noe, Akron*	.905	25	1	18	2	21	0
Norman, Scott, New Haven	1.000	29	2	10	0	12	1
Norris, Joe, Portland	1.000	9	0	1	0	1	0
Osteen, Gavin, Bowie*	1.000	18	2	5	0	7	0

Player, Team	Pct.	G	PO	A	E	TC	DP
Parisi, Mike, Portland	1.000	9	4	11	0	15	2
Parrish, John, Bowie*	.500	1	0	1	1	2	0
Peever, Lloyd, New Haven	.957	20	4	18	1	23	0
Pena, Juan, Trenton	1.000	16	3	14	0	17	0
Percibal, Billy, Bowie	1.000	1	0	2	0	2	0
Perez, Julio, Akron	1.000	9	0	2	0	2	0
Perez, Yorkis, Binghamtom*	1.000	12	2	2	0	4	0
Perkins, Dan, New Britain	.911	24	11	30	4	45	1
Peterson, Dean, Trenton	1.000	33	4	10	0	14	1
Phelps, Tom, Harrisburg*	1.000	18	6	16	0	22	0
Pierson, Jason, Binghamtom*	1.000	13	0	4	0	4	0
Ponson, Sidney, Bowie	1.000	13	3	8	0	11	1
Pool, Matt, New Haven	.938	29	6	9	1	16	2
Press, Gregg, Portland	.909	28	8	22	3	33	1
Price, Tom, New Haven*	1.000	48	5	9	0	14	0
Pulsipher, Bill, Binghamtom*	1.000	10	0	2	0	2	0
Rakers, Jason, Akron	.889	7	0	8	1	9	0
Ramirez, Felix, Trenton*	1.000	18	1	7	0	8	0
Rath, Fred, New Britain	1.000	33	5	7	0	12	0
Rector, Bobby, Portland	.875	6	5	2	1	8	1
Resz, Greg, Norwich	.800	25	6	6	3	15	0
Ricken, Ray, Norwich	1.000	2	1	1	0	2	0
Roberts, Chris, Binghamtom*	1.000	19	4	16	0	20	0
Roque, Rafael, Binghamtom*	.667	16	0	2	1	3	0
Rose, Brian, Trenton	1.000	15	0	5	0	5	0
Rose, Scott, Norwich	1.000	21	2	9	0	11	3
Rushing, Will, New Britain*	1.000	3	1	1	0	2	0
Ryan, Ken, Reading	1.000	2	0	1	0	1	0
Saberhagen, Bret, Trenton	1.000	2	1	0	0	1	0
Saipe, Mike, New Haven	.943	19	9	24	2	35	4
Sampson, Ben, New Britain*	.923	25	3	9	1	13	2
Sanchez, Jesus, Binghamtom*	.925	26	10	27	3	40	1
Saneaux, Francisco, Bowie	1.000	8	0	2	0	2	0
Sauerbeck, Scott, Binghamtom*	.933	27	5	23	2	30	1
Schlomann, Brett, Norwich	.667	10	2	2	2	6	0
Sexton, Jeff, Akron	1.000	16	0	14	0	14	0
Shepherd, Alvie, Bowie	.913	22	7	14	2	23	0
Shoemaker, Stephen, New Haven	.960	14	10	14	1	25	0
Short, Barry, Binghamtom	.500	6	0	1	1	2	0
Shuey, Paul, Akron	1.000	3	1	2	0	3	0
Smart, J.D., Harrisburg	1.000	12	5	10	0	15	0
Smetana, Steve, Trenton*	1.000	18	0	5	0	5	0
Smith, Hut, Bowie	.963	14	7	19	1	27	2

Player, Team	Pct.	G	PO	A	E	TC	DP
Snyder, Matt, Bowie	.889	67	7	9	2	18	1
Steph, Rod, Bowie	1.000	7	0	5	0	5	0
Stidham, Phil, New Haven	1.000	8	1	2	0	3	0
Tessmer, Jay, Norwich	.905	55	0	19	2	21	0
Thomas, Evan, Reading	.786	15	6	5	3	14	1
Thurman, Mike, Harrisburg	1.000	20	16	16	0	32	0
Tolar, Kevin, Binghamtom*	1.000	22	2	2	0	4	0
Townsend, Dave, Portland	.955	15	9	12	1	22	2
Trinidad, Hector, New Britain	1.000	6	0	3	0	3	0
Troutman, Keith, Reading	1.000	57	3	27	0	30	3
Turrentine, Rich, Binghamtom	1.000	61	2	11	0	13	1
Tweedlie, Brad, Trenton	.929	41	4	9	1	14	2
Urso, Sal, Norwich*	1.000	7	1	3	0	4	0
Vasquez, Leoner, Binghamtom*	1.000	1	0	2	0	2	0
Vaught, Jay, Akron	1.000	29	4	13	0	17	1
Vavrek, Mike, New Haven*	.950	17	5	14	1	20	1
Vazquez, Javier, Harrisburg	1.000	6	2	4	0	6	0
Walker, Pete, Trenton	.800	8	2	2	1	5	0
Ward, Bryan, Portland*	.882	12	5	10	2	17	0
Warrecker, Teddy, Akron	.667	10	0	4	2	6	1
Watkins, Scott, New Haven*	1.000	13	2	2	0	4	0
Weber, Lenny, Akron	1.000	6	1	1	0	2	0
Weber, Neil, Harrisburg*	.875	18	3	11	2	16	0
Wertz, Bill, Akron	1.000	11	0	2	0	2	0
Westbrook, Destry, Reading	.750	26	2	4	2	8	0
Whiteman, Greg, Reading*	1.000	9	1	15	0	16	0
Whitten, Casey, Akron*	1.000	4	0	2	0	2	0
Wilson, Pookie, Portland*	1.000	1	0	1	0	1	0
Winchester, Scott, Akron	.000	6	0	0	1	1	0
Wright, Jaret, Akron	.875	8	3	11	2	16	0
Yarnall, Ed, Binghamtom*	.333	5	0	1	2	3	0
Yennaco, Jay, Trenton	1.000	21	11	18	0	29	1
Zolecki, Mike, New Haven	.929	16	4	9	1	14	1

PITCHERS WITH TWO OR MORE TEAMS

Player, Team	Pct.	G	PO	A	E	TC	DP
Carter, John, Binghamtom	1.000	9	0	2	0	2	0
Carter, John, Akron	.818	10	1	8	2	11	0
Cumberland, Chris, Norwich*	.849	25	11	34	8	53	4
Cumberland, Chris, New Britain*	1.000	1	1	1	0	2	0
Haynes, Heath, Trenton	.833	14	2	3	1	6	0
Haynes, Heath, New Haven	1.000	5	1	2	0	3	0
Haynes, Heath, Portland	1.000	28	0	4	0	4	0

The following players did not have any fielding statistics at the positions indicated or appeared only as a designated hitter, pinch-hitter or pinch-runner: Berry, 2b; Brinkley, p; Buddie, p; Carvajal, of; Cedarblad, p; Checo, p; Donato, ss, of; Gibralter, of; Guiliano, p; Haas, p; Hall, of; Hastings, c; Hubbard, p; Hudler, 2b; Hurst, p; Irabu, p; Kammerer, p; LeCronier, p; Lobaton, of; Long, 3b; Lopez, p; Luzinski, 3b; Maine, p; Mantei, p; Merloni, ss; Mott, p; Paxton, p; D. Perez, p; Raleigh, of; Roberts, of; S. Rose, of; T. Saunders, p; Seefried, 2b; Stevenson, p; Strawberry, of; Wesemann, of; P. Wilson, 3b; T. Young, p.

LEAGUE CHAMPIONS

Year	Team	Pct.
1923—	Williamsport	.661
1924—	Williamsport	.654
1925—	York§	.583
	Williamsport§	.583
1926—	Scranton	.627
1927—	Harrisburg	.630
1928—	Harrisburg	.603
1929—	Binghamton	.597
1930—	Wilkes-Barre	.572
1931—	Harrisburg	.597
1932—	Wilkes-Barre	.561
1933—	Binghamton	.690
1934—	Binghamton	.694
	Williamsport*	.603
1935—	Scranton	.657
	Binghamton*	.580
1936—	Scranton*	.609
	Elmira	.629
1937—	Elmira†	.622
1938—	Binghamton	.622
	Elmira (3rd)‡	.522
1939—	Scranton†	.571
1940—	Scranton	.568
	Binghamton (2nd)‡	.554
1941—	Wilkes-Barre	.630
	Elmira (3rd)‡	.514
1942—	Albany	.600
	Scranton (2nd)‡	.593
1943—	Scranton	.630
	Elmira (2nd)‡	.568

Year	Team	Pct.
1944—	Hartford	.723
	Binghamton (4th)‡	.474
1945—	Utica	.615
	Albany (3rd)‡	.564
1946—	Scranton†	.691
1947—	Utica†	.652
1948—	Scranton†	.636
1949—	Albany	.664
	Binghamton (4th)‡	.500
1950—	Wilkes-Barre‡	.652
1951—	Wilkes-Barre‡	.612
	Scranton (2nd)†	.562
1952—	Albany	.603
	Binghamton (2nd)‡	.562
1953—	Reading	.682
	Binghamton (2nd)‡	.636
1954—	Wilkes-Barre	.576
	Albany (3rd)‡	.540
1955—	Reading	.613
	Allentown (2nd)‡	.565
1956—	Schenectady†	.609
1957—	Binghamton	.607
	Reading (3rd)‡	.529
1958—	Lancaster∞	.568
	Binghamton (6th)‡	.493
1959—	Springfield†	.607
1960—	Williamsport▲	.551
	Springfield (3rd)▲	.496
1961—	Springfield	.612
1962—	Williamsport	.593
	Elmira (2nd)‡	.514

Year	Team	Pct.
1963—	Charleston	.593
1964—	Elmira	.586
1965—	Pittsfield	.607
1966—	Elmira	.633
1967—	Binghamton◆	.586
	Elmira	.532
1968—	Pittsfield	.604
	Reading (2nd)‡	.579
1969—	York	.640
1970—	Waterbury■	.560
	Reading■	.553
1971—	Three Rivers	.569
	Elmira▼	.561
1972—	West Haven▼	.600
	Three Rivers	.559
1973—	Reading▼	.551
	Pittsfield	.551
1974—	Thetford Miners (2nd)•	.536
	Pittsfield (2nd)	.496
1975—	Reading	.613
	Bristol*	.587
1976—	Three Rivers	.601
	West Haven††	.576
1977—	West Haven‡‡	.623
	Three Rivers	.551
1978—	Reading	.642
	Bristol*	.580
1979—	West Haven§§	.597
1980—	Holyoke*	.561
	Waterbury	.540

Year	Team	Pct.	Year	Team	Pct.	Year	Team	Pct.
1981—	Glens Falls	.615	1987—	Pittsfield	.630	1993—	Harrisburg‡	.681
	Bristol*	.577		Harrisburg‡	.550		Canton/Akron	.543
1982—	West Haven*	.614	1988—	Glens Falls	.584	1994—	Harrisburg	.633
	Lynn	.590		Albany‡	.522		Binghamton‡	.582
1983—	Lynn	.554	1989—	Albany‡	.657	1995—	New Haven	.556
	New Britain‡	.518		Harrisburg	.522		Reading‡	.514
1984—	Waterbury	.543	1990—	Albany	.568	1996—	Portland	.589
	Vermont‡	.536		London‡	.547		Harrisburg‡	.521
1985—	Albany	.540	1991—	Harrisburg	.621	1997—	Harrisburg‡	.606
	Vermont‡	.514		Albany‡	.543		Portland	.556
1986—	Reading	.566	1992—	Canton/Akron	.580			
	Vermont‡	.554		Binghamton‡	.572			

*Won split-season playoff. †Won championship and four-team playoff. ‡Won four-team playoff. §Tied for pennant, York winning playoff. ∞League was divided into Northern, Southern divisions and played a split season; Lancaster was overall season leader. ▲Playoff finals canceled after one game because of rain with Williamsport and Springfield declared playoff co-champions. ◆League was divided into Eastern, Western divisions; Binghamton won playoff. ■Tied for pennant, Waterbury winning playoff. ▼League was divided into American, National divisions; won playoff. •League was divided into American and National divisions; won four-team playoff. ††League was divided into Northern, Southern divisions, won playoff. ‡‡League was divided into New England and Canadian-American divisions; won playoff. §§Won both halves of split season (no playoffs). (NOTE—Known as New York-Pennsylvania League prior to 1938.)

CLASS AA Eastern League

SOUTHERN LEAGUE

LEAGUE OFFICE

President/secretary-treasurer
Arnold Fielkow

Address
1 Depot St., Suite 300
Marietta, GA 30060

Phone
770-428-4749

TEAMS

BIRMINGHAM BARONS

General manager
Tony Ensor
Manager
Dave Huppert
Ballpark (capacity, surface)
Hoover Metropolitan Stadium (10,800, grass)
Affiliation
White Sox
Address
P.O. Box 360007
Birmingham, AL 35236
Phone
205-988-3200

CAROLINA MUDCATS

General manager
Joe Kremer
Manager
To be announced
Ballpark (capacity, surface)
Five County Stadium (6,000, grass)
Affiliation
Pirates
Address
P.O. Drawer 1218
Zebulon, NC 27597
Phone
919-269-2287

CHATTANOOGA LOOKOUTS

President/general manager
J. Frank Burke
Manager
Mark Berry
Ballpark (capacity, surface)
Historic Engel Stadium (7,500, grass)
Affiliation
Reds
Address
P.O. Box 11002
Chattanooga, TN 37401
Phone
423-267-2208

GREENVILLE BRAVES

General manager
Steve DeSalvo
Manager
Randy Ingle

Ballpark (capacity, surface)
Greenville Municipal Stadium (7,027, grass)
Affiliation
Braves
Address
P.O. Box 16683
Greenville, SC 29606
Phone
864-299-3456

HUNTSVILLE STARS

President/general manager
Don Mincher
Manager
Jeffrey Leonard
Ballpark (capacity, surface)
Joe W. Davis Stadium (10,400, grass)
Affiliation
Athletics
Address
P.O. Box 2769
Huntsville, AL 35804
Phone
205-882-2562

JACKSONVILLE SUNS

Vice president/general manager
Peter Bragan Jr.
Manager
Dave Anderson
Ballpark (capacity, surface)
Wolfson Park (8,200, grass)
Affiliation
Tigers
Address
P.O. Box 4756
Jacksonville, FL 32201
Phone
904-358-2846

KNOXVILLE SMOKIES

General manager
Dan Rajkowski
Manager
Omar Malave
Ballpark (capacity, surface)
Bill Meyer Stadium (6,412, grass)
Affiliation
Blue Jays
Address
633 Jessamine St.

Knoxville, TN 37917
Phone
423-637-9494

MOBILE BAYBEARS

General manager
Tom Simmons
Manager
Mike Ramsey
Ballpark (capacity, surface)
Hank Aaron Stadium (6,000, grass)
Affiliation
Padres
Address
P.O. Box 161663
Mobile, AL 36616
Phone
334-476-2287

ORLANDO RAYS

General manager
Tom Ramsberger
Manager
Dan Rohn
Ballpark (capacity, surface)
Tinker Field (6,000, grass)
Affiliation
Mariners
Address
287 S. Tampa Ave.
Orlando, FL 32805
Phone
407-245-2827

WEST TENN DIAMOND JAXX

Assistant general manager
Jarrod Coates
Manager
Dave Trembly
Ballpark (capacity, surface)
Pringles Park (6,000, grass)
Affiliation
Cubs
Address
To be announced
Phone
901-664-2020

FIRST HALF

EAST DIVISION

Team	W	L	T	Pct.	GB
Knoxville (Blue Jays)	41	27	1	.603	....
Jacksonville (Tigers)	34	35	0	.493	7½
Greenville (Braves)	34	36	0	.486	8
Carolina (Pirates)	26	42	0	.382	15
Orlando (Cubs)	25	44	0	.362	16½

WEST DIVISION

Team	W	L	T	Pct.	GB
Mobile (Padres)	39	29	0	.574	....
Memphis (Mariners)	37	32	0	.536	2½
Chattanooga (Reds)	37	32	0	.536	2½
Birmingham (White Sox)	36	32	1	.529	3
Huntsville (Athletics)	35	35	0	.500	5

SECOND HALF

EAST DIVISION

Team	W	L	T	Pct.	GB
Greenville (Braves)	40	30	0	.571	....
Orlando (Cubs)	38	31	0	.551	1½
Knoxville (Blue Jays)	34	36	0	.486	6
Jacksonville (Tigers)	32	38	0	.457	8
Carolina (Pirates)	29	40	0	.420	10½

WEST DIVISION

Team	W	L	T	Pct.	GB
Huntsville (Athletics)	42	27	0	.609	....
Birmingham (White Sox)	40	30	0	.571	2½
Chattanooga (Reds)	33	37	0	.471	9½
Mobile (Padres)	30	39	0	.435	12
Memphis (Mariners)	30	40	0	.429	12½

COMPOSITE

Team	Hun.	Bir.	Knx.	Grn.	Mob.	Chat.	Mem.	Jax.	Orl.	Caro.	W	L	T	Pct.	GB
Huntsville (Athletics)	....	7	7	8	8	9	8	10	11	9	77	62	0	.554	....
Birmingham (White Sox)	8	....	8	12	5	7	11	6	10	9	76	62	1	.551	½
Knoxville (Blue Jays)	8	7	....	9	6	9	9	8	9	10	75	63	1	.543	1½
Greenville (Braves)	8	3	6	....	13	9	7	9	9	10	74	66	0	.529	3½
Mobile (Padres)	8	11	9	2	....	8	8	8	6	9	69	68	0	.504	7
Chattanooga (Reds)	6	8	7	7	7	....	6	11	7	11	70	69	0	.504	7
Memphis (Mariners)	8	5	7	9	6	9	....	8	7	8	67	72	0	.482	10
Jacksonville (Tigers)	6	9	7	7	8	5	8	....	7	9	66	73	0	.475	11
Orlando (Cubs)	5	6	7	7	8	9	6	9	....	7	63	75	0	.457	13½
Carolina (Pirates)	5	6	5	5	7	5	6	7	9	....	55	82	0	.401	21

Carolina's home games played in Zebulon, N.C.

Major league affiliations in parentheses.

PLAYOFFS: Greenville defeated Knoxville, three games to one; Huntsville defeated Mobile, three games to two; Greenville defeated Huntsville, three games to two, to win league championship.

REGULAR-SEASON ATTENDANCE: Birmingham, 302,144; Carolina, 265,219; Chattanooga, 228,391; Greenville, 254,049; Huntsville, 285,580; Jacksonville, 238,238; Knoxville, 138,389; Memphis, 113,183; Mobile, 332,639; Orlando, 147,241. Total—2,305,073. Playoffs (14 games)—41,107. Class AA All-Star Game at San Antonio—7,114.

MANAGERS: Birmingham, Dave Huppert; Carolina, Marc Hill (through June 18) and Jeff Banister (June 19 through end of season); Chattanooga, Mark Berry; Greenville, Randy Ingle; Huntsville, Mike Quade; Jacksonville, Dave Anderson; Knoxville, Omar Malave; Memphis, Dave Brundage; Mobile, Mike Ramsey; Orlando, Dave Trembley. Managerial record of team with more than one manager: Carolina, Hill 26-42, Banister, 29-40.

ALL-STAR TEAM: 1B—D.T. Cromer, Huntsville; 2B—Frank Menechino, Birmingham; 3B—Mike Coolbaugh, Huntsville; SS—Miguel Tejada, Huntsville; OF—Juan Encarnacion, Jacksonville; Ben Grieve, Huntsville; Mike Neill, Huntsville; Chris Prieto, Mobile; Anthony Sanders, Knoxville; C—Justin Towle, Chattanooga; DH—Luis Raven, Birmingham; Utility—Kevin Witt, Knoxville; RHP—Ken Cloude, Memphis; LHP—Scott Eyre, Birmingham; Most Valuable Player—Ben Grieve, Huntsville; Most Outstanding Pitcher—Scott Eyre, Birmingham; Hustler of the Year—Brian Simmons, Birmingham; Manager of the Year—Randy Ingle, Greenville.

1997 BATTING

TEAM

Team	Avg.	G	TPA	AB	R	H	TB	2B	3B	HR	RBI	SH	SF	HP	BB	IBB	SO	SB	CS	GDP	LOB	ShO	Slg.	OBP
Huntsville	.286	139	5605	4818	942	1380	2221	281	34	164	871	19	50	54	664	12	1036	121	59	108	1057	0	.461	.376
Chattanooga	.284	139	5374	4766	744	1354	2078	274	33	128	677	40	47	37	484	22	826	94	71	98	1015	6	.436	.352
Birmingham	.279	139	5452	4761	793	1330	2069	287	40	124	729	47	44	60	540	25	1015	70	45	104	1044	3	.435	.357
Mobile	.277	137	5400	4676	768	1297	1954	255	39	108	702	28	48	52	596	23	887	126	62	109	1053	10	.418	.362
Greenville	.273	140	5344	4701	711	1283	1993	225	22	147	640	69	35	61	478	26	832	92	84	126	957	4	.424	.345
Knoxville	.272	139	5259	4669	727	1269	2067	255	42	153	661	28	40	56	466	23	933	76	73	107	938	7	.443	.342
Orlando	.272	138	5217	4570	733	1242	1929	244	37	123	651	37	41	69	500	33	846	123	76	114	929	2	.422	.350
Memphis	.272	139	5183	4563	672	1239	1792	229	36	84	603	22	40	63	495	18	853	109	68	108	987	8	.393	.348
Jacksonville	.267	139	5335	4730	699	1263	1947	245	29	127	630	45	36	57	467	16	918	115	38	111	973	4	.412	.338
Carolina	.264	137	5337	4745	688	1255	1983	253	44	129	631	43	35	58	456	25	1024	112	66	81	989	7	.418	.334

INDIVIDUAL

TOP QUALIFIERS FOR BATTING CHAMPIONSHIP

Minimum 378 plate appearances. *Lefthanded batter. †Switch-hitter.

Player, Team	Avg.	G	TPA	AB	R	H	TB	2B	3B	HR	RBI	SH	SF	HP	BB	IBB	SO	SB	CS	GDP	Slg.	OBP
Neill, Mike, Huntsville*	.340	122	568	486	129	165	241	30	2	14	80	3	4	3	72	0	113	16	7	8	.496	.427
Raven, Luis, Birmingham	.336	117	514	456	88	153	279	30	3	30	112	0	7	5	46	7	126	4	3	5	.612	.397
Grieve, Ben, Huntsville*	.328	100	466	372	100	122	227	29	2	24	108	0	4	9	81	0	75	5	1	8	.610	.455
Pearson, Eddie, Birmingham†	.327	95	410	382	59	125	175	33	1	5	59	0	3	2	23	1	50	1	1	13	.458	.366
Cromer, D.T., Huntsville*	.323	134	614	545	100	176	273	40	6	15	121	0	6	3	60	4	102	12	7	8	.501	.389
Encarnacion, Juan, Jack.	.323	131	561	493	91	159	276	31	4	26	90	0	6	19	43	6	86	17	3	8	.560	.394
Prieto, Chris, Mobile*	.320	109	463	388	80	124	170	22	9	2	58	1	5	10	59	0	55	26	6	2	.438	.418
Ramirez, Angel, Knoxville	.309	85	384	369	55	114	167	24	7	5	37	0	2	3	10	0	48	11	6	4	.453	.331

CLASS AA Southern League

Player, Team	Avg.	G	TPA	AB	R	H	TB	2B	3B	HR	RBI	SH	SF	HP	BB	IBB	SO	SB	CS	GDP	Slg.	OBP
Towle, Justin, Chattanooga......	.309	119	478	418	62	129	209	37	5	11	70	0	3	2	55	1	77	5	5	7	.500	.389
Rose, Pete, Chattanooga*........	.308	112	486	445	75	137	243	31	0	25	98	1	3	2	63	0	1	5		5	.546	.359
Coolbaugh, Mike, Huntsville	.308	139	628	559	100	172	303	37	2	30	132	2	8	7	52	3	105	8	3	17	.542	.369
Monahan, Shane, Memphis* ...	.302	107	436	401	52	121	193	24	6	12	76	1	2	2	30	2	100	14	7	4	.481	.352
Alvarez, Gabe, Mobile	.300	114	489	427	71	128	202	28	2	14	78	0	6	5	51	2	64	1	1	21	.473	.376
Menechino, Frankie, Birmingham	.299	90	415	318	78	95	167	28	4	12	60	1	6	11	79	0	77	7	3	7	.525	.447
Roberts, David, Jacksonville*..	.296	105	473	415	76	123	163	24	2	4	41	9	2	2	45	1	62	23	5	5	.393	.366

DEPARTMENTAL LEADERS: G—M. Coolbaugh, 139; AB—M. Coolbaugh, 559; R—Neill, 129; H—D. Cromer, 176; TB—M. Coolbaugh, 303; 2B—D. Cromer, 40; 3B—B. Simmons, 12; HR—M. Coolbaugh, Raven, Witt, 30 each; RBI—M. Coolbaugh, 132; SH—Moore, 21; SF—Maxwell, 9; HP—Encarnacion, 19; BB—B. Simmons, 88; IBB—Raven, Witt, 7 each; SO—Hermansen, 136; SB—E. Johnson, 42; CS—Sturdivant, 17; GIDP—G. Alvarez, 21; Slg.—Raven, .612; OBP—Grieve, .455.

ALL PLAYERS
*Lefthanded batter. †Switch-hitter.

Player, Team	Avg.	G	TPA	AB	R	H	TB	2B	3B	HR	RBI	SH	SF	HP	BB	IBB	SO	SB	CS	GDP	Slg.	OBP
Adriana, Sharnol, Knoxville....	.236	99	375	314	50	74	105	11	1	6	39	5	4	5	47	2	66	9	7	11	.334	.341
Allen, Dustin, Mobile.............	.253	131	559	475	85	120	207	28	4	17	75	0	3	0	81	0	116	1	4	12	.436	.360
Allen, Marlon, Chattanooga.....	.255	62	229	196	27	50	81	15	2	4	23	0	4	3	26	1	39	0	1	2	.413	.345
Almanzar, Richard, Jack.........	.243	103	438	387	55	94	133	20	2	5	35	11	0	3	37	0	43	20	6	11	.344	.314
Alvarez, Clemente, Bir...........	.202	79	278	242	29	49	70	10	1	3	23	3	1	5	27	0	49	0	0	17	.289	.295
Alvarez, Gabe, Mobile	.300	114	489	427	71	128	202	28	2	14	78	0	6	5	51	2	64	1	1	21	.473	.376
Anderson, Jimmy, Carolina* ..	.000	4	4	4	0	0	0	0	0	0	0	0	0	0	0	0	1	0	0	0	.000	.000
Ardoin, Danny, Huntsville........	.231	57	230	208	26	48	72	10	1	4	23	0	2	3	17	0	38	2	3	7	.346	.296
Asche, Mike, Carolina	.214	15	47	42	2	9	12	1	1	0	2	1	0	0	4	0	6	0	0	0	.286	.283
Atchley, Justin, Chattanooga*	.167	13	8	6	0	1	1	0	0	0	1	0	0	0	2	0	2	0	0	1	.167	.375
Ayrault, Joe, Greenville	.242	13	41	33	6	8	16	2	0	2	4	1	1	0	6	0	8	0	0	0	.485	.350
Ballara, Juan, Orlando............	.194	15	37	31	2	6	6	0	0	0	2	0	1	0	5	0	10	2	0	0	.194	.297
Barker, Glen, Jacksonville	.280	69	302	257	47	72	106	8	4	6	29	8	3	5	29	0	72	17	8	4	.412	.361
Barker, Richie, Orlando	.500	19	2	2	1	1	1	0	0	0	0	0	0	0	0	0	0	0	0	0	.500	.500
Baron, Jim, Mobile*..............	.000	19	1	1	0	0	0	0	0	0	0	0	0	0	0	0	0	0	0	0	.000	.000
Bautista, Juan, Birmingham.....	.239	12	50	46	6	11	14	3	0	0	4	1	0	0	3	0	15	0	1	2	.304	.286
Beasley, Tony, Carolina	.274	31	126	117	15	32	37	5	0	0	12	0	1	1	7	1	16	2	1	3	.316	.317
Beatty, Blaine, Carolina*	.455	20	15	11	1	5	7	0	1	0	0	2	0	0	2	0	1	0	0	0	.636	.538
Benbow, Lou, Greenville	.232	117	358	315	39	73	116	14	1	9	34	4	2	3	34	1	80	4	8	7	.368	.311
Benson, Kris, Carolina............	.000	14	11	9	0	0	0	0	0	0	0	1	2	0	0	0	2	0	0	0	.000	.000
Boggs, Robert, Chattanooga..	.125	9	8	8	0	1	1	0	0	0	0	0	0	0	0	0	2	0	0	0	.125	.125
Bonifay, Ken, Carolina*	.176	22	85	68	11	12	21	4	1	1	7	0	0	0	17	1	23	1	0	0	.309	.341
Bowie, Jim, Mobile*	.241	32	67	54	4	13	18	2	0	1	10	0	2	1	10	2	5	0	0	3	.333	.358
Bowie, Micah, Greenville*	.083	8	14	12	1	1	1	0	0	0	1	2	0	0	0	0	5	0	0	0	.083	.083
Bream, Scott, Jacksonville†....	.273	19	70	55	12	15	22	1	0	2	3	1	0	0	14	0	12	1	0	1	.400	.420
Bridges, Kary, Carolina*........	.336	66	297	283	43	95	123	17	1	3	29	3	2	0	9	0	10	9	5	1	.435	.354
Briggs, Anthony, Greenville.....	.235	19	20	17	3	4	4	0	0	0	2	0	0	1	4	0	4	0	0	0	.235	.278
Brinkley, Darryl, Mobile...........	.307	55	246	215	41	66	97	14	1	5	33	0	0	5	26	1	30	10	9	6	.451	.394
Brito, Luis, Greenville†	.289	97	360	336	35	97	112	12	0	1	36	6	3	0	15	1	25	4	5	11	.333	.316
Broach, Donald, Chattanooga	.274	105	449	402	62	110	133	15	4	0	31	4	2	6	35	1	47	12	15	6	.331	.339
Brown, Adrian, Carolina†	.303	37	168	145	29	44	62	4	4	2	15	3	0	2	18	1	12	9	5	1	.428	.388
Brown, Darold, Orlando*	.000	18	1	1	0	0	0	0	0	0	0	0	0	0	0	0	1	0	0	0	.000	.000
Brown, Ray, Mobile*	.352	57	214	179	28	63	91	16	0	4	30	0	1	1	33	1	33	1	0	6	.508	.453
Bruno, Julio, Jacksonville	.265	120	480	438	51	116	162	22	3	6	57	0	1	3	38	1	70	6	3	9	.370	.327
Bussa, Todd, Huntsville...........	.000	19	2	0	0	0	0	0	0	0	0	0	0	0	0	0	0	0	0	0	.000	.000
Butler, Adam, Greenville*	.000	46	1	1	0	0	0	0	0	0	0	0	0	0	0	0	0	0	0	0	.000	.000
Byrd, Matt, Greenville†	.000	28	2	2	0	0	0	0	0	0	0	0	0	0	0	0	1	0	0	0	.000	.000
Byrne, Earl, Orlando*	.083	32	28	24	3	2	2	0	0	0	0	0	0	0	4	0	6	0	0	1	.083	.214
Candelaria, Ben, Knoxville*....	.294	120	529	472	81	139	226	32	5	15	67	4	6	5	42	2	89	4	3	9	.479	.354
Caruthers, Clay, Chat.†..........	.250	9	5	4	1	1	1	0	0	0	1	0	0	0	1	0	2	0	0	0	.250	.400
Castro, Jose, Huntsville†........	.385	5	18	13	4	5	5	0	0	0	1	0	0	1	4	0	2	0	0	0	.385	.556
Cather, Mike, Greenville	.000	22	1	1	0	0	0	0	0	0	0	0	0	0	0	0	1	0	0	0	.000	.000
Christenson, Ryan, Huntsville	.367	29	145	120	39	44	65	9	3	2	18	0	1	0	24	0	23	5	4	3	.542	.469
Christian, Eddie, Memphis†....	.336	68	281	238	50	80	112	20	0	4	39	2	3	1	36	6	24	8	3	11	.471	.421
Christiansen, Jason, Carolina..	.000	8	2	2	0	0	0	0	0	0	0	0	0	0	0	0	0	0	0	0	.000	.000
Clement, Matt, Mobile............	.200	13	15	10	1	2	2	0	0	0	1	5	0	0	0	0	5	0	0	0	.200	.200
Cline, Pat, Orlando	.255	78	305	271	39	69	109	19	0	7	37	0	2	5	27	1	78	2	2	5	.402	.331
Conger, Jeff, Carolina*	.196	58	161	138	15	27	43	5	1	3	12	2	0	2	19	1	53	4	0	2	.312	.302
Conner, Decomba, Jack..........	.208	47	187	154	22	32	56	6	3	4	17	0	1	2	30	1	45	5	1	4	.364	.342
Cook, Jason, Memphis	.216	53	191	162	23	35	42	7	0	0	19	2	3	1	21	0	24	2	1	9	.259	.312
Coolbaugh, Mike, Huntsville....	.308	139	628	559	100	172	303	37	2	30	132	2	8	7	52	3	105	8	3	17	.542	.369
Coolbaugh, Scott, Bir.............	.289	68	280	235	35	68	119	18	0	11	50	0	4	4	37	3	60	0	0	3	.506	.389
Cordero, Edward, Greenville ..	.400	3	6	5	1	2	2	0	0	0	0	1	0	0	0	0	1	0	0	0	.400	.400
Correa, Miguel, Memphis†......	.260	68	272	250	33	65	96	13	0	6	31	2	2	2	16	0	49	2	2	5	.384	.307
Cortes, David, Greenville........	.000	3	1	1	0	0	0	0	0	0	0	0	0	0	0	0	0	0	0	0	.000	.000
Cotton, John, Birmingham* ...	.290	33	136	124	23	36	71	0	2	7	26	0	1	2	9	0	33	1	2	3	.573	.346
Coughlin, Kevin, Chat.*..........	.292	54	186	168	22	49	65	7	0	3	15	1	1	1	15	1	20	0	2	3	.387	.351
Courtright, John, Chat............	.000	20	13	10	0	0	0	0	0	0	0	3	0	0	0	0	5	0	0	0	.000	.000
Cox, Darron, Orlando	.222	3	11	9	2	2	6	1	0	1	4	0	1	0	1	0	0	0	1	0	.667	.273
Cradle, Rickey, Knoxville	.214	84	308	257	50	55	103	16	1	10	34	2	1	7	41	0	67	5	6	5	.401	.337
Crawford, Carlos, Carolina	.200	29	5	5	0	1	1	0	0	0	0	0	0	0	0	0	0	0	0	0	.200	.200
Cromer, Brandon, Carolina*...	.228	55	228	193	23	44	76	12	4	4	14	4	2	0	29	0	50	1	0	5	.394	.326
Cromer, D.T., Huntsville*	.323	134	614	545	100	176	273	40	6	15	121	0	6	3	60	4	102	12	7	8	.501	.389
Crowell, Jim, Chattanooga*....	.000	3	7	7	0	0	0	0	0	0	0	0	0	0	0	0	2	0	0	0	.000	.000
Curl, John, Knoxville*	.207	10	32	29	0	6	7	1	0	0	1	0	0	0	3	0	6	0	0	0	.241	.281
Davis, Kane, Carolina.............	.200	6	7	5	0	1	1	0	0	0	0	1	0	0	1	0	3	1	0	0	.200	.333
Dean, Chris, Memphis†..........	.253	67	267	237	24	60	90	11	5	3	18	2	1	2	25	2	37	3	5	6	.380	.328
DeBoer, Rob, Huntsville	.243	91	359	288	55	70	142	16	1	18	48	3	1	7	60	0	111	8	5	6	.493	.385

Player, Team	Avg.	G	TPA	AB	R	H	TB	2B	3B	HR	RBI	SH	SF	HP	BB	IBB	SO	SB	CS	GDP	Slg.	OBP
DeLaCruz, Lorenzo, Knoxville	.336	39	166	146	32	49	81	7	2	7	26	0	1	5	14	1	38	2	2	2	.555	.410
Devarez, Cesar, Orlando	.281	34	105	96	13	27	48	4	1	5	17	1	0	0	8	2	15	1	0	2	.500	.337
Diaz, Cesar, Knoxville	.200	7	20	15	2	3	7	1	0	1	3	0	0	0	5	0	2	0	0	0	.467	.400
Dillinger, John, Carolina	.000	23	13	13	0	0	0	0	0	0	0	0	0	0	0	0	6	0	0	0	.000	.000
Dismuke, Jamie, Chat.*	.286	36	118	98	21	28	45	5	0	4	25	0	0	2	18	0	10	0	1	0	.459	.407
Dixon, Bubba, Mobile	.000	56	4	4	0	0	0	0	0	0	0	0	0	0	0	0	0	0	0	0	.000	.000
Donnelly, Brendan, Chat.	.000	62	2	2	0	0	0	0	0	0	0	0	0	0	0	0	0	0	0	1	.000	.000
Dowler, Dee, Orlando	.253	52	209	178	32	45	61	7	0	3	19	4	1	5	21	2	23	8	4	10	.343	.346
Doyle, Tom, Chattanooga*	.000	65	7	5	1	0	0	0	0	0	0	2	0	0	0	0	1	0	0	0	.000	.000
Duncan, Courtney, Orlando*	.000	8	7	6	0	0	0	0	0	0	0	1	0	0	0	0	4	0	0	0	.000	.000
Eaglin, Mike, Greenville	.288	126	462	396	62	114	150	15	3	5	47	13	3	9	41	4	66	15	10	5	.379	.365
Ebert, Derrin, Greenville	.217	27	30	23	3	5	5	0	0	0	3	2	1	0	4	0	1	0	0	1	.217	.321
Eddie, Steve, Chattanooga	.287	118	426	394	57	113	170	25	4	8	49	3	7	1	21	4	64	3	2	10	.431	.319
Ellis, Kevin, Orlando	.255	104	363	330	41	84	131	15	4	8	41	1	2	5	25	1	66	6	1	7	.397	.315
Encarnacion, Juan, Jack.	.323	131	561	493	91	159	276	31	4	26	90	0	6	19	43	6	86	17	3	8	.560	.394
Espinosa, Ramon, Carolina	.278	19	75	72	10	20	27	2	1	1	10	0	0	3	0	0	15	0	2	3	.375	.307
Evans, Jason, Birmingham†	.305	63	255	223	33	68	101	16	1	5	25	3	1	0	28	4	51	2	2	2	.453	.381
Fagley, Dan, Birmingham	.368	20	20	19	1	7	8	1	0	0	0	0	0	0	1	0	5	0	0	1	.421	.400
Finley, Steve, Mobile*	.500	1	5	4	1	2	5	0	0	1	2	0	0	0	1	0	2	0	0	0	1.250	.600
Finn, John, Birmingham	.276	73	298	246	49	68	83	15	0	0	27	4	1	8	39	0	28	13	2	5	.337	.391
Font, Franklin, Orlando	.300	10	22	20	3	6	6	0	0	0	2	0	0	0	2	0	1	0	1	1	.300	.364
Forkerway, Trey, Orlando	.199	75	198	166	19	33	42	6	0	1	10	2	3	2	25	3	30	4	4	6	.253	.306
Freel, Ryan, Knoxville	.202	33	116	94	18	19	22	1	1	0	4	1	0	2	19	0	13	5	3	3	.234	.348
Freeman, Ricky, Orlando	.312	81	344	308	58	96	167	19	2	16	73	0	2	5	29	6	51	8	5	3	.542	.378
French, Anton, Knoxville†	.333	2	6	6	2	2	4	0	1	0	1	0	0	0	0	0	2	0	0	0	.667	.333
Gama, Rick, Mobile	.288	88	355	295	56	85	123	16	2	6	43	1	6	2	51	0	41	9	3	3	.417	.390
Garcia, Al, Orlando	.091	12	14	11	1	1	1	0	0	0	1	1	0	0	2	0	6	0	0	0	.091	.231
Garcia, Freddy, Carolina	.291	73	310	282	47	82	164	17	4	19	57	0	4	6	18	2	56	0	1	11	.582	.342
Garcia, Guillermo, Chat.	.284	20	83	74	11	21	36	1	1	4	19	0	1	0	8	0	13	0	0	1	.486	.349
Garcia, Luis, Jacksonville	.268	126	481	456	55	122	158	19	1	5	48	6	6	3	10	0	59	3	2	15	.346	.284
Gazarek, Marty, Orlando	.331	76	317	290	55	96	149	23	0	10	52	0	2	5	20	2	31	10	3	3	.514	.382
Giard, Ken, Greenville	.000	25	5	3	1	0	0	0	0	0	0	0	0	0	1	0	1	0	0	1	.000	.250
Gibralter, Steve, Chattanooga	.258	30	116	97	20	25	40	9	0	2	12	1	3	2	13	1	22	0	0	0	.412	.348
Gipson, Charles, Memphis	.247	88	371	320	56	79	99	9	4	1	28	2	1	13	34	2	71	31	6	4	.309	.342
Gonzalez, Wikleman, Mobile	.273	47	156	143	15	39	60	7	1	4	25	0	1	2	10	0	12	1	1	5	.420	.327
Gordon, Keith, Chattanooga	.167	4	15	12	2	2	5	0	0	1	2	0	0	0	3	0	7	1	1	0	.417	.333
Gower, Tim, Chattanooga	.000	24	3	3	1	0	0	0	0	0	0	1	0	0	0	0	0	0	0	0	.000	.000
Grall, Gregory, Chattanooga	.250	2	4	4	0	1	1	0	0	0	0	0	0	0	0	0	2	0	0	1	.250	.250
Grieve, Ben, Huntsville*	.328	100	466	372	100	122	227	29	2	24	108	0	4	9	81	0	75	5	1	8	.610	.455
Griffey, Craig, Mem.-Chat.	.223	90	345	300	48	67	79	8	2	0	20	5	2	0	37	2	63	14	8	9	.263	.307
Grijak, Kevin, Greenville*	.250	72	267	240	35	60	113	12	1	13	48	1	3	5	18	2	35	0	1	8	.471	.312
Guevara, Giomar, Memphis	.263	65	249	228	30	60	90	10	4	4	28	0	1	0	20	0	42	5	5	3	.395	.321
Guiel, Aaron, Mobile*	.385	8	32	26	9	10	15	2	0	1	9	0	0	1	5	0	4	1	0	0	.577	.500
Hall, Billy, Chattanooga†	.256	58	241	215	31	55	72	4	2	3	19	1	0	1	24	0	35	13	8	9	.335	.333
Halperin, Mike, Carolina*	.250	17	13	12	0	3	3	0	0	0	1	0	0	0	2	0	4	0	0	1	.250	.250
Hammack, Brandon, Orlando	.000	39	1	0	1	0	0	0	0	0	0	0	0	1	0	0	0	0	0	0	.000	1.000
Hanel, Marcus, Carolina	.237	56	187	173	15	41	52	5	0	2	12	3	0	2	9	3	39	0	0	5	.301	.283
Hart, Jason, Orlando	.000	14	1	1	0	0	0	0	0	0	0	0	0	0	1	0	0	0	0	0	.000	.000
Harvey, Bryan, Greenville	.000	22	1	0	0	0	0	0	0	0	0	1	0	0	0	0	0	0	0	0	.000	.000
Hazlett, Steve, Carolina	.235	45	171	153	22	36	55	7	3	2	17	0	0	4	14	0	31	1	6	2	.359	.316
Helms, Wes, Greenville	.296	86	356	314	50	93	142	14	1	11	44	0	3	6	33	2	50	3	4	14	.452	.371
Henry, Santiago, Knoxville	.291	52	204	196	25	57	84	10	1	5	26	0	3	1	4	1	35	3	2	3	.429	.304
Hermansen, Chad, Carolina	.275	129	571	487	87	134	233	31	4	20	70	0	5	10	69	5	136	18	6	3	.478	.373
Hernandez, Elvin, Carolina	.000	17	18	14	2	0	0	0	0	0	0	3	0	0	1	0	5	0	0	0	.000	.067
Hernandez, Ramon, Hun.	.193	44	185	161	27	31	46	3	0	4	24	0	3	3	18	0	23	0	0	8	.286	.281
Hicks, Jamie, Greenville	.294	8	19	17	3	5	8	0	0	1	1	0	0	0	2	0	3	1	0	0	.471	.368
Hightower, Vee, Orlando†	.233	87	332	283	35	66	96	8	2	6	29	0	2	4	43	0	66	16	11	10	.339	.340
Hills, Rich, Mobile	.250	71	249	216	37	54	83	12	1	5	30	0	3	3	25	1	34	2	0	8	.384	.332
Hines, Rich, Greenville*	.333	41	4	3	0	1	1	0	0	0	0	1	0	0	0	0	1	0	0	0	.333	.333
Holdridge, David, Memphis	.000	31	1	0	0	0	0	0	0	0	0	1	0	0	0	0	0	0	0	0	.000	1.000
Holifield, Rick, Carolina*	.216	51	202	185	27	40	77	12	5	5	23	1	1	1	14	1	59	8	3	2	.416	.274
Hughes, Troy, Huntsville	.209	72	285	258	37	54	81	12	0	5	33	0	3	1	23	0	50	2	1	8	.314	.274
Hurst, Jimmy, Jacksonville	.471	5	21	17	5	8	16	2	0	2	6	0	1	0	3	0	6	0	0	0	.941	.524
Ibarra, Jesse, Jacksonville†	.283	115	504	441	73	125	226	24	1	25	91	0	5	3	55	4	85	3	2	9	.512	.355
Jacobs, Ryan, Greenville	.333	28	5	3	0	1	1	0	0	0	0	2	0	0	0	0	2	0	0	0	.333	.333
Jimenez, Manny, Greenville	.291	115	465	430	59	125	168	24	2	5	45	5	2	6	22	0	70	3	10	20	.391	.333
Johnson, Earl, Mob.-Jack.	.245	114	497	453	76	111	142	14	4	3	35	9	4	1	30	0	75	42	14	6	.313	.291
Johnson, Jason, Carolina	.182	9	11	11	0	2	3	1	0	0	2	0	0	0	0	0	2	0	0	0	.273	.182
Jones, Ryan, Knoxville	.256	86	362	328	44	84	145	19	3	12	51	0	4	3	27	1	63	0	1	5	.442	.315
Jordan, Ricky, Carolina	.314	52	201	188	25	59	93	9	2	7	33	0	3	2	8	0	25	0	0	2	.495	.343
Jorgensen, Randy, Memphis*	.291	129	530	477	66	139	206	28	3	11	70	0	7	8	38	2	58	1	2	10	.432	.349
Joseph, Terry, Orlando	.277	134	530	452	80	125	202	22	11	11	68	1	4	14	59	1	87	17	16	11	.447	.374
Kaufman, Brad, Mobile	.217	22	25	23	0	5	6	1	0	0	3	1	0	0	1	0	9	1	0	1	.261	.250
Keefe, Jamie, Mobile	.268	16	49	41	4	11	15	2	1	0	3	2	0	1	5	0	12	2	1	0	.366	.362
Kelly, Jeff, Carolina*	.250	31	20	20	2	5	5	0	0	0	3	0	0	0	0	0	11	0	0	0	.250	.250
Kelly, Mike, Chattanooga	.350	15	64	60	14	21	37	7	0	3	12	0	1	0	3	0	16	3	2	0	.617	.375
Killeen, Tim, Mobile*	.202	66	224	168	23	34	59	8	1	5	21	1	1	1	53	0	60	0	1	2	.351	.395
King, Raymond, Greenville*	.143	12	8	7	1	1	1	0	0	0	0	1	0	0	0	0	4	0	0	0	.143	.143
Koelling, Brian, Chattanooga	.280	73	312	279	50	78	102	9	3	3	22	2	1	2	28	2	49	18	9	5	.366	.348
Koppe, Clint, Chattanooga	.167	13	12	12	0	2	2	0	0	0	1	0	0	0	0	0	7	0	0	0	.167	.167
Lackey, Steve, Jacksonville	.077	5	14	13	1	1	1	0	0	0	0	1	0	0	0	0	1	1	0	2	.077	.077
Ladell, Cleveland, Chat.	.344	14	35	32	3	11	12	1	0	0	4	0	1	2	0	0	3	1	1	0	.375	.371
Lanza, Mike, Memphis	.250	21	61	56	8	14	16	2	0	0	6	0	0	1	4	0	13	2	0	0	.286	.311

Player, Team	Avg.	G	TPA	AB	R	H	TB	2B	3B	HR	RBI	SH	SF	HP	BB	IBB	SO	SB	CS	GDP	Slg.	OBP
LaRocca, Greg, Mobile..........	.267	76	339	300	44	80	109	16	2	3	31	0	5	8	26	0	46	8	3	4	.363	.336
Larson, Brandon, Chat.	.268	11	43	41	4	11	18	5	1	0	6	0	1	0	1	0	10	0	0	1	.439	.279
LeBlanc, Eric, Chattanooga* ..	.000	8	12	11	2	0	0	0	0	0	0	1	0	0	0	0	5	0	0	0	.000	.000
LeRoy, John, Greenville	.250	29	6	4	0	1	1	0	0	0	1	1	0	0	1	0	2	0	0	0	.250	.400
Lewis, Marc, Greenville..........	.273	135	551	512	64	140	214	17	3	17	67	4	2	8	25	3	84	21	14	9	.418	.316
Lidle, Kevin, Jacksonville	.151	59	210	186	18	28	38	7	0	1	16	3	2	2	17	0	77	0	0	4	.204	.227
Liefer, Jeff, Birmingham*.......	.238	119	524	474	67	113	200	24	9	15	71	1	4	7	38	3	115	2	0	10	.422	.302
Ligtenberg, Kerry, Greenville..	1.000	31	1	1	0	1	2	1	0	0	1	0	0	0	0	0	0	0	0	0	2.000	1.000
Livsey, Shawn, Orlando†........	.267	13	37	30	6	8	13	2	0	1	2	0	0	0	7	1	4	2	0	0	.433	.405
Lott, Brian, Chattanooga	.200	25	14	10	0	2	2	0	0	0	2	4	0	0	0	0	5	0	0	0	.200	.200
Lyons, Curt, Orlando.............	.000	2	2	1	0	0	0	0	0	0	0	1	0	0	0	0	1	0	0	0	.000	.000
Magdaleno, Ricky, Chat..........	.262	61	232	187	33	49	88	13	1	8	34	1	1	1	42	1	51	1	1	11	.471	.398
Magee, Danny, Greenville.......	.273	7	24	22	1	6	9	0	0	1	3	0	0	1	1	0	6	0	1	1	.409	.333
Mahoney, Mike, Greenville	.228	87	336	298	46	68	109	17	0	8	46	5	2	3	28	1	75	1	0	10	.366	.299
Marine, Del, Jacksonville	.238	99	384	328	45	78	138	22	1	12	43	0	1	7	48	1	92	0	1	11	.421	.346
Marquez, Jesus, Jack.*..........	.267	114	498	465	56	124	192	24	4	12	74	3	5	3	22	2	77	9	5	12	.413	.301
Martin, Al, Carolina*	.111	3	9	9	0	1	1	0	0	0	0	0	0	0	0	0	0	0	0	0	.111	.111
Martins, Eric, Huntsville.........	.259	61	236	205	33	53	78	10	3	3	31	3	2	2	23	0	31	2	1	9	.380	.336
Mashore, Justin, Mobile	.238	90	324	281	53	67	120	10	5	11	41	3	3	5	32	2	70	11	8	8	.427	.324
Mathews, Del, Carolina*	.125	21	8	8	1	1	1	0	0	0	0	0	0	0	0	0	1	0	0	0	.125	.125
Matthews, Gary, Mobile†	.244	28	108	90	14	22	34	4	1	2	12	0	2	1	15	1	29	3	1	1	.378	.352
Maxwell, Jason, Orlando........	.279	122	509	409	87	114	190	22	6	14	58	5	9	4	82	1	72	12	9	6	.465	.397
Maynard, Scott, Memphis......	.158	14	40	38	3	6	6	0	0	0	3	0	0	1	1	0	12	0	0	0	.158	.200
McBride, Charles, Greenville..	.244	45	143	127	24	31	51	5	0	5	15	1	2	2	11	1	20	0	1	3	.402	.310
McCall, Rod, Orlando*...........	.300	19	83	70	11	21	41	2	0	6	20	0	1	2	10	0	24	0	0	0	.586	.398
McKenzie, Scott, Chat.	.000	30	3	3	0	0	0	0	0	0	0	0	0	0	0	0	2	0	0	0	.000	.000
McKinnon, Sandy, Bir.............	.271	96	373	332	58	90	124	20	1	4	31	5	3	2	31	1	68	13	6	3	.373	.334
McNichol, Brian, Orlando*	.417	22	16	12	4	5	7	2	0	0	2	1	0	0	3	0	5	0	0	0	.583	.533
Melhuse, Adam, Knoxville†....	.230	31	108	87	14	20	32	3	0	3	10	1	1	0	19	1	19	0	0	1	.368	.364
Melo, Juan, Mobile†	.287	113	487	456	52	131	178	22	2	7	67	0	2	0	29	4	90	7	9	16	.390	.329
Mendez, Sergio, Carolina	.233	49	158	146	17	34	52	10	1	2	12	0	2	4	6	1	33	1	1	10	.356	.278
Menechino, Frankie, Bir..........	.299	90	415	318	78	95	167	28	4	12	60	1	6	11	79	0	77	7	3	7	.525	.447
Micucci, Mike, Orlando*	.000	4	6	6	0	0	0	0	0	0	0	0	0	0	0	0	1	0	0	0	.000	.000
Miller, Orlando, Jacksonville ..	.364	3	13	11	2	4	8	1	0	1	3	0	0	1	1	0	1	0	0	0	.727	.462
Millette, Joe, Memphis..........	.304	57	213	191	36	58	80	11	1	3	22	0	0	8	14	0	35	2	5	4	.419	.376
Millwood, Kevin, Greenville....	.167	11	8	6	1	1	1	0	0	0	0	2	0	0	0	0	3	0	0	0	.167	.167
Mitchell, Tony, Carolina†	.091	4	12	11	0	1	1	0	0	0	1	0	0	0	1	0	4	0	0	0	.091	.167
Miyake, Chris, Carolina	.000	5	10	9	1	0	0	0	0	0	0	1	0	0	0	0	4	0	0	0	.000	.000
Molina, Jose, Orlando	.172	37	117	99	10	17	23	3	0	1	15	1	3	2	12	5	28	0	1	4	.232	.267
Monahan, Shane, Memphis* .	.302	107	436	401	52	121	193	24	6	12	76	1	2	2	30	2	100	14	7	4	.481	.352
Monds, Wonderful, Greenville	.315	27	111	89	21	28	57	5	0	8	15	1	1	0	20	0	23	6	3	1	.640	.436
Moore, Brandon, Birmingham	.256	125	485	414	58	106	126	15	1	1	47	21	4	1	45	0	48	4	7	11	.304	.328
Morales, Willie, Huntsville......	.272	36	156	136	19	37	57	11	0	3	24	0	3	0	17	0	24	1	0	2	.419	.346
Morgan, Dave, Knoxville	.273	21	55	44	6	12	14	2	0	0	4	0	0	1	10	0	14	0	0	0	.318	.418
Morris, Bobby, Orlando*.........	.313	4	18	16	3	5	6	1	0	0	1	0	0	0	2	0	3	0	0	0	.375	.389
Mosquera, Julio, Knoxville.....	.291	87	341	309	47	90	130	23	1	5	50	2	3	5	22	0	56	3	4	10	.421	.345
Moss, Damian, Greenville	.071	21	16	14	1	1	1	0	0	0	0	0	0	1	1	0	6	0	0	0	.071	.188
Moten, Scott, Orlando...........	1.000	4	1	1	0	1	1	0	0	0	0	0	0	0	0	0	0	0	0	0	1.000	1.000
Mottola, Chad, Chattanooga...	.362	46	197	174	35	63	93	9	3	5	32	1	5	1	16	1	23	7	1	3	.534	.408
Mouton, Lyle, Birmingham.....	.182	3	12	11	1	2	5	0	0	1	1	0	0	0	1	0	4	0	0	0	.455	.250
Murray, Glenn, Chattanooga ..	.283	94	396	329	66	93	191	16	2	26	73	0	6	4	56	2	91	7	5	5	.581	.387
Neill, Mike, Huntsville*	.340	122	568	486	129	165	241	30	2	14	80	3	3	4	72	0	113	16	7	8	.496	.427
Nelson, Bry, Orlando†...........	.288	110	435	382	51	110	171	33	2	8	58	1	6	1	45	4	43	5	7	15	.448	.359
Newhan, David, Huntsville* ...	.316	57	245	212	40	67	99	13	2	5	35	1	2	2	28	2	59	5	5	4	.467	.398
Nix, James, Chattanooga	.000	28	1	0	0	0	0	0	0	0	0	1	0	0	0	0	0	0	0	0	.000	.000
Norris, Dax, Greenville	.333	2	9	9	3	3	6	0	0	1	3	0	0	0	0	0	1	0	0	0	.667	.333
Norton, Phillip, Orlando	.000	2	2	2	0	0	0	0	0	0	0	0	0	0	0	0	1	0	0	0	.000	.000
Nunez, Abraham, Carolina†....	.328	47	223	198	31	65	76	6	1	1	14	2	3	0	20	1	28	10	5	2	.384	.385
Nunez, Raymond, Orlando	.296	106	371	351	59	104	171	13	3	16	65	1	1	3	15	2	65	1	2	5	.487	.330
Orie, Kevin, Orlando..............	.385	3	15	13	3	5	13	2	0	2	6	0	0	0	2	1	1	0	0	1	1.000	.467
Parris, Steve, Chattanooga.....	.091	14	14	11	2	1	1	0	0	0	1	3	0	0	0	0	4	0	0	0	.091	.091
Paul, Josh, Birmingham.........	.296	34	131	115	18	34	42	5	0	1	16	3	0	1	12	0	25	6	2	4	.365	.367
Pearson, Eddie, Birmingham†	.327	95	410	382	59	125	175	33	1	5	59	0	3	2	23	1	50	1	1	13	.458	.366
Peterson, Charles, Carolina....	.251	126	488	442	59	111	166	26	4	7	68	1	1	4	40	4	105	20	11	11	.376	.318
Peterson, Mark, Orlando*	.000	9	1	0	0	0	0	0	0	0	0	0	0	0	1	0	0	0	0	0	.000	1.000
Pett, Jose, Carolina...............	.067	14	16	15	1	1	1	0	0	0	0	0	0	0	1	0	8	0	0	0	.067	.125
Phillips, Jason, Carolina.........	.000	4	6	4	0	0	0	0	0	0	0	1	0	0	1	0	3	0	0	0	.000	.200
Pickford, Kevin, Carolina*......	.667	21	4	3	0	2	3	1	0	0	1	0	0	0	1	0	0	0	0	0	1.000	.750
Pierce, Jeff, Orlando..............	.000	5	3	2	0	0	0	0	0	0	0	1	0	0	0	0	0	0	0	0	.000	.000
Poe, Charles, Mobile.............	.311	53	209	193	30	60	84	7	4	3	35	0	3	2	11	3	43	5	1	2	.435	.349
Polcovich, Kevin, Carolina......	.320	17	64	50	13	16	30	5	0	3	7	2	0	2	10	0	4	4	2	1	.600	.452
Polidor, Wil, Birmingham†	.269	33	96	93	11	25	29	2	1	0	13	1	0	1	1	0	16	0	2	1	.312	.284
Pool, Matt, Orlando†.............	.000	9	3	2	0	0	0	0	0	0	0	1	0	0	0	0	2	0	0	0	.000	.000
Porter, Bo, Orlando	.258	8	32	31	4	8	12	1	0	1	3	0	0	1	0	0	11	0	1	1	.387	.281
Powers, John, Mobile*	.250	14	60	48	8	12	15	0	0	1	8	0	2	2	8	0	9	2	0	1	.313	.367
Presto, Nick, Chattanooga......	.226	9	35	31	2	7	8	1	0	0	6	0	1	1	2	0	7	1	0	1	.258	.286
Price, Corey, Chattanooga†....	.333	1	4	3	0	1	1	0	0	0	0	0	0	0	1	0	1	0	0	0	.333	.500
Priest, Eddie, Chattanooga.....	.000	14	19	15	0	0	0	0	0	0	1	1	0	0	3	0	7	0	0	0	.000	.167
Prieto, Chris, Mobile*	.320	109	463	388	80	124	170	22	9	2	58	1	5	10	59	0	55	26	6	2	.438	.418
Ramirez, Angel, Knoxville	.309	85	384	369	55	114	167	24	7	5	37	0	2	3	10	0	48	11	6	4	.453	.331
Ramirez, Roberto, Huntsville .	.318	19	68	66	7	21	25	4	0	0	6	1	0	1	0	0	16	2	0	0	.379	.328
Ratliff, Jon, Orlando..............	.308	18	14	13	0	4	4	0	0	0	3	0	0	0	1	0	4	0	0	0	.308	.357
Raven, Luis, Birmingham.......	.336	117	514	456	88	153	279	30	3	30	112	0	7	5	46	7	126	4	3	5	.612	.397

Player, Team	Avg.	G	TPA	AB	R	H	TB	2B	3B	HR	RBI	SH	SF	HP	BB	IBB	SO	SB	CS	GDP	Slg.	OBP
Reed, Chris, Chattanooga	.136	23	24	22	1	3	3	0	0	0	2	2	0	0	0	0	4	0	0	0	.136	.136
Rivette, Scott, Huntsville†	.000	7	3	3	0	0	0	0	0	0	0	0	0	0	0	0	2	0	0	0	.000	.000
Roberts, David, Jacksonville*	.296	105	473	415	76	123	163	24	2	4	41	9	2	2	45	1	62	23	5	5	.393	.366
Roberts, Lonell, Knoxville†	.190	7	27	21	5	4	6	0	1	0	0	2	0	2	2	0	3	0	2	0	.286	.320
Rocker, John, Greenville	.278	22	22	18	3	5	7	2	0	0	3	3	0	0	1	0	7	0	0	0	.389	.316
Rodarte, Raul, Greenville	.221	55	201	172	29	38	69	8	1	7	22	1	0	2	26	0	30	10	6	4	.401	.330
Rodriguez, Adam, Jack.	.200	2	7	5	0	1	1	0	0	0	0	0	0	0	2	0	0	0	0	0	.200	.429
Rodriguez, Luis, Knoxville......	.269	24	82	78	6	21	26	3	1	0	6	0	0	1	3	0	20	0	1	1	.333	.305
Rogers, Bryan, Greenville	.000	19	2	2	0	0	0	0	0	0	0	0	0	0	0	0	0	0	0	0	.000	.000
Romero, Mandy, Mobile†	.320	61	263	222	50	71	132	22	0	13	52	0	1	2	38	3	31	0	1	4	.595	.422
Rose, Pete, Chattanooga*	.308	112	486	445	75	137	243	31	0	25	98	1	3	3	34	1	63	0	1	5	.546	.359
Rumfield, Toby, Chattanooga .	.287	101	357	331	35	95	134	22	1	5	38	4	2	2	18	3	32	0	1	12	.405	.326
Runyan, Sean, Mobile*	.667	40	3	3	0	2	3	1	0	0	0	0	0	0	0	0	0	0	0	0	1.000	.667
Russell, LaGrande, Orlando ...	.000	25	10	7	1	0	0	0	0	0	0	2	0	0	1	0	3	0	0	0	.000	.125
Ryan, Matt, Carolina	.500	48	2	2	0	1	2	1	0	0	0	0	0	0	0	0	0	0	0	0	1.000	.500
Samuels, Scott, Orlando*	.283	34	147	127	30	36	58	7	3	3	17	1	0	1	18	0	34	5	4	4	.457	.377
Sanders, Anthony, Knoxville ..	.266	111	484	429	68	114	220	20	4	26	69	4	4	3	44	3	121	20	12	9	.513	.335
Sanders, Reggie, Chat.	.545	3	13	11	3	6	12	1	1	1	3	0	0	1	1	0	2	0	0	0	1.091	.615
Sanders, Tracy, Carolina*	.271	116	460	376	77	102	190	23	1	21	78	1	3	6	74	0	88	7	6	2	.505	.397
Sanford, Chance, Carolina*	.262	44	177	149	30	39	80	10	2	9	36	2	4	2	20	1	39	3	1	1	.537	.349
Saunders, Doug, Memphis	.259	73	283	232	33	60	81	15	0	2	28	2	3	0	46	2	44	0	3	5	.349	.377
Sawkiw, Warren, Bir.†	.286	4	7	7	1	2	5	0	0	1	3	0	0	0	0	0	1	0	0	0	.714	.286
Schmidt, Tom, Jacksonville ...	.258	82	323	291	37	75	121	17	1	9	44	0	1	2	29	0	81	2	0	9	.416	.328
Schwenke, Matt, Mobile†	.000	1	1	1	0	0	0	0	0	0	0	0	0	0	0	0	0	0	0	0	.000	.000
Sealy, Scot, Memphis	.238	45	163	143	17	34	61	9	0	6	20	1	0	4	15	0	33	1	2	2	.427	.327
Seitzer, Brad, Memphis	.329	17	78	70	14	23	39	8	1	2	13	0	1	1	6	0	13	1	0	4	.557	.385
Shaw, Curtis, Carolina*	.000	27	4	2	0	0	0	0	0	0	0	2	0	0	0	0	1	0	0	0	.000	.000
Simmons, Brian, Bir.†	.262	138	641	546	108	143	240	28	12	15	72	2	3	2	88	5	124	15	12	10	.440	.365
Skett, Will, Knoxville	.273	30	117	110	18	30	47	6	1	3	15	1	1	1	4	0	31	4	4	2	.427	.302
Skrmetta, Matt, Mobile†	.000	21	1	1	0	0	0	0	0	0	0	0	0	0	0	0	0	0	0	0	.000	.000
Smith, Cam, Mobile	.267	26	18	15	0	4	6	2	0	0	8	2	0	0	1	0	3	0	0	0	.400	.313
Smith, Demond, Huntsville† ..	.279	87	398	323	79	90	146	20	6	8	39	3	2	4	65	0	76	31	9	3	.452	.404
Smith, Ira, Jacksonville	.308	53	208	172	29	53	86	14	2	5	20	0	0	1	35	0	30	1	1	4	.500	.428
Smith, Mark, Carolina	.417	3	12	12	5	5	15	1	0	3	4	0	0	0	0	0	1	0	0	0	1.250	.417
Smith, Scott, Memphis	.249	123	506	453	58	113	178	19	2	14	67	0	4	5	44	1	132	4	7	12	.393	.320
Solano, Fausto, Knoxville	.265	115	424	378	52	100	162	24	4	10	56	4	4	1	37	2	47	8	14	11	.429	.329
Soriano, Fred, Knoxville†	.059	7	22	17	3	1	1	0	0	0	0	0	0	2	3	0	4	1	1	0	.059	.273
Speier, Justin, Orlando	.000	50	8	8	0	0	0	0	0	0	0	0	0	0	0	0	3	0	0	0	.000	.000
Staton, T.J., Carolina*	.290	58	229	207	33	60	93	11	2	6	33	3	2	5	12	1	60	8	4	3	.449	.341
Stephenson, Brian, Orlando ...	.000	6	1	1	0	0	0	0	0	0	0	0	0	0	0	0	1	0	0	0	.000	.000
Stewart, Chaad, Greenville* ...	.000	6	4	3	0	0	0	0	0	0	0	0	0	0	1	0	3	0	0	0	.000	.250
Strange, Mike, Knoxville	.095	12	24	21	1	2	4	0	1	0	0	0	0	0	3	0	4	0	0	0	.190	.208
Sturdivant, Marcus, Memphis*	.271	112	501	432	71	117	151	18	5	2	35	2	3	1	63	0	61	21	17	9	.350	.363
Swann, Pedro, Greenville*	.286	124	519	465	78	133	238	29	2	24	83	0	1	4	49	5	75	5	5	14	.512	.358
Sweet, Jon, Carolina*	.245	82	291	273	22	67	87	15	1	1	27	1	1	1	15	2	20	1	1	8	.319	.286
Taylor, Kerry, Mobile	.000	5	5	3	0	0	0	0	0	0	0	1	0	0	1	0	2	0	0	0	.000	.250
Tejada, Miguel, Huntsville	.275	128	568	502	85	138	230	20	3	22	97	1	8	7	50	0	99	15	11	9	.458	.344
Thobe, Steve, Carolina	.293	53	200	181	21	53	84	10	0	7	32	1	1	4	13	0	52	4	1	4	.464	.352
Thomas, Juan, Birmingham	.302	80	342	311	50	94	144	16	2	10	55	0	4	4	23	1	92	1	2	4	.463	.354
Thompson, Andy, Knoxville	.286	124	522	448	75	128	204	25	3	15	71	1	4	6	63	3	76	0	5	18	.455	.378
Thompson, Karl, Memphis	.230	42	169	148	18	34	56	10	0	4	21	4	2	4	11	0	25	2	0	5	.378	.297
Tollberg, Brian, Mobile	.000	31	13	9	1	0	0	0	0	0	0	3	0	0	1	0	5	0	0	0	.000	.100
Topham, Ryan, Birmingham*.	.213	17	57	47	6	10	17	5	1	0	8	1	1	2	6	0	15	1	0	0	.362	.321
Torres, Paul, Memphis	.344	62	263	218	40	75	107	8	3	6	55	0	4	2	38	1	30	3	1	6	.491	.439
Toth, Dave, Greenville	.245	58	213	184	23	45	75	9	0	7	24	0	0	4	25	0	35	2	2	7	.408	.347
Towle, Justin, Chattanooga	.309	119	478	418	62	129	209	37	5	11	70	0	3	2	55	1	77	5	5	7	.500	.389
Tredaway, Chad, Mobile†	.083	4	14	12	2	1	1	0	0	0	0	0	0	0	2	0	1	0	0	0	.083	.214
Tryon, Eric, Chattanooga	.000	6	4	3	0	0	0	0	0	0	0	0	0	0	1	0	1	0	0	0	.000	.250
Twiggs, Greg, Orlando*	.000	48	5	4	0	0	0	0	0	0	0	1	0	0	0	0	1	0	0	0	.000	.000
Van De Weg, Ryan, Mobile	.130	27	24	23	1	3	3	0	0	0	1	1	0	0	0	0	7	0	0	0	.130	.130
Ventura, Robin, Birmingham*	.294	4	18	17	3	5	9	1	0	1	2	0	0	0	1	0	1	0	0	2	.529	.333
Wade, Terrell, Greenville*	.333	8	5	3	0	1	1	0	0	0	1	1	0	0	1	0	1	0	0	0	.333	.500
Wagner, Mark, Chattanooga ...	.250	2	4	4	0	1	1	0	0	0	1	0	0	0	0	0	0	0	0	0	.250	.250
Wagner, Paul, Carolina	.000	12	1	1	0	0	0	0	0	0	0	0	0	0	0	0	1	0	0	0	.000	.000
Walker, Dane, Huntsville*	.241	106	434	361	62	87	131	17	3	7	52	2	2	0	68	0	87	7	2	8	.363	.360
Walker, Wade, Orlando	.000	4	5	4	0	0	0	0	0	0	1	1	0	0	0	0	1	0	0	0	.000	.000
Wallace, Jeff, Carolina*	.500	38	2	2	0	1	1	0	0	0	0	0	0	0	0	0	1	0	0	0	.500	.500
Walters, Brett, Mobile	.200	33	20	20	1	4	4	0	0	0	1	0	0	0	0	0	6	0	0	1	.200	.200
Warner, Mike, Greenville*	.320	91	371	303	58	97	146	22	3	7	35	3	3	1	61	6	61	12	9	1	.482	.432
Wathan, Dusty, Memphis†	.268	49	174	149	20	40	58	4	1	4	19	0	1	5	19	0	28	1	1	4	.389	.368
Watkins, Pat, Chattanooga	.350	46	195	177	35	62	100	15	1	7	30	0	1	2	15	1	16	9	3	3	.565	.405
Whatley, Gabe, Greenville*	.303	95	376	310	60	94	166	17	5	15	57	4	6	6	50	0	42	5	5	9	.535	.403
White, Rick, Orlando	.154	39	14	13	1	2	3	1	0	0	0	1	0	0	0	0	4	0	0	0	.231	.154
Whitmore, Darrell, Carolina* ..	.333	2	9	9	1	3	5	2	0	0	2	0	0	0	0	0	2	0	0	0	.556	.333
Williams, Harold, Orlando*	.352	26	94	88	13	31	46	12	0	1	11	0	0	0	6	1	15	1	1	2	.523	.394
Williams, Jason, Chattanooga	.310	69	293	271	38	84	122	21	1	5	28	1	3	0	18	0	35	5	5	7	.450	.349
Williams, Todd, Chattanooga .	.000	48	1	1	0	0	0	0	0	0	0	0	0	0	0	0	1	0	0	0	.000	.000
Wilson, Gary, Carolina	.000	7	4	4	0	0	0	0	0	0	0	0	0	0	0	0	3	0	0	0	.000	.000
Wimmer, Chris, Orlando	.275	102	412	371	62	102	129	15	3	2	28	7	1	10	23	0	37	23	4	13	.348	.333
Witt, Kevin, Knoxville*	.289	127	551	501	76	145	270	27	4	30	91	1	2	3	44	7	109	1	0	13	.539	.349
Wood, Kerry, Orlando	.348	19	24	23	3	8	11	3	0	0	4	1	0	0	0	0	5	0	0	1	.478	.348
Worrell, Steve, Birm.-Orl.*	.400	44	5	5	0	2	3	1	0	0	2	0	0	0	0	0	0	0	0	0	.600	.400
Wrona, Rick, Birmingham	.252	29	110	103	11	26	41	7	1	2	24	1	1	2	3	0	12	0	0	1	.398	.284
Zancanaro, Dave, Mobile†	.261	31	24	23	5	6	14	2	0	2	3	1	0	0	0	0	7	0	0	0	.609	.261

GRAND SLAMS: Monahan, 4; Correa, Helms, Ibarra, Mahoney, Mosquera, Raven, Tejada, 2 each; Adriana, G. Barker, R. Brown, Bruno, Candelaria, Christenson, M. Coolbaugh, Cradle, D. Cromer, DeLaCruz, Devarez, Dowler, Gipson, Grieve, Grijak, Jones, Joseph, Koelling, Marquez, Murray, Poe, Rose, Sanford, Schmidt, S. Smith, Swann, A. Thompson, 1 each.

AWARDED FIRST BASE ON CATCHER'S INTERFERENCE: Hills 2 (Lidle 2); Christian (Morgan); Gipson (Devarez); Griffey (Lidle); Martins (Marine); Murray (Ardoin); D. Smith (Morgan); Torres (Marine); D. Walker (Romero).

PLAYERS WITH TWO OR MORE TEAMS

Player, Team	Avg.	G	TPA	AB	R	H	TB	2B	3B	HR	RBI	SH	SF	HP	BB	IBB	SO	SB	CS	GDP	Slg.	OBP
Griffey, Craig, Memphis	.217	35	138	120	20	26	31	3	1	0	5	2	2	0	13	0	22	6	1	5	.258	.289
Griffey, Craig, Chattanooga	.228	55	207	180	28	41	48	5	1	0	15	3	0	0	24	2	41	8	7	4	.267	.319
Johnson, Earl, Mobile	.254	78	336	307	52	78	98	11	3	1	22	6	2	0	21	0	56	35	13	3	.319	.300
Johnson, Earl, Jacksonville	.226	36	161	146	24	33	44	3	1	2	13	3	2	1	9	0	19	7	1	3	.301	.272
Worrell, Steve, Birmingham*	.000	18	0	0	0	0	0	0	0	0	0	0	0	0	0	0	0	0	0	0	.000	.000
Worrell, Steve, Orlando*	.400	26	5	5	0	2	3	1	0	0	2	0	0	0	0	0	0	0	0	0	.600	.400

1997 PITCHING

TEAM

Team	W	L	Pct.	ERA	G	CG	ShO	Sv.	IP	H	TBF	R	ER	HR	SH	SF	HB	BB	IBB	SO	WP	Bk.
Memphis	67	72	.482	4.43	139	13	8	28	1171.0	1187	5089	657	577	130	24	40	63	486	14	910	79	6
Birmingham	76	62	.551	4.49	139	6	8	36	1211.0	1266	5407	744	604	95	34	39	67	559	15	941	79	11
Mobile	69	68	.504	4.52	137	8	3	33	1197.2	1261	5303	687	602	116	45	32	57	507	19	975	81	8
Knoxville	75	63	.543	4.60	139	9	6	40	1202.1	1307	5351	723	615	113	43	35	67	480	26	980	89	14
Jacksonville	66	73	.475	4.75	139	14	7	29	1218.2	1270	5352	741	643	161	33	51	57	482	4	869	70	9
Carolina	55	82	.401	4.77	137	3	2	27	1205.0	1281	5464	786	639	116	50	40	73	569	36	933	80	8
Greenville	74	66	.529	4.89	140	1	4	49	1228.1	1283	5433	755	667	157	38	43	43	531	17	994	104	10
Orlando	63	75	.457	4.91	138	2	9	34	1184.0	1255	5239	759	646	122	40	45	42	515	34	927	90	20
Huntsville	77	62	.554	5.16	139	3	1	36	1209.0	1443	5445	816	693	134	35	47	47	477	22	827	78	8
Chattanooga	70	69	.504	5.26	139	2	2	41	1205.1	1359	5433	809	704	143	36	44	51	540	36	814	71	7

INDIVIDUAL

TOP QUALIFIERS FOR EARNED-RUN AVERAGE TITLE

Minimum 112 innings. *Lefthanded pitcher.

Pitcher, Team	W	L	Pct.	ERA	G	GS	CG	ShO	GF	Sv.	IP	H	TBF	R	ER	HR	SH	SF	HB	BB	IBB	SO	WP	Bk.
Herbert, Russ, Birmingham	13	5	.722	3.63	27	26	3	1	0	0	158.2	136	681	72	64	14	3	6	14	80	0	126	7	0
Tollberg, Brian, Mobile	6	3	.667	3.72	31	13	1	0	5	0	123.1	123	512	60	51	15	2	1	4	24	2	108	4	0
Eyre, Scott, Birmingham*	13	5	.722	3.84	22	22	0	0	0	0	126.2	110	538	61	54	14	1	1	5	55	1	127	9	1
Cloude, Ken, Memphis	11	7	.611	3.87	22	22	3	2	0	0	132.2	131	567	62	57	15	1	2	11	48	2	124	7	0
Byrne, Earl, Orlando*	5	5	.500	3.95	32	20	0	0	2	0	130.0	102	554	62	57	16	5	2	2	73	1	128	6	7
Ebert, Derrin, Greenville*	11	8	.579	4.10	27	25	0	0	0	0	175.2	191	743	95	80	24	9	6	4	48	1	101	10	0
King, Bill, Huntsville	9	7	.563	4.19	28	27	1	0	0	0	176.0	216	762	99	82	18	8	3	10	28	0	103	7	0
Stevenson, Jason, Knoxville	12	9	.571	4.27	26	26	2	2	0	0	149.2	166	640	88	71	18	5	5	7	43	1	101	7	1
Zancanaro, Dave, Mobile*	10	8	.556	4.44	27	19	3	0	3	1	133.2	140	581	69	66	15	5	3	4	57	0	66	10	1
Hinchliffe, Brett, Memphis	10	10	.500	4.45	24	24	5	1	0	0	145.2	159	627	81	72	20	3	4	9	45	2	107	2	1
Walters, Brett, Mobile	10	7	.588	4.47	31	19	0	0	1	0	145.0	169	625	85	72	17	6	2	11	30	0	98	3	1
Wooten, Greg, Memphis	11	10	.524	4.47	26	26	0	0	0	0	155.0	166	681	91	77	14	5	6	6	59	1	98	12	0
Reed, Brandon, Jacksonville	11	9	.550	4.55	27	27	2	0	0	0	176.0	190	754	100	89	25	6	10	8	54	0	90	9	0
Snyder, John, Birmingham	7	8	.467	4.64	20	20	2	1	0	0	114.1	130	510	76	59	9	1	3	6	43	0	90	6	2
Kelly, Jeff, Carolina*	6	11	.353	4.65	31	19	0	0	3	0	127.2	134	593	79	66	7	9	9	12	85	5	83	7	2

DEPARTMENTAL LEADERS: W—Eyre, Herbert, 13 each; L—Roberts, 15; Pct.—C. Nelson, Price, .750; G—Doyle, 65; GS—Greisinger, 28; CG—Hinchliffe, 5; ShO—Franklin, Cloude, Stevenson, 2 each; GF—Erdos, 50; Sv.—T. Williams, 31; IP—B. Reed, W. King, 176 each; H—W. King, 216; TBF—W. King, 762; R—Roberts, 120; ERA—Roberts 104; HR—Greisinger, 29; SH—Olsen, 11; SF—Kaufman, 11; HB—Drews, 16; BB—Kelly, 85; IBB—Freeman, 7; SO—Byrne, 128; WP—Rocker, 17; BK—Byrne, 7.

ALL PITCHERS

*Lefthanded pitcher.

Pitcher, Team	W	L	Pct.	ERA	G	GS	CG	ShO	GF	Sv.	IP	H	TBF	R	ER	HR	SH	SF	HB	BB	IBB	SO	WP	Bk.
Almanzar, Carlos, Knoxville	1	1	.500	4.91	21	0	0	0	19	8	25.2	30	109	14	14	2	2	2	0	5	1	25	0	0
Anderson, Bill, Mobile	0	0	.000	1.86	7	0	0	0	3	0	9.2	8	43	3	2	0	0	0	2	6	0	6	1	0
Anderson, Jimmy, Carolina*	2	1	.667	1.46	4	4	0	0	0	0	24.2	16	98	6	4	1	0	0	2	9	0	23	1	0
Apana, Matt, Memphis	3	9	.250	5.83	17	16	1	0	0	0	80.1	78	365	59	52	14	1	2	6	47	0	45	6	0
Arnold, Jamie, Greenville	0	1	.000	11.57	1	1	0	0	0	0	4.2	10	27	6	6	3	0	0	1	2	0	3	1	0
Atchley, Justin, Chattanooga*	4	2	.667	4.70	13	13	1	0	0	0	67.0	75	289	45	35	8	2	5	1	14	0	48	5	0
Baez, Benito, Huntsville*	2	4	.333	9.14	15	7	0	0	2	0	42.1	64	206	47	43	8	2	4	1	22	1	27	3	2
Barcelo, Lorenzo, Bir.	2	1	.667	4.86	6	6	0	0	0	0	33.1	36	147	20	18	2	0	1	4	9	0	29	1	0
Barker, Richie, Orlando	0	1	.000	3.30	19	0	0	0	7	2	30.0	25	121	17	11	5	0	1	2	7	0	19	2	0
Baron, Jim, Mobile*	2	4	.333	4.54	19	1	0	0	4	0	33.2	35	152	21	17	3	2	0	3	13	1	30	3	0
Baxter, Bob, Huntsville*	1	1	.500	11.57	6	0	0	0	4	0	4.2	15	32	10	6	0	2	0	0	3	1	3	1	0
Beatty, Blaine, Carolina*	0	5	.000	5.38	19	9	0	0	3	0	82.0	104	366	61	49	12	2	3	3	27	4	41	4	0
Beck, Chris, Memphis	0	0	.000	1.93	5	1	0	0	1	0	9.1	8	43	3	2	0	0	1	0	2	1	0	0	0
Beirne, Kevin, Birmingham	6	4	.600	4.92	13	12	0	0	1	0	75.0	76	336	51	41	4	2	3	4	41	0	49	2	1
Bennett, Bob, Huntsville	4	3	.571	7.17	23	1	0	0	3	1	42.2	64	204	38	34	7	0	3	0	15	2	32	3	0
Benson, Kris, Carolina	3	5	.375	4.98	14	14	0	0	0	0	68.2	81	316	49	38	11	0	2	2	32	1	66	2	0
Bere, Jason, Birmingham	0	1	.000	7.71	2	2	0	0	0	0	7.0	8	33	7	6	2	0	0	1	2	0	7	0	0
Boggs, Robert, Chattanooga	1	3	.250	7.59	9	9	0	0	0	0	40.1	53	193	36	34	6	2	0	5	21	1	35	2	0
Bogott, Kurtiss, Knoxville*	2	1	.667	3.90	35	1	0	0	14	2	64.2	66	284	32	28	10	1	3	6	25	2	77	6	1
Bowie, Micah, Greenville*	3	2	.600	3.50	8	7	0	0	0	0	43.2	34	193	19	17	3	1	2	3	26	1	41	2	0

Pitcher, Team	W	L	Pct.	ERA	G	GS	CG	ShO	GF	Sv.	IP	H	TBF	R	ER	HR	SH	SF	HB	BB	IBB	SO	WP	Bk.
Bradley, Bert, Huntsville	0	0	.000	0.00	1	0	0	0	1	0	1.0	0	0	0	0	0	0	0	0	0	0	0	0	0
Briggs, Anthony, Greenville	6	3	.667	5.44	19	13	0	0	0	0	94.1	91	413	64	57	11	4	2	0	43	0	59	4	2
Brooks, Antone, Greenville*	1	0	1.000	4.79	14	0	0	0	3	0	20.2	21	93	14	11	3	0	2	2	8	1	10	1	0
Brosnan, Jason, Memphis*	2	3	.400	2.53	40	0	0	0	21	5	53.1	44	213	16	15	7	2	1	4	11	1	62	2	1
Brown, Chad, Knoxville*	6	4	.600	3.72	32	0	0	0	14	4	55.2	46	231	25	23	4	5	1	2	16	0	40	2	0
Brown, Darold, Orlando*	0	0	.000	4.20	18	0	0	0	5	0	30.0	28	134	15	14	1	0	0	1	18	1	24	1	0
Brown, Michael, Carolina*	0	0	.000	18.00	1	0	0	0	0	0	2.0	5	13	5	4	0	0	0	0	1	0	2	1	0
Bryant, Adam, Chattanooga	1	0	1.000	7.00	6	0	0	0	1	0	9.0	15	43	8	7	2	0	0	3	1	1	4	0	0
Bussa, Todd, Huntsville	2	1	.667	4.22	19	0	0	0	13	7	21.1	20	99	13	10	2	0	0	4	12	0	27	3	1
Buteaux, Shane, Birmingham	2	2	.500	4.19	44	0	0	0	16	2	73.0	74	328	41	34	4	1	6	7	34	1	34	5	1
Butler, Adam, Greenville*	5	1	.833	2.57	46	0	0	0	38	22	49.0	40	203	16	14	3	3	2	4	15	2	56	1	0
Byrd, Matt, Greenville	3	2	.600	6.00	28	0	0	0	12	0	45.0	58	210	31	30	9	3	2	2	21	1	38	7	1
Byrne, Earl, Orlando*	5	5	.500	3.95	32	20	0	0	2	0	130.0	102	554	62	57	16	5	2	73	1	128	6	7
Carter, John, Carolina	0	0	.000	54.00	1	0	0	0	0	0	1.0	4	9	6	6	1	0	1	0	2	0	0	0	0
Caruthers, Clay, Chattanooga	2	4	.333	9.09	9	6	0	0	1	0	34.2	63	175	36	35	4	1	0	1	17	1	30	2	1
Castillo, Marino, Mobile	0	1	.000	4.32	8	0	0	0	5	1	8.1	14	43	4	4	0	1	0	0	5	1	10	1	0
Cather, Mike, Greenville	5	2	.714	4.34	22	0	0	0	2	1	37.1	37	153	18	18	2	1	2	6	7	1	29	0	0
Chaves, Rafael, Carolina	0	2	.000	8.59	5	0	0	0	4	0	7.1	12	39	8	7	1	0	0	0	4	2	6	0	0
Christiansen, Jason, Car.*	0	1	.000	4.20	8	1	0	0	3	1	15.0	17	63	7	7	1	0	0	5	0	25	0	1
Christman, Scott, Bir.*	2	7	.222	9.05	15	14	0	0	0	0	63.2	100	325	74	64	8	1	1	5	38	0	39	5	0
Clayton, Craig, Mobile	0	0	.000	0.00	3	0	0	0	1	0	2.1	1	11	0	0	0	0	0	1	3	0	2	0	0
Clement, Matt, Mobile	6	5	.545	2.56	13	13	1	1	0	0	88.0	83	382	37	25	4	4	1	12	32	0	92	12	0
Cloude, Ken, Memphis	11	7	.611	3.87	22	22	3	2	0	0	132.2	131	567	62	57	15	1	2	11	48	2	124	7	0
Connelly, Steve, Huntsville	3	3	.500	3.75	43	0	0	0	22	7	69.2	74	297	33	29	3	2	1	4	20	2	49	5	0
Cook, O.J., Carolina	0	0	.000	20.25	1	0	0	0	0	0	1.1	5	10	3	3	1	0	0	1	0	2	0	1
Corey, Bryan, Jacksonville	3	8	.273	4.76	52	0	0	0	36	9	68.0	74	298	42	36	8	5	3	1	21	3	37	4	0
Cortes, David, Greenville	1	0	1.000	1.80	3	0	0	0	1	0	5.0	4	20	1	1	1	0	0	1	0	7	0	0
Courtright, John, Chat.*	5	7	.417	6.82	20	16	0	0	1	0	92.1	137	447	79	70	8	3	3	2	42	1	42	2	1
Crawford, Carlos, Carolina	3	2	.600	4.19	29	3	0	0	10	4	62.1	62	273	34	29	4	1	1	2	25	2	39	4	0
Crowell, Jim, Chattanooga*	2	1	.667	2.84	3	3	0	0	0	0	19.0	19	75	6	6	2	1	1	0	5	0	14	0	0
Curl, John, Knoxville	0	0	.000	0.00	1	0	0	0	1	0	2.0	3	10	0	0	0	0	0	1	0	0	1	0
Cushman, Dwayne, Chat.	0	0	.000	16.20	1	0	0	0	0	0	1.2	4	10	3	3	0	0	0	1	0	1	0	0
Czajkowski, Jim, Knoxville	2	2	.500	6.47	25	0	0	0	18	5	32.0	43	149	27	23	5	2	1	2	11	1	33	0	0
Dale, Carl, Huntsville	6	4	.600	5.38	20	16	0	0	2	0	85.1	95	389	61	51	10	1	3	8	43	0	57	4	0
Davey, Tom, Knoxville	6	7	.462	5.83	20	16	0	0	1	0	92.1	108	429	65	60	5	1	1	6	50	0	72	14	0
Davis, Kane, Carolina	0	3	.000	3.77	6	6	0	0	0	0	28.2	22	128	17	12	2	2	1	3	16	1	23	2	0
Dillinger, John, Carolina	6	4	.600	6.00	23	11	0	0	3	0	81.0	88	382	66	54	8	3	4	5	52	0	64	7	1
Dixon, Bubba, Mobile*	7	2	.778	3.45	56	0	0	0	25	1	75.2	67	329	31	29	4	6	3	1	37	3	88	11	1
Doman, Roger, Knoxville	7	3	.700	3.67	48	1	0	0	13	4	100.2	99	425	46	41	5	4	2	8	29	6	71	9	1
Donnelly, Brendan, Chat.	6	4	.600	3.27	62	0	0	0	21	6	82.2	71	359	43	30	6	4	3	4	37	4	64	9	0
Doyle, Tom, Chattanooga*	7	3	.700	3.51	65	0	0	0	21	6	66.2	62	298	32	26	5	4	0	11	38	5	46	6	1
Drews, Matt, Jacksonville	8	11	.421	5.49	24	24	4	1	0	0	144.1	160	652	109	88	23	1	6	16	50	0	85	3	0
Drumright, Mike, Jacksonville	1	1	.500	1.57	5	5	0	0	0	0	28.2	16	112	7	5	0	1	3	13	0	24	2	0
Dunbar, Matt, Huntsville*	1	0	1.000	5.40	5	0	0	0	2	0	5.0	8	23	3	3	0	0	0	1	0	7	0	0
Duncan, Courtney, Orlando	2	2	.500	3.40	8	8	0	0	0	0	45.0	37	196	28	17	2	1	2	1	29	5	45	4	0
Duran, Roberto, Jacksonville*	4	2	.667	2.37	50	0	0	0	34	16	60.2	41	265	19	16	2	2	5	2	39	0	95	11	0
Ebert, Derrin, Greenville*	11	8	.579	4.10	27	25	0	0	0	0	175.2	191	743	95	80	24	9	6	4	48	1	101	10	0
Eddie, Steve, Chattanooga	0	0	.000	12.00	3	0	0	0	3	0	3.0	4	13	4	4	2	0	0	1	0	0	0	0
Erdos, Todd, Mobile	1	4	.200	3.36	55	0	0	0	50	27	59.0	45	244	22	22	4	2	1	0	22	4	49	2	1
Escobar, Kelvim, Knoxville	2	1	.667	3.70	5	5	1	0	0	0	24.1	20	108	13	10	1	0	2	1	16	0	31	1	2
Etler, Todd, Chattanooga	0	3	.000	6.57	23	0	0	0	6	0	37.0	38	172	29	27	6	1	1	1	24	4	29	5	0
Eyre, Scott, Birmingham*	13	5	.722	3.84	22	22	0	0	0	0	126.2	110	538	61	54	14	1	1	5	55	2	127	9	1
Fernandez, Osvaldo, Memphis*0		.000	2.08	1	1	0	0	0	0	4.1	2	18	1	1	0	0	0	0	4	0	4	1	1
Folkers, Kenneth, Knoxville	1	0	1.000	0.00	1	0	0	0	1	0	4.1	1	15	0	0	0	0	0	0	0	4	0	0
Franklin, Ryan, Memphis	4	2	.667	3.03	11	8	2	2	2	0	59.1	45	234	22	20	4	0	3	1	14	1	49	1	0
Fredrickson, Scott, Carolina	0	3	.000	6.08	19	0	0	0	8	1	23.2	22	117	21	16	3	1	1	3	19	1	17	0	0
Freeman, Chris, Knoxville	3	3	.500	2.48	47	2	0	0	21	8	83.1	71	362	32	23	8	6	2	3	36	7	86	4	0
Freitas, Mike, Carolina	1	0	1.000	13.50	6	0	0	0	4	1	5.1	8	30	8	8	1	1	0	2	4	1	2	0	0
Gallaher, Kevin, Jacksonville	4	3	.571	6.47	10	10	2	0	0	0	57.0	70	271	45	41	10	1	3	6	32	0	33	5	0
Garcia, Al, Orlando	4	4	.500	3.48	12	12	0	0	0	0	72.1	87	315	39	28	6	2	2	4	23	1	27	1	1
Garrett, Hal, Carolina	1	2	.333	8.78	6	0	0	0	0	0	13.1	19	64	14	13	0	0	6	1	7	2	0	0
Gentile, Scott, Jacksonville	1	5	.167	5.23	43	0	0	0	27	2	63.2	69	273	41	37	8	3	3	0	21	0	52	2	0
Giard, Ken, Greenville	3	0	1.000	1.96	25	0	0	0	9	6	36.2	30	152	9	8	1	0	1	0	11	1	39	2	0
Goldsmith, Gary, Jacksonville	4	5	.444	4.07	31	8	1	1	5	1	97.1	97	415	48	44	16	2	4	5	30	0	45	1	0
Gordon, Mike, Knoxville	2	3	.400	5.33	33	6	0	0	7	2	72.2	91	341	46	43	5	3	2	1	40	3	64	6	0
Gower, Tim, Chattanooga	2	0	1.000	4.57	24	0	0	0	11	0	45.1	52	194	24	23	6	3	2	3	12	4	28	0	1
Graterol, Beiker, Knoxville	2	1	.667	5.40	3	3	0	0	0	0	16.2	24	81	12	10	1	0	1	9	0	11	0	0
Greisinger, Seth, Jacksonville	10	6	.625	5.20	28	28	1	0	0	0	159.1	194	710	103	92	29	3	6	3	53	0	105	12	2
Grijak, Kevin, Greenville	0	0	.000	0.00	1	0	0	0	1	0	1.0	3	7	2	0	0	0	0	0	0	0	0	0
Halladay, Roy, Knoxville	2	3	.400	5.40	7	7	0	0	0	0	36.2	46	165	26	22	4	1	0	0	11	0	30	4	0
Halperin, Mike, Carolina*	6	7	.462	3.87	17	17	0	0	0	0	93.0	102	419	54	40	8	1	1	8	40	0	66	8	0
Hammack, Brandon, Orlando	0	6	.000	7.29	39	0	0	0	28	8	42.0	58	212	43	34	5	1	2	1	28	3	36	7	0
Hancock, Lee, Orlando*	0	0	.000	16.62	3	2	0	0	0	0	4.1	12	32	13	8	3	1	1	0	4	0	2	2	0
Harikkala, Tim, Memphis	3	1	.750	3.74	5	5	1	0	0	0	33.2	39	146	18	14	3	0	1	3	4	0	26	1	0
Harris, D.J., Knoxville	1	1	.500	1.64	5	2	0	0	0	0	11.0	6	43	2	2	1	0	0	6	0	8	1	0
Hart, Jason, Orlando	0	1	.000	6.62	14	0	0	0	7	0	17.2	20	75	13	13	0	2	1	0	12	1	21	2	0
Harvey, Bryan, Greenville	1	1	.500	5.18	22	8	0	0	5	0	24.1	23	110	15	14	5	0	0	16	0	18	3	1
Hasselhoff, Derek, Bir.	5	2	.714	2.41	18	0	0	0	10	3	33.2	35	141	10	9	3	0	1	1	11	0	22	1	0
Haught, Gary, Huntsville	0	1	.000	5.59	6	0	0	0	0	0	9.2	15	44	6	6	2	0	0	2	1	6	0	0
Hazlett, Steve, Carolina	0	0	.000	9.00	1	0	0	0	1	0	1.0	4	7	1	1	0	0	0	0	1	0	0
Heathcott, Mike, Birmingham	3	1	.750	1.83	30	1	0	0	12	7	59.0	50	247	20	12	2	3	0	1	25	0	47	3	0
Herbert, Russ, Birmingham	13	5	.722	3.63	27	26	3	1	0	0	158.2	136	681	72	64	14	3	6	14	80	0	126	7	0
Hernandez, Elvin, Carolina	2	7	.222	5.73	17	17	0	0	0	0	92.1	104	409	67	59	11	2	2	3	26	2	66	4	0

Pitcher, Team	W	L	Pct.	ERA	G	GS	CG	ShO	GF	Sv.	IP	H	TBF	R	ER	HR	SH	SF	HB	BB	IBB	SO	WP	Bk.
Hinchliffe, Brett, Memphis	10	10	.500	4.45	24	24	5	1	0	0	145.2	159	627	81	72	20	3	4	9	45	2	107	2	1
Hines, Rich, Greenville*	4	0	1.000	6.58	41	0	0	0	13	1	67.0	85	308	56	49	10	4	5	1	22	1	49	4	0
Holdridge, David, Memphis	0	3	.000	3.34	30	0	0	0	27	17	35.0	31	149	14	13	2	1	1	2	17	1	37	2	0
Hollins, Stacy, Huntsville	5	4	.556	5.37	32	17	0	0	4	2	114.0	110	514	77	68	11	3	3	5	72	4	68	15	0
Howry, Bob, Birmingham	0	0	.000	2.84	12	0	0	0	6	2	12.2	16	54	4	4	1	0	0	0	3	0	3	0	0
Jacobs, Ryan, Greenville*	1	8	.111	7.21	28	6	0	0	3	1	68.2	84	328	61	55	8	1	5	2	43	1	52	6	0
Jarvis, Jason, Knoxville	0	2	.000	9.78	4	4	1	0	0	0	19.1	28	95	24	21	7	1	2	0	9	0	11	1	0
Jean, Domingo, Chattanooga	1	1	.500	9.75	10	0	0	0	4	1	12.0	17	69	20	13	2	0	2	1	15	1	9	1	0
Jimenez, Miguel, Huntsville	7	6	.538	5.86	24	18	1	0	2	0	101.1	127	475	83	66	15	0	3	2	50	1	64	4	1
Johnson, Jason, Carolina	3	3	.500	4.08	9	9	1	0	0	0	57.1	56	244	31	26	6	1	1	1	16	0	63	1	0
Kaufman, Brad, Mobile	5	13	.278	6.18	22	22	1	0	0	0	125.1	138	585	97	86	10	9	11	5	66	0	103	3	0
Kelly, Jeff, Carolina*	6	11	.353	4.65	31	19	0	0	3	0	127.2	134	593	79	66	7	9	9	12	85	5	83	7	2
King, Bill, Huntsville	9	7	.563	4.19	28	27	1	0	0	0	176.0	216	762	99	82	18	8	3	10	28	0	103	7	0
King, Raymond, Greenville*	5	5	.500	6.85	12	9	0	0	0	0	65.2	85	305	53	50	9	0	0	1	24	2	42	4	0
Konuszewski, Dennis, Car.	1	0	1.000	4.43	15	0	0	0	5	0	22.1	20	103	12	11	3	0	1	1	15	2	21	2	0
Koppe, Clint, Chattanooga	2	5	.286	7.38	13	13	0	0	0	0	68.1	82	331	58	56	12	1	3	2	44	2	33	4	0
LeBlanc, Eric, Chattanooga	2	4	.333	5.58	8	8	0	0	0	0	50.0	53	216	35	31	3	2	3	1	21	0	25	2	2
LeRoy, John, Greenville	5	5	.500	5.03	29	14	0	0	9	1	98.1	105	444	59	55	20	1	2	5	43	1	84	15	1
Ligtenberg, Kerry, Greenville	3	1	.750	2.04	31	0	0	0	27	16	35.1	20	140	8	8	3	0	0	1	14	1	43	1	0
Lott, Brian, Chattanooga	6	7	.462	6.77	25	14	0	0	2	0	91.2	108	429	76	69	21	2	8	2	50	0	62	5	0
Lowe, Benny, Knoxville*	3	1	.750	5.54	18	0	0	0	8	0	26.0	33	124	21	16	6	1	1	2	14	1	29	2	2
Luce, Robert, Memphis	5	2	.714	3.93	13	13	1	0	0	0	75.2	90	315	40	33	5	2	0	1	14	0	41	3	0
Lukasiewicz, Mark, Knx.*	2	0	1.000	3.65	27	0	0	0	8	7	37.0	26	149	17	15	2	1	1	1	14	1	43	4	0
Lundquist, David, Bir.	0	0	.000	8.78	7	0	0	0	5	0	13.1	26	73	20	13	3	0	1	0	5	0	15	0	0
Lyons, Curt, Orlando	0	0	.000	7.50	2	2	0	0	0	0	6.0	6	26	5	5	0	0	1	1	2	0	8	1	0
Manning, Derek, Huntsville*	1	2	.333	5.93	21	0	0	0	8	2	44.0	57	195	31	29	7	1	3	1	12	0	27	2	0
Manzanillo, Josias, Memphis	0	0	.000	3.00	2	0	0	0	1	0	3.0	1	10	1	1	1	0	0	0	0	0	6	0	0
Marrero, Kenny, Jacksonville	4	3	.571	2.94	37	0	0	0	12	0	64.1	45	275	32	21	4	2	0	1	37	1	60	2	0
Maskivish, Joe, Carolina	0	1	.000	6.19	15	0	0	0	9	0	16.0	20	73	11	11	2	2	2	1	4	1	7	0	0
Mathews, Del, Carolina*	5	2	.714	3.04	21	1	0	0	5	1	50.1	53	225	25	17	5	4	2	1	20	1	51	2	1
Maurer, Mike, Huntsville	8	7	.533	3.83	52	5	0	0	24	2	84.2	86	371	48	36	10	5	4	2	31	3	61	5	1
McBride, Chris, Knoxville	4	4	.500	3.71	10	10	0	0	0	0	60.2	61	256	30	25	5	2	1	3	14	0	33	3	1
McKenzie, Scott, Chat.	2	0	1.000	5.77	30	0	0	0	9	0	53.0	74	251	37	34	8	1	5	4	19	2	30	2	0
McNichol, Brian, Orlando*	7	10	.412	5.81	22	22	0	0	0	0	119.1	153	544	89	77	18	3	7	2	42	6	97	9	0
Meiners, Doug, Knoxville	9	5	.643	5.43	23	23	3	0	0	0	122.2	161	554	85	74	13	4	3	8	31	0	81	4	0
Meinershagen, Adam, Knx.	0	0	.000	3.71	7	7	0	0	0	0	17.0	16	72	8	7	0	0	1	0	6	0	7	0	0
Melendez, Dave, Jacksonville	6	4	.600	5.33	12	11	2	0	0	0	72.2	77	314	47	43	10	0	2	5	24	0	55	0	0
Millwood, Kevin, Greenville	3	5	.375	4.11	11	11	0	0	0	0	61.1	59	264	37	28	8	2	0	2	24	0	61	7	0
Montane, Ivan, Memphis	0	8	.000	7.53	22	12	0	0	6	0	71.2	83	347	70	60	16	1	5	6	51	0	63	11	0
Morgan, Dave, Knoxville	0	0	.000	0.00	1	0	0	0	1	0	1.0	0	4	0	0	0	0	0	0	1	0	0	0	0
Moss, Damian, Greenville*	6	8	.429	5.35	21	19	1	0	0	0	112.2	111	498	73	67	13	1	8	9	58	0	116	14	2
Moten, Scott, Orlando	0	1	.000	13.50	4	1	0	0	2	0	6.2	9	33	10	10	2	0	0	1	6	0	1	0	0
Nelson, Chris, Huntsville	9	3	.750	4.97	20	15	1	1	0	0	99.2	116	430	60	55	10	3	3	1	25	1	71	4	2
Nelson, Erick, Greenville*	0	1	.000	4.50	5	0	0	0	3	0	6.0	9	28	4	3	1	0	0	0	4	0	4	0	0
Newman, Alan, Birmingham*	7	3	.700	2.49	44	0	0	0	33	10	72.1	55	314	34	20	0	4	2	0	40	4	64	9	0
Nix, James, Chattanooga	6	1	.857	3.13	28	0	0	0	6	0	37.1	31	160	15	13	7	0	1	0	20	2	32	4	0
Norton, Phillip, Orlando*	1	0	1.000	2.57	2	1	0	0	1	0	7.0	8	28	2	2	0	0	0	0	2	1	7	0	0
Nunez, Maximo, Birmingham	0	0	.000	7.64	14	0	0	0	3	0	17.2	19	85	18	15	1	0	1	1	13	0	14	3	2
Olsen, Jason, Birmingham	9	14	.391	4.88	28	27	1	1	0	0	160.1	183	709	101	87	14	11	5	3	58	2	121	9	0
Olszewski, Eric, Greenville	0	0	.000	6.00	4	0	0	0	1	0	6.0	9	34	6	4	0	2	1	0	8	0	7	0	0
Pacheco, Alexander, Memphis	1	1	.500	3.75	9	0	0	0	6	0	12.0	7	50	5	5	0	0	0	0	9	0	13	2	0
Parris, Steve, Chattanooga	6	2	.750	4.13	14	14	0	0	0	0	80.2	78	345	44	37	9	1	1	1	29	0	68	2	0
Paugh, Rick, Carolina*	0	0	.000	5.63	5	0	0	0	2	0	8.0	8	31	5	5	2	1	0	0	1	0	3	0	0
Peterson, Mark, Orlando*	0	2	.000	9.88	9	0	0	0	2	0	13.2	26	68	15	15	1	2	1	0	4	1	8	1	0
Pett, Jose, Carolina	4	4	.500	3.51	14	14	0	0	0	0	74.1	76	313	37	29	5	2	0	1	25	1	39	1	0
Phillips, Jason, Carolina	1	2	.333	2.32	4	4	2	1	0	0	31.0	21	127	8	8	1	1	2	4	9	0	22	2	0
Phoenix, Steve, Huntsville	0	3	.000	5.80	29	0	0	0	23	9	35.2	43	156	25	23	3	0	2	2	11	1	25	4	0
Pickford, Kevin, Carolina*	1	2	.333	7.36	21	1	0	0	7	1	29.1	48	152	29	24	3	1	1	3	15	3	24	0	0
Pierce, Jeff, Orlando	0	0	.000	9.87	5	4	0	0	1	0	17.1	28	85	21	19	6	0	0	0	7	0	8	1	0
Pool, Matt, Orlando	4	2	.667	4.60	9	8	1	0	0	0	47.0	47	207	28	24	6	4	3	1	21	1	38	6	0
Price, Jamey, Huntsville	9	3	.750	5.30	20	20	0	0	0	0	110.1	153	502	71	65	16	1	0	3	38	0	80	2	0
Priest, Eddie, Chattanooga*	4	6	.400	3.44	14	14	1	0	0	0	91.2	101	379	39	35	7	2	2	0	17	1	63	3	1
Rain, Steve, Orlando	1	2	.333	3.07	14	0	0	0	12	4	14.2	16	69	7	5	2	0	0	1	8	0	11	0	0
Rajotte, Jason, Huntsville*	2	6	.250	4.40	55	0	0	0	21	3	57.1	67	264	35	28	5	3	8	1	29	4	35	3	0
Ratliff, Jon, Orlando	6	4	.600	4.35	18	15	0	0	1	0	101.1	112	443	59	49	10	5	2	1	32	3	68	12	1
Reed, Brandon, Jacksonville	11	9	.550	4.55	27	27	2	0	0	0	176.0	190	754	100	89	25	6	10	8	54	0	90	9	0
Reed, Chris, Chattanooga	6	8	.429	5.34	23	23	0	0	0	0	129.2	140	585	93	77	11	3	1	7	68	4	96	3	0
Rhine, Kendall, Knoxville	0	0	.000	10.32	8	0	0	0	2	0	11.1	13	61	13	13	1	2	2	2	15	1	6	1	0
Ricketts, Chad, Orlando	0	0	.000	18.00	2	0	0	0	0	0	2.0	7	15	4	4	0	0	0	0	2	0	3	0	0
Rivera, Rafael, Memphis	0	0	.000	2.57	6	0	0	0	3	0	7.0	7	33	3	2	0	0	0	0	7	0	8	0	0
Rivette, Scott, Huntsville	3	1	.750	6.69	7	6	0	0	0	0	39.0	52	180	29	29	3	2	3	0	19	0	33	3	1
Roberts, Willis, Jacksonville	6	15	.286	6.28	26	26	2	0	0	0	149.0	181	685	120	104	18	6	7	6	64	0	86	6	6
Rocker, John, Greenville*	5	6	.455	4.86	22	18	0	0	1	0	113.0	119	507	69	61	12	3	1	0	61	0	96	17	2
Rogers, Bryan, Greenville	2	3	.400	3.08	19	0	0	0	11	1	26.1	20	109	11	9	2	2	1	0	12	3	14	3	1
Runyan, Sean, Mobile*	5	2	.714	2.34	40	1	0	0	15	1	61.2	54	261	25	16	4	2	1	3	28	3	52	1	1
Russell, LaGrande, Orlando	6	4	.600	6.22	25	9	1	0	2	0	81.0	102	365	66	56	8	3	2	3	27	1	43	6	3
Ryan, Matt, Carolina	4	3	.571	2.22	48	0	0	0	39	14	52.2	32	229	18	13	2	4	1	12	21	4	43	9	0
Santana, Marino, Jacksonville	4	1	.800	3.28	39	0	0	0	10	1	74.0	55	317	28	27	8	1	1	1	43	0	98	13	1
Schroeder, Chad, Jax.	0	0	.000	0.00	2	0	0	0	1	0	3.2	1	11	0	0	0	0	0	0	1	0	4	0	0
Shaw, Curtis, Carolina*	1	1	.500	2.81	27	0	0	0	6	0	41.2	30	189	23	13	1	3	0	1	28	1	46	9	1
Simmons, Scott, Memphis*	8	4	.667	3.28	40	7	0	0	6	1	90.2	77	380	40	33	10	3	1	4	40	3	85	5	2
Skrmetta, Matt, Mobile	2	3	.400	5.23	21	0	0	0	7	1	32.2	32	154	21	19	4	0	1	2	21	3	30	3	0
Smith, Brian, Knoxville	0	0	.000	0.00	1	0	0	0	0	0	1.0	0	4	0	0	0	0	0	0	1	0	1	0	0

Pitcher, Team	W	L	Pct.	ERA	G	GS	CG	ShO	GF	Sv.	IP	H	TBF	R	ER	HR	SH	SF	HB	BB	IBB	SO	WP	Bk.
Smith, Cam, Mobile..................	3	5	.375	7.03	26	15	0	0	4	1	79.1	85	390	70	62	5	1	1	3	73	0	88	14	0
Smith, Chuck, Birmingham	2	2	.500	3.16	25	0	0	0	6	0	62.2	63	280	35	22	4	1	2	5	27	5	57	8	3
Smith, Roy, Memphis................	0	0	.000	10.38	4	0	0	0	3	0	4.1	6	20	5	5	0	0	1	0	1	0	6	0	0
Smith, Ryan, Memphis.............	3	6	.333	5.60	41	4	0	0	9	1	80.1	97	356	53	50	6	3	5	4	22	1	50	7	0
Snyder, John, Birmingham	7	8	.467	4.64	20	20	2	1	0	0	114.1	130	510	76	59	9	1	3	6	43	0	90	6	2
Speier, Justin, Orlando	6	5	.545	4.48	50	0	0	0	20	6	78.1	77	328	46	39	8	4	2	3	23	0	63	2	2
Stein, Blake, Huntsville............	3	2	.600	5.71	7	7	0	0	0	0	34.2	36	157	24	22	3	0	1	0	20	1	25	6	0
Stephenson, Brian, Orlando	0	2	.000	9.64	6	0	0	0	2	0	9.1	10	42	10	10	4	0	1	0	5	0	9	4	0
Stevenson, Jason, Knoxville	12	9	.571	4.27	26	26	2	2	0	0	149.2	166	640	88	71	18	5	5	7	43	1	101	7	1
Stewart, Chaad, Greenville*	1	2	.333	8.50	6	3	0	0	1	0	18.0	20	84	18	17	3	1	1	0	12	0	11	1	0
Tapani, Kevin, Orlando	0	0	.000	4.50	1	1	0	0	0	0	4.0	3	16	2	2	2	0	0	0	2	0	2	0	0
Taylor, Kerry, Mobile................	2	1	.667	4.85	5	5	0	0	0	0	26.0	27	117	14	14	4	0	0	1	13	0	30	2	0
Telemaco, Amaury, Orlando	1	0	1.000	2.25	1	1	0	0	0	0	8.0	9	34	2	2	0	0	0	0	2	0	6	1	0
Theodile, Robert, Bir................	2	0	1.000	5.45	19	9	0	0	3	1	57.1	72	272	43	35	2	2	2	5	35	0	41	5	0
Thompson, John, Memphis	3	2	.600	4.62	45	0	0	0	30	4	60.1	59	278	33	31	6	1	5	3	48	0	44	13	1
Tollberg, Brian, Mobile	6	3	.667	3.72	31	13	1	0	5	0	123.1	123	512	60	51	15	2	1	4	24	2	108	4	0
Tryon, Eric, Chattanooga *	0	4	.000	8.31	6	6	0	0	0	0	26.0	35	124	27	24	7	1	1	0	16	0	7	7	0
Twiggs, Greg, Orlando*............	2	4	.333	4.31	48	1	0	0	14	1	62.2	79	285	33	30	4	2	2	2	24	3	38	2	0
Van De Weg, Ryan, Mobile........	9	8	.529	5.43	27	27	2	0	0	0	159.0	198	708	105	96	20	5	6	5	55	1	81	7	2
Veniard, Jay, Knoxville*	3	8	.273	5.85	17	15	2	0	0	0	75.1	97	369	59	49	6	2	2	8	37	2	54	14	2
Veras, Dario, Mobile................	0	0	.000	9.00	5	2	0	0	2	0	5.0	8	25	5	5	1	0	0	0	3	0	5	0	0
Wade, Terrell, Greenville*.........	0	2	.000	4.97	8	6	0	0	0	0	12.2	15	60	10	7	3	0	0	0	8	0	14	1	0
Wagner, Bret, Huntsville*	0	0	.000	20.25	3	0	0	0	1	0	2.2	7	24	11	6	0	1	0	1	6	0	3	2	0
Wagner, Paul, Carolina............	0	1	.000	10.13	12	3	0	0	1	0	16.0	25	90	20	18	3	1	1	1	16	0	20	3	1
Walker, Dane, Huntsville..........	0	0	.000	0.00	1	0	0	0	1	0	1.0	0	5	0	0	0	0	0	0	1	0	0	0	0
Walker, Wade, Orlando	2	2	.500	8.64	4	4	0	0	0	0	16.2	19	80	17	16	0	0	1	1	13	1	11	1	0
Wallace, Jeff, Carolina*	4	8	.333	5.40	38	0	0	0	15	3	43.1	43	207	37	26	3	5	0	1	36	3	39	9	1
Walters, Brett, Mobile..............	10	7	.588	4.47	31	19	0	0	1	0	145.0	169	625	85	72	17	6	2	11	30	0	98	3	1
Weinberg, Todd, Huntsville*	2	1	.667	2.33	20	0	0	0	5	3	27.0	18	114	12	7	1	2	1	1	17	0	24	2	0
White, Rick, Orlando	5	7	.417	4.71	39	8	0	0	22	12	86.0	93	370	55	45	7	4	3	2	22	2	65	6	2
Whiteside, Sean, Memphis*.......	3	4	.429	5.34	36	0	0	0	11	0	57.1	57	252	40	34	7	1	4	2	35	2	40	2	0
Williams, Jeff, Carolina............	0	0	.000	10.80	3	0	0	0	1	0	3.1	6	21	5	4	1	0	0	4	3	0	0	0	0
Williams, Todd, Chattanooga	3	3	.500	2.10	48	0	0	0	44	31	55.2	38	231	16	13	1	0	2	25	2	45	6	0	
Wilson, Gary, Carolina.............	1	2	.333	5.65	7	4	0	0	1	1	28.2	34	124	19	18	1	2	4	1	5	0	19	1	0
Winchester, Scott, Chat............	2	1	.667	1.69	9	4	0	0	7	3	10.2	9	45	4	2	0	2	0	3	1	3	1	0	
Wolff, Bryan, Mobile................	1	2	.333	4.80	20	0	0	0	5	0	30.0	34	141	18	16	6	0	1	0	19	1	37	4	1
Wood, Kerry, Orlando..............	6	7	.462	4.50	19	19	0	0	0	0	94.0	58	416	49	47	2	0	6	10	79	2	106	10	4
Woods, Brian, Birmingham	5	5	.167	6.31	35	0	0	0	31	10	45.2	49	223	41	32	3	6	0	8	28	1	35	4	0
Wooten, Greg, Memphis	11	10	.524	4.47	26	26	0	0	0	0	155.0	166	681	91	77	14	5	5	6	59	1	98	12	0
Worrell, Steve, Bir.-Orl.*	7	4	.636	3.47	44	0	0	0	15	2	62.1	52	257	25	24	6	3	3	2	20	1	54	5	1
Young, Joe, Knoxville..............	2	4	.556	4.42	19	11	0	0	2	0	59.0	52	271	38	29	4	0	3	5	40	0	62	6	3
Zancanaro, Dave, Mobile *	10	8	.556	4.44	27	19	3	0	3	1	133.2	140	581	69	66	15	5	3	4	57	0	66	10	1

COMBINATION SHUTOUTS: **Birmingham (5)**—Herbert-Buteaux-Newman, Eyre-Woods, Herbert-Buteaux, Beirne-Hasselhoff, Herbert-Heathcott. **Carolina (2)**—Halperin-Wagner-Ryan, Halperin-Fredrickson-Ryan. **Chattanooga (2)**—Courtright-Donnelly-Nix, Priest-Williams. **Greenville (4)**—Ebert-Ligtenberg, Rocker-Cather-Butler-Ligtenberg, Bowie-Giard-Butler, Briggs-Butler. **Huntsville (0)**—None. **Jacksonville (5)**—Reed-Marrero-Duran, Roberts-Marrero-Duran-Corey, Roberts-Marrero-Corey, Goldsmith-Gentile, Melendez-Marrero. **Knoxville (4)**—Veniard-Lukasiewicz, Young-Lukasiewicz, Stevenson-Gordon-Lukasiewicz-Czajkowski, McBride-Doman. **Memphis (3)**—Hinchliffe-Brosnan-Holdridge, Franklin-Simmons-Holdridge, Harikkala-Brosnan. **Mobile (2)**—Clement-Erdos, Zancanaro-Tollberg. **Orlando (9)**—Russell-Twiggs-Speier, Wood-Brown-Hammack, Wood-Byrne, Garcia-Byrne-Hammack, Wood-Twiggs-Speier, Wood-Worrell, Wood-Hammack, Byrne-White, Ratliff-Barker-Rain.

NO-HIT GAMES: Franklin, Memphis, defeated Carolina, 6-0 (first game), April 21.

PITCHERS WITH TWO OR MORE TEAMS

Pitcher, Team	W	L	Pct.	ERA	G	GS	CG	ShO	GF	Sv.	IP	H	TBF	R	ER	HR	SH	SF	HB	BB	IBB	SO	WP	Bk.
Worrell, Steve, Birmingham*......	2	2	.500	5.47	18	0	0	0	7	1	24.2	28	111	16	15	5	0	1	0	12	0	21	2	1
Worrell, Steve, Orlando*..........	5	2	.714	2.15	26	0	0	0	8	1	37.2	24	146	9	9	1	3	2	2	8	1	33	3	0

1997 FIELDING

TEAM

Team	Pct.	G	PO	A	E	TC	DP	PB	Team	Pct.	G	PO	A	E	TC	DP	PB
Orlando	.973	138	3552	1481	140	5173	120	15	Birmingham.....	.967	139	3633	1443	174	5250	134	23
Memphis	.972	139	3513	1473	141	5127	147	21	Huntsville	.966	139	3627	1602	184	5413	157	12
Greenville	.969	140	3685	1426	161	5272	111	10	Knoxville..........	.965	139	3607	1502	186	5295	116	14
Mobile	.969	137	3593	1391	158	5142	112	15	Carolina...........	.960	137	3615	1515	211	5341	125	11
Chattanooga	.969	139	3616	1491	164	5271	133	21	TRIPLE PLAYS: None.								
Jacksonville.....	.968	139	3656	1566	170	5392	145	24									

INDIVIDUAL

FIRST BASEMEN

NOTE: All caps denotes fielding-percentage leader based on 72 games for catchers, 96 for all other non-pitchers and 144 innings for pitchers. *Throws lefthanded.

Player, Team	Pct.	G	PO	A	E	TC	DP
Adriana, Sharnol, Knoxville	.963	7	49	3	2	54	6
Allen, Dustin, Mobile	.980	76	585	53	13	651	43
Allen, Marlon, Chattanooga	.984	57	463	26	8	497	52
Asche, Mike, Carolina	1.000	2	14	1	0	15	0
Benbow, Lou, Greenville	.992	61	357	20	3	380	35
Bonifay, Ken, Carolina	1.000	10	105	2	0	107	5

Player, Team	Pct.	G	PO	A	E	TC	DP
Bowie, Jim, Mobile*	1.000	7	36	2	0	38	3
Brown, Ray, Mobile	.974	35	287	18	8	313	23
Cromer, D.T., Huntsville*	.986	131	1167	100	18	1285	129
Dismuke, Jamie, Chattanooga	.995	24	190	17	1	208	16
Eddie, Steve, Chattanooga	.981	30	193	16	4	213	17
Ellis, Kevin, Orlando	.975	19	144	14	4	162	9
Freeman, Ricky, Orlando	.989	81	718	63	9	790	67
Garcia, Freddy, Carolina	1.000	6	41	3	0	44	6
Garcia, Guillermo, Chattanooga ..	1.000	1	10	0	0	10	2
Grijak, Kevin, Greenville	.992	46	323	32	3	358	27

Player, Team	Pct.	G	PO	A	E	TC	DP
Hanel, Marcus, Carolina	.846	2	10	1	2	13	1
Hernandez, Ramon, Huntsville	1.000	4	34	2	0	36	2
Hicks, Jamie, Greenville	.941	2	16	0	1	17	2
Hills, Rich, Mobile	.995	23	187	19	1	207	29
Ibarra, Jesse, Jacksonville	.985	109	925	104	16	1045	90
Jimenez, Manny, Greenville	1.000	1	2	0	0	2	0
Jones, Ryan, Knoxville	.985	62	546	26	9	581	44
Jordan, Ricky, Carolina	.996	24	211	13	1	225	19
JORGENSEN, Randy, Memphis*	.990	120	998	78	11	1087	106
Killeen, Tim, Mobile	1.000	6	30	2	0	32	1
Marine, Del, Jacksonville	.975	13	105	11	3	119	12
McCall, Rod, Orlando*	.978	15	125	7	3	135	16
Melhuse, Adam, Knoxville	.982	8	48	6	1	55	1
Mendez, Sergio, Carolina	.985	17	125	6	2	133	7
Morales, Willie, Huntsville	.980	5	43	7	1	51	6
Morgan, Dave, Huntsville	1.000	3	14	2	0	16	2
Nunez, Raymond, Orlando	.992	23	112	10	1	123	12
Pearson, Eddie, Birmingham	.988	89	737	60	10	807	68
Raven, Luis, Birmingham	1.000	4	33	3	0	36	2
Rodarte, Raul, Greenville	.984	16	115	7	2	124	12
Rumfield, Toby, Chattanooga	.981	40	324	31	7	362	32
Sanders, Tracy, Carolina	.992	65	553	35	5	593	58
Saunders, Doug, Memphis	.987	9	70	5	1	76	11
Schmidt, Tom, Jacksonville	.974	21	176	11	5	192	24
Seitzer, Brad, Memphis	1.000	5	28	1	0	29	4
Thobe, Steve, Carolina	.982	22	196	18	4	218	16
Thomas, Juan, Birmingham	.983	47	400	13	7	420	56
Torres, Paul, Memphis	1.000	9	73	7	0	80	8
Towle, Justin, Chattanooga	1.000	5	37	3	0	40	4
Whatley, Gabe, Greenville	.997	51	354	20	1	375	27
Williams, Harold, Orlando	1.000	16	114	6	0	120	11
Witt, Kevin, Knoxville	.992	66	529	60	5	594	43

SECOND BASEMEN

Player, Team	Pct.	G	PO	A	E	TC	DP
Adriana, Sharnol, Knoxville	.955	79	157	223	18	398	45
Almanzar, Richard, Jacksonville	.969	103	237	292	17	546	85
Asche, Mike, Carolina	1.000	3	6	8	0	14	1
Beasley, Tony, Carolina	.949	12	29	45	4	78	6
Benbow, Lou, Greenville	1.000	8	4	8	0	12	3
Bream, Scott, Jacksonville	.983	12	20	38	1	59	13
Bridges, Kary, Carolina	.953	65	123	180	15	318	55
Brito, Luis, Greenville	.975	31	58	57	3	118	11
Bruno, Julio, Jacksonville	.957	26	53	59	5	117	15
Cook, Jason, Memphis	.976	31	59	62	3	124	20
Coolbaugh, Mike, Huntsville	1.000	1	1	1	0	2	0
Cotton, John, Birmingham	.948	24	60	50	6	116	17
Cromer, Brandon, Carolina	.983	11	29	28	1	58	7
Dean, Chris, Memphis	.955	65	142	176	15	333	57
Eaglin, Mike, Greenville	.961	120	237	306	22	565	58
Eddie, Steve, Chattanooga	1.000	2	1	1	0	2	0
Finn, John, Birmingham	.982	12	17	37	1	55	8
Font, Franklin, Orlando	1.000	1	2	1	0	3	0
Forkerway, Trey, Orlando	.979	40	58	85	3	146	19
Gama, Rick, Mobile	.978	68	138	127	6	271	25
Garcia, Guillermo, Chattanooga	1.000	3	7	8	0	15	2
Gipson, Charles, Memphis	.936	17	41	47	6	94	12
Hall, Billy, Chattanooga	.973	29	59	83	4	146	16
Hazlett, Steve, Carolina	1.000	2	2	0	0	2	0
Henry, Santiago, Knoxville	.947	35	87	108	11	206	25
Hermansen, Chad, Carolina	.913	22	39	45	8	92	10
Hills, Rich, Mobile	.944	4	9	8	1	18	2
Keefe, Jamie, Mobile	1.000	2	0	2	0	2	0
Koelling, Brian, Chattanooga	.954	42	80	107	9	196	28
Lackey, Steve, Jacksonville	.929	4	8	18	2	28	2
LaRocca, Greg, Mobile	.990	68	132	164	3	299	38
Livsey, Shawn, Orlando	.897	9	11	15	3	29	3
Martins, Eric, Huntsville	.967	57	126	168	10	304	46
Maxwell, Jason, Orlando	1.000	3	3	7	0	10	1
Menechino, Frankie, Birm.	.972	78	167	211	11	389	58
Millette, Joe, Memphis	1.000	9	28	25	0	53	5
Miyake, Chris, Carolina	1.000	1	2	1	0	3	0
Moore, Brandon, Birmingham	1.000	12	35	27	0	62	13
Morris, Bobby, Orlando	1.000	4	7	9	0	16	3
Newhan, David, Huntsville	.934	48	96	129	16	241	27
Polcovich, Kevin, Carolina	.846	4	3	8	2	13	0
Polidor, Wil, Birmingham	.941	17	27	37	4	68	6
Powers, John, Mobile	1.000	2	3	5	0	8	1
Presto, Nick, Chattanooga	1.000	1	3	2	0	5	0
Price, Corey, Chattanooga	1.000	1	1	4	0	5	1
Sanford, Chance, Carolina	.984	23	53	71	2	126	10
Saunders, Doug, Memphis	1.000	20	32	55	0	87	12

Player, Team	Pct.	G	PO	A	E	TC	DP
Schmidt, Tom, Jacksonville	.750	2	1	2	1	4	0
Solano, Fausto, Knoxville	.987	23	30	44	1	75	10
Soriano, Fred, Knoxville	.947	4	12	6	1	19	1
Strange, Mike, Knoxville	.971	8	15	19	1	35	2
Tredaway, Chad, Mobile	1.000	2	7	6	0	13	2
Walker, Dane, Huntsville	.932	39	74	104	13	191	28
Williams, Jason, Chattanooga	.988	65	140	180	4	324	50
WIMMER, Chris, Orlando	.982	97	190	246	8	444	66

THIRD BASEMEN

Player, Team	Pct.	G	PO	A	E	TC	DP
Adriana, Sharnol, Knoxville	.900	5	1	8	1	10	0
Alvarez, Gabe, Mobile	.892	107	65	200	32	297	17
Ardoin, Danny, Huntsville	1.000	3	1	2	0	3	0
Asche, Mike, Carolina	.684	4	2	11	6	19	0
Beasley, Tony, Carolina	.900	7	7	11	2	20	1
Benbow, Lou, Greenville	.875	25	20	36	8	64	4
Bonifay, Ken, Carolina	.949	11	11	26	2	39	0
Bream, Scott, Jacksonville	1.000	2	1	1	0	2	0
Bruno, Julio, Jacksonville	.935	91	51	207	18	276	16
Cook, Jason, Memphis	.922	21	9	38	4	51	1
COOLBAUGH, Mike, Huntsville	.943	131	94	302	24	420	35
Coolbaugh, Scott, Birmingham	.960	62	42	124	7	173	16
Cotton, John, Birmingham	.556	5	1	4	4	9	0
Eddie, Steve, Chattanooga	.933	36	24	73	7	104	6
Finn, John, Birmingham	.922	20	9	38	4	51	4
Garcia, Freddy, Carolina	.903	68	52	152	22	226	12
Gipson, Charles, Memphis	.934	30	23	62	6	91	8
Helms, Wes, Greenville	.950	86	60	147	11	218	10
Hernandez, Ramon, Huntsville	1.000	2	2	2	0	4	0
Hills, Rich, Mobile	.923	13	5	31	3	39	2
Jimenez, Manny, Greenville	.958	33	16	52	3	71	6
Keefe, Jamie, Mobile	1.000	2	0	5	0	5	1
Koelling, Brian, Chattanooga	.778	6	1	6	2	9	0
Lanza, Mike, Memphis	.880	11	6	16	3	25	1
LaRocca, Greg, Mobile	1.000	1	1	2	0	3	0
Magee, Danny, Greenville	.667	5	3	9	6	18	1
Marine, Del, Jacksonville	1.000	2	1	2	0	3	1
Martins, Eric, Huntsville	.000	1	0	0	1	1	0
Mashore, Justin, Mobile	.833	7	4	11	3	18	0
Menechino, Frankie, Birm.	1.000	12	9	26	0	35	5
Millette, Joe, Memphis	1.000	3	0	1	0	1	0
Nelson, Bry, Orlando	.884	96	50	179	30	259	13
Nunez, Raymond, Orlando	.919	49	23	91	10	124	9
Polcovich, Kevin, Carolina	.906	11	7	22	3	32	1
Polidor, Wil, Birmingham	.696	10	1	15	7	23	1
Powers, John, Mobile	.935	12	7	22	2	31	1
Raven, Luis, Birmingham	.800	39	19	73	23	115	4
Rodarte, Raul, Greenville	.750	1	0	3	1	4	0
Rose, Pete, Chattanooga	.917	102	81	217	27	325	31
Rumfield, Toby, Chattanooga	.750	1	0	3	1	4	0
Sanford, Chance, Carolina	.905	19	5	52	6	63	4
Saunders, Doug, Memphis	.954	24	17	45	3	65	4
Schmidt, Tom, Jacksonville	.948	48	25	103	7	135	9
Seitzer, Brad, Memphis	1.000	9	4	21	0	25	2
Smith, Scott, Memphis	.500	1	0	1	1	2	0
Thobe, Steve, Carolina	.888	26	20	59	10	89	6
Thompson, Andy, Knoxville	.898	104	72	202	31	305	9
Torres, Paul, Memphis	.900	51	36	99	15	150	8
Tredaway, Chad, Mobile	1.000	2	2	0	0	2	0
Ventura, Robin, Birmingham	.714	4	2	3	2	7	0
Wagner, Mark, Chattanooga	1.000	1	1	1	0	2	0
Walker, Dane, Huntsville	.842	8	5	11	3	19	1
Whatley, Gabe, Greenville	.778	2	1	6	2	9	0
Witt, Kevin, Knoxville	.885	34	19	58	10	87	9

SHORTSTOPS

Player, Team	Pct.	G	PO	A	E	TC	DP
Alvarez, Gabe, Mobile	.933	4	5	9	1	15	4
Bautista, Juan, Birmingham	.912	12	20	32	5	57	6
Beasley, Tony, Carolina	.955	11	14	28	2	44	5
Benbow, Lou, Greenville	.948	23	28	45	4	77	8
Bream, Scott, Jacksonville	1.000	5	6	9	0	15	1
Bridges, Kary, Carolina	1.000	1	0	1	0	1	0
Brito, Luis, Greenville	.951	54	69	124	10	203	27
Castro, Jose, Huntsville	.913	5	4	17	2	23	6
Cook, Jason, Memphis	1.000	2	5	7	0	12	2
Coolbaugh, Mike, Huntsville	.950	8	11	27	2	40	5
Cordero, Edward, Greenville	.909	2	4	6	1	11	0
Cromer, Brandon, Carolina	.948	44	65	137	11	213	34
Eddie, Steve, Chattanooga	.929	36	51	106	12	169	26
Finn, John, Birmingham	.936	13	17	27	3	47	4

Player, Team	Pct.	G	PO	A	E	TC	DP
Font, Franklin, Orlando	1.000	7	7	16	0	23	4
Forkerway, Trey, Orlando	.963	26	29	50	3	82	14
Freel, Ryan, Knoxville	.913	33	44	92	13	149	17
Garcia, Guillermo, Chattanooga	1.000	1	3	4	0	7	0
Garcia, Luis, Jacksonville	.948	125	176	370	30	576	74
Gipson, Charles, Memphis	.931	30	49	100	11	160	22
Guevara, Giomar, Memphis	.958	64	80	217	13	310	55
Hall, Billy, Chattanooga	.919	8	16	18	3	37	5
Hazlett, Steve, Carolina	.800	1	2	2	1	5	1
Henry, Santiago, Knoxville	.938	17	27	63	6	96	9
Hermansen, Chad, Carolina	.839	33	43	77	23	143	14
Hills, Rich, Mobile	.967	19	27	62	3	92	5
Jimenez, Manny, Greenville	.943	88	103	228	20	351	40
Koelling, Brian, Chattanooga	.938	20	31	60	6	97	13
Lanza, Mike, Memphis	1.000	1	2	2	0	4	1
LaRocca, Greg, Mobile	.970	7	8	24	1	33	5
Larson, Brandon, Chattanooga	.891	11	19	22	5	46	5
Magdaleno, Ricky, Chattanooga	.941	58	116	171	18	305	28
Maxwell, Jason, Orlando	.951	118	173	369	28	570	67
Melo, Juan, Mobile	.946	112	182	307	28	517	61
Miller, Orlando, Jacksonville	.846	3	3	8	2	13	1
Millette, Joe, Memphis	.962	44	57	121	7	185	25
Miyake, Chris, Carolina	1.000	2	3	5	0	8	0
MOORE, Brandon, Birmingham	.960	112	177	354	22	553	70
Nelson, Bry, Orlando	.893	6	14	11	3	28	3
Nunez, Abraham, Carolina	.949	47	76	129	11	216	25
Polcovich, Kevin, Carolina	1.000	2	2	3	0	5	1
Polidor, Wil, Birmingham	.833	8	6	19	5	30	1
Presto, Nick, Chattanooga	.917	8	8	14	2	24	2
Saunders, Doug, Memphis	1.000	1	4	4	0	8	1
Schmidt, Tom, Jacksonville	.882	9	8	22	4	34	4
Solano, Fausto, Knoxville	.950	93	151	267	22	440	53
Soriano, Fred, Knoxville	.900	2	5	4	1	10	1
Strange, Mike, Knoxville	1.000	1	0	3	0	3	0
Tejada, Miguel, Huntsville	.948	128	229	423	36	688	97

OUTFIELDERS

Player, Team	Pct.	G	PO	A	E	TC	DP
Allen, Dustin, Mobile	.971	56	66	1	2	69	0
Asche, Mike, Carolina	1.000	3	2	0	0	2	0
Barker, Glen, Jacksonville	.988	64	154	6	2	162	2
Brinkley, Darryl, Mobile	.946	50	68	2	4	74	0
Brito, Luis, Greenville	1.000	6	4	0	0	4	0
Broach, Donald, Chattanooga	.987	99	215	9	3	227	1
Brown, Adrian, Carolina	.956	37	63	2	3	68	1
Brown, Ray, Mobile	.800	8	12	0	3	15	0
Candelaria, Ben, Knoxville	.974	102	174	13	5	192	1
Christenson, Ryan, Huntsville	.988	29	81	1	1	83	0
Christian, Eddie, Memphis*	1.000	26	38	1	0	39	0
Conger, Jeff, Carolina*	.984	39	57	6	1	64	1
Conner, Decomba, Jacksonville	.960	47	96	1	4	101	0
Correa, Miguel, Memphis	.969	53	89	6	3	98	1
Cotton, John, Birmingham	1.000	4	5	0	0	5	0
Coughlin, Kevin, Chattanooga*	.986	45	68	4	1	73	0
Cradle, Rickey, Knoxville	.982	73	104	5	2	111	0
Cromer, D.T., Huntsville*	1.000	1	2	1	0	3	0
Curl, John, Knoxville	1.000	1	2	0	0	2	0
DeBoer, Rob, Huntsville	.714	4	5	0	2	7	0
DeLaCruz, Lorenzo, Knoxville	.957	11	20	2	1	23	0
Dowler, Dee, Orlando	.983	52	114	3	2	119	0
Eddie, Steve, Chattanooga	.947	10	18	0	1	19	0
Ellis, Kevin, Orlando	.955	54	63	1	3	67	0
Encarnacion, Juan, Jacksonville	.987	112	208	12	3	223	3
Espinosa, Ramon, Carolina	.950	17	19	0	1	20	0
Evans, Jason, Birmingham	.920	61	89	3	8	100	0
Finn, John, Birmingham	1.000	15	26	3	0	29	0
French, Anton, Knoxville	1.000	2	1	0	0	1	0
Gazarek, Marty, Orlando	.994	75	145	10	1	156	2
Gibralter, Steve, Chattanooga	.972	19	35	0	1	36	0
Gipson, Charles, Memphis	1.000	11	30	2	0	32	0
Gordon, Keith, Chattanooga	1.000	4	6	0	0	6	0
Grieve, Ben, Huntsville	.961	98	193	6	8	207	2
Griffey, Craig, Mem.-Chat.	.980	83	139	8	3	150	2
Guiel, Aaron, Mobile	1.000	8	8	0	0	8	0
Hall, Billy, Chattanooga	.962	12	25	0	1	26	0
Hazlett, Steve, Carolina	1.000	38	59	6	0	65	0
Hermansen, Chad, Carolina	.935	59	112	3	8	123	0
Hightower, Vee, Orlando	1.000	82	156	2	0	158	0
Hills, Rich, Mobile	.857	8	11	1	2	14	0
Holifield, Rick, Carolina*	.972	50	100	3	3	106	2
Hughes, Troy, Huntsville	.974	50	67	9	2	78	2
Hurst, Jimmy, Jacksonville	1.000	3	3	0	0	3	0

Player, Team	Pct.	G	PO	A	E	TC	DP
Johnson, Earl, Mob.-Jack.	.985	105	258	12	4	274	4
Joseph, Terry, Orlando	.972	133	206	3	6	215	0
Keefe, Jamie, Mobile	1.000	8	13	3	0	16	2
Kelly, Mike, Chattanooga	1.000	15	32	2	0	34	0
Killeen, Tim, Mobile	1.000	2	2	0	0	2	0
Ladell, Cleveland, Chattanooga	1.000	1	22	0	0	22	0
Lewis, Marc, Greenville	.982	133	275	4	5	284	3
Liefer, Jeff, Birmingham	.955	106	166	2	8	176	0
Marquez, Jesus, Jacksonville*	.965	106	182	11	7	200	1
Martin, Al, Carolina*	1.000	3	2	0	0	2	0
Mashore, Justin, Mobile	.985	64	120	11	2	133	3
Matthews, Gary, Mobile	.960	26	45	3	2	50	1
McBride, Charles, Greenville	.977	32	39	3	1	43	0
McKinnon, Sandy, Birmingham	.972	88	170	6	5	181	1
Melhuse, Adam, Knoxville	1.000	5	10	2	0	12	0
Mitchell, Tony, Carolina	.800	3	4	0	1	5	0
Monahan, Shane, Memphis	.980	92	139	10	3	152	1
Monds, Wonderful, Greenville	.941	27	61	3	4	68	0
Mottola, Chad, Chattanooga	.963	44	74	5	3	82	0
Mouton, Lyle, Birmingham	1.000	3	5	0	0	5	0
Murray, Glenn, Chattanooga	.974	75	146	6	4	156	0
Neill, Mike, Huntsville*	.982	119	212	12	4	228	2
Peterson, Charles, Carolina	.967	116	186	17	7	210	6
Poe, Charles, Mobile	.961	31	47	2	2	51	0
Porter, Bo, Orlando	.938	8	13	2	1	16	0
PRIETO, Chris, Mobile*	.991	98	212	11	2	225	3
Ramirez, Angel, Knoxville	.954	82	131	15	7	153	5
Ramirez, Roberto, Huntsville	.935	17	25	4	2	31	1
Roberts, David, Jacksonville*	.954	34	82	1	4	87	1
Roberts, Lonell, Knoxville	.941	7	16	0	1	17	0
Rodarte, Raul, Greenville	.955	36	61	2	3	66	1
Rumfield, Toby, Chattanooga	1.000	6	11	2	0	13	0
Samuels, Scott, Orlando	.974	33	70	4	2	76	0
Sanders, Anthony, Knoxville	.983	109	224	7	4	235	3
Sanders, Reggie, Chattanooga	1.000	3	11	0	0	11	0
Sanders, Tracy, Carolina	.881	27	50	2	7	59	1
Simmons, Brian, Birmingham	.985	136	322	7	5	334	1
Skett, Will, Knoxville	.977	30	40	2	1	43	0
Smith, Demond, Huntsville	.971	84	167	2	5	174	0
Smith, Ira, Jacksonville	.980	29	48	2	1	51	0
Smith, Mark, Carolina	.800	3	4	0	1	5	0
Smith, Scott, Memphis	.974	105	173	15	5	193	1
Staton, T.J., Carolina*	.965	50	79	4	3	86	1
Sturdivant, Marcus, Memphis*	.983	106	231	6	4	241	0
Swann, Pedro, Greenville	.957	94	150	4	7	161	1
Topham, Ryan, Birmingham*	.968	13	30	0	1	31	0
Walker, Dane, Huntsville	1.000	29	38	6	0	44	0
Warner, Mike, Greenville*	.962	89	167	10	7	184	1
Watkins, Pat, Chattanooga	1.000	43	78	3	0	81	1
Whatley, Gabe, Greenville	.978	59	88	3	2	93	0
Witt, Kevin, Knoxville	1.000	4	5	0	0	5	0

OUTFIELDERS WITH TWO OR MORE TEAMS

Player, Team	Pct.	G	PO	A	E	TC	DP
Griffey, Craig, Memphis	.979	31	44	2	1	47	1
Griffey, Craig, Chattanooga	.981	52	95	6	2	103	1
Johnson, Earl, Mobile	.985	76	189	8	3	200	2
Johnson, Earl, Jacksonville	.986	29	69	4	1	74	2

CATCHERS

Player, Team	Pct.	G	PO	A	E	TC	DP	PB
ALVAREZ, Clemente, Birm.	.998	78	500	49	1	550	5	10
Ardoin, Danny, Huntsville	.972	51	301	43	10	354	6	8
Ayrault, Joe, Greenville	1.000	11	62	4	0	66	0	0
Ballara, Juan, Orlando	1.000	14	53	11	0	64	1	1
Cline, Pat, Orlando	.989	71	416	35	5	456	1	8
Cox, Darron, Orlando	1.000	3	20	4	0	24	0	1
DeBoer, Rob, Huntsville	.942	42	205	24	5	234	3	2
Devarez, Cesar, Orlando	.985	31	182	20	3	205	1	1
Diaz, Cesar, Knoxville	1.000	5	26	1	0	27	0	0
Ellis, Kevin, Orlando	1.000	5	5	1	0	6	0	1
Fagley, Dan, Birmingham	.933	20	40	2	3	45	0	0
Garcia, Guillermo, Chat.	.988	11	75	7	1	83	2	0
Gonzalez, Wikleman, Mobile	.989	41	250	24	3	277	0	6
Hanel, Marcus, Carolina	.984	51	326	39	6	371	2	2
Hernandez, Ramon, Hunt.	.996	34	238	23	1	262	1	0
Hicks, Jamie, Greenville	1.000	2	9	2	0	11	0	0
Killeen, Tim, Mobile	.982	53	313	20	6	339	4	2
Lidle, Kevin, Jacksonville	.980	58	336	51	8	395	8	7
Mahoney, Mike, Greenville	.985	85	589	58	10	657	6	8
Marine, Del, Jacksonville	.984	85	550	59	10	619	6	17
Maynard, Scott, Memphis	1.000	14	64	8	0	72	1	4

Player, Team	Pct.	G	PO	A	E	TC	DP	PB
Melhuse, Adam, Knoxville	.992	18	114	18	1	133	3	4
Mendez, Sergio, Carolina	1.000	22	137	10	0	147	0	4
Micucci, Mike, Orlando	1.000	4	10	0	0	10	0	0
Molina, Jose, Orlando	.993	36	237	28	2	267	1	3
Morales, Willie, Huntsville	.991	17	102	10	1	113	2	2
Morgan, Dave, Knoxville	.984	16	118	9	2	129	2	2
Mosquera, Julio, Knoxville	.989	86	587	56	7	650	6	4
Norris, Dax, Greenville	1.000	2	9	1	0	10	1	0
Paul, Josh, Birmingham	.988	32	221	17	3	241	0	7
Rodriguez, Adam, Jack.	1.000	2	10	0	0	10	0	0
Rodriguez, Luis, Knoxville	.983	24	153	19	3	175	2	4
Romero, Mandy, Mobile	.987	57	436	33	6	475	2	7
Rumfield, Toby, Chat.	.988	34	219	23	3	245	4	3
Sawkiw, Warren, Birm.	1.000	1	6	0	0	6	0	2
Sealy, Scot, Memphis	.991	41	295	19	3	317	2	7
Sweet, Jon, Carolina	.995	75	505	46	3	554	7	5
Thompson, Karl, Memphis	.981	42	283	26	6	315	5	3
Toth, Dave, Greenville	.995	47	333	35	2	370	5	2
Towle, Justin, Chattanooga	.984	96	537	68	10	615	4	18
Wathan, Dusty, Memphis	.987	48	290	23	4	317	4	7
Wrona, Rick, Birmingham	.987	29	199	28	3	230	4	4

PITCHERS

Player, Team	Pct.	G	PO	A	E	TC	DP
Almanzar, Carlos, Knoxville	1.000	21	2	6	0	8	0
Anderson, Bill, Mobile	1.000	7	0	1	0	1	1
Anderson, Jimmy, Carolina*	1.000	4	5	9	0	14	1
Apana, Matt, Memphis	.909	17	4	6	1	11	0
Arnold, Jamie, Greenville	1.000	1	0	2	0	2	0
Atchley, Justin, Chattanooga*	.833	13	3	7	2	12	0
Baez, Benito, Huntsville*	1.000	15	1	4	0	5	0
Barcelo, Lorenzo, Birmingham	1.000	6	2	8	0	10	0
Barker, Richie, Orlando	1.000	19	4	4	0	8	0
Baron, Jim, Mobile*	.875	19	3	4	1	8	0
Baxter, Bob, Huntsville*	.500	6	0	2	2	4	1
Beatty, Blaine, Carolina*	1.000	19	3	18	0	21	0
Beck, Chris, Memphis	1.000	5	2	1	0	3	0
Beirne, Kevin, Birmingham	.938	13	5	10	1	16	0
Bennett, Bob, Huntsville	1.000	23	4	6	0	10	0
Benson, Kris, Carolina	1.000	14	2	5	0	7	0
Boggs, Robert, Chattanooga	1.000	9	3	3	0	6	0
Bogott, Kurtiss, Knoxville*	.917	35	0	11	1	12	0
Bowie, Micah, Greenville*	1.000	8	0	6	0	6	1
Briggs, Anthony, Greenville	.964	19	11	16	1	28	1
Brooks, Antone, Greenville*	1.000	14	4	4	0	8	0
Brosnan, Jason, Memphis*	1.000	40	1	6	0	7	1
Brown, Chad, Knoxville*	1.000	32	9	4	0	13	1
Brown, Darold, Orlando*	1.000	18	1	4	0	5	0
Bryant, Adam, Chattanooga	1.000	6	1	1	0	2	0
Bussa, Todd, Huntsville	1.000	19	3	1	0	4	0
Buteaux, Shane, Birmingham	1.000	44	5	7	0	12	0
Butler, Adam, Greenville*	1.000	46	1	6	0	7	0
Byrd, Matt, Greenville	.857	28	0	6	1	7	0
Byrne, Earl, Orlando*	.962	32	3	22	1	26	0
Caruthers, Clay, Chattanooga	1.000	9	2	8	0	10	1
Castillo, Marino, Mobile	.833	8	3	2	1	6	1
Cather, Mike, Greenville	1.000	22	4	7	0	11	0
Chaves, Rafael, Carolina	1.000	5	0	1	0	1	0
Christiansen, Jason, Carolina*	.000	8	0	0	1	1	0
Christman, Scott, Birmingham*	1.000	15	6	10	0	16	1
Clement, Matt, Mobile	1.000	13	6	10	0	16	0
Cloude, Ken, Memphis	.903	22	5	23	3	31	3
Connelly, Steve, Huntsville	.944	43	8	9	1	18	1
Corey, Bryan, Jacksonville	.958	52	13	10	1	24	0
Cortes, David, Greenville	1.000	3	1	1	0	2	0
Courtright, John, Chattanooga*	.962	20	6	19	1	26	0
Crawford, Carlos, Carolina	1.000	29	5	12	0	17	2
Crowell, Jim, Chattanooga*	1.000	3	1	1	0	2	0
Curl, John, Knoxville	1.000	1	0	1	0	1	0
Cushman, Dwayne, Chattanooga	1.000	1	1	1	0	2	0
Czajkowski, Jim, Knoxville	1.000	25	1	2	0	3	0
Dale, Carl, Huntsville	1.000	20	6	18	0	24	2
Davey, Tom, Knoxville	.864	20	8	11	3	22	1
Davis, Kane, Carolina	.667	6	2	4	3	9	0
Dillinger, John, Carolina	.889	23	7	9	2	18	0
Dixon, Bubba, Mobile*	.947	56	2	16	1	19	0
Doman, Roger, Knoxville	.906	48	6	23	3	32	1
Donnelly, Brendan, Chattanooga	1.000	62	6	7	0	13	1
Doyle, Tom, Chattanooga*	.889	65	11	13	3	27	2
Drews, Matt, Jacksonville	.933	24	14	14	2	30	2
Drumright, Mike, Jacksonville	.800	5	3	5	2	10	1
Dunbar, Matt, Huntsville*	1.000	5	1	0	0	1	1
Duncan, Courtney, Orlando	.889	8	3	5	1	9	0
Duran, Roberto, Jacksonville*	1.000	50	1	9	0	10	0
EBERT, Derrin, Greenville*	1.000	27	10	41	0	51	2
Erdos, Todd, Mobile	1.000	55	2	7	0	9	1
Escobar, Kelvim, Knoxville	1.000	5	0	2	0	2	0
Etler, Todd, Chattanooga	1.000	23	5	3	0	8	0
Eyre, Scott, Birmingham*	1.000	22	3	20	0	23	1
Fernandez, Osvaldo, Memphis*	1.000	1	0	1	0	1	0
Folkers, Kenneth, Knoxville	1.000	1	0	1	0	1	0
Franklin, Ryan, Memphis	.929	11	6	7	1	14	0
Fredrickson, Scott, Carolina	1.000	19	2	2	0	4	0
Freeman, Chris, Knoxville	1.000	47	10	9	0	19	0
Freitas, Mike, Carolina	1.000	6	0	2	0	2	0
Gallaher, Kevin, Jacksonville	.867	10	6	7	2	15	0
Garcia, Al, Orlando	.957	12	4	18	1	23	1
Garrett, Hal, Carolina	1.000	6	0	3	0	3	0
Gentile, Scott, Jacksonville	.938	43	7	8	1	16	2
Giard, Ken, Greenville	1.000	25	6	1	0	7	0
Goldsmith, Gary, Jacksonville	.885	31	11	12	3	26	0
Gordon, Mike, Knoxville	.933	33	4	10	1	15	0
Gower, Tim, Chattanooga	1.000	24	0	7	0	7	0
Graterol, Beiker, Knoxville	1.000	3	0	3	0	3	0
Greisinger, Seth, Jacksonville	.974	28	12	25	1	38	4
Grijak, Kevin, Greenville	1.000	1	0	1	0	1	0
Halladay, Roy, Knoxville	.929	7	4	9	1	14	2
Halperin, Mike, Carolina*	.923	17	5	19	2	26	0
Hammack, Brandon, Orlando	.800	39	2	2	1	5	0
Hancock, Lee, Orlando*	1.000	3	1	1	0	2	0
Harikkala, Tim, Memphis	1.000	5	1	6	0	7	0
Harris, D.J., Knoxville	1.000	2	0	1	0	1	0
Hart, Jason, Orlando	1.000	14	2	0	0	2	0
Harvey, Bryan, Greenville	1.000	22	1	2	0	3	1
Hasselhoff, Derek, Birmingham	1.000	18	4	3	0	7	0
Haught, Gary, Huntsville	1.000	6	2	3	0	5	1
Heathcott, Mike, Birmingham	1.000	30	4	9	0	13	1
Herbert, Russ, Birmingham	.938	27	9	21	2	32	0
Hernandez, Elvin, Carolina	1.000	17	3	12	0	15	0
Hinchliffe, Brett, Memphis	.933	24	8	20	2	30	1
Hines, Rich, Greenville*	.867	41	3	10	2	15	0
Holdridge, David, Memphis	.800	30	3	1	1	5	0
Hollins, Stacy, Huntsville	1.000	32	15	12	0	27	1
Howry, Bob, Birmingham	1.000	12	0	2	0	2	1
Jacobs, Ryan, Greenville*	.857	28	4	8	2	14	1
Jarvis, Jason, Knoxville	1.000	4	3	3	0	6	0
Jean, Domingo, Chattanooga	1.000	10	2	1	0	3	1
Jimenez, Miguel, Huntsville	.846	24	12	10	4	26	0
Johnson, Jason, Carolina	.750	9	1	5	2	8	0
Kaufman, Brad, Mobile	.878	22	7	29	5	41	3
Kelly, Jeff, Carolina*	.833	31	1	24	5	30	0
King, Bill, Huntsville	.868	28	15	18	5	38	1
King, Raymond, Greenville*	.950	12	5	14	1	20	1
Konuszewski, Dennis, Carolina	1.000	15	2	2	0	4	0
Koppe, Clint, Chattanooga	.900	13	4	5	1	10	0
LeBlanc, Eric, Chattanooga	.889	8	1	7	1	9	0
LeRoy, John, Greenville	.857	29	4	14	3	21	0
Ligtenberg, Kerry, Greenville	1.000	31	0	1	0	1	0
Lott, Brian, Chattanooga	.813	25	4	9	3	16	1
Lowe, Benny, Knoxville*	1.000	18	1	3	0	4	0
Luce, Robert, Memphis	.964	13	11	16	1	28	3
Lukasiewicz, Mark, Knoxville*	1.000	27	4	4	0	8	0
Lundquist, David, Birmingham	1.000	7	0	1	0	1	0
Lyons, Curt, Orlando	1.000	2	1	0	0	1	0
Manning, Derek, Huntsville*	1.000	21	5	8	0	13	2
Manzanillo, Josias, Memphis	1.000	2	1	0	0	1	0
Marrero, Kenny, Jacksonville	.944	37	5	12	1	18	0
Maskivish, Joe, Carolina	.750	15	1	2	1	4	0
Mathews, Del, Carolina*	.938	21	4	11	1	16	1
Maurer, Mike, Huntsville	.923	52	7	17	2	26	1
McBride, Chris, Knoxville	.750	10	3	3	2	8	0
McKenzie, Scott, Chattanooga	1.000	30	4	4	0	8	0
McNichol, Brian, Orlando*	1.000	22	5	15	0	20	2
Meiners, Doug, Knoxville	.905	23	5	14	2	21	0
Meinershagen, Adam, Knoxville	.500	7	0	1	1	2	0
Melendez, Dave, Jacksonville	1.000	12	8	10	0	18	1
Millwood, Kevin, Greenville	.909	11	4	6	1	11	1
Montane, Ivan, Memphis	.846	22	3	8	2	13	1
Moss, Damian, Greenville*	.840	21	3	18	4	25	1
Moten, Scott, Orlando	1.000	4	0	1	0	1	0
Nelson, Chris, Huntsville	.882	20	6	9	2	17	0
Nelson, Erick, Greenville*	.667	5	1	1	1	3	0
Newman, Alan, Birmingham*	.783	44	2	16	5	23	1
Nix, James, Chattanooga	1.000	28	3	3	0	6	0
Norton, Phillip, Orlando*	1.000	2	1	0	0	1	0

Player, Team	Pct.	G	PO	A	E	TC	DP
Nunez, Maximo, Birmingham	1.000	14	2	1	0	3	0
Olsen, Jason, Birmingham	.955	28	14	28	2	44	0
Olszewski, Eric, Greenville	1.000	4	1	2	0	3	0
Pacheco, Alexander, Memphis	1.000	9	0	1	0	1	0
Parris, Steve, Chattanooga	.947	14	6	12	1	19	0
Paugh, Rick, Carolina*	1.000	4	0	2	0	2	0
Peterson, Mark, Orlando*	1.000	9	2	2	0	4	0
Pett, Jose, Carolina	1.000	14	1	10	0	11	0
Phillips, Jason, Carolina	1.000	4	3	7	0	10	0
Phoenix, Steve, Huntsville	1.000	29	0	2	0	2	0
Pickford, Kevin, Carolina*	.833	21	2	3	1	6	0
Pierce, Jeff, Orlando	.857	5	1	5	1	7	0
Pool, Matt, Orlando	1.000	9	3	10	0	13	1
Price, Jamey, Huntsville	1.000	20	4	24	0	28	1
Priest, Eddie, Chattanooga*	1.000	14	2	13	0	15	0
Rain, Steve, Orlando	1.000	14	2	0	0	2	0
Rajotte, Jason, Huntsville*	1.000	55	8	13	0	21	1
Ratliff, Jon, Orlando	1.000	18	12	19	0	31	0
Reed, Brandon, Jacksonville	1.000	27	15	22	0	37	2
Reed, Chris, Chattanooga	.977	23	14	28	1	43	1
Rhine, Kendall, Knoxville	1.000	8	0	2	0	2	0
Rivera, Rafael, Memphis	1.000	6	1	2	0	3	0
Rivette, Scott, Huntsville	.889	7	3	5	1	9	0
Roberts, Willis, Jacksonville	.882	26	22	23	6	51	3
Rocker, John, Greenville*	.905	22	4	15	2	21	2
Rogers, Bryan, Greenville	1.000	19	1	5	0	6	0
Runyan, Sean, Mobile*	1.000	40	5	10	0	15	4
Russell, LaGrande, Orlando	.966	25	11	17	1	29	1
Ryan, Matt, Carolina	.923	48	4	8	1	13	0
Santana, Marino, Jacksonville	1.000	39	5	5	0	10	0
Shaw, Curtis, Carolina*	.833	27	3	7	2	12	1
Simmons, Scott, Memphis*	1.000	40	3	19	0	22	2
Skrmetta, Matt, Mobile	1.000	21	3	1	0	4	1
Smith, Cam, Mobile	1.000	26	5	12	0	17	0
Smith, Chuck, Birmingham	.909	25	4	6	1	11	2
Smith, Ryan, Memphis	1.000	41	6	11	0	17	4
Snyder, John, Birmingham	.926	20	8	17	2	27	1
Speier, Justin, Orlando	.944	50	8	9	1	18	0
Stein, Blake, Huntsville	1.000	7	2	2	0	4	0
Stephenson, Brian, Orlando	1.000	6	0	1	0	1	0
Stevenson, Jason, Knoxville	.893	26	7	18	3	28	1
Stewart, Chaad, Greenville*	.667	6	0	2	1	3	0
Tapani, Kevin, Orlando	1.000	1	0	1	0	1	0
Taylor, Kerry, Mobile	1.000	5	3	1	0	4	0
Telemaco, Amaury, Orlando	1.000	1	0	1	0	1	0
Theodile, Robert, Birmingham	.800	19	4	4	2	10	0
Thompson, John, Memphis	1.000	45	6	5	0	11	0
Tollberg, Brian, Mobile	1.000	31	11	16	0	27	5
Tryon, Eric, Chattanooga*	.917	6	4	7	1	12	1
Twiggs, Greg, Orlando*	.923	48	4	8	1	13	0
Van De Weg, Ryan, Mobile	.958	27	16	30	2	48	2
Veniard, Jay, Knoxville*	.957	17	5	17	1	23	1
Wade, Terrell, Greenville*	1.000	8	0	2	0	2	0
Wagner, Paul, Carolina	1.000	12	1	4	0	5	0
Walker, Wade, Orlando	1.000	4	5	3	0	8	0
Wallace, Jeff, Carolina*	1.000	38	1	12	0	13	0
Walters, Brett, Mobile	.875	31	10	25	5	40	1
Weinberg, Todd, Huntsville*	1.000	20	2	3	0	5	0
White, Rick, Orlando	1.000	39	3	15	0	18	0
Whiteside, Sean, Memphis*	.923	36	2	10	1	13	1
Williams, Jeff, Carolina	1.000	3	1	1	0	2	0
Williams, Todd, Chattanooga	1.000	48	6	20	0	26	0
Wilson, Gary, Carolina	.800	7	1	3	1	5	0
Winchester, Scott, Chattanooga	1.000	9	1	4	0	5	0
Wolff, Bryan, Mobile	.667	20	0	2	1	3	0
Wood, Kerry, Orlando	.938	19	4	11	1	16	2
Woods, Brian, Birmingham	.900	35	1	8	1	10	0
Wooten, Greg, Memphis	.971	26	11	22	1	34	2
Worrell, Steve, Birm.-Orl.*	.889	44	2	6	1	9	0
Young, Joe, Knoxville	.833	19	4	1	1	6	0
Zancanaro, Dave, Mobile*	1.000	27	5	27	0	32	2

PITCHERS WITH TWO OR MORE TEAMS

Player, Team	Pct.	G	PO	A	E	TC	DP
Worrell, Steve, Birmingham*	1.000	18	2	2	0	4	0
Worrell, Steve, Orlando*	.800	26	0	4	1	5	0

The following players did not have any fielding statistics at the positions indicated or appeared only as a designated hitter, pinch-hitter or pinch-runner: Benbow, of; Bere, p; Bradley, p; M. Brown, p; Bruno, of; Carter, p; Castro, 2b; Clayton, p; Cook, p; Eddie, p; Finley, dh; Forkerway, 3b; Grall, dh; Hazlett, p; Lidle, of; Livesy, of; Morgan, p; Orie, dh; Ricketts, p; Schroeder, p; Schwenke, ph; B. Smith, p; Roy Smith, p; Sweet, 1b, 2b, 3b; Toth, 1b; Towle, of; Veras, p; B. Wagner, p; D. Walker, p; Whitmore, dh; Witt, ss.

LEAGUE CHAMPIONS

Year	Team	Pct.
1904—	Macon	.598
1905—	Macon	.625
1906—	Savannah	.637
1907—	Charleston	.620
1908—	Jacksonville	.694
1909—	Chattanooga*	.738
	Augusta	.702
1910—	Columbus	.588
1911—	Columbus*	.681
	Columbia	.710
1912—	Jacksonville*	.679
	Columbus	.632
1913—	Savannah	.754
	Savannah	.593
1914—	Savannah*	.667
	Albany	.650
1915—	Macon	.588
	Columbus*	.686
1916—	Augusta*	.617
	Columbia	.631
1917—	Charleston	.741
	Columbia*	.667
1918—	Did not operate.	
1919—	Columbia	.585
1920—	Columbia	.633
1921—	Columbia	.642
1922—	Charleston	.625
1923—	Charlotte*	.653
	Macon	.580
1924—	Augusta	.612
1925—	Spartanburg	.620
1926—	Greenville	.662
1927—	Greenville	.622
1928—	Asheville	.664
1929—	Asheville	.605
	Knoxville*	.634
1930—	Greenville*	.620
	Macon	.643
1931-35—	Did not operate.	
1936—	Jacksonville	.652
	Columbus*	.650
1937—	Columbus	.572
	Savannah (3rd)†	.565
1938—	Savannah	.574
	Macon (2nd)†	.570
1939—	Columbus	.601
	Augusta (2nd)†	.597
1940—	Savannah	.627
	Columbus (2nd)†	.583
1941—	Macon	.643
	Columbia (2nd)†	.636
1942—	Charleston	.620
	Macon (2nd)†	.585
1943-45—	Did not operate.	
1946—	Columbus	.568
	Augusta (4th)†	.547
1947—	Columbus	.575
	Savannah (2nd)†	.563
1948—	Charleston	.572
	Greenville (3rd)†	.549
1949—	Macon‡	.623
1950—	Macon‡	.588
1951—	Montgomery	.607
1952—	Columbia	.649
	Montgomery (3rd)†	.558
1953—	Jacksonville	.679
	Savannah (2nd)†	.571
1954—	Jacksonville	.593
	Savannah (2nd)†	.571
1955—	Columbia	.636
	Augusta (3rd)†	.543
1956—	Jacksonville‡	.621
1957—	Augusta	.636
	Charlotte (2nd)†	.562
1958—	Augusta	.550
	Macon (3rd)†	.500
1959—	Knoxville	.557
	Gastonia (4th)†	.504
1960—	Columbia	.597
	Savannah (3rd)†	.561
1961—	Asheville	.635
1962—	Savannah	.662
	Macon (3rd)†	.576
1963—	Augusta*	.661
	Lynchburg	.662
1964—	Lynchburg	.579
1965—	Columbus	.572
1966—	Mobile	.629
1967—	Birmingham	.604
1968—	Asheville	.614
1969—	Charlotte	.579
1970—	Columbus	.569
1971—	Did not operate as league—clubs were members of Dixie Association.	
1972—	Asheville	.583
	Montgomery§	.561
1973—	Montgomery§	.580
	Jacksonville	.559
1974—	Jacksonville	.565
	Knoxville§	.533
1975—	Orlando	.587
	Montgomery§	.545
1976—	Montgomery∞	.591
	Orlando	.540

Year	Team	Pct.	Year	Team	Pct.	Year	Team	Pct.
1977—	Montgomery∞	.628	1984—	Charlotte∞	.510	1991—	Greenville	.611
	Jacksonville	.522		Knoxville	.483		Orlando∞	.535
1978—	Knoxville∞	.611	1985—	Charlotte	.545	1992—	Greenville∞	.699
	Savannah	.500		Huntsville∞	.542		Chattanooga	.629
1979—	Columbus	.587	1986—	Huntsville	.553	1993—	Birmingham∞	.549
	Nashville∞	.576		Columbus∞	.500		Knoxville	.500
1980—	Memphis	.576	1987—	Charlotte	.586	1994—	Huntsville∞	.587
	Charlotte∞	.500		Birmingham∞	.476		Carolina	.529
1981—	Nashville	.566	1988—	Greenville	.604	1995—	Carolina∞	.618
	Orlando∞	.556		Chattanooga∞	.566		Chattanooga	.580
1982—	Jacksonville	.576	1989—	Birmingham∞	.615	1996—	Chattanooga	.579
	Nashville∞	.535		Greenville	.504		Jacksonville∞	.543
1983—	Birmingham∞	.628	1990—	Orlando	.590	1997—	Huntsville	.554
	Jacksonville	.531		Memphis∞	.507		Greenville∞	.529

*Won split season playoff. †Won four-club playoff. ‡Won championship and four-club playoff. §League was divided into Eastern and Western divisions; won playoff. ∞League was divided into Eastern and Western divisions and played split season; won playoff.

CLASS AA *Southern League*

TEXAS LEAGUE

TEAMS

ARKANSAS TRAVELERS

General manager
Bill Valentine

Manager
Chris Maloney

Ballpark (capacity, surface)
Ray Winder Field (6,089, grass)

Affiliation
Cardinals

Address
P.O. Box 55066
Little Rock, AR 72215

Phone
501-664-1555

EL PASO DIABLOS

Associate general managers
Andrew Wheeler, Rob Sesish

Manager
Ed Romero

Ballpark (capacity, surface)
Cohen Stadium (9,765, grass)

Affiliation
Brewers

Address
P.O. Drawer 4797
El Paso, TX 79914

Phone
915-755-2000

JACKSON GENERALS

General manager
Bill Blackwell

Manager
Jim Pankovits

Ballpark (capacity, surface)
Smith-Wills Stadium (5,200, grass)

Affiliation
Astros

Address
P.O. Box 4209
Jackson, MS 39296

Phone
601-981-4664

MIDLAND ANGELS

General manager
Monty Hoppel

Manager
Don Long

Ballpark (capacity, surface)
Christensen Stadium (5,000, grass)

Affiliation
Angels

Address
P.O. Box 51187
Midland, TX 79710

Phone
915-683-4251

SAN ANTONIO MISSIONS

General manager
Dave Oldham

Manager
Ron Roenicke

Ballpark (capacity, surface)
Nelson Wolf Stadium (6,300, grass)

Affiliation
Dodgers

Address
5757 Highway 90 West
San Antonio, TX 78227

Phone
210-675-7275

SHREVEPORT CAPTAINS

General manager
Daniel Robinson

Manager
Mike Hart

Ballpark (capacity, surface)
Fair Grounds Field (6,200, grass)

Affiliation
Giants

Address
P.O. Box 3448
Shreveport, LA 71133

Phone
318-636-5555

TULSA DRILLERS

Executive v.p./general manager
Chuck Lamson

Manager
Bobby Jones

Ballpark (capacity, surface)
Drillers Stadium (11,000, grass)

Affiliation
Rangers

Address
P.O. Box 4448
Tulsa, OK 74159

Phone
918-744-5998

WICHITA WRANGLERS

General manager
Lance Deckinger

Manager
John Mizerock

Ballpark (capacity, surface)
Lawrence-Dumont Stadium (6,067, artificial infield, grass outfield)

Affiliation
Royals

Address
P.O. Box 1420
Wichita, KS 67201

Phone
316-267-3372

1997 FINAL STANDINGS

FIRST HALF

EAST DIVISION

Team	W	L	T	Pct.	GB
Shreveport (Giants)	37	30	0	.552	....
Arkansas (Cardinals)	37	31	0	.544	1/2
Jackson (Astros)	32	36	0	.471	5 1/2
Tulsa (Rangers)	23	44	0	.343	14

WEST DIVISION

Team	W	L	T	Pct.	GB
San Antonio (Dodgers)	44	23	0	.657	....
El Paso (Brewers)	35	33	0	.515	9 1/2
Midland (Angels)	32	35	0	.478	12
Wichita (Royals)	30	38	0	.441	14 1/2

SECOND HALF

EAST DIVISION

Team	W	L	T	Pct.	GB
Shreveport (Giants)	39	32	0	.549	....
Tulsa (Rangers)	38	34	0	.528	1 1/2
Jackson (Astros)	34	37	0	.479	5
Arkansas (Cardinals)	31	41	0	.431	8 1/2

WEST DIVISION

Team	W	L	T	Pct.	GB
San Antonio (Dodgers)	40	32	0	.556	....
El Paso (Brewers)	39	33	0	.542	1
Wichita (Royals)	34	38	0	.472	6
Midland (Angels)	32	40	0	.444	8

CLASS AA *Texas League*

COMPOSITE

Team	S.A.	Shr.	E.P.	Ark.	Jac.	Mid.	Wch.	Tul.	W	L	T	Pct.	G.B.
San Antonio (Dodgers)	....	4	16	8	7	19	22	8	84	55	0	.604	....
Shreveport (Giants)	6	....	7	19	15	7	5	17	76	62	0	.551	7½
El Paso (Brewers)	16	5	....	6	6	17	18	6	74	66	0	.529	10½
Arkansas (Cardinals)	4	13	4	....	17	6	4	20	68	72	0	.486	16½
Jackson (Astros)	5	16	4	15	....	4	5	17	66	73	0	.475	18
Midland (Angels)	12	5	15	4	6	....	19	3	64	75	0	.460	20
Wichita (Royals)	10	5	14	8	7	13	....	7	64	76	0	.457	20½
Tulsa (Rangers)	2	14	6	12	15	9	3	....	61	78	0	.439	23

Arkansas' home games played in Little Rock, Ark.

Major league affiliations in parentheses.

PLAYOFFS: San Antonio defeated Shreveport, four games to three, to win league championship.

REGULAR-SEASON ATTENDANCE: Arkansas, 195,935; El Paso, 302,894; Jackson, 160,587; Midland, 185,532; San Antonio, 336,542; Shreveport, 164,922; Tulsa, 333,019; Wichita, 151,205. Total—1,830,636. Playoffs (7 games)—20,941. Class AA All-Star Game at San Antonio—7,114.

MANAGERS: Arkansas, Rick Mahler; El Paso, Dave Machemer; Jackson, Gary Allenson; Midland, Mitch Seoane; San Antonio, Ron Roenicke; Shreveport, Carlos Lezcano; Tulsa, Bobby Jones; Wichita, Ron Johnson.

ALL-STAR TEAM: 1B—Daryle Ward, Jackson; 2B—Placido Polanco, Arkansas; 3B—Mike Kinkade, El Paso; Fernando Tatis, Tulsa; SS—Danny Klassen, El Paso; OF—Kevin Gibbs, San Antonio; Scott Krause, El Paso; Kerry Robinson, Arkansas; Keith Williams, Shreveport; C—Paul LoDuca, San Antonio; DH—Dan Collier, Jackson; Starting Pitcher—Troy Brohawn, Shreveport; Enrique Calero, Wichita; Scott Elarton, Jackson; Travis Smith, El Paso; Scott Woodard, El Paso; Relief Pitcher—Bob Howry, Shreveport; Player of the Year—Mike Kinkade, El Paso; Pitcher of the Year—Steve Woodard, El Paso; Manager of the Year—Ron Roenicke, San Antonio.

1997 BATTING

TEAM

Team	Avg.	G	TPA	AB	R	H	TB	2B	3B	HR	RBI	SH	SF	HP	BB	IBB	SO	SB	CS	GDP	LOB	ShO	Slg.	OBP
El Paso	.309	140	5406	4822	851	1489	2274	300	76	111	777	46	56	72	410	10	881	139	59	117	987	6	.472	.368
San Antonio	.283	139	5160	4548	736	1289	1947	245	49	105	679	59	41	60	452	20	773	161	85	103	913	7	.428	.353
Midland	.282	139	5346	4687	792	1324	2127	315	43	134	728	49	39	56	515	13	841	70	60	112	966	7	.454	.358
Shreveport	.278	138	5253	4610	735	1282	1958	249	47	111	673	44	50	31	518	20	821	133	54	112	971	6	.425	.352
Wichita	.275	140	5269	4658	723	1282	1897	240	21	111	665	37	51	58	465	14	824	121	70	108	954	4	.407	.345
Arkansas	.271	140	5141	4565	643	1238	1699	208	35	61	581	62	38	29	447	14	753	111	79	106	941	4	.372	.337
Tulsa	.268	139	5259	4619	712	1237	2004	272	24	149	652	22	33	53	532	19	1025	66	49	99	1003	6	.434	.348
Jackson	.266	139	5210	4583	638	1220	1802	210	18	112	586	63	30	46	488	20	844	85	59	107	954	4	.393	.341

INDIVIDUAL

TOP QUALIFIERS FOR BATTING CHAMPIONSHIP

Minimum 367 plate appearances. *Lefthanded batter. †Switch-hitter.

Player, Team	Avg.	G	TPA	AB	R	H	TB	2B	3B	HR	RBI	SH	SF	HP	BB	IBB	SO	SB	CS	GDP	Slg.	OBP
Kinkade, Mike, El Paso	.385	125	540	468	112	180	275	35	12	12	109	1	6	13	52	0	66	17	4	13	.588	.455
Krause, Scott, El Paso	.361	125	512	474	97	171	274	33	11	16	88	4	7	7	20	3	108	13	4	7	.578	.390
Gibbs, Kevin, San Antonio†	.335	101	445	358	89	120	159	21	6	2	34	6	3	6	72	3	48	49	19	3	.444	.451
Klassen, Danny, El Paso	.331	135	585	519	112	172	256	30	6	14	81	4	4	10	48	1	104	16	9	13	.493	.396
Burke, Jamie, Midland	.329	116	479	428	77	141	209	44	3	6	72	0	3	8	40	0	46	2	3	12	.488	.395
Ward, Daryle, Jackson*	.329	114	472	422	72	139	221	25	0	19	90	0	1	3	46	4	68	4	2	12	.524	.398
Guiel, Aaron, Midland*	.329	116	501	419	91	138	255	37	7	22	85	2	3	18	59	3	94	14	10	9	.609	.431
LoDuca, Paul, San Antonio	.327	105	443	385	63	126	179	28	2	7	69	4	5	3	46	3	27	16	8	17	.465	.399
Mendez, Carlos, Wichita	.325	129	536	507	72	165	235	32	1	12	90	0	8	1	19	2	43	4	7	19	.464	.346
Roberge, J.P., San Antonio	.322	134	569	516	94	166	251	26	4	17	105	2	5	7	39	3	70	18	9	13	.486	.374
Robinson, Kerry, Arkansas*	.321	135	586	523	80	168	196	16	3	2	62	5	2	2	54	1	64	40	23	7	.375	.386
Williams, Keith, Shreveport	.320	131	549	493	83	158	275	37	7	22	106	0	7	3	46	3	94	3	0	12	.558	.377
Martinez, Ramon, Shreveport	.319	105	454	404	72	129	184	32	4	5	54	4	3	3	40	1	48	4	5	6	.455	.382
Singleton, Christopher, Shr.*	.317	126	500	464	85	147	220	26	10	9	61	2	9	1	22	4	50	27	11	7	.474	.343
Nicholas, Darrell, El Paso	.315	127	556	518	79	163	262	47	5	14	68	6	3	2	27	1	116	17	6	14	.506	.349

DEPARTMENTAL LEADERS: G—Vessel, 138; AB—K. Robinson, 523; R—Kinkade, Klassen, 112 each; H—Kinkade, 180; TB—K. Williams, 275 each; 2B—Nicholas, 47; 3B—B. Richardson, 13; HR—Collier, 26; RBI—Kinkade, 109; SH—Mitchell, 12; SF—C. Singleton, 9; HP—Guiel, 18; BB—Simonton, 81; IBB—Several players tied with 4 each; SO—Herrick, 141; SB—Murray, 52; CS—K. Robinson, 23; GIDP—Ordaz, 19; Slg.—Guiel, .609; OBP—Kinkade, .455.

ALL PLAYERS

*Lefthanded batter. †Switch-hitter.

Player, Team	Avg.	G	TPA	AB	R	H	TB	2B	3B	HR	RBI	SH	SF	HP	BB	IBB	SO	SB	CS	GDP	Slg.	OBP
Abreu, Bob, Jackson*	.167	3	13	12	2	2	3	1	0	0	0	0	0	0	1	0	5	0	0	0	.250	.231
Ahearne, Pat, San Antonio	.000	14	9	5	0	0	0	0	0	0	0	4	0	0	0	0	1	0	0	0	.000	.000
Almond, Greg, Arkansas†	.203	69	194	158	23	32	38	4	1	0	16	4	2	1	29	1	38	0	0	2	.241	.326
Anderson, Mike, San Antonio	1.000	19	1	1	0	1	1	0	0	0	0	0	0	0	0	0	0	0	0	0	1.000	1.000
Andreopoulos, Alex, El Paso*	.154	7	27	26	1	4	5	1	0	0	3	0	0	0	1	0	2	0	0	1	.192	.185
Barcelo, Lorenzo, Shreveport	.000	5	2	2	0	0	0	0	0	0	0	0	0	0	0	0	2	0	0	0	.000	.000
Barker, Kevin, El Paso*	.277	65	273	238	37	66	123	15	6	10	63	0	5	2	28	0	40	3	3	5	.517	.352
Barkett, Andy, Tulsa*	.299	130	542	471	82	141	215	34	8	6	65	1	2	5	63	2	86	1	3	15	.456	.386
Battle, Howard, San Antonio	.242	16	36	33	2	8	9	1	0	1	1	0	0	2	0	0	7	0	0	0	.273	.289
Bell, David, Arkansas	.219	9	34	32	3	7	12	2	0	1	3	0	0	0	2	0	2	1	0	1	.375	.265
Bell, Mike, Tulsa	.285	33	146	123	17	35	70	11	0	8	23	2	2	4	15	0	28	0	0	1	.569	.375
Bess, Johnny, Shreveport†	.143	12	32	28	1	4	7	3	0	0	6	0	0	1	3	0	9	0	0	1	.250	.250
Betten, Randy, Midland	.291	57	248	220	39	64	92	13	3	3	24	4	1	1	22	0	45	7	3	5	.418	.357

Player, Team	Avg.	G	TPA	AB	R	H	TB	2B	3B	HR	RBI	SH	SF	HP	BB	IBB	SO	SB	CS	GDP	Slg.	OBP
Bilderback, Ty, Midland*	.227	21	72	66	7	15	20	5	0	0	5	0	0	0	6	1	17	1	3	2	.303	.292
Blair, Brian, Tulsa*	.262	86	314	260	46	68	95	9	3	4	28	1	3	1	49	2	64	11	2	4	.365	.377
Blanco, Alberto, Jackson*	.250	1	4	4	1	1	2	1	0	0	0	0	0	0	0	0	1	0	0	0	.500	.250
Blood, Darin, Shreveport†	.211	27	28	19	4	4	9	2	0	1	5	5	0	0	4	0	5	0	0	1	.474	.348
Bokemeier, Matt, Tulsa†	.231	105	437	394	51	91	130	18	3	5	43	3	3	0	37	2	73	1	6	7	.330	.295
Bolick, Frank, Midland†	.330	28	124	97	26	32	63	5	1	8	27	0	0	1	26	0	18	0	0	1	.649	.476
Brohawn, Troy, Shreveport*	.148	27	33	27	4	4	8	1	0	1	3	4	1	0	1	0	7	0	0	1	.296	.172
Brooks, Rayme, Wichita	.229	56	164	140	19	32	49	5	0	4	16	0	1	4	19	0	45	2	2	2	.350	.335
Brown, Alvin, San Antonio	.000	16	4	3	0	0	0	0	0	0	0	1	0	0	0	0	3	0	0	0	.000	.000
Brunson, William, San Ant.*	.000	17	5	4	0	0	0	0	0	0	0	1	0	0	0	0	2	0	0	0	.000	.000
Burke, Jamie, Midland	.329	116	479	428	77	141	209	44	3	6	72	0	3	8	40	0	46	2	3	12	.488	.395
Burton, Essex, Tulsa	.206	17	67	63	8	13	17	2	1	0	2	0	0	1	3	0	7	3	2	4	.270	.254
Buxbaum, Danny, Midland	.288	130	570	514	78	148	224	42	2	10	70	0	3	2	51	3	91	1	1	9	.436	.353
Byington, Jimmie, Wichita	.235	92	220	196	30	46	60	8	0	2	16	3	2	4	15	0	39	5	6	3	.306	.300
Canizaro, Jay, Shreveport	.256	50	206	176	36	45	87	9	0	11	38	0	2	2	26	0	44	2	2	4	.494	.354
Carr, Jeremy, Wichita	.306	91	403	340	76	104	149	19	1	8	40	3	1	9	50	1	53	39	8	4	.438	.408
Carter, Cale, Midland*	.167	7	27	24	3	4	4	0	0	0	2	0	0	0	3	0	7	1	0	0	.167	.259
Carter, Mike, Midland	.277	15	68	65	9	18	23	3	1	0	2	1	0	0	2	0	8	5	2	1	.354	.299
Cedeno, Domingo, Tulsa†	.444	2	9	9	0	4	6	0	1	0	0	0	0	0	0	0	3	0	0	0	.667	.444
Charles, Frank, Tulsa	.230	95	364	335	38	77	126	18	2	9	49	1	1	3	24	1	81	2	2	9	.376	.287
Chavarria, David, Arkansas*	.200	28	9	5	1	1	2	1	0	0	1	4	0	0	0	0	1	0	0	0	.400	.200
Christopherson, Eric, Tulsa	.244	39	151	123	26	30	57	9	0	6	34	0	3	0	25	0	22	1	1	4	.463	.364
Collier, Dan, Tulsa	.257	115	451	389	60	100	198	20	0	26	79	1	3	14	44	1	134	1	2	3	.509	.351
Cooney, Kyle, San Antonio	.290	72	275	252	39	73	117	16	2	8	49	1	2	13	7	0	44	4	2	5	.464	.339
Cora, Alex, San Antonio*	.234	127	484	448	52	105	142	20	4	3	48	7	1	3	25	4	60	12	9	17	.317	.279
Corps, Edwin, Shreveport	1.000	43	4	3	1	3	3	0	0	0	0	0	0	0	1	0	0	0	0	0	1.000	1.000
Cossins, Tim, Tulsa	.296	36	120	108	11	32	51	5	1	4	17	2	2	0	8	0	24	2	0	1	.472	.339
Coughlin, Kevin, Arkansas*	.300	26	101	90	15	27	38	6	1	1	8	0	1	1	9	0	12	0	0	3	.422	.356
Creek, Ryan, Jackson	.000	19	20	18	1	0	0	0	0	0	0	2	0	0	0	0	7	0	0	1	.000	.000
Croushore, Rick, Arkansas	.143	17	19	14	1	2	3	1	0	0	2	2	0	0	3	0	5	0	0	1	.214	.294
Dalton, Dee, Arkansas	.228	116	408	360	52	82	110	16	0	4	43	2	5	3	38	0	66	2	5	10	.306	.303
Dalton, Jed, Midland	.225	94	405	360	63	81	136	18	2	11	48	4	1	5	35	0	58	7	12	6	.378	.302
Davalillo, David, Midland	.250	49	188	176	21	44	57	6	2	1	12	6	0	0	6	0	26	1	2	8	.324	.275
Davis, Eddie, San Antonio	.209	74	230	206	30	43	88	8	2	11	34	5	1	3	15	0	69	2	3	8	.427	.271
Dawsey, Jason, El Paso*	.000	11	0	0	1	0	0	0	0	0	0	0	0	0	0	0	0	0	0	0	.000	.000
DeBerry, Joe, Wichita*	.244	30	93	82	9	20	28	5	0	1	5	0	0	1	10	3	20	3	0	0	.341	.333
Detmers, Kris, Arkansas†	.000	15	15	13	1	0	0	0	0	0	0	1	0	0	1	0	10	0	0	0	.000	.071
Diaz, Edwin, Tulsa	.275	105	485	440	65	121	199	31	1	15	46	2	2	8	33	0	102	6	9	6	.452	.335
Diaz, Freddie, Midland†	.267	43	158	135	21	36	51	9	0	2	18	2	2	1	18	0	30	0	3	3	.378	.353
Diaz, Lino, Wichita	.284	92	326	289	36	82	120	26	3	2	51	3	3	7	23	0	27	3	6	7	.415	.348
Difelice, Mike, Arkansas	.333	1	4	3	0	1	2	1	0	0	0	0	0	0	0	0	0	0	0	0	.667	.500
Dobrolsky, Bill, El Paso	.264	102	357	303	44	80	118	23	0	5	45	6	2	8	38	0	63	1	3	7	.389	.359
Durkin, Chris, San Antonio*	.272	38	141	125	18	34	57	11	0	4	18	1	1	1	13	0	33	8	2	1	.456	.343
Elarton, Scott, Jackson	.273	20	24	22	3	6	10	1	0	1	1	2	0	0	0	0	1	0	0	0	.455	.273
Fasano, Sal, Wichita	.237	40	161	131	27	31	75	5	0	13	27	0	3	7	20	0	35	0	2	2	.573	.360
Felix, Lauro, El Paso	.258	49	157	128	27	33	49	9	2	1	17	2	3	4	20	0	24	1	2	6	.383	.368
Fick, Chris, Shreveport*	.000	4	6	5	1	0	0	0	0	0	0	0	0	0	1	0	4	0	0	0	.000	.167
Flora, Kevin, Jackson	.000	1	5	5	0	0	0	0	0	0	0	0	0	0	0	0	3	0	0	0	.000	.000
Flores, Ignacio, San Antonio	.000	27	15	14	0	0	0	0	0	0	0	0	0	0	0	0	8	0	0	0	.000	.000
Fontenot, Joe, Shreveport	.100	26	33	30	1	3	3	0	0	0	1	0	0	0	2	0	11	0	0	0	.100	.156
Forkner, Tim, Jackson*	.261	116	467	398	52	104	150	23	1	7	46	1	5	2	60	1	68	4	0	14	.377	.357
Frontera, Chad, Shreveport	.000	15	17	16	1	0	0	0	0	0	0	0	0	0	0	0	3	0	0	1	.000	.059
Fultz, Aaron, Shreveport*	.000	49	3	3	0	0	0	0	0	0	0	0	0	0	0	0	1	0	0	0	.000	.000
Garcia, Frank, Arkansas	.333	28	3	3	1	1	4	0	0	1	1	0	0	0	0	0	1	0	0	0	1.333	.333
Giambi, Jeremy, Wichita*	.321	74	322	268	50	86	136	15	1	11	52	0	4	6	44	3	47	4	4	7	.507	.422
Gibbs, Kevin, San Antonio†	.335	101	445	358	89	120	159	21	6	2	34	6	3	6	72	3	48	49	19	3	.444	.451
Gonzalez, Jimmy, Jackson	.254	97	390	342	49	87	147	18	0	14	58	0	3	8	37	1	91	2	1	8	.430	.338
Gonzalez, Raul, Wichita	.285	129	501	452	66	129	206	30	4	13	74	3	8	2	36	0	52	12	8	12	.456	.335
Gorecki, Rick, San Antonio	.000	7	8	7	0	0	0	0	0	0	0	1	0	0	0	0	5	0	0	0	.000	.125
Green, Scarborough, Ark.†	.307	76	293	251	45	77	105	14	4	2	29	3	1	2	36	4	48	11	5	2	.418	.397
Groppuso, Mike, El Paso	.345	29	99	87	15	30	64	6	2	8	23	0	1	1	10	1	19	1	1	4	.736	.404
Grzanich, Mike, Jackson	.214	38	16	14	1	3	3	0	0	0	1	2	0	0	0	0	6	0	0	0	.214	.214
Guiel, Aaron, Midland*	.329	116	501	419	91	138	255	37	7	22	85	2	3	18	59	3	94	14	10	9	.609	.431
Guillen, Carlos, Jackson†	.254	115	436	390	47	99	147	16	1	10	39	4	2	2	38	1	78	6	5	9	.377	.322
Gutierrez, Jim, Jackson	.143	52	9	7	0	1	1	0	0	0	0	2	0	0	0	0	5	0	0	1	.143	.143
Guzman, Edwards, Shr.*	.284	118	422	380	52	108	140	15	4	3	42	5	3	1	33	4	57	3	1	6	.368	.341
Haas, David, Jackson	1.000	13	2	1	0	1	2	1	0	0	2	1	0	0	0	0	0	0	0	0	2.000	1.000
Harkrider, Timothy, Midland†	.287	69	284	251	39	72	93	12	3	1	24	7	4	0	22	0	17	1	2	7	.371	.339
Hartvigson, Chad, Shr.*	.000	4	1	1	0	0	0	0	0	0	0	0	0	0	0	0	0	0	0	0	.000	.000
Hatcher, Chris, Wichita	.262	11	47	42	7	11	26	0	0	5	7	0	0	1	4	0	16	1	0	0	.619	.340
Heiserman, Rick, Arkansas	.118	34	19	17	0	2	2	0	0	0	1	2	0	0	0	0	6	0	0	0	.118	.118
Hemphill, Bret, Midland†	.308	78	325	266	46	82	131	15	2	10	63	1	5	6	47	2	56	0	2	6	.492	.417
Hernandez, Carlos, Jackson	.292	92	409	363	62	106	132	12	1	4	33	6	3	4	33	2	59	17	8	10	.364	.355
Hernandez, Santos, Shr.	.000	11	1	1	0	0	0	0	0	0	0	0	0	0	0	0	0	0	0	0	.000	.000
Herrick, Jason, Midland*	.252	118	460	416	60	105	200	27	4	20	67	6	2	2	34	3	141	9	6	7	.481	.311
Howry, Bob, Shreveport*	.000	48	2	1	0	0	0	0	0	0	0	0	0	0	0	0	0	0	0	0	.000	.000
Iglesias, Mike, San Antonio	.000	42	1	1	0	0	0	0	0	0	0	0	0	0	0	0	1	0	0	0	.000	.000
Ingram, Garey, San Antonio	.299	92	392	348	68	104	182	28	7	12	52	1	2	4	37	1	50	16	6	5	.523	.371
Jarvis, Matt, Arkansas	.333	50	6	6	1	2	3	1	0	0	0	0	0	0	0	0	3	0	0	0	.500	.333
Johnson, Jack, Midland	.200	5	16	15	2	3	8	2	0	1	3	0	0	0	1	0	4	0	0	0	.533	.250
Johnson, Keith, San Antonio	.268	96	330	298	43	80	122	9	3	9	52	8	3	4	17	0	48	7	6	4	.409	.314
Judd, Mike, San Antonio	.000	12	9	8	0	0	0	0	0	0	0	0	0	0	1	0	2	0	0	0	.000	.111
Kennedy, Darryl, Shreveport	.268	22	77	71	11	19	29	4	0	2	10	0	0	0	6	1	8	0	0	2	.408	.325

Player, Team	Avg.	G	TPA	AB	R	H	TB	2B	3B	HR	RBI	SH	SF	HP	BB	IBB	SO	SB	CS	GDP	Slg.	OBP
Kester, Tim, Jackson	.000	47	5	3	1	0	0	0	0	0	0	1	0	0	1	0	1	0	0	0	.000	.250
King, Brett, Shreveport	.216	79	227	194	28	42	68	6	1	6	20	1	1	1	30	1	55	4	5	3	.351	.323
King, Cesar, Tulsa	.356	14	50	45	6	16	20	1	0	1	8	0	0	0	5	0	3	0	1	2	.444	.420
King, Curt, Arkansas	.000	32	1	1	0	0	0	0	0	0	0	0	0	0	0	0	0	0	0	0	.000	.000
Kinkade, Mike, El Paso	.385	125	540	468	112	180	275	35	12	12	109	1	6	13	52	0	66	17	4	13	.588	.455
Kirkpatrick, Jay, San Ant.*	.260	62	223	215	22	56	89	9	0	8	42	0	0	0	8	0	53	0	1	5	.414	.287
Klassen, Danny, El Paso	.331	135	585	519	112	172	256	30	6	14	81	4	4	10	48	1	104	16	9	13	.493	.396
Kleiner, Stacy, Arkansas	.255	16	57	55	7	14	25	4	2	1	10	0	0	0	2	0	14	0	0	2	.455	.281
Krause, Scott, El Paso	.361	125	512	474	97	171	274	33	11	16	88	4	7	7	20	3	108	13	4	7	.578	.390
Kubenka, Jeff, San Antonio	.000	19	1	1	0	0	0	0	0	0	0	0	0	0	0	0	1	0	0	0	.000	.000
Lagarde, Joe, San Antonio	.500	53	2	2	0	1	1	0	0	0	0	0	0	0	0	0	0	0	0	0	.500	.500
Landry, Todd, El Paso	.315	106	377	346	43	109	160	24	3	7	69	2	8	6	15	1	52	5	5	16	.462	.347
LaRiviere, Jason, Arkansas	.274	118	412	372	50	102	154	24	5	6	60	3	4	0	33	1	69	4	3	16	.414	.330
Lock, Dan, Jackson	.250	35	6	4	1	1	2	1	0	0	2	0	0	0	2	0	2	0	0	0	.500	.500
LoDuca, Paul, San Antonio	.327	105	443	385	63	126	179	28	2	7	69	4	5	3	46	3	27	16	8	17	.465	.399
Logan, Marcus, Arkansas	.281	27	35	32	3	9	10	1	0	0	6	2	0	0	1	0	11	0	0	1	.313	.303
Looper, Braden, Arkansas	.000	19	1	0	0	0	0	0	0	0	0	0	0	0	1	0	0	0	0	0	.000	1.000
Lopez, Johann, Jackson	.111	35	21	18	1	2	2	0	0	0	1	3	0	0	0	0	4	0	0	0	.111	.111
Lopez, Mendy, Wichita	.232	101	406	357	56	83	120	16	3	5	42	5	5	3	36	0	70	7	5	8	.336	.304
Lopez, Mickey, El Paso†	.300	134	550	483	79	145	195	21	10	3	58	9	5	5	48	2	60	20	10	10	.404	.366
Lopez, Pedro, Jackson	.295	27	93	88	9	26	37	5	0	2	13	0	0	1	4	0	16	0	1	2	.420	.333
Lovingier, Kevin, Arkansas*	.000	59	3	2	0	0	0	0	0	0	0	1	0	0	0	0	1	0	0	1	.000	.000
Luuloa, Keith, Midland	.273	120	478	421	67	115	181	29	5	9	59	10	6	5	36	0	59	7	4	18	.430	.333
Martin, Jeff, Shreveport	.000	26	2	2	0	0	0	0	0	0	0	0	0	0	0	0	2	0	0	0	.000	.000
Martin, Jim, Jackson*	.274	39	139	117	15	32	59	4	1	7	22	0	1	5	16	0	42	8	4	0	.504	.381
Martinez, Greg, El Paso†	.291	95	427	381	75	111	144	10	10	1	29	9	2	3	32	0	55	39	7	5	.378	.349
Martinez, Ramon, Shreveport	.319	105	454	404	72	129	184	32	4	5	54	4	3	3	40	1	48	4	5	6	.455	.382
Matvey, Mike, Arkansas	.221	57	161	136	16	30	37	4	0	1	9	3	1	0	21	0	33	1	1	3	.272	.323
Mayes, Craig, Shreveport*	.273	86	311	293	27	80	104	8	5	2	38	0	3	1	14	1	29	1	0	17	.355	.305
McDonald, Keith, Arkansas	.240	79	268	233	32	56	87	16	0	5	30	1	0	3	31	0	56	0	1	6	.373	.337
McEwing, Joe, Arkansas	.259	103	292	263	33	68	92	6	3	4	35	3	2	1	19	4	39	2	4	6	.350	.309
McNabb, Buck, Jackson*	.258	112	448	395	65	102	125	16	2	1	30	7	0	4	42	0	58	10	9	11	.316	.336
McNally, Sean, Wichita	.245	18	64	53	9	13	17	4	0	0	2	0	0	0	11	0	12	1	2	2	.321	.375
Medrano, Tony, Wichita	.246	108	389	349	45	86	109	9	1	4	42	9	4	1	26	1	32	8	2	10	.312	.297
Melendez, Dan, San Antonio*	.256	87	310	258	40	66	93	19	1	2	24	4	3	1	44	2	42	4	2	3	.360	.363
Meluskey, Mitch, Jackson†	.340	73	278	241	49	82	142	18	0	14	46	0	3	3	31	4	39	1	3	7	.589	.417
Mendez, Carlos, Wichita	.325	129	536	507	72	165	235	32	1	12	90	0	8	1	19	2	43	4	7	19	.464	.346
Merchant, Mark, Wichita†	.340	49	174	147	27	50	86	9	0	9	38	0	2	2	23	0	35	0	1	3	.585	.431
Miller, Ryan, Jackson	.200	20	62	55	6	11	18	0	2	1	8	1	1	0	5	0	10	1	0	1	.327	.262
Mitchell, Donovan, Jackson*	.256	128	553	477	64	122	166	17	6	5	44	12	0	3	61	4	48	22	11	9	.348	.344
Mlicki, Doug, Jackson	.600	9	6	5	1	3	3	0	0	0	0	1	0	0	0	0	0	0	0	0	.600	.600
Molina, Ben, Midland	.330	29	118	106	18	35	61	8	0	6	30	0	2	0	10	0	7	0	0	2	.575	.381
Morillo, Cesar, Tulsa†	.264	84	321	288	38	76	99	18	1	1	23	4	1	0	28	2	53	0	4	3	.344	.328
Mounce, Tony, Jackson*	.043	25	28	23	0	1	1	0	0	0	0	4	0	0	1	0	12	0	0	0	.043	.083
Munoz, Juan, Arkansas*	.279	58	235	215	28	60	91	9	2	6	31	2	1	1	16	0	26	6	10	2	.423	.330
Murphy, Mike, Tulsa	.256	46	195	156	30	40	64	10	1	4	19	0	0	4	35	0	45	6	3	3	.410	.405
Murray, Calvin, Shreveport	.272	122	492	419	83	114	175	25	3	10	56	1	2	4	66	0	73	52	6	7	.418	.375
Myers, Rod, Wichita*	.313	4	19	16	3	5	7	2	0	0	3	0	0	0	3	0	3	0	1	0	.438	.421
Newson, Warren, Tulsa*	.143	2	9	7	1	1	4	0	0	1	2	0	0	0	2	0	1	0	0	0	.571	.333
Nicholas, Darrell, El Paso	.315	127	556	518	79	163	262	47	5	14	68	6	3	2	27	1	116	17	6	14	.506	.349
Norton, Chris, Midland	.265	58	237	200	40	53	111	8	1	16	47	0	2	0	35	0	57	2	1	8	.555	.371
Nunez, Sergio, Wichita	.277	34	144	137	18	38	44	1	1	1	11	1	0	0	6	0	17	12	3	3	.321	.308
O'Neal, Troy, El Paso	.287	40	132	122	18	35	39	1	0	1	11	1	1	4	4	0	29	0	0	3	.320	.328
O'Neill, Doug, Tulsa	.277	118	470	412	69	114	195	21	0	20	64	1	4	4	49	2	122	12	4	4	.473	.356
Ordaz, Luis, Arkansas	.287	115	427	390	44	112	156	20	6	4	58	7	6	2	22	1	39	11	10	19	.400	.324
Oropesa, Eddie, Shreveport*	.211	43	21	19	1	4	4	0	0	0	1	1	0	0	1	0	8	0	0	0	.211	.250
Ortiz, Hector, Wichita	.250	59	209	180	20	45	51	3	0	1	25	4	2	2	21	0	15	1	2	10	.283	.332
Ortiz, Russ, Shreveport	.000	12	9	6	0	0	0	0	0	0	0	2	0	0	1	0	4	0	0	0	.000	.143
Ozorio, Yudith, Arkansas†	.208	84	158	144	23	30	34	2	1	0	9	2	0	0	12	0	44	6	2	0	.236	.269
Pagnozzi, Tom, Arkansas	.317	21	68	63	8	20	35	0	0	5	17	0	1	0	4	0	8	0	0	0	.556	.353
Pecorilli, Aldo, Arkansas	.360	31	124	111	21	40	62	10	0	4	22	0	4	2	7	0	15	2	3	2	.559	.395
Pellow, Kit, Wichita	.249	68	269	241	40	60	104	12	1	10	41	2	3	2	21	1	72	5	2	5	.432	.311
Perez, Jhonny, Jackson	.253	48	171	154	16	39	55	7	0	3	17	1	0	1	12	0	26	4	3	2	.357	.311
Perez, Richard, El Paso	.300	14	35	30	5	9	13	2	1	0	4	0	0	0	5	0	1	0	0	2	.433	.400
Peterson, Nate, Jackson*	.301	49	164	143	19	43	66	11	0	4	24	1	1	2	17	0	21	2	2	3	.462	.380
Phillips, Randy, Shreveport	.000	11	2	1	0	0	0	0	0	0	0	1	0	0	0	0	0	0	0	0	.000	.000
Pledger, Kinnis, Wichita*	.081	12	42	37	3	3	6	1	1	0	0	0	0	0	5	0	14	0	0	0	.162	.190
Polanco, Placido, Arkansas	.291	129	549	508	71	148	176	16	3	2	51	6	3	3	29	1	51	19	5	11	.346	.331
Politte, Cliff, Arkansas	.000	6	9	8	0	0	0	0	0	0	0	0	0	0	1	0	3	0	0	0	.000	.111
Pote, Lou, Arkansas	.333	7	4	3	0	1	1	0	0	0	0	1	0	0	0	0	0	0	0	0	.333	.333
Probst, Alan, Jackson	.333	8	27	24	2	8	13	2	0	1	7	0	0	0	3	0	7	0	0	0	.542	.407
Quinn, Mark, Wichita	.375	26	114	96	26	36	55	13	0	2	19	0	0	3	15	0	19	1	1	2	.573	.474
Ramirez, Peto, Shreveport	.177	41	122	113	8	20	29	6	0	1	9	0	1	1	7	2	37	0	0	4	.257	.230
Ramos, Edgar, Jackson	.200	4	5	5	0	1	2	1	0	0	0	0	0	0	0	0	1	0	0	0	.400	.200
Rennhack, Mike, El Paso†	.276	106	417	369	59	102	171	28	7	9	64	2	6	2	38	1	81	4	3	5	.463	.342
Reyes, Dennis, San Antonio*	.000	12	7	6	1	0	0	0	0	0	0	0	0	0	1	0	2	0	0	0	.000	.143
Richard, Chris, Arkansas*	.269	113	458	390	62	105	168	24	3	11	58	0	3	5	60	1	59	6	4	8	.431	.371
Richards, Rowan, Tulsa	.286	11	41	35	5	10	11	1	0	0	5	0	0	0	5	0	9	0	0	3	.314	.375
Richardson, Brian, San Ant.	.297	134	545	488	73	145	233	23	13	13	90	2	5	8	42	0	99	3	6	13	.477	.359
Richardson, Scott, San Ant.	.283	91	352	300	49	85	123	15	1	7	38	1	3	2	46	4	52	6	5	6	.410	.379
Rios, Armando, Shreveport*	.289	127	534	461	86	133	217	30	6	14	79	4	6	0	63	1	85	17	7	11	.471	.370
Roach, Petie, San Antonio*	.000	13	5	5	0	0	0	0	0	0	0	0	0	0	0	0	1	0	0	0	.000	.000
Roberge, J.P., San Antonio	.322	134	569	516	94	166	251	26	4	17	105	2	5	7	39	3	70	18	9	13	.486	.374

Player, Team	Avg.	G	TPA	AB	R	H	TB	2B	3B	HR	RBI	SH	SF	HP	BB	IBB	SO	SB	CS	GDP	Slg.	OBP
Robinson, Hassan, Jackson	.174	9	24	23	3	4	5	1	0	0	1	0	1	0	0	0	2	0	0	1	.217	.167
Robinson, Kerry, Arkansas*...	.321	135	586	523	80	168	196	16	3	2	62	5	2	54	1	64	40	23	7	.375	.386
Rodriguez, Noel, Jackson ...	.235	33	103	85	12	20	35	3	0	4	17	0	4	2	11	1	18	0	2	1	.412	.324
Rogue, Francisco, El Paso	.125	13	25	24	3	3	4	1	0	0	1	0	0	0	1	0	5	0	0	0	.167	.160
Romero, Willie, San Antonio..	.324	30	132	108	22	35	48	8	1	1	16	2	5	2	15	0	11	7	4	1	.444	.400
Rumer, Tim, Jackson*	.125	7	8	8	0	1	1	0	0	0	0	0	0	0	0	0	2	0	0	0	.125	.125
Rupp, Brian, Arkansas	.295	36	141	122	18	36	48	9	0	1	15	2	1	3	13	0	16	0	3	2	.393	.374
Ryder, Derek, Midland	.231	25	82	78	4	18	20	2	0	0	6	1	1	0	2	0	6	1	0	2	.256	.247
Sanchez, Victor, Jackson	.211	69	202	175	22	37	65	4	0	8	35	1	1	2	23	1	42	1	2	6	.371	.308
Saylor, Jamie, Jackson*.......	.254	63	230	205	24	52	85	12	3	5	21	3	0	3	19	1	43	3	2	1	.415	.326
Sbrocco, Jon, Shreveport* ...	.262	97	323	271	32	71	98	15	3	2	27	7	2	3	40	0	21	7	8	7	.362	.361
Schramm, Carl, Shreveport.....	.000	3	1	1	0	0	0	0	0	0	0	0	0	0	0	0	1	0	0	0	.000	.000
Shirley, Al, Wichita...............	.271	81	267	240	31	65	89	10	1	4	25	2	2	2	21	1	92	9	7	3	.371	.332
Sikorski, Brian, Jackson.........	.053	17	21	19	0	1	1	0	0	0	0	2	0	0	0	0	3	0	0	0	.053	.053
Simonton, Benji, Shreveport..	.256	116	479	387	73	99	178	15	2	20	79	0	5	6	81	1	120	7	5	15	.460	.388
Singleton, Christopher, Shr.*..	.317	126	500	464	85	147	220	26	10	9	61	2	9	1	22	4	50	27	11	7	.474	.343
Singleton, Duane, Midland*...	.309	13	62	55	15	17	30	5	1	2	6	1	0	6	0	8	4	0	0	.545	.371
Sisco, Steve, Wichita	.286	55	209	182	34	52	73	8	2	3	24	1	2	0	24	0	29	3	1	5	.401	.365
Small, Mark, Jackson.............	.000	37	1	0	0	0	0	0	0	0	0	0	0	0	0	0	0	0	0	0	.000	.000
Smith, Matt, Wichita*	.227	52	192	176	19	40	52	7	1	1	15	1	1	1	13	2	37	1	0	1	.295	.283
Spearman, Vernon, San Ant.*	.279	41	162	136	31	38	50	3	3	1	7	4	2	1	19	0	25	9	3	2	.368	.367
Stefanski, Mike, Arkansas	.250	1	4	4	1	1	3	0	1	0	0	0	0	0	0	0	0	0	0	1	.750	.250
Stein, Blake, Arkansas...........	.083	22	31	24	3	2	3	1	0	0	4	5	1	0	1	0	8	0	0	0	.125	.115
Stone, Ricky, San Antonio......	.333	25	4	3	0	1	1	0	0	0	0	1	0	0	0	0	1	0	0	0	.333	.333
Tatis, Fernando, Tulsa†	.314	102	433	382	73	120	220	26	1	24	61	0	2	3	46	4	72	17	8	16	.576	.390
Taulbee, Andy, Shreveport	.231	14	16	13	2	3	3	0	0	0	3	1	2	0	0	0	6	0	0	2	.231	.200
Tettleton, Mickey, Tulsa†	.182	3	15	11	4	2	5	0	0	1	2	0	0	0	4	0	2	0	0	2	.455	.400
Thurmond, Travis, Shr.	.000	2	1	1	0	0	0	0	0	0	0	0	0	0	0	0	0	0	0	0	.000	.000
Trammell, Gary, Jackson*	.264	110	349	314	38	83	101	10	1	2	28	6	4	1	24	0	53	0	4	9	.322	.315
Unrat, Chris, Tul.-Shre.*	.238	25	81	63	6	15	19	4	0	0	11	0	0	1	17	1	7	0	0	3	.302	.407
Urbina, Dan, San Antonio	.000	9	1	1	0	0	0	0	0	0	0	0	0	0	0	0	1	0	0	0	.000	.000
Vessel, Andrew, Tulsa	.261	138	573	517	78	135	208	35	1	12	75	4	5	6	41	2	87	3	1	8	.402	.320
Wachter, Derek, El Paso.........	.306	13	55	49	8	15	18	0	0	1	8	0	0	2	4	0	7	0	1	2	.367	.382
Walter, Daryle, Jackson	.000	34	3	0	0	0	0	0	0	0	0	0	0	0	1	0	2	0	0	0	.000	.250
Ward, Daryle, Jackson*	.329	114	472	422	72	139	221	25	0	19	90	0	1	3	46	4	68	4	2	12	.524	.398
Weaver, Eric, San Antonio......	.250	13	5	4	0	1	1	0	0	0	0	0	0	0	1	0	0	0	0	0	.250	.250
Westbrook, Destry, Arkansas.	.000	14	1	1	0	0	0	0	0	0	0	0	0	0	0	0	0	0	0	0	.000	.000
White, Derrick, Midland	.189	10	43	37	2	7	9	2	0	0	3	0	0	1	5	0	6	1	0	1	.243	.302
Williams, Drew, El Paso*	.237	71	282	257	36	61	104	14	1	9	36	0	2	4	19	0	49	2	1	4	.405	.298
Williams, Jeff, San Antonio.....	.167	5	9	6	0	1	1	0	0	0	1	0	0	2	0	5	0	0	0	.167	.375
Williams, Keith, Shreveport.....	.320	131	549	493	83	158	275	37	7	22	106	0	7	3	46	3	94	3	0	12	.558	.377
Windham, Mike, Arkansas	.154	29	15	13	0	2	2	0	0	0	0	1	0	0	1	0	4	0	0	0	.154	.214
Wingate, Ervan, San Antonio .	.000	1	5	3	0	0	0	0	0	0	0	0	0	0	2	0	1	0	0	0	.000	.400
Woods, Ken, Shreveport.........	.300	104	331	293	41	88	112	14	2	2	32	4	3	3	28	0	40	6	4	6	.382	.364
Young, Kevin, Midland	.284	103	401	338	64	96	149	23	6	6	53	5	3	6	49	1	40	6	9	5	.441	.381

GRAND SLAMS: Mendez, Munoz, 2 each; J. Dalton, Fasano, Forkner, R. Gonzalez, Green, Lariviere, Merchant, Miller, Nicholas, O'Neill, Pagnozzi, Pellow, Rennhack, B. Richardson, Rios, Roberge, 1 each.

AWARDED FIRST BASE ON CATCHER'S INTERFERENCE: McEwing 4 (O'Neal 2, Bess, Charles); J. Perez 3 (Mayes, Ramirez, Almond); C. Singleton 2 (Sanchez, J. Gonzalez); L. Diaz (Burke); Forkner (Mayes); Mendez (Almond); R. Richards (McDonald); Rodriguez (Cossins).

PLAYERS WITH TWO OR MORE TEAMS

Player, Team	Avg.	G	TPA	AB	R	H	TB	2B	3B	HR	RBI	SH	SF	HP	BB	IBB	SO	SB	CS	GDP	Slg.	OBP
Unrat, Chris, Tulsa*	.216	19	67	51	4	11	14	3	0	0	7	0	0	0	16	1	7	0	0	3	.275	.403
Unrat, Chris, Shreveport*	.333	6	14	12	2	4	5	1	0	0	4	0	0	1	1	0	0	0	0	0	.417	.429

1997 PITCHING

TEAM

Team	W	L	Pct.	ERA	G	CG	ShO	Sv.	IP	H	TBF	R	ER	HR	SH	SF	HB	BB	IBB	SO	WP	Bk.
San Antonio	84	55	.604	3.97	139	11	11	34	1183.1	1166	5039	592	522	88	49	33	40	438	5	901	85	11
Arkansas............	68	72	.486	4.10	140	5	9	35	1184.1	1221	5438	639	539	120	56	29	44	469	21	868	63	11
Shreveport	76	62	.551	4.23	138	5	7	39	1187.2	1195	5147	651	558	106	51	40	37	514	7	743	68	21
Jackson.............	66	73	.475	4.54	139	3	0	37	1205.2	1282	5379	722	608	112	54	33	60	523	34	939	69	10
Tulsa.................	61	78	.439	4.64	139	14	5	16	1175.0	1252	5163	727	606	108	40	62	33	445	7	850	79	13
El Paso..............	74	66	.529	4.99	140	7	1	29	1195.0	1439	5398	797	663	98	48	46	52	455	14	800	93	15
Wichita..............	64	76	.457	5.15	140	5	3	32	1190.0	1370	5362	781	681	136	48	36	64	477	35	815	58	9
Midland.............	64	75	.460	6.05	139	18	2	35	1192.0	1436	5432	921	801	130	36	59	75	506	7	846	98	19

INDIVIDUAL

TOP QUALIFIERS FOR EARNED-RUN AVERAGE TITLE

Minimum 109 innings. *Lefthanded pitcher.

Pitcher, Team	W	L	Pct.	ERA	G	GS	CG	ShO	GF	Sv.	IP	H	TBF	R	ER	HR	SH	SF	HB	BB	IBB	SO	WP	Bk.
Brohawn, Troy, Shreveport*.....	13	5	.722	2.56	26	26	1	1	0	0	169.0	148	695	57	48	10	3	1	2	64	0	98	4	3
Woodard, Steve, El Paso.........	14	3	.824	3.17	19	19	6	1	0	0	136.1	136	561	56	48	8	8	0	2	25	2	97	9	0
Elarton, Scott, Jackson	7	4	.636	3.24	20	20	2	0	0	0	133.1	103	544	57	48	6	3	1	2	47	3	141	14	0
Flores, Ignacio, San Antonio	10	7	.588	3.25	27	18	0	0	3	1	133.0	125	547	59	48	5	3	2	3	39	0	102	14	2
Oropesa, Eddie, Shreveport* ...	7	7	.500	3.92	43	9	1	0	12	0	124.0	122	531	58	54	7	7	4	4	64	0	65	6	6
Silva, Ted, Tulsa	13	10	.565	4.09	26	25	4	0	1	0	171.2	178	728	88	78	21	9	7	3	42	1	121	7	1

Pitcher, Team	W	L	Pct.	ERA	G	GS	CG	ShO	GF	Sv.	IP	H	TBF	R	ER	HR	SH	SF	HB	BB	IBB	SO	WP	Bk.
Logan, Marcus, Arkansas	11	7	.611	4.12	27	25	1	1	1	0	153.0	152	663	75	70	15	9	2	7	64	1	101	4	2
Smith, Travis, El Paso	16	3	.842	4.15	28	28	5	1	0	0	184.1	210	805	106	85	12	7	5	7	58	2	107	7	3
Heiserman, Rick, Arkansas	5	8	.385	4.17	34	20	1	1	9	4	131.2	151	569	73	61	19	6	2	8	36	2	90	8	0
Stein, Blake, Arkansas	8	7	.533	4.24	22	22	1	0	0	0	133.2	128	557	67	63	17	5	1	1	49	2	114	5	0
Blood, Darin, Shreveport	8	10	.444	4.33	27	27	0	0	0	0	156.0	152	698	89	75	12	7	8	8	83	0	90	14	2
Lopez, Johann, Jackson	6	8	.429	4.38	35	19	0	0	5	1	133.2	131	586	79	65	18	7	2	6	57	3	109	11	4
Calero, Enrique, Wichita	11	9	.550	4.44	23	22	2	0	0	0	127.2	120	541	78	63	15	4	6	4	44	0	100	2	2
Bonanno, Rob, Midland	5	10	.333	4.60	21	21	3	0	0	0	125.1	125	536	83	64	9	5	10	8	34	0	64	5	0
Estrada, Horacio, El Paso*	8	10	.444	4.74	29	23	1	0	2	1	153.2	174	694	93	81	11	4	4	4	70	0	127	8	3

DEPARTMENTAL LEADERS: W—Tr. Smith, 16; L—Brower, Washburn, 12 each; Pct.—Tr. Smith, .842; G—Prihoda, 70; GS—Washburn, 29; CG—Woodard, 6; ShO—Several pitchers tied with 1 each; GF—Howry, 39; Sv.—Howry, 22; IP—Washburn, 189.1; H—Washburn, 211; TBF—Washburn, 818; R—Washburn, 115; ER—Washburn, 101; HR—Washburn, 23; SH—Several pitchers tied with 9 each; SF—Bonanno, 10; HB—Fontenot, 12; BB—Blood, 83; IBB—Prihoda, 8; SO—Washburn, 146; WP—Gardner, 17; BK—Oropesa, 6.

ALL PITCHERS

*Lefthanded pitcher.

Pitcher, Team	W	L	Pct.	ERA	G	GS	CG	ShO	GF	Sv.	IP	H	TBF	R	ER	HR	SH	SF	HB	BB	IBB	SO	WP	Bk.
Ahearne, Pat, San Antonio	4	5	.444	4.50	14	14	3	0	0	0	84.0	109	364	48	42	1	6	2	2	13	0	45	4	0
Alvarez, Juan, Midland*	4	1	.800	8.27	24	0	0	0	6	0	37.0	63	199	42	34	5	0	1	3	22	1	27	0	3
Anderson, Mike, San Antonio...	4	2	.667	6.33	19	2	0	0	8	0	42.2	47	185	31	30	6	3	3	0	13	0	30	4	0
Barber, Brian, Arkansas	0	1	.000	10.47	3	3	0	0	0	0	16.1	28	80	19	19	2	2	3	5	0	15	0	1	1
Barcelo, Lorenzo, Shreveport	2	0	1.000	4.02	5	5	0	0	0	0	31.1	30	132	19	14	4	1	0	0	8	0	20	0	2
Beaumont, Matt, Midland*	0	2	.000	25.14	4	3	0	0	0	0	9.2	24	62	27	27	5	0	0	0	10	0	11	1	0
Beck, Greg, El Paso	1	5	.167	6.52	18	6	0	0	3	0	48.1	75	232	46	35	8	2	3	5	15	2	37	5	1
Bene, Bill, Midland	0	3	.000	6.31	25	0	0	0	5	0	41.1	42	202	33	29	5	1	4	2	40	0	41	11	0
Benes, Andy, Arkansas	1	0	1.000	1.29	1	1	0	0	0	0	7.0	2	26	1	1	0	0	0	0	2	0	6	0	0
Bevil, Brian, Wichita	0	0	.000	5.63	4	2	0	0	2	0	8.0	11	38	8	5	0	0	1	1	4	0	10	1	0
Blanco, Alberto, Jackson*	1	0	1.000	2.57	1	1	0	0	0	0	7.0	5	30	2	2	1	0	1	3	4	0	4	2	0
Bland, Nate, San Antonio*	1	2	.600	7.02	10	8	0	0	1	0	41.0	47	190	34	32	5	3	1	3	24	0	30	3	1
Blood, Darin, Shreveport	8	10	.444	4.33	27	27	0	0	0	0	156.0	152	698	89	75	12	7	8	8	83	0	90	14	2
Bonanno, Rob, Midland	5	10	.333	4.60	21	21	3	0	0	0	125.1	125	536	83	64	9	5	10	8	34	0	64	5	0
Bovee, Mike, Midland	8	2	.800	4.24	20	13	3	0	1	0	102.0	117	424	53	48	7	3	5	4	23	0	61	7	0
Brewington, Jamie, Wichita	2	5	.286	6.71	10	10	0	0	0	0	51.0	68	245	43	38	12	0	1	4	28	0	31	2	0
Brixey, Dusty, Wichita	0	4	.000	6.98	5	3	0	0	2	0	19.1	23	92	15	15	1	2	1	4	9	1	5	1	1
Brohawn, Troy, Shreveport*	13	5	.722	2.56	26	26	1	1	0	0	169.0	148	695	57	48	10	3	1	2	64	0	98	4	3
Brower, Jim, Tulsa	5	12	.294	5.21	23	23	1	0	0	0	140.0	156	602	99	81	13	4	7	3	42	1	103	15	1
Brown, Alvin, San Antonio	6	5	.545	3.74	16	16	2	1	0	0	96.1	83	406	48	40	9	2	2	5	33	0	67	9	2
Browne, Byron, El Paso	0	1	.000	7.50	1	1	0	0	0	0	6.0	8	27	5	5	1	0	0	0	3	0	3	1	0
Brunson, William, San Ant.*	5	5	.500	3.47	17	11	2	1	4	0	72.2	68	299	30	28	8	3	1	6	13	0	71	2	0
Buckles, Bucky, Tulsa	2	2	.500	7.00	34	0	0	0	19	1	45.0	59	204	38	35	5	0	2	1	20	0	29	2	0
Byington, Jimmie, Wichita	0	0	.000	0.00	3	0	0	0	2	0	3.0	1	14	0	0	0	0	0	0	3	0	3	0	0
Calero, Enrique, Wichita	11	9	.550	4.44	23	22	2	0	0	0	127.2	120	541	78	63	15	4	6	4	44	0	100	2	2
Chavarria, David, Arkansas	3	6	.333	4.50	28	14	0	0	4	2	90.0	85	394	56	45	10	4	5	3	41	1	62	13	2
Chavez, Anthony, Midland*	1	2	.333	4.21	33	1	0	0	15	6	47.0	53	200	23	22	1	3	2	3	15	1	35	4	0
Collier, Dan, Tulsa	0	0	.000	9.00	1	0	0	0	1	0	1.0	2	6	1	1	0	0	0	0	1	0	0	0	0
Corps, Edwin, Shreveport	5	3	.625	4.35	43	1	0	0	20	6	72.1	66	306	38	35	6	5	4	0	35	2	24	4	0
Creek, Ryan, Jackson	10	5	.667	4.11	19	19	0	0	0	0	105.0	95	471	57	48	10	5	1	3	74	1	88	14	0
Croushore, Rick, Arkansas	7	5	.583	4.18	17	16	1	0	1	0	92.2	111	421	52	43	7	1	5	4	37	0	67	8	2
Davalillo, David, Midland	0	0	.000	27.00	1	0	0	0	1	0	1.0	2	8	3	3	0	0	1	2	0	2	0	0
Davis, Eddie, San Antonio	0	1	.000	13.50	1	0	0	0	1	0	2.0	1	12	3	3	0	0	0	5	0	1	1	0
Davis, Jeff, Tulsa	4	6	.400	3.65	11	11	2	1	0	0	69.0	76	299	41	28	5	4	6	2	17	0	25	2	1
Dawsey, Jason, El Paso*	2	2	.500	6.81	8	7	0	0	0	0	38.1	50	182	30	29	3	0	1	2	23	0	14	4	1
DeClue, Jon, Jackson*	0	2	.000	12.96	9	0	0	0	5	0	8.1	13	48	13	12	2	1	0	1	11	2	7	2	0
Dedrick, Jim, Tulsa	1	0	1.000	2.35	12	0	0	0	2	0	23.0	26	100	9	6	0	1	0	9	0	16	5	0
De La Cruz, Fernando, Mid...	2	5	.286	7.79	13	13	0	0	0	0	71.2	81	348	70	62	10	3	3	10	46	0	44	8	2
De Los Santos, Valerio, El Paso*	6	10	.375	5.75	26	16	1	0	3	2	114.1	146	516	83	73	6	5	4	4	38	2	61	7	1
Detmers, Kris, Arkansas*	5	7	.417	5.77	15	15	0	0	0	0	78.0	99	346	54	50	11	3	2	2	27	0	44	1	0
Diorio, Mike, Jackson	1	3	.250	9.53	8	0	0	0	2	1	11.1	18	63	17	12	1	1	0	2	6	1	9	1	2
Eddy, Chris, Tulsa*	4	0	1.000	3.18	41	0	0	0	24	5	51.0	48	222	24	18	1	1	4	1	24	0	45	2	0
Elarton, Scott, Jackson	7	4	.636	3.24	20	20	2	0	0	0	133.1	103	544	57	48	6	3	1	2	47	3	141	5	0
Estrada, Horacio, El Paso*	8	10	.444	4.74	29	23	1	0	2	1	153.2	174	694	93	81	11	4	4	4	70	0	127	8	3
Evans, Bart, Wichita	1	2	.333	4.59	32	0	0	0	22	6	33.1	45	148	20	17	4	2	1	0	8	2	16	0	0
Farrar, Terry, Tulsa*	1	2	.333	4.95	6	3	0	0	1	0	20.0	18	92	12	11	1	1	0	2	15	0	16	0	0
Felix, Lauro, El Paso	0	0	.000	0.00	1	0	0	0	1	0	1.0	1	4	0	0	0	0	0	0	0	0	1	0	0
Fieldbinder, Mick, El Paso	2	3	.400	5.73	6	6	0	0	0	0	37.2	55	176	32	24	3	1	0	12	0	20	4	0
Flores, Ignacio, San Antonio	10	7	.588	3.25	27	18	0	0	3	1	133.0	125	547	59	48	5	2	3	39	0	102	14	2
Flury, Pat, Wichita	8	3	.727	3.58	42	0	0	0	19	5	48.0	47	215	26	19	4	2	3	4	18	3	47	1	0
Fontenot, Joe, Shreveport	10	11	.476	5.53	26	26	1	0	0	0	151.1	171	688	105	93	12	8	1	12	65	0	103	10	0
Freehill, Mike, Midland	0	7	.000	7.05	35	0	0	0	28	10	37.0	46	177	33	29	4	3	4	3	20	0	32	8	2
Frontera, Chad, Shreveport	4	4	.500	5.86	15	15	0	0	0	0	70.2	78	312	48	46	15	4	2	4	31	1	42	2	1
Fultz, Aaron, Shreveport*	6	3	.667	2.83	49	0	0	0	20	1	70.0	65	293	30	22	5	2	5	19	0	60	4	1
Gamboa, Javier, Wichita	0	3	.000	8.69	6	6	0	0	0	0	29.0	49	139	30	28	3	1	1	0	16	1	0
Gamez, Robert, Midland*	7	2	.778	5.10	51	0	0	0	14	0	47.2	62	221	37	27	4	0	1	3	20	1	46	4	1
Garcia, Frank, Arkansas	1	3	.250	6.63	28	0	0	0	7	0	38.0	43	183	38	28	6	0	2	2	24	0	25	0	1
Garcia, Jose, San Antonio	3	1	.750	3.15	10	0	0	0	5	0	20.0	19	82	8	7	1	2	1	3	4	1	14	1	0
Gardner, Scott, Tulsa	7	8	.467	5.10	29	22	1	0	4	0	139.1	166	625	93	79	8	7	8	8	56	1	89	17	1
Glauber, Keith, Arkansas	5	7	.417	2.75	50	0	0	0	22	3	59.0	48	245	22	18	3	2	2	5	53	5	0
Glynn, Ryan, Tulsa	1	1	.500	3.38	3	3	0	0	0	0	21.1	21	94	9	8	1	2	2	10	0	18	2	0
Gorecki, Rick, San Antonio	4	2	.667	1.39	7	7	0	0	0	0	45.1	26	174	8	7	3	1	1	15	0	33	2	0
Grieve, Tim, Wichita	3	1	.750	3.38	17	0	0	0	4	1	37.1	30	160	15	14	3	1	0	3	21	0	36	4	0
Grundy, Phillip, Wichita	9	11	.450	5.70	28	24	2	0	1	0	156.1	194	712	108	99	17	6	5	6	53	3	117	12	1

Pitcher, Team	W	L	Pct.	ERA	G	GS	CG	ShO	GF	Sv.	IP	H	TBF	R	ER	HR	SH	SF	HB	BB	IBB	SO	WP	Bk.
Grzanich, Mike, Jackson	7	6	.538	4.96	38	13	0	0	21	12	101.2	114	472	68	56	10	4	5	8	46	2	73	2	0
Gutierrez, Jim, Jackson	4	4	.500	2.93	52	3	0	0	26	5	89.0	96	376	33	29	4	1	1	6	23	5	51	4	0
Haas, David, Jackson	1	1	.500	5.03	13	0	0	0	4	0	19.2	23	89	14	11	0	3	1	1	4	2	5	0	0
Haney, Chris, Wichita*	0	1	.000	2.70	2	2	0	0	0	0	6.2	5	24	3	2	1	0	1	0	0	0	2	0	0
Harris, Bryan, Midland*	0	2	.000	11.29	10	1	0	0	4	1	18.1	28	98	26	23	3	0	1	4	15	0	15	1	2
Hartvigson, Chad, Shre.*	1	0	1.000	3.55	4	1	1	0	1	0	12.2	11	53	8	5	3	0	0	0	5	0	9	2	0
Heiserman, Rick, Arkansas	5	8	.385	4.17	34	20	1	1	9	4	131.2	151	569	73	61	19	6	2	8	36	2	90	8	0
Herges, Matt, San Antonio	0	1	.000	8.80	4	3	0	0	0	0	15.1	22	74	15	15	2	0	0	2	10	0	12	3	0
Hernandez, Santos, Shre.	1	1	.500	2.30	11	0	0	0	11	6	15.2	13	62	4	4	1	0	1	3	0	14	3	0
Hill, Ken, Tulsa	0	0	.000	0.00	1	1	0	0	0	0	5.2	2	16	0	0	0	1	0	1	0	3	0	0
Hook, Chris, Midland	1	4	.200	7.07	22	2	0	0	7	2	35.2	41	169	34	28	6	2	3	2	19	1	24	3	0
Howry, Bob, Shreveport	6	3	.667	4.91	48	0	0	0	39	22	55.0	58	240	35	30	6	1	3	0	21	0	43	3	1
Huber, Jeff, El Paso*	3	1	.750	3.46	19	0	0	0	7	1	26.0	35	121	14	10	2	2	0	1	11	2	20	2	1
Humphrey, Rich, Jackson	0	1	.000	32.40	3	0	0	0	1	0	1.2	7	16	9	6	0	2	0	1	3	0	0	0	0
Huntsman, Scott, El Paso	4	4	.500	7.20	42	0	0	0	13	3	55.0	76	272	56	44	5	0	5	4	21	2	37	4	2
Iglesias, Jose, San Antonio	6	2	.750	3.64	42	0	0	0	20	8	59.1	51	247	25	24	7	2	1	0	26	1	55	5	1
Janicki, Pete, Midland	0	0	.000	0.00	2	0	0	0	1	0	1.2	3	10	3	0	0	0	0	0	2	0	2	1	0
Jarvis, Matt, Arkansas*	8	5	.615	1.91	50	4	0	0	16	2	80.0	70	344	24	17	0	9	1	3	45	4	52	4	0
Johnson, Jonathan, Tulsa	5	4	.556	3.52	10	10	4	0	0	0	71.2	70	297	35	28	3	1	3	2	15	0	47	4	0
Judd, Mike, San Antonio	4	2	.667	2.73	12	12	0	0	0	0	79.0	69	323	27	24	0	0	3	0	33	0	65	8	2
Kell, Rob, Tulsa*	0	2	.000	5.88	28	2	0	0	8	1	41.1	60	197	32	27	7	1	2	1	14	2	35	4	0
Kester, Tim, Jackson	4	6	.400	5.23	47	4	0	0	18	2	82.2	107	375	53	48	9	2	4	8	26	3	50	2	0
King, Curt, Arkansas	2	3	.400	4.46	32	0	0	0	27	16	36.1	38	154	19	18	7	2	0	1	10	1	29	1	0
Knight, Brandon, Tulsa	6	4	.600	4.50	14	14	2	1	0	0	90.0	83	383	52	45	12	0	4	2	35	0	84	9	4
Knudsen, Kurt, Midland	0	4	.000	8.68	35	4	0	0	8	0	57.0	88	284	63	55	9	3	5	7	25	1	35	15	0
Kojima, Keiichi, Tulsa*	1	8	.111	8.83	13	10	0	0	1	0	53.0	83	258	55	52	6	3	1	0	18	0	40	1	1
Kolb, Danny, Tulsa	0	2	.000	4.76	2	2	0	0	0	0	11.1	7	50	7	6	1	0	0	0	11	0	6	4	0
Kubenka, Jeff, San Antonio*	3	0	1.000	0.70	19	0	0	0	17	4	25.2	10	93	2	2	1	0	1	0	6	0	38	1	0
Lagarde, Joe, San Antonio	4	4	.500	3.76	53	0	0	0	36	17	69.1	68	301	34	29	6	4	3	1	31	0	65	5	0
Linares, Rich, San Antonio	2	1	.667	7.23	18	0	0	0	8	0	23.2	37	112	21	19	3	1	0	0	6	1	11	1	0
Lock, Dan, Jackson*	2	2	.500	6.15	35	0	0	0	8	0	33.2	43	159	29	23	1	3	2	0	17	0	20	5	0
Logan, Marcus, Arkansas	11	7	.611	4.12	27	25	1	1	1	0	153.0	152	663	75	70	15	9	2	7	64	1	101	4	2
Looper, Braden, Arkansas	1	4	.200	5.91	19	0	0	0	14	5	21.1	24	94	14	14	2	1	1	1	7	2	20	1	2
Lopez, Johann, Jackson	6	8	.429	4.38	35	19	0	0	5	1	133.2	131	586	79	65	18	7	2	6	57	3	109	11	4
Lovingier, Kevin, Arkansas*	4	3	.571	2.54	59	0	0	0	22	3	74.1	68	314	27	21	4	3	0	1	26	2	82	5	1
Macey, Fausto, Midland	6	9	.400	8.03	17	17	1	0	0	0	96.1	141	464	93	86	15	3	7	7	46	1	38	5	2
Manning, David, Tulsa	4	7	.364	4.88	13	12	1	0	1	0	75.2	77	324	46	41	8	2	3	0	27	0	55	5	0
Martin, Jeff, Shreveport	0	2	.000	4.26	26	0	0	0	10	1	38.0	33	160	20	18	3	1	2	2	15	2	24	3	0
McDill, Allen, Wichita*	0	1	.000	3.12	16	0	0	0	7	3	17.1	18	72	7	6	0	1	0	0	7	1	14	1	0
McEwing, Joe, Arkansas	0	0	.000	27.00	1	0	0	0	1	0	0.1	1	2	1	1	0	0	0	0	0	1	0	0
Mlicki, Doug, Jackson	4	4	.500	5.36	9	9	0	0	0	0	48.2	69	229	36	29	7	0	1	3	20	0	35	3	0
Moody, Ritchie, Tulsa*	2	4	.333	5.88	30	0	0	0	13	0	49.0	52	243	41	32	2	4	4	4	41	1	38	8	0
Moore, Bobby, Tulsa	4	6	.400	5.35	35	7	0	0	11	2	72.1	74	327	50	43	8	3	3	2	34	0	41	3	1
Morvay, Joe, Wichita	1	2	.333	10.94	9	2	0	0	1	0	26.1	39	118	32	32	9	0	0	1	7	0	13	1	0
Mounce, Tony, Jackson*	8	9	.471	5.03	25	25	1	0	0	0	145.0	165	645	91	81	18	6	5	2	66	3	116	7	0
Mull, Blaine, Wichita	1	2	.333	6.65	8	8	0	0	0	0	44.2	66	225	41	33	4	0	1	0	23	0	16	1	1
Mullins, Greg, El Paso*	1	1	.500	2.70	25	0	0	0	22	13	23.1	19	100	8	7	2	2	1	1	11	1	21	2	0
Myers, Jason, Shreveport*	1	0	1.000	0.75	7	0	0	0	2	0	12.0	14	50	7	1	1	0	1	0	0	0	12	0	0
Neal, Billy, San Antonio	2	4	.333	6.10	25	0	0	0	10	0	31.0	35	145	25	21	1	3	2	1	16	1	12	2	0
Olsen, Steve, Wichita	2	0	1.000	0.00	3	2	0	0	0	0	14.2	11	56	1	0	0	1	0	0	2	0	7	0	0
O'Malley, Paul, Jackson	0	2	.000	6.45	28	0	0	0	7	0	44.2	53	211	32	32	4	1	5	5	21	1	25	4	0
Oropesa, Eddie, Shreveport*	7	7	.500	3.92	43	9	1	0	12	0	124.0	122	531	58	54	7	7	4	4	64	0	65	6	6
Ortiz, Russ, Shreveport	2	3	.400	4.13	12	12	0	0	0	0	56.2	52	249	28	26	3	4	1	1	37	0	50	2	1
Pace, Scotty, El Paso*	0	5	.000	5.92	41	2	0	0	18	0	65.1	86	305	52	43	12	2	3	3	31	0	38	5	0
Patterson, Danny, Tulsa	0	0	.000	4.50	2	2	0	0	0	0	2.0	5	13	4	1	0	0	1	0	0	0	0	0	0
Pavlik, Roger, Tulsa	0	0	.000	3.60	1	1	0	0	0	0	5.0	3	19	2	2	0	0	2	0	2	0	4	0	0
Pennington, Brad, Wichita*	0	0	.000	0.75	12	0	0	0	8	3	12.0	7	50	1	1	0	0	0	0	8	0	14	3	0
Perisho, Matt, Midland*	5	2	.714	2.96	10	10	3	1	0	0	73.0	60	299	26	24	5	0	1	0	26	1	62	1	2
Peterson, Mark, Jackson*	0	0	.000	5.40	6	0	0	0	5	0	5.0	7	23	3	3	0	0	1	0	2	1	6	0	0
Phillips, Randy, Shreveport	2	0	1.000	2.66	11	0	0	0	3	1	20.1	17	78	6	6	1	0	1	0	3	0	8	1	0
Politte, Cliff, Arkansas	4	1	.800	2.15	6	6	0	0	0	0	37.2	35	152	15	9	3	6	1	0	9	1	26	0	0
Pote, Lou, Arkansas	0	0	.000	1.54	7	3	0	0	1	0	23.1	15	94	10	4	1	1	0	0	8	0	21	2	0
Powell, John, Tulsa	4	3	.571	2.56	43	0	0	0	34	5	63.1	54	265	22	18	8	2	4	2	23	2	56	2	1
Prihoda, Stephen, Wichita*	0	3	.000	3.24	70	0	0	0	32	10	89.0	87	391	34	32	9	1	4	0	40	8	68	3	1
Quirico, Rafael, Midland*	3	3	.500	6.91	20	5	0	0	4	0	54.2	73	255	47	42	8	2	1	4	22	0	37	2	3
Ramos, Edgar, Jackson	0	2	.000	4.82	4	3	0	0	0	0	18.2	24	88	12	10	0	2	0	2	7	1	12	3	0
Rawitzer, Kevin, Wichita*	5	1	.833	5.75	44	9	0	0	6	0	97.0	125	457	68	62	10	2	1	6	44	4	75	1	1
Rennhack, Mike, El Paso	0	0	.000	0.00	1	0	0	0	1	0	0.1	1	1	0	0	0	0	0	0	0	0	0	0	0
Reyes, Dennis, San Antonio*	8	1	.889	3.02	12	12	1	0	0	0	80.1	79	335	33	27	6	3	1	1	28	1	66	2	2
Roach, Petie, San Antonio*	7	4	.636	3.73	13	13	1	0	0	0	82.0	76	351	39	34	14	3	2	1	35	0	56	7	0
Rodriguez, Frankie, El Paso.	2	2	.500	3.40	31	0	0	0	16	4	50.1	46	210	23	19	2	2	7	3	13	0	40	4	0
Rossiter, Mike, El Paso*	1	0	1.000	2.61	8	0	0	0	4	0	20.2	22	87	6	6	0	1	1	1	8	0	11	1	0
Rumer, Tim, Jackson*	1	2	.333	3.63	7	6	0	0	0	0	34.2	32	147	21	14	3	0	2	1	10	1	31	2	0
Sadler, Al, El Paso	6	6	.500	6.62	35	4	0	0	21	4	66.2	102	327	59	49	5	2	2	3	28	0	58	10	2
Saier, Matt, Wichita	7	5	.583	4.90	17	17	0	0	0	0	101.0	112	452	66	55	6	5	4	7	48	4	53	7	0
Santiago, Jose, Wichita	2	1	.667	4.00	12	0	0	0	8	0	27.0	32	120	13	12	1	1	2	1	8	1	12	0	0
Schoeneweis, Scott, Mid.*	7	5	.583	5.96	20	20	3	0	0	0	113.1	145	510	84	75	7	1	5	1	39	0	94	8	1
Schramm, Carl, Shreveport	1	0	1.000	6.43	3	1	0	0	0	0	7.0	10	30	6	5	1	0	0	0	5	0	5	0	0
Sikorski, Brian, Jackson	5	5	.500	4.63	17	17	0	0	0	0	93.1	91	402	55	48	8	5	2	4	31	2	74	0	2
Silva, Ted, Tulsa	13	10	.565	4.09	26	25	4	0	1	0	171.2	178	728	88	78	21	9	7	3	42	1	121	7	1
Skuse, Nick, Midland	0	0	.000	6.27	30	0	0	0	27	16	33.0	31	148	26	23	4	0	1	4	15	0	30	5	0
Small, Mark, Jackson	3	4	.429	3.14	37	0	0	0	25	9	43.0	46	196	20	15	1	4	1	1	19	2	40	0	1
Smith, Dan, Tulsa*	1	1	.500	3.64	5	5	0	0	0	0	29.2	25	128	18	12	3	0	2	0	15	0	27	1	0

Pitcher, Team	W	L	Pct.	ERA	G	GS	CG	ShO	GF	Sv.	IP	H	TBF	R	ER	HR	SH	SF	HB	BB	IBB	SO	WP	Bk.
Smith, Toby, Wichita	2	3	.400	4.91	8	8	0	0	0	0	44.0	49	195	30	24	7	1	2	2	11	0	29	4	2
Smith, Travis, El Paso	16	3	.842	4.15	28	28	5	1	0	0	184.1	210	805	106	85	12	7	5	7	58	2	107	7	3
Springer, Russ, Jackson	0	0	.000	9.00	1	0	0	0	0	0	1.0	2	5	1	1	0	0	0	0	0	0	2	0	0
Stein, Blake, Arkansas	8	7	.533	4.24	22	22	1	0	0	0	133.2	128	557	67	63	17	5	1	1	49	2	114	5	0
Stone, Ricky, San Antonio	0	3	.000	5.47	25	5	0	0	10	3	52.2	63	245	33	32	4	4	1	3	30	0	46	3	0
Taulbee, Andy, Shreveport	4	8	.333	5.17	14	14	1	0	0	0	85.1	104	376	59	49	9	3	6	1	32	0	46	5	3
Telgheder, Jim, Wichita	4	7	.364	6.28	28	12	0	0	5	0	86.0	104	393	66	60	22	2	1	2	30	4	47	6	0
Thurmond, Travis, Shre.	0	1	.000	6.00	2	1	0	0	0	0	6.0	10	36	9	4	1	1	1	0	9	0	4	1	0
Toth, Robert, Wichita	4	8	.333	5.82	20	9	1	0	5	0	68.0	82	303	47	44	9	5	2	2	26	2	47	3	0
Urbina, Dan, San Antonio	0	0	.000	3.86	9	0	0	0	5	0	14.0	19	67	8	6	0	1	1	0	13	0	6	3	0
Van Poppel, Todd, Tulsa	3	3	.500	5.06	7	7	0	0	0	0	42.2	53	197	27	24	2	3	3	1	15	0	26	2	1
Venafro, Michael, Tulsa*	0	1	.000	3.45	11	0	0	0	9	1	15.2	13	75	12	6	1	0	2	2	12	0	13	1	0
Villano, Mike, Shreveport	3	1	.750	6.29	30	0	0	0	15	2	34.1	41	158	25	24	5	2	0	0	20	2	26	4	1
Wagner, Joe, El Paso	1	2	.333	9.32	19	1	0	0	0	11	28.0	32	153	35	29	6	1	1	4	32	0	19	3	0
Walker, Jamie, Wichita*	0	0	.000	9.45	5	0	0	0	0	0	6.2	6	32	8	7	1	1	1	2	5	0	6	0	0
Walter, Michael, Jackson	2	3	.400	3.63	34	0	0	0	14	7	44.2	38	204	20	18	6	4	0	3	30	1	41	4	1
Washburn, Jarrod, Midland*	15	12	.556	4.80	29	29	5	1	0	0	189.1	211	818	115	101	23	7	4	9	65	0	146	9	1
Watts, Brandon, San Ant.*	0	0	.000	9.00	1	0	0	0	0	0	1.0	2	5	1	1	0	0	0	0	0	0	2	0	0
Weaver, Eric, San Antonio	7	2	.778	3.61	13	13	2	1	0	0	84.2	80	363	43	34	4	1	4	5	38	0	60	2	0
Westbrook, Destry, Arkansas	0	2	.000	2.74	14	0	0	0	6	0	23.0	16	104	11	7	1	3	1	1	17	2	16	2	0
Williams, Jeff, San Antonio*	2	1	.667	5.40	5	5	0	0	0	0	28.1	30	119	17	17	2	2	2	0	7	0	14	3	1
Windham, Mike, Arkansas	3	3	.500	5.48	29	11	1	1	8	0	88.2	107	396	61	54	11	1	0	5	37	1	44	4	0
Wolff, Bryan, Wichita	1	1	.500	6.52	12	0	0	0	8	1	9.2	18	50	7	7	2	1	1	1	5	1	8	1	0
Woodard, Steve, El Paso	14	3	.824	3.17	19	19	6	1	0	0	136.1	136	561	56	48	8	8	0	2	25	2	97	9	0
York, Mike, Tulsa	0	0	.000	5.06	1	1	0	0	0	0	5.1	7	24	3	3	0	0	2	0	2	0	2	0	2
Zimmerman, Mike, Wichita	1	2	.333	3.67	11	4	0	0	3	0	27.0	21	120	14	11	2	1	0	7	17	1	11	2	0

COMBINATION SHUTOUTS: **Arkansas (6)**—Heiserman-Jarvis, Heiserman-Glauber, Politte-Looper, Stein-Lovingier-Chavarria, Politte-Jarvis, Jarvis-Lovingier. **El Paso (5)**—Estrada-Huntsman, DeLosSantos-Pace, DeLosSantos-Mullins, Sadler-Pace, Gardner-DeLosSantos. **Jackson (0)**—None. **Midland (0)**—None. **San Antonio (8)**—Roach-Linares-Lagarde, Reyes-Neal, Reyes-Flores, Flores-Neal-Iglesias, Flores-Neal-Lagarde, Roach-Lagarde-Stone-Iglesias, Gorecki-Lagarde, Gorecki-Garcia-Lagarde. **Shreveport (6)**—Blood-Fultz-Villano, Brohawn-Corps, Brohawn-Martin, Brohawn-Corps-Oropesa, Fontenot-Corps, Brohawn-Hernandez. **Tulsa (3)**—Hill-Kojima-Powell, Manning-Eddy, Van Poppel-Buckles. **Wichita (3)**—Telgheder-Pennington-Wolff-Prihoda, Rawitzer-Prihoda-Santiago-Evans, Olsen-Grieve-Telgheder.

NO-HIT GAMES: None.

1997 FIELDING
TEAM

Team	Pct.	G	PO	A	E	TC	DP	PB
San Antonio	.976	139	3550	1578	127	5255	122	15
Arkansas	.976	140	3553	1535	127	5215	157	23
Shreveport	.972	138	3563	1623	151	5337	149	23
Midland	.968	139	3576	1634	175	5385	141	34
Jackson	.966	139	3617	1523	183	5323	128	11
Tulsa	.965	139	3525	1462	179	5166	104	23
Wichita	.965	140	3570	1524	186	5280	129	13
El Paso	.962	140	3585	1668	207	5460	148	23

TRIPLE PLAY: El Paso.

INDIVIDUAL

FIRST BASEMEN

NOTE: All caps denotes fielding-percentage leader based on 68 games for catchers, 91 for all other non-pitchers and 136 innings for pitchers. *Throws lefthanded.

Player, Team	Pct.	G	PO	A	E	TC	DP
Barker, Kevin, El Paso*	.982	49	455	30	9	494	44
Barkett, Andy, Tulsa*	.988	130	1114	76	15	1205	92
Battle, Howard, San Antonio	1.000	4	46	1	0	47	3
Betten, Randy, Midland	1.000	1	9	0	0	9	2
Blair, Brian, Tulsa*	1.000	2	6	2	0	8	0
Burke, Jamie, Midland	1.000	4	45	2	0	47	5
BUXBAUM, Danny, Midland	.9911	118	1022	92	10	1124	102
Byington, Jimmie, Wichita	1.000	1	2	1	0	3	0
Charles, Frank, Tulsa	.984	11	56	4	1	61	5
Cooney, Kyle, San Antonio	1.000	1	3	0	0	3	0
Coughlin, Kevin, Arkansas*	1.000	1	9	0	0	9	1
Dalton, Dee, Arkansas	1.000	1	3	0	0	3	1
Diaz, Lino, Wichita	.982	9	49	6	1	56	6
Fasano, Sal, Wichita	1.000	2	15	0	0	15	0
Forkner, Tim, Jackson	1.000	4	15	2	0	17	3
Gonzalez, Jimmy, Jackson	.965	12	75	7	3	85	6
Groppuso, Mike, El Paso	1.000	1	11	0	0	11	0
King, Brett, Shreveport	1.000	5	23	1	0	24	4
Kirkpatrick, Jay, San Antonio	.989	29	244	24	3	271	17
Krause, Scott, El Paso	1.000	1	1	0	0	1	0
Landry, Todd, El Paso*	.996	63	510	42	2	554	52
LaRiviere, Jason, Arkansas	.988	18	152	14	2	168	14
Lopez, Pedro, Jackson	.992	16	120	4	1	125	15
LoDuca, Paul, San Antonio	1.000	7	60	7	0	67	2
McEwing, Joe, Arkansas	1.000	2	24	0	0	24	3
Melendez, Dan, San Antonio*	.985	72	614	45	10	669	53
Mendez, Carlos, Wichita	.990	84	738	67	8	813	67
Merchant, Mark, Wichita	1.000	1	4	0	0	4	0
Morillo, Cesar, Tulsa	.946	4	34	1	2	37	2
Norton, Chris, Midland	.994	17	170	8	1	179	14
Pecorilli, Aldo, Arkansas	.980	13	88	10	2	100	12
Ramirez, Peto, Shreveport	1.000	2	1	0	0	1	0
Richard, Chris, Arkansas*	.990	104	921	68	10	999	103
Richardson, Brian, San Antonio	.946	6	32	3	2	37	3
Richardson, Scott, San Antonio	1.000	2	5	0	0	5	1
Roberge, J.P., San Antonio	.993	33	257	11	2	270	31
Rupp, Brian, Arkansas	1.000	9	42	3	0	45	7
Sanchez, Victor, Jackson	1.000	10	61	2	0	63	6
Simonton, Benji, Shreveport	.9906	113	1079	77	11	1167	110
Smith, Matt, Wichita*	.988	51	448	37	6	491	41
Ward, Daryle, Jackson*	.988	108	951	76	12	1039	84
Williams, Drew, El Paso	.986	36	332	26	5	363	35
Williams, Keith, Shreveport	.989	11	81	5	1	87	5
Woods, Ken, Shreveport	1.000	14	136	11	0	147	12

TRIPLE PLAYS: Mendez, D. Williams.

SECOND BASEMEN

Player, Team	Pct.	G	PO	A	E	TC	DP
Bell, David, Arkansas	1.000	1	0	5	0	5	0
Betten, Randy, Midland	.963	6	11	15	1	27	4
Bokemeier, Matt, Tulsa	.667	1	1	1	1	3	0
Burton, Essex, Tulsa	.915	16	27	38	6	71	3
Byington, Jimmie, Wichita	.973	17	32	40	2	74	8
Canizaro, Jay, Shreveport	.974	38	63	85	4	152	22
Dalton, Dee, Arkansas	.952	5	4	16	1	21	5
Davalillo, David, Midland	.982	10	30	25	1	56	10
Diaz, Edwin, Tulsa	.962	105	170	312	19	501	58
Diaz, Freddie, Midland	.967	12	21	38	2	61	7
Diaz, Lino, Wichita	1.000	6	14	11	0	25	4
Felix, Lauro, El Paso	.964	11	21	33	2	56	8
Guiel, Aaron, Midland	.943	6	12	21	2	35	3
Hernandez, Carlos, Jackson	.983	91	187	269	8	464	56
Ingram, Garey, San Antonio	.962	69	118	186	12	316	27
Johnson, Keith, San Antonio	.970	36	63	99	5	167	22
King, Brett, Shreveport	.985	23	26	41	1	68	9

CLASS AA Texas League

Player, Team	Pct.	G	PO	A	E	TC	DP
Kleiner, Stacy, Arkansas	1.000	4	6	11	0	17	3
Lopez, Mickey, El Paso	.976	131	290	397	17	704	110
Luuloa, Keith, Midland	.965	92	210	260	17	487	65
Matvey, Mike, Arkansas	1.000	6	9	9	0	18	1
McEwing, Joe, Arkansas	1.000	5	9	10	0	19	2
Medrano, Tony, Wichita	.982	70	129	190	6	325	40
Miller, Ryan, Jackson	.988	18	34	48	1	83	10
Mitchell, Donovan, Jackson	.971	9	15	19	1	35	4
Morillo, Cesar, Tulsa	.955	20	25	60	4	89	11
Nunez, Sergio, Wichita	.943	33	56	93	9	158	16
Perez, Jhonny, Jackson	1.000	2	3	7	0	10	3
Perez, Richard, El Paso	1.000	2	2	4	0	6	1
POLANCO, Placido, Arkansas	.979	128	240	425	14	679	110
Roberge, J.P., San Antonio	.979	39	71	117	4	192	21
Saylor, Jamie, Jackson	.956	26	50	58	5	113	11
Sbrocco, Jon, Shreveport	.955	65	124	175	14	313	47
Sisco, Steve, Wichita	.993	27	50	83	1	134	18
Wingate, Ervan, San Antonio	1.000	1	2	2	0	4	0
Woods, Ken, Shreveport	.978	33	57	78	3	138	18
Young, Kevin, Midland	.987	17	34	42	1	77	12

TRIPLE PLAY: Medrano.

THIRD BASEMEN

Player, Team	Pct.	G	PO	A	E	TC	DP
Battle, Howard, San Antonio	1.000	1	0	2	0	2	0
Bell, David, Arkansas	.929	8	3	10	1	14	0
Bell, Mike, Tulsa	.902	33	28	55	9	92	2
Betten, Randy, Midland	.930	24	14	66	6	86	3
Bokemeier, Matt, Tulsa	1.000	1	3	0	0	3	0
Bolick, Frank, Midland	.872	13	6	28	5	39	4
Burke, Jamie, Midland	.925	84	64	195	21	280	20
Buxbaum, Danny, Midland	1.000	2	2	1	0	3	1
Canizaro, Jay, Shreveport	.947	7	3	15	1	19	0
Charles, Frank, Tulsa	1.000	1	0	1	0	1	0
Dalton, Dee, Arkansas	.939	70	51	134	12	197	14
Davalillo, David, Midland	.931	10	10	17	2	29	2
Diaz, Freddie, Midland	.977	12	9	34	1	44	2
Diaz, Lino, Wichita	.912	45	22	82	10	114	8
Dobrolsky, Bill, El Paso	1.000	1	1	5	0	6	1
Felix, Lauro, El Paso	.887	17	11	36	6	53	7
Forkner, Tim, Jackson	.906	110	56	195	26	277	16
Groppuso, Mike, El Paso	.979	16	5	41	1	47	4
Guiel, Aaron, Midland	.875	7	3	18	3	24	3
Guzman, Edwards, Shreveport	.935	113	73	199	19	291	17
Ingram, Garey, San Antonio	.900	5	3	6	1	10	0
Johnson, Keith, San Antonio	.765	8	2	11	4	17	0
King, Brett, Shreveport	1.000	24	9	39	0	48	0
Kinkade, Mike, El Paso	.845	106	79	249	60	388	17
Kleiner, Stacy, Arkansas	1.000	4	2	4	0	6	1
Matvey, Mike, Arkansas	.943	46	22	77	6	105	11
McEwing, Joe, Arkansas	1.000	2	2	3	0	5	1
McNally, Sean, Wichita	.891	16	17	24	5	46	3
Mitchell, Donovan, Jackson	1.000	2	1	1	0	2	0
Morillo, Cesar, Tulsa	1.000	9	5	16	0	21	0
Pecorilli, Aldo, Arkansas	1.000	1	0	3	0	3	0
Pellow, Kit, Wichita	.898	65	51	161	24	236	13
Perez, Jhonny, Jackson	.941	8	4	12	1	17	1
Perez, Richard, El Paso	.905	8	3	16	2	21	0
RICHARDSON, Brian, San Ant.	.946	130	62	268	19	349	19
Rupp, Brian, Arkansas	.947	31	20	51	4	75	7
Sanchez, Victor, Jackson	.867	12	6	20	4	30	1
Saylor, Jamie, Jackson	.902	20	7	48	6	61	2
Sisco, Steve, Wichita	.917	18	9	35	4	48	2
Tatis, Fernando, Tulsa	.921	100	53	193	21	267	15
Woods, Ken, Shreveport	.809	14	7	31	9	47	2

SHORTSTOPS

Player, Team	Pct.	G	PO	A	E	TC	DP
Betten, Randy, Midland	.957	6	6	16	1	23	3
Bokemeier, Matt, Tulsa	.931	97	145	248	29	422	45
Byington, Jimmie, Wichita	.886	9	11	20	4	35	5
Canizaro, Jay, Shreveport	.974	8	14	24	1	39	5
Cedeno, Domingo, Tulsa	.923	2	3	9	1	13	3
CORA, Alex, San Antonio	.9682	127	197	412	20	629	88
Dalton, Dee, Arkansas	.964	39	55	105	6	166	30
Davalillo, David, Midland	.960	28	34	85	5	124	10
Diaz, Freddie, Midland	.970	15	22	43	2	67	12
Diaz, Lino, Wichita	.857	1	4	2	1	7	1
Felix, Lauro, El Paso	.932	9	19	22	3	44	6
Groppuso, Mike, El Paso	1.000	1	2	2	0	4	2
Guillen, Carlos, Jackson	.932	109	169	313	35	517	68

Player, Team	Pct.	G	PO	A	E	TC	DP
Harkrider, Timothy, Midland	.951	68	98	232	17	347	48
Johnson, Keith, San Antonio	.931	13	14	40	4	58	5
King, Brett, Shreveport	.902	22	30	62	10	102	15
Klassen, Danny, El Paso	.920	131	177	399	50	626	79
Lopez, Mendy, Wichita	.961	101	193	296	20	509	59
Luuloa, Keith, Midland	.941	29	35	77	7	119	17
Martinez, Ramon, Shreveport	.9676	104	167	370	18	555	80
Matvey, Mike, Arkansas	1.000	3	0	3	0	3	0
Medrano, Tony, Wichita	.945	34	56	100	9	165	24
Mitchell, Donovan, Jackson	.907	10	17	32	5	54	4
Morillo, Cesar, Tulsa	.943	43	65	118	11	194	31
Ordaz, Luis, Arkansas	.935	111	149	327	33	509	79
Perez, Jhonny, Jackson	.904	11	13	34	5	52	8
Perez, Richard, El Paso	.800	3	1	3	1	5	1
Roberge, J.P., San Antonio	.500	1	2	0	2	4	0
Saylor, Jamie, Jackson	.909	15	18	42	6	66	9
Woods, Ken, Shreveport	.940	15	21	42	4	67	8

TRIPLE PLAYS: Klassen, Lopez.

OUTFIELDERS

Player, Team	Pct.	G	PO	A	E	TC	DP
Abreu, Bob, Jackson	1.000	3	1	0	0	1	0
Betten, Randy, Midland	.968	15	30	0	1	31	0
Bilderback, Ty, Midland*	.978	19	43	1	1	45	0
Blair, Brian, Tulsa*	.981	71	154	4	3	161	1
Burke, Jamie, Midland	1.000	5	10	1	0	11	0
Byington, Jimmie, Wichita	1.000	59	75	2	0	77	1
Carr, Jeremy, Wichita	.972	91	161	10	5	176	0
Carter, Cale, Midland	1.000	7	12	0	0	12	0
Carter, Mike, Midland	1.000	15	26	2	0	28	0
Collier, Dan, Tulsa	.969	51	91	4	3	98	0
Coughlin, Kevin, Arkansas*	1.000	18	25	2	0	27	1
Dalton, Jed, Midland	.972	93	197	11	6	214	2
Davis, Eddie, San Antonio	.965	68	104	7	4	115	0
DeBerry, Joe, Wichita*	.950	18	19	0	1	20	0
Durkin, Chris, San Antonio*	.961	31	67	6	3	76	1
Felix, Lauro, El Paso	1.000	4	2	0	0	2	0
Fick, Chris, Shreveport	.667	1	2	0	1	3	0
Flora, Kevin, Jackson	1.000	1	2	0	0	2	0
Giambi, Jeremy, Wichita*	.975	57	117	2	3	122	0
Gibbs, Kevin, San Antonio	.982	98	215	2	4	221	1
Gonzalez, Raul, Wichita	.926	101	167	9	14	190	2
Green, Scarborough, Arkansas	.994	75	170	8	1	179	1
Guiel, Aaron, Midland	.973	63	103	6	3	112	1
Hatcher, Chris, Wichita	.900	6	9	0	1	10	0
Herrick, Jason, Midland*	.983	116	216	12	4	232	2
Ingram, Garey, San Antonio	1.000	18	33	0	0	33	0
Johnson, Keith, San Antonio	.974	27	36	1	1	38	0
Krause, Scott, Wichita	.967	119	195	13	7	215	3
Landry, Todd, El Paso*	1.000	18	20	4	0	24	0
LaRiviere, Jason, Arkansas	.991	62	103	5	1	109	0
Martin, Jim, Jackson	.979	25	42	4	1	47	1
MARTINEZ, Greg, El Paso	.995	95	193	13	1	207	4
McEwing, Joe, Arkansas	.982	62	98	11	2	111	1
McNabb, Buck, Jackson	.957	106	211	12	10	233	2
McNally, Sean, Wichita	1.000	1	1	0	0	1	0
Mendez, Carlos, Wichita	1.000	3	4	0	0	4	0
Merchant, Mark, Wichita	1.000	11	24	0	0	24	0
Mitchell, Donovan, Jackson	.973	109	205	9	6	220	0
Munoz, Juan, Arkansas*	1.000	55	107	11	0	118	3
Murphy, Mike, Tulsa	.991	44	108	2	1	111	0
Murray, Calvin, Shreveport	.978	107	214	9	5	228	4
Myers, Rod, Wichita*	1.000	4	8	0	0	8	0
Nicholas, Darrell, El Paso	.963	118	220	11	9	240	2
Norton, Chris, Midland	.833	6	9	1	2	12	0
O'Neill, Doug, Tulsa	.973	111	246	3	7	256	0
Ozorio, Yudith, Arkansas	.982	45	53	3	1	57	0
Perez, Jhonny, Jackson	.970	25	31	1	1	33	0
Peterson, Nate, Jackson	.986	42	70	3	1	74	1
Pledger, Kinnis, Wichita	1.000	8	9	1	0	10	0
Quinn, Mark, Wichita	.972	26	35	0	1	36	0
Rennhack, Mike, El Paso	.981	72	97	6	2	105	0
Richard, Chris, Arkansas*	1.000	3	3	0	0	3	0
Richards, Rowan, Tulsa	1.000	11	18	3	0	21	0
Richardson, Scott, San Antonio	.967	83	115	2	4	121	1
Rios, Armando, Shreveport*	.972	115	191	17	6	214	3
Roberge, J.P., San Antonio	1.000	49	70	8	0	78	1
Robinson, Hassan, Jackson	1.000	7	9	0	0	9	0
Robinson, Kerry, Arkansas*	.966	129	193	6	7	206	1
Rodriguez, Noel, Jackson	1.000	19	26	2	0	28	0
Romero, Willie, San Antonio	1.000	24	37	2	0	39	0
Sanchez, Victor, Jackson	.971	21	33	0	1	34	0

– 464 –

Player, Team	Pct.	G	PO	A	E	TC	DP
Saylor, Jamie, Jackson	1.000	5	3	0	0	3	0
Sbrocco, Jon, Shreveport	1.000	1	2	0	0	2	0
Shirley, Al, Wichita	.948	71	104	6	6	116	1
Singleton, Christopher, Shr.*	.974	119	253	11	7	271	4
Singleton, Duane, Midland	.960	13	23	1	1	25	0
Sisco, Steve, Wichita	1.000	11	7	0	0	7	0
Spearman, Vernon, San Ant.*	.975	39	73	4	2	79	1
Trammell, Gary, Jackson	.946	98	134	6	8	148	0
Vessel, Andrew, Tulsa	.967	133	225	9	8	242	1
Wachter, Derek, El Paso	1.000	11	18	2	0	20	0
White, Derrick, Midland	1.000	2	3	0	0	3	0
Williams, Keith, Shreveport	.972	85	163	9	5	177	2
Woods, Ken, Shreveport	1.000	3	2	0	0	2	0
Young, Kevin, Midland	.965	84	103	7	4	114	1

TRIPLE PLAY: Rennhack.

CATCHERS

Player, Team	Pct.	G	PO	A	E	TC	DP	PB
Almond, Greg, Arkansas	.986	68	332	20	5	357	2	7
Andreopoulos, Alex, El Paso	1.000	7	34	5	0	39	0	4
Bess, Johnny, Shreveport	.987	12	65	10	1	76	0	1
Brooks, Rayme, Wichita	.979	47	244	30	6	280	1	5
Burke, Jamie, Midland	.969	26	134	22	5	161	2	8
Charles, Frank, Tulsa	.975	59	339	46	10	395	0	9
Christopherson, Eric, Tulsa	.977	37	237	19	6	262	0	2
Cooney, Kyle, San Antonio	.983	53	325	26	6	357	2	6
Cossins, Tim, Tulsa	.979	35	206	22	5	233	0	11
Difelice, Mike, Arkansas	1.000	1	6	2	0	8	0	0
Dobrolsky, Bill, El Paso	.989	101	585	64	7	656	9	15
Fasano, Sal, Wichita	.983	39	217	21	4	242	4	5
Gonzalez, Jimmy, Jackson	.974	71	471	53	14	538	4	4
Hemphill, Bret, Midland	.985	67	425	48	7	480	4	9
Johnson, Jack, Midland	1.000	5	28	4	0	32	1	0
Kennedy, Darryl, Shreveport	.951	18	104	12	6	122	4	0
King, Cesar, Tulsa	.969	13	85	8	3	96	3	1
Kirkpatrick, Jay, San Antonio	1.000	3	9	2	0	11	0	0
Kleiner, Stacy, Arkansas	.983	10	57	1	1	59	0	1
Lopez, Pedro, Jackson	.985	9	61	6	1	68	0	1
LoDUCA, Paul, San Antonio	.990	88	576	84	7	667	7	9
Mayes, Craig, Shreveport	.986	84	363	54	6	423	2	11
McDonald, Keith, Arkansas	.988	68	384	29	5	418	6	9
McEwing, Joe, Arkansas	1.000	1	1	0	0	1	0	0
Meluskey, Mitch, Jackson	.985	54	356	43	6	405	5	4
Mendez, Carlos, Wichita	.979	8	42	4	1	47	0	0
Molina, Ben, Midland	.978	13	74	15	2	91	3	2
Norton, Chris, Midland	.963	13	75	3	3	81	0	9
O'Neal, Troy, El Paso	.962	40	166	39	8	213	6	4
Ortiz, Hector, Wichita	.962	59	340	40	15	395	0	3
Pagnozzi, Tom, Arkansas	.986	14	68	4	1	73	1	1
Pecorilli, Aldo, Arkansas	1.000	10	55	7	0	62	1	5
Probst, Alan, Jackson	1.000	7	36	11	0	47	2	0
Ramirez, Peto, Shreveport	.975	35	208	22	6	236	3	10
Roberge, J.P., San Antonio	1.000	1	1	0	0	1	0	0
Rogue, Francisco, El Paso	.980	13	43	5	1	49	0	0
Ryder, Derek, Midland	.993	25	125	20	1	146	3	6
Sanchez, Victor, Jackson	.979	9	40	7	1	48	0	2
Stefanski, Mike, Arkansas	1.000	1	4	1	0	5	0	0
Unrat, Chris, Tul.-Shrev.	1.000	6	18	1	0	19	1	1

CATCHERS WITH TWO OR MORE TEAMS

Player, Team	Pct.	G	PO	A	E	TC	DP	PB
Unrat, Chris, Tulsa	1.000	1	6	0	0	6	0	0
Unrat, Chris, Shreveport	1.000	5	12	1	0	13	1	1

PITCHERS

Player, Team	Pct.	G	PO	A	E	TC	DP
Ahearne, Pat, San Antonio	1.000	14	7	16	0	23	1
Alvarez, Juan, Midland*	1.000	24	2	5	0	7	0
Anderson, Mike, San Antonio	1.000	19	5	5	0	10	1
Barber, Brian, Arkansas	1.000	3	0	1	0	1	0
Barcelo, Lorenzo, Shreveport	1.000	5	3	5	0	8	0
Beaumont, Matt, Midland*	1.000	4	0	2	0	2	1
Beck, Greg, El Paso	.929	18	3	10	1	14	1
Bene, Bill, Midland	.600	25	1	2	2	5	0
Benes, Andy, Arkansas	1.000	1	0	1	0	1	0
Bevil, Brian, Wichita	1.000	4	0	2	0	2	0
Bland, Nate, San Antonio*	1.000	10	4	10	0	14	0
Blood, Darin, Shreveport	.974	27	9	28	1	38	1
Bonanno, Rob, Midland	.853	21	13	16	5	34	0
Bovee, Mike, Midland	.957	20	7	15	1	23	1
Brewington, Jamie, Wichita	.833	10	1	4	1	6	0
Brixey, Dusty, Wichita	1.000	5	0	3	0	3	0
Brohawn, Troy, Shreveport*	.945	26	10	42	3	55	1
Brower, Jim, Tulsa	.970	23	9	23	1	33	1
Brown, Alvin, San Antonio	.920	16	8	15	2	25	1
Browne, Byron, El Paso	1.000	1	1	0	0	1	0
Brunson, William, San Antonio*	1.000	17	4	18	0	22	1
Buckles, Bucky, Tulsa	1.000	34	2	12	0	14	4
Byington, Jimmie, Wichita	1.000	3	1	1	0	2	0
Calero, Enrique, Wichita	.920	23	9	14	2	25	0
Chavarria, David, Arkansas	.955	28	10	11	1	22	0
Chavez, Anthony, Midland	1.000	33	1	6	0	7	0
Corps, Edwin, Shreveport	1.000	43	4	14	0	18	3
Creek, Ryan, Jackson	1.000	19	10	8	0	18	1
Croushore, Rick, Arkansas	.833	17	8	7	3	18	1
Davis, Jeff, Tulsa	.963	11	9	17	1	27	1
Dawsey, Jason, El Paso*	.857	8	1	5	1	7	0
DeClue, Jon, Jackson*	1.000	9	0	1	0	1	0
Dedrick, Jim, Tulsa	1.000	12	1	4	0	5	0
Delacruz, Fernando, Midland	.760	13	5	14	6	25	1
De Los Santos, Valerio, El Paso*	.957	26	5	17	1	23	0
Detmers, Kris, Arkansas*	1.000	15	2	11	0	13	0
Diorio, Mike, Jackson	1.000	8	0	4	0	4	0
Eddy, Chris, Tulsa*	1.000	41	0	8	0	8	0
Elarton, Scott, Jackson	1.000	20	11	16	0	27	0
Estrada, Horacio, El Paso*	.969	29	8	23	1	32	2
Evans, Bart, Wichita	.909	32	5	5	1	11	0
Farrar, Terry, Tulsa*	1.000	6	0	2	0	2	0
Felix, Lauro, El Paso	1.000	1	0	1	0	1	0
Fieldbinder, Mick, El Paso	1.000	6	2	7	0	9	0
Flores, Ignacio, San Antonio	1.000	27	15	19	0	34	3
Flury, Pat, Wichita	.833	42	2	3	1	6	0
Fontenot, Joe, Shreveport	.935	26	13	30	3	46	3
Freehill, Mike, Midland	1.000	35	2	6	0	8	1
Frontera, Chad, Shreveport	1.000	15	7	10	0	17	1
Fultz, Aaron, Shreveport*	.938	49	3	12	1	16	1
Gamboa, Javier, Wichita	1.000	6	3	4	0	7	0
Gamez, Robert, Midland*	.909	51	4	6	1	11	0
Garcia, Frank, Arkansas	1.000	28	1	6	0	7	0
Garcia, Jose, San Antonio	1.000	10	2	4	0	6	1
Gardner, Scott, El Paso	.950	29	16	22	2	40	2
Glauber, Keith, Arkansas	1.000	50	6	9	0	15	2
Glynn, Ryan, Tulsa	1.000	3	1	4	0	5	0
Gorecki, Rick, San Antonio	1.000	7	3	10	0	13	1
Grieve, Tim, Wichita	1.000	17	2	4	0	6	0
Grundy, Phillip, Wichita	.862	28	12	13	4	29	2
Grzanich, Mike, Jackson	.968	38	6	24	1	31	1
Gutierrez, Jim, Jackson	1.000	52	5	12	0	17	0
Haas, David, Jackson	1.000	13	1	3	0	4	0
Haney, Chris, Wichita*	1.000	2	1	0	0	1	0
Harris, Bryan, Midland*	1.000	10	1	3	0	4	0
Hartvigson, Chad, Shreveport*	1.000	4	2	2	0	4	0
Heiserman, Scott, Arkansas	1.000	34	12	11	0	23	3
Herges, Matt, San Antonio	1.000	4	0	3	0	3	0
Hernandez, Santos, Shreveport	1.000	11	2	1	0	3	0
Hill, Ken, Tulsa	1.000	1	2	0	0	2	0
Hook, Chris, Midland	.750	22	1	2	1	4	0
Howry, Bob, Shreveport	.875	48	0	7	1	8	2
Huber, Jeff, El Paso*	1.000	19	1	4	0	5	0
Humphrey, Rich, Jackson	.333	3	1	0	2	3	0
Huntsman, Scott, El Paso	1.000	42	2	5	0	7	0
Iglesias, Mike, San Antonio	.900	42	4	5	1	10	0
Jarvis, Matt, Arkansas*	.960	50	7	17	1	25	0
Johnson, Jonathan, Tulsa	1.000	10	9	6	0	15	0
Judd, Mike, San Antonio	1.000	12	9	12	0	21	2
Kell, Rob, Tulsa*	1.000	28	0	4	0	4	0
Kester, Tim, Jackson	.929	47	2	11	1	14	0
King, Curt, Arkansas	1.000	32	1	9	0	10	0
Knight, Brandon, Tulsa	.824	14	2	12	3	17	0
Knudsen, Kurt, Midland	1.000	35	0	2	0	2	0
Kojima, Keiichi, Tulsa*	1.000	13	0	16	0	16	0
Kolb, Danny, Tulsa	1.000	2	0	3	0	3	0
Kubenka, Jeff, San Antonio*	1.000	19	0	3	0	3	0
Lagarde, Joe, San Antonio	1.000	53	3	10	0	13	3
Linares, Rich, San Antonio	1.000	18	1	5	0	6	0
Lock, Dan, Jackson*	.833	35	6	9	3	18	2
Logan, Marcus, Arkansas	.962	27	15	10	1	26	3
Looper, Braden, Arkansas	1.000	19	0	1	0	1	0
Lopez, Johann, Jackson	.903	35	8	20	3	31	0
Lovingier, Kevin, Arkansas*	1.000	59	2	8	0	10	1
Macey, Fausto, Midland	.938	17	6	24	2	32	2
Manning, David, Tulsa	.929	13	7	19	2	28	2
Martin, Jeff, Shreveport	1.000	26	2	0	0	2	0
McDill, Allen, Wichita*	1.000	16	1	2	0	3	0
Mlicki, Doug, Jackson	1.000	9	4	6	0	10	0

CLASS AA *Texas League*

Player, Team	Pct.	G	PO	A	E	TC	DP	Player, Team	Pct.	G	PO	A	E	TC	DP
Moody, Ritchie, Tulsa*	.833	30	3	12	3	18	2	Saier, Matt, Wichita	1.000	17	9	14	0	23	2
Moore, Bobby, Tulsa	.955	35	7	14	1	22	0	Santiago, Jose, Wichita	1.000	22	1	3	0	4	0
Morvay, Joe, Wichita	1.000	9	0	5	0	5	1	Schoeneweis, Scott, Midland*	.950	20	8	11	1	20	0
Mounce, Tony, Jackson*	.957	25	5	17	1	23	1	Sikorski, Brian, Jackson	1.000	17	12	9	0	21	0
Mull, Blaine, Wichita	.875	8	3	4	1	8	0	Silva, Ted, Tulsa	.977	26	11	31	1	43	0
Mullins, Greg, El Paso*	1.000	25	0	1	0	1	0	Skuse, Nick, Midland	1.000	30	0	3	0	3	1
Neal, Billy, San Antonio	1.000	25	7	7	0	14	2	Small, Mark, Jackson	.952	37	9	11	1	21	1
Olsen, Steve, Wichita	.750	3	1	2	1	4	0	Smith, Dan, Tulsa*	1.000	5	1	4	0	5	0
O'Malley, Paul, Jackson	1.000	28	3	7	0	10	0	Smith, Toby, Wichita	.909	8	7	3	1	11	0
OROPESA, Eddie, Shreveport*	1.000	43	4	44	0	48	3	Smith, Travis, El Paso	.966	28	20	37	2	59	2
Ortiz, Russ, Shreveport	.857	12	5	7	2	14	1	Stein, Blake, Arkansas	.957	22	9	13	1	23	0
Pace, Scotty, El Paso*	.955	41	5	16	1	22	4	Stone, Ricky, San Antonio	.900	25	3	6	1	10	0
Patterson, Danny, Tulsa	1.000	2	0	1	0	1	0	Taulbee, Andy, Shreveport	.933	14	3	11	1	15	1
Pavlik, Roger, Tulsa	1.000	1	0	1	0	1	0	Telgheder, Jim, Wichita	.923	28	2	10	1	13	0
Pennington, Brad, Wichita*	1.000	12	0	2	0	2	0	Toth, Robert, Wichita	1.000	20	6	7	0	13	0
Perisho, Matt, Midland*	.875	10	7	7	2	16	0	Urbina, Dan, San Antonio	.750	9	2	4	2	8	1
Peterson, Mark, Jackson*	1.000	6	1	3	0	4	1	Van Poppel, Todd, Tulsa	1.000	7	4	3	0	7	0
Phillips, Randy, Shreveport	1.000	11	0	5	0	5	1	Venafro, Michael, Tulsa*	1.000	11	4	2	0	6	0
Politte, Cliff, Arkansas	.875	6	1	6	1	8	0	Villano, Mike, Shreveport	1.000	30	3	5	0	8	1
Pote, Lou, Arkansas	.889	7	2	6	1	9	0	Wagner, Joe, El Paso	.750	19	6	3	3	12	0
Powell, John, Tulsa	.833	43	2	8	2	12	0	Walker, Jamie, Wichita*	1.000	5	0	2	0	2	0
Prihoda, Stephen, Wichita*	.923	70	10	14	2	26	0	Walter, Michael, Jackson	1.000	34	0	10	0	10	0
Quirico, Rafael, Midland*	.850	20	3	14	3	20	0	Washburn, Jarrod, Midland*	.867	29	12	27	6	45	0
Ramos, Edgar, Jackson	1.000	4	0	1	0	1	0	Weaver, Eric, San Antonio	.909	13	7	13	2	22	4
Rawitzer, Kevin, Wichita*	.933	44	9	19	2	30	0	Westbrook, Destry, Arkansas	1.000	14	1	3	0	4	0
Reyes, Dennis, San Antonio*	1.000	12	3	15	0	18	0	Williams, Jeff, San Antonio*	1.000	5	2	6	0	8	0
Roach, Petie, San Antonio*	1.000	13	5	14	0	19	1	Windham, Mike, Arkansas	.813	29	6	7	3	16	0
Rodriguez, Frankie, El Paso	1.000	31	6	10	0	16	0	Wolff, Bryan, Wichita	.667	12	1	1	1	3	0
Rossiter, Mike, El Paso	1.000	8	1	1	0	2	0	Woodard, Steve, El Paso	.977	19	10	32	1	43	1
Rumer, Tim, Jackson*	.714	7	0	5	2	7	0	York, Mike, Tulsa	1.000	1	1	2	0	3	0
Sadler, Al, El Paso	.923	35	5	7	1	13	0	Zimmerman, Mike, Wichita	.917	11	1	10	1	12	2

The following players did not have any fielding statistics at the positions indicated or appeared only as a designated hitter, pinch-hitter or pinch-runner: Almond, of; Blanco, p; Charles, of; Collier, p; Davalillo, p; E. Davis, p; L. Diaz, of; Forkner, 2b; Giambi, 1b; Groppuso, of; Janicki, p; B. King, p; P. Lopez, 3b; McEwing, ss, p; Morillo, of; J. Myers, p; Newson, dh; Rennhack, p; Schramm, p; Sisco, ss; Springer, p; Tettleton, dh; Thurmond, p; Watts, p; A. Williams, of.

LEAGUE CHAMPIONS

Year	Team	Pct.	Year	Team	Pct.	Year	Team	Pct.
1888—	Dallas	.671	1921—	Fort Worth	.691	1950—	Beaumont	.595
1889—	Houston	.551		Fort Worth	.662		San Antonio (4th)§	.513
1890—	Galveston	.705	1922—	Fort Worth	.694	1951—	Houston‡	.619
1892—	Houston	.741		Fort Worth	.711	1952—	Dallas	.571
	Houston	.613	1923—	Fort Worth	.632		Shreveport (3rd)§	.522
1895—	Dallas	.754	1924—	Fort Worth	.689	1953—	Dallas‡	.571
	Fort Worth*	.750		Fort Worth	.763	1954—	Shreveport	.559
1896—	Fort Worth	.757	1925—	Fort Worth	.711		Houston (2nd)§	.553
	Houston*	.679		Fort Worth▲	.653	1955—	Dallas	.581
	Galveston	.548	1926—	Dallas	.574		Shreveport (3rd)§	.540
1897—	San Antonio†	.657	1927—	Wichita Falls	.654	1956—	Houston‡	.623
	Galveston†	.717	1928—	Houston*	.679	1957—	Dallas	.662
1898—	League disbanded.			Wichita Falls	.731		Houston (2nd)§	.630
1899—	Galveston	.632	1929—	Dallas*	.588	1958—	Fort Worth	.582
	Galveston	.762		Wichita Falls	.620		Cor. Christi (3rd)§	.507
1900-01—	Did not operate.		1930—	Wichita Falls	.697	1959—	Victoria	.589
1902—	Corsicana	.866		Fort Worth*	.632		Austin (2nd)§	.548
	Corsicana	.682	1931—	Houston♦	.625	1960—	Rio Grande Valley	.590
1903—	Paris-Waco	.615		Houston	.734		Tulsa (3rd)	.528
	Dallas*	.648	1932—	Beaumont*	.640	1961—	Amarillo	.643
1904—	Corsicana*	.615		Dallas	.727		San Antonio (3rd)§	.532
	Fort Worth	.800	1933—	Houston	.623	1962—	El Paso	.571
1905—	Fort Worth	.545		San Antonio (4th)§	.523		Tulsa (2nd)§	.550
1906—	Fort Worth	.677	1934—	Galveston‡	.579	1963—	San Antonio	.564
	Cleburne∞	.609	1935—	Oklahoma City‡	.590		Tulsa (3rd)§	.529
1907—	Austin	.629	1936—	Dallas	.604	1964—	San Antonio‡	.607
1908—	San Antonio	.664		Tulsa (3rd)§	.519	1965—	Tulsa	.574
1909—	Houston	.601	1937—	Oklahoma City	.635		Albuquerque■	.550
1910—	Dallas†	.586		Fort Worth (3rd)§	.535	1966—	Arkansas	.579
	Houston†	.586	1938—	Beaumont	.635	1967—	Albuquerque	.557
1911—	Austin	.575	1939—	Houston	.606	1968—	Arkansas	.586
1912—	Houston	.626		Fort Worth (4th)§	.540		El Paso■	.562
1913—	Houston	.620	1940—	Houston‡	.652	1969—	Amarillo	.593
1914—	Houston†	.671	1941—	Houston	.673		Memphis■	.504
	Waco†	.671		Dallas (4th)§	.519	1970—	Albuquerque♦	.615
1915—	Waco	.592	1942—	Beaumont	.605		Memphis	.507
1916—	Waco	.587		Shreveport (2nd)§	.576	1971—	Did not operate as league—clubs
1917—	Dallas	.600	1943-44-45—	Did not operate.			were members of Dixie Association.
1918—	Dallas	.584	1946—	Fort Worth	.656	1972—	Alexandria	.600
1919—	Shreveport*	.677		Dallas (2nd)§	.591		El Paso■	.557
	Fort Worth	.651	1947—	Houston‡	.623	1973—	San Antonio	.590
1920—	Fort Worth	.703	1948—	Fort Worth‡	.601		Memphis■	.558
	Fort Worth	.750	1949—	Fort Worth	.649	1974—	Victoria■	.581
				Tulsa (2nd)§	.584		El Paso	.555

CLASS AA Texas League

Year	Team	Pct.	Year	Team	Pct.	Year	Team	Pct.
1975—	Lafayette▼	.558	1983—	Jackson	.507	1991—	Shreveport•	.632
	Midland▼	.604		Beaumont•	.500		El Paso	.596
1976—	Amarillo■	.600	1984—	Beaumont	.654	1992—	Shreveport	.566
	Shreveport	.515		Jackson•	.610		Wichita•	.515
1977—	El Paso	.600	1985—	El Paso	.632	1993—	El Paso	.563
	Arkansas•	.485		Jackson•	.537		Jackson•	.541
1978—	El Paso•	.593	1986—	El Paso•	.630	1994—	El Paso•	.647
	Jackson	.567		Jackson	.533		Jackson	.548
1979—	Arkansas•	.571	1987—	Wichita•	.515	1995—	Shreveport•	.652
	Midland	.563		Jackson	.515		Midland	.485
1980—	Arkansas•	.596	1988—	El Paso	.552	1996—	Jackson•	.547
	San Antonio	.544		Tulsa•	.522		Wichita	.500
1981—	San Antonio	.571	1989—	Arkansas•	.585	1997—	San Antonio•	.604
	Jackson•	.507		Wichita	.537		Shreveport	.551
1982—	El Paso	.559	1990—	San Antonio	.582			
	Tulsa•	.515		Shreveport•	.489			

*Won split-season playoff. †Won playoff for title. ‡Finished first and won four-club playoff. §Won four-club playoff. ∞Title to Cleburne by default. ▲Tied with Dallas in second half and won playoff for championship. ◆Tied with Beaumont at end of first half and won title in best-of-five series played as part of second-half schedule. ■League divided into Eastern, Western divisions; won two-team playoff. ▼League divided into Eastern, Western divisions; declared co-champions when playoffs were not completed. •League divided into Eastern and Western divisions and played split-season; won playoffs. NOTE—Championship awarded to winner of four-team playoff, 1933-51; first-place team and playoff winner co-champions, 1952-64.

CLASS AA *Texas League*

CALIFORNIA LEAGUE

LEAGUE OFFICE

President
Joe Gagliardi

Address
2380 S. Bascom Ave., Suite 200
Campbell, CA 95008

Phone
408-369-8038

Teams (affiliation)
Bakersfield Blaze (Giants)
High Desert Mavericks (Diamondbacks)
Lake Elsinore Storm (Angels)
Modesto A's (A's)
Rancho Cucamonga Quakes (Padres)
Lancaster Jethawks (Mariners)

San Bernardino Stampede (Dodgers)
San Jose Giants (Giants)
Stockton Ports (Brewers)
Visalia Oaks (A's)

1997 FINAL STANDINGS

FIRST HALF

VALLEY DIVISION						FREEWAY DIVISION					
Team	W	L	T	Pct.	GB	Team	W	L	T	Pct.	GB
Stockton (Brewers)	40	30	0	.571	....	San Bernardino (Dodgers)	40	30	0	.571	....
High Desert (Diamondbacks)	38	32	0	.543	2	Rancho Cucamonga (Padres)	38	32	0	.543	2
Lancaster (Mariners)	33	37	0	.471	7	Visalia (Athletics)	35	35	0	.500	5
Modesto (Athletics)	32	38	0	.457	8	Lake Elsinore (Angels)	33	37	0	.471	7
San Jose (Giants)	30	40	0	.429	10	Bakersfield (Giants)	31	39	0	.443	9

SECOND HALF

VALLEY DIVISION						FREEWAY DIVISION					
Team	W	L	T	Pct.	GB	Team	W	L	T	Pct.	GB
High Desert (Diamondbacks)	45	25	0	.643	....	Rancho Cucamonga (Padres)	39	31	0	.557	....
Modesto (Athletics)	42	29	0	.592	3½	Visalia (Athletics)	36	34	0	.514	3
Lancaster (Mariners)	42	29	0	.592	3½	Bakersfield (Giants)	31	39	0	.443	8
Stockton (Brewers)	30	40	0	.429	15	San Bernardino (Dodgers)	28	42	0	.400	11
San Jose (Giants)	30	40	0	.429	15	Lake Elsinore (Angels)	28	42	0	.400	11

COMPOSITE

Team	H.D.	R.C.	Lan.	Mod.	Vis.	Stk.	S.B.	Bak.	L.E.	S.J.	W	L	T	Pct.	GB
High Desert (Diamondbacks)	....	12	13	5	4	7	13	9	10	10	83	57	0	.593	....
Rancho Cucamonga (Padres)	8	....	12	6	8	7	7	8	12	9	77	63	0	.550	6
Lancaster (Mariners)	7	7	....	8	6	8	14	7	11	7	75	66	0	.532	8½
Modesto (Athletics)	8	6	5	....	12	9	8	11	5	10	74	67	0	.525	9½
Visalia (Athletics)	8	4	7	7	....	14	7	10	5	9	71	69	0	.507	12
Stockton (Brewers)	5	5	5	11	6	....	6	10	8	14	70	70	0	.500	13
San Bernardino (Dodgers)	6	13	5	4	6	7	....	7	13	8	68	72	0	.486	15
Bakersfield (Giants)	3	5	5	9	9	9	6	....	8	8	62	78	0	.443	21
Lake Elsinore (Angels)	9	8	9	7	8	4	7	4	....	5	61	79	0	.436	22
San Jose (Giants)	3	3	5	10	10	6	4	12	7	....	60	80	0	.429	23

Major league affiliations in parentheses.

High Desert played home games in Adelanto, Calif.

PLAYOFFS: San Bernardino defeated Visalia, two games to none; Lancaster defeated Stockton, two games to one; High Desert defeated Lancaster, three games to none; San Bernardino defeated Rancho Cucamonga, three games to two; High Desert defeated San Bernardino, three games to none, to win league championship.

REGULAR-SEASON ATTENDANCE: Bakersfield, 117,818; High Desert, 157,605; Lake Elsinore, 341,393; Lancaster, 298,465; Modesto, 140,861; Rancho Cucamonga, 404,525; San Bernardino, 273,739; San Jose, 146,151; Stockton, 101,254; Visalia, 80,078. Total—2,061,889. Playoffs (16 games)—40,964. All-Star Game (California and Carolina Leagues) at Durham, N.C.—6,419.

MANAGERS: Bakersfield, Glenn Tufts (through June 24) and Keith Bodie (June 25 to end of season); High Desert, Chris Speier; Lake Elsinore, Don Long; Lancaster, Rick Burleson; Modesto, Jeffrey Leonard; Rancho Cucamonga, Mike Basso; San Bernardino, Del Crandall (through July 21) and Dino Ebel (July 22 to end of season); San Jose, Frank Cacciatore; Stockton, Greg Mahlberg; Visalia, Tony DeFrancesco. Managerial record of teams with more than one manager: Bakersfield, Tufts 33-43, Bodie 29-35; San Bernardino, Crandall 50-51, Ebel 18-21.

ALL-STAR TEAM: 1B—Travis Lee, High Desert; 2B—Mike Metcalfe, San Bernardino; 3B—Eric Chavez, Visalia; SS—Mike Caruso, San Jose; OF—Mike Stoner, High Desert; Mike Darr, Rancho Cucamonga; Stanton Cameron, High Desert; Mike Glendenning, Bakersfield; Justin Bowles, Modesto; C—Ramon Hernandez, Visalia; DH—Mike Mitchell, Rancho Cucamonga; LHP—Ted Lilly, San Bernardino; RHP—Matt Clement, Rancho Cucamonga; Mick Fieldbinder, Stockton; Relief Pitcher—James Sak, Rancho Cucamonga; Most Valuable Player—Mike Stoner, High Desert; Rookie of the Year—Mike Stoner, High Desert; Pitcher of the Year—Ted Lilly, San Bernardino; Manager of the Year—Chris Speier, High Desert.

1997 BATTING

TEAM

Team	Avg.	G	TPA	AB	R	H	TB	2B	3B	HR	RBI	SH	SF	HP	BB	IBB	SO	SB	CS	GDP	LOB	ShO	Slg.	OBP
High Desert	.286	140	5657	4933	890	1411	2260	274	40	165	808	19	50	49	606	20	1055	79	46	108	1057	3	.458	.366
R. Cucamonga	.276	140	5581	4914	783	1354	2098	298	37	124	718	45	39	67	516	10	1077	95	45	96	1076	4	.427	.350
Lancaster	.271	141	5533	4873	842	1319	2204	282	60	161	759	30	36	10	584	17	1146	101	77	97	1036	5	.452	.348
Stockton	.267	140	5326	4762	622	1272	1835	251	48	72	543	55	34	82	393	13	1000	151	101	104	976	11	.385	.331
San Bernardino	.266	140	5382	4727	748	1256	2029	290	57	123	648	47	39	80	489	17	1098	195	143	63	912	5	.429	.342
San Jose	.266	140	5413	4736	656	1258	1816	241	40	79	610	44	31	76	530	23	964	150	85	115	1035	7	.383	.347
Visalia	.265	140	5516	4772	763	1264	1930	246	36	116	670	47	36	46	615	11	1065	157	96	94	1025	5	.404	.352

Team	Avg.	G	TPA	AB	R	H	TB	2B	3B	HR	RBI	SH	SF	HP	BB	IBB	SO	SB	CS	GDP	LOB	ShO	Slg.	OBP
Lake Elsinore ...	.263	140	5409	4759	703	1250	1941	265	57	104	635	63	47	80	460	24	1105	250	99	66	942	8	.408	.335
Bakersfield	.262	140	5382	4825	678	1264	1918	229	28	123	599	35	30	64	428	13	1023	61	60	99	978	9	.398	.328
Modesto...........	.259	141	5478	4704	769	1218	2039	277	50	148	692	48	41	76	609	26	1238	137	76	68	1016	11	.433	.350

INDIVIDUAL

TOP QUALIFIERS FOR BATTING CHAMPIONSHIP

Minimum 378 plate appearances. *Lefthanded batter. †Switch-hitter.

Player, Team	Avg.	G	TPA	AB	R	H	TB	2B	3B	HR	RBI	SH	SF	HP	BB	IBB	SO	SB	CS	GDP	Slg.	OBP
Hernandez, Ramon, Visalia	.361	86	384	332	57	120	190	21	2	15	85	0	8	9	35	1	47	2	4	5	.572	.427
Stoner, Mike, High Desert	.358	136	618	567	115	203	356	44	5	33	142	1	11	3	36	4	91	6	4	17	.628	.392
Mitchell, Michael, Rancho Cuca.*	.350	109	486	440	78	154	243	36	1	17	106	0	5	6	35	0	83	2	0	8	.552	.401
Wilson, Todd, San Jose	.345	130	547	502	66	173	229	35	3	5	88	1	3	9	32	2	60	7	3	23	.456	.392
Darr, Mike, Rancho Cuca.*	.344	134	587	521	104	179	278	32	11	15	94	0	5	4	57	1	90	23	7	19	.534	.409
Shockey, Greg, Rancho Cuca.*	.339	103	454	401	60	136	214	28	4	14	78	0	7	5	36	0	67	0	2	7	.534	.394
Caruso, Michael, San Jose†...	.333	108	492	441	76	147	199	24	11	2	50	4	3	6	38	3	19	11	16	3	.451	.391
Bowles, Justin, Modesto*	.327	107	465	394	66	129	207	39	9	7	51	5	5	5	56	2	85	6	3	3	.525	.413
Tyler, Josh, Stockton	.310	114	454	416	63	129	177	28	4	4	46	5	3	10	20	0	54	21	7	7	.425	.354
Hinch, A.J., Modesto..........	.309	95	394	333	70	103	194	25	3	20	73	4	4	11	42	3	68	8	3	9	.583	.400
Maddox, Garry, High Desert*..	.306	101	465	409	89	125	192	22	12	7	44	3	0	0	52	2	94	25	8	8	.469	.384
Proctor, Murph, San Bern.†...	.304	107	455	381	66	116	192	33	2	13	70	0	5	4	65	1	66	1	7	3	.504	.407
Kominek, Toby, Stockton	.300	128	553	476	83	143	230	28	7	15	72	1	2	24	50	3	107	22	14	8	.483	.393
Goligoski, Jason, High Desert*	.300	123	523	437	92	131	163	17	3	3	58	5	2	3	76	0	91	15	6	2	.373	.405
Cameron, Stanton, High Desert	.300	139	623	514	103	154	290	31	3	33	113	0	9	7	93	1	127	1	0	13	.564	.408

DEPARTMENTAL LEADERS: G—Minor, 140; AB—Garland, 577; R—Stoner, 115; H—Stoner, 203; TB—Stoner, 356; 2B—Stoner, 44; 3B—Mathis, 15; HR—Stoner, Cameron, Glendenning, 33 each; RBI—Stoner, 142; SH—Reynoso, 18; SF—Stoner, 11; HP—Kominek, 24; BB—Cameron, 93; IBB—Minor, 8; SO—Vandergriend, 153; SB—Baughman, 68; CS—Metcalfe, 32; GIDP—T. Wilson, 23; Slg.—Stoner, .628; OBP—R. Hernandez, .427.

ALL PLAYERS

*Lefthanded batter. †Switch-hitter.

Player, Team	Avg.	G	TPA	AB	R	H	TB	2B	3B	HR	RBI	SH	SF	HP	BB	IBB	SO	SB	CS	GDP	Slg.	OBP
Alguacil, Jose, San Jose†	.207	122	445	392	53	81	121	15	2	7	42	10	1	10	32	2	98	13	13	4	.309	.283
Anderson, Cliff, San Bern.*.....	.273	132	522	458	77	125	238	40	5	21	79	6	7	20	31	2	137	3	11	7	.520	.341
Ardoin, Danny, Visalia..........	.234	43	171	145	16	34	52	7	1	3	19	1	0	4	21	0	39	0	1	3	.359	.347
Avila, Rolo, San Bernardino ...	.290	134	589	507	94	147	196	25	3	6	47	7	7	5	63	4	63	52	24	7	.387	.369
Baeza, Art, Bakersfield	.258	86	334	310	51	80	152	18	3	16	60	3	0	3	18	0	73	2	3	8	.490	.305
Baltzell, Beau, High Desert.....	.100	8	23	20	3	2	5	0	0	1	4	0	0	0	3	0	10	0	0	3	.250	.217
Barajas, Rodrigo, High Desert	.266	57	209	199	24	53	85	11	0	7	30	0	1	1	8	0	41	0	2	7	.427	.297
Barker, Kevin, Stockton*	.303	70	293	267	47	81	150	20	5	13	45	0	1	0	25	4	60	4	3	6	.562	.362
Barlok, Todd, S.B.-L.E.	.248	93	336	286	46	71	114	11	7	6	34	2	4	10	34	0	83	17	9	4	.399	.344
Barnes, Larry, Lake Elsinore*	.287	115	500	446	68	128	203	32	2	13	71	1	5	5	43	4	84	3	4	6	.455	.353
Baughman, Justin, Lk. Elsinore	.274	134	547	478	71	131	157	14	3	2	48	11	5	13	40	3	79	68	15	5	.328	.343
Beck, Greg, Stockton	.000	27	1	0	0	0	0	0	0	0	0	0	0	1	0	0	0	0	0	0	.000	1.000
Bergeron, Peter, San Bern.*....	.250	7	8	8	1	2	2	0	0	0	1	0	0	0	0	0	2	2	0	0	.250	.250
Bess, Johnny, San Jose†	.239	44	175	155	29	37	63	9	1	5	26	1	2	2	15	2	41	4	2	3	.406	.310
Betten, Randy, Lake Elsinore..	.345	35	139	116	18	40	55	5	2	2	27	4	0	3	16	1	29	7	5	1	.474	.437
Bilderback, Ty, Lake Elsinore*	.316	62	250	209	38	66	91	13	3	2	30	0	1	4	36	2	42	11	5	2	.435	.424
Blanco, Dany, San Jose	.164	33	77	73	8	12	16	2	1	0	4	0	0	4	0	0	25	0	0	2	.219	.208
Bonds, Bobby, San Jose	.317	79	325	268	46	85	118	12	3	5	44	2	2	5	48	0	55	17	10	7	.440	.427
Boston, D.J., Visalia*	.224	14	55	49	7	11	17	3	0	1	4	0	0	1	5	0	13	0	0	1	.347	.309
Boughton, Mike, High Desert†..	.178	20	47	45	6	8	13	3	1	0	2	0	0	2	0	0	11	1	0	0	.289	.213
Bournigal, Rafael, Modesto.....	.238	7	24	21	0	5	6	1	0	0	2	0	0	3	0	0	2	0	0	1	.286	.333
Bowles, Justin, Modesto*.......	.327	107	465	394	66	129	207	39	9	7	51	5	5	5	56	2	85	6	3	3	.525	.413
Brito, Tilson, Modesto..........	.333	4	13	9	3	3	7	1	0	1	3	0	0	2	2	0	1	0	0	0	.778	.538
Brock, Tarrik, Lancaster*	.269	132	492	402	88	108	174	21	12	7	47	6	0	6	78	1	106	40	8	7	.433	.395
Brosius, Scott, Modesto	.333	2	6	3	1	1	1	0	0	0	1	0	1	1	1	0	1	0	0	0	.333	.500
Brown, Jason, San Bern.	.255	30	114	102	15	26	36	10	0	0	13	3	2	4	3	0	26	0	3	2	.353	.297
Buhner, Shawn, Lancaster	.257	111	456	397	66	102	159	22	1	11	53	0	3	7	49	3	126	4	1	5	.401	.346
Byers, MacGregor, Visalia	.226	18	59	53	8	12	19	5	1	0	9	0	0	6	0	0	15	2	1	1	.358	.305
Cameron, Stanton, High Desert	.300	139	623	514	103	154	290	31	3	33	113	0	9	7	93	1	127	1	0	13	.564	.408
Campusano, Carlos, Bak.	.199	61	207	191	17	38	55	8	3	1	15	3	2	4	7	0	49	2	0	3	.288	.240
Cana, Nelson, Stockton*........	.500	4	2	2	0	1	1	0	0	0	0	0	0	0	0	0	0	0	0	0	.500	.500
Cancel, Robinson, Stockton....	.280	64	234	211	25	59	73	11	0	1	16	7	1	2	13	0	40	9	3	6	.346	.326
Carter, Cale, Lake Elsinore* ...	.228	25	91	79	19	18	23	2	0	1	5	1	0	2	9	2	15	2	0	3	.291	.322
Caruso, Michael, San Jose†...	.333	108	492	441	76	147	199	24	11	2	50	4	3	6	38	3	19	11	16	3	.451	.391
Castro, Jose, Modesto†	.212	112	439	368	67	78	118	17	4	5	28	11	0	2	58	0	125	27	13	2	.321	.322
Cesar, Dionys, Visalia†	.239	97	335	285	60	68	91	16	2	1	11	6	0	1	43	1	79	10	12	5	.319	.340
Chavez, Eric, Rancho Cuca.* ...	.271	134	564	520	67	141	231	30	3	18	100	3	2	2	37	1	91	13	7	20	.444	.321
Chavez, Steven, R. Cuca.*	.197	88	316	274	34	54	86	17	0	5	30	5	4	5	28	0	77	1	0	7	.314	.280
Chiaramonte, Giuseppe, S.J...	.229	64	255	223	29	51	100	11	1	12	44	0	3	4	25	1	58	0	0	7	.448	.314
Christenson, Ryan, Visalia	.292	83	384	308	69	90	163	18	8	13	54	3	1	2	70	1	72	20	11	4	.529	.425
Clark, Kevin, High Desert	.234	13	51	47	4	11	18	4	1	1	3	0	0	0	3	0	13	0	0	1	.383	.280
Clifford, Jim, Lancaster*	.232	122	541	453	73	105	206	20	3	25	82	0	6	22	60	4	109	0	6	10	.455	.346
Connors, Greg, Lancaster	.243	10	41	37	5	9	14	2	0	1	5	0	0	0	4	0	10	0	1	0	.378	.317
Conti, Jason, High Desert*	.356	14	70	59	15	21	34	5	1	2	8	0	0	1	10	0	12	1	2	0	.576	.457
Cooper, Tim, Bakersfield	.223	34	137	112	15	25	36	5	0	2	18	0	4	0	24	0	38	2	2	9	.321	.365
Correa, Miguel, Lancaster†	.329	51	232	213	46	70	144	21	4	15	47	0	2	17	4		43	3		3	.676	.375
Corujo, Rey, San Jose	.202	30	105	94	10	19	33	6	1	2	11	0	1	0	10	0	19	0	0	1	.351	.276
Cruz, Cirilo, Lancaster..........	.270	43	183	152	22	41	56	10	1	1	25	0	1	6	24	0	33	0	3	2	.368	.388

CLASS A *California League*

Player, Team	Avg.	G	TPA	AB	R	H	TB	2B	3B	HR	RBI	SH	SF	HP	BB	IBB	SO	SB	CS	GDP	Slg.	OBP
Curtis, Matt, Lake Elsinore†	.330	74	292	264	58	87	179	25	8	17	55	0	1	2	25	1	54	3	1	2	.678	.390
Darr, Mike, Rancho Cuca.*	.344	134	587	521	104	179	278	32	11	15	94	0	5	4	57	1	90	23	7	19	.534	.409
Davalillo, David, Lk. Elsinore	.222	37	136	126	15	28	38	6	2	0	9	2	1	0	7	0	33	3	1	1	.302	.261
DaVanon, Jeff, Visalia†	.255	119	501	408	70	104	145	17	3	6	38	10	2	0	81	1	101	23	14	7	.355	.377
Davis, Ben, Rancho Cuca.†	.278	122	509	474	67	132	215	30	1	17	76	2	3	2	28	2	107	3	1	11	.454	.320
Davis, Glenn, San Bern.†	.246	64	276	228	44	56	99	16	0	9	36	0	0	2	46	0	77	7	3	3	.434	.377
Davis, Reggie, High Desert	.266	44	168	154	24	41	73	8	0	8	35	0	0	1	12	0	26	0	2	3	.474	.323
Dean, Chris, Lancaster†	.335	68	317	263	59	88	145	23	5	8	38	3	2	8	41	1	51	15	10	2	.551	.436
Delgado, Reymundo, Bak.*	.265	50	183	166	21	44	69	8	1	5	29	1	1	0	15	1	27	3	4	3	.416	.324
Denbow, Don, San Jose	.248	107	435	339	58	84	136	20	1	10	50	1	4	5	86	0	138	19	12	6	.401	.403
Dilone, Juan, Modesto†	.225	97	372	325	54	73	157	15	6	19	51	3	0	0	44	1	112	7	1	6	.483	.317
Donati, John, Lancaster	.000	4	16	14	0	0	0	0	0	0	0	0	0	2	0	0	4	0	0	1	.000	.125
Dougherty, Jeb, Lake Elsinore	.231	12	27	26	2	6	6	0	0	0	1	0	0	1	0	0	5	3	2	0	.231	.259
Durkac, Bo, High Desert†	.282	137	578	510	76	144	203	27	4	8	71	2	2	1	63	2	70	1	0	10	.398	.361
Durkin, Chris, San Bern.*	.167	3	12	12	1	2	2	0	0	0	0	0	0	0	0	0	4	0	0	0	.167	.167
Durrington, Trent, Lk. Elsinore†	.247	123	491	409	60	101	137	21	3	3	36	17	3	11	51	1	90	52	18	8	.335	.344
Ehmann, Kurt, San Jose	.238	50	171	147	15	35	38	0	0	1	13	2	0	2	20	2	33	3	2	5	.259	.337
Elliott, David, Stockton	.195	25	95	82	8	16	26	5	1	1	8	0	0	1	12	0	18	1	1	6	.317	.305
Encarnacion, Mario, Modesto	.297	111	413	364	70	108	197	17	9	18	78	0	1	6	42	1	121	14	11	7	.541	.378
Espada, Josue, Visalia	.274	118	536	445	90	122	144	7	3	3	39	7	3	9	72	1	69	46	17	6	.324	.384
Failla, Paul, Lake Elsinore†	.228	103	431	360	43	82	107	20	1	1	42	11	4	1	55	3	89	21	10	9	.297	.329
Faircloth, Chad, Bakersfield*	.260	19	82	73	8	19	27	5	0	1	7	3	0	0	6	0	22	1	0	1	.370	.316
Faircloth, Kevin, San Bern.	.226	63	179	159	28	36	53	9	1	2	16	5	0	9	6	1	49	10	4	3	.333	.293
Felix, Pedro, Bakersfield	.272	135	551	515	59	140	215	25	4	14	56	3	3	7	23	0	90	5	7	15	.417	.310
Fernandez, Antonio, Stockton	.235	118	462	412	46	97	133	24	0	4	49	5	5	5	35	0	83	2	4	7	.323	.300
Fick, Chris, High Desert*	.241	17	69	54	12	13	22	3	0	2	10	0	2	2	11	1	12	1	0	1	.407	.377
Figueroa, Jose, Modesto	.182	7	16	11	2	2	5	0	0	1	3	0	0	1	4	0	3	1	0	0	.455	.438
Filchner, Duane, Visalia*	.257	126	508	432	59	111	180	30	3	11	55	3	4	3	66	1	76	6	3	6	.417	.356
Finley, Steve, Rancho Cuca.*	.286	4	18	14	3	4	10	0	0	2	3	0	0	1	3	0	2	1	0	0	.714	.444
Fuentes, Joel, San Jose†	.200	5	7	5	1	1	1	0	0	0	1	0	0	0	2	0	2	0	1	0	.200	.429
Gama, Rick, Rancho Cuca.	.252	25	123	115	17	29	44	9	0	2	12	2	0	0	6	0	12	4	2	3	.383	.289
Gann, Jamie, High Desert	.225	91	289	267	33	60	94	12	2	6	32	2	2	1	17	2	71	2	1	6	.352	.272
Garcia, Juan, High Desert	.000	3	3	3	0	0	0	0	0	0	0	0	0	0	0	0	1	0	0	0	.000	.000
Garland, Tim, San Jose	.298	135	631	577	106	172	227	28	9	3	39	3	3	14	34	1	88	65	15	6	.393	.350
Geronimo, Cesar, Lk. Elsinore	.571	3	8	7	1	4	4	0	0	0	2	0	0	1	0	0	0	0	0	1	.571	.625
Glasser, Scott, High Desert	.248	57	136	121	23	30	38	5	0	1	11	0	1	0	14	0	19	3	4	2	.314	.324
Glendenning, Mike, Bak.	.258	134	577	503	95	130	256	27	0	33	100	0	7	4	63	1	150	1	4	15	.509	.341
Goligoski, Jason, High Desert*	.300	123	523	437	92	131	163	17	3	3	58	5	2	3	76	0	91	15	6	2	.373	.405
Gonzalez, Santos, R. Cuca.†	.111	6	20	18	3	2	2	0	0	0	1	0	1	0	1	0	7	0	1	0	.111	.150
Gonzalez, Wikleman, R. Cuca.	.300	33	119	110	18	33	59	9	1	5	26	1	1	0	7	1	25	1	1	1	.536	.339
Green, Chad, Stockton†	.250	127	567	513	78	128	188	26	14	2	43	11	4	2	37	2	138	37	16	3	.366	.300
Guerrero, Sergio, Stockton	.220	76	270	241	23	53	61	6	1	0	25	3	6	1	14	0	31	1	6	6	.253	.277
Gulseth, Mark, San Jose*	.317	95	377	325	47	103	164	25	3	10	58	2	3	1	46	5	49	1	0	11	.505	.400
Guse, Bryan, Bakersfield*	.253	26	101	87	7	22	28	3	0	1	6	0	0	2	12	0	16	0	1	3	.322	.356
Hardy, Brett, High Desert*	.114	12	37	35	3	4	5	1	0	0	0	1	0	0	1	0	14	1	0	2	.143	.139
Hartman, Ron, High Desert*	.292	75	333	291	43	85	149	22	0	14	65	0	4	8	30	0	57	0	2	3	.512	.357
Hernandez, Carlos, R. Cuca.	.250	1	4	4	0	1	1	0	0	0	0	0	0	0	0	0	1	0	0	1	.250	.250
Hernandez, Ramon, Visalia	.361	86	384	332	57	120	190	21	2	15	85	0	9	8	35	1	47	2	4	5	.572	.427
Hills, Rich, Rancho Cuca.	.273	40	150	128	19	35	45	8	1	0	15	1	1	2	18	0	31	1	1	2	.352	.369
Hinch, A.J., Modesto	.309	95	394	333	70	103	194	25	3	20	73	4	4	11	42	3	68	8	3	9	.583	.400
Hollandsworth, Todd, San Bern.*	.250	2	9	8	1	2	4	0	1	0	2	0	0	1	1	2	4	0	0	0	.500	.333
Horner, Jim, Lancaster	.258	45	182	163	26	42	75	6	0	9	27	0	1	2	16	0	48	2	0	4	.460	.330
Horton, Conan, San Bern.†	.100	14	36	30	3	3	3	0	0	0	0	0	0	4	2	0	10	0	1	0	.100	.250
Hutchins, Norm, Lk. Elsinore*.	.289	132	604	564	87	163	263	31	12	15	69	5	6	6	23	4	147	39	17	2	.466	.321
Iapoce, Anthony, Stockton†	.266	99	434	387	48	103	127	13	4	1	27	9	2	6	30	0	71	22	12	3	.328	.327
Jones, Jack, San Bernardino*	.227	123	449	388	53	88	148	21	3	11	52	11	4	6	40	0	112	10	7	4	.381	.306
Jones, Tim, Modesto*	.239	119	363	309	45	74	122	18	3	8	47	4	2	2	46	2	120	8	3	1	.395	.340
Kent, Robbie, Rancho Cuca.	.247	81	328	295	35	73	103	18	0	4	32	3	4	4	22	0	65	0	2	4	.349	.305
Kim, Yuni, Lancaster	.242	89	332	289	52	70	139	12	6	15	58	0	1	13	28	0	93	3	1	10	.481	.335
Kjos, Ryan, Modesto	.000	35	0	0	1	0	0	0	0	0	0	0	0	0	0	0	0	0	0	0	.000	.000
Koerner, Michael, Visalia*	.188	32	100	85	13	16	29	3	2	2	12	3	1	3	8	0	27	2	3	2	.341	.278
Kominek, Toby, Stockton	.300	128	553	476	83	143	230	28	7	15	72	1	2	24	50	3	107	22	14	8	.483	.393
Lara, Edward, Vis.-Mod.†	.222	15	50	45	10	10	17	4	0	1	3	0	0	1	4	0	9	1	1	0	.378	.300
Leach, Nick, San Bernardino*	.367	16	67	60	11	22	42	6	1	4	12	0	0	2	5	0	11	0	1	1	.700	.433
Lee, Travis, High Desert*	.363	61	279	226	63	82	156	18	1	18	63	0	3	3	47	6	36	5	1	8	.690	.473
Lennon, Patrick, Modesto	.188	5	19	16	3	3	7	1	0	1	4	0	0	0	3	1	5	0	0	0	.438	.316
Livingstone, Scott, R. Cuca.*.	.250	3	11	8	2	2	2	0	0	0	0	0	0	1	2	0	1	0	0	0	.250	.455
Macalutas, Jon, Stockton	.268	42	178	164	18	44	70	10	2	4	35	0	2	3	9	0	13	2	2	6	.427	.315
Maddox, Garry, High Desert*	.306	101	465	409	89	125	192	22	12	7	44	3	0	0	52	2	94	25	8	8	.469	.384
Malave, Joshua, San Bern.	.250	1	4	4	0	1	1	0	0	0	0	0	0	0	0	0	0	0	0	0	.250	.250
Manning, Brian, Bakersfield	.282	105	459	394	56	111	162	21	3	8	41	1	3	7	34	2	74	6	5	10	.411	.347
Marcinczyk, T.R., Modesto	.276	133	552	463	89	128	242	41	2	23	91	1	6	11	71	5	107	4	4	7	.523	.381
Martin, Mike, Lancaster*	.236	34	138	110	17	26	34	5	0	1	16	1	1	1	25	0	15	1	1	5	.309	.380
Marval, Raul, Bakersfield	.256	115	459	437	41	112	139	15	3	2	42	6	3	2	11	0	66	8	6	3	.318	.276
Mathis, Joe, Lancaster*	.283	134	615	562	94	159	259	28	15	14	82	3	5	7	38	1	94	25	16	3	.461	.333
Matthews, Gary, R. Cuca.†.	.302	69	320	268	66	81	128	15	4	8	40	0	0	3	49	2	57	10	4	4	.478	.416
McAninch, John, Lk. Elsinore	.250	61	214	188	24	47	73	12	1	4	21	1	4	6	15	0	43	1	1	3	.388	.319
McCarty, Matt, San Bern.	.087	12	29	23	5	2	2	0	0	0	1	0	0	1	5	1	5	3	0	0	.087	.276
McKay, Cody, Modesto*	.249	125	459	390	47	97	140	20	1	7	50	3	4	16	46	2	69	4	2	9	.359	.349
Melendez, Angel, San Jose*	.207	62	221	203	16	42	66	11	2	3	15	1	0	3	14	0	58	0	1	6	.325	.268
Mensik, Todd, Visalia*	.200	15	53	45	3	9	13	1	0	1	6	0	1	1	6	0	11	0	0	2	.289	.302
Metcalfe, Mike, San Bern.	.283	132	585	519	83	147	198	28	7	3	47	6	1	4	55	0	79	67	32	5	.382	.356
Mikesell, Steve, San Bern.	.000	2	2	1	0	0	0	0	0	0	0	0	0	0	0	0	0	0	0	0	.000	.500

Player, Team	Avg.	G	TPA	AB	R	H	TB	2B	3B	HR	RBI	SH	SF	HP	BB	IBB	SO	SB	CS	GDP	Slg.	OBP
Minor, Damon, Bakersfield*	.289	140	629	532	98	154	283	34	1	31	99	0	5	5	87	8	143	2	1	6	.532	.391
Miranda, Alex, Visalia*	.174	11	26	23	2	4	7	1	1	0	4	0	0	0	3	0	9	0	1	0	.304	.269
Mitchell, Michael, R. Cuca.*	.350	109	486	440	78	154	243	36	1	17	106	0	5	6	35	0	83	2	0	8	.552	.401
Molina, Ben, Lake Elsinore	.282	36	159	149	18	42	68	10	2	4	33	0	3	0	7	2	9	0	1	5	.456	.308
Molina, Luis, Lancaster	.229	105	367	328	47	75	115	11	4	7	46	2	7	4	26	0	63	0	5	8	.351	.288
Moore, Vince, Rancho Cuca.*	.234	100	361	325	43	76	128	23	1	9	38	1	2	3	30	1	118	13	3	5	.394	.303
Morales, Alex, San Jose	.217	29	90	83	8	18	20	2	0	0	6	1	1	1	4	0	28	4	5	2	.241	.258
Morris, Greg, Lake Elsinore	.288	74	311	278	38	80	117	26	1	3	30	1	1	2	29	0	47	1	3	5	.421	.358
Mosier, Mark, San Jose	.262	25	97	84	8	22	27	2	0	1	13	1	1	1	10	0	13	1	0	4	.321	.344
Mota, Gary, High Desert	.252	31	123	107	23	27	45	3	0	5	16	0	0	1	15	0	25	2	3	2	.421	.350
Mota, Pedro, San Jose*	.161	13	32	31	2	5	6	1	0	0	2	0	0	0	1	0	13	1	1	0	.194	.188
Mota, Tony, San Bernardino†	.240	111	462	420	53	101	153	14	13	4	49	6	2	4	30	2	97	11	8	9	.364	.296
Murray, Eddie, Lake Elsinore†	.500	2	8	8	1	4	7	0	0	1	2	0	0	0	0	0	0	0	0	0	.875	.500
Newhan, David, Visalia*	.278	67	295	241	52	67	107	15	2	7	48	2	5	3	44	2	58	9	3	5	.444	.389
Nicholson, Kevin, R. Cuca.†	.323	17	73	65	7	21	29	5	0	1	9	2	0	2	4	0	15	2	1	1	.446	.380
Norton, Chris, Lake Elsinore	.275	37	163	138	34	38	82	7	2	11	35	0	1	2	22	1	41	0	1	2	.594	.380
O'Neal, Troy, Stockton	.467	4	18	15	0	7	8	1	0	0	3	1	0	2	0	0	1	0	0	0	.533	.529
Ortiz, Jose, Modesto	.245	128	570	497	92	122	209	25	7	16	58	3	4	6	60	2	107	22	14	7	.421	.332
Osborne, Mark, High Desert*	.190	15	53	42	6	8	14	1	1	1	5	1	0	0	10	0	14	0	0	1	.333	.346
Owen, Andy, San Bernardino*	.269	112	387	357	46	96	166	30	5	10	49	0	1	3	26	1	77	11	13	1	.465	.323
Panaro, Carmen, High Desert*	.212	51	105	104	7	22	25	1	1	0	3	0	0	0	1	0	31	0	1	4	.240	.219
Parker, Allan, Lake Elsinore	.182	8	12	11	2	2	5	0	0	1	3	0	0	1	0	0	3	0	0	0	.455	.250
Paulino, Arturo, Modesto	.207	88	243	217	26	45	63	12	0	2	22	4	2	3	17	0	70	1	5	6	.290	.272
Pena, Angel, San Bernardino	.276	86	358	322	53	89	167	22	4	16	64	0	2	2	32	4	84	3	5	9	.519	.344
Penix, Troy, Mod.-Vis.*	.217	107	341	314	25	68	107	15	0	8	41	2	3	3	19	1	86	0	2	1	.341	.265
Perez, Richard, Stockton	.265	35	117	102	3	27	32	5	0	0	13	1	3	3	8	0	18	0	6	2	.314	.328
Pernalete, Marco, Bak.†	.270	17	41	37	6	10	10	0	0	0	2	1	0	1	2	0	7	0	1	0	.270	.325
Phair, Kelly, Stockton	.258	121	468	415	48	107	135	21	2	1	31	5	2	4	42	0	84	6	10	10	.325	.330
Plantier, Phil, Rancho Cuca.*	.235	4	17	17	1	4	7	1	1	0	3	0	0	0	0	0	1	1	0	0	.412	.235
Polanco, Juan, Modesto	.234	68	160	137	19	32	57	3	2	6	19	0	1	1	21	1	39	7	2	0	.416	.338
Poor, Jeff, San Jose	.186	52	146	118	11	22	29	7	0	0	14	0	0	0	28	0	18	0	0	6	.246	.342
Powers, John, Rancho Cuca.*	.254	107	486	402	77	102	170	28	5	10	44	5	3	11	63	0	90	7	8	9	.423	.367
Prieto, Chris, Rancho Cuca.*	.280	22	104	82	21	23	39	4	0	4	12	3	0	0	19	1	16	4	3	0	.476	.416
Prieto, Rick, Rancho Cuca.†	.292	68	333	281	47	82	115	12	3	5	31	2	0	6	44	0	45	11	6	0	.409	.399
Proctor, Murph, San Bern.†	.304	107	455	381	66	116	192	33	2	13	70	0	5	4	65	1	66	1	7	3	.504	.407
Prospero, Ted, San Jose	.262	29	69	65	6	17	27	2	1	2	11	1	0	0	3	0	23	1	0	0	.415	.294
Ramirez, Joel, Lancaster	.280	91	360	328	41	92	132	26	4	2	39	8	5	7	12	0	51	1	3	6	.402	.315
Ramirez, Peto, San Jose	.267	43	154	135	17	36	64	7	0	7	26	2	1	1	15	1	31	0	0	3	.474	.342
Ramirez, Roberto, Visalia	.298	63	264	242	28	72	95	12	1	3	29	0	2	1	19	1	46	4	3	5	.393	.348
Rand, Ian, Bakersfield	.232	29	89	82	9	19	26	4	0	1	7	1	0	2	4	0	28	2	2	2	.317	.284
Rauer, Troy, Visalia	.221	90	331	299	37	66	107	14	3	7	31	4	2	1	25	0	100	5	5	4	.358	.281
Ready, Randy, Lake Elsinore	.182	7	31	22	6	4	11	1	0	2	4	0	0	1	8	0	6	0	0	0	.500	.419
Regan, Jason, Lancaster	.281	69	311	260	50	73	163	20	2	22	54	0	0	6	45	2	79	2	2	2	.627	.399
Reynoso, Benjamin, R. Cuca.	.192	120	476	407	48	78	98	13	2	1	35	18	1	9	41	0	92	6	2	10	.241	.279
Rivera, Ruben, Rancho Cuca.	.174	6	27	23	6	4	8	1	0	1	3	0	1	0	3	0	9	1	0	0	.348	.259
Rodriguez, Guillermo, San Jose	.148	13	29	27	2	4	9	3	1	0	2	2	0	0	0	0	9	0	0	1	.333	.148
Rodriguez, Miguel, Stockton	.275	95	373	346	41	95	139	16	2	8	35	3	1	6	17	2	68	16	5	13	.402	.319
Ryder, Derek, Lake Elsinore	.231	36	103	91	12	21	33	5	2	1	13	3	1	0	8	0	17	1	2	1	.363	.290
Sankey, Brian, San Bern.*	.257	55	199	179	21	46	64	10	1	2	22	1	1	2	16	0	28	3	10	1	.358	.323
Schwenke, Matt, R. Cuca.†	.202	69	266	242	27	49	74	9	2	4	30	0	1	4	19	2	67	4	0	4	.306	.271
Shockey, Greg, R. Cuca.*	.339	103	454	401	60	136	214	28	4	14	78	0	7	5	36	0	67	0	2	7	.534	.394
Skeels, David, Lancaster	.278	59	195	180	26	50	59	7	1	0	21	3	0	3	9	0	40	0	2	10	.328	.323
Slemmer, Dave, Visalia	.280	115	453	404	70	113	170	25	1	10	64	1	1	3	44	1	83	11	3	9	.421	.354
Snow, Casey, San Bern.†	.197	43	139	132	10	26	40	5	3	1	10	1	0	2	4	0	35	2	3	1	.303	.232
Soriano, Jose, Modesto	.228	124	415	360	51	82	116	13	3	5	44	6	7	5	37	0	95	28	11	5	.322	.303
Spivey, Ernest, High Desert	.273	136	576	491	88	134	188	24	6	6	53	2	3	11	69	2	115	14	9	9	.383	.373
Steverson, Todd, High Desert	.229	24	107	83	16	19	35	4	0	4	15	0	2	3	19	0	34	0	1	1	.422	.383
Stoner, Mike, High Desert	.358	136	618	567	115	203	356	44	5	33	142	1	11	3	36	4	91	6	4	17	.628	.392
Stuart, Rich, Lake Elsinore	.230	45	187	165	25	38	79	11	6	6	33	1	5	3	13	0	50	6	4	3	.479	.290
Swinton, Jermaine, Stockton	.222	93	387	352	41	78	132	14	2	12	41	0	1	2	32	0	152	2	5	6	.375	.289
Thompson, Karl, Lancaster	.273	6	26	22	5	6	8	2	0	0	1	1	0	0	3	1	5	0	0	1	.364	.360
Thurston, Jerrey, Lk. Elsinore	.500	2	6	6	1	3	4	1	0	0	1	0	0	0	0	0	2	0	0	0	.667	.500
Tinoco, Luis, Lancaster	.163	12	49	43	9	7	15	2	0	2	5	0	0	1	5	0	12	0	1	3	.349	.265
Torrealba, Yorvit, Bakersfield	.274	119	486	446	52	122	155	15	3	4	40	1	3	5	31	0	58	4	2	8	.348	.326
Turner, Chris, Lake Elsinore	.083	3	12	12	0	1	3	0	1	0	1	0	0	0	0	0	3	0	0	1	.250	.083
Twist, Jeff, Bakersfield	.137	18	56	51	4	7	9	2	0	0	1	0	0	1	4	0	18	0	0	1	.176	.214
Tyler, Josh, Stockton	.310	114	454	416	63	129	177	28	4	4	46	5	3	10	20	0	54	21	7	7	.425	.354
Unrat, Chris, San Jose*	.244	59	192	160	18	39	57	9	0	3	19	0	1	1	30	4	38	0	1	4	.356	.365
Urso, Joe, Lake Elsinore	.000	2	1	1	0	0	0	0	0	0	0	0	0	0	0	0	0	0	0	0	.000	.000
Ussery, Brian, Lake Elsinore†	.241	10	32	29	1	7	8	1	0	0	4	0	1	0	2	0	11	0	0	0	.276	.281
Valenti, Jon, Modesto	.293	105	328	283	43	83	117	17	1	5	43	2	2	2	39	2	55	0	3	5	.413	.380
Vandergriend, Jon, Lk. Elsinore*	.182	118	450	402	45	73	136	17	2	14	45	3	3	10	32	0	153	19	5	4	.338	.257
Van Rossum, Chris, Bak.*	.261	125	521	441	72	115	148	17	5	2	40	5	3	15	57	1	98	9	12	6	.336	.362
Vaz, Roberto, Visalia*	.356	19	83	73	9	26	40	5	0	3	13	2	0	0	8	0	10	2	5	4	.548	.420
Ventura, Wilfredo, Visalia	.196	62	198	184	23	36	59	5	0	6	23	2	2	1	9	0	64	1	0	5	.321	.235
Villalobos, Carlos, Lancaster	.341	86	365	296	71	101	160	22	2	11	53	2	0	7	60	0	42	4	6	7	.541	.463
Vina, Fernando, Stockton*	.444	3	9	9	2	4	6	0	1	0	3	0	0	0	0	0	0	0	2	0	.667	.444
Wachter, Derek, Stockton	.311	49	206	177	21	55	77	7	3	3	28	0	0	3	26	1	24	2	4	11	.435	.408
Wathan, Dusty, Lancaster†	.297	56	232	202	27	60	89	17	0	4	35	1	1	7	21	0	51	0	1	7	.441	.381
Watson, Jon, Bakersfield	.259	119	490	448	67	116	148	22	2	2	36	7	0	5	30	0	66	14	10	10	.330	.313
Watts, Josh, Lancaster*	.220	56	184	159	18	35	58	5	0	6	25	0	1	1	23	0	71	1	3	3	.365	.321
Weekley, Jason, San Bern.	.281	101	363	313	58	88	161	15	5	16	59	1	5	3	41	0	102	3	6	5	.514	.365
Welles, Robby, Lake Elsinore	.000	3	6	5	0	0	0	0	0	0	0	0	0	0	1	0	2	0	0	0	.000	.167

Player, Team	Avg.	G	TPA	AB	R	H	TB	2B	3B	HR	RBI	SH	SF	HP	BB	IBB	SO	SB	CS	GDP	Slg.	OBP
Williams, Drew, Stockton*	.257	48	205	175	27	45	70	16	0	3	23	1	4	3	22	1	37	4	1	4	.400	.343
Williams, George, Modesto†	.318	13	52	44	8	14	21	4	0	1	6	0	1	0	7	2	14	0	1	0	.477	.404
Wilson, Keith, High Desert	.230	60	174	148	22	34	57	8	0	5	25	1	4	7	14	0	40	1	0	5	.385	.318
Wilson, Todd, San Jose	.345	130	547	502	66	173	229	35	3	5	88	1	3	9	32	2	60	7	3	23	.456	.392
Zuniga, Tony, San Jose	.183	97	341	289	24	53	66	10	0	1	32	6	2	11	33	0	48	3	3	11	.228	.290

GRAND SLAMS: Baeza, 5; Marcinczyk, 4; Cameron, R. Hernandez, Lee, Stoner, Villalobos, 2 each; Baltzell, Chiarmonte, Christenson, Hinch, Hutchins, Kominek, Manning, Matthews, Minor, Penix, Polanco, Proctor, P. Ramirez, Regan, Stuart, Valenti, Weekley.

AWARDED FIRST BASE ON CATCHER'S INTERFERENCE: Shockey 5 (R. Davis, Hinch, Figueroa, Snow, Ussery); Powers 2 (An. Pena, Ussery); R. Davis (Ryder); Kim (Snow); Maddox (Skeels); Manning (Cancel).

PLAYERS WITH TWO OR MORE TEAMS

Player, Team	Avg.	G	TPA	AB	R	H	TB	2B	3B	HR	RBI	SH	SF	HP	BB	IBB	SO	SB	CS	GDP	Slg.	OBP
Barlok, Todd, San Bernardino..	.302	44	138	116	25	35	62	6	3	5	19	0	2	3	17	0	32	7	5	2	.534	.399
Barlok, Todd, Lake Elsinore	.212	49	198	170	21	36	52	5	4	1	15	2	2	7	17	0	51	10	4	2	.306	.306
Lara, Edward, Visalia†	.222	13	50	45	10	10	17	4	0	1	3	0	1	4	0	0	9	1	1	0	.378	.300
Lara, Edward, Modesto†	.000	2	0	0	0	0	0	0	0	0	0	0	0	0	0	0	0	0	0	0	.000	.000
Penix, Troy, Modesto*	.225	58	175	160	12	36	53	8	0	3	18	2	1	2	10	1	40	0	0	0	.331	.277
Penix, Troy, Visalia*	.208	49	166	154	13	32	54	7	0	5	23	0	2	1	9	0	46	0	2	1	.351	.253

1997 PITCHING

TEAM

Team	W	L	Pct.	ERA	G	CG	ShO	Sv.	IP	H	TBF	R	ER	HR	SH	SF	HB	BB	IBB	SO	WP	Bk.
R. Cucamonga	77	63	.550	4.09	140	3	12	35	1247.0	1156	5405	683	566	105	42	31	71	556	11	1292	102	9
Modesto	74	67	.525	4.14	141	3	4	33	1233.2	1309	5444	737	568	114	46	46	60	466	36	1076	91	14
Stockton	70	70	.500	4.28	140	9	9	38	1243.1	1207	5426	672	591	116	63	35	97	576	6	953	99	11
San Jose	60	80	.429	4.44	140	4	8	35	1231.2	1314	5389	706	608	95	38	37	59	483	19	1210	96	23
High Desert	83	57	.593	4.53	140	2	5	34	1251.0	1300	5485	766	629	156	39	32	87	438	14	984	80	10
Lake Elsinore	61	79	.436	4.53	140	6	4	29	1248.1	1327	5498	758	628	113	45	32	99	437	18	998	78	19
San Bernardino	68	72	.486	4.74	140	3	9	35	1238.2	1218	5482	760	652	114	37	48	65	630	14	1097	127	19
Lancaster	75	66	.532	4.74	141	3	4	37	1255.2	1341	5549	773	661	153	46	51	77	518	17	1130	97	12
Visalia	71	69	.507	4.89	140	2	3	38	1244.0	1355	5627	809	676	125	38	38	57	572	25	1058	126	14
Bakersfield	62	78	.443	4.90	140	3	10	35	1233.2	1339	5483	790	671	124	35	33	58	554	14	973	107	12

INDIVIDUAL

TOP QUALIFIERS FOR EARNED-RUN AVERAGE TITLE

Minimum 112 innings. *Lefthanded pitcher.

Pitcher, Team	W	L	Pct.	ERA	G	GS	CG	ShO	GF	Sv.	IP	H	TBF	R	ER	HR	SH	SF	HB	BB	IBB	SO	WP	Bk.
Lilly, Ted, San Bernardino*	7	8	.467	2.81	23	21	2	1	0	0	144.0	116	540	52	42	9	5	3	4	32	0	158	7	5
Fieldbinder, Mick, Stockton	11	6	.647	2.83	21	21	4	1	0	0	143.1	141	594	58	45	9	4	3	3	38	2	68	10	0
Laxton, Brett, Visalia	11	5	.688	2.99	29	22	0	0	2	0	138.2	141	606	62	46	7	4	0	11	50	0	121	14	0
Leese, Brandon, San Jose	7	5	.583	3.05	19	19	0	0	0	0	112.0	99	475	44	38	11	1	0	4	46	2	99	15	0
Williams, Jeff, San Bernardino*	10	4	.714	3.10	18	18	0	0	0	0	116.0	101	472	52	40	8	4	2	2	34	0	72	7	3
Grote, Jason, Bakersfield	12	8	.600	3.45	25	25	0	0	0	0	156.1	156	659	77	60	11	1	3	2	59	1	116	15	0
Wunsch, Kelly, Stockton*	7	9	.438	3.46	24	22	2	2	0	0	143.0	141	627	65	55	11	10	4	14	62	0	98	9	2
Cooper, Brian, Lake Elsinore	7	3	.700	3.54	17	17	1	0	0	0	117.0	111	497	56	46	7	6	2	10	27	0	104	6	0
Rivette, Scott, Modesto	9	9	.500	3.57	20	20	3	0	0	0	126.0	147	533	65	50	12	3	2	7	31	1	96	8	1
Noriega, Ray, Modesto*	5	8	.385	4.04	28	28	0	0	0	0	156.0	161	698	101	70	17	8	2	4	69	1	119	10	3
Marte, Damaso, Lancaster*	8	8	.500	4.13	25	25	2	1	0	0	139.1	144	609	75	64	15	4	4	8	62	1	127	8	4
Newman, Eric, Rancho Cuca.	13	6	.684	4.15	35	15	0	0	3	0	123.2	104	542	64	57	12	1	3	7	73	1	141	12	0
Thurmond, Travis, L.E.-S.J.	8	8	.429	4.21	21	21	2	1	0	0	130.1	124	567	74	61	14	5	4	10	50	0	114	11	0
Vining, Kenneth, San Jose*	9	6	.600	4.21	23	23	1	1	0	0	136.2	140	592	77	64	9	1	6	5	60	0	142	3	1
Brester, Jason, San Jose*	9	9	.500	4.24	26	26	0	0	0	0	142.1	164	625	80	67	4	4	3	3	52	0	172	10	7

DEPARTMENTAL LEADERS: W—Sobkoviak, Pearsall, 14 each; L—Bermudez, 14; Pct.—Luce, .909; G—Pageler, 61; GS—Malloy, 29; CG—Fieldbinder, 4; ShO—Wunsch, Agosto, 2 each; GF—Pageler, 53; Sv.—Pageler, 29; IP—Malloy, 167.1; H—Malloy, 184; TBF—Malloy, 755; R—Pincavitch, 128; ER—Pincavitch, 102; HR—Nunez, 36; SH—Hardwick, 12; SF—Gryboski, 8; HB—Pincavitch, 19; BB—Pincavitch, 112; IBB—Wallace, 9; SO—Brester, 172; WP—Gregg, 28; BK—Bermudez, 10.

ALL PITCHERS

*Lefthanded pitcher.

Pitcher, Team	W	L	Pct.	ERA	G	GS	CG	ShO	GF	Sv.	IP	H	TBF	R	ER	HR	SH	SF	HB	BB	IBB	SO	WP	Bk.
Abbott, Todd, Visalia	11	10	.524	5.93	31	21	0	0	1	0	121.1	146	575	100	80	17	4	5	3	63	2	70	11	0
Abreu, Oscar, Visalia	0	1	.000	14.66	5	2	0	0	0	0	11.2	19	65	23	19	6	0	0	0	14	1	0	0	0
Agosto, Stevenson, L.E.-R.C.*	7	8	.467	4.98	27	24	2	2	0	0	159.0	173	692	98	88	25	5	2	3	56	0	109	12	3
Alguacil, Jose, San Jose	0	0	.000	0.00	1	0	0	0	1	0	1.0	0	4	0	0	0	0	0	0	0	0	1	0	0
Alvarez, Juan, Lake Elsinore*	4	2	.667	1.40	27	0	0	0	10	3	51.1	33	196	9	8	2	1	4	13	1	2	46	2	2
Anderson, Bill, Rancho Cuca.	8	4	.667	4.01	29	14	0	0	6	1	101.0	78	429	53	45	9	2	2	6	51	0	118	6	2
Anderson, Mike, San Bernardino	1	0	1.000	4.00	4	0	0	0	1	0	9.0	7	39	5	4	1	1	0	0	5	0	13	1	0
Andra, Jeff, San Jose*	1	4	.200	6.98	6	6	0	0	0	0	29.2	36	142	25	23	2	3	0	4	11	0	29	2	2
Apana, Matt, Lancaster	1	1	.500	5.40	3	3	0	0	0	0	11.2	13	54	7	7	3	0	2	1	8	0	7	0	0
Arias, Wagner, Stockton	2	6	.250	6.13	20	14	0	0	3	0	86.2	89	402	63	59	18	3	6	7	64	1	74	10	0
Ashworth, Kym, San Bern.*	0	3	.000	6.46	9	5	0	0	2	0	30.2	34	146	27	22	4	0	1	3	24	0	26	8	0
Backlund, Brett, High Desert	4	2	.667	3.67	17	0	0	0	4	0	34.1	23	137	19	14	4	5	0	1	11	1	38	1	0
Backowski, Lance, San Bern.	0	0	.000	13.50	4	0	0	0	2	0	6.0	10	39	11	9	0	0	1	2	9	0	3	0	0

Pitcher, Team	W	L	Pct.	ERA	G	GS	CG	ShO	GF	Sv.	IP	H	TBF	R	ER	HR	SH	SF	HB	BB	IBB	SO	WP	Bk.
Baez, Benito, Visalia*	5	5	.500	3.54	16	15	1	0	0	0	96.2	83	393	40	38	8	1	2	3	28	0	87	0	1
Bailey, Philip, San Jose*	0	9	.000	7.35	25	10	0	0	5	0	60.0	70	273	54	49	12	1	2	6	33	0	42	11	1
Barcelo, Lorenzo, San Jose	5	4	.556	3.94	16	16	1	1	0	0	89.0	91	378	45	39	13	1	3	1	30	2	89	1	2
Baron, Jim, Rancho Cuca.*	1	7	.125	3.38	14	14	0	0	0	0	85.1	89	371	50	32	2	4	7	2	28	1	64	4	1
Beaumont, Matt, Lake Elsinore*.	0	0	.000	6.75	1	1	0	0	0	0	1.1	2	7	1	1	0	0	0	0	1	0	1	0	1
Beck, Chris, Lancaster	1	4	.200	9.00	8	7	0	0	0	0	33.0	53	171	37	33	8	3	1	3	15	0	23	3	0
Beck, Greg, Stockton	4	4	.500	2.45	27	1	0	0	11	0	55.0	33	222	16	15	4	2	1	3	23	2	46	2	0
Bedinger, Doug, High Desert	0	0	.000	40.50	1	0	0	0	0	0	0.2	3	8	5	3	0	1	0	0	2	0	0	2	0
Bennett, Tom, Modesto	6	9	.400	5.71	25	24	0	0	0	0	112.0	118	521	84	71	8	2	7	5	73	2	116	16	0
Bermudez, Manuel, S.J.-Bak.	10	14	.417	5.42	28	27	3	0	0	0	156.0	182	690	104	94	16	3	5	5	63	2	98	11	10
Berninger, Darren, Stockton	3	2	.600	4.35	18	0	0	0	8	1	31.0	33	143	20	15	1	5	1	2	17	1	20	3	2
Bice, Justin, High Desert	2	0	1.000	4.13	4	4	0	0	0	0	24.0	18	95	12	11	1	0	3	9	0	22	0	1	
Bishop, Joshua, Stockton	2	3	.400	8.51	11	8	0	0	0	0	37.0	56	188	38	35	6	3	0	5	24	0	39	4	0
Blumenstock, Brad, Visalia	0	0	.000	13.89	9	0	0	0	3	0	11.2	22	67	18	18	1	0	0	0	11	1	3	2	0
Blyleven, Todd, Stockton	1	0	1.000	0.00	1	0	0	0	0	0	3.1	2	13	0	0	0	0	0	0	2	0	4	0	0
Bond, Jason, Lancaster*	5	7	.417	3.76	36	9	0	0	11	2	110.0	99	472	54	46	17	1	2	8	45	0	123	5	1
Bonilla, Denys, Lancaster*	9	6	.600	2.84	40	0	0	0	28	6	76.0	67	307	29	24	6	5	2	2	18	4	92	3	3
Brea, Leslie, Lancaster	0	0	.000	13.50	1	0	0	0	0	0	2.0	5	13	5	3	1	0	0	1	1	0	1	1	0
Brester, Jason, San Jose*	9	9	.500	4.24	26	26	0	0	0	0	142.1	164	625	80	67	4	4	3	3	52	0	172	10	7
Brewer, Billy, Visalia*	0	0	.000	0.00	2	2	0	0	0	0	3.0	1	15	1	0	0	1	0	4	0	5	0	0	
Browne, Byron, Stockton	1	3	.250	3.58	8	7	0	0	1	0	27.2	22	120	12	11	0	0	3	22	0	24	4	0	
Bussa, Todd, Modesto	5	4	.556	1.75	30	0	0	0	19	6	46.1	34	192	15	9	2	4	2	2	16	2	61	2	0
Cairncross, Cameron, R. Cuca.*	1	3	.250	5.63	40	0	0	0	17	1	64.0	81	291	46	40	5	4	1	5	15	0	70	4	1
Cana, Nelson, Stockton*	6	1	.857	3.44	44	0	0	0	14	1	91.2	91	396	46	35	7	4	2	4	34	0	69	12	0
Carlson, Dan, Bakersfield	0	0	.000	0.00	2	2	0	0	0	0	6.0	3	22	0	0	0	0	0	1	0	7	0	0	
Carmody, Brian, Rancho Cuca.*.	0	1	.000	8.59	4	3	0	0	0	0	14.2	18	75	16	14	4	1	0	1	15	0	7	1	0
Castillo, Alberto, San Jose*	2	2	.500	5.61	18	1	0	0	8	0	33.2	41	162	26	21	2	2	2	4	15	0	30	7	0
Cervantes, Peter, San Bern.	0	0	.000	0.00	1	0	0	0	1	0	1.0	1	3	0	0	0	0	0	0	0	0	0	0	0
Cesar, Dionys, Visalia	0	0	.000	9.00	1	0	0	0	1	0	1.0	2	6	1	1	0	0	0	0	0	0	1	0	0
Chavez, Carlos, Stockton	0	0	.000	5.40	4	0	0	0	1	0	3.1	5	15	2	2	1	0	0	0	0	5	0	0	
Christianson, Robby, Lancaster..	0	1	.000	7.20	6	0	0	0	4	0	10.0	15	51	12	8	2	0	0	3	4	0	4	1	0
Cintron, Jose, Lake Elsinore	2	3	.400	6.11	28	6	0	0	7	0	63.1	76	281	44	43	8	1	2	7	22	2	50	3	1
Clayton, Craig, Rancho Cuca.	2	1	.667	6.57	10	0	0	0	6	1	12.1	14	57	10	9	1	2	0	5	1	15	3	0	
Clement, Matt, Rancho Cuca.	6	3	.667	1.60	14	14	2	1	0	0	101.0	74	410	30	18	3	2	1	9	31	1	109	6	0
Cooper, Brian, Lake Elsinore	7	3	.700	3.54	17	17	1	0	0	0	117.0	111	497	56	46	7	6	2	10	27	0	104	6	0
Crabtree, Robert, Bakersfield	7	7	.500	5.13	45	9	1	0	9	1	112.1	124	506	77	64	10	1	0	5	59	1	116	12	1
Crossan, Clayton, High Desert	0	0	.000	6.00	2	1	0	0	0	0	6.0	8	30	8	4	0	0	1	2	0	0	0	0	
D'Amico, Jeffrey, Modesto	7	3	.700	3.80	20	13	0	0	5	1	97.0	115	442	57	41	5	1	4	7	34	1	89	9	1
Davis, John, San Bernardino	0	2	.000	7.83	17	4	0	0	3	0	43.2	50	214	48	38	8	1	4	2	34	1	44	6	0
Davis, Keith, Rancho Cuca.	8	10	.444	5.74	35	14	0	0	4	0	125.1	141	575	92	80	13	2	3	15	65	0	103	12	0
Davis, Mark, High Desert*	3	1	.750	2.66	16	0	0	0	5	0	20.1	17	82	6	6	1	0	0	4	0	28	3	0	
Deakman, Josh, Lake Elsinore ...	8	11	.421	4.75	26	25	0	0	0	0	165.0	182	723	107	87	17	1	4	14	42	0	99	9	3
De La Cruz, Fernando, Lk. Elsinore	2	2	.500	4.54	8	6	0	0	1	0	37.2	36	165	22	19	3	1	2	2	17	0	26	1	2
Della Ratta, Pete, Modesto	6	7	.462	3.33	45	0	0	0	19	3	83.2	73	362	45	31	5	5	4	6	31	8	81	6	0
Deskins, Casey, San Bern.*	6	5	.545	5.07	37	6	1	0	11	2	97.2	110	425	56	55	11	4	3	5	34	3	65	11	3
Drumheller, Al, Rancho Cuca.*...	5	6	.455	4.56	38	6	0	0	8	1	81.0	76	355	48	41	5	5	1	0	37	2	107	4	1
DuBose, Eric, Visalia*	1	3	.250	7.04	10	9	0	0	0	0	38.1	43	194	37	30	4	2	0	5	28	0	39	6	3
Eden, Bill, High Desert*	1	0	1.000	5.23	6	0	0	0	3	0	10.1	7	45	6	6	2	1	0	0	8	0	12	0	1
Emerson, Scott, High Desert*	0	0	.000	6.75	3	1	0	0	1	0	4.0	4	21	4	3	0	0	2	4	0	6	1	0	
Enochs, Chris, Modesto	3	0	1.000	2.78	10	9	0	0	1	0	45.1	51	203	20	14	0	3	2	12	0	45	7	0	
Ervin, Kent, Rancho Cuca.	0	0	.000	6.00	2	0	0	0	1	0	3.0	3	14	2	2	1	0	0	0	2	4	0	0	
Estrella, Luis, San Jose	5	5	.500	3.39	42	0	0	0	15	2	77.0	84	332	39	29	3	1	0	2	25	3	59	7	6
Farnsworth, Jeff, Lancaster	1	1	.500	6.97	5	5	0	0	0	0	20.2	24	93	20	16	2	1	1	3	8	0	18	2	0
Fesh, Sean, Rancho Cuca.*	0	1	.000	11.57	4	0	0	0	1	0	4.2	10	28	7	6	2	1	0	1	3	0	5	0	0
Fieldbinder, Mick, Stockton	11	6	.647	2.83	21	21	4	1	0	0	143.1	141	594	58	45	9	4	3	3	38	2	68	10	0
Filchner, Duane, Visalia*	0	0	.000	22.50	2	0	0	0	2	0	2.0	7	15	5	5	1	0	1	2	0	3	0	0
Finley, Chuck, Lake Elsinore*	0	0	.000	2.00	2	2	0	0	0	0	9.0	5	36	3	2	0	0	0	0	4	0	12	0	0
Fleming, John, High Desert	0	0	.000	16.88	1	1	0	0	0	0	2.2	7	17	5	5	0	0	0	0	3	0	1	0	0
Franklin, Wayne, San Bern.*	0	0	.000	0.00	1	0	0	0	0	0	2.0	2	7	0	0	0	0	0	0	0	0	1	0	0
Freehill, Mike, Lake Elsinore	0	0	.000	1.99	21	0	0	0	18	8	22.2	18	89	7	5	1	0	0	8	0	20	1	0	
Goedhart, Darrell, Lake Elsinore.	0	2	.000	8.44	8	3	0	0	3	0	16.0	29	92	18	15	1	2	0	1	11	1	12	2	1
Gogolin, Al, Modesto	0	0	.000	18.00	4	0	0	0	2	0	4.0	9	24	8	8	0	0	1	2	0	3	4	0
Gomez, Dennys, Bakersfield	0	4	.000	7.22	32	2	0	0	10	1	57.1	61	272	52	46	9	3	1	8	34	0	50	7	0
Gorecki, Rick, San Bernardino	2	3	.400	3.88	14	14	0	0	0	0	51.0	38	215	22	22	4	0	2	2	32	0	58	4	0
Gregg, Kevin, Visalia	6	8	.429	5.70	25	24	0	0	0	0	115.1	116	534	81	73	8	2	3	5	74	0	136	28	0
Grote, Jason, Bakersfield	12	8	.600	3.45	25	25	0	0	0	0	156.1	156	659	77	60	11	1	3	2	59	1	116	4	0
Gryboski, Kevin, Lancaster	0	7	.000	9.89	21	15	0	0	4	0	67.1	113	332	82	74	13	2	8	1	26	0	41	7	0
Gubicza, Mark, Lake Elsinore	0	1	.000	15.75	2	2	0	0	0	0	4.0	12	22	7	7	1	0	0	0	1	0	4	0	0
Gunther, Kevin, Modesto	7	2	.778	3.38	42	0	0	0	35	17	53.1	53	223	24	20	7	2	3	11	2	43	2	0	
Gutierrez, Javier, Lancaster	1	1	.500	6.40	14	8	0	0	3	0	52.0	60	250	39	37	8	0	1	4	36	0	51	7	2
Guzman, Domingo, R. Cuca.	3	2	.600	5.45	6	6	0	0	0	0	38.0	42	168	23	23	6	2	1	2	16	0	39	2	0
Hardwick, Bubba, Stockton*	8	6	.571	4.66	31	18	1	1	2	0	133.1	138	570	75	69	10	12	3	7	51	0	80	5	0
Harris, Bryan, Lake Elsinore*	5	5	.500	3.98	31	0	0	0	12	0	43.0	35	184	23	19	4	2	0	2	23	3	39	2	0
Hartvigson, Chad, Bak.*	1	1	.500	3.00	5	4	0	0	0	0	27.0	22	103	9	9	2	1	1	5	0	22	1	0	
Harville, Chad, Visalia	0	0	.000	5.79	14	0	0	0	9	0	18.2	25	92	14	12	2	1	0	13	1	24	1	3	
Hause, Brendan, Modesto	0	0	.000	3.86	2	0	0	0	0	0	4.2	6	20	2	2	1	0	0	0	3	0	4	2	0
Hecker, Doug, Stockton	0	1	.000	4.24	12	0	0	0	3	0	17.0	12	70	9	8	1	0	0	8	0	11	0	2	
Helmer, Chad, Stockton	2	0	1.000	3.09	7	0	0	0	3	1	11.2	12	50	4	4	0	0	1	4	0	10	0	0	
Henderson, Juan, Lk. Elsinore.	1	1	.500	10.45	1	0	0	0	0	0	10.1	20	54	13	12	4	0	0	1	6	0	6	0	0
Henderson, Kenny, R. Cuca.	1	2	.333	4.38	7	7	0	0	0	0	24.2	17	106	14	12	5	1	0	2	17	0	26	0	0
Hernandez, Santos, San Jose	2	6	.250	3.47	47	0	0	0	39	15	57.0	51	237	26	22	7	4	1	14	2	87	4	0	
Hill, Jason, Lake Elsinore*	3	7	.300	4.23	54	0	0	0	37	15	66.0	71	313	43	31	2	10	1	5	34	4	73	4	0

Pitcher, Team	W	L	Pct.	ERA	G	GS	CG	ShO	GF	Sv.	IP	H	TBF	R	ER	HR	SH	SF	HB	BB	IBB	SO	WP	Bk.
Hoff, Steve, Rancho Cuca.*	4	5	.444	6.24	14	13	0	0	1	0	66.1	73	319	56	46	6	2	2	2	48	0	59	13	0
Holmes, Mike, Visalia	2	1	.667	3.81	16	0	0	0	11	3	28.1	28	116	13	12	5	0	0	0	4	0	20	1	0
Hommel, Brian, Stockton*	7	2	.778	3.15	55	0	0	0	34	14	71.1	45	296	25	25	5	4	3	8	39	0	76	6	0
Humphreys, Kevin, Lk. Elsinore	0	1	.000	3.50	16	0	0	0	4	0	18.0	19	77	9	7	2	1	0	3	2	0	15	1	0
Hutzler, Jeff, Bakersfield	2	7	.222	5.30	47	3	1	0	12	1	88.1	92	391	59	52	7	6	3	5	41	1	70	12	0
Ishee, Gabe, Stockton	2	3	.400	6.57	21	3	0	0	6	0	49.1	55	232	38	36	8	2	2	2	29	0	52	5	2
Jensen, Ryan, Bakersfield	0	0	.000	13.50	1	1	0	0	0	0	1.1	3	7	2	2	1	0	1	0	0	0	2	0	0
Johnson, Gregory, Lk. Elsinore*	1	0	1.000	3.43	34	0	0	0	8	0	44.2	46	197	21	17	2	2	3	5	9	2	35	1	0
Jordan, Jason, High Desert	2	0	1.000	6.14	6	4	0	0	0	0	14.2	16	70	12	10	0	0	1	0	13	0	10	1	0
Kazmirski, Robert, Visalia	1	1	.500	16.62	5	0	0	0	3	1	4.1	11	30	9	8	3	0	0	0	5	2	6	1	0
Keith, Jeff, Bakersfield*	1	2	.333	5.73	37	0	0	0	12	0	44.0	45	205	29	28	9	1	3	6	32	0	35	4	0
Kern, Brian, Visalia	3	0	1.000	7.60	23	0	0	0	9	1	34.1	42	178	38	29	5	1	1	2	28	1	39	7	3
Kjos, Ryan, Modesto	2	2	.500	3.82	34	0	0	0	16	0	61.1	57	272	38	26	6	2	5	3	30	1	73	7	0
Knoll, Brian, Bakersfield	3	6	.333	5.69	49	0	0	0	23	2	68.0	88	323	50	43	6	1	2	35	3	56	10	0	
Knudsen, Kurt, Lake Elsinore	1	2	.333	6.97	7	0	0	0	7	3	10.1	13	46	9	8	1	0	0	4	0	10	1	0	
Kolb, Brandon, Rancho Cuca.	3	2	.600	3.00	10	10	0	0	0	0	63.0	60	261	29	21	0	1	1	2	22	0	49	5	0
Konieczki, Dom, Stockton*	1	1	.500	2.77	12	0	0	0	5	1	13.0	11	56	5	4	0	2	0	1	10	0	16	1	0
Kramer, Matthew, San Bern.	0	0	.000	5.94	10	0	0	0	2	0	16.2	18	79	12	11	1	0	2	0	16	0	16	0	0
Kubenka, Jeff, San Bernardino*	5	1	.833	0.92	34	0	0	0	32	19	39.0	24	152	4	4	1	4	2	1	11	1	62	3	0
Lagattuta, Rico, Modesto*	0	0	.000	9.00	3	0	0	0	2	0	1.0	3	9	1	1	0	0	0	3	0	1	0	0	
Langston, Mark, Lake Elsinore*	0	2	.000	3.21	3	3	0	0	0	0	14.0	11	53	7	5	1	0	1	2	0	10	0	0	
Larreal, Guillermo, Bakersfield	2	0	1.000	6.12	32	0	0	0	12	1	50.0	63	222	40	34	9	2	3	4	14	0	37	1	1
Laxton, Brett, Visalia	11	5	.688	2.99	29	22	0	0	2	0	138.2	141	606	62	46	7	4	0	11	50	0	121	14	0
Leese, Brandon, San Jose	7	5	.583	3.05	19	19	0	0	0	0	112.0	99	475	44	38	11	1	0	4	46	2	99	15	0
Leyva, Julian, Modesto	4	9	.308	4.92	28	19	0	0	6	2	139.0	148	596	99	76	21	3	3	6	38	1	90	5	1
Lilly, Ted, San Bernardino*	7	8	.467	2.81	23	21	2	1	0	0	134.2	116	540	52	42	9	5	3	4	32	0	158	7	5
Linares, Rich, San Bernardino	1	0	1.000	3.41	26	0	0	0	23	10	29.0	36	130	11	11	3	0	1	1	7	0	33	1	0
Linebrink, Scott, San Jose	2	1	.667	3.18	6	6	0	0	0	0	28.1	29	120	11	10	2	0	0	0	10	0	40	2	0
Luce, Robert, Lancaster	10	1	.909	2.81	14	14	0	0	0	0	86.1	100	372	43	27	8	0	2	5	24	0	57	4	0
Malloy, William, Bakersfield	7	9	.438	4.79	29	29	0	0	0	0	167.1	184	755	106	89	11	5	3	7	83	1	124	23	1
Manwiller, Tim, Modesto	1	1	.500	3.05	7	0	0	0	2	0	20.2	21	85	8	7	1	2	3	0	7	2	18	1	1
Marenghi, Matt, High Desert	4	3	.571	3.07	38	0	0	0	14	2	73.1	81	326	38	25	8	0	1	2	23	1	45	4	0
Marte, Damaso, Lancaster*	8	8	.500	4.13	25	25	2	1	0	0	139.1	144	609	75	64	15	4	4	8	62	1	127	8	4
Martin, Jeff, San Jose	0	4	.000	5.40	20	0	0	0	14	6	26.2	36	125	18	16	2	2	1	3	11	3	25	1	0
Martinez, Ramon, San Bern.	0	1	.000	1.15	4	4	0	0	0	0	15.2	10	58	2	2	0	0	1	4	0	16	0	0
Mayer, Aaron, Lake Elsinore	2	3	.400	7.29	36	0	0	0	14	0	58.0	69	282	57	47	4	3	5	6	41	1	38	6	0
Mayo, Blake, San Bernardino	1	1	.500	5.16	20	0	0	0	5	0	29.2	36	141	18	17	0	1	1	1	17	2	29	6	0
Mays, Joe, Lancaster	7	4	.636	4.86	15	15	1	0	0	0	96.1	108	420	55	52	9	2	6	5	34	0	82	2	0
McMullen, Mike, San Jose	6	4	.600	2.67	56	0	0	0	23	7	91.0	85	377	37	27	1	9	4	5	33	3	71	6	0
McNeely, Mitch, San Bern.*	1	3	.250	7.55	18	0	0	0	8	0	39.1	61	196	36	33	9	3	3	0	20	1	28	3	3
Medina, Rafael, Rancho Cuca.	2	0	1.000	2.00	3	3	0	0	0	0	18.0	13	68	4	4	1	1	0	0	5	0	14	1	0
Michalak, Chris, High Desert*	3	7	.300	2.65	49	0	0	0	17	4	85.0	76	362	36	25	4	3	0	9	31	1	74	6	1
Middlebrook, Jason, R. Cuca.	0	2	.000	4.03	6	6	0	0	0	0	22.1	29	105	15	10	1	1	3	0	12	1	18	2	1
Miranda, Angel, Stockton*	0	0	.000	0.00	1	1	0	0	0	0	2.0	0	8	0	0	0	0	0	0	2	0	2	0	0
Mitchell, Dean, San Bernardino	0	0	.000	0.00	1	0	0	0	1	0	1.0	0	4	0	0	0	0	0	1	0	1	0	0	
Mlodik, Kevin, Visalia	8	9	.471	5.44	35	19	0	0	3	0	129.0	164	580	86	78	17	3	5	4	42	1	91	7	2
Montane, Ivan, Lancaster	1	2	.333	5.29	6	6	0	0	0	0	32.1	40	150	25	19	2	1	2	2	13	1	34	8	1
Moore, Vince, Rancho Cuca.*	0	0	.000	0.00	1	0	0	0	1	0	1.0	1	7	2	0	0	0	0	2	0	0	0	0	
Morgan, Eric, Lancaster	4	3	.571	5.42	24	13	0	0	3	0	89.2	98	413	59	54	9	6	3	7	56	2	56	12	0
Morrison, Chris, Visalia	3	3	.500	3.84	48	0	0	0	21	2	79.2	92	366	46	34	2	6	4	6	39	4	43	8	0
Mullins, Greg, Stockton*	0	2	.000	2.18	30	0	0	0	30	19	33.0	22	131	9	8	2	0	0	1	12	0	52	4	0
Myers, Jason, Bakersfield*	4	3	.571	6.42	10	9	0	0	0	0	47.2	64	221	43	34	7	1	2	1	14	0	32	3	0
Narcisse, Tyrone, Rancho Cuca.	2	0	1.000	3.41	22	0	0	0	9	0	34.1	21	140	13	13	3	2	2	2	22	0	38	4	0
Nash, Damon, Rancho Cuca.	0	0	.000	0.00	1	0	0	0	1	0	0.0	1	3	1	0	0	0	0	2	0	1	0	0	
Neal, Billy, San Bernardino	0	5	.000	4.24	24	0	0	0	9	1	46.2	50	207	30	22	4	3	1	17	0	31	2	0	
Nelson, Chris, Modesto	3	3	.500	3.83	8	8	0	0	0	0	47.0	55	198	23	20	4	0	1	1	7	0	53	2	2
Newman, Eric, Rancho Cuca.	13	6	.684	4.15	35	15	0	0	3	0	123.2	104	542	64	57	12	1	3	7	73	1	141	12	0
Niles, Randy, Modesto	4	0	1.000	2.60	7	5	0	0	0	0	34.2	32	148	13	10	3	1	0	6	9	0	20	0	0
Noriega, Ray, Modesto*	5	8	.385	4.04	28	28	0	0	0	0	156.0	161	698	101	70	17	8	2	4	69	1	119	10	3
Nunez, Vladimir, High Desert	8	5	.615	5.17	28	28	1	1	0	0	158.1	169	682	102	91	36	1	3	14	40	1	142	10	2
Ochsenfeld, Chris, San Bern.*	1	1	.500	5.87	13	0	0	0	7	0	15.1	18	80	13	10	0	1	1	0	14	1	12	4	0
O'Dell, Jacob, Visalia	8	5	.615	4.54	27	27	1	1	0	0	150.2	159	648	86	76	17	4	2	11	47	0	117	10	0
Oleksik, George, High Desert	2	2	.500	8.63	17	0	0	0	3	0	24.0	32	128	28	23	3	1	0	3	22	0	13	1	0
Ontiveros, Steve, Lake Elsinore	0	1	.000	27.00	1	1	0	0	0	0	0.1	0	2	1	1	0	0	0	0	1	0	0	0	0
Oquist, Mike, Modesto	0	0	.000	4.91	2	2	0	0	0	0	3.2	5	17	2	2	1	0	0	0	1	0	5	0	0
Pageler, Mick, Bakersfield	2	5	.286	4.68	61	0	0	0	53	29	65.1	69	291	39	34	8	2	1	5	26	3	68	4	0
Paluk, Jeff, San Bernardino	1	3	.250	7.57	28	0	0	0	10	0	44.0	63	218	39	37	6	0	4	1	25	1	38	6	0
Pasqualicchio, Mike, Stockton*	1	10	.091	6.43	17	15	1	0	1	1	85.1	93	389	67	61	10	4	3	7	44	0	58	12	3
Passini, Brian, Stockton*	1	5	.167	4.76	8	8	1	0	0	0	45.1	40	185	28	24	7	3	1	3	21	0	34	1	0
Paulino, Jose, Visalia	3	2	.600	4.54	39	0	0	0	7	2	83.1	89	363	48	42	7	1	2	1	32	1	67	6	0
Pearsall, J.J., San Bernardino*	14	11	.560	4.54	31	28	0	0	1	0	160.2	145	696	91	81	12	4	4	8	93	0	112	9	2
Pena, Alex, High Desert	2	1	.667	6.49	33	3	0	0	7	0	69.1	80	310	56	50	15	1	2	3	30	0	39	6	1
Percival, Troy, Lake Elsinore	0	0	.000	0.00	2	1	0	0	0	0	2.0	1	7	0	0	0	0	0	0	0	0	3	0	0
Perez, Juan, Visalia*	3	6	.333	7.28	29	0	0	0	25	8	64.2	47	266	30	20	6	2	6	1	24	4	66	7	1
Petcka, Joe, Visalia	0	1	.000	23.63	4	0	0	0	0	0	2.2	8	22	8	7	1	0	0	6	0	1	1	0	
Peters, Don, High Desert	1	2	.333	1.62	21	0	0	0	15	7	33.1	20	134	10	6	2	1	0	1	13	0	25	3	0
Pincavitch, Kevin, San Bern.	6	9	.400	6.78	28	27	0	0	1	0	135.1	135	665	128	102	18	3	6	19	112	0	130	27	1
Proctor, Murph, San Bern.*	0	0	.000	0.00	2	0	0	0	2	0	1.2	0	6	0	0	0	0	0	0	0	0	0	0	0
Quirico, Rafael, Lake Elsinore*	8	4	.667	2.83	14	13	0	0	0	0	92.1	94	399	43	29	5	4	5	7	29	0	74	5	2
Rector, Bobby, Bakersfield	2	4	.333	4.10	8	8	0	0	0	0	48.1	52	199	27	22	8	1	1	1	12	1	32	1	1
Remington, Jake, Rancho Cuca.	2	1	.667	7.45	6	0	0	0	2	0	9.2	12	43	9	8	0	0	0	3	1	9	2	0	
Rice, Nathan, Bakersfield*	2	0	1.000	1.96	8	1	0	0	4	0	18.1	13	77	4	4	0	0	0	1	9	0	9	0	0

Pitcher, Team	W	L	Pct.	ERA	G	GS	CG	ShO	GF	Sv.	IP	H	TBF	R	ER	HR	SH	SF	HB	BB	IBB	SO	WP	Bk.
Riggan, Jerrod, Lake Elsinore	2	5	.286	6.07	8	8	0	0	0	0	43.0	60	202	36	29	1	4	2	4	16	0	31	6	2
Riley, Michael, Bakersfield*	1	2	.333	8.41	6	4	0	0	0	0	20.1	25	94	20	19	4	0	1	0	8	0	17	0	0
Rivera, Rafael, Lancaster............	1	3	.250	3.51	24	1	0	0	15	3	48.2	47	209	27	19	3	4	2	3	17	4	46	4	0
Rivette, Scott, Modesto	9	9	.500	3.50	20	20	3	0	0	0	126.0	147	533	65	50	12	3	2	7	31	1	96	8	1
Robbins, Jason, High Desert	7	5	.583	4.42	23	23	1	0	0	0	128.1	125	549	74	63	15	1	2	8	42	0	127	6	1
Robertson, Doug, Modesto........	0	0	.000	0.00	1	0	0	0	0	0	1.0	1	4	0	0	0	0	0	0	0	0	0	0	0
Rogers, Kevin, San Jose*	0	0	.000	2.76	8	8	0	0	0	0	29.1	29	118	9	9	1	0	1	1	6	0	27	1	0
Rossiter, Mike, Stockton	8	1	.889	2.72	34	8	0	0	9	0	86.0	83	368	31	26	6	2	2	15	27	0	79	3	0
Sabel, Erik, High Desert	11	11	.500	5.32	31	22	0	0	4	1	143.2	174	646	101	85	21	10	6	10	40	0	86	6	0
Sak, James, Rancho Cuca.	6	3	.667	2.93	57	3	0	0	50	27	70.2	42	286	28	23	5	1	3	5	30	2	113	4	1
Scheffer, Aaron, Lancaster	11	3	.786	5.44	37	3	0	0	9	4	92.2	93	410	58	56	17	4	3	7	42	1	103	10	0
Schramm, Carl, San Jose..........	4	4	.500	4.94	36	4	0	0	9	0	93.0	103	410	54	51	10	2	3	3	33	0	75	6	0
Scutero, Brian, Lake Elsinore	0	1	.000	11.25	5	0	0	0	2	0	8.0	16	42	11	10	2	0	0	0	6	1	8	1	0
Skrmetta, Matt, Rancho Cuca.	0	1	.000	1.59	17	0	0	0	8	0	28.1	27	122	7	5	2	1	0	1	10	0	36	4	0
Skuse, Nick, Lake Elsinore	0	0	.000	2.03	17	0	0	0	7	0	26.2	23	113	13	6	2	1	0	3	8	0	40	6	1
Smith, Andy, Visalia	3	7	.300	3.82	42	0	0	0	14	1	70.2	77	330	40	30	7	4	1	4	39	6	67	9	1
Sobkoviak, Jeff, High Desert	14	6	.700	4.28	28	28	0	0	0	0	160.0	167	683	88	76	12	6	4	11	37	0	101	9	1
Spencer, Sean, Lancaster*	2	3	.400	1.64	39	0	0	0	32	18	60.1	41	227	12	11	4	4	1	2	15	0	72	2	0
Spencer, Stan, Rancho Cuca.	3	1	.750	3.35	7	7	0	0	0	0	40.1	37	164	18	15	6	0	1	2	5	0	46	1	0
Stark, Dennis, Lancaster	1	1	.500	3.24	3	3	0	0	0	0	16.2	13	71	7	6	1	1	0	2	10	0	17	0	0
Steed, Rick, High Desert	6	1	.857	2.79	46	0	0	0	21	1	77.1	58	325	28	24	5	3	2	6	31	7	64	10	0
Stephens, Jason, Lake Elsinore..	7	11	.389	5.40	24	22	1	0	1	0	126.2	149	569	86	76	14	1	2	16	42	2	101	4	1
Stone, Ricky, San Bernardino	3	3	.500	3.35	8	8	0	0	0	0	53.2	40	206	22	20	4	2	1	2	10	0	40	2	0
Stoops, Jim, San Jose	2	5	.286	5.20	50	0	0	0	16	4	91.2	92	401	56	53	3	2	3	7	45	2	114	7	1
Sweeney, Brian, Lancaster	6	3	.667	3.80	40	0	0	0	13	1	85.1	83	358	39	36	11	2	4	2	21	1	73	8	0
Takahashi, Kurt, San Jose	1	1	.500	5.95	10	0	0	0	6	1	19.2	20	90	17	13	1	1	3	4	8	1	21	2	0
Telgheder, David, Modesto	0	0	.000	3.38	2	2	0	0	0	0	5.1	3	21	2	2	0	0	0	0	2	0	4	0	0
Thompson, Frank, San Bern......	5	2	.714	5.69	39	0	0	0	12	2	55.1	58	258	39	35	6	1	3	3	35	2	40	5	1
Thompson, John, Lancaster..........	1	0	1.000	2.25	3	0	0	0	3	0	4.0	4	19	1	1	1	0	0	0	2	0	3	0	0
Thurmond, Travis, L.E.-S.J.	6	8	.429	4.21	21	21	2	1	0	0	130.1	124	567	74	61	14	5	4	10	50	0	114	11	0
Torres, Luis, Rancho Cuca.	2	2	.500	4.34	31	0	0	0	16	2	56.0	53	239	30	27	7	2	0	4	24	1	46	7	1
Tranbarger, Mark, High Desert* .	1	0	1.000	4.70	5	0	0	0	2	0	7.2	9	36	4	4	1	1	1	0	5	0	4	1	0
Tuttle, Dave, High Desert...........	4	3	.571	2.43	50	0	0	0	42	19	63.0	54	262	22	17	4	3	3	0	23	3	57	5	0
Tyler, Josh, Stockton	0	0	.000	0.00	2	0	0	0	2	0	1.2	0	6	0	0	0	0	1	0	1	0	0	0	0
Urbina, Dan, San Bernardino	3	2	.600	2.57	13	2	0	0	2	0	35.0	26	150	14	10	2	0	2	4	22	2	33	5	1
Valenti, Jon, Modesto.................	0	0	.000	0.00	1	0	0	0	1	0	1.0	1	4	0	0	0	0	0	0	0	0	1	0	0
Veras, Dario, Rancho Cuca..........	0	0	.000	6.00	2	0	0	0	1	1	3.0	3	13	3	2	1	0	0	1	0	0	3	1	0
Verplancke, Joe, High Desert	7	2	.778	5.81	17	17	0	0	0	0	74.1	91	345	53	48	15	1	2	12	30	0	64	4	2
Victory, Joe, Lancaster	5	4	.556	4.34	28	14	0	0	5	0	102.1	98	460	70	55	9	5	7	7	53	3	86	9	1
Vining, Kenneth, San Jose*	9	6	.600	4.21	23	23	1	1	0	0	136.2	140	592	77	64	9	1	6	5	60	0	142	3	1
Vizcaino, Luis, Modesto	0	3	.000	13.19	7	0	0	0	3	0	14.1	24	76	24	21	4	1	0	0	13	4	15	0	2
Wagner, Joe, Stockton	3	5	.375	6.72	14	14	0	0	0	0	72.1	83	345	61	54	10	3	11	44	0	36	6	0	
Wallace, Flint, Modesto	10	4	.714	3.73	35	8	0	0	9	1	99.0	105	437	53	41	12	6	6	3	34	9	59	4	2
Warrecker, Teddy, San Bern.	1	5	.167	7.76	10	3	0	0	3	0	29.0	29	136	28	25	3	0	1	3	20	0	36	10	0
Weinberg, Todd, Visalia*	3	2	.600	4.26	38	0	0	0	35	20	38.0	33	166	23	18	1	2	4	0	22	2	39	5	0
Wells, Matt, Bakersfield	8	12	.400	4.45	29	25	0	0	2	0	143.2	154	654	87	71	10	6	7	6	81	2	109	8	0
Westfall, Allan, Lancaster	0	3	.000	6.16	15	0	0	0	8	3	19.0	23	88	17	13	4	1	0	2	8	0	14	1	0
Williams, Jeff, San Bernardino* ..	10	4	.714	3.10	18	18	0	0	0	0	116.0	101	472	52	40	8	4	2	2	34	0	72	7	3
Winkleman, Greg, Modesto*	2	2	.500	5.70	39	1	0	0	19	0	60.0	71	284	44	38	4	3	2	37	2	54	7	1	
Witasick, Jay, Modesto	0	1	.000	4.15	9	2	0	0	1	1	17.1	16	75	9	8	1	0	1	5	0	29	1	0	
Wolff, Bryan, Rancho Cuca.	3	0	1.000	1.62	9	2	0	0	3	1	33.1	19	125	6	6	2	0	0	3	6	0	39	2	1
Wunsch, Kelly, Stockton	7	9	.438	3.46	24	22	2	2	0	0	143.0	141	627	65	55	11	10	4	14	62	0	98	9	2
Zerbe, Chad, High Desert*	1	6	.143	7.43	9	8	0	0	0	0	36.1	61	192	49	30	7	0	3	1	15	0	26	1	0

COMBINATION SHUTOUTS: Bakersfield (10)—Carlson-Hartvigson-Crabtree, Myers-Crabtree, Myers-Crabtree-Hutzler, Grote-Crabtree, Malloy-Hutzler, Grote-Pageler, Bermudez-Crabtree-Pageler, Rector-Pageler, Malloy-Pageler, Bermudez-Pageler. **High Desert (4)**—Robbins-Pena, Bice-Zerbe-Tuttle, Sobkoviak-Michalak-Steed, Sobkoviak-Peters. **Lake Elsinore (2)**—Stephens-Mayer-Hill, Cooper-Humphreys. **Lancaster (3)**—Mays-Rivera, Marte-Spencer, Mays-Sweeney-Spencer. **Modesto (4)**—Leyva-D'Amico, Bennett-Della Ratta, D'Amico-Bussa, Noriega-Della Ratta-Gunther. **Rancho Cucamonga (10)**—Kolb-Cairncross, Kolb-Sak, Clement-Cairncross, Henderson-Cairncross-Newman, Middlebrook-Wolff, Wolff-Cairncross, Anderson-Veras, Newman-Torres, Hoff-Cairncross, Anderson-Davis. **San Bernardino (8)**—Williams-Kubenka, Williams-Kubenka, Pearsall-Thompson-Kubenka, Lilly-Thompson-Neal, Gorecki-Deskins, Lilly-Paluk-Deskins, Lilly-Neal, Deskins-Cervantes-Franklin-Mitchell. **San Jose (6)**—Brester-Hernandez-Martin, Vining-Stoops-Martin, Brester-Hernandez, Brester-McMullen-Schramm, Linebrink-Estrella, Linebrink-McMullen-Stoops. **Stockton (5)**—Wunsch-Cana-Beck-Hommel-Mullins, Miranda-Wunsch-Berninger-Mullins, Browne-Hommel-Beck-Mullins, Pasqualicchio-Hommel-Mullins, Browne-Rossiter-Hommel. **Visalia (2)**—Laxton-Morrison-Weinberg, DuBose-Morrison-Abbott-Perez-Holmes.

NO-HIT GAMES: Lilly, San Bernardino, defeated Lake Elsinore, 8-0, May 10.

PITCHERS WITH TWO OR MORE TEAMS

Pitcher, Team	W	L	Pct.	ERA	G	GS	CG	ShO	GF	Sv.	IP	H	TBF	R	ER	HR	SH	SF	HB	BB	IBB	SO	WP	Bk.
Agosto, Stevenson, Lk. Elsinore*	5	8	.385	5.32	24	21	1	1	0	0	137.0	155	603	91	81	23	2	2	3	50	0	91	11	3
Agosto, Stevenson, R. Cuca.* ...	2	0	1.000	2.86	3	3	1	1	0	0	22.0	18	89	7	7	2	3	0	0	6	0	18	1	0
Bermudez, Manuel, San Jose	2	6	.250	6.75	9	9	2	0	0	0	44.0	61	208	35	33	4	1	3	1	22	1	27	5	2
Bermudez, Manuel, Bakersfield..	8	8	.500	4.90	19	18	1	0	0	0	112.0	121	482	69	61	12	2	2	4	41	1	71	6	8
Thurmond, Travis, Lk. Elsinore..	3	3	.500	2.52	9	9	2	1	0	0	60.2	41	247	21	17	6	2	1	5	22	0	53	5	0
Thurmond, Travis, San Jose......	3	5	.375	5.68	12	12	0	0	0	0	69.2	83	320	53	44	8	3	3	5	28	0	61	6	0

1997 FIELDING

TEAM

Team	Pct.	G	PO	A	E	TC	DP	PB	Team	Pct.	G	PO	A	E	TC	DP	PB
Stockton	.973	140	3730	1567	148	5445	125	36	Bakersfield...............	.969	140	3701	1742	175	5618	160	22
San Bernardino........	.970	140	3716	1519	163	5398	112	41	R. Cucamonga..........	.969	140	3741	1425	168	5334	107	19

Team	Pct.	G	PO	A	E	TC	DP	PB
Lancaster	.968	141	3767	1446	171	5384	113	22
High Desert	.967	140	3753	1616	183	5552	104	37
San Jose	.967	140	3695	1494	179	5368	116	18
Lake Elsinore	.967	140	3745	1609	185	5539	106	25
Visalia	.963	140	3732	1584	207	5523	92	25
Modesto	.958	141	3701	1534	227	5462	135	25

TRIPLE PLAY: Modesto.

INDIVIDUAL

FIRST BASEMEN

NOTE: All caps denotes fielding-percentage leader based on 70 games for catchers, 93 for all other non-pitchers and 140 innings for pitchers. *Throws lefthanded.

Player, Team	Pct.	G	PO	A	E	TC	DP
Alguacil, Jose, San Jose	1.000	2	3	0	0	3	0
Ardoin, Danny, Visalia	1.000	3	21	3	0	24	1
Baeza, Art, Bakersfield	.971	9	93	7	3	103	11
Barajas, Rodrigo, High Desert	1.000	2	17	1	0	18	2
Barker, Kevin, Stockton*	.988	61	476	31	6	513	41
BARNES, Larry, Lake Elsinore*	.993	113	1048	87	8	1143	72
Betten, Randy, Lake Elsinore	1.000	1	11	1	0	12	3
Boston, D.J., Visalia*	.979	14	131	11	3	145	15
Buhner, Shawn, Lancaster	.983	64	487	33	9	529	48
Byers, MacGregor, Visalia	.962	4	25	0	1	26	2
Cameron, Stanton, High Desert	1.000	1	8	1	0	9	1
Clifford, Jim, Lancaster*	.985	71	604	36	10	650	49
Cooper, Tim, Bakersfield	1.000	2	19	5	0	24	2
Cruz, Cirilo, Lancaster	1.000	15	106	5	0	111	5
Davis, Ben, Rancho Cuca.	1.000	1	1	0	0	1	0
Davis, Glenn, San Bernardino*	.990	58	530	39	6	575	43
Dilone, Juan, Modesto	.988	20	148	14	2	164	14
Donati, John, Lancaster	.857	1	5	1	1	7	1
Durkac, Bo, High Desert	.983	69	591	61	11	663	39
Failla, Paul, Lake Elsinore	.971	15	124	10	4	138	10
Faircloth, Kevin, San Bernardino	.971	9	32	2	1	35	0
Glasser, Scott, High Desert	1.000	6	21	0	0	21	2
Gulseth, Mark, San Jose	.989	84	671	53	8	732	57
Hernandez, Ramon, Visalia	1.000	2	13	3	0	16	0
Hills, Rich, Rancho Cuca.	.978	5	39	6	1	46	3
Hinch, A.J., Modesto	1.000	1	7	1	0	8	0
Horton, Conan, San Bernardino	1.000	1	3	0	0	3	0
Kent, Robbie, Rancho Cuca.	1.000	2	8	0	0	8	1
Leach, Nick, San Bernardino	.952	4	38	2	2	42	3
Lee, Travis, High Desert*	.998	55	553	67	1	621	37
Macalutas, Jon, Stockton	.978	21	205	13	5	223	10
Marcinczyk, T.R., Modesto	.987	100	747	75	11	833	74
Martin, Mike, Lancaster	.667	1	1	1	1	3	0
McAninch, John, Lake Elsinore	.977	15	117	9	3	129	8
McCarty, Matt, San Bernardino	1.000	1	1	0	0	1	0
Mensik, Todd, Visalia*	.974	13	101	10	3	114	4
Minor, Damon, Bakersfield*	.984	129	1261	88	22	1371	127
Miranda, Alex, Visalia*	1.000	11	61	6	0	67	3
Mitchell, Michael, Rancho Cuca.	.984	108	877	62	15	954	75
Morris, Jon, Lake Elsinore	1.000	1	14	0	0	14	1
Penix, Troy, Mod.-Vis.*	.987	77	501	34	7	542	48
Poor, Jeff, San Jose	.889	3	8	0	1	9	1
Proctor, Murph, San Bern.*	.992	27	213	22	2	237	15
Ramirez, Peto, San Jose	1.000	1	7	0	0	7	0
Reynoso, Benjamin, R. Cuca.	.667	1	2	0	1	3	0
Rodriguez, Guillermo, San Jose	1.000	10	58	7	0	65	6
Sankey, Brian, San Bernardino*	.994	51	424	42	3	469	40
Schwenke, Matt, Rancho Cuca.	.980	29	237	10	5	252	16
Slemmer, Dave, Visalia	.987	72	510	41	7	558	33
Swinton, Jermaine, Stockton	.975	20	148	11	4	163	15
Unrat, Chris, San Jose	.952	16	107	11	6	124	11
Valenti, Jon, Modesto	.989	20	83	3	1	87	6
Ventura, Wilfredo, Visalia	.966	13	79	6	3	88	3
Williams, Drew, Stockton	.993	44	380	38	3	421	41
Wilson, Keith, High Desert	.994	19	151	15	1	167	13
Wilson, Todd, San Jose	.990	48	353	34	4	391	24

TRIPLE PLAY: Marcinczyk.

FIRST BASEMEN WITH TWO OR MORE TEAMS

Player, Team	Pct.	G	PO	A	E	TC	DP
Penix, Troy, Modesto*	.981	34	197	15	4	216	24
Penix, Troy, Visalia*	.991	43	304	19	3	326	24

SECOND BASEMEN

Player, Team	Pct.	G	PO	A	E	TC	DP
Alguacil, Jose, San Jose	.963	44	73	81	6	160	19
Anderson, Cliff, San Bernardino	1.000	3	10	10	0	20	5
Betten, Randy, Lake Elsinore	1.000	1	3	1	0	4	0
Boughton, Mike, High Desert	1.000	2	1	2	0	3	1
Castro, Jose, Modesto	.949	109	202	279	26	507	66

Player, Team	Pct.	G	PO	A	E	TC	DP
Cesar, Dionys, Visalia	.972	52	89	122	6	217	17
Davalillo, David, Lake Elsinore	1.000	4	5	11	0	16	1
Dean, Chris, Lancaster	.953	65	125	201	16	342	40
Durrington, Trent, Lake Elsinore	.968	111	205	310	17	532	56
Ehmann, Kurt, San Jose	.913	4	10	11	2	23	4
Failla, Paul, Lake Elsinore	.952	26	45	55	5	105	10
Faircloth, Kevin, San Bernardino	1.000	15	17	37	0	54	4
Fuentes, Joel, San Jose	1.000	3	4	1	0	5	1
Gama, Rick, Rancho Cuca.	.938	22	57	64	8	129	18
Glasser, Scott, High Desert	.968	11	10	20	1	31	6
Gonzalez, Santos, Rancho Cuca.	1.000	2	3	7	0	10	1
Guerrero, Sergio, Stockton	.977	76	168	178	8	354	40
Hills, Rich, Rancho Cuca.	1.000	1	4	3	0	7	2
Kent, Robbie, Rancho Cuca.	.970	22	37	59	3	99	15
Lara, Edward, Vis.-Mod.	.909	12	17	23	4	44	3
Marval, Raul, Bakersfield	.966	26	51	93	5	149	25
METCALFE, Mike, San Bern.	.979	129	228	324	12	564	70
Mosier, Mark, San Jose	1.000	1	2	2	0	4	1
Newhan, David, Visalia	.966	60	123	157	10	290	28
Ortiz, Jose, Modesto	.931	6	16	11	2	29	2
Parker, Allan, Lake Elsinore	.833	2	2	3	1	6	0
Paulino, Arturo, Modesto	.961	40	66	81	6	153	23
Perez, Richard, Stockton	.944	5	6	11	1	18	2
Pernalete, Marco, Bakersfield	.945	14	19	33	3	55	11
Powers, John, Rancho Cuca.	.976	98	187	252	11	450	39
Prospero, Ted, San Jose	.962	15	19	31	2	52	6
Ramirez, Joel, Lancaster	.950	40	63	108	9	180	17
Ready, Randy, Lake Elsinore	.500	1	1	1	2	4	0
Regan, Jason, Lancaster	.983	45	66	109	3	178	23
Reynoso, Benjamin, R. Cuca.	1.000	1	0	3	0	3	0
Slemmer, Dave, Visalia	.975	38	63	91	4	158	20
Spivey, Ernest, High Desert	.949	136	226	394	33	653	59
Tyler, Josh, Stockton	.976	70	165	161	8	334	44
Valenti, Jon, Modesto	1.000	3	1	4	0	5	1
Vina, Fernando, Stockton	1.000	3	2	7	0	9	1
Watson, Jon, Bakersfield	.972	109	217	378	17	612	80
Zuniga, Tony, San Jose	.968	95	135	253	13	401	41

TRIPLE PLAY: Castro.

SECOND BASEMEN WITH TWO OR MORE TEAMS

Player, Team	Pct.	G	PO	A	E	TC	DP
Lara, Edward, Visalia	.907	10	17	22	4	43	3
Lara, Edward, Modesto	1.000	2	0	1	0	1	0

THIRD BASEMEN

Player, Team	Pct.	G	PO	A	E	TC	DP
Alguacil, Jose, San Jose	.952	47	28	71	5	104	5
Anderson, Cliff, San Bernardino	.937	127	71	241	21	333	24
Ardoin, Danny, Visalia	.667	1	2	0	1	3	0
Barlok, Todd, S.B.-L.E.	.893	45	35	82	14	131	7
Betten, Randy, Lake Elsinore	1.000	11	11	22	0	33	2
Brosius, Scott, Modesto	.667	2	1	1	1	3	0
Cesar, Dionys, Visalia	.881	14	9	28	5	42	3
Chavez, Eric, Visalia	.917	118	84	268	32	384	10
Chavez, Steven, Rancho Cuca.	.882	76	60	126	25	211	14
Cooper, Tim, Bakersfield	1.000	4	6	4	0	10	2
Cruz, Cirilo, Lancaster	.890	27	22	43	8	73	1
Curtis, Matt, Lake Elsinore	.923	5	0	12	1	13	0
Davalillo, David, Lake Elsinore	.929	26	12	40	4	56	2
Durkac, Bo, High Desert	.920	64	35	138	15	188	5
Durrington, Trent, Lake Elsinore	1.000	1	5	1	0	6	0
Ehmann, Kurt, San Jose	.927	32	9	42	4	55	4
Failla, Paul, Lake Elsinore	.870	19	12	35	7	54	1
Faircloth, Kevin, San Bernardino	.762	7	2	14	5	21	0
FELIX, Pedro, Bakersfield	.950	135	112	322	23	457	39
Fernandez, Antonio, Stockton	.933	118	77	259	24	360	23
Glasser, Scott, High Desert	.909	7	2	8	1	11	1
Hartman, Ron, High Desert	.939	75	50	120	11	181	6
Hills, Rich, Rancho Cuca.	.976	20	14	27	1	42	2
Kent, Robbie, Rancho Cuca.	.935	53	26	89	8	123	7
Lara, Edward, Visalia	1.000	1	0	4	0	4	1
Marcinczyk, T.R., Modesto	.914	20	15	38	5	58	6
Martin, Mike, Lancaster	.954	26	24	38	3	65	3
McCarty, Matt, San Bernardino	1.000	1	0	1	0	1	0

CLASS A California League

Player, Team	Pct.	G	PO	A	E	TC	DP
McKay, Cody, Modesto	.923	64	33	98	11	142	9
Morris, Greg, Lake Elsinore	.901	57	39	125	18	182	10
Mosier, Mark, San Jose	.881	24	13	39	7	59	2
Parker, Allan, Lake Elsinore	1.000	3	2	6	0	8	0
Paulino, Arturo, Modesto	.875	12	4	17	3	24	3
Perez, Richard, Stockton	.971	13	8	25	1	34	3
Pernalete, Marco, Bakersfield	.000	1	0	0	1	1	0
Powers, John, Rancho Cuca.	1.000	5	2	11	0	13	1
Prospero, Ted, San Jose	1.000	6	0	7	0	7	0
Ramirez, Joel, Lancaster	.000	2	0	0	1	1	0
Ready, Randy, Lake Elsinore	1.000	1	0	2	0	2	0
Regan, Jason, Lancaster	.902	27	12	25	4	41	1
Reynoso, Benjamin, R. Cuca.	1.000	1	0	1	0	1	0
Slemmer, Dave, Visalia	.889	11	2	14	2	18	0
Tyler, Josh, Stockton	.941	18	15	49	4	68	8
Valenti, Jon, Modesto	.930	74	50	124	13	187	11
Villalobos, Carlos, Lancaster	.923	73	40	129	14	183	13
Watson, Jon, Bakersfield	1.000	1	0	3	0	3	0
Wilson, Keith, High Desert	.889	3	2	6	1	9	1
Wilson, Todd, San Jose	.992	57	31	97	1	129	13

TRIPLE PLAY: McKay.

THIRD BASEMEN WITH TWO OR MORE TEAMS

Player, Team	Pct.	G	PO	A	E	TC	DP
Barlok, Todd, San Bernardino	.875	20	11	24	5	40	2
Barlok, Todd, Lake Elsinore	.901	25	24	58	9	91	5

SHORTSTOPS

Player, Team	Pct.	G	PO	A	E	TC	DP
Alguacil, Jose, San Jose	.934	32	45	68	8	121	16
Baughman, Justin, Lake Elsinore..	.953	129	239	403	32	674	64
Betten, Randy, Lake Elsinore	1.000	1	1	5	0	6	1
Boughton, Mike, High Desert	.907	15	12	27	4	43	4
Bournigal, Rafael, Modesto	1.000	5	5	7	0	12	0
Brito, Tilson, Modesto	.846	4	5	6	2	13	3
Campusano, Carlos, Bakersfield	.920	56	87	166	22	275	38
Caruso, Michael, San Jose	.934	106	168	300	33	501	51
Castro, Jose, Modesto	1.000	1	2	0	0	2	0
Cesar, Dionys, Visalia	.893	28	44	65	13	122	14
Davalillo, David, Lake Elsinore	.964	7	8	19	1	28	1
Espada, Josue, Visalia	.944	117	196	346	32	574	50
Failla, Paul, Lake Elsinore	.950	7	13	25	2	40	4
Faircloth, Kevin, San Bernardino	.909	27	37	73	11	121	15
Glasser, Scott, High Desert	.906	25	27	69	10	106	10
Goligoski, James, Visalia	.958	121	192	337	23	552	59
Gonzalez, Santos, Rancho Cuca.	.778	1	1	6	2	9	1
Hills, Rich, Rancho Cuca.	.950	12	13	25	2	40	5
Jones, Jack, San Bernardino	.946	122	160	335	28	523	53
Kent, Robbie, Rancho Cuca.	1.000	3	5	2	0	7	0
Lara, Edward, Visalia	.909	3	4	6	1	11	2
Marval, Raul, Bakersfield	.945	90	151	281	25	457	63
Molina, Luis, Lancaster	.950	101	157	226	20	403	42
Nicholson, Kevin, Rancho Cuca.	.887	14	21	26	6	53	3
Ortiz, Jose, Modesto	.909	116	170	362	53	585	80
Paulino, Arturo, Modesto	.889	27	36	52	11	99	8
Perez, Richard, Stockton	1.000	19	23	47	0	70	10
PHAIR, Kelly, Stockton	.969	121	213	349	18	580	53
Prospero, Ted, San Jose	.750	4	0	3	1	4	0
Ramirez, Joel, Lancaster	.949	50	84	140	12	236	30
Reynoso, Benjamin, R. Cuca.	.960	117	131	301	18	450	50
Tyler, Josh, Stockton	1.000	10	15	16	0	31	3
Valenti, Jon, Modesto	1.000	1	1	1	0	2	1
Wilson, Todd, San Jose	1.000	4	4	7	0	11	2

OUTFIELDERS

Player, Team	Pct.	G	PO	A	E	TC	DP
Alguacil, Jose, San Jose	1.000	2	2	0	0	2	0
Anderson, Cliff, San Bernardino..	1.000	2	1	0	0	1	0
Avila, Rolo, San Bernardino	.968	134	264	10	9	283	1
Baeza, Art, Bakersfield	.714	3	4	1	2	7	0
Barlok, Todd, S.B.-L.E.	.966	24	27	1	1	29	0
Bergeron, Peter, San Bernardino	1.000	2	5	1	0	6	1
Bess, Johnny, San Jose	1.000	7	8	1	0	9	0
Betten, Randy, Lake Elsinore	.974	17	33	4	1	38	1
Bilderback, Ty, Lake Elsinore*	.950	30	54	3	3	60	1
Blanco, Dany, San Jose	.931	27	24	3	2	29	1
Bonds, Bobby, San Jose	.955	27	39	3	2	44	0
Bowles, Justin, Modesto*	.959	102	157	8	7	172	2
Brock, Tarrik, Lancaster*	.979	131	225	11	5	241	2
Buhner, Shawn, Lancaster	1.000	7	8	0	0	8	0
Byers, MacGregor, Visalia	1.000	10	13	1	0	14	0

Player, Team	Pct.	G	PO	A	E	TC	DP
Cameron, Stanton, High Desert ..	.941	105	135	8	9	152	3
Cancel, Robinson, Stockton	1.000	1	2	0	0	2	0
Carter, Cale, Lake Elsinore	1.000	22	37	2	0	39	1
Cesar, Dionys, Visalia	1.000	2	3	1	0	4	0
Christensen, Ryan, Visalia	.982	81	164	4	3	171	0
Connors, Greg, Lancaster	.889	8	7	1	1	9	0
Conti, Jason, High Desert	.853	14	27	2	5	34	0
Cooper, Tim, Bakersfield	.833	6	5	0	1	6	0
Correa, Miguel, Lancaster	.948	49	70	3	4	77	0
Corujo, Rey, San Jose	.980	27	47	2	1	50	0
Cruz, Cirilo, Lancaster	1.000	6	6	0	0	6	0
Curtis, Matt, Lake Elsinore	1.000	8	12	2	0	14	1
Darr, Mike, Rancho Cuca.	.959	132	176	12	8	196	1
DaVanon, Jeff, Visalia	.948	107	166	17	10	193	3
Delgado, Reymundo, Bak.*	1.000	14	17	3	0	20	1
Denbow, Don, San Jose	.954	103	162	5	8	175	2
Dilone, Juan, Modesto	.932	24	41	0	3	44	0
Dougherty, Jeb, Lake Elsinore	.889	9	8	0	1	9	0
Durkin, Chris, San Bernardino* ..	1.000	3	3	0	0	3	0
Durrington, Trent, Lake Elsinore	1.000	6	12	0	0	12	0
Ehmann, Kurt, San Jose	1.000	7	4	0	0	4	0
Elliott, David, Stockton	.968	23	26	4	1	31	0
Encarnacion, Mario, Modesto	.927	92	145	7	12	164	0
Failla, Paul, Lake Elsinore	.923	29	35	1	3	39	0
Faircloth, Chad, Bakersfield	.906	18	27	2	3	32	0
Fick, Chris, High Desert	1.000	5	5	0	0	5	0
Filchner, Duane, Visalia*	.984	56	60	2	1	63	0
Gann, Jamie, High Desert	.945	89	127	11	8	146	3
Garland, Tim, San Jose	.973	133	238	14	7	259	6
Glasser, Scott, High Desert	1.000	3	2	0	0	2	0
Glendenning, Mike, Bakersfield	.969	132	173	13	6	192	0
Green, Chad, Stockton	.971	126	291	11	9	311	3
Hardy, Brett, High Desert*	.750	3	3	0	1	4	0
Hollandsworth, Todd, San Bern.*	1.000	2	2	1	0	3	0
Horner, Jim, Lancaster	.500	2	2	0	2	4	0
Hutchins, Norm, Lake Elsinore*	.955	130	266	9	13	288	2
Iapoce, Anthony, Stockton*	.962	93	168	9	7	184	1
Jones, Tim, Modesto	.918	100	113	10	11	134	2
Kim, Yuni, Lancaster	.950	70	87	8	5	100	2
Koerner, Michael, Visalia*	1.000	31	45	3	0	48	0
KOMINEK, Toby, Stockton	.996	127	222	13	1	236	2
Lennon, Patrick, Modesto	1.000	1	2	0	0	2	0
Maddox, Garry, High Desert	.990	97	199	5	2	206	1
Manning, Brian, Bakersfield	.960	105	135	9	6	150	1
Mathis, Joe, Lancaster	.973	134	279	7	8	294	1
Matthews, Gary, Rancho Cuca. ..	.959	68	110	6	5	121	2
McCarty, Matt, San Bernardino	.833	8	5	0	1	6	0
Melendez, Angel, San Jose	.987	60	72	2	1	75	0
Moore, Vince, Rancho Cuca.*	.976	87	111	10	3	124	2
Morales, Alex, San Jose	.980	27	45	3	1	49	0
Mota, Gary, High Desert	1.000	8	9	1	0	10	0
Mota, Pedro, San Jose*	.778	9	7	0	2	9	0
Mota, Tony, San Bernardino	.984	110	225	15	4	244	4
Owen, Andy, San Bernardino*	.966	98	137	7	5	149	2
Plantier, Phil, Rancho Cuca.	1.000	4	5	0	0	5	0
Polanco, Juan, Modesto	.950	50	54	3	3	60	0
Powers, John, Rancho Cuca.	.750	2	3	0	1	4	0
Prieto, Chris, Rancho Cuca.*	1.000	20	33	2	0	35	0
Prieto, Rick, Rancho Cuca.	.967	68	136	9	5	150	0
Prospero, Ted, San Jose	.000	1	0	0	1	1	0
Ramirez, Roberto, Visalia	.964	61	100	7	4	111	2
Rand, Ian, Bakersfield	.900	26	48	6	6	60	2
Rauer, Troy, Visalia	.931	80	116	6	9	131	0
Shockey, Greg, Rancho Cuca.* ..	1.000	52	67	3	0	70	0
Soriano, Jose, Modesto	.978	116	212	15	5	232	6
Stoner, Mike, High Desert	.972	127	201	6	6	213	0
Stuart, Rich, Lake Elsinore	.913	43	60	3	6	69	1
Swinton, Jermaine, Stockton	.750	7	6	0	2	8	0
Tyler, Josh, Stockton	1.000	20	30	2	0	32	0
Unrat, Chris, San Jose	1.000	2	2	0	0	2	0
Valenti, Jon, Modesto	1.000	9	13	0	0	13	0
Van Rossum, Chris, Bakersfield*	.957	124	210	14	10	234	2
Vandergriend, Jon, Lk. Elsinore ..	.941	117	193	16	13	222	4
Vaz, Roberto, Visalia*	.976	19	37	3	1	41	0
Villalobos, Carlos, Lancaster	1.000	5	3	1	0	4	0
Wachter, Derek, Stockton	1.000	34	46	4	0	50	0
Watson, Jon, Bakersfield	1.000	6	11	0	0	11	0
Watts, Josh, Lancaster	.956	52	62	3	3	68	0
Weekley, Jason, San Bernardino	.955	85	101	5	5	111	0
Welles, Robby, Lake Elsinore	1.000	2	3	0	0	3	0
Wilson, Keith, High Desert	.875	7	7	0	1	8	0
Wilson, Todd, San Jose	.976	27	37	3	1	41	1

OUTFIELDERS WITH TWO OR MORE TEAMS

Player, Team	Pct.	G	PO	A	E	TC	DP
Barlok, Todd, San Bernardino	.... 1.000	2	2	0	0	2	0
Barlok, Todd, Lake Elsinore	.963	22	25	1	1	27	0

CATCHERS

Player, Team	Pct.	G	PO	A	E	TC	DP	PB
Ardoin, Danny, Visalia	.988	41	308	35	4	347	2	6
Baltzell, Beau, High Desert	.957	4	18	4	1	23	0	3
Barajas, Rodrigo, High Desert	.992	54	357	37	3	397	1	10
Bess, Johnny, San Jose	.976	22	179	28	5	212	2	3
Brown, Jason, San Bernardino	.980	29	178	22	4	204	1	3
Cancel, Robinson, Stockton	.981	62	434	72	10	516	8	9
Chiaramonte, Giuseppe, S.J.	.993	56	476	59	4	539	5	5
Clark, Kevin, High Desert	1.000	13	102	8	0	110	0	5
Connors, Greg, Lancaster	.947	2	15	3	1	19	0	0
Curtis, Matt, Lake Elsinore	.986	47	255	32	4	291	3	9
Davis, Ben, Rancho Cuca.	.987	110	992	103	14	1109	9	13
Davis, Reggie, High Desert	.979	41	265	21	6	292	2	10
Figueroa, Jose, Modesto	.935	5	27	2	2	31	1	2
Gonzalez, Wikleman, R. Cuca.	.985	15	117	17	2	136	2	4
Guse, Bryan, Bakersfield	.992	17	103	14	1	118	1	5
Hernandez, Carlos, R. Cuca.	1.000	1	11	1	0	12	0	0
Hernandez, Ramon, Visalia	.976	80	564	77	16	657	5	11
HINCH, A.J., Modesto	.996	86	615	65	3	683	6	9
Horner, Jim, Lancaster	.991	37	312	24	3	339	4	10
Horton, Conan, San Bern.	.984	9	57	5	1	63	0	0
Malave, Joshua, San Bern.	1.000	1	4	1	0	5	0	0
Martin, Mike, Lancaster	1.000	8	61	7	0	68	0	1
McAninch, John, Lake Elsinore	.990	30	194	12	2	208	0	2
McKay, Cody, Modesto	.979	59	386	44	9	439	4	11
Mikesell, Steve, San Bern.	1.000	2	3	0	0	3	0	0
Molina, Ben, Lake Elsinore	.996	33	239	36	1	276	3	3
Norton, Chris, Lake Elsinore	1.000	3	17	2	0	19	1	1
O'Neal, Troy, Stockton	.978	4	37	7	1	45	1	0
Osborne, Mark, High Desert	.957	15	81	9	4	94	0	2
Panaro, Carmen, High Desert	.971	51	175	27	6	208	3	7
Pena, Angel, San Bernardino	.987	81	661	83	10	754	5	31
Poor, Jeff, San Jose	.986	34	196	22	3	221	1	4
Ramirez, Peto, San Jose	.981	41	317	46	7	370	4	4
Rodriguez, Guillermo, S.J.	1.000	1	3	0	0	3	0	0
Rodriguez, Miguel, Stockton	.982	75	464	69	10	543	6	23
Ryder, Derek, Lake Elsinore	.992	35	199	37	2	238	3	7
Schwenke, Matt, Rancho Cuca.	.985	19	181	12	3	196	1	2
Skeels, David, Lancaster	.988	52	364	35	5	404	2	6
Snow, Casey, San Bernardino	.964	29	202	15	8	225	2	7
Thompson, Karl, Lancaster	1.000	4	23	3	0	26	0	1
Thurston, Jerry, Lake Elsinore	1.000	2	17	3	0	20	0	1
Torrealba, Yorvit, Bakersfield	.993	114	779	119	6	904	10	15
Turner, Chris, Lake Elsinore	.963	3	25	1	1	27	0	1
Twist, Jeff, Lake Elsinore	1.000	17	88	12	0	100	0	2
Tyler, Josh, Stockton	1.000	4	17	1	0	18	0	2
Unrat, Chris, San Jose	.800	4	11	1	3	15	0	2
Ussery, Brian, Lake Elsinore	.957	9	53	13	3	69	1	1
Valenti, Jon, Modesto	.800	4	3	1	1	5	0	1
Ventura, Wilfredo, Visalia	.958	33	186	21	9	216	0	8
Wathan, Dusty, Lancaster	.984	52	384	60	7	451	3	4
Williams, Drew, Stockton	1.000	2	7	0	0	7	0	2
Williams, George, Modesto	1.000	8	53	9	0	62	1	2

PITCHERS

Player, Team	Pct.	G	PO	A	E	TC	DP
Abbott, Todd, Visalia	.964	31	14	13	1	28	1
Abreu, Oscar, Visalia	.400	5	1	1	3	5	0
AGOSTO, Stevenson, L.E.-R.C.*	1.000	27	4	26	0	30	0
Alvarez, Juan, Lake Elsinore*	.944	27	6	11	1	18	2
Anderson, Bill, Rancho Cuca.	.960	29	9	15	1	25	0
Andra, Jeff, San Jose*	1.000	6	2	6	0	8	0
Apana, Matt, Lancaster	1.000	3	0	1	0	1	1
Arias, Wagner, Stockton	.867	20	6	7	2	15	0
Ashworth, Kym, San Bern.*	.846	9	1	10	2	13	0
Backlund, Brett, High Desert	.857	17	0	6	1	7	0
Baez, Benito, Visalia*	1.000	16	1	22	0	23	0
Bailey, Philip, San Jose*	.929	25	3	10	1	14	1
Barcelo, Lorenzo, San Jose	.923	16	8	4	1	13	1
Baron, Jim, Rancho Cuca.*	.909	14	5	15	2	22	1
Beck, Chris, Lancaster	1.000	8	3	4	0	7	0
Beck, Greg, Stockton	.909	27	4	6	1	11	0
Bedinger, Doug, High Desert	1.000	1	0	1	0	1	0
Bennett, Tom, Modesto	1.000	25	13	15	0	28	2
Bermudez, Manuel, S.J.-Bak.	.974	28	13	24	1	38	1
Berninger, Darren, Stockton	.667	18	1	3	2	6	0

Player, Team	Pct.	G	PO	A	E	TC	DP
Bice, Justin, High Desert	1.000	4	0	4	0	4	0
Bishop, Joshua, Stockton	1.000	11	0	6	0	6	0
Blyleven, Todd, Stockton	.500	1	1	0	1	2	0
Bond, Jason, Lancaster*	.941	36	4	12	1	17	0
Bonilla, Denys, Lancaster*	1.000	40	1	11	0	12	0
Brester, Jason, San Jose*	.879	26	7	22	4	33	1
Browne, Byron, Stockton	1.000	8	1	3	0	4	1
Bussa, Todd, Modesto	.923	30	5	7	1	13	2
Cairncross, Cameron, R.Cuca.*	.933	40	3	11	1	15	0
Cana, Nelson, Stockton*	.909	44	9	11	2	22	0
Carlson, Dan, Bakersfield	1.000	2	0	1	0	1	0
Carmody, Brian, Rancho Cuca.*	1.000	4	0	2	0	2	0
Castillo, Alberto, San Jose*	.833	18	1	4	1	6	0
Christianson, Robby, Lancaster	1.000	6	0	3	0	3	0
Cintron, Jose, Lake Elsinore	1.000	28	2	4	0	6	1
Clayton, Craig, Rancho Cuca.	1.000	10	1	2	0	3	0
Clement, Matt, Rancho Cuca.	.913	14	9	12	2	23	3
Cooper, Brian, Lake Elsinore	.957	17	7	15	1	23	1
Crabtree, Robert, Bakersfield	.941	45	3	13	1	17	0
Crossan, Clayton, High Desert	1.000	2	0	1	0	1	0
D'Amico, Jeffrey, Modesto	.938	20	6	9	1	16	2
Davis, John, San Bernardino	1.000	17	5	2	0	7	0
Davis, Keith, Rancho Cuca.	.955	35	9	12	1	22	1
Davis, Mark, High Desert*	1.000	16	1	3	0	4	0
Deakman, Josh, Lake Elsinore	.938	26	12	33	3	48	3
Delacruz, Fernando, Lk. Elsinore	.875	8	3	11	2	16	0
Della Ratta, Pete, Modesto	.933	45	5	9	1	15	1
Deskins, Casey, San Bern.*	1.000	37	12	14	0	26	4
Drumheller, Al, Rancho Cuca.*	.800	38	1	11	3	15	0
DuBose, Eric, Visalia*	.900	10	3	6	1	10	0
Eden, Bill, High Desert*	1.000	6	1	1	0	2	0
Emerson, Scott, High Desert*	1.000	3	1	1	0	2	1
Enochs, Chris, Modesto	1.000	10	2	4	0	6	0
Estrella, Luis, San Jose	.941	42	12	20	2	34	1
Farnsworth, Jeff, Lancaster	.800	5	0	4	1	5	0
Fesh, Sean, Rancho Cuca.*	1.000	4	1	1	0	2	0
Fieldbinder, Mick, Stockton	.950	21	12	26	2	40	5
Finley, Chuck, Lake Elsinore*	1.000	2	1	2	0	3	0
Fleming, John, High Desert	1.000	1	1	0	0	1	0
Freehill, Mike, Lake Elsinore	.833	21	1	4	1	6	0
Goedhart, Darrell, Lake Elsinore	.500	8	0	1	1	2	0
Gogolin, Al, Modesto	1.000	4	3	0	0	3	0
Gomez, Dennys, Bakersfield	1.000	32	7	11	0	18	0
Gorecki, Rick, San Bernardino	1.000	15	1	3	0	4	0
Gregg, Kevin, Visalia	.769	25	2	8	3	13	1
Grote, Jason, Bakersfield	.897	25	9	17	3	29	2
Gryboski, Kevin, Lancaster	.875	21	5	9	2	16	1
Gunther, Kevin, Modesto	1.000	42	5	7	0	12	0
Gutierrez, Javier, Lancaster	.800	14	1	3	1	5	0
Guzman, Domingo, R.Cuca.	.889	6	2	6	1	9	0
Hardwick, Bubba, Stockton*	.976	31	12	28	1	41	3
Harris, Bryan, Lake Elsinore*	1.000	31	3	7	0	10	1
Hartvigson, Chad, Bakersfield*	1.000	5	2	3	0	5	0
Harville, Chad, Visalia	1.000	14	3	2	0	5	0
Hause, Brendan, Modesto*	1.000	2	0	1	0	1	0
Hecker, Doug, Stockton	1.000	12	1	3	0	4	0
Helmer, Chad, Stockton	1.000	7	2	0	0	2	0
Henderson, Juan, Lake Elsinore	1.000	9	0	3	0	3	0
Henderson, Kenny, R.Cuca.	1.000	7	1	1	0	2	0
Hernandez, Santos, San Bern.	.833	47	0	5	1	6	0
Hill, Jason, Lake Elsinore*	.941	54	4	12	1	17	0
Hoff, Steve, Rancho Cuca.*	.750	14	2	10	4	16	0
Holmes, Mike, Visalia	.857	16	3	3	1	7	1
Hommel, Brian, Stockton*	.933	55	3	11	1	15	0
Humphreys, Kevin, Lk. Elsinore	1.000	16	1	4	0	5	0
Hutzler, Jeff, Bakersfield	.964	47	9	18	1	28	0
Ishee, Gabe, Stockton	.765	21	4	9	4	17	0
Johnson, Gregory, Lk. Elsinore*	1.000	34	4	7	0	11	0
Jordan, Jason, High Desert	.857	6	2	4	1	7	1
Kazmirski, Robert, Visalia	1.000	5	1	0	0	1	0
Keith, Jeff, Bakersfield*	1.000	37	8	7	0	15	0
Kern, Brian, Visalia	1.000	23	2	5	0	7	0
Kjos, Ryan, Modesto	.917	34	3	8	1	12	1
Knoll, Brian, Bakersfield	.909	49	6	4	1	11	0
Knudsen, Kurt, Lake Elsinore	1.000	7	0	1	0	1	0
Kolb, Brandon, Rancho Cuca.	.952	10	5	15	1	21	3
Konieczki, Dom, Stockton*	1.000	12	1	3	0	4	0
Kramer, Matthew, San Bern.	.500	10	0	1	1	2	0
Kubenka, Jeff, San Bernardino*	1.000	34	3	8	0	11	0
Langston, Mark, Lake Elsinore*	.750	3	1	2	1	4	0
Larreal, Guillermo, Bakersfield	1.000	32	3	9	0	12	1
Laxton, Brett, Visalia	.929	29	13	26	3	42	0

Player, Team	Pct.	G	PO	A	E	TC	DP
Leese, Brandon, San Jose	.909	19	9	11	2	22	0
Leyva, Julian, Modesto	.879	28	11	18	4	33	1
Lilly, Ted, San Bernardino*	.917	23	7	15	2	24	0
Linares, Rich, San Bernardino	1.000	26	0	2	0	2	0
Linebrink, Scott, San Jose	.667	6	0	2	1	3	0
Luce, Robert, Lancaster	.947	14	8	10	1	19	0
Malloy, William, Bakersfield	.875	29	6	22	4	32	1
Manwiller, Tim, Modesto	.833	7	1	4	1	6	0
Marenghi, Matt, High Desert	.947	38	8	10	1	19	0
Marte, Damaso, Lancaster*	.906	25	3	26	3	32	1
Martin, Jeff, San Jose	1.000	20	1	5	0	6	0
Martinez, Ramon, San Bern.	1.000	4	1	1	0	2	0
Mayer, Aaron, Lake Elsinore	.824	36	3	11	3	17	2
Mayo, Blake, San Bernardino	.571	20	4	0	3	7	1
Mays, Joe, Lancaster	.969	15	12	19	1	32	2
McMullen, Mike, San Jose	.923	56	5	19	2	26	1
McNeely, Mitch, San Bern.*	.929	18	1	12	1	14	0
Medina, Rafael, Rancho Cuca.	1.000	3	2	3	0	5	1
Michalak, Chris, High Desert*	.917	49	6	27	3	36	2
Middlebrook, Jason, R.Cuca.	1.000	6	2	2	0	4	0
Mitchell, Dean, San Bernardino	1.000	1	0	1	0	1	0
Mlodik, Kevin, Visalia	.923	35	8	16	2	26	1
Montane, Ivan, Lancaster	.714	6	1	4	2	7	0
Moore, Vince, Rancho Cuca.*	1.000	1	0	1	0	1	0
Morgan, Eric, Lancaster	.960	24	6	18	1	25	2
Morrison, Chris, Visalia	.968	48	10	20	1	31	0
Mullins, Greg, Stockton*	.800	30	2	2	1	5	0
Myers, Jason, Bakersfield*	1.000	10	3	9	0	12	0
Narcisse, Tyrone, Rancho Cuca.	1.000	22	1	4	0	5	0
Neal, Billy, San Bernardino	1.000	24	4	5	0	9	0
Nelson, Chris, Modesto	.889	8	5	3	1	9	0
Newman, Eric, Rancho Cuca.	.882	35	5	10	2	17	0
Niles, Randy, Modesto	1.000	7	1	8	0	9	1
Noriega, Ray, Modesto*	.895	28	13	38	6	57	0
Nunez, Vladimir, High Desert	.980	28	22	26	1	49	0
Ochsenfeld, Chris, San Bern.*	.667	13	1	3	2	6	0
O'Dell, Jacob, Visalia	.944	27	11	23	2	36	0
Oleksik, George, High Desert	.917	17	5	6	1	12	0
Ontiveros, Steve, Lake Elsinore	1.000	1	0	1	0	1	0
Pageler, Mick, Bakersfield	.909	61	7	3	1	11	1
Paluk, Jeff, San Bernardino	.917	28	1	10	1	12	0
Pasqualicchio, Mike, Stockton*..	.958	17	2	21	1	24	1
Passini, Brian, Stockton*	.857	8	1	5	1	7	0
Paulino, Jose, Visalia	.938	39	6	9	1	16	0
Pearsall, J.J., San Bernardino* ..	.978	31	17	27	1	45	4
Pena, Alex, High Desert	.964	33	9	18	1	28	1
Perez, Juan, Visalia*	.941	53	5	11	1	17	1
Petcka, Joe, Visalia	1.000	4	1	1	0	2	0
Peters, Don, High Desert	1.000	21	2	3	0	5	0
Pincavitch, Kevin, San Bern.	.947	28	9	27	2	38	0
Proctor, Murph, San Bern.* ..	1.000	2	0	1	0	1	1
Quirico, Rafael, Lake Elsinore* ..	1.000	14	1	16	0	17	0
Rector, Bobby, Bakersfield	.917	8	4	7	1	12	0
Remington, Jake, Rancho Cuca.	.500	6	0	1	1	2	0
Rice, Nathan, Bakersfield*	1.000	8	1	4	0	5	1
Riggan, Jerrod, Lake Elsinore	.889	8	3	5	1	9	0
Riley, Michael, Bakersfield*	1.000	6	1	4	0	5	0
Rivera, Rafael, Lancaster	.800	24	0	12	3	15	0
Rivette, Scott, Modesto	.964	20	9	18	1	28	8
Robbins, Jason, High Desert	1.000	23	13	11	0	24	1
Rogers, Kevin, San Jose*	.857	8	2	4	1	7	1
Rossiter, Mike, Stockton	1.000	34	6	8	0	14	2
Sabel, Erik, High Desert	.938	31	10	20	2	32	1
Sak, James, Rancho Cuca.	.917	57	3	8	1	12	1
Scheffer, Aaron, Lancaster	1.000	37	6	8	0	14	0
Schramm, Carl, San Jose	.885	36	11	12	3	26	0
Scutero, Brian, Lake Elsinore	1.000	5	0	1	0	1	0
Skrmetta, Matt, Rancho Cuca.	1.000	17	0	3	0	3	1
Skuse, Nick, Lake Elsinore	1.000	17	1	0	0	1	0
Smith, Andy, Visalia	.950	42	5	14	1	20	0
Sobkoviak, Jeff, High Desert	.962	28	24	27	2	53	1
Spencer, Sean, Lancaster*	1.000	39	3	11	0	14	2
Spencer, Stan, Rancho Cuca.	1.000	7	7	6	0	13	1
Stark, Dennis, Lancaster	1.000	3	0	2	0	2	0
Steed, Rick, High Desert	1.000	46	13	14	0	27	3
Stephens, Jason, Lake Elsinore ..	.909	24	9	11	2	22	1
Stone, Ricky, San Bernardino	.857	8	3	3	1	7	0
Stoops, Jim, San Jose	.833	50	5	10	3	18	0
Sweeney, Brian, Lancaster	1.000	40	3	10	0	13	0
Takahashi, Kurt, San Jose	1.000	10	1	4	0	5	0
Thompson, Frank, San Bern.	.917	39	3	8	1	12	0
Thompson, John, Lancaster	1.000	3	1	0	0	1	0
THURMOND, Travis, L.E.-S.J.	1.000	21	5	25	0	30	1
Torres, Luis, Rancho Cuca.	.923	31	2	10	1	13	0
Tranbarger, Mark, High Desert*..	.600	5	1	2	2	5	0
Tuttle, Dave, High Desert	1.000	50	10	14	0	24	1
Urbina, Dan, San Bernardino	1.000	13	6	4	0	10	0
Veras, Dario, Rancho Cuca.	1.000	2	0	1	0	1	0
Verplancke, Joe, High Desert	.833	17	6	9	3	18	1
Victery, Joe, Lancaster	1.000	28	6	16	0	22	1
Vining, Kenneth, San Jose*	.794	23	5	22	7	34	1
Vizcaino, Luis, Modesto	1.000	7	0	4	0	4	1
Wagner, Joe, Stockton	.867	14	5	8	2	15	1
Wallace, Flint, Modesto	.955	35	5	16	1	22	0
Warrecker, Teddy, San Bern.	.667	10	2	2	0	6	0
Weinberg, Todd, Visalia*	1.000	38	3	5	0	8	0
Wells, Matt, Bakersfield	.963	29	6	20	1	27	2
Westfall, Allan, Lancaster	1.000	15	0	2	0	2	0
Williams, Jeff, San Bernardino*..	.974	18	8	30	1	39	2
Winkleman, Greg, Modesto*	.929	39	4	9	1	14	1
Witasick, Jay, Modesto	1.000	9	0	2	0	2	0
Wolff, Bryan, Rancho Cuca.	1.000	9	3	3	0	6	0
Wunsch, Kelly, Stockton*	.867	24	6	20	4	30	0
Zerbe, Chad, High Desert*	.909	9	7	3	1	11	0

PITCHERS WITH TWO OR MORE TEAMS

Player, Team	Pct.	G	PO	A	E	TC	DP
Agosto, Stevenson, Lk. Elsinore*	1.000	24	3	21	0	24	0
Agosto, Stevenson, R.Cuca.*	1.000	3	1	5	0	6	0
Bermudez, Manuel, San Jose..	.909	9	3	7	1	11	0
Bermudez, Manuel, Bakersfield ..	1.000	19	10	17	0	27	1
Thurmond, Travis, Lake Elsinore	1.000	9	2	8	0	10	0
Thurmond, Travis, San Jose	1.000	12	3	17	0	20	1

The following players did not have any fielding statistics at the positions indicated or appeared only as a designated hitter, pinch-hitter, or pinch-runner: Alguacil, p; C. Anderson, ss; M. Anderson, p; Ardoin, of; Backowski, p; Barlock, 2b; Barnes, of; Beaumont, p; Blumenstock, p; Brea, p; Brewer, p; Bussa, of; Cervantes, p; Cesar, p; Chavez, p; Ehmann, ss; Ervin, p; Filchner, p; Finley, of; W. Franklin, p; Garcia, of; Geronimo, of; Goligoski, 3b; Gubicza, of; Hecker, of; Jensen, p; Kent, of; Lagattuta, p; Livingstone, dh; Marcinczyk, of; Miranda, p; Murray, dh; Nash, p; Oquist, p; Owen, 1b; Parker, ss; Percival, p; R. Rivera, dh; Robertson, p; Pernalete, of; Polanco, 3b; Regan, of; Slemmer, of; Steverson, dh; Telgheder, p; Tinoco, dh; Tyler, p; Urso, ph, or; Valenti, p; Wathan, 1b; Weekley, 3b; K. Wilson, c.

LEAGUE CHAMPIONS

Year	Team	Pct.
1914—	Fresno	.571
1915—	Modesto	.857
1916-40—	Did not operate.	
1941—	Fresno	.643
	Santa Barbara (2nd)*	.597
1942—	Santa Barbara†	.642
1943-44-45—	Did not operate.	
1946—	Stockton‡	.600
1947—	Stockton‡	.679
1948—	Fresno	.607
	Santa Barbara (3rd)*	.529
1949—	Bakersfield	.612
	San Jose (4th)*	.543
1950—	Ventura	.607
	Modesto (2nd)*	.586
1951—	Santa Barbara‡	.599
1952—	Fresno‡	.629
1953—	San Jose‡	.664
1954—	Modesto‡	.623
1955—	Stockton	.733
	Fresno§	.718
1956—	Fresno§	.650
1957—	Visalia∞	.622
	Salinas (4th)*	.504
1958—	Fresno*	.639
	Bakersfield	.672
1959—	Bakersfield	.592
	Modesto§	.643
1960—	Reno	.614
	Reno	.657
1961—	Reno	.743
	Reno	.643
1962—	San José§	.686
	Reno	.587
1963—	Modesto	.589
	Stockton§	.687
1964—	Fresno	.638
	Fresno	.600
1965—	San Jose	.586
	Stockton§	.614
1966—	Modesto	.577
	Modesto	.671
1967—	San José§	.676
	Modesto	.586

CLASS A California League

Year	Team	Pct.	Year	Team	Pct.	Year	Team	Pct.
1968—	San Jose	.629	1978—	Visalia§	.698	1988—	Stockton	.657
	Fresno§	.623		Lodi	.607		Riverside§	.599
1969—	Stockton§	.600	1979—	San Jose§	.636	1989—	Stockton	.627
	Visalia	.614		Reno	.525		Bakersfield§	.577
1970—	Bakersfield	.667	1980—	Stockton§	.638	1990—	Visalia	.638
	Bakersfield	.671		Visalia	.507		Stockton§	.582
1971—	Visalia§	.583	1981—	Visalia	.621	1991—	San Jose	.676
	Fresno	.500		Lodi§	.521		High Desert§	.537
1972—	Modesto§	.547	1982—	Modesto§	.671	1992—	Stockton§	.610
	Bakersfield	.629		Visalia	.586		Visalia	.551
1973—	Lodi§	.657	1983—	Visalia	.621	1993—	High Desert§	.620
	Bakersfield	.571		Redwood§	.529		Modesto	.529
1974—	Fresno§	.607	1984—	Modesto§	.597	1994—	Modesto	.706
	San Jose	.579		Bakersfield	.486		Rancho Cucamonga§	.566
1975—	Reno	.614	1985—	Fresno§	.575	1995—	San Bernardino§	.612
	Reno	.614		Stockton	.566		San Jose	.550
1976—	Salinas	.650	1986—	Palm Springs	.613	1996—	San Jose	.636
	Reno§	.547		Stockton§	.585		Lake Elsinore‡	.550
1977—	Salinas	.564	1987—	Fresno§	.559	1997—	High Desert▲	.593
	Lodi§	.579		Reno	.535		San Bernardino	.486

*Won four-club playoff. †League disbanded June 28. ‡Won championship and four-club playoff. §Won split-season playoff. ∞Won both halves of split season. ▲Played split season and won six-club playoff.

CAROLINA LEAGUE

LEAGUE OFFICE

President/treasurer
John Hopkins
Address
P.O. Box 9503
Greensboro, NC 27429
Phone
910-691-9030

Teams (affiliation)
Danville 97s (Braves)
Frederick Keys (Orioles)
Kinston Indians (Indians)
Lynchburg Hillcats (Pirates)
Prince William Cannons (Cardinals)
Salem Avalanche (Rockies)

Wilmington Blue Rocks (Royals)
Winston-Salem Warthogs (White Sox)

1997 FINAL STANDINGS

FIRST HALF

NORTHERN DIVISION

Team	W	L	T	Pct.	GB
Frederick (Orioles)	45	25	0	.643	....
Lynchburg (Pirates)	40	30	0	.571	5
Wilmington (Royals)	34	36	0	.486	11
Prince William (Cardinals)	30	39	0	.435	14½

SOUTHERN DIVISION

Team	W	L	T	Pct.	GB
Kinston (Indians)	46	24	0	.657	....
Durham (Braves)	30	39	0	.435	15½
Salem (Rockies)	27	41	0	.397	18
Winston-Salem (White Sox)	26	44	0	.371	20

SECOND HALF

NORTHERN DIVISION

Team	W	L	T	Pct.	GB
Lynchburg (Pirates)	42	28	0	.600	....
Prince William (Cardinals)	39	31	0	.557	3
Wilmington (Royals)	28	42	0	.400	14
Frederick (Orioles)	24	46	0	.343	18

SOUTHERN DIVISION

Team	W	L	T	Pct.	GB
Kinston (Indians)	41	29	0	.586	....
Winston-Salem (White Sox)	37	33	0	.529	4
Salem (Rockies)	36	34	0	.514	5
Durham (Braves)	33	37	0	.471	8

COMPOSITE

Team	Kin.	Lyn.	P.W.	Fre.	Sal.	Dur.	W.S.	Wil.	W	L	T	Pct.	GB
Kinston (Indians)	....	13	13	15	11	11	12	12	87	53	0	.621	....
Lynchburg (Pirates)	7	....	12	15	12	10	15	11	82	58	0	.586	5
Prince William (Cardinals)	7	8	....	15	7	12	9	11	69	70	0	.496	17½
Frederick (Orioles)	5	5	5	....	13	15	15	11	69	71	0	.493	18
Salem (Rockies)	9	8	12	7	....	9	8	10	63	75	0	.457	23
Durham (Braves)	9	10	8	5	10	....	12	9	63	76	0	.453	23½
Winston-Salem (White Sox)	8	5	11	5	12	8	....	14	63	77	0	.450	24
Wilmington (Royals)	8	9	9	9	10	11	6	....	62	78	0	.443	25

Major league affiliations in parentheses.

PLAYOFFS: Lynchburg defeated Frederick, two games to none; Lynchburg defeated Kinston, three games to one, to win league championship.

REGULAR-SEASON ATTENDANCE: Durham, 381,589; Frederick, 274,894; Kinston, 151,953; Lynchburg, 112,363; Prince William, 214,037; Salem, 188,023; Wilmington, 326,201; Winston-Salem, 156,285. Total—1,805,345. Playoffs (6 games)—11,967. All-Star Game (California and Carolina Leagues) at Durham—6,419.

MANAGERS: Durham, Paul Runge; Frederick, Dave Hilton; Kinston, Joel Skinner; Lynchburg, Jeff Banister (through June 18) and Jeff Richardson (June 19 to end of season); Prince William, Roy Silver; Salem, Bill McGuire; Wilmington, John Mizerock; Winston-Salem, Mike Heath (through July 10) and Mark Haley (July 11 to end of season). Managerial records of teams with more than one manager: Lynchburg, Banister 40-30, Richardson 42-28; Winston-Salem, Heath 38-53, Haley 25-24.

ALL-STAR TEAM: 1B—Nate Dishington, Prince William; 2B—Rick Short, Frederick; 3B—Aramis Ramirez, Lynchburg; SS—John McDonald, Kinston; Utility—Carlos Lee, Winston-Salem; OF—Adam Johnson, Durham; Scott Morgan, Kinston; Danny Peoples, Kinston; Mark Quinn, Wilmington; C—Heath Hayes, Kinston; Ben Petrick, Salem; DH—Russ Branyan, Kinston; Starting Pitcher—Cliff Politte, Prince William; Relief Pitcher—Armando Almanza, Prince William; Most Valuable Player—Aramis Ramirez, Lynchburg; Pitcher of the Year—Cliff Politte, Prince William; Manager of the Year—Joel Skinner, Kinston.

1997 BATTING

TEAM

Team	Avg.	G	TPA	AB	R	H	TB	2B	3B	HR	RBI	SH	SF	HP	BB	IBB	SO	SB	CS	GDP	LOB	ShO	Slg.	OBP
Kinston	.268	140	5419	4715	775	1265	2142	270	26	185	715	25	43	48	588	21	1037	92	46	99	1040	4	.454	.352
Lynchburg	.260	140	5317	4670	683	1215	1874	253	38	110	625	42	39	66	500	27	1061	147	66	87	1001	9	.401	.338
Prince William	.260	139	5352	4700	689	1221	1830	246	45	91	631	33	40	53	526	35	1020	116	61	112	1001	7	.389	.338
Durham	.258	139	5257	4642	657	1199	1859	270	27	112	599	31	47	69	468	32	1015	154	85	98	922	6	.400	.332
Frederick	.256	140	5374	4665	670	1194	1813	248	19	111	597	70	30	75	534	25	964	94	57	119	1036	5	.389	.340
Winston-Salem	.254	140	5178	4595	615	1168	1802	268	45	92	552	39	37	42	465	11	1045	128	71	83	947	13	.392	.326
Salem	.244	138	5073	4439	588	1084	1571	227	22	72	522	73	35	59	467	20	980	191	92	77	892	4	.354	.322
Wilmington	.242	140	5281	4591	652	1109	1691	203	29	107	589	53	34	54	549	21	1062	147	70	86	958	10	.368	.327

INDIVIDUAL

TOP QUALIFIERS FOR BATTING CHAMPIONSHIP

Minimum 378 plate appearances. *Lefthanded batter. †Switch-hitter.

Player, Team	Avg.	G	TPA	AB	R	H	TB	2B	3B	HR	RBI	SH	SF	HP	BB	IBB	SO	SB	CS	GDP	Slg.	OBP
Short, Rick, Frederick	.319	126	538	480	73	153	214	29	1	10	72	7	1	12	38	2	44	10	7	20	.446	.382
Lee, Carlos, Winston-Salem	.317	139	593	546	81	173	282	50	4	17	82	2	7	2	36	2	65	11	5	12	.516	.357

Player, Team	Avg.	G	TPA	AB	R	H	TB	2B	3B	HR	RBI	SH	SF	HP	BB	IBB	SO	SB	CS	GDP	Slg.	OBP
Morgan, Scott, Kinston	.315	95	424	368	86	116	223	32	3	23	67	0	4	5	47	3	87	4	2	8	.606	.396
Asche, Mike, Lynchburg	.306	107	463	409	70	125	200	34	4	11	70	1	8	4	41	0	77	33	3	5	.489	.368
Wells, Forry, Salem*	.299	93	382	321	58	96	162	27	3	11	52	3	1	9	48	2	64	19	7	9	.505	.404
Hernandez, Alexander, Lyn.*	.290	131	558	520	75	151	211	37	4	5	68	2	7	2	27	2	140	13	8	6	.406	.324
Stumberger, Darren, Kinston	.283	133	573	502	72	142	217	30	0	15	79	0	5	3	60	6	88	1	0	13	.432	.360
Johnson, Adam, Durham*	.281	133	572	502	80	141	264	39	3	26	92	0	16	4	50	9	94	18	8	10	.526	.341
Ramirez, Aramis, Lynchburg	.278	137	579	482	85	134	249	24	2	29	114	0	5	12	80	9	103	5	3	12	.517	.390
Gomez, Ramon, Win.-Salem	.277	118	532	477	78	132	185	23	12	2	42	8	2	3	42	0	132	53	21	9	.388	.338
LeCronier, Jason, Frederick*	.273	117	460	421	68	115	201	25	2	19	59	5	1	2	31	1	112	6	0	13	.477	.325
Scutaro, Marcos, Kinston	.272	97	427	378	58	103	162	17	6	10	59	2	3	9	35	0	72	23	7	3	.429	.346
Dishington, Nate, Prin.William*	.272	133	543	448	75	122	238	20	6	28	106	1	6	7	81	11	121	8	5	3	.531	.387
Trippy, Joe, Durham*	.272	120	521	437	62	119	163	24	4	4	45	10	4	9	61	0	76	34	20	8	.373	.370
DeRosa, Mark, Durham	.269	92	387	346	51	93	134	11	3	8	37	2	4	10	25	2	73	6	8	12	.387	.332

DEPARTMENTAL LEADERS: G—Lee, 139; AB—Lee, 546; R—Morgan, 86; H—Lee, 173; TB—Lee, 282; 2B—Lee, 50; 3B—Gomez, 12; HR—Peoples, 34; RBI—Ramirez, 114; SH—Pena, 14; SF—A. Johnson, 16; HP—Wilson, 15; BB—M. Johnson, 106; IBB—Dishington, 11; SO—Coffee, 157; SB—Gomez, 53; CS—Gomez, 21; GIDP—Short, 20; Slg.—Morgan, .606; OBP—M. Johnson, .420.

ALL PLAYERS

*Lefthanded batter. †Switch-hitter.

Player, Team	Avg.	G	TPA	AB	R	H	TB	2B	3B	HR	RBI	SH	SF	HP	BB	IBB	SO	SB	CS	GDP	Slg.	OBP
Akins, Carlos, Frederick	.212	110	403	335	53	71	93	16	0	2	30	4	3	7	54	0	79	14	4	2	.278	.331
Albert, Rashad, Winston-Salem	.181	24	82	72	10	13	28	1	1	4	9	2	0	0	8	0	25	3	5	0	.389	.263
Almond, Greg, Prince William	.327	18	58	52	5	17	27	7	0	1	2	0	1	0	5	1	11	1	2	2	.519	.379
Almonte, Wady, Frederick	.257	57	226	202	34	52	99	13	2	10	36	1	3	4	16	4	59	4	1	8	.490	.320
Alvarez, Clemente, Winston-Salem	.250	2	5	4	0	1	1	0	0	0	1	0	0	1	0	0	2	0	0	0	.250	.400
Ametller, Jesus, Prince William*	.270	60	234	215	26	58	81	10	2	3	26	4	0	0	15	1	12	3	1	5	.377	.317
Antczak, Chuck, Winston-Salem	.143	5	15	14	0	2	2	0	0	0	0	0	0	0	0	0	3	0	0	0	.143	.143
Antigua, Nilson, Lynchburg	.243	46	156	148	18	36	44	5	0	1	17	1	0	2	5	0	24	2	2	5	.297	.277
Asche, Mike, Lynchburg	.306	107	463	409	70	125	200	34	4	11	70	1	8	4	41	0	77	33	3	5	.489	.368
Bair, Rod, Salem	.273	16	50	44	5	12	15	3	0	0	6	3	1	2	0	0	6	2	0	1	.341	.298
Bass, Jayson, Durham†	.256	75	310	277	48	71	111	20	4	4	34	2	0	2	29	1	57	8	4	6	.401	.331
Baugh, Darren, Winston-Salem	.225	101	365	325	41	73	101	11	4	3	22	9	2	2	27	0	100	13	3	4	.311	.287
Bello, Jilberto, Frederick	.286	2	8	7	0	2	3	1	0	0	1	0	0	0	1	0	2	0	0	0	.429	.375
Beltran, Carlos, Wilmington†	.229	120	473	419	57	96	152	15	4	11	46	3	1	4	46	3	96	17	7	10	.363	.311
Betances, Junior, Kinston	.278	74	263	230	34	64	90	10	2	4	26	3	3	3	24	0	34	8	4	5	.391	.350
Boulware, Ben, Winston-Salem	.256	43	189	176	24	45	70	12	2	3	16	0	1	5	7	0	29	9	8	2	.398	.302
Branyan, Russell, Kinston*	.290	83	359	297	59	86	197	26	2	27	75	0	5	5	52	4	94	3	1	9	.663	.398
Bronson, Ben, Wilmington*	.175	34	75	57	9	10	13	3	0	0	4	3	1	3	11	1	17	2	2	0	.228	.333
Bryant, Chris, Frederick	.274	91	343	317	53	87	127	17	1	7	36	3	1	4	47	2	65	6	3	7	.401	.374
Bryant, Clint, Salem	.227	52	205	185	15	42	57	9	0	2	18	2	0	2	14	0	36	4	4	2	.308	.289
Budzinski, Mark, Kinston*	.286	68	292	241	43	69	109	13	3	7	39	2	0	1	48	1	61	6	4	3	.452	.407
Carney, Bartt, Frederick†	.000	4	8	6	2	0	0	0	0	0	0	0	0	0	2	0	0	0	0	0	.000	.250
Caruso, Michael, Winston-Salem†	.227	28	125	119	12	27	34	3	2	0	14	0	0	2	4	0	8	3	0	0	.286	.264
Cepeda, Jose, Wilmington	.282	28	86	71	9	20	20	0	0	0	8	0	0	3	12	0	10	1	0	1	.282	.386
Chavez, Eric, Frederick	.188	82	302	272	29	51	100	16	0	11	34	0	4	4	22	0	69	1	3	6	.368	.255
Clapp, Stubby, Prince William†	.318	78	333	267	51	85	130	21	6	4	46	4	4	6	52	2	41	9	4	2	.487	.435
Claudio, Patricio, Kinston	.303	24	94	89	14	27	35	5	0	1	9	3	0	0	2	0	16	1	2	1	.393	.319
Clifford, John, Salem	.235	17	36	34	3	8	8	0	0	0	3	0	0	1	1	0	7	0	1	1	.235	.278
Coffee, Gary, Wilmington	.222	120	493	427	58	95	141	11	1	11	56	0	4	7	55	0	157	6	4	13	.330	.318
Conger, Jeff, Lynchburg*	.213	24	71	61	12	13	23	3	2	1	5	1	0	3	6	0	18	2	1	0	.377	.314
Connacher, Kevin, Winston-Salem†	.288	70	278	243	32	70	99	16	2	3	27	2	3	2	28	0	50	12	8	2	.407	.362
Cordero, Edward, Durham	.224	57	189	165	19	37	49	6	0	2	15	2	3	4	15	1	45	7	4	1	.297	.299
Davis, Albert, Lynchburg	.167	18	70	60	9	10	15	2	0	1	3	2	1	0	7	0	13	2	1	2	.250	.250
Delaney, Donovan, Wilmington	.235	124	471	434	53	102	150	25	4	5	60	6	6	1	24	0	112	15	7	4	.346	.273
Delgado, Jose, Durham†	.264	129	542	492	72	130	165	27	1	2	45	6	4	1	39	1	72	8	10	11	.335	.317
DeRosa, Mark, Durham	.269	92	387	346	51	93	134	11	3	8	37	2	4	10	25	2	73	6	8	12	.387	.332
Diaz, Maikell, Durham†	.000	7	19	15	2	0	0	0	0	0	0	1	0	0	3	0	3	0	1	0	.000	.167
Dishington, Nate, Prince William*	.272	133	543	448	75	122	238	20	6	28	106	1	6	7	81	11	121	8	5	3	.531	.387
Downs, Brian, Winston-Salem	.260	33	112	100	13	26	44	7	0	1	11	1	1	0	8	1	22	0	0	3	.440	.324
Drizos, Justin, Salem*	.185	57	170	151	13	28	52	7	1	5	19	2	1	1	15	2	56	1	1	2	.344	.262
Duverge, Salvadore, Salem	.186	42	127	113	9	21	26	5	0	0	9	1	2	2	9	0	32	1	4	6	.230	.254
Elam, Brett, Salem	.200	6	17	15	0	3	3	0	0	0	1	0	1	0	1	0	1	0	2	1	.200	.250
Escamilla, Roman, Wilmington	.235	57	200	167	19	42	52	7	0	1	21	4	1	0	28	0	30	0	6	4	.311	.357
Escandon, Emiliano, Wilmington†	.273	80	303	238	40	65	86	9	3	2	32	5	2	1	57	3	54	9	4	3	.361	.413
Evans, Michael, Wilmington*	.227	108	411	352	55	80	147	14	1	17	55	1	3	1	54	0	97	3	2	3	.418	.329
Evans, Pat, Kinston†	.203	26	80	69	5	14	17	3	0	0	2	1	1	1	8	0	21	0	1	1	.246	.291
Falciglia, Tony, Prince William	.197	64	160	147	16	29	43	8	0	2	17	1	1	2	9	1	31	1	1	7	.293	.252
Farley, Cordell, Prince William	.261	61	231	211	34	55	79	9	3	3	32	3	1	1	15	1	46	24	5	2	.374	.286
Farris, Mark, Lynchburg*	.232	116	402	367	40	85	120	17	3	4	39	0	5	4	26	5	71	4	1	8	.327	.286
Febles, Carlos, Wilmington	.237	122	504	438	78	104	152	27	6	3	29	0	12	5	51	2	95	49	11	5	.347	.333
Feuerstein, Dave, Salem	.232	94	361	327	47	76	98	13	3	1	34	7	2	4	21	3	45	20	6	8	.300	.285
Figueroa, Luis, Lynchburg†	.281	26	96	89	12	25	30	5	0	0	2	0	0	0	7	0	6	1	2	5	.337	.333
Foote, Derek, Durham*	.240	68	242	217	28	52	80	10	0	6	33	0	1	6	18	3	73	0	1	2	.369	.314
Foster, Jim, Frederick	.350	61	255	200	48	70	132	12	1	16	65	0	3	7	45	7	24	8	0	5	.660	.478
Gambill, Chad, Salem	.247	124	495	450	61	111	166	18	2	11	53	0	4	4	37	4	125	6	11	7	.369	.307
Garcia, Luis, Winston-Salem	.257	130	523	498	55	128	210	29	7	13	81	4	5	0	16	0	93	4	8	9	.422	.277
Garcia, Ossie, Prince William	.239	104	283	247	38	59	77	12	3	0	20	6	2	3	25	0	41	10	5	9	.312	.314
Garcia, Vicente, Salem	.257	98	376	319	49	82	118	22	1	4	37	5	2	6	44	2	51	11	5	8	.370	.356
Germosen, Julio, Lynchburg	.167	3	7	6	0	1	1	0	0	0	0	0	0	0	0	0	2	0	0	0	.167	.286
Gomez, Ramon, Winston-Salem	.277	118	532	477	78	132	185	23	12	2	42	8	2	3	42	0	132	53	21	9	.388	.338
Gonzalez, Richard, Kinston	.254	44	161	142	17	36	48	6	0	2	17	2	3	1	13	0	25	0	0	2	.338	.314

Player, Team	Avg.	G	TPA	AB	R	H	TB	2B	3B	HR	RBI	SH	SF	HP	BB	IBB	SO	SB	CS	GDP	Slg.	OBP
Gresham, Kris, Frederick	.237	43	157	131	17	31	47	7	0	3	19	5	0	6	15	0	30	3	2	2	.359	.342
Gross, Rafael, Kinston	.267	73	302	266	53	71	118	20	0	9	36	0	2	4	30	0	68	17	10	7	.444	.348
Haas, Chris, Prince William*	.238	100	410	361	58	86	142	10	2	14	54	1	2	4	42	2	144	1	1	7	.393	.323
Hall, Andy, Prince William†	.193	23	97	83	13	16	24	1	2	1	7	3	0	1	10	0	22	4	1	2	.289	.287
Hallmark, Patrick, Wilmington	.300	27	118	100	22	30	41	5	0	2	11	1	2	3	12	0	16	8	3	0	.410	.385
Hayes, Heath, Kinston	.254	103	422	378	54	96	190	22	0	24	59	0	2	2	40	3	107	2	3	7	.503	.327
Hendricks, Ryan, Frederick*	.194	77	258	222	21	43	70	9	0	6	25	1	3	2	30	0	71	1	4	4	.315	.292
Hernandez, Alexander, Lynchburg*	.290	131	558	520	75	151	211	37	4	5	68	2	7	2	27	2	140	13	8	6	.406	.324
Houser, Kyle, Salem	.217	110	432	383	36	83	103	18	1	0	28	10	4	2	33	1	61	11	8	6	.269	.280
Huelsmann, Mike, Kinston†	.246	90	343	289	50	71	94	9	4	2	19	4	0	2	48	0	56	12	4	8	.325	.357
Jarrett, Link, Salem†	.160	9	27	25	1	4	4	0	0	0	1	1	0	0	1	0	5	0	0	1	.160	.192
Jimenez, Ruben, Prince William†	.146	17	48	41	5	6	7	1	0	0	1	0	1	0	6	0	7	2	0	0	.171	.250
Johnson, Adam, Durham*	.281	133	572	502	80	141	264	39	3	26	92	0	16	4	50	9	94	18	8	10	.526	.341
Johnson, Mark, Winston-Salem*	.253	120	491	375	59	95	142	27	4	4	46	0	5	5	106	2	85	4	2	7	.379	.420
Jorgensen, Tim, Kinston*	.284	91	369	334	49	95	172	19	2	18	65	0	6	1	28	0	47	0	1	9	.515	.336
Keck, Brian, Salem	.281	48	142	121	22	34	38	4	0	0	11	5	2	3	11	1	21	17	3	3	.314	.350
Kelley, Erskine, Lynchburg	.214	39	124	112	19	24	48	8	2	4	16	2	0	1	9	0	31	1	2	7	.429	.279
Kennedy, Adam, Prince William*	.312	35	163	154	24	48	66	9	3	1	27	1	0	2	6	1	17	4	3	3	.429	.346
Kilburg, Joe, Kinston*	.233	9	35	30	5	7	12	2	0	1	5	0	0	0	5	0	6	1	0	0	.400	.343
Kleiner, Stacy, Prince William	.313	91	344	310	37	97	139	22	4	4	32	1	1	4	28	2	69	1	1	11	.448	.376
Kurtz, Tony, Frederick*	.218	81	307	262	35	57	85	11	4	3	17	5	1	1	38	2	90	7	2	1	.324	.318
Lamb, David, Frederick†	.261	70	286	249	30	65	94	21	1	2	39	3	3	6	25	2	32	3	1	10	.378	.339
Lankford, Ray, Prince William*	.308	4	18	13	3	4	5	1	0	0	4	0	1	0	4	0	5	1	1	0	.385	.444
Lanza, Mike, Frederick	.224	23	72	67	4	15	19	4	0	0	5	0	1	1	3	0	13	1	2	2	.284	.264
Lawrence, Chip, Frederick	.268	57	186	164	18	44	55	5	0	2	14	6	0	3	13	0	19	2	4	1	.335	.333
Lee, Carlos, Winston-Salem	.317	139	593	546	81	173	282	50	4	17	82	2	7	2	36	2	65	11	5	12	.516	.357
LeCronier, Jason, Frederick*	.273	117	460	421	68	115	201	25	2	19	59	5	1	2	31	1	112	6	0	13	.477	.325
Light, Tal, Salem	.265	104	440	373	57	99	167	19	2	15	65	0	4	4	59	2	144	0	1	6	.448	.368
Lombard, George, Durham*	.264	131	541	462	65	122	203	25	7	14	72	2	2	9	66	9	145	35	7	4	.439	.365
Long, Garrett, Lynchburg	.207	9	32	29	1	6	12	3	0	1	5	0	0	0	3	0	10	0	0	3	.414	.281
Longueira, Tony, Wilmington	.241	62	222	195	27	47	60	7	0	2	23	3	0	3	21	0	34	2	3	1	.308	.324
Luzinski, Ryan, Frederick	.667	1	4	3	1	2	2	0	0	0	0	0	0	0	1	0	0	0	0	0	.667	.750
Manning, Brian, Winston-Salem	.292	28	116	106	13	31	43	6	0	2	12	0	0	2	8	1	14	1	2	3	.406	.353
Marnell, Dean, Salem	.192	17	58	52	4	10	12	2	0	0	7	2	0	1	3	0	1	0	0	0	.231	.250
Martin, Lincoln, Frederick†	.194	79	298	253	42	49	71	6	5	2	23	9	2	1	33	0	52	11	2	3	.281	.287
Martinez, Eddy, Frederick	.241	54	200	174	14	42	51	6	0	1	14	3	2	2	19	0	43	6	7	9	.293	.320
Matos, Pascual, Durham	.242	117	447	430	51	104	182	18	3	18	50	0	1	2	14	3	122	4	5	12	.423	.268
Matvey, Mike, Prince William	.228	32	142	123	22	28	49	12	0	3	22	0	4	0	15	1	28	1	0	3	.398	.303
Mazurek, Brian, Prince William*	.281	97	352	324	39	91	137	17	1	9	47	1	3	3	21	0	53	0	2	12	.423	.328
McBride, Charles, Durham	.111	5	20	18	1	2	3	1	0	0	1	0	0	0	2	0	4	1	0	0	.167	.200
McDonald, John, Kinston	.259	130	603	541	77	140	188	27	3	5	53	7	2	2	51	0	75	6	5	12	.348	.324
McHugh, Ryan, Prince William	.265	116	485	442	68	117	172	27	2	8	61	1	7	3	32	4	117	4	7	11	.389	.314
McKinnis, Leroy, Frederick	.288	88	345	319	36	92	130	24	1	4	39	1	0	5	20	0	62	3	3	14	.408	.340
McNally, Sean, Wilmington	.266	95	369	323	51	86	163	22	2	17	68	3	1	2	40	4	98	2	1	6	.505	.350
McNally, Shawn, Prince William	.217	47	168	138	12	30	39	7	1	0	18	1	0	2	27	3	22	3	2	6	.283	.353
Mejia, Miguel, Prince William	.213	39	147	136	17	29	31	2	0	0	9	0	0	1	10	0	25	7	8	3	.228	.272
Mendez, Sergio, Lynchburg	.141	17	67	64	5	9	17	2	0	2	6	0	0	2	1	0	18	0	1	2	.266	.179
Miyake, Chris, Lynchburg	.250	79	322	288	40	72	94	14	1	2	20	5	0	1	28	1	57	3	2	6	.326	.319
Morgan, Scott, Kinston	.315	95	424	368	86	116	223	32	3	23	67	0	4	5	47	3	87	4	2	8	.606	.396
Morris, Bobby, Kinston*	.156	10	39	32	6	5	12	1	0	2	10	0	1	2	4	0	6	0	0	2	.375	.282
Morseman, Bob, Frederick*	.000	39	1	1	0	0	0	0	0	0	0	0	0	0	0	0	1	0	0	0	.000	.000
Motley, Mel, Kinston	.211	7	19	19	3	4	8	1	0	1	1	0	0	0	0	0	5	0	0	0	.421	.211
Munoz, Juan, Prince William*	.313	66	279	256	41	80	122	16	7	4	48	0	4	0	19	3	25	3	1	5	.477	.355
Neubart, Garrett, Salem	.256	133	590	527	66	135	164	23	3	0	34	10	2	12	39	0	90	50	18	3	.311	.321
Norris, Dax, Durham	.237	95	377	338	29	80	120	19	0	7	45	0	3	4	32	1	49	2	5	10	.355	.308
Nunez, Abraham, Lynchburg†	.260	78	338	304	45	79	105	9	4	3	32	9	1	1	23	0	47	29	14	5	.345	.313
Ojeda, Augie, Frederick†	.344	34	151	128	25	44	60	11	1	1	20	4	0	1	18	1	18	2	5	1	.469	.429
Ortega, William, Prince William	.229	73	271	249	23	57	71	14	0	0	15	1	0	0	21	1	42	1	2	10	.285	.289
O'Toole, Bobby, Frederick	.276	12	37	29	5	8	13	2	0	1	4	1	0	0	7	0	4	0	0	0	.448	.417
Paxton, Chris, Frederick*	.267	4	15	15	1	4	7	0	0	1	1	0	0	0	0	0	5	0	0	1	.467	.267
Pena, Elvis, Salem†	.222	93	335	279	41	62	78	9	2	1	30	14	3	2	37	0	53	16	6	1	.280	.315
Peoples, Daniel, Kinston	.249	121	505	409	82	102	227	21	1	34	84	0	6	6	84	4	145	8	1	6	.555	.380
Petke, Jonathan, Kinston	.168	41	112	101	8	17	23	6	0	0	10	1	0	1	9	0	24	0	1	3	.228	.243
Petrick, Ben, Salem	.248	121	482	412	68	102	176	23	3	15	56	4	2	2	62	2	100	30	11	6	.427	.347
Pitts, Rick, Wilmington	.216	15	41	37	6	8	15	1	0	2	5	1	0	0	3	0	14	3	1	0	.405	.275
Polidor, Wil, Winston-Salem†	.248	41	153	149	14	37	44	7	0	0	11	1	0	1	2	0	16	6	1	4	.295	.263
Prieto, Alejandro, Wilmington	.215	129	497	437	52	94	122	13	3	3	38	11	6	2	41	1	59	20	8	6	.279	.282
Pryor, Pete, Winston-Salem*	.210	124	479	391	51	82	121	15	0	8	44	3	5	9	71	4	97	3	0	11	.309	.340
Quinn, Mark, Wilmington	.308	87	355	299	51	92	168	22	3	16	71	0	6	8	42	4	47	3	2	10	.562	.400
Ramirez, Aramis, Lynchburg	.278	137	579	482	85	134	249	24	2	29	114	0	5	12	80	9	103	5	3	12	.517	.390
Randolph, Edward, Win.-Salem†	.220	72	261	241	21	53	79	12	1	4	27	3	2	2	13	1	68	0	1	2	.328	.264
Redman, Julian, Lynchburg*	.251	125	476	415	55	104	144	18	5	4	45	8	1	7	45	0	82	21	8	8	.347	.333
Reyes, Jose, Lynchburg	.000	2	5	5	0	0	0	0	0	0	0	0	0	0	0	0	2	0	0	0	.000	.000
Rice, Charles, Lynchburg*	.211	33	110	95	10	20	30	2	1	2	13	0	1	2	10	0	28	2	0	3	.316	.296
Rivera, Roberto, Frederick	.226	16	57	53	8	12	16	1	0	1	8	0	0	1	3	0	16	1	1	0	.302	.281
Robinson, Tony, Lynchburg	.295	77	297	254	40	75	103	16	3	2	33	5	3	7	28	0	37	12	6	3	.406	.377
Rocha, Juan, Wilmington	.256	97	373	340	43	87	135	16	1	10	42	0	1	5	27	1	67	6	3	8	.397	.319
Rust, Brian, Durham	.258	122	482	430	67	111	180	29	2	12	71	1	5	3	43	0	104	10	4	8	.419	.326
Salzano, Jerry, Durham	.279	68	267	226	29	63	86	20	0	1	24	2	1	12	26	2	42	6	4	10	.381	.381
Schmidt, Dave, Prince William*	.195	82	272	231	23	45	54	9	0	0	19	3	1	9	28	0	66	2	2	9	.234	.305
Scutaro, Marcos, Kinston	.272	97	427	378	58	103	162	17	6	10	59	2	3	9	35	0	72	23	7	3	.429	.346
Short, Rick, Frederick	.319	126	538	480	73	153	214	29	1	10	72	7	1	12	38	2	44	10	7	20	.446	.382
Stumberger, Darren, Kinston	.283	133	573	502	72	142	217	30	0	15	79	0	5	3	60	6	88	1	0	13	.432	.360

Player, Team	Avg.	G	TPA	AB	R	H	TB	2B	3B	HR	RBI	SH	SF	HP	BB	IBB	SO	SB	CS	GDP	Slg.	OBP
Swafford, Derek, Lynchburg*	.250	38	141	112	16	28	33	5	0	0	5	3	0	1	25	0	28	8	3	1	.295	.391
Taylor, Jamie, Salem*	.263	23	96	80	13	21	30	4	1	1	9	1	0	2	13	0	27	2	2	2	.375	.379
Thobe, Steve, Lynchburg	.148	12	31	27	1	4	5	1	0	0	2	1	1	1	1	0	10	1	0	0	.185	.200
Thomas, Allen, Winston-Salem*	.169	31	92	77	11	13	20	4	0	1	11	0	1	1	13	0	27	1	3	2	.260	.293
Thomas, Juan, Winston-Salem	.262	45	182	164	28	43	89	7	0	13	28	0	0	1	17	0	61	1	1	5	.543	.335
Topham, Ryan, Winston-Salem*	.238	58	220	193	26	46	75	13	2	4	21	0	2	1	24	0	53	0	2	1	.389	.323
Treanor, Matt, Wilmington	.198	80	290	257	22	51	74	6	1	5	25	6	0	2	25	0	59	1	6	4	.288	.275
Trippy, Joe, Durham*	.272	120	521	437	62	119	163	24	4	4	45	10	4	9	61	0	76	34	20	8	.373	.370
Turlais, John, Lynchburg*	.167	14	35	30	2	5	9	1	0	1	5	0	0	0	5	0	9	0	1	0	.300	.286
Utting, Ben, Durham*	.216	67	173	148	18	32	37	5	0	0	5	4	1	0	20	0	26	6	4	2	.250	.308
Vavrek, Mike, Salem*	.500	10	2	2	0	1	1	0	0	0	0	0	0	0	0	0	1	0	0	0	.500	.500
Vidal, Carlos, Salem	.239	80	252	226	20	54	93	21	0	6	30	2	5	0	19	1	54	1	2	4	.412	.292
Walker, Morgan, Lynchburg	.270	29	95	89	15	24	39	6	0	3	8	0	0	0	6	1	19	0	0	2	.438	.316
Walker, Shon, Lynchburg*	.261	100	386	303	59	79	151	15	6	15	48	1	4	1	77	3	131	2	3	1	.498	.408
Walton, Jerome, Frederick	.211	7	24	19	1	4	7	0	0	1	2	0	0	0	5	0	0	1	1	0	.368	.375
Welch, Travis, Prince William	.000	58	1	1	0	0	0	0	0	0	0	0	0	0	0	0	0	0	0	0	.000	.000
Wells, Forry, Salem*	.299	93	382	321	58	96	162	27	3	11	52	3	1	9	48	2	64	19	7	9	.505	.404
Whatley, Gabe, Durham*	.273	43	187	154	37	42	82	16	0	8	30	0	2	3	28	0	33	9	1	2	.532	.390
Whittaker, Jerry, Winston-Salem	.271	52	186	170	24	46	82	17	2	5	20	2	0	0	14	0	62	3	1	2	.482	.326
Wilhelm, Brent, Winston-Salem	.206	48	180	155	22	32	51	8	1	3	26	2	1	1	21	0	33	1	0	5	.329	.303
Wilson, Craig, Lynchburg	.264	117	458	401	54	106	191	26	1	19	69	1	2	15	39	6	98	6	5	3	.476	.350
Wolff, Mike, Frederick*	.252	112	386	321	50	81	117	12	0	8	34	11	2	6	45	4	47	4	4	10	.364	.353
Woolf, Jason, Prince William†	.247	70	313	251	59	62	97	11	3	6	18	1	1	5	55	1	75	26	5	0	.386	.391

GRAND SLAMS: Dishington 3; L. Garcia, Peoples, Ramirez, 2 each; Albert, M. Evans, Foster, Gambill, Hayes, Hendricks, A. Johnson, Jorgensen, Kleiner, Light, Lombard, L. Martin, Matos, Sean McNally, McDonald, Munoz, Randolph, 1 each.

AWARDED FIRST BASE ON CATCHER'S INTERFERENCE: Stumberger 3 (McKinnis, Turlais, Wilson); Rice 2 (Falciglia, Randolph); Cl. Bryant 2 (Hayes, Antigua); Antczak (Almond); M. Wolff (Petrick).

1997 PITCHING

TEAM

Team	W	L	Pct.	ERA	G	CG	ShO	Sv.	IP	H	TBF	R	ER	HR	SH	SF	HB	BB	IBB	SO	WP	Bk.
Kinston	87	53	.621	3.80	140	5	8	47	1218.2	1114	5157	597	514	107	46	22	49	470	18	1046	68	7
Lynchburg	82	58	.586	3.84	140	9	7	45	1224.2	1154	5187	607	523	103	50	23	56	410	22	1093	83	6
Salem	63	75	.457	3.89	138	11	12	26	1190.1	1143	5112	612	515	99	41	53	81	431	12	985	71	7
Winston-Salem	63	77	.450	4.03	140	9	5	34	1198.1	1081	5200	653	537	115	37	45	51	567	23	1075	91	16
Prince William	69	70	.496	4.26	139	2	7	42	1224.0	1189	5377	698	579	132	34	28	45	559	7	1007	73	13
Frederick	69	71	.493	4.30	140	4	7	35	1220.1	1195	5386	706	583	122	47	38	59	605	23	1096	66	14
Wilmington	62	78	.443	4.36	140	1	9	30	1216.1	1317	5337	701	589	86	51	46	49	435	57	856	66	12
Durham	63	76	.453	4.79	139	1	3	30	1218.2	1262	5504	755	649	116	60	50	76	620	30	1026	85	8

INDIVIDUAL

TOP QUALIFIERS FOR EARNED-RUN AVERAGE TITLE
Minimum 112 innings. *Lefthanded pitcher.

Pitcher, Team	W	L	Pct.	ERA	G	GS	CG	ShO	GF	Sv.	IP	H	TBF	R	ER	HR	SH	SF	HB	BB	IBB	SO	WP	Bk.
Politte, Cliff, Prince William	11	1	.917	2.24	19	19	0	0	0	0	120.1	89	475	37	30	11	0	3	2	31	0	118	2	2
Crowell, Jim, Kinston*	9	4	.692	2.37	17	17	0	0	0	0	114.0	96	461	41	30	4	3	2	8	26	0	94	3	0
Kusiewicz, Mike, Salem*	8	6	.571	2.52	19	18	1	1	0	0	117.2	99	480	44	33	5	4	5	9	32	0	107	7	1
Martinez, William, Kinston	8	2	.800	3.09	23	23	1	0	0	0	137.0	125	568	61	47	13	4	3	4	42	2	120	4	0
Jimenez, Jose, Prince William	9	7	.563	3.09	24	24	2	0	0	0	145.2	128	609	73	50	12	2	2	9	42	2	81	10	2
Arroyo, Bronson, Lynchburg	12	4	.750	3.31	24	24	3	1	0	0	160.1	154	658	69	59	17	7	0	3	33	0	121	9	0
Estes, Eric, Frederick	9	8	.529	3.47	26	25	1	0	0	0	148.0	142	608	70	57	8	2		6	30	0	124	4	0
Atkins, Ross, Kinston	8	4	.667	3.62	27	16	0	0	3	0	117.0	98	501	53	47	10	2	3	2	62	2	84	11	2
Phillips, Jason, Lynchburg	11	6	.647	3.76	23	23	2	1	0	0	138.2	129	577	66	58	10	4	2	6	35	0	140	9	1
Randall, Scott, Salem	9	10	.474	3.84	27	26	2	1	1	0	176.0	167	763	95	75	8		6	11	66	3	128	14	0
Chapman, Jake, Wilmington*	8	9	.471	3.85	27	26	0	0	1	0	154.1	163	673	83	66	7	3	5	5	59	5	122	4	0
Sanders, Frankie, Kinston	11	5	.688	4.06	25	25	2	0	0	0	146.1	130	611	72	66	10	6	2	2	66	1	127	8	0
Secoda, Jason, Winston-Salem	7	4	.636	4.14	29	15	1	0	5	2	119.2	118	525	67	55	11	3	5	4	57	1	85	16	1
Stepka, Tom, Salem	11	14	.440	4.15	28	27	4	3	0	0	182.1	205	766	100	84	25	2	5	9	28	0	120	3	0
Reed, Dan, Frederick*	10	10	.500	4.21	28	27	2	0	0	0	173.1	189	772	104	81	14	4	3	1	75	2	108	2	0

DEPARTMENTAL LEADERS: W—Arroyo, Weibl, 12 each; L—Stepka, 14; Pct.—Politte, .917; G—Almanza, Nestor, Welch, 58 each; GS—Weibl, 29; CG—Stepka, 4; ShO—Stepka, 3; GF—Almanza, 47; Sv.—Almanza, 36; IP—Stepka, 182.3; H—Stepka, 205; TBF—D. Reed, 772; R—D. Reed, 104; ER—Ambrose, 91; HR—Stepka, 25; SH—Mull, 9; SF—Ambrose, 9; HB—Mays, 13; BB—Ambrose, 117; IBB—Bernal, 10; SO—Chantres, 158; WP—Saneaux, 24; BK—Thorn, Ambrose, 5 each.

ALL PITCHERS
*Lefthanded pitcher.

Pitcher, Team	W	L	Pct.	ERA	G	GS	CG	ShO	GF	Sv.	IP	H	TBF	R	ER	HR	SH	SF	HB	BB	IBB	SO	WP	Bk.
Ah Yat, Paul, Lynchburg*	5	1	.833	1.31	6	6	3	1	0	0	48.0	37	182	8	7	2	2	0	1	4	0	38	1	0
Almanza, Armando, Prince Wm.*	2	3	.400	1.67	58	0	0	0	47	36	64.2	38	259	18	12	3	1		4	32	1	83	8	1
Ambrose, John, Winston-Salem	8	13	.381	5.47	27	27	1	1	0	0	149.2	136	688	102	91	17	5	9	8	117	2	137	16	5
Anderson, Eric, Wilmington	1	2	.333	4.89	14	6	0	0	0	0	38.2	37	169	25	21	3	2	4	1	16	0	11	2	0
Arnold, Jamie, Durham	2	2	.500	5.92	5	5	0	0	0	0	24.1	25	115	21	16	2	2	0	1	13	0	21	2	0
Arroyo, Bronson, Lynchburg	12	4	.750	3.31	24	24	3	1	0	0	160.1	154	658	69	59	17	7	0	3	33	0	121	9	0
Atkins, Ross, Kinston	8	4	.667	3.62	27	16	0	0	3	0	117.0	98	501	53	47	10	2	3	2	62	2	84	11	2

CLASS A Carolina League

Pitcher, Team	W	L	Pct.	ERA	G	GS	CG	ShO	GF	Sv.	IP	H	TBF	R	ER	HR	SH	SF	HB	BB	IBB	SO	WP	Bk.
Avrard, Corey, Prince William	0	3	.000	5.36	8	8	0	0	0	0	40.1	30	190	28	24	1	0	0	2	44	0	50	4	1
Ayers, Mike, Lynchburg*	5	4	.556	5.00	39	0	0	0	13	4	63.0	54	288	38	35	8	4	2	6	44	6	62	4	0
Barber, Brian, Prince William	1	1	.500	4.09	2	2	0	0	0	0	11.0	10	44	5	5	3	0	0	0	5	0	13	0	0
Beirne, Kevin, Winston-Salem	4	4	.500	3.05	13	13	1	0	0	0	82.2	66	338	38	28	7	1	2	7	28	1	75	5	0
Benes, Adam, Prince William	3	3	.500	6.27	33	5	0	0	9	0	70.1	92	326	54	49	15	3	2	2	29	0	44	4	0
Benes, Andy, Prince William	0	0	.000	0.00	1	1	0	0	0	0	5.0	3	19	1	0	0	0	0	0	1	0	9	0	0
Benson, Kris, Lynchburg	5	2	.714	2.58	10	10	0	0	0	0	59.1	49	241	20	17	1	3	1	2	13	0	72	3	1
Bernal, Manuel, Wilmington	6	8	.429	4.33	45	3	0	0	25	8	97.2	108	424	51	47	5	4	2	5	27	10	55	2	2
Bevel, Bobby, Salem*	4	7	.364	4.64	50	0	0	0	18	3	66.0	69	290	37	34	5	2	7	9	17	0	57	3	0
Blanco, Roger, Durham	3	3	.500	7.64	36	0	0	0	11	0	68.1	91	336	64	58	15	6	3	12	33	1	33	3	0
Bost, Heath, Salem	1	0	1.000	2.40	13	0	0	0	10	3	15.0	9	57	4	4	1	1	0	0	2	0	9	0	0
Bowie, Micah, Durham*	2	2	.500	3.66	9	6	0	0	0	0	39.1	29	167	16	16	2	0	2	0	27	0	44	2	0
Bradford, Chad, Winston-Salem	3	7	.300	3.95	46	0	0	0	41	15	54.2	51	247	30	24	2	4	0	5	25	5	43	2	0
Brewer, Ryan, Wilmington	5	4	.556	3.34	47	0	0	0	19	7	105.0	100	439	41	39	5	6	0	3	29	4	93	4	0
Briggs, Anthony, Durham	1	2	.333	4.50	17	0	0	0	10	3	30.0	27	129	16	15	2	1	1	0	13	2	25	3	0
Brixey, Dusty, Wilmington	0	4	.000	3.83	24	0	0	0	9	1	42.1	49	192	29	18	1	2	1	2	22	7	22	5	0
Bullock, Derek, Lynchburg	2	0	1.000	4.81	15	2	0	0	2	0	33.2	27	152	20	18	5	0	1	4	21	0	34	3	1
Byrdak, Tim, Wilmington*	4	3	.571	3.51	22	2	0	0	15	3	41.0	34	169	17	16	3	5	1	2	12	4	47	4	0
Caldwell, David, Kinston*	2	1	.667	4.33	9	3	0	0	3	0	27.0	31	127	16	13	2	1	1	2	10	0	16	2	0
Camp, Jared, Kinston	5	4	.556	3.79	13	12	0	0	0	0	73.2	57	297	36	31	11	5	1	2	20	0	64	1	1
Chantres, Carlos, Winston-Salem	9	11	.450	4.70	26	26	2	0	0	0	164.2	152	712	94	86	21	6	5	4	71	1	158	10	2
Chapman, Jake, Wilmington*	8	9	.471	3.85	27	26	0	0	0	0	154.1	163	673	83	66	7	3	5	5	59	5	122	4	0
Chavez, Eric, Frederick	0	1	.000	27.00	1	0	0	0	1	0	1.0	2	6	3	3	1	0	0	0	1	1	1	0	0
Colmenares, Luis, Salem	6	1	.857	3.92	32	3	0	0	15	2	66.2	60	283	34	29	5	6	4	4	30	3	70	6	2
Conway, Keith, Prince William*	1	0	1.000	2.79	15	0	0	0	2	0	19.1	18	83	6	6	2	1	0	1	8	0	22	0	0
Corn, Chris, Lynchburg	3	4	.429	3.20	28	1	0	0	11	2	64.2	54	265	30	23	8	4	2	1	23	2	66	1	0
Cortes, David, Durham	2	0	1.000	2.33	19	0	0	0	16	8	19.1	15	76	5	5	1	0	1	0	5	0	16	1	0
Crowell, Jim, Kinston*	9	4	.692	2.37	17	17	0	0	0	0	114.0	96	461	41	30	4	3	2	8	26	0	94	3	0
Cruz, Charlie, Durham*	5	0	1.000	3.16	49	0	0	0	23	1	85.1	80	379	37	30	5	7	4	5	44	3	76	6	0
Daniels, David, Lynchburg	1	1	.500	1.80	10	0	0	0	8	4	10.0	6	36	2	2	1	0	0	0	1	0	6	1	0
Deschenes, Marc, Kinston	2	0	1.000	0.81	20	0	0	0	19	10	22.1	9	79	2	2	2	0	0	0	4	0	39	1	0
Dietrich, Jason, Salem	3	2	.600	3.26	21	0	0	0	11	2	30.1	15	121	11	11	2	1	2	0	16	0	38	1	1
Dixon, Jim, Winston-Salem	0	1	.000	4.05	16	0	0	0	6	0	33.1	29	139	16	15	2	0	2	1	10	0	29	1	0
Donnelly, Robert, Prince William	5	0	1.000	3.51	37	0	0	0	12	0	51.1	44	232	33	20	5	2	0	2	26	0	54	7	0
Duncan, Sean, Winston-Salem*	0	1	.000	8.68	6	0	0	0	2	0	9.1	16	53	12	9	4	0	1	0	7	0	9	1	0
Duverge, Salvadore, Salem	0	0	.000	27.00	1	0	0	0	1	0	0.2	3	6	2	2	1	0	0	0	1	0	0	0	0
Dyess, Todd, Frederick	4	2	.667	3.28	10	10	0	0	0	0	46.2	32	195	19	17	3	1	1	6	23	1	50	3	3
Dykhoff, Radhames, Frederick	3	3	.500	2.42	31	0	0	0	18	5	67.0	48	282	19	18	4	6	1	0	38	3	98	0	1
Edwards, Jon, Kinston	6	4	.600	6.60	33	0	0	0	16	2	61.1	65	286	48	45	13	3	2	2	38	1	55	3	0
Estes, Eric, Frederick	9	8	.529	3.47	26	25	1	0	1	0	148.0	142	608	70	57	8	2	2	6	30	0	124	4	0
Evans, Bart, Wilmington	0	1	.000	6.53	16	2	0	0	8	0	20.2	22	101	18	15	1	0	2	3	15	0	22	3	0
Franks, Lance, Prince William	1	0	1.000	2.08	2	0	0	0	0	0	4.1	3	16	1	1	1	0	0	0	1	0	4	0	0
Freedberg, Todd, Frederick	0	0	.000	3.00	1	0	0	0	0	0	3.0	1	11	1	1	1	0	0	0	1	0	3	0	0
Fussell, Chris, Frederick	3	3	.500	3.96	9	9	1	1	0	0	50.0	42	218	23	22	5	2	3	3	31	2	54	3	0
Garcia, Frank, Prince William	2	2	.500	9.00	18	0	0	0	5	0	24.0	36	122	30	24	2	0	2	1	12	0	14	5	0
Garrett, Hal, Lynchburg	2	5	.286	4.82	29	5	0	0	11	5	56.0	56	250	36	30	5	4	3	4	22	3	45	5	0
Garza, Alberto, Kinston	1	0	1.000	3.38	1	1	0	0	0	0	8.0	5	33	3	3	0	0	0	0	4	1	4	1	0
Giard, Ken, Durham	2	2	.500	2.33	30	0	0	0	28	12	38.2	28	175	14	10	2	2	2	2	35	2	47	5	0
Gonzalez, Lariel, Salem	5	0	1.000	2.53	44	0	0	0	25	8	57.0	42	237	19	16	3	2	2	3	23	1	79	4	0
Granata, Chris, Kinston	0	1	.000	10.02	9	1	0	0	5	1	20.2	30	95	23	23	5	0	0	0	7	0	11	1	0
Granger, Greg, Kinston	4	6	.400	4.40	18	0	0	0	9	0	30.2	39	141	17	15	0	5	2	1	18	4	18	4	0
Gresham, Kris, Frederick	0	0	.000	108.00	1	0	0	0	0	0	0.2	9	11	8	8	2	0	0	0	0	0	2	0	0
Grieve, Tim, Wilmington	4	1	.800	1.88	26	0	0	0	19	7	38.1	24	154	11	8	3	4	1	0	20	4	34	1	0
Hackman, Luther, Salem	1	4	.200	5.80	15	15	2	0	0	0	80.2	99	384	60	52	14	4	5	9	37	0	59	8	0
Hall, Yates, Prince William	6	7	.462	4.77	26	21	0	0	0	0	109.1	89	500	70	58	13	1	4	4	94	0	75	12	1
Hasselhoff, Derek, Winston-Salem	3	2	.600	1.56	20	0	0	0	11	3	34.2	22	138	10	6	1	2	1	0	15	3	41	4	0
Haynie, Jason, Lynchburg*	2	5	.286	3.25	13	13	1	0	0	0	83.0	68	337	42	30	8	1	2	1	23	0	69	6	0
Hernandez, Elvin, Lynchburg	0	0	.000	1.80	3	0	0	0	2	1	5.0	4	20	1	1	0	0	0	0	1	0	5	0	0
Hernandez, Francis, Frederick	4	4	.500	2.31	49	0	0	0	46	24	58.1	51	244	23	15	8	3	3	1	21	1	51	1	0
Hodges, Kevin, Wilmington	8	11	.421	4.48	28	20	0	0	4	1	124.2	150	563	78	62	11	3	6	5	44	7	63	5	2
Horgan, Joe, Kinston*	1	2	.333	7.27	4	2	0	0	0	0	17.1	23	83	15	14	1	1	0	1	9	0	9	0	0
Horn, Keith, Kinston	0	0	.000	9.60	9	0	0	0	5	1	15.0	20	76	16	16	3	0	0	1	8	0	11	1	0
Hunt, Jon, Winston-Salem*	0	2	.000	4.35	25	2	0	0	11	0	31.0	32	143	21	15	3	0	2	1	14	0	26	4	0
Jacobs, Dwayne, Durham	4	8	.333	5.01	25	24	1	1	0	0	116.2	112	527	78	65	8	4	5	4	85	0	115	20	0
Jimenez, Jose, Prince William	9	7	.563	3.09	24	24	2	0	0	0	145.2	128	609	73	50	12	2	2	9	42	2	81	10	2
Johnson, Jason, Lynchburg	8	4	.667	3.71	17	17	0	0	0	0	99.1	98	411	43	41	4	4	2	6	30	1	92	7	0
Kammerer, James, Salem*	0	0	.000	2.87	6	1	0	0	2	0	15.2	10	57	5	5	0	0	0	0	3	0	12	0	0
King, Raymond, Durham*	6	9	.400	5.40	24	6	0	0	6	3	71.2	89	335	54	43	6	7	1	4	26	4	60	4	0
Koeman, Matt, Kinston	1	1	.500	7.63	7	0	0	0	3	0	15.1	20	70	14	13	3	1	0	0	4	0	12	2	0
Kown, John, Prince William	2	6	.250	6.92	20	10	0	0	1	0	66.1	83	310	60	51	10	2	4	3	25	0	32	2	0
Kusiewicz, Mike, Salem*	8	6	.571	2.52	19	18	1	1	0	0	117.2	99	480	44	33	5	4	5	9	32	0	107	7	1
Leskanic, Curt, Salem	0	0	.000	3.86	2	1	0	0	0	0	2.1	5	12	2	1	0	0	0	0	1	0	3	0	0
Looper, Braden, Prince William	3	6	.333	4.48	12	12	0	0	0	0	64.1	71	287	38	32	6	1	1	3	25	0	58	1	2
Lundquist, David, Winston-Salem	3	1	.750	6.75	20	6	0	0	6	0	48.0	65	228	41	36	7	1	2	3	23	3	39	2	2
Marache, Luis, Frederick*	0	2	.000	10.13	2	2	0	0	0	0	8.0	12	44	14	9	4	1	0	0	7	0	6	1	0
Markham, Andy, Frederick	4	0	1.000	3.03	20	0	0	0	9	1	29.2	31	130	13	10	3	2	1	0	12	1	22	1	0
Martin, Chandler, Salem	1	5	.167	3.97	16	5	0	0	8	1	45.1	46	205	25	20	1	1	0	3	25	0	30	7	0
Martin, Jeffrey, Lynchburg	8	10	.444	5.77	24	21	0	0	1	0	115.1	139	527	86	74	8	3	2	6	48	1	101	9	2
Martinez, Johnny, Kinston	1	2	.333	2.21	9	0	0	0	3	1	20.1	16	80	5	5	2	1	2	0	6	1	14	2	0
Martinez, William, Kinston	8	2	.800	3.09	23	23	1	0	0	0	137.0	125	568	61	47	13	4	3	4	42	2	120	4	0
Maskivish, Joe, Lynchburg	2	0	1.000	2.97	32	0	0	0	27	17	33.1	31	141	12	11	1	1	2	4	13	2	24	4	1
Mathews, Del, Lynchburg*	2	5	.286	3.51	18	5	0	0	6	1	48.2	48	209	25	19	3	4	1	3	13	3	48	3	0
Mattson, Craig, Lynchburg	0	0	.000	6.23	4	0	0	0	3	1	4.1	6	20	3	3	3	1	0	0	2	0	3	1	0

CLASS A *Carolina League*

Pitcher, Team	W	L	Pct.	ERA	G	GS	CG	ShO	GF	Sv.	IP	H	TBF	R	ER	HR	SH	SF	HB	BB	IBB	SO	WP	Bk.
Mays, Jarrod, Kinston	7	5	.583	4.13	20	19	0	0	0	0	100.1	94	435	53	46	8	1	1	13	42	0	64	5	0
McClinton, Pat, Frederick*	0	1	.000	27.00	1	0	0	0	1	0	0.1	1	5	1	1	0	0	0	1	2	0	0	0	1
McDade, Neal, Lynchburg	2	0	1.000	2.89	3	3	0	0	0	0	18.2	16	77	8	6	3	1	0	1	6	0	15	2	0
McGlinchy, Kevin, Durham	3	7	.300	4.90	26	26	0	0	0	0	139.2	145	595	78	76	14	2	4	9	39	2	113	4	2
McLaughlin, Denis, Durham	0	1	.000	15.00	11	0	0	0	8	0	9.0	23	62	20	15	4	0	2	1	11	1	4	3	0
McNeill, Kevin, Prince William*	2	6	.250	4.96	55	1	0	0	14	1	69.0	66	303	43	38	3	6	0	2	28	1	58	1	0
Merrick, Brett, Kinston*	0	1	.000	1.08	8	0	0	0	4	1	8.1	7	39	4	1	0	2	0	1	5	0	3	0	1
Million, Doug, Salem	5	9	.357	5.12	18	17	1	0	0	0	96.2	104	436	59	55	13	3	3	8	55	1	58	5	0
Mitchell, Kendrick, Winston-Salem	0	0	.000	4.50	5	0	0	0	5	0	6.0	7	28	3	3	0	0	0	2	2	0	5	2	0
Morseman, Bob, Frederick*	0	5	.000	4.81	38	0	0	0	23	2	63.2	61	303	37	34	4	6	2	6	46	3	61	3	0
Mull, Blaine, Wilmington	8	6	.571	3.56	19	19	0	0	0	0	111.1	126	485	55	44	6	9	5	4	33	3	64	5	0
Mullen, Scott, Wilmington*	4	4	.500	4.55	11	11	0	0	0	0	59.1	64	260	35	30	5	1	2	1	26	4	43	5	2
Murphy, Sean, Salem	1	3	.250	4.58	15	0	0	0	5	0	19.2	21	93	16	10	0	1	3	2	12	0	11	5	0
Nelson, Erick, Durham*	6	8	.429	4.76	41	1	0	0	14	1	70.0	76	326	49	37	6	6	4	3	30	4	42	6	1
Nelson, Joe, Durham	10	6	.625	4.76	25	24	0	0	0	0	124.2	114	543	74	66	17	5	4	12	61	1	99	5	0
Nestor, Joe, Prince William	3	7	.300	3.87	58	0	0	0	27	3	76.2	77	339	39	33	10	6	1	3	29	1	63	6	0
Norman, Scott, Salem	0	1	.000	3.96	18	0	0	0	11	1	25.0	29	109	12	11	4	0	0	0	8	1	13	0	0
Nunez, Maximo, Winston-Salem	0	2	.000	1.73	28	0	0	0	19	8	52.0	35	210	15	10	5	3	2	1	21	1	53	2	0
O'Connor, Brian, Lynchburg*	2	1	.667	3.46	11	0	0	0	6	2	13.0	11	55	5	5	0	0	0	1	6	1	14	3	0
Olszewski, Tim, Frederick	3	1	.750	5.43	34	0	0	0	7	1	64.2	75	293	48	39	14	2	4	4	29	2	41	2	0
Onley, Shawn, Durham	5	11	.313	4.92	27	27	0	0	0	0	133.2	158	614	86	73	11	2	7	4	59	5	112	6	1
Paredes, Carlos, Wilmington	5	9	.357	6.19	23	21	0	0	0	0	112.0	130	511	90	77	10	3	3	6	49	2	93	7	1
Parque, Jim, Winston-Salem*	7	2	.778	2.77	11	11	0	0	0	0	61.2	29	231	19	19	3	0	1	0	23	0	76	2	2
Parrish, John, Frederick*	1	3	.250	6.04	5	5	0	0	0	0	22.1	23	103	18	15	3	1	0	2	16	0	17	3	0
Paugh, Rick, Lynchburg*	0	2	.000	7.85	24	0	0	0	10	5	18.1	18	89	17	16	6	0	0	2	11	2	18	2	0
Peever, Lloyd, Salem	0	0	.000	3.27	4	1	0	0	0	0	11.0	13	49	6	4	0	1	1	0	3	0	10	0	0
Percibal, Billy, Frederick	1	3	.250	5.74	7	6	0	0	0	0	26.2	28	118	18	17	1	1	1	0	18	0	28	1	2
Perez, Julio, Kinston	6	1	.857	4.84	27	0	0	0	8	0	48.1	58	210	35	26	4	2	1	0	17	2	35	7	2
Phillips, Jason, Lynchburg	11	6	.647	3.76	23	23	2	1	0	0	138.2	129	577	66	58	10	4	2	6	35	0	140	9	1
Phillips, Marc, Wilmington*	0	3	.000	5.19	40	0	0	0	21	1	60.2	72	276	39	35	5	4	3	3	23	3	44	8	0
Pickford, Kevin, Lynchburg*	3	4	.429	3.56	14	10	0	0	1	1	73.1	72	296	31	29	3	4	1	2	11	0	50	2	0
Politte, Cliff, Prince William	11	1	.917	2.24	19	19	0	0	0	0	120.1	89	475	37	30	11	0	3	2	31	0	118	2	2
Rakers, Jason, Kinston	8	5	.615	3.07	17	17	2	2	0	0	102.2	93	405	41	35	10	1	0	1	18	0	105	2	1
Randall, Scott, Salem	9	10	.474	3.84	27	26	2	1	1	0	176.0	167	763	93	75	8	8	6	11	66	3	128	14	0
Reed, Dan, Frederick*	10	10	.500	4.21	28	27	2	0	0	0	173.1	189	772	104	81	14	4	3	1	75	2	108	2	0
Reed, Steve, Prince William	2	2	.500	4.31	7	7	0	0	0	0	39.2	45	176	24	19	6	0	1	0	12	0	25	2	2
Rhodes, Joey, Frederick	7	11	.389	5.45	28	22	0	0	2	0	117.1	130	530	86	71	16	8	7	4	61	3	75	5	1
Riske, David, Kinston	4	4	.500	2.25	39	0	0	0	23	2	72.0	58	299	22	18	3	6	1	2	33	4	90	0	0
Robbins, Michael, Wilmington*	0	0	.000	7.18	20	0	0	0	9	0	31.1	41	146	26	25	3	1	3	1	14	1	24	2	0
Roberts, Mark, Winston-Salem	5	9	.357	4.04	14	14	3	0	0	0	91.1	78	379	48	41	10	1	3	3	45	0	64	4	0
Rocker, John, Durham*	1	1	.500	4.33	11	1	0	0	3	0	35.1	33	157	21	17	3	2	1	2	22	0	39	5	1
Rogers, Jason, Frederick*	5	3	.625	5.73	36	5	0	0	8	0	70.2	68	320	46	45	6	1	2	5	48	1	57	2	3
Ruiz, Rafael, Winston-Salem*	0	1	.000	8.31	10	0	0	0	5	0	8.2	16	54	10	8	2	0	1	2	10	1	9	1	1
Saier, Matt, Wilmington	2	2	.500	1.69	9	9	0	0	0	0	42.2	31	173	11	8	4	0	2	0	15	0	47	2	0
Sanders, Frankie, Kinston	11	5	.688	4.06	25	25	2	0	0	0	146.1	130	611	72	66	10	6	2	2	66	1	127	8	0
Saneaux, Francisco, Frederick	2	6	.250	4.50	32	5	0	0	10	0	74.0	56	358	48	37	8	2	5	8	84	3	89	24	0
Santiago, Jose, Wilmington	1	1	.500	4.91	4	0	0	0	4	2	3.2	3	18	3	2	0	1	0	1	1	0	1	0	0
Schmack, Brian, Winston-Salem	2	5	.286	2.75	42	0	0	0	18	6	75.1	65	325	32	23	0	5	3	2	36	4	71	6	1
Schroeffel, Scott, Salem	1	4	.200	8.16	16	3	0	0	6	0	28.2	34	140	27	26	3	1	2	5	17	1	24	0	0
Seaver, Mark, Frederick	3	2	.600	3.05	11	10	0	0	0	0	62.0	57	258	29	21	6	2	0	6	17	0	68	6	1
Secoda, Jason, Winston-Salem	7	4	.636	4.14	29	15	1	0	5	2	119.2	118	525	67	55	11	3	5	4	57	1	85	16	1
Shoemaker, Stephen, Salem	3	3	.500	2.77	9	9	1	0	0	0	52.0	31	215	21	16	3	2	1	5	25	0	76	2	3
Smith, Hut, Frederick	4	1	.800	3.87	16	11	0	0	1	1	79.0	63	323	42	34	7	2	2	3	27	0	77	3	1
Stepka, Tom, Salem	11	14	.440	4.15	28	28	4	3	0	0	182.1	205	766	100	84	25	2	5	9	28	0	120	3	0
Stewart, Chaad, Durham*	1	0	1.000	2.90	8	5	0	0	0	0	31.0	26	137	12	10	3	0	0	2	15	0	19	1	1
Swift, Billy, Salem	0	1	.000	6.75	1	1	0	0	0	0	4.0	4	16	3	3	1	0	0	0	0	0	1	0	0
Temple, Jason, Lynchburg	2	0	1.000	4.14	28	0	0	0	15	1	37.0	39	171	21	17	4	1	1	2	24	0	34	7	0
Theodile, Robert, Winston-Salem	7	3	.700	2.94	13	12	0	0	1	0	82.2	66	344	34	27	6	2	4	6	33	0	75	5	0
Thorn, Todd, Wilmington*	6	10	.375	5.16	27	21	1	0	4	0	132.2	163	584	89	76	14	3	6	7	30	3	71	7	5
Towers, Josh, Frederick	6	2	.750	4.86	25	3	0	0	8	1	53.2	74	252	36	29	4	1	1	3	18	0	64	2	1
Vavrek, Mike, Salem*	2	2	.500	2.15	10	9	0	0	0	0	62.2	55	255	21	15	3	1	4	3	18	0	48	3	0
Villegas, Ismael, Durham	2	5	.286	5.07	30	1	0	0	5	1	55.0	60	255	33	31	5	2	2	4	32	0	44	5	0
Vining, Kenneth, Winston-Salem*	2	2	.500	2.86	5	5	0	0	0	0	34.2	36	153	17	11	2	3	0	0	11	0	38	2	0
Virchis, Adam, Winston-Salem	3	7	.300	4.78	14	9	1	0	1	0	58.1	62	265	44	31	12	1	2	2	19	1	42	6	2
Walker, Morgan, Lynchburg*	0	0	.000	36.00	1	0	0	0	1	0	1.0	2	7	4	4	1	0	0	0	2	0	1	0	0
Wallace, Jeff, Lynchburg*	5	0	1.000	1.65	9	0	0	0	6	1	16.1	9	65	3	3	0	1	0	0	10	1	13	1	0
Warrecker, Teddy, Kinston	1	0	1.000	5.18	6	4	0	0	0	0	24.1	19	115	14	14	1	2	0	6	20	0	26	7	0
Weibl, Clint, Prince William	12	11	.522	4.64	29	29	0	0	0	0	163.0	185	718	90	84	18	5	2	9	62	2	135	3	1
Welch, Travis, Prince William	4	5	.444	4.88	58	0	0	0	20	2	79.1	82	369	48	43	11	4	2	1	53	0	69	6	1
Winchester, Scott, Kinston	2	1	.667	1.47	34	0	0	0	34	29	36.2	21	146	6	6	2	0	1	1	11	0	45	3	0
Winkelsas, Joseph, Durham	1	4	.200	7.11	13	0	0	0	8	1	19.0	24	93	18	15	0	5	2	4	11	1	17	1	0
Wolff, Mike, Frederick*	0	0	.000	0.00	1	0	0	0	1	0	0.1	0	2	0	0	0	0	0	0	0	0	0	0	0
Wright, Jamey, Salem	0	1	.000	9.00	1	1	0	0	0	0	1.0	1	5	1	1	0	0	0	0	1	0	1	0	0
Young, Danny, Lynchburg*	0	0	.000	5.92	15	0	0	0	8	0	24.1	27	113	17	16	2	1	1	1	14	0	22	0	0
Zolecki, Mike, Salem	2	2	.500	2.65	22	0	0	0	14	6	34.0	22	133	10	10	2	1	3	1	11	2	31	3	0
Zwirchitz, Andy, Durham	7	5	.583	4.26	33	13	0	0	6	0	107.2	107	483	59	51	10	7	5	7	59	4	100	3	2

COMBINATION SHUTOUTS: **Durham (2)**—McGlinchy-Cruz, Zwirchitz-Villegas. **Frederick (6)**—Reed-Smith-Hernandez, Seaver-Saneaux-Dykhoff, Smith-Morseman, Estes-Dykhoff, Rhodes-Percibal-Dykhoff, Fussell-Morseman. **Kinston (6)**—Sanders-Edwards, Atkins-Winchester, Rakers-Winchester, Sanders-Winchester, Crowell-Atkins, Sanders-Riske. **Lynchburg (4)**—Benson-Wallace-Maskivash, Arroyo-Young, Johnson-Ayers-Garrett, Ah Yat-Temple. **Prince William (7)**—Jimenez-Almanza-Nestor, Weibl-Welch-Almanza, Politte-Welch, Looper-Nestor-Almanza, Jimenez-McNeill-Welch-Nestor, Hall-McNeill-Welch-Almanza, Hall-Garcia-Adam Benes. **Salem (7)**—Randall-Gonzalez, Shoemaker-Zolecki, Randall-Gonzalez, Kusiewicz-Bevel, Kusiewicz-Gonzalez, Stepka-Bevel-Norman-Colmenares. **Wilmington (9)**—Hodges-Grieve, Chapman-Bernal, Saier-Brewer-Grieve, Hodges-Anderson-Phillips, Saier-Brewer, Thorn-Bernal-Evans, Chapman-Bernal, Mull-Brewer-Byrdak, Mullen-Anderson-Phillips-Brixey. **Winston-Salem (4)**—Secoda-Bradford, Roberts-Hunt-Nunez, Theodile-Bradford, Ambrose-Secoda.

NO-HIT GAMES: Rakers, Kinston, defeated Durham, 8-0 (first game), June 4.

1997 FIELDING

TEAM

Team	Pct.	G	PO	A	E	TC	DP	PB
Kinston	.975	140	3656	1508	131	5295	143	14
Salem	.972	138	3571	1491	145	5207	103	23
Lynchburg	.970	140	3674	1539	159	5372	120	32
Durham	.967	139	3656	1461	174	5291	96	29
Frederick	.967	140	3661	1461	177	5299	117	19
Winston-Salem	.964	140	3595	1397	188	5180	91	21
Prince William	.964	139	3672	1428	193	5293	100	19
Wilmington	.962	140	3649	1698	212	5559	153	16

TRIPLE PLAY: Wilmington.

INDIVIDUAL

FIRST BASEMEN

NOTE: All caps denotes fielding-percentage leader based on 70 games for catchers, 93 for all other non-pitchers and 140 innings for pitchers. *Throws lefthanded.

Player, Team	Pct.	G	PO	A	E	TC	DP
Bryant, Chris, Frederick	1.000	2	11	0	0	11	1
Chavez, Eric, Frederick	.987	12	69	5	1	75	5
Clifford, John, Salem	1.000	10	44	4	0	48	3
Coffee, Gary, Wilmington	.981	119	1116	86	23	1225	125
Dishington, Nate, Prince William	.982	100	855	65	17	937	64
Downs, Brian, Winston-Salem	.973	8	71	2	2	75	3
Drizos, Justin, Salem*	.988	53	380	41	5	426	23
Evans, Michael, Wilmington	.980	27	221	18	5	244	19
Farris, Mark, Lynchburg	.993	107	845	49	6	900	80
Foote, Derek, Durham	.988	58	473	32	6	511	33
Gresham, Kris, Frederick	.857	3	6	0	1	7	1
Hayes, Heath, Kinston	.966	3	26	2	1	29	1
Hendricks, Ryan, Frederick	.979	42	289	36	7	332	28
Johnson, Adam, Durham*	1.000	1	2	0	0	2	0
Jorgensen, Tim, Kinston	1.000	5	36	1	0	37	4
Light, Tal, Salem	.949	14	102	10	6	118	10
Long, Garrett, Lynchburg	1.000	4	28	4	0	32	3
Mazurek, Brian, Prince William*	.975	46	329	20	9	358	27
McKinnis, Leroy, Frederick	1.000	8	38	2	0	40	3
McNally, Sean, Wilmington	1.000	1	11	0	0	11	0
McNally, Shawn, Prince William	1.000	5	34	3	0	37	2
Mendez, Sergio, Lynchburg	.976	13	116	7	3	126	9
Norris, Dax, Durham	.968	10	58	3	2	63	7
Pryor, Pete, Winston-Salem*	.978	99	753	52	18	823	48
Randolph, Edward, Win.-Salem	.981	6	50	1	1	52	6
Rust, Brian, Durham	.979	55	414	46	10	470	26
Salzano, Jerry, Durham	.982	14	102	7	2	111	9
STUMBERGER, Darren, Kinston	.994	133	1137	108	8	1253	125
Taylor, Jamie, Salem	1.000	7	61	7	0	68	4
Thobe, Steve, Lynchburg	1.000	6	38	1	0	39	2
Thomas, Juan, Winston-Salem	.992	26	227	9	2	238	14
Utting, Ben, Durham	1.000	8	32	3	0	35	5
Walker, Morgan, Lynchburg*	.984	21	172	15	3	190	12
Walker, Shon, Lynchburg*	1.000	8	75	0	0	75	6
Walton, Jerome, Frederick	1.000	1	4	0	0	4	0
Wells, Forry, Salem	.990	70	630	40	7	677	51
Whatley, Gabe, Durham	.986	9	62	7	1	70	8
Wilhelm, Brent, Winston-Salem	1.000	7	43	3	0	46	4
Wolff, Mike, Frederick*	.986	103	714	85	11	810	68

TRIPLE PLAY: Coffee.

SECOND BASEMEN

Player, Team	Pct.	G	PO	A	E	TC	DP
Ametller, Jesus, Prince William	.974	52	77	114	5	196	26
Asche, Mike, Lynchburg	.867	14	18	21	6	45	6
Baugh, Darren, Winston-Salem	.857	3	1	5	1	7	1
Betances, Junior, Kinston	1.000	44	82	126	0	208	37
Boulware, Ben, Winston-Salem	.956	41	60	112	8	180	16
Bryant, Chris, Frederick	1.000	2	6	2	0	8	1
Cepeda, Jose, Wilmington	1.000	1	3	1	0	4	0
Clapp, Stubby, Prince William	.961	42	73	101	7	181	22
Connacher, Kevin, Win.-Salem	.975	68	94	184	7	285	31
Cordero, Edward, Durham	.943	19	29	54	5	88	7
Delgado, Jose, Durham	.963	122	223	267	19	509	54
Elam, Brett, Salem	1.000	2	5	7	0	12	2
Escandon, Emiliano, Wilmington	.972	17	26	43	2	71	14
Febles, Carlos, Wilmington	.961	120	212	355	23	590	85
Figueroa, Luis, Lynchburg	.990	23	46	58	1	105	16
GARCIA, Vicente, Salem	.970	97	199	282	15	496	61
Hall, Andy, Prince William	.933	22	31	67	7	105	10
Jarrett, Link, Salem	1.000	5	9	9	0	18	1
Jimenez, Ruben, Prince William	.800	2	2	2	1	5	1
Jorgensen, Tim, Kinston	1.000	11	17	27	0	44	6
Kilburg, Joe, Kinston	.974	8	15	23	1	39	3
Kleiner, Stacy, Prince William	.967	33	43	76	4	123	8

Player, Team	Pct.	G	PO	A	E	TC	DP
Lamb, David, Frederick	.969	61	114	167	9	290	34
Lawrence, Chip, Frederick	.946	20	32	55	5	92	13
Longueira, Tony, Wilmington	.961	20	26	47	3	76	13
Martin, Lincoln, Frederick	.938	8	8	7	1	16	2
Miyake, Chris, Lynchburg	1.000	19	35	43	0	78	9
Morris, Bobby, Kinston	.892	9	11	22	4	37	4
Pena, Elvis, Salem	.972	38	70	101	5	176	8
Polidor, Wil, Winston-Salem	.975	16	28	51	2	81	12
Robinson, Tony, Lynchburg	.974	74	115	186	8	309	37
Scutaro, Marcos, Kinston	.980	74	128	209	7	344	55
Short, Rick, Frederick	.965	63	117	129	9	255	31
Swafford, Derek, Lynchburg	.935	34	45	70	8	123	20
Utting, Ben, Durham	.920	7	13	10	2	25	3
Wilhelm, Brent, Winston-Salem	.956	18	34	53	4	91	6

TRIPLE PLAY: Escandon.

THIRD BASEMEN

Player, Team	Pct.	G	PO	A	E	TC	DP
Asche, Mike, Lynchburg	.833	6	3	7	2	12	1
Baugh, Darren, Winston-Salem	1.000	1	1	2	0	3	1
Betances, Junior, Kinston	.891	12	12	29	5	46	2
Branyan, Russell, Kinston	.897	69	64	118	21	203	8
Bryant, Chris, Frederick	.890	71	45	109	19	173	13
Bryant, Clint, Salem	.848	39	16	68	15	99	4
Cepeda, Jose, Wilmington	.963	27	15	62	3	80	5
Chavez, Eric, Frederick	.931	12	6	21	2	29	2
Cordero, Edward, Durham	.833	4	1	4	1	6	0
Elam, Brett, Salem	.833	3	0	5	1	6	1
Escandon, Emiliano, Wilmington	.841	27	20	49	13	82	3
Farris, Mark, Lynchburg	.889	6	2	6	1	9	0
Gresham, Kris, Frederick	1.000	7	4	15	0	19	1
Gross, Rafael, Kinston	.750	4	1	2	1	4	0
HAAS, Chris, Prince William	.935	97	89	183	19	291	16
Hallmark, Patrick, Wilmington	1.000	1	0	2	0	2	0
Hayes, Heath, Kinston	.875	2	1	6	1	8	0
Jarrett, Link, Salem	1.000	2	2	5	0	7	1
Jorgensen, Tim, Kinston	.942	40	29	68	6	103	8
Keck, Brian, Salem	.984	28	8	55	1	64	3
Kleiner, Stacy, Prince William	.937	22	13	61	5	79	2
Lamb, David, Frederick	1.000	3	3	8	0	11	0
Lawrence, Chip, Frederick	.857	4	3	3	1	7	2
Lee, Carlos, Winston-Salem	.906	133	93	233	34	360	18
Light, Tal, Salem	.908	53	22	86	11	119	3
Longueira, Tony, Wilmington	.879	17	5	24	4	33	3
Matvey, Mike, Prince William	.818	14	14	22	8	44	1
McNally, Sean, Wilmington	.916	86	58	192	23	273	24
McNally, Shawn, Prince William	.895	10	6	11	2	19	0
Pena, Elvis, Salem	.892	19	11	22	4	37	1
Polidor, Wil, Winston-Salem	1.000	3	1	4	0	5	0
Ramirez, Aramis, Lynchburg	.897	131	75	265	39	379	21
Rust, Brian, Durham	.898	67	50	126	20	196	11
Salzano, Jerry, Durham	.912	51	37	98	13	148	5
Scutaro, Marcos, Kinston	.922	19	14	33	4	51	5
Short, Rick, Frederick	.919	54	45	103	13	161	9
Taylor, Jamie, Salem	.958	6	3	20	1	24	1
Thobe, Steve, Lynchburg	1.000	4	3	11	0	14	0
Utting, Ben, Durham	.913	23	12	30	4	46	1
Whatley, Gabe, Durham	1.000	5	1	3	0	4	0
Wilhelm, Brent, Winston-Salem	1.000	5	1	5	0	6	0

TRIPLE PLAY: Longueira.

SHORTSTOPS

Player, Team	Pct.	G	PO	A	E	TC	DP
Baugh, Darren, Winston-Salem	.925	91	147	246	32	425	37
Betances, Junior, Kinston	1.000	14	10	25	0	35	2
Bryant, Chris, Frederick	.882	4	4	11	2	17	3
Bryant, Clint, Salem	1.000	1	0	1	0	1	0
Caruso, Michael, Winston-Salem	.941	26	44	67	7	118	12

CLASS A Carolina League

Player, Team	Pct.	G	PO	A	E	TC	DP
Cordero, Edward, Durham	.938	31	50	85	9	144	12
DeRosa, Mark, Durham	.948	91	136	245	21	402	44
Diaz, Maikell, Frederick	.944	6	3	14	1	18	4
Elam, Brett, Salem	1.000	2	1	3	0	4	1
Escandon, Emiliano, Wilmington	.914	9	8	24	3	35	7
Figueroa, Luis, Lynchburg	.947	6	7	11	1	19	2
Garcia, Ossie, Prince William	1.000	3	1	0	0	1	0
Germosen, Julio, Lynchburg	1.000	3	2	9	0	11	1
Houser, Kyle, Salem	.960	110	154	297	19	470	61
Jarrett, Link, Salem	.857	1	1	5	1	7	0
Jimenez, Ruben, Prince William	.891	12	15	26	5	46	5
Keck, Brian, Salem	1.000	2	2	5	0	7	0
Kennedy, Adam, Prince William	.939	35	63	92	10	165	16
Kleiner, Stacy, Prince William	.960	10	4	20	1	25	5
Lamb, David, Frederick	1.000	7	2	8	0	10	1
Lanza, Mike, Frederick	.938	23	25	51	5	81	8
Lawrence, Chip, Frederick	.941	31	39	57	6	102	13
Longueira, Tony, Wilmington	.948	16	24	49	4	77	11
Martinez, Eddy, Frederick	.918	53	100	112	19	231	28
Matvey, Mike, Prince William	.914	19	26	48	7	81	7
McDONALD, John, Kinston	.961	130	209	413	25	647	105
McNally, Sean, Wilmington	1.000	3	3	8	0	11	2
Miyake, Chris, Lynchburg	.978	59	82	188	6	276	36
Nunez, Abraham, Lynchburg	.955	78	100	219	15	334	43
Ojeda, Augie, Frederick	.966	34	36	108	5	149	14
Pena, Elvis, Salem	.917	29	46	76	11	133	14
Polidor, Wil, Winston-Salem	.962	18	28	47	3	78	5
Prieto, Alejandro, Wilmington	.940	129	199	383	37	619	82
Robinson, Tony, Lynchburg	1.000	5	4	8	0	12	2
Utting, Ben, Durham	.943	24	28	55	5	88	7
Wilhelm, Brent, Winston-Salem	.929	9	6	7	1	14	1
Woolf, Jason, Prince William	.939	70	90	207	20	326	33

OUTFIELDERS

Player, Team	Pct.	G	PO	A	E	TC	DP
AKINS, Carlos, Frederick	.990	109	185	10	2	197	2
Albert, Rashad, Winston-Salem	.956	22	42	1	2	45	0
Almond, Greg, Prince William	1.000	1	2	0	0	2	0
Almonte, Wady, Frederick	.953	47	70	12	4	86	0
Asche, Mike, Lynchburg	.965	89	129	7	5	141	0
Bair, Rod, Salem	.875	5	7	0	1	8	0
Bass, Jayson, Durham	.959	50	65	6	3	74	0
Baugh, Darren, Winston-Salem	1.000	1	1	0	0	1	0
Beltran, Carlos, Wilmington	.968	119	236	7	8	251	0
Bronson, Ben, Wilmington	1.000	32	38	0	0	38	0
Bryant, Chris, Frederick	1.000	13	21	0	0	21	0
Budzinski, Mark, Kinston*	.984	65	119	2	2	123	0
Carney, Bartt, Frederick	1.000	3	4	0	0	4	0
Clapp, Stubby, Prince William	.980	34	44	6	1	51	1
Claudio, Patricio, Kinston	1.000	15	30	3	0	33	1
Conger, Jeff, Lynchburg*	.958	21	22	1	1	24	0
Cordero, Edward, Durham	1.000	4	3	0	0	3	0
Davis, Albert, Lynchburg	.967	16	27	2	1	30	0
Delaney, Donovan, Wilmington	.968	121	230	12	8	250	2
Dishington, Nate, Prince William	1.000	4	4	0	0	4	0
Duverge, Salvadore, Salem	.925	41	46	3	4	53	0
Evans, Michael, Wilmington	.963	37	47	5	2	54	0
Farley, Cordell, Prince William	.958	58	110	4	5	119	0
Feuerstein, Dave, Salem	.972	91	164	7	5	176	1
Gambill, Chad, Salem	.974	123	214	7	6	227	3
Garcia, Luis, Winston-Salem	.984	113	175	13	3	191	2
Garcia, Ossie, Prince William	.980	97	189	6	4	199	0
Gomez, Ramon, Winston-Salem	.940	113	213	8	14	235	1
Gross, Rafael, Kinston	.976	66	114	6	3	123	0
Hallmark, Patrick, Wilmington	1.000	5	7	1	0	8	0
Hernandez, Alexander, Lynch.*	.962	130	212	15	9	236	2
Huelsman, Mike, Kinston	.976	87	152	9	4	165	2
Johnson, Adam, Durham*	.989	123	255	11	3	269	0
Keck, Brian, Salem	1.000	7	6	1	0	7	0
Kelley, Erskine, Lynchburg	.964	37	52	1	2	55	0
Kilburg, Joe, Kinston	1.000	2	2	0	0	2	0
Kurtz, Tony, Frederick	.978	79	128	6	3	137	1
Lankford, Ray, Prince William*	1.000	2	6	0	0	6	0
Lawrence, Chip, Frederick	1.000	2	3	0	0	3	0
LeCronier, Jason, Frederick	.971	105	160	9	5	174	1
Lombard, George, Durham	.968	125	270	5	9	284	0
Long, Garrett, Lynchburg	1.000	2	4	0	0	4	0
Manning, Brian, Winston-Salem	1.000	22	43	1	0	44	0
Marnell, Dean, Salem	1.000	17	36	1	0	37	0
Martin, Lincoln, Frederick	.960	61	70	2	3	75	0
McBride, Charles, Durham	1.000	2	3	0	0	3	0
McHugh, Ryan, Prince William	.930	83	117	3	9	129	0

Player, Team	Pct.	G	PO	A	E	TC	DP
McKinnis, Leroy, Frederick	.970	17	29	3	1	33	1
McNally, Shawn, Prince William	.980	31	49	1	1	51	0
Mejia, Miguel, Prince William	.975	38	70	7	2	79	0
Morgan, Scott, Kinston	.987	86	143	7	2	152	2
Motley, Mel, Kinston	1.000	7	11	2	0	13	1
Munoz, Juan, Prince William*	.976	64	115	7	3	125	1
Neubart, Garrett, Salem	.985	132	254	13	4	271	1
Ortega, William, Prince William	.931	56	89	5	7	101	0
Peoples, Daniel, Kinston	.957	76	86	2	4	92	2
Petke, Jonathan, Kinston	.959	40	45	2	2	49	0
Pitts, Rick, Wilmington	.962	14	25	0	1	26	0
Quinn, Mark, Wilmington	.932	64	75	7	6	88	1
Randolph, Edward, Win.-Salem	.955	42	80	4	4	88	1
Redman, Julian, Lynchburg*	.975	124	227	8	6	241	3
Rivera, Roberto, Frederick	.941	15	31	1	2	34	0
Rocha, Juan, Wilmington	.923	61	82	2	7	91	0
Salzano, Jerry, Durham	.667	3	2	0	1	3	0
Thomas, Allen, Winston-Salem*	1.000	23	33	2	0	35	0
Topham, Ryan, Winston-Salem*	1.000	49	75	8	0	83	1
Trippy, Joe, Durham*	.979	112	174	13	4	191	2
Walker, Shon, Lynchburg*	.938	22	26	4	2	32	0
Walton, Jerome, Frederick	1.000	5	11	0	0	11	0
Wells, Forry, Salem	1.000	14	21	1	0	22	0
Whatley, Gabe, Durham	.947	8	15	3	1	19	1
Whittaker, Jerry, Winston-Salem	.983	46	105	8	2	115	4

CATCHERS

Player, Team	Pct.	G	PO	A	E	TC	DP	PB
Almond, Greg, Prince William	.970	16	116	13	4	133	0	2
Alvarez, Clemente, Win.-Salem	.900	2	8	1	1	10	0	0
Antczak, Chuck, Win.-Salem	.974	5	37	1	1	39	0	2
Antigua, Nilson, Lynchburg	.982	46	335	44	7	386	0	10
Bello, Jilberto, Frederick	1.000	1	9	0	0	9	0	0
Bryant, Chris, Frederick	.889	3	8	1	1	9	0	0
Chavez, Eric, Frederick	.975	32	233	40	7	280	5	9
Downs, Brian, Winston-Salem	.992	16	110	11	1	122	2	2
Escamilla, Roman, Wilmington	.993	45	263	27	2	292	2	6
Evans, Michael, Wilmington	.818	3	8	1	2	11	0	0
Evans, Pat, Kinston	.991	15	101	10	1	112	0	1
Falciglia, Tony, Prince William	.991	48	205	23	2	230	1	7
Foote, Derek, Durham	1.000	2	14	2	0	16	0	0
Foster, Jim, Frederick	.989	41	309	35	4	348	5	0
Gonzalez, Richard, Kinston	.997	41	271	23	1	295	2	4
Gresham, Kris, Frederick	.992	28	204	35	2	241	3	4
Hallmark, Patrick, Wilmington	1.000	23	129	20	0	149	1	3
Hayes, Heath, Kinston	.987	91	681	70	10	761	5	9
JOHNSON, Mark, Win.-Salem	.989	117	899	90	11	1000	8	14
Kleiner, Stacy, Prince William	.995	24	165	18	1	184	1	3
Luzinski, Ryan, Frederick	1.000	1	12	1	0	13	0	0
Matos, Pascual, Durham	.986	109	783	109	13	905	8	26
McKinnis, Leroy, Frederick	.989	35	250	19	3	272	0	5
McNally, Shawn, Prince Wm.	1.000	1	9	0	0	9	0	0
Norris, Dax, Kinston	.993	33	253	18	2	273	0	3
O'Toole, Bobby, Frederick	.973	10	65	7	2	74	0	1
Paxton, Chris, Frederick	1.000	4	29	1	0	30	0	0
Petrick, Ben, Durham	.988	107	754	91	10	855	6	12
Randolph, Edward, Win.-Salem	.952	8	35	5	2	42	0	3
Reyes, Jose, Lynchburg	1.000	2	10	4	0	14	0	0
Schmidt, Dave, Prince William	.983	82	533	53	10	596	4	7
Treanor, Matt, Wilmington	.978	80	460	68	12	540	3	7
Turlais, John, Lynchburg	.962	5	25	0	1	26	0	1
Vidal, Carlos, Salem	.988	41	218	26	3	247	1	11
Wilson, Craig, Lynchburg	.985	98	714	76	12	802	7	21
Woolf, Jason, Prince William	1.000	1	1	0	0	1	0	0

PITCHERS

Player, Team	Pct.	G	PO	A	E	TC	DP
Ah Yat, Paul, Lynchburg*	.917	6	2	9	1	12	0
Almanza, Armando, Prince Wm.*	1.000	58	0	9	0	9	0
Ambrose, John, Winston-Salem	.944	27	3	14	1	18	0
Anderson, Eric, Wilmington	1.000	14	2	6	0	8	2
Arnold, Jamie, Durham	.909	5	2	8	1	11	1
Arroyo, Bronson, Lynchburg	.974	24	11	26	1	38	1
Atkins, Ross, Kinston	.943	27	18	15	2	35	0
Avrard, Corey, Prince William	.846	8	2	9	2	13	1
Ayers, Mike, Lynchburg*	1.000	39	5	15	0	20	0
Beirne, Kevin, Winston-Salem	.842	13	5	11	3	19	0
Benes, Adam, Prince William*	1.000	33	6	10	0	16	1
Benson, Kris, Lynchburg	.833	10	6	4	2	12	0
Bernal, Manuel, Wilmington	1.000	45	13	14	0	27	1
Bevel, Bobby, Salem*	.950	50	5	14	1	20	5
Blanco, Roger, Durham	.947	36	7	11	1	19	1

Player, Team	Pct.	G	PO	A	E	TC	DP
Bost, Heath, Salem	1.000	13	0	3	0	3	0
Bowie, Micah, Durham*	1.000	9	1	5	0	6	2
Bradford, Chad, Winston-Salem	.913	46	4	17	2	23	1
Brewer, Ryan, Wilmington	.968	47	8	22	1	31	0
Briggs, Anthony, Durham	1.000	17	5	6	0	11	1
Brixey, Dusty, Wilmington	.929	24	1	12	1	14	2
Bullock, Derek, Lynchburg	1.000	15	1	3	0	4	0
Byrdak, Tim, Wilmington*	1.000	22	3	7	0	10	0
Caldwell, David, Kinston*	1.000	9	1	3	0	4	0
Camp, Jared, Kinston	.938	13	3	12	1	16	0
Chantres, Carlos, Win.-Salem	.939	26	10	21	2	33	1
Chapman, Jake, Wilmington*	.957	27	11	33	2	46	2
Colmenares, Luis, Salem	1.000	32	3	14	0	17	0
Conway, Keith, Prince William*	1.000	15	1	4	0	5	2
Corn, Chris, Lynchburg	1.000	28	4	6	0	10	1
Cortes, David, Durham	.800	19	2	2	1	5	0
Crowell, Jim, Kinston*	.913	17	5	16	2	23	2
Cruz, Charlie, Durham*	1.000	49	2	20	0	22	0
Deschenes, Marc, Kinston	1.000	20	1	3	0	4	0
Dietrich, Jason, Salem	1.000	21	0	3	0	3	0
Dixon, Jim, Winston-Salem	1.000	16	2	5	0	7	0
Donnelly, Robert, Prince William	.900	37	3	6	1	10	0
Duncan, Sean, Winston-Salem*	1.000	6	0	2	0	2	0
Dyess, Todd, Frederick	.917	10	4	7	1	12	0
Dykhoff, Radhames, Frederick*	1.000	31	8	6	0	14	0
Edwards, Jon, Kinston	.813	33	7	6	3	16	0
Estes, Eric, Frederick	.935	26	14	15	2	31	0
Evans, Bart, Wilmington	1.000	16	2	2	0	4	0
Franks, Lance, Prince William	1.000	2	0	1	0	1	0
Fussell, Chris, Frederick	1.000	9	3	4	0	7	0
Garcia, Frank, Prince William	1.000	18	4	4	0	8	1
Garrett, Hal, Lynchburg	1.000	29	4	10	0	14	0
Garza, Alberto, Kinston	1.000	1	0	1	0	1	0
Giard, Ken, Durham	1.000	30	2	5	0	7	0
Gonzalez, Lariel, Salem	1.000	44	3	2	0	5	0
Granata, Chris, Kinston	1.000	9	2	1	0	3	0
Granger, Greg, Kinston	.800	18	1	3	1	5	0
Grieve, Tim, Wilmington	1.000	26	3	5	0	8	0
Hackman, Luther, Salem	.944	15	9	8	1	18	0
Hall, Yates, Prince William	.880	26	13	9	3	25	2
Hasselhoff, Derek, Win.-Salem	.833	20	2	8	2	12	1
Haynie, Jason, Lynchburg*	1.000	13	2	15	0	17	1
Hernandez, Elvin, Lynchburg	1.000	3	1	0	0	1	0
Hernandez, Francis, Frederick	.909	49	7	3	1	11	1
Hodges, Kevin, Wilmington	.921	28	13	22	3	38	2
Horgan, Jose, Kinston*	1.000	4	1	3	0	4	1
Horn, Keith, Kinston	1.000	9	2	3	0	5	0
Hunt, Jon, Winston-Salem*	.625	25	2	3	3	8	0
Jacobs, Dwayne, Durham	.923	25	10	26	3	39	0
Jimenez, Jose, Prince William	.915	24	7	36	4	47	0
Johnson, Jason, Lynchburg	.870	17	8	12	3	23	1
Kammerer, James, Salem*	1.000	6	0	2	0	2	0
King, Raymond, Durham*	.840	24	3	18	4	25	0
Koeman, Matt, Kinston	1.000	7	2	0	0	2	0
Kown, John, Prince William	1.000	20	5	7	0	12	0
Kusiewicz, Mike, Salem*	.966	19	6	22	1	29	0
Looper, Braden, Prince William	.917	12	4	7	1	12	1
Lundquist, David, Win.-Salem	1.000	20	2	6	0	8	0
Marache, Luis, Frederick*	1.000	2	0	2	0	2	0
Markham, Andy, Frederick	.800	20	0	4	1	5	0
Martin, Chandler, Salem	.900	16	2	7	1	10	0
Martin, Jeffrey, Lynchburg	.947	24	3	15	1	19	1
Martinez, Johnny, Kinston	1.000	9	1	2	0	3	0
Martinez, William, Kinston	.925	23	14	23	3	40	2
Maskivish, Joe, Lynchburg	1.000	32	2	8	0	10	1
Mathews, Del, Lynchburg*	.889	18	2	14	2	18	0
Mattson, Craig, Lynchburg	1.000	4	0	1	0	1	0
Mays, Jarrod, Kinston	.905	20	7	12	2	21	1
McDade, Neal, Lynchburg	1.000	3	1	3	0	4	0
McGlinchy, Kevin, Durham	1.000	26	11	10	0	21	3
McLaughlin, Denis, Durham	1.000	11	0	1	0	1	0
McNeill, Kevin, Prince William*	1.000	55	1	4	0	5	0
Merrick, Brett, Kinston*	.667	8	1	1	1	3	1
Million, Doug, Salem*	1.000	18	2	18	0	20	0
Morseman, Bob, Frederick*	1.000	38	3	16	0	19	0
Mull, Blaine, Wilmington	.857	19	7	17	4	28	2
Mullen, Scott, Wilmington*	.875	11	4	10	2	16	0
Murphy, Sean, Salem	.750	15	2	1	1	4	0
Nelson, Erick, Durham*	.955	41	6	15	1	22	0
Nelson, Joe, Durham*	.980	25	20	30	1	51	5
Nestor, Joe, Prince William	.938	58	6	9	1	16	1
Norman, Scott, Salem	1.000	18	1	6	0	7	0
Nunez, Maximo, Winston-Salem	.786	28	7	4	3	14	0
O'Connor, Brian, Lynchburg*	1.000	11	0	2	0	2	0
Olszewski, Tim, Frederick	1.000	34	4	6	0	10	1
Onley, Shawn, Durham	.919	27	9	25	3	37	2
Paredes, Carlos, Wilmington	.828	23	9	15	5	29	2
Parque, Jim, Winston-Salem*	.909	11	1	9	1	11	0
Parrish, John, Frederick*	1.000	5	0	1	0	1	0
Paugh, Rick, Lynchburg*	1.000	24	0	5	0	5	0
Peever, Lloyd, Salem	1.000	4	1	5	0	6	0
Percibal, Billy, Frederick	.929	7	7	6	1	14	0
Perez, Julio, Kinston	1.000	27	6	7	0	13	1
Phillips, Jason, Lynchburg	.927	23	16	22	3	41	1
Phillips, Mark, Wilmington*	.923	40	4	8	1	13	1
Pickford, Kevin, Lynchburg*	.944	14	5	12	1	18	2
Politte, Cliff, Prince William	1.000	19	7	13	0	20	0
Rakers, Jason, Kinston	.923	17	12	12	2	26	1
Randall, Scott, Salem	.943	27	18	32	3	53	4
Reed, Dan, Frederick*	.919	28	16	41	5	62	4
Reed, Steve, Prince William	.909	7	2	8	1	11	0
Rhodes, Joey, Frederick	.929	28	14	12	2	28	1
Riske, David, Kinston	1.000	39	4	11	0	15	2
Robbins, Michael, Wilmington*	1.000	20	5	3	0	8	0
Roberts, Mark, Winston-Salem	.889	14	3	13	2	18	1
Rocker, John, Durham*	1.000	11	0	6	0	6	0
Rogers, Jason, Frederick*	.957	36	7	15	1	23	2
Ruiz, Rafael, Winston-Salem*	1.000	10	0	1	0	1	0
Saier, Matt, Wilmington	1.000	9	3	5	0	8	0
Sanders, Frankie, Kinston	.976	25	17	23	1	41	1
Saneaux, Francisco, Frederick	.800	32	2	6	2	10	0
Schmack, Brian, Winston-Salem	.875	42	5	9	2	16	0
Schroeffel, Scott, Salem	1.000	16	3	7	0	10	0
Seaver, Mark, Frederick	1.000	11	6	9	0	15	2
Secoda, Jason, Winston-Salem	1.000	29	8	14	0	22	1
Shoemaker, Stephen, Salem	.833	9	3	7	2	12	0
Smith, Hut, Frederick	.833	16	11	14	5	30	0
STEPKA, Tom, Salem	1.000	28	18	27	0	45	3
Stewart, Chaad, Durham*	.857	8	2	4	1	7	0
Swift, Billy, Salem	1.000	1	1	1	0	2	0
Temple, Jason, Lynchburg	1.000	28	4	8	0	12	0
Theodile, Robert, Win.-Salem	.833	13	1	9	2	12	0
Thorn, Todd, Wilmington*	.950	27	14	24	2	40	3
Towers, Josh, Frederick	1.000	25	1	5	0	6	0
Vavrek, Mike, Salem*	1.000	10	6	7	0	13	0
Villegas, Ismael, Durham	1.000	30	5	8	0	13	0
Vining, Kenneth, Win.-Salem*	.857	5	0	6	1	7	0
Virchis, Adam, Winston-Salem	.917	14	2	9	1	12	0
Wallace, Jeff, Lynchburg*	1.000	9	1	4	0	5	0
Warrecker, Teddy, Kinston	1.000	6	0	1	0	1	0
Weibl, Clint, Prince William	.875	29	6	22	4	32	3
Welch, Travis, Prince William	1.000	58	7	6	0	13	0
Winchester, Scott, Kinston	1.000	34	4	2	0	6	0
Winkelsas, Joseph, Durham	.875	13	4	3	1	8	0
Wright, Jamey, Salem	1.000	1	0	1	0	1	0
Young, Danny, Lynchburg*	1.000	15	2	5	0	7	0
Zolecki, Mike, Salem	1.000	22	2	5	0	7	0
Zwirchitz, Andy, Durham	.955	33	5	16	1	22	0

The following players did not have any fielding statistics at the positions indicated or appeared only as a designated hitter, pinch-hitter or pinch-runner: Barber, p; Andy Benes, p; Chavez, p; C. Cruz, of; D. Daniels, p; Drizos, of; Duverge, p; Freedberg, p; Gresham, p; Gross, 2b; Hendricks, of; Leskanic, p; McClinton, p; K. Mitchell, p; Miyake, 3b; R. Morris, 1b; Petke, 1b; Redman, 1b; Rice, of, c; Santiago, p; Walker, p; M. Wolff, p.

LEAGUE CHAMPIONS

Year	Team	Pct.	Year	Team	Pct.	Year	Team	Pct.
1945—	Danville	.681	1948—	Raleigh	.592	1951—	Durham	.600
1946—	Greensboro	.599		Martinsville (2nd)†	.570		Winston-Salem (2nd)†	.583
	Raleigh (2nd)†	.563	1949—	Danville	.601	1952—	Raleigh	.581
1947—	Burlington	.613		Burlington (4th)†	.500		Reidsville (4th)†	.536
	Raleigh (3rd)†	.574	1950—	Winston-Salem*	.693			

Year	Team	Pct.
1953—	Raleigh	.593
	Danville (2nd)†	.572
1954—	Fayetteville*	.628
1955—	HP-Thomasville	.580
	Danville (2nd)†	.533
1956—	HP-Thomasville	.591
	Fayetteville (4th)§	.523
1957—	Durham	.632
	HP-Thomasville	.622
1958—	Danville	.576
	Burlington (4th)†	.511
1959—	Raleigh	.600
	Wilson (2nd)†	.550
1960—	Greensboro‡	.636
	Burlington	.586
1961—	Wilson	.594
1962—	Durham	.636
	Wilson	.600
	Kinston (2nd)†	.593
1963—	Kinston§	.538
	Greensboro§	.590
	Wilson (2nd)†	.535
1964—	Kinston§	.572
	Winston-Salem§†	.590
1965—	Peninsula§	.597
	Durham§	.580
	Tidewater†	.528
1966—	Kinston§	.547
	Winston-Salem§	.586
	Rocky Mount†	.533
1967—	Durham∞(West.)	.536
	Raleigh (East.)	.542

Year	Team	Pct.
1968—	Salem (West.)	.607
	Ral-Dur (East.)	.597
	HP-Thom.▲(W.)	.493
1969—	Rocky M (East.)	.569
	Salem (West.)	.542
	Ral-Dur◆(East.)	.560
1970—	Winston-Salem‡	.586
	Burlington	.597
1971—	Peninsula‡	.647
	Kinston	.623
1972—	Salem‡	.657
	Burlington	.632
1973—	Lynchburg	.588
	Winston-Salem‡	.557
1974—	Salem	.671
	Salem	.582
1975—	Rocky Mount	.667
	Rocky Mount	.614
1976—	Winston-Salem	.618
	Winston-Salem	.551
1977—	Lynchburg	.591
	Peninsula‡	.556
1978—	Peninsula	.696
	Lynchburg‡	.614
1979—	Winston-Salem■	.607
1980—	Peninsula‡	.714
	Durham	.600
1981—	Peninsula	.522
	Hagerstown‡	.507
1982—	Alexandria‡	.597
	Durham	.588

Year	Team	Pct.
1983—	Lynchburg‡	.691
	Winston-Salem	.529
1984—	Lynchburg‡	.645
	Durham	.486
1985—	Lynchburg	.679
	Winston-Salem‡	.417
1986—	Hagerstown	.655
	Winston-Salem‡	.594
1987—	Salem‡	.576
	Kinston	.536
1988—	Kinston§	.629
	Lynchburg	.486
1989—	Durham	.609
	Prince William‡	.522
1990—	Kinston	.652
	Frederick‡	.544
1991—	Kinston‡	.645
	Lynchburg	.482
1992—	Lynchburg	.570
	Peninsula‡	.536
1993—	Wilmington	.532
	Winston-Salem‡	.514
1994—	Wilmington‡	.681
	Winston-Salem	.555
1995—	Wilmington	.601
	Kinston‡	.591
1996—	Wilmington▼	.571
	Kinston	.551
1997—	Kinston	.621
	Lynchburg†	.586

*Won championship and four-club playoff. †Won four-club playoff. ‡Won split-season playoff. §League was divided into Eastern, Western divisions. ∞Won eight-club, two-division playoff. sWon eight-club, two-division playoff against Raleigh-Durham. ◆Won eight-club, two-division playoff against Burlington. ■Won both halves of split season (no playoffs). ▼League divided into Northern and Southern Divisions and played a split-season, won playoffs.

CLASS A *Carolina League*

FLORIDA STATE LEAGUE

LEAGUE OFFICE

President
Chuck Murphy
Address
P.O. Box 349
Daytona Beach, FL 32115
Phone
904-252-7479

Teams (affiliation)
Brevard County Manatees (Marlins)
Charlotte Rangers (Rangers)
Clearwater Phillies (Phillies)
Daytona Cubs (Cubs)
Dunedin Blue Jays (Blue Jays)
Fort Myers Miracle (Twins)
Jupiter Hammerheads (Expos)

Kissimmee Cobras (Astros)
Lakeland Tigers (Tigers)
St. Lucie Mets (Mets)
St. Petersburg Devil Rays (Devil Rays)
Sarasota Red Sox (Red Sox)
Tampa Yankees (Yankees)
Vero Beach Dodgers (Dodgers)

1997 FINAL STANDINGS

FIRST HALF

EAST DIVISION

Team	W	L	T	Pct.	GB
Vero Beach (Dodgers)	38	31	0	.551	....
West Palm Beach (Expos)	34	34	0	.500	3¹/₂
Brevard County (Marlins)	33	35	0	.485	4¹/₂
St. Lucie (Mets)	28	39	0	.418	9
Daytona (Cubs)	29	41	0	.414	9¹/₂
Kissimmee (Astros)	28	40	0	.412	9¹/₂

WEST DIVISION

Team	W	L	T	Pct.	GB
St. Petersburg (Devil Rays)	42	26	0	.618	....
Tampa (Yankees)	41	26	0	.612	¹/₂
Fort Myers (Twins)	41	28	0	.594	1¹/₂
Lakeland (Tigers)	38	32	0	.543	5
Sarasota (Red Sox)	34	34	0	.500	8
Dunedin (Blue Jays)	32	38	0	.457	11
Clearwater (Phillies)	31	38	0	.449	11¹/₂
Charlotte (Rangers)	31	38	0	.449	11¹/₂

SECOND HALF

EAST DIVISION

Team	W	L	T	Pct.	GB
Kissimmee (Astros)	43	26	0	.623	....
Daytona (Cubs)	36	32	0	.529	6¹/₂
West Palm Beach (Expos)	35	32	0	.522	7
Vero Beach (Dodgers)	32	36	0	.471	10¹/₂
Brevard County (Marlins)	29	41	0	.414	14¹/₂
St. Lucie (Mets)	26	42	0	.382	16¹/₂

WEST DIVISION

Team	W	L	T	Pct.	GB
Lakeland (Tigers)	43	25	0	.632	....
Fort Myers (Twins)	40	30	0	.571	4
St. Petersburg (Devil Rays)	39	30	0	.565	4¹/₂
Clearwater (Phillies)	39	30	0	.565	4¹/₂
Charlotte (Rangers)	37	33	0	.529	7
Tampa (Yankees)	29	40	0	.420	14¹/₂
Sarasota (Red Sox)	29	41	0	.414	15
Dunedin (Blue Jays)	25	44	0	.362	18¹/₂

COMPOSITE

Team	St.P.	Lak.	Ft.M.	Kis.	Tam.	WPB	V.B.	Clw.	Char.	Day.	Sar.	B.C.	Dun.	StL	W	L	T	Pct.	GB
St. Petersburg (Devil Rays)	....	4	4	5	9	1	6	8	8	7	6	6	11	6	81	56	0	.591	....
Lakeland (Tigers)	8	....	6	6	6	5	3	9	7	4	11	5	8	3	81	57	0	.587	¹/₂
Fort Myers (Twins)	8	6	....	7	6	4	5	6	9	6	10	5	6	3	81	58	0	.583	1
Kissimmee (Astros)	3	1	1	....	4	9	8	8	2	9	5	10	4	7	71	66	0	.518	10
Tampa (Yankees)	6	6	6	3	....	7	7	3	7	5	8	2	6	4	70	66	0	.515	10¹/₂
West Palm Beach (Expos)	5	3	3	7	1	....	8	6	2	5	2	7	6	14	69	66	0	.511	11
Vero Beach (Dodgers)	2	4	3	6	1	8	....	2	5	7	4	12	4	12	70	67	0	.511	11
Clearwater (Phillies)	6	3	6	0	11	2	5	....	6	6	7	2	10	6	70	68	0	.507	11¹/₂
Charlotte (Rangers)	4	9	7	5	5	6	3	6	....	4	5	4	5	5	68	71	0	.489	14
Daytona (Cubs)	1	4	2	7	3	7	7	2	4	....	5	10	5	8	65	73	0	.471	16¹/₂
Sarasota (Red Sox)	6	5	6	3	4	6	4	5	7	3	....	4	7	3	63	75	0	.457	18¹/₂
Brevard County (Marlins)	2	3	3	6	5	7	4	6	4	6	4	....	4	8	62	76	0	.449	19¹/₂
Dunedin (Blue Jays)	3	4	6	4	7	2	4	6	7	3	5	4	....	2	57	82	0	.410	25
St. Lucie (Mets)	2	5	5	7	4	2	3	1	3	8	3	5	6	....	54	81	0	.400	26

Brevard County played home games in Melbourne, Fla.

Charlotte played home games in Port Charlotte, Fla.

Major league affiliations in parentheses.

PLAYOFFS: Vero Beach defeated Kissimmee, two games to one; St. Petersburg defeated Lakeland, two games to none; St. Petersburg defeated Vero Beach, three games to two, to win league championship.

REGULAR-SEASON ATTENDANCE: Brevard County, 132,608; Charlotte, 69,072; Clearwater, 97,687; Daytona, 86,704; Dunedin, 54,544; Fort Myers, 88,266; Kissimmee, 37,989; Lakeland, 21,198; St. Lucie, 60,210; St. Petersburg, 154,670; Sarasota, 69,813; Tampa, 149,191; Vero Beach, 59,511; West Palm Beach, 51,747. Total—1,133,210. Playoffs (10 games)—6,173. All-Star Game—2,104.

MANAGERS: Brevard County, Lorenzo Bundy; Charlotte, Butch Wynegar; Clearwater, Roy Majtyka; Daytona, Steve Roadcap; Dunedin, Dennis Holmberg (through July 25) and Ernie Whitt (July 26 to end of season); Fort Myers, John Russell; Kissimmee, John Tamargo; Lakeland, Mark Meleski; St. Lucie, John Gibbons; St. Petersburg, Bill Evers; Sarasota, Rob Derksen; Tampa, Lee Mazzilli; Vero Beach, John Shoemaker; West Palm Beach, Doug Sisson. Managerial record of teams with more than one manager: Dunedin, Holmberg 42-61; Whitt 15-21.

ALL-STAR TEAM: 1B—Alejandro Freire, Lakeland; 2B—Warren Morris, Charlotte; 3B—Adrian Beltre, Vero Beach; SS—Joe Funaro, Brevard County; Utility INF—Ramon Valette, Daytona; LF—Jacque Jones, Fort Myers; CF—Bo Porter, Daytona; RF—Gabe Kapler, Lakeland; Utility OF—Ruben Mateo, Charlotte; C—Ramon Castro, Kissimmee; Cesar King, Charlotte; DH—Jaime Torres, Tampa; RHP—Brian Powell, Lakeland; Courtney Duncan, Daytona; LHP—Corey Lee, Charlotte; Eddie Yarnall, St. Lucie; Relief Pitcher—John Daniels, St. Petersburg; Dan Ricabal, Vero Beach; Most Valuable Player—Adrian Beltre, Vero Beach; Manager of the Year—Mark Meleski, Lakeland; Coach of the Year—Butch Wynegar, Charlotte; John Tamargo, Kissimmee.

CLASS A *Florida State League*

1997 BATTING

TEAM

Team	Avg.	G	TPA	AB	R	H	TB	2B	3B	HR	RBI	SH	SF	HP	BB	IBB	SO	SB	CS	GDP	LOB	ShO	Slg.	OBP
Daytona	.274	138	5150	4601	698	1262	1860	247	33	95	628	28	43	73	405	8	979	177	89	83	932	11	.404	.340
Lakeland	.271	138	5151	4608	650	1251	1891	216	44	112	583	44	45	42	412	21	926	123	67	82	955	7	.410	.334
Vero Beach	.268	137	5198	4551	728	1220	1814	225	24	107	644	37	61	49	500	17	796	245	89	82	944	6	.399	.343
Fort Myers........	.267	139	5127	4636	635	1239	1759	231	23	81	581	36	39	39	377	16	834	132	79	101	918	7	.379	.325
Kissimmee	.266	137	5156	4618	615	1230	1716	214	43	62	533	40	40	43	415	17	823	122	63	108	984	11	.372	.330
St. Petersburg ...	.266	137	5237	4517	655	1201	1690	227	35	64	580	53	44	51	559	24	661	148	83	93	1017	6	.374	.352
Brevard County..	.263	138	5211	4632	617	1220	1747	234	34	75	544	39	42	56	442	14	956	149	63	101	978	12	.377	.332
Sarasota	.260	138	5056	4506	608	1171	1655	199	39	69	545	49	35	44	422	17	861	164	113	80	876	9	.367	.327
Charlotte	.259	138	5186	4598	653	1193	1763	228	48	82	583	24	36	62	466	11	968	167	100	88	927	4	.383	.333
Tampa...............	.255	136	5165	4543	621	1159	1700	210	29	91	531	40	43	68	471	27	1003	136	85	83	927	10	.374	.331
W. Palm Beach ..	.253	135	4890	4402	583	1112	1645	218	30	85	508	28	41	47	372	22	870	154	105	56	822	9	.374	.315
Dunedin	.250	138	5382	4644	662	1160	1770	229	24	111	590	48	42	81	567	17	1109	168	88	72	1034	8	.381	.339
Clearwater	.245	138	5043	4503	583	1104	1601	199	32	78	507	49	36	54	401	17	906	105	63	87	886	7	.356	.312
St. Lucie	.241	135	4901	4400	512	1059	1551	214	34	70	460	35	27	40	399	22	996	122	78	77	892	18	.353	.308

INDIVIDUAL

TOP QUALIFIERS FOR BATTING CHAMPIONSHIP

Minimum 378 plate appearances. *Lefthanded batter. †Switch-hitter.

Player, Team	Avg.	G	TPA	AB	R	H	TB	2B	3B	HR	RBI	SH	SF	HP	BB	IBB	SO	SB	CS	GDP	Slg.	OBP
Valette, Ramon, Daytona	.332	106	406	371	54	123	170	25	2	6	50	5	4	6	20	1	49	20	6	6	.458	.372
Freire, Alejandro, Lakeland	.323	130	547	477	85	154	260	30	2	24	92	0	7	12	50	1	84	13	4	10	.545	.396
Funaro, Joe, Brevard County	.319	125	535	470	67	150	190	16	6	4	53	3	6	7	49	3	65	9	5	8	.404	.387
Beltre, Adrian, Vero Beach............	.317	123	519	435	95	138	244	24	2	26	104	0	11	6	67	12	66	25	9	9	.561	.407
Mateo, Ruben, Calgary	.314	99	416	385	63	121	196	23	8	12	67	1	2	6	22	0	55	20	5	16	.509	.359
Allen, Chad, Fort Myers	.309	105	447	401	66	124	159	18	4	3	45	2	2	2	40	2	51	27	15	9	.397	.373
Fernandez, Jose, W. Palm Beach ...	.309	97	394	350	49	108	162	21	3	9	58	0	0	7	37	3	76	22	14	8	.463	.386
Porter, Bo, Daytona	.307	122	508	440	87	135	218	20	6	17	65	1	3	3	61	1	115	23	13	8	.495	.393
Morris, Warren, Calgary*	.306	128	567	494	78	151	232	27	9	12	75	3	1	7	62	3	100	16	5	6	.470	.390
Romano, Scott, St. Petersburg	.298	99	414	359	54	107	155	25	1	7	67	3	3	7	42	1	55	5	3	8	.432	.380
Jones, Jacque, Fort Myers*	.297	131	577	539	84	160	250	33	6	15	82	0	2	3	33	3	110	24	12	9	.464	.340
Fraraccio, Dan, St. Petersburg.......	.296	129	541	463	67	137	180	34	3	1	63	5	6	14	53	0	50	7	7	11	.389	.381
Fortin, Troy, Fort Myers	.295	111	434	383	58	113	172	20	0	13	59	3	4	10	34	1	37	1	2	11	.449	.364
Kapler, Gabe, Lakeland	.295	137	588	519	87	153	262	40	6	19	87	0	10	5	54	4	68	8	6	8	.505	.361
Torres, Jaime, Tampa....................	.294	115	449	408	48	120	178	28	0	10	56	2	1	10	28	2	30	0	2	13	.436	.353

DEPARTMENTAL LEADERS: G—Brumbaugh, 139; AB—R. Taylor, 545; R—Stuckenschneider, 100; H—Jacque Jones, 160; TB—Kapler, 262; 2B—Kapler, 40; 3B—Lugo, 14; HR—Beltre, 26; RBI—Beltre, 104; SH—Zorrilla, 16; SF—Seguignol, 14; HP—Skett, 19; BB—Stuckenschneider, 101; IBB—Beltre, 12; SO—Rolison, 143; SB—V. Brown, 55; CS—R. Taylor, 23; GIDP—Paez, 18; Slg.—Beltre, .561; OBP—Stuckenschneider, .419.

ALL PLAYERS

*Lefthanded batter. †Switch-hitter.

Player, Team	Avg.	G	TPA	AB	R	H	TB	2B	3B	HR	RBI	SH	SF	HP	BB	IBB	SO	SB	CS	GDP	Slg.	OBP
Acevedo, Luis, Calgary	.000	1	3	3	0	0	0	0	0	0	0	0	0	0	0	0	2	0	0	0	.000	.000
Adams, Jason, Kissimmee.............	.211	31	109	95	9	20	26	6	0	0	9	1	1	1	11	0	13	0	0	2	.274	.296
Adolfo, Carlos, W. Palm Beach	.225	120	491	448	62	101	153	15	2	11	50	3	0	2	38	1	91	9	18	8	.342	.289
Airoso, Kurt, Lakeland	.194	22	75	62	12	12	17	1	2	0	7	1	0	1	11	0	23	0	0	2	.274	.324
Alexander, Chad, Kissimmee.........	.271	129	534	469	67	127	182	31	6	4	46	2	3	4	56	1	91	11	8	15	.388	.352
Alexander, Manny, St. Lucie...........	.250	1	4	4	0	1	1	0	0	0	0	0	0	0	0	0	1	0	0	0	.250	.250
Allen, Chad, Fort Myers	.309	105	447	401	66	124	159	18	4	3	45	2	2	2	40	2	51	27	15	9	.397	.373
Allison, Chris, Sarasota.................	.293	109	413	365	51	107	137	10	7	2	52	7	4	5	32	2	28	13	11	10	.375	.355
Alvarez, Rafael, Fort Myers	.270	47	143	122	13	33	47	9	1	1	15	3	1	0	17	0	27	6	2	1	.385	.357
Amezcua, Adan, Kissimmee...........	.400	9	24	20	3	8	11	3	0	0	5	0	1	0	3	1	3	0	0	0	.550	.458
Andrews, Shane, W. Palm Beach ...	.176	5	20	17	2	3	8	2	0	1	5	0	1	0	2	0	7	0	1	0	.471	.250
August, Brian, Tampa....................	.209	23	75	67	5	14	21	4	0	1	11	1	2	0	5	0	14	0	2	2	.313	.257
Baker, Derek, Calgary*	.344	8	33	32	2	11	15	1	0	1	5	0	0	0	1	0	7	0	0	0	.469	.364
Balfe, Ryan, Lakeland†	.269	86	346	312	40	84	140	13	2	13	48	1	6	3	24	3	75	1	1	7	.449	.322
Barker, Glen, Lakeland	.316	13	64	57	9	18	25	4	0	1	11	3	0	0	4	0	17	7	1	0	.439	.361
Barnes, Kelvin, Daytona	.261	123	463	433	64	113	165	26	7	4	51	2	1	2	25	1	82	22	6	12	.381	.304
Barrett, Michael, W. Palm Beach....	.284	119	476	423	52	120	174	30	0	8	61	2	10	5	36	1	49	7	4	11	.411	.340
Bass, Jayson, Sarasota.................	.258	108	423	376	58	97	162	18	4	13	53	0	4	2	41	5	130	17	7	4	.431	.331
Bates, Fletcher, St. Lucie†.............	.300	70	293	253	49	76	150	19	11	11	38	0	2	4	33	6	66	7	6	4	.593	.387
Bautista, Jorge, Brevard County	.000	10	17	15	2	0	0	0	0	0	0	1	0	1	1	0	7	0	0	1	.000	.118
Bautista, Rayner, Lakeland............	.167	6	12	12	1	2	2	0	0	0	0	0	0	0	0	0	2	0	0	1	.167	.167
Bazzani, Matt, Sarasota.................	.195	58	195	169	21	33	56	5	0	6	18	5	2	8	11	0	51	4	2	0	.331	.274
Beltre, Adrian, Vero Beach	.317	123	519	435	95	138	244	24	2	26	104	0	11	6	67	12	66	25	9	9	.561	.407
Bennett, Ryan, St. Lucie	.000	2	2	2	0	0	0	0	0	0	0	0	0	0	0	0	1	0	0	0	.000	.000
Bentley, Kevin, Daytona	.228	26	89	79	12	18	28	2	1	2	14	0	1	1	8	0	26	1	2	3	.354	.303
Berkman, Lance, Kissimmee†........	.293	53	223	184	31	54	100	10	0	12	35	0	0	2	37	4	38	2	1	2	.543	.417
Bess, Johnny, W. Palm Beach†.......	.145	23	66	62	2	9	9	0	0	0	1	0	0	1	3	1	21	1	1	1	.145	.185
Blake, Casey, Dunedin	.238	129	507	449	56	107	149	21	0	7	39	2	2	6	48	2	91	19	9	5	.332	.319
Blosser, Greg, St. Petersburg*	.312	52	226	189	40	59	108	9	2	12	32	0	2	0	35	5	42	7	9	3	.571	.416
Bovender, Andy, Lakeland	.215	52	195	177	16	38	57	8	1	3	16	0	0	2	16	0	56	3	0	3	.322	.287
Bowers, R.J., Kissimmee...............	.206	10	40	34	3	7	8	1	0	0	3	0	1	0	5	0	7	0	0	0	.235	.300
Braughler, Matt, Brevard County*..	.240	26	83	75	5	18	23	2	0	1	10	0	1	1	6	0	17	0	0	2	.307	.301

Player, Team	Avg.	G	TPA	AB	R	H	TB	2B	3B	HR	RBI	SH	SF	HP	BB	IBB	SO	SB	CS	GDP	Slg.	OBP
Bravo, Danny, W. Palm Beach†	.162	15	39	37	3	6	9	1	1	0	0	0	0	0	2	0	5	0	0	0	.243	.205
Bream, Scott, Lakeland†	.216	11	42	37	5	8	11	1	1	0	6	1	1	0	3	0	11	0	0	1	.297	.268
Brinkley, Josh, W. Palm Beach	.260	69	241	227	24	59	84	12	2	3	20	0	2	3	9	1	44	3	1	6	.370	.295
Brooks, Eddie, St. Lucie	.193	41	133	119	12	23	32	3	0	2	9	1	1	2	10	1	39	1	3	3	.269	.265
Brown, Nate, W. Palm Beach*	.225	15	44	40	7	9	13	1	0	1	5	0	0	1	3	2	16	2	0	2	.325	.295
Brown, Ron, Tampa	.059	5	19	17	1	1	3	0	1	0	3	0	0	0	2	0	4	1	1	0	.176	.158
Brown, Roosevelt, B.C.*	.246	33	123	114	8	28	40	7	1	1	12	1	1	0	7	0	31	0	3	4	.351	.287
Brown, Vick, Tampa	.292	123	523	463	77	135	168	19	4	2	42	6	5	11	38	0	78	55	13	6	.363	.356
Brumbaugh, Cliff, Calgary	.261	139	579	522	78	136	216	27	4	15	70	0	4	6	47	2	99	13	11	7	.414	.326
Brumfield, Jacob, Dunedin	.160	6	25	25	2	4	4	0	0	0	2	0	0	0	0	0	6	1	1	0	.160	.160
Buccheri, Jim, St. Petersburg	.245	58	238	204	29	50	59	9	0	0	13	3	3	1	27	0	20	25	7	2	.289	.332
Bustos, Saul, W. Palm Beach	.264	39	115	106	10	28	35	5	1	0	12	2	1	0	6	0	23	1	3	5	.330	.301
Byrd, Tony, W. Palm Beach†	.111	6	22	18	2	2	2	0	0	0	1	0	0	0	4	0	5	1	0	0	.111	.273
Cabrera, Orlando, W. Palm Beach..	.276	69	307	279	56	77	115	19	2	5	26	1	0	0	27	0	33	32	12	1	.412	.340
Camilli, Jason, W. Palm Beach	.128	15	50	47	1	6	9	3	0	0	1	1	0	0	2	0	12	0	1	1	.191	.163
Camilo, Jose, Brevard County*	.235	107	425	371	53	87	127	12	2	8	51	1	6	1	46	3	62	20	9	5	.342	.316
Campos, Jesus, W. Palm Beach	.190	28	86	84	11	16	21	3	1	0	7	0	1	0	1	0	9	0	1	2	.250	.198
Caravelli, Mike, Brevard County	.000	40	1	0	0	0	0	0	0	0	0	0	0	0	0	0	0	0	0	0	.000	.000
Cardona, Javier, Lakeland	.289	85	314	284	28	82	118	15	0	7	38	2	2	1	25	1	51	1	3	8	.415	.346
Carroll, Doug, St. Petersburg*	.248	73	237	222	17	55	79	14	2	2	31	1	1	0	13	0	25	0	2	4	.356	.288
Carroll, Jamey, W. Palm Beach	.243	121	466	407	56	99	120	19	1	0	38	8	4	4	43	0	48	17	11	4	.295	.319
Carter, Bart, St. Petersburg	.182	6	15	11	3	2	2	0	0	0	1	0	0	2	2	0	3	0	0	0	.182	.400
Castro, Ramon, Kissimmee	.280	115	476	410	53	115	163	22	1	8	65	0	11	2	53	3	73	1	0	17	.398	.357
Cey, Dan, Fort Myers	.284	127	567	521	84	148	213	34	5	7	60	3	4	5	34	1	85	23	9	11	.409	.332
Chapman, Scott, Kissimmee	.286	2	7	7	1	2	2	0	0	0	0	0	0	0	0	0	0	0	0	0	.286	.286
Chevalier, Virgil, Sarasota	.208	94	316	289	31	60	93	13	1	6	37	2	3	3	19	0	43	8	7	6	.322	.261
Choi, Kyung, Sarasota*	.232	85	258	228	26	53	73	9	1	3	25	3	4	0	23	1	35	4	3	5	.320	.298
Clark, Kevin, Sarasota	.600	3	6	5	0	3	3	0	0	0	1	0	0	1	0	0	2	0	0	0	.600	.667
Coe, Ryan, Kissimmee	.217	52	179	161	21	35	50	6	0	3	19	1	0	3	14	0	36	0	1	4	.311	.292
Colina, Roberto, St. Petersburg* ..	.248	96	404	351	48	87	121	13	3	5	49	1	2	5	45	3	40	4	5	9	.345	.340
Colon, Jose, Daytona	.210	52	111	100	11	21	27	4	1	0	7	0	0	3	8	0	31	1	2	3	.270	.288
Conner, Decomba, Lakeland	.318	56	226	201	35	64	100	7	4	7	29	3	1	0	21	1	47	9	2	1	.498	.381
Coquillette, Trace, W. Palm Beach .	.319	53	223	188	34	60	106	18	2	8	33	1	1	6	27	0	27	8	7	1	.564	.419
Cornelius, Jonathon, Clearwater	.141	33	77	71	4	10	14	1	0	1	4	1	1	1	3	0	29	2	0	1	.197	.184
Corps, Erick, St. Petersburg†	.240	39	148	121	16	29	36	5	1	0	14	2	1	1	23	1	29	0	2	5	.298	.363
Costello, Brian, Clearwater	.241	87	305	282	37	68	113	11	2	10	43	0	3	5	15	0	73	8	3	3	.401	.289
Crane, Todd, Clearwater	.143	2	8	7	0	1	2	1	0	0	1	0	0	1	0	0	1	0	0	0	.286	.250
Cranford, Joe, Fort Myers	.200	112	381	355	39	71	85	9	1	1	22	3	1	1	21	0	90	4	6	4	.239	.246
Cruz, Alain, Tampa	.111	10	29	27	3	3	5	2	0	0	2	0	0	0	2	0	13	0	0	1	.185	.172
Curl, John, Dunedin*	.255	74	256	231	36	59	118	14	0	15	48	0	1	0	24	4	53	3	2	4	.511	.324
Dallimore, Brian, Kissimmee	.000	1	3	3	0	0	0	0	0	0	0	0	0	0	0	0	2	0	0	0	.000	.000
Dandridge, Brad, Vero Beach	.260	112	434	388	45	101	148	21	1	8	65	1	5	7	33	1	42	4	6	10	.381	.326
Darden, Tony, Brevard County	.286	107	432	392	50	112	170	32	4	6	48	1	3	4	32	0	72	7	3	12	.434	.343
Delarosa, Tomas, W. Palm Beach ..	.222	4	11	9	1	2	2	0	0	0	0	0	0	0	2	0	3	2	0	0	.222	.364
Demetral, Chris, Vero Beach*	.277	86	334	278	52	77	132	13	3	12	45	2	4	2	48	0	40	5	2	6	.475	.383
Dennis, Les, Tampa	.260	85	202	177	24	46	50	4	0	0	17	6	1	1	16	0	36	1	6	6	.282	.323
Deshazer, Jeremy, Kissimmee†	.200	2	7	5	2	1	1	0	0	0	0	0	0	0	2	0	2	0	0	0	.200	.429
Diaz, Cesar, Dunedin	.290	108	423	379	50	110	171	23	1	12	56	5	3	0	36	2	108	4	7	5	.451	.349
Diaz, Jose, Vero Beach	.250	1	4	4	0	1	1	0	0	0	0	0	0	0	0	0	3	0	0	0	.250	.250
Diaz, Juan, Vero Beach	.667	1	4	3	2	2	5	0	0	1	3	0	0	1	0	0	1	0	0	0	1.667	.750
Dransfeldt, Kelly, Calgary	.227	135	519	466	64	106	158	20	7	6	58	4	3	3	42	0	115	25	16	8	.339	.294
Duffy, James, Kissimmee	.146	19	46	41	1	6	7	1	0	0	4	1	0	0	4	0	9	0	2	2	.171	.222
Dukart, Derek, Tampa*	.273	37	122	110	10	30	35	2	0	1	10	1	2	1	8	0	9	1	1	3	.318	.322
Elliott, Zach, Clearwater	.263	129	510	448	65	118	157	21	3	4	45	6	4	6	46	1	63	7	6	11	.350	.337
Ellis, John, Calgary	.000	1	2	2	0	0	0	0	0	0	0	0	0	0	0	0	1	0	0	0	.000	.000
Emmons, Scott, Tampa	.178	51	136	118	19	21	32	5	0	2	14	2	1	6	9	0	28	0	0	2	.271	.269
Engle, Beau, St. Lucie	.192	28	87	78	3	15	24	6	0	1	3	0	0	4	5	0	22	1	1	1	.308	.276
Epperson, Chad, Sarasota†	.272	107	402	367	45	100	151	25	1	8	48	1	1	1	32	3	95	13	8	8	.411	.332
Erickson, Corey, St. Lucie	.201	46	162	134	10	27	39	3	0	3	11	1	2	3	22	0	43	0	2	1	.291	.323
Escalona, Felix, Kissimmee	.222	3	13	9	6	2	2	0	0	0	0	0	0	0	3	1	0	2	0	0	.222	.462
Espinal, Juan, Sarasota	.248	109	384	322	49	80	125	20	2	7	45	2	3	6	50	0	79	4	5	2	.388	.359
Evans, Tom, Dunedin	.262	15	58	42	8	11	19	2	0	2	4	0	1	4	11	0	10	0	0	1	.452	.448
Faggett, Ethan, Sarasota*	.293	114	468	410	56	120	166	19	9	3	46	4	4	7	43	4	87	23	12	4	.405	.366
Fagley, Dan, Brevard County	.214	6	17	14	3	3	4	1	0	0	1	0	0	2	1	0	6	0	0	0	.286	.353
Fernandez, Jose, W. Palm Beach ...	.309	97	394	350	49	108	162	21	3	9	58	0	0	7	37	3	76	22	14	8	.463	.386
Font, Franklin, Daytona	.220	19	64	59	8	13	17	2	1	0	2	1	0	0	4	0	13	2	1	0	.288	.270
Fortin, Troy, Fort Myers	.295	111	434	383	58	113	172	20	0	13	59	3	4	10	34	1	37	1	2	11	.449	.364
Foster, Quincy, Brevard County	.247	61	205	186	25	46	61	8	2	1	11	2	0	3	14	0	47	12	4	0	.328	.310
Francia, David, Clearwater*	.280	21	85	75	5	21	26	3	1	0	10	3	0	1	6	0	7	5	2	1	.347	.341
Fraraccio, Dan, St. Petersburg	.296	129	541	463	67	137	180	34	3	1	63	5	6	14	53	0	50	7	7	11	.389	.381
Freel, Ryan, Dunedin	.282	61	243	181	42	51	72	8	2	3	17	6	1	9	46	2	28	24	5	3	.398	.447
Freeman, Sean, Lakeland*	.226	13	56	53	3	12	15	0	0	1	5	0	0	0	3	0	12	0	0	2	.283	.268
Freire, Alejandro, Lakeland	.323	130	547	477	85	154	260	30	2	24	92	0	7	12	50	1	84	13	4	10	.545	.396
French, Anton, Dunedin†	.222	78	295	261	34	58	78	5	3	3	17	5	2	2	25	1	51	35	15	4	.299	.293
Fuentes, Javier, Sarasota	.286	47	162	147	16	42	58	6	2	2	24	0	1	0	12	0	19	4	3	4	.395	.344
Fuller, Brian, Lakeland	.217	45	144	129	13	28	38	2	1	2	18	3	2	3	7	0	26	0	0	5	.295	.270
Funaro, Joe, Brevard County	.319	125	535	470	67	150	190	16	6	4	53	3	6	7	49	3	65	9	5	8	.404	.387
Gainey, Bryon, St. Lucie*	.240	117	432	405	33	97	158	22	0	13	51	0	3	6	18	2	133	0	2	7	.390	.280
Gallagher, Shawn, Calgary	.141	27	106	99	7	14	18	4	0	0	8	0	1	5	0	0	35	0	0	0	.182	.189
Garcia, Amaury, Brevard County	.288	124	550	479	77	138	193	30	2	7	44	14	3	5	49	2	97	45	11	4	.403	.358
Garcia, Carlos, Fort Myers	.136	69	165	147	11	20	23	3	0	0	7	4	0	0	11	0	31	8	6	4	.156	.196
Garcia, Miguel, Vero Beach	.000	48	0	0	0	0	0	0	0	0	0	0	0	0	0	0	0	0	0	0	.000	.000
Garcia, Neil, St. Petersburg†	.226	75	238	195	33	44	58	10	2	0	21	5	5	2	31	3	20	2	3	7	.297	.330

Player, Team	Avg.	G	TPA	AB	R	H	TB	2B	3B	HR	RBI	SH	SF	HP	BB	IBB	SO	SB	CS	GDP	Slg.	OBP
Gargiulo, Mike, St. Lucie*	.224	19	53	49	4	11	14	0	0	1	5	0	0	2	2	0	10	0	0	1	.286	.283
Gil, Geronimo, Vero Beach	.249	66	233	213	30	53	86	13	1	6	24	1	0	4	15	0	41	3	0	5	.404	.310
Gonzalez, Jimmy, Kissimmee	.341	12	49	44	7	15	31	6	2	2	6	0	1	3	1	0	9	0	0	1	.705	.388
Goodell, Steve, Brevard County	.270	117	468	381	48	103	158	18	2	11	61	6	7	14	60	0	67	1	1	7	.415	.383
Goodwin, Joe, Calgary	.238	61	212	185	18	44	61	9	1	2	22	2	0	5	20	0	18	2	2	6	.330	.329
Gorecki, Ryan, Calgary*	.273	101	432	388	52	106	123	13	2	0	24	5	1	9	28	3	12	6	7	8	.317	.336
Guerrero, Vladimir, W. Palm Beach	.400	3	11	10	0	4	6	2	0	0	2	0	0	1	0	0	1	0	0	1	.600	.455
Gunderson, Shane, Fort Myers	.280	14	58	50	5	14	18	4	0	0	5	0	0	1	7	0	8	3	1	2	.360	.379
Guzman, Cristian, Tampa	.286	4	15	14	4	4	4	0	0	0	1	0	0	0	1	0	1	0	1	0	.286	.333
Haas, Matt, W. Palm Beach*	.234	72	231	201	17	47	57	5	1	1	16	4	1	1	24	2	34	7	3	1	.284	.317
Hall, Noah, W. Palm Beach	.000	1	1	1	0	0	0	0	0	0	0	0	0	0	0	0	1	0	0	0	.000	.000
Hall, Ronnie, Daytona	.271	125	527	450	65	122	184	23	3	11	78	0	3	18	47	1	80	21	14	6	.409	.361
Hamilton, Joe, Sarasota*	.278	104	362	317	51	88	147	17	3	12	52	1	1	0	43	0	89	14	3	8	.464	.363
Harkrider, Kip, Vero Beach*	.282	33	111	103	18	29	34	5	0	0	14	2	0	1	5	0	13	2	1	2	.330	.321
Harvey, Aaron, Brevard County*	.270	115	493	455	65	123	170	17	6	6	47	3	4	1	30	0	78	30	15	5	.374	.314
Hawkins, Kraig, Tampa	.300	9	38	30	2	9	10	1	0	0	4	0	0	0	8	0	2	3	2	1	.333	.447
Haws, Scott, Clearwater*	.203	39	135	123	5	25	26	1	0	0	5	1	0	0	11	0	13	0	0	6	.211	.269
Hayes, Chris, Dunedin	.230	60	160	139	20	32	45	5	1	2	20	2	0	4	15	0	27	2	1	4	.324	.323
Hernaiz, Juan, Lakeland	.279	118	465	438	58	122	183	13	6	12	56	1	1	3	22	1	107	29	13	0	.418	.317
Hillenbrand, Shea, Sarasota	.295	57	232	220	25	65	83	12	0	2	28	1	2	2	7	1	29	9	8	4	.377	.320
Hudler, Rex, Clearwater	.324	9	35	34	8	11	24	2	1	3	6	0	1	0	0	0	8	1	0	0	.706	.314
Jaime, Angel, St. Lucie	.240	80	289	258	25	62	80	9	0	3	27	1	0	1	29	0	43	15	4	2	.310	.319
Jasco, Elinton, Daytona	.335	84	321	281	50	94	115	10	4	1	22	4	2	3	31	0	61	32	11	2	.409	.404
Jimenez, D'Angelo, Tampa†	.281	94	413	352	52	99	143	14	6	6	48	3	6	2	50	4	50	8	14	3	.406	.368
Johnson, Ric, Sarasota	.280	121	487	453	47	127	149	11	4	1	40	3	4	6	21	0	67	21	8	8	.329	.318
Johnson, Travis, Fort Myers*	.242	73	264	227	29	55	94	16	1	7	36	0	2	4	30	2	77	2	1	4	.414	.338
Jones, Jacque, Fort Myers*	.297	131	577	539	84	160	250	33	6	15	82	0	2	3	33	3	110	24	12	9	.464	.340
Jones, Jaime, Brevard County*	.271	95	422	373	63	101	166	27	4	10	60	0	4	1	44	2	86	6	1	7	.445	.346
Kane, Ryan, Tampa	.224	95	350	303	36	68	95	8	2	5	20	2	1	7	37	1	66	1	1	7	.314	.322
Kapler, Gabe, Lakeland	.295	137	588	519	87	153	262	40	6	19	87	0	10	5	54	4	68	8	6	8	.505	.361
Keel, David, Tampa*	.267	92	343	300	50	80	143	15	0	16	48	1	1	2	39	2	57	9	3	4	.477	.354
Kelley, Erskine, Daytona	.257	35	125	113	24	29	50	6	0	5	19	0	0	1	11	1	38	2	1	3	.442	.328
Kelly, Roberto, Fort Myers	.364	4	15	11	2	4	7	0	0	1	3	0	0	0	4	0	1	0	0	0	.636	.533
Kennedy, Gus, Daytona	.261	113	424	368	63	96	158	20	0	14	57	0	5	5	46	1	89	15	8	6	.429	.347
Keppen, Jeffrey, Vero Beach	.000	33	1	1	0	0	0	0	0	0	0	0	0	0	0	0	1	0	0	0	.000	.000
Key, Jeff, Clearwater*	.282	136	561	522	85	147	257	37	11	17	87	1	3	6	29	5	112	15	9	9	.492	.325
King, Andre, St. Petersburg	.193	48	130	114	16	22	29	2	1	1	11	3	1	2	10	0	29	8	3	1	.254	.268
King, Cesar, Calgary	.296	91	350	307	51	91	131	14	4	6	37	3	4	1	35	0	58	8	6	5	.427	.366
Knowles, Eric, St. Lucie*	.167	24	92	84	8	14	22	5	0	1	10	0	1	0	7	0	16	3	1	3	.262	.228
Knupfer, Jason, Clearwater	.258	108	430	365	56	94	112	15	0	1	40	7	5	4	49	1	70	5	6	7	.307	.348
Koehler, Jason, Dunedin	.000	1	2	1	0	0	0	0	0	0	0	0	0	0	1	0	0	0	0	0	.000	.500
Kofler, Eric, Tampa*	.232	39	158	151	12	35	51	8	1	2	22	0	2	0	5	0	25	0	4	4	.338	.253
Kuilan, Hector, Brevard County	.226	77	282	265	18	60	76	16	0	0	25	3	4	7	0	0	41	0	1	12	.287	.254
Lackey, Steve, Lakeland	.223	71	266	247	24	55	69	14	0	0	22	6	2	1	10	0	58	5	4	3	.279	.254
Lambert, Clark, St. Lucie	.000	2	2	2	0	0	0	0	0	0	0	0	0	0	0	0	0	0	0	1	.000	.000
Langaigne, Selwyn, Dunedin*	.189	42	104	90	9	17	23	3	0	1	7	4	0	0	10	0	26	4	1	4	.256	.270
Leidens, Enrique, W. Palm Beach	.143	4	7	7	1	1	1	0	0	0	0	0	0	0	0	0	1	0	0	0	.143	.143
Lewis, Jeremy, Daytona	.279	72	246	233	31	65	98	15	3	4	30	1	2	1	9	0	45	2	1	1	.421	.306
Lewis, Keith, Daytona†	.213	62	107	94	11	20	27	4	0	1	10	3	1	1	8	0	25	1	1	1	.287	.279
Lindstrom, David, Lakeland	.207	76	247	213	25	44	61	8	0	3	14	5	2	3	24	0	25	1	0	9	.286	.293
Liniak, Cole, Sarasota	.336	64	247	217	32	73	107	16	0	6	42	3	2	3	22	1	31	1	2	2	.493	.402
Lobaton, Jose, Tampa	.130	7	27	23	0	3	3	0	0	0	5	1	1	0	2	0	6	0	0	2	.130	.192
Long, Terrence, St. Lucie*	.251	126	516	470	52	118	185	29	7	8	61	0	4	2	40	4	102	24	8	6	.394	.310
Lopez, Jose, St. Lucie	.195	23	91	87	14	17	34	3	1	4	13	0	0	1	3	0	25	2	0	1	.391	.231
Lopez, Pedro, Kissimmee	.203	25	75	69	7	14	20	4	1	0	8	0	1	0	4	0	11	0	1	4	.290	.243
Lopez, Pee Wee, St. Lucie	.248	113	416	375	40	93	121	19	0	3	30	1	1	0	39	3	56	3	2	10	.323	.318
Lugo, Julio, Kissimmee	.267	125	565	505	89	135	206	22	14	7	61	8	4	2	46	1	99	35	8	8	.408	.329
Macias, Jose, Lakeland	.267	122	488	424	54	113	141	18	2	2	21	8	2	2	52	1	33	10	14	10	.333	.348
Maness, Dwight, St. Lucie	.296	45	194	179	29	53	75	9	2	3	19	0	0	3	12	0	29	12	6	1	.419	.351
Manfredi, Joel, Vero Beach	.000	6	3	3	1	0	0	0	0	0	0	0	0	0	0	0	0	0	0	0	.000	.000
Manning, Nate, Daytona	.244	120	480	454	51	111	161	29	0	7	54	0	6	4	14	0	93	5	4	12	.355	.273
Mansavage, Jay, Kissimmee†	.273	9	36	33	4	9	14	0	1	1	1	0	1	0	2	0	6	2	0	4	.424	.333
Marino, Lawrence, Sarasota	.091	4	12	11	2	1	2	1	0	0	0	0	0	0	1	0	2	0	0	0	.182	.167
Marsh, Roy, Sarasota	.230	107	266	230	47	53	68	4	4	1	14	8	4	1	23	0	44	19	8	2	.296	.298
Marshall, Monte, Vero Beach†	.269	18	27	26	4	7	8	1	0	0	2	0	0	1	0	0	4	0	0	0	.308	.296
Marsters, Brandon, Clearwater	.184	44	163	141	10	26	29	3	0	0	18	1	2	4	15	0	26	1	0	3	.206	.278
Martin, Chris, St. Petersburg	.260	105	472	393	72	102	149	20	0	9	49	5	4	7	62	1	66	23	7	13	.379	.367
Martinez, Rafael, St. Lucie*	.196	66	224	204	24	40	58	11	2	1	13	1	2	2	15	1	54	0	1	5	.284	.256
Mateo, Ruben, Calgary	.314	99	416	385	63	121	196	23	8	12	67	1	2	6	22	0	55	20	5	16	.509	.359
McCain, Marcus, St. Petersburg	.284	84	332	306	47	87	106	13	3	0	36	4	4	8	10	1	30	19	7	8	.346	.320
McCartney, Sommer, B.C.	.245	16	58	53	3	13	18	2	0	1	12	0	1	1	3	1	19	0	0	3	.340	.293
McDonald, Donzell, Tampa†	.296	77	351	297	69	88	136	23	8	3	23	1	1	4	48	0	75	39	18	3	.458	.400
McLemore, Mark, Calgary	.571	2	9	7	1	4	5	1	0	0	3	0	0	0	2	0	1	1	0	1	.714	.667
McMullen, Jon, Clearwater*	.195	21	84	77	7	15	18	3	0	0	8	0	0	2	5	1	19	0	0	1	.234	.262
Mejia, Juan, Daytona*	.179	26	91	78	9	14	16	0	1	0	6	0	0	0	6	0	16	3	1	1	.205	.238
Mendez, Donaldo, Kissimmee	.188	5	17	16	0	3	3	0	0	0	0	0	0	1	0	0	4	1	1	0	.188	.235
Meulens, Hensley, W. Palm Beach	.250	1	4	4	0	1	2	1	0	0	1	0	0	0	0	0	2	0	0	1	.500	.250
Micucci, Mike, Daytona*	.250	54	154	140	15	35	43	5	0	1	24	1	0	1	12	1	27	1	4	3	.307	.314
Millan, Adan, Clearwater	.291	13	61	55	7	16	24	3	1	1	8	0	1	0	5	0	8	1	0	1	.436	.344
Miller, Orlando, Lakeland	.190	5	22	21	1	4	7	1	1	0	0	0	0	0	1	0	4	0	0	1	.333	.227
Miller, Ryan, St.L.-Kis.	.256	74	250	227	32	58	78	12	1	2	29	4	2	1	16	0	41	6	5	3	.344	.305
Molina, Jose, Daytona	.251	55	201	179	17	45	56	9	1	0	23	5	2	1	14	0	25	4	0	5	.313	.306
Monroe, Craig, Calgary	.235	92	379	328	54	77	123	23	1	7	41	0	6	0	44	1	80	24	1	5	.375	.320

Player, Team	Avg.	G	TPA	AB	R	H	TB	2B	3B	HR	RBI	SH	SF	HP	BB	IBB	SO	SB	CS	GDP	Slg.	OBP
Morales, Eric, St. Lucie†	.238	38	117	101	12	24	31	7	0	0	6	0	1	1	14	2	24	1	2	2	.307	.333
Morales, Francisco, W.P.B.	.283	45	138	127	15	36	57	7	1	4	13	1	0	0	10	1	37	0	2	2	.449	.336
Morenz, Shea, Tampa*	.236	117	439	403	43	95	132	14	1	7	44	6	5	7	18	3	101	2	3	7	.328	.277
Morgan, Dave, Dunedin	.208	20	61	53	8	11	18	1	0	2	7	1	0	1	6	0	11	2	2	1	.340	.300
Morimoto, Ken, Vero Beach	.176	34	99	85	13	15	16	1	0	0	5	2	1	0	11	0	29	11	1	0	.188	.268
Morris, Warren, Calgary*	.306	128	567	494	78	151	232	27	9	12	75	3	1	7	62	3	100	16	5	6	.470	.390
Morrow, Nick, St. Petersburg	.269	108	433	379	51	102	168	23	5	11	53	5	3	3	43	5	78	20	7	2	.443	.346
Mucker, Kelcey, Fort Myers*	.239	114	437	389	43	93	134	26	3	3	48	4	7	4	33	1	80	1	5	5	.344	.300
Mulvehill, Brandon, St. Lucie	.000	2	6	6	0	0	0	0	0	0	0	0	0	0	0	0	2	0	0	0	.000	.000
Myers, Adrian, Calgary	.247	90	328	287	40	71	86	7	4	0	21	1	1	3	36	0	73	18	15	5	.300	.336
Nelson, Charles, Vero Beach*	.281	113	482	417	73	117	149	12	1	6	42	11	3	1	50	0	62	53	16	5	.357	.357
Nevin, Phil, Lakeland	.556	3	12	9	3	5	9	1	0	1	4	0	0	0	3	0	2	0	0	0	1.000	.667
Nichols, Kevin, Clearwater	.000	4	14	12	0	0	0	0	0	0	0	0	0	0	2	0	2	0	0	0	.000	.000
Nieves, Jose, Daytona	.275	85	362	331	51	91	125	20	1	4	42	4	6	4	17	0	55	16	6	7	.378	.313
Northeimer, Jamie, Clearwater	.254	20	83	71	13	18	33	6	0	3	8	1	0	2	9	0	13	0	0	0	.465	.354
Nunez, Juan, Calgary†	.197	21	76	61	7	12	15	1	1	0	6	3	1	3	8	0	18	5	7	0	.246	.315
Ortiz, David, Fort Myers*	.331	61	265	239	45	79	133	15	0	13	58	0	3	1	22	3	53	2	1	3	.556	.385
Ovalles, Homy, W. Palm Beach	.000	2	1	1	2	0	0	0	0	0	0	0	0	0	0	0	0	0	0	0	.000	.000
Owens, Billy, Kissimmee†	.283	96	405	381	51	108	160	18	2	10	60	0	3	3	18	5	68	4	2	10	.420	.319
Padilla, Roy, Sarasota*	.246	130	513	463	66	114	144	16	4	2	38	4	0	5	41	1	80	24	19	14	.311	.314
Paez, Israel, Fort Myers†	.253	135	522	478	56	121	137	11	1	1	39	5	3	1	35	1	66	26	16	18	.287	.304
Parra, Franklin, St. Lucie†	.261	56	226	199	23	52	74	10	3	2	25	0	2	3	22	0	33	11	5	4	.372	.341
Parra, Jose, Calgary†	.115	15	29	26	3	3	3	0	0	0	1	0	0	0	3	0	14	0	2	0	.115	.207
Parsons, Jeff, St. Lucie	.209	45	153	134	13	28	28	0	0	0	5	0	1	0	18	0	31	7	6	1	.209	.301
Patel, Manny, St. Petersburg*	.267	129	583	505	66	135	178	17	7	4	54	7	4	6	61	0	51	24	15	10	.352	.351
Patton, Greg, Sarasota	.250	4	18	16	2	4	5	1	0	0	1	0	0	1	0	0	2	1	2	0	.313	.333
Peck, Tom, Dunedin*	.190	50	124	105	12	20	26	4	1	0	4	4	1	1	14	0	21	0	1	2	.248	.289
Peeples, Michael, Dunedin	.256	129	550	477	73	122	161	29	2	2	42	9	7	3	54	1	83	26	16	8	.338	.331
Perez, Jhonny, Kissimmee	.264	69	292	273	40	72	107	16	5	3	22	2	3	1	12	0	38	8	6	5	.392	.294
Perez, Santiago, Lakeland†	.274	111	480	445	66	122	178	20	12	4	46	8	5	2	20	1	98	21	9	6	.400	.305
Pierce, Kirk, Clearwater	.265	24	75	68	9	18	24	1	1	1	5	1	0	3	3	0	13	0	0	3	.353	.324
Pierzynski, A.J., Fort Myers*	.279	118	439	412	49	115	167	23	1	9	64	1	4	6	16	1	59	2	1	9	.405	.313
Pimentel, Jose, Vero Beach	.259	110	366	344	56	89	119	13	1	5	40	2	1	2	17	0	67	41	19	8	.346	.297
Polanco, Enohel, St. Lucie	.252	43	147	131	20	33	44	9	1	0	12	4	1	1	10	0	33	2	5	4	.336	.308
Pomierski, Joe, St. Petersburg*	.265	119	474	422	64	112	180	25	5	11	49	2	3	4	43	4	78	4	3	5	.427	.337
Porter, Bo, Daytona	.307	122	508	440	87	135	218	20	6	17	65	1	3	3	61	1	115	23	13	8	.495	.393
Quero, Pedro, W. Palm Beach	.000	1	2	2	0	0	0	0	0	0	0	0	0	0	0	0	0	0	0	0	.000	.000
Raifstanger, John, Sarasota	.230	95	289	256	26	59	81	8	1	4	28	3	2	1	27	0	51	7	9	2	.316	.304
Raines, Tim, Tampa†	.343	11	46	35	8	12	18	0	0	2	5	0	0	0	11	2	1	1	0	0	.514	.500
Raynor, Mark, Clearwater	.235	136	543	469	54	110	135	12	2	3	45	3	2	9	60	1	58	8	6	10	.288	.331
Redmond, Mike, Brevard County	.000	5	19	17	2	0	0	0	0	0	0	0	0	0	2	0	2	0	0	0	.000	.105
Reynoso, Ismael, Brevard County	.000	2	4	3	0	0	0	0	0	0	0	0	0	0	1	0	2	0	0	0	.000	.250
Ricabal, Dan, Vero Beach	.000	75	1	1	0	0	0	0	0	0	0	0	0	0	0	0	0	0	0	0	.000	.000
Richards, Rowan, Calgary	.264	60	205	178	18	47	70	12	1	3	26	1	1	3	22	1	54	5	2	4	.393	.353
Rivera, Luis, W. Palm Beach	.000	1	1	1	0	0	0	0	0	0	0	0	0	0	0	0	0	0	0	0	.000	.000
Rivero, Eddie, Clearwater*	.288	132	516	455	61	131	210	30	2	15	74	1	7	4	49	4	107	1	2	8	.462	.357
Rivers, Jonathan, Dunedin	.269	132	522	457	62	123	189	21	3	13	75	0	7	5	53	0	107	24	8	8	.414	.347
Robinson, Hassan, Kissimmee	.252	35	121	115	12	29	33	4	0	0	12	1	1	1	3	0	14	3	3	1	.287	.275
Robles, Oscar, Kissimmee*	.225	66	290	236	39	53	57	4	0	0	21	8	2	1	43	0	28	0	1	4	.242	.344
Rodriguez, Maximo, B.C.	.203	42	131	118	14	24	38	4	2	2	10	2	0	1	10	0	30	0	1	5	.322	.271
Rodriguez, Noel, Kissimmee	.316	65	256	228	26	72	101	15	1	4	36	1	1	3	23	0	24	1	5	8	.443	.384
Rodriques, Cecil, W. Palm Beach	.146	15	44	41	9	6	10	1	0	1	3	0	0	0	3	1	14	2	0	0	.244	.205
Rolison, Nate, Brevard County*	.256	122	514	473	59	121	191	22	0	16	65	0	1	2	38	1	143	1	1	16	.404	.313
Romano, Scott, St. Petersburg	.298	99	414	359	54	107	155	25	1	7	67	3	3	7	42	1	55	5	3	8	.432	.380
Roney, Chad, Vero Beach	.171	58	38	35	0	6	9	3	0	0	2	1	0	0	2	0	7	0	0	2	.257	.216
Roper, Chad, Fort Myers	.203	66	170	148	19	30	42	3	0	3	9	0	0	0	22	1	23	1	0	7	.284	.306
Ross, Tony, Kissimmee	.256	74	238	215	30	55	70	6	3	1	19	4	0	1	18	2	40	11	7	5	.326	.316
Rowson, James, Tampa	.060	25	56	50	2	3	5	2	0	0	4	1	0	1	4	1	29	2	1	0	.100	.145
Salzano, Jerry, Lakeland	.222	40	160	135	20	30	42	4	1	2	8	1	0	2	22	2	27	1	1	1	.311	.340
Samboy, Nelson, Kissimmee	.316	48	201	190	20	60	76	9	2	1	13	2	0	2	7	0	34	9	6	5	.400	.347
Samuel, Cody, Tampa	.232	92	371	323	39	75	144	15	3	16	61	1	6	9	32	2	121	2	0	5	.446	.314
Sanchez, Orlando, Sarasota	.182	41	106	99	10	18	23	3	1	0	9	1	0	0	6	0	29	2	1	2	.232	.229
Sandberg, Jared, St. Petersburg	.333	2	5	3	1	1	1	0	0	0	2	0	0	0	2	0	0	0	0	0	.333	.600
Sanders, Anthony, Dunedin	.200	1	5	5	0	1	2	1	0	0	1	0	0	0	0	0	1	0	1	0	.400	.333
Sanderson, David, St. Lucie*	.228	97	330	267	41	61	73	8	2	0	14	8	0	1	54	0	76	11	3	5	.273	.360
Santo, Jose, Calgary	.000	2	6	6	0	0	0	0	0	0	0	0	0	0	0	0	4	0	0	0	.000	.000
Schifano, Anthony, B.C.	.000	1	1	1	0	0	0	0	0	0	0	0	0	0	0	0	1	0	0	0	.000	.000
Schramm, Kevin, Calgary	.225	88	325	284	37	64	100	18	0	6	45	1	5	2	33	0	80	5	1	6	.352	.306
Schwab, Chris, W. Palm Beach	.188	58	233	207	22	39	73	7	0	9	28	0	3	1	22	0	82	3	1	1	.353	.266
Seguignol, Fernando, W.P.B.†	.254	124	505	456	70	116	207	27	5	18	83	0	14	5	30	3	129	5	5	1	.454	.299
Sell, Chip, Vero Beach*	.284	111	380	342	50	97	153	21	7	7	46	2	3	4	29	2	67	25	8	4	.447	.344
Shores, Scott, Clearwater	.268	27	108	97	20	26	42	7	0	3	7	0	0	0	11	0	23	6	3	2	.433	.343
Shumpert, Derek, Tampa	.260	44	195	169	24	44	55	6	1	1	3	6	0	3	20	0	49	6	8	1	.325	.349
Skett, Will, Dunedin	.269	98	433	361	63	97	182	22	3	19	71	3	5	19	45	3	100	12	7	7	.504	.374
Smith, Jeff, Fort Myers*	.281	49	139	121	17	34	51	5	0	4	26	0	6	0	12	0	18	0	2	4	.421	.331
Smith, Sloan, Tampa†	.220	65	225	186	32	41	64	9	1	4	23	0	4	2	33	5	64	4	2	2	.344	.338
Snusz, Chris, Clearwater	.200	36	110	105	12	21	28	7	0	0	3	3	0	0	2	0	22	0	0	3	.267	.215
Soriano, Fred, Dunedin	.308	26	94	78	18	24	37	5	1	2	12	3	1	4	8	0	17	3	0	1	.474	.396
Sosa, John, Vero Beach	.220	92	272	250	32	55	79	5	2	5	29	3	2	2	14	0	39	20	8	6	.316	.264
Sotelo, Danilo, Vero Beach	.196	23	70	56	13	11	18	1	0	2	11	1	3	0	10	0	17	1	1	2	.321	.304
Stone, Craig, Dunedin	.235	113	439	404	56	95	167	28	1	14	59	0	2	8	25	1	109	1	2	9	.413	.292
Stowers, Chris, W. Palm Beach*	.273	111	455	414	56	113	150	15	5	4	30	2	2	7	30	5	77	19	14	0	.362	.331
Strange, Mike, Dunedin	.264	48	124	106	15	28	35	5	1	0	7	3	0	1	14	0	39	1	1	0	.330	.355

Player, Team	Avg.	G	TPA	AB	R	H	TB	2B	3B	HR	RBI	SH	SF	HP	BB	IBB	SO	SB	CS	GDP	Slg.	OBP
Strawberry, Darryl, Tampa*	.438	4	17	16	2	7	8	1	0	0	4	0	0	0	1	0	3	0	0	1	.500	.471
Stricklin, Scott, St. Petersburg*	.259	85	305	243	28	63	69	6	0	0	29	7	1	2	52	0	32	0	3	4	.284	.393
Stuckenschneider, Eric, V.B.	.279	131	574	452	100	126	175	25	3	6	45	4	5	12	101	1	79	40	11	4	.387	.419
Suplee, Ray, St. Petersburg	.077	4	13	13	0	1	1	0	0	0	0	0	0	0	0	0	5	0	0	0	.077	.077
Taylor, Greg, Clearwater	.193	32	98	83	7	16	20	4	0	0	6	2	0	2	11	0	16	0	2	2	.241	.302
Taylor, Reggie, Clearwater*	.244	134	590	545	73	133	199	18	6	12	47	5	6	4	30	4	130	40	23	3	.365	.285
Tebbs, Nate, Sarasota†	.261	111	407	375	52	98	133	14	3	5	39	2	3	0	27	3	65	15	9	9	.355	.309
Tomberlin, Andy, St. Lucie*	.000	1	4	3	0	0	0	0	0	0	0	1	0	0	0	0	2	0	0	0	.000	.250
Torres, Jaime, Tampa	.294	115	449	408	48	120	178	28	0	10	56	2	1	10	28	2	30	0	2	13	.436	.353
Torti, Michael, Clearwater	.220	70	259	232	29	51	77	12	1	4	27	0	1	0	26	0	57	1	0	9	.332	.297
Treanor, Matt, Brevard County	.214	23	85	70	11	15	21	4	1	0	3	1	0	2	12	0	14	0	0	1	.300	.345
Troilo, Jason, Tampa	.333	3	10	9	0	3	3	0	0	0	0	0	0	0	1	0	5	0	0	0	.333	.400
Truby, Chris, Kissimmee	.246	57	216	199	23	49	66	11	0	2	29	4	3	2	8	0	40	8	3	4	.332	.278
Tucker, Jon, Vero Beach*	.291	121	470	422	59	123	189	27	0	13	78	0	10	3	35	1	85	5	3	7	.448	.343
Twombley, Dennis, Tampa	.333	4	9	9	1	3	3	0	0	0	0	0	0	0	0	0	4	1	0	0	.333	.333
Valdez, Trovin, W. Palm Beach	.234	55	206	188	19	44	60	4	3	2	14	2	1	5	10	1	24	12	6	0	.319	.289
Valette, Ramon, Daytona	.332	106	406	371	54	123	170	25	2	6	50	5	4	6	20	1	49	20	6	6	.458	.372
Vaughn, Lateef, Fort Myers	.269	36	105	93	15	25	27	2	0	0	8	5	0	1	6	0	18	2	0	0	.290	.320
Vieira, Scott, Daytona	.275	134	571	476	84	131	218	27	3	18	80	1	7	17	70	1	125	9	7	5	.458	.382
Villalobos, Carlos, Lakeland	.252	39	161	147	19	37	45	5	0	1	15	1	0	2	11	0	25	0	1	3	.306	.313
Voita, Sam, St. Petersburg†	.250	14	30	24	3	6	11	2	0	1	6	0	0	1	5	0	6	0	0	1	.458	.400
Walbeck, Matt, Lakeland†	.500	4	14	10	4	5	6	1	0	0	3	0	0	0	4	1	1	0	1	0	.600	.643
Warriax, Brandon, Calgary	.000	1	4	4	0	0	0	0	0	0	0	0	0	0	0	0	1	0	0	1	.000	.000
Watkins, Sean, Calgary*	.222	21	79	72	5	16	21	3	1	0	10	0	0	1	6	1	25	0	0	2	.292	.291
Wesemann, Jason, Clearwater	.159	38	102	88	7	14	15	1	0	0	4	4	0	0	10	0	20	1	0	2	.170	.245
Wheeler, Mike, Kissimmee	.417	8	13	12	2	5	5	0	0	0	2	0	0	0	1	0	3	1	0	0	.417	.462
White, Walter, Brevard County	.202	54	179	163	18	33	44	8	0	1	15	0	1	1	14	1	41	0	1	4	.270	.268
Whitlock, Mike, Dunedin*	.193	107	405	322	41	62	109	14	0	11	48	0	5	9	69	1	132	1	1	3	.339	.346
Wilcox, Luke, Tampa*	.300	12	49	40	7	12	16	4	0	0	4	0	1	1	7	2	6	1	1	0	.400	.408
Willis, Symmion, Dunedin	.220	56	175	164	18	36	49	5	1	2	16	1	0	0	10	0	37	2	1	1	.299	.264
Wilson, Preston, St. Lucie	.245	63	258	245	32	60	107	12	1	11	48	0	4	1	8	0	66	3	4	4	.437	.267
Wilson, Steve, Vero Beach	.210	84	251	233	21	49	74	14	1	3	21	1	3	3	11	0	63	4	0	3	.318	.252
Wingate, Ervan, Vero Beach	.228	84	257	224	26	51	74	12	1	3	24	3	3	0	27	0	51	3	2	6	.330	.307
Winn, Randy, Brevard County†	.315	36	167	143	26	45	57	8	2	0	15	2	1	5	16	1	28	16	8	3	.399	.400
Woodward, Chris, Dunedin	.293	91	378	314	38	92	116	13	4	1	38	3	4	5	52	0	52	4	8	3	.369	.397
Yard, Bruce, Vero Beach*	.309	71	268	236	37	73	101	14	1	4	44	1	6	1	24	0	19	3	2	3	.428	.367
Yedo, Carlos, Tampa*	.242	131	499	446	51	108	175	26	1	13	54	3	3	1	46	3	126	1	0	10	.392	.313
Zorrilla, Julio, St. Lucie†	.251	118	462	418	41	105	132	18	3	1	31	16	0	2	26	3	50	14	12	8	.316	.298
Zywica, Michael, Calgary	.258	126	530	462	75	119	190	25	5	12	64	0	6	12	50	0	116	19	19	10	.411	.342

GRAND SLAMS: Barrett, Cardona, Costello, Dransfeldt, Emmons, Hamilton, Kapler, C. King, Ortiz, Padilla, Rolison, Samuel, Seguignol, Skett, Sotelo, Stone, 1 each.
AWARDED FIRST BASE ON CATCHER'S INTERFERENCE: R. Hall 9 (Fortin, Gil, E. Morales, Castro, S. Wilson, Marsters, Pierzynski, Goodwin, Emmons); Peck 2 (C. King, Millan); Bates (Emmons); Dennis (Snusz); Dransfeldt (Torres); Freire (Gil); Gorecki (Emmons); T. Johnson (Goodwin); P. Lopez (Torres); Martin (C. Diaz); Monroe (J. Smith); J. Perez (F. Morales).

PLAYERS WITH TWO OR MORE TEAMS

Player, Team	Avg.	G	TPA	AB	R	H	TB	2B	3B	HR	RBI	SH	SF	HP	BB	IBB	SO	SB	CS	GDP	Slg.	OBP
Miller, Ryan, St. Lucie	.254	61	209	193	27	49	69	12	1	2	28	2	2	1	11	0	38	5	5	3	.358	.295
Miller, Ryan, Kissimmee	.265	13	41	34	5	9	9	0	0	0	1	2	0	0	5	0	3	1	0	0	.265	.359

1997 PITCHING

TEAM

Team	W	L	Pct.	ERA	G	CG	ShO	Sv.	IP	H	TBF	R	ER	HR	SH	SF	HB	BB	IBB	SO	WP	Bk.
Kissimmee	71	66	.518	3.36	137	16	15	36	1192.0	1134	5061	562	445	54	36	43	57	385	25	862	46	24
Lakeland	81	57	.587	3.43	138	17	9	30	1192.2	1122	5064	569	454	63	32	42	49	430	11	829	63	13
Fort Myers	81	58	.583	3.54	139	12	16	39	1204.0	1138	5069	563	473	71	42	52	40	384	11	911	54	6
St. Petersburg	81	56	.591	3.63	137	13	8	36	1200.2	1169	5055	564	484	81	32	37	63	349	13	869	47	18
Clearwater	70	68	.507	3.66	138	7	7	37	1193.2	1156	5101	584	486	72	38	30	44	476	6	957	96	17
Tampa	70	66	.515	3.69	136	3	5	35	1207.0	1145	5103	594	495	81	48	39	43	458	45	939	64	17
West Palm Beach	69	66	.511	3.71	135	8	13	29	1159.1	1162	4956	583	478	75	45	36	63	376	1	883	97	11
St. Lucie	54	81	.400	3.77	135	12	11	24	1151.2	1137	4961	574	483	69	34	33	51	411	23	829	80	28
Vero Beach	70	67	.511	4.19	137	6	11	37	1178.1	1113	5159	653	549	92	40	39	56	566	18	1064	94	20
Dunedin	57	82	.410	4.29	139	5	4	22	1216.0	1332	5432	760	580	88	32	39	72	522	26	921	105	22
Charlotte	68	71	.489	4.30	139	24	7	35	1202.2	1198	5211	666	574	115	48	38	55	502	10	937	103	10
Daytona	65	73	.471	4.33	138	15	8	26	1173.2	1250	5170	696	565	109	39	49	51	440	27	913	88	13
Brevard County	62	76	.449	4.38	138	10	11	26	1197.2	1312	5255	731	583	102	41	44	85	388	19	835	65	10
Sarasota	63	75	.457	4.41	138	10	5	24	1184.2	1213	5277	721	580	110	43	52	34	521	15	939	82	20

INDIVIDUAL

TOP QUALIFIERS FOR EARNED-RUN AVERAGE TITLE

Minimum 112 innings. *Lefthanded pitcher.

Pitcher, Team	W	L	Pct.	ERA	G	GS	CG	ShO	GF	Sv.	IP	H	TBF	R	ER	HR	SH	SF	HB	BB	IBB	SO	WP	Bk.
Duncan, Courtney, Daytona	8	4	.667	1.63	19	19	1	0	0	0	121.2	90	489	35	22	3	6	1	8	35	0	120	8	1
Vazquez, Javier, W. Palm Beach	6	3	.667	2.16	19	19	1	0	0	0	112.2	98	461	40	27	8	1	2	6	28	0	100	2	2
Lincoln, Mike, Fort Myers	13	4	.765	2.28	20	20	1	1	0	0	134.0	130	553	41	34	4	5	3	4	25	0	75	4	2
Powell, Brian, Lakeland	13	9	.591	2.50	27	27	8	2	0	0	183.1	153	732	70	51	9	4	5	6	35	2	122	5	0

Pitcher, Team	W	L	Pct.	ERA	G	GS	CG	ShO	GF	Sv.	IP	H	TBF	R	ER	HR	SH	SF	HB	BB	IBB	SO	WP	Bk.
Garcia, Freddy, Kissimmee	10	8	.556	2.56	27	27	5	2	0	0	179.0	165	741	63	51	6	4	3	4	49	3	131	3	2
Radlosky, Rob, Fort Myers	9	5	.643	2.59	23	22	3	1	1	0	128.1	87	510	42	37	10	5	4	5	37	0	109	2	0
Blanco, Alberto, Kissimmee*	7	4	.636	2.83	19	19	1	1	0	0	114.1	83	467	45	36	4	5	4	11	45	0	95	6	2
Haigler, Phil, Fort Myers	11	9	.550	2.84	25	25	4	1	0	0	158.1	172	652	57	50	7	3	4	2	32	0	80	2	0
Powell, Jeremy, W. Palm Beach	9	10	.474	3.02	26	26	1	0	0	0	155.0	162	675	75	52	3	9	5	12	62	0	121	12	2
Johnson, Mark, Kissimmee	8	9	.471	3.07	26	26	3	1	0	0	155.1	150	652	67	53	8	7	5	6	39	1	127	4	6
Callaway, Michael, St. Petersburg	11	7	.611	3.22	28	28	3	0	0	0	170.2	162	696	74	61	9	2	3	5	39	0	109	7	7
Santos, Victor, Lakeland	10	5	.667	3.23	26	26	4	2	0	0	145.0	136	623	74	52	10	4	6	6	59	1	108	12	1
Getz, Rod, Brevard County	9	12	.429	3.23	27	26	4	1	1	0	164.1	166	689	84	59	12	6	8	10	39	1	92	8	1
Kaufman, John, St. Petersburg*	9	5	.643	3.37	26	26	2	1	0	0	149.2	138	649	62	56	9	4	3	7	66	1	121	3	1
Murray, Dan, St. Lucie	12	10	.545	3.45	30	24	4	2	3	0	156.1	150	682	75	60	4	5	3	10	55	3	91	13	0

DEPARTMENTAL LEADERS: W—C. Lee, 15; L—Root, 14; Pct.—Darwin, .909; G—Ricabal, 75; GS—Callaway, Manias, 28 each; CG—B. Powell, 8; ShO—Several tied with 2 each; GF—Ricabal, 71; Sv.—Daniels, 29; IP—B. Powell, 183.1; H—Hartshorn, 197; TBF—F. Garcia, 741; R—Ryan, 105; ER—Dempster, 90; HR—Ryan, 22; SH—J. Powell, 9; SF—Lyons, 12; HB—Stephens, 14; BB—Burger, 93; IBB—Einerston, 8; SO—Burger, 154; WP—Coggin, 24; BK—Stewart, Callaway, Lyons, 7 each.

ALL PITCHERS

*Lefthanded pitcher.

Pitcher, Team	W	L	Pct.	ERA	G	GS	CG	ShO	GF	Sv.	IP	H	TBF	R	ER	HR	SH	SF	HB	BB	IBB	SO	WP	Bk.
Adkins, Tim, Dunedin*	1	1	.500	4.71	39	0	0	0	10	3	49.2	52	252	43	26	1	2	3	3	58	0	55	9	2
Aguiar, Douglas, Clearwater	0	1	.000	6.75	1	1	0	0	0	0	4.0	4	17	3	3	1	0	0	0	1	0	2	0	0
Alejo, Nigel, Brevard County	1	0	1.000	2.13	7	0	0	0	0	0	12.2	8	47	4	3	1	0	2	2	1	0	11	0	0
Alvord, Aaron, Lakeland	0	0	.000	2.89	5	0	0	0	2	0	9.1	9	39	3	3	0	0	0	0	2	0	4	0	0
Aquino, Julio, St. Petersburg	3	5	.375	2.85	50	0	0	0	8	1	60.0	53	240	21	19	3	2	2	3	8	0	39	3	1
Armas, Tony, Tam.-Sar.	5	2	.714	4.24	12	12	0	0	0	0	63.2	61	272	36	30	3	5	5	3	28	3	35	5	0
Arrojo, Rolando, St. Petersburg	5	6	.455	3.43	16	16	4	1	0	0	89.1	73	349	40	34	6	1	3	10	13	0	73	5	1
Arroyo, Luis, St. Lucie*	3	3	.500	2.09	36	2	0	0	11	0	56.0	37	231	21	13	2	3	1	3	23	2	57	1	3
Aucoin, Derek, W. Palm Beach	0	0	.000	7.58	17	0	0	0	9	0	19.0	13	102	17	16	1	2	1	6	27	0	21	15	0
Avery, Steve, Sarasota*	0	0	.000	0.00	1	1	0	0	0	0	3.0	2	11	0	0	0	0	0	0	1	0	3	0	0
Babineaux, Darrin, Vero Beach	7	3	.700	4.41	18	12	0	0	0	0	81.2	82	350	46	40	7	1	3	3	32	0	63	6	1
Bailey, Ben, Lakeland	4	4	.500	3.87	15	14	1	1	0	0	93.0	102	394	49	40	5	0	2	3	24	0	61	5	1
Baker, Jason, W. Palm Beach	3	4	.429	6.00	15	14	1	1	0	0	72.0	90	326	55	48	10	4	3	2	31	0	47	11	2
Barcelo, Marc, Daytona	3	3	.500	5.48	23	3	0	0	5	1	42.2	45	200	35	26	5	5	6	3	27	5	30	6	0
Barker, Richie, Daytona	2	1	.667	3.35	29	1	0	0	10	1	51.0	49	220	27	19	3	2	1	3	15	1	38	7	1
Barksdale, Shane, Kissimmee	0	0	.000	0.00	3	0	0	0	1	0	5.0	5	22	2	0	1	1	0	1	2	0	3	1	0
Barnes, Keith, Sarasota*	2	3	.400	5.57	28	5	0	0	9	1	64.2	72	306	48	40	4	2	4	3	38	0	39	9	0
Barnett, Marty, Clearwater	5	6	.455	3.69	17	15	1	0	0	0	97.2	102	411	50	40	10	1	1	0	29	0	62	6	2
Bauer, Chris, Lakeland	3	2	.600	4.63	19	0	0	0	7	2	35.0	43	164	31	18	2	0	0	2	11	1	19	3	2
Becker, Tom, Tampa	2	1	.667	5.02	25	0	0	0	9	0	43.0	45	192	29	24	2	1	2	0	26	4	26	6	1
Beech, Matt, Clearwater*	0	0	.000	0.00	1	1	0	0	0	0	5.2	1	22	1	0	0	0	0	0	4	0	9	0	0
Bell, Mike, W. Palm Beach*	5	4	.556	3.10	41	3	0	0	15	4	81.1	60	328	30	28	2	4	2	5	27	0	56	2	0
Benz, Jacob, W. Palm Beach*	0	2	.000	2.63	14	0	0	0	3	0	24.0	18	94	9	7	1	1	1	2	6	0	28	3	0
Berry, Jason, St. Petersburg	4	2	.667	4.99	35	0	0	0	16	4	48.2	65	225	32	27	3	2	2	4	11	1	40	2	2
Bess, Johnny, W. Palm Beach	0	0	.000	0.00	1	0	0	0	1	0	0.1	0	1	0	0	0	0	0	0	0	0	0	0	0
Bettencourt, Justin, Lakeland*	7	10	.412	4.14	25	25	1	0	0	0	143.1	143	624	78	66	10	1	8	4	68	0	112	9	0
Beverlin, Jason, Tampa	1	3	.250	4.79	7	6	0	0	0	0	41.1	37	167	26	22	4	2	2	4	13	1	24	6	0
Birsner, Roark, Daytona	0	0	.000	4.76	8	0	0	0	6	0	11.1	15	52	6	6	2	0	0	1	3	0	12	1	0
Blanco, Alberto, Kissimmee*	7	4	.636	2.83	19	19	1	1	0	0	114.1	83	467	45	36	4	5	4	11	45	0	95	6	2
Bland, Nate, Vero Beach*	7	7	.500	3.38	17	14	0	0	0	0	82.2	85	356	35	31	7	4	3	1	38	0	67	5	0
Blazier, Ron, Clearwater	2	3	.400	2.93	15	0	0	0	9	3	30.2	24	123	11	10	0	1	1	0	8	1	45	7	1
Boehringer, Brian, Tampa	0	1	.000	5.00	3	3	0	0	0	0	9.0	9	40	5	5	1	1	0	0	5	0	8	0	0
Bogle, Sean, Daytona	1	1	.500	6.75	8	0	0	0	5	2	6.2	11	38	7	5	1	0	0	0	7	1	3	3	0
Bosio, Chris, Sarasota	0	0	.000	1.93	1	1	0	0	0	0	4.2	6	21	2	1	0	0	0	0	0	0	5	0	0
Bowen, Ryan, Tampa	0	2	.000	4.02	4	4	0	0	0	0	15.2	17	66	7	7	1	0	0	1	5	0	15	1	1
Bowles, Brian, Dunedin	0	2	.000	7.53	7	1	0	0	3	0	14.1	20	68	14	12	2	0	1	0	7	1	9	3	1
Brackeen, Colin, Dunedin*	0	2	.000	3.60	6	0	0	0	4	0	10.0	13	43	4	4	0	0	0	1	3	1	11	0	0
Bradford, Josh, Dunedin	8	8	.500	4.99	28	23	2	1	3	0	158.2	173	701	104	88	11	0	5	11	65	3	92	18	5
Brandenburg, Mark, Sarasota	0	0	.000	0.00	1	0	0	0	1	0	3.0	3	12	0	0	0	0	0	0	0	0	1	0	0
Brannan, Ryan, Clearwater	0	0	.000	0.33	21	0	0	0	18	10	27.1	20	108	2	1	0	5	0	0	8	0	25	2	2
Brittan, Corey, St. Lucie	3	5	.375	3.58	51	1	0	0	18	3	78.0	91	338	35	31	5	4	0	1	21	4	57	2	0
Brown, Charlie, Tampa	4	3	.571	4.76	28	0	0	0	14	0	39.2	44	191	24	21	4	3	0	6	25	3	26	5	1
Brown, Darold, Daytona*	2	3	.400	2.79	29	1	0	0	6	1	38.2	33	166	16	12	3	0	1	2	20	1	32	3	2
Bryant, Chris, Daytona*	0	1	.000	9.53	8	1	0	0	1	0	11.1	20	59	12	12	5	1	1	0	8	0	10	3	0
Bullinger, Kirk, W. Palm Beach	2	0	1.000	0.00	2	0	0	0	0	0	3.2	3	15	0	0	0	0	0	0	0	0	7	1	0
Burger, Rob, Clearwater	11	9	.550	3.59	28	27	1	1	0	0	160.2	131	682	79	64	8	2	3	13	93	0	154	17	3
Bustos, Saul, W. Palm Beach	0	1	.000	27.00	1	0	0	0	1	0	1.0	2	6	3	3	1	0	0	0	1	0	0	0	0
Cafaro, Rocco, St. Petersburg	2	2	.500	1.99	19	2	0	0	8	0	40.2	35	163	10	9	0	2	1	0	5	1	28	1	1
Cain, Travis, St. Petersburg	1	4	.200	5.06	9	8	0	0	0	0	42.2	44	200	33	24	2	1	2	1	30	0	21	2	0
Callaway, Michael, St. Petersburg	11	7	.611	3.22	28	28	3	0	0	0	170.2	162	696	74	61	9	2	3	5	39	0	109	7	7
Cannon, Jon, Daytona*	1	0	1.000	1.32	2	2	0	0	0	0	13.2	7	55	2	2	1	2	1	0	10	1	13	0	0
Cannon, Kevan, Sarasota*	5	0	1.000	4.15	32	0	0	0	20	5	43.1	41	195	27	20	1	2	1	3	26	0	35	5	0
Caravelli, Mike, Brevard County*	3	5	.375	4.70	40	0	0	0	18	3	61.1	81	279	44	32	3	3	3	2	12	2	35	4	1
Carrasco, Troy, Fort Myers*	3	3	.500	5.37	12	8	0	0	3	0	55.1	61	241	37	33	5	3	2	0	18	2	36	4	1
Carroll, David, St. Petersburg*	4	1	.800	1.78	47	0	0	0	9	0	50.2	50	218	15	10	1	1	2	2	20	3	34	2	0
Carroll, Doug, St. Petersburg	0	0	.000	0.00	1	0	0	0	1	0	1.0	0	3	0	0	0	0	0	0	0	0	0	0	0
Castro, Tony, Brevard County	1	0	1.000	5.76	14	0	0	0	6	1	25.0	29	111	18	16	3	1	2	2	7	0	16	2	1
Chambers, Scott, Vero Beach*	5	5	.500	3.30	56	2	0	0	16	6	84.2	67	359	40	31	5	2	1	0	48	0	89	10	1
Chapman, Walker, Fort Myers	6	5	.545	5.80	27	14	0	0	4	1	90.0	121	405	64	58	7	2	5	3	32	0	65	1	1
Checo, Robinson, Sarasota	1	4	.200	5.30	11	11	0	0	0	0	56.0	54	250	37	33	9	3	5	1	27	0	63	4	5
Civit, Xavier, W. Palm Beach	3	0	1.000	1.64	4	0	0	0	1	0	11.0	5	42	2	2	0	1	0	0	4	0	9	2	0
Cobb, Trevor, Fort Myers*	7	0	1.000	2.97	15	7	1	1	0	0	60.2	49	246	29	20	2	3	1	2	16	0	48	2	0
Coggin, David, Clearwater	11	8	.579	4.70	27	27	3	2	0	0	155.0	160	697	96	81	12	5	7	9	86	0	110	24	1

Pitcher, Team	W	L	Pct.	ERA	G	GS	CG	ShO	GF	Sv.	IP	H	TBF	R	ER	HR	SH	SF	HB	BB	IBB	SO	WP	Bk.
Cole, Jason, W. Palm Beach	2	1	.667	2.37	11	0	0	0	5	2	19.0	21	80	7	5	1	0	0	1	4	0	8	2	0
Collins, Ed, Brevard County	2	3	.400	5.16	26	1	0	0	7	2	45.1	49	209	33	26	2	1	4	4	24	0	29	2	0
Cook, Derrick, Charlotte	5	2	.714	2.30	8	8	2	0	0	0	58.2	54	243	21	15	5	0	1	2	15	0	35	4	0
Coronado, Osvaldo, St. Lucie	0	0	.000	4.32	5	0	0	0	2	0	8.1	9	42	7	4	1	0	0	0	4	0	4	1	0
Correa, Ed, Vero Beach	0	0	.000	3.18	5	1	0	0	2	0	5.2	2	23	3	2	0	1	0	1	3	0	7	1	1
Correa, Ramser, Vero Beach	2	3	.400	1.77	9	9	0	0	0	0	45.2	45	199	19	9	0	0	1	0	18	0	31	2	2
Crawford, Paxton, Sarasota	4	8	.333	4.55	12	11	2	1	0	0	65.1	69	289	42	33	6	4	2	1	27	2	56	3	0
Cressend, Jack, Sarasota	8	11	.421	3.80	28	25	2	1	1	0	165.2	163	718	98	70	15	8	6	2	56	1	149	14	4
Crowther, John, Dunedin	1	2	.333	5.88	19	0	0	0	10	0	26.0	36	130	23	17	2	1	2	2	15	0	30	7	0
Dace, Derek, Lakeland*	0	0	.000	3.86	2	0	0	0	1	0	2.1	2	9	1	1	1	0	0	0	1	0	0	0	0
Daniels, John, St. Petersburg	4	4	.500	2.64	55	0	0	0	44	29	61.1	53	255	24	18	4	3	1	3	14	3	72	3	0
Danner, Adam, Brevard County	1	1	.500	7.43	17	0	0	0	3	0	26.2	50	141	28	22	3	3	1	4	11	1	14	1	2
Darwin, David, Lakeland*	10	1	.909	2.50	12	12	1	0	0	0	82.2	70	326	23	23	2	3	2	0	18	0	41	1	1
DaSilva, Fernando, W.P.B.	8	5	.615	5.28	30	4	0	0	11	0	59.2	73	259	38	35	4	2	1	1	12	1	59	3	1
Davey, Tom, Dunedin	1	3	.250	4.31	7	6	0	0	0	0	39.2	44	172	21	19	4	0	2	0	15	0	36	5	1
Davis, Doug, Charlotte*	5	3	.625	3.10	9	8	1	0	0	0	49.1	29	205	19	17	2	4	2	0	33	1	52	8	3
Davis, Jason, Clearwater*	2	1	.667	1.49	24	0	0	0	6	2	42.1	31	169	11	7	0	2	0	1	17	0	36	4	1
Davis, John, Vero Beach	3	5	.375	5.40	11	10	0	0	0	0	50.0	50	228	38	30	6	3	1	5	26	2	39	5	0
DeClue, Jon, Kissimmee*	2	0	1.000	1.80	7	0	0	0	5	0	15.0	10	64	4	3	2	0	1	1	9	0	13	0	0
DeJesus, Javier, Daytona*	3	1	.750	5.17	8	5	0	0	0	0	31.1	32	131	19	18	4	1	1	1	12	0	21	1	0
DeLaCruz, Francisco, Tampa	0	2	.000	6.87	8	8	0	0	0	0	36.2	39	174	30	28	5	3	2	1	29	1	22	2	0
Dellamano, Anthony, Charlotte	2	3	.400	12.31	15	0	0	0	7	4	22.2	23	125	33	31	3	2	2	6	29	1	15	14	0
De Los Santos, Luis, Tampa	5	0	1.000	2.34	10	10	0	0	0	0	61.2	49	240	19	16	4	0	3	2	8	0	39	0	1
Dempster, Ryan, Brevard County	10	9	.526	4.90	28	26	2	1	0	0	165.1	190	721	100	90	19	3	4	13	46	1	131	8	1
DeWitt, Chris, Daytona	1	8	.111	5.88	38	2	0	0	14	3	64.1	89	302	55	42	4	1	2	2	20	4	42	10	0
DeWitt, Scott, Brevard County*	4	10	.286	4.16	25	24	0	0	1	0	132.0	145	585	80	61	13	6	3	8	51	0	121	3	1
Dickey, R.A., Charlotte	1	4	.200	6.94	8	6	0	0	2	0	35.0	51	162	32	27	8	0	0	12	1	32	5	3
Dingman, Craig, Tampa	0	4	.000	5.24	19	0	0	0	11	6	22.1	15	92	14	13	2	1	0	0	14	2	26	3	0
Dinyar, Eric, Lakeland	0	0	.000	5.63	15	0	0	0	8	1	16.0	9	78	10	10	1	1	0	5	22	1	12	0	0
Diorio, Mike, Kissimmee	3	2	.600	2.97	36	0	0	0	30	19	39.1	33	161	15	13	1	1	0	1	10	1	30	1	1
Dollar, Toby, Vero Beach	0	0	.000	0.00	1	0	0	0	0	0	1.0	1	4	0	0	0	0	0	0	0	0	2	0	0
Dotel, Octavio, St. Lucie	5	2	.714	2.52	9	8	1	1	1	0	50.0	44	212	18	14	2	0	1	1	23	0	39	5	1
Dudeck, Dave, Tampa	0	0	.000	3.00	5	0	0	0	3	0	9.0	9	36	3	3	1	0	1	2	5	0	5	0	0
Duncan, Courtney, Daytona	8	4	.667	1.63	19	19	1	0	0	0	121.2	90	489	35	22	3	6	1	8	35	0	120	8	1
Durkovic, Peter, Lakeland*	6	4	.600	2.47	40	0	0	0	25	10	65.2	50	263	21	18	4	3	2	5	14	1	53	2	0
Durocher, Jayson, W. Palm Beach	6	4	.600	3.83	25	17	0	0	2	0	87.0	84	385	58	37	6	3	3	4	39	1	71	10	2
Duvall, Mike, Brevard County*	1	0	1.000	0.73	11	0	0	0	11	6	12.1	7	45	1	1	0	0	0	3	1	9	0	0
Ehlers, Corey, Brevard County	0	0	.000	2.38	6	0	0	0	4	0	11.1	9	45	3	3	2	0	0	3	1	3	0	1
Eiland, Dave, Tampa	1	0	1.000	3.75	3	3	0	0	0	0	12.0	11	48	5	5	0	0	1	0	0	11	0	0
Einerston, Darrell, Tampa	5	4	.556	2.15	45	0	0	0	24	6	71.0	63	287	24	17	2	5	0	1	19	8	55	1	0
Escobar, Kelvim, Dunedin	0	1	.000	3.75	3	2	0	0	0	0	12.0	16	55	9	5	0	1	1	3	0	16	1	0
Estavil, Mauricio, Clearwater	1	0	1.000	3.92	9	2	0	0	2	0	20.2	23	96	11	9	1	0	0	1	13	0	6	1	0
Evans, Keith, W. Palm Beach	4	4	.333	4.37	7	7	2	2	0	0	43.2	42	185	23	21	4	2	2	5	11	0	20	1	0
Farnsworth, Kyle, Daytona	10	10	.500	4.09	27	27	2	0	0	0	156.1	178	684	91	71	13	6	2	6	47	1	105	5	1
Faulkner, Neal, Daytona	3	7	.300	6.83	36	0	0	0	20	5	55.1	65	251	44	42	7	1	1	1	19	4	40	3	1
Feliciano, Pedro, Vero Beach*	0	0	.000	4.50	1	0	0	0	0	0	2.0	3	7	1	1	1	0	0	0	0	1	0	0
Fidge, Darren, Fort Myers	0	3	.000	6.34	24	0	0	0	13	0	38.1	44	175	29	27	3	3	6	2	20	0	25	4	0
Flores, Pedro, Vero Beach*	0	0	.000	5.79	3	0	0	0	1	0	4.2	10	26	6	3	1	0	0	0	4	0	1	0	0
Ford, Ben, Tampa	4	0	1.000	1.93	32	0	0	0	30	18	37.1	27	155	8	8	1	2	0	6	14	1	37	4	0
Foster, Kris, Vero Beach	6	3	.667	5.32	17	17	2	0	0	0	89.2	97	414	69	53	8	3	3	7	44	1	77	5	1
Garcia, Freddy, Kissimmee	10	8	.556	2.56	27	27	5	2	0	0	179.0	165	741	63	51	6	4	3	4	49	3	131	3	2
Garcia, Miguel, Vero Beach	10	3	.769	3.73	45	5	1	1	8	0	111.0	110	478	53	46	10	2	3	7	36	4	105	3	2
Getz, Rod, Brevard County	9	12	.429	3.23	27	26	4	1	1	0	164.1	166	689	84	59	12	6	8	10	39	1	92	8	1
Gillian, Charlie, Fort Myers	1	1	.500	2.30	10	0	0	0	3	0	15.2	10	65	5	4	1	0	0	5	5	0	11	3	0
Glynn, Ryan, Charlotte	8	7	.533	4.97	23	22	5	1	1	1	134.0	148	579	81	74	13	2	7	4	44	0	96	9	1
Gomez, Miguel, Dunedin	4	3	.571	4.93	21	0	0	0	9	2	34.2	41	154	26	19	1	0	4	10	1	30	6	1
Gonzalez, Juan, Brevard County	3	2	.600	2.39	26	0	0	0	20	6	37.2	32	155	13	10	3	2	3	7	0	28	2	0
Gorecki, Ryan, Charlotte	0	0	.000	0.00	1	0	0	0	1	0	1.0	0	3	0	0	0	0	0	0	0	0	0	0	0
Graterol, Beiker, Dunedin	4	7	.364	4.22	17	10	1	0	1	1	81.0	86	352	46	38	9	5	2	5	26	1	54	0	1
Green, Jason, Kissimmee	0	3	.000	5.19	8	0	0	0	4	0	8.2	11	50	12	5	0	0	0	0	10	1	3	2	0
Gulin, Lindsay, St. Lucie*	0	3	.000	9.23	6	6	0	0	0	0	26.1	36	136	31	27	2	0	2	1	21	1	11	6	1
Guzman, Juan, Dunedin	0	0	.000	0.00	2	2	0	0	0	0	4.0	3	15	0	0	0	0	0	0	1	0	3	0	0
Haigler, Phil, Fort Myers	11	9	.550	2.84	25	25	4	1	0	0	158.1	172	652	57	50	7	3	4	2	32	0	80	2	0
Hale, Chad, Kissimmee*	2	4	.333	4.82	46	0	0	0	18	7	52.1	56	225	30	28	2	4	3	1	11	4	46	3	1
Hall, Billy, Kissimmee	0	0	.000	3.86	4	0	0	0	1	0	7.0	7	34	5	3	0	0	1	5	0	5	1	0
Hammack, Brandon, Daytona	2	3	.400	2.37	16	0	0	0	7	1	19.0	25	89	11	5	0	2	1	0	7	0	20	2	1
Handy, Russell, W. Palm Beach	0	0	.000	22.50	2	0	0	0	1	0	2.0	6	15	6	5	2	0	0	0	1	0	1	0	0
Hanson, Erik, Dunedin	0	0	.000	1.29	2	2	0	0	0	0	7.0	7	28	5	1	1	0	0	0	1	0	5	0	0
Harnisch, Pete, St. Lucie	1	0	1.000	3.00	2	2	0	0	0	0	12.0	5	45	5	4	1	0	1	0	4	0	7	0	0
Harris, D.J., Dunedin	8	4	.667	3.22	42	3	0	0	24	5	78.1	64	344	41	28	5	1	2	4	45	4	66	7	4
Harris, Jeff, Fort Myers	2	4	.333	2.14	24	0	0	0	6	1	42.0	30	164	11	10	4	3	1	0	15	2	32	1	0
Hart, Len, Daytona	1	2	.333	5.19	8	8	0	0	0	0	9.1	10	44	6	6	0	1	0	1	7	0	12	1	0
Hartshorn, Tyson, Dunedin	5	13	.278	4.44	26	24	2	1	1	0	160.0	197	711	102	79	19	3	4	12	40	3	101	1	0
Harvey, Bryan, Brevard County	0	1	.000	4.91	4	4	0	0	0	0	11.0	11	48	9	6	2	1	0	0	1	0	11	2	1
Harvey, Terry, St. Petersburg	3	2	.600	7.71	18	3	0	0	7	0	35.0	39	167	33	30	6	1	2	6	26	0	15	5	1
Henry, Butch, Sarasota*	0	1	.000	5.40	2	2	0	0	0	0	8.1	8	33	5	5	1	0	0	0	7	0	0	0
Hollis, Ron, Sarasota	1	1	.500	2.84	13	0	0	0	9	4	19.0	13	77	8	6	2	1	1	2	7	0	21	2	0
Howard, Chris, St. Lucie*	1	1	.500	7.15	10	0	0	0	2	1	11.1	12	52	9	9	1	0	0	2	6	0	10	0	0
Howatt, Jeff, St. Lucie	1	2	.333	4.31	39	0	0	0	14	2	64.2	78	305	41	31	4	2	3	8	20	1	41	6	1
Hower, Dan, Charlotte*	0	1	.000	4.50	2	0	0	0	1	0	2.0	2	9	1	1	0	0	0	2	0	0	0	0
Hurtado, Victor, Brevard County	4	7	.364	4.89	17	16	2	0	0	0	92.0	102	405	54	50	9	2	5	7	34	1	58	7	0
Iddon, Brent, Sarasota	1	2	.333	4.95	37	2	0	0	19	3	56.1	63	260	39	31	4	1	0	2	28	3	50	3	0
Irabu, Hideki, Tampa	1	0	1.000	0.00	2	2	0	0	0	0	9.0	4	29	0	0	0	0	0	0	0	0	12	0	3

Pitcher, Team	W	L	Pct.	ERA	G	GS	CG	ShO	GF	Sv.	IP	H	TBF	R	ER	HR	SH	SF	HB	BB	IBB	SO	WP	Bk.
Isringhausen, Jason, St. Lucie	1	0	1.000	0.00	2	2	0	0	0	0	12.0	8	47	1	0	0	0	0	0	5	0	15	1	0
Jarvis, Jason, Dunedin	6	11	.353	5.19	35	7	0	0	19	1	85.0	92	400	64	49	3	4	3	4	47	5	70	16	1
Johnson, Mark, Kissimmee	8	9	.471	3.07	26	26	3	1	0	0	155.1	150	652	67	53	8	7	5	6	39	1	127	4	6
Judd, Mike, Vero Beach	6	5	.545	3.53	14	14	1	0	0	0	86.2	67	361	37	34	4	3	3	1	39	1	104	4	1
Julio, Jorge, W. Palm Beach	0	0	.000	0.00	1	0	0	0	0	0	0.0	2	2	1	1	0	0	0	0	0	0	0	0	0
Kaufman, John, St. Petersburg*	9	5	.643	3.37	26	26	2	1	0	0	149.2	138	649	62	56	9	4	3	7	66	1	121	3	1
Keppen, Jeffrey, Vero Beach	2	3	.400	3.93	32	8	0	0	14	0	68.2	61	304	37	30	3	2	3	8	43	0	54	7	2
Kershner, Jason, Clearwater*	5	10	.333	3.90	22	16	0	0	3	1	99.1	113	417	49	43	9	2	4	4	21	0	51	2	0
Kimbrell, Michael, St. Petersburg*	0	0	.000	7.71	3	0	0	0	2	0	9.1	10	44	8	8	2	1	0	0	7	0	7	1	0
Kimsey, Keith, Lakeland	2	5	.286	5.04	26	12	0	0	8	1	80.1	92	377	57	45	5	4	3	6	42	1	42	6	2
Knight, Brandon, Charlotte	7	4	.636	2.23	14	12	3	1	1	0	92.2	82	380	33	23	9	3	2	1	22	0	91	0	2
Knoll, Randy, Clearwater	1	2	.333	4.45	5	5	0	0	0	0	30.1	33	127	18	15	0	0	1	2	7	0	20	3	1
Koch, Bill, Dunedin	0	1	.000	2.08	3	3	0	0	0	0	21.2	27	88	10	5	1	1	1	0	3	0	20	1	1
Kojima, Keiichi, Charlotte	0	1	.000	1.73	11	0	0	0	11	4	26.0	24	104	5	5	1	1	1	0	5	0	25	0	0
Kolb, Danny, Charlotte	4	10	.286	4.87	24	23	3	0	0	0	133.0	146	600	91	72	10	8	5	8	62	1	83	12	0
Lail, Denny, Tampa	3	5	.375	3.90	44	1	0	0	13	1	62.1	67	267	38	27	2	1	5	0	23	7	40	4	0
Largusa, Levon, Daytona*	0	0	.000	8.31	14	0	0	0	4	0	8.2	16	51	11	8	0	0	1	0	8	2	5	1	0
LaRosa, Tom, Fort Myers	8	6	.571	4.31	25	23	3	1	0	0	135.2	120	592	73	65	10	1	5	7	66	0	118	6	0
Larson, Toby, St. Lucie	0	1	.000	7.20	4	0	0	0	1	0	5.0	9	25	6	4	2	0	0	0	1	0	3	0	0
Lee, Corey, Charlotte*	15	5	.750	3.47	23	23	6	2	0	0	160.2	132	654	66	62	9	5	3	7	60	0	147	7	0
Lee, Jeremy, Dunedin	8	9	.471	4.64	28	22	0	0	3	1	153.1	179	678	95	79	12	4	6	8	54	0	90	12	1
Leslie, Sean, W. Palm Beach*	0	0	.000	27.00	1	0	0	0	0	0	0.2	2	5	2	2	0	0	0	0	1	0	0	0	0
Lincoln, Mike, Fort Myers	13	4	.765	2.28	20	20	1	1	0	0	134.0	130	553	41	34	4	5	3	4	25	0	75	4	2
Lisio, Joseph, St. Lucie	2	6	.250	4.56	48	0	0	0	44	16	47.1	48	209	27	24	4	4	0	4	19	5	42	3	2
Lock, Dan, Kissimmee*	0	2	.000	2.67	17	0	0	0	6	1	27.0	28	123	17	8	0	1	1	1	11	1	23	0	1
Loiz, Niuman, Kissimmee	1	1	.500	3.82	11	3	1	0	2	0	33.0	37	141	19	14	4	1	3	2	8	0	19	2	0
Loubier, Scott, W. Palm Beach	0	0	.000	12.60	4	0	0	0	3	0	5.0	10	27	7	7	1	0	0	1	2	0	3	0	1
Lowe, Benny, Dunedin*	2	1	.667	1.84	13	0	0	0	13	5	14.2	7	57	3	3	0	0	1	1	3	0	19	1	0
Lyons, Jonathan, Sarasota	3	12	.200	6.05	25	14	0	0	6	0	96.2	125	462	79	65	11	3	12	1	45	2	47	5	7
Mahaffey, Alan, Fort Myers*	1	2	.333	4.10	38	0	0	0	11	1	48.1	46	200	27	22	2	3	2	1	8	0	55	1	0
Mairena, Oswaldo, Tampa*	0	0	.000	4.15	3	0	0	0	0	0	4.1	6	19	2	2	1	0	0	0	0	0	6	0	0
Malenfant, David, Lakeland	0	0	.000	15.00	6	0	0	0	2	0	6.0	18	46	12	10	1	1	1	1	7	0	3	1	0
Manias, James, St. Petersburg*	13	5	.722	3.78	28	28	2	2	0	0	171.1	163	710	84	72	16	3	4	11	40	0	119	6	0
Mann, Jim, Dunedin	1	0	1.000	6.00	12	0	0	0	4	0	18.0	27	88	12	12	2	0	1	1	6	1	13	1	0
Manning, David, Charlotte	0	0	.000	1.50	1	1	0	0	0	0	6.0	4	26	1	1	1	0	0	0	4	0	4	0	0
Manning, Len, Clearwater*	0	0	.000	0.00	5	0	0	0	2	0	6.0	2	22	0	0	0	0	0	0	0	0	7	1	0
Mantei, Matt, Brevard County	0	0	.000	6.00	4	0	0	0	0	0	6.0	4	27	4	4	1	0	0	0	6	0	11	1	0
Markey, Barry, Daytona	5	7	.417	5.55	22	21	2	0	1	0	120.0	144	537	81	74	13	2	5	8	41	1	67	4	2
Marquez, Robert, W. Palm Beach	1	1	.500	2.57	21	0	0	0	13	6	28.0	28	117	12	8	3	1	0	0	3	0	22	0	0
Marshall, Gary, Daytona*	0	0	.000	4.79	22	0	0	0	11	6	20.2	23	92	13	11	4	0	1	0	8	2	23	1	0
Marsonek, Sam, Charlotte	0	2	.000	7.56	2	2	0	0	0	0	8.1	14	41	10	7	3	0	0	1	2	0	7	3	0
Martinez, Javier, Daytona	2	6	.250	5.79	9	9	2	0	0	0	51.1	65	238	40	33	8	1	3	3	26	0	34	3	2
Martinez, Jose, Charlotte	3	1	.750	3.75	26	0	0	0	13	2	57.2	52	229	25	24	6	3	0	0	13	0	48	4	1
Masaoka, Onan, Vero Beach*	6	8	.429	3.87	28	24	2	1	3	1	148.2	113	612	72	64	16	6	4	10	55	1	132	10	1
Mattes, Troy, W. Palm Beach	6	9	.400	4.94	20	16	2	2	3	1	102.0	123	441	61	56	8	3	5	5	20	0	61	11	1
McBride, Chris, Dunedin	3	0	1.000	6.10	10	4	0	0	1	0	31.0	44	153	25	21	4	0	0	3	17	0	25	5	0
McClellan, Sean, Dunedin	0	0	.000	10.80	3	0	0	0	2	0	3.1	5	20	4	4	0	0	1	0	5	0	4	0	0
McDonald, Matt, Vero Beach*	8	8	.500	3.72	57	3	0	0	3	0	109.0	93	484	53	45	9	6	4	2	67	2	123	10	1
McEntire, Ethan, St. Lucie*	0	1	.000	6.17	3	3	0	0	0	0	11.2	16	54	9	8	0	0	1	0	7	0	8	0	0
McHugh, Mike, Charlotte*	0	1	.000	7.62	18	0	0	0	10	0	26.0	32	137	25	22	4	3	3	3	27	2	23	3	0
McMullen, Jerry, Sarasota*	2	4	.333	5.23	33	0	0	0	18	2	51.2	61	243	33	30	5	2	3	3	28	0	37	6	0
McNeely, Mitch, Vero Beach*	1	1	.500	5.33	14	1	0	0	4	2	27.0	36	122	18	16	5	2	1	0	7	0	15	0	3
McNichol, Brian, Daytona*	2	2	.500	2.31	6	6	0	0	0	0	39.0	32	161	14	10	1	1	2	3	10	1	40	1	0
Meinershagen, Adam, Dunedin	0	1	.000	5.00	3	2	0	0	0	0	9.0	12	41	5	5	0	1	1	1	1	0	4	0	0
Mejia, Javier, Clearwater	6	3	.667	3.09	52	0	0	0	26	7	64.0	68	276	22	22	1	3	2	1	24	0	54	5	0
Melendez, Dave, Lakeland	8	4	.667	1.76	15	15	2	1	0	0	102.1	70	409	28	20	5	0	3	7	32	0	79	3	3
Merrill, Ethan, Sarasota*	2	0	1.000	6.32	12	0	0	0	6	1	15.2	27	82	11	11	0	3	1	2	8	2	8	1	1
Miles, Chad, Brevard County*	3	4	.429	4.50	42	0	0	0	18	5	64.0	63	291	46	32	4	2	1	2	31	4	59	6	0
Miller, Kurt, Brevard County	0	0	.000	1.80	2	2	0	0	0	0	5.0	6	22	1	1	1	0	0	0	2	0	7	0	0
Miller, Wade, Kissimmee	10	2	.833	1.80	14	14	4	1	0	0	100.0	79	395	28	20	3	3	5	4	14	1	76	4	1
Milton, Eric, Tampa*	8	3	.727	3.09	14	14	1	0	0	0	93.1	78	371	35	32	8	2	1	3	14	0	95	4	3
Miranda, Walter, Brevard County	2	3	.400	5.19	10	9	0	0	0	0	34.2	45	170	32	20	2	0	1	2	26	0	15	4	0
Mitchell, Scott, W. Palm Beach	5	3	.625	2.57	39	3	0	0	15	3	73.2	61	291	21	21	4	3	1	3	18	0	56	4	0
Mlicki, Doug, Kissimmee	0	0	.000	0.00	1	1	0	0	0	0	4.0	4	17	0	0	0	0	0	0	0	0	2	0	0
Moraga, David, W. Palm Beach*	1	4	.200	4.91	13	7	0	0	3	0	47.2	50	207	27	26	3	1	2	1	18	0	37	6	0
Morales, Eric, St. Lucie	0	0	.000	0.00	1	0	0	0	1	0	1.0	0	3	0	0	0	0	0	0	0	0	0	0	0
Morris, Alex, Brevard County	0	0	.000	0.00	2	0	0	0	2	0	3.0	1	12	1	0	0	0	0	2	0	0	2	0	0
Mota, Henry, Charlotte	2	5	.286	5.23	31	3	0	0	11	2	74.0	84	330	51	43	14	2	2	5	29	2	45	4	0
Mott, Tom, Fort Myers	2	0	1.000	3.19	14	0	0	0	3	0	31.0	25	127	13	11	1	1	2	2	12	0	23	6	0
Mudd, Scott, Charlotte	0	1	.000	4.91	4	0	0	0	2	0	3.2	5	19	2	2	0	0	0	0	4	0	3	1	0
Murray, Dan, St. Lucie	12	10	.545	3.45	30	24	4	2	3	0	156.1	150	682	75	60	4	5	3	10	55	3	91	13	0
Nakashima, Tony, Vero Beach*	1	0	1.000	10.91	10	0	0	0	2	0	15.2	23	80	19	19	2	0	1	0	11	1	17	2	1
Niedermaier, Brad, Fort Myers	2	3	.400	1.47	32	0	0	0	29	17	36.2	27	154	15	6	2	2	4	0	12	2	47	4	0
Norton, Phillip, Daytona*	3	2	.600	2.34	7	6	3	0	0	0	42.1	40	171	11	11	5	1	0	0	12	0	44	0	0
Nyari, Pete, Clearwater	0	4	.000	2.70	31	0	0	0	18	5	43.1	29	181	20	13	1	2	0	2	21	2	35	3	1
Oakley, Matt, Lakeland	1	2	.333	5.98	27	0	0	0	8	0	43.2	54	211	35	29	2	2	3	2	26	1	34	3	0
Olson, Phillip, St. Lucie	3	3	.500	3.30	47	0	0	0	16	1	71.0	74	307	32	26	4	4	3	7	26	4	57	10	0
O'Malley, Paul, Kissimmee	2	2	.500	2.80	24	0	0	0	13	5	35.1	24	145	12	11	3	1	2	1	19	3	20	1	0
Orta, Juan, W. Palm Beach	0	0	.000	0.00	1	0	0	0	1	0	0.2	2	4	0	0	0	0	1	0	0	0	0	0	0
Ovalle, Bonelly, Charlotte	2	2	.500	5.87	14	0	0	0	7	2	23.0	26	108	20	15	3	1	1	1	15	0	16	5	0
Paige, Carey, Dunedin	1	3	.250	3.02	12	9	0	0	2	1	44.2	36	191	21	15	3	2	2	0	22	1	39	1	0
Pailthorpe, Bob, Brevard County	6	4	.600	4.86	35	3	0	0	13	1	74.0	88	327	50	40	6	2	2	2	24	1	53	4	1
Paniagua, Jose, W. Palm Beach	1	0	1.000	0.00	2	2	0	0	0	0	10.0	5	36	0	0	0	0	0	0	2	0	11	0	0

Pitcher, Team	W	L	Pct.	ERA	G	GS	CG	ShO	GF	Sv.	IP	H	TBF	R	ER	HR	SH	SF	HB	BB	IBB	SO	WP	Bk.
Parker, Christian, W. Palm Beach..	0	1	.000	3.32	3	3	0	0	0	0	19.0	22	81	7	7	0	0	0	0	5	0	10	2	0
Parotte, Frisco, Daytona	0	0	.000	0.00	5	0	0	0	5	0	5.1	1	20	0	0	0	1	0	0	4	1	4	2	0
Patino, Leonardo, Lakeland*	6	4	.600	2.63	40	3	0	0	23	8	72.0	61	289	25	21	3	4	2	0	20	0	75	3	3
Pena, Juan, Sarasota	4	6	.400	2.96	13	13	3	0	0	0	91.1	67	359	39	30	8	1	2	2	23	1	88	1	0
Phillips, Ben, Tampa	8	11	.421	4.41	25	25	0	0	0	0	136.2	135	608	83	67	9	4	5	4	79	0	97	11	1
Pierson, Jason, St. Lucie	0	1	.000	2.30	7	1	0	0	0	0	15.2	13	59	4	4	2	0	0	2	6	0	6	0	0
Powell, Brian, Lakeland	13	9	.591	2.50	27	27	8	2	0	0	183.1	153	732	70	51	9	4	5	6	35	2	122	5	0
Powell, Jeremy, W. Palm Beach	9	10	.474	3.02	26	26	1	0	0	0	155.0	162	675	75	52	3	9	5	12	62	0	121	12	2
Pujals, Denis, St. Petersburg	9	4	.692	4.43	24	24	2	1	0	0	140.1	156	588	74	69	14	6	8	8	27	1	69	1	0
Pulsipher, Bill, St. Lucie*	1	4	.200	5.89	12	7	0	0	2	0	36.2	29	178	27	24	1	2	1	4	35	0	35	14	5
Radlosky, Rob, Fort Myers	9	5	.643	2.59	23	22	3	1	1	0	128.1	87	510	42	37	10	5	4	5	37	0	109	2	0
Raifstanger, John, Sarasota	0	0	.000	0.00	1	0	0	0	1	0	0.2	0	2	0	0	0	0	0	0	0	0	1	0	0
Rama, Shelby, St. Petersburg	0	0	.000	18.00	1	0	0	0	0	0	1.0	1	5	2	2	0	0	0	1	0	1	0	0	0
Ramirez, Felix, Sarasota*	2	1	.667	1.53	19	0	0	0	9	1	35.1	39	153	10	6	3	4	1	0	12	1	31	1	0
Ramos, Edgar, Clearwater	0	0	.000	3.60	2	2	0	0	0	0	5.0	3	19	3	2	0	0	0	2	0	3	0	0	0
Ramsay, Robert, Sarasota*	9	9	.500	4.78	23	22	1	0	0	0	135.2	134	603	90	72	16	1	3	5	63	0	115	7	0
Randolph, Stephen, Tampa*	4	7	.364	3.87	34	13	1	0	6	1	95.1	74	417	55	41	8	7	3	3	63	5	108	4	1
Rath, Fred, Fort Myers	4	0	1.000	1.64	17	0	0	0	11	2	22.0	18	87	4	4	2	1	1	0	3	1	22	1	0
Resz, Greg, Tampa	1	0	1.000	3.18	1	1	0	0	0	0	5.2	5	23	2	2	1	0	0	1	2	0	5	0	0
Reynoso, Armando, St. Lucie	1	1	.500	2.70	2	2	0	0	0	0	10.0	9	38	3	3	0	0	0	0	1	0	6	0	0
Rhine, Kendall, Dunedin	0	0	.000	12.46	4	0	0	0	2	0	4.1	9	26	7	6	1	0	0	1	4	1	2	0	0
Ricabal, Dan, Vero Beach	4	5	.444	4.25	75	0	0	0	71	28	84.2	79	373	44	40	1	4	4	7	39	5	79	5	2
Richardson, Kasey, Fort Myers*	1	3	.250	4.46	7	7	0	0	0	0	34.1	35	156	23	17	1	3	3	0	18	0	17	5	0
Ricketts, Chad, Daytona	3	1	.750	0.44	20	0	0	0	17	8	20.1	13	82	4	1	0	0	0	1	6	0	18	1	0
Risley, Bill, Dunedin	0	2	.000	4.50	8	6	0	0	0	0	12.0	9	49	9	6	0	1	1	0	3	0	11	0	1
Rivera, Marco, W. Palm Beach	0	1	.000	22.50	2	0	0	0	1	0	2.0	4	11	5	5	0	1	0	0	2	0	1	0	0
Robbins, Jake, Tampa	1	1	.500	5.06	3	3	0	0	0	0	16.0	18	73	14	9	2	0	2	0	10	1	5	2	0
Rodriguez, Maximo, B.C.	0	0	.000	18.00	3	0	0	0	1	0	2.0	6	14	5	4	1	0	1	0	2	0	2	0	0
Romero, Juan, Fort Myers	1	1	.500	4.38	7	1	0	0	3	0	12.1	11	50	6	6	1	0	0	1	4	0	9	0	0
Root, Derek, Kissimmee*	4	14	.222	4.19	26	22	2	0	0	0	129.0	131	555	76	60	10	4	7	7	42	1	68	7	5
Roper, Chad, Fort Myers	1	2	.333	2.72	27	1	0	0	10	0	39.2	32	159	20	12	1	1	0	0	13	1	27	1	0
Roque, Rafael, St. Lucie*	2	10	.167	4.29	17	13	1	0	1	0	77.2	81	325	42	37	8	3	4	1	25	0	54	2	1
Rose, Brian, Sarasota	4	1	.800	3.00	21	0	0	0	17	7	33.0	35	145	16	11	1	2	1	0	12	0	34	1	0
Rushing, Will, Fort Myers*	1	5	.167	7.51	12	7	0	0	0	0	38.1	54	191	41	32	4	1	5	0	22	0	34	1	0
Ryan, Jay, Daytona	9	8	.529	4.44	27	27	5	0	0	0	170.1	168	740	105	84	22	3	10	6	55	2	140	12	0
St. Pierre, Bob, Tampa	3	5	.375	3.86	27	3	0	0	7	1	51.1	66	225	27	22	5	3	1	1	18	4	37	0	0
Santiago, Derek, Brevard County..	3	2	.600	4.45	10	1	0	0	4	0	28.1	20	123	14	14	2	2	0	4	19	4	17	2	0
Santoro, Gary, Brevard County	0	0	.000	3.38	20	0	0	0	16	2	26.2	32	112	11	10	2	1	0	2	3	0	14	3	0
Santos, Victor, Lakeland	10	5	.667	3.23	26	26	4	2	0	0	145.0	136	623	74	52	10	4	6	6	59	1	108	12	1
Sasaki, Junichi, W. Palm Beach	0	0	.000	0.00	1	0	0	0	1	0	0.1	1	2	0	0	0	0	0	0	0	0	0	0	0
Schlomann, Brett, Tampa	8	4	.667	3.65	19	18	1	1	0	0	118.1	129	503	55	48	8	3	2	2	29	0	86	2	0
Schroeder, Chad, Lakeland	0	3	.000	4.76	12	1	0	0	5	0	22.2	25	98	14	12	1	1	2	0	8	1	8	1	0
Sekany, Jason, Sarasota	4	4	.500	5.57	10	9	0	0	1	0	64.2	56	290	43	40	8	2	2	2	41	0	32	3	2
Shelby, Anthony, Tampa*	4	3	.571	2.60	48	0	0	0	11	2	69.1	68	285	23	20	4	4	4	0	16	5	57	3	1
Shumaker, Anthony, Clearwater*	5	4	.556	2.13	61	0	0	0	28	9	72.0	64	295	22	17	1	2	0	2	17	1	77	5	0
Sievert, Mark, Dunedin	1	0	1.000	3.27	3	2	0	0	0	0	11.0	10	44	5	4	0	0	0	1	5	0	7	2	1
Sikorski, Brian, Kissimmee	8	2	.800	3.06	11	11	0	0	0	0	67.2	64	279	29	23	2	0	1	6	16	0	46	0	3
Sinclair, Steve, Dunedin*	2	5	.286	2.94	43	0	0	0	20	3	68.1	63	296	36	22	4	4	1	2	26	3	66	4	1
Smart, J.D., W. Palm Beach	5	4	.556	3.26	17	13	1	0	1	1	102.0	105	422	45	37	10	2	3	2	21	0	65	3	0
Smetana, Steve, Sarasota*	0	1	.000	4.71	10	1	0	0	3	0	21.0	25	90	12	11	1	0	1	0	7	0	20	2	0
Smith, Dan, Charlotte	8	10	.444	4.43	26	25	2	0	0	0	160.2	169	705	93	79	17	6	4	11	66	1	113	9	0
Smith, Eric, Kissimmee	2	2	.500	4.41	32	6	0	0	10	1	79.2	84	347	44	39	5	3	2	2	23	3	59	6	1
Smith, Keilan, Lakeland	9	2	.818	2.57	40	3	0	0	24	7	77.0	65	314	23	22	4	2	3	2	27	2	46	7	0
Smith, Ottis, Charlotte	2	3	.400	3.94	27	0	0	0	21	5	48.0	34	204	21	21	2	2	0	4	27	0	34	12	0
Smith, Sloan, Tampa	0	0	.000	0.00	5	0	0	0	3	0	8.0	4	33	0	0	0	0	0	0	3	0	10	0	0
Sobik, Trad, Lakeland	0	1	.000	40.50	2	0	0	0	0	0	0.2	4	9	3	3	0	0	0	0	3	0	1	1	0
Spence, Cam, Tampa	1	2	.333	2.37	15	5	0	0	2	0	49.1	42	191	16	13	2	1	1	0	10	0	31	1	2
Spinelli, Mike, Sarasota*	0	4	.000	5.40	5	5	0	0	0	0	26.2	34	127	22	16	3	0	3	1	12	0	11	4	0
Splittorff, Jamie, Fort Myers	0	0	.000	9.53	2	2	0	0	0	0	5.2	11	29	6	6	0	0	0	1	0	0	3	0	0
Spoljaric, Paul, Dunedin*	0	0	.000	1.69	4	3	0	0	1	0	10.2	10	43	3	2	1	0	0	2	0	0	10	1	0
Spykstra, Dave, Vero Beach	2	6	.250	5.91	25	14	0	0	7	0	70.0	79	335	54	46	5	1	4	4	51	1	48	19	1
Stachler, Eric, Kissimmee	4	4	.500	4.13	48	0	0	0	22	4	65.1	76	291	38	30	2	1	2	3	21	3	43	2	0
Steinmetz, Earl, Kissimmee	0	0	.000	12.00	4	0	0	0	0	0	6.0	8	28	8	8	0	1	0	0	3	0	4	1	0
Stentz, Brent, Fort Myers	7	2	.778	2.47	49	1	0	0	30	17	69.1	53	285	20	19	4	2	3	2	24	3	70	5	2
Stephens, Shannon, B.C.	8	13	.381	4.81	27	25	2	2	0	0	149.2	162	647	93	80	11	7	10	14	34	2	90	5	0
Stevens, Kris, Clearwater	6	3	.667	4.56	13	13	0	0	0	0	71.0	80	319	42	36	4	3	4	3	30	0	53	3	0
Stevenson, Rodney, W.P.B.	3	3	.500	1.78	26	0	0	0	12	3	35.1	31	158	13	7	2	1	1	6	0	39	0	0	
Stewart, Scott, St. Lucie*	5	10	.333	4.01	22	18	4	0	1	0	123.1	114	496	62	55	8	3	7	4	18	1	64	4	7
Strange, Mike, Dunedin	0	0	.000	0.00	1	0	0	0	0	0	1.0	1	4	0	0	0	0	0	0	1	0	0	0	0
Stumpf, Brian, Clearwater	0	0	.000	5.92	17	0	0	0	6	0	24.1	31	118	18	16	7	1	0	0	9	1	23	3	0
Tapani, Kevin, Daytona	0	0	.000	3.86	1	1	0	0	0	0	4.2	5	21	2	2	0	0	0	0	2	0	4	0	0
Thomas, Evan, Clearwater	5	5	.500	2.44	13	12	2	0	0	0	84.2	68	340	30	23	7	1	3	1	23	0	89	3	2
Thompson, Chris, Sarasota	5	2	.714	3.69	29	6	0	0	8	0	61.0	68	289	35	25	7	1	3	1	29	2	36	6	0
Tolar, Kevin, St. Lucie*	0	0	.000	2.03	9	0	0	0	3	1	13.1	9	54	3	3	0	0	0	0	6	0	8	1	0
Tribe, Byron, Daytona	0	0	.000	7.32	18	0	0	0	7	0	19.2	21	102	20	16	0	1	1	1	22	0	19	7	0
Trinidad, Hector, Fort Myers	1	0	1.000	0.00	2	0	0	0	2	0	8.0	2	28	0	0	0	0	0	0	1	0	5	1	0
Trumpour, Andy, St. Lucie	8	10	.444	4.11	27	27	0	0	0	0	144.2	159	632	75	66	12	2	5	3	57	2	86	8	2
Tucker, Julien, Kissimmee	8	7	.533	5.22	33	8	0	0	7	0	69.0	79	324	48	40	1	0	3	5	42	3	49	2	1
Urbina, Dan, Vero Beach	0	0	.000	8.68	3	3	0	0	0	0	9.1	11	44	9	9	0	1	0	0	5	0	10	0	0
Valette, Ramon, Daytona	0	0	.000	7.71	3	0	0	0	3	0	2.1	2	11	2	2	1	0	0	0	2	0	1	0	0
Vandemark, John, Clearwater*	2	1	.667	2.88	14	0	0	0	4	0	25.0	21	106	11	8	2	1	1	0	12	1	22	1	1
Van Poppel, Todd, Charlotte	0	4	.000	4.04	6	6	2	0	0	0	35.2	36	152	19	16	3	2	1	0	4	0	33	2	0
Vazquez, Javier, W. Palm Beach	6	3	.667	2.16	19	19	1	0	0	0	112.2	98	461	40	27	8	1	2	6	28	0	100	2	0

Pitcher, Team	W	L	Pct.	ERA	G	GS	CG	ShO	GF	Sv.	IP	H	TBF	R	ER	HR	SH	SF	HB	BB	IBB	SO	WP	Bk.
Venafro, Michael, Charlotte*	4	2	.667	3.43	35	0	0	0	27	10	44.2	51	196	17	17	2	4	3	1	21	1	35	1	0
Veniard, Jay, Dunedin*	1	3	.250	1.88	10	8	0	0	1	0	52.2	49	229	23	11	2	2	4	35	1	32	4	1	
Verdin, Cesar, Tampa*	3	4	.429	5.40	8	8	0	0	0	0	43.1	41	180	27	26	3	1	2	4	13	0	37	1	2
Viano, Jake, St. Petersburg	3	4	.429	3.15	31	2	0	0	14	1	60.0	62	253	23	21	2	1	2	0	18	0	68	2	1
Wagner, Matt, W. Palm Beach	0	0	.000	54.00	1	1	0	0	0	0	0.2	4	8	4	4	0	0	1	1	0	0	2	0	
Wallace, Derek, St. Lucie	0	0	.000	6.43	5	0	0	0	3	0	7.0	7	30	6	5	0	0	0	0	2	0	8	1	1
Weidert, Chris, W. Palm Beach	0	1	.000	0.00	4	0	0	0	0	0	6.0	5	26	1	0	0	0	1	0	3	0	7	0	0
Westover, Richard, W.P.B.	0	0	.000	15.00	3	0	0	0	3	0	3.0	10	21	7	5	1	1	0	0	2	0	2	1	0
Whisenant, Matt, B.C.*	0	0	.000	8.10	2	1	0	0	0	0	3.1	3	15	3	3	0	0	0	0	3	0	4	1	0
Whiteman, Greg, Clearwater	3	3	.500	4.59	11	11	0	0	0	0	51.0	57	228	30	26	3	0	2	0	26	0	32	2	1
Williams, Matt, St. Petersburg*	9	5	.643	2.97	43	0	0	0	15	1	63.2	57	267	26	21	4	2	0	2	24	3	50	3	3
Wilson, Paul, St. Lucie	0	0	.000	2.57	1	1	0	0	0	0	7.0	6	26	2	2	1	0	0	0	0	0	5	0	0
Winslett, Dax, Daytona	4	3	.571	6.19	9	7	0	0	1	0	36.1	51	164	27	25	4	2	4	1	7	0	16	3	2
Woodring, Jason, W. Palm Beach	1	1	.500	2.76	16	0	0	0	14	5	16.1	12	67	6	5	0	0	1	3	5	0	8	4	0
Yarnall, Ed, St. Lucie*	5	8	.385	2.48	18	18	2	0	0	0	105.1	93	435	33	29	5	2	1	2	30	0	114	2	4
Ybarra, Jamie, St. Petersburg	1	0	1.000	5.06	3	0	0	0	0	0	5.1	8	23	3	3	0	0	2	1	0	0	3	1	0
Yeager, Gary, Clearwater	5	5	.500	6.11	39	6	0	0	9	0	73.2	91	334	55	50	5	5	3	3	25	0	42	4	1
Yennaco, Jay, Sarasota	4	0	1.000	2.23	7	7	2	1	0	0	44.1	30	179	12	11	3	1	0	1	19	1	41	2	1
Young, Tim, W. Palm Beach	0	0	.000	0.57	11	0	0	0	8	5	15.2	8	56	1	1	0	2	0	1	4	0	13	0	0
Zaleski, Kevin, Brevard County	1	0	1.000	0.00	3	0	0	0	3	0	4.0	3	15	0	0	0	0	0	0	0	0	3	0	0
Zamarripa, Mark, Lakeland	2	1	.667	8.03	11	0	0	0	8	1	12.1	16	59	12	11	0	0	0	0	11	0	9	1	0

COMBINATION SHUTOUTS: **Brevard County (7)**—Getz-Gonzalez, Miranda-Gonzalez-Duvall, DeWitt-Collins-Caravelli, Stephens-Alejo-Gonzalez, Hurtado-Pailthorpe-Caravelli, Dempster-Mantei-Santoro, DeWitt-Danner-Alejo-Pailthorpe. **Charlotte (3)**—Lee-Mota, Davis-McHugh, Davis-Kojima. **Clearwater (4)**—Thomas-Brannan, Kershner-Brannan, Barnett-Mejia-Shumaker, Whiteman-Mejia-Shumaker. **Daytona (3)**—Farnsworth-Barker-Faulkner-Marshall, Winslett-DeWitt, Duncan-DeWitt. **Dunedin (2)**—Davey-Sinclair, Graterol-Mann-Sinclair. **Fort Myers (11)**—Haigler-Harris-Rath, Chapman-Harris-Mahaffey-Niedermaier, Haigler-Mahaffey-Niedermaier, Cobb-Harris, Radlosky-Harris-Rath, Radlosky-Harris-Niedermaier, LaRosa-Mahaffey-Stentz, LaRosa-Mott, Richardson-Gillian-Stentz, Radlosky-Chapman-Stentz, Radlosky-Stentz. **Kissimmee (10)**—Blanco-Hall-Stachler, Blanco-Diorio, Garcia-Stachler-Hale, Garcia-Diorio, Johnson-Diorio, Garcia-Diorio, Garcia-O'Malley-Diorio, Miller-Hale, Smith-O'Malley-Hale-Diorio, Garcia-DeClue. **Lakeland (3)**—Melendez-Dinyar-Durkovic, Powell-Patino-Zamarripa, Smith-Zamarripa. **St. Lucie (8)**—Yarnall-Brittan, Dotel-Brittan, Yarnall-Arroyo-Howatt, Murray-Arroyo-Brittan-Lisio, Yarnall-Arroyo-Lisio, Trumpour-Pulsipher, Yarnall-Howatt-Lisio, Isringhausen-Pierson-Lisio. **St. Petersburg (3)**—Kaufman-Aquino-Viano, Manias-Williams-Aquino-Daniels, Callaway-Aquino. **Sarasota (2)**—Ramsay-McMullen-Cannon, Sekany-Ramirez. **Tampa (4)**—Schlomann-Randolph-Ford, Phillips-Einerston, Schlomann-Randolph, Phillips-Becker-Brown. **Vero Beach (9)**—Correa-McDonald-Ricabal, Davis-Garcia-Chambers-McDonald-Ricabal, Davis-McDonald-Chambers-Ricabal, Masaoka-Davis-McDonald-Spykstra, Garcia-McDonald, Babineaux-Keppen, Keppen-McDonald-Correa-Ricabal, Babineaux-Chambers-Ricabal, Bland-Ricabal. **West Palm Beach (8)**—Paniagua-Smart-Cole, Powell-Weidert-Bell-Woodring, Paniagua-Weidert-Woodring, Powell-Mitchell, Mitchell-Bullinger-Bell, DaSilva-Mattes, Bell-Moraga-Young, Durocher-Civit-Aucoin.

NO-HIT GAMES: Blanco, Kissimmee, defeated Daytona, 7-0, June 25.

PITCHERS WITH TWO OR MORE TEAMS

Pitcher, Team	W	L	Pct.	ERA	G	GS	CG	ShO	GF	Sv.	IP	H	TBF	R	ER	HR	SH	SF	HB	BB	IBB	SO	WP	Bk.
Armas, Tony, Tampa	3	1	.750	3.33	9	9	0	0	0	0	46.0	43	191	23	17	1	3	4	1	16	3	26	2	0
Armas, Tony, Sarasota	2	1	.667	6.62	3	3	0	0	0	0	17.2	18	81	13	13	2	2	1	2	12	0	9	3	0

1997 FIELDING

TEAM

Team	Pct.	G	PO	A	E	TC	DP	PB	Team	Pct.	G	PO	A	E	TC	DP	PB
St. Petersburg	.972	137	3602	1363	141	5106	95	13	Brev. County	.966	138	3593	1529	180	5302	123	45
Charlotte	.969	139	3608	1450	160	5218	130	27	W.Palm Beach	.965	135	3478	1412	175	5065	94	28
Fort Myers	.969	139	3612	1490	163	5265	115	22	St. Lucie	.963	135	3455	1492	190	5137	109	35
Tampa	.969	136	3621	1530	166	5317	110	21	Dunedin	.960	139	3648	1584	220	5452	107	27
Vero Beach	.969	137	3535	1335	157	5027	111	35	Sarasota	.959	138	3554	1340	207	5101	108	33
Clearwater	.968	138	3581	1522	168	5271	110	33	Daytona	.959	138	3521	1456	214	5191	97	28
Kissimmee	.968	137	3576	1581	172	5329	110	21	TRIPLE PLAY: Dunedin.								
Lakeland	.966	138	3578	1550	178	5306	109	15									

INDIVIDUAL

FIRST BASEMEN

NOTE: All caps denotes fielding-percentage leader based on 69 games for catchers, 92 for all other non-pitchers and 138 innings for pitchers. *Throws lefthanded.

Player, Team	Pct.	G	PO	A	E	TC	DP
Bovender, Andy, Kissimmee	.971	4	32	2	1	35	3
Braughler, Matt, Brevard County	.917	2	9	2	1	12	0
Bravo, Danny, W. Palm Beach	1.000	1	1	0	0	1	0
Brooks, Eddie, St. Lucie	.947	4	18	0	1	19	1
Brown, Nate, W. Palm Beach*	1.000	8	68	3	0	71	2
Brumbaugh, Cliff, Calgary	1.000	8	50	0	0	50	3
Camilo, Jose, Brevard County*	.500	1	1	0	1	2	0
Chevalier, Virgil, Sarasota	.994	24	152	13	1	166	11
Coe, Ryan, Kissimmee	1.000	27	232	8	0	240	18
Colina, Roberto, St. Petersburg*	.988	96	783	43	10	836	60
Curl, John, Dunedin	.980	23	173	22	4	199	15
Dandridge, Brad, Vero Beach	.989	26	162	20	2	184	8
Diaz, Juan, Vero Beach	1.000	1	8	1	0	9	1
Duffy, James, Kissimmee	.991	17	107	8	1	116	6
Dukart, Derek, Tampa	1.000	3	19	1	0	20	3
Elliott, Zach, Clearwater	.994	81	628	41	4	673	54
Emmons, Scott, Tampa	.667	1	1	1	1	3	0

Player, Team	Pct.	G	PO	A	E	TC	DP
Epperson, Chad, Sarasota	1.000	30	206	24	0	230	19
Espinal, Juan, Sarasota	.981	55	386	26	8	420	37
Fernandez, Jose, W. Palm Beach	1.000	2	9	1	0	10	0
Fortin, Troy, Fort Myers	.989	72	611	43	7	661	42
Fraraccio, Dan, St. Petersburg	.993	17	126	11	1	138	14
Freire, Alejandro, Lakeland	.986	124	1114	76	17	1207	87
Gainey, Bryon, St. Lucie	.984	79	679	56	12	747	50
Gallagher, Shawn, Calgary	.984	27	232	10	4	246	18
Garcia, Neil, St. Petersburg	1.000	2	2	0	0	2	0
Gonzalez, Jimmy, Kissimmee	.961	8	67	7	3	77	7
Goodell, Steve, Brevard County	.990	20	184	5	2	191	14
Gunderson, Shane, Fort Myers	1.000	1	8	0	0	8	0
Haas, Matt, W. Palm Beach	.983	16	105	10	2	117	15
Hamilton, Joe, Sarasota	1.000	3	2	0	0	2	0
Haws, Scott, Clearwater	.973	8	67	5	2	74	6
Hayes, Chris, Dunedin	1.000	11	63	4	0	67	4
Hillenbrand, Shea, Sarasota	.967	22	170	6	6	182	13
Johnson, Travis, Fort Myers	.800	1	4	0	1	5	1
Knowles, Eric, St. Lucie	1.000	1	5	3	0	8	0
Knupfer, Jason, Clearwater	1.000	1	3	0	0	3	1
Lindstrom, David, Lakeland	.986	19	132	10	2	144	6

Player, Team	Pct.	G	PO	A	E	TC	DP
Manning, Nate, Daytona	.982	13	103	8	2	113	5
Martinez, Rafael, St. Lucie*	.989	59	524	29	6	559	42
McMullen, Jon, Clearwater	.977	21	162	10	4	176	15
Millan, Adan, Clearwater	.966	8	75	10	3	88	3
Nevin, Phil, Lakeland	1.000	1	9	1	0	10	2
Ortiz, David, Fort Myers*	.984	59	524	44	9	577	52
Owens, Billy, Kissimmee	.991	84	759	53	7	819	61
Pierzynski, A.J., Fort Myers	1.000	2	16	0	0	16	1
Pomierski, Joe, St. Petersburg	.996	30	247	18	1	266	14
Raifstanger, John, Sarasota	.978	29	171	7	4	182	14
Redmond, Mike, Brevard County	1.000	1	8	0	0	8	1
Rivero, Eddie, Clearwater*	.965	16	134	2	5	141	14
Rodriguez, Maximo, B.C.	1.000	1	10	0	0	10	2
Rodriguez, Noel, Kissimmee	1.000	9	67	12	0	79	5
Rolison, Nate, Brevard County	.985	115	1036	69	17	1122	89
Ross, Tony, Kissimmee	1.000	1	2	0	0	2	1
Salzano, Jerry, Lakeland	1.000	1	9	0	0	9	1
Samuel, Cody, Tampa	1.000	12	81	8	0	89	8
Schramm, Kevin, Calgary	.984	82	683	58	12	753	63
Seguignol, Fernando, W.P.B.	.986	115	962	91	15	1068	71
Smith, Jeff, Fort Myers	.980	8	47	3	1	51	4
Stone, Craig, Dunedin	.981	39	229	27	5	261	14
Torres, Jaime, Tampa	1.000	2	17	0	0	17	1
Torti, Michael, Clearwater	.984	14	117	9	2	128	10
Truby, Chris, Kissimmee	1.000	5	22	2	0	24	2
TUCKER, Jon, Vero Beach*	.991	113	869	62	8	939	76
Valette, Ramon, Daytona	1.000	1	3	0	0	3	1
Vieira, Scott, Daytona	.987	126	1114	63	15	1192	79
Villalobos, Carlos, Lakeland	1.000	1	12	1	0	13	1
Watkins, Sean, Calgary*	.989	20	173	11	2	186	19
White, Walter, Brevard County	1.000	3	33	1	0	34	4
Whitlock, Mike, Dunedin	.976	86	743	70	20	833	63
Wingate, Ervan, Vero Beach	1.000	12	61	4	0	65	8
Yedo, Carlos, Tampa*	.983	130	1116	91	21	1228	86
Zywica, Michael, Calgary	1.000	7	42	3	0	45	5

TRIPLE PLAY: Stone.

Player, Team	Pct.	G	PO	A	E	TC	DP
Mansavage, Jay, Kissimmee	.882	4	6	9	2	17	1
Marino, Lawrence, Sarasota	.875	2	2	5	1	8	0
Marsh, Roy, Sarasota	1.000	1	1	0	0	1	0
Marshall, Monte, Vero Beach	.950	11	6	13	1	20	2
McLemore, Mark, Calgary	1.000	2	3	3	0	6	1
Mejia, Juan, Clearwater	.947	23	49	58	6	113	13
Miller, Ryan, St.L.-Kis.	.956	20	43	44	4	91	12
Morimoto, Ken, Vero Beach	1.000	2	0	1	0	1	0
Morris, Warren, Calgary	.962	99	192	241	17	450	60
Nieves, Jose, Daytona	.960	18	48	49	4	101	12
Paez, Israel, Fort Myers	.989	33	71	110	2	183	23
Parra, Franklin, St. Lucie	1.000	2	4	3	0	7	0
Parra, Jose, Calgary	1.000	1	2	0	0	2	0
Parsons, Jeff, St. Lucie	1.000	3	7	7	0	14	2
Patel, Manny, St. Petersburg	.980	127	209	335	11	555	55
Peeples, Michael, Dunedin	.961	124	219	341	23	583	61
Perez, Jhonny, Kissimmee	.842	4	3	13	3	19	0
Raifstanger, John, Sarasota	.977	16	20	23	1	44	4
Robles, Oscar, Kissimmee	.973	65	119	170	8	297	35
Samboy, Nelson, Kissimmee	.978	48	92	126	5	223	21
Sanchez, Orlando, Sarasota	.857	2	3	3	1	7	2
Sandberg, Jared, St. Petersburg	1.000	2	4	5	0	9	0
Santo, Jose, Calgary	.833	2	4	6	2	12	1
Skett, Will, Dunedin	1.000	3	3	5	0	8	1
Soriano, Fred, Dunedin	1.000	3	4	6	0	10	2
Sosa, Juan, Vero Beach	.971	32	63	72	4	139	16
Sotelo, Danilo, Vero Beach	.988	22	30	53	1	84	10
Strange, Mike, Dunedin	.900	15	16	20	4	40	3
Taylor, Greg, Clearwater	.985	12	32	33	1	66	12
Tebbs, Nate, Sarasota	.977	26	35	51	2	88	12
Truby, Chris, Kissimmee	1.000	1	2	3	0	5	1
Valette, Ramon, Daytona	.987	20	29	47	1	77	11
Vaughn, Lateef, Fort Myers	1.000	1	1	2	0	3	1
White, Walter, Brevard County	.984	15	22	40	1	63	9
Wingate, Ervan, Vero Beach	.975	14	16	23	1	40	3
Zorrilla, Julio, St. Lucie	.975	116	234	313	14	561	74

TRIPLE PLAY: Peeples.

SECOND BASEMEN

Player, Team	Pct.	G	PO	A	E	TC	DP
Adams, Jason, Kissimmee	1.000	4	6	16	0	22	4
Allison, Chris, Sarasota	.973	106	185	277	13	475	59
August, Brian, Tampa	.955	6	11	10	1	22	6
Bautista, Rayner, Lakeland	1.000	3	1	2	0	3	0
Bravo, Danny, W. Palm Beach	.902	12	18	19	4	41	8
Bream, Scott, Lakeland	1.000	4	11	14	0	25	2
Brinkley, Josh, W. Palm Beach	.961	18	34	40	3	77	4
Brooks, Eddie, St. Lucie	.966	9	11	17	1	29	3
Brown, Ron, Tampa	.864	5	9	10	3	22	2
Brown, Vick, Tampa	.974	122	236	319	15	570	53
Brumbaugh, Cliff, Calgary	1.000	2	3	8	0	11	2
Bustos, Saul, W. Palm Beach	.979	23	28	65	2	95	11
Cabrera, Orlando, W.P.B.	1.000	3	4	5	0	9	1
Camilli, Jason, W. Palm Beach	.870	5	13	7	3	23	1
Carroll, Jamey, W. Palm Beach	.965	36	56	108	6	170	22
Cey, Dan, Fort Myers	1.000	14	25	23	0	48	5
Coquillette, Trace, W.P.B.	.966	44	90	109	7	206	18
Corps, Erick, St. Petersburg	.938	8	11	19	2	32	5
Cranford, Joe, Fort Myers	.954	100	178	280	22	480	57
Dallimore, Brian, Kissimmee	1.000	1	2	0	0	2	0
Darden, Tony, Brevard County	1.000	6	7	10	0	17	2
Demetral, Chris, Vero Beach	.973	80	134	159	8	301	38
Dennis, Les, Tampa	1.000	8	9	17	0	26	3
Elliott, Zach, Clearwater	.900	9	10	17	3	30	2
Escalona, Felix, Kissimmee	.833	3	7	8	3	18	0
Font, Franklin, Daytona	.800	1	2	2	1	5	0
Fraraccio, Dan, St. Petersburg	1.000	4	7	8	0	15	2
Freel, Ryan, Dunedin	.862	7	11	14	4	29	3
Fuentes, Javier, Sarasota	1.000	6	15	15	0	30	5
Garcia, Amaury, Brevard County	.973	124	246	329	16	591	66
Garcia, Carlos, Fort Myers	1.000	4	2	3	0	5	0
Garcia, Neil, St. Petersburg	1.000	1	0	1	0	1	0
Gorecki, Ryan, Calgary	.981	36	64	94	3	161	24
Hudler, Rex, Clearwater	1.000	2	3	2	0	5	1
Jasco, Elinton, Daytona	.946	81	148	202	20	370	36
Knowles, Eric, St. Lucie	1.000	4	6	15	0	21	3
Knupfer, Jason, Clearwater	.960	99	190	291	20	501	51
Lackey, Steve, Lakeland	.947	18	45	44	5	94	8
Leidens, Enrique, WP.B.	1.000	4	3	2	0	5	0
Lewis, Keith, Daytona	.983	26	44	71	2	119	6
Lobaton, Jose, Tampa	1.000	2	1	3	0	4	0
Lugo, Julio, Kissimmee	.969	9	10	21	1	32	3
MACIAS, Jose, Lakeland	.989	120	255	349	7	611	65

SECOND BASEMEN WITH TWO OR MORE TEAMS

Player, Team	Pct.	G	PO	A	E	TC	DP
Miller, Ryan, St. Lucie	.947	14	28	26	3	57	7
Miller, Ryan, Kissimmee	.971	6	15	18	1	34	5

THIRD BASEMEN

Player, Team	Pct.	G	PO	A	E	TC	DP
Adams, Jason, Kissimmee	.884	23	9	52	8	69	3
Andrews, Shane, W. Palm Beach	.917	2	2	9	1	12	1
August, Brian, Tampa	.853	13	7	22	5	34	1
Balfe, Ryan, Lakeland	.907	75	44	161	21	226	14
Barnes, Kelvin, Daytona	.849	55	28	96	22	146	4
Bautista, Jorge, Brevard County	.950	9	4	15	1	20	1
Bazzani, Matt, Sarasota	.000	1	0	0	1	1	0
Beltre, Adrian, Vero Beach	.895	121	83	231	37	351	26
Blake, Casey, Dunedin	.895	121	98	235	39	372	23
Bovender, Andy, Kissimmee	.883	48	28	100	17	145	5
Braughler, Matt, Brevard County	1.000	1	0	2	0	2	0
Bravo, Danny, W. Palm Beach	1.000	1	1	2	0	3	0
Bream, Scott, Lakeland	.824	5	1	13	3	17	0
Brinkley, Josh, W. Palm Beach	.882	31	16	44	8	68	1
Brooks, Eddie, St. Lucie	.959	21	12	35	2	49	6
BRUMBAUGH, Cliff, Calgary	.958	128	93	271	16	380	19
Bustos, Saul, W. Palm Beach	.929	14	6	20	2	28	0
Coe, Ryan, Kissimmee	.882	6	3	12	2	17	0
Coquillette, Trace, W.P.B.	1.000	1	0	2	0	2	0
Corps, Erick, St. Petersburg	1.000	1	1	1	0	2	0
Cranford, Joe, Fort Myers	1.000	3	0	2	0	2	0
Cruz, Alain, Tampa	.944	6	5	12	1	18	0
Dandridge, Brad, Vero Beach	1.000	1	3	0	0	3	0
Darden, Tony, Brevard County	.921	90	58	187	21	266	10
Dennis, Les, Tampa	.882	28	3	12	2	17	0
Dransfeldt, Kelly, Calgary	1.000	3	0	6	0	6	0
Dukart, Derek, Tampa	.908	24	8	51	6	65	2
Elliott, Zach, Clearwater	.934	47	34	79	8	121	6
Erickson, Corey, St. Lucie	.891	44	27	88	14	129	8
Espinal, Juan, Sarasota	.876	41	21	71	13	105	5
Evans, Tom, Dunedin	.900	4	6	12	2	20	1
Fernandez, Jose, W. Palm Beach	.948	92	80	192	15	287	14
Fraraccio, Dan, St. Petersburg	.953	53	49	92	7	148	5
Freel, Ryan, Dunedin	.667	4	2	0	1	3	0
Garcia, Carlos, Fort Myers	1.000	1	0	1	0	1	0
Garcia, Neil, St. Petersburg	1.000	3	4	2	0	6	1
Goodell, Steve, Brevard County	.853	36	26	61	15	102	4

Player, Team	Pct.	G	PO	A	E	TC	DP
Gorecki, Ryan, Calgary	.895	7	4	13	2	19	3
Hayes, Chris, Dunedin	.722	6	3	10	5	18	0
Hillenbrand, Shea, Sarasota	.843	34	28	47	14	89	4
Jaime, Angel, St. Lucie	.545	3	2	4	5	11	1
Kane, Ryan, Tampa	.928	91	65	181	19	265	15
King, Cesar, Calgary	1.000	1	1	0	0	1	0
Knowles, Eric, St. Lucie	.895	11	7	27	4	38	2
Knupfer, Jason, Clearwater	.833	10	6	24	6	36	3
Lackey, Steve, Lakeland	.838	26	13	44	11	68	4
Lewis, Jeremy, Daytona	.500	1	1	0	1	2	0
Lewis, Keith, Daytona	.800	32	6	10	4	20	0
Liniak, Cole, Sarasota	.895	60	38	116	18	172	8
Lobaton, Jose, Tampa	.900	5	3	6	1	10	0
Lopez, Jose, St. Lucie	1.000	3	7	4	0	11	1
Lopez, Pee Wee, St. Lucie	.905	12	4	15	2	21	1
Lugo, Julio, Kissimmee	1.000	1	0	2	0	2	0
Manning, Nate, Daytona	.865	69	47	113	25	185	12
Mansavage, Jay, Kissimmee	.846	4	1	10	2	13	1
Marino, Lawrence, Sarasota	.800	2	1	3	1	5	0
Marsh, Roy, Sarasota	1.000	1	1	0	0	1	0
Meulens, Hensley, W.P.B.	1.000	1	0	2	0	2	0
Miller, Ryan, St.L.-Kis.	.855	29	16	43	10	69	5
Morris, Warren, Calgary	.875	2	1	6	1	8	1
Nevin, Phil, Lakeland	.750	1	0	3	1	4	0
Nichols, Keith, Clearwater	.667	4	1	3	2	6	1
Paez, Israel, Fort Myers	.938	99	70	185	17	272	17
Parra, Jose, Calgary	1.000	1	1	2	0	3	0
Parsons, Jeff, St. Lucie	.895	34	16	69	10	95	5
Pomierski, Joe, St. Petersburg	.889	5	4	12	2	18	2
Raifstanger, John, Sarasota	.333	3	0	1	2	3	0
Romano, Scott, St. Petersburg	.925	80	58	165	18	241	11
Roper, Chad, Fort Myers	.916	39	19	79	9	107	5
Salzano, Jerry, Lakeland	.897	11	10	16	3	29	0
Sanchez, Orlando, Sarasota	1.000	2	0	2	0	2	1
Schramm, Kevin, Calgary	.667	3	0	2	1	3	0
Soriano, Fred, Dunedin	.500	2	0	1	1	2	0
Sosa, Juan, Vero Beach	1.000	10	2	9	0	11	1
Stone, Craig, Dunedin	1.000	6	4	9	0	13	1
Strange, Mike, Dunedin	1.000	6	3	6	0	9	0
Taylor, Greg, Clearwater	.700	3	2	5	3	10	1
Tebbs, Nate, Sarasota	.972	13	9	26	1	36	3
Torti, Michael, Clearwater	.929	52	38	93	10	141	10
Truby, Chris, Kissimmee	.897	54	25	114	16	155	8
Valette, Ramon, Daytona	.902	27	12	34	5	51	5
Villalobos, Carlos, Lakeland	.879	28	22	58	11	91	6
Wesemann, Jason, Clearwater	.968	37	19	42	2	63	2
Wheeler, Mike, Kissimmee	.750	5	1	2	1	4	0
White, Walter, Brevard County	.962	18	9	41	2	52	3
Wingate, Ervan, Vero Beach	.903	22	12	16	3	31	4

Player, Team	Pct.	G	PO	A	E	TC	DP
Goodell, Steve, Brevard County	.889	4	5	11	2	18	2
Guzman, Cristian, Tampa	.889	4	6	10	2	18	3
Harkrider, Kip, Vero Beach	.971	33	46	55	3	104	17
Jaime, Angel, St. Lucie	.833	9	6	19	5	30	1
Jasco, Elinton, Daytona	1.000	1	0	2	0	2	0
Jimenez, D'Angelo, Tampa	.953	93	147	283	21	451	49
Knowles, Eric, St. Lucie	.941	9	13	19	2	34	2
Knupfer, Jason, Clearwater	1.000	2	3	4	0	7	1
Lackey, Steve, Lakeland	.942	28	32	82	7	121	13
Lewis, Keith, Daytona	.750	3	4	8	4	16	2
Lugo, Julio, Kissimmee	.936	114	176	410	40	626	64
MARTIN, Chris, St. Petersburg	.958	102	194	242	19	455	50
Mejia, Juan, Clearwater	1.000	2	2	5	0	7	0
Mendez, Donaldo, Kissimmee	.960	5	12	12	1	25	0
Miller, Orlando, Lakeland	.933	3	3	11	1	15	1
Miller, Ryan, St.L.-Kis.	.941	26	26	54	5	85	7
Nieves, Jose, Daytona	.922	65	103	169	23	295	28
Paez, Israel, Fort Myers	1.000	2	1	2	0	3	0
Parra, Franklin, St. Lucie	.935	51	70	147	15	232	21
Parra, Jose, Calgary	.958	10	12	11	1	24	4
Parsons, Jeff, St. Lucie	1.000	2	4	9	0	13	3
Patel, Manny, St. Petersburg	.857	2	1	5	1	7	0
Patton, Greg, Sarasota	1.000	4	10	15	0	25	4
Perez, Jhonny, Kissimmee	.931	12	18	36	4	58	6
Perez, Santiago, Lakeland	.933	109	148	322	34	504	50
Polanco, Enohel, St. Lucie	.943	43	65	150	13	228	20
Raynor, Mark, Clearwater	.951	136	186	421	31	638	69
Reynoso, Ismael, B.C>	1.000	2	2	2	0	4	0
Sanchez, Orlando, Sarasota	.891	34	38	77	14	129	14
Schifano, Anthony, B.C.	1.000	1	0	1	0	1	0
Soriano, Fred, Dunedin	.949	18	27	48	4	79	3
Sosa, Juan, Vero Beach	.922	48	65	112	15	192	19
Strange, Mike, Dunedin	.867	15	18	34	8	60	4
Taylor, Greg, Clearwater	1.000	1	0	1	0	1	0
Tebbs, Nate, Sarasota	.952	76	109	188	15	312	40
Truby, Chris, Kissimmee	1.000	2	3	3	0	6	0
Valette, Ramon, Daytona	.944	61	77	192	16	285	22
Vaughn, Lateef, Fort Myers	.933	34	39	87	9	135	16
Warriax, Brandon, Calgary	.750	1	2	1	1	4	0
White, Walter, Brevard County	.917	21	29	48	7	84	5
Wingate, Ervan, Vero Beach	1.000	4	2	1	0	3	0
Woodward, Chris, Dunedin	.972	89	145	267	12	424	48
Yard, Bruce, Vero Beach	.947	65	95	175	15	285	27

TRIPLE PLAY: Soriano.

SHORTSTOPS WITH TWO OR MORE TEAMS

Player, Team	Pct.	G	PO	A	E	TC	DP
Miller, Ryan, St. Lucie	.940	25	26	52	5	83	7
Miller, Ryan, Kissimmee	1.000	1	0	2	0	2	0

THIRD BASEMEN WITH TWO OR MORE TEAMS

Player, Team	Pct.	G	PO	A	E	TC	DP
Miller, Ryan, St. Lucie	.860	22	12	37	8	57	4
Miller, Ryan, Kissimmee	.833	7	4	6	2	12	1

SHORTSTOPS

Player, Team	Pct.	G	PO	A	E	TC	DP
Acevedo, Luis, Calgary	.750	1	2	4	2	8	1
Adams, Jason, Kissimmee	.935	6	13	16	2	31	3
Alexander, Manny, St. Lucie	1.000	1	1	4	0	5	0
August, Brian, Tampa	.909	3	3	7	1	11	1
Bautista, Rayner, Lakeland	.846	3	4	7	2	13	2
Bream, Scott, Lakeland	1.000	1	1	3	0	4	0
Brooks, Eddie, St. Lucie	.933	8	10	18	2	30	5
Brumbaugh, Cliff, Calgary	1.000	1	0	1	0	1	0
Bustos, Saul, W. Palm Beach	.800	3	1	7	2	10	0
Cabrera, Orlando, WP.B.	.925	61	88	157	20	265	29
Camilli, Jason, W. Palm Beach	.921	10	18	17	3	38	4
Carroll, Jamey, W. Palm Beach	.943	59	86	180	16	282	31
Cey, Dan, Fort Myers	.913	68	84	178	25	287	39
Corps, Erick, St. Petersburg	.947	17	26	45	4	75	10
Darden, Tony, Brevard County	.912	7	9	22	3	34	7
Delarosa, Tomas, WP.B.	.917	4	5	6	1	12	0
Dennis, Les, Tampa	.949	43	68	120	10	198	21
Dransfeldt, Kelly, Calgary	.942	133	227	363	36	626	85
Espinal, Juan, Sarasota	.667	2	1	1	1	3	0
Font, Franklin, Sarasota	.950	17	16	41	3	60	6
Fraraccio, Dan, St. Petersburg	.973	19	29	42	2	73	8
Freel, Ryan, Dunedin	.899	27	37	79	13	129	10
Fuentes, Javier, Sarasota	.901	39	54	83	15	152	13
Funaro, Joe, Brevard County	.952	112	185	350	27	562	65
Garcia, Carlos, Fort Myers	.966	52	58	140	7	205	25

OUTFIELDERS

Player, Team	Pct.	G	PO	A	E	TC	DP
Adolfo, Carlos, W. Palm Beach	.955	117	226	8	11	245	2
Airoso, Kurt, Lakeland	.957	16	21	1	1	23	0
Alexander, Chad, Kissimmee	.992	128	231	8	2	241	2
Allen, Chad, Fort Myers	.977	105	206	10	5	221	1
Alvarez, Rafael, Fort Myers*	.966	29	55	1	2	58	1
Barker, Glen, Lakeland	1.000	13	34	0	0	34	0
Barnes, Kelvin, Daytona	.902	23	35	2	4	41	1
Bass, Jayson, Lakeland*	.962	86	146	7	6	159	0
Bates, Fletcher, St. Lucie	.945	63	100	4	6	110	1
Bentley, Kevin, Daytona	.976	24	40	0	1	41	0
Berkman, Lance, Kissimmee*	1.000	44	70	2	0	72	1
Bess, Johnny, W. Palm Beach	1.000	1	2	0	0	2	0
Blosser, Greg, St. Petersburg*	.976	44	75	5	2	82	0
Bowers, R.J., Kissimmee	.864	10	17	2	3	22	0
Brinkley, Josh, W. Palm Beach	.929	16	12	1	1	14	0
Brown, Nate, W. Palm Beach*	1.000	7	9	1	0	10	0
Brown, Roosevelt, B.C.	.980	31	44	5	1	50	0
Brumfield, Jacob, Dunedin	.900	6	7	2	1	10	0
Buccheri, Jim, St. Petersburg	.965	46	106	3	4	113	0
Byrd, Tony, W. Palm Beach	1.000	5	8	0	0	8	0
Camilo, Jose, Brevard County*	.977	86	167	2	4	173	1
Campos, Jesus, W. Palm Beach	1.000	28	50	2	0	52	0
Carroll, Doug, St. Petersburg	.988	45	81	4	1	86	1
Choi, Kyung, Sarasota*	.963	49	75	2	3	80	0
Colon, Jose, Daytona	1.000	50	64	2	0	66	0
Conner, Decomba, Lakeland	1.000	56	133	1	0	134	0
Cornelius, Jonathon, Clearwater	1.000	17	16	2	0	18	0
Costello, Brian, Clearwater	.973	82	139	7	4	150	2
Crane, Todd, Clearwater	1.000	2	2	0	0	2	0
Curl, John, Dunedin	1.000	3	0	1	0	1	0

Player, Team	Pct.	G	PO	A	E	TC	DP
Dandridge, Brad, Vero Beach	1.000	20	21	1	0	22	0
Darden, Tony, Brevard County	1.000	4	4	0	0	4	0
Deshazer, Jeremy, Kissimmee	1.000	2	3	0	0	3	0
Duffy, James, Kissimmee	1.000	2	4	0	0	4	0
Faggett, Ethan, Sarasota*	.946	111	184	9	11	204	3
Foster, Quincy, Brevard County	.967	60	142	3	5	150	3
Francia, David, Clearwater*	.947	21	36	0	2	38	0
Fraraccio, Dan, St. Petersburg	1.000	14	17	0	0	17	0
Freel, Ryan, Dunedin	1.000	18	38	0	0	38	0
French, Anton, Dunedin	.950	75	168	2	9	179	0
Funaro, Joe, Brevard County	1.000	1	2	0	0	2	0
Goodell, Steve, Brevard County	.976	54	74	6	2	82	0
Guerrero, Vladimir, W.P.B.	1.000	3	4	1	0	5	0
Gunderson, Shane, Fort Myers	1.000	13	23	1	0	24	1
Haas, Matt, W. Palm Beach	.979	30	45	2	1	48	0
Hall, Ronnie, Daytona	.936	123	182	7	13	202	0
Hamilton, Joe, Sarasota	.967	76	115	1	4	120	0
HARVEY, Aaron, Brevard County	.994	94	155	9	1	165	2
Hawkins, Kraig, Tampa	.882	9	14	1	2	17	0
Hayes, Chris, Dunedin	.941	32	45	3	3	51	0
Hernaiz, Juan, Lakeland	.976	104	197	3	5	205	1
Hudler, Rex, Clearwater	1.000	3	7	0	0	7	0
Jaime, Angel, St. Lucie	.942	61	96	2	6	104	0
Johnson, Ric, Kissimmee	.983	121	274	7	5	286	1
Johnson, Travis, Fort Myers	.984	36	58	4	1	63	0
Jones, Jacque, Fort Myers*	.979	131	313	8	7	328	2
Jones, Jaime, Brevard County*	.935	61	100	1	7	108	0
Kapler, Gabe, Lakeland	.978	137	252	14	6	272	3
Keel, David, Tampa	.966	53	84	2	3	89	0
Kelley, Erskine, Daytona	.978	26	44	0	1	45	0
Kelly, Roberto, Fort Myers	1.000	4	6	0	0	6	0
Kennedy, Gus, Daytona	.980	97	138	8	3	149	0
Key, Jeff, Clearwater	.971	102	157	8	5	170	0
King, Andre, St. Petersburg	.943	40	64	2	4	70	0
Kofler, Eric, Tampa*	.973	39	68	4	2	74	0
Langaigne, Selwyn, Dunedin*	1.000	41	67	1	0	68	0
Long, Terrence, St. Lucie*	.972	117	235	7	7	249	1
Maness, Dwight, St. Lucie	.989	41	85	2	1	88	0
Marsh, Roy, Sarasota	.975	92	150	7	4	161	2
Martinez, Rafael, St. Lucie*	1.000	1	3	0	0	3	0
Mateo, Ruben, Calgary	.958	91	174	10	8	192	0
McCain, Marcus, St. Petersburg	.966	82	195	4	7	206	0
McDonald, Donzell, Tampa	.978	77	173	3	4	180	1
Monroe, Craig, Calgary	.959	90	151	13	7	171	5
Morenz, Shea, Tampa	.957	116	169	10	8	187	1
Morrow, Nick, St. Petersburg	.979	107	266	13	6	285	3
Mucker, Kelcey, Fort Myers	.984	103	187	2	3	192	0
Mulvehill, Brandon, St. Lucie	1.000	2	2	1	0	3	0
Myers, Adrian, Calgary	.994	73	168	3	1	172	0
Nelson, Charles, Vero Beach*	.987	99	146	3	2	151	1
Nunez, Juan, Calgary	.917	21	21	1	2	24	0
Padilla, Roy, Sarasota*	.968	126	327	9	11	347	3
Parsons, Jeff, St. Lucie	1.000	7	7	2	0	9	0
Peck, Tom, Dunedin	.920	26	22	1	2	25	0
Perez, Jhonny, Kissimmee	1.000	6	12	1	0	13	0
Pimentel, Jose, Vero Beach	.979	99	174	16	4	194	2
Pomierski, Joe, St. Petersburg	.987	56	74	1	1	76	1
Porter, Bo, Daytona	.984	118	237	10	4	251	0
Raifstanger, John, Sarasota	.963	17	26	0	1	27	0
Raines, Tim, Tampa	1.000	7	13	1	0	14	0
Richards, Rowan, Calgary	1.000	40	64	1	0	65	0
Rivero, Eddie, Clearwater*	.906	53	55	3	6	64	0
Rivers, Jonathan, Dunedin	.959	130	198	14	9	221	4
Robinson, Hassan, Kissimmee	.961	32	45	4	2	51	0
Rodriguez, Noel, Kissimmee	1.000	14	15	1	0	16	0
Rodriques, Cecil, W. Palm Beach	1.000	13	15	1	0	16	0
Ross, Tony, Kissimmee	.990	60	99	1	1	101	0
Rowson, James, Tampa	.958	18	22	1	1	24	0
Salzano, Jerry, Lakeland	1.000	6	7	0	0	7	0
Sanders, Anthony, Dunedin	1.000	1	1	0	0	1	0
Sanderson, David, St. Lucie*	.968	67	119	2	4	125	0
Schwab, Chris, W. Palm Beach	.951	44	76	2	4	82	0
Seguignol, Fernando, W.P.B.	1.000	4	5	0	0	5	0
Sell, Chip, Vero Beach	.973	105	168	10	5	183	2
Shores, Scott, Clearwater	.947	22	34	2	2	38	0
Shumpert, Derek, Tampa	.970	43	98	0	3	101	0
Skett, Will, Dunedin	.979	95	176	10	4	190	1
Smith, Sloan, Tampa	.990	59	97	7	1	105	0
Stowers, Chris, W. Palm Beach*	.975	109	223	7	6	236	0
Stuckenschneider, Eric, V.B.	.991	117	208	4	2	214	0
Suplee, Ray, St. Petersburg	1.000	2	2	0	0	2	0
Taylor, Greg, Clearwater	1.000	2	2	0	0	2	0
Taylor, Reggie, Clearwater	.969	132	324	19	11	354	1
Valdez, Trovin, W. Palm Beach	.990	53	89	7	1	97	2
Wilcox, Luke, Tampa	1.000	12	10	0	0	10	0
Willis, Symmion, Dunedin	.975	52	75	4	2	81	0
Wilson, Preston, St. Lucie	.973	61	104	5	3	112	2
Wingate, Ervan, Vero Beach	1.000	6	1	0	0	1	0
Winn, Randy, Brevard County	1.000	36	95	0	0	95	0
Zywica, Michael, Calgary	.977	113	202	13	5	220	5

CATCHERS

Player, Team	Pct.	G	PO	A	E	TC	DP	PB
Amezcua, Adan, Kissimmee	.958	7	23	0	1	24	0	1
Barrett, Michael, W.P.B.	.982	96	629	78	13	720	1	19
Bazzani, Matt, Sarasota	.975	49	291	20	8	319	3	7
Bess, Johnny, W. Palm Beach	.990	14	83	13	1	97	2	1
Braughler, Matt, B.C.	.953	15	77	5	4	86	1	4
Cardona, Javier, Lakeland	.979	80	498	75	12	585	7	12
Carter, Bart, St. Petersburg	1.000	1	1	0	0	1	0	0
CASTRO, Ramon, Kissimmee	.992	104	630	88	6	724	6	15
Chapman, Scott, Kissimmee	1.000	2	12	2	0	14	0	1
Chevalier, Virgil, Sarasota	.981	65	376	37	8	421	2	11
Clark, Kevin, Sarasota	.933	1	12	2	1	15	0	0
Coe, Ryan, Kissimmee	.981	9	47	5	1	53	0	2
Cruz, Alain, Tampa	1.000	1	1	0	0	1	0	0
Dandridge, Brad, Vero Beach	.950	5	35	3	2	40	3	0
Diaz, Cesar, Dunedin	.982	96	656	97	14	767	3	14
Ellis, John, Calgary	1.000	1	2	1	0	3	0	1
Emmons, Scott, Tampa	.982	49	239	34	5	278	2	8
Engle, Beau, St. Lucie	1.000	8	29	2	0	31	1	4
Epperson, Chad, Sarasota	.977	42	265	31	7	303	0	14
Fagley, Dan, Brevard County	1.000	3	6	0	0	6	0	0
Fortin, Troy, Fort Myers	.971	22	151	14	5	170	1	2
Fuller, Brian, Lakeland	1.000	18	75	11	0	86	0	2
Garcia, Neil, St. Petersburg	.985	59	367	34	6	407	3	9
Gargiulo, Mike, St. Lucie	.972	12	58	11	2	71	1	3
Gil, Geronimo, Vero Beach	.975	63	457	58	13	528	8	18
Gonzalez, Jimmy, Kissimmee	.957	5	19	3	1	23	0	0
Goodwin, Joe, Calgary	.978	61	394	41	10	445	4	8
Haas, Matt, W. Palm Beach	1.000	2	14	0	0	14	0	0
Haws, Scott, Clearwater	.986	27	182	28	3	213	4	5
King, Cesar, Calgary	.985	85	552	84	10	646	10	18
Koehler, Jason, Dunedin	1.000	1	1	0	0	1	0	0
Kuilan, Hector, B.C.	.982	77	455	78	10	543	5	32
Lambert, Clark, St. Lucie	1.000	2	7	0	0	7	0	1
Lewis, Jeremy, Daytona	.970	51	310	44	11	365	4	10
Lindstrom, David, Lakeland	.977	53	250	49	7	306	2	1
Lopez, Pedro, Kissimmee	.987	24	145	12	2	159	0	2
Lopez, Pee Wee, St. Lucie	.982	95	532	70	11	613	8	20
Manfredi, Joel, Vero Beach	1.000	5	7	1	0	8	0	0
Marsters, Brandon, Clearwater	.986	44	305	55	5	365	1	7
McCartney, Sommer, B.C.	1.000	1	1	0	0	1	0	1
Micucci, Mike, Daytona	.987	47	275	31	4	310	3	5
Millan, Adan, Clearwater	.971	4	30	4	1	35	0	2
Molina, Jose, Daytona	.981	55	341	71	8	420	1	13
Montero, Luis, Calgary	1.000	1	2	0	0	2	0	0
Morales, Eric, St. Lucie	.979	35	215	23	5	243	2	7
Morales, Francisco, WP.B.	.985	26	180	15	3	198	0	8
Morgan, Dave, Dunedin	.965	13	75	7	3	85	4	4
Northeimer, Jamie, Clearwater	.993	18	135	13	1	149	1	5
Pierce, Kirk, Clearwater	.993	22	128	23	1	152	1	4
Pierzynski, A.J., Fort Myers	.987	105	661	78	10	749	6	18
Raifstanger, John, Sarasota	1.000	2	4	0	0	4	0	0
Rodriguez, Maximo, B.C.	.990	29	183	16	2	201	1	8
Roney, Chad, Vero Beach	1.000	13	50	2	0	52	1	1
Rowson, James, Tampa	.000	1	0	0	1	1	0	0
Smith, Jeff, Fort Myers	.984	18	120	5	2	127	0	2
Snusz, Chris, Clearwater	.982	36	192	22	4	218	1	10
Stone, Craig, Dunedin	.962	43	213	37	10	260	3	9
Stricklin, Scott, St. Petersburg	.990	85	511	77	6	594	8	3
Torres, Jaime, Tampa	.989	104	700	109	9	818	7	11
Treanor, Matt, Brevard County	1.000	22	127	14	0	141	3	1
Troilo, Jason, Tampa	.933	3	11	3	0	14	0	1
Twombley, Dennis, Tampa	1.000	4	26	2	0	28	0	1
Voita, Sam, St. Petersburg	.938	9	29	1	2	32	0	1
Walbeck, Matt, Lakeland	.933	3	14	0	1	15	0	0
Wilson, Steve, Vero Beach	.985	84	533	60	9	602	4	16

PITCHERS

Player, Team	Pct.	G	PO	A	E	TC	DP
Adkins, Tim, Dunedin*	.929	39	4	9	1	14	1
Aguiar, Douglas, Clearwater	1.000	1	1	1	0	2	0
Aquino, Julio, St. Petersburg	.933	50	3	11	1	15	1
Armas, Tony, Tam.-Sar.	1.000	12	4	12	0	16	0
Arrojo, Rolando, St. Petersburg	.952	16	2	18	1	21	0

Player, Team	Pct.	G	PO	A	E	TC	DP
Arroyo, Luis, St. Lucie*	1.000	36	10	11	0	21	0
Aucoin, Derek, W. Palm Beach	1.000	17	2	3	0	5	0
Avery, Steve, Sarasota*	1.000	1	1	1	0	2	0
Babineaux, Darrin, Vero Beach	.786	18	4	7	3	14	1
Bailey, Ben, Lakeland	.933	15	4	10	1	15	0
Baker, Jason, W. Palm Beach	.905	15	10	9	2	21	0
Barcelo, Marc, Daytona	.818	23	3	6	2	11	0
Barker, Richie, Daytona	.917	29	4	7	1	12	1
Barksdale, Shane, Kissimmee	1.000	3	0	3	0	3	0
Barnes, Keith, Sarasota*	1.000	28	5	13	0	18	1
Barnett, Marty, Clearwater	.955	17	6	15	1	22	0
Bauer, Chris, Lakeland	.833	19	3	7	2	12	0
Becker, Tom, Tampa	.889	25	2	6	1	9	1
Beech, Matt, Clearwater*	1.000	1	0	1	0	1	0
Bell, Mike, W. Palm Beach*	.903	41	13	15	3	31	1
Benz, Jacob, W. Palm Beach*	1.000	14	2	4	0	6	1
Berry, Jason, St. Petersburg	1.000	35	4	8	0	12	2
Bettencourt, Justin, Lakeland*	.833	25	3	17	4	24	1
Beverlin, Jason, Tampa	1.000	7	4	8	0	12	1
Birsner, Roark, Daytona	1.000	8	0	2	0	2	0
Blanco, Alberto, Kissimmee*	.939	19	9	22	2	33	3
Bland, Nate, Vero Beach*	.913	17	2	19	2	23	2
Blazier, Ron, Clearwater	.875	15	2	5	1	8	1
Boehringer, Brian, Tampa	1.000	3	0	5	0	5	0
Bogle, Sean, Daytona	1.000	9	0	2	0	2	0
Bowen, Ryan, Tampa	.600	4	0	3	2	5	0
Bowles, Brian, Dunedin	1.000	7	1	4	0	5	1
Brackeen, Colin, Dunedin*	1.000	6	0	3	0	3	0
Bradford, Josh, Dunedin	.938	28	19	26	3	48	3
Brannan, Ryan, Clearwater	1.000	21	3	8	0	11	0
Brittan, Corey, St. Lucie	.920	51	7	16	2	25	0
Brown, Charlie, Tampa	1.000	28	3	6	0	9	1
Brown, Darold, Daytona*	1.000	29	0	8	0	8	1
Bryant, Chris, Daytona*	1.000	8	0	4	0	4	0
Burger, Rob, Clearwater	.909	28	7	13	2	22	0
Cafaro, Rocco, St. Petersburg	1.000	19	0	4	0	4	0
Cain, Travis, St. Petersburg	.538	9	1	6	6	13	0
Callaway, Michael, St. Petersburg	.872	28	9	25	5	39	3
Cannon, Jon, Daytona*	1.000	2	2	3	0	5	0
Cannon, Kevan, Sarasota*	1.000	32	3	8	0	11	0
Caravelli, Mike, Brevard County*	.880	40	2	20	3	25	1
Carrasco, Troy, Fort Myers*	.850	12	4	13	3	20	0
Carroll, David, St. Petersburg*	.909	47	1	9	1	11	3
Castro, Tony, Brevard County	.667	14	1	3	2	6	0
Chambers, Scott, Vero Beach*	1.000	56	4	8	0	12	0
Chapman, Walker, Fort Myers	.714	27	3	7	4	14	1
Checo, Robinson, Sarasota	.875	11	1	6	1	8	0
Civit, Xavier, W. Palm Beach	1.000	4	1	1	0	2	0
Cobb, Trevor, Fort Myers*	.905	15	7	12	2	21	1
COGGIN, David, Clearwater	1.000	27	15	28	0	43	4
Cole, Jason, W. Palm Beach	1.000	11	0	7	0	7	0
Collins, Ed, Brevard County	.833	26	1	4	1	6	0
Cook, Derrick, Calgary	.882	8	8	7	2	17	0
Correa, Ed, Vero Beach	1.000	5	0	2	0	2	0
Correa, Ramser, Vero Beach	1.000	9	2	6	0	8	0
Crawford, Paxton, Sarasota	.667	12	2	2	2	6	0
Cressend, Jack, Sarasota	.972	28	13	22	1	36	0
Crowther, John, Dunedin	1.000	19	0	5	0	5	0
Daniels, John, St. Petersburg	.824	55	6	8	3	17	0
Danner, Adam, Brevard County	1.000	17	2	4	0	6	1
Darwin, David, Lakeland*	.957	12	9	13	1	23	3
DaSilva, Fernando, W.P.B.	1.000	30	3	8	0	11	0
Davey, Tom, Dunedin	.875	7	2	5	1	8	0
Davis, Doug, Calgary*	.900	9	4	5	1	10	0
Davis, Jason, Clearwater	1.000	24	2	10	0	12	1
Davis, John, Vero Beach	.714	11	1	4	2	7	0
DeJesus, Javier, Daytona*	1.000	8	0	4	0	4	0
DeLaCruz, Francisco, Tampa	.833	8	4	6	2	12	0
Dellamano, Anthony, Calgary	.714	15	2	3	2	7	0
DeLosSantos, Luis, Tampa	1.000	10	4	10	0	14	0
Dempster, Ryan, Brevard County	.848	28	10	18	5	33	1
DeWitt, Chris, Daytona	1.000	38	2	8	0	10	0
DeWitt, Scott, Brevard County*	.917	25	10	23	3	36	2
Dickey, R.A., Calgary	1.000	8	2	3	0	5	0
Dingman, Craig, Tampa	1.000	19	2	1	0	3	0
Dinyar, Eric, Lakeland	1.000	15	1	4	0	5	1
Diorio, Mike, Kissimmee	1.000	36	3	12	0	15	1
Dotel, Octavio, St. Lucie	1.000	22	2	10	0	12	0
Dudeck, Dave, Tampa	1.000	5	0	1	0	1	0
Duncan, Courtney, Daytona	.921	19	11	24	3	38	2
Durkovic, Peter, Lakeland*	1.000	40	8	10	0	18	2
Durocher, Jayson, W.P.B.	.750	25	11	7	6	24	1
Duvall, Mike, Brevard County*	1.000	11	3	1	0	4	0
Ehlers, Corey, Brevard County	.667	6	2	0	1	3	0
Einerston, Darrell, Tampa	.889	45	4	12	2	18	1
Escobar, Kelvim, Dunedin	1.000	3	0	3	0	3	0
Estavil, Mauricio, Clearwater*	1.000	9	3	4	0	7	2
Evans, Keith, W. Palm Beach	.950	7	2	17	1	20	2
Farnsworth, Kyle, Daytona	.963	27	9	17	1	27	2
Faulkner, Neal, Daytona	1.000	36	4	7	0	11	0
Fidge, Darren, Fort Myers	1.000	24	4	8	0	12	1
Ford, Ben, Tampa	1.000	32	2	8	0	10	0
Foster, Kris, Vero Beach	.737	17	4	10	5	19	0
Garcia, Freddy, Kissimmee	.949	27	10	27	2	39	5
Garcia, Miguel, Vero Beach	.957	45	12	10	1	23	2
Getz, Rod, Brevard County	.902	27	17	38	6	61	1
Gillian, Charlie, Fort Myers	1.000	10	1	1	0	2	0
Glynn, Ryan, Calgary	.966	23	14	14	1	29	2
Gomez, Miguel, Dunedin	1.000	21	4	3	0	7	1
Gonzalez, Juan, Brevard County	1.000	26	3	7	0	10	1
Graterol, Beiker, Dunedin	1.000	17	12	13	0	25	3
Green, Jason, Kissimmee	.857	8	2	4	1	7	0
Gulin, Lindsay, St. Lucie*	.900	9	5	4	1	10	0
Haigler, Phil, Fort Myers	.959	25	15	32	2	49	2
Hale, Chad, Kissimmee*	1.000	46	3	8	0	11	0
Hall, Billy, Kissimmee	1.000	6	0	1	0	1	0
Hammack, Brandon, Daytona	.750	16	2	1	1	4	0
Hanson, Erik, Dunedin	1.000	2	3	2	0	5	0
Harnisch, Pete, St. Lucie	1.000	2	0	1	0	1	0
Harris, D.J., Dunedin	.895	42	7	10	2	19	0
Harris, Jeff, Fort Myers	.917	24	3	8	1	12	2
Hart, Len, Daytona*	1.000	8	0	1	0	1	0
Hartshorn, Tyson, Dunedin	.927	26	13	25	3	41	2
Harvey, Bryan, Brevard County ..	1.000	4	0	3	0	3	0
Harvey, Terry, St. Petersburg	1.000	18	1	8	0	9	0
Henry, Butch, Sarasota*	1.000	2	0	2	0	2	0
Hollis, Ron, Sarasota	1.000	13	0	2	0	2	0
Howard, Chris, St. Lucie*	1.000	10	1	1	0	2	0
Howatt, Jeff, St. Lucie	.875	39	4	3	1	8	0
Hower, Dan, Calgary*	1.000	2	0	2	0	2	0
Hurtado, Victor, Brevard County	1.000	17	2	11	0	13	1
Iddon, Brent, Sarasota	.800	37	5	7	3	15	1
Irabu, Hideki, Tampa	1.000	2	0	1	0	1	0
Isringhausen, Jason, St. Lucie	.667	2	0	2	1	3	0
Jarvis, Jason, Dunedin	.941	35	6	10	1	17	0
Johnson, Mark, Kissimmee	.913	26	13	29	4	46	2
Judd, Mike, Vero Beach	.941	14	5	11	1	17	0
Kaufman, John, St. Petersburg*	.929	26	3	23	2	28	0
Keppen, Jeffrey, Vero Beach	.947	32	5	13	1	19	1
Kershner, Jason, Clearwater*	.941	22	7	9	1	17	0
Kimbrell, Michael, St. Petersburg*	1.000	3	0	2	0	2	0
Kimsey, Keith, Lakeland	1.000	26	7	13	0	20	2
Knight, Brandon, Calgary	.947	14	4	14	1	19	2
Knoll, Randy, Clearwater	1.000	5	3	6	0	9	0
Koch, Bill, Dunedin	.889	3	2	6	1	9	1
Kojima, Keiichi, Calgary*	1.000	11	1	4	0	5	0
Kolb, Danny, Calgary	.969	24	6	25	1	32	0
Lail, Denny, Tampa	.955	44	3	18	1	22	2
Largusa, Levon, Daytona*	1.000	14	0	3	0	3	0
LaRosa, Tom, Fort Myers	.893	25	8	17	3	28	1
Larson, Toby, St. Lucie	1.000	4	1	0	0	1	0
Lee, Corey, Calgary*	1.000	23	9	21	0	30	2
Lee, Jeremy, Dunedin	.939	28	13	18	2	33	3
Lincoln, Mike, Fort Myers	.975	20	10	29	1	40	2
Lisio, Joseph, St. Lucie	1.000	48	4	8	0	12	0
Lock, Dan, Kissimmee*	.889	17	2	6	1	9	1
Loiz, Niuman, Kissimmee	1.000	11	2	2	0	4	0
Loubier, Scott, W. Palm Beach*	1.000	4	1	0	0	1	0
Lyons, Jonathan, Sarasota	.897	35	11	15	3	29	0
Mahaffey, Alan, Fort Myers*	1.000	38	3	7	0	10	0
Mairena, Oswaldo, Tampa*	1.000	3	0	1	0	1	0
Manias, James, St. Petersburg*	.900	28	8	19	3	30	0
Mann, Jim, Dunedin	1.000	12	0	1	0	1	0
Manning, Len, Clearwater*	1.000	5	0	1	0	1	0
Markey, Barry, Daytona	.907	22	17	22	4	43	3
Marquez, Robert, W.P.B.	.857	21	3	3	1	7	0
Marshall, Gary, Daytona*	1.000	22	0	2	0	2	0
Marsonek, Sam, Calgary	.500	2	0	1	1	2	0
Martinez, Javier, Daytona	.800	9	1	3	1	5	0
Martinez, Jose, Calgary	1.000	26	3	8	0	11	1
Masaoka, Onan, Vero Beach*	.960	28	17	31	2	50	1
Mattes, Troy, W. Palm Beach	.926	20	11	14	2	27	1
McBride, Chris, Dunedin	.889	10	1	7	1	9	2
McDonald, Matt, Vero Beach*	.944	57	2	15	1	18	1
McEntire, Ethan, St. Lucie*	1.000	3	0	6	0	6	0
McHugh, Mike, Calgary*	.875	18	2	5	1	8	1

Player, Team	Pct.	G	PO	A	E	TC	DP
McMullen, Jerry, Sarasota*	.900	33	3	6	1	10	1
McNeely, Mitch, Vero Beach*	.833	14	0	10	2	12	0
McNichol, Brian, Daytona*	1.000	6	1	6	0	7	0
Meinershagen, Adam, Dunedin	1.000	3	3	0	0	3	0
Mejia, Javier, Clearwater	1.000	52	8	8	0	16	0
Melendez, Dave, Lakeland	.960	15	6	18	1	25	1
Merrill, Ethan, Sarasota*	1.000	12	0	3	0	3	0
Miles, Chad, Brevard County*	.846	42	0	11	2	13	0
Miller, Wade, Kissimmee	1.000	14	13	16	0	29	1
Milton, Eric, Tampa*	1.000	14	6	10	0	16	1
Miranda, Walter, Brevard County	1.000	10	0	7	0	7	2
Mitchell, Scott, W. Palm Beach	1.000	39	5	10	0	15	2
Mlicki, Doug, Kissimmee	1.000	1	0	2	0	2	0
Moraga, David, W. Palm Beach*	.938	13	5	10	1	16	2
Morris, Alex, Brevard County	1.000	2	0	1	0	1	0
Mota, Henry, Calgary	.923	31	3	9	1	13	1
Mott, Tom, Fort Myers	1.000	14	2	3	0	5	0
Mudd, Scott, Calgary	1.000	4	0	1	0	1	0
Murray, Dan, St. Lucie	.886	30	9	22	4	35	1
Nakashima, Tony, Vero Beach*	1.000	10	1	2	0	3	0
Niedermaier, Brad, Fort Myers	.857	32	1	5	1	7	0
Norton, Phillip, Daytona*	1.000	7	1	6	0	7	0
Nyari, Pete, Clearwater	.875	31	1	6	1	8	0
O'Malley, Paul, Kissimmee	1.000	24	0	5	0	5	1
Oakley, Matt, Lakeland	1.000	27	3	3	0	6	0
Olson, Phillip, St. Lucie	.857	47	3	9	2	14	0
Ovalle, Bonelly, Calgary	.800	14	2	2	1	5	0
Paige, Carey, Dunedin	1.000	12	1	6	0	7	0
Pailthorpe, Bob, Brevard County	.917	35	9	13	2	24	1
Parker, Christian, W. Palm Beach	1.000	3	1	3	0	4	1
Parotte, Frisco, Daytona	1.000	5	0	2	0	2	0
Patino, Leonardo, Lakeland*	.923	40	3	9	1	13	0
Pena, Juan, Sarasota	.923	13	5	7	1	13	0
Phillips, Ben, Tampa	.903	25	13	15	3	31	1
Pierson, Jason, St. Lucie*	1.000	7	1	3	0	4	1
Powell, Brian, Lakeland	.962	27	24	26	2	52	1
Powell, Jeremy, W. Palm Beach	.950	26	15	23	2	40	1
Pujals, Denis, St. Petersburg	.968	24	11	19	1	31	3
Pulsipher, Bill, St. Lucie*	.833	12	2	8	2	12	0
Radlosky, Rob, Fort Myers	.952	23	5	15	1	21	0
Ramirez, Felix, Sarasota*	1.000	19	1	7	0	8	0
Ramsay, Robert, Sarasota*	.857	23	4	14	3	21	0
Randolph, Stephen, Tampa*	.944	34	4	13	1	18	1
Rath, Fred, Fort Myers	1.000	17	0	3	0	3	0
Reynoso, Armando, St. Lucie	1.000	2	1	2	0	3	1
Rhine, Kendall, Dunedin	1.000	4	1	2	0	3	0
Ricabal, Dan, Vero Beach	1.000	75	10	13	0	23	0
Richardson, Kasey, Fort Myers*	1.000	7	1	9	0	10	1
Ricketts, Chad, Daytona	1.000	20	1	6	0	7	0
Risley, Bill, Dunedin	1.000	8	1	2	0	3	0
Robbins, Jake, Tampa	.818	3	4	5	2	11	0
Romero, Juan, Fort Myers*	1.000	7	0	1	0	1	0
Root, Derek, Kissimmee*	.964	26	8	19	1	28	0
Roper, Chad, Fort Myers	.857	27	3	3	1	7	0
Roque, Rafael, St. Lucie*	.810	17	1	16	4	21	1
Rose, Brian, Sarasota	1.000	21	0	4	0	4	0
Rushing, Will, Fort Myers*	1.000	12	0	5	0	5	1
Ryan, Jay, Daytona	.912	27	6	25	3	34	0
St. Pierre, Bob, Tampa	1.000	27	6	10	0	16	1
Santiago, Derek, Brevard County	1.000	10	0	1	0	1	0
Santoro, Gary, Brevard County	1.000	20	4	2	0	6	1
Santos, Victor, Lakeland	.971	26	8	26	1	35	2
Schlomann, Brett, Tampa	.947	19	2	16	1	19	2
Schroeder, Chad, Lakeland	.750	12	2	1	1	4	0
Sekany, Jason, Sarasota	1.000	10	5	7	0	12	0
Shelby, Anthony, Tampa*	.955	48	5	16	1	22	0
Shumaker, Anthony, Clearwater*	1.000	61	4	8	0	12	0
Sievert, Mark, Dunedin	1.000	3	1	2	0	3	0
Sikorski, Brian, Kissimmee	.842	11	5	11	3	19	3
Sinclair, Steve, Dunedin*	.875	43	6	15	3	24	0
Smart, J.D., W. Palm Beach	.923	17	10	14	2	26	0
Smetana, Steve, Sarasota*	1.000	10	0	5	0	5	0
Smith, Dan, Calgary	.889	26	9	15	3	27	0
Smith, Eric, Kissimmee	.958	32	8	15	1	24	0
Smith, Keilan, Lakeland	1.000	40	4	11	0	15	1
Smith, Ottis, Calgary*	.909	27	5	15	2	22	0
Spence, Cam, Tampa	.923	15	6	6	1	13	1
Spinelli, Mike, Sarasota*	1.000	5	0	1	0	1	0
Splittorff, Jamie, Fort Myers	1.000	2	1	1	0	2	0
Spoljaric, Paul, Dunedin*	1.000	4	0	1	0	1	0
Spykstra, Dave, Vero Beach	.867	25	7	6	2	15	0
Stachler, Eric, Kissimmee	.857	48	4	2	1	7	0
Steinmetz, Earl, Kissimmee	1.000	4	1	1	0	2	1
Stentz, Brent, Fort Myers	1.000	49	2	5	0	7	0
Stephens, Shannon, B.C>	.927	27	12	26	3	41	2
Stevens, Kris, Clearwater*	.947	13	3	15	1	19	3
Stevenson, Rodney, W.P.B.	.833	26	2	3	1	6	0
Stewart, Scott, St. Lucie*	.963	22	2	24	1	27	0
Stumpf, Brian, Clearwater	1.000	17	3	2	0	5	1
Thomas, Evan, Clearwater	.909	13	5	5	1	11	0
Thompson, Chris, Sarasota	.846	29	6	5	2	13	0
Tolar, Kevin, St. Lucie*	1.000	9	0	3	0	3	1
Tribe, Byron, Daytona	.833	18	1	4	1	6	0
Trinidad, Hector, Fort Myers	1.000	2	1	1	0	2	0
Trumpour, Andy, St. Lucie	.943	27	6	27	2	35	0
Tucker, Julien, Kissimmee	.846	34	4	7	2	13	0
Urbina, Dan, Vero Beach	1.000	3	2	3	0	5	0
Valette, Ramon, Daytona	1.000	3	0	1	0	1	0
Vandemark, John, Clearwater*	.833	14	1	4	1	6	0
Van Poppel, Todd, Calgary	1.000	6	5	4	0	9	0
Vazquez, Javier, W. Palm Beach	.962	19	12	13	1	26	1
Venafro, Michael, Calgary*	1.000	35	8	11	0	19	1
Veniard, Jay, Dunedin*	1.000	2	17	0	0	19	0
Verdin, Cesar, Tampa*	.889	8	3	5	1	9	0
Viano, Jason, St. Petersburg	1.000	31	4	4	0	8	0
Wagner, Matt, W. Palm Beach	1.000	1	1	0	0	1	0
Wallace, Derek, St. Lucie	1.000	5	0	1	0	1	0
Weidert, Chris, W. Palm Beach	1.000	4	0	1	0	1	0
Westover, Richard, W.P.B.	.333	3	0	1	2	3	0
Whisenant, Matt, B.C.*	1.000	2	0	1	0	1	0
Whiteman, Greg, Clearwater*	.900	11	0	9	1	10	0
Williams, Matt, St. Petersburg*	1.000	43	5	8	0	13	0
Winslett, Dax, Daytona	1.000	9	3	0	0	3	0
Woodring, Jason, W.P.B.	1.000	16	1	7	0	8	0
Yarnall, Ed, St. Lucie*	.960	18	6	18	1	25	0
Ybarra, Jamie, St. Petersburg	1.000	3	1	1	0	2	0
Yeager, Gary, Clearwater	.962	39	2	23	1	26	0
Yennaco, Jay, Sarasota	1.000	7	6	0	0	6	0
Young, Tim, W. Palm Beach*	1.000	11	3	3	0	6	1
Zamarripa, Mark, Lakeland	.800	11	0	4	1	5	0

PITCHERS WITH TWO OR MORE TEAMS

Player, Team	Pct.	G	PO	A	E	TC	DP
Armas, Tony, Tampa	1.000	9	4	7	0	11	0
Armas, Tony, Sarasota	1.000	3	0	5	0	5	0

The following players did not have any fielding statistics at the positions indicated or appeared only as a designated hitter, pinch-hitter or pinch-runner: Alejo, p; Alvord, p; C. Alexander, 3b; D. Baker, dh; Bazzani, 1b, of; Beltre, of; Bennett, c; Bess, p; Blake, ss; Bosio, p; Brandenburg, p; Bravo, of; V. Brown, ss; Brumbaugh, c; Bullinger, p; Bustos, of, p; Doug Carroll, p; J. Carroll, 3b; Clark, of; Coquillette, of; Coronado, p; Corps, of; Cranford, of; Dace, p; DeClue, p; Jose Diaz, dh; Dollar, p; Eiland, p; Elliott, of; Feliciano, p; Flores, p; Fortin, 3b; Freeman, dh; C. Garcia, of; N. Garcia, of; Goodwin, 3b; Gorecki, p; J. Guzman, p; Handy, p; N. Hall, ph; Julio, p; Leslie, p; Lowe, p; Macias, of; Malenfant, p; D. Manning, p; Mantei, p; Markey, of; McClellan, p; Micucci, 2b; K. Miller, p; H. Morales, p; Morimoto, ss; Orta, of; Ovalles, 2b; Paniagua, of; Peeples, of; Porter, 2b; Quero, dh; Raifstanger, ss, p; Ramos, p; Resz, p; L. Rivera, ph; M. Rivera, p; M. Rodriguez, p; Sanchez, of; Sasaki, p; Sell, 1b; Skett, 3b; S. Smith, p; Sobik, p; Sotelo, ss; Strange, p; Strawberry, dh; Tapani, p; Tomberlin, dh; P. Wilson, p; Zaleski, p.

LEAGUE CHAMPIONS

Year	Team	Pct.	Year	Team	Pct.	Year	Team	Pct.
1919—	Sanford*	.605	1923—	Orlando	.667	1926—	Sanford	.647
	Orlando*	.703		Orlando	.678		Sanford	.623
1920—	Tampa	.654	1924—	Lakeland	.695	1927—	Orlando†	.600
	Tampa	.722		Lakeland	.683		Miami	.661
1921—	Orlando	.635	1925—	St. Petersburg	.667	1928-35—Did not operate.		
1922—	St. Petersburg	.503		Tampa†	.696	1936—	Gainesville	.542
	St. Petersburg	.618					St. Augustine (4th)†	.492

Year	Team	Pct.
1937—	Gainesville§	.616
1938—	Leesburg	.626
	Gainesville (2nd)‡	.615
1939—	Sanford§	.787
1940—	Daytona Beach	.619
	Orlando (4th)‡	.507
1941—	St. Augustine	.659
	Leesburg (4th)‡	.488
1942-45—	Did not operate.	
1946—	Orlando§	.681
1947—	St. Augustine	.625
	Gainesville (2nd)‡	.584
1948—	Orlando	.643
	Daytona Beach (2nd)‡	.616
1949—	Gainesville	.635
	St. Augustine (3rd)‡	.556
1950—	Orlando	.629
	DeLand (3rd)‡	.590
1951—	DeLand§	.643
1952—	DeLand∞	.704
	Palatka (3rd)‡	.569
1953—	Daytona Beach†	.657
	DeLand	.703
1954—	Jacksonville Beach	.629
	Lakeland†	.594
1955—	Orlando	.671
	Orlando	.643
1956—	Cocoa	.614
	Cocoa	.671
1957—	Palatka	.629
	Tampa†	.681
1958—	St. Petersburg	.732
	St. Petersburg	.681
1959—	Tampa	.591
	St. Petersburg†	.612
1960—	Lakeland	.731
	Palatka†	.614
1961—	Tampa†	.710
	Sarasota	.696

Year	Team	Pct.
1962—	Sarasota	.689
	Fort Lauderdale†	.623
1963—	Sarasota	.645
	Sarasota	.667
1964—	Fort Lauderdale†	.629
	St. Petersburg	.594
1965—	Fort Lauderdale	.627
	Fort Lauderdale	.634
1966—	Leesburg†	.781
	St. Petersburg	.700
1967—	St. Petersburg▲	.691
	Orlando	.638
1968—	Miami	.613
	Orlando◆	.579
1969—	Miami■	.606
	Orlando	.606
1970—	Miami▼	.662
	St. Petersburg	.600
1971—	Miami▼	.667
	Daytona Beach	.586
1972—	Miami•	.562
	Daytona Beach	.606
1973—	St. Petersburg††	.575
	West Palm Beach	.580
1974—	West Palm Beach††	.598
	Fort Lauderdale	.626
1975—	St. Petersburg††	.652
	Miami	.581
1976—	Tampa	.559
	Lakeland††	.536
1977—	Lakeland††	.616
	West Palm Beach	.583
1978—	Lakeland	.565
	Miami§	.539
1979—	Fort Lauderdale	.643
	Winter Haven‡‡	.577
1980—	Daytona Beach	.628
	Fort Lauderdale††	.606

Year	Team	Pct.
1981—	Fort Myers	.554
	Daytona Beach§§	.504
1982—	Fort Lauderdale§§	.621
	Tampa	.546
1983—	Daytona Beach	.634
	Vero Beach§§	.515
1984—	Tampa	.532
	Fort Lauderdale§§	.521
1985—	Fort Myers∞∞	.590
	Fort Lauderdale	.550
1986—	St. Petersburg∞∞	.647
	West Palm Beach	.593
1987—	Fort Lauderdale∞∞	.616
	Osceola	.576
1988—	Osceola	.606
	St. Lucie▲▲	.532
1989—	Port Charlotte▲▲	.540
	St. Petersburg	.540
1990—	West Palm Beach	.697
	Vero Beach▲▲	.585
1991—	Clearwater	.623
	West Palm Beach▲▲	.550
1992—	Sarasota	.639
	Lakeland◆◆	.530
1993—	St. Lucie	.600
	Clearwater§§	.556
1994—	Tampa§§	.606
	Brevard County	.561
1995—	Daytona§§	.644
	Fort Myers	.577
1996—	Tampa	.627
	St. Lucie§§	.534
1997—	St. Petersburg■ ■	.591
	Vero Beach	.511

*Split-season playoff abandoned after each team won three games. †Won split-season playoff. ‡Won four-club playoff. §Won championship and four-club playoff. ∞Won both halves of split season. ▲League divided into Eastern and Western divisions with split season. St. Petersburg and Orlando won both halves of split season; St. Petersburg won playoff. ◆League divided into Eastern and Western divisions. Miami won regular-season pennant on basis of highest won-lost percentage. Orlando won four-club playoff involving first two teams in each division. ■League divided into Southern and Central divisions. Miami won playoff between division leaders. (NOTE—Pennant awarded to playoff winner in 1936.) ▼League divided into Eastern and Western divisions. Miami won regular-season pennant on basis of highest won-loss percentage, and also won four-club playoff involving first two teams in each division. •League divided into Eastern and Western divisions. Won four-club playoff involving first two teams in each division. ††League divided into Northern and Southern divisions. Won four-club playoff involving first two teams in each division. ‡‡League divided into Northern and Southern divisions. Same two clubs won both halves; won playoffs. §§Won split-season playoff. ∞∞League divided into Western, Central and Southern divisions. Won four-club playoff. ▲▲League divided into Eastern, Western and Central divisions; played split-season. Won six-club playoff. ◆◆League divided into Eastern, Western and Central divisions; played split-season. Won eight-club playoff. ■ ■League divided into East and West divisions and played split season; won four-club playoff.

MIDWEST LEAGUE

LEAGUE OFFICE

President
George H. Spelius
Address
P.O. Box 936
Beloit, WI 53512
Phone
608-364-1188

Teams (affiliation)
Beloit Snappers (Brewers)
Burlington Bees (Reds)
Cedar Rapids Kernels (Angels)
Clinton Lumber Kings (Padres)
Fort Wayne Wizards (Twins)
Kane County Cougars (Marlins)
Lansing Lugnuts (Royals)

Michigan Battle Cats (Red Sox)
Peoria Chiefs (Cardinals)
Quad City River Bandits (Astros)
Rockford Cubbies (Cubs)
South Bend Silver Hawks (Diamondbacks)
West Michigan Whitecaps (Tigers)
Wisconsin Timber Rattlers (Mariners)

1997 FINAL STANDINGS

FIRST HALF

EASTERN DIVISION

Team	W	L	T	Pct.	GB
West Michigan (Tigers)	46	17	0	.730	....
Michigan (Red Sox)	38	31	0	.551	11
Lansing (Royals)	34	34	0	.500	14½
Fort Wayne (Twins)	32	33	0	.492	15
South Bend (Diamondbacks)	24	43	0	.358	24

CENTRAL DIVISION

Team	W	L	T	Pct.	GB
Wisconsin (Mariners)	40	29	0	.580	....
Beloit (Brewers)	32	32	0	.500	5½
Rockford (Cubs)	32	32	0	.500	5½
Peoria (Cardinals)	34	35	0	.493	6
Kane County (Marlins)	33	37	0	.471	7½

WESTERN DIVISION

Team	W	L	T	Pct.	GB
Burlington (Reds)	39	31	0	.557	....
Clinton (Padres)	33	34	0	.493	4½
Quad City (Astros)	26	38	0	.406	10
Cedar Rapids (Angels)	26	43	0	.377	12½

SECOND HALF

EASTERN DIVISION

Team	W	L	T	Pct.	GB
West Michigan (Tigers)	46	22	0	.676	....
Fort Wayne (Twins)	36	34	0	.514	11
Lansing (Royals)	35	34	0	.507	11½
Michigan (Red Sox)	32	36	0	.471	14
South Bend (Diamondbacks)	30	40	0	.429	17

CENTRAL DIVISION

Team	W	L	T	Pct.	GB
Kane County (Marlins)	37	31	0	.544	....
Wisconsin (Mariners)	36	34	0	.514	2
Peoria (Cardinals)	36	34	0	.514	2
Rockford (Cubs)	34	34	0	.500	3
Beloit (Brewers)	28	41	0	.406	9½

WESTERN DIVISION

Team	W	L	T	Pct.	GB
Cedar Rapids (Angels)	36	33	0	.522	....
Quad City (Astros)	33	37	0	.471	3½
Burlington (Reds)	33	37	0	.471	3½
Clinton (Padres)	32	37	0	.464	4

COMPOSITE

Team	W.M.	Wis.	Bur.	Mch.	K.C.	F.W.	Lan.	Peo.	Rck.	Cln.	Bel.	C.R.	Q.C.	S.B.	W	L	T	Pct.	GB
West Michigan (Tigers)	....	3	5	11	6	9	10	7	6	7	4	6	4	14	92	39	0	.702	....
Wisconsin (Mariners)	4	....	4	6	6	8	6	3	8	7	3	12	6	5	76	63	0	.547	20
Burlington (Reds)	3	4	....	4	2	3	3	4	3	15	6	11	10	4	72	68	0	.514	24½
Michigan (Red Sox)	4	2	4	....	3	10	12	3	4	3	5	4	6	10	70	67	0	.511	25
Kane County (Marlins)	2	10	6	5	....	4	4	12	6	3	6	3	6	3	70	68	0	.507	25½
Fort Wayne (Twins)	7	2	5	8	4	....	7	4	2	2	4	5	4	14	68	67	0	.504	26
Lansing (Royals)	8	5	5	6	3	9	....	3	3	2	4	6	4	11	69	68	0	.504	26
Peoria (Cardinals)	1	8	4	4	6	4	5	....	10	4	11	4	3	6	70	69	0	.504	26
Rockford (Cubs)	2	11	5	3	9	4	3	8	....	2	6	3	6	4	66	66	0	.500	26½
Clinton (Padres)	0	5	5	5	5	6	4	6	4	....	3	11	7	4	65	71	0	.478	29½
Beloit (Brewers)	1	6	2	3	12	3	4	5	10	5	....	4	2	3	60	73	0	.451	33
Cedar Rapids (Angels)	2	2	9	4	5	3	2	4	5	8	4	....	14	0	62	76	0	.449	33½
Quad City (Astros)	1	2	10	2	2	4	4	5	1	13	4	6	....	5	59	75	0	.440	34½
South Bend (Diamondbacks)	4	3	4	6	5	4	4	5	2	4	4	7	3	....	54	83	0	.394	41

Quad City's home games played in Davenport, Iowa.

Kane County's home games played in Geneva, Ill.

Michigan's home games played in Battle Creek, Mich.

West Michigan's home games played in Comstock Park, Mich.

Major league affiliations in parentheses.

PLAYOFFS: Cedar Rapids defeated Burlington, two games to none; Kane County defeated Wisconsin, two games to none; Fort Wayne defeated West Michigan, two games to none; Lansing defeated Michigan, two games to one; Kane County defeated Cedar Rapids, two games to none; Lansing defeated Fort Wayne, two games to none; Lansing defeated Kane County, three games to two, to win league championship.

REGULAR-SEASON ATTENDANCE: Beloit, 81,564; Burlington, 52,152; Cedar Rapids, 124,629; Clinton, 50,597; Fort Wayne, 230,210; Kane County, 436,505; Lansing, 523,443; Michigan, 126,947; Peoria, 148,585; Quad City, 130,932; Rockford, 86,716; South Bend, 197,864; West Michigan, 536,029; Wisconsin, 227,104. Total—2,953,277. Playoffs (18 games)—43,348. All-Star Game at Lansing, Mich.—10,060.

MANAGERS: Beloit, Luis Salazar; Burlington, Phillip Wellman; Cedar Rapids, Mario Mendoza; Clinton, Tom LeVasseur; Fort Wayne, Mike Boulanger; Kane County, Lynn Jones; Lansing, Bob Herold; Michigan, Billy Gardner; Peoria, Joe Cunningham; Quad City, Manny Acta; Rockford, Ruben Amaro; South Bend, Dickie Scott; West Michigan, Bruce Fields; Wisconsin, Gary Varsho.

ALL-STAR TEAM: 1B—Robert Fick, West Michigan; 2B—Jim Chamblee, Michigan; 3B—Jose Leon, Peoria; SS—Brent Butler, Peoria; OF—Jason Conti, South Bend; Julio Ramirez, Kane County; Brady Clark, Burlington; C—Chad Moeller, Fort Wayne; DH—Tyrone Horne, Kane County; LHP—Phillip Norton, Rockford; RHP—David Borkowski, West Michigan; LH Reliever—Chris Garza, Fort Wayne; RH Reliever—Francisco Cordero, West Michigan; Most Valuable Player—Robert Fick, West Michigan; Prospect of the Year—Brent Butler, Peoria; Manager of the Year—Bruce Fields, West Michigan.

CLASS A Midwest League

1997 BATTING
TEAM

Team	Avg.	G	TPA	AB	R	H	TB	2B	3B	HR	RBI	SH	SF	HP	BB	IBB	SO	SB	CS	GDP	LOB	SHO	Slg.	OBP
Lansing	.278	137	5364	4731	772	1316	1918	276	52	74	685	29	62	0	542	14	889	162	52	106	1105	5	.405	.348
West Michigan	.273	131	5103	4505	698	1229	1820	249	42	86	619	36	41	66	455	29	980	168	67	76	980	2	.404	.345
Burlington	.270	140	5292	4646	785	1255	2006	238	42	143	699	43	32	44	527	14	1158	162	76	89	906	2	.432	.348
Michigan	.264	137	5227	4591	725	1212	1826	231	37	103	640	20	44	91	481	17	965	103	46	97	995	9	.398	.343
Beloit	.261	133	4921	4480	619	1170	1726	218	34	90	550	41	31	2	367	12	853	95	81	102	914	3	.385	.315
Rockford	.261	132	4926	4339	594	1133	1584	228	38	49	503	39	38	72	438	17	1025	197	103	84	902	7	.365	.336
Wisconsin	.259	139	5198	4585	625	1187	1752	250	39	79	541	58	23	52	480	17	972	102	90	109	943	12	.382	.334
Fort Wayne	.255	135	5125	4568	627	1164	1671	203	38	76	548	45	32	58	422	14	973	173	82	96	920	9	.366	.324
Kane County	.254	138	5301	4541	667	1152	1636	196	27	78	596	69	40	53	598	37	944	137	64	102	1066	12	.360	.345
Quad City	.252	134	4898	4371	586	1103	1594	190	17	89	529	32	36	60	399	18	848	102	60	105	881	13	.365	.321
Peoria	.252	139	5216	4611	662	1160	1818	244	27	120	579	36	34	63	472	22	1079	125	69	87	947	5	.394	.327
South Bend	.251	137	5143	4499	591	1131	1627	223	45	61	527	34	37	47	526	17	1113	92	49	107	988	14	.362	.334
Cedar Rapids	.251	138	5180	4520	685	1135	1771	220	40	112	619	44	35	50	531	14	1080	135	71	99	910	8	.392	.334
Clinton	.245	136	5149	4422	644	1084	1584	184	56	68	557	28	42	55	602	21	1085	191	96	91	1003	5	.358	.340

INDIVIDUAL
TOP QUALIFIERS FOR BATTING CHAMPIONSHIP
Minimum 378 plate appearances. *Lefthanded batter. †Switch-hitter.

Player, Team	Avg.	G	TPA	AB	R	H	TB	2B	3B	HR	RBI	SH	SF	HP	BB	IBB	SO	SB	CS	GDP	Slg.	OBP
Fick, Robert, West Michigan*	.341	122	546	463	100	158	262	50	3	16	90	0	7	1	75	11	74	13	4	10	.566	.429
Miranda, Tony, Lansing	.341	104	456	387	85	132	192	35	5	5	72	0	5	10	54	2	62	11	10	10	.496	.430
Lopiccolo, Jamie, Beloit	.332	112	462	410	72	136	220	27	3	17	80	1	4	9	38	2	76	5	6	10	.537	.397
Clark, Brady, Burlington	.325	126	544	459	108	149	225	29	7	11	63	1	3	4	76	3	71	31	18	10	.490	.423
Abreu, Dennis, Rockford	.321	126	541	483	71	155	183	19	3	1	37	5	1	7	45	2	99	36	26	8	.379	.386
Harrison, Adonis, Wisconsin	.318	125	481	412	61	131	190	26	6	7	62	5	3	6	55	2	74	25	18	11	.461	.403
Ryan, Rob, South Bend*	.314	121	517	421	71	132	201	35	5	8	73	0	5	2	89	5	58	12	1	7	.477	.431
Sollmann, Scott, W. Mich.*	.313	121	560	460	89	144	165	13	4	0	33	8	3	11	79	5	81	40	14	1	.359	.423
Conti, Jason, South Bend*	.310	117	521	458	78	142	193	22	10	3	43	4	3	11	45	2	99	30	18	10	.421	.383
Butler, Brent, Peoria	.306	129	553	480	81	147	233	37	2	15	71	0	5	4	63	6	69	6	4	9	.485	.388
Horne, Tyrone, Kane County*	.306	133	566	489	89	143	234	24	2	21	91	0	1	3	104	18	88	18	7	13	.500	.434
Barnes, John, Michigan	.304	130	566	490	80	149	196	19	5	6	73	0	6	5	65	3	42	19	5	7	.400	.387
Meyers, Chad, Rockford	.301	125	536	439	89	132	180	28	4	4	58	6	7	10	74	5	72	54	16	4	.410	.408
Chamblee, James, Michigan	.300	133	562	487	112	146	251	29	5	22	73	0	5	17	53	3	107	18	4	8	.515	.384
Walther, Chris, Beloit	.300	113	474	437	55	131	164	25	4	0	38	3	1	5	28	0	41	5	7	16	.375	.348

DEPARTMENTAL LEADERS: G—Podsednik, 135; AB—Podsednik, 531; R—Chamblee, 112; H—Fick, 158; TB—Fick, 262; 2B—Fick, 50; 3B—Y. Sanchez, 12; HR—Freitas, 33; RBI—Ingram, 97; SH—J. Rodriguez, 18; SF—Garrett, 9; HP—Dallimore, 20; BB—Horne, 104; IBB—Horne, 18; SO—Ingram, 195; SB—Lindsey, 70; CS—D. Abreu, 26; GIDP—Veras, 19; Slg.—Fick, .566; OBP—Horne, .434.

ALL PLAYERS
*Lefthanded batter. †Switch-hitter.

Player, Team	Avg.	G	TPA	AB	R	H	TB	2B	3B	HR	RBI	SH	SF	HP	BB	IBB	SO	SB	CS	GDP	Slg.	OBP
Abbott, Chuck, C.R.†	.231	133	593	520	86	120	172	21	5	7	54	6	2	3	62	0	170	34	12	7	.331	.315
Abell, Antonio, Peoria	.160	13	30	25	4	4	4	0	0	0	2	0	1	4	0	12	2	2	0	.160	.300	
Abreu, Dennis, Rockford	.321	126	541	483	71	155	183	19	3	1	37	5	1	7	45	2	99	36	26	8	.379	.386
Abreu, Nelson, Rockford	.240	63	205	179	27	43	63	4	5	2	20	6	1	0	19	0	52	9	6	6	.352	.312
Adams, John, South Bend	.259	60	223	216	22	56	95	7	1	10	36	0	1	1	5	1	71	3	0	8	.440	.278
Agnoly, Earl, Kane County	.210	34	113	100	9	21	29	0	1	2	10	3	0	4	6	0	23	3	1	0	.290	.282
Ahumada, Alejandro, Mich.	.250	3	12	12	1	3	6	1	1	0	1	0	0	0	0	0	3	0	0	0	.500	.250
Airoso, Kurt, West Michigan	.297	14	44	37	6	11	16	5	0	0	2	0	1	0	6	0	15	0	0	0	.432	.386
Alaimo, Jason, Kane County	.244	36	99	90	7	22	33	5	0	2	10	0	2	2	5	1	25	1	2	0	.367	.293
Alfano, Jeff, Beloit	.231	37	139	121	14	28	41	3	2	2	16	1	1	7	9	0	32	3	1	4	.339	.319
Allen, Marlon, Burlington	.310	69	283	242	42	75	133	20	1	12	52	0	2	3	36	2	61	5	3	5	.550	.403
Alleyne, Roberto, Quad City	.260	63	230	215	24	56	81	10	0	5	30	1	0	2	12	0	55	1	3	6	.377	.306
Allison, Bradley, South Bend	.133	55	180	166	5	22	25	3	0	0	9	0	0	3	11	0	52	1	0	9	.151	.200
Amado, Jose, Lansing	.342	61	268	234	49	80	119	25	1	4	45	0	6	4	24	1	18	10	2	8	.509	.403
Amerson, Gordon, Clinton*	.235	34	130	102	13	24	37	7	3	0	16	0	2	1	25	0	31	6	2	0	.363	.385
Andersen, Ryan, Rockford	.264	19	60	53	2	14	17	3	0	0	4	1	0	0	6	0	10	1	0	2	.321	.339
Aversa, Joe, Kane County†	.202	63	243	203	17	41	48	3	2	0	17	6	3	1	30	1	58	3	1	4	.236	.304
Baderdeen, Kevin, Burlington	.220	39	145	127	18	28	40	3	0	3	8	2	0	2	14	0	61	3	1	0	.315	.308
Barnes, John, Michigan	.304	130	566	490	80	149	196	19	5	6	73	0	6	5	65	3	42	19	5	7	.400	.387
Barr, Tucker, Quad City	.207	93	353	309	42	64	106	10	1	10	36	0	1	4	39	0	91	0	2	4	.343	.303
Bautista, Jorge, Kane County	.149	20	76	67	9	10	13	3	0	0	7	1	2	1	5	0	18	2	2	2	.194	.213
Bautista, Juan, South Bend	.130	31	102	92	12	12	15	1	1	0	4	1	0	3	6	0	32	1	0	1	.163	.208
Bearden, Doug, Beloit	.221	56	172	163	15	36	41	3	1	0	14	4	0	3	2	0	37	1	1	4	.252	.244
Berger, Brandon, Lansing	.293	107	446	393	64	115	185	22	6	12	73	0	4	7	42	1	79	13	1	8	.471	.368
Blosser, Doug, Lansing*	.214	38	128	103	13	22	34	3	0	3	17	1	4	0	20	3	29	0	0	2	.330	.331
Bly, Derrick, Rockford	.242	109	438	392	48	95	148	19	5	8	43	2	2	6	35	0	131	6	3	7	.378	.313
Bolivar, Papo, Fort Wayne	.262	91	343	324	30	85	130	12	6	7	42	2	3	3	11	0	82	18	9	7	.401	.290
Boughton, Mike, S.Bend†	.098	15	57	51	2	5	7	2	0	0	2	2	0	0	4	0	11	0	0	0	.137	.164
Bovender, Andy, Quad City	.218	15	60	55	10	12	18	3	0	1	6	0	0	2	1	0	15	1	0	0	.327	.250
Boyette, Tony, Burlington	.273	4	14	11	1	3	6	0	0	1	4	0	0	1	0	0	4	0	0	0	.545	.286
Britt, Bryan, Peoria	.225	123	464	413	58	93	166	23	1	16	59	0	4	8	39	3	104	5	3	9	.402	.302
Brown, Roosevelt, K.C.*	.237	61	234	211	29	50	71	7	1	4	30	0	0	1	22	2	52	5	4	5	.336	.312
Buchman, Tom, Fort Wayne	.143	13	47	42	7	6	7	1	0	0	5	0	1	0	4	0	14	0	0	0	.167	.213

CLASS A Midwest League

Player, Team	Avg.	G	TPA	AB	R	H	TB	2B	3B	HR	RBI	SH	SF	HP	BB	IBB	SO	SB	CS	GDP	Slg.	OBP
Burns, Kevin, Quad City*	.270	131	540	477	72	129	219	28	1	20	86	0	4	6	53	8	114	1	2	12	.459	.348
Burrows, Mike, Wisconsin*	.249	102	419	389	55	97	173	24	8	12	54	1	2	6	21	3	91	17	14	8	.445	.297
Butler, Brent, Peoria	.306	129	553	480	81	147	233	37	2	15	71	0	5	4	63	6	69	6	4	9	.485	.388
Calloway, Ronald, S. Bend*	.280	9	27	25	3	7	8	1	0	0	1	0	0	0	2	0	8	1	0	1	.320	.333
Cameron, Ken, Peoria*	.260	105	372	323	51	84	118	20	4	2	27	6	3	5	35	1	50	21	8	6	.365	.339
Cancel, Robinson, Beloit	.300	17	60	50	9	15	18	3	0	0	4	0	0	3	7	0	9	0	2	1	.360	.417
Capellan, Rene, W. Michigan	.287	100	424	383	61	110	156	26	4	4	48	4	1	11	25	0	60	7	9	13	.407	.348
Carmona, Cesarin, Clinton†	.252	65	251	234	33	59	103	7	2	11	32	0	1	2	14	0	69	15	5	4	.440	.299
Carter, Cale, Cedar Rapids*	.221	30	100	86	18	19	22	3	0	0	8	1	1	4	8	0	16	2	1	2	.256	.313
Carter, Quincy, Rockford	.211	105	445	388	61	82	118	26	2	2	34	1	4	4	48	0	100	17	10	3	.304	.302
Castro, Jose, Wisconsin*	.242	64	263	248	29	60	77	12	1	1	19	1	0	1	13	0	50	3	4	6	.310	.282
Catlett, David, Rockford	.250	42	157	132	21	33	53	11	3	1	21	1	0	6	17	0	37	4	2	2	.402	.361
Cedeno, Jesus, W.Michigan	.270	110	458	429	42	116	170	24	3	8	63	2	6	3	18	0	77	13	5	9	.396	.300
Cepeda, Jose, Lansing	.279	89	380	326	40	91	116	17	1	2	35	5	4	3	42	0	35	4	2	10	.356	.363
Chamblee, James, Michigan	.300	133	562	487	112	146	251	29	5	22	73	0	5	17	53	3	107	18	4	8	.515	.384
Chavera, Arnie, Quad City*	.262	80	305	263	35	69	127	14	1	14	44	0	5	1	36	3	69	2	0	2	.483	.348
Clark, Brady, Burlington	.325	126	544	459	108	149	225	29	7	11	63	1	3	4	76	3	71	31	18	10	.490	.423
Clark, Chris, Kane County	.170	21	55	47	7	8	11	3	0	0	2	0	0	2	6	0	12	2	1	0	.234	.291
Colon, Jose, Rockford	.246	56	221	195	16	48	70	14	1	2	28	1	2	2	21	2	35	1	3	6	.359	.323
Conti, Jason, South Bend*	.310	117	521	458	78	142	193	22	10	3	43	4	3	11	45	2	99	30	18	10	.421	.383
Craig, Benjamin, Burlington†	.275	61	263	240	43	66	118	16	3	10	45	0	1	0	22	1	70	6	3	3	.492	.335
Cronin, Shane, Clinton	.239	69	267	230	21	55	73	1	1	5	33	1	5	6	25	0	37	4	0	6	.317	.323
Cross, Adam, Clinton	.226	59	178	155	22	35	44	5	2	0	16	3	1	5	14	0	28	9	7	2	.284	.309
Cruz, Cirilo, Wisconsin	.299	69	280	241	26	72	86	12	1	0	19	13	1	4	21	1	50	1	6	7	.357	.363
Cuntz, Casey, South Bend	.272	49	202	169	19	46	60	11	0	1	14	4	0	2	27	2	34	3	4	4	.355	.379
Curtis, Matt, Cedar Rapids†	.248	34	134	113	21	28	50	8	1	4	18	0	2	2	17	0	16	0	0	3	.442	.351
Dallimore, Brian, Quad City	.260	130	561	492	80	128	175	23	3	6	48	6	5	20	38	0	76	24	8	19	.356	.335
Davidson, Cleatus, Ft.Wayne†	.255	124	540	478	80	122	172	16	8	6	52	5	4	1	52	1	100	39	9	7	.360	.327
Davis, James, Burlington	.292	91	346	319	37	93	128	18	1	5	46	4	2	4	17	1	46	3	0	8	.401	.333
Davis, Josh, Clinton	.189	60	195	180	13	34	41	5	1	0	18	0	2	0	13	0	45	4	3	4	.228	.241
Deck, Billy, Peoria*	.269	114	442	383	51	103	142	30	0	3	53	1	2	4	51	2	89	2	5	11	.371	.359
DeLeon, Jorge, Michigan	.271	20	63	59	10	16	19	3	0	0	4	1	3	0	0	0	19	2	0	3	.322	.258
Derenches, Albert, Wis.†	.000	30	1	0	0	0	0	0	0	0	0	1	0	0	0	0	0	0	0	0	.000	.000
Doezie, Troy, Lansing	.157	19	55	51	3	8	10	2	0	0	1	1	1	0	2	0	14	0	0	2	.196	.185
Dubose, Brian, W. Michigan*	.268	105	432	358	72	96	167	12	7	15	79	3	2	3	66	3	87	17	2	2	.466	.385
Duffy, James, Quad City	.250	12	48	44	4	11	14	3	0	0	7	0	1	0	3	0	9	0	0	1	.318	.292
Dunn, Nathan, Clinton	.268	104	462	399	58	107	164	22	7	7	48	5	2	2	54	1	112	8	11	11	.411	.357
Elliott, David, Beloit	.277	76	306	267	44	74	126	12	2	12	48	1	2	6	30	3	60	13	7	3	.472	.361
Ellison, Tony, Rockford	.195	34	135	118	21	23	47	5	2	5	13	1	1	1	14	0	25	1	1	2	.398	.284
Espino, Fernando, Wisconsin.	.250	3	10	8	2	2	8	0	0	2	5	0	0	0	2	0	2	0	0	0	1.000	.400
Farraez, Jesus, Quad City	.219	80	254	228	30	50	73	6	1	5	24	0	1	6	19	0	61	9	8	10	.320	.295
Faurot, Adam, Beloit	.238	100	339	298	38	71	87	11	1	1	19	14	0	10	17	0	56	9	11	4	.292	.302
Fefee, Theo, Cedar Rapids*	.240	110	387	367	40	88	122	13	6	3	35	0	1	1	18	1	90	10	9	9	.332	.276
Felston, Anthony, Ft. Wayne*	.278	94	409	338	63	94	114	10	2	2	29	11	1	4	55	1	53	45	15	6	.337	.384
Fick, Robert, West Michigan*	.341	122	546	463	100	158	262	50	3	16	90	0	7	1	75	11	74	13	4	10	.566	.429
Figueroa, Luis, Wisconsin	.286	125	524	482	56	138	178	27	2	3	60	2	1	6	33	1	21	3	3	18	.369	.339
Fink, Marc, Beloit*	.148	10	33	27	4	4	10	0	0	2	3	0	0	0	6	1	10	0	0	0	.370	.303
Freitas, Joe, Peoria	.250	122	504	436	78	109	226	16	1	33	86	0	3	7	58	1	148	6	1	6	.518	.345
Fuentes, Javier, Michigan	.169	30	92	77	10	13	16	1	1	0	8	2	0	4	7	0	18	1	1	2	.208	.273
Gann, Jamie, South Bend	.167	12	38	36	4	6	7	1	0	0	3	1	0	0	1	0	9	0	1	0	.194	.189
Gargiulo, Jimmy, Peoria	.239	96	345	305	39	73	93	14	0	2	29	6	1	2	31	0	54	1	3	4	.305	.313
Garrett, Jason, Kane County	.275	128	528	476	72	131	180	28	3	5	68	3	9	5	35	2	101	3	2	11	.378	.326
Garrick, Matt, Cedar Rapids	.221	28	110	95	11	21	29	6	1	0	14	1	0	2	12	0	23	1	0	7	.305	.321
Geronimo, Cesar, Cedar Rapids	.167	17	46	42	5	7	7	0	0	0	1	1	0	1	2	0	10	1	0	0	.167	.222
Giambi, Jeremy, Lansing*	.336	31	143	116	33	39	67	11	1	5	21	0	1	2	23	2	16	5	1	1	.578	.451
Gillespie, Eric, Cedar Rapids*	.254	122	485	421	78	107	201	26	7	18	72	0	4	4	55	0	80	8	0	7	.477	.343
Gjerde, Jeff, South Bend*	.202	31	118	104	9	21	21	0	0	0	3	1	1	0	12	0	34	0	1	1	.202	.282
Glozier, Larry, Kane County	.176	55	182	159	21	28	33	5	0	0	16	0	1	6	16	1	29	2	2	8	.208	.275
Goodhart, Steve, Burlington	.185	19	76	54	11	10	13	3	0	0	4	5	0	1	16	0	13	3	0	1	.241	.380
Graves, Bryan, Cedar Rapids	.204	68	226	191	14	39	54	12	0	1	17	0	0	3	32	0	32	1	2	4	.283	.327
Griffis, Cade, Lansing*	.300	10	35	30	4	9	12	3	0	0	5	0	1	0	4	0	8	2	1	0	.400	.371
Guiel, Jeff, Cedar Rapids*	.318	41	172	132	32	42	79	7	0	10	26	0	2	3	35	5	28	13	2	0	.598	.465
Gunderson, Shane, Ft. Wayne	.267	13	50	45	3	12	13	1	0	0	7	1	1	0	3	0	3	1	1	2	.289	.306
Gutierrez, Alfredo, Beloit	.000	19	0	0	0	0	0	0	0	0	0	0	0	0	0	0	0	0	1	0	.000	.000
Haas, Chris, Peoria*	.313	36	142	115	23	36	62	11	0	5	22	0	2	3	22	1	38	3	0	4	.539	.430
Hall, Doug, Rockford*	.290	115	447	407	49	118	150	19	2	3	46	2	2	2	33	0	106	26	13	8	.369	.345
Hallmark, Patrick, Lansing	.284	88	347	306	49	87	112	13	6	0	39	1	5	7	28	0	43	22	5	8	.366	.353
Halloran, Matt, Clinton	.201	46	169	154	19	31	41	7	0	1	22	1	2	4	8	0	37	9	3	5	.266	.256
Ham, Kevin, Cedar Rapids	.281	123	494	441	67	124	197	26	1	15	73	3	6	3	41	0	127	9	9	15	.447	.342
Hampton, Mike, Burlington	.241	77	292	228	52	55	108	8	3	13	42	1	4	12	47	1	58	18	4	3	.474	.392
Harris, Rodger, Peoria†	.228	85	278	250	30	57	77	7	5	1	15	6	1	2	19	0	62	12	6	3	.308	.287
Harrison, Adonis, Wisconsin*	.318	125	481	412	61	131	190	26	6	7	62	5	3	6	55	2	74	25	18	11	.461	.403
Hartman, Ron, South Bend	.254	53	225	197	25	50	80	17	2	3	37	0	2	1	25	1	35	1	0	12	.406	.338
Heinrichs, Jon, Kane County	.268	60	258	235	35	63	82	12	2	1	36	3	1	0	19	1	34	8	5	7	.349	.322
Hillenbrand, Shea, Michigan	.290	64	238	224	28	65	93	13	3	3	39	0	4	1	9	1	20	1	3	2	.415	.315
Hogan, Todd, Peoria	.247	112	492	449	57	111	153	18	3	6	37	3	3	11	26	2	104	28	16	7	.341	.303
Horne, Tyrone, Kane County*	.306	133	576	468	89	143	234	24	2	21	91	0	1	3	104	18	88	18	7	13	.500	.434
Horner, Jim, Wisconsin	.248	47	185	161	19	40	67	10	1	5	24	1	1	5	17	0	53	0	1	4	.416	.337
Houston, Tyler, Rockford*	.500	2	6	6	1	3	4	1	0	0	1	0	0	0	0	0	0	0	0	0	.667	.500
Hudson, Bert, South Bend	.147	28	101	95	5	14	16	2	0	0	9	0	1	0	5	0	36	1	2	0	.168	.188
Huls, Steve, Fort Wayne†	.190	56	173	158	20	30	37	7	0	0	16	2	1	0	12	0	37	2	1	2	.234	.246
Hyers, Matt, Quad City*	.248	81	300	270	32	67	81	8	3	0	18	2	0	3	25	1	46	7	6	4	.300	.319
Ingram, Darron, Burlington	.265	134	559	510	74	135	255	25	4	29	97	0	3	0	46	1	195	8	5	9	.500	.324

Player, Team	Avg.	G	TPA	AB	R	H	TB	2B	3B	HR	RBI	SH	SF	HP	BB	IBB	SO	SB	CS	GDP	Slg.	OBP
Jefferson, Dave, Rockford	.200	18	60	55	7	11	15	2	1	0	2	1	0	1	3	0	12	3	1	0	.273	.254
Jenkins, Corey, Michigan	.239	111	468	426	68	102	181	17	4	18	62	0	3	11	28	1	129	5	5	9	.425	.301
Johnson, Gary, Rockford	.000	1	4	3	0	0	0	0	0	0	0	0	0	0	1	0	1	1	0	1	.000	.250
Johnson, Heath, Fort Wayne*	.209	22	82	67	10	14	27	4	0	3	11	1	1	0	13	0	29	0	1	0	.403	.333
Johnson, Rontrez, Michigan	.241	118	494	411	87	99	136	10	6	5	40	6	3	9	65	0	96	29	12	2	.331	.355
Jones, Jay, Kane County*	.295	64	222	210	20	62	80	6	0	4	31	1	0	3	8	1	29	0	2	7	.381	.330
Kennison, Kyle, Wisconsin	.000	40	1	1	0	0	0	0	0	0	0	0	0	0	0	0	0	0	0	0	.000	.000
King, Brad, Rockford	.250	68	237	204	31	51	88	14	1	7	29	2	4	8	19	2	35	4	4	5	.431	.332
Kleinz, Larry, Kane County	.242	107	423	364	50	88	139	16	1	11	44	2	3	4	48	2	63	1	2	8	.382	.334
Klimek, Josh, Beloit*	.266	121	495	443	62	118	191	31	3	12	66	2	6	5	39	1	56	4	8	8	.431	.329
Knauss, Tom, Fort Wayne	.190	14	64	58	3	11	15	1	0	1	7	0	0	0	6	0	18	1	0	1	.259	.266
Kratochvil, Tim, Michigan	.264	44	142	129	11	34	40	4	1	0	19	0	2	2	9	0	35	0	0	4	.310	.317
Landry, Jacques, W.Mich.	.274	103	403	369	51	101	177	18	5	16	52	0	5	8	21	1	99	15	3	6	.480	.323
Layne, Jason, Lansing*	.276	98	403	337	54	93	148	22	3	9	68	0	3	9	54	3	85	0	0	5	.439	.387
LeBron, Juan, Lansing	.212	35	116	113	12	24	40	7	0	3	20	0	2	1	0	0	32	0	0	4	.354	.216
Lemonis, Chris, W.Mich.*	.304	48	168	158	27	48	69	10	1	3	30	0	0	1	9	1	31	2	5	3	.437	.345
Leon, Jose, Peoria	.231	118	444	399	50	92	177	21	2	20	54	2	2	9	32	1	122	6	5	10	.444	.301
Lewis, Keith, Rockford†	.171	15	46	41	5	7	9	2	0	0	5	1	0	1	3	0	9	1	0	1	.220	.244
Lindsey, Rodney, Clinton	.213	130	576	502	80	107	156	15	8	6	49	3	2	7	62	0	161	70	23	8	.311	.307
Lisanti, Bob, Rockford	.236	66	207	182	18	43	51	8	0	0	21	1	4	5	15	0	42	1	3	0	.280	.306
Liverziani, Claudio, Wis.*	.254	108	419	346	73	88	133	22	4	5	31	2	0	3	68	0	93	11	4	7	.384	.381
LoCurto, Gary, Michigan†	.236	120	489	419	64	99	138	27	0	4	63	3	2	2	63	2	93	8	5	13	.329	.337
Lofton, James, Burlington†	.265	129	553	483	83	128	164	18	3	4	45	9	3	4	54	1	89	20	12	9	.340	.342
Lomasney, Steve, Michigan	.275	102	371	324	50	89	158	27	3	12	51	3	3	9	32	0	98	3	4	8	.488	.353
Longmire, Marcel, Rockford	.218	84	284	266	20	58	78	7	2	3	21	1	1	2	14	0	77	6	5	13	.293	.261
Lopez, Henry, Fort Wayne	.245	87	364	327	43	80	116	13	4	5	29	4	0	4	29	1	76	10	9	11	.355	.314
Lopiccolo, Jamie, Beloit	.332	112	462	410	72	136	220	27	3	17	80	1	4	9	38	2	76	5	6	10	.537	.397
Lorenzo, Juan, Fort Wayne†	.143	4	9	7	0	1	1	0	0	0	0	1	0	1	0	0	1	0	0	0	.143	.250
Loyd, Brian, Clinton	.274	73	301	259	35	71	87	10	0	2	33	4	5	8	25	2	41	6	4	12	.336	.350
Macalutas, Jon, Beloit	.313	59	248	211	45	66	111	13	1	10	36	1	1	11	24	1	19	6	5	6	.526	.409
Madera, Wil, South Bend*	.248	70	230	210	22	52	71	8	4	1	20	1	2	1	16	0	66	6	3	2	.338	.301
Madonna, Chris, Michigan*	.147	16	42	34	4	5	7	2	0	0	1	0	1	1	6	0	9	1	0	0	.206	.286
Maldonado, Carlos, Wis.	.190	97	347	316	15	60	72	8	2	0	25	8	3	3	17	1	33	2	3	8	.228	.236
Marchiano, Mike, Wisconsin	.111	3	11	9	1	1	1	0	0	0	0	0	0	1	1	0	0	0	0	0	.111	.273
Martin, Jared, South Bend†	.247	34	111	97	13	24	32	6	1	0	10	2	2	1	9	0	30	2	1	0	.330	.312
Martinez, David E., Beloit	.216	30	94	88	10	19	22	1	1	0	5	1	0	0	5	0	33	1	3	0	.250	.258
Martinez, Tony, South Bend	.272	108	455	404	54	110	151	21	1	6	62	3	8	3	37	1	85	1	3	15	.374	.332
Martinez, Victor, Wisconsin	.200	30	106	95	9	19	23	2	1	0	6	6	0	1	4	0	19	3	3	4	.242	.240
McAffee, Josh, South Bend	.196	50	186	168	16	33	56	9	1	4	17	0	0	6	12	0	67	0	1	5	.333	.274
McClendon, Travis, Peoria	.214	6	17	14	1	3	3	0	0	0	2	0	0	0	3	0	4	0	0	0	.214	.353
McClure, Brian, Clinton*	.276	118	516	416	75	115	167	18	11	4	55	3	6	1	90	4	64	12	11	7	.401	.402
McCutcheon, Mike, S. Bend*	.000	32	0	0	1	0	0	0	0	0	0	0	0	0	0	0	0	0	0	0	.000	.000
McNeal, Pepe, Peoria	.246	56	169	142	18	35	59	9	0	5	25	3	5	1	18	1	32	0	1	4	.415	.325
Medrano, Steve, Lansing†	.221	97	364	321	35	71	88	7	5	0	29	3	3	3	34	0	39	10	5	8	.274	.299
Mejia, Marlon, Quad City	.241	21	59	54	4	13	14	1	0	0	2	0	0	2	3	0	7	0	0	0	.259	.305
Melconian, Alex, Kane County	.100	3	12	10	0	1	1	0	0	0	0	0	0	1	1	0	2	0	0	1	.100	.250
Meyer, Brad, Fort Wayne*	.300	12	27	20	5	6	9	1	1	0	3	3	0	0	4	0	6	1	0	0	.450	.417
Meyers, Chad, Rockford	.301	125	536	439	89	132	180	28	4	4	58	6	7	10	74	5	72	54	16	4	.410	.408
Miles, Aaron, Quad City†	.262	97	413	370	55	97	117	13	2	1	35	7	4	2	30	0	45	18	11	8	.316	.318
Miranda, Tony, Lansing	.341	104	456	387	85	132	192	35	5	5	72	0	5	10	54	2	62	11	10	10	.496	.430
Mitchell, Derek, W. Michigan	.198	110	419	353	47	70	91	14	2	1	31	8	3	5	50	1	91	11	8	5	.258	.304
Moeller, Chad, Fort Wayne	.289	108	448	384	58	111	162	18	3	9	39	2	1	13	48	0	76	11	8	8	.422	.386
Montas, Ricardo, Lansing	.300	4	11	10	0	3	3	0	0	0	1	0	1	0	0	0	2	0	0	0	.300	.273
Monzon, Jose, Cedar Rapids	.225	34	124	111	12	25	40	3	0	4	14	1	0	0	12	1	14	0	0	8	.360	.301
Moore, Donnie, Beloit	.223	47	179	157	19	35	38	3	0	0	11	2	1	6	13	0	53	8	4	0	.242	.305
Moore, Jason, South Bend	.143	59	221	196	21	28	57	5	0	8	16	1	3	2	19	3	80	2	2	6	.291	.223
Moore, Kenderick, Lansing	.285	112	527	456	105	130	180	16	8	6	42	2	5	19	45	0	78	43	14	5	.395	.370
Morgan, James, S.Bend	.000	5	7	6	1	0	0	0	0	0	0	0	0	0	1	0	1	0	0	0	.000	.143
Moss, Rick, Fort Wayne*	.278	133	581	508	76	141	186	28	4	3	77	2	8	2	61	4	57	3	3	10	.366	.352
Murphy, Nate, Cedar Rapids*	.221	51	171	149	21	33	41	4	2	0	13	0	1	1	19	1	43	4	2	2	.275	.312
Myers, Mickey, Wisconsin*	.200	20	58	55	4	11	19	3	1	1	4	0	0	0	3	0	18	0	1	0	.345	.241
Nieves, Wilbert, Clinton	.218	18	63	55	6	12	18	1	1	1	7	1	1	0	6	0	10	2	1	0	.327	.290
Nunez, Jose, South Bend	.276	108	424	351	58	97	138	16	11	1	45	7	3	3	59	0	67	4	1	7	.393	.382
Olmeda, Jose, Michigan†	.191	61	207	194	24	37	47	7	0	1	21	1	0	1	11	0	63	5	0	3	.242	.238
Ortiz, Asbel, Michigan†	.280	43	148	143	19	40	59	8	1	3	6	1	0	1	3	0	32	1	0	2	.413	.299
Osborne, Mark, South Bend*	.264	96	379	333	38	88	141	25	2	8	51	1	1	1	43	1	98	2	2	6	.423	.349
Ozarowski, Richard, W.Mich.†	.216	36	146	134	14	29	38	7	1	0	13	2	1	1	8	0	35	2	1	2	.284	.264
Paciorek, Peter, Clinton†	.234	126	515	435	70	102	164	19	11	7	52	1	5	4	70	5	113	10	4	6	.377	.342
Parent, Jerry, Clinton*	.260	87	358	304	37	79	94	13	1	0	38	2	1	1	50	3	75	5	4	8	.309	.365
Parker, Allan, Cedar Rapids	.250	15	51	48	4	12	14	2	0	0	5	0	0	0	3	0	10	3	3	0	.292	.294
Patterson, Jacob, Ft.Wayne*	.215	121	524	469	61	101	181	16	2	20	80	2	3	12	38	1	131	11	2	10	.386	.289
Pellow, Kit, Lansing	.297	65	290	256	39	76	130	17	2	11	52	0	4	6	24	1	74	2	0	5	.508	.366
Pernell, Brandon, Clinton	.282	95	392	340	63	96	164	26	3	12	41	2	1	5	44	1	77	15	5	5	.482	.372
Peterman, Tommy, Ft.Wayne*	.293	113	452	417	46	122	165	22	0	7	57	1	5	1	28	4	69	0	4	9	.396	.335
Peters, Tony, Beloit	.235	113	413	375	50	88	143	16	6	9	43	5	1	1	31	0	110	21	7	8	.381	.294
Pitts, Rick, Lansing	.155	35	69	58	7	9	14	3	1	0	6	1	0	2	8	0	16	2	0	3	.241	.279
Podsednik, Scott, K.C.*	.277	135	611	531	80	147	187	23	4	3	49	14	3	3	60	2	72	28	11	5	.352	.352
Poepard, Scott, Fort Wayne†	.233	36	115	103	16	24	36	9	0	1	8	1	0	1	10	0	30	3	1	4	.350	.307
Prada, Nelson, Fort Wayne	.245	29	102	98	8	24	38	5	0	3	11	0	1	0	3	0	22	0	1	3	.388	.265
Pratt, Wes, Quad City	.257	124	480	435	65	112	174	26	0	12	51	2	4	4	35	2	56	10	5	7	.400	.316
Presto, Nick, Burlington	.213	27	102	94	14	20	27	7	0	0	8	0	0	1	7	0	15	3	2	1	.287	.275
Prodanov, Peter, Michigan	.184	55	165	141	24	26	48	5	1	5	21	2	1	3	18	1	30	1	1	3	.340	.288
Radcliff, Victor, Lansing	.269	81	289	253	40	68	108	25	3	3	33	2	6	9	19	0	56	3	0	5	.427	.334

CLASS A Midwest League

Player, Team	Avg.	G	TPA	AB	R	H	TB	2B	3B	HR	RBI	SH	SF	HP	BB	IBB	SO	SB	CS	GDP	Slg.	OBP
Ramirez, Julio, Kane County†	.255	99	434	376	70	96	170	18	7	14	53	14	2	5	37	1	122	41	6	1	.452	.329
Reeder, Jim, Quad City*	.244	92	336	312	35	76	98	12	2	2	21	1	1	2	20	3	29	2	4	11	.314	.293
Regan, Jason, Wisconsin	.254	51	207	177	31	45	88	14	1	9	23	0	3	4	23	0	55	2	0	1	.497	.348
Rexrode, Jackie, S.Bend*	.282	92	395	330	60	93	119	10	5	2	27	5	3	2	55	0	47	15	5	3	.361	.385
Reyes, Freddy, Fort Wayne	.261	85	330	306	37	80	127	19	2	8	45	1	0	11	12	1	79	0	0	11	.415	.313
Reynoso, Ismael, K.C.>	.132	34	102	91	4	12	12	0	0	0	10	2	0	1	8	0	21	1	2	5	.132	.210
Rivas, Luis, Fort Wayne	.239	121	465	419	61	100	135	20	6	1	30	6	2	5	33	1	90	28	18	5	.322	.301
Rivera, Miguel, Peoria	.149	49	123	114	8	17	19	0	1	0	13	1	0	1	7	0	20	1	2	0	.167	.205
Robertson, Ryan, K.C.*	.285	116	471	376	64	107	164	22	1	11	71	0	7	3	85	4	69	0	3	9	.436	.414
Robles, Juan, Lansing	.207	51	161	145	11	30	44	6	1	2	17	0	1	1	14	0	40	1	2	1	.303	.280
Roche, Marlon, Burlington	.219	72	260	233	30	51	67	5	1	3	36	1	3	2	21	0	57	7	3	9	.288	.286
Rodriguez, Juan, C.R.†	.281	111	481	416	66	117	187	18	8	12	55	18	3	1	43	0	106	11	12	4	.450	.348
Rogue, Francisco, Beloit	.170	17	57	53	1	9	11	2	0	0	7	0	0	0	4	0	7	0	0	1	.208	.228
Rojas, Christian, Burlington	.239	101	388	348	53	83	154	17	3	16	56	3	3	1	33	0	106	7	3	4	.443	.304
Rose, Mike, Quad City†	.256	79	277	234	22	60	77	6	1	3	27	8	3	4	28	0	62	3	1	1	.329	.342
Ruotsinoja, Jacob, Clinton*	.186	54	216	188	19	35	48	10	0	1	16	0	2	2	24	2	51	2	2	4	.255	.282
Rupcich, Larry, Kane County*	.216	33	135	111	13	24	25	1	0	0	8	5	0	2	17	0	21	2	0	4	.225	.331
Rutherford, Daryl, Clinton	.220	21	63	59	9	13	19	3	0	1	5	0	0	0	4	0	19	2	1	1	.322	.270
Ryan, Rob, South Bend*	.314	121	517	421	71	132	201	35	5	8	73	0	5	2	89	5	58	12	1	7	.477	.431
Sachse, Matt, Wisconsin*	.268	110	404	373	37	100	145	21	3	6	51	1	2	2	26	1	110	5	3	10	.389	.318
Salazar, Juan, Rockford†	.267	54	176	161	16	43	61	9	0	3	17	1	0	1	13	0	36	2	1	3	.379	.326
Samboy, Nelson, Quad City	.353	14	54	51	2	18	21	3	0	0	8	1	0	0	2	0	8	1	1	0	.412	.377
Sanchez, Marcos, Clinton†	.291	63	254	206	42	60	88	6	5	4	39	1	2	3	42	3	53	9	4	5	.427	.415
Sanchez, Orlando, Michigan	.180	21	70	61	3	11	18	2	1	1	10	0	0	0	9	0	15	0	0	2	.295	.286
Sanchez, Yuri, Burlington*	.255	101	402	364	66	93	168	12	12	13	48	2	1	0	35	0	116	7	3	9	.462	.320
Sandoval, Jhensy, S.Bend	.264	19	75	72	9	19	25	3	0	1	4	0	0	1	2	0	19	4	3	0	.347	.293
Santana, Pedro, W.Michigan	.261	74	310	287	36	75	106	10	6	3	28	3	0	6	14	0	55	20	3	8	.369	.309
Sasser, Rob, Cedar Rapids	.272	134	577	497	103	135	222	26	5	17	77	0	3	8	69	6	92	37	13	11	.447	.367
Saturria, Luis, Peoria	.274	122	498	445	81	122	184	19	5	11	51	3	3	3	44	3	95	23	10	5	.413	.341
Saylor, Jamie, Quad City*	.246	20	74	61	10	15	20	5	0	0	2	5	0	2	2	0	11	1	16	3	2	.328	.361
Schafer, Brett, Lansing	.191	21	66	47	16	9	14	3	1	0	6	0	1	3	15	0	8	3	0	2	.298	.409
Schaub, Greg, Beloit	.226	108	419	394	35	89	139	18	4	8	45	0	4	4	17	1	90	5	3	13	.353	.263
Schmidt, Todd, Peoria†	.000	1	1	0	0	0	0	0	0	0	0	0	0	0	1	0	0	0	0	0	.000	1.000
Scott, Tom, Burlington	.301	50	195	183	30	55	91	16	1	6	34	2	1	0	9	0	57	10	1	2	.497	.332
Seal, Scott, Clinton*	.254	29	127	114	20	29	50	6	0	5	23	0	1	2	10	0	37	2	1	3	.439	.323
Sharp, Scott, Burlington	.149	30	102	87	9	13	15	2	0	0	10	1	0	2	12	1	36	0	2	2	.172	.267
Smith, Jason, Rockford*	.182	9	35	33	4	6	8	0	1	0	3	0	0	0	2	0	11	1	0	1	.242	.229
Smith, Matt, Lansing*	.278	62	251	227	33	63	85	4	3	4	33	0	2	0	21	1	45	4	2	2	.374	.336
Sollmann, Scott, W.Mich.*	.313	121	561	460	89	144	165	13	4	0	33	8	3	11	79	5	81	40	14	1	.359	.423
Sorg, Jay, Burlington*	.283	112	463	399	62	113	174	18	2	13	72	2	2	4	56	3	65	13	7	10	.436	.375
Sosa, Franklin, W.Michigan	.256	57	218	195	24	50	54	4	0	0	16	3	2	9	10	1	24	2	3	3	.277	.319
Speed, Dorian, Rockford	.248	44	183	157	27	39	51	7	1	1	18	3	1	4	18	0	45	18	4	5	.325	.339
Steinmann, Scott, Wis.*	.213	72	258	225	26	48	55	7	0	0	20	5	0	4	24	1	60	5	3	5	.244	.300
Stenson, Dernell, Michigan*	.291	131	570	471	79	137	221	35	2	15	80	0	8	19	72	6	105	6	4	10	.469	.400
Stevenson, Chad, W.Michigan	.220	72	283	259	32	57	90	10	1	7	32	2	1	1	20	1	77	2	4	3	.347	.278
Stewart, Keith, Wisconsin*	.143	4	14	14	0	2	3	1	0	0	2	0	0	0	0	0	2	0	0	1	.214	.143
Suero, Ignacio, Beloit	.226	85	323	297	32	67	104	14	1	7	41	0	4	8	14	1	49	1	3	12	.350	.276
Sweeney, Kevin, South Bend*	.263	68	277	232	36	61	91	16	1	4	37	0	2	4	39	1	56	1	0	9	.392	.375
Taft, Brett, Lansing	.249	85	327	269	41	67	100	21	0	4	30	5	2	4	47	0	60	5	4	9	.372	.366
Tanner, Paul, Peoria	.233	104	344	318	31	74	102	19	3	1	33	5	0	2	19	1	76	9	3	9	.321	.280
Taveras, Jose, South Bend	.186	15	45	43	5	8	11	0	0	1	2	0	0	0	2	0	11	2	1	0	.256	.222
Thoen, E.J., Cedar Rapids	.203	123	432	384	41	78	112	19	3	3	46	7	3	7	31	0	114	2	3	7	.292	.273
Thrower, Jake, Clinton	.254	19	79	63	8	16	19	3	0	0	12	1	0	2	13	0	15	1	3	0	.302	.397
Truby, Chris, Quad City	.280	68	294	268	34	75	112	14	1	7	46	1	2	1	22	0	32	13	4	8	.418	.334
Ullery, David, Lansing*	.159	18	59	44	5	7	15	1	2	1	10	0	1	1	13	0	16	0	0	2	.341	.356
Ussery, Brian, Cedar Rapids†	.000	1	1	1	0	0	0	0	0	0	0	0	0	0	0	0	0	0	0	0	.000	.000
Valdez, Trovin, Burlington	.252	33	140	119	22	30	35	3	1	0	11	4	1	0	16	0	28	14	4	2	.294	.338
Valentin, Jose, Beloit†	.500	2	8	6	3	3	4	1	0	0	1	0	0	2	0	1	0	0	0	0	.667	.625
Valera, Gregori, South Bend	.185	8	28	27	2	5	7	2	0	0	2	1	0	0	0	0	7	0	0	1	.259	.185
Valera, Ramon, Wisconsin†	.176	13	40	34	6	6	8	2	0	0	2	2	0	0	4	0	6	1	4	0	.235	.263
Vallone, Gar, Cedar Rapids†	.236	41	110	89	13	21	25	1	0	1	8	2	1	0	18	0	20	0	2	3	.281	.361
Vazquez, Ramon, Wisconsin*	.269	131	567	479	79	129	188	25	5	8	49	4	3	3	78	2	93	16	10	8	.392	.373
Venghaus, Jeff, K.C.†	.236	128	529	416	71	98	124	20	3	0	43	15	6	6	86	1	105	17	11	12	.298	.370
Veras, Wilton, Michigan	.288	131	530	489	51	141	192	21	3	8	68	1	3	6	31	0	51	3	2	19	.393	.336
Wakeland, Chris, W.Mich.*	.285	111	468	414	64	118	181	38	2	7	75	0	7	4	43	5	120	20	6	3	.437	.353
Walker, Ron, Rockford	.333	4	18	15	1	5	8	0	0	1	5	0	0	0	3	0	2	0	0	0	.533	.444
Walther, Chris, Beloit	.300	113	474	437	55	131	164	25	4	0	38	3	1	5	28	0	41	5	7	16	.375	.348
Washam, Jason, Beloit	.283	88	328	276	44	78	123	15	3	8	46	0	3	16	33	0	31	4	2	5	.446	.387
Watkins, Sean, Clinton*	.148	10	37	27	1	4	7	0	0	1	2	0	1	0	9	0	10	0	2	0	.259	.351
Watts, Josh, Wisconsin*	.278	51	196	162	37	45	83	10	2	8	24	0	1	0	33	3	55	3	7	5	.512	.398
Welles, Robby, Cedar Rapids	.266	20	71	64	10	17	25	2	0	2	9	2	0	0	5	0	18	2	0	2	.391	.329
Wetmore, Michael, Beloit†	.253	114	472	407	67	103	133	20	2	2	27	6	3	8	48	2	83	9	10	7	.327	.341
Whitehead, Braxton, Burl.	.187	34	135	123	11	23	29	6	0	0	13	1	1	1	9	0	27	2	2	5	.236	.246
Williams, Jason, Burlington	.324	68	291	256	49	83	123	17	1	7	41	6	3	5	21	0	40	9	6	6	.480	.382
Williams, Micah, Lansing	.333	65	275	249	34	83	102	13	3	0	30	8	0	9	9	0	34	22	3	6	.410	.378
Wooten, Shawn, C.R.	.289	108	417	353	43	102	172	23	1	15	75	3	6	6	49	0	71	0	1	9	.487	.379
Zachmann, Rob, Wisconsin	.260	107	407	358	59	93	155	24	1	12	61	6	3	3	37	2	87	5	6	7	.433	.332
Zapata, Alexis, W.Michigan	.223	64	223	206	33	46	78	3	6	3	27	2	2	1	11	0	54	4	0	8	.379	.267
Zuleta, Julio, Rockford	.288	119	488	430	59	124	182	30	5	6	77	3	8	12	35	6	88	5	5	7	.423	.353

GRAND SLAMS: T. Martinez, Osborne, 2 each; Alfano, Bolivar, Brown, Butler, Capellan, Chamblee, Dubose, Halloran, Ham, Jenkins, Kleinz, LeBron, Leon, Lindsey, Liverziani, Patterson, Podsednik, Ramirez, Roche, Sachse, Y. Sanchez, Sasser, Saturria, Thoen, Truby, Wooten, Zachmann, 1 each.

AWARDED FIRST BASE ON CATCHER'S INTERFERENCE: Fuentes 2 (Alfano, Doezie); Kleinz 2 (Gargiulo, Jo. Davis); Bly (Alfano); Butler (King); Catlett (Alfano); B. Clark (Osborne); Deck (R. Robertson); Giambi (Suero); Gillespie (Osborne); Hall (Alfano); Murphy (Suero); Nunez (Barr); M. Smith (King).

1997 PITCHING

TEAM

Team	W	L	Pct.	ERA	G	CG	ShO	Sv.	IP	H	TBF	R	ER	HR	SH	SF	HB	BB	IBB	SO	WP	Bk.
West Michigan	92	39	.702	2.67	131	11	13	47	1169.1	984	4861	456	347	57	31	33	53	386	10	916	79	15
South Bend	54	83	.394	3.76	137	1	6	27	1178.2	1158	5195	653	493	72	42	41	76	524	33	972	109	14
Clinton	65	71	.478	3.83	136	17	5	26	1168.1	1154	5101	626	497	81	37	40	63	459	8	1042	90	23
Wisconsin	76	63	.547	3.87	139	2	13	32	1217.2	1084	5236	612	524	82	35	34	64	555	23	1220	106	27
Fort Wayne	68	67	.504	3.88	135	5	12	29	1195.2	1191	5189	638	516	51	36	36	55	480	7	1003	96	23
Kane County	70	68	.507	4.03	138	10	8	29	1192.0	1164	5148	620	534	82	56	32	96	439	23	1090	98	19
Michigan	70	67	.511	4.11	137	11	5	28	1168.0	1155	5149	672	533	83	40	39	67	448	22	1018	119	16
Rockford	66	66	.500	4.31	132	9	4	34	1142.0	1133	5106	665	547	79	35	33	58	572	23	1031	112	23
Quad City	59	75	.440	4.31	134	8	4	28	1134.2	1095	5010	682	544	100	29	28	72	509	32	963	84	18
Burlington	72	68	.514	4.49	140	4	2	28	1199.2	1230	5325	709	598	80	46	43	59	529	14	924	82	14
Beloit	60	73	.451	4.50	133	5	5	21	1151.1	1173	5051	715	576	100	39	36	59	487	9	947	88	31
Lansing	69	68	.504	4.65	137	3	5	27	1197.0	1335	5286	730	618	127	50	42	64	400	12	910	67	10
Peoria	70	69	.504	4.69	139	6	10	38	1202.2	1284	5387	746	627	89	47	54	61	578	34	1001	91	18
Cedar Rapids	62	76	.449	4.89	138	18	7	27	1189.0	1251	5214	756	646	145	31	36	66	474	13	927	93	28

INDIVIDUAL

TOP QUALIFIERS FOR EARNED-RUN AVERAGE TITLE

Minimum 112 innings. *Lefthanded pitcher.

Pitcher, Team	W	L	Pct.	ERA	G	GS	CG	ShO	GF	Sv.	IP	H	TBF	R	ER	HR	SH	SF	HB	BB	IBB	SO	WP	Bk.
Quintal, Craig, West Michigan	11	6	.647	1.96	23	23	3	2	0	0	156.1	133	634	48	34	3	4	6	13	31	0	88	2	0
Bruner, Clayton, West Michigan	15	3	.833	2.38	24	24	3	2	0	0	166.1	134	664	52	44	11	2	7	4	48	1	135	9	1
Hooten, David, Fort Wayne	11	8	.579	2.61	28	27	2	2	0	0	165.2	134	675	57	48	5	4	2	9	54	0	138	4	6
Penny, Brad, South Bend	10	5	.667	2.73	25	25	0	0	0	0	118.2	91	489	44	36	4	5	0	4	43	2	116	10	2
Spear, Russell, West Michigan	11	6	.647	2.96	23	23	1	1	0	0	139.2	126	605	63	46	9	3	3	11	61	0	112	9	0
Billingsley, Brent, Kane County*	14	7	.667	3.01	26	26	3	1	0	0	170.2	146	697	67	57	9	7	1	11	50	0	175	13	1
Richardson, Kasey, Fort Wayne*	7	5	.583	3.07	19	19	1	1	0	0	114.1	100	476	47	39	5	4	3	4	46	0	84	10	0
Cannon, Jon, Rockford*	9	6	.600	3.13	24	20	1	0	3	0	129.1	110	548	53	45	13	2	3	7	50	1	130	16	3
Lopez, Rodrigo, Clinton	6	8	.429	3.18	37	14	2	0	19	9	121.2	103	508	49	43	6	7	4	3	42	1	123	3	4
Passini, Brian, Beloit*	9	5	.643	3.22	19	19	1	0	0	0	123.0	114	505	48	44	14	2	1	4	35	0	116	3	3
Borkowski, David, West Michigan	15	3	.833	3.46	25	25	4	2	0	0	164.0	143	670	79	63	15	3	7		31	0	104	7	0
Kinney, Matt, Michigan	8	5	.615	3.43	22	22	2	1	0	0	117.1	93	514	59	46	4	5	2	0	78	2	123	6	0
Romo, Greg, West Michigan	12	6	.667	3.54	24	24	0	0	0	0	139.2	128	595	65	55	7	3	5	0	51	0	124	14	3
Fuentes, Brian, Wisconsin*	6	7	.462	3.56	22	22	1	1	0	0	118.2	84	486	52	47	6	3	3	8	59	0	153	11	3
Ortiz, Ramon, Cedar Rapids*	11	10	.524	3.58	27	27	8	4	0	0	123.0	113	533	54	49	8	3	8	12	53	0	225	14	5

DEPARTMENTAL LEADERS: W—Borkowski, Bruner, 15 each; L—G. Garcia, Stockstill, 14 each; Pct.—Borkowski, Bruner, .833 each; G—West, 62; GS—Several pitchers tied with 27 each; CG—Ortiz, 8; ShO—Ortiz, 4; GF—Cordero, 47; Sv.—Cordero, 35; IP—Darrell, 191.2; H—Darrell, 212; TBF—Darrell, 810; R—Kaye, 113; ER—Kaye, 103; HR—Stockstill, 25; SH—Reames, 9; SF—McCall, 9; HB—Welch, 17; BB—Kaye, 104; IBB—Crafton, Crews, 7 each; SO—Ortiz, 225; WP—Montgomery, 27; BK—Levrault, 12.

ALL PITCHERS

*Lefthanded pitcher.

Pitcher, Team	W	L	Pct.	ERA	G	GS	CG	ShO	GF	Sv.	IP	H	TBF	R	ER	HR	SH	SF	HB	BB	IBB	SO	WP	Bk.
Akin, Jay, Beloit*	1	5	.167	3.17	9	9	0	0	0	0	48.1	52	211	32	17	3	4	2	3	11	0	25	0	1
Allison, Bradley, South Bend	0	0	.000	15.88	3	0	0	0	2	0	5.2	13	33	10	10	1	0	0	1	2	0	4	1	0
Almonte, Hector, Kane County	0	1	.000	3.86	8	1	0	0	3	1	14.0	11	59	6	6	1	1	2	1	6	0	10	2	0
Andrews, Jeff, South Bend	1	5	.167	5.24	23	4	0	0	7	0	55.0	52	237	37	32	4	2	1	2	27	1	32	3	0
Aversa, Joe, Kane County	0	0	.000	0.00	1	0	0	0	0	0	2.0	2	9	0	0	0	0	0	1	0	0	0	0	0
Avrard, Corey, Peoria	4	5	.444	6.36	20	20	0	0	0	0	93.1	97	437	76	66	5	4	4	4	69	1	94	9	0
Ayala, Julio, Wisconsin*	11	3	.786	3.87	36	9	0	0	13	0	103.0	114	443	47	42	4	2	1	4	30	4	81	7	2
Baird, Brandon, Lansing*	10	7	.588	3.01	55	0	0	0	36	7	77.2	74	336	31	26	2	5	3	5	28	6	83	2	0
Barksdale, Shane, Quad City	0	0	.000	7.30	8	0	0	0	6	1	12.1	22	64	12	10	3	0	0	1	5	0	8	1	0
Barnes, Larry, Beloit	3	6	.333	5.73	13	13	0	0	0	0	66.0	61	294	47	42	4	1	2	4	47	1	58	12	0
Bauder, Mike, Fort Wayne*	6	4	.600	3.72	40	10	0	0	5	1	104.0	94	435	51	43	5	1	4	1	33	0	96	10	3
Bauer, Chris, West Michigan	0	2	.000	4.07	18	0	0	0	15	1	24.1	30	111	15	11	1	1	1	3	10	1	11	1	0
Beale, Chuck, Michigan	2	7	.222	3.73	39	9	1	0	28	12	89.1	111	405	58	37	5	3	2	2	17	2	86	9	2
Bedinger, Doug, South Bend	0	1	.000	2.49	11	0	0	0	6	1	21.2	19	91	6	6	3	0	0	2	8	0	26	0	0
Bell, Matthew, South Bend	2	3	.400	6.75	14	0	0	0	4	0	22.2	27	111	27	17	4	3	1	2	9	3	22	2	2
Betancourt, Rafael, Michigan	0	3	.000	1.95	27	0	0	0	22	11	32.1	26	125	9	7	2	1	0	0	2	0	52	3	1
Bierbrodt, Nick, South Bend*	2	4	.333	5.04	15	15	0	0	0	0	75.2	77	340	43	34	4	3	1	9	37	0	64	6	1
Billingsley, Brent, Kane County*	14	7	.667	3.01	26	26	3	1	0	0	170.2	146	697	67	57	9	7	1	11	50	0	175	13	1
Birsner, Roark, Rockford	0	2	.000	3.73	18	0	0	0	5	2	31.1	33	155	19	13	3	1	0	3	24	1	33	1	0
Bishop, Joshua, Beloit	5	7	.417	5.99	21	11	1	0	5	1	79.2	79	354	62	53	10	1	5	6	34	0	61	8	1
Blair, Willie, West Michigan	0	0	.000	0.00	1	1	0	0	0	0	5.0	1	16	0	0	0	0	0	0	0	0	7	0	0
Boring, Richard, Lansing	0	0	.000	20.25	3	0	0	0	2	0	2.2	6	16	6	6	0	0	0	4	0	2	0	0	0
Borkowski, David, West Michigan	15	3	.833	3.46	25	25	4	2	0	0	164.0	143	670	79	63	15	3	7		31	0	104	7	0
Boughton, Mike, South Bend	0	0	.000	0.00	2	0	0	0	1	0	0.1	0	1	0	0	0	0	0	0	0	0	0	0	0
Braswell, Bryan, Quad City*	6	6	.500	3.79	19	19	1	0	0	0	116.1	107	495	70	49	10	0	4	2	32	0	118	2	5
Brookens, Casey, Rockford	3	2	.600	3.18	28	0	0	0	9	3	51.0	48	218	20	18	6	1	1	1	21	2	51	2	0
Bruner, Clayton, West Michigan	15	3	.833	2.38	24	24	3	2	0	0	166.1	134	664	52	44	11	2	7	4	48	1	135	9	1
Callahan, Damon, Burlington	2	2	.500	3.86	11	7	0	0	0	0	37.1	33	155	17	16	1	1	1	1	15	0	29	3	0
Cames, Aaron, Kane County	8	10	.444	3.91	26	26	3	3	0	0	149.2	143	627	67	65	11	6	6	15	43	0	157	10	6
Cannon, Jon, Rockford*	9	6	.600	3.13	24	20	1	0	3	0	129.1	110	548	53	45	13	2	3	7	50	1	130	16	3
Carmody, Brian, Clinton*	0	0	.000	1.56	8	1	0	0	2	1	17.1	14	69	7	3	0	0	0	8	1	19	2	1

CLASS A *Midwest League*

Pitcher, Team	W	L	Pct.	ERA	G	GS	CG	ShO	GF	Sv.	IP	H	TBF	R	ER	HR	SH	SF	HB	BB	IBB	SO	WP	Bk.
Carnes, Matt, Fort Wayne	0	1	.000	9.00	1	1	0	0	0	0	4.0	2	18	4	4	1	0	0	0	5	0	3	1	1
Caruthers, Clay, Burlington	3	7	.300	5.84	17	13	0	0	3	0	74.0	103	353	63	48	6	4	5	5	26	0	44	0	1
Cedeno, Blas, Rockford	3	3	.500	2.90	22	0	0	0	13	0	40.1	36	168	19	13	3	1	1	1	14	2	25	0	0
Cintron, Jose, Cedar Rapids	0	0	.000	5.40	2	0	0	0	0	0	5.0	3	20	3	3	2	0	0	1	0	0	4	0	0
Clark, Chris, Clinton	5	5	.500	4.15	32	11	0	0	5	3	89.0	89	395	50	41	5	0	0	3	46	0	91	15	0
Clark, Greg, Fort Wayne	0	1	.000	4.41	6	1	0	0	1	0	16.1	16	69	9	8	0	0	2	0	8	1	7	2	0
Collins, Ed, Beloit	0	0	.000	10.80	2	0	0	0	0	0	1.2	3	12	3	2	0	0	1	0	3	0	3	3	0
Cordero, Francisco, W.Michigan	6	1	.857	0.99	50	0	0	0	47	35	54.1	36	208	13	6	2	4	2	0	15	2	67	5	0
Cowsill, Brendon, Cedar Rapids	3	5	.375	4.75	26	0	0	0	18	3	36.0	41	160	24	19	4	0	2	3	16	1	32	2	0
Crafton, Kevin, Peoria	7	2	.778	1.96	50	0	0	0	45	29	55.0	40	219	16	12	2	5	2	2	18	7	59	2	1
Crane, Randy, Rockford	3	6	.333	5.74	21	12	0	0	4	0	73.2	68	346	51	47	7	2	1	9	55	3	62	8	1
Crews, Jason, South Bend	4	6	.400	3.18	50	0	0	0	32	9	82.0	78	354	39	29	5	4	3	2	27	7	74	4	1
Cushman, Dwayne, Burlington	1	4	.200	3.02	47	0	0	0	39	19	50.2	45	229	22	17	2	5	0	5	25	4	54	3	0
Dace, Derek, West Michigan*	1	0	1.000	0.72	10	2	0	0	3	2	25.0	23	100	2	2	0	0	0	1	4	0	24	0	0
D'Amico, Jeff, Beloit	0	0	.000	0.00	1	1	0	0	0	0	3.0	0	10	0	0	0	0	0	0	1	0	7	0	0
Danner, Adam, Kane County	1	4	.200	4.12	10	0	0	0	2	0	19.2	26	92	12	9	2	3	1	0	8	4	16	2	2
Darrell, Tommy, Cedar Rapids	12	10	.545	4.04	27	26	5	0	0	0	191.2	212	810	108	86	18	7	0	6	40	1	106	7	2
Darwin, David, West Michigan*	1	0	1.000	0.89	21	4	0	0	10	3	40.1	23	164	7	4	2	0	2	2	20	2	31	0	1
Davis, Lance, Burlington*	4	6	.400	6.59	30	13	0	0	8	0	97.0	121	452	78	71	6	4	3	1	55	0	51	8	3
De La Cruz, Fernando, C.R.	0	2	.000	11.48	10	0	0	0	4	1	13.1	19	80	22	17	1	1	2	6	14	0	10	2	0
DeLeon, Jose, Peoria	11	3	.786	5.01	60	0	0	0	28	8	73.2	79	329	46	41	8	3	3	3	35	5	76	3	0
Derenches, Albert, Wisconsin*	3	2	.600	4.53	29	0	0	0	12	2	43.2	46	214	36	22	3	4	3	5	25	4	50	2	0
DeWitt, Matt, Peoria	9	9	.500	4.09	27	27	1	0	0	0	158.1	152	672	84	72	16	7	8	9	57	2	121	6	1
Dose, Gary, Fort Wayne	1	4	.200	4.70	45	4	0	0	25	3	67.0	52	313	44	35	3	2	3	5	61	0	73	7	2
Downs, Scott, Rockford*	3	0	1.000	1.25	5	5	0	0	0	0	36.0	17	128	5	5	1	1	0	1	8	0	43	2	2
Duchscherer, Justin, Michigan	1	1	.500	5.63	4	4	0	0	0	0	24.0	26	109	17	15	1	0	1	3	10	0	19	0	0
Duncan, Geoff, Kane County	7	2	.778	4.07	44	2	0	0	13	1	86.1	85	375	46	39	7	7	2	5	30	5	96	4	0
Duncan, Sean, Quad City*	6	0	1.000	2.89	34	0	0	0	14	3	46.2	39	193	19	15	4	2	1	4	15	5	46	4	0
Durbin, Chad, Lansing	5	8	.385	4.79	26	26	0	0	0	0	144.2	157	642	85	77	15	6	6	11	53	0	116	12	1
Espinal, Jose, Rockford	10	10	.500	4.92	24	24	1	0	0	0	120.2	147	545	83	66	7	2	4	2	41	1	107	4	7
Etler, Todd, Burlington	2	3	.400	2.09	25	0	0	0	12	3	43.0	34	175	13	10	2	2	0	2	14	2	40	2	0
Festa, Chris, Michigan	4	5	.444	4.04	37	10	0	0	11	0	93.2	109	418	50	42	8	1	3	5	34	1	53	7	2
Fidge, Darren, Fort Wayne	2	2	.500	2.84	8	0	0	0	5	0	12.2	15	61	4	4	0	3	1	5	4	1	8	1	0
Fitzgerald, Brian, Wisconsin*	3	1	.750	1.94	41	0	0	0	28	10	69.2	63	281	16	15	4	1	0	0	19	2	68	2	1
Fleming, John, South Bend	0	0	.000	3.86	5	0	0	0	2	0	9.1	11	44	6	4	0	0	0	0	7	1	5	2	0
Foran, John, West Michigan	2	2	.500	3.71	29	0	0	0	6	1	53.1	51	242	27	22	2	1	2	6	29	0	45	12	0
Fuentes, Brian, Wisconsin*	6	7	.462	3.56	22	22	0	0	0	0	118.2	84	486	52	47	6	3	3	8	59	0	153	11	3
Fulcher, John, Beloit*	0	4	.000	4.06	34	0	0	0	17	0	51.0	56	236	33	23	3	6	4	2	25	2	43	3	4
Gadway, Christopher, C.R.	0	1	.000	4.56	15	0	0	0	3	0	23.2	23	101	12	12	1	0	0	3	9	0	14	3	1
Gallagher, Keith, Peoria	2	1	.667	5.79	31	1	0	0	7	0	56.0	68	269	45	36	6	0	2	11	29	1	43	3	0
Gandy, Josh, Fort Wayne*	2	4	.333	5.40	8	5	0	0	1	0	20.0	25	93	19	12	0	1	0	1	12	0	14	2	1
Garcia, Apostol, West Michigan	7	2	.778	3.02	33	5	0	0	10	1	65.2	48	275	26	22	2	1	0	4	31	0	52	10	2
Garcia, Eddy, Burlington	6	6	.500	5.58	22	6	0	0	7	0	69.1	84	321	49	43	4	2	2	6	21	0	60	5	5
Garcia, Gabe, Quad City	5	14	.263	4.40	26	25	2	0	0	0	149.1	153	668	86	73	11	3	0	8	75	4	112	14	0
Garcia, Jose, Beloit	6	11	.353	4.00	27	26	2	0	0	0	155.1	145	682	89	69	9	7	3	5	70	1	126	12	4
Garrett, Josh, Michigan	8	10	.444	4.80	22	22	2	0	0	0	138.2	164	619	94	74	13	7	4	13	35	0	64	23	3
Garza, Chris, Fort Wayne*	5	2	.714	1.99	60	0	0	0	32	15	95.0	67	385	28	21	2	3	2	3	38	1	90	11	0
Gillian, Charlie, Fort Wayne	0	0	.000	3.16	22	0	0	0	7	3	25.2	21	114	11	9	1	1	0	6	13	0	24	2	0
Gissell, Christopher, Rockford	6	11	.353	4.45	26	24	3	1	1	0	143.2	155	646	89	71	7	5	4	11	62	1	105	11	3
Giuliano, Joe, Burlington	6	5	.545	4.91	32	15	0	0	7	0	113.2	123	503	74	62	9	7	5	8	44	2	76	3	0
Gnirk, Mark, Beloit	3	2	.600	3.87	38	0	0	0	14	1	76.2	95	333	46	33	2	2	2	2	18	0	63	9	0
Gonzalez, Edwin, Lansing	3	5	.375	3.65	11	11	0	0	0	0	69.0	67	283	32	28	4	2	4	3	15	0	58	3	0
Gonzalez, Jose, Wisconsin	2	2	.500	2.77	8	7	0	0	0	0	39.0	35	170	15	12	4	0	2	4	15	0	43	2	1
Gooding, Jason, Lansing*	0	1	.000	5.79	1	1	0	0	0	0	4.2	6	24	5	3	0	0	1	1	1	0	3	2	0
Green, Jason, Quad City	7	12	.368	4.58	23	22	1	0	1	0	125.2	126	548	79	64	9	5	2	8	53	2	96	12	2
Greene, Danny, Cedar Rapids	1	1	.500	0.45	24	0	0	0	18	12	39.2	27	156	7	2	1	1	0	1	11	0	42	1	0
Gutierrez, Alfredo, Beloit	4	3	.571	4.19	19	6	0	0	6	0	62.1	64	269	38	29	6	6	1	2	22	1	35	4	2
Gutierrez, Javier, Wisconsin	2	3	.400	2.83	13	3	0	0	2	0	35.0	29	149	13	11	2	1	0	1	19	1	36	4	2
Guzman, Domingo, Clinton	4	5	.444	3.19	12	12	5	0	0	0	79.0	66	320	36	28	7	2	2	3	25	0	91	5	2
Harriger, Mark, Cedar Rapids	1	6	.143	7.82	12	11	1	1	1	0	50.2	70	251	50	44	4	3	3	1	33	1	50	10	4
Hart, Len, Rockford*	2	1	.667	2.09	27	0	0	0	5	0	47.1	30	194	11	11	0	1	0	2	28	1	55	5	0
Harvell, Pete, South Bend*	4	5	.444	2.90	50	0	0	0	39	13	62.0	50	276	27	20	2	1	0	3	36	6	57	5	0
Hawkins, Alsharik, Beloit	1	4	.200	10.58	6	6	0	0	0	0	24.2	46	133	33	29	8	0	1	5	12	0	17	2	1
Hazlett, Andy, Michigan*	1	0	1.000	5.25	2	2	0	0	0	0	12.0	15	50	7	7	2	0	0	0	1	0	12	0	0
Hecht, Brian, Quad City	0	0	.000	2.16	5	0	0	0	4	1	8.1	4	32	3	2	0	0	0	0	2	0	5	1	0
Henderson, Juan, Cedar Rapids	1	4	.200	9.13	20	7	0	0	4	1	45.1	70	224	55	46	9	1	5	4	17	0	21	5	2
Hite, Kevin, Clinton	5	5	.500	3.31	38	4	1	0	17	1	87.0	86	354	38	32	6	0	4	1	11	0	85	2	1
Hoff, Steve, Clinton*	7	1	.875	2.71	12	12	1	0	0	0	76.1	72	318	28	23	4	2	4	5	18	0	78	5	0
Hooten, David, Fort Wayne	11	8	.579	2.61	28	27	2	2	0	0	165.2	134	675	57	48	5	4	2	9	54	0	138	4	6
Hueston, Stephen, Lansing	2	2	.500	7.44	34	7	0	0	5	0	71.1	95	345	65	59	6	6	3	6	49	1	42	5	2
Huls, Steve, Fort Wayne	0	0	.000	18.00	1	0	0	0	1	0	1.0	4	6	2	2	0	0	0	0	0	0	1	0	0
Humphreys, Kevin, Cedar Rapids	5	1	.833	5.62	30	0	0	0	16	2	65.2	75	283	45	41	9	2	3	7	9	0	40	5	3
Hunter, Germaine, Michigan	5	4	.556	3.64	52	0	0	0	21	1	71.2	65	322	40	29	8	3	4	2	42	4	68	10	6
Hurst, Doug, Burlington	2	1	.667	3.13	22	0	0	0	9	1	46.0	44	194	19	16	4	0	3	2	18	1	23	3	2
Ishee, Gabe, Beloit	3	1	.750	3.77	13	0	0	0	4	1	28.2	20	122	12	12	3	0	0	3	18	1	24	2	1
Jacobs, Russell, Wisconsin	4	2	.667	4.44	21	9	0	0	2	1	77.0	62	339	41	38	7	3	4	3	58	1	76	14	1
Johannsen, Jeff, Kane County*	0	0	.000	7.15	7	0	0	0	3	0	11.1	13	55	10	9	2	0	2	0	7	0	10	3	0
Karnuth, Jason, Peoria	0	3	.000	6.65	4	4	0	0	0	0	23.0	29	102	19	17	1	1	1	1	7	1	12	2	1
Kaye, Justin, Wisconsin	8	12	.400	7.30	28	26	0	0	2	0	127.0	129	618	113	103	13	6	5	16	104	0	115	21	6
Kelley, Jason, Rockford	1	0	1.000	4.97	22	0	0	0	12	2	29.0	29	148	20	16	2	1	0	1	27	1	20	10	0
Kennison, Kyle, Wisconsin	2	3	.400	2.13	40	0	0	0	18	6	80.1	54	324	24	19	5	1	2	2	38	1	112	6	4
Kiess, Barry, South Bend	3	4	.429	5.12	19	0	0	0	8	1	31.2	29	140	19	18	3	3	0	3	19	1	34	5	2
King, Brad, Rockford	0	0	.000	9.00	1	0	0	0	1	0	2.0	4	13	2	2	0	0	1	0	3	0	2	0	0

Pitcher, Team	W	L	Pct.	ERA	G	GS	CG	ShO	GF	Sv.	IP	H	TBF	R	ER	HR	SH	SF	HB	BB	IBB	SO	WP	Bk.
Kinney, Matt, Michigan	8	5	.615	3.53	22	22	2	1	0	0	117.1	93	514	59	46	4	5	2	0	78	2	123	6	0
Knotts, Gary, Kane County	1	5	.167	13.05	7	7	0	0	0	0	20.0	33	113	34	29	2	2	0	3	17	0	19	8	1
Koehler, Harold, Wisconsin	3	2	.600	4.47	23	0	0	0	10	2	48.1	50	214	30	24	6	1	1	4	15	4	33	1	1
Lara, Nelson, Kane County	1	2	.333	3.99	29	0	0	0	18	3	38.1	37	169	20	17	1	3	3	1	14	0	43	3	1
Leese, Brandon, Kane County	3	1	.750	3.83	7	6	0	0	0	0	42.1	27	171	18	18	0	1	2	3	18	0	32	3	1
Levan, Matt, Kane County	2	3	.400	3.09	11	9	0	0	0	0	43.2	44	183	16	15	5	1	0	3	16	0	45	5	2
Levrault, Allen, Beloit	3	10	.231	5.28	24	24	1	0	0	0	131.1	141	561	89	77	18	1	2	6	40	1	112	3	12
Lewis, Keith, Rockford	0	0	.000	0.00	1	0	0	0	1	0	1.0	0	4	0	0	0	0	0	0	1	0	0	0	0
Leyva, Edgar, Cedar Rapids	8	6	.571	4.69	22	21	0	0	1	1	121.0	118	529	73	63	13	3	3	9	58	1	77	3	3
Lindberg, Frederick, Fort Wayne*	0	0	.000	3.65	5	0	0	0	2	0	12.1	16	53	5	5	0	0	0	0	5	0	8	2	1
Lineweaver, Aaron, Lansing	7	1	.875	3.33	21	9	0	0	3	0	83.2	89	359	38	31	4	2	2	3	28	1	73	6	1
Lister, Martin, South Bend*	0	0	.000	16.20	3	0	0	0	2	0	3.1	6	18	6	6	1	0	1	0	2	0	1	1	0
Loiz, Niuman, Quad City	2	5	.286	4.87	18	9	0	0	4	0	64.2	63	282	37	35	8	3	3	5	29	1	49	10	0
Loonam, Rick, Fort Wayne	3	2	.600	5.66	34	1	0	0	6	0	49.1	63	245	36	31	3	1	2	1	33	0	35	8	2
Lopez, Rodrigo, Clinton	6	8	.429	3.18	37	14	2	0	19	9	121.2	103	508	49	43	6	7	4	3	42	1	123	3	4
Lynch, Jim, Quad City	3	3	.500	4.63	37	0	0	0	14	1	58.1	44	280	37	30	4	1	1	10	46	4	68	5	2
Lynch, Ryan, Fort Wayne*	2	2	.500	3.15	15	2	0	0	5	0	34.1	38	155	20	12	2	1	1	3	10	0	39	0	0
MacRae, Scott, Burlington	11	4	.733	3.82	27	26	4	1	0	0	160.1	159	694	76	68	9	7	4	9	57	0	89	18	1
Maldonado, Esteban, Quad City	4	4	.500	3.54	39	4	0	0	24	9	68.2	51	294	38	27	3	2	3	2	32	1	56	2	1
Malko, Bryan, Fort Wayne	4	4	.500	3.78	14	13	0	0	1	0	64.1	68	271	29	27	2	1	4	2	22	0	59	3	1
Marshall, Gary, Rockford*	4	1	.800	3.82	29	0	0	0	7	2	33.0	34	154	20	14	3	2	2	2	17	1	21	1	0
Martinez, Javier, Rockford	1	7	.125	5.70	17	17	1	0	0	0	79.0	85	369	61	50	7	3	2	3	50	1	70	10	0
Martinez, Romulo, W.Michigan	6	4	.600	2.39	36	0	0	0	12	2	79.0	73	329	28	21	3	6	0	0	21	0	51	4	3
Maurer, Dave, Clinton*	0	4	.000	2.88	25	0	0	0	10	3	34.1	24	142	15	11	1	2	1	0	15	0	43	3	1
Mays, Joe, Wisconsin	9	3	.750	2.09	13	13	1	0	0	0	81.2	62	322	20	19	3	1	2	6	23	1	79	1	0
McBride, Rodney, Fort Wayne	3	4	.429	6.31	31	0	0	0	11	0	45.2	57	232	40	32	3	0	1	4	32	0	54	7	1
McCall, Travis, South Bend*	7	6	.538	3.87	25	22	0	0	0	0	121.0	140	537	74	52	6	2	9	11	35	0	86	6	1
McCarter, Jason, Quad City	1	0	1.000	4.82	5	0	0	0	2	0	9.1	10	50	7	5	1	2	1	1	9	0	7	4	0
McClaskey, Tim, Kane County	2	1	.667	3.16	18	2	0	0	7	1	37.0	29	151	18	13	3	1	2	3	8	2	38	3	1
McCutcheon, Mike, South Bend*	7	5	.583	3.41	31	17	0	0	6	1	105.2	104	464	55	40	5	3	5	5	49	1	67	9	2
McFerrin, Chris, Quad City	1	3	.250	5.79	37	0	0	0	18	3	56.0	55	269	42	36	7	1	2	11	49	1	47	10	0
McKnight, Tony, Quad City	4	9	.308	4.68	20	20	0	0	0	0	115.1	116	504	71	60	7	6	3	5	55	5	92	6	3
Meady, Todd, Lansing	0	1	.000	4.85	4	2	0	0	1	0	13.0	25	64	10	7	0	1	1	0	6	0	5	2	0
Meche, Gil, Wisconsin	0	2	.000	3.00	2	2	0	0	0	0	12.0	12	51	5	4	1	0	0	1	4	0	14	2	1
Middlebrook, Jason, Clinton	6	4	.600	3.98	14	14	2	1	0	0	81.1	76	353	46	36	4	3	1	1	39	0	86	6	5
Miller, Wade, Quad City	5	3	.625	3.36	10	8	2	0	1	0	59.0	45	235	27	22	7	0	1	0	10	0	50	4	0
Montgomery, Greg, Peoria	2	8	.200	8.53	40	11	0	0	5	1	82.1	103	424	89	78	6	1	5	8	69	4	68	27	3
Moore, Jason, South Bend	0	0	.000	0.00	1	0	0	0	0	0	0.0	0	3	0	0	0	0	0	0	3	0	0	0	0
Moreno, Orber, Lansing	4	8	.333	4.81	27	25	0	0	0	0	138.1	150	603	83	74	15	6	4	8	45	0	128	9	0
Morris, Alex, Kane County	4	0	1.000	5.34	19	0	0	0	5	0	32.0	39	149	24	19	3	2	1	1	19	2	22	6	1
Mullen, Scott, Lansing*	5	2	.714	3.70	16	16	0	0	0	0	92.1	90	391	46	38	14	0	3	4	31	0	78	2	1
Musgrave, Scott, Michigan*	4	5	.444	5.61	15	11	0	0	2	0	78.2	96	357	59	49	11	4	2	5	17	2	51	3	1
Myers, Taylor, Lansing	1	1	.500	9.26	8	2	0	0	3	1	23.1	29	116	24	24	10	1	1	4	13	0	19	0	0
Nash, Damon, Clinton	1	1	.500	3.86	4	0	0	0	1	0	7.0	5	33	3	3	0	0	0	2	5	0	6	2	0
Neiman, Josh, Clinton	0	0	.000	12.91	5	0	0	0	2	0	7.2	16	44	11	11	2	1	1	1	4	1	5	1	0
Norris, Ben, South Bend*	1	8	.111	4.03	14	13	0	0	0	0	60.1	69	291	44	27	7	2	2	6	31	0	40	2	1
Norris, Mac, Beloit	1	1	.500	8.62	4	4	0	0	0	0	15.2	20	81	18	15	0	0	0	2	13	0	10	2	0
Norton, Phillip, Rockford*	9	3	.750	3.22	18	18	3	0	0	0	109.0	92	460	51	39	4	3	3	1	44	1	114	12	1
Nussbeck, Mark, Peoria	8	12	.400	4.58	27	27	2	2	0	0	151.1	181	683	92	77	14	4	8	3	56	3	132	6	4
Oleksik, George, South Bend	3	2	.600	2.52	24	0	0	0	6	1	50.0	52	223	26	14	3	2	4	2	29	1	44	3	0
Onofrei, Tim, Peoria	5	5	.500	4.78	42	9	0	0	4	0	98.0	111	442	66	52	6	4	5	5	45	1	69	4	0
Opipari, Mario, Fort Wayne	6	7	.462	3.44	53	2	0	0	27	8	70.2	71	307	45	27	2	5	3	3	24	3	61	7	1
O'Quinn, Jimmy, Cedar Rapids*	0	1	.000	8.22	14	0	0	0	7	0	15.1	17	71	14	14	4	1	1	0	11	1	17	1	0
O'Reilly, John, Beloit	9	2	.818	3.64	36	7	0	0	16	2	101.1	95	433	51	41	4	3	2	5	43	0	106	6	2
Ortiz, Ramon, Cedar Rapids	11	10	.524	3.58	27	27	8	4	0	0	181.0	156	740	78	72	22	2	1	7	53	0	225	14	5
O'Toole, Ryan, Burlington	1	1	.500	1.93	3	0	0	0	1	0	9.1	9	41	4	2	1	0	1	0	3	0	4	0	0
Palki, Jeromy, Wisconsin	9	3	.750	2.78	44	0	0	0	35	8	64.2	50	255	22	20	2	5	2	2	18	2	75	2	0
Paredes, Carlos, Lansing	0	1	.000	9.00	5	0	0	0	3	0	7.0	8	36	7	7	0	0	0	1	8	0	9	3	0
Paredes, Roberto, Beloit	5	4	.556	2.86	46	0	0	0	44	15	50.1	36	225	19	16	2	2	4	4	33	2	49	5	0
Parent, Jerry, Clinton	0	0	.000	0.00	2	0	0	0	2	0	2.0	0	8	0	0	0	0	0	0	2	0	1	0	0
Partenheimer, Brian, Michigan*	1	1	.500	6.65	17	0	0	0	4	0	21.2	32	104	16	16	1	0	2	3	9	3	16	4	0
Passini, Brian, Beloit*	9	5	.643	3.22	19	19	1	0	0	0	123.0	114	505	48	44	14	2	1	4	35	0	116	3	3
Patterson, John, South Bend	1	9	.100	3.23	18	18	0	0	0	0	78.0	63	327	32	28	3	1	2	5	34	0	95	8	0
Penny, Brad, South Bend	10	5	.667	2.73	25	25	0	0	0	0	118.2	91	489	44	36	4	5	0	4	43	2	116	10	2
Penny, Tony, Lansing	4	1	.800	5.21	22	2	0	0	6	0	38.0	46	179	30	22	8	3	0	0	15	1	25	5	1
Perry, Tim, Clinton	1	0	1.000	4.32	6	0	0	0	3	0	8.1	9	47	7	4	0	1	1	1	10	0	13	2	1
Peters, Don, South Bend	0	2	.000	2.93	13	0	0	0	5	0	15.1	19	65	7	5	0	1	0	1	4	0	8	1	0
Peterson, Jay, Burlington	14	6	.700	4.48	26	26	0	0	0	0	144.2	139	646	88	72	12	3	2	4	79	0	112	10	0
Phillips, Jon, Burlington	4	5	.444	3.95	37	1	0	0	14	0	70.2	63	306	33	31	3	3	5	6	33	1	66	2	0
Poepard, Scott, Fort Wayne	0	0	.000	0.00	1	0	0	0	0	0	1.0	0	5	0	0	0	0	0	0	2	0	2	0	0
Polanco, Elvis, Rockford	2	5	.286	8.60	16	5	0	0	4	0	45.0	66	235	53	43	4	1	5	1	36	2	34	7	0
Prempas, Lyle, Michigan*	2	1	.667	7.79	13	1	0	0	4	0	17.1	27	98	17	15	2	3	0	3	20	2	15	5	0
Puffer, Brandon, Cedar Rapids	0	0	.000	2.60	10	0	0	0	2	0	17.1	8	66	6	5	0	0	0	0	10	0	11	3	1
Quintal, Craig, West Michigan	11	6	.647	1.96	23	23	3	2	0	0	156.1	133	634	48	34	3	4	6	13	31	0	88	2	0
Reames, Jay, Peoria	6	9	.400	3.98	27	24	2	1	1	0	133.1	132	599	77	59	6	9	6	5	86	3	83	12	0
Rector, Bobby, Kane County	1	0	1.000	0.86	3	3	1	1	0	0	21.0	11	76	2	2	1	1	0	0	4	0	24	0	0
Reed, Steve, Peoria	4	3	.571	5.95	38	6	0	0	7	0	75.2	107	349	56	50	7	4	1	5	16	0	64	4	2
Reitsma, Chris, Michigan	4	1	.800	2.90	9	9	0	0	0	0	49.2	57	217	23	16	4	0	2	2	13	0	41	3	0
Richards, Mark, Kane County	1	1	.500	2.38	18	0	0	0	5	1	34.0	34	142	13	9	3	2	0	1	7	3	27	1	0
Richardson, Kasey, Fort Wayne*	7	5	.583	3.07	19	19	1	1	0	0	114.1	100	476	47	39	5	4	3	4	46	0	84	10	0
Ricketts, Chad, Rockford	4	0	1.000	2.48	16	0	0	0	10	3	29.0	19	116	9	8	1	1	1	1	11	2	32	1	0
Riedling, John, Burlington	7	6	.538	5.26	35	16	0	0	11	0	102.2	101	461	70	60	8	3	5	7	47	0	104	10	0
Riegert, Tim, Peoria*	4	2	.667	3.11	55	0	0	0	19	0	75.1	79	324	35	26	5	0	5	1	31	0	69	2	4

Pitcher, Team	W	L	Pct.	ERA	G	GS	CG	ShO	GF	Sv.	IP	H	TBF	R	ER	HR	SH	SF	HB	BB	IBB	SO	WP	Bk.
Riggan, Jerrod, Cedar Rapids	9	8	.529	4.89	19	19	3	1	0	0	116.0	132	506	70	63	15	3	7	2	36	2	65	12	2
Rijo, Jose, Quad City	3	6	.333	4.40	35	0	0	0	19	2	59.1	63	275	43	29	6	2	3	7	27	6	41	3	2
Rivera, Miguel, Peoria	0	0	.000	0.00	1	0	0	0	1	0	1.0	1	4	0	0	0	0	0	0	1	0	0	0	0
Robbins, Jason, South Bend	2	0	1.000	0.87	5	4	0	0	0	0	20.2	7	78	2	2	1	1	0	3	10	0	26	1	0
Robertson, Jeromie, Quad City*	11	8	.579	4.07	26	25	2	1	1	1	146.0	151	647	86	66	12	1	4	8	56	1	135	5	3
Rodgers, Bobby, Kane County	8	10	.444	3.86	27	27	2	0	0	0	165.2	154	699	81	71	9	6	4	14	61	0	138	7	1
Rodriguez, Chad, Lansing	5	3	.625	4.01	48	0	0	0	37	12	60.2	66	256	29	27	5	4	1	4	11	0	48	3	0
Rodriguez, Hector, Cedar Rapids	1	0	1.000	12.19	9	0	0	0	4	0	10.1	14	58	15	14	4	0	1	0	13	0	15	1	0
Rodriguez, Juan, Cedar Rapids*	0	0	.000	54.00	1	0	0	0	1	0	1.0	6	12	7	6	1	0	0	0	2	0	0	1	0
Rodriguez, Larry, South Bend	4	11	.267	3.62	19	19	1	0	0	0	104.1	102	458	56	42	6	6	6	8	37	3	72	10	0
Rolocut, Brian, Rockford	0	1	.000	6.16	14	0	0	0	1	1	30.2	43	148	23	21	2	3	1	1	15	0	20	8	0
Romboli, Curtis, Michigan*	5	2	.714	3.00	46	1	0	0	20	1	69.0	60	293	29	23	3	5	5	3	25	2	69	6	0
Romo, Greg, West Michigan	12	6	.667	3.54	24	24	0	0	0	0	139.2	128	595	65	55	7	3	5	0	51	0	124	14	3
Rose, Brian, Michigan	4	1	.800	1.76	10	0	0	0	1	0	15.1	12	60	3	3	0	1	1	2	2	0	19	1	0
Rupcich, Larry, Kane County	0	0	.000	0.00	1	0	0	0	1	0	1.0	1	3	0	0	0	0	0	0	0	0	0	0	0
Sanchez, Martin, Kane County	3	5	.375	4.50	51	0	0	0	44	22	54.0	40	237	31	27	2	4	0	5	32	2	57	11	0
Sanders, Allen, Lansing	12	7	.632	3.78	32	18	2	1	7	2	140.1	143	594	72	59	15	3	6	2	32	0	79	8	1
Santiago, Derek, Kane County	1	6	.143	8.02	12	8	0	0	0	0	46.0	72	224	46	41	6	1	3	2	18	0	30	3	1
Santiago, Jose, Lansing	1	0	1.000	2.08	9	0	0	0	6	1	13.0	10	57	6	3	0	0	1	0	6	1	8	0	0
Schaffer, Trevor, Rockford	2	3	.400	2.47	46	0	0	0	42	21	47.1	44	206	16	13	3	2	0	5	19	2	46	7	0
Schroeder, Chad, West Michigan	2	3	.400	3.71	18	0	0	0	8	0	26.2	22	120	14	11	0	1	1	0	16	2	24	3	1
Scutero, Brian, Cedar Rapids	0	1	.000	0.87	10	0	0	0	9	1	10.1	14	54	5	1	0	1	0	0	6	3	11	1	0
Sekany, Jason, Michigan	5	6	.455	4.08	16	16	3	0	0	0	106.0	92	448	55	48	5	2	4	4	41	1	103	14	0
Serrano, Wascar, Clinton	0	1	.000	6.00	1	1	1	0	0	0	6.0	6	24	5	4	0	0	0	0	2	1	2	1	0
Simontacchi, Jason, Lansing	3	7	.300	6.97	29	1	0	0	11	2	60.2	93	295	56	47	7	3	4	4	15	1	38	1	2
Smetana, Steve, Michigan*	2	1	.667	2.35	18	0	0	0	6	2	30.2	23	132	16	8	1	1	3	1	12	0	29	2	0
Smith, Roy, Wisconsin	3	4	.429	5.59	18	11	0	0	4	0	66.0	81	304	50	41	3	1	2	2	31	0	38	14	2
Soriano, Jacobo, Cedar Rapids	1	4	.200	7.75	25	0	0	0	12	1	33.2	43	169	33	29	5	2	0	4	23	1	28	6	1
Sparks, Jeff, Burlington	2	5	.286	5.72	22	9	0	0	5	0	61.1	61	281	49	39	7	2	3	0	39	1	72	6	1
Spear, Russell, West Michigan	11	6	.647	2.96	23	23	1	1	0	0	139.2	126	605	63	46	9	3	3	11	61	0	112	9	0
Spiers, Corey, Fort Wayne*	5	9	.357	4.86	24	23	0	0	0	0	120.1	154	530	83	65	5	4	5	2	33	0	94	12	1
Stark, Dennis, Wisconsin	6	3	.667	1.97	16	15	1	0	0	0	91.1	52	361	27	20	3	4	1	2	33	0	105	5	1
Stein, Ethan, Lansing	6	10	.375	4.69	39	10	1	0	13	2	124.2	150	549	83	65	19	8	1	8	24	1	72	4	1
Steinmann, Scott, Wisconsin	0	1	.000	13.50	1	0	0	0	1	0	0.2	1	4	1	1	0	0	0	0	1	0	0	1	0
Stockstill, Jason, Cedar Rapids*	7	14	.333	5.38	27	27	1	0	0	0	160.2	167	706	111	96	25	3	5	5	86	1	116	10	4
Sullivan, Brendan, Clinton	7	5	.583	3.90	47	0	0	0	35	6	62.1	55	283	33	27	1	4	3	7	34	2	54	2	0
Szymborski, Thomas, Clinton	5	7	.417	3.88	22	22	1	1	0	0	134.2	141	591	67	58	11	3	4	12	46	0	74	7	1
Tank, Travis, Beloit	6	3	.667	3.87	41	0	0	0	18	1	79.0	80	339	42	34	6	3	1	3	33	0	45	7	0
Tanksley, Scott, Fort Wayne	0	1	.000	4.05	5	0	0	0	1	0	6.2	4	28	5	3	0	2	0	1	4	0	2	0	0
Tapani, Kevin, Rockford	1	0	1.000	0.82	2	2	0	0	0	0	11.0	5	37	1	1	0	0	0	0	0	0	7	0	0
Teut, Nate, Rockford*	0	1	.000	10.13	2	2	0	0	0	0	10.2	18	52	12	12	1	0	0	1	2	0	6	0	0
Thompson, Chris, Michigan	0	1	.000	1.15	8	0	0	0	3	0	15.2	11	62	7	2	1	1	0	0	1	1	13	1	0
Torres, Luis, Clinton	1	0	1.000	1.17	5	0	0	0	1	0	7.2	3	39	5	1	0	2	1	2	9	1	8	5	0
Townsend, Dave, Kane County	5	1	.833	2.40	12	11	1	0	0	0	63.2	54	260	20	17	4	0	2	8	16	0	51	5	1
Tranbarger, Mark, South Bend*	2	2	.500	4.14	32	0	0	0	9	0	54.1	56	239	29	25	3	3	1	4	27	4	39	6	1
Tribe, Byron, Rockford	2	2	.500	5.40	13	0	0	0	4	0	21.2	20	100	14	13	1	3	2	1	20	1	30	1	3
Tryon, Eric, Burlington*	2	0	1.000	3.53	7	7	0	0	0	0	35.2	37	163	15	14	1	0	3	2	19	0	25	1	0
Vanwormer, Marc, South Bend	0	5	.000	5.54	39	0	0	0	7	1	76.1	90	356	63	47	7	0	5	5	45	1	56	23	1
Verplancke, Joe, South Bend	1	0	1.000	1.93	2	0	0	0	0	0	4.2	3	20	1	1	0	0	0	0	3	0	3	1	0
Viegas, Randy, Clinton*	1	1	.500	2.70	18	0	0	0	6	2	26.2	18	120	11	8	1	1	1	1	24	0	21	7	0
Villafana, Jose, Peoria	5	3	.625	2.82	10	10	1	0	0	0	60.2	59	260	22	19	5	2	2	1	26	2	28	8	2
Volkman, Keith, Cedar Rapids*	2	2	.500	2.45	38	0	0	0	20	5	51.1	36	218	18	14	7	1	3	7	27	1	43	6	0
Walker, Kevin, Clinton*	6	10	.375	4.88	19	19	3	1	0	0	110.2	133	495	80	60	9	2	5	4	37	0	80	5	2
Ward, Brandon, Rockford	1	2	.333	11.95	9	3	0	0	1	0	20.1	30	116	33	27	4	0	2	4	24	0	18	6	3
Watson, Mark, Beloit*	0	3	.000	6.68	8	7	0	0	0	0	32.1	40	153	33	24	3	0	3	1	20	0	33	3	0
Welch, Robb, Michigan	13	10	.565	4.22	26	26	3	1	0	0	153.2	142	678	88	72	8	3	4	17	80	2	158	19	1
West, Adam, Peoria*	3	4	.429	3.02	62	0	0	0	16	0	65.2	46	274	23	22	2	3	2	3	33	4	83	3	0
Westfall, Allan, Wisconsin	0	2	.000	3.62	18	0	0	0	10	3	32.1	26	142	14	13	2	0	2	1	20	2	41	4	0
Weymouth, Marty, Wisconsin	5	7	.417	5.06	23	19	0	0	0	0	110.1	116	484	75	62	14	2	3	3	33	1	83	5	2
Widerski, Jon, Kane County	2	4	.333	5.71	17	10	0	0	0	0	64.2	76	307	46	41	5	1	1	14	30	0	45	5	0
Williamson, Jeremy, Lansing*	1	1	.500	4.22	8	7	0	0	1	0	32.0	31	141	22	15	3	0	1	0	16	0	24	0	0
Wimberly, Larry, Michigan*	1	3	.250	6.89	13	4	0	0	4	1	31.1	34	138	25	24	4	0	0	2	9	0	27	3	0
Witte, Dominic, Clinton	1	4	.200	3.58	40	1	0	0	16	1	65.1	77	295	44	26	7	6	0	5	10	1	55	0	0
Workman, Widd, Clinton	9	10	.474	4.94	25	25	1	0	0	0	144.0	161	663	91	79	17	1	8	12	72	0	107	17	5
Wright, Scott, Burlington	5	7	.417	3.11	42	1	0	0	20	5	84.0	74	351	39	29	5	3	1	1	34	3	75	8	1
Wyckoff, Travis, Kane County*	4	2	.667	2.68	40	0	0	0	14	0	50.1	50	226	23	15	2	3	0	5	22	1	36	3	0
Yanez, Luis, Quad City	1	2	.333	4.81	27	2	0	0	18	7	39.1	46	174	25	21	8	1	0	0	14	2	33	1	0
Yeskie, Nate, Fort Wayne	11	7	.611	4.84	27	27	2	0	0	0	165.1	190	718	99	89	12	3	3	5	41	1	111	7	3
Zaleski, Kevin, Kane County	2	3	.400	5.47	21	0	0	0	13	0	24.2	37	124	20	15	4	4	0	1	12	4	19	1	0
Zamarripa, Mark, West Michigan	3	1	.750	2.12	20	0	0	0	9	2	29.2	13	128	17	7	0	2	1	2	18	2	41	3	4
Zapata, Juan, Beloit	1	2	.333	6.86	12	0	0	0	4	0	21.0	26	98	20	16	5	1	2	2	9	0	14	4	0
Zimmerman, Jordan, Wisconsin*	0	1	.000	5.82	3	3	0	0	0	0	17.0	18	75	11	11	0	0	1	0	10	0	18	2	0

COMBINATION SHUTOUTS: **Beloit (5)**—Garcia-Ishee, Garcia-O'Reilly, Barnes-Tank, Akin-Zapata-Paredes, O'Reilly-Tank-Paredes. **Burlington (1)**—Peterson-Hurst-Sparks-Cushman. **Cedar Rapids (1)**—Leyva-Humphreys. **Clinton (2)**—Szymborski-Hite, Workman-Viegas. **Fort Wayne (9)**—Richardson-Hooten-Gillian-Bauder-Fidge, Malko-Gillian-Opipari, Hooten-Dose, Richardson-Garza, Spiers-Gillian, Spiers-Garza-Opipari-Lynch, Bauder-Opipari, Hooten-Opipari, Hooten-Dose-Garza. **Kane County (5)**—Billingsley-Sanchez, Duncan-Johannsen-Sanchez, Billingsley-McClaskey, Leese-Levan-Duncan-Sanchez, Levan-McClaskey-Richards. **Lansing (4)**—Hueston-Stein, Gonzalez-Penny-Stein-Rodriguez, Sanders-Stein, Sanders-Stein-Rodriguez. **Michigan (3)**—Sekany-Romboli-Hunter-Thompson, Kinney-Beale, Welch-Romboli-Festa. **Peoria (7)**—Nussbeck-Onofrei-Crafton-West, Gallagher-Riegert, DeWitt-Reed-West-Crafton, DeWitt-West-Montgomery-DeLeon, Villafana-Montgomery-Crafton, DeWitt-Crafton, Nussbeck-Riegert-DeLeon. **Quad-City (3)**—Garcia-Miller-Robertson, McKnight-Duncan-Maldonado, Yanez-Rijo. **Rockford (8)**—Espinal-Hart-Kelly, Espinal-Ricketts, Cannon-Crane, Norton-Hart-Schaffer, Cannon-Cedeno, Downs-Brookens-Schaffer, Downs-Schaffer, Downs-Brookens. **South Bend (6)**—McCall-Verplancke-Bell-Harvell, Penny-McCutcheon-Crews, Penny-Oleksik-Crews, Penny-Crews, Penny-McCutcheon, Penny-Bedinger. **West Michigan (6)**—Bruner-Foran-Darwin, Quintal-Foran-Garcia, Darwin-Zamarripa, Dace-Garcia-Cordero, Romo-Cordero, Bruner-Garcia. **Wisconsin (13)**—Mays-Kennison, Kaye-Fitzgerald, Weymouth-Kennison, Weymouth-Palki, Fuentes-Kennison, Mays-Kennison, Mays-Kennison-Fitzgerald, Kaye-Westfall, Fuentes-Westfall, Ayala-Koehler, Gonzalez-Fitzgerald-Palki, Weymouth-Fitzgerald, Gonzalez-Fitzgerald.

NO-HIT GAMES: Borkowski, West Michigan, defeated Kane County, 6-0, April 20; Ortiz, Cedar Rapids, defeated Quad City, 12-0, August 7; Cames, Kane County, defeated Peoria, 1-0, August 24.

1997 FIELDING

TEAM

Team	Pct.	G	PO	A	E	TC	DP	PB
Kane County	.969	138	3576	1463	159	5198	115	17
Cedar Rapids	.967	138	3567	1552	174	5293	138	22
Burlington	.967	140	3599	1482	176	5257	134	25
Wisconsin	.967	139	3653	1454	177	5284	111	25
Lansing	.966	137	3591	1456	176	5223	120	13
Fort Wayne	.965	135	3587	1635	187	5409	145	14
West Michigan...	.965	131	3508	1550	182	5240	126	20
Peoria	.962	139	3608	1436	198	5242	123	22
Beloit	.962	133	3454	1426	192	5072	128	18
Quad City..........	.959	134	3404	1381	203	4988	104	22
Rockford........	.958	132	3426	1403	210	5039	122	20
Clinton	.958	136	3505	1493	220	5218	104	20
South Bend.......	.958	137	3536	1505	223	5264	121	26
Michigan........	.957	137	3504	1389	218	5111	117	19

TRIPLE PLAYS: Quad City 2, Peoria.

INDIVIDUAL

FIRST BASEMEN

NOTE: All caps denotes fielding-percentage leader based on 70 games for catchers, 93 for all other non-pitchers and 144 innings for pitchers. *Throws lefthanded.

Player, Team	Pct.	G	PO	A	E	TC	DP
Agnoly, Earl, Kane County	1.000	9	64	4	0	68	5
Allen, Marlon, Burlington	.983	51	420	33	8	461	37
Alleyne, Roberto, Quad City.......	1.000	1	2	1	0	3	0
Allison, Bradley, South Bend	1.000	3	18	1	0	19	0
Amado, Jose, Lansing	.981	12	91	10	2	103	13
Blosser, Doug, Lansing	1.000	7	32	2	0	34	1
Bly, Derrick, Rockford	1.000	7	36	1	0	37	3
Britt, Bryan, Peoria	.989	71	498	41	6	545	48
Burns, Kevin, Quad City*	.984	129	1128	68	20	1216	94
Catlett, David, Rockford.............	.972	19	128	13	4	145	14
Chavera, Arnie, Quad City	1.000	5	42	2	0	44	0
Cruz, Cirilo, Wisconsin..............	.974	18	142	9	4	155	10
Curtis, Matt, Cedar Rapids.........	1.000	5	47	2	0	49	0
Deck, Billy, Peoria*	.992	79	645	56	6	707	61
Dubose, Brian, West Michigan.....	.997	33	314	22	1	337	26
Duffy, James, Quad City..............	1.000	1	3	0	0	3	0
Dunn, Nathan, Clinton	.986	7	62	8	1	71	2
Fick, Robert, West Michigan	.990	96	970	60	10	1040	88
Fuentes, Javier, Michigan...........	.875	1	6	1	1	8	0
Garrett, Jason, Kane County	.992	123	1084	76	9	1169	90
Gillespie, Eric, Cedar Rapids	.991	101	905	64	9	978	91
Gjerde, Jeff, South Bend	.980	31	266	21	6	293	26
Hampton, Mike, Burlington	1.000	1	3	0	0	3	0
Hartman, Ron, South Bend	.974	4	37	1	1	39	2
Hillenbrand, Shea, Michigan	.979	16	133	6	3	142	10
Ingram, Darron, Burlington	.987	23	213	15	3	231	22
Jones, Jay, Kane County	1.000	10	74	4	0	78	6
Landry, Jacques, West Michigan	1.000	4	20	1	0	21	2
Layne, Jason, Lansing	.984	56	474	26	8	508	49
Leon, Jose, Peoria	1.000	1	1	0	0	1	0
Lopiccolo, Jamie, Beloit..............	1.000	3	28	1	0	29	2
LoCurto, Gary, Michigan	.981	112	909	63	19	991	83
Macalutas, Jon, Beloit...............	.983	43	333	22	6	361	38
Madonna, Chris, Michigan	1.000	2	12	0	0	12	3
Martinez, Tony, South Bend	.984	42	353	26	6	385	26
Martinez, Victor, Wisconsin	1.000	1	2	0	0	2	0
Mejia, Marlon, Quad City	1.000	1	4	2	0	6	0
Miranda, Tony, Lansing	1.000	2	22	0	0	22	2
Montas, Ricardo, Lansing	1.000	1	2	0	0	2	0
Moore, Jason, South Bend	.981	51	427	34	9	470	39
Osborne, Mark, South Bend........	.975	13	103	12	3	118	8
Paciorek, Peter, Clinton*	.987	125	1148	64	16	1228	87
Patterson, Jacob, Fort Wayne* ..	.997	57	566	35	2	603	54
Pellow, Kit, Lansing	.986	18	132	8	2	142	16
Peterman, Tommy, Fort Wayne*	.988	31	247	10	3	260	27
Peters, Tony, Beloit	1.000	2	8	1	0	9	0
Prodanov, Peter, Michigan	.970	13	89	7	3	99	10
Regan, Jason, Wisconsin............	.935	5	26	3	2	31	1
Reyes, Freddy, Fort Wayne	.984	52	504	35	9	548	48
Rodriguez, Juan, Cedar Rapids*	.981	22	147	8	3	158	11
Salazar, Juan, Rockford	.987	19	143	4	2	149	8
Smith, Matt, Lansing*	.990	54	468	29	5	502	26
Sorg, Jay, Burlington	.994	64	582	40	4	626	60
Steinmann, Scott, Wisconsin.......	.988	30	228	20	3	251	17
Vallone, Gar, Cedar Rapids	1.000	5	31	0	0	31	3
Walther, Chris, Beloit	.992	48	362	30	3	395	35
Washam, Jason, Beloit	.993	53	426	27	3	456	35
Watkins, Sean, Clinton*	1.000	8	53	6	0	59	5
Welles, Robby, Cedar Rapids......	.989	11	87	6	1	94	10
Whitehead, Braxton, Burlington ..	1.000	6	41	2	0	43	4
Wooten, Shawn, Cedar Rapids ..	1.000	9	66	6	0	72	5
ZACHMANN, Rob, Wisconsin	.996	96	774	51	3	828	70
Zuleta, Julio, Rockford..............	.985	100	828	62	14	904	80

TRIPLE PLAYS: Britt, Burns.

SECOND BASEMEN

Player, Team	Pct.	G	PO	A	E	TC	DP
Abbott, Chuck, Cedar Rapids	.973	113	196	339	15	550	69
Abreu, Dennis, Rockford	.985	39	57	72	2	131	13
Ahumada, Alejandro, Michigan ...	.857	1	2	4	1	7	0
Aversa, Joe, Kane County	1.000	1	0	1	0	1	1
Capellan, Rene, West Michigan ..	.960	77	141	245	16	402	50
Cepeda, Jose, Lansing	.984	43	69	119	3	191	15
Chamblee, James, Michigan	.959	104	194	278	20	492	63
Cross, Adam, Clinton	.972	23	25	44	2	71	3
Cruz, Cirilo, Wisconsin..............	.833	5	4	11	3	18	1
Dallimore, Brian, Quad City	.934	24	43	56	7	106	15
Davidson, Cleatus, Fort Wayne ..	.971	121	271	405	20	696	98
Davis, Josh, Clinton	1.000	1	3	1	0	4	0
Dunn, Nathan, Clinton	.950	7	12	26	2	40	3
Faurot, Adam, Beloit	.938	46	66	100	11	177	23
Fuentes, Javier, Michigan...........	.929	3	4	9	1	14	2
Glozier, Larry, Kane County	.979	12	17	30	1	48	4
Goodhart, Steve, Burlington........	.955	19	27	57	4	88	13
Harris, Rodger, Peoria	.930	51	74	98	13	185	21
Harrison, Adonis, Wisconsin	.950	119	198	294	26	518	63
Huls, Steve, Fort Wayne.............	.961	17	26	48	3	77	2
Hyers, Matt, Quad City	.956	23	35	52	4	91	12
Lewis, Keith, Rockford	.952	11	15	25	2	42	5
Lofton, James, Burlington	.968	75	146	216	12	374	38
Lorenzo, Juan, Fort Wayne	1.000	1	1	2	0	3	0
Martin, Jared, South Bend	.949	26	35	59	5	99	12
Martinez, David E., Beloit...........	.944	16	31	37	4	72	6
Martinez, Victor, Wisconsin	.955	6	7	14	1	22	3
McCLURE, Brian, Clinton	.978	116	178	319	11	508	60
Mejia, Marlon, Quad City	1.000	3	4	7	0	11	0
Meyers, Chad, Rockford	.951	97	176	249	22	447	51
Miles, Aaron, Quad City	.961	82	135	206	14	355	41
Montas, Ricardo, Lansing	1.000	1	0	1	0	1	0
Moore, Kenderick, Lansing	.971	57	124	142	8	274	30
Nunez, Jose, South Bend	.957	28	44	67	5	116	9
Ortiz, Asbel, Michigan	.945	30	43	77	7	127	17
Ozarowski, Richard, W.Michigan	.979	11	17	30	1	48	3
Presto, Nick, Burlington	.980	26	67	82	3	152	22
Prodanov, Peter, Michigan	.913	17	19	23	4	46	3
Regan, Jason, Wisconsin............	1.000	1	1	2	0	3	0
Rexrode, Jackie, South Bend	.949	92	204	257	25	486	54
Rivera, Miguel, Peoria	1.000	22	29	39	0	68	6
Rupcich, Larry, Kane County	1.000	6	7	12	0	19	0
Samboy, Nelson, Quad City	.950	9	16	22	2	40	4
Sanchez, Orlando, Michigan	.909	4	5	5	1	11	2
Sanchez, Yuri, Burlington	1.000	1	3	2	0	5	0
Santana, Pedro, West Michigan..	.926	45	84	155	19	258	27
Schafer, Brett, Lansing...............	1.000	4	5	7	0	12	2
Schmidt, Todd, Peoria	1.000	1	0	1	0	1	0
Steinmann, Scott, Wisconsin.......	.750	1	1	2	1	4	0
Taft, Brett, Lansing.....................	.955	47	101	130	11	242	31
Tanner, Paul, Peoria	.967	85	168	213	13	394	44
Thoen, E.J., Cedar Rapids	.963	18	35	42	3	80	15
Valera, Ramon, Wisconsin	1.000	4	6	12	0	18	4
Vallone, Gar, Cedar Rapids	1.000	11	16	20	0	36	4
Venghaus, Jeff, Kane County	.958	125	234	313	24	571	77
Wetmore, Michael, Beloit............	.981	89	155	257	8	420	54
Williams, Jason, Burlington.........	1.000	23	33	64	0	97	10

TRIPLE PLAY: Dallimore.

CLASS A Midwest League

THIRD BASEMEN

Player, Team	Pct.	G	PO	A	E	TC	DP
Abreu, Nelson, Rockford	.882	26	22	45	9	76	1
Amado, Jose, Lansing	.953	27	26	55	4	85	7
Andersen, Ryan, Rockford	.952	8	4	16	1	21	0
Baderdeen, Kevin, Burlington	.883	35	25	81	14	120	12
Bautista, Jorge, Kane County	.833	20	12	28	8	48	2
Bautista, Juan, South Bend	1.000	5	3	15	0	18	1
Bly, Derrick, Rockford	.914	92	63	191	24	278	22
Bovender, Andy, Quad City	.829	14	10	19	6	35	4
Capellan, Rene, West Michigan	1.000	3	2	6	0	8	0
Cepeda, Jose, Lansing	.923	37	22	50	6	78	2
Cronin, Shane, Clinton	.881	55	29	104	18	151	7
Cross, Adam, Clinton	.938	6	4	11	1	16	3
Dallimore, Brian, Quad City	.909	35	34	66	10	110	8
Dunn, Nathan, Clinton	.899	77	40	138	20	198	8
Faurot, Adam, Beloit	.900	6	5	13	2	20	0
Fick, Robert, West Michigan	1.000	3	4	3	0	7	0
Figueroa, Luis, Wisconsin	.912	115	69	202	26	297	15
Fuentes, Javier, Michigan	1.000	1	0	3	0	3	0
Gillespie, Eric, Cedar Rapids	.895	12	4	13	2	19	2
Glozier, Larry, Kane County	.875	3	0	7	1	8	1
Haas, Chris, Peoria	.919	26	16	52	6	74	7
Hampton, Mike, Burlington	.892	16	6	27	4	37	3
Hartman, Ron, South Bend	.925	48	34	89	10	133	9
Hillenbrand, Shea, Michigan	.737	8	4	10	5	19	0
Huls, Steve, Fort Wayne	.938	18	12	49	4	65	4
King, Brad, Rockford	1.000	1	1	2	0	3	1
Kleinz, Larry, Kane County	.909	106	52	217	27	296	16
Klimek, Josh, Beloit	.905	111	77	209	30	316	22
Landry, Jacques, West Michigan	.883	92	60	173	31	264	9
Layne, Jason, Lansing	.948	17	15	40	3	58	6
Lemonis, Chris, West Michigan	.875	26	14	42	8	64	4
Leon, Jose, Peoria	.902	107	68	163	25	256	21
Lofton, James, Burlington	.895	51	32	70	12	114	5
Lorenzo, Juan, Fort Wayne	1.000	1	0	3	0	3	0
Martinez, David E., Beloit	1.000	3	0	1	0	1	0
Martinez, Tony, South Bend	.918	43	33	79	10	122	10
Martinez, Victor, Wisconsin	.941	13	12	36	3	51	2
Mejia, Marlon, Quad City	.881	17	4	33	5	42	0
Meyers, Chad, Rockford	.789	10	2	13	4	19	2
Miranda, Tony, Lansing	.800	5	5	11	4	20	2
Montas, Ricardo, Lansing	.667	2	2	0	1	3	0
Moore, Jason, South Bend	.833	4	0	5	1	6	0
Moss, Rick, Fort Wayne	.909	119	67	244	31	342	18
Nunez, Jose, South Bend	.929	40	20	84	8	112	3
Ozarowski, Richard, W.Michigan	.915	20	14	51	6	71	5
Parker, Allan, Cedar Rapids	1.000	1	0	3	0	3	0
Pellow, Kit, Lansing	.805	51	38	90	31	159	5
Prodanov, Peter, Michigan	.750	4	3	3	2	8	0
Radcliff, Victor, Lansing	.750	1	1	2	1	4	0
Regan, Jason, Wisconsin	.905	10	2	17	2	21	2
Rivera, Miguel, Peoria	.960	17	11	37	2	50	0
Rupcich, Larry, Kane County	.879	12	5	24	4	33	4
Samboy, Nelson, Quad City	.750	4	1	5	2	8	0
Sasser, Rob, Cedar Rapids	.936	133	104	303	28	435	22
Saylor, Jamie, Quad City	1.000	1	1	0	0	1	0
Schafer, Brett, Lansing	.944	6	8	9	1	18	2
Sharp, Scott, Burlington	.800	3	3	1	1	5	0
Sorg, Jay, Burlington	.897	43	25	62	10	97	4
Steinmann, Scott, Wisconsin	1.000	6	1	8	0	9	2
Tanner, Paul, Peoria	1.000	4	1	4	0	5	0
Taveras, Jose, South Bend	.765	8	5	8	4	17	0
Thrower, Jake, Clinton	.917	4	7	4	1	12	0
Truby, Chris, Quad City	.926	67	39	149	15	203	10
Valera, Ramon, Wisconsin	1.000	3	2	4	0	6	1
VERAS, Wilton, Michigan	.944	130	99	220	19	338	29
Walker, Ron, Rockford	.750	4	1	5	2	8	1
Walther, Chris, Beloit	.892	24	16	42	7	65	4

SHORTSTOPS

Player, Team	Pct.	G	PO	A	E	TC	DP
Abbott, Chuck, Cedar Rapids	.923	19	33	51	7	91	13
Abreu, Dennis, Rockford	.915	95	140	256	37	433	47
Abreu, Nelson, Rockford	.920	33	40	75	10	125	16
Ahumada, Alejandro, Michigan	1.000	2	2	4	0	6	1
Andersen, Ryan, Rockford	.885	10	6	17	3	26	2
Aversa, Joe, Kane County	.966	62	83	175	9	267	39
Baderdeen, Kevin, Burlington	.929	4	3	10	1	14	1
Bautista, Juan, South Bend	.935	25	34	82	8	124	21
Bearden, Doug, Beloit	.923	55	76	105	15	196	24
Boughton, Mike, South Bend	.927	15	22	54	6	82	8
Butler, Brent, Peoria	.942	129	220	345	35	600	71
Carmona, Cesarin, Clinton	.899	64	90	205	33	328	38
Cepeda, Jose, Lansing	.872	10	9	32	6	47	5
Chamblee, James, Michigan	.933	27	29	69	7	105	10
Cross, Adam, Clinton	.830	14	14	30	9	53	4
Cuntz, Casey, South Bend	.945	48	71	119	11	201	28
Dallimore, Brian, Quad City	.910	68	108	185	29	322	25
DeLeon, Jorge, Michigan	.873	18	17	38	8	63	6
Dunn, Nathan, Clinton	.833	2	0	5	1	6	0
Faurot, Adam, Beloit	.907	51	78	127	21	226	29
Fuentes, Javier, Michigan	.936	25	31	57	6	94	12
Gillespie, Eric, Cedar Rapids	1.000	2	2	4	0	6	0
Glozier, Larry, Kane County	.936	41	54	93	10	157	21
Halloran, Matt, Clinton	.894	46	70	107	21	198	30
Huls, Steve, Fort Wayne	.939	16	12	50	4	66	7
Hyers, Matt, Quad City	.918	52	71	143	19	233	34
Klimek, Josh, Beloit	.958	7	13	10	1	24	1
Lewis, Keith, Rockford	.875	3	2	5	1	8	1
Lorenzo, Juan, Fort Wayne	1.000	2	1	3	0	4	1
Martin, Jared, South Bend	.778	4	3	4	2	9	1
Martinez, David E., Beloit	.914	9	13	19	3	35	4
Martinez, Victor, Wisconsin	1.000	3	0	3	0	3	1
Medrano, Steve, Lansing	.953	95	140	263	20	423	52
Meyers, Chad, Rockford	1.000	1	1	2	0	3	0
MITCHELL, Derek, W.Michigan	.959	110	156	380	23	559	73
Nunez, Jose, South Bend	.953	43	64	99	8	171	17
Olmeda, Jose, Michigan	.874	59	80	135	31	246	21
Ortiz, Asbel, Michigan	.857	8	12	18	5	35	6
Ozarowski, Richard, W.Michigan	.769	4	2	8	3	13	2
Parker, Allan, Cedar Rapids	.983	13	24	35	1	60	6
Presto, Nick, Burlington	1.000	1	2	3	0	5	1
Regan, Jason, Wisconsin	.955	7	5	16	1	22	3
Reynoso, Ismael, Kane County	.926	34	33	79	9	121	11
Rivas, Luis, Fort Wayne	.907	119	169	394	58	621	92
Rivera, Miguel, Peoria	.923	7	2	10	1	13	3
Rupcich, Larry, Kane County	.942	16	19	46	4	69	7
Sanchez, Orlando, Michigan	.922	16	26	57	7	90	17
Sanchez, Yuri, Burlington	.923	93	135	272	34	441	58
Santana, Pedro, West Michigan	.869	19	36	50	13	99	12
Saylor, Jamie, Quad City	.926	19	34	54	7	95	9
Smith, Jason, Rockford	.884	9	14	24	5	43	5
Steinmann, Scott, Wisconsin	.778	2	4	3	2	9	1
Taft, Brett, Lansing	.950	41	64	107	9	180	16
Tanner, Paul, Peoria	.944	16	25	26	3	54	5
Taveras, Jose, South Bend	.931	7	13	14	2	29	2
Thoen, E.J., Cedar Rapids	.899	102	141	269	46	456	65
Thrower, Jake, Clinton	.949	13	18	38	3	59	10
Valentin, Jose, Beloit	1.000	2	1	8	0	9	1
Valera, Gregori, South Bend	.839	8	7	19	5	31	1
Valera, Ramon, Wisconsin	.867	6	4	9	2	15	1
Vallone, Gar, Cedar Rapids	.865	10	10	22	5	37	5
Vazquez, Ramon, Wisconsin	.935	131	170	333	35	538	61
Wetmore, Michael, Beloit	.949	28	43	87	7	137	17
Williams, Jason, Burlington	.948	45	60	123	10	193	27

TRIPLE PLAYS: Butler, Dallimore, Hyers.

OUTFIELDERS

Player, Team	Pct.	G	PO	A	E	TC	DP
Abell, Antonio, Peoria	.938	11	15	0	1	16	0
Abreu, Nelson, Rockford	1.000	7	6	0	0	6	0
Adams, John, South Bend	.920	57	85	7	8	100	2
Agnoly, Earl, Kane County	.929	20	26	0	2	28	0
Airoso, Kurt, West Michigan	1.000	10	11	0	0	11	0
Alleyne, Roberto, Quad City	.948	59	90	1	5	96	0
Amerson, Gordon, Clinton*	.944	34	51	0	3	54	0
Barnes, John, Michigan	.974	113	213	8	6	227	1
Berger, Brandon, Lansing	.979	87	136	7	3	146	0
Bolivar, Papo, Fort Wayne	.958	90	110	4	5	119	1
Brown, Roosevelt, Kane County	.930	59	75	5	6	86	1
Burrows, Mike, Wisconsin*	.969	102	177	10	6	193	3
Calloway, Ronald, South Bend*	.846	8	10	1	2	13	0
Cameron, Ken, Peoria*	.977	96	166	5	4	175	0
Capellan, Rene, West Michigan	1.000	1	1	0	0	1	0
Carter, Cale, Cedar Rapids	.946	22	34	1	2	37	0
Carter, Quincy, Rockford	.977	104	169	3	4	176	1
Castro, Jose, Wisconsin*	.991	63	106	2	1	109	1
Catlett, David, Rockford	.750	9	6	0	2	8	0
Cedeno, Jesus, West Michigan	.961	109	163	10	7	180	1
Chavera, Arnie, Quad City	.913	23	20	1	2	23	0
Clark, Brady, Burlington	.986	117	265	9	4	278	2
Clark, Chris, Kane County	.920	19	23	0	2	25	0
Colon, Jose, Rockford	.961	56	91	8	4	103	5
Conti, Jason, South Bend	.981	117	240	13	5	258	6

Player, Team	Pct.	G	PO	A	E	TC	DP
Craig, Benjamin, Burlington	.939	40	44	2	3	49	0
Cruz, Cirilo, Wisconsin	.938	18	15	0	1	16	0
Curtis, Matt, Cedar Rapids	.946	17	31	4	2	37	1
Davidson, Cleatus, Fort Wayne	1.000	1	1	0	0	1	0
Deck, Billy, Peoria*	.926	31	50	0	4	54	0
Duffy, James, Quad City	1.000	5	12	0	0	12	0
Elliott, David, Beloit	.961	75	119	5	5	129	1
Ellison, Tony, Rockford	.970	22	31	1	1	33	1
Espino, Fernando, Wisconsin	1.000	2	7	0	0	7	0
Farraez, Jesus, Quad City	.961	79	119	4	5	128	0
Faurot, Adam, Beloit	.800	3	4	0	1	5	0
Fefee, Theo, Cedar Rapids*	.976	99	159	7	4	170	1
Felston, Anthony, Fort Wayne*	.974	91	143	5	4	152	2
Freitas, Joe, Peoria	.921	52	65	5	6	76	1
Gann, Jamie, South Bend	.895	9	15	2	2	19	0
Garrick, Matt, Cedar Rapids	1.000	1	1	0	0	1	0
Geronimo, Cesar, Cedar Rapids	1.000	13	21	0	0	21	0
Giambi, Jeremy, Lansing*	1.000	17	30	2	0	32	0
Guiel, Jeff, Cedar Rapids	.933	41	65	5	5	75	1
Gunderson, Shane, Fort Wayne	1.000	13	21	0	0	21	0
HALL, Doug, Rockford*	.991	111	210	7	2	219	2
Hallmark, Patrick, Lansing	.974	20	35	2	1	38	0
Ham, Kevin, Cedar Rapids	.971	121	220	16	7	243	5
Hampton, Mike, Burlington	.949	39	72	3	4	79	1
Harris, Rodger, Peoria	.973	29	35	1	1	37	0
Heinrichs, Jon, Kane County	1.000	60	81	4	0	85	0
Hogan, Todd, Peoria	.980	112	240	6	5	251	2
Horne, Tyrone, Kane County	.981	34	50	2	1	53	0
Horner, Jim, Wisconsin	1.000	1	1	0	0	1	0
Hudson, Bert, South Bend	.897	26	35	0	4	39	0
Huls, Steve, Fort Wayne	1.000	1	1	0	0	1	0
Ingram, Darron, Burlington	.963	86	127	3	5	135	0
Jefferson, Dave, Rockford	.966	17	27	1	1	29	0
Jenkins, Corey, Michigan	.941	72	104	7	7	118	2
Johnson, Heath, Fort Wayne	.964	22	26	1	1	28	0
Johnson, Rontrez, Michigan	.972	109	237	6	7	250	0
Knauss, Tom, Fort Wayne	1.000	14	20	2	0	22	0
LeBron, Juan, Lansing	.959	31	45	2	2	49	1
Leon, Jose, Peoria	1.000	2	1	1	0	2	0
Lindsey, Rodney, Clinton	.947	129	206	8	12	226	2
Liverziani, Claudio, Wisconsin	.992	75	114	10	1	125	2
Lofton, James, Burlington	1.000	3	6	0	0	6	0
Longmire, Marcel, Rockford	.938	70	89	2	6	97	2
Lopez, Henry, Fort Wayne	.956	87	145	8	7	160	0
Lopiccolo, Jamie, Beloit	.977	33	40	2	1	43	1
Macalutas, Jon, Beloit	1.000	4	7	0	0	7	0
Madera, Wil, South Bend*	.918	56	74	4	7	85	1
Marchiano, Mike, Wisconsin	1.000	3	2	0	0	2	0
Martinez, Tony, South Bend	.882	17	13	2	0	15	0
Martinez, Victor, Wisconsin	1.000	4	3	1	0	4	0
Melconian, Alex, Kane County	1.000	3	7	0	0	7	0
Meyer, Brad, Fort Wayne	1.000	10	13	0	0	13	0
Meyers, Chad, Rockford	1.000	24	26	2	0	28	0
Miranda, Tony, Lansing	.992	73	107	14	1	122	3
Moore, Donnie, Beloit	.935	44	80	6	6	92	1
Moore, Kenderick, Lansing	.982	57	106	4	2	112	1
Moss, Rick, Fort Wayne	1.000	3	3	0	0	3	0
Murphy, Nate, Cedar Rapids*	.969	18	30	1	1	32	0
Ortiz, Asbel, Michigan	1.000	1	1	0	0	1	0
Ozarowski, Richard, W.Michigan	1.000	1	3	0	0	3	0
Paciorek, Peter, Clinton*	1.000	3	6	0	0	6	0
Parent, Jerry, Clinton	.960	80	113	8	5	126	1
Pernell, Brandon, Clinton	.939	91	136	3	9	148	1
Peterman, Tommy, Fort Wayne*	.949	60	71	3	4	78	0
Peters, Tony, Beloit	.964	107	228	14	9	251	6
Pitts, Rick, Lansing	.952	25	39	1	2	42	0
Podsednik, Scott, Kane County*	.977	133	202	10	5	217	1
Poepard, Scott, Fort Wayne	.982	34	53	3	1	57	1
Pratt, Wes, Quad City	.983	118	228	10	4	242	3
Prodanov, Peter, Michigan	1.000	18	30	0	0	30	0
Radcliff, Victor, Lansing	.966	68	105	9	4	118	0
Ramirez, Julio, Kane County	.979	99	179	8	4	191	2
Reeder, Jim, Quad City	.945	81	117	3	7	127	0
Regan, Jason, Wisconsin	1.000	9	11	0	0	11	0
Roche, Marlon, Quad City	.971	68	96	4	3	103	0
Rodriguez, Juan, Cedar Rapids*	.979	96	174	10	4	188	3
Rojas, Christian, Burlington	.975	67	107	9	3	119	2
Ruotsinoja, Jacob, Clinton	1.000	34	50	4	0	54	1
Rutherford, Daryl, Clinton	.964	15	26	1	1	28	0
Ryan, Rob, South Bend*	.966	111	188	11	7	206	4
Sachse, Matt, Wisconsin*	.953	107	170	13	9	192	1
Sanchez, Marcos, Clinton	1.000	2	2	0	0	2	0
Sandoval, Jhensy, South Bend	1.000	19	29	1	0	30	0
Saturria, Luis, Peoria	.961	115	196	24	9	229	3
Schafer, Brett, Lansing	1.000	9	14	1	0	15	1
Schaub, Greg, Beloit	.953	107	190	14	10	214	2
Scott, Tom, Burlington	.987	44	74	2	1	77	0
Seal, Scott, Clinton*	.981	29	49	2	1	52	0
Sollmann, Scott, W.Michigan*	.982	119	264	6	5	275	1
Speed, Dorian, Rockford	1.000	8	11	0	0	11	0
Steinman, Scott, Wisconsin	1.000	7	14	0	0	14	0
Stenson, Dernell, Michigan*	.918	108	145	11	14	170	0
Stewart, Keith, Wisconsin	.857	4	6	0	1	7	0
Sweeney, Kevin, South Bend*	1.000	2	2	0	0	2	0
Tanner, Paul, Peoria	1.000	1	1	0	0	1	0
Valdez, Trovin, Burlington	.982	33	50	4	1	55	1
Vallone, Gar, Cedar Rapids	1.000	3	1	0	0	1	0
Venghaus, Jeff, Kane County	1.000	5	9	0	0	9	0
Wakeland, Chris, W.Michigan*	.972	111	169	7	5	181	3
Walther, Chris, Beloit	.935	52	54	4	4	62	0
Watts, Josh, Wisconsin	.952	44	54	5	3	62	1
Welles, Robby, Cedar Rapids	1.000	3	7	0	0	7	0
Williams, Micah, Lansing	.992	63	126	2	1	129	1
Zapata, Alexis, West Michigan	.951	51	76	2	4	82	0

CATCHERS

Player, Team	Pct.	G	PO	A	E	TC	DP	PB
Alaimo, Jason, Kane County	.995	33	185	20	1	206	5	5
Alfano, Jeff, Beloit	.962	32	226	29	10	265	7	9
Allison, Bradley, South Bend	.995	48	345	39	2	386	2	2
Barr, Tucker, Quad City	.981	66	457	53	10	520	2	13
Boyette, Tony, Burlington	.967	4	27	2	1	30	0	3
Buchman, Tom, Fort Wayne	.952	5	16	4	1	21	1	0
Cancel, Robinson, Beloit	.992	16	111	15	1	127	0	2
Curtis, Matt, Cedar Rapids	1.000	7	35	4	0	39	1	2
Davis, James, Burlington	.989	90	584	63	7	654	9	12
Davis, Josh, Clinton	.983	52	298	44	6	348	2	10
Doezie, Troy, Lansing	.932	17	74	8	6	88	1	1
Fick, Robert, West Michigan	.974	9	69	5	2	76	1	2
Gargiulo, Jimmy, Peoria	.983	95	636	97	13	746	3	19
Garrick, Matt, Cedar Rapids	.970	23	145	15	5	165	2	1
Gillespie, Eric, Cedar Rapids	.975	7	36	3	1	40	1	1
Graves, Bryan, Cedar Rapids	.982	64	368	61	8	437	6	5
Griffis, Cade, Lansing	.973	10	67	6	2	75	1	2
Hallmark, Patrick, Lansing	.980	62	398	43	9	450	2	7
Horner, Jim, Wisconsin	1.000	25	202	18	0	220	0	6
Houston, Tyler, Rockford	1.000	1	5	0	0	5	0	0
Jones, Jay, Kane County	.993	23	142	10	1	153	1	3
King, Brad, Rockford	.985	62	461	60	8	529	11	9
Kratochvil, Tim, Michigan	.990	40	279	25	3	307	3	3
Lisanti, Bob, Rockford	.975	66	412	50	12	474	2	6
Lomasney, Steve, Michigan	.983	94	623	83	12	718	3	12
Longmire, Marcel, Rockford	1.000	2	1	0	0	1	0	0
Loyd, Brian, Clinton	.977	60	457	47	12	516	5	4
Madonna, Chris, Michigan	.976	9	34	7	1	42	0	2
Maldonado, Carlos, Wis.	.989	97	857	105	11	973	6	10
McAffee, Josh, South Bend	.969	36	215	37	8	260	1	1
McClendon, Travis, Peoria	.938	5	28	2	2	32	1	1
McNeal, Pepe, Peoria	.987	54	345	33	5	383	2	2
Moeller, Chad, Fort Wayne	.984	107	824	90	15	929	7	8
Monzon, Jose, Cedar Rapids	.996	32	228	36	1	265	1	6
Morgan, James, South Bend	.875	3	7	0	1	8	0	0
Nieves, Wilbert, Clinton	.952	18	125	14	7	146	1	0
Osborne, Mark, South Bend	.979	58	411	55	10	476	9	16
Peters, Tony, Beloit	1.000	4	10	3	0	13	0	1
Prada, Nelson, Fort Wayne	.985	29	174	21	3	198	2	6
Prodanov, Peter, Michigan	1.000	12	67	12	0	79	0	2
ROBERTSON, Ryan, K.C.	.991	98	793	90	8	891	5	9
Robles, Juan, Lansing	.992	48	321	30	3	354	2	2
Rogue, Francisco, Beloit	.993	17	117	17	1	135	4	2
Rose, Mike, Quad City	.983	71	502	65	10	577	4	9
Salazar, Juan, Rockford	.982	24	142	18	3	163	0	5
Sanchez, Marcos, Clinton	.973	22	169	14	5	188	0	6
Sharp, Scott, Burlington	.986	27	189	21	3	213	2	7
Sosa, Franklin, West Michigan	.988	57	369	32	5	406	1	7
Steinmann, Scott, Wisconsin	.979	28	165	22	4	191	0	9
Stevenson, Chad, W.Michigan	.989	70	486	48	6	540	3	11
Suero, Ignacio, Beloit	.986	70	468	83	8	559	7	3
Ullery, David, Lansing	.989	18	77	12	1	90	1	1
Washam, Jason, Beloit	1.000	2	2	6	0	8	0	1
Whitehead, Braxton, Burl.	1.000	26	139	23	0	162	2	3
Wooten, Shawn, C.R.	1.000	19	100	13	0	113	0	7

CLASS A *Midwest League*

PITCHERS

Player, Team	Pct.	G	PO	A	E	TC	DP
Akin, Jay, Beloit*	.909	9	1	9	1	11	0
Almonte, Hector, Kane County	1.000	8	0	2	0	2	0
Andrews, Jeff, South Bend	.600	23	2	4	4	10	1
Avrard, Corey, Peoria	.833	20	6	14	4	24	2
Ayala, Julio, Wisconsin*	1.000	36	8	18	0	26	3
Baird, Brandon, Lansing*	.857	55	0	6	1	7	1
Barksdale, Shane, Quad City	1.000	8	1	1	0	2	0
Barnes, Larry, Beloit	1.000	13	0	11	0	11	1
Bauder, Mike, Fort Wayne*	.963	40	10	16	1	27	1
Bauer, Chris, West Michigan	1.000	18	3	3	0	6	1
Beale, Chuck, Michigan	.944	39	2	15	1	18	1
Bedinger, Doug, South Bend	1.000	11	1	0	0	1	0
Bell, Matthew, South Bend	.778	14	3	4	2	9	0
Betancourt, Rafael, Michigan	1.000	27	1	5	0	6	0
Bierbrodt, Nick, South Bend*	.931	15	8	19	2	29	0
Billingsley, Brent, Kane County*	.962	26	3	22	1	26	1
Birsner, Roark, Rockford	.500	18	0	1	1	2	0
Bishop, Joshua, Beloit	1.000	21	5	7	0	12	0
Blair, Willie, West Michigan	1.000	1	0	1	0	1	0
Borkowski, David, W.Michigan	.917	25	5	28	3	36	2
Braswell, Bryan, Quad City*	.895	19	5	12	2	19	0
Brookens, Casey, Rockford	1.000	28	3	7	0	10	0
Bruner, Clayton, West Michigan..	.933	24	9	33	3	45	5
Callahan, Damon, Burlington	.600	11	1	2	2	5	0
Cames, Aaron, Kane County	.912	26	6	25	3	34	0
Cannon, Jon, Rockford*	.927	24	10	28	3	41	0
Carnes, Matt, Fort Wayne	1.000	1	0	1	0	1	0
Caruthers, Clay, Burlington	.857	17	11	7	3	21	1
Cedeno, Blas, Rockford	1.000	22	1	7	0	8	0
Clark, Chris, Clinton	.857	32	6	12	3	21	1
Collins, Ed, Beloit	1.000	2	2	0	0	2	0
Cordero, Francisco, W.Michigan	.769	50	2	8	3	13	0
Cowsill, Brendon, Cedar Rapids..	.857	26	0	6	1	7	1
Crafton, Kevin, Peoria	.923	50	5	7	1	13	0
Crane, Randy, Rockford	.833	21	4	6	2	12	1
Crews, Jason, South Bend	.895	50	3	14	2	19	0
Cushman, Dwayne, Burlington...	.917	47	2	9	1	12	0
Dace, Derek, West Michigan*	1.000	10	3	5	0	8	0
Danner, Adam, Kane County	1.000	10	1	2	0	3	1
Darrell, Tommy, Cedar Rapids	.867	27	11	28	6	45	1
Darwin, David, West Michigan*..	1.000	21	3	13	0	16	4
Davis, Lance, Burlington*	.872	30	7	27	5	39	2
Delacruz, Fernando, C.R.	.857	10	2	4	1	7	0
DeLeon, Jose, Peoria	.929	60	3	10	1	14	3
Derenches, Albert, Wisconsin* ..	.833	29	1	4	1	6	0
DeWitt, Matt, Peoria	.939	27	12	19	2	33	1
Dose, Gary, Fort Wayne	1.000	45	5	5	0	10	0
Downs, Scott, Rockford*	1.000	5	0	11	0	11	1
Duchscherer, Justin, Michigan....	.750	4	0	3	1	4	0
Duncan, Geoff, Kane County	.875	44	7	14	3	24	0
Duncan, Sean, Quad City*	1.000	34	0	8	0	8	0
Durbin, Chad, Lansing	.926	26	5	20	2	27	1
Espinal, Jose, Rockford	.889	24	4	12	2	18	0
Etler, Todd, Burlington	1.000	25	5	14	0	19	3
Festa, Chris, Michigan	.889	37	8	16	3	27	2
Fidge, Darren, Fort Wayne	1.000	8	0	6	0	6	1
Fitzgerald, Brian, Wisconsin*......	.857	41	3	15	3	21	1
Fleming, John, South Bend	1.000	5	1	1	0	2	0
Foran, John, West Michigan	1.000	29	7	5	0	12	0
Fuentes, Brian, Wisconsin*	.867	22	4	22	4	30	0
Fulcher, John, Beloit*	.875	34	7	7	2	16	0
Gadway, Christopher, C.R.	1.000	15	2	4	0	6	1
Gallagher, Keith, Peoria	1.000	31	4	4	0	8	1
Gandy, Josh, Fort Wayne*	.750	8	1	2	1	4	0
Garcia, Apostol, West Michigan..	.929	33	5	8	1	14	1
Garcia, Eddy, Burlington	.824	22	2	12	3	17	0
Garcia, Gabe, Quad City	.968	26	5	25	1	31	1
Garcia, Jose, Beloit	.889	27	11	13	3	27	3
Garrett, Josh, Michigan	.868	22	8	25	5	38	4
Garza, Chris, Fort Wayne*	.964	60	9	18	1	28	2
Gillian, Charlie, Fort Wayne	1.000	22	0	1	0	1	0
Gissell, Christopher, Rockford	.921	26	10	25	3	38	1
Giuliano, Joe, Burlington	.800	32	3	21	6	30	1
Gnirk, Mark, Beloit	1.000	38	6	16	0	22	2
Gonzalez, Edwin, Lansing	.947	11	10	8	1	19	0
Gonzalez, Jose, Wisconsin	1.000	8	2	3	0	5	0
Gooding, Jason, Lansing*	1.000	1	0	1	0	1	0
Green, Jason, Quad City	.966	23	3	25	1	29	1
Greene, Danny, Cedar Rapids	1.000	24	3	8	0	11	0
Gutierrez, Alfredo, Beloit	.800	19	1	7	2	10	0
Gutierrez, Javier, Wisconsin......	1.000	13	1	8	0	9	1
Guzman, Domingo, Clinton	1.000	12	4	14	0	18	2
Harriger, Mark, Cedar Rapids....	1.000	12	8	8	0	16	1
Hart, Len, Rockford*	1.000	27	3	7	0	10	1
Harvell, Pete, South Bend*	.833	50	1	9	2	12	0
Hawkins, Alsharik, Beloit	.833	6	0	5	1	6	0
Hecht, Brian, Quad City	1.000	5	0	3	0	3	0
Henderson, Juan, Cedar Rapids..	1.000	20	2	7	0	9	2
Hite, Kevin, Clinton	.950	38	8	11	1	20	0
Hoff, Steve, Clinton*	.933	12	2	12	1	15	0
Hooten, David, Fort Wayne	.983	28	22	36	1	59	1
Hueston, Stephen, Lansing	.952	34	2	18	1	21	1
Humphreys, Kevin, C.R.	.963	30	7	19	1	27	1
Hunter, Germaine, Michigan	1.000	52	8	13	0	21	1
Hurst, Doug, Burlington	.909	22	5	5	1	11	0
Ishee, Gabe, Beloit	.750	13	2	4	2	8	0
Jacobs, Russell, Wisconsin	.951	21	4	15	1	20	0
Johannsen, Jeff, Kane County* ..	1.000	7	1	1	0	2	0
Karnuth, Jason, Peoria	.800	4	2	2	1	5	2
Kaye, Justin, Wisconsin	1.000	28	7	16	0	23	1
Kelley, Jason, Rockford	1.000	22	1	2	0	3	0
Kennison, Kyle, Wisconsin	1.000	40	7	10	0	17	2
Kiess, Barry, South Bend	1.000	19	1	5	0	6	0
Kinney, Matt, Michigan	1.000	22	5	13	0	18	0
Knotts, Gary, Kane County	.667	7	0	4	2	6	0
Koehler, Harold, Wisconsin	.867	23	2	11	2	15	1
Lara, Nelson, Kane County	1.000	29	1	5	0	6	0
Leese, Brandon, Kane County	1.000	7	1	3	0	4	0
Levan, Matt, Kane County*	1.000	11	2	6	0	8	0
Levrault, Allen, Beloit	1.000	24	10	15	0	25	2
Leyva, Edgar, Cedar Rapids	1.000	22	4	10	0	14	2
Lindberg, Frederick, Ft.Wayne* ..	1.000	5	0	1	0	1	0
Lineweaver, Aaron, Lansing	.933	21	3	11	1	15	0
Lister, Martin, South Bend*	1.000	3	0	1	0	1	0
Loiz, Niuman, Quad City	.917	18	4	7	1	12	1
Loonam, Rick, Fort Wayne	1.000	34	4	6	0	10	2
Lopez, Rodrigo, Clinton	.931	37	4	23	2	29	1
Lynch, Jim, Quad City	.857	37	3	3	1	7	1
Lynch, Ryan, Fort Wayne*	1.000	15	1	2	0	3	0
MacRae, Scott, Burlington	1.000	27	21	18	0	39	2
Maldonado, Esteban, Quad City ..	.867	39	3	10	2	15	0
Malko, Bryan, Fort Wayne	.947	14	3	15	1	19	3
Marshall, Gary, Rockford*	1.000	29	3	7	0	10	2
Martinez, Javier, Rockford	.875	17	5	9	2	16	1
Martinez, Romulo, W.Michigan ..	.926	36	6	17	2	25	2
Maurer, Dave, Clinton*	1.000	25	2	6	0	8	1
Mays, Joe, Wisconsin	.950	13	7	12	1	20	4
McBride, Rodney, Fort Wayne	1.000	31	4	4	0	8	1
McCall, Travis, South Bend	.935	25	5	24	2	31	3
McCarter, Jason, Quad City	1.000	5	1	1	0	2	0
McClaskey, Tim, Kane County	1.000	18	0	7	0	7	0
McCutcheon, Mike, South Bend*	.906	31	3	26	3	32	0
McFerrin, Chris, Quad City	.917	37	2	9	1	12	0
McKnight, Tony, Quad City	.963	20	6	20	1	27	4
Meche, Gil, Wisconsin	.667	2	2	0	1	3	0
Middlebrook, Jason, Clinton	.955	14	5	16	1	22	0
Miller, Wade, Quad City	.950	10	7	12	1	20	2
Montgomery, Greg, Peoria	.864	40	8	11	3	22	0
Moreno, Orber, Lansing	.952	27	4	16	1	21	1
Morris, Alex, Kane County	.905	19	5	14	2	21	1
Mullen, Scott, Lansing*	1.000	16	5	17	0	22	1
Musgrave, Scott, Michigan*	.929	15	2	11	1	14	0
Myers, Taylor, Lansing	1.000	8	1	3	0	4	0
Neiman, Josh, Clinton	1.000	5	0	2	0	2	0
Norris, Ben, South Bend*	.833	14	7	8	3	18	0
Norris, Mac, Beloit	1.000	4	0	1	0	1	0
Norton, Phillip, Rockford*	.839	18	5	21	5	31	2
Nussbeck, Mark, Peoria	.926	27	8	17	2	27	1
Oleksik, George, South Bend	.929	24	7	6	1	14	0
Onofrei, Tim, Peoria	.857	42	4	20	4	28	1
Opipari, Mario, Fort Wayne	.850	53	2	15	3	20	1
O'Quinn, Jimmy, Cedar Rapids*	1.000	14	1	3	0	4	1
O'Reilly, John, Beloit	1.000	36	8	5	0	13	2
Ortiz, Ramon, Cedar Rapids	.960	27	4	20	1	25	1
O'Toole, Ryan, Burlington	.750	3	1	2	1	4	0
Palki, Jeromy, Wisconsin	.909	44	2	8	1	11	0
Paredes, Carlos, Lansing	1.000	5	0	2	0	2	0
Paredes, Roberto, Beloit	1.000	46	7	2	0	9	0
Parent, Jerry, Clinton	1.000	2	0	1	0	1	0
Partenheimer, Brian, Michigan*..	1.000	17	1	1	0	2	0
Passini, Brian, Beloit*	.950	19	2	17	1	20	0
Patterson, John, South Bend	.923	18	2	10	1	13	1
Penny, Brad, South Bend	1.000	25	10	19	0	29	1
Penny, Tony, Lansing	1.000	22	6	4	0	10	0
Perry, Clint, Clinton	1.000	6	0	2	0	2	0
Peters, Don, South Bend	1.000	13	1	2	0	3	0
Peterson, Jay, Burlington	.968	26	10	20	1	31	2
Phillips, Jon, Clinton	.923	37	1	11	1	13	1
Poepard, Scott, Fort Wayne	1.000	1	0	1	0	1	0

Player, Team	Pct.	G	PO	A	E	TC	DP	Player, Team	Pct.	G	PO	A	E	TC	DP
Polanco, Elvis, Rockford	.909	16	5	5	1	11	0	Spiers, Corey, Fort Wayne*	.943	24	8	25	2	35	3
Prempas, Lyle, Michigan*	.600	13	0	3	2	5	1	Stark, Dennis, Wisconsin	.841	16	12	25	7	44	2
Puffer, Brandon, Cedar Rapids	1.000	10	1	3	0	4	1	Stein, Ethan, Lansing	.962	39	9	16	1	26	1
Quintal, Craig, West Michigan	.980	23	9	39	1	49	2	STOCKSTILL, Jason, C.R.*	1.000	27	6	43	0	49	2
Reames, Jay, Peoria	.820	27	10	31	9	50	6	Sullivan, Brendan, Clinton	.955	48	7	14	1	22	0
Rector, Bobby, Kane County	1.000	3	0	1	0	1	0	Szymborski, Thomas, Clinton	.957	22	10	35	2	47	2
Reed, Steve, Peoria	.923	38	2	10	1	13	0	Tank, Travis, Beloit	.818	41	4	5	2	11	0
Reitsma, Chris, Michigan	.714	9	2	3	2	7	0	Tanksley, Scott, Fort Wayne	1.000	5	2	2	0	4	0
Richards, Mark, Kane County	.923	18	4	8	1	13	0	Tapani, Kevin, Rockford	1.000	2	0	2	0	2	0
Richardson, Kasey, Fort Wayne*	.972	19	7	28	1	36	3	Teut, Nate, Rockford*	.667	2	0	2	1	3	0
Ricketts, Chad, Rockford	1.000	16	1	3	0	4	0	Thompson, Chris, Michigan	1.000	8	0	4	0	4	0
Riedling, John, Burlington	1.000	35	12	12	0	24	0	Torres, Luis, Clinton	1.000	5	1	2	0	3	0
Riegert, Tim, Peoria*	.774	55	5	19	7	31	1	Townsend, Dave, Kane County	1.000	12	3	11	0	14	3
Riggan, Jerrod, Cedar Rapids	.864	19	10	9	3	22	0	Tranbarger, Mark, South Bend*	1.000	32	3	7	0	10	1
Rijo, Jose, Quad City	1.000	35	3	8	0	11	0	Tribe, Byron, Rockford	1.000	13	0	2	0	2	0
Robbins, Jason, South Bend	1.000	5	1	2	0	3	0	Tryon, Eric, Burlington*	1.000	7	1	6	0	7	1
Robertson, Jeromie, Quad City*	.852	26	5	18	4	27	2	Van Wormer, Marc, South Bend	.667	39	5	3	4	12	0
Rodgers, Bobby, Kane County	.935	27	12	31	3	46	3	Verplancke, Joe, South Bend	1.000	2	0	3	0	3	0
Rodriguez, Chad, Lansing	1.000	48	2	9	0	11	0	Viegas, Randy, Clinton*	1.000	18	1	3	0	4	0
Rodriguez, Hector, Cedar Rapids	1.000	9	0	1	0	1	0	Villafana, Jose, Peoria	.857	10	2	4	1	7	0
Rodriguez, Larry, South Bend	.800	19	7	17	6	30	0	Volkman, Keith, Cedar Rapids*	1.000	38	3	12	0	15	1
Rolocut, Brian, Rockford	.929	14	1	12	1	14	0	Walker, Kevin, Clinton*	.960	19	6	42	2	50	4
Romboli, Curtis, Michigan*	1.000	46	4	13	0	17	0	Ward, Brandon, Rockford	.667	9	2	2	2	6	0
Romo, Greg, West Michigan	.966	24	3	25	1	29	1	Watson, Mark, Beloit*	1.000	8	0	5	0	5	0
Rose, Brian, Michigan	1.000	10	2	2	0	4	0	Welch, Robb, Michigan	.750	26	6	9	5	20	1
Rupcich, Larry, Kane County	1.000	1	0	1	0	1	0	West, Adam, Peoria*	.833	62	1	9	2	12	2
Sanchez, Martin, Kane County	.875	51	5	9	2	16	0	Westfall, Allan, Wisconsin	1.000	18	0	3	0	3	0
Sanders, Allen, Lansing	.912	32	9	22	3	34	1	Weymouth, Marty, Wisconsin	.950	23	5	14	1	20	0
Santiago, Derek, Kane County	.938	12	3	12	1	16	2	Widerski, Jon, Kane County	.864	17	6	13	3	22	0
Santiago, Jose, Lansing	1.000	9	0	2	0	2	1	Williamson, Jeremy, Lansing*	1.000	8	3	8	0	11	1
Schaffer, Trevor, Rockford	.714	46	2	3	2	7	0	Wimberly, Larry, Michigan*	1.000	13	3	4	0	7	0
Schroeder, Chad, West Michigan	1.000	18	2	6	0	8	1	Witte, Dominic, Clinton	.923	40	5	19	2	26	1
Scutero, Brian, Cedar Rapids	1.000	10	0	1	0	1	0	Workman, Widd, Clinton	.857	25	1	23	4	28	0
Sekany, Jason, Michigan	1.000	16	12	15	0	27	0	Wright, Scott, Burlington	1.000	42	5	10	0	15	1
Serrano, Wascar, Clinton	.750	1	2	1	1	4	0	Wyckoff, Travis, Kane County*	.941	40	5	11	1	17	0
Simontacchi, Jason, Lansing	.864	29	2	17	3	22	0	Yanez, Luis, Quad City	.818	27	1	8	2	11	0
Smetana, Steve, Michigan*	.778	18	4	3	2	9	0	Yeskie, Nate, Fort Wayne	.978	27	12	32	1	45	2
Smith, Roy, Wisconsin	1.000	18	5	12	0	17	1	Zaleski, Kevin, Kane County	.800	21	1	3	1	5	0
Soriano, Jacobo, Cedar Rapids	.750	25	0	3	1	4	0	Zamarripa, Mark, West Michigan	.750	20	2	4	2	8	0
Sparks, Jeff, Burlington	1.000	22	2	5	0	7	0	Zapata, Juan, Beloit	.800	12	1	3	1	5	1
Spear, Russell, West Michigan	.958	23	4	19	1	24	3	Zimmerman, Jordan, Wis.*	1.000	3	1	2	0	3	0

The following players did not have any fielding statistics at the positions indicated or appeared only as a designated hitter, pinch-hitter, or pinch-runner: N. Abreu, 2b; Allison, p; Aversa, p; Boring, p; Boughton, p; Britt, of; Carmody, p; Cintron, p; G. Clark, p; Cross, of; Cruz, 3b, ss; D'Amico, p; DeLeon, 2b; Fink, 1b; Graves, of; Hartman, ss; Hazlett, p; Houston, 3b; Huls, p; G. Johnson, dh; Kratochvil, of; Layne, of; Lewis, p; Meady, p; J. Moore, p; M. Myers, c; Nash, p; A. Ortiz, 3b; Rivera, of, p; J. Rodriguez, p; Sasser, ss; Steinmann, p; Ussery, ph.

LEAGUE CHAMPIONS

Year	Team	Pct.	Year	Team	Pct.	Year	Team	Pct.
1947—	Belleville	.667	1966—	Fox Cities◆	.689	1983—	Appleton•	.635
	Belleville	.672		Cedar Rapids	.762		Springfield	.576
1948—	West Frankfort*	.708	1967—	Wisconsin Rapids	.685	1984—	Appleton•	.640
1949—	Centralia	.627		Appleton◆	.587		Springfield	.504
	Paducah (4th)†	.454	1968—	Decatur	.656	1985—	Kenosha▼	.568
1950—	Centralia‡	.675		Quad Cities◆	.648		Peoria	.536
1951—	Paris§	.700	1969—	Appleton	.648	1986—	Springfield	.621
	Danville (4th)†	.432		Appleton	.690		Waterloo▼	.557
1952—	Danville∞	.685	1970—	Quincy◆	.691	1987—	Springfield	.671
	Decatur (3rd)†	.584		Quad Cities	.581		Kenosha▼	.586
1953—	Decatur*	.576	1971—	Appleton	.642	1988—	Cedar Rapids■	.621
1954—	Decatur	.587		Quad Cities■	.548		Kenosha	.579
	Danville (2nd)‡	.528	1972—	Appleton	.598	1989—	South Bend■	.644
1955—	Dubuque*	.587		Danville■	.584		Springfield	.541
1956—	Paris▲	.656	1973—	Wisconsin Rapids■	.562	1990—	Cedar Rapids	.657
	Dubuque	.603		Danville	.537		Quad City■	.579
1957—	Decatur▲	.683	1974—	Appleton	.593	1991—	Clinton■	.583
	Clinton	.623		Danville■	.517		Madison	.558
1958—	Michigan City	.623	1975—	Waterloo■	.727	1992—	Quad City	.664
	Waterloo◆	.613		Quad Cities	.624		Cedar Rapids■	.594
1959—	Waterloo	.613	1976—	Waterloo■	.600	1993—	Clinton	.597
	Waterloo	.613		Cedar Rapids	.595		South Bend■	.566
1960—	Waterloo	.629	1977—	Waterloo	.580	1994—	Rockford	.640
	Waterloo	.677		Burlington■	.511		Cedar Rapids■	.554
1961—	Waterloo	.613	1978—	Appleton■	.708	1995—	Beloit††	.633
	Quincy◆	.594		Burlington	.500		Michigan	.543
1962—	Dubuque◆	.667	1979—	Waterloo	.600	1996—	Wisconsin	.570
	Waterloo	.625		Quad Cities■	.579		West Michigan††	.558
1963—	Clinton	.710	1980—	Waterloo■	.610	1997—	Kane County	.507
	Clinton	.629		Quad Cities	.532		Lansing**	.504
1964—	Clinton	.667	1981—	Wausau■	.636			
	Fox Cities◆	.667		Quad Cities	.570			
1965—	Burlington	.667	1982—	Madison■	.626			
	Burlington	.677		Appleton▼	.579			

*Won championship and four-club playoff. †Won four-club playoff. ‡Playoff finals canceled because of bad weather. §Won both halves of split season. ∞Won first half of split season and tied Paris for second-half title. ◆Won split season playoff. ■League divided into Northern and Southern divisions and played split season. Playoff winner. ▼League divided into Northern, Central and Southern divisions. Playoff winner. •League divided into Northern, Central and Southern divisions; regular season and playoff winner. ††League divided into Eastern, Central and Western divisions; regular season and playoff winner. **League divided into Eastern, Central and Western divisions, playoff winner. (NOTE—Known as Illinois State League in 1947-48 and Mississippi-Ohio Valley League from 1949 through 1955.)

CLASS A *Midwest League*

NEW YORK-PENN LEAGUE

LEAGUE OFFICE

President
Bob Julian
Address
1629 Oneida St.
Utica, NY 13501
Phone
315-733-8036

Teams (affiliation)
Auburn Doubledays (Astros)
Batavia Muck Dogs (Phillies)
Erie SeaWolves (Pirates)
Hudson Valley Renegades (Devil Rays)
Jamestown Jammers (Tigers)
Lowell Spinners (Red Sox)
New Jersey Cardinals (Cardinals)

Oneonta Yankees (Yankees)
Pittsfield Mets (Mets)
St. Catharines Stompers (Blue Jays)
Utica Blue Sox (Marlins)
Vermont Expos (Expos)
Watertown Indians (Indians)
Williamsport Cubs (Cubs)

1997 FINAL STANDINGS

McNAMARA DIVISION

Team	W	L	T	Pct.	GB
Pittsfield (Mets)	42	32	0	.568	....
Lowell (Red Sox)	38	38	0	.500	5
New Jersey (Cardinals)	35	39	0	.473	7
Hudson Valley (Devil Rays)	35	40	0	.467	7½
Vermont (Expos)	35	41	0	.461	8

PINCKNEY DIVISION

Team	W	L	T	Pct.	GB
Oneonta (Yankees)	49	25	0	.662	....
Watertown (Indians)	39	36	0	.520	10½
Utica (Marlins)	36	38	0	.486	13
Williamsport (Cubs)	29	46	0	.387	20½
Auburn (Astros)	29	47	0	.382	21

STEDLER DIVISION

Team	W	L	T	Pct.	GB
Erie (Pirates)	50	26	0	.658	....
Batavia (Phillies)	47	27	0	.635	2
St. Catharines (Blue Jays)	35	40	0	.467	14½
Jamestown (Tigers)	25	49	0	.338	24

COMPOSITE

Team	One.	Erie	Bat.	Pit.	Wat.	Low.	Uti.	N.J.	St.C.	H.V.	Ver.	Wpt.	Aub.	Jam.	W	L	T	Pct.	GB
Oneonta (Yankees)	....	2	1	1	9	1	6	2	1	4	1	6	11	4	49	25	0	.662	....
Erie (Pirates)	4	....	8	1	3	2	2	3	6	3	4	2	4	8	50	26	0	.658	....
Batavia (Phillies)	1	4	....	2	3	4	3	2	8	2	2	4	4	8	47	27	0	.635	2
Pittsfield (Mets)	1	3	2	....	1	7	2	6	2	8	4	0	2	4	42	32	0	.568	7
Watertown (Indians)	2	1	1	1	....	1	8	1	2	1	1	9	9	2	39	36	0	.520	10½
Lowell (Red Sox)	1	2	0	5	3	....	2	5	3	7	7	0	0	3	38	38	0	.500	12
Utica (Marlins)	6	0	2	2	4	0	....	1	4	1	2	8	5	1	36	38	0	.486	13
New Jersey (Cardinals)	0	1	2	5	1	7	0	....	3	4	7	2	0	3	35	39	0	.473	14
St. Catharines (Blue Jays)	1	6	3	2	2	1	2	1	....	1	3	3	3	1	35	40	0	.467	14½
Hudson Valley (Devil Rays)	0	1	2	4	1	5	1	8	3	....	6	2	1	1	35	40	0	.467	14½
Vermont (Expos)	1	0	2	8	1	5	0	5	1	6	....	2	1	3	35	41	0	.461	15
Williamsport (Cubs)	6	2	0	1	3	2	4	2	1	0	0	....	6	2	29	46	0	.387	20½
Auburn (Astros)	1	0	0	0	3	2	7	2	2	1	3	6	....	2	29	47	0	.382	21
Jamestown (Tigers)	1	4	4	0	2	1	1	1	4	2	1	2	2	....	25	49	0	.338	24

Major league affiliations in parentheses.

Hudson Valley home games played in Fishkill, N.Y.

New Jersey home games played in Augusta, N.J.

Vermont home games played in Winooski, Vt.

PLAYOFFS: Batavia defeated Oneonta, two games to none; Pittsfield defeated Erie, two games to none; Pittsfield defeated Batavia, two games to one, to win league championship.

REGULAR-SEASON ATTENDANCE: Auburn, 51,260; Batavia, 41,192; Erie, 196,212; Hudson Valley, 161,771; Jamestown, 51,775; Lowell, 106,862; New Jersey, 171,244; Oneonta, 53,447; Pittsfield, 82,935; St. Catharines, 53,520; Utica, 52,185; Vermont, 91,694; Watertown, 36,359; Williamsport, 58,795. Total—1,209,251. Playoffs (7 games)—9,765.

MANAGERS: Auburn, Mike Rojas; Batavia, Gregg Legg; Erie, Marty Brown; Hudson Valley, Julio Garcia; Jamestown, Dwight Lowry and Matt Martin; Lowell, Dick Berardino; New Jersey, Jeff Shireman; Oneonta, Joe Arnold; Pittsfield, Doug Davis; St. Catharines, Rocket Wheeler; Utica, Juan Bustabad; Vermont, Kevin Higgins; Watertown, Ted Kubiak; Williamsport, Bob Zalston. Managerial record of team with more than one manager: Jamestown, Lowry 9-13 and Martin 16-36.

ALL-STAR TEAM: 1B—Andy Dominique, Batavia; 2B—Raul Franco, Utica; 3B—Ron Walker, Williamsport; SS—Kevin Haverbusch, Erie; Reserve INF—Rusty McNamara, Batavia; OF—Alexander Steele, Jamestown; Dustan Mohr, Watertown; Vernon Wells, St. Catharines; Kenny James, Vermont; Milton Bradley, Vermont; Andy Bevins, New Jersey; C—Scott Chapman, Auburn; Johnny Estrada, Batavia; DH—Gary Burnham, Batavia; RHP—Zach Day, Oneonta; Derek Adair, Batavia; LHP—Kris Lambert, Erie; Scott Comer, Pittsfield; Manager of the Year—Marty Brown, Erie; Most Valuable Player—Kevin Haverbusch, Erie; Executive of the Year—Shawn Smith, Lowell.

1997 BATTING

TEAM

Team	Avg.	G	TPA	AB	R	H	TB	2B	3B	HR	RBI	SH	SF	HP	BB	IBB	SO	SB	CS	GDP	LOB	ShO	Slg.	OBP
Batavia	.279	74	2881	2553	414	713	1002	127	21	40	368	26	29	48	225	5	472	89	30	48	545	0	.392	.345
Erie	.266	76	2884	2525	410	672	1019	124	26	57	356	23	30	52	254	10	595	93	59	44	516	3	.404	.342
Auburn	.263	76	2808	2503	332	658	959	129	20	44	289	20	15	40	230	8	586	55	52	67	502	5	.383	.333
Utica	.262	74	2773	2392	334	627	822	102	12	23	280	26	31	42	282	14	486	68	39	59	554	8	.344	.346
Watertown	.257	75	2833	2491	383	640	944	136	15	46	331	15	20	30	277	8	588	74	33	37	534	7	.379	.336
Oneonta	.254	74	2739	2384	359	606	827	99	25	24	299	17	27	35	276	11	568	103	47	42	490	4	.347	.337

Team	Avg.	G	TPA	AB	R	H	TB	2B	3B	HR	RBI	SH	SF	HP	BB	IBB	SO	SB	CS	GDP	LOB	ShO	Slg.	OBP
Jamestown	.254	74	2786	2503	336	636	913	111	17	44	287	11	16	37	219	5	565	42	23	61	528	7	.365	.321
Vermont	.253	76	2903	2546	361	644	879	100	36	21	304	23	26	45	263	11	524	156	59	35	558	4	.345	.331
Hudson Valley	.252	75	2816	2532	363	639	905	130	23	30	317	8	22	30	224	4	558	57	31	43	490	3	.357	.318
New Jersey	.252	74	2755	2441	375	615	885	106	22	40	326	13	23	48	230	4	559	75	34	46	490	3	.363	.326
Williamsport	.251	75	2756	2490	275	625	849	91	23	29	246	15	15	21	215	17	581	68	32	57	520	6	.341	.314
St. Catharines	.249	75	2813	2499	368	623	898	121	14	42	303	14	23	31	246	5	511	72	44	37	505	6	.359	.322
Pittsfield	.244	74	2738	2457	343	600	826	108	20	26	293	21	23	39	198	7	536	107	28	31	479	2	.336	.308
Lowell	.239	76	2860	2529	334	604	874	117	12	43	285	41	13	55	222	3	618	71	24	46	548	5	.346	.313

INDIVIDUAL

TOP QUALIFIERS FOR BATTING CHAMPIONSHIP

Minimum 205 plate appearances. *Lefthanded batter. †Switch-hitter.

Player, Team	Avg.	G	TPA	AB	R	H	TB	2B	3B	HR	RBI	SH	SF	HP	BB	IBB	SO	SB	CS	GDP	Slg.	OBP
Franco, Raul, Utica	.352	72	319	293	41	103	131	19	0	3	38	2	5	2	17	3	24	10	4	11	.447	.385
Walker, Ron, Williamsport	.349	54	215	189	30	66	105	10	1	9	39	0	2	5	17	7	48	0	1	6	.556	.413
Erickson, Matt, Utica*	.328	69	303	238	44	78	103	10	0	5	44	2	4	11	48	3	36	9	3	7	.433	.455
Chapman, Scott, Auburn	.327	53	212	205	32	67	96	11	0	6	39	0	1	0	6	0	23	1	2	14	.468	.344
Burnham, Gary, Batavia*	.325	73	327	289	44	94	139	22	4	5	45	1	2	5	30	0	47	3	1	8	.481	.396
Langaigne, Selwyn, St.C.*	.320	74	319	266	50	85	111	15	4	1	39	0	3	2	48	1	46	19	9	5	.417	.423
Nunnari, Talmadge, Vermont*	.318	62	274	236	30	75	104	11	3	4	42	0	4	3	31	4	37	6	3	4	.441	.398
Estrada, Johnny, Batavia†	.314	58	240	223	28	70	109	17	2	6	43	2	5	1	9	1	15	0	0	9	.489	.336
Freeman, Terrance, Erie†	.313	63	272	217	56	68	87	9	2	2	19	5	1	11	38	0	38	46	11	2	.401	.438
McNamara, Rusty, Batavia	.312	72	326	295	55	92	127	17	0	6	54	0	6	10	15	0	33	3	3	4	.431	.359
Steele, Alexander, Jamestown	.311	72	304	257	51	80	145	15	4	14	43	0	1	9	37	2	61	6	3	5	.564	.414
Haverbusch, Kevin, Erie	.311	67	265	241	37	75	124	15	2	10	55	2	4	4	13	1	37	4	4	6	.515	.351
Young, Michael, St. Catharines	.308	74	319	276	49	85	136	18	3	9	48	0	3	7	33	1	59	9	5	6	.493	.392
Lankford, Derrick, Erie*	.308	58	231	195	36	60	107	11	3	10	55	0	2	1	33	4	57	2	0	1	.549	.407
Wells, Vernon, St. Catharines	.307	66	297	264	52	81	133	20	1	10	31	0	2	1	30	1	44	8	6	2	.504	.377

DEPARTMENTAL LEADERS: G—Cutshall, 76; AB—Mota, 311; R—James, 61; H—Franco, 103; TB—Steele, 145; 2B—Cutshall, 23; 3B—N. Hall, 8; HR—Steele, Dominique, 14 each; RBI—Haverbusch, Lankford, 55 each; SH—Eckstein, Izturis, Schifano, 8 each; SF—Several tied with 6 each; HP—Melconian, 15; BB—Benefield, 49; IBB—Walker, 7; SO—Howard, 78; SB—Freeman, 46; CS—Freeman, Darjean, Mateo, 11 each; GIDP—Chapman, 14; Slg.—Steele, .564; OBP—Erickson, .455.

ALL PLAYERS

*Lefthanded batter. †Switch-hitter.

Player, Team	Avg.	G	TPA	AB	R	H	TB	2B	3B	HR	RBI	SH	SF	HP	BB	IBB	SO	SB	CS	GDP	Slg.	OBP
Abell, Antonio, New Jersey	.225	10	44	40	11	9	12	0	0	1	4	1	0	0	3	0	16	1	1	0	.300	.279
Abreu, Nelson, Williamsport	.306	14	61	49	8	15	20	1	2	0	3	2	0	1	9	0	17	6	3	0	.408	.424
Ahumada, Alejandro, Lowell	.222	57	225	203	25	45	54	4	1	1	13	1	2	4	15	0	49	5	1	5	.266	.286
Alayon, Elvis, Lowell*	.207	32	121	111	12	23	32	4	1	1	7	4	0	1	5	0	16	1	2	1	.288	.248
Albaral, Randy, St. Catharines	.225	56	245	218	39	49	56	5	1	0	23	3	2	2	20	0	27	14	3	1	.257	.293
Alevras, Chad, Lowell	.145	22	67	55	8	8	13	2	0	1	5	1	0	1	10	0	13	1	1	0	.236	.288
Allison, Cody, Watertown*	.265	51	202	181	25	48	61	10	0	1	23	1	0	0	20	2	34	7	3	4	.337	.338
Alvarez, Carlos, Watertown	.300	22	88	80	15	24	47	5	0	6	17	0	1	5	2	0	21	3	2	0	.588	.352
Amrhein, Michael, Williamsport	.278	62	253	237	17	66	82	11	1	1	31	0	4	2	10	1	19	0	2	11	.346	.308
Arrendondo, Hernando, H.V.	.275	50	219	200	24	55	74	14	1	1	27	0	1	3	15	0	44	1	3	5	.370	.333
Austin, Peter, Erie	.154	5	16	13	1	2	2	0	0	0	1	0	0	2	1	0	4	0	0	0	.154	.313
Aybar, Ramon, Jamestown*	.200	40	145	125	20	25	25	0	0	0	3	1	0	1	13	2	32	5	2	3	.200	.289
Bagley, Lorenzo, St. Catharines	.264	58	212	197	25	52	79	10	1	5	21	0	1	2	12	0	55	3	4	5	.401	.311
Bagley, Sean, Vermont	.182	39	133	121	17	22	27	2	0	1	9	0	1	2	9	0	36	7	3	3	.223	.248
Banks, Tony, Williamsport*	.259	37	143	116	21	30	53	11	3	2	11	0	0	0	27	1	23	4	1	2	.457	.399
Barnett, Brian, St. Catharines	.230	45	144	122	18	28	39	9	1	0	8	0	0	0	22	0	36	3	3	0	.320	.347
Baston, Stanley, St. Catharines	.161	44	154	137	10	22	24	2	0	0	14	1	4	1	11	0	32	1	3	1	.175	.222
Bautista, Jorge, Utica	.244	58	229	201	19	49	70	10	1	3	27	0	2	1	25	1	55	5	3	3	.348	.328
Bender, Heath, Watertown*	.231	62	206	186	19	43	55	6	0	2	20	1	1	8	10	1	38	1	1	2	.296	.298
Benefield, Brian, Watertown	.287	69	318	285	47	76	99	9	1	4	19	2	1	1	49	3	40	23	7	3	.374	.399
Bernhardt, Tom, Williamsport	.205	38	134	122	8	25	39	3	4	1	8	1	1	0	10	1	39	2	1	1	.320	.263
Bevins, Andy, New Jersey	.272	65	259	235	35	64	110	9	5	9	44	0	3	3	18	1	66	2	1	3	.468	.328
Blakeney, Mo, Vermont	.284	32	128	116	9	33	49	3	2	3	11	1	1	2	8	1	25	4	4	2	.422	.339
Bly, Derrick, Williamsport	.149	13	54	47	2	7	9	2	0	0	3	0	0	1	5	0	20	0	0	2	.191	.245
Bradley, Milton, Vermont†	.300	50	220	200	29	60	86	7	5	3	30	1	2	0	17	1	34	7	7	6	.430	.352
Bronikowski, William, Oneonta	.000	1	2	2	0	0	0	0	0	0	0	0	0	0	0	0	2	0	0	0	.000	.000
Brooks, Ali, Erie	.000	6	13	11	3	0	0	0	0	0	0	0	0	0	2	0	2	1	0	1	.000	.154
Bruce, Maurice, Pittsfield	.348	29	130	115	26	40	65	7	3	4	14	0	0	2	11	0	23	12	2	4	.565	.408
Burkhart, Lance, Vermont*	.168	38	161	143	15	24	32	6	1	0	12	0	0	1	17	0	40	3	3	3	.224	.261
Burnham, Gary, Batavia*	.325	73	327	289	44	94	139	22	4	5	45	1	2	5	30	0	47	3	1	8	.481	.396
Burns, Xavier, Erie	.274	63	251	226	33	62	100	13	2	7	27	0	1	6	18	0	62	4	4	5	.442	.343
Butler, Allen, Oneonta*	.280	68	267	214	40	60	88	11	4	3	30	2	2	3	46	2	57	4	3	4	.411	.411
Carey, Orlando, Oneonta	.248	71	266	238	40	59	77	4	4	2	17	2	2	1	23	1	59	20	6	4	.324	.314
Carr, Dustin, Hudson Valley	.288	74	328	281	46	81	112	12	2	5	47	0	3	2	42	2	42	4	2	10	.399	.381
Carter, Bart, Hudson Valley	.214	10	33	28	2	6	7	1	0	0	2	1	0	1	7	0	0	1	0	0	.250	.313
Cathey, Joseph, Auburn†	.268	70	308	269	36	72	85	7	3	0	13	4	1	4	30	2	56	13	6	6	.316	.339
Chabot, Kevin, New Jersey*	.154	12	40	39	2	6	9	1	0	1	4	0	0	0	1	0	14	0	0	0	.231	.175
Chambliss, Russ, Oneonta*	.132	29	59	53	4	7	8	1	0	0	2	0	1	1	4	0	24	4	0	1	.151	.203
Chapman, Scott, Auburn	.327	53	212	205	32	67	96	11	0	6	39	0	1	0	6	0	23	1	2	14	.468	.344
Chiaffredo, Paul, St. Catharines	.239	48	183	163	20	39	55	8	1	2	15	1	1	1	9	0	42	5	2	1	.337	.313
Clark, Chris C., Utica	.063	6	18	16	1	1	2	1	0	0	1	0	0	0	2	0	8	0	0	0	.125	.167
Clark, Chris L., Erie	.256	28	99	90	14	23	36	4	0	3	13	0	1	1	8	0	13	0	0	2	.400	.316
Clark, Jason, Hudson Valley*	.231	62	234	216	25	50	69	12	2	1	28	0	4	1	8	0	10	3	5	5	.319	.267
Cleto, Ambioris, Erie	.182	8	27	22	0	4	4	0	0	0	2	1	0	1	3	0	11	0	3	0	.182	.308

Player, Team	Avg.	G	TPA	AB	R	H	TB	2B	3B	HR	RBI	SH	SF	HP	BB	IBB	SO	SB	CS	GDP	Slg.	OBP
Cole, Eric, Auburn	.275	71	251	222	29	61	111	20	3	8	34	2	3	5	19	1	46	4	4	3	.500	.341
Collins, Francis, Batavia*	.267	63	238	206	35	55	64	5	2	0	16	5	1	3	23	0	46	16	4	4	.311	.348
Connell, Gerald, Williamsport	.281	55	228	203	25	57	85	7	6	3	18	0	1	4	20	0	55	4	3	2	.419	.355
Copeland, Brandon, Pittsfield	.256	27	108	90	24	23	32	6	0	1	7	0	3	2	13	0	30	0	0	1	.356	.352
Cota, Humberto, Hudson Valley	.222	3	9	9	0	2	2	0	0	0	2	0	0	0	0	0	1	0	0	0	.222	.222
Cripps, Bobby, St. Catharines*	.125	14	46	40	4	5	10	0	1	1	3	0	0	2	4	0	11	0	0	1	.250	.239
Cutshall, Patrick, Auburn	.297	76	317	273	54	81	130	23	1	8	34	3	2	8	31	1	23	5	6	11	.476	.382
Darjean, John, Oneonta	.291	58	205	189	30	55	65	4	3	0	13	5	0	3	8	0	36	27	11	1	.344	.330
Davis, Jerry, Erie	.077	4	13	13	1	1	1	0	0	0	0	0	0	0	0	0	4	0	0	0	.077	.077
DeCelle, Mike, Hudson Valley*	.259	73	300	270	41	70	111	18	7	3	28	0	1	4	25	1	69	3	4	5	.411	.330
Dehaan, Korwin, Erie*	.239	58	255	205	43	49	72	8	6	1	18	6	4	2	38	2	43	14	9	4	.351	.357
Delarosa, Tomas, Vermont	.266	69	312	271	46	72	104	14	6	2	40	3	4	2	32	0	47	19	6	1	.384	.343
DeLeon, Jorge, Lowell	.333	3	12	12	1	4	4	0	0	0	2	0	0	0	0	0	0	0	0	0	.333	.333
Diaz, Diogenes, Erie	.179	10	33	28	4	5	8	3	0	0	4	0	1	0	4	0	12	0	0	1	.286	.273
Dominique, Andy, Batavia	.278	72	318	277	52	77	136	17	0	14	48	0	5	10	26	0	60	4	1	6	.491	.355
Donaldson, Rhodney, Utica*	.264	70	313	269	49	71	81	3	2	1	16	3	2	2	37	0	42	21	6	5	.301	.355
Drizos, Justin, Hudson Valley*	.215	43	173	149	23	32	57	8	1	5	26	0	1	2	21	0	39	0	0	1	.383	.318
Duffy, James, Auburn	.276	48	201	185	28	51	89	9	1	9	25	0	0	2	14	0	47	4	4	4	.481	.333
Dunn, Ryan, Auburn*	.183	60	177	142	16	26	45	9	2	2	15	1	2	6	26	0	58	2	1	2	.317	.330
Eckstein, David, Lowell	.301	68	303	249	43	75	106	11	4	4	39	8	1	12	33	1	29	21	5	2	.426	.407
Elliott, Dawan, Erie*	.250	57	184	172	14	43	62	13	0	2	18	0	2	1	9	2	32	1	1	1	.360	.288
Erickson, Matt, Utica*	.328	69	303	238	44	78	103	10	0	5	44	2	4	11	48	3	36	9	3	7	.433	.455
Espada, Angel, Pittsfield	.305	20	90	82	15	25	26	1	0	0	7	1	1	1	5	0	5	7	3	2	.317	.348
Estrada, Johnny, Batavia†	.314	58	240	223	28	70	109	17	2	6	43	2	5	1	9	1	15	0	0	9	.489	.336
Evans, Lee, Erie†	.298	40	156	141	20	42	63	6	0	5	16	1	1	2	11	1	30	1	2	3	.447	.355
Fajardo, Alejandro, Batavia	.270	52	214	200	35	54	75	7	4	2	29	3	1	3	7	1	34	9	2	5	.375	.303
Farley, Cordell, New Jersey	.368	6	22	19	6	7	7	0	0	0	1	0	0	1	2	0	6	1	0	0	.368	.455
Fereday, Todd, Williamsport	.209	32	125	115	13	24	37	5	1	2	11	0	1	2	7	0	20	2	4	4	.322	.264
Fischer, Mark, Lowell	.330	48	198	179	25	59	91	15	1	5	25	0	1	3	15	0	38	13	2	4	.508	.389
Fitzgerald, Jason, Watertown*	.196	34	132	112	11	22	33	8	0	1	13	1	2	0	17	0	31	2	0	4	.295	.298
Fitzpatrick, Eddie, Batavia	.143	25	65	63	5	9	9	0	0	0	7	0	0	0	2	0	23	0	0	1	.143	.169
Flores, Jose, Lowell†	.221	37	129	122	13	27	34	4	0	1	9	0	0	1	6	0	36	4	1	4	.279	.264
Font, Franklin, Williamsport	.311	33	147	135	13	42	52	6	2	0	12	1	2	2	7	0	20	10	4	2	.385	.349
Forbes, Kevin, Vermont	.200	30	111	100	13	20	21	1	0	0	8	3	0	3	5	0	22	8	1	2	.210	.259
Franco, Raul, Utica	.352	72	319	293	41	103	131	19	0	3	38	2	5	2	17	3	24	10	4	11	.447	.385
Freeman, Terrance, Erie†	.313	63	272	217	56	68	87	9	2	2	19	5	1	11	38	0	38	46	11	2	.401	.438
Fritz, Jim, Batavia	.267	35	111	90	10	24	37	8	1	1	13	1	1	5	14	0	25	4	1	1	.411	.391
Gancasz, Michael, Lowell	.210	34	98	81	10	17	21	4	0	0	6	1	0	3	13	0	25	0	2	1	.259	.340
Garff, Jeff, Watertown	.000	6	1	1	0	0	0	0	0	0	0	0	0	0	0	0	1	0	0	0	.000	.000
Gentry, Aaron, New Jersey	.249	64	254	225	30	56	85	8	3	6	32	1	2	6	20	1	58	4	7	4	.378	.324
Germosen, Julio, Erie	.200	42	125	115	21	23	41	3	3	3	16	1	1	1	7	0	34	2	3	1	.357	.250
Gick, Brady, New Jersey*	.216	32	112	102	9	22	29	4	0	1	20	0	1	1	8	0	4	1	1	4	.284	.277
Gload, Ross, Utica*	.261	68	280	245	28	64	92	15	2	3	43	0	5	2	28	0	57	1	1	5	.376	.336
Goodwin, Keith, Lowell	.228	67	265	241	23	55	72	11	0	2	25	4	1	5	14	0	50	4	0	5	.299	.284
Gray, Travis, Lowell*	.198	45	143	116	18	23	35	3	0	3	12	2	1	3	21	1	41	2	1	0	.302	.333
Green, Kevin, Utica	.238	10	25	21	2	5	5	0	0	0	2	0	0	0	4	0	6	2	0	0	.238	.360
Grimmett, Ryan, Jamestown	.324	17	80	68	14	22	35	5	1	2	9	0	0	1	11	0	9	11	2	4	.515	.425
Grubbs, Chris, Williamsport	.204	23	65	54	5	11	12	1	0	0	2	0	0	0	11	0	17	0	0	1	.222	.338
Haad, Yamid, Erie	.290	43	169	155	27	45	61	7	3	1	19	1	6	0	7	0	27	3	3	5	.394	.310
Haas, Danny, Lowell*	.179	9	33	28	6	5	8	3	0	0	4	0	0	1	2	0	8	3	0	0	.286	.258
Haley, Ryan, Watertown*	.000	12	15	13	4	0	0	0	0	0	0	0	0	2	0	0	4	1	1	1	.000	.133
Hall, Noah, Vermont	.274	73	316	266	43	73	107	12	8	2	45	0	2	3	45	2	48	22	5	1	.402	.383
Hall, Toby, Hudson Valley	.250	55	218	200	25	50	56	3	0	1	27	1	3	1	13	1	33	0	0	3	.280	.295
Halper, Jason, Oneonta†	.063	11	18	16	0	1	1	0	0	0	3	0	1	1	0	0	4	0	0	1	.063	.111
Harper, Brandon, Utica	.257	47	176	152	27	39	56	7	2	2	22	0	2	1	19	2	32	1	1	9	.368	.339
Harrell, Ken, Oneonta	.167	11	26	24	1	4	5	1	0	0	2	0	0	0	2	0	8	5	0	0	.208	.231
Harris, Brian, Batavia*	.311	51	187	148	31	46	55	7	1	0	19	3	1	4	31	0	27	11	6	1	.372	.440
Haverbusch, Kevin, Erie	.311	67	265	241	37	75	124	15	2	10	55	2	4	4	13	1	37	4	4	6	.515	.351
Hernandez, Jesus, Watertown*	.222	16	53	45	4	10	14	4	0	0	3	0	0	2	6	0	10	1	0	1	.311	.302
Hernandez, Rafael, Vermont	.234	22	81	77	8	18	22	1	0	1	5	0	0	1	3	0	18	0	2	3	.286	.272
Hervey, Brennan, Jamestown†	.243	58	242	222	24	54	76	10	0	4	35	1	2	0	17	0	62	1	2	9	.342	.293
Howard, Marcus, Lowell	.208	70	258	221	38	46	85	10	1	9	25	0	2	6	29	1	78	2	5	2	.385	.314
Hubbard, Jeremy, Williamsport	.125	6	8	8	0	1	2	1	0	0	1	0	0	0	0	0	2	0	0	0	.250	.125
Hunter, Travis, Utica	.226	19	58	53	3	12	16	4	0	0	4	0	1	0	4	0	12	0	0	0	.302	.276
Izturis, Cesar, St. Catharines†	.190	70	257	231	32	44	50	3	0	1	11	8	2	1	15	0	27	6	3	3	.216	.241
Jacomino, Mandy, Watertown*	.301	62	255	229	32	69	90	9	0	4	26	1	0	0	24	0	44	0	1	9	.393	.368
James, Kennoth, Vermont†	.233	71	330	301	61	70	90	4	5	2	23	2	1	11	13	1	52	37	4	0	.299	.288
Jefferies, Daryl, Williamsport	.289	10	41	38	7	11	13	2	0	0	2	0	0	1	2	0	6	1	0	1	.342	.341
Jimenez, Felipe, Williamsport	.115	10	27	26	3	3	3	0	0	0	0	0	0	0	1	0	8	0	0	0	.115	.148
Joffrion, Jack, Hudson Valley	.240	73	278	258	41	62	106	13	2	9	37	2	3	2	13	0	61	2	1	2	.411	.279
Johnson, Jason A., Erie	.320	28	117	103	19	33	48	7	1	2	19	0	2	1	11	0	21	2	2	1	.466	.385
Johnson, Jason B., Batavia	.294	60	266	238	40	70	91	14	5	0	28	3	5	3	17	0	26	20	7	3	.382	.342
Johnson, Thomas, Pittsfield	.234	57	229	209	28	49	79	15	0	5	38	0	1	4	14	1	51	12	3	3	.378	.294
Jones, Aaron, Oneonta*	.241	63	212	166	25	40	52	8	2	0	17	1	0	2	43	3	40	4	6	5	.313	.403
Kane, Kevin, Oneonta	.125	4	9	8	1	1	1	0	0	0	0	0	0	0	1	0	4	0	0	0	.125	.222
Keaveney, Jeff, Lowell	.204	51	212	191	26	39	72	12	0	7	29	0	0	3	18	0	58	0	0	2	.377	.283
Keech, Erik, Oneonta*	.270	12	37	37	3	10	11	1	0	0	5	0	0	0	0	0	5	0	0	1	.297	.270
Kennedy, Adam, New Jersey*	.342	29	132	114	20	39	51	6	3	0	19	1	2	2	13	0	10	9	1	3	.447	.412
Kidd, Scott, Oneonta	.263	74	306	281	38	74	109	14	3	5	45	2	3	2	18	2	62	7	2	5	.388	.309
Kiefer, Dax, Williamsport	.244	70	268	234	28	57	76	5	1	4	18	4	2	0	28	0	61	7	1	7	.325	.322
Kim, David, New Jersey	.278	58	234	205	38	57	92	16	2	5	35	0	1	11	17	0	39	5	2	3	.449	.363
Kingsbury, Willy, Lowell*	.169	23	86	77	6	13	20	4	0	1	7	0	0	0	9	0	32	0	0	1	.260	.259
Koehler, Jason, St. Catharines	.231	10	43	39	4	9	16	4	0	1	7	0	0	0	4	0	11	0	1	0	.410	.302

– 524 –

Player, Team	Avg.	G	TPA	AB	R	H	TB	2B	3B	HR	RBI	SH	SF	HP	BB	IBB	SO	SB	CS	GDP	Slg.	OBP
Kurilla, Kevin, Batavia	.239	60	231	209	27	50	74	7	1	5	36	3	1	1	17	3	59	7	1	3	.354	.298
Langaigne, Selwyn, St. C*	.320	74	319	266	50	85	111	15	4	1	39	0	2	2	48	1	46	19	9	5	.417	.423
Lankford, Derrick, Erie*	.308	58	231	195	36	60	107	11	3	10	55	0	2	1	33	4	57	2	0	1	.549	.407
Lara, Felix, Erie*	.248	50	184	165	24	41	54	8	1	1	16	2	0	0	17	0	55	8	8	1	.327	.319
Lauterhahn, Daniel, Jamestown....	.247	53	205	186	18	46	56	7	0	1	14	2	1	2	14	0	39	2	4	2	.301	.305
Lawler, Scott, Auburn	.236	39	120	106	16	25	37	3	0	3	10	2	1	2	9	0	35	2	0	3	.349	.305
Lebron, Ruben, Lowell†	.305	51	182	167	25	51	65	9	1	1	24	7	1	1	6	0	30	13	3	4	.389	.331
Lee, Jason, New Jersey*	.239	60	250	226	34	54	79	10	0	5	37	0	0	3	21	0	69	8	2	6	.350	.312
Lignitz, Jeremiah, Jamestown*....	.280	41	162	150	16	42	57	7	1	2	27	0	0	3	9	0	47	0	2	6	.380	.333
Logan, Stephen, Auburn*	.292	71	281	260	27	76	100	16	4	0	29	0	0	1	20	3	60	5	10	3	.385	.345
Lopez-Cao, Mike, Hudson Valley*.	.295	14	48	44	6	13	19	3	0	1	7	0	1	0	3	0	10	2	0	2	.432	.333
Mackowiak, Robert, Erie*	.286	61	235	203	26	58	79	14	2	1	25	3	1	7	21	0	47	1	7	5	.389	.371
MaCrory, Robert, New Jersey	.306	67	273	248	52	76	92	9	2	1	26	3	2	2	18	0	27	23	3	3	.371	.356
Maduro, Remy, Utica*	.217	49	175	157	16	34	45	5	3	0	12	1	1	1	15	0	27	2	5	2	.287	.287
Maier, Taber, New Jersey	.213	50	181	155	19	33	50	9	1	2	22	1	1	2	20	0	30	6	2	2	.323	.309
Mansavage, Jay, Auburn†	.325	10	45	40	7	13	18	3	1	0	2	0	0	0	5	0	2	1	1	0	.450	.400
Martine, Chris, New Jersey	.211	47	169	142	22	30	35	5	0	0	12	0	3	2	22	0	37	0	0	3	.246	.320
Mateo, Henry, Vermont†	.246	67	270	228	32	56	74	9	3	1	31	3	2	7	30	1	44	21	11	4	.325	.348
Maxwell, Keith, Erie	.209	42	154	134	23	28	51	3	1	6	24	0	3	7	10	0	38	1	1	4	.381	.292
Maxwell, Vernon, Oneonta	.196	50	168	148	14	29	39	6	2	0	22	0	6	1	13	0	49	7	2	3	.264	.256
McCarthy, Kevin, Pittsfield*	.204	57	217	201	20	41	54	9	2	0	20	1	0	1	14	2	55	4	2	1	.269	.259
McCladdie, Tony, Pittsfield	.236	52	208	178	30	42	53	9	1	0	22	2	2	1	25	0	30	11	4	2	.298	.330
McKinney, Antonio, Jamestown	.155	35	129	116	12	18	26	6	1	0	3	0	0	3	10	0	41	3	1	0	.224	.240
McNamara, Rusty, Batavia	.312	72	326	295	55	92	127	17	0	6	54	0	6	10	15	0	33	3	3	4	.431	.359
McNeal, Aaron, Auburn	.250	12	44	40	5	10	13	3	0	0	3	0	0	0	4	0	10	1	0	1	.325	.318
Medina, Robert, St. Catharines	.228	34	130	123	18	28	41	5	1	2	16	0	0	0	7	0	32	1	0	4	.333	.269
Mejia, Marlon, Auburn	.304	9	25	23	5	7	8	1	0	0	2	0	0	0	2	0	5	1	1	0	.348	.360
Mejia, Miguel, New Jersey	.331	30	132	124	22	41	51	8	1	0	14	0	2	0	6	0	27	11	3	2	.411	.356
Melconian, Alex, Utica	.279	62	253	215	37	60	76	6	2	2	22	4	1	15	18	0	48	6	6	5	.353	.373
Meran, Jorge, Jamestown	.175	51	195	183	21	32	55	11	0	4	15	0	1	0	11	1	50	2	1	3	.301	.221
Mercedes, Carlos, Auburn	.000	29	1	0	0	0	0	0	0	0	0	0	0	0	1	0	0	0	0	0	.000	1.000
Metzger, Erik, Lowell	.195	41	152	128	15	25	38	7	0	2	21	3	4	6	11	0	40	0	1	4	.297	.282
Miller, Kenny, Pittsfield	.226	26	104	93	16	21	24	3	0	0	14	1	2	2	6	0	13	4	1	1	.258	.282
Miller, Travis, Hudson Valley	.167	37	127	120	16	20	27	7	0	0	7	0	0	1	6	0	44	1	2	3	.225	.213
Miner, Tony, Watertown	.274	49	181	164	26	45	67	8	1	4	23	1	1	0	15	0	30	1	2	2	.409	.333
Mirizzi, Marc, Oneonta†	.261	74	292	245	40	64	74	5	1	1	33	3	3	3	38	0	36	12	7	4	.302	.363
Mohr, Dustan, Watertown	.291	74	314	275	52	80	125	20	2	7	53	0	4	4	31	1	76	3	6	1	.455	.366
Moreno, Juan, Pittsfield	.289	71	300	287	35	83	114	17	4	2	41	0	1	0	12	2	60	19	6	6	.397	.317
Mota, Cristian, Watertown†	.238	75	333	311	51	74	105	21	2	2	33	0	1	3	18	1	67	13	4	5	.338	.285
Murray, Doug, Auburn*	.165	34	95	79	4	13	14	1	0	0	5	3	1	4	8	0	18	0	1	6	.177	.272
Morris, Jeremy, Oneonta	.280	68	276	239	44	67	94	19	1	2	28	0	3	5	29	0	47	10	3	0	.393	.366
Nieves, Juan, St. Catharines	.230	64	254	243	29	56	76	14	0	2	30	1	1	2	7	1	41	3	5	3	.313	.257
Nolte, Bruce, Pittsfield	.230	47	177	161	22	37	48	3	4	0	18	2	1	2	11	0	37	4	0	2	.298	.286
Nunnari, Talmadge, Vermont*	.318	62	274	236	30	75	104	11	3	4	42	0	4	3	31	4	37	6	3	4	.441	.398
Olmeda, Jose, Lowell†	.289	54	206	187	24	54	78	8	2	4	27	1	0	2	16	0	42	2	2	4	.417	.351
Otero, Oscar, Williamsport	.161	19	67	62	3	10	11	1	0	0	7	0	1	1	3	0	10	0	0	1	.177	.209
Ovalles, Homy, Vermont	.214	29	98	84	6	18	25	4	0	1	12	4	0	1	9	0	23	3	2	0	.298	.298
Ozarowski, Richard, Jamestown†.	.286	7	32	28	5	8	12	2	1	0	2	1	0	2	1	0	8	0	0	1	.429	.355
Pandolfini, Ryan, Hudson Valley*.	.238	40	145	130	12	31	37	4	1	0	9	0	0	1	13	0	28	2	4	2	.285	.306
Parker, Clark, Jamestown†	.080	9	28	25	1	2	2	0	0	0	0	0	1	2	0	0	7	0	1	0	.080	.179
Patton, Cory, Pittsfield	.211	56	220	199	27	42	53	2	3	1	18	4	1	2	14	0	51	16	1	0	.266	.269
Pedersoli, Bernard, Jamestown	.162	32	117	105	11	17	19	2	0	0	6	1	1	3	7	0	28	1	0	1	.181	.233
Phillips, Blaine, Oneonta	.109	31	53	46	6	5	7	0	1	0	1	1	0	1	5	0	12	1	0	2	.152	.212
Phillips, Jason, Pittsfield	.206	48	175	155	15	32	47	9	0	2	17	1	2	4	13	0	24	4	0	2	.303	.282
Pigott, Anthony, Hudson Valley....	.000	1	4	4	0	0	0	0	0	0	0	0	0	0	0	0	0	0	0	0	.000	.000
Pinto, Rene, Oneonta	.289	52	208	187	31	54	78	8	2	4	29	1	4	5	11	1	37	1	3	5	.417	.338
Pointer, Corey, Erie	.116	18	51	43	5	5	11	0	0	2	7	0	1	4	3	0	22	3	1	0	.256	.235
Polonia, Israel, Utica	.173	37	132	110	13	19	29	7	0	1	8	3	1	3	15	0	51	1	1	3	.264	.287
Pressley, Kasey, Williamsport*	.193	44	149	140	15	27	43	7	0	3	13	0	0	1	8	2	56	1	2	4	.307	.242
Purkiss, Matt, Oneonta*	.277	65	242	213	31	59	91	14	0	6	41	0	2	6	21	2	53	0	2	3	.427	.355
Quaccia, Luke, New Jersey*	.230	60	233	204	27	47	67	5	0	5	23	0	3	11	15	1	52	2	3	4	.328	.313
Quero, Pedro, Vermont	.275	13	44	40	2	11	12	1	0	0	3	1	0	0	3	0	14	1	0	0	.300	.326
Reding, Josh, Vermont	.167	8	27	24	2	4	8	2	1	0	0	0	0	0	3	0	11	0	0	2	.333	.259
Reese, Nate, Utica	.205	13	47	44	5	9	11	2	0	0	5	0	1	0	2	0	14	0	1	1	.250	.234
Reyes, Jose, Erie	.152	10	35	33	3	5	8	0	0	1	3	0	0	0	2	0	6	0	0	1	.242	.200
Ribaudo, Mike, Williamsport	.170	30	92	88	6	15	26	2	0	3	8	2	0	0	2	1	25	1	0	4	.295	.189
Rijo-Berger, Jose, Pittsfield†	.296	36	160	135	20	40	45	5	0	0	9	3	1	2	19	1	11	7	2	2	.333	.389
Rios, Brian, Jamestown	.263	45	187	167	23	44	64	6	1	4	23	0	2	4	14	0	22	3	0	6	.383	.332
Rivera, Luis, Vermont	.252	40	151	135	17	34	50	12	2	0	13	0	3	3	10	0	37	1	1	2	.370	.311
Roach, Jason, Pittsfield	.213	64	252	235	26	50	79	11	0	6	28	1	3	5	8	0	70	0	0	1	.336	.251
Robinson, Joseph, Auburn	.227	39	80	75	6	17	20	1	1	0	3	1	0	0	4	0	30	1	1	2	.267	.275
Rodriguez, Aurelio, Watertown	.305	51	224	203	34	62	81	11	1	2	22	3	2	0	16	0	32	5	1	2	.399	.353
Rodriguez, Mike, St. Catharines ...	.286	2	7	7	0	2	3	1	0	0	1	0	0	0	0	0	1	0	0	0	.429	.286
Rodriguez, Sammy, Pittsfield	.245	36	136	110	15	27	52	6	2	5	20	1	2	2	21	1	33	2	1	1	.473	.370
Rosa, Erick, Watertown	.188	28	96	85	6	16	20	2	1	0	6	3	1	1	6	0	27	2	4	2	.235	.258
Rowson, James, Oneonta	.195	12	45	41	8	8	14	2	2	0	4	0	0	0	4	0	17	1	0	2	.341	.267
Ruecker, Dion, Lowell	.219	50	169	160	16	35	46	6	1	1	11	4	0	1	4	0	32	0	0	6	.288	.242
Russell, Jake, Watertown	.000	2	2	2	0	0	0	0	0	0	0	0	0	0	0	0	1	0	0	0	.000	.000
Salazar, Juan, Williamsport†....	.200	29	115	105	12	21	30	6	0	1	11	0	1	1	8	1	20	1	0	2	.286	.261
Santiago, Jorge, Pittsfield	.255	48	163	145	16	37	42	5	0	0	17	3	1	6	8	0	24	5	3	2	.290	.319
Schaffer, Jake, Jamestown	.293	55	240	215	39	63	103	14	4	6	26	2	2	2	19	0	35	5	2	5	.479	.353
Schesser, Heath, Jamestown	.284	67	299	271	30	77	102	12	2	3	39	1	2	4	21	0	40	3	2	2	.376	.342
Schifano, Anthony, Utica	.261	48	178	153	26	40	50	7	0	1	14	8	1	2	11	0	28	5	5	3	.327	.317

– 525 –

Player, Team	Avg.	G	TPA	AB	R	H	TB	2B	3B	HR	RBI	SH	SF	HP	BB	IBB	SO	SB	CS	GDP	Slg.	OBP
Schmidt, Todd, New Jersey†	.211	15	44	38	2	8	10	2	0	0	2	0	0	0	6	1	12	0	1	0	.263	.318
Schnabel, Matthew, Utica*	.191	67	272	225	23	43	55	6	0	2	22	3	5	2	37	5	46	5	4	5	.244	.305
Scioneaux, Damian, H.V.*	.300	70	313	273	48	82	103	13	4	0	23	3	0	5	31	0	45	22	10	2	.377	.382
Sencion, Pablo, St. Catharines†	.220	51	203	173	18	38	69	7	0	8	36	0	4	2	24	1	47	0	0	5	.399	.315
Smith, Jason, Williamsport*	.288	51	215	205	25	59	68	5	2	0	11	0	0	0	10	0	44	9	2	0	.332	.321
Spear, Chad, Hudson Valley	.298	18	66	57	13	17	30	5	1	2	13	0	1	0	8	0	13	1	0	0	.526	.379
Speckhardt, Mike, New Jersey	.185	51	152	135	15	25	32	5	1	0	6	2	1	2	12	0	39	3	5	4	.237	.260
Stanton, Rob, Watertown	.270	55	211	189	21	51	85	11	4	5	34	0	1	1	20	0	72	4	2	5	.450	.341
Steele, Alexander, Jamestown	.311	72	304	257	51	80	145	15	4	14	43	0	1	9	37	2	61	6	3	5	.564	.414
Stewart, Courteney, Williamsport	.243	54	192	181	13	44	49	5	0	0	26	0	0	0	11	0	50	8	5	3	.271	.286
Taylor, Adam, Watertown	.221	50	182	149	27	33	66	8	2	7	33	3	1	4	25	0	54	1	0	1	.443	.346
Terrell, Jeffrey, Batavia*	.220	52	182	159	20	35	41	4	1	0	17	5	1	1	16	0	38	3	1	3	.258	.294
Terry, Tony, Auburn†	.178	53	173	157	14	28	36	0	1	2	17	3	2	0	11	0	56	3	4	4	.229	.229
Thomas, Don, Auburn*	.125	17	8	8	0	1	1	0	0	0	1	0	0	0	0	0	0	0	0	0	.125	.125
Thomas, James, Auburn	.265	66	249	211	29	56	80	15	0	3	31	1	1	6	30	1	72	4	6	7	.379	.371
Thompson, Nick, Batavia	.200	4	19	15	4	3	5	2	0	0	4	0	0	1	3	0	3	0	0	0	.333	.368
Tiller, Brad, Watertown	.245	29	113	98	15	24	36	6	0	2	10	0	1	2	12	0	25	6	2	1	.367	.336
Twombley, Dennis, Oneonta	.243	15	48	37	3	9	13	1	0	1	7	0	0	1	10	0	12	0	1	1	.351	.417
Upshaw, Ryan, Watertown	.242	41	162	132	26	32	50	7	1	3	21	0	2	1	27	0	31	3	0	1	.379	.370
Valentine, Anthony, Pittsfield	.177	17	70	62	8	11	13	2	0	0	3	1	0	3	4	0	19	0	0	1	.210	.261
Vazquez, Roberto, New Jersey	.122	19	55	49	3	6	10	1	0	1	4	2	0	0	4	0	13	0	0	1	.204	.189
Verrall, Jared, Hudson Valley	.138	7	31	29	4	4	8	1	0	1	4	0	1	1	0	0	14	0	0	0	.276	.161
Villalobos, Noe, Lowell	.000	24	1	1	0	0	0	0	0	0	0	0	0	0	0	0	1	0	0	0	.000	.000
Voita, Sam, Hudson Valley†	.291	32	128	117	19	34	47	10	0	1	16	0	0	0	11	0	20	2	1	1	.402	.352
Walker, Ron, Williamsport	.349	54	215	189	30	66	105	10	1	9	39	0	2	5	17	7	48	0	1	6	.556	.413
Ware, Ryan, Hudson Valley	.204	44	166	147	18	30	40	6	2	0	13	1	2	2	14	0	40	7	1	1	.272	.279
Watson, Al, Williamsport†	.250	45	162	136	21	34	34	0	0	0	11	5	0	0	19	1	21	10	5	2	.250	.342
Wells, Vernon, St. Catharines	.307	66	297	264	52	81	133	20	1	10	31	0	2	1	30	1	44	8	6	2	.504	.377
Wesson, Barry, Auburn	.260	58	221	208	24	54	76	7	3	3	26	1	1	1	10	0	45	8	4	1	.365	.295
Whitner, Keith, Jamestown	.237	46	167	156	19	37	46	5	2	0	12	0	2	2	7	0	40	0	0	5	.295	.275
Wilson, Scott, New Jersey	.248	44	171	141	28	35	64	9	1	6	21	2	2	2	24	0	36	0	2	4	.454	.361
Worthy, Thomas, Batavia	.241	56	157	141	28	34	40	3	0	1	9	0	0	1	15	0	36	9	3	0	.284	.318
Young, Michael, St. Catharines	.308	74	319	276	49	85	136	18	3	9	48	0	3	7	33	1	59	9	5	6	.493	.392
Zech, Scott, Vermont	.265	63	250	204	31	54	68	11	0	1	20	5	6	7	27	1	36	17	7	4	.333	.361

GRAND SLAMS: Chris C. Clark 2; Alevras, Bautista, Dominique, Duffy, Erickson, Franco, Fritz, Haverbusch, Joffrion, Lankford, Maier, Purkiss, Sencion, R. Walker, 1 each.

AWARDED FIRST BASE ON CATCHER'S INTERFERENCE: Schifano 3 (S. Bagley 2, Ribaudo); J. Clark 2 (Martine, Burkhart); Harper 2 (Ribaudo, Amrhein); James 2 (Martine, A. Taylor); Maier 2 (S. Rodriguez 2); R. Walker 2 (Twombley, Martine); Watson 2 (Chapman, Twombley); Bly (A. Taylor); Haverbusch (Pinto); Jacomino (Grubbs); T. Johnson (Bagley); Pandolfini (Martine); Scioneaux (Martine); Zech (Gick).

1997 PITCHING

TEAM

Team	W	L	Pct.	ERA	G	CG	ShO	Sv.	IP	H	TBF	R	ER	HR	SH	SF	HB	BB	IBB	SO	WP	Bk.
Pittsfield	42	32	.568	2.82	74	5	3	20	644.1	546	2708	284	202	28	20	13	39	193	3	586	36	9
Oneonta	49	25	.662	3.12	74	8	8	21	638.1	596	2698	275	221	20	8	17	23	226	5	610	30	7
Batavia	47	27	.635	3.14	74	1	9	19	651.0	641	2740	296	227	42	10	14	39	156	5	551	35	8
Lowell	38	38	.500	3.58	76	3	5	19	658.2	609	2824	341	262	33	24	26	37	219	20	590	47	8
Erie	50	26	.658	3.58	76	1	7	27	663.1	595	2810	323	264	42	20	17	30	230	1	558	51	6
New Jersey	35	39	.473	3.75	74	4	5	12	629.1	630	2690	314	262	27	18	21	31	202	2	520	58	14
Hudson Valley	35	40	.467	3.84	75	1	4	17	654.2	610	2889	379	279	34	23	17	46	277	0	579	51	25
Williamsport	29	46	.387	3.86	75	1	4	17	646.1	656	2907	378	277	34	30	25	31	340	7	529	71	13
Utica	36	38	.486	4.12	74	3	4	14	629.1	653	2713	359	288	42	17	21	40	192	6	549	38	4
Watertown	39	36	.520	4.20	75	5	3	18	642.2	632	2828	361	300	41	25	28	26	292	26	553	48	11
St. Catharines	35	40	.467	4.27	75	0	1	21	645.1	652	2854	399	306	47	12	26	52	244	9	558	69	12
Vermont	35	41	.461	4.39	76	4	1	15	658.2	669	2925	401	321	41	21	37	42	259	0	546	52	9
Auburn	29	47	.382	4.45	76	7	5	15	650.2	717	2920	405	322	32	27	15	65	249	24	534	61	8
Jamestown	25	49	.338	5.20	74	7	2	11	627.2	696	2861	472	363	46	18	36	52	282	4	484	64	17

INDIVIDUAL

TOP QUALIFIERS FOR EARNED-RUN AVERAGE TITLE

Minimum 61 innings. *Lefthanded pitcher.

Pitcher, Team	W	L	Pct.	ERA	G	GS	CG	ShO	GF	Sv.	IP	H	TBF	R	ER	HR	SH	SF	HB	BB	IBB	SO	WP	Bk.
Blank, Matt, Vermont*	6	4	.600	1.69	16	15	2	0	0	0	95.2	74	375	26	18	2	1	3	2	14	0	84	0	0
Choate, Randy, Oneonta*	5	1	.833	1.73	10	10	0	0	0	0	62.1	49	242	12	12	1	0	0	2	12	1	61	0	2
Comer, Scott, Pittsfield*	7	1	.875	1.74	14	14	1	0	0	0	93.1	71	359	25	18	4	1	1	1	12	0	98	0	0
Adair, Derek, Batavia	7	3	.700	2.11	13	12	1	0	0	0	76.2	71	308	29	18	4	0	3	2	4	0	53	0	0
Day, Zach, Oneonta	7	2	.778	2.15	14	14	0	0	0	0	92.0	82	372	26	22	2	2	4	1	23	0	92	3	0
Lambert, Kristopher, Erie*	11	2	.846	2.33	15	14	0	0	0	0	81.0	59	330	28	21	5	2	0	2	21	0	94	7	1
Rizzo, Nick, Utica	4	1	.800	2.36	15	10	0	0	3	1	68.2	64	278	30	18	3	0	5	1	12	1	54	3	0
Heath, Woody, St. Catharines	7	4	.636	2.42	15	12	0	0	1	0	78.0	63	316	29	21	4	0	1	5	19	1	72	3	3
McDougal, Mike, New Jersey	4	4	.500	2.49	13	11	2	2	0	0	68.2	62	272	24	19	1	3	2	9	23	0	63	1	0
Henry, Jason, Oneonta	5	4	.556	2.56	12	12	0	0	0	0	63.1	61	270	27	18	2	1	1	3	23	0	57	6	1
Wiggins, Scott, Oneonta*	6	2	.750	2.56	13	13	1	1	0	0	63.1	58	261	25	18	1	0	0	2	22	0	44	0	0
Bacci, Anthony, Erie*	8	3	.727	2.56	15	14	0	0	0	0	84.1	68	350	34	24	5	0	1	3	36	0	50	2	1
Cotton, Joseph, Batavia	7	4	.636	2.99	15	15	0	0	0	0	96.1	90	402	38	32	10	2	2	7	29	0	74	6	0
Wheeler, Daniel, Hudson Valley	6	7	.462	3.00	15	15	0	0	0	0	84.0	75	351	38	28	2	1	1	3	17	0	81	4	2
Estrella, Leoncio, Pittsfield	7	6	.538	3.03	15	15	0	0	0	0	92.0	91	395	48	31	0	2	1	3	27	0	55	3	2

DEPARTMENTAL LEADERS: W—Lambert, 11; L—Fennell, Johnson, 10 each; Pct.—Comer, .875; G—Cook, 34; GS—Bowles, Ireland, 16 each; CG—Johnson, Beebe, 3 each; ShO—McDougal, Shearn, 2 each; GF—Reyes, 29; Sv.—Mota, 17; IP—Ireland, 107; H—Ireland, 111; TBF—Ireland, 458; R—J. Wallace, Persails, 64 each; ER—Persails, 54; HR—Diebolt, 12; SH—Vael, 6; SF—J. Thomas, 8; HB—Ireland, 12; BB—Polanco, 46; IBB—Mercedes, Hayden, Swinburson, 5 each; SO—Comer, 98; WP—Burchart, 20; BK—Madison, 6.

ALL PITCHERS

*Lefthanded pitcher.

Pitcher, Team	W	L	Pct.	ERA	G	GS	CG	ShO	GF	Sv.	IP	H	TBF	R	ER	HR	SH	SF	HB	BB	IBB	SO	WP	Bk.
Adair, Derek, Batavia	7	3	.700	2.11	13	12	1	0	0	0	76.2	71	308	29	18	4	0	3	2	4	0	53	0	0
Aguiar, Douglas, Batavia	1	0	1.000	3.57	7	3	0	0	1	0	22.2	24	108	15	9	1	1	0	2	15	1	15	3	1
Alkire, John, Jamestown	0	3	.000	8.51	9	7	1	0	1	0	37.0	61	185	42	35	2	1	2	4	14	0	33	5	0
Alvarez, Danny, Watertown	0	0	.000	13.50	3	0	0	0	2	0	3.1	9	20	6	5	2	0	0	0	0	0	2	0	1
Arnold, Neal, New Jersey	0	2	.000	3.93	23	0	0	0	4	0	36.2	35	154	21	16	2	4	1	3	9	0	27	4	0
Arteaga, Juan, Pittsfield*	4	2	.667	2.67	12	3	0	0	2	0	30.1	32	129	15	9	0	1	0	1	4	0	29	1	0
Bacci, Anthony, Erie*	8	3	.727	2.56	15	14	0	0	0	0	84.1	68	350	34	24	5	0	1	3	36	0	50	2	1
Baez, Miguel, Watertown	0	1	.000	1.93	3	0	0	0	3	1	4.2	5	21	2	1	1	1	0	0	1	1	6	0	0
Bair, Andy, Utica*	1	6	.143	6.32	12	12	0	0	0	0	52.2	54	228	42	37	8	3	1	7	17	0	32	2	0
Barksdale, Shane, Auburn	3	3	.500	5.55	22	1	0	0	4	0	35.2	49	159	28	22	3	1	2	1	12	1	22	3	0
Barry, Shawn, Pittsfield*	3	4	.400	1.73	22	0	0	0	9	0	26.0	14	105	6	5	0	0	0	0	10	1	35	4	1
Bass, Randall, Hudson Valley*	6	1	.857	3.18	17	3	0	0	4	0	45.1	34	194	22	16	1	2	1	2	27	0	31	3	2
Bausher, Andrew, Erie*	4	3	.571	3.88	15	10	0	0	1	1	65.0	62	278	32	28	3	2	2	3	19	1	44	2	1
Beck, Matthew, Jamestown	1	0	1.000	6.91	17	0	0	0	6	0	28.2	41	141	30	22	3	1	3	5	9	0	17	0	0
Becks, Ryan, Vermont*	2	8	.200	5.83	15	15	1	0	0	0	78.2	92	368	61	51	4	4	2	7	33	0	57	12	1
Beebe, Hans, Pittsfield*	6	6	.500	3.90	15	15	3	0	0	0	90.0	90	382	49	39	9	4	3	3	22	0	71	1	0
Belitz, Todd, Hudson Valley*	4	5	.444	3.53	15	15	0	0	0	0	74.0	65	315	41	29	4	1	2	5	18	0	78	0	0
Benzing, Skipp, Lowell	0	1	.000	5.91	2	2	0	0	0	0	10.2	11	45	8	7	1	0	0	0	2	1	6	1	0
Bergan, Thomas, Hudson Valley	0	5	.000	6.35	27	0	0	0	11	0	39.2	48	193	34	28	1	3	1	1	20	0	32	8	1
Black, Brett, Batavia	3	0	1.000	1.32	28	0	0	0	23	15	41.0	23	149	7	6	2	1	0	0	2	1	66	0	1
Blank, Matt, Vermont*	6	4	.600	1.69	16	15	2	0	0	0	95.2	74	375	26	18	2	1	3	2	14	0	84	0	0
Booker, Chris, Williamsport	1	5	.167	3.35	24	3	0	0	11	1	45.2	39	200	20	17	2	3	4	0	25	0	60	9	0
Borges, Reece, Utica	7	5	.583	4.80	15	15	2	0	0	0	80.2	92	358	54	43	6	3	1	3	28	0	58	4	0
Bowles, Brian, St. Catharines	5	8	.385	5.03	16	16	0	0	0	0	78.2	76	351	53	44	6	0	3	11	35	0	64	4	1
Bradley, Ryan, Oneonta	3	1	.750	1.35	14	0	0	0	9	1	26.2	22	103	5	4	1	0	0	0	5	1	22	0	1
Brand, Scott, Oneonta	4	3	.571	7.32	10	2	0	0	2	0	19.2	24	92	17	16	1	1	1	2	8	0	18	1	0
Brown, Jamie, Watertown	10	2	.833	3.08	13	13	1	0	0	0	73.0	66	303	35	25	6	1	2	4	15	0	57	1	1
Brunette, Justin, New Jersey*	1	0	1.000	7.94	6	0	0	0	2	0	5.2	13	29	6	5	0	0	0	0	6	1	1	1	0
Bryant, Chris, Williamsport*	0	0	.000	6.75	4	0	0	0	0	0	6.2	13	38	8	5	0	0	0	5	3	8	3	0	
Burchart, Kyle, St. Catharines	3	4	.429	4.78	14	14	0	0	0	0	69.2	75	314	49	37	6	2	5	7	23	2	56	20	0
Burnett, Allan, Pittsfield	3	1	.750	4.70	9	9	0	0	0	0	44.0	28	192	26	23	3	0	2	6	35	0	48	9	0
Cali, Joe, Watertown	1	0	1.000	9.00	2	0	0	0	2	0	3.0	4	13	3	3	2	0	0	0	0	0	3	1	0
Calvert, Klae, Lowell	1	0	1.000	8.36	3	3	0	0	0	0	14.0	16	64	13	13	3	1	1	5	3	0	8	3	0
Cammack, Eric, Pittsfield	0	1	.000	0.86	23	0	0	0	17	8	31.1	9	117	4	3	1	3	1	1	14	1	32	1	1
Carpenter, Justin, Oneonta	3	1	.750	4.60	24	0	0	0	8	0	29.1	32	140	17	15	1	1	1	0	20	0	36	4	0
Carter, Bart, Hudson Valley	0	0	.000	0.00	1	0	0	0	0	0	1.0	3	9	4	0	0	0	0	1	0	0	1	0	
Casey, Joseph, St. Catharines	7	4	.636	4.36	14	11	0	0	1	0	64.0	59	279	42	31	6	0	1	3	23	0	43	11	0
Casey, Shaw, Utica	0	2	.000	12.00	8	0	0	0	3	0	11.0	28	73	21	16	1	1	0	6	8	0	10	3	0
Charbonneau, Marc, St.C.*	0	1	.000	7.20	6	0	0	0	2	1	10.0	9	46	9	8	1	0	1	4	0	15	2	0	
Choate, Randy, Oneonta*	5	1	.833	1.73	10	10	0	0	0	0	62.1	49	242	12	12	1	0	2	12	1	61	0	2	
Coco, Pascual, St. Catharines	1	4	.200	4.89	10	8	0	0	1	0	46.0	48	199	32	25	5	4	2	16	1	44	6	1	
Combs, Chris, Erie	2	1	.667	0.73	21	0	0	0	19	9	24.2	13	92	2	2	0	0	1	3	0	36	1	0	
Comer, Scott, Pittsfield*	7	1	.875	1.74	14	14	1	0	0	0	93.1	71	359	25	18	4	1	1	12	0	98	0	0	
Coogan, Patrick, New Jersey	2	5	.286	3.70	10	10	0	0	0	0	56.0	56	231	27	23	4	1	0	3	14	0	37	0	2
Cook, O.J., Erie	5	2	.714	2.08	34	0	0	0	26	10	39.0	37	168	14	9	2	0	0	20	0	43	7	0	
Cotton, Joseph, Batavia	7	4	.636	2.99	15	15	0	0	0	0	96.1	90	402	38	32	10	2	2	7	29	0	74	6	0
Crabtree, Tim, St. Catharines	0	0	.000	3.00	2	1	0	0	0	0	3.0	3	12	2	1	1	0	0	0	0	3	0	0	
Cummins, Jon, Hudson Valley	1	0	1.000	6.43	21	1	0	0	4	0	35.0	37	175	30	25	3	0	1	0	32	0	35	6	2
Curtis, Mark, St. Catharines*	1	0	1.000	4.76	4	0	0	0	1	0	5.2	6	27	4	3	0	0	0	0	5	0	5	2	0
Daniels, Ronney, Vermont*	0	0	.000	3.60	3	0	0	0	0	0	5.0	5	20	2	2	0	0	0	0	2	0	1	0	0
Davis, Mike, Pittsfield	1	2	.333	3.34	24	1	0	0	16	4	35.0	31	162	17	13	0	3	1	7	16	1	20	2	0
Day, Zach, Oneonta	7	2	.778	2.15	14	14	0	0	0	0	92.0	82	372	26	22	2	2	4	1	23	0	92	3	0
DePaula, Sean, Watertown	1	1	.500	2.84	9	0	0	0	2	0	19.0	21	86	6	6	1	1	1	1	8	0	17	0	0
Diebolt, Michael, Jamestown*	3	6	.333	4.30	15	13	0	0	1	0	81.2	87	355	50	39	12	1	2	4	38	0	63	8	5
Doan, Zachary, Utica	2	2	.500	5.65	13	0	0	0	10	1	28.2	34	127	18	18	2	0	1	0	13	1	22	3	0
Downs, Scott, Williamsport*	0	2	.000	2.74	5	5	0	0	0	0	23.0	15	93	11	7	0	1	1	0	7	0	28	0	2
Drew, Tim, Watertown	0	0	.000	1.93	1	1	0	0	0	0	4.2	4	20	1	1	0	0	0	0	3	0	4	0	0
Driscoll, Patrick, Batavia*	0	0	.000	3.72	11	0	0	0	0	0	9.2	14	48	5	4	0	0	0	2	4	0	10	0	1
Eason, Clay, Batavia	0	1	.000	0.92	20	0	0	0	9	0	29.1	16	119	6	3	1	0	1	1	11	0	29	2	1
Ehlers, Corey, Utica	1	0	1.000	1.47	10	0	0	0	6	1	19.1	16	73	3	3	1	0	1	0	1	0	17	0	0
Ellison, Jason, Oneonta	0	1	.000	1.74	11	0	0	0	3	0	20.2	19	82	6	4	0	0	0	1	4	0	19	2	0
Erwin, David, Watertown	3	1	.750	5.25	18	2	0	0	9	1	36.0	36	163	24	21	2	1	1	6	23	2	36	2	0
Estrella, Leoncio, Pittsfield	7	6	.538	3.03	15	15	0	0	0	0	92.0	91	395	48	31	0	2	1	3	27	0	55	3	2
Eversgerd, Randy, St.C.*	0	1	.000	2.66	15	0	0	0	4	0	23.2	30	107	16	7	2	1	0	0	5	1	34	1	1
Fennell, Barry, Williamsport*	2	10	.167	6.11	17	10	0	0	1	0	66.1	92	306	51	45	5	3	3	29	0	50	4	1	
Fenus, Justin, Batavia	3	5	.375	4.45	15	7	0	0	1	0	54.2	54	245	34	27	2	2	3	5	30	0	26	6	1
Fisher, Louis, Williamsport	1	3	.250	4.69	11	9	0	0	0	0	40.1	41	188	27	21	2	0	0	2	32	0	31	8	0
Fisher, Ryan, Erie*	0	0	.000	5.79	2	2	0	0	0	0	9.1	11	40	7	6	1	0	2	0	2	0	6	1	1
Flores, Randy, Oneonta*	4	4	.500	3.25	13	13	2	1	0	0	74.2	64	308	32	27	3	0	1	4	23	1	70	5	1
Folkers, Kenneth, St. Catharines	1	0	1.000	3.03	14	0	0	0	5	0	29.2	27	124	16	10	3	2	2	1	7	0	28	3	0
Fowler, Blair, Utica	2	2	.500	4.00	18	1	0	0	8	0	36.0	40	160	23	16	2	2	1	7	29	1	29	1	0
Fraser, Joe, Vermont	0	3	.000	6.11	10	3	0	0	2	0	17.2	22	95	21	12	1	0	3	2	17	0	7	1	0
Frush, Jimmy, Batavia	6	1	.857	2.85	26	0	0	0	7	1	41.0	34	166	14	13	5	1	1	4	6	2	37	3	0
Fuduric, Tony, Watertown	0	1	.000	8.22	2	1	0	0	0	0	7.2	8	37	8	7	0	0	1	0	3	0	6	0	1
Gagliano, Steve, Utica	0	1	.000	9.82	1	1	0	0	0	0	3.2	6	20	4	4	0	0	1	0	3	0	6	0	1

CLASS A *New York-Pennsylvania League*

Pitcher, Team	W	L	Pct.	ERA	G	GS	CG	ShO	GF	Sv.	IP	H	TBF	R	ER	HR	SH	SF	HB	BB	IBB	SO	WP	Bk.
Garff, Jeff, Watertown	3	0	1.000	2.81	6	4	0	0	0	0	25.2	31	114	12	8	0	0	1	1	7	3	18	1	0
Gaskill, Derek, Pittsfield	3	2	.600	2.58	21	3	0	0	2	0	45.1	41	187	23	13	3	2	4	2	5	0	39	3	0
Geis, John, New Jersey*	0	0	.000	3.00	3	0	0	0	0	0	3.0	2	14	1	1	0	0	0	0	3	0	3	0	0
Gonzalez, Ignacio, H.V>	1	5	.167	2.35	26	0	0	0	2	0	38.1	35	164	16	10	1	2	2	3	16	0	40	2	1
Greene, Joel, Jamestown*	4	1	.800	2.40	20	0	0	0	4	1	30.0	26	135	14	8	1	1	1	2	19	0	22	5	1
Gresko, Michael, Erie*	1	2	.333	7.66	7	5	0	0	0	0	24.2	29	119	26	21	0	1	0	2	17	0	14	1	0
Guilmet, John, Jamestown	0	6	.000	5.26	17	6	0	0	5	1	49.2	68	235	44	29	4	1	4	4	10	0	29	4	3
Guy, Bradley, Erie	5	1	.833	1.88	25	0	0	0	6	1	52.2	37	201	12	11	3	3	0	2	7	0	53	9	1
Guzman, Wilson, Erie*	1	2	.333	5.06	5	5	0	0	0	0	26.2	26	112	20	15	4	2	1	1	6	0	25	0	0
Hayden, Terry, Lowell*	0	6	.000	3.19	16	5	0	0	4	0	53.2	42	216	21	19	2	5	0	3	14	5	52	1	0
Hazlett, Andy, Lowell*	5	0	1.000	1.61	19	3	0	0	12	4	50.1	44	206	16	9	1	0	1	0	7	0	66	0	0
Heath, Woody, St. Catharines	7	4	.636	2.42	15	12	0	0	1	0	78.0	63	316	29	21	4	0	1	5	19	1	72	3	3
Hecht, Brian, Auburn	2	2	.500	1.69	26	0	0	0	25	11	37.1	35	151	10	7	0	1	0	1	8	2	35	1	2
Heffernan, Greg, New Jersey	0	2	.000	2.57	26	0	0	0	26	9	28.0	23	115	9	8	0	2	2	0	7	1	31	3	2
Henderson, Scott, Utica	5	1	.833	2.27	15	1	0	0	6	4	39.2	28	151	11	10	1	2	1	1	7	0	51	3	0
Henry, Jason, Oneonta	5	4	.556	2.56	12	12	0	0	0	0	63.1	61	270	27	18	2	1	1	3	23	0	57	6	1
Hill, T.J., Hudson Valley	2	2	.500	5.00	11	11	0	0	0	0	45.0	53	216	36	25	2	3	0	7	22	0	31	3	2
Hlodan, George, Erie	1	0	1.000	6.15	15	1	1	0	3	2	33.2	39	151	24	23	3	2	3	1	11	0	21	3	0
Holobinko, Mike, Williamsport*	0	0	.000	3.29	12	0	0	0	6	0	13.2	16	66	6	5	1	1	0	3	7	0	10	3	0
Horgan, Joe, Watertown*	0	1	.000	6.10	15	4	0	0	2	0	38.1	48	179	31	26	4	2	2	1	18	1	31	4	1
Howard, Jason, Jamestown	4	3	.571	5.24	13	1	0	0	3	0	22.1	21	110	22	13	1	0	3	7	14	0	21	3	0
Huber, John, Auburn	0	4	.000	6.50	4	4	1	0	0	0	18.0	27	88	20	13	0	2	0	1	5	1	5	1	0
Huff, Tim, St. Catharines*	1	1	.500	5.34	15	0	0	0	3	0	32.0	38	139	20	19	3	0	1	1	13	1	20	1	0
Huffaker, Michael, New Jersey	1	4	.200	2.40	33	0	0	0	4	1	45.0	40	192	17	12	0	1	0	3	16	0	36	3	0
Huggins, David, St. Catharines	0	3	.000	3.28	27	2	0	0	18	11	35.2	33	159	18	13	1	0	2	4	15	1	42	1	2
Hughes, Mike, Watertown*	5	3	.625	3.51	13	13	2	0	0	0	77.0	69	325	37	30	4	0	3	4	25	2	80	7	0
Hunter, Travis, Utica	0	0	.000	20.25	2	0	0	0	2	0	1.1	5	11	3	3	0	0	1	0	2	0	1	0	0
Ireland, Eric, Auburn	5	7	.417	3.70	16	16	2	0	0	0	107.0	111	458	55	44	4	2	0	12	21	1	78	3	0
Jacquez, Thomas, Batavia*	2	1	.667	2.42	4	4	0	0	0	0	22.1	20	93	6	6	0	0	2	3	2	0	20	0	0
Jerue, Tristan, New Jersey	5	4	.556	3.52	13	13	0	0	0	0	71.2	73	310	35	28	3	2	5	5	21	0	55	4	1
Jimenez, Jason, H.V.*	3	0	1.000	0.28	19	0	0	0	5	0	31.2	16	121	5	1	1	0	0	2	10	0	31	0	1
Johnson, Craig, Jamestown	3	10	.231	4.43	14	14	3	0	0	0	83.1	88	349	59	41	4	1	6	6	10	0	66	1	2
Karnuth, Jason, New Jersey	4	1	.800	1.86	7	7	0	0	0	0	38.2	33	158	8	8	0	1	1	2	9	0	23	2	0
Keller, Kris, Jamestown	0	2	.000	8.67	16	0	0	0	10	0	27.0	37	143	33	26	3	1	3	3	20	0	18	5	2
Kelley, Jason, Williamsport	2	2	.500	7.16	27	0	0	0	18	10	27.2	28	144	31	22	3	4	1	4	32	0	16	12	1
Kimbrell, Michael, H.V.*	1	3	.250	4.54	26	0	0	0	12	2	39.2	34	177	32	20	5	4	2	1	18	0	43	1	1
Knotts, Gary, Utica	3	5	.375	3.62	12	12	1	0	0	0	69.2	70	304	34	28	3	1	2	8	27	1	65	3	0
Koch, Jack, Oneonta	0	0	.000	0.00	1	0	0	0	0	0	2.0	1	8	0	0	0	0	0	0	1	0	2	0	0
Koehler, Jason, St. Catharines	0	0	.000	0.00	1	0	0	0	1	0	1.0	0	3	0	0	0	0	0	0	0	0	1	0	0
Lacefield, Timothy, St.C.	2	0	1.000	4.99	25	0	0	0	9	2	39.2	52	177	26	22	5	3	1	5	5	1	33	1	1
Lambert, Kristopher, Erie*	11	2	.846	2.33	15	14	0	0	0	0	81.0	59	330	28	21	5	2	0	2	21	0	94	7	1
Lanzetta, Tobin, Vermont	1	4	.200	5.61	23	5	0	0	5	1	43.1	60	206	36	27	5	0	3	2	8	0	43	4	0
Levan, Matt, Utica*	0	0	.000	6.75	1	1	0	0	0	0	4.0	5	20	3	3	1	0	0	1	1	0	6	1	0
Levey, Joshua, New Jersey	1	3	.250	5.35	18	3	0	0	3	0	33.2	31	149	21	20	1	1	3	7	14	0	25	10	0
Licciardi, Ron, Williamsport*	4	1	.800	4.98	17	9	0	0	1	0	65.0	84	305	41	36	6	2	2	0	25	1	56	6	1
Lima, Cory, Utica	3	1	.750	2.03	17	2	0	0	7	1	40.0	31	160	11	9	1	0	0	2	11	0	40	2	2
Lohrman, David, Pittsfield	1	2	.333	2.91	22	0	0	0	13	4	34.0	25	146	18	11	2	0	0	5	12	0	42	3	1
Loubier, Scott, Vermont	3	2	.600	3.08	7	6	0	0	0	0	38.0	32	155	16	13	3	1	1	1	10	0	29	3	1
Love, Farley, Auburn	0	0	.000	0.00	3	0	0	0	1	1	3.0	1	11	0	0	0	1	0	0	1	0	2	0	0
Luttig, Christopher, Erie*	1	2	.333	3.32	11	0	0	0	5	0	19.0	18	85	12	7	0	0	1	0	8	0	16	1	0
Lynde, Jerry, Vermont	0	2	.000	9.24	12	2	0	0	4	0	12.2	17	74	17	13	1	0	1	1	18	0	12	1	0
Mackowiak, Robert, Erie	0	0	.000	0.00	2	0	0	0	2	0	1.1	1	5	0	0	0	0	0	0	0	0	1	0	0
Madison, Scott, Hudson Valley*	6	4	.600	3.74	15	15	1	0	0	0	86.2	87	362	43	36	9	1	3	2	28	0	54	5	6
Magers, Mathew, Williamsport*	4	4	.500	3.58	27	0	0	0	14	5	50.1	46	231	28	20	0	3	5	1	35	3	48	4	1
Manbeck, Mark, Batavia	1	2	.333	4.76	5	5	0	0	0	0	28.1	36	116	16	15	1	0	0	0	4	0	27	1	0
Mangieri, John, Pittsfield	0	0	.000	20.25	2	0	0	0	1	0	1.1	3	9	3	3	0	0	0	2	0	0	0	0	0
Markwell, Diegomar, St.C.*	1	6	.143	4.99	16	11	0	0	1	0	48.2	50	240	35	27	1	3	0	8	40	0	33	5	1
Marriott, Mike, Utica	1	2	.333	5.52	7	7	0	0	0	0	29.1	31	134	25	18	1	0	1	2	14	0	21	2	0
Martin, Trey, Vermont	1	0	1.000	6.20	11	0	0	0	1	0	24.2	30	110	19	17	3	1	2	2	7	0	13	1	0
McBride, Jason, Oneonta	0	0	.000	0.00	2	0	0	0	0	0	2.2	1	15	1	0	0	0	0	2	3	0	2	0	0
McCarter, Jason, Auburn	0	0	.000	3.74	16	0	0	0	5	0	21.2	23	113	12	9	1	0	4	10	17	0	20	3	0
McClaskey, Tim, Utica	1	0	1.000	0.00	1	0	0	0	1	0	5.0	1	16	0	0	0	0	0	0	0	0	8	0	0
McCleary, Marty, Lowell	3	6	.333	3.75	13	13	0	0	0	0	62.1	53	275	38	26	2	3	3	5	36	1	43	6	2
McConnell, John, Erie*	2	2	.500	5.06	17	10	0	0	0	0	58.2	56	261	38	33	7	1	3	3	24	0	45	6	0
McDougal, Mike, New Jersey	4	4	.500	2.49	13	11	2	2	0	0	68.2	62	272	24	19	1	3	0	2	9	0	63	1	0
McNally, Andrew, Watertown	2	3	.400	2.87	23	0	0	0	18	8	31.1	23	127	10	10	2	2	0	0	13	1	37	2	0
Mear, Richard, Jamestown*	1	1	.500	12.54	8	0	0	0	2	0	9.1	6	62	18	13	0	0	1	1	28	0	7	8	0
Medina, Tomas, Auburn	0	0	.000	8.46	15	0	0	0	5	0	22.1	33	125	24	21	5	0	1	7	21	1	19	8	0
Mercedes, Carlos, Auburn	2	4	.333	4.47	28	1	0	0	10	2	44.1	47	193	26	22	2	4	0	1	19	5	43	4	1
Messman, Joseph, Auburn	1	2	.333	3.21	25	0	0	0	10	1	28.0	26	132	13	10	1	3	0	6	21	3	31	8	0
Meyers, Mike, Williamsport	0	0	.000	0.00	1	1	0	0	0	0	4.0	3	15	0	0	0	1	0	0	1	0	2	0	0
Miller, Tom, Lowell*	1	3	.250	2.77	24	0	0	0	9	1	39.0	38	183	24	12	2	3	3	3	20	3	42	2	0
Minter, Matt, Watertown*	0	0	.000	4.70	7	0	0	0	5	0	7.2	6	35	4	4	0	0	2	1	5	0	12	3	0
Mobley, Kevin, Jamestown	2	1	.667	3.16	18	0	0	0	9	0	25.2	27	115	10	9	1	4	2	1	11	1	24	0	0
Mondello, Peter, Batavia	0	1	.000	3.71	27	0	0	0	13	0	34.0	32	157	20	14	5	1	0	3	17	1	41	3	0
Montemayor, Humberto, Lowell.	0	1	.000	13.50	1	0	0	0	1	0	0.2	2	6	1	1	0	1	0	1	1	1	0	0	0
Mota, Daniel, Oneonta	1	0	1.000	2.22	27	0	0	0	25	17	28.1	21	119	8	7	0	1	0	0	16	0	40	0	0
Navarro, Jason, New Jersey*	1	6	.143	6.85	10	10	1	0	0	0	44.2	60	211	40	34	4	0	1	1	22	0	41	7	3
Negrette, Richard, Watertown	2	3	.400	3.66	17	0	0	0	7	1	39.1	25	171	17	16	0	5	2	3	29	2	30	6	1
O'Dette, Rick, Lowell*	5	3	.625	3.47	13	10	1	0	1	0	59.2	64	268	30	23	1	1	1	0	28	3	61	4	2
Oswalt, Roy, Auburn	2	4	.333	4.53	9	9	1	1	0	0	51.2	50	220	29	26	1	0	1	6	15	1	44	3	1
Palma, Ricardo, Williamsport*	4	7	.364	3.48	14	14	1	0	0	0	77.2	77	336	36	30	6	1	3	2	36	1	47	2	5
Parker, Eric, Lowell*	3	0	1.000	3.24	23	0	0	0	11	1	41.2	32	180	20	15	3	4	1	1	23	0	41	6	0

Pitcher, Team	W	L	Pct.	ERA	G	GS	CG	ShO	GF	Sv.	IP	H	TBF	R	ER	HR	SH	SF	HB	BB	IBB	SO	WP	Bk.
Partenheimer, Brian, Lowell*	2	1	.667	0.68	5	0	0	0	3	1	13.1	9	51	1	1	0	1	0	0	1	0	11	0	0
Pascarella, Josh, Auburn	0	0	.000	3.00	1	1	0	0	0	0	6.0	8	27	5	2	1	0	0	0	2	0	0	0	0
Pelton, Brad, Watertown	1	5	.167	5.10	9	9	0	0	0	0	47.2	54	211	31	27	2	0	0	0	18	1	29	3	1
Perez, Julio, Vermont	0	1	.000	5.68	3	1	0	0	0	0	6.1	12	35	8	4	1	0	0	0	2	0	5	1	0
Persails, Mark, Jamestown	3	7	.300	5.74	15	14	2	0	1	0	84.2	103	384	64	54	5	1	3	3	33	1	56	13	0
Pitt, Jye, Williamsport	0	1	.000	4.26	4	0	0	0	0	0	6.1	9	37	11	3	1	0	0	0	5	0	9	0	0
Plummer, Raymond, Vermont*	4	3	.571	5.26	28	0	0	0	4	0	39.1	39	179	28	23	5	3	4	3	17	0	28	3	1
Polanco, Elvis, Williamsport	2	5	.286	3.23	15	15	0	0	0	0	83.2	71	364	45	30	5	4	1	9	46	0	64	6	1
Poupart, Melvin, Pittsfield	0	0	.000	2.70	8	1	0	0	0	0	10.0	10	56	8	3	2	0	3	14	0	9	2	1
Prater, Andrew, Erie	3	2	.600	4.40	15	14	0	0	0	0	73.2	82	320	37	36	6	2	2	7	26	0	40	4	0
Prempas, Lyle, Lowell*	0	0	.000	10.80	3	0	0	0	2	0	3.1	1	15	4	4	1	0	0	0	4	0	2	1	0
Putnicki, William, Utica	3	4	.429	2.47	21	0	0	0	13	4	43.2	44	184	17	12	3	1	2	3	10	1	33	2	1
Pyrtle, Joe, Pittsfield	3	2	.600	0.75	23	0	0	0	9	4	36.0	13	137	7	3	0	1	0	3	8	0	44	3	0
Queen, Mike, Pittsfield*	5	4	.556	3.24	13	13	1	1	0	0	75.0	86	326	33	27	3	3	0	2	13	0	63	3	3
Quintana, Urbano, Batavia	1	0	1.000	2.16	6	0	0	0	2	0	8.1	9	36	5	2	0	0	1	1	5	0	4	0	0
Rahilly, Michael, Vermont	2	0	1.000	2.30	9	0	0	0	5	1	15.2	9	60	4	4	1	0	0	0	4	0	18	2	1
Ramirez, Jose, Jamestown*	3	4	.429	3.90	15	15	1	0	0	0	94.2	84	398	49	41	4	4	4	4	38	0	75	5	2
Rayborn, Kenny, Lowell	2	2	.500	2.74	11	7	0	0	1	1	46.0	39	197	18	14	0	1	2	6	15	0	35	8	0
Regalado, Frank, Hudson Valley	0	0	.000	2.08	5	0	0	0	5	0	4.1	5	16	1	1	0	0	0	0	0	0	3	0	0
Reyes, Eddy, Hudson Valley	0	2	.000	2.76	31	0	0	0	29	14	32.2	24	144	12	10	1	2	0	4	18	0	29	0	5
Richards, Mark, Utica	0	0	.000	0.00	2	0	0	0	2	0	2.0	1	7	0	0	0	0	0	0	0	0	3	0	0
Rizzo, Nick, Utica	4	1	.800	2.36	15	10	0	0	3	1	68.2	64	278	30	18	3	0	5	1	12	1	54	3	0
Roberson, Charles, Watertown	3	1	.750	3.09	18	2	0	0	6	2	43.2	39	183	18	15	4	0	2	0	17	2	35	4	0
Rosario, Ruben, New Jersey	5	5	.500	4.28	14	14	1	0	0	0	73.2	64	315	42	35	3	0	5	2	37	0	66	11	1
Rupp, Michael, Lowell	0	1	.000	3.55	2	2	0	0	0	0	12.2	8	49	5	5	1	0	0	3	0	0	10	0	0
Rutherford, Mark, Batavia	2	1	.667	0.75	3	2	0	0	0	0	12.0	10	47	5	1	0	0	1	0	3	0	11	3	0
Saberhagen, Bret, Lowell	0	0	.000	0.00	1	1	0	0	0	0	3.0	1	10	0	0	0	0	0	0	0	0	2	0	0
Sadler, Carl, Vermont*	2	2	.500	4.21	7	6	0	0	0	0	36.1	33	167	20	17	2	1	2	2	23	0	27	4	1
Salyers, Jeremy, Vermont	3	4	.429	5.00	16	14	0	0	0	0	77.1	87	346	53	43	4	3	6	5	31	0	32	6	2
Santamaria, Juan, Jamestown	0	0	.000	9.49	8	4	0	0	0	0	24.2	28	123	29	26	5	0	2	6	18	0	11	6	1
Santana, Johan, Auburn*	0	0	.000	2.25	1	1	0	0	0	0	4.0	1	19	1	1	0	0	1	0	6	0	5	0	0
Santana, Pedro, Lowell	6	3	.667	4.09	15	15	2	0	0	0	88.0	90	364	47	40	6	0	5	6	17	1	65	3	1
Santiago, Antonio, Wpt.*	3	1	.750	1.55	26	0	0	0	13	1	46.1	41	204	15	8	1	5	1	3	21	1	33	5	0
Sasaki, Junichi, Vermont	1	0	1.000	3.24	11	0	0	0	6	1	16.2	14	70	7	6	0	1	1	4	0	19	2	1
Saylor, Ryan, Vermont	3	0	1.000	2.37	16	0	0	0	14	2	19.0	17	82	7	5	0	1	1	8	0	29	2	0
Schnautz, Brad, Oneonta*	0	1	.000	9.39	4	0	0	0	1	0	7.2	16	43	14	8	1	0	0	2	0	9	1	0
Seabury, Jaron, St. Catharines	2	0	1.000	4.50	8	0	0	0	7	4	8.0	7	37	4	4	0	0	0	6	1	11	1	0
Shearn, Thomas, Auburn	4	6	.400	3.50	14	14	2	2	0	0	82.1	79	349	42	32	4	1	4	9	26	3	59	7	1
Shipp, Kevin, Batavia	5	3	.625	2.83	13	7	0	0	4	0	47.2	44	188	17	15	1	1	0	2	6	0	41	1	2
Shockley, Keith, Batavia*	1	3	.250	6.82	27	2	0	0	12	2	31.2	48	146	30	24	3	1	2	3	6	0	10	3	1
Siciliano, Jess, Erie	2	0	1.000	4.24	16	0	0	0	8	3	23.1	22	107	16	11	2	3	1	2	10	0	20	6	1
Smith, Andy, Oneonta	3	2	.600	2.93	26	0	0	0	11	1	40.0	30	164	13	13	0	1	2	1	13	1	55	1	1
Snyder, William, Jamestown	1	3	.250	2.17	25	0	0	0	25	9	29.0	19	126	8	7	1	2	0	2	20	2	42	1	1
Sparks, Eric, Vermont*	0	4	.000	4.29	28	0	0	0	10	2	42.0	34	189	22	20	2	4	3	26	0	46	3	0
Stabile, Paul, Erie*	4	4	.500	2.72	22	0	0	0	5	1	43.0	32	174	17	13	1	2	1	16	0	50	1	0
Stechschulte, Gene, New Jersey	1	1	.500	3.22	30	0	0	0	9	1	36.1	45	164	16	13	2	0	2	1	16	0	28	3	0
Strickland, Scott, Vermont	5	2	.714	3.82	15	9	1	0	5	0	61.1	56	255	27	26	5	3	2	6	20	1	69	3	1
Stutz, Shawn, Hudson Valley	1	0	1.000	8.10	6	0	0	0	1	1	13.1	16	83	21	12	1	1	2	4	21	0	9	8	1
Swinburnson, Tyler, Watertown	2	0	.600	4.62	25	0	0	0	12	5	39.0	40	176	26	20	1	3	1	2	24	5	38	1	4
Taglienti, Jeff, Lowell	3	4	.429	4.91	17	4	0	0	11	6	36.2	30	150	22	20	2	0	0	13	0	34	3	2
Taylor, Mark, Watertown*	3	7	.300	4.67	15	13	1	1	1	0	71.1	68	320	45	37	5	2	6	2	45	2	58	6	1
Tejera, Michael, Utica*	3	5	.500	3.76	12	12	0	0	0	0	69.1	65	279	36	29	8	3	1	2	11	0	67	6	0
Teut, Nate, Williamsport*	3	4	.429	2.57	9	9	0	0	0	0	49.0	55	203	23	14	0	1	2	0	6	1	37	2	1
Thomas, Don, Auburn*	6	4	.600	4.53	15	15	1	0	0	0	87.1	93	374	50	44	5	5	0	6	21	1	72	9	0
Thomas, Joe, Lowell*	4	5	.444	3.84	18	11	0	0	6	2	75.0	71	327	43	32	3	3	8	6	19	1	61	3	0
Tisone, Jason, Oneonta	1	0	1.000	6.39	18	0	0	0	5	2	31.0	42	150	27	22	2	0	2	3	13	0	27	6	0
Vael, Robert, Watertown	1	4	.200	4.62	12	12	1	0	0	0	62.1	63	279	38	32	5	6	3	0	30	2	47	4	1
Van Gilder, Ryan, Vermont*	2	1	.667	2.61	19	0	0	0	11	8	20.2	17	88	9	6	0	0	2	1	9	0	19	1	0
Vasquez, Antonio, Watertown	1	1	.500	6.75	3	0	0	0	1	0	8.0	13	45	7	6	0	0	0	2	6	1	0	0	0
Villafana, Jose, New Jersey	4	0	1.000	2.63	5	5	0	0	0	0	27.1	20	109	10	8	1	0	0	9	0	20	2	0
Villalobos, Noe, Lowell	3	2	.600	4.25	24	0	0	0	12	3	48.2	58	218	30	23	5	1	1	13	4	51	6	1
Vizcaino, Edward, Wpt.	1	1	.500	2.75	11	0	0	0	5	0	19.2	15	78	13	6	1	0	1	4	0	14	0	0
Vogt, Robert, Erie*	0	0	.000	10.80	1	1	0	0	0	0	3.1	3	17	4	4	0	0	0	4	0	0	1	0
Walker, Tyler, Pittsfield	0	0	.000	13.50	1	1	0	0	0	0	2.0	2	6	2	1	1	0	0	1	0	1	1	0
Wallace, Christopher, Oneonta	2	1	.667	3.63	10	2	0	0	1	0	22.1	22	98	13	9	2	1	1	2	8	0	13	0	0
Wallace, Jim, Auburn	3	8	.273	7.13	14	14	0	0	0	0	65.2	98	328	64	52	2	5	2	3	37	1	47	8	3
Ward, Brandon, Williamsport	2	0	1.000	3.86	19	0	0	0	5	0	21.0	11	99	12	9	1	1	1	4	24	0	16	7	0
Weimer, Matthew, St.C.	2	2	.500	3.57	23	0	0	0	15	0	35.1	35	150	21	14	1	1	2	3	4	0	22	3	0
Westover, Richard, Vermont	0	1	.000	15.12	7	0	0	0	3	0	8.1	19	51	18	14	2	0	3	6	0	8	0	0
Wheeler, Daniel, Hudson Valley	6	7	.462	3.40	15	15	0	0	0	0	84.0	75	351	38	28	2	1	1	3	17	0	81	4	2
White, Matt, Hudson Valley	4	6	.400	4.07	15	15	0	0	0	0	84.0	78	369	44	38	3	2	11	29	0	82	11	1
White, Samuel, Oneonta	5	2	.714	4.47	17	8	0	0	6	0	52.1	52	231	32	26	3	0	3	1	30	1	43	1	1
Whiteman, Trevor, Auburn*	1	3	.250	4.21	30	0	0	0	9	0	36.1	36	173	26	17	3	0	0	18	4	50	3	0
Wiggins, Scott, Oneonta*	6	2	.750	2.56	13	13	1	1	0	0	63.1	58	261	25	18	1	0	0	2	22	0	44	0	0
Williams, Henry, Utica	0	3	.000	7.66	18	0	0	0	10	2	24.2	38	130	24	21	1	1	2	18	1	26	2	0
Wingerd, Joshua, New Jersey	4	1	.800	6.43	20	1	0	0	2	0	28.0	43	130	23	20	3	0	0	6	0	20	4	3
Wolf, Randy, Batavia*	1	0	1.000	1.58	7	7	0	0	0	0	40.0	29	153	8	7	1	0	1	2	8	0	53	0	0
Woodards, Orlando, St.C.	2	2	.500	5.15	21	0	0	0	6	2	36.2	41	174	23	21	2	0	3	1	24	0	32	5	2
Woodward, Finley, New Jersey	2	1	.667	3.34	29	0	0	0	20	1	32.1	30	137	14	12	3	0	1	2	10	1	39	3	1
Zawatski, Geoff, Batavia	4	2	.667	5.04	15	10	0	0	1	0	55.1	87	259	41	31	6	0	1	0	33	4	0		

COMBINATION SHUTOUTS: **Auburn (2)**—Oswalt-Hecht, Thomas-Hecht. **Batavia (9)**—Zawatski-Frush-Mondello, Aguiar-Mondello, Jacquez-Black, Fenus-Black, Shipp-Eason-Shockley, Cotton-Frush-Black, Adair-Eason, Wolf-Eason-Black, Adair-Shockley-Mondello. **Erie (7)**—Lambert-Combs, Bacci-Hlodan, Bausher-Hlodan-Combs, Lambert-Stabile-Siciliano, Prater-Luttig-Combs, Lambert-Stabile, Bacci-Stabile-Cook. **Hudson Valley (4)**—Madison-Bergan, Belitz-Gonzalez-Reyes, Wheeler-Gonzalez-Bergan-Reyes, Madison-Bergan-Kimbrell. **Jamestown (2)**—Johnson-Snyder, Alkire-Mobley. **Lowell (5)**—McLeary-Parker, Thomas-Hazlett, O'Dette-Parker-Taglienti, Hazlett-Miller, Santana-Parker. **New Jersey (3)**—Karnuth-Stechschulte-Heffernan, Wingerd-Levey-Huffaker, Rosario-Woodward. **Oneonta (6)**—White-Wallace-Ellison, Choate-Ellison-Smith, Wallace-Carpenter-Mota, Day-Mota, Choate-White, Henry-Bradley. **Pittsfield (2)**—Burnett-Pyrtle-Cammack, Estrella-Cammack. **St. Catharines (1)**—Heath-Markwell-Lacefield. **Utica (4)**—Rizzo-Putnicki, Rizzo-Ehlers, Borges-Doan, Borges-Williams-Putnicki. **Vermont (1)**—Blank-Rahilly-Van Gilder. **Watertown (2)**—Brown-McNally-DePaula-Cali, Hughes-Swinburnson. **Williamsport (4)**—Licciardi-Magers-Kelley, Fisher-Fennell-Kelley, Fennell-Magers, Meyers-Santiago.

NO-HIT GAMES: None.

1997 FIELDING

TEAM

Team	Pct.	G	PO	A	E	TC	DP	PB	Team	Pct.	G	PO	A	E	TC	DP	PB
Oneonta	.967	74	1915	809	94	2818	69	15	Williamsport	.952	75	1939	870	143	2952	59	23
New Jersey	.965	74	1888	822	97	2807	69	14	Erie	.952	76	1990	760	140	2890	69	15
Batavia	.963	74	1953	765	104	2822	64	8	Hudson Valley	.952	75	1964	764	139	2867	39	14
Watertown	.958	75	1928	832	122	2882	71	14	Vermont	.950	76	1976	764	144	2884	55	32
Utica	.958	74	1888	799	119	2806	56	12	Jamestown	.949	74	1883	819	145	2847	73	19
Auburn	.956	76	1952	819	129	2900	73	15	Pittsfield	.949	74	1933	751	145	2829	53	12
Lowell	.954	76	1976	729	131	2836	55	13									
St. Catharines	.952	75	1936	777	136	2849	73	19									

TRIPLE PLAY: Pittsfield.

INDIVIDUAL

FIRST BASEMEN

NOTE: All caps denotes fielding-percentage leader based on 38 games for catchers, 51 for all other non-pitchers and 76 innings for pitchers. *Throws lefthanded.

Player, Team	Pct.	G	PO	A	E	TC	DP
Allison, Cody, Watertown	.987	19	140	11	2	153	16
Amrhein, Michael, Williamsport	.978	10	78	12	2	92	7
Bagley, Sean, Vermont	.949	6	34	3	2	39	1
Bautista, Jorge, Utica	.976	14	120	3	3	126	9
Bender, Heath, Watertown*	.985	61	480	32	8	520	49
Burnham, Gary, Batavia*	.989	12	87	7	1	95	12
Carter, Bart, Hudson Valley	.938	3	13	2	1	16	0
Chabot, Kevin, New Jersey	.962	7	47	3	2	52	2
Chiaffredo, Paul, St. Catharines	1.000	1	11	0	0	11	1
Cole, Eric, Auburn	1.000	2	1	0	0	1	0
Dominique, Andy, Batavia	.990	63	540	36	6	582	44
Drizos, Justin, Hudson Valley*	.987	43	366	23	5	394	24
Duffy, James, Auburn	.990	31	267	18	3	288	19
Estrada, Johnny, Batavia	1.000	1	12	1	0	13	0
Fereday, Todd, Williamsport	.971	5	31	2	1	34	3
Fritz, Jim, Batavia	1.000	2	3	0	0	3	0
Gload, Ross, Utica*	.973	63	546	37	16	599	38
Gray, Travis, Lowell	.994	20	138	15	1	154	7
Hervey, Brennan, Jamestown	.978	56	496	30	12	538	50
Jones, Aaron, Oneonta*	.995	26	177	17	1	195	16
Keaveney, Jeff, Lowell	.973	48	371	28	11	410	37
Kingsbury, Willy, Lowell	1.000	7	60	0	0	60	3
Koehler, Jason, St. Catharines	1.000	6	49	1	0	50	6
Kurilla, Kevin, Batavia	1.000	1	1	0	0	1	0
Langaigne, Selwyn, St.C.*	.989	63	510	54	6	570	59
Lankford, Derrick, Erie	.978	49	376	33	9	418	37
Lawler, Scott, Auburn	1.000	2	5	0	0	5	0
Lignitz, Jeremiah, Jamestown	.984	19	181	6	3	190	18
Mackowiak, Robert, Erie	1.000	1	1	1	0	2	0
Maxwell, Keith, Erie	.988	30	236	14	3	253	21
McCarthy, Kevin, Pittsfield*	.977	33	282	16	7	305	20
McNeal, Aaron, Auburn	.980	10	88	8	2	98	11
Medina, Robert, St. Catharines	.900	4	17	1	2	20	0
Miner, Tony, Watertown	.926	3	25	0	2	27	1
Mota, Cristian, Watertown	1.000	1	6	0	0	6	0
Morris, Jeremy, Oneonta	1.000	1	3	1	0	4	1
Nolte, Bruce, Pittsfield	1.000	5	21	3	0	24	0
Nunnari, Talmadge, Vermont*	.989	61	507	35	6	548	44
Otero, Oscar, Williamsport	.972	8	65	4	2	71	2
Pandolfini, Ryan, Hudson Valley	.982	31	256	18	5	279	10
Pressley, Kasey, Williamsport	.985	31	258	8	4	270	17
PURKISS, Matt, Oneonta	.992	54	472	21	4	497	45
Quaccia, Luke, New Jersey	.991	60	538	38	5	581	47
Quero, Pedro, Vermont	.961	13	121	3	5	129	7
Reyes, Jose, Erie	1.000	4	25	0	0	25	3
Roach, Jason, Pittsfield	.973	27	201	12	6	219	13
Rodriguez, Aurelio, Watertown	1.000	1	11	1	0	12	0
Ruecker, Dion, Lowell	1.000	9	44	3	0	47	0
Salazar, Juan, Williamsport	.993	26	245	24	2	271	22
Sencion, Pablo, St. Catharines	1.000	4	34	1	0	35	2

Player, Team	Pct.	G	PO	A	E	TC	DP
Thomas, Don, Auburn*	1.000	1	7	0	0	7	1
Thomas, James, Auburn	.989	41	337	11	4	352	32
Valentine, Anthony, Pittsfield	1.000	17	128	14	0	142	10
Voita, Sam, Hudson Valley	.857	1	6	0	1	7	0
Ware, Ryan, Hudson Valley	.889	1	7	1	1	9	1
Wilson, Scott, New Jersey	1.000	14	113	7	0	120	10

TRIPLE PLAY: McCarthy.

SECOND BASEMEN

Player, Team	Pct.	G	PO	A	E	TC	DP
Ahumada, Alejandro, Lowell	.921	9	18	17	3	38	4
Aybar, Ramon, Jamestown	.953	13	21	40	3	64	6
Barnett, Brian, St. Catharines	1.000	5	3	8	0	11	0
Baston, Stanley, St. Catharines	.938	5	7	8	1	16	1
Benefield, Brian, Watertown	.951	69	137	176	16	329	45
Brooks, Ali, Erie	1.000	8	14	0	0	22	3
Bruce, Maurice, Pittsfield	.933	24	64	62	9	135	13
Carr, Dustin, Hudson Valley	.925	71	142	154	24	320	21
Cathey, Joseph, Auburn	.983	12	18	41	1	60	8
Cutshall, Patrick, Auburn	.978	34	57	75	3	135	23
ECKSTEIN, David, Lowell	.971	66	139	166	9	314	34
Erickson, Matt, Utica	1.000	5	7	18	0	25	2
Espada, Angel, Pittsfield	.961	18	28	45	3	76	8
Fereday, Todd, Williamsport	.926	16	24	39	5	68	5
Font, Franklin, Williamsport	.966	22	29	55	3	87	5
Franco, Raul, Utica	.953	67	124	182	15	321	37
Freeman, Terrance, Erie	.961	60	130	141	11	282	32
Gentry, Aaron, New Jersey	.833	1	0	5	1	6	1
Germosen, Julio, Erie	.933	20	39	44	6	89	13
Haley, Ryan, Watertown	1.000	3	4	7	0	11	0
Harris, Brian, Batavia	.958	28	48	67	5	120	19
Izturis, Cesar, St. Catharines	.970	40	61	98	5	164	26
Jefferies, Daryl, Williamsport	1.000	3	6	7	0	13	1
Kane, Kevin, Oneonta	1.000	4	4	3	0	7	0
Kidd, Scott, Oneonta	.954	73	140	231	18	389	52
Lauterhahn, Daniel, Jamestown	.967	39	73	104	6	183	33
Lebron, Ruben, Lowell	.929	7	13	13	2	28	4
Mackowiak, Robert, Erie	.923	3	7	5	1	13	1
Maier, Taber, New Jersey	1.000	7	6	15	0	21	3
Mansavage, Jay, Auburn	.965	10	20	35	2	57	7
Mateo, Henry, Vermont	.956	64	134	173	14	321	33
MaCrory, Robert, New Jersey	.952	66	130	167	15	312	41
McCladdie, Tony, Pittsfield	.886	8	9	22	4	35	4
McNamara, Rusty, Batavia	1.000	8	16	14	0	30	3
Mejia, Marlon, Auburn	.938	5	7	8	1	16	2
Nolte, Bruce, Pittsfield	.962	16	24	27	2	53	5
Olmeda, Jose, Lowell	1.000	1	1	2	0	3	0
Ovalles, Homy, Vermont	.966	6	14	14	1	29	5
Parker, Clark, Jamestown	.778	4	1	6	2	9	0
Robinson, Joseph, Auburn	.927	32	43	58	8	109	11
Rodriguez, Aurelio, Watertown	.875	4	8	13	3	24	3
Santiago, Jorge, Pittsfield	.909	15	18	32	5	55	2
Schaffer, Jake, Jamestown	.895	6	8	9	2	19	4

Player, Team	Pct.	G	PO	A	E	TC	DP
Schesser, Heath, Jamestown	.987	16	31	44	1	76	8
Schifano, Anthony, Utica	1.000	5	3	9	0	12	3
Terrell, Jeffrey, Batavia	.949	45	76	93	9	178	19
Vazquez, Roberto, New Jersey	1.000	5	6	7	0	13	0
Ware, Ryan, Hudson Valley	1.000	5	5	9	0	14	4
Watson, Al, Williamsport	.965	38	71	96	6	173	18
Young, Michael, St. Catharines	.976	28	45	78	3	126	18
Zech, Scott, Vermont	.893	6	15	10	3	28	2

THIRD BASEMEN

Player, Team	Pct.	G	PO	A	E	TC	DP
Ahumada, Alejandro, Lowell	.824	22	11	31	9	51	1
Arrendondo, Hernando, H.V>	.877	49	32	111	20	163	5
Barnett, Brian, St. Catharines	.750	10	9	12	7	28	1
Baston, Stanley, St. Catharines	.906	23	13	45	6	64	5
Bautista, Jorge, Utica	.708	12	4	13	7	24	0
Bly, Derrick, Williamsport	.917	12	11	33	4	48	1
Burkhart, Lance, Vermont	.824	8	3	11	3	17	1
Burns, Xavier, Erie	.836	61	33	110	28	171	10
Butler, Allen, Oneonta	.919	66	38	109	13	160	9
Cole, Eric, Auburn	.832	57	49	100	30	179	13
Cutshall, Patrick, Auburn	.881	27	19	40	8	67	4
DeLeon, Jorge, Lowell	1.000	2	1	3	0	4	0
ERICKSON, Matt, Utica	.942	61	39	140	11	190	11
Fereday, Todd, Williamsport	.947	6	6	12	1	19	1
Fritz, Jim, Batavia	.822	20	16	21	8	45	1
Gentry, Aaron, New Jersey	.928	49	31	98	10	139	7
Germosen, Julio, Erie	1.000	2	0	2	0	2	0
Gray, Travis, Lowell	.848	22	9	19	5	33	2
Haverbusch, Kevin, Erie	1.000	1	1	1	0	2	0
Hernandez, Rafeal, Vermont	1.000	2	1	4	0	5	0
Jefferies, Daryl, Williamsport	.905	6	7	12	2	21	0
Lebron, Ruben, Lowell	1.000	5	3	8	0	11	0
Mackowiak, Robert, Erie	.927	16	6	32	3	41	1
Maier, Taber, New Jersey	1.000	2	1	0	0	1	0
McCladdie, Tony, Pittsfield	.839	29	18	60	15	93	1
McNamara, Rusty, Batavia	.899	61	42	127	19	188	10
Mejia, Marlon, Auburn	.800	1	2	2	1	5	0
Miner, Tony, Watertown	.910	44	30	91	12	133	10
Mota, Cristian, Watertown	.915	20	12	42	5	59	4
Morris, Jeremy, Oneonta	.710	15	5	17	9	31	2
Nieves, Juan, St. Catharines	.667	2	2	2	2	6	0
Nolte, Bruce, Pittsfield	.778	17	8	20	8	36	2
Otero, Oscar, Williamsport	.933	11	7	21	2	30	2
Ovalles, Homy, Vermont	.867	14	5	21	4	30	1
Reding, Josh, Vermont	1.000	4	2	9	0	11	2
Rios, Brian, Jamestown	.935	45	43	101	10	154	12
Roach, Jason, Pittsfield	.851	35	19	78	17	114	4
Rodriguez, Aurelio, Watertown	.946	15	9	26	2	37	0
Ruecker, Dion, Lowell	.882	38	26	56	11	93	3
Russell, Jake, Watertown	.000	2	0	1	1	0	0
Schaffer, Jake, Jamestown	.600	2	0	3	2	5	1
Schesser, Heath, Jamestown	.942	29	22	59	5	86	7
Schifano, Anthony, Utica	1.000	2	4	4	0	8	0
Sencion, Pablo, St. Catharines	.893	45	22	86	13	121	7
Vazquez, Roberto, New Jersey	.842	6	6	10	3	19	3
Walker, Ron, Williamsport	.872	42	28	81	16	125	4
Ware, Ryan, Hudson Valley	.889	30	19	53	9	81	1
Wilson, Scott, New Jersey	.951	18	15	43	3	61	5
Zech, Scott, Vermont	.881	50	33	100	18	151	5

SHORTSTOPS

Player, Team	Pct.	G	PO	A	E	TC	DP
Abreu, Nelson, Williamsport	.889	14	18	38	7	63	5
Ahumada, Alejandro, Lowell	.917	24	29	81	10	120	13
Barnett, Brian, St. Catharines	.333	1	0	2	4	6	0
Brooks, Ali, Erie	.833	2	2	3	1	6	2
Bruce, Maurice, Pittsfield	.885	5	9	14	3	26	2
Butler, Allen, Oneonta	1.000	1	1	2	0	3	1
CATHEY, Joseph, Auburn	.962	59	71	180	10	261	40
Cleto, Ambioris, Erie	.889	8	9	23	4	36	5
Cutshall, Patrick, Auburn	.943	20	27	55	5	87	11
Delarosa, Tomas, Vermont	.932	69	85	201	21	307	32
DeLeon, Jorge, Lowell	1.000	1	0	1	0	1	0
Font, Franklin, Williamsport	.892	11	20	38	7	65	11
Freeman, Terrance, Erie	.875	2	3	4	1	8	1
Gentry, Aaron, New Jersey	.869	13	11	42	8	61	8
Germosen, Julio, Erie	.895	21	23	54	9	86	14
Haley, Ryan, Watertown	.500	1	2	0	2	4	0
Harris, Brian, Batavia	.913	16	23	50	7	80	9
Haverbusch, Kevin, Erie	.915	55	70	114	17	201	23
Izturis, Cesar, St. Catharines	.932	30	54	96	11	161	20

Player, Team	Pct.	G	PO	A	E	TC	DP
Joffrion, Jack, Hudson Valley	.901	73	89	213	33	335	26
Kennedy, Adam, New Jersey	.951	26	41	96	7	144	15
Kidd, Scott, Oneonta	1.000	1	1	0	0	1	0
Kurilla, Kevin, Batavia	.920	57	85	178	23	286	34
Lauterhahn, Daniel, Jamestown	.893	11	18	32	6	56	8
Lebron, Ruben, Lowell	.833	3	4	1	1	6	0
Maier, Taber, New Jersey	.962	37	46	104	6	156	17
Miller, Kenny, Pittsfield	.941	26	29	66	6	101	15
Mirizzi, Marc, Oneonta	.957	74	120	232	16	368	49
Mota, Cristian, Watertown	.908	50	65	142	21	228	25
Nolte, Bruce, Pittsfield	.959	12	14	33	2	49	4
Olmeda, Jose, Lowell	.904	52	63	134	21	218	26
Ovalles, Homy, Vermont	.789	5	5	10	4	19	0
Polonia, Israel, Utica	.910	37	42	99	14	155	19
Reding, Josh, Vermont	1.000	1	3	1	0	4	0
Ruecker, Dion, Lowell	1.000	2	1	5	0	6	1
Santiago, Jorge, Pittsfield	.854	35	39	78	20	137	16
Schaffer, Jake, Jamestown	.940	42	66	136	13	215	26
Schesser, Heath, Jamestown	.833	21	27	58	17	102	13
Schifano, Anthony, Utica	.938	42	72	110	12	194	18
Smith, Jason, Williamsport	.930	51	95	158	19	272	30
Terrell, Jeffrey, Batavia	1.000	2	0	2	0	2	0
Tiller, Brad, Watertown	.956	25	44	85	6	135	17
Ware, Ryan, Hudson Valley	.800	2	1	3	1	5	1
Young, Michael, St. Catharines	.927	44	70	121	15	206	31
Zech, Scott, Vermont	1.000	2	6	6	0	12	5

TRIPLE PLAY: Bruce.

OUTFIELDERS

Player, Team	Pct.	G	PO	A	E	TC	DP
Abell, Antonio, New Jersey	.895	10	13	4	2	19	1
Alayon, Elvis, Lowell	.965	31	53	2	2	57	1
Albaral, Randy, St. Catharines	.907	55	88	9	10	107	0
Alvarez, Carlos, Watertown	.943	22	31	2	2	35	0
Austin, Peter, Erie	1.000	5	10	0	0	10	0
Aybar, Ramon, Jamestown	1.000	16	17	2	0	19	0
Bagley, Lorenzo, St. Catharines	.873	38	56	6	9	71	1
Bagley, Sean, Vermont	1.000	3	2	0	0	2	0
Banks, Tony, Williamsport*	.968	21	29	1	1	31	0
Barnett, Brian, St. Catharines	.857	5	6	0	1	7	0
Baston, Stanley, St. Catharines	.889	7	7	1	1	9	0
Bernhardt, Tom, Williamsport	.909	23	24	6	3	33	0
Bevins, Andy, New Jersey	.938	43	43	2	3	48	0
Blakeney, Mo, Vermont	.978	26	44	1	1	46	0
Bradley, Milton, Vermont	.967	50	113	3	4	120	0
Bruce, Maurice, Pittsfield	1.000	1	1	0	0	1	0
Burnham, Gary, Batavia*	.975	27	36	3	1	40	0
Carey, Orlando, Oneonta	.962	70	95	6	4	105	1
Chambliss, Russ, Oneonta	1.000	19	13	0	0	13	0
Clark, Chris C., Erie	1.000	25	32	0	0	32	0
Clark, Chris L., Utica	.857	5	6	0	1	7	0
Clark, Jason, Hudson Valley*	.942	60	105	9	7	121	1
Collins, Francis, Batavia*	.957	61	106	6	5	117	0
Connell, Gerald, Williamsport	.969	55	85	9	3	97	1
Copeland, Brandon, Pittsfield	.927	24	36	2	3	41	1
Darjean, John, Oneonta	.980	47	48	1	1	50	0
DeCelle, Mike, Hudson Valley	.990	71	103	1	1	105	0
Dehaan, Korwin, Erie	.991	54	105	0	1	106	0
Donaldson, Rhodney, Utica	.954	68	121	3	6	130	1
Duffy, James, Auburn	.952	24	19	1	1	21	1
Dunn, Ryan, Auburn	.980	49	44	5	1	50	1
Elliott, Dawan, Erie*	.899	45	61	1	7	69	1
Fajardo, Alejandro, Batavia	.941	51	78	2	5	85	1
Farley, Cordell, New Jersey	1.000	5	7	1	0	8	0
Fischer, Mark, Lowell	.976	41	76	6	2	84	0
Fitzgerald, Jason, Watertown*	.890	33	60	5	8	73	2
Flores, Jose, Lowell	.984	36	59	2	1	62	0
Forbes, Kevin, Vermont	.894	20	41	1	5	47	0
Goodwin, Keith, Lowell	.936	65	100	3	7	110	1
Green, Kevin, Utica	1.000	10	9	0	0	9	0
Grimmett, Ryan, Jamestown	.976	17	40	0	1	41	0
Haas, Danny, Lowell	1.000	4	6	0	0	6	0
Hall, Noah, Vermont	.963	60	100	5	4	109	3
Halper, Jason, Oneonta	1.000	7	6	0	0	6	0
Harrell, Ken, Oneonta	.889	5	7	1	1	9	0
Haverbusch, Kevin, Erie	1.000	1	1	0	0	1	0
Hernandez, Jesus, Watertown*	1.000	14	30	2	0	32	0
Hernandez, Rafael, Vermont	.857	7	6	0	1	7	0
Howard, Marcus, Lowell	.903	65	107	5	12	124	0
Jacomino, Mandy, Jamestown	.866	44	65	6	11	82	0
James, Kennoth, Vermont	.972	70	137	1	4	142	0
Jimenez, Felipe, Williamsport	.889	10	15	1	2	18	0
Johnson, Jason A., Batavia	.985	60	124	8	2	134	0

Player, Team	Pct.	G	PO	A	E	TC	DP
Johnson, Jason B., Erie	.957	19	43	2	2	47	0
Johnson, Thomas, Pittsfield	.965	55	108	2	4	114	0
Kiefer, Dax, Williamsport	.957	70	128	6	6	140	3
Kim, David, New Jersey	1.000	45	71	4	0	75	0
Langaigne, Selwyn, St.C.*	1.000	13	28	3	0	31	1
Lara, Felix, Erie*	.936	48	83	5	6	94	1
Lebron, Ruben, Lowell	1.000	4	1	0	0	1	0
Lee, Jason, New Jersey	.943	59	90	9	6	105	0
Logan, Stephen, Auburn	.889	68	85	11	12	108	2
Mackowiak, Robert, Erie	.958	40	64	4	3	71	0
Maduro, Remy, Utica	.917	40	62	4	6	72	0
Maxwell, Vernon, Oneonta	.972	43	68	2	2	72	1
McCarthy, Kevin, Pittsfield*	1.000	18	31	3	0	34	1
McKinney, Antonio, Jamestown..	.892	33	63	3	8	74	0
Mejia, Miguel, New Jersey	.935	30	55	3	4	62	2
Melconian, Alex, Utica	.891	41	55	2	7	64	0
Miller, Travis, Hudson Valley	.980	28	46	3	1	50	0
MOHR, Dustan, Watertown	.993	74	140	11	1	152	2
Moreno, Juan, Pittsfield	.957	49	62	4	3	69	0
Mota, Cristian, Watertown	1.000	5	11	0	0	11	0
Murray, Doug, Auburn	.000	1	0	0	2	2	0
Morris, Jeremy, Oneonta	.971	51	60	6	2	68	0
Nieves, Juan, St. Catharines	.945	57	97	7	6	110	2
Ozarowski, Richard, Jamestown	.889	6	8	0	1	9	0
Patton, Cory, Pittsfield	.988	48	81	1	1	83	0
Pigott, Anthony, Hudson Valley ..	1.000	1	2	0	0	2	0
Pointer, Corey, Erie	.903	18	26	2	3	31	0
Ribaudo, Mike, Williamsport	.667	2	2	0	1	3	0
Rijo-Berger, Jose, Pittsfield	.988	32	74	5	1	80	0
Roach, Jason, Pittsfield	1.000	1	1	0	0	1	0
Rowson, James, Oneonta	.950	11	19	0	1	20	0
Schifano, Anthony, Utica	1.000	1	1	0	0	1	0
Schnabel, Matthew, Utica	.971	65	96	3	3	102	0
Scioneaux, Damian, H.V.	.966	70	137	3	5	145	1
Speckhardt, Mike, New Jersey	.946	44	52	1	3	56	0
Stanton, Rob, Watertown	.909	47	45	5	5	55	0
Steele, Alexander, Jamestown	.964	71	126	6	5	140	2
Stewart, Courteney, Williamsport	.949	52	69	5	4	78	0
Terry, Tony, Auburn	.968	47	89	3	3	95	2
Thomas, James, Auburn	.833	5	4	1	1	6	0
Upshaw, Ryan, Watertown	.936	40	42	2	3	47	1
Verrall, Jared, Hudson Valley	.800	2	4	0	1	5	0
Wells, Vernon, St. Catharines	.953	61	135	6	7	148	1
Wesson, Barry, Auburn	.956	57	103	6	5	114	0
Whitner, Keith, Jamestown	.926	40	60	3	5	68	1
Worthy, Thomas, Batavia	.983	47	54	3	1	58	1

CATCHERS

Player, Team	Pct.	G	PO	A	E	TC	DP	PB
Alevras, Chad, Lowell	1.000	21	140	13	0	153	2	6
Allison, Cody, Watertown	.955	3	21	0	1	22	0	0
Amrhein, Michael, Wpt.	.974	39	273	30	8	311	4	14
Bagley, Sean, Vermont	.953	28	174	29	10	213	0	15
Burkhart, Lance, Vermont	.982	15	101	10	2	113	0	8
Carter, Bart, Hudson Valley	1.000	1	2	0	0	2	0	0
Chapman, Scott, Auburn	.979	51	346	36	8	390	4	9
Chiaffredo, Paul, St.C.	.995	45	320	42	2	364	5	8
Cota, Humberto, H.V.>	1.000	3	29	0	0	29	0	0
Cripps, Bobby, St. Catharines .	.946	9	82	5	5	92	0	4
Diaz, Diogenes, Erie	.917	6	50	5	5	60	0	0
ESTRADA, Johnny, Batavia	1.000	51	391	43	0	434	5	3
Evans, Lee, Erie	.982	30	188	30	4	222	3	8
Fitzpatrick, Eddie, Batavia	.992	23	111	19	1	131	2	4
Fritz, Jim, Batavia	1.000	7	43	2	0	45	0	1
Gancasz, Michael, Lowell	.991	34	206	17	2	225	1	3
Gick, Brady, New Jersey	.985	28	174	24	3	201	2	4
Grubbs, Chris, Williamsport	.967	23	125	22	5	152	0	5
Haad, Yamid, Erie	.990	38	267	30	3	300	3	7
Hall, Toby, Hudson Valley	.989	31	243	21	3	267	1	0
Harper, Brandon, Utica	.978	46	337	54	9	400	1	6
Harrell, Ken, Oneonta	1.000	4	13	1	0	14	0	0
Hubbard, Jeremy, Wpt.	.900	6	17	1	2	20	0	0
Keech, Erik, Oneonta	1.000	12	74	16	0	90	0	0
Kingsbury, Willy, Lowell	1.000	5	43	6	0	49	0	1
Koehler, Jason, St. Catharines	1.000	2	15	0	0	15	0	0
Lawler, Scott, Auburn	1.000	2	8	1	0	9	0	1
Lignitz, Jeremiah, Jamestown	.982	9	48	8	1	57	0	1
Lopez-Cao, Mike, H.V.	.957	6	39	5	2	46	0	0
Mackowiak, Robert, Erie	1.000	1	3	0	0	3	0	0
Martine, Chris, New Jersey	.981	47	322	38	7	367	8	9
Medina, Robert, St.C.	.959	20	133	9	6	148	0	7
Melconian, Alex, Utica	.994	19	130	25	1	156	0	4
Meran, Jorge, Jamestown	.966	46	291	55	12	358	0	15

Player, Team	Pct.	G	PO	A	E	TC	DP	PB
Metzger, Erik, Lowell	.982	31	209	10	4	223	0	3
Murray, Doug, Auburn	.995	33	199	15	1	215	1	5
Pedersoli, Bernard, Jam	.976	25	145	16	4	165	0	3
Phillips, Blaine, Oneonta	.977	29	117	9	3	129	0	3
Phillips, Jason, Pittsfield	.990	46	353	43	4	400	4	4
Pinto, Rene, Oneonta	.994	36	304	45	2	351	4	8
Reese, Nate, Utica	1.000	11	70	8	0	78	1	2
Reyes, Jose, Erie	1.000	6	50	8	0	58	1	0
Ribaudo, Mike, Wpt.	.940	19	110	15	8	133	2	4
Rivera, Luis, Vermont	.961	36	255	19	11	285	2	9
Rodriguez, Mike, St.C.	1.000	2	10	0	0	10	0	0
Rodriguez, Sammy, Pittsfield..	.973	30	239	17	7	263	2	8
Rosa, Erick, Watertown	.991	28	193	18	2	213	3	6
Salazar, Juan, Williamsport	1.000	2	23	3	0	25	0	0
Schmidt, Todd, New Jersey	1.000	6	29	4	0	33	1	1
Spear, Chad, Hudson Valley	.993	18	124	12	1	137	1	3
Taylor, Adam, Watertown	.970	48	344	47	12	403	3	9
Thompson, Nick, Batavia	.957	4	20	2	1	23	0	0
Twombley, Dennis, Oneonta	.980	15	95	5	2	102	0	4
Voita, Sam, Hudson Valley	.984	22	164	16	3	183	0	2

PITCHERS

Player, Team	Pct.	G	PO	A	E	TC	DP
Adair, Derek, Batavia	.800	13	4	8	3	15	1
Aguilar, Douglas, Batavia	.857	7	1	5	1	7	1
Alkire, John, Jamestown	.500	9	1	1	2	4	0
Arnold, Neal, New Jersey	1.000	23	0	7	0	7	1
Arteaga, Juan, Pittsfield*	.727	12	0	8	3	11	2
Bacci, Anthony, Erie*	.875	15	4	17	3	24	0
Baez, Miguel, Watertown	1.000	3	0	1	0	1	0
Bair, Andy, Utica*	1.000	12	2	15	0	17	1
Barksdale, Shane, Auburn	.778	23	3	4	2	9	1
Barry, Shawn, Pittsfield*	.667	22	1	1	1	3	0
Bass, Randall, Hudson Valley*	1.000	17	0	4	0	4	0
Bausher, Andrew, Erie*	.889	15	7	9	2	18	0
Beck, Matthew, Jamestown	.800	17	1	3	1	5	0
Becks, Ryan, Vermont*	.920	15	8	15	2	25	1
Beebe, Hans, Pittsfield*	.958	15	8	15	1	24	1
Belitz, Todd, Hudson Valley*	.833	15	1	9	2	12	0
Benzing, Skipp, Lowell	1.000	2	1	3	0	4	0
Bergan, Thomas, Hudson Valley	1.000	27	6	9	0	15	0
Black, Brett, Batavia	1.000	28	2	2	0	4	0
Blank, Matt, Vermont*	.857	16	6	12	3	21	0
Booker, Chris, Williamsport	.889	24	2	6	1	9	1
BORGES, Reece, Utica	1.000	15	10	10	0	20	1
Bowles, Brian, St. Catharines	1.000	16	10	7	0	17	2
Bradley, Ryan, Oneonta	.833	14	1	4	1	6	0
Brand, Scott, Oneonta	.500	10	2	0	2	4	0
Brown, Jamie, Watertown	.938	13	7	8	1	16	0
Bryant, Chris, Williamsport*	1.000	4	0	1	0	1	0
Burchart, Kyle, St. Catharines	.750	14	7	8	5	20	2
Burnett, Allan, Pittsfield	1.000	9	1	7	0	8	0
Cali, Joe, Watertown	1.000	2	0	1	0	1	0
Calvert, Klae, Lowell	1.000	3	0	2	0	2	0
Cammack, Eric, Pittsfield	.833	23	0	5	1	6	0
Carpenter, Justin, Oneonta	.778	24	0	7	2	9	0
Casey, Joseph, St. Catharines	1.000	14	6	5	0	11	2
Casey, Shaw, Utica	1.000	9	0	1	0	1	0
Charbonneau, Marc, St.C.*	1.000	6	1	1	0	2	0
Choate, Randy, Oneonta*	1.000	10	0	14	0	14	1
Coco, Pascual, St. Catharines	.600	10	2	1	2	5	0
Combs, Chris, Erie	1.000	21	1	1	0	2	0
Comer, Scott, Pittsfield*	1.000	14	2	10	0	12	1
Coogan, Patrick, New Jersey	1.000	5	5	10	0	15	0
Cook, O.J., Erie	1.000	34	4	2	0	6	2
Cotton, Joseph, Batavia	.958	15	7	16	1	24	1
Cummins, Jon, Hudson Valley	1.000	21	2	1	0	3	1
Curtis, Mark, St. Catharines*	1.000	4	0	1	0	1	0
Daniels, Ronney, Vermont*	.000	3	0	0	1	1	0
Davis, Mike, Pittsfield	.889	24	4	4	1	9	0
Day, Zach, Oneonta	.900	14	3	15	2	20	0
DePaula, Sean, Watertown	.600	9	0	3	2	5	0
Diebolt, Michael, Jamestown*	.950	15	3	16	1	20	2
Doan, Zachary, Utica	1.000	13	1	4	0	5	0
Downs, Scott, Williamsport*	1.000	5	0	9	0	9	0
Driscoll, Patrick, Batavia*	1.000	11	0	4	0	4	0
Eason, Clay, Batavia	1.000	20	5	3	0	8	1
Ehlers, Corey, Utica	1.000	9	5	1	0	6	0
Ellison, Jason, Oneonta	1.000	11	1	2	0	3	0
Erwin, David, Watertown	1.000	18	1	3	0	4	0
Estrella, Leoncio, Pittsfield	.923	15	10	14	2	26	2
Eversgerd, Randy, St. Catharines	1.000	13	2	1	0	3	0

CLASS A *New York-Pennsylvania League*

Player, Team	Pct.	G	PO	A	E	TC	DP
Fennell, Barry, Williamsport*	.933	17	3	11	1	15	0
Fenus, Justin, Batavia	.941	15	2	14	1	17	0
Fisher, Louis, Williamsport	1.000	11	2	9	0	11	0
Fisher, Ryan, Erie*	1.000	2	1	0	0	1	0
Flores, Randy, Oneonta*	1.000	13	0	11	0	11	1
Folkers, Kenneth, St. Catharines	1.000	14	0	5	0	5	1
Fowler, Blair, Utica	.833	19	2	3	1	6	0
Fraser, Joe, Vermont	.500	10	0	3	3	6	0
Frush, Jimmy, Batavia	1.000	26	1	2	0	3	0
Fuduric, Tony, Watertown	1.000	2	1	0	0	1	0
Garff, Jeff, Watertown	.833	6	0	5	1	6	1
Gaskill, Derek, Pittsfield	.846	22	2	9	2	13	0
Gonzalez, Ignacio, H.V.	.800	26	1	7	2	10	0
Greene, Joel, Jamestown*	1.000	20	0	4	0	4	0
Gresko, Michael, Erie*	1.000	7	2	2	0	4	1
Guilmet, John, Jamestown	.875	17	4	3	1	8	0
Guy, Bradley, Erie	1.000	25	4	8	0	12	0
Guzman, Wilson, Erie*	1.000	5	3	4	0	7	0
Hayden, Terry, Lowell*	.875	16	5	9	2	16	1
Hazlett, Andy, Lowell*	1.000	19	2	9	0	11	0
Heath, Woody, St. Catharines	.882	15	8	7	2	17	2
Hecht, Brian, Auburn	1.000	26	2	5	0	7	0
Heffernan, Greg, New Jersey	.889	26	3	5	1	9	0
Henderson, Scott, Utica	.889	15	1	7	1	9	0
Henry, Jason, Oneonta	.800	12	5	7	3	15	2
Hill, T.J., Hudson Valley	1.000	11	2	8	0	10	0
Hlodan, George, Erie	1.000	15	3	4	0	7	0
Holobinko, Mike, Williamsport*	.714	12	2	3	2	7	1
Horgan, Joe, Watertown*	.889	15	3	5	1	9	0
Howard, Jason, Jamestown	.667	13	0	2	1	3	0
Huber, John, Auburn	1.000	4	2	3	0	5	1
Huff, Tim, St. Catharines*	1.000	15	0	6	0	6	1
Huffaker, Michael, New Jersey	1.000	33	2	4	0	6	0
Huggins, David, St. Catharines	1.000	27	3	6	0	9	1
HUGHES, Mike, Watertown*	1.000	13	4	16	0	20	0
Ireland, Eric, Auburn	.870	16	11	29	6	46	3
Jacquez, Thomas, Batavia*	.750	4	1	2	1	4	0
Jerue, Tristan, New Jersey	.909	13	3	7	1	11	0
Jimenez, Jason, Hudson Valley*	1.000	19	2	8	0	10	1
Johnson, Craig, Jamestown	.824	14	4	10	3	17	1
Karnuth, Jason, New Jersey	.944	7	4	13	1	18	1
Keller, Kris, Jamestown	.833	16	2	3	1	6	0
Kelley, Jason, Williamsport	1.000	27	1	4	0	5	0
Kimbrell, Michael, H.V.*	.824	26	3	11	3	17	0
Knotts, Gary, Utica	.889	12	1	7	1	9	0
Koch, Jack, Oneonta	1.000	1	0	1	0	1	0
Lacefield, Timothy, St.C.	.857	25	2	10	2	14	0
Lambert, Kristopher, Erie*	.727	15	1	7	3	11	0
Lanzetta, Tobin, Vermont	.875	23	1	6	1	8	0
Levan, Matt, Utica*	1.000	1	0	1	0	1	0
Levey, Joshua, New Jersey	.714	18	1	4	2	7	0
Licciardi, Ron, Williamsport*	.933	17	4	10	1	15	1
Lima, Cory, Utica	1.000	17	1	4	0	5	1
Lohrman, David, Pittsfield	.667	22	2	0	1	3	0
Loubier, Scott, Vermont	1.000	7	1	1	0	2	0
Love, Farley, Auburn	1.000	3	1	0	0	1	0
Luttig, Christopher, Erie*	1.000	11	1	1	0	2	0
Lynde, Jerry, Vermont	.500	12	1	1	2	4	0
Madison, Scott, Hudson Valley*	.893	15	4	21	3	28	0
Magers, Mathew, Williamsport*	.737	27	2	12	5	19	2
Manbeck, Mark, Batavia	.750	5	0	3	1	4	0
Markwell, Diegomar, St.C.*	.769	16	4	6	3	13	1
Marriott, Mike, Utica	.600	7	2	4	4	10	1
Martin, Trey, Vermont	1.000	11	0	4	0	4	0
McBride, Jason, Oneonta	.000	2	0	0	1	1	0
McCarter, Jason, Auburn	.500	16	1	0	1	2	0
McClaskey, Tim, Utica	1.000	1	1	1	0	2	0
McCleary, Marty, Lowell	.760	13	5	14	6	25	0
McConnell, John, Erie*	1.000	17	2	6	0	8	0
McDougal, Mike, New Jersey	1.000	13	5	10	0	15	0
McNally, Andrew, Watertown	1.000	23	2	7	0	9	1
Mear, Richard, Jamestown*	1.000	8	1	1	0	2	0
Medina, Tomas, Auburn	1.000	15	3	3	0	6	0
Mercedes, Carlos, Auburn	1.000	28	0	8	0	8	0
Messman, Joseph, Auburn	1.000	25	2	9	0	11	0
Meyers, Mike, Williamsport	1.000	1	0	2	0	2	0
Miller, Tom, Lowell*	.727	24	3	5	3	11	0
Minter, Matt, Watertown*	1.000	7	0	2	0	2	0
Mobley, Kevin, Jamestown	1.000	18	5	2	0	7	0
Mondello, Peter, Batavia	1.000	27	2	4	0	6	0
Montemayor, Humberto, Lowell..	1.000	1	0	1	0	1	0
Mota, Daniel, Oneonta	1.000	27	2	1	0	3	0
Navarro, Jason, New Jersey*	1.000	10	2	8	0	10	0
Negrette, Richard, Watertown	1.000	17	2	13	0	15	1
O'Dette, Rick, Lowell*	.900	13	3	6	1	10	1
Oswalt, Roy, Auburn	1.000	9	4	5	0	9	1
Palma, Ricardo, Williamsport*	.944	14	4	13	1	18	0
Parker, Eric, Lowell*	1.000	23	2	5	0	7	1
Partenheimer, Brian, Lowell*	1.000	5	2	1	0	3	0
Pelton, Brad, Watertown	1.000	9	3	5	0	8	0
Persails, Mark, Jamestown	.826	15	5	14	4	23	4
Pitt, Jye, Williamsport	1.000	4	0	1	0	1	0
Plummer, Raymond, Vermont*	.923	28	3	9	1	13	2
Polanco, Elvis, Williamsport	.931	15	9	18	2	29	1
Poupart, Melvin, Pittsfield	.333	8	0	1	2	3	0
Prater, Andrew, Erie	.875	15	3	11	2	16	1
Putnicki, William, Utica	1.000	21	3	5	0	8	0
Pyrtle, Joe, Pittsfield	1.000	23	1	4	0	5	0
Queen, Mike, Pittsfield*	.950	13	5	14	1	20	2
Quintana, Urbano, Batavia	.000	6	0	0	1	1	0
Rahilly, Michael, Vermont	1.000	9	0	1	0	1	0
Ramirez, Jose, Jamestown*	.962	15	5	20	1	26	0
Rayborn, Kenny, Lowell	.800	11	4	4	2	10	0
Reyes, Eddy, Hudson Valley	1.000	31	2	5	0	7	1
Rizzo, Nick, Utica	1.000	15	5	8	0	13	0
Roberson, Charles, Watertown	1.000	18	5	6	0	11	0
Rosario, Ruben, New Jersey	.905	14	4	15	2	21	3
Rupp, Michael, Lowell	1.000	2	2	1	0	3	0
Saberhagen, Bret, Lowell	1.000	1	2	2	0	4	0
Sadler, Carl, Vermont*	1.000	7	4	6	0	10	0
Salyers, Jeremy, Vermont	.714	16	4	11	6	21	0
Santamaria, Juan, Jamestown	1.000	8	2	3	0	5	0
Santana, Pedro, Lowell	.882	15	7	8	2	17	0
Santiago, Antonio, Wpt.*	.938	26	4	11	1	16	0
Sasaki, Junichi, Vermont	1.000	11	0	1	0	1	0
Saylor, Ryan, Vermont	1.000	16	0	5	0	5	0
Seabury, Jaron, St. Catharines....	1.000	8	1	2	0	3	0
Shearn, Thomas, Auburn	.929	14	2	11	1	14	1
Shipp, Kevin, Batavia	.917	13	2	9	1	12	3
Shockley, Keith, Batavia*	1.000	27	2	4	0	6	1
Siciliano, Jess, Erie	.857	16	1	5	1	7	1
Smith, Andy, Oneonta	1.000	26	1	3	0	4	0
Snyder, William, Jamestown	1.000	25	3	4	0	7	0
Sparks, Eric, Vermont*	.800	28	2	2	1	5	1
Stabile, Paul, Erie*	.333	22	0	1	2	3	0
Stechschulte, Gene, New Jersey	.875	30	5	2	1	8	0
Strickland, Scott, Vermont	.947	15	3	15	1	19	0
Stutz, Shawn, Hudson Valley	1.000	6	0	6	0	6	0
Swinburnson, Tyler, Watertown ..	1.000	25	1	13	0	14	0
Taglienti, Jeff, Lowell	1.000	17	1	3	0	4	0
Taylor, Mark, Watertown*	.895	15	4	13	2	19	0
Tejera, Michael, Utica*	.941	12	5	11	1	17	2
Teut, Nate, Williamsport*	.947	9	3	15	1	19	1
Thomas, Don, Auburn*	.889	15	4	20	3	27	2
Thomas, Joe, Lowell*	.778	18	4	3	2	9	0
Tisone, Jason, Oneonta	1.000	18	6	2	0	8	1
Vael, Robert, Watertown	1.000	12	5	10	0	15	0
Van Gilder, Ryan, Vermont	1.000	19	2	1	0	3	0
Vasquez, Antonio, Watertown	.750	3	0	3	1	4	0
Villafana, Jose, New Jersey	1.000	5	1	5	0	6	1
Villalobos, Noe, Lowell	1.000	24	2	6	0	8	0
Vizcaino, Edward, Williamsport	.875	11	4	3	1	8	0
Vogt, Robert, Erie*	1.000	1	1	1	0	2	0
Wallace, Christopher, Oneonta	1.000	10	1	2	0	3	1
Wallace, Jim, Auburn	.733	14	2	9	4	15	1
Ward, Brandon, Williamsport	.800	19	1	3	1	5	0
Weimer, Matthew, St. Catharines	1.000	23	5	5	0	10	1
Westover, Richard, Vermont	1.000	7	0	1	0	1	0
Wheeler, Daniel, Hudson Valley ..	.938	15	3	12	1	16	0
White, Matt, Hudson Valley	.714	15	4	6	4	14	0
White, Samuel, Oneonta	.923	17	6	6	1	13	0
Whiteman, Trevor, Auburn*	1.000	30	0	3	0	3	1
Wiggins, Scott, Oneonta*	.842	13	7	9	3	19	1
Williams, Henry, Utica	1.000	18	1	4	0	5	0
Wingerd, Joshua, New Jersey	.800	20	3	1	1	5	0
Wolf, Randy, Batavia*	1.000	7	5	4	0	9	0
Woodards, Orlando, St.C.	1.000	21	1	5	0	6	0
Woodward, Finley, New Jersey ..	1.000	29	3	6	0	9	0
Zawatski, Geoff, Batavia	1.000	15	7	1	0	8	0

The following players did not have any fielding statistics at the positions indicated or appeared only as a designated hitter, pinch-hitter or pinch-runner: Alvarez, p; Arrendondo, 1b; Bronikowski, dh, ph; Brunette, p; Butler, of; Carter, p; Crabtree, p; J. Davis, dh; Drew, p; Duffy, 3b; Gagliano, p; Geis, p; Haley, of; Hunter, of, p; Jason B. Johnson, 2b; Jones, of; Koehler, p; Mackowiak, p; Mangieri, p; C. Parker, of; Pascarella, p; J. Perez, p; Prempas, p; Purkiss, of; Regalado, p; Richards, p; Robinson, ss; Rutherford, p; J. Santana, p; J. Santiago, 3b; Schnautz, p; Vazquez, ss; T. Walker, p; Watson, of.

LEAGUE CHAMPIONS

Year	Team	Pct.	Year	Team	Pct.	Year	Team	Pct.
1939—	Olean*	.631	1962—	Jamestown	.580	1983—	Utica▲	.649
1940—	Olean*	.625		Auburn (3rd)†	.521		Newark	.649
1941—	Jamestown	.618	1963—	Auburn	.585	1984—	Newark	.622
	Bradford (2nd)†	.549		Batavia (3rd)†	.485		Little Falls▲	.587
1942—	Jamestown*	.672	1964—	Auburn§	.622	1985—	Oneonta*	.705
1943—	Lockport	.591	1965—	Binghamton	.677		Auburn	.603
	Wellsville (3rd)†	.532		Binghamton	.607	1986—	Oneonta	.766
1944—	Lockport	.608	1966—	Auburn∞	.620		St. Catharines◆	.632
	Jamestown (2nd)†	.565		Binghamton	.646	1987—	Geneva▲	.632
1945—	Batavia*	.677	1967—	Auburn	.667		Watertown	.579
1946—	Jamestown‡	.672	1968—	Auburn	.645	1988—	Oneonta▲	.632
	Batavia‡	.672		Oneonta (2nd)*	.558		Jamestown	.618
1947—	Jamestown*	.690	1969—	Oneonta	.662	1989—	Pittsfield	.697
1948—	Lockport*	.603	1970—	Auburn	.623		Jamestown▲	.579
1949—	Bradford*	.635	1971—	Oneonta	.662	1990—	Oneonta■	.667
1950—	Hornell	.653	1972—	Niagara Falls	.686		Geneva	.662
	Olean (2nd)†	.568	1973—	Auburn	.667	1991—	Pittsfield	.662
1951—	Olean	.622	1974—	Oneonta	.768		Jamestown■	.654
	Hornell (3rd)†	.568	1975—	Newark	.688	1992—	Hamilton	.737
1952—	Hamilton	.659		Newark	.714		Geneva▼	.547
	Jamestown (2nd)†	.643	1976—	Elmira	.727	1993—	Niagara Falls▼	.603
1953—	Jamestown*	.704		Elmira	.703		Pittsfield	.533
1954—	Corning*	.621	1977—	Oneonta▲	.671	1994—	Auburn	.592
1955—	Hamilton*	.656		Batavia	.600		New Jersey▼	.573
1956—	Wellsville*	.617	1978—	Oneonta	.729	1995—	Vermont	.645
1957—	Wellsville	.632		Geneva◆	.718		Watertown▼	.630
	Erie (2nd)†	.598	1979—	Geneva	.725	1996—	Vermont▼	.649
1958—	Wellsville	.556		Oneonta◆	.618		St. Catharines	.579
	Geneva (2nd)†	.548	1980—	Oneonta▲	.662	1997—	Batavia	.635
1959—	Wellsville†	.635		Geneva	.649		Pittsfield▼	.568
1960—	Erie	.643	1981—	Oneonta▲	.658			
	Wellsville (2nd)†	.535		Jamestown	.649			
1961—	Geneva	.616	1982—	Oneonta	.566			
	Olean (4th)†	.512		Niagara Falls▲	.553			

*Won championship and four-club playoff. †Won four-club playoff. ‡Jamestown and Batavia declared co-champions; Batavia defeated Jamestown in final of four-club playoff. §Won championship and two-club playoff. ∞Won split-season playoff. ▲League divided into Eastern and Western divisions; won playoff. League divided into Wrigley and Yawkey divisions; won playoff. ■League divided into Eastern, Western and Stedler divisions; won playoff. ▼League divided into McNamara, Pinckney and Stedler divisions; won playoff. (NOTE—Known as Pennsylvania-Ontario-New York League from 1939 through 1956.)

CLASS A *New York-Pennsylvania League*

NORTHWEST LEAGUE

LEAGUE OFFICE

President/treasurer
Bob Richmond
Address
P.O. Box 4941
Scottsdale, AZ 85261
Phone
602-483-8224

Teams (affiliation)
Boise Hawks (Angels)
Eugene Emeralds (Braves)
Everett AquaSox (Mariners)
Portland Rockies (Rockies)
Salem-Keizer Volcanoes (Giants)
Southern Oregon Timberjacks (A's)

Spokane Indians (Royals)
Yakima Bears (Dodgers)

1997 FINAL STANDINGS

NORTH DIVISION

Team	W	L	T	Pct.	GB
Boise (Angels)	51	25	0	.671	....
Spokane (Royals)	45	31	0	.592	6
Everett (Mariners)	29	47	0	.382	22
Yakima (Dodgers)	23	53	0	.303	28

SOUTH DIVISION

Team	W	L	T	Pct.	GB
Portland (Rockies)	44	32	0	.579	....
Southern Oregon (Athletics)	41	35	0	.539	3
Salem-Keizer (Giants)	40	36	0	.526	4
Eugene (Braves)	31	45	0	.408	13

COMPOSITE

Team	Boi.	Spo.	Port.	S.O.	S-K	Eug.	Ever.	Yak.	W	L	T	Pct.	GB
Boise (Angels)	....	8	6	5	6	6	10	10	51	25	0	.671	....
Spokane (Royals)	4	....	5	5	8	7	8	8	45	31	0	.592	6
Portland (Rockies)	4	5	....	10	7	4	7	7	44	32	0	.579	7
Southern Oregon (Athletics)	5	5	2	....	5	9	7	8	41	35	0	.539	10
Salem-Keizer (Giants)	4	2	5	7	....	9	5	8	40	36	0	.526	11
Eugene (Braves)	4	3	8	3	3	....	6	4	31	45	0	.408	20
Everett (Mariners)	2	4	3	3	5	4	....	8	29	47	0	.382	22
Yakima (Dodgers)	2	4	3	2	2	6	4	....	23	53	0	.303	28

Major league affiliations in parentheses.

Southern Oregon played home games in Medford, Ore.

PLAYOFFS: Portland defeated Boise, three games to two, to win league championship.

REGULAR-SEASON ATTENDANCE: Boise, 154,819; Eugene, 135,926; Everett, 79,918; Portland, 213,242; Salem-Keizer, 136,836; Southern Oregon, 68,757; Spokane, 185,304; Yakima, 80,003. Total—1,054,805; Playoffs (5 games)—14,298.

MANAGERS: Boise, Tom Kotchman; Eugene, Jim Saul; Everett, Orlando Gomez; Portland, Jim Eppard; Salem-Keizer, Shane Turner; Southern Oregon, John Kuehl; Spokane, Jeff Garber; Yakima, Joe Vavra.

ALL-STAR TEAM: 1B—Mark Burke, Eugene; Nick Leach, Yakima; 2B—Travis Young, Salem-Keizer; 3B—Adam Piatt, Southern Oregon; SS—Nelson Castro, Boise; OF—Dermal Brown, Spokane; Casey Child, Boise; Juan Lebron, Spokane; C—Jason Dewey, Boise; DH—Mike Marchiano, Everett; LHP—Michael Riley, Salem-Keizer; RHP—Matt Wise, Boise; LH Relief Pitcher—Robert Chrysler, Everett; RH Relief Pitcher—Ara Petrosian, Portland; Most Valuable Player—Dermal Brown, Spokane; Manager of the Year—Jim Eppard, Portland.

1997 BATTING

TEAM

Team	Avg.	G	TPA	AB	R	H	TB	2B	3B	HR	RBI	SH	SF	HP	BB	IBB	SO	SB	CS	GDP	LOB	ShO	Slg.	OBP
Boise	.290	76	3213	2777	550	804	1201	172	15	65	457	9	24	40	363	12	585	92	27	63	628	2	.432	.377
Spokane	.281	76	3163	2741	514	771	1186	149	28	70	435	26	19	36	341	14	628	97	27	50	614	1	.433	.366
Everett	.276	76	3132	2755	457	761	1137	143	25	61	397	21	22	39	295	9	729	127	36	49	635	0	.413	.352
Southern Oregon	.275	76	3151	2675	496	736	1104	147	31	53	416	14	28	47	387	10	714	138	46	47	626	1	.413	.373
Salem-Keizer	.263	76	3024	2607	434	686	972	112	24	42	354	9	26	37	345	5	613	173	36	49	599	1	.373	.354
Eugene	.256	76	3018	2649	383	677	953	111	27	37	328	27	29	38	275	10	610	58	28	47	601	6	.360	.331
Portland	.255	76	2983	2562	394	653	915	117	26	31	337	33	31	45	312	14	681	80	35	38	596	1	.357	.342
Yakima	.252	76	3005	2678	365	674	983	139	28	38	316	20	15	41	251	9	658	107	26	48	574	2	.367	.324

INDIVIDUAL

TOP QUALIFIERS FOR BATTING CHAMPIONSHIP

Minimum 205 plate appearances. *Lefthanded batter. †Switch-hitter.

Player, Team	Avg.	G	TPA	AB	R	H	TB	2B	3B	HR	RBI	SH	SF	HP	BB	IBB	SO	SB	CS	GDP	Slg.	OBP
Tomlinson, Goefrey, Spokane*	.338	58	256	210	49	71	99	16	0	4	28	4	2	8	32	0	20	19	1	1	.471	.440
Martin, Casey, Boise	.337	50	211	181	30	61	99	14	0	8	48	0	3	1	23	0	45	1	0	4	.547	.409
Clark, Jermaine, Everett*	.337	59	241	199	42	67	93	13	2	3	29	3	2	3	34	1	31	22	3	1	.467	.437
Espino, Fernando, Everett	.336	64	296	256	48	86	127	17	3	6	36	1	2	4	33	2	44	9	4	7	.496	.417
Young, Travis, Salem-Keizer	.334	76	359	320	80	107	133	11	6	1	34	1	3	5	30	0	50	40	8	3	.416	.397
Stewart, Paxton, Boise*	.333	72	329	282	59	94	135	16	2	7	45	1	3	2	41	3	55	8	5	6	.479	.418
Brown, Dermal, Spokane*	.326	73	340	298	67	97	168	20	6	13	73	0	1	2	38	5	65	17	4	5	.564	.404
Child, Casey, Boise	.325	68	323	274	69	89	152	26	2	11	57	1	5	8	34	0	47	18	2	7	.555	.408
Martinez, Hipolito, So. Oregon	.324	65	260	222	45	72	120	13	4	9	44	1	1	2	34	2	65	3	2	2	.541	.417
Dewey, Jason, Boise	.324	68	318	272	55	88	148	17	2	13	64	1	2	2	41	4	70	5	2	2	.544	.413
Alviso, Jerome, Portland†	.319	69	308	270	48	86	113	15	3	2	45	6	6	7	19	1	46	12	5	3	.419	.371

Player, Team	Avg.	G	TPA	AB	R	H	TB	2B	3B	HR	RBI	SH	SF	HP	BB	IBB	SO	SB	CS	GDP	Slg.	OBP
Valera, Ramon, Everett	.317	58	265	221	43	70	94	12	3	2	23	5	1	1	37	2	65	24	6	0	.425	.415
Leach, Nick, Yakima*	.313	54	231	192	33	60	101	18	1	7	47	0	1	6	32	4	37	5	0	4	.526	.424
LeBron, Juan, Spokane	.306	69	308	288	49	88	138	27	1	7	45	0	1	2	17	2	74	8	4	5	.479	.347
Burke, Mark, Eugene*	.305	62	280	236	37	72	110	17	0	7	45	1	2	5	36	3	41	1	1	4	.466	.405

DEPARTMENTAL LEADERS: G—Young, 76; AB—Young, 320; R—Young, 80; H—Young, 107; TB—D. Brown, 168; 2B—LeBron, 27; 3B—Riley, 7; HR—Marchiano, 15; RBI—D. Brown, 73; SH—Caruso, 8; SF—Ankrum, 7; HP—Ankrum, 11; BB—Sosa, 55; IBB—Sears, 7; SO—Mitchell, 102; SB—Byas, 51; CS—Robinson, 11; GIDP—Eady, 10; Slg.—D. Brown, .564; OBP—Tomlinson, .440.

ALL PLAYERS

*Lefthanded batter. †Switch-hitter.

Player, Team	Avg.	G	TPA	AB	R	H	TB	2B	3B	HR	RBI	SH	SF	HP	BB	IBB	SO	SB	CS	GDP	Slg.	OBP
Alamo, Efrain, Portland	.216	69	288	255	27	55	78	13	2	2	33	3	6	2	22	0	88	12	4	4	.306	.277
Alcala, Juan, Everett	.152	9	34	33	3	5	6	1	0	0	1	0	0	0	1	0	15	1	0	1	.182	.176
Allen, Shane, Yakima	.000	12	31	26	2	0	0	0	0	0	0	0	0	0	5	0	13	1	0	2	.000	.161
Alviso, Jerome, Portland†	.319	69	308	270	48	86	113	15	3	2	45	6	6	7	19	1	46	12	5	3	.419	.371
Ankrum, C.J., Salem-Keizer*	.266	74	330	263	44	70	101	14	1	5	64	0	7	11	49	1	44	6	5	6	.384	.394
Arnold, John, Eugene	.245	50	191	159	25	39	65	9	1	5	30	0	2	2	28	0	50	0	1	4	.409	.361
Ashley, Steve, Eugene	.267	4	17	15	3	4	5	1	0	0	0	0	0	0	2	0	3	0	0	1	.333	.353
Backowski, Lance, Yakima	.000	16	1	1	0	0	0	0	0	0	0	0	0	0	0	0	1	0	0	0	.000	.000
Baeza, Art, Salem-Keizer	.313	6	19	16	5	5	12	1	0	2	5	0	0	1	2	0	3	0	1	0	.750	.421
Balbuena, Mike, Yakima†	.208	15	52	48	2	10	13	1	1	0	4	0	0	1	3	0	15	1	0	0	.271	.269
Bautista, Francisco, Spokane	.278	29	41	36	11	10	15	3	1	0	2	0	0	0	5	0	14	4	1	1	.417	.366
Bell, Ricky, Yakima	.258	66	289	264	42	68	91	15	1	2	24	3	3	4	15	0	52	9	0	7	.345	.304
Betancourt, Oscar, Boise	.286	68	301	266	47	76	121	16	1	9	46	1	1	3	30	0	70	2	2	8	.455	.363
Blosser, Doug, Spokane*	.296	65	264	213	43	63	115	14	1	12	50	0	3	1	47	2	61	2	1	5	.540	.420
Brambilla, Michael, Spokane	.226	36	132	115	16	26	45	5	1	4	21	1	1	3	12	0	34	1	2	3	.391	.313
Brown, Bobby, Spokane	.059	14	19	17	1	1	1	0	0	0	1	0	0	0	2	0	9	0	0	0	.059	.158
Brown, Dermal, Spokane*	.326	73	340	298	67	97	168	20	6	13	73	0	1	2	38	5	65	17	4	5	.564	.404
Brown, Jason, Spokane	.203	18	70	59	6	12	15	0	0	1	5	1	0	4	6	0	13	0	0	0	.254	.319
Burke, Mark, Eugene*	.305	62	280	236	37	72	110	17	0	7	45	1	2	5	36	3	41	1	1	4	.466	.405
Byas, Michael, Salem-Keizer	.276	71	341	290	68	80	91	9	1	0	16	1	0	2	48	0	44	51	9	4	.314	.382
Camilo, Juan, So. Oregon*	.231	4	14	13	0	3	3	0	0	0	2	0	0	0	1	0	4	0	1	0	.231	.286
Caruso, Joe, Spokane	.299	57	237	194	48	58	91	12	3	5	36	8	0	6	29	1	30	10	4	1	.469	.406
Casper, Brett, Salem-Keizer	.223	61	264	229	31	51	88	14	1	7	34	0	1	3	31	0	86	17	3	2	.384	.322
Castro, Al, Eugene†	.199	71	263	226	20	45	62	8	3	1	23	4	3	6	24	0	56	7	1	5	.274	.290
Castro, Nelson, Boise†	.294	69	338	293	74	86	125	16	1	7	37	1	1	4	38	1	53	26	6	1	.427	.381
Child, Casey, Boise	.325	68	323	274	69	89	152	26	2	11	57	1	5	8	34	0	47	18	2	7	.555	.408
Clark, Jermaine, Everett*	.337	59	241	199	42	67	93	13	2	3	29	3	2	3	34	1	31	22	3	1	.467	.437
Clark, John, Portland	.204	17	64	54	8	11	16	3	1	0	3	1	0	0	9	0	16	0	0	1	.296	.317
Clifford, John, Portland	.059	6	18	17	2	1	1	0	0	0	1	1	0	0	0	0	3	0	2	0	.059	.059
Clifton, Rodney, So. Oregon	.270	69	320	256	66	69	107	13	5	5	31	2	3	5	54	0	76	14	3	2	.418	.403
Connors, Greg, Everett	.291	54	253	230	41	67	105	18	1	6	43	0	4	3	16	0	44	6	2	3	.457	.340
Delgado, Ariel, Boise*	.242	60	224	207	30	50	65	10	1	1	22	0	1	0	16	3	43	6	1	1	.314	.295
Dewey, Jason, Boise	.324	68	318	272	55	88	148	17	2	13	64	1	2	2	41	4	70	5	2	2	.544	.413
Dillon, Joe, Spokane	.214	19	76	70	6	15	24	3	0	2	6	0	0	1	5	0	13	1	0	2	.343	.276
Dishman, Richard, Eugene	.000	19	1	1	0	0	0	0	0	0	0	0	0	0	0	0	1	0	0	0	.000	.000
Dougherty, Jeb, Boise	.304	25	103	92	20	28	35	5	1	0	8	0	0	3	8	0	10	3	0	2	.380	.379
Eady, Gerald, Everett	.234	67	278	248	32	58	82	11	2	3	33	1	4	3	22	0	89	13	4	10	.331	.300
Espino, Fernando, Everett	.336	64	296	256	48	86	127	17	3	6	36	1	2	4	33	2	44	9	4	7	.496	.417
Faircloth, Chad, Salem-Keizer*	.284	31	118	102	13	29	38	5	2	0	13	0	1	1	14	0	30	2	0	3	.373	.373
Farris, Ed, So. Oregon*	.267	66	282	255	33	68	106	19	2	5	56	0	3	2	22	3	76	4	1	6	.416	.326
Figueroa, Jose, So. Oregon	.237	41	147	131	16	31	47	8	1	2	16	0	1	4	11	0	40	3	0	3	.359	.313
Flach, Jason, Eugene	.000	23	1	1	0	0	0	0	0	0	0	0	0	0	0	0	0	0	0	0	.000	.000
Flaherty, Tim, Salem-Keizer	.227	32	129	110	16	25	43	6	0	4	17	1	2	1	15	0	44	1	0	1	.391	.320
Flores, Eric, Yakima	.221	33	115	104	17	23	50	5	2	6	17	1	0	0	10	0	48	1	1	1	.481	.289
Flores, Javier, So. Oregon	.331	45	190	160	25	53	73	11	3	1	25	1	3	9	17	0	22	2	1	2	.456	.418
Folmar, Ryan, Portland*	.180	19	71	61	8	11	19	5	0	1	9	0	0	1	9	0	19	2	1	4	.311	.296
Franklin, Jason, Portland	.237	63	259	211	37	50	83	13	1	6	37	2	4	5	37	2	60	4	1	5	.393	.358
Fuentes, Joel, Salem-Keizer†	.218	20	72	55	7	12	14	2	0	0	2	0	0	1	17	0	12	1	1	2	.255	.403
Garrick, Matt, Boise	.300	5	23	20	1	6	6	0	0	0	4	0	0	0	3	0	2	0	0	1	.300	.391
Geronimo, Cesar, Boise	.286	54	211	192	32	55	76	11	2	2	29	1	2	1	15	0	29	3	2	5	.396	.338
Gonzales, Jose, Portland	.241	48	196	166	18	40	58	9	0	3	16	0	1	3	25	0	30	1	1	3	.349	.349
Goris, Braulio, So. Oregon*	.067	5	19	15	3	1	2	1	0	0	0	0	0	0	4	0	11	0	0	0	.133	.263
Gorrie, Brad, So. Oregon	.302	59	237	205	48	62	86	11	2	3	29	1	1	2	28	0	50	19	3	2	.420	.390
Goudie, Jaime, Salem-Keizer	.239	56	249	230	33	55	77	10	6	0	16	1	0	2	16	0	38	21	5	2	.335	.294
Greene, Clay, Salem-Keizer	.225	33	96	89	11	20	26	4	1	0	5	0	0	0	7	0	19	21	3	1	.292	.281
Griffis, Cade, Spokane*	.107	24	33	28	1	3	3	0	0	0	0	0	0	0	5	0	13	0	0	0	.107	.242
Hargrove, Harvey, Everett	.271	69	300	256	40	70	113	21	5	4	34	2	1	9	30	0	74	8	2	7	.438	.366
Haynes, Nathan, So. Oregon*	.280	24	111	82	18	23	26	1	1	0	9	0	1	2	26	0	21	19	3	1	.317	.459
Hernandez, John, Yakima	.182	29	88	77	7	14	20	3	0	1	8	1	0	1	9	0	22	1	1	3	.260	.276
Hernandez, Victor, So. Oregon	.149	43	139	121	14	18	25	5	1	0	18	3	0	3	12	0	43	5	0	2	.207	.243
Hill, Jeremy, Spokane	.283	60	218	187	35	53	76	12	1	3	29	0	3	1	25	0	53	1	0	6	.406	.366
Hines, Pooh, Eugene	.274	69	316	266	40	73	100	10	4	3	35	3	4	3	40	1	52	5	6	2	.376	.371
Horton, Conan, Yakima†	.333	1	4	3	0	1	2	1	0	0	0	0	0	0	1	0	0	0	0	0	.667	.500
Illig, Brett, Yakima	.000	1	2	2	0	0	0	0	0	0	0	0	0	0	0	0	2	0	0	0	.000	.000
Jackson, Jeremy, Portland*	.284	68	317	289	45	82	105	12	4	1	26	3	0	5	20	1	70	13	4	4	.363	.341
Johns, Michael, Portland	.232	62	242	220	28	51	70	4	3	3	27	6	5	0	11	0	66	2	2	5	.318	.263
Johnson, Duan, Everett	.251	46	186	171	31	43	53	4	3	0	14	1	1	1	12	0	26	10	1	4	.310	.303
Kenna, David, Salem-Keizer*	.198	64	262	242	24	48	81	8	2	7	33	0	0	3	17	1	86	1	1	8	.335	.260
King, Willie, Yakima*	.219	50	186	155	14	34	52	4	1	4	20	1	2	1	27	0	43	11	1	5	.335	.335
Kirkpatrick, Brian, Portland	.286	2	8	7	1	2	2	0	0	0	0	0	0	0	1	0	3	0	0	0	.286	.375

Player, Team	Avg.	G	TPA	AB	R	H	TB	2B	3B	HR	RBI	SH	SF	HP	BB	IBB	SO	SB	CS	GDP	Slg.	OBP
Koerner, Michael, So. Oregon*	.340	24	117	106	21	36	56	12	1	2	19	0	0	0	11	2	30	7	3	1	.528	.402
Kokinda, Steven, Everett*	.286	34	116	98	18	28	39	3	1	2	14	3	0	0	15	1	27	1	1	2	.398	.381
Lara, Edward, So. Oregon†	.274	65	296	252	45	69	97	12	5	2	43	3	5	4	32	0	28	25	7	3	.385	.358
Leach, Nick, Yakima*	.313	54	231	192	33	60	101	18	1	7	47	0	1	6	32	4	37	5	0	4	.526	.424
LeBron, Juan, Spokane	.306	69	308	288	49	88	138	27	1	7	45	0	1	2	17	2	74	8	4	5	.479	.347
Leggett, Adam, Boise†	.224	62	262	219	47	49	72	16	2	1	32	0	3	6	34	1	54	8	1	7	.329	.340
Ligons, Merrell, Spokane†	.224	44	176	143	25	32	40	2	0	2	11	1	0	0	32	0	54	12	2	4	.280	.366
Lopez, Luis, Salem-Keizer	.000	1	4	4	0	0	0	0	0	0	0	1	0	0	0	0	0	1	0	0	1	.000	.000
Marchiano, Mike, Everett	.292	63	286	257	52	75	140	20	0	15	64	0	1	5	22	2	42	6	4	4	.545	.358
Marnell, Dean, Portland	.300	19	82	70	13	21	22	1	0	0	9	2	1	2	7	0	8	1	1	1	.314	.375
Martin, Casey, Boise	.337	50	211	181	30	61	99	14	0	8	48	0	3	1	23	0	45	1	0	4	.547	.409
Martinez, Hipolito, So. Oregon	.324	65	260	222	45	72	120	13	4	9	44	1	1	2	34	2	65	3	2	2	.541	.417
Martinez, Victor, Portland	.241	20	67	58	10	14	18	2	1	0	9	1	0	0	8	0	16	0	1	2	.310	.333
Maynard, Scott, Everett	.221	24	93	86	11	19	28	3	0	2	13	2	0	0	5	0	30	3	0	0	.326	.264
McCrotty, William, Yakima	.200	43	150	135	12	27	32	2	0	1	10	2	1	3	9	0	19	2	0	3	.237	.264
Medosch, Keith, Boise†	.220	45	161	132	25	29	34	5	0	0	9	0	0	3	26	0	31	5	3	5	.258	.360
Mendoza, Carlos, Salem-Keizer†	.208	33	122	106	10	22	22	0	0	0	6	4	0	1	11	0	19	6	0	3	.208	.288
Metzler, Rod, Spokane†	.228	62	250	224	37	51	75	5	5	3	31	5	2	1	18	0	48	9	2	1	.335	.286
Mitchell, Andres, Portland	.230	69	314	265	57	61	90	5	6	4	20	5	2	6	36	0	102	21	8	2	.340	.333
Montas, Ricardo, Spokane	.300	66	258	217	42	65	82	5	3	2	20	2	2	2	35	1	39	5	3	5	.378	.398
Mortimer, Mark, Eugene	.305	53	194	174	25	53	70	7	2	2	21	0	2	2	16	0	24	1	1	3	.402	.366
Mosier, Mark, Salem-Keizer	.306	19	75	62	10	19	21	2	0	0	7	1	2	1	9	0	13	0	2	1	.339	.392
Myers, Mickey, Everett*	.143	4	7	7	1	1	1	0	0	0	0	0	0	0	0	0	2	0	0	0	.143	.143
Nelson, Brian, Everett	.270	13	41	37	5	10	12	2	0	0	3	0	0	1	3	0	15	0	0	0	.324	.341
Newton, Kimani, Yakima	.269	56	230	201	34	54	72	7	1	3	14	1	1	4	23	1	63	20	6	0	.358	.354
Nunley, Jay, Boise	.282	60	249	216	34	61	94	16	1	5	39	1	2	4	26	0	37	5	3	8	.435	.367
Oquendo, Nelvin, Salem-Keizer	.200	4	6	5	1	1	1	0	0	0	0	0	0	0	1	0	2	0	0	0	.200	.333
Otero, William, Salem-Keizer	.238	46	169	147	22	35	50	3	0	4	12	0	1	4	17	1	32	2	1	4	.340	.331
Pagan, Carlos, Spokane	.279	26	73	68	13	19	24	2	0	1	10	0	0	1	4	0	13	0	0	3	.353	.329
Paterson, Joe, Yakima	.231	47	167	156	13	36	50	12	1	0	15	0	4	2	5	0	51	2	2	2	.321	.257
Peckham, Chris, Boise	.257	17	46	35	7	9	12	0	0	1	6	0	1	0	10	0	10	0	0	1	.343	.413
Peoples, Derrick, Yakima	.229	47	161	144	14	33	44	7	2	0	16	2	0	2	13	0	44	7	0	5	.306	.302
Petersen, Mike, Portland	.235	13	56	51	8	12	14	2	0	0	5	0	0	1	4	0	12	0	1	0	.275	.304
Petru, Rich, Spokane	.273	33	115	99	25	27	45	5	2	3	17	2	1	2	11	0	15	2	1	5	.455	.354
Philip-Guide, Sheldon, Boise	.235	19	60	51	7	12	16	4	0	0	5	1	0	1	7	0	16	2	0	1	.314	.339
Phoenix, Wynter, Yakima*	.253	56	218	186	29	47	74	14	2	3	17	5	1	3	23	2	36	11	4	1	.398	.343
Piatt, Adam, So. Oregon	.292	57	253	216	63	63	113	9	1	13	35	0	1	1	35	1	58	19	4	4	.523	.391
Pierce, Brett, Eugene	.278	57	207	176	23	49	61	7	1	1	19	1	3	4	22	2	25	3	3	4	.347	.366
Priess, Matthew, Salem-Keizer	.273	46	188	172	22	47	68	8	2	3	31	0	1	2	12	0	30	0	1	3	.395	.319
Pugh, Josh, Eugene	.148	30	94	88	10	13	16	3	0	0	5	0	0	2	4	1	23	0	0	1	.182	.202
Riley, Cash, Yakima	.265	65	279	253	36	67	114	12	7	7	43	0	0	5	21	0	77	14	3	7	.451	.333
Robinson, Adam, So. Oregon	.272	68	290	250	41	68	94	13	2	3	27	2	3	6	28	0	68	13	11	8	.376	.355
Rodriguez, Chris, Portland	.264	23	81	72	7	19	22	1	1	0	4	1	0	2	6	0	12	0	1	0	.306	.338
Rodriguez, Guillermo, S-K	.231	11	44	39	3	9	12	3	0	0	3	0	0	0	5	0	12	0	1	1	.308	.318
Russoniello, Michael, Boise	.000	2	5	3	1	0	0	0	0	0	0	1	0	0	2	0	2	0	0	0	.000	.400
Saitta, Rich, Yakima	.311	44	201	183	37	57	77	13	2	1	15	1	1	2	14	0	27	6	2	0	.421	.365
Sanchez, Manuel, Eugene*	.288	58	256	229	46	66	89	6	4	3	27	4	2	9	12	0	39	14	5	2	.389	.345
Schwartzbauer, Whitey, Portland*	.256	50	200	156	22	40	60	7	2	3	29	0	2	5	37	1	47	2	2	1	.385	.410
Sears, Todd, Portland*	.270	55	243	200	37	54	75	13	1	2	29	1	1	0	41	7	49	2	0	4	.375	.393
Seifert, Ryan, Portland	.000	16	0	0	0	0	0	0	0	0	0	0	0	0	0	0	0	1	0	0	.000	.000
Silvestre, Juan, Everett	.315	14	61	54	9	17	31	3	1	3	9	0	1	2	4	0	19	1	0	0	.574	.377
Slater, Wayne, Yakima*	.235	29	79	68	11	16	22	3	0	1	7	0	0	0	11	2	11	2	0	2	.324	.342
Smith, Brian, Everett†	.232	33	108	95	9	22	30	3	1	1	7	1	0	0	12	0	29	6	4	0	.316	.318
Smothers, Stewart, Eugene	.275	59	258	233	31	64	93	11	6	2	27	3	0	1	21	0	57	12	4	5	.399	.337
Sosa, Nicolas, So. Oregon	.230	62	256	196	29	45	62	7	2	2	26	0	3	2	55	0	80	0	3	3	.316	.398
Soverel, Bret, Eugene	.111	13	40	36	1	4	7	0	0	1	3	0	0	1	3	1	13	1	1	1	.194	.200
Spencer, Jeff, Eugene	.262	67	308	275	46	72	126	14	2	12	54	0	5	1	27	1	83	4	2	8	.458	.325
Spiezio, Scott, So. Oregon†	.556	2	12	9	1	5	5	0	0	0	2	0	1	0	2	1	0	0	0	0	.556	.583
Stewart, Keith, Everett*	.268	38	143	127	19	34	44	3	2	1	11	0	0	0	16	0	46	15	3	0	.346	.350
Stewart, Paxton, Boise*	.333	72	329	282	59	94	135	16	2	7	45	1	3	2	41	3	55	8	5	6	.479	.418
Strangfeld, Aaron, Eugene†	.068	11	46	44	0	3	4	1	0	0	1	0	0	0	2	0	13	0	0	2	.091	.109
Strickland, Gregory, Eugene*	.284	55	226	204	33	58	72	8	3	0	16	5	3	0	14	0	62	9	2	0	.353	.326
Taylor, Kirk, Spokane	.254	23	69	59	9	15	29	3	1	3	13	0	2	0	8	1	14	1	0	2	.492	.333
Tegland, Ron, So. Oregon	.231	37	124	108	17	25	42	6	1	3	19	1	1	4	8	0	37	0	1	2	.389	.306
Terhune, Mike, Eugene†	.213	14	67	61	4	13	14	1	0	0	3	2	0	0	4	1	6	0	0	2	.230	.262
Tomlinson, Goefrey, Spokane*	.338	58	256	210	49	71	99	16	0	4	28	4	2	8	32	0	20	19	1	5	.471	.440
Ullery, David, Spokane*	.217	12	29	23	1	5	8	0	0	1	4	0	0	1	5	1	5	0	0	1	.348	.379
Underwood, Jake, Everett	.103	12	38	29	4	3	3	0	0	0	3	1	2	3	3	0	11	0	0	0	.103	.243
Ussery, Brian, Boise†	.262	15	54	42	5	11	11	0	0	0	5	1	0	0	11	0	11	0	0	4	.262	.415
Valderrama, Carlos, Salem-Keizer.	.319	41	152	138	21	44	66	7	3	3	28	0	2	0	12	0	29	22	0	2	.478	.368
Valera, Ramon, Everett	.317	58	265	221	43	70	94	12	3	2	23	5	1	1	37	2	65	24	6	0	.425	.415
Vaz, Roberto, So. Oregon*	.321	22	87	78	11	25	40	6	0	3	15	0	1	1	7	1	4	5	3	6	.513	.379
Warren, Lance, Yakima*	.400	2	6	5	0	2	2	0	0	0	1	0	0	0	1	0	1	0	0	0	.400	.500
Wells, Zachary, Salem-Keizer	.284	62	274	218	47	62	105	9	2	10	43	1	4	3	48	2	57	3	1	3	.482	.414
Williams, Patrick, Everett	.267	64	280	255	38	68	111	7	0	12	48	0	3	3	19	0	93	1	0	6	.435	.321
Willis, Dave, Spokane	.286	65	272	252	36	72	108	15	3	5	36	3	1	5	11	1	54	5	2	3	.429	.317
Wise, Jamie, Eugene*	.000	22	1	0	0	0	0	0	0	0	0	0	1	0	0	0	0	0	0	0	.000	.000
Wissen, Collin, Eugene*	.204	73	292	260	40	53	66	8	1	1	22	3	3	3	21	1	75	2	2	4	.254	.273
Wyatt, Ben, Eugene*	.000	15	1	1	0	0	0	0	0	0	0	0	0	0	0	0	0	0	0	0	.000	.000
Young, Travis, Salem-Keizer	.334	76	359	320	80	107	133	11	6	1	34	1	5	3	30	0	50	40	8	3	.416	.397
Zaun, Brian, Yakima	.312	46	196	186	23	58	75	12	1	1	37	1	1	0	8	0	45	3	1	4	.403	.338
Zweifel, Kent, Portland	.288	57	237	198	28	57	87	14	2	4	44	2	3	5	29	2	50	7	2	1	.439	.387

GRAND SLAMS: N. Castro, Farris, Piatt, 2 each; Ankrum, Burke, Child, Connors, Eady, Gonzales, Kenna, Leach, H. Martinez, Nunley, Zaun, 1 each.

AWARDED FIRST BASE ON CATCHER'S INTERFERENCE: Martin 3 (Tegland 3); Hill 2 (Maynard, Dewey); Tegland 2 (Nelson, Dewey); D. Brown (Fegueroa); N. Castro (J. Brown); Child (Figueroa); Gonzales (Figueroa); Marchiano (Tegland); Robinson (Ussery); Pierce (Ussery).

CLASS A Northwest League

1997 PITCHING

TEAM

Team	W	L	Pct.	ERA	G	CG	ShO	Sv.	IP	H	TBF	R	ER	HR	SH	SF	HB	BB	IBB	SO	WP	Bk.
Spokane	45	31	.592	4.02	76	0	2	17	685.0	701	3055	420	306	50	12	27	36	272	9	683	70	10
Portland	44	32	.579	4.12	76	1	3	23	670.1	728	2956	382	307	39	17	17	41	240	2	547	47	10
Boise	51	25	.671	4.27	76	0	0	23	693.0	692	3100	421	329	30	25	27	38	292	14	730	88	12
Salem-Keizer	40	36	.526	4.35	76	1	1	20	666.2	682	2992	408	322	63	26	16	40	295	7	644	60	13
Southern Oregon	41	35	.539	4.85	76	1	2	15	679.1	694	3097	464	366	52	20	24	42	334	5	678	96	22
Everett	29	47	.382	4.88	76	1	3	12	672.2	726	3142	480	365	64	18	27	38	380	12	735	75	19
Eugene	31	45	.408	5.24	76	0	3	16	671.2	781	3194	495	391	53	17	25	40	384	14	602	76	14
Yakima	23	53	.303	5.29	76	1	0	9	673.2	758	3167	523	396	46	24	31	48	372	20	599	65	18

INDIVIDUAL

TOP QUALIFIERS FOR EARNED-RUN AVERAGE TITLE

Minimum 61 innings. *Lefthanded pitcher.

Pitcher, Team	W	L	Pct.	ERA	G	GS	CG	ShO	GF	Sv.	IP	H	TBF	R	ER	HR	SH	SF	HB	BB	IBB	SO	WP	Bk.
Miller, Justin, Portland	4	2	.667	2.14	14	11	0	0	1	0	67.1	68	288	26	16	3	2	2	4	20	0	54	6	0
Nathan, Joe, Salem-Keizer	2	1	.667	2.47	18	5	0	0	4	0	62.0	53	254	22	17	7	4	2	4	26	0	44	2	0
Cummings, Ryan, Boise	6	2	.750	3.09	14	13	0	0	0	0	70.0	73	297	38	24	3	2	1	7	10	0	79	4	2
Key, Scott, Spokane	3	3	.500	3.23	25	1	0	0	8	3	69.2	55	296	33	25	5	0	2	4	31	1	66	9	0
Schurman, Ryan, Eugene	4	6	.400	3.23	16	15	0	0	0	0	86.1	75	379	46	31	8	1	2	5	43	0	95	2	1
Wise, Matt, Boise	9	1	.900	3.25	15	15	0	0	0	0	83.0	62	342	37	30	5	0	1	2	34	0	86	7	3
Pederson, Justin, Spokane	5	3	.625	3.44	15	13	0	0	0	0	65.1	61	280	34	25	4	0	2	4	24	0	84	2	2
Kringen, Jake, Portland*	6	5	.545	3.46	15	15	1	1	0	0	83.1	84	349	40	32	6	1	1	2	20	0	72	4	2
Riley, Michael, Salem-Keizer*	9	2	.818	3.46	15	15	1	0	0	0	88.1	76	375	39	34	9	2	2	4	28	0	96	6	1
Meady, Todd, Spokane	2	3	.400	3.72	21	4	0	0	4	0	65.1	68	283	38	27	4	2	4	3	18	1	39	8	0
Meche, Gil, Everett	3	4	.429	3.98	12	12	1	0	0	0	74.2	75	316	40	33	7	3	2	3	24	0	62	7	0
Fish, Steve, Boise	5	2	.714	4.08	24	4	0	0	2	0	75.0	69	314	41	34	4	6	3	3	23	3	79	5	0
Thompson, Travis, Portland	5	5	.500	4.32	50	18	11	0	0	2	74.0	88	328	51	37	6	2	2	6	16	0	51	2	0
Wilson, Kris, Spokane	5	3	.625	4.52	15	15	0	0	0	0	73.2	101	345	50	37	6	0	3	5	21	1	72	1	2
Alexander, Jordy, Spokane*	7	3	.700	4.59	16	12	0	0	2	1	86.1	82	366	59	44	10	0	4	6	18	2	83	4	0
Greene, Ryan, Eugene	3	7	.300	4.59	15	15	0	0	0	0	84.1	90	381	52	43	2	2	4	6	30	1	72	10	6

DEPARTMENTAL LEADERS: W—M. Wise, Riley, 9 each; L—Backowski, 12; Pct.—M. Wise, .900; G—Shields, 30; GS—Gangemi, R. Jensen, 16 each; CG—Several pitchers tied with 1 each; ShO—Kringen, 1; GF—Travis, 27; Sv.—Travis, 16; IP—Riley, 88.1; H—Roberts, 104; TBF—Greene, 381; R—Backowski, 72; ER—Roberts, 59; HR—Wyatt, R. Jensen, Alexander, 10 each; SH—Fish, Hannah, 6 each; SF—Roberts, 6; HB—Backowski, 10; BB—Nogowski, 57; IBB—Everly, 6; SO—Riley, 96; WP—Harriger, 15; BK—Greene, 6.

ALL PITCHERS

*Lefthanded pitcher.

Pitcher, Team	W	L	Pct.	ERA	G	GS	CG	ShO	GF	Sv.	IP	H	TBF	R	ER	HR	SH	SF	HB	BB	IBB	SO	WP	Bk.
Abreu, Oscar, So. Oregon	2	2	.500	8.31	20	0	0	0	9	1	26.0	26	133	28	24	6	0	1	1	25	0	47	9	1
Alexander, Jordy, Spokane*	7	3	.700	4.59	16	12	0	0	2	1	86.1	82	366	59	44	10	0	4	6	18	2	83	4	0
Allen, Rodney, Eugene	1	1	.500	6.28	20	1	0	0	7	2	43.0	56	213	35	30	4	1	1	0	27	2	29	5	0
Anderson, Jason A., Boise	1	0	1.000	19.80	5	0	0	0	2	0	5.0	15	37	13	11	1	0	1	0	6	0	3	0	0
Anderson, Jason P., So. Oregon*	3	3	.500	4.99	14	9	0	0	1	0	52.1	63	238	38	29	4	3	0	5	19	0	38	8	2
Andra, Jeff, Salem-Keizer*	3	1	.750	2.03	8	8	0	0	0	0	44.1	39	185	21	10	3	1	1	1	10	0	58	4	0
Arnold, John, Eugene	0	0	.000	27.00	1	0	0	0	1	0	1.0	3	6	3	3	1	0	0	0	0	0	2	1	0
Ashworth, Kym, Yakima*	0	1	.000	3.63	4	4	0	0	0	0	17.1	13	73	7	7	2	1	1	1	10	0	15	2	0
Austin, Shawn, Salem-Keizer*	1	1	.500	1.06	13	0	0	0	2	0	17.0	12	73	7	2	1	0	1	1	6	0	18	0	0
Backowski, Lance, Yakima	2	12	.143	6.40	15	15	1	0	0	0	71.2	85	357	72	51	2	1	3	10	53	0	61	9	0
Barber, Andrew, Portland	6	1	.857	2.48	22	0	0	0	8	1	32.2	23	132	10	9	0	3	0	1	18	0	39	3	5
Bello, Emerson, Everett	2	4	.333	4.03	22	3	0	0	10	1	44.2	52	209	27	20	9	0	1	3	15	1	65	4	4
Bloomfield, Shane, Yakima	0	0	.000	0.00	1	0	0	0	0	0	1.0	1	3	0	0	0	0	0	0	0	0	0	0	0
Blumenstock, Brad, So. Oregon	0	4	.000	9.33	19	7	0	0	2	0	45.1	61	227	51	47	4	0	1	3	30	1	28	7	0
Boring, Richard, Spokane	2	1	.667	3.20	26	0	0	0	19	7	25.1	32	121	15	9	2	1	1	1	7	0	17	4	1
Brea, Lesli, Everett	2	4	.333	7.99	23	0	0	0	14	3	32.2	34	162	29	29	3	2	1	3	29	4	49	6	0
Burnside, Adrian, Yakima	6	3	.667	4.93	15	13	0	0	0	0	65.2	67	314	53	36	9	1	3	5	49	1	66	4	4
Burton, Jamie, Salem-Keizer*	0	0	.000	1.29	7	0	0	0	6	0	7.0	4	31	2	1	0	0	0	0	5	0	9	1	0
Carter, Aaron, Spokane	2	1	.667	2.06	24	0	0	0	7	2	35.0	23	155	12	8	0	1	2	0	27	2	52	11	0
Christianson, Robby, Everett	2	2	.500	5.66	20	2	0	0	1	0	41.1	48	195	31	26	4	1	1	7	23	1	46	4	0
Chrysler, Clint, Everett	3	0	1.000	0.79	18	0	0	0	10	2	22.2	11	83	3	2	0	0	0	0	7	0	25	3	0
Clark, Richard, Salem-Keizer	0	0	.000	7.50	6	0	0	0	2	0	6.0	6	32	6	5	0	1	0	0	7	0	5	2	0
Cummings, Ryan, Boise	6	2	.750	3.09	14	13	0	0	0	0	70.0	73	297	38	24	3	2	1	7	10	0	79	4	2
DeAbreu, Milton, Salem-Keizer	0	0	.000	14.09	7	0	0	0	2	0	7.2	17	45	12	12	1	0	0	0	6	1	8	1	0
DeJesus, Tony, Everett*	2	6	.250	5.89	14	14	0	0	0	0	62.2	68	300	51	41	7	1	3	5	48	0	53	6	1
Dishman, Richard, Eugene	2	2	.500	3.00	19	1	0	0	6	3	51.0	47	213	19	17	2	1	0	7	13	0	60	5	1
Dobson, Dwayne, Boise	0	0	.000	6.45	12	0	0	0	3	0	22.1	28	106	17	16	1	0	0	1	8	0	17	2	0
Donaldson, Bo, Boise	3	1	.750	1.21	27	0	0	0	25	15	52.0	31	208	10	7	0	3	1	2	20	1	88	10	2
DuBose, Eric, So. Oregon*	1	0	1.000	0.00	15	1	0	0	0	0	10.0	5	39	0	0	0	0	0	0	6	0	15	0	0
Dunham, Pat, Everett	0	3	.000	4.13	17	0	0	0	10	0	28.1	26	127	19	13	3	1	0	1	12	1	39	5	3
Enochs, Chris, So. Oregon	0	0	.000	3.48	3	3	0	0	0	0	10.1	12	45	4	4	0	0	0	1	2	0	10	1	0
Everly, Bill, Yakima	2	3	.400	3.41	28	1	0	0	0	0	58.0	48	259	26	22	4	2	3	9	33	6	63	5	1
Farley, Joseph, Salem-Keizer*	0	1	.000	4.50	10	0	0	0	3	0	14.0	16	68	7	7	2	0	0	1	16	1	17	5	2
Faust, Jason, So. Oregon*	5	0	1.000	2.91	16	2	0	0	4	2	46.1	37	205	22	15	1	2	1	1	25	0	62	5	0
Fish, Steve, Boise	5	2	.714	4.08	24	4	0	0	2	0	75.0	69	314	41	34	4	6	3	3	23	3	79	5	0
Fitzpatrick, Ken, Spokane	2	1	.667	4.24	12	0	0	0	5	0	17.0	15	69	8	8	2	0	2	0	6	0	26	3	0

Pitcher, Team	W	L	Pct.	ERA	G	GS	CG	ShO	GF	Sv.	IP	H	TBF	R	ER	HR	SH	SF	HB	BB	IBB	SO	WP	Bk.
Flach, Jason, Eugene	4	3	.571	2.97	23	0	0	0	18	5	39.1	40	180	18	13	2	4	1	1	24	5	51	2	0
Gallagher, Bryan, So. Oregon*	0	1	.000	3.86	2	0	0	0	0	0	2.1	1	11	2	1	0	0	0	0	3	1	3	0	0
Gangemi, Joseph, Boise*	7	2	.778	5.47	16	16	0	0	0	0	79.0	97	369	56	48	2	3	1	6	31	0	61	0	2
Gilfillan, Jason, Spokane	2	1	.667	5.06	16	0	0	0	5	0	16.0	16	82	13	9	0	1	0	1	16	1	22	3	0
Glaze, Randy, So. Oregon	1	2	.333	4.21	21	1	0	0	6	1	36.1	30	174	21	17	4	2	3	7	21	0	38	7	3
Gonzalez, Jose, Everett	1	3	.250	1.76	6	6	0	0	0	0	30.2	35	152	20	6	3	0	2	2	19	0	38	3	0
Gooding, Jason, Spokane*	4	0	1.000	2.26	11	11	0	0	0	0	55.2	44	220	16	14	2	0	0	3	11	0	58	3	0
Gorrell, Chris, So. Oregon	5	3	.625	4.65	18	10	1	0	0	0	71.2	86	326	50	37	8	4	1	3	28	0	60	5	2
Graham, Kyle, Yakima*	0	3	.000	3.88	21	3	0	0	10	0	46.1	46	217	28	20	3	1	5	1	26	1	52	3	2
Greene, Ryan, Eugene	3	7	.300	4.59	15	15	0	0	0	0	84.1	96	381	52	43	2	2	4	6	30	1	72	10	6
Gutierrez, Javier, Everett	0	1	.000	9.82	1	1	0	0	0	0	3.2	4	21	4	4	1	0	2	1	5	0	4	3	0
Hannah, Neal, Yakima	2	7	.222	5.57	22	2	0	0	4	0	63.0	84	300	57	39	4	6	1	3	27	2	44	6	0
Harriger, Mark, Boise	3	4	.429	7.94	13	12	0	0	0	0	51.0	51	243	52	45	2	1	5	1	36	1	42	15	0
Harville, Chad, So. Oregon	1	0	1.000	0.00	3	0	0	0	1	0	5.0	3	23	0	0	0	1	0	2	3	0	6	0	0
Holmes, Mike, So. Oregon	2	0	1.000	2.51	7	0	0	0	2	0	14.1	14	57	8	4	2	0	0	0	4	0	16	0	0
Hudson, Tim, So. Oregon	3	1	.750	2.51	8	4	0	0	1	0	28.2	12	111	8	8	0	0	1	1	15	2	37	3	2
Hughes, Michael, Boise	0	2	.000	7.56	11	3	0	0	3	0	16.2	20	81	16	14	2	0	0	2	12	0	18	4	0
Husted, Brent, Yakima	1	5	.167	6.98	10	6	0	0	1	0	29.2	45	145	32	23	0	0	0	1	11	3	22	2	0
Hutchings, Mark, Salem-Keizer	1	0	1.000	8.56	11	0	0	0	1	0	13.2	24	72	15	13	2	1	0	3	8	1	5	1	0
Jensen, Jared, So. Oregon	4	2	.667	3.71	23	0	0	0	18	6	26.2	27	113	13	11	1	1	0	0	8	0	34	3	0
Jensen, Ryan, Salem-Keizer	7	3	.700	5.15	16	16	0	0	0	0	80.1	87	353	55	46	10	2	2	4	32	0	67	2	1
Johnson, David, Portland	0	1	.000	3.24	18	0	0	0	12	5	16.2	10	81	8	6	0	2	1	0	20	1	21	7	0
Johnson, Eric, Salem-Keizer	0	0	.000	11.88	10	0	0	0	1	0	8.1	7	49	12	11	0	0	0	1	18	0	8	2	2
Jones, Greg, Boise	2	2	.500	3.62	21	4	0	0	4	2	37.1	35	172	19	15	1	2	4	3	19	1	39	5	1
Jones, Marcus, So. Oregon	3	3	.500	4.50	14	10	0	0	0	0	56.0	58	246	37	28	4	0	3	2	22	0	49	4	0
Joseph, Kevin, Salem-Keizer	3	5	.375	5.40	17	6	0	0	5	1	45.0	44	208	35	27	4	1	2	2	26	0	45	10	3
Kalinowski, Josh, Portland*	0	1	.000	2.41	6	6	0	0	0	0	18.2	15	78	6	5	0	0	0	0	10	0	27	3	0
Karabinus, Chris, Yakima	0	0	.000	15.00	2	0	0	0	0	0	3.0	6	19	7	5	1	0	0	1	1	0	5	0	0
Kawahara, Orin, Everett	0	1	.000	4.76	23	0	0	0	5	0	45.1	50	219	29	24	3	0	3	1	33	0	52	5	3
Kennedy, Ryan, Portland	0	0	.000	12.27	6	0	0	0	0	0	7.1	10	40	10	10	0	0	1	4	4	0	5	1	1
Key, Scott, Spokane	3	3	.500	3.23	25	1	0	0	8	3	69.2	55	296	33	25	5	0	2	4	31	1	66	9	0
Kimball, Andrew, So. Oregon	3	2	.600	3.62	13	7	0	0	0	0	54.2	37	230	29	22	4	1	1	3	17	0	75	8	2
Knickerbocker, Tom, So. Oregon*	1	0	1.000	2.81	4	4	0	0	0	0	16.0	20	72	7	5	0	0	2	0	6	0	18	0	0
Kringen, Jake, Portland*	6	5	.545	3.46	15	15	1	1	0	0	83.1	84	349	40	32	6	1	1	2	20	0	72	4	2
Lagattuta, Rico, So. Oregon*	2	1	.667	4.97	16	0	0	0	9	2	29.0	35	138	21	16	2	2	3	1	14	1	17	7	0
Lagrandeur, Yan, Eugene	1	1	.500	7.91	21	0	0	0	10	0	33.0	41	169	34	29	2	0	2	3	21	1	35	11	0
Lamber, Justin, Spokane*	1	1	.500	4.28	25	0	0	0	12	4	27.1	24	126	14	13	1	0	1	1	20	0	40	10	0
Larreal, Guillermo, Salem-Keizer	1	2	.333	5.51	13	0	0	0	7	1	16.1	23	75	12	10	1	2	0	0	3	0	16	0	0
Lebejko, David, Eugene	0	3	.000	6.19	20	0	0	0	9	0	32.0	44	175	32	22	2	2	2	2	31	1	27	6	1
Linebrink, Scott, Salem-Keizer	0	0	.000	4.50	3	3	0	0	0	0	10.0	7	42	5	5	1	0	0	0	6	0	6	1	0
Lira, Felipe, Everett	1	0	1.000	3.60	1	1	0	0	0	0	5.0	6	24	3	2	0	0	1	0	2	0	9	0	0
Maestas, Mickey, Yakima	1	4	.200	6.61	21	3	0	0	6	0	47.2	65	239	44	35	2	0	2	4	30	1	50	6	0
Mahlberg, John, Portland	2	4	.333	6.65	18	7	0	0	6	0	46.0	69	225	47	34	3	2	3	5	14	1	31	1	0
Malerich, William, Salem-Keizer*	2	1	.667	3.04	21	0	0	0	5	0	26.2	26	130	14	9	2	1	0	3	21	1	43	4	0
Manwiller, Tim, So. Oregon	2	0	1.000	1.86	12	3	0	0	5	2	29.0	19	115	8	6	0	2	1	0	10	0	30	1	2
Matos, Josue, Everett	0	0	.000	2.08	2	0	0	0	1	0	4.1	5	20	2	1	0	0	0	0	2	0	6	1	1
Maynard, Scott, Everett	0	0	.000	18.00	1	0	0	0	1	0	1.0	1	5	2	2	1	0	0	0	1	0	1	0	0
Meady, Todd, Spokane	2	3	.400	3.72	21	4	0	0	4	0	65.1	68	283	38	27	4	2	4	3	18	1	39	8	0
Mears, Chris, Everett	3	5	.375	5.34	12	12	0	0	0	0	62.1	82	283	47	37	5	3	1	1	20	0	47	3	1
Meche, Gil, Everett	3	4	.429	3.98	12	12	1	0	0	0	74.2	75	316	40	33	7	3	2	3	24	0	62	7	0
Miller, Justin, Portland	4	2	.667	2.14	14	11	0	0	1	0	67.1	68	288	26	16	3	2	2	4	20	0	54	6	0
Montero, Agus, So. Oregon	0	0	.000	6.75	2	0	0	0	1	0	2.2	4	15	2	2	0	0	0	2	3	0	1	0	0
Montgomery, Matthew, Yakima	2	2	.500	2.44	11	9	0	0	0	0	55.1	48	229	23	15	3	2	0	1	17	0	38	2	2
Moon, Jared, Yakima	2	2	.500	5.79	11	6	0	0	0	0	37.1	45	168	29	24	4	0	3	1	17	0	32	3	0
Nathan, Joe, Salem-Keizer	2	1	.667	2.47	18	5	0	0	4	2	62.0	53	254	22	17	7	4	2	4	26	0	44	2	0
Newell, Brett, Eugene	2	1	.667	2.62	19	0	0	0	11	4	34.1	17	140	12	10	1	1	0	1	18	1	46	3	0
Nickle, Douglas, Boise	0	1	.000	6.41	17	2	0	0	7	0	19.2	27	96	17	14	3	0	2	1	8	1	22	0	0
Nielsen, Thomas, Salem-Keizer*	1	1	.500	4.82	7	0	0	0	4	0	9.1	10	42	5	5	0	0	0	0	4	1	12	2	1
Niles, Randy, So. Oregon	0	1	.000	1.99	7	4	0	0	0	0	22.2	14	98	12	5	0	1	1	4	12	0	15	4	5
Nina, Elvin, So. Oregon	1	3	.250	5.23	18	2	0	0	8	1	31.0	36	150	24	18	4	0	0	2	18	1	26	2	2
Noe, Matthew, Everett*	0	1	.000	2.72	23	0	0	0	7	1	36.1	38	170	20	11	4	1	1	1	18	1	35	8	0
Nogowski, Brandon, Everett*	4	5	.444	6.64	16	9	0	0	0	0	59.2	67	313	67	44	8	5	5	2	57	2	60	7	0
Ochsenfeld, Chris, Yakima*	2	0	1.000	2.08	12	0	0	0	7	3	21.2	13	89	6	5	0	1	0	2	13	0	18	3	1
Olivo, Gary, Salem-Keizer*	0	0	.000	24.00	3	0	0	0	3	0	3.0	4	21	11	8	2	1	0	1	6	0	3	0	0
Parker, Beau, Yakima	0	8	.000	9.35	15	12	0	0	1	0	51.0	63	252	59	53	4	3	3	4	32	1	44	10	4
Parker, Brandon, Everett	0	0	.000	9.00	2	1	0	0	0	0	3.0	7	16	3	3	1	0	0	0	0	0	5	1	2
Pederson, Justin, Spokane	5	3	.625	3.44	15	13	0	0	0	0	65.1	61	280	34	25	4	0	2	4	24	0	84	2	2
Petrosian, Ara, Portland	3	1	.750	2.40	29	0	0	0	21	13	45.0	42	190	18	12	1	0	1	3	14	0	37	3	1
Pineiro, Joel, Everett	4	2	.667	5.33	18	6	0	0	9	2	49.0	54	223	33	29	2	0	0	3	18	1	59	3	2
Pohl, Jeff, Salem-Keizer	5	4	.556	4.65	18	8	0	0	3	0	71.2	88	329	51	37	8	3	3	6	20	0	47	6	2
Price, Chris, Portland	3	1	.750	6.06	26	0	0	0	18	1	32.2	41	146	25	22	4	0	1	2	5	0	22	1	0
Puffer, Brandon, Boise	0	0	.000	2.35	6	0	0	0	2	1	15.1	10	63	5	4	0	0	1	1	2	0	15	1	0
Quigley, Donald, Spokane	4	2	.667	5.40	22	1	0	0	6	0	45.0	56	212	35	27	5	2	0	0	21	0	21	2	1
Rawls, Mike, Yakima*	0	2	.000	5.21	22	2	0	0	9	2	38.0	38	176	27	22	4	2	4	3	28	2	27	6	1
Reichert, Dan, Spokane	3	4	.429	2.84	9	9	0	0	0	0	38.0	40	178	25	12	2	0	2	3	16	0	39	2	2
Rice, Nathan, Salem-Keizer*	1	2	.333	5.40	13	0	0	0	4	0	18.1	22	85	13	11	0	0	1	2	7	0	26	5	0
Riley, Michael, Salem-Keizer*	9	2	.818	3.46	15	15	1	0	0	0	88.1	76	375	39	34	9	2	2	4	28	0	96	6	1
Rivera, Alvin, Portland	3	0	1.000	4.99	13	6	0	0	0	0	39.2	41	171	23	22	3	1	1	1	13	0	19	3	1
Roberts, Mike, Eugene	7	6	.538	7.08	15	15	0	0	0	0	75.0	104	359	63	59	7	2	6	7	33	2	33	3	3
Rodriguez, Hector, Boise	5	1	.833	2.38	25	0	0	0	6	2	41.2	35	194	16	11	0	0	3	3	30	1	55	9	0
Roeder, Jason, Spokane	2	1	.667	7.23	9	0	0	0	2	0	18.2	29	93	20	15	3	2	1	0	6	1	14	1	0
Rosa, Cristy, Portland	4	2	.667	5.56	21	0	0	0	2	1	43.2	54	200	32	27	4	3	0	2	14	0	35	2	0

Pitcher, Team	W	L	Pct.	ERA	G	GS	CG	ShO	GF	Sv.	IP	H	TBF	R	ER	HR	SH	SF	HB	BB	IBB	SO	WP	Bk.
Schmalz, Darin, Yakima............	3	1	.750	5.13	22	0	0	0	14	1	33.1	45	163	27	19	2	2	1	12	1	29	2	2
Schmidt, Donnie, Portland	4	2	.667	4.97	22	0	0	0	5	2	41.2	47	189	24	23	0	1	0	5	23	0	32	6	0
Schurman, Ryan, Eugene...........	4	6	.400	3.23	16	15	0	0	0	0	86.1	75	379	46	31	8	1	2	5	43	0	95	2	1
Sebring, Jeffrey, Portland*........	2	0	1.000	3.20	13	0	0	0	1	0	25.1	28	110	10	9	1	0	0	1	8	0	27	1	0
Seifert, Ryan, Portland	1	7	.125	4.84	16	15	0	0	0	0	74.1	89	337	49	40	8	0	4	4	31	0	52	3	0
Shields, Scot, Boise	7	2	.778	2.94	30	0	0	0	13	2	52.0	45	225	20	17	1	3	2	3	24	4	61	9	1
Shumate, Jacob, Eugene............	0	2	.000	10.89	19	0	0	0	7	0	20.2	19	126	32	25	1	0	0	2	43	0	23	7	0
Simpson, Allan, Everett.............	0	3	.000	6.84	16	0	0	0	6	0	26.1	26	127	23	20	1	1	1	2	24	1	26	3	0
Snellings, Ryan, Boise*.............	1	2	.333	6.37	12	6	0	0	1	1	29.2	44	147	28	21	5	1	1	0	11	1	27	5	1
Soriano, Jacobo, Boise..............	0	0	.000	6.75	3	0	0	0	3	0	4.0	3	20	3	3	0	0	0	1	4	0	3	0	0
Takahashi, Kurt, Salem-Keizer ...	0	1	.000	3.71	10	1	0	0	2	0	17.0	22	82	9	7	1	1	0	1	8	1	19	1	0
Thieme, Richard, Eugene*..........	5	3	.625	5.81	14	14	0	0	0	0	69.2	92	332	50	45	8	1	3	2	39	0	51	4	0
Thompson, Travis, Portland	5	5	.500	4.50	18	11	0	0	2	0	74.0	88	328	51	37	6	2	2	6	16	0	51	2	0
Thurman, Corey, Spokane	1	2	.333	5.16	5	5	0	0	0	0	22.2	23	106	19	13	2	0	2	2	13	0	24	2	1
Travis, Jesse, Salem-Keizer	0	1	.000	2.45	28	0	0	0	27	16	29.1	24	125	9	8	3	0	1	0	12	0	19	5	0
Verdugo, Jason, Salem-Keizer.....	4	8	.333	4.83	16	14	0	0	0	0	78.1	85	347	48	42	7	5	1	6	25	1	82	1	1
Verigood, Steve, Yakima	0	0	.000	5.35	21	0	0	0	12	0	33.2	46	164	26	20	2	2	1	1	13	2	33	2	1
Vizcaino, Luis, So. Oregon	1	6	.143	7.93	22	5	0	0	7	0	47.2	62	237	51	42	5	1	5	3	27	0	42	14	0
Wagner, Denny, So. Oregon	1	1	.500	15.43	10	4	0	0	1	0	14.0	29	86	27	24	3	0	0	1	14	0	11	8	1
Waites, David, So. Oregon	0	0	.000	6.75	1	0	0	0	0	0	1.1	3	8	1	1	0	0	0	0	0	0	0	0	0
Walls, Doug, Portland	1	0	1.000	1.23	5	5	0	0	0	0	22.0	19	92	3	3	0	0	1	0	10	0	23	1	0
Williams, Kris, Boise	2	3	.400	3.43	19	1	0	0	4	1	39.1	47	186	33	15	0	4	1	2	14	1	35	12	0
Wilson, Kris, Spokane	5	3	.625	4.52	15	15	0	0	0	0	73.2	101	345	50	37	6	0	3	5	21	1	72	1	2
Wise, Jim, Eugene*..................	2	0	1.000	3.77	22	0	0	0	7	2	43.0	59	210	34	18	3	2	0	3	20	0	31	4	1
Wise, Matt, Boise	9	1	.900	3.25	15	15	0	0	0	0	83.0	62	342	37	30	5	0	1	2	34	0	86	7	3
Wyatt, Ben, Eugene*................	0	10	.000	7.02	15	15	0	0	0	0	59.0	88	311	65	46	10	0	4	1	42	1	47	13	1
Yanz, Eric, Spokane	0	2	.000	12.18	8	5	0	0	0	0	17.0	28	92	27	23	2	3	1	3	12	0	17	4	1
Zimmerman, Jordan, Everett*.....	2	3	.400	4.15	11	9	0	0	1	0	39.0	37	177	32	18	2	0	3	3	23	0	54	1	2

COMBINATION SHUTOUTS: **Boise (0)**—None. **Eugene (3)**—Schurman-Allen, Schurman-Wise, Greene-Newell. **Everett (3)**—Meche-Simpson-Bello, Mears-Christianson-Noe, Gonzalez-Christianson-Noe. **Portland (2)**—Miller-Rosa, Thompson-Petrosian. **Salem-Keizer (1)**—Pohl-Joseph. **Southern Oregon (2)**—DuBose-Manwiller-Nina, Jones-Faust-Jensen. **Spokane (2)**—Alexander-Quigley, Wilson-Lamber. **Yakima (0)**—None.

NO-HIT GAMES: None.

1997 FIELDING

TEAM

Team	Pct.	G	PO	A	E	TC	DP	PB	Team	Pct.	G	PO	A	E	TC	DP	PB
Portland	.959	76	2011	821	122	2954	73	27	Southern Oregon ...	.949	76	2038	905	158	3101	64	47
Boise......................	.953	76	2079	865	144	3088	47	25	Yakima...................	.944	76	2021	853	171	3045	72	50
Salem-Keizer..........	.951	76	2000	737	142	2879	65	25	Everett...................	.942	76	2018	769	173	2960	53	37
Spokane.................	.950	76	2055	830	153	3038	56	36	TRIPLE PLAYS: None.								
Eugene..................	.949	76	2015	842	152	3009	65	25									

INDIVIDUAL

FIRST BASEMEN

NOTE: All caps denotes fielding-percentage leader based on 38 games for catchers, 51 for all other non-pitchers and 76 innings for pitchers. *Throws lefthanded.

Player, Team	Pct.	G	PO	A	E	TC	DP
Ankrum, C.J., Salem-Keizer*	.991	73	609	49	6	664	53
Arnold, John, Eugene................	.960	4	23	1	1	25	3
Blosser, Doug, Spokane.............	.962	35	274	7	11	292	17
Brambilla, Michael, Spokane.......	.939	10	87	5	6	98	8
BURKE, Mark, Eugene*	.993	62	521	26	4	551	47
Clifford, John, Portland	.950	3	18	1	1	20	0
Connors, Greg, Everett..............	.980	31	229	20	5	254	17
Delgado, Ariel, Boise*	.989	10	88	3	1	92	6
Faircloth, Chad, Salem-Keizer	1.000	4	32	2	0	34	2
Farris, Ed, So. Oregon	.988	34	300	28	4	332	23
Johnson, Duan, Everett	.983	17	114	3	2	119	7
King, Willie, Yakima	.972	35	300	10	9	319	31
Kirkpatrick, Brian, Portland	1.000	1	9	0	0	9	0
Kokinda, Steven, Everett	.974	18	134	13	4	151	11
Leach, Nick, Yakima	.975	45	356	33	10	399	35
Martin, Casey, Boise	.982	12	107	4	2	113	11
Maynard, Scott, Everett	.944	9	57	10	4	71	3
Montas, Ricardo, Spokane	1.000	3	3	1	0	4	0
Mosier, Mark, Salem-Keizer	1.000	1	2	0	0	2	0
Petersen, Mike, Portland	.990	11	97	7	1	105	8
Piatt, Adam, So. Oregon	1.000	1	3	0	0	3	0
Pierce, Brett, Eugene	1.000	1	1	0	0	1	0
Rodriguez, Guillermo, S.-K.	1.000	1	2	0	0	2	1
Schwartzbauer, Whitey, Portland	1.000	1	1	0	0	1	1
Sears, Todd, Portland	.989	55	509	23	6	538	49
Sosa, Nicolas, So. Oregon	.984	47	398	28	7	433	34
Stewart, Paxton, Boise	.991	61	551	29	5	585	29
Strangfeld, Aaron, Eugene	.975	11	111	4	3	118	9
Williams, Patrick, Everett...........	.958	10	67	2	3	72	6
Willis, Dave, Spokane	.985	44	302	18	5	325	28
Zaun, Brian, Yakima..................	1.000	1	7	0	0	7	0
Zweifel, Kent, Portland...............	.974	8	71	3	2	76	8

SECOND BASEMEN

Player, Team	Pct.	G	PO	A	E	TC	DP
Allen, Shane, Yakima	.941	4	6	10	1	17	3
Alviso, Jerome, Portland	.975	43	81	116	5	202	31
Caruso, Joe, Spokane	.959	51	97	137	10	244	22
Clark, Jermaine, Everett	.957	55	81	119	9	209	17
Clark, John, Portland	.907	9	18	21	4	43	5
Franklin, Jason, Portland	.923	3	5	7	1	13	0
Gorrie, Brad, So. Oregon	.918	20	30	37	6	73	6
GOUDIE, Harvey, Yakima............	.971	51	122	143	8	273	38
Hargrove, Harvey, Everett	.900	3	1	8	1	10	2
Hernandez, Victor, So. Oregon......	.882	6	15	15	4	34	7
Hines, Pooh, Eugene	.989	16	45	45	1	91	8
Johns, Michael, Portland	.900	23	35	64	11	110	13
Lara, Edward, So. Oregon	.985	25	63	70	2	135	12
Leggett, Adam, Boise	.939	59	95	167	17	279	24
Martinez, Victor, Everett............	.950	5	6	13	1	20	2
Medosch, Keith, Boise	.971	21	43	56	3	102	6
Metzler, Rod, Spokane	.971	30	68	67	4	139	11
Montas, Ricardo, Spokane	1.000	1	1	0	0	1	0
Petru, Rich, Spokane	.800	5	4	4	2	10	1
Pierce, Brett, Eugene	1.000	1	1	0	0	1	0
Robinson, Adam, So. Oregon	.993	34	61	90	1	152	16
Saitta, Rich, Yakima	.945	24	53	68	7	128	12
Sanchez, Manuel, Eugene	.933	54	123	140	19	282	32
Smith, Brian, Everett	.948	21	39	53	5	97	9
Spiezio, Scott, So. Oregon	.875	1	3	4	1	8	1
Terhune, Mike, Eugene..............	.977	7	20	23	1	44	11

Player, Team	Pct.	G	PO	A	E	TC	DP
Valera, Ramon, Everett	1.000	1	2	3	0	5	0
Young, Travis, Salem-Keizer	.953	76	173	193	18	384	43

THIRD BASEMEN

Player, Team	Pct.	G	PO	A	E	TC	DP
Baeza, Art, Salem-Keizer	.917	4	2	9	1	12	1
Balbuena, Mike, Yakima	.881	15	10	27	5	42	0
Betancourt, Oscar, Boise	.873	68	37	142	26	205	5
Clark, Jermaine, Everett	1.000	1	1	0	0	1	0
Faircloth, Chad, Salem-Keizer	.758	12	8	17	8	33	2
Flores, Eric, Yakima	.846	9	10	12	4	26	3
Flores, Javier, So. Oregon	1.000	3	1	7	0	8	0
Franklin, Jason, Portland	.888	43	36	91	16	143	12
Goris, Braulio, So. Oregon*	.800	1	1	3	1	5	0
Gorrie, Brad, So. Oregon	.896	15	10	33	5	48	1
Hargrove, Harvey, Everett	.870	44	21	66	13	100	4
Hernandez, Victor, So. Oregon..	1.000	8	5	13	0	18	0
Hines, Pooh, Eugene	.857	25	15	51	11	77	2
Johnson, Duan, Everett	.833	32	18	37	11	66	0
Kenna, David, Salem-Keizer	.817	32	28	48	17	93	3
Kirkpatrick, Brian, Portland	1.000	1	2	0	0	2	0
Lara, Edward, So. Oregon	.750	1	1	2	1	4	0
Martinez, Victor, Everett	.870	12	4	16	3	23	0
Medosch, Keith, Boise	.875	3	2	5	1	8	0
Metzler, Rod, Spokane	.750	6	1	2	1	4	1
Mitchell, Andres, Portland	.667	2	0	2	1	3	0
MONTAS, Ricardo, Spokane	.884	56	33	97	17	147	9
Mortimer, Mark, Eugene	1.000	4	0	2	0	2	0
Mosier, Mark, Salem-Keizer	.778	16	6	15	6	27	2
Oquendo, Nelvin, Salem-Keizer ..	1.000	3	1	2	0	3	0
Otero, William, Salem-Keizer	.902	19	10	27	4	41	1
Peckham, Chris, Boise	.792	13	4	15	5	24	1
Petru, Rich, Spokane	1.000	1	1	1	0	2	0
Piatt, Adam, So. Oregon	.861	50	23	107	21	151	7
Pierce, Brett, Eugene	.800	1	0	4	1	5	0
Saitta, Rich, Yakima	.944	12	8	26	2	36	3
Sanchez, Manuel, Eugene	1.000	1	0	1	0	1	0
Schwartzbauer, Whitey, Portland	.976	31	25	57	2	84	5
Smith, Brian, Everett	1.000	3	0	1	0	1	0
Spencer, Jeff, Eugene	.861	44	33	116	24	173	9
Tegland, Ron, So. Oregon	.667	3	1	7	4	12	0
Terhune, Mike, Eugene	.842	7	3	13	3	19	0
Willis, Dave, Spokane	.843	28	22	53	14	89	2
Zaun, Brian, Yakima	.869	44	23	96	18	137	13

SHORTSTOPS

Player, Team	Pct.	G	PO	A	E	TC	DP
Alviso, Jerome, Portland	.961	26	53	95	6	154	19
Baeza, Art, Salem-Keizer	1.000	2	2	4	0	6	1
Bell, Ricky, Yakima	.900	66	99	189	32	320	36
Castro, Al, Eugene	.916	69	74	219	27	320	36
CASTRO, Nelson, Boise	.923	68	80	218	25	323	32
Clark, John, Portland	.920	8	20	26	4	50	7
Flores, Eric, Yakima	.913	9	13	29	4	46	7
Fuentes, Joel, Salem-Keizer	.900	20	32	49	9	90	7
Gorrie, Brad, So. Oregon	.857	8	10	20	5	35	3
Hargrove, Harvey, Everett	.923	17	27	57	7	91	13
Hines, Pooh, Eugene	.500	2	1	1	2	4	1
Illig, Brett, Yakima	1.000	1	3	2	0	5	0
Johns, Michael, Portland	.911	38	54	131	18	203	20
Lara, Edward, So. Oregon	.913	40	60	140	19	219	26
Ligons, Merrell, Spokane	.897	44	70	130	23	223	22
Martinez, Victor, Everett	.778	2	2	5	2	9	0
Medosch, Keith, Boise	.889	12	12	36	6	54	3
Mendoza, Carlos, Salem-Keizer ..	.932	33	48	88	10	146	18
Mitchell, Andres, Portland	.824	6	10	4	3	17	1
Montas, Ricardo, Spokane	.920	13	14	32	4	50	2
Otero, William, Salem-Keizer	.888	28	33	70	13	116	18
Petru, Rich, Spokane	.924	29	31	79	9	119	7
Pierce, Brett, Eugene	.881	13	12	25	5	42	6
Robinson, Adam, So. Oregon	.915	37	32	119	14	165	18
Saitta, Rich, Yakima	.778	2	5	2	2	9	1
Smith, Brian, Everett	.429	2	1	2	4	7	1
Valera, Ramon, Everett	.862	56	109	153	42	304	27

OUTFIELDERS

Player, Team	Pct.	G	PO	A	E	TC	DP
Alamo, Efrain, Portland	.935	68	104	11	8	123	2
Bautista, Francisco, Spokane	.933	12	13	1	1	15	0
Brown, Bobby, Spokane	1.000	10	0	1	0	1	0
Brown, Dermal, Spokane	.921	70	80	2	7	89	0
BYAS, Michael, Salem-Keizer	.980	71	140	6	3	149	0
Camilo, Juan, So. Oregon	.500	4	2	0	2	4	0
Casper, Brett, Salem-Keizer	.910	61	86	5	9	100	2
Child, Casey, Boise	.951	64	94	4	5	103	0
Clifton, Rodney, So. Oregon	.931	69	89	5	7	101	1
Connors, Greg, Everett	1.000	2	1	0	0	1	0
Delgado, Ariel, Boise*	.900	49	58	5	7	70	0
Dougherty, Jeb, Boise	1.000	24	29	4	0	33	0
Eady, Gerald, Everett	.937	67	97	7	7	111	0
Espino, Fernando, Everett	.944	61	94	7	6	107	2
Faircloth, Chad, Salem-Keizer	1.000	15	20	0	0	20	0
Farris, Ed, So. Oregon	.875	9	7	0	1	8	0
Geronimo, Cesar, Boise	.926	49	59	4	5	68	1
Gorrie, Brad, So. Oregon	1.000	14	10	2	0	12	0
Greene, Clay, Salem-Keizer	.974	27	37	0	1	38	0
Hargrove, Harvey, Everett	.833	7	4	1	1	6	0
Haynes, Nathan, So. Oregon*	.970	22	32	0	1	33	0
Hernandez, Victor, So. Oregon	.944	28	32	2	2	36	0
Hines, Pooh, Eugene	1.000	18	26	2	0	28	0
Jackson, Jeremy, Portland	.953	67	139	2	7	148	0
Koerner, Michael, So. Oregon* ..	.961	24	45	4	2	51	0
LeBron, Juan, Spokane	.934	65	104	9	8	121	4
Marchiano, Mike, Everett	.937	47	54	5	4	63	2
Marnell, Dean, Portland	1.000	16	16	0	0	16	0
Martinez, Hipolito, So. Oregon	.955	62	59	4	3	66	0
Medosch, Keith, Boise	.857	9	6	0	1	7	0
Metzler, Rod, Spokane	.963	24	24	2	1	27	0
Mitchell, Andres, Portland	.930	63	100	6	8	114	0
Mortimer, Mark, Eugene	.857	3	6	0	1	7	0
Newton, Kimani, Yakima	.965	55	78	5	3	86	0
Nunley, Jay, Boise	.980	45	47	1	1	49	0
Paterson, Joe, Yakima	.966	37	53	3	2	58	1
Peoples, Derrick, Yakima	.929	37	47	5	4	56	2
Philip-Guide, Sheldon, Boise	.889	15	8	0	1	9	0
Phoenix, Wynter, Yakima	.930	49	89	4	7	100	1
Pierce, Brett, Eugene	.951	35	36	3	2	41	0
Riley, Cash, Yakima	.904	57	96	7	11	114	1
Silvestre, Juan, Everett	.867	14	12	1	2	15	0
Slater, Wayne, Yakima*	.944	14	16	1	1	18	0
Smith, Brian, Everett	.000	2	0	0	1	1	0
Smothers, Stewart, Eugene	.950	58	104	9	6	119	1
Soverel, Bret, Everett	1.000	4	7	0	0	7	0
Stewart, Keith, Everett	.948	37	54	1	3	58	1
Stewart, Paxton, Boise	.750	6	3	0	1	4	0
Strickland, Gregory, Eugene*	.935	52	84	2	6	92	0
Taylor, Kirk, Spokane	.917	21	22	0	2	24	0
Tegland, Ron, So. Oregon	.800	9	8	0	2	10	0
Tomlinson, Goefrey, Spokane*	.972	55	99	6	3	108	2
Underwood, Jake, Everett	1.000	3	4	0	0	4	0
Valderrama, Carlos, S.-K.	.963	20	25	1	1	27	0
Vaz, Roberto, So. Oregon*	.909	13	9	1	1	11	0
Wells, Zachary, Salem-Keizer	.894	42	38	4	5	47	0
Wissen, Collin, Eugene*	.958	72	136	1	6	143	0
Zweifel, Kent, Portland	.970	19	31	1	1	33	0

CATCHERS

Player, Team	Pct.	G	PO	A	E	TC	DP	PB
Alcala, Juan, Everett	.989	9	87	6	1	94	0	2
Arnold, John, Eugene	.992	20	117	11	1	129	1	5
Ashley, Steve, Eugene	1.000	4	31	2	0	33	0	2
Brown, Jason, Yakima	.972	18	127	11	4	142	1	6
Connors, Greg, Everett	.995	21	195	25	1	221	3	6
Dewey, Jason, Boise	.990	52	483	36	5	524	0	19
Figueroa, Jose, So. Oregon	.957	36	291	22	14	327	1	17
Flaherty, Tim, Salem-Keizer	.992	28	225	17	2	244	0	11
Flores, Eric, Yakima	.958	11	79	12	4	95	0	13
Flores, Javier, So. Oregon	.974	36	295	39	9	343	2	12
Folmar, Ryan, Portland	.963	12	69	10	3	82	0	7
Garrick, Matt, Boise	.970	4	28	4	1	33	0	0
Gonzales, Jose, Portland	.977	47	348	30	9	387	3	11
Griffis, Cade, Spokane	1.000	4	5	1	0	6	0	0
Hernandez, John, Yakima	.972	17	94	12	3	109	1	8
Hill, Jeremy, Spokane	.985	60	462	60	8	530	2	29
Horton, Conan, Yakima	1.000	1	5	2	0	7	0	2
Kenna, David, Salem-Keizer	.889	3	7	1	1	9	0	2
Martin, Casey, Boise	.966	14	126	14	5	145	0	3
Maynard, Scott, Everett	.981	12	98	7	2	107	2	5
McCrotty, William, Yakima	.974	41	273	28	8	309	0	23
MORTIMER, Mark, Eugene	.992	43	326	32	3	361	3	10
Nelson, Brian, Everett	.977	10	73	11	2	86	1	3
Pagan, Carlos, Spokane	.989	25	164	17	2	183	1	6
Priess, Matthew, S.-K.	.983	42	316	35	6	357	1	10

CLASS A Northwest League

Player, Team	Pct.	G	PO	A	E	TC	DP	PB
Pugh, Josh, Eugene	.960	21	126	18	6	150	1	8
Rodriguez, Chris, Portland	1.000	20	136	18	0	154	0	9
Rodriguez, Guillermo, S.-K.	.989	9	80	10	1	91	0	2
Russoniello, Michael, Boise	1.000	2	11	2	0	13	0	0
Tegland, Ron, So. Oregon	.933	18	87	11	7	105	1	18
Ullery, David, Spokane	1.000	6	38	5	0	43	0	1
Underwood, Jake, Everett	.979	9	83	11	2	96	2	12
Ussery, Brian, Boise	.964	11	74	7	3	84	0	3
Warren, Lance, Yakima	.875	2	17	4	3	24	0	0
Williams, Patrick, Everett	.991	23	203	15	2	220	1	9

PITCHERS

Player, Team	Pct.	G	PO	A	E	TC	DP
Abreu, Oscar, So. Oregon	.667	20	2	0	1	3	0
ALEXANDER, Jordy, Spokane*	1.000	16	3	13	0	16	2
Allen, Rodney, Eugene	.909	20	4	6	1	11	0
Anderson, Jason P., So. Ore.*	.895	14	4	13	2	19	2
Andra, Jeff, Salem-Keizer*	.900	8	3	6	1	10	1
Ashworth, Kym, Yakima*	.833	4	0	5	1	6	0
Austin, Shawn, Salem-Keizer*	1.000	13	2	3	0	5	1
Backowski, Lance, Yakima	.938	15	5	10	1	16	0
Barber, Andrew, Portland	.889	22	2	6	1	9	0
Bello, Emerson, Everett	1.000	22	2	8	0	10	0
Blumenstock, Brad, So. Oregon	.909	19	4	6	1	11	1
Boring, Richard, Spokane	1.000	26	1	1	0	2	0
Brea, Lesli, Everett	1.000	23	1	2	0	3	0
Burnside, Adrian, Yakima	.857	15	2	10	2	14	0
Burton, Jamie, Spokane*	1.000	7	0	2	0	2	0
Carter, Aaron, Spokane	.800	24	1	3	1	5	0
Christianson, Robby, Everett	.857	20	2	4	1	7	0
Chrysler, Clint, Everett*	1.000	18	3	2	0	5	1
Clark, Richard, Salem-Keizer	1.000	6	0	3	0	3	0
Cummings, Ryan, Boise	.857	14	5	7	2	14	1
DeAbreu, Milton, Salem-Keizer ..	1.000	7	0	1	0	1	0
DeJesus, Tony, Everett*	.727	14	3	5	3	11	0
Dishman, Richard, Eugene	.900	19	2	7	1	10	1
Dobson, Dwayne, Boise	1.000	12	1	1	0	2	0
Donaldson, Bo, Boise	.917	27	4	7	1	12	0
Dunham, Pat, Everett	.667	17	1	1	1	3	0
DuBose, Eric, So. Oregon*	1.000	3	2	3	0	5	1
Enochs, Chris, So. Oregon	1.000	3	1	0	0	1	0
EVERLY, Bill, Yakima	1.000	28	5	11	0	16	1
Farley, Joseph, Salem-Keizer*	.000	10	0	0	2	2	0
Faust, Jason, So. Oregon*	1.000	16	5	5	0	10	1
Fish, Steve, Boise	.889	24	2	14	2	18	2
Fitzpatrick, Ken, Spokane	1.000	12	2	4	0	6	0
Flach, Jason, Eugene	1.000	23	1	6	0	7	0
Gangemi, Joseph, Boise*	.875	16	3	25	4	32	2
Gilfillan, Jason, Spokane	.600	16	1	2	2	5	0
Glaze, Randy, So. Oregon	1.000	21	2	6	0	8	0
Gonzalez, Jose, Everett	.889	6	2	6	1	9	1
Gooding, Jason, Spokane*	.929	11	3	10	1	14	1
Gorrell, Chris, So. Oregon	.889	18	4	4	1	9	0
Graham, Kyle, Yakima*	.875	21	1	6	1	8	0
Greene, Ryan, Eugene	.938	15	5	10	1	16	0
Hannah, Neal, Yakima	.923	22	3	9	1	13	1
Harriger, Mark, Boise	.923	13	4	8	1	13	0
Holmes, Mike, So. Oregon	1.000	7	0	3	0	3	2
Hudson, Tim, So. Oregon	1.000	8	2	3	0	5	0
Hughes, Michael, Boise	.750	11	1	2	1	4	0
Husted, Brent, Yakima	.778	10	1	6	2	9	0
Hutchings, Mark, Salem-Keizer ..	1.000	11	0	1	0	1	0
Jensen, Jared, So. Oregon	.000	23	0	4	0	4	0
Jensen, Ryan, Salem-Keizer	.862	16	6	19	4	29	2
Johnson, David, Portland	.500	18	0	1	1	2	0
Johnson, Eric, Salem-Keizer	.000	10	0	0	1	1	0
Jones, Greg, Boise	.889	21	1	7	1	9	0
Jones, Marcus, So. Oregon	1.000	14	4	7	0	11	0
Joseph, Kevin, Salem-Keizer	.600	17	4	2	4	10	0
Kalinowski, Josh, Portland*	1.000	6	0	2	0	2	0
Karabinus, Chris, Yakima	1.000	2	1	1	0	2	0
Kawahara, Orin, Everett	.700	23	4	3	3	10	1
Kennedy, Ryan, Portland	1.000	6	0	1	0	1	0
Key, Scott, Spokane	.824	25	2	12	3	17	0
Kimball, Andrew, So. Oregon	.824	13	6	8	3	17	0
Knickerbocker, Tom, So. Ore.*	1.000	4	0	4	0	4	1
KRINGEN, Jake, Portland*	1.000	15	4	12	0	16	3
Lagattuta, Rico, So. Oregon*	.667	16	1	1	1	3	0
Lagrandeur, Yan, Eugene	1.000	21	5	3	0	8	0
Lamber, Justin, Spokane*	.750	25	0	3	1	4	0
Larreal, Guillermo, Salem-Keizer	.889	13	2	6	1	9	0
Lebejko, David, Eugene	.900	20	2	7	1	10	1
Linebrink, Scott, Salem-Keizer....	1.000	3	1	0	0	1	0
Lira, Felipe, Everett	1.000	1	0	1	0	1	0
Maestas, Mickey, Yakima	.800	21	2	6	2	10	1
Mahlberg, John, Portland	.909	18	3	7	1	11	0
Malerich, William, S.-K.*	1.000	21	1	3	0	4	0
Manwiller, Tim, So. Oregon	.917	12	4	7	1	12	0
Maynard, Scott, Everett	1.000	1	0	1	0	1	0
Meady, Todd, Spokane	1.000	21	3	8	0	11	1
Mears, Chris, Everett	.800	12	5	7	3	15	0
Meche, Gil, Everett	.967	12	10	19	1	30	3
Miller, Justin, Portland	1.000	14	2	10	0	12	0
Montero, Agus, So. Oregon	1.000	2	0	1	0	1	0
Montgomery, Matthew, Yakima ..	1.000	11	6	9	0	15	1
Moon, Jared, Yakima	.875	11	1	6	1	8	0
Nathan, Joe, Salem-Keizer	.846	18	2	9	2	13	0
Newell, Brett, Eugene	1.000	19	1	3	0	4	0
Nickle, Douglas, Boise	.875	17	0	7	1	8	0
Nielsen, Thomas, Salem-Keizer*	1.000	7	1	2	0	3	1
Niles, Randy, So. Oregon	.900	7	3	6	1	10	1
Nina, Elvin, So. Oregon	.889	18	4	4	1	9	0
Noe, Matthew, Everett*	.857	23	1	5	1	7	0
Nogowski, Brandon, Everett*	.733	16	3	8	4	15	0
Ochsenfeld, Chris, Yakima*	.800	12	2	2	1	5	0
Parker, Beau, Yakima	.786	11	5	10	3	14	0
Pederson, Justin, Spokane	.714	15	1	4	2	7	0
Petrosian, Ara, Portland	.857	29	1	5	1	7	0
Pineiro, Joel, Everett	.818	18	1	8	2	11	2
Pohl, Jeff, Salem-Keizer	1.000	18	3	11	0	14	2
Price, Chris, Portland	1.000	26	1	3	0	4	0
Puffer, Brandon, Boise	1.000	6	2	1	0	3	0
Quigley, Donald, Spokane	.909	22	4	6	1	11	0
Rawls, Mike, Yakima*	.875	22	0	7	1	8	0
Reichert, Dan, Spokane	.900	9	4	5	1	10	0
Rice, Nathan, Salem-Keizer*	.333	13	0	1	2	3	0
Riley, Michael, Salem-Keizer*	.833	15	5	5	2	12	0
Rivera, Alvin, Portland	1.000	13	2	4	0	6	0
Roberts, Mike, Eugene	.762	15	5	11	5	21	0
Rodriguez, Hector, Boise	1.000	25	2	2	0	4	0
Roeder, Jason, Spokane	.667	9	0	2	1	3	0
Rosa, Cristy, Portland	1.000	21	3	4	0	7	0
Schmalz, Darin, Salem-Keizer	.750	22	1	8	3	12	0
Schmidt, Donnie, Portland	1.000	22	2	8	0	10	0
Schurman, Ryan, Eugene	.875	16	3	11	2	16	0
Sebring, Jeffrey, Portland*	1.000	13	0	7	0	7	2
Seifert, Ryan, Portland	1.000	16	3	12	0	15	0
Shields, Scot, Boise	1.000	30	5	10	0	15	0
Shumate, Jacob, Eugene	.750	19	2	1	1	4	0
Simpson, Allan, Everett	1.000	16	1	3	0	4	0
Snellings, Ryan, Boise*	1.000	12	1	6	0	7	1
Soriano, Jacobo, Boise	1.000	3	0	2	0	2	0
Takahashi, Kurt, Salem-Keizer	1.000	10	0	2	0	2	0
Thieme, Richard, Eugene*	.889	14	3	13	2	18	1
Thompson, Travis, Portland	.917	18	1	10	1	12	0
Thurman, Corey, Spokane	1.000	5	4	3	0	7	0
Travis, Jesse, Salem-Keizer	.833	28	3	2	1	6	1
Verdugo, Jason, Salem-Keizer	.933	16	5	9	1	15	1
Verigood, Steve, Yakima*	1.000	21	1	6	0	7	0
Vizcaino, Luis, So. Oregon	1.000	22	5	6	0	11	1
Wagner, Denny, Eugene	1.000	10	2	1	0	3	0
Walls, Doug, Portland	1.000	5	0	3	0	3	0
Williams, Kris, Boise	.625	19	1	4	3	8	0
Wilson, Kris, Spokane	.941	15	4	12	1	17	2
Wise, Jamie, Eugene*	.800	22	6	6	3	15	1
Wise, Matt, Boise	.800	15	2	6	2	10	0
Wyatt, Ben, Eugene*	.800	15	1	7	2	10	0
Yanz, Eric, Spokane	.833	8	3	2	1	6	1
Zimmerman, Jordan, Everett*	.727	11	0	8	3	11	0

The following players did not have any fielding statistics at the positions indicated or appeared only as a designated hitter, pinch-hitter or pinch-runner: Jason A. Anderson, p; Arnold, ss, p; Baeza, c; Bloomfield, p; Clifford, of; Dillon, dh; E. Flores, of; Gallagher, p; Greene, 2b; Griffis, 3b; of; Gutierrez, p; Hargrove, 1b; Harville, p; J. Hernandez, 1b; Du. Johnson, of; Kokinda, of; Lopez, dh; Matos, p; Olivo, p; Br. Parker, p; Pugh, of; Schwartzbauer, 2b; Waites, p.

LEAGUE CHAMPIONS

Year	Team	Pct.
1901—	Portland	.675
1902—	Butte	.608
1903—	Butte	.578
1904—	Boise	.625
1905—	Vancouver	.586
	Everett*	.667
1906—	Tacoma	.600
1907—	Aberdeen	.625
1908—	Vancouver	.578
1909—	Seattle	.653
1910—	Spokane	.596
1911—	Vancouver	.628
1912—	Seattle	.600
1913—	Vancouver	.600
1914—	Vancouver	.632
1915—	Seattle	.564
1916—	Spokane	.622
1917—	Great Falls	.592
1918—	Seattle	.588
1919—	Seattle	.590
1920—	Victoria	.600
1921—	Yakima	.710
	Yakima	.660
1922—	Calgary‡	.600
1923-36—	Did not operate.	
1937—	Wenatchee	.603
	Tacoma*	.627
1938—	Yakima	.583
	Bellingham (2nd)†	.511
1939—	Wenatchee	.601
	Tacoma (2nd)†	.533
1940—	Spokane	.587
	Tacoma (4th)†	.500
1941—	Spokane	.669
1942—	Vancouver	.594
1943-45—	Did not operate.	
1946—	Wenatchee	.622
1947—	Vancouver	.566
1948—	Spokane	.614
1949—	Yakima	.660
	Vancouver (2nd)†	.615
1950—	Yakima	.613
1951—	Spokane	.655
1952—	Victoria	.631
1953—	Salem	.635
	Spokane*	.590
1954—	Vancouver*	.636
	Lewiston	.629
1955—	Salem	.646
	Eugene*	.639
1956—	Yakima	.691
	Yakima	.619
1957—	Eugene	.576
	Wenatchee*	.647
1958—	Lewiston	.621
	Yakima*	.594
1959—	Salem	.623
	Yakima*	.563
1960—	Yakima	.638
	Yakima	.562
1961—	Lewiston*	.621
	Yakima	.600
1962—	Wenatchee*	.574
	Tri-City	.580
1963—	Lewiston	.594
	Yakima*	.613
1964—	Eugene	.636
	Yakima*	.611
1965—	Lewiston	.667
	Tri-City*	.681
1966—	Tri-City	.679
1967—	Medford	.607
1968—	Tri-City	.600
1969—	Rogue Valley	.633
1970—	Lewiston§	.538
	Coos Bay-No. Bend	.563
1971—	Tri-City§	.625
	Bend	.538
1972—	Lewiston§	.675
	Walla Walla	.513
1973—	Walla Walla∞	.638
	Portland	.563
1974—	Bellingham	.619
	Eugene▲	.571
1975—	Portland	.545
	Eugene◆	.684
1976—	Portland	.556
	Walla Walla◆	.639
1977—	Bellingham■	.618
	Portland	.667
1978—	Grays Harbor▼	.671
	Eugene	.514
1979—	Central Oregon◆	.606
	Walla Walla	.571
1980—	Bellingham•	.643
	Eugene•	.529
1981—	Medford◆	.600
	Bellingham	.557
1982—	Medford	.757
	Salem◆	.486
1983—	Medford††	.735
	Bellingham	.588
1984—	Tri-Cities††	.622
	Medford	.608
1985—	Everett††	.541
	Eugene	.541
1986—	Bellingham††	.608
	Eugene	.608
1987—	Spokane▲	.711
	Everett	.653
1988—	Southern Oregon	.605
	Spokane▲	.553
1989—	Southern Oregon	.600
	Spokane◆	.547
1990—	Boise	.697
	Spokane◆	.645
1991—	Boise◆	.658
	Yakima	.579
1992—	Bellingham◆	.566
	Bend	.566
1993—	Bellingham	.579
	Boise◆	.539
1994—	Yakima	.645
	Boise◆	.579
1995—	Boise◆	.640
	Bellingham	.566
1996—	Eugene	.645
	Yakima§	.526
1997—	Boise	.671
	Portland◆	.579

*Won split-season playoff. †Won four-club playoff. ‡League disbanded June 18. §League divided into Northern and Southern divisions, declared champion under league rules. ∞League divided into Eastern and Western divisions, declared champion under league rules. ▲League divided into Eastern and Western divisions; won two-team playoff. ◆League divided into North and South divisions; won two-team playoff. ■League divided into Affiliate and Independent divisions; won two-team playoff. ▼Declared league champion after winning one-game playoff. Balance of playoff canceled due to rain and wet grounds. •Declared co-champion after winning one game. Balance of playoff canceled due to rain and wet grounds. ††League divided into Washington and Oregon divisions; won two-team playoff. (NOTE—Known as Pacific Northwest League 1901-02, Pacific National League 1903-04, Northwestern League 1905-18, Pacific Coast International League 1919-22 and Western International League 1937-54.)

CLASS A *Northwest League*

SOUTH ATLANTIC LEAGUE

LEAGUE OFFICE

President/secretary-treasurer
John Moss

Address
P.O. Box 38
Kings Mountain, NC 28086

Phone
704-739-3466

Teams (affiliation)
Asheville Tourists (Rockies)
Augusta Greenjackets (Pirates)
Capital City Bombers (Mets)
Charleston (S.C.) Riverdogs (Devil Rays)
Charleston (W.Va.) Alley Cats (Reds)
Columbus Redstixx (Indians)
Delmarva Shorebirds (Orioles)

Fayetteville Crocks (Expos)
Greensboro Bats (Yankees)
Hagerstown Suns (Blue Jays)
Hickory Crawdads (White Sox)
Macon Braves (Braves)
Piedmont Bollweevils (Phillies)
Savannah Sand Gnats (Dodgers)

1997 FINAL STANDINGS

FIRST HALF

NORTHERN DIVISION

Team	W	L	T	Pct.	GB
Charleston, W.Va. (Reds)	39	30	0	.565	....
Delmarva (Orioles)	40	31	0	.563	....
Cape Fear (Expos)	36	34	0	.514	3½
Hagerstown (Blue Jays)	31	38	0	.449	8

CENTRAL DIVISION

Team	W	L	T	Pct.	GB
Greensboro (Yankees)	39	29	0	.574	....
Hickory (White Sox)	39	31	0	.557	1
Piedmont (Phillies)	36	35	0	.507	4½
Columbia (Mets)	34	35	0	.493	5½
Charleston, S.C. (Devil Rays)	31	39	0	.443	9
Asheville (Rockies)	27	42	0	.391	12½

SOUTHERN DIVISION

Team	W	L	T	Pct.	GB
Macon (Braves)	42	28	0	.600	....
Augusta (Pirates)	34	37	0	.479	8½
Columbus (Indians)	31	39	0	.443	11
Savannah (Dodgers)	30	41	0	.423	12½

SECOND HALF

NORTHERN DIVISION

Team	W	L	T	Pct.	GB
Charleston, W.Va. (Reds)	37	32	0	.536	....
Delmarva (Orioles)	37	34	0	.521	1
Hagerstown (Blue Jays)	34	35	0	.493	3
Cape Fear (Expos)	30	40	0	.429	7½

CENTRAL DIVISION

Team	W	L	T	Pct.	GB
Columbia (Mets)	43	28	0	.606	....
Hickory (White Sox)	37	33	0	.529	5½
Asheville (Rockies)	35	34	1	.507	7
Greensboro (Yankees)	36	36	1	.500	7½
Piedmont (Phillies)	34	37	0	.479	9
Charleston, S.C. (Devil Rays)	29	43	0	.403	14½

SOUTHERN DIVISION

Team	W	L	T	Pct.	GB
Macon (Braves)	38	32	0	.543	....
Augusta (Pirates)	37	34	0	.521	1½
Savannah (Dodgers)	33	36	0	.478	4½
Columbus (Indians)	31	37	0	.456	6

COMPOSITE

Team	Mac.	CWV	Clb.	Hck.	Del.	Gbr.	Aug.	Pie.	C.F.	Hag.	Sav.	Clm.	Ash.	CSC	W	L	T	Pct.	GB
Macon (Braves)	....	1	6	5	3	4	12	7	1	4	13	13	5	6	80	60	0	.571	....
Charleston, W.Va. (Reds)	2	....	4	5	14	5	1	3	14	13	4	3	2	6	76	62	0	.551	3
Columbia (Mets)	2	4	....	6	4	8	5	9	2	4	7	6	10	10	77	63	0	.550	3
Hickory (White Sox)	3	1	9	....	4	9	3	10	4	6	5	4	9	9	76	64	0	.543	4
Delmarva (Orioles)	1	12	4	4	....	3	2	3	14	18	2	2	6	6	77	65	0	.543	4
Greensboro (Yankees)	4	3	7	7	5	....	3	7	5	5	4	7	13	75	65	1	.536	5
Augusta (Pirates)	14	3	3	5	2	5	....	3	3	2	14	14	2	1	71	71	0	.500	10
Piedmont (Phillies)	1	5	7	6	5	8	5	....	5	2	6	3	7	10	70	72	0	.493	11
Cape Fear (Expos)	2	12	5	4	12	3	1	3	....	10	2	2	5	5	66	74	0	.471	14
Hagerstown (Blue Jays)	0	13	3	2	8	3	2	6	16	....	1	2	5	4	65	73	0	.471	14
Savannah (Dodgers)	13	0	1	3	2	3	12	2	2	1	....	16	6	2	63	77	0	.450	17
Columbus (Indians)	13	0	2	4	2	3	12	5	2	2	10	....	4	3	62	76	0	.449	17
Asheville (Rockies)	3	6	6	6	2	8	6	9	3	2	2	2	....	7	62	76	1	.449	17
Charleston, S.C. (Devil Rays)	2	2	6	7	2	3	7	5	3	4	6	5	8	....	60	82	0	.423	21

Major league affiliations in parentheses.

PLAYOFFS: Delmarva defeated Hickory, two games to none; Charleston, W.Va. defeated Cape Fear, two games to none; Greensboro defeated Columbia, two games to none; Macon defeated Augusta, two games to one; Delmarva defeated Charleston, W.Va., two games to one; Greensboro defeated Macon, two games to none; Delmarva defeated Greensboro, two games to none, to win league championship.

REGULAR-SEASON ATTENDANCE: Asheville, 143,351; Augusta, 152,270; Cape Fear, 69,873; Charleston, S.C., 231,006; Charleston, W.Va., 88,378; Columbia, 135,670; Columbus, 119,646; Delmarva, 324,412; Greensboro, 146,987; Hagerstown, 115,011; Hickory, 196,394; Macon, 129,723; Piedmont, 114,646; Savannah, 125,729. Total—2,093,096. Playoffs (16 games)—21,906. All-Star Game at Augusta—4,153.

MANAGERS: Asheville, Ron Gideon; Augusta, Jeff Richardson (through June 15) and Scott Little (June 16 to end of season); Cape Fear, Phil Stephenson; Charleston, S.C., Scott Fletcher; Charleston, W.Va., Barry Lyons; Columbia, Doug Mansolino (through June 15) and John Stephenson (June 18 to end of season); Columbus, Jack Mull (through July 20) and Boyd Coffie (July 21-August 13) and Harry Spilman (August 14 to end of season); Delmarva, Tommy Shields; Greensboro, Tom Nieto; Hagerstown, J.J. Cannon; Hickory, Chris Cron; Macon, Brian Snitker; Piedmont, Ken Oberkfell; Savannah, John Shelby. Managerial record of teams with more than one manager: Augusta, Richardson 34-37, Little 37-34; Columbia, Mansolino 11-13, Stephenson 66-50; Columbus, Mull 44-53, Coffie 6-17, Spilman 12-6.

ALL-STAR TEAM: 1B—Luis Lopez, Hagerstown; 2B—Brent Abernathy, Hagerstown; 3B—Ryan Minor, Delmarva; SS—Jimmy Rollins, Piedmont; Utility INF—Jason Parsons, Charleston, W.Va.; OF—Jeff Inglin, Hickory; Alex Sanchez, Charleston, S.C.; Mark Hamlin, Asheville; Utility OF—McKay Christensen, Hickory; C—Jason LaRue, Charleston, W.Va.; DH—Steve Hacker, Macon; RHP—Grant Roberts, Columbia; LHP—Bruce Chen, Macon; Manager of the Year—Brian Snitker, Macon; Coach of the Year—Glenn Hubbard, Macon; Marc Ross, Macon; Most Valuable Player—Luis Lopez, Hagerstown; Most Outstanding Pitcher—Grant Roberts, Columbia; Most Outstanding Major League Prospect—Ryan Minor, Delmarva; General Manager of the Year—Keith Lupton, Delmarva.

TEAM

Team	Avg.	G	TPA	AB	R	H	TB	2B	3B	HR	RBI	SH	SF	HP	BB	IBB	SO	SB	CS	GDP	LOB	ShO	Slg.	OBP
Hickory	.278	140	5383	4771	748	1327	1950	272	39	91	666	37	61	68	446	8	940	127	73	84	961	4	.409	.344
Hagerstown	.272	138	5119	4617	644	1254	1881	293	23	96	583	28	44	59	371	11	1032	118	73	83	920	6	.407	.331
Charl. (W.Va.)	.264	138	5150	4533	695	1198	1734	235	35	77	631	44	47	61	465	8	1074	192	69	55	924	4	.383	.338
Cape Fear	.259	140	5245	4712	634	1222	1777	230	38	83	575	37	43	49	404	12	848	181	85	101	909	6	.377	.322
Macon	.255	140	5300	4757	689	1213	1920	222	31	141	623	31	33	56	423	10	1101	162	69	72	954	6	.404	.321
Greensboro	.252	141	5187	4667	641	1174	1794	233	33	107	570	19	42	68	391	5	1162	147	68	67	914	6	.384	.316
Delmarva	.250	142	5394	4729	668	1182	1772	241	38	91	589	48	37	70	510	18	1148	232	97	89	963	11	.375	.330
Piedmont	.250	142	5313	4786	624	1195	1670	216	35	63	556	52	36	70	369	12	967	173	51	77	952	9	.349	.311
Asheville	.249	139	5196	4569	599	1136	1581	207	14	70	531	89	23	78	437	8	940	180	78	114	938	12	.346	.323
Columbus	.248	138	5332	4696	658	1163	1827	201	47	123	598	52	29	64	491	6	1278	99	43	80	1011	11	.389	.325
Charl. (S.C.)	.243	142	5219	4662	563	1132	1563	213	25	56	498	45	42	37	433	17	977	255	125	70	895	14	.335	.310
Augusta	.242	142	5308	4635	642	1120	1606	193	31	77	554	54	39	63	517	15	1111	218	91	79	940	6	.346	.324
Columbia	.239	140	4979	4457	564	1067	1540	190	26	77	515	35	31	45	411	7	1124	172	75	60	885	15	.346	.308
Savannah	.229	140	5026	4507	560	1034	1574	174	42	94	488	25	29	55	410	10	1164	111	58	78	870	14	.349	.300

INDIVIDUAL

TOP QUALIFIERS FOR BATTING CHAMPIONSHIP

Minimum 383 plate appearances. *Lefthanded batter. †Switch-hitter.

Player, Team	Avg.	G	TPA	AB	R	H	TB	2B	3B	HR	RBI	SH	SF	HP	BB	IBB	SO	SB	CS	GDP	Slg.	OBP
Lopez, Luis, Hagerstown	.358	136	577	503	96	180	268	47	4	11	99	0	6	8	60	4	45	5	8	14	.533	.430
Giles, Tim, Hagerstown*	.334	112	435	380	54	127	195	32	0	12	56	0	7	2	46	4	95	2	2	8	.513	.402
Inglin, Jeff, Hickory	.334	135	598	536	100	179	273	34	6	16	102	0	9	4	49	4	87	31	8	12	.509	.388
Hacker, Steve, Macon	.324	117	508	460	80	149	285	35	1	33	119	0	9	5	34	7	91	1	0	5	.620	.370
LaRue, Jason, Cha. (W.Va.)	.315	132	534	473	78	149	229	50	3	8	81	1	8	5	47	0	90	14	4	8	.484	.377
Parsons, Jason, Cha. (W.Va.)	.311	131	541	460	87	143	237	34	0	20	102	0	5	14	62	5	99	5	1	5	.515	.405
Pickering, Calvin, Delmarva*	.311	122	509	444	88	138	246	31	1	25	79	0	1	9	53	2	139	6	3	14	.554	.394
Abernathy, Brent, Hagerstown	.309	99	423	379	69	117	151	27	2	1	26	6	2	6	30	0	32	22	13	6	.398	.367
Minor, Ryan, Delmarva	.307	134	558	488	83	150	266	42	1	24	97	0	4	15	51	2	102	7	3	8	.545	.387
Sheppard, Greg, Hickory	.307	102	400	342	54	105	172	27	2	12	62	2	4	6	46	1	81	4	2	7	.503	.394
Ramirez, Daniel, Columbia	.305	130	532	478	82	146	181	24	4	1	42	3	4	4	44	0	104	51	25	4	.379	.367
Konrady, Dennis, Columbus*	.301	107	444	365	60	110	145	23	3	2	43	7	5	5	62	0	60	15	7	6	.397	.405
Francia, David, Piedmont*	.300	112	480	424	72	127	192	24	7	9	65	4	8	19	25	2	61	39	12	5	.453	.359
Camilli, Jason, Cape Fear	.298	98	441	396	57	118	166	35	2	3	43	7	2	5	31	0	64	22	11	7	.419	.355
Hamlin, Mark, Asheville	.290	134	576	497	79	144	229	31	0	18	74	1	8	15	55	1	107	6	3	13	.461	.372

DEPARTMENTAL LEADERS: G—Rollins, 139; AB—Rollins, 560; R—Inglin, 100; H—Lopez, 180; TB—Hacker, 285; 2B—LaRue, 50; 3B—Christensen, 12; HR—Hacker, 33; RBI—Hacker, 119; SH—Hutchison, 16; SF—Becker, Inglin, Hacker, 9 each; HP—Francia, 19; BB—DeCinces, 97; IBB—Hacker, 7; SO—Hessman, 167; SB—Sanchez, 92; CS—Sanchez, 40; GIDP—Pond, 22; Slg.—Hacker, .620; OBP—Lopez, .430.

ALL PLAYERS

*Lefthanded batter. †Switch-hitter.

Player, Team	Avg.	G	TPA	AB	R	H	TB	2B	3B	HR	RBI	SH	SF	HP	BB	IBB	SO	SB	CS	GDP	Slg.	OBP
Abernathy, Brent, Hagerstown	.309	99	423	379	69	117	151	27	2	1	26	6	2	6	30	0	32	22	13	6	.398	.367
Acevedo, Jose, Cha. (W.Va.)	.000	15	1	1	0	0	0	0	0	0	0	0	0	0	0	0	0	0	0	0	.000	.000
Alamo, Efrain, Asheville	.232	34	134	125	17	29	41	9	0	1	14	2	0	1	6	0	49	2	3	3	.328	.273
Allen, Brandon, Piedmont*	1.000	25	3	1	1	1	1	0	0	0	0	1	0	0	1	0	0	0	0	0	1.000	1.000
Alley, Chip, Delmarva†	.236	82	296	250	19	59	87	17	1	3	32	1	2	8	34	3	45	7	2	5	.348	.344
Anderson, Blake, Asheville†	.267	73	281	247	30	66	100	9	2	7	31	1	0	0	32	2	50	2	5	7	.405	.351
Anderson, Christopher, CSC	.188	68	241	223	27	42	71	17	0	4	28	2	1	2	13	1	87	3	1	5	.318	.238
Antczak, Chuck, Hickory	1.000	1	2	1	0	1	1	0	0	0	1	0	1	0	0	0	0	0	0	0	1.000	.500
Anthony, Brian, Asheville*	.257	83	322	296	41	76	131	17	1	12	49	1	0	2	23	0	75	4	4	6	.443	.315
Antrim, Pat, Greensboro†	.225	68	180	173	23	39	42	3	0	0	13	0	0	0	7	0	40	3	2	1	.243	.256
Arias, Rogelio, Asheville	.239	72	267	251	23	60	70	4	0	2	19	5	0	1	10	0	21	4	2	6	.279	.271
Arnold, John, Macon	.429	2	8	7	2	3	6	0	0	1	1	0	0	0	1	0	0	0	0	0	.857	.500
Arrendondo, Hernando, CSC	.235	6	17	17	0	4	5	1	0	0	1	0	0	0	0	0	0	0	0	1	.294	.235
Aylor, Brian, Greensboro*	.160	61	201	181	25	29	71	7	4	9	28	0	4	0	16	0	90	3	0	2	.392	.224
Bain, Tyler, Cha. (S.C.)*	.242	118	504	429	56	104	134	17	2	3	42	5	1	3	66	4	79	33	19	2	.312	.347
Bair, Rod, Asheville	.281	91	384	356	50	100	146	20	1	8	51	3	1	11	13	1	51	9	6	11	.410	.325
Baksh, Ray, Greensboro	.167	4	6	6	1	1	1	0	0	0	2	0	0	0	0	0	2	0	0	0	.167	.167
Barner, Doug, Cha. (S.C.)	.222	93	355	302	35	67	107	17	1	7	40	1	2	7	43	0	87	1	3	4	.354	.331
Baston, Stanley, Hagerstown	.212	19	78	66	8	14	18	2	1	0	9	1	2	1	8	0	17	3	1	0	.273	.299
Batts, Rodney, Piedmont	.224	24	80	67	8	15	23	3	1	1	7	1	1	0	11	0	19	1	1	0	.343	.329
Becker, Brian, Cha. (S.C.)	.235	135	561	494	55	116	184	31	2	11	70	0	9	4	53	3	120	12	1	12	.372	.309
Bellenger, Butch, Augusta	.167	4	13	12	1	2	3	1	0	0	0	0	0	0	1	0	4	0	0	0	.250	.231
Benjamin, Al, Augusta	.143	5	15	14	2	2	2	0	0	0	1	1	0	0	0	0	3	1	0	0	.143	.143
Bennett, Ryan, Columbia	.190	19	47	42	6	8	9	1	0	0	3	0	0	0	5	0	15	0	0	1	.214	.277
Bergeron, Peter, Savannah*	.280	131	569	492	89	138	181	18	5	5	36	5	3	2	67	3	110	32	21	5	.368	.367
Bishop, Tim, Columbia	.204	14	57	49	4	10	12	2	0	0	2	1	0	1	6	0	16	7	2	0	.245	.304
Blakeney, Mo, Cape Fear	.265	17	52	49	10	13	26	1	0	4	7	0	0	0	3	0	12	3	1	2	.531	.308
Blandford, Paul, Cape Fear	.289	113	447	398	63	115	161	23	4	5	40	4	3	2	40	1	50	20	13	11	.405	.354
Borges, Alex, Macon	.195	39	132	118	14	23	34	2	0	3	14	4	0	2	8	0	45	1	0	3	.288	.258
Bramlett, Jeff, Savannah	.187	102	396	326	49	61	126	11	6	14	42	0	3	12	49	1	122	2	1	7	.387	.313
Bravo, Danny, Cape Fear†	.269	73	272	253	28	68	88	9	1	3	34	3	3	4	9	0	31	3	4	4	.348	.301

CLASS A *South Atlantic League*

Player, Team	Avg.	G	TPA	AB	R	H	TB	2B	3B	HR	RBI	SH	SF	HP	BB	IBB	SO	SB	CS	GDP	Slg.	OBP
Broach, Donald, Cha. (W.Va.)	.300	18	78	60	15	18	18	0	0	0	8	0	2	5	11	0	9	8	1	1	.300	.436
Brown, Eric, Savannah	.242	61	233	211	26	51	88	10	3	7	22	0	3	1	17	0	74	12	1	3	.417	.297
Brown, Gavin, Macon	.233	66	262	227	27	53	73	7	2	3	25	0	2	3	30	0	40	8	4	11	.322	.328
Bruce, Robert, Columbus	.248	69	281	234	42	58	101	8	1	11	36	3	1	10	33	0	69	6	0	5	.432	.363
Bryant, Clint, Asheville	.268	63	252	220	30	59	77	12	0	2	25	4	3	5	19	0	62	9	3	4	.350	.336
Burress, Andy, Cha. (W.Va.)	.207	38	93	87	12	18	24	0	0	2	14	0	2	0	4	0	26	1	0	3	.276	.237
Butler, Garrett, Greensboro†	.194	82	257	237	31	46	65	14	1	1	14	4	1	4	11	0	58	11	5	4	.274	.241
Camilli, Jason, Cape Fear	.298	98	441	396	57	118	166	35	2	3	43	7	2	5	31	0	64	22	11	7	.419	.355
Campbell, Wylie, Cha. (W.Va.)†	.272	121	515	453	73	123	149	18	4	0	36	10	3	8	41	0	80	34	12	2	.329	.341
Carney, Bartt, Delmarva†	.100	14	36	30	3	3	4	1	0	0	1	1	0	0	5	0	10	4	1	0	.133	.229
Casimiro, Carlos, Delmarva	.243	122	494	457	54	111	175	21	8	9	51	4	2	5	26	1	108	20	13	11	.383	.290
Chancey, Bailey, Columbia†	.247	30	104	85	12	21	21	0	0	0	7	4	1	1	13	0	19	5	2	0	.247	.350
Charles, Curtis, Delmarva	.193	95	264	244	29	47	72	12	2	3	8	2	0	2	16	0	104	20	10	0	.295	.248
Chatman, Karl, Cape Fear	.233	121	495	443	65	103	152	19	6	6	50	0	5	6	41	0	131	26	4	9	.343	.303
Chavez, Eric, Delmarva	.224	24	99	85	10	19	26	4	0	1	12	1	2	1	10	2	23	1	0	4	.306	.306
Christensen, McKay, Hickory*	.280	127	578	503	95	141	192	12	12	5	47	4	6	11	52	0	61	28	20	2	.382	.357
Clark, Kirby, Piedmont*	.175	42	155	143	18	25	33	8	0	0	10	1	1	0	10	0	50	0	1	0	.231	.227
Claybrook, Steve, Cha. (W.Va.)*	.241	95	282	249	38	60	75	6	3	1	21	3	0	2	28	1	68	22	10	1	.301	.323
Coffie, Evanon, Delmarva*	.275	90	341	305	41	84	117	14	5	3	48	1	6	4	23	1	45	19	10	5	.384	.328
Cooley, Shannon, Piedmont*	.266	90	319	304	35	81	102	16	1	1	28	2	1	2	10	1	57	5	4	4	.336	.293
Corps, Erick, Cha. (S.C.)†	.229	57	237	188	28	43	55	9	0	1	22	4	1	2	42	0	49	14	6	0	.293	.373
Cortes, David, Macon	.000	27	1	1	0	0	0	0	0	0	0	0	0	0	0	0	0	0	0	0	.000	.000
Crane, Todd, Piedmont	.290	80	357	314	50	91	119	13	0	5	35	6	3	4	30	1	57	26	6	4	.379	.356
Crawford, Marty, Piedmont*	.226	108	429	389	37	88	117	15	1	4	51	2	4	4	30	3	51	3	1	10	.301	.286
Crede, Bradley, Piedmont	.214	110	450	402	52	86	136	18	1	10	47	1	3	12	32	1	145	0	3	3	.338	.290
Crede, Joe, Hickory	.271	113	433	402	45	109	149	25	0	5	62	0	2	5	24	0	83	3	1	6	.371	.319
Cuevas, Trent, Savannah	.233	90	334	313	42	73	119	10	3	10	41	1	2	5	13	1	59	3	1	10	.380	.273
Daedelow, Craig, Delmarva	.267	101	310	277	37	74	96	17	1	1	35	5	4	0	24	1	46	11	5	9	.347	.321
Davis, Albert, Augusta	.240	77	339	279	51	67	104	13	3	6	40	5	1	5	49	1	67	27	8	2	.373	.362
DeCelle, Mike, Cha. (S.C.)*	.223	48	186	157	23	35	47	7	1	1	17	0	4	4	21	2	39	8	8	6	.299	.323
DeCinces, Tim, Delmarva*	.257	127	520	416	65	107	166	20	0	13	70	1	3	0	97	1	117	3	4	10	.399	.395
Dellaero, Jason, Hickory†	.277	55	214	191	37	53	87	10	3	6	29	0	3	3	17	0	49	3	1	6	.455	.341
Delossantos, Eddy, Cha. (S.C.)	.234	127	463	432	46	101	122	11	2	2	40	5	4	2	20	0	101	8	9	3	.282	.269
Denning, Wes, Cape Fear*	.248	137	604	557	77	138	197	24	10	5	50	5	1	10	31	0	97	34	13	5	.354	.299
Dent, Darrell, Delmarva*	.234	128	521	441	69	103	131	17	4	1	37	7	6	4	63	2	110	60	15	2	.297	.331
Diaz, Juan, Savannah	.230	127	517	460	63	106	209	24	2	25	83	1	4	4	48	2	155	2	2	10	.454	.306
Downs, Brian, Hickory	.232	25	85	82	8	19	35	4	0	4	7	0	0	0	3	0	22	0	0	0	.427	.259
Duverge, Salvadore, Asheville	.223	28	114	94	7	21	32	3	1	2	8	1	0	6	13	0	23	4	1	2	.340	.354
Edmondson, Tracy, Columbia	.191	50	150	131	16	25	36	6	1	1	12	1	1	1	16	0	38	1	1	0	.275	.282
Edwards, Lamont, Piedmont	.249	106	424	386	48	96	124	16	3	2	53	7	1	1	29	0	68	18	7	9	.321	.302
Edwards, Randy, Augusta	.067	6	19	15	2	1	1	0	0	0	0	0	0	0	4	0	2	0	0	1	.067	.263
Elam, Brett, Asheville	.243	96	387	337	44	82	102	12	1	2	30	9	3	2	35	0	58	8	5	8	.303	.316
Emmons, Scott, Greensboro	.286	3	8	7	1	2	3	1	0	0	0	0	0	1	0	0	1	0	0	0	.429	.375
Engle, Beau, Columbia	.300	6	13	10	0	3	3	0	0	0	2	0	0	1	2	0	3	0	0	0	.300	.462
Erickson, Corey, Columbia	.214	49	189	173	18	37	58	11	2	2	16	1	3	1	11	0	49	3	1	2	.335	.261
Espada, Angel, Columbia	.324	30	116	102	17	33	39	6	0	0	7	5	0	0	9	0	9	8	4	0	.382	.378
Evans, Lee, Augusta†	.194	54	202	186	19	36	55	9	2	2	23	0	1	1	14	1	52	6	3	5	.296	.252
Evans, Pat, Columbus†	.181	32	104	83	13	15	20	3	1	0	5	3	1	0	17	0	19	0	2	2	.241	.317
Fagley, Dan, Hickory	.200	9	25	20	4	4	6	2	0	0	2	1	0	0	4	0	9	0	0	0	.300	.333
Fauske, Joshua, Hickory	.235	98	398	344	56	81	150	24	0	15	60	0	5	10	38	0	76	1	0	4	.436	.325
Figueroa, Franky, Delmarva	.179	7	28	28	2	5	6	1	0	0	3	0	0	0	0	0	8	0	0	2	.214	.179
Figueroa, Luis, Augusta†	.226	71	295	248	38	56	64	8	0	0	21	9	2	1	35	0	29	22	6	2	.258	.322
Flores, Eric, Savannah	.077	5	17	13	0	1	1	0	0	0	0	0	0	0	4	0	7	0	0	1	.077	.294
Foulks, Brian, Savannah	.105	20	59	57	2	6	11	2	0	1	3	0	0	0	2	0	21	1	1	0	.193	.136
Fowler, Ben, Columbus†	.183	19	63	60	5	11	15	1	0	1	7	0	0	1	2	0	26	1	0	0	.250	.222
Fowler, Maleke, Delmarva	.230	105	367	339	49	78	91	9	2	0	18	4	0	4	20	0	69	36	16	5	.268	.281
Francia, David, Piedmont*	.300	112	480	424	72	127	192	24	7	9	65	4	8	19	25	2	61	39	12	5	.453	.359
Freedberg, Todd, Delmarva†	.000	9	1	1	0	0	0	0	0	0	0	0	0	0	0	0	1	0	0	0	.000	.000
Frias, Ovidio, Hickory	.231	33	118	108	10	25	30	3	1	0	11	1	2	1	6	0	20	1	2	3	.278	.274
Garavito, Eddy, Delmarva†	.000	2	4	4	0	0	0	0	0	0	0	0	0	0	0	0	0	0	0	0	.000	.000
Garrett, Scott, Cha. (W.Va.)	.257	33	108	101	9	26	30	4	0	0	14	2	0	1	4	0	39	1	1	1	.297	.292
Giles, Tim, Hagerstown*	.334	112	435	380	54	127	195	32	0	12	56	0	7	2	46	4	95	2	2	8	.513	.402
Glassey, Josh, Savannah*	.184	73	246	207	17	38	43	5	0	0	20	3	1	0	35	0	72	3	1	3	.208	.300
Glavine, Michael, Columbus*	.239	114	481	397	62	95	195	16	0	28	75	0	1	3	80	1	127	0	1	9	.491	.370
Gonzalez, Manuel, Hickory†	.275	116	510	469	70	129	187	21	2	11	54	7	5	1	28	1	78	31	12	11	.399	.314
Goodhart, Steve, Cha. (W.Va.)	.226	81	299	252	26	57	69	5	2	1	28	8	5	2	32	0	66	7	3	4	.274	.313
Gordon, Gary, Asheville	.199	79	282	231	34	46	53	5	1	0	18	11	0	8	32	0	73	21	10	6	.229	.317
Guthrie, David, Cha. (W.Va.)	.215	73	264	233	27	50	70	7	2	3	26	3	1	7	20	0	75	6	2	5	.300	.295
Guzman, Cristian, Greensboro†	.273	124	528	495	68	135	176	21	4	4	52	4	2	10	17	0	105	23	12	3	.356	.309
Hacker, Steve, Macon	.324	117	508	460	80	149	285	35	1	33	119	0	9	5	34	7	91	1	0	5	.620	.370
Haltiangber, Garrick, Columbia	.261	125	499	441	59	115	180	19	2	14	73	1	2	10	45	0	107	20	7	4	.408	.341
Hamlin, Mark, Asheville	.290	134	576	497	79	144	229	31	0	18	74	1	8	15	55	1	107	6	3	13	.461	.372
Hampton, Robby, Hagerstown	.211	100	364	337	32	71	122	22	1	9	34	0	3	1	23	0	124	9	3	6	.362	.261
Harkrider, Kip, Savannah*	.183	18	75	71	8	13	13	0	0	0	4	1	1	0	2	0	6	0	0	1	.183	.203
Heintz, Chris, Hickory	.284	107	432	388	57	110	146	28	1	2	54	2	5	9	28	0	57	1	3	6	.376	.342
Heredia, Maximo, Delmarva	1.000	38	1	1	0	1	1	0	0	0	0	0	0	0	0	0	0	0	0	0	1.000	1.000
Hessman, Michael, Macon	.235	122	508	459	69	108	196	25	0	21	74	0	2	6	41	0	167	0	2	6	.427	.305
Hines, Pooh, Macon	.163	32	122	104	19	17	24	3	2	0	7	0	0	2	16	0	29	3	2	2	.231	.287
Holliday, Hugh, Cha. (W.Va.)*	.333	15	4	3	1	1	1	0	0	0	0	0	0	0	1	0	1	0	0	0	.333	.500
Hollins, Darontaye, Hickory	.235	42	134	115	22	27	48	9	0	4	13	1	2	1	15	0	37	3	1	1	.417	.323
Hooper, Daren, Delmarva	.000	7	17	15	1	0	0	0	0	0	0	0	1	0	1	0	7	1	0	0	.000	.118
Huff, Brent, Columbia	.253	99	389	363	49	92	143	20	5	7	41	1	2	4	19	1	78	11	3	8	.394	.296
Huffman, Ryan, Greensboro	.125	4	10	8	0	1	1	0	0	0	0	0	0	0	2	0	3	0	1	0	.125	.300

Player, Team	Avg.	G	TPA	AB	R	H	TB	2B	3B	HR	RBI	SH	SF	HP	BB	IBB	SO	SB	CS	GDP	Slg.	OBP
Hundt, Bo, Augusta†	.246	111	448	407	56	100	143	21	2	6	42	3	4	10	24	1	109	18	7	9	.351	.301
Hutchison, Bernard, Asheville	.232	108	472	419	59	97	111	10	2	0	30	16	0	2	35	0	91	81	18	2	.265	.294
Illig, Brett, Savannah	.203	51	185	158	16	32	42	4	0	2	11	0	2	5	20	0	49	1	3	3	.266	.308
Inglin, Jeff, Hickory	.334	135	598	536	100	179	273	34	6	16	102	0	9	4	49	4	87	31	8	12	.509	.388
Jaroncyk, Ryan, Columbia†	.174	29	101	86	5	15	20	1	2	0	7	1	3	0	11	0	25	4	4	1	.233	.260
Jefferson, Dave, Cape Fear	.195	28	96	87	12	17	24	1	0	2	6	1	1	0	7	0	14	6	2	3	.276	.253
Johnson, Damon, Hagerstown	.325	84	320	302	44	98	159	21	5	10	55	0	5	13	0	0	65	11	6	5	.526	.363
Johnson, Jason, Augusta	.228	20	69	57	9	13	17	1	0	1	7	0	0	0	12	0	17	4	0	0	.298	.362
Johnson, Nick, Greensboro*	.273	127	534	433	77	118	191	23	1	16	75	0	6	18	76	1	99	16	3	5	.441	.398
Kastelic, Matthew, Cha. (S.C.)*	.301	50	204	183	19	55	67	10	1	0	14	2	1	0	18	1	19	13	10	1	.366	.361
Katz, Jason, Macon†	.234	74	263	222	36	52	79	9	0	6	24	4	2	3	32	0	41	11	4	5	.356	.336
Keck, Brian, Asheville	.234	37	140	124	8	29	32	3	0	0	8	7	0	0	9	0	22	5	2	5	.258	.286
Keech, Erik, Greensboro*	.250	26	76	72	5	18	25	1	0	2	9	0	1	0	3	0	15	0	0	1	.347	.276
Kehoe, John, Hagerstown	.172	14	62	58	9	10	15	3	1	0	4	0	0	0	4	0	19	2	0	1	.259	.226
Keller, Jeremy, Cha. (W.Va.)*	.262	117	440	386	55	101	149	19	1	9	66	0	3	3	48	0	93	3	0	4	.386	.345
Kent, Troy, Columbus	.274	117	509	463	61	127	203	22	6	14	71	2	5	8	31	0	91	13	4	7	.438	.327
Kiil, Harry, Piedmont	.226	82	315	261	48	59	101	15	3	7	34	3	3	13	35	1	74	13	2	0	.387	.343
King, Michael, Cha. (S.C.)	.196	60	210	199	16	39	55	7	0	3	16	3	0	1	7	0	36	6	1	4	.276	.227
Klee, Charles, Hickory	.270	119	450	400	55	108	135	18	3	1	48	8	3	8	31	1	78	5	8	8	.338	.333
Koehler, Jason, Hagerstown	.203	26	75	69	7	14	23	0	0	3	12	2	0	1	3	0	19	1	3	1	.333	.247
Kofler, Eric, Greensboro*	.275	73	274	262	23	72	108	17	2	5	39	0	5	0	7	0	54	3	2	1	.412	.288
Konrady, Dennis, Columbus*	.301	107	444	365	60	110	145	23	3	2	43	7	5	5	62	0	60	15	7	6	.397	.405
Kurtz, Tony, Delmarva	.244	38	135	119	13	29	43	6	4	0	9	2	2	1	11	0	49	4	0	0	.361	.308
Landstad, Rob, Columbus*	.224	96	364	331	41	74	139	12	7	13	56	1	2	3	27	0	91	5	3	7	.420	.287
Larkin, Stephen, Cha. (W.Va.)*	.278	129	526	464	88	129	211	23	10	13	79	0	5	5	52	1	83	28	9	6	.455	.354
LaRue, Jason, Cha. (W.Va.)	.315	132	534	473	78	149	229	50	3	8	81	1	8	5	47	0	90	14	4	8	.484	.377
Lasater, Chris, Delmarva	.181	25	80	72	6	13	24	5	0	2	11	0	0	1	7	0	16	0	0	1	.333	.263
Lawrence, Joe, Hagerstown	.229	116	505	446	63	102	152	24	1	8	38	3	2	5	49	0	107	10	12	3	.341	.311
Leach, Nick, Savannah*	.267	37	150	131	14	35	41	6	0	0	13	0	0	4	14	0	23	1	2	2	.313	.356
Leon, Donny, Greensboro†	.254	137	545	516	45	131	201	32	1	12	74	2	7	5	15	2	106	6	4	13	.390	.278
Lindsey, John, Asheville	.236	110	443	399	54	94	154	20	2	12	67	1	3	11	29	1	110	3	2	14	.386	.303
Livingston, Doug, Asheville	.263	128	533	468	53	123	168	30	3	3	61	15	0	5	45	1	82	8	5	12	.359	.334
Long, Garrett, Augusta	.300	83	343	280	50	84	119	10	2	7	41	0	1	1	61	2	78	5	2	3	.425	.426
Lopez, Luis, Hagerstown	.358	136	577	503	96	180	268	47	4	11	99	0	6	8	60	4	45	5	8	14	.533	.430
Lorenzana, Luis, Augusta	.236	92	326	288	36	68	81	11	1	0	20	4	1	2	31	0	66	4	5	5	.281	.314
Lunar, Fernando, Macon	.261	105	406	380	41	99	150	26	2	7	37	2	1	5	18	1	42	0	1	11	.395	.302
MacKay, Tripp, Cape Fear†	.238	68	228	189	25	45	53	6	1	0	12	7	1	2	29	0	20	5	9	2	.280	.344
Malave, Joshua, Savannah	.252	58	213	206	23	52	92	11	1	9	32	1	1	1	4	0	54	2	1	2	.447	.269
Maloney, Jeff, Hagerstown	.258	101	424	395	49	102	146	19	2	7	38	1	3	2	23	2	98	19	9	7	.370	.300
Marquis, Jason, Macon*	.000	28	2	2	0	0	0	0	0	0	0	0	0	0	0	0	0	0	0	0	.000	.000
Marsters, Brandon, Piedmont	.203	61	236	212	25	43	57	8	0	2	20	2	0	0	22	2	51	0	0	4	.269	.278
Martinez, Luis, Savannah	.231	75	307	294	26	68	87	7	3	2	23	3	2	3	5	0	48	1	0	6	.296	.250
Martinez, Rafael, Columbia*	.268	44	167	149	20	40	66	7	2	5	25	0	1	17	2	44	10	2	1	.443	.347
Matos, Luis, Delmarva	.210	36	133	119	10	25	30	1	2	0	13	2	1	2	9	0	21	8	5	2	.252	.275
May, Freddy, Augusta*	.235	107	408	358	51	84	123	13	7	4	33	6	1	0	43	1	84	16	18	6	.344	.316
May, Scott, Augusta*	.250	19	49	44	5	11	14	3	0	0	2	2	0	0	3	0	8	1	2	0	.318	.298
McCain, Marcus, Cha. (S.C.)	.222	9	22	18	8	4	4	0	0	0	3	1	1	0	2	0	0	7	1	0	.222	.286
McCarthy, Kevin, Columbia*	.194	31	106	98	6	19	23	1	0	1	9	0	0	0	8	0	21	1	1	0	.235	.255
McKinnon, Tom, Cha. (S.C.)*	.228	108	443	412	52	94	154	19	4	11	53	0	3	1	26	3	100	13	7	7	.374	.274
Mejia, Juan, Piedmont	.250	36	116	112	15	28	38	6	2	0	12	1	2	1	0	0	32	7	0	3	.339	.252
Melendez, Jorge, Columbus	.233	57	168	146	15	34	45	9	1	0	12	8	1	1	11	0	37	0	0	1	.308	.289
Mendes, Jaime, Piedmont	.000	42	2	2	0	0	0	0	0	0	0	0	0	0	0	0	0	0	0	0	.000	.000
Meyer, Travis, Savannah	.289	13	47	45	4	13	15	2	0	0	2	0	0	1	1	0	6	1	1	2	.333	.319
Minor, Ryan, Delmarva	.307	134	558	488	83	150	266	42	1	24	97	0	4	15	51	2	102	7	3	8	.545	.387
Molina, Gabe, Delmarva	.000	46	2	2	0	0	0	0	0	0	0	0	0	0	0	0	1	0	0	0	.000	.000
Montgomery, Andre, CWV	.190	20	62	58	6	11	14	3	0	0	5	1	0	1	2	0	23	7	2	1	.241	.230
Morrison, Scott, Savannah	.233	61	246	219	30	51	82	13	3	4	34	5	1	4	17	0	45	4	1	2	.374	.294
Motley, Mel, Columbus	.217	28	107	92	18	20	35	4	1	3	10	1	0	0	14	0	29	4	2	1	.380	.321
Murphy, Robbie, Cha. (W.Va.)†	.184	53	185	174	19	32	42	10	0	0	7	3	1	0	7	0	38	7	2	0	.241	.214
Myers, Aaron, Asheville	.075	12	47	40	3	3	4	1	0	0	3	1	1	4	0	8	0	0	4	.100	.174
Needham, Kevin, CWV*	.000	35	1	1	0	0	0	0	0	0	0	0	0	0	0	0	0	0	0	0	.000	.000
Newman, Howard, Cha. (W.Va.)	.161	12	39	31	3	5	9	1	0	1	4	0	1	1	6	0	10	2	0	2	.290	.308
Nichols, Kevin, Piedmont	.293	81	333	321	21	94	129	16	2	5	46	0	3	0	9	0	46	1	1	7	.402	.309
Nunnari, Talmadge, Cape Fear*	.371	9	36	35	8	13	19	1	1	1	6	0	0	0	1	0	5	2	0	0	.543	.389
O'Hearn, Brandon, Cha. (W.Va.)	.242	65	242	215	27	52	89	13	3	6	32	1	2	1	23	1	69	6	2	4	.414	.315
Oliveros, Leonardo, Piedmont†	.171	38	137	129	6	22	25	3	0	0	5	2	0	1	5	0	18	0	0	6	.194	.207
Olsen, D.C., Cape Fear	.256	51	171	160	18	41	69	9	2	5	29	0	1	0	9	0	37	2	1	1	.431	.298
Olson, Dan, Hickory*	.286	98	395	350	59	100	164	31	3	9	47	1	5	3	36	1	120	4	1	4	.469	.353
Oropeza, Willie, Cape Fear	.233	78	288	270	28	63	93	9	0	7	32	3	5	2	8	0	46	1	2	10	.344	.256
Owens-Bragg, Luke, Cha. (S.C.)†	.226	53	190	164	29	37	46	6	0	1	14	4	0	1	21	0	37	14	2	2	.280	.317
Parsons, Jason, Cha. (W.Va.)†	.311	131	541	460	87	143	237	34	0	20	102	0	5	14	62	5	99	5	1	5	.515	.405
Parsons, Jeff, Columbia	.270	52	183	152	25	41	43	2	0	0	11	4	0	1	26	0	41	16	2	1	.283	.380
Paz, Richard, Delmarva	.242	111	451	389	60	94	122	14	4	2	48	15	4	5	38	1	60	15	5	8	.314	.314
Pena, Alex, Augusta	.244	111	378	356	34	87	118	12	2	5	40	0	1	3	18	0	81	11	10	8	.331	.286
Penalver, Juan, Columbia	.273	9	27	22	1	6	7	1	0	0	1	2	0	0	3	0	3	0	1	1	.318	.360
Pendergrass, Tyrone, Macon†	.260	127	565	489	81	127	171	16	5	6	37	8	3	5	60	0	101	70	15	5	.350	.344
Perez, Edwin, Columbus	.278	52	206	187	30	52	79	10	1	5	24	1	0	1	17	0	41	2	2	4	.422	.341
Perez, Jersen, Columbia	.667	2	7	6	3	4	7	3	0	0	2	0	0	1	0	0	0	1	0	0	1.167	.714
Perez, Richard, Delmarva	.235	27	79	68	9	16	25	5	2	0	8	1	0	1	9	0	21	5	2	3	.368	.333
Phelps, Josh, Hagerstown	.210	68	258	233	26	49	81	9	1	7	24	0	2	8	15	0	72	3	2	6	.348	.279
Pickering, Calvin, Delmarva*	.311	122	509	444	88	138	246	31	1	25	79	0	1	9	53	2	139	6	3	14	.554	.394
Pinto, Rene, Greensboro	.286	35	111	105	20	30	47	9	1	2	10	0	2	1	3	0	34	0	0	0	.448	.306
Pointer, Corey, Augusta	.190	84	289	248	38	47	77	9	0	7	26	3	3	9	26	0	116	23	3	1	.310	.287

Player, Team	Avg.	G	TPA	AB	R	H	TB	2B	3B	HR	RBI	SH	SF	HP	BB	IBB	SO	SB	CS	GDP	Slg.	OBP
Pond, Simon, Cape Fear*	.270	118	488	444	48	120	140	11	0	3	47	1	4	2	37	1	46	12	8	22	.315	.326
Presto, Nick, Cha. (W.Va.)	.287	83	346	300	57	86	118	19	2	3	44	9	8	3	26	0	60	16	2	0	.393	.341
Price, Corey, Cha. (W.Va.)†	.258	22	71	62	7	16	17	1	0	0	10	0	0	0	9	0	16	4	3	2	.274	.352
Prokopec, Luke, Savannah*	.232	61	179	164	11	38	57	7	3	2	20	0	1	2	12	1	49	3	1	2	.348	.291
Quatraro, Matthew, Cha. (S.C.)	.299	78	320	294	35	88	131	18	2	7	42	1	5	2	18	0	55	15	5	7	.446	.339
Ramirez, Daniel, Columbia	.305	130	532	482	82	146	181	24	4	1	42	3	3	4	44	0	104	51	25	4	.379	.367
Rice, Charles, Augusta†	.250	51	176	156	24	39	77	6	1	10	30	0	1	2	16	2	37	3	1	5	.494	.326
Rigoli, David, Cape Fear	.188	17	57	48	5	9	13	2	1	0	3	0	1	0	8	0	6	1	0	1	.271	.298
Rijo-Berger, Jose, Columbia†	.229	17	55	48	4	11	13	2	0	0	1	1	0	0	6	0	12	2	1	0	.271	.315
Riley, Cash, Savannah	.207	27	92	87	6	18	27	3	3	0	3	0	0	2	3	0	27	4	2	4	.310	.250
Rivera, Carlos, Augusta*	.272	120	453	415	52	113	166	16	5	9	65	0	6	10	19	2	82	4	1	9	.400	.336
Rivera, Roberto, Delmarva	.153	17	60	59	6	9	9	1	0	1	2	5	0	0	1	0	20	1	2	0	.288	.167
Robinson, Tony, Augusta	.210	18	71	62	11	13	19	4	1	0	8	1	1	2	5	0	6	3	2	2	.306	.286
Rodriguez, Chris, Asheville	.000	2	4	4	0	0	0	0	0	0	0	0	0	0	0	0	1	0	0	0	.000	.000
Rodriguez, Liu, Hickory†	.289	129	537	450	72	130	166	21	6	1	62	10	7	5	65	0	56	12	13	13	.369	.380
Rodriguez, Luis, Hagerstown	.266	27	102	94	13	25	37	6	0	2	14	3	2	1	2	0	20	3	0	2	.394	.283
Rodriguez, Mike, Hagerstown	.228	43	148	123	17	28	31	3	0	0	12	3	3	1	18	0	25	0	2	1	.252	.324
Rodriguez, Gary, Columbus*	.257	116	545	482	73	124	149	12	5	1	37	11	2	4	46	1	94	22	8	5	.309	.326
Rollins, Jimmy, Piedmont†	.270	139	624	560	94	151	207	22	8	6	59	9	3	0	52	2	80	46	6	4	.370	.330
Rolls, Damian, Savannah	.211	130	528	475	57	100	142	17	5	5	47	3	4	5	38	0	83	11	3	9	.299	.274
Ross, Jason, Macon	.258	112	479	430	70	111	168	20	5	9	59	0	3	9	37	0	121	16	7	7	.391	.328
Rowson, James, Greensboro	.286	8	27	21	1	6	7	1	0	0	2	1	0	0	5	0	8	0	0	0	.333	.423
Saffer, Jeff, Greensboro	.206	90	313	267	40	55	106	13	1	12	39	2	3	6	35	0	79	0	3	6	.397	.309
Salinas, Hector, Cha. (S.C.)	.276	90	354	322	33	89	126	19	3	4	44	1	4	3	24	0	52	4	6	6	.391	.329
Sanchez, Alex, Cha. (S.C.)*	.289	131	593	537	73	155	182	15	6	0	34	12	4	3	37	2	72	92	40	7	.339	.336
Sankey, Brian, Savannah*	.267	63	237	210	25	56	82	11	0	5	27	0	1	2	24	1	37	5	2	6	.390	.344
Scharrer, Jim, Macon	.245	121	484	444	67	109	192	19	2	20	57	0	1	2	37	1	136	0	3	1	.432	.306
Schneider, Brian, Cape Fear*	.252	113	449	381	46	96	130	20	1	4	49	6	5	4	53	2	45	3	6	9	.341	.345
Schreiber, Stan, Augusta	.214	115	427	345	51	74	89	10	1	1	26	10	4	3	65	0	83	40	11	7	.258	.341
Schwab, Chris, Cape Fear	.268	54	238	209	29	56	112	19	2	11	42	0	2	1	26	2	70	3	3	3	.536	.349
Scott, Tom, Cha. (W.Va.)	.250	60	231	212	27	53	95	14	2	8	28	0	1	1	17	0	82	6	6	1	.448	.307
Seabol, Scott, Greensboro	.265	48	151	136	11	36	58	12	2	2	15	0	2	4	9	0	26	3	1	1	.426	.325
Sharpe, Grant, Columbus*	.130	33	125	108	10	14	24	4	0	2	9	1	1	0	15	0	46	0	0	3	.222	.234
Shatley, Andy, Hagerstown	.242	117	435	401	51	97	161	28	0	12	46	4	3	9	17	0	114	6	3	6	.401	.286
Sheppard, Greg, Hickory	.307	102	400	342	54	105	172	27	2	12	62	2	4	6	46	1	81	4	2	7	.503	.394
Shipp, Skip, Augusta	.252	81	286	254	29	64	83	15	2	0	23	2	0	4	26	0	53	12	5	2	.327	.331
Shumpert, Derek, Greensboro	.301	86	357	322	49	97	149	22	6	6	39	0	1	7	27	1	91	12	6	5	.463	.367
Sikes, Jason, Piedmont	.000	2	2	2	0	0	0	0	0	0	0	0	0	0	0	0	0	0	0	0	.000	.000
Simpson, Jeramie, Columbia*	.241	10	30	29	4	7	9	0	1	0	2	0	0	0	1	0	15	1	1	0	.310	.267
Smith, Casey, Columbus	.333	13	45	36	6	12	15	0	0	1	3	0	0	1	8	0	15	0	0	0	.417	.467
Smith, Rod, Greensboro†	.248	137	605	528	96	131	207	25	6	13	50	2	1	5	69	0	148	54	20	5	.392	.340
Solano, Angel, Hickory	.095	11	22	21	0	2	3	1	0	0	3	0	1	0	0	0	7	0	0	0	.143	.091
Soriano, Carlos, Columbia	.208	101	353	318	37	66	92	14	0	4	41	3	7	1	24	1	52	5	2	8	.289	.260
Soriano, Fred, Hagerstown†	.242	38	129	120	18	29	38	9	0	0	6	2	0	2	5	0	27	8	2	5	.317	.283
Springfield, Bo, Augusta*	.242	12	42	33	7	8	8	0	0	0	2	1	1	0	7	0	5	5	1	0	.242	.366
Stanton, Thomas, Columbia†	.189	60	223	190	29	36	67	10	0	7	31	0	2	7	24	0	79	0	1	2	.353	.300
Staubach, Jeff, Greensboro	.000	1	4	4	0	0	0	0	0	0	0	0	0	0	0	0	1	0	0	0	.000	.000
Stearns, Randy, Savannah*	.226	94	336	301	41	68	90	10	3	2	18	2	0	2	31	1	96	21	14	1	.299	.302
Stephens, Joel, Delmarva	.224	33	96	76	14	17	27	4	0	2	4	4	1	0	7	0	12	8	4	1	.355	.291
Streicher, Robert, Cape Fear	.111	15	51	45	0	5	5	0	0	0	4	0	0	0	6	0	10	0	0	0	.111	.216
Stromsborg, Ryan, Hagerstown	.288	56	203	184	22	53	75	10	0	4	24	1	3	2	13	0	37	5	1	2	.408	.337
Suriel, Miguel, Cha. (S.C.)	.153	26	93	85	7	13	15	2	0	0	4	2	2	1	5	0	9	1	0	1	.176	.204
Swafford, Derek, Augusta*	.217	21	86	69	12	15	20	2	0	1	9	4	2	3	8	0	20	6	2	0	.290	.317
Tamargo, John, Columbia†	.249	113	446	393	44	98	122	17	2	1	47	5	1	2	45	2	72	13	7	9	.310	.329
Taylor, Adam, Columbus	.187	47	155	123	14	23	35	3	3	1	16	0	2	6	24	1	66	1	0	0	.285	.342
Taylor, Greg, Piedmont	.278	41	136	115	15	32	41	7	1	0	14	4	0	2	15	0	11	1	2	8	.357	.371
Terhune, Mike, Macon†	.226	92	366	328	33	74	96	11	4	1	28	6	2	5	25	0	45	8	3	4	.293	.289
Tessmar, Timothy, Columbia†	.244	120	473	430	53	105	151	14	4	8	55	0	4	2	36	1	93	10	3	7	.351	.303
Thames, Marcus, Greensboro	.313	4	16	16	2	5	6	1	0	0	2	0	0	0	0	0	3	1	0	0	.375	.313
Thomas, Allen, Hickory*	.082	27	55	49	4	4	6	2	0	0	2	0	1	1	4	0	19	0	1	1	.122	.164
Thompson, Nick, Piedmont	.258	58	240	225	32	58	81	8	3	3	21	2	1	4	8	0	33	1	1	4	.360	.294
Thorpe, A.D., Macon†	.249	97	397	350	52	87	104	9	1	2	29	4	0	1	42	0	46	29	17	5	.297	.331
Tidwell, David, Cha. (W.Va.)	.264	65	288	258	40	68	88	8	3	2	26	3	0	2	25	0	47	15	9	6	.341	.333
Tober, Dave, Piedmont	.000	46	1	0	1	0	0	0	0	0	0	0	0	0	0	0	0	0	0	0	.000	.000
Torti, Michael, Piedmont	.250	49	209	176	19	44	76	12	1	6	31	1	0	4	28	0	47	1	0	3	.432	.365
Tracy, Andrew, Cape Fear*	.300	59	236	210	31	63	100	9	2	8	43	0	2	3	21	4	47	6	1	4	.476	.369
Tucci, Peter, Hagerstown	.264	127	513	466	60	123	191	28	5	10	75	1	6	5	35	1	95	9	5	9	.410	.318
Turlais, John, Augusta*	.292	33	119	106	8	31	48	5	0	4	18	0	3	0	10	1	20	2	1	3	.453	.345
Twombley, Dennis, Greensboro	.194	15	40	36	4	7	10	0	0	1	2	0	1	0	3	0	12	0	0	1	.278	.250
Valencia, Victor, Greensboro	.221	107	406	353	42	78	131	12	1	13	43	0	1	10	42	0	116	2	1	6	.371	.317
Valera, Willy, Columbus	.267	117	459	431	47	115	166	15	6	8	40	5	3	0	20	0	91	8	4	10	.385	.297
Valera, Yohanny, Columbia	.191	94	322	293	32	56	94	14	0	8	33	2	1	5	21	0	101	2	0	4	.321	.256
Vazquez, Manny, Cha. (S.C.)*	.233	61	198	176	20	41	49	6	1	0	11	4	0	1	17	1	26	9	6	2	.278	.304
Velazquez, Jose, Greensboro*	.280	137	539	489	77	137	189	19	3	9	62	2	5	1	42	1	71	10	8	15	.387	.335
Verrall, Jared, Cha. (S.C.)	.167	8	30	30	1	5	9	1	0	1	4	0	0	0	0	0	9	2	0	0	.300	.167
Vickers, Randy, Columbus	.171	72	257	245	22	42	84	10	1	10	26	0	1	2	9	0	99	1	4	5	.343	.206
Walker, Morgan, Augusta	.275	76	318	295	40	81	144	16	7	14	64	0	3	3	17	2	70	3	2	7	.488	.318
Ware, Jeremy, Cape Fear	.263	138	584	529	84	139	229	32	5	16	77	0	6	6	43	2	114	32	7	8	.433	.322
Warren, Lance, Savannah*	.240	11	28	25	5	6	9	1	1	0	1	0	0	0	3	0	5	2	0	0	.360	.321
Wesemann, Jason, Piedmont	.250	44	116	104	16	26	32	1	1	1	12	3	1	0	8	0	23	1	0	3	.308	.301
Whipple, Boomer, Augusta	.222	40	141	108	16	24	31	7	0	0	13	3	0	2	4	0	19	2	1	2	.287	.310
Whitaker, Chad, Columbus*	.273	109	462	432	48	118	183	25	2	12	72	0	2	5	23	3	144	3	0	6	.424	.316
White, John, Cape Fear	.000	3	12	9	0	0	0	0	0	0	1	0	1	1	1	0	3	0	0	0	.000	.167
Whitley, Matt, Asheville	.232	129	561	461	67	107	131	21	0	1	43	11	4	8	77	2	57	14	9	11	.284	.349

Player, Team	Avg.	G	TPA	AB	R	H	TB	2B	3B	HR	RBI	SH	SF	HP	BB	IBB	SO	SB	CS	GDP	Slg.	OBP
Whitlock, Brian, Columbus	.263	92	369	327	56	86	147	14	7	11	41	6	2	6	28	0	92	5	4	5	.450	.331
Williams, Errick, Piedmont	.206	37	149	136	12	28	36	5	0	1	6	0	1	3	9	0	44	10	4	0	.265	.268
Williams, Glenn, Macon†	.266	77	331	297	52	79	143	18	2	14	52	1	4	5	24	1	105	9	6	4	.481	.327
Williams, Jewell, Columbus	.188	113	446	399	57	75	131	20	3	10	40	3	1	10	33	0	140	14	6	9	.328	.266
Willis, Symmion, Hagerstown	.246	25	69	61	6	15	18	3	0	0	11	1	0	0	7	0	21	0	1	1	.295	.324
Wong, Jerrod, Macon*	.278	118	467	439	46	122	199	22	5	15	60	2	4	4	18	0	92	6	5	3	.453	.310
Zamora, Junior, Columbia	.250	36	134	124	16	31	60	5	0	8	19	0	0	0	10	0	29	0	1	2	.484	.306
Zaun, Brian, Savannah................	.238	13	43	42	6	10	17	2	1	1	6	0	0	1	0	0	16	0	0	0	.405	.256

GRAND SLAMS: Minor, 4; Hacker, 3; Bruce, Glavine, Stanton, 2 each; C. Anderson, Becker, Bramlett, Chavez, B. Crede, Diaz, Hessman, Huff, Inglin, Katz, Kent, LaRue, Lawrence, Leon, Lopez, Olsen, Pena, Pendergrass, Ross, Scharrer, R. Smith, Ware, Whitlock, Zamora, 1 each.

AWARDED FIRST BASE ON CATCHER'S INTERFERENCE: Bramlett 6 (Alley, A. Taylor, P. Evans, Shipp, S. May 2); DeCinces 3 (M. Rodriguez, Lunar, Schneider); C. Rivera 3 (Phelps, Glassey, P. Evans); Rolls 3 (Lunar 2, Turlais); Christensen 2 (Valencia, Phelps); Coffie 2 (Phelps, Oliveros); Pickering 2 (Lunar, C. Anderson); Alley (Melendez); B. Anderson (Melendez); Becker (Heintz); E. Brown (A. Taylor); Bryant (Quatraro); Elam (Quatraro); Fauske (Quatraro); N. Johnson (Arias); Leach (Alley); Melendez (Koehler); McKinnon (Bennett); Pendergrass (Suriel); Rice (Melendez); Shatley (Arias); Tessmar (C. Anderson), 1 each.

1997 PITCHING

TEAM

Team	W	L	Pct.	ERA	G	CG	ShO	Sv.	IP	H	TBF	R	ER	HR	SH	SF	HB	BB	IBB	SO	WP	Bk.
Columbia	77	63	.550	3.17	140	14	19	29	1181.2	1020	4944	495	416	71	45	27	66	455	13	1113	85	8
Macon................	80	60	.571	3.39	140	2	14	39	1226.1	1106	5170	573	462	96	42	38	56	411	8	1206	54	5
Charleston (S.C.)...	60	82	.423	3.44	142	4	9	27	1243.0	1136	5248	617	475	81	51	37	57	381	7	1088	86	9
Delmarva	77	65	.542	3.62	142	2	12	46	1261.0	1129	5343	625	507	79	40	39	45	495	21	1139	79	10
Cape Fear	66	74	.471	3.82	140	6	8	32	1231.0	1208	5251	630	522	80	40	42	77	405	3	947	84	8
Augusta	71	70	.500	3.82	142	3	9	42	1249.2	1225	5388	656	531	84	37	34	60	417	20	1174	88	18
Piedmont	70	72	.493	3.85	142	10	10	31	1242.1	1238	5252	632	531	94	47	27	69	363	5	929	61	10
Greensboro	75	65	.536	3.92	141	9	7	41	1216.0	1125	5266	683	530	88	41	40	53	516	14	1026	87	13
Hickory	76	64	.543	3.95	140	9	3	29	1229.2	1255	5305	669	540	90	50	49	50	411	7	962	102	12
Hagerstown	65	73	.471	3.96	138	5	8	32	1187.1	1159	5172	646	523	70	42	37	58	472	7	1119	94	13
Asheville	62	76	.449	4.07	139	8	5	33	1215.0	1225	5249	651	549	112	41	41	70	445	6	1022	69	12
Charleston (W.Va.)	76	62	.551	4.07	138	9	6	37	1182.2	1262	5083	650	535	83	46	42	50	325	15	934	81	16
Savannah.............	63	77	.450	4.19	140	10	6	31	1195.1	1162	5181	660	556	104	48	30	50	451	6	1079	112	13
Columbus.............	62	76	.449	4.79	138	2	8	38	1213.0	1167	5335	742	645	114	26	53	82	531	15	1128	104	9

INDIVIDUAL

TOP QUALIFIERS FOR EARNED-RUN AVERAGE TITLE

Minimum 114 innings. *Lefthanded pitcher.

Pitcher, Team	W	L	Pct.	ERA	G	GS	CG	ShO	GF	Sv.	IP	H	TBF	R	ER	HR	SH	SF	HB	BB	IBB	SO	WP	Bk.
Heredia, Maximo, Delmarva	10	5	.667	2.13	37	6	0	0	13	1	114.0	97	441	29	27	4	3	3	0	20	0	73	2	0
Roberts, Grant, Columbia	11	3	.786	2.36	22	22	2	1	0	0	129.2	98	530	37	34	1	3	8	44	0	122	5	0
Rose, Ted, Cha. (W.Va.)..........	11	6	.647	2.51	38	13	2	2	9	4	129.1	108	525	44	36	7	9	3	6	27	0	132	3	2
Evans, Keith, Cape Fear	12	7	.632	2.61	21	21	3	1	0	0	138.0	113	551	56	40	6	2	4	10	18	0	102	1	0
Kessel, Kyle, Columbia*	11	11	.500	2.72	27	27	5	1	0	0	168.2	131	685	63	51	8	9	5	9	53	3	151	8	0
Carlyle, Buddy, Cha. (W.Va.)......	14	5	.737	2.77	23	23	4	1	0	0	143.0	130	579	51	44	9	4	4	3	27	0	111	5	1
Shiell, Jason, Macon	10	5	.667	2.86	27	24	0	0	0	0	129.0	113	523	53	41	12	3	5	8	32	0	101	6	0
Ortega, Pablo, Cha. (S.C.)	12	10	.545	2.86	29	29	3	0	0	0	188.2	173	778	87	60	10	7	6	10	30	0	142	4	1
Mitchell, Dean, Savannah	11	5	.688	2.88	52	7	1	0	38	16	122.0	110	499	50	39	6	5	3	1	25	1	118	2	1
Pumphrey, Kenny, Columbia	12	6	.667	3.10	27	27	3	2	0	0	165.2	137	708	70	57	11	7	3	20	72	0	133	11	1
Parker, Christian, Cape Fear	11	10	.524	3.12	25	25	0	0	0	0	153.0	146	640	72	53	5	9	6	7	49	0	106	9	2
Leon, Scott, Cha. (S.C.)...........	6	12	.333	3.17	27	25	1	0	1	0	156.1	151	654	70	55	13	5	8	7	41	0	109	10	1
Bowers, Cedrick, Cha. (S.C.)*	10	10	.444	3.21	28	28	0	0	0	0	157.0	119	657	74	56	11	4	3	3	78	0	164	15	1
LaChapelle, Yan, Hagerstown	7	7	.500	3.26	26	15	1	1	8	3	118.2	73	503	54	43	7	6	4	6	74	0	115	12	1
Chen, Bruce, Macon*	12	7	.632	3.51	28	28	1	1	0	0	146.1	120	602	67	57	19	4	5	7	44	0	182	5	1

DEPARTMENTAL LEADERS: W—Several pitchers tied with 14 each; L—Glover, 17; Pct.—G. Roberts, .786; G—D. Mitchell, 52; GS—Ortega, 29; CG—Kessel, 5; ShO—Stevens, 3; GF—Lee, 49; Sv.—Kohlmeier, 24; IP—Ortega, 188.2; H—Lara, 199; TBF—Ortega, 778; R—Lara, 107; ER—Brammer, 91; HR—Chen, 19; SH—Farley, 10; SF—Lara, 9; HB—Pumphrey, 20; BB—Coble, 96; IBB—Several pitchers tied with 5 each; SO—Chen, 182; WP—Lakman, 24; BK—Altman, 6.

ALL PITCHERS

*Lefthanded pitcher.

Pitcher, Team	W	L	Pct.	ERA	G	GS	CG	ShO	GF	Sv.	IP	H	TBF	R	ER	HR	SH	SF	HB	BB	IBB	SO	WP	Bk.
Acevedo, Jose, Cha. (W.Va.) ..	3	3	.500	3.92	15	8	0	0	3	0	57.1	61	245	29	25	8	2	1	5	9	0	34	4	1
Achilles, Matt, Delmarva	0	0	.000	9.53	3	0	0	0	1	1	5.2	11	36	9	6	0	0	2	3	0	4	2	0
Ah Yat, Paul, Augusta*	5	1	.833	2.90	29	9	0	0	5	0	90.0	82	366	34	29	7	3	0	3	16	1	119	4	0
Allen, Brandon, Piedmont*	11	8	.579	3.54	25	24	4	2	1	0	152.2	153	631	78	60	12	9	2	11	38	0	91	4	1
Allen, Craig, Savannah	0	1	.000	7.53	10	0	0	0	6	2	14.1	13	71	14	12	1	0	0	1	13	0	14	5	0
Altman, Gene, Cha. (W.Va.).....	1	4	.200	7.79	17	1	0	0	5	0	32.1	45	156	31	28	1	2	2	3	10	0	35	4	6
Alvarado, Carlos, Augusta	6	5	.545	3.27	29	20	0	0	2	0	113.0	114	499	58	41	4	3	8	11	45	0	109	9	4
Andrews, Clayton, Hag.*	7	7	.500	4.55	28	15	0	0	7	0	114.2	120	512	70	58	8	4	5	47	1	112	4	2
Armas, Tony, Greensboro	5	2	.714	1.05	9	9	2	1	0	0	51.2	36	207	13	6	3	1	1	3	13	0	64	1	1
Arminio, Steven, CWV	2	3	.400	3.80	46	2	0	0	15	6	90.0	113	392	45	38	6	1	2	3	20	3	58	5	1
Arteaga, Juan, Columbia*	1	0	1.000	0.00	1	1	0	0	0	0	6.0	3	20	0	0	0	0	0	4	0	4	0	0
Averette, Robert, CWV	2	2	.500	7.86	11	5	0	0	2	0	26.1	42	131	28	23	3	3	1	0	12	0	20	2	0
Bacci, Anthony, Augusta*	1	3	.250	4.76	6	6	1	1	0	0	28.1	31	127	20	15	3	0	0	0	14	0	24	2	0
Bacsik, Mike, Columbus*	4	14	.222	5.44	28	28	0	0	0	0	139.0	163	622	94	84	16	7	3	9	47	1	100	12	2
Bale, John, Hagerstown*	7	7	.500	4.30	25	25	0	0	0	0	140.1	130	603	83	67	11	4	3	1	63	1	155	11	0

CLASS A South Atlantic League

Pitcher, Team	W	L	Pct.	ERA	G	GS	CG	ShO	GF	Sv.	IP	H	TBF	R	ER	HR	SH	SF	HB	BB	IBB	SO	WP	Bk.
Bales, Joseph, Hickory	0	0	.000	6.48	11	0	0	0	4	1	25.0	29	117	19	18	4	0	3	2	16	0	28	0	0
Barnett, Marty, Piedmont	2	1	.667	3.16	6	6	0	0	0	0	37.0	34	154	16	13	1	1	2	2	11	0	28	1	0
Bauer, Richard, Delmarva	0	0	.000	0.00	1	0	0	0	1	1	2.0	0	7	0	0	0	0	0	0	1	0	2	0	0
Bauldree, Joe, Macon	3	1	.750	4.62	39	2	0	0	13	0	60.1	65	271	40	31	5	2	5	5	25	0	66	2	0
Beasley, Raymond, Macon*	3	4	.429	2.65	49	0	0	0	30	8	71.1	52	294	28	21	4	4	3	5	26	2	102	2	0
Beebe, Hans, Columbia*	0	0	.000	9.95	6	0	0	0	1	0	12.2	21	64	15	14	3	1	2	0	6	0	6	0	0
Bell, Rob, Macon	14	7	.667	3.68	27	27	1	0	0	0	146.2	144	614	72	60	15	5	5	3	41	1	140	7	0
Benesh, Edward, Cha. (S.C.)	4	4	.500	1.95	46	0	0	0	40	15	50.2	44	210	16	11	2	4	0	1	14	1	39	6	0
Bere, Jason, Hickory	0	0	.000	6.00	1	1	0	0	0	0	3.0	4	13	2	2	0	0	0	0	0	0	2	0	0
Berry, Jason, Cha. (S.C.)	1	1	.500	5.40	8	0	0	0	5	0	10.0	11	43	10	6	1	1	0	0	1	0	2	1	1
Biddle, Rocky, Hickory	0	1	.000	4.64	13	0	0	0	4	1	21.1	22	96	18	11	2	0	1	2	10	0	25	5	0
Bleazard, David, Hagerstown	5	0	1.000	3.32	10	10	0	0	0	0	59.2	52	250	25	22	1	1	2	5	20	0	58	5	4
Blythe, Billy, Macon	2	5	.286	5.22	35	1	0	0	13	0	58.2	54	279	40	34	2	6	1	5	38	1	57	4	0
Boggs, Robert, Cha. (W.Va.)	1	1	.500	7.34	15	1	0	0	7	0	34.1	44	165	30	28	5	0	5	4	20	0	25	1	0
Bogle, Sean, Cha. (S.C.)	3	0	1.000	1.98	20	0	0	0	10	0	36.1	24	149	11	8	0	1	1	2	17	0	38	2	1
Bourbakis, Michael, Sav.	0	6	.000	7.82	23	13	0	0	2	0	58.2	70	286	57	51	9	1	2	6	39	0	47	11	3
Bowers, Cedrick, Cha. (S.C.)*	8	10	.444	3.21	28	28	0	0	0	0	157.0	119	657	74	56	11	4	3	3	78	0	164	15	1
Bowles, Brian, Hagerstown	1	0	1.000	6.97	4	0	0	0	1	0	10.1	14	49	10	8	2	0	1	1	5	0	9	1	0
Brammer, John, Columbus	6	10	.375	7.02	28	23	0	0	1	1	116.2	132	542	102	91	11	2	7	18	50	0	105	9	4
Brand, Scott, Greensboro	2	0	1.000	3.43	8	0	0	0	6	1	21.0	21	88	8	8	2	0	0	0	5	0	22	2	0
Bravo, Franklin, Augusta	0	0	.000	2.35	7	3	0	0	0	0	15.1	12	67	9	4	1	0	1	1	5	0	14	0	1
Brooks, Wyatt, Augusta*	5	3	.625	3.14	16	4	0	0	2	1	51.2	49	220	26	18	3	2	1	1	18	1	49	5	0
Brown, Derek, Delmarva	0	0	.000	0.00	2	0	0	0	0	0	2.0	2	9	0	0	0	0	0	0	1	0	2	0	0
Brown, Elliot, Cha. (S.C.)	5	8	.385	4.32	33	16	0	0	6	3	118.2	117	525	73	57	11	4	2	8	45	0	86	12	0
Brown, Trent, Cha. (S.C.)*	3	1	.750	2.02	33	0	0	0	13	1	49.0	36	190	12	11	2	1	2	2	7	0	43	0	0
Brueggemann, Dean, Ashe.*	2	8	.200	4.25	34	12	0	0	7	3	110.0	116	482	62	52	11	6	5	1	44	2	99	6	2
Buckman, Tom, Hickory	5	8	.385	5.69	24	19	1	0	3	0	112.1	140	503	83	71	12	3	8	14	29	0	64	8	1
Bullock, Derek, Augusta	2	4	.333	4.54	8	6	0	0	0	0	33.2	32	142	21	17	6	1	0	1	8	0	30	2	0
Caldwell, David, Columbus*	2	1	.667	4.18	5	5	0	0	0	0	23.2	25	104	13	11	0	1	1	1	4	0	22	1	1
Calmus, Lance, Columbus	1	5	.167	5.83	23	15	0	0	2	0	88.0	94	400	64	57	12	0	7	4	41	0	78	8	0
Campbell, Tedde, Augusta	2	1	.667	3.86	5	0	0	0	2	1	4.2	6	22	3	2	0	1	0	0	2	0	4	0	0
Cardona, Steve, Hickory	4	5	.444	4.33	32	0	0	0	12	1	60.1	62	265	41	29	5	4	6	5	16	0	40	17	0
Carlyle, Buddy, Cha. (W.Va.)	14	5	.737	2.77	23	23	4	1	0	0	143.0	130	579	51	44	9	4	4	3	27	0	111	5	1
Cervantes, Peter, Savannah	8	8	.500	3.84	21	20	1	0	0	0	103.0	113	438	48	44	9	2	3	4	22	0	84	1	0
Chacon, Shawn, Asheville	11	7	.611	3.89	28	27	1	0	0	0	162.0	155	701	80	70	13	5	3	14	63	1	149	15	1
Chaney, Michael, Augusta*	8	7	.533	3.52	31	14	0	0	2	0	125.1	129	525	58	49	8	4	4	5	28	1	95	7	0
Charbonneau, Marc, Hag.*	1	1	.500	9.28	6	1	0	0	1	0	10.2	18	58	14	11	2	2	0	0	7	0	13	2	0
Chen, Bruce, Macon*	12	7	.632	3.51	28	28	1	1	0	0	146.1	120	602	67	57	19	4	5	7	44	0	182	5	1
Christman, Tim, Asheville*	7	3	.700	3.41	29	0	0	0	11	3	63.1	55	263	32	24	8	5	3	3	18	1	87	7	4
Civit, Xavier, Cape Fear	4	3	.571	3.55	39	0	0	0	17	3	63.1	59	270	28	25	9	2	4	2	18	0	60	5	0
Coble, Jason, Greensboro*	2	11	.154	4.94	24	23	1	0	0	0	120.1	93	552	84	66	6	3	3	3	96	1	99	14	0
Cooley, Shannon, Piedmont	0	0	.000	0.00	1	0	0	0	1	0	1.0	0	3	0	0	0	0	0	0	0	0	0	0	0
Corey, Mark, Cha. (W.Va.)	8	13	.381	4.57	26	26	1	0	0	0	136.0	169	602	87	69	7	8	5	4	42	3	97	14	0
Coronado, Osvaldo, Columbia	2	4	.333	2.64	26	0	0	0	9	0	47.2	42	195	18	14	5	0	1	0	15	0	42	4	0
Cortes, David, Macon	3	0	1.000	0.57	27	0	0	0	24	15	31.1	16	114	3	2	0	2	1	2	4	0	32	0	0
Cutchins, Todd, Columbia*	0	1	.000	5.40	3	1	0	0	1	0	6.2	7	31	4	4	1	0	0	0	5	0	6	0	0
Daedelow, Craig, Delmarva	0	0	.000	0.00	3	0	0	0	3	0	2.1	1	10	0	0	0	0	0	0	1	0	2	0	0
D'Alessandro, Marc, Ashe.*	0	2	.000	5.62	29	0	0	0	12	1	65.2	87	296	47	41	6	2	2	1	19	0	46	3	0
Daniels, David, Augusta	6	3	.667	2.62	44	0	0	0	39	18	55.0	51	231	22	16	0	1	0	1	13	3	51	0	1
Danner, Andy, Cha. (W.Va.)	1	2	.333	2.66	22	0	0	0	9	2	44.0	38	186	23	13	2	2	0	2	15	2	35	4	0
Davenport, Joe, Hagerstown	4	6	.400	3.68	37	0	0	0	29	10	51.1	43	225	26	21	0	4	1	4	24	2	43	8	0
Davis, Jason, Piedmont*	1	0	1.000	0.61	17	0	0	0	7	1	29.1	10	102	3	2	1	2	0	0	6	0	34	0	0
DeLaCruz, Francisco, Grn.	5	4	.556	3.30	13	13	1	0	0	0	84.2	71	359	41	31	6	2	2	4	36	1	75	3	2
Delgado, Ernie, Hagerstown	5	10	.333	5.23	32	17	0	0	5	1	134.1	163	618	96	78	10	6	6	10	56	0	103	12	0
De Los Santos, Luis, Grn.	5	6	.455	3.05	14	14	1	0	0	0	88.2	91	377	45	30	3	3	6	7	13	0	62	4	0
DePaula, Sean, Columbus	4	5	.444	5.20	29	1	0	0	7	0	71.0	71	336	56	41	4	3	7	4	43	3	75	9	0
Deschenes, Marc, Columbus	2	2	.500	1.90	40	0	0	0	39	19	42.2	31	180	11	9	2	0	1	1	21	0	69	3	0
Dingman, Craig, Greensboro	2	0	1.000	1.91	30	0	0	0	27	19	33.0	19	131	7	7	0	2	1	1	12	0	41	3	0
Dixon, Jim, Hickory	1	3	.250	3.63	16	0	0	0	13	6	22.1	17	97	12	9	0	2	1	1	7	1	22	6	1
Dollar, Toby, Savannah	7	2	.778	2.60	20	8	3	1	7	1	90.0	78	359	33	26	7	2	0	5	12	0	67	6	0
Dudeck, Dave, Greensboro	3	4	.429	3.60	25	1	0	0	7	0	50.0	48	221	29	20	6	4	1	5	16	1	43	6	0
Duff, Matt, Augusta	0	1	.000	1.50	2	1	0	0	1	0	6.0	6	26	1	1	0	0	0	1	2	0	6	0	0
Dykhoff, Radhames, Delmarva*	0	0	.000	0.00	1	0	0	0	1	1	3.0	3	12	0	0	0	0	0	0	0	0	3	0	0
Eaton, Adam, Piedmont	5	6	.455	4.16	14	14	0	0	0	0	71.1	81	318	38	33	2	0	2	4	30	0	57	4	2
Eibey, Scott, Delmarva*	10	4	.714	1.83	47	0	0	0	19	7	93.1	65	371	25	19	3	7	0	2	33	5	82	4	0
Ellison, Jason, Greensboro	1	0	1.000	4.85	9	0	0	0	4	1	13.0	16	60	10	7	1	0	0	1	3	0	11	1	0
Elmore, Jason, Augusta	2	1	.667	10.20	10	1	0	0	0	0	15.0	17	77	17	17	3	0	1	0	14	1	15	3	0
Emiliano, James, Asheville	0	1	.000	5.85	18	0	0	0	12	0	20.0	24	96	15	13	1	0	0	0	12	0	20	3	0
Enders, Trevor, Cha. (S.C.)*	4	3	.571	1.88	44	0	0	0	24	2	67.0	55	271	18	14	2	2	1	2	17	3	73	2	1
Evans, Keith, Cape Fear	12	7	.632	2.61	21	21	3	1	0	0	138.0	113	551	56	40	6	2	4	10	18	0	102	1	0
Eversgerd, Randy, Hag.	0	0	.000	4.50	5	0	0	0	3	0	8.0	13	38	4	4	0	0	0	0	2	0	2	1	1
Falkenborg, Brian, Delmarva	7	9	.438	4.46	25	25	0	0	0	0	127.0	122	547	73	63	6	3	2	13	46	2	107	17	0
Farley, Joe, Hickory*	14	6	.700	4.30	28	27	3	2	0	0	173.2	190	742	94	83	16	10	5	3	48	0	94	11	1
Farson, Bryan, Augusta*	0	0	.000	3.60	7	0	0	0	0	0	10.0	5	44	6	4	1	0	0	1	8	0	7	1	0
Feliciano, Pedro, Savannah*	3	7	.300	2.64	36	9	1	0	8	4	105.2	90	437	45	31	11	3	3	1	39	0	94	6	4
Feliz, Bienvenido, Columbus	3	0	1.000	2.28	6	4	0	0	0	0	27.2	21	110	7	7	1	0	0	0	8	0	20	0	0
Finol, Ricardo, Augusta	1	2	.333	6.65	11	0	0	0	5	0	21.2	21	98	17	16	2	1	1	2	13	1	16	0	1
Fisher, Ryan, Augusta*	0	1	.000	14.85	4	1	0	0	0	0	6.2	15	38	11	11	3	0	0	0	3	0	5	0	0
Folkers, Kenneth, Hag.	0	0	.000	0.00	5	0	0	0	2	0	6.1	3	22	0	0	0	0	0	0	2	0	4	1	0
Forbes, Cameron, Delmarva	6	7	.462	3.74	34	17	1	0	10	1	130.0	108	557	68	54	6	2	6	6	64	0	111	9	0
Fortune, Peter, Cape Fear*	1	1	.500	7.66	12	0	0	0	2	0	22.1	23	113	19	19	1	1	2	5	20	2	21	3	0
France, Aaron, Augusta	7	4	.636	3.52	26	17	1	0	2	0	107.1	98	458	48	42	5	0	2	8	44	0	89	6	3
Franklin, Wayne, Savannah*	5	3	.625	3.18	28	7	1	0	10	2	82.0	79	362	41	29	10	1	1	4	35	0	58	2	1

Pitcher, Team	W	L	Pct.	ERA	G	GS	CG	ShO	GF	Sv.	IP	H	TBF	R	ER	HR	SH	SF	HB	BB	IBB	SO	WP	Bk.
Freedberg, Todd, Delmarva	0	1	.000	3.26	9	0	0	0	3	0	19.1	19	93	9	7	1	2	0	3	15	1	12	2	0
Garcia, Ariel, Hickory	0	1	.000	13.50	1	1	0	0	0	0	2.2	6	17	5	4	0	0	1	0	2	0	0	0	0
Garcia, Eddy, Cha. (W.Va.)	1	1	.500	7.88	6	0	0	0	0	0	16.0	16	70	16	14	0	1	1	0	5	0	10	0	0
Garrett, Hal, Savannah	0	3	.000	8.44	8	1	0	0	4	0	16.0	21	78	15	15	0	1	0	2	7	0	13	4	0
Garza, Alberto, Columbus	8	3	.727	3.13	18	18	2	1	0	0	95.0	72	380	34	33	7	0	2	9	32	0	107	5	0
Giron, Roberto, Cha. (W.Va.)	1	1	.500	8.64	7	0	0	0	1	0	8.1	14	45	8	8	1	0	0	0	6	0	5	3	0
Glover, Gary, Hagerstown	6	17	.261	3.73	28	28	3	0	0	0	173.2	165	751	94	72	9	3	5	10	58	1	155	20	4
Gomez, Miguel, Hagerstown	1	1	.500	8.04	12	0	0	0	5	0	15.2	27	82	19	14	2	0	0	0	9	0	17	4	0
Gonzalez, Dicky, Columbia	1	4	.200	4.94	10	7	1	0	2	0	47.1	50	204	28	26	8	2	1	1	15	0	49	2	0
Gonzalez, Michael, Augusta*	1	1	.500	1.86	4	3	0	0	1	0	19.1	11	76	5	4	1	1	0	0	8	0	22	3	0
Gower, Tim, Cha. (W.Va.)	4	2	.667	2.68	35	0	0	0	32	13	37.0	31	154	13	11	1	4	1	2	9	2	30	3	0
Granger, Greg, Columbus	2	0	1.000	0.82	5	0	0	0	0	0	11.0	8	44	3	1	0	0	0	1	3	0	6	2	0
Graterol, Beiker, Hagerstown	1	0	1.000	0.00	4	0	0	0	4	2	11.0	7	45	1	0	0	0	0	1	3	0	12	1	0
Gresko, Michael, Augusta*	1	0	1.000	3.60	1	1	0	0	0	0	5.0	7	23	2	2	0	0	0	0	3	0	3	0	0
Griffiths, Everard, Cha. (S.C.)	6	13	.316	4.24	30	21	0	0	2	1	140.0	138	593	87	66	9	8	4	7	31	0	107	9	0
Gulin, Lindsay, Columbia*	8	1	.889	2.91	17	15	1	1	2	0	99.0	77	421	37	32	2	2	2	5	60	0	118	9	1
Hacen, Abraham, Delmarva	7	5	.583	4.25	23	23	0	0	0	0	112.1	95	481	59	53	9	2	4	2	58	1	103	9	3
Hafer, Jeffrey, Columbia	6	5	.545	2.99	37	2	0	0	18	7	69.1	59	284	29	23	2	3	1	2	21	3	74	10	1
Hale, Mark, Cha. (S.C.)	1	2	.333	2.93	18	0	0	0	13	4	30.2	26	126	12	10	2	4	1	1	10	0	39	2	1
Halla, Ryan, Augusta	1	1	.500	1.75	32	0	0	0	22	8	46.1	26	176	10	9	2	2	1	2	10	1	51	3	0
Hamilton, Jimmy, Columbus*	5	7	.417	4.46	22	22	0	0	0	0	123.0	123	547	68	61	10	3	2	0	66	0	137	11	0
Handy, Russell, Cape Fear	1	0	1.000	5.00	19	1	0	0	8	0	27.0	20	128	22	15	2	0	1	3	29	0	22	7	0
Harrison, Scott, Columbus	0	1	.000	21.00	1	1	0	0	0	0	3.0	8	19	7	7	1	0	1	1	1	0	1	0	0
Haynie, Jason, Augusta*	6	5	.545	3.43	14	14	1	0	0	0	86.2	77	360	39	33	5	2	2	3	24	1	81	8	2
Herbison, Brett, Columbia	7	14	.333	3.99	28	27	2	0	0	0	160.0	166	690	86	71	13	7	2	9	63	0	146	11	2
Heredia, Maximo, Delmarva	10	5	.667	2.13	37	6	0	0	13	1	114.0	97	441	29	27	4	3	3	0	20	0	73	2	0
Hibbard, Billy, Hagerstown	0	0	.000	5.19	11	0	0	0	5	0	17.1	23	75	10	10	1	0	0	0	3	0	13	2	0
Hill, T.J., Cha. (S.C.)	0	0	.000	4.50	7	0	0	0	0	0	16.0	15	69	10	8	0	1	0	1	8	0	15	4	0
Hlodan, George, Augusta	1	2	.333	5.58	12	6	0	0	2	1	40.1	40	180	31	25	7	3	3	5	15	0	33	3	2
Holliday, Hugh, Cha. (W.Va.)*	0	0	.000	2.40	14	0	0	0	7	1	15.0	10	59	4	4	0	0	0	0	6	1	15	2	2
Hunt, Jon, Hickory*	2	3	.400	4.21	10	9	0	0	0	0	47.0	65	234	33	22	1	1	2	2	23	0	28	3	0
Iglesias, Mario, Hickory	8	4	.667	3.41	36	0	0	0	27	10	68.2	64	289	29	26	4	3	2	1	26	5	64	7	2
Irvine, Kirk, Hickory	3	3	.500	3.39	29	5	0	0	13	0	63.2	80	282	34	24	5	3	2	0	18	0	51	1	0
Jacobson, Brian, Savannah*	1	4	.200	4.04	23	0	0	0	18	3	35.2	36	159	24	16	2	2	0	2	10	2	35	6	1
Jacquez, Thomas, Piedmont*	2	4	.333	4.97	8	8	0	0	0	0	41.2	45	183	29	23	2	2	3	3	13	0	26	1	0
Kammerer, James, Asheville*	0	2	.000	2.82	12	3	1	0	2	0	38.1	37	162	15	12	1	0	1	1	20	0	27	1	0
Kawabata, Kyle, Piedmont	9	5	.643	1.44	44	0	0	0	41	16	62.2	45	242	14	10	2	6	0	2	13	2	75	5	0
Kelly, John, Augusta	0	0	.000	27.00	1	0	0	0	0	0	0.2	4	6	2	2	0	0	0	0	0	0	2	0	0
Kessel, Kyle, Columbia*	11	11	.500	2.72	27	27	5	1	0	0	168.2	131	685	63	51	8	9	5	9	53	3	151	8	0
Key, Calvin, Piedmont	0	0	.000	3.77	3	1	0	0	1	0	14.1	19	61	6	6	3	1	1	0	2	0	9	0	0
Kimbrell, Michael, CSC*	0	0	.000	0.00	1	0	0	0	1	0	3.0	0	10	0	0	0	0	0	0	1	0	4	0	0
Koehler, Luther, Macon*	3	7	.300	4.48	26	7	0	0	6	0	62.1	60	278	44	31	6	3	1	1	24	0	46	3	0
Koeman, Matt, Columbus	4	5	.444	2.62	34	0	0	0	9	2	58.1	38	235	17	17	8	0	2	2	23	1	63	4	0
Kohlmeier, Ryan, Delmarva	2	2	.500	2.65	50	0	0	0	41	24	74.2	48	276	22	22	8	2	2	1	17	1	99	2	1
Koppe, Clint, Cha. (W.Va.)	0	1	.000	7.57	23	1	0	0	16	4	27.1	38	129	23	23	4	0	1	0	10	0	23	2	0
Krall, Eric, Greensboro*	2	2	.500	3.86	15	1	0	0	9	0	35.0	37	157	23	15	3	1	1	1	14	1	26	2	0
Kramer, Matthew, Savannah	6	4	.600	5.85	23	8	0	0	3	0	64.2	62	290	49	42	7	6	1	1	31	1	62	9	0
Kraus, Tim, Hickory	0	2	.000	4.99	15	0	0	0	6	0	30.2	37	143	22	17	1	0	3	1	13	0	29	0	0
LaChapelle, Yan, Hagerstown	7	7	.500	3.26	26	15	1	1	8	3	118.2	73	503	54	43	7	6	6	6	74	0	115	12	1
Lakman, Jason, Hickory	10	9	.526	3.90	27	27	3	0	0	0	154.2	139	667	82	67	11	5	1	4	70	0	168	24	1
Landstad, Rob, Columbus	0	0	.000	0.00	1	0	0	0	1	0	1.0	0	4	0	0	0	0	0	1	0	0	0	0	0
Lara, Giovanny, Cape Fear	9	12	.429	4.55	28	27	1	0	0	0	170.0	199	742	107	86	13	9	9	9	45	0	100	13	1
Lawrence, Clint, Hag.*	13	10	.565	3.54	27	27	1	1	0	0	170.1	179	718	76	67	8	4	4	6	40	0	149	3	1
LeBlanc, Eric, Cha. (W.Va.)	10	7	.588	3.36	24	13	2	0	2	1	107.0	98	440	51	40	7	0	5	6	29	1	77	7	2
Lee, David, Asheville	4	8	.333	4.08	51	0	0	0	49	22	53.0	61	239	30	24	5	3	1	1	23	0	59	4	0
Leon, Scott, Cha. (S.C.)	6	12	.333	3.17	27	25	1	0	1	0	156.1	151	654	70	55	13	5	8	7	41	0	109	10	1
Leslie, Sean, Cape Fear*	0	5	.000	5.02	34	1	0	0	14	0	61.0	75	284	40	34	8	5	2	2	27	0	42	6	0
Loubier, Scott, Cape Fear	1	1	.500	2.89	10	2	0	0	2	0	28.0	19	114	9	9	1	1	1	4	12	0	20	2	0
Lowe, Benny, Hagerstown*	0	0	.000	0.00	2	0	0	0	2	0	2.0	3	10	3	0	0	0	0	0	0	0	4	0	0
Lyons, Mike, Columbia	6	2	.750	1.86	44	0	0	0	32	14	58.0	40	228	15	12	3	4	0	1	20	4	55	2	0
Mackey, Jason, Columbus	2	8	.200	5.01	18	17	0	0	1	0	93.1	86	411	61	52	14	0	4	11	45	1	69	8	2
MacKay, Tripp, Cape Fear	0	0	.000	0.00	1	0	0	0	1	0	1.0	2	6	0	0	0	0	0	0	0	0	0	0	0
Madison, Scott, Cha. (S.C.)*	0	1	.000	4.50	2	0	0	0	0	0	4.0	7	23	6	2	0	0	1	0	2	0	4	1	0
Mahlberg, John, Asheville	0	0	.000	5.03	12	0	0	0	8	2	19.2	29	96	15	11	1	0	1	0	8	0	16	2	0
Mairena, Oswaldo, Grn.*	6	1	.857	2.54	49	0	0	0	20	8	60.1	43	241	24	17	2	3	1	1	16	3	75	0	3
Mallard, Randi, Cha. (W.Va.)	3	3	.500	3.83	13	12	0	0	0	0	56.1	51	238	25	24	0	2	3	5	23	0	61	8	0
Mann, Jim, Hagerstown	0	1	.000	5.06	19	0	0	0	16	4	26.2	35	122	18	15	4	0	1	1	11	0	30	2	0
Manon, Julio, Cha. (S.C.)	3	5	.375	4.47	27	9	0	0	4	0	88.2	95	392	53	44	8	5	3	3	22	1	98	7	0
Marquez, Robert, Cape Fear	0	0	.000	2.95	12	0	0	0	5	2	18.1	15	81	6	6	0	0	0	1	12	0	18	0	2
Marquis, Jason, Macon	14	10	.583	4.38	28	28	0	0	0	0	141.2	156	627	78	69	10	2	7	2	55	1	121	8	2
Martinez, Caleb, Piedmont*	5	10	.333	4.66	20	19	0	0	0	0	110.0	117	487	70	57	11	7	5	10	38	0	89	3	3
Martinez, Dennis, Columbus	0	2	.000	23.40	6	0	0	0	2	0	5.0	7	32	13	13	2	0	0	3	8	0	2	2	0
Matcuk, Steven, Asheville	5	12	.294	4.45	28	27	3	0	1	1	159.2	157	674	86	79	15	2	5	10	55	1	100	2	1
Matz, Brian, Cape Fear*	4	6	.400	4.39	44	5	1	1	12	0	96.1	102	424	54	47	9	5	6	8	41	0	64	13	1
McClellan, Sean, Hagerstown	3	2	.600	1.66	35	0	0	0	26	11	65.0	49	271	21	12	3	5	3	1	26	1	80	4	0
McCrary, Scott, Columbia	3	2	.600	0.96	13	0	0	0	5	0	28.0	20	104	4	3	1	1	1	0	5	1	24	2	0
McDade, Neal, Augusta	10	4	.714	2.80	36	12	0	0	8	3	112.1	105	466	42	35	4	3	3	5	24	3	104	5	2
McNatt, Joshua, Delmarva*	6	2	.750	3.63	28	11	0	0	2	1	96.2	97	425	48	39	4	2	6	1	45	1	73	4	0
Mendes, Jaime, Piedmont	4	5	.444	4.45	42	2	0	0	10	0	85.0	103	368	48	42	7	8	3	2	20	2	47	2	1
Merrick, Brett, Columbus*	2	2	.500	4.94	23	0	0	0	11	0	31.0	29	144	24	17	4	1	1	1	21	1	25	2	0
Milburn, Robert, Macon*	4	1	.800	3.34	46	0	0	0	18	4	70.0	71	301	29	26	6	2	1	3	23	2	51	2	0
Miller, Brian, Piedmont	1	2	.333	4.94	29	7	0	0	6	1	74.2	91	338	44	41	10	1	2	4	24	1	63	2	1
Minter, Matt, Columbus*	5	3	.625	4.26	30	0	0	0	13	2	57.0	57	242	29	27	6	3	3	2	18	0	49	3	0

Pitcher, Team	W	L	Pct.	ERA	G	GS	CG	ShO	GF	Sv.	IP	H	TBF	R	ER	HR	SH	SF	HB	BB	IBB	SO	WP	Bk.
Mitchell, Courtney, Pied.*	7	4	.636	2.41	47	0	0	0	29	3	78.1	60	306	25	21	3	0	2	1	19	0	68	7	1
Mitchell, Dean, Savannah	11	5	.688	2.88	52	7	1	0	38	16	122.0	110	499	50	39	6	5	3	1	25	1	118	2	1
Molina, Gabe, Delmarva	8	6	.571	2.18	46	0	0	0	31	7	91.0	59	364	24	22	3	6	1	3	32	5	119	7	2
Morseman, Bob, Delmarva*	0	1	.000	4.73	7	0	0	0	3	0	13.1	13	65	11	7	2	0	0	0	11	0	18	1	2
Mota, Daniel, Greensboro	2	0	1.000	1.82	20	0	0	0	9	1	29.2	17	111	6	6	1	0	0	0	11	1	30	0	0
Mota, Guillermo, Cape Fear	5	10	.333	4.36	25	23	0	0	0	0	126.0	135	528	65	61	8	2	3	4	33	0	112	1	2
Musachio, John, Hickory*	1	0	1.000	3.66	11	0	0	0	5	1	19.2	21	82	8	8	1	1	0	1	4	0	19	0	0
Myette, Aaron, Hickory	3	1	.750	1.14	5	5	0	0	0	0	31.2	19	121	6	4	1	1	0	2	11	0	27	2	2
Needham, Kevin, CWV*	4	3	.571	4.81	35	11	0	0	13	2	78.2	93	354	58	42	5	4	4	3	28	0	51	8	1
Negrette, Richard, Columbus	2	1	.667	4.46	16	0	0	0	8	1	36.1	24	155	23	18	2	2	1	6	16	0	21	5	0
Nichols, James, Hickory	12	6	.667	4.14	28	27	1	0	1	0	158.2	161	681	85	73	12	8	8	6	49	0	112	7	0
Nicholson, John, Asheville	8	9	.471	3.78	25	25	0	0	0	0	135.2	128	570	70	57	13	8	7	7	36	0	115	4	3
Obando, Omar, Greensboro	5	7	.417	4.65	45	0	0	0	23	7	60.0	61	267	36	31	5	2	1	4	26	2	41	8	0
O'Connor, Brian, Augusta*	2	7	.222	4.41	25	14	0	0	3	0	85.2	90	385	54	42	6	4	1	2	39	1	91	11	0
Ojeda, Erick, C'bia-Aug.*	3	8	.273	4.80	44	0	0	0	18	1	75.0	77	318	46	40	4	6	3	3	20	5	66	6	1
Olivier, Rich, Greensboro	8	5	.615	4.13	35	13	0	0	6	2	106.2	111	471	61	49	8	4	2	8	51	1	79	6	0
Olszewski, Tim, Delmarva	0	0	.000	3.18	3	0	0	0	0	0	5.2	4	21	3	2	1	0	0	0	0	0	7	0	0
Ortega, Pablo, Cha. (S.C.)	12	10	.545	2.86	29	29	3	0	0	0	188.2	173	778	87	60	10	7	6	10	30	0	142	4	1
O'Shaughnessy, Jay, Sav.	6	12	.333	4.44	27	24	0	0	1	0	115.2	87	509	64	57	10	2	1	2	83	0	150	13	1
Osting, Jimmy, Macon*	2	3	.400	3.28	15	15	0	0	0	0	57.2	54	251	28	21	3	1	0	2	29	0	62	5	0
Pacheco, Delvis, Macon	1	3	.250	4.05	35	4	0	0	7	2	80.0	77	335	39	36	8	1	2	3	23	0	74	1	0
Paluk, Brian, Savannah	3	8	.273	5.78	27	20	1	1	0	0	118.1	141	527	82	76	10	7	1	9	35	0	61	11	0
Parker, Christian, Cape Fear	11	10	.524	3.12	25	25	0	0	0	0	153.0	146	640	72	53	5	9	6	7	49	0	106	9	2
Paronto, Chad, Delmarva	6	9	.400	4.74	28	23	0	0	2	0	127.1	133	569	95	67	9	5	5	1	56	1	93	6	0
Parotte, Frisco, Greensboro	1	1	.500	4.19	18	0	0	0	11	2	38.2	48	174	27	18	6	0	3	0	14	2	28	5	0
Parrish, John, Delmarva*	3	3	.500	3.84	23	10	0	0	5	1	72.2	69	315	39	31	7	2	3	2	32	3	76	9	0
Paugh, Rick, Augusta*	1	2	.333	2.43	24	0	0	0	18	8	29.2	24	122	9	8	3	1	0	0	7	0	40	0	0
Peguero, Americo, Delmarva	11	10	.524	4.87	27	26	1	0	0	0	142.1	152	631	97	77	14	2	6	8	53	1	133	7	2
Pena, Jesus, Hickory*	5	3	.625	2.22	43	0	0	0	32	8	65.0	55	263	24	16	3	4	3	0	19	1	57	3	0
Perez, Odalis, Macon*	4	5	.444	1.65	36	0	0	0	12	5	87.1	67	358	31	16	4	4	1	5	27	1	100	3	0
Prater, Andrew, Augusta	0	0	.000	10.95	6	3	0	0	1	0	12.1	21	64	16	15	3	0	0	1	6	0	9	2	0
Presley, Kirk, Columbia	0	1	.000	10.80	2	0	0	0	0	0	3.1	5	15	4	4	0	0	1	0	0	0	5	0	0
Priest, Eddie, Cha. (W.Va.)*	5	3	.625	3.62	14	14	0	0	0	0	77.0	79	321	38	31	6	2	3	2	10	0	70	5	0
Prokopec, Luke, Savannah	3	1	.750	4.07	13	6	0	0	5	0	42.0	37	175	21	19	8	1	3	1	12	0	45	1	0
Pumphrey, Kenny, Columbia	12	6	.667	3.10	27	27	3	2	0	0	165.2	137	708	70	57	11	7	3	20	72	0	133	11	1
Quezada, Edward, Cape Fear	8	6	.571	4.27	30	19	0	0	5	2	141.1	143	589	73	67	12	1	1	11	31	0	87	4	0
Quintana, Urbano, Piedmont	0	0	.000	18.47	3	0	0	0	2	0	6.1	12	34	13	13	2	0	2	1	3	0	2	1	0
Ramagli, Matt, Delmarva	1	1	.500	5.63	4	0	0	0	0	0	8.0	13	40	6	5	1	1	0	1	5	0	6	0	0
Rangel, Julio, Greensboro	12	9	.571	3.57	26	26	4	1	0	0	163.2	147	681	80	65	17	7	5	6	49	0	122	9	5
Reichow, Robert, Columbus	3	2	.600	3.39	20	2	0	0	4	2	61.0	54	254	32	23	4	1	2	4	11	5	50	5	0
Rivera, Alvin, Asheville	0	1	.000	0.00	1	1	0	0	0	0	2.1	2	13	1	0	0	0	0	0	4	0	0	0	0
Rivera, Luis, Macon	2	0	1.000	1.29	4	4	0	0	0	0	21.0	13	81	4	3	1	0	1	1	7	0	27	2	0
Robbins, Jake, Greensboro	6	4	.600	5.77	20	19	0	0	0	0	101.1	114	462	81	65	6	2	3	2	55	1	72	7	0
Roberson, Charles, Col.	0	0	.000	4.50	1	0	0	0	0	0	2.0	1	7	1	1	0	0	0	0	1	0	2	1	0
Roberts, Grant, Columbia	11	3	.786	2.36	22	22	2	1	0	0	129.2	98	530	37	34	1	3	3	8	44	0	122	5	0
Roberts, Mark, Hickory	0	2	.000	3.68	4	4	0	0	0	0	22.0	23	96	12	9	3	1	1	0	9	0	14	1	0
Rolocut, Brian, Cha. (S.C.)	0	1	.000	7.27	10	1	0	0	4	0	17.1	23	85	20	14	3	0	1	2	7	0	14	3	0
Romero, Alejandro, Savannah	0	1	.000	10.38	5	0	0	0	2	0	4.1	12	28	10	5	0	0	0	0	1	0	5	0	0
Romine, Jason, Asheville	4	2	.667	4.02	28	0	0	0	15	1	47.0	45	201	23	21	6	0	3	4	14	0	53	4	0
Rose, Ted, Cha. (W.Va.)	11	6	.647	2.51	38	13	2	2	9	4	129.1	108	525	44	36	7	9	3	6	27	0	132	3	2
Rutherford, Mark, Piedmont	1	4	.200	2.47	9	9	0	0	0	0	58.1	42	225	17	16	4	2	0	1	9	0	47	3	0
Sanchez, Mike, Savannah	1	5	.167	4.68	40	0	0	0	16	0	75.0	72	321	43	39	10	6	5	3	32	2	74	21	1
Santamaria, Bill, Columbia	2	1	.667	3.33	14	0	0	0	8	0	24.1	22	109	11	9	0	0	1	2	16	1	18	1	1
Saylor, Ryan, Cape Fear	2	1	.667	4.30	10	0	0	0	7	1	14.2	17	70	9	7	2	1	0	0	9	0	19	2	0
Schaffner, Eric, Greensboro	5	2	.714	3.45	28	7	0	0	9	0	78.1	73	329	35	30	1	1	5	4	23	0	73	3	2
Schroeffel, Scott, Asheville	2	3	.400	3.74	19	2	0	0	5	0	45.2	31	185	23	19	5	2	1	4	20	1	40	5	0
Scott, Brian, Hickory	6	3	.667	2.16	13	13	1	0	0	0	83.1	57	321	26	20	4	4	0	1	23	0	69	2	3
Seay, Robert, Cha. (S.C.)*	3	4	.429	4.55	13	13	0	0	0	0	61.1	56	269	35	31	2	2	2	3	37	0	64	6	0
Shepard, David, Cha. (W.Va.)	5	2	.714	4.95	18	10	0	0	8	3	67.1	82	292	46	37	11	2	1	2	17	3	45	1	0
Shiell, Jason, Macon	10	5	.667	2.86	27	24	0	0	0	0	129.0	113	523	53	41	12	3	5	8	32	0	101	6	0
Siciliano, Jess, Augusta	0	0	.000	4.66	11	0	0	0	6	1	19.1	22	88	12	10	2	1	1	2	5	0	9	1	0
Sikes, Jason, Piedmont	4	5	.444	5.63	27	11	0	0	7	0	96.0	124	432	67	60	16	1	2	5	31	0	63	5	0
Simon, Benjamin, Savannah	7	5	.583	3.09	18	17	2	1	1	0	93.1	84	398	35	32	2	6	4	7	27	0	93	3	0
Slamka, John, Asheville*	1	3	.250	3.75	26	2	0	0	8	0	57.2	61	250	31	24	7	3	2	5	27	0	48	8	0
Soto, Seferino, Savannah	2	2	.500	3.79	26	0	0	0	9	3	54.2	57	244	29	23	2	3	3	1	28	0	59	11	1
Spence, Cam, Greensboro	2	2	.500	3.38	8	7	0	0	0	0	48.0	43	195	23	18	4	3	3	3	10	0	35	0	0
Spiegel, Mike, Columbus*	0	0	.000	3.60	2	2	0	0	0	0	10.0	6	39	4	4	1	0	0	1	5	0	6	0	0
Splawn, Matt, Columbia	0	0	.000	0.93	7	0	0	0	5	0	9.2	7	40	4	1	1	0	0	1	1	0	10	0	0
Stevens, Kris, Piedmont*	6	4	.600	2.22	14	14	3	3	0	0	89.1	66	361	30	22	2	1	1	3	31	0	72	4	0
Stevenson, Rodney, Cape Fear	1	1	.500	0.53	16	0	0	0	15	5	17.0	7	66	3	1	0	0	0	0	6	1	20	1	0
Strickland, Scott, Cape Fear	0	1	.000	6.35	3	1	0	0	2	1	5.2	8	26	7	4	0	0	0	0	1	0	8	1	0
Taylor, Brien, Greensboro*	1	4	.200	14.33	8	7	0	0	1	0	27.0	31	162	47	43	6	3	2	0	52	0	20	13	0
Taylor, Mark, Columbus*	1	1	.500	7.50	20	0	0	0	11	0	30.0	37	147	29	25	1	1	4	1	26	0	28	7	0
Temple, Jason, Augusta	0	4	.000	5.54	11	5	0	0	1	0	37.1	46	185	29	23	2	0	3	1	22	0	38	7	1
Thompson, Mark, Asheville	0	2	.000	2.70	4	4	0	0	0	0	13.1	11	58	5	4	0	0	0	2	5	0	9	0	0
Tilton, Ira, Piedmont	7	13	.350	4.78	28	27	3	1	0	0	152.2	171	674	100	81	10	2	0	17	50	0	103	14	0
Tober, Dave, Piedmont	5	1	.833	3.42	46	0	0	0	27	10	81.2	65	333	34	31	6	4	0	3	25	0	55	5	1
Towers, Josh, Delmarva	0	0	.000	3.44	9	1	0	0	5	1	18.1	18	73	8	7	1	1	1	0	2	0	16	0	0
Tucker, Julien, Hickory	0	0	.000	3.68	4	0	0	0	1	0	7.1	11	35	7	3	1	0	1	1	2	0	7	0	0
Turman, Jimmy, Cape Fear	5	7	.417	4.18	19	15	1	0	1	0	88.1	84	374	45	41	4	1	1	6	35	0	72	8	0
Van Gilder, Ryan, Cape Fear	1	2	.333	3.18	4	0	0	0	2	0	5.2	8	31	3	2	0	0	0	3	4	0	8	0	0
Vasquez, Leoner, Columbia*	4	5	.444	5.14	22	8	0	0	8	1	56.0	63	250	37	32	4	1	2	3	22	1	49	7	1
Verdin, Cesar, Greensboro*	0	1	.000	1.80	1	1	0	0	0	0	5.0	5	21	3	1	2	0	0	0	1	0	8	0	0

Pitcher, Team	W	L	Pct.	ERA	G	GS	CG	ShO	GF	Sv.	IP	H	TBF	R	ER	HR	SH	SF	HB	BB	IBB	SO	WP	Bk.
Villafuerte, Brandon, Col.	3	1	.750	2.38	47	3	0	0	31	7	75.2	58	308	23	20	6	2	1	4	33	0	88	12	0
Virchis, Adam, Hickory	2	3	.400	3.86	15	2	0	0	4	1	44.1	42	183	20	19	3	0	1	3	11	0	34	3	1
Volkert, Oreste, Hagerstown	4	4	.500	3.68	34	0	0	0	19	1	51.1	42	220	22	21	2	3	1	7	22	1	45	1	0
Wagner, Ken, Columbus	6	4	.600	4.96	47	0	0	0	25	11	85.1	80	373	50	47	8	2	5	2	37	3	92	7	0
Walker, Morgan, Augusta*	0	1	.000	13.50	1	0	0	0	1	0	0.2	2	5	1	1	0	1	0	0	2	1	0	0	1
Walls, Doug, Asheville	4	2	.667	2.96	10	9	0	0	1	0	51.2	50	227	23	17	4	0	1	2	22	0	62	2	1
Westbrook, Jake, Asheville	14	11	.560	4.29	28	27	3	2	0	0	170.0	176	736	93	81	16	5	6	15	55	0	92	3	0
Whipple, Boomer, Augusta	0	0	.000	9.00	2	0	0	0	2	0	2.0	3	10	2	2	0	0	0	0	1	0	0	1	0
Whitley, Garry, Hickory*	0	1	.000	3.65	9	0	0	0	6	0	12.1	11	58	7	5	1	0	0	1	5	0	8	2	0
Whitlock, Brian, Columbus	0	0	.000	0.00	2	0	0	0	2	0	2.0	0	8	0	0	0	0	0	0	4	0	1	0	0
Whitson, Eric, Cha. (S.C.)	1	7	.125	4.10	30	0	0	0	15	1	48.1	46	204	23	22	5	2	2	5	13	2	47	2	2
Winkelsas, Joseph, Macon	3	2	.600	2.01	38	0	0	0	15	5	62.2	44	242	17	14	1	3	0	4	13	0	45	4	2
Young, Danny, Augusta*	0	2	.000	9.82	3	2	0	0	0	0	7.1	16	42	15	8	1	0	0	2	5	0	5	0	0
Young, Tim, Cape Fear*	1	1	.500	1.50	45	0	0	0	41	18	54.0	33	214	12	9	0	1	2	2	15	0	66	8	0

COMBINATION SHUTOUTS: **Asheville (3)**—Nicholson-Romine, Westbrook-Romine, Westbrook-Lee. **Augusta (8)**—O'Connor-McDade-Paugh, Alvarado-Elmore-Temple-Daniels, O'Connor-Halla, Ah Yat-Halla, McDade-Halla, Alvarado-Ojeda-Siciliano, Alvarado-Ojeda-Halla, Bullock-Siciliano. **Cape Fear (6)**—Lara-Young, Mota-Civit, Evans-Young, Turman-Quezada-Young, Parker-Handy, Quezada-Saylor. **Charleston, S.C. (9)**—Ortega-Enders-Whitson, Leon-Hill-Benesh, Seay-Brown-Manon-Benesh, Bowers-Hill-Benesh, Ortega-Hale, Griffiths-Brown, Brown-Brown-Benesh, Ortega-Benesh, Bowers-Manon-Enders. **Charleston, W.Va. (3)**—Mallard-LeBlanc-Needham, Corey-Rose, Carlyle-Arminio. **Columbia (14)**—Pumphrey-Lyons 2, Pumphrey-Coronado-Lyons, Kessel-Beebe-Lyons, Gonzalez-Lyons, Pumphrey-Coronado-Ojeda, Hafer-Coronado-Lyons, Roberts-Santamaria-Splawn, Kessel-Hafer, Roberts-Lyons, Roberts-Lyons-Hafer, Roberts-Vasquez, Kessel-Lyons, Arteaga-Santamaria-McCrary. **Columbus (7)**—Garza-Wagner, Feliz-Koeman-Deschenes, Feliz-Koeman-Deschenes, Feliz-Koeman-Deschenes, Garza-DePaula-Koeman-Deschenes, Bacsik-Deschenes, Mackey-Koeman-Deschenes. **Delmarva (12)**—Peguero-Kohlmeier, Forbes-Morseman-Molina, Forbes-Eibey-Molina, Falkenborg-Eibey-Kohlmeier, Falkenborg-Parrish-Kohlmeier, Falkenborg-Eibey, Falkenborg-Kohlmeier, Heredia-Dykhoff, Paronto-Kohlmeier, Paronto-Heredia, Peguero-Kohlmeier, McNatt-Molina. **Greensboro (5)**—Armas-Olivier, Armas-Mairena, Rangel-Mairena-Dingman, Spence-Parotte, Coble-Obando. **Hagerstown (6)**—Bale-McClellan, Andrews-Volkert-Davenport, LaChapelle-Delgado, Lawrence-Davenport, Glover-Lowe, Lawrence-McClellan. **Hickory (1)**—Scott-Whitley. **Macon (6)**—Marquis-Winkelsas, Bell-Perez-Cortes, Marquis-Winkelsas-Cortes, Shiell-Perez, Bell-Cortes, Bell-Winkelsas-Cortes, Marquis-Cortes, Chen-Winkelsas, Osting-Koehler-Milburn-Beasley-Winkelsas, Chen-Blythe-Milburn, Osting-Pacheco-Beasley-Winkelsas, Bell-Milburn, Rivera-Perez-Bauldree-Milburn. **Piedmont (4)**—Allen-Tober, Sikes-Mendes-Miller, Eaton-Tober, Sikes-Mitchell. **Savannah (3)**—Simon-Mitchell-Jacobson, Cervantes-Mitchell, O'Shaughnessy-Mitchell.

NO-HIT GAMES: Carlyle, Charleston, W.Va., defeated Asheville, 2-0 (first game), May 4; Bacci, Augusta, defeated Savanna, 2-0 (first game), May 26; Gulin, Columbus, defeated Columbia, 3-0 (first game), June 7.

PITCHERS WITH TWO OR MORE TEAMS

Pitcher, Team	W	L	Pct.	ERA	G	GS	CG	ShO	GF	Sv.	IP	H	TBF	R	ER	HR	SH	SF	HB	BB	IBB	SO	WP	Bk.
Ojeda, Erick, Columbia*	0	2	.000	5.79	7	0	0	0	4	0	14.0	14	58	10	9	2	3	1	1	4	0	13	1	1
Ojeda, Erick, Augusta*	3	6	.333	4.57	37	0	0	0	14	1	61.0	63	260	36	31	2	3	2	2	16	5	53	5	0

1997 FIELDING

TEAM

Team	Pct.	G	PO	A	E	TC	DP	PB
Columbia	.972	140	3545	1504	144	5193	96	21
Piedmont	.969	142	3727	1626	173	5526	104	17
Asheville	.967	139	3645	1608	177	5430	115	24
Cape Fear	.967	140	3693	1588	183	5464	101	33
Cha. (W.Va.)	.966	138	3548	1440	175	5163	113	7
Delmarva	.965	142	2783	1504	190	5477	112	24
Columbus	.965	138	3639	1421	182	5242	99	21
Savannah	.964	140	3586	1418	185	5189	99	28
Augusta	.963	142	3749	1479	203	5431	100	41
Hagerstown	.963	138	3562	1371	192	5125	96	36
Hickory	.962	140	3689	1509	207	5405	125	59
Macon	.961	140	3679	1376	205	5260	105	11
Greensboro	.959	141	3648	1528	220	5396	115	29
Charleston (S.C.)	.959	142	3729	1531	225	5485	94	25

TRIPLE PLAY: Charleston (W.Va.).

INDIVIDUAL

FIRST BASEMEN

NOTE: All caps denotes fielding-percentage leader based on 71 games for catchers, 94 for all other non-pitchers and 142 innings for pitchers. *Throws lefthanded.

Player, Team	Pct.	G	PO	A	E	TC	DP
Anthony, Brian, Asheville	.993	60	510	38	4	552	44
Baksh, Ray, Greensboro	.952	4	19	1	1	21	0
Becker, Brian, Cha. (S.C.)	.990	132	1161	106	13	1280	83
Bramlett, Jeff, Savannah	.993	16	142	9	1	152	9
Bruce, Robert, Columbus	.978	38	291	18	7	316	19
Chavez, Eric, Delmarva	.972	5	34	1	1	36	3
Clark, Kirby, Piedmont	1.000	1	13	0	0	13	1
Crede, Bradley, Piedmont	.989	109	1025	70	12	1107	67
Daedelow, Craig, Delmarva	1.000	1	1	0	0	1	0
DeCinces, Tim, Delmarva	.981	8	47	5	1	53	4
Diaz, Juan, Savannah	.977	70	608	23	15	646	49
Edmondson, Tracy, Columbia	1.000	1	1	0	0	1	0
Elam, Brett, Asheville	1.000	1	1	0	0	1	1
Figueroa, Franky, Delmarva	.986	7	71	2	1	74	6
Giles, Tim, Hagerstown	.987	51	417	22	6	445	25
Glavine, Michael, Columbus*	.991	71	620	40	6	666	51
Hacker, Steve, Macon	.990	49	372	38	4	414	34
Heintz, Chris, Hickory	.994	69	614	42	4	660	51
Huffman, Ryan, Greensboro	1.000	1	5	0	0	5	0
Johnson, Nick, Greensboro*	.987	126	1176	59	16	1251	99
Keller, Jeremy, Cha. (W.Va.)	.975	22	151	6	4	161	9
Kent, Troy, Columbus	.986	27	199	14	3	216	12
King, Michael, Cha. (S.C.)	1.000	7	36	2	0	38	2
Klee, Charles, Hickory	.979	8	41	6	1	48	5
Larkin, Stephen, Cha. (W.Va.)*	.971	32	220	16	7	243	15
LaRue, Jason, Cha. (W.Va.)	.933	7	41	1	3	45	6
Lasater, Chris, Delmarva	1.000	1	5	0	0	5	0
Leach, Nick, Savannah	.987	26	201	19	3	223	9
Lindsey, John, Asheville	.985	84	789	49	13	851	59
Long, Garrett, Augusta	.971	34	287	17	9	313	24
Lopez, Luis, Hagerstown	1.000	87	749	47	0	796	53
Martinez, Rafael, Columbia*	.969	17	142	13	5	160	11
Minor, Ryan, Delmarva	1.000	14	95	3	0	98	7
Nichols, Kevin, Piedmont	1.000	9	76	6	0	82	6
Nunnari, Talmadge, Cape Fear*	1.000	8	73	7	0	80	7
O'Hearn, Brandon, Cha. (W.Va.)	1.000	1	8	0	0	8	0
Olsen, D.C., Cape Fear	.990	21	185	13	2	200	10
Olson, Dan, Hickory*	.935	5	29	0	2	31	1
Oropeza, Willie, Cape Fear	.983	51	434	36	8	478	30
Parsons, Jason, Cha. (W.Va.)	.989	89	784	46	9	839	67
Pickering, Calvin, Delmarva*	.974	115	940	70	27	1037	73
Pond, Simon, Cape Fear	.993	16	135	10	1	146	12
Quatraro, Matthew, Cha. (S.C.)	.981	5	49	2	1	52	1
RIVERA, Carlos, Augusta*	.993	97	798	59	6	863	56
Saffer, Jeff, Greensboro	.978	7	45	0	1	46	2
Salinas, Hector, Cha. (S.C.)	.900	1	9	0	1	10	0

CLASS A South Atlantic League

Player, Team	Pct.	G	PO	A	E	TC	DP
Sankey, Brian, Savannah*	.996	32	262	19	1	282	20
Scharrer, Jim, Macon	.984	90	741	39	13	793	52
Sharpe, Grant, Columbus	.989	11	83	10	1	94	5
Shatley, Andy, Hagerstown	1.000	4	19	1	0	20	2
Sheppard, Greg, Hickory	.973	68	601	23	17	641	50
Shipp, Skip, Augusta	1.000	2	2	0	0	2	0
Suriel, Miguel, Cha. (S.C.)	1.000	1	9	0	0	9	0
Tessmar, Timothy, Columbia*	.991	103	877	77	9	963	61
Torti, Michael, Piedmont	.996	26	227	15	1	243	15
Tracy, Andrew, Cape Fear	.985	52	483	37	8	528	27
Turlais, John, Augusta	1.000	1	3	0	0	3	0
Velazquez, Jose, Greensboro*	.990	14	99	3	1	103	7
Vickers, Randy, Columbia	.991	24	192	17	2	211	12
Walker, Morgan, Augusta*	.981	17	139	15	3	157	5
Wesemann, Jason, Piedmont	1.000	1	2	0	0	2	0
Whipple, Boomer, Augusta	1.000	3	11	0	0	11	1
Wong, Jerrod, Macon*	.923	3	23	1	2	26	3

TRIPLE PLAY: Larkin.

SECOND BASEMEN

Player, Team	Pct.	G	PO	A	E	TC	DP
Abernathy, Brent, Hagerstown	.973	99	178	258	12	448	45
Antrim, Pat, Greensboro	.926	13	16	34	4	54	5
Bain, Tyler, Cha. (S.C.)	.948	115	203	289	27	519	45
Baston, Stanley, Hagerstown	.882	4	10	5	2	17	2
Batts, Rodney, Piedmont	1.000	3	1	10	0	11	0
Bellenger, Butch, Augusta	.500	1	0	2	2	4	0
Blandford, Paul, Cape Fear	.962	101	222	280	20	522	44
Borges, Alex, Macon	1.000	1	4	2	0	6	0
Bravo, Danny, Cape Fear	.931	7	15	12	2	29	2
Campbell, Wylie, Cha. (W.Va.)	.964	15	28	25	2	55	4
Casimiro, Carlos, Delmarva	.959	115	204	287	21	512	49
Cuevas, Trent, Savannah	.963	57	86	145	9	240	27
Daedelow, Craig, Delmarva	.987	18	33	45	1	79	11
Edmondson, Tracy, Columbia	.913	11	7	14	2	23	0
Edwards, Lamont, Piedmont	.949	106	203	332	29	564	48
Elam, Brett, Asheville	.857	3	2	4	1	7	0
Erickson, Corey, Columbia	.983	46	54	123	3	180	15
Espada, Angel, Columbia	.978	30	41	92	3	136	13
Figueroa, Luis, Augusta	1.000	3	9	14	0	23	3
Fowler, Maleke, Delmarva	1.000	2	0	1	0	1	0
Frias, Ovidio, Hickory	.875	5	2	9	2	16	0
Goodhart, Steve, Cha. (W.Va.)	.970	80	146	210	11	367	42
Hines, Pooh, Macon	.936	20	37	51	6	94	11
Katz, Jason, Macon	.931	34	63	71	10	144	18
Kehoe, John, Hagerstown	1.000	14	19	35	0	54	4
Kent, Troy, Columbus	.963	91	161	233	15	409	46
Klee, Charles, Hickory	.956	11	18	25	2	45	5
Konrady, Dennis, Columbus	1.000	8	9	25	0	34	4
Livingston, Doug, Asheville	.967	121	227	365	20	612	70
Lorenzana, Luis, Augusta	.968	41	61	92	5	158	18
MacKay, Tripp, Cape Fear	.968	36	61	91	5	157	19
Martinez, Luis, Savannah	.972	74	128	187	9	324	35
Mejia, Juan, Piedmont	.947	3	8	10	1	19	1
Montgomery, Andre, Cha. (W.Va.)	.952	15	28	31	3	62	8
Morrison, Scott, Savannah	.978	15	9	35	1	45	2
Owens-Bragg, Luke, Cha. (S.C.)	.961	31	62	87	6	155	17
Parsons, Jeff, Columbia	.970	8	13	19	1	33	3
Paz, Richard, Delmarva	.964	20	36	44	3	83	9
Penalver, Juan, Columbia	1.000	8	11	15	0	26	2
Perez, Edwin, Columbus	.939	23	42	50	6	98	9
Perez, Jersen, Columbia	1.000	2	2	9	0	11	4
Presto, Nick, Cha. (W.Va.)	1.000	20	35	66	0	101	10
Price, Corey, Cha. (W.Va.)	.966	13	26	31	2	59	8
RODRIGUEZ, Liu, Hickory	.989	126	225	332	6	563	69
Schreiber, Stan, Augusta	.957	82	150	210	16	376	44
Shatley, Andy, Hagerstown	1.000	3	4	4	0	8	4
Smith, Rod, Greensboro	.950	134	244	387	33	664	79
Solano, Angel, Hickory	.960	9	9	15	1	25	3
Soriano, Carlos, Columbia	.959	34	52	66	5	123	12
Soriano, Fred, Hagerstown	.965	17	23	32	2	57	6
Stromsborg, Ryan, Hagerstown	.980	12	25	23	1	49	6
Swafford, Derek, Augusta	.938	20	38	52	6	96	7
Tamargo, John, Columbia	.978	21	38	52	2	92	11
Taylor, Greg, Piedmont	.983	33	70	99	3	172	21
Terhune, Mike, Macon	.945	58	86	139	13	238	21
Thorpe, A.D., Macon	.951	38	47	90	7	144	17
Whipple, Boomer, Augusta	1.000	5	5	3	0	8	0
Whitley, Matt, Asheville	.989	17	28	61	1	90	6
Whitlock, Brian, Columbus	.969	24	41	54	3	98	12

TRIPLE PLAY: Goodhart.

THIRD BASEMEN

Player, Team	Pct.	G	PO	A	E	TC	DP
Antrim, Pat, Greensboro	.813	5	2	11	3	16	1
Arrendondo, Hernando, Cha. (S.C.)	.895	6	7	10	2	19	3
Barner, Doug, Cha. (S.C.)	.904	79	45	162	22	229	7
Baston, Stanley, Hagerstown	.889	10	12	20	4	36	2
Batts, Rodney, Piedmont	.912	14	11	20	3	34	1
Bellenger, Butch, Augusta	1.000	2	2	2	0	4	0
Blandford, Paul, Cape Fear	1.000	2	1	3	0	4	0
Bravo, Danny, Cape Fear	.895	24	8	43	6	57	4
Bruce, Robert, Columbus	.938	9	1	14	1	16	1
Bryant, Clint, Asheville	.902	50	35	103	15	153	9
Campbell, Wylie, Cha. (W.Va.)	.914	95	46	178	21	245	15
Coffie, Evanon, Delmarva	.933	7	8	6	1	15	0
Corps, Erick, Cha. (S.C.)	.913	53	30	96	12	138	9
Crede, Joe, Hickory	.905	112	84	232	33	349	23
Cuevas, Trent, Savannah	1.000	2	0	5	0	5	1
Daedelow, Craig, Delmarva	.800	5	3	5	2	10	2
Edmondson, Tracy, Columbia	.932	22	9	32	3	44	3
Elam, Brett, Asheville	.941	48	39	73	7	119	6
Erickson, Corey, Columbia	1.000	3	1	7	0	8	0
Frias, Ovidio, Hickory	.907	20	11	28	4	43	3
Hessman, Michael, Macon	.899	116	74	184	29	287	17
Hundt, Bo, Augusta	.898	102	68	170	27	265	9
Katz, Jason, Macon	.909	6	5	5	1	11	0
Keck, Brian, Asheville	.976	31	16	65	2	83	1
Keller, Jeremy, Cha. (W.Va.)	.900	40	27	63	10	100	3
Klee, Charles, Hickory	.875	14	12	16	4	32	2
Konrady, Dennis, Columbus	.948	72	51	114	9	174	12
LaRue, Jason, Cha. (W.Va.)	.750	5	3	3	2	8	0
Lasater, Chris, Delmarva	1.000	1	1	3	0	4	0
Leon, Donny, Greensboro	.885	136	80	229	40	349	13
Long, Garrett, Augusta	1.000	1	1	1	0	2	0
Lopez, Luis, Hagerstown	.875	7	4	17	3	24	1
Lorenzana, Luis, Augusta	1.000	1	1	0	0	1	0
MacKay, Tripp, Cape Fear	1.000	1	0	1	0	1	0
Malave, Joshua, Savannah	1.000	1	1	5	0	6	1
May, Scott, Augusta	.833	3	1	4	1	6	0
Mejia, Juan, Piedmont	.911	21	14	37	5	56	2
Minor, Ryan, Delmarva	.899	113	98	206	34	338	13
Myers, Aaron, Asheville	.879	12	7	22	4	33	2
Nichols, Kevin, Piedmont	.901	56	35	93	14	142	5
Oropeza, Willie, Cape Fear	.882	7	3	12	2	17	1
Owens-Bragg, Luke, Cha. (S.C.)	.800	8	4	8	3	15	0
Parsons, Jeff, Columbia	.900	4	3	6	1	10	0
Paz, Richard, Delmarva	.932	24	17	38	4	59	5
Penalver, Juan, Columbia	1.000	2	0	2	0	2	1
Perez, Edwin, Columbus	.972	13	11	24	1	36	2
POND, Simon, Cape Fear	.925	100	49	209	21	279	9
Presto, Nick, Cha. (W.Va.)	.727	10	4	12	6	22	0
Price, Corey, Cha. (W.Va.)	1.000	1	0	1	0	1	0
Rigoli, David, Cape Fear	.882	12	6	24	4	34	0
Rodriguez, Luis, Hagerstown	1.000	2	0	2	0	2	0
Rolls, Damian, Savannah	.920	130	111	246	31	388	14
Schreiber, Stan, Augusta	.821	22	8	38	10	56	2
Seabol, Scott, Greensboro	.826	10	8	11	4	23	1
Shatley, Andy, Hagerstown	.882	107	80	190	36	306	18
Soriano, Carlos, Columbia	.941	65	31	113	9	153	7
Soriano, Fred, Hagerstown	.857	8	4	8	2	14	2
Stromsborg, Ryan, Hagerstown	.957	12	8	14	1	23	0
Suriel, Miguel, Cha. (S.C.)	1.000	2	0	1	0	1	0
Taylor, Greg, Piedmont	1.000	6	4	2	0	6	0
Terhune, Mike, Macon	.902	23	8	47	6	61	1
Torti, Michael, Piedmont	.871	23	14	47	9	70	8
Vickers, Randy, Columbia	.889	25	15	41	7	63	3
Wesemann, Jason, Piedmont	.896	42	21	65	10	96	1
Whipple, Boomer, Augusta	.931	32	20	61	6	87	5
Whitlock, Brian, Columbus	.876	55	35	85	17	137	8
Zamora, Junior, Columbia	.969	36	22	72	3	97	5
Zaun, Brian, Savannah	.929	9	10	16	2	28	2

SHORTSTOPS

Player, Team	Pct.	G	PO	A	E	TC	DP
Antrim, Pat, Greensboro	.890	24	37	60	12	109	8
Bravo, Danny, Cape Fear	.969	29	33	90	4	127	14
Camilli, Jason, Cape Fear	.924	94	138	290	35	463	42
Campbell, Wylie, Cha. (W.Va.)	.977	11	13	29	1	43	7
Coffie, Evanon, Delmarva	.946	79	118	197	18	333	38
Corps, Erick, Cha. (S.C.)	1.000	3	6	8	0	14	0
Cuevas, Trent, Savannah	.925	32	43	68	9	120	18
Daedelow, Craig, Delmarva	.959	28	39	79	5	123	16
Dellaero, Jason, Hickory	.942	55	79	150	14	243	23

Player, Team	Pct.	G	PO	A	E	TC	DP
Delossantos, Eddy, Cha. (S.C.)	.923	127	158	348	42	548	52
Edmondson, Tracy, Columbia	.952	15	19	21	2	42	4
Elam, Brett, Asheville	.930	32	48	99	11	158	16
Figueroa, Luis, Augusta	.936	68	98	182	19	299	34
Frias, Ovidio, Hickory	.839	7	6	20	5	31	5
Guthrie, David, Cha. (W.Va.)	.938	73	115	216	22	353	45
Guzman, Cristian, Greensboro	.936	122	173	364	37	574	68
Harkrider, Kip, Savannah	.962	18	28	47	3	78	8
Illig, Brett, Savannah	.966	51	67	132	7	206	15
Jaroncyk, Ryan, Columbia	.902	29	26	85	12	123	15
Keck, Brian, Asheville	1.000	3	3	9	0	12	1
Klee, Charles, Hickory	.915	80	125	239	34	398	41
Konrady, Dennis, Columbus	.940	27	39	71	7	117	13
Lawrence, Joe, Hagerstown	.926	115	134	278	33	445	46
Lorenzana, Luis, Augusta	.956	52	59	136	9	204	19
MacKay, Tripp, Cape Fear	.910	19	24	47	7	78	8
Mejia, Juan, Piedmont	.824	5	3	11	3	17	2
Morrison, Scott, Savannah	.921	45	42	121	14	177	18
Owens-Bragg, Luke, Cha. (S.C.)	.954	13	19	43	3	65	7
Parsons, Jeff, Columbia	.869	17	25	48	11	84	6
Paz, Richard, Delmarva	.969	50	77	110	6	193	23
Perez, Edwin, Columbus	.917	3	4	7	1	12	2
Presto, Nick, Cha. (W.Va.)	.962	54	83	171	10	264	24
Price, Corey, Cha. (W.Va.)	.882	4	2	13	2	17	1
Robinson, Tony, Augusta	.964	18	27	53	3	83	9
Rodriguez, Liu, Hickory	1.000	2	0	4	0	4	0
ROLLINS, Jimmy, Piedmont	.960	138	201	421	26	648	67
Schreiber, Stan, Augusta	.977	10	18	25	1	44	2
Seabol, Scott, Greensboro	.875	2	4	3	1	8	1
Shatley, Andy, Hagerstown	1.000	7	9	22	0	31	1
Soriano, Fred, Hagerstown	.940	10	13	34	3	50	3
Stromsborg, Ryan, Hagerstown	.967	8	7	22	1	30	2
Tamargo, John, Columbia	.944	84	122	197	19	338	34
Taylor, Greg, Piedmont	1.000	1	1	0	0	1	0
Terhune, Mike, Macon	.984	13	18	42	1	61	8
Thorpe, A.D., Macon	.896	58	85	138	26	249	30
Valera, Willy, Columbus	.944	116	161	326	29	516	54
Wesemann, Jason, Piedmont	1.000	1	4	2	0	6	0
Whitley, Matt, Asheville	.944	106	174	351	31	556	61
Williams, Glenn, Macon	.944	74	113	171	17	301	39

OUTFIELDERS

Player, Team	Pct.	G	PO	A	E	TC	DP
Alamo, Efrain, Asheville	.914	31	60	4	6	70	1
Anderson, Christopher, CSC	.889	4	8	0	1	9	0
Antrim, Pat, Greensboro	1.000	12	18	2	0	20	0
Aylor, Brian, Greensboro*	.971	59	95	4	3	102	0
Bair, Rod, Asheville	.969	87	105	19	4	128	5
Baston, Stanley, Hagerstown	1.000	3	10	0	0	10	0
Batts, Rodney, Piedmont	1.000	3	3	0	0	3	0
Benjamin, Al, Augusta	1.000	5	8	0	0	8	0
Bergeron, Peter, Savannah	.984	131	240	8	4	252	3
Bishop, Tim, Columbia	.957	14	22	0	1	23	0
Blakeney, Mo, Cape Fear	.920	12	22	1	2	25	0
Blandford, Paul, Cape Fear	1.000	3	3	0	0	3	0
Bramlett, Jeff, Savannah	.980	56	94	2	2	98	1
Broach, Donald, Cha. (W.Va.)	1.000	17	28	0	0	28	0
Brown, Eric, Savannah	.989	58	79	8	1	88	2
Brown, Gavin, Macon	.976	53	83	0	2	85	0
Burress, Andy, Cha. (W.Va.)	.909	11	10	0	1	11	0
Butler, Garrett, Greensboro	.965	74	110	1	4	115	0
Carney, Bartt, Delmarva	1.000	14	12	0	0	12	0
Chancey, Bailey, Columbia	.949	18	35	2	2	39	0
Charles, Curtis, Delmarva	.965	87	127	9	5	141	2
Chatman, Karl, Cape Fear	.986	116	197	7	3	207	3
Christensen, McKay, Hickory*	.969	124	280	5	9	294	4
Clark, Kirby, Piedmont	1.000	6	5	0	0	5	0
Claybrook, Steve, Cha. (W.Va.)	.973	84	103	4	3	110	0
Cooley, Shannon, Piedmont	.975	77	143	10	4	157	0
Crane, Todd, Piedmont	.978	80	124	12	3	139	4
Crawford, Marty, Piedmont	.956	30	39	4	2	45	0
Daedelow, Craig, Delmarva	1.000	18	20	0	0	20	0
Davis, Albert, Augusta	.959	74	111	5	5	121	0
DeCelle, Mike, Cha. (S.C.)	1.000	47	56	5	0	61	0
Denning, Wes, Cape Fear	.983	133	272	10	5	287	3
Dent, Darrell, Delmarva*	.957	127	232	15	11	258	2
Duverge, Salvadore, Asheville	1.000	28	44	6	0	50	0
Edmondson, Tracy, Columbia	1.000	3	3	0	0	3	0
Edwards, Randy, Augusta	.667	1	2	0	1	3	0
Foulks, Brian, Savannah	.962	17	24	1	1	26	0
FOWLER, Maleke, Delmarva	.9939	97	152	12	1	165	3
Francia, David, Piedmont*	.987	110	228	7	3	238	3
Gonzalez, Manuel, Hickory	.976	114	222	22	6	250	4
Gordon, Gary, Asheville	1.000	60	94	7	0	101	2
Haltiwanger, Garrick, Columbia*	.975	113	148	7	4	159	1
Hamlin, Mark, Asheville	.973	113	138	7	4	149	1
Hampton, Robby, Hagerstown	.952	98	156	2	8	166	0
Hines, Pooh, Macon	1.000	5	7	0	0	7	0
Hollins, Darontaye, Hickory	.978	27	40	4	1	45	0
Hooper, Daren, Delmarva	1.000	6	3	0	0	3	0
Huff, Brent, Columbia	.993	83	139	2	1	142	1
Hundt, Bo, Augusta	1.000	12	18	1	0	19	0
Hutchison, Bernard, Asheville	.958	100	200	5	9	214	0
Inglin, Jeff, Hickory	.972	88	124	14	4	142	4
Jefferson, Dave, Cape Fear	1.000	22	38	1	0	39	0
Johnson, Damon, Hagerstown	.934	81	121	7	9	137	2
Johnson, Jason, Augusta	.977	18	37	5	1	43	0
Kastelic, Matthew, Cha. (S.C.)*	.937	50	83	6	6	95	1
Katz, Jason, Macon	1.000	25	32	1	0	33	0
Kiil, Harry, Piedmont	1.000	80	141	9	0	150	0
King, Michael, Cha. (S.C.)	.931	44	63	4	5	72	0
Kofler, Eric, Greensboro*	.962	62	95	6	4	105	0
Kurtz, Tony, Delmarva	1.000	37	56	1	0	57	0
Landstad, Rob, Columbus	.944	58	65	3	4	72	2
Larkin, Stephen, Cha. (W.Va.)*	.980	100	184	9	4	197	2
Long, Garrett, Augusta	.969	28	30	1	1	32	0
MacKay, Tripp, Cape Fear	1.000	3	1	1	0	2	0
Maloney, Jeff, Hagerstown	.951	95	167	6	9	182	0
Martinez, Rafael, Columbia*	1.000	18	28	1	0	29	0
Matos, Luis, Delmarva	.972	36	66	3	2	71	1
May, Freddy, Augusta*	.966	105	190	6	7	203	0
May, Scott, Augusta	1.000	2	2	0	0	2	0
McCain, Marcus, Cha. (S.C.)	1.000	5	8	0	0	8	0
McCarthy, Kevin, Columbia*	.966	27	26	2	1	29	0
McKinnon, Tom, Cha. (S.C.)	.976	41	77	4	2	83	2
Motley, Mel, Columbus	.979	24	45	1	1	47	0
Murphy, Robbie, Cha. (W.Va.)	.954	50	98	5	5	108	2
O'Hearn, Brandon, Cha. (W.Va.)	.983	61	108	5	2	115	0
Olson, Dan, Hickory*	.974	63	105	6	3	114	1
Parsons, Jeff, Columbia	.941	13	13	3	1	17	0
Paz, Richard, Delmarva	1.000	1	2	1	0	3	0
Pena, Alex, Augusta	.949	107	176	11	10	197	5
Pendergrass, Tyrone, Macon	.960	127	251	16	11	278	4
Perez, Richard, Delmarva	1.000	25	34	3	0	37	0
Pointer, Corey, Augusta	.902	72	102	9	12	123	2
Prokopec, Luke, Savannah	.977	47	77	8	2	87	1
Ramirez, Daniel, Columbia	.959	125	196	17	9	222	4
Rice, Charles, Augusta	.921	35	33	2	3	38	0
Rijo-Berger, Jose, Columbia	1.000	15	13	0	0	13	0
Riley, Cash, Savannah	.941	26	31	1	· 2	34	0
Rivera, Roberto, Delmarva	.900	13	18	0	2	20	0
Rodriguez, Mike, Hagerstown	1.000	5	8	1	0	9	0
Rodriquez, Gary, Columbus	.987	116	226	7	3	236	3
Ross, Jason, Macon	.972	111	199	6	6	211	2
Rowson, James, Greensboro	.938	8	13	2	1	16	0
Saffer, Jeff, Greensboro	.857	12	12	0	2	14	0
Salinas, Hector, Cha. (S.C.)	.950	62	94	1	5	100	0
Sanchez, Alex, Cha. (S.C.)*	.963	131	279	6	11	296	2
Sankey, Brian, Savannah*	1.000	11	16	1	0	17	0
Schwab, Chris, Cape Fear*	1.000	15	17	0	0	17	0
Scott, Tom, Cha. (W.Va.)	.947	60	85	5	5	95	0
Seabol, Scott, Greensboro	.955	17	21	0	1	22	0
Sheppard, Greg, Hickory	1.000	4	2	0	0	2	0
Shumpert, Derek, Greensboro	.986	86	144	2	2	148	0
Simpson, Jeramie, Columbia	.909	10	10	0	1	11	0
Springfield, Bo, Augusta	1.000	9	10	0	0	10	0
Stearns, Randy, Savannah	.967	90	139	6	5	150	1
Stephens, Joel, Delmarva	.914	29	30	2	3	35	0
Stromsborg, Ryan, Hagerstown	1.000	23	43	2	0	45	1
Suriel, Miguel, Cha. (S.C.)	1.000	1	1	0	0	1	0
Thames, Marcus, Greensboro	1.000	4	6	0	0	6	0
Thomas, Allen, Hickory*	.966	20	28	0	1	29	0
Thompson, Nick, Piedmont	.896	17	40	3	5	48	0
Tidwell, David, Cha. (W.Va.)	.982	64	158	2	3	163	0
Tucci, Peter, Hagerstown	.9937	108	147	11	1	159	1
Vazquez, Manny, Cha. (S.C.)*	.990	52	89	8	1	98	2
Velazquez, Jose, Greensboro*	.970	115	158	5	5	166	0
Verrall, Jared, Cha. (S.C.)	1.000	3	6	0	0	6	0
Ware, Jeremy, Cape Fear	.955	130	218	14	11	243	4
Whitaker, Chad, Columbus	.964	107	183	3	7	193	0
Whitlock, Brian, Columbus	1.000	10	13	2	0	15	0
Williams, Errick, Piedmont	.955	37	58	5	3	66	3
Williams, Jewell, Columbus	.943	110	160	6	10	176	0
Willis, Symmion, Hagerstown	1.000	15	26	0	0	26	0
Wong, Jerrod, Macon*	.948	110	157	6	9	172	2

CLASS A South Atlantic League

CATCHERS

Player, Team	Pct.	G	PO	A	E	TC	DP	PB
Alley, Chip, Delmarva	.980	72	503	79	12	594	6	17
Anderson, Blake, Asheville	.986	69	442	57	7	506	2	9
Anderson, Christopher, CSC	.963	60	405	60	18	483	4	9
Antczak, Chuck, Hickory	1.000	1	1	0	0	1	0	0
Arias, Rogelio, Asheville	.978	72	589	66	15	670	5	15
Arnold, John, Macon	1.000	2	14	3	0	17	1	1
Bennett, Ryan, Columbia	.984	18	108	13	2	123	0	2
Borges, Alex, Macon	.979	37	296	23	7	326	1	8
Brown, Gavin, Macon	1.000	1	4	0	0	4	0	0
Burress, Andy, Cha. (W.Va.)	1.000	4	3	0	0	3	0	0
Chavez, Eric, Delmarva	.969	16	108	16	4	128	2	4
Clark, Kirby, Piedmont	.991	16	105	10	1	116	0	1
DeCinces, Tim, Delmarva	.990	53	371	39	4	414	5	2
Downs, Brian, Hickory	.950	25	149	22	9	180	3	6
Emmons, Scott, Greensboro	1.000	3	16	2	0	18	0	0
Engle, Beau, Columbia	1.000	4	10	1	0	11	0	0
Evans, Lee, Augusta	.983	41	317	39	6	362	3	17
Evans, Pat, Columbus	.977	31	229	22	6	257	1	2
Fagley, Dan, Hickory	1.000	7	42	4	0	46	0	1
Fauske, Joshua, Hickory	.971	78	504	70	17	591	7	26
Flores, Eric, Savannah	.917	3	9	2	1	12	0	1
Fowler, Ben, Columbus	.946	16	98	7	6	111	1	5
Garrett, Scott, Cha. (W.Va.)	.983	30	214	21	4	239	2	1
Glassey, Josh, Savannah	.983	73	533	53	10	596	2	15
Heintz, Chris, Hickory	.980	43	252	35	6	293	3	26
Keech, Erik, Greensboro	1.000	12	63	8	0	71	1	2
Koehler, Jason, Hagerstown	.974	26	166	21	5	192	2	6
Landstad, Rob, Columbus	1.000	2	8	0	0	8	0	0
LaRue, Jason, Cha. (W.Va.)	.982	106	667	80	14	761	7	4
Lasater, Chris, Delmarva	1.000	17	135	17	0	152	1	1
Lunar, Fernando, Macon	.987	105	888	135	13	1036	7	2
Malave, Joshua, Savannah	.969	56	403	40	14	457	1	12
Marsters, Brandon, Piedmont	.985	61	398	55	7	460	8	7
May, Scott, Augusta	.966	11	51	5	2	58	1	7
Melendez, Jorge, Columbus	.972	57	367	47	12	426	2	7
Meyer, Travis, Savannah	.966	13	128	12	5	145	1	0
Munson, Mike, Greensboro	1.000	1	2	0	0	2	0	0
Newman, Howard, CWV	.985	11	61	6	1	68	1	3
Oliveros, Leonardo, Piedmont	.990	26	162	32	2	196	3	5
Olsen, D.C., Cape Fear	.968	7	29	1	1	31	0	2
Oropeza, Willie, Cape Fear	.991	18	92	23	1	116	2	10
O'Toole, Bobby, Delmarva	1.000	1	2	1	0	3	1	0
Phelps, Josh, Hagerstown	.965	66	519	56	21	596	7	14
Pinto, Rene, Greensboro	.991	28	211	18	2	231	1	5
Pointer, Corey, Augusta	.905	6	36	2	4	42	1	5
Quatraro, Matthew, CSC	.970	47	378	45	13	436	1	11
Rodriguez, Chris, Asheville	1.000	2	13	0	0	16	1	0
Rodriguez, Luis, Hagerstown	.966	25	199	28	8	235	0	5
Rodriguez, Mike, Hagerstown	.975	31	221	12	6	239	0	11
Salinas, Hector, Cha. (S.C.)	.955	22	157	12	8	177	1	2
Schneider, Brian, Cape Fear	.988	108	724	99	10	833	5	19
Sheppard, Greg, Hickory	1.000	6	9	0	0	9	0	0
SHIPP, Skip, Augusta	.989	71	550	71	7	628	5	9
Smith, Casey, Columbus	.962	13	117	8	5	130	0	1
Stanton, Thomas, Columbia	.995	43	338	39	2	379	4	8
Streicher, Robert, Cape Fear	.979	13	85	7	2	94	1	1
Suriel, Miguel, Cha. (S.C.)	.959	19	147	15	7	169	0	3
Taylor, Adam, Columbus	.983	45	307	48	6	361	2	6
Thompson, Nick, Piedmont	.978	42	279	29	7	315	0	4
Turlais, John, Augusta	.986	26	204	15	3	222	2	3
Twombley, Dennis, Grn.	1.000	8	38	3	0	41	1	4
Valencia, Victor, Greensboro	.970	100	680	105	24	809	5	18
Valera, Yohanny, Columbia	.987	89	651	107	10	768	4	11
White, John, Cape Fear	1.000	3	22	2	0	24	0	1

PITCHERS

Player, Team	Pct.	G	PO	A	E	TC	DP
Acevedo, Jose, Cha. (W.Va.)	.909	15	2	8	1	11	0
Achilles, Matt, Delmarva	1.000	3	3	5	0	8	0
Ah Yat, Paul, Augusta*	.923	29	2	10	1	13	0
Allen, Brandon, Piedmont*	.935	25	7	36	3	46	1
Allen, Craig, Savannah	1.000	10	1	0	0	1	0
Altman, Gene, Cha. (W.Va.)	1.000	17	1	4	0	5	0
Alvarado, Carlos, Augusta	.960	29	8	16	1	25	1
Andrews, Clayton, Hagerstown*	1.000	28	1	14	0	15	2
Armas, Tony, Greensboro	1.000	9	4	8	0	12	0
Arminio, Samuel, Cha. (W.Va.)	.958	46	8	15	1	24	4
Arteaga, Juan, Columbia*	1.000	1	1	0	0	1	0
Averette, Robert, Cha. (W.Va.)	1.000	11	0	4	0	4	0
Bacci, Anthony, Augusta*	1.000	6	1	4	0	5	0
Bacsik, Mike, Columbus*	.978	28	11	34	1	46	0
Bale, John, Hagerstown*	.963	25	6	20	1	27	2
Bales, Joseph, Hickory	1.000	11	0	1	0	1	0

Player, Team	Pct.	G	PO	A	E	TC	DP
Barnett, Marty, Piedmont	1.000	6	3	3	0	6	1
Bauldree, Joe, Macon	.800	39	2	10	3	15	1
Beasley, Raymond, Macon*	.923	49	2	10	1	13	1
Beebe, Hans, Columbia*	.667	6	0	2	1	3	0
Bell, Rob, Macon	.875	27	10	11	3	24	0
Benesh, Edward, Cha. (S.C.)	1.000	46	5	12	0	17	2
Bere, Jason, Hickory	1.000	1	1	0	0	1	0
Biddle, Rocky, Hickory	.500	13	0	1	1	2	0
Bleazard, David, Hagerstown	.857	10	3	15	3	21	0
Blythe, Billy, Macon	.941	35	7	9	1	17	1
Boggs, Robert, Cha. (W.Va.)	1.000	15	0	4	0	4	0
Bogle, Sean, Cha. (S.C.)	1.000	20	1	10	0	11	1
Bourbakis, Michael, Savannah	1.000	23	2	5	0	7	0
Bowers, Cedrick, Cha. (S.C.)*	.867	28	5	21	4	30	0
Brammer, John, Columbus	.913	28	1	20	2	23	0
Brand, Scott, Greensboro	1.000	8	5	4	0	9	1
Bravo, Franklin, Augusta	.750	7	1	2	1	4	0
Brooks, Wyatt, Augusta*	.818	17	4	5	2	11	0
Brown, Elliot, Cha. (S.C.)	.929	33	7	19	2	28	1
Brown, Trent, Cha. (S.C.)*	.933	33	4	10	1	15	1
Brueggemann, Dean, Asheville*	.971	34	8	25	1	34	3
Buckman, Tom, Hickory	.947	24	6	12	1	19	2
Bullock, Derek, Augusta	.857	8	2	4	1	7	0
Caldwell, David, Columbus*	.833	5	3	2	1	6	0
Calmus, Lance, Columbus	.923	23	3	9	1	13	1
Cardona, Steve, Hickory	.909	32	4	6	1	11	1
Carlyle, Buddy, Cha. (W.Va.)	.905	23	12	26	4	42	1
Cervantes, Peter, Savannah	.871	21	9	18	4	31	0
Chacon, Shawn, Asheville	.912	28	12	19	3	34	1
Chaney, Michael, Augusta*	.957	31	6	16	1	23	0
Charbonneau, Marc, Hagerstown*	.667	6	1	1	1	3	0
Chen, Bruce, Macon*	1.000	28	3	22	0	25	0
Christman, Tim, Asheville*	.786	29	2	9	3	14	0
Civit, Xavier, Cape Fear	.833	39	4	6	2	12	0
Coble, Jason, Greensboro*	.786	24	3	19	6	28	0
Corey, Mark, Cha. (W.Va.)	.903	26	6	22	3	31	2
Coronado, Osvaldo, Columbia	.857	26	3	3	1	7	0
Cortes, David, Macon	.933	27	4	10	1	15	2
Cutchins, Todd, Columbia*	1.000	3	1	1	0	2	0
Daedelow, Craig, Delmarva	1.000	3	0	1	0	1	0
D'Alessandro, Marc, Asheville*	.952	29	3	17	1	21	1
Daniels, David, Augusta	1.000	44	3	11	0	14	0
Danner, Andy, Cha. (W.Va.)	1.000	22	2	11	0	13	1
Davenport, Joe, Hagerstown	.938	37	3	12	1	16	1
Davis, Jason, Piedmont*	1.000	17	0	7	0	7	1
DeLaCruz, Francisco, Greensboro	1.000	13	3	12	0	15	0
Delgado, Ernie, Hagerstown	.947	32	8	28	2	38	2
Delossantos, Luis, Greensboro	1.000	14	4	19	0	23	2
DePaula, Sean, Columbus	.962	29	9	16	1	26	0
Deschenes, Marc, Columbus	1.000	40	1	6	0	7	0
Dingman, Craig, Greensboro	1.000	30	1	4	0	5	0
Dixon, Jim, Hickory	1.000	16	1	2	0	3	0
Dollar, Toby, Savannah	1.000	20	4	19	0	23	1
Dudeck, Dave, Greensboro	.818	25	0	9	2	11	0
Duff, Matt, Augusta	1.000	2	1	1	0	2	0
Eaton, Adam, Piedmont	.692	14	6	3	4	13	0
Eibey, Scott, Delmarva	.931	47	9	18	2	29	1
Ellison, Jason, Greensboro	1.000	9	1	0	0	1	0
Elmore, Jason, Augusta	.500	10	0	1	1	2	0
Emiliano, James, Asheville	1.000	18	4	2	0	6	1
Enders, Trevor, Cha. (S.C.)*	.947	44	2	16	1	19	0
Evans, Keith, Cape Fear	.974	21	7	30	1	38	0
Falkenborg, Brian, Delmarva	.966	25	5	23	1	29	3
Farley, Joe, Hickory*	.960	28	11	37	2	50	4
Farson, Bryan, Augusta*	1.000	7	1	1	0	2	0
Feliciano, Pedro, Savannah*	.854	37	5	30	6	41	2
Feliz, Bienvenido, Columbus	1.000	6	4	3	0	7	0
Finol, Ricardo, Augusta	1.000	11	0	1	0	1	0
Fisher, Ryan, Augusta*	.500	4	0	1	1	2	0
Folkers, Kenneth, Hagerstown	1.000	5	0	1	0	1	0
Forbes, Cameron, Delmarva	.938	34	6	24	2	32	2
Fortune, Peter, Cape Fear*	.857	12	2	4	1	7	0
France, Aaron, Augusta	1.000	26	10	9	0	19	2
Franklin, Wayne, Savannah*	.889	28	0	16	2	18	0
Freedberg, Todd, Delmarva	1.000	9	1	6	0	7	0
Garcia, Eddy, Cha. (W.Va.)	.600	6	2	1	2	5	0
Garrett, Hal, Savannah	1.000	9	4	8	0	12	0
Garza, Alberto, Columbus	.933	18	6	8	1	15	2
Giron, Roberto, Cha. (W.Va.)	1.000	7	1	1	0	2	0
Glover, Gary, Hagerstown	.942	28	23	26	3	52	1
Gomez, Miguel, Hagerstown	1.000	12	1	4	0	5	0
Gonzalez, Dicky, Columbia	1.000	10	6	9	0	15	1
Gonzalez, Michael, Augusta*	1.000	4	0	4	0	4	1
Gower, Tim, Cha. (W.Va.)	.900	35	0	9	1	10	1

Player, Team	Pct.	G	PO	A	E	TC	DP
Granger, Greg, Columbus	1.000	5	0	1	0	1	0
Graterol, Beiker, Hagerstown	1.000	4	1	1	0	2	0
Gresko, Michael, Augusta*	1.000	1	0	1	0	1	0
Griffiths, Everard, Cha. (S.C.)	.886	30	9	22	4	35	0
Gulin, Lindsay, Columbia*	.900	17	5	13	2	20	1
Hacen, Abraham, Delmarva	.810	23	8	9	4	21	1
Hafer, Jeffrey, Columbia	1.000	37	5	9	0	14	0
Hale, Mark, Cha. (S.C.)	1.000	18	1	6	0	7	0
Halla, Ryan, Augusta	.875	32	0	7	1	8	0
Hamilton, Jimmy, Columbus*	1.000	22	2	13	0	15	1
Handy, Russell, Cape Fear	.800	19	5	3	2	10	1
Harrison, Scott, Columbus	1.000	1	0	1	0	1	1
Haynie, Jason, Augusta*	1.000	14	6	18	0	24	0
Herbison, Brett, Columbia	.972	28	8	27	1	36	3
Heredia, Maximo, Delmarva	.976	37	11	29	1	41	0
Hibbard, Billy, Hagerstown	1.000	11	0	2	0	2	0
Hill, T.J., Cha. (S.C.)	1.000	7	3	2	0	5	0
Hlodan, George, Augusta	1.000	12	2	5	0	7	0
Holliday, Hugh, Cha. (W.Va.)*	1.000	14	1	2	0	3	0
Hunt, Jon, Hickory*	.786	10	1	10	3	14	1
Iglesias, Mario, Hickory	1.000	36	2	13	0	15	0
Irvine, Kirk, Hickory	1.000	29	3	5	0	8	0
Jacobson, Brian, Savannah*	.600	23	2	4	4	10	0
Jacquez, Thomas, Piedmont*	1.000	8	1	6	0	7	0
Kammerer, James, Asheville*	1.000	12	3	4	0	7	0
Kawabata, Kyle, Piedmont	.857	44	3	9	2	14	1
Kessel, Kyle, Columbia*	.936	27	14	30	3	47	2
Key, Calvin, Piedmont	1.000	3	0	3	0	3	0
Koehler, Luther, Macon*	.867	26	5	8	2	15	0
Koeman, Matt, Columbus	1.000	34	3	9	0	12	1
Kohlmeier, Ryan, Delmarva	1.000	50	4	8	0	12	1
Koppe, Clint, Cha. (W.Va.)	1.000	23	3	2	0	5	1
Krall, Eric, Greensboro*	.833	15	0	5	1	6	0
Kramer, Matthew, Savannah	.895	23	5	12	2	19	2
Kraus, Tim, Hickory	.857	15	1	5	1	7	0
LaChapelle, Yan, Hagerstown	.909	26	4	16	2	22	0
Lakman, Jason, Hickory	.879	27	12	17	4	33	0
Landstad, Rob, Columbus	1.000	1	1	0	0	1	0
Lara, Giovanny, Cape Fear	.875	28	17	32	7	56	3
Lawrence, Clint, Hagerstown*	.944	27	8	26	2	36	0
LeBlanc, Eric, Cha. (W.Va.)	.905	24	6	13	2	21	3
Lee, David, Asheville	.900	51	2	7	1	10	0
LEON, Scott, Cha. (S.C.)	1.000	27	18	30	0	48	2
Leslie, Sean, Cape Fear*	1.000	34	2	12	0	14	0
Loubier, Scott, Cape Fear	1.000	10	2	3	0	5	0
Lyons, Mike, Columbia	1.000	44	6	5	0	11	0
Mackey, Jason, Columbus	.850	18	8	9	3	20	0
Madison, Scott, Cha. (S.C.)*	1.000	2	1	0	0	1	0
Mahlberg, John, Asheville	1.000	12	2	1	0	3	0
Mairena, Oswaldo, Greensboro*	.909	49	2	8	1	11	1
Mallard, Randi, Cha. (W.Va.)	1.000	13	4	8	0	12	0
Mann, Jim, Hagerstown	1.000	19	1	2	0	3	0
Manon, Julio, Cha. (S.C.)	1.000	27	4	9	0	13	0
Marquez, Robert, Cape Fear	.500	12	0	1	1	2	0
Marquis, Jason, Macon	.920	28	8	15	2	25	1
Martinez, Caleb, Piedmont*	1.000	20	2	17	0	19	0
Matcuk, Steven, Asheville	.912	28	10	21	3	34	2
Matz, Brian, Cape Fear*	1.000	44	7	29	0	36	2
McClellan, Sean, Hagerstown	.824	35	2	12	3	17	0
McCrary, Scott, Columbia	1.000	13	3	7	0	10	1
McDade, Neil, Augusta	.885	36	7	16	3	26	2
McNatt, Joshua, Delmarva*	.967	28	6	23	1	30	0
Mendes, Jaime, Piedmont	1.000	42	6	21	0	27	1
Merrick, Brett, Columbus*	1.000	23	6	0	0	6	0
Milburn, Robert, Macon*	1.000	46	2	13	0	15	0
Miller, Brian, Piedmont	.889	29	6	10	2	18	0
Minter, Matt, Columbus*	1.000	30	3	16	0	19	2
Mitchell, Courtney, Piedmont*	1.000	47	2	12	0	14	0
Mitchell, Dean, Savannah	.844	52	11	16	5	32	3
Molina, Gabe, Delmarva	.909	46	10	10	2	22	0
Morseman, Bob, Delmarva*	1.000	7	1	2	0	3	0
Mota, Daniel, Greensboro	1.000	20	1	4	0	5	0
Mota, Guillermo, Cape Fear	1.000	25	14	24	0	38	1
Musachio, John, Hickory*	1.000	11	2	3	0	5	0
Myette, Aaron, Hickory	1.000	5	2	4	0	6	1
Needham, Kevin, Cha. (W.Va.)*	.923	35	4	8	1	13	0
Negrete, Richard, Columbus	1.000	16	4	10	0	14	0
Nichols, James, Hickory	.939	28	8	23	2	33	2
Nicholson, John, Asheville	.974	25	8	30	1	39	3
Obando, Omar, Greensboro	.895	45	3	14	2	19	1
O'Connor, Brian, Augusta*	.947	25	4	14	1	19	0
Ojeda, Erick, C'bia-Aug.*	.933	44	2	12	1	15	0
Olivier, Rich, Greensboro	.920	35	2	21	2	25	3
Olszewski, Tim, Delmarva	1.000	3	0	1	0	1	0
Ortega, Pablo, Cha. (S.C.)	.979	29	18	29	1	48	1
O'Shaughnessy, Jay, Savannah	.955	27	7	14	1	22	0
Osting, Jimmy, Macon*	.941	15	4	12	1	17	0
Pacheco, Delvis, Macon	1.000	35	9	4	0	13	1
Paluk, Brian, Savannah	.878	27	10	26	5	41	1
Parker, Christian, Cape Fear	.925	25	17	32	4	53	1
Paronto, Chad, Delmarva	.935	28	10	19	2	31	1
Parotte, Frisco, Greensboro	1.000	18	1	6	0	7	0
Parrish, John, Delmarva*	.800	23	1	15	4	20	0
Paugh, Rick, Augusta*	1.000	24	2	3	0	5	0
Peguero, Americo, Delmarva	.882	27	7	8	2	17	1
Pena, Jesus, Hickory	.895	43	4	13	2	19	2
Perez, Odalis, Macon*	.889	36	4	12	2	18	1
Priest, Eddie, Cha. (W.Va.)*	.947	14	7	11	1	19	0
Prokopec, Luke, Savannah	1.000	13	2	3	0	5	0
Pumphrey, Kenny, Columbia	.980	27	20	30	1	51	2
Quezada, Edward, Cape Fear	.973	30	12	24	1	37	0
Quintana, Urbano, Piedmont	1.000	3	0	1	0	1	0
Ramagli, Matt, Delmarva	1.000	4	0	3	0	3	2
Rangel, Julio, Greensboro	.958	26	10	36	2	48	1
Reichow, Robert, Columbus	.813	20	2	11	3	16	0
Rivera, Alvin, Asheville	1.000	1	0	1	0	1	0
Rivera, Luis, Macon	.800	4	4	0	1	5	0
Robbins, Jake, Greensboro	.933	20	7	21	2	30	1
Roberts, Grant, Columbia	1.000	22	15	25	0	40	0
Roberts, Mark, Hickory	.500	4	0	2	2	4	0
Rolocut, Brian, Cha. (S.C.)	.500	10	0	1	1	2	0
Romine, Jason, Asheville	.857	28	1	5	1	7	0
Rose, Ted, Cha. (W.Va.)	.971	38	8	25	1	34	1
Rutherford, Mark, Piedmont	1.000	9	6	6	0	12	0
Sanchez, Mike, Savannah	.938	40	4	11	1	16	1
Santamaria, Bill, Columbia	.833	14	3	2	1	6	0
Saylor, Ryan, Cape Fear	.333	10	0	1	2	3	0
Schaffner, Eric, Greensboro	.923	28	5	7	1	13	0
Schroeffel, Scott, Asheville	.900	19	3	6	1	10	1
Scott, Brian, Hickory	.926	13	9	16	2	27	2
Seay, Robert, Cha. (S.C.)*	.909	13	1	9	1	11	0
Shepard, David, Cha. (W.Va.)	.929	18	2	11	1	14	1
Shiell, Jason, Macon	.818	27	4	14	4	22	1
Siciliano, Jess, Augusta	.857	11	2	4	1	7	0
Sikes, Jason, Piedmont	.875	27	8	20	4	32	1
Simon, Benjamin, Savannah	.926	18	7	18	2	27	0
Slamka, John, Asheville*	.765	26	2	11	4	17	2
Soto, Seferino, Savannah	.909	26	5	5	1	11	0
Spence, Cam, Greensboro	1.000	8	4	7	0	11	0
Spiegel, Mike, Columbus*	1.000	2	1	1	0	2	0
Splawn, Matt, Columbia	1.000	7	0	2	0	2	0
Stevens, Kris, Piedmont*	.957	14	6	16	1	23	1
Stevenson, Rodney, Cape Fear	.833	16	2	3	1	6	0
Strickland, Scott, Cape Fear	1.000	3	1	0	0	1	0
Taylor, Brien, Greensboro*	1.000	8	2	5	0	7	0
Taylor, Mark, Columbus*	1.000	20	3	5	0	8	0
Temple, Jason, Augusta	.778	11	2	5	2	9	1
Thompson, Mark, Asheville	1.000	4	0	3	0	3	0
Tilton, Ira, Piedmont	.906	28	4	25	3	32	0
Tober, Dave, Piedmont	.960	46	9	15	1	25	1
Towers, Josh, Delmarva	1.000	9	3	0	0	3	0
Tucker, Julien, Hickory	1.000	4	1	3	0	4	1
Turman, Jimmy, Cape Fear	1.000	19	8	8	0	16	1
Van Gilder, Ryan, Cape Fear	1.000	4	0	1	0	1	0
Vasquez, Leoner, Columbia*	1.000	22	6	11	0	17	0
Verdin, Cesar, Greensboro*	1.000	1	0	1	0	1	0
Villafuerte, Brandon, Columbia	.941	47	5	11	1	17	0
Virchis, Adam, Hickory	1.000	15	2	11	0	13	0
Volkert, Oreste, Hagerstown	.929	34	2	11	1	14	0
Wagner, Ken, Columbus	.769	48	2	8	3	13	0
Walker, Morgan, Augusta*	1.000	1	0	1	0	1	0
Walls, Doug, Asheville	1.000	10	7	1	0	8	0
Westbrook, Jake, Asheville	.922	28	14	33	4	51	4
Whipple, Boomer, Augusta	1.000	2	0	1	0	1	0
Whitley, Garry, Hickory*	.800	9	2	2	1	5	0
Whitson, Eric, Cha. (S.C.)	.889	30	1	7	1	9	0
Winkelsas, Joseph, Macon	.957	38	4	18	1	23	3
Young, Danny, Augusta*	1.000	3	1	0	0	1	0
Young, Tim, Cape Fear*	.875	45	3	4	1	8	0

PITCHERS WITH TWO OR MORE TEAMS

Player, Team	Pct.	G	PO	A	E	TC	DP
Ojeda, Erick, Columbia*	1.000	7	1	2	0	3	0
Ojeda, Erick, Augusta*	.917	37	1	10	1	12	0

The following players did not have any fielding statistics at the positions indicated or appeared only as a designated hitter, pinch-hitter or pinch-runner: Bauer, p; Berry, p; Blandford, c; Bowles, p; Bramlett, 3b; D. Brown, p; T. Campbell, p; Cooley, p; Dykhoff, p; L. Evans, 3b; Eversgerd, p; Frias, of; Garavito, dh; A. Garcia, p; Heredia, of; Huffman, of; Keech, of; Kelly, p; Kimbrell, p; LaRue, of; Lowe, p; Mackay, p; D. Martinez, p; Owens-Bragg, of; J. Perez, ss; Prater, p; Presley, p; C. Rivera, of; Roberson, p; Romero, p; Schreiber, of; Solano, ss; Staubach, dh; Warren, dh; Whitlock, p.

LEAGUE CHAMPIONS

Year	Team	Pct.	Year	Team	Pct.	Year	Team	Pct.
1948—	Lincolnton*	.627	1970—	Greenville	.576	1985—	Florence‡	.599
1949—	Newton-Conover	.667		Greenville	.619		Greensboro	.540
	Rutherford Co. (2nd)†	.627	1971—	Greenwood	.631	1986—	Columbia‡	.682
1950—	Newton-Conover	.627		Greenwood	.759		Asheville	.643
	Lenoir (2nd)†	.626	1972—	Spartanburg‡	.788	1987—	Asheville	.655
1951—	Morganton	.645		Greenville	.652		Myrtle Beach‡	.597
	Shelby (2nd)†	.604	1973—	Spartanburg‡	.646	1988—	Charleston (S.C.)	.616
1952—	Lincolnton	.649		Gastonia	.619		Spartanburg‡	.500
	Shelby (2nd)†	.645	1974—	Gastonia	.606	1989—	Gastonia	.657
1953-59—	League inactive.			Gastonia	.672		Augusta‡	.535
1960—	Lexington	.707	1975—	Spartanburg	.543	1990—	Columbia	.580
	Salisbury (2nd)†	.650		Spartanburg	.614		Charleston (W.Va.)‡	.538
1961—	Salisbury	.627	1976—	Asheville	.544	1991—	Charleston (W.Va.)	.648
	Shelby (4th)†	.481		Greenwood‡	.600		Columbia‡	.614
1962—	Statesville	.563	1977—	Greenwood	.557	1992—	Columbia	.572
	Statesville	.700		Gastonia‡	.590		Myrtle Beach‡	.522
1963—	Greenville†	.576	1978—	Greenwood	.614	1993—	Savannah‡	.662
	Salisbury	.631		Greenwood	.565		Greensboro	.603
1964—	Rock Hill	.672	1979—	Greenwood‡	.565	1994—	Columbus	.630
	Salisbury‡	.631		Spartanburg	.525		Savannah‡	.599
1965—	Salisbury	.641	1980—	Greensboro	.590	1995—	Piedmont	.586
	Rock Hill‡	.603		Charleston	.561		Augusta‡	.551
1966—	Spartanburg	.682	1981—	Greensboro‡	.695	1996—	Delmarva	.585
	Spartanburg	.767		Greenwood	.549		Savannah†	.511
1967—	Spartanburg	.730	1982—	Greensboro‡	.681	1997—	Delmarva§	.543
	Spartanburg	.567		Florence	.546		Greensboro	.536
1968—	Spartanburg	.597	1983—	Columbia	.620			
	Greenwood‡	.597		Gastonia‡	.587			
1969—	Greenwood‡	.587	1984—	Charleston	.549			
	Shelby	.565		Asheville‡	.510			

*Won championship and four-club playoff. †Won four-club playoff. ‡Won split-season playoff. §Won split season, eight-club playoff. (NOTE—Known as Western Carolina League from 1948 through 1962 and known as Western Carolinas League through 1979.)

APPALACHIAN LEAGUE

LEAGUE OFFICE

President
Lee Landers

Address
283 Deerchase Circle
Statesville, NC 28625

Phone
704-873-5300

Teams (affiliation)
Bluefield Orioles (Orioles)
Bristol White Sox (White Sox)
Burlington Indians (Indians)
Danville Braves (Braves)
Elizabethton Twins (Twins)
Johnson City Cardinals (Cardinals)

Kingsport Mets (Mets)
Martinsville Phillies (Phillies)
Princeton Devil Rays (Devil Rays)
Pulaski Rangers (Rangers)

1997 FINAL STANDINGS

NORTH DIVISION

Team	W	L	T	Pct.	GB
Bluefield (Orioles)	40	29	0	.580	....
Princeton (Devil Rays)	39	30	0	.565	1
Burlington (Indians)	32	36	0	.471	7 1/2
Danville (Braves)	30	38	0	.441	9 1/2
Martinsville (Phillies)	29	39	0	.426	10 1/2

SOUTH DIVISION

Team	W	L	T	Pct.	GB
Pulaski (Rangers)	43	25	0	.632	....
Elizabethton (Twins)	38	30	0	.559	5
Kingsport (Mets)	37	31	0	.544	6
Bristol (White Sox)	30	38	0	.441	13
Johnson City (Cardinals)	23	45	0	.338	20

COMPOSITE

Team	Pul.	Blu.	Pri.	Elz.	Kng.	Bur.	Dan.	Brs.	Mar.	J.C.	W	L	T	Pct.	GB
Pulaski (Rangers)	....	5	4	4	3	5	4	6	7	5	43	25	0	.632	....
Bluefield (Orioles)	5	....	7	2	4	3	5	6	4	4	40	29	0	.580	3 1/2
Princeton (Devil Rays)	6	6	....	4	5	4	2	3	4	5	39	30	0	.565	4 1/2
Elizabethton (Twins)	2	4	2	....	3	3	4	6	5	9	38	30	0	.559	5
Kingsport (Mets)	3	2	1	7	....	5	4	7	3	5	37	31	0	.544	6
Burlington (Indians)	1	3	6	3	1	....	6	1	8	3	32	36	0	.471	11
Danville (Braves)	2	5	4	2	2	6	....	2	4	3	30	38	0	.441	13
Bristol (White Sox)	0	0	3	4	5	5	4	....	3	6	30	38	0	.441	13
Martinsville (Phillies)	5	2	2	1	3	2	6	3	....	5	29	39	0	.426	14
Johnson City (Cardinals)	1	2	1	3	3	5	3	4	1	....	23	45	0	.338	20

Major league affiliations in parentheses.

PLAYOFFS: Bluefield defeated Pulaski, two games to none, to win league championship.

REGULAR-SEASON ATTENDANCE: Bluefield, 43,300; Bristol, 25,105; Burlington, 46,915; Danville, 75,745; Elizabethton, 17,397; Johnson City, 43,300; Kingsport, 48,396; Martinsville, 39,947; Princeton, 36,481; Pulaski, 23,898. Total—400,484. Playoffs (2 games)—2,013.

MANAGERS: Bluefield, Bobby Dickerson; Bristol, Nick Capra; Burlington, Harry Spilman (through August 11) and Joe Mikulik (August 12 to end of season); Danville, Rick Albert; Elizabethton, Jose Marzan; Johnson City, Steve Turco; Kingsport, Ken Berry; Martinsville, Kelly Heath; Princeton, Charlie Montoyo; Pulaski, Julio Cruz. Managerial record of team with more than one manager: Burlington, Spilman 22-31, Mikulik 10-5.

ALL-STAR TEAM: 1B—Robert Berns, Princeton; 2B—Jared Sandberg, Princeton; 3B—Matt Berger, Bristol; SS—Pablo Ozuna, Johnson City; Utility INF—Joe Kilburg, Burlington; OF—Brandon Copeland, Kingsport; Robert Stratton, Kingsport; Derek Feramisco, Johnson City; Utility OF—Joe McHenry, Elizabethton; C—Joe Sutton, Bristol; DH—Dave Orndorff, Elizabethton; RHP—Dan DeYoung, Pulaski; LHP—Trey Poland, Pulaski; Relief Pitcher—Dave Mastrolonardo, Bluefield; Player of the Year—Jared Sandberg, Princeton; Pitcher of the Year—Trey Poland, Pulaski; Manager of the Year—Julio Cruz, Pulaski.

1997 BATTING

TEAM

Team	Avg.	G	TPA	AB	R	H	TB	2B	3B	HR	RBI	SH	SF	HP	BB	IBB	SO	SB	CS	GDP	LOB	ShO	Slg.	OBP
Elizabethton	.295	68	2754	2387	469	704	1066	130	8	72	402	23	31	40	273	14	518	50	26	45	548	4	.447	.372
Bristol	.279	68	2642	2302	440	642	1018	121	15	75	389	17	22	36	265	10	558	84	31	51	466	2	.442	.359
Princeton	.272	69	2792	2447	408	666	1077	138	27	73	420	11	23	48	263	5	606	70	27	47	498	3	.440	.351
Pulaski	.270	68	2694	2331	440	629	986	130	25	59	351	22	21	25	295	5	538	132	36	36	489	1	.423	.355
Kingsport	.267	68	2639	2327	414	621	941	109	20	57	356	32	11	39	230	7	560	87	47	36	455	4	.404	.341
Johnson City	.265	68	2593	2326	384	617	961	139	17	57	291	18	13	39	197	4	598	62	30	42	482	2	.413	.331
Bluefield	.265	69	2655	2325	389	615	905	120	22	42	334	16	19	48	247	9	520	116	53	42	485	6	.389	.345
Burlington	.263	68	2665	2320	403	609	924	120	18	53	350	8	25	36	276	10	611	116	41	26	490	3	.398	.347
Martinsville	.252	68	2577	2324	345	585	842	111	10	42	287	10	13	50	198	2	620	72	45	35	454	3	.362	.318
Danville	.252	68	2598	2277	360	573	866	113	21	46	310	14	17	50	240	3	642	64	30	50	479	3	.380	.334

INDIVIDUAL

TOP QUALIFIERS FOR BATTING CHAMPIONSHIP

Minimum 184 plate appearances. *Lefthanded batter. †Switch-hitter.

Player, Team	Avg.	G	TPA	AB	R	H	TB	2B	3B	HR	RBI	SH	SF	HP	BB	IBB	SO	SB	CS	GDP	Slg.	OBP
Orndorff, Dave, Elizabethton	.368	55	260	228	62	84	134	15	1	11	42	2	2	6	22	0	25	18	4	1	.588	.434
Giles, Marcus, Danville	.348	55	246	207	53	72	115	13	3	8	45	1	3	3	32	0	47	5	2	4	.556	.437
Feramisco, Derek, J.C.	.342	53	205	184	34	63	99	12	3	6	36	0	0	4	16	0	37	8	2	2	.538	.407
Zapp, A.J., Danville*	.338	65	277	234	34	79	127	23	2	7	56	0	1	7	35	0	78	0	1	3	.543	.437
Kilburg, Joe, Brevard Cty.*	.335	52	233	182	59	61	92	8	7	3	30	3	2	7	39	0	46	29	5	1	.505	.465
Lamb, Michael, Pulaski†	.335	60	276	233	59	78	130	19	3	9	47	2	6	4	31	2	18	7	2	5	.558	.412
Pena, Jose, Pulaski	.333	51	220	204	45	68	97	14	3	3	31	1	1	2	12	0	40	17	6	5	.475	.374
Schaeffer, Jon, Elizabethton	.333	48	204	165	35	55	86	13	0	6	34	0	2	4	33	3	32	0	1	5	.521	.451

Player, Team	Avg.	G	TPA	AB	R	H	TB	2B	3B	HR	RBI	SH	SF	HP	BB	IBB	SO	SB	CS	GDP	Slg.	OBP
Sutton, Joe, Bristol	.332	56	227	190	46	63	118	18	2	11	43	0	1	1	35	2	51	7	0	4	.621	.436
Hairston, Jerry, Bluefield	.330	59	258	221	44	73	100	13	4	2	36	4	2	10	21	0	29	13	9	4	.452	.409
Sergio, Thomas, Pulaski*	.327	58	270	226	57	74	123	14	4	9	40	1	1	4	38	0	42	25	6	1	.544	.431
Berns, Robert, Princeton........	.327	64	287	245	53	80	143	34	1	9	61	0	3	5	34	0	44	2	4	3	.584	.415
Lutz, Manuel, Bristol*	.325	65	275	249	50	81	137	11	3	13	61	0	3	4	19	0	71	6	3	3	.550	.378
Ozuna, Pablo, Johnson City ...	.323	56	251	232	40	75	105	13	1	5	24	6	1	1	10	0	24	23	5	2	.453	.351
Gallagher, Shawn, Pulaski......	.322	50	217	199	41	64	128	13	3	15	52	0	4	4	10	0	49	2	0	1	.643	.359

DEPARTMENTAL LEADERS: G—Sandberg, Neuberger, Brooks, 67 each; AB—Sandberg, 268; R—Orndorff, 62; H—Orndorff, 84; TB—Sandberg, 157; 2B—Berns, 34; 3B—Kilburg, 7; HR—Berger, 18; RBI—Sandberg, 68; SH—Ozuna, Brett, 6 each; SF—Garavito, 7; HP—Casillas, 12; BB—Hamilton, 51; IBB—Sandberg, 5; SO—Sandberg, Stratton, 94 each; SB—Kilburg, 29; CS—Garavito, Je. Hairston, Collier, 9 each; GIDP—Lopes, 9; Slg.—Gallagher, .643; OBP—Kilburg, .465.

ALL PLAYERS

*Lefthanded batter. †Switch-hitter.

Player, Team	Avg.	G	TPA	AB	R	H	TB	2B	3B	HR	RBI	SH	SF	HP	BB	IBB	SO	SB	CS	GDP	Slg.	OBP
Albert, Rashad, Bristol	.235	4	18	17	2	4	7	0	0	1	2	0	0	0	1	0	7	2	0	0	.412	.278
Alfonso, Eliezer, Johnson City	.275	38	133	120	15	33	52	11	1	2	15	0	0	6	7	0	34	0	1	1	.433	.346
Allen, Troy, Danville*............	.214	43	154	131	16	28	39	5	0	2	12	0	3	1	19	2	44	1	1	2	.298	.312
Araujo, Danilo, Johnson City..	.251	54	227	187	33	47	63	7	3	1	24	5	0	3	32	0	42	8	7	2	.337	.369
Arias, Jeison, Princeton	.167	5	20	18	5	3	3	0	0	0	0	0	0	1	1	0	5	0	0	0	.167	.250
Ashley, Steve, Danville	.162	26	81	74	7	12	17	2	0	1	5	1	0	1	5	0	15	1	0	4	.230	.225
Ayuso, Julio, Elizabethton	.224	39	125	107	13	24	35	8	0	1	12	0	0	1	17	0	39	0	1	0	.327	.336
Benavidez, Eric, Princeton......	.311	52	229	206	50	64	84	12	4	0	27	3	1	8	11	0	25	14	5	5	.408	.367
Berger, Matt, Bristol	.289	66	279	232	51	67	134	11	1	18	56	0	4	3	40	1	72	1	0	7	.578	.394
Berns, Robert, Princeton........	.327	64	287	245	53	80	143	34	1	9	61	0	3	5	34	0	44	2	4	3	.584	.415
Beverly, Shomari, Martinsville	.256	34	131	125	13	32	43	5	0	2	13	0	0	1	5	0	37	9	5	2	.344	.290
Bonilla, Elin, Martinsville	.207	36	129	121	16	25	39	4	2	2	20	2	0	0	6	0	46	1	1	0	.322	.244
Borrego, Ramon, Elz.†	.280	55	248	211	43	59	83	12	0	4	34	5	2	4	26	0	44	7	5	3	.393	.366
Bosch, Bryon, Brev.	.067	13	31	30	1	2	3	1	0	0	0	0	0	1	0	0	17	0	0	2	.100	.097
Bowring, Jason, Kingsport	.248	61	235	218	32	54	84	10	1	6	35	0	1	4	12	0	43	8	3	3	.385	.298
Brett, Jason, Kingsport	.271	49	196	170	25	46	55	3	3	0	18	6	0	0	20	0	42	6	2	2	.324	.347
Brignac, Junior, Danville	.244	59	262	225	47	55	77	10	0	4	25	1	0	7	29	0	70	12	4	2	.342	.349
Brooks, Anthony, Danville	.271	67	248	229	43	62	88	12	1	4	24	3	3	5	8	0	59	15	5	5	.384	.306
Bruce, Maurice, Kingsport	.367	34	146	128	35	47	70	8	3	3	21	0	0	2	16	0	20	14	4	1	.547	.445
Burns, Patrick, Kingsport†......	.246	60	248	224	32	55	72	11	3	0	30	5	1	1	17	1	67	7	4	2	.321	.300
Bushman, Jonathan, Mar.	.211	12	19	19	3	4	5	1	0	0	0	0	0	0	0	0	8	0	0	0	.263	.211
Caines, Franklyn, Martinsville	.274	53	215	197	26	54	78	12	0	4	30	0	0	1	17	0	58	6	0	3	.396	.335
Cameron, Troy, Danville†	.216	56	236	208	28	45	72	5	2	6	24	0	0	3	25	1	80	1	3	3	.346	.309
Caradonna, Brett, Bristol*	.313	22	94	80	16	25	31	3	0	1	12	0	0	1	13	1	16	3	2	3	.388	.415
Carrion, Jorge, Pulaski..........	.198	43	125	111	19	22	32	7	0	1	10	0	2	0	12	0	26	8	0	2	.288	.272
Casillas, Uriel, Martinsville	.268	60	260	220	42	59	76	12	1	1	26	3	2	12	23	0	29	5	3	6	.345	.366
Castro, Martires, Pulaski........	.256	53	237	211	33	54	78	13	1	3	27	1	0	2	23	1	53	7	2	4	.370	.335
Chavez, Endy, Kingsport*	.301	19	88	73	16	22	26	4	0	0	4	2	0	0	13	0	10	5	2	2	.356	.407
Cody, Ryan, Martinsville	.237	26	85	76	9	18	25	4	0	1	8	0	0	1	8	0	21	0	1	1	.329	.318
Collier, Lamonte, Martinsville.	.252	62	275	222	49	56	73	7	2	2	23	3	1	2	47	0	50	14	9	2	.329	.386
Cook, Josh, Kingsport	.150	9	26	20	0	3	3	0	0	0	2	0	1	0	5	0	10	0	1	0	.150	.346
Copeland, Brandon, Kng........	.338	41	179	148	31	50	83	10	1	7	37	1	2	5	23	0	33	6	3	1	.561	.438
Crespo, Jesse, Danville	.286	14	45	42	11	12	21	0	3	0	7	0	0	3	0	0	8	0	0	2	.500	.333
Cruz, Andres, Princeton	.231	3	14	13	3	3	4	1	0	0	4	1	0	0	0	0	2	0	1	0	.308	.231
Cruz, Edgar, Brevard County ..	.211	46	186	171	18	36	58	7	0	5	29	0	0	1	14	1	54	0	1	4	.339	.274
Cruz, Luis, Princeton..............	.282	18	86	78	16	22	33	2	0	3	14	0	0	3	5	0	16	2	2	2	.423	.314
Dampeer, Kelly, Brev.	.255	53	234	212	37	54	82	19	0	3	24	1	2	4	15	0	32	9	3	2	.387	.313
Darr, Ryan, Johnson City	.297	54	220	192	35	57	113	22	2	10	33	0	1	0	27	1	55	0	0	1	.589	.382
Davis, Tim, Johnson City	.059	13	36	34	4	2	2	0	0	0	0	0	0	1	1	0	12	2	0	1	.059	.111
Davison, Ashanti, Bluefield	.247	49	188	162	31	40	64	10	4	2	25	0	2	7	17	1	39	8	4	3	.395	.340
De La Rosa, Miguel, Pulaski...	.172	22	67	58	9	10	20	1	0	3	8	1	0	1	7	0	28	1	1	2	.345	.269
Diaz, Miguel, Johnson City	.283	59	236	223	33	63	94	17	1	4	28	0	4	2	7	0	32	1	3	7	.422	.305
Duncan, Carlos, Martinsville ...	.260	54	222	204	38	53	108	8	4	13	33	0	2	2	14	0	62	11	5	3	.529	.311
Durick, Chad, Kingsport.........	.302	31	136	126	23	38	66	13	0	5	25	0	1	2	7	0	35	1	0	4	.524	.346
Eckelman, Alex, Johnson City	.321	49	185	165	30	53	89	13	1	7	27	1	2	7	10	0	23	3	1	3	.539	.380
Edwards, Michael, Brev..........	.288	60	277	236	50	68	100	16	2	4	41	0	2	1	38	1	53	10	5	2	.424	.386
Ellis, John, Pulaski................	.289	37	139	128	19	37	50	6	2	1	21	2	0	1	8	0	22	1	1	2	.391	.336
Escobar, Alex, Kingsport	.194	10	40	36	6	7	10	3	0	0	3	0	1	0	3	0	8	1	0	3	.278	.250
Fennell, Jason, Bristol†..........	.284	48	215	190	39	54	78	9	0	5	36	1	2	4	18	1	38	6	3	6	.411	.355
Feramisco, Derek, J.C.	.342	53	205	184	34	63	99	12	3	6	36	0	0	4	16	0	37	8	2	2	.538	.407
Figueroa, Franky, Bluefield	.267	63	260	243	32	65	105	14	1	8	41	0	1	2	14	0	70	4	2	3	.432	.312
Fisher, Anthony, Pulaski	.193	30	124	109	23	21	36	5	2	2	13	1	0	0	14	0	43	6	2	1	.330	.285
Folkers, Brandon, J.C.*	.293	53	179	150	20	44	65	8	2	3	20	0	1	3	25	3	62	3	2	1	.433	.402
Frias, Ovidio, Bristol..............	.299	35	129	117	15	35	45	7	0	1	20	2	1	2	7	0	12	3	2	1	.385	.346
Gallagher, Shawn, Pulaski......	.322	50	217	199	41	64	128	13	3	15	52	0	4	4	10	0	49	2	0	1	.643	.359
Garavito, Eddy, Bluefield†	.303	61	264	231	47	70	103	12	3	5	44	2	7	3	21	0	30	26	9	5	.446	.359
Garcia, Sandy, Princeton	.255	58	238	216	38	55	85	14	2	4	28	1	1	9	11	0	75	13	2	1	.394	.316
Garmon, Adrian, Kingsport	.000	18	1	1	0	0	0	0	0	0	0	0	0	0	0	0	0	0	0	0	.000	.000
Giles, Marcus, Danville..........	.348	55	246	207	53	72	115	13	3	8	45	1	3	3	32	0	47	5	2	4	.556	.437
Giron, Alejandro, Martinsville.	.302	54	221	202	26	61	81	15	1	1	20	2	0	3	11	0	40	6	5	3	.401	.342
Gonzalez, Jean, Princeton	.306	24	95	85	10	26	33	5	1	0	8	1	0	1	8	0	19	1	1	1	.388	.372
Gooden, Carl, Johnson City ...	.234	43	127	107	17	25	42	5	0	4	12	1	0	3	16	0	38	7	2	3	.393	.349
Grabowski, Jason, Pulaski* ...	.293	50	217	174	36	51	77	14	0	4	24	1	0	2	40	0	32	6	1	2	.443	.423
Guzman, Martin, Princeton	.324	21	84	74	22	24	42	7	1	3	15	0	0	0	10	0	20	2	0	3	.568	.405
Hairston, Jason, Danville	.243	52	207	177	21	43	71	4	3	6	33	1	1	9	19	0	42	7	3	3	.401	.344
Hairston, Jerry, Bluefield........	.330	59	258	221	44	73	100	13	4	2	36	4	2	10	21	0	29	13	9	4	.452	.409
Haley, Ryan, Brevard County*	.250	8	27	24	4	6	7	1	0	0	1	0	1	0	1	0	5	2	0	1	.292	.269
Haman, Mack, Bluefield	.226	47	166	133	28	30	51	6	0	5	17	1	0	7	24	0	51	6	5	1	.383	.370

Player, Team	Avg.	G	TPA	AB	R	H	TB	2B	3B	HR	RBI	SH	SF	HP	BB	IBB	SO	SB	CS	GDP	Slg.	OBP
Hamilton, Jonathan, Brev.*	.243	64	306	247	50	60	89	11	3	4	20	1	2	5	51	3	69	25	5	0	.360	.380
Harding, Todd, Brev.	.177	24	85	79	8	14	20	1	1	1	4	0	0	2	4	1	33	3	2	1	.253	.235
Hernandez, Jesus, Brev.*	.302	50	225	192	37	58	91	12	0	7	40	0	4	4	25	1	36	7	2	1	.474	.387
Hollins, Darontaye, Bristol	.240	54	227	196	42	47	68	10	1	3	18	5	2	4	20	1	47	21	7	3	.347	.320
Hooper, Daren, Bluefield	.125	10	38	32	4	4	8	1	0	1	4	0	0	0	6	0	11	0	1	0	.250	.263
Hoover, Paul, Princeton	.303	66	285	251	55	76	112	16	4	4	37	3	4	6	20	0	37	7	4	3	.446	.363
Jaramillo, Francisco, Pulaski	.295	46	188	156	26	46	72	14	0	4	22	3	1	3	25	0	44	8	4	1	.462	.400
Jaworowski, Aaron, Elz.*	.292	64	288	264	46	77	134	18	0	13	66	0	5	5	14	2	65	1	0	4	.508	.333
Johnson, Anthony, Kingsport	.333	15	54	45	10	15	27	3	0	3	9	0	0	0	9	0	17	1	1	1	.600	.444
Johnson, Doug, Princeton	.201	34	152	139	19	28	51	7	2	4	19	0	1	4	8	0	56	2	0	2	.367	.263
Johnson, Duane, Martinsville	.139	35	84	79	9	11	11	0	0	0	3	0	0	0	5	0	35	5	2	0	.139	.190
Kalcounos, Andy, J.C.	.130	9	30	23	4	3	4	1	0	0	2	0	0	0	7	0	10	0	0	0	.174	.333
Kennedy, Brian, Elizabethton*	.293	55	222	191	26	56	68	9	0	1	25	1	4	4	22	2	43	3	4	2	.356	.371
Kilburg, Joe, Brev.*	.335	52	233	182	59	61	92	8	7	3	30	3	2	7	39	0	46	29	5	1	.505	.465
Lamb, Michael, Pulaski†	.335	60	276	233	59	78	130	19	3	9	47	2	6	4	31	2	18	7	2	5	.558	.412
Lasater, Chris, Bluefield	.257	11	39	35	8	9	19	4	0	2	9	0	0	1	3	1	6	0	1	1	.543	.333
Ledbetter, Blake, J.C.	.119	16	43	42	2	5	6	1	0	0	2	0	0	1	0	0	15	0	0	0	.143	.140
Lina, Estivinson, Pulaski	.176	14	57	51	5	9	13	1	0	1	4	0	0	1	5	0	19	1	0	3	.255	.263
Llibre, Brian, Johnson City	.267	33	115	105	17	28	50	10	0	4	22	0	1	2	7	0	25	1	1	2	.476	.322
Lopes, Omar, Bristol	.276	49	200	170	29	47	60	4	0	3	23	2	2	2	24	1	22	7	3	9	.353	.369
Lopez-Cao, Mike, Princeton*	.226	17	60	53	7	12	17	0	1	1	7	0	1	0	5	0	8	0	0	0	.321	.288
Lorenzo, Juan, Elizabethton†	.300	52	231	210	41	63	98	10	2	7	34	3	0	6	12	1	38	4	2	6	.467	.355
Lugo, Ursino, Brev.†	.271	13	53	48	8	13	15	2	0	0	5	0	0	0	5	0	7	9	4	0	.313	.340
Lutz, Manuel, Bristol*	.325	65	275	249	50	81	137	11	3	13	61	0	3	4	19	0	71	6	3	3	.550	.378
Maberry, Mark, Kingsport	1.000	23	1	1	0	1	1	0	0	0	0	0	0	0	0	0	0	0	0	0	1.000	1.000
Majcherek, Matthew, Pulaski	.194	24	77	62	11	12	13	1	0	0	2	0	0	0	15	0	17	5	0	1	.210	.351
Malloy, Patrick, Brev.	.000	17	1	1	0	0	0	0	0	0	0	0	0	0	0	0	1	0	0	0	.000	.000
Marchant, Nick, Martinsville	.093	23	80	75	3	7	7	0	0	0	3	0	1	1	3	0	32	2	0	1	.093	.138
Martin, Tommy, Bluefield	.289	40	100	90	17	26	34	3	1	1	9	0	1	1	8	0	31	9	3	0	.378	.350
Matos, Luis, Bluefield	.275	61	266	240	37	66	85	7	3	2	35	1	1	4	20	0	36	26	4	5	.354	.340
McGee, Thomas, Bluefield	.244	27	102	86	14	21	29	5	0	1	8	0	0	5	11	0	22	2	1	3	.337	.363
McGehee, Michael, Pri.†	.215	33	131	107	16	23	40	5	0	4	9	0	0	4	20	0	33	2	0	6	.374	.359
McGrath, Sean, Kingsport	.256	26	95	78	18	20	24	4	0	0	6	3	2	5	7	0	26	4	4	2	.308	.348
McHenry, Joe, Elizabethton*	.321	51	196	168	40	54	78	6	0	6	31	2	3	1	22	0	48	5	3	1	.464	.397
McIntyre, Remer, J.C.	.187	39	117	107	11	20	27	3	2	0	3	2	0	1	7	0	38	0	2	2	.252	.243
Melson, Bryant, Elizabethton	.263	28	92	80	18	21	26	3	1	0	9	3	1	1	7	0	22	1	0	3	.325	.326
Messner, Jake, Brev.*	.251	49	195	179	28	45	82	10	0	9	26	0	3	1	8	1	47	7	3	3	.458	.283
Morales, Domingo, Bluefield	.000	4	6	6	2	0	0	0	0	0	0	0	0	0	0	0	0	0	0	0	.000	.000
Mortimer, Mark, Danville	.077	5	19	13	1	1	1	0	0	0	3	1	1	0	4	0	1	0	0	1	.077	.278
Neuberger, Scott, Princeton	.276	67	289	254	46	70	112	11	2	9	53	0	3	2	30	0	59	7	1	5	.441	.353
Newkirk, Jeff, Bristol*	.298	48	219	188	46	56	97	14	3	7	24	1	0	2	28	2	29	6	4	2	.516	.394
Norrell, Troy, Martinsville	.192	36	138	120	17	23	44	6	0	5	18	0	0	3	15	0	55	4	3	3	.367	.297
Nova, Fernando, Bristol	.266	42	165	143	29	38	55	9	1	2	23	1	1	6	14	0	35	8	3	3	.385	.354
Nunez, Jose, Kingsport	.000	2	7	6	1	0	0	0	0	0	0	1	0	0	0	0	2	0	0	0	.000	.000
Nunez, Juan, Pulaski†	.189	37	148	122	19	23	36	1	3	2	14	3	1	1	21	0	39	21	4	0	.295	.310
Orndorff, Dave, Elizabethton	.368	55	260	228	62	84	134	15	1	11	42	2	2	6	22	0	25	18	4	1	.588	.434
Ozuna, Pablo, Johnson City	.323	56	251	232	40	75	105	13	1	5	24	6	2	1	10	0	24	23	5	2	.453	.351
Pacheco, Juan, Bluefield	.197	47	148	132	21	26	34	3	1	1	12	2	1	2	11	0	32	2	4	2	.258	.267
Pagan, Felix, Elizabethton	.291	59	266	227	48	66	113	18	1	9	41	1	5	2	31	2	59	4	1	4	.498	.374
Parra, Jose, Pulaski†	.161	51	194	161	18	26	34	3	1	1	19	4	1	2	26	0	44	8	3	5	.211	.284
Paxton, Chris, Bluefield*	.303	38	132	109	19	33	50	8	0	3	22	0	1	3	19	3	26	0	0	2	.459	.417
Pena, Francisco, Elizabethton	.260	37	146	131	21	34	58	4	1	6	25	0	0	1	14	0	27	0	0	6	.443	.336
Pena, Jose, Pulaski	.333	51	220	204	45	68	97	14	3	3	31	1	1	2	12	0	40	17	6	5	.475	.374
Penalver, Juan, Kingsport	.317	51	220	180	37	57	73	8	1	2	28	2	1	5	32	1	32	7	6	1	.406	.431
Perez, Jersen, Kingsport	.267	65	270	258	45	69	92	10	2	3	29	0	2	3	7	0	41	12	7	4	.357	.293
Perez, Richard, Bluefield	.173	20	58	52	11	9	12	3	0	0	5	0	0	0	6	0	17	6	0	0	.231	.259
Pigott, Anthony, Princeton	.232	46	162	151	20	35	41	4	1	0	14	1	1	1	8	0	34	2	1	3	.272	.273
Piniella, Juan, Pulaski	.270	33	139	126	20	34	47	4	3	1	17	3	2	0	8	0	22	9	4	1	.373	.309
Ramos, Kelly, Kingsport†	.224	50	192	170	25	38	64	3	1	7	32	4	0	1	17	3	33	2	3	5	.376	.298
Rapp, Travis, Bristol	.185	26	94	81	9	15	25	4	0	2	12	1	2	1	9	0	33	0	1	1	.309	.269
Rivera, Roberto, Bluefield	.318	50	209	192	28	61	94	20	2	3	27	2	1	1	13	1	43	6	6	3	.490	.362
Rodriguez, Mark, Kingsport	.149	26	100	87	12	13	23	1	0	3	14	5	0	0	8	0	25	0	0	1	.264	.221
Rodriguez, Miguel, J.C.	.105	8	19	19	1	2	2	0	0	0	0	0	0	0	0	0	8	0	0	2	.105	.105
Rojas, Alejandro, Mar.†	.180	15	51	50	4	9	10	1	0	0	0	0	0	0	1	0	18	1	2	0	.200	.196
Romans, Billy, Martinsville	.176	19	71	68	7	12	16	4	0	0	3	0	0	0	3	0	16	3	2	2	.235	.211
Romero, Marty, Bristol*	.500	2	3	2	0	1	1	0	0	0	0	0	0	0	1	0	1	0	0	0	.500	.667
Russell, Jake, Brev.	.256	27	106	86	20	22	33	2	0	3	17	0	2	4	14	0	21	0	0	4	.384	.377
Ryan, Mike, Elizabethton*	.300	62	266	220	44	66	85	10	0	3	29	1	4	3	38	3	39	2	2	8	.386	.404
Sandberg, Jared, Princeton	.302	67	312	268	61	81	157	15	5	17	68	0	0	2	42	5	94	12	3	4	.586	.401
Schaeffer, Jon, Elizabethton	.333	48	204	165	35	55	86	13	0	6	34	0	2	4	33	3	32	0	1	5	.521	.451
Schlicher, B.J., Martinsville†	.295	58	245	217	33	64	95	16	0	5	34	0	0	0	28	2	59	2	3	6	.438	.376
Secoda, Joe, Johnson City	.251	52	209	187	21	47	61	5	0	3	16	1	1	3	17	0	56	4	3	3	.326	.322
Sergio, Thomas, Pulaski*	.327	58	270	226	57	74	123	14	4	9	40	1	1	4	38	0	42	25	6	1	.544	.431
Sharpe, Grant, Brev.*	.253	64	277	245	29	62	106	12	1	10	51	0	1	2	29	2	86	0	0	4	.433	.336
Smith, Casey, Brevard County	.351	19	83	77	8	27	35	2	0	2	9	0	1	2	3	0	22	1	0	0	.455	.386
Smith, Marcus, Elizabethton*	.228	44	166	145	22	33	53	1	2	5	15	4	3	2	12	1	32	4	2	2	.366	.290
Smith, Shane, Kingsport	.221	37	135	113	15	25	41	7	0	3	13	3	0	4	15	0	22	2	1	2	.363	.333
Spear, Chad, Princeton	.176	9	25	17	8	3	4	1	0	0	3	0	1	3	4	0	6	0	0	2	.235	.400
Stephens, Joel, Bluefield	.167	6	20	18	3	3	3	0	0	0	1	0	0	0	2	0	2	2	1	1	.167	.250
Stratton, Robert, Kingsport	.249	63	270	245	51	61	127	11	5	15	50	0	0	6	19	1	94	11	6	2	.518	.319
Suriel, Miguel, Princeton	.272	58	228	202	40	55	89	3	2	9	38	2	2	1	21	0	29	2	2	7	.441	.341
Sutton, Joe, Bristol	.332	56	227	190	46	63	118	18	2	11	43	0	1	1	35	2	51	7	0	4	.621	.436
Taveras, Frank, Brev.*	.263	56	215	194	29	51	73	10	3	2	34	1	4	0	16	0	56	11	8	1	.376	.313

Player, Team	Avg.	G	TPA	AB	R	H	TB	2B	3B	HR	RBI	SH	SF	HP	BB	IBB	SO	SB	CS	GDP	Slg.	OBP
Terrell, Jim, Bristol*	.216	47	197	176	30	38	47	4	1	1	22	1	2	1	17	0	40	5	0	5	.267	.286
Torrealba, Steve, Danville.......	.227	44	171	150	17	34	49	9	0	2	18	2	2	2	15	0	27	0	1	6	.327	.302
Torres, Reynaldo, J.C.	.140	34	113	107	4	15	19	1	0	1	4	0	0	0	6	0	58	0	0	6	.178	.186
Utting, Andy, Bluefield†	.230	51	186	152	22	35	56	7	1	4	18	3	0	1	30	2	41	2	4	3	.368	.361
Valdez, Jerry, Martinsville	.272	34	136	125	21	34	44	7	0	1	11	0	0	4	7	0	27	0	2	2	.352	.331
Van Iten, Bob, Martinsville* ...	.309	55	215	204	29	63	87	9	0	5	35	0	3	3	5	0	27	3	2	1	.426	.330
Vanasselberg, Ricky, Blu.* ...	.210	27	68	62	5	13	18	2	0	1	7	0	0	0	6	0	9	1	0	5	.290	.279
Vaughn, Lateef, Elizabethton..	.300	10	44	40	10	12	15	3	0	0	5	1	0	0	3	0	5	1	1	0	.375	.349
Ventura, Frankie, Brev.	.256	35	135	117	17	30	38	6	1	0	18	1	1	3	13	0	26	3	3	0	.325	.343
Villar, Jose, Danville	.222	54	219	203	34	45	69	10	4	2	16	0	2	1	12	0	69	16	5	3	.340	.266
Wallace, Derek, Bristol	.242	50	206	186	26	45	82	12	2	7	29	2	2	4	11	1	65	8	2	3	.441	.296
Wilder, Paul, Princeton*	.206	44	192	155	25	32	60	6	2	6	23	0	2	2	33	0	63	3	2	1	.387	.349
Williams, Jovany, J.C.	.246	41	149	142	25	35	68	10	1	7	23	2	1	2	2	0	29	2	1	4	.479	.265
Wilson, Cliff, Bluefield*	.240	46	147	129	16	31	40	2	2	1	14	1	1	1	15	1	35	3	1	1	.310	.322
Wilson, Travis, Danville	.215	61	256	233	29	50	76	14	6	0	27	1	0	8	14	0	60	4	1	5	.326	.282
Zapp, A.J., Danville*	.338	65	277	234	34	79	127	23	2	7	56	0	1	7	35	0	78	0	1	3	.543	.437
Zydowsky, John, Danville........	.232	43	178	151	19	35	44	6	0	1	15	3	1	3	20	0	42	2	4	7	.291	.331

GRAND SLAMS: Berns, Berger, Sandberg, 2 each; Brooks, Caines, Darr, Figueroa, Garavito, Grabowski, Ja. Hairston, Jaramillo, Jaworowski, Lutz, Schlicher, Torrealba, Wallace, Zydowsky, 1 each.

AWARDED FIRST BASE ON CATCHER'S INTERFERENCE: Messner 4 (Norrell 2, Rapp, Suriel); Feramisco (Cruz); Grabowski (Norrell); Hoover (J. Cook); Lopez-Cao (Alfonso); Villar (F. Pena); Wallace (Cruz).

1997 PITCHING
TEAM

Team	W	L	Pct.	ERA	G	CG	ShO	Sv.	IP	H	TBF	R	ER	HR	SH	SF	HB	BB	IBB	SO	WP	Bk.
Pulaski	43	25	.632	3.33	68	4	4	15	600.2	538	2575	309	222	43	10	7	33	199	0	663	65	15
Bluefield	40	29	.580	4.20	69	1	4	16	595.2	564	2598	337	278	51	7	25	30	255	10	628	55	13
Princeton ...	39	30	.565	4.34	69	1	4	10	607.0	640	2666	392	293	55	14	19	29	210	3	565	52	17
Burlington....	32	36	.471	4.41	68	0	5	10	592.0	605	2674	393	290	48	23	21	52	261	2	522	67	12
Martinsville...	29	39	.426	4.62	68	1	3	13	588.1	608	2611	399	302	60	21	26	33	215	10	503	53	11
Elizabethton .	38	30	.559	5.11	68	2	3	12	582.2	639	2648	416	331	65	27	10	37	229	3	562	63	10
Danville......	30	38	.441	5.13	68	1	3	14	583.2	601	2666	428	333	49	16	17	56	275	5	621	92	9
Kingsport	37	31	.544	5.32	68	2	1	16	592.0	683	2677	479	350	75	27	18	45	208	19	578	50	7
Bristol........	30	38	.441	5.91	68	2	4	9	574.0	655	2715	465	377	52	15	23	43	312	7	560	67	16
Johnson City..	23	45	.338	6.60	68	1	0	14	578.1	728	2796	537	424	78	11	28	36	320	10	569	57	17

INDIVIDUAL

TOP QUALIFIERS FOR EARNED-RUN AVERAGE TITLE
Minimum 54 innings. *Lefthanded pitcher.

Pitcher, Team	W	L	Pct.	ERA	G	GS	CG	ShO	GF	Sv.	IP	H	TBF	R	ER	HR	SH	SF	HB	BB	IBB	SO	WP	Bk.
DeYoung, Daniel, Pulaski	4	1	.800	1.91	19	8	1	0	9	3	61.1	52	250	16	13	1	0	1	2	12	0	69	3	0
Poland, Robert, Pulaski*........	7	3	.700	2.00	13	13	3	2	0	0	85.1	57	333	29	19	9	2	0	3	18	0	106	4	3
Manbeck, Mark, Martinsville ..	3	1	.750	2.22	9	9	0	0	0	0	56.2	51	227	16	14	4	0	0	2	3	0	64	0	0
Bond, Aaron, Pulaski............	5	2	.714	2.45	14	14	0	0	0	0	77.0	56	311	29	21	5	4	1	1	22	0	64	9	2
Turnbow, Mark, Burlington	8	2	.800	2.78	13	13	0	0	0	0	74.1	49	297	25	23	1	4	2	4	18	0	53	2	0
Bauer, Richard, Bluefield........	8	3	.727	2.86	13	13	0	0	0	0	72.1	58	294	31	23	1	0	4	4	20	0	67	8	0
Seberino, Ronni, Princeton* ..	4	4	.500	3.17	14	14	0	0	0	0	65.1	71	292	39	23	3	0	1	1	28	0	57	6	2
Perez, Norberto, Bluefield	3	5	.375	3.46	10	10	0	0	0	0	54.2	52	231	29	21	5	0	2	2	16	0	58	5	1
Perez, Pablo, Elizabethton......	10	0	1.000	3.52	17	10	0	0	3	0	79.1	79	327	37	31	10	3	1	1	12	0	69	4	0
Quevedo, Ruben, Danville	1	5	.167	3.56	13	11	0	0	0	0	68.1	46	286	37	27	6	3	5	4	27	0	78	3	1
Layne, Roger, Burlington	1	4	.200	3.62	11	11	0	0	0	0	59.2	55	257	39	24	5	3	2	1	21	0	52	11	0
Harrison, Scott, Burlington	3	5	.375	3.71	12	12	0	0	0	0	63.0	62	276	37	26	6	0	2	3	24	0	50	6	0
Marshall, Lee, Elizabethton	5	3	.625	3.86	14	14	1	0	0	0	84.0	93	369	56	36	6	4	1	5	16	0	41	2	0
Pugmire, Robert, Burlington	1	2	.333	3.92	14	14	0	0	0	0	66.2	72	302	42	29	4	3	4	4	29	0	62	7	2
Achilles, Matt, Bluefield..........	7	2	.778	3.95	14	13	0	0	0	0	73.0	60	301	37	32	9	1	2	2	33	0	68	7	2

DEPARTMENTAL LEADERS: W—P. Perez, 10; L—Taylor, Lanfranco, 8 each; Pct.—P. Perez, 1.000; G—D. Gooden, 31; GS—Several pitchers tied with 14 each; CG—Poland, 3; ShO—Poland 2; GF—Franks, 23; Sv.—Franks, Mastrolonardo, 12 each; IP—Poland, 85.1; H—Marshall, 93; TBF—Marshall, 369; R—T. Guzman, 75; ER—T. Guzman, 60; HR—Lanfranco, 14; SH—Reimers, Lunney, Montero, 5 each; SF—Turnbow, 6 each; HB—Lyons, 12; BB—Bales, 49; IBB—Maberry, Santana, 4 each; SO—Poland, 106; WP—Lyons, 24; BK—T. Guzman, 6.

ALL PITCHERS
*Lefthanded pitcher.

Pitcher, Team	W	L	Pct.	ERA	G	GS	CG	ShO	GF	Sv.	IP	H	TBF	R	ER	HR	SH	SF	HB	BB	IBB	SO	WP	Bk.
Achilles, Matt, Bluefield	7	2	.778	3.95	14	13	0	0	0	0	73.0	60	301	37	32	9	1	2	2	33	0	68	7	2
Albaugh, Chad, Martinsville	1	2	.333	5.79	20	0	0	0	4	1	32.2	38	154	27	21	3	1	3	4	15	1	27	0	0
Alvarez, Danny, Burlington..........	0	2	.000	6.75	3	1	0	0	0	0	6.2	10	33	6	5	0	2	1	0	4	0	6	0	0
Andrade, Jancy, Bluefield............	0	0	.000	2.51	4	4	0	0	0	0	14.1	9	62	5	4	1	0	0	0	11	0	13	1	1
Aracena, Juan, Burlington	1	4	.200	4.89	19	0	0	0	8	2	38.2	45	176	32	21	4	1	1	0	16	0	31	3	2
Baez, Miguel, Burlington	1	3	.250	2.15	19	0	0	0	15	2	29.1	21	131	17	7	4	3	4	4	14	0	33	3	0
Bales, Joseph, Bristol	8	3	.727	4.12	14	14	1	1	0	0	83.0	73	356	50	38	7	0	1	1	49	1	86	4	1
Bauer, Richard, Bluefield............	8	3	.727	2.86	13	13	0	0	0	0	72.1	58	294	31	23	1	0	4	4	20	0	67	8	0
Birrell, Simon, Danville	4	3	.571	4.71	13	9	0	0	0	0	49.2	59	232	36	26	6	1	1	8	27	0	25	8	0
Bond, Aaron, Pulaski	5	2	.714	2.45	14	14	0	0	0	0	77.0	56	311	29	21	5	4	1	1	22	0	64	9	2
Borkowski, Robert, Kingsport......	2	0	1.000	16.88	5	0	0	0	4	2	5.1	13	33	10	10	1	0	0	0	5	0	5	0	0

Pitcher, Team	W	L	Pct.	ERA	G	GS	CG	ShO	GF	Sv.	IP	H	TBF	R	ER	HR	SH	SF	HB	BB	IBB	SO	WP	Bk.
Bowring, Jason, Kingsport	0	0	.000	9.00	2	0	0	0	2	0	4.0	7	18	4	4	1	0	0	1	0	4	2	0
Box, John, Princeton*	4	1	.800	2.35	25	0	0	0	12	3	38.1	29	152	15	10	2	1	1	10	0	53	1	3
Bray, Chris, Bluefield	0	0	.000	15.75	3	0	0	0	0	0	4.0	1	20	7	7	0	0	0	3	4	0	5	0
Brown, Derek, Bluefield	2	5	.286	5.01	17	5	1	0	2	1	41.1	44	180	26	23	3	1	1	0	13	0	48	3	1
Brummitt, Travis, Danville	0	0	.000	13.05	12	0	0	0	4	0	20.0	34	118	36	29	4	1	1	7	16	0	24	5	1
Cali, Joe, Burlington	1	2	.333	11.07	14	0	0	0	8	0	20.1	37	120	36	25	4	0	1	2	20	0	24	8	2
Canciobello, Anthony, Dan.	0	0	.000	12.27	3	0	0	0	0	0	3.2	6	24	6	5	0	0	1	0	6	0	4	2	0
Carnes, Matt, Elizabethton	3	0	1.000	3.08	8	7	1	0	0	0	38.0	33	156	17	13	3	2	0	1	5	0	42	7	1
Carrion, Jorge, Pulaski	5	5	.500	4.74	13	13	0	0	0	0	76.0	75	356	64	40	9	0	0	10	44	0	78	7	1
Carter, Chris, Princeton	2	0	1.000	3.31	26	0	0	0	13	2	35.1	40	147	16	13	1	0	1	0	5	0	24	0	3
Carter, Roger, Princeton	5	2	.714	4.61	13	13	0	0	0	0	56.2	61	247	36	29	6	2	4	5	17	0	50	7	1
Ciravolo, Jon, Danville	4	2	.667	5.06	19	0	0	0	5	1	37.1	48	176	31	21	4	0	0	4	13	0	42	4	0
Clark, Greg, Elizabethton	1	0	1.000	5.08	16	0	0	0	7	0	28.1	34	124	21	16	5	2	1	0	8	0	22	0	0
Cook, Derrick, Pulaski	2	2	.500	3.74	6	6	0	0	0	0	33.2	32	141	15	14	1	0	1	2	12	0	32	4	0
Cook, Steven, Martinsville	0	0	.000	5.00	7	0	0	0	3	0	9.0	11	47	6	5	1	0	0	2	7	1	8	2	0
Corcoran, Tim, Kingsport	2	0	1.000	4.24	7	0	0	0	3	0	17.0	12	75	10	8	2	0	2	3	8	2	14	2	1
Cosgrove, Michael, Elz.	1	1	.500	4.76	12	1	0	0	6	2	22.2	25	107	16	12	1	1	1	0	6	1	31	1	0
Cox, Robert, Kingsport	1	2	.333	4.71	21	0	0	0	11	2	42.0	49	188	25	22	2	3	3	3	16	2	24	3	2
Currens, Timothy, Bristol	0	4	.000	4.88	20	0	0	0	12	1	27.2	29	130	21	15	0	2	0	2	13	1	23	3	2
Daneker, Patrick, Bristol	3	6	.333	6.50	12	12	0	0	0	0	63.2	83	294	55	46	5	2	3	5	20	1	53	4	5
Davies, Robert, Elizabethton	0	1	.000	40.50	1	1	0	0	0	0	0.2	2	7	3	3	0	0	0	0	3	0	1	1	0
De La Cruz, Ynocencio, Kin.	2	3	.400	6.61	6	6	0	0	0	0	31.1	46	151	30	23	4	0	1	4	8	1	31	1	0
DeLeon, Julio, Princeton	1	1	.500	5.26	11	0	0	0	6	0	25.2	26	116	21	15	0	3	0	10	15	0	15	2	0
DeYoung, Daniel, Pulaski	4	1	.800	1.91	19	8	1	0	9	3	61.1	52	250	16	13	1	0	1	2	12	0	69	3	0
Dolby, Lawrence, Danville	0	0	.000	5.87	3	0	0	0	0	0	7.2	7	35	5	5	2	0	0	0	5	0	6	1	0
Drew, Tim, Burlington	0	1	.000	6.17	4	4	0	0	0	0	11.2	16	63	15	8	0	0	0	6	4	0	14	4	1
Driscoll, Patrick, Martinsville*	2	2	.500	2.57	8	0	0	0	1	0	14.0	12	55	4	4	1	2	0	0	4	2	17	1	0
Durick, Chad, Kingsport	1	0	1.000	1.17	6	0	0	0	5	0	7.2	3	31	2	1	1	0	0	0	3	0	11	0	0
Elder, David, Pulaski	2	2	.500	1.95	20	0	0	0	17	6	32.1	18	127	8	7	2	0	0	0	12	0	57	4	0
Embry, Byron, Danville	2	1	.667	1.97	20	1	0	0	14	3	32.0	14	125	7	7	0	3	1	0	15	0	56	4	0
Enloe, Mark, Kingsport*	1	1	.500	6.45	15	4	0	0	4	0	44.2	57	208	37	32	7	3	3	2	21	0	36	6	1
Espina, Rendy, Elizabethton	0	3	.000	7.94	6	3	0	0	1	0	17.0	25	86	21	15	2	0	3	9	0	15	3	1
Felix, Miguel, Bristol	2	5	.286	7.51	11	-10	0	0	0	0	50.1	78	256	52	42	7	0	4	7	22	0	38	5	2
Fleck, William, Danville	2	3	.400	3.57	23	0	0	0	18	6	35.1	36	158	17	14	2	1	1	1	17	3	56	3	1
Fleming, Emar, Pulaski	1	1	.500	2.12	23	1	0	0	10	3	51.0	36	206	16	12	4	1	0	2	16	0	75	2	3
Folkers, Brandon, Johnson City*	0	0	.000	4.15	4	0	0	0	4	0	4.1	8	21	2	2	1	0	0	0	4	0	6	2	0
Fontaine, Tom, Bluefield	5	1	.833	6.02	21	2	0	0	2	0	40.1	44	196	31	27	3	0	5	28	2	50	6	3	
Franks, Lance, Johnson City	0	0	.000	1.17	26	0	0	0	23	12	30.2	16	113	4	4	1	0	0	7	1	40	2	0
Freedberg, Todd, Bluefield	2	1	.667	1.98	11	1	0	0	1	0	27.1	29	131	14	6	0	3	2	12	3	29	7	0
Fry, Jeff, Danville*	1	1	.500	4.12	21	0	0	0	10	1	19.2	19	99	12	9	3	1	1	3	20	1	16	1	0
Gandy, Josh, Elizabethton*	3	0	1.000	5.91	8	6	0	0	0	0	35.0	36	160	26	23	3	1	0	1	19	0	47	0	0
Garcia, Wilson, Johnson City	0	2	.000	6.66	25	3	0	0	3	0	48.2	78	258	59	36	4	2	3	2	21	1	44	5	3
Garff, Jeff, Burlington	1	1	.500	4.50	5	0	0	0	5	1	8.0	9	34	4	4	2	0	0	0	2	0	9	1	0
Garmon, Adam, Kingsport	2	2	.500	7.71	18	5	0	0	10	3	42.0	50	200	43	36	10	0	0	5	21	1	39	6	0
Geis, John, Johnson City*	3	4	.429	3.98	30	0	0	0	12	0	40.2	44	188	27	18	4	1	2	1	15	1	57	1	0
Gholar, Antonio, Elizabethton	2	2	.500	6.04	24	0	0	0	7	2	44.2	49	225	41	30	5	0	5	3	32	0	50	7	0
Gonzalez, Dicky, Kingsport	3	6	.333	4.36	12	12	1	0	0	0	66.0	70	282	38	32	7	4	2	4	10	0	76	0	0
Gooden, Carl, Johnson City	1	0	1.000	0.00	1	0	0	0	0	0	2.0	1	7	0	0	0	0	0	1	0	3	1	0
Gooden, Derek, Johnson City	2	2	.500	3.72	31	0	0	0	17	1	36.1	41	171	22	15	1	1	2	0	21	1	48	2	0
Granadillo, Adel, Burlington	6	4	.600	5.44	15	4	0	0	2	0	48.0	55	224	30	29	5	1	1	10	23	1	44	4	0
Gray, Jason, Bristol	0	3	.000	18.29	4	3	0	0	0	0	10.1	22	61	21	21	4	0	0	0	8	0	11	2	0
Guzman, Ambiorix, Pulaski	3	1	.750	2.27	10	2	0	0	4	2	35.2	40	146	10	9	1	0	0	3	3	0	26	2	0
Guzman, Toribio, Johnson City	1	7	.125	8.44	13	13	0	0	0	0	64.0	91	308	75	60	9	1	6	1	26	0	49	7	6
Halpin, Jeremy, Bluefield	1	0	1.000	3.24	15	0	0	0	8	0	25.0	30	108	14	9	0	0	2	0	4	0	22	1	1
Hamilton, Randy, Kingsport*	5	3	.625	2.53	21	0	0	0	9	4	46.1	38	192	18	13	0	3	3	1	15	2	44	1	0
Harrison, Scott, Burlington	3	5	.375	3.71	12	12	0	0	0	0	63.0	62	276	37	26	6	0	2	3	24	0	50	6	0
Hodges, Reid, Bristol	0	2	.000	5.13	27	0	0	0	17	2	26.1	30	125	16	15	2	1	0	0	19	1	32	8	0
Hogge, Shawn, Johnson City	0	1	.000	5.11	3	3	0	0	0	0	12.1	16	55	9	7	3	0	0	6	0	10	0	0
Hootselle, Jeff, Martinsville*	1	1	.500	5.05	14	12	1	1	1	0	66.0	62	286	43	37	8	1	1	2	28	0	69	5	2
Hopson, Craig, Johnson City	1	3	.250	9.93	15	4	0	0	0	0	29.0	44	169	43	32	8	0	3	5	32	1	23	11	0
Humphries, Christopher, Mar.	1	0	1.000	8.38	5	0	0	0	1	0	9.2	14	50	14	9	1	2	0	0	8	0	7	2	0
Izquierdo, Hansel, Bristol	2	2	.500	4.30	9	2	0	0	2	0	23.0	25	104	14	11	5	0	0	4	8	0	24	0	1
Jacobson, Andrew, Bristol	1	2	.333	6.98	14	7	0	0	1	0	49.0	57	249	51	38	1	0	3	2	46	2	47	9	2
James, Delvin, Princeton	4	4	.500	4.94	20	5	0	0	4	0	58.1	71	276	57	32	11	4	2	4	24	1	46	4	2
Jurgena, Matt, Elizabethton	2	4	.333	5.06	23	5	0	0	10	4	42.2	46	194	28	24	8	1	0	5	18	0	57	7	0
Kertis, John, Pulaski	2	0	1.000	2.95	14	0	0	0	1	0	21.1	14	97	9	7	0	0	0	4	11	0	22	4	0
Key, Calvin, Martinsville	5	2	.714	4.83	14	6	0	0	3	0	50.1	56	227	35	27	5	0	2	3	13	1	53	5	1
Kofler, Ed, Princeton	5	6	.455	5.57	13	13	0	0	0	0	63.0	63	280	46	39	9	1	1	7	28	0	66	5	2
Kvasnicka, Jonathon, Bristol	1	2	.333	6.08	4	4	0	0	0	0	23.2	22	108	18	16	3	1	0	4	12	0	19	0	1
Lambert, Jeremy, Johnson City	1	1	.500	9.19	27	0	0	0	4	1	32.1	46	181	42	33	3	1	1	5	37	1	29	6	0
Lanfranco, Otoniel, Johnson City	2	8	.200	7.64	14	14	0	0	0	0	68.1	85	319	60	58	14	1	1	6	31	0	69	1	0
Layne, Roger, Burlington	1	4	.200	3.62	11	11	0	0	0	0	59.2	55	257	39	24	5	3	2	1	21	0	52	11	0
Lee, Chris, Bluefield	2	0	1.000	4.06	23	0	0	0	10	2	31.0	24	128	17	14	4	3	2	2	14	1	32	2	1
Lee, Garrett, Danville	5	5	.500	4.93	14	14	1	1	0	0	84.0	87	360	57	46	8	3	2	7	17	1	72	3	1
Lewis, Derrick, Danville	2	4	.333	6.34	16	9	0	0	2	0	49.2	59	241	48	35	5	1	1	2	31	0	46	8	0
Lopez, Jose, Bristol	3	1	.750	7.01	20	0	0	0	6	0	43.2	62	213	42	34	1	2	4	1	18	0	33	1	0
Lovingood, Ray, Kingsport*	6	4	.600	5.86	13	13	0	0	0	0	63.0	80	294	48	41	11	1	1	5	30	2	65	7	0
Lunney, Barry, Elizabethton*	1	3	.250	9.00	22	0	0	0	12	1	25.0	30	132	26	25	3	5	0	3	22	1	21	11	0
Lyons, Timothy, Danville	0	0	.000	32.40	10	0	0	0	5	0	8.1	14	70	31	30	0	0	1	12	19	0	13	24	1
Maberry, Mark, Kingsport	2	2	.500	1.80	22	0	0	0	13	5	35.0	36	158	14	7	3	3	1	0	13	4	51	2	0
Malloy, Patrick, Burlington	0	1	.000	6.83	17	0	0	0	6	1	29.0	35	138	24	22	3	1	1	5	14	0	26	2	0

Pitcher, Team	W	L	Pct.	ERA	G	GS	CG	ShO	GF	Sv.	IP	H	TBF	R	ER	HR	SH	SF	HB	BB	IBB	SO	WP	Bk.
Manbeck, Mark, Martinsville	3	1	.750	2.22	9	9	0	0	0	0	56.2	51	227	16	14	4	0	0	2	3	0	64	0	0
Marshall, Lee, Elizabethton	5	3	.625	3.86	14	14	1	0	0	0	84.0	93	369	56	36	6	4	1	5	16	0	41	2	0
Marsonek, Sam, Pulaski	7	3	.700	5.02	12	11	0	0	0	0	71.2	90	331	57	40	4	2	3	3	20	0	65	13	3
Martinez, Caleb, Martinsville*	1	3	.250	3.69	7	7	0	0	0	0	39.0	37	167	21	16	3	0	2	2	18	0	27	1	3
Mason, Chris, Princeton	2	1	.667	3.64	19	1	0	0	7	1	42.0	43	174	17	17	3	2	1	2	5	0	45	4	0
Mastrolonardo, David, Bluefield	4	0	1.000	1.08	26	0	0	0	22	12	33.1	15	130	5	4	3	0	1	0	12	1	45	1	0
Mattson, John, Kingsport	1	0	1.000	4.63	6	4	0	0	1	0	23.1	25	98	12	12	2	1	0	2	5	0	25	3	0
McDermott, Ryan, Burlington	3	3	.500	6.49	8	8	0	0	0	0	34.2	45	168	29	25	2	0	1	4	25	0	22	7	0
McDermott, Toby, Princeton*	0	0	.000	2.25	17	0	0	0	6	0	24.0	16	97	9	6	3	1	1	0	11	0	23	3	0
McGee, Thomas, Bluefield	0	1	.000	54.00	1	0	0	0	1	0	0.1	2	3	2	2	1	0	0	0	0	0	0	0	0
Meyer, Jake, Bristol	1	1	.500	2.25	17	0	0	0	15	5	20.0	15	84	7	5	3	1	0	0	7	0	25	4	0
Miller, Aaron, Elizabethton*	2	1	.667	6.30	23	0	0	0	7	0	30.0	25	140	25	21	4	1	0	5	25	0	43	6	0
Miller, Matt, Johnson City	2	2	.500	7.88	20	3	0	0	2	0	40.0	62	200	43	35	4	0	1	2	16	2	32	3	1
Molta, Salvatore, Martinsville	0	2	.000	9.53	13	0	0	0	10	0	17.0	25	89	18	18	2	1	2	3	13	0	12	7	0
Montada, Joaquin, Kingsport	3	2	.600	6.90	13	11	0	0	0	0	60.0	78	282	55	46	11	2	1	6	22	1	52	5	1
Montero, Francisco, Martinsville	3	5	.375	4.09	14	14	0	0	0	0	77.0	79	342	49	35	4	5	2	3	22	0	47	2	1
Murphy, Darren, Bluefield*	1	3	.250	5.82	23	1	0	0	6	0	38.2	48	182	28	25	8	1	0	3	18	2	42	3	0
Myers, Rob, Elizabethton	0	1	.000	15.43	3	0	0	0	0	0	4.2	9	35	11	8	0	0	0	1	11	1	6	4	1
Myette, Aaron, Bristol	4	3	.571	3.61	9	8	1	0	0	0	47.1	39	215	28	19	9	0	0	7	20	0	50	2	1
Nation, Joey, Danville*	1	2	.333	2.73	8	8	0	0	0	0	26.1	24	107	11	8	1	0	0	1	5	0	41	1	0
Norris, Stephen, Johnson City*	4	7	.364	5.90	14	14	0	0	0	0	71.2	84	340	64	47	8	0	4	9	42	0	72	7	2
Ortega, Franklin, Johnson City	3	4	.429	7.30	18	7	1	0	1	0	49.1	62	241	46	40	6	1	3	2	39	1	46	2	4
Ovalle, Bonelly, Pulaski	3	4	.429	4.91	26	0	0	0	17	1	33.0	27	149	23	18	4	0	1	3	15	0	39	4	0
Payne, Tony, Kingsport*	3	0	1.000	5.26	10	0	0	0	2	0	25.2	31	120	17	15	3	4	0	4	14	0	28	2	0
Pena, Francisco, Elizabethton	0	0	.000	0.00	1	0	0	0	1	0	0.1	0	1	0	0	0	0	0	0	0	0	0	0	0
Perez, Norberto, Bluefield	3	5	.375	3.46	10	10	0	0	0	0	54.2	52	231	29	21	5	0	2	2	16	0	58	5	1
Perez, Pablo, Elizabethton	10	0	1.000	3.52	17	10	0	0	3	0	79.1	79	327	37	31	10	3	1	1	12	0	69	4	0
Perez, Sam, Burlington*	1	1	.500	5.96	16	1	0	0	9	0	22.2	26	100	19	15	3	1	0	1	10	0	14	2	1
Phelps, Travis, Princeton	4	3	.571	4.88	14	13	1	0	0	0	62.2	73	279	42	34	4	3	1	2	23	0	60	4	1
Phipps, Jeff, Bluefield	0	2	.000	10.80	4	2	0	0	1	0	10.0	12	50	13	12	2	0	2	1	8	0	6	1	0
Poland, Robert, Pulaski*	7	3	.700	2.00	13	13	3	2	0	0	85.1	57	333	29	19	9	2	0	3	18	0	106	4	3
Pruett, Matthew, Princeton	3	2	.600	4.38	24	0	0	0	19	4	24.2	26	111	19	12	1	1	1	1	10	1	22	2	0
Pugmire, Robert, Burlington	1	2	.333	3.92	14	14	0	0	0	0	66.2	72	302	42	29	4	3	4	4	29	0	62	7	2
Quevedo, Ruben, Danville	1	5	.167	3.56	13	11	0	0	0	0	68.1	46	286	37	27	6	3	5	4	27	0	78	3	1
Ramos, Fernando, Martinsville	2	3	.400	2.05	24	0	0	0	21	9	26.1	13	106	8	6	0	2	0	1	12	3	25	1	0
Reimers, Tom, Bristol	3	2	.600	6.38	12	4	0	0	1	0	42.1	47	212	35	30	3	5	2	4	28	0	47	18	0
Reyes, Arquimedes, Martinsville	4	1	.800	2.31	20	0	0	0	7	0	39.0	32	170	17	10	3	1	2	1	15	1	39	8	0
Reynolds, Chris, Princeton	1	0	1.000	5.49	12	0	0	0	3	0	19.2	21	88	13	12	2	0	2	0	6	0	18	4	0
Rincon, Juan, Elizabethton	0	1	.000	3.86	2	1	0	0	0	0	9.1	11	41	4	4	0	0	0	0	3	0	7	2	0
Rivera, Luis, Danville	3	1	.750	2.41	9	9	0	0	0	0	41.0	28	169	15	11	2	1	1	1	17	0	57	5	0
Roberts, Marquis, Princeton*	2	0	1.000	4.91	3	3	0	0	0	0	18.1	20	78	10	10	2	0	0	1	4	0	15	2	0
Rodgers, Marcus, Bristol	0	1	.000	9.43	6	4	0	0	0	0	21.0	35	113	26	22	1	1	4	0	16	0	14	3	1
Rodriguez, Jose, Johnson City*	0	0	.000	4.05	4	0	0	0	1	0	6.2	4	27	3	3	1	1	0	1	3	1	8	1	0
Rojas, Francisco, Johnson City	1	1	.500	5.40	6	0	0	0	0	0	10.0	11	49	8	6	2	0	0	0	8	0	9	2	1
Romero, Jordan, Bluefield	1	3	.250	6.51	12	5	0	0	3	0	27.2	31	131	20	20	0	0	3	1	17	0	38	6	0
Romero, Juan, Elizabethton*	3	2	.600	4.88	18	0	0	0	12	3	24.0	27	110	16	13	4	1	0	4	7	0	29	0	4
Ruiz, Rafael, Bristol*	2	1	.667	4.26	23	0	0	0	10	1	38.0	34	169	21	18	0	0	2	6	18	1	56	1	0
Santana, Humberto, Kingsport*	3	6	.333	5.28	13	13	1	0	0	0	76.2	87	329	51	45	9	3	1	6	16	4	71	10	2
Seberino, Ronni, Princeton*	4	4	.500	3.17	14	14	0	0	0	0	65.1	71	292	39	23	3	0	1	1	28	0	57	6	2
Serrano, Elio, Martinsville	1	5	.167	5.93	21	0	0	0	8	1	41.0	46	187	34	27	10	2	1	2	16	0	40	3	1
Shanklin, Paul, Danville	4	3	.571	4.95	17	0	0	0	5	3	43.2	51	195	27	24	2	0	0	4	9	0	44	9	3
Silva, Carlos, Martinsville	2	2	.500	5.15	11	11	0	0	0	0	57.2	66	252	46	33	9	3	2	1	14	0	31	6	3
Silva, Troy, Burlington	1	1	.500	3.54	20	0	0	0	9	3	40.2	35	181	22	16	4	2	1	4	18	0	50	5	2
Sims, Kenny, Bluefield	1	2	.333	3.06	18	2	0	0	10	1	35.1	30	158	18	12	2	0	1	3	22	0	33	1	1
Smith, Ryan, Pulaski*	2	1	.667	8.87	15	0	0	0	6	0	22.1	41	128	33	22	3	1	0	0	14	0	30	9	3
Smith, Shane, Kingsport	0	0	.000	13.50	2	0	0	0	2	0	2.0	1	11	4	3	1	0	0	0	3	0	2	0	0
Stephens, John, Bluefield	2	0	1.000	2.25	4	4	0	0	0	0	24.0	17	93	6	6	4	0	0	1	5	0	34	1	1
Spurgeon, Jay, Bluefield	1	1	.500	3.34	9	7	0	0	1	0	35.0	35	146	13	13	4	0	1	1	14	1	32	1	1
Taylor, Aaron, Danville	1	8	.111	5.53	15	7	0	0	2	0	55.1	65	261	49	34	4	1	1	2	31	0	38	11	1
Theodile, Simeon, Bluefield	0	0	.000	21.86	4	0	0	0	0	0	7.0	21	49	20	17	1	0	1	0	4	0	6	0	3
Thomas, Ben, Elizabethton*	2	4	.333	7.43	7	7	0	0	0	0	26.2	37	127	25	22	6	3	2	1	12	0	28	0	1
Thomas, Brad, Elizabethton*	3	4	.429	4.48	14	13	0	0	0	0	70.1	78	307	43	35	5	3	0	3	21	0	53	8	2
Turnbow, Mark, Burlington	8	2	.800	2.78	13	13	0	0	0	0	74.1	49	297	25	23	1	4	2	4	18	0	53	2	0
Turnbow, Thomas, Martinsville	1	3	.250	7.40	7	7	0	0	0	0	24.1	34	121	29	20	5	0	6	3	16	1	7	5	0
Tuttle, John, Johnson City	2	3	.400	7.88	7	7	0	0	0	0	32.0	35	148	30	28	9	2	2	2	15	0	24	4	0
Vasquez, Antonio, Burlington	2	0	1.000	2.81	12	0	0	0	5	1	25.2	23	118	13	8	1	2	0	2	13	1	20	1	2
Walker, Adam, Martinsville*	0	5	.000	6.28	21	2	0	0	8	2	28.2	32	131	28	20	1	1	3	4	11	0	30	5	0
Wheeler, Johnnie, Burlington*	2	0	1.000	2.08	6	0	0	0	1	0	13.0	10	56	3	3	0	0	0	2	6	0	12	1	0
Williams, Thomas, Bristol	0	0	.000	13.50	4	0	0	0	2	0	4.2	4	26	8	7	1	0	0	0	8	0	2	3	0
Wilson, Cliff, Bluefield	0	0	.000	9.00	1	0	0	0	1	0	1.0	2	5	1	1	0	0	0	0	0	0	0	1	0
Wright, Christopher, Princeton	2	4	.333	7.27	14	7	0	0	0	0	43.1	62	203	39	35	7	2	0	1	20	0	35	6	2
Zambrano, Victor, Princeton	0	2	.000	1.82	20	0	0	0	6	0	29.2	18	126	13	6	1	0	0	4	9	1	36	2	1
Zydowsky, John, Danville	0	0	.000	10.80	2	0	0	0	2	0	1.2	4	10	3	2	0	0	0	0	0	0	3	0	0

COMBINATION SHUTOUTS: **Bluefield (4)**—Perez-Lee, Spurgeon-Fontaine-Lee, Spurgeon-Halpin-Sims, Stephens-Mastrolonardo. **Bristol (3)**—Myette-Hodges-Meyer, Reimers-Felix-Currens, Bales-Hodges. **Burlington (5)**—Turnbow-Baez, Granadillo-Aracena-Baez, Turnbow-Vasquez, Drew-Granadillo-Vasquez, Turnbow-Silva. **Danville (2)**—Rivera-Fleck-Embry, Rivera-Shanklin. **Elizabethton (3)**—Marshall-Carnes-Romero-Lunney, Carnes-Jurgena, Perez-Cosgrove. **Johnson City (0)**—None. **Kingsport (1)**—Lovingood-Garmon. **Martinsville (2)**—Manbeck-Albaugh, Manbeck-Walker-Ramos. **Princeton (4)**—Seberino-James-Reynolds, Phelphs-Box, Seberino-Carter, Seberino-Carter-Box. **Pulaski (2)**—Cook-Ovalle, Poland-Fleming-Ovalle.

NO-HIT GAMES: None.

1997 FIELDING

TEAM

Team	Pct.	G	PO	A	E	TC	DP	PB
Bluefield	.958	69	1787	641	106	2534	48	10
Burlington	.953	68	1776	790	126	2692	58	30
Princeton	.953	69	1821	760	127	2708	48	18
Kingsport	.951	68	1776	713	129	2618	56	13
Pulaski	.948	68	1802	673	137	2612	45	24
Elizabethton	.947	68	1748	710	138	2596	56	20

Team	Pct.	G	PO	A	E	TC	DP	PB
Bristol	.944	68	1722	685	144	2551	57	17
Martinsville	.943	68	1765	754	151	2670	57	23
Johnson City	.941	68	1735	643	148	2526	52	27
Danville	.939	68	1751	638	155	2544	43	20

TRIPLE PLAYS: None.

INDIVIDUAL

FIRST BASEMEN

NOTE: All caps denotes fielding-percentage leader based on 34 games for catchers, 45 for all other non-pitchers and 68 innings for pitchers. *Throws lefthanded.

Player, Team	Pct.	G	PO	A	E	TC	DP
Allen, Troy, Danville	.933	4	28	0	2	30	1
Berger, Matt, Bristol	1.000	7	59	2	0	61	5
Berns, Robert, Princeton*	.981	52	451	52	10	513	34
Bruce, Maurice, Kingsport	1.000	1	9	0	0	9	0
Burns, Patrick, Kingsport*	.981	49	388	19	8	415	38
Caines, Franklyn, Martinsville	1.000	3	18	1	0	19	3
De La Rosa, Miguel, Pulaski	1.000	3	18	1	0	19	0
Durick, Chad, Kingsport	1.000	8	66	11	0	77	5
Edwards, Michael, Brev.	1.000	3	19	2	0	21	0
Ellis, John, Pulaski	1.000	1	3	1	0	4	1
Fennell, Jason, Bristol	.911	10	72	10	8	90	5
FIGUEROA, Franky, Bluefield	.989	63	489	32	6	527	41
Folkers, Brandon, Johnson City*	.973	47	339	22	10	371	24
Gallagher, Shawn, Pulaski	.982	50	419	11	8	438	30
Jaramillo, Francisco, Pulaski	1.000	13	101	14	0	115	6
Jaworowski, Aaron, Elizabethton	.979	64	529	33	12	574	43
Lasater, Chris, Bluefield	1.000	1	15	0	0	15	1
Lina, Estivinson, Pulaski	.905	3	18	1	2	21	0
Llibre, Brian, Johnson City	.973	6	35	1	1	37	4
Lutz, Manuel, Bristol	.975	52	434	26	12	472	38
Majcherek, Matthew, Pulaski	1.000	6	26	0	0	26	2
McGee, Thomas, Bluefield	1.000	3	29	3	0	32	0
McGehee, Michael, Princeton	1.000	20	134	5	0	139	8
Pagan, Felix, Elizabethton	.978	8	40	4	1	45	8
Paxton, Chris, Bluefield	1.000	3	15	0	0	15	1
Rodriguez, Mark, Kingsport	.983	8	55	2	1	58	3
Russell, Jake, Brevard County	.973	5	34	2	1	37	1
Schaeffer, Jon, Elizabethton	1.000	1	3	0	0	3	0
Schlicher, B.J., Martinsville	.983	53	464	43	9	516	39
Sharpe, Grant, Brevard County	.986	61	547	32	8	587	51
Smith, Shane, Kingsport	1.000	3	26	0	0	26	0
Spear, Chad, Princeton	1.000	1	7	0	0	7	1
Suriel, Miguel, Princeton	1.000	1	0	1	0	1	0
Taveras, Frank, Brevard County	.944	3	16	1	1	18	2
Torres, Reynaldo, Johnson City	.957	27	152	3	7	162	19
Vanasselberg, Ricky, Bluefield	1.000	3	20	0	0	20	2
Van Iten, Bob, Martinsville	.983	16	105	12	2	119	12
Zapp, A.J., Danville	.978	65	497	37	12	546	40

SECOND BASEMEN

Player, Team	Pct.	G	PO	A	E	TC	DP
Araujo, Danilo, Johnson City	.947	51	59	118	10	187	23
Benavidez, Eric, Princeton	.983	11	19	38	1	58	6
Borrego, Ramon, Elizabethton	.941	35	72	87	10	169	21
Bowring, Jason, Kingsport	.983	14	25	34	1	60	6
Brett, Jason, Kingsport	.942	28	56	58	7	121	17
Bruce, Maurice, Kingsport	.969	6	17	14	1	32	5
Casillas, Uriel, Martinsville	.956	45	82	135	10	227	31
Collier, Lamonte, Martinsville	1.000	11	18	30	0	48	3
Cruz, Andres, Princeton	.857	1	2	4	1	7	0
Cruz, Luis, Princeton	.926	17	19	31	4	54	3
Dampeer, Kelly, Brevard County	.968	31	62	87	5	154	20
Eckelman, Alex, Johnson City	.971	14	28	40	2	70	10
Frias, Ovidio, Bristol	.955	8	8	13	1	22	3
GARAVITO, Eddy, Bluefield	.956	60	97	143	11	251	28
Giles, Marcus, Danville	.962	42	86	92	7	185	17
Gonzalez, Jose, Bristol	.967	9	16	13	1	30	1
Haley, Ryan, Brevard County	1.000	3	1	10	0	11	1
Jaramillo, Francisco, Pulaski	.963	4	14	12	1	27	2
Kilburg, Joe, Brevard County	.951	35	84	89	9	182	20
Lopes, Omar, Bristol	.962	8	7	18	1	26	3
Majcherek, Matthew, Pulaski	.957	10	21	23	2	46	4
McGrath, Sean, Kingsport	.955	7	21	21	2	44	7
Orndorff, Dave, Elizabethton	.935	29	56	74	9	139	16
Pacheco, Juan, Bluefield	.939	9	11	20	2	33	2
Pagan, Felix, Elizabethton	1.000	8	17	13	0	30	6
Parra, Jose, Pulaski	1.000	1	0	1	0	1	0
Penalver, Juan, Kingsport	.958	9	9	14	1	24	2
Perez, Jersen, Kingsport	.889	7	14	18	4	36	2
Rojas, Alejandro, Martinsville	.894	14	18	24	5	47	4
Sandberg, Jared, Princeton	.957	40	73	127	9	209	25
Secoda, Joe, Johnson City	.938	6	9	6	1	16	1
Sergio, Thomas, Pulaski	.946	55	75	151	13	239	19
Terrell, Jim, Bristol	.918	47	76	114	17	207	29
Zydowsky, John, Danville	.968	27	49	71	4	124	14

THIRD BASEMEN

Player, Team	Pct.	G	PO	A	E	TC	DP
Benavidez, Eric, Princeton	.938	11	10	20	2	32	2
Berger, Matt, Bristol	.863	59	52	105	25	182	11
Bowring, Jason, Kingsport	.791	15	5	29	9	43	4
Caines, Franklyn, Martinsville	.824	5	6	8	3	17	0
Casillas, Uriel, Martinsville	1.000	5	4	9	0	13	2
Collier, Lamonte, Martinsville	.878	43	29	100	18	147	9
Dampeer, Kelly, Brevard County	1.000	5	1	8	0	9	0
Darr, Ryan, Johnson City	.887	52	35	91	16	142	7
Durick, Chad, Kingsport	1.000	3	0	5	0	5	0
Eckelman, Alex, Johnson City	.813	11	6	20	6	32	4
EDWARDS, Michael, Brev.	.890	46	40	130	21	191	13
Frias, Ovidio, Bristol	1.000	6	2	4	0	6	0
Gonzalez, Jose, Bristol	1.000	2	1	4	0	5	1
Harding, Todd, Brevard County	.902	18	8	38	5	51	3
Jaramillo, Francisco, Pulaski	.636	5	2	5	4	11	0
Johnson, Doug, Princeton	.812	33	19	50	16	85	2
Kalcounos, Andy, Johnson City	.750	9	3	15	6	24	2
Lamb, Michael, Pulaski	.862	58	38	118	25	181	10
Lasater, Chris, Bluefield	1.000	1	0	1	0	1	1
Lopes, Omar, Bristol	.944	7	3	14	1	18	2
Lorenzo, Juan, Elizabethton	1.000	3	0	5	0	5	0
Majcherek, Matthew, Pulaski	.600	2	0	3	2	5	0
Martin, Tommy, Bluefield	.900	20	15	21	4	40	3
McGrath, Sean, Kingsport	.914	11	6	26	3	35	0
Pacheco, Juan, Bluefield	.935	22	10	33	3	46	2
Pagan, Felix, Elizabethton	.805	16	4	29	8	41	2
Parra, Jose, Pulaski	.875	3	2	5	1	8	1
Penalver, Juan, Kingsport	.908	38	29	100	13	142	12
Perez, Jersen, Kingsport	1.000	2	0	1	0	1	0
Rodriguez, Mark, Kingsport	1.000	4	3	5	0	8	0
Romans, Billy, Martinsville	.813	18	11	28	9	48	2
Ryan, Mike, Elizabethton	.825	56	37	95	28	160	9
Sandberg, Jared, Princeton	.913	18	11	31	4	46	0
Secoda, Joe, Johnson City	.800	3	0	4	1	5	0
Stephens, Joel, Bluefield	.000	1	0	0	1	1	0
Suriel, Miguel, Princeton	.909	10	2	18	2	22	2
Wilson, Cliff, Bluefield	.864	38	31	58	14	103	4
Wilson, Travis, Danville	.818	56	29	88	26	143	5
Zydowsky, John, Danville	.865	14	10	22	5	37	1

SHORTSTOPS

Player, Team	Pct.	G	PO	A	E	TC	DP
Benavidez, Eric, Princeton	.941	6	6	10	1	17	2
Borrego, Ramon, Elizabethton	.895	17	20	48	8	76	6
Brett, Jason, Kingsport	.792	8	16	22	10	48	4
Brignac, Junior, Danville	.866	33	55	81	21	157	12
Cameron, Troy, Danville	.906	35	58	96	16	170	18
Casillas, Uriel, Martinsville	.961	13	15	34	2	51	4
Collier, Lamonte, Martinsville	.800	3	2	10	3	15	2
Cruz, Luis, Princeton	1.000	1	0	2	0	2	0

SUMMER CLASS A Appalachian League

– 565 –

Player, Team	Pct.	G	PO	A	E	TC	DP
Dampeer, Kelly, Brevard County	.983	12	18	40	1	59	7
Duncan, Carlos, Martinsville	.888	54	74	157	29	260	29
Eckelman, Alex, Johnson City	.918	17	15	41	5	61	7
Edwards, Michael, Brev.	1.000	1	0	4	0	4	0
Frias, Ovidio, Bristol	.879	21	33	54	12	99	13
Gonzalez, Jose, Bristol	.917	14	15	29	4	48	5
HAIRSTON, Jerry, Bluefield	.949	58	84	174	14	272	28
Haley, Ryan, Brevard County	1.000	2	2	4	0	6	2
Hoover, Paul, Princeton	.904	65	111	199	33	343	35
Jaramillo, Francisco, Pulaski	.867	21	34	57	14	105	10
Kilburg, Joe, Brevard County	.833	2	4	6	2	12	2
Lopes, Omar, Bristol	.921	34	59	104	14	177	20
Lorenzo, Juan, Elizabethton	.884	46	48	128	23	199	24
Majcherek, Matthew, Pulaski	.875	2	4	10	2	16	3
Martin, Tommy, Bluefield	.500	3	0	4	4	8	0
McGrath, Sean, Kingsport	.500	2	2	1	3	6	1
Ozuna, Pablo, Johnson City	.898	56	80	139	25	244	22
Pacheco, Juan, Bluefield	.911	16	22	29	5	56	6
Parra, Jose, Pulaski	.907	46	66	120	19	205	15
Penalver, Juan, Kingsport	1.000	5	3	11	0	14	1
Perez, Jersen, Kingsport	.912	52	98	130	22	250	27
Romans, Billy, Martinsville	1.000	1	0	2	0	2	1
Taveras, Frank, Brevard County	.883	54	68	180	33	281	23
Vaughn, Lateef, Elizabethton	.922	10	11	36	4	51	5
Wilson, Cliff, Bluefield	1.000	1	1	0	0	1	1

OUTFIELDERS

Player, Team	Pct.	G	PO	A	E	TC	DP
Albert, Rashad, Bristol	.750	4	5	1	2	8	0
Allen, Troy, Danville	.911	38	40	1	4	45	0
Arias, Jeison, Princeton	.500	4	3	0	3	6	0
Ayuso, Julio, Elizabethton	.938	32	29	1	2	32	0
Benavidez, Eric, Princeton	1.000	17	20	1	0	21	0
Beverly, Shomari, Martinsville	.962	30	73	3	3	79	1
Bonilla, Elin, Martinsville	.903	36	55	1	6	62	0
Borrego, Ramon, Elizabethton	1.000	2	4	0	0	4	0
Bowring, Jason, Kingsport	1.000	28	25	4	0	29	2
Brett, Jason, Kingsport	1.000	3	4	0	0	4	0
Brooks, Anthony, Danville	.927	67	111	4	9	124	1
Bruce, Maurice, Kingsport	.953	23	39	2	2	43	1
Burns, Patrick, Kingsport*	.882	8	15	0	2	17	0
Bushman, Jonathan, Mar.	1.000	8	3	0	0	3	0
Caines, Franklyn, Martinsville	.938	44	72	4	5	81	1
Caradonna, Brett, Bristol	.960	18	23	1	1	25	0
Castro, Martires, Pulaski	.863	50	57	6	10	73	1
Chavez, Endy, Kingsport*	.957	18	43	2	2	47	1
Collier, Lamonte, Martinsville	.909	5	8	2	1	11	1
Copeland, Brandon, Kingsport	.909	40	51	9	6	66	0
Cox, Robert, Kingsport	1.000	1	0	1	0	1	0
Crespo, Jesse, Danville	1.000	13	11	0	0	11	0
Davis, Tim, Johnson City	.923	13	11	1	1	13	0
Davison, Ashanti, Bluefield	.966	44	55	2	2	59	0
De La Rosa, Miguel, Pulaski	.917	18	20	2	2	24	1
Diaz, Miguel, Johnson City	.940	57	101	9	7	117	1
Durick, Chad, Kingsport	.958	14	21	2	1	24	0
Eckelman, Alex, Johnson City	1.000	4	2	0	0	2	0
Escobar, Alex, Kingsport	.905	10	19	0	2	21	0
Fennell, Jason, Bristol	.714	3	4	1	2	7	0
Feramisco, Derek, Johnson City	.905	26	34	4	4	42	1
Fisher, Anthony, Pulaski	.957	30	42	2	2	46	0
Folkers, Brandon, Johnson City*	1.000	4	5	1	0	6	0
Garcia, Sandy, Princeton	.921	57	91	2	8	101	0
Giron, Alejandro, Martinsville	.955	54	100	5	5	110	0
Gooden, Carl, Johnson City	.890	39	70	3	9	82	0
Hairston, Jason, Danville	.850	45	32	2	6	40	0
Haman, Mack, Bluefield	.891	38	40	1	5	46	0
Hamilton, Jonathan, Brev.*	.964	64	122	10	5	137	2
Hernandez, Jesus, Brev.*	.911	48	51	0	5	56	0
Hollins, Darontaye, Bristol	.981	52	97	6	2	105	2
Hooper, Daren, Bluefield	.857	8	6	0	1	7	0
Jaramillo, Francisco, Pulaski	1.000	4	6	0	0	6	0
Johnson, Anthony, Kingsport	.750	8	6	0	2	8	0
Johnson, Duane, Martinsville	.786	26	31	2	9	42	0
Kennedy, Brian, Elizabethton	.970	50	62	2	2	66	0
Kilburg, Joe, Brevard County	1.000	10	13	0	0	13	0
Lugo, Ursino, Brevard County	1.000	13	18	1	0	19	0
Marchant, Nick, Martinsville	.903	19	28	0	3	31	0
Matos, Luis, Bluefield	.977	61	125	4	3	132	0
McHenry, Joe, Elizabethton	.948	46	70	3	4	77	1
McIntyre, Remer, Johnson City	.963	36	51	1	2	54	0
Messner, Jake, Brevard County*	.953	45	79	2	4	85	1
Morales, Domingo, Bluefield	.714	3	5	0	2	7	0
Neuberger, Scott, Princeton	.962	65	115	11	5	131	2
Newkirk, Jeff, Bristol*	.974	45	71	3	2	76	1
Nova, Fernando, Bristol	.983	40	53	4	1	58	1
Nunez, Juan, Pulaski	.949	34	54	2	3	59	0
Orndorff, Dave, Elizabethton	.947	16	18	0	1	19	0
Pagan, Felix, Elizabethton	.894	28	40	2	5	47	0
Pena, Jose, Pulaski	.981	46	49	3	1	53	0
Perez, Richard, Bluefield	.929	13	13	0	1	14	0
Pigott, Anthony, Princeton	.986	44	65	6	1	72	1
Piniella, Juan, Pulaski	1.000	33	49	0	0	49	0
Rivera, Roberto, Bluefield	.913	44	40	2	4	46	0
Schaeffer, Jon, Elizabethton	.750	7	3	0	1	4	0
SECODA, Joe, Johnson City	.990	45	89	7	1	97	0
Smith, Marcus, Elizabethton	.960	42	93	3	4	100	0
Stephens, Joel, Bluefield	.833	5	10	0	2	12	0
Stratton, Robert, Kingsport	.953	63	100	2	5	107	0
Suriel, Miguel, Princeton	1.000	2	3	1	0	4	0
Ventura, Frankie, Brev.	1.000	27	35	0	0	35	0
Villar, Jose, Danville	.926	54	85	3	7	95	0
Wallace, Derek, Bristol	.943	46	64	2	4	70	0
Wilder, Paul, Princeton	.891	34	41	0	5	46	0
Wilson, Travis, Danville	1.000	5	4	0	0	4	0

CATCHERS

Player, Team	Pct.	G	PO	A	E	TC	DP	PB
Alfonso, Eliezer, Johnson City	.980	24	177	17	4	198	0	6
Ashley, Steve, Danville	.976	26	175	30	5	210	0	2
Bosch, Bryon, Brevard County	.942	11	44	5	3	52	0	3
Cody, Ryan, Martinsville	.989	13	83	10	1	94	1	4
Cook, Josh, Kingsport	.970	5	30	2	1	33	0	0
Cruz, Andres, Princeton	1.000	1	2	0	0	2	0	0
Cruz, Edgar, Brevard County	.977	38	294	42	8	344	2	20
Ellis, John, Pulaski	.993	27	244	23	2	269	5	7
Grabowski, Jason, Pulaski	.982	43	386	40	8	434	1	15
Guzman, Martin, Princeton	.975	5	35	4	1	40	1	4
Hairston, Jason, Danville	1.000	4	17	1	0	18	0	3
Lasater, Chris, Bluefield	.971	5	32	2	1	35	0	0
Ledbetter, Blake, Johnson City	1.000	5	10	0	0	10	0	3
Lina, Estivinson, Pulaski	.967	3	29	0	1	30	0	2
Llibre, Brian, Johnson City	.925	11	70	4	6	80	1	8
Lopez-Cao, Mike, Princeton	.990	15	93	7	1	101	0	2
McGee, Thomas, Bluefield	1.000	16	113	15	0	128	1	2
McGehee, Michael, Princeton	.980	6	43	5	1	49	0	0
Melson, Bryant, Elizabethton	.989	22	157	21	2	180	1	5
Mortimer, Mark, Danville	1.000	5	33	5	0	38	0	0
Norrell, Troy, Martinsville	.959	23	172	15	8	195	1	7
Paxton, Chris, Bluefield	1.000	11	80	4	0	84	0	1
Pena, Francisco, Elizabethton	.988	28	214	28	3	245	1	10
Ramos, Kelly, Kingsport	.980	45	386	47	9	442	4	7
Rapp, Travis, Bristol	.970	26	172	22	6	200	2	4
Romero, Marty, Bristol	.889	2	8	0	1	9	0	0
Russell, Jake, Brevard County	.982	15	100	9	2	111	0	5
Schaeffer, Jon, Elizabethton	.980	26	185	12	4	201	1	5
Smith, Casey, Brevard County	.978	11	76	11	2	89	0	2
Smith, Shane, Kingsport	.985	25	162	29	3	194	1	6
Spear, Chad, Princeton	.973	7	35	1	1	37	0	1
SURIEL, Miguel, Princeton	.983	45	364	45	7	416	1	11
Sutton, Joe, Bristol	.979	45	354	61	9	424	3	13
Torrealba, Steve, Danville	.961	42	398	41	18	457	0	15
Utting, Andy, Bluefield	.976	44	375	27	10	412	0	6
Valdez, Jerry, Martinsville	.976	21	140	23	4	167	1	8
Vanasselberg, Ricky, Bluefield	1.000	3	24	1	0	25	0	1
Van Iten, Bob, Martinsville	.992	15	109	12	1	122	0	4
Williams, Jovany, Johnson City	.980	39	324	27	7	358	1	10

PITCHERS

Player, Team	Pct.	G	PO	A	E	TC	DP
Achilles, Matt, Bluefield	.944	14	7	10	1	18	1
Albaugh, Chad, Martinsville	.625	20	2	3	3	8	0
Alvarez, Danny, Brevard County	1.000	3	0	3	0	3	0
Andrade, Jancy, Bluefield	1.000	4	0	2	0	2	0
Aracena, Juan, Brevard County	.818	19	2	7	2	11	0
Baez, Miguel, Brevard County	.889	19	4	4	1	9	0
Bales, Joseph, Bristol	1.000	14	6	5	0	11	0
Bauer, Richard, Bluefield	.875	13	4	10	2	16	0
Birrell, Simon, Danville	.846	13	5	6	2	13	0
Bond, Aaron, Pulaski	.875	14	1	6	1	8	0
Borkowski, Robert, Kingsport	1.000	5	0	2	0	2	0
Box, John, Princeton*	.933	25	5	9	1	15	3
Brown, Derek, Bluefield	.636	17	2	5	4	11	0
Brummitt, Travis, Danville	.800	12	0	4	1	5	0
Cali, Joe, Brevard County	.500	14	0	1	1	2	0
Canciobello, Anthony, Danville	1.000	3	1	0	0	1	0
Carnes, Matt, Elizabethton	1.000	8	4	9	0	13	1

Player, Team	Pct.	G	PO	A	E	TC	DP
Carrion, Jorge, Pulaski	.667	13	3	9	6	18	0
Carter, Chris, Princeton	1.000	26	2	6	0	8	0
Carter, Roger, Princeton	.833	13	4	6	2	12	0
Ciravolo, Jon, Danville	1.000	19	5	1	0	6	0
Clark, Greg, Elizabethton	1.000	16	2	3	0	5	2
Cook, Derrick, Pulaski	1.000	6	1	7	0	8	0
Cook, Steven, Martinsville	1.000	7	3	0	0	3	0
Corcoran, Tim, Kingsport	1.000	7	1	2	0	3	0
Cosgrove, Michael, Elizabethton	1.000	12	3	4	0	7	1
Cox, Robert, Kingsport	.900	21	3	6	1	10	0
Currens, Timothy, Bristol	.875	20	1	6	1	8	0
Daneker, Patrick, Bristol	.964	12	8	19	1	28	2
De La Cruz, Ynocencio, Kin.	1.000	6	2	0	0	2	0
DeLeon, Julio, Princeton	1.000	11	0	7	0	7	0
DeYoung, Daniel, Pulaski	.875	19	2	5	1	8	0
Dolby, Lawrence, Danville	1.000	3	1	0	0	1	0
Drew, Tim, Brevard County	1.000	4	3	0	0	3	0
Driscoll, Patrick, Martinsville*	1.000	8	1	4	0	5	0
Durick, Chad, Kingsport	1.000	6	0	1	0	1	0
Elder, David, Pulaski	1.000	20	2	2	0	4	0
Embry, Byron, Danville	1.000	20	0	3	0	3	0
Enloe, Mark, Kingsport*	.846	15	0	11	2	13	0
Espina, Rendy, Elizabethton*	1.000	6	0	4	0	4	0
Felix, Miguel, Bristol	.500	11	1	4	5	10	0
Fleck, William, Danville	1.000	23	0	4	0	4	0
Fleming, Emar, Pulaski	.833	23	1	4	1	6	0
Fontaine, Tom, Bluefield	1.000	21	1	2	0	3	0
Franks, Lance, Johnson City	1.000	26	4	6	0	10	1
Freedberg, Todd, Bluefield	1.000	11	1	3	0	4	1
Fry, Jeff, Danville*	.750	21	1	5	2	8	0
Gandy, Josh, Elizabethton*	1.000	8	1	1	0	2	0
Garcia, Wilson, Johnson City	.333	25	0	1	2	3	0
Garff, Jeff, Brevard County	1.000	5	1	1	0	2	0
Garmon, Adam, Kingsport	.750	18	1	2	1	4	0
Geis, John, Johnson City*	1.000	30	0	4	0	4	0
Gholar, Antonio, Elizabethton	1.000	24	4	7	0	11	0
Gonzalez, Dicky, Kingsport	.933	12	4	10	1	15	2
Gooden, Carl, Johnson City	1.000	1	1	1	0	2	0
Gooden, Derek, Johnson City	.692	31	5	4	4	13	0
Granadillo, Adel, Brevard County	1.000	15	3	6	0	9	0
Gray, Jason, Bristol	1.000	4	2	1	0	3	1
Guzman, Ambiorix, Pulaski	.889	10	3	5	1	9	0
Guzman, Toribio, Johnson City	.813	13	5	8	3	16	1
Halpin, Jeremy, Bluefield	1.000	15	1	2	0	3	1
Hamilton, Randy, Kingsport*	1.000	21	2	5	0	7	1
Harrison, Scott, Brevard County	.875	12	1	6	1	8	0
Hogge, Shawn, Johnson City	1.000	3	1	1	0	2	0
Hootselle, Jeff, Martinsville*	.667	14	2	8	5	15	0
Hopson, Craig, Johnson City	1.000	15	2	0	0	2	0
Humphries, Christopher, Mar.	1.000	5	0	3	0	3	1
Izquierdo, Hansel, Bristol	.889	9	1	7	1	9	0
Jacobson, Andrew, Bristol	.909	14	4	6	1	11	0
James, Delvin, Princeton	.895	20	5	12	2	19	0
Jurgena, Matt, Elizabethton	1.000	23	1	3	0	4	0
Kertis, John, Pulaski	.875	14	5	2	1	8	0
Key, Calvin, Martinsville	1.000	14	1	7	0	8	0
Kofler, Ed, Princeton	.778	13	0	7	2	9	2
Kvasnicka, Jonathon, Bristol	1.000	4	1	3	0	4	0
Lambert, Jeremy, Johnson City ..	1.000	27	2	5	0	7	1
Lanfranco, Otoniel, Johnson City	.800	14	2	6	2	10	0
Layne, Roger, Brevard County	.900	11	3	6	1	10	1
Lee, Chris, Bluefield	1.000	23	1	2	0	3	0
Lee, Garrett, Danville	.867	14	5	8	2	15	1
Lewis, Derrick, Danville	.867	16	4	9	2	15	0
Lopez, Jose, Bristol	.857	20	1	5	1	7	1
Lovingood, Ray, Kingsport*	.875	13	1	6	1	8	0
Lunney, Barry, Elizabethton*	.875	22	1	6	1	8	1
Maberry, Mark, Kingsport	1.000	22	1	4	0	5	0
Malloy, Patrick, Brevard County..	1.000	17	2	5	0	7	1
Manbeck, Mark, Martinsville	1.000	9	5	8	0	13	1
Marshall, Lee, Elizabethton	.926	14	12	13	2	27	1
Marsonek, Sam, Pulaski	.882	12	5	10	2	17	0
Martinez, Caleb, Martinsville*	1.000	7	6	5	0	11	0
Mason, Chris, Princeton	1.000	19	5	4	0	9	0
Mastrolonardo, David, Bluefield..	.750	26	2	1	1	4	0
Mattson, John, Kingsport	1.000	6	1	3	0	4	0
McDermott, Ryan, Brev.	1.000	8	3	4	0	7	0
McDermott, Toby, Princeton*	1.000	17	3	3	0	6	0
Meyer, Jake, Bristol	.833	17	4	1	1	6	0
Miller, Aaron, Elizabethton*	.800	23	0	4	1	5	0
Miller, Matt, Johnson City	1.000	20	1	7	0	8	0
Molta, Salvatore, Martinsville	1.000	13	3	2	0	5	0
Montada, Joaquin, Kingsport	.889	13	3	13	2	18	0
Montero, Francisco, Martinsville	.885	14	6	17	3	26	3
Murphy, Darren, Bluefield*	1.000	23	0	5	0	5	0
Myette, Aaron, Bristol	1.000	9	2	8	0	10	1
Nation, Joey, Danville*	1.000	8	0	1	0	1	0
Norris, Stephen, Johnson City*..	.727	14	5	11	6	22	0
Ortega, Franklin, Johnson City...	1.000	18	0	8	0	8	0
Ovalle, Bonelly, Pulaski	.800	26	0	4	1	5	0
Payne, Tony, Kingsport*	1.000	10	0	3	0	3	1
Perez, Norberto, Bluefield	1.000	10	5	9	0	14	1
Perez, Pablo, Elizabethton	.833	17	2	3	1	6	0
Perez, Sam, Brevard County*	1.000	16	1	2	0	3	0
Phelps, Travis, Princeton	1.000	14	6	6	0	12	1
Poland, Robert, Pulaski*	.889	13	2	6	1	9	0
Pruett, Matthew, Princeton	1.000	24	2	1	0	3	0
Pugmire, Robert, Brev.	.867	14	5	8	2	15	1
Quevedo, Ruben, Danville	.846	13	3	8	2	13	0
Ramos, Fernando, Martinsville ..	.800	24	1	3	1	5	1
Reimers, Tom, Bristol	1.000	12	1	7	0	8	0
Reyes, Arquimedes, Martinsville	.875	20	2	5	1	8	0
Reynolds, Chris, Princeton	1.000	12	5	1	0	6	0
Rincon, Juan, Elizabethton..	1.000	2	0	2	0	2	0
Rivera, Luis, Danville	1.000	9	2	5	0	7	0
Roberts, Marquis, Princeton*	1.000	3	0	6	0	6	1
Rodgers, Marcus, Bristol	.200	6	0	1	4	5	0
Rodriguez, Jose, Johnson City*	1.000	4	0	1	0	1	0
Rojas, Francisco, Johnson City ..	1.000	6	1	1	0	2	0
Romero, Jordan, Bluefield	.500	12	1	1	2	4	0
Romero, Juan, Elizabethton*	1.000	18	0	2	0	2	0
Ruiz, Rafael, Bristol*	.500	23	2	1	3	6	1
SANTANA, Humberto, Kin.*	1.000	13	7	24	0	31	2
Seberino, Ronni, Princeton*	.895	14	4	13	2	19	0
Serrano, Elio, Martinsville	.833	21	3	2	1	6	0
Shanklin, Paul, Danville	1.000	17	4	5	0	9	0
Silva, Carlos, Martinsville	.938	11	9	6	1	16	1
Silva, Troy, Brevard County	.846	20	6	5	2	13	0
Sims, Kenny, Bluefield	.833	18	0	5	1	6	0
Smith, Ryan, Pulaski*	1.000	15	0	2	0	2	0
Smith, Shane, Kingsport	.500	2	1	0	1	2	0
Stephens, John, Bluefield	1.000	4	2	1	0	3	0
Spurgeon, Jay, Bluefield	1.000	9	2	7	0	9	1
Taylor, Aaron, Danville	.778	15	2	5	2	9	0
Theodile, Simeon, Bluefield	1.000	4	1	0	0	1	0
Thomas, Ben, Elizabethton	.833	7	0	5	1	6	0
Thomas, Brad, Elizabethton*	.963	14	6	20	1	27	1
Turnbow, Mark, Brevard County	.947	13	5	13	1	19	0
Turnbow, Thomas, Martinsville ..	1.000	7	0	3	0	3	0
Tuttle, John, Johnson City	1.000	7	1	5	0	6	0
Vasquez, Antonio, Brev.	1.000	12	0	3	0	3	0
Walker, Adam, Martinsville*	1.000	21	1	8	0	9	0
Wheeler, Johnnie, Brev.*	1.000	6	1	3	0	4	0
Wright, Christopher, Princeton	.917	14	5	6	1	12	0
Zambrano, Victor, Princeton	.750	20	1	2	1	4	0

The following players did not have any fielding statistics at the positions indicated or appeared only as a designated hitter, pinch-hitter or pinch-runner: Bowring, p; Bray, p; Darr, ss; Davies, of; Edwards, of; Folkers, p; Harding, 2b; Hodges, p; Lina, of; Lyons, p; Martin, 2b; McGee, of, p; McHenry, c; Melson, of; Myers, p; Jo. Nunez, ss; F. Pena, p; Phipps, p; Pigott, 3b; Mi. Rodriguez, of; Secoda, ss; Van Iten, of; T. Williams, of; C. Wilson, 1b, p; Zydowsky, p.

LEAGUE CHAMPIONS

Year	Team	Pct.	Year	Team	Pct.	Year	Team	Pct.
1921—	Greenville	.608	1925—	Greenville	.667	1939—	Elizabethton‡	.597
	Johnson City*	.627	1926-36—Did not operate.			1940—	Johnson City§	.726
1922—	Bristol	.557	1937—	Elizabethton	.559		Elizabethton	.750
1923—	Knoxville	.635		Pennington Gap*	.580	1941—	Johnson City	.614
1924—	Knoxville*	.642	1938—	Elizabethton	.664		Elizabethton*	.661
	Bristol	.607		Greenville (3rd)†	.571			

Year	Team	Pct.	Year	Team	Pct.	Year	Team	Pct.
1942—	Bristol	.667	1963—	Bluefield	.652	1983—	Paintsville	.653
	Bristol∞	.660	1964—	Johnson City	.662	1984—	Elizabethton•	.580
1943—	Bristol	.755	1965—	Salem	.614		Pulaski	.536
	Bristol▲	.617	1966—	Marion	.623	1985—	Bristol††	.638
1944—	Kingsport‡	.575	1967—	Bluefield	.627	1986—	Johnson City	.667
1945—	Kingsport‡	.670	1968—	Marion	.583		Pulaski•	.621
1946—	New River‡	.675	1969—	Pulaski▼	.576	1987—	Burlington•	.729
1947—	Pulaski	.648		Johnson City	.544		Johnson City	.609
	New River (3rd)†	.516	1970—	Bluefield	.638	1988—	Kingsport•	.644
1948—	Pulaski‡	.680	1971—	Bluefield▼	.609		Burlington	.529
1949—	Bluefield‡	.721		Kingsport	.559	1989—	Elizabethton•	.691
1950—	Bluefield	.600	1972—	Bristol▼	.588		Pulaski	.618
	Bluefield◆	.745		Covington	.586	1990—	Elizabethton	.761
1951—	Kingsport‡	.659	1973—	Kingsport	.757	1991—	Pulaski•	.662
1952—	Johnson City	.595	1974—	Bristol▼	.754		Burlington	.597
	Welch (3rd)†	.509		Bluefield	.536	1992—	Elizabethton	.742
1953—	Welch*	.705	1975—	Marion	.515		Bluefield•	.597
	Johnson City	.672		Johnson City▼	.603	1993—	Burlington•	.647
1954—	Bluefield‡	.619	1976—	Johnson City▼	.714		Elizabethton	.552
1955—	Salem■	.689		Bluefield	.600	1994—	Princeton•	.621
1956—Did not operate.			1977—	Kingsport	.623		Johnson City	.618
1957—	Bluefield	.701	1978—	Elizabethton	.594	1995—	Bluefield	.754
1958—	Johnson City	.662	1979—	Paintsville	.800		Kingsport•	.727
1959—	Morristown	.603	1980—	Paintsville	.657	1996—	Kingsport	.716
1960—	Wytheville	.614	1981—	Paintsville	.657		Bluefield▼	.618
1961—	Middlesboro	.591	1982—	Bluefield▼	.681	1997—	Pulaski	.632
1962—	Bluefield	.671		Johnson City	.478		Bluefield•	.580

*Won split-season playoff. †Won four-team playoff. ‡Won championship and four-team playoff. §Johnson City, first-half winner, won playoff involving six clubs. ∞Won both halves and defeated second-place Elizabethton in playoff. ▲Won both halves, but Erwin won four-team playoff. ◆Won both halves, but Bristol won two-club playoff. ■Salem and Johnson City declared playoff co-champions when weather forced cancellation of final series. ▼League was divided into Northern, Southern divisions; declared league champion based on highest won-lost percentage. •League was divided into North and South divisions; won playoff. ††Bristol declared league champion based on regular-season record.

SUMMER CLASS A *Appalachian League*

ARIZONA LEAGUE

LEAGUE OFFICE

President/treasurer
Bob Richmond
Address
P.O. Box 4941
Scottsdale, AZ 85261
Phone
602-483-8224

Teams*
Athletics
Cubs
Diamondbacks
Mariners
Padres
Rockies

White Sox
TBA

*Teams play their games in Mesa, Peoria, Phoenix and other Arizona sites to be announced.

1997 FINAL STANDINGS
COMPOSITE

Team	Cubs	Mar.	Ath.	Dia.	Pad.	Rck.	W	L	T	Pct.	GB
Cubs	....	8	7	9	6	4	34	21	0	.618	....
Mariners	3	....	6	5	9	7	30	26	0	.536	4½
Athletics	4	5	....	7	7	6	29	27	0	.518	5½
Diamondbacks	2	6	5	....	6	8	27	29	0	.482	7½
Padres	4	3	4	5	....	9	25	30	0	.455	9
Rockies	8	4	5	3	2	....	22	34	0	.393	12½

Games played in Chandler, Mesa, Peoria and Scottsdale.

Club names are major league affiliations.

PLAYOFFS: No playoffs scheduled.

REGULAR-SEASON ATTENDANCE: No total official attendance figures reported.

MANAGERS: Athletics, Juan Navarette; Cubs, Terry Kennedy; Diamondbacks, Brian Butterfield and Don Wakamatsu; Mariners, Darrin Garner; Padres, Randy Whisler; Rockies, Tim Blackwell.

ALL-STAR TEAM: 1B—Lance Downing, Diamondbacks; 2B—Jose Nunez, Rockies; 3B—Todd Fereday, Cubs; SS—Jose Moreno, Mariners; OF—Jesus Basabe, Athletics; Kevin Burford, Padres; Juan Camilo, Athletics; C—Brad Ramsey, Cubs; DH—Juan Silvestre, Mariners; LHP—Travis Jones, Padres; RHP—Todd Noel, Cubs; LH Reliever—Miguel Frias, Diamondbacks; RH Reliever—Jake Kidd, Rockies; Shane Sullivan, Cubs; Most Valuable Player—Kevin Burford, Padres; Manager of the Year—Terry Kennedy, Cubs.

1997 BATTING
TEAM

Team	Avg.	G	TPA	AB	R	H	TB	2B	3B	HR	RBI	SH	SF	HP	BB	IBB	SO	SB	CS	GDP	LOB	ShO	Slg.	OBP
Mariners	.278	56	2291	1956	364	543	739	90	20	22	295	19	24	28	264	3	510	114	43	29	462	1	.378	.368
Athletics	.269	56	2345	1931	407	520	768	91	23	37	321	13	17	52	332	0	442	137	31	41	492	1	.398	.388
Padres	.265	55	2287	1939	335	513	705	106	16	18	280	8	16	28	296	1	464	85	41	41	480	1	.364	.367
Rockies	.263	56	2221	1977	297	519	688	82	21	15	231	15	12	38	179	2	388	112	39	36	416	1	.348	.334
Cubs	.262	55	2216	1886	345	495	672	75	27	16	265	13	28	67	222	0	410	109	36	31	426	1	.356	.356
Diamndbcks	.262	56	2212	1937	324	507	699	105	21	15	260	14	13	22	226	1	469	47	27	45	405	2	.361	.343

INDIVIDUAL
TOP QUALIFIERS FOR BATTING CHAMPIONSHIP
Minimum 151 plate appearances. *Lefthanded batter. †Switch-hitter.

Player, Team	Avg.	G	TPA	AB	R	H	TB	2B	3B	HR	RBI	SH	SF	HP	BB	IBB	SO	SB	CS	GDP	Slg.	OBP
Burford, Kevin, Padres*	.389	47	226	167	42	65	96	15	2	4	50	0	5	4	49	1	25	12	5	3	.575	.524
Downing, Lance, Diamndbcks*	.381	55	254	215	48	82	102	12	1	2	40	0	1	1	37	0	26	10	4	3	.474	.472
Nunez, Jose, Rockies	.365	52	237	208	31	76	108	17	3	3	32	1	5	4	19	2	31	12	2	4	.519	.419
Moreno, Jose, Mariners	.363	51	223	190	56	69	81	12	0	0	36	4	2	2	25	0	18	31	10	2	.426	.438
Camilo, Juan, Athletics*	.346	50	235	191	48	66	111	11	5	8	47	0	0	2	41	0	41	12	2	6	.581	.466
Silvestre, Juan, Mariners	.341	34	155	135	32	46	84	11	3	7	36	0	3	2	15	1	31	4	2	1	.622	.406
Davis, Monty, Athletics	.329	47	209	173	34	57	84	12	0	5	34	1	1	7	25	0	25	5	2	2	.486	.432
Parker, Hubert, Mariners†	.317	38	158	123	23	39	45	6	0	0	17	2	3	0	26	1	21	5	2	1	.366	.428
Dunham, Traylon, Padres*	.317	35	157	139	20	44	65	13	1	2	32	0	0	1	17	0	42	0	2	1	.468	.395
Ramsey, Brad, Cubs	.315	51	237	200	50	63	103	10	3	8	34	0	2	13	22	0	33	8	0	3	.515	.414
Basabe, Jesus, Athletics	.313	55	250	201	51	63	115	11	4	11	43	1	1	7	40	0	76	6	2	1	.572	.442
Carroll, Mark, Mariners	.306	36	155	121	15	37	41	4	0	0	26	0	1	6	27	0	30	3	1	1	.339	.432
Cust, Jack, Diamondbacks*	.306	35	152	121	26	37	59	11	1	3	33	0	0	0	31	0	39	2	0	4	.488	.447
Nunez, Abraham, Diamndbcks†	.305	54	244	213	52	65	90	17	4	0	21	2	1	2	26	0	40	3	3	4	.423	.384
Williams, Patrick, Mariners	.305	47	196	177	28	54	65	9	1	0	27	0	3	0	15	0	43	17	2	1	.367	.354

DEPARTMENTAL LEADERS: G—O. Rosario, 56; AB—Eaddy, 221; R—Moreno, 56; H—Downing, 82; TB—Basabe, 115; 2B—Gordon, 18; 3B—Figgins, 6; HR—Basabe, 11; RBI—Burford, 50; SH—L. Haynes, 6; SF—Payne, 6; HP—Johnson, 14; BB—Minor, 52; IBB—Jose Nunez, 2; SO—Basabe, 76; SB—O. Rosario, 40; CS—Figgins, 13; GIDP—Luderer, 6; Slg.—Silvestre, .622; OBP—Burford, .524.

ALL PLAYERS
*Lefthanded batter. †Switch-hitter.

Player, Team	Avg.	G	TPA	AB	R	H	TB	2B	3B	HR	RBI	SH	SF	HP	BB	IBB	SO	SB	CS	GDP	Slg.	OBP
Acosta, Jhon, Cubs†	.000	14	1	0	0	0	0	0	0	0	0	1	0	0	0	0	0	0	0	0	.000	.000
Alcala, Juan, Mariners	.228	29	101	92	15	21	29	5	0	1	7	2	0	0	7	0	26	0	0	2	.315	.283

Player, Team	Avg.	G	TPA	AB	R	H	TB	2B	3B	HR	RBI	SH	SF	HP	BB	IBB	SO	SB	CS	GDP	Slg.	OBP
Aldrup, Morey, Cubs	.192	36	138	125	13	24	33	6	0	1	12	2	0	3	8	0	43	4	3	2	.264	.257
Basabe, Jesus, Athletics	.313	55	250	201	51	63	115	11	4	11	43	1	1	7	40	0	76	6	2	1	.572	.442
Beltran, Francis, Cubs	.000	16	2	2	0	0	0	0	0	0	0	0	0	0	0	0	2	0	0	0	.000	.000
Bernhardt, Tom, Cubs	.267	8	39	30	11	8	13	3	1	0	5	0	1	2	6	0	6	2	1	0	.433	.410
Brooks, Jeffrey, Diamndbcks	.225	54	224	204	22	46	55	9	0	0	27	3	1	4	12	0	50	3	1	5	.270	.281
Burford, Kevin, Padres*	.389	47	226	167	42	65	96	15	2	4	50	0	5	4	49	1	25	12	5	3	.575	.524
Camilo, Juan, Athletics*	.346	50	235	191	48	66	111	11	5	8	47	0	0	2	41	0	41	12	2	6	.581	.466
Carroll, Mark, Mariners	.306	36	155	121	15	37	41	4	0	0	26	0	1	6	27	0	30	3	1	1	.339	.452
Castro, Juan, Rockies	.171	33	139	129	13	22	37	4	1	3	13	2	1	2	5	0	42	3	3	0	.287	.212
Cintron, Alexander, Dia.†	.197	43	179	152	23	30	38	6	1	0	20	3	1	2	21	0	32	1	4	3	.250	.301
Cochrane, Christopher, Athl.	.000	2	8	8	0	0	0	0	0	0	1	0	0	0	0	0	1	0	0	0	.000	.000
Connell, Brian, Cubs*	.000	12	2	0	1	0	0	0	0	0	0	0	0	0	2	0	0	0	0	0	.000	1.000
Corniel, Henry, Athletics	.143	22	7	7	0	1	2	1	0	0	0	0	0	0	0	0	2	0	0	0	.286	.143
Cosentino, Anthony, Padres	.274	33	125	106	11	29	37	3	1	1	14	0	0	1	18	0	20	1	0	6	.349	.384
Cosme, Caonabo, Athletics	.215	37	153	130	28	28	39	6	1	1	17	1	1	2	19	0	28	7	1	2	.300	.322
Curry, Jesse, Padres*	.234	39	168	145	17	34	51	9	1	2	21	1	1	2	19	0	62	1	1	1	.352	.329
Cust, Jack, Diamondbacks*	.306	35	152	121	26	37	59	11	1	3	33	0	0	0	31	0	39	2	0	4	.488	.447
Davis, Monty, Athletics	.329	47	209	173	34	57	84	12	0	5	34	1	1	7	25	0	25	5	2	2	.486	.432
Declet, Miguel, Athletics†	.300	13	37	30	7	9	11	2	0	0	4	0	1	4	2	0	6	2	0	4	.367	.405
De La Cruz, Henry, Cubs	.138	25	98	80	11	11	13	2	0	0	3	0	0	2	16	0	32	5	3	0	.163	.296
Delano, Michael, Cubs*	.000	8	1	1	0	0	0	0	0	0	0	0	0	0	0	0	1	0	0	0	.000	.000
DeMarco, Joey, Padres†	.154	7	32	26	7	4	6	2	0	0	2	0	0	1	5	0	6	1	0	0	.231	.313
Downing, Lance, Dia.*	.381	55	254	215	48	82	102	12	1	2	40	0	1	1	37	0	26	10	4	3	.474	.472
Dunaway, Michael, Padres	.260	44	203	177	30	46	60	14	0	0	21	1	1	5	19	0	38	8	2	4	.339	.347
Dunham, Traylon, Padres*	.317	35	157	139	20	44	65	13	1	2	32	0	0	1	17	0	42	0	2	1	.468	.395
Eaddy, Deon, Cubs	.281	53	248	221	43	62	72	5	1	1	25	2	5	2	18	0	17	2	3	4	.326	.333
Encarnacion, Bernaldo, Roc.	.261	43	169	142	27	37	55	9	0	3	23	0	1	7	19	0	37	2	1	2	.387	.373
Estrella, Gorky, Mariners	.250	54	237	188	40	47	71	6	0	6	34	0	5	3	41	0	57	6	4	2	.378	.384
Fereday, Todd, Cubs	.374	24	103	91	19	34	55	12	3	1	23	0	4	0	8	0	14	5	1	3	.604	.408
Figgins, Desmond, Rockies†	.280	54	255	214	41	60	80	5	6	1	23	0	2	3	35	0	51	30	13	2	.374	.386
Folmar, Ryan, Rockies*	.304	11	50	46	5	14	20	6	0	0	7	0	0	1	3	0	2	0	2	4	.435	.360
Garcia, Alex, Padres	.269	21	89	78	10	21	27	3	0	1	10	0	1	1	9	0	14	1	1	3	.346	.348
Garcia, Cipriano, Mariners	.205	41	180	156	29	32	49	9	1	2	21	0	1	3	19	1	43	3	1	1	.314	.302
Garcia, Expeddy, Athletics*	.000	8	1	1	0	0	0	0	0	0	0	0	0	0	0	0	0	0	0	0	.000	.000
Garcia, Sandro, Padres	.214	28	124	103	22	22	34	8	2	0	16	0	2	3	16	0	10	4	0	5	.330	.331
German, Franklin, Cubs	.172	35	140	116	22	20	28	3	1	1	22	3	1	3	16	0	40	8	3	2	.241	.287
German, Manuel, Dia.	.223	34	131	112	21	25	37	5	2	1	11	1	0	2	16	0	36	2	2	4	.330	.331
Gonzalez, Franklin, Padres	.273	24	106	99	12	27	34	4	0	1	9	1	0	1	5	0	22	7	4	4	.343	.314
Gordon, Brian, Diamndbcks*	.247	54	232	219	27	54	92	18	4	4	46	0	4	0	9	1	62	8	3	4	.420	.272
Guerrero, Joel, Padres†	.264	41	169	140	25	37	41	2	1	0	10	0	0	1	28	0	35	22	5	3	.293	.391
Guzman, Julio, Diamndbcks	.222	12	40	36	4	8	11	0	0	1	5	0	0	0	4	0	11	1	0	1	.306	.300
Hargreaves, Brad, Cubs	.240	32	120	104	11	25	27	2	0	0	12	1	2	5	8	0	26	1	0	1	.260	.319
Haynes, Larry, Mariners	.206	45	163	136	26	28	47	6	2	3	13	6	1	0	20	0	66	10	3	0	.346	.306
Haynes, Nathan, Athletics*	.278	17	64	54	8	15	16	1	0	0	6	1	0	2	7	0	9	5	1	3	.296	.381
Hemmings, Brandon, Padres	.202	28	116	104	18	21	36	8	2	1	11	1	1	2	8	0	33	4	0	1	.346	.270
Hunter, Andrew, Padres	.273	5	24	22	3	6	9	1	1	0	4	0	0	0	2	1	5	0	0	1	.409	.333
Jimenez, Felipe, Cubs	.248	41	156	137	23	34	48	3	4	1	22	2	2	8	7	0	37	17	1	1	.350	.318
Johnson, Gary, Cubs	.288	52	236	198	40	57	84	14	5	1	31	0	1	14	23	0	26	9	3	4	.424	.398
Kirkpatrick, Brian, Rockies	.254	45	187	173	23	44	60	5	1	3	25	3	0	2	9	0	28	2	1	4	.347	.299
Landaeta, Luis, Rockies*	.291	38	157	148	25	43	55	6	3	0	13	1	0	1	7	0	9	4	3	5	.372	.327
Lina, Donald, Rockies	.232	30	103	95	15	22	25	1	1	0	8	0	0	1	7	0	28	8	2	3	.263	.291
Lopez, Jose, Diamondbacks	.265	41	166	155	17	41	55	7	2	1	22	1	2	1	7	0	22	1	4	5	.355	.297
Lopez, Miguel, Diamndbcks	.267	29	115	105	14	28	42	4	2	2	9	0	0	2	8	0	32	1	0	2	.400	.330
Luderer, Brian, Athletics	.268	39	148	123	21	33	46	4	0	3	26	1	1	6	17	0	12	3	4	6	.374	.381
Mahoney, Ricardo, Rockies	.282	32	132	124	15	35	38	3	0	0	17	1	0	1	6	0	20	8	6	3	.306	.321
Martinez, Belvani, Diamndbcks	.321	30	144	134	25	43	58	11	2	0	11	2	2	3	3	0	18	7	2	3	.433	.345
Mashore, Justin, Padres	.269	7	32	26	4	7	10	3	0	0	3	1	0	0	5	1	13	1	1	1	.385	.387
Mauck, Matt, Cubs*	.285	40	171	144	28	41	60	8	4	1	19	0	2	4	21	0	46	8	3	5	.417	.386
Meeks, Eric, Athletics	.000	15	1	1	0	0	0	0	0	0	0	0	0	0	0	0	1	0	0	0	.000	.000
Minor, Damon, Padres*	.295	42	204	146	46	43	49	2	2	0	18	0	2	4	52	0	36	12	10	0	.336	.485
Montilla, Alvin, Diamndbcks	.185	20	62	54	4	10	11	1	0	0	3	0	0	1	7	0	20	0	0	2	.204	.290
Moreno, Jose, Mariners	.363	51	223	190	56	69	81	12	0	0	36	4	2	2	25	0	18	31	10	2	.426	.438
Morgan, James, Diamndbcks	.000	4	10	9	1	0	0	0	0	0	0	0	0	0	1	0	4	0	0	1	.000	.100
Motley, Brittan, Padres†	.240	39	164	150	27	36	44	4	2	0	14	2	1	0	10	0	38	9	5	2	.293	.286
Moye, Melvin, Diamondbacks	.203	28	97	79	10	16	20	1	0	1	5	0	1	3	14	0	16	2	1	2	.253	.340
Nicholson, Kevin, Padres†	.265	7	36	34	7	9	16	1	0	2	8	0	0	0	2	0	5	0	2	2	.471	.306
Nielsen, Bret, Mariners*	.245	48	197	163	23	40	58	8	2	2	29	0	3	1	30	0	64	10	3	5	.356	.360
Nieves, Wilbert, Padres	.296	8	33	27	2	8	10	2	0	0	2	1	0	0	5	0	5	1	0	0	.370	.406
Nova, Kelvin, Athletics	.244	33	147	123	19	30	40	1	3	1	20	0	3	2	19	0	27	18	4	1	.325	.347
Nunez, Abraham, Dia.†	.305	54	244	213	52	65	90	17	4	0	21	2	1	2	26	0	40	3	3	4	.423	.384
Nunez, Jose M., Athletics	.282	51	232	181	39	51	85	10	3	6	42	0	2	2	47	0	47	2	2	6	.470	.431
Nunez, Jose, Rockies	.365	52	237	208	31	76	108	17	3	3	32	1	5	4	19	2	31	12	2	4	.519	.419
Pacheco, Domingo, Mariners†	.305	26	112	105	16	32	44	4	4	0	12	1	0	4	2	0	17	6	3	1	.419	.342
Parker, Hubert, Mariners†	.317	38	158	123	23	39	45	6	0	0	17	2	3	0	26	1	21	5	2	1	.366	.428
Payne, Ronald, Cubs*	.279	53	230	179	28	50	61	6	1	1	31	2	6	6	37	0	31	16	10	3	.341	.408
Pena, Juan, Athletics*	1.000	14	2	1	0	1	1	0	0	0	0	1	0	0	0	0	0	0	0	0	1.000	1.000
Petersen, Mike, Rockies	.220	33	129	118	18	26	35	7	1	0	13	0	1	3	7	0	20	2	2	1	.297	.279
Pimentel, Hector, Athletics	.211	41	146	123	17	26	28	2	0	0	13	0	2	0	21	0	21	4	1	4	.228	.322
Pinson, Brian, Mariners*	.200	32	110	100	16	20	28	3	1	1	7	0	1	0	9	0	20	6	1	3	.280	.264
Pitt, Jye, Cubs*	.333	14	3	3	0	1	1	0	0	0	0	0	0	0	0	0	2	0	0	0	.333	.333
Porter, Jamie, Athletics	.253	33	112	95	23	24	40	11	1	1	11	0	1	5	11	0	31	5	1	1	.421	.357
Proctor, Jerry, Diamndbcks	.083	3	12	12	2	1	3	0	1	0	0	0	0	0	0	0	6	1	0	1	.250	.083
Ramsey, Brad, Cubs	.315	51	237	200	50	63	103	10	3	8	34	0	2	13	22	0	33	8	0	3	.515	.414

Player, Team	Avg.	G	TPA	AB	R	H	TB	2B	3B	HR	RBI	SH	SF	HP	BB	IBB	SO	SB	CS	GDP	Slg.	OBP
Randolph, Jaisen, Cubs	.266	53	251	218	42	58	67	1	4	0	26	0	2	5	26	0	45	24	5	3	.307	.355
Rosario, Carlos, Rockies†	.284	46	183	169	29	48	58	7	0	1	18	2	1	1	10	0	22	14	3	5	.343	.326
Rosario, Felix, Mariners†	.270	26	71	63	15	17	21	0	2	0	4	0	0	1	7	0	20	6	5	1	.333	.352
Rosario, Omar, Athletics*	.241	56	265	216	48	52	67	9	3	0	28	1	3	7	38	0	51	40	3	1	.310	.367
Sanchez, Augustin, Rockies†.	.271	36	139	118	15	32	36	2	1	0	15	4	1	1	15	0	24	15	0	1	.305	.356
Sawai, Ryosuke, Padres........	.100	3	14	10	3	1	1	0	0	0	1	0	0	0	4	0	3	1	0	0	.100	.357
Silvestre, Juan, Mariners	.341	34	155	135	32	46	84	11	3	7	36	0	3	2	15	1	31	4	2	1	.622	.406
Smith, Sam, Rockies............	.235	52	231	200	27	47	63	9	2	1	18	0	0	7	24	0	38	6	1	2	.315	.338
Soriano, Rafael, Mariners	.269	38	137	119	19	32	39	3	2	0	12	3	0	1	14	0	31	7	4	6	.328	.351
Sosa, Jorge, Rockies†	.140	29	111	93	13	13	18	1	2	0	6	1	0	4	13	0	36	6	0	0	.194	.273
Soto, Luis, Padres...............	.286	35	157	140	20	40	66	12	1	4	32	0	2	0	15	0	33	0	2	3	.471	.350
Sullivan, Shane, Cubs..........	.000	21	3	3	0	0	0	0	0	0	0	0	0	0	0	0	3	0	0	0	.000	.000
Thomas, Gary, Athletics.......	.228	28	106	92	17	21	30	2	2	1	7	1	0	3	9	0	25	6	2	2	.326	.317
Tolbert, Ernest, Mariners......	.368	5	19	19	1	7	7	0	0	0	3	0	0	0	0	0	7	0	0	0	.368	.368
Tripp, Terry, Padres............	.130	28	110	100	9	13	13	0	0	0	2	0	0	2	8	0	19	0	1	1	.130	.209
Underwood, Jake, Mariners ...	.319	22	83	69	10	22	30	4	2	0	11	1	1	5	7	0	16	0	2	2	.435	.415
Urquiola, Carlos, Dia.*	.000	2	3	2	1	0	0	0	0	0	0	1	0	0	0	0	1	1	0	0	.000	.000
Weichard, Paul, Dia.†	.183	36	147	115	27	21	26	3	1	0	7	1	0	1	30	0	54	4	3	1	.226	.356
Williams, Patrick, Mariners....	.305	47	196	177	28	54	65	9	1	0	27	0	3	0	15	0	43	17	2	1	.367	.354
Yoshida, Kota, Athletics†	.238	48	228	181	47	43	53	8	1	0	22	5	1	3	36	0	39	22	6	2	.293	.371

GRAND SLAMS: Jose Nunez, Silvestre, 2 each; Basabe, Encarnacion, Gordon, 1 each.

AWARDED FIRST BASE ON CATCHER'S INTERFERENCE: Parker 4 (Luderer, M. Lopez, Soto 2); Davis 2 (Soto 2); Yoshida 2 (Mahoney 2); Burford (Jose Nunez); Camilo (Mahoney); Figgins (J. Lopez); C. Garcia (Luderer); F. German (J. Lopez); Motley (Jose Nunez); Thomas (Soto); Williams (Jose Nunez).

1997 PITCHING
TEAM

Team	W	L	Pct.	ERA	G	CG	ShO	Sv.	IP	H	TBF	R	ER	HR	SH	SF	HB	BB	IBB	SO	WP	Bk.
Cubs..................	34	21	.618	3.43	55	0	4	20	488.0	493	2212	294	186	14	10	12	29	255	0	464	42	26
Diamondbacks......	27	29	.482	4.17	56	0	1	13	494.1	530	2210	309	229	21	14	20	38	200	3	399	33	15
Rockies	22	34	.393	4.51	56	0	0	12	499.0	532	2338	376	250	17	13	20	41	258	0	449	60	17
Mariners	30	26	.536	4.61	56	1	1	11	492.0	485	2249	344	252	22	14	16	56	268	1	458	71	22
Athletics	29	27	.518	4.87	56	0	1	13	484.1	526	2263	349	262	22	18	21	38	260	3	441	55	25
Padres...............	25	30	.455	5.61	55	0	0	9	487.1	531	2316	400	304	27	13	21	33	278	2	472	74	29

INDIVIDUAL

TOP QUALIFIERS FOR EARNED-RUN AVERAGE TITLE
Minimum 45 innings. *Lefthanded pitcher.

Pitcher, Team	W	L	Pct.	ERA	G	CG	ShO	GF	Sv.	IP	H	TBF	R	ER	HR	SH	SF	HB	BB	IBB	SO	WP	Bk.
Noel, Todd, Cubs...................	5	1	.833	1.98	12	11	0	0	1	1	59.0	39	245	27	13	1	2	1	1	30	0	63	6	1
Pena, Juan, Athletics*..............	6	2	.750	2.91	14	13	0	1	0	65.0	54	290	38	21	0	5	0	2	33	0	67	5	5
Lohse, Kyle, Cubs..................	2	2	.500	3.02	12	11	0	0	0	47.2	46	210	22	16	0	1	1	1	22	0	49	3	0
Jones, Travis, Padres*............	4	3	.571	3.04	21	2	0	3	0	53.1	53	238	28	18	0	1	1	3	23	0	51	2	3
Cook, Aaron, Rockies..............	1	3	.250	3.13	9	8	0	0	0	46.0	48	208	27	16	1	2	0	5	17	0	35	3	3
Serrano, Wascar, Rockies........	6	3	.667	3.18	12	11	0	0	1	70.2	60	301	43	25	4	0	4	4	22	0	75	8	3
Mateo, Julio, Mariners............	3	1	.750	3.30	13	6	0	4	1	60.0	45	254	32	22	1	2	2	8	23	0	54	10	1
Price, Ryan, Rockies	2	7	.222	3.51	14	14	0	0	0	77.0	69	338	49	30	2	1	2	5	28	0	98	10	4
Montero, Agus, Athletics..........	3	2	.600	3.59	14	13	0	0	1	72.2	72	327	38	29	3	0	0	8	31	0	88	9	9
Royer, Jason, Diamondbacks	3	0	1.000	3.71	13	13	0	0	0	51.0	53	222	29	21	2	1	2	3	22	0	40	3	2
Rincones, Gabriel, Mariners......	5	4	.556	3.82	13	11	1	0	2	68.1	60	302	37	29	4	2	2	9	36	0	67	6	1
Kohl, Doug, Diamondbacks	1	2	.333	3.96	14	14	0	0	0	61.1	62	270	33	27	5	1	3	5	25	0	46	3	1
Matos, Josue, Mariners...........	1	0	1.000	4.17	14	1	0	5	1	45.1	48	190	27	21	4	1	1	0	6	0	50	3	4
Mallory, Andrew, Cubs............	3	4	.429	4.24	12	10	0	0	0	51.0	63	235	38	24	3	0	2	9	22	0	32	8	3
Herndon, Harry, Padres...........	3	2	.600	4.42	14	14	0	0	0	77.1	80	348	51	38	2	3	5	3	32	0	65	6	2

DEPARTMENTAL LEADERS: W—Heams, Pena, Serrano, 6 each; L—Price, 7; Pct.—Heams, Pena, .750 each; G—F. Gonzalez, 26; GS—Several pitchers tied with 14 each; CG—Rincones, 1; ShO—none; GF—Sullivan, 20; Sv.—Sullivan, 9; IP—Herndon, 77.1; H—Herndon, 80; TBF—Herndon, 348; R—Darr, 59; ER—Howard, 45; HR—Kohl, 5; SH—Pena, 5; SF—B. Garcia, Serrano, Walton, 4 each; HB—Torres, 11; BB—Howard, 63; IBB—F. Gonzalez, 2; SO—Price, 98; WP—Howard, Walton, 19 each; BK—Montero, 9.

ALL PITCHERS
*Lefthanded pitcher.

Pitcher, Team	W	L	Pct.	ERA	G	GS	CG	ShO	GF	Sv.	IP	H	TBF	R	ER	HR	SH	SF	HB	BB	IBB	SO	WP	Bk.
Abbott, Paul, Mariners	0	0	.000	0.93	3	3	0	0	0	0	9.2	0	35	2	1	0	1	0	7	0	13	3	0
Abeyta, Scott, Diamondbacks*...	1	1	.500	3.29	17	0	0	0	6	1	27.1	29	110	12	10	1	1	0	0	9	0	25	0	1
Acosta, Jhon, Cubs................	1	0	1.000	2.53	14	0	0	0	5	1	21.1	27	96	10	6	1	2	0	0	6	0	15	2	1
Barboza, Carlos, Rockies..........	1	1	.500	4.03	16	0	0	0	7	1	29.0	29	146	23	13	1	2	2	3	25	0	18	6	2
Batts, Nathan, Cubs*..............	2	0	1.000	7.45	8	1	0	0	1	0	9.2	11	48	9	8	0	2	1	1	10	0	9	2	0
Bedinger, Doug, Diamondbacks .	0	0	.000	0.00	1	0	0	0	1	0	2.0	0	6	0	0	0	0	0	0	0	0	5	0	0
Bell, Matthew, Diamondbacks	3	2	.600	2.88	18	0	0	0	7	2	34.1	31	152	18	11	1	1	2	2	16	0	36	5	3
Beltran, Francis, Cubs	0	1	.000	3.42	15	0	0	0	5	1	23.2	27	111	18	9	1	1	1	3	8	0	17	3	2
Bido, Jose, Diamondbacks	0	1	.000	27.00	1	1	0	0	0	0	1.0	5	7	3	3	0	0	0	1	0	0	0	0	0
Boughton, Mike, Diamondbacks..	3	3	.500	3.96	15	1	0	0	2	0	38.2	51	179	24	17	4	0	2	4	11	0	31	4	2
Cepeda, Wellington, Diamndbcks	4	0	1.000	1.64	15	1	0	0	0	0	38.1	31	158	16	7	1	0	0	0	12	0	32	3	0
Connell, Brian, Cubs*..............	3	5	.375	3.76	12	9	0	0	0	0	38.1	46	190	31	16	0	0	3	3	29	0	32	2	4
Cook, Aaron, Rockies..............	1	3	.250	3.13	9	8	0	0	0	0	46.0	48	208	27	16	1	2	0	5	17	0	35	3	3
Corniel, Henry, Athletics..........	2	1	.667	6.46	20	0	0	0	11	3	30.2	42	142	27	22	1	0	2	1	11	0	25	4	0
Crawford, Jeremy, Athletics*	1	3	.250	6.75	15	0	0	0	6	2	22.2	29	114	19	17	3	4	1	3	14	1	20	1	0

Pitcher, Team	W	L	Pct.	ERA	G	GS	CG	ShO	GF	Sv.	IP	H	TBF	R	ER	HR	SH	SF	HB	BB	IBB	SO	WP	Bk.
Cueto, Jose, Mariners	1	3	.250	6.00	17	0	0	0	15	1	27.0	40	134	24	18	4	1	1	6	9	0	28	0	0
Darr, Jerry, Padres	4	6	.400	6.49	14	13	0	0	0	0	59.2	67	292	59	43	3	2	3	7	33	0	62	10	1
Delano, Michael, Cubs*	0	1	.000	12.41	8	1	0	0	1	0	12.1	22	69	21	17	1	0	0	1	9	0	13	3	1
Delgado, Dan, Mariners	0	0	.000	5.19	6	0	0	0	1	0	8.2	11	44	5	5	2	0	0	0	7	0	8	0	0
Diaz, Antonio, Padres	1	1	.500	3.00	22	0	0	0	12	4	39.0	45	172	22	13	3	2	0	0	4	0	41	5	3
Duprey, Peter, Mariners*	4	2	.667	1.45	15	0	0	0	7	2	43.1	29	175	10	7	1	0	2	0	20	1	55	4	5
Frias, Miguel, Diamondbacks*	4	2	.667	2.25	21	0	0	0	18	8	32.0	35	137	11	8	1	3	0	1	5	0	38	1	2
Gallagher, Bryan, Athletics*	1	3	.250	2.94	17	0	0	0	9	2	33.2	29	141	14	11	2	1	2	2	10	1	27	3	0
Garcia, Bryan, Athletics	4	2	.667	5.67	15	7	0	0	2	0	46.0	50	219	36	29	2	2	4	3	34	0	45	4	1
Garcia, Expeddy, Athletics*	1	3	.250	7.82	8	1	0	0	0	0	12.2	20	65	13	11	0	1	3	3	7	0	9	2	2
Garcia, Sandro, Padres	0	0	.000	0.00	3	0	0	0	3	0	2.1	0	8	0	0	0	0	0	0	0	0	3	0	0
Garey, Daniel, Mariners	2	2	.500	5.91	7	7	0	0	0	0	35.0	46	163	28	23	1	0	1	6	7	0	16	0	0
Garland, Jon, Cubs	3	2	.600	2.70	10	7	0	0	0	0	40.0	37	161	14	12	3	0	0	1	10	0	39	3	3
Gonzalez, Armando, Rockies	1	3	.250	2.57	13	4	0	0	1	0	42.0	33	171	27	12	2	0	3	1	13	0	33	1	1
Gonzalez, Francisco, Padres	4	4	.500	5.48	26	2	0	0	19	2	47.2	55	229	36	29	4	1	1	5	26	2	40	7	3
Guttormson, Ricky, Padres	1	1	.500	4.91	5	0	0	0	4	1	11.0	17	55	11	6	3	0	1	0	4	0	19	0	0
Guzman, Julio, Diamondbacks	0	0	.000	0.00	1	0	0	0	1	0	1.0	1	5	1	0	0	0	0	0	2	0	1	0	0
Hause, Brendan, Athletics*	3	1	.750	3.86	6	0	0	0	1	0	11.2	13	49	7	5	1	1	1	0	1	0	11	0	0
Haverstick, David, Diamndbcks	2	5	.286	5.56	14	14	0	0	0	0	56.2	71	261	42	35	3	0	3	4	20	0	39	4	4
Heams, Shane, Mariners	6	2	.750	1.70	21	0	0	0	14	2	37.0	30	168	20	7	2	3	0	5	22	0	42	7	0
Herndon, Harry, Padres	3	2	.600	4.42	14	14	0	0	0	0	77.1	80	348	51	38	2	3	3	5	32	0	65	6	2
Herrera, Misael, Padres	1	2	.333	8.05	11	0	0	0	3	1	19.0	27	97	19	17	1	2	2	1	10	0	15	0	1
Hohenstein, Andrew, Padres	0	0	.000	6.94	9	0	0	0	2	0	11.2	15	59	9	9	0	0	0	2	8	0	13	3	1
Howard, Ben, Padres	1	4	.200	7.45	13	12	0	0	1	0	54.1	54	281	53	45	3	1	0	2	63	0	59	19	7
Iannacone, Steve, Rockies	1	2	.333	4.19	11	0	0	0	4	1	19.1	24	92	11	9	1	2	1	1	14	0	13	3	0
Iida, Masashi, Padres	0	2	.000	11.25	11	1	0	0	4	0	20.0	25	106	29	25	3	1	2	2	18	0	11	8	2
Ishimaru, Taisuke, Mariners	1	1	.500	10.57	7	0	0	0	1	0	7.2	3	44	10	9	0	0	0	2	16	0	5	5	2
Jacobs, Frankey, Athletics	0	2	.000	7.12	15	3	0	0	4	0	36.2	52	182	37	29	2	1	3	2	17	0	22	7	0
Jimenez, Mario, Mariners	3	1	.750	6.27	7	6	0	0	0	0	33.0	44	158	32	23	0	2	2	2	19	0	18	3	2
Jones, Charlie, Diamondbacks	0	1	.000	7.50	7	0	0	0	4	1	12.0	14	59	12	10	1	1	2	0	8	1	10	1	0
Jones, Travis, Padres*	4	3	.571	3.04	21	2	0	0	3	0	53.1	53	238	28	18	0	1	1	3	23	0	51	2	3
Kidd, Jake, Rockies	5	0	1.000	1.62	19	0	0	0	11	3	39.0	37	163	14	7	0	2	0	1	10	0	27	0	0
Kohl, Doug, Diamondbacks	1	2	.333	3.96	14	14	0	0	0	0	61.1	62	270	33	27	5	1	3	5	25	0	46	3	1
Labitzke, Jesse, Rockies*	0	1	.000	10.27	12	4	0	0	1	0	23.2	41	131	33	27	3	0	1	2	21	0	22	2	1
Little, Rodney, Rockies	3	1	.750	7.36	15	1	0	0	4	0	25.2	29	132	26	21	4	0	1	5	19	0	21	2	0
Little, Roger, Rockies	2	1	.667	5.45	14	4	0	0	4	1	33.0	30	156	24	20	1	0	1	4	23	0	31	6	1
Lohse, Kyle, Cubs	2	2	.500	3.02	12	11	0	0	0	0	47.2	46	210	22	16	0	1	1	1	22	0	49	3	0
Lora, Edison, Rockies	0	0	.000	6.75	11	0	0	0	1	0	21.1	31	108	20	16	1	0	2	3	9	0	8	3	0
Mahoney, Ricardo, Rockies	0	0	.000	13.50	1	0	0	0	1	0	1.1	2	7	2	2	0	0	1	0	1	0	0	0	0
Mallory, Andrew, Cubs	3	4	.429	4.24	12	10	0	0	0	0	51.0	63	235	38	24	3	0	2	9	22	0	32	8	3
Mangum, Mark, Rockies	4	6	.400	4.80	14	14	0	0	0	0	65.2	67	305	45	35	1	0	3	7	38	0	77	9	1
Mateo, Julio, Mariners	3	1	.750	3.30	13	6	0	0	4	1	60.0	45	254	32	22	1	2	2	8	23	0	54	10	1
Matos, Josue, Mariners	1	0	1.000	4.17	14	1	0	0	5	1	45.1	48	190	27	21	4	1	1	0	6	0	50	3	4
Medina, Eleazer, Cubs	0	0	.000	6.23	8	0	0	0	1	0	13.0	17	67	11	9	0	0	1	0	17	0	2	2	3
Medina, Jaime, Rockies	1	1	.500	7.20	10	0	0	0	4	0	15.0	19	82	17	12	0	1	1	2	10	0	8	4	1
Meeks, Eric, Athletics	1	2	.333	5.35	15	3	0	0	2	1	38.2	40	185	30	23	2	0	1	4	26	0	24	6	0
Mendoza, Hatuey, Diamndbcks	1	5	.167	7.58	17	0	0	0	5	0	29.2	29	151	27	25	0	2	0	8	25	1	24	3	0
Mercedes, Jose, Athletics	5	1	.833	5.53	14	12	0	0	0	0	57.0	68	266	43	35	3	3	2	5	30	0	35	1	0
Meyers, Mike, Cubs	3	1	.750	1.41	12	2	0	0	4	3	38.1	34	166	15	6	2	1	1	2	13	0	45	0	0
Montero, Agus, Athletics	3	2	.600	3.59	14	13	0	0	1	0	72.2	72	327	38	29	3	0	0	8	31	0	88	9	9
Morel, Francis, Diamondbacks	0	0	.000	18.00	1	0	0	0	1	0	1.0	3	5	2	2	0	0	0	0	0	0	0	0	0
Manzueta, Roberto, Diamndbcks.	0	0	.000	1.54	7	0	0	0	3	0	11.2	6	46	3	2	0	2	0	3	2	1	4	0	0
Newton, Geronimo, Mariners*	0	0	.000	0.00	4	0	0	0	3	3	4.0	0	12	0	0	0	0	0	0	0	0	6	0	0
Nix, Wayne, Athletics	1	3	.250	5.85	15	4	0	0	1	0	32.1	32	162	28	21	2	0	1	2	29	1	32	8	4
Noel, Todd, Cubs	5	1	.833	1.98	12	11	0	0	1	1	59.0	39	245	27	13	1	2	1	1	30	0	63	6	1
Nova, Kelvin, Athletics	0	0	.000	27.00	2	0	0	0	1	0	0.2	0	4	2	2	0	0	0	0	2	0	0	0	0
Paredes, Vladimir, Diamndbcks*	2	0	1.000	3.78	12	0	0	0	5	0	16.2	18	69	10	7	0	0	3	0	7	0	12	0	0
Parent, Jerry, Padres	0	0	.000	4.26	5	0	0	0	1	0	6.1	6	25	3	3	0	0	1	0	1	0	7	2	1
Pena, Juan, Athletics*	6	2	.750	2.91	14	13	0	0	0	0	65.0	54	290	38	21	0	5	0	2	33	0	67	5	5
Piersoll, Christopher, Cubs	4	0	1.000	2.08	15	0	0	0	3	2	34.2	26	142	12	8	0	0	0	2	9	0	41	2	4
Pimentel, Hector, Athletics	0	0	.000	40.50	1	0	0	0	1	0	0.2	1	8	3	3	0	0	0	1	4	0	1	0	0
Pineiro, Joel, Mariners	1	0	1.000	0.00	1	0	0	0	0	0	3.0	1	11	0	0	0	0	0	1	0	0	4	0	0
Pinson, Brian, Mariners	0	0	.000	45.00	1	0	0	0	1	0	1.0	3	9	5	5	0	0	0	0	3	0	1	0	0
Pitt, Jye, Cubs	3	0	1.000	2.66	13	1	0	0	1	1	23.2	14	105	9	7	1	0	0	1	17	0	28	2	0
Powalski, Richard, Cubs*	0	0	.000	1.59	6	0	0	0	0	0	11.1	11	51	4	2	0	0	0	0	7	0	13	0	0
Precinal, Huilberto, Padres	0	2	.000	21.00	13	0	0	0	2	0	15.0	27	105	37	35	1	0	3	2	34	0	11	4	2
Price, Ryan, Rockies	2	7	.222	3.51	14	14	0	0	0	0	77.0	69	338	49	30	2	1	2	5	28	0	98	10	4
Prouty, Scott, Mariners	0	1	.000	18.00	3	0	0	0	0	0	5.0	11	35	10	10	1	0	0	1	9	0	3	2	0
Rincones, Gabriel, Mariners	5	4	.556	3.82	13	11	1	0	2	0	68.1	60	302	37	29	4	2	2	9	36	0	67	6	1
Royer, Jason, Diamondbacks	3	0	1.000	3.71	13	13	0	0	0	0	51.0	53	222	29	21	2	1	2	3	22	0	40	3	2
Sanchez, Simon, Diamndbcks	3	5	.375	5.05	14	12	0	0	0	0	57.0	66	266	45	32	2	1	3	6	25	0	44	2	0
Serrano, Wascar, Padres	6	3	.667	3.18	12	11	0	0	1	1	70.2	60	301	43	25	4	0	4	4	22	0	75	8	3
Sullivan, Shane, Cubs	1	2	.333	2.70	21	0	0	0	20	9	23.1	21	99	11	7	1	0	1	0	8	0	22	0	1
Tate, Seth, Diamondbacks	0	2	.000	4.76	11	0	0	0	4	1	22.2	25	107	21	12	0	1	0	1	11	0	12	4	0
Torres, Melqui, Mariners	2	6	.250	6.59	13	10	0	0	2	1	54.2	60	266	53	40	1	1	0	11	38	0	42	9	4
Vargas, Derrick, Rockies*	0	3	.000	6.03	11	7	0	0	2	0	31.1	40	159	33	21	0	1	0	0	23	0	28	9	3
Vracar, Paul, Cubs	0	1	.000	6.75	7	2	0	0	2	0	10.2	17	60	11	8	0	0	3	1	10	0	9	2	2
Waites, David, Athletics	1	2	.333	3.09	21	0	0	0	17	5	23.1	24	109	14	8	1	0	1	2	11	0	35	5	1
Waldrum, Kevin, Cubs	1	1	.500	7.36	8	0	0	0	0	0	7.1	10	47	15	6	0	0	0	1	13	0	6	1	1
Waligora, Thomas, Cubs	3	0	1.000	5.16	16	0	0	0	11	2	22.2	25	110	16	13	0	1	0	2	15	0	29	1	0
Walton, Samuel, Mariners*	1	3	.250	5.84	13	12	0	0	0	0	49.1	54	249	49	32	1	2	4	5	46	0	46	19	3
Woodard, Brad, Rockies	1	5	.167	2.73	19	0	0	0	16	6	29.2	33	140	25	9	0	2	2	2	7	0	30	2	0

COMBINATION SHUTOUTS: **Athletics (1)**—Mercedes-Gallagher-Waites. **Cubs (4)**—Batts-Mallory-Powalski-Acosta, Noel-Waldrum-Pitt-Sullivan, Vracar-Pitt-Sullivan, Meyers-Noel. **Diamondbacks (1)**—Haverstick-Cepeda-Manzueta. **Mariners (1)**—Mateo-Heams. **Padres (0)**—None. **Rockies (0)**—None.

NO-HIT GAMES: None.

TEAM

Team	Pct.	G	PO	A	E	TC	DP	PB	Team	Pct.	G	PO	A	E	TC	DP	PB
Mariners	.949	56	1476	594	111	2181	40	30	Rockies	.929	56	1497	641	163	2301	56	26
Diamondbacks	.944	56	1483	616	124	2223	43	8	Padres	.926	55	1462	590	165	2217	55	19
Athletics	.942	56	1453	594	126	2173	44	21	TRIPLE PLAY: Cubs.								
Cubs	.941	55	1464	530	126	2120	51	18									

INDIVIDUAL

FIRST BASEMEN

NOTE: All caps denotes fielding-percentage leader based on 28 games for catchers, 37 for all other non-pitchers and 56 innings for pitchers. *Throws lefthanded.

Player, Team	Pct.	G	PO	A	E	TC	DP
Bernhardt, Tom, Cubs	.982	6	50	4	1	55	7
Camilo, Juan, Athletics	.923	2	12	0	1	13	0
Cosme, Caonabo, Athletics	.857	1	5	1	1	7	1
Curry, Jesse, Padres*	.956	39	347	26	17	390	40
Davis, Monty, Athletics	.981	12	98	4	2	104	8
Downing, Lance, Diamondbacks	.989	53	500	28	6	534	36
Dunham, Traylon, Padres	.942	17	133	13	9	155	11
Estrella, Gorky, Mariners	.994	20	149	7	1	157	8
Folmar, Ryan, Rockies	1.000	1	6	0	0	6	1
Garcia, Cipriano, Mariners	.975	19	151	4	4	159	14
Guzman, Julio, Diamondbacks	1.000	1	4	0	0	4	0
Hargreaves, Brad, Cubs	.972	4	34	1	1	36	1
JOHNSON, Gary, Cubs	.995	45	360	25	2	387	31
Kirkpatrick, Brian, Rockies	.974	40	348	22	10	380	33
Lina, Donald, Rockies	1.000	1	3	0	0	3	0
Luderer, Brian, Athletics	1.000	2	25	1	0	26	5
Mahoney, Ricardo, Rockies	.950	2	19	0	1	20	2
Mauck, Matt, Cubs	.714	2	5	0	2	7	0
Moye, Melvin, Diamondbacks	.929	3	24	2	2	28	4
Nunez, Jose, Athletics	.947	3	34	2	2	38	0
Petersen, Mike, Rockies	.982	17	150	14	3	167	16
Pimentel, Hector, Athletics	1.000	2	8	0	0	8	0
Rosario, Omar, Athletics*	.976	40	307	15	8	330	24
Soriano, Rafael, Mariners	.971	21	160	9	5	174	12
Underwood, Jake, Mariners	1.000	3	23	1	0	24	0

SECOND BASEMEN

Player, Team	Pct.	G	PO	A	E	TC	DP
Aldrup, Morey, Cubs	.922	23	37	58	8	103	15
Davis, Monty, Athletics	.956	20	41	46	4	91	14
DeMarco, Joey, Padres	.920	4	9	14	2	25	8
Dunaway, Michael, Padres	.929	4	6	7	1	14	1
Eaddy, Deon, Cubs	1.000	1	4	4	0	8	2
Fereday, Todd, Cubs	.958	5	11	12	1	24	3
Garcia, Alex, Padres	1.000	1	2	3	0	5	1
Garcia, Sandro, Padres	.953	7	14	27	2	43	6
German, Franklin, Cubs	.901	29	33	76	12	121	6
German, Manuel, Diamndbcks	.836	14	16	35	10	61	4
Guerrero, Joel, Padres	.952	36	63	94	8	165	21
Lina, Donald, Rockies	.959	16	27	44	3	74	11
Martinez, Belvani, Diamndbcks	.968	28	53	99	5	157	19
Moreno, Jose, Mariners	1.000	4	7	4	0	11	1
Moye, Melvin, Diamondbacks	.928	16	26	38	5	69	4
Nova, Kelvin, Athletics	.924	14	25	36	5	66	6
NUNEZ, Jose, Rockies	.929	42	77	120	15	212	24
Parker, Hubert, Mariners	.957	24	33	56	4	93	10
Pinson, Brian, Mariners	.943	23	28	38	4	70	9
Rosario, Felix, Mariners	.908	17	26	33	6	65	4
Tripp, Terry, Padres	.970	8	17	15	1	33	1
Yoshida, Kota, Athletics	.971	27	40	59	3	102	11

TRIPLE PLAY: F. German.

THIRD BASEMEN

Player, Team	Pct.	G	PO	A	E	TC	DP
Aldrup, Morey, Cubs	.762	6	4	12	5	21	0
Brooks, Jeffrey, Diamondbacks	.807	53	32	77	26	135	12
Cosme, Caonabo, Athletics	.917	4	0	11	1	12	3
Davis, Monty, Athletics	.864	8	10	9	3	22	1
DeMarco, Joey, Padres	1.000	1	0	2	0	2	1
Downing, Lance, Diamondbacks	1.000	3	1	3	0	4	0
Dunaway, Michael, Padres	1.000	1	3	1	0	4	0
Estrella, Gorky, Mariners	.896	34	22	73	11	106	6
Fereday, Todd, Cubs	.964	11	5	22	1	28	3
Garcia, Alex, Padres	.793	20	9	37	12	58	1
Garcia, Sandro, Padres	.824	18	12	30	9	51	3

Player, Team	Pct.	G	PO	A	E	TC	DP
German, Franklin, Cubs	.800	5	5	3	2	10	1
Guerrero, Joel, Padres	1.000	1	0	2	0	2	1
Kirkpatrick, Brian, Rockies	.706	7	2	10	5	17	0
Lina, Donald, Rockies	.667	5	1	5	3	9	0
Mauck, Matt, Cubs	.783	36	19	53	20	92	2
Moreno, Jose, Mariners	1.000	1	1	0	0	1	0
Moye, Melvin, Diamondbacks	.750	4	1	2	1	4	1
Nova, Kelvin, Athletics	.922	17	18	29	4	51	2
Pacheco, Domingo, Mariners	.848	23	14	42	10	66	3
Pimentel, Hector, Athletics	.858	34	26	71	16	113	5
Sawai, Ryosuke, Padres	.556	3	2	3	4	9	0
SMITH, Sam, Rockies	.838	48	34	85	23	142	8
Tripp, Terry, Padres	.743	12	5	21	9	35	0

SHORTSTOPS

Player, Team	Pct.	G	PO	A	E	TC	DP
Aldrup, Morey, Cubs	.909	4	3	7	1	11	2
Cintron, Alexander, Diamndbcks	.931	43	85	118	15	218	26
Cosme, Caonabo, Athletics	.903	34	46	84	14	144	14
Declet, Miguel, Athletics	.800	12	8	24	8	40	2
DeMarco, Joey, Padres	.500	1	0	1	1	2	0
Dunaway, Michael, Padres	.862	39	78	109	30	217	28
Eaddy, Deon, Cubs	.911	51	97	107	20	224	33
Figgins, Desmond, Rockies	.867	51	97	164	40	301	35
German, Manuel, Diamondbacks	.952	14	25	34	3	62	4
Hargreaves, Brad, Cubs	1.000	1	2	1	0	3	1
Lina, Donald, Rockies	.871	8	4	23	4	31	3
MORENO, Jose, Mariners	.945	44	82	125	12	219	21
Moye, Melvin, Diamondbacks	.833	1	1	4	1	6	1
Nicholson, Kevin, Padres	.923	7	11	25	3	39	5
Pacheco, Domingo, Mariners	.933	3	3	11	1	15	2
Parker, Hubert, Mariners	.909	11	16	34	5	55	5
Tripp, Terry, Padres	.917	10	10	34	4	48	7
Yoshida, Kota, Athletics	.923	21	21	63	7	91	11

TRIPLE PLAY: Eaddy.

OUTFIELDERS

Player, Team	Pct.	G	PO	A	E	TC	DP
Aldrup, Morey, Cubs	1.000	1	2	0	0	2	0
Basabe, Jesus, Athletics	.924	52	81	4	7	92	1
Bernhardt, Tom, Cubs	1.000	2	5	0	0	5	0
Burford, Kevin, Padres*	.880	35	41	3	6	50	1
Camilo, Juan, Athletics	.932	47	65	4	5	74	1
Cust, Jack, Diamondbacks	.902	34	46	0	5	51	0
De La Cruz, Henry, Cubs	.875	14	12	2	2	16	0
Dunham, Traylon, Padres	1.000	1	1	0	0	1	0
Encarnacion, Bernaldo, Rockies	.898	38	47	6	6	59	0
Gonzalez, Franklin, Padres	.978	24	42	3	1	46	1
Gordon, Brian, Diamondbacks	.885	49	64	5	9	78	0
Guerrero, Joel, Padres	1.000	2	1	1	0	2	0
Guzman, Julio, Diamondbacks	.818	6	8	1	2	11	1
Hargreaves, Brad, Cubs	1.000	3	1	0	0	1	0
Haynes, Larry, Mariners	.970	45	57	8	2	67	0
Haynes, Nathan, Athletics*	.955	13	21	0	1	22	0
Hemmings, Brandon, Padres	.967	24	29	0	1	30	0
Hunter, Andrew, Padres	1.000	3	2	0	0	2	0
Jimenez, Felipe, Cubs	.958	40	90	2	4	96	0
Johnson, Gary, Cubs	1.000	9	16	2	0	18	0
Landaeta, Luis, Rockies*	.904	32	43	4	5	52	0
Mashore, Justin, Padres	1.000	2	3	0	0	3	0
Minor, Damon, Padres*	.984	41	63	0	1	64	0
Montilla, Alvin, Diamondbacks	.964	17	26	1	1	28	0
Motley, Brittan, Padres	.918	37	53	3	5	61	1
Nielsen, Bret, Mariners	.914	46	71	3	7	81	0
Nieves, Wilbert, Padres	1.000	3	3	0	0	3	0
NUNEZ, Abraham, Diamndbcks	.990	53	94	8	1	103	0
Payne, Ronald, Cubs*	.916	51	73	3	7	83	1
Petersen, Mike, Rockies	1.000	11	17	1	0	18	0
Pimentel, Hector, Athletics	1.000	2	2	0	0	2	0

Player, Team	Pct.	G	PO	A	E	TC	DP
Porter, Jamie, Athletics	.977	26	38	4	1	43	0
Randolph, Jaisen, Cubs	.966	52	76	8	3	87	4
Rosario, Carlos, Rockies	.926	41	68	7	6	81	0
Rosario, Omar, Athletics*	.923	17	23	1	2	26	1
Sanchez, Augustin, Rockies	.961	34	48	1	2	51	0
Silvestre, Juan, Mariners	.938	31	52	8	4	64	2
Soriano, Rafael, Mariners	.966	17	27	1	1	29	0
Sosa, Jorge, Rockies	.892	26	31	2	4	37	0
Thomas, Gary, Athletics	1.000	27	40	2	0	42	0
Weichard, Paul, Diamondbacks*	.902	19	34	3	4	41	0
Williams, Patrick, Mariners	.976	45	77	5	2	84	0

CATCHERS

Player, Team	Pct.	G	PO	A	E	TC	DP	PB
Alcala, Juan, Mariners	.964	20	132	28	6	166	2	7
Camilo, Juan, Athletics	1.000	1	2	1	0	3	0	0
Carroll, Mark, Mariners	.973	22	180	37	6	223	2	10
Castro, Juan, Rockies	.983	29	207	28	4	239	1	16
Cosentino, Anthony, Padres	.983	26	211	17	4	232	0	6
Dunham, Traylon, Padres	.966	7	48	8	2	58	2	3
Folmar, Ryan, Rockies	1.000	2	17	0	0	17	0	2
Garcia, Cipriano, Mariners	.989	12	83	8	1	92	2	10
Hargreaves, Brad, Cubs	.991	16	105	10	1	116	2	3
Lopez, Jose, Diamondbacks	.972	32	242	38	8	288	1	6
Lopez, Miguel, Diamondbacks	.963	23	154	26	7	187	1	1
Luderer, Brian, Athletics	.960	35	228	37	11	276	4	8
Mahoney, Ricardo, Rockies	.965	26	220	30	9	259	1	8
Morgan, James, Diamndbcks	.947	4	16	2	1	19	0	1
Nunez, Jose, Athletics	.963	29	212	20	9	241	1	13
RAMSEY, Brad, Cubs	.990	41	358	39	4	401	6	15
Soto, Luis, Padres	.928	26	216	29	19	264	3	10
Underwood, Jake, Mariners	1.000	8	62	5	0	67	0	3

PITCHERS

Player, Team	Pct.	G	PO	A	E	TC	DP
Abbott, Paul, Mariners	.500	3	0	1	1	2	0
Abeyta, Scott, Diamondbacks*	.833	17	1	9	2	12	0
Acosta, Jhon, Cubs	1.000	14	0	3	0	3	0
Barboza, Carlos, Rockies	.800	16	2	6	2	10	1
Batts, Nathan, Cubs*	1.000	8	1	4	0	5	0
Bell, Matthew, Diamondbacks	.889	18	3	5	1	9	0
Beltran, Francis, Cubs	.833	16	2	3	1	6	0
Boughton, Mike, Diamondbacks	1.000	15	3	10	0	13	1
Cepeda, Wellington, Diamndbcks	.917	15	5	6	1	12	0
Connell, Brian, Cubs*	.529	12	4	5	8	17	0
Cook, Aaron, Rockies	.789	9	5	10	4	19	1
Corniel, Henry, Athletics	1.000	20	1	5	0	6	0
Crawford, Jeremy, Athletics*	.750	15	0	3	1	4	0
Cueto, Jose, Mariners	.800	17	1	3	1	5	1
Darr, Jerry, Padres	.864	14	5	14	3	22	0
Delano, Michael, Cubs*	1.000	8	0	1	0	1	1
Delgado, Dan, Mariners	1.000	6	1	0	0	1	0
Diaz, Antonio, Padres	.800	22	1	3	1	5	0
Duprey, Peter, Mariners*	.600	15	1	2	2	5	0
Frias, Miguel, Diamondbacks*	1.000	21	2	4	0	6	1
Gallagher, Bryan, Athletics*	.800	17	0	4	1	5	0
Garcia, Bryan, Athletics	1.000	15	1	3	0	4	0
Garcia, Expeddy, Athletics*	1.000	8	0	1	0	1	0
Garey, Daniel, Mariners	1.000	7	1	6	0	7	0
Garland, Jon, Cubs	.909	11	4	6	1	11	0

Player, Team	Pct.	G	PO	A	E	TC	DP
Gonzalez, Armando, Rockies	1.000	13	5	6	0	11	0
Gonzalez, Francisco, Padres	.857	26	3	3	1	7	0
Guttormson, Ricky, Padres	.500	5	0	1	1	2	0
Hause, Brendan, Athletics*	1.000	6	1	3	0	4	0
Haverstick, David, Diamndbcks	.882	14	5	10	2	17	0
Heams, Shane, Mariners	.857	21	2	4	1	7	1
Herndon, Harry, Padres	.828	14	5	19	5	29	1
Herrera, Misael, Padres	1.000	11	2	1	0	3	0
Howard, Ben, Padres	.750	13	4	5	3	12	1
Iannacone, Steve, Rockies	.333	13	0	1	2	3	0
Iida, Masashi, Padres	1.000	11	0	2	0	2	1
Ishimaru, Taisuke, Mariners	1.000	7	1	0	0	1	0
Jacobs, Frankey, Athletics	1.000	15	3	4	0	7	0
Jimenez, Mario, Mariners	.625	7	0	5	3	8	0
Jones, Charlie, Diamondbacks	1.000	7	1	1	0	2	0
Jones, Travis, Padres*	1.000	21	2	6	0	8	1
Kidd, Jake, Rockies	.909	19	1	9	1	11	2
KOHL, Doug, Diamondbacks	1.000	14	4	14	0	18	0
Labitzke, Jesse, Rockies*	.714	12	1	4	2	7	0
Little, Rodney, Rockies	1.000	15	1	1	0	2	0
Little, Roger, Rockies	1.000	14	3	1	0	4	0
Lohse, Kyle, Cubs	1.000	12	7	3	0	10	0
Lora, Edison, Rockies	1.000	11	0	3	0	3	0
Mallory, Andrew, Cubs	.833	11	7	13	4	24	3
Mangum, Mark, Rockies	.913	14	6	15	2	23	1
Mateo, Julio, Mariners	.800	13	2	6	2	10	1
Matos, Josue, Mariners	.800	14	1	3	1	5	0
Medina, Eleazer, Cubs	1.000	8	0	1	0	1	0
Medina, Jaime, Rockies	.500	10	3	0	3	6	0
Meeks, Eric, Athletics	.625	15	1	4	3	8	0
Mendoza, Hatuey, Diamndbcks	1.000	17	1	5	0	6	0
Mercedes, Jose, Athletics	.933	14	2	12	1	15	1
Meyers, Mike, Cubs	.667	12	1	3	2	6	2
Montero, Agus, Athletics	1.000	14	5	7	0	12	0
Manzueta, Roberto, Diamndbcks	1.000	7	0	3	0	3	1
Newton, Geronimo, Mariners*	1.000	4	1	1	0	2	0
Nix, Wayne, Athletics	.667	15	1	1	1	3	0
Noel, Todd, Cubs	.750	12	5	7	4	16	1
Paredes, Vladimir, Diamondbacks*	1.000	10	2	0	0	2	0
Parent, Jerry, Padres	1.000	5	0	1	0	1	0
Pena, Juan, Athletics*	.857	14	1	17	3	21	1
Piersoll, Christopher, Cubs	.875	15	0	7	1	8	2
Pitt, Jye, Cubs	1.000	14	0	1	0	1	0
Powalski, Richard, Cubs*	.750	6	0	3	1	4	0
Precinal, Huilberto, Padres	1.000	13	1	0	0	1	0
Price, Ryan, Rockies	.786	14	0	11	3	14	1
Prouty, Scott, Mariners	1.000	3	1	0	0	1	0
Rincones, Gabriel, Mariners	.842	13	5	11	3	19	0
Royer, Jason, Diamondbacks	.929	13	1	12	1	14	0
Sanchez, Simon, Diamondbacks	.813	14	4	9	3	16	0
Serrano, Wascar, Padres	1.000	12	5	7	0	12	0
Sullivan, Shane, Cubs	1.000	21	1	5	0	6	0
Tate, Seth, Diamondbacks	.600	11	1	2	2	5	0
Torres, Melqui, Mariners	.778	13	2	5	2	9	1
Vargas, Derrick, Rockies*	.875	11	3	4	1	8	0
Vracar, Paul, Cubs	.500	7	0	1	1	2	0
Waites, David, Athletics	.750	21	1	2	1	4	0
Waldrum, Kevin, Cubs	1.000	8	1	2	0	3	0
Waligora, Thomas, Cubs	.667	16	0	2	1	3	0
Walton, Samuel, Mariners*	.727	13	1	7	3	11	0
Woodard, Brad, Rockies	1.000	19	1	4	0	5	0

The following players did not have any fielding statistics at the positions indicated or appeared only as a designated hitter, pinch-hitter, or pinch-runner:
Bedinger, p; Bido, p; Cochrane, dh; Corniel, of; Cosentino, 1b; S. Garcia, p; M. German, 3b; Guzman, p; Hohenstein, p; J. Lopez, 3b, of; Mahoney, p; Morel, p; Nova, p; Parker, 1b, 3b; Payne, 1b; Pimentel, p; Pineiro, p; Pinson, p; Proctor, dh; F. Rosario, ss, of; Thomas, 2b; Tolbert, dh; Urquiola, dh.

LEAGUE CHAMPIONS

Year	Team	Pct.	Year	Team	Pct.	Year	Team	Pct.
1988—	Peoria Brewers	.690	1992—	Scottsdale A's	.607	1996—	Padres	.643
1989—	Peoria Brewers	.732	1993—	Scottsdale A's	.636	1997—	Cubs	.618
1990—	Peoria Brewers	.679	1994—	Chandler Cardinals	.607			
1991—	Scottsdale A's	.650	1995—	Scottsdale A's	.661			

GULF COAST LEAGUE

LEAGUE OFFICE

President
Tom Saffell

Address
1503 Clower Creek Dr., H-262
Sarasota, FL 34231

Phone
941-966-6407

Teams*
Astros
Braves
Devil Rays
Expos
Marlins
Mets
Orioles
Pirates
Rangers
Red Sox

Royals
Tigers
Twins
White Sox
Yankees

*Teams play their games in Bradenton, Dunedin, Fort Myers, Kissimmee, Lakeland, Melbourne, Orlando, Port Charlotte, Port St. Lucie, St. Petersburg, Sarasota, Tampa and West Palm Beach, Fla.

1997 FINAL STANDINGS

EASTERN DIVISION

Team	W	L	T	Pct.	GB
Mets	42	18	0	.700	....
Marlins	31	28	0	.525	10½
Expos	25	35	0	.417	17
Braves	21	38	0	.356	20½

WESTERN DIVISION

Team	W	L	T	Pct.	GB
Yankees	40	20	0	.667	....
Tigers	31	29	0	.517	9
Devil Rays	25	35	0	.417	15
Astros	24	36	0	.400	16

NORTHWEST DIVISION

Team	W	L	T	Pct.	GB
Royals	36	24	0	.600	....
Rangers	34	26	0	.567	2
Red Sox	31	28	0	.525	4½
Twins	28	32	0	.467	8
Pirates	27	32	0	.458	8½
Orioles	27	33	0	.450	9
White Sox	26	34	0	.433	10

COMPOSITE

Team	Mets	Yan.	Ryl.	Rng.	R.S.	Mrl.	Tig.	Twi.	Pir.	Ori.	W.S.	Exp.	Dev.	Ast.	Brv.	W	L	T	Pct.	GB
Mets	....	0	0	0	0	12	0	0	0	0	0	14	0	0	16	42	18	0	.700	....
Yankees	0	....	0	0	0	0	14	0	0	0	0	0	13	13	0	40	20	0	.667	2
Royals	0	0	....	6	5	0	0	4	8	9	4	0	0	0	0	36	24	0	.600	6
Rangers	0	0	4	....	7	0	0	4	6	8	5	0	0	0	0	34	26	0	.567	8
Red Sox	0	0	5	3	....	0	0	7	4	5	7	0	0	0	0	31	28	0	.525	10½
Marlins	8	0	0	0	0	....	0	0	0	0	0	11	0	0	12	31	28	0	.525	10½
Tigers	0	6	0	0	0	0	....	0	0	0	0	0	10	15	0	31	29	0	.517	11
Twins	0	0	6	6	3	0	0	....	4	4	5	0	0	0	0	28	32	0	.467	14
Pirates	0	0	2	4	5	0	0	6	....	5	5	0	0	0	0	27	32	0	.458	14½
Orioles	0	0	1	2	5	0	0	6	5	....	8	0	0	0	0	27	33	0	.450	15
White Sox	0	0	6	5	3	0	0	5	5	2	....	0	0	0	0	26	34	0	.433	16
Expos	6	0	0	0	0	9	0	0	0	0	0	....	0	0	10	25	35	0	.417	17
Devil Rays	0	7	0	0	0	0	10	0	0	0	0	0	....	8	0	25	35	0	.417	17
Astros	0	7	0	0	0	0	5	0	0	0	0	0	12	....	0	24	36	0	.400	18
Braves	4	0	0	0	0	7	0	0	0	0	0	10	0	0	....	21	38	0	.356	20½

Games played in Bradenton, Dunedin, Fort Myers, Melbourne, Osceola, Port Charlotte, St. Lucie County, Sarasota, Tampa and West Palm Beach, Fla.

Club names are major league affiliations.

PLAYOFFS: Mets defeated Yankees, one game to none; Rangers defeated Royals, one game to none; Mets defeated Rangers, two games to none, to win league championship.

REGULAR-SEASON ATTENDANCE: No official attendance figures reported.

MANAGERS: Astros, Julio Linares; Braves, Frank Howard; Devil Rays, Bobby Ramos; Expos, Luis Dorante; Marlins, John Deeble; Mets, Mickey Brantley (through July 17) and Doug Flynn (July 18 to end of season); Orioles, Butch Davis; Pirates, Woody Huyke; Rangers, James Byrd; Red Sox, Luis Aguayo; Royals, Al Pedrique; Tigers, Kevin Bradshaw; Twins, Steve Liddle; White Sox, Roly de Armas; Yankees, Ken Dominguez. Managerial records of team with more than one manager: Mets, Brantley 18-7, Flynn 24-11.

ALL-STAR TEAM: 1B—Travis Hafner, Rangers; 2B—Willy Ruiz, Royals; 3B—Erick Almonte, Yankees; SS—Rayner Bautista, Tigers; OF—Juan Mora, Tigers; Jose Taveras, Royals; Marcus Thames, Yankees; C—Michael Rivera, Tigers; Starting Pitcher—Marquis Roberts, Devil Rays; Relief Pitcher—Jake Jacobs, Twins; Co-Managers of the Year—Mickey Brantley and Doug Flynn, Mets.

1997 BATTING

TEAM

Team	Avg.	G	TPA	AB	R	H	TB	2B	3B	HR	RBI	SH	SF	HP	BB	IBB	SO	SB	CS	GDP	LOB	ShO	Slg.	OBP
Yankees	.275	60	2293	2002	349	550	785	91	30	28	293	12	25	29	225	4	414	74	18	38	457	4	.392	.352
Royals	.269	60	2170	1916	293	516	698	73	17	25	241	27	18	34	175	4	411	67	28	46	408	1	.364	.338
Mets	.264	60	2132	1862	308	491	697	105	28	15	234	8	18	34	210	0	392	43	25	30	419	3	.374	.346
Rangers	.251	60	2110	1872	267	470	644	78	21	18	199	13	15	19	191	2	446	120	43	37	362	4	.344	.324
Red Sox	.251	59	2045	1818	213	456	608	82	23	8	181	16	16	19	176	1	404	68	26	36	389	7	.334	.321
Pirates	.251	59	2102	1883	226	472	638	91	12	17	187	11	17	25	166	5	445	49	34	46	387	7	.339	.317
Tigers	.249	60	2218	1916	310	477	684	81	18	30	264	11	23	33	235	3	476	69	21	41	423	2	.357	.338
White Sox	.244	60	2094	1865	218	455	606	76	18	13	189	19	19	28	163	5	390	66	24	43	392	6	.325	.311

SUMMER CLASS A Gulf Coast League

Team	Avg.	G	TPA	AB	R	H	TB	2B	3B	HR	RBI	SH	SF	HP	BB	IBB	SO	SB	CS	GDP	LOB	ShO	Slg.	OBP
Braves	.244	58	2056	1819	244	443	613	75	10	25	208	2	10	19	206	0	432	31	12	29	406	6	.337	.325
Twins	.242	60	2231	1970	220	476	585	62	13	7	165	17	15	30	199	2	418	110	41	39	433	5	.297	.318
Expos	.241	59	2053	1822	241	439	597	91	14	13	166	17	9	20	185	1	385	92	40	23	366	4	.328	.316
Devil Rays	.238	60	2129	1850	255	440	610	73	20	19	202	11	9	27	232	0	443	71	40	45	387	4	.330	.330
Marlins	.233	59	2056	1779	225	414	539	75	10	10	176	16	14	27	220	3	459	77	29	35	407	4	.303	.324
Orioles	.230	60	2123	1856	226	427	571	70	19	12	187	13	18	35	201	4	481	85	33	33	400	8	.308	.314
Astros	.225	60	2118	1895	236	427	591	83	6	23	198	16	13	29	165	3	429	65	37	31	366	8	.312	.295

INDIVIDUAL

TOP QUALIFIERS FOR BATTING CHAMPIONSHIP

Minimum 162 plate appearances. *Lefthanded batter. †Switch-hitter.

Player, Team	Avg.	G	TPA	AB	R	H	TB	2B	3B	HR	RBI	SH	SF	HP	BB	IBB	SO	SB	CS	GDP	Slg.	OBP
Ruiz, Willy, Royals	.360	54	216	197	33	71	75	4	0	0	14	4	0	6	9	0	19	20	11	6	.381	.406
Mora, Juan, Tigers*	.348	43	175	155	26	54	85	9	5	4	31	0	2	0	18	0	43	9	2	3	.548	.411
Thames, Marcus, Yankees	.344	57	219	195	51	67	113	17	4	7	36	1	4	3	16	0	26	6	4	3	.579	.394
Durham, Chad, White Sox	.328	49	208	189	24	62	76	5	3	1	17	3	1	3	12	1	17	22	3	4	.402	.376
Taveras, Jose, Royals	.327	57	237	205	46	67	110	14	4	7	39	4	1	3	24	1	42	14	4	1	.537	.403
Gomez, Erick, Royals*	.320	50	187	169	18	54	79	16	0	3	29	0	2	0	16	0	36	0	0	6	.467	.374
Quero, Pedro, Expos	.311	56	209	190	28	59	84	14	4	1	21	3	3	1	12	0	31	6	0	6	.442	.350
Torres, Rafael, Braves	.306	44	176	160	20	49	60	2	0	3	33	0	3	6	7	1	16	2	1	5	.375	.352
Washington, Dion, Yankees	.303	52	210	165	35	50	71	10	1	3	33	0	2	6	36	0	39	2	0	1	.430	.440
Lehr, Ryan, Braves	.300	54	218	207	30	62	93	15	2	4	34	0	2	0	9	0	32	1	0	6	.449	.326
Rodriguez, John, Yankees*	.299	46	190	157	31	47	70	10	2	3	23	0	3	0	30	1	32	7	0	3	.446	.405
Bautista, Rayner, Tigers	.299	49	179	164	33	49	67	11	2	1	17	3	0	1	11	0	33	7	1	2	.409	.347
Mejias, Oliver, Pirates†	.293	44	168	157	20	46	60	12	1	0	9	2	0	2	7	0	26	8	7	2	.382	.319
McNeal, Aaron, Astros	.293	46	177	164	22	48	69	12	0	3	26	0	2	0	11	0	28	0	5	4	.421	.333
Hill, Bobby, Mets*	.292	41	170	144	27	42	64	9	2	3	24	1	1	7	17	0	37	3	5	2	.444	.391

DEPARTMENTAL LEADERS: G—Nolasco, 58; AB—C. Myers, 217; R—Thames, 51; H—Ruiz, 71; TB—Thames, 113; 2B—Thames, 17; 3B—Olivares, 7; HR—M. Rivera, 10; RBI—J. Taveras, 39; SH—Herrera, 6; SF—Nolasco, 6; HP—B. Hill, 7; BB—Oropeza, 37; IBB—Several players tied with 2 each; SO—C. Myers, 58; SB—C. Myers, 24; CS—Mann, Ruiz, Wright, 11 each; GIDP—J. Ramirez, 11; Slg.—Thames, .579; OBP—D. Washington, .440.

ALL PLAYERS

*Lefthanded batter. †Switch-hitter.

Player, Team	Avg.	G	TPA	AB	R	H	TB	2B	3B	HR	RBI	SH	SF	HP	BB	IBB	SO	SB	CS	GDP	Slg.	OBP
Abreu, Miguel, Marlins	.213	37	101	94	10	20	24	2	1	0	6	0	2	1	4	0	28	2	2	1	.255	.248
Acevedo, Luis, Rangers	.181	51	174	155	16	28	34	3	0	1	7	0	3	3	13	0	46	8	3	3	.219	.253
Aceves, Jonathan, White Sox	.184	30	87	76	9	14	18	4	0	0	4	0	0	2	9	0	18	0	0	5	.237	.287
Ackerman, Scott, Expos	.239	43	159	142	17	34	48	6	1	2	18	2	0	1	14	0	26	3	4	1	.338	.312
Adorno, Wilson, Pirates†	.179	15	44	39	7	7	7	0	0	0	4	0	0	1	4	0	12	0	0	2	.179	.273
Aguila, Chris, Marlins	.217	46	183	157	12	34	44	7	0	1	17	2	2	1	21	0	49	2	1	3	.280	.309
Airoso, Kurt, Tigers	.000	4	14	10	1	0	0	0	0	0	0	0	0	1	3	0	3	0	0	0	.000	.286
Aldridge, Claudio, Braves*	.278	46	184	169	26	47	66	8	1	3	37	0	0	1	14	0	37	1	0	1	.391	.337
Alfaro, Jason, Astros	.265	34	113	102	8	27	38	5	0	2	13	2	0	1	8	0	14	6	0	2	.373	.324
Alleyne, Roberto, Astros	.385	3	14	13	1	5	8	1	1	0	3	0	0	0	1	0	0	3	0	0	.615	.429
Almonte, Claudio, Twins	.287	57	205	188	19	54	68	7	2	1	25	1	2	2	12	0	36	16	5	0	.362	.333
Almonte, Erick, Yankees	.283	52	204	180	32	51	72	4	4	3	31	1	2	0	21	1	27	8	2	5	.400	.355
Alvarez, Jimmy, Twins	.249	52	209	185	25	46	59	5	4	0	14	1	1	1	21	0	46	12	5	4	.319	.327
Alvarez, Julio, Tigers†	.167	6	20	18	1	3	3	0	0	0	0	0	0	0	2	0	5	0	0	0	.167	.250
Alvarez, Nelson, Tigers	.247	34	101	85	21	21	27	3	0	1	10	0	1	3	12	0	16	4	3	8	.318	.356
Arias, Jeison, Devil Rays	.190	39	144	126	14	24	42	4	4	2	10	0	0	2	16	0	41	7	4	2	.333	.292
August, Brian, Yankees	.277	17	52	47	8	13	28	2	2	3	7	0	0	0	5	0	7	0	1	0	.596	.346
Austin, Peter, Pirates	.245	17	58	53	3	13	15	2	0	0	6	0	1	0	4	0	10	2	3	3	.283	.293
Bailey, Jeff, Marlins	.143	5	8	7	0	1	1	0	0	0	0	0	0	1	1	0	2	1	0	1	.143	.250
Baker, Derek, Rangers*	.364	12	47	44	7	16	26	4	0	2	7	0	0	1	2	0	10	0	1	1	.591	.404
Balfe, Ryan, Tigers†	.571	2	8	7	2	4	7	0	0	1	1	0	0	0	1	0	1	0	0	0	1.000	.625
Batista, Angel, Devil Rays*	.205	37	127	117	14	24	28	4	0	0	11	1	0	0	9	0	35	2	2	1	.239	.262
Bautista, Jose, Twins†	.107	14	36	28	2	3	3	0	0	0	0	0	0	0	8	0	9	2	0	2	.107	.306
Bautista, Juan, Orioles	.111	3	12	9	3	1	1	0	0	0	0	0	0	2	1	0	2	1	1	0	.111	.333
Bautista, Rayner, Tigers	.299	49	179	164	33	49	67	11	2	1	17	3	0	1	11	0	33	7	1	2	.409	.347
Bello, Jilberto, Orioles	.245	33	110	102	8	25	32	5	1	0	14	0	0	0	8	1	29	2	2	2	.314	.300
Beltres, Manuel, Yankees†	.223	29	122	103	13	23	24	1	0	0	11	5	0	1	13	0	27	9	4	1	.233	.316
Benes, Richard, Royals†	.205	34	42	39	15	8	10	0	1	0	1	0	0	0	3	0	11	3	1	0	.256	.262
Benjamin, Al, Pirates	.322	39	160	152	18	49	73	14	2	2	21	1	2	1	4	0	26	7	1	3	.480	.340
Betemit, Wilson, Braves†	.212	32	122	113	12	24	32	6	1	0	15	0	0	0	9	0	32	0	0	3	.283	.270
Bethea, Larry, Orioles	.164	36	131	116	6	19	26	1	0	0	15	0	0	4	11	0	32	2	1	6	.224	.260
Boone, Matthew, Tigers	.204	48	170	152	13	31	42	11	0	0	15	0	2	3	13	0	37	2	1	7	.276	.276
Borges, Elio, White Sox†	.288	28	96	80	9	23	31	6	1	0	15	1	2	1	12	0	14	4	0	1	.388	.379
Boscan, Jean, Braves	.202	36	123	104	7	21	29	5	0	1	16	0	1	2	16	0	21	0	1	2	.279	.317
Bradley, Milton, Expos†	.200	9	30	25	6	5	10	2	0	1	2	0	0	1	4	0	4	2	2	0	.400	.333
Brito, Alen, Royals	.250	11	26	24	3	6	6	0	0	0	3	0	0	1	1	0	7	1	0	0	.250	.269
Brito, Juan, Royals	.314	25	77	70	14	22	35	4	0	3	15	0	1	5	5	0	13	0	0	1	.500	.368
Brosam, Eric, Twins*	.241	44	160	141	13	34	41	3	2	0	9	1	3	3	14	0	31	3	0	0	.291	.321
Brown, Richard, Yankees*	.367	10	36	30	7	11	14	3	0	0	5	0	0	1	5	0	6	0	0	2	.467	.444
Burke, Mark, Braves*	.433	9	34	30	9	13	25	3	0	3	7	0	0	0	4	0	2	1	0	2	.833	.500
Byrd, Brandon, Astros	.192	45	164	146	12	28	48	5	0	5	18	0	2	2	14	0	49	2	2	3	.329	.268
Bystrowski, Robert, Astros	.226	51	206	177	28	40	57	8	0	3	22	0	1	6	22	0	47	5	6	4	.322	.330
Calderon, Henry, Royals	.245	43	155	139	17	34	48	5	3	1	15	2	2	2	10	0	31	3	1	3	.345	.301

Player, Team	Avg.	G	TPA	AB	R	H	TB	2B	3B	HR	RBI	SH	SF	HP	BB	IBB	SO	SB	CS	GDP	Slg.	OBP
Canaguacan, Oscar, Yankees†	.313	7	18	16	3	5	6	1	0	0	2	0	0	0	2	0	3	1	0	0	.375	.389
Candelaria, Vidal, Yankees* ...	.263	35	129	114	12	30	33	3	0	0	16	3	2	2	8	0	28	3	0	4	.289	.317
Capista, Aaron, Red Sox†	.239	38	152	134	16	32	40	6	1	0	14	0	2	0	16	1	17	6	2	3	.299	.316
Caracciolo, Anthony, Expos	.199	40	172	156	17	31	38	4	0	1	10	2	0	0	14	0	35	16	9	0	.244	.265
Caradonna, Brett, White Sox*	.276	36	138	123	15	34	51	5	3	2	16	0	3	1	11	1	21	3	0	2	.415	.333
Cardona, Luis, Mets	.143	2	7	7	0	1	1	0	0	0	2	0	0	0	0	0	1	0	0	0	.143	.143
Carter, Shannon, Orioles*	.195	50	175	159	22	31	38	3	2	0	11	0	0	4	12	0	45	13	5	1	.239	.269
Castillo, Geramel, Rangers†...	.237	44	145	139	20	33	47	2	3	2	10	0	1	1	4	0	33	11	2	3	.338	.262
Chaidez, Juan, Red Sox†	.147	14	40	34	1	5	5	0	0	0	2	0	1	0	5	0	16	0	0	0	.147	.250
Charles, Curtis, Orioles	.250	6	22	20	4	5	9	1	0	1	3	0	0	0	2	0	5	0	0	0	.450	.318
Chavez, Endy, Mets*	.277	33	140	119	26	33	45	6	3	0	15	0	1	0	20	0	10	1	2	2	.378	.379
Cleto, Ambioris, Pirates	.188	35	122	101	9	19	26	4	0	1	3	1	0	5	15	0	27	1	7	1	.257	.322
Cochran, Ed, White Sox	.116	28	75	69	12	8	9	1	0	0	5	1	0	1	4	1	14	2	0	3	.130	.176
Colina, Roberto, Devil Rays* .	.000	1	3	2	0	0	0	0	0	0	0	0	0	0	1	0	0	0	0	0	.000	.333
Collier, Marc, Orioles.............	.183	24	86	71	10	13	15	2	0	0	6	1	3	1	10	0	16	2	0	1	.211	.282
Colson, Julian, Astros	.100	7	11	10	1	1	2	1	0	0	0	0	0	0	1	0	4	0	0	1	.200	.182
Conway, Scott, Marlins*	.000	2	6	4	0	0	0	0	0	0	1	0	1	0	1	0	1	0	0	1	.000	.167
Cook, Josh, Astros	.222	4	11	9	0	2	3	1	0	0	1	0	1	0	1	0	3	0	0	0	.333	.273
Cordero, Ellery, White Sox	.259	29	89	81	12	21	31	5	1	1	6	0	0	3	5	1	18	2	1	1	.383	.326
Cordero, Willy, Rangers	.227	26	76	66	6	15	17	2	0	0	8	1	1	0	8	0	12	7	2	1	.258	.307
Cota, Humberto, Devil Rays ...	.241	44	157	133	14	32	46	6	1	2	20	1	3	3	17	0	27	3	1	1	.346	.333
Crespo, Jesse, Braves	.327	16	56	52	5	17	22	2	0	1	8	0	1	0	3	0	5	2	0	1	.423	.357
Cruz, Alain, Yankees...............	.000	1	1	1	0	0	0	0	0	0	0	0	0	0	0	0	1	0	0	0	.000	.000
Cruz, Andres, Devil Rays.........	.277	28	89	83	7	23	29	4	1	0	6	0	0	0	6	0	16	3	2	5	.349	.326
Cruz, Geronimo, Rangers†.....	.243	27	81	70	6	17	24	3	2	0	6	0	1	0	10	0	23	4	2	1	.343	.333
Cruz, Luis, Devil Rays	.362	34	134	116	25	42	66	8	2	4	20	0	2	0	16	0	26	17	4	3	.569	.433
Dasher, Melvin, Royals...........	.201	49	170	154	20	31	42	8	0	1	10	0	2	3	11	0	47	3	1	2	.273	.265
Davila, Angel, Mets	.231	5	19	13	4	3	5	0	1	0	1	0	1	0	5	0	1	0	0	1	.385	.421
Davis, Jerry, Pirates	.255	45	184	165	19	42	59	10	2	1	18	0	3	2	14	2	44	0	0	4	.358	.315
DeArmas, Fran, White Sox	.224	17	54	49	5	11	16	3	1	0	2	1	0	0	4	0	12	0	0	2	.327	.283
DeJesus, Wilmer, Expos	.294	13	39	34	5	10	11	1	0	0	5	1	0	0	4	0	6	0	1	2	.324	.368
De La Cruz, Raul, Pirates	.239	28	97	92	6	22	30	0	1	2	11	0	1	1	3	1	25	5	0	4	.326	.268
De La Cruz, Ruddi, Mets	.171	38	141	129	16	22	27	3	1	0	6	0	0	4	8	0	25	3	2	0	.209	.241
De La Espada, Miguel, Astros	.204	49	177	162	20	33	49	7	0	3	14	0	1	5	9	0	45	8	2	1	.302	.266
Delgado, Christopher, W. Sox	.275	51	198	189	24	52	66	12	1	0	19	0	1	1	7	0	40	0	1	4	.349	.303
Dellaero, Jason, White Sox†..	.200	5	17	15	1	3	5	2	0	0	1	0	1	0	1	0	2	0	0	1	.333	.235
Deshazer, Jeremy, Astros†.....	.250	46	176	164	23	41	59	11	2	1	18	1	0	0	11	1	23	3	4	1	.360	.297
Devarez, Cesar, Devil Rays.....	.000	4	10	6	0	0	0	0	0	0	0	0	0	0	4	0	2	0	0	0	.000	.400
Diaz, Christian, Royals	.200	9	18	15	3	3	4	1	0	0	2	0	0	2	1	0	3	0	0	0	.267	.333
Diaz, Diogenes, Pirates	.288	34	126	111	19	32	51	7	0	4	20	2	2	2	9	0	30	0	0	3	.459	.347
Diaz, Maikell, Orioles.............	.255	46	161	137	19	35	47	5	2	1	15	3	1	0	20	0	30	18	2	1	.343	.348
Dodson, Bo, Red Sox*	.417	12	41	36	6	15	23	5	0	1	9	0	1	0	4	0	5	0	0	1	.639	.463
Durham, Chad, White Sox.......	.328	49	208	189	24	62	76	5	3	1	17	3	1	3	12	1	17	22	3	4	.402	.376
Durick, Chad, Mets	.318	25	93	88	13	28	49	10	1	3	24	0	2	1	2	0	15	3	1	2	.557	.333
Edge, Michael, Mets	.139	50	174	144	17	20	21	1	0	0	4	1	1	0	28	0	42	20	1	1	.146	.277
Edwards, Randy, Pirates	.455	4	17	11	3	5	8	3	0	0	1	0	0	1	5	0	4	0	0	0	.727	.647
Escalante, Jaime, Orioles†	.273	50	165	143	12	39	50	9	1	0	17	2	1	1	18	2	34	0	1	4	.350	.356
Escalona, Felix, Astros	.206	51	216	189	27	39	51	9	0	1	9	4	0	3	20	0	49	11	3	1	.270	.292
Escobar, Alex, Mets	.247	26	85	73	12	18	27	4	1	1	11	0	1	1	10	0	17	0	0	1	.370	.341
Ewan, Benjamin, Braves	.307	36	141	127	9	39	53	3	1	3	15	0	1	1	12	0	33	2	2	4	.417	.369
Fafard, Mathias, Mets	.159	23	83	69	11	11	18	3	2	0	2	0	0	3	11	0	17	1	0	2	.261	.301
Fatheree, Danny, Astros	.237	21	43	38	4	9	10	1	0	0	3	1	1	0	3	0	0	0	1	0	.263	.286
Feliz, Joselyn, Marlins............	.294	34	108	102	9	30	34	4	0	0	9	0	0	0	6	0	17	0	1	0	.333	.333
Ferguson, Dwight, Red Sox* .	.253	33	106	95	13	24	31	5	1	0	9	1	0	5	5	0	33	8	1	1	.326	.324
Fernandez, Winston, Rangers*	.310	18	65	58	10	18	25	5	1	0	2	0	0	0	7	0	14	7	2	0	.431	.385
Fisher, Anthony, Rangers	.314	22	86	70	11	22	32	5	1	1	12	1	0	0	15	0	17	4	1	2	.457	.435
Flora, Kevin, Astros	.200	3	10	10	1	2	2	0	0	0	0	0	0	0	0	0	1	0	0	0	.200	.200
Flores, Jose, Red Sox†	.289	29	108	90	18	26	39	4	3	1	8	2	2	1	13	0	20	9	6	1	.433	.377
Forbes, Kevin, Expos..............	.234	22	87	77	8	18	30	3	3	1	10	0	0	2	8	0	26	1	2	1	.390	.322
Franklin, Toby, Twins*............	.091	3	11	11	1	1	1	0	0	0	0	0	0	0	0	0	6	0	0	0	.091	.091
Frawley, Scott, Braves............	.104	26	89	77	6	8	8	1	0	0	2	0	0	1	11	0	30	0	0	2	.104	.225
Freeman, Terrance, Pirates†.....	.455	3	13	11	1	5	5	0	0	0	4	0	0	0	2	0	1	1	1	0	.455	.538
Fuentes, Omar, Yankees	.211	32	109	90	8	19	24	5	0	0	11	0	3	5	11	0	16	0	1	4	.267	.321
Furcal, Rafael, Braves†...........	.258	50	212	190	31	49	65	5	4	1	9	0	0	2	20	0	21	15	2	1	.342	.335
Garcia, Douglas, Rangers*.....	.261	35	122	119	11	31	37	6	0	0	12	1	0	0	2	0	21	4	3	2	.311	.273
Garcia, Rafael, Royals	.252	37	131	115	19	29	30	1	0	0	10	2	3	0	11	0	33	9	4	1	.261	.310
Garza, Rolando, White Sox	.248	36	117	109	2	27	34	5	1	0	10	0	0	1	7	0	22	2	1	2	.312	.299
Gomez, Erick, Royals*	.320	50	187	169	18	54	79	16	0	3	29	0	2	0	16	0	36	0	0	6	.467	.374
Graham, Tarik, Royals............	.143	28	69	42	10	6	8	0	1	0	4	3	0	4	20	0	25	1	2	0	.190	.455
Gray, Travis, Red Sox*	.261	8	28	23	0	6	8	2	0	0	4	0	0	0	5	0	4	0	0	0	.348	.393
Guerrero, Francisco, D. Rays .	.210	34	110	100	10	21	27	4	1	0	6	2	2	1	5	0	24	5	2	3	.270	.250
Guerrero, Jason, Devil Rays ..	.111	28	84	72	3	8	9	1	0	0	3	0	0	1	11	0	22	2	0	4	.125	.238
Gunner, Chie, Devil Rays*	.285	46	167	144	18	41	56	3	3	2	23	0	0	1	22	0	34	3	2	3	.389	.383
Gutierrez, Victor, Pirates	.237	43	181	156	28	37	43	1	1	1	12	1	2	2	20	0	27	10	3	2	.276	.328
Guzman, Juan, Orioles...........	.149	15	48	47	1	7	8	1	0	0	4	0	0	0	1	0	18	0	0	1	.170	.167
Guzman, Martin, Devil Rays...	.263	18	49	38	10	10	16	1	1	1	6	0	0	0	11	0	7	3	1	1	.421	.429
Hafner, Travis, Rangers*	.286	55	216	189	38	54	83	14	0	5	24	0	0	3	24	1	45	7	2	3	.439	.375
Hahn, Cameron, Astros	.194	31	80	72	8	14	19	2	0	1	7	0	0	1	7	0	22	1	1	1	.264	.275
Harper, Brandon, Marlins	.000	2	6	6	0	0	0	0	0	0	0	0	0	0	0	0	1	0	0	1	.000	.000
Harris, Kevin, Rangers	.163	32	103	98	10	16	19	1	1	0	8	0	1	1	3	0	31	11	2	1	.194	.194
Harrison, Jamal, Twins...........	.246	39	144	126	12	31	39	6	1	0	17	0	0	3	15	0	22	5	3	4	.310	.340
Hasbun, Andy, Tigers	.231	21	68	52	7	12	14	2	0	0	5	1	1	6	8	0	9	2	0	2	.269	.388

Player, Team	Avg.	G	TPA	AB	R	H	TB	2B	3B	HR	RBI	SH	SF	HP	BB	IBB	SO	SB	CS	GDP	Slg.	OBP
Haselman, Bill, Red Sox	.125	4	16	16	2	2	2	0	0	0	1	0	0	0	0	0	1	1	0	0	.125	.125
Hazelton, Justin, Tigers	.257	35	132	105	21	27	40	3	2	2	17	0	1	1	25	0	36	3	1	1	.381	.402
Heffernan, Christian, Braves*	.174	36	128	121	7	21	24	1	1	0	9	0	0	1	6	0	52	3	3	1	.198	.219
Hernandez, Rafeal, Expos	.378	29	93	82	17	31	50	10	0	3	20	2	0	0	9	0	12	0	2	0	.610	.440
Herrera, Pedro, Royals	.297	36	115	101	15	30	32	2	0	0	7	6	1	0	7	0	22	2	1	1	.317	.339
Hill, Bobby, Mets*	.292	41	170	144	27	42	64	9	2	3	24	1	1	7	17	0	37	3	5	2	.444	.391
Hill, Jason, Astros	.208	8	30	24	7	5	5	0	0	0	5	0	0	1	5	0	5	3	0	1	.208	.367
Hill, Michael, White Sox	.142	46	161	134	16	19	27	3	1	1	15	2	2	2	21	0	47	5	2	2	.201	.264
Hodges, Scott, Expos*	.235	57	225	196	26	46	69	13	2	2	23	1	3	2	23	1	47	2	2	2	.352	.317
Holifield, Rick, Pirates*	.333	4	17	15	2	5	9	1	0	1	3	0	0	0	2	0	3	1	0	1	.600	.412
Hooper, Daren, Orioles	.323	19	72	62	7	20	30	5	1	1	5	0	0	1	9	0	20	1	1	1	.484	.417
Hoshina, Koji, Expos†	.322	19	64	59	8	19	19	0	0	0	5	1	0	0	4	0	7	1	0	0	.322	.365
Hyde, Brandon, White Sox	.195	28	92	77	10	15	22	4	0	1	14	1	1	2	11	0	24	0	0	2	.286	.308
Ide, Antoine, Orioles	.207	33	108	92	13	19	19	0	0	0	6	1	3	4	8	0	21	12	4	1	.207	.290
Iglesias, Rigoberto, White Sox†	.220	48	183	159	20	35	57	8	4	2	20	1	4	0	19	0	24	2	2	2	.358	.297
Infante, Danny, Rangers	.304	41	156	148	18	45	58	7	0	2	24	1	2	0	5	0	34	7	2	4	.392	.323
Jackson, Quantaa, Marlins	.230	41	137	126	17	29	43	8	0	2	13	0	0	3	8	0	52	6	1	3	.341	.292
Jenkins, Brian, Mets	.349	36	114	109	17	38	49	6	1	1	15	0	1	0	4	0	16	1	1	3	.450	.368
Jones, Andrew, Pirates	.220	29	104	91	9	20	21	1	0	0	6	1	0	1	11	0	21	3	4	2	.231	.311
Jordan, Yustin, Pirates	.269	30	109	93	15	25	31	6	0	0	7	1	0	1	14	0	24	3	1	1	.333	.370
Kaplan, Brett, Pirates	.053	19	61	57	5	3	4	1	0	0	4	0	1	0	3	0	20	0	0	2	.070	.098
Kelly, Kenneth, Devil Rays	.212	27	112	99	21	21	31	2	1	2	7	0	0	2	11	0	24	6	3	1	.313	.304
Kingsale, Eugene, Orioles†	.294	6	20	17	2	5	5	0	0	0	1	0	0	1	2	0	2	1	0	0	.294	.400
Kirkpatrick, Michael, Orioles*	.252	38	132	115	18	29	44	6	3	1	12	1	2	5	9	0	22	7	0	1	.383	.328
LaForest, Pierre Luc, D. Rays*	.262	34	119	107	21	28	48	7	2	3	21	0	1	1	10	0	18	4	3	1	.449	.328
Lambert, Clark, Mets	.228	35	127	114	12	26	31	5	0	0	11	0	0	1	12	0	18	0	0	2	.272	.307
Lara, Balmes, Tigers	.238	43	175	151	26	36	64	4	3	6	29	0	2	2	20	0	51	0	3	1	.424	.331
Lawler, Scott, Astros	.500	1	5	4	2	2	3	1	0	0	2	0	0	0	1	0	0	0	0	0	.750	.600
Lebron, Hector, Devil Rays*	.255	40	114	98	7	25	29	4	0	0	19	1	1	1	13	0	16	2	1	5	.296	.345
Ledee, Ricky, Yankees*	.333	7	24	21	3	7	8	1	0	0	2	0	0	1	2	1	4	0	0	1	.381	.417
Lehr, Ryan, Braves	.300	54	218	207	30	62	93	15	2	4	34	0	2	0	9	0	32	1	0	6	.449	.326
Leidens, Enrique, Expos	.317	19	44	41	6	13	18	5	0	0	3	0	0	0	3	0	9	2	2	0	.439	.364
Leon, Carlos, Red Sox†	.246	44	144	126	18	31	42	5	3	0	15	3	0	1	14	0	25	10	3	4	.333	.326
Linares, Rodney, Tigers	.228	25	67	57	5	13	15	0	1	0	10	1	3	0	6	0	23	0	2	1	.263	.288
Little, Josh, Devil Rays*	.206	28	74	63	8	13	15	0	1	0	4	3	0	2	6	0	22	1	2	4	.238	.296
Mann, Derek, Devil Rays*	.286	50	204	168	34	48	55	2	1	1	17	2	0	5	29	0	24	8	11	3	.327	.406
Marino, Lawrence, Red Sox	.283	47	164	145	15	41	51	7	0	1	19	0	2	2	15	0	19	0	0	4	.352	.354
Martinez, Andres, Mets	.240	31	108	96	18	23	39	8	4	0	7	2	1	0	9	0	33	1	1	0	.406	.302
Martinez, Gabby, Yankees	.400	2	6	5	3	2	2	0	0	0	1	2	0	0	1	0	0	2	0	0	1.000	.500
Mateo, Victor, Yankees†	.269	26	101	93	18	25	28	3	0	0	10	0	1	1	6	0	14	4	0	1	.301	.317
McCorvey, Kenneth, Twins	.291	42	143	134	19	39	56	6	1	3	11	1	0	2	5	0	24	10	6	3	.418	.326
McDonald, Ryan, Royals*	.281	26	69	57	9	16	22	1	1	1	9	0	0	2	10	0	8	1	0	1	.386	.406
McKinley, Michael, Red Sox	.268	22	62	56	5	15	18	3	0	0	6	2	0	1	3	0	8	1	1	2	.321	.317
McKinney, Antonio, Tigers	.246	18	76	65	16	16	28	3	0	3	12	1	0	0	10	0	13	5	2	0	.431	.347
McLaughlin, Eric, Braves	.286	10	30	21	5	6	13	1	0	2	6	0	1	2	6	0	6	0	0	0	.619	.467
McNeal, Aaron, Astros	.293	46	177	164	22	48	69	12	0	3	26	0	2	0	11	0	28	0	5	4	.421	.333
Meadows, Mike, Mets	.291	43	153	134	28	39	64	12	2	3	22	0	1	2	16	0	35	0	0	2	.478	.373
Medrano, Jesus, Marlins	.279	40	134	111	20	31	35	4	0	0	16	1	1	2	19	0	18	16	3	0	.315	.391
Medrano, Ricardo, White Sox†	.231	29	101	91	10	21	27	4	1	0	8	0	0	2	8	1	21	2	1	3	.297	.307
Meier, Bob, Yankees	.400	5	6	5	1	2	2	0	0	0	0	0	0	0	1	0	2	0	0	1	.400	.500
Mejia, Renato, Marlins	.229	35	127	109	15	25	37	9	0	1	8	0	0	4	14	2	27	2	1	2	.339	.339
Mejias, Oliver, Pirates†	.293	44	168	157	20	46	60	12	1	0	9	2	2	0	7	0	26	8	7	2	.382	.319
Melian, Jackson, Yankees	.263	57	237	213	32	56	80	11	2	3	36	0	2	0	20	0	52	9	1	8	.376	.323
Mendez, Donaldo, Astros	.193	48	171	150	16	29	36	4	0	1	13	3	3	2	13	0	32	9	6	2	.240	.262
Mendoza, Angel, Red Sox	.271	49	180	170	18	46	60	6	4	0	17	0	0	1	9	0	36	13	1	4	.353	.311
Meyer, Brad, Twins*	.256	16	47	39	6	10	13	1	1	0	4	1	0	1	6	1	5	0	0	0	.333	.370
Milton, Prinz, Braves	.253	26	95	83	12	21	29	5	0	1	8	0	1	4	7	0	29	1	1	3	.349	.337
Monds, Wonderful, Braves	.250	2	5	4	2	1	4	0	0	1	1	0	0	0	1	0	1	0	0	0	1.000	.400
Montero, Jose, Rangers	.393	15	41	28	5	11	16	0	1	1	6	0	1	2	9	0	5	2	0	2	.571	.550
Mora, Juan, Tigers*	.348	43	175	155	26	54	85	9	5	4	31	0	2	0	18	0	43	9	2	3	.548	.411
Morales, Domingo, Orioles	.255	33	111	98	8	25	29	4	0	0	9	1	3	9	0	0	11	5	2	5	.296	.333
Morales, Stephen, Marlins†	.210	20	71	62	7	13	20	1	0	2	13	0	2	1	6	0	10	1	1	3	.323	.282
Morgan, Todd, Orioles	.000	9	17	16	1	0	0	0	0	0	0	0	0	0	1	0	11	0	0	0	.000	.059
Mounts, Alfonso, White Sox†	.241	41	170	145	18	35	55	5	0	5	22	2	3	5	15	0	54	9	4	4	.379	.327
Mulvehill, Brandon, Mets	.260	49	191	169	20	44	54	7	0	1	19	1	3	5	13	0	30	7	2	3	.320	.326
Myers, Tootie, Expos	.230	54	233	217	26	50	63	9	2	0	13	1	0	4	11	0	58	24	8	3	.290	.280
Myles, Dion, Devil Rays	.091	5	13	11	0	1	1	0	0	0	1	0	0	0	2	0	5	1	0	0	.091	.231
Nanita, Emmanuel, Twins	.258	22	68	62	4	16	18	2	0	0	2	1	0	0	5	0	14	2	0	1	.290	.313
Ndungidi, Ntema, Orioles†	.185	18	67	54	10	10	20	2	1	2	7	0	0	1	12	0	15	4	0	1	.370	.343
Nicley, Dru, Astros	.119	26	66	59	5	7	7	0	0	0	3	3	0	0	4	0	30	0	0	2	.119	.175
Nicolas, Jose, Pirates	.241	40	156	141	17	34	46	6	3	0	11	0	1	1	13	0	44	3	2	2	.326	.310
Nolasco, Regino, Orioles	.224	58	196	165	17	37	50	10	0	1	18	3	6	1	21	0	33	3	7	3	.303	.306
Nova, Geraldo, Red Sox†	.287	40	142	122	8	35	44	5	2	0	17	0	2	0	18	0	33	1	3	6	.361	.373
Nunez, Jose A., Royals	.207	52	200	174	22	36	61	8	4	3	22	2	1	2	21	1	53	2	0	5	.351	.298
Nunez, Jose M., Mets	.333	5	16	15	3	5	6	1	0	0	2	0	0	0	1	0	4	0	1	0	.400	.375
Nunez, Sergio, Royals	.286	5	15	14	4	4	6	0	1	0	1	0	0	1	0	0	2	2	0	1	.429	.333
Ochoa, Javier, Astros	.198	30	91	81	7	16	20	2	1	0	14	1	0	2	7	0	13	1	1	1	.247	.278
Olivares, Teuris, Yankees	.261	38	168	153	33	40	58	4	7	0	17	0	0	1	14	0	40	7	2	1	.379	.327
Oropeza, Asdrubal, Braves	.228	50	211	167	38	38	58	8	0	4	22	1	1	4	37	0	27	3	0	1	.347	.378
Ortiz, Miguel, Yankees	.228	36	132	123	19	28	39	6	1	1	12	2	2	0	5	0	31	4	2	0	.317	.254
Otanez, Willis, Orioles	.320	8	28	25	5	8	16	2	0	2	3	0	0	1	2	0	4	0	0	1	.640	.393
O'Toole, Bobby, Orioles	.286	6	22	21	1	6	9	0	0	1	3	0	0	0	1	0	5	0	0	0	.429	.318
Parker, Chris, Tigers	.161	31	103	87	6	14	15	1	0	0	7	0	2	4	10	0	33	0	1	3	.172	.272

Player, Team	Avg.	G	TPA	AB	R	H	TB	2B	3B	HR	RBI	SH	SF	HP	BB	IBB	SO	SB	CS	GDP	Slg.	OBP
Pascual, Edison, Pirates*	.429	5	21	21	1	9	11	2	0	0	1	0	0	0	0	0	3	1	0	1	.524	.429
Pass, Patrick, Marlins	.222	19	57	45	7	10	14	1	0	1	8	0	2	0	10	0	16	3	1	0	.311	.351
Paul, Josh, White Sox	.429	5	16	14	3	6	8	0	0	0	0	1	0	0	1	0	3	1	0	1	.571	.467
Pena, Jose, Devil Rays	.126	36	104	87	12	11	19	3	1	1	3	0	0	5	12	0	41	0	0	1	.218	.269
Pena, Rodolfo, Red Sox	.306	44	137	124	7	38	45	5	1	0	12	0	0	3	10	0	21	1	2	2	.363	.372
Pender, Darrell, Tigers	.178	37	112	101	16	18	20	2	0	0	4	2	0	0	9	0	38	11	0	2	.198	.245
Peniche, Fray, Tigers	.264	35	122	106	19	28	32	4	0	0	9	1	1	0	14	0	16	7	3	2	.302	.347
Perez, Alejandro, Red Sox	.272	48	162	151	19	41	68	12	3	3	10	1	1	1	8	0	33	1	2	2	.450	.311
Perez, Jesse, Orioles†	.227	35	121	110	12	25	28	1	1	0	7	1	0	3	7	0	39	1	4	2	.255	.292
Persails, Michael, Red Sox	.190	10	27	21	3	4	7	0	0	1	4	0	1	1	4	0	5	1	0	0	.333	.333
Petru, Rich, Royals	.000	1	2	1	0	0	0	0	0	0	0	1	0	1	0	0	0	0	0	0	.000	.000
Pimentel, Eddie, Marlins†	.256	44	148	133	23	34	45	7	2	0	17	4	0	1	10	0	39	8	3	2	.338	.313
Pittman, Thomas, Expos	.152	15	53	46	7	7	9	2	0	0	2	0	0	1	6	0	9	0	0	1	.196	.264
Preciado, Victor, Yankees†	.251	54	208	187	21	47	75	9	5	3	29	0	2	4	15	1	37	6	1	2	.401	.317
Proctor, Mark, Mets	.267	16	49	45	7	12	15	3	0	0	3	0	0	1	3	0	14	1	1	0	.333	.327
Prosper, Gerard, Mets*	.283	39	153	120	26	34	48	8	3	0	13	1	0	2	30	0	22	7	5	3	.400	.434
Perini, Mike, Red Sox*	.220	39	134	118	12	26	32	4	1	0	9	2	0	0	14	0	33	2	0	1	.271	.303
Quero, Pedro, Expos	.311	56	209	190	28	59	84	14	4	1	21	3	3	1	12	0	31	6	0	6	.442	.350
Raines, Tim, Yankees†	.250	1	5	4	0	1	1	0	0	0	2	0	0	0	1	0	1	0	0	0	.250	.400
Rains, Nick, Mets	.220	30	108	100	11	22	28	4	1	0	8	1	0	0	7	0	39	4	1	3	.280	.271
Ramirez, Edgar, Devil Rays	.227	42	154	128	15	29	39	8	1	0	8	1	0	3	22	0	31	2	2	6	.305	.353
Ramirez, Juan, Royals	.203	46	142	133	11	27	38	5	0	2	14	2	1	0	6	0	18	0	1	11	.286	.236
Ramirez, Luis, Orioles	.237	45	172	156	24	37	55	5	5	1	24	1	0	3	12	1	49	5	2	4	.353	.304
Ramon, Ricardo, White Sox*	.265	38	143	132	10	35	37	2	0	0	5	1	0	0	10	0	16	4	5	1	.280	.317
Reding, Josh, Expos	.255	56	226	196	34	50	69	11	1	2	19	2	2	4	22	0	31	14	3	3	.352	.339
Redmond, Mike, Marlins	.345	16	67	55	7	19	22	3	0	0	5	0	0	3	9	0	5	2	0	1	.400	.463
Reed, Brian, Marlins	.199	48	203	166	22	33	40	3	2	0	10	3	1	6	27	0	48	16	5	3	.241	.330
Reese, Nate, Marlins	.241	11	33	29	3	7	8	1	0	0	3	0	0	1	3	0	9	0	1	1	.276	.333
Reyes, Deurys, Tigers*	.257	38	142	113	24	29	42	8	1	1	14	0	2	2	25	1	32	7	1	1	.372	.394
Reyes, Jose, Pirates	.344	12	35	32	4	11	15	2	1	0	4	1	1	0	1	0	5	1	0	1	.469	.353
Reynoso, Ismael, Marlins	.284	48	189	162	19	46	63	11	0	2	19	2	1	1	23	0	30	8	2	1	.389	.374
Rivera, Luis, Expos	.206	50	182	165	15	34	43	7	1	0	7	1	0	3	13	0	34	0	0	3	.261	.276
Rivera, Michael, Tigers	.286	47	177	154	34	44	87	9	2	10	36	0	2	3	18	2	25	0	0	2	.565	.367
Rockow, Jeremy, Pirates*	.233	23	82	73	7	17	31	5	0	3	15	0	0	2	7	0	18	0	2	1	.425	.317
Rodriguez, John, Yankees*	.299	46	190	157	31	47	70	10	2	3	23	0	3	0	30	1	32	7	0	3	.446	.405
Rojas, Mo, Red Sox	.286	39	122	112	16	32	45	7	3	0	6	0	1	2	7	0	16	1	1	1	.402	.336
Roman, John, White Sox†	.250	38	147	132	18	33	34	1	0	0	10	5	1	3	6	0	23	8	4	3	.258	.296
Romano, Jason, Rangers	.257	34	127	109	27	28	45	5	3	2	11	1	3	1	13	0	19	13	4	1	.413	.349
Roneberg, Brett, Marlins*	.265	53	215	185	25	49	64	11	2	0	13	1	1	0	28	1	35	6	5	7	.346	.360
Ruiz, Willy, Royals	.360	54	216	197	33	71	75	4	0	0	14	4	0	6	9	0	19	20	11	6	.381	.406
Runnells, T.J., Tigers	.226	48	184	159	19	36	43	5	1	0	23	2	3	3	17	0	28	7	1	3	.270	.308
Saenz, Olmedo, White Sox...	1.000	2	2	1	0	1	2	1	0	0	0	0	0	1	0	0	0	0	0	0	2.000	1.000
St. Pierre, Maxim, Tigers	.244	20	47	41	3	10	11	1	0	0	3	0	0	3	3	0	8	2	0	3	.268	.340
Samboy, Nelson, Astros	.400	2	6	5	1	2	2	0	0	0	1	0	0	0	1	0	0	0	0	0	.400	.500
Santo, Jose, Rangers	.269	28	115	93	17	25	35	5	1	1	10	0	0	1	21	0	30	12	1	3	.376	.409
Santos, Ramon, Red Sox†	.183	17	70	60	8	11	12	1	0	0	7	1	2	0	7	0	11	8	3	0	.200	.261
Sassanella, Jeremy, Tigers†	.221	32	120	113	12	25	32	4	0	1	17	0	1	1	5	0	24	3	0	0	.283	.258
Schaffer, Jake, Tigers	.333	6	26	21	5	7	10	1	1	0	4	0	0	0	5	0	2	0	0	0	.476	.462
Sevillano, Jose, Pirates†	.000	1	1	1	0	0	0	0	0	0	0	0	0	0	0	0	0	0	0	1	.000	.000
Shuck, Jason, Mets	.274	25	90	73	10	20	28	6	1	0	8	2	1	2	12	0	13	2	1	1	.384	.386
Smith, Marcus, Twins*	.071	6	17	14	0	1	1	0	0	0	1	0	0	0	3	0	8	1	0	0	.071	.235
Southward, Deshawn, Twins..	.260	57	185	154	24	40	42	2	0	0	6	2	0	0	29	1	43	14	4	3	.273	.377
Stevens, Tony, Twins†	.241	47	184	170	23	41	47	3	0	1	17	1	2	2	9	0	21	9	2	8	.276	.284
Strangfeld, Aaron, Braves†	.237	11	42	38	4	9	13	1	0	1	4	0	0	0	4	0	10	0	0	0	.342	.310
Sutton, Bruce, Twins	.240	35	116	96	13	23	28	5	0	0	4	1	1	5	13	0	31	1	2	0	.292	.357
Swafford, Derek, Pirates*	.200	1	5	5	1	1	4	0	0	1	1	0	0	0	0	0	0	0	0	0	.800	.200
Tancred, Lachlan, Expos	.231	22	63	52	4	12	15	3	0	0	4	0	0	1	10	0	8	1	4	0	.288	.365
Taveras, Jose, Rangers	.327	57	237	205	46	67	110	14	4	7	39	4	1	3	24	1	42	14	4	1	.537	.403
Taveras, Luis, Rangers	.241	37	93	83	10	20	26	3	0	1	10	0	1	0	9	1	21	1	0	2	.313	.312
Terni, Chas, Red Sox	.184	27	86	76	12	14	17	3	0	0	4	2	0	1	7	0	23	2	0	3	.224	.262
Thames, Marcus, Yankees	.344	57	219	195	51	67	113	17	4	7	36	1	4	3	16	0	26	6	4	3	.579	.394
Tillis, Cameron, Royals†	.225	34	116	102	14	23	32	2	2	1	12	1	0	1	12	0	28	4	1	2	.314	.313
Tolbert, William, Pirates*	.245	31	108	94	10	23	26	3	0	0	7	1	0	1	12	1	23	1	1	2	.277	.333
Tomberlin, Andy, Mets*	.318	7	25	22	6	7	13	0	0	2	7	0	0	0	3	0	7	1	0	1	.591	.400
Torres, Franklin, Twins	.258	48	179	155	18	40	52	7	1	1	18	2	3	2	17	0	31	7	3	1	.335	.333
Torres, Gabriel, Twins	.257	45	182	152	17	39	46	5	1	0	16	3	2	6	19	0	21	18	3	7	.303	.358
Torres, Jason, Rangers*	.220	31	93	82	13	18	29	5	3	0	17	1	1	1	8	0	10	1	2	1	.354	.293
Torres, Rafael, Royals	.306	44	176	160	20	49	60	2	0	3	33	0	3	6	7	1	16	2	1	5	.375	.352
Valdez, Angel, Yankees	.260	41	119	100	19	26	34	1	2	1	10	0	1	5	13	0	21	6	0	1	.340	.370
Valentine, Anthony, Mets	.326	30	110	92	19	30	39	7	1	0	14	0	2	1	15	0	12	3	0	1	.424	.418
Valerio, Denny, Twins	.182	28	49	44	8	8	10	2	0	0	1	1	0	0	4	0	13	6	1	2	.227	.250
Vasquez, Alejandro, Astros* ..	.269	53	211	186	30	50	67	9	1	2	20	0	2	5	18	2	23	8	3	5	.360	.346
Vazquez, Alex, Rangers	.100	4	14	10	2	1	2	1	0	0	0	0	0	1	3	0	6	1	0	0	.200	.357
Vazquez, Carlos, Devil Rays	.257	46	161	152	22	39	54	12	0	1	17	0	0	0	9	0	28	2	0	1	.355	.298
Velazquez, Juan, Braves†	.219	30	115	96	14	21	24	3	0	0	8	0	1	0	18	0	26	2	2	1	.250	.342
Viera, Rob, Pirates	.200	10	21	20	2	4	7	3	0	0	1	0	0	0	1	0	5	0	1	0	.350	.238
Vilorio, Leonel, Twins	.195	50	178	169	8	33	39	6	0	0	6	1	0	2	6	0	31	3	4	4	.231	.230
Wade, Chip, Twins	.167	33	119	102	8	17	22	2	0	1	14	1	2	1	13	0	26	1	1	2	.216	.263
Walker, Javon, Marlins	.106	16	55	47	7	5	5	0	0	0	3	0	0	0	8	0	21	0	0	0	.106	.236
Ward, Gregory, Braves	.215	48	181	163	20	35	42	7	0	0	10	0	2	0	16	0	46	0	0	1	.258	.282
Warriax, Brandon, Rangers	.217	47	186	166	21	36	45	5	2	0	14	4	2	1	13	0	47	6	3	6	.271	.275
Washington, Cory, Marlins	.224	27	88	76	14	17	27	3	2	1	10	0	2	6	36	0	19	3	1	0	.355	.330
Washington, Dion, Yankees ...	.303	52	210	165	35	50	71	10	1	3	33	0	2	6	36	0	39	2	0	1	.430	.440

Player, Team	Avg.	G	TPA	AB	R	H	TB	2B	3B	HR	RBI	SH	SF	HP	BB	IBB	SO	SB	CS	GDP	Slg.	OBP
Washington, Enrico, Pirates* .	.245	28	107	98	12	24	33	6	0	1	11	0	1	4	4	1	13	1	0	2	.337	.299
Washington, Kelly, Marlins.....	.107	35	120	103	8	11	13	0	1	0	6	3	1	3	10	0	32	2	1	3	.126	.205
Washington, Maurice, Pirates	.202	31	106	94	8	19	23	2	1	0	7	1	0	0	11	0	34	1	1	6	.245	.286
Werth, Jayson, Orioles..........	.295	32	111	88	16	26	35	6	0	1	8	0	1	0	22	0	22	7	1	0	.398	.432
Wheeler, Mike, Astros	.208	41	141	130	13	27	36	4	1	1	6	1	0	1	8	0	41	5	3	3	.277	.259
Wilson, Heath, Braves............	.193	21	71	57	7	11	13	2	0	0	5	0	0	1	13	0	22	0	1	0	.228	.352
Woods, James, Royals†	.000	2	7	5	0	0	0	0	0	0	0	0	0	1	1	0	5	0	0	0	.000	.286
Wright, Corey, Rangers*	.248	43	171	145	19	36	44	2	3	0	11	3	0	1	22	0	25	14	11	1	.303	.351
Yancy, Michael, Mets	.252	38	150	131	22	33	47	3	4	1	20	0	3	4	12	0	26	5	2	1	.359	.327
Zapata, Wilson, Red Sox	.110	47	124	109	16	12	19	2	1	1	8	2	1	0	12	0	45	3	1	1	.174	.197
Ziths, Deshawn, Orioles	.152	17	36	33	7	5	5	0	0	0	3	0	0	0	3	0	16	1	0	0	.152	.222

GRAND SLAMS: Mounts, 2; Byrd, Bystrowski, Durick, J. Ramirez, J. Taveras, Tomberlin, R. Torres, 1 each.

AWARDED FIRST BASE ON CATCHER'S INTERFERENCE: Melian 2 (Fatheree 2); McCorvey (J. Brito); Montero (Herrera); Nicolas (Herrera).

1997 PITCHING

TEAM

Team	W	L	Pct.	ERA	G	CG	ShO	Sv.	IP	H	TBF	R	ER	HR	SH	SF	HB	BB	IBB	SO	WP	Bk.
Mets	42	18	.700	2.50	60	1	8	21	479.1	406	2019	189	133	14	16	7	21	183	4	462	38	11
Red Sox	31	28	.525	2.57	59	5	5	12	484.0	437	2040	213	138	7	22	9	23	146	5	522	37	13
Rangers	34	26	.567	2.93	60	4	7	18	500.0	441	2077	215	163	19	11	14	13	171	6	429	23	21
Twins	28	32	.467	2.95	60	2	7	12	527.0	482	2203	225	173	7	8	17	32	168	8	450	52	11
Royals	36	24	.600	3.12	60	7	9	10	493.0	461	2094	225	171	11	13	13	36	170	1	385	45	8
Marlins	31	28	.525	3.35	59	6	5	9	473.1	428	2061	256	176	16	13	10	39	194	0	410	31	13
Yankees	40	20	.667	3.41	60	3	5	15	507.1	468	2164	266	192	27	13	14	21	191	3	405	65	12
Orioles	27	33	.450	3.41	60	2	5	15	496.1	489	2155	251	188	22	15	24	26	210	1	394	46	18
Expos	25	35	.417	3.50	59	0	4	13	478.2	462	2070	231	186	14	8	16	27	181	0	366	28	4
Devil Rays . . .	25	35	.417	3.63	60	0	4	9	491.1	436	2145	258	198	20	16	26	35	214	4	460	58	14
White Sox	26	34	.433	3.64	60	1	5	11	487.2	473	2144	261	197	17	19	18	23	217	0	412	32	12
Tigers	31	29	.517	3.70	60	2	5	10	495.2	474	2163	278	204	33	10	10	29	180	3	459	65	17
Pirates	27	32	.458	3.78	59	3	4	10	493.1	489	2165	273	207	17	23	23	37	189	2	403	46	16
Astros	24	36	.400	4.71	60	4	4	13	498.2	516	2290	348	261	20	11	20	33	272	0	438	70	26
Braves	21	38	.356	5.02	58	0	0	6	462.2	491	2148	342	258	19	6	18	13	263	0	430	46	7

INDIVIDUAL

TOP QUALIFIERS FOR EARNED-RUN AVERAGE TITLE

Minimum 48 innings.   *Lefthanded pitcher.

Pitcher, Team	W	L	Pct.	ERA	G	GS	CG	ShO	GF	Sv.	IP	H	TBF	R	ER	HR	SH	SF	HB	BB	IBB	SO	WP	Bk.
Roberts, Marquis, Devil Rays* .	6	1	.857	0.51	12	10	0	0	1	0	53.1	27	206	8	3	1	2	0	1	19	0	68	2	0
Rupp, Michael, Red Sox........	1	4	.200	1.22	11	9	3	0	0	0	59.0	51	246	23	8	0	2	0	3	17	1	56	4	0
Rodriguez, Cristobol, Expos....	3	3	.500	1.65	13	10	0	0	3	1	54.2	45	220	15	10	1	0	2	1	16	0	61	2	1
Dougherty, James, Mets*	6	1	.857	1.93	11	8	0	0	1	0	51.1	42	214	18	11	0	1	1	0	13	0	51	6	0
Sheets, Matt, Twins................	2	2	.500	2.38	15	5	0	0	5	2	53.0	49	215	17	14	1	1	2	4	10	1	24	2	0
Myers, Taylor, Royals............	5	4	.556	2.41	11	10	2	2	1	0	59.2	48	248	21	16	3	2	1	5	20	0	48	6	0
Blevins, Jeremy, Yankees.........	5	3	.625	2.43	11	11	0	0	0	0	55.2	50	235	27	15	1	0	4	23	1	46	4	0
Suggs, Willie, Mets	5	3	.625	2.49	10	8	1	0	1	0	54.1	34	200	21	14	1	1	1	4	22	0	32	5	0
Moore, Christopher, Marlins	3	2	.600	2.65	10	9	1	0	0	0	54.1	39	225	23	16	1	1	3	2	29	0	40	1	0
Ratliff, Craig, Orioles..............	2	5	.286	2.75	12	12	0	0	0	0	59.0	60	260	26	18	2	2	3	0	32	0	50	10	3
Casteel, Raymond, Orioles........	2	3	.400	2.77	15	9	0	0	2	1	65.0	63	287	31	20	2	1	1	7	30	1	37	9	0
Reith, Brian, Yankees.............	4	2	.667	2.86	12	11	1	0	0	0	63.0	70	270	28	20	1	2	2	3	14	0	40	8	0
Perez, Julio, Expos	3	2	.600	2.88	10	9	0	0	1	0	50.0	38	205	18	16	0	1	2	4	13	0	38	1	0
Forti, Eugene, White Sox*	4	1	.800	2.91	11	8	0	0	1	0	52.2	42	224	21	17	1	3	2	2	30	4	44	9	2
Padua, Geraldo, Yankees.........	8	0	1.000	2.92	11	8	1	1	1	0	61.2	46	237	24	20	5	2	0	1	8	0	36	5	1

DEPARTMENTAL LEADERS: W—Vanderhorst, Padua, W. Rodriguez, 8 each; L—Crabow, Mendoza, E. Perez, 7 each; Pct.—Padua, 1.000; G—Jacobs, Hamulack, 23 each; GS—Standridge, 13; CG—Rupp, 3; ShO—Hlodan, T. Myers, 2 each; GF—Jacobs, 20; Sv.—Jacobs, 10; IP—W. Rodriguez, 68.0; H—Balfour, 73; TBF—Colon, 289; R—Colon, 47; ER—Blackmore, 33; HR—Stowe, Padua, 5 each; SH—Mendoza, Parkerson, 5 each; SF—Harden, Jimenez, Standridge, 5 each; HB—Blackmore, 9; BB—E. Perez, 44; IBB—Fitts, Gaerte, Mundine, Tynan, 2 each; SO—M. Martinez, 78; WP—Blackmore, 17; BK—P. Blanco, Centeno, Knowles, Morales, 6 each.

ALL PITCHERS

*Lefthanded pitcher.

Pitcher, Team	W	L	Pct.	ERA	G	GS	CG	ShO	GF	Sv.	IP	H	TBF	R	ER	HR	SH	SF	HB	BB	IBB	SO	WP	Bk.
Acosta, Alberto, Yankees........	1	1	.500	3.28	9	3	0	0	2	0	24.2	24	105	14	9	1	0	0	0	10	0	11	3	0
Affeldt, Jeremy, Royals*	2	0	1.000	4.50	10	9	0	0	0	0	40.0	34	171	24	20	3	2	3	5	21	0	36	4	2
Akin, Aaron, Marlins	0	0	.000	2.31	4	4	0	0	0	0	11.2	13	52	5	3	0	0	0	2	3	0	5	1	0
Alfaro, Jason, Astros.............	1	0	1.000	1.50	4	0	0	0	0	0	6.0	5	28	2	1	0	0	1	1	3	0	6	1	0
Almonte, Hector, Marlins	2	0	1.000	0.76	8	0	0	0	7	3	23.2	12	89	3	2	0	0	1	2	6	0	25	1	0
Alvarado, David, Pirates	1	6	.143	3.80	12	6	0	0	0	0	47.1	51	213	32	20	4	2	3	3	23	0	34	3	0
Alvord, Aaron, Tigers	0	3	.000	4.30	9	5	0	0	0	0	29.1	36	141	28	14	4	1	0	0	13	0	24	4	0
Andujar, Jesse, Expos............	1	2	.333	7.99	17	0	0	0	6	2	23.2	27	134	25	21	1	0	0	6	30	0	18	4	0
Arias, Rafael, Red Sox	3	3	.500	3.96	11	5	2	0	5	1	45.0	46	216	26	22	1	4	2	0	7	1	37	1	1
Arnold, Jamie, Braves	1	0	1.000	2.84	5	5	0	0	0	0	19.0	13	74	6	6	1	0	0	0	6	0	21	0	0
Arthurs, Shane, Expos	0	3	.000	9.82	8	1	0	0	2	0	25.2	37	128	31	28	1	0	3	2	14	0	12	1	1
Avery, Steve, Red Sox*	0	0	.000	1.50	1	1	0	0	0	0	6.0	5	25	3	1	1	0	0	0	8	0	0	0	0
Baker, Jason, Expos	0	0	.000	0.00	2	2	0	0	0	0	7.0	4	28	0	0	0	1	0	3	0	0	0	0
Balfour, Grant, Twins.............	2	4	.333	3.76	13	12	0	0	0	0	67.0	73	275	31	28	1	0	1	4	20	0	43	3	2

Pitcher, Team	W	L	Pct.	ERA	G	GS	CG	ShO	GF	Sv.	IP	H	TBF	R	ER	HR	SH	SF	HB	BB	IBB	SO	WP	Bk.
Beatty, Blaine, Pirates*	1	0	1.000	1.52	4	3	1	0	1	0	23.2	23	96	8	4	0	0	0	1	2	0	14	2	0
Becker, Keith, Red Sox	0	1	.000	4.70	5	0	0	0	5	0	7.2	7	34	5	4	0	1	0	1	4	1	7	1	0
Benoit, Joaquin, Rangers	3	3	.500	2.05	10	10	1	0	0	0	44.0	40	177	14	10	0	1	0	1	11	0	38	1	0
Benzing, Skipp, Red Sox	0	3	.000	5.51	6	2	0	0	3	1	16.1	16	80	16	10	2	1	0	1	9	0	17	2	0
Bere, Jason, White Sox	0	0	.000	0.00	2	2	0	0	0	0	5.0	2	16	0	0	0	0	0	0	0	0	5	0	0
Betti, Rich, Red Sox*	1	0	1.000	1.00	4	0	0	0	3	0	9.0	4	31	1	1	0	0	0	1	0	0	14	0	0
Blackmore, John, Astros	4	2	.667	7.75	15	4	0	0	3	0	38.1	35	200	40	33	1	1	2	9	42	0	32	17	3
Blais, Mike, Red Sox	1	0	1.000	0.00	3	1	0	0	2	0	5.0	2	17	0	0	0	0	0	0	0	0	5	0	0
Blanco, Alberto, Astros*	0	0	.000	0.00	2	2	0	0	0	0	5.0	1	19	0	0	0	0	0	1	1	0	11	0	0
Blanco, Pablo, Marlins	2	5	.286	4.06	11	9	1	0	1	0	51.0	41	231	31	23	2	1	2	6	36	0	44	6	6
Blevins, Jeremy, Yankees	5	3	.625	2.43	11	9	0	0	0	0	55.2	50	235	27	15	1	0	4	23	1	46	4	0
Boehringer, Brian, Yankees	0	0	.000	0.00	1	1	0	0	0	0	2.0	1	7	0	0	0	0	0	0	2	0	2	0	0
Bogeajis, Daniel, Astros	1	1	.500	5.23	7	0	0	0	5	1	10.1	14	50	6	6	1	0	1	2	4	0	6	1	1
Bosio, Chris, Red Sox	0	0	.000	0.00	2	2	0	0	0	0	5.0	2	18	0	0	0	0	0	0	2	0	4	0	0
Bowers, Jason, Braves*	2	3	.400	9.10	12	0	0	0	10	0	29.2	40	152	32	30	3	0	1	0	28	0	21	6	1
Bravo, Franklin, Pirates	0	1	.000	8.00	4	4	0	0	0	0	9.0	16	45	10	8	1	0	0	1	5	0	5	1	1
Brazoban, Melvin, Rangers	1	3	.250	4.20	14	0	0	0	9	2	30.0	28	133	16	14	1	1	2	14	1	36	1	3
Bridges, Donald, Expos	0	2	.000	6.30	5	2	0	0	0	0	10.0	14	49	9	7	0	0	1	2	5	0	6	0	0
Brown, Michael, Pirates*	0	0	.000	4.15	2	0	0	0	0	0	4.1	3	18	2	2	1	0	1	0	3	0	6	0	0
Budsky, Pavel, Royals	2	1	.667	5.23	6	0	0	0	0	0	10.1	17	47	6	6	0	0	0	1	1	0	7	1	0
Burnett, Allan, Mets	0	1	.000	3.18	3	2	0	0	0	0	11.1	8	54	8	4	0	0	0	2	8	0	15	3	0
Cafaro, Robert, Devil Rays	0	0	.000	1.64	4	4	0	0	0	0	11.0	9	45	2	2	0	1	0	0	2	0	8	1	2
Cain, Travis, Devil Rays	1	2	.333	6.00	4	0	0	0	2	0	6.0	8	28	6	4	1	0	0	0	4	0	6	2	0
Calvert, Klae, Red Sox	6	0	1.000	2.31	12	4	0	0	5	1	46.2	52	191	16	12	1	0	1	1	7	0	37	4	0
Casteel, Raymond, Orioles	2	3	.400	2.77	15	9	0	0	2	1	65.0	63	287	31	20	2	1	1	7	30	1	37	9	0
Castillo, Jose, Tigers	4	5	.444	3.25	12	10	1	0	1	0	55.1	50	224	28	20	3	1	1	3	7	0	47	5	4
Ceasar, Donald, Braves	1	1	.500	7.11	10	0	0	0	7	2	19.0	27	102	24	15	1	1	0	8	0	12	3	0
Cederblad, Brett, Red Sox	0	0	.000	0.00	1	0	0	0	0	0	2.0	0	7	0	0	0	0	0	1	0	1	0	0	0
Celta, Nicolas, Astros*	0	1	.000	6.59	8	0	0	0	4	1	13.2	14	64	13	10	0	2	1	0	9	0	16	3	1
Centeno, Juan, Astros	1	5	.167	3.46	7	6	1	0	1	0	26.0	21	107	18	10	1	1	1	1	6	0	17	1	6
Chivers, Jason, Mets*	1	0	1.000	5.25	11	0	0	0	5	1	12.0	10	57	7	7	1	0	0	1	11	0	14	2	0
Colon, Roman, Braves	3	4	.429	4.29	14	12	0	0	1	0	63.0	68	289	47	30	2	4	3	2	28	0	44	3	0
Connolly, Sean, White Sox	2	1	.667	2.86	15	0	0	0	11	3	22.0	21	102	12	7	0	3	1	2	15	0	17	3	1
Converse, Jim, Yankees	0	0	.000	1.93	3	3	0	0	0	0	4.2	5	21	1	1	0	0	0	0	1	0	8	0	0
Conway, Scott, Marlins*	0	0	.000	0.00	1	0	0	0	1	0	0.2	0	2	0	0	0	0	0	0	0	0	0	0	0
Coppinger, Rocky, Orioles	0	0	.000	1.80	3	3	0	0	0	0	10.0	7	36	3	2	0	0	0	0	0	0	13	0	0
Corcoran, Tim, Mets	3	0	1.000	3.00	10	0	0	0	4	3	21.0	16	94	8	7	0	2	0	0	15	0	20	4	0
Coriolan, Roberto, Yankees	4	1	1.000	3.50	10	0	0	0	0	0	18.0	19	83	14	7	1	0	1	2	10	0	10	2	0
Corominas, Mike, Astros*	1	1	.500	4.58	8	2	0	0	1	0	19.2	31	94	16	10	1	0	1	1	4	0	8	2	3
Corsi, Jim, Red Sox	1	0	1.000	0.00	3	2	0	0	0	0	4.0	2	14	1	0	0	0	0	0	0	0	6	0	0
Cremer, Richard, Yankees*	4	2	.667	3.96	10	9	1	1	0	0	38.2	30	170	24	17	4	0	1	1	25	0	47	9	0
Crutchley, Rickey, Royals*	1	1	.500	2.41	11	1	0	0	3	0	18.2	14	84	6	5	0	0	0	1	14	0	19	1	0
Cruz, Charlie, Orioles	2	2	.500	9.41	15	0	0	0	10	1	22.0	36	112	23	23	4	0	1	1	14	0	7	2	0
Cubillan, Darwin, Yankees	0	0	.000	0.00	1	1	0	0	0	0	1.2	1	7	0	0	0	0	0	0	1	0	2	0	0
Curtice, John, Red Sox*	2	0	1.000	0.79	4	3	0	0	0	0	11.1	6	45	2	1	0	0	0	1	5	0	11	0	2
Curtis, Gregory, Orioles	1	2	.333	4.57	15	4	0	0	1	0	41.1	54	199	29	21	1	3	4	0	23	0	28	2	1
Daniels, Ronney, Expos*	0	0	.000	0.00	8	0	0	0	2	0	12.0	2	44	0	0	0	0	0	1	5	0	7	0	0
Davis, Casey, Devil Rays*	0	1	.000	4.88	13	2	0	0	5	0	24.0	13	112	15	13	0	0	3	5	24	0	26	8	1
Davis, Doug, Devil Rays*	3	1	.750	1.71	4	4	0	0	0	0	21.0	14	88	5	4	0	0	1	2	15	0	27	1	1
Deckard, Edward, Devil Rays	1	0	1.000	7.27	4	2	0	0	0	0	8.2	15	48	13	7	1	0	0	1	5	0	3	2	0
De La Cruz, Ynocencio, Mets	3	3	.500	1.15	6	5	0	0	1	0	39.0	31	154	12	5	0	0	0	3	4	0	42	0	0
DeLeon, Julio, Devil Rays	0	1	.000	2.89	9	0	0	0	5	0	18.2	18	77	7	6	1	1	2	2	5	1	10	2	0
Desrosiers, Erik, White Sox	0	1	.000	3.32	7	6	0	0	0	0	21.2	19	88	8	8	1	0	0	3	0	18	1	0
Diaz, Billy, Rangers	2	3	.400	5.02	9	9	1	0	0	0	43.0	49	182	28	24	4	0	1	0	7	0	31	2	2
Dinyar, Eric, Tigers	0	0	.000	19.64	7	0	0	0	0	0	3.2	4	30	9	8	0	0	2	6	9	0	1	2	0
Doan, Zachary, Marlins	0	0	.000	0.00	1	0	0	0	1	0	2.0	1	8	0	0	0	0	0	0	1	0	1	0	0
Dolby, Lawrence, Braves	1	5	.167	6.43	10	6	0	0	2	1	35.0	41	166	34	25	4	0	2	1	16	0	33	4	0
Dotel, Octavio, Mets	0	0	.000	0.96	3	2	0	0	1	1	9.1	9	39	1	1	0	0	0	1	2	0	7	0	2
Dougherty, James, Mets*	6	1	.857	1.93	11	8	0	0	1	0	51.1	42	214	18	11	0	1	1	0	13	0	51	6	0
Douglass, Ryan, Royals	5	1	.833	3.05	12	9	1	1	1	0	56.0	66	237	21	19	0	0	0	2	12	0	35	2	0
Douglass, Sean, Orioles	1	3	.250	6.11	9	1	0	0	5	0	17.2	20	80	14	12	2	4	0	2	9	0	10	1	0
Duchscherer, Justin, Red Sox	2	3	.400	1.81	10	8	0	0	0	0	44.2	34	190	18	9	0	2	1	3	17	0	59	5	4
Durick, Chad, Mets	0	0	.000	0.00	1	0	0	0	1	1	2.0	0	7	0	0	0	0	0	0	0	0	3	1	0
Eavenson, Samuel, Yankees	1	1	.500	6.75	10	0	0	0	7	0	13.1	18	64	10	10	1	2	0	0	8	0	11	3	0
Ehlers, Corey, Marlins	0	1	.000	4.70	2	2	0	0	0	0	7.2	11	38	6	4	0	0	0	0	5	0	2	0	0
Eiland, Dave, Yankees	0	1	.000	9.00	2	1	0	0	0	0	7.0	12	34	8	7	0	0	0	0	0	0	5	0	0
Encarnacion, Orlando, Mets	4	2	.667	2.45	13	0	0	0	9	1	22.0	23	93	8	6	1	2	0	0	5	1	27	0	0
Ericks, John, Pirates	0	0	.000	3.46	9	8	0	0	0	0	13.0	5	50	5	5	0	0	0	0	5	0	18	1	1
Escalante, Jaime, Orioles	0	0	.000	0.00	1	0	0	0	1	0	1.0	0	3	0	0	0	0	0	0	1	0	1	0	0
Espina, Rendy, Twins*	2	2	.500	1.30	8	7	0	0	0	0	34.2	24	132	11	5	0	1	2	6	0	34	4	0
Farizo, Brad, Marlins	3	6	.333	3.71	11	11	2	0	0	0	60.2	55	260	34	25	1	1	1	2	21	0	52	2	1
Farson, Bryan, Pirates*	0	0	.000	7.63	8	0	0	0	3	0	15.1	19	78	15	13	2	1	2	2	12	0	9	3	0
Felix, Miguel, White Sox	1	0	1.000	1.50	3	2	0	0	1	0	12.0	10	45	3	2	0	0	0	0	2	0	10	1	0
Figueroa, Carlos, Rangers*	0	0	.000	3.18	5	1	0	0	1	1	5.2	7	27	2	2	1	1	0	0	2	0	9	0	1
Figueroa, Juan, White Sox	1	4	.200	3.36	11	10	0	0	0	0	64.1	66	274	31	24	4	0	3	7	14	0	43	1	0
Finol, Ricardo, Pirates	1	1	.500	3.15	6	1	0	0	2	1	20.0	19	85	13	7	0	1	1	2	4	0	20	0	0
Fitts, Brian, Twins	4	2	.667	2.83	10	3	0	0	0	0	28.2	29	125	15	9	0	0	1	6	2	31	2	0
Flock, Rick, Twins	2	1	.667	2.89	12	0	0	0	4	0	18.2	21	80	9	6	0	1	2	0	6	0	17	2	1
Forti, Eugene, White Sox*	4	1	.800	2.91	11	8	0	0	1	0	52.2	42	224	21	17	1	3	2	30	0	44	9	2
Fraser, Joe, Expos	0	1	.000	2.89	3	1	0	0	0	0	9.1	8	37	3	3	0	0	0	0	6	0	9	1	0
Fretwell, Joseph, Expos	2	0	1.000	3.94	8	0	0	0	3	1	16.0	19	66	8	7	3	1	0	0	2	0	14	0	0
Frias, Yovany, White Sox	0	0	.000	3.65	7	0	0	0	5	0	12.1	14	56	12	5	1	0	0	0	7	0	2	1	1

Pitcher, Team	W	L	Pct.	ERA	G	GS	CG	ShO	GF	Sv.	IP	H	TBF	R	ER	HR	SH	SF	HB	BB	IBB	SO	WP	Bk.
Gaerte, Travis, Pirates	1	2	.333	2.73	18	0	0	0	12	2	29.2	26	129	19	9	1	4	3	4	10	2	22	3	1
Gagliano, Steve, Marlins	3	4	.429	3.70	12	12	1	0	0	0	56.0	56	234	28	23	1	2	1	3	16	0	50	4	1
Gamboa, Javier, Royals	0	0	.000	1.13	2	2	0	0	0	0	8.0	4	26	1	1	0	0	0	1	1	0	7	0	1
Garcia, Ariel, White Sox	2	1	.667	2.57	10	1	0	0	5	2	28.0	23	117	11	8	0	0	2	0	11	0	28	0	0
Garcia, Luis, Red Sox	1	2	.333	2.87	8	1	0	0	5	1	15.2	12	70	10	5	0	1	0	0	10	0	18	3	0
Garvin, James, Marlins	4	3	.571	1.62	14	0	0	0	12	1	33.1	28	138	20	6	4	1	1	1	4	0	27	2	1
Glaser, Eric, Red Sox	1	2	.333	3.97	7	6	0	0	0	0	22.2	29	102	13	10	0	1	1	0	5	0	22	4	0
Goetz, Geoff, Mets*	0	2	.000	2.73	8	6	0	0	1	1	26.1	23	112	11	8	0	1	2	0	18	0	28	1	2
Gomez, Rafael, Mets	0	0	.000	0.90	4	2	0	0	1	0	10.0	9	41	2	1	0	1	0	1	2	0	6	2	0
Gomez, Ricardo, Pirates	0	2	.000	6.16	5	4	0	0	0	0	19.0	20	97	17	13	0	0	1	4	17	0	11	2	1
Gonzalez, Edwin, Royals	2	1	.667	1.93	3	3	1	0	0	0	18.2	16	75	8	4	0	2	0	1	3	0	12	4	0
Gonzalez, Michael, Pirates*	2	0	1.000	2.48	7	3	0	0	0	0	29.0	21	115	9	8	0	1	0	1	8	0	33	3	3
Gorman, Pat, Mets	1	1	.500	1.80	11	0	0	0	10	5	15.0	10	57	3	3	0	2	0	0	4	1	13	0	0
Grabow, John, Pirates*	2	7	.222	4.57	11	8	0	0	0	0	45.1	57	204	32	23	0	1	2	0	14	0	28	3	0
Gray, Jason, White Sox	3	2	.600	4.66	10	5	0	0	3	0	36.2	43	165	20	19	4	2	2	0	12	0	34	3	0
Gresko, Michael, Pirates*	1	1	.500	5.12	6	2	0	0	1	1	19.1	22	82	11	11	2	1	0	1	3	0	21	2	0
Guzman, Ambiorix, Rangers	2	0	1.000	0.00	5	2	0	0	3	1	15.0	10	57	1	0	0	1	0	0	2	0	15	0	2
Guzman, Wilson, Pirates*	4	1	.800	2.90	9	8	0	0	0	0	40.1	43	173	15	13	1	1	2	3	8	0	48	2	1
Hall, Billy, Astros	2	5	.286	2.68	7	7	0	0	0	0	37.0	39	159	17	11	2	1	2	0	9	0	26	2	1
Hamulack, Timothy, Astros*	1	1	.500	4.20	23	0	0	0	17	9	45.0	56	198	31	21	3	0	0	0	18	0	38	2	2
Harden, Nathan, Braves	1	6	.143	5.36	11	9	0	0	1	0	47.0	46	220	40	28	1	1	5	3	30	0	36	7	2
Harnisch, Pete, Mets	0	0	.000	12.00	1	1	0	0	0	0	3.0	7	16	4	4	1	0	0	0	0	0	5	2	0
Harvey, Terry, Devil Rays	2	0	1.000	3.75	5	0	0	0	1	0	12.0	5	47	6	5	0	0	0	0	5	0	11	3	0
Hayden, Terry, Red Sox*	1	0	1.000	2.25	3	0	0	0	2	0	8.0	6	32	2	2	0	0	0	0	1	0	8	0	0
Hecker, Doug, Red Sox	0	0	.000	0.00	1	0	0	0	0	0	1.0	0	4	0	0	0	0	0	0	1	0	1	0	0
Hlodan, George, Pirates	3	0	1.000	0.49	3	3	2	2	0	0	18.1	12	69	1	1	0	0	0	2	4	0	12	0	1
Hohenstein, Andrew, Pirates	1	1	.500	8.38	3	2	0	0	0	0	9.2	11	45	10	9	1	0	1	1	6	0	4	0	0
Hollins, Jessie, Yankees	2	0	1.000	12.00	4	1	0	0	0	0	6.0	13	37	8	8	0	0	0	0	8	0	5	5	0
Hollis, Ron, Red Sox	0	0	.000	1.29	4	0	0	0	2	1	7.0	7	27	1	1	0	2	0	0	0	0	7	0	0
Holzbauer, Joseph, Braves	2	2	.500	7.71	15	0	0	0	11	1	25.2	30	135	25	22	1	0	0	0	29	0	22	5	0
Howard, Chris, Mets*	0	1	.000	5.14	4	2	0	0	0	0	7.0	7	29	4	4	0	0	0	0	2	0	11	0	0
Huntsman, Brandon, Orioles	0	0	.000	0.00	2	0	0	0	1	0	4.2	3	19	0	0	0	0	0	0	1	0	6	0	1
Isringhausen, Jason, Mets	1	0	1.000	1.93	1	0	0	0	0	0	4.2	2	17	1	1	0	0	0	0	1	0	7	0	0
Izquierdo, Hansel, White Sox	0	0	.000	3.48	5	0	0	0	2	0	10.1	9	45	4	4	0	1	0	0	8	0	15	1	0
Jacobs, Jake, Twins	1	1	.500	0.29	23	0	0	0	20	10	31.1	16	128	7	1	0	0	0	3	11	1	55	3	0
Jaime, Wilson, Astros	2	0	1.000	4.66	18	0	0	0	9	0	36.2	37	177	25	19	0	1	3	3	29	0	43	10	2
Janssen, Mike, Astros	0	1	.000	9.36	13	0	0	0	6	1	25.0	28	129	27	26	2	0	1	1	23	0	20	5	0
Jimenez, Ricardo, Orioles	3	1	.750	3.46	8	6	0	0	2	1	39.0	30	168	22	15	1	0	5	3	21	0	27	1	1
Johnson, Jeremiah, Orioles	2	1	.667	2.84	6	0	0	0	3	1	6.1	4	27	2	2	0	0	1	0	4	0	4	0	0
Johnston, Bruce, Tigers	1	1	.500	4.00	18	2	0	0	4	0	36.0	37	157	22	16	2	0	1	3	11	0	29	4	2
Jones, Sean, Orioles	0	0	.000	3.00	9	0	0	0	6	0	15.0	18	66	7	5	0	0	0	1	7	0	7	1	1
Jones, Stacy, White Sox	0	0	.000	0.00	2	1	0	0	1	1	3.0	2	10	0	0	0	0	0	0	0	0	4	0	0
Julio, Jorge, Expos	5	6	.455	3.58	15	8	0	0	4	1	55.1	57	248	25	22	0	1	2	1	21	0	42	3	0
Klein, Cody, Yankees*	1	0	1.000	0.51	10	0	0	0	3	1	17.2	13	73	1	1	0	0	0	0	9	0	17	2	0
Knowles, Michael, Yankees	2	2	.500	4.85	9	8	0	0	0	0	39.0	41	168	30	21	2	4	2	1	14	0	24	3	6
Koch, Jack, Yankees	0	0	.000	16.20	2	0	0	0	0	0	1.2	6	13	3	3	0	0	0	0	2	0	0	0	0
Kvasnicka, Jonathon, W. Sox	2	3	.400	5.45	8	7	0	0	1	1	36.1	43	158	24	22	2	0	1	0	6	0	44	3	0
Kyzar, Cory, Royals	0	0	.000	2.45	3	0	0	0	0	0	3.2	2	14	2	1	0	0	0	0	0	0	3	0	0
Langston, David, Yankees	2	1	.667	3.60	11	0	0	0	3	0	20.0	19	89	11	8	2	0	1	1	9	0	11	6	0
Larson, Toby, Mets	1	0	1.000	2.25	2	1	0	0	0	0	4.0	4	16	1	1	0	0	0	0	0	0	4	0	0
Ledden, Ryan, Devil Rays	1	0	1.000	6.35	8	0	0	0	3	0	11.1	11	59	9	8	0	0	2	0	16	0	4	10	0
Leidens, Enrique, Expos	0	0	.000	9.00	1	0	0	0	1	0	1.0	4	6	1	1	0	0	0	0	0	0	0	0	0
Lopez, Carlos, Expos	2	4	.333	3.38	14	6	0	0	2	0	42.2	47	195	28	16	2	1	1	1	14	0	24	7	0
Lopez, Gustavo, Marlins	0	3	.000	4.13	7	6	1	0	0	0	32.2	33	140	20	15	0	3	1	1	10	0	25	3	1
Loux, Shane, Tigers	4	1	.800	0.84	10	9	1	1	0	0	43.0	19	158	7	4	0	0	0	1	10	0	33	2	1
Love, Farley, Astros	0	0	.000	0.00	2	0	0	0	0	0	3.0	1	12	0	0	0	0	0	0	2	0	7	0	0
Lowe, Matthew, Mets	2	0	1.000	1.13	5	0	0	0	2	1	8.0	4	37	1	1	0	0	0	0	9	1	15	1	0
Lundberg, David, Rangers	1	1	.500	0.84	14	1	0	0	11	5	32.1	13	115	4	3	1	0	1	0	11	0	32	0	1
Luttig, Christopher, Pirates*	1	1	.500	2.49	12	0	0	0	8	3	21.2	23	102	9	6	0	0	0	1	9	0	21	1	0
Lyons, Timothy, Braves	0	0	.000	0.00	1	0	0	0	1	0	1.0	1	5	0	0	0	0	0	0	1	0	3	0	0
Maine, Dalton, Orioles	0	0	.000	0.00	2	0	0	0	1	1	3.0	1	9	0	0	0	0	0	0	0	0	4	0	0
Malenfant, David, Tigers	0	0	.000	27.00	1	0	0	0	0	0	0.2	1	5	2	2	0	0	0	0	2	0	1	0	0
Mancha, Tony, Royals	2	6	.250	3.28	13	7	0	0	4	2	49.1	53	216	28	18	1	0	1	4	11	0	47	2	0
Maness, Nicholas, Mets	3	2	.600	3.02	11	6	0	0	2	0	44.2	52	205	25	15	3	1	1	1	20	0	54	2	2
Mangieri, John, Mets	2	0	1.000	7.08	13	0	0	0	3	1	20.1	28	101	16	16	3	0	1	1	14	0	15	2	2
Marache, Luis, Orioles*	4	6	.400	3.14	11	10	1	1	0	0	57.1	48	232	26	20	4	0	1	2	17	0	45	2	2
Marino, Lawrence, Red Sox	1	0	1.000	4.15	3	0	0	0	3	0	4.1	3	21	2	2	0	0	0	0	5	0	2	2	0
Martinez, Carlos, Royals*	1	0	1.000	1.97	14	1	1	1	6	4	32.0	24	128	8	7	0	3	2	1	14	1	19	1	1
Martinez, Mark, Red Sox*	4	2	.667	2.64	14	4	0	0	1	0	47.2	35	199	18	14	1	0	1	1	18	0	78	4	2
McCormick, Terry, D. Rays*	2	5	.286	4.60	10	9	0	0	0	0	43.0	37	192	26	22	3	1	2	4	24	0	41	7	0
McCrary, Scott, Mets	1	0	1.000	0.00	5	0	0	0	4	2	9.0	5	36	3	0	0	0	0	1	2	0	15	2	1
Medrano, Juan, Royals	1	3	.250	4.55	15	2	0	0	9	1	29.2	33	132	21	15	0	3	2	3	9	0	17	7	1
Mejia, Luis, Yankees	1	2	.333	1.14	13	0	0	0	9	2	23.2	8	88	4	3	0	0	1	3	9	1	31	2	1
Mejias, Oliver, Pirates	0	0	.000	54.00	1	0	0	0	1	0	0.2	2	7	4	4	0	0	0	0	3	0	0	0	1
Melson, Nate, Twins	0	4	.000	5.63	12	7	0	0	1	0	38.1	52	190	35	24	1	0	3	2	22	0	29	15	2
Mendoza, Geronimo, W. Sox	2	7	.222	3.67	12	8	0	0	1	0	54.0	51	241	32	22	3	5	2	3	28	0	41	4	0
Mercado, Hector, Tigers	3	3	.500	3.79	15	5	0	0	1	0	40.1	45	181	23	17	2	3	2	0	12	0	32	4	0
Mikkola, Shaun, Mets	5	0	1.000	1.17	14	4	0	0	3	0	38.1	25	154	11	5	0	2	1	4	16	0	23	2	2
Miller, Greg, Red Sox*	0	2	.000	3.72	4	4	0	0	0	0	9.2	8	40	6	4	0	0	0	0	6	0	6	0	2
Miller, Tom, Red Sox*	0	1	.000	6.75	1	0	0	0	0	0	1.1	2	8	1	1	0	1	0	0	2	0	3	0	0
Minaya, Pedro, Marlins	3	1	.750	1.88	12	6	0	0	4	0	38.1	30	164	14	8	0	0	0	6	15	0	39	1	0
Mitchell, Kendrick, White Sox	0	0	.000	0.00	4	0	0	0	0	0	8.2	3	36	0	0	0	0	0	0	6	0	12	2	0

Pitcher, Team	W	L	Pct.	ERA	G	GS	CG	ShO	GF	Sv.	IP	H	TBF	R	ER	HR	SH	SF	HB	BB	IBB	SO	WP	Bk.
Molina, Primitivo, Red Sox	2	0	1.000	0.00	15	0	0	0	11	4	19.2	12	72	0	0	0	1	0	1	2	0	22	0	0
Montanez, Jorge, Red Sox	0	1	.000	1.80	5	0	0	0	2	0	5.0	5	20	2	1	0	1	0	0	2	1	1	0	0
Montemayor, Humberto, R.S.	1	0	1.000	4.19	9	0	0	0	4	1	19.1	29	87	13	9	1	3	2	0	2	1	19	0	1
Moore, Christopher, Marlins ..	3	2	.600	2.65	10	9	1	1	0	0	54.1	39	225	23	16	1	1	3	2	29	0	40	1	0
Morales, Johnny, Orioles*	3	4	.429	4.23	18	1	0	0	7	1	38.1	40	169	21	18	2	2	2	5	12	0	47	7	6
Morel, Jose, Pirates*	2	0	1.000	2.93	7	0	0	0	3	0	15.1	11	60	5	5	2	2	1	0	6	0	10	1	0
Morrobel, Juan, Pirates*........	1	0	1.000	0.00	3	0	0	0	1	0	8.0	7	33	1	0	0	0	0	0	2	0	4	0	0
Moylan, Peter, Twins.............	4	2	.667	4.05	12	7	0	0	2	0	40.0	46	178	21	18	0	0	1	4	10	0	40	3	0
Mundine, John, Twins............	1	1	.500	1.69	15	0	0	0	7	0	32.0	20	125	7	6	1	2	0	1	9	2	32	1	0
Myers, Rob, Twins	1	1	.500	0.63	9	0	0	0	6	0	14.1	5	53	2	1	0	0	0	2	5	0	13	0	0
Myers, Taylor, Royals	5	4	.556	2.41	11	10	2	2	1	0	59.2	48	248	21	16	3	2	1	5	20	0	48	6	0
Naulty, Dan, Twins	0	0	.000	2.25	2	2	0	0	0	0	4.0	2	15	1	1	0	0	1	0	3	0	3	0	0
Neal, Blaine, Marlins	4	1	.800	3.63	10	0	0	0	5	1	22.1	24	102	11	9	1	0	0	1	11	0	19	2	0
O'Dette, Rick, Red Sox*	0	1	.000	2.25	3	0	0	0	0	0	8.0	6	31	3	2	0	0	0	0	1	0	6	0	0
Orellano, Rafael, Red Sox*	1	0	1.000	1.29	2	1	0	0	0	0	7.0	2	23	1	1	0	0	0	0	1	0	9	0	0
Orta, Juan, Expos	0	4	.000	3.10	19	0	0	0	16	4	29.0	27	118	12	10	0	1	2	2	7	0	12	1	1
Oswalt, Roy, Astros...............	1	1	.500	0.64	5	5	0	0	0	0	28.1	25	117	7	2	2	0	0	0	7	0	28	0	0
Padua, Geraldo, Yankees........	8	0	1.000	2.92	11	8	1	1	1	0	61.2	46	237	24	20	5	2	0	1	8	0	36	5	1
Paraqueima, Jesus, Yankees..	0	1	.000	8.44	3	0	0	0	0	0	5.1	14	32	11	5	1	1	1	1	0	0	2	1	0
Parkerson, Michael, Pirates*	2	3	.400	4.28	14	0	0	0	9	3	27.1	27	124	15	13	1	5	3	4	10	0	25	7	3
Pascarella, Josh, Astros	2	2	.500	2.55	10	6	1	0	2	1	42.1	37	178	19	12	3	1	2	3	15	0	33	5	0
Pavlik, Roger, Rangers	0	0	.000	1.29	2	2	0	0	0	0	7.0	8	29	1	1	1	0	0	0	0	0	5	0	0
Peguero, Darwin, Astros*......	0	4	.000	5.57	9	8	0	0	0	0	32.1	30	155	26	20	1	0	0	4	23	0	36	6	1
Peguero, Radhame, D. Rays ..	1	1	.500	8.74	3	2	0	0	0	0	11.1	19	55	11	11	2	1	0	1	3	0	9	0	3
Peniche, Fray, Tigers.............	0	0	.000	9.00	1	0	0	0	1	0	2.0	3	9	2	2	1	0	0	0	1	0	1	0	0
Percibal, Billy, Orioles	0	0	.000	0.90	4	3	0	0	0	0	10.0	11	38	1	1	0	0	0	0	2	0	12	0	0
Perez, Elvis, White Sox*	3	7	.300	4.19	12	8	1	0	1	0	58.0	57	281	41	27	0	3	1	5	44	0	50	2	5
Perez, Julio, Expos	3	2	.600	2.88	10	9	0	0	1	0	50.0	38	205	18	16	0	1	2	4	13	0	38	1	0
Peterson, Dean, Red Sox	0	0	.000	0.00	2	0	0	0	1	1	2.0	1	8	0	0	0	0	0	1	1	0	1	0	0
Petique, Marino, Devil Rays ..	2	2	.500	4.15	22	0	0	0	13	3	39.0	48	180	21	18	2	1	3	5	11	0	38	2	0
Phillips, Randy, Braves*	0	1	.000	4.50	4	0	0	0	3	0	4.0	6	19	3	2	0	0	1	0	2	0	4	0	1
Pidgeon, Matt, Marlins	2	1	.667	4.56	16	0	0	0	13	4	25.2	25	126	21	13	1	2	0	5	15	0	21	1	0
Pierson, Jason, Mets*	0	0	.000	0.00	1	0	0	0	1	0	2.0	0	7	0	0	0	0	0	0	1	0	3	0	0
Ponson, Sidney, Orioles	1	0	1.000	0.00	1	0	0	0	0	0	2.0	0	6	0	0	0	0	0	0	0	0	1	0	0
Porter, Bobby, Braves*	0	1	.000	9.19	7	0	0	0	1	0	15.2	23	94	20	16	1	0	0	0	15	0	20	4	3
Price, Thomas, Devil Rays	3	3	.500	2.77	15	4	0	0	2	0	39.0	31	167	16	12	0	1	2	3	17	0	29	3	3
Pulsipher, Bill, Mets*	0	0	.000	1.80	2	2	0	0	0	0	5.0	3	18	1	1	0	0	0	0	1	0	4	0	0
Quintero, Jose, Rangers*	4	4	.500	3.64	12	9	0	0	1	1	59.1	49	245	29	24	1	1	1	2	26	0	45	1	2
Quiros, Misael, Pirates	2	4	.333	3.65	13	3	0	0	7	0	37.0	42	172	20	15	0	3	1	6	14	0	24	6	2
Rahilly, Michael, Expos	4	0	1.000	3.18	12	0	0	0	4	2	28.1	25	119	11	10	0	1	2	3	7	0	19	3	0
Raino, Brian, Pirates	0	0	.000	40.50	1	0	0	0	0	0	0.2	3	6	3	3	0	0	0	0	1	0	2	0	0
Ramirez, Horacio, Braves*	3	3	.500	2.25	11	8	0	0	2	0	44.0	30	175	13	11	1	0	1	0	18	0	61	4	0
Ramirez, Juan, Royals	0	0	.000	0.00	1	0	0	0	1	0	1.0	0	2	0	0	0	0	0	0	0	0	1	0	1
Ratliff, Craig, Orioles.............	2	5	.286	2.75	12	12	0	0	0	0	59.0	60	260	26	18	2	2	3	0	32	0	50	10	3
Reed, Aaron, Tigers	2	2	.500	2.66	13	0	0	0	5	0	23.2	18	98	7	7	2	0	0	1	6	1	24	3	0
Regalado, Frank, Devil Rays ..	2	3	.400	1.76	18	1	0	0	10	3	30.2	31	132	15	6	0	1	1	0	11	0	31	4	0
Reith, Brian, Yankees	4	2	.667	2.86	12	11	1	0	0	0	63.0	70	270	28	20	1	2	2	3	14	0	40	8	0
Reynolds, Chris, Devil Rays ..	0	1	.000	5.02	8	0	0	0	5	2	14.1	12	61	9	8	2	2	1	0	4	1	16	1	1
Ridenour, Jeffrey, Rangers	3	1	.750	2.56	12	0	0	0	5	2	31.2	26	134	10	9	2	0	0	1	14	1	30	2	0
Rincon, Juan, Twins	3	3	.500	2.95	11	10	1	0	1	0	58.0	55	245	21	19	0	2	3	4	24	0	46	7	1
Rios, Romualdo, Rangers......	1	2	.333	5.72	10	2	0	0	6	1	28.1	31	131	24	18	0	2	2	2	15	0	31	4	1
Rivera, Homero, Tigers*	4	4	.500	4.94	15	9	0	0	1	0	51.0	67	231	36	28	3	1	0	3	10	0	47	6	1
Rivera, Marco, Expos*	1	4	.200	2.25	19	0	0	0	11	0	28.0	28	116	10	7	1	1	0	0	6	0	17	2	0
Rivera, Raul, Tigers...............	2	1	.667	2.73	15	2	0	0	7	2	29.2	20	130	15	9	2	0	0	3	21	1	36	4	0
Roberts, Marquis, D. Rays* ..	6	1	.857	0.51	12	10	0	0	1	0	53.1	27	206	8	3	1	2	0	1	19	0	68	2	0
Roberts, Richard, Tigers*......	2	2	.500	4.24	11	10	0	0	0	0	34.0	35	159	22	16	0	0	1	1	19	0	40	9	2
Rodriguez, Cristobol, Expos ..	3	3	.500	1.65	13	10	0	0	3	1	54.2	45	220	15	10	1	0	2	1	16	0	61	2	1
Rodriguez, Jorge, Yankees	0	3	.000	4.91	17	0	0	0	11	4	25.2	31	117	19	14	2	1	2	2	8	1	12	1	2
Rodriguez, Wilfredo, Astros*	8	2	.800	3.04	12	12	1	1	0	0	68.0	54	279	30	23	1	1	1	2	32	0	71	6	4
Rojas, Cesar, Rangers...........	2	0	1.000	2.21	10	0	0	0	5	3	20.1	20	85	8	5	1	0	1	0	2	0	15	0	1
Roller, Adam, Red Sox	1	1	.500	3.18	10	0	0	0	2	0	17.0	7	78	9	6	0	1	1	6	14	0	21	5	0
Rolocut, Brian, Devil Rays	1	0	1.000	0.00	3	0	0	0	2	0	7.0	5	27	0	0	0	0	0	0	1	0	10	0	0
Rosario, Rafael, Tigers	1	1	.500	3.22	22	0	0	0	11	0	36.1	37	165	19	13	3	1	1	4	18	0	28	3	1
Rosario, Reynaldo, Tigers......	2	2	.500	3.94	21	0	0	0	12	4	32.0	32	135	15	14	3	1	0	0	13	0	39	3	0
Rupp, Michael, Red Sox	1	4	.200	1.22	11	9	3	0	0	0	59.0	51	246	23	8	0	2	0	3	17	1	56	4	0
Ryba, Jason, Orioles.............	3	4	.429	4.60	14	8	1	0	3	1	43.0	51	200	33	22	3	0	3	4	19	0	30	10	1
Sadler, Carl, Expos*	0	2	.000	4.35	9	3	0	0	0	0	20.2	26	91	11	10	0	0	1	2	5	0	14	2	0
Santana, Alfredo, Tigers	3	3	.500	3.44	19	0	0	0	13	3	36.2	37	166	20	14	3	1	2	2	11	1	20	10	1
Santana, Fausto, White Sox ..	3	3	.500	4.05	13	0	0	0	12	2	20.0	16	85	10	9	0	1	1	1	9	0	10	1	0
Santana, Johan, Astros*........	0	4	.000	7.93	9	5	1	0	0	0	36.1	49	176	36	32	2	3	1	2	18	0	25	5	1
Santos, Juan, Orioles	0	1	.000	1.50	3	0	0	0	1	0	6.0	6	28	4	1	0	0	1	0	2	0	5	0	0
Sasaki, Junichi, Expos	1	0	1.000	0.52	11	0	0	0	6	2	17.1	15	67	2	1	0	0	0	0	3	0	13	0	1
Schmidt, Patrick, Braves*......	2	3	.400	4.03	12	1	0	0	5	0	38.0	52	182	29	17	0	0	2	2	20	0	23	2	0
Sheets, Matt, Twins...............	2	2	.500	2.38	15	5	0	0	5	2	53.0	49	215	17	14	1	1	2	4	10	1	24	2	0
Shields, Drew, Marlins	3	1	.750	5.93	10	0	0	0	5	0	30.1	42	143	24	20	3	2	0	3	10	0	27	2	1
Shourds, Anthony, Rangers ..	3	1	.750	1.05	13	1	0	0	10	1	34.1	25	134	7	4	0	1	0	2	5	1	24	0	1
Siegel, Justin, Rangers*	0	1	.000	1.17	4	0	0	0	3	1	7.2	6	36	5	1	0	0	0	0	6	0	6	1	0
Silva, Douglas, Rangers	5	4	.556	3.77	11	9	1	0	1	0	62.0	69	271	34	26	4	1	2	0	18	1	46	4	3
Simpson, Cory, Braves	1	3	.250	4.73	12	2	0	0	8	1	26.2	29	133	20	14	2	0	0	1	22	0	27	1	0
Solano, Francisco, Royals......	4	1	.800	3.81	12	7	1	1	4	0	49.2	53	213	25	21	2	2	0	4	9	0	30	1	0
Sordo, Fernando, Mets	3	1	.750	3.58	11	3	0	0	3	0	27.2	26	116	12	11	2	1	0	2	7	0	12	3	0
Spinelli, Mike, Red Sox*	0	2	.000	11.37	3	3	0	0	0	0	6.1	15	42	16	8	0	1	0	1	4	0	15	1	1

Pitcher, Team	W	L	Pct.	ERA	G	GS	CG	ShO	GF	Sv.	IP	H	TBF	R	ER	HR	SH	SF	HB	BB	IBB	SO	WP	Bk.
Splittorff, Jamie, Twins	0	1	.000	2.08	2	0	0	0	2	0	4.1	2	19	1	1	0	0	0	1	4	0	6	0	0
Standridge, Jason, D. Rays....	0	6	.000	3.59	13	13	0	0	0	0	57.2	56	246	30	23	3	2	5	2	13	1	55	2	2
Stenger, Pat, Twins	0	2	.000	4.54	15	2	0	0	3	0	35.2	41	155	21	18	3	0	3	3	10	1	22	6	3
Stephens, John, Orioles	3	0	1.000	0.82	9	3	0	0	3	1	33.0	15	121	3	3	1	3	2	0	9	0	43	0	0
Stinson, Kevin, White Sox.....	1	2	.333	6.59	10	0	0	0	6	0	13.2	21	64	10	10	0	1	1	8	0	12	0	1
Stowe, Chris, Expos	2	1	.667	3.23	9	9	0	0	0	0	39.0	32	163	19	14	5	1	0	1	20	0	36	0	0
Sturdy, Tim, Twins	1	1	.500	0.75	9	2	1	1	3	0	24.0	12	88	4	2	0	0	0	6	0	14	0	2
Stutz, Shawn, Devil Rays	0	0	.000	4.50	2	0	0	0	0	0	4.0	3	16	2	2	0	0	2	1	0	2	1	0
Suggs, Willie, Mets	5	3	.625	2.49	10	8	1	0	1	0	50.2	34	200	21	14	1	1	1	4	22	0	32	5	0
Sullivan, Peter, Astros..........	0	6	.000	9.51	14	3	0	0	2	0	23.2	39	141	35	25	0	0	3	3	26	0	14	4	1
Sylvester, Billy, Braves	3	4	.429	3.91	12	9	0	0	1	0	53.0	45	225	25	23	2	0	0	3	28	0	58	6	0
Tanksley, Scott, Twins...........	0	2	.000	2.08	4	0	0	0	0	0	8.2	5	31	2	2	0	0	0	1	0	7	1	0
Tellez, Eloy, White Sox	0	0	.000	2.25	2	2	0	0	0	0	4.0	2	19	2	1	0	0	2	3	0	2	0	1
Tetz, Kristofer, Expos	0	0	.000	4.15	3	0	0	0	0	0	4.1	2	17	2	2	0	0	0	0	3	0	5	1	0
Theodile, Simeon, Orioles	0	1	.000	1.99	15	0	0	0	13	6	22.2	22	95	6	5	0	0	0	7	0	17	1	2
Thomas, Gaige, Marlins	2	0	1.000	3.52	12	0	0	0	4	0	23.0	18	109	16	9	2	0	3	17	0	30	5	0
Thurman, Corey, Royals	2	1	.667	2.38	8	8	1	0	0	0	34.0	28	149	12	9	1	1	0	2	22	0	42	1	0
Torres, Michael, Royals.........	1	1	.500	3.53	15	0	0	0	8	1	35.2	32	155	19	14	0	2	1	4	12	0	27	10	1
Tucker, Thomas, Expos	1	0	1.000	1.93	3	2	0	0	0	0	4.2	5	19	1	1	0	0	0	1	0	11	0	0
Tynan, Christopher, Rangers..	4	2	.667	2.93	11	10	1	0	1	0	58.1	46	233	27	19	3	2	3	1	23	2	39	6	3
Tyrrell, Jim, Red Sox*..........	0	0	.000	5.40	3	0	0	0	0	0	3.1	5	16	3	2	0	0	0	1	0	6	1	0
Valle, Yoiset, Yankees*	1	1	.500	0.45	11	0	0	0	6	0	20.0	8	76	1	1	1	0	1	4	0	20	0	0
Vallis, Jamie, Twins*..............	5	3	.625	4.76	14	3	0	0	3	0	34.0	30	147	20	18	0	1	1	14	1	34	3	0
Vanderhorst, Francisco, Royals	8	4	.667	2.72	18	1	0	0	13	2	43.0	35	179	20	13	1	1	3	1	17	0	34	5	1
Verdin, Cesar, Yankees*	1	0	1.000	1.50	3	3	0	0	0	0	12.0	5	42	2	2	0	0	2	0	1	0	17	1	1
Viera, Rob, Pirates	0	0	.000	0.00	4	0	0	0	4	0	5.1	3	20	0	0	0	0	1	1	0	2	0	0
Vogt, Robert, Pirates*...........	2	2	.500	3.97	12	4	0	0	4	0	34.0	23	142	17	15	1	1	2	0	19	0	40	2	1
Wade, Chip, Twins	0	0	.000	0.00	1	0	0	0	1	0	0.1	0	2	0	0	0	0	0	0	1	0	0	0	0
Walker, Pete, Red Sox	0	0	.000	0.96	4	3	0	0	0	0	9.1	5	36	1	1	0	0	0	1	1	0	14	0	0
Walker, Tyler, Mets	0	0	.000	1.00	5	0	0	0	5	3	9.0	8	37	1	1	0	1	0	2	1	9	0	0
Wallace, Derek, Mets	0	1	.000	3.38	8	5	0	0	0	0	8.0	6	31	3	3	2	0	0	1	2	0	8	0	0
Walsh, Steven, Royals	0	0	.000	4.91	4	0	0	0	3	0	3.2	2	18	3	2	0	0	1	4	0	1	0	0
Webb, Alan, Tigers*..............	3	1	.750	3.74	9	8	0	0	0	0	33.2	27	139	17	14	3	1	0	2	11	0	46	4	4
Wheeler, Mike, Astros	0	0	.000	0.00	2	0	0	0	2	0	2.0	0	7	0	0	0	0	0	0	1	0	1	0	0
Whitley, Garry, White Sox*	1	1	.500	6.23	3	0	0	0	1	0	4.1	7	21	4	3	0	0	0	2	0	6	0	0
Williams, Bradford, Yankees* ..	1	0	1.000	5.75	11	2	0	0	1	0	20.1	16	97	19	13	2	1	2	1	19	0	27	9	1
Williams, Thomas, White Sox ..	2	1	.667	3.92	11	0	0	0	8	2	20.2	22	97	16	9	1	1	1	0	9	0	15	0	1
Willoughby, Justin, Braves* ..	0	2	.000	4.07	13	6	0	0	5	1	42.0	40	177	24	19	0	0	3	1	12	0	45	1	0
Wilson, Paul, Mets	1	0	1.000	1.45	4	3	0	0	1	1	18.2	14	77	7	3	0	1	0	3	4	0	18	0	0
Wimberly, Larry, Red Sox*	1	0	1.000	3.00	1	0	0	0	0	0	3.0	2	10	1	1	0	0	0	0	1	0	1	0	0
Wood, Stanton, Yankees	2	0	1.000	2.45	17	0	0	0	14	8	25.2	18	99	7	7	3	0	1	0	7	0	21	1	0
Wright, Barrett, Devil Rays	2	5	.286	3.47	13	11	0	0	1	0	49.1	40	215	27	19	0	3	3	22	0	33	3	1
Wright, Jason, Devil Rays......	1	2	.333	6.75	14	1	0	0	3	0	24.0	27	117	21	18	2	0	1	3	18	1	31	1	0
Young, Spencer, Devil Rays ..	1	1	.500	4.13	14	1	0	0	7	1	24.0	20	105	14	11	2	0	1	3	9	0	27	4	1
Zamarripa, Mark, Tigers	0	0	.000	6.48	4	0	0	0	1	1	8.1	6	35	6	6	2	0	0	6	0	11	2	1
Zambrano, Victor, Devil Rays	0	0	.000	0.00	2	0	0	0	0	0	3.0	1	10	0	0	0	0	0	0	0	2	0	0

COMBINATION SHUTOUTS: **Astros (3)**—Hall-Hamulack-Pascarella, Pascarella-Corominas-Bogeajis, Pascarella-Corominas-Hamulack. **Braves (0)**—None. Devil Rays (4)—Standridge-Rolocut, Roberts-Wright-Regalado, McCormick-Price, Roberts-Regalado. **Expos (4)**—Baker-Rahilly-Rodriguez, Perez-Rahilly-Rivera, Rodriguez-Rivera-Orta, Bridges-Julio. **Marlins (4)**—Moore-Garvin, Lopez-Shields, Minaya-Garvin, Blanco-Pidgeon. **Mets (8)**—De La Cruz-McCrary, Dougherty-Corcoran, Dougherty-Maness, Howard-Sordo, Wallace-Dougherty-Mikkola-Chivers-Encarcion-Gorman, Dougherty-Sordo-Mikkola-Lowe, Suggs-Mangiera-Encarcion-Chivers, Mikkola-Goetz. **Orioles (4)**—Marache-Curtis-Jones-Theodile, Marache-Curtis, Ratliff-Theodile, Stephens-Theodile. **Pirates (2)**—Ericks-Guzman-Gresko, Ericks-Alvarado-Gaerte. **Rangers (7)**—Benoit-Quintero-Lundberg, Davis-Guzman, Guzman-Figueroa-Ridenour, Benoit-Lundberg, Quintero-Lundberg, Pavlik-Silva-Siegel, Benoit-Ridenour. **Red Sox (5)**—Rupp-Roller-Hayden-Garcia, Duchscherer-Molina, Walker-Hollis-Betti, Miller-Martinez-Molina, Martinez-Cederblad-Montanez-Peterson. **Royals (4)**—Thurman-Crutchley-Medrano, Thurman-Crutchley-Torres, Mancha-Solano, Affeldt-Martinez-Vanderhorst. **Tigers (4)**—Webb-Rivera-Santana, Roberts-Mercado-Rivera, Loux-Reed, Loux-Mercado-Rosario. **Twins (6)**—Balfour-Tanksley-Jacobs, Rincon-Vallis-Jacobs, Espina-Rincon, Melson-Sheets-Jacobs, Espina-Flock-Sturdy, Rincon-Vallis-Meyer. **White Sox (1)**—Desrosiers-Garcia. **Yankees (3)**—Padua-Paraqueima-Valle, Padua-Wood, Boehringer-Blevins-Langston.

NO-HIT GAME: Sturdy, Twins, defeated Rangers, 5-0 (second game), August 16.

1997 FIELDING

TEAM

Team	Pct.	G	PO	A	E	TC	DP	PB	Team	Pct.	G	PO	A	E	TC	DP	PB
Twins..............	.963	60	1581	758	91	2430	48	12	Rangers.............	.954	60	1500	631	103	2234	53	17
Orioles.............	.961	60	1489	628	86	2203	58	18	Pirates.............	.951	59	1480	632	108	2220	37	8
Yankees..........	.961	60	1522	620	88	2230	49	14	White Sox.........	.951	60	1463	611	108	2182	53	16
Royals.............	.959	60	1479	659	91	2229	51	14	Tigers...............	.948	60	1487	606	114	2207	33	23
Expos	.958	59	1436	583	88	2107	34	10	Astros...............	.947	60	1496	594	118	2208	60	17
Devil Rays	.956	60	1474	555	94	2123	47	19	Red Sox............	.946	59	1452	588	117	2157	56	17
Mets	.956	60	1438	611	95	2144	37	16	Braves..............	.943	58	1388	514	114	2016	48	20
Marlins	.955	59	1420	633	97	2150	30	17									

TRIPLE PLAYS: Orioles, Rangers.

INDIVIDUAL

FIRST BASEMEN

NOTE: All caps denotes fielding-percentage leader based on 30 games for catchers, 40 for all other non-pitchers and 59 innings for pitchers. *Throws lefthanded.

Player, Team	Pct.	G	PO	A	E	TC	DP
Acevedo, Luis, Rangers	.983	7	51	6	1	58	5
Bethea, Larry, Orioles	.960	29	205	13	9	227	17
Brosam, Eric, Twins	.988	39	371	25	5	401	25
Burke, Mark, Braves*.................	1.000	9	81	3	0	84	7
Byrd, Brandon, Astros	.971	27	212	19	7	238	21
Chaidez, Juan, Red Sox	.952	11	78	2	4	84	10

– 584 –

Player, Team	Pct.	G	PO	A	E	TC	DP
Conway, Scott, Marlins*	1.000	1	7	1	0	8	0
Crespo, Jesse, Braves	.957	4	40	4	2	46	3
Cruz, Andres, Devil Rays	.982	9	51	5	1	57	5
DeJesus, Wilmer, Expos	1.000	2	15	1	0	16	0
De La Cruz, Raul, Pirates	.956	8	56	9	3	68	4
Delgado, Christopher, White Sox	.973	51	403	22	12	437	37
Diaz, Christian, Royals	1.000	1	2	0	0	2	0
Dodson, Bo, Red Sox*	.939	7	29	2	2	33	5
Durick, Chad, Mets	.985	15	122	13	2	137	10
Escalante, Jaime, Orioles	.986	27	207	10	3	220	19
Ewan, Benjamin, Braves	.985	16	123	8	2	133	13
Frawley, Scott, Braves	.986	10	69	3	1	73	7
Gomez, Erick, Royals	.955	13	78	6	4	88	5
Hafner, Travis, Rangers	.994	35	306	23	2	331	22
Harrison, Jamal, Twins	.981	31	238	18	5	261	19
Hazelton, Justin, Tigers	1.000	1	1	0	0	1	0
Hernandez, Rafael, Expos	.900	3	9	0	1	10	1
Hodges, Scott, Expos	.994	18	148	8	1	157	10
Hyde, Brandon, White Sox	.964	7	48	5	2	55	5
Iglesias, Rigoberto, White Sox	.982	5	51	4	1	56	2
Infante, Danny, Rangers	1.000	20	171	10	0	181	21
Kaplan, Brett, Pirates	.993	18	138	7	1	146	13
Lara, Balmes, Tigers	1.000	5	39	1	0	40	0
Lebron, Hector, Devil Rays	.989	39	252	11	3	266	24
Lehr, Ryan, Braves	.909	1	9	1	1	11	0
McNeal, Aaron, Astros	.983	35	279	16	5	300	32
Meadows, Mike, Mets	.987	27	213	13	3	229	13
Mejia, Renato, Marlins	1.000	8	61	7	0	68	3
Montero, Jose, Rangers	.800	1	4	0	1	5	0
Mulvehill, Brandon, Mets	1.000	2	17	0	0	17	1
Nunez, Jose, Royals	.988	11	78	6	1	85	11
Pascual, Edison, Pirates*	.979	5	44	2	1	47	3
Peniche, Fray, Tigers	.996	32	256	10	1	267	13
Pittman, Thomas, Expos	.989	12	86	8	1	95	2
Preciado, Victor, Yankees	.988	54	458	20	6	484	38
Perini, Michael, Red Sox	.968	36	264	12	9	285	27
Quero, Pedro, Expos	.986	17	129	7	2	138	12
Rains, Nick, Mets	1.000	1	4	1	0	5	0
Ramirez, Juan, Royals	.990	43	349	29	4	382	26
Ramirez, Luis, Orioles	.981	9	49	3	1	53	6
Rivera, Luis, Expos	.972	15	98	6	3	107	7
Rivera, Michael, Tigers	1.000	3	21	1	0	22	0
Rockow, Jeremy, Pirates*	.882	3	15	0	2	17	0
Rojas, Mo, Red Sox	.986	8	64	5	1	70	4
RONEBERG, Brett, Marlins*	.994	53	481	29	3	513	26
Sassanella, Jeremy, Tigers	.991	25	212	12	2	226	13
Strangfeld, Aaron, Braves	.988	11	77	7	1	85	8
Tolbert, William, Pirates	.981	31	240	13	5	258	14
Valdez, Angel, Yankees	.990	11	92	5	1	98	6
Valentine, Anthony, Mets	.984	22	171	11	3	185	9
Vazquez, Carlos, Devil Rays	.974	26	181	9	5	195	14
Werth, Jayson, Orioles	.936	8	42	2	3	47	6
Wilson, Heath, Braves	.964	10	53	1	2	56	8
Zapata, Wilson, Red Sox	.971	8	33	0	1	34	3

TRIPLE PLAYS: Hafner, L. Ramirez.

SECOND BASEMEN

Player, Team	Pct.	G	PO	A	E	TC	DP
Acevedo, Luis, Rangers	.959	13	32	39	3	74	5
Alfaro, Jason, Astros	.920	5	10	13	2	25	6
Alvarez, Julio, Tigers	.800	2	2	6	2	10	0
August, Brian, Yankees	.975	12	13	26	1	40	7
Bautista, Jose, Twins	.857	1	2	4	1	7	1
Beltres, Manuel, Yankees	1.000	3	7	8	0	15	1
Benes, Richard, Royals	.947	15	19	35	3	57	6
Canaguacan, Oscar, Yankees	.929	3	7	6	1	14	1
Caracciolo, Anthony, Expos	.931	8	16	11	2	29	3
Castillo, Geramel, Rangers	.917	4	5	6	1	12	1
Collier, Marc, Orioles	.958	7	9	14	1	24	1
Cordero, Willy, Rangers	.930	17	29	37	5	71	8
Cruz, Luis, Devil Rays	.915	26	43	65	10	118	13
Diaz, Maikell, Orioles	.938	3	3	12	1	16	2
Durham, Chad, White Sox	.945	37	84	105	11	200	20
Escalona, Felix, Astros	.969	50	94	127	7	228	37
Freeman, Terrance, Pirates	.933	2	6	8	1	15	1
Furcal, Rafael, Braves	.961	49	122	125	10	257	30
Garcia, Rafael, Royals	.917	3	5	6	1	12	0
Gutierrez, Victor, Pirates	.965	17	33	49	3	85	9
Hasbun, Andy, Tigers	.714	1	1	4	2	7	2
Hill, Bobby, Mets	.982	17	20	36	1	57	7
Hoshina, Koji, Expos	.976	9	22	18	1	41	3
Infante, Danny, Rangers	1.000	1	1	3	0	4	1

Player, Team	Pct.	G	PO	A	E	TC	DP
Leidens, Enrique, Expos	.965	14	23	32	2	57	8
Leon, Carlos, Red Sox	.951	42	73	101	9	183	28
Linares, Rodney, Tigers	.927	13	18	20	3	41	5
Mann, Derek, Devil Rays	.992	29	58	73	1	132	14
Marino, Lawrence, Red Sox	.833	4	3	2	1	6	1
Martinez, Andres, Mets	.882	13	15	30	6	51	7
Martinez, Gabby, Yankees	1.000	2	3	5	0	8	0
Mateo, Victor, Yankees	.972	19	32	37	2	71	8
McDonald, Ryan, Royals	.957	7	11	11	1	23	5
Medrano, Jesus, Marlins	.952	38	69	89	8	166	12
Medrano, Ricardo, White Sox	.990	24	41	63	1	105	14
Mejias, Oliver, Pirates	.973	38	82	98	5	185	15
Mendoza, Angel, Red Sox	1.000	1	0	1	0	1	1
Myers, Tootie, Expos	.919	31	55	70	11	136	6
Nolasco, Regino, Orioles	.971	55	108	127	7	242	28
Nunez, Jose, Mets	.941	5	8	8	1	17	2
Nunez, Sergio, Royals	.941	4	11	5	1	17	1
Oropeza, Asdrubal, Braves	.947	8	22	14	2	38	6
Ortiz, Miguel, Yankees	.949	27	33	60	5	98	10
Pena, Jose, Devil Rays	.943	10	13	20	2	35	3
Perez, Jesse, Orioles	1.000	4	3	3	0	6	1
Proctor, Mark, Mets	.941	5	6	10	1	17	3
Ramirez, Edgar, Devil Rays	1.000	1	2	1	0	3	1
Reynoso, Ismael, Marlins	.958	8	10	13	1	24	2
Roman, Junior, White Sox	1.000	1	5	2	0	7	1
Ruiz, Willy, Royals	.968	43	85	96	6	187	20
Runnells, T.J., Tigers	.965	48	66	100	6	172	14
Samboy, Nelson, Astros	1.000	1	2	2	0	4	1
Santo, Jose, Rangers	.982	24	47	64	2	113	18
Shuck, Jason, Mets	.939	23	36	41	5	82	6
STEVENS, Tony, Twins	.977	41	73	96	4	173	18
Swafford, Derek, Pirates	.750	1	2	1	1	4	0
Terni, Chas, Red Sox	.903	19	29	36	7	72	7
Torres, Franklin, Twins	.931	25	43	78	9	130	11
Velazquez, Juan, Braves	.000	1	0	0	1	1	0
Warriax, Brandon, Rangers	1.000	7	11	14	0	25	4
Washington, Cory, Marlins	.947	14	25	29	3	57	4
Washington, Enrico, Pirates	.800	3	2	6	2	10	1
Washington, Kelley, Marlins	.833	3	3	7	2	12	0
Wheeler, Mike, Astros	.929	7	14	12	2	28	3

TRIPLE PLAYS: Acevedo, Diaz.

THIRD BASEMEN

Player, Team	Pct.	G	PO	A	E	TC	DP
Acevedo, Luis, Rangers	.897	14	9	26	4	39	2
Adorno, Wilson, Pirates	.500	1	0	1	1	2	0
Aguila, Chris, Marlins	.843	45	25	93	22	140	6
Alfaro, Jason, Astros	.923	16	7	17	2	26	2
Almonte, Erick, Yankees	.890	51	53	92	18	163	7
Alvarez, Julio, Tigers	.000	1	0	0	2	2	0
August, Brian, Yankees	1.000	3	1	6	0	7	1
Balfe, Ryan, Tigers	1.000	1	0	1	0	1	0
Beltres, Manuel, Yankees	1.000	2	1	1	0	2	0
Boone, Matthew, Tigers	.845	48	30	95	23	148	5
Borges, Elio, White Sox	.885	22	13	41	7	61	5
Calderon, Henry, Royals	.951	21	15	43	3	61	3
Caracciolo, Anthony, Expos	.908	21	22	37	6	65	3
Collier, Marc, Orioles	.889	6	1	7	1	9	1
Cordero, Ellery, White Sox	.855	26	23	42	11	76	6
Cruz, Andres, Devil Rays	.333	1	0	1	2	3	0
Cruz, Luis, Devil Rays	1.000	2	0	2	0	2	0
Davila, Angel, Mets	.833	3	1	4	1	6	0
Diaz, Christian, Royals	1.000	2	2	1	0	3	1
Durick, Chad, Mets	1.000	6	4	6	0	10	0
Escalante, Jaime, Orioles	1.000	3	1	2	0	3	0
Fafard, Mathias, Mets	.906	21	14	34	5	53	2
Feliz, Joselyn, Marlins	1.000	2	0	1	0	1	0
Garcia, Rafael, Royals	.750	2	0	3	1	4	0
Garza, Rolando, White Sox	.906	11	9	20	3	32	2
Gray, Travis, Red Sox	1.000	7	4	10	0	14	0
Gutierrez, Victor, Pirates	.800	1	3	1	1	5	0
Hasbun, Andy, Tigers	.857	3	1	5	1	7	0
Hernandez, Rafael, Expos	.929	5	4	9	1	14	1
Hodges, Scott, Expos	.918	35	30	71	9	110	1
Infante, Danny, Rangers	.906	20	19	29	5	53	4
Jordan, Yustin, Pirates	.833	30	23	52	15	90	3
LaForest, Pierre Luc, Devil Rays	.909	33	21	49	7	77	5
Lehr, Ryan, Braves	.741	19	10	30	14	54	2
Linares, Rodney, Tigers	.900	14	4	14	2	20	2
Marino, Lawrence, Red Sox	.927	40	28	74	8	110	10
Martinez, Andres, Mets	.900	16	10	26	4	40	3
Meadows, Mike, Mets	.850	8	4	13	3	20	0

Player, Team	Pct.	G	PO	A	E	TC	DP
Medrano, Ricardo, White Sox	.769	6	1	9	3	13	1
Mejias, Oliver, Pirates	.667	2	0	2	1	3	0
Nicley, Dru, Astros	.795	24	7	28	9	44	0
Nova, Geraldo, Red Sox	.837	19	7	34	8	49	6
NUNEZ, Jose, Royals	.944	40	33	84	7	124	4
Oropeza, Asdrubal, Braves	.905	39	20	75	10	105	8
Ortiz, Miguel, Yankees	.900	7	6	21	3	30	0
Pena, Jose, Devil Rays	.827	21	11	32	9	52	4
Perez, Jesse, Orioles	.861	34	18	69	14	101	4
Petru, Rich, Royals	1.000	1	0	1	0	1	0
Proctor, Mark, Mets	.968	10	9	21	1	31	1
Ramirez, Edgar, Devil Rays	.913	10	7	14	2	23	1
Ramirez, Juan, Royals	1.000	1	0	1	0	1	0
Ramirez, Luis, Orioles	.944	26	23	28	3	54	2
Reynoso, Ismael, Marlins	.886	13	9	22	4	35	1
Romano, Jason, Rangers	.810	29	14	50	15	79	3
Samboy, Nelson, Astros	1.000	1	1	0	0	1	0
Schaffer, Jake, Tigers	.778	5	3	11	4	18	0
Torres, Franklin, Twins	.960	12	4	20	1	25	2
Valentine, Anthony, Mets	.667	1	1	1	1	3	0
Valerio, Denny, Twins	1.000	2	1	0	0	1	0
Vilorio, Leonel, Twins	.907	49	28	89	12	129	4
Wade, Chip, Twins	.957	9	4	18	1	23	0
Washington, Enrico, Pirates	.812	24	18	38	13	69	1
Washington, Maurice, Pirates	.909	2	1	9	1	11	1
Wheeler, Mike, Astros	.884	29	23	38	8	69	3

TRIPLE PLAY: Infante.

SHORTSTOPS

Player, Team	Pct.	G	PO	A	E	TC	DP
Acevedo, Luis, Rangers	.926	17	32	55	7	94	14
Alfaro, Jason, Astros	.887	13	18	29	6	53	8
Alvarez, Jimmy, Twins	.952	51	78	178	13	269	33
Bautista, Jose, Twins	.795	12	7	24	8	39	2
Bautista, Juan, Orioles	.813	3	2	11	3	16	2
Bautista, Rayner, Tigers	.915	49	45	137	17	199	17
Beltres, Manuel, Yankees	.922	20	32	51	7	90	9
Betemit, Wilson, Braves	.856	32	48	71	20	139	7
Borges, Elio, White Sox	.875	3	3	4	1	8	2
Brito, Alen, Royals	.769	3	4	6	3	13	1
Calderon, Henry, Royals	.923	22	28	68	8	104	10
Canaguacan, Oscar, Yankees	.667	3	4	2	3	9	0
Capista, Aaron, Red Sox	.915	31	32	76	10	118	17
Caracciolo, Anthony, Expos	.864	5	8	11	3	22	0
Cleto, Ambioris, Pirates	.958	34	52	108	7	167	16
Collier, Marc, Orioles	.950	13	18	39	3	60	10
Cordero, Willy, Rangers	.857	9	5	19	4	28	4
Cruz, Luis, Devil Rays	1.000	1	0	3	0	3	0
De La Cruz, Ruddi, Mets	.908	38	48	129	18	195	19
Dellaero, Jason, White Sox	.846	4	5	6	2	13	1
DIAZ, Maikell, Orioles	.978	42	65	117	4	186	24
Escobar, Alex, Mets	.875	1	1	6	1	8	1
Garcia, Rafael, Royals	.889	30	40	88	16	144	14
Garza, Rolando, White Sox	.896	20	24	36	7	67	7
Guerrero, Jason, Devil Rays	.884	25	29	47	10	86	12
Gutierrez, Victor, Pirates	.935	25	31	70	7	108	5
Hasbun, Andy, Tigers	.905	17	21	36	6	63	3
Hill, Bobby, Mets	.928	20	25	39	5	69	4
Hoshina, Koji, Expos	.902	9	12	25	4	41	3
Leidens, Enrique, Expos	1.000	1	2	0	0	2	0
Mann, Derek, Devil Rays	.963	7	8	18	1	27	5
Mateo, Victor, Yankees	1.000	2	2	1	0	3	0
Mendez, Donaldo, Astros	.924	47	62	157	18	237	31
Mendoza, Angel, Red Sox	.863	23	27	61	14	102	14
Nolasco, Regino, Orioles	.875	3	3	11	2	16	2
Olivares, Teuris, Yankees	.930	38	65	121	14	200	27
Ramirez, Edgar, Devil Rays	.872	32	29	73	15	117	12
Reding, Josh, Royals	.944	46	69	132	12	213	20
Reynoso, Ismael, Marlins	.958	29	47	90	6	143	14
Roman, Junior, White Sox	.943	36	57	108	10	175	26
Ruiz, Willy, Royals	.951	9	11	28	2	41	7
Santos, Ramon, Red Sox	.964	8	10	17	1	28	2
Schaffer, Jake, Tigers	1.000	1	0	1	0	1	0
Shuck, Jason, Mets	1.000	1	1	3	0	4	1
Stevens, Tony, Twins	.905	7	5	14	2	21	3
Velazquez, Juan, Braves	.915	26	37	71	10	118	20
Warriax, Brandon, Rangers	.931	38	29	106	10	145	13
Washington, Enrico, Pirates	.500	1	1	2	3	6	1
Washington, Kelley, Marlins	.887	33	45	89	17	151	6
Wheeler, Mike, Astros	.895	5	7	10	2	19	5

TRIPLE PLAY: Nolasco.

OUTFIELDERS

Player, Team	Pct.	G	PO	A	E	TC	DP
Abreu, Miguel, Marlins	.935	27	28	1	2	31	0
Airoso, Kurt, Tigers	1.000	3	2	0	0	2	0
Aldridge, Cory, Braves	.955	29	21	0	1	22	0
Alleyne, Roberto, Astros	1.000	2	4	1	0	5	1
Almonte, Claudio, Twins	.981	50	53	0	1	54	0
Arias, Jeison, Devil Rays	.981	34	52	1	1	54	0
Austin, Peter, Pirates	1.000	17	26	0	0	26	0
Batista, Angel, Devil Rays*	.969	35	61	1	2	64	0
Benjamin, Al, Pirates	.949	24	36	1	2	39	0
Bradley, Milton, Expos	.938	9	15	0	1	16	0
Brown, Richard, Yankees*	.900	5	9	0	1	10	0
Bystrowski, Robert, Astros	.990	51	92	3	1	96	0
Caradonna, Brett, White Sox	.981	31	49	3	1	53	0
Carter, Shannon, Orioles*	.978	48	85	4	2	91	1
Castillo, Geramel, Rangers	.970	40	60	4	2	66	1
Charles, Curtis, Orioles	1.000	6	9	1	0	10	0
Chavez, Endy, Mets*	.967	33	50	8	2	60	1
Cochran, Ed, White Sox	.923	7	12	0	1	13	0
Colson, Julian, Astros	1.000	4	2	0	0	2	0
Crespo, Jesse, Braves	1.000	12	13	0	0	13	0
Cruz, Geronimo, Rangers*	.931	25	24	3	2	29	0
DASHER, Melvin, Royals	1.000	47	65	1	0	66	0
Davis, Jerry, Pirates	1.000	23	42	1	0	43	0
De La Cruz, Raul, Pirates	.955	15	20	1	1	22	0
De La Espada, Miguel, Astros	.976	48	77	3	2	82	1
Deshazer, Jeremy, Astros	.976	33	38	3	1	42	0
Durham, Chad, White Sox	.952	12	19	1	1	21	0
Edge, Michael, Expos	.935	50	96	4	7	107	0
Edwards, Randy, Pirates	1.000	3	6	0	0	6	0
Escobar, Alex, Mets	.966	19	26	2	1	29	0
Ferguson, Dwight, Red Sox*	.957	28	41	4	2	47	1
Fernandez, Winston, Rangers* ..	1.000	17	33	0	0	33	0
Fisher, Anthony, Rangers	1.000	4	4	0	0	4	0
Flora, Kevin, Astros	1.000	2	2	0	0	2	0
Flores, Jose, Red Sox	.977	27	41	1	1	43	0
Forbes, Kevin, Expos	.944	22	32	2	2	36	1
Franklin, Toby, Twins	1.000	3	3	1	0	4	0
Garcia, Douglas, Rangers*	.980	32	45	3	1	49	1
Graham, Tarik, Royals*	1.000	23	36	3	0	39	1
Guerrero, Francisco, Devil Rays..	.939	34	58	4	4	66	1
Guerrero, Jason, Devil Rays	1.000	3	8	0	0	8	0
Gunner, Chie, Devil Rays	1.000	40	42	3	0	45	1
Hafner, Travis, Rangers	.909	10	9	1	1	11	0
Harris, Kevin, Rangers	.909	27	29	1	3	33	0
Harrison, Jamal, Twins	1.000	4	6	0	0	6	0
Hazelton, Justin, Tigers	.979	31	45	2	1	48	0
Heffernan, Christian, Braves	.938	36	58	3	4	65	0
Hernandez, Rafeal, Expos	1.000	21	26	1	0	27	0
Hill, Michael, White Sox	.964	44	50	3	2	55	0
Holifield, Rick, Pirates*	1.000	4	8	0	0	8	0
Hooper, Daren, Orioles	1.000	19	23	1	0	24	1
Hoshina, Koji, Expos	1.000	1	1	0	0	1	0
Ide, Antoine, Orioles	1.000	29	47	2	0	49	2
Iglesias, Rigoberto, White Sox..	.967	42	52	6	2	60	2
Jackson, Quantaa, Marlins	1.000	19	27	1	0	28	0
Jones, Andrew, Pirates	.983	25	55	4	1	60	0
Kelly, Kenneth, Devil Rays	.958	26	43	3	2	48	0
Kingsale, Eugene, Orioles	.941	6	16	0	1	17	0
Kirkpatrick, Michael, Orioles*	.973	26	34	2	1	37	1
Lara, Balmes, Tigers	.912	35	59	3	6	68	1
Ledee, Ricky, Yankees*	1.000	1	1	0	0	1	0
Lehr, Ryan, Mets	.960	28	23	1	1	25	1
Little, Josh, Devil Rays*	1.000	21	21	1	0	22	0
McCorvey, Kenneth, Twins	.944	35	48	3	3	54	0
McKinley, Michael, Red Sox.	.929	18	13	0	1	14	0
McKinney, Antonio, Tigers	.971	18	33	0	1	34	0
Mejia, Renato, Marlins	.842	23	16	0	3	19	0
Melian, Jackson, Yankees	.975	53	110	7	3	120	0
Mendoza, Angel, Red Sox	.923	24	31	5	3	39	1
Meyer, Brad, Twins	1.000	14	14	1	0	15	0
Milton, Prinz, Braves	.727	23	16	0	6	22	0
Mora, Juan, Tigers*	.963	41	48	4	2	54	0
Morales, Domingo, Orioles	1.000	20	24	0	0	24	0
Morgan, Todd, Orioles	1.000	7	9	0	0	9	0
Mounts, Alfonso, White Sox	1.000	22	43	0	0	43	0
Mulvehill, Brandon, Mets	.966	39	49	7	2	58	1
Myers, Tootie, Expos	.967	18	28	1	1	30	0
Myles, Dion, Devil Rays	1.000	5	2	0	0	2	0
Ndungidi, Ntema, Orioles	.938	18	28	2	2	32	1
Nicolas, Jose, Pirates	.935	34	56	2	4	62	2
Nova, Geraldo, Red Sox	.923	11	10	2	1	13	0

Player, Team	Pct.	G	PO	A	E	TC	DP
Pass, Patrick, Marlins	1.000	15	11	1	0	12	0
Pender, Darrell, Tigers	.978	33	44	1	1	46	0
Perez, Alejandro, Red Sox	.952	44	55	5	3	63	0
Persails, Michael, Red Sox	1.000	8	7	1	0	8	0
Pimentel, Eddie, Marlins	.930	37	39	1	3	43	0
Prosper, Gerard, Mets*	1.000	36	32	2	0	34	0
Quero, Pedro, Expos	1.000	42	49	6	0	55	0
Raines, Tim, Yankees	1.000	1	2	0	0	2	0
Rains, Nick, Mets	.964	25	25	2	1	28	0
Ramirez, Luis, Orioles	1.000	18	26	1	0	27	1
Ramon, Ricardo, White Sox*	.927	26	37	1	3	41	0
Reed, Brian, Marlins	1.000	42	54	3	0	57	0
Reyes, Deurys, Tigers*	.942	37	61	4	4	69	2
Rockow, Jeremy, Pirates*	.958	13	23	0	1	24	0
Rodriguez, John, Yankees*	.985	36	62	2	1	65	0
Roman, Junior, White Sox	1.000	1	2	0	0	2	0
Smith, Marcus, Twins	.917	6	9	2	1	12	0
Southward, Deshawn, Twins	.986	55	64	6	1	71	3
Sutton, Bruce, Twins	1.000	30	36	0	0	36	0
Tancred, Lachlan, Expos	1.000	21	41	2	0	43	0
Taveras, Jose, Royals	.978	57	84	4	2	90	0
Thames, Marcus, Yankees	.978	55	86	4	2	92	1
Tillis, Cameron, Royals	.925	23	33	4	3	40	1
Tomberlin, Andy, Mets*	1.000	2	5	1	0	6	0
TORRES, Rafael, Royals	1.000	43	60	5	0	65	2
Valdez, Angel, Yankees	.842	26	16	0	3	19	0
Valerio, Denny, Twins	1.000	16	9	0	0	9	0
Vasquez, Alejandro, Astros*	.918	49	74	4	7	85	0
Vazquez, Alex, Rangers	.833	4	4	1	1	6	1
Vilorio, Leonel, Twins	1.000	5	2	0	0	2	0
Walker, Javon, Marlins	.889	15	24	0	3	27	0
Ward, Gregory, Braves	.947	48	89	1	5	95	0
Washington, Cory, Marlins	1.000	12	12	0	0	12	0
Washington, Dion, Yankees	.962	27	24	1	1	26	0
Washington, Maurice, Pirates	.966	25	27	1	1	29	0
Wilson, Heath, Braves	1.000	3	2	1	0	3	0
Wright, Corey, Rangers*	.983	39	55	2	1	58	1
Yancy, Michael, Mets	.971	34	32	2	1	35	0
Zapata, Wilson, Red Sox	.929	40	46	6	4	56	2
Ziths, Deshawn, Orioles	1.000	12	6	1	0	7	0

CATCHERS

Player, Team	Pct.	G	PO	A	E	TC	DP	PB
Aceves, Jonathan, White Sox	.962	27	157	22	7	186	3	4
Ackerman, Scott, Expos	.969	29	160	27	6	193	2	7
Adorno, Wilson, Pirates	.958	14	82	10	4	96	0	3
Alvarez, Julio, Tigers	1.000	2	8	4	0	12	0	1
Alvarez, Nelson, Tigers	.991	19	103	10	1	114	0	1
Bello, Jilberto, Orioles	.977	13	67	18	2	87	2	2
Boscan, Jean, Braves	.981	35	234	27	5	266	0	13
Brito, Alen, Royals	1.000	3	22	4	0	26	0	2
Brito, Juan, Royals	.980	23	128	17	3	148	2	1
CANDELARIA, Vidal, Yankees	.991	35	199	29	2	230	3	7
Cardona, Luis, Mets	.857	2	12	0	2	14	0	5
Chaidez, Juan, Red Sox	.909	3	9	1	1	11	1	0
Cook, Josh, Astros	1.000	2	7	0	0	9	0	1
Cota, Humberto, Devil Rays	.985	42	294	26	5	325	4	10
Cruz, Andres, Devil Rays	1.000	4	8	1	0	9	0	1
Devarez, Cesar, Devil Rays	1.000	2	7	0	0	7	0	1
DeArmas, Fran, White Sox	.950	16	97	17	6	120	2	10
DeJesus, Wilmer, Expos	.986	11	63	10	1	74	1	0
Diaz, Christian, Royals	1.000	4	9	2	0	11	0	2
Diaz, Diogenes, Pirates	.980	33	216	33	5	254	3	1
Escalante, Jaime, Orioles	.966	15	89	23	4	116	1	9
Ewan, Benjamin, Braves	.991	11	98	11	1	110	0	4
Fatheree, Danny, Astros	.926	17	59	4	5	68	0	6
Feliz, Joselyn, Marlins	.988	32	204	42	3	249	1	5
Frawley, Scott, Braves	1.000	10	67	2	0	69	0	1
Fuentes, Omar, Yankees	.986	31	175	40	3	218	1	7
Guzman, Juan, Orioles	.989	15	79	15	1	95	1	3
Guzman, Martin, Devil Rays	.970	10	61	3	2	66	0	1
Hahn, Cameron, Astros	.964	28	152	10	6	168	0	4
Harper, Brandon, Marlins	1.000	2	12	2	0	14	0	1
Herrera, Pedro, Royals	.965	36	221	28	9	258	1	9
Hill, Jason, Astros	1.000	2	12	0	0	12	0	1
Hyde, Brandon, White Sox	.980	21	136	12	3	151	1	2
Jenkins, Brian, Mets	.966	30	198	31	8	237	1	9
Lambert, Clark, Mets	.989	34	243	32	3	278	2	2
Meier, Bob, Yankees	1.000	3	10	1	0	11	0	0
Montero, Jose, Rangers	.976	13	77	5	2	84	0	3
Morales, Stephen, Marlins	.972	20	121	17	4	142	2	6
Nanita, Emmanuel, Twins	.900	6	16	2	2	20	0	1

Player, Team	Pct.	G	PO	A	E	TC	DP	PB
Ochoa, Javier, Astros	.970	30	198	31	7	236	0	5
O'Toole, Bobby, Orioles	1.000	4	18	3	0	21	0	0
Parker, Chris, Tigers	.963	18	84	21	4	109	1	3
Paul, Josh, White Sox	.900	5	21	6	3	30	0	0
Pena, Rodolfo, Red Sox	.985	43	348	36	6	390	4	8
Reese, Nate, Marlins	.973	11	62	11	2	75	0	1
Reyes, Jose, Pirates	.976	12	67	15	2	84	0	4
Rivera, Luis, Expos	.988	22	151	20	2	173	1	3
Rivera, Michael, Tigers	.995	27	189	22	1	212	3	3
Rojas, Mo, Red Sox	.976	23	151	14	4	169	3	9
St. Pierre, Maxim, Tigers	.956	15	55	10	3	68	0	6
Sassanella, Jeremy, Tigers	1.000	3	9	1	0	10	0	3
Taveras, Luis, Rangers	.960	33	177	15	8	200	2	8
Torres, Gabriel, Twins	.979	41	309	62	8	379	0	7
Torres, Jason, Rangers	.968	29	192	21	7	220	0	6
Valentine, Anthony, Mets	1.000	2	1	0	0	1	0	0
Vazquez, Carlos, Devil Rays	.980	16	90	7	2	99	1	6
Viera, Rob, Pirates	.980	6	44	5	1	50	0	0
Wade, Chip, Twins	.993	22	119	27	1	147	3	4
Werth, Jayson, Orioles	.964	21	144	18	6	168	4	4
Wilson, Heath, Braves	1.000	5	35	2	0	37	0	2
Woods, James, Royals	.909	2	10	0	1	11	0	0

PITCHERS

Player, Team	Pct.	G	PO	A	E	TC	DP
Acosta, Alberto, Yankees	.500	9	0	1	1	2	1
Affeldt, Jeremy, Royals*	.833	10	1	4	1	6	1
Akin, Aaron, Marlins	1.000	4	0	3	0	3	0
Alfaro, Jason, Astros	1.000	4	2	1	0	3	0
Almonte, Hector, Marlins	1.000	8	2	4	0	6	0
Alvarado, David, Pirates	.750	12	3	6	3	12	1
Alvord, Aaron, Tigers	.333	9	0	1	2	3	0
Andujar, Jesse, Expos	.778	17	2	5	2	9	1
Arias, Rafael, Red Sox	.778	11	4	10	4	18	1
Arnold, Jamie, Braves	1.000	5	3	3	0	6	0
Arthurs, Shane, Expos	1.000	8	2	1	0	3	0
Avery, Steve, Red Sox*	.500	1	0	1	1	2	0
Balfour, Grant, Twins	.952	13	3	17	1	21	0
Beatty, Blaine, Pirates*	1.000	4	3	6	0	9	0
Becker, Keith, Red Sox	1.000	5	1	0	0	1	0
Benoit, Joaquin, Rangers	.929	10	4	9	1	14	2
Benzing, Skipp, Red Sox	.857	6	1	5	1	7	0
Betti, Rich, Red Sox*	1.000	4	1	2	0	3	0
Blackmore, John, Astros	.875	15	1	6	1	8	1
Blais, Mike, Red Sox	1.000	3	1	0	0	1	0
Blanco, Alberto, Astros*	1.000	2	0	2	0	2	0
Blanco, Pablo, Marlins	.857	11	0	6	1	7	0
Blevins, Jeremy, Yankees	1.000	11	1	6	0	7	0
Bogeajis, Daniel, Astros	.800	7	1	3	1	5	1
Bowers, Jason, Braves*	1.000	12	2	2	0	4	0
Brazoban, Melvin, Rangers	.800	14	0	4	1	5	0
Bridges, Donald, Expos	1.000	5	1	1	0	2	0
Brown, Michael, Pirates*	1.000	3	0	1	0	1	0
Budsky, Pavel, Royals	1.000	6	2	2	0	4	0
Burnett, Allan, Mets	1.000	3	4	0	0	4	0
Cafaro, Robert, Devil Rays	1.000	4	1	1	0	2	0
Cain, Travis, Devil Rays	1.000	4	0	2	0	2	0
Calvert, Klae, Red Sox	.923	12	3	9	1	13	3
Casteel, Raymond, Orioles	.929	15	6	7	1	14	1
Castillo, Jose, Tigers	1.000	12	0	13	0	13	0
Ceasar, Donald, Braves	.857	10	2	4	1	7	0
Celta, Nicolas, Astros*	.778	8	3	4	2	9	0
Centeno, Juan, Astros	.692	7	3	6	4	13	0
Chivers, Jason, Mets*	1.000	11	1	0	0	1	0
Colon, Roman, Braves	.889	14	2	6	1	9	0
Connolly, Sean, White Sox	.800	15	1	3	1	5	0
Converse, Jim, Yankees	.000	3	0	1	1	1	0
Coppinger, Rocky, Orioles	1.000	3	1	1	0	2	1
Corcoran, Tim, Mets	1.000	10	2	3	0	5	0
Coriolan, Roberto, Yankees	1.000	10	0	4	0	4	1
Corominas, Mike, Astros*	1.000	8	3	2	0	5	0
Corsi, Jim, Astros	1.000	3	0	1	0	1	0
Cremer, Richard, Yankees*	.917	10	2	9	1	12	0
Crutchley, Rickey, Royals*	1.000	15	1	4	0	5	0
Cruz, Charlie, Orioles	1.000	15	0	3	0	3	1
Curtice, John, Red Sox*	1.000	4	0	5	0	5	1
Curtis, Gregory, Orioles	.889	15	2	6	1	9	0
Daniels, Ronney, Expos*	1.000	8	1	4	0	5	0
Davis, Casey, Devil Rays*	1.000	13	1	3	0	4	0
Davis, Doug, Rangers*	.750	4	1	2	1	4	0
De La Cruz, Ynocencio, Mets	.846	6	2	9	2	13	0
Deckard, Edward, Devil Rays	1.000	4	1	2	0	3	1

Player, Team	Pct.	G	PO	A	E	TC	DP
DeLeon, Julio, Devil Rays	.800	9	0	4	1	5	0
Desrosiers, Erik, White Sox	1.000	7	1	3	0	4	0
Diaz, Billy, Rangers	.909	9	4	6	1	11	1
Dinyar, Eric, Tigers	1.000	7	0	1	0	1	0
Dolby, Lawrence, Braves	.750	10	1	2	1	4	0
Dotel, Octavio, Mets	1.000	3	1	0	0	1	0
Dougherty, James, Mets*	1.000	11	4	11	0	15	0
Douglass, Ryan, Royals	1.000	12	7	8	0	15	1
Douglass, Sean, Orioles	1.000	9	1	4	0	5	1
Duchscherer, Justin, Red Sox	.833	10	0	10	2	12	0
Eavenson, Samuel, Yankees	.750	10	1	2	1	4	0
Ehlers, Corey, Marlins	.500	2	0	1	1	2	0
Eiland, Dave, Mets	1.000	2	1	0	0	1	0
Encarnacion, Orlando, Mets	1.000	13	0	3	0	3	0
Ericks, John, Pirates	1.000	9	0	2	0	2	0
Espina, Rendy, Twins*	.818	8	3	6	2	11	1
Farizo, Brad, Marlins	1.000	11	6	9	0	15	3
Farson, Bryan, Pirates*	.500	8	1	0	1	2	0
Felix, Miguel, White Sox	1.000	3	1	3	0	4	0
Figueroa, Carlos, Rangers*	1.000	5	1	2	0	3	0
Figueroa, Juan, White Sox	.733	11	3	8	4	15	0
Finol, Ricardo, Pirates	1.000	6	1	5	0	6	2
Fitts, Brian, Twins	.778	10	2	5	2	9	0
Flock, Rick, Twins	.750	12	0	3	1	4	1
Forti, Eugene, White Sox*	1.000	11	0	13	0	13	0
Fraser, Joe, Expos	1.000	3	0	1	0	1	1
Fretwell, Joseph, Expos	1.000	8	1	1	0	2	0
Frias, Yovany, White Sox	1.000	7	0	1	0	1	0
Gaerte, Travis, Pirates	.833	18	2	8	2	12	0
Gagliano, Steve, Marlins	.958	12	8	15	1	24	0
Gamboa, Javier, Royals	1.000	2	0	1	0	1	0
Garcia, Ariel, White Sox	1.000	10	0	1	0	1	0
Garcia, Luis, Red Sox	1.000	8	1	6	0	7	0
Garvin, James, Marlins	.900	14	1	8	1	10	1
Glaser, Eric, Red Sox	1.000	7	0	2	0	2	0
Goetz, Geoff, Mets*	1.000	8	3	6	0	9	0
Gomez, Rafael, Mets	1.000	4	1	4	0	5	0
Gomez, Ricardo, Pirates	1.000	5	1	2	0	3	0
Gonzalez, Edwin, Royals	.833	3	3	2	1	6	1
Gonzalez, Michael, Pirates*	.909	7	2	8	1	11	1
Gorman, Pat, Mets	1.000	11	2	4	0	6	0
Grabow, John, Pirates*	.875	11	2	5	1	8	0
Gray, Jason, White Sox	1.000	10	3	4	0	7	0
Gresko, Michael, Pirates*	1.000	6	0	3	0	3	0
Guzman, Ambiorix, Rangers	.800	5	0	4	1	5	0
Guzman, Wilson, Pirates*	1.000	9	1	6	0	7	0
Hall, Billy, Astros	1.000	7	2	3	0	5	0
Hamulack, Timothy, Astros*	.769	23	5	5	3	13	0
Harden, Nathan, Braves	.545	11	1	5	5	11	0
Harvey, Terry, Devil Rays	.750	5	0	3	1	4	0
Hlodan, George, Pirates	1.000	3	0	4	0	4	0
Hohenstein, Andrew, Pirates	1.000	3	1	1	0	2	0
Hollins, Jessie, Yankees	1.000	4	0	1	0	1	1
Hollis, Ron, Red Sox	1.000	4	1	1	0	2	0
Holzbauer, Joseph, Braves	.000	15	0	0	1	1	0
Isringhausen, Jason, Mets	1.000	1	1	0	0	1	0
Izquierdo, Hansel, White Sox	1.000	5	0	2	0	2	0
Jacobs, Jake, Twins	.333	23	0	1	2	3	0
Jaime, Wilson, Astros	1.000	18	2	1	0	3	0
Janssen, Mike, Astros	1.000	13	2	4	0	6	0
Jimenez, Ricardo, Orioles	1.000	8	1	7	0	8	0
Johnson, Jeremiah, Orioles	1.000	6	0	3	0	3	0
Johnston, Bruce, Tigers	.909	18	4	6	1	11	0
Jones, Sean, Orioles	1.000	9	2	1	0	3	0
Julio, Jorge, Expos	1.000	15	3	4	0	7	0
Klein, Cody, Yankees*	1.000	10	0	4	0	4	1
Knowles, Michael, Yankees	.917	9	1	10	1	12	0
Kvasnicka, Jonathon, White Sox	1.000	8	3	4	0	7	0
Kyzar, Cory, Royals	1.000	3	1	0	0	1	0
Langston, David, Yankees	1.000	11	3	2	0	5	2
Ledden, Ryan, Devil Rays	1.000	8	0	1	0	1	0
Lopez, Carlos, Expos	.857	14	1	5	1	7	0
Lopez, Gustavo, Marlins	1.000	7	2	7	0	9	0
Loux, Shane, Tigers	1.000	10	3	4	0	7	0
Lundberg, David, Rangers	1.000	14	1	12	0	13	0
Luttig, Christopher, Pirates*	.500	12	1	0	1	2	0
Mancha, Tony, Royals	.882	13	9	6	2	17	1
Maness, Nicholas, Mets	.688	11	4	7	5	16	0
Mangieri, John, Mets	1.000	6	4	3	0	7	0
Marache, Luis, Orioles*	.833	11	2	13	3	18	1
Martinez, Carlos, Royals*	.833	14	0	5	1	6	0
Martinez, Mark, Red Sox*	1.000	14	1	5	0	6	0
McCormick, Terry, Devil Rays*	.923	10	4	8	1	13	0
Medrano, Juan, Royals	.667	15	3	3	3	9	0
Mejia, Luis, Yankees	1.000	13	1	2	0	3	0
Melson, Nate, Twins	.750	12	3	3	2	8	0
Mendoza, Geronimo, White Sox	.857	12	2	4	1	7	0
Mercado, Hector, Tigers	.909	15	2	8	1	11	0
Mikkola, Shaun, Mets	.909	14	3	7	1	11	1
Miller, Greg, Red Sox*	1.000	4	0	1	0	1	0
Minaya, Pedro, Marlins	.818	12	2	7	2	11	0
Mitchell, Kendrick, White Sox	1.000	4	0	2	0	2	0
Molina, Primitivo, Red Sox	1.000	15	0	2	0	2	0
Montanez, Jorge, Red Sox	1.000	5	0	1	0	1	0
Montemayor, Humberto, Red Sox	.500	9	0	1	1	2	0
Moore, Christopher, Marlins	.941	10	0	16	1	17	1
Morales, Johnny, Orioles*	.833	18	2	3	1	6	1
Morel, Jose, Pirates*	1.000	7	1	1	0	2	0
Morrobel, Juan, Pirates*	1.000	3	0	1	0	1	0
Moylan, Peter, Twins	1.000	12	3	5	0	8	0
Mundine, John, Twins	1.000	15	3	1	0	4	0
Myers, Rob, Twins	1.000	8	2	3	0	5	0
MYERS, Taylor, Royals	1.000	11	7	18	0	25	1
Naulty, Dan, Twins	1.000	2	0	1	0	1	0
Neal, Blaine, Marlins	.250	10	1	0	3	4	0
Orellano, Rafael, Red Sox*	1.000	2	1	2	0	3	1
Orta, Juan, Expos	.917	19	2	9	1	12	0
Oswalt, Roy, Astros	.833	5	1	4	1	6	0
Padua, Geraldo, Yankees	.818	11	5	4	2	11	1
Paraqueima, Jesus, Yankees	.500	3	0	1	1	2	0
Parkerson, Michael, Pirates*	1.000	14	1	11	0	12	0
Pascarella, Josh, Astros	.778	10	4	3	2	9	0
Pavlik, Roger, Rangers	1.000	2	2	1	0	3	0
Peguero, Darwin, Astros*	.818	9	1	8	2	11	0
Peguero, Radhame, Devil Rays	1.000	3	3	3	0	6	0
Percibal, Billy, Orioles	1.000	4	0	3	0	3	0
Perez, Elvis, White Sox*	.889	12	3	13	2	18	1
Perez, Julio, Expos	.944	10	7	10	1	18	2
Petique, Marino, Devil Rays	.667	22	0	2	1	3	0
Phillips, Randy, Braves*	1.000	4	0	1	0	1	1
Pidgeon, Matt, Marlins	.833	16	1	4	1	6	0
Pierson, Jason, Mets*	1.000	1	0	1	0	1	0
Porter, Bobby, Braves*	.333	7	0	1	2	3	0
Price, Thomas, Devil Rays	.857	15	1	5	1	7	0
Pulsipher, Bill, Mets*	1.000	2	0	5	0	5	0
Quintero, Jose, Rangers*	.895	12	1	16	2	19	1
Quiros, Misael, Pirates	.833	13	3	7	2	12	0
Rahilly, Michael, Expos	1.000	12	0	1	0	1	0
Ramirez, Horacio, Braves*	.900	11	3	6	1	10	0
Ratliff, Craig, Orioles	.789	12	3	12	4	19	0
Reed, Aaron, Tigers	.800	13	2	2	1	5	0
Regalado, Frank, Devil Rays	1.000	18	0	4	0	4	2
Reith, Brian, Yankees	.875	12	3	11	2	16	2
Reynolds, Chris, Devil Rays	1.000	8	0	4	0	4	0
Ridenour, Jeffrey, Rangers	.750	12	3	3	2	8	1
Rincon, Juan, Twins	1.000	11	3	13	0	16	1
Rios, Romualdo, Rangers	.857	10	0	6	1	7	0
Rivera, Homero, Tigers*	.833	15	5	10	3	18	0
Rivera, Marco, Expos*	.714	19	1	4	2	7	0
Rivera, Raul, Expos	.714	15	1	4	2	7	0
Roberts, Marquis, Devil Rays*	.947	12	4	14	1	19	2
Roberts, Richard, Tigers*	.800	11	1	3	1	5	0
Rodriguez, Cristobal, Expos	1.000	13	0	7	0	7	0
Rodriguez, Jorge, Yankees	1.000	17	1	4	0	5	3
Rodriguez, Wilfredo, Astros*	.875	12	7	7	2	16	0
Rojas, Cesar, Rangers	1.000	10	1	1	0	2	0
Roller, Adam, Red Sox	1.000	10	0	2	0	2	0
Rolocut, Brian, Devil Rays	1.000	3	0	2	0	2	0
Rosario, Rafael, Tigers	.769	22	4	6	3	13	0
Rosario, Reynaldo, Tigers	.800	21	2	2	1	5	0
Rupp, Michael, Red Sox	.842	11	4	12	3	19	0
Ryba, Jason, Orioles	.600	14	1	2	2	5	0
Sadler, Carl, Expos*	1.000	9	0	4	0	4	0
Santana, Alfredo, Tigers	.778	19	2	5	2	9	1
Santana, Fausto, White Sox	1.000	13	3	5	0	8	0
Santana, Johan, Astros*	.800	9	1	7	2	10	0
Santos, Juan, Orioles	1.000	3	1	0	0	1	0
Sasaki, Junichi, Expos	1.000	11	0	4	0	4	0
Schmidt, Patrick, Braves*	.667	12	1	1	1	3	0
Sheets, Matt, Twins	.889	15	6	10	2	18	0
Shields, Drew, Marlins	1.000	10	3	3	0	6	0
Shourds, Anthony, Rangers	1.000	13	1	6	0	7	1
Siegel, Justin, Rangers*	1.000	4	2	1	0	3	0
Silva, Douglas, Rangers	.889	11	2	6	1	9	0

Player, Team	Pct.	G	PO	A	E	TC	DP
Simpson, Cory, Braves	.909	12	4	6	1	11	0
Solano, Francisco, Royals	.882	12	3	12	2	17	0
Sordo, Fernando, Mets	1.000	11	4	4	0	8	0
Spinelli, Mike, Red Sox*	.000	3	0	0	3	3	0
Standridge, Jason, Devil Rays	.941	13	4	12	1	17	1
Stenger, Pat, Twins	1.000	15	5	6	0	11	0
Stephens, John, Orioles	1.000	9	3	2	0	5	0
Stinson, Kevin, White Sox	1.000	10	0	2	0	2	0
Stowe, Chris, Expos	.875	9	4	3	1	8	1
Sturdy, Tim, Twins	.923	9	3	9	1	13	0
Stutz, Shawn, Devil Rays	1.000	2	0	3	0	3	1
Suggs, Willie, Mets	.625	10	1	9	6	16	2
Sullivan, Peter, Astros	.800	14	3	1	1	5	1
Sylvester, Billy, Braves	.929	12	2	11	1	14	6
Tanksley, Scott, Twins	1.000	4	0	1	0	1	0
Tellez, Eloy, White Sox	1.000	2	0	1	0	1	0
Tetz, Kristofer, Expos	.500	3	1	0	1	2	0
Theodile, Simeon, Orioles	1.000	15	3	2	0	5	0
Thomas, Gaige, Marlins	1.000	12	2	1	0	3	0
Thurman, Corey, Royals	.833	8	3	2	1	6	0
Torres, Michael, Royals	1.000	15	1	5	0	6	0
Tynan, Christopher, Rangers	.750	11	3	6	3	12	0
Tyrrell, Jim, Red Sox*	1.000	3	0	1	0	1	0
Valle, Yoiset, Yankees*	.750	11	0	3	1	4	0
Vallis, Jamie, Twins*	1.000	14	3	6	0	9	0
Vanderhorst, Francisco, Royals	.500	18	0	1	1	2	0
Verdin, Cesar, Yankees*	1.000	3	0	3	0	3	0
Vogt, Robert, Pirates*	.800	12	2	6	2	10	1
Walker, Pete, Red Sox	1.000	4	0	1	0	1	0
Walker, Tyler, Mets	1.000	5	1	1	0	2	0
Wallace, Derek, Mets	1.000	8	0	1	0	1	0
Walsh, Steven, Royals	1.000	4	0	1	0	1	0
Webb, Alan, Tigers*	.714	9	1	4	2	7	1
Whitley, Garry, White Sox*	1.000	3	0	1	0	1	0
Williams, Bradford, Yankees*	1.000	11	0	5	0	5	0
Williams, Thomas, White Sox	1.000	11	1	3	0	4	0
Willoughby, Justin, Braves*	1.000	13	0	5	0	5	0
Wilson, Paul, Mets	1.000	4	0	2	0	2	0
Wood, Stanton, Yankees	1.000	17	0	2	0	2	0
Wright, Barrett, Devil Rays	.875	13	1	6	1	8	0
Wright, Jason, Devil Rays	1.000	14	1	2	0	3	0
Young, Spencer, Devil Rays	1.000	14	1	1	0	2	0
Zamarripa, Mark, Tigers	1.000	4	0	1	0	1	0

The following players did not have any fielding statistics at the positions indicated or appeared only as a designated hitter, pinch-hitter or pinch-runner: August, ss; Bailey, of; D. Baker, dh; J. Baker, p; Bello, 2b; Bere, p; Boehringer, p; Bosio, p; Bravo, p; Cederblad, p; Colina, dh; Conway, p; Al. Cruz, c; Cubillan, p; Doan, p; Durick, p; Escalante, p; Escalona, 3b; Freeman, of; Furcal, of; Harnisch, p; Haselman, dh; Hayden, p; Hecker, p; Hodges, of; Howard, p; Huntsman, of; St. Jones, p; Koch, p; Larson, p; Lawler, dh; Leidens, c, p; Love, p; Lowe, p; Lyons, p; Maine, p; Malenfant, p; Marino, p; McCrary, p; McLaughlin, of; Mejias, of, p; Mendez, 3b; Meyer, p; T. Miller, p; Monds, of; J.A. Nunez, of; O'Dette, p; Ortiz, ss; Otanez, dh; Pass, 1b; J. Pena, ss; Peniche, p; Peterson, p; Ponson, p; Raino, p; J. Ramirez, p; Reding, 2b; Redmond, dh; Rojas, of; Saenz, dh; Sevillano, ss; Splittorff, p; Terni, 3b; F. Torres, ss; Tucker, p; Velazquez, of; Viera, p; Wade, p; Wer

LEAGUE CHAMPIONS

Year	Team	Pct.	Year	Team	Pct.	Year	Team	Pct.
1964—	Sarasota Braves	.610	1980—	Kansas City-Blue	.635	1990—	Expos	.635
1965—	Bradenton Astros	.632	1981—	Kansas City-Gold	.688		Dodgers‡	.603
1966—	New York AL	.667	1982—	New York AL	.667	1991—	Orioles	.593
1967—	Kansas City	.614	1983—	Texas	.645		Expos∞	.533
1968—	Oakland	.650		Los Angeles†	.617	1992—	Royals∞	.695
1969—	Montreal	.585	1984—	White Sox	.651		Expos	.593
1970—	Chicago AL	.600		Rangers†	.571	1993—	Rangers▲	.667
1971—	Kansas City	.755	1985—	Yankees§	.705		Astros	.593
1972—	Chicago NL*	.651		Rangers	.532	1994—	Royals◆	.797
	Kansas City*	.651	1986—	Reds	.548		Astros	.695
1973—	Texas	.732		Dodgers†	.541	1995—	Royals■	.649
1974—	Chicago NL	.702	1987—	Dodgers†	.683		Tigers	.579
1975—	Texas	.774		Royals	.635	1996—	Yankees◆	.638
1976—	Texas	.704	1988—	Yankees†	.714		Rangers	.617
1977—	Chicago AL	.731		Royals	.619	1997—	Mets▼	.700
1978—	Texas	.600	1989—	Yankees‡	.651		Rangers	.567
1979—	Houston	.635		Dodgers	.635			

*Declared co-champions; no playoff. †League divided into Northern and Southern divisions; won one-game playoff for league championship. ‡League divided into Northern and Southern divisions; won best-of-three playoff for league championship. §Yankees declared champion based on winning percentage when one-game playoff against Rangers was rained out. ∞League divided into Northern, Southern and Central divisions; won best-of-three playoff for league championship. ▲League divided into Eastern, Central and Western divisions; won three-team playoff. ◆League divided into Eastern, Northern and Western divisions; won three-team playoff. ■League divided into Eastern, Northern, Northwest and Southwest divisions; won four-team playoff. ▼League divided into Eastern, Western and Northwest divisions; won four-club playoff. (Note—Known as Sarasota Rookie League in 1964 and Florida Rookie League in 1965.)

PIONEER LEAGUE

LEAGUE OFFICE

President
Jim McCurdy
Address
P.O. Box 2564
Spokane, WA 99220
Phone
509-456-7615

Teams (affiliation)
Billings Mustangs (Reds)
Butte Copper Kings (Angels)
Great Falls Dodgers (Dodgers)
Helena Brewers (Brewers)

Idaho Falls Braves (Padres)
Lethbridge Black Diamonds (Arizona Diamondbacks)
Medicine Hat Blue Jays (Blue Jays)
Ogden Raptors (Brewers)

1997 FINAL STANDINGS
FIRST HALF

NORTHERN DIVISION

Team	W	L	T	Pct.	GB
Great Falls (Dodgers)	21	15	0	.583	....
Medicine Hat (Blue Jays)	17	19	0	.472	4
Lethbridge (Diamondbacks)	17	19	0	.472	4
Helena (Brewers)	16	20	0	.444	5

SOUTHERN DIVISION

Team	W	L	T	Pct.	GB
Ogden (Brewers)	21	15	0	.583	....
Billings (Reds)	21	15	0	.583	....
Idaho Falls (Padres)	18	18	0	.500	3
Butte (Angels)	13	23	0	.361	8

SECOND HALF

NORTHERN DIVISION

Team	W	L	T	Pct.	GB
Lethbridge (Diamondbacks)	22	14	0	.611	....
Helena (Brewers)	21	14	0	.600	1/2
Great Falls (Dodgers)	19	17	0	.528	3
Medicine Hat (Blue Jays)	9	27	0	.250	13

SOUTHERN DIVISION

Team	W	L	T	Pct.	GB
Idaho Falls (Padres)	21	15	0	.583	....
Billings (Reds)	18	17	0	.514	2 1/2
Butte (Angels)	17	19	0	.472	4
Ogden (Brewers)	16	20	0	.444	5

COMPOSITE

Team	G.F.	Bil.	Let.	I.F.	Hel.	Ogd.	But.	M.H.	W	L	T	Pct.	GB
Great Falls (Dodgers)	....	5	7	0	7	4	8	9	40	32	0	.556	....
Billings (Reds)	3	....	3	6	4	8	8	7	39	32	0	.549	1/2
Lethbridge (Diamondbacks)	6	5	....	5	7	4	4	8	39	33	0	.542	1
Idaho Falls (Padres)	8	7	3	....	3	6	7	5	39	33	0	.542	1
Helena (Brewers)	7	3	6	5	....	3	4	9	37	34	0	.521	2 1/2
Ogden (Brewers)	4	5	4	8	5	....	8	3	37	35	0	.514	3
Butte (Angels)	0	6	4	6	4	5	....	5	30	42	0	.417	10
Medicine Hat (Blue Jays)	4	1	6	3	4	5	3	....	26	46	0	.361	14

Major league affiliations in parentheses.

PLAYOFFS: Billings defeated Idaho Falls, two games to none; Great Falls defeated Lethbridge, two games to none; Billings defeated Great Falls, two games to none, to win league championship.

REGULAR-SEASON ATTENDANCE: Billings, 97,708; Butte, 32,854; Great Falls, 58,595; Helena, 35,161; Idaho Falls, 56,039; Lethbridge, 46,909; Medicine Hat, 46,770; Ogden, 101,256. Total—475,292. Playoffs (6 games)—7,348.

MANAGERS: Billings, Donnie Scott; Butte, Bill Lachemann; Great Falls, Mickey Hatcher; Helena, Alex Morales; Idaho Falls, Don Werner; Lethbridge, Rod Allen; Medicine Hat, Marty Pevey; Ogden, Bernie Moncallo.

ALL-STAR TEAM: 1B—Jake Kraus, Ogden-Helena; 2B—Clay Snellgrove, Idaho Falls; 3B—Luke Allen, Great Falls; SS—Travis Dawkins, Billings; OF—Greg Morrison, Medicine Hat; Mike Frank, Billings; DeWayne Wise, Billings; C—Bobby Darula, Ogden; DH—Antuan Bunkley, Helena; RHP—Scott Williamson, Billings; LHP—Derek Lee, Ogden; Craig Taczy, Great Falls; Relief Pitcher—Shawn Camp, Idaho Falls; Most Valuable Player—Greg Morrison, Medicine Hat; Manager of the Year—Don Werner, Idaho Falls.

1997 BATTING
TEAM

Team	Avg.	G	TPA	AB	R	H	TB	2B	3B	HR	RBI	SH	SF	HP	BB	IBB	SO	SB	CS	GDP	LOB	ShO	Slg.	OBP
Idaho Falls	.291	72	2950	2552	465	743	1060	132	37	37	395	7	26	35	330	15	524	95	46	58	598	0	.415	.376
Ogden	.288	72	2907	2528	478	727	1080	156	22	51	416	23	18	51	287	5	548	69	38	33	563	3	.427	.369
Billings	.287	71	2810	2482	446	713	1059	127	21	59	390	7	31	33	257	10	516	76	50	51	507	2	.427	.358
Butte	.286	72	2912	2549	478	728	1094	132	21	64	414	16	28	43	276	6	558	71	27	50	558	3	.429	.362
Helena	.285	71	2842	2501	434	712	1025	131	10	54	379	14	21	40	266	11	506	63	44	52	555	1	.410	.360
Lethbridge	.274	72	2849	2492	439	683	1056	107	25	72	377	13	20	43	281	7	603	66	33	52	542	3	.424	.355
Great Falls	.274	72	2701	2441	376	669	943	101	31	37	307	37	13	22	188	3	527	103	76	36	437	2	.386	.330
Medicine Hat	.262	72	2786	2492	378	654	956	110	15	54	339	20	19	22	233	2	538	79	43	32	518	4	.384	.329

INDIVIDUAL

TOP QUALIFIERS FOR BATTING CHAMPIONSHIP
Minimum 194 plate appearances. *Lefthanded batter. †Switch-hitter.

Player, Team	Avg.	G	TPA	AB	R	H	TB	2B	3B	HR	RBI	SH	SF	HP	BB	IBB	SO	SB	CS	GDP	Slg.	OBP
Morrison, Greg, Med. Hat*	.448	69	264	241	63	108	199	16	3	23	88	0	6	3	14	1	29	2	3	3	.826	.473
Kraus, Jake, Og.-Hel.	.390	69	300	246	51	96	150	22	1	10	69	0	4	12	38	3	15	8	4	12	.610	.487

Player, Team	Avg.	G	TPA	AB	R	H	TB	2B	3B	HR	RBI	SH	SF	HP	BB	IBB	SO	SB	CS	GDP	Slg.	OBP
Bunkley, Antuan, Helena	.381	70	309	270	52	103	177	23	0	17	67	0	3	4	32	5	37	2	4	8	.656	.450
Frank, Mike, Billings*...........	.376	69	307	266	62	100	164	22	6	10	62	0	3	2	35	5	24	18	8	7	.617	.448
Alfano, Jeff, Ogden	.360	46	197	175	39	63	104	12	4	7	29	0	1	4	17	1	31	9	4	4	.594	.426
Hagins, Steve, Butte	.351	64	298	268	59	94	167	20	1	17	56	1	1	10	17	2	53	13	3	5	.623	.409
Suarez, Marc, Billings	.347	64	259	219	42	76	120	17	0	9	37	0	2	5	33	0	51	2	1	5	.548	.440
Snellgrove, Clayton, Idaho Falls	.345	66	310	281	52	97	136	19	7	2	48	2	6	3	18	2	39	3	2	7	.484	.383
Allen, Luke, Great Falls*	.345	67	278	258	50	89	134	12	6	7	40	1	0	0	19	1	53	12	11	3	.519	.390
Moreta, Ramon, Great Falls ...	.336	68	290	265	45	89	102	6	2	1	20	6	0	1	18	0	38	29	17	5	.385	.380
Llanos, Alex, Butte*	.335	49	201	179	41	60	97	9	2	8	43	1	1	3	17	1	30	3	1	6	.542	.400
Darula, Bobby, Ogden*	.332	69	314	262	61	87	139	26	4	6	52	1	4	5	42	0	23	11	2	5	.531	.428
Dean, Aaron, Great Falls*	.330	60	194	179	28	59	87	14	1	4	27	0	0	2	13	0	41	4	4	1	.486	.381
Jacobsen, Bucky, Ogden	.328	67	286	238	57	78	123	17	2	8	52	0	4	3	41	0	44	6	6	4	.517	.427
Welsh, Eric, Billings*	.315	67	283	260	41	82	132	13	2	11	54	0	3	2	18	1	38	2	4	3	.508	.360

DEPARTMENTAL LEADERS: G—Knight, James, 72 each; AB—Knight, 293; R—Kirby, 65; H—Morrison, 108; TB—Morrison, 199; 2B—Darula, 26; 3B—Wise, 9; HR—Morrison, 23; RBI—Morrison, 88; SH—Marshall, Moreta, 6 each; SF—Dawkins, Snellgrove, Morrison, 6 each; HP—Kraus, 12; BB—Kirby, 53; IBB—Frank, Bunkley, 5 each; SO—James, 79; SB—Moreta, 29; CS—Moreta, 17; GIDP—Kraus, 12; Slg.—Morrison, .826; OBP—Kraus, .487.

ALL PLAYERS

*Lefthanded batter. †Switch-hitter.

Player, Team	Avg.	G	TPA	AB	R	H	TB	2B	3B	HR	RBI	SH	SF	HP	BB	IBB	SO	SB	CS	GDP	Slg.	OBP
Adams, Lawrence, Med. Hat ..	.179	47	133	117	9	21	31	7	0	1	13	0	1	4	11	0	44	1	3	2	.265	.271
Adams, Tim, Butte	.260	38	144	131	20	34	43	4	1	1	17	0	1	4	8	0	43	0	1	4	.328	.319
Alfano, Jeff, Ogden	.360	46	197	175	39	63	104	12	4	7	29	0	1	4	17	1	31	9	4	4	.594	.426
Allen, Jake, Great Falls	.000	1	1	1	0	0	0	0	0	0	0	0	0	0	0	0	1	0	0	0	.000	.000
Allen, Luke, Great Falls*	.345	67	278	258	50	89	134	12	6	7	40	1	0	0	19	1	53	12	11	3	.519	.390
Allen, Shane, Great Falls	.194	24	33	31	5	6	6	0	0	0	2	0	0	1	1	0	14	0	0	0	.194	.242
Alvarez, Victor, Great Falls	.000	12	1	0	0	0	0	0	0	0	0	0	0	1	0	0	0	0	0	0	.000	1.000
Armenta, Jason, Billings*	.237	44	105	97	17	23	28	5	0	0	5	0	0	1	7	0	27	2	2	3	.289	.295
Auterson, Jeffrey, Great Falls .	.173	60	185	156	28	27	46	8	1	3	17	3	0	4	21	0	58	6	6	3	.295	.287
Baez, Juan, Ogden	.289	52	145	128	19	37	53	7	0	3	21	0	1	1	15	0	45	2	2	4	.414	.366
Balbuena, Mike, Great Falls*	.151	18	55	53	5	8	9	1	0	0	4	0	0	0	2	0	3	1	1	2	.170	.182
Barrett, Andrew, Med. Hat	.233	43	110	103	4	24	27	3	0	0	14	0	0	1	6	0	30	1	1	1	.262	.282
Battle, Rohn, Butte	.250	2	8	8	2	2	4	0	1	0	1	0	0	0	0	0	3	0	0	0	.500	.250
Bautista, Juan, Lethbridge	.206	43	156	136	23	28	36	3	1	1	14	2	2	4	12	0	35	4	1	4	.265	.286
Beatriz, Ramy, Helena*	.267	55	217	187	35	50	80	12	3	4	27	1	2	3	24	1	43	9	7	4	.428	.356
Bejarano, Brian, Medicine Hat	.290	53	211	193	26	56	82	8	0	6	29	0	0	0	18	0	38	1	3	5	.425	.351
Bernhardt, Jossephany, M.H. ...	.176	60	214	199	20	35	40	2	0	1	13	5	1	1	8	0	55	3	2	4	.201	.211
Brackeen, Colin, Medicine Hat*	.000	19	1	1	0	0	0	0	0	0	0	0	0	0	0	0	1	0	0	0	.000	.000
Brewer, Brad, Butte	.239	19	85	67	14	16	18	2	0	0	8	2	2	0	14	0	17	0	2	2	.269	.361
Brown, Billy, Medicine Hat	.287	70	312	272	63	78	126	16	4	8	39	1	3	0	36	1	66	22	4	2	.463	.367
Brown, Kent, Idaho Falls*	.270	36	149	126	22	34	38	4	0	0	19	0	0	1	22	0	29	10	7	1	.302	.383
Bunkley, Antuan, Helena	.381	70	309	270	52	103	177	23	0	17	67	0	3	4	32	5	37	2	4	8	.656	.450
Burford, Kevin, Idaho Falls*....	.207	7	30	29	2	6	11	0	1	1	3	0	0	0	1	0	5	0	0	1	.379	.233
Burress, Andy, Billings	.304	27	108	102	13	31	53	7	0	5	18	0	0	0	6	0	20	1	1	4	.520	.343
Caceres, Wilmy, Billings..........	.263	15	41	38	10	10	12	2	0	0	9	0	0	1	2	0	3	1	1	0	.316	.317
Caiazzo, Nick, Helena	.269	63	256	234	31	63	89	15	1	3	37	0	2	4	16	1	34	2	0	5	.380	.324
Calloway, Ronald, Lethbridge*	.250	43	167	148	23	37	42	5	0	0	9	0	2	3	14	0	29	5	8	4	.284	.323
Candela, Frank, Ogden	.267	25	82	75	9	20	25	0	1	1	10	2	0	1	4	0	17	3	1	1	.333	.313
Castillo, Alex, Helena	.214	5	15	14	0	3	5	2	0	0	0	0	0	0	1	0	5	0	0	0	.357	.267
Cintron, Alexander, Lethbridge†	.333	1	4	3	0	1	1	0	0	0	0	0	0	1	0	0	1	0	0	0	.333	.333
Collier, Marc, Butte................	.071	5	16	14	0	1	1	0	0	0	0	1	0	0	1	0	6	0	0	0	.071	.133
Condon, Mike, Butte	.304	49	199	181	38	55	72	12	1	1	19	0	0	4	14	0	19	4	1	7	.398	.367
Cripps, Bobby, Great Falls*	.310	47	158	145	19	45	73	6	5	4	25	1	2	3	7	1	26	4	4	3	.503	.350
Cronin, Shane, Idaho Falls	.336	32	143	128	21	43	61	10	1	2	24	0	0	4	11	1	18	0	4	3	.477	.406
Dallin, Spencer, Idaho Falls.....	.000	1	1	1	0	0	0	0	0	0	0	0	0	0	0	0	1	0	0	0	.000	.000
Darula, Bobby, Ogden*	.332	69	314	262	61	87	139	26	4	6	52	1	4	5	42	0	23	11	2	5	.531	.428
Dawkins, Travis, Billings	.241	70	292	253	47	61	78	5	0	4	37	3	6	0	30	0	38	16	6	6	.308	.315
Dean, Aaron, Great Falls*	.330	60	194	179	28	59	87	14	1	4	27	0	0	2	13	0	41	4	4	1	.486	.381
Deardorff, Jeff, Ogden	.275	63	252	222	33	61	90	17	3	2	27	1	0	5	24	0	74	2	2	1	.405	.359
DeJesus, Eddie, Butte	.297	57	250	219	38	65	93	14	1	4	35	0	5	3	23	0	58	4	4	0	.425	.364
DeMarco, Joey, Idaho Falls† ..	.280	32	141	125	21	35	45	5	1	1	20	0	0	0	16	0	14	9	3	2	.360	.362
Dempsey, Nicholas, Great Falls	.000	6	9	8	0	0	0	0	0	0	0	1	0	0	0	0	2	0	0	1	.000	.111
Doherty, Steven, Lethbridge*..	.286	53	211	185	38	53	82	12	1	5	29	1	0	2	22	0	28	5	4	4	.443	.368
Dunham, Traylon, Idaho Falls	.400	1	5	5	0	2	2	0	0	0	0	0	0	0	0	0	0	0	0	0	.400	.400
Encarnacion, Bienvenido, Butte†	.259	26	86	81	11	21	26	5	0	0	9	2	0	1	2	0	14	2	2	2	.321	.286
Falcon, Edwin, Great Falls	.241	50	152	133	20	32	55	6	1	5	22	1	3	0	15	0	39	0	1	4	.414	.311
Fernandez, Ramon, Helena	.265	59	218	196	36	52	74	8	1	4	28	1	2	0	19	0	53	2	1	2	.378	.327
Fortin, Blaine, Medicine Hat ...	.329	55	172	164	21	54	80	5	0	7	26	0	1	2	5	0	12	1	3	3	.488	.355
Fox, Brian, Lethbridge*	.295	64	260	220	30	65	105	9	2	9	44	0	3	3	34	1	45	1	0	6	.477	.392
Frank, Mike, Billings*...........	.376	69	307	266	62	100	164	22	6	10	62	0	3	2	35	5	24	18	8	7	.617	.448
Gallo, Ismael, Great Falls*	.251	61	220	199	31	50	72	9	5	1	34	3	2	0	16	0	44	4	3	5	.362	.304
Gomera, Rafael, Great Falls....	.258	59	231	209	36	54	89	11	3	6	29	1	2	3	16	0	67	13	5	3	.426	.317
Gonzalez, Santos, Idaho Falls†	.297	46	217	192	41	57	93	9	6	5	34	1	1	4	19	0	44	17	7	3	.484	.370
Guillen, Jose, Helena†	.216	25	63	51	6	11	14	0	0	1	6	1	0	2	9	0	17	4	2	0	.275	.355
Guthrie, Kendal, Ogden	.276	63	270	239	38	66	90	19	1	1	34	5	1	5	20	1	57	4	5	2	.377	.343
Guzman, Elpidio, Butte*	.302	17	48	43	12	13	26	2	1	3	10	0	0	0	5	0	5	3	0	0	.605	.375
Guzman, Julio, Lethbridge	.217	22	66	60	11	13	23	3	2	1	12	0	1	0	5	0	23	2	0	0	.383	.273
Hagins, Steve, Butte	.351	64	298	268	59	94	167	20	1	17	56	1	1	10	17	2	53	13	3	5	.623	.409
Hilliker, Tracey, Great Falls	.212	38	107	99	14	21	29	2	0	2	10	0	1	2	5	0	29	3	2	2	.293	.262
Horsman, Brent, Idaho Falls*	.305	52	226	213	36	65	81	9	2	1	24	1	0	1	10	1	35	9	2	8	.380	.338

Player, Team	Avg.	G	TPA	AB	R	H	TB	2B	3B	HR	RBI	SH	SF	HP	BB	IBB	SO	SB	CS	GDP	Slg.	OBP
Hubbel, Travis, Medicine Hat .	.160	42	133	119	10	19	24	3	1	0	10	1	2	1	10	0	43	1	2	5	.202	.227
Hudson, Bert, Lethbridge......	.256	60	243	219	28	56	94	11	0	9	34	0	2	3	19	1	57	5	3	5	.429	.321
Hueda, Alejandro, Med. Hat ...	.000	18	0	0	0	0	0	0	0	0	0	0	0	0	0	0	0	0	1	0	.000	.000
Hunter, Johnny, Idaho Falls	.269	21	81	67	19	18	34	4	0	4	15	0	1	1	12	0	24	1	0	3	.507	.383
Jacobsen, Bucky, Ogden	.328	67	286	238	57	78	123	17	2	8	52	0	4	3	41	0	44	6	6	4	.517	.427
James, Brandon, Ogden*.......	.285	72	304	267	51	76	124	14	2	10	58	2	3	3	29	2	79	8	3	3	.464	.358
Jergenson, Brian, Idaho Falls*.	.260	54	226	196	34	51	67	8	1	2	32	0	3	4	23	2	49	6	1	4	.342	.345
Johnson, Patrick, Butte........	.250	47	190	160	31	40	58	9	0	3	21	1	2	3	24	0	32	1	1	3	.363	.354
Jones, Keith, Lethbridge	.257	58	233	214	27	55	80	8	1	5	28	0	2	2	15	1	76	3	3	4	.374	.309
Kelleher, Pat, Great Falls*	.290	57	170	145	22	42	50	8	0	0	10	5	0	1	19	0	27	6	10	2	.345	.376
Kirby, Scott, Helena...............	.262	68	312	248	65	65	110	10	1	11	47	0	4	7	53	0	65	8	6	5	.444	.401
Knight, Marcus, Butte†........	.294	72	349	293	51	86	135	15	5	8	43	1	3	8	44	2	62	8	3	4	.461	.397
Kraus, Jake, Og.-Hel...........	.390	69	300	246	51	96	150	22	1	10	69	0	4	12	38	3	15	4	1	12	.610	.487
Landingham, James, Med. Hat*	.302	21	48	43	10	13	18	3	1	0	3	2	0	0	3	0	5	3	3	0	.419	.348
Langdon, Trajan, Idaho Falls...	.189	22	103	90	11	17	30	7	0	2	10	0	1	1	11	0	36	0	1	1	.333	.282
Lawrence, Mike, Butte..........	.259	69	308	263	43	68	88	10	2	2	46	4	4	1	36	0	40	4	2	9	.335	.345
Lawrence, Tony, Idaho Falls ...	.267	56	249	210	40	56	89	8	2	7	36	0	3	2	34	3	48	7	3	2	.424	.369
Llanos, Alex, Butte*..........	.335	49	201	179	41	60	97	9	2	8	43	1	1	3	17	1	30	3	1	6	.542	.400
Madera, Wil, Lethbridge*.......	.297	33	107	101	15	30	43	4	0	3	11	1	0	1	4	0	29	5	0	2	.426	.330
Markray, Thad, Billings	.143	46	139	119	11	17	20	3	0	0	5	2	0	3	15	0	44	3	0	3	.168	.255
Marshall, Monte, Great Falls†	.289	60	200	184	29	53	67	8	3	0	21	6	1	1	8	0	34	12	6	0	.364	.320
Martin, Jared, Lethbridge†.....	.231	25	96	78	12	18	27	3	3	0	5	0	1	2	15	1	19	1	0	1	.346	.365
Martinez, Belvani, Lethbridge.	.344	25	101	90	21	31	55	4	1	6	13	1	1	4	5	0	13	4	1	2	.611	.400
Mathis, Jared, Ogden	.279	54	212	197	30	55	69	14	0	0	29	4	1	4	6	0	20	7	3	3	.350	.313
McAfee, Josh, Lethbridge	.198	36	122	101	26	20	41	5	2	4	18	2	1	5	13	0	32	0	1	3	.406	.317
McDaniel, Ryan, Idaho Falls...	.189	22	84	74	5	14	23	4	1	1	7	0	1	2	7	0	31	0	1	6	.311	.274
Montgomery, Andre, Billings .	.314	51	227	207	43	65	99	18	2	4	31	0	3	2	15	2	47	6	4	1	.478	.361
Moon, Brian, Helena†..........	.282	49	189	170	15	48	53	5	0	0	22	4	2	5	8	0	23	2	1	4	.312	.330
Moreta, Ramon, Great Falls ...	.336	68	290	265	45	89	102	6	2	1	20	6	0	1	18	0	38	29	17	5	.385	.380
Morillo, Luis, Medicine Hat*...	.314	8	39	35	5	11	13	3	0	0	4	0	0	0	4	0	6	6	1	0	.400	.385
Morrison, Greg, Medicine Hat*	.448	69	264	241	63	108	199	16	3	23	88	0	6	3	14	1	29	2	3	3	.826	.473
Morrow, Alvin, Ogden	.250	2	5	4	1	1	1	0	0	0	0	0	0	0	1	0	2	0	0	0	.250	.400
Newman, Howard, Billings	.295	17	46	44	7	13	19	3	0	1	7	0	1	1	0	0	14	0	0	1	.432	.304
Nizov, Alexander, Butte..........	.276	27	98	87	12	24	34	5	1	1	8	1	0	2	8	0	21	1	2	1	.391	.351
Nunez, Abraham, Lethbridge†	.167	2	7	6	2	1	1	0	0	0	0	0	0	0	1	0	0	0	0	0	.167	.286
Oliver, Johnny, Billings	.091	6	13	11	1	1	1	0	0	0	0	0	0	1	1	0	3	0	0	1	.091	.231
Ortiz, Carlos, Medicine Hat	.200	31	77	70	5	14	16	2	0	0	9	1	0	1	6	0	17	0	0	1	.229	.273
Osilka, Garret, Ogden	.255	64	274	231	41	59	72	9	2	0	19	5	0	6	32	1	50	10	4	0	.312	.361
Pascual, Edison, Billings*......	.071	10	16	14	2	1	1	0	0	0	0	0	0	0	2	0	5	0	0	1	.071	.188
Patten, Chris, Og.-Hel...........	.270	49	205	189	27	51	61	6	2	0	19	0	1	0	15	1	38	4	3	2	.323	.327
Patterson, Marty, Helena.......	.237	51	189	169	24	40	58	9	0	3	23	0	3	4	13	0	56	4	2	3	.343	.302
Pearson, Ryan, Helena†.........	.209	44	145	134	17	28	41	5	1	2	14	0	1	1	9	0	33	2	3	3	.306	.262
Perez, Angelo, Medicine Hat ..	.238	70	298	269	37	64	107	15	5	6	33	5	2	3	19	0	62	8	3	0	.398	.294
Philip-Guide, Sheldon, Butte..	.260	17	61	50	10	13	15	2	0	0	2	0	0	1	11	0	17	3	0	2	.300	.393
Pichardo, Gilbert, Butte†........	.217	8	28	23	7	5	9	1	0	1	5	0	0	0	5	0	10	0	1	0	.391	.357
Price, Corey, Billings†............	.267	19	71	60	11	16	17	1	0	0	8	0	0	4	7	0	14	0	1	1	.283	.324
Quire, Jeremy, Lethbridge......	.293	30	62	58	11	17	22	5	0	0	7	0	0	1	3	0	8	0	0	2	.379	.339
Quittner, Peter, Butte*.........	.284	36	139	134	21	38	51	2	1	3	13	2	1	0	2	0	26	3	1	2	.381	.292
Rakers, Jason, Idaho Falls* ...	.200	5	23	20	3	4	5	1	0	0	3	0	0	0	3	0	5	0	0	1	.250	.304
Rexrode, Jackie, Lethbridge*..	.337	26	122	89	29	30	39	2	2	1	14	2	1	1	29	0	17	7	3	0	.438	.500
Richey, Mikal, Great Falls	.215	32	69	65	10	14	19	0	1	1	13	0	2	1	1	0	29	1	1	1	.292	.239
Riggio, Robert, Ogden	.178	29	80	73	13	13	15	2	0	0	10	0	0	0	7	0	9	0	0	3	.205	.250
Rios, Fernando, Billings	.333	41	168	153	19	51	61	8	1	0	18	0	1	3	11	0	22	1	5	1	.399	.387
Rivera, Francisco, Billings*.....	.239	26	54	46	4	11	16	2	0	1	5	0	2	0	6	0	13	0	0	3	.348	.315
Rodriguez, Felipe, Med. Hat ...	.253	54	225	190	48	48	55	7	0	0	12	3	0	3	29	0	38	18	6	1	.289	.360
Rodriguez, John, Idaho Falls..	.296	32	129	115	17	34	39	5	0	0	11	2	0	2	10	0	26	1	4	2	.339	.362
Rojas, Eliezer, Helena	.268	47	160	149	26	40	46	3	0	1	16	2	0	1	8	0	19	5	2	3	.309	.310
Rowan, Chris, Ogden	.251	55	244	211	46	53	96	10	3	9	34	2	0	4	27	0	65	2	5	1	.455	.347
Ruotsinoja, Jacob, Idaho Falls.	.303	31	140	109	20	33	51	10	1	2	17	0	1	1	29	1	21	5	0	1	.468	.450
Rutherford, Daryl, Idaho Falls	.375	15	69	64	13	24	34	4	3	0	10	0	2	0	3	0	9	8	1	0	.531	.391
Ryden, Karl, Idaho Falls	.263	57	250	198	48	52	67	6	3	1	20	1	4	4	45	2	38	9	6	3	.338	.404
Saitta, Rich, Great Falls	.241	16	60	58	4	14	17	3	0	0	4	0	0	0	2	0	9	1	0	1	.293	.267
Sanchez, Toby, Billings	.219	62	228	178	37	39	59	5	0	5	35	0	2	9	39	2	76	4	6	5	.331	.382
Sanchez, Wellington, Helena..	.271	61	254	236	46	64	83	13	0	2	20	3	0	1	14	0	47	10	7	3	.352	.315
Sandoval, Jhensy, Lethbridge	.375	40	173	160	33	60	100	14	1	8	37	1	1	3	8	1	36	7	3	1	.625	.413
Santos, Jose, Butte	.229	21	83	70	11	16	22	3	0	1	9	0	3	1	9	0	20	1	1	1	.314	.313
Seal, Scott, Idaho Falls*	.358	30	144	120	18	43	66	8	3	3	30	0	1	1	22	1	24	0	3	4	.550	.458
Skeens, Jeremy, Helena.........	.204	23	63	49	12	10	13	0	0	1	9	1	1	0	12	0	15	2	0	0	.265	.355
Snellgrove, Clayton, Idaho Falls	.345	66	310	281	52	97	136	19	7	2	48	2	6	3	18	2	39	3	2	7	.484	.383
Snow, Casey, Great Falls†......	.321	17	65	53	5	17	26	3	0	2	9	3	0	1	8	1	10	2	0	0	.491	.419
Solano, Manny, Billings..........	.224	42	108	98	14	22	30	3	1	1	9	0	0	1	9	0	15	0	3	4	.306	.296
Steelmon, Wyley, Lethbridge*	.271	53	207	166	29	45	76	5	1	8	26	0	0	0	41	1	50	3	0	1	.458	.415
Suarez, Marc, Billings	.347	64	259	219	42	76	120	17	0	9	37	0	2	5	33	0	51	2	1	5	.548	.440
Sykes, Jamie, Lethbridge........	.305	58	252	223	45	68	100	18	6	4	37	1	0	3	25	0	40	9	2	6	.448	.382
Talbott, Benjamin, Butte†.......	.200	22	79	65	13	13	17	1	0	1	13	0	1	1	12	1	29	0	0	0	.262	.329
Taveras, Jose, Lethbridge.......	.234	67	261	235	36	55	89	6	2	8	38	1	3	3	19	1	65	5	4	7	.379	.296
Thrower, Jared, Idaho Falls† ...	.340	35	177	141	37	48	75	10	4	3	28	0	1	4	31	2	16	10	1	2	.532	.469
Tolentino, Juan, Butte	.300	61	243	213	44	64	118	16	4	10	53	0	4	2	24	0	53	21	2	2	.554	.370
Torres, Bernie, Great Falls	.251	57	196	175	23	44	57	4	3	1	23	5	2	2	12	0	27	6	4	2	.326	.304
Tucent, Francisco, Ogden†......	.248	42	132	117	22	29	33	4	0	0	16	1	1	4	9	0	23	2	0	1	.282	.321
Umbria, Jose, Medicine Hat.....	.175	49	136	126	4	22	24	2	0	0	15	1	3	0	6	0	24	2	1	2	.190	.207
Warren, Lance, Great Falls*....	.200	3	6	5	0	1	1	0	0	0	0	0	0	0	1	0	3	0	0	2	.200	.333

Player, Team	Avg.	G	TPA	AB	R	H	TB	2B	3B	HR	RBI	SH	SF	HP	BB	IBB	SO	SB	CS	GDP	Slg.	OBP
Warren, Thomas, Helena†	.278	33	120	97	21	27	30	3	0	0	8	2	0	1	20	0	30	4	3	1	.309	.407
Watley, Clarence, Med. Hat†	.303	10	37	33	3	10	12	2	0	0	6	0	0	0	4	0	13	3	0	0	.364	.378
Welsh, Eric, Billings*	.315	67	283	260	41	82	132	13	2	11	54	0	3	2	18	1	38	2	4	3	.508	.360
Wise, Dewayne, Billings*	.313	62	283	268	53	84	136	13	9	7	41	1	3	2	9	0	47	18	8	2	.507	.337
Zamora, Pete, Great Falls*	.200	29	22	20	2	4	4	0	0	0	0	0	0	0	2	0	3	0	0	0	.200	.273
Zeber, Ryan, Medicine Hat	.198	43	113	101	11	20	25	2	0	1	7	0	0	0	12	0	26	1	2	2	.248	.283
Zepeda, Jesse, Medicine Hat†	.264	64	263	216	39	57	76	14	1	1	23	2	0	3	42	0	29	6	5	1	.352	.391
Zucha, Jason, Idaho Falls	.208	13	53	48	5	10	13	1	1	0	5	1	1	0	3	0	10	0	0	4	.271	.250

GRAND SLAMS: Jacobsen, 2; Dawkins, Darula, Gomera, E. Guzman, Hagins, Morrison, Ruotsinoja, Snow, Suarez, 1 each.

AWARDED FIRST BASE ON CATCHER'S INTERFERENCE: Auterson (Fox); Doherty (Hilliker); Frank (Fox); Hagins (McDaniel).

PLAYERS WITH TWO OR MORE TEAMS

Player, Team	Avg.	G	TPA	AB	R	H	TB	2B	3B	HR	RBI	SH	SF	HP	BB	IBB	SO	SB	CS	GDP	Slg.	OBP
Kraus, Jake, Ogden	.365	18	81	63	16	23	40	5	0	4	21	0	2	6	10	0	4	3	0	2	.635	.481
Kraus, Jake, Helena	.399	51	219	183	35	73	110	17	1	6	48	0	2	6	28	3	11	5	4	10	.601	.489
Patten, Chris, Ogden	.231	8	29	26	2	6	6	0	0	0	3	0	0	0	3	0	5	0	1	1	.231	.310
Patten, Chris, Helena	.276	41	176	163	25	45	55	6	2	0	16	0	0	1	12	1	33	4	2	1	.337	.330

1997 PITCHING

TEAM

Team	W	L	Pct.	ERA	G	CG	ShO	Sv.	IP	H	TBF	R	ER	HR	SH	SF	HB	BB	IBB	SO	WP	Bk.
Great Falls	40	32	.556	3.77	72	2	5	17	635.0	660	2806	348	266	40	12	20	33	252	6	563	41	8
Billings	39	32	.549	4.03	71	4	3	18	623.2	675	2802	389	279	38	15	18	32	264	14	548	69	10
Lethbridge	39	33	.542	4.22	72	2	3	14	624.1	652	2745	379	293	49	16	16	35	209	3	550	31	1
Helena	37	34	.521	4.87	71	2	2	20	616.2	664	2799	430	334	51	22	25	25	292	5	536	42	5
Medicine Hat	26	46	.361	4.96	72	4	1	7	621.0	696	2863	469	342	60	18	18	44	294	5	530	65	14
Ogden	37	35	.514	5.05	72	2	1	11	623.1	732	2882	468	350	67	17	27	44	238	7	573	41	5
Idaho Falls	39	33	.542	5.92	72	2	2	24	632.0	756	2931	482	416	72	16	23	32	294	13	550	62	3
Butte	30	42	.417	5.93	72	10	1	7	620.1	794	2933	529	409	51	21	29	44	275	6	470	78	5

INDIVIDUAL

TOP QUALIFIERS FOR EARNED-RUN AVERAGE TITLE

Minimum 58 innings. *Lefthanded pitcher.

Pitcher, Team	W	L	Pct.	ERA	G	GS	CG	ShO	GF	Sv.	IP	H	TBF	R	ER	HR	SH	SF	HB	BB	IBB	SO	WP	Bk.
Sneed, John, Medicine Hat	6	1	.857	1.29	15	10	2	0	1	0	69.2	42	275	19	10	5	2	1	7	20	0	79	2	0
Williamson, Scott, Billings	8	2	.800	1.78	13	13	2	1	0	0	86.0	66	346	25	17	5	1	2	4	23	0	101	12	2
Puorto, Jamie, Lethbridge*	4	2	.667	2.43	20	6	0	0	4	2	59.1	44	236	26	16	5	0	1	3	9	0	58	0	0
Stover, C.D., Great Falls	7	2	.778	2.56	12	12	1	0	0	0	77.1	71	324	36	22	4	1	3	2	14	0	61	3	1
Zamora, Pete, Great Falls*	2	5	.286	2.58	13	10	1	0	2	2	69.2	59	289	27	20	3	1	1	3	30	0	73	3	1
Rojas, Renney, Butte	8	4	.667	3.51	15	15	5	0	0	0	110.1	113	454	54	43	7	2	5	1	19	0	65	5	0
Robinson, Dustin, Billings	6	2	.750	3.68	16	9	2	0	5	4	73.1	91	311	38	30	5	3	1	1	6	0	48	6	0
Lee, Derek, Ogden*	4	4	.500	3.87	14	13	0	0	0	0	74.1	89	325	49	32	3	2	6	3	20	0	71	8	1
Harris, Josh, Billings	4	6	.400	4.02	14	14	0	0	1	0	85.0	103	385	51	38	3	2	3	2	26	4	56	1	2
Merrell, Philip, Billings	2	6	.250	4.33	14	14	0	0	0	0	72.2	72	313	51	35	6	3	1	2	27	1	62	2	0
Johnston, Doug, Helena	6	2	.750	4.36	13	13	0	0	0	0	74.1	64	318	39	36	5	1	1	6	34	0	66	5	0
Fleming, John, Lethbridge	3	6	.333	4.50	12	12	0	0	0	0	64.0	80	282	37	32	6	2	0	3	25	0	32	3	0
Steele, Brandon, Butte	3	4	.429	4.52	13	13	1	0	0	0	69.2	83	326	53	35	8	2	2	4	42	0	55	9	1
Goure, Sam, Medicine Hat	2	6	.250	4.71	15	15	1	0	0	0	80.1	99	360	61	42	7	3	2	7	20	0	66	5	0
Hernandez, Pedro, Great Falls	5	5	.500	4.76	15	14	0	0	1	1	75.2	98	333	44	40	10	0	3	7	12	1	50	5	0

DEPARTMENTAL LEADERS: W—Williamson, Rojas, 8 each; L—Hawkins, 8; Pct.—Sneed, .857; G—Camp, 30; GS—Goure, Stewart, Rojas, 15 each; CG—Rojas, 5; ShO—Gourlay, Perry, Stewart, Williamson, 1 each; GF—Camp, 24; Sv.—Camp, 12; IP—Rojas, 110.1; H—Rojas, Hawkins, 113 each; TBF—Rojas, 454; R—Hawkins, 74; ER—Hawkins, 53; HR—Stewart, 13; SH—Guttormson, 5; SF—Ryan, 8; HB—Kirst, 10; BB—Steele, 42; IBB—Harris, Smith, 4 each; SO—Williamson, 101; WP—Williamson, E. Miller, Porter, 12 each; BK—Alvarez, F. Rodriguez, 3 each.

ALL PITCHERS

*Lefthanded pitcher.

Pitcher, Team	W	L	Pct.	ERA	G	GS	CG	ShO	GF	Sv.	IP	H	TBF	R	ER	HR	SH	SF	HB	BB	IBB	SO	WP	Bk.
Akin, Jay, Helena*	2	0	1.000	1.00	5	5	1	0	0	0	27.0	16	99	5	3	1	0	0	0	5	0	19	1	0
Altman, Gene, Billings	3	2	.600	7.83	20	5	0	0	9	3	33.1	48	163	36	29	2	0		4	19	0	34	2	1
Alvarez, Victor, Great Falls	4	1	.800	3.35	12	8	0	0	3	0	48.1	49	212	30	18	0	4		3	17	0	50	2	3
Anderson, Dallas, Lethbridge	0	0	.000	9.00	10	0	0	0	3	0	11.0	10	52	12	11	0	0		0	11	0	13	1	1
Andrews, Jeff, Lethbridge	3	3	.500	3.26	9	9	1	0	0	0	49.2	55	219	27	18	3	1		3	10	0	50	3	0
Arroyo, Joel, Ogden	0	1	.000	10.89	16	0	0	0	9	0	20.2	33	127	37	25	1	0	1	8	21	0	18	2	0
Averette, Robert, Billings	0	0	.000	0.00	2	1	0	0	1	0	2.2	3	11	0	0	0	0	0		1		3	0	0
Baker, Jason, Great Falls*	0	0	.000	5.87	9	0	0	0	1	0	15.1	24	82	10	10	1	2	1	1	12	1	22	3	1
Bane, Jaymie, Butte*	3	2	.600	5.80	24	0	0	0	15	6	40.1	43	180	33	26	6	0	4	2	16	3	47	4	0
Barrera, Iran, Medicine Hat	3	1	.750	5.79	17	0	0	0	7	0	18.2	27	95	22	12	2	0	1	2	7	0	15	1	2
Barrett, Scott, Medicine Hat	0	6	.000	5.53	19	8	0	0	6	0	53.2	69	261	42	33	6	2		5	16	0	46	6	2
Bell, Matthew, Lethbridge	1	0	1.000	0.00	2	0	0	0	1	0	4.1	4	19	0	0	0	0	0	0	4	0	9	1	0
Bloomer, Christopher, Leth.	5	2	.714	1.76	27	0	0	0	23	9	30.2	19	130	14	6	2	0	0	4	9	1	38	2	0
Bornyk, Matthew, Great Falls	0	3	.000	5.79	13	2	0	0	5	1	23.1	21	105	16	15	3	0	0	2	15	0	29	4	0

Pitcher, Team	W	L	Pct.	ERA	G	GS	CG	ShO	GF	Sv	IP	H	TBF	R	ER	HR	SH	SF	HB	BB	IBB	SO	WP	Bk.
Bost, Ronald, Medicine Hat*	0	2	.000	7.71	14	0	0	0	3	0	16.1	22	84	20	14	1	1	0	0	17	1	17	1	0
Brackeen, Colin, Medicine Hat*	1	1	.500	1.40	18	0	0	0	14	5	19.1	11	83	4	3	0	1	0	4	8	1	20	2	1
Brewer, Clint, Billings	3	5	.375	3.29	22	0	0	0	13	4	41.0	33	180	21	15	0	1	2	3	20	2	37	11	1
Brown, Zay, Billings	0	0	.000	5.73	8	0	0	0	3	0	11.0	22	64	14	7	0	0	0	1	9	0	12	0	0
Bunkley, Antuan, Helena	0	0	.000	0.00	1	0	0	0	1	0	0.2	1	3	0	0	0	0	0	0	0	0	1	0	0
Byrd, Ben, Ogden	3	1	.750	4.46	18	0	0	0	8	1	38.1	42	173	27	19	4	3	1	2	13	0	35	3	0
Caddell, Carl, Billings*	1	1	.500	0.93	4	1	0	0	1	0	9.2	7	38	1	1	0	1	0	0	3	0	5	1	0
Camp, Shawn, Idaho Falls	2	1	.667	5.51	30	0	0	0	24	12	32.2	41	150	22	20	3	1	1	2	14	0	41	4	0
Cavanagh, Andrew, Helena	2	1	.667	4.29	18	2	0	0	7	3	35.2	32	155	22	17	2	2	0	1	18	1	37	3	0
Childers, Jason, Helena	1	1	.500	3.31	10	0	0	0	6	2	16.1	14	69	9	6	2	2	0	0	7	0	25	0	0
Childers, Matthew, Helena	1	4	.200	6.20	14	10	0	0	1	1	61.0	81	285	49	42	5	2	4	0	24	0	19	1	0
Correa, Elvis, Great Falls	3	0	1.000	1.61	21	0	0	0	5	0	28.0	20	111	8	5	2	0	1	0	8	0	38	3	0
Cronin, Shane, Idaho Falls	0	1	.000	27.00	1	0	0	0	1	0	0.1	2	3	1	1	0	1	0	0	0	0	0	0	0
Dotel, Melido, Great Falls	3	7	.300	8.08	14	11	0	0	1	0	42.1	59	230	54	38	3	1	2	5	39	0	26	5	1
Elias, Javier, Butte	0	2	.000	7.09	18	0	0	0	10	0	26.2	47	144	36	21	2	3	2	3	16	1	18	2	0
Ervin, Kent, Idaho Falls	5	6	.455	5.33	16	14	1	0	0	0	82.2	107	377	57	49	10	2	4	5	26	0	59	7	0
Eye, Jacob, Ogden	0	0	.000	0.00	1	1	0	0	0	0	3.0	2	12	1	0	0	0	0	0	1	0	2	0	0
Figueroa, Claudio, Butte	1	0	1.000	5.79	4	0	0	0	1	0	4.2	7	22	3	3	0	0	0	0	2	0	4	0	0
Fleming, John, Lethbridge	3	6	.333	4.50	12	12	0	0	0	0	64.0	80	282	37	32	6	2	0	3	25	0	32	3	0
Flores, Pedro, Great Falls*	2	1	.667	3.55	22	0	0	0	9	1	38.0	36	176	18	15	2	3	0	2	27	3	51	1	0
Fontanes, Reuben, Lethbridge	1	0	1.000	9.00	5	0	0	0	3	0	6.0	8	32	6	6	0	0	3	0	7	0	8	0	0
Frias, Miguel, Lethbridge	0	0	.000	0.00	1	0	0	0	1	0	1.1	2	5	0	0	0	0	0	0	0	0	3	0	0
Galvez, Randy, Great Falls	3	1	.750	3.64	16	1	0	0	5	0	29.2	29	128	14	12	0	0	1	3	10	0	29	1	0
Gooda, David, Ogden*	3	2	.600	5.69	16	5	0	0	4	0	61.2	78	283	49	39	7	2	0	6	20	1	62	4	1
Goure, Sam, Medicine Hat	2	6	.250	4.71	15	15	1	0	0	0	80.1	99	360	61	42	7	3	2	7	20	0	68	6	1
Gourlay, Matthew, Med. Hat	2	6	.250	5.72	14	14	1	1	0	0	67.2	72	298	56	43	7	1	1	6	28	1	35	9	0
Gutierrez, Jose, Ogden	0	0	.000	18.00	1	1	0	0	0	0	1.0	3	6	2	2	0	0	0	0	0	0	1	0	0
Guttormson, Ricky, Idaho Falls	3	2	.600	6.43	18	2	0	0	8	3	28.0	34	129	25	20	2	5	2	1	11	2	19	5	0
Guzman, Jonathan, Helena*	2	1	.667	2.61	19	1	0	0	9	1	31.0	32	146	23	9	3	0	1	1	20	0	21	4	0
Hannah, Neal, Great Falls	1	0	1.000	6.75	2	0	0	0	0	0	2.2	2	11	2	2	1	0	0	0	3	0	3	0	0
Haring, Brett, Billings*	0	2	.000	4.63	14	0	0	0	4	0	23.1	30	106	14	12	0	2	0	0	9	0	16	1	0
Harper, David, Lethbridge	2	0	1.000	6.08	8	0	0	0	3	0	13.1	16	64	9	9	2	0	0	1	6	0	13	2	0
Harris, Josh, Billings	4	6	.400	4.02	14	14	0	0	0	0	85.0	103	385	51	38	3	2	3	2	26	4	56	1	2
Haverstick, David, Lethbridge	0	1	.000	16.20	1	0	0	0	0	0	1.2	3	9	3	3	1	0	0	0	2	0	1	1	0
Hawkins, Alsharik, Ogden	2	8	.200	5.89	14	14	0	0	0	0	81.0	113	394	74	53	8	0	2	4	24	0	47	5	0
Helmer, Chad, Helena	0	2	.000	2.08	14	0	0	0	4	2	30.1	27	132	12	7	2	2	2	4	9	0	33	1	0
Hernandez, Pedro, Great Falls	5	5	.500	4.76	15	14	0	0	1	0	75.2	98	333	44	40	10	0	3	7	12	1	50	5	0
Herndon, Harry, Idaho Falls	0	0	.000	0.00	1	0	0	0	0	0	5.0	2	20	0	0	0	0	0	1	3	0	3	0	0
Herrera, Misael, Idaho Falls	0	1	.000	11.30	6	3	0	0	0	0	14.1	25	78	22	18	7	0	0	1	8	0	8	0	0
Hueda, Alejandro, Med. Hat	1	4	.200	5.71	16	0	0	0	4	0	52.0	59	240	41	33	6	1	0	1	28	2	32	4	0
Hunter, Johnny, Idaho Falls	0	0	.000	1.69	4	0	0	0	3	1	5.1	4	25	1	1	0	1	0	0	2	0	0	0	0
Hurst, Doug, Billings	0	0	.000	4.50	1	0	0	0	1	0	2.0	2	9	1	1	0	0	0	0	1	0	2	0	1
Incantalupo, Todd, Helena*	5	4	.556	5.12	14	11	0	0	0	0	65.0	76	295	48	37	7	1	1	2	24	1	51	2	2
Jensen, Jason, Lethbridge*	4	3	.571	4.97	14	14	0	0	0	0	63.1	73	282	43	35	3	2	1	3	23	0	46	0	0
Johnston, Doug, Helena	6	2	.750	4.36	13	13	0	0	0	0	74.1	64	318	39	36	5	1	6	34	6	0	66	5	0
Jones, Charlie, Lethbridge	0	3	.000	6.23	16	0	0	0	4	0	21.2	23	108	21	15	3	1	1	2	17	0	18	0	0
Jones, Chauncey, Hel.-Og.	0	1	.000	7.20	14	0	0	0	10	0	15.0	18	81	13	12	3	1	0	0	18	0	17	0	0
Jones, Keith, Lethbridge	0	0	.000	0.00	1	0	0	0	1	0	1.0	2	7	1	0	0	0	0	0	2	0	0	0	0
Keathley, Davan, Med. Hat*	3	4	.429	6.48	20	0	0	0	8	0	25.0	24	121	24	18	1	1	1	2	20	0	19	6	1
Kendall, Phil, Helena	3	4	.429	5.45	14	14	0	0	0	0	76.0	84	347	55	46	6	2	4	6	37	0	73	8	2
Kirst, Mark, Ogden	4	4	.500	5.00	16	10	0	0	1	0	66.2	88	307	49	37	7	1	4	10	14	1	56	4	0
Knott, Eric, Lethbridge*	4	0	1.000	2.87	21	3	0	0	7	3	47.0	41	195	21	15	4	2	1	0	9	1	62	2	0
Lancaster, Roger, Medicine Hat	1	2	.333	4.82	18	0	0	0	3	1	28.0	33	133	20	15	1	2	1	0	15	0	18	2	2
Lee, Derek, Ogden*	4	4	.500	3.87	14	13	0	0	0	0	74.1	89	325	49	32	3	2	6	3	20	0	71	8	1
Leshay, Manny, Helena	1	0	1.000	18.56	5	2	0	0	1	0	5.1	11	35	12	11	1	0	0	0	10	0	5	0	0
Levy, Tye, Billings*	1	1	.500	3.60	18	2	0	0	5	0	30.0	32	131	14	12	2	0	0	1	9	1	32	3	2
Lynch, Pat, Medicine Hat	3	3	.500	5.26	12	11	0	0	0	0	49.2	64	231	40	29	8	1	2	1	24	0	34	8	0
Mallette, Brian, Helena	6	2	.750	4.33	23	0	0	0	13	5	35.1	33	156	19	17	1	3	2	1	20	2	58	7	0
Martines, Jason, Lethbridge	3	3	.500	3.14	22	0	0	0	6	0	43.0	45	180	15	15	4	1	1	2	11	0	34	1	0
Martinez, Francisco, Helena	0	2	.000	5.61	16	0	0	0	6	0	25.2	30	129	26	16	2	0	1	1	18	0	20	1	0
Mathis, Jared, Ogden	0	0	.000	0.00	1	0	0	0	0	0	0.1	0	1	0	0	0	0	0	0	0	0	0	0	0
McClellan, Matthew, Med. Hat.	2	5	.286	6.92	14	6	0	0	1	0	39.0	50	192	36	30	7	0	3	3	24	0	43	2	0
McGuire, Brandon, Butte	3	4	.429	9.79	17	2	0	0	5	0	34.0	55	185	43	37	5	3	1	5	25	0	20	1	0
Merrell, Philip, Billings	2	6	.250	4.33	14	14	0	0	0	0	72.2	72	313	51	35	6	3	1	2	27	1	62	2	0
Miller, Ernie, Butte*	1	4	.200	8.01	20	2	0	0	7	1	39.1	53	204	41	35	1	0	2	2	26	0	39	12	0
Miller, Jim, Helena	5	7	.417	5.99	16	13	1	0	0	0	70.2	88	324	56	47	9	2	5	2	24	0	51	3	1
Montgomery, Matthew, Gr. Falls	1	1	.500	3.91	4	4	0	0	0	0	23.0	24	92	11	10	1	0	0	3	6	1	0	0	0
Myers, Rob, Helena	1	3	.250	9.43	18	0	0	0	6	0	27.2	43	155	42	29	4	1	2	4	24	1	24	6	0
Naff, Todd, Idaho Falls	3	3	.500	5.45	24	0	0	0	5	1	38.0	43	180	31	23	5	0	0	1	25	2	29	6	0
Nash, Damon, Idaho Falls	3	2	.600	6.60	14	10	0	0	0	0	60.0	79	279	48	44	9	0	1	3	29	0	65	4	0
Needle, Chad, Medicine Hat	0	1	.000	2.70	10	0	0	0	7	0	16.2	17	68	6	5	1	1	0	0	5	0	17	1	0
Norris, Ben, Lethbridge*	7	3	.700	4.86	14	14	0	0	0	0	83.1	93	373	61	45	6	1	3	8	23	0	54	4	0
Oiseth, Jon, Idaho Falls*	3	1	.750	4.39	18	0	0	0	2	1	26.2	22	113	15	13	2	0	1	1	13	2	27	4	0
O'Toole, Ryan, Billings	1	0	1.000	2.37	11	1	0	0	4	1	19.0	20	84	12	5	1	1	0	7	0	6	0	1
Padilla, Charly, Butte	0	2	.000	6.62	20	0	0	0	6	0	34.0	44	155	31	25	2	1	1	1	12	0	24	8	1
Patterson, Marty, Helena	0	0	.000	0.00	1	0	0	0	1	0	1.0	0	5	0	0	0	0	0	0	2	0	1	0	0
Perozo, Felix, Butte	1	6	.143	5.81	14	14	2	0	0	0	79.0	106	374	63	51	5	2	8	35	1	54	7	2
Perry, Tim, Idaho Falls	5	3	.625	5.40	15	14	1	1	0	0	78.1	84	356	52	47	6	1	1	7	38	1	84	6	0
Peterson, Kyle, Ogden.	0	0	.000	0.87	3	3	0	0	0	0	10.1	5	40	2	1	1	0	0	1	4	0	11	0	0
Porter, Aaron, Butte	2	2	.500	7.47	13	4	0	0	3	0	37.1	53	181	34	31	3	1	2	7	15	0	25	12	1
Pozo, Jason, Ogden	0	0	.000	21.00	2	0	0	0	1	0	3.0	7	19	7	7	1	0	1	1	3	0	2	1	0
Priebe, Kevin, Helena*	2	1	.667	1.61	19	0	0	0	12	6	28.0	24	115	7	5	0	2	0	0	9	0	25	0	0

– 594 –

Pitcher, Team	W	L	Pct.	ERA	G	GS	CG	ShO	GF	Sv.	IP	H	TBF	R	ER	HR	SH	SF	HB	BB	IBB	SO	WP	Bk.
Puorto, Jamie, Lethbridge*....	4	2	.667	2.43	20	6	0	0	4	2	59.1	44	236	26	16	5	0	1	3	9	0	58	0	0
Regalado, Maximo, Gr. Falls ..	2	1	.667	1.96	9	6	0	0	0	0	36.2	27	158	12	8	0	1	2	1	21	0	24	1	0
Reyes, Nate, Great Falls*	3	3	.500	2.51	24	0	0	0	22	8	28.2	26	120	9	8	1	1	0	0	15	1	30	2	0
Ricks, Ronald, Butte	5	3	.625	5.23	17	8	2	0	7	0	62.0	80	301	48	36	2	3	1	5	22	1	48	9	0
Robinson, Dustin, Billings.......	6	2	.750	3.68	16	9	2	0	5	4	73.1	91	311	38	30	5	3	1	1	6	0	48	6	0
Rodriguez, Franklin, Med. Hat*	0	0	.000	10.24	7	0	0	0	1	0	9.2	22	56	13	11	1	0	1	0	7	0	9	2	3
Rodriguez, Hector, Butte	1	0	1.000	1.93	2	0	0	0	0	0	4.2	5	24	1	1	1	0	0	0	4	0	7	0	0
Rojas, Renney, Butte	8	4	.667	3.51	15	15	5	0	0	0	110.1	113	454	54	43	7	2	5	1	19	0	65	5	0
Romero, Alejandro, Gr. Falls ..	2	1	.667	4.01	25	0	0	0	9	0	42.2	50	193	28	19	7	0	3	1	11	0	27	3	1
Romero, John, Butte	0	3	.000	10.07	15	1	0	0	7	0	22.1	33	122	34	25	3	2	2	3	22	0	17	5	0
Rooney, Mike, Lethbridge	5	2	.714	5.49	13	13	1	0	0	0	62.1	72	282	42	38	4	2	3	5	24	0	40	3	0
Roundtree, Monte, Billings* ..	1	2	.333	5.06	13	5	0	0	2	1	37.1	37	186	38	21	5	1	1	0	33	0	40	5	0
Runk, David, Billings	0	0	.000	8.10	10	0	0	0	4	0	13.1	13	69	14	12	3	0	1	1	16	0	8	6	0
Ryan, Patrick, Idaho Falls	2	1	.667	4.77	14	10	0	0	0	0	60.1	64	260	42	32	8	2	8	2	17	0	47	3	0
Salley, Anthony, Med. Hat*	2	2	.500	4.46	24	0	0	0	8	1	36.1	32	165	27	18	5	0	4	3	24	0	28	5	1
Santa, Jeffrey, Medicine Hat..	0	0	.000	4.68	18	1	0	0	6	0	25.0	27	113	19	13	2	2	1	1	8	1	28	2	0
Satterfield, Jeremy, Med. Hat	0	1	.000	8.46	16	0	0	0	5	0	22.1	29	127	29	21	2	1	1	2	27	1	26	7	0
Schubmehl, Brian, Ogden	4	3	.571	5.40	19	0	0	0	17	4	30.0	32	139	23	18	6	3	1	0	15	2	38	4	0
Seale, Dustin, Medicine Hat*	1	0	.000	2.30	10	0	0	0	2	0	15.2	21	68	8	4	0	1	0	0	3	0	24	1	1
Sellers, Justin, Idaho Falls	5	1	.833	5.56	24	0	0	0	6	4	43.2	58	194	28	27	7	1	2	9	19	1	32	0	0
Serrano, Wascar, Idaho Falls..	0	1	.000	11.88	2	2	0	0	0	0	8.1	13	43	12	11	2	0	0	1	4	0	13	0	0
Smith, Josh, Idaho Falls*	2	2	.500	10.13	26	0	0	0	10	0	26.2	35	146	33	30	1	1	0	0	31	4	24	9	1
Sneed, John, Medicine Hat	6	1	.857	1.29	15	10	2	0	1	0	69.2	42	275	19	10	5	2	1	7	20	0	79	2	0
Sokol, Trad, Ogden*	2	0	1.000	4.19	17	0	0	0	6	3	38.2	44	177	18	18	6	1	1	1	16	0	43	2	1
Steele, Brandon, Butte	3	4	.429	4.52	13	13	1	0	0	0	69.2	83	326	53	35	8	2	2	4	42	0	55	9	1
Stewart, Paul, Ogden	5	6	.455	5.31	15	15	1	1	0	0	81.1	88	370	59	48	13	1	3	6	30	0	82	3	2
Stover, C.D., Great Falls	7	2	.778	2.56	12	12	1	1	0	0	77.1	71	324	36	22	4	1	3	2	14	0	61	3	1
Stumbo, Wes, Billings	3	2	.600	4.19	15	2	0	0	4	1	34.1	33	157	21	16	0	0	2	4	22	2	40	7	0
Taczy, Craig, Great Falls*	2	1	.667	4.02	18	4	0	0	6	3	53.2	65	242	29	24	2	2	0	2	15	0	44	4	0
Timm, Dan, Billings................	4	1	.800	4.66	20	0	0	0	11	4	38.2	47	190	24	20	2	0	0	6	26	2	36	9	0
Timmerman, Heath, Butte	0	2	.000	6.35	7	6	0	0	0	0	17.0	26	88	21	12	3	1	0	0	10	0	10	2	0
Tokarse, Brian, Butte	2	4	.333	6.87	8	7	0	0	0	0	36.2	44	162	33	28	3	1	4	2	8	0	34	2	0
Torrealba, Aquiles, Butte	0	0	.000	3.86	2	0	0	0	1	0	2.1	2	11	1	1	0	1	1	1	3	0	3	0	0
Viator, Dustin, Idaho Falls	2	2	.500	5.01	23	5	0	0	6	1	50.1	57	236	34	28	7	1	0	2	24	1	42	3	0
Viegas, Randy, Idaho Falls* ..	1	1	.500	2.35	5	0	0	0	2	0	7.2	2	39	4	2	0	0	1	1	11	0	12	4	1
Wasinger, Mark, Idaho Falls ..	0	0	.000	3.00	1	0	0	0	1	0	3.0	2	14	2	1	0	1	0	0	2	0	1	0	0
Watson, Mark, Ogden*	4	3	.571	4.15	10	10	1	0	0	0	47.2	44	202	26	22	4	1	2	0	19	0	49	2	0
Werner, Don, Idaho Falls........	0	1	.000	108.00	1	1	0	0	0	0	1.0	10	15	12	12	1	0	0	0	2	0	0	0	0
Whitesides, John, Billings	2	1	.667	7.36	9	0	0	0	4	0	11.0	16	59	14	9	2	1	2	1	7	1	10	3	0
Williamson, Scott, Billings	8	2	.800	1.78	13	13	2	1	0	0	86.0	66	346	25	17	5	1	2	4	23	0	101	12	2
Wilson, Jeffrey, Lethbridge* ..	1	1	.500	4.46	22	0	0	0	9	0	36.1	35	157	22	18	4	2	1	0	12	0	49	5	0
Wooten, Brandon, Ogden*	4	1	.800	5.29	18	0	0	0	10	1	34.0	43	164	33	20	3	2	4	2	14	1	27	1	0
Young, Douglas, Idaho Falls ..	3	4	.429	5.58	15	10	0	0	3	1	59.2	69	274	41	37	2	0	1	2	27	0	44	7	1
Zamora, Pete, Great Falls*	2	5	.286	2.58	13	10	1	0	2	0	69.2	59	289	27	20	3	1	3	3	30	0	73	3	1
Zapata, Juan, Ogden	2	1	.667	1.23	8	0	0	0	2	0	22.0	11	93	5	3	1	1	0	1	13	2	19	2	0
Zepeda, Jesse, Medicine Hat..	0	0	.000	9.00	1	0	0	0	1	0	1.0	3	6	1	1	0	0	0	0	0	0	1	0	0

COMBINATION SHUTOUTS: **Billings (2)**—Williamson-Timm, Williamson-Stumbo-Altman. **Butte (1)**—Porter-Rodriguez-Bane. **Great Falls (5)**—Stover-Reyes, Zamora-Baker-Correa, Regalado-Zamora, Alvarez-Bornyk, Montgomery-Romero-Galvez-Correa. **Helena (2)**—Incantalupo-Childers, Johnston-Childers. **Idaho Falls (1)**—Viator-Oiseth-Young. **Lethbridge (3)**—Andrews-Martines-Knott, Jenson-Martines, Rooney-Knott-Jones. **Medicine Hat (0)**—None. **Ogden (0)**—None.

NO-HIT GAMES: None.

PITCHERS WITH TWO OR MORE TEAMS

Pitcher, Team	W	L	Pct.	ERA	G	GS	CG	ShO	GF	Sv.	IP	H	TBF	R	ER	HR	SH	SF	HB	BB	IBB	SO	WP	Bk.
Jones, Chauncey, Helena	0	0	.000	9.53	5	0	0	0	3	0	5.2	8	31	6	6	1	1	0	0	7	0	7	0	0
Jones, Chauncey, Ogden	0	1	.000	5.79	9	0	0	0	7	0	9.1	10	50	7	6	2	0	0	0	11	0	10	0	0

1997 FIELDING

TEAM

Team	Pct.	G	PO	A	E	TC	DP	PB	Team	Pct.	G	PO	A	E	TC	DP	PB
Idaho Falls.......	.957	72	1896	823	123	2842	65	25	Billings	.943	71	1871	751	158	2780	57	26
Great Falls	.952	72	1905	826	138	2869	73	14	Butte................	.942	72	1861	854	168	2883	70	26
Ogden..............	.950	72	1870	784	141	2795	57	11	Medicine Hat ...	.938	72	1863	777	174	2814	61	14
Lethbridge........	.949	72	1873	846	146	2865	62	14	TRIPLE PLAYS: None.								
Helena	.948	71	1850	791	145	2786	59	13									

INDIVIDUAL

FIRST BASEMEN

NOTE: All caps denotes fielding-percentage leader based on 36 games for catchers, 48 for all other non-pitchers and 72 innings for pitchers. *Throws lefthanded.

Player, Team	Pct.	G	PO	A	E	TC	DP
Adams, Tim, Butte	.980	34	316	20	7	343	29
Alfano, Jeff, Ogden	1.000	3	23	2	0	25	1
Bejarano, Brian, Medicine Hat ...	.974	20	161	24	5	190	19
Bunkley, Antuan, Helena	.971	26	216	16	7	239	22
Caiazzo, Nick, Helena	.889	4	16	0	2	18	3
Castillo, Alex, Helena	.940	4	41	6	3	50	0
Cronin, Shane, Idaho Falls	.983	12	108	6	2	116	13
Darula, Bobby, Ogden	.944	2	17	0	1	18	1
Dean, Aaron, Great Falls*	.982	58	454	27	9	490	38
Dempsey, Nicholas, Great Falls ..	1.000	2	2	0	0	2	1
Falcon, Edwin, Great Falls	.963	35	246	16	10	272	24
Fortin, Blaine, Medicine Hat........	.921	5	31	4	3	38	0

Player, Team	Pct.	G	PO	A	E	TC	DP
Fox, Brian, Lethbridge	.988	25	241	12	3	256	14
Guthrie, Kendal, Ogden	.988	41	372	39	5	416	26
James, Brandon, Ogden	1.000	6	48	2	0	50	2
Jergenson, Brian, Idaho Falls*	.983	53	473	41	9	523	38
Jones, Keith, Lethbridge	.989	30	264	16	3	283	22
KRAUS, Jake, Og.-Hel.	.994	57	492	38	3	533	41
Lawrence, Tony, Idaho Falls	1.000	3	23	1	0	24	0
Llanos, Alex, Butte	.946	4	33	2	2	37	4
Morrison, Greg, Medicine Hat*	.988	45	282	37	4	323	27
Ortiz, Carlos, Medicine Hat	.971	24	121	11	4	136	9
Pascual, Edison, Billings*	.900	5	8	1	1	10	0
Patterson, Marty, Helena	.952	5	18	2	1	21	0
Quittner, Peter, Butte	.986	25	202	13	3	218	19
Riggio, Robert, Ogden	1.000	7	40	2	0	42	5
Ryden, Karl, Idaho Falls	1.000	2	0	1	0	1	0
Sanchez, Toby, Billings	.977	26	195	16	5	216	17
Seal, Scott, Idaho Falls*	.974	7	73	3	2	78	5
Steelmon, Wyley, Lethbridge	.965	8	52	3	2	57	2
Talbott, Benjamin, Butte	.986	13	124	12	2	138	13
Taveras, Jose, Lethbridge	.966	17	135	8	5	148	14
Welsh, Eric, Billings*	.981	48	394	23	8	425	36
Zamora, Pete, Great Falls*	1.000	2	3	0	0	3	0

FIRST BASEMEN WITH TWO OR MORE TEAMS

Player, Team	Pct.	G	PO	A	E	TC	DP
Kraus, Jake, Ogden	.994	18	156	14	1	171	12
Kraus, Jake, Helena	.994	39	336	24	2	362	29

SECOND BASEMEN

Player, Team	Pct.	G	PO	A	E	TC	DP
Allen, Shane, Great Falls	.871	16	9	18	4	31	5
Bautista, Juan, Lethbridge	1.000	1	3	3	0	6	0
Brewer, Brad, Butte	1.000	2	1	8	0	9	0
Caceres, Wilmy, Billings	.939	10	18	28	3	49	11
Collier, Marc, Butte	.950	3	9	10	1	20	3
Condon, Mike, Butte	.942	17	42	56	6	104	16
DeMarco, Joey, Idaho Falls	.935	10	13	30	3	46	6
Doherty, Steven, Lethbridge	.929	35	64	107	13	184	22
Gallo, Ismael, Great Falls	.982	26	40	71	2	113	10
Gonzalez, Santos, Idaho Falls	.950	13	19	38	3	60	8
Guillen, Jose, Helena	.855	21	22	43	11	76	8
Llanos, Alex, Butte	.938	34	64	88	10	162	17
Marshall, Monte, Great Falls	.962	41	61	117	7	185	22
Martin, Jared, Lethbridge	.867	6	11	15	4	30	2
Martinez, Belvani, Lethbridge	.882	21	34	41	10	85	9
Mathis, Jared, Ogden	1.000	2	3	1	0	4	0
Montgomery, Andre, Billings	.924	46	84	122	17	223	25
Nizov, Alexander, Butte	.917	26	51	60	10	121	13
Osilka, Garret, Ogden	.778	2	2	5	2	9	2
Patten, Chris, Og.-Hel.	.941	25	41	71	7	119	14
Price, Corey, Billings	.923	19	33	39	6	78	4
Rexrode, Jackie, Lethbridge	.912	11	28	24	5	57	8
Riggio, Robert, Ogden	.750	5	2	4	2	8	0
RODRIGUEZ, Felipe, Med. Hat	.929	52	104	119	17	240	26
Rodriguez, John, Idaho Falls	.909	5	9	11	2	22	2
Rojas, Eliezer, Helena	.960	45	92	123	9	224	28
Rowan, Chris, Ogden	.902	39	54	84	15	153	24
Saitta, Rich, Great Falls	1.000	7	6	16	0	22	4
Snellgrove, Clayton, Idaho Falls	.981	39	84	126	4	214	25
Solano, Manny, Billings	.933	7	4	10	1	15	2
Taveras, Jose, Lethbridge	1.000	1	1	3	0	4	0
Thrower, Jake, Idaho Falls	.973	6	17	19	1	37	3
Torres, Bernie, Great Falls	.895	5	10	7	2	19	2
Tucent, Francisco, Ogden	.919	36	38	75	10	123	11
Zeber, Ryan, Medicine Hat	.833	4	4	1	1	6	0
Zepeda, Jesse, Medicine Hat	.938	24	55	50	7	112	10

SECOND BASEMEN WITH TWO OR MORE TEAMS

Player, Team	Pct.	G	PO	A	E	TC	DP
Patten, Chris, Ogden	.909	4	0	10	1	11	0
Patten, Chris, Helena	.944	21	41	61	6	108	14

THIRD BASEMEN

Player, Team	Pct.	G	PO	A	E	TC	DP
Allen, Luke, Great Falls	.866	63	35	107	22	164	10
Balbuena, Mike, Great Falls	.871	12	8	19	4	31	1
Barrett, Andrew, Medicine Hat	.000	2	0	0	1	1	0
Bejarano, Brian, Medicine Hat	.912	20	11	20	3	34	2
Caceres, Wilmy, Billings	1.000	1	0	1	0	1	0
Cronin, Shane, Idaho Falls	.925	18	7	30	3	40	5
Deardorff, Jeff, Ogden	.845	63	37	110	27	174	4

Player, Team	Pct.	G	PO	A	E	TC	DP
DeMarco, Joey, Idaho Falls	.875	8	4	17	3	24	2
Doherty, Steven, Lethbridge	.839	13	6	20	5	31	4
Gonzalez, Santos, Idaho Falls	1.000	1	0	1	0	1	0
Hubbel, Travis, Medicine Hat	.819	37	28	67	21	116	9
Jones, Keith, Lethbridge	.869	23	7	46	8	61	3
Kirby, Scott, Helena	.817	66	47	118	37	202	10
Langdon, Trajan, Idaho Falls	.831	19	12	37	10	59	4
LAWRENCE, Mike, Butte	.935	69	52	163	15	230	20
Llanos, Alex, Butte	.769	5	2	8	3	13	1
Markray, Thad, Billings	.879	44	27	53	11	91	4
Montgomery, Andre, Billings	.688	7	2	9	5	16	1
Osilka, Garret, Ogden	.800	1	0	4	1	5	0
Patten, Chris, Og.-Hel.	.810	11	3	14	4	21	0
Riggio, Robert, Ogden	.800	11	3	17	5	25	1
Rodriguez, John, Idaho Falls	.885	24	16	38	7	61	8
Saitta, Rich, Great Falls	1.000	3	5	3	0	8	2
Sanchez, Toby, Billings	.905	11	6	13	2	21	0
Snellgrove, Clayton, Idaho Falls	1.000	1	0	2	0	2	0
Solano, Manny, Billings	.863	31	13	31	7	51	2
Taveras, Jose, Lethbridge	.881	42	23	88	15	126	5
Thrower, Jake, Idaho Falls	.778	4	1	6	2	9	0
Tucent, Francisco, Ogden	.750	2	1	2	1	4	0
Umbria, Jose, Medicine Hat	1.000	3	1	5	0	6	0
Watley, Clarence, Medicine Hat	.625	3	2	3	3	8	0
Zepeda, Jesse, Medicine Hat	.891	24	7	34	5	46	4

THIRD BASEMEN WITH TWO OR MORE TEAMS

Player, Team	Pct.	G	PO	A	E	TC	DP
Patten, Chris, Ogden	.625	4	1	4	3	8	0
Patten, Chris, Helena	.923	7	2	10	1	13	0

SHORTSTOPS

Player, Team	Pct.	G	PO	A	E	TC	DP
Barrett, Andrew, Medicine Hat	.850	8	4	13	3	20	3
Bautista, Juan, Lethbridge	.907	41	56	119	18	193	21
Bernhardt, Jossephang, Med. Hat	.860	60	86	153	39	278	28
Brewer, Brad, Butte	.948	18	32	59	5	96	12
Caceres, Wilmy, Billings	.667	4	4	2	3	9	1
Cintron, Alexander, Lethbridge	.857	1	3	3	1	7	0
Collier, Marc, Butte	1.000	2	0	4	0	4	0
Condon, Mike, Butte	.882	33	44	98	19	161	15
Dawkins, Travis, Billings	.908	70	118	216	34	368	36
DeMarco, Joey, Idaho Falls	.952	10	11	29	2	42	4
Encarnacion, Bienvenido, Butte	.883	26	33	58	12	103	13
Gallo, Ismael, Great Falls	.902	28	40	79	13	132	14
Gonzalez, Santos, Idaho Falls	.888	26	30	81	14	125	13
Guillen, Jose, Helena	.800	3	3	5	2	10	1
Marshall, Monte, Great Falls	1.000	1	1	0	0	1	0
Martin, Jared, Lethbridge	.918	19	33	56	8	97	13
Martinez, Belvani, Lethbridge	.933	4	8	20	2	30	3
Mathis, Jared, Ogden	.933	6	5	9	1	15	1
Osilka, Garret, Ogden	.909	61	96	174	27	297	32
Patten, Chris, Og.-Hel.	.927	13	14	37	4	55	4
Rowan, Chris, Ogden	.883	13	22	31	7	60	9
Sanchez, Wellington, Helena	.934	60	90	181	19	290	37
Snellgrove, Clayton, Idaho Falls	.969	19	26	67	3	96	12
Solano, Manny, Billings	.857	2	2	4	1	7	1
Taveras, Jose, Lethbridge	.895	12	13	38	6	57	4
Thrower, Jake, Idaho Falls	.929	18	29	63	7	99	5
TORRES, Bernie, Great Falls	.942	52	73	172	15	260	34
Tucent, Francisco, Ogden	1.000	1	1	1	0	2	0
Zepeda, Jesse, Medicine Hat	.905	14	17	40	6	63	4

SHORTSTOPS WITH TWO OR MORE TEAMS

Player, Team	Pct.	G	PO	A	E	TC	DP
Patten, Chris, Ogden	1.000	1	0	2	0	2	0
Patten, Chris, Helena	.925	12	14	35	4	53	4

OUTFIELDERS

Player, Team	Pct.	G	PO	A	E	TC	DP
Adams, Lawrence, Medicine Hat	.969	33	24	7	1	32	0
Allen, Luke, Great Falls	1.000	2	3	0	0	3	0
Armenta, Jason, Billings*	.947	37	34	2	2	38	1
Auterson, Jeffrey, Great Falls	.963	56	75	2	3	80	0
Baez, Juan, Ogden	.934	50	53	4	4	61	2
Barrett, Andrew, Medicine Hat	.929	25	24	2	2	28	1
Battle, Rohn, Butte	.600	2	2	1	2	5	0
Beatriz, Ramy, Helena*	.933	53	80	4	6	90	0
Bejarano, Brian, Medicine Hat	1.000	1	1	0	0	2	0
Brown, Billy, Medicine Hat	.954	50	96	7	5	108	1
Brown, Kent, Idaho Falls*	.932	35	52	3	4	59	0

Player, Team	Pct.	G	PO	A	E	TC	DP
Burford, Kevin, Idaho Falls*	1.000	7	11	0	0	11	0
Burress, Andy, Billings	1.000	7	6	0	0	6	0
Caiazzo, Nick, Helena	.966	50	54	2	2	58	0
Calloway, Ronald, Lethbridge*	.954	40	61	1	3	65	0
Candela, Frank, Ogden	.961	23	48	1	2	51	0
DeJesus, Eddie, Butte	.946	57	66	4	4	74	1
Fernandez, Ramon, Helena	.940	54	72	6	5	83	0
Frank, Mike, Billings*	.970	69	118	11	4	133	3
Gomera, Rafael, Great Falls	.904	58	88	6	10	104	4
Guzman, Elpidio, Butte*	.852	17	23	0	4	27	0
Guzman, Julio, Lethbridge	.958	17	21	2	1	24	1
Horsman, Brent, Idaho Falls	.922	47	66	5	6	77	1
Hudson, Bert, Lethbridge	.957	50	60	6	3	69	1
Hunter, Johnny, Idaho Falls	.885	9	21	2	3	26	0
Jacobsen, Bucky, Ogden	.925	62	82	4	7	93	0
James, Brandon, Ogden	.980	66	100	0	2	102	0
Kelleher, Pat, Great Falls	.949	43	34	3	2	39	0
Knight, Marcus, Butte	.921	70	101	4	9	114	1
Landingham, James, Med. Hat*	.941	14	15	1	1	17	0
Lawrence, Tony, Idaho Falls	1.000	1	1	0	0	1	0
Madera, Wil, Lethbridge*	.889	30	31	1	4	36	0
Mathis, Jared, Ogden	1.000	41	56	3	0	59	2
Moreta, Ramon, Great Falls	.919	67	110	4	10	124	1
Morillo, Luis, Medicine Hat*	1.000	8	16	0	0	16	0
Morrison, Greg, Medicine Hat*	.824	23	28	0	6	34	0
Nunez, Abraham, Lethbridge	1.000	2	1	1	0	2	0
Oliver, Johnny, Billings	1.000	3	2	0	0	2	0
Patten, Chris, Helena	1.000	3	6	0	0	6	0
Patterson, Marty, Helena	.929	10	12	1	1	14	0
Pearson, Ryan, Helena	.929	41	50	2	4	56	0
Perez, Angelo, Medicine Hat	.925	70	115	9	10	134	1
Philip-Guide, Sheldon, Butte	1.000	16	30	1	0	31	0
Pichardo, Gilbert, Butte	.917	7	11	0	1	12	0
Richey, Mikal, Great Falls	.875	21	6	1	1	8	0
Rios, Fernando, Billings	.958	41	64	5	3	72	1
Ruotsinoja, Jacob, Idaho Falls	.939	31	42	4	3	49	1
Rutherford, Daryl, Idaho Falls	.957	14	22	0	1	23	0
RYDEN, Karl, Idaho Falls	.989	53	85	2	1	88	1
Saitta, Rich, Great Falls	1.000	7	5	1	0	6	0
Sandoval, Jhensy, Lethbridge	.943	40	63	3	4	70	1
Seal, Scott, Idaho Falls*	1.000	22	29	2	0	31	1
Skeens, Jeremy, Billings	.962	23	25	0	1	26	0
Sykes, Jamie, Lethbridge	.956	55	79	8	4	91	0
Thrower, Jake, Idaho Falls	1.000	1	1	0	0	1	0
Tolentino, Juan, Butte	.920	59	113	2	10	125	0
Tucent, Francisco, Ogden	1.000	3	2	0	0	2	0
Warren, Lance, Great Falls	1.000	1	1	1	0	2	0
Warren, Thomas, Helena	.929	33	51	1	4	56	0
Watley, Clarence, Medicine Hat	1.000	8	9	1	0	10	0
Wise, Dewayne, Billings*	.907	62	118	9	13	140	1
Zeber, Ryan, Medicine Hat	1.000	5	1	0	0	1	0
Zepeda, Jesse, Medicine Hat	1.000	8	10	0	0	10	0

CATCHERS

Player, Team	Pct.	G	PO	A	E	TC	DP	PB
Alfano, Jeff, Ogden	.980	23	160	32	4	196	3	5
Burress, Andy, Billings	1.000	1	3	0	0	3	0	2
Caiazzo, Nick, Helena	.981	11	50	2	1	53	0	5
Cripps, Bobby, Great Falls	.981	46	318	34	7	359	3	6
Darula, Bobby, Ogden	.991	41	311	24	3	338	1	5
Dunham, Traylon, Idaho Falls	1.000	1	10	0	0	10	0	1
Falcon, Edwin, Great Falls	1.000	3	6	0	0	6	0	1
Fortin, Blaine, Medicine Hat	.987	25	137	20	2	159	2	2
Fox, Brian, Lethbridge	.987	30	194	31	3	228	0	3
Guthrie, Kendal, Ogden	1.000	10	77	5	0	82	1	1
Hilliker, Tracey, Great Falls	.976	24	146	17	4	167	0	7
Johnson, Patrick, Butte	.988	47	294	30	4	328	2	13
Lawrence, Tony, Idaho Falls	.975	41	308	46	9	363	2	16
Mathis, Jared, Ogden	1.000	7	17	0	0	17	1	0
McAFFEE, Josh, Lethbridge	.996	36	216	30	1	247	3	7
McDaniel, Ryan, Idaho Falls	.958	21	163	18	8	189	0	6
Moon, Brian, Helena	.987	48	326	51	5	382	5	4
Newman, Howard, Billings	.987	13	62	13	1	76	0	2
Ortiz, Carlos, Medicine Hat	1.000	1	2	0	0	2	0	1
Patterson, Marty, Helena	.978	20	163	16	4	183	0	4
Quire, Jeremy, Lethbridge	.993	28	138	13	1	152	1	4
Quittner, Peter, Butte	1.000	8	47	7	0	54	1	4
Rivera, Francisco, Billings	.981	13	48	3	1	52	0	1
Santos, Jose, Butte	.959	21	119	21	6	146	2	9
Snow, Casey, Great Falls	.981	15	95	8	2	105	1	0
Suarez, Marc, Billings	.973	62	439	64	14	517	1	21

Player, Team	Pct.	G	PO	A	E	TC	DP	PB
Umbria, Jose, Medicine Hat	.975	44	245	33	7	285	3	8
Zeber, Ryan, Medicine Hat	.984	28	163	20	3	186	1	3
Zucha, Jason, Idaho Falls	1.000	11	72	4	0	76	1	2

PITCHERS

Player, Team	Pct.	G	PO	A	E	TC	DP
Akin, Jay, Helena*	1.000	5	1	11	0	12	0
Altman, Gene, Great Falls	.857	20	3	3	1	7	0
Alvarez, Victor, Great Falls	.846	12	2	9	2	13	0
Anderson, Dallas, Lethbridge	.000	10	0	0	1	1	0
Andrews, Jeff, Lethbridge	1.000	9	3	7	0	10	0
Arroyo, Joel, Ogden	.667	16	1	1	1	3	0
Averette, Robert, Billings	1.000	2	0	1	0	1	0
Baker, Jason, Great Falls*	1.000	9	1	6	0	7	0
Bane, Jaymie, Butte*	1.000	24	3	8	0	11	0
Barrera, Iran, Medicine Hat	.750	17	2	1	1	4	1
Barrett, Scott, Medicine Hat	.826	19	6	13	4	23	1
Bloomer, Christopher, Lethbridge	.900	27	2	7	1	10	1
Bornyk, Matthew, Great Falls	1.000	13	0	2	0	2	0
Bost, Ronald, Medicine Hat*	.667	14	1	1	1	3	0
Brackeen, Colin, Medicine Hat*	.800	18	2	2	1	5	0
Brewer, Clint, Billings	.750	22	2	1	1	4	0
Brown, Zay, Billings	.000	8	0	0	1	1	0
Byrd, Ben, Ogden	.000	18	3	13	0	16	1
Caddell, Carl, Billings*	1.000	4	2	1	0	3	0
Camp, Shawn, Idaho Falls	1.000	30	4	7	0	11	0
Cavanagh, Andrew, Helena	1.000	18	4	4	0	8	0
Childers, Jason, Helena	1.000	10	0	2	0	2	0
Childers, Matthew, Helena	1.000	14	6	17	0	23	1
Correa, Elvis, Great Falls	1.000	21	0	1	0	1	0
Cronin, Shane, Idaho Falls	1.000	1	0	1	0	1	0
Dotel, Melido, Great Falls	.789	14	4	11	4	19	0
Elias, Javier, Butte	.900	18	0	9	1	10	0
Ervin, Kent, Idaho Falls	.913	16	5	16	2	23	1
Eye, Jacob, Ogden	1.000	1	1	1	0	2	0
Fleming, John, Lethbridge	.909	12	3	17	2	22	3
Flores, Pedro, Great Falls*	1.000	22	2	9	0	11	1
Fontanes, Reuben, Lethbridge	1.000	5	0	1	0	1	0
Frias, Miguel, Lethbridge*	1.000	1	0	1	0	1	0
Galvez, Randy, Great Falls	1.000	16	1	4	0	5	0
Gooda, David, Ogden*	.909	16	1	9	1	11	0
Goure, Sam, Medicine Hat	.895	15	6	11	2	19	1
Gourlay, Matthew, Medicine Hat	.950	14	8	11	1	20	1
Guttormson, Ricky, Idaho Falls	.875	18	3	4	1	8	0
Guzman, Jonathan, Helena*	1.000	19	2	0	0	2	0
Hannah, Neal, Great Falls	1.000	2	0	1	0	1	0
Haring, Brett, Billings*	1.000	14	2	3	0	5	0
Harper, David, Lethbridge	1.000	8	1	5	0	6	0
Harris, Josh, Billings	.900	14	13	14	3	30	1
Hawkins, Alsharik, Ogden	.938	14	8	22	2	32	1
Helmer, Chad, Helena	.833	14	4	1	1	6	0
Hernandez, Pedro, Great Falls	1.000	15	1	5	0	6	0
Herndon, Harry, Idaho Falls	1.000	1	0	2	0	2	0
Herrera, Misael, Idaho Falls	.833	6	0	5	1	6	1
Hueda, Alejandro, Medicine Hat	.944	16	9	8	1	18	2
Hunter, Johnny, Idaho Falls	1.000	4	1	2	0	3	0
Hurst, Doug, Billings	1.000	1	0	1	0	1	0
Incantalupo, Todd, Helena*	.917	14	2	9	1	12	0
Jensen, Jason, Lethbridge*	.938	14	0	15	1	16	1
Johnston, Doug, Helena	.929	13	5	8	1	14	0
Jones, Charlie, Lethbridge	1.000	16	1	2	0	3	0
Jones, Chauncey, Hel.-Og.	1.000	14	1	3	0	4	0
Keathley, Davan, Medicine Hat*	.875	20	3	4	1	8	0
Kendall, Phil, Helena	1.000	14	10	9	0	19	0
Kirst, Mark, Ogden	.944	16	7	10	1	18	1
Knott, Eric, Lethbridge*	.909	21	2	8	1	11	0
Lancaster, Roger, Medicine Hat	1.000	18	4	6	0	10	0
LEE, Derek, Ogden*	1.000	14	9	21	0	30	3
Levy, Tye, Billings*	1.000	18	0	1	0	1	0
Lynch, Pat, Medicine Hat	.941	12	6	10	1	17	2
Mallette, Brian, Helena	.800	23	1	3	1	5	0
Martines, Jason, Lethbridge	1.000	22	1	7	0	8	0
Martinez, Francisco, Helena	.875	16	5	2	1	8	0
McClellan, Matthew, Med. Hat	1.000	14	2	4	0	6	0
McGuire, Brandon, Butte	.714	17	2	3	2	7	0
Merrell, Philip, Lethbridge	.933	14	6	8	1	15	1
Miller, Ernie, Butte*	.900	20	3	6	1	10	1
Miller, Jim, Helena	.786	16	4	7	3	14	0
Montgomery, Matthew, Great Falls	1.000	4	1	5	0	6	1
Myers, Rob, Helena	.500	18	0	1	1	2	0
Naff, Todd, Idaho Falls	1.000	24	5	4	0	9	1

Player, Team	Pct.	G	PO	A	E	TC	DP
Nash, Damon, Idaho Falls	.909	14	6	4	1	11	1
Needle, Chad, Medicine Hat	1.000	10	1	4	0	5	1
Norris, Ben, Lethbridge*	.808	14	5	16	5	26	0
Oiseth, Jon, Idaho Falls*	.667	18	1	1	1	3	1
O'Toole, Ryan, Billings	1.000	11	2	2	0	4	0
Padilla, Charly, Butte	.929	20	4	9	1	14	0
Perozo, Felix, Butte	.900	14	8	19	3	30	3
Perry, Tim, Idaho Falls	.929	15	5	8	1	14	0
Peterson, Kyle, Ogden	1.000	3	2	1	0	3	1
Porter, Aaron, Butte	.833	13	4	6	2	12	0
Priebe, Kevin, Helena*	1.000	19	4	6	0	10	1
Puorto, Jamie, Lethbridge*	1.000	20	2	9	0	11	0
Regalado, Maximo, Great Falls	.800	9	2	2	1	5	0
Reyes, Nate, Great Falls*	.933	24	0	14	1	15	0
Ricks, Ronald, Butte	.722	17	5	8	5	18	0
Robinson, Dustin, Billings	1.000	16	1	8	0	9	0
Rodriguez, Franklin, Med. Hat*	1.000	7	1	2	0	3	0
Rojas, Renney, Butte	.857	15	8	28	6	42	2
Romero, Alejandro, Great Falls	1.000	25	3	2	0	5	0
Romero, John, Butte	.714	15	1	4	2	7	0
Rooney, Mike, Lethbridge	.967	13	5	24	1	30	1
Roundtree, Monte, Billings*	.500	13	1	2	3	6	0
Runk, David, Billings	.333	10	0	1	2	3	0
Ryan, Patrick, Idaho Falls	.952	14	10	10	1	21	1
Salley, Anthony, Medicine Hat*	.909	24	6	4	1	11	0
Santa, Jeffrey, Lethbridge*	.750	18	0	3	1	4	0
Satterfield, Jeremy, Med. Hat	.833	16	3	2	1	6	0
Schubmehl, Brian, Ogden	1.000	19	0	4	0	4	0
Seale, Dustin, Medicine Hat*	1.000	10	0	1	0	1	0
Sellers, Justin, Idaho Falls	1.000	24	5	1	0	6	0
Smith, Josh, Idaho Falls*	.750	26	1	5	2	8	0
Sneed, John, Medicine Hat	1.000	15	3	11	0	14	1
Sokol, Trad, Ogden*	.889	17	4	4	1	9	0
Steele, Brandon, Butte	.800	13	3	17	5	25	1
Stewart, Paul, Ogden	.917	15	6	5	1	12	0
Stover, C.D., Great Falls	.667	12	1	5	3	9	0
Stumbo, Wes, Billings	.750	15	1	5	2	8	0
Taczy, Craig, Great Falls*	1.000	18	1	3	0	4	0
Timm, Dan, Billings	1.000	20	1	7	0	8	0
Timmerman, Heath, Butte	.625	7	4	1	3	8	0
Tokarse, Brian, Butte	.846	8	5	6	2	13	0
Torrealba, Aquiles, Butte	1.000	2	0	1	0	1	0
Viator, Dustin, Idaho Falls	1.000	23	7	5	0	12	0
Viegas, Randy, Idaho Falls*	1.000	5	1	0	0	1	0
Watson, Mark, Ogden	.846	10	0	11	2	13	0
Werner, Don, Idaho Falls	1.000	1	1	0	0	1	0
Whitesides, John, Billings	.750	9	1	2	1	4	0
Williamson, Scott, Billings	1.000	13	9	16	0	25	0
Wilson, Jeffrey, Lethbridge*	.889	22	2	6	1	9	1
Wooten, Brandon, Ogden*	.917	18	0	11	1	12	0
Young, Douglas, Idaho Falls	.947	15	3	15	1	19	3
Zamora, Pete, Great Falls*	1.000	13	6	18	0	24	1
Zapata, Juan, Ogden	1.000	8	0	5	0	5	0

PITCHERS WITH TWO OR MORE TEAMS

Player, Team	Pct.	G	PO	A	E	TC	DP
Jones, Chauncey, Helena	1.000	5	0	2	0	2	0
Jones, Chauncey, Ogden	1.000	9	1	1	0	2	0

The following players did not have any fielding statistics at the positions indicated or appeared only as a designated hitter, pinch-hitter or pinch-runner: Ja. Allen, ph; Jo. Allen, of; S. Barrett, 1b; Bell, p; Bunkley, 2b, p; Dallin, 2b; Figueroa, p; Fortin, of; Gallo, of; Gutierrez, p; Hagins, 2b, c; Haverstick, p; Hudson, 3b; K. Jones, p; Landingham, 1b; Leshay, p; Martin, c; Mathis, p; McDaniel, 2b; Morrow, of; Ortiz, 3b; Patterson, p; Pozo, p; Rakers, dh; Fe. Rodriguez, of; H. Rodriguez, p; Serrano, p; Solano, of; Wasinger, p; Zeber, 3b; Zepeda, c, p.

LEAGUE CHAMPIONS

Year Team	Pct.	Year Team	Pct.	Year Team	Pct.
1939— Twin Falls*	.581	1959— Boise	.633	1983— Billings▲	.614
1940— Salt Lake City	.608	Billings (2nd)*	.523	Calgary	.600
Ogden (4th)*	.492	1960— Boise†	.686	1984— Billings	.691
1941— Boise	.623	Idaho Falls	.650	Helena▲	.647
Ogden (2nd)*	.598	1961— Boise	.638	1985— Great Falls	.771
1942— Pocatello†	.690	Great Falls*	.571	Salt Lake City▲	.657
Boise	.683	1962— Boise§	.565	1986— Salt Lake City♦	.643
1943-44-45—Did not operate.		Billings†	.706	Great Falls	.571
1946— Twin Falls‡	.585	1963— Idaho Falls	.702	1987— Salt Lake City♦	.700
Salt Lake City†	.585	Magic Valley†	.643	Helena	.657
1947— Salt Lake City	.618	1964— Treasure Valley	.615	1988— Great Falls♦	.754
Twin Falls†	.600	1965— Treasure Valley	.530	Butte	.629
1948— Pocatello	.611	1966— Ogden	.591	1989— Great Falls♦	.791
Twin Falls (2nd)*	.595	1967— Ogden	.621	Butte	.621
1949— Twin Falls	.624	1968— Ogden	.609	1990— Great Falls♦	.706
Pocatello (3rd)*	.595	1969— Ogden	.620	Salt Lake	.618
1950— Pocatello	.635	1970— Idaho Falls	.629	1991— Salt Lake City♦	.700
Billings (3rd)*	.571	1971— Great Falls	.643	Great Falls	.657
1951— Salt Lake City	.618	1972— Billings	.694	1992— Salt Lake	.697
Great Falls (3rd)*	.559	1973— Billings	.629	Billings♦	.697
1952— Pocatello	.595	1974— Idaho Falls	.569	1993— Billings♦	.653
Idaho Falls (2nd)*	.573	1975— Billings	.577	Helena	.589
1953— Ogden	.679	1976— Great Falls	.577	1994— Billings♦	.694
Salt Lake City (4th)*	.527	1977— Lethbridge	.629	Helena	.611
1954— Salt Lake City	.595	1978— Billings∞	.735	1995— Billings	.710
Great Falls (4th)*	.530	1979— Helena	.623	Helena■	.690
1955— Boise	.588	Lethbridge▲	.559	1996— Helena■	.597
Magic Valley (4th)*	.489	1980— Lethbridge▲	.743	Ogden	.583
1956— Boise	.561	Billings	.629	1997— Great Falls	.556
1957— Salt Lake City	.650	1981— Calgary	.657	Billings■	.549
Billings†	.582	Butte▲	.557		
1958— Great Falls	.582	1982— Medicine Hat▲	.629		
Boise†	.615	Idaho Falls	.600		

*Won four-club playoff. †Won split-season playoff. ‡Ended first half in tie with Salt Lake City and won one-game playoff. §Ended first half in tie with Billings and Great Falls and won playoff. ∞Billings (first place) defeated Idaho Falls (second place) in first place-second place playoff. ▲League divided into Northern and Southern divisions; won two-club playoff. ♦Won two-club playoff. ■League divided into Northern and Southern divisions; won four-club playoff.

SUMMER CLASS A *Pioneer League*

MINOR LEAGUE INDEX

TEAMS AND CITIES

MINOR LEAGUE INDEX